Index

1991 SCHEDULE AND NOTE CALENDAR

(All Times Local Except Tokyo, London, and Berlin Which Are EDT)
Nationally televised games in parentheses.

Preseason/First Week

Friday, July 26	Chicago ___ at Miami ___	8:00
Saturday, July 27	Hall of Fame Game at Canton, Ohio Denver ___ vs. Detroit ___	(ABC) 12:30
	San Francisco ___ at Los Angeles Raiders ___	1:00
Sunday, July 28	American Bowl '91 at London Buffalo ___ vs. Philadelphia ___	(NBC) 1:00*
Friday, August 2	Cincinnati ___ at Detroit ___	7:30
	Indianapolis ___ at Denver ___	7:00
Saturday, August 3	American Bowl '91 at Berlin Chicago ___ vs. San Francisco ___	(NBC) 1:30*
	Dallas ___ at Kansas City ___	8:00
	Houston ___ at San Diego ___	7:00
	American Bowl '91 at Tokyo Los Angeles Raiders ___ vs. Miami ___	(ESPN) 10:00*
	Los Angeles Rams ___ vs. Atlanta ___ at Jacksonville, Fla.	8:00
	Minnesota ___ at New Orleans	7:00
	New England ___ at Green Bay ___	6:00
	Philadelphia ___ at New York Jets ___	8:00
	Phoenix ___ at Seattle ___	7:30
Sunday, August 4	Washington ___ at Pittsburgh ___	(TNT) 8:00
Monday, August 5	Buffalo ___ at New York Giants ___	(ABC) 8:00
	Tampa Bay ___ at Cleveland ___	8:30

*(London game actual kickoff 6:00 P.M. July 28; Berlin game actual kickoff 7:30 P.M. August 3; Tokyo game actual kickoff 11:00 A.M. August 4)

Preseason/Second Week

Wednesday, August 7	Denver ___ at San Francisco ___	6:00
Friday, August 9	Atlanta ___ at Houston ___	7:00
Saturday, August 10	Detroit ___ at Buffalo ___	6:30
	Green Bay ___ at New Orleans ___	7:00
	Kansas City ___ vs. New York Jets ___ at St. Louis	7:00
	Miami ___ at Tampa Bay ___	7:00
	New York Giants ___ at Cleveland ___	(CBS) 9:00
	Philadelphia ___ at Cincinnati ___	7:30
	Pittsburgh ___ at Minnesota ___	8:00
	Seattle ___ at Indianapolis ___	7:30
	Washington ___ at New England ___	7:30
Sunday, August 11	Phoenix ___ at Chicago ___	(TNT) 7:00
Monday, August 12	Los Angeles Raiders ___ at Dallas ___	(ABC) 7:00
	San Diego ___ at Los Angeles Rams ___	7:00

Preseason/Third Week

Friday, August 16	Cleveland ___ at Washington ___	8:00
Saturday, August 17	Buffalo ___ vs. Green Bay ___ at Madison, Wis.	(CBS) 12:00
	Chicago ___ at Los Angeles Raiders ___	1:00
	Detroit ___ at Kansas City ___	7:00
	Minnesota ___ at Cincinnati ___	7:30
	New England ___ at Phoenix ___	7:30
	New Orleans ___ at Indianapolis ___	7:30
	New York Jets ___ at New York Giants ___	(ESPN) 8:00
	Pittsburgh ___ at Philadelphia ___	7:30
	Seattle ___ at Los Angeles Rams ___	7:00
	Tampa Bay ___ at Atlanta ___	7:00
Sunday, August 18	Dallas ___ at Houston ___	(TNT) 7:00
Monday, August 19	Miami ___ at Denver ___	(ABC) 6:00
	San Diego ___ at San Francisco ___	6:00

Preseason/Fourth Week

Thursday, August 22	Los Angeles Rams ___ vs. Houston ___ at Memphis, Tenn.	(ESPN) 7:00
Friday, August 23	Atlanta ___ at Dallas ___	8:00
	Cleveland ___ at Minnesota ___	7:00
	Denver ___ at Phoenix ___	7:30
	Indianapolis ___ at Philadelphia ___	7:30
	Kansas City ___ at Tampa Bay ___	8:00
	Los Angeles Raiders ___ at San Diego ___	7:00
	Pittsburgh ___ at Detroit ___	7:30
	San Francisco ___ at Seattle ___	(NBC) 5:00
Saturday, August 24	Buffalo ___ at Chicago ___	(CBS) 8:00
	Cincinnati ___ at Green Bay ___	6:00
	New Orleans ___ at Miami ___	8:00
	New York Giants ___ at New England ___	4:00
	New York Jets ___ vs. Washington ___ at Columbia, S.C.	7:00

First Week

Sunday, September 1 (CBS-TV National Weekend)	Atlanta ___ at Kansas City ___	12:00
	Cincinnati ___ at Denver ___	2:00
	Dallas ___ at Cleveland ___	1:00
	Los Angeles Raiders ___ at Houston ___	3:00
	Miami ___ at Buffalo ___	4:00
	Minnesota ___ at Chicago ___	(CBS) 3:00
	New England ___ at Indianapolis ___	3:00
	Philadelphia ___ at Green Bay ___	12:00
	Phoenix ___ at Los Angeles Rams ___	1:00
	San Diego ___ at Pittsburgh ___	4:00
	Seattle ___ at New Orleans ___	12:00
	Tampa Bay ___ at New York Jets ___	1:00
Sunday Night	Detroit ___ at Washington ___	(TNT) 8:00
Monday, September 2	San Francisco ___ at New York Giants ___	(ABC) 9:00

Second Week

Sunday, September 8 (NBC-TV National Weekend)	Chicago ___ at Tampa Bay ___	1:00
	Cleveland ___ at New England ___	1:00
	Denver ___ at Los Angeles Raiders ___	(NBC) 1:00
	Green Bay ___ at Detroit ___	1:00
	Indianapolis ___ at Miami ___	1:00
	Los Angeles Rams ___ at New York Giants ___	1:00
	Minnesota ___ at Atlanta ___	1:00
	New Orleans ___ at Kansas City ___	12:00
	New York Jets ___ at Seattle ___	1:00
	Phoenix ___ at Philadelphia ___	1:00
	Pittsburgh ___ at Buffalo ___	1:00
	San Diego ___ at San Francisco ___	1:00
Sunday Night	Houston ___ at Cincinnati ___	(TNT) 8:00
Monday, September 9	Washington ___ at Dallas ___	(ABC) 8:00

Third Week

Sunday, September 15 (NBC-TV National Weekend)	Atlanta ___ at San Diego ___	1:00
	Buffalo ___ at New York Jets ___	4:00
	Cincinnati ___ at Cleveland ___	1:00
	Indianapolis ___ at Los Angeles Raiders ___	(NBC) 1:00
	Miami ___ at Detroit ___	1:00
	New England ___ at Pittsburgh ___	1:00
	New York Giants ___ at Chicago ___	12:00
	Philadelphia ___ at Dallas ___	12:00
	Phoenix ___ at Washington ___	1:00
	San Francisco ___ at Minnesota ___	12:00
	Seattle ___ at Denver ___	2:00
	Tampa Bay ___ at Green Bay ___	12:00
Sunday Night	Los Angeles Rams ___ at New Orleans ___	(TNT) 7:00
Monday, September 16	Kansas City ___ at Houston ___	(ABC) 8:00

Fourth Week

Sunday, September 22 (CBS-TV National Weekend)	Buffalo ___ at Tampa Bay ___	4:00
	Cleveland ___ at New York Giants ___	1:00
	Detroit ___ at Indianapolis ___	12:00
	Green Bay ___ at Miami ___	1:00
	Houston ___ at New England ___	1:00
	Los Angeles Raiders ___ at Atlanta ___	1:00
	Los Angeles Rams ___ at San Francisco ___	(CBS) 1:00
	Minnesota ___ at New Orleans ___	12:00
	Pittsburgh ___ at Philadelphia ___	1:00
	San Diego ___ at Denver ___	2:00
	Seattle ___ at Kansas City ___	3:00
	Washington ___ at Cincinnati ___	1:00
Sunday Night	Dallas ___ at Phoenix ___	(TNT) 5:00
Monday, September 23	New York Jets ___ at Chicago ___	(ABC) 8:00

Fifth Week

Open Date: Four AFC Central Teams

Sunday, September 29 (CBS-TV National Weekend)	Chicago ___ at Buffalo ___	1:00
	Green Bay ___ at Los Angeles Rams ___	1:00
	Indianapolis ___ at Seattle ___	1:00
	Kansas City ___ at San Diego ___	1:00
	Miami ___ at New York Jets ___	4:00
	New England ___ at Phoenix ___	1:00
	New Orleans ___ at Atlanta ___	1:00
	New York Giants ___ at Dallas ___	12:00
	San Francisco ___ at Los Angeles Raiders ___	(CBS) 1:00
	Tampa Bay ___ at Detroit ___	1:00
Sunday Night	Denver ___ at Minnesota ___	(TNT) 7:00
Monday, September 30	Philadelphia ___ at Washington ___	(ABC) 9:00

Sixth Week

Open Date: Four NFC West Teams

Sunday, October 6 (NBC-TV National Weekend)	Dallas ___ vs. Green Bay ___ at Milwaukee	12:00
	Denver ___ at Houston ___	12:00
	Miami ___ at New England ___	1:00
	Minnesota ___ at Detroit ___	1:00
	New York Jets ___ at Cleveland ___	1:00
	Philadelphia ___ at Tampa Bay ___	1:00
	Phoenix ___ at New York Giants ___	4:00
	San Diego ___ at Los Angeles Raiders ___	(NBC) 1:00
	Seattle ___ at Cincinnati ___	1:00
	Washington ___ at Chicago ___	12:00
Sunday Night	Pittsburgh ___ at Indianapolis ___	(TNT) 7:00
Monday, October 7	Buffalo ___ at Kansas City ___	(ABC) 8:00

Seventh Week

Open Date: Four NFC Central and Two AFC Fifth Place Teams

Sunday, October 13 (NBC-TV National Weekend)	Cincinnati ___ at Dallas ___	12:00
	Cleveland ___ at Washington ___	1:00
	Houston ___ at New York Jets ___	4:00
	Indianapolis ___ at Buffalo ___	1:00
	Miami ___ at Kansas City ___	(NBC) 3:00
	New Orleans ___ at Philadelphia ___	1:00
	Phoenix ___ at Minnesota ___	12:00
	San Diego ___ at Los Angeles Rams ___	1:00
	San Francisco ___ at Atlanta ___	1:00
Sunday Night	Los Angeles Raiders ___ at Seattle ___	(TNT) 4:30
Monday, October 14	New York Giants ___ at Pittsburgh ___	(ABC) 9:00

Eighth Week
Open Date: Four NFC East Teams

Thursday, October 17	Chicago ___ at Green Bay ___	(TNT) 6:30
Sunday, October 20	Atlanta ___ at Phoenix ___	1:00
(CBS-TV National Weekend)	Cleveland ___ at San Diego ___	1:00
	Detroit ___ at San Francisco ___	1:00
	Houston ___ at Miami ___	1:00
	Kansas City ___ at Denver ___	2:00
	L.A. Rams ___ at L.A. Raiders ___	(CBS) 1:00
	Minnesota ___ at New England ___	1:00
	New York Jets ___ at Indianapolis ___	12:00
	Seattle ___ at Pittsburgh ___	1:00
	Tampa Bay ___ at New Orleans ___	12:00
Monday, October 21	Cincinnati ___ at Buffalo ___	(ABC) 9:00

Ninth Week
Open Date: Four AFC East Teams

Sunday, October 27	Chicago ___ at New Orleans ___	12:00
(NBC-TV National Weekend)	Cincinnati ___ at Houston ___	12:00
	Dallas ___ at Detroit ___	4:00
	Denver ___ at New England ___	4:00
	Green Bay ___ at Tampa Bay ___	1:00
	Los Angeles Rams ___ at Atlanta ___	1:00
	Minnesota ___ at Phoenix ___	2:00
	Pittsburgh ___ at Cleveland ___	4:00
	San Diego ___ at Seattle ___	(NBC) 1:00
	San Francisco ___ at Philadelphia ___	1:00
Sunday Night	Washington ___ at New York Giants ___	(ESPN) 7:30
Monday, October 28	Los Angeles Raiders ___ at Kansas City ___	(ABC) 8:00

Tenth Week
Open Date: Four AFC West Teams

Sunday, November 3	Atlanta ___ at San Francisco ___	1:00
(CBS-TV National Weekend)	Cleveland ___ at Cincinnati ___	1:00
	Detroit ___ at Chicago ___	12:00
	Green Bay ___ at New York Jets ___	1:00
	Houston ___ at Washington ___	1:00
	Miami ___ at Indianapolis ___	4:00
	New England ___ at Buffalo ___	1:00
	New Orleans ___ at Los Angeles Rams ___	(CBS) 1:00
	Phoenix ___ at Dallas ___	12:00
	Tampa Bay ___ at Minnesota ___	12:00
Sunday Night	Pittsburgh ___ at Denver ___	(ESPN) 6:00
Monday, November 4	New York Giants ___ at Philadelphia ___	(ABC) 9:00

Eleventh Week

Sunday, November 10	Atlanta ___ at Washington ___	1:00
(NBC-TV National Weekend)	Buffalo ___ vs. Green Bay ___ at Milwaukee	12:00
	Dallas ___ at Houston ___	12:00
	Detroit ___ at Tampa Bay ___	1:00
	Indianapolis ___ at New York Jets ___	1:00
	Kansas City ___ at Los Angeles Rams ___	(NBC) 1:00
	Los Angeles Raiders ___ at Denver ___	2:00
	New York Giants ___ at Phoenix ___	2:00
	Philadelphia ___ at Cleveland ___	1:00
	Pittsburgh ___ at Cincinnati ___	1:00
	San Francisco ___ at New Orleans ___	12:00
	Seattle ___ at San Diego ___	1:00
Sunday Night	New England ___ at Miami ___	(ESPN) 8:00
Monday, November 11	Chicago ___ at Minnesota ___	(ABC) 8:00

Twelfth Week

Sunday, November 17	Chicago ___ at Indianapolis ___	1:00
(CBS-TV National Weekend)	Cincinnati ___ at Philadelphia ___	1:00
	Dallas ___ at New York Giants ___	(CBS) 4:00
	Denver ___ at Kansas City ___	12:00
	Los Angeles Rams ___ at Detroit ___	4:00
	Minnesota ___ at Green Bay ___	12:00
	New Orleans ___ at San Diego ___	1:00
	New York Jets ___ at New England ___	1:00
	Phoenix ___ at San Francisco ___	1:00
	Seattle ___ at Los Angeles Raiders ___	1:00
	Tampa Bay ___ at Atlanta ___	1:00
	Washington ___ at Pittsburgh ___	1:00
Sunday Night	Cleveland ___ at Houston ___	(ESPN) 7:00
Monday, November 18	Buffalo ___ at Miami ___	(ABC) 9:00

Thirteenth Week

Sunday, November 24	Buffalo ___ at New England ___	1:00
(NBC-TV National Weekend)	Dallas ___ at Washington ___	1:00
	Denver ___ at Seattle ___	(NBC) 1:00
	Detroit ___ at Minnesota ___	12:00
	Houston ___ at Pittsburgh ___	1:00
	Indianapolis ___ vs. Green Bay ___ at Milwaukee	12:00
	Kansas City ___ at Cleveland ___	1:00
	Los Angeles Raiders ___ at Cincinnati ___	1:00
	Miami ___ at Chicago ___	12:00
	New York Giants ___ at Tampa Bay ___	1:00
	Philadelphia ___ at Phoenix ___	2:00
	San Diego ___ at New York Jets ___	4:00
Sunday Night	Atlanta ___ at New Orleans ___	(ESPN) 7:00
Monday, November 25	San Francisco ___ at Los Angeles Rams ___	(ABC) 6:00

Fourteenth Week

Open Date: Two NFC Fifth Place Teams

Thursday, November 28	Chicago ___ at Detroit ___	(CBS) 12:30
Thanksgiving Day	Pittsburgh ___ at Dallas ___	(NBC) 3:00
Sunday, December 1	Cleveland ___ at Indianapolis ___	1:00
(CBS-TV National Weekend)	Green Bay ___ at Atlanta ___	1:00
	Kansas City ___ at Seattle ___	1:00
	New England ___ at Denver ___	2:00
	New Orleans ___ at San Francisco ___	1:00
	New York Giants ___ at Cincinnati ___	4:00
	New York Jets ___ at Buffalo ___	1:00
	Tampa Bay ___ at Miami ___	1:00
	Washington ___ at Los Angeles Rams ___	(CBS) 1:00
Sunday Night	Los Angeles Raiders ___ at San Diego ___	(ESPN) 5:00
Monday, December 2	Philadelphia ___ at Houston ___	(ABC) 8:00

Fifteenth Week

Sunday, December 8	Atlanta ___ at Los Angeles Rams ___	1:00
(NBC-TV National Weekend)	Buffalo ___ at Los Angeles Raiders ___	(NBC) 1:00
	Denver ___ at Cleveland ___	1:00
	Green Bay ___ at Chicago ___	12:00
	Indianapolis ___ at New England ___	1:00
	New Orleans ___ at Dallas ___	12:00
	New York Jets ___ at Detroit ___	4:00
	Philadelphia ___ at New York Giants ___	1:00
	Pittsburgh ___ at Houston ___	12:00
	San Diego ___ at Kansas City ___	12:00
	San Francisco ___ at Seattle ___	1:00
	Washington ___ at Phoenix ___	2:00
Sunday Night	Minnesota ___ at Tampa Bay ___	(ESPN) 8:00
Monday, December 9	Cincinnati ___ at Miami ___	(ABC) 9:00

Sixteenth Week

Saturday, December 14	Kansas City ___ at San Francisco ___	(NBC) 1:00
	Tampa Bay ___ at Chicago ___	(CBS) 11:30
Sunday, December 15 (CBS-TV National Weekend)	Cincinnati ___ at Pittsburgh ___	1:00
	Dallas ___ at Philadelphia ___	1:00
	Detroit ___ at Green Bay ___	12:00
	Houston ___ at Cleveland ___	1:00
	Los Angeles Rams ___ at Minnesota ___	12:00
	Miami ___ at San Diego ___	1:00
	New England ___ at New York Jets ___	1:00
	New York Giants ___ at Washington ___	(CBS) 4:00
	Phoenix ___ at Denver ___	2:00
	Seattle ___ at Atlanta ___	1:00
Sunday Night	Buffalo ___ at Indianapolis ___	(ESPN) 8:00
Monday, December 16	Los Angeles Raiders ___ at New Orleans ___	(ABC) 8:00

Seventeenth Week

Saturday, December 21	Green Bay ___ at Minnesota ___	(CBS) 3:00
	Houston ___ at New York Giants ___	(NBC) 12:30
Sunday, December 22 (NBC-TV National Weekend)	Atlanta ___ at Dallas ___	12:00
	Cleveland ___ at Pittsburgh ___	1:00
	Denver ___ at San Diego ___	1:00
	Detroit ___ at Buffalo ___	1:00
	Indianapolis ___ at Tampa Bay ___	1:00
	Kansas City ___ at Los Angeles Raiders ___	(NBC) 1:00
	New England ___ at Cincinnati ___	1:00
	New Orleans ___ at Phoenix ___	2:00
	New York Jets ___ at Miami ___	1:00
	Washington ___ at Philadelphia ___	4:00
Sunday Night	Los Angeles Rams ___ at Seattle ___	(ESPN) 5:00
Monday, December 23	Chicago ___ at San Francisco ___	(ABC) 6:00

Wild Card Playoff Games

Site Priorities
Three Wild Card teams (division non-champions with best three records) from each conference and the division champion with the third-best record in each conference will enter the first round of the playoffs. The division champion with the third-best record will play host to the Wild Card team with the third-best record. The Wild Card team with the best record will play host to the Wild Card team with the second-best record. There are no restrictions on intra-division games.

Saturday, December 28, 1991

American Football Conference

__________ at __________ (ABC)

National Football Conference

__________ at __________ (ABC)

Sunday, December 29, 1991

American Football Conference

__________ at __________ (NBC)

National Football Conference

__________ at __________ (CBS)

Divisional Playoff Games

Site Priorities
In each conference, the two division champions with the highest won-lost-tied percentage during the regular season will play host to the Wild Card winners. The division champion with the best record in each conference is assured of playing the Wild Card survivor with the poorest record. There are no restrictions on intra-division games.

Saturday, January 4, 1992

American Football Conference

__________ at __________ (NBC)

National Football Conference

__________ at __________ (CBS)

Sunday, January 5, 1992

American Football Conference

__________ at __________ (NBC)

National Football Conference

__________ at __________ (CBS)

Conference Championship Games, Super Bowl XXVI, and AFC-NFC Pro Bowl

Site Priorities for Championship Games
The home teams will be the surviving playoff winners with the best won-lost-tied percentage during the regular season. A Wild Card team cannot play host unless two Wild Card teams are in the game, in which case the Wild Card team with the best record will play host.

Sunday, January 12, 1992 American Football Conference Championship Game

________________ at ________________ (NBC)

National Football Conference Championship Game

________________ at ________________ (CBS)

Sunday, January 26, 1992 Super Bowl XXVI at Metrodome, Minneapolis, Minnesota

________________ vs. ________________ (CBS)

Sunday, February 2, 1992 AFC-NFC Pro Bowl at Honolulu, Hawaii

AFC ________________ vs. NFC ________________ (ESPN)

Postseason Games

Saturday, December 28	AFC and NFC Wild Card Playoffs (ABC)
Sunday, December 29	AFC and NFC Wild Card Playoffs (NBC and CBS)
Saturday, January 4	AFC and NFC Divisional Playoffs (NBC and CBS)
Sunday, January 5	AFC and NFC Divisional Playoffs (NBC and CBS)
Sunday, January 12	AFC and NFC Championship Games (NBC and CBS)
Sunday, January 26	Super Bowl XXVI at Metrodome, Minneapolis, Minnesota (CBS)
Sunday, February 2	AFC-NFC Pro Bowl at Honolulu, Hawaii (ESPN)

1991 Nationally Televised Games

(All games carried on CBS Radio Network.)

Regular Season

Sunday, September 1	Minnesota at Chicago (day, CBS)
	Detroit at Washington (night, TNT)
Monday, September 2	San Francisco at New York Giants (night, ABC)
Sunday, September 8	Denver at Los Angeles Raiders (day, NBC)
	Houston at Cincinnati (night, TNT)
Monday, September 9	Washington at Dallas (night, ABC)
Sunday, September 15	Indianapolis at Los Angeles Raiders (day, NBC)
	Los Angeles Rams at New Orleans (night, TNT)
Monday, September 16	Kansas City at Houston (night, ABC)
Sunday, September 22	Los Angeles Rams at San Francisco (day, CBS)
	Dallas at Phoenix (night, TNT)
Monday, September 23	New York Jets at Chicago (night, ABC)
Sunday, September 29	San Francisco at Los Angeles Raiders (day, CBS)
	Denver at Minnesota (night, TNT)
Monday, September 30	Philadelphia at Washington (night, ABC)
Sunday, October 6	San Diego at Los Angeles Raiders (day, NBC)
	Pittsburgh at Indianapolis (night, TNT)
Monday, October 7	Buffalo at Kansas City (night, ABC)
Sunday, October 13	Miami at Kansas City (day, NBC)
	Los Angeles Raiders at Seattle (night, TNT)
Monday, October 14	New York Giants at Pittsburgh (night, ABC)
Thursday, October 17	Chicago at Green Bay (night, TNT)
Sunday, October 20	Los Angeles Rams at Los Angeles Raiders (day, CBS)
Monday, October 21	Cincinnati at Buffalo (night, ABC)
Sunday, October 27	San Diego at Seattle (day, NBC)
	Washington at New York Giants (night, ESPN)
Monday, October 28	Los Angeles Raiders at Kansas City (night, ABC)
Sunday, November 3	New Orleans at Los Angeles Rams (day, CBS)
	Pittsburgh at Denver (night, ESPN)
Monday, November 4	New York Giants at Philadelphia (night, ABC)
Sunday, November 10	Kansas City at Los Angeles Rams (day, NBC)
	New England at Miami (night, ESPN)
Monday, November 11	Chicago at Minnesota (night, ABC)
Sunday, November 17	Dallas at New York Giants (day, CBS)
	Cleveland at Houston (night, ESPN)
Monday, November 18	Buffalo at Miami (night, ABC)
Sunday, November 24	Denver at Seattle (day, NBC)
	Atlanta at New Orleans (night, ESPN)
Monday, November 25	San Francisco at Los Angeles Rams (night, ABC)
Thursday, November 28	Chicago at Detroit (day, CBS)
	Pittsburgh at Dallas (day, NBC)
Sunday, December 1	Washington at Los Angeles Rams (day, CBS)
	Los Angeles Raiders at San Diego (night, ESPN)
Monday, December 2	Philadelphia at Houston (night, ABC)
Sunday, December 8	Buffalo at Los Angeles Raiders (day, NBC)
	Minnesota at Tampa Bay (night, ESPN)
Monday, December 9	Cincinnati at Miami (night, ABC)
Saturday, December 14	Kansas City at San Francisco (day, NBC)
	Tampa Bay at Chicago (day, CBS)
Sunday, December 15	New York Giants at Washington (day, CBS)
	Buffalo at Indianapolis (night, ESPN)
Monday, December 16	Los Angeles Raiders at New Orleans (night, ABC)
Saturday, December 21	Green Bay at Minnesota (day, CBS)
	Houston at New York Giants (day, NBC)
Sunday, December 22	Kansas City at Los Angeles Raiders (day, NBC)
	Los Angeles Rams at Seattle (night, ESPN)
Monday, December 23	Chicago at San Francisco (night, ABC)

1991 AFC-NFC Interconference Games

(All times local.)

September 1	Atlanta at Kansas City	12:00
	Dallas at Cleveland	1:00
	Seattle at New Orleans	12:00
	Tampa Bay at New York Jets	1:00
September 8	New Orleans at Kansas City	12:00
	San Diego at San Francisco	1:00
September 15	Atlanta at San Diego	1:00
	Miami at Detroit	1:00
September 22	Buffalo at Tampa Bay	4:00
	Cleveland at New York Giants	1:00
	Detroit at Indianapolis	12:00
	Green Bay at Miami	1:00
	L.A. Raiders at Atlanta	1:00
	Pittsburgh at Philadelphia	1:00
	Washington at Cincinnati	1:00
September 23	New York Jets at Chicago	8:00
September 29	Chicago at Buffalo	1:00
	New England at Phoenix	1:00
	San Francisco at L.A. Raiders	1:00
	Denver at Minnesota	7:00
October 13	Cincinnati at Dallas	12:00
	Cleveland at Washington	1:00
	San Diego at L.A. Rams	1:00
October 14	N.Y. Giants at Pittsburgh	9:00
October 20	L.A. Rams at L.A. Raiders	1:00
	Minnesota at New England	1:00
November 3	Green Bay at New York Jets	1:00
	Houston at Washington	1:00
November 10	Buffalo vs. Green Bay at Milwaukee	12:00
	Dallas at Houston	12:00
	Kansas City at L.A. Rams	1:00
	Philadelphia at Cleveland	1:00
November 17	Chicago at Indianapolis	1:00
	Cincinnati at Philadelphia	1:00
	New Orleans at San Diego	1:00
	Washington at Pittsburgh	1:00

November 24	Indianapolis vs. Green Bay at Milw. . .	12:00
	Miami at Chicago	12:00
November 28	Pittsburgh at Dallas	3:00
December 1	New York Giants at Cincinnati	4:00
	Tampa Bay at Miami	1:00
December 2	Philadelphia at Houston	8:00
December 8	New York Jets at Detroit	4:00
	San Francisco at Seattle	1:00
December 14	Kansas City at San Francisco	1:00
December 15	Phoenix at Denver	2:00
	Seattle at Atlanta	1:00
December 16	L.A. Raiders at New Orleans	8:00
December 21	Houston at New York Giants	12:30
December 22	Detroit at Buffalo	1:00
	Indianapolis at Tampa Bay	1:00
	L.A. Rams at Seattle	5:00

Thursday, Sunday, and Monday Night Television Games at a Glance

(All games carried on CBS Radio Network.)

Sunday, September 1	Detroit at Washington (TNT)	8:00
Monday, September 2	San Francisco at N.Y. Giants (ABC) . .	9:00
Sunday, September 8	Houston at Cincinnati (TNT)	8:00
Monday, September 9	Washington at Dallas (ABC)	8:00
Sunday, September 15	L.A. Rams at New Orleans (TNT)	7:00
Monday, September 16	Kansas City at Houston (ABC)	8:00
Sunday, September 22	Dallas at Phoenix (TNT)	5:00
Monday, September 23	New York Jets at Chicago (ABC)	8:00
Sunday, September 29	Denver at Minnesota (TNT)	7:00
Monday, September 30	Philadelphia at Washington (ABC) . . .	9:00
Sunday, October 6	Pittsburgh at Indianapolis (TNT)	7:00
Monday, October 7	Buffalo at Kansas City (ABC)	8:00
Sunday, October 13	L.A. Raiders at Seattle (TNT)	4:30
Monday, October 14	N.Y. Giants at Pittsburgh (ABC)	9:00
Thursday, October 17	Chicago at Green Bay (TNT)	6:30
Monday, October 21	Cincinnati at Buffalo (ABC)	9:00
Sunday, October 27	Washington at N.Y. Giants (ESPN) . . .	7:30
Monday, October 28	L.A. Raiders at Kansas City (ABC) . . .	8:00
Sunday, November 3	Pittsburgh at Denver (ESPN)	6:00
Monday, November 4	N.Y. Giants at Philadelphia (ABC) . . .	9:00
Sunday, November 10	New England at Miami (ESPN)	8:00
Monday, November 11	Chicago at Minnesota (ABC)	8:00
Sunday, November 17	Cleveland at Houston (ESPN)	7:00
Monday, November 18	Buffalo at Miami (ABC)	9:00
Sunday, November 24	Atlanta at New Orleans (ESPN)	7:00
Monday, November 25	San Francisco at L.A. Rams (ABC) . .	6:00
Sunday, December 1	L.A. Raiders at San Diego (ESPN) . . .	5:00
Monday, December 2	Philadelphia at Houston (ABC)	8:00
Sunday, December 8	Minnesota at Tampa Bay (ESPN)	8:00
Monday, December 9	Cincinnati at Miami (ABC)	9:00
Sunday, December 15	Buffalo at Indianapolis (ESPN)	8:00
Monday, December 16	L.A. Raiders at New Orleans (ABC) . .	8:00
Sunday, December 22	L.A. Rams at Seattle (ESPN)	5:00
Monday, December 23	Chicago at San Francisco (ABC)	6:00

Important Dates

1991 Season

July 5	Claiming period of 24 hours begins in waiver system. All waiver requests for the rest of the year are no-recall and no-withdrawal.
Mid-July	Preseason training camps open.
July 27	Hall of Fame Game, Canton, Ohio: Denver vs. Detroit.
July 28	American Bowl '91, London, England: Buffalo vs. Philadelphia.
August 2-5	First preseason weekend.
August 3	American Bowl '91, Berlin, Germany: Chicago vs. San Francisco.
August 3	American Bowl '91, Tokyo, Japan: Los Angeles Raiders vs. Miami.
August 7-12	Second preseason weekend.
August 16-19	Third preseason weekend.
August 20	Roster cutdown to maximum of 60 players.
August 22-24	Fourth preseason weekend.
August 26	Roster cutdown to maximum of 47 players. Clubs may dress 45 players for each regular-season game. No later than 1:15 prior to kickoff of each game, clubs must establish an Inactive List of two players.
September 1-2	Regular season opens.
September 17	Priority on multiple waiver claims is now based on the current season's standings.
October 8	Trading of player contracts/rights ends at 4 P.M. New York Time.
October 23-24	NFL Fall Meeting, Dallas, Texas.
November 23	Deadline for reinstatement of players in Reserve List categories of Retired, Did Not Report, and Veteran Free Agent Asked to Re-Sign.
December 16-17	Balloting for AFC-NFC Pro Bowl.
December 20	Deadline for waiver requests in 1991 for non-playoff teams.
December 28-29	AFC and NFC Wild Card Playoff Games.
January 4-5	AFC and NFC Divisional Playoff Games.
January 12	AFC and NFC Championship Games.
January 26	Super Bowl XXVI, Metrodome, Minneapolis, Minnesota.
January 27	Trading period begins.
February 1	Deadline for establishing Protected List of 37 players. All players who are not on Protected List will be eligible to sign as free agents with any other club through April 1.
February 2	AFC-NFC Pro Bowl at Aloha Stadium, Honolulu, Hawaii.

1992 Season

February 3	Waiver system begins for 1992.
February 5-10	Combine timing and testing of college players, Hoosier Dome, Indianapolis, Indiana.
March 15-20	NFL Annual Meeting, Phoenix, Arizona.
April 1	Deadline for signing of offer sheets by protected veteran free agents and new clubs.
April 1	Expiration of free agency period for unprotected players.
April 26-27	57th Annual NFL Selection Meeting, New York, New York.
May 19-20	NFL Spring Meeting, Laguna Niguel, California.
August 1	Hall of Fame Game, Canton, Ohio: New York Jets vs. Philadelphia.
August 7-9	First preseason weekend.
September 6-7	Regular season opens.
January 4	Regular season closes.
January 9-10	AFC and NFC Wild Card Playoff Games.
January 16-17	AFC and NFC Divisional Playoff Games.
January 24	AFC and NFC Championship Games.
January 31	Super Bowl XXVII at Rose Bowl, Pasadena, California.
February 7	AFC-NFC Pro Bowl.

Future Pro Football Hall of Fame Games

1993	Los Angeles Raiders (AFC) vs. Green Bay Packers (NFC)
1994	Denver Broncos (AFC) vs. Dallas Cowboys (NFC)
1995	San Diego Chargers (AFC) vs. Atlanta Falcons (NFC)
1996	Indianapolis Colts (AFC) vs. New Orleans Saints (NFC)
1997	Seattle Seahawks (AFC) vs. Minnesota Vikings (NFC)
1998	Pittsburgh Steelers (AFC) vs. Tampa Bay Buccaneers (NFC)

Waivers

The waiver system is a procedure by which player contracts or NFL rights to players are made available by a club to other clubs in the League. During the procedure, the 27 other clubs either file claims to obtain the players or waive the opportunity to do so—thus the term "waiver." Claiming clubs are assigned players on a priority based on the inverse of won-and-lost standing. The claiming period normally is 10 days during the offseason and 24 hours from early July through December. In some circumstances, another 24 hours is added on to allow the original club to rescind its action (known as a recall of a waiver request) and/or the claiming club to do the same (known as withdrawal of a claim). If a player passes through waivers unclaimed and is not recalled by the original club, he becomes a free agent. All waivers from July through December are no recall and no withdrawal. Under the Collective Bargaining Agreement, from the beginning of the waiver system each year on the day after the Pro Bowl through the trading deadline (October 8, 1991), any veteran who has acquired four years of pension credit may, if about to be assigned to another club through the waiver system, reject such assignment and become a free agent.

Active List

The Active List is the principal status for players participating for a club. It consists of all players under contract, including option, who are eligible for preseason, regular season, and postseason games. In 1991, teams will be permitted to open training camp with no more than 80 players under contract and thereafter must meet a series of mandatory roster reductions prior to the season opener. Teams will be permitted an Active List of 45 players and an Inactive List of two players for each regular-season and postseason game during the 1991 season. Provided that a club has only two quarterbacks on its 45-player Active List, a third quarterback from its Inactive List is permitted to dress for the game, but if he participates in the game, the other two quarterbacks are thereafter prohibited from playing.

August 20 . . . . active list of 60 players
August 26 . . . . active list of 45 players (plus two-player Inactive List)

In addition to the Active List limits described above, there also is an overall roster limit of 80 players that is applicable to players on a club's Active, Inactive, or Exempt Lists, and any players on Reserve as Injured, Physically Unable to Perform, Non-Football Illness/Injury, and Suspended.

Reserve List

The Reserve List is a status for players who, for reasons of injury, retirement, military service, or other circumstances, are not immediately available for participation with a club. Players on Reserve/Injured are not eligible to practice or return to the Active List until four regular-season games have been played.

Each club will have five free activations for players placed on Reserve/Injured after the final cutdown. Players also can be returned to the club's Active List if they clear Procedural Recall waivers. Any player placed on Reserve/Injured prior to or concurrent with the final cutdown on August 26 may not return to the club nor practice with the team that year. Clubs participating in postseason competition will be granted an additional activation for each postseason game, provided they have exhausted all previous activations.

Players in the category of Reserve/Retired, Reserve/Did Not Report, or Reserve/Veteran Free Agent Asked to Re-Sign may not be reinstated during the period from 30 days before the end of the regular season through the postseason.

Trades

Unrestricted trading between the AFC and NFC is allowed in 1991 through October 8, after which trading will end until January 27, 1992.

Annual Active Player Limits

NFL

Year(s)	Limit
1985-91	45
1983-84	49
1982	45†–49
1978–81	45
1975–77	43
1974	47
1964–73	40
1963	37
1961–62	36
1960	38
1959	36
1957–58	35
1951–56	33
1949–50	32
1948	35
1947	35*–34
1945–46	33
1943–44	28
1940–42	33
1938–39	30
1936–37	25
1935	24
1930–34	20
1926–29	18
1925	16

†45 for first two games
*35 for first three games

AFL

Year(s)	Limit
1966–69	40
1965	38
1964	34
1962–63	33
1960–61	35

Tie-Breaking Procedures

The following procedures will be used to break standings ties for postseason playoffs and to determine regular-season schedules.

To Break a Tie Within a Division

If, at the end of the regular season, two or more clubs in the same division finish with identical won-lost-tied percentages, the following steps will be taken until a champion is determined.

Two Clubs

1. Head-to-head (best won-lost-tied percentage in games between the clubs).
2. Best won-lost-tied percentage in games played within the division.
3. Best won-lost-tied percentage in games played within the conference.
4. Best won-lost-tied percentage in common games, if applicable.
5. Best net points in division games.
6. Best net points in all games.
7. Strength of schedule.
8. Best net touchdowns in all games.
9. Coin toss.

Three or More Clubs

(Note: If one team wins multiple-team tiebreaker to advance to playoff round, remaining teams revert to step 1 of applicable two-club format, i.e., either in division tiebreaker or Wild Card tiebreaker. If two teams in a multiple-team tie possess superior marks in a tiebreaking step, this pair of teams revert to top of applicable two-club format to break tie. One team advances to playoff round, while other returns to original group and step 1 of applicable tiebreaker).

1. Head-to-head (best won-lost-tied percentage in games among the clubs).
2. Best won-lost-tied percentage in games played within the division.
3. Best won-lost-tied percentage in games played within the conference.
4. Best won-lost-tied percentage in common games.
5. Best net points in division games.
6. Best net points in all games.
7. Strength of schedule.
8. Best net touchdowns in all games.
9. Coin toss.

To Break a Tie for the Wild Card Team

If it is necessary to break ties to determine the three Wild Card clubs from each conference, the following steps will be taken.

1. If the tied clubs are from the same division, apply division tiebreaker.
2. If the tied clubs are from different divisions, apply the following steps.

Two Clubs

1. Head-to-head, if applicable.
2. Best won-lost-tied percentage in games played within the conference.
3. Best won-lost-tied percentage in common games, minimum of four.
4. Best average net points in conference games.
5. Best net points in all games.
6. Strength of schedule.
7. Best net touchdowns in all games.
8. Coin toss.

Three or More Clubs

(Note: If two clubs remain tied after third or other clubs are eliminated, tiebreaker reverts to step 1 of applicable two-club format.)

When the first Wild Card team has been identified, the procedure is repeated to name the second Wild Card, i.e., eliminate all but the highest-ranked club in each division prior to proceeding to step two, and repeated a third time, if necessary, to identify the third Wild Card. In situations where three or more teams from the same division are involved in the procedure, the original seeding of the teams remains the same for subsequent applications of the tiebreaker if the top-ranked team in that division qualifies for a Wild Card berth.

1. Apply division tiebreaker to eliminate all but highest-ranked club in each division prior to proceeding to step 2. The original seeding within a division upon application of the division tiebreaker remains the same for all subsequent applications of the procedure that are necessary to identify the three Wild Card participants.
2. Head-to-head sweep (Applicable only if one club has defeated each of the others or one club has lost to each of the others.)
3. Best won-lost-tied percentage in games played within the conference.
4. Best won-lost-tied percentage in common games, minimum of four.
5. Best average net points in conference games.
6. Best net points in all games.
7. Strength of schedule.
8. Best net touchdowns in all games.
9. Coin toss.

Tie-Breaking Procedure for Selection Meeting

If two or more clubs are tied for selection order, the conventional strength of schedule tiebreaker will be applied, subject to the following exceptions for all playoff teams.

1. The Super Bowl winner will be last and the Super Bowl loser will be next-to-last.
2. Any non-Super Bowl playoff team involved in the tie moves down in drafting priority as follows:
   A. Participation by a club in the playoffs without a victory adds one-half victory to the club's regular-season won-lost-tied record.
   B. For each victory in the playoffs, one full victory will be added to the club's regular-season won-lost-tied record.
3. Clubs with the best won-lost-tied records after these steps are applied will drop to their appropriate spots at the bottom of the tied segment. In no case will the above process move a club lower than the segment in which it was initially tied.
4. Tied clubs will alternate priority throughout the 12 rounds of the draft. In case of a tie involving three or more teams, the club with priority in the first round will drop to the bottom of the tied segment in the second round and move its way back to the top of the segment in each succeeding round.

Instant Replay Approved for 1991

For the sixth consecutive season, NFL clubs have approved a limited system of Instant Replay on a one-year basis.

All replay reviews which involve contact to the field from the Replay Booth will be a maximum of two minutes in duration, timed from the moment when the Umpire signals timeout.

The Replay Official will be assigned to a regular officiating crew and will attend crew meetings the day before each game.

The following table outlines the number of reversals and plays closely reviewed by instant replay in each of the previous five regular seasons.

	Games	Reversals	Plays Closely Reviewed
1986	224	38	374
1987	210	57	490
1988	224	53	537
1989	224	65	492
1990	224	73	504

In 1986, the system was approved by a 23-4-1 vote and in 1987 the vote was 21-7. In 1988, replay was cleared by a 23-5 margin. In 1989, the vote was 24-4. In 1990, the vote was 21-7. In 1991, Instant Replay was approved by a 21-7 vote.

The NFL has discussed Instant Replay in some degree or other since the early 1970s. The League experimented in 1976 and 1978 using two basic frameworks—an independent system using cameras, replay machines, and technicians separate from the network covering the games, and a "no-frills" approach using existing TV coverage.

In 1985, the NFL used the network feed of the nine nationally televised preseason games to experiment with the basic system which later was adopted and has been used since 1986. A total of 28 plays (17 confirmed calls, 4 inconclusive, 1 reversed, and 6 no replay shown) were closely examined in the 1985 experiment.

Q—What is the objective of this system?

A—The clubs feel that on certain plays the telecast viewed by the general public should be used to correct an indisputable error. The system will be used to reverse an on-field decision only when the Replay Official has **indisputable visual evidence** available to him that warrants the change.

Q—Who will be involved?

A—The Replay Official (a former NFL or collegiate official) will be positioned in a sideline Replay Booth, which will house two TV monitors and two high-speed VCRs plus radio communications to the on-field officials. The Replay Official makes the decision although a Communicator (normally a member of the League Office staff) and a Technician also will be there to lend logistical help.

Q—Why is the system referred to as "limited" Instant Replay?

A—This system will concentrate on plays of **possession** or **touching** (e.g. fumbles, receptions, interceptions, muffs) and most plays governed by the **sidelines, goal lines, end lines,** and **line of scrimmage** (e.g. receiver or runner in or out of bounds, forward or backward passes, breaking the plane of the goal line). It also will be used to determine whether there are more than 11 men on the field.

Q—Why aren't most fouls included in this system?

A—It is recognized that in most circumstances the on-field officials have the best vantage points involving fouls. It is for this reason that Instant Replay **will not review** a list of the following 26 fouls:

1. Clipping
2. Encroachment and offsides
3. Grasp of facemask
4. False start
5. Defensive pass interference
6. Offensive pass interference
7. Offensive holding and illegal use of hands
8. Illegal batting or punching ball
9. Illegal block on free kick or scrimmage kick
10. Illegal crackback
11. Illegal motion
12. Illegal use of forearm or elbow
13. Illegal use of hands by defense
14. Illegally kicking ball
15. Illegally snapping ball
16. Intentional grounding
17. Member of punting team downfield early
18. Illegal formation
19. Palpably unfair act
20. Piling on
21. Roughing the passer
22. Running into/roughing kicker
23. Striking, kicking, or kneeing
24. Unnecessary roughness
25. Unsportsmanlike conduct
26. Use of helmet as a weapon

Q—Is the television network carrying the game part of the review process?

A—No. Although the Replay Official will be viewing the live network feed, there is no communication to television personnel as to which plays to show or not to show. The Replay Official does not hear the TV commentators.

Q—What is the step-by-step procedure of a play review?

A—The Replay Official will view game action and a play will be replayed immediately on one of the two monitors, while the other one continues to record the live feed.

The Replay Official makes a determination if further study of the play is needed. If not, there is no contact with the field and play continues without interruption.

If the Replay Official believes an error may have been made the Umpire will be contacted via a headset.

The Replay Official will watch replay(s) on one or both monitors and complete his review within two minutes after the Umpire signals timeout.

The Replay Official will inform the Umpire of his decision, and the Referee will make the appropriate announcement on the wireless microphone.

Figuring the 1992 NFL Schedule

As soon as the final game of the 1991 NFL regular season (Chicago at San Francisco on December 23) has been completed, it will be possible to determine the 1992 opponents of the 28 teams.

At the March, 1990, Owners' Meeting, the NFL announced it will play its 16-game schedule over 17 weeks in 1990 and 1991, and a 16-game schedule over 18 weeks in 1992 and 1993.

The 16-over-17 format provided each team one open weekend. The 16-over-18 format will provide each team two open weekends.

Each 1992 team schedule is based on a "common opponent" formula initiated for the 1978 season and most recently modified in 1987. Under the common opponent format, the first- through fourth-place teams in a division play at least 12 of their 16 games the following season against common opponents, and the fifth-place team in the division plays at least 10 common opponent games. It is not a position scheduling format in which the strong play the strong and the weak play the weak.

For years, the NFL had been seeking a more easily understood and balanced schedule that would provide both competitive equality and a variety of opponents. Under the old rotation scheduling system in effect from 1970-77, non-division opponents were determined by a pre-set formula. This often resulted in competitive imbalances.

With common opponents as the basis for scheduling, a more competitive and equitable method of determining division champions and postseason playoff representatives has developed. Teams battling for a division title are playing at least 75 percent of their games against common opponents.

In 1987, NFL owners passed a bylaw proposal designed to modify the common opponent scheduling format in the hopes of creating even more equity. Since then, the pairings with non-division opponents have been:

Prior Year's Finish in Division	Pairings in Non-Division Games Within Conference	Previous Pairings 1978-86
1	1-1-2-3	1-1-4-4
2	1-2-2-4	2-2-3-3
3	1-3-3-4	2-2-3-3
4	2-3-4-4	1-1-4-4

Under the common opponent format, schedules of any NFL team are figured according to one of the following three formulas. (The reference point for the figuring is the team's final division standing. Ties for a position in divisions are broken according to the tie-breaking procedures outlined on page 14. The chart on the following page is included for use as you go through each step.)

A. First- through fourth-place teams in a five-team division (AFC East, AFC West, NFC East, NFC Central).

1. Home-and-home round-robin within the division (8 games).
2. One game each with the first- through fourth-place teams in a division of the other conference (4 games). In 1992, the AFC East will play the NFC West, the AFC Central will play the NFC Central, and the AFC West will play the NFC East.
3. The first-place team plays the first-place teams in the other divisions within the conference plus a second- and third-place team within the conference. The second-place team plays the second-place teams in the other divisions within the conference plus a first- and fourth-place team within the conference. The third-place team plays the third-place teams in the other divisions within the conference plus a first- and fourth-place team within the conference. The fourth-place team plays the fourth-place teams in the other divisions within the conference plus a second- and third-place team within the conference (4 games).

This completes the 16-game schedule.

B. First- through fourth-place teams in a four-team division (AFC Central, NFC West).

1. Home-and-home round-robin within the division (6 games).
2. One game with each of the fifth-place teams in the conference (2 games).
3. The same procedure that is listed in step A2 (4 games).
4. The same procedure that is listed in step A3 (4 games).

This completes the 16-game schedule.

C. The fifth-place teams in a division (AFC East, AFC West, NFC East, NFC Central).

1. Home-and-home round-robin within the division (8 games).
2. One game with each team in the four-team division of the conference (4 games).
3. A home-and-home with the other fifth-place team in the conference (2 games).
4. One game each with the fifth-place teams in the other conference (2 games).

This completes the 16-game schedule.

The 1992 Opponent Breakdown chart on the following page does not include the round-robin games within the division. Those are automatically scheduled on a home-and-away basis.

1991 NFL Standings

AFC

EAST AE

1 ________________
2 ________________
3 ________________
4 ________________
5 ________________

CENTRAL AC

1 ________________
2 ________________
3 ________________
4 ________________

WEST AW

1 ________________
2 ________________
3 ________________
4 ________________
5 ________________

NFC

EAST NE

1 ________________
2 ________________
3 ________________
4 ________________
5 ________________

WEST NW

1 ________________
2 ________________
3 ________________
4 ________________

CENTRAL NC

1 ________________
2 ________________
3 ________________
4 ________________
5 ________________

A Team's 1992 Schedule

Team Name ________________

1992 Opponent Breakdown

(Certain game sites for interconference opponents subject to change under NFL scheduling formulas.)

AE — AFC East

Team	Home	Away
AE1	AW1	AC1
	AC2	AW3
	NW2	NW1
	NW4	NW3
AE2	AW2	AC2
	AC4	AW1
	NW1	NW2
	NW3	NW4
AE3	AW3	AC3
	AC1	AW4
	NW2	NW1
	NW4	NW3
AE4	AW4	AC4
	AC3	AW2
	NW1	NW2
	NW3	NW4
AE5	AC1	AC2
	AC3	AC4
	AW5	AW5
	NE5	NC5

AC — AFC Central

Team	Home	Away
AC1	AE1	AW1
	AW2	AE3
	AW5	AE5
	NC2	NC1
	NC4	NC3
AC2	AE2	AW2
	AW4	AE1
	AE5	AW5
	NC1	NC2
	NC3	NC4
AC3	AE3	AW3
	AW1	AE4
	AW5	AE5
	NC2	NC1
	NC4	NC3
AC4	AE4	AW4
	AW3	AE2
	AE5	AW5
	NC1	NC2
	NC3	NC4

AW — AFC West

Team	Home	Away
AW1	AC1	AE1
	AE2	AC3
	NE2	NE1
	NE4	NE3
AW2	AC2	AE2
	AE4	AC1
	NE1	NE2
	NE3	NE4
AW3	AC3	AE3
	AE1	AC4
	NE2	NE1
	NE4	NE3
AW4	AC4	AE4
	AE3	AC2
	NE1	NE2
	NE3	NE4
AW5	AC2	AC1
	AC4	AC3
	AE5	AE5
	NC5	NE5

NE — NFC East

Team	Home	Away
NE1	NC1	NW1
	NW2	NC3
	AW1	AW2
	AW3	AW4
NE2	NC2	NW2
	NW4	NC1
	AW2	AW1
	AW4	AW3
NE3	NC3	NW3
	NW1	NC4
	AW1	AW2
	AW3	AW4
NE4	NC4	NW4
	NW3	NC2
	AW2	AW1
	AW4	AW3
NE5	NW1	NW2
	NW3	NW4
	NC5	NC5
	AW5	AE5

NC — NFC Central

Team	Home	Away
NC1	NW1	NE1
	NE2	NW3
	AC1	AC2
	AC3	AC4
NC2	NW2	NE2
	NE4	NW1
	AC2	AC1
	AC4	AC3
NC3	NW3	NE3
	NE1	NW4
	AC1	AC2
	AC3	AC4
NC4	NW4	NE4
	NE3	NW2
	AC2	AC1
	AC4	AC3
NC5	NW2	NW1
	NW4	NW3
	NE5	NE5
	AE5	AW5

NW — NFC West

Team	Home	Away
NW1	NE1	NC1
	NC2	NE3
	NC5	NE5
	AE1	AE2
	AE3	AE4
NW2	NE2	NC2
	NC4	NE1
	NE5	NC5
	AE2	AE1
	AE4	AE3
NW3	NE3	NC3
	NC1	NE4
	NC5	NE5
	AE1	AE2
	AE3	AE4
NW4	NE4	NC4
	NC3	NE2
	NE5	NC5
	AE2	AE1
	AE4	AE3

AFC ACTIVE STATISTICAL LEADERS

LEADING ACTIVE PASSERS, AMERICAN FOOTBALL CONFERENCE

1,000 or more attempts

	Yrs.	Att.	Comp.	Pct. Comp.	Yards	Avg. Gain	TD	Pct. TD	Had Int.	Pct. Int.	Rate Pts.
Dan Marino, Mia.	8	4181	2480	59.3	31416	7.51	241	5.8	136	3.3	88.5
Jim Kelly, Buff.	5	2088	1251	59.9	15730	7.53	105	5.0	72	3.4	85.8
Boomer Esiason, Cin.	7	2687	1520	56.6	21381	7.96	150	5.6	98	3.6	85.8
Dave Krieg, Sea.	11	3291	1909	58.0	24052	7.31	184	5.6	136	4.1	82.3
Ken O'Brien, N.Y.J.	7	2878	1697	59.0	20444	7.10	109	3.8	78	2.7	82.2
Bernie Kosar, Clev.	6	2363	1364	57.7	16450	6.96	85	3.6	62	2.6	80.3
Warren Moon, Hou.	7	3025	1701	56.2	22989	7.60	134	4.4	112	3.7	79.9
John Elway, Den.	8	3572	1959	54.8	24721	6.92	135	3.8	128	3.6	74.3
Steve DeBerg, K.C.	13	4179	2376	56.9	28490	6.82	166	4.0	175	4.2	73.7
Jay Schroeder, Raiders	6	1801	903	50.1	13683	7.60	79	4.4	72	4.0	73.5
Bubby Brister, Pitt.	5	1171	610	52.1	8035	6.86	40	3.4	43	3.7	70.2
Jack Trudeau, Ind.	5	1186	620	52.3	7365	6.21	35	3.0	46	3.9	65.2
Vince Evans, Raiders	10	1039	506	48.7	6888	6.63	36	3.5	57	5.5	59.0

TOP 10 ACTIVE RUSHERS, AFC

2,000 or more yards

	Yrs.	Att.	Yards	TD
1. Eric Dickerson, Ind.	8	2616	11903	86
2. Marcus Allen, Raiders	9	1960	7957	75
3. Freeman McNeil, N.Y.J.	10	1704	7604	36
4. James Brooks, Cin.	10	1515	7347	47
5. Roger Craig, Raiders	8	1686	7064	50
6. Greg Bell, Raiders	7	1204	4959	51
7. Johnny Hector, N.Y.J.	8	965	3868	41
8. Kevin Mack, Clev.	6	915	3821	31
9. James Jones, Sea.	8	965	3472	23
10. Thurman Thomas, Buff.	3	776	3422	19

Other Leading Rushers

	Yrs.	Att.	Yards	TD
Christian Okoye, K.C.	4	877	3418	25
John L. Williams, Sea.	5	764	3128	9
John Stephens, N.E.	3	753	2809	13
Bo Jackson, Raiders	4	515	2782	16
Albert Bentley, Ind.	6	526	2355	19
Bobby Humphrey, Den.	2	582	2353	14
Merril Hoge, Pitt.	4	562	2106	18

TOP 10 ACTIVE PASS RECEIVERS, AFC

200 or more receptions

	Yrs.	No.	Yards	TD
1. James Lofton, Buff.	13	642	11963	61
2. Stanley Morgan, Ind.	14	557	10716	72
3. Roger Craig, Raiders	8	508	4442	16
4. Drew Hill, Hou.	11	450	7715	53
5. Mark Clayton, Mia.	8	437	6971	66
6. Al Toon, N.Y.J.	6	412	5331	29
7. Marcus Allen, Raiders	9	403	3850	17
8. Mark Duper, Mia.	9	397	7022	47
9. Andre Reed, Buff.	6	388	5353	39
10. Stephone Paige, K.C.	8	368	6230	49

Other Leading Receivers

	Yrs.	No.	Yards	TD
James Brooks, Cin.	10	341	3274	28
Pete Holohan, K.C.	10	330	3698	14
Vance Johnson, Den.	6	322	4506	27
Eddie Brown, Cin.	6	304	5307	39
Louis Lipps, Pitt.	7	303	5347	37
Ernest Givins, Hou.	5	301	4744	26
Bill Brooks, Ind.	5	295	4462	23
James Jones, Sea.	8	287	2348	10
Brian Brennan, Clev.	7	284	3823	18
Willie Gault, Raiders	8	278	5717	36
John L. Williams, Sea.	5	278	2646	12
Freeman McNeil, N.Y.J.	10	272	2751	12
Rodney Holman, Cin.	9	261	3618	30
Jeff Chadwick, Sea.	8	241	3932	21
Webster Slaughter, Clev.	5	241	3928	24
Irving Fryar, N.E.	7	240	3921	31
Reggie Langhorne, Clev.	6	222	3092	13
Eric Dickerson, Ind.	8	220	1725	4
Albert Bentley, Ind.	6	219	2203	8
Eric Sievers, Mia.	10	214	2485	16
Jim Jensen, Mia.	10	208	1988	17

TOP 10 ACTIVE SCORERS, AFC

250 or more points

	Yrs.	TD	FG	PAT	TP
1. Pat Leahy, N.Y.J.	17	0	278	528	1362
2. Nick Lowery, K.C.	12	0	259	375	1152
3. Jim Breech, Cin.	12	0	201	459	1062
4. Gary Anderson, Pitt.	9	0	206	292	910
5. Norm Johnson, Sea.	9	0	159	333	810
6. Scott Norwood, Buff.	6	0	115	215	560
7. Marcus Allen, Raiders	9	93	0	0	558
8. Eric Dickerson, Ind.	8	90	0	0	540
9. Dean Biasucci, Ind.	6	0	103	165	474
10. James Brooks, Cin.	10	75	0	0	450

Other Leading Scorers

	Yrs.	TD	FG	PAT	TP
Stanley Morgan, Ind.	14	73	0	0	438
Mark Clayton, Mia.	8	67	0	0	402
Roger Craig, Raiders	8	66	0	0	396
James Lofton, Buff.	13	62	0	0	372
Greg Bell, Raiders	7	58	0	0	348
Drew Hill, Hou.	11	54	0	0	324
Stephone Paige, K.C.	8	49	0	0	294
Freeman McNeil, N.Y.J.	10	48	0	0	288
Mark Duper, Mia.	9	47	0	0	282
Johnny Hector, N.Y.J.	8	44	0	0	264
Louis Lipps, Pitt.	7	44	0	0	264
Jeff Jaeger, Raiders	3	0	52	107	263

TOP 10 ACTIVE INTERCEPTORS, AFC

20 or more interceptions

	Yrs.	No.	Yards	TD
1. Ronnie Lott, Raiders	10	51	643	5
2. Deron Cherry, K.C.	10	46	657	1
3. Dwayne Woodruff, Pitt.	11	37	689	3
4. Raymond Clayborn, Clev.	14	36	555	1
5. Gill Byrd, S.D.	8	32	410	2
6. Terry Kinard, Hou.	8	31	649	2
Vann McElroy, Sea.	9	31	296	1
8. Roland James, N.E.	11	29	383	0
9. Albert Lewis, K.C.	8	28	247	0
10. Fred Marion, N.E.	9	27	424	1

Other Leading Interceptors

	Yrs.	No.	Yards	TD
Kevin Ross, K.C.	7	26	403	1
David Fulcher, Cin.	5	24	195	1
Ronnie Lippett, N.E.	7	22	393	2
Eugene Daniel, Ind.	7	22	201	1
Lloyd Burruss, K.C.	10	21	426	4
Mark Kelso, Buff.	5	21	306	1
Lionel Washington, Raiders	8	21	249	2

TOP 10 ACTIVE QUARTERBACK SACKERS, AFC

Official statistic since 1982

	No.
1. Jacob Green, Sea.	91.5
2. Greg Townsend, Raiders	82
3. Bruce Smith, Buff.	76.5
4. Andre Tippett, N.E.	76
5. Howie Long, Raiders	66
6. Lee Williams, S.D.	65.5
7. Sean Jones, Hou.	57
8. Ezra Johnson, Hou.	55.5
9. Jeff Bryant, Sea.	54.5
10. Bill Pickel, N.Y.J.	53

Other Leading Sackers

	No.
Karl Mecklenburg, Den.	52
Keith Willis, Pitt.	52

TOP 10 ACTIVE PUNT RETURNERS, AFC

40 or more punt returns

	Yrs.	No.	Yards	Avg.	TD
1. Clarence Verdin, Ind.	5	76	931	12.3	2
2. Louis Lipps, Pitt.	7	107	1212	11.3	3
3. James Brooks, Cin.	10	52	565	10.9	0
4. JoJo Townsell, N.Y.J.	6	127	1360	10.7	2
5. Stanley Morgan, Ind.	14	92	960	10.4	1
6. Irving Fryar, N.E.	7	204	2045	10.0	3
7. Kevin Clark, Den.	3	52	507	9.8	1
8. Scott Schwedes, Mia.	4	80	765	9.6	1
9. Roland James, N.E.	11	42	400	9.5	1
10. Mark Clayton, Mia.	8	52	485	9.3	1

Other Leading Punt Returners

	Yrs.	No.	Yards	Avg.	TD
Vance Johnson, Den.	6	57	515	9.0	0
Paul Skansi, Sea.	8	95	858	9.0	0
Gerald McNeil, Hou.	5	191	1717	9.0	1
Tim Brown, Raiders	3	87	782	9.0	0
Rod Woodson, Pitt.	4	116	1021	8.8	1
Ricky Nattiel, Den.	4	45	378	8.4	0
Nesby Glasgow, Sea.	12	80	651	8.1	1
Brian Brennan, Clev.	7	53	424	8.0	1
Stefon Adams, Raiders	5	43	321	7.5	0
Cliff Hicks, Buff.	4	42	293	7.0	0
Bill Brooks, Ind.	5	43	292	6.8	0

TOP 10 ACTIVE KICKOFF RETURNERS, AFC

40 or more kickoff returns

	Yrs.	No.	Yards	Avg.	TD
1. Ray Clayborn, Clev.	14	57	1538	27.0	3
2. Tim Brown, Raiders	3	44	1161	26.4	1
3. Anthony Miller, S.D.	3	47	1194	25.4	2
4. Rod Woodson, Pitt.	4	121	2886	23.9	2
5. Bobby Humphery, S.D.	7	130	2974	22.9	2
6. Sammy Martin, N.E.	3	80	1834	22.9	1
7. Vance Johnson, Den.	6	45	1027	22.8	0
8. Ron Brown, Raiders	7	187	4237	22.7	4
9. Nesby Glasgow, Sea.	12	85	1906	22.4	0
10. Albert Bentley, Ind.	6	148	3175	21.5	0
Jamie Holland, Raiders	4	111	2385	21.5	1
Tim McGee, Cin.	5	58	1249	21.5	0
Gaston Green, Den.	3	42	905	21.5	1

Other Leading Kickoff Returners

	Yrs.	No.	Yards	Avg.	TD
Marc Logan, Mia.	4	51	1091	21.4	1
James Brooks, Cin.	10	118	2523	21.4	0
Steve Tasker, Buff.	6	42	896	21.3	0
Eric Metcalf, Clev.	2	83	1770	21.3	2
Leonard Harris, Hou.	5	55	1159	21.1	0
Ronnie Harmon, S.D.	5	48	1009	21.0	0
Dwight Stone, Pitt.	4	69	1442	20.9	1
JoJo Townsell, N.Y.J.	6	98	2048	20.9	1
Brent Fullwood, Mia.	4	62	1293	20.9	0
Donnie Elder, S.D.	4	123	2505	20.4	0
Gerald McNeil, Hou.	5	91	1852	20.4	1
Don Smith, Mia.	3	41	831	20.3	0
Stanford Jennings, Cin.	7	136	2752	20.2	1
Drew Hill, Hou.	11	172	3460	20.1	1
Clarence Verdin, Ind.	5	68	1350	19.9	0
Allen Pinkett, Hou.	5	54	1069	19.8	0
Stefon Adams, Raiders	5	65	1240	19.1	0
Terance Mathis, N.Y.J.	1	43	787	18.3	0

TOP 10 ACTIVE PUNTERS, AFC

50 or more punts

	Yrs.	No.	Avg.	LG
1. Rohn Stark, Ind.	9	664	44.1	72
2. Reggie Roby, Mia.	8	466	43.2	77
3. Rick Donnelly, Sea.	5	363	42.2	71
4. Mike Horan, Den.	7	448	42.1	75
5. Brian Hansen, Clev.	6	453	42.0	69
6. Greg Montgomery, Hou.	3	155	41.8	63
7. Lee Johnson, Cin.	6	377	41.0	70
8. Jeff Gossett, Raiders	9	558	40.6	64
9. John Kidd, S.D.	7	507	40.4	67
10. Rick Tuten, Buff.	2	60	39.4	55
Joe Prokop, N.Y.J.	5	304	39.4	76

Other Leading Punters

	Yrs.	No.	Avg.	LG
Bryan Barker, K.C.	1	64	38.7	56
Dan Stryzinski, Pitt.	1	65	37.8	51

NFC ACTIVE STATISTICAL LEADERS

LEADING ACTIVE PASSERS, NATIONAL FOOTBALL CONFERENCE

1,000 or more attempts

	Yrs.	Att.	Comp.	Pct. Comp.	Yards	Avg. Gain	TD	Pct. TD	Had Int.	Pct. Int.	Rate Pts.
Joe Montana, S.F.	12	4579	2914	63.6	34998	7.64	242	5.3	123	2.7	93.4
Jim Everett, Rams	5	2038	1154	56.6	15345	7.53	101	5.0	73	3.6	82.2
Jim McMahon, Phil.	9	1840	1056	57.4	13398	7.28	77	4.2	66	3.6	79.3
Randall Cunningham, Phil.	6	2253	1230	54.6	15399	6.83	107	4.7	71	3.2	78.8
Phil Simms, N.Y.G.	11	3969	2164	54.5	28519	7.19	171	4.3	141	3.6	77.0
Don Majkowski, G.B.	4	1326	736	55.5	9237	6.97	51	3.8	46	3.5	75.7
Wade Wilson, Minn.	9	1543	857	55.5	11310	7.33	63	4.1	65	4.2	75.0
Chris Miller, Atl.	4	1357	725	53.4	8879	6.54	45	3.3	45	3.3	71.1
Vinny Testaverde, T.B.	4	1476	754	51.1	10272	6.96	55	3.7	81	5.5	63.2

TOP 10 ACTIVE RUSHERS, NFC

2,000 or more yards

	Yrs.	Att.	Yards	TD
1. Ottis Anderson, N.Y.G.	12	2499	10101	80
2. Gerald Riggs, Wash.	9	1911	7940	58
3. James Wilder, Det.	10	1586	6008	37
4. Herschel Walker, Minn.	5	1155	4827	36
5. Earnest Byner, Wash.	7	1103	4512	36
6. Neal Anderson, Chi.	5	947	4191	36
7. Mike Rozier, Atl.	6	1063	4101	30
8. Randall Cunningham, Phil.	6	486	3437	23
9. Rueben Mayes, N.O.	4	837	3408	23
10. Dalton Hilliard, N.O.	5	882	3302	30

Other Leading Rushers

	Yrs.	Att.	Yards	TD
Gary Anderson, T.B.	5	714	2896	14
Barry Sanders, Det.	2	535	2774	27
Mosi Tatupu, Rams	13	612	2415	18
Anthony Toney, Phil.	5	639	2294	14
Alfred Anderson, Minn.	7	600	2256	21
Keith Byars, Phil.	5	615	2113	15

TOP 10 ACTIVE PASS RECEIVERS, NFC

200 or more receptions

	Yrs.	No.	Yards	TD
1. Art Monk, Wash.	11	730	9935	52
2. Roy Green, Phx.	12	522	8496	66
3. Mickey Shuler, Phil.	13	456	5009	37
4. Jerry Rice, S.F.	6	446	7866	79
5. James Wilder, Det.	10	431	3500	10
6. Henry Ellard, Rams	8	421	7037	40
7. Gary Clark, Wash.	6	415	6940	43
8. Ottis Anderson, N.Y.G.	12	365	3021	5
9. Mike Quick, Phil.	9	363	6464	61
10. Steve Jordan, Minn.	9	354	4710	23

Other Leading Receivers

	Yrs.	No.	Yards	TD
Eric Martin, N.O.	6	332	5060	36
Anthony Carter, Minn.	6	326	5728	40
Earnest Byner, Wash.	7	289	2771	11
Mark Bavaro, N.Y.G.	6	266	3722	28
Herschel Walker, Minn.	5	264	2795	11
Ricky Sanders, Wash.	5	260	3929	24
Keith Byars, Phil.	5	253	2466	8
Don Warren, Wash.	12	235	2460	7
Gary Anderson, T.B.	5	232	2442	14
Hoby Brenner, N.O.	10	228	3338	20
Mark Carrier, T.B.	4	218	3628	21
Sterling Sharpe, G.B.	3	212	3319	19
Stacey Bailey, Rams	9	206	3422	18
Tom Rathman, S.F.	5	206	1775	4
Gerald Riggs, Wash.	9	200	1511	0

TOP 10 ACTIVE SCORERS, NFC

250 or more points

	Yrs.	TD	FG	PAT	TP
1. Eddie Murray, Det.	11	0	225	341	1016
2. Matt Bahr, N.Y.G.	12	0	199	378	975
3. Morten Andersen, N.O.	9	0	192	276	852
4. Rich Karlis, Atl.	9	0	172	283	799
5. Kevin Butler, Chi.	6	0	134	231	633
6. Tony Zendejas, Rams	6	0	117	197	548
7. Al Del Greco, Phx.	7	0	101	221	524
8. Ottis Anderson, N.Y.G.	12	85	0	0	510
9. Jerry Rice, S.F.	6	83	0	0	498
10. Donald Igwebuike, Minn.	6	0	108	153	477

Other Leading Scorers

	Yrs.	TD	FG	PAT	TP
Roy Green, Phx.	12	69	0	0	414
Fuad Reveiz, Minn.	5	0	66	187	385
Mike Cofer, S.F.	4	0	81	133	376
Mike Quick, Phil.	9	61	0	0	366
Chip Lohmiller, Wash.	3	0	78	122	356
Gerald Riggs, Wash.	9	58	0	0	348
Roger Ruzek, Phil.	4	0	68	126	330
Art Monk, Wash.	11	52	0	0	312
Greg Davis, Phx.	4	0	67	96	297
Earnest Byner, Wash.	7	48	0	0	288
Herschel Walker, Minn.	5	48	0	0	288
Neal Anderson, Chi.	5	47	0	0	282
James Wilder, Det.	10	47	0	0	282
Henry Ellard, Rams	8	44	0	0	264
Gary Clark, Wash.	6	43	0	0	258

TOP 10 ACTIVE INTERCEPTORS, NFC

20 or more interceptions

	Yrs.	No.	Yards	TD
1. Everson Walls, N.Y.G.	10	50	471	1
2. Dave Waymer, S.F.	11	44	459	0
3. Joey Browner, Minn.	8	32	368	3
4. Mark Lee, G.B.	11	31	249	0
6. Felix Wright, Minn.	6	26	469	2
7. Jerry Holmes, G.B.	9	24	306	2
Scott Case, Atl.	7	24	229	1
Darrell Green, Wash.	8	24	214	2
10. Carl Lee, Minn.	8	23	309	2
Harry Hamilton, T.B.	7	23	300	0

Other Leading Interceptors

	Yrs.	No.	Yards	TD
Wes Hopkins, Phil.	7	21	209	1
Cedric Mack, Phx.	8	20	178	0
Tim McKyer, Atl.	5	20	102	1

TOP 10 ACTIVE QUARTERBACK SACKERS, NFC

Official statistic since 1982

	No.
1. Lawrence Taylor, N.Y.G.	114.5
2. Reggie White, Phil.	95
3. Richard Dent, Chi.	93
4. Dexter Manley, Phx.	91
5. Rickey Jackson, N.O.	78.5
6. Steve McMichael, Chi.	67
7. Jim Jeffcoat, Dall.	66
8. Charles Mann, Wash.	65
9. Leonard Marshall, N.Y.G.	64.5
10. Mike Cofer, Det.	59.5
Kevin Greene, Rams	59.5

Other Leading Sackers

	No.
Charles Haley, S.F.	56.5
Tim Harris, G.B.	55
Chris Doleman, Minn.	54.5
Keith Millard, Minn.	53
Freddie Joe Nunn, Phx.	49
Pat Swilling, N.O.	49
Keith Ferguson, Det.	47

TOP 10 ACTIVE PUNT RETURNERS, NFC

40 or more punt returns

	Yrs.	No.	Yards	Avg.	TD
1. David Meggett, N.Y.G.	2	89	1049	11.8	2
2. Mel Gray, Det.	5	94	1094	11.6	1
3. Henry Ellard, Rams	8	133	1509	11.3	4
4. Vai Sikahema, G.B.	5	193	2152	11.2	3
John Taylor, S.F.	4	107	1194	11.2	2
6. Darrell Green, Wash.	8	50	549	11.0	0
7. Deion Sanders, Atl.	2	57	557	9.8	2
Darryl Henley, Rams	2	47	461	9.8	0
9. Leo Lewis, Minn.	10	171	1643	9.6	1
10. Walter Stanley, Wash.	6	147	1392	9.5	1

Other Leading Punt Returners

	Yrs.	No.	Yards	Avg.	TD
Jeff Query, G.B.	2	62	555	9.0	0
Don Griffin, S.F.	5	68	598	8.8	1
Kelvin Martin, Dall.	4	75	654	8.7	0
Ron Pitts, G.B.	5	50	436	8.7	2
Willie Drewrey, T.B.	6	106	900	8.5	0
Eric Martin, N.O.	6	46	368	8.0	0
Rod Harris, Phil.	2	55	410	7.5	0

TOP 10 ACTIVE KICKOFF RETURNERS, NFC

40 or more kickoff returns

	Yrs.	No.	Yards	Avg.	TD
1. Mel Gray, Det.	5	158	3751	23.7	1
2. Herschel Walker, Minn.	5	57	1340	23.5	1
3. Dennis Gentry, Chi.	9	163	3796	23.3	3
4. James Dixon, Dall.	2	83	1917	23.1	1
5. Roy Green, Phx.	12	84	1932	23.0	1
6. Gene Atkins, N.O.	4	51	1140	22.4	0
7. David Meggett, N.Y.G.	2	48	1069	22.3	0
8. Joe Howard, Wash.	2	43	949	22.1	1
9. Vai Sikahema, G.B.	5	164	3501	21.3	0
Deion Sanders, Atl.	2	74	1576	21.3	0

Other Leading Kickoff Returners

	Yrs.	No.	Yards	Avg.	TD
Willie Drewrey, T.B.	6	75	1558	20.8	0
Robert Delpino, Rams	3	51	1056	20.7	0
Gary Anderson, T.B.	5	65	1340	20.6	1
Herman Fontenot, G.B.	6	50	997	19.9	0
Alfred Anderson, Minn.	7	41	796	19.4	0
Thomas Sanders, Phil.	6	94	1796	19.1	1
Mark Lee, G.B.	11	45	859	19.1	0
Dexter Carter, S.F.	1	41	783	19.1	0
Walter Stanley, Wash.	6	60	1129	18.8	0
Terrence Flagler, Phx.	4	45	841	18.7	0
Vince Workman, G.B.	2	47	757	16.1	0

TOP 10 ACTIVE PUNTERS, NFC

50 or more punts

	Yrs.	No.	Avg.	LG
1. Sean Landeta, N.Y.G.	6	376	43.4	71
2. Rich Camarillo, Phx.	10	651	42.5	76
3. Jim Arnold, Det.	8	608	42.2	69
4. Harry Newsome, Minn.	6	453	41.6	64
5. Tommy Barnhardt, N.O.	4	157	41.5	65
6. Maury Buford, Chi.	8	508	41.4	71
7. Mike Saxon, Dall.	6	473	41.2	63
8. Scott Fulhage, Atl.	4	250	40.9	65
9. Mark Royals, T.B.	2	83	40.2	62
10. John Teltschik, Phil.	4	345	40.1	70

Other Leading Punters

	Yrs.	No.	Avg.	LG
Kelly Goodburn, Wash.	4	230	40.0	59
Don Bracken, G.B.	6	368	39.7	65
Jeff Feagles, Phil.	3	226	39.4	74
Keith English, Rams	1	68	39.2	58
Barry Helton, S.F.	3	202	38.8	56

NFL Passer Rating System

The NFL rates its forward passers for statistical purposes against a pre-fixed performance standard based on statistical achievements of all qualified pro passers since 1960. The system now being used replaced one that rated passers in relation to their position in a total group based on various criteria. The current system, which was adopted in 1973, removes inequities that existed in the former method and, at the same time, provides a means of comparing passing performances from one season to the next.

It is important to remember that the system is used to rate **passers,** not **quarterbacks.** Statistics do not reflect leadership, play-calling, and other intangible factors that go into making a successful professional quarterback. Four categories are used as a basis for compiling a rating:

—Percentage of touchdown passes per attempt
—Percentage of completions per attempt
—Percentage of interceptions per attempt
—Average yards gained per attempt

The base, or **average** standard, is 1.000. The bottom is .000. To earn a 2.000 rating, a passer must perform at exceptional levels, i.e., 70 percent in completions, 10 percent in touchdowns, 1.5 percent in interceptions, and 11 yards average gain per pass attempt. The **maximum** a passer can receive in any category is 2.375.

For example, to gain a 2.375 in completion percentage, a passer would have to complete 77.5 percent of his passes. The NFL record is 70.55 by Ken Anderson (Cincinnati, 1982). To gain 2.375 in percentage of interceptions, a passer would have to go the entire season without an interception. The 2.375 figure in average yards is 12.50, compared with the NFL record of 11.17 by Tommy O'Connell (Cleveland, 1957). To earn a 2.375 in percentage of touchdowns, a passer would have to achieve an 11.9. The record is 13.9 by Sid Luckman (Chicago, 1943).

In order to make the rating more understandable, the point rating is then converted into a scale of 100. For instance, if a passer completes 11 of 23 passes for 114 yards, with one touchdown and no interceptions, the four components would be:

—**Percentage of Completions**—11 of 23 is 47.8 percent. The point rating is 0.890.

—**Percentage of Touchdown Passes**—1 touchdown in 23 attempts works out to 4.3 percent for a rating of 0.860.

—**Percentage of Interceptions**—You can't do better than zero, so the passer receives a maximum rating of 2.375.

—**Average Yards Gained Per Attempt**—23 attempts divided into 114 yards equals 4.96 yards per attempt for a corresponding rating of 0.490.

The sum of the four components is 4.615, which converts to a rating of 76.9. In order for a passer to achieve 100, his points would have to total 6.000. In rare cases, where statistical performance has been superior, it is possible for a passer to go over 100. However, such an instance is rare. The leading passers each year were checked from 1932 when the NFL began keeping official statistics, and only 11 passers in history have scored over 100 in the year they led the league in passing. The most recent passer to lead the league and score over 100 was Buffalo quarterback Jim Kelly, who achieved a 101.2 rating in 1990.

Active Coaches' Career Records (Order Based on Career Victories)

Start of 1991 Season

Coach	Team(s)	Regular Season					Postseason				Career			
		Yrs.	Won	Lost	Tied	Pct.	Won	Lost	Tied	Pct.	Won	Lost	Tied	Pct.
Don Shula	Baltimore Colts, Miami Dolphins	28	281	123	6	.693	17	14	0	.548	298	137	6	.683
Chuck Noll	Pittsburgh Steelers	22	186	139	1	.572	16	8	0	.667	202	147	1	.579
Chuck Knox	Los Angeles Rams, Buffalo Bills, Seattle Seahawks	18	164	105	1	.609	7	11	0	.389	171	116	1	.595
Joe Gibbs	Washington Redskins	10	101	51	0	.664	12	4	0	.750	113	55	0	.673
Mike Ditka	Chicago Bears	9	90	46	0	.662	6	5	0	.545	96	51	0	.653
Dan Reeves	Denver Broncos	10	90	61	1	.595	6	5	0	.545	96	66	1	.590
Marv Levy	Kansas City Chiefs, Buffalo Bills	10	74	69	0	.517	3	3	0	.500	77	72	0	.517
John Robinson	Los Angeles Rams	8	72	55	0	.567	4	6	0	.400	76	61	0	.555
Marty Schottenheimer	Cleveland Browns, Kansas City Chiefs	7	63	39	1	.617	2	5	0	.286	65	44	1	.595
Sam Wyche	Cincinnati Bengals	7	58	53	0	.523	3	2	0	.600	61	55	0	.526
Ron Meyer	New England Patriots, Indianapolis Colts	8	54	45	0	.545	0	2	0	.000	54	47	0	.535
Jack Pardee	Chicago Bears, Washington Redskins, Houston Oilers	7	53	53	0	.500	0	2	0	.000	53	55	0	.491
Jerry Burns	Minnesota Vikings	5	44	35	0	.557	3	3	0	.500	47	38	0	.553
Jim Mora	New Orleans Saints	5	46	33	0	.582	0	2	0	.000	46	35	0	.568
Jerry Glanville	Houston Oilers, Atlanta Falcons	6	38	43	0	.469	2	3	0	.400	40	46	0	.465
Dan Henning	Atlanta Falcons, San Diego Chargers	6	34	61	1	.359	0	0	0	.000	34	61	1	.359
George Seifert	San Francisco 49ers	2	28	4	0	.875	4	1	0	.800	32	5	0	.865
Lindy Infante	Green Bay Packers	3	20	28	0	.417	0	0	0	.000	20	28	0	.417
Art Shell	Los Angeles Raiders	2	19	9	0	.679	1	1	0	.500	20	10	0	.667
Wayne Fontes	Detroit Lions	2	15	22	0	.405	0	0	0	.000	15	22	0	.405
Jimmy Johnson	Dallas Cowboys	2	8	24	0	.250	0	0	0	.000	8	24	0	.250
Bruce Coslet	New York Jets	1	6	10	0	.375	0	0	0	.000	6	10	0	.375
Joe Bugel	Phoenix Cardinals	1	5	11	0	.313	0	0	0	.000	5	11	0	313
Richard Williamson	Tampa Bay Buccaneers	1	1	2	0	.333	0	0	0	.000	1	2	0	.333
Bill Belichick	Cleveland Browns	0	0	0	0	.000	0	0	0	.000	0	0	0	.000
Ray Handley	New York Giants	0	0	0	0	.000	0	0	0	.000	0	0	0	.000
Rich Kotite	Philadelphia Eagles	0	0	0	0	.000	0	0	0	.000	0	0	0	.000
Dick MacPherson	New England Patriots	0	0	0	0	.000	0	0	0	.000	0	0	0	.000

Coaches With 100 Career Victories (Order Based on Career Victories)

Start of 1991 Season

Coach	Team(s)	Regular Season					Postseason				Career			
		Yrs.	Won	Lost	Tied	Pct.	Won	Lost	Tied	Pct.	Won	Lost	Tied	Pct.
George Halas	Chicago Bears	40	319	148	31	.672	6	3	0	.667	325	151	31	.672
Don Shula	Baltimore Colts, Miami Dolphins	28	281	123	6	.693	17	14	0	.548	298	137	6	.683
Tom Landry	Dallas Cowboys	29	250	162	6	.605	20	16	0	.556	270	178	6	.601
Earl (Curly) Lambeau	Green Bay Packers, Chicago Cardinals, Washington Redskins	33	226	132	22	.624	3	2	0	.600	229	134	22	.623
Chuck Noll	Pittsburgh Steelers	22	186	139	1	.572	16	8	0	.667	202	147	1	.579
Chuck Knox	Los Angeles Rams, Buffalo Bills, Seattle Seahawks	18	164	105	1	.609	7	11	0	.389	171	116	1	.595
Paul Brown	Cleveland Browns, Cincinnati Bengals	21	166	100	6	.621	4	8	0	.333	170	108	6	.609
Bud Grant	Minnesota Vikings	18	158	96	5	.620	10	12	0	.455	168	108	5	.607
Steve Owen	New York Giants	23	151	100	17	.595	2	8	0	.200	153	108	17	.581
Hank Stram	Kansas City Chiefs, New Orleans Saints	17	131	97	10	.571	5	3	0	.625	136	100	10	.573
Weeb Ewbank	Baltimore Colts, New York Jets	20	130	129	7	.502	4	1	0	.800	134	130	7	.507
Sid Gillman	Los Angeles Rams, Los Angeles-San Diego Chargers, Houston Oilers	18	122	99	7	.550	1	5	0	.167	123	104	7	.541
George Allen	Los Angeles Rams, Washington Redskins	12	116	47	5	.705	2	7	0	.222	118	54	5	.681
Don Coryell	St. Louis Cardinals, San Diego Chargers	14	111	83	1	.572	3	6	0	.333	114	89	1	.561
Joe Gibbs	Washington Redskins	10	101	51	0	.664	12	4	0	.750	113	55	0	.673
John Madden	Oakland Raiders	10	103	32	7	.750	9	7	0	.563	112	39	7	.731
Ray (Buddy) Parker	Chicago Cardinals, Detroit Lions, Pittsburgh Steelers	15	104	75	9	.577	3	1	0	.750	107	76	9	.581
Vince Lombardi	Green Bay Packers, Washington Redskins	10	96	34	6	.728	9	1	0	.900	105	35	6	.740
Bill Walsh	San Francisco 49ers	10	92	59	1	.609	10	4	0	.714	102	63	1	.617

DRAFT LIST FOR 1991

56th Annual NFL Draft, April 21-22, 1991

Atlanta Falcons (Drafted alternately 3-6-5-4)

1. Bruce Pickens—3, DB, Nebraska
   Mike Pritchard—13, WR, Colorado, from Indianapolis
2. Brett Favre—33, QB, Southern Mississippi
3. Choice to Miami
4. Moe Gardner—87, NT, Illinois
5. James Goode—114, LB, Oklahoma
6. Erric Pegram—145, RB, North Texas State
7. Brian Mitchell—172, DB, Brigham Young
   Mark Tucker—186, C, Southern California, from Seattle
8. Randy Austin—199, TE, UCLA
9. Ernie Logan—226, DE, East Carolina
10. Walter Sutton—256, WR, Southwest Minnesota
    Pete Lucas—258, T, Wisconsin-Stevens Point, from Detroit
11. Joe Sims—283, NT, Nebraska
12. Bob Christian—310, RB, Northwestern

Buffalo Bills (Drafted 27th)

1. Henry Jones—26, DB, Illinois
2. Phil Hansen—54, DE, North Dakota State
3. Darryl Wren—82, DB, Pittsburg, Kan.
4. Choice to Dallas through New England
5. Shawn Wilbourn—138, DB, Long Beach State
6. Millard Hamilton—166, WR, Clark
7. Amir Rasul—194, RB, Florida A&M
8. Brad Lamb—222, WR, Anderson, Ind.
9. Mark Maddox—249, LB, Northern Michigan
10. Tony De Lorenzo—277, G, New Mexico State
11. Dean Kirkland—305, G, Washington
12. Stephen Clark—333, TE, Texas

Chicago Bears (Drafted alternately 23-22)

1. Stan Thomas—22, T, Texas
2. Chris Zorich—49, DT, Notre Dame
3. Chris Gardocki—78, P-K, Clemson
4. Joe Johnson—105, DB, North Carolina State
5. Anthony Morgan—134, WR, Tennessee
6. Darren Lewis—161, RB, Texas A&M
7. Paul Justin—190, QB, Arizona State
8. Larry Horton—217, DB, Texas A&M
9. Mike Stonebreaker—245, LB, Notre Dame
10. Tom Backes—272, DE, Oklahoma
11. Stacy Long—301, G, Clemson
12. John Cook—328, DT, Washington

Cincinnati Bengals (Drafted alternately 19-18-17-16)

1. Alfred Williams—18, LB, Colorado
2. Choice to San Francisco
   Lamar Rogers—52, DT, Auburn, from Miami through San Francisco
3. Bob Dahl—72, DT, Notre Dame
4. Donald Hollas—99, QB, Rice
   Rob Carpenter—109, WR, Syracuse, from San Francisco
5. Mike Arthur—130, C, Texas A&M
6. Richard Fain—157, DB, Florida
7. Fernandus Vinson—184, DB, North Carolina State
8. Mike Dingle—211, RB, South Carolina
9. Shane Garrett—241, WR, Texas A&M
10. Jim Lavin—268, G, Georgia Tech
11. Chris Smith—295, TE, Brigham Young
12. Antoine Bennett—322, DB, Florida A&M

Cleveland Browns (Drafted 2nd)

1. Eric Turner—2, DB, UCLA
2. Ed King—29, G, Auburn
3. James Jones—57, NT, Northern Iowa
4. Pio Sagapolutele—85, NT, San Diego State
5. Choice to Miami
6. Michael Jackson—141, WR, Southern Mississippi
7. Chioce to Green Bay
8. Frank Conover—197, DT, Syracuse
9. Raymond Irvin—225, DB, Central Florida
   Shawn Wiggins—239, WR, Wyoming, from Seattle
10. Brian Greenfield—252, P, Pittsburgh
11. Todd Jones—280, G, Henderson, Ark.
12. Elijah Austin—308, NT, North Carolina State

Dallas Cowboys (Drafted alternately 13-14)

1. Russell Maryland—1, DT, Miami, from New England
   Alvin Harper—12, WR, Tennessee
   Kelvin Pritchett—20, DT, Mississippi, from Washington
2. Dixon Edwards—37, LB, Michigan State, from Detroit
   Choice to New England
3. Godfrey Myles—62, LB, Florida, from San Diego
   James Richards—64, G, California, from Detroit
   Choice to Minnesota
   Eric Williams—70, T, Central State, Ohio, from New Orleans
4. Curvin Richards—97, RB, Pittsburgh
   Bill Musgrave—106, QB, Oregon, from Kansas City
   Tony Hill—108, DE, Tennessee-Chattanooga, from Miami through Washington and Detroit
   Kevin Harris—110, DE, Texas Southern, from Buffalo through New England
5. Choice to New England through Los Angeles Raiders
   Darrick Brownlow—132, LB, Illinois, from Washington
6. Mike Sullivan—153, G, Miami
7. Leon Lett—173, DT, Emporia State, from Denver
   Choice to Minnesota through Los Angeles Raiders
8. Choice to Phoenix
9. Damon Mays—235, WR, Missouri
10. Sean Love—264, G, Penn State
11. Tony Boles—291, RB, Michigan
12. Larry Brown—320, DB, Texas Christian

Denver Broncos (Drafted alternately 4-3-6-5)

1. Mike Croel—4, LB, Nebraska
2. Reggie Johnson—30, TE, Florida State
3. Keith Traylor—61, LB, Central State, Okla.
4. Choice to Pittsburgh through New England
   Derek Russell—89, WR, Arkansas, from Los Angeles Rams
5. Greg Lewis—115, RB, Washington
6. Nick Subis—142, T, San Diego State
7. Choice to Dallas
8. Kenny Walker—200, DE, Nebraska
9. Don Gibson—227, NT, Southern California
10. Curtis Mayfield—253, WR, Oklahoma State
11. Shawn Moore—284, QB, Virginia
12. Choice to Los Angeles Rams

Detroit Lions (Drafted alternately 11-10-9-8-7-12)

1. Herman Moore—10, WR, Virginia
2. Choice to Dallas
3. Reggie Barrett—58, WR, Texas-El Paso, from Los Angeles Rams
   Choice to Dallas
4. Kevin Scott—91, DB, Stanford
5. Scott Conover—118, G, Purdue
6. Richie Andrews—151, K, Florida State
7. Franklin Thomas—178, TE, Grambling
8. Cedric Jackson—205, RB, Texas Christian
9. Darryl Milburn—231, DE, Grambling
10. Choice to Atlanta
11. Slip Watkins—285, KR, Louisiana State
12. Zeno Alexander—318, LB, Arizona

Green Bay Packers (Drafted alternately 9-8-7-12-11-10)

1. Choice to Philadelphia
   Vinnie Clark—19, DB, Ohio State, from Philadelphia
2. Esera Tuaolo—35, NT, Oregon State
3. Choice to N.Y. Jets
   Don Davey—67, DE, Wisconsin, from New York Jets
   Chuck Webb—81, RB, Tennessee, from San Francisco
4. Choice to San Francisco
5. Choice to San Francisco
   Jeff Fite—135, P, Memphis State, from Miami
6. Walter Dean—149, RB, Grambling
   Joe Garten—164, C, Colorado, from Miami
7. Frank Blevins—169, LB, Oklahoma, from Cleveland
   Reggie Burnette—176, LB, Houston
8. Johnny Walker—203, WR, Texas
9. Dean Witkowski—229, LB, North Dakota
10. Rapier Porter—262, TE, Arkansas-Pine Bluff
11. J.J. Wierenga—289, DE, Central Michigan
12. Linzy Collins—316, WR, Missouri

Houston Oilers (Drafted alternately 18-17-16-19)

1. Choice to Washington through New England and Dallas
2. Mike Dumas—28, DB, Indiana, from New England
   Darryl Lewis—38, DB, Arizona, from Minnesota through Dallas
   John Flannery—44, C, Syracuse
3. Steve Jackson—71, DB, Purdue
   Kevin Donnalley—79, T, North Carolina, from Miami
4. David Rocker—101, DT, Auburn, from Seattle through New England
   Marcus Robertson—102, DB, Iowa State
5. Gary Wellman—129, WR, Southern California
6. Choice to Philadelphia
7. Kyle Freeman—183, LB, Angelo State
8. Gary Brown—214, RB, Penn State
9. Shawn Jefferson—240, WR, Central Florida
10. Curtis Moore—267, LB, Kansas
11. James Smith—294, DB, Richmond
12. Alex Johnson—325, WR, Miami

Indianapolis Colts (Drafted alternately 14-13)

1. Choice to Atlanta
2. Shane Curry—40, DE, Miami
3. Dave McCloughan—69, DB, Colorado
4. Mark Vander Poel—96, T, Colorado
5. Kerry Cash—125, TE, Texas
6. Mel Agee—152, DT, Illinois
7. James Bradley—181, WR, Michigan State
8. Tim Bruton—208, TE, Missouri
9. Howard Griffith—236, RB, Illinois
10. Frank Giannetti—263, DE, Penn State
11. Jerry Crafts—292, T, Louisville
12. Rob Luedeke—319, C, Penn State

Kansas City Chiefs (Drafted alternately 22-23)

1. Harvey Williams—21, RB, Louisiana State
2. Joe Valerio—50, T, Pennsylvania
3. Tim Barnett—77, WR, Jackson State
4. Choice to Dallas
5. Charles Mincy—133, DB, Washington
6. Darrell Malone—162, DB, Jacksonville State
7. Bernard Ellison—189, DB, Nevada-Reno
8. Tom Dohring—218, T, Michigan
9. Robbie Keen—244, K, California
10. Eric Ramsey—273, DB, Auburn
11. Bobby Olive—300, WR, Ohio State
12. Ron Shipley—329, G, New Mexico

Los Angeles Raiders (Drafted alternately 25-24)

1. Todd Marinovich—24, QB, Southern California
2. Nick Bell—43, RB, Iowa, from Seattle
   Choice to Seattle
3. Choice to Tampa Bay
4. Raghib Ismail—100, WR, Notre Dame, from Pittsburgh through New England
   Choice to Los Angeles Rams
5. Choice to Tampa Bay
6. Nolan Harrison—146, DT, Indiana, from Minnesota
   Choice to Minnesota
7. Choice to San Diego
8. Brian Jones—213, LB, Texas, from Seattle
   Todd Woulard—219, LB, Alabama A&M
9. Tahaun Lewis—247, DB, Nebraska
10. Andrew Glover—274, TE, Grambling
11. Choice to New England through San Diego
12. Dennis Johnson—330, WR, Winston-Salem State

Los Angeles Rams (Drafted alternately 5-4-3-6)

1. Todd Lyght—5, DB, Notre Dame
2. Roman Phifer—31, LB, UCLA
3. Choice to Detroit
4. Choice to Denver
   Robert Bailey—107, DB, Miami, from Los Angeles Raiders
5. Robert Young—116, DE, Mississippi State
6. Neal Fort—143, T, Brigham Young
7. Tyrone Shelton—170, RB, William & Mary
8. Pat Tyrance—201, LB, Nebraska
9. Jeff Fields—228, NT, Arkansas State
10. Choice to San Diego
11. Terry Crews—281, LB, Western Michigan
12. Jeff Pahukoa—311, T, Washington, from Denver
    Ernie Thompson—312, RB, Indiana

Miami Dolphins (Drafted alternately 24-25)

1. Randal Hill—23, WR, Miami
2. Choice to Cincinnati through San Francisco
3. Aaron Craver—60, RB, Fresno State, from Atlanta
   Choice to Houston
4. Choice to Dallas through Washington and Detroit
5. Bryan Cox—113, LB, Western Illinois, from Cleveland
   Gene Williams—121, G, Iowa State, from New York Jets through Green Bay
   Choice to Green Bay
6. Choice to Green Bay
7. Chris Green—191, DB, Illinois
8. Roland Smith—220, DB, Miami
9. Scott Miller—246, WR, UCLA
10. Michael Titley—275, TE, Iowa
11. Ernie Rogers—302, G, California
12. Joe Brunson—331, DT, Tennessee-Chattanooga

Minnesota Vikings (Drafted alternately 12-11-10-9-8-7)

1. Choice to New England through Dallas
2. Choice to Houston through Dallas
3. Carlos Jenkins—65, LB, Michigan State
   Jake Reed—68, WR, Grambling, from Dallas
4. Randy Baldwin—92, RB, Mississippi
5. Chris Thome—119, C, Minnesota
6. Choice to Los Angeles Raiders
   Todd Scott—163, DB, Southwestern Louisiana, from Los Angeles Raiders
7. Scotty Reagan—179, DT, Humboldt State
   Tripp Welborne—180, DB, Michigan, from Dallas through Los Angeles Raiders
8. Reggie Johnson—206, DE, Arizona
9. Gerald Hudson—232, RB, Oklahoma State
10. Brady Pierce—259, T, Wisconsin
11. Ivan Caesar—286, LB, Boston College
12. Darren Hughes—313, WR, Carson-Newman

New England Patriots (Drafted 1st)

1. Choice to Dallas
   Pat Harlow—11, T, Southern California, from Minnesota through Dallas
   Leonard Russell—14, RB, Arizona State, from New Orleans through Dallas
2. Choice to Houston
   Jerome Henderson—41, DB, Clemson, from Dallas
3. Calvin Stephens—56, G, South Carolina
4. Scott Zolak—84, QB, Maryland
5. Jon Vaughn—112, RB, Michigan
   Ben Coates—124, TE, Livingstone, from Dallas through Los Angeles Raiders
6. David Key—140, DB, Michigan
7. Blake Miller—168, C, Louisiana State
8. Harry Colon—196, DB, Missouri
9. O'Neil Glenn—224, G, Maryland
10. Randy Bethel—251, TE, Miami
11. Vince Moore—279, WR, Tennessee
    Paul Alsbury—303, P, Southwest Texas State, from Los Angeles Raiders through San Diego
12. Tim Edwards—307, DT, Delta State

New Orleans Saints (Drafted 15th)

1. Choice to New England through Dallas
2. Wesley Carroll—42, WR, Miami
3. Choice to Dallas
4. Choice to Seattle through Los Angeles Raiders
5. Reginald Jones—126, DB, Memphis State
6. Fred McAfee—154, RB, Mississippi College
7. Hayward Haynes—182, G, Florida State
8. Frank Wainright—210, TE, Northern Colorado
9. Anthony Wallace—237, RB, California
10. Choice to Tampa Bay
11. Scott Ross—293, LB, Southern California
12. Mark Drabczak—321, G, Minnesota

New York Giants (Drafted 28th)

1. Jarrod Bunch—27, RB, Michigan
2. Kanavis McGhee—55, LB, Colorado
3. Ed McCaffrey—83, WR, Stanford
4. Clarence Jones—111, T, Maryland
5. Anthony Moss—139, LB, Florida State
6. Corey Miller—167, LB, South Carolina
7. Simmie Carter—195, DB, Southern Mississippi
8. Lamar McGriggs—223, DB, Western Illinois
9. Jerry Bouldin—250, WR, Mississippi State
10. Luis Cristobal—278, G, Miami
11. Ted Popson—306, TE, Portland State
12. Larry Wanke—334, QB, John Carroll

New York Jets (Drafted alternately 8-7-12-11-10-9)

1. Choice exercised in 1990 Supplemental Draft for Rob Moore, WR, Syracuse
2. Browning Nagle—34, QB, Louisville
3. Morris Lewis—63, LB, Georgia, from Green Bay
   Chioce to Green Bay
4. Mark Gunn—94, DT, Pittsburgh
5. Choice to Miami through Green Bay
6. Blaise Bryant—148, RB, Iowa State
   Mike Riley—160, DB, Tulane, from Philadelphia
7. Doug Parrish—175, DB, San Francisco State
8. Tim James—202, DB, Colorado
9. Paul Glonek—234, DT, Arizona
10. Al Baker—261, RB, Kentucky
11. Rocen Keeton—288, LB, UCLA
12. Mark Hayes—315, T, Arizona State

Philadelphia Eagles (Drafted alternately 20-21)

1. Antone Davis—8, T, Tennessee, from Green Bay
   Choice to Green Bay
2. Jesse Campbell—48, DB, North Carolina State
3. Rob Selby—75, T, Auburn
4. William Thomas—104, LB, Texas A&M
5. Craig Erickson—131, QB, Miami
6. Andy Harmon—156, DE, Kent State, from Houston
   Choice to New York Jets
7. James Joseph—187, RB, Auburn
8. Scott Kowalkowski—216, LB, Notre Dame
9. Chuck Weatherspoon—242, RB, Houston
10. Eric Harmon—271, G, Clemson
11. Mike Flores—298, DE, Louisville
12. Darrell Beavers—327, DB, Morehead State

Phoenix Cardinals (Drafted alternately 6-5-4-3)

1. Eric Swann—6, DE, No College
2. Mike Jones—32, DE, North Carolina State
3. Aeneas Williams—59, DB, Southern University
4. Dexter Davis—86, DB, Clemson
5. Vance Hammond—117, DT, Clemson
6. Eduardo Vega—144, T, Memphis State
7. Ivory Lee Brown—171, RB, Arkansas-Pine Bluff
8. Greg Amsler—198, RB, Tennessee
   Jerry Evans—204, TE, Toledo, from San Diego
   Scott Evans—209, DT, Oklahoma, from Dallas
9. Choice exercised in 1990 Supplemental Draft for Willie Williams, TE, Louisiana State
10. Herbie Anderson—255, DB, Texas A&I
11. Nathan LaDuke—282, DB, Arizona State
12. Jeff Bridewell—309, QB, Cal-Davis

Pittsburgh Steelers (Drafted alternately 16-19-18-17)

1. Huey Richardson—15, DE, Florida
2. Jeff Graham—46, WR, Ohio State
3. Ernie Mills—73, WR, Florida
4. Sammy Walker—88, DB, Texas Tech, from Denver through New England
   Choice to Los Angeles Raiders through New England
   Adrian Cooper—103, TE, Oklahoma, from Washington
5. Choice to San Diego through New England
6. Leroy Thompson—158, RB, Penn State
7. Andre Jones—185, LB, Notre Dame
8. Dean Dingman—212, G, Michigan
9. Bruce McGonnigal—238, TE, Virginia
10. Ariel Solomon—269, T, Colorado
11. Efrum Thomas—296, DB, Alabama
12. Jeff Brady—323, LB, Kentucky

San Diego Chargers (Drafted alternately 10-9-8-7-12-11)

1. Stanley Richard—9, DB, Texas
2. George Thornton—36, DT, Alabama
   Eric Bieniemy—39, RB, Colorado, from Tampa Bay
   Eric Moten—47, G, Michigan State, from Washington
3. Choice to Dallas
4. Yancey Thigpen—90, WR, Winston-Salem State
5. Duane Young—123, TE, Michigan State
   Floyd Fields—127, DB, Arizona State, from Pittsburgh through New England
6. Jimmy Laister—150, T, Oregon Tech
7. David Jones—177, WR, Delaware State
   Terry Beauford—192, G, Florida A&M, from Los Angeles Raiders
8. Choice to Phoenix
9. Andy Katoa—230, LB, Southern Oregon
10. Ronald Poles—254, RB, Tennessee, from Los Angeles Rams
    Mike Heldt—257, C, Notre Dame
11. Joachim Weinberg—290, WR, Johnson C. Smith
12. Chris Samuels—317, RB, Texas

San Francisco 49ers (Drafted 26th)

1. Ted Washington—25, DT, Louisville
2. Ricky Watters—45, RB, Notre Dame, from Cincinnati
   John Johnson—53, LB, Clemson
3. Choice to Green Bay
4. Mitch Donahue—95, LB, Wyoming, from Green Bay
   Choice to Cincinnati
5. Merton Hanks—122, DB, Iowa, from Green Bay
   Harry Boatswain—137, T, New Haven
6. Scott Bowles—165, T, North Texas State
7. Sheldon Canley—193, RB, San Jose State
8. Tony Hargain—221, WR, Oregon
9. Louis Riddick—248, DB, Pittsburgh
10. Byron Holdbrooks—276, NT, Alabama
11. Bobby Slaughter—304, WR, Louisiana Tech
12. Cliff Confer—332, DE, Michigan State

Seattle Seahawks (Drafted alternately 17-16-19-18)

1. Dan McGwire—16, QB, San Diego State
2. Choice to Los Angeles Raiders
   Doug Thomas—51, WR, Clemson, from Los Angeles Raiders
3. David Daniels—74, WR, Penn State
4. John Kasay—98, K, Georgia, from New Orleans through Los Angeles Raiders
   Choice to Houston through New England
5. Harlan Davis—128, DB, Tennessee
6. Mike Sinclair—155, DE, Eastern New Mexico
7. Choice to Atlanta
8. Choice to Los Angeles Raiders
9. Choice to Cleveland
10. Erik Ringoen—266, LB, Hofstra
11. Tony Stewart—297, RB, Iowa
12. Ike Harris—324, G, South Carolina

Tampa Bay Buccaneers (Drafted alternately 7-12-11-10-9-8)

1. Charles McRae—7, T, Tennessee
2. Choice to San Diego
3. Lawrence Dawsey—66, WR, Florida State
   Robert Wilson—80, RB, Texas A&M, from Los Angeles Raiders
4. Tony Covington—93, DB, Virginia
5. Terry Bagsby—120, LB, East Texas State
   Tim Ryan—136, G, Notre Dame, from Los Angeles Raiders
6. Rhett Hall—147, DT, California
7. Calvin Tiggle—174, LB, Georgia Tech
8. Marty Carter—207, DB, Middle Tennessee State
9. Treamelle Taylor—233, WR, Nevada-Reno
10. Pat O'Hara—260, QB, Southern California
    Hyland Hickson—265, RB, Michigan State, from New Orleans
11. Mike Sunvold—287, DT, Minnesota
12. Al Chamblee—314, LB, Virginia Tech

Washington Redskins (Drafted alternately 21-20)

1. Bobby Wilson—17, DT, Michigan State, from Houston through New England and Dallas
   Choice to Dallas
2. Choice to San Diego
3. Ricky Ervins—76, RB, Southern California
4. Choice to Pittsburgh
5. Choice to Dallas
6. Dennis Ransom—159, TE, Texas A&M
7. Keith Cash—188, WR, Texas
8. Jimmy Spencer—215, DB, Florida
9. Charles Bell—243, DB, Baylor
10. Cris Shale—270, P, Bowling Green
11. David Gulledge—299, DB, Jacksonville State
12. Keenan McCardell—326, WR, Nevada-Las Vegas

Look for in 1991

Things that could happen in 1991

• **Don Shula,** Miami head coach, needs two victories to reach 300 in his career and join George Halas (325) as the only coaches in NFL history to achieve the 300-victory mark. Shula currently has 298 wins.

• **Mike Ditka,** Chicago head coach, needs 10 wins to register his 100th regular-season victory. He has a 90-46 record in his nine seasons as Bears' coach.

• **Chuck Noll,** Pittsburgh head coach, needs 10 victories to become the third-active NFL coach to achieve nine 10-win seasons, joining Don Shula (18) and Chuck Knox (9). If the Steelers win the AFC Central Division in 1991, Noll would become the first NFL coach to win 10 division titles since the 1970 merger.

• **Dan Reeves,** Denver head coach, needs four victories for 100 career wins. In his 10 seasons, he has recorded a 96-77-1 record.

• **Gary Anderson,** Pittsburgh, needs two extra points to surpass Roy Gerela's team career record (293). Anderson currently has 292.

• **Morten Andersen,** New Orleans, needs two field goals of 50 yards or more to tie Kansas City's Nick Lowery as the NFL's all-time leader. Lowery holds the NFL record with 18.

• **Neal Anderson,** Chicago, needs four rushing touchdowns to overtake Gale Sayers for third place on the Bears' career list.

• **Joey Browner,** Minnesota, needs one interception returned for a touchdown to set the Vikings' club career record with four. Browner (3) currently shares the club record with three other players.

• **Kevin Butler,** Chicago, needs 117 points to surpass Walter Payton as the Bears' all-time leading scorer.

• **Anthony Carter,** Minnesota, needs 673 receiving yards to break the club record of 6,400 held by Sammy White. Carter currently has 5,728 yards receiving. He also needs 11 touchdown receptions to break the club record of 50, also held by White.

• **John Elway,** Denver, needs 279 passing yards to reach 25,000 for his career. Elway also needs 67 yards rushing to reach 2,000.

• **Roland James,** New England, needs eight interceptions to break Raymond Clayborn's club record of 36 career interceptions. James currently has 29.

• **Pat Leahy,** New York Jets, needs 20 points to become the fourth-leading scorer in NFL history, surpassing Mark Moseley. Leahy currently has 1,362 points in 17 seasons.

• **Dan Marino,** Miami, and **Joe Montana,** San Francisco, need more than 3,000 yards passing in 1991 to achieve eight 3,000-yard seasons and extend their NFL record. Both players have thrown for more than 3,000 yards seven times in their careers.

• Marino also needs 20-or-more touchdown passes in 1991 to become the NFL's all-time leader. He currently shares the NFL record with Johnny Unitas at eight seasons with 20-or-more touchdown passes.

• **Art Monk,** Washington, needs 21 receptions to surpass Charlie Joiner for second place on the NFL's all-time receiving list. Monk currently has 730 career receptions.

• **Stephone Paige,** Kansas City, needs 49 receptions to break Henry Marshall's club record of 416 career catches. Paige currently has 368 career receptions.

• **Barry Sanders,** Detroit, has rushed for more than 1,000 yards in each of the last two seasons (1989 and 1990). If he rushes for more than 1,000 yards in 1991, he will become the first player in Lions' history to record three consecutive 1,000-yard rushing seasons.

• **Deion Sanders,** Atlanta, needs 29 combined return yards to surpass Ron Smith's club record of 2,161. Sanders currently has 2,133 yards in two seasons.

• **Vinny Testaverde,** Tampa Bay, needs 19 touchdown passes to break Doug Williams's club record of 73 career touchdown passes. Testaverde currently has 55. He needs 2,377 yards passing to break Williams's club career mark of 12,648.

• **Lee Williams,** San Diego, needs two sacks to become the Chargers' all-time sack leader with 67.5, surpassing Gary Johnson's 67. Williams currently has 65.5 career sacks.

• **Rod Woodson,** Pittsburgh, needs 24 return yards to break the club record held by Theo Bell (139). Woodson currently has 116 yards.

THE AFC

American Football Conference
Eastern Division

Team Colors: Royal Blue, Scarlet Red, and White

One Bills Drive
Orchard Park, New York 14127
Telephone: (716) 648-1800

Club Officials

President: Ralph C. Wilson, Jr.
Executive Vice President: David N. Olsen
General Manager and Vice President-Administration: Bill Polian
Vice President-Head Coach: Marv Levy
Treasurer: Jeffrey C. Littmann
Asst. G.M./Director of Pro Personnel: Bob Ferguson
Asst. G.M./Business Operations: Bill Munson
Director of Administration: Ed Stillwell
Business Manager: Jim Overdorf
Director of Player Personnel: John Butler
Asst. Dir./Collegiate Scouting: A.J. Smith
Director of Marketing/Sales: Jerry Foran
Director of Public/Community Relations: Denny Lynch
Director of Stadium Operations: Steve Champlin
Box Office Comptroller: June Foran
Manager of Media Relations: Scott Berchtold
Equipment Manager: Dave Hojnowski
Strength/Conditioning Coordinator: Rusty Jones
Trainers: Ed Abramoski, Bud Carpenter
Video Director: Henry Kunttu

Stadium: Rich Stadium • **Capacity:** 80,290
One Bills Drive
Orchard Park, New York 14127

Playing Surface: AstroTurf

Training Camp: Fredonia State University
Fredonia, New York 14063

1991 Schedule

Preseason

July 28	vs. Philadelphia at London	1:00*
Aug. 5	at New York Giants	6:00
Aug. 10	**Detroit**	6:30
Aug. 17	vs. Green Bay at Madison, Wis.	12:00
Aug. 24	at Chicago	8:00

*P.M. Eastern Time

Regular Season

Sept. 1	**Miami**	4:00
Sept. 8	**Pittsburgh**	1:00
Sept. 15	at New York Jets	4:00
Sept. 22	at Tampa Bay	4:00
Sept. 29	**Chicago**	1:00
Oct. 7	at Kansas City (Monday)	8:00
Oct. 13	**Indianapolis**	1:00
Oct. 21	**Cincinnati** (Monday)	9:00
Oct. 27	**Open Date**	
Nov. 3	**New England**	1:00
Nov. 10	vs. Green Bay at Milwaukee	12:00
Nov. 18	at Miami (Monday)	9:00
Nov. 24	at New England	1:00
Dec. 1	**New York Jets**	1:00
Dec. 8	at Los Angeles Raiders	1:00
Dec. 15	at Indianapolis	8:00
Dec. 22	**Detroit**	1:00

Bills Coaching History
(204-254-8)

1960-61	Buster Ramsey	11-16-1
1962-65	Lou Saban	38-18-3
1966-68	Joe Collier*	13-17-1
1968	Harvey Johnson	1-10-1
1969-70	John Rauch	7-20-1
1971	Harvey Johnson	1-13-0
1972-76	Lou Saban**	32-29-1
1976-77	Jim Ringo	3-20-0
1978-82	Chuck Knox	38-38-0
1983-84	Kay Stephenson***	10-26-0
1985-86	Hank Bullough****	4-17-0
1986-90	Marv Levy	46-30-0

*Released after two games in 1968
**Resigned after five games in 1976
***Released after four games in 1985
****Released after nine games in 1986

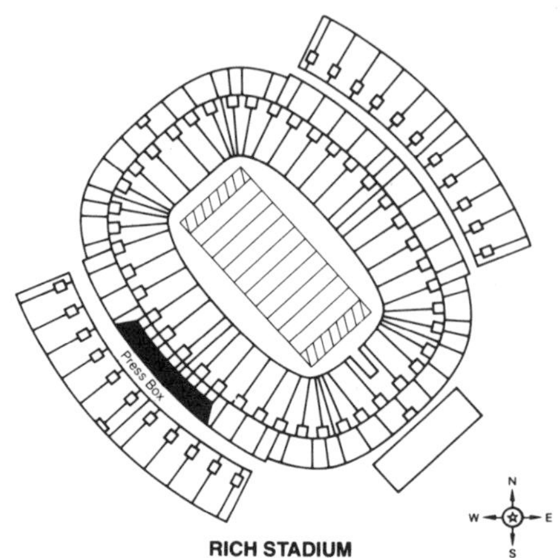

RICH STADIUM

Record Holders
Individual Records—Career

Category	Name	Performance
Rushing (Yds.)	O.J. Simpson, 1969-1977	10,183
Passing (Yds.)	Joe Ferguson, 1973-1984	27,590
Passing (TDs)	Joe Ferguson, 1973-1984	181
Receiving (No.)	Andre Reed, 1985-1990	388
Receiving (Yds.)	Andre Reed, 1985-1990	5,353
Interceptions	George (Butch) Byrd, 1964-1970	40
Punting (Avg.)	Paul Maguire, 1964-1970	42.1
Punt Return (Avg.)	Keith Moody, 1976-79	10.5
Kickoff Return (Avg.)	Wallace Francis, 1973-74	27.2
Field Goals	Scott Norwood, 1985-1990	115
Touchdowns (Tot.)	O.J. Simpson, 1969-1977	70
Points	Scott Norwood, 1985-1990	560

Individual Records—Single Season

Category	Name	Performance
Rushing (Yds.)	O.J. Simpson, 1973	2,003
Passing (Yds.)	Joe Ferguson, 1981	3,652
Passing (TDs)	Joe Ferguson, 1983	26
Receiving (No.)	Andre Reed, 1989	88
Receiving (Yds.)	Andre Reed, 1989	1,312
Interceptions	Billy Atkins, 1961	10
	Tom Janik, 1967	10
Punting (Avg.)	Billy Atkins, 1961	44.5
Punt Return (Avg.)	Keith Moody, 1977	13.1
Kickoff Return (Avg.)	Ed Rutkowski, 1963	30.2
Field Goals	Scott Norwood, 1988	32
Touchdowns (Tot.)	O.J. Simpson, 1975	23
Points	O.J. Simpson, 1975	138

Individual Records—Single Game

Category	Name	Performance
Rushing (Yds.)	O.J. Simpson, 11-25-76	273
Passing (Yds.)	Joe Ferguson, 10-9-83	419
Passing (TDs)	Joe Ferguson, 9-23-79	5
	Joe Ferguson, 10-9-83	5
	Jim Kelly, 9-24-89	5
Receiving (No.)	Greg Bell, 9-8-85	13
	Andre Reed, 9-18-89	13
Receiving (Yds.)	Jerry Butler, 9-23-79	255
Interceptions	Many Times	3
	Last time by Jeff Nixon, 9-7-80	
Field Goals	Pete Gogolak, 12-5-65	5
	Scott Norwood, 9-25-88	5
Touchdowns (Tot.)	Cookie Gilchrist, 12-8-63	5
Points	Cookie Gilchrist, 12-8-63	30

1990 Team Record

Preseason (0-4)

Date	Result		Opponents
8/13	L	6-20	N.Y. Giants
8/17	L	13-24	at Detroit
8/25	L	23-28	at New Orleans
8/30	L	7-35	vs. Chicago at Columbia, S.C.
		49-107	

Regular Season (13-3)

Date	Result		Opponents	Att.
9/9	W	26-10	Indianapolis	78,899
9/16	L	7-30	at Miami	68,142
9/24	W	30- 7	at N.Y. Jets	69,927
9/30	W	29-28	Denver	74,393
10/7	W	38-24	L.A. Raiders	80,076
10/21	W	30-27	N.Y. Jets	79,002
10/28	W	27-10	at New England	51,959
11/4	W	42- 0	at Cleveland	78,331
11/11	W	45-14	Phoenix	74,904
11/18	W	14- 0	New England	74,720
11/26	L	24-27	at Houston	60,130
12/2	W	30-23	Philadelphia	79,320
12/9	W	31- 7	at Indianapolis	53,268
12/15	W	17-13	at N.Y. Giants	66,893
12/23	W	24-14	Miami	80,235
12/30	L	14-29	at Washington	52,397

Postseason (2-1)

Date	Result		Opponent	Att.
1/12	W	44-34	Miami	77,087
1/20	W	51- 3	L.A. Raiders	80,324
1/27	L	19-20	N.Y. Giants	73,813

Score by Periods

Bills	83	116	69	160	0	—	428
Opponents	55	74	72	62	0	—	263

Attendance

Home 598,788 Away 501,065 Total 1,099,853
Single-game home record, 80,235 (12-23-90)
Single-season home record, 622,793 (1988)*
*NFL record

1990 Team Statistics

	Bills	Opp.
Total First Downs	302	288
Rushing	123	105
Passing	161	159
Penalty	18	24
Third Down: Made/Att.	81/184	89/208
Third Down: Pct.	44.0	42.8
Fourth Down: Made/Att.	5/11	10/19
Fourth Down: Pct.	45.5	52.6
Total Net Yards	5276	4607
Avg. Per Game	329.8	287.9
Total Plays	931	981
Avg. Per Play	5.7	4.7
Net Yards Rushing	2080	1808
Avg. Per Game	130.0	113.0
Total Rushes	479	483
Net Yards Passing	3196	2799
Avg. Per Game	199.8	174.9
Sacked/Yards Lost	27/208	43/326
Gross Yards	3404	3125
Att./Completions	425/263	455/254
Completion Pct.	61.9	55.8
Had Intercepted	11	18
Punts/Avg.	58/39.3	66/38.2
Net Punting Avg.	33.6	34.0
Penalties/Yards Lost	92/683	107/839
Fumbles/Ball Lost	17/10	33/17
Touchdowns	53	30
Rushing	20	13
Passing	28	17
Returns	5	0
Avg. Time of Possession	28:39	31:21

1990 Individual Statistics

Scoring	TD R	TD P	TD Rt	PAT	FG	Saf	TP
Norwood	0	0	0	50/52	20/29	0	110
Thomas	11	2	0	0/0	0/0	0	78
Reed	0	8	0	0/0	0/0	0	48
K. Davis	4	1	0	0/0	0/0	0	30
McKeller	0	5	0	0/0	0/0	0	30
Lofton	0	4	0	0/0	0/0	0	24
Mueller	2	1	0	0/0	0/0	0	18
Rolle	0	3	0	0/0	0/0	0	18
D. Smith	2	0	0	0/0	0/0	0	12
Tasker	0	2	0	0/0	0/0	0	12
Beebe	0	1	0	0/0	0/0	0	6
Bennett	0	0	1	0/0	0/0	0	6
Kinnebrew	1	0	0	0/0	0/0	0	6
Metzelaars	0	1	0	0/0	0/0	0	6
Odomes	0	0	1	0/0	0/0	0	6
L. Smith	0	0	1	0/0	0/0	0	6
Talley	0	0	1	0/0	0/0	0	6
Williams	0	0	1	0/0	0/0	0	6
Bills	20	28	5	50/53	20/29	0	428
Opponents	13	17	0	29/30	18/24	0	263

Passing	Att.	Comp.	Yds.	Pct.	TD	Int.	Tkld.	Rate
Kelly	346	219	2829	63.3	24	9	20/158	101.2
Reich	63	36	469	57.1	2	0	6/41	91.3
Gilbert	15	8	106	53.3	2	2	1/9	76.0
D. Smith	1	0	0	0.0	0	0	0/0	39.6
Bills	425	263	3404	61.9	28	11	27/208	98.2
Opponents	455	254	3125	55.8	17	18	43/326	73.2

Rushing	Att.	Yds.	Avg.	LG	TD
Thomas	271	1297	4.8	80t	11
K. Davis	64	302	4.7	47	4
Mueller	59	207	3.5	20	2
D. Smith	20	82	4.1	13	2
Kelly	22	63	2.9	15	0
Gardner	15	41	2.7	14	0
Reich	15	24	1.6	9	0
Beebe	1	23	23.0	23	0
Reed	3	23	7.7	26	0
Kinnebrew	9	18	2.0	4	1
Bills	479	2080	4.3	80t	20
Opponents	483	1808	3.7	51	13

Receiving	No.	Yds.	Avg.	LG	TD
Reed	71	945	13.3	56t	8
Thomas	49	532	10.9	63	2
Lofton	35	712	20.3	71	4
McKeller	34	464	13.6	43	5
D. Smith	21	225	10.7	39	0
Mueller	16	106	6.6	30	1
Beebe	11	221	20.1	49	1
Metzelaars	10	60	6.0	12	1
K. Davis	9	78	8.7	16	1
Rolle	3	6	2.0	3t	3
Tasker	2	44	22.0	24t	2
Edwards	2	11	5.5	6	0
Bills	263	3404	12.9	71	28
Opponents	254	3125	12.3	95t	17

Interceptions	No.	Yds.	Avg.	LG	TD
Jackson	3	16	5.3	14	0
Talley	2	60	30.0	60t	1
L. Smith	2	39	19.5	39t	1
Hagy	2	23	11.5	23	0
Kelso	2	0	0.0	0	0
Williams	2	0	0.0	0	0
Bentley	1	13	13.0	13	0
Hicks	1	0	0.0	0	0
Odomes	1	0	0.0	0	0
Pool	1	0	0.0	0	0
Seals	1	0	0.0	0	0
Bills	18	151	8.4	60t	2
Opponents	11	156	14.2	61	0

Punting	No.	Yds.	Avg.	In 20	LG
Tuten	53	2107	39.8	12	55
Nies	5	174	34.8	0	39
Bills	58	2281	39.3	12	55
Opponents	66	2523	38.2	18	61

Punt Returns	No.	FC	Yds.	Avg.	LG	TD
Edwards	14	5	92	6.6	16	0
Hale	10	4	76	7.6	25	0
Odomes	1	0	9	9.0	9	0
Bills	25	9	177	7.1	25	0
Opponents	31	12	251	8.1	21	0

Kickoff Returns	No.	Yds.	Avg.	LG	TD
D. Smith	32	643	20.1	38	0
Edwards	11	256	23.3	54	0
Beebe	6	119	19.8	27	0
Rolle	2	22	11.0	11	0
Bills	51	1040	20.4	54	0
Opponents	72	1129	15.7	35	0

Sacks	No.
B. Smith	19.0
Wright	5.0
Bennett	4.0
Seals	4.0
Talley	4.0
Bailey	2.0
Lodish	2.0
Conlan	1.0
Hicks	1.0
Garner	0.5
Patton	0.5
Bills	43.0
Opponents	27.0

1991 Draft Choices

Round	Name	Pos.	College
1.	Henry Jones	DB	Illinois
2.	Phil Hansen	DE	North Dakota State
3.	Darryl Wren	DB	Pittsburg, Kan.
5.	Shawn Wilbourn	DB	Long Beach State
6.	Millard Hamilton	WR	Clark
7.	Amir Rasul	RB	Florida A&M
8.	Brad Lamb	WR	Anderson, Ind.
9.	Mark Maddox	LB	Northern Michigan
10.	Tony De Lorenzo	G	New Mexico State
11.	Dean Kirkland	G	Washington
12.	Stephen Clark	TE	Texas

Buffalo Bills 1991 Veteran Roster

No.	Name	Pos.	Ht.	Wt.	Birth-date	NFL Exp.	College	Hometown	How Acq.	'90 Games/ Starts
54	Bailey, Carlton	LB	6-2	237	12/15/64	4	North Carolina	Baltimore, Md.	D9-'88	16/6
92	Baldinger, Gary	NT	6-3	270	10/4/63	5	Wake Forest	Massapequa, N.Y.	FA-'90	9/0
75	Ballard, Howard	T	6-6	315	11/3/63	4	Alabama A&M	Ashland, Ala.	D11-'87	16/16
52	Bavaro, David	LB	6-0	235	3/27/67	2	Syracuse	Danvers, Mass.	PB(Phx)-'91#	14/0*
82	Beebe, Don	WR	5-11	177	12/18/64	3	Chadron, Neb.	Sugar Grove, Ill.	D3-'89	12/4
97	Bennett, Cornelius	LB	6-2	235	8/25/66	5	Alabama	Birmingham, Ala.	T(Ind)-'87	16/16
50	Bentley, Ray	LB	6-2	235	11/25/60	6	Central Michigan	Grand Rapids, Mich.	FA-'86	16/9
61	†Burton, Leonard	C	6-3	277	6/18/64	5	South Carolina	Memphis, Tenn.	D3-'86	0*
58	Conlan, Shane	LB	6-3	235	4/3/64	5	Penn State	Frewsburg, N.Y.	D1-'87	16/16
65	†Davis, John	T	6-4	310	8/22/65	5	Georgia Tech	Ellijay, Ga.	PB(Hou)-'89#	16/15
23	Davis, Kenneth	RB	5-10	209	4/10/62	6	Texas Christian	Temple, Tex.	PB(GB)-'89#	16/0
45	Drane, Dwight	S	6-2	205	5/6/62	6	Oklahoma	Miami, Fla.	SD1-'84	12/0
85	Edwards, Al	WR	5-8	168	5/18/67	2	Northwestern Louisiana	Kenner, La.	D11-'90	14/2
59	Frerotte, Mitch	G	6-3	280	3/30/65	3	Penn State	Kittanning, Pa.	FA-'88	16/0
35	Gardner, Carwell	RB	6-2	235	11/27/66	2	Louisville	Louisville, Ky.	D2-'90	7/0
99	Garner, Hal	LB	6-4	235	1/18/62	5	Utah State	Logan, Utah	D3b-'85	10/0
7	Gilbert, Gale	QB	6-3	210	12/20/61	4	California	Red Bluff, Calif.	FA-'89	1/0
26	Hale, Chris	CB	5-7	161	1/4/66	3	Southern California	Monrovia, Calif.	D7b-'89	8/0
27	Hicks, Clifford	CB	5-10	188	8/18/64	5	Oregon	San Diego, Calif.	FA-'90	4/0
67	Hull, Kent	C	6-5	275	1/13/61	6	Mississippi State	Greenwood, Miss.	FA-'86	16/16
47	Jackson, Kirby	CB	5-10	180	2/2/65	5	Mississippi State	Sturgis, Miss.	FA-'87	12/11
12	Kelly, Jim	QB	6-3	218	2/14/60	6	Miami	East Brady, Pa.	D1b-'83	14/14
38	†Kelso, Mark	S	5-11	185	7/23/63	6	William & Mary	Pittsburgh, Pa.	FA-'86	6/5
63	Lingner, Adam	C	6-4	268	11/2/60	9	Illinois	Rock Island, Ill.	FA-'89	16/0
73	Lodish, Mike	NT	6-3	260	8/11/67	2	UCLA	Birmingham, Mich.	D10-'90	12/0
80	Lofton, James	WR	6-3	190	7/5/56	14	Stanford	Los Angeles, Calif.	FA-'89	16/14
42	Manuel, Lionel	WR	5-11	180	4/13/62	8	Pacific	Los Angeles, Calif.	FA-'91	14/0*
84	McKeller, Keith	TE	6-4	245	7/9/64	4	Jacksonville State	Fairfield, Ala.	D9-'87	16/14
88	Metzelaars, Pete	TE	6-7	250	5/24/60	10	Wabash	Portage, Mich.	T(Sea)-'85	16/4
57	Monger, Matt	LB	6-1	235	11/15/61	6	Oklahoma State	Denver, Colo.	FA-'89	4/0
41	Mueller, Jamie	RB	6-1	230	10/4/64	5	Benedictine	Fairview Park, Ohio	D3b-'87	16/8
11	Norwood, Scott	K	6-0	207	7/17/60	7	James Madison	Alexandria, Va.	FA-'85	16/0
37	†Odomes, Nate	CB	5-10	188	8/25/65	5	Wisconsin	Columbus, Ga.	D2a-'87	16/16
74	Parker, Glenn	G	6-5	301	4/22/66	2	Arizona	Huntington Beach, Calif.	D3-'90	16/3
28	Paterra, Greg	RB	5-11	220	5/11/67	3	Slippery Rock	McKeesport, Pa.	FA-'91	0*
53	Patton, Marvcus	LB	6-2	216	5/1/67	2	UCLA	Lawndale, Calif.	D8-'90	16/0
94	†Pike, Mark	DE	6-4	272	12/27/63	5	Georgia Tech	Villa Hills, Ky.	D7b-'86	16/0
29	Pool, David	CB	5-9	188	12/20/66	2	Carson-Newman	Cincinnati, Ohio	FA-'90	9/1
83	Reed, Andre	WR	6-1	190	1/29/64	7	Kutztown State	Allentown, Pa.	D4a-'85	16/16
14	Reich, Frank	QB	6-4	210	12/4/61	7	Maryland	Lebanon, Pa.	D3a-'85	16/2
51	Ritcher, Jim	G	6-3	273	5/21/58	12	North Carolina State	Medina, Ohio	D1-'80	16/16
77	Rogers, Reggie	DE	6-6	280	1/21/64	3	Washington	Sacramento, Calif.	FA-'91	0*
87	Rolle, Butch	TE	6-4	245	8/19/64	6	Michigan State	Hallandale, Fla.	D7c-'86	16/0
96	Seals, Leon	DE	6-5	267	1/30/64	5	Jackson State	Baton Rouge, La.	D4b-'87	16/16
78	Smith, Bruce	DE	6-4	280	6/18/63	7	Virginia Tech	Norfolk, Va.	D1a-'85	16/16
46	Smith, Leonard	S	5-11	202	9/2/60	9	McNeese State	Baton Rouge, La.	T(Phx)-'88	16/16
56	Talley, Darryl	LB	6-4	235	7/10/60	9	West Virginia	Cleveland, Ohio	D2-'83	16/16
89	Tasker, Steve	WR	5-9	185	4/10/62	7	Northwestern	Leoti, Ky.	W(Hou)-'86	16/0
21	Taylor, Brian	CB	5-10	195	10/1/67	2	Oregon State	New Orleans, La.	FA-'91	0*
34	Thomas, Thurman	RB	5-10	198	5/16/66	4	Oklahoma State	Missouri City, Tex.	D2-'88	16/16
10	Tuten, Rick	P	6-2	218	1/5/65	3	Florida State	Ocala, Fla.	PB(Phil)-'90#	14/0
31	Williams, James	CB	5-10	172	3/30/67	2	Fresno State	Coalinga, Calif.	D1-'90	16/5
69	Wolford, Will	T	6-5	290	5/18/64	6	Vanderbilt	Louisville, Ky.	D1b-'86	14/14
91	Wright, Jeff	NT	6-2	270	6/13/63	4	Central Missouri State	Lawrence, Kan.	D8b-'88	16/16

* Bavaro played 14 games with Phoenix in '90; Burton missed '90 season due to injury; Manuel played 14 games with New York Giants; Paterra last active with Atlanta in '89; Rogers last active with Detroit in '87; Taylor last active with Chicago in '89.

† Option playout; subject to developments.

Plan B unconditional free agent.

Players lost through Plan B (4): G Brent Griffith (NO; active for one game in '90, but did not play), S John Hagy (Hou; 16), CB Carl Mims (Minn; 0), RB Don Smith (Mia; 16).

Also played with Bills in '90—CB-S Richard Carey (3 games), DE Jeff Hunter (3), RB Larry Kinnebrew (2).

COACHING STAFF

Head Coach, Marv Levy

Pro Career: Begins his fifth full season as Bills head coach. Led the Bills to their first AFC championship and their third consecutive AFC East title last season. Under Levy, the Bills recorded a 13-3 record in 1990, the best regular-season mark in club history. He guided the Bills to AFC East title with 9-7 record in 1989. Finished 1988 with a 12-4 record and a berth in the AFC Championship Game. In his first full year in 1987, Levy led Bills to a 7-8 record. He replaced Hank Bullough on November 3, 1986, and compiled a 2-5 record over the final seven weeks of the season. Previously served as head coach of the Kansas City Chiefs from 1978-82 and produced a 31-42 mark. Levy began his pro coaching career in 1969 as an assistant with the Philadelphia Eagles. He joined George Allen and the Los Angeles Rams as an assistant one year later and followed Allen to Washington, where he remained through the 1972 season when the Redskins played in Super Bowl VII. He was named head coach of the Montreal Alouettes (CFL) in 1973 and posted a 50-34-4 record and two Grey Cup victories (1974, 1977) in five seasons in Canada. After two years away from football, he became head coach of the Chicago Blitz of the USFL in 1984, the team's only year in existence. No pro playing experience. Career record: 77-72.

Background: Running back Coe College 1948-50. Coached at high school level for two years before returning to alma mater from 1953-55. Joined New Mexico staff in 1956 where he served as head coach in 1958-59. Head coach at California from 1960-63 before becoming head coach at William & Mary from 1964-68.

Personal: Born August 3, 1928, Chicago, Ill. Levy was Phi Beta Kappa at Coe College and earned master's degree in English history from Harvard. Marv lives in Orchard Park, N.Y.

Assistant Coaches

Tom Bresnahan, offensive line; born January 21, 1935, Springfield, Mass., lives in Hamburg, N.Y. Tackle Holy Cross 1953-55. No pro playing experience. College coach: Williams 1963-67, Columbia 1968-72, Navy 1973-80. Pro coach: Kansas City Chiefs 1981-82, New York Giants 1983-84, Phoenix Cardinals 1986-88, joined Bills in 1989.

Walt Corey, defensive coordinator, linebackers; born May 9, 1938, Latrobe, Pa., lives in West Seneca, N.Y. Defensive end Miami 1957-59. Pro linebacker Kansas City Chiefs 1960-66. College coach: Utah State 1967-69, Miami 1970-71. Pro coach: Kansas City Chiefs 1971-74, 1978-86, Cleveland Browns 1975-77, joined Bills in 1987.

Bruce DeHaven, special teams; born September 6, 1948, Trousdale, Kan., lives in East Aurora, N.Y. No college or pro playing experience. College coach: Kansas 1979-81, New Mexico State 1982. Pro coach: New Jersey Generals (USFL) 1983, Pittsburgh Maulers (USFL) 1984, Orlando Renegades (USFL) 1985, joined Bills in 1987.

Chuck Dickerson, defensive line; born August 1, 1937, Hammond, Ind., lives in East Aurora, N.Y. Defensive tackle Florida 1955-56, Illinois 1961. Pro defensive lineman Montreal Alouettes (CFL) 1962-64. College coach: Eastern Illinois 1967-70, 1981-82, Minnesota 1983. Pro coach: Toronto Rifles (Continental League) 1964-66, Chicago Fire (WFL) 1974-75, Toronto Argonauts (CFL) 1976-79, Memphis Showboats (USFL) 1984-86, joined Bills in 1987.

Rusty Jones, strength and conditioning; born August 14, 1953, Berwick, Maine, lives in Lakeview, N.Y. No college or pro playing experience. College coach: Springfield 1978-79. Pro coach: Pittsburgh Maulers (USFL) 1983-84, joined Bills in 1985.

Buffalo Bills 1991 First-Year Roster

Name	Pos.	Ht.	Wt.	Birth-date	College	Hometown	How Acq.
Bill, Tom	QB	6-0	204	7/7/68	Penn State	Flemington, N.J.	FA
Chapman, Keith	K	5-8	165	7/12/67	North Texas State	Farmersville, Tex.	FA
Clark, Steve	TE	6-6	244	11/28/67	Texas	New Orleans, La.	D12
Collins, Brent	LB	6-2	235	4/27/68	Carson-Newman	Dandridge, Tenn.	D7b-'90
DeLorenzo, Tony	T	6-3	285	11/8/67	New Mexico State	San Antonio, Tex.	D10
Dugan, Chris	K	5-11	170	5/4/65	Arizona State	Indianapolis, Ind.	FA
Fuller, Eddie (1)	RB	5-9	199	6/22/68	Louisiana State	Leesville, La.	D4-'90
Glover, Deval (1)	WR	5-11	184	9/12/66	Syracuse	Troy, N.Y.	FA-'90
Haggins, Odell (1)	NT	6-2	278	2/27/67	Florida State	Bartow, Fla.	FA
Hamilton, Millard	WR	5-10	185	12/30/67	Clark	Ridgeland, S.C.	D6
Hansen, Phil	DE	6-5	271	5/20/68	North Dakota State	Ellendale, N.D.	D2
Kalal, Tim	P	6-3	205	9/13/67	Miami	Longview, Wash.	FA
Kirkland, Dean	G	6-2	290	1/4/68	Washington	Vancouver, Wash.	D11
Lamb, Brad	WR	5-10	171	10/7/67	Anderson	Middletown, Ohio	D8
Maddox, Mark	LB	6-1	220	3/23/68	Northern Michigan	Milwaukee, Wis.	D9
Pool, David (1)	CB	5-9	188	12/20/66	Carson-Newman	Cincinnati, Ohio	FA-'90
Rasul, Amir	RB	5-11	190	7/3/69	Florida A&M	Tallahassee, Fla.	D7
Smiley, Tim (1)	S	6-0	190	5/11/66	Arkansas State	Wynne, Ark.	FA-'90
Staysniak, Joe (1)	T	6-5	295	12/8/66	Ohio State	Elyria, Ohio	FA
Tucker, Brett (1)	S	5-11	195	9/6/67	Northern Illinois	Sycamore, Ill.	FA
Turner, Vernon (1)	WR	5-8	185	1/6/67	Carson-Newman	Brooklyn, N.Y.	FA
Wilbourn, Shawn	S	6-3	205	7/22/67	Long Beach State	Visalia, Calif.	D5
Wren, Darryl	CB	6-0	186	1/25/67	Pittsburg State	Tulsa, Okla.	D3
Young, Brett (1)	S	5-10	195	6/3/67	Oregon	Wilmington, Calif.	SD8-'89

The term NFL Rookie is defined as a player who is in his first season of professional football and has not been on the roster of another professional football team for any regular-season or postseason games. A Rookie is designated by an "R" on NFL rosters. Players who have been active in another professional football league or players who have NFL experience, including either preseason training camp or being on an active roster for fewer than three regular-season or postseason games, are termed NFL First-Year Players. An NFL First-Year Player is designated by a "1" on NFL rosters. Thereafter, a player on an NFL active roster for at least three regular-season or postseason games is credited with an additional year of NFL playing experience.

NOTES

Don Lawrence, offensive quality control, tight ends; born June 4, 1937, Cleveland, Ohio, lives in Orchard Park, N.Y. Offensive-defensive lineman Notre Dame 1957-59. Pro offensive-defensive lineman Washington Redskins 1959-61. College coach: Notre Dame 1961-63, Kansas State 1964-65, Cincinnati 1966, Virginia 1970-73 (head coach 1971-73), Texas Christian 1974-75, Missouri 1976-77. Pro coach: British Columbia Lions (CFL) 1978-79, Kansas City Chiefs 1980-82, 1987-88, Buffalo Bills 1983-84, Tampa Bay Buccaneers 1985-86, Winnipeg Blue Bombers (CFL) 1989, rejoined Bills in 1990.

Chuck Lester, defensive quality control, administrative assistant; born May 18, 1955, Chicago, Ill., lives in Orchard Park, N.Y. Linebacker Oklahoma 1974. No pro playing experience. College coach: Iowa State 1980-81, Oklahoma 1982-84. Pro scout: Kansas City Chiefs 1984-87. Pro coach: Joined Bills in 1987.

Ted Marchibroda, offensive coordinator; born March 15, 1931, Franklin, Pa., lives in East Aurora, N.Y. Quarterback St. Bonaventure 1950-51, Detroit 1952. Pro quarterback Pittsburgh Steelers 1953, 1955-56, Chicago Cardinals 1957. Pro coach: Washington Redskins 1961-65, 1971-74, Los Angeles Rams 1966-70, Baltimore Colts 1975-79 (head coach), Chicago Bears 1981, Detroit Lions 1982-83, Philadelphia Eagles 1984-85, joined Bills in 1987.

Nick Nicolau, receivers; born May 5, 1933, New York, N.Y., lives in Orchard Park, N.Y. Running back Southern Connecticut 1957-59. No pro playing experience. College coach: Southern Connecticut 1960, Springfield 1961, Bridgeport 1962-69 (head coach 1965-69), Massachusetts 1970, Connecticut 1971-72, Kentucky 1973-75, Kent State 1976. Pro coach: Hamilton Tiger-Cats (CFL) 1977, Montreal Alouettes (CFL) 1978-79, New Orleans Saints 1980, Denver Broncos 1981-87, Los Angeles Raiders 1988, joined Bills in 1989.

Elijah Pitts, running backs; born February 3, 1938, Mayflower, Ark., lives in Orchard Park, N.Y. Running back Philander Smith 1957-60. Pro running back Green Bay Packers 1961-69, 1971, Los Angeles Rams 1970, Chicago Bears 1970, New Orleans Saints 1970. Pro coach: Los Angeles Rams 1974-77, Buffalo Bills 1978-80, Houston Oilers 1981-83, Hamilton Tiger-Cats (CFL) 1984, rejoined Bills in 1985.

Dick Roach, defensive backs; born August 23, 1937, Rapid City, S.D., lives in West Seneca, N.Y. Defensive back Black Hills State 1952-55. No pro playing experience. College coach: Montana State 1966-69, Oregon State 1970, Wyoming 1971-72, Fresno State 1973, Washington State 1974-75. Pro coach: Montreal Alouettes (CFL) 1976-77, Kansas City Chiefs 1978-80, New England Patriots 1981, Michigan Panthers (USFL) 1983-84, Tampa Bay Buccaneers 1985-86, joined Bills in 1987.

American Football Conference Central Division

Team Colors: Black, Orange, and White

200 Riverfront Stadium
Cincinnati, Ohio 45202
Telephone: (513) 621-3550

Club Officials

President: John Sawyer
General Manager: Paul E. Brown
Assistant General Manager: Michael Brown
Business Manager: Bill Connelly
Director of Public Relations: Allan Heim
Director of Player Personnel: Pete Brown
Accountant: Jay Reis
Ticket Manager: Paul Kelly
Consultant: John Murdough
Trainer: Marv Pollins, Paul Sparling
Equipment Manager: Tom Gray
Video Director: Al Davis

Stadium: Riverfront Stadium • **Capacity:** 60,389
200 Riverfront Stadium
Cincinnati, Ohio 45202

Playing Surface: AstroTurf-8

Training Camp: Wilmington College
Wilmington, Ohio 45177

1991 Schedule

Preseason

Aug. 2	at Detroit	7:30
Aug. 10	**Philadelphia**	7:30
Aug. 17	**Minnesota**	7:30
Aug. 24	at Green Bay	6:00

Regular Season

Sept. 1	at Denver	2:00
Sept. 8	**Houston**	8:00
Sept. 15	at Cleveland	1:00
Sept. 22	**Washington**	1:00
Sept. 29	**Open Date**	
Oct. 6	**Seattle**	1:00
Oct. 13	at Dallas	12:00
Oct. 21	at Buffalo (Monday)	9:00
Oct. 27	at Houston	12:00
Nov. 3	**Cleveland**	1:00
Nov. 10	**Pittsburgh**	1:00
Nov. 17	at Philadelphia	1:00
Nov. 24	**Los Angeles Raiders**	1:00
Dec. 1	**New York Giants**	4:00
Dec. 9	at Miami (Monday)	9:00
Dec. 15	at Pittsburgh	1:00
Dec. 22	**New England**	1:00

Bengals Coaching History

(176-175-1)

1968-75	Paul Brown	55-59-1
1976-78	Bill Johnson*	18-15-0
1978-79	Homer Rice	8-19-0
1980-83	Forrest Gregg	34-27-0
1984-90	Sam Wyche	61-55-0

*Resigned after five games in 1978

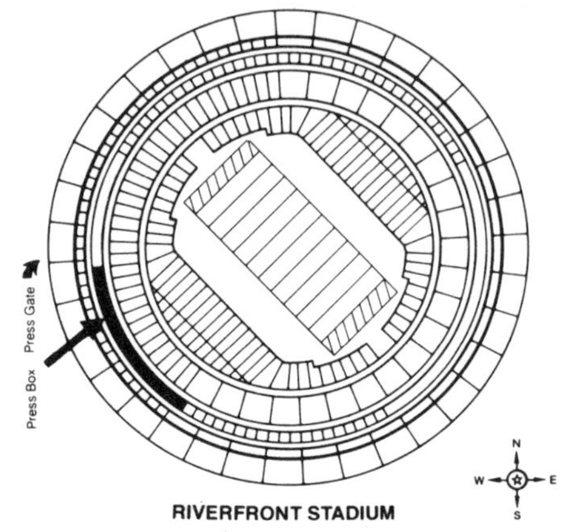

RIVERFRONT STADIUM

Record Holders

Individual Records—Career

Category	Name	Performance
Rushing (Yds.)	James Brooks, 1984-1990	5,605
Passing (Yds.)	Ken Anderson, 1971-1986	32,838
Passing (TDs)	Ken Anderson, 1971-1986	197
Receiving (No.)	Isaac Curtis, 1973-1984	420
Receiving (Yds.)	Isaac Curtis, 1973-1984	7,106
Interceptions	Ken Riley, 1969-1983	63
Punting (Avg.)	Dave Lewis, 1970-73	43.9
Punt Return (Avg.)	Mike Martin, 1983-89	9.9
Kickoff Return (Avg.)	Lemar Parrish, 1970-78	24.7
Field Goals	Jim Breech, 1980-89	184
Touchdowns (Tot.)	Pete Johnson, 1977-1983	70
Points	Jim Breech, 1980-89	875

Individual Records—Single Season

Category	Name	Performance
Rushing (Yds.)	James Brooks, 1989	1,239
Passing (Yds.)	Boomer Esiason, 1986	3,959
Passing (TDs)	Ken Anderson, 1981	29
Receiving (No.)	Dan Ross, 1981	71
Receiving (Yds.)	Eddie Brown, 1988	1,273
Interceptions	Ken Riley, 1976	9
Punting (Avg.)	Dave Lewis, 1970	46.2
Punt Return (Avg.)	Mike Martin, 1984	15.7
Kickoff Return (Avg.)	Lemar Parrish, 1980	30.2
Field Goals	Horst Muhlmann, 1972	27
Touchdowns (Tot.)	Pete Johnson, 1981	16
Points	Jim Breech, 1985	120

Individual Records—Single Game

Category	Name	Performance
Rushing (Yds.)	James Brooks, 12-23-90	201
Passing (Yds.)	Boomer Esiason, 10-7-90	490
Passing (TDs)	Boomer Esiason, 12-21-86	5
Receiving (No.)	Tim McGee, 11-9-89	11
Receiving (Yds.)	Eddie Brown, 11-6-88	216
Interceptions	Many times	3
	Last time by David Fulcher, 12-16-89	
Field Goals	Horst Muhlmann, 11-8-70	5
	Horst Muhlmann, 9-24-72	5
	Jim Breech, 11-1-87	5
Touchdowns (Tot.)	Larry Kinnebrew, 10-28-84	4
Points	Larry Kinnebrew, 10-28-84	24

1990 Team Record

Preseason (1-3)

Date	Result		Opponents
8/11	L	17-30	at Tampa Bay
8/18	L	17-34	at Atlanta
8/24	W	13-10	at New England (OT)
8/31	L	24-26	Detroit
		71-100	

Regular Season (9-7)

Date	Result		Opponents	Att.
9/9	W	25-20	N.Y. Jets	56,467
9/16	W	21-16	at San Diego	48,098
9/23	W	41- 7	New England	56,470
10/1	L	16-31	at Seattle	60,135
10/7	W	34-31	at L.A. Rams (OT)	62,619
10/14	L	17-48	at Houston	53,501
10/22	W	34-13	at Cleveland	78,567
10/28	L	17-38	at Atlanta	53,214
11/4	L	7-21	New Orleans	60,067
11/18	W	27- 3	Pittsburgh	60,064
11/25	L	20-34	Indianapolis	60,051
12/2	W	16-12	at Pittsburgh	58,200
12/9	L	17-20	San Fran. (OT)	60,084
12/16	L	7-24	at L.A. Raiders	54,132
12/23	W	40-20	Houston	60,044
12/30	W	21-14	Cleveland	60,041

(OT) Overtime

Postseason (1-1)

Date	Result		Opponent	Att.
1/6	W	41-14	Houston	60,012
1/13	L	10-20	at L.A. Raiders	92,045

Score by Periods

Bengals	79	110	78	90	3	—	360
Opponents	70	115	101	63	3	—	352

Attendance

Home 473,288 Away 468,466 Total 941,754
Single-game home record, 60,284 (10-17-71)
Single-season home record, 473,288 (1990)

1990 Team Statistics

	Bengals	Opp.
Total First Downs	277	308
Rushing	107	116
Passing	151	180
Penalty	19	12
Third Down: Made/Att.	79/196	93/213
Third Down: Pct.	40.3	43.7
Fourth Down: Made/Att.	12/19	2/12
Fourth Down: Pct.	63.2	16.7
Total Net Yards	5063	5605
Avg. Per Game	316.4	350.3
Total Plays	943	1010
Avg. Per Play	5.4	5.5
Net Yards Rushing	2120	2085
Avg. Per Game	132.5	130.3
Total Rushes	485	442
Net Yards Passing	2943	3520
Avg. Per Game	183.9	220.0
Sacked/Yards Lost	33/209	25/205
Gross Yards	3152	3725
Att./Completions	425/237	543/300
Completion Pct.	55.8	55 2
Had Intercepted	23	15
Punts/Avg.	65/42.1	63/41.8
Net Punting Avg.	34.0	36.5
Penalties/Yards Lost	83/627	101/824
Fumbles/Ball Lost	25/12	32/16
Touchdowns	44	41
Rushing	16	15
Passing	25	24
Returns	3	2
Avg. Time of Possession	29:21	30:39

1990 Individual Statistics

Scoring	TD R	TD P	TD Rt	PAT	FG	Saf	TP
Breech	0	0	0	41/44	17/21	0	92
Brooks	5	4	0	0/0	0/0	0	54
Brown	0	9	0	0/0	0/0	0	54
Woods	6	0	0	0/0	0/0	0	36
Holman	0	5	0	0/0	0/0	0	30
Taylor	2	1	0	0/0	0/0	0	18
Ball	1	1	0	0/0	0/0	0	12
Green	1	1	0	0/0	0/0	0	12
Kattus	0	2	0	0/0	0/0	0	12
Francis	0	0	1	0/0	0/0	1	8
Barber	0	1	0	0/0	0/0	0	6
Bussey	0	0	1	0/0	0/0	0	6
Jennings	1	0	0	0/0	0/0	0	6
McGee	0	1	0	0/0	0/0	0	6
Price	0	0	1	0/0	0/0	0	6
Fulcher	0	0	0	0/0	0/0	1	2
Bengals	16	25	3	41/44	17/21	2	360
Opponents	15	24	2	40/41	22/29	0	352

Passing	Att.	Comp.	Yds.	Pct.	TD	Int.	Tkld.	Rate
Esiason	402	224	3031	55.7	24	22	30/198	77.0
Wilhelm	19	12	117	63.2	0	0	1/2	80.4
Philcox	2	0	0	0.0	0	1	2/9	0.0
James	1	0	0	0.0	0	0	0/0	39.6
Johnson	1	1	4	100.0	1	0	0/0	122.9
Bengals	425	237	3152	55.8	25	23	33/209	76.5
Opponents	543	300	3725	55.2	24	15	25/205	79.9

Rushing	Att.	Yds.	Avg.	LG	TD
Brooks	195	1004	5.1	56t	5
Green	83	353	4.3	39	1
Woods	64	268	4.2	32	6
Taylor	51	216	4.2	24	2
Esiason	50	157	3.1	21	0
Ball	22	72	3.3	15	1
Jennings	12	46	3.8	13	1
James	1	11	11.0	11	0
Wilhelm	6	6	1.0	4	0
Barber	1	−13	−13.0	−13	0
Bengals	485	2120	4.4	56t	16
Opponents	442	2085	4.7	88	15

Receiving	No.	Yds.	Avg.	LG	TD
Brown	44	706	16.0	50t	9
McGee	43	737	17.1	52	1
Holman	40	596	14.9	53	5
Brooks	26	269	10.3	35	4
Woods	20	162	8.1	22	0
Barber	14	196	14.0	28	1
Green	12	90	7.5	22	1
Kattus	11	145	13.2	31	2
Riggs	8	79	9.9	21	0
Smith	7	45	6.4	11	0
Jennings	4	23	5.8	13	0
James	3	36	12.0	16	0
Taylor	3	22	7.3	20	1
Ball	2	46	23.0	48t	1
Bengals	237	3152	13.3	53	25
Opponents	300	3725	12.4	75	24

Interceptions	No.	Yds.	Avg.	LG	TD
Bussey	4	37	9.3	18	0
Fulcher	4	20	5.0	18	0
Billups	3	39	13.0	29	0
White	1	21	21.0	21	0
Francis	1	17	17.0	17t	1
Zander	1	12	12.0	12	0
Price	1	0	0.0	0	0
Bengals	15	146	9.7	29	1
Opponents	23	233	10.1	30t	1

Punting	No.	Yds.	Avg.	In 20	LG
Johnson	64	2705	42.3	12	70
Breech	1	34	34.0	0	34
Bengals	65	2739	42.1	12	70
Opponents	63	2634	41.8	19	65

Punt Returns	No.	FC	Yds.	Avg.	LG	TD
Price	29	14	251	8.7	66t	1
Smith	1	0	4	4.0	4	0
Bengals	30	14	255	8.5	66t	1
Opponents	36	11	352	9.8	79t	1

Kickoff Returns	No.	Yds.	Avg.	LG	TD
Jennings	29	584	20.1	33	0
Ball	16	366	22.9	38	0
Price	10	191	19.1	33	0
Smith	2	35	17.5	20	0
Barber	1	14	14.0	14	0
James	1	43	43.0	43	0
Kattus	1	10	10.0	10	0
Riggs	1	7	7.0	7	0
Taylor	1	16	16.0	16	0
Bengals	62	1266	20.4	43	0
Opponents	43	945	22.0	64	0

Sacks	No.
Francis	8.0
Tuatagaloa	4.5
Bussey	2.0
Hammerstein	2.0
Krumrie	2.0
McClendon	2.0
Fulcher	1.0
Grant	1.0
Walker	1.0
White	1.0
Buck	0.5
Bengals	25.0
Opponents	33.0

1991 Draft Choices

Round	Name	Pos.	College
1.	Alfred Williams	LB	Colorado
2.	Lamar Rogers	DT	Auburn
3.	Bob Dahl	DT	Notre Dame
4.	Donald Hollas	QB	Rice
	Rob Carpenter	WR	Syracuse
5.	Mike Arthur	C	Texas A&M
6.	Richard Fain	DB	Florida
7.	Fernandus Vinson	DB	North Carolina St.
8.	Mike Dingle	RB	South Carolina
9.	Shane Garrett	WR	Texas A&M
10.	Jim Lavin	G	Georgia Tech
11.	Chris Smith	TE	Brigham Young
12.	Antoine Bennett	DB	Florida A&M

Cincinnati Bengals 1991 Veteran Roster

No.	Name	Pos.	Ht.	Wt.	Birth-date	NFL Exp.	College	Hometown	How Acq.	'90 Games/ Starts
42	Ball, Eric	RB	6-2	214	7/1/66	3	UCLA	Ypsilanti, Mich.	D2-'89	13/1
86	Barber, Mike	WR	5-11	172	6/19/67	3	Marshall	Charleston, W. Va.	PB (Phx)-'90#	16/1
53	Barker, Leo	LB	6-2	230	11/7/59	8	New Mexico State	Cristobal, Panama	D7-'84	14/1
24	Billups, Lewis	CB	5-11	182	10/10/63	6	North Alabama	Fort Walton Beach, Fla.	D2-'86	15/14
74	†Blados, Brian	G	6-5	296	1/11/62	8	North Carolina	Arlington, Va.	D1b-'84	4/4
55	Brady, Ed	LB	6-2	236	6/17/60	8	Illinois	Morris, Ill.	FA-'86	16/0
3	Breech, Jim	K	5-6	161	4/11/56	13	California	Sacramento, Calif.	FA-'89	16/0
60	Brennan, Mike	T	6-5	275	3/22/67	2	Notre Dame	Los Angeles, Calif.	D4-'90	16/0
21	Brooks, James	RB	5-10	180	12/28/58	11	Auburn	Warner Robins, Ga.	T(SD)-'84	16/15
81	Brown, Eddie	WR	6-0	185	12/17/62	7	Miami	Miami, Fla.	D1-'85	14/12
99	†Buck, Jason	DE	6-5	264	7/27/63	5	Brigham Young	St. Anthony, Idaho	D1-'87	16/6
27	†Bussey, Barney	S	6-0	210	5/20/62	6	South Carolina State	Lincolnton, Ga.	D5-'84	16/5
45	Carter, Carl	CB	5-11	180	3/7/64	6	Texas Tech	Fort Worth, Tex.	T(Phx)-'90	15/11
57	Clark, Bernard	LB	6-2	248	1/12/67	2	Miami	Tampa, Fla.	D3-'90	14/0
29	Dixon, Rickey	S	5-11	191	12/26/66	4	Oklahoma	Dallas, Tex.	D1-'88	13/5
7	Esiason, Boomer	QB	6-5	220	4/17/61	8	Maryland	East Islip, N.Y.	D2-'84	16/16
50	Francis, James	LB	6-5	252	8/4/68	2	Baylor	Houston, Tex.	D1-'90	16/16
33	†Fulcher, David	S	6-3	238	9/28/64	6	Arizona State	Los Angeles, Calif.	D3b-'86	13/12
58	Gordon, Alex	LB	6-5	245	9/14/64	5	Cincinnati	Jacksonville, Fla.	PB(Raid)-'91#	10/0*
98	†Grant, David	NT	6-5	278	9/17/65	4	West Virginia	Belleville, N.J.	D4-'88	16/9
28	Green, Harold	RB	6-2	222	1/29/68	2	South Carolina	Ladson, S.C.	D2-'90	12/9
82	Holman, Rodney	TE	6-3	238	4/20/60	10	Tulane	Ypsilanti, Mich.	D3-'82	16/15
80	James, Lynn	WR	6-0	191	1/25/67	2	Arizona State	Navasota, Tex.	D5-'90	11/0
36	Jennings, Stanford	RB	6-1	212	3/12/62	8	Furman	Summerville, S.C.	D3-'84	16/0
68	Jetton, Paul	G	6-4	288	10/6/64	3	Texas	Houston, Tex.	D6-'88	15/0
11	†Johnson, Lee	P-K	6-2	200	11/27/61	7	Brigham Young	Conroe, Tex.	FA-'88	16/0
25	Jones, Rod	CB	6-0	185	3/31/64	6	Southern Methodist	Dallas, Tex.	T(TB)-'90	16/6
84	Kattus, Eric	TE	6-5	251	3/4/63	6	Michigan	Cincinnati, Ohio	D4-'86	16/3
64	Kozerski, Bruce	C	6-4	287	4/2/62	8	Holy Cross	Plains, Pa.	D9-'84	16/16
69	Krumrie, Tim	NT	6-2	274	5/20/60	9	Wisconsin	Eau Claire, Wis.	D10-'83	16/15
72	McClendon, Skip	DE	6-7	287	4/9/64	5	Arizona State	Detroit, Mich.	D3a-'87	15/13
85	McGee, Tim	WR	5-10	183	8/7/64	6	Tennessee	Cleveland, Ohio	D1a-'86	16/15
73	†Moyer, Ken	T	6-7	297	11/19/66	3	Toledo	Temperance, Mich.	FA-'89	16/16
78	Muñoz, Anthony	T	6-6	284	8/19/58	12	Southern California	Ontario, Calif.	D1-'80	16/16
52	Ogletree, Craig	LB	6-2	236	4/2/68	2	Auburn	Barnesville, Ga.	D7-'90	11/0
32	Price, Mitchell	CB	5-9	181	5/10/67	2	Tulane	San Antonio, Tex.	D9-'90	16/1
75	Reimers, Bruce	T	6-7	298	9/18/60	8	Iowa State	Humboldt, Iowa	D8-'84	12/12
87	Riggs, Jim	TE	6-5	245	9/29/63	5	Clemson	Laurinburg, N.C.	D4-'87	16/0
76	Scrafford, Kirk	T	6-6	255	3/16/67	2	Montana	Billings, Mont.	FA-'90	2/0
83	Smith, Kendal	WR	5-10	189	11/23/65	3	Utah State	Redwood City, Calif.	D6-'89	9/2
97	Stewart, Andrew	DE	6-5	265	11/20/65	2	Cincinnati	West Hempstead, N.Y.	FA-'91	0*
20	†Taylor, Craig	RB	6-0	228	1/3/66	3	West Virginia	Linden, N.J.	D6-'89	12/1
22	†Thomas, Eric	CB	5-11	181	9/11/64	5	Tulane	Sacramento, Calif.	D2-'87	4/2
96	Tuatagaloa, Natu	DE	6-4	274	5/25/66	3	California	San Rafael, Calif.	D5-'89	16/7
59	Walker, Kevin	LB	6-3	244	12/24/65	4	Maryland	West Milford, N.J.	D3-'88	16/15
63	Walter, Joe	T	6-7	292	6/18/63	7	Texas Tech	Dallas, Tex.	D7a-'85	16/16
51	White, Leon	LB	6-3	242	10/4/63	6	Brigham Young	La Mesa, Calif.	D5-'86	16/13
4	Wilhelm, Erik	QB	6-3	217	11/19/65	3	Oregon State	Lake Oswego, Ore.	D3-'89	7/0
30	Woods, Ickey	RB	6-2	232	2/28/66	3	Nevada-Las Vegas	Fresno, Calif.	D2-'88	10/6
91	†Zander, Carl	LB	6-2	235	3/23/63	7	Tennessee	Mendham, N.J.	D2-'85	16/13

* Gordon played 10 games with Raiders in '90; Stewart last active with Cleveland in '89.

† Option playout; subject to developments.

Plan B unconditional free agent.

Players lost through Plan B (3): DE Mike Hammerstein (Minn; 15 games in '90), QB Todd Philcox (Clev; 2), S Solomon Wilcots (Minn; 16).

COACHING STAFF

Head Coach, Sam Wyche

Pro Career: Bengals finished first in AFC Central Division in 1990. Wyche also led Cincinnati to AFC championship in 1988 with 12-4 regular-season record before coming within 34 seconds of defeating San Francisco (20-16 loss) in Super Bowl XXIII. Became the fifth head coach in Cincinnati history when he was named to lead the Bengals on December 28, 1983. Played quarterback with Bengals 1968-70, Washington Redskins 1971-73, Detroit Lions 1974-75, St. Louis Cardinals 1976, and Buffalo Bills 1977. Quarterback coach with San Francisco 49ers 1979-82. Career record: 61-55.

Background: Attended North Fulton High School in Atlanta and Furman University where he was the quarterback from 1962-65. Assistant coach at South Carolina in 1967. Head coach at Indiana University in 1983.

Personal: Born January 5, 1945, in Atlanta, Ga. Sam and his wife, Jane, have two children—Zak and Kerry. They live in Cincinnati.

Assistant Coaches

Jim Anderson, running backs; born March 27, 1948, Harrisburg, Pa., lives in Cincinnati. Linebacker-defensive end Cal Western (U.S. International) 1969-70. No pro playing experience. College coach: Cal Western 1970-71, Scottsdale Community College 1973, Nevada-Las Vegas 1974-75, Southern Methodist 1977-80, Stanford 1981-83. Pro coach: Joined Bengals in 1984.

Dana Bible, quarterbacks; born October 30, 1953, Erie, Pa., lives in Cincinnati. Defensive back Cincinnati 1972-75. No pro playing experience. College coach: Cincinnati 1976-80, Miami, Ohio 1981-82, 1989, North Carolina State 1983-85, San Diego State 1986-88. Pro coach: Joined Bengals in 1990.

Marv Braden, special teams; born January 25, 1938, Kansas City, Mo., lives in Cincinnati. Linebacker Southwest Missouri State 1956-59. No pro playing experience. College coach: Parsons 1963-66, Northeast Missouri State 1967-68 (head coach), U.S. International 1969-72, Iowa State 1973, Southern Methodist 1974-75, Michigan State 1976. Pro coach: Denver Broncos 1977-80, San Diego Chargers 1981-85, St. Louis-Phoenix Cardinals 1986-89, joined Bengals in 1990.

Dick LeBeau, defensive coordinator-defensive backs; born September 9, 1937, London, Ohio, lives in Cincinnati. Halfback Ohio State 1957-59. Pro defensive back Detroit Lions 1959-72. Pro coach: Philadelphia Eagles 1973-75, Green Bay Packers 1976-79, joined Bengals in 1980.

Jim McNally, offensive line-running game; born December 13, 1943, Buffalo, N.Y., lives in Cincinnati. Guard Buffalo 1961-64. No pro playing experience. College coach: Buffalo 1965-70, Marshall 1971-74, Boston College 1975-77, Wake Forest 1978-79. Pro coach: Joined Bengals in 1980.

Dick Selcer, linebackers; born August 22, 1937, Cincinnati, Ohio, lives in Cincinnati. Running back Notre Dame 1955-58. No pro playing experience. College coach: Xavier, Ohio 1962-64, 1970-71 (head coach), Cincinnati 1965-66, Brown 1967-69, Wisconsin 1972-74, Kansas State 1975-77, Southwestern Louisiana 1978-80. Pro coach: Houston Oilers 1981-83, joined Bengals in 1984.

David Shula, wide receivers; born May 28, 1959, Lexington, Ky., lives in Cincinnati. Wide receiver Dartmouth 1978-80. Pro wide receiver Baltimore Colts 1981. Pro coach: Miami Dolphins 1982-88, Dallas Cowboys 1989-90, joined Bengals in 1991.

Mike Stock, tight ends; born September 29, 1939, Barberton, Ohio, lives in Cincinnati. Fullback Northwestern 1958-60. No pro playing experience. College coach: Northwestern 1961, Buffalo 1966-67, Navy 1968, Notre Dame 1969-75, 1983-86, Wisconsin 1976-77, Eastern Michigan 1978-82 (head coach). Pro coach: Joined Bengals in 1987.

Chuck Studley, defensive line; born January 17, 1929, Maywood, Ill., lives in Cincinnati. Guard Illinois 1949-51. No pro playing experience. College coach: Illinois 1955-59, Massachusetts 1960 (head coach), Cincinnati 1961-68 (head coach). Pro coach: Cincinnati Bengals 1969-78, San Francisco 49ers 1979-82, Houston Oilers 1983 (interim head coach for last 10 games), Miami Dolphins 1984-88, rejoined Bengals in 1989.

Kim Wood, strength; born July 12, 1945, Barrington, Ill., lives in Cincinnati. Running back Wisconsin 1965-68. No pro playing experience. Pro coach: Joined Bengals in 1975.

Cincinnati Bengals 1991 First-Year Roster

Name	Pos.	Ht.	Wt.	Birthdate	College	Hometown	How Acq.
Arey, Dennis	WR	5-11	183	8/18/68	San Diego State	Fountain Valley, Calif.	FA
Arthur, Mike	C	6-3	271	5/7/68	Texas A&M	Minneapolis, Minn.	D5
Bennett, Antoine	CB	5-11	185	11/29/67	Florida A&M	Miami, Fla.	D12
Carpenter, Rob	WR	6-2	215	8/1/68	Syracuse	Amityville, N.Y.	D4a
Crigler, Eric (1)	T	6-5	295	6/3/67	Murray State	Louisville, Ky.	D10-'90
Dahl, Bob	DE	6-5	290	11/5/68	Notre Dame	Chicago, Ill.	D3
Dingle, Mike	RB	6-2	240	1/30/69	South Carolina	Moncks, S.C.	D8
Fain, Richard	CB	5-10	183	2/29/68	Florida	North Fort Myers, Fla.	D6
Garrett, Shane	WR	5-11	185	11/16/67	Texas A&M	Lafayette, La.	D9
Hollas, Donald	QB	6-3	215	11/22/67	Rice	Kingsville, Tex.	D4
Jones, Jerry	WR	5-10	175	5/9/66	Central State, Ohio	Cleveland, Ohio	FA
Langeloh, John	K	6-1	192	12/20/67	Michigan State	Sterling Heights, Mich.	FA
Lavin, Jim	T	6-3	282	12/25/68	Georgia Tech	New Orleans, La.	D10
McKay, Ken	TE	6-3	237	5/7/68	Louisville	Chicago, Ill.	FA
Rembert, Reggie (1)	WR	6-5	200	12/25/66	West Virginia	Okeechobee, Fla.	T(NYJ)-'90
Rogers, Lamar	DE	6-4	290	11/5/67	Auburn	Opp, Ala.	D2
Senczyszyn, David	T	6-5	285	3/5/68	Wisconsin	Milwaukee, Wis.	FA
Smith, Chris	TE	6-3	236	6/27/66	Brigham Young	Littleton, Colo.	D11
Swartz, Chris	QB	6-2	205	3/24/68	Morehead State	Owingsville, Ky.	FA
Trumbull, Rick	T	6-6	300	12/4/67	Missouri	St. Louis, Mo.	FA
Vallin, Travis	WR	6-1	187	11/9/68	Kearney State	Long Island, Kan.	FA
Vinson, Fernandus	S	5-10	197	11/3/68	North Carolina State	Montgomery, Ala.	D7
Williams, Alfred	LB	6-6	240	11/6/68	Colorado	Houston, Tex.	D1

The term NFL Rookie is defined as a player who is in his first season of professional football and has not been on the roster of another professional football team for any regular-season or postseason games. A Rookie is designated by an "R" on NFL rosters. Players who have been active in another professional football league or players who have NFL experience, including either preseason training camp or being on an active roster for fewer than three regular-season or postseason games, are termed NFL First-Year Players. An NFL First-Year Player is designated by a "1" on NFL rosters. Thereafter, a player on an NFL active roster for at least three regular-season or postseason games is credited with an additional year of NFL playing experience.

NOTES

American Football Conference Central Division

Team Colors: Seal Brown, Orange, and White

Offices:
Tower B, Cleveland Stadium
Cleveland, Ohio 44114
Telephone: (216) 696-5555

Practice Facility:
80 First Street, Berea, Ohio 44017
Telephone: (216) 891-5000

Club Officials

President and Owner: Arthur B. Modell
Executive Vice President/Legal and Administrative: Jim Bailey
Executive Vice President/Football Operations: Ernie Accorsi
Vice President/Marketing and Assistant to President: David Modell
Vice President/Public Relations: Kevin Byrne
Vice President/Finance: Mike Poplar
Treasurer: Mike Srsen
Director of Operations/Information: Bob Eller
Player Relations/Media Services: Dino Lucarelli
Asst. Director of Public Relations: Francine Lubera
Director of Pro Personnel: Mike Lombardi
Director of Player Personnel: Jim Shofner
Scouts: Dom Anile, Milt Davis, Tom Dimitroff, Gary Horton, Ozzie Newsome
Head Trainer: Bill Tessendorf
Facilities Manager: Charley Cusick
Equipment Manager: Ed Carroll

Stadium: Cleveland Stadium • **Capacity:** 80,098
West 3rd Street
Cleveland, Ohio 44114

Playing Surface: Grass

Training Camp: Lakeland Community College
Mentor, Ohio 44060

1991 Schedule

Preseason

Aug. 5	**Tampa Bay**	8:30
Aug. 10	**New York Giants**	9:00
Aug. 16	at Washington	8:00
Aug. 23	at Minnesota	7:30

Regular Season

Sept. 1	**Dallas**	1:00
Sept. 8	at New England	1:00
Sept. 15	**Cincinnati**	1:00
Sept. 22	at New York Giants	1:00
Sept. 29	**Open Date**	
Oct. 6	**New York Jets**	1:00
Oct. 13	at Washington	1:00
Oct. 20	at San Diego	1:00
Oct. 27	**Pittsburgh**	4:00
Nov. 3	at Cincinnati	1:00
Nov. 10	**Philadelphia**	1:00
Nov. 17	at Houston	7:00
Nov. 24	**Kansas City**	1:00
Dec. 1	at Indianapolis	1:00
Dec. 8	**Denver**	1:00
Dec. 15	**Houston**	1:00
Dec. 22	at Pittsburgh	1:00

Browns Coaching History

(348-240-10)

1950-62	Paul Brown	115-49-5
1963-70	Blanton Collier	79-38-2
1971-74	Nick Skorich	30-26-2
1975-77	Forrest Gregg*	18-23-0
1977	Dick Modzelewski	0-1-0
1978-84	Sam Rutigliano**	47-52-0
1984-88	Marty Schottenheimer	46-31-0
1989-90	Bud Carson***	12-14-1
1990	Jim Shofner	1-6-0

*Resigned after 13 games in 1977
**Released after eight games in 1984
***Released after nine games in 1990

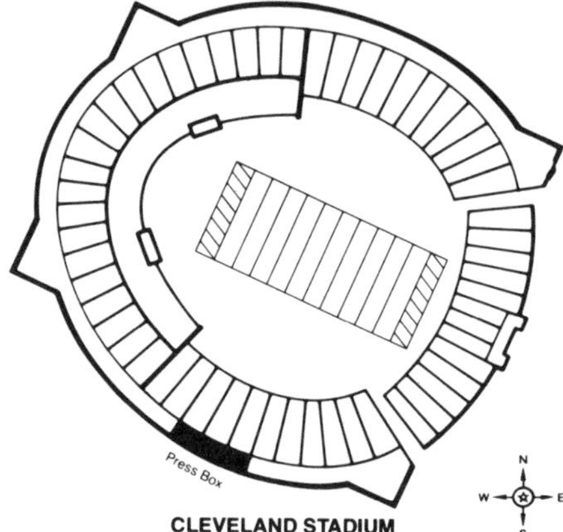

CLEVELAND STADIUM

Record Holders

Individual Records—Career

Category	Name	Performance
Rushing (Yds.)	Jim Brown, 1957-1965	12,312
Passing (Yds.)	Brian Sipe, 1974-1983	23,713
Passing (TDs)	Brian Sipe, 1974-1983	154
Receiving (No.)	Ozzie Newsome, 1978-1990	662
Receiving (Yds.)	Ozzie Newsome, 1978-1990	7,980
Interceptions	Thom Darden, 1972-74, 1976-1981	45
Punting (Avg.)	Horace Gillom, 1950-56	43.8
Punt Return (Avg.)	Greg Pruitt, 1973-1981	11.8
Kickoff Return (Avg.)	Greg Pruitt, 1973-1981	26.3
Field Goals	Lou Groza, 1950-59, 1961-67	234
Touchdowns (Tot.)	Jim Brown, 1957-1965	*126
Points	Lou Groza, 1950-59, 1961-67	1,349

Individual Records—Single Season

Category	Name	Performance
Rushing (Yds.)	Jim Brown, 1963	1,863
Passing (Yds.)	Brian Sipe, 1980	4,132
Passing (TDs)	Brian Sipe, 1980	30
Receiving (No.)	Ozzie Newsome, 1983	89
	Ozzie Newsome, 1984	89
Receiving (Yds.)	Webster Slaughter, 1989	1,236
Interceptions	Thom Darden, 1978	10
Punting (Avg.)	Gary Collins, 1965	46.7
Punt Return (Avg.)	Leroy Kelly, 1965	15.6
Kickoff Return (Avg.)	Billy Reynolds, 1954	29.5
Field Goals	Matt Bahr, 1984	24
	Matt Bahr, 1988	24
Touchdowns (Tot.)	Jim Brown, 1965	21
Points	Jim Brown, 1965	126

Individual Records—Single Game

Category	Name	Performance
Rushing (Yds.)	Jim Brown, 11-24-57	237
	Jim Brown, 11-19-61	237
Passing (Yds.)	Bernie Kosar, 1-3-87	489
Passing (TDs)	Frank Ryan, 12-12-64	5
	Bill Nelson, 11-2-69	5
	Brian Sipe, 10-7-79	5
Receiving (No.)	Ozzie Newsome, 10-14-84	14
Receiving (Yds.)	Ozzie Newsome, 10-14-84	191
Interceptions	Many times	3
	Last time by Frank Minnifield, 11-22-87	
Field Goals	Don Cockroft, 10-19-75	5
Touchdowns (Tot.)	Dub Jones, 11-25-51	*6
Points	Dub Jones, 11-25-51	36

*NFL Record

1990 Team Record

Preseason (1-4)

Date	Result		Opponents
8/4	L	0-13	vs. Chicago at Canton, Ohio
8/11	W	25-10	at Green Bay
8/19	L	20-23	Minnesota
8/25	L	13-31	Washington
9/1	L	10-28	at N.Y. Giants
		68-105	

Regular Season (3-13)

Date	Result		Opponents	Att.
9/9	W	13- 3	Pittsburgh	78,298
9/16	L	21-24	at N.Y. Jets	67,354
9/23	L	14-24	San Diego	77,429
9/30	L	0-34	at Kansas City	75,462
10/8	W	30-29	at Denver	74,814
10/14	L	20-25	at New Orleans	68,608
10/22	L	13-34	Cincinnati	78,567
10/28	L	17-20	at San Francisco	63,672
11/4	L	0-42	Buffalo	78,331
11/18	L	23-35	Houston	76,726
11/25	L	13-30	Miami	70,225
12/2	L	23-38	L.A. Rams	61,981
12/9	L	14-58	at Houston	54,469
12/16	W	13-10	Atlanta	46,536
12/23	L	0-35	at Pittsburgh	51,665
12/30	L	14-21	at Cincinnati	60,041

Score by Periods

Browns	32	57	71	68	0	—	228
Opponents	107	182	61	112	0	—	462

Attendance

Home 568,093 Away 516,086 Total 1,084,179
Single-game home record, 85,073 (9-21-70)
Single-season home record, 620,496 (1980)

1990 Team Statistics

	Browns	Opp.
Total First Downs	259	314
Rushing	74	117
Passing	167	169
Penalty	18	28
Third Down: Made/Att.	81/207	104/211
Third Down: Pct.	39.1	49.3
Fourth Down: Made/Att.	7/19	2/3
Fourth Down: Pct.	36.8	66.7
Total Net Yards	4367	5190
Avg. Per Game	272.9	324.4
Total Plays	960	987
Avg. Per Play	4.5	5.3
Net Yards Rushing	1220	2105
Avg. Per Game	76.3	131.6
Total Rushes	345	512
Net Yards Passing	3147	3085
Avg. Per Game	196.7	192.8
Sacked/Yards Lost	42/260	31/211
Gross Yards	3407	3296
Att./Completions	573/301	444/253
Completion Pct.	52.5	57.0
Had Intercepted	23	13
Punts/Avg.	78/36.9	68/38.1
Net Punting Avg.	30.9	33.8
Penalties/Yards Lost	122/922	95/684
Fumbles/Ball Lost	37/23	24/9
Touchdowns	27	59
Rushing	10	21
Passing	13	32
Returns	4	6
Avg. Time of Possession	27:12	32:49

1990 Individual Statistics

Scoring	TD R	TD P	TD Rt	PAT	FG	Saf	TP
Kauric	0	0	0	24/27	14/20	0	66
Mack	5	2	0	0/0	0/0	0	42
Metcalf	1	1	2	0/0	0/0	0	24
Slaughter	0	4	0	0/0	0/0	0	24
Hoard	3	0	0	0/0	0/0	0	18
Brennan	0	2	0	0/0	0/0	0	12
Langhorne	0	2	0	0/0	0/0	0	12
Newsome	0	2	0	0/0	0/0	0	12
Blaylock	0	0	1	0/0	0/0	0	6
Fullwood, G.B.-Clev.	1	0	0	0/0	0/0	0	6
Gainer	1	0	0	0/0	0/0	0	6
M. Johnson	0	0	1	0/0	0/0	0	6
Browns	10	13	4	24/27	14/20	0	228
Opponents	21	32	6	56/59	16/27	2	462

Passing	Att.	Comp.	Yds.	Pct.	TD	Int.	Tkld.	Rate
Kosar	423	230	2562	54.4	10	15	37/220	65.7
Pagel	148	69	819	46.6	3	8	5/40	48.2
Francis	2	2	26	100.0	0	0	0/0	118.8
Browns	573	301	3407	52.5	13	23	42/260	61.5
Opponents	444	253	3296	57.0	32	13	31/211	92.3

Rushing	Att.	Yds.	Avg.	LG	TD
Mack	158	702	4.4	26	5
Metcalf	80	248	3.1	17	1
Hoard	58	149	2.6	42	3
Fullwood, G.B.-Clev.	44	124	2.8	16	1
Gainer	30	81	2.7	9	1
Slaughter	5	29	5.8	17	0
Kosar	10	13	1.3	5	0
Pagel	3	−1	−0.3	0	0
Redden	1	−1	−1.0	−1	0
Browns	345	1220	3.5	42	10
Opponents	512	2105	4.1	39	21

Receiving	No.	Yds.	Avg.	LG	TD
Slaughter	59	847	14.4	50	4
Metcalf	57	452	7.9	35	1
Langhorne	45	585	13.0	39	2
Brennan	45	568	12.6	28	2
Mack	42	360	8.6	30	2
Newsome	23	240	10.4	38	2
Hoard	10	73	7.3	17	0
Gainer	7	85	12.1	20	0
Joines	6	86	14.3	24	0
Galbraith	4	62	15.5	28	0
Fullwood, G.B.-Clev.	3	17	5.7	10	0
Talley	2	28	14.0	19	0
Kauric	1	21	21.0	21	0
Browns	301	3407	11.3	50	13
Opponents	253	3296	13.0	59	32

Interceptions	No.	Yds.	Avg.	LG	TD
Wright	3	56	18.7	36	0
Blaylock	2	45	22.5	45	0
Braggs	2	13	6.5	11	0
Minnifield	2	0	0.0	0	0
M. Johnson	1	64	64.0	64t	1
Gash	1	16	16.0	16	0
Waiters	1	15	15.0	15	0
Grayson	1	3	3.0	3	0
Browns	13	212	16.3	64t	1
Opponents	23	422	18.3	67	3

Punting	No.	Yds.	Avg.	In 20	LG
Wagner	74	2879	38.9	13	65
Browns	78	2879	36.9	13	65
Opponents	68	2589	38.1	16	70

Punt Returns	No.	FC	Yds.	Avg.	LG	TD
Adams	13	4	81	6.2	25	0
Brennan	9	4	72	8.0	15	0
Lewis	8	7	56	7.0	18	0
Waiters	1	0	0	0.0	0	0
Browns	31	15	209	6.7	25	0
Opponents	41	13	425	10.4	37	0

Kickoff Returns	No.	Yds.	Avg.	LG	TD
Metcalf	52	1052	20.2	101t	2
Fullwood	6	119	19.8	27	0
Adams	3	33	11.0	15	0
Galbraith	3	16	5.3	10	0
Hoard	2	18	9.0	10	0
E. Johnson	2	17	8.5	11	0
Barnett	1	15	15.0	15	0
Gainer	1	0	0.0	0	0
Talley	1	6	6.0	6	0
Browns	71	1276	18.0	101t	2
Opponents	45	805	17.9	39	0

Sacks	No.
Perry	11.5
Matthews	3.5
Baker	3.0
Braggs	2.5
Pleasant	2.5
Burnett	2.0
M. Johnson	2.0
Blaylock	1.0
Gibson	1.0
Grayson	1.0
Buczkowski	0.5
Waiters	0.5
Browns	31.0
Opponents	42.0

1991 Draft Choices

Round	Name	Pos.	College
1.	Eric Turner	DB	UCLA
2.	Ed King	G	Auburn
3.	James Jones	NT	Northern Iowa
4.	Pio Sagapolutele	NT	San Diego State
6.	Michael Jackson	WR	So. Mississippi
8.	Frank Conover	DT	Syracuse
9.	Raymond Irvin	DB	Central Florida
	Shawn Wiggins	WR	Wyoming
10.	Brian Greenfield	P	Pittsburgh
11.	Todd Jones	G	Henderson, Ark.
12.	Elijah Austin	NT	North Carolina St.

Cleveland Browns 1991 Veteran Roster

No.	Name	Pos.	Ht.	Wt.	Birth-date	NFL Exp.	College	Hometown	How Acq.	'90 Games/ Starts
61	†Baab, Mike	C	6-4	275	12/6/59	10	Texas	Fort Worth, Tex.	PB(NE)-'90#	16/16
37	Barnett, Harlon	S	5-11	200	1/2/67	2	Michigan State	Cincinnati, Ohio	D4-'90	6/0
24	Blaylock, Tony	CB	5-11	190	2/21/65	4	Winston-Salem State	Raleigh, N.C.	D4-'88	16/7
36	Braggs, Stephen	CB	5-9	180	8/29/65	5	Texas	Houston, Tex.	D6-'87	15/2
58	Brandon, David	LB	6-4	230	2/9/65	4	Memphis State	Memphis, Tenn.	PB(SD)-'91#	0*
86	Brennan, Brian	WR	5-10	185	2/15/62	8	Boston College	Bloomfield, Mich.	D4b-'84	16/5
52	Brown, Richard	LB	6-3	240	9/21/65	4	San Diego State	Westminster, Calif.	PB(SD)-'91#	11/0*
90	Burnett, Rob	DT-DE	6-4	270	8/27/67	2	Syracuse	Coram, N.Y.	D5-'90	16/6
26	†Clayborn, Raymond	CB	6-1	190	1/2/55	15	Texas	Fort Worth, Tex.	PB(NE)-'90#	16/16
74	Farren, Paul	T-G	6-6	270	12/24/60	9	Boston University	Cohasset, Mass.	D12-'83	16/16
69	†Fike, Dan	G	6-7	285	6/16/61	7	Florida	Pensacola, Fla.	FA-'85	10/0
27	Gainer, Derrick	RB	5-11	235	8/15/66	2	Florida A&M	Plant City, Fla.	FA-'90	16/1
81	Galbraith, Scott	TE	6-3	260	1/7/67	2	Southern California	Sacramento, Calif.	D7-'90	16/1
30	Gash, Thane	S	6-0	195	9/1/65	4	East Tennessee State	Hendersonville, N.C.	D7-'88	16/16
71	Gibson, Tom	DT-DE	6-8	275	12/20/63	3	Northern Arizona	Saugus, Calif.	FA-'89	12/3
56	Grayson, David	LB	6-3	230	2/27/64	5	Fresno State	San Diego, Calif.	FA-'87	16/8
11	Hansen, Brian	P	6-4	220	10/26/60	7	Sioux Falls	Hawarden, Iowa	PB(NE)-'91#	16/0*
23	Harper, Mark	CB	5-9	185	11/5/61	6	Alcorn State	Memphis, Tenn.	FA-'86	5/2
39	Hilliard, Randy	CB	5-11	160	6/2/67	2	Northwestern Louisiana	Metairie, La.	D6-'90	15/0
33	Hoard, Leroy	RB	5-11	230	5/5/68	2	Michigan	New Orleans, La.	D2-'90	14/5
62	Jefferson, Ben	T	6-9	330	1/15/66	2	Maryland	New Rochelle, N.Y.	FA-'90	4/4
51	†Johnson, Eddie	LB	6-1	235	2/3/59	11	Louisville	Albany, Ga.	D7-'81	16/0
29	Johnson, Flip	WR	5-9	181	7/13/63	3	McNeese State	Beaumont, Tex.	FA-'91	0*
59	Johnson, Mike	LB	6-1	230	11/26/62	6	Virginia Tech	Hyattsville, Md.	D1b-'84	16/15
80	†Joines, Vernon	WR	6-2	210	6/20/65	2	Maryland	Baltimore, Md.	FA-'90	16/0
55	Jones, Jock	LB	6-2	230	3/13/68	2	Virginia Tech	Ashland, Va.	D8-'90	11/0
66	Jones, Tony	T	6-5	290	5/24/66	4	Western Carolina	Cannesville, Ga.	FA-'88	16/16
19	Kosar, Bernie	QB	6-5	215	11/25/63	7	Miami	Boardman, Ohio	SD1-'85	13/13
40	†Kramer, Kyle	S	6-3	190	1/12/67	2	Bowling Green	Kettering, Ohio	D5a-'89	0*
88	Langhorne, Reggie	WR	6-2	205	4/7/63	7	Elizabeth City State	Carrollton, Va.	D7-'85	12/11
49	Lyons, Robert	S	6-2	200	5/16/66	2	Akron	St. Clairesville, Ohio	FA-'91	0*
34	Mack, Kevin	RB	6-0	230	8/9/62	7	Clemson	Kings Mountain, N.C.	SD1-'84	14/14
57	Matthews, Clay	LB	6-2	245	3/15/56	14	Southern California	New Trier, Ill.	D1a-'78	16/16
21	Metcalf, Eric	RB	5-10	190	1/23/68	3	Texas	Arlington, Va.	D1-'89	16/10
31	Minnifield, Frank	CB	5-9	180	1/1/60	8	Louisville	Lexington, Ky.	FA-'84	9/8
20	Morris, Joe	RB	5-7	195	9/15/60	9	Syracuse	Ayer, Mass.	FA-'91	0*
67	†Morris, Mike	C	6-5	285	2/22/61	4	Northeast Missouri State	Centerville, Iowa	FA-'90	10/0
22	†Newsome, Vince	S	6-1	185	1/22/61	9	Washington	Vacaville, Calif.	PB(Rams)-'91#	16/16*
89	Oliphant, Mike	WR-KR	5-9	171	5/19/63	2	Puget Sound	Federal Way, Wash.	T(Wash)-'89	0*
92	Perry, Michael Dean	DT	6-1	285	8/27/65	4	Clemson	Aiken, S.C.	D2-'88	16/16
17	Philcox, Todd	QB	6-4	225	9/25/66	2	Syracuse	Norwalk, Conn.	PB(Cin)-'91#	1/0*
98	Pleasant, Anthony	DE	6-5	258	1/27/68	2	Tennessee State	Century, Fla.	D3-'90	16/7
73	Rakoczy, Gregg	G-C	6-5	295	5/18/65	5	Miami	Medford Lakes, N.J.	D2-'87	16/12
77	Reeves, Ken	T-G	6-5	277	10/4/61	7	Texas A&M	Pittsburg, Tex.	T(Phil)-'90	16/0
70	Rienstra, John	G	6-5	275	3/22/63	6	Temple	Bryn Athyne, Pa.	PB(Pitt)-'91#	6/3*
72	Robbins, Kevin	T-G	6-6	295	12/12/66	2	Michigan State	Washington, D.C.	FA-'89	6/4
44	Rouson, Lee	RB	6-1	222	10/18/62	7	Colorado	Greensboro, N.C.	PB(NYG)-'91#	16/0*
83	Rowell, Eugene	WR	6-1	180	6/12/68	2	Southern Mississippi	Auburn, Ala.	D9-'90	3/0
84	Slaughter, Webster	WR	6-1	170	10/19/64	6	San Diego State	Stockton, Calif.	D2-'86	16/16
87	Talley, John	TE	6-5	245	12/19/64	2	West Virginia	Cleveland, Ohio	FA-'90	14/2
65	Tamm, Ralph	G-C	6-4	280	3/11/66	2	West Chester	Bensalem, Pa.	PB(Wash)-'90#	16/12
85	Tillman, Lawyer	WR	6-5	230	5/20/66	2	Auburn	Mobile, Ala.	D2-'89	0*
50	Waiters, Van	LB	6-4	250	2/27/65	4	Indiana	Coral Gables, Fla.	D3-'88	16/6
91	†Weston, Rhondy	DT-DE	6-5	280	6/7/66	2	Florida	Belle Glade, Fla.	PB(TB)-'90#	0*

* Brandon, Kramer, Oliphant, Tillman, and Weston missed '90 season due to injury; Brown played 11 games with San Diego in '90; Hansen played 16 games with New England; F. Johnson last active with Buffalo in '89; Lyons last active with Cleveland in '89; J. Morris last active with N.Y. Giants in '88; Newsome played 16 games with L.A. Rams; Philcox played 1 game with Cincinnati; Rienstra played 6 games with Pittsburgh; Rouson played 16 games with N.Y. Giants.

† Option playout; subject to developments.

Plan B unconditional free agent.

Traded—DE Bob Buczkowski to Seattle.

Players lost through Plan B (6): DE Robert Banks (Hou; 15 games in '90), LB Marcus Cotton (Sea; 7), DT Marlon Jones (TB; 0), RB Tim Manoa (NO; 0), DT Chris Pike (SD; 12), S Felix Wright (Minn; 16).

Also played with Browns in '90—CB Stefon Adams (10 games), DE Al Baker (9), S Keith Bostic (4), RB Brent Fullwood (1), K Jerry Kauric (14), CB Leo Lewis (3), TE Ozzie Newsome (16), QB Mike Pagel (16), RB Barry Redden (5), LB Ken Rose (7), P Bryan Wagner (16).

COACHING STAFF

Head Coach, Bill Belichick

Pro Career: Became the Browns' eighth head coach on February 5, 1991. Is the youngest head coach in the NFL. Most recently was defensive coordinator of the New York Giants, who defeated the Buffalo Bills 20-19 in Super Bowl XXV. Also coordinated the Giants' defense that won Super Bowl XXI in 1986. Began coaching career at the age of 23 as special assistant to Ted Marchibroda for 1975 Baltimore Colts. He tutored the Detroit Lions' tight ends, wide receivers, and special teams in 1976-77, before joining the Denver Broncos in 1978. He joined the Giants in 1979 as defensive assistant and special teams coach, moved to linebackers in 1981-82, and became defensive coordinator in 1983.

Background: Attended Annapolis (Maryland) High School and Phillips Academy in Andover, Massachusetts. Played football and lacrosse at Wesleyan (Connecticut) University. Earned a bachelor's degree in economics in 1975.

Personal: Born April 16, 1952, in Nashville, Tenn. Bill and his wife, Debby, have two children, Amanda and Stephen.

Assistant Coaches

Ernie Adams, offensive assistant; born March 31, 1953, Waltham, Mass., lives in Berea, Ohio. No college or pro playing experience. College coach: Northwestern 1972-75. Pro coach: New England Patriots 1975-78, New York Giants 1979-81 (Pro Personnel Director 1982-85), joined Browns in 1991.

Jim Bates, inside linebackers; born May 31, 1946, Pontiac, Mich., lives in Berea, Ohio. Linebacker Tennessee 1964-67. No pro playing experience. College coach: Tennessee 1968, 1989, Southern Mississippi 1972, Villanova 1973-74, Kansas State 1975-76, West Virginia 1977, Texas Tech 1978-83, Florida 1990. Pro coach: San Antonio Gunslingers (USFL) 1984-85 (head coach 1985), Arizona Wranglers (USFL) 1986, Detroit Drive (Arena Football) 1988, joined Browns in 1991.

Don Blackmon, outside linebackers; born March 14, 1958, Pompano Beach, Fla., lives in Berea, Ohio. Linebacker Tulsa 1977-80. Pro linebacker New England Patriots 1981-87. No college coaching experience. Pro coach: New England Patriots 1988-90, joined Browns in 1991.

Steve Crosby, running backs; born July 3, 1950, Great Bend, Kan., lives in Berea, Ohio. Running back Fort Hays College 1969-72. Pro running back New York Giants 1974-76. No college coaching experience. Pro coach: Miami Dolphins 1979-82, Atlanta Falcons 1983-84, 1986-89, Cleveland Browns 1985, New England Patriots 1990, rejoined Browns in 1991.

Hal Hunter, offensive line; born June 3, 1934, Canonsburg, Pa., lives in Hinckley, Ohio. Linebacker/guard Pittsburgh 1953-55. Pro guard Pittsburgh Steelers 1956. College coach: Richmond 1958-61, West Virginia 1962-63, Maryland 1964-65, Duke 1966-70, Kentucky 1971-72, Indiana 1973-76, California State (Pa.) 1977-80. Pro coach: Hamilton Tiger-Cats (CFL) 1981, Baltimore/Indianapolis Colts 1982-84, (interim head coach, final 1984 game), Pittsburgh Steelers 1985-88, joined Browns in 1989.

Richard Mann, receivers; born April 20, 1947, Aliquippa, Pa., lives in Strongsville, Ohio. Wide receiver Arizona State 1966-68. No pro playing experience. College coach: Arizona State 1974-79, Louisville 1980-81. Pro coach: Baltimore/Indianapolis Colts 1982-84; joined Browns in 1985.

John Mitchell, defensive line; born October 14, 1950, Mobile, Ala., lives in Berea, Ohio. Defensive end Eastern Arizona J.C. 1969-70, Alabama 1971-72. College coach: Alabama 1973-76, Arkansas 1977-82, Temple 1986, Louisiana State 1987-90. Pro coach: Birmingham Stallions (USFL) 1983-85, joined Browns in 1991.

Cleveland Browns 1991 First-Year Roster

Name	Pos.	Ht.	Wt.	Birth-date	College	Hometown	How Acq.
Arbuckle, Charles (1)	TE	6-2	240	9/13/68	UCLA	Houston, Tex.	FA
Austin, Elijah	NT	6-2	290	10/3/67	North Carolina State	Attapulgus, Ga.	D12
Bolton, Nathaniel	WR	5-10	199	7/1/68	Mississippi College	McClain, Miss.	FA
Chatman, Terrill	T	6-3	350	2/27/68	Alabama	Childersburg, Ala.	FA
Conover, Frank	T	6-5	317	4/6/68	Syracuse	Monmouth, N.J.	D8
Cunningham, Ed (1)	T	6-7	295	5/10/66	Texas	Fritch, Tex.	FA
Ellis, Theron	LB	6-1	243	1/2/69	West Virginia	Morristown, Pa.	FA
Florence, Anthony (1)	CB	6-0	185	12/11/66	Bethune-Cookman	Delray Beach, Fla.	FA
Fontennette, Dwayne	LB	6-2	235	7/9/68	S.W. Louisiana	Lafayette, La.	FA
Francis, Jeff (1)	QB	6-4	225	7/7/66	Tennessee	Mt. Prospect, Ill.	FA-'90
Greenfield, Brian	P	5-11	227	6/6/69	Pittsburgh	Sepulveda, Calif.	D10
Hawthorne, George (1)	T	6-6	275	11/23/67	Iowa	Chicago, Ill.	FA
Hemmingway, George	RB	6-0	236	5/3/68	Colorado	Colton, Calif.	FA
Herring, Archie	RB	5-7	170	9/16/67	Youngstown State	Massilon, Ohio	FA
Hines, John (1)	DE	6-4	260	5/1/66	Alabama State	Opp, Ala.	FA
Irvin, Ray	CB	5-11	176	1/21/67	Central Florida	Daytona Beach, Fla.	D9a
Jackson, Michael	WR	6-4	195	4/12/69	Southern Mississippi	Kentwood, La.	D6
Jones, James	DT-DE	6-2	294	2/6/69	Northern Iowa	Davenport, Iowa	D3
Jones, Todd	T-G	6-3	297	7/3/67	Henderson State	Little Rock, Ark.	D11
King, Ed	G	6-4	303	12/3/69	Auburn	Phenix City, Ala.	D2
Mitchell, Ben	G	6-3	318	9/18/68	Toledo	Detroit, Mich.	FA
Moore, Doug	LB	6-1	235	8/6/67	East Stroudsburg	Queens, N.Y.	FA
Oliver, Charlie	S	6-0	190	9/20/69	Idaho	Spokane, Wash.	FA
Sagapolutele, Pio	T-G	6-6	297	11/28/69	San Diego State	Honolulu, Hawaii	D4
Sanders, Terrence (1)	G-T	6-7	319	8/8/66	Grambling	Detroit, Mich.	FA
Shavers, Tyrone (1)	WR	6-3	210	2/9/68	Lamar	Texarkana, Tex.	FA
Smith, Billy (1)	P	5-11	190	9/30/66	Tenn.-Chattanooga	Chattanooga, Tenn.	FA
Stover, Matt (1)	K	5-11	178	1/27/68	Louisiana Tech	Dallas, Tex.	FA
Strong, Terrence	RB	5-9	201	9/20/68	Cincinnati	Flint, Mich.	FA
Turner, Eric	S	6-1	207	9/20/68	UCLA	Ventura, Calif.	D1
Wiggins, Shawn	WR	5-10	165	8/15/68	Wyoming	Oak Lawn, Ill.	D9b
Williams, Marlin (1)	DE	6-3	255	4/12/65	Western Illinois	Tampa, Fla.	FA
Woods, Rob (1)	T	6-5	295	10/3/65	Arizona	Santa Barbara, Calif.	FA
Word, Fred	RB	6-1	226	10/4/66	Delta State	Cleveland, Miss.	FA

The term NFL Rookie is defined as a player who is in his first season of professional football and has not been on the roster of another professional football team for any regular-season or postseason games. A Rookie is designated by an "R" on NFL rosters. Players who have been active in another professional football league or players who have NFL experience, including either preseason training camp or being on an active roster for fewer than three regular-season or postseason games, are termed NFL First-Year Players. An NFL First-Year Player is designated by a "1" on NFL rosters. Thereafter, a player on an NFL active roster for at least three regular-season or postseason games is credited with an additional year of NFL playing experience.

NOTES

Scott O'Brien, special teams; born June 25, 1957, Superior, Wis., lives in Berea, Ohio. Defensive end Wisconsin-Superior 1975-78. Pro defensive end Green Bay Packers 1979, Toronto Argonauts 1979. College coach: Wisconsin-Superior 1980-82, Nevada-Las Vegas 1983-85, Rice 1986, Pittsburgh 1987-90. Pro coach: Joined Browns in 1991.

Nick Saban, defensive coordinator; born October 31, 1951, Fairmont, W.Va., lives in Berea, Ohio. Defensive back Kent State 1969-72. No pro playing experience. College coach: Kent State 1973-76, Syracuse 1977, West Virginia 1978-79, Ohio State 1980-81, Navy 1982, Michigan State 1983-87, Toledo 1990 (head coach). Pro coach: Houston Oilers 1988-89, joined Browns in 1991.

Jerry Simmons, strength and conditioning; born June 15, 1954, Elkhart, Kan., lives in Berea, Ohio. Linebacker Fort Hays State 1976-77. No pro playing experience. College coach: Fort Hays State 1978, Clemson 1980, Rice 1981-82, Southern California 1983-87. Pro coach: New England Patriots 1988-90, joined Browns in 1991.

Gary Tranquill, quarterbacks; born April 13, 1940, Avella, Pa., lives in Berea, Ohio. Quarterback Wittenberg 1959-62. College coach: Wittenberg 1963-69, Ball State 1970, Bowling Green 1971-72, Navy 1973-76, Ohio State 1977-78, West Virginia 1979-81, Navy 1982-86 (head coach), Virginia 1987-90. Pro coach: Joined Browns in 1991.

American Football Conference Western Division

Team Colors: Orange, Royal Blue, and White

13655 Broncos Parkway
Englewood, Colorado 80112
Telephone: (303) 649-9000

Club Officials

President-Chief Executive Officer: Pat Bowlen
Vice President-Head Coach: Dan Reeves
General Manager: John Beake
Chief Financial Officer-Treasurer: Robert M. Hurley
Director of Administration: Sandy Waters
Director of Football Operations: Lide Huggins
Director of Player Personnel: Reed Johnson
Director of Media Relations: Jim Saccomano
Ticket Manager: Gail Stuckey
Director of Operations: Bill Harpole
Video Director: Rusty Nail
Director of Player and Community Relations: Charlie Lee
Equipment Manager: Dan Bill
Trainer: Steve Antonopulos

Stadium: Denver Mile High Stadium • **Capacity:** 76,273
1900 West Eliot
Denver, Colorado 80204

Playing Surface: Grass (PAT)

Training Camp: University of Northern Colorado
Greeley, Colorado 80639

1991 Schedule

Preseason

July 27	vs. Detroit at Canton, Ohio	12:30
Aug. 2	**Indianapolis**	7:00
Aug. 7	at San Francisco	6:00
Aug. 19	**Miami**	6:00
Aug. 23	at Phoenix	7:30

Regular Season

Sept. 1	**Cincinnati**	2:00
Sept. 8	at Los Angeles Raiders	1:00
Sept. 15	**Seattle**	2:00
Sept. 22	**San Diego**	2:00
Sept. 29	at Minnesota	7:00
Oct. 6	at Houston	12:00
Oct. 13	**Open Date**	
Oct. 20	**Kansas City**	2:00
Oct. 27	at New England	4:00
Nov. 3	**Pittsburgh**	6:00
Nov. 10	**Los Angeles Raiders**	2:00
Nov. 17	at Kansas City	12:00
Nov. 24	at Seattle	1:00
Dec. 1	**New England**	2:00
Dec. 8	at Cleveland	1:00
Dec. 15	**Phoenix**	2:00
Dec. 22	at San Diego	1:00

Broncos Coaching History

(220-238-10)

1960-61	Frank Filchock	7-20-1
1962-64	Jack Faulkner*	9-22-1
1964-66	Mac Speedie**	6-19-1
1966	Ray Malavasi	4-8-0
1967-71	Lou Saban***	20-42-3
1971	Jerry Smith	2-3-0
1972-76	John Ralston	34-33-3
1977-80	Robert (Red) Miller	42-25-0
1981-90	Dan Reeves	96-66-1

*Released after four games in 1964
**Resigned after two games in 1966
***Resigned after nine games in 1971

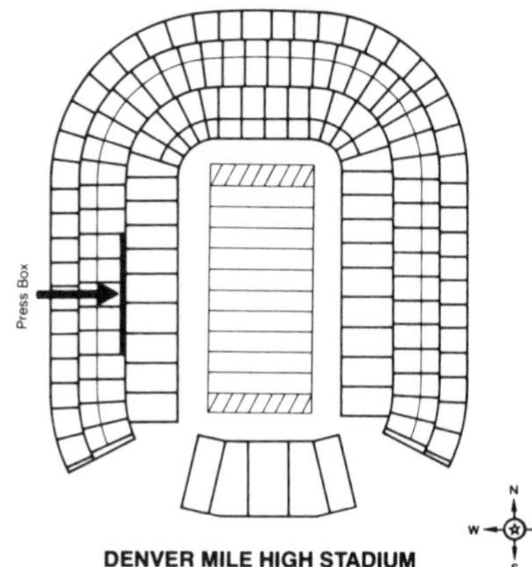

DENVER MILE HIGH STADIUM

Record Holders

Individual Records—Career

Category	Name	Performance
Rushing (Yds.)	Floyd Little, 1967-1975	6,323
Passing (Yds.)	John Elway, 1983-1990	24,721
Passing (TDs)	John Elway, 1983-1990	135
Receiving (No.)	Lionel Taylor, 1960-66	543
Receiving (Yds.)	Lionel Taylor, 1960-66	6,872
Interceptions	Steve Foley, 1976-1986	44
Punting (Avg.)	Jim Fraser, 1962-64	45.2
Punt Return (Avg.)	Rick Upchurch, 1975-1983	12.1
Kickoff Return (Avg.)	Abner Haynes, 1965-66	26.3
Field Goals	Jim Turner, 1971-79	151
Touchdowns (Tot.)	Floyd Little, 1967-1975	54
Points	Jim Turner, 1971-79	742

Individual Records—Single Season

Category	Name	Performance
Rushing (Yds.)	Otis Armstrong, 1974	1,407
Passing (Yds.)	John Elway, 1985	3,891
Passing (TDs)	Frank Tripucka, 1960	24
Receiving (No.)	Lionel Taylor, 1961	100
Receiving (Yds.)	Steve Watson, 1981	1,244
Interceptions	Goose Gonsoulin, 1960	11
Punting (Avg.)	Jim Fraser, 1963	46.1
Punt Return (Avg.)	Floyd Little, 1967	16.9
Kickoff Return (Avg.)	Bill Thompson, 1969	28.5
Field Goals	Gene Mingo, 1962	27
	David Treadwell, 1989	27
Touchdowns (Tot.)	Sammy Winder, 1986	14
Points	Gene Mingo, 1962	137

Individual Records—Single Game

Category	Name	Performance
Rushing (Yds.)	Otis Armstrong, 12-8-74	183
Passing (Yds.)	Frank Tripucka, 9-15-62	447
Passing (TDs)	Frank Tripucka, 10-28-62	5
	John Elway, 11-18-84	5
Receiving (No.)	Lionel Taylor, 11-29-64	13
	Bobby Anderson, 9-30-73	13
Receiving (Yds.)	Lionel Taylor, 11-27-60	199
Interceptions	Goose Gonsoulin, 9-18-60	*4
	Willie Brown, 11-15-64	*4
Field Goals	Gene Mingo, 10-6-63	5
	Rich Karlis, 11-20-83	5
Touchdowns (Tot.)	Many times	3
	Last time by Gerald Willhite, 11-16-86	
Points	Gene Mingo, 12-10-60	21

*NFL Record

1990 Team Record

Preseason (3-2)

Date	Result		Opponents
8/4	W	10- 7	vs. Seattle at Tokyo
8/11	W	16- 7	at Indianapolis
8/20	L	24-27	San Francisco
8/25	L	16-17	at Miami
8/31	W	25-14	Phoenix
		91-72	

Regular Season (5-11)

Date	Result		Opponents	Att.
9/9	L	9-14	at L.A. Raiders	54,206
9/17	W	24-23	Kansas City	75,277
9/23	W	34-31	Seattle (OT)	75,290
9/30	L	28-29	at Buffalo	74,393
10/8	L	29-30	Cleveland	74,814
10/14	L	17-34	Pittsburgh	74,285
10/21	W	27-17	at Indianapolis	59,850
11/4	L	22-27	at Minnesota	57,331
11/11	L	7-19	at San Diego	59,557
11/18	L	13-16	Chicago (OT)	75,013
11/22	L	27-40	at Detroit	73,896
12/2	L	20-23	L.A. Raiders	74,162
12/9	L	20-31	at Kansas City	74,347
12/16	W	20-10	San Diego	64,919
12/23	L	12-17	at Seattle	55,845
12/30	W	22-13	Green Bay	46,943

(OT) Overtime

Score by Periods

Broncos	87	120	46	75	3	—	331
Opponents	60	85	95	131	3	—	374

Attendance

Home 561,703 Away 509,425 Total 1,071,128
Single-game home record, 76,105 (1-4-87)
Single-season home record, 598,224 (1981)

1990 Team Statistics

	Broncos	Opp.
Total First Downs	323	306
Rushing	126	110
Passing	170	181
Penalty	27	15
Third Down: Made/Att.	86/207	84/195
Third Down: Pct.	41.5	43.1
Fourth Down: Made/Att.	7/14	7/12
Fourth Down: Pct.	50.0	58.3
Total Net Yards	5213	5345
Avg. Per Game	325.8	334.1
Total Plays	1035	969
Avg. Per Play	5.0	5.5
Net Yards Rushing	1872	1963
Avg. Per Game	117.0	122.7
Total Rushes	462	456
Net Yards Passing	3341	3382
Avg. Per Game	208.8	211.4
Sacked/Yards Lost	46/330	34/289
Gross Yards	3671	3671
Att./Completions	527/305	479/284
Completion Pct.	57.9	59.3
Had Intercepted	18	10
Punts/Avg.	60/43.5	62/41.4
Net Punting Avg.	38.5	35.6
Penalties/Yards Lost	108/775	105/824
Fumbles/Ball Lost	30/14	36/15
Touchdowns	36	43
Rushing	19	16
Passing	15	22
Returns	2	5
Avg. Time of Possession	30:50	29:10

1990 Individual Statistics

Scoring	TD R	TD P	TD Rt	PAT	FG	Saf	TP
Treadwell	0	0	0	34/36	25/34	0	109
Humphrey	7	0	0	0/0	0/0	0	42
Jackson	1	4	0	0/0	0/0	0	30
Bratton	3	1	0	0/0	0/0	0	24
Young	0	4	0	0/0	0/0	0	24
Elway	3	0	0	0/0	0/0	0	18
Johnson	0	3	0	0/0	0/0	0	18
Sewell	3	0	0	0/0	0/0	0	18
Nattiel	0	2	0	0/0	0/0	0	12
Winder	2	0	0	0/0	0/0	0	12
Mecklenburg	0	0	1	0/0	0/0	1	8
Henderson	0	0	1	0/0	0/0	0	6
Sharpe	0	1	0	0/0	0/0	0	6
Fletcher	0	0	0	0/0	0/0	1	2
Broncos	19	15	2	34/36	25/34	3	331
Opponents	16	22	5	38/43	26/33	0	374

Passing	Att.	Comp.	Yds.	Pct.	TD	Int.	Tkld.	Rate
Elway	502	294	3526	58.6	15	14	43/311	78.5
Kubiak	22	11	145	50.0	0	4	3/19	31.6
Humphrey	2	0	0	0.0	0	0	0.0	39.6
Sewell	1	0	0	0.0	0	0	0/0	39.6
Broncos	527	305	3671	57.9	15	18	46/330	74.6
Opponents	479	284	3671	59.3	22	10	34/289	90.0

Rushing	Att.	Yds.	Avg.	LG	TD
Humphrey	288	1202	4.2	37t	7
Elway	50	258	5.2	21	3
Winder	42	120	2.9	19	2
Bratton	27	82	3.0	10	3
Ezor	23	81	3.5	15	0
Kubiak	9	52	5.8	18	0
Sewell	17	46	2.7	8	3
Jackson	5	28	5.6	16t	1
Porter	1	3	3.0	3	0
Broncos	462	1872	4.1	37t	19
Opponents	456	1963	4.3	62t	16

Receiving	No.	Yds.	Avg.	LG	TD
Jackson	57	926	16.2	66	4
Johnson	54	747	13.8	49	3
Kay	29	282	9.7	22	0
Bratton	29	276	9.5	63	1
Young	28	385	13.8	42	4
Sewell	26	268	10.3	36	0
Humphrey	24	152	6.3	26	0
Nattiel	18	297	16.5	52t	2
Winder	17	145	8.5	17	0
Mobley	8	41	5.1	9	0
Sharpe	7	99	14.1	33	1
Porter	4	44	11.0	16	0
Verhulst	3	13	4.3	6	0
Lanier	1	−4	−4.0	−4	0
Broncos	305	3671	12.0	66	15
Opponents	284	3671	12.9	90	22

Interceptions	No.	Yds.	Avg.	LG	TD
Henderson	2	71	35.5	49t	1
Montgomery	2	43	21.5	24	0
Atwater	2	32	16.0	27	0
Plummer	1	16	16.0	16	0
D. Smith	1	13	13.0	13	0
Braxton	1	10	10.0	10	0
Lang	1	5	5.0	5	0
Broncos	10	190	19.0	49t	1
Opponents	18	169	9.4	39t	3

Punting	No.	Yds.	Avg.	In 20	LG
Horan	58	2575	44.4	14	67
Elway	1	37	37.0	0	37
Broncos	60	2612	43.5	14	67
Opponents	62	2565	41.4	15	59

Punt Returns	No.	FC	Yds.	Avg.	LG	TD
Clark	21	1	159	7.6	32	0
Johnson	11	11	92	8.4	29	0
Nattiel	1	0	5	5.0	5	0
Broncos	33	12	256	7.8	32	0
Opponents	22	9	159	7.2	22	0

Kickoff Returns	No.	Yds.	Avg.	LG	TD
Clark	20	505	25.3	75	0
Montgomery	14	286	20.4	59	0
Ezor	13	214	16.5	50	0
Johnson	6	126	21.0	39	0
Winder	4	55	13.8	24	0
Bratton	3	37	12.3	18	0
Kay	2	10	5.0	7	0
Atwater	1	0	0.0	0	0
Jackson	1	18	18.0	18	0
Mobley	1	9	9.0	9	0
Nattiel	1	0	0.0	0	0
Broncos	66	1260	19.1	75	0
Opponents	69	1319	19.1	71	0

Sacks	No.
Fletcher	11.0
Mecklenburg	5.0
Powers	4.0
Holmes	3.0
Brooks	2.0
Galloway	2.0
Kragen	2.0
Atwater	1.0
Dennison	1.0
Lucas	1.0
Townsend	1.0
Broncos	34.0
Opponents	46.0

1991 Draft Choices

Round	Name	Pos.	College
1.	Mike Croel	LB	Nebraska
2.	Reggie Johnson	TE	Florida State
3.	Keith Traylor	LB	Central State, Okla.
4.	Derek Russell	WR	Arkansas
5.	Greg Lewis	RB	Washington
6.	Nick Subis	T	San Diego State
8.	Kenny Walker	DE	Nebraska
9.	Don Gibson	NT	Southern California
10.	Curtis Mayfield	WR	Oklahoma State
11.	Shawn Moore	QB	Virginia

Denver Broncos 1991 Veteran Roster

No.	Name	Pos.	Ht.	Wt.	Birth-date	NFL Exp.	College	Hometown	How Acq.	'90 Games/ Starts
27	Atwater, Steve	S	6-3	213	10/28/66	3	Arkansas	Chicago, Ill.	D1-'89	15/15
64	Beavers, Scott	T-G	6-4	277	2/17/67	2	Georgia Tech	Fairburn, Ga.	FA-'90	2/0
32	†Bratton, Melvin	RB	6-1	225	2/2/65	3	Miami	Miami, Fla.	D7-'89	16/3
34	Braxton, Tyrone	CB	5-11	185	12/17/64	5	North Dakota State	Madison, Wis.	D12-'87	3/2
56	†Brooks, Michael	LB	6-1	235	10/2/64	5	Louisiana State	Rustin, La.	D3-'87	16/16
92	Carreker, Alphonso	DE	6-6	272	5/25/62	7	Florida State	Marietta, Ga.	FA-'89	0*
20	Clark, Kevin	CB-S	5-10	185	6/8/64	4	San Jose State	Sacramento, Calif.	FA-'90	8/0
25	Corrington, Kip	S	6-0	175	4/12/65	3	Texas A&M	Ames, Iowa	T(Det)-'88	16/1
58	Curtis, Scott	LB	6-1	230	12/26/64	4	New Hampshire	Lynnfield, Mass.	FA-'89	9/1
62	Davidson, Jeff	G	6-5	309	10/3/67	2	Ohio State	Akron, Ohio	D5a-'90	12/0
55	Dennison, Rick	LB	6-3	220	6/22/58	10	Colorado State	Kalispel, Mont.	FA-'82	13/0
29	Dimry, Charles	CB	6-0	175	1/31/66	4	Nevada-Las Vegas	San Diego, Calif.	PB(Atl)-'91#	16/2*
7	Elway, John	QB	6-3	215	6/28/60	9	Stanford	Port Angeles, Wash.	T(Balt)-'83	16/16
35	Ezor, Blake	RB	5-9	183	10/11/66	2	Michigan State	Las Vegas, Nev.	FA-'90	9/0
63	Farrell, Sean	G	6-3	260	5/25/60	10	Penn State	Southhampton, N.Y.	W(NE)-'90	5/0
73	Fletcher, Simon	LB	6-5	240	2/18/62	7	Houston	Bay City, Tex.	D2b-'85	16/16
99	Galloway, David	DE	6-3	265	2/16/59	10	Florida	Tampa, Fla.	T(Phx)-'90	10/0
28	t-Green, Gaston	RB	5-11	192	8/1/66	5	UCLA	Los Angeles, Calif.	T(Rams)-'91	15/2*
93	Haliburton, Ronnie	LB	6-4	230	4/14/68	2	Louisiana State	Port Arthur, Tex.	D6-'90	9/0
69	Hamilton, Darrell	T	6-5	298	5/11/65	3	North Carolina	Washington, D.C.	D3-'89	15/8
24	†Henderson, Wymon	CB	5-9	186	12/15/61	5	Nevada-Las Vegas	North Miami Beach, Fla.	FA-'89	15/15
90	Holmes, Ron	DE	6-4	265	8/26/63	7	Washington	Seattle, Wash.	T(TB)-'89	14/10
2	Horan, Mike	P	5-11	190	2/1/59	8	Long Beach State	Orange, Calif.	FA-'86	15/0
26	Humphrey, Bobby	RB	6-1	201	10/11/66	3	Alabama	Birmingham, Ala.	SD1-'89	15/14
80	Jackson, Mark	WR	5-9	180	7/23/63	6	Purdue	Chicago, Ill.	D6b-'86	16/15
82	Johnson, Vance	WR	5-11	185	3/13/63	7	Arizona	Trenton, N.J.	D2a-'85	16/13
66	Juriga, Jim	G-T	6-6	275	9/12/64	4	Illinois	Fort Wayne, Ind.	D4-'86	12/11
72	Kartz, Keith	C	6-4	270	5/5/63	5	California	Las Vegas, Nev.	FA-'87	16/16
88	Kay, Clarence	TE	6-2	237	7/30/61	8	Georgia	Seneca, S.C.	D7-'84	16/14
68	Ker, Crawford	G	6-3	285	5/5/62	7	Florida	Philadelphia, Pa.	PB(Dall)-'91#	14/14*
71	Kragen, Greg	NT	6-3	265	3/4/62	7	Utah State	Chicago, Ill.	FA-'85	16/16
8	Kubiak, Gary	QB	6-0	192	8/15/61	9	Texas A&M	Houston, Tex.	D8-'83	16/0
21	Lang, Le-Lo	CB-S	5-11	185	1/23/67	2	Washington	Los Angeles, Calif.	D5b-'90	6/0
76	Lanier, Ken	T	6-3	290	7/8/59	11	Florida State	Columbus, Ohio	D5-'81	16/16
59	Lucas, Tim	LB	6-3	230	4/3/61	5	California	Stockton, Calif.	FA-'87	11/5
77	Mecklenburg, Karl	LB	6-3	240	9/1/60	9	Minnesota	Edina, Minn.	D12-'83	16/16
52	Mills, Jeff	LB	6-3	238	10/8/68	2	Nebraska	Montclair, N.J.	W(SD)-'90	2/0
22	Montgomery, Alton	CB-S	6-0	195	6/16/68	2	Houston	Griffin, Ga.	D2-'90	15/4
84	†Nattiel, Ricky	WR	5-9	180	1/25/66	5	Florida	Gainesville, Fla.	D1-'87	15/3
33	Perryman, Robert	RB	6-2	233	10/16/64	5	Michigan	Raleigh, N.C.	PB(NE)-'91#	8/7*
91	Powers, Warren	DE	6-6	287	2/4/65	3	Maryland	Baltimore, Md.	D2b-'89	16/16
48	†Robbins, Randy	S	6-2	189	9/14/62	8	Arizona	Casa Grande, Ariz.	D4-'84	16/9
30	†Sewell, Steve	RB	6-3	210	4/2/63	7	Oklahoma	San Francisco, Calif.	D1-'85	12/1
81	Sharpe, Shannon	WR	6-2	225	6/26/68	2	Savannah State	Glennville, Ga.	D7-'90	16/2
49	Smith, Dennis	S	6-3	200	2/3/59	11	Southern California	Santa Monica, Calif.	D1-'81	15/15
65	Smith, Monte	G	6-4	270	4/24/67	2	North Dakota	Madison, Wis.	D9a-'89	0*
94	Szymanski, Jim	DE	6-5	268	9/7/67	2	Michigan State	Warren, Mich.	D10a-'90	6/6
53	Thompson, Anthony	LB	6-1	227	6/19/67	2	East Carolina	Stantonsburg, N.C.	D10b-'90	10/0
61	Townsend, Andre	DE-NT	6-3	265	10/8/62	8	Mississippi	Chicago, Ill.	D2-'84	15/0
9	Treadwell, David	K	6-1	175	2/27/67	3	Clemson	Columbia, S.C.	T(Phx)-'89	16/0
86	Verhulst, Chris	TE	6-2	249	5/16/66	3	Chico State	Sacramento, Calif.	FA-'90	11/1
79	Widell, Dave	T	6-6	292	5/14/65	4	Boston College	Hartford, Conn.	T(Dall)-'90	16/5
67	Widell, Doug	G	6-4	287	9/23/66	3	Boston College	Hartford, Conn.	D2a-'89	16/16
83	Young, Mike	WR	6-1	183	2/21/62	7	UCLA	Hanford, Calif.	FA-'89	16/1

* Carreker and M. Smith missed '90 season due to injury; Dimry played 16 games with Atlanta in '90; Green played 16 games with L.A. Rams; Ker played 14 games with Dallas; Perryman played 8 games with New England.

† Option playout; subject to developments.

Traded—T Gerald Perry to L.A. Rams.

t- Broncos traded for Green (L.A. Rams).

Retired—Running back Sammy Winder, nine-year veteran, 15 games in '90.

Plan B unconditional free agent.

Players lost through Plan B (2): LB Marc Munford (KC; 13 games in '90), RB Kerry Porter (Hou; 13).

Also played with Broncos in '90—LB Ty Allert (7 games), DE Jake McCullough (6), TE Orson Mobley (9), CB Elliot Smith (9).

Coaching Staff

Head Coach, Dan Reeves

Pro Career: Became ninth head coach in Broncos history on February 28, 1981, after spending entire pro career as both player and coach with Dallas Cowboys. Denver was 5-11 in 1990, but Reeves's Broncos won the AFC Western Division title and AFC championship in 1986, 1987, and 1989, making Denver the only AFC team to reach three Super Bowls during the decade of the 1980s. Denver posted regular-season records of 11-5 (1986), 10-4-1 (1987), and 11-5 (1989) in those championship seasons. Reeves has played or coached in eight Super Bowls, the most by any single participant in the NFL Championship Game. Led Denver to an 11-5 record in 1985, barely missing a playoff berth. Guided Broncos to AFC West championship with a 13-3 record in 1984, and a 9-7 mark and playoff berth in 1983. His teams were 10-6 in 1981 and 2-7 in 1982. He joined the Cowboys as a free agent running back in 1965 and became a member of the coaching staff in 1970 when he undertook the dual role of player-coach for two seasons. Was Cowboys offensive backfield coach in 1972 and from 1974-76, and became offensive coordinator in 1977. Was an all-purpose running back during his eight seasons as a player, rushing for 1,990 yards and catching 129 passes for 1,693. Career record: 96-66-1.

Background: Quarterback at South Carolina from 1962-64. He was inducted into the school's Hall of Fame in 1978.

Personal: Born January 19, 1944, Rome, Ga. Dan and his wife, Pam, live in Denver and have three children—Dana, Laura, and Lee.

Assistant Coaches

Marvin Bass, special assistant; born August 28, 1919, Norfolk, Va., lives in Denver. Tackle William & Mary 1940-42. No pro playing experience. College coach: William & Mary 1944-48, 1950-51 (head coach), North Carolina 1949, 1953-55, South Carolina 1956-59, 1961-65, Georgia Tech 1960, Richmond 1973. Pro coach: Washington Redskins 1952, Montreal Beavers (Continental League) 1966-67, Montreal Alouettes (CFL) 1968, Buffalo Bills 1969-71, Birmingham Americans (WFL) 1974-75, joined Broncos in 1982.

Barney Chavous, defensive assistant; born March 22, 1951, Aiken, S.C., lives in Denver. Defensive end South Carolina State 1969-72. Pro defensive end Denver Broncos 1973-85. Pro coach: Joined Broncos in 1989.

Joe DeCamillis, defensive quality control; born June 29, 1965, Denver, Colo., lives in Denver. No college or pro playing experience. Wrestler Wyoming 1983-87. Pro coach: Joined Broncos in 1989.

Mo Forte, running backs; born March 1, 1947, Hannibal, Mo., lives in Denver. Running back Minnesota 1965-68. No pro playing experience. College coach: Minnesota 1970-75, Duke 1976-77, Michigan State 1978-79, Arizona State 1980-81, North Carolina A&T 1982-87 (head coach). Pro coach: Joined Broncos in 1988.

George Henshaw, wide receivers; born January 22, 1948, Richmond, Va., lives in Denver. Defensive tackle West Virginia 1967-69. No pro playing experience. College coach: West Virginia 1970-75, Florida State 1976-82, Alabama 1983-86, Tulsa 1987 (head coach). Pro coach: Joined Broncos in 1988.

Pete Mangurian, offensive line; born June 17, 1955, Los Angeles, Calif., lives in Denver. Defensive lineman Louisiana State 1975-78. No pro playing experience. College coach: Southern Methodist 1979-80, New Mexico State 1981, Stanford 1982-83, Louisiana State 1984-87. Pro coach: Joined Broncos in 1988.

Al Miller, strength and conditioning; born August 29, 1947, El Dorado, Ark., lives in Denver. Wide receiver Northeast Louisiana 1966-69. No pro playing experience. College coach: Northwestern Louisiana 1974-78, Mississippi State 1980, Northeast Louisiana 1981, Alabama 1982-84. Pro coach: Joined Broncos in 1985.

Denver Broncos 1991 First-Year Roster

Name	Pos.	Ht.	Wt.	Birth-date	College	Hometown	How Acq.
Alford, Tony	RB	5-10	200	11/27/68	Colorado State	Akron, Ohio	FA
Bennett, Tracy	K	6-0	175	6/29/68	Mesa, Colo.	Grand Junction, Colo.	FA
Cochran, Paul	T-G	6-5	322	6/15/68	Ferris State	Detroit, Mich.	FA
Croel, Mike	LB	6-3	231	6/6/69	Nebraska	Detroit, Mich.	D1
Foggie, Fred	CB-S	6-0	180	6/10/69	Minnesota	Lauren, S.C.	FA
Gibson, Don	NT-DE	6-2	270	3/4/68	Southern California	Atlanta, Ga.	D9
Hanes, Norris	WR	5-11	175	12/15/67	Maryland	Indianapolis, Ind.	FA
Hopkins, Marcus	CB-S	5-11	196	9/11/69	Southern California	San Diego, Calif.	FA
Jacobs, Doug	NT-DE	6-7	278	1/3/68	Mississippi	Mocksville, N.C.	FA
Johnson, Barry	WR	6-2	197	2/1/68	Maryland	Baltimore, Md.	FA
Johnson, Reggie	TE	6-2	256	1/27/68	Florida State	Pensacola, Fla.	D2
Lewis, Greg	RB	5-10	214	8/10/69	Washington	Port St. Joe, Fla.	D5
Mayfield, Curtis	WR	5-11	174	3/23/68	Oklahoma State	Dallas, Tex.	D10
McCall, Matt	T-G	6-6	306	1/4/69	Texas A&M	Lufkin, Tex.	FA
McCurdy, Paris (1)	LB	6-6	220	3/25/67	Ball State	Detroit, Mich.	FA
Moore, Shawn	QB	6-2	214	4/4/68	Virginia	Martinsville, Va.	D11
Morgan, Eric	WR	5-10	187	6/23/68	New Mexico	Chicago, Ill.	FA
Murray, Mark	LB	6-2	240	10/15/67	Florida	Orlando, Fla.	FA
Parkinson, Brent (1)	G-T	6-5	267	5/26/67	Southern California	Canyon Country, Calif.	FA-'90
Priester, Ernest	WR	5-8	183	9/5/67	Edinboro State	Cleveland, Ohio	FA
Rivers, Reggie	RB	6-1	206	2/22/68	Southwest Texas St.	Dayton, Ohio	FA
Russell, Derek	WR	6-0	179	7/22/69	Arkansas	Little Rock, Ark.	D4
Story, John	WR	5-11	170	10/13/66	Indiana State	Chicago, Ill.	FA
Subis, Nick	T-G	6-4	278	12/24/67	San Diego State	Inglewood, Calif.	D6
Tobler, Evins	CB-S	5-11	195	5/23/65	No College	Caguas, Puerto Rico	FA
Traylor, Keith	LB	6-2	260	9/3/69	Central Oklahoma	Little Rock, Ark.	D3
Walker, Kenny	DE-NT	6-3	246	3/4/68	Nebraska	Crane, Tex.	D8
Wilson, Sean	P	5-11	212	2/14/68	Texas A&M	Kansas City, Mo.	FA
Wood, Jon	DE-NT	6-7	280	5/6/67	Texas Tech	Glendale, Calif.	FA

The term NFL Rookie is defined as a player who is in his first season of professional football and has not been on the roster of another professional football team for any regular-season or postseason games. A Rookie is designated by an "R" on NFL rosters. Players who have been active in another professional football league or players who have NFL experience, including either preseason training camp or being on an active roster for fewer than three regular-season or postseason games, are termed NFL First-Year Players. An NFL First-Year Player is designated by a "1" on NFL rosters. Thereafter, a player on an NFL active roster for at least three regular-season or postseason games is credited with an additional year of NFL playing experience.

NOTES

Mike Nolan, linebackers; born March 7, 1959, Baltimore, Md., lives in Denver. Safety Oregon 1977-80. No pro playing experience. College coach: Stanford 1982-83, Rice 1984-85, Louisiana State 1986. Pro coach: Joined Broncos in 1987.

Wade Phillips, defensive coordinator; born June 21, 1947, Orange, Tex., lives in Denver. Linebacker Houston 1966-68. No pro playing experience. College coach: Houston 1969, Oklahoma State 1973-74, Kansas 1975. Pro coach: Houston Oilers 1976-80, New Orleans Saints 1981-85 (head coach last four games of 1985), Philadelphia Eagles 1986-88, joined Broncos in 1989.

Harold Richardson, tight ends/special teams; born September 27, 1944, Houston, Tex., lives in Denver. Tight end Southern Methodist 1964-67. No pro playing experience. College coach: Southern Methodist 1971-72, Oklahoma State 1973-76, Texas Christian 1977-78, North Texas State 1979-80, Colorado State 1986-88. Pro coach: New Orleans Saints 1981-85, joined Broncos in 1989.

Mike Shanahan, offensive coordinator/quarterbacks; born August 24, 1952, Oak Park, Ill., lives in Denver. Quarterback Eastern Illinois 1970-73. No pro playing experience. College coach: Oklahoma 1975-76, Northern Arizona 1977, Eastern Illinois 1978, Minnesota 1979, Florida 1980-83. Pro coach: Denver Broncos 1984-87, Los Angeles Raiders 1988-89 (head coach), rejoined Broncos in 1989.

Ernie Stautner, defensive line; born April 20, 1925, Cham, Bavaria, lives in Denver. Tackle Boston College 1946-49. Pro defensive tackle Pittsburgh Steelers 1950-63 (player-coach 1963). Pro coach: Pittsburgh Steelers 1964, Washington Redskins 1965, Dallas Cowboys 1966-88, Dallas Texans (Arena Football League, head coach) 1990, joined Broncos in 1991.

Charlie Waters, defensive backs; born September 10, 1948, Miami, Fla., lives in Denver. Safety Clemson 1967-69. Pro safety Dallas Cowboys 1970-81. Pro coach: Joined Broncos in 1988.

American Football Conference Central Division

Team Colors: Columbia Blue, Scarlet, and White

6910 Fannin Street
Houston, Texas 77030
Telephone: (713) 797-9111

Club Officials

President: K. S. (Bud) Adams, Jr.
Executive Vice President/General Manager: Mike Holovak
Executive Vice President/Administration: Mike McClure
Executive Assistant to President: Thomas S. Smith
Vice President/Marketing and Broadcasting: Don MacLachlan
Assistant General Manager: Floyd Reese
Director of College Scouting: Dick Corrick
Director of Business Operations: Lewis Mangum
Director of Accounting Services: Marilan Logan
Director of Media Services: Chip Namias
Director of Ticket Administration Services: Mike Mullis
Assistant Ticket Manager: Ralph Stolarski
Head Trainer: Brad Brown
Assistant Trainer: Don Moseley
Equipment Manager: Gordon Batty
Video Coordinator: Ken Sparacino

Stadium: Astrodome • **Capacity:** 60,502
Loop 610, Kirby and Fannin Streets
Houston, Texas 77054

Playing Surface: AstroTurf-8

Training Camp: Prassel Residence Hall
Trinity University
San Antonio, Texas 78212

1991 Schedule

Preseason

Aug. 3	at San Diego	7:00
Aug. 9	**Atlanta**	7:00
Aug. 18	**Dallas**	7:00
Aug. 22	vs. Los Angeles Rams at Memphis, Tenn.	7:00

Regular Season

Sept. 1	**Los Angeles Raiders**	3:00
Sept. 8	at Cincinnati	8:00
Sept. 16	**Kansas City** (Monday)	8:00
Sept. 22	at New England	1:00
Sept. 29	**Open Date**	
Oct. 6	**Denver**	12:00
Oct. 13	at New York Jets	4:00
Oct. 20	at Miami	1:00
Oct. 27	**Cincinnati**	12:00
Nov. 3	at Washington	1:00
Nov. 10	**Dallas**	12:00
Nov. 17	**Cleveland**	7:00
Nov. 24	at Pittsburgh	1:00
Dec. 2	**Philadelphia** (Monday)	8:00
Dec. 8	**Pittsburgh**	12:00
Dec. 15	at Cleveland	1:00
Dec. 21	at N.Y. Giants (Saturday)	12:30

Oilers Coaching History

(209-255-6)

1960-61	Lou Rymkus*	12-7-1
1961	Wally Lemm	10-0-0
1962-63	Frank (Pop) Ivy	17-12-0
1964	Sammy Baugh	4-10-0
1965	Hugh Taylor	4-10-0
1966-70	Wally Lemm	28-40-4
1971	Ed Hughes	4-9-1
1972-73	Bill Peterson**	1-18-0
1973-74	Sid Gillman	8-15-0
1975-80	O.A. (Bum) Phillips	59-38-0
1981-83	Ed Biles***	8-23-0
1983	Chuck Studley	2-8-0
1984-85	Hugh Campbell****	8-22-0
1985-89	Jerry Glanville	35-35-0
1990	Jack Pardee	9-8-0

*Released after five games in 1961
**Released after five games in 1973
***Resigned after six games in 1983
****Released after 14 games in 1985

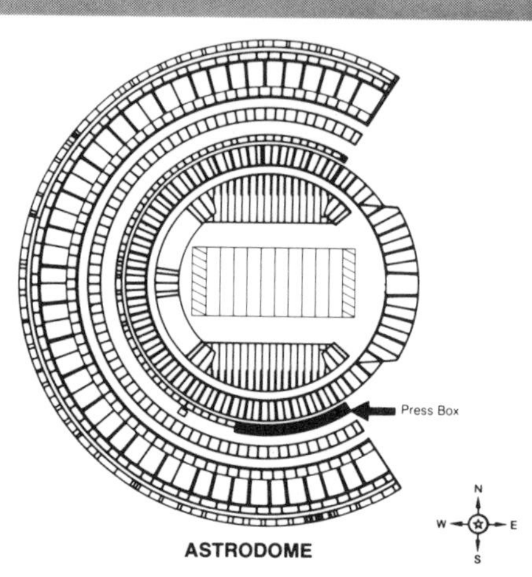

Record Holders

Individual Records—Career

Category	Name	Performance
Rushing (Yds.)	Earl Campbell, 1978-1984	8,574
Passing (Yds.)	Warren Moon, 1984-1990	22,989
Passing (TDs)	George Blanda, 1960-66	165
Receiving (No.)	Charley Hennigan, 1960-66	410
Receiving (Yds.)	Ken Burrough, 1971-1981	6,907
Interceptions	Jim Norton, 1960-68	45
Punting (Avg.)	Jim Norton, 1960-68	42.3
Punt Return (Avg.)	Billy Johnson, 1974-1980	13.2
Kickoff Return (Avg.)	Bobby Jancik, 1962-67	26.4
Field Goals	Tony Zendejas, 1985-1990	117
Touchdowns (Tot.)	Earl Campbell, 1978-1984	73
Points	George Blanda, 1960-66	596

Individual Records—Single Season

Category	Name	Performance
Rushing (Yds.)	Earl Campbell, 1980	1,934
Passing (Yds.)	Warren Moon, 1990	4,689
Passing (TDs)	George Blanda, 1961	36
Receiving (No.)	Charley Hennigan, 1964	101
Receiving (Yds.)	Charley Hennigan, 1961	*1,746
Interceptions	Fred Glick, 1963	12
	Mike Reinfeldt, 1979	12
Punting (Avg.)	Greg Montgomery, 1990	45.0
Punt Return (Avg.)	Billy Johnson, 1977	15.4
Kickoff Return (Avg.)	Ken Hall, 1960	31.2
Field Goals	Tony Zendejas, 1989	25
Touchdowns (Tot.)	Earl Campbell, 1979	19
Points	George Blanda, 1960	115
	Tony Zendejas, 1989	115

Individual Records—Single Game

Category	Name	Performance
Rushing (Yds.)	Billy Cannon, 12-10-61	216
Passing (Yds.)	Warren Moon, 12-16-91	527
Passing (TDs)	George Blanda, 11-19-61	*7
Receiving (No.)	Charley Hennigan, 10-13-61	13
Receiving (Yds.)	Charley Hennigan, 10-13-61	272
Interceptions	Many times	3
	Last time by Willie Alexander, 11-14-71	
Field Goals	Skip Butler, 10-12-75	6
Touchdowns (Tot.)	Billy Cannon, 12-10-61	5
Points	Billy Cannon, 12-10-61	30

*NFL Record

1990 Team Record

Preseason (1-3)

Date	Result		Opponents
8/9	L	10-34	Detroit
8/18	L	10-13	N.Y. Giants
8/26	L	21-22	at Minnesota
9/1	W	27- 6	at Dallas
		68-75	

Regular Season (9-7)

Date	Result		Opponents	Att.
9/9	L	27-47	at Atlanta	56,222
9/16	L	9-20	at Pittsburgh	54,814
9/23	W	24-10	Indianapolis	50,093
9/30	W	17- 7	at San Diego	48,762
10/7	L	21-24	San Francisco	59,931
10/14	W	48-17	Cincinnati	53,501
10/21	W	23-10	New Orleans	57,908
10/28	L	12-17	N.Y. Jets	56,337
11/4	L	13-17	at L.A. Rams	52,628
11/18	W	35-23	at Cleveland	76,726
11/26	W	27-24	Buffalo	60,130
12/2	L	10-13	at Seattle (OT)	57,592
12/9	W	58-14	Cleveland	54,469
12/16	W	27-10	at Kansas City	61,756
12/23	L	20-40	at Cincinnati	60,044
12/30	W	34-14	Pittsburgh	56,906

(OT) Overtime

Postseason (0-1)

Date	Result		Opponent	Att.
1/6	L	14-41	at Cincinnati	60,012

Score by Periods

Oilers	83	152	70	100	0	—	405
Opponents	54	95	71	84	3	—	307

Attendance

Home 449,275 Away 468,904 Total 918,179
Single-game home record, 60,694 (11-13-89)
Single-season home record, 451,027 (1989)

1990 Team Statistics

	Oilers	Opp.
Total First Downs	376	279
Rushing	97	88
Passing	251	160
Penalty	28	31
Third Down: Made/Att.	94/180	69/177
Third Down: Pct.	52.2	39.0
Fourth Down: Made/Att.	3/12	6/13
Fourth Down: Pct.	25.0	46.2
Total Net Yards	6222	4635
Avg. Per Game	388.9	289.7
Total Plays	1006	890
Avg. Per Play	6.2	5.2
Net Yards Rushing	1417	1575
Avg. Per Game	88.6	98.4
Total Rushes	328	392
Net Yards Passing	4805	3060
Avg. Per Game	300.3	191.3
Sacked/Yards Lost	39/267	38/272
Gross Yards	5072	3332
Att./Completions	639/399	460/267
Completion Pct.	62.4	58.0
Had Intercepted	15	21
Punts/Avg.	34/45.0	62/38.7
Net Punting Avg.	36.6	35.0
Penalties/Yards Lost	135/1009	134/1015
Fumbles/Ball Lost	34/21	22/12
Touchdowns	49	37
Rushing	10	12
Passing	37	18
Returns	2	7
Avg. Time of Possession	31:35	28:25

1990 Individual Statistics

Scoring	TD R	TD P	TD Rt	PAT	FG	Saf	TP
White	8	4	0	0/0	0/0	0	72
Garcia	0	0	0	26/28	14/20	0	68
Givins	0	9	0	0/0	0/0	0	54
Jeffires	0	8	0	0/0	0/0	0	48
Zendejas	0	0	0	20/21	7/12	0	41
T. Jones	0	6	0	0/0	0/0	0	36
Hill	0	5	0	0/0	0/0	0	30
Harris	0	3	0	0/0	0/0	0	18
Moon	2	0	0	0/0	0/0	0	12
Duncan	0	1	0	0/0	0/0	0	6
Ford	0	1	0	0/0	0/0	0	6
R. Johnson	0	0	1	0/0	0/0	0	6
Kinard	0	0	1	0/0	0/0	0	6
Childress	0	0	0	0/0	0/0	1	2
Oilers	10	37	2	46/49	21/32	1	405
Opponents	12	18	7	34/37	17/21	0	307

Passing	Att.	Comp.	Yds.	Pct.	TD	Int.	Tkld.	Rate
Moon	584	362	4689	62.0	33	13	36/252	96.8
Carlson	55	37	383	67.3	4	2	3/15	96.3
Oilers	639	399	5072	62.4	37	15	39/267	96.7
Opponents	460	267	3332	58.0	18	21	38/272	74.7

Rushing	Att.	Yds.	Avg.	LG	TD
White	168	702	4.2	22	8
Pinkett	66	268	4.1	19	0
Moon	55	215	3.9	17	2
V. Jones	14	75	5.4	14	0
Givins	3	65	21.7	31	0
Carlson	11	52	4.7	16	0
Rozier	10	42	4.2	11	0
T. Jones	1	−2	−2.0	−2	0
Oilers	328	1417	4.3	31	10
Opponents	392	1575	4.0	56t	12

Receiving	No.	Yds.	Avg.	LG	TD
Jeffires	74	1048	14.2	87t	8
Hill	74	1019	13.8	57	5
Givins	72	979	13.6	80t	9
Duncan	66	785	11.9	37t	1
White	39	368	9.4	29	4
T. Jones	30	409	13.6	47	6
Harris	13	172	13.2	42t	3
Pinkett	11	85	7.7	38	0
Ford	10	98	9.8	24	1
McNeil	5	63	12.6	16	0
Rozier	5	46	9.2	24	0
Oilers	399	5072	12.7	87t	37
Opponents	267	3332	12.5	78t	18

Interceptions	No.	Yds.	Avg.	LG	TD
R. Johnson	8	100	12.5	35	1
Kinard	4	75	18.8	47	0
Dishman	4	50	12.5	42	0
McDowell	2	11	5.5	11	0
Meads	1	32	32.0	32	0
Allen	1	27	27.0	27	0
Knight	1	0	0.0	0	0
Oilers	21	295	14.0	47	1
Opponents	15	237	15.8	82t	2

Punting	No.	Yds.	Avg.	In 20	LG
Gr. Montgomery	34	1530	45.0	7	60
Oilers	34	1530	45.0	7	60
Opponents	62	2402	38.7	20	55

Punt Returns	No.	FC	Yds.	Avg.	LG	TD
McNeil	30	20	172	5.7	26	0
Duncan	0	1	0	—	0	0
Oilers	30	21	172	5.7	26	0
Opponents	23	0	186	8.1	52t	1

Kickoff Returns	No.	Yds.	Avg.	LG	TD
McNeil	27	551	20.4	64	0
Ford	14	219	15.6	23	0
Pinkett	4	91	22.8	28	0
Norgard	2	0	0.0	0	0
Oilers	47	861	18.3	64	0
Opponents	71	1329	18.7	101t	1

Sacks	No.
S. Jones	12.5
Childress	8.0
Fuller	8.0
E. Johnson	2.5
Meads	2.5
D. Smith	2.0
A. Smith	1.0
Alm	0.5
Gl. Montgomery	0.5
McDowell	0.5
Oilers	38.0
Opponents	39.0

1991 Draft Choices

Round	Name	Pos.	College
2.	Mike Dumas	DB	Indiana
	Darryl Lewis	DB	Arizona
	John Flannery	C	Syracuse
3.	Steve Jackson	DB	Purdue
	Kevin Donnalley	T	North Carolina
4.	David Rocker	DT	Auburn
	Marcus Robertson	DB	Iowa State
5.	Gary Wellman	WR	Southern California
7.	Kyle Freeman	LB	Angelo State
8.	Gary Brown	RB	Penn State
9.	Shawn Jefferson	WR	Central Florida
10.	Curtis Moore	LB	Kansas
11.	James Smith	DB	Richmond
12.	Alex Johnson	WR	Miami

Houston Oilers 1991 Veteran Roster

No.	Name	Pos.	Ht.	Wt.	Birth-date	NFL Exp.	College	Hometown	How Acq.	'90 Games/ Starts
76	Alm, Jeff	DT	6-6	269	3/31/68	2	Notre Dame	Orland Park, Ill.	D2-'90	16/0
75	Banes, Joey	T	6-6	290	4/7/67	2	Houston	Houston, Tex.	FA-'91	1/0*
97	Banks, Robert	DE-DT	6-5	260	12/10/63	4	Notre Dame	Hampton, Va.	PB(Clev)-'91#	15/9*
37	Bergeson, Eric	S	5-11	192	1/1/66	2	Brigham Young	Salt Lake City, Utah	PB(Atl)-'91#	13/0*
71	Byrd, Richard	DT	6-4	278	3/20/62	6	Southern Mississippi	Jackson, Miss.	FA-'91	0*
14	†Carlson, Cody	QB	6-3	202	11/5/63	5	Baylor	San Antonio, Tex.	D3-'87	6/1
79	Childress, Ray	DT-DE	6-6	272	10/20/62	7	Texas A&M	Richardson, Tex.	D1a-'85	16/16
66	†Dawson, Doug	G-C	6-3	288	12/27/61	4	Texas	Houston, Tex.	FA-'90	16/1
28	†Dishman, Cris	CB	6-0	178	8/13/65	4	Purdue	Louisville, Ky.	D5a-'88	16/16
80	Duncan, Curtis	WR	5-11	184	1/26/65	5	Northwestern	Detroit, Mich.	D10-'87	16/16
51	Fairs, Eric	LB	6-3	244	2/17/64	6	Memphis State	Memphis, Tenn.	FA-'86	16/1
88	Ford, Bernard	WR	5-10	171	2/27/66	3	Central Florida	Cordele, Ga.	PB(Dall)-'90#	14/0
95	Fuller, William	DE	6-3	265	3/8/62	6	North Carolina	Chesapeake, Va.	T(Rams)-'86	16/16
8	Garcia, Teddy	K	5-9	172	6/4/64	4	Northeast Louisiana	Lewisville, Tex.	FA-'90	9/0
81	Givins, Ernest	WR	5-9	172	9/3/64	6	Louisville	St. Petersburg, Fla.	D2-'86	16/16
93	Graf, Rick	LB	6-5	250	8/29/63	5	Wisconsin	Madison, Wis.	PB(Mia)-'91#	8/0*
22	Hagy, John	S	6-0	190	12/9/65	4	Texas	San Antonio, Tex.	PB(Buff)-'91#	16/11*
83	†Harris, Leonard	WR	5-8	162	11/27/60	6	Texas Tech	McKinney, Tex.	FA-'87	14/0
85	Hill, Drew	WR	5-9	172	10/5/56	12	Georgia Tech	Newnan, Ga.	T(Rams)-'85	16/16
84	†Jeffires, Haywood	WR	6-2	201	12/12/64	5	North Carolina State	Greensboro, N.C.	D1b-'87	16/16
90	Johnson, Ezra	DE	6-4	257	10/2/55	15	Morris Brown	Shreveport, La.	PB(Ind)-'90#	16/3
23	Johnson, Richard	CB	6-1	195	9/16/63	7	Wisconsin	Dixmoor, Ill.	D1b-'85	16/16
87	Johnson, Richard L.	WR	5-8	182	10/19/61	3	Colorado	San Pedro, Calif.	PB(Det)-'91#	16/16*
86	Jones, Cedric	WR	6-1	184	6/1/60	10	Duke	Weldon, N.C.	PB(NE)-'91#	14/2*
96	†Jones, Sean	DE	6-7	264	12/19/62	8	Northeastern	Montclair, N.J.	T(Raid)-'88	16/16
82	Jones, Tony	WR	5-7	139	12/30/65	2	Texas	Grapeland, Tex.	D6-'90	15/0
32	Jordan, Tony	RB	6-2	220	5/8/65	3	Kansas State	Rochester, N.Y.	FA-'91	0*
27	Kinard, Terry	S	6-1	198	11/24/59	9	Clemson	Sumter, S.C.	PB(NYG)-'90#	16/16
21	Knight, Leander	CB-S	6-1	192	2/16/63	3	Montclair State	East Orange, N.J.	PB(NYJ)-'90#	16/1
56	Kozak, Scott	LB	6-3	222	11/28/65	3	Oregon	Colton, Ore.	D2-'89	16/0
57	Lathon, Lamar	LB	6-3	244	12/23/67	2	Houston	Wharton, Tex.	D1-'90	11/1
78	Maggs, Don	T-G	6-5	290	11/1/61	5	Tulane	Youngstown, Ohio	SD2-'84	16/16
74	Matthews, Bruce	G-C	6-5	291	8/8/61	9	Southern California	Arcadia, Calif.	D1-'83	16/16
25	McDowell, Bubba	S	6-1	198	11/4/66	3	Miami	Merritt Island, Fla.	D3-'89	15/15
89	McNeil, Gerald	WR-KR	5-8	142	3/27/62	6	Baylor	Killeen, Tex.	PB(Clev)-'90#	16/0
91	†Meads, Johnny	LB	6-2	226	6/25/61	8	Nicholls State	Napoleonville, La.	D3-'84	16/16
94	†Montgomery, Glenn	DT	6-0	268	3/31/67	3	Houston	Gretna, La.	D5-'89	15/0
9	†Montgomery, Greg	P	6-4	215	10/29/64	4	Michigan State	Red Bank, N.J.	D3-'88	16/0
1	Moon, Warren	QB	6-3	212	11/18/56	8	Washington	Los Angeles, Calif.	FA-'84	15/15
63	Munchak, Mike	G	6-3	284	3/5/60	10	Penn State	Scranton, Pa.	D1-'82	16/16
64	Norgard, Erik	C-G	6-1	278	11/4/65	2	Colorado	Arlington, Wash.	FA-'90	16/0
26	Orlando, Bo	S	5-10	180	4/3/66	2	West Virginia	Berwick, Pa.	D6-'89	16/0
72	Peguese, Willis	DE	6-4	267	12/18/66	2	Miami	Miami, Fla.	D3-'90	2/0
52	†Pennison, Jay	C	6-1	274	9/9/61	6	Nicholls State	Houma, La.	FA-'86	15/15
20	Pinkett, Allen	RB	5-9	196	1/25/64	6	Notre Dame	Sterling, Va.	D3-'86	15/0
31	Porter, Kerry	RB	6-1	220	9/23/64	4	Washington State	Great Falls, Mont.	PB(Den)-'91#	13/3*
53	Seale, Eugene	LB	5-10	253	6/3/64	5	Lamar	Jasper, Tex.	FA-'87	15/0
54	Smith, Al	LB	6-1	244	11/26/64	5	Utah State	Los Angeles, Calif.	D6a-'87	15/15
99	Smith, Doug	DT	6-6	314	6/13/59	7	Auburn	Bayboro, N.C.	D2a-'84	14/13
70	Steinkuhler, Dean	T	6-3	287	1/27/61	8	Nebraska	Burr, Neb.	D1-'84	15/7
36	Thomas, Dee	CB-S	5-10	176	11/7/67	2	Nicholls State	Morgan City, La.	D10-'90	6/0
44	†White, Lorenzo	RB	5-11	222	4/12/66	4	Michigan State	Ft. Lauderdale, Fla.	D1-'88	16/16
73	Williams, David	T	6-5	292	6/21/66	3	Florida	Lakeland, Fla.	D1-'89	15/9

* Banes played 1 game with Indianapolis in '90; Banks played 15 games with Cleveland; Bergeson played 13 games with Atlanta; Byrd last active with Houston in '89; Graf played 8 games with Miami; Hagy played 16 games with Buffalo; R.L. Johnson played 16 games with Detroit; C. Jones played 14 games with New England; Jordan last active with Phoenix in '89; Porter played 13 games with Denver.

† Option playout; subject to developments.

Plan B unconditional free agent.

Players lost through Plan B (4): CB Steve Brown (SF; 16 games in '90), RB Victor Jones (NE; 10), S Brett Tucker (Buff; 0), K Tony Zendejas (Rams; 7).

Also played with Oilers in '90—CB-S Patrick Allen (16 games), LB John Grimsley (15), S Quintin Jones (1), LB Robert Lyles (3), RB Mike Rozier (3).

COACHING STAFF

Head Coach, Jack Pardee

Pro Career: Named the Oilers' fourteenth head coach on January 9, 1990. Accepted post after serving three years (1987-89) as head coach at University of Houston. While at Houston, Cougars set over 100 NCAA/Southwest Conference records in 1988 and 1989. In 1986, was a scout for the Green Bay Packers. Prior to that, was head coach of successful Houston Gamblers of the USFL from 1984-85 as team led league in total offense and scoring in both seasons. Spent 1982 in private business after serving as defensive coordinator for San Diego Chargers in 1981. That season, Chargers won AFC's Western Division and advanced to AFC Championship Game. From 1978-80, was head coach of the Washington Redskins, earning NFL Coach of the Year honors in 1979. Was head coach of the Chicago Bears from 1975-77, earning NFC Coach of the Year accolades in 1976 and leading the club in 1977 to its first playoff berth in 14 years. Was general manager/head coach for Florida Blazers of the World Football League in 1974, winning division title and advancing to WFL title game. Began coaching career as Washington Redskins' assistant in 1973. Drafted by Los Angeles Rams in second round in 1957 and played 15 seasons at linebacker for Rams (1957-64, 1966-70) and Washington Redskins (1971-72). Was an all-pro selection in 1963 and 1971, and is a member of Rams' all-time fortieth anniversary team. Career record: 53-55.

Background: Played linebacker and fullback in All-America and Academic All-America career for coach Paul "Bear" Bryant at Texas A&M (1953-56). Is a member of the Texas A&M Hall of Fame, National Football Foundation Hall of Fame, College Football Hall of Fame, Texas Sports Hall of Fame, and Senior Bowl Hall of Fame.

Personal: Born April 19, 1936, Exira, Iowa. Jack and his wife, Phyllis, live in Missouri City, Tex., and have two sons, Steven and Ted, and three daughters, Judee, Anne, and Susan.

Assistant Coaches

Jim Eddy, defensive coordinator; born May 2, 1939, Checotah, Okla., lives in Houston. Defensive back/running back New Mexico State 1956-59. No pro playing experience. College coach: New Mexico State 1965-70, Texas-El Paso 1971-72, Houston 1987-89. Pro coach: Saskatchewan Roughriders (CFL) 1974-78 (head coach 1977-78), Hamilton Tiger-Cats (CFL) 1979-80, Montreal Alouettes (CFL) 1981 (head coach), Toronto Argonauts (CFL) 1982-83, Houston Gamblers (USFL) 1984-85, joined Oilers in 1990.

Kevin Gilbride, offensive coordinator; born August 27, 1951, New Haven, Conn., lives in Missouri City, Tex. Quarterback/tight end Southern Connecticut State 1970-73. No pro playing experience. College coach: Idaho State 1974-75, Tufts 1976-77, American International 1978-79, Southern Connecticut State 1980-84 (head coach), East Carolina 1987-88. Pro coach: Ottawa Rough Riders (CFL) 1985-86, joined Oilers in 1989.

Frank Novak, running backs; born May 18, 1938, Worcester, Mass., lives in Missouri City, Tex. Quarterback Northern Michigan 1959-61. No pro playing experience. College coach: Northern Michigan 1966-72, East Carolina 1973, Virginia 1974-75, Western Illinois 1976-77, Holy Cross 1978-83, Massachusetts 1986, Missouri 1988. Pro coach: Oklahoma Outlaws (USFL) 1984, Birmingham Stallions (USFL) 1985, joined Oilers in 1989.

Chris Palmer, receivers; born September 23, 1949, Mt. Kisco, N.Y., lives in Missouri City, Tex. Quarterback Southern Connecticut State 1968-71. No pro playing experience. College coach: Connecticut 1972-74, Lehigh 1975, Colgate 1976-82, New Haven 1986-87 (head coach), Boston University 1988-89 (head coach). Pro coach: Montreal Concordes (CFL) 1983, New Jersey Generals (USFL) 1984-85, joined Oilers in 1990.

Houston Oilers 1991 First-Year Roster

Name	Pos.	Ht.	Wt.	Birth-date	College	Hometown	How Acq.
Brown, Gary	RB	5-11	218	7/1/69	Penn State	Williamsport, Pa.	D8
Coleman, Pat (1)	WR	5-7	173	4/8/67	Mississippi	Cleveland, Miss.	D9-'90
Donnalley, Kevin	T	6-5	290	6/10/68	North Carolina	Raleigh, N.C.	D3b
Dumas, Mike	S	5-11	178	3/18/69	Indiana	Lowell, Mich.	D2a
Flannery, John	C	6-3	304	1/13/69	Syracuse	Pottsville, Pa.	D2c
Freeman, Kyle	LB	6-1	234	11/22/65	Angelo State	Snyder, Tex.	D7
Friberg, Keith (1)	DE-LB	6-4	258	11/21/66	Syracuse	Farrell, N.Y.	FA
Hough, Scott (1)	T	6-5	295	5/14/66	Maine	Weston, Mass.	FA
Jackson, Steve	CB	5-8	182	4/8/69	Purdue	Houston, Tex.	D3a
Jefferson, Shawn	WR	5-11	172	2/22/69	Central Florida	Jacksonville, Fla.	D9
Johnson, Alex	WR	5-9	167	8/18/68	Miami	Homestead, Fla.	D12
Levine, Marion	CB-S	6-3	215	10/26/67	Louisiana State	Galveston, Tex.	FA
Lewis, Darryl	CB	5-9	193	12/16/68	Arizona	La Puente, Calif.	D2b
Miotke, Frank (1)	WR	6-0	175	12/22/65	Grand Valley State	Hartland, Mich.	FA
Moore, Curtis	LB	6-1	247	11/2/67	Kansas	Wichita, Kan.	D10
Robertson, Marcus	CB	5-11	197	10/2/69	Iowa	Pasadena, Calif.	D4b
Rocker, David	DT	6-4	267	3/12/69	Auburn	Atlanta, Ga.	D4a
Smith, James	S	6-2	211	11/18/69	Richmond	Bumpass, Va.	D11
Wellman, Gary	WR	5-9	173	8/9/67	Southern California	Westlake, Calif.	D5

The term NFL Rookie is defined as a player who is in his first season of professional football and has not been on the roster of another professional football team for any regular-season or postseason games. A Rookie is designated by an "R" on NFL rosters. Players who have been active in another professional football league or players who have NFL experience, including either preseason training camp or being on an active roster for fewer than three regular-season or postseason games, are termed NFL First-Year Players. An NFL First-Year Player is designated by a "1" on NFL rosters. Thereafter, a player on an NFL active roster for at least three regular-season or postseason games is credited with an additional year of NFL playing experience.

NOTES

Richard Smith, special teams-linebackers; born October 17, 1955, Los Angeles, lives in Richmond, Tex. Offensive lineman Rio Hondo (Calif.) J.C. 1975-76, Fresno State 1977-78. No pro playing experience. College coach: Rio Hondo (Calif.) J.C. 1979-80, Cal State-Fullerton 1981-83, California 1984-86, Arizona 1987. Pro coach: Joined Oilers in 1988.

Jim Stanley, defensive line; born June 22, 1934, Dunham, Ky., lives in Houston. Guard/defensive tackle Texas A&M 1954-57. No pro playing experience. College coach: Southern Methodist 1961, Texas-El Paso 1962, Oklahoma State 1963-68, 1972-78 (head coach 1973-78), Navy 1969-70. Pro coach: Winnipeg Blue Bombers (CFL) 1971, New York Giants 1979, Atlanta Falcons 1980-82, Michigan Panthers (USFL) 1983-84 (head coach), Tampa Bay Buccaneers 1986, joined Oilers in 1990.

Pat Thomas, defensive backs; born September 1, 1954, Plano, Tex., lives in Houston. Cornerback Texas A&M 1972-75. Pro cornerback Los Angeles Rams 1976-82. College coach: Houston 1987-89. Pro coach: Houston Gamblers (USFL) 1984-85, joined Oilers in 1990.

Steve Watterson, strength and rehabilitation; born November 27, 1956, Newport, R.I., lives in Sugar Land, Tex. Attended Rhode Island. No college or pro playing experience. Pro coach: Philadelphia Eagles 1984-85 (assistant trainer), joined Oilers in 1986 (elevated to assistant coach in 1988).

Bob Young, offensive line; born September 3, 1942, Marshall, Tex., lives in Sugar Land, Tex. Guard Texas 1960-61, Howard Payne 1962-63. Pro guard Denver Broncos 1966-70, Houston Oilers 1971, 1980, St. Louis Cardinals 1972-79, New Orleans Saints 1981. College coach: Houston 1987-89. Pro coach: Houston Gamblers (USFL) 1984-85, joined Oilers in 1990.

American Football Conference Eastern Division

Team Colors: Royal Blue and White

P.O. Box 535000
Indianapolis, Indiana 46253
Telephone: (317) 297-2658

Club Officials

President-Treasurer: Robert Irsay
Vice President-General Manager: James Irsay
Vice President-General Counsel: Michael G. Chernoff
Assistant General Manager: Bob Terpening
Director of Player Personnel: Jack Bushofsky
Controller: Kurt Humphrey
Director of Operations: Pete Ward
Director of Public Relations: Craig Kelley
Ticket Manager: Larry Hall
Assistant Director of Public Relations: Rod St. Clair
Purchasing Administrator: David Filar
Administrative Assistant/Coaching: Todd Stewart
Equipment Manager: Jon Scott
Assistant Equipment Manager: Chris Matlock
Video Director: Marty Heckscher
Assistant Video Director: John Starliper
Head Trainer: Hunter Smith
Assistant Trainer: Dave Hammer
Team Physician and Orthopedic Surgeon: K. Donald Shelbourne
Orthopedic Surgeon: Arthur C. Rettig

Stadium: Hoosier Dome • **Capacity:** 60,129
100 South Capitol Avenue
Indianapolis, Indiana 46225

Playing Surface: AstroTurf

Training Camp: Anderson University
Anderson, Indiana 46011

1991 Schedule

Preseason

Aug. 2	at Denver	7:00
Aug. 10	**Seattle**	7:30
Aug. 17	**New Orleans**	7:30
Aug. 23	at Philadelphia	7:30

Regular Season

Sept. 1	**New England**	3:00
Sept. 8	at Miami	1:00
Sept. 15	at Los Angeles Raiders	1:00
Sept. 22	**Detroit**	12:00
Sept. 29	at Seattle	1:00
Oct. 6	**Pittsburgh**	7:00
Oct. 13	at Buffalo	1:00
Oct. 20	**New York Jets**	12:00
Oct. 27	**Open Date**	
Nov. 3	**Miami**	4:00
Nov. 10	at New York Jets	1:00
Nov. 17	**Chicago**	1:00
Nov. 24	vs. Green Bay at Milwaukee	12:00
Dec. 1	**Cleveland**	1:00
Dec. 8	at New England	1:00
Dec. 15	**Buffalo**	8:00
Dec. 22	at Tampa Bay	1:00

Colts Coaching History

Baltimore 1953-83
(275-268-7)

1953	Keith Molesworth	3-9-0
1954-62	Weeb Ewbank	61-52-1
1963-69	Don Shula	73-26-4
1970-72	Don McCafferty*	26-11-1
1972	John Sandusky	4-5-0
1973-74	Howard Schnellenberger**	4-13-0
1974	Joe Thomas	2-9-0
1975-79	Ted Marchibroda	41-36-0
1980-81	Mike McCormack	9-23-0
1982-84	Frank Kush***	11-28-1
1984	Hal Hunter	0-1-0
1985-86	Rod Dowhower****	5-24-0
1986-90	Ron Meyer	36-31-0

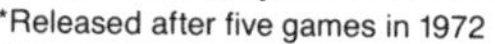

*Released after five games in 1972
**Released after three games in 1974
***Resigned after 15 games in 1984
****Released after 13 games in 1986

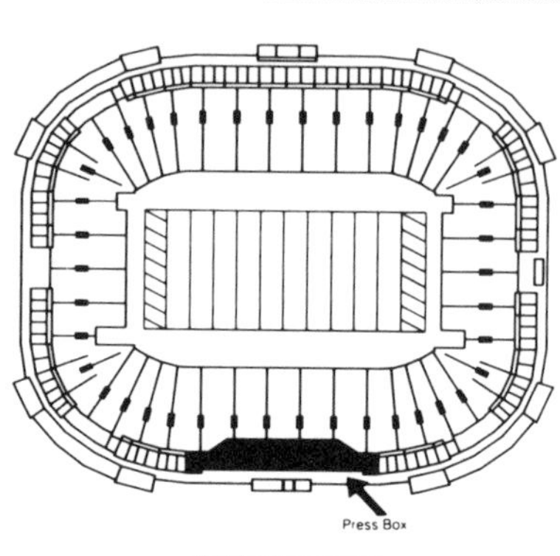

HOOSIER DOME

Record Holders

Individual Records—Career

Category	Name	Performance
Rushing (Yds.)	Lydell Mitchell, 1972-77	5,487
Passing (Yds.)	Johnny Unitas, 1956-1972	39,768
Passing (TDs)	Johnny Unitas, 1956-1972	287
Receiving (No.)	Raymond Berry, 1955-1967	631
Receiving (Yds.)	Raymond Berry, 1955-1967	9,275
Interceptions	Bob Boyd, 1960-68	57
Punting (Avg.)	Rohn Stark, 1982-1990	44.1
Punt Return (Avg.)	Wendell Harris, 1964	12.6
Kickoff Return (Avg.)	Jim Duncan, 1969-1971	32.5
Field Goals	Lou Michaels, 1964-69	107
Touchdowns (Tot.)	Lenny Moore, 1956-1967	113
Points	Lenny Moore, 1956-1967	678

Individual Records—Single Season

Category	Name	Performance
Rushing (Yds.)	Eric Dickerson, 1988	1,659
Passing (Yds.)	Johnny Unitas, 1963	3,481
Passing (TDs)	Johnny Unitas, 1959	32
Receiving (No.)	Joe Washington, 1979	82
Receiving (Yds.)	Raymond Berry, 1960	1,298
Interceptions	Tom Keane, 1953	11
Punting (Avg.)	Rohn Stark, 1985	45.9
Punt Return (Avg.)	Clarence Verdin, 1989	12.9
Kickoff Return (Avg.)	Jim Duncan, 1970	35.4
Field Goals	Raul Allegre, 1983	30
Touchdowns (Tot.)	Lenny Moore, 1964	20
Points	Lenny Moore, 1964	120

Individual Records—Single Game

Category	Name	Performance
Rushing (Yds.)	Norm Bulaich, 9-19-71	198
Passing (Yds.)	Johnny Unitas, 9-17-67	401
Passing (TDs)	Gary Cuozzo, 11-14-65	5
	Gary Hogeboom, 10-4-87	5
Receiving (No.)	Lydell Mitchell, 12-15-74	13
	Joe Washington, 9-2-79	13
Receiving (Yds.)	Raymond Berry, 11-10-57	224
Interceptions	Many times	3
	Last time by Leonard Coleman, 10-12-86	
Field Goals	Many times	5
	Last time by Dean Biasucci, 9-25-88	
Touchdowns (Tot.)	Many times	4
	Last time by Eric Dickerson, 10-31-88	
Points	Many times	24
	Last time by Eric Dickerson, 10-31-88	

1990 Team Record

Preseason (0-4)

Date	Result		Opponents
8/11	L	7-16	Denver
8/17	L	10-13	at Seattle
8/27	L	16-17	Philadelphia
8/31	L	14-17	at New Orleans
		47-63	

Regular Season (7-9)

Date	Result		Opponents	Att.
9/9	L	10-26	at Buffalo	78,899
9/16	L	14-16	New England	49,256
9/23	L	10-24	at Houston	50,093
9/30	W	24-23	at Philadelphia	62,067
10/7	W	23-19	Kansas City	54,950
10/21	L	17-27	Denver	59,850
10/28	L	7-27	Miami	59,213
11/5	L	7-24	N.Y. Giants	58,688
11/11	W	13-10	at New England	28,924
11/18	W	17-14	N.Y. Jets	47,283
11/25	W	34-20	at Cincinnati	60,051
12/2	L	17-20	at Phoenix	31,885
12/9	L	7-31	Buffalo	53,268
12/16	W	29-21	at N.Y. Jets	41,423
12/22	W	35-28	Washington	58,173
12/30	L	17-23	at Miami	59,547

Score by Periods

Colts	47	68	85	81	0	—	281
Opponents	87	128	43	95	0	—	353

Attendance

Home 440,700 Away 412,889 Total 853,589
Single-game home record, 61,479 (11-13-83)
Single-season home record, 481,305 (1984)

1990 Team Statistics

	Colts	Opp.
Total First Downs	245	320
Rushing	81	130
Passing	142	176
Penalty	22	14
Third Down: Made/Att.	56/185	87/204
Third Down: Pct.	30.3	42.6
Fourth Down: Made/Att.	11/18	7/14
Fourth Down: Pct.	61.1	50.0
Total Net Yards	4155	5614
Avg. Per Game	259.7	350.9
Total Plays	874	1034
Avg. Per Play	4.8	5.4
Net Yards Rushing	1282	2212
Avg. Per Game	80.1	138.3
Total Rushes	335	513
Net Yards Passing	2873	3402
Avg. Per Game	179.6	212.6
Sacked/Yards Lost	51/424	29/203
Gross Yards	3297	3605
Att./Completions	488/269	492/301
Completion Pct.	55.1	61.2
Had Intercepted	21	9
Punts/Avg.	72/42.8	58/42.0
Net Punting Avg.	37.4	34.4
Penalties/Yards Lost	78/590	104/781
Fumbles/Ball Lost	23/10	25/15
Touchdowns	33	36
Rushing	9	12
Passing	22	20
Returns	2	4
Avg. Time of Possession	26:27	33:33

1990 Individual Statistics

Scoring	TD R	TD P	TD Rt	PAT	FG	Saf	TP
Biasucci	0	0	0	32/33	17/24	0	83
Bentley	4	2	0	0/0	0/0	0	36
Hester	0	6	0	0/0	0/0	0	36
Brooks	0	5	0	0/0	0/0	0	30
Morgan	0	5	0	0/0	0/0	0	30
Dickerson	4	0	0	0/0	0/0	0	24
Johnson	0	2	0	0/0	0/0	0	12
Beach	0	1	0	0/0	0/0	0	6
George	1	0	0	0/0	0/0	0	6
Goode	0	0	1	0/0	0/0	0	6
Grant	0	0	1	0/0	0/0	0	6
Verdin	0	1	0	0/0	0/0	0	6
Colts	9	22	2	32/33	17/24	0	281
Opponents	12	20	4	35/36	32/43	3	353

Passing	Att.	Comp.	Yds.	Pct.	TD	Int.	Tkld.	Rate
George	334	181	2152	54.2	16	13	37/320	73.8
Trudeau	144	84	1078	58.3	6	6	14/104	78.4
Ferguson	8	2	21	25.0	0	2	0/0	0.0
Herrmann	1	1	6	100.0	0	0	0/0	91.7
Stark	1	1	40	100.0	0	0	0/0	118.8
Colts	488	269	3297	55.1	22	21	51/424	73.3
Opponents	492	301	3605	61.2	20	9	29/203	89.5

Rushing	Att.	Yds.	Avg.	LG	TD
Dickerson	166	677	4.1	43	4
Bentley	137	556	4.1	26t	4
Trudeau	10	28	2.8	9	0
Clark	7	10	1.4	11	0
Hester	4	9	2.3	10	0
George	11	2	0.2	6	1
Colts	335	1282	3.8	43	9
Opponents	513	2212	4.3	32	12

Receiving	No.	Yds.	Avg.	LG	TD
Bentley	71	664	9.4	73	2
Brooks	62	823	13.3	75	5
Hester	54	924	17.1	64t	6
Morgan	23	364	15.8	42t	5
Dickerson	18	92	5.1	17	0
Verdin	14	178	12.7	45	1
Beach	12	124	10.3	21	1
Mobley, Den.-Ind.	8	41	5.1	9	0
Johnson	5	32	6.4	15t	2
Clark	5	23	4.6	11	0
Simmons	4	33	8.3	12	0
Prior	1	40	40.0	40	0
Colts	269	3297	12.3	75	22
Opponents	301	3605	12.0	66	20

Interceptions	No.	Yds.	Avg.	LG	TD
Prior	3	66	22.0	36	0
Taylor	2	51	25.5	40	0
Grant	1	25	25.0	25t	1
Herrod	1	12	12.0	12	0
Goode	1	10	10.0	10	0
Bickett	1	9	9.0	9	0
Colts	9	173	19.2	40	1
Opponents	21	221	10.5	35t	1

Punting	No.	Yds.	Avg.	In 20	LG
Stark	71	3084	43.4	24	61
Colts	72	3084	42.8	24	61
Opponents	58	2435	42.0	13	68

Punt Returns	No.	FC	Yds.	Avg.	LG	TD
Verdin	31	3	396	12.8	36	0
Grant	2	0	6	3.0	6	0
Prior	2	6	0	0.0	0	0
Daniel	1	0	0	0.0	0	0
Colts	36	9	402	11.2	36	0
Opponents	42	15	334	8.0	32	0

Kickoff Returns	No.	Yds.	Avg.	LG	TD
Simmons	19	348	18.3	34	0
Verdin	18	350	19.4	44	0
Grant	15	280	18.7	29	0
Bentley	11	211	19.2	36	0
Ball	1	0	0.0	0	0
Jarvis	1	0	0.0	0	0
Mobley, Den.-Ind.	1	9	9.0	9	0
Colts	65	1189	18.3	44	0
Opponents	49	961	19.6	38	0

Sacks	No.
Clancy	7.5
Banks	4.5
Bickett	4.5
Herrod	4.0
Hand	3.0
Faulkner	2.0
Thompson	1.5
Siragusa	1.0
Colts	29.0
Opponents	51.0

1991 Draft Choices

Round	Name	Pos.	College
2.	Shane Curry	DE	Miami
3.	Dave McCloughan	DB	Colorado
4.	Mark Vander Poel	T	Colorado
5.	Kerry Cash	TE	Texas
6.	Mel Agee	DT	Illinois
7.	James Bradley	WR	Michigan State
8.	Tim Bruton	TE	Missouri
9.	Howard Griffith	RB	Illinois
10.	Frank Giannetti	DE	Penn State
11.	Jerry Crafts	T	Louisville
12.	Rob Luedeke	C	Penn State

Indianapolis Colts 1991 Veteran Roster

No.	Name	Pos.	Ht.	Wt.	Birth-date	NFL Exp.	College	Hometown	How Acq.	'90 Games/ Starts
79	Armstrong, Harvey	NT	6-3	282	12/29/59	9	Southern Methodist	Houston, Tex.	FA-'86	12/10
62	Baldinger, Brian	G	6-4	278	1/7/59	9	Duke	Massapequa Park, N.Y.	FA-'88	16/16
31	†Ball, Michael	CB-S	6-0	220	8/5/64	4	Southern	New Orleans, La.	D4-'88	16/0
51	†Banks, Chip	LB	6-4	254	9/18/59	9	Southern California	Augusta, Ga.	T(SD)-'89	16/16
36	Baylor, John	CB-S	6-0	203	3/5/65	3	Southern Mississippi	Meridian, Miss.	D5-'88	10/0
81	Beach, Pat	TE	6-4	249	12/28/59	9	Washington State	Grant's Pass, Wash.	D6-'82	16/11
20	Bentley, Albert	RB	5-11	217	8/15/60	7	Miami	Immokalee, Fla.	SD2-'84	16/15
4	Biasucci, Dean	K	6-0	190	7/25/62	7	Western Carolina	Niagara Falls, N.Y.	FA-'86	16/0
50	Bickett, Duane	LB	6-5	251	12/1/62	7	Southern California	Los Angeles, Calif.	D1-'85	15/15
80	Brooks, Bill	WR	6-0	189	4/6/64	6	Boston University	Milton, Mass.	D4-'86	16/16
71	Call, Kevin	T	6-7	308	11/13/61	8	Colorado State	Boulder, Colo.	D5b-'84	8/8
76	†Clancy, Sam	DE	6-7	290	5/29/58	8	Pittsburgh	Pittsburgh, Pa.	PB(Clev)-'89	16/8
66	†Conlin, Chris	G-T	6-4	287	6/7/65	3	Penn State	Philadelphia, Pa.	FA-'90	16/0
38	†Daniel, Eugene	CB-S	5-11	188	5/4/61	8	Louisiana State	Baton Rouge, La.	D8-'84	15/15
95	Davis, Travis	DT	6-2	274	5/10/66	2	Michigan State	Warren, Ohio	PB(NO)-'91#	2/0*
29	Dickerson, Eric	RB	6-3	224	9/2/60	9	Southern Methodist	Sealy, Tex.	T(Rams)-'87	11/8
69	Dixon, Randy	G	6-3	302	3/12/65	5	Pittsburgh	Clewiston, Fla.	D4-'87	15/14
53	Donaldson, Ray	C	6-3	300	5/18/58	12	Georgia	Rome, Ga.	D2a-'80	16/16
58	Figaro, Cedric	LB	6-2	250	8/17/66	4	Notre Dame	Lafayette, La.	PB(SD)-'91#	16/1*
11	George, Jeff	QB	6-4	221	12/8/67	2	Illinois	Indianapolis, Ind.	D1-'90	13/12
37	†Goode, Chris	CB-S	6-0	196	9/17/63	5	Alabama	Town Creek, Ala.	D10-'87	16/10
26	Grant, Alan	CB-S	5-10	187	10/1/66	2	Stanford	Pasadena, Calif.	D4c-'90	16/7
78	Hand, Jon	DE	6-7	301	11/13/63	6	Alabama	Sylacauga, Ala.	D1-'86	12/12
9	†Herrmann, Mark	QB	6-4	220	1/8/59	10	Purdue	Carmel, Ind.	W(Rams)-'90	3/0
54	Herrod, Jeff	LB	6-0	246	7/29/66	4	Mississippi	Birmingham, Ala.	D9-'88	13/13
84	†Hester, Jessie	WR	5-11	172	1/21/63	6	Florida State	Belle Glade, Fla.	FA-'90	16/14
7	Hilger, Rusty	QB	6-4	209	5/9/62	6	Oklahoma State	Oklahoma City, Okla.	FA-'90	0*
25	Holloway, Cornell	CB-S	5-11	182	1/30/66	2	Pittsburgh	Alliance, Ohio	FA-'90	15/0
23	Johnson, Anthony	RB	6-0	222	10/25/67	2	Notre Dame	Indianapolis, Ind.	D2-'90	16/0
96	McDonald, Quintus	LB	6-3	263	12/14/66	3	Penn State	Rockingham, N.C.	D6-'89	9/1
87	†Mobley, Orson	TE	6-5	259	3/6/63	6	Salem College	Brooksville, Fla.	W(Den)-'90	0*
86	Morgan, Stanley	WR	5-11	185	2/17/55	15	Tennessee	Easley, S.C.	FA-'90	16/6
73	Moss, Zefross	T	6-6	338	8/17/66	3	Alabama State	Tuscaloosa, Ala.	T(Dall)-'89	16/16
39	Prior, Mike	S	6-0	210	11/14/63	6	Illinois State	Chicago Heights, Ill.	FA-'87	16/16
52	Radecic, Scott	LB	6-3	236	6/14/62	8	Penn State	Pittsburgh, Pa.	W(Buff)-'90	15/1
74	Schultz, William	T	6-5	293	5/1/67	2	Southern California	Granada Hills, Calif.	D4b-'90	12/0
85	Simmons, Stacey	WR	5-9	183	8/5/68	2	Florida	Clearwater, Fla.	D4a-'90	14/1
98	Siragusa, Tony	NT	6-3	291	5/14/67	2	Pittsburgh	Kenilworth, N.J.	FA-'90	13/6
3	Stark, Rohn	P	6-3	203	5/4/59	10	Florida State	Minneapolis, Minn.	D2b-'82	16/0
27	†Taylor, Keith	CB-S	5-11	206	12/21/64	4	Illinois	Pennsauken, N.J.	FA-'88	16/16
99	Thompson, Donnell	DE	6-4	280	10/27/58	11	North Carolina	Lumberton, N.C.	D1b-'81	12/12
68	Tomberlin, Pat	T	6-2	330	1/29/66	2	Florida State	Jacksonville, Fla.	D4-'89	16/10
10	Trudeau, Jack	QB	6-3	219	9/9/62	6	Illinois	Livermore, Calif.	D2-'86	6/4
83	Verdin, Clarence	WR	5-8	162	6/14/63	6	Southwest Louisiana	New Orleans, La.	T(Wash)-'88	15/5
92	Walker, Tony	LB	6-3	235	4/2/68	2	Southeastern Missouri	Birmingham, Ala.	D6-'90	14/0

* Davis played 2 games with New Orleans in '90; Figaro played 16 games with San Diego; Hilger active for 9 games but did not play; Mobley last active with Denver in '89.

† Option playout; subject to developments.

Plan B unconditional free agent.

Retired—Fredd Young, 7-year linebacker, 11 games in '90.

Players lost through Plan B (6): LB O'Brien Alston (Raid; 0 games in '90), DE Jeff Faulkner (Phx; 7), RB Ivy Joe Hunter (NE; 16), LB Kurt Larson (GB; 16), TE Eugene Riley (Det; 1), DE Matt Vanderbeek (Minn; 16).

Also played with Colts in '90—NT Gary Baldinger (1 game), T Joey Banes (1), NT Mitchell Benson (9), RB Ken Clark (5), QB Joe Ferguson (1), DE Ralph Jarvis (8), DE Sean McNanie (1), DE Ray Seals (1).

COACHING STAFF

Head Coach, Ron Meyer

Pro Career: Named Colts' twelfth head coach on December 1, 1986. Led Colts to AFC Eastern Division championship in 1987 with a 9-6 record. Has won 36 of 66 games with the Colts. Served as head coach of the New England Patriots from 1982-84. Compiled 18-15 regular-season record with one playoff game following the 1982 season. Scout for Dallas Cowboys 1971-72. Career record: 54-47.

Background: Entered coaching ranks at Penn High School in Mishawauka, Indiana, in 1964. Joined staff at Purdue (where he played defensive back 1959-62) in 1965 in charge of the offensive backfield, receivers, and overall passing game. Remained at Purdue through 1970. Named head coach at Nevada-Las Vegas in 1973, directing the Rebels to a three-year 27-8 mark, including an undefeated (11-0) regular season in 1974 before losing in the national semifinals in the NCAA Division II playoffs. Named head coach at Southern Methodist in 1976, where he coached until 1981. The Mustangs had a 34-31-1 record during Meyer's tenure and won the Southwestern Conference championship his final year.

Personal: Born February 17, 1941, in Westerville, Ohio. Ron and his wife, Cindy, live in Indianapolis with their daughters Kathryn and Elizabeth. Ron's sons, Ron, Jr., and Ralph, reside in Dallas.

Assistant Coaches

Leon Burtnett, offensive coordinator, quarterbacks; born May 30, 1943, Fresno, Calif., lives in Indianapolis. Fullback Southwestern (Kan.) University 1961-65. No pro playing experience. College coach: Montana State 1970, Washington State 1971, Wyoming 1972-73, San Jose State 1974-75, Michigan State 1976, Purdue 1977-86 (head coach 1982-86). Pro coach: Joined Colts in 1987.

George Catavolos, secondary; born May 8, 1945, Chicago, Ill., lives in Indianapolis. Defensive back Purdue 1964-66. No pro playing experience. College coach: Purdue 1967-68, 1971-76, Middle Tennessee State 1969, Louisville 1970, Kentucky 1977-81, Tennessee 1982-83. Pro coach: Joined Colts in 1984.

Sylvester Crooms, running backs; born September 25, 1954, Tuscaloosa, Ala., lives in Indianapolis. Center Alabama 1971-74. Pro center New Orleans Saints 1975. College coach: Alabama 1976-86. Pro coach: Tampa Bay Buccaneers 1987-90, joined Colts in 1991.

Steve Furness, defensive line; born December 5, 1950, Warwick, R.I., lives in Indianapolis. Defensive tackle Rhode Island 1968-71. Pro defensive tackle Pittsburgh Steelers 1972-80, Detroit Lions 1981. College coach: Michigan State 1982-90. Pro coach: Philadelphia Stars (USFL) 1981, joined Colts in 1991.

Milt Jackson, receivers; born October 16, 1943, Groesbeck, Tex., lives in Indianapolis. Defensive back Tulsa 1965-66. Pro defensive back San Francisco 49ers 1967. College coach: Oregon State 1973, Rice 1974, California 1975-76, Oregon 1977-78, UCLA 1979. Pro coach: San Francisco 49ers 1980-82, Buffalo Bills 1983-84, Philadelphia Eagles 1985, Houston Oilers 1986-88, joined Colts in 1989.

Bill Muir, assistant head coach, offensive line; born October 26, 1942, Pittsburgh, Pa., lives in Indianapolis. Tackle Susquehanna 1962-64. No pro playing experience. College coach: Susquehanna 1965, Delaware Valley 1966-67, Rhode Island 1970-71, Idaho State 1972-73, Southern Methodist 1976-77. Pro coach: Orlando (Continental Football League) 1968-69, Houston-Shreveport Steamer (WFL) 1975, New England Patriots 1982-84, Detroit Lions 1985-88, joined Colts in 1989.

Brad Seely, special teams, tight ends; born September 6, 1956, Vinton, Iowa, lives in Indianapolis. Tackle/guard South Dakota State 1974-77. No pro playing experience. College coach: Colorado State 1980, Southern Methodist 1981, North Carolina State 1982, Pacific 1983, Oklahoma State 1984-88. Pro coach: Joined Colts in 1989.

Rick Venturi, defensive coordinator, linebackers; born February 23, 1946, Taylorville, Ill., lives in Indianapolis. Quarterback Northwestern 1965-67. No pro playing experience. College coach: Northwestern 1968-72, 1978-80 (head coach), Purdue 1973-76, Illinois 1977. Pro coach: Joined Colts in 1982.

Tom Zupancic, strength and conditioning; born September 14, 1955, Indianapolis, lives in Indianapolis. Defensive tackle-offensive tackle Indiana Central 1975-78. No pro playing experience. Pro coach: Joined Colts in 1984.

Indianapolis Colts 1991 First-Year Roster

Name	Pos.	Ht.	Wt.	Birth-date	College	Hometown	How Acq.
Agee, Mel	DE	6-5	282	11/22/68	Illinois	Chicago, Ill.	D6
Bates, Stephen (1)	NT	6-4	245	6/28/66	James Madison	Pittsburgh, Pa.	FA
Bradley, James	WR	5-11	193	11/24/68	Michigan State	Orrville, Ohio	D7
Bruton, Tim	TE	6-3	252	6/14/67	Missouri	Nacogdoches, Tex.	D8
Cash, Kerry	TE	6-4	247	8/7/69	Texas	San Antonio, Tex.	D5
Cline, Michael (1)	LB	6-4	283	7/28/63	Arkansas State	Pine Bluff, Ark.	FA
Crafts, Jerry	T	6-5	331	1/6/68	Louisville	Tulsa, Okla.	D11
Cunningham, Pat (1)	T	6-6	295	1/4/69	Texas A&M	Los Angeles, Calif.	D4d-'90
Curry, Shane	DE	6-4	259	4/7/68	Miami	Cincinnati, Ohio	D2
Davis, Willie (1)	CB-S	5-11	198	1/6/67	Southern Illinois	Ft. Benning, Ga.	FA
Giannetti, Frank	LB	6-2	255	3/14/68	Penn State	Toms River, N.J.	D10
Griffith, Howard	RB	5-11	219	11/17/67	Illinois	Chicago, Ill.	D9
Huffman, Darvell (1)	WR	5-7	158	5/5/67	Boston University	Boston, Mass.	FA
Jaworski, Matthew (1)	LB	6-1	228	10/23/67	Colgate	Blasdell, N.Y.	FA
Lattimore, Brian (1)	RB	6-1	202	10/29/66	Southeastern Missouri	St. Petersburg, Fla.	FA
Luedeke, Rob	C	6-4	271	9/20/67	Penn State	Bridgewater, N.J.	D12
McCloughan, Dave	CB	6-0	180	11/20/66	Colorado	San Leandro, Calif.	D3
Thornton, Reggie (1)	WR	5-10	170	9/26/67	Bowling Green	Detroit, Mich.	FA
Vander Poel, Mark	T	6-7	303	3/5/68	Colorado	Upland, Calif.	D4
Weir, Robert (1)	DT-DE	6-3	250	2/4/61	Southern Methodist	Birmingham, England	FA
Williams, Kyle (1)	CB-S	5-10	170	11/11/66	Southeastern Missouri	St. Petersburg, Fla.	FA

The term NFL Rookie is defined as a player who is in his first season of professional football and has not been on the roster of another professional football team for any regular-season or postseason games. A Rookie is designated by an "R" on NFL rosters. Players who have been active in another professional football league or players who have NFL experience, including either preseason training camp or being on an active roster for fewer than three regular-season or postseason games, are termed NFL First-Year Players. An NFL First-Year Player is designated by a "1" on NFL rosters. Thereafter, a player on an NFL active roster for at least three regular-season or postseason games is credited with an additional year of NFL playing experience.

NOTES

American Football Conference Western Division

Team Colors: Red, Gold, and White

One Arrowhead Drive
Kansas City, Missouri 64129
Telephone: (816) 924-9300

Club Officials

Founder: Lamar Hunt
Chairman of the Board: Jack Steadman
President/General Manager and Chief Operating Officer: Carl Peterson
Executive Vice President of Administration: Tim Connolly
Assistant General Manager: Dennis Thum
Secretary: Jim Seigfreid
Director of Finance/Treasurer: Dale Young
Director of Public Relations: Bob Moore
Director of Operations: Bill Dickerson
Director of Marketing & Sales: Dennis Watley
Director of Development: Ken Blume
Player Personnel Director: Whitey Dovell
Assistant Director of Public Relations: Jim Carr
Director of Promotions: Phil Thomas
Community Relations Manager: Brenda Boatright
Ticket Manager: Phil Youtsey
Equipment Manager: Mike Davidson
Assistant Equipment Manager: Albert Veytia
Trainer: Dave Kendall
Assistant Trainer: Bud Epps
Video Coordinator: Mike Dennis
Assistant Video Coordinator: Mike Kirk

Stadium: Arrowhead Stadium • **Capacity:** 78,067
One Arrowhead Drive
Kansas City, Missouri 64129

Playing Surface: AstroTurf-8

Training Camp: Wisconsin-River Falls
River Falls, Wisconsin 54022

1991 Schedule

Preseason

Aug. 3	**Dallas**	8:00
Aug. 10	vs. N.Y. Jets at St. Louis	7:00
Aug. 17	**Detroit**	7:00
Aug. 23	at Tampa Bay	8:00

Regular Season

Sept. 1	**Atlanta**	12:00
Sept. 8	**New Orleans**	12:00
Sept. 16	at Houston (Monday)	8:00
Sept. 22	**Seattle**	3:00
Sept. 29	at San Diego	1:00
Oct. 7	**Buffalo** (Monday)	8:00
Oct. 13	**Miami**	3:00
Oct. 20	at Denver	2:00
Oct. 28	**L.A. Raiders** (Monday)	8:00
Nov. 3	**Open Date**	
Nov. 10	at Los Angeles Rams	1:00
Nov. 17	**Denver**	12:00
Nov. 24	at Cleveland	1:00
Dec. 1	at Seattle	1:00
Dec. 8	**San Diego**	12:00
Dec. 14	at San Francisco (Saturday)	1:00
Dec. 22	at Los Angeles Raiders	1:00

Chiefs Coaching History

Dallas Texans 1960-62
(229-221-12)

1960-74	Hank Stram	129-79-10
1975-77	Paul Wiggin*	11-24-0
1977	Tom Bettis	1-6-0
1978-82	Marv Levy	31-42-0
1983-86	John Mackovic	30-35-0
1987-88	Frank Gansz	8-22-1
1989-90	Marty Schottenheimer	19-13-1

*Released after seven games in 1977

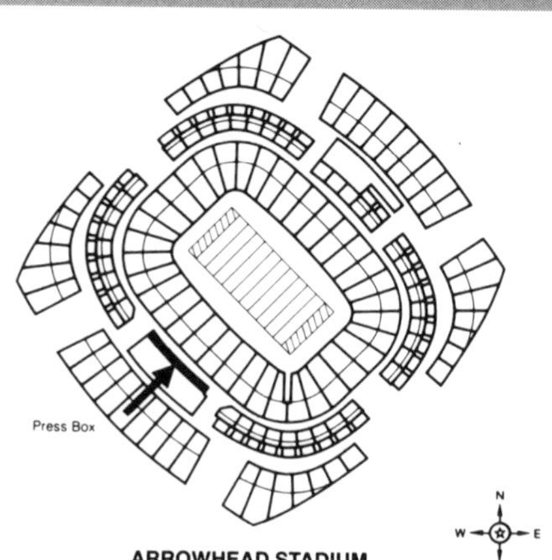

ARROWHEAD STADIUM

Record Holders

Individual Records—Career

Category	Name	Performance
Rushing (Yds.)	Ed Podolak, 1969-1977	4,451
Passing (Yds.)	Len Dawson, 1962-1975	28,507
Passing (TDs)	Len Dawson, 1962-1975	237
Receiving (No.)	Henry Marshall, 1976-1987	416
Receiving (Yds.)	Otis Taylor, 1965-1975	7,306
Interceptions	Emmitt Thomas, 1966-1978	58
Punting (Avg.)	Jerrel Wilson, 1963-1977	43.5
Punt Return (Avg.)	J.T. Smith, 1979-1984	10.6
Kickoff Return (Avg.)	Noland Smith, 1967-69	26.8
Field Goals	Jan Stenerud, 1967-1979	279
Touchdowns (Tot.)	Otis Taylor, 1965-1975	60
Points	Jan Stenerud, 1967-1979	1,231

Individual Records—Single Season

Category	Name	Performance
Rushing (Yds.)	Christian Okoye, 1989	1,480
Passing (Yds.)	Bill Kenney, 1983	4,348
Passing (TDs)	Len Dawson, 1964	30
Receiving (No.)	Carlos Carson, 1983	80
Receiving (Yds.)	Carlos Carson, 1983	1,351
Interceptions	Emmitt Thomas, 1974	12
Punting (Avg.)	Jerrel Wilson, 1965	46.0
Punt Return (Avg.)	Abner Haynes, 1960	15.4
Kickoff Return (Avg.)	Dave Grayson, 1962	29.7
Field Goals	Nick Lowery, 1990	34
Touchdowns (Tot.)	Abner Haynes, 1962	19
Points	Nick Lowery, 1990	139

Individual Records—Single Game

Category	Name	Performance
Rushing (Yds.)	Barry Word, 10-14-90	200
Passing (Yds.)	Len Dawson, 11-1-64	435
Passing (TDs)	Len Dawson, 11-1-64	6
Receiving (No.)	Ed Podolak, 10-7-73	12
Receiving (Yds.)	Stephone Paige, 12-22-85	309
Interceptions	Bobby Ply, 12-16-62	*4
	Bobby Hunt, 12-4-64	*4
	Deron Cherry, 9-29-85	*4
Field Goals	Many times	5
	Last time by Nick Lowery, 12-29-90	
Touchdowns (Tot.)	Abner Haynes, 11-26-61	5
Points	Abner Haynes, 11-26-61	30

*NFL Record

1990 Team Record

Preseason (1-3)

Date	Result		Opponents
8/11	L	3-19	vs. L.A. Rams at Berlin
8/18	L	0-20	N.Y. Jets
8/24	L	21-35	at Detroit
8/31	W	27-14	Green Bay
		51-88	

Regular Season (11-5)

Date	Result		Opponents	Att.
9/9	W	24-21	Minnesota	68,363
9/17	L	23-24	at Denver	75,277
9/23	W	17- 3	at Green Bay	58,817
9/30	W	34- 0	Cleveland	75,462
10/7	L	19-23	at Indianapolis	54,950
10/14	W	43-24	Detroit	74,312
10/21	L	7-19	at Seattle	60,358
11/4	W	9- 7	L.A. Raiders	70,951
11/11	L	16-17	Seattle	71,285
11/18	W	27-10	San Diego	63,717
11/25	W	27-24	at L.A. Raiders	65,710
12/2	W	37- 7	at New England	26,280
12/9	W	31-20	Denver	74,347
12/16	L	10-27	Houston	61,756
12/23	W	24-21	at San Diego	45,135
12/29	W	21-10	at Chicago	60,262

Postseason (0-1)

Date	Result		Opponent	Att.
1/5	L	16-17	at Miami	67,276

Score by Periods

Chiefs	86	123	71	89	0	—	369
Opponents	48	66	62	81	0	—	257

Attendance

Home 560,193 Away 446,789 Total 1,006,982
Single-game home record, 82,094 (11-5-72)
Single-season home record, 560,193 (1990)

1990 Team Statistics

	Chiefs	Opp.
Total First Downs	280	268
Rushing	115	85
Passing	142	164
Penalty	23	19
Third Down: Made/Att.	91/222	81/204
Third Down: Pct.	41.0	39.7
Fourth Down: Made/Att.	7/10	3/15
Fourth Down: Pct.	70.0	20.0
Total Net Yards	5215	4881
Avg. Per Game	325.9	305.1
Total Plays	975	945
Avg. Per Play	5.3	5.2
Net Yards Rushing	1948	1640
Avg. Per Game	121.8	102.5
Total Rushes	504	373
Net Yards Passing	3267	3241
Avg. Per Game	204.2	202.6
Sacked/Yards Lost	22/191	60/421
Gross Yards	3458	3662
Att./Completions	449/260	512/267
Completion Pct.	57.9	52.1
Had Intercepted	5	20
Punts/Avg.	81/38.7	72/37.0
Net Punting Avg.	32.9	32.3
Penalties/Yards Lost	111/886	122/859
Fumbles/Ball Lost	30/14	38/25
Touchdowns	38	30
Rushing	11	12
Passing	23	16
Returns	4	2
Avg. Time of Possession	31:30	28:30

1990 Individual Statistics

Scoring	TD R	TD P	TD Rt	PAT	FG	Saf	TP
Lowery	0	0	0	37/38	34/37	0	139
Okoye	7	0	0	0/0	0/0	0	42
B. Jones	0	5	0	0/0	0/0	0	30
Paige	0	5	0	0/0	0/0	0	30
R. Thomas	0	4	0	0/0	0/0	0	24
Word	4	0	0	0/0	0/0	0	24
Birden	0	3	0	0/0	0/0	0	18
Harry	0	2	0	0/0	0/0	0	12
McNair	0	2	0	0/0	0/0	0	12
Hayes	0	1	0	0/0	0/0	0	6
C. Martin	0	0	1	0/0	0/0	0	6
Petry	0	0	1	0/0	0/0	0	6
Ross	0	0	1	0/0	0/0	0	6
Saleaumua	0	0	1	0/0	0/0	0	6
Whitaker	0	1	0	0/0	0/0	0	6
Maas	0	0	0	0/0	0/0	1	2
Chiefs	11	23	4	37/38	34/37	1	369
Opponents	12	16	2	29/30	16/20	0	257

Passing	Att.	Comp.	Yds.	Pct.	TD	Int.	Tkld.	Rate
DeBerg	444	258	3444	58.1	23	4	22/191	96.3
Pelluer	5	2	14	40.0	0	1	0/0	8.3
Chiefs	449	260	3458	57.9	23	5	22/191	94.9
Opponents	512	267	3662	52.1	16	20	60/421	69.5

Rushing	Att.	Yds.	Avg.	LG	TD
Word	204	1015	5.0	53t	4
Okoye	245	805	3.3	32	7
McNair	14	61	4.4	13	0
B. Jones	10	47	4.7	14	0
Saxon	3	15	5.0	8	0
Pelluer	5	6	1.2	5	0
Goodburn	1	5	5.0	5	0
F. Jones	1	−1	−1.0	−1	0
DeBerg	21	−5	−0.2	6	0
Chiefs	504	1948	3.9	53t	11
Opponents	373	1640	4.4	42	12

Receiving	No.	Yds.	Avg.	LG	TD
Paige	65	1021	15.7	86t	5
R. Thomas	41	545	13.3	47t	4
Harry	41	519	12.7	60	2
McNair	40	507	12.7	65	2
B. Jones	19	137	7.2	19	5
Birden	15	352	23.5	90t	3
Roberts	11	119	10.8	27	0
Hayes	9	83	9.2	21	1
Mandley	7	97	13.9	24	0
Word	4	28	7.0	10	0
Okoye	4	23	5.8	8	0
Whitaker	2	17	8.5	16	1
F. Jones	1	5	5.0	5	0
Saxon	1	5	5.0	5	0
Chiefs	260	3458	13.3	90t	23
Opponents	267	3662	13.7	87t	16

Interceptions	No.	Yds.	Avg.	LG	TD
Ross	5	97	19.4	40	0
Cherry	3	40	13.3	21	0
Petry	3	33	11.0	33t	1
Donaldson	3	28	9.3	14	0
Lewis	2	15	7.5	15	0
Burruss	1	14	14.0	14	0
Porter	1	13	13.0	13	0
Pearson	1	10	10.0	10	0
Snow	1	0	0.0	0	0
Chiefs	20	250	12.5	40	1
Opponents	5	86	17.2	40	0

Punting	No.	Yds.	Avg.	In 20	LG
Barker	64	2479	38.7	16	56
Goodburn	17	653	38.4	6	58
Chiefs	81	3132	38.7	22	58
Opponents	72	2662	37.0	19	58

Punt Returns	No.	FC	Yds.	Avg.	LG	TD
Worthen	25	3	180	7.2	37	0
Birden	10	3	72	7.2	22	0
Harry	1	0	2	2.0	2	0
Whitaker	1	0	0	0.0	0	0
Chiefs	37	6	254	6.9	37	0
Opponents	44	19	411	9.3	95t	2

Kickoff Returns	No.	Yds.	Avg.	LG	TD
McNair	14	227	16.2	23	0
Worthen	11	226	20.5	32	0
F. Jones	9	175	19.4	46	0
Saxon	5	81	16.2	23	0
Mandley	4	51	12.8	23	0
Birden	1	14	14.0	14	0
Roberts	1	0	0.0	0	0
Word	1	10	10.0	10	0
Chiefs	46	784	17.0	46	0
Opponents	81	1391	17.2	50	0

Sacks	No.
D. Thomas	20.0
Smith	9.5
Saleaumua	7.0
C. Martin	5.5
Maas	5.5
Griffin	3.5
Hackett	3.0
Cooper	2.0
Snow	2.0
Bell	1.0
Meisner	1.0
Chiefs	60.0
Opponents	22.0

1991 Draft Choices

Round	Name	Pos.	College
1.	Harvey Williams	RB	Louisiana State
2.	Joe Valerio	T	Pennsylvania
3.	Tim Barnett	WR	Jackson State
5.	Charles Mincy	DB	Washington
6.	Darrell Malone	DB	Jacksonville State
7.	Bernard Ellison	DB	Nevada-Reno
8.	Tom Dohring	T	Michigan
9.	Robbie Keen	K	California
10.	Eric Ramsey	DB	Auburn
11.	Bobby Olive	WR	Ohio State
12.	Ron Shipley	G	New Mexico

Kansas City Chiefs 1991 Veteran Roster

No.	Name	Pos.	Ht.	Wt.	Birth-date	NFL Exp.	College	Hometown	How Acq.	'90 Games/ Starts
76	Alt, John	T	6-8	296	6/30/62	8	Iowa	Columbia Heights, Minn.	D1b-'84	16/16
77	Baldinger, Rich	T	6-4	291	12/31/59	10	Wake Forest	Long Island, N.Y.	FA-'83	16/16
4	Barker, Bryan	P	6-1	187	6/28/64	2	Santa Clara	Kirkland, Wash.	FA-'90	13/0
3	Barnes, Lew	WR-KR	5-8	170	12/27/62	3	Oregon	San Diego, Calif.	FA-'91	0*
99	Bell, Mike	DE	6-4	266	8/30/57	11	Colorado State	Wichita, Kan.	D1a-'79	16/2
26	Bell, Richard	RB	6-0	200	5/3/67	2	Nebraska	Altadena, Calif.	PB(Pitt)-'91#	16/1*
88	Birden, J.J.	WR-KR	5-9	160	6/16/66	2	Oregon	Portland, Ore.	FA-'90	11/0
34	Burruss, Lloyd	S	6-0	211	10/31/57	11	Maryland	Charlottesville, N.C.	D3c-'81	16/1
55	Charlton, Clifford	LB	6-3	245	2/16/65	3	Florida	Tallahassee, Fla.	FA-'91	0*
20	Cherry, Deron	S	5-11	205	9/12/59	11	Rutgers	Palmyra, N.J.	FA-'81	9/6
17	†DeBerg, Steve	QB	6-3	214	1/19/54	15	San Jose State	Anaheim, Calif.	T(TB)-'88	16/16
19	Dixon, Titus	WR	5-6	152	6/15/66	2	Troy State	Clewiston, Fla.	FA-'91	0*
91	Fears, Willie	DE-NT	6-4	287	6/4/64	3	Northwestern Louisiana	Barton, Ark.	FA-'91	2/0*
22	Gamble, Kenny	RB-KR	5-10	206	3/8/65	2	Colgate	Holyoke, Mass.	D10-'88	1/0
74	Graham, Derrick	T	6-4	306	3/18/67	2	Appalachian State	Groveland, Fla.	D6a-'90	6/0
98	Griffin, Leonard	DE	6-4	275	9/22/62	6	Grambling	Lake Providence, La.	D3-'86	16/2
61	Grunhard, Tim	C	6-2	302	5/17/68	2	Notre Dame	Chicago, Ill.	D2-'90	14/9
56	Hackett, Dino	LB	6-3	230	6/28/64	6	Appalachian State	Greensboro, N.C.	D2-'86	16/15
86	Harry, Emile	WR	5-11	188	4/5/63	5	Stanford	Los Angeles, Calif.	FA-'86	16/1
85	Hayes, Jonathan	TE	6-5	254	8/11/62	7	Iowa	Pittsburgh, Pa.	D2-'85	12/11
92	Henry, Maurice	LB	5-11	220	3/12/67	2	Kansas State	Salina, Kan.	FA-'91	7/0*
89	Holohan, Pete	TE	6-4	236	7/25/59	11	Notre Dame	Liverpool, N.Y.	PB(Rams)-'91#	16/10*
43	Jones, Bill	RB	5-11	228	9/10/66	2	Southwest Texas State	Corsicana, Tex.	FA-'90	16/5
80	Jones, Fred	WR-KR	5-9	175	3/6/67	2	Grambling	Decatur, Ga.	D4-'90	6/0
29	Lewis, Albert	CB	6-2	190	10/6/60	9	Grambling	Mansfield, La.	D3-'83	15/14
8	Lowery, Nick	K	6-4	205	5/27/56	12	Dartmouth	Washington, D.C.	FA-'80	16/0
72	Lutz, David	G	6-6	305	12/30/59	9	Georgia Tech	Peachland, N.C.	D2-'83	16/15
63	†Maas, Bill	DE	6-5	270	12/19/62	8	Pittsburgh	Newtown Square, Pa.	D1a-'84	16/15
57	Martin, Chris	LB	6-2	245	12/19/60	9	Auburn	Huntsville, Ala.	FA-'88	16/16
48	†McNair, Todd	RB-KR	6-1	197	10/7/65	3	Temple	Pennsauken, N.J.	D8b-'89	15/1
69	Meisner, Greg	NT-DE	6-3	267	4/23/59	11	Pittsburgh	New Kensington, Pa.	PB(Rams)-'89#	16/0
30	Mitchell, Stump	RB	5-9	194	3/15/59	10	Citadel	St. Mary's, Ga.	FA-'91	0*
50	Munford, Marc	LB	6-2	231	2/14/65	5	Nebraska	Lincoln, Neb.	PB(Den)-'91#	13/10*
35	Okoye, Christian	RB	6-1	260	8/16/61	5	Azusa Pacific	Enugu, Nigeria	D2-'87	14/13
83	Paige, Stephone	WR	6-2	188	10/15/61	9	Fresno State	Long Beach, Calif.	FA-'83	16/16
24	†Pearson, Jayice	CB	5-11	180	8/17/63	6	Washington	Oceanside, Calif.	FA-'86	16/5
11	†Pelluer, Steve	QB	6-4	212	7/29/62	8	Washington	Bellevue, Wash.	T(Dall)-'89	13/0
45	Petry, Stan	CB	5-11	180	8/14/66	3	Texas Christian	Manuel, Tex.	D3-'89	16/2
27	†Porter, Kevin	S	5-10	214	4/11/66	4	Auburn	Warner Robins, Ga.	D3-'88	16/14
52	Rogers, Tracy	LB	6-2	241	8/13/67	2	Fresno State	Taft, Calif.	FA-'90	10/0
31	Ross, Kevin	CB	5-9	182	1/16/62	8	Temple	Camden, N.J.	D7-'84	16/15
87	Sadowski, Troy	TE	6-6	265	12/8/65	2	Georgia	Chamblee, Ga.	PB(Atl)-'91#	13/1*
97	Saleaumua, Dan	NT	6-0	286	11/11/65	5	Arizona State	San Diego, Calif.	PB(Det)-'89#	16/16
21	Saxon, James	RB	5-11	226	3/23/66	4	San Jose State	Buford, S.C.	D6-'88	6/0
93	Shaw, Ricky	LB	6-4	240	7/28/65	4	Oklahoma State	Fayetteville, N.C.	PB(Phil)-'91#	8/0*
90	Smith, Neil	DE	6-4	275	4/10/66	4	Nebraska	New Orleans, La.	D1-'88	16/15
59	Snow, Percy	LB	6-2	248	11/5/67	2	Michigan State	Canton, Ohio	D1-'90	15/14
96	t-Stallworth, Ron	DE	6-5	260	2/25/66	3	Auburn	Pensacola, Fla.	T(NYJ)-'91	16/16
26	Stradford, Troy	RB	5-9	192	9/11/64	5	Boston College	Linden, N.J.	PB(Mia)-'91#	14/0*
79	Szott, David	G	6-4	278	12/12/67	2	Penn State	Clifton, N.J.	D7-'90	16/11
58	Thomas, Derrick	LB	6-3	244	1/1/67	3	Alabama	Miami, Fla.	D1-'89	15/15
81	Thomas, Robb	WR	5-11	174	3/29/66	3	Oregon State	Corvallis, Ore.	D6-'89	16/12
13	Vlasic, Mark	QB	6-3	206	10/25/63	4	Iowa	Monaca, Pa.	PB(SD)-'91#	6/1*
46	Washington, Charles	CB	6-1	210	10/8/66	3	Cameron	Shreveport, La.	PB(Ind)-'90#	6/0
82	Whitaker, Danta	TE	6-4	248	3/14/64	2	Mississippi Valley State	Atlanta, Ga.	FA-'90	16/3
70	Williams, Larry	G	6-5	290	7/3/63	4	Notre Dame	Santa Ana, Calif.	FA-'91	0*
66	Winters, Frank	G-C	6-3	285	1/23/64	5	Western Illinois	Union City, N.J.	PB(NYG)-'90#	16/6
23	†Word, Barry	RB	6-2	240	7/17/64	3	Virginia	Long Island, Va.	FA-'90	16/3

* Barnes last active with Atlanta in '88; R. Bell played 16 games with Pittsburgh in '90; Charlton last active with Cleveland in '89; Dixon last active with N.Y. Jets in '89; Fears played 2 games with Minnesota; Henry played 7 games with Philadelphia; Holohan played 16 games with L.A. Rams; Mitchell last active with Phoenix in '88; Munford played 13 games with Denver; Sadowski played 13 games with Atlanta; Shaw played 8 games with Philadelphia; Stradford played 14 games with Miami; Vlasic played 6 games with San Diego; Williams last active with San Diego in '89.

† Option playout; subject to developments.

Plan B unconditional free agent.

Retired—Mike Webster, 17-year center, 9 games in 1990.

t- Chiefs traded for Stallworth (New York Jets).

Traded—T Irv Eatman to New York Jets.

Players lost through Plan B (7): LB Louis Cooper (Mia; 16 games in '90), CB Danny Copeland (Wash; 14), S Jeff Donaldson (Atl; 16), LB Rob McGovern (Pitt; 11), TE Alfredo Roberts (Dall; 16), WR Naz Worthen (Atl; 9), T Rob Woods (Clev; 0).

Also played with Chiefs in '90—P Kelly Goodburn (3 games), WR Pete Mandley (5).

COACHING STAFF

Head Coach, Marty Schottenheimer

Pro Career: In six full seasons as an NFL head coach, Marty Schottenheimer has never experienced a losing season. Since 1985, he is the only coach in the league that has not had at least one losing season. After four-and-a-half years as the Cleveland Browns head coach, Schottenheimer took over the Chiefs on January 24, 1989. He has a 19-12-1 regular-season record as Chiefs' head coach. His .617 career winning percentage is the fourth-highest among active NFL head coaches with at least three years experience. He has coached Kansas City to two of its four winning seasons since 1974. In 1990, Schottenheimer guided the Chiefs to an 11-5 regular-season record, the club's finest in 21 years. He also directed the team to postseason play for just the second time since 1971 and the first time since 1986. As head coach of the Cleveland Browns from midseason in 1984 through 1988, he led his teams to four playoff berths, three AFC Central Division titles, two AFC Championship Game appearances, and captured AFC coach of the year honors (1986). He first joined the Browns in 1980 as defensive coordinator after serving as linebacker coach of the Detroit Lions in 1978-79. His first NFL coaching job came with the New York Giants, where he was linebacker coach and offensive coordinator from 1975-77. He served as an assistant coach with the Portland Storm (WFL) in 1974. A seventh-round draft choice of the Buffalo Bills in 1965, he played linebacker with the Bills until 1968 and finished his pro playing career with the Boston Patriots in 1969-70. Career record: 65-44-1.

Background: All-America linebacker at University of Pittsburgh 1962-64. Following retirement from pro football, he worked as a real estate developer in both Miami and Denver from 1971-74.

Personal: Born September 23, 1943, Canonsburg, Pa. Marty and his wife, Patricia, live in Overland Park, Kan., and have one daughter, Kristen, and one son, Brian.

Assistant Coaches

Bruce Arians, running backs; born October 3, 1952, York, Pa., lives in Kansas City. Quarterback Virginia Tech 1971-74. No pro playing experience. College coach: Virginia Tech 1975-77, Mississippi State 1978-80, Alabama 1981-82, Temple 1983-88 (head coach). Pro coach: Joined Chiefs in 1989.

Russ Ball, assistant strength and conditioning; born August 28, 1959, Moberly, Mo., lives in Kansas City. Center Central Missouri State 1977-80. No pro playing experience. College coach: Missouri 1981-88. Pro coach: Joined Chiefs in 1989.

Bill Cowher, defensive coordinator-linebackers; born May 8, 1957, Pittsburgh, Pa., lives in Overland Park, Kan. Linebacker North Carolina State 1975-78. Pro linebacker Cleveland Browns 1980-82, Philadelphia Eagles 1983-84. Pro coach: Cleveland Browns 1985-88, joined Chiefs in 1989.

Tony Dungy, defensive backs; born October 6, 1955, Jackson, Mich., lives in Kansas City. Quarterback Minnesota 1973-76. Pro safety Pittsburgh Steelers 1977-78, San Francisco 49ers 1979. College coach: Minnesota 1980. Pro coach: Pittsburgh Steelers 1981-88, joined Chiefs in 1989.

Jim Erkenbeck, offensive assistant/tight ends; born September 10, 1931, Los Angeles, lives in Mission, Kan. Fullback San Diego State 1949-52. No pro playing experience. College coach: San Diego State 1960-63, Grossmont (Calif.) J.C. 1964-67, Utah State 1968, Washington State 1969-71, California 1972-76. Pro coach: Winnipeg Blue-Bombers (CFL) 1977, Montreal Alouettes (CFL) 1978-81, Calgary Stampeders (CFL) 1982, Philadelphia/Baltimore Stars (USFL) 1983-85, New Orleans Saints 1986, Dallas Cowboys 1987-88, joined Chiefs in 1990.

Kansas City Chiefs 1991 First-Year Roster

Name	Pos.	Ht.	Wt.	Birth-date	College	Hometown	How Acq.
Anders, Kimble (1)	RB	5-11	210	9/10/66	Houston	Galveston, Tex.	FA
Barnett, Tim	WR	6-1	209	4/19/68	Jackson State	Rosedale, Miss.	D3
Boysaw, Greg (1)	CB-S	6-1	207	12/11/66	Illinois	Urbana, Ill.	FA
Davis, Willie (1)	WR	6-0	159	10/10/67	Central Arkansas	Little Rock, Ark.	FA
Dohring, Tom	T	6-6	290	5/24/68	Michigan	Dearborn, Mich.	D8
Dunn, Chris (1)	LB	6-3	235	2/1/66	Cal Poly-SLO	Whittier, Calif.	FA
Elkins, Mike (1)	QB	6-3	225	7/20/66	Wake Forest	Greensboro, N.C.	D2-'89
Ellison, Bernard	CB	6-0	192	1/2/67	Nevada-Reno	Milpitas, Calif.	D7
Ford, Herman (1)	CB	5-9	185	5/11/65	No College	Norfolk, Va.	FA
Henry, Maurice (1)	LB	5-11	220	3/12/67	Kansas State	Salina, Kan.	FA
Hoskins, Eric (1)	CB-S	5-11	175	12/30/63	Missouri Western	Kansas City, Mo.	FA
Keen, Robbie	P-K	6-3	213	8/2/68	California	Orangeville, Calif.	D9
Malone, Darrell	CB-S	5-10	182	11/23/67	Jacksonville State	Jacksonville, Ala.	D6
Mincy, Charles	CB-S	5-11	187	12/16/69	Washington	Los Angeles, Calif.	D5
Olive, Bobby	WR	5-11	158	4/22/69	Ohio State	Atlanta, Ga.	D11
Owens, Michael (1)	RB	5-11	218	4/7/68	Syracuse	Carlisle, Pa.	FA
Ramsey, Eric	CB-S	5-11	189	7/1/68	Auburn	Homewood, Ala.	D10
Shipley, Ron	G	6-4	298	8/17/68	New Mexico	Ramona, Calif.	D12
Simien, Tracy (1)	LB	6-1	245	5/21/67	Texas Christian	Bay City, Tex.	FA
Thompson, Ernest (1)	RB	6-2	236	3/25/67	Georgia Southern	Louisville, Ga.	FA
Valerio, Joe	T	6-5	293	2/11/69	Pennsylvania	Ridley, Pa.	D2
Williams, Harvey	RB	6-2	216	4/22/67	Louisiana State	Hempstead, Tex.	D1

The term NFL Rookie is defined as a player who is in his first season of professional football and has not been on the roster of another professional football team for any regular-season or postseason games. A Rookie is designated by an "R" on NFL rosters. Players who have been active in another professional football league or players who have NFL experience, including either preseason training camp or being on an active roster for fewer than three regular-season or postseason games, are termed NFL First-Year Players. An NFL First-Year Player is designated by a "1" on NFL rosters. Thereafter, a player on an NFL active roster for at least three regular-season or postseason games is credited with an additional year of NFL playing experience.

NOTES

Howard Mudd, offensive line; born February 10, 1942, Midland, Mich., lives in Kansas City. Guard Hillsdale 1961-63. Pro guard San Francisco 49ers 1964-69, Chicago Bears 1970-71. College coach: California 1972-73. Pro coach: San Diego Chargers 1974-76, San Francisco 49ers 1977, Seattle Seahawks 1978-82, Cleveland Browns 1983-88, joined Chiefs in 1989.

Joe Pendry, offensive coordinator-quarterbacks; born August 5, 1947, Matheny, W. Va., lives in Lakewood, Mo. Tight end West Virginia 1966-67. No pro playing experience. College coach: West Virginia 1967-74, 1976-77, Kansas State 1975, Pittsburgh 1978-79, Michigan State 1980-81. Pro coach: Philadelphia Stars (USFL) 1983, Pittsburgh Maulers (USFL) 1984 (head coach), Cleveland Browns 1985-88, joined Chiefs in 1989.

Tom Pratt, defensive line; born June 21, 1935, Edgerton, Wis., lives in Overland Park, Kan. Linebacker Miami 1953-56. College coach: Miami 1957-59, Southern Mississippi 1960-62. No pro playing experience. Pro coach: Kansas City Chiefs 1963-77, New Orleans Saints 1978-80, Cleveland Browns 1981-88, rejoined Chiefs in 1989.

Dave Redding, strength and conditioning; born June 14, 1952, North Platte, Neb., lives in Kansas City. Defensive end Nebraska 1972-75. No pro playing experience. College coach: Nebraska 1976, Washington State 1977, Missouri 1978-81. Pro coach: Cleveland Browns 1982-88, joined Chiefs in 1989.

Al Saunders, receivers; born February 1, 1947, London, England, lives in Kansas City. Defensive back San Jose State 1966-68. No pro playing experience. College coach: Southern California 1970-71, Missouri 1972, Utah State 1973-75, California 1976-81, Tennessee 1982. Pro coach: San Diego Chargers 1983-88 (head coach 1986-88), joined Chiefs in 1989.

Kurt Schottenheimer, special teams; born October 1, 1949, McDonald, Pa., lives in Kansas City. Defensive back Miami 1969-70. No pro playing experience. College coach: William Patterson 1974, Michigan State 1978-82, Tulane 1983, Louisiana State 1984-85, Notre Dame 1986. Pro coach: Cleveland Browns 1987-88, joined Chiefs in 1989.

Darvin Wallis, special assistant-quality control; born February 14, 1949, Ft. Branch, Ind., lives in Overland Park, Kan. Defensive end Arizona 1970-71. No pro playing experience. College coach: Adams State 1976-77, Tulane 1978-79, Mississippi 1980-81. Pro coach: Cleveland Browns 1982-88, joined Chiefs in 1989.

American Football Conference Western Division

Team Colors: Silver and Black

332 Center Street
El Segundo, California 90245
Telephone: (213) 322-3451

Club Officials

President of the Managing General Partner: Al Davis
Executive Assistant: Al LoCasale
Pro Football Scout: George Karras
Finance: Gary Huff
Legal Affairs: Jeff Birren, Amy Trask
Senior Executive: John Herrera
Senior Administrator: Morris Bradshaw
Business Manager: Jack Novak
Administrative Assistant: John Walsh
Publications: Mike Taylor
Ticket Operations: Peter Eiges
Trainers: George Anderson, H. Rod Martin, Todd Sperber
Equipment Manager: Richard Romanski
Assistant Equipment Manager: Bob Romanski

Stadium: Los Angeles Memorial Coliseum • **Capacity:** 92,488
3911 South Figueroa Street
Los Angeles, California 90037

Playing Surface: Grass

Training Camp: Radisson Hotel
Oxnard, California 93030

1991 Schedule

Preseason

July 27	**San Francisco**	1:00
Aug. 3	vs. Miami at Tokyo	10:00*
Aug. 12	at Dallas	7:00
Aug. 17	**Chicago**	1:00
Aug. 23	at San Diego	7:00

*P.M. Eastern Time

Regular Season

Sept. 1	at Houston	3:00
Sept. 8	**Denver**	1:00
Sept. 15	**Indianapolis**	1:00
Sept. 22	at Atlanta	1:00
Sept. 29	**San Francisco**	1:00
Oct. 6	**San Diego**	1:00
Oct. 13	at Seattle	4:30
Oct. 20	**Los Angeles Rams**	1:00
Oct. 28	at Kansas City (Monday)	8:00
Nov. 3	**Open Date**	
Nov. 10	at Denver	2:00
Nov. 17	**Seattle**	1:00
Nov. 24	at Cincinnati	1:00
Dec. 1	at San Diego	5:00
Dec. 8	**Buffalo**	1:00
Dec. 16	at New Orleans (Monday)	8:00
Dec. 22	**Kansas City**	1:00

Raiders Coaching History

Oakland 1960-81
(298-176-11)

1960-61	Eddie Erdelatz*	6-10-0
1961-62	Marty Feldman**	2-15-0
1962	Red Conkright	1-8-0
1963-65	Al Davis	23-16-3
1966-68	John Rauch	35-10-1
1969-78	John Madden	112-39-7
1979-87	Tom Flores	91-56-0
1988-89	Mike Shanahan***	8-12-0
1989-90	Art Shell	20-10-0

*Released after two games in 1961
**Released after five games in 1962
***Released after four games in 1989

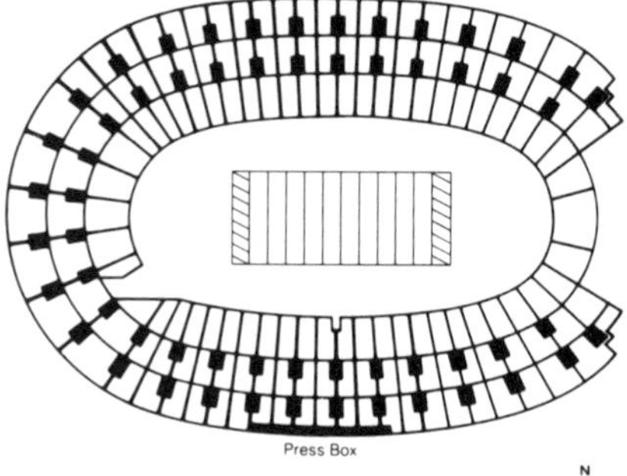

MEMORIAL COLISEUM

Record Holders

Individual Records—Career

Category	Name	Performance
Rushing (Yds.)	Marcus Allen, 1982-1990	7,957
Passing (Yds.)	Ken Stabler, 1970-79	19,078
Passing (TDs)	Ken Stabler, 1970-79	150
Receiving (No.)	Fred Biletnikoff, 1965-1978	589
Receiving (Yds.)	Fred Biletnikoff, 1965-1978	8,974
Interceptions	Willie Brown, 1967-1978	39
	Lester Hayes, 1977-1986	39
Punting (Avg.)	Ray Guy, 1973-1986	42.5
Punt Return (Avg.)	Claude Gibson, 1963-65	12.6
Kickoff Return (Avg.)	Jack Larscheid, 1960-61	28.4
Field Goals	George Blanda, 1967-1975	156
Touchdowns (Tot.)	Marcus Allen, 1982-1990	93
Points	George Blanda, 1967-1975	863

Individual Records—Single Season

Category	Name	Performance
Rushing (Yds.)	Marcus Allen, 1985	1,759
Passing (Yds.)	Ken Stabler, 1979	3,615
Passing (TDs)	Daryle Lamonica, 1969	34
Receiving (No.)	Todd Christensen, 1986	95
Receiving (Yds.)	Art Powell, 1964	1,361
Interceptions	Lester Hayes, 1980	13
Punting (Avg.)	Ray Guy, 1973	45.3
Punt Return (Avg.)	Claude Gibson, 1964	14.4
Kickoff Return (Avg.)	Harold Hart, 1975	30.5
Field Goals	George Blanda,1973	23
Touchdowns (Tot.)	Marcus Allen, 1984	18
Points	George Blanda, 1968	117

Individual Records—Single Game

Category	Name	Performance
Rushing (Yds.)	Bo Jackson, 11-30-87	221
Passing (Yds.)	Cotton Davidson, 10-25-64	427
Passing (TDs)	Tom Flores, 12-22-63	6
	Daryle Lamonica, 10-19-69	6
Receiving (No.)	Dave Casper, 10-3-76	12
Receiving (Yds.)	Art Powell, 12-22-63	247
Interceptions	Many times	3
	Last time by Charles Phillips, 12-8-75	
Field Goals	Many times	4
	Last time by Jeff Jaeger, 11-12-89	
Touchdowns (Tot.)	Art Powell, 12-22-63	4
	Marcus Allen, 9-24-84	4
Points	Art Powell, 12-22-63	24
	Marcus Allen, 9-24-84	24

1990 Team Record

Preseason (4-1)

Date	Result		Opponents
8/5	L	10-17	vs. New Orleans at London
8/11	W	23-13	at San Francisco
8/18	W	16-14	Dallas
8/24	W	20- 3	at Chicago
9/1	W	34- 7	San Diego
		103-54	

Regular Season (12-4)

Date	Result		Opponents	Att.
9/9	W	14- 9	Denver	54,206
9/16	W	17-13	at Seattle	61,889
9/23	W	20- 3	Pittsburgh	50,657
9/30	W	24-10	Chicago	80,156
10/7	L	24-38	at Buffalo	80,076
10/14	W	24-17	Seattle	50,624
10/21	W	24- 9	at San Diego	60,569
11/4	L	7- 9	at Kansas City	70,951
11/11	L	16-29	Green Bay	50,855
11/19	W	13-10	at Miami	70,553
11/25	L	24-27	Kansas City	65,710
12/2	W	23-20	at Denver	74,162
12/10	W	38-31	at Detroit	72,190
12/16	W	24- 7	Cincinnati	54,132
12/22	W	28-24	at Minnesota	53,899
12/30	W	17-12	San Diego	62,593

Postseason (1-1)

Date	Result		Opponent	Att.
1/13	W	20-10	Cincinnati	92,045
1/20	L	3-51	at Buffalo	80,324

Score by Periods

Raiders	82	84	76	95	0	—	337
Opponents	59	89	33	87	0	—	268

Attendance

Home 468,933 Away 545,289 Total 1,014,222
Single-game home record, 92,045 (1-13-91)
Single-season home record, 516,205 (1986)

1990 Team Statistics

	Raiders	Opp.
Total First Downs	258	266
Rushing	110	95
Passing	133	152
Penalty	15	19
Third Down: Made/Att.	86/180	75/201
Third Down: Pct.	47.8	37.3
Fourth Down: Made/Att.	2/7	9/19
Fourth Down: Pct.	28.6	47.4
Total Net Yards	4716	4413
Avg. Per Game	294.8	275.8
Total Plays	861	924
Avg. Per Play	5.5	4.8
Net Yards Rushing	2028	1716
Avg. Per Game	126.8	107.3
Total Rushes	496	439
Net Yards Passing	2688	2697
Avg. Per Game	168.0	168.6
Sacked/Yards Lost	29/197	48/335
Gross Yards	2885	3032
Att./Completions	336/183	437/246
Completion Pct.	54.5	56.3
Had Intercepted	10	13
Punts/Avg.	62/37.3	64/38.2
Net Punting Avg.	33.6	31.8
Penalties/Yards Lost	97/682	86/710
Fumbles/Ball Lost	24/14	21/9
Touchdowns	42	26
Rushing	20	4
Passing	19	20
Returns	3	2
Avg. Time of Possession	29:28	30:32

1990 Individual Statistics

Scoring	TD R	TD P	TD Rt	PAT	FG	Saf	TP
Jaeger	0	0	0	40/42	15/20	0	85
Allen	12	1	0	0/0	0/0	0	78
Fernandez	0	5	0	0/0	0/0	0	30
Jackson	5	0	0	0/0	0/0	0	30
Smith	2	3	0	0/0	0/0	0	30
T. Brown	0	3	0	0/0	0/0	0	18
Gault	0	3	0	0/0	0/0	0	18
Horton	0	3	0	0/0	0/0	0	18
Bell	1	0	0	0/0	0/0	0	6
Graddy	0	1	0	0/0	0/0	0	6
McDaniel	0	0	1	0/0	0/0	0	6
Robinson	0	0	1	0/0	0/0	0	6
Townsend	0	0	1	0/0	0/0	0	6
Raiders	20	19	3	40/42	15/20	0	337
Opponents	4	20	2	25/26	29/33	0	268

Passing	Att.	Comp.	Yds.	Pct.	TD	Int.	Tkld.	Rate
Schroeder	334	182	2849	54.5	19	9	29/197	90.8
Allen	1	0	0	0.0	0	1	0/0	0.0
Evans	1	1	36	100.0	0	0	0/0	118.8
Raiders	336	183	2885	54.5	19	10	29/197	89.7
Opponents	437	246	3032	56.3	20	13	48/335	80.8

Rushing	Att.	Yds.	Avg.	LG	TD
Jackson	125	698	5.6	88	5
Allen	179	682	3.8	28	12
Smith	81	327	4.0	17	2
Bell	47	164	3.5	21	1
Schroeder	37	81	2.2	17	0
Mueller	13	43	3.3	12	0
McCallum	10	25	2.5	6	0
Fernandez	3	10	3.3	9	0
Evans	1	−2	−2.0	−2	0
Raiders	496	2028	4.1	88	20
Opponents	439	1716	3.9	41	4

Receiving	No.	Yds.	Avg.	LG	TD
Fernandez	52	839	16.1	66t	5
Gault	50	985	19.7	68t	3
Horton	33	404	12.2	36	3
T. Brown	18	265	14.7	51	3
Allen	15	189	12.6	30	1
Jackson	6	68	11.3	18	0
Smith	4	30	7.5	17t	3
Dyal	3	51	17.0	29	0
Graddy	1	47	47.0	47t	1
Bell	1	7	7.0	7	0
Raiders	183	2885	15.8	68t	19
Opponents	246	3032	12.3	80t	20

Interceptions	No.	Yds.	Avg.	LG	TD
Anderson	3	49	16.3	31	0
McDaniel	3	20	6.7	15	0
Harden	3	19	6.3	15	0
Ellison	1	7	7.0	7	0
Robinson	1	5	5.0	5t	1
Washington	1	2	2.0	2	0
Townsend	1	0	0.0	0	0
Raiders	13	102	7.8	31	1
Opponents	10	100	10.0	32	0

Punting	No.	Yds.	Avg.	In 20	LG
Gossett	60	2315	38.6	18	57
Raiders	62	2315	37.3	18	57
Opponents	64	2447	38.2	10	59

Punt Returns	No.	FC	Yds.	Avg.	LG	TD
T. Brown	34	8	295	8.7	39	0
Raiders	34	8	295	8.7	39	0
Opponents	24	6	153	6.4	33	0

Kickoff Returns	No.	Yds.	Avg.	LG	TD
Holland	32	655	20.5	87	0
R. Brown	30	575	19.2	34	0
McCallum	1	0	0.0	0	0
Turk	1	7	7.0	7	0
Raiders	64	1237	19.3	87	0
Opponents	49	1026	20.9	90	0

Sacks	No.
Townsend	12.5
Davis	10.0
Wallace	9.0
Long	6.0
Golic	4.0
McDaniel	2.0
Robinson	2.0
Pickel	1.5
Wise	1.0
Raiders	48.0
Opponents	29.0

1991 Draft Choices

Round	Name	Pos.	College
1.	Todd Marinovich	QB	Southern California
2.	Nick Bell	RB	Iowa
4.	Raghib Ismail	WR	Notre Dame
6.	Nolan Harrison	DT	Indiana
8.	Brian Jones	LB	Texas
	Todd Woulard	LB	Alabama A&M
9.	Tahaun Lewis	DB	Nebraska
10.	Andrew Glover	TE	Grambling
12.	Dennis Johnson	WR	Winston-Salem St.

Los Angeles Raiders 1991 Veteran Roster

No.	Name	Pos.	Ht.	Wt.	Birth-date	NFL Exp.	College	Hometown	How Acq.	'90 Games/ Starts
44	Adams, Stefon	WR	5-10	185	8/11/63	6	East Carolina	High Point, N.C.	PB(Mia)-'91#	12/0*
80	Alexander, Mike	WR	6-3	190	3/19/65	2	Penn State	Piscataway, N.J.	D8-'88	0*
32	†Allen, Marcus	RB	6-2	210	3/26/60	10	Southern California	San Diego, Calif.	D1-'82	16/15
59	Alston, O'Brien	LB	6-6	240	12/21/65	3	Maryland	New Haven, Conn.	PB(Ind)-'91#	0*
33	†Anderson, Eddie	S	6-1	205	7/22/63	6	Fort Valley State	Warner Robins, Ga.	FA-'87	16/16
28	Bell, Greg	RB	5-10	210	8/1/62	8	Notre Dame	Columbus, Ohio	T(Rams)-'90	6/0
54	Benson, Tom	LB	6-2	240	9/6/61	8	Oklahoma	Ardmore, Tex.	PB(NE)-'89#	16/16
7	†Beuerlein, Steve	QB	6-2	210	3/7/65	3	Notre Dame	Fullerton, Calif.	D4-'87	0*
24	Brown, Ron	CB	5-11	185	3/31/61	8	Arizona State	Baldwin Park, Calif.	PB(Rams)-'90#	16/0
81	Brown, Tim	WR	6-0	195	7/22/66	3	Notre Dame	Dallas, Tex.	D1-'88	16/0
97	Burton, Ron	LB	6-1	245	5/2/64	5	North Carolina	Highland Springs, Va.	PB(Phx)-'90#	5/0
95	Charles, Mike	DT	6-4	305	9/23/62	9	Syracuse	Newark, N.J.	FA-'91	10/0*
55	Cofield, Tim	LB	6-2	240	5/18/63	5	Elizabeth City State	Murfreesboro, N.C.	FA-'91	0*
22	Craig, Roger	RB	6-0	225	7/10/60	9	Nebraska	Davenport, Iowa	PB(SF)-'91#	11/11*
70	†Davis, Scott	DE	6-7	275	8/7/65	4	Illinois	Plainfield, Ill.	D1-'88	16/16
46	Dorn, Torin	CB	6-0	195	2/29/68	2	North Carolina	Southfield, Mich.	D4-'90	16/0
84	Dyal, Mike	TE	6-2	240	5/20/66	3	Texas A&I	Kerrville, Tex.	FA-'88	3/2
50	Ellison, Riki	LB	6-2	230	8/15/60	8	Southern California	Tucson, Ariz.	FA-'90	16/15
11	†Evans, Vince	QB	6-2	210	6/14/55	12	Southern California	Greensboro, N.C.	FA-'90	5/0
86	†Fernandez, Mervyn	WR	6-3	205	12/29/59	5	San Jose State	San Jose, Calif.	D10-'83	16/15
73	FitzPatrick, James	T	6-7	330	2/1/64	6	Southern California	Beaverton, Ore.	PB(SD)-'90#	11/1
83	Gault, Willie	WR	6-1	180	9/5/60	9	Tennessee	Griffin, Ga.	T(Chi)-'88	16/16
26	Glenn, Vencie	S	6-0	190	10/26/64	6	Indiana State	Terre Haute, Ind.	PB(SD)-'91#	14/14*
79	†Golic, Bob	DT	6-2	275	10/26/57	12	Notre Dame	Cleveland, Ohio	PB(Clev)-'89#	16/16
6	†Gossett, Jeff	P	6-2	195	1/25/57	10	Eastern Illinois	Charleston, Ill.	T(Hou)-'88	16/0
85	†Graddy, Sam	WR	5-10	175	2/10/64	4	Tennessee	Gaffney, S.C.	PB(Den)-'89	16/0
60	Graves, Rory	T	6-6	295	7/21/63	4	Ohio State	Decatur, Ga.	FA-'88	15/15
82	Holland, Jamie	WR	6-1	195	2/1/64	5	Ohio State	Wake Forest, N.C.	T(SD)-'90	16/0
88	Horton, Ethan	TE	6-4	240	12/19/62	5	North Carolina	Kannapolis, N.C.	FA-'89	16/14
34	Jackson, Bo	RB	6-1	230	11/30/62	5	Auburn	Bessemer, Ala.	D7-'87	10/0
18	Jaeger, Jeff	K	5-11	195	11/26/64	4	Washington	Kent, Wash.	PB(Clev)-'89#	16/0
58	Jimerson, A.J.	LB	6-3	235	5/12/68	2	Norfolk State	Chesapeake, Va.	D8-'90	4/0
92	King, Emanuel	DE	6-4	265	8/15/63	6	Alabama	Leroy, Ala.	FA-'91	0*
53	Klostermann, Bruce	LB	6-4	230	4/17/63	4	South Dakota State	Dubuque, Iowa	PB(Rams)-'91#	5/1*
25	†Land, Dan	S	6-0	195	7/3/65	3	Albany State	Donalsonville, Ga.	FA-'89	16/0
49	Lee, Zeph	S	6-3	215	6/17/63	3	Southern California	San Francisco, Calif.	FA-'91	0*
21	Lewis, Garry	CB	5-11	180	8/25/67	2	Alcorn State	Vicksburg, Miss.	D7-'90	12/5
75	Long, Howie	DE	6-5	270	1/6/60	11	Villanova	Charleston, Mass.	D2-'81	12/11
42	Lott, Ronnie	S	6-0	200	5/8/59	11	Southern California	Rialto, Calif.	PB(SF)-'91#	11/11*
91	Mark, Greg	DE	6-3	260	7/7/67	2	Miami	Pennsauken, N.J.	FA-'91	6/0*
41	McCallum, Napoleon	RB	6-2	220	10/6/63	3	Navy	Milford, Ohio	T(SD)-'90	16/0
36	McDaniel, Terry	CB	5-10	180	2/8/65	3	Tennessee	Saginaw, Mich.	D1-'88	16/13
77	McElroy, Reggie	T	6-6	275	3/4/60	9	West Texas State	Beaumont, Tex.	FA-'91	0*
65	Montoya, Max	G	6-5	290	5/12/56	13	UCLA	La Puente, Calif.	PB(Cin)-'90#	16/16
72	†Mosebar, Don	C	6-6	280	9/11/61	9	Southern California	Visalia, Calif.	D1-'83	16/16
99	t-Moss, Winston	LB	6-3	235	12/24/65	5	Miami	Miami, Fla.	T(TB)-'91	16/15*
31	Mueller, Vance	RB	6-0	220	5/5/64	6	Occidental	Jackson, Calif.	D4-'86	16/1
71	Patten, Joel	T	6-7	305	2/7/58	7	Duke	Fairfax, Va.	PB(SD)-'91#	8/0*
43	†Patterson, Elvis	CB	5-11	195	10/21/60	8	Kansas	Houston, Tex.	PB(SD)-'90#	16/1
64	Peat, Todd	G	6-2	315	5/20/64	4	Northern Illinois	Champaign, Ill.	FA-'90	16/1
57	Robinson, Jerry	LB	6-2	230	12/18/56	13	UCLA	Santa Rosa, Calif.	T(Phil)-'85	16/16
78	†Rother, Tim	DT	6-7	280	9/28/65	3	Nebraska	Bellevue, Neb.	D4-'88	4/0
13	†Schroeder, Jay	QB	6-4	215	6/28/61	8	UCLA	Pacific Palisades, Calif.	T(Wash)-'88	16/16
35	Smith, Steve	RB	6-1	240	8/30/64	5	Penn State	Clinton, Md.	D3-'87	16/15
93	Townsend, Greg	DE	6-3	270	11/3/61	9	Texas Christian	Compton, Calif.	D4-'83	16/16
67	†Turk, Dan	C	6-4	275	6/25/62	6	Wisconsin	Milwaukee, Wis.	FA-'89	16/0
89	Tyler, Rob	TE	6-5	255	10/12/65	2	South Carolina State	Salley, N.C.	FA-'91	0*
51	Wallace, Aaron	LB	6-3	235	4/17/67	2	Texas A&M	Dallas, Tex.	D2-'90	16/0
40	Washington, Lionel	CB	6-0	185	10/21/60	9	Tulane	New Orleans, La.	T(StL)-'87	15/15
68	†Wilkerson, Bruce	T	6-5	295	7/28/64	5	Tennessee	Philadelphia, Tenn.	D2-'87	8/1
90	†Wise, Mike	DE	6-7	270	6/5/64	5	California-Davis	Novato, Calif.	D4-'86	13/2
76	Wisniewski, Steve	G	6-4	280	4/7/67	3	Penn State	Houston, Tex.	D2-'89	16/16
66	Wright, Steve	G	6-6	280	4/8/59	9	Northern Illinois	Wayzata, Minn.	FA-'88	16/16

* Adams played 10 games with Cleveland, 2 with Miami in '90; Alexander missed '90 season due to injury; Alston last active with Indianapolis in '89; Beuerlein last active with Raiders in '89; Charles played 10 games with Raiders; Cofield last active with Buffalo in '89; Craig played 11 games with San Francisco; Glenn played 14 games with San Diego; King last active with Raiders in '89; Klostermann played 5 games with L.A. Rams; Lee last active with Raiders in '89; Lott played 11 games with San Francisco; Mark played 4 games with Miami, 2 with Philadelphia; McElroy last active with N.Y. Jets in '89; Moss played 16 games with Tampa Bay; Patten played 8 games with San Diego; Tyler last active with Seattle in '89.

† Option playout; subject to developments.

Plan B unconditional free agent.

t- Raiders traded for Moss (Tampa Bay).

Players lost through Plan B (3): LB Alex Gordon (Cin; 10 games in '90), LB Darin Jordan (SF; 0), DT Bill Pickel (NYJ; 14).

Also played with Raiders in '90—TE Rich Bartlewski (4 games), S Mike Harden (15), LB Ricky Hunley (11), S Vann McElroy (3), TE Andy Parker (5).

COACHING STAFF

Head Coach, Art Shell

Pro Career: Named ninth head coach in Raiders' history on October 3, 1989. Had been Raiders' offensive line coach for seven years, including 1983 world championship season. He first joined the coaching staff in 1983 after 15 seasons as one of the greatest offensive tackles in pro football history. Came to Raiders in 1968 as a third-round draft choice out of Maryland State. Went on to play in 207 league games, including first 156 in a row, and 24 playoff games for the Raiders. Starting left tackle in Super Bowl XI and XV victories. Selected to Pro Bowl eight times—most by any Raiders player. Inducted into Pro Football Hall of Fame on August 5, 1989. Also named to state of South Carolina Sports Hall of Fame. Career record: 20-10.

Background: All-America tackle as junior and senior and three-year All-Conference on both offense and defense at Maryland State 1965-1967. Also lettered in basketball.

Personal: Born November 26, 1946, Charleston, S.C. Art and wife, Janice, live in Palos Verdes, California with their sons Arthur III and Christopher.

Assistant Coaches

Dave Adolph, defensive coordinator, linebackers; born June 6, 1937, Akron, Ohio, lives in El Segundo, Calif. Guard-linebacker Akron 1955-58. No pro playing experience. College coach: Akron 1963-64, Connecticut 1965-68, Kentucky 1969-72, Illinois 1973-76, Ohio State 1977-78. Pro coach: Cleveland Browns 1979-84, 1986-88, San Diego Chargers 1985, joined Raiders in 1989.

Fred Biletnikoff, wide receivers; born February 23, 1943, Erie, Pa., lives in El Segundo, Calif. Wide receiver Florida State 1962-64. Pro wide receiver Oakland Raiders 1965-78, Montreal Alouettes (CFL) 1980. College coach: Palomar, Calif., J.C. 1983, Diablo Valley, Calif., J.C. 1984, 1986. Pro coach: Oakland Invaders (USFL) 1985, Arizona Outlaws (USFL) 1986, Calgary Stampeders (CFL) 1987-88, joined Raiders in 1989.

Gunther Cunningham, linebackers; born June 19, 1946, Munich, Germany, lives in El Segundo, Calif. Linebacker Oregon 1965-67. No pro playing experience. College coach: Oregon 1969-71, Arkansas 1972, Stanford 1973-76, California 1977-80. Pro coach: Hamilton Tiger-Cats (CFL) 1981, Indianapolis Colts 1982-84, San Diego Chargers 1985-90, joined Raiders in 1991.

Kim Helton, offensive line; born July 28, 1948, Pensacola, Fla., lives in El Segundo, Calif. Center Florida 1967-69. No pro playing experience. College coach: Florida 1972-78, Miami 1979-82. Pro coach: Tampa Bay Buccaneers 1983-86, Houston Oilers 1987-89, joined Raiders in 1990.

Earl Leggett, defensive line; born May 5, 1933, Jacksonville, Fla., lives in El Segundo, Calif. Tackle Hinds J.C. 1953-54, Louisiana State 1955-56. Pro defensive tackle Chicago Bears 1957-65, Los Angeles Rams 1966, New Orleans Saints 1967-68. College coach: Nicholls State 1971, Texas Christian 1972-73. Pro coach: Southern California Sun (WFL) 1974-75, Seattle Seahawks 1976-77, San Francisco 49ers 1978, Los Angeles Raiders 1980-88, Denver Broncos 1989-90, rejoined Raiders in 1991.

Steve Ortmayer, football operations, special teams; born February 13, 1944, Painesville, Ohio, lives in El Segundo, Calif. LaVerne College 1966. No college or pro playing experience. College coach: Colorado 1967-73, Georgia Tech 1974. Pro coach: Kansas City Chiefs 1975-77, Oakland-Los Angeles Raiders 1978-86, San Diego Chargers 1987-89 (Director of Football Operations), rejoined Raiders in 1990.

Terry Robiskie, tight ends; born November 12, 1954, New Orleans, La., lives in Beverly Hills, Calif. Running back Louisiana State 1973-76. Pro running back Oakland Raiders 1977-79, Miami Dolphins 1980-81. Pro coach: Joined Raiders in 1982.

Los Angeles Raiders 1991 First-Year Roster

Name	Pos.	Ht.	Wt.	Birth-date	College	Hometown	How Acq.
Bell, Nick	RB	6-2	250	8/19/68	Iowa	Las Vegas, Nev.	D2
Flory, Rob	T	6-4	300	1/5/67	Arizona	Huntington Beach, Calif.	FA
Glover, Andrew	TE	6-6	225	8/12/67	Grambling	Geismar, La.	D10
Grimes, Jeff	G	6-6	290	9/23/68	Texas-El Paso	Garland, Tex.	FA
Harrell, Newt (1)	G	6-5	285	9/17/64	West Texas State	Canyon, Tex.	D10-'88
Harrison, Nolan	DT	6-5	290	1/25/69	Indiana	Flossmoor, Ill.	D6
Hopper, Darrell (1)	WR	6-1	210	3/14/64	Southern California	Los Angeles, Calif.	FA
Johnson, Dennis	CB	6-1	200	7/22/67	Winston-Salem State	Harrels, N.C.	D12
Jones, Brian	LB	6-1	240	1/22/68	Texas	Lubbock, Tex.	D8
Jones, Mike	LB	6-1	220	4/15/69	Missouri	Kansas City, Mo.	FA
Lewis, Tahaun	CB	5-10	175	9/29/68	Nebraska	Colorado Springs, Colo.	D9
Lloyd, Doug (1)	RB	6-1	220	8/31/65	North Dakota State	Beaver Dam, Wis.	D6-'89
Marinovich, Todd	QB	6-4	220	7/4/69	Southern California	Mission Viejo, Calif.	D1
Mayo, Lyniel	LB	6-0	235	1/29/68	San Jose State	St. Anne, Ill.	FA
Moore, Sean	RB	5-10	200	5/23/69	Missouri	Springfield, Mo.	FA
Sap, Brian	RB	6-1	195	2/10/66	Eastern Oregon	Lakeport, Calif.	FA
Showell, Malcolm	DE	6-6	255	10/1/68	Delaware State	Baltimore, Md.	FA
Smith, Anthony (1)	DE	6-3	265	6/28/67	Arizona	Elizabeth, N.C.	D1-'90
Smith, Sean	WR	6-1	185	1/22/68	Iowa	San Pedro, Calif.	FA
Taotoai, Josh	C	6-6	315	1/20/68	Florida	Wilmington, Calif.	FA
Tunney, Jono	LB	6-2	235	10/1/68	Stanford	Mill Valley, Calif.	FA
White, Frank	WR	5-7	170	6/16/65	Azusa Pacific	Spring Valley, Calif.	FA
Wilson, Marcus (1)	S	6-1	200	4/16/68	Virginia	Rochester, N.Y.	D6-'90
Wright, Keith (1)	WR	6-0	185	2/10/64	Cal State-Northridge	Hawthorne, Calif.	FA
Woulard, Todd	LB	6-1	230	8/15/69	Alabama A&M	Gainesville, Fla.	D8
Young, Charles	RB	6-0	200	8/21/68	Stanford	Glencoe, Ill.	FA

The term NFL Rookie is defined as a player who is in his first season of professional football and has not been on the roster of another professional football team for any regular-season or postseason games. A Rookie is designated by an "R" on NFL rosters. Players who have been active in another professional football league or players who have NFL experience, including either preseason training camp or being on an active roster for fewer than three regular-season or postseason games, are termed NFL First-Year Players. An NFL First-Year Player is designated by a "1" on NFL rosters. Thereafter, a player on an NFL active roster for at least three regular-season or postseason games is credited with an additional year of NFL playing experience.

NOTES

Joe Scannella, offensive backfield; born May 22, 1932, Passaic, N.J., lives in El Segundo, Calif. Quarterback Lehigh 1947-50. Pro safety Saskatchewan Roughriders (CFL) 1951-52. College coach: Cornell 1960, C.W. Post 1963-68 (head coach 1964-68), Vermont 1970-71. Pro coach: Montreal Alouettes (CFL) 1969, 1978-81 (head coach), Oakland Raiders 1972-77, Cleveland Browns 1982-84, rejoined Raiders in 1987.

Jack Stanton, defensive backs; born June 6, 1938, Bridgeville, Pa., lives in El Segundo, Calif. Running back North Carolina State 1959-60. Pro running back Pittsburgh Steelers 1961, Toronto Argonauts (CFL) 1962-63. College coach: George Washington 1966, North Carolina State 1968-72, Florida State 1973, 1976-83, North Carolina 1974-75, Purdue 1986, New Mexico 1987-88. Pro coach: Atlanta Falcons 1984-85, joined Raiders in 1989.

Tom Walsh, offense; born April 16, 1949, Vallejo, Calif., lives in Manhattan Beach, Calif. UC-Santa Barbara 1971. No college or pro playing experience. College coach: University of San Diego 1972-76, U.S. International 1979, Murray State 1980, Cincinnati 1981. Pro coach: Joined Raiders in 1982.

Mike White, quarterbacks; born January 4, 1936, Berkeley, Calif., lives in El Segundo, Calif. Offensive end California 1955-57. No pro playing experience. College coach: California 1958-63, 1972-77 (head coach), Stanford 1964-71, Illinois 1980-87 (head coach). Pro coach: San Francisco 49ers 1978-79, joined Raiders in 1990.

MIAMI DOLPHINS

American Football Conference Eastern Division

Team Colors: Aqua, Coral, and White

Joe Robbie Stadium
2269 N.W. 199th Street
Miami, Florida 33056
Telephone: (305) 620-5000

Club Officials

President: Timothy J. Robbie
Executive Vice President: Daniel T. Robbie
Executive Vice President: Janet Robbie
Executive V.P./General Manager: Eddie J. Jones
Vice President: Elizabeth Robbie
Assistant General Manager: Bryan Wiedmeier
Head Coach: Don Shula
Director of Player Personnel: Charley Winner
Director of College Scouting: Tom Heckert
Director of Media Relations: Harvey Greene
Media Relations Assistants: Scott Stone, Fudge Browne
Vice President, Marketing: Kevin McHale
Marketing Director: David Evans
Treasurer: Jill R. Strafaci
Trainer: Bob Lundy
Equipment Manager: Bob Monica

Stadium: Joe Robbie Stadium • **Capacity:** 73,000
2269 N.W. 199th Street
Miami, Florida 33056

Playing Surface: Grass (PAT)

Training Camp: St. Thomas University
16400-D N.W. 32nd Avenue
Miami, Florida 33054

1991 Schedule

Preseason

July 26	**Chicago**	8:00
Aug. 3	vs. L.A. Raiders at Tokyo	10:00*
Aug. 10	at Tampa Bay	7:00
Aug. 19	at Denver	6:00
Aug. 24	**New Orleans**	8:00

*P.M. Eastern Time

Regular Season

Sept. 1	at Buffalo	4:00
Sept. 8	**Indianapolis**	1:00
Sept. 15	at Detroit	1:00
Sept. 22	**Green Bay**	1:00
Sept. 29	at New York Jets	4:00
Oct. 6	at New England	1:00
Oct. 13	at Kansas City	3:00
Oct. 20	**Houston**	1:00
Oct. 27	**Open Date**	
Nov. 3	at Indianapolis	4:00
Nov. 10	**New England**	8:00
Nov. 18	**Buffalo** (Monday)	9:00
Nov. 24	at Chicago	12:00
Dec. 1	**Tampa Bay**	1:00
Dec. 9	**Cincinnati** (Monday)	9:00
Dec. 15	at San Diego	1:00
Dec. 22	**New York Jets**	1:00

Dolphins Coaching History

(240-150-4)

1966-69	George Wilson	15-39-2
1970-90	Don Shula	225-111-2

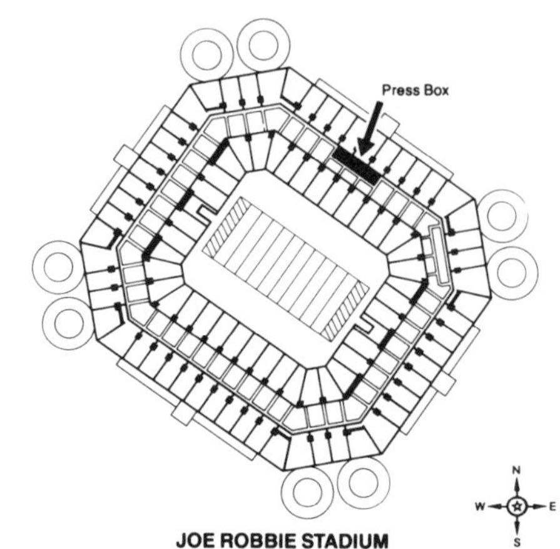

JOE ROBBIE STADIUM

Record Holders

Individual Records—Career

Category	Name	Performance
Rushing (Yds.)	Larry Csonka, 1968-1974, 1979	6,737
Passing (Yds.)	Dan Marino, 1983-1990	31,416
Passing (TDs)	Dan Marino, 1983-1990	241
Receiving (No.)	Nat Moore, 1974-1986	510
Receiving (Yds.)	Nat Moore, 1974-1986	7,547
Interceptions	Jake Scott, 1970-75	35
Punting (Avg.)	Reggie Roby, 1983-1990	43.2
Punt Return (Avg.)	Freddie Solomon, 1975-77	11.4
Kickoff Return (Avg.)	Mercury Morris, 1969-1975	26.5
Field Goals	Garo Yepremian, 1970-78	165
Touchdowns (Tot.)	Nat Moore, 1974-1986	75
Points	Garo Yepremian, 1970-78	830

Individual Records—Single Season

Category	Name	Performance
Rushing (Yds.)	Delvin Williams, 1978	1,258
Passing (Yds.)	Dan Marino, 1984	*5,084
Passing (TDs)	Dan Marino, 1984	*48
Receiving (No.)	Mark Clayton, 1988	86
Receiving (Yds.)	Mark Clayton, 1984	1,389
Interceptions	Dick Westmoreland, 1967	10
Punting (Avg.)	Reggie Roby, 1984	44.7
Punt Return (Avg.)	Freddie Solomon, 1975	12.3
Kickoff Return (Avg.)	Duriel Harris, 1976	32.9
Field Goals	Garo Yepremian, 1971	28
Touchdowns (Tot.)	Mark Clayton, 1984	18
Points	Garo Yepremian, 1971	117

Individual Records—Single Game

Category	Name	Performance
Rushing (Yds.)	Mercury Morris, 9-30-73	197
Passing (Yds.)	Dan Marino, 10-23-88	521
Passing (TDs)	Bob Griese, 11-24-77	6
	Dan Marino, 9-21-86	6
Receiving (No.)	Jim Jensen, 11-6-88	12
Receiving (Yds.)	Mark Duper, 11-10-85	217
Interceptions	Dick Anderson, 12-3-73	*4
Field Goals	Garo Yepremian, 9-26-71	5
Touchdowns (Tot.)	Paul Warfield, 12-15-73	4
Points	Paul Warfield, 12-15-73	24

*NFL Record

1990 Team Record

Preseason (1-3)

Date	Result		Opponents
8/11	L	6-10	at Chicago
8/18	L	14-23	at Philadelphia
8/25	W	17-16	Denver
8/31	L	17-20	Minnesota
		54-69	

Regular Season (12-4)

Date	Result		Opponents	Att.
9/9	W	27-24	at New England	45,305
9/16	W	30- 7	Buffalo	68,142
9/23	L	3-20	at N.Y. Giants	76,483
9/30	W	28- 6	at Pittsburgh	54,691
10/7	W	20-16	N.Y. Jets	69,678
10/18	W	17-10	New England	62,630
10/28	W	27- 7	at Indianapolis	59,213
11/4	W	23- 3	Phoenix	54,924
11/11	W	17- 3	at N.Y. Jets	68,362
11/19	L	10-13	L.A. Raiders	70,553
11/25	W	30-13	at Cleveland	70,225
12/2	L	20-42	at Washington	53,599
12/9	W	23-20	Philadelphia (OT)	67,034
12/16	W	24-17	Seattle	57,851
12/23	L	14-24	at Buffalo	80,235
12/30	W	23-17	Indianapolis	59,547

(OT) Overtime

Postseason (1-1)

Date	Result		Opponent	Att.
1/5	W	17-16	Kansas City	67,276
1/12	L	34-44	at Buffalo	77,087

Score by Periods

Dolphins	60	113	77	83	3	—	336
Opponents	30	108	39	65	0	—	242

Attendance

Home 510,359 Away 508,113 Total 1,018,472
Single-game home record, 70,553 (11-19-90)
Single-season home record, 510,359 (1990)

1990 Team Statistics

	Dolphins	Opp.
Total First Downs	303	268
Rushing	90	110
Passing	190	145
Penalty	23	13
Third Down: Made/Att.	88/206	79/207
Third Down: Pct.	42.7	38.2
Fourth Down: Made/Att.	10/13	7/18
Fourth Down: Pct.	76.9	38.9
Total Net Yards	5047	4547
Avg. Per Game	315.4	284.2
Total Plays	975	968
Avg. Per Play	5.2	4.7
Net Yards Rushing	1535	1831
Avg. Per Game	95.9	114.4
Total Rushes	420	461
Net Yards Passing	3512	2716
Avg. Per Game	219.5	169.8
Sacked/Yards Lost	16/99	45/348
Gross Yards	3611	3064
Att./Completions	539/310	462/257
Completion Pct.	57.5	55.6
Had Intercepted	12	19
Punts/Avg.	72/42.0	75/40.0
Net Punting Avg.	35.6	34.8
Penalties/Yards Lost	64/486	95/759
Fumbles/Ball Lost	33/15	23/8
Touchdowns	39	26
Rushing	13	11
Passing	21	14
Returns	5	1
Avg. Time of Possession	30:10	29:50

1990 Individual Statistics

Scoring	TD R	TD P	TD Rt	PAT	FG	Saf	TP
Stoyanovich	0	0	0	37/37	21/25	0	100
Smith	8	1	0	0/0	0/0	0	54
Paige	2	4	0	0/0	0/0	0	36
Duper	0	5	0	0/0	0/0	0	30
Clayton	0	3	0	0/0	0/0	0	18
Pruitt	0	3	0	0/0	0/0	0	18
Logan	2	0	0	0/0	0/0	0	12
Martin	0	2	0	0/0	0/0	0	12
Edmunds	0	1	0	0/0	0/0	0	6
Glenn	0	0	1	0/0	0/0	0	6
Higgs	0	0	1	0/0	0/0	0	6
Jensen	0	1	0	0/0	0/0	0	6
McKinnon, Dall.-Mia.	0	1	0	0/0	0/0	0	6
Odom	0	0	1	0/0	0/0	0	6
Schwedes	0	1	0	0/0	0/0	0	6
Sochia	0	0	1	0/0	0/0	0	6
Stradford	1	0	0	0/0	0/0	0	6
Williams	0	0	1	0/0	0/0	0	6
Dolphins	13	21	5	37/37	21/25	1	336
Opponents	11	14	1	26/26	20/29	0	242

Passing	Att.	Comp.	Yds.	Pct.	TD	Int.	Tkld.	Rate
Marino	531	306	3563	57.6	21	11	15/90	82.6
Secules	7	3	17	42.9	0	1	1/9	10.7
Jensen	1	1	31	100.0	0	0	0/0	118.8
Dolphins	539	310	3611	57.5	21	12	16/99	81.6
Opponents	462	257	3064	55.6	14	19	45/348	69.0

Rushing	Att.	Yds.	Avg.	LG	TD
Smith	226	831	3.7	33	8
Logan	79	317	4.0	17	2
Stradford	37	138	3.7	15	1
Paige	32	95	3.0	11	2
Higgs	10	67	6.7	27	0
Secules	8	34	4.3	17	0
Marino	16	29	1.8	15	0
Limbrick	5	14	2.8	5	0
Martin	1	8	8.0	8	0
Jensen	4	6	1.5	2	0
Banks	1	3	3.0	3	0
Edmunds	1	−7	−7.0	−7	0
McKinnon, Dall.-Mia.	1	−8	−8.0	−8	0
Dolphins	420	1535	3.7	33	13
Opponents	461	1831	4.0	39	11

Receiving	No.	Yds.	Avg.	LG	TD
Duper	52	810	15.6	69t	5
Jensen	44	365	8.3	18	1
Paige	35	247	7.1	17t	4
Clayton	32	406	12.7	43	3
Edmunds	31	446	14.4	35	1
Stradford	30	257	8.6	23	0
Martin	29	388	13.4	45	2
McKinnon, Dall.-Mia.	14	172	12.3	28t	1
Pruitt	13	235	18.1	35t	3
Banks	13	131	10.1	23	0
Smith	11	134	12.2	53t	1
Logan	7	54	7.7	12	0
Schwedes	6	66	11.0	19	1
Limbrick	4	23	5.8	9	0
A. Brown	3	49	16.3	24	0
Dolphins	310	3611	11.6	69t	21
Opponents	257	3064	11.9	64t	14

Interceptions	No.	Yds.	Avg.	LG	TD
Oliver	5	87	17.4	35	0
Williams	5	82	16.4	42t	1
McKyer	4	40	10.0	21	0
Glenn	2	31	15.5	31t	1
Offerdahl	1	28	28.0	28	0
Hobley	1	15	15.0	15	0
Kumerow	1	5	5.0	5	0
Dolphins	19	288	15.2	42t	2
Opponents	12	184	15.3	73	0

Punting	No.	Yds.	Avg.	In 20	LG
Roby	72	3022	42.0	20	62
Dolphins	72	3022	42.0	20	62
Opponents	75	3001	40.0	19	63

Punt Returns	No.	FC	Yds.	Avg.	LG	TD
Martin	26	9	140	5.4	35	0
Schwedes, S.D.-Mia.	14	3	122	8.7	23	0
Schwedes, Mia.	9	2	89	9.9	23	0
Adams, Clev.-Mia.	13	4	81	6.2	25	0
Stradford	3	2	4	1.3	4	0
McKinnon, Dall.-Mia.	2	1	20	10.0	20	0
Williams	1	5	0	0.0	0	0
Dolphins	39	18	233	6.0	35	0
Opponents	40	15	397	9.9	36	0

Kickoff Returns	No.	Yds.	Avg.	LG	TD
Logan	20	367	18.4	35	0
Higgs	10	210	21.0	30	0
Adams, Clev.-Mia.	5	49	9.8	15	0
Adams, Mia.	2	16	8.0	10	0
Stradford	3	56	18.7	21	0
Collins	2	30	15.0	30	0
Schwedes	2	52	26.0	30	0
Graf	1	6	6.0	6	0
Kinchen	1	16	16.0	16	0
Paige	1	18	18.0	18	0
Sims	1	9	9.0	9	0
Martin	0	0	0.0	0	0
Dolphins	43	780	18.1	35	0
Opponents	53	1092	20.6	38	0

Sacks	No.
Cross	11.5
Junior	6.0
Griggs	5.5
Wilson	4.0
Hobley	3.0
Oglesby	2.5
Green	2.0
Williams	2.0
Lee	1.5
J. Brown	1.0
Glenn	1.0
Odom	1.0
Offerdahl	1.0
Oliver	1.0
Sochia	1.0
Turner	1.0
Dolphins	45.0
Opponents	16.0

1991 Draft Choices

Round	Name	Pos.	College
1.	Randal Hill	WR	Miami
3.	Aaron Craver	RB	Fresno State
5.	Bryan Cox	LB	Western Illinois
	Gene Williams	G	Iowa State
7.	Chris Green	DB	Illinois
8.	Roland Smith	DB	Miami
9.	Scott Miller	WR	UCLA
10.	Michael Titley	TE	Iowa
11.	Ernie Rogers	G	California
12.	Joe Brunson	DT	Tenn.-Chattanooga

Miami Dolphins 1991 Veteran Roster

No.	Name	Pos.	Ht.	Wt.	Birth-date	NFL Exp.	College	Hometown	How Acq.	'90 Games/ Starts
86	†Banks, Fred	WR	5-10	185	5/26/62	6	Liberty	Columbus, Ga.	FA-'87	8/1
84	Baty, Greg	TE	6-5	240	8/28/64	4	Stanford	Sparta, N.J.	FA-'90	12/0
53	Bolcar, Ned	LB	6-1	235	1/12/67	2	Notre Dame	Phillipsburg, N.J.	PB(Sea)-'91#	5/0*
82	Brown, Andre	WR	6-3	210	8/21/66	3	Miami	Chicago, Ill.	FA-'89	6/0
37	†Brown, J.B.	CB	6-0	192	1/5/67	3	Maryland	Washington, D.C.	D12-'89	16/16
83	Clayton, Mark	WR	5-9	185	4/8/61	9	Louisville	Indianapolis, Ind.	D8-'83	10/10
50	Cooper, Louis	LB	6-2	238	8/5/63	7	Western Carolina	Marion, S.C.	PB(KC)-'91#	16/0*
91	Cross, Jeff	DE	6-4	272	3/25/66	4	Missouri	Blythe, Calif.	D9-'88	16/16
65	Dellenbach, Jeff	T-C	6-6	285	2/14/63	7	Wisconsin	Wausau, Wis.	D4b-'85	15/0
74	†Dennis, Mark	T	6-6	295	4/15/65	5	Illinois	Washington, Ill.	D8b-'87	16/16
85	Duper, Mark	WR	5-9	192	1/25/59	10	Northwestern Louisiana	Moreauville, La.	D2-'82	16/15
80	†Edmunds, Ferrell	TE	6-6	254	4/16/65	4	Maryland	Danville, Va.	D3-'88	16/16
34	Fullwood, Brent	RB	5-11	210	10/10/63	5	Auburn	St. Cloud, Fla.	FA-'91	6/4*
62	†Galbreath, Harry	G	6-2	275	1/1/65	4	Tennessee	Clarksville, Tenn.	D8a-'88	16/16
35	Glenn, Kerry	CB	5-9	178	1/3/62	5	Minnesota	East St. Louis, Ill.	PB(NYJ)-'90#	16/0
55	†Green, Hugh	LB	6-2	230	7/27/59	11	Pittsburgh	Natchez, Miss.	T(TB)-'85	16/16
92	Griggs, David	LB	6-3	248	2/5/67	3	Virginia	Pennsauken, N.J.	FA-'89	16/16
59	Grimsley, John	LB	6-2	238	2/25/62	8	Kentucky	Canton, Ohio	T(Hou)-'91	15/13*
21	Higgs, Mark	RB	5-7	195	4/11/66	4	Kentucky	Owensboro, Ky.	PB(Phil)-'90#	12/0
29	Hobley, Liffort	S	6-0	202	5/12/62	6	Louisiana State	Shreveport, La.	FA-'87	14/0
24	t-Jackson, Vestee	CB	6-0	186	8/14/63	6	Washington	Fresno, Calif.	T(Chi)-'91	16/8*
11	Jensen, Jim	WR	6-4	224	11/14/58	11	Boston University	Doylestown, Pa.	D11-'81	15/2
54	Junior, E.J.	LB	6-3	242	12/8/59	11	Alabama	Nashville, Tenn.	PB(Phx)-'89#	16/0
58	Krauss, Barry	LB	6-3	250	3/17/57	12	Alabama	Pompano Beach, Fla.	W(Clev)-'89	0*
44	Lankford, Paul	CB	6-1	191	6/15/58	10	Penn State	Farmingdale, N.Y.	D3-'82	7/0
98	†Lee, Shawn	NT	6-2	285	10/24/66	4	North Alabama	Brooklyn, N.Y.	T(Atl)-'90	13/10
32	Limbrick, Garrett	RB	6-2	240	11/16/65	2	Oklahoma State	Northbrook, Tex.	FA-'90	7/2
20	†Logan, Marc	RB	5-11	222	5/9/65	5	Kentucky	Lexington, Ky.	PB(Cin)-'89#	16/0
13	Marino, Dan	QB	6-4	224	9/15/61	9	Pittsburgh	Pittsburgh, Pa.	D1-'83	16/16
89	Martin, Tony	WR	6-0	180	9/5/65	2	Mesa, Colo.	Miami, Fla.	FA-'89	16/5
27	Moore, Stevon	S	5-11	204	2/9/67	2	Mississippi	Wiggins, Miss.	FA-'90	7/0
93	Odom, Cliff	LB	6-2	243	8/15/58	11	Texas-Arlington	Beaumont, Tex.	PB(Ind)-'90#	16/16
56	Offerdahl, John	LB	6-3	238	8/17/64	6	Western Michigan	Fort Atkinson, Wis.	D2-'86	16/16
96	Oglesby, Alfred	NT	6-3	278	1/27/67	2	Houston	Weimer, Tex.	D3-'90	13/6
25	Oliver, Louis	S	6-2	226	3/9/66	3	Florida	Belle Glade, Fla.	D1b-'89	16/16
49	Paige, Tony	RB	5-10	235	10/14/62	8	Virginia Tech	Washington, D.C.	PB(Det)-'90#	13/13
90	Price, Terry	DE	6-4	272	4/5/68	2	Texas A&M	Atlanta, Ga.	PB(Chi)-'91#	2/0*
52	Reichenbach, Mike	LB	6-2	240	9/14/61	8	East Stroudsburg	Bethlehem, Pa.	PB(Phil)-'90#	16/0
4	Roby, Reggie	P	6-2	246	7/30/61	9	Iowa	East Waterloo, Iowa	D6-'83	16/0
81	Schwedes, Scott	WR	6-0	185	6/30/65	5	Syracuse	DeWitt, N.Y.	FA-'90	9/0
9	Secules, Scott	QB	6-3	220	11/8/64	4	Virginia	Centreville, Va.	T(Dall)-'89	16/0
88	Sievers, Eric	TE	6-4	238	11/9/57	11	Maryland	Arlington, Va.	PB(NE)-'91#	8/1*
69	Sims, Keith	G	6-2	305	6/17/67	2	Iowa State	Watchung, N.J.	D2-'90	14/13
30	Smith, Don	RB	5-11	200	10/30/63	4	Mississippi State	Hamilton, Miss.	PB(Buff)-'91#	16/2*
33	Smith, Sammie	RB	6-2	230	5/16/67	3	Florida State	Zellwood, Fla.	D1a-'89	16/16
70	†Sochia, Brian	NT	6-3	278	7/21/61	9	Northwestern Oklahoma	Brasher Falls, N.Y.	FA-'86	5/2
10	†Stoyanovich, Pete	K	5-10	185	4/28/67	3	Indiana	Oberlin, Ohio	D8-'89	16/0
95	†Turner, T.J.	DE	6-4	280	5/16/63	6	Houston	Lufkin, Tex.	D5-'88	14/12
63	†Uhlenhake, Jeff	C	6-3	284	1/28/66	3	Ohio State	Newark, Ohio	D3-'86	16/16
78	Webb, Richmond	T	6-6	298	1/11/67	2	Texas A&M	Dallas, Tex.	D1-'90	16/16
60	Weidner, Bert	C	6-3	284	11/20/66	2	Kent State	Eden, N.Y.	D11-'89	8/0
26	Williams, Jarvis	S	5-11	200	5/16/65	4	Florida	Palatka, Fla.	D2-'88	16/16

* Bolcar played 5 games with Seattle in '90; Cooper played 16 games with Kansas City; Fullwood played 5 games with Green Bay, 1 game with Cleveland; Grimsley played 15 games with Houston; Jackson played 16 games with Chicago; Krauss missed '90 season due to injury; Price played 2 games with Chicago; Sievers played 8 games with New England; D. Smith played 16 games with Buffalo.

† Option playout; subject to developments.

Plan B unconditional free agent.

t- Dolphins traded for Jackson (Chicago).

Traded—CB Tim McKyer to Atlanta.

Players lost through Plan B (10): S Stefon Adams (Raid; 2 games in '90), DE John Bosa (Jets; 0), G Roy Foster (SF; 16), LB Rick Graf (Hou; 8), TE Brian Kinchen (GB; 4), WR James Pruitt (Minn; 6), RB Troy Stradford (KC; 14), CB Rodney Thomas (Rams; 15), CB Sean Vanhorse (Det; 0). DE Karl Wilson (Rams; 16).

Also played with Dolphins in '90: RB Tony Collins (1 game in '90), S African Grant (4), DE Greg Mark (4).

COACHING STAFF

Head Coach, Don Shula

Pro Career: Begins his twenty-ninth season as an NFL head coach, and twenty-second with the Dolphins. Miami has won or shared first place in the AFC East in 13 of his 21 years and has earned 13 playoff berths in that span. Has most wins (298) among active NFL coaches and is second only to George Halas's 325. Captured back-to-back NFL championships, defeating Washington 14-7 in Super Bowl VII and Minnesota 24-7 in Super Bowl VIII. Lost to Dallas 24-3 in Super Bowl VI, to Washington 27-17 in Super Bowl XVII, and to San Francisco 38-16 in Super Bowl XIX. His 1972 17-0 club is the only team in NFL history to go undefeated throughout the regular season and postseason. Started his pro playing career with Cleveland Browns as defensive back in 1951. After two seasons with Browns, spent 1953-56 with Baltimore Colts and 1957 with Washington Redskins. Joined Detroit Lions as defensive coach in 1960 and was named head coach of the Colts in 1963. Baltimore had a 13-1 record in 1968 and captured NFL championship before losing to New York Jets in Super Bowl III. Career record: 298-137-6.

Background: Outstanding offensive player at John Carroll University in Cleveland before becoming defensive specialist as a pro. His alma mater gave him doctorate in Humanities in May, 1973. Served as assistant coach at Virginia in 1958 and at Kentucky in 1959.

Personal: Born January 4, 1930, in Painesville, Ohio. Don lives in Miami Lakes, Fla., and has five children—David, Donna, Sharon, Annie, and Mike. David is Cincinnati's receivers coach and Mike is a coaches' assistant with Miami.

Assistant Coaches

George Hill, linebackers; born April 28, 1933, Bay Village, Ohio, lives in Miami. Tackle-fullback Denison 1954-57. No pro playing experience. College coach: Findlay 1959, Denison 1960-64, Cornell 1965, Duke 1966-70, Ohio State 1971-78. Pro coach: Philadelphia Eagles 1979-84, Indianapolis Colts 1985-88, joined Dolphins in 1989.

Tony Nathan, coaches' assistant; born December 14, 1956, Birmingham, Ala., lives in Miami. Running back Alabama 1975-78. Pro running back Miami Dolphins 1979-87. Pro coach: Joined Dolphins in 1988.

Tom Olivadotti, defense; born September 22, 1945, Long Branch, N.J., lives in Cooper City, Fla. Defensive back-wide receiver Upsala 1963-66. No pro playing experience. College coach: Princeton 1975-77, Boston College 1978-79, Miami 1980-83. Pro coach: Cleveland Browns 1985-86, joined Dolphins in 1987.

Mel Phillips, defensive backs; born January 6, 1942, Shelby, N.C., lives in Miami Lakes, Fla. Defensive back-running back North Carolina A&T 1964-65. Pro defensive back San Francisco 49ers 1966-77. Pro coach: Detroit Lions 1980-84, joined Dolphins in 1985.

John Sandusky, assistant head coach, offensive line-run offense; born December 28, 1925, Philadelphia, lives in Hollywood, Fla. Tackle Villanova 1946-49. Pro tackle Cleveland Browns 1950-55, Green Bay Packers 1956. College coach: Villanova 1957-58. Pro coach: Baltimore Colts 1959-72 (head coach 1972), Philadelphia Eagles 1973-75, joined Dolphins in 1976.

Larry Seiple, receivers; born February 14, 1945, Allentown, Pa., lives in Miami Lakes, Fla. Running back-receiver-punter Kentucky 1964-66. Pro punter-tight end-receiver-running back Miami Dolphins 1967-77. College coach: Miami 1978-79. Pro coach: Detroit Lions 1980-84, Tampa Bay Buccaneers 1985-86, joined Dolphins in 1988.

Dan Sekanovich, defensive line; born July 27, 1933, West Hazleton, Pa., lives in Cooper City, Fla. End Tennessee 1951-53. Pro defensive end Montreal Alouettes (CFL) 1954. College coach: Susquehanna 1961-63, Connecticut 1964-67, Pittsburgh 1968, Navy 1969-70, Kentucky 1971-72. Pro coach: Montreal Alouettes (CFL) 1973-76, New York Jets 1977-82, Atlanta Falcons 1983-85, joined Dolphins in 1986.

Mike Shula, coaches assistant; born June 23, 1965, Baltimore, Md., lives in Miami. Quarterback Alabama 1984-87. Pro quarterback Tampa Bay Buccaneers 1987. Pro coach: Tampa Bay Buccaneers 1988-90, joined Dolphins in 1991.

Gary Stevens, quarterbacks-pass offense; born March 19, 1943, Cleveland, Ohio, lives in Kendall, Fla. Running back John Carroll 1963-65. No pro playing experience. College coach: Louisville 1971-74, Kent State 1975, West Virginia 1976-79, Miami 1980-88. Pro coach: Joined Dolphins in 1989.

Carl Taseff, offensive backs; born September 28, 1928, Cleveland, Ohio, lives in Miami. Back John Carroll 1947-50. Pro defensive back Cleveland Browns 1951, Baltimore Colts 1953-61, Philadelphia Eagles 1961, Buffalo Bills 1962. Pro coach: Boston Patriots 1964, Detroit Lions 1965-66, joined Dolphins in 1970.

Junior Wade, strength-conditioning; born February 2, 1947, Bath, S.C., lives in Miami. South Carolina State 1969. No college or pro playing experience. Pro coach: Joined Dolphins in 1975, coach since 1983.

Mike Westhoff, special teams; born January 10, 1948, Pittsburgh, Pa., lives in Ft. Lauderdale, Fla. Center-linebacker Wichita State 1967-69. No pro playing experience. College coach: Indiana 1974-75, Dayton 1976, Indiana State 1977, Northwestern 1978-80, Texas Christian 1981. Pro coach: Baltimore/Indianapolis Colts 1982-84, Arizona Outlaws (USFL) 1985, joined Dolphins in 1986.

Miami Dolphins 1991 First-Year Roster

Name	Pos.	Ht.	Wt.	Birth-date	College	Hometown	How Acq.
Balkcom, Tom	S	5-10	174	1/6/68	Georgia Tech	Miami, Fla.	FA
Brown, Eddie	CB	5-10	180	2/27/69	Michigan State	Muskegon, Mich.	FA
Brown, Tim	DE	6-2	272	10/2/69	Georgia Southern	Madison, Ga.	FA
Brunson, Joe	NT	6-4	270	10/15/68	Tenn.-Chattanooga	Elberton, Ga.	D12
Buchanan, Richard	WR	5-10	173	5/8/69	Northwestern	Chicago, Ill.	FA
Champ, Clifford	LB	6-1	232	10/14/66	S.W. Louisiana	St. Martinville, La.	FA
Cox, Bryan	LB	6-3	235	2/17/68	Western Illinois	St. Louis, Mo.	D5a
Craver, Aaron	RB	5-11	215	12/18/69	Fresno State	Compton, Calif.	D3
Duffy, Pat	G	6-2	277	7/16/67	Penn State	Canton, Ohio	FA
Fleece, Rick	NT	6-3	265	11/29/67	Maryland	Laurel, N.J.	FA
Flores, Sam	K	6-0	198	11/8/61	C.W. Post	Uniondale, N.Y.	FA
Green, Chris	CB	5-11	188	2/26/68	Illinois	Lawrenceburg, Ind.	D6
Handy, Darren	C	6-1	273	9/26/68	Miami	Miami, Fla.	FA
Harden, Bobby (1)	S	6-0	192	2/8/67	Miami	Ft. Lauderdale, Fla.	D12-'90
Henry, Charles (1)	TE	6-4	230	4/18/64	Miami	St. Petersburg, Fla.	FA
Hill, Randal	WR	5-10	177	9/21/69	Miami	Miami, Fla.	D1
Holt, Leroy (1)	RB	5-10	224	2/7/67	Southern California	Brenham, Tex.	D5-'90
Iaquaniello, Mike	S	6-3	208	2/13/68	Michigan State	Dearborn, Mich.	FA
Jenkins, Eric	RB	5-10	220	3/22/69	Southwest Missouri	Dunedin, Fla.	FA
Jessup, Jason	T	6-3	290	2/12/68	Houston	Garland, Tex.	FA
Johnson, Joe	LB	6-2	223	4/28/65	Texas A&M	Miami, Fla.	FA
Klingbeil, Chuck (1)	NT	6-1	260	11/2/65	Northern Michigan	Houghton, Mich.	FA
Linn, Jack (1)	T	6-5	278	6/10/67	West Virginia	Rochester, Pa.	FA
McGruder, Michael (1)	CB	5-11	190	5/6/62	Kent State	Cleveland Hts., Ohio	FA-'90
Miller, Scott	WR	5-10	179	10/20/68	UCLA	El Toro, Calif.	D9
Miller, Scott	DE	6-4	275	4/22/68	Rutgers	Patterson, N.J.	FA
Mitchell, Scott (1)	QB	6-6	236	1/2/68	Utah	Springville, Utah	D4-'90
Parrish, James	T	6-5	292	5/19/68	Temple	Baltimore, Md.	FA
Pavelec, Mike	T	6-6	290	2/9/68	Calgary	Boise, Idaho	FA
Pederson, Doug	QB	6-3	200	1/31/68	Northeast Louisiana	Monroe, La.	FA
Pelham, Dwayne	LB	6-1	230	3/4/68	Appalachian State	Boone, N.C.	FA
Ray, Pat (1)	CB	5-10	180	2/11/66	Missouri	Columbia, Mo.	FA
Rogers, Ernie	T	6-5	290	1/3/68	California	Newport Beach, Calif.	D11
Rose, Blaine (1)	G	6-5	271	6/13/66	Maryland	Stanton, Ohio	FA
Sander, Mark	LB	6-2	232	3/21/68	Louisville	Louisville, Ky.	FA
Scotton, Stefen	RB	5-11	226	2/15/69	Georgia Tech	Cleveland, Tenn.	FA
Smith, Roland	CB	5-9	180	9/14/69	Miami	Miami, Fla.	D8
Taylor, Joel	WR	5-10	175	2/3/68	Franklin	New Carlisle, Ind.	FA
Titley, Michael	TE	6-3	235	5/5/68	Iowa	Brooklyn, N.Y.	D10
Williams, Gene	G	6-2	308	10/14/68	Iowa State	Omaha, Neb.	D5
Wood, Gordy	TE	6-3	228	2/3/68	Wyoming	Merced, Calif.	FA

The term NFL Rookie is defined as a player who is in his first season of professional football and has not been on the roster of another professional football team for any regular-season or postseason games. A Rookie is designated by an "R" on NFL rosters. Players who have been active in another professional football league or players who have NFL experience, including either preseason training camp or being on an active roster for fewer than three regular-season or postseason games, are termed NFL First-Year Players. An NFL First-Year Player is designated by a "1" on NFL rosters. Thereafter, a player on an NFL active roster for at least three regular-season or postseason games is credited with an additional year of NFL playing experience.

NOTES

American Football Conference
Eastern Division

Team Colors: Red, White, and Blue

Foxboro Stadium
Route 1
Foxboro, Massachusetts 02035
Telephone: (508) 543-8200

Club Officials

Chairman: Victor K. Kiam II
Vice Chairman: Francis W. Murray
President: William H. Sullivan, Jr.
Chief Executive Officer: Sam Jankovich
Vice President-Public Relations/Player Asst.: Tom Bass
Vice President-Administration: Patrick Forte
Vice President: Francis J. Kilroy
Vice President-Player Operations: Joe Mendes
Director of Pro Scouting: Rod Rust
National Scout: Norm Pollom
Personnel Scouts: Larry Cook, Charles Garcia, Ralph Goldston, Mike Pollom, Bob Teahan
Director of Sales and Marketing: David Wintergrass
Director of Ticket Sales: Ken Sternfeld
Director of Public Relations: Pat Hanlon
Assistant Director of Public Relations: Mike Hanson
Ticket Office Manager: Frank Napoli
Trainer: Ron O'Neil
Equipment Manager: George Luongo
Video Director: Ken Deininger

Stadium: Foxboro Stadium • **Capacity:** 60,794
Route 1
Foxboro, Massachusetts 02035

Playing Surface: Grass

Training Camp: Bryant College
Route 7
Smithfield, Rhode Island 02917

1991 Schedule

Preseason

Aug. 3	at Green Bay	6:00
Aug. 10	**Washington**	7:00
Aug. 17	at Phoenix	7:30
Aug. 24	**New York Giants**	4:00

Regular Season

Sept. 1	at Indianapolis	3:00
Sept. 8	**Cleveland**	1:00
Sept. 15	at Pittsburgh	1:00
Sept. 22	**Houston**	1:00
Sept. 29	at Phoenix	1:00
Oct. 6	**Miami**	1:00
Oct. 13	**Open Date**	
Oct. 20	**Minnesota**	1:00
Oct. 27	**Denver**	4:00
Nov. 3	at Buffalo	1:00
Nov. 10	at Miami	8:00
Nov. 17	**New York Jets**	1:00
Nov. 24	**Buffalo**	1:00
Dec. 1	at Denver	2:00
Dec. 8	**Indianapolis**	1:00
Dec. 15	at New York Jets	1:00
Dec. 22	at Cincinnati	1:00

Patriots Coaching History

Boston 1960-70
(212-241-9)

1960-61	Lou Saban*	7-12-0
1961-68	Mike Holovak	53-47-9
1969-70	Clive Rush**	5-16-0
1970-72	John Mazur***	9-21-0
1972	Phil Bengtson	1-4-0
1973-78	Chuck Fairbanks****	46-41-0
1978	Hank Bullough-Ron Erhardt#	0-1-0
1979-81	Ron Erhardt	21-27-0
1982-84	Ron Meyer##	18-16-0
1984-89	Raymond Berry	51-41-0
1990	Rod Rust	1-15-0

*Released after five games in 1961
**Released after seven games in 1970
***Resigned after nine games in 1972
****Suspended for final regular season game in 1978
#Co-coaches
##Released after eight games in 1984

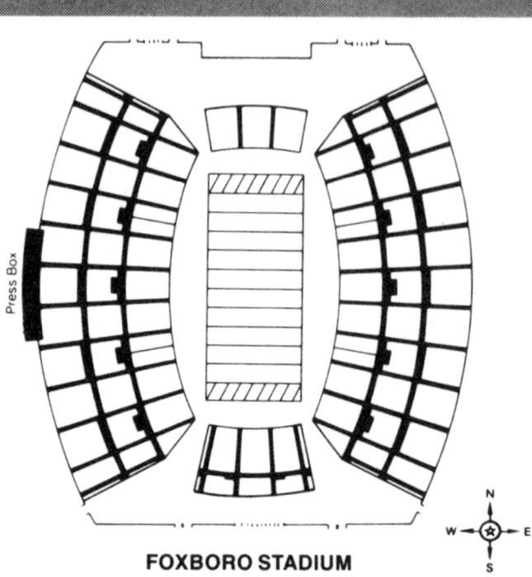

FOXBORO STADIUM

Record Holders

Individual Records—Career

Category	Name	Performance
Rushing (Yds.)	Sam Cunningham, 1973-79, 1981-82	5,453
Passing (Yds.)	Steve Grogan, 1975-1990	26,886
Passing (TDs)	Steve Grogan, 1975-1990	182
Receiving (No.)	Stanley Morgan, 1977-1989	534
Receiving (Yds.)	Stanley Morgan, 1977-1989	10,352
Interceptions	Raymond Clayborn, 1977-1989	36
Punting (Avg.)	Rich Camarillo, 1981-87	42.6
Punt Return (Avg.)	Mack Herron, 1973-75	12.0
Kickoff Return (Avg.)	Horace Ivory, 1977-1981	27.6
Field Goals	Gino Cappelletti, 1960-1970	176
Touchdowns (Tot.)	Stanley Morgan, 1977-1989	68
Points	Gino Cappelletti, 1960-1970	1,130

Individual Records—Single Season

Category	Name	Performance
Rushing (Yds.)	Jim Nance, 1966	1,458
Passing (Yds.)	Vito (Babe) Parilli, 1964	3,465
Passing (TDs)	Vito (Babe) Parilli, 1964	31
Receiving (No.)	Stanley Morgan, 1986	84
Receiving (Yds.)	Stanley Morgan, 1986	1,491
Interceptions	Ron Hall, 1964	11
Punting (Avg.)	Rich Camarillo, 1983	44.6
Punt Return (Avg.)	Mack Herron, 1974	14.8
Kickoff Return (Avg.)	Raymond Clayborn, 1977	31.0
Field Goals	Tony Franklin, 1986	32
Touchdowns (Tot.)	Steve Grogan, 1976	13
	Stanley Morgan, 1979	13
Points	Gino Cappelletti, 1964	155

Individual Records—Single Game

Category	Name	Performance
Rushing (Yds.)	Tony Collins, 9-18-83	212
Passing (Yds.)	Tony Eason, 9-21-86	414
Passing (TDs)	Vito (Babe) Parilli, 11-15-64	5
	Vito (Babe) Parilli, 10-15-67	5
	Steve Grogan, 9-9-79	5
Receiving (No.)	Art Graham, 11-20-66	11
	Tony Collins, 11-29-87	11
Receiving (Yds.)	Stanley Morgan, 11-8-81	182
Interceptions	Many times	3
	Last time by Roland James, 10-23-83	
Field Goals	Gino Cappelletti, 10-4-64	6
Touchdowns (Tot.)	Many times	3
	Last time by Stanley Morgan, 9-21-86	
Points	Gino Cappelletti, 12-18-65	28

1990 Team Record

Preseason (0-4)

Date	Result		Opponents
8/9	L	14-30	vs. Pittsburgh at Montreal
8/18	L	10-44	vs. Tampa Bay at Jacksonville
8/24	L	10-13	Cincinnati
8/31	L	17-20	Atlanta
		48-132	

Regular Season (1-15)

Date	Result		Opponents	Att.
9/9	L	24-27	Miami	45,305
9/16	W	16-14	at Indianapolis	49,256
9/23	L	7-41	at Cincinnati	56,470
9/30	L	13-37	N.Y. Jets	36,724
10/7	L	20-33	Seattle	39,735
10/18	L	10-17	at Miami	62,630
10/28	L	10-27	Buffalo	51,959
11/4	L	20-48	at Philadelphia	65,514
11/11	L	10-13	Indianapolis	28,924
11/18	L	0-14	at Buffalo	74,720
11/25	L	14-34	at Phoenix	30,110
12/2	L	7-37	Kansas City	26,280
12/9	L	3-24	at Pittsburgh	48,354
12/15	L	10-25	Washington	22,286
12/23	L	7-42	at N.Y. Jets	30,250
12/30	L	10-13	N.Y. Giants	60,410

Score by Periods

Patriots	30	81	30	40	0	—	181
Opponents	120	128	88	110	0	—	446

Attendance

Home 311,623 Away 417,305 Total 728,928
Single-game home record, 61,457 (12-5-71)
Single-season home record, 482,572 (1986)

1990 Team Statistics

	Patriots	Opp.
Total First Downs	239	307
Rushing	65	151
Passing	156	139
Penalty	18	17
Third Down: Made/Att.	86/227	84/192
Third Down: Pct.	37.9	43.8
Fourth Down: Made/Att.	2/12	7/13
Fourth Down: Pct.	16.7	53.8
Total Net Yards	4163	5697
Avg. Per Game	260.2	356.1
Total Plays	955	972
Avg. Per Play	4.4	5.9
Net Yards Rushing	1398	2676
Avg. Per Game	87.4	167.3
Total Rushes	383	565
Net Yards Passing	2765	3021
Avg. Per Game	172.8	188.8
Sacked/Yards Lost	58/443	33/224
Gross Yards	3208	3245
Att./Completions	514/274	374/218
Completion Pct.	53.3	58.3
Had Intercepted	20	14
Punts/Avg.	92/40.8	56/40.8
Net Punting Avg.	33.6	36.6
Penalties/Yards Lost	99/742	73/488
Fumbles/Ball Lost	33/16	25/18
Touchdowns	19	52
Rushing	4	29
Passing	14	21
Returns	1	2
Avg. Time of Possession	28:21	31:39

1990 Individual Statistics

Scoring	TD R	TD P	TD Rt	PAT	FG	Saf	TP
Staurovsky	0	0	0	19/19	16/22	0	67
Cook	0	5	0	0/0	0/0	0	30
Fryar	0	4	0	0/0	0/0	0	24
Stephens	2	1	0	0/0	0/0	0	18
Dykes	0	2	0	0/0	0/0	0	12
Adams	0	1	0	0/0	0/0	0	6
Allen	1	0	0	0/0	0/0	0	6
Martin	0	1	0	0/0	0/0	0	6
Perryman	1	0	0	0/0	0/0	0	6
B. Williams	0	0	1	0/0	0/0	0	6
Patriots	4	14	1	19/19	16/22	0	181
Opponents	29	21	2	51/52	27/31	1	446

Passing	Att.	Comp.	Yds.	Pct.	TD	Int.	Tkld.	Rate
Wilson	265	139	1625	52.5	6	11	29/228	61.6
Hodson	156	85	968	54.5	4	5	20/147	68.5
Grogan	92	50	615	54.3	4	3	9/68	76.1
Stephens	1	0	0	0.0	0	1	0/0	0.0
Patriots	514	274	3208	53.3	14	20	58/443	65.4
Opponents	374	218	3245	58.3	21	14	33/224	89.9

Rushing	Att.	Yds.	Avg.	LG	TD
Stephens	212	808	3.8	26	2
Allen	63	237	3.8	29	1
Adams	28	111	4.0	13	0
Perryman	32	97	3.0	13	1
Hodson	12	79	6.6	23	0
Tatupu	16	56	3.5	15	0
Overton	5	8	1.6	6	0
Wilson	5	7	1.4	6	0
Morris	2	4	2.0	3	0
Gannon	1	0	0.0	0	0
Hansen	1	0	0.0	0	0
Fryar	2	−4	−2.0	−1	0
Grogan	4	−5	−1.3	0	0
Patriots	383	1398	3.7	29	4
Opponents	565	2676	4.7	80t	29

Receiving	No.	Yds.	Avg.	LG	TD
Fryar	54	856	15.9	56	4
Cook	51	455	8.9	35t	5
Dykes	34	549	16.1	35t	2
Stephens	28	196	7.0	43	1
McMurtry	22	240	10.9	26	0
Jones	21	301	14.3	26	0
Adams	16	146	9.1	28	1
Perryman	15	88	5.9	15	0
Sievers	8	77	9.6	25	0
Mowatt	6	67	11.2	16	0
Allen	6	48	8.0	19	0
Timpson	5	91	18.2	42	0
Martin	4	65	16.3	19t	1
Overton	2	19	9.5	15	0
Tatupu	2	10	5.0	6	0
Patriots	274	3208	11.7	56	14
Opponents	218	3245	14.9	86t	21

Interceptions	No.	Yds.	Avg.	LG	TD
Lippett	4	94	23.5	73	0
Hurst	4	61	15.3	36	0
Marion	4	17	4.3	16	0
Rembert	2	22	11.0	11	0
Patriots	14	194	13.9	73	0
Opponents	20	143	7.2	42	0

Punting	No.	Yds.	Avg.	In 20	LG
Hansen	90	3752	41.7	18	69
Patriots	92	3752	40.8	18	69
Opponents	56	2282	40.8	17	70

Punt Returns	No.	FC	Yds.	Avg.	LG	TD
Fryar	28	10	133	4.8	17	0
Martin	1	0	1	1.0	1	0
Patriots	29	10	134	4.6	17	0
Opponents	50	13	503	10.1	34	0

Kickoff Returns	No.	Yds.	Avg.	LG	TD
Martin	25	515	20.6	38	0
Allen	11	168	15.3	34	0
Morris	11	202	18.4	22	0
Robinson	11	211	19.2	27	0
Overton	10	188	18.8	23	0
Timpson	3	62	20.7	26	0
P. Coleman	2	18	9.0	12	0
Jones	2	24	12.0	13	0
Adams	1	7	7.0	7	0
Gordon, Atl.-N.E.	1	43	43.0	43	0
McSwain	1	0	0.0	0	0
Patriots	77	1395	18.1	38	0
Opponents	38	665	17.5	38	0

Sacks	No.
B. Williams	6.0
Tippett	3.5
Hobby	3.0
Singleton	3.0
Agnew	2.5
Brown	2.5
Goad	2.5
McSwain	2.0
Veris	2.0
E. Williams	2.0
Smith	1.5
Rembert	1.0
Reynolds	1.0
Gannon	0.5
Patriots	33.0
Opponents	58.0

1991 Draft Choices

Round	Name	Pos.	College
1.	Pat Harlow	T	Southern California
	Leonard Russell	RB	Arizona State
2.	Jerome Henderson	DB	Clemson
3.	Calvin Stephens	G	South Carolina
4.	Scott Zolak	QB	Maryland
5.	Jon Vaughn	RB	Michigan
	Ben Coates	TE	Livingstone
6.	David Key	DB	Michigan
7.	Blake Miller	C	Louisiana State
8.	Harry Colon	DB	Missouri
9.	O'Neil Glenn	G	Maryland
10.	Randy Bethel	TE	Miami
11.	Vince Moore	WR	Tennessee
	Paul Alsbury	P	Southwest Texas St.
12.	Tim Edwards	DT	Delta State

New England Patriots 1991 Veteran Roster

No.	Name	Pos.	Ht.	Wt.	Birth-date	NFL Exp.	College	Hometown	How Acq.	'90 Games/ Starts
33	Adams, George	RB	6-1	225	12/22/62	6	Kentucky	Lexington, Ky.	PB(NYG)-'90#	16/7
92	Agnew, Ray	DE	6-3	272	12/9/67	2	North Carolina State	Winston-Salem, N.C.	D1b-'90	12/9
39	Allen, Marvin	RB	5-10	208	11/23/65	4	Tulane	Wichita Falls, Tex.	D11-'88	8/3
78	Armstrong, Bruce	T	6-4	284	9/7/65	5	Louisville	Miami, Fla.	D1-'87	16/16
59	Brown, Vincent	LB	6-2	245	1/9/65	4	Mississippi Valley State	Decatur, Ga.	D2-'88	16/14
63	Chilton, Gene	C	6-3	286	3/27/64	4	Texas	Houston, Tex.	FA-'90	4/3
76	Clayton, Stan	T-G	6-3	265	1/31/65	4	Penn State	Cherry Hill, N.J.	FA-'90	11/3
22	Coleman, Eric	CB	6-0	190	12/27/66	3	Wyoming	Denver, Colo.	D2-'89	7/0
46	Cook, Marv	TE	6-4	234	2/24/66	3	Iowa	West Branch, Iowa	D3a-'89	16/16
65	Crawford, Elbert	C-G	6-3	280	6/20/66	2	Arkansas	Little Rock, Ark.	FA-'90	14/0
88	Dykes, Hart Lee	WR	6-4	218	9/2/66	3	Oklahoma State	Bay City, Tex.	D1-'89	10/10
28	t-Francis, Ron	CB	5-9	186	4/7/64	5	Baylor	La Marque, Tex.	T(Dall)-'91	15/0
80	Fryar, Irving	WR-KR	6-0	200	9/28/62	8	Nebraska	Mt. Holly, N.J.	D1-'84	16/15
74	Gambol, Chris	G-T	6-6	303	9/4/64	4	Iowa	Oxford, Mich.	PB(Det)-'90#	16/15
91	Gannon, Chris	DE	6-6	260	1/20/66	3	Southwestern Louisiana	Orange Park, Fla.	PB(SD)-'90#	6/2
43	Gibson, Ernest	CB	5-10	185	10/3/61	7	Furman	Jacksonville, Fla.	PB(Mia)-'90#	0*
72	Goad, Tim	NT	6-3	280	2/28/66	4	North Carolina	Stuart, Va.	D4a-'88	16/16
28	Gordon, Tim	S	6-0	188	5/7/65	5	Tulsa	Ardmore, Okla.	FA-'90	0*
58	Harvey, Richard	LB	6-1	227	9/11/66	2	Tulane	Gautier, Miss.	PB(Buff)-'90#	16/9
60	Hobby, Marion	DE	6-4	277	11/7/66	2	Tennessee	Birmingham, Ala.	FA-'90	16/5
13	Hodson, Tom	QB	6-3	195	1/28/67	2	Louisiana State	Matthews, La.	D3-'90	7/6
99	t-Howard, David	LB	6-1	230	12/8/61	7	Long Beach State	Long Beach, Calif.	T(Dall)-'91	16/0
45	Hunter, Ivy Joe	RB	6-1	248	11/16/66	3	Kentucky	Gainesville, Fla.	PB(Ind)-'91#	16/1*
37	Hurst, Maurice	CB	5-10	185	9/17/67	3	Southern	New Orleans, La.	D4a-'89	16/16
38	James, Roland	S	6-2	191	2/18/58	12	Tennessee	Xenia, Ohio	D1a-'80	6/4
50	Jarostchuk, Ilia	LB	6-3	245	8/1/64	5	New Hampshire	Utica, N.Y.	PB(Phx)-'90#	12/1
68	Johnson, Damian	G-T	6-5	290	12/18/62	6	Kansas State	Great Bend, Kan.	PB(NYG)-'90#	16/16
30	Jones, Victor	RB	5-8	212	12/5/67	2	Louisiana State	Zachary, La.	PB(Hou)-'91#	10/0*
42	Lippett, Ronnie	CB	5-11	180	12/10/60	8	Miami	Sebring, Fla.	D3-'83	16/16
51	t-Lockhart, Eugene	LB	6-2	233	3/8/61	8	Houston	Crockett, Tex.	T(Dall)-'91	16/16
31	Marion, Fred	S	6-2	191	1/2/59	10	Miami	Gainesville, Fla.	D5-'82	16/16
82	Martin, Sammy	WR	5-11	175	8/21/65	4	Louisiana State	New Orleans, La.	D4b-'88	10/0
86	McMurtry, Greg	WR	6-2	207	10/15/67	2	Michigan	Brockton, Mass.	D4-'90	13/5
23	McSwain, Rod	CB	6-1	198	1/28/62	8	Clemson	Forest City, N.C.	T(Atl)-'84	13/12
7	Millen, Hugh	QB	6-5	216	11/22/63	4	Washington	Seattle, Wash.	PB(Atl)-'91#	3/2*
81	Mowatt, Zeke	TE	6-3	240	3/5/61	8	Florida State	Wauchula, Fla.	PB(NYG)-'90#	10/0
52	Rembert, Johnny	LB	6-3	234	1/19/61	9	Clemson	DeSoto, Fla.	D4-'83	5/5
95	Reynolds, Ed	LB	6-5	242	9/23/61	9	Virginia	Ridgeway, Va.	FA-'83	12/12
27	Robinson, Junior	CB	5-9	181	2/3/68	2	East Carolina	High Point, N.C.	D5a-'89	16/0
55	Singleton, Chris	LB	6-2	247	2/20/67	2	Arizona	Parsippany, N.J.	D1a-'90	13/4
97	Smith, Sean	DE	6-7	280	5/29/67	2	Georgia Tech	Cincinnati, Ohio	D11-'90	15/0
4	Staurovsky, Jason	K	5-9	170	3/23/63	4	Tulsa	Tulsa, Okla.	FA-'88	16/0
44	Stephens, John	RB	6-1	215	2/23/66	4	Northwestern Louisiana	Springhill, La.	D1-'88	16/14
34	Strachan, Steve	RB	6-1	225	3/22/63	6	Boston College	Burlington, Mass.	FA-'91	0*
45	Timpson, Michael	WR	5-10	175	6/6/67	2	Penn State	Hialeah, Fla.	D4-'89	5/0
56	Tippett, Andre	LB	6-3	241	12/27/59	9	Iowa	Newark, N.J.	D2b-'82	13/13
90	Veris, Garin	DE	6-4	255	2/27/63	6	Stanford	Chillicothe, Ohio	D2a-'85	7/2
70	Viaene, David	T	6-5	300	7/14/65	3	Minnesota-Duluth	Kaukauna, Wis.	PB(Hou)-'89#	4/4
75	Villa, Danny	C-T	6-5	305	9/21/64	5	Arizona State	Nogales, Ariz.	D5a-'87	16/16
21	Washington, Mickey	CB	5-9	187	7/8/68	2	Texas A&M	Beaumont, Tex.	FA-'90	9/0
96	Williams, Brent	DE	6-4	275	10/23/64	6	Toledo	Flint, Mich.	D7b-'86	16/16

* Gibson and Gordon missed '90 season due to injury; Hunter played 16 games with Indianapolis in '90; Jones played 10 games with Houston; Millen played 3 games in Atlanta; Strachan last active with Raiders in '89.

† Option playout; subject to developments.

Plan B unconditional free agent.

Patriots traded for Francis (Dallas), Howard (Dallas), and Lockhart (Dallas).

Retired—Marc Wilson, 11-year quarterback, 16 games in '90.

Players lost through Plan B (8): CB Ventson Donelson (GB; 0 games in '90), P Brian Hansen (Clev; 16), S Tim Hauck (GB; 10), WR Cedric Jones (Hou; 14), RB Jamie Lawson (TB; 1), RB Jamie Morris (Minn; 5), TE Eric Sievers (Mia; 8), RB Mosi Tatupu (Rams; 15).

Also played with Patriots in '90—WR Pat Coleman (1 game), TE Lin Dawson (3), QB Steve Grogan (4), S Brian Hutson (2), RB Don Overton (7), RB Robert Perryman (8).

COACHING STAFF

Head Coach, Dick MacPherson

Pro Career: Named the Patriots' eleventh head coach on January 7, 1991. Accepted post after serving 10 years (1981-90) as head coach at Syracuse University. While at Syracuse, MacPherson compiled a record of 66-46-4 (.586) and appeared in five bowl games, including the 1990 Aloha Bowl. Was linebackers coach with Cleveland Browns under Sam Rutigliano from 1978-80. Prior to that, was head coach at Massachusetts and led Minutemen to 45-27-1 record in seven years (1971-77). Was defensive backs coach and later defensive coordinator with Denver Broncos from 1967-70. Before that, was assistant coach at Maryland (1966) and Cincinnati (1961-65). Began coaching career at Massachusetts as freshman coach from 1959-60. Compiled collegiate coaching record of 111-73-5 (.600).

Background: Entered Maine Maritime Academy in 1948, but left after two years to join the Air Force. Spent four years in the service, then enrolled at Springfield (Massachusetts) College and received bachelor of science degree in 1958. Was center on football team at Springfield and earned three letters. Was standout on 1956 undefeated squad and was team captain as a senior. Received master's degree in 1959 from Illinois.

Personal: Born November 4, 1930, Old Town, Maine. Dick and his wife, Sandra, live in Foxboro, Mass., and have two daughters—Maureen and Janet.

Assistant Coaches

Joe Collier, defensive coordinator; born June 7, 1932, Rock Island, Ill., lives in Foxboro, Mass. Defensive end Northwestern 1950-53. No pro playing experience. Pro coach: Boston Patriots 1960-61, Buffalo Bills 1962-68 (head coach 1966-68), Denver Broncos 1969-88, rejoined Patriots in 1991.

Joel Collier, assistant running backs, assistant wide receivers; born December 25, 1963, Buffalo, N.Y., lives in Foxboro, Mass. Linebacker Northern Colorado 1983-86. No pro playing experience. College coach: Syracuse 1988-89 (graduate assistant). Pro coach: Tampa Bay Buccaneers 1990, joined Patriots in 1991.

Dick Coury, offensive coordinator; born September 29, 1929, Athens, Ohio, lives in Foxboro, Mass. Quarterback Notre Dame 1950-54. No pro playing experience. College coach: Southern California 1967-69, Cal State-Fullerton 1970-71. Pro coach: Denver Broncos 1972-73, Portland Storm (WFL) 1974, San Diego Chargers 1975, Philadelphia Eagles 1976-82, Boston/New Orleans/Portland Breakers (USFL) 1983-85 (head coach), Los Angeles Rams 1986-90, joined Patriots in 1991.

Ivan Fears, wide receivers; born November 15, 1954, Portsmouth, Va., lives in Foxboro, Mass. Running back William and Mary 1973-75. No pro playing experience. College coach: William and Mary 1977-80, Syracuse 1981-90. Pro coach: Joined Patriots in 1991.

Norm Gerber, inside linebackers; born August 11, 1935, Manchester, N.H., lives in Foxboro, Mass. Tackle Connecticut 1953-56. No pro playing experience. College coach: Central Connecticut State 1965-69, Columbia 1969-73, Boston College 1974-77, Dartmouth 1978-80, Syracuse 1980-90. Pro coach: Joined Patriots in 1991.

Bobby Grier, running backs; born November 10, 1942, Detroit, Mich., lives in Holliston, Mass. Running back Iowa 1961-64. No pro playing experience. College coach: Eastern Michigan 1974-77, Boston College 1978-80. Pro coach: New England Patriots 1981-91 (scout 1982-84).

Rod Humenuik, offensive line; born June 17, 1938, Detroit, Mich., lives in Foxboro, Mass. Guard Southern California 1956-58. Pro guard Winnipeg Blue Bombers (CFL) 1960-62. College coach: Fullerton, Calif., J.C. 1964-65, Southern California 1966-70, Cal State-Northridge 1971-72 (head coach). Pro coach: Toronto Argonauts (CFL) 1973-74, Cleveland Browns 1975-82, Kansas City Chiefs 1983-84, New England Patriots 1985-88, New York Jets 1989, rejoined Patriots in 1990.

Stan Jones, defensive line; born November 24, 1931, Altoona, Pa., lives in Walpole, Mass. Tackle Maryland 1949-53. Pro guard/defensive tackle Chicago Bears 1954-65, Washington Redskins 1966. Pro coach: Denver Broncos 1967-71, 1976-88, Buffalo Bills 1972-75, Cleveland Browns 1989-90, joined Patriots in 1991.

Myrel Moore, outside linebackers; born March 9, 1934, Sebastopole, Calif., lives in Foxboro, Mass. Tight end/linebacker California-Davis 1954-57. Pro linebacker Washington Redskins 1958-59. College coach: Santa Ana, Calif., J.C. 1959, California 1963. Pro coach: Denver Broncos 1972, 1981-88 (scout 1981), Oakland Raiders 1978-80, joined Patriots in 1991.

Dante Scarnecchia, tight ends, offensive tackles, special teams; born February 15, 1948, Los Angeles, Calif., lives in Wrentham, Mass. Center/guard California Western 1968-70. No pro playing experience. College coach: California Western 1970-72, Iowa State 1973, Southern Methodist 1975-76, 1980-81, Pacific 1977-78, Northern Arizona 1979. Pro coach: New England Patriots 1982-89, Indianapolis Colts 1990, rejoined Patriots in 1991.

Dave Uyrus, assistant defensive line, assistant special teams; born August 19, 1952, Adams, Mass., lives in Wrentham, Mass. Tackle Middlebury College 1970-74. No pro playing experience. College coach: Middlebury College 1974-76, Massachusetts 1977-78, American International 1979, Merchant Marine Academy 1980, Syracuse 1981-90. Pro coach: Joined Patriots in 1991.

Charlie West, defensive backs; born August 31, 1946, Terrell, Tex., lives in North Attleboro, Mass. Defensive back Texas-El Paso 1965-68. Pro defensive back Minnesota Vikings 1968-73, Detroit Lions 1974-77, Denver Broncos 1978-79. College coach: Macalester College 1981, California 1982, Howard 1989. Pro coach: Denver Broncos 1983-88, joined Patriots in 1991.

New England Patriots 1991 First-Year Roster

Name	Pos.	Ht.	Wt.	Birth-date	College	Hometown	How Acq.
Alsbury, Paul	P	6-1	203	9/15/68	S.W. Texas State	Edinburg, Tex.	D11b
Bethel, Randy	TE	6-1	235	9/6/69	Miami	Vero Beach, Fla.	D10
Clark, Reggie	LB	6-2	226	10/17/67	North Carolina	Charlotte, N.C.	FA
Coates, Ben	TE	6-4	245	8/16/69	Livingstone	Greenwood, S.C.	D5b
Colon, Harry	S	5-11	203	2/14/69	Missouri	Kansas City, Kan.	D8
Crimm, Ben	T	6-4	285	12/27/68	Southern Mississippi	Pascagoula, Miss.	FA
Edwards, Timothy	DE	6-1	270	8/29/68	Delta State	Nesoba, Miss.	D12
Foster, Sean	WR	5-11	184	12/22/67	Long Beach State	Los Angeles, Calif.	FA
Glenn, O'Neil	G	6-2	290	1/27/68	Maryland	Bronx, N.Y.	D9
Harlow, Pat	T	6-6	290	3/16/69	Southern California	Norco, Calif.	D1a
Henderson, Jerome	CB	5-10	189	8/8/69	Clemson	Statesville, N.C.	D2
Key, David	CB	5-10	198	3/27/68	Michigan	Columbus, Ohio	D6
McGee, Reggie	WR	5-11	170	11/8/69	Jackson State	Tupelo, Miss.	FA
Melander, Jon (1)	T	6-7	280	12/27/66	Minnesota	Fridley, Minn.	D5a-'90
Miller, Blake	C	6-1	285	8/23/68	Louisiana State	Alexandria, La.	D7
Moore, Vincent	WR	5-10	198	11/7/67	Tennessee	Memphis, Tenn.	FA
Russell, Leonard	RB	6-2	235	11/17/69	Arizona State	Long Beach, Calif.	D1b
Ryder, Brian	LB	6-2	230	7/10/69	Tulane	Nantucket, Mass.	FA
Stephens, Robert	C	6-3	265	5/16/69	Brigham Young	La Mirada, Calif.	FA
Stephens, Calvin	G	6-2	285	10/25/67	South Carolina	Kings Mountain, N.C.	D3
Tardits, Richard (1)	LB	6-2	235	7/30/65	Georgia	Biarritz, France	FA-'90
Thomson, Rob	S	6-2	200	4/13/67	Syracuse	Southington, Conn.	FA
Vaughn, Jon	RB	5-9	203	3/12/70	Michigan	Florissant, Mo.	D5a
Warner, Kirk (1)	TE	6-4	225	11/24/67	Georgia	Cochran, Ga.	FA-'90
Wiggins, Brian	WR	5-11	185	6/14/68	Texas Southern	San Antonio, Tex.	FA
Zolak, Scott	QB	6-5	222	12/13/67	Maryland	Monongahela, Pa.	D4
Zackery, Tony	S	6-2	195	11/20/66	Washington	Seattle, Wash.	FA-'90

The term NFL Rookie is defined as a player who is in his first season of professional football and has not been on the roster of another professional football team for any regular-season or postseason games. A Rookie is designated by an "R" on NFL rosters. Players who have been active in another professional football league or players who have NFL experience, including either preseason training camp or being on an active roster for fewer than three regular-season or postseason games, are termed NFL First-Year Players. An NFL First-Year Player is designated by a "1" on NFL rosters. Thereafter, a player on an NFL active roster for at least three regular-season or postseason games is credited with an additional year of NFL playing experience.

NOTES

NEW YORK JETS

American Football Conference Eastern Division

Team Colors: Kelly Green and White

1000 Fulton Avenue
Hempstead, New York 11550
Telephone: (516) 538-6600

Club Officials

Chairman of the Board: Leon Hess
President: Steve Gutman
Vice President & General Manager: Dick Steinberg
Director of Player Personnel: Ron Wolf
Pro Personnel Director: Jim Royer
Talent Scouts: Joe Collins, Don Grammer, Daryl Gross, Sid Hall, Ron Nay, Marv Sunderland
College Scouting Assistant: John Griffin
Director of Public Relations: Frank Ramos
Director of Promotions: Ron Cohen
Public Relations Assistant: Eileen Walker
Public Relations Assistant: Brooks Thomas
Comptroller: Mike Gerstle
Director of Operations: Mike Kensil
Director of Business Relations: Bob Parente
Ticket Manager: Gerry Parravano
Video Director: Jim Pons
Assistant Video Director: John Seiter
Trainer: Bob Reese
Assistant Trainers: Pepper Burruss, Joe Patten
Equipment Manager: Bill Hampton
Assistant Equipment Managers: Bill Hampton, Jr., Mickey Rendine

Stadium: Giants Stadium • **Capacity:** 76,891
East Rutherford, New Jersey 07073

Playing Surface: AstroTurf

Training Center: 1000 Fulton Avenue
Hempstead, New York 11550
(516) 538-6600

1991 Schedule

Preseason

Aug. 3	**Philadelphia**	8:00
Aug. 10	vs. Kansas City at St. Louis	7:00
Aug. 17	at New York Giants	8:00
Aug. 24	vs. Washington at Columbia, S.C.	7:00

Regular Season

Sept. 1	**Tampa Bay**	1:00
Sept. 8	at Seattle	1:00
Sept. 15	**Buffalo**	4:00
Sept. 23	at Chicago (Monday)	8:00
Sept. 29	**Miami**	4:00
Oct. 6	at Cleveland	1:00
Oct. 13	**Houston**	4:00
Oct. 20	at Indianapolis	12:00
Oct. 27	**Open Date**	
Nov. 3	**Green Bay**	1:00
Nov. 10	**Indianapolis**	1:00
Nov. 17	at New England	1:00
Nov. 24	**San Diego**	4:00
Dec. 1	at Buffalo	1:00
Dec. 8	at Detroit	4:00
Dec. 15	**New England**	1:00
Dec. 22	at Miami	1:00

Jets Coaching History

New York Titans 1960-62
(206-248-8)

1960-61	Sammy Baugh	14-14-0
1962	Clyde (Bulldog) Turner	5-9-0
1963-73	Weeb Ewbank	73-78-6
1974-75	Charley Winner*	9-14-0
1975	Ken Shipp	1-4-0
1976	Lou Holtz**	3-10-0
1976	Mike Holovak	0-1-0
1977-82	Walt Michaels	41-49-1
1983-89	Joe Walton	54-59-1
1990	Bruce Coslet	6-10-0

*Released after nine games in 1975
**Resigned after 13 games in 1976

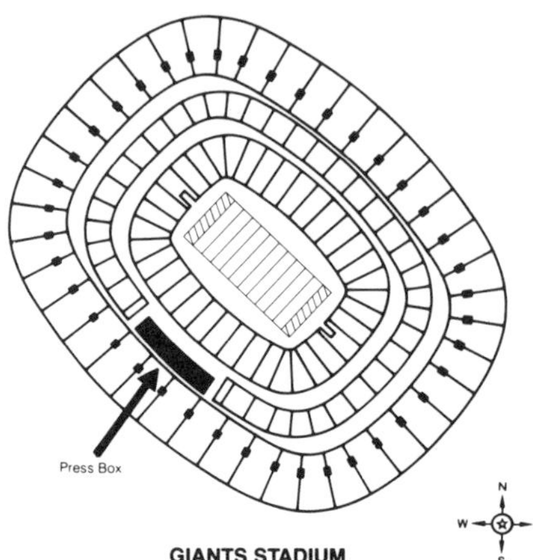

GIANTS STADIUM

Record Holders

Individual Records—Career

Category	Name	Performance
Rushing (Yds.)	Freeman McNeil, 1981-1990	7,604
Passing (Yds.)	Joe Namath, 1965-1976	27,057
Passing (TDs)	Joe Namath, 1965-1976	170
Receiving (No.)	Don Maynard, 1960-1972	627
Receiving (Yds.)	Don Maynard, 1960-1972	11,732
Interceptions	Bill Baird, 1963-69	34
Punting (Avg.)	Curley Johnson, 1961-68	42.8
Punt Return (Avg.)	Dick Christy, 1961-63	16.2
Kickoff Return (Avg.)	Bobby Humphery, 1984-89	22.8
Field Goals	Pat Leahy, 1974-1990	278
Touchdowns (Tot.)	Don Maynard, 1960-1972	88
Points	Pat Leahy, 1974-1990	1,362

Individual Records—Single Season

Category	Name	Performance
Rushing (Yds.)	Freeman McNeil, 1985	1,331
Passing (Yds.)	Joe Namath, 1967	4,007
Passing (TDs)	Al Dorow, 1960	26
	Joe Namath, 1967	26
Receiving (No.)	Al Toon, 1988	93
Receiving (Yds.)	Don Maynard, 1967	1,434
Interceptions	Dainard Paulson, 1964	12
Punting (Avg.)	Curley Johnson, 1965	45.3
Punt Return (Avg.)	Dick Christy, 1961	21.3
Kickoff Return (Avg.)	Bobby Humphery, 1984	30.7
Field Goals	Jim Turner, 1968	34
Touchdowns (Tot.)	Art Powell, 1960	14
	Don Maynard, 1965	14
	Emerson Boozer, 1972	14
Points	Jim Turner, 1968	145

Individual Records—Single Game

Category	Name	Performance
Rushing (Yds.)	Freeman McNeil, 9-15-85	192
Passing (Yds.)	Joe Namath, 9-24-72	496
Passing (TDs)	Joe Namath, 9-24-72	6
Receiving (No.)	Clark Gaines, 9-21-80	17
Receiving (Yds.)	Don Maynard, 11-17-68	228
Interceptions	Many times	3
	Last time by Erik McMillan, 10-23-88	
Field Goals	Jim Turner, 11-3-68	6
	Bobby Howfield, 12-3-72	6
Touchdowns (Tot.)	Wesley Walker, 9-21-86	4
Points	Jim Turner, 11-3-68	19
	Pat Leahy, 9-16-84	19

1990 Team Record

Preseason (2-2)

Date	Result		Opponents
8/11	W	17- 6	at Philadelphia
8/18	W	20- 0	at Kansas City
8/25	L	7-17	at N.Y. Giants
8/30	L	14-23	at Tampa Bay
		58-46	

Regular Season (6-10)

Date	Result		Opponents	Att.
9/9	L	20-25	at Cincinnati	56,467
9/16	W	24-21	Cleveland	67,354
9/24	L	7-30	Buffalo	69,927
9/30	W	37-13	at New England	36,724
10/7	L	16-20	at Miami	69,678
10/14	L	3-39	San Diego	63,311
10/21	L	27-30	at Buffalo	79,002
10/28	W	17-12	at Houston	56,337
11/4	W	24- 9	Dallas	68,086
11/11	L	3-17	Miami	68,362
11/18	L	14-17	at Indianapolis	47,283
11/25	L	7-24	Pittsburgh	57,806
12/2	L	17-38	at San Diego	40,877
12/16	L	21-29	Indianapolis	41,423
12/23	W	42- 7	New England	30,250
12/30	W	16-14	at Tampa Bay	46,543

Score by Periods

Jets	61	131	46	57	0	—	295
Opponents	38	100	90	117	0	—	345

Attendance

Home 458,519 Away 432,911 Total 891,430
Single-game home record, 74,975 (12-2-84)
Single-season home record, 541,832 (1985)

1990 Team Statistics

	Jets	Opp.
Total First Downs	295	318
Rushing	128	112
Passing	143	186
Penalty	24	20
Third Down: Made/Att.	74/193	88/199
Third Down: Pct.	38.3	44.2
Fourth Down: Made/Att.	5/21	10/14
Fourth Down: Pct.	23.8	71.4
Total Net Yards	4886	5455
Avg. Per Game	305.4	340.9
Total Plays	967	977
Avg. Per Play	5.1	5.6
Net Yards Rushing	2127	2018
Avg. Per Game	132.9	126.1
Total Rushes	476	423
Net Yards Passing	2759	3437
Avg. Per Game	172.4	214.8
Sacked/Yards Lost	40/300	38/308
Gross Yards	3059	3745
Att./Completions	451/246	516/311
Completion Pct.	54.5	60.3
Had Intercepted	11	18
Punts/Avg.	61/39.3	56/41.4
Net Punting Avg.	33.9	33.6
Penalties/Yards Lost	101/848	106/874
Fumbles/Ball Lost	28/13	29/11
Touchdowns	32	39
Rushing	16	15
Passing	14	23
Returns	2	1
Avg. Time of Possession	30:05	29:55

1990 Individual Statistics

Scoring	TD R	TD P	TD Rt	PAT	FG	Saf	TP
Leahy	0	0	0	32/32	23/26	0	101
Baxter	6	0	0	0/0	0/0	0	36
F. McNeil	6	0	0	0/0	0/0	0	36
Moore	0	6	0	0/0	0/0	0	36
Toon	0	6	0	0/0	0/0	0	36
Hector	2	0	0	0/0	0/0	0	12
Thomas	1	1	0	0/0	0/0	0	12
Boyer	0	1	0	0/0	0/0	0	6
Davis	0	0	1	0/0	0/0	0	6
Mathis	0	0	1	0/0	0/0	0	6
Taylor	1	0	0	0/0	0/0	0	6
Byrd	0	0	0	0/0	0/0	1	2
Jets	16	14	2	32/32	23/26	1	295
Opponents	15	23	1	35/39	24/32	2	345

Passing	Att.	Comp.	Yds.	Pct.	TD	Int.	Tkld.	Rate
O'Brien	411	226	2855	55.0	13	10	34/262	77.3
Eason	28	13	155	46.4	0	1	4/35	49.0
Taylor	10	7	49	70.0	1	0	2/3	114.2
Toon	2	0	0	0.0	0	0	0/0	39.6
Jets	451	246	3059	54.5	14	11	40/300	76.0
Opponents	516	311	3745	60.3	23	18	38/308	82.9

Rushing	Att.	Yds.	Avg.	LG	TD
Thomas	123	620	5.0	41	1
Baxter	124	539	4.3	28t	6
F. McNeil	99	458	4.6	29	6
Hector	91	377	4.1	22	2
O'Brien	21	72	3.4	15	0
Eason	7	29	4.1	24	0
Taylor	2	20	10.0	15	1
Mathis	2	9	4.5	10	0
Brown	1	8	8.0	8	0
Prokop	3	2	0.7	8	0
Wellsandt	1	−3	−3.0	−3	0
Moore	2	−4	−2.0	4	0
Jets	476	2127	4.5	41	16
Opponents	423	2018	4.8	60	15

Receiving	No.	Yds.	Avg.	LG	TD
Toon	57	757	13.3	46t	6
Moore	44	692	15.7	69t	6
Boyer	40	334	8.4	25	1
Thomas	20	204	10.2	55	1
Mathis	19	245	12.9	23	0
F. McNeil	16	230	14.4	59	0
Burkett	14	204	14.6	46	0
Baxter	8	73	9.1	22	0
Hector	8	72	9.0	25	0
Dressel	6	66	11.0	21	0
Dawkins	5	68	13.6	31	0
Wellsandt	5	57	11.4	20	0
Townsell	4	57	14.3	18	0
Jets	246	3059	12.4	69t	14
Opponents	311	3745	12.0	69t	23

Interceptions	No.	Yds.	Avg.	LG	TD
McMillan	5	92	18.4	25	0
Clifton	3	49	16.3	39	0
B. Washington	3	22	7.3	13	0
Curtis	2	45	22.5	23	0
Hasty	2	0	0.0	0	0
Stargell	2	−3	−1.5	0	0
Mayes	1	0	0.0	0	0
Jets	18	205	11.4	39	0
Opponents	11	186	16.9	36	0

Punting	No.	Yds.	Avg.	In 20	LG
Prokop	59	2363	40.1	18	58
O'Brien	1	23	23.0	0	23
Leahy	1	12	12.0	0	12
Jets	61	2398	39.3	18	58
Opponents	56	2321	41.4	14	69

Punt Returns	No.	FC	Yds.	Avg.	LG	TD
Townsell	17	4	154	9.1	20	0
Mathis	11	7	165	15.0	98t	1
Hasty	1	0	0	0.0	0	0
Odegard	1	0	0	0.0	0	0
Jets	30	11	319	10.6	98t	1
Opponents	35	8	269	7.7	35	0

Kickoff Returns	No.	Yds.	Avg.	LG	TD
Mathis	43	787	18.3	35	0
Townsell	7	158	22.6	38	0
Odegard	5	89	17.8	25	0
Nichols	2	3	1.5	3	0
Boyer	1	14	14.0	14	0
Brown	1	63	63.0	63	0
Dressel	1	7	7.0	7	0
Duffy	1	8	8.0	8	0
Jets	61	1129	18.5	63	0
Opponents	61	1185	19.4	98t	1

Sacks	No.
Byrd	13.0
Davis	5.0
Mersereau	4.5
M. Washington	4.5
Lageman	4.0
Nichols	3.5
T. Johnson	1.0
Stallworth	1.0
B. Washington	1.0
Clifton	0.5
Jets	38.0
Opponents	40.0

1991 Draft Choices

Round	Name	Pos.	College
2.	Browning Nagle	QB	Louisville
3.	Morris Lewis	LB	Georgia
4.	Mark Gunn	DT	Pittsburgh
6.	Blaise Bryant	RB	Iowa State
	Mike Riley	DB	Tulane
7.	Doug Parrish	DB	San Francisco St.
8.	Tim James	DB	Colorado
9.	Paul Glonek	DT	Arizona
10.	Al Baker	RB	Kentucky
11.	Rocen Keeton	LB	UCLA
12.	Mark Hayes	T	Arizona State

New York Jets 1991 Veteran Roster

No.	Name	Pos.	Ht.	Wt.	Birth-date	NFL Exp.	College	Hometown	How Acq.	'90 Games/ Starts
30	Baxter, Brad	RB	6-1	235	5/5/67	2	Alabama State	Slocomb, Ala.	FA-'89	16/9
99	Bosa, John	DE	6-4	275	1/10/64	4	Boston College	Keene, N.H.	PB(Mia)-'91#	0*
80	Boyer, Mark	TE	6-4	242	9/16/62	7	Southern California	Huntington Beach, Calif.	PB(Ind)-'90#	16/16
43	Brim, Mike	CB	6-0	188	1/23/66	4	Virginia Union	Queens, N.Y.	PB(Minn)-'91#	16/2*
29	Brown, A.B.	RB	5-9	215	12/4/65	2	West Virginia	Salem, N.J.	D8-'89	1/0
87	†Burkett, Chris	WR	6-4	200	8/21/62	7	Jackson State	Collins, Miss.	FA-'89	16/4
90	Byrd, Dennis	DE	6-5	270	10/5/66	3	Tulsa	Mustang, Okla.	D2-'89	16/16
66	Cadigan, Dave	G-T	6-4	285	4/6/65	4	Southern California	Newport Beach, Calif.	D1-'88	5/5
59	Clifton, Kyle	LB	6-4	236	8/23/62	8	Texas Christian	Bridgeport, Tex.	D3-'84	16/16
69	Criswell, Jeff	T	6-7	291	3/7/64	5	Graceland	Searsboro, Iowa	FA-'88	16/16
49	Curtis, Travis	S	5-10	180	9/27/65	5	West Virginia	Potomac, Md.	PB(Minn)-'90#	14/3
98	Davis, Darrell	DE	6-2	258	3/10/66	2	Texas Christian	Midland, Tex.	D12-'90	15/0
89	Dawkins, Dale	WR	6-1	190	10/30/66	2	Miami	Vero Beach, Fla.	D9-'90	11/0
84	Dressel, Chris	TE	6-4	239	2/7/61	8	Stanford	Placentia, Calif.	W(KC)-'89	15/4
62	Duffy, Roger	C	6-3	285	7/16/67	2	Penn State	Canton, Ohio	D8-'90	16/2
75	t-Eatman, Irv	T	6-7	298	1/1/61	6	UCLA	Dayton, Ohio	T(KC)-'91	12/0
44	Egu, Patrick	RB	5-11	206	2/20/67	2	Nevada-Reno	Richmond, Calif.	PB(NE)-'90#	0*
91	Frase, Paul	DE-DT	6-5	260	5/5/65	3	Syracuse	Barrington, N.H.	D6-'88	0*
52	Galvin, John	LB	6-3	230	7/9/65	4	Boston College	Lowell, Mass.	W(Minn)-'90	16/0
79	Haight, Mike	G	6-4	279	10/6/62	6	Iowa	Dyersville, Iowa	D1-'86	14/14
40	Hasty, James	CB	6-0	201	5/23/65	4	Washington State	Seattle, Wash.	D3b-'88	16/16
34	Hector, Johnny	RB	5-11	207	11/26/60	9	Texas A&M	New Iberia, La.	D2-'83	15/4
26	Johnson, Kenneth	S	6-2	208	9/14/66	2	Florida A&M	Thomaston, Ga.	FA-'90	4/0
95	Johnson, Troy	LB	6-2	236	11/10/64	4	Oklahoma	Houston, Tex.	W(Cin)-'90	16/4
58	Kelly, Joe	LB	6-2	235	12/11/64	6	Washington	Los Angeles, Calif.	T(Cin)-'90	12/12
82	Kelly, Pat	TE	6-6	252	10/29/65	3	Syracuse	Webster, N.Y.	PB(Den)-'90#	1/0
56	Lageman, Jeff	DE	6-5	255	7/18/67	3	Virginia	Great Falls, Va.	D1-'89	16/16
5	Leahy, Pat	K	6-0	200	3/19/51	18	St. Louis	St. Louis, Mo.	FA-'74	16/0
81	Mathis, Terance	WR-KR	5-10	170	6/7/67	2	New Mexico	Stone Mountain, Ga.	D6-'90	16/1
64	Matich, Trevor	C-T-G	6-4	282	10/9/61	7	Brigham Young	Sacramento, Calif.	PB(Det)-'90#	16/6
70	Mattes, Ron	T	6-6	302	8/8/63	5	Virginia	Ringtown, Pa.	T(Sea)-'90	16/8
23	Mayes, Mike	CB	5-10	173	8/17/66	2	Louisiana State	DeRidder, La.	FA-'90	16/2
22	McMillan, Erik	S	6-2	200	5/3/65	4	Missouri	Silver Spring, Md.	D3a-'88	16/16
24	McNeil, Freeman	RB	5-11	208	4/22/59	11	UCLA	Carson, Calif.	D1-'81	16/4
94	†Mersereau, Scott	DT	6-3	273	4/8/65	5	Southern Connecticut	Riverhead, N.Y.	FA-'87	16/16
72	Miller, Brett	T	6-7	293	10/2/58	9	Iowa	Glendale, Calif.	PB(SD)-'90#	16/16
85	Moore, Rob	WR	6-3	205	9/27/68	2	Syracuse	Hempstead, N.Y.	SD1-'90	15/13
51	Mott, Joe	LB	6-4	243	10/6/65	3	Iowa	Endicott, N.Y.	D3-'89	16/14
77	Nichols, Gerald	DT-DE	6-2	260	2/10/64	5	Florida State	St. Louis, Mo.	D7-'87	15/0
7	O'Brien, Ken	QB	6-4	212	11/27/60	9	California-Davis	Sacramento, Calif.	D1-'83	16/16
21	Odegard, Don	CB	6-0	180	11/22/66	2	Nevada-Las Vegas	Kennewick, Wash.	FA-'90	14/0
71	Pickel, Bill	DT	6-5	260	11/5/59	9	Rutgers	Brooklyn, N.Y.	PB(Raid)-'91#	14/3*
20	Price, Dennis	CB	6-1	175	6/14/65	3	UCLA	Long Beach, Calif.	T(Raid)-'90	0*
6	Prokop, Joe	P	6-2	225	7/7/60	6	Cal Poly-Pomona	White Bear Lake, Minn.	FA-'88	16/0
15	Schonert, Turk	QB	6-1	196	1/15/57	9	Stanford	Placentia, Calif.	FA-'91	0*
45	Stargell, Tony	CB	5-11	190	8/7/66	2	Tennessee State	LaGrange, Ga.	D3-'90	16/16
57	Stephens, Mac	LB	6-3	220	1/20/68	2	Minnesota	Akron, Ohio	FA-'90	2/0
53	Sweeney, Jim	C-G	6-4	275	8/8/62	8	Pittsburgh	Pittsburgh, Pa.	D2a-'84	16/16
14	Taylor, Troy	QB	6-4	200	4/5/68	2	California	Sacramento, Calif.	D4-'90	4/0
32	Thomas, Blair	RB	5-10	195	10/7/67	2	Penn State	Philadelphia, Pa.	D1-'90	15/11
88	Toon, Al	WR	6-4	205	4/30/63	7	Wisconsin	Newport News, Va.	D1-'85	14/12
83	Townsell, JoJo	WR-KR	5-9	182	11/4/60	7	UCLA	Reno, Nev.	FA-'85	9/1
48	†Washington, Brian	S	6-1	220	9/10/65	3	Nebraska	Richmond, Va.	W(Clev)-'89	14/13
97	†Washington, Marvin	DE-DT	6-6	276	10/22/65	3	Idaho	Dallas, Tex.	D6a-'89	16/2
86	Wellsandt, Doug	TE	6-3	248	2/9/67	2	Washington State	Ritzville, Wash.	W(Cin)-'90	16/0
67	White, Dwayne	G	6-2	312	2/10/67	2	Alcorn State	Philadelphia, Pa.	D7a-'90	11/5
63	Zawatson, Dave	G-T	6-5	287	4/13/66	3	California	Concord, Calif.	PB(Chi)-'90#	16/0

* Bosa, Egu, and Price missed '90 season due to injury; Brim played 16 games with Minnesota in '90; Frase last active with Jets in '89; Pickel played 14 games with L.A. Raiders; Schonert last active with Bengals in '88.

† Option playout; subject to developments.

t- Jets traded for Eatman (Kansas City).

Plan B unconditional free agent.

Players lost through Plan B (2): CB-S John Booty (Phil; 13 games in '90), T Scott Jones (GB; 3).

Also played with Jets in '90—QB Tony Eason (16 games), DE Ron Stallworth (16), CB Carl Howard (1).

COACHING STAFF

Head Coach, Bruce Coslet

Pro Career: Begins second year as head coach of the Jets. In his first season, the Jets posted a 6-10 record with a squad that had 23 players with a year or less of NFL experience. Of the five new NFL coaches last year, he had the second best record (only Houston's Jack Pardee, who took over a playoff team, had a better record). With Coslet serving as offensive coordinator, the Jets finished second in the AFC and fourth in NFL in rushing (132.9 yards per game) and reduced the offensive turnovers from 24 in 1989 to 11. Entered pro coaching ranks as tight ends and special teams coach with the San Francisco 49ers in 1980. Joined the Cincinnati Bengals in 1981 as tight ends and special teams coach. In 1983, was given the added responsibility of the Bengals' passing game. Tutored the Cincinnati receivers in 1984-85 before being named offensive coordinator (1986-89). The Bengals had the NFL's top-ranked offense in three of those years and went to Super Bowl XXIII. Played tight end for Cincinnati in 1969-76.

Background: Played tight end at the University of the Pacific from 1965-67.

Personal: Born August 5, 1946, in Oakdale, Calif. Bruce and his wife, Kathy, live in Long Island, and have two children—J.J. and Amy.

Assistant Coaches

Larry Beightol offensive line; born November 21, 1942, Morrisdale, Pa., lives in Long Island. Guard-linebacker Catawba College 1961-63. No pro playing experience. College coach: William & Mary 1968-71, North Carolina State 1972-75, Auburn 1976, Arkansas 1977-78, 1980-82, Louisiana Tech 1979 (head coach), Missouri 1983-84. Pro coach: Atlanta Falcons 1985-86, Tampa Bay Buccaneers 1987-88, San Diego Chargers 1989, joined Jets in 1990.

Kippy Brown, running backs; born March 6, 1955, Sweetwater, Tenn., lives in Long Island. Quarterback Memphis State 1973-77. No pro playing experience. College coach: Memphis State 1978-80, Louisville 1981, Tennessee 1982-89. Pro coach: Joined Jets in 1990.

Pete Carroll, defensive coordinator; born September 15, 1951, San Francisco, Calif., lives in Long Island. Defensive back Pacific 1969-72. No pro playing experience. College coach: Arkansas 1977, Iowa State 1978, Ohio State 1979, North Carolina State 1980-82, Pacific 1983. Pro coach: Buffalo Bills 1984, Minnesota Vikings 1985-89, joined Jets in 1990.

Joe Daniels, quarterbacks; born November 15, 1942, Pittsburgh, Pa., lives in Long Island. Running back Slippery Rock 1961-64. No pro playing experience. College coach: Boston College 1968-77, West Virginia 1978-79, Pittsburgh 1980-82, Akron 1989. Pro coach: Cleveland Browns 1983-84, Buffalo Bills 1986, joined Jets in 1990.

Ed Donatell, defensive assistant, secondary; born February 4, 1957, Akron, Ohio, lives in Long Island. Safety Glenville State 1975-78. No pro playing experience. College coach: Kent State 1979-80, Washington 1981-82, Pacific 1983-85, Idaho 1986-88, Cal State-Fullerton 1989. Pro coach: Joined Jets in 1990.

Foge Fazio, linebackers; born February 22, 1939, Dawmont, W. Va., lives in Long Island. Linebacker-center Pittsburgh 1957-60. Pro linebacker Boston Patriots 1961. College coach: Boston University 1967, Harvard 1968, Pittsburgh 1969-72, 1977-81 (head coach), Cincinnati 1973-76, Notre Dame 1986-87. Pro coach: Atlanta Falcons 1988-89, joined Jets in 1990.

Greg Mackrides, strength and conditioning; born July 9, 1954, Philadelphia, Pa., lives in Long Island. No pro playing experience. College coach: Villanova 1985-86, Fairfield 1986-88. U.S. Olympic Wrestling team 1988, U.S. Pan Am and World touring teams 1986-88. Pro coach: New York Knicks (NBA) 1987-90, joined Jets in 1990.

New York Jets 1991 First-Year Roster

Name	Pos.	Ht.	Wt.	Birth-date	College	Hometown	How Acq.
Baker, Al	RB	6-0	225	4/2/68	Kentucky	Cadiz, Ky.	D10
Balistrieri, Pete	WR	5-11	180	8/18/69	Wisconsin-Eau Claire	Whitefish Bay, Wis.	FA
Beach, Kip	T	6-5	300	10/13/66	Indiana State	Chicago, Ill.	FA
Bell, Grantis (1)	WR-KR	5-9	156	8/11/66	West Virginia	Oakland Park, Fla.	FA-'90
Bryant, Blaise	RB	5-11	203	11/23/69	Iowa State	Huntington Beach, Calif.	D6a
Glonek, Paul	DT	6-5	272	12/11/67	Arizona	Chicago, Ill.	D9
Goetz, Chris (1)	G	6-2	272	3/13/67	Pittsburgh	Queens, N.Y.	FA
Gunn, Mark	DT	6-5	292	7/24/68	Pittsburgh	Cleveland, Ohio	D4
Hayes, Mark	T	6-6	295	6/19/68	Arizona State	San Diego, Calif.	D12
Holmes, Bruce (1)	LB	6-2	241	10/24/65	Minnesota	Detroit, Mich.	FA
Houston, Bobby (1)	LB	6-2	235	10/26/67	North Carolina State	Hyattsville, Md.	FA
Isaiah, Rick	WR	5-11	175	7/17/68	Toledo	Akron, Ohio	FA
James, Tim	S	6-1	210	12/11/67	Colorado	San Dimas, Calif.	D8
Jenkins, Pepper	LB	6-4	216	3/7/68	Long Beach State	Los Angeles, Calif.	FA
Keeton, Rocen	LB	6-2	245	5/31/68	UCLA	Los Angeles, Calif.	D11
Kinard, Leroy	RB	5-9	200	2/24/69	Liberty	Oakland, Fla.	FA
Kors, R.J. (1)	S	6-0	195	6/27/66	Long Beach State	Woodland Hills, Calif.	FA
Levelis, John (1)	LB	6-2	236	4/19/67	C.W. Post	Lindenhurst, N.Y.	T(SF)-'91
Lewis, Mo	LB	6-3	240	10/21/69	Georgia	Peachtree, Ga.	D3
Logan, Phil	WR	6-2	190	3/7/69	Kentucky	Louisville, Ky.	FA
McNeil, Emanuel (1)	DT	6-3	277	6/9/67	Tennessee-Martin	Richmond, Va.	FA-'90
Moore, Reggie	WR	5-9	175	3/23/68	UCLA	Houston, Tex.	FA
Nagle, Browning	QB	6-3	225	4/29/68	Louisville	Largo, Fla.	D2
Parrish, Doug	CB-KR	6-0	200	2/25/68	San Francisco State	Madison, Wis.	D7
Riley, Mike	CB	5-11	175	3/30/68	Tulane	Marrero, La.	D6b
Scully, Jim	LB	6-2	235	9/26/68	Hofstra	Franklin Square, N.Y.	FA
Swinson, Matt	TE	6-5	242	5/5/68	Maine	Bay Shore, N.Y.	FA
Young, Ron	WR	6-3	210	3/7/69	Washington State	San Diego, Calif.	FA

The term NFL Rookie is defined as a player who is in his first season of professional football and has not been on the roster of another professional football team for any regular-season or postseason games. A Rookie is designated by an "R" on NFL rosters. Players who have been active in another professional football league or players who have NFL experience, including either preseason training camp or being on an active roster for fewer than three regular-season or postseason games, are termed NFL First-Year Players. An NFL First-Year Player is designated by a "1" on NFL rosters. Thereafter, a player on an NFL active roster for at least three regular-season or postseason games is credited with an additional year of NFL playing experience.

NOTES

Chip Myers, receivers; born July 9, 1945, Panama City, Fla., lives in Long Island. Receiver Northwest Oklahoma 1964-66. Pro receiver San Francisco 49ers 1967, Cincinnati Bengals 1969-76. College coach: Illinois 1980-82. Pro coach: Tampa Bay Buccaneers 1983-84, Indianapolis Colts 1985-88, joined Jets in 1990.

Al Roberts, special teams coordinator; born January 6, 1944, Fresno, Calif., lives in Long Island. Running back Washington 1964-65, Puget Sound 1967-68. No pro playing experience. College coach: Washington 1977-82, Purdue 1986, Wyoming 1987. Pro coach: Los Angeles Express (USFL) 1983-84, Houston Oilers 1984-85, Philadelphia Eagles 1988-90, joined Jets in 1991.

Greg Robinson, defensive line; born October 9, 1951, Los Angeles, Calif., lives in Long Island. Linebacker-tight end Pacific 1972-73. No pro playing experience. College coach: Cal State-Fullerton 1977-79, North Carolina State 1980-81, UCLA 1982-89. Pro coach: Joined Jets in 1990.

Bob Wylie, offensive assistant, tight ends; born February 16, 1951, Providence, R.I., lives in Long Island. Linebacker Colorado 1969-71. No pro playing experience. College coach: Brown 1980-82, Holy Cross 1983-84, Ohio University 1985-87, Colorado State 1988-89. Pro coach: Joined Jets in 1990.

American Football Conference Central Division

Team Colors: Black and Gold

Three Rivers Stadium
300 Stadium Circle
Pittsburgh, Pennsylvania 15212
Telephone: (412) 323-1200

Club Officials

President: Daniel M. Rooney
Vice President: John R. McGinley
Vice President: Arthur J. Rooney, Jr.
Director of Communications: Joe Gordon
Controller: Dan McGrogan
Assistant Controller/Business: Dan Ferens
Public Relations Director: Dan Edwards
Director of Player Personnel: Dick Haley
Director of Football Development: Tom Donahoe
Football Business Manager: James A. Boston
College Scouting Coordinator: Tom Modrak
Talent Scout: Bob Schmitz
Talent Scout: Max McCartney
Talent Scout: Charles Bailey
Talent Scout: Bob Lane
Ticket Sales Manager: Geraldine R. Glenn
Assistant Controller/Office: Jim Ellenberger
Trainers: Ralph Berlin, Francis Feld
Equipment Manager: Anthony Parisi

Stadium: Three Rivers Stadium • **Capacity:** 59,492
300 Stadium Circle
Pittsburgh, Pennsylvania 15212

Playing Surface: AstroTurf

Training Camp: St. Vincent College
Latrobe, Pennsylvania 15650

1991 Schedule

Preseason

Aug. 4	**Washington**	8:00
Aug. 10	at Minnesota	8:00
Aug. 17	at Philadelphia	7:30
Aug. 23	at Detroit	7:30

Regular Season

Sept. 1	**San Diego**	4:00
Sept. 8	at Buffalo	1:00
Sept. 15	**New England**	1:00
Sept. 22	at Philadelphia	1:00
Sept. 29	**Open Date**	
Oct. 6	at Indianapolis	7:00
Oct. 14	**New York Giants** (Monday)	9:00
Oct. 20	**Seattle**	1:00
Oct. 27	at Cleveland	4:00
Nov. 3	at Denver	6:00
Nov. 10	at Cincinnati	1:00
Nov. 17	**Washington**	1:00
Nov. 24	**Houston**	1:00
Nov. 28	at Dallas (Thanksgiving)	3:00
Dec. 8	at Houston	12:00
Dec. 15	**Cincinnati**	1:00
Dec. 22	**Cleveland**	1:00

Steelers Coaching History

Pittsburgh Pirates 1933-40
(363-402-20)

1933	Forrest (Jap) Douds	3-6-2
1934	Luby DiMelio	2-10-0
1935-36	Joe Bach	10-14-0
1937-39	Johnny Blood (McNally)*	6-19-0
1939-40	Walt Kiesling	3-13-3
1941	Bert Bell**	0-2-0
	Aldo (Buff) Donelli***	0-5-0
1941-44	Walt Kiesling****	13-20-2
1945	Jim Leonard	2-8-0
1946-47	Jock Sutherland	13-10-1
1948-51	Johnny Michelosen	20-26-2
1952-53	Joe Bach	11-13-0
1954-56	Walt Kiesling	14-22-0
1957-64	Raymond (Buddy) Parker	51-47-6
1965	Mike Nixon	2-12-0
1966-68	Bill Austin	11-28-3
1969-90	Chuck Noll	202-147-1

*Released after three games in 1939
**Resigned after two games in 1941
***Released after five games in 1941
****Co-coach with Earle (Greasy) Neale in Philadelphia-Pittsburgh merger in 1943 and with Phil Handler in Chicago Cardinals-Pittsburgh merger in 1944

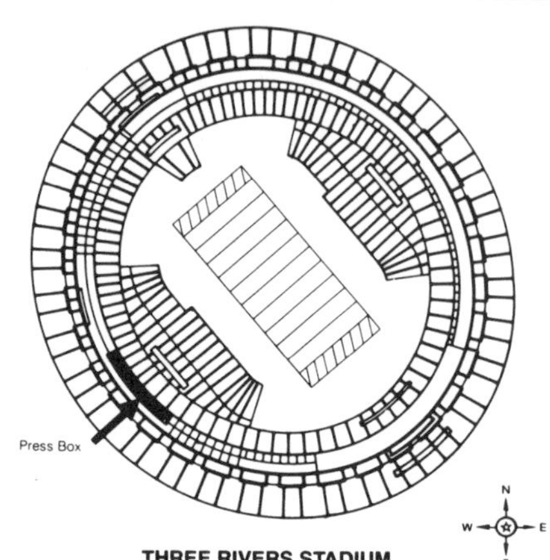

THREE RIVERS STADIUM

Record Holders

Individual Records—Career

Category	Name	Performance
Rushing (Yds.)	Franco Harris, 1972-1983	11,950
Passing (Yds.)	Terry Bradshaw, 1970-1983	27,989
Passing (TDs)	Terry Bradshaw, 1970-1983	212
Receiving (No.)	John Stallworth, 1974-1987	537
Receiving (Yds.)	John Stallworth, 1974-1987	8,723
Interceptions	Mel Blount, 1970-1983	57
Punting (Avg.)	Bobby Joe Green, 1960-61	45.7
Punt Return (Avg.)	Bobby Gage, 1949-1950	14.9
Kickoff Return (Avg.)	Lynn Chandnois, 1950-56	29.6
Field Goals	Gary Anderson, 1982-1990	206
Touchdowns (Tot.)	Franco Harris, 1972-1983	100
Points	Gary Anderson, 1982-1990	910

Individual Records—Single Season

Category	Name	Performance
Rushing (Yds.)	Franco Harris, 1975	1,246
Passing (Yds.)	Terry Bradshaw, 1979	3,724
Passing (TDs)	Terry Bradshaw, 1978	28
Receiving (No.)	John Stallworth, 1984	80
Receiving (Yds.)	John Stallworth, 1984	1,395
Interceptions	Mel Blount, 1975	11
Punting (Avg.)	Bobby Joe Green, 1961	47.0
Punt Return (Avg.)	Bobby Gage, 1949	16.0
Kickoff Return (Avg.)	Lynn Chandnois, 1952	35.2
Field Goals	Gary Anderson, 1985	33
Touchdowns (Tot.)	Louis Lipps, 1985	15
Points	Gary Anderson, 1985	139

Individual Records—Single Game

Category	Name	Performance
Rushing (Yds.)	John Fuqua, 12-20-70	218
Passing (Yds.)	Bobby Layne, 12-3-58	409
Passing (TDs)	Terry Bradshaw, 11-15-81	5
	Mark Malone, 9-8-85	5
Receiving (No.)	J.R. Wilburn, 10-22-67	12
Receiving (Yds.)	Buddy Dial, 10-22-61	235
Interceptions	Jack Butler, 12-13-53	*4
Field Goals	Gary Anderson, 10-23-88	6
Touchdowns (Tot.)	Ray Mathews, 10-17-54	4
	Roy Jefferson, 11-3-68	4
Points	Ray Mathews, 10-17-54	24
	Roy Jefferson, 11-3-68	24

*NFL Record

1990 Team Record

Preseason (2-2)

Date	Result		Opponents
8/9	W	30-14	vs. New England at Montreal
8/17	L	24-27	at Washington
8/25	L	9-20	at Dallas
9/1	W	20-10	Philadelphia
		83-71	

Regular Season (9-7)

Date	Result		Opponents	Att.
9/9	L	3-13	at Cleveland	78,298
9/16	W	20- 9	Houston	54,814
9/23	L	3-20	at L.A. Raiders	50,657
9/30	L	6-28	Miami	54,691
10/7	W	36-14	San Diego	53,486
10/14	W	34-17	at Denver	74,285
10/21	L	7-27	at San Francisco	64,301
10/29	W	41-10	L.A. Rams	56,466
11/4	W	21- 9	Atlanta	57,093
11/18	L	3-27	at Cincinnati	60,064
11/25	W	24- 7	at N.Y. Jets	57,806
12/2	L	12-16	Cincinnati	58,200
12/9	W	24- 3	New England	48,354
12/16	W	9- 6	at New Orleans	68,582
12/23	W	35- 0	Cleveland	51,665
12/30	L	14-34	at Houston	56,906

Score by Periods

Steelers	64	71	54	103	0	—	292
Opponents	58	86	56	40	0	—	240

Attendance

Home 434,770 Away 510,899 Total 945,669
Single-game home record, 59,541 (9-30-85)
Single-season home record, 462,567 (1983)

1990 Team Statistics

	Steelers	Opp.
Total First Downs	263	257
Rushing	93	102
Passing	150	130
Penalty	20	25
Third Down: Made/Att.	76/189	81/204
Third Down: Pct.	40.2	39.7
Fourth Down: Made/Att.	4/10	6/17
Fourth Down: Pct.	40.0	35.3
Total Net Yards	4525	4115
Avg. Per Game	282.8	257.2
Total Plays	897	940
Avg. Per Play	5.0	4.4
Net Yards Rushing	1880	1615
Avg. Per Game	117.5	100.9
Total Rushes	456	446
Net Yards Passing	2645	2500
Avg. Per Game	165.3	156.3
Sacked/Yards Lost	33/242	34/228
Gross Yards	2887	2728
Att./Completions	408/237	460/236
Completion Pct.	58.1	51.3
Had Intercepted	15	24
Punts/Avg.	66/37.2	64/40.9
Net Punting Avg.	34.1	33.7
Penalties/Yards Lost	110/928	89/719
Fumbles/Ball Lost	40/17	33/18
Touchdowns	33	26
Rushing	11	13
Passing	20	9
Returns	2	4
Avg. Time of Possession	30:06	29:54

1990 Individual Statistics

Scoring	TD R	TD P	TD Rt	PAT	FG	Saf	TP
Anderson	0	0	0	32/32	20/25	0	92
Hoge	7	3	0	0/0	0/0	0	60
Green	0	7	0	0/0	0/0	0	42
W. Williams	3	1	0	0/0	0/0	0	24
Lipps	0	3	0	0/0	0/0	0	18
Mularkey	0	3	0	0/0	0/0	0	18
Bell	0	1	0	0/0	0/0	0	6
Calloway	0	1	0	0/0	0/0	0	6
Foster	1	0	0	0/0	0/0	0	6
Johnson	0	0	1	0/0	0/0	0	6
Stone	0	1	0	0/0	0/0	0	6
Woodson	0	0	1	0/0	0/0	0	6
Stowe	0	0	0	0/0	0/0	1	2
Steelers	11	20	2	32/33	20/25	1	292
Opponents	13	9	4	26/26	18/28	2	240

Passing	Att.	Comp.	Yds.	Pct.	TD	Int.	Tkld.	Rate
Brister	387	223	2725	57.6	20	14	28/213	81.6
Strom	21	14	162	66.7	0	1	5/29	69.9
Steelers	408	237	2887	58.1	20	15	33/242	81.0
Opponents	460	236	2728	51.3	9	24	34/228	54.3

Rushing	Att.	Yds.	Avg.	LG	TD
Hoge	203	772	3.8	41t	7
Worley	109	418	3.8	38	0
W. Williams	68	389	5.7	70t	3
Foster	36	203	5.6	38	1
Brister	25	64	2.6	11	0
Bell	5	18	3.6	12	0
Stryzinski	3	17	5.7	9	0
Strom	4	10	2.5	10	0
Lipps	1	−5	−5.0	−5	0
Stone	2	−6	−3.0	10	0
Steelers	456	1880	4.1	70t	11
Opponents	446	1615	3.6	31	13

Receiving	No.	Yds.	Avg.	LG	TD
Lipps	50	682	13.6	37	3
Hoge	40	342	8.6	27	3
Green	34	387	11.4	46	7
Mularkey	32	365	11.4	28	3
Hill	25	391	15.6	66	0
Stone	19	332	17.5	90	1
Bell	12	137	11.4	43	1
Calloway	10	124	12.4	20t	1
Worley	8	70	8.8	27	0
W. Williams	5	42	8.4	13	1
O'Shea	1	13	13.0	13	0
Foster	1	2	2.0	2	0
Steelers	237	2887	12.2	90	20
Opponents	236	2728	11.6	66t	9

Interceptions	No.	Yds.	Avg.	LG	TD
Woodson	5	67	13.4	34	0
Griffin	4	75	18.8	36	0
Woodruff	3	110	36.7	59	0
Everett	3	2	0.7	2	0
Johnson	2	60	30.0	34	1
Little	1	35	35.0	35	0
Hinkle	1	19	19.0	19	0
Lloyd	1	9	9.0	9	0
Willis	1	5	5.0	5	0
A. Jones	1	3	3.0	3	0
Hall	1	0	0.0	0	0
Lake	1	0	0.0	0	0
Steelers	24	385	16.0	59	1
Opponents	15	124	8.3	24	0

Punting	No.	Yds.	Avg.	In 20	LG
Stryzinski	65	2454	37.8	18	51
Steelers	66	2454	37.2	18	51
Opponents	64	2616	40.9	13	62

Punt Returns	No.	FC	Yds.	Avg.	LG	TD
Woodson	38	8	398	10.5	52t	1
Hill	1	0	0	0.0	0	0
Steelers	39	8	398	10.2	52t	1
Opponents	16	32	105	6.6	39	0

Kickoff Returns	No.	Yds.	Avg.	LG	TD
Woodson	35	764	21.8	49	0
Stone	5	91	18.2	24	0
Foster	3	29	9.7	13	0
J. Williams	3	31	10.3	20	0
Griffin	2	16	8.0	14	0
Green	1	16	16.0	16	0
Lipps	1	9	9.0	9	0
Olsavsky	0	0	—	0	0
Steelers	50	956	19.1	49	0
Opponents	56	1245	22.2	99t	1

Sacks	No.
G. Williams	6.0
Willis	5.0
Lloyd	4.5
Davidson	3.5
Evans	3.0
Freeman	2.0
Hinkle	2.0
A. Jones	2.0
Jenkins	2.0
Nickerson	2.0
Lake	1.0
J. Williams	1.0
Steelers	34.0
Opponents	33.0

1991 Draft Choices

Round	Name	Pos.	College
1.	Huey Richardson	DE	Florida
2.	Jeff Graham	WR	Ohio State
3.	Ernie Mills	WR	Florida
4.	Sammy Walker	DB	Texas Tech
	Adrian Cooper	TE	Oklahoma
6.	Leroy Thompson	RB	Penn State
7.	Andre Jones	LB	Notre Dame
8.	Dean Dingman	G	Michigan
9.	Bruce McGonnigal	TE	Virginia
10.	Ariel Solomon	T	Colorado
11.	Efrum Thomas	DB	Alabama
12.	Jeff Brady	LB	Kentucky

Pittsburgh Steelers 1991 Veteran Roster

No.	Name	Pos.	Ht.	Wt.	Birth-date	NFL Exp.	College	Hometown	How Acq.	'90 Games/ Starts
1	Anderson, Gary	K	5-11	184	7/16/59	10	Syracuse	Durban, South Africa	W(Buff)-'82	16/0
60	Blankenship, Brian	G	6-1	280	4/7/63	5	Nebraska	Omaha, Neb.	FA-'87	16/13
6	Brister, Bubby	QB	6-3	208	8/15/62	6	Northeast Louisiana	Alexandria, La.	D3-'86	16/16
88	Calloway, Chris	WR	5-10	185	3/29/68	2	Michigan	Chicago, Ill.	D4-'90	16/2
64	Davidson, Kenny	DE	6-5	272	8/17/67	2	Louisiana State	Shreveport, La.	D2-'90	14/0
89	Davis, Lorenzo	WR	5-11	185	2/12/68	2	Youngstown State	Ft. Lauderdale, Fla.	FA-'90	4/0
63	Dawson, Dermontti	C	6-2	279	6/17/65	4	Kentucky	Lexington, Ky.	D2-'88	16/16
66	Evans, Donald	DE	6-2	265	3/14/64	3	Winston-Salem State	Raleigh, N.C.	FA-'90	16/16
27	Everett, Thomas	S	5-9	182	11/21/64	5	Baylor	Daingerfield, Tex.	D4-'87	15/14
29	Foster, Barry	RB	5-10	223	12/8/68	2	Arkansas	Duncanville, Tex.	D5-'90	16/1
68	Freeman, Lorenzo	NT	6-5	319	5/23/64	5	Pittsburgh	Camden, N.J.	FA-'87	11/1
86	Green, Eric	TE	6-5	274	6/22/67	2	Liberty	Savannah, Ga.	D1-'90	13/7
22	Griffin, Larry	S	6-0	202	1/11/63	6	North Carolina	Chesapeake, Va.	FA-'87	16/3
35	†Hall, Delton	CB	6-1	208	1/16/65	5	Clemson	Greensboro, N.C.	D2-'87	12/1
77	Haselrig, Carlton	G	6-1	291	1/22/66	2	Pittsburgh-Johnstown	Johnstown, Pa.	D12-'89	16/0
53	Hinkle, Bryan	LB	6-2	220	6/4/59	10	Oregon	Silverdale, Wash.	D6-'81	16/16
33	Hoge, Merril	RB	6-2	229	1/26/65	5	Idaho State	Pocatello, Idaho	D10-'87	16/15
62	Ilkin, Tunch	T	6-3	274	9/23/57	12	Indiana State	Highland Park, Ill.	D6-'80	13/13
65	Jackson, John	T	6-6	290	1/4/65	4	Eastern Kentucky	Cincinnati, Ohio	D10-'88	16/16
99	Jenkins, A.J.	LB-DE	6-2	237	4/12/66	3	Cal State-Fullerton	Havelock, N.C.	D9-'89	5/0
44	Johnson, David	CB	6-0	185	4/14/66	3	Kentucky	Louisville, Ky.	D7-'89	16/15
97	Jones, Aaron	DE	6-5	269	12/18/66	4	Eastern Kentucky	Orlando, Fla.	D1-'88	7/1
25	Jones, Gary	S	6-1	203	11/30/67	2	Texas A&M	Tyler, Tex.	D9-'90	16/1
37	Lake, Carnell	S	6-1	207	7/15/67	3	UCLA	Inglewood, Calif.	D2-'89	16/16
51	Lanza, Chuck	C	6-2	265	9/20/64	3	Notre Dame	Pittsburgh, Pa.	D3-'88	0*
83	Lipps, Louis	WR	5-10	186	8/9/62	8	Southern Mississippi	Reserve, La.	D1-'84	14/14
50	†Little, David	LB	6-1	236	1/3/59	11	Florida	Miami, Fla.	D7-'81	16/14
95	Lloyd, Greg	LB	6-2	225	5/26/65	4	Fort Valley State	Fort Valley, Ga.	D6b-'87	15/14
74	Long, Terry	G	5-11	278	7/21/59	8	East Carolina	Columbia, S.C.	D4b-'84	16/16
56	McGovern, Rob	LB	6-2	234	10/1/66	3	Holy Cross	Oradell, N.J.	PB(KC)-'91#	11/0*
84	Mularkey, Mike	TE	6-4	238	11/19/61	9	Florida	Ft. Lauderdale, Fla.	PB(Minn)-'89#	16/15
54	Nickerson, Hardy	LB	6-2	225	9/1/65	5	California	Los Angeles, Calif.	D5-'87	16/14
14	O'Donnell, Neil	QB	6-3	221	7/3/66	2	Maryland	Madison, N.J.	D3a-'90	0*
55	Olsavsky, Jerry	LB	6-1	218	3/29/67	3	Pittsburgh	Youngstown, Ohio	D10-'89	15/0
85	O'Shea, Terry	TE	6-4	238	12/3/66	3	California, Pa.	Pittsburgh, Pa.	FA-'89	16/0
71	Ricketts, Tom	T	6-5	293	11/21/65	3	Pittsburgh	Murrysville, Pa.	D1b-'89	16/3
20	Stone, Dwight	WR-RB	6-0	190	1/28/64	5	Middle Tennessee State	Florala, Ala.	FA-'87	16/2
11	Strom, Rick	QB	6-2	201	3/11/65	3	Georgia Tech	Pittsburgh, Pa.	FA-'89	6/0
4	Stryzinski, Dan	P	6-1	193	5/15/65	2	Indiana	Indianapolis, Ind.	FA-'90	16/0
73	Strzelczyk, Justin	T	6-5	291	8/18/68	2	Maine	Seneca, N.Y.	D11-'90	16/0
91	Veasey, Craig	DT-DE	6-2	280	12/25/66	2	Houston	Clear Lake City, Tex.	D3b-'90	10/0
98	Williams, Gerald	NT	6-3	291	9/8/63	6	Auburn	Lanett, Ala.	D2-'86	16/15
57	Williams, Jerrol	LB	6-5	244	7/5/67	3	Purdue	Las Vegas, Nev.	D4-'89	16/1
42	Williams, Warren	RB	6-0	201	7/29/65	4	Miami	Fort Myers, Fla.	D6-'88	14/4
93	Willis, Keith	DE	6-1	263	7/29/59	9	Northeastern	Newark, N.J.	FA-'82	16/16
49	Woodruff, Dwayne	CB	6-0	196	2/18/57	12	Louisville	New Richmond, Ohio	D6b-'79	15/1
26	†Woodson, Rod	CB	6-0	197	3/10/65	5	Purdue	Fort Wayne, Ind.	D1-'87	16/16
38	Worley, Tim	RB	6-2	223	9/24/66	3	Georgia	Lumberton, N.C.	D1a-'89	11/8
76	Wyatt, Willie	NT	6-0	275	9/27/67	2	Alabama	Birmingham, Ala.	PB(TB)-'91#	7/3*

* Lanza missed '90 season due to injury; McGovern played 11 games with Kansas City in '90; O'Donnell active for 3 games but did not play; Wyatt played 7 games with Tampa Bay.

† Option playout; subject to developments.

\# Plan B unconditional free agent.

Players lost through Plan B (4): RB Richard Bell (KC; 16 games in '90), WR Derek Hill (Phx; 16), G John Rienstra (Clev; 6), LB Tyronne Stowe (Phx; 16).

Also played with Steelers in '90—CB Richard Shelton (2 games).

COACHING STAFF

Head Coach, Chuck Noll

Pro Career: Became only NFL coach to win four Super Bowls when Steelers defeated Los Angeles Rams 31-19 in Super Bowl XIV. Put together 13 consecutive non-losing seasons and has guided Steelers into postseason play 12 of last 19 years. Led Pittsburgh to consecutive NFL championships twice (1974-75, 1978-79). With 202 career wins, is second among active NFL coaches behind Don Shula (298). Has eighth-highest winning percentage (.579) among active coaches and is fifth among the NFL's all-time winningest coaches with a 202-147-1 career record. Noll is one of only four coaches in NFL history to lead a team for 23 or more consecutive seasons—Curly Lambeau (29), Tom Landry (29), and Steve Owen (23) are the others. Played pro football as guard-linebacker for Cleveland Browns from 1953-59. At age 28, he started coaching career as defensive coach with Los Angeles (San Diego) Chargers in 1960. Left after 1965 season to become defensive backfield coach in Baltimore. Remained with Colts until taking over Pittsburgh as head coach in 1969. Career record: 202-147-1.

Background: Was an all-state star at Benedictine High in Cleveland. Captained the University of Dayton team, playing both tackle and linebacker. He was drafted by the Browns in 1953.

Personal: Born in Cleveland on January 5, 1932. He and his wife, Marianne, live in Pittsburgh and have one son—Chris.

Assistant Coaches

Ron Blackledge, offensive line; born April 15, 1938, Canton, Ohio, lives in Pittsburgh. Tight end-defensive end Bowling Green 1957-59. No pro playing experience. College coach: Ashland 1968-69, Cincinnati 1970-72, Kentucky 1973-75, Princeton 1976, Kent State 1977-81 (head coach 1979-81). Pro coach: Joined Steelers in 1982.

Dave Brazil, defensive coordinator; born March 25, 1936, Detroit, lives in Pittsburgh. No college or pro playing experience. College coach: Holy Cross 1968-69, Tulsa 1970-71, Eastern Michigan 1972-74, Boston College 1978-79, Kent State 1980-82. Pro coach: Detroit Wheel (WFL) 1975, Chicago Fire (WFL) 1976, Kansas City Chiefs 1984-88, joined Steelers in 1989.

John Fox, defensive backs; born February 8, 1955, Virginia Beach, Va., lives in Pittsburgh. Defensive back San Diego State 1975-77. No pro playing experience. College coach: U.S. International 1979, Boise State 1980, Long Beach State 1981, Utah 1982, Kansas 1983, 1985, Iowa State 1984, Pittsburgh 1986-88. Pro coach: Los Angeles Express (USFL) 1985, joined Steelers in 1989.

Joe Greene, defensive line; born September 24, 1946, Temple, Tex., lives in Pittsburgh. Defensive tackle North Texas State 1966-68. Pro defensive tackle Pittsburgh Steelers 1969-81. Inducted into Pro Football Hall of Fame in 1987. Pro coach: Joined Steelers in 1987.

Jack Henry, offensive line; born March 14, 1946, Houston, Pa., lives in Indiana, Pa. Linebacker Penn State 1964-65, guard Indiana (Pa.) 1967-68. No pro playing experience. College coach: West Virginia 1970, 1978, Edinboro State 1973, Louisville 1974, Millersville State 1975-76, Southern Illinois 1977, Appalachian State 1979, Wake Forest 1980-86, Indiana (Pa.) 1986-89. Pro coach: Joined Steelers in 1990.

Dick Hoak, offensive backfield; born December 8, 1939, Jeannette, Pa., lives in Greensburg, Pa. Halfback-quarterback Penn State 1958-60. Pro running back Pittsburgh Steelers 1961-70. Pro coach: Joined Steelers in 1972.

Jon Kolb, tight ends, conditioning; born August 30, 1947, Ponca City, Okla., lives in Pittsburgh. Center-linebacker Oklahoma State 1966-68. Pro tackle Pittsburgh Steelers 1969-81. Pro coach: Joined Steelers in 1982.

Pittsburgh Steelers 1991 First-Year Roster

Name	Pos.	Ht.	Wt.	Birth-date	College	Hometown	How Acq.
Bernard, Mike	G-T	6-2	281	12/27/67	Syracuse	Williamstown, N.Y.	FA
Brady, Jeff	LB	6-1	220	11/9/68	Kentucky	Melbourne, Ky.	D12
Byrd, Ricky	G	6-1	288	1/21/67	Mississippi State	Natchez, Miss.	FA
Cooper, Adrian	TE	6-5	253	4/27/68	Oklahoma	Denver, Colo.	D4b
Cullinane, Gene (1)	C	6-4	278	11/10/66	Washburn	Omaha, Neb.	FA-'90
Davis, Scott	RB	6-2	208	7/17/67	North Texas State	Richardson, Tex.	FA
Dingman, Dean	G	6-2	286	9/27/68	Michigan	Troy, Wis.	D8
Drayton, Rich	WR	5-11	190	6/22/69	Temple	Philadelphia, Pa.	FA
Dunbar, Karl (1)	DE	6-4	275	5/18/67	Louisiana State	Opelousas, La.	D8-'90
Fair, Ron (1)	WR	5-11	190	10/28/66	Arizona State	Asheville, N.C.	FA-'90
Graham, Jeff	WR	6-1	198	2/14/69	Ohio State	Dayton, Ohio	D2
Herds, Tyreese (1)	CB	5-11	205	5/9/68	Kansas State	Tampa, Fla.	FA
Holleran, Randy	LB	6-0	240	12/24/68	Kentucky	McKeesport, Pa.	FA
Howe, Garry	NT	6-1	290	6/20/68	Colorado	Spencer, Iowa	FA
Johnson, Jarrod	C	6-1	280	3/29/69	Lehigh	West Orange, N.J.	FA
Jones, Andre	LB	6-3	226	5/15/69	Notre Dame	Hyattsville, Md.	D7
LeBaron, Brian	LB	6-4	238	3/12/68	Syracuse	Corning, N.Y.	FA
Mannery, Sam	QB	6-2	193	7/21/69	California, Pa.	McClellandtown, Pa.	FA
McGonnigal, Bruce	TE	6-4	229	5/1/68	Virginia	Baltimore, Md.	D9
Mills, Ernie	WR	5-11	176	10/28/68	Florida	Dunnellon, Fla.	D3
Richardson, Huey	LB	6-5	238	2/2/68	Florida	Atlanta, Ga.	D1
Smith, Kevin	S	5-11	190	4/2/67	Rhode Island	Newport, R.I.	FA
Solomon, Ariel	T	6-5	273	7/16/68	Colorado	Boulder, Colo.	D10
Thomas, Efrum	S	5-11	186	7/18/69	Alabama	Long Beach, Calif.	D11
Thompson, Leroy	RB	5-10	210	2/3/69	Penn State	Knoxville, Tenn.	D6
Vincent, Shawn	CB	5-10	175	6/2/68	Akron	St. Clairsville, Ohio	FA
Walker, Jeff	TE	6-4	248	4/10/66	Rice	Austin, Tex.	FA
Walker, Sammy	CB	5-11	192	1/20/69	Texas Tech	McKinney, Tex.	D4a
Walsh, Dan (1)	RB	6-0	215	2/14/66	Montclair State	Hazlet, N.J.	FA

The term NFL Rookie is defined as a player who is in his first season of professional football and has not been on the roster of another professional football team for any regular-season or postseason games. A Rookie is designated by an "R" on NFL rosters. Players who have been active in another professional football league or players who have NFL experience, including either preseason training camp or being on an active roster for fewer than three regular-season or postseason games, are termed NFL First-Year Players. An NFL First-Year Player is designated by a "1" on NFL rosters. Thereafter, a player on an NFL active roster for at least three regular-season or postseason games is credited with an additional year of NFL playing experience.

NOTES

Dwain Painter, receivers; born February 13, 1942, Monroeville, Pa., lives in Pittsburgh. Quarterback-defensive back Rutgers 1961-64. No pro playing experience. College coach: San Jose State 1971-72, College of San Mateo 1973, Brigham Young 1974-75, UCLA 1976-78, Northern Arizona 1979-81 (head coach), Georgia Tech 1982-85, Texas 1986, Illinois 1987. Pro coach: Joined Steelers in 1988.

George Stewart, special teams; born December 29, 1958, Little Rock, Ark., lives in Pittsburgh. Guard Arkansas 1977-80. No pro playing experience. College coach: Minnesota 1984-85, Notre Dame 1986-88. Pro coach: Joined Steelers in 1989.

Bob Valesente, linebackers; born July 19, 1940, Seneca Falls, N.Y., lives in Pittsburgh. Halfback Ithaca College 1958-61. No pro playing experience. College coach: Cornell 1964-74, Cincinnati 1975-76, Arizona 1977-79, Mississippi State 1980-81, Kansas 1984-87 (head coach 1986-87), Maryland 1988, Pittsburgh 1989. Pro coach: Baltimore Colts 1982-83, joined Steelers in 1990.

Joe Walton, offensive coordinator; born December 15, 1935, Beaver Falls, Pa., lives in Pittsburgh. Tight end-linebacker Pittsburgh 1953-56. Pro tight end Washington Redskins 1957-60, New York Giants 1961-63. Pro coach: New York Giants 1969-73, Washington Redskins 1974-80, New York Jets 1981-89 (head coach 1983-89), joined Steelers in 1990.

SAN DIEGO CHARGERS

American Football Conference Western Division

Team Colors: Navy Blue, White, and Gold

San Diego Jack Murphy Stadium
P.O. Box 609609
San Diego, California 92160-9609
Telephone: (619) 280-2111

Club Officials

Chairman of the Board/President: Alex G. Spanos
Vice Chairman: Dean A. Spanos
General Manager: Bobby Beathard
Special Assistant to Chairman of the Board: Warren B. Jones, Jr.
Assistant General Manager: Dick Daniels
Director of Player Personnel: Billy Devaney
Director of Pro Personnel: Rudy Feldman
Director of College Scouting: John Hinek
Director of Public Relations: Bill Johnston
Business Manager: Pat Curran
Director of Marketing: Rich Israel
Director of Ticket Operations: Joe Scott
Assistant Director of Public Relations: Rob Boulware
Chief Financial Officer: Jeremiah T. Murphy
Head Trainer: Keoki Kamau
Equipment Manager: Sid Brooks

Stadium: San Diego Jack Murphy Stadium • **Capacity:** 60,835
9449 Friars Road
San Diego, California 92108

Playing Surface: Grass

Training Camp: University of California-San Diego
Third College
La Jolla, California 92037

1991 Schedule

Preseason

Aug. 3	**Houston**	7:00
Aug. 12	at Los Angeles Rams	7:00
Aug. 19	at San Francisco	6:00
Aug. 23	**Los Angeles Raiders**	7:00

Regular Season

Sept. 1	at Pittsburgh	4:00
Sept. 8	at San Francisco	1:00
Sept. 15	**Atlanta**	1:00
Sept. 22	at Denver	2:00
Sept. 29	**Kansas City**	1:00
Oct. 6	at Los Angeles Raiders	1:00
Oct. 13	at Los Angeles Rams	1:00
Oct. 20	**Cleveland**	1:00
Oct. 27	at Seattle	1:00
Nov. 3	**Open Date**	
Nov. 10	**Seattle**	1:00
Nov. 17	**New Orleans**	1:00
Nov. 24	at New York Jets	4:00
Dec. 1	**Los Angeles Raiders**	5:00
Dec. 8	at Kansas City	12:00
Dec. 15	**Miami**	1:00
Dec. 22	**Denver**	1:00

Chargers Coaching History

(226-227-11)

1960-69	Sid Gillman*	83-51-6
1969-70	Charlie Waller	9-7-3
1971	Sid Gillman**	4-6-0
1971-73	Harland Svare***	7-17-2
1973	Ron Waller	1-5-0
1974-78	Tommy Prothro****	21-39-0
1978-86	Don Coryell#	72-60-0
1986-88	Al Saunders	17-22-0
1989-90	Dan Henning	12-20-0

*Retired after nine games in 1969
**Resigned after 10 games in 1971
***Resigned after eight games in 1973
****Resigned after four games in 1978
#Resigned after eight games in 1986

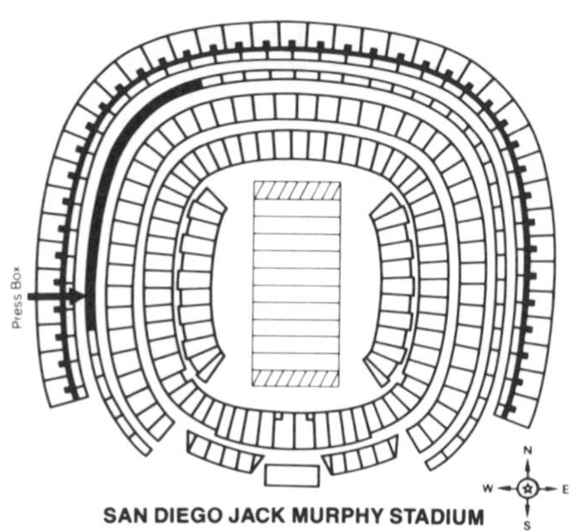

SAN DIEGO JACK MURPHY STADIUM

Record Holders

Individual Records—Career

Category	Name	Performance
Rushing (Yds.)	Paul Lowe, 1960-67	4,963
Passing (Yds.)	Dan Fouts, 1973-1987	43,040
Passing (TDs)	Dan Fouts, 1973-1987	254
Receiving (No.)	Charlie Joiner, 1976-1986	586
Receiving (Yds.)	Lance Alworth, 1962-1970	9,585
Interceptions	Gill Byrd, 1983-1990	32
Punting (Avg.)	Maury Buford, 1982-84	42.7
Punt Return (Avg.)	Leslie (Speedy) Duncan, 1964-1970	12.3
Kickoff Return (Avg.)	Leslie (Speedy) Duncan, 1964-1970	25.2
Field Goals	Rolf Benirschke, 1977-1986	146
Touchdowns (Tot.)	Lance Alworth, 1962-1970	83
Points	Rolf Benirschke, 1977-1986	766

Individual Records—Single Season

Category	Name	Performance
Rushing (Yds.)	Marion Butts, 1990	1,225
Passing (Yds.)	Dan Fouts, 1981	4,802
Passing (TDs)	Dan Fouts, 1981	33
Receiving (No.)	Kellen Winslow, 1980	89
Receiving (Yds.)	Lance Alworth, 1965	1,602
Interceptions	Charlie McNeil, 1961	9
Punting (Avg.)	Dennis Partee, 1969	44.6
Punt Return (Avg.)	Leslie (Speedy) Duncan, 1965	15.5
Kickoff Return (Avg.)	Keith Lincoln, 1962	28.4
Field Goals	Rolf Benirschke, 1980	24
Touchdowns (Tot.)	Chuck Muncie, 1981	19
Points	Rolf Benirschke, 1980	118

Individual Records—Single Game

Category	Name	Performance
Rushing (Yds.)	Gary Anderson, 12-18-88	217
Passing (Yds.)	Dan Fouts, 10-19-80	444
	Dan Fouts, 12-11-82	444
Passing (TDs)	Dan Fouts, 11-22-81	6
Receiving (No.)	Kellen Winslow, 10-7-84	15
Receiving (Yds.)	Wes Chandler, 12-20-82	260
Interceptions	Many times Last time by Pete Shaw, 11-2-80	3
Field Goals	Many times Last time by John Carney, 11-11-90	4
Touchdowns (Tot.)	Kellen Winslow, 11-22-81	5
Points	Kellen Winslow, 11-22-81	30

1990 Team Record

Preseason (3-1)

Date	Result		Opponents
8/11	W	28-16	Dallas
8/18	W	30-27	at L.A. Rams
8/25	W	29-28	San Francisco
9/1	L	7-34	at L.A. Raiders
		94-105	

Regular Season (6-10)

Date	Result		Opponents	Att.
9/9	L	14-17	at Dallas	48,063
9/16	L	16-21	Cincinnati	48,098
9/23	W	24-14	at Cleveland	77,429
9/30	L	7-17	Houston	48,762
10/7	L	14-36	at Pittsburgh	53,486
10/14	W	39- 3	at N.Y. Jets	63,311
10/21	L	9-24	L.A. Raiders	60,569
10/28	W	41-10	Tampa Bay	40,653
11/4	W	31-14	at Seattle	59,646
11/11	W	19- 7	Denver	59,557
11/18	L	10-27	at Kansas City	63,717
11/25	L	10-13	Seattle (OT)	50,097
12/2	W	38-17	N.Y. Jets	40,877
12/16	L	10-20	at Denver	64,919
12/23	L	21-24	Kansas City	45,135
12/30	L	12-17	at L.A. Raiders	62,593

(OT) Overtime

Score by Periods

Chargers	69	102	75	69	0	—	315
Opponents	54	111	27	86	3	—	281

Attendance

Home 393,748 Away 493,164 Total 886,912
Single-game home record, 61,880 (11-29-87)
Single-season home record, 415,626 (1985)

1990 Team Statistics

	Chargers	Opp.
Total First Downs	272	268
Rushing	112	92
Passing	142	152
Penalty	18	24
Third Down: Made/Att.	101/223	86/203
Third Down: Pct.	45.3	42.4
Fourth Down: Made/Att.	6/20	6/14
Fourth Down: Pct.	30.0	42.9
Total Net Yards	4940	4425
Avg. Per Game	308.8	276.6
Total Plays	976	931
Avg. Per Play	5.1	4.8
Net Yards Rushing	2257	1515
Avg. Per Game	141.1	94.7
Total Rushes	484	424
Net Yards Passing	2683	2910
Avg. Per Game	167.7	181.9
Sacked/Yards Lost	20/157	45/345
Gross Yards	2840	3255
Att./Completions	472/246	462/254
Completion Pct.	52.1	55.0
Had Intercepted	19	19
Punts/Avg.	62/39.4	70/41.2
Net Punting Avg.	36.6	35.0
Penalties/Yards Lost	103/886	87/720
Fumbles/Ball Lost	24/13	26/11
Touchdowns	36	33
Rushing	14	10
Passing	18	22
Returns	4	1
Avg. Time of Possession	30:19	29:41

1990 Individual Statistics

Scoring	TD R	TD P	TD Rt	PAT	FG	Saf	TP
Carney	0	0	0	27/28	19/21	0	84
Butts	8	0	0	0/0	0/0	0	48
A. Miller	0	7	0	0/0	0/0	0	42
Bernstine	4	0	0	0/0	0/0	0	24
Lewis	1	1	1	0/0	0/0	0	18
McEwen	0	3	0	0/0	0/0	0	18
Reveiz	0	0	0	7/8	2/7	0	13
Harmon	0	2	0	0/0	0/0	0	12
L. Miller	0	0	2	0/0	0/0	0	12
Plummer	1	1	0	0/0	0/0	0	12
Caravello	0	1	0	0/0	0/0	0	6
Cox	0	1	0	0/0	0/0	0	6
Early	0	1	0	0/0	0/0	0	6
Taylor	0	0	1	0/0	0/0	0	6
Walker	0	1	0	0/0	0/0	0	6
Grossman	0	0	0	0/0	0/0	1	2
Chargers	14	18	4	34/36	21/28	1	315
Opponents	10	22	1	33/33	16/21	1	281

Passing	Att.	Comp.	Yds.	Pct.	TD	Int.	Tkld.	Rate
Tolliver	410	216	2574	52.7	16	16	19/150	68.9
Vlasic	40	19	168	47.5	1	2	0/0	46.7
Friesz	22	11	98	50.0	1	1	1/7	58.5
Chargers	472	246	2840	52.1	18	19	20/157	66.5
Opponents	462	254	3255	55.0	22	19	45/345	76.0

Rushing	Att.	Yds.	Avg.	LG	TD
Butts	265	1225	4.6	52	8
Bernstine	124	589	4.8	40t	4
Harmon	66	363	5.5	41	0
Lewis	4	25	6.3	10t	1
Tolliver	14	22	1.6	14	0
Nelson	3	14	4.7	5	0
A. Miller	3	13	4.3	10	0
Friesz	1	3	3.0	3	0
Plummer	2	3	1.5	2	1
Vlasic	1	0	0.0	0	0
Wilson	1	0	0.0	0	0
Chargers	484	2257	4.7	52	14
Opponents	424	1515	3.6	27	10

Receiving	No.	Yds.	Avg.	LG	TD
A. Miller	63	933	14.8	31t	7
Harmon	46	511	11.1	36t	2
McEwen	29	325	11.2	32	3
Walker	23	240	10.4	23	1
Butts	16	117	7.3	26	0
Early	15	238	15.9	45t	1
Lewis	14	192	13.7	40	1
Cox	14	93	6.6	12	1
Wilson	10	87	8.7	20	0
Bernstine	8	40	5.0	11	0
Nelson	4	29	7.3	10	0
Caravello	2	21	10.5	17t	1
Hendrickson	1	12	12.0	12	0
Plummer	1	2	2.0	2t	1
Chargers	246	2840	11.5	45t	18
Opponents	254	3255	12.8	90t	22

Interceptions	No.	Yds.	Avg.	LG	TD
Byrd	7	63	9.0	24	0
Seale	2	14	7.0	14	0
Smith	2	12	6.0	12	0
Frank	2	8	4.0	4	0
Rolling	1	67	67.0	67	0
Lyles	1	19	19.0	19	0
Fuller	1	5	5.0	5	0
Bayless	1	0	0.0	0	0
Elder	1	0	0.0	0	0
Glenn	1	0	0.0	0	0
Chargers	19	188	9.9	67	0
Opponents	19	310	16.3	64t	1

Punting	No.	Yds.	Avg.	In 20	LG
Kidd	61	2442	40.0	14	59
Chargers	62	2442	39.4	14	59
Opponents	70	2886	41.2	15	67

Punt Returns	No.	FC	Yds.	Avg.	LG	TD
Lewis	13	8	117	9.0	63t	1
Mays	7	4	30	4.3	17	0
Taylor	6	3	112	18.7	55t	1
Schwedes	5	1	33	6.6	12	0
Nelson	3	0	44	14.7	33	0
Lyles	1	0	0	0.0	0	0
Chargers	35	16	336	9.6	63t	2
Opponents	28	15	131	4.7	18	0

Kickoff Returns	No.	Yds.	Avg.	LG	TD
Elder	24	571	23.8	90	0
Lewis	17	383	22.5	39	0
Frank	8	172	21.5	31	0
Nelson	4	36	9.0	26	0
A. Miller	1	13	13.0	13	0
Orr	1	13	13.0	13	0
Chargers	55	1188	21.6	90	0
Opponents	62	1048	16.9	75	0

Sacks	No.
O'Neal	13.5
Grossman	10.0
Williams	7.5
Rolling	3.5
Bayless	3.0
Robinson	2.0
L. Miller	1.0
Seau	1.0
Smith	1.0
Elder	0.5
Hinkle	0.5
Phillips	0.5
Chargers	45.0
Opponents	20.0

1991 Draft Choices

Round	Name	Pos.	College
1.	Stanley Richard	DB	Texas
2.	George Thornton	DT	Alabama
	Eric Bieniemy	RB	Colorado
	Eric Moten	G	Michigan State
4.	Yancey Thigpen	WR	Winston-Salem St.
5.	Duane Young	TE	Michigan State
	Floyd Fields	DB	Arizona State
6.	Jimmy Laister	T	Oregon Tech
7.	David Jones	WR	Delaware State
	Terry Beauford	G	Florida A&M
9.	Andy Katoa	LB	Southern Oregon
10.	Roland Poles	RB	Tennessee
	Mike Heldt	C	Notre Dame
11.	Joachim Weinberg	WR	Johnson C. Smith
12.	Chris Samuels	RB	Texas

San Diego Chargers 1991 Veteran Roster

No.	Name	Pos.	Ht.	Wt.	Birth-date	NFL Exp.	College	Hometown	How Acq.	'90 Games/ Starts
44	Bayless, Martin	S	6-2	212	10/11/62	8	Bowling Green	Dayton, Ohio	T(Buff)-'87	14/14
95	Benson, Mitchell	DT	6-4	300	5/30/67	3	Texas Christian	Ft. Worth, Tex.	FA-'91	11/0*
82	†Bernstine, Rod	RB	6-3	238	2/8/65	5	Texas A&M	Bryan, Tex.	D1-'87	12/1
35	Butts, Marion	RB	6-1	248	8/1/66	3	Florida State	Sylvester, Ga.	D7a-'89	14/13
22	Byrd, Gill	CB-S	5-11	198	2/20/61	9	San Jose State	San Francisco, Calif.	D1c-'83	16/16
46	Caravello, Joe	RB	6-3	262	6/6/63	5	Tulane	El Segundo, Calif.	PB(Wash)-'89#	7/7
3	Carney, John	K	5-11	170	4/20/64	3	Notre Dame	West Palm Beach, Fla.	FA-'90	12/0
29	Carrington, Darren	CB-S	6-2	200	10/10/66	3	Northern Arizona	Bronx, N.Y.	PB(Det)-'91#	14/0*
63	Cornish, Frank	C-G	6-4	295	9/24/67	2	UCLA	Chicago, Ill.	D6b-'90	16/16
88	Cox, Arthur	TE	6-2	277	2/5/61	9	Texas Southern	Plant City, Fla.	FA-'88	16/14
28	Elder, Donnie	CB	5-9	178	12/13/63	6	Memphis State	Chattanooga, Tenn.	FA-'90	12/0
61	Floyd, Eric	G-T	6-5	300	10/28/65	2	Auburn	Rome, Ga.	FA-'90	16/6
27	Frank, Donald	CB	6-0	200	10/24/65	2	Winston-Salem State	Tarboro, N.C.	FA-'90	16/2
16	Gagliano, Bob	QB	6-3	205	9/5/58	5	Utah	Glendale, Calif.	PB(Det)-'91#	9/4*
67	Goeas, Leo	G-T	6-4	285	8/15/66	2	Hawaii	Honolulu, Hawaii	D3b-'90	15/9
92	Grossman, Burt	DE	6-4	255	4/10/67	3	Pittsburgh	Bala-Cynwyd, Pa.	D1-'89	15/15
53	Hall, Courtney	G-C	6-1	269	8/26/68	3	Rice	Wilmington, Calif.	D2a-'89	16/16
33	Harmon, Ronnie	RB	5-11	200	5/7/64	6	Iowa	Queens, N.Y.	PB(Buff)-'90#	16/2
34	†Hendrickson, Steve	LB-RB	6-0	250	8/30/66	3	California	Napa, Calif.	FA-'90	14/0
97	†Hinkle, George	DE	6-5	269	3/17/65	4	Arizona	Pacific, Mo.	D11b-'88	16/3
48	Humphery, Bobby	CB-S	5-11	180	8/23/61	9	New Mexico State	Lubbock, Tex.	PB(Rams)-'91#	16/10*
10	Kidd, John	P	6-3	208	8/22/61	8	Northwestern	Findlay, Ohio	PB(Buff)-'90#	16/0
80	Kyles, Troy	WR	6-1	188	8/13/68	2	Howard	Detroit, Mich.	PB(NYG)-'91#	9/0*
81	Lewis, Nate	WR	5-11	189	10/19/66	2	Oregon Tech	Moultrie, Ga.	D7c-'90	12/3
73	May, Mark	G-T	6-6	290	11/2/59	10	Pittsburgh	Oneonta, N.Y.	PB(Wash)-'91#	0*
31	McEwen, Craig	RB	6-1	220	12/16/65	5	Utah	Northport, N.Y.	FA-'89	16/5
83	Miller, Anthony	WR	5-11	185	4/15/65	4	Tennessee	Pasadena, Calif.	D1-'88	16/16
20	†Nelson, Darrin	RB	5-9	185	1/2/59	10	Stanford	Downey, Calif.	FA-'90	14/0
91	O'Neal, Leslie	LB	6-4	259	5/7/64	5	Oklahoma State	Little Rock, Ark.	D1a-'86	16/16
37	†Orr, Terry	RB	6-2	235	9/27/61	6	Texas	Abilene, Tex.	FA-'90	14/0*
75	†Phillips, Joe	NT	6-5	315	7/15/63	6	Southern Methodist	Vancouver, Wash.	FA-'87	3/3
50	Plummer, Gary	LB	6-2	240	1/26/60	6	California	Fremont, Calif.	FA-'86	16/15
25	Radachowsky, George	S	6-0	195	9/7/62	7	Boston College	Danbury, Conn.	FA-'91	0*
65	†Richards, David	G-T	6-4	310	4/11/66	4	UCLA	Dallas, Tex.	D4c-'88	16/16
64	Rodenhauser, Mark	C	6-5	263	6/1/61	4	Illinois State	Addison, Ill.	PB(Minn)-'90#	16/0
57	Rolling, Henry	LB	6-2	225	9/8/65	4	Nevada-Reno	Henderson, Nev.	FA-'90	16/8
30	Seale, Sam	CB	5-9	185	10/6/62	8	Western State, Colo.	Orange, N.J.	FA-'88	16/13
55	Seau, Junior	LB	6-3	250	1/19/69	2	Southern California	Oceanside, Calif.	D1-'90	16/15
23	Shelton, Anthony	CB	6-1	195	9/4/67	2	Tennessee State	Fayetteville, Tenn.	W(SF)-'90	14/0
68	Simmonds, Mike	G	6-4	295	8/12/64	2	Indiana State	Belleville, Ill.	PB(TB)-'90#	0*
54	Smith, Billy Ray	LB	6-3	236	8/10/61	9	Arkansas	Plano, Tex.	D1a-'83	11/10
43	†Spencer, Tim	RB	6-1	223	12/10/60	7	Ohio State	St. Clairsville, Ohio	FA-'90	4/0
72	Swayne, Harry	T	6-5	290	2/2/65	5	Rutgers	Philadelphia, Pa.	PB(TB)-'91#	10/0*
85	†Taylor, Kitrick	WR	5-11	191	7/22/64	4	Washington State	Pomona, Calif.	FA-'90	3/0
56	Thaxton, Galand	LB	6-1	240	10/23/64	2	Wyoming	Denver, Colo.	PB(Atl)-'91#	0*
76	†Thompson, Broderick	G-T	6-4	295	8/14/60	7	Kansas	Cerritos, Calif.	FA-'87	16/16
11	†Tolliver, Billy Joe	QB	6-1	218	2/7/66	3	Texas Tech	Boyd, Tex.	D2b-'89	15/14
89	Walker, Derrick	TE	6-0	244	6/23/67	2	Michigan	Chicago Heights, Ill.	D6d-'90	16/12
99	Williams, Lee	DE	6-5	271	10/15/62	8	Bethune-Cookman	Ft. Lauderdale, Fla.	SD1-'84	16/16
84	Wilson, Walter	WR	5-10	185	10/6/66	2	East Carolina	Baltimore, Md.	D3c-'90	14/3
70	Zandofsky, Mike	G	6-2	285	11/30/65	3	Washington	Corvallis, Ore.	T(Phx)-'90	13/0

* Benson played 11 games with Indianapolis in '90; Carrington played 12 games with Detroit, 2 with Denver; Gagliano played 9 games with Detroit; Humphery played 16 games with L.A. Rams; Kyles played 9 games with N.Y. Giants; May last active with Washington in '89; Orr played 5 games with Washington; Radachowsky last active with N.Y. Jets in '89; Simmonds missed '90 season due to injury; Swayne played 10 games with Tampa Bay; Thaxton last active with Atlanta in '89.

† Option playout; subject to developments.

\# Plan B unconditional free agent.

Players lost through Plan B (11): LB David Brandon (Clev; 0 games in '90), LB Richard Brown (Clev; 11), WR Quinn Early (NO; 14), LB Cedric Figaro (Ind; 16), S Vencie Glenn (Raid; 14), CB Sam Lilly (Rams; 2), DT Les Miller (NO; 14), T Joel Patten (Raid; 8), DE Gerald Robinson (Rams; 11), QB Mark Vlasic (KC; 6), WR Wayne Walker (Minn; 0).

Also played with Chargers in '90—S Michael Brooks (1 game), CB Joe Fuller (4), LB Antonio Goss (2), RB Jerry Mays (2), RB Joe Mickles (1), LB Jeff Mills (5), K Fuad Reveiz (4), WR Scott Schwedes (5), G Tom Toth (1).

COACHING STAFF

Head Coach, Dan Henning

Pro Career: Begins third season as San Diego's head coach. Named eighth head coach in Chargers' history on February 9, 1989, replacing Al Saunders. Previously served as head coach of Atlanta Falcons from 1983-86, producing 22-41-1 record. Henning began his pro coaching career in 1972 as an assistant with Houston Oilers. Also was assistant with New York Jets 1976-78 and Miami Dolphins 1979-80. Served as assistant head coach with Washington Redskins 1981-82 and helped lead Washington to a Super Bowl victory following the 1982 season. Returned to Washington as receivers coach in 1987-88. Played quarterback with Chargers 1964-67. Career record: 34-61-1.

Background: Played quarterback for William & Mary 1960-63. College assistant coach at Florida State 1968-70, 1974, and Virginia Tech 1971-73.

Personal: Born June 21, 1942, Bronx, N.Y. Attended St. Francis Prep in Brooklyn before attending William & Mary. Dan and his wife, Sandy, live in La Mesa, Calif., and have five children—Mary K., Patty, Danny, Terry, and Mike.

Assistant Coaches

Chuck Clausen, defensive line; born June 23, 1940, Anamosa, Iowa, lives in Roswell, Ga. Defensive lineman New Mexico 1961-63. No pro playing experience. College coach: William & Mary 1969-70, Ohio State 1971-75. Pro coach: Philadelphia Eagles 1976-85, Atlanta Falcons 1986-88, joined Chargers in 1991.

John Dunn, strength and conditioning; born July 22, 1956, Great Barrington, Mass., lives in San Diego. Guard Penn State 1975-77. No pro playing experience. College coach: Penn State 1978. Pro coach: Washington Redskins 1984-86, Los Angeles Raiders 1987-89, joined Chargers in 1990.

Alex Gibbs, offensive line; born February 11, 1941, Morganton, N.C., lives in San Diego. Running back-defensive back Davidson College 1959-63. No pro playing experience. College coach: Duke 1969-70, Kentucky 1971-72, West Virginia 1973-74, Ohio State 1975-78, Auburn 1979-81, Georgia 1982-83. Pro coach: Denver Broncos 1984-87, Los Angeles Raiders 1988-89, joined Chargers in 1990.

Mike Haluchak, linebackers; born November 28, 1949, Concord, Calif., lives in San Diego. Linebacker Southern California 1967-70. No pro playing experience. College coach: Southern California 1976-77, Cal State-Fullerton 1978, Pacific 1979-80, California 1981, North Carolina State 1982. Pro coach: Oakland Invaders (USFL) 1983-85, joined Chargers in 1986.

Bobby Jackson, running backs; born February 16, 1940, Forsyth, Ga., lives in San Diego. Linebacker-running back Samford (Ga.) 1959-62. No pro playing experience. College coach: Florida State 1965-69, Kansas State 1970-74, Louisville 1975-76, Tennessee 1977-82. Pro coach: Atlanta Falcons 1983-86, joined Chargers in 1987.

Charlie Joiner, receivers; born October 14, 1947, Many, La., lives in San Diego. Wide receiver Grambling 1965-68. Defensive back-wide receiver Houston Oilers 1969-72, Cincinnati Bengals 1972-75, San Diego Chargers 1976-86. Pro coach: Joined Chargers in 1987.

Ron Lynn, defensive coordinator; born December 6, 1944, Youngstown, Ohio, lives in San Diego. Quarterback-defensive back Mount Union (Ohio) 1963-65. No pro playing experience. College coach: Toledo 1966, Mount Union (Ohio) 1967-73, Kent State 1974-76, San Jose State 1977-78, Pacific 1979, California 1980-82. Pro coach: Oakland Invaders (USFL) 1983-85, joined Chargers in 1986.

LeCharls McDaniel, assistant to special teams coordinator; born October 15, 1958, Fort Bragg, N.C., lives in San Diego. Defensive back Cal Poly-SLO 1976-80. Defensive back Washington Redskins 1981-82, New York Giants 1983-84. College coach: Hartnell Community College 1986-88. Pro coach: Joined Chargers in 1989.

San Diego Chargers 1991 First-Year Roster

Name	Pos.	Ht.	Wt.	Birth-date	College	Hometown	How Acq.
Anderson, LeAndre	DE	6-4	265	9/19/68	Nebraska	Chicago, Ill.	FA
Barnett, Joaquin	LB	6-1	235	1/15/68	Hawaii	Carson, Calif.	FA
Beauford, Terry	G	6-1	281	3/27/68	Florida A&M	Ft. Pierce, Fla.	D7b
Bieniemy, Eric	RB	5-7	204	8/15/69	Colorado	West Covina, Calif.	D2b
Brown, Dean (1)	T	6-3	311	9/7/68	Notre Dame	Canton, Ohio	FA-'90
Burgermeister, Duncan	RB	6-3	245	6/26/67	Wyoming	Boulder, Colo.	FA
Cook, Geoff	TE	6-4	257	9/16/68	Santa Clara	Duarte, Calif.	FA
Davis, Mike	LB	6-3	255	1/5/68	North Texas State	Denton, Tex.	FA
Delgardo, Curtis	RB	5-6	172	10/19/67	Portland State	Renton, Wash.	FA
Fields, Floyd	S	6-0	208	1/7/69	Arizona State	South Holland, Ill.	D5b
Fitisemanu, Alema	LB	6-1	235	5/29/66	Brigham Young	American Samoa	FA
Friesz, John (1)	QB	6-4	209	5/19/67	Idaho	Coeur d'Alene, Idaho	D6a-'90
Heard, Ron (1)	WR	5-10	180	8/20/67	Bowling Green	Detroit, Mich.	FA-'90
Heldt, Mike	C	6-2	270	1/2/70	Notre Dame	Tampa, Fla.	D10b
Jenkins, Darryl	T	6-4	290	5/3/67	Georgia Tech	Jacksonville, Fla.	FA
Jones, David	WR	6-2	217	11/9/68	Delaware State	Hillside, N.J.	D7a
Katoa, Andy	LB	6-2	238	8/18/65	Southern Oregon St.	Millbrae, Calif.	D9
Kaufusi, Rich	DE	6-4	255	7/16/66	Brigham Young	Salt Lake City, Utah	FA
Kelson, Derrick (1)	CB-S	6-0	187	5/14/68	Purdue	Warren, Ohio	FA
Laister, Jimmy	T	6-5	300	4/12/69	Oregon Tech	Maplesville, Ala.	D6
Lashley, Craig	DE	6-3	284	12/11/65	No College	La Habra, Calif.	FA
McCall, Kris	CB	6-0	188	8/26/69	Idaho	Alameda, Calif.	FA
McCloud, Kim	CB	6-0	185	5/8/68	Hawaii	Los Angeles, Calif.	FA
McGill, Reggie	RB	5-9	195	7/11/69	Arizona	Phoenix, Ariz.	FA
Moten, Eric	G	6-2	292	4/11/68	Michigan State	Cleveland Heights, Ohio	D2c
Murphy, Dan	CB	6-3	210	8/28/68	Acadia, Nova Scotia	Richmond, Ontario	FA
Odom, DeWayne	LB	6-3	235	8/10/68	California	San Diego, Calif.	FA
Poles, Roland	RB	6-0	251	9/9/66	Tennessee	Caledonia, N.Y.	D10a
Richard, Stanley	S	6-2	197	10/21/67	Texas	Hawkins, Tex.	D1
Samuels, Chris	RB	5-10	198	8/15/69	Texas	San Antonio, Tex.	D12
Savage, Tony (1)	NT	6-3	300	7/7/67	Washington State	San Francisco, Calif.	FA-'90
Thigpen, Yancey	WR	6-0	208	8/15/69	Winston-Salem State	Tarboro, N.C.	D4
Thornton, George	DT	6-3	300	4/28/68	Alabama	Montgomery, Ala.	D2a
Weatherspoon, Stephan	LB	6-2	245	6/15/68	Texas Tech	Lubbock, Tex.	FA
Weinberg, Joe	WR	6-1	185	10/17/67	Johnson C. Smith	Newport News, Va.	D11
Wyche, John	S	6-1	207	4/10/68	Florida State	Thomasville, Ga.	FA
Young, Duane	TE	6-1	276	5/29/68	Michigan State	Kalamazoo, Mich.	D5

The term NFL Rookie is defined as a player who is in his first season of professional football and has not been on the roster of another professional football team for any regular-season or postseason games. A Rookie is designated by an "R" on NFL rosters. Players who have been active in another professional football league or players who have NFL experience, including either preseason training camp or being on an active roster for fewer than three regular-season or postseason games, are termed NFL First-Year Players. An NFL First-Year Player is designated by a "1" on NFL rosters. Thereafter, a player on an NFL active roster for at least three regular-season or postseason games is credited with an additional year of NFL playing experience.

NOTES

Jim Mora, secondary; born November 19, 1961, Los Angeles, lives in San Diego. Defensive back Washington 1980-83. No pro playing experience. College coach: Washington 1984. Pro coach: Joined Chargers in 1986.

Larry Pasquale, special teams coordinator; born April 21, 1941, Brooklyn, N.Y., lives in San Diego. Quarterback Bridgeport 1961-63. No pro playing experience. College coach: Slippery Rock State 1967, Boston University 1968, Navy 1969-70, Massachusetts 1971-75, Idaho State 1976. Pro coach: Montreal Alouettes (CFL) 1977-78, Detroit Lions 1979, New York Jets 1980-89, joined Chargers in 1990.

Jack Reilly, offensive assistant; born May 22, 1945, Boston, Mass., lives in San Diego. Quarterback Washington State 1963, Santa Monica City College 1964, Long Beach State 1965-66. No pro playing experience. College coach: El Camino (Calif.) J.C. 1980-84, Utah 1985-89 (head coach). Pro coach: Joined Chargers in 1990.

Ted Tollner, assistant head coach/quarterbacks; born May 29, 1940, San Francisco, lives in San Diego. Quarterback Cal Poly-SLO 1959-61. No pro playing experience. College coach: College of San Mateo 1971-72 (head coach), San Diego State 1973-80, Brigham Young 1981, Southern California 1982-86 (head coach 1983-86). Pro coach: Buffalo Bills 1987-88, joined Chargers in 1989.

Ed White, tight ends; born April 4, 1947, San Diego, Calif., lives in Alpine, Calif. Defensive lineman California 1965-68. Guard-tackle Minnesota 1969-77, San Diego Chargers 1978-85. Pro coach: San Diego Chargers 1986-87, Los Angeles Rams 1988, rejoined Chargers in 1989.

SEATTLE SEAHAWKS

American Football Conference Western Division

Team Colors: Blue, Green, and Silver

11220 N.E. 53rd Street
Kirkland, Washington 98033
Telephone: (206) 827-9777

Club Officials

Owner: Ken Behring
President/General Manager: Tom Flores
Vice President/Assistant General Manager: Chuck Allen
Player Personnel Director: Mike Allman
Vice President/Public Relations: Gary Wright
Publicity Director: Dave Neubert
Community Relations Director: Sandy Gregory
Sales and Marketing Director: Reggie McKenzie
Business Manager: Mickey Loomis
Data Processing Director: Tom Monroe
Ticket Manager: James Nagaoka
Trainer: Jim Whitesel
Equipment Manager: Walt Loeffler

Stadium: Kingdome • **Capacity:** 64,984
201 South King Street
Seattle, Washington 98104

Playing Surface: AstroTurf

Training Camp: 11220 N.E. 53rd Street
Kirkland, Washington 98033

1991 Schedule

Preseason

Aug. 3	**Phoenix**	7:30
Aug. 10	at Indianapolis	7:30
Aug. 17	at Los Angeles Rams	7:00
Aug. 23	**San Francisco**	5:00

Regular Season

Sept. 1	at New Orleans	12:00
Sept. 8	**New York Jets**	1:00
Sept. 15	at Denver	2:00
Sept. 22	at Kansas City	3:00
Sept. 29	**Indianapolis**	1:00
Oct. 6	at Cincinnati	1:00
Oct. 13	**Los Angeles Raiders**	4:30
Oct. 20	at Pittsburgh	1:00
Oct. 27	**San Diego**	1:00
Nov. 3	**Open Date**	
Nov. 10	at San Diego	1:00
Nov. 17	at Los Angeles Raiders	1:00
Nov. 24	**Denver**	1:00
Dec. 1	**Kansas City**	1:00
Dec. 8	**San Francisco**	1:00
Dec. 15	at Atlanta	1:00
Dec. 22	**Los Angeles Rams**	5:00

Seahawks Coaching History

(115-120-0)

1976-82	Jack Patera*	35-59-0
1982	Mike McCormack	4-3-0
1983-90	Chuck Knox	76-58-0

*Released after two games in 1982

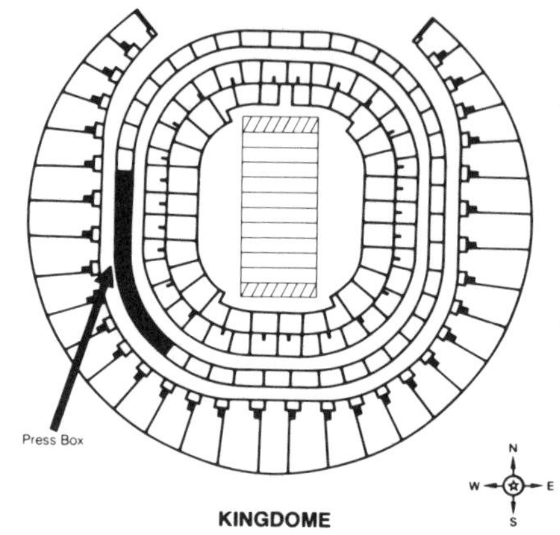

Record Holders

Individual Records—Career

Category	Name	Performance
Rushing (Yds.)	Curt Warner, 1983-89	6,705
Passing (Yds.)	Dave Krieg, 1980-1990	24,052
Passing (TDs)	Dave Krieg, 1980-1990	184
Receiving (No.)	Steve Largent, 1976-1989	*819
Receiving (Yds.)	Steve Largent, 1976-1989	*13,089
Interceptions	Dave Brown, 1976-1986	50
Punting (Avg.)	Ruben Rodriguez, 1987-89	40.3
Punt Return (Avg.)	Paul Johns, 1981-84	11.4
Kickoff Return (Avg.)	Bobby Joe Edmonds, 1986-88	22.1
Field Goals	Norm Johnson, 1982-1990	159
Touchdowns (Tot.)	Steve Largent, 1976-1989	101
Points	Norm Johnson, 1982-1990	810

Individual Records—Single Season

Category	Name	Performance
Rushing (Yds.)	Curt Warner, 1986	1,481
Passing (Yds.)	Dave Krieg, 1984	3,671
Passing (TDs)	Dave Krieg, 1984	32
Receiving (No.)	Steve Largent, 1985	79
Receiving (Yds.)	Steve Largent, 1985	1,287
Interceptions	John Harris, 1981	10
	Kenny Easley, 1984	10
Punting (Avg.)	Herman Weaver, 1980	41.8
Punt Return (Avg.)	Bobby Joe Edmonds, 1987	12.6
Kickoff Return (Avg.)	Al Hunter, 1978	24.1
Field Goals	Norm Johnson, 1990	23
Touchdowns (Tot.)	David Sims, 1978	15
	Sherman Smith, 1979	15
	Derrick Fenner, 1990	15
Points	Norm Johnson, 1984	110

Individual Records—Single Game

Category	Name	Performance
Rushing (Yds.)	Curt Warner, 11-27-83	207
Passing (Yds.)	Dave Krieg, 11-20-83	418
Passing (TDs)	Dave Krieg, 12-2-84	5
	Dave Krieg, 9-15-85	5
	Dave Krieg, 11-28-88	5
Receiving (No.)	Steve Largent, 10-18-87	15
Receiving (Yds.)	Steve Largent, 10-18-87	261
Interceptions	Kenny Easley, 9-3-84	3
Field Goals	Norm Johnson, 9-20-87	5
	Norm Johnson, 12-18-88	5
Touchdowns (Tot.)	Daryl Turner, 9-15-85	4
	Curt Warner, 12-11-88	4
Points	Daryl Turner, 9-15-85	24
	Curt Warner, 12-11-88	24

*NFL Record

1990 Team Record

Preseason (4-1)

Date	Result		Opponents
8/4	L	7-10	vs. Denver at Tokyo
8/11	W	34- 9	at Phoenix
8/17	W	13-10	Indianapolis
8/24	W	10- 3	Tampa Bay
8/31	W	30-10	at San Francisco
		94-42	

Regular Season (9-7)

Date	Result		Opponents	Att.
9/9	L	0-17	at Chicago	64,400
9/16	L	13-17	L.A. Raiders	61,889
9/23	L	31-34	at Denver (OT)	75,290
10/1	W	31-16	Cincinnati	60,135
10/7	W	33-20	at New England	39,735
10/14	L	17-24	at L.A. Raiders	50,624
10/21	W	19- 7	Kansas City	60,358
11/4	L	14-31	San Diego	59,646
11/11	W	17-16	at Kansas City	71,285
11/18	L	21-24	Minnesota	59,735
11/25	W	13-10	at San Diego (OT)	50,097
12/2	W	13-10	Houston (OT)	57,592
12/9	W	20-14	at Green Bay	52,015
12/16	L	17-24	at Miami	57,851
12/23	W	17-12	Denver	55,845
12/30	W	30-10	Detroit	50,681

(OT) Overtime

Score by Periods

Seahawks	50	94	60	96	6	—	306
Opponents	50	112	53	68	3	—	286

Attendance

Home 466,241 Away 461,297 Total 927,538
Single-game home record, 64,411 (12-15-84)
Single-season home record, 494,103 (1988)

1990 Team Statistics

	Seahawks	Opp.
Total First Downs	284	280
Rushing	111	86
Passing	155	171
Penalty	18	23
Third Down: Made/Att.	87/200	83/207
Third Down: Pct.	43.5	40.1
Fourth Down: Made/Att.	6/7	7/11
Fourth Down: Pct.	85.7	63.6
Total Net Yards	4583	4609
Avg. Per Game	286.4	288.1
Total Plays	945	950
Avg. Per Play	4.8	4.9
Net Yards Rushing	1749	1605
Avg. Per Game	109.3	100.3
Total Rushes	457	413
Net Yards Passing	2834	3004
Avg. Per Game	177.1	187.8
Sacked/Yards Lost	40/360	33/252
Gross Yards	3194	3256
Att./Completions	448/265	504/300
Completion Pct.	59.2	59.5
Had Intercepted	20	12
Punts/Avg.	67/40.6	77/41.9
Net Punting Avg.	34.4	36.2
Penalties/Yards Lost	89/746	108/766
Fumbles/Ball Lost	32/16	32/18
Touchdowns	34	32
Rushing	18	7
Passing	15	19
Returns	1	6
Avg. Time of Possession	30:47	29:13

1990 Individual Statistics

Scoring	TD R	TD P	TD Rt	PAT	FG	Saf	TP
Johnson	0	0	0	33/34	23/32	0	102
Fenner	14	1	0	0/0	0/0	0	90
Chadwick	0	4	0	0/0	0/0	0	24
Kane	0	4	0	0/0	0/0	0	24
Blades	0	3	0	0/0	0/0	0	18
Williams	3	0	0	0/0	0/0	0	18
Skansi	0	2	0	0/0	0/0	0	12
Heller	0	1	0	0/0	0/0	0	6
Robinson	0	0	1	0/0	0/0	0	6
Warren	1	0	0	0/0	0/0	0	6
Seahawks	18	15	1	33/34	23/32	0	306
Opponents	7	19	6	32/32	20/27	1	286

Passing	Att.	Comp.	Yds.	Pct.	TD	Int.	Tkld.	Rate
Krieg	448	265	3194	59.2	15	20	40/360	73.6
Seahawks	448	265	3194	59.2	15	20	40/360	73.6
Opponents	504	300	3256	59.5	19	12	33/252	81.3

Rushing	Att.	Yds.	Avg.	LG	TD
Fenner	215	859	4.0	36	14
Williams	187	714	3.8	25	3
Krieg	32	115	3.6	25	0
Jones	5	20	4.0	5	0
Blades	3	19	6.3	12	0
Loville	7	12	1.7	4	0
Warren	6	11	1.8	4	1
McNeal	1	2	2.0	2	0
Chadwick	1	−3	−3.0	−3	0
Seahawks	457	1749	3.8	36	18
Opponents	413	1605	3.9	58t	7

Receiving	No.	Yds.	Avg.	LG	TD
Williams	73	699	9.6	60	0
Kane	52	776	14.9	63t	4
Blades	49	525	10.7	24	3
Chadwick	27	478	17.7	54t	4
Skansi	22	257	11.7	25t	2
Fenner	17	143	8.4	50	1
Heller	13	157	12.1	23	1
McNeal	10	143	14.3	30	0
Jones	1	22	22.0	22	0
Krieg	1	−6	−6.0	−6	0
Seahawks	265	3194	12.1	63t	15
Opponents	300	3256	10.9	46	19

Interceptions	No.	Yds.	Avg.	LG	TD
Robinson	3	89	29.7	39	0
Harper	3	69	23.0	47	0
Wyman	2	24	12.0	22	0
Bolcar	1	0	0.0	0	0
Hunter	1	0	0.0	0	0
Jefferson	1	0	0.0	0	0
Jenkins	1	0	0.0	0	0
Seahawks	12	182	15.2	47	0
Opponents	20	252	12.6	42	0

Punting	No.	Yds.	Avg.	In 20	LG
Donnelly	67	2722	40.6	18	54
Seahawks	67	2722	40.6	18	54
Opponents	77	3225	41.9	22	67

Punt Returns	No.	FC	Yds.	Avg.	LG	TD
Warren	28	16	269	9.6	39	0
Jefferson	8	0	68	8.5	14	0
Seahawks	36	16	337	9.4	39	0
Opponents	29	21	254	8.8	66t	2

Kickoff Returns	No.	Yds.	Avg.	LG	TD
Warren	23	478	20.8	71	0
Loville	18	359	19.9	29	0
Jefferson	4	96	24.0	26	0
Jones	2	21	10.5	13	0
McNeal	2	29	14.5	17	0
Glasgow	1	2	2.0	2	0
Seahawks	50	985	19.7	71	0
Opponents	51	910	17.8	39	0

Sacks	No.
Green	12.5
Bryant	5.5
Porter	5.0
Woods	3.0
Glasgow	2.0
Comeaux	1.0
Kennedy	1.0
McElroy	1.0
Nash	1.0
Wyman	1.0
Seahawks	33.0
Opponents	40.0

1991 Draft Choices

Round	Name	Pos.	College
1.	Dan McGwire	QB	San Diego State
2.	Doug Thomas	WR	Clemson
3.	David Daniels	WR	Penn State
4.	John Kasay	K	Georgia
5.	Harlan Davis	DB	Tennessee
6.	Mike Sinclair	DE	E. New Mexico
10.	Erik Ringoen	LB	Hofstra
11.	Tony Stewart	RB	Iowa
12.	Ike Harris	G	South Carolina

Seattle Seahawks 1991 Veteran Roster

No.	Name	Pos.	Ht.	Wt.	Birth-date	NFL Exp.	College	Hometown	How Acq.	'90 Games/ Starts
50	Ahrens, Dave	LB	6-4	247	12/5/58	11	Wisconsin	Oregon, Wis.	FA-'90	10/3
51	Allert, Ty	LB	6-2	238	7/23/63	6	Texas	Houston, Tex.	W(Den)-'90	8/0*
52	Andrews, Ricky	LB	6-2	236	4/14/66	2	Washington	Mililani, Hawaii	FA-'90	15/0
65	Bailey, Edwin	G	6-4	279	5/15/59	11	South Carolina State	Savannah, Ga.	D5-'81	11/11
25	Blackmon, Robert	S	6-0	198	5/12/67	2	Baylor	Van Vleck, Tex.	D2b-'90	15/5
89	Blades, Brian	WR	5-11	191	7/24/65	4	Miami	Ft. Lauderdale, Fla.	D2-'88	16/16
64	Brilz, Darrick	G	6-3	281	2/14/64	5	Oregon State	Pinole Valley, Calif.	FA-'89	16/5
77	Bryant, Jeff	DT	6-5	281	5/22/60	10	Clemson	Decatur, Ga.	D1-'82	15/14
	t-Buczkowski, Bob	DT-DE	6-5	260	5/15/64	3	Pittsburgh	Pittsburgh, Pa.	T(Clev)-'91	15/3*
59	Cain, Joe	LB	6-1	233	6/11/65	3	Oregon Tech	Compton, Calif.	FA-'89	16/5
88	†Chadwick, Jeff	WR	6-3	189	12/16/60	9	Grand Valley State	Dearborn, Mich.	FA-'89	16/0
84	Clark, Louis	WR	6-0	198	7/3/64	5	Mississippi State	Shannon, Miss.	D10-'87	4/0
52	Comeaux, Darren	LB	6-1	239	4/15/60	10	Arizona State	San Diego, Calif.	W(SF)-'88	9/9
55	Cotton, Marcus	LB	6-3	237	8/11/66	4	Southern California	Oakland, Calif.	PB(Clev)-'91#	14/1*
34	†Davis, Brian	CB	6-2	190	8/31/63	5	Nebraska	Phoenix, Ariz.	W(Wash)-'90	7/0*
3	Donnelly, Rick	P	6-0	209	2/17/62	6	Wyoming	Miller Place, N.Y.	PB(Atl)-'90#	16/0
75	Dyko, Chris	T	6-6	295	3/16/66	2	Washington State	Spokane, Wash.	FA-'90	0*
54	Feasel, Grant	C	6-7	279	6/28/60	7	Abilene Christian	Barstow, Calif.	FA-'87	16/16
44	†Fenner, Derrick	RB	6-3	228	4/6/67	3	North Carolina	Oxon Hill, Md.	D10-'89	16/15
7	Ford, John	WR	6-2	204	7/31/66	2	Virginia	Belle Glade, Fla.	FA-'91	0*
22	Glasgow, Nesby	S	5-10	187	4/15/57	13	Washington	Gardena, Calif.	FA-'88	16/13
79	Green, Jacob	DE	6-3	256	1/21/57	12	Texas A&M	Houston, Tex.	D1-'80	16/16
29	Harper, Dwayne	CB	5-11	174	3/29/66	4	South Carolina State	Orangeburg, S.C.	D11b-'88	16/16
78	Hayes, Eric	DT	6-3	297	11/12/67	2	Florida State	Tampa, Fla.	D5-'90	16/0
66	Heck, Andy	T	6-6	286	1/1/67	3	Notre Dame	Fairfax, Va.	D1-'89	16/16
85	†Heller, Ron	TE	6-3	242	9/18/63	5	Oregon State	Clark Fork, Idaho	PB(Atl)-'90#	16/5
27	Hunter, Patrick	CB	5-11	186	10/24/64	6	Nevada-Reno	San Francisco, Calif.	D3-'86	16/16
26	Jefferson, James	CB	6-1	199	11/18/63	3	Texas A&I	Kingville, Tex.	FA-'89	15/2
9	†Johnson, Norm	K	6-2	203	5/31/60	10	UCLA	Garden Grove, Calif.	FA-'82	16/0
30	†Jones, James	RB	6-2	232	3/21/61	9	Florida	Pompano Beach, Fla.	T(Det)-'89	16/0
83	Junkin, Trey	TE	6-2	240	1/23/61	9	Louisiana Tech	Winfield, La.	FA-'90	12/0
81	Kane, Tommy	WR	5-11	181	1/14/64	4	Syracuse	Montreal, Canada	D3-'88	16/11
15	Kemp, Jeff	QB	6-0	201	7/11/59	11	Dartmouth	Bethesda, Md.	T(SF)-'87	15/0
96	Kennedy, Cortez	DT	6-3	293	8/23/68	2	Miami	Rivercrest, Ark.	D1-'90	16/2
17	Krieg, Dave	QB	6-1	192	10/20/58	12	Milton	Schofield, Wis.	FA-'80	16/16
63	Lee, Ronnie	T	6-3	295	12/24/56	13	Baylor	Tyler, Tex.	T(Atl)-'90	15/9
20	Loville, Derek	RB	5-9	196	7/4/68	2	Oregon	Pacifica, Calif.	FA-'90	11/1
31	†McElroy, Vann	S	6-2	190	1/13/60	10	Baylor	Uvalde, Tex.	T(Raid)-'90	10/0
86	McNeal, Travis	TE	6-3	244	1/10/67	3	Tennessee-Chattanooga	Birmingham, Ala.	D4a-'89	16/14
71	Millard, Bryan	G	6-5	277	12/2/60	8	Texas	Dumas, Tex.	FA-'84	16/16
99	Miller, Donald	LB	6-2	223	4/6/64	2	Idaho State	Chicago, Ill.	FA-'90	7/0
72	Nash, Joe	DT	6-3	278	10/11/60	10	Boston College	Dorchester, Mass.	FA-'82	16/16
58	Newbill, Richard	LB	6-1	240	2/8/68	2	Miami	Clearview, N.J.	FA-'90	3/0*
97	Porter, Rufus	LB	6-1	226	5/18/65	4	Southern	Baton Rouge, La.	FA-'89	12/12
41	Robinson, Eugene	S	6-0	190	5/28/63	7	Colgate	Hartford, Conn.	FA-'85	16/16
73	Singer, Curt	T	6-5	292	11/4/61	4	Tennessee	Aliquippa, Pa.	FA-'91	0*
82	Skansi, Paul	WR	5-11	187	1/11/61	9	Washington	Gig Harbor, Wash.	FA-'85	16/0
94	Stephens, Rod	LB	6-1	237	6/14/66	3	Georgia Tech	Atlanta, Ga.	FA-'90	4/0
11	Stouffer, Kelly	QB	6-3	207	7/6/64	3	Colorado State	Rushville, Neb.	T(Phx)-'88	0*
87	Tice, Mike	TE	6-7	247	2/2/59	11	Maryland	Central Islip, N.Y.	FA-'90	5/2
56	Tofflemire, Joe	C	6-2	273	7/7/65	3	Arizona	Post Falls, Idaho	D2-'89	16/0
42	Warren, Chris	RB	6-2	225	1/24/67	2	Ferrum	Burke, Va.	D4-'90	16/0
74	Wheat, Warren	G	6-6	274	5/13/67	2	Brigham Young	Phoenix, Ariz.	W(Rams)-'89	0*
32	Williams, John L.	RB	5-11	231	11/23/64	6	Florida	Palatka, Fla.	D1-'86	16/16
90	Wooden, Terry	LB	6-3	232	1/14/67	2	Syracuse	Farmingham, Conn.	D2a-'90	8/8
57	Woods, Tony	DE	6-4	269	9/11/65	5	Pittsburgh	Newark, N.J.	D1-'87	16/15
92	Wyman, David	LB	6-2	250	3/31/64	5	Stanford	Reno, Nev.	D2-'87	8/8

* Allert played in 7 games with Denver in '90; Buczkowski played 15 games with Cleveland; Cotton played in 7 games with Atlanta and 7 games with Cleveland; Davis played 7 games with Washington; Dyko missed '90 season due to injury; Ford last active with Detroit in '89; Newbill played 2 games with Minnesota; Singer active for 1 game but did not play; Stouffer active for 1 game but did not play; Wheat active for 5 games but did not play.

† Option playout; subject to developments.

Plan B unconditional free agent.

t- Seahawks traded for Buczkowski (Cleveland).

Players lost through Plan B (4): LB Ned Bolcar (Mia; 5 games in '90), CB Melvin Jenkins (Det; 16), S Thom Kaumeyer (NYG; 7), S R.J. Kors (NYJ; 0).

Also played with Seahawks in '90: WR Willie Bouyer (1 game); T Ron Mattes (15); T Michael Morris (4).

COACHING STAFF

Head Coach, Chuck Knox

Pro Career: Named head coach of Seahawks on January 26, 1983, after five seasons as head coach at Buffalo, where he led Bills to AFC East title in 1980. Led Los Angeles Rams to five straight NFC West titles before taking over Bills in 1978. Pro assistant with New York Jets 1963-66, coaching offensive line, before moving to Detroit in 1967. Served Lions in same capacity until named head coach of Rams in 1973. No pro playing experience. Career record: 171-116-1.

Background: Played tackle for Juniata College in Huntingdon, Pa., 1950-53. Was assistant coach at his alma mater in 1954, then spent 1955 season at Tyrone High in Tyrone, Pennsylvania, and was head coach at Ellwood City High School in Pennsylvania from 1956-58. Moved to Wake Forest as an assistant coach in 1959-60, then Kentucky in 1961-62.

Personal: Born April 27, 1932, Sewickley, Pa. Chuck and his wife, Shirley, live in Bellevue, Wash., and have four children—Chris, Kathy, Colleen, and Chuck.

Assistant Coaches

John Becker, offensive coordinator-receivers; born February 16, 1943, Alexandria, Va., lives in Redmond, Wash. Cal State-Northridge 1965. No college or pro playing experience. College coach: UCLA 1970, New Mexico State 1971, New Mexico 1972-73, Los Angeles Valley J.C. (head coach) 1974-76, Oregon 1977-79. Pro coach: Philadelphia Eagles 1980-83, Buffalo Bills 1984, Indianapolis Colts 1985-88, joined Seahawks in 1989.

Tom Catlin, assistant head coach-defensive coordinator; born September 8, 1931, Ponca City, Okla., lives in Redmond, Wash. Center-linebacker Oklahoma 1950-52. Pro linebacker Cleveland Browns 1953-54, 1957-58, Philadelphia Eagles 1959. College coach: Army 1956. Pro coach: Dallas Texans-Kansas City Chiefs 1960-65, Los Angeles Rams 1966-77, Buffalo Bills 1978-82, joined Seahawks in 1983.

George Dyer, defensive line; born May 4, 1940, Alhambra, Calif., lives in Redmond, Wash. Center-linebacker U.C. Santa Barbara 1961-63. No pro playing experience. College coach: Humboldt State 1964-66, Coalinga, Calif., J.C. 1967 (head coach), Portland State 1968-71, Idaho 1972, San Jose State 1973, Michigan State 1977-79, Arizona State 1980-81. Pro coach: Winnipeg Blue Bombers (CFL) 1974-76, Buffalo Bills 1982, joined Seahawks in 1983.

Chick Harris, offensive backfield; born September 21, 1945, Durham, N.C., lives in Redmond, Wash. Running back Northern Arizona 1966-69. No pro playing experience. College coach: Colorado State 1970-72, Long Beach State 1973-74, Washington 1975-80. Pro coach: Buffalo Bills 1981-82, joined Seahawks in 1983.

Ken Meyer, quarterbacks; born July 14, 1926, Erie, Pa., lives in Bellevue, Wash. Quarterback Denison 1947-50. No pro playing experience. College coach: Denison 1952-57, Wake Forest 1958-59, Florida State 1960-62, Alabama 1963-67, Tulane 1981-82. Pro coach: San Francisco 49ers 1968, 1977 (head coach), New York Jets 1969-72, Los Angeles Rams 1973-76, Chicago Bears 1978-80, joined Seahawks in 1983.

Paul Moyer, staff assistant; born July 26, 1961, Villa Park, Calif., lives in Renton, Wash. Safety Fullerton, Calif., J.C., Arizona State 1979-82. Pro safety Seattle Seahawks 1983-89. Pro coach: Joined Seahawks in 1990.

Rod Perry, defensive backfield; born September 11, 1953, Fresno, Calif., lives in Kirkland, Wash. Defensive back Fresno City College, Colorado 1971-74. Pro cornerback Los Angeles Rams 1975-82, Cleveland Browns 1983-84. College coach: Columbia 1985, Fresno City College 1986, Fresno State 1987-88. Pro coach: Joined Seahawks in 1989.

Russ Purnell, tight ends-assistant special teams; born June 12, 1948, Chicago, Ill., lives in Bellevue, Wash. Center Orange Coast, Calif., J.C., Whittier College 1966-69. No pro playing experience. College coach: Whittier 1970-71, Southern California 1982-85. Pro coach: Joined Seahawks in 1986.

Frank Raines, strength and conditioning; born November 29, 1960, Portsmouth, Va., lives in Kirkland, Wash. No college or pro playing experience. Pro coach: Washington Redskins 1986-89, joined Seahawks in 1990.

Kent Stephenson, offensive line; born February 4, 1942, Anita, Iowa, lives in Redmond, Wash. Guard-nose tackle Northern Iowa 1962-64. No pro playing experience. College coach: Wayne State 1965-68, North Dakota 1969-71, Southern Methodist 1972-73, Iowa 1974-76, Oklahoma State 1977-78, Kansas 1979-82. Pro coach: Michigan Panthers (USFL) 1983-84, joined Seahawks in 1985.

Rusty Tillman, special teams-assistant linebackers; born February 27, 1948, Beloit, Wis., lives in Bellevue, Wash. Linebacker Northern Arizona 1967-69. Pro linebacker Washington Redskins 1970-77. Pro coach: Joined Seahawks in 1979.

Joe Vitt, special assignments; born August 23, 1954, Camden, N.J., lives in Redmond, Wash. Linebacker Towson State 1973-75. No pro playing experience. Pro coach: Baltimore Colts 1979-81, joined Seahawks in 1982.

Seattle Seahawks 1991 First-Year Roster

Name	Pos.	Ht.	Wt.	Birth-date	College	Hometown	How Acq.
Brewer, Derwin	WR	5-8	165	5/26/68	Middle Tennessee St.	La Grange, Ga.	FA
Bromley, Chris	C	6-4	257	4/8/68	Florida	Pensacola, Fla.	FA
Chirico, Robert	DT	6-4	255	2/5/68	Colorado State	Aurora, Colo.	FA
Craft, Douglas	S	5-11	195	7/23/68	Southern	Haughton, La.	FA
Daniels, David	WR	6-1	190	9/16/69	Penn State	Sarasota, Fla.	D3
Danley, Stacy	RB	6-3	216	7/19/68	Auburn	Douglasville, Ala.	FA
Davis, Harlan	CB	6-0	191	8/4/67	Tennessee	Metairie, La.	D5
Frank, Malcolm	CB	5-8	182	12/5/68	Baylor	Beaumont, Tex.	FA
Garrett, Murray	DT	6-4	265	7/28/69	Eastern New Mexico	Houston, Tex.	FA
Gasser, Howard	QB	6-3	221	9/3/67	Texas-El Paso	Laguna Hills, Calif.	FA
Griggs, Calvin	WR	5-10	178	6/26/67	Washington State	Rome, N.Y.	FA
Harris, Ike	T	6-4	272	12/24/67	South Carolina	Columbia, S.C.	D12
Hitchcock, Bill (1)	T	6-6	308	8/26/65	Purdue	Kirkland, Canada	FA
Hochertz, Martin	DE	6-5	245	10/21/68	Southern Illinois	Cary, Ill.	FA
Kasay, John	K	5-10	186	10/27/69	Georgia	Athens, Ga.	D4
Keller, Matt	G	6-4	282	6/12/68	Michigan State	Austintown, Ohio	FA
Mazzoli, Nick	WR	5-11	185	8/22/68	Simon Fraser	Ontario, Canada	FA
McGwire, Dan	QB	6-8	243	12/18/67	San Diego State	Claremont, Calif.	D1
McManus, Curtis	WR	5-8	169	1/6/67	Purdue	Benton Harbor, Mich.	FA
Moore, Mark	DT	6-4	271	8/7/69	Tennessee	Charleston, W. Va.	FA
Morris, Robert (1)	DE	6-6	279	5/12/68	Valdosta State	Brunswick, Ga.	FA
Purter, Shawn	S	6-0	178	1/14/68	Ohio University	Belmont, Ohio	FA
Ragans, Bill	S	6-3	206	12/31/68	Florida State	Suwanee County, Fla.	FA
Ringoen, Erik	LB	6-3	236	7/1/68	Hofstra	Newark, Del.	D10
Ruffin, Aaron	CB	5-10	160	5/17/69	Nicholls State	Hammond, La.	FA
Sims, Turnell	G	6-3	292	7/13/68	Syracuse	Cleveland, Ohio	FA
Sinclair, Michael	DE	6-4	250	1/31/68	Eastern New Mexico	Beaumont, Tex.	D6
Speer, James	LB	6-1	223	12/26/68	Florida	Miami, Fla.	FA
Stewart, Tony	RB	6-0	201	1/3/68	Iowa	Union, N.J.	D11
Thomas, Doug	WR	5-10	178	9/18/69	Clemson	Hamlet, N.C.	D2
Thomas, Willie	CB	5-9	180	12/8/69	Penn State	Coral Springs, Fla.	FA
Thompson, Kevin (1)	S	5-10	190	4/17/66	Oklahoma	Houston, Tex.	FA
Waits, Alex	P	6-2	204	6/21/68	Texas	Plano, Tex.	FA
Wilson, Cecil	RB	5-10	226	10/11/67	Oklahoma State	Ft. Worth, Tex.	FA

The term NFL Rookie is defined as a player who is in his first season of professional football and has not been on the roster of another professional football team for any regular-season or postseason games. A Rookie is designated by an "R" on NFL rosters. Players who have been active in another professional football league or players who have NFL experience, including either preseason training camp or being on an active roster for fewer than three regular-season or postseason games, are termed NFL First-Year Players. An NFL First-Year Player is designated by a "1" on NFL rosters. Thereafter, a player on an NFL active roster for at least three regular-season or postseason games is credited with an additional year of NFL playing experience.

NOTES

THE NFC

ATLANTA FALCONS

National Football Conference Western Division

Team Colors: Black, Red, Silver, and White

Suwanee Road at I-85
Suwanee, Georgia 30174
Telephone: (404) 945-1111

Club Officials

Chairman of the Board: Rankin M. Smith, Sr.
President: Taylor Smith
Vice President & Chief Financial Officer: Jim Hay
Vice President of Player Personnel: Ken Herock
Director of Marketing: Tommy Nobis
Director of Public Relations: Charlie Taylor
Asst. Director of Public Relations: Frank Kleha
Public Relations Assistant: Todd Marble
Director of Community Relations: Carol Breeding
Director of Ticket Operations: Jack Ragsdale
Asst. Director of Ticket Operations: Luci Bailey
Administrative Assistant/Player Personnel: Danny Mock
Scouts: Charley Armey, Bill Baker, Scott Campbell, Elbert Dubenion, Bill Groman
Director of Pro Personnel: Chuck Connor
Controller: Wallace Norman
Trainer: Jerry Rhea
Assistant Trainer: Billy Brooks
Equipment Manager: Whitey Zimmerman
Assistant Equipment Manager: Horace Daniel
Video Director: Tom Atcheson

Stadium: Atlanta-Fulton County Stadium •
Capacity: 59,643
521 Capitol Avenue, S.W.
Atlanta, Georgia 30312

Playing Surface: Grass (PAT)

Training Camp: Suwanee Road at I-85
Suwanee, Georgia 30174

1991 Schedule

Preseason

Aug. 3	vs. Los Angeles Rams at Jacksonville, Fla.	8:00
Aug. 9	at Houston	7:00
Aug. 17	**Tampa Bay**	7:00
Aug. 23	at Dallas	8:00

Regular Season

Sept. 1	at Kansas City	12:00
Sept. 8	**Minnesota**	1:00
Sept. 15	at San Diego	1:00
Sept. 22	**Los Angeles Raiders**	1:00
Sept. 29	**New Orleans**	1:00
Oct. 6	**Open Date**	
Oct. 13	**San Francisco**	1:00
Oct. 20	at Phoenix	1:00
Oct. 27	**Los Angeles Rams**	1:00
Nov. 3	at San Francisco	1:00
Nov. 10	at Washington	1:00
Nov. 17	**Tampa Bay**	1:00
Nov. 24	at New Orleans	7:00
Dec. 1	**Green Bay**	1:00
Dec. 8	at Los Angeles Rams	1:00
Dec. 15	**Seattle**	1:00
Dec. 22	at Dallas	12:00

Falcons Coaching History

(135-232-5)

1966-68	Norb Hecker*	4-26-1
1968-74	Norm Van Brocklin**	37-49-3
1974-76	Marion Campbell***	6-19-0
1976	Pat Peppler	3-6-0
1977-82	Leeman Bennett	47-44-0
1983-86	Dan Henning	22-41-1
1987-89	Marion Campbell****	11-32-0
1989	Jim Hanifan	0-4-0
1990	Jerry Glanville	5-11-0

*Released after three games in 1968
**Released after eight games in 1974
***Released after five games in 1976
****Retired after 12 games in 1989

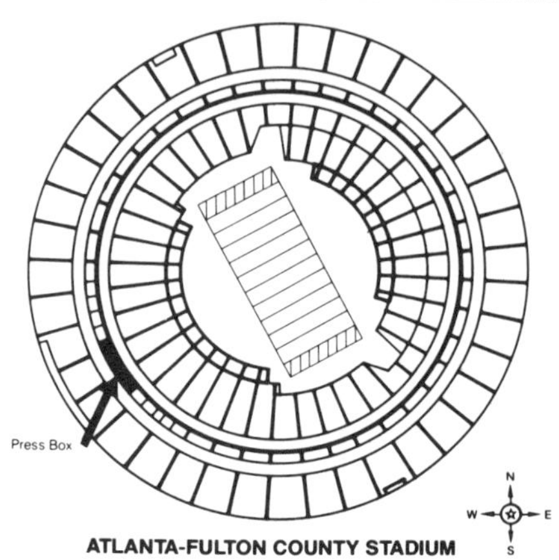

ATLANTA-FULTON COUNTY STADIUM

Record Holders

Individual Records—Career

Category	Name	Performance
Rushing (Yds.)	Gerald Riggs, 1982-88	6,631
Passing (Yds.)	Steve Bartkowski, 1975-1985	23,468
Passing (TDs)	Steve Bartkowski, 1975-1985	154
Receiving (No.)	Alfred Jenkins, 1975-1983	359
Receiving (Yds.)	Alfred Jenkins, 1975-1983	6,257
Interceptions	Rolland Lawrence, 1973-1980	39
Punting (Avg.)	Rick Donnelly, 1985-89	42.6
Punt Return (Avg.)	Al Dodd, 1973-74	11.8
Kickoff Return (Avg.)	Ron Smith, 1966-67	24.3
Field Goals	Mick Luckhurst, 1981-87	115
Touchdowns (Tot.)	Gerald Riggs, 1982-88	48
Points	Mick Luckhurst, 1981-87	558

Individual Records—Single Season

Category	Name	Performance
Rushing (Yds.)	Gerald Riggs, 1985	1,719
Passing (Yds.)	Steve Bartkowski, 1981	3,830
Passing (TDs)	Steve Bartkowski, 1980	31
Receiving (No.)	Andre Rison, 1990	82
Receiving (Yds.)	Alfred Jenkins, 1981	1,358
Interceptions	Scott Case, 1988	10
Punting (Avg.)	Billy Lothridge, 1968	44.3
Punt Return (Avg.)	Gerald Tinker, 1974	13.9
Kickoff Return (Avg.)	Sylvester Stamps, 1987	27.5
Field Goals	Nick Mike-Mayer, 1973	26
Touchdowns (Tot.)	Alfred Jenkins, 1981	13
	Gerald Riggs, 1984	13
Points	Mick Luckhurst, 1981	114

Individual Records—Single Game

Category	Name	Performance
Rushing (Yds.)	Gerald Riggs, 9-2-84	202
Passing (Yds.)	Steve Bartkowski, 11-15-81	416
Passing (TDs)	Randy Johnson, 11-16-69	4
	Steve Bartkowski, 10-19-80	4
	Steve Bartkowski, 10-18-81	4
Receiving (No.)	William Andrews, 11-15-81	15
Receiving (Yds.)	Alfred Jackson, 12-2-84	193
Interceptions	Many times	2
	Last time by Tim Gordon, 11-19-89	
Field Goals	Nick Mike-Mayer, 11-4-73	5
	Tim Mazzetti, 10-30-78	5
Touchdowns (Tot.)	Many times	3
	Last time by Gerald Riggs, 11-17-85	
Points	Many times	18
	Last time by Gerald Riggs, 11-17-85	

1990 Team Record

Preseason (4-0)

Date	Result		Opponents
8/11	W	31-27	vs. Washington at Chapel Hill, N.C.
8/18	W	34-17	Cincinnati
8/25	W	17-14	vs. Green Bay at Milwaukee
8/31	W	45-14	at New England
		127-72	

Regular Season (5-11)

Date	Result		Opponents	Att.
9/9	W	47-27	Houston	56,222
9/16	L	14-21	at Detroit	48,961
9/23	L	13-19	at San Francisco	62,858
10/7	W	28-27	New Orleans	57,401
10/14	L	35-45	San Francisco	57,921
10/21	L	24-44	at L.A. Rams	54,761
10/28	W	38-17	Cincinnati	53,214
11/4	L	9-21	at Pittsburgh	57,093
11/11	L	24-30	at Chicago	62,855
11/18	L	23-24	Philadelphia	53,755
11/25	L	7-10	at New Orleans	68,629
12/2	L	17-23	at Tampa Bay	42,839
12/9	L	13-24	Phoenix	36,222
12/16	L	10-13	at Cleveland	46,536
12/23	W	20-13	L.A. Rams	30,021
12/30	W	26- 7	Dallas	50,097

Score by Periods

Falcons	94	74	68	112	0	—	348
Opponents	35	143	72	115	0	—	365

Attendance

Home 394,853 Away 447,935 Total 842,788
Single-game home record, 59,257 (10-30-77)
Single-season home record, 442,457 (1980)

1990 Team Statistics

	Falcons	Opp.
Total First Downs	274	300
Rushing	85	79
Passing	168	179
Penalty	21	42
Third Down: Made/Att.	78/209	68/197
Third Down: Pct.	37.3	34.5
Fourth Down: Made/Att.	9/21	5/14
Fourth Down: Pct.	42.9	35.7
Total Net Yards	5055	5270
Avg. Per Game	315.9	329.4
Total Plays	994	983
Avg. Per Play	5.1	5.4
Net Yards Rushing	1594	1357
Avg. Per Game	99.6	84.8
Total Rushes	420	413
Net Yards Passing	3461	3913
Avg. Per Game	216.3	244.6
Sacked/Yards Lost	46/265	33/214
Gross Yards	3726	4127
Att./Completions	528/293	537/297
Completion Pct.	55.5	55.3
Had Intercepted	18	17
Punts/Avg.	70/41.6	74/40.2
Net Punting Avg.	36.0	34.5
Penalties/Yards Lost	125/1004	95/811
Fumbles/Ball Lost	40/21	26/18
Touchdowns	40	44
Rushing	11	11
Passing	21	31
Returns	8	2
Avg. Time of Possession	31:05	28:55

1990 Individual Statistics

Scoring	TD R	TD P	TD Rt	PAT	FG	Saf	TP
Davis	0	0	0	40/40	22/33	0	106
Rison	0	10	0	0/0	0/0	0	60
Broussard	4	0	0	0/0	0/0	0	24
Dixon	0	4	0	0/0	0/0	0	24
Johnson	3	1	0	0/0	0/0	0	24
Rozier	3	0	0	0/0	0/0	0	18
Sanders	0	0	3	0/0	0/0	0	18
Butler	0	0	2	0/0	0/0	0	12
Collins	0	2	0	0/0	0/0	0	12
Wilkins	0	2	0	0/0	0/0	0	12
Case	0	0	1	0/0	0/0	0	6
Jones	0	0	1	0/0	0/0	0	6
Miller	1	0	0	0/0	0/0	0	6
Milling	0	1	0	0/0	0/0	0	6
Thomas	0	1	0	0/0	0/0	0	6
Tuggle	0	0	1	0/0	0/0	0	6
Green	0	0	0	0/0	0/0	1	2
Falcons	11	21	8	40/40	22/33	1	348
Opponents	11	31	2	42/44	19/28	1	365

Passing	Att.	Comp.	Yds.	Pct.	TD	Int.	Tkld.	Rate
Miller	388	222	2735	57.2	17	14	26/167	78.7
Campbell	76	36	527	47.4	3	4	9/55	61.7
Millen	63	34	427	54.0	1	0	11/43	80.6
Jones	1	1	37	100.0	0	0	0/0	118.8
Falcons	528	293	3726	55.5	21	18	46/265	76.8
Opponents	537	297	4127	55.3	31	17	33/214	86.2

Rushing	Att.	Yds.	Avg.	LG	TD
Rozier, Hou.-Atl.	163	717	4.4	67	3
Rozier, Atl.	153	675	4.4	67	3
Broussard	126	454	3.6	50t	4
Jones	49	185	3.8	22	0
Johnson	30	106	3.5	12	3
Miller	26	99	3.8	18	1
Campbell	9	38	4.2	20	0
Lang	9	24	2.7	9	0
Settle	9	16	1.8	4	0
Pringle	2	9	4.5	9	0
Millen	7	−12	−1.7	2	0
Falcons	420	1594	3.8	67	11
Opponents	413	1357	3.3	70t	11

Receiving	No.	Yds.	Avg.	LG	TD
Rison	82	1208	14.7	75t	10
Dixon	38	399	10.5	34	4
Collins	34	503	14.8	61	2
Haynes	31	445	14.4	60	0
Broussard	24	160	6.7	18	0
Thomas	18	383	21.3	72	1
Milling	18	161	8.9	24	1
Rozier, Hou.-Atl.	13	105	8.1	24	0
Rozier, Atl.	8	59	7.4	20	0
Jones	13	103	7.9	16	0
Wilkins	12	175	14.6	37	2
Johnson	10	79	7.9	16	1
Bailey	4	44	11.0	13	0
Lang	1	7	7.0	7	0
Falcons	293	3726	12.7	75t	21
Opponents	297	4127	13.9	89t	31

Interceptions	No.	Yds.	Avg.	LG	TD
Sanders	3	153	51.0	82t	2
Case	3	38	12.7	36t	1
Dimry	3	16	5.3	13	0
Jordan	3	14	4.7	14	0
Butler	3	0	0.0	0	0
Mitchell	2	16	8.0	16	0
Falcons	17	237	13.9	82t	3
Opponents	18	368	20.4	59	2

Punting	No.	Yds.	Avg.	In 20	LG
Fulhage	70	2913	41.6	15	59
Falcons	70	2913	41.6	15	59
Opponents	74	2974	40.2	18	62

Punt Returns	No.	FC	Yds.	Avg.	LG	TD
Sanders	29	13	250	8.6	79t	1
Jordan	2	4	19	9.5	10	0
Rison	2	0	10	5.0	8	0
Mitchell	1	0	0	0.0	0	0
Reid	1	0	0	0.0	0	0
Falcons	35	17	279	8.0	79t	1
Opponents	39	12	314	8.1	39	0

Kickoff Returns	No.	Yds.	Avg.	LG	TD
Sanders	39	851	21.8	50	0
Jones	8	236	29.5	76t	1
Broussard	3	45	15.0	23	0
Johnson	2	2	1.0	6	0
Case	1	13	13.0	13	0
Dixon	1	0	0.0	0	0
Gordon	1	43	43.0	43	0
Lang	1	18	18.0	18	0
Pringle	1	14	14.0	14	0
Wilkins	1	7	7.0	7	0
Falcons	58	1229	21.2	76t	1
Opponents	49	814	16.6	37	0

Sacks	No.
Green	6.0
Tuggle	5.0
Bruce	4.0
Gann	3.5
Case	3.0
Epps	3.0
Reid	3.0
Conner	2.0
Lyles	1.5
Bryan	1.0
Casillas	1.0
Falcons	33.0
Opponents	46.0

1991 Draft Choices

Round	Name	Pos.	College
1.	Bruce Pickens	DB	Nebraska
	Mike Pritchard	WR	Colorado
2.	Brett Favre	QB	So. Mississippi
4.	Moe Gardner	NT	Illinois
5.	James Goode	LB	Oklahoma
6.	Erric Pegram	RB	North Texas State
7.	Brian Mitchell	DB	Brigham Young
	Mark Tucker	C	Southern California
8.	Randy Austin	TE	UCLA
9.	Ernie Logan	DE	East Carolina
10.	Walter Sutton	WR	S.W. Minnesota
	Pete Lucas	T	Wis-Steven's Point
11.	Joe Sims	NT	Nebraska
12.	Bob Christian	RB	Northwestern

Atlanta Falcons 1991 Veteran Roster

No.	Name	Pos.	Ht.	Wt.	Birth-date	NFL Exp.	College	Hometown	How Acq.	'90 Games/ Starts
72	Barnett, Oliver	NT	6-3	288	4/9/66	2	Kentucky	Louisville, Ky.	D3-'90	15/1
65	†Bingham, Guy	C	6-3	260	2/25/58	12	Montana	Aberdeen, Wash.	T(Jets)-'89	16/0
63	Brinkley, Lester	DE	6-6	255	5/16/65	2	Mississippi	Drew, Miss.	FA-'91	6/0*
34	Broussard, Steve	RB	5-7	201	2/22/67	2	Washington State	Los Angeles, Calif.	D1-'90	13/10
93	Bruce, Aundray	LB	6-5	248	4/30/66	4	Auburn	Montgomery, Ala.	D1-'88	16/3
77	Bryan, Rick	DE	6-4	265	3/20/62	7	Oklahoma	Coweta, Okla.	D1-'84	16/5
23	†Butler, Bobby	CB	5-11	175	5/28/59	11	Florida State	Delray Beach, Fla.	D1-'81	16/6
20	Carey, Richard	CB	5-9	185	5/6/68	3	Idaho	Seattle, Wash.	FA-'91	3/0*
25	Case, Scott	S	6-0	188	5/17/62	8	Oklahoma	Edmond, Okla.	D2a-'84	16/16
75	Casillas, Tony	NT	6-3	280	10/26/63	6	Oklahoma	Norman, Okla.	D1a-'86	9/0
85	Collins, Shawn	WR	6-2	207	2/20/67	3	Northern Arizona	San Diego, Calif.	D1b-'89	16/6
56	Conner, Darion	LB	6-2	256	9/28/67	2	Jackson State	Prairie Point, Miss.	D2-'90	16/7
86	†Dixon, Floyd	WR	5-9	170	4/9/64	6	Stephen F. Austin	Beaumont, Tex.	D6a-'86	16/2
42	Donaldson, Jeff	S	6-0	188	4/19/62	8	Colorado	Ft. Collins, Colo.	PB(KC)-'91#	16/9*
64	Dukes, Jamie	C	6-1	285	6/14/64	6	Florida State	Orlando, Fla.	FA-'86	16/16
32	Eaton, Tracey	S	6-1	195	7/19/65	4	Portland State	Medford, Ore.	PB(Phx)-'91#	11/0*
74	Epps, Tory	NT	6-0	280	5/28/67	2	Memphis State	Uniontown, Pa.	D8-'90	16/15
79	Fralic, Bill	G	6-5	280	10/31/62	7	Pittsburgh	Penn Hills, Pa.	D1-'85	16/16
17	Fulhage, Scott	P	5-10	193	11/17/61	5	Kansas State	Beloit, Kan.	FA-'89	16/0
76	Gann, Mike	DE	6-5	270	10/19/63	7	Notre Dame	Lakewood, Colo.	D2-'85	16/15
99	†Green, Tim	DE	6-2	245	12/16/63	6	Syracuse	Liverpool, N.Y.	D1b-'86	16/16
81	Haynes, Michael	WR	6-0	180	12/24/65	4	Northern Arizona	New Orleans, La.	D7-'88	13/10
71	Hinton, Chris	T	6-4	300	7/31/61	9	Northwestern	Chicago, Ill.	T(Ind)-'90	15/12
69	Hoover, Houston	G	6-2	290	2/6/65	4	Jackson State	Yazoo City, Miss.	D6-'88	16/12
68	Hunter, John	T	6-8	296	8/16/65	3	Brigham Young	Northbend, Ore.	FA-'89	15/3
43	Johnson, Tracy	RB	6-0	230	3/13/66	3	Clemson	Kannapolis, N.C.	PB(Hou)-'90#	16/5
38	Jones, Keith	RB	6-1	210	3/20/66	3	Illinois	Rock Hill, Mo.	D3-'89	15/10
40	Jordan, Brian	S	5-11	202	3/29/67	3	Richmond	Baltimore, Md.	FA-'89	16/15
3	Karlis, Rich	K	6-0	180	5/23/59	10	Cincinnati	Salem, Ohio	FA-'91	6/0*
78	Kenn, Mike	T	6-7	277	2/9/56	14	Michigan	Evanston, Ill.	D1-'78	16/16
88	Le Bel, Harper	TE	6-4	245	7/14/63	3	Colorado State	Sherman Oaks, Calif.	PB(Phil)-'91#	16/0*
54	Lyles, Robert	LB	6-1	230	3/21/61	8	Texas Christian	Sugarland, Tex.	FA-'90	11/11
22	t-McKyer, Tim	CB	6-0	174	9/5/63	6	Texas-Arlington	Port Arthur, Tex.	T(Mia)-'91	16/16*
12	Miller, Chris	QB	6-2	200	8/9/65	5	Oregon	Eugene, Ore.	D1-'87	12/12
97	Phillips, Jason	WR	5-7	168	10/11/68	3	Houston	Houston, Tex.	PB(Det)-'91#	13/2*
24	Pringle, Mike	RB	5-8	186	10/1/67	2	Cal State-Fullerton	Los Angeles, Calif.	D6-'90	3/0
59	Rade, John	LB	6-1	240	8/31/60	9	Boise State	Sierra Vista, Ariz.	D8-'83	16/15
95	Reid, Michael	LB	6-2	235	6/25/64	5	Wisconsin	Albany, Ga.	D7-'87	6/4
14	Renfroe, Gilbert	QB	6-1	195	2/18/63	2	Tennessee State	Streamwood, Ill.	FA-'90	0*
80	Rison, Andre	WR	6-0	191	3/18/67	3	Michigan State	Flint, Mich.	T(Ind)-'90	16/15
92	Roland, Benji	NT-DE	6-3	260	4/4/67	2	Auburn	Eastman, Ga.	PB(TB)-'91#	3/1*
30	†Rozier, Mike	RB	5-10	213	3/1/61	7	Nebraska	Camden, N.J.	W(Hou)-'90	13/5
55	Ruether, Mike	C	6-4	275	9/20/62	6	Texas	Denver, Colo.	FA-'90	16/0
21	Sanders, Deion	CB	6-0	187	8/8/67	3	Florida State	Ft. Myers, Fla.	D1a-'89	16/16
61	Scully, John	G	6-6	270	8/2/58	10	Notre Dame	Huntington, N.Y.	D4-'81	10/5
37	Shelley, Elbert	S	5-11	180	12/24/64	5	Arkansas State	Trumann, Ark.	D11-'87	12/0
89	†Thomas, George	WR	5-9	169	7/11/64	3	Nevada-Las Vegas	Riverside, Calif.	D6-'88	13/2
52	Tippins, Ken	LB	6-1	230	7/22/66	3	Middle Tennessee State	Adel, Ga.	FA-'90	16/2
58	†Tuggle, Jessie	LB	5-11	230	2/14/65	5	Valdosta State	Griffin, Ga.	FA-'87	16/14
87	Wilkins, Gary	TE	6-2	235	11/23/63	6	Georgia Tech	West Palm Beach, Fla.	FA-'90	16/13
94	Worthen, Naz	WR	5-8	177	3/27/66	3	North Carolina State	Jacksonville, Fla.	PB(KC)-'91#	9/0*

* Brinkley played 6 games with Dallas in '90; Carey played 3 games with Buffalo; Donaldson played 16 games with Kansas City; Eaton played 11 games with Phoenix; Karlis played 6 games with Detroit; Le Bel played 16 games with Philadelphia; McKyer played 16 games with Miami; Phillips played 13 games with Detroit; Renfroe active for 2 games, but did not play; Roland played 3 games with Tampa Bay; Worthen played 9 games with Kansas City.

† Option playout; subject to developments.

\# Plan B unconditional free agent.

t- Falcons traded for McKyer (Miami).

Players lost through Plan B (10): CB Eric Bergeson (Hou; 13 games in '90), K Greg Davis (Phx; 16), CB Charles Dimry (Den; 16), LB Bobby Houston (NYJ; did not play in '90), QB Hugh Millen (NE; 3), WR James Milling (NYG; 13), CB Roland Mitchell (GB; 13), TE Troy Sadowski (KC; 13), RB John Settle (Wash; 6), LB Galand Thaxton (SD; 0).

Also played with Falcons in '90—WR Stacey Bailey (3 games), QB Scott Campbell (7), LB Marcus Cotton (1), CB William Evers (2), S Tim Gordon (5), RB Gene Lang (3), CB Rickey Royal (1).

COACHING STAFF

Head Coach, Jerry Glanville

Pro Career: Named Atlanta's head coach on January 14, 1990, after serving as Houston's head coach since the last two games of the 1985 season. Guided Oilers to three consecutive playoff berths (1987-89), posting a 28-19 mark in the process. Under his direction, Houston was one of only four NFL teams to make the playoffs during those years. The 48-year-old Glanville took over a team that had suffered five consecutive losing seasons and turned the club into winners in his second season at the helm. As an assistant coach, he was part of three playoff teams and one division title winner in Atlanta. He helped the 1977 team establish the modern-day record for fewest points allowed in a season (129 over 14 games) with his attacking "Gritz Blitz" defense. Career record: 40-46.

Background: Attended Montana State in 1960 before transferring to Northern Michigan, where he played linebacker from 1961-63. He coached in the Ohio high school system from 1964-66 before accepting an assistant coaching post at Western Kentucky in 1967. From 1968-73, he was an assistant at Georgia Tech, helping the Yellow Jackets to three bowl games.

Personal: Born October 14, 1941, in Detroit, Mich. Jerry and his wife, Brenda, live in Roswell, Ga., with their son, Justin.

Assistant Coaches

Bobby April, Jr., special teams, tight ends; born April 15, 1953, New Orleans, La., lives in Atlanta. Linebacker Nicholls State 1972-75. No pro playing experience. College coach: Tulane 1979, Arizona 1980-86, Southern California 1987-90. Pro coach: Joined Falcons in 1991.

Jimmy Carr, secondary; born March 25, 1933, Kayford, W. Va., lives in Atlanta. Running back-defensive back-linebacker Morris Harvey (now Univ. of Charleston, W. Va.) 1951-54. Pro running back-defensive back-linebacker Chicago Cardinals 1955-57, Montreal Alouettes (CFL) 1958, Philadelphia Eagles 1959-63, Washington Redskins 1964-65. Pro coach: Minnesota Vikings 1966-68, 1979-81, Chicago Bears 1969, 1973-74, Philadelphia Eagles 1970-72, Detroit Lions 1975-76, Buffalo Bills 1977, San Francisco 49ers 1978, Denver Gold (USFL) 1983-84, New England Patriots 1985-89, joined Falcons in 1990.

June Jones, assistant head coach-offense; born February 19, 1953, Portland, Ore., lives in Atlanta. Quarterback, Hawaii 1973-74, Portland State 1975-76. Pro quarterback Atlanta Falcons 1977-81, Toronto Argonauts (CFL) 1982. College coach: Hawaii 1983. Pro coach: Toronto Argonauts (CFL) 1982, Houston Gamblers (USFL) 1984, Denver Gold (USFL) 1985, Houston Oilers 1987-88, Detroit Lions 1989-90, joined Falcons in 1991.

Tim Jorgensen, strength and conditioning; born April 21, 1955, St. Louis, Mo., lives in Snellville, Ga. Guard Southwest Missouri State 1974-76. No pro playing experience. College coach: Southwest Missouri State 1977-78, Alabama 1979, Louisiana State 1980-83. Pro coach: Philadelphia Eagles 1984-86, joined Falcons in 1987.

Bill Kollar, defensive line; born November 12, 1952, Warren, Ohio, lives in Atlanta. Defensive end Montana State 1971-74. Pro defensive end Cincinnati Bengals 1974-76, Tampa Bay Buccaneers 1977-81. College coach: Illinois 1985-87, Purdue 1988-89. Pro coach: Tampa Bay Buccaneers 1984, joined Falcons in 1990.

Jimmy Robinson, wide receivers; born January 3, 1953, Atlanta, lives in Atlanta. Wide receiver Georgia Tech 1972-74. Pro wide receiver Atlanta Falcons 1975, New York Giants 1976-79, San Francisco 49ers 1980, Denver Broncos 1981. College coach: Georgia Tech 1986-89. Pro coach: Memphis Showboats (USFL) 1984-85, joined Falcons in 1990.

Atlanta Falcons 1991 First-Year Roster

Name	Pos.	Ht.	Wt.	Birth-date	College	Hometown	How Acq.
Austin, Randy	TE	6-2	245	12/14/67	UCLA	Canyon Country, Calif.	D10b
Bartlewski, Rich (1)	TE	6-5	255	8/15/67	Fresno State	Chowchilla, Calif.	FA
Borgognone, Dirk (1)	K	6-2	220	1/9/68	Pacific	Reno, Nev.	FA
Chaffey, Pat (1)	RB	6-1	218	4/19/67	Oregon State	McMinnville, Ore.	FA
Christian, Bob	RB	5-10	215	11/4/68	Northwestern	Florissant, Mo.	D12
Conley, Leonard	RB	5-7	165	10/18/68	Miami	Tarpon Springs, Fla.	FA
Evers, William (1)	CB	5-10	175	9/24/68	Florida A&M	Cairo, Ga.	FA
Favre, Brett	QB	6-2	220	10/10/69	Southern Mississippi	Kiln, Miss.	D2
Fishback, Joe (1)	S	5-11	198	11/29/67	Carson-Newman	Knoxville, Tenn.	FA
Freeman, Corien	LB	6-3	221	8/16/68	Florida State	Jacksonville, Fla.	FA
Gardner, Moe	NT	6-2	258	8/10/68	Illinois	Indianapolis, Ind.	D4
Giles, Oscar	DE	6-2	246	9/27/68	Texas	Palacios, Tex.	FA
Goode, James	LB	6-2	246	1/21/68	Oklahoma	Houston, Tex.	D5
Jackson, Jacque (1)	LB	6-2	228	12/11/67	Jackson State	Varnado, La.	FA
Jackson, Pat (1)	WR	5-8	165	8/12/68	Stephen F. Austin	Dallas, Tex.	FA
Koonce, George	LB	6-1	237	10/15/68	East Carolina	New Bern, N.C.	FA
Logan, Ernie	DE	6-3	271	5/18/68	East Carolina	Fayetteville, N.C.	D9
Lucas, Pete	T	6-3	320	3/15/66	Wis.-Stevens Point	Fort Atkinson, Wis.	D10b
McKenzie, Brian	LB	6-3	230	8/22/68	Georgetown, Ky.	Hopkinsville, Ky.	FA
Miles, Eddie (1)	LB	6-1	233	9/13/68	Minnesota	Miami, Fla.	FA
Miller, Karl	WR	5-10	183	1/24/69	Georgia Southern	College Park, Ga.	FA
Mitchell, Brian	CB	5-9	164	12/13/68	Brigham Young	Waco, Tex.	D7a
Pegram, Erric	RB	5-9	188	1/7/69	North Texas State	Dallas, Tex.	D6
Pickens, Bruce	CB	5-11	190	5/9/68	Nebraska	Kansas City, Mo.	D1
Pritchard, Mike	WR	5-11	180	10/25/69	Colorado	Las Vegas, Nev.	D1b
Pritchett, Wes (1)	LB	6-4	234	7/7/67	Notre Dame	Atlanta, Ga.	FA
Redding, Reggie (1)	T	6-3	281	9/22/68	Cal State-Fullerton	Cincinnati, Ohio	D5-'90
Rhodes, Mike (1)	QB	6-7	230	1/22/66	Georgia Tech	Smyrna, Ga.	FA
Sims, Joe	DT-DE	6-3	294	3/1/69	Nebraska	Sudbury, Mass.	D11
Truitt, Leroy	T	6-3	308	5/23/69	Houston	LaMarque, Tex.	FA
Tucker, Mark	G	6-2	279	4/29/68	Southern California	Los Angeles, Calif.	D7b
White, Reggie	G	6-4	280	12/27/67	William & Mary	Bradenton, Fla.	FA
Williams, Mike (1)	WR	5-10	177	10/9/66	Northeastern	Katonah, N.Y.	FA

The term NFL Rookie is defined as a player who is in his first season of professional football and has not been on the roster of another professional football team for any regular-season or postseason games. A Rookie is designated by an "R" on NFL rosters. Players who have been active in another professional football league or players who have NFL experience, including either preseason training camp or being on an active roster for fewer than three regular-season or postseason games, are termed NFL First-Year Players. An NFL First-Year Player is designated by a "1" on NFL rosters. Thereafter, a player on an NFL active roster for at least three regular-season or postseason games is credited with an additional year of NFL playing experience.

NOTES

Keith Rowen, offensive line; born September 2, 1952, New York, N.Y., lives in Atlanta. Offensive tackle Stanford 1972-74. No pro playing experience. College coach: Stanford 1975-76, Long Beach State 1977-78, Arizona 1979-82. Pro coach: Boston/New Orleans Breakers (USFL) 1983-84, Cleveland Browns 1984, Indianapolis Colts 1985-88, New England Patriots 1989, joined Falcons in 1990.

Doug Shively, assistant head coach-defense; born March 18, 1938, Lexington, Ky., lives in Atlanta. End Kentucky 1955-58. No pro playing experience. College coach: Virginia Tech 1960-66, Kentucky 1967-70, Clemson 1971-72, North Carolina 1973. Pro coach: New Orleans Saints 1974-76, Atlanta Falcons 1977-82, Arizona Wranglers (USFL) 1983 (head coach), San Diego Chargers 1984, Tampa Bay Buccaneers 1985, Houston Oilers 1986-89, rejoined Falcons in 1990.

Ollie Wilson, running backs; born March 31, 1951, Worcester, Mass., lives in Atlanta. Wide receiver Springfield 1971-73. No pro playing experience. College coach: Springfield 1975, Northeastern 1976-82, California 1983-90. Pro coach: Joined Falcons in 1991.

National Football Conference Central Division

Team Colors: Navy Blue, Orange, and White

Corporate Headquarters:
Halas Hall, 250 North Washington
Lake Forest, Illinois 60045
Telephone: (708) 295-6600

Club Officials

Chairman of the Board: Edward W. McCaskey
President and CEO: Michael B. McCaskey
Secretary: Virginia H. McCaskey
Vice President-Player Personnel: Bill Tobin
Director of Administration: Tim LeFevour
Director of Community Involvement: Pat McCaskey
Director of Finance: Ted Phillips
Director of Marketing and Communications: Ken Valdiserri
Director of Public Relations: Bryan Harlan
Asst. Director of Public Relations: John Bostrom
Ticket Manager: Gary Christenson
Computer Systems: Greg Gershuny
Video Director: Mitch Friedman
Trainer: Fred Caito
Assistant Trainer: Brian McCaskey
Strength Coordinator: Clyde Emrich
Equipment Manager: Gary Haeger
Assistant Equipment Manager: Tony Medlin
Scouts: Jim Parmer, Rod Graves, Ken Geiger, Jeff Shiver, Charlie MacKey

Stadium: Soldier Field • **Capacity:** 66,946
425 McFetridge Place
Chicago, Illinois 60605

Playing Surface: Grass

Training Camp: Wisconsin-Platteville
Platteville, Wisconsin 53818

1991 Schedule

Preseason

July 26	at Miami	8:00
Aug. 3	vs. San Francisco at Berlin	7:30*
Aug. 11	**Phoenix**	7:00
Aug. 17	at Los Angeles Raiders	1:00
Aug. 24	**Buffalo**	8:00

*P.M. Eastern Time

Regular Season

Sept. 1	**Minnesota**	3:00
Sept. 8	at Tampa Bay	1:00
Sept. 15	**New York Giants**	12:00
Sept. 23	**New York Jets** (Monday)	8:00
Sept. 29	at Buffalo	1:00
Oct. 6	**Washington**	12:00
Oct. 13	**Open Date**	
Oct. 17	at Green Bay (Thursday)	6:30
Oct. 27	at New Orleans	12:00
Nov. 3	**Detroit**	12:00
Nov. 11	at Minnesota (Monday)	8:00
Nov. 17	at Indianapolis	1:00
Nov. 24	**Miami**	12:00
Nov. 28	at Detroit (Thanksgiving)	12:30
Dec. 8	**Green Bay**	12:00
Dec. 14	**Tampa Bay** (Saturday)	11:30
Dec. 23	at San Francisco (Monday)	6:00

Bears Coaching History

Decatur Staleys 1920
Chicago Staleys 1921
(563-358-42)

1920-29	George Halas	84-31-19
1930-32	Ralph Jones	24-10-7
1933-42	George Halas*	89-24-4
1942-45	Hunk Anderson-Luke Johnsos**	18-11-2
1946-55	George Halas	76-43-2
1956-57	John (Paddy) Driscoll	14-10-1
1958-67	George Halas	76-53-6
1968-71	Jim Dooley	20-36-0
1972-74	Abe Gibron	11-30-1
1975-77	Jack Pardee	20-23-0
1978-81	Neill Armstrong	30-35-0
1982-90	Mike Ditka	96-51-0

*Retired after six games to enter U.S. Navy
**Co-coaches

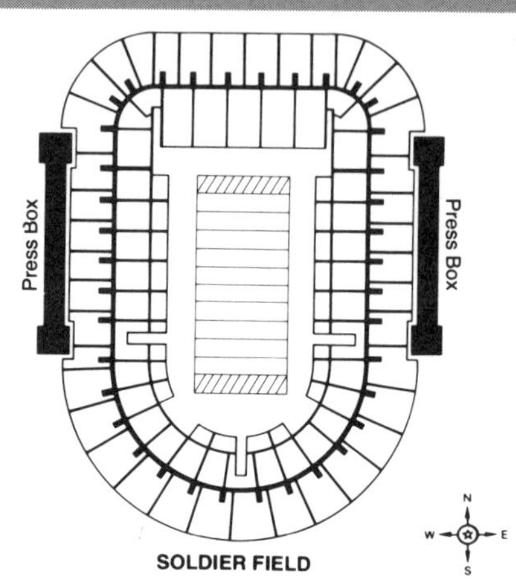

SOLDIER FIELD

Record Holders

Individual Records—Career

Category	Name	Performance
Rushing (Yds.)	Walter Payton, 1975-1987	*16,726
Passing (Yds.)	Sid Luckman, 1939-1950	14,686
Passing (TDs)	Sid Luckman, 1939-1950	137
Receiving (No.)	Walter Payton, 1975-1987	492
Receiving (Yds.)	Johnny Morris, 1958-1967	5,059
Interceptions	Gary Fencik, 1976-1987	38
Punting (Avg.)	George Gulyanics, 1947-1952	44.5
Punt Return (Avg.)	Ray (Scooter) McLean, 1940-47	14.8
Kickoff Return (Avg.)	Gale Sayers, 1965-1971	30.6
Field Goals	Kevin Butler, 1985-1990	134
Touchdowns (Tot.)	Walter Payton, 1975-1987	125
Points	Walter Payton, 1975-1987	750

Individual Records—Single Season

Category	Name	Performance
Rushing (Yds.)	Walter Payton, 1977	1,852
Passing (Yds.)	Bill Wade, 1962	3,172
Passing (TDs)	Sid Luckman, 1943	28
Receiving (No.)	Johnny Morris, 1964	93
Receiving (Yds.)	Johnny Morris, 1964	1,200
Interceptions	Mark Carrier, 1990	10
Punting (Avg.)	Bobby Joe Green, 1963	46.5
Punt Return (Avg.)	Harry Clark, 1943	15.8
Kickoff Return (Avg.)	Gale Sayers, 1967	37.7
Field Goals	Kevin Butler, 1985	31
Touchdowns (Tot.)	Gale Sayers, 1965	**22
Points	Kevin Butler, 1985	**144

Individual Records—Single Game

Category	Name	Performance
Rushing (Yds.)	Walter Payton, 11-20-77	*275
Passing (Yds.)	Johnny Lujack, 12-11-49	468
Passing (TDs)	Sid Luckman, 11-14-43	*7
Receiving (No.)	Jim Keane, 10-23-49	14
Receiving (Yds.)	Harlon Hill, 10-31-54	214
Interceptions	Many times	3
	Last time by Mark Carrier, 12-9-90	
Field Goals	Roger LeClerc, 12-3-61	5
	Mac Percival, 10-20-68	5
Touchdowns (Tot.)	Gale Sayers, 12-12-65	*6
Points	Gale Sayers, 12-12-65	36

*NFL Record
**NFL Rookie Record

1990 Team Record

Preseason (3-1)

Date	Result		Opponents
8/11	W	13- 0	Miami
8/18	W	10- 6	at Phoenix
8/24	W	17- 9	L.A. Raiders
8/30	L	3-20	vs. Buffalo at Columbia, S.C.
		78-42	

Regular Season (11-5)

Date	Result		Opponents	Att.
9/9	W	17- 0	Seattle	64,400
9/16	W	31-13	at Green Bay	58,938
9/23	W	19-16	Minnesota	65,420
9/30	L	10-24	at L.A. Raiders	80,156
10/7	W	27-13	Green Bay	59,929
10/14	W	38- 9	L.A. Rams	59,383
10/28	W	31-21	at Phoenix	71,233
11/4	W	26- 6	at Tampa Bay	68,555
11/11	W	30-24	Atlanta	62,855
11/18	W	16-13	at Denver (OT)	75,013
11/25	L	13-41	at Minnesota	58,866
12/2	W	23-17	Detroit (OT)	62,313
12/9	L	9-10	at Washington	53,920
12/16	L	21-38	at Detroit	67,759
12/23	W	27-14	Tampa Bay	46,456
12/29	L	10-21	Kansas City	60,262

(OT) Overtime

Postseason (1-1)

Date	Result		Opponent	Att.
1/6	W	16- 6	New Orleans	60,767
1/13	L	3-31	at N.Y. Giants	77,025

Score by Periods

Bears	54	156	70	59	9	—	348
Opponents	59	80	53	88	0	—	280

Attendance

Home 481,018 Away 534,440 Total 1,015,458
Single-game home record, 66,475 (9-17-89)
Single-season home record, 495,484 (1986)

1990 Team Statistics

	Bears	Opp.
Total First Downs	295	256
Rushing	142	102
Passing	134	136
Penalty	19	18
Third Down: Made/Att.	81/221	65/188
Third Down: Pct.	36.7	34.6
Fourth Down: Made/Att.	5/13	6/11
Fourth Down: Pct.	38.5	54.5
Total Net Yards	4980	4492
Avg. Per Game	311.3	280.8
Total Plays	1024	927
Avg. Per Play	4.9	4.8
Net Yards Rushing	2436	1572
Avg. Per Game	152.3	98.3
Total Rushes	551	391
Net Yards Passing	2544	2920
Avg. Per Game	159.0	182.5
Sacked/Yards Lost	43/283	41/300
Gross Yards	2827	3220
Att./Completions	430/229	495/258
Completion Pct.	53.3	52.1
Had Intercepted	12	31
Punts/Avg.	78/39.4	74/37.9
Net Punting Avg.	33.5	31.7
Penalties/Yards Lost	75/615	84/676
Fumbles/Ball Lost	29/14	38/14
Touchdowns	39	31
Rushing	22	10
Passing	14	19
Returns	3	2
Avg. Time of Possession	33:06	26:54

1990 Individual Statistics

Scoring	TD R	TD P	TD Rt	PAT	FG	Saf	TP
Butler	0	0	0	36/37	26/37	0	114
Anderson	10	3	0	0/0	0/0	0	78
Muster	6	0	0	0/0	0/0	0	36
Harbaugh	4	0	0	0/0	0/0	0	24
Davis	0	3	0	0/0	0/0	0	18
Morris	0	3	0	0/0	0/0	0	18
Gentry	0	2	0	0/0	0/0	0	12
Tomczak	2	0	0	0/0	0/0	0	12
Bailey	0	0	1	0/0	0/0	0	6
Boso	0	1	0	0/0	0/0	0	6
Dent	0	0	1	0/0	0/0	0	6
Green	0	1	0	0/0	0/0	0	6
Jackson	0	0	1	0/0	0/0	0	6
Thornton	0	1	0	0/0	0/0	0	6
Bears	22	14	3	36/38	26/37	0	348
Opponents	10	19	2	28/31	22/28	0	280

Passing	Att.	Comp.	Yds.	Pct.	TD	Int.	Tkld.	Rate
Harbaugh	312	180	2178	57.7	10	6	31/206	81.9
Tomczak	104	39	521	37.5	3	5	11/70	43.8
Willis	13	9	106	69.2	1	1	1/7	87.3
Bailey	1	1	22	100.0	0	0	0/0	118.8
Bears	430	229	2827	53.3	14	12	43/283	73.1
Opponents	495	258	3220	52.1	19	31	41/300	59.3

Rushing	Att.	Yds.	Avg.	LG	TD
Anderson	260	1078	4.1	52	10
Muster	141	664	4.7	28	6
Harbaugh	51	321	6.3	17	4
Green	27	126	4.7	14	0
Bailey	26	86	3.3	9	0
Rouse	16	56	3.5	10	0
Gentry	11	43	3.9	11	0
Tomczak	12	41	3.4	14	2
Morris	2	26	13.0	16	0
L. Tate	3	5	1.7	4	0
Perry	1	−1	−1.0	−1	0
Buford	1	−9	−9.0	−9	0
Bears	551	2436	4.4	52	22
Opponents	391	1572	4.0	25	10

Receiving	No.	Yds.	Avg.	LG	TD
Muster	47	452	9.6	48	0
Anderson	42	484	11.5	50t	3
Davis	39	572	14.7	51	3
Morris	31	437	14.1	67t	3
Gentry	23	320	13.9	80t	2
Thornton	19	254	13.4	32	1
Boso	11	135	12.3	25	1
Kozlowski	7	83	11.9	32	0
Green	4	26	6.5	10t	1
Waddle	2	32	16.0	23	0
Smith	2	20	10.0	12	0
Coley	1	7	7.0	7	0
Tomczak	1	5	5.0	5	0
Bears	229	2827	12.3	80t	14
Opponents	258	3220	12.5	76t	19

Interceptions	No.	Yds.	Avg.	LG	TD
Carrier	10	39	3.9	14	0
Stinson	6	66	11.0	30	0
Dent	3	21	7.0	15	0
Woolford	3	18	6.0	9	0
Paul	2	49	24.5	26	0
Rivera	2	13	6.5	13	0
Morrissey	2	12	6.0	12	0
Gayle	2	5	2.5	5	0
Jackson	1	45	45.0	45t	1
Bears	31	268	8.6	45t	1
Opponents	12	164	13.7	46	0

Punting	No.	Yds.	Avg.	In 20	LG
Buford	76	3073	40.4	22	59
Bears	78	3073	39.4	22	59
Opponents	74	2804	37.9	13	56

Punt Returns	No.	FC	Yds.	Avg.	LG	TD
Bailey	36	13	399	11.1	95t	1
Bears	36	13	399	11.1	95t	1
Opponents	39	6	322	8.3	30	0

Kickoff Returns	No.	Yds.	Avg.	LG	TD
Bailey	23	363	15.8	30	0
Gentry	18	388	21.6	59	0
Green	7	112	16.0	20	0
Rouse	3	17	5.7	10	0
Roper	1	0	0.0	0	0
Ryan	1	−1	−1.0	−1	0
L. Tate	1	0	0.0	0	0
Bears	54	879	16.3	59	0
Opponents	73	1494	20.5	64	0

Sacks	No.
Dent	12.0
Armstrong	10.0
McMichael	4.0
Perry	4.0
Cox	3.0
Jones	2.0
Woolford	2.0
Gayle	1.0
Pruitt	1.0
Roper	1.0
Singletary	1.0
Bears	41.0
Opponents	43.0

1991 Draft Choices

Round	Name	Pos.	College
1.	Stan Thomas	T	Texas
2.	Chris Zorich	DT	Notre Dame
3.	Chris Gardocki	P-K	Clemson
4.	Joe Johnson	DB	North Carolina St.
5.	Anthony Morgan	WR	Tennessee
6.	Darren Lewis	RB	Texas A&M
7.	Paul Justin	QB	Arizona State
8.	Larry Horton	DB	Texas A&M
9.	Mike Stonebreaker	LB	Notre Dame
10.	Tom Backes	DE	Oklahoma
11.	Stacy Long	G	Clemson
12.	John Cook	DT	Washington

Chicago Bears 1991 Veteran Roster

No.	Name	Pos.	Ht.	Wt.	Birth-date	NFL Exp.	College	Hometown	How Acq.	'90 Games/ Starts
35	Anderson, Neal	RB	5-11	210	8/14/64	6	Florida	Graceville, Fla.	D1-'86	15/14
93	Armstrong, Trace	DE	6-4	259	10/5/65	3	Florida	Birmingham, Ala.	D1b-'89	16/16
22	Bailey, Johnny	RB	5-8	180	3/17/67	2	Texas A&I	Houston, Tex.	D9-'90	16/1
79	Becker, Kurt	G	6-5	269	12/22/58	10	Michigan	Aurora, Ill.	PB(Rams)-'90#	10/0
62	Bortz, Mark	G	6-6	272	2/12/61	9	Iowa	Pardeeville, Wis.	D8-'83	16/16
86	Boso, Cap	TE	6-4	240	9/10/63	5	Illinois	Kansas City, Mo.	FA-'87	13/1
8	Buford, Maury	P	6-0	198	2/18/60	10	Texas Tech	Mount Pleasant, Tex.	W(GB)-'89	16/0
6	†Butler, Kevin	K	6-1	190	7/24/62	7	Georgia	Atlanta, Ga.	D4-'84	16/0
20	Carrier, Mark	S	6-1	180	4/28/68	2	Southern California	Long Beach, Calif.	D1-'90	16/16
89	Coley, James	TE	6-3	270	4/13/67	2	Clemson	Jacksonville, Fla.	FA-'89	16/0
74	Covert, Jim	T	6-4	278	3/22/60	9	Pittsburgh	Conway, Pa.	D1-'83	15/15
54	Cox, Ron	LB	6-2	242	2/27/68	2	Fresno State	Fresno, Calif.	D2b-'90	13/0
82	Davis, Wendell	WR	5-11	188	1/3/66	4	Louisiana State	Shreveport, La.	D1-'88	14/12
95	Dent, Richard	DE	6-5	268	12/13/60	9	Tennessee State	Atlanta, Ga.	D8-'83	16/16
37	Douglass, Maurice	CB	5-11	200	2/12/64	6	Kentucky	Dayton, Ohio	D8-'86	11/0
67	Fontenot, Jerry	G	6-3	272	11/21/66	3	Texas A&M	Lafayette, La.	D3-'89	16/2
23	Gayle, Shaun	S	5-11	194	3/8/62	8	Ohio State	Hampton, Va.	D10-'84	16/16
29	Gentry, Dennis	WR	5-8	180	2/10/59	10	Baylor	Lubbock, Tex.	D4-'82	14/5
31	Green, Mark	RB	5-11	195	3/22/67	3	Notre Dame	Riverside, Calif.	D5a-'89	12/1
4	†Harbaugh, Jim	QB	6-3	220	12/23/64	5	Michigan	Kalamazoo, Mich.	D1-'87	14/14
63	Hilgenberg, Jay	C	6-3	260	3/21/59	11	Iowa	Iowa City, Iowa	FA-'81	14/14
53	Jones, Dante	LB	6-1	236	3/23/65	4	Oklahoma	Dallas, Tex.	D2-'88	2/0
88	Kozlowski, Glen	WR	6-1	205	12/31/62	5	Brigham Young	Honolulu, Hawaii	D11-'86	12/0
70	t-Kumerow, Eric	DE-DT	6-7	260	4/17/65	4	Ohio State	Oak Park, Ill.	T(Mia)-'91	10/0
26	Mangum, John	CB	5-10	173	3/16/67	2	Alabama	Magee, Miss.	FA-'90	16/7
76	McMichael, Steve	DT	6-2	268	10/17/57	12	Texas	Houston, Tex.	FA-'81	15/15
84	†Morris, Ron	WR	6-1	195	11/4/64	5	Southern Methodist	Cooper, Tex.	D2-'87	16/16
51	Morrissey, Jim	LB	6-3	227	12/24/62	7	Michigan State	Flint, Mich.	D11-'85	16/15
25	†Muster, Brad	RB	6-3	231	4/11/65	4	Stanford	Marin, Calif.	D1-'88	16/15
36	Paul, Markus	S	6-2	199	4/1/66	3	Syracuse	Kissimmee, Fla.	D4-'89	16/0
72	Perry, William	DT	6-2	325	12/16/62	7	Clemson	Aiken, S.C.	D1-'85	16/16
52	Pruitt, Mickey	LB	6-1	215	1/10/65	4	Colorado	Chicago, Ill.	FA-'88	16/2
59	†Rivera, Ron	LB	6-3	240	1/7/62	8	California	Monterey, Calif.	D2-'84	14/14
55	Roper, John	LB	6-1	228	10/4/65	3	Texas A&M	Houston, Tex.	D2a-'89	14/0
30	Rouse, James	RB	6-0	220	12/18/66	2	Arkansas	Little Rock, Ark.	D8b-'90	16/0
96	Ryan, Tim	DE	6-4	268	9/8/67	2	Southern California	Memphis, Tenn.	D3a-'90	15/0
50	Singletary, Mike	LB	6-0	230	10/9/58	11	Baylor	Houston, Tex.	D2-'81	16/16
85	Smith, Quintin	WR	5-10	172	8/17/68	2	Kansas	Houston, Tex.	FA-'90	4/0
32	†Stinson, Lemuel	CB	5-9	159	5/10/66	4	Texas Tech	Houston, Tex.	D6-'88	10/10
49	Tate, David	S	6-0	177	11/22/64	4	Colorado	Denver, Colo.	D8-'88	16/1
57	†Thayer, Tom	G	6-4	270	8/16/61	7	Notre Dame	Joliet, Ill.	D4-'83	16/16
80	†Thornton, James	TE	6-2	242	2/8/65	4	Cal State-Fullerton	Santa Rosa, Calif.	D4-'88	16/16
78	†Van Horne, Keith	T	6-6	283	11/6/57	11	Southern California	Mt. Lebanon, Pa.	D1-'81	16/16
87	Waddle, Tom	WR	6-0	181	2/20/67	3	Boston College	Cincinnati, Ohio	FA-'89	5/0
10	Willis, Peter Tom	QB	6-2	188	1/4/67	2	Florida State	Morris, Ala.	D3b-'90	3/0
73	Wojciechowski, John	G	6-4	270	7/30/63	5	Michigan State	Detroit, Mich.	FA-'87	13/1
21	Woolford, Donnell	CB	5-9	187	1/6/66	3	Clemson	Fayetteville, N.C.	D1a-'89	13/13

† Option playout; subject to developments.

Plan B unconditional free agent.

Retired—Dan Hampton, 12-year defensive tackle-end, 14 games in '90.

t- Bears traded for Kumerow (Miami).

Traded—CB Vestee Jackson to Miami.

Players lost through Plan B (2): DT Terry Price (Mia; 2 games in '90), QB Mike Tomczak (GB; 16).

Also played with Bears in '90—CB Vestee Jackson (16 games in '90), RB Lars Tate (2).

COACHING STAFF

Head Coach, Mike Ditka

Pro Career: Became Bears' tenth head coach on January 20, 1982, after serving nine years as an offensive assistant with Dallas. Led Bears to first Super Bowl title following 15-1 1985 season. Bears shut out New York Giants and Los Angeles Rams in playoffs before routing New England 46-10 in Super Bowl XX. Rebounded from 6-10 season in 1989 and led Bears to 11-5 mark in 1990 which won NFC Central Division for sixth time in seven years. Under his leadership, the Bears have qualified for the postseason in six of his nine seasons and have advanced to the NFC Championship Game on three occasions. Ditka is a 29-year veteran of the NFL as both a player and coach. Had 12-year playing career as a tight end with Chicago (1961-66), Philadelphia (1967-68), and Dallas (1969-72). A first-round draft choice by Chicago in 1961, Ditka was NFL rookie of the year, all-NFL (1961-64), and played in five Pro Bowls (1962-66). He joined Cowboys coaching staff in 1973. In addition to working with Dallas special teams, Ditka coached Cowboys' receivers. During his NFL career, he has been in the playoffs 16 times and has been a member of five NFC champions and three NFL champions. He became the first tight end to be inducted into the Pro Football Hall of Fame in July, 1988. Career record: 96-51.

Background: Played at University of Pittsburgh from 1958-60 and was a unanimous All-America his senior year. A two-way performer, he played both tight end and linebacker. He also was one of the nation's leading punters with a 40-plus-yard average over three years.

Personal: Born October 18, 1939, Carnegie, Pa. Mike and his wife, Diana, live in Bannockburn, Ill., and have four children—Michael, Mark, Megan, and Matt.

Assistant Coaches

Steve Kazor, special teams/tight ends; born February 24, 1948, New Kensington, Pa., lives in Vernon Hills, Ill. Nose tackle Westminister College 1967-70. No pro playing experience. College coach: Emporia State 1973 (head coach), Texas-Arlington 1974, Colorado State 1975, Wyoming 1976, Texas 1977-78, Texas-El Paso 1979-80. Pro coach: Joined Bears in 1982.

Greg Landry, offensive coordinator; born December 18, 1946, Nashua, N.H., lives in Libertyville, Ill. Quarterback Massachusetts 1965-67. Pro quarterback Detroit Lions 1968-78, Baltimore Colts 1979-81, Chicago Blitz/Arizona Wranglers (USFL) 1983-84, Chicago Bears 1984. Pro coach: Cleveland Browns 1985, joined Bears in 1986.

Jim LaRue, research and quality control; born August 11, 1925, Clinton, Okla., lives in Libertyville, Ill. Halfback Carson-Newman 1943, Duke 1944-45, Maryland 1947-49. No pro playing experience. College coach: Maryland 1950, Kansas State 1951-54, Houston 1955-56, Southern Methodist 1957-58, Arizona 1959-66 (head coach), Utah 1967-73, Wake Forest 1974-75. Pro coach: Buffalo Bills 1976-77, joined Bears in 1978.

John Levra, defensive line; born October 2, 1937, Arma, Kan., lives in Libertyville, Ill. Guard-linebacker Pittsburg (Kan.) State 1963-65. No pro playing experience. College coach: Stephen F. Austin 1971-74, Kansas 1975-78, North Texas State 1979. Pro coach: British Columbia Lions (CFL) 1980, New Orleans Saints 1981-85, joined Bears in 1986.

David McGinnis, linebackers; born August 7, 1951, Independence, Kan., lives in Lake Forest, Ill. Defensive back Texas Christian 1970-72. No pro playing experience. College coach: Texas Christian 1973-74, 1982, Missouri 1975-77, Indiana State 1978-81, Kansas State 1983-85. Pro coach: Joined Bears in 1986.

Chicago Bears 1991 First-Year Roster

Name	Pos.	Ht.	Wt.	Birth-date	College	Hometown	How Acq.
Asman, Scott	TE	6-0	249	6/28/69	West Chester State	Philadelphia, Pa.	FA
Backes, Tom	DE	6-4	273	3/19/68	Oklahoma	El Paso, Tex.	D10
Beckton, Sean	WR	5-11	172	9/9/68	Central Florida	Daytona Beach, Fla.	FA
Booker, Richard	LB	6-1	236	5/21/68	Texas Christian	Clifton, Tex.	FA
Brantley, Peter	LB	6-4	235	10/27/68	Oregon	Detroit, Mich.	FA
Brown, Steve	WR	6-1	188	1/6/69	Wake Forest	Washington, D.C.	FA
Codrington, Nigel	WR	6-2	189	8/20/68	Rice	Trinadad, Tobago	FA
Cook, John	DT	6-4	269	5/27/68	Washington	Spokane, Wash.	D12
Cross, Tim	RB	6-2	239	8/29/68	Tennessee State	Clarksville, Tenn.	FA
Ferguson, Ron	CB	5-9	168	12/23/67	Texas Tech	Houston, Tex.	FA
Gardocki, Chris	P-K	6-1	194	2/7/70	Clemson	Stone Mountain, Ga.	D3
Giller, Tre	T	6-4	292	6/10/67	Southern Methodist	Cincinnati, Ohio	FA
Hardy, John	CB	5-10	166	6/11/68	California	Pasadena, Calif.	FA
Horton, Larry	CB	5-11	179	1/2/69	Texas A&M	Henderson, Tex.	D8
Ihnat, Eric	TE	6-3	239	8/18/68	Marshall	Columbus, Ohio	FA
Johnson, Joe	CB	5-8	186	10/6/67	North Carolina State	Hackensack, N.J.	D4
Johnson, Michael	WR	6-0	190	1/14/69	Cal State-Sacramento	Fairfield, Calif.	FA
Justin, Paul	QB	6-4	202	5/19/68	Arizona State	Schaumburg, Ill.	D7
Lance, Tim	S	6-0	202	1/22/69	Eastern Illinois	Peoria, Ill.	FA
Lewis, Darren	RB	5-10	219	11/7/68	Texas A&M	Henderson, Tex.	D6
Long, Stacy	G	6-1	294	9/30/67	Clemson	Griffin, Ga.	D11
Montgomery, Steve	RB	6-1	238	7/8/66	Michigan State	Cincinnati, Ohio	FA
Moore, Patrick	DE	6-2	262	5/16/68	Cal Poly-SLO	Gresham, Ore.	FA
Morgan, Anthony	WR	6-0	195	11/15/67	Tennessee	Cleveland, Ohio	D5
Parker, Quintin	S	6-0	195	1/23/68	Illinois	St. Louis, Mo.	FA
Reed, Chris	G	6-3	272	3/25/68	S.W. Missouri	St. Louis, Mo.	FA
Rowe, Charles	LB	6-1	220	3/8/68	Texas Tech	Columbus, Ga.	FA
Stonebreaker, Mike	LB	6-0	226	1/14/67	Notre Dame	Baltimore, Md.	D9
Thomas, Stan	T	6-5	302	10/28/68	Texas	El Centro, Calif.	D1
Wenckowski, Eric	C	6-2	265	7/21/68	Northern Illinois	Franklin, Pa.	FA
Wiley, John	S	6-0	190	8/6/69	Auburn	Tuskegee, Ala.	FA
Williams, James	DT	6-7	295	3/29/68	Cheyney State	Pittsburgh, Pa.	FA
Wright, Eric	WR	6-0	197	8/4/69	Stephen F. Austin	Pittsburgh, Pa.	FA
Zorich, Chris	DT	6-1	267	3/13/69	Notre Dame	Chicago, Ill.	D2

The term NFL Rookie is defined as a player who is in his first season of professional football and has not been on the roster of another professional football team for any regular-season or postseason games. A Rookie is designated by an "R" on NFL rosters. Players who have been active in another professional football league or players who have NFL experience, including either preseason training camp or being on an active roster for fewer than three regular-season or postseason games, are termed NFL First-Year Players. An NFL First-Year Player is designated by a "1" on NFL rosters. Thereafter, a player on an NFL active roster for at least three regular-season or postseason games is credited with an additional year of NFL playing experience.

NOTES

Vic Rapp, wide receivers; born December 23, 1935, Marionville, Mo., lives in Rochester, Mich. Running back Southwest Missouri State 1954-57. No pro playing experience. College coach: Arizona 1965-66, Missouri 1967-71. Pro coach: Edmonton Eskimos (CFL) 1972-76, British Columbia Lions (CFL) 1977-82 (head coach), Houston Oilers 1983, Los Angeles Rams 1984, Tampa Bay Buccaneers 1985-86, Detroit Lions 1987, joined Bears in 1989.

Johnny Roland, running backs; born May 21, 1943, Corpus Christi, Tex., lives in Vernon Hills, Ill. Running back Missouri 1963-65. Pro running back St. Louis Cardinals 1966-72, New York Giants 1973. College coach: Notre Dame 1975. Pro coach: Green Bay Packers 1974, Philadelphia Eagles 1976-78, joined Bears in 1983.

Dick Stanfel, offensive line; born July 20, 1927, San Francisco, Calif., lives in Libertyville, Ill. Guard San Francisco 1948-51. Pro guard Detroit Lions 1952-55, Washington Redskins 1956-58. College coach: Notre Dame 1959-62, California 1963. Pro coach: Philadelphia Eagles 1964-70, San Francisco 49ers 1971-75, New Orleans Saints 1976-80 (head coach, 4 games in 1980), joined Bears in 1981.

Vince Tobin, defensive coordinator; born September 29, 1943, in Burlington Junction, Mo., lives in Libertyville, Ill. Defensive back-running back Missouri 1961-64. No pro playing experience. College coach: Missouri 1967-76. Pro coach: British Columbia Lions (CFL) 1977-82, Philadelphia/Baltimore Stars (USFL) 1983-85, joined Bears in 1986.

Zaven Yaralian, defensive backs; born February 5, 1952, Syria, lives in Lake Forest, Ill. Defensive back Nebraska 1972-73. Pro defensive back Green Bay Packers 1974, Philadelphia Bell (WFL) 1975. College coach: Nebraska 1975, Washington State 1976-77, Missouri 1978-83, Florida 1984-87, Colorado 1988-89. Pro coach: Joined Bears in 1990.

National Football Conference Eastern Division

Team Colors: Royal Blue, Metallic Silver Blue, and White

Cowboys Center
One Cowboys Parkway
Irving, Texas 75063
Telephone: (214) 556-9900

Club Officials

Owner/President/General Manager: Jerry Jones
Director of Player Personnel: Bob Ackles
Director of College Scouting: Dick Mansperger
Treasurer: Jack Dixon
Director of Administrative Personnel: Steve Orsini
Public Relations Director: Rich Dalrymple
Football Facility Coordinator: Bruce Mays
Ticket Manager: Marcia Lavine
Trainers: Kevin O'Neill, Jim Maurer, Don Cochren
Equipment Managers: Buck Buchanan, Jerry Fowler
Video Directors: Robert Blackwell, Randy Tinsley
Cheerleaders Director: Leslie Haynes

Stadium: Texas Stadium • **Capacity:** 65,024
Irving, Texas 75062

Playing Surface: Texas Turf

Training Camp: St. Edward's University
Austin, Texas 78704

1991 Schedule

Preseason

Aug. 3	at Kansas City	8:00
Aug. 12	**Los Angeles Raiders**	7:00
Aug. 18	at Houston	7:00
Aug. 23	**Atlanta**	8:00

Regular Season

Sept. 1	at Cleveland	1:00
Sept. 9	**Washington** (Monday)	8:00
Sept. 15	**Philadelphia**	12:00
Sept. 22	at Phoenix	5:00
Sept. 29	**New York Giants**	12:00
Oct. 6	vs. Green Bay at Milwaukee	12:00
Oct. 13	**Cincinnati**	12:00
Oct. 20	**Open Date**	
Oct. 27	at Detroit	4:00
Nov. 3	**Phoenix**	12:00
Nov. 10	at Houston	12:00
Nov. 17	at New York Giants	4:00
Nov. 24	at Washington	1:00
Nov. 28	**Pittsburgh** (Thanksgiving)	3:00
Dec. 8	**New Orleans**	12:00
Dec. 15	at Philadelphia	1:00
Dec. 22	**Atlanta**	12:00

Cowboys Coaching History

(278-202-6)

1960-88	Tom Landry	270-178-6
1989-90	Jimmy Johnson	8-24-0

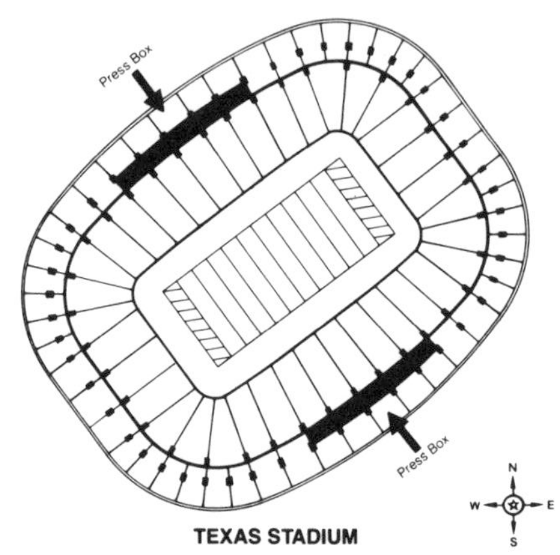

TEXAS STADIUM

Record Holders

Individual Records—Career

Category	Name	Performance
Rushing (Yds.)	Tony Dorsett, 1977-1987	12,036
Passing (Yds.)	Roger Staubach, 1969-1979	22,700
Passing (TDs)	Danny White, 1976-1988	155
Receiving (No.)	Drew Pearson, 1973-1983	489
Receiving (Yds.)	Tony Hill, 1977-1986	7,988
Interceptions	Mel Renfro, 1964-1977	52
Punting (Avg.)	Mike Saxon, 1985-1990	41.2
Punt Return (Avg.)	Bob Hayes, 1965-1974	11.1
Kickoff Return (Avg.)	Mel Renfro, 1964-1977	26.4
Field Goals	Rafael Septien, 1978-1986	162
Touchdowns (Tot.)	Tony Dorsett, 1977-1987	86
Points	Rafael Septien, 1978-1986	874

Individual Records—Single Season

Category	Name	Performance
Rushing (Yds.)	Tony Dorsett, 1981	1,646
Passing (Yds.)	Danny White, 1983	3,980
Passing (TDs)	Danny White, 1983	29
Receiving (No.)	Herschel Walker, 1985	76
Receiving (Yds.)	Bob Hayes, 1966	1,232
Interceptions	Everson Walls, 1981	11
Punting (Avg.)	Sam Baker, 1962	45.4
Punt Return (Avg.)	Bob Hayes, 1968	20.8
Kickoff Return (Avg.)	Mel Renfro, 1965	30.0
Field Goals	Rafael Septien, 1981	27
Touchdowns (Tot.)	Dan Reeves, 1966	16
Points	Rafael Septien, 1983	123

Individual Records—Single Game

Category	Name	Performance
Rushing (Yds.)	Tony Dorsett, 12-4-77	206
Passing (Yds.)	Don Meredith, 11-10-63	460
Passing (TDs)	Many times	5
	Last time by Danny White, 10-30-83	
Receiving (No.)	Lance Rentzel, 11-19-67	13
Receiving (Yds.)	Bob Hayes, 11-13-66	246
Interceptions	Herb Adderley, 9-26-71	3
	Lee Roy Jordan, 11-4-73	3
	Dennis Thurman, 12-13-81	3
Field Goals	Roger Ruzek, 12-21-87	5
Touchdowns (Tot.)	Many times	4
	Last time by Emmitt Smith, 11-18-90	
Points	Many times	24
	Last time by Emmitt Smith, 11-18-90	

1990 Team Record

Preseason (1-3)

Date	Result		Opponents
8/11	L	16-28	at San Diego
8/18	L	14-16	at L.A. Raiders
8/25	W	20- 9	Pittsburgh
9/1	L	6-27	Houston
		56-80	

Regular Season (7-9)

Date	Result		Opponents	Att.
9/9	W	17-14	San Diego	48,063
9/16	L	7-28	N.Y. Giants	61,090
9/23	L	15-19	at Washington	53,804
9/30	L	17-31	at N.Y. Giants	75,923
10/7	W	14-10	Tampa Bay	60,076
10/14	L	3-20	at Phoenix	45,235
10/21	W	17-13	at Tampa Bay	68,315
10/28	L	20-21	Philadelphia	62,605
11/4	L	9-24	at N.Y. Jets	68,086
11/11	L	6-24	San Francisco	62,966
11/18	W	24-21	at L.A. Rams	58,589
11/22	W	27-17	Washington	60,355
12/2	W	17-13	New Orleans	60,087
12/16	W	41-10	Phoenix	60,190
12/23	L	3-17	at Philadelphia	63,895
12/30	L	7-26	at Atlanta	50,097

Score by Periods

Cowboys	50	46	40	108	0	—	244
Opponents	54	102	52	100	0	—	308

Attendance

Home 475,062 Away 475,944 Total 951,006
Single-game home record, 80,259 (11-24-66)
Single-season home record, 511,541 (1981)

1990 Team Statistics

	Cowboys	Opp.
Total First Downs	250	281
Rushing	88	110
Passing	135	153
Penalty	27	18
Third Down: Made/Att.	67/198	86/208
Third Down: Pct.	33.8	41.3
Fourth Down: Made/Att.	5/10	8/16
Fourth Down: Pct.	50.0	50.0
Total Net Yards	4081	4615
Avg. Per Game	255.1	288.4
Total Plays	911	988
Avg. Per Play	4.5	4.7
Net Yards Rushing	1500	1976
Avg. Per Game	93.8	123.5
Total Rushes	393	482
Net Yards Passing	2581	2639
Avg. Per Game	161.3	164.9
Sacked/Yards Lost	43/317	36/292
Gross Yards	2898	2931
Att./Completions	475/254	470/271
Completion Pct.	53.5	57.7
Had Intercepted	24	11
Punts/Avg.	79/43.2	70/40.9
Net Punting Avg.	35.6	36.2
Penalties/Yards Lost	98/729	104/911
Fumbles/Ball Lost	27/9	32/19
Touchdowns	27	36
Rushing	13	18
Passing	12	12
Returns	2	6
Avg. Time of Possession	28:44	31:16

1990 Individual Statistics

Scoring	TD R	TD P	TD Rt	PAT	FG	Saf	TP
Willis	0	0	0	26/26	18/25	0	80
E. Smith	11	0	0	0/0	0/0	0	66
Irvin	0	5	0	0/0	0/0	0	30
Novacek	0	4	0	0/0	0/0	0	24
Johnston	1	1	0	0/0	0/0	0	12
Agee	0	1	0	0/0	0/0	0	6
Aikman	1	0	0	0/0	0/0	0	6
Holt	0	0	1	0/0	0/0	0	6
McKinnon	0	1	0	0/0	0/0	0	6
Perryman, N.E.-Dall.	1	0	0	0/0	0/0	0	6
Wright	0	0	1	0/0	0/0	0	6
Cowboys	13	12	2	26/26	18/25	1	244
Opponents	18	12	6	36/36	18/26	1	308

Passing	Att.	Comp.	Yds.	Pct.	TD	Int.	Tkld.	Rate
Aikman	399	226	2579	56.6	11	18	39/288	66.6
Laufenberg	67	24	279	35.8	1	6	4/29	16.9
Walsh	9	4	40	44.4	0	0	0/0	57.6
Cowboys	475	254	2898	53.5	12	24	43/317	59.4
Opponents	470	271	2931	57.7	12	11	36/292	74.9

Rushing	Att.	Yds.	Avg.	LG	TD
E. Smith	241	937	3.9	48t	11
Agee	53	213	4.0	28	0
Aikman	40	172	4.3	20	1
Perryman, N.E.-Dall.	32	97	3.0	13	1
Highsmith	19	48	2.5	7	0
Dixon	11	43	3.9	18	0
Johnston	10	35	3.5	8	1
Wright	3	26	8.7	14	0
Saxon	1	20	20.0	20	0
Laufenberg	2	6	3.0	5	0
T. Smith	6	6	1.0	3	0
Bates	1	4	4.0	4	0
Walsh	1	0	0.0	0	0
Martin	4	−2	−0.5	3	0
McKinnon	1	−8	−8.0	−8	0
Cowboys	393	1500	3.8	48t	13
Opponents	482	1976	4.1	67	18

Receiving	No.	Yds.	Avg.	LG	TD
Martin	64	732	11.4	45	0
Novacek	59	657	11.1	41	4
Agee	30	272	9.1	30	1
E. Smith	24	228	9.5	57	0
Irvin	20	413	20.7	61t	5
Perryman, N.E.-Dall.	15	88	5.9	15	0
McKinnon	14	172	12.3	28t	1
Johnston	14	148	10.6	26	1
Awalt	13	133	10.2	25	0
Wright	11	104	9.5	20	0
Highsmith	3	13	4.3	7	0
Dixon	2	26	13.0	21	0
Cowboys	254	2898	11.4	61t	12
Opponents	271	2931	10.8	58t	12

Interceptions	No.	Yds.	Avg.	LG	TD
Holt	3	72	24.0	64t	1
Washington	3	24	8.0	13	0
Gant	1	26	26.0	26	0
Bates	1	4	4.0	4	0
Hendrix	1	0	0.0	0	0
Horton	1	0	0.0	0	0
Williams	1	0	0.0	0	0
Cowboys	11	126	11.5	64t	1
Opponents	24	353	14.7	61t	4

Punting	No.	Yds.	Avg.	In 20	LG
Saxon	79	3413	43.2	20	62
Cowboys	79	3413	43.2	20	62
Opponents	70	2866	40.9	15	62

Punt Returns	No.	FC	Yds.	Avg.	LG	TD
Shepard	20	1	121	6.1	13	0
Harris	12	6	63	5.3	12	0
Martin	5	3	46	9.2	17	0
McKinnon	2	1	20	10.0	20	0
Cowboys	39	11	250	6.4	20	0
Opponents	43	8	438	10.2	98t	1

Kickoff Returns	No.	Yds.	Avg.	LG	TD
Dixon	36	736	20.4	47	0
Wright	12	276	23.0	90t	1
Shepard	4	75	18.8	22	0
Harris	1	0	0.0	0	0
Stepnoski	1	15	15.0	15	0
Cowboys	54	1102	20.4	90t	1
Opponents	55	1136	20.7	76t	1

Sacks	No.
Jones	7.5
Stubbs	7.5
Tolbert	5.5
Noonan	4.5
Jeffcoat	3.5
Norton	2.5
Del Rio	1.5
Hamel	1.5
Lockhart	1.0
Solomon	1.0
Cowboys	36.0
Opponents	43.0

1991 Draft Choices

Round	Name	Pos.	College
1.	Russell Maryland	DT	Miami
	Alvin Harper	WR	Tennessee
	Kelvin Pritchett	DT	Mississippi
2.	Dixon Edwards	LB	Michigan State
3.	Godfrey Myles	LB	Florida
	James Richards	G	California
	Eric Williams	T	Central State, Ohio
4.	Curvin Richards	RB	Pittsburgh
	Bill Musgrave	QB	Oregon
	Tony Hill	DE	Tenn.-Chattanooga
	Kevin Harris	DE	Texas Southern
5.	Darrick Brownlow	LB	Illinois
6.	Mike Sullivan	G	Miami
7.	Leon Lett	DT	Emporia State
9.	Damon Mays	WR	Missouri
10.	Sean Love	G	Penn State
11.	Tony Boles	RB	Michigan
12.	Larry Brown	DB	Texas Christian

Dallas Cowboys 1991 Veteran Roster

No.	Name	Pos.	Ht.	Wt.	Birth-date	NFL Exp.	College	Hometown	How Acq.	'90 Games/ Starts
34	Agee, Tommie	RB	6-0	223	2/22/64	4	Auburn	Maplesville, Ala.	PB(KC)-'90#	16/11
8	Aikman, Troy	QB	6-4	218	11/21/66	3	UCLA	Henryetta, Okla.	D1-'89	15/15
36	Albritton, Vince	S	6-2	212	7/23/62	8	Washington	Oakland, Calif.	FA-'84	8/8
89	Awalt, Rob	TE	6-5	238	4/9/64	5	San Diego State	Sacramento, Calif.	T(Phx)-'90	13/1
40	Bates, Bill	S	6-1	204	6/6/61	9	Tennessee	Knoxville, Tenn.	FA-'83	16/0
44	Brooks, Michael	CB	6-0	195	3/12/67	2	North Carolina State	Greensboro, N.C.	FA-'90	3/0
79	Broughton, Willie	DT	6-5	280	9/9/64	5	Miami	Ft. Pierce, Fla.	FA-'89	4/0
90	Crockett, Willis	LB	6-3	234	8/25/66	2	Georgia Tech	Douglas, Ga.	D5b-'89	13/0
55	†Del Rio, Jack	LB	6-4	232	4/4/63	7	Southern California	Castro Valley, Calif.	W(KC)-'89	16/16
21	Dixon, James	WR	5-10	184	2/2/67	3	Houston	Vernon, Tex.	FA-'89	15/1
85	†Folsom, Steve	TE	6-5	240	3/21/58	6	Utah	Santa Fe Springs, Calif.	FA-'87	1/0
29	Gant, Kenneth	CB	5-11	181	4/18/67	2	Albany State	Lakeland, Fla.	D9-'90	12/0
63	†Gesek, John	G	6-5	283	2/18/63	5	Cal State-Sacramento	Danville, Calif.	T(Raid)-'90	15/12
66	Gogan, Kevin	T	6-7	311	11/2/64	5	Washington	Pacifica, Calif.	D8-'87	16/4
78	†Hamel, Dean	DT	6-3	271	7/7/61	7	Tulsa	Warren, Mich.	T(Wash)-'89	12/11
50	Harper, Dave	LB	6-1	220	5/5/66	2	Humboldt State	Eureka, Calif.	D11-'90	6/0
25	Harris, Odie	CB-S	6-0	190	4/1/66	4	Sam Houston State	Bryan, Tex.	PB(TB)-'91#	16/0*
70	Hellestrae, Dale	C-G	6-5	275	7/11/62	5	Southern Methodist	Scottsdale, Ariz.	T(Raid)-'90	16/0
45	Hendrix, Manny	CB	5-10	185	10/20/64	6	Utah	Phoenix, Ariz.	FA-'86	16/11
32	†Highsmith, Alonzo	RB	6-1	237	2/28/65	5	Miami	Miami, Fla.	T(Hou)-'90	7/5
30	Holt, Issiac	CB	6-2	198	10/4/62	7	Alcorn State	Birmingham, Ala.	T(Minn)-'89	15/15
20	Horton, Ray	S	5-11	186	4/12/60	9	Washington	Tacoma, Wash.	PB(Cin)-'89#	14/14
88	Irvin, Michael	WR	6-2	199	3/5/66	4	Miami	Ft. Lauderdale, Fla.	D1-'88	12/7
77	Jeffcoat, Jim	DE	6-5	264	4/1/61	9	Arizona State	Cliffwood, N.J.	D1-'83	16/13
48	Johnston, Daryl	RB	6-2	238	2/10/66	3	Syracuse	Youngstown, N.Y.	D2-'89	16/0
97	Jones, Jimmie	DT	6-4	272	1/9/66	2	Miami	Okeechobee, Fla.	D3-'90	16/6
26	Jones, Keith	RB	5-10	180	2/5/66	2	Nebraska	Omaha, Neb.	PB(Clev)-'90#	0*
15	†Laufenberg, Babe	QB	6-3	214	12/5/59	6	Indiana	Encino, Calif.	FA-'89	4/1
83	Martin, Kelvin	WR	5-9	163	5/14/65	5	Boston College	Jacksonville, Fla.	D4-'87	16/16
61	Newton, Nate	G	6-3	322	12/20/61	6	Florida A&M	Orlando, Fla.	FA-'86	16/16
73	†Noonan, Danny	DT-DE	6-4	266	7/14/65	5	Nebraska	Lincoln, Neb.	D1-'87	16/15
51	Norton, Ken	LB	6-2	237	9/29/66	4	UCLA	Los Angeles, Calif.	D2-'88	15/15
84	Novacek, Jay	TE	6-4	230	10/24/62	7	Wyoming	Gothenburg, Neb.	PB(Phx)-'90#	16/15
86	Roberts, Alfredo	TE	6-3	246	3/1/65	4	Miami	Hollywood, Fla.	PB(KC)-'91#	16/13*
4	Saxon, Mike	P	6-3	200	7/10/62	7	San Diego State	Arcadia, Calif.	FA-'85	16/0
87	Shepard, Derrick	WR	5-10	181	1/22/64	4	Oklahoma	Odessa, Tex.	W(NO)-'89	8/0
42	Smagala, Stan	CB	5-10	184	4/6/68	2	Notre Dame	Burbank, Ill.	D5-'90	3/0
22	Smith, Emmitt	RB	5-9	203	5/15/69	2	Florida	Escambia, Fla.	D1-'90	16/15
57	Smith, Vinson	LB	6-2	225	7/3/65	3	East Carolina	Statesville, N.C.	PB(Pitt)-'90#	16/1
54	Solomon, Jesse	LB	6-0	235	11/4/63	6	Florida State	Madison, Fla.	T(Minn)-'89	9/0
53	Stepnoski, Mark	C	6-2	266	1/20/67	3	Pittsburgh	Erie, Pa.	D3a-'89	16/16
18	Stoudt, Cliff	QB	6-4	222	3/27/55	12	Youngstown State	Oberlin, Ohio	FA-'90	0*
96	†Stubbs, Daniel	DE	6-4	264	1/3/65	4	Miami	Red Bank, N.J.	T(SF)-'90	16/15
92	Tolbert, Tony	DE	6-6	254	12/29/67	3	Texas-El Paso	Englewood, N.J.	D4-'89	16/4
71	Tuinei, Mark	T	6-5	293	3/31/60	9	Hawaii	Honolulu, Hawaii	FA-'83	13/13
75	Veingrad, Alan	T	6-5	277	7/24/63	5	East Texas State	Miami, Fla.	PB(GB)-'91#	16/4*
37	Washington, James	S	6-1	195	1/10/65	4	UCLA	Los Angeles, Calif.	PB(Rams)-'90#	15/10
23	Williams, Robert	CB	5-10	186	10/2/62	5	Baylor	Galveston, Tex.	FA-'87	16/6
1	Willis, Ken	K	5-11	189	10/6/66	2	Kentucky	Owensboro, Ky.	FA-'90	16/0
81	Wright, Alexander	WR	6-0	189	7/19/67	2	Auburn	Albany, Ga.	D2-'90	15/1
76	†Zimmerman, Jeff	G	6-3	332	1/10/65	5	Florida	Orlando, Fla.	D3-'87	6/0

* Harris played 16 games with Tampa Bay in '90; K. Jones missed '90 season due to injury; Roberts played 16 games with Kansas City; Stoudt active for 1 game, but did not play; Veingrad played 16 games with Green Bay.

† Option playout; subject to developments.

Plan B unconditional free agent.

Traded—CB Ron Francis, LB David Howard, and LB Eugene Lockhart to New England.

Players lost through Plan B (2): G Crawford Ker (Den; 15 games in '90), RB Robert Perryman (Den; 8 games with N.E.; 0 with Dall).

COACHING STAFF

Head Coach, Jimmy Johnson

Pro Career: Named second head coach in Cowboys' history on February 25, 1989. Youngest head coach in the NFC. No pro playing experience. Career NFL record: 8-24.

Background: All-Southwest Conference defensive lineman on Arkansas's 1964 undefeated national championship team. Began coaching career in 1965 at Louisiana Tech. Moved on as an assistant at Wichita State 1967, Iowa State 1968-69, Oklahoma 1970-72, Arkansas 1973-76, and Pittsburgh 1977-78. Head coach at Oklahoma State from 1979-83. Compiled 52-9 (.853) record in five seasons as head coach at the University of Miami. Under Johnson, the Hurricanes won the national championship in 1987 and 34 of 36 games from 1986-88. Career collegiate record: 81-34-3.

Personal: Born July 16, 1943, Port Arthur, Tex. Jimmy lives in Irving, Tex., and has two sons, Brent and Chad.

Assistant Coaches

Hubbard Alexander, wide receivers; born February 14, 1939, Winston-Salem, N.C., lives in Coppell, Tex. Center Tennessee State 1958-61. No pro playing experience. College coach: Tennessee State 1962-63, Vanderbilt 1974-78, Miami 1979-88. Pro coach: Joined Cowboys in 1989.

Joe Avezzano, special teams; born November 17, 1943, Yonkers, N.Y., lives in Coppell, Tex. Guard Florida State 1961-65. Pro center Boston Patriots 1966. College coach: Florida State 1968, Iowa State 1969-72, Pittsburgh 1973-76, Tennessee 1977-79, Oregon State 1980-84 (head coach), Texas 1985-88. Pro coach: Joined Cowboys in 1990.

Joe Brodsky, running backs; born June 9, 1934, Miami, Fla., lives in Irving, Tex. Fullback/linebacker Florida 1953-56. No pro playing experience. College coach: Miami 1978-88. Pro coach: Joined Cowboys in 1989.

Dave Campo, defensive backs; born July 18, 1947, New London, Conn., lives in Coppell, Tex. Defensive back Central Connecticut State 1967-70. No pro playing experience. College coach: Central Connecticut State 1971-72, Albany State 1973, Bridgeport 1974, Pittsburgh 1975, Washington State 1976, Boise State 1977-79, Oregon State 1980, Weber State 1981-82, Iowa State 1983, Syracuse 1984-86, Miami 1987-88. Pro coach: Joined Cowboys in 1989.

Butch Davis, defensive line; born November 17, 1951, Tahlequah, Okla., lives in Coppell, Tex. Defensive end Arkansas 1971-74. No pro playing experience. College coach: Oklahoma State 1979-83, Miami 1984-88. Pro coach: Joined Cowboys in 1989.

Robert Ford, tight ends; born June 21, 1951, Belton, Tex., lives in Irving, Tex. Wide receiver Houston 1970-72. No pro playing experience. College coach: Western Illinois 1974-76, New Mexico 1977-79, Oregon State 1980-81, Mississippi State 1982-83, Kansas 1986, Texas Tech 1987-88, Texas A&M 1989-90. Pro coach: Houston Gamblers (USFL) 1985, joined Cowboys in 1991.

Steve Hoffman, kickers/research and development; born September 8, 1958, Camden, N.J., lives in Coppell, Tex. Quarterback-running back-wide receiver Dickinson College 1979-82. Pro punter Washington Federals (USFL) 1983. College coach: Miami 1985-87. Pro coach: Joined Cowboys in 1989.

Ron Meeks, defensive assistant; born August 27, 1954, Jacksonville, Fla., lives in Irving, Tex. Defensive back Arkansas State 1975-76. Pro defensive back Hamilton Tiger-Cats (CFL) 1977-79, Ottawa Roughriders (CFL) 1979, Toronto Argonauts (CFL) 1980-81. College coach: Arkansas State 1984-85, Miami 1986-87, New Mexico State 1988, Fresno State 1989-90. Pro coach: Joined Cowboys in 1991.

Dallas Cowboys 1991 First-Year Roster

Name	Pos.	Ht.	Wt.	Birth-date	College	Hometown	How Acq.
Blanchard, Cary	K	6-1	225	11/5/68	Oklahoma State	Hurst, Tex.	FA
Boles, Tony	RB	6-1	196	12/11/67	Michigan	Detroit, Mich.	D11
Brown, Larry	CB-S	5-11	184	11/30/69	Texas Christian	Los Angeles, Calif.	D11
Brownlow, Darrick	LB	5-10	245	12/28/68	Illinois	Indianapolis, Ind.	D5
Childress, Freddie (1)	G	6-4	334	9/17/66	Arkansas	West Helena, Ark.	FA
Cooper, Reggie	LB	6-2	214	7/11/68	Nebraska	Slidell, La.	FA
Edwards, Dixon	LB	6-1	220	3/25/68	Michigan State	Cincinnati, Ohio	D2
Gicewicz, Rich (1)	TE	6-4	245	12/4/65	Michigan State	Buffalo, N.Y.	FA
Harper, Alvin	WR	6-3	204	7/6/67	Tennessee	Frostproof, Fla.	D1b
Harris, Kevin	DE	6-5	248	10/21/69	Texas Southern	Dallas, Tex.	D4d
Hill, Tony	DE	6-6	250	10/23/68	Tenn.-Chattanooga	Warren County, Ga.	D4c
Hudson, Craig (1)	TE	6-3	245	5/1/67	Wisconsin	East Aurora, Ill.	FA
Lett, Leon	DT-DE	6-6	273	10/12/68	Emporia State	Fair Hope, Ala.	D7
Love, Sean	G	6-3	285	9/6/68	Penn State	Tamaqua, Pa.	D10
Martin, Ricky	RB	5-10	184	8/1/69	Middle Tennessee St.	Chattoogaville, Ga.	FA
Maryland, Russell	DT	6-1	274	3/22/69	Miami	Chicago, Ill.	D1a
Mays, Damon	WR	5-9	166	5/20/68	Missouri	Phoenix, Ariz.	D9
Musgrave, Bill	QB	6-2	196	11/11/67	Oregon	Grand Junction, Colo.	D4b
Myles, Godfrey	LB	6-1	242	9/22/68	Florida	Miami, Fla.	D3a
Powe, Keith	LB	6-3	251	6/5/69	Texas-El Paso	Houston, Tex.	FA
Richards, Curvin	RB	5-9	200	12/26/68	Pittsburgh	LaPorte, Tex.	D4a
Richards, James	G	6-4	289	11/7/69	California	Antelope Valley, Calif.	D3b
Warnsley, Reginald (1)	RB	5-10	215	4/5/68	Southern Mississippi	Bay Springs, Miss.	FA
Williams, Erik	T	6-5	304	9/7/68	Central State, Ohio	Philadelphia, Pa.	D3c
Zeno, Lance	G-C	6-4	279	4/15/67	UCLA	Fountain Valley, Calif.	FA

The term NFL Rookie is defined as a player who is in his first season of professional football and has not been on the roster of another professional football team for any regular-season or postseason games. A Rookie is designated by an "R" on NFL rosters. Players who have been active in another professional football league or players who have NFL experience, including either preseason training camp or being on an active roster for fewer than three regular-season or postseason games, are termed NFL First-Year Players. An NFL First-Year Player is designated by a "1" on NFL rosters. Thereafter, a player on an NFL active roster for at least three regular-season or postseason games is credited with an additional year of NFL playing experience.

NOTES

Norval Turner, offensive coordinator/quarterbacks; born May 17, 1952, Martinez, Calif., lives in Irving, Tex. Quarterback Oregon 1972-74. No pro playing experience. College coach: Oregon 1975, Southern California 1976-84. Pro coach: L.A. Rams 1985-90, joined Cowboys in 1991.

Dave Wannstedt, defensive coordinator/linebackers; born May 21, 1952, Pittsburgh, Pa., lives in Coppell, Tex. Offensive tackle Pittsburgh 1970-73. No pro playing experience. College coach: Pittsburgh 1975-78, Oklahoma State 1979-82, Southern California 1983-85, Miami 1986-88. Pro coach: Joined Cowboys in 1989.

Tony Wise, offensive line; born December 28, 1951, Albany, N.Y., lives in Coppell, Tex. Offensive lineman Ithaca College 1971-72. No pro playing experience. College coach: Albany State 1973, Bridgeport 1974, Central Connecticut State 1975, Washington State 1976, Pittsburgh 1977-78, Oklahoma State 1979-83, Syracuse 1984, Miami 1985-88. Pro coach: Joined Cowboys in 1989.

Mike Woicik, strength and conditioning; born September 26, 1956, Westwood, Mass., lives in Coppell, Tex. Boston College 1974-78. No college or pro playing experience. College coach: Springfield 1978-80, Syracuse 1980-89. Pro coach: Joined Cowboys in 1990.

National Football Conference
Central Division

Team Colors: Honolulu Blue and Silver

Pontiac Silverdome
1200 Featherstone Road
Pontiac, Michigan 48342
Telephone: (313) 335-4131

Club Officials

President-Owner: William Clay Ford
Executive Vice President-CEO: Chuck Schmidt
Director of Player Personnel: Ron Hughes
Director of Pro Personnel: Kevin Colbert
Scouts: Dirk Dierking, Allen Hughes, Scott McEwen, Jim Owens, Rick Spielman, John Trump
Director of Player Relations: Otis Canty
Controller/Travel Coordinator: Tom Lesnau
Director of Marketing, Broadcasting, and Communications: Bill Keenist
Director of Marketing, Sales, and Ticket Operations: Fred Otto
Director of Community Relations and Detroit Lions Charities: Tim Pendell
Media Relations Coordinator: Mike Murray
Media Relations Assistant: James Petrylka
Strength and Conditioning: Bert Hill
Trainer: Kent Falb
Equipment Manager: Dan Jaroshewich
Video Director: Steve Hermans

Stadium: Pontiac Silverdome • **Capacity:** 80,500
1200 Featherstone Road
Pontiac, Michigan 48342

Playing Surface: AstroTurf

Training Camp: Pontiac Silverdome
1200 Featherstone Road
Pontiac, Michigan 48342

1991 Schedule

Preseason

July 27	vs. Denver at Canton, Ohio	12:30
Aug. 2	**Cincinnati**	7:30
Aug. 10	at Buffalo	6:30
Aug. 17	at Kansas City	7:00
Aug. 23	**Pittsburgh**	7:30

Regular Season

Sept. 1	at Washington	8:00
Sept. 8	**Green Bay**	1:00
Sept. 15	**Miami**	1:00
Sept. 22	at Indianapolis	12:00
Sept. 29	**Tampa Bay**	1:00
Oct. 6	**Minnesota**	1:00
Oct. 13	**Open Date**	
Oct. 20	at San Francisco	1:00
Oct. 27	**Dallas**	4:00
Nov. 3	at Chicago	12:00
Nov. 10	at Tampa Bay	1:00
Nov. 17	**Los Angeles Rams**	4:00
Nov. 24	at Minnesota	12:00
Nov. 28	**Chicago** (Thanksgiving)	12:30
Dec. 8	**New York Jets**	4:00
Dec. 15	at Green Bay	12:00
Dec. 22	at Buffalo	1:00

Portsmouth Spartans 1930-33
(381-398-32)

1930	Hal (Tubby) Griffen	5-6-3
1931-36	George (Potsy) Clark	49-20-6
1937-38	Earl (Dutch) Clark	14-8-0
1939	Elmer (Gus) Henderson	6-5-0
1940	George (Potsy) Clark	5-5-1
1941-42	Bill Edwards*	4-9-1
1942	John Karcis	0-8-0
1943-47	Charles (Gus) Dorais	20-31-2
1948-50	Alvin (Bo) McMillin	12-24-0
1951-56	Raymond (Buddy) Parker	50-24-2
1957-64	George Wilson	55-45-6
1965-66	Harry Gilmer	10-16-2
1967-72	Joe Schmidt	43-35-7
1973	Don McCafferty	6-7-1
1974-76	Rick Forzano**	15-17-0
1976-77	Tommy Hudspeth	11-13-0
1978-84	Monte Clark	43-63-1
1985-88	Darryl Rogers***	18-40-0
1988-90	Wayne Fontes	15-22-0

*Released after three games in 1942
**Resigned after four games in 1976
***Released after 11 games in 1988

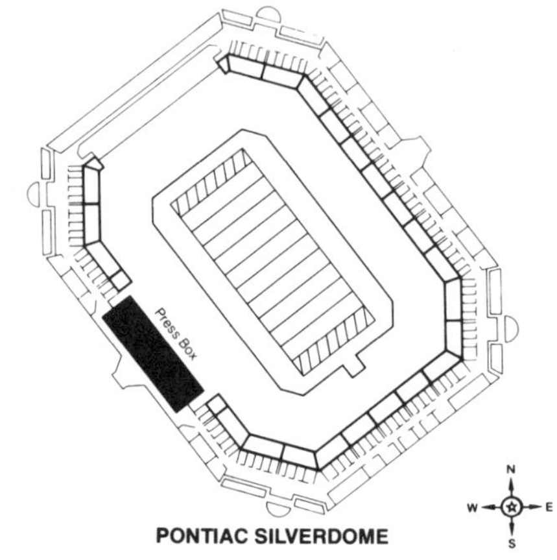

PONTIAC SILVERDOME

Record Holders

Individual Records—Career

Category	Name	Performance
Rushing (Yds.)	Billy Sims, 1980-84	5,106
Passing (Yds.)	Bobby Layne, 1950-58	15,710
Passing (TDs)	Bobby Layne, 1950-58	118
Receiving (No.)	Charlie Sanders, 1968-1977	336
Receiving (Yds.)	Gail Cogdill, 1960-68	5,220
Interceptions	Dick LeBeau, 1959-1972	62
Punting (Avg.)	Yale Lary, 1952-53, 1956-1964	44.3
Punt Return (Avg.)	Jack Christiansen, 1951-58	12.8
Kickoff Return (Avg.)	Pat Studstill, 1961-67	25.7
Field Goals	Eddie Murray, 1980-89	212
Touchdowns (Tot.)	Billy Sims, 1980-84	47
Points	Eddie Murray, 1980-89	943

Individual Records—Single Season

Category	Name	Performance
Rushing (Yds.)	Barry Sanders, 1989	1,470
Passing (Yds.)	Gary Danielson, 1980	3,223
Passing (TDs)	Bobby Layne, 1951	26
Receiving (No.)	James Jones, 1984	77
Receiving (Yds.)	Pat Studstill, 1966	1,266
Interceptions	Don Doll, 1950	12
	Jack Christiansen, 1953	12
Punting (Avg.)	Yale Lary, 1963	48.9
Punt Return (Avg.)	Jack Christiansen, 1952	21.5
Kickoff Return (Avg.)	Tom Watkins, 1965	34.4
Field Goals	Eddie Murray, 1980	27
Touchdowns (Tot.)	Billy Sims, 1980	16
	Barry Sanders, 1990	16
Points	Doak Walker, 1950	128

Individual Records—Single Game

Category	Name	Performance
Rushing (Yds.)	Bob Hoernschemeyer, 11-23-50	198
Passing (Yds.)	Bobby Layne, 11-5-50	374
Passing (TDs)	Gary Danielson, 12-9-78	5
Receiving (No.)	Cloyce Box, 12-3-50	12
	James Jones, 9-28-86	12
Receiving (Yds.)	Cloyce Box, 12-3-50	302
Interceptions	Don Doll, 10-23-49	*4
Field Goals	Garo Yepremian, 11-13-66	6
Touchdowns (Tot.)	Cloyce Box, 12-3-50	4
Points	Cloyce Box, 12-3-50	24

*NFL Record

1990 Team Record

Preseason (4-0)

Date	Result		Opponents
8/9	W	34-10	at Houston
8/17	W	24-13	Buffalo
8/24	W	35-21	Kansas City
8/31	W	26-24	at Cincinnati
		119-68	

Regular Season (6-10)

Date	Result		Opponents	Att.
9/9	L	21-38	Tampa Bay	56,692
9/16	W	21-14	Atlanta	48,961
9/23	L	20-23	at Tampa Bay	55,075
9/30	L	21-24	Green Bay	64,509
10/7	W	34-27	at Minnesota	57,586
10/14	L	24-43	at Kansas City	74,312
10/28	W	27-10	at New Orleans	64,368
11/4	L	38-41	Washington (OT)	69,326
11/11	L	7-17	Minnesota	68,264
11/18	L	0-20	at N.Y. Giants	76,109
11/22	W	40-27	Denver	73,896
12/2	L	17-23	at Chicago (OT)	62,313
12/10	L	31-38	L.A. Raiders	72,190
12/16	W	38-21	Chicago	67,759
12/22	W	24-17	at Green Bay	46,700
12/30	L	10-30	at Seattle	50,681

(OT) Overtime

Score by Periods

Lions	111	102	65	95	0	—	373
Opponents	86	122	83	113	9	—	413

Attendance

Home 521,597 Away 487,144 Total 1,008,741
Single-game home record, 80,444 (12-20-81)
Single-season home record, 622,593 (1980)

1990 Team Statistics

	Lions	Opp.
Total First Downs	278	334
Rushing	112	141
Passing	152	174
Penalty	14	19
Third Down: Made/Att.	55/164	106/222
Third Down: Pct.	33.5	47.7
Fourth Down: Made/Att.	7/14	12/18
Fourth Down: Pct.	50.0	66.7
Total Net Yards	4977	5734
Avg. Per Game	311.1	358.4
Total Plays	870	1080
Avg. Per Play	5.7	5.3
Net Yards Rushing	1927	2388
Avg. Per Game	120.4	149.3
Total Rushes	366	532
Net Yards Passing	3050	3346
Avg. Per Game	190.6	209.1
Sacked/Yards Lost	44/278	41/279
Gross Yards	3328	3625
Att./Completions	460/242	507/319
Completion Pct.	52.6	62.9
Had Intercepted	20	17
Punts/Avg.	63/40.6	62/40.8
Net Punting Avg.	35.3	33.0
Penalties/Yards Lost	88/711	97/788
Fumbles/Ball Lost	29/16	31/18
Touchdowns	46	49
Rushing	19	22
Passing	24	21
Returns	3	6
Avg. Time of Possession	25:33	34:27

1990 Individual Statistics

Scoring	TD R	TD P	TD Rt	PAT	FG	Saf	TP
B. Sanders	13	3	0	0/0	0/0	0	96
Murray	0	0	0	34/34	13/19	0	73
Clark	0	8	0	0/0	0/0	0	48
Johnson	0	6	0	0/0	0/0	0	36
Peete	6	0	0	0/0	0/0	0	36
Karlis	0	0	0	12/12	4/7	0	24
Greer	0	3	0	0/0	0/0	0	18
Campbell	0	2	0	0/0	0/0	0	12
Crockett	0	0	1	0/0	0/0	0	6
Matthews	0	1	0	0/0	0/0	0	6
J. Williams	0	0	1	0/0	0/0	0	6
W. White	0	0	1	0/0	0/0	0	6
Wilder	0	1	0	0/0	0/0	0	6
Lions	19	24	3	46/46	17/26	0	373
Opponents	22	21	6	48/48	23/30	1	413

Passing	Att.	Comp.	Yds.	Pct.	TD	Int.	Tkld.	Rate
Peete	271	142	1974	52.4	13	8	27/173	79.8
Gagliano	159	87	1190	54.7	10	10	13/83	73.6
Ware	30	13	164	43.3	1	2	4/22	44.3
Lions	460	242	3328	52.6	24	20	44/278	75.3
Opponents	507	319	3625	62.9	21	17	41/279	84.1

Rushing	Att.	Yds.	Avg.	LG	TD
B. Sanders	255	1304	5.1	45t	13
Peete	47	363	7.7	37	6
Gagliano	46	145	3.2	22	0
Ware	7	64	9.1	30	0
Wilder	11	51	4.6	13	0
Lions	366	1927	5.3	45t	19
Opponents	532	2388	4.5	55t	22

Receiving	No.	Yds.	Avg.	LG	TD
Johnson	64	727	11.4	44t	6
Clark	52	914	17.6	57	8
B. Sanders	36	480	13.3	47t	3
Matthews	30	349	11.6	52	1
Greer	20	332	16.6	68t	3
Campbell	19	236	12.4	51	2
Farr	12	170	14.2	44	0
Phillips	8	112	14.0	29	0
Wilder	1	8	8.0	8t	1
Lions	242	3328	13.8	68t	24
Opponents	319	3625	11.4	68t	21

Interceptions	No.	Yds.	Avg.	LG	TD
W. White	5	120	24.0	48	1
Crockett	3	17	5.7	9	0
Blades	2	25	12.5	21	0
McNorton	1	33	33.0	33	0
Oldham	1	28	28.0	28	0
Irvin	1	22	22.0	22	0
Welch	1	16	16.0	16	0
Spielman	1	12	12.0	12	0
Cofer	1	0	0.0	0	0
Jones	1	0	0.0	0	0
Lions	17	273	16.1	48	1
Opponents	20	346	17.3	62t	3

Punting	No.	Yds.	Avg.	In 20	LG
Arnold	63	2560	40.6	10	59
Lions	63	2560	40.6	10	59
Opponents	62	2530	40.8	9	57

Punt Returns	No.	FC	Yds.	Avg.	LG	TD
Gray	34	7	361	10.6	39	0
Campbell	1	0	0	0.0	0	0
Lions	35	7	361	10.3	39	0
Opponents	29	10	233	8.0	24	0

Kickoff Returns	No.	Yds.	Avg.	LG	TD
Gray	41	939	22.9	65	0
Oldham	13	234	18.0	42	0
Campbell	12	238	19.8	38	0
Phillips	2	43	21.5	23	0
Andolsek	1	12	12.0	12	0
McKnight	1	0	0.0	0	0
Lions	70	1466	20.9	65	0
Opponents	70	1229	17.6	76t	1

Sacks	No.
Cofer	10.0
Hayworth	4.0
Duckens	3.0
Ferguson	3.0
Hunter	3.0
Owens	3.0
J. Williams	3.0
Ball	2.0
Jamison	2.0
Spielman	2.0
Blades	1.0
Brooks	1.0
Cline	1.0
Crockett	1.0
Jones	1.0
Spindler	1.0
Lions	41.0
Opponents	44.0

1991 Draft Choices

Round	Name	Pos.	College
1.	Herman Moore	WR	Virginia
3.	Reggie Barrett	WR	Texas-El Paso
4.	Kevin Scott	DB	Stanford
5.	Scott Conover	G	Purdue
6.	Richie Andrews	K	Florida State
7.	Franklin Thomas	TE	Grambling
8.	Cedric Jackson	RB	Texas Christian
9.	Darryl Milburn	DE	Grambling
11.	Slip Watkins	KR	Louisiana State
12.	Zeno Alexander	LB	Arizona

Detroit Lions 1991 Veteran Roster

No.	Name	Pos.	Ht.	Wt.	Birth-date	NFL Exp.	College	Hometown	How Acq.	'90 Games/ Starts
32	Alexander, Bruce	CB	5-9	169	9/17/65	2	Stephen F. Austin	Lufkin, Tex.	FA-'89	1/0
65	Andolsek, Eric	G	6-2	286	8/22/66	4	Louisiana State	Thibodaux, La.	D5-'88	16/16
6	Arnold, Jim	P	6-3	211	1/31/61	9	Vanderbilt	Dalton, Ga.	FA-'86	16/0
93	Ball, Jerry	NT	6-1	298	12/15/64	5	Southern Methodist	Beaumont, Tex.	D3-'87	15/15
36	Blades, Bennie	S	6-1	221	9/3/66	4	Miami	Ft. Lauderdale, Fla.	D1-'88	12/12
75	Brown, Lomas	T	6-4	287	3/30/63	7	Florida	Miami, Fla.	D1-'85	16/16
52	†Brown, Mark	LB	6-2	240	7/18/61	9	Purdue	Inglewood, Calif.	W(Mia)-'89	15/0
87	Campbell, Jeff	WR	5-8	167	3/29/68	2	Colorado	Vail, Colo.	D5-'90	16/8
50	Caston, Toby	LB	6-1	243	7/17/65	5	Louisiana State	Monroe, La.	PB(Hou)-'89#	12/4
82	†Clark, Robert	WR	5-11	173	8/6/65	4	North Carolina Central	Richmond, Va.	PB(NO)-'89#	16/15
55	Cofer, Michael	LB	6-5	244	4/7/60	9	Tennessee	Knoxville, Tenn.	D3-'83	16/16
39	Crockett, Ray	CB	5-9	181	1/5/67	3	Baylor	Duncanville, Tex.	D4-'89	16/6
67	Dallafior, Ken	G-C	6-4	279	8/26/59	7	Minnesota	Madison Heights, Mich.	PB(SD)-'89#	16/15
91	Duckens, Mark	DE	6-4	270	3/4/65	3	Arizona State	Wichita, Kan.	PB(NYG)-'90#	15/0
81	Farr, Mike	WR	5-10	192	8/8/67	2	UCLA	Birmingham, Mich.	FA-'90	12/8
77	Ferguson, Keith	DE	6-5	276	4/3/59	11	Ohio State	Miami, Fla.	W(SD)-'85	16/14
98	Gibson, Dennis	LB	6-2	243	2/8/64	5	Iowa State	Ankeny, Iowa	D8-'87	11/11
53	Glover, Kevin	C	6-2	282	6/17/63	7	Maryland	Upper Marlboro, Md.	D2-'85	16/16
23	Gray, Mel	WR-KR	5-9	162	3/16/61	6	Purdue	Williamsburg, Va.	PB(NO)-'89#	16/0
74	Graybill, Michael	T	6-7	280	10/14/66	2	Boston University	Washington, D.C.	PB(Phx)-'91#	0*
89	Greer, Terry	WR	6-1	192	9/27/57	6	Alabama State	Memphis, Tenn.	PB(SF)-'90#	15/10
99	Hayworth, Tracy	LB	6-3	250	12/18/67	2	Tennessee	Franklin, Tenn.	D7-'90	16/0
97	Hunter, Jeff	DE	6-5	285	4/12/66	2	Albany State	Augusta, Ga.	FA-'90	6/0
58	Jamison, George	LB	6-1	228	9/30/62	5	Cincinnati	Bridgeton, N.J.	SD2-'84	14/7
24	Jenkins, Melvin	CB	5-10	173	3/16/62	5	Cincinnati	Jackson, Miss.	PB(Sea)-'91#	16/0*
57	†Jones, Victor	LB	6-2	240	10/19/66	4	Virginia Tech	Rockville, Md.	PB(TB)-'89#	16/5
12	Kramer, Erik	QB	6-1	195	11/6/64	2	North Carolina State	Madison, Wis.	FA-'90	0*
83	Matthews, Aubrey	WR	5-7	165	9/15/62	6	Delta State	Jacksonville, Fla.	PB(GB)-'90	12/7
29	McNorton, Bruce	CB	5-11	175	2/28/59	10	Georgetown, Ky.	Daytona Beach, Fla.	D4-'82	12/8
3	Murray, Eddie	K	5-10	180	8/29/56	12	Tulane	Halifax, Nova Scotia	D7-'80	11/0
51	†Noga, Niko	LB	6-1	235	3/1/62	8	Hawaii	Honolulu, Hawaii	FA-'89	16/0
28	Oldham, Chris	CB	5-9	183	10/26/68	2	Oregon	Sacramento, Calif.	D4b-'90	16/0
90	Owens, Dan	DE	6-3	268	3/16/67	2	Southern California	Whittier, Calif.	D2-'90	16/12
9	Peete, Rodney	QB	6-0	193	3/16/66	3	Southern California	Tucson, Ariz.	D6-'89	11/11
96	†Pete, Lawrence	NT	6-0	282	1/18/66	3	Nebraska	Wichita, Kan.	D5-'89	6/0
4	Pillow, Frank	WR	5-11	170	3/11/65	4	Tennessee State	Nashville, Tenn.	PB(TB)-'91#	16/2*
73	Salem, Harvey	T-G	6-6	289	1/15/61	9	California	El Cerrito, Calif.	T(Hou)-'86	15/13
20	Sanders, Barry	RB	5-8	203	7/16/68	3	Oklahoma State	Wichita, Kan.	D1-'89	16/16
64	†Sanders, Eric	T-G	6-7	286	10/22/58	11	Nevada-Reno	Reno, Nev.	W(Atl)-'86	16/2
54	Spielman, Chris	LB	6-0	247	10/11/65	4	Ohio State	Canton, Ohio	D2b-'88	12/12
92	Spindler, Marc	DT-DE	6-5	277	11/28/69	2	Pittsburgh	West Scranton, Pa.	D3-'90	3/2
60	Utley, Mike	G-T	6-6	279	12/20/65	3	Washington State	Seattle, Wash.	D3-'89	16/1
11	Ware, Andre	QB	6-2	205	7/31/68	2	Houston	Dickinson, Tex.	D1-'90	4/1
27	Welch, Herb	S	5-11	180	1/12/61	6	UCLA	Watchung, N.J.	PB(Wash)-'90#	16/4
25	†White, Sheldon	CB	5-11	188	3/1/65	4	Miami, Ohio	Dayton, Ohio	W(NYG)-'90	3/0
35	White, William	CB	5-10	191	2/19/66	4	Ohio State	Lima, Ohio	D4-'88	16/16
34	Wilder, James	RB	6-3	225	5/12/58	11	Missouri	Sikeston, Mo.	T(Wash)-'90	15/0

* Graybill active for one game, but did not play for Phoenix in '90; Jenkins played 16 games with Seattle; Kramer missed '90 season due to injury; Pillow played 16 games with Tampa Bay.

† Option playout; subject to developments.

Plan B unconditional free agent.

Players lost through Plan B (6): CB Darren Carrington (SD; 12 games in '90), QB Bob Gagliano (SD; 9), WR Richard Johnson (Hou; 16), C-G Dennis McKnight (Phil; 14), WR Jason Phillips (Atl; 13), DE Derrell Robertson (TB; 0).

Retired—LeRoy Irvin, 12-year, 16 games in '90.

Also played with the Lions in '90—DE Kevin Brooks (6 games), DE Jackie Cline (5), K Rich Karlis (6), S John Miller (4), CB Terry Taylor (2).

COACHING STAFF

Head Coach, Wayne Fontes

Pro Career: Became Lions' seventeenth head coach on December 22, 1988, after serving five weeks as interim head coach (2-3 record). Fontes led the Lions to a 7-9 record in 1989, including five consecutive season-ending wins, and a 6-10 record in 1990. He began the 1988 season as Detroit's defensive coordinator and secondary coach, following a nine-year stint with the Tampa Bay Buccaneers. A former defensive back with the New York Jets, Fontes advanced from secondary coach to defensive coordinator to assistant head coach of the Buccaneers during his years at Tampa Bay. As a player with the Jets, his brief pro career was cut short by a broken leg after two seasons (1963-64). However, his 83-yard interception return against Houston (12-15-63) did stand as the Jets' team record until it was broken in 1989 by Erik McMillan's 93-yard return. Career record: 15-22.

Background: A former two-sport star (football and baseball) at Michigan State, Fontes earned all-Big Ten honors at defensive back for the Spartans. He earned his bachelor's degree in education and biological science and later earned his master's degree in administration, all from Michigan State. After directing the freshman team at Michigan State in 1965, Fontes became defensive backfield coach at Dayton in 1968. He also served in the same capacity at Iowa (1969-71) and Southern California (1972-75).

Personal: Born February 17, 1939, New Bedford, Mass. Fontes and his wife, Evelyn, live in Rochester Hills, Mich., and have three children—Mike, Scott, and Kim.

Assistant Coaches

Raymond Berry, quarterbacks; born February 27, 1933, Corpus Christi, Tex., lives in Pontiac, Mich. Receiver Southern Methodist 1951-54. Pro receiver Baltimore Colts 1955-67. College coach: Arkansas 1970-72. Pro coach: Dallas Cowboys 1968-69, Detroit Lions 1973-75, Cleveland Browns 1976-77, New England Patriots 1978-81, 1984-89 (head coach 1984-89), rejoined Lions in 1991.

Don Clemons, administrative assistant; born February 15, 1954, Newark, N.J., lives in Rochester, Mich. Defensive end Muehlenberg College 1973-76. No pro playing experience. College coach: Kutztown State 1977-78, New Mexico 1979, Arizona State 1980-84. Pro coach: Detroit Lions 1985-90.

Len Fontes, defensive backs; born March 8, 1938, New Bedford, Mass., lives in Pontiac, Mich. Defensive back Ohio State 1958-59. No pro playing experience. College coach: Eastern Michigan 1968, Dayton 1969-72, Navy 1973, Miami 1974-79. Pro coach: Cleveland Browns 1980-82, New York Giants 1983-88, joined Lions in 1990.

Frank Gansz, special teams; born November 22, 1938, Altoona, Pa., lives in Auburn Hills, Mich. Center-linebacker Navy 1957-59. No pro playing experience. College coach: Air Force 1964, Colgate 1968, Navy 1969, Oklahoma State 1973, 1975, Army 1974, UCLA 1976-77. Pro coach: San Francisco 49ers 1978, Cincinnati Bengals 1979-80, Kansas City Chiefs 1981-82, 1986-88 (head coach 1987-88), Philadelphia Eagles 1983-85, joined Lions in 1989.

Lamar Leachman, defensive line; born August 7, 1934, Cartersville, Ga., lives in Pontiac, Mich. Center-linebacker Tennessee 1952-55. No pro playing experience. College coach: Richmond 1966-67, Georgia Tech 1968-71, Memphis State 1972, South Carolina 1973. Pro coach: New York Stars (WFL) 1974, Toronto Argonauts (CFL) 1975-77, Montreal Alouettes (CFL) 1978-79, New York Giants 1980-89, joined Lions in 1990.

Dave Levy, offensive coordinator; born October 25, 1932, Carrollton, Mo., lives in Lake Orion, Mich. Guard UCLA 1952-53. No pro playing experience. College coach: UCLA 1954, Long Beach City College 1955, Southern California 1960-75. Pro coach: San Diego Chargers 1980-88, joined Lions in 1989.

Billie Matthews, defensive backs; born March 15, 1930, Houston, Tex., lives in Rochester, Mich. Quarterback Southern University 1948-51. No pro playing experience. College coach: Kansas 1970, UCLA 1971-78. Pro coach: San Francisco 49ers 1979-82, Philadelphia Eagles 1983-84, Indianapolis Colts 1985-86, Kansas City Chiefs 1987-88, joined Lions in 1989.

Herb Paterra, inside linebackers; born November 8, 1940, Glassport, Pa., lives in Rochester Hills, Mich. Offensive guard-linebacker Michigan State 1960-62. Pro linebacker Buffalo Bills 1963-64, Hamilton Tiger-Cats (CFL) 1965-68. College coach: Michigan State 1969-71, Wyoming 1972-74. Pro coach: Charlotte Hornets (WFL) 1975, Hamilton Tiger-Cats (CFL) 1978-79, Los Angeles Rams 1980-82, Edmonton Eskimos (CFL) 1983, Green Bay Packers 1984-85, Buffalo Bills 1986, Tampa Bay Buccaneers 1987-88, joined Lions in 1989.

Charlie Sanders, receivers; born August 25, 1946, Greensboro, N.C., lives in Rochester, Mich. Tight end Minnesota 1966-67. Pro tight end Detroit Lions 1968-77. Pro coach: Joined Lions in 1989.

Jerry Wampfler, offensive line; born August 6, 1932, New Philadelphia, Ohio, lives in Lake Orion, Mich. Tackle Miami, Ohio 1951-54. No pro playing experience. College coach: Presbyterian 1955, Miami, Ohio 1963-65, Notre Dame 1966-69, Colorado State 1970-72 (head coach). Pro coach: Philadelphia Eagles 1973-75, 1979-83, Buffalo Bills 1976-77, New York Giants 1978, Green Bay Packers 1984-87, San Diego Chargers 1988, joined Lions in 1989.

Woody Widenhofer, defensive coordinator, outside linebackers; born January 20, 1943, Riverview, Mich., lives in Rochester Hills, Mich. Linebacker Missouri 1961-64. No pro playing experience. College coach: Michigan State 1969-70, Eastern Michigan 1971, Minnesota 1972, Missouri 1985-88 (head coach). Pro coach: Pittsburgh Steelers 1973-83, Oklahoma Outlaws (USFL) 1984 (head coach), joined Lions in 1989.

Detroit Lions 1991 First-Year Roster

Name	Pos.	Ht.	Wt.	Birth-date	College	Hometown	How Acq.
Alexander, Zeno	LB	6-1	224	3/13/68	Arizona	Houston, Tex.	D12
Andrews, Rich	K	5-10	160	3/11/69	Florida State	Coral Springs, Fla.	D6
Barrett, Reggie	WR	6-3	215	8/14/69	Texas-El Paso	Corpus Christi, Tex.	D3
Chesley, Delmar (1)	LB	6-2	235	1/13/66	Southern California	Washington, D.C.	FA
Conover, Scott	G	6-4	276	8/27/68	Purdue	Freehold, N.J.	D5
Fortin, Roman (1)	T	6-5	270	2/26/67	San Diego State	Columbus, Ohio	D8b-'90
Green, Willie (1)	WR	6-2	179	4/2/66	Mississippi	Athens, Ga.	D8a-'90
Hinckley, Rob (1)	LB	6-4	241	7/19/67	Stanford	Walnut Creek, Calif.	D4-'90
Jackson, Cedric	RB	5-11	229	1/13/68	Texas Christian	Texarkana, Tex.	D8
Jones, Greg	QB	6-2	208	7/1/67	West Virginia	Miami, Fla.	FA
Kramer, Erik (1)	QB	6-1	195	11/6/64	North Carolina State	Madison, Ky.	FA
Milburn, Darryl	DE	6-3	255	10/25/68	Grambling	Baton Rouge, La.	D9
Moore, Herman	WR	6-3	205	10/20/69	Virginia	Danville, Va.	D1
Patrick, Greg	CB-S	6-0	215	6/12/69	Brown	Canton, Ohio	FA
Pettaway, Claude	CB-S	5-10	198	10/17/68	Maine	Washington, D.C.	FA
Pritchett, Kelvin	DE	6-2	281	10/24/69	Mississippi	Atlanta, Ga.	T(Dall)-'91
Scott, Kevin	CB	5-9	175	5/19/69	Stanford	Phoenix, Ariz.	D4
Thomas, Franklin	TE	6-4	245	4/22/68	Grambling	New Orleans, La.	D7
Valerie, Kerry	S	5-10	190	10/31/68	Southern Mississippi	Mobile, Ala.	FA
Van Horse, Sean (1)	CB	5-10	180	7/22/68	Howard	Baltimore, Md.	FA
Wallace, Darrell	RB-WR	5-9	180	9/27/65	Missouri	Nashville, Tenn.	FA
Ware, Riley	CB	5-9	175	9/19/66	Western Kentucky	Ft. Myers, Fla.	FA
Watkins, Slip	KR-WR	5-9	173	9/29/67	Louisiana State	Ft. Lauderdale, Fla.	D11

The term NFL Rookie is defined as a player who is in his first season of professional football and has not been on the roster of another professional football team for any regular-season or postseason games. A Rookie is designated by an "R" on NFL rosters. Players who have been active in another professional football league or players who have NFL experience, including either preseason training camp or being on an active roster for fewer than three regular-season or postseason games, are termed NFL First-Year Players. An NFL First-Year Player is designated by a "1" on NFL rosters. Thereafter, a player on an NFL active roster for at least three regular-season or postseason games is credited with an additional year of NFL playing experience.

NOTES

GREEN BAY PACKERS

National Football Conference Central Division

Team Colors: Dark Green, Gold, and White

1265 Lombardi Avenue
P.O. Box 10628
Green Bay, Wisconsin 54307-0628
Telephone: (414) 496-5700

Club Officials

Chairman of the Board: Robert J. Parins
President, CEO: Bob Harlan
Vice President: John Fabry
Secretary: Peter M. Platten III
Treasurer: John R. Underwood
Chief Financial Officer: Michael R. Reinfeldt
Exec. Vice President, Football Operations: Tom Braatz
Exec. Assistant to the President: Phil Pionek
Exec. Director of Public Relations: Lee Remmel
Director of Marketing/Community Relations: Jeff Cieply
Asst. Director of Public Relations: Jeff Blumb
Green Bay Ticket Director: Mark Wagner
Milwaukee Ticket Director: Marge Paget
Controller: Dick Blasczyk
Video Director: Al Treml
Trainer: Domenic Gentile
Equipment Manager: Bob Noel

Stadium: Lambeau Field • **Capacity:** 59,543
P.O. Box 10628
1265 Lombardi Avenue
Green Bay, Wisconsin 54307-0628

Milwaukee County Stadium • **Capacity:** 56,051
Highway I-94
Milwaukee, Wisconsin 53214

Playing Surfaces: Grass

Training Camp: St. Norbert College
West DePere, Wisconsin 54115

1991 Schedule

Preseason

Aug. 3	**New England**	6:00
Aug. 10	at New Orleans	7:00
Aug. 17	vs. Buffalo at Madison, Wis.	12:00
Aug. 24	**Cincinnati**	6:00

Regular Season

Sept. 1	**Philadelphia**	12:00
Sept. 8	at Detroit	1:00
Sept. 15	**Tampa Bay**	12:00
Sept. 22	at Miami	1:00
Sept. 29	at Los Angeles Rams	1:00
Oct. 6	**Dallas** at Milwaukee	12:00
Oct. 13	**Open Date**	
Oct. 17	**Chicago** (Thursday)	6:30
Oct. 27	at Tampa Bay	1:00
Nov. 3	at New York Jets	1:00
Nov. 10	**Buffalo** at Milwaukee	12:00
Nov. 17	**Minnesota**	12:00
Nov. 24	**Indianapolis** at Milwaukee	12:00
Dec. 1	at Atlanta	1:00
Dec. 8	at Chicago	12:00
Dec. 15	**Detroit**	12:00
Dec. 21	at Minnesota (Saturday)	3:00

Packers Coaching History

(485-401-36)

1921-49	Earl (Curly) Lambeau	212-106-21
1950-53	Gene Ronzani*	14-31-1
1953	Hugh Devore- Ray (Scooter) McLean**	0-2-0
1954-57	Lisle Blackbourn	17-31-0
1958	Ray (Scooter) McLean	1-10-1
1959-67	Vince Lombardi	98-30-4
1968-70	Phil Bengtson	20-21-1
1971-74	Dan Devine	25-28-4
1975-83	Bart Starr	53-77-3
1984-87	Forrest Gregg	25-37-1
1988-90	Lindy Infante	20-28-0

*Released after 10 games in 1953
**Co-coaches

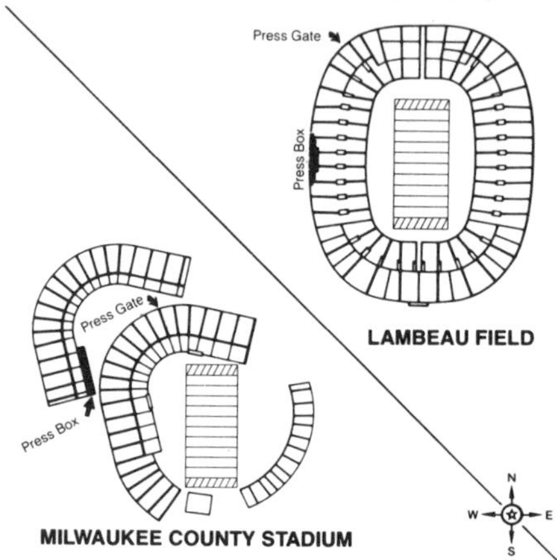

Record Holders

Individual Records—Career

Category	Name	Performance
Rushing (Yds.)	Jim Taylor, 1958-1966	8,207
Passing (Yds.)	Bart Starr, 1956-1971	23,718
Passing (TDs)	Bart Starr, 1956-1971	152
Receiving (No.)	James Lofton, 1978-1986	530
Receiving (Yds.)	James Lofton, 1978-1986	9,656
Interceptions	Bobby Dillon, 1952-59	52
Punting (Avg.)	Dick Deschaine, 1955-57	42.6
Punt Return (Avg.)	Billy Grimes, 1950-52	13.2
Kickoff Return (Avg.)	Travis Williams, 1967-1970	26.7
Field Goals	Chester Marcol, 1972-1980	120
Touchdowns (Tot.)	Don Hutson, 1935-1945	105
Points	Don Hutson, 1935-1945	823

Individual Records—Single Season

Category	Name	Performance
Rushing (Yds.)	Jim Taylor, 1962	1,407
Passing (Yds.)	Lynn Dickey, 1983	4,458
Passing (TDs)	Lynn Dickey, 1983	32
Receiving (No.)	Sterling Sharpe, 1989	90
Receiving (Yds.)	Sterling Sharpe, 1989	1,423
Interceptions	Irv Comp, 1943	10
Punting (Avg.)	Jerry Norton, 1963	44.7
Punt Return (Avg.)	Billy Grimes, 1950	19.1
Kickoff Return (Avg.)	Travis Williams, 1967	41.1
Field Goals	Chester Marcol, 1972	33
Touchdowns (Tot.)	Jim Taylor, 1962	19
Points	Paul Hornung, 1960	*176

Individual Records—Single Game

Category	Name	Performance
Rushing (Yds.)	Jim Taylor, 12-3-61	186
Passing (Yds.)	Lynn Dickey, 10-12-80	418
Passing (TDs)	Many times Last time by Lynn Dickey, 9-4-83	5
Receiving (No.)	Don Hutson, 11-22-42	14
Receiving (Yds.)	Bill Howton, 10-21-56	257
Interceptions	Bobby Dillon, 11-26-53	*4
	Willie Buchanon, 9-24-78	*4
Field Goals	Chris Jacke, 11-11-90	5
Touchdowns (Tot.)	Paul Hornung, 12-12-65	5
Points	Paul Hornung, 10-8-61	33

*NFL Record

1990 Team Record

Preseason (1-3)

Date	Result		Opponents
8/11	L	10-25	Cleveland
8/18	W	27-13	vs. New Orleans at Madison, Wis.
8/25	L	14-17	vs. Atlanta at Milwaukee
8/31	L	14-27	at Kansas City
		65-82	

Regular Season (6-10)

Date	Result		Opponents	Att.
9/9	W	36-24	L.A. Rams	57,685
9/16	L	13-31	Chicago	58,938
9/23	L	3-17	Kansas City	58,817
9/30	W	24-21	at Detroit	64,509
10/7	L	13-27	at Chicago	59,929
10/14	L	14-26	at Tampa Bay	67,472
10/28	W	24-10	Minnesota	55,125
11/4	L	20-24	San Francisco	58,835
11/11	W	29-16	at L.A. Raiders	50,855
11/18	W	24-21	at Phoenix	46,878
11/25	W	20-10	Tampa Bay	53,677
12/2	L	7-23	at Minnesota	62,058
12/9	L	14-20	Seattle	52,015
12/16	L	0-31	at Philadelphia	65,627
12/22	L	17-24	Detroit	46,700
12/30	L	13-22	at Denver	46,943

Score by Periods

Packers	36	76	57	102	0	—	271
Opponents	64	103	88	92	0	—	347

Attendance

Home 441,792 Away 464,271 Total 906,063
Single-game home record, 56,895 (11-3-85, Lambeau Field), 56,258 (9-28-80, Milwaukee County Stadium)
Single-season home record, 445,335 (1989)

1990 Team Statistics

	Packers	Opp.
Total First Downs	276	286
Rushing	72	113
Passing	183	160
Penalty	21	13
Third Down: Made/Att.	76/196	85/210
Third Down: Pct.	38.8	40.5
Fourth Down: Made/Att.	5/14	3/9
Fourth Down: Pct.	35.7	33.3
Total Net Yards	4675	5442
Avg. Per Game	292.2	340.1
Total Plays	953	981
Avg. Per Play	4.9	5.5
Net Yards Rushing	1369	2059
Avg. Per Game	85.6	128.7
Total Rushes	350	475
Net Yards Passing	3306	3383
Avg. Per Game	206.6	211.4
Sacked/Yards Lost	62/390	27/172
Gross Yards	3696	3555
Att./Completions	541/302	479/256
Completion Pct.	55.8	53.4
Had Intercepted	21	16
Punts/Avg.	65/37.4	69/39.1
Net Punting Avg.	32.7	31.7
Penalties/Yards Lost	84/674	109/854
Fumbles/Ball Lost	37/22	26/14
Touchdowns	29	40
Rushing	5	16
Passing	20	20
Returns	4	4
Avg. Time of Possession	29:34	30:26

1990 Individual Statistics

Scoring	TD R	TD P	TD Rt	PAT	FG	Saf	TP
Jacke	0	0	0	28/29	23/30	0	97
Sharpe	0	6	0	0/0	0/0	0	36
West	0	5	0	0/0	0/0	0	30
Query	0	2	1	0/0	0/0	0	18
Haddix	0	2	0	0/0	0/0	0	12
Kemp	0	2	0	0/0	0/0	0	12
Thompson	1	0	1	0/0	0/0	0	12
Fontenot	0	1	0	0/0	0/0	0	6
Fullwood	1	0	0	0/0	0/0	0	6
Greene	0	0	1	0/0	0/0	0	6
Kiel	1	0	0	0/0	0/0	0	6
Majkowski	1	0	0	0/0	0/0	0	6
Patterson	0	0	1	0/0	0/0	0	6
Weathers	0	1	0	0/0	0/0	0	6
Woodside	1	0	0	0/0	0/0	0	6
Workman	0	1	0	0/0	0/0	0	6
Packers	5	20	4	28/29	23/30	0	271
Opponents	16	20	4	39/40	22/34	1	347

Passing	Att.	Comp.	Yds.	Pct.	TD	Int.	Tkld.	Rate
Majkowski	264	150	1925	56.8	10	12	32/178	73.5
Dilweg	192	101	1267	52.6	8	7	22/150	72.1
Kiel	85	51	504	60.0	2	2	8/62	74.8
Packers	541	302	3696	55.8	20	21	62/390	73.2
Opponents	479	256	3555	53.4	20	16	27/172	77.5

Rushing	Att.	Yds.	Avg.	LG	TD
Haddix	98	311	3.2	13	0
Thompson	76	264	3.5	37	1
Majkowski	29	186	6.4	24	1
Woodside	46	182	4.0	21	1
Fullwood	44	124	2.8	16	1
Dilweg	21	114	5.4	22	0
Fontenot	17	76	4.5	18	0
Workman	8	51	6.4	31	0
Query	3	39	13.0	18	0
Sharpe	2	14	7.0	10	0
Kiel	5	9	1.8	4	1
Kemp	1	−1	−1.0	−1	0
Packers	350	1369	3.9	37	5
Opponents	475	2059	4.3	52	16

Receiving	No.	Yds.	Avg.	LG	TD
Sharpe	67	1105	16.5	76t	6
Kemp	44	527	12.0	29	2
Query	34	458	13.5	47t	2
Weathers	33	390	11.8	29	1
Fontenot	31	293	9.5	59	1
West	27	356	13.2	50	5
Woodside	24	184	7.7	25	0
Haddix	13	94	7.2	28	2
J. Harris	12	157	13.1	26	0
Wilson	7	84	12.0	18	0
Workman	4	30	7.5	9	1
Fullwood	3	17	5.7	10	0
Thompson	3	1	0.3	1	0
Packers	302	3696	12.2	76t	20
Opponents	256	3555	13.9	74	20

Interceptions	No.	Yds.	Avg.	LG	TD
Butler	3	42	14.0	28	0
Holmes	3	39	13.0	24	0
Murphy	3	6	2.0	4	0
Stephen	2	26	13.0	26	0
Holland	1	32	32.0	32	0
Patterson	1	9	9.0	9t	1
Cecil	1	0	0.0	0	0
Lee	1	0	0.0	0	0
Pitts	1	0	0.0	0	0
Packers	16	154	9.6	32	1
Opponents	21	293	14.0	47	2

Punting	No.	Yds.	Avg.	In 20	LG
Bracken	64	2431	38.0	17	59
Packers	65	2431	37.4	17	59
Opponents	69	2698	39.1	16	61

Punt Returns	No.	FC	Yds.	Avg.	LG	TD
Query	32	7	308	9.6	25	0
Pitts	0	2	0	—	0	0
Packers	32	9	308	9.6	25	0
Opponents	34	13	266	7.8	30	0

Kickoff Returns	No.	Yds.	Avg.	LG	TD
Wilson	35	798	22.8	36	0
Workman	14	210	15.0	26	0
Bland	7	104	14.9	24	0
Fontenot	3	88	29.3	50	0
Thompson	3	103	34.3	76t	1
West	1	0	0.0	0	0
Packers	63	1303	20.7	76t	1
Opponents	56	1125	20.1	87	0

Sacks	No.
T. Harris	7.0
Brock	4.0
Patterson	4.0
Bennett	3.0
Brown	3.0
Dent	1.0
Holmes	1.0
Murphy	1.0
Nelson	1.0
Noble	1.0
Stephen	1.0
Packers	27.0
Opponents	62.0

1991 Draft Choices

Round	Name	Pos.	College
1.	Vinnie Clark	DB	Ohio State
2.	Esera Tuaolo	NT	Oregon State
3.	Don Davey	DE	Wisconsin
	Chuck Webb	RB	Tennessee
5.	Jeff Fite	P	Memphis State
6.	Walter Dean	RB	Grambling
	Joe Garten	C	Colorado
7.	Frank Blevins	LB	Oklahoma
	Reggie Burnette	LB	Houston
8.	Johnny Walker	WR	Texas
9.	Dean Witkowski	LB	North Dakota
10.	Rapier Porter	TE	Ark.-Pine Bluff
11.	J.J. Wierenga	DE	Central Michigan
12.	Linzy Collins	WR	Missouri

Green Bay Packers 1991 Veteran Roster

No.	Name	Pos.	Ht.	Wt.	Birth-date	NFL Exp.	College	Hometown	How Acq.	'90 Games/ Starts
74	Archambeau, Lester	DE	6-4	270	6/27/67	2	Stanford	Montville, N.J.	D7-'90	4/0
67	Ard, Billy	G	6-3	273	3/12/59	11	Wake Forest	Watchung, N.J.	PB(NYG)-'89#	15/15
76	Ariey, Mike	T	6-5	287	3/12/64	2	San Diego State	Bakersfield, Calif.	FA-'91	0*
90	Bennett, Tony	LB	6-2	233	7/1/67	2	Mississippi	Alligator, Miss.	D1a-'90	14/0
83	Bland, Carl	WR	5-11	179	8/17/61	8	Virginia Union	Richmond, Va.	FA-'90	14/0
17	Bracken, Don	P	6-1	218	2/16/62	7	Michigan	Thermopolis, Wyo.	FA-'85	16/0
62	†Brock, Matt	DE-NT	6-5	285	1/14/66	3	Oregon	San Diego, Calif.	D3a-'89	16/16
93	Brown, Robert	DE	6-3	270	5/21/60	10	Virginia Tech	Edenton, N.C.	D4-'82	16/16
51	Bush, Blair	C	6-3	273	11/25/56	14	Washington	Palos Verdes, Calif.	PB(Sea)-'89#	16/0
36	Butler, LeRoy	CB	6-0	192	7/19/68	2	Florida State	Jacksonville, Fla.	D2-'90	16/0
63	†Campen, James	C	6-2	275	6/11/64	5	Tulane	Sacramento, Calif.	PB(NO)-'89#	16/16
26	†Cecil, Chuck	S	6-0	188	11/8/64	4	Arizona	San Diego, Calif.	D4a-'88	9/8
78	Cheek, Louis	G-T	6-6	295	10/6/64	4	Texas A&M	Fairfield, Tex.	PB(Phil)-'91#	5/1*
55	Clark, Greg	LB	6-0	232	3/5/65	4	Arizona State	Torrance, Calif.	PB(Rams)-'91#	11/0*
56	†Dent, Burnell	LB	6-1	234	3/16/63	6	Tulane	New Orleans, La.	D6-'86	15/2
60	Derby, Glenn	T-G	6-6	290	6/27/64	3	Wisconsin	Oconomowoc, Wis.	PB(NO)-'91#	4/0*
8	†Dilweg, Anthony	QB	6-3	198	3/28/65	3	Duke	Bethesda, Md.	D3b-'89	9/7
27	†Fontenot, Herman	RB	6-0	205	9/12/63	7	Louisiana State	Beaumont, Tex.	T(Clev)-'89	14/0
23	Greene, Tiger	S	6-0	192	2/15/62	7	Western Carolina	Flat Rock, N.C.	FA-'86	16/8
35	Haddix, Michael	RB	6-1	230	12/27/61	9	Mississippi State	Walnut, Miss.	PB(Phil)-'89#	16/12
72	Hall, Mark	DE	6-4	280	8/21/65	3	Southwestern Louisiana	Patterson, La.	FA-'89	3/0
65	Hallstrom, Ron	G	6-6	297	6/11/59	10	Iowa	Moline, Ill.	D1-'82	16/4
80	Harris, Jackie	TE	6-3	240	1/4/68	2	Northeast Louisiana	Pine Bluff, Ark.	D4-'90	16/3
97	†Harris, Tim	LB	6-6	258	9/10/64	6	Memphis State	Memphis, Tenn.	D4a-'86	16/16
89	Harris, William	TE	6-5	255	2/10/65	4	Bishop College	Houston, Tex.	FA-'91	4/0*
24	Hauck, Tim	S	5-11	185	12/20/66	2	Montana	Big Timbers, Mont.	PB(NE)-'91#	10/0*
50	†Holland, Johnny	LB	6-1	233	3/11/65	5	Texas A&M	Hempstead, Tex.	D2-'87	16/16
44	Holmes, Jerry	CB	6-1	176	12/22/57	10	West Virginia	Hampton, Va.	PB(Det)-'90#	16/16
13	†Jacke, Chris	K	6-0	197	3/12/66	3	Texas-El Paso	Richardson, Tex.	D6-'89	16/0
71	Jones, Scott	T	6-5	282	3/20/66	3	Washington	Port Angeles, Wash.	PB(NYJ)-'91#	3/0*
81	Kemp, Perry	WR	5-11	165	12/31/61	5	California, Pa.	McDonald, Pa.	FA-'88	16/16
10	Kiel, Blair	QB	6-0	203	11/29/61	7	Notre Dame	Columbus, Ind.	FA-'89	3/1
48	Kinchen, Brian	TE	6-2	232	8/6/65	4	Louisiana State	Baton Rouge, La.	PB(Mia)-'91#	4/0*
59	Larson, Kurt	LB	6-4	244	2/25/66	3	Michigan State	Waukesha, Wis.	PB(Ind)-'91#	16/0*
22	Lee, Mark	CB	6-0	195	3/20/58	12	Washington	Hanford, Calif.	D2-'80	16/16
7	†Majkowski, Don	QB	6-2	208	2/25/64	5	Virginia	DePew, N.Y.	D10-'87	9/8
77	Mandarich, Tony	T	6-5	295	9/23/66	3	Michigan State	Kent, Ohio	D1-'89	16/16
47	Mitchell, Roland	CB	5-11	180	3/15/64	5	Texas Tech	Bay City, Tex.	PB(Atl)-'91#	13/2*
57	Moran, Rich	G	6-2	283	3/19/62	7	San Diego State	Pleasanton, Calif.	D3-'85	16/1
37	Murphy, Mark	S	6-2	203	4/22/58	10	West Liberty State	Canton, Ohio	FA-'80	16/16
79	Nelson, Bob	NT	6-4	275	3/3/59	5	Miami	Baltimore, Md.	FA-'88	14/14
43	Neubert, Keith	TE	6-6	250	9/13/64	2	Nebraska	Fort Atkinson, Wis.	FA-'91	0*
91	Noble, Brian	LB	6-4	243	9/6/62	7	Arizona State	Anaheim, Calif.	D5-'85	14/14
4	Norseth, Mike	QB	6-3	202	8/22/64	3	Kansas	La Crescenta, Calif.	FA-'90	0*
96	†Patterson, Shawn	DE	6-4	270	6/13/64	4	Arizona State	Tempe, Ariz.	D2-'88	11/0
95	Paup, Bryce	LB	6-5	245	2/29/68	2	Northern Iowa	Scranton, Iowa	D6-'90	5/0
28	†Pitts, Ron	CB	5-10	183	10/14/62	6	UCLA	Orchard Park, N.Y.	FA-'88	16/0
85	†Query, Jeff	WR	6-0	167	3/7/67	3	Millikin	Maroa, Ill.	D5a-'89	16/0
31	Rice, Allen	RB	5-10	206	4/5/62	8	Baylor	Houston, Tex.	PB(Minn)-'91#	15/0*
75	Ruettgers, Ken	T	6-5	288	8/20/62	7	Southern California	Bakersfield, Calif.	D1-'85	11/11
84	Sharpe, Sterling	WR	6-0	202	4/6/65	4	South Carolina	Glennville, Ga.	D1-'88	16/16
45	Sikahema, Vai	RB-KR	5-9	191	8/29/62	6	Brigham Young	Mesa, Ariz.	PB(Phx)-'91#	16/0*
54	†Stephen, Scott	LB	6-2	243	6/18/64	5	Arizona State	Los Angeles, Calif.	D3b-'87	16/16
39	Thompson, Darrell	RB	6-0	215	11/23/67	2	Minnesota	Rochester, Minn.	D1b-'90	16/0
18	Tomczak, Mike	QB	6-1	195	10/23/62	7	Ohio State	Calumet City, Ill.	PB(Chi)-'91#	16/2*
70	Uecker, Keith	G-T	6-5	295	6/29/60	8	Auburn	Hollywood, Fla.	W(Den)-'84	13/13
87	Weathers, Clarence	WR	5-8	182	1/10/62	9	Delaware State	Fort Pierce, Fla.	PB(KC)-'90#	14/0
52	Weddington, Mike	LB	6-3	243	10/9/60	6	Oklahoma	Temple, Tex.	FA-'86	6/0
86	West, Ed	TE	6-1	240	8/2/61	8	Auburn	Leighton, Ala.	FA-'84	16/16
88	Wilson, Charles	WR	5-9	174	7/1/68	2	Memphis State	Godby, Fla.	D5-'90	15/0
68	Winter, Blaise	DE	6-4	282	1/31/62	7	Syracuse	Blauvelt, N.Y.	FA-'90	13/0
29	Woods, Jerry	S	5-8	193	2/13/66	2	Northern Michigan	Racine, Wis.	FA-'90	16/0
33	Woodside, Keith	RB	6-0	200	7/29/64	4	Texas A&M	Vidalia, La.	D3-'88	16/13
46	†Workman, Vince	RB	5-10	195	5/9/68	3	Ohio State	Dublin, Ohio	D5b-'89	15/0

* Ariey last active with Green Bay in '89; Cheek played 5 games with Philadelphia in '90; Clark played 11 games with L.A. Rams; Derby played 4 games with New Orleans; W. Harris played 4 games with Green Bay; Hauck played 10 games with New England; Jones played 3 games with N.Y. Jets; Kinchen played 4 games with Miami; Larson played 16 games with Indianapolis; Mitchell played 13 games with Atlanta; Neubert last active with N.Y. Jets in '89; Norseth active for 2 games but did not play; Rice played 15 games with Minnesota; Sikahema played 16 games with Phoenix; Tomczak played 16 games with Chicago.

† Option playout; subject to developments.

Plan B unconditional free agent.

Players lost through Plan B (2): TE Craig Hudson (Dall; 9 games in '90), T Alan Veingrad (Dall; 16).

Also played with Packers in '90—RB Brent Fullwood (5 games), LB Bobby Houston (1).

COACHING STAFF

Head Coach, Lindy Infante

Pro Career: Named Packers' head coach on February 3, 1988, after serving as offensive coordinator of Cleveland Browns in 1986-87. In that two-year span the Browns won more games (22) than any other team in the AFC. Was previously head coach of the Jacksonville Bulls (USFL) in 1984-85, compiling a 15-21 record. Earlier had been quarterback, receivers coach of the Cincinnati Bengals in 1980-81 and offensive coordinator in 1982, helping Bengals gain Super Bowl XVI berth in 1981 and compile the best record in the NFL over the 1981-82 seasons (19-6). Began pro coaching career with Charlotte Hornets (WFL) in 1975, later moving into the NFL with the New York Giants in 1978. Career record: 20-28.

Background: Running back and defensive back at University of Florida 1960-62, winning second-team All-Southeastern Conference honors as senior, when he also was a team captain. Entered coaching at Miami High School 1965. College assistant at Florida 1966-71, Memphis State 1972-74, and Tulane 1976, 1979.

Personal: Born May 27, 1940, in Miami, Fla. Attended Miami High School. He and his wife, Stephanie, live in Green Bay and have two sons, Brett and Brad.

Assistant Coaches

Greg Blache, defensive line; born March 9, 1949, New Orleans, La., lives in Green Bay. No college or pro playing experience. College coach: Notre Dame 1973-75, 1981-83, Tulane 1976-80, Southern University 1986, Kansas 1987. Pro coach: Jacksonville Bulls (USFL) 1984-85, joined Packers in 1988.

Hank Bullough, defensive coordinator; born January 24, 1934, Scranton, Pa., lives in Green Bay. Offensive guard Michigan State 1952-54. Pro offensive guard Green Bay Packers 1955, 1958. College coach: Michigan State 1959-69. Pro coach: Baltimore Colts 1970-72, New England Patriots 1973-79, Cincinnati Bengals 1980-83, Pittsburgh Maulers (USFL) 1984-85, Buffalo Bills 1985-86 (compiled 4-17 record as head coach from October 1, 1985, through November 3, 1986), joined Packers in 1988.

Joe B. Clark, general offensive assistant; born December 22, 1932, Los Angeles, Calif., lives in Green Bay. Quarterback Santa Clara 1951-52. No pro playing experience. College coach: Wooster College 1958-59, Detroit 1960-64, Tulane 1965-70, Memphis State 1974, Nicholls State 1981-83, Southeastern Louisiana 1985, Southern University 1986. Pro coach: Charlotte Hornets (WFL) 1975, Jacksonville Bulls (USFL) 1984-85, joined Packers in 1988.

Charlie Davis, offensive line; born August 7, 1944, San Diego, Calif., lives in Green Bay. Linebacker San Diego City College 1961, UCLA 1962-64. No pro playing experience. College coach: San Francisco State 1967-70, Xavier 1971-73, Ball State 1974-75, Tulane 1976-80. Pro coach: Jacksonville Bulls (USFL) 1984-85, Cleveland Browns 1986-87, joined Packers in 1988.

Buddy Geis, receivers; born September 16, 1946, Altoona, Pa., lives in Green Bay. Running back Lock Haven State 1967-69. No pro playing experience. College coach: Arizona 1973-76, Tulane 1977-82, Memphis State 1986-87. Pro coach: Jacksonville Bulls (USFL) 1984-85, joined Packers in 1988.

Dick Jauron, defensive backfield; born October 7, 1950, Peoria, Ill., lives in Green Bay. Defensive back Yale 1970-72. Pro defensive back Detroit Lions 1973-77, Cincinnati Bengals 1978-80. Pro coach: Buffalo Bills 1985, joined Packers in 1986.

Virgil Knight, tight ends; born January 30, 1948, Clarksville, Ark., lives in Green Bay. Tight end Northeastern Oklahoma 1968-70. No pro playing experience. College coach: Arkansas Tech 1975-78, Florida 1979-80, Auburn 1981-83. Pro coach: Joined Packers in 1984.

Green Bay Packers 1991 First-Year Roster

Name	Pos.	Ht.	Wt.	Birth-date	College	Hometown	How Acq.
Affholter, Erik (1)	WR	6-0	182	4/10/66	Southern California	Agoura, Calif.	D4-'89
Blevins, Frank	LB	6-4	232	12/31/68	Oklahoma	Killeen, Tex.	D7a
Burnett, Reggie	LB	6-1	235	10/4/68	Houston	Rayville, La.	D7b
Clark, Vinnie	CB	5-11	189	1/22/69	Ohio State	Cincinnati, Ohio	D1
Collins, Linzy	WR	6-0	185	1/24/69	Missouri	St. Louis, Mo.	D12
Cromer, Steve	G	6-3	287	7/16/68	Washington State	Lewiston, Idaho	FA
Daluiso, Brad	K	6-2	207	12/31/67	UCLA	San Diego, Calif.	FA
Davey, Don	DE	6-3	269	4/8/68	Wisconsin	Manitowoc, Wis.	D3a
Dean, Walter	RB	5-9	211	5/1/68	Grambling	Grambling, La.	D6a
Donelson, Ventson (1)	CB	5-11	180	2/2/68	Michigan State	Detroit, Mich.	FA
Douglas, Derrick (1)	RB	5-10	205	8/10/68	Louisiana Tech	Shreveport, La.	FA
Finn, Michael	DE	6-5	290	9/26/67	Arkansas-Pine Bluff	Texarkana, Tex.	FA
Fite, Jeff	P	6-0	206	2/1/69	Memphis State	Memphis, Tenn.	D5
Garten, Joe	C-G	6-2	286	8/13/68	Colorado	Placentia, Calif.	D6b
Greathouse, Art	RB	5-9	200	7/20/68	Arizona	Tempe, Ariz.	FA
Hester, Joey (1)	P	6-1	195	5/7/66	Georgia	Cairo, Ga.	FA
Hutson, Brian (1)	S	6-1	200	2/20/65	Mississippi State	Brandon, Miss.	FA
Jurkovic, John (1)	NT	6-2	282	8/18/67	Eastern Illinois	Calumet City, Ill.	FA
Labbe, Rico (1)	S	6-0	210	6/16/67	Boston College	Rockville, Md.	FA-'90
McCutcheon, Mark	S	6-2	196	1/19/68	Tennessee State	Washington, D.C.	FA
Neta, Rob	WR	6-0	187	6/12/65	Wisconsin-Oshkosh	Shawano, Wis.	FA
Porter, Rapier	TE	6-3	275	8/14/66	Arkansas-Pine Bluff	Mobile, Ala.	D10
Ray, Billy	QB	6-2	201	1/17/68	Duke	Atlanta, Ga.	FA
Shorts, Pete (1)	DE	6-7	280	7/12/66	Illinois State	Clinton, Wis.	FA
Stewart, Reggie	LB	6-1	245	5/28/69	Mississippi State	Eupora, Miss.	FA
Tuaolo, Esera	NT	6-2	280	7/11/68	Oregon State	Chino, Calif.	D2
Walker, Johnny	WR	5-11	188	11/18/68	Texas	San Antonio, Tex.	D8
Webb, Chuck	RB	5-9	209	11/17/69	Tennessee	Toledo, Ohio	D3b
Wierenga, J.J.	DE	6-3	276	11/12/67	Central Michigan	Lowell, Mich.	D11
Witkowski, Dean	LB	6-1	238	7/7/68	North Dakota	North Fond du Lac, Wis.	D9

The term NFL Rookie is defined as a player who is in his first season of professional football and has not been on the roster of another professional football team for any regular-season or postseason games. A Rookie is designated by an "R" on NFL rosters. Players who have been active in another professional football league or players who have NFL experience, including either preseason training camp or being on an active roster for fewer than three regular-season or postseason games, are termed NFL First-Year Players. An NFL First-Year Player is designated by a "1" on NFL rosters. Thereafter, a player on an NFL active roster for at least three regular-season or postseason games is credited with an additional year of NFL playing experience.

NOTES

Dick Moseley, outside linebackers; born August 1, 1933, Detroit, Mich., lives in Green Bay. Running back-defensive back Eastern Michigan 1953-55. No pro playing experience. College coach: Eastern Michigan 1968-70, Wichita State 1971, Minnesota 1972-78, Colorado 1979-81. Pro coach: New Jersey Generals (USFL) 1982, Pittsburgh Maulers (USFL) 1983, Buffalo Bills 1984-85, Chicago Bruisers (Arena Football) 1987, joined Packers in 1988.

Willie Peete, offensive backfield; born July 14, 1937, Mesa, Ariz., lives in Green Bay. Fullback Arizona 1956-59. No pro playing experience. College coach: Arizona 1960-62, 1971-82. Pro coach: Kansas City Chiefs 1983-86, joined Packers in 1987.

Russell Riederer, strength and conditioning; born August 5, 1957, Holton, Kan., lives in Green Bay. Linebacker Kansas State 1975-78. No pro playing experience. College coach: Kansas State 1979-86, Purdue 1987-90. Pro coach: Joined Packers in 1991.

Howard Tippett, special teams; born September 23, 1938, Tallassee, Ala., lives in Green Bay. Quarterback-safety East Tennessee State 1956-58. No pro playing experience. College coach: Tulane 1963-65, West Virginia 1966, 1970-71, Houston 1967-69, Wake Forest 1972, Mississippi State 1973, 1979, Washington State 1976, Oregon 1977-78, UCLA 1980, Illinois 1987. Pro coach: Jacksonville Express (WFL) 1974-75, Tampa Bay Buccaneers 1981-86, joined Packers in 1988.

LOS ANGELES RAMS

National Football Conference Western Division

Team Colors: Royal Blue, Gold, and White

Business Address:
2327 West Lincoln Avenue
Anaheim, California 92801
Telephone: (714) 535-7267

Ticket Office:
Anaheim Stadium
1900 State College Boulevard
Anaheim, California 92806
Telephone: (714) 937-6767

Club Officials

President: Georgia Frontiere
Executive Vice President: John Shaw
Senior Vice President: Jay Zygmunt
Vice President-Media and Community Relations: Marshall Klein
Administrator, Football Operations: Jack Faulkner
Director of Operations: Dick Beam
General Counsel: Steve Novak
Director of Player Personnel: John Math
Administrative Assistant/Consultant: Paul (Tank) Younger
Director of Promotions/Sales: Pete Donovan
Director of Public Relations: John Oswald
Trainers: George Menefee, Jim Anderson, Blynn DeNiro
Equipment Managers: Don Hewitt, Todd Hewitt

Stadium: Anaheim Stadium • **Capacity:** 69,008
Anaheim, California 92806

Playing Surface: Grass

Training Camp: California-Irvine
Irvine, California 92717

1991 Schedule

Preseason

Aug. 3	vs. Atlanta at Jacksonville, Fla.	8:00
Aug. 12	**San Diego**	7:00
Aug. 17	**Seattle**	7:00
Aug. 22	vs. Houston at Memphis, Tenn.	7:00

Regular Season

Sept. 1	**Phoenix**	1:00
Sept. 8	at New York Giants	1:00
Sept. 15	at New Orleans	7:00
Sept. 22	at San Francisco	1:00
Sept. 29	**Green Bay**	1:00
Oct. 6	**Open Date**	
Oct. 13	**San Diego**	1:00
Oct. 20	at Los Angeles Raiders	1:00
Oct. 27	at Atlanta	1:00
Nov. 3	**New Orleans**	1:00
Nov. 10	**Kansas City**	1:00
Nov. 17	at Detroit	4:00
Nov. 25	**San Francisco** (Monday)	6:00
Dec. 1	**Washington**	1:00
Dec. 8	**Atlanta**	1:00
Dec. 15	at Minnesota	12:00
Dec. 22	at Seattle	5:00

Rams Coaching History

Cleveland 1937-45
(393-323-20)

1937-38	Hugo Bezdek*	1-13-0
1938	Art Lewis	4-4-0
1939-42	Earl (Dutch) Clark	16-26-2
1944	Aldo (Buff) Donelli	4-6-0
1945-46	Adam Walsh	16-5-1
1947	Bob Snyder	6-6-0
1948-49	Clark Shaughnessy	14-8-3
1950-52	Joe Stydahar**	19-9-0
1952-54	Hamp Pool	23-11-2
1955-59	Sid Gillman	28-32-1
1960-62	Bob Waterfield***	9-24-1
1962-65	Harland Svare	14-31-3
1966-70	George Allen	49-19-4
1971-72	Tommy Prothro	14-12-2
1973-77	Chuck Knox	57-20-1
1978-82	Ray Malavasi	43-36-0
1983-90	John Robinson	76-61-0

*Released after three games in 1938
**Resigned after one game in 1952
***Resigned after eight games in 1962

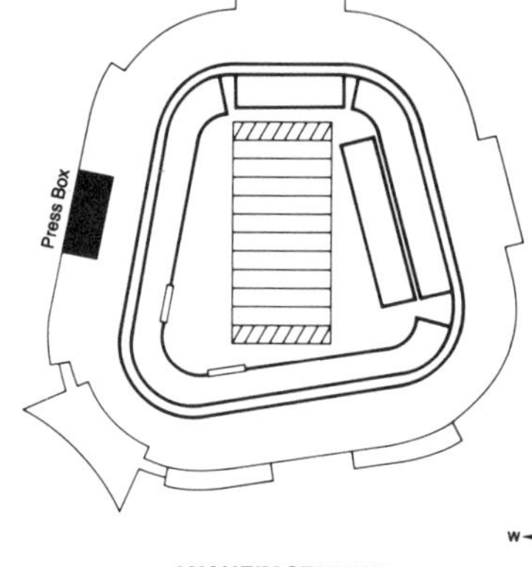

ANAHEIM STADIUM

Record Holders

Individual Records—Career

Category	Name	Performance
Rushing (Yds.)	Eric Dickerson, 1983-87	7,245
Passing (Yds.)	Roman Gabriel, 1962-1972	22,223
Passing (TDs)	Roman Gabriel, 1962-1972	154
Receiving (No.)	Henry Ellard, 1983-1990	421
Receiving (Yds.)	Henry Ellard, 1983-1990	7,037
Interceptions	Ed Meador, 1959-1970	46
Punting (Avg.)	Danny Villanueva, 1960-64	44.2
Punt Return (Avg.)	Henry Ellard, 1983-1990	11.3
Kickoff Return (Avg.)	Tom Wilson, 1956-1961	27.1
Field Goals	Mike Lansford, 1982-1990	158
Touchdowns (Tot.)	Eric Dickerson, 1983-87	58
Points	Mike Lansford, 1982-1990	789

Individual Records—Single Season

Category	Name	Performance
Rushing (Yds.)	Eric Dickerson, 1984	*2,105
Passing (Yds.)	Jim Everett, 1989	4,310
Passing (TDs)	Jim Everett, 1988	31
Receiving (No.)	Henry Ellard, 1988	86
Receiving (Yds.)	Elroy (Crazylegs) Hirsch, 1951	1,425
Interceptions	Dick (Night Train) Lane, 1952	*14
Punting (Avg.)	Danny Villanueva, 1962	45.5
Punt Return (Avg.)	Woodley Lewis, 1952	18.5
Kickoff Return (Avg.)	Verda (Vitamin T) Smith, 1950	33.7
Field Goals	David Ray, 1973	30
Touchdowns (Tot.)	Eric Dickerson, 1983	20
Points	David Ray, 1973	130

Individual Records—Single Game

Category	Name	Performance
Rushing (Yds.)	Eric Dickerson, 1-4-86	248
Passing (Yds.)	Norm Van Brocklin, 9-28-51	*554
Passing (TDs)	Many times	5
	Last time by Jim Everett, 9-25-88	
Receiving (No.)	Tom Fears, 12-3-50	*18
Receiving (Yds.)	Willie Anderson, 11-26-89	*336
Interceptions	Many times	3
	Last time by Pat Thomas, 10-7-79	
Field Goals	Bob Waterfield, 12-9-51	5
Touchdowns (Tot.)	Bob Shaw, 12-11-49	4
	Elroy (Crazylegs) Hirsch, 9-28-51	4
	Harold Jackson, 10-14-73	4
Points	Bob Shaw, 12-11-49	24
	Elroy (Crazylegs) Hirsch, 9-28-51	24
	Harold Jackson, 10-14-73	24

*NFL Record

1990 Team Record

Preseason (2-2)

Date	Result		Opponents
8/11	W	19- 3	vs. Kansas City at Berlin
8/18	L	27-30	San Diego
8/25	W	27- 7	Phoenix
8/31	L	10-37	at Washington
		83-77	

Regular Season (5-11)

Date	Result		Opponents	Att.
9/9	L	24-36	at Green Bay	57,685
9/16	W	35-14	at Tampa Bay	59,705
9/23	L	21-27	Philadelphia	63,644
10/7	L	31-34	Cincinnati (OT)	62,619
10/14	L	9-38	at Chicago	59,383
10/21	W	44-24	Atlanta	54,761
10/29	L	10-41	at Pittsburgh	56,466
11/4	W	17-13	Houston	52,628
11/11	L	7-31	N.Y. Giants	64,632
11/18	L	21-24	Dallas	58,589
11/25	W	28-17	at San Francisco	62,633
12/2	W	38-23	at Cleveland	61,981
12/9	L	20-24	New Orleans	56,864
12/17	L	10-26	San Francisco	65,619
12/23	L	13-20	at Atlanta	30,021
12/31	L	17-20	at New Orleans	68,647

(OT) Overtime

Score by Periods

Rams	62	130	85	68	0	—	345
Opponents	98	123	74	114	3	—	412

Attendance

Home 479,356 Away 456,521 Total 935,877
Single-game home record, 67,037 (12-23-84)
Single-season home record, 500,403 (1980)

1990 Team Statistics

	Rams	Opp.
Total First Downs	311	287
Rushing	89	93
Passing	191	176
Penalty	31	18
Third Down: Made/Att.	78/204	86/201
Third Down: Pct.	38.2	42.8
Fourth Down: Made/Att.	6/18	3/10
Fourth Down: Pct.	33.3	30.0
Total Net Yards	5430	5411
Avg. Per Game	339.4	338.2
Total Plays	1013	949
Avg. Per Play	5.4	5.7
Net Yards Rushing	1612	1649
Avg. Per Game	100.8	103.1
Total Rushes	422	418
Net Yards Passing	3818	3762
Avg. Per Game	238.6	235.1
Sacked/Yards Lost	30/198	30/180
Gross Yards	4016	3942
Att./Completions	561/310	501/296
Completion Pct.	55.3	59.1
Had Intercepted	17	12
Punts/Avg.	69/38.6	66/41.4
Net Punting Avg.	31.9	34.7
Penalties/Yards Lost	87/632	109/968
Fumbles/Ball Lost	25/14	32/19
Touchdowns	43	49
Rushing	17	17
Passing	24	30
Returns	2	2
Avg. Time of Possession	29:59	30:01

1990 Individual Statistics

Scoring	TD R	TD P	TD Rt	PAT	FG	Saf	TP
Gary	14	1	0	0/0	0/0	0	90
Lansford	0	0	0	42/43	15/24	0	87
McGee	1	4	0	0/0	0/0	0	30
Anderson	0	4	0	0/0	0/0	0	24
Delpino	0	4	0	0/0	0/0	0	24
Ellard	0	4	0	0/0	0/0	0	24
Johnson	0	3	0	0/0	0/0	0	18
Green	0	1	1	0/0	0/0	0	12
Holohan	0	2	0	0/0	0/0	0	12
Everett	1	0	0	0/0	0/0	0	6
Faison	0	1	0	0/0	0/0	0	6
Humphery	0	0	1	0/0	0/0	0	6
Warner	1	0	0	0/0	0/0	0	6
Rams	17	24	2	42/43	15/24	0	345
Opponents	17	30	2	46/49	24/31	0	412

Passing	Att.	Comp.	Yds.	Pct.	TD	Int.	Tkld.	Rate
Everett	554	307	3989	55.4	23	17	30/198	79.3
Long	5	1	4	20.0	0	0	0/0	39.6
McGee	2	2	23	100.0	1	0	0/0	154.2
Rams	561	310	4016	55.3	24	17	30/198	79.6
Opponents	501	296	3942	59.1	30	12	30/180	94.1

Rushing	Att.	Yds.	Avg.	LG	TD
Gary	204	808	4.0	48	14
Green	68	261	3.8	31	0
McGee	44	234	5.3	19	1
Warner	49	139	2.8	9	1
Dupree	19	72	3.8	13	0
Delpino	13	52	4.0	13	0
Everett	20	31	1.6	15	1
Ellard	2	21	10.5	13	0
Anderson	1	13	13.0	13	0
English	2	−19	−9.5	−8	0
Rams	422	1612	3.8	48	17
Opponents	418	1649	3.9	74t	17

Receiving	No.	Yds.	Avg.	LG	TD
Ellard	76	1294	17.0	50t	4
Anderson	51	1097	21.5	55t	4
Holohan	49	475	9.7	28	2
McGee	47	388	8.3	25	4
Gary	30	150	5.0	22t	1
A. Cox	17	266	15.6	32	0
Delpino	15	172	11.5	42t	4
Johnson	12	66	5.5	11	3
Carter	8	58	7.3	16	0
Faison	3	27	9.0	12	1
Green	2	23	11.5	16t	1
Rams	310	4016	13.0	55t	24
Opponents	296	3942	13.3	71t	30

Interceptions	No.	Yds.	Avg.	LG	TD
Humphery	4	52	13.0	44t	1
Newsome	4	47	11.8	22	0
Newman	2	0	0.0	0	0
Terrell	1	6	6.0	6	0
Henley	1	0	0.0	0	0
Rams	12	105	8.8	44t	1
Opponents	17	204	12.0	50t	2

Punting	No.	Yds.	Avg.	In 20	LG
English	68	2663	39.2	8	58
Rams	69	2663	38.6	8	58
Opponents	66	2733	41.4	20	57

Punt Returns	No.	FC	Yds.	Avg.	LG	TD
Henley	19	4	195	10.3	26	0
Sutton	14	3	136	9.7	22	0
Ellard	2	0	15	7.5	8	0
Rams	35	7	346	9.9	26	0
Opponents	46	11	420	9.1	33	0

Kickoff Returns	No.	Yds.	Avg.	LG	TD
Green	25	560	22.4	99t	1
Delpino	20	389	19.5	38	0
Berry	17	315	18.5	29	0
McDonald	1	15	15.0	15	0
Rams	63	1279	20.3	99t	1
Opponents	68	1406	20.7	50	0

Sacks	No.
Greene	13.0
Piel	5.0
Hawkins	3.0
Bethune	2.0
Faryniarz	2.0
Reed	2.0
B. Smith	1.0
Wilcher	1.0
Wright	1.0
Rams	30.0
Opponents	30.0

1991 Draft Choices

Round	Name	Pos.	College
1.	Todd Lyght	DB	Notre Dame
2.	Roman Phifer	LB	UCLA
4.	Robert Bailey	DB	Miami
5.	Robert Young	DE	Mississippi State
6.	Neal Fort	T	Brigham Young
7.	Tyrone Shelton	RB	William & Mary
8.	Pat Tyrance	LB	Nebraska
9.	Jeff Fields	NT	Arkansas State
11.	Terry Crews	LB	Western Michigan
12.	Jeff Pahukoa	T	Washington
	Ernie Thompson	RB	Indiana

Los Angeles Rams 1991 Veteran Roster

No.	Name	Pos.	Ht.	Wt.	Birth-date	NFL Exp.	College	Hometown	How Acq.	'90 Games/ Starts
83	Anderson, Willie	WR	6-0	172	3/7/65	4	UCLA	Paulsboro, N.J.	D2b-'88	16/11
82	Bailey, Stacey	WR	6-1	163	2/10/60	10	San Jose State	San Rafael, Calif.	FA-'91	3/1*
42	Barry, Latin	CB	5-10	196	1/13/67	2	Oregon	Lakeview Terrace, Calif.	D3-'90	16/0
57	†Bethune, George	LB	6-4	240	3/30/67	3	Alabama	Fort Walton Beach, Fla.	D7-'89	16/0
61	Brostek, Bern	G-C	6-3	295	9/11/66	2	Washington	Honolulu, Hawaii	D1-'90	16/2
59	Butcher, Paul	LB	6-0	230	11/8/63	5	Wayne State	Detroit, Mich.	FA-'90	16/1
88	Carter, Pat	TE	6-4	250	6/1/66	4	Florida State	Sarasota, Fla.	T(Det)-'89	16/4
84	Cox, Aaron	WR	5-9	178	3/13/65	4	Arizona State	Los Angeles, Calif.	D1b-'88	14/2
72	†Cox, Robert	T	6-5	285	12/30/63	5	UCLA	Dublin, Calif.	D6-'86	11/0
39	†Delpino, Robert	RB	6-0	205	11/2/65	4	Missouri	Dodge City, Kan.	D5a-'88	15/3
22	Dupree, Marcus	RB	6-2	225	7/21/61	2	Oklahoma	Meridian, Miss.	FA-'90	7/1
80	Ellard, Henry	WR	5-11	182	7/21/61	9	Fresno State	Fresno, Calif.	D2-'83	15/15
8	English, Keith	P	6-3	220	3/10/66	2	Colorado	Greeley, Colo.	T(SD)-'90	16/0
11	Everett, Jim	QB	6-5	212	1/3/63	6	Purdue	Albuquerque, N.M.	T(Hou)-'86	16/16
89	Faison, Derrick	WR	6-4	200	8/24/67	2	Howard	Lake City, S.C.	FA-'90	15/0
51	†Faryniarz, Brett	LB	6-3	235	7/23/65	4	San Diego State	Sacramento, Calif.	FA-'88	16/3
43	Gary, Cleveland	RB	6-0	226	5/4/66	3	Miami	Indiantown, Fla.	D1b-'89	15/7
25	†Gray, Jerry	CB	6-0	185	12/2/62	7	Texas	Austin, Tex.	D1-'85	12/12
91	Greene, Kevin	DE	6-3	250	7/31/62	7	Auburn	Granite City, Ill.	D5-'85	15/15
5	Hatcher, Dale	P	6-2	220	4/5/63	7	Clemson	Cheraw, S.C.	FA-'91	0*
70	Hawkins, Bill	DE	6-6	268	5/9/66	3	Miami	Miami, Fla.	D1a-'89	15/0
20	Henley, Darryl	CB	5-9	170	10/30/66	3	UCLA	La Verne, Calif.	D2c-'89	9/6
31	Jackson, Alfred	CB	6-0	177	7/10/67	3	San Diego State	Tulare, Calif.	FA-'91	5/0
86	Johnson, Damone	TE	6-4	250	3/2/62	5	Cal Poly-SLO	Santa Monica, Calif.	D6-'85	13/9
52	Kelm, Larry	LB	6-4	240	11/29/64	5	Texas A&M	Corpus Christi, Tex.	D4-'87	11/10
27	Lilly, Sammy	CB	5-9	178	2/12/65	3	Georgia Tech	Augusta, Ga.	PB(SD)-'91	10/0*
16	Long, Chuck	QB	6-4	221	2/18/63	6	Iowa	Wheaton, Ill.	T(Det)-'90	4/0
67	†Love, Duval	G	6-3	287	6/24/63	7	UCLA	Fountain Valley, Calif.	D10-'85	16/16
24	†McGee, Buford	RB	6-0	210	8/16/60	8	Mississippi	Durant, Miss.	T(SD)-'87	16/15
71	Milinichik, Joe	G	6-5	275	3/30/63	5	North Carolina State	Macungie, Pa.	PB(Det)-'90#	8/0
66	†Newberry, Tom	C-G	6-2	285	12/20/62	6	Wisconsin-LaCrosse	Onalaska, Wis.	D2-'86	15/15
26	Newman, Anthony	S	6-0	199	11/25/65	4	Oregon	Beaverton, Ore.	D2a-'88	16/6
75	†Pankey, Irv	T	6-5	295	2/15/58	11	Penn State	Aberdeen, Pa.	D2-'80	16/16
60	t-Perry, Gerald	T	6-6	305	11/12/64	4	Southern	Columbia, S.C.	T(Den)-'91	11/0*
95	Piel, Mike	DT	6-4	263	9/21/65	3	Illinois	El Toro, Calif.	D3-'88	16/11
93	Reed, Doug	DT	6-3	265	7/16/60	8	San Diego State	San Diego, Calif.	D4-'83	16/16
97	Robinson, Gerald	DE	6-3	262	5/4/63	4	Auburn	Notasulga, Ala.	PB(SD)-'91#	10/1*
55	Sanders, Glenell	LB	6-0	224	11/4/66	2	Louisiana Tech	Clinton, La.	PB(Chi)-'91#	2/0*
78	Slater, Jackie	T	6-4	285	5/27/54	16	Jackson State	Meridian, Miss.	D3-'76	15/15
96	Smith, Brian	DE	6-6	242	4/23/66	3	Auburn	Pelicka, Ala.	D2b-'89	16/4
56	Smith, Doug	C	6-3	272	11/25/56	14	Bowling Green	Columbus, Ohio	FA-'78	16/16
50	Stams, Frank	LB	6-2	240	7/17/65	3	Notre Dame	Akron, Ohio	D2a-'89	14/13
23	Stewart, Michael	S	6-0	195	7/12/65	5	Fresno State	Bakersfield, Calif.	D8-'87	16/11
53	†Strickland, Fred	LB	6-2	250	8/15/66	4	Purdue	Lakeland, N.J.	D2c-'88	5/5
30	Tatupu, Mosi	RB	6-0	227	4/26/55	14	Southern California	Honolulu, Hawaii	PB(NE)-'91#	15/0*
37	Terrell, Pat	S	6-0	195	3/18/68	2	Notre Dame	St. Petersburg, Fla.	D2-'90	15/1
94	Thomas, Ben	DE	6-3	275	7/2/61	5	Auburn	Auburn, Ala.	FA-'91	0*
21	Thomas, Rodney	CB	5-10	190	12/21/65	4	Brigham Young	Ontario, Calif.	PB(Mia)-'91#	15/0*
54	Wilcher, Mike	LB	6-3	245	3/20/60	9	North Carolina	Washington, D.C.	D2-'83	16/15
77	Wilson, Karl	DE	6-4	275	9/10/64	5	Louisiana State	Baton Rouge, La.	PB(Mia)-'91#	16/2*
99	Wright, Alvin	DT	6-2	285	2/5/61	6	Jacksonville State	Wedonee, Ala.	FA-'86	16/16
10	Zendejas, Tony	K	5-8	165	5/15/60	7	Nevada-Reno	Chino, Calif.	PB(Hou)-'91#	7/0*

* Bailey played 3 games with Atlanta in '90; Hatcher last active with Rams in '89; Lilly played 8 games with Philadelphia, 2 with San Diego; Perry played 11 games with Denver; Robinson played 10 games with San Diego; Sanders played 2 games with Chicago; Tatupu played 15 games with New England; B. Thomas last active with Atlanta in '89; R. Thomas played 15 games with Miami; Wilson played 16 games with Miami; Zendejas played 7 games with Houston.

† Option playout; subject to developments.

Plan B unconditional free agent.

t- Rams traded for Perry (Denver).

Traded—Running back Gaston Green to Denver.

Players lost through Plan B (6): LB Greg Clark (GB; 11 games in '90), TE Pete Holohan (KC; 16), CB Bobby Humphery (SD; 16), LB Bruce Klostermann (Raiders; 5), K Mike Lansford (Clev; 16), S Vince Newsome (Clev; 16).

Also played with Rams in '90—TE Richard Ashe (1 game), K John Carney (1), CB Clifford Hicks (1), WR Tony Lomack (3), LB Mike McDonald (16), G Jeff Mickel (1), CB-S Mickey Sutton (7), RB Curt Warner (7).

COACHING STAFF

Head Coach, John Robinson

Pro Career: Robinson is in his ninth season as head coach of the Rams. He is the winningest coach in club history and has led the Rams to six playoff appearances in eight years, including two trips to the NFC Championship Game (1985, 1990). Has guided the Rams to 10 or more wins in six different seasons. Entering this season, his 76 career victories rank ninth among active NFL head coaches. Became the seventeenth head coach in Rams' history on February 14, 1983. Arrived with 23 years of experience, including one on the professional level with the Raiders in 1975. No pro playing experience. Career record: 76-61.

Background: Played end at Oregon 1955-58. Began coaching career with his alma mater from 1960-71. Became an assistant at Southern California from 1972-74. Returned as head coach in 1976 before resigning after the 1982 season. Compiled seven-year .819 winning percentage at Southern California with 67 wins, 14 losses, and 2 ties.

Personal: Born July 25, 1935, Chicago, Ill. John and his wife, Linda, live in Yorba Linda, Calif.

Assistant Coaches

Tom Bettis, defensive backs; born March 17, 1933, Chicago Ill., lives in Anaheim, Calif. Linebacker-guard Purdue 1952-54. Pro linebacker Green Bay Packers 1955-61, Pittsburgh Steelers 1962, Chicago Bears 1963. Pro coach: Chicago Bears 1964-65 (scout), Kansas City Chiefs 1966-77, 1988, St. Louis Cardinals 1978-84, Cleveland Browns 1985, Houston Oilers 1986-87, Philadelphia Eagles 1989-90, joined Rams in 1991.

Jeff Fisher, defensive coordinator; born February 25, 1958, Culver City, Calif., lives in LaVerne, Calif. Defensive back Southern California 1978-80. Pro defensive back-punt returner Chicago Bears 1981-85. Pro coach: Philadelphia Eagles 1986-90, joined Rams in 1991.

Garrett Giemont, strength and conditioning; born August 31, 1957, Fullerton, Calif., lives in Irvine, Calif. No college or pro playing experience. Pro coach: Joined Rams in 1990.

Marv Goux, defensive line, administrative assistant; born September 8, 1932, Santa Barbara, Calif., lives in Long Beach, Calif. Linebacker Southern California 1952, 1954-55. No pro playing experience. College coach: Southern California 1957-82. Pro coach: Joined Rams in 1983.

Gil Haskell, special teams, tight ends; born September 24, 1943, San Francisco, lives in Anaheim, Calif. Defensive back San Francisco State 1961, 1963-65. No pro playing experience. College coach: Southern California 1978-82. Pro coach: Joined Rams in 1983.

Hudson Houck, offensive line; born January 7, 1943, Los Angeles, lives in Newport Beach, Calif. Center Southern California 1962-64. No pro playing experience. College coach: Southern California 1970-72, 1976-82, Stanford 1973-75. Pro coach: Joined Rams in 1983.

Ronnie Jones, linebackers; born October 17, 1955, Dumas, Tex., lives in Anaheim, Calif. Running back Northwestern State (Okla.) 1974-77. No pro playing experience. College coach: Northeastern State (Okla.) 1979-83, Tulsa 1984, Arizona State 1985-86. Pro coach: Philadelphia Eagles 1987-90, joined Rams in 1991.

Jimmy Raye, wide receivers, passing game coordinator; born March 26, 1946, Fayetteville, N.C., lives in Anaheim, Calif. Quarterback Michigan State 1965-67. Pro defensive back Philadelphia Eagles 1969. College coach: Michigan State 1971-75, Wyoming 1976. Pro coach: San Francisco 49ers 1977, Detroit Lions 1978-79, Atlanta Falcons 1980-82, 1987-89, Los Angeles Rams 1983-84, Tampa Bay Buccaneers 1985-86, New England Patriots 1990, rejoined Rams in 1991.

Los Angeles Rams 1991 First-Year Roster

Name	Pos.	Ht.	Wt.	Birth-date	College	Hometown	How Acq.
Anthony, Corwin	TE	6-3	235	10/8/68	UCLA	Bakersfield, Calif.	FA
Bailey, Robert	CB	5-9	176	9/3/68	Miami	Miami, Fla.	D4
Carr, Derrick (1)	DE	6-6	270	1/30/67	Bowling Green	Detroit, Mich.	FA
Crews, Terry	LB	6-2	237	7/30/68	Western Michigan	Flint, Mich.	D11
Delaney, Jarrod (1)	WR	6-5	196	12/1/66	Texas Christian	Houston, Tex.	FA
Emanuel, Aaron (1)	RB	6-2	235	1/10/67	Southern California	Palmdale, Calif.	FA
Fields, Jeff	DT	6-1	298	7/7/67	Arkansas State	Jackson, Miss.	D9
Fort, Neal	T	6-5	279	4/12/68	Brigham Young	El Centro, Calif.	D6
Goldberg, Bill (1)	DT	6-3	266	12/27/66	Georgia	Tulsa, Okla.	FA
Grudt, Darren	T	6-5	330	10/14/67	Texas A&M	Fountain Valley, Calif.	FA
James, Danny	WR	5-10	175	11/22/65	Morehouse	Jacksonville, Fla.	FA
Lang, David	RB	5-11	201	3/28/67	Northern Arizona	San Bernardino, Calif.	D12-'90
Lyght, Todd	CB	6-0	186	2/9/69	Notre Dame	Germantown, Md.	D1
McKinnon, David	G	6-5	280	11/26/67	Long Beach State	Fullerton, Calif.	FA
Pahukoa, Jeff	G-T	6-2	298	2/2/69	Washington	Vancouver, Wash.	D12a
Phifer, Roman	LB	6-2	230	3/5/68	UCLA	Pineville, N.C.	D2
Price, Jim (1)	TE	6-4	247	10/2/62	Stanford	Englewood, N.J.	FA
San Jose, Bobby	QB	6-1	188	8/25/67	Long Beach State	Long Beach, Calif.	FA
Shelton, Tyrone	RB	5-11	219	12/30/68	William & Mary	Wheaton, Md.	D7
Slack, Ron	RB	5-10	208	12/7/66	San Diego State	Pasadena, Calif.	FA
Thompson, Ernie	RB	5-11	238	1/25/69	Indiana	Terre Haute, Ind.	D12b
Tucker, Peter	G	6-4	280	4/23/68	Occidental	Huntington Beach, Calif.	FA
Tyrance, Pat	LB	6-1	240	7/30/68	Nebraska	Omaha, Neb.	D8
Young, Robert	DT	6-6	273	1/29/69	Mississippi State	Jackson, Miss.	D5

The term NFL Rookie is defined as a player who is in his first season of professional football and has not been on the roster of another professional football team for any regular-season or postseason games. A Rookie is designated by an "R" on NFL rosters. Players who have been active in another professional football league or players who have NFL experience, including either preseason training camp or being on an active roster for fewer than three regular-season or postseason games, are termed NFL First-Year Players. An NFL First-Year Player is designated by a "1" on NFL rosters. Thereafter, a player on an NFL active roster for at least three regular-season or postseason games is credited with an additional year of NFL playing experience.

NOTES

Clarence Shelmon, running backs; born September 17, 1952, Bossier, La., lives in Los Angeles. Running back Houston 1971-75. No pro playing experience. College coach: Army 1978-80, Indiana 1981-83, Arizona 1984-86, Southern California 1987-90. Pro coach: Joined Rams in 1991.

John Teerlinck, defensive line; born April 9, 1951, Rochester, N.Y., lives in Anaheim, Calif. Defensive lineman Western Illinois 1970-73. Pro defensive tackle San Diego Chargers 1974-76. College coach: Iowa Lakes J.C. 1977, Eastern Illinois 1978-79, Illinois 1980-82. Pro coach: Chicago Blitz (USFL) 1983, Arizona Wranglers (USFL) 1984, Cleveland Browns 1989-90, joined Rams in 1991.

Ernie Zampese, offensive coordinator; born March 12, 1936, Santa Barbara, Calif., lives in El Toro, Calif. Halfback Southern California 1956-58. No pro playing experience. College coach: Hancock, Calif., J.C. 1962-65, Cal Poly-SLO 1966, San Diego State 1967-75. Pro coach: San Diego Chargers 1976, 1979-86, New York Jets 1977-78 (scout), joined Rams in 1987.

National Football Conference Central Division

Team Colors: Purple, Gold, and White

9520 Viking Drive
Eden Prairie, Minnesota 55344
Telephone: (612) 828-6500

Club Officers

Chairman of the Board: John C. Skoglund
President: Roger L. Headrick
Senior Vice President: Jack Steele
Senior Vice President, Secretary, and Treasurer: Jaye F. Dyer

Club Officials

President, CEO: Roger L. Headrick
Vice President and Assistant General Manager/Finance and Administration: Jeff Diamond
Assistant G.M./Football: Bob Hollway
Director of Finance: Harley Peterson
Ticket Manager: Harry Randolph
Director of Football Operations: Jerry Reichow
Director of Player Personnel: Frank Gilliam
Head Scout: Ralph Kohl
Assistant Head Scout: Don Deisch
Regional Scout: John Carson
Regional Scout: Conrad Cardano
Director of Public Relations: Merrill Swanson
Director of Marketing and Community Relations: Kernal Buhler
Director of Communications: Daniel Endy
Trainer: Fred Zamberletti
Equipment Manager: Dennis Ryan

Stadium: Hubert H. Humphrey Metrodome • **Capacity:** 63,000
500 11th Avenue South
Minneapolis, Minnesota 55415

Playing Surface: AstroTurf

Training Camp: Mankato State University
Mankato, Minnesota 56001

1991 Schedule

Preseason

Aug. 3	at New Orleans	7:00
Aug. 10	**Pittsburgh**	8:00
Aug. 17	at Cincinnati	7:30
Aug. 23	**Cleveland**	7:00

Regular Season

Sept. 1	at Chicago	3:00
Sept. 8	at Atlanta	1:00
Sept. 15	**San Francisco**	12:00
Sept. 22	at New Orleans	12:00
Sept. 29	**Denver**	7:00
Oct. 6	at Detroit	1:00
Oct. 13	**Phoenix**	12:00
Oct. 20	at New England	1:00
Oct. 27	at Phoenix	2:00
Nov. 3	**Tampa Bay**	12:00
Nov. 11	**Chicago** (Monday)	8:00
Nov. 17	at Green Bay	12:00
Nov. 24	**Detroit**	12:00
Dec. 1	**Open Date**	
Dec. 8	at Tampa Bay	8:00
Dec. 15	**Los Angeles Rams**	12:00
Dec. 21	**Green Bay** (Saturday)	3:00

Vikings Coaching History

(247-210-9)

1961-66	Norm Van Brocklin	29-51-4
1967-83	Bud Grant	161-99-5
1984	Les Steckel	3-13-0
1985	Bud Grant	7-9-0
1986-90	Jerry Burns	47-38-0

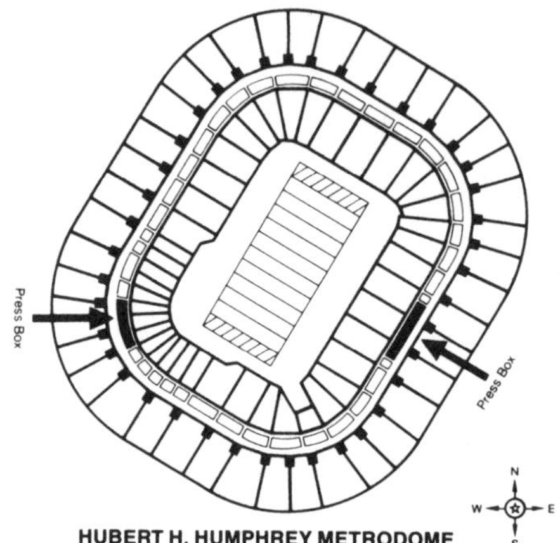

HUBERT H. HUMPHREY METRODOME

Record Holders

Individual Records—Career

Category	Name	Performance
Rushing (Yds.)	Chuck Foreman, 1973-79	5,879
Passing (Yds.)	Fran Tarkenton, 1961-66, 1972-78	33,098
Passing (TDs)	Fran Tarkenton, 1961-66, 1972-78	239
Receiving (No.)	Ahmad Rashad, 1976-1982	400
Receiving (Yds.)	Sammy White, 1976-1985	5,925
Interceptions	Paul Krause, 1968-1979	53
Punting (Avg.)	Bobby Walden, 1964-67	42.9
Punt Return (Avg.)	Tommy Mason, 1961-66	10.4
Kickoff Return (Avg.)	Bob Reed, 1962-63	27.1
Field Goals	Fred Cox, 1963-1977	282
Touchdowns (Tot.)	Bill Brown, 1962-1974	76
Points	Fred Cox, 1963-1977	1,365

Individual Records—Single Season

Category	Name	Performance
Rushing (Yds.)	Chuck Foreman, 1976	1,155
Passing (Yds.)	Tommy Kramer, 1981	3,912
Passing (TDs)	Tommy Kramer, 1981	26
Receiving (No.)	Rickey Young, 1978	88
Receiving (Yds.)	Anthony Carter, 1988	1,225
Interceptions	Paul Krause, 1975	10
Punting (Avg.)	Bobby Walden, 1964	46.4
Punt Return (Avg.)	Leo Lewis, 1987	12.5
Kickoff Return (Avg.)	John Gilliam, 1972	26.3
Field Goals	Rich Karlis, 1989	31
Touchdowns (Tot.)	Chuck Foreman, 1975	22
Points	Chuck Foreman, 1975	132

Individual Records—Single Game

Category	Name	Performance
Rushing (Yds.)	Chuck Foreman, 10-24-76	200
Passing (Yds.)	Tommy Kramer, 11-2-86	490
Passing (TDs)	Joe Kapp, 9-28-69	*7
Receiving (No.)	Rickey Young, 12-16-79	15
Receiving (Yds.)	Sammy White, 11-7-76	210
Interceptions	Many times	3
	Last time by Willie Teal, 11-28-82	
Field Goals	Rich Karlis, 11-5-89	*7
Touchdowns (Tot.)	Chuck Foreman, 12-20-75	4
	Ahmad Rashad, 9-2-79	4
Points	Chuck Foreman, 12-20-75	24
	Ahmad Rashad, 9-2-79	24

*NFL Record

1990 Team Record

Preseason (3-1)

Date	Result		Opponents
8/11	L	10-13	New Orleans
8/19	W	23-20	at Cleveland
8/26	W	22-21	Houston
8/31	W	20-17	at Miami
		75-71	

Regular Season (6-10)

Date	Result		Opponents	Att.
9/9	L	21-24	at Kansas City	68,363
9/16	W	32- 3	New Orleans	56,272
9/23	L	16-19	at Chicago	65,420
9/30	L	20-23	Tampa Bay (OT)	54,462
10/7	L	27-34	Detroit	57,586
10/15	L	24-32	at Philadelphia	66,296
10/28	L	10-24	at Green Bay	55,125
11/4	W	27-22	Denver	57,331
11/11	W	17- 7	at Detroit	68,264
11/18	W	24-21	at Seattle	59,735
11/25	W	41-13	Chicago	58,866
12/2	W	23- 7	Green Bay	62,058
12/9	L	15-23	at N.Y. Giants	76,121
12/16	L	13-26	at Tampa Bay	47,272
12/22	L	24-28	L.A. Raiders	53,899
12/30	L	17-20	San Francisco	51,590

(OT) Overtime

Score by Periods

Vikings	54	131	80	86	0	—	351
Opponents	76	76	66	105	3	—	326

Attendance

Home 452,064 Away 506,596 Total 958,660
Single-game home record, 62,851 (10-19-86)
Single-season home record, 464,902 (1983)

1990 Team Statistics

	Vikings	Opp.
Total First Downs	288	257
Rushing	106	107
Passing	164	136
Penalty	18	14
Third Down: Made/Att.	81/215	71/207
Third Down: Pct.	37.7	34.3
Fourth Down: Made/Att.	6/15	5/11
Fourth Down: Pct.	40.0	45.5
Total Net Yards	5034	4717
Avg. Per Game	314.6	294.8
Total Plays	1001	972
Avg. Per Play	5.0	4.9
Net Yards Rushing	1867	2074
Avg. Per Game	116.7	129.6
Total Rushes	455	503
Net Yards Passing	3167	2643
Avg. Per Game	197.9	165.2
Sacked/Yards Lost	49/278	47/277
Gross Yards	3445	2920
Att./Completions	497/265	422/218
Completion Pct.	53.3	51.7
Had Intercepted	24	22
Punts/Avg.	79/41.8	77/39.4
Net Punting Avg.	33.2	35.4
Penalties/Yards Lost	83/565	100/787
Fumbles/Ball Lost	30/13	25/11
Touchdowns	39	34
Rushing	10	12
Passing	25	20
Returns	4	2
Avg. Time of Possession	29:34	30:26

1990 Individual Statistics

Scoring	TD R	TD P	TD Rt	PAT	FG	Saf	TP
Reveiz, S.D.-Minn.	0	0	0	26/27	13/19	0	65
Reveiz, Minn.	0	0	0	19/19	11/12	0	52
Igwebuike	0	0	0	19/19	14/16	0	61
Walker	5	4	0	0/0	0/0	0	54
A. Carter	0	8	0	0/0	0/0	0	48
H. Jones	0	7	0	0/0	0/0	0	42
C. Carter	0	3	0	0/0	0/0	0	18
Jordan	0	3	0	0/0	0/0	0	18
Anderson	2	0	0	0/0	0/0	0	12
Fenney	2	0	0	0/0	0/0	0	12
Noga	0	0	2	0/0	0/0	0	12
Browner	0	0	1	0/0	0/0	0	6
Gannon	1	0	0	0/0	0/0	0	6
Merriweather	0	0	1	0/0	0/0	0	6
J. Williams, Det.-Minn.	0	0	1	0/0	0/0	0	6
Doleman	0	0	0	0/0	0/0	1	2
Dusbabek	0	0	0	0/0	0/0	1	2
Vikings	10	25	4	38/39	25/28	2	351
Opponents	12	20	2	32/34	30/36	0	326

Passing	Att.	Comp.	Yds.	Pct.	TD	Int.	Tkld.	Rate
Gannon	349	182	2278	52.1	16	16	34/188	68.9
Wilson	146	82	1155	56.2	9	8	15/90	79.6
Walker	2	1	12	50.0	0	0	0/0	68.8
Vikings	497	265	3445	53.3	25	24	49/278	72.0
Opponents	422	218	2920	51.7	20	22	47/277	68.0

Rushing	Att.	Yds.	Avg.	LG	TD
Walker	184	770	4.2	58t	5
Fenney	87	376	4.3	27	2
Gannon	52	268	5.2	27	1
Anderson	59	207	3.5	14	2
Wilson	12	79	6.6	24	0
Rice	22	74	3.4	13	0
Clark	16	49	3.1	11	0
Smith	9	19	2.1	7	0
A. Carter	3	16	5.3	11	0
Dozier	6	12	2.0	4	0
C. Carter	2	6	3.0	8	0
Newsome	2	−2	−1.0	0	0
H. Jones	1	−7	−7.0	−7	0
Vikings	455	1867	4.1	58t	10
Opponents	503	2074	4.1	48t	12

Receiving	No.	Yds.	Avg.	LG	TD
A. Carter	70	1008	14.4	56t	8
H. Jones	51	810	15.9	75t	7
Jordan	45	636	14.1	38	3
Walker	35	315	9.0	32	4
C. Carter	27	413	15.3	78t	3
Fenney	17	112	6.6	17	0
Anderson	13	80	6.2	17	0
Rice	4	46	11.5	24	0
Dozier	1	12	12.0	12	0
Lewis	1	9	9.0	9	0
Clark	1	4	4.0	4	0
Vikings	265	3445	13.0	78t	25
Opponents	218	2920	13.4	61	20

Interceptions	No.	Yds.	Avg.	LG	TD
Browner	7	103	14.7	31	1
Merriweather	3	108	36.0	73	0
McMillian	3	20	6.7	20	0
Lee	2	29	14.5	25	0
Rutland	2	21	10.5	16	0
Brim	2	11	5.5	11	0
Doleman	1	30	30.0	30	0
Noga	1	26	26.0	26t	1
Fullington	1	10	10.0	10	0
Vikings	22	358	16.3	73	2
Opponents	24	260	10.8	37	1

Punting	No.	Yds.	Avg.	In 20	LG
Newsome	78	3299	42.3	19	61
Vikings	79	3299	41.8	19	61
Opponents	77	3030	39.4	24	67

Punt Returns	No.	FC	Yds.	Avg.	LG	TD
Lewis, Clev.-Minn.	33	22	236	7.2	30	0
Lewis, Minn.	25	15	180	7.2	30	0
Hillary	8	4	45	5.6	12	0
A. Carter	0	5	0	—	0	0
Vikings	33	24	225	6.8	30	0
Opponents	44	12	513	11.7	39	0

Kickoff Returns	No.	Yds.	Avg.	LG	TD
Walker	44	966	22.0	64	0
Rice	12	176	14.7	24	0
Anderson	3	44	14.7	24	0
Lewis	3	39	13.0	15	0
Hillary	1	6	6.0	6	0
Jordan	1	−3	−3.0	−3	0
Schreiber	1	5	5.0	5	0
Smith	1	16	16.0	16	0
Vikings	66	1249	18.9	64	0
Opponents	62	1350	21.8	63	0

Sacks	No.
Doleman	11.0
Thomas	8.5
Clarke	7.0
Noga	6.0
Strauthers	4.0
Browner	3.0
J. Williams, Det.-Minn.	3.0
Merriweather	2.5
Millard	2.0
Fullington	1.0
Randle	1.0
Vikings	47.0
Opponents	49.0

1991 Draft Choices

Round	Name	Pos.	College
3.	Carlos Jenkins	LB	Michigan State
	Jake Reed	WR	Grambling
4.	Randy Baldwin	RB	Mississippi
5.	Chris Thome	C	Minnesota
6.	Todd Scott	DB	S.W. Louisiana
7.	Scotty Reagan	DT	Humboldt State
	Tripp Welborne	DB	Michigan
8.	Reggie Johnson	DE	Arizona
9.	Gerald Hudson	RB	Oklahoma State
10.	Brady Pierce	T	Wisconsin
11.	Ivan Caesar	LB	Boston College
12.	Darren Hughes	WR	Carson-Newman

Minnesota Vikings 1991 Veteran Roster

No.	Name	Pos.	Ht.	Wt.	Birth-date	NFL Exp.	College	Hometown	How Acq.	'90 Games/ Starts
46	Anderson, Alfred	RB	6-1	214	8/4/61	8	Baylor	Waco, Tex.	D3-'84	11/6
50	Berry, Ray	LB	6-2	226	10/28/63	5	Baylor	Abilene, Tex.	D2-'87	16/3
47	Browner, Joey	S	6-2	228	5/15/60	9	Southern California	Atlanta, Ga.	D1-'83	16/16
81	Carter, Anthony	WR	5-11	178	9/17/60	7	Michigan	Riviera Beach, Fla.	T(Mia)-'85	15/14
80	†Carter, Cris	WR	6-3	200	11/25/65	5	Ohio State	Middletown, Ohio	W(Phil)-'90	16/5
71	†Clarke, Ken	DT	6-2	280	8/28/56	14	Syracuse	Boston, Mass.	FA-'90	12/0
56	†Doleman, Chris	DE	6-5	263	10/16/61	7	Pittsburgh	York, Pa.	D1-'85	16/16
42	†Dozier, D.J.	RB	6-0	205	9/21/65	5	Penn State	Virginia Beach, Va.	D1-'87	6/1
59	†Dusbabek, Mark	LB	6-3	230	6/23/64	3	Minnesota	Faribault, Minn.	FA-'89	14/11
24	Eilers, Pat	S	5-11	195	9/3/66	2	Notre Dame	St. Paul, Minn.	FA-'90	8/0
31	Fenney, Rick	RB	6-1	231	12/7/64	5	Washington	Everett, Wash.	D8-'87	12/5
62	†Foote, Chris	C	6-4	266	12/2/56	9	Southern California	Boulder, Colo.	T(NYG)-'87	16/3
29	Fullington, Darrell	S	6-1	195	4/17/64	4	Miami	New Smyrna Beach, Fla.	D5-'88	16/11
16	†Gannon, Rich	QB	6-3	202	12/20/65	5	Delaware	Philadelphia, Pa.	T(NE)-'87	14/12
74	†Habib, Brian	T	6-7	288	12/2/64	3	Washington	Ellensburg, Wash.	D10-'88	16/0
77	Hammerstein, Mike	T	6-4	272	3/3/63	5	Michigan	Wapakoneta, Ohio	PB(Cin)-'91#	16/3*
25	Hampton, Alonzo	CB	5-10	191	1/19/67	2	Pittsburgh	Denver, Colo.	D4-'90	10/0
4	Igwebuike, Donald	K	5-9	184	12/27/60	7	Clemson	Anambra, Nigeria	W(TB)-'90	8/0
76	Irwin, Tim	T	6-7	295	12/13/58	11	Tennessee	Knoxville, Tenn.	D3-'81	16/16
84	†Jones, Hassan	WR	6-0	195	7/2/64	6	Florida State	Clearwater, Fla.	D5-'85	15/10
82	Jones, Mike	TE	6-3	255	11/10/66	2	Texas A&M	Bridgeport, Conn.	D3-'90	11/0
83	Jordan, Steve	TE	6-3	240	1/10/61	10	Brown	Phoenix, Ariz.	D7-'82	16/16
69	†Kalis, Todd	G	6-5	286	5/10/65	4	Arizona State	Phoenix, Ariz.	D4-'88	15/14
52	Kirksey, William	LB	6-2	221	1/29/66	2	Southern Mississippi	Leeds, Ala.	PB(Atl)-'90#	9/0
39	Lee, Carl	CB	5-11	184	2/6/61	9	Marshall	South Charleston, W.Va.	D7-'83	16/16
87	†Lewis, Leo	WR	5-8	166	9/17/56	11	Missouri	Columbia, Mo.	FA-'90	11/0
63	†Lowdermilk, Kirk	C	6-3	263	4/10/63	7	Ohio State	Canton, Ohio	D3a-'85	15/13
91	Manusky, Greg	LB	6-1	242	8/12/66	4	Colgate	Wilkes-Barre, Pa.	PB(Wash)-'90#	16/8*
64	†McDaniel, Randall	G	6-3	270	12/19/64	4	Arizona State	Avondale, Ariz.	D1-'88	16/16
26	†McMillian, Audray	CB	6-0	189	8/13/62	6	Houston	Carthage, Tex.	PB(Hou)-'89#	15/2
57	Merriweather, Mike	LB	6-2	222	11/26/60	9	Pacific	Vallejo, Calif.	T(Pitt)-'89	16/16
75	Millard, Keith	DT	6-5	263	3/18/62	7	Washington State	Pleasanton, Calif.	D1-'84	4/4
20	Morris, Jamie	RB	5-7	188	6/6/65	4	Michigan	Southern Pines, N.C.	PB(NE)-'90#	5/0*
18	Newsome, Harry	P	6-0	188	1/25/63	7	Wake Forest	Cheraw, S.C.	PB(Pitt)-'90#	16/0
99	Noga, Al	DE	6-1	248	9/16/65	4	Hawaii	Honolulu, Hawaii	D3-'88	16/16
85	Novoselsky, Brent	TE	6-2	238	1/8/66	4	Pennsylvania	Niles, Ill.	FA-'90	16/3
86	Pruitt, James	WR	6-3	201	1/29/64	6	Cal State-Fullerton	Los Angeles, Calif.	PB(Mia)-'91#	6/0*
93	Randle, John	DE	6-1	248	12/12/67	2	Texas A&I	Hearne, Tex.	FA-'90	16/0
7	Reveiz, Fuad	K	5-11	216	2/24/63	6	Tennessee	Miami, Fla.	FA-'90	9/0
48	†Rutland, Reggie	CB	6-1	192	6/20/64	5	Georgia Tech	East Point, Ga.	D4-'87	16/16
12	Salisbury, Sean	QB	6-5	208	3/9/63	4	Southern California	Escondido, Calif.	FA-'90	0*
60	Schreiber, Adam	C-G	6-4	288	2/20/62	8	Texas	Huntsville, Ala.	PB(NYJ)-'90#	16/0
30	Smith, Cedric	RB	5-10	223	5/27/68	2	Florida	Enterprise, Ala.	D5-'90	15/1
27	†Stills, Ken	S	5-10	186	9/6/63	7	Wisconsin	Oceanside, Calif.	PB(GB)-'90#	12/3
94	†Strauthers, Thomas	DE	6-4	262	4/6/61	8	Jackson State	Brookhaven, Miss.	FA-'89	13/2
97	Thomas, Henry	NT	6-2	268	1/12/65	5	Louisiana State	Houston, Tex.	D3-'87	16/16
54	Vanderbeek, Matt	LB	6-3	258	8/16/67	2	Michigan State	Holland, Mich.	PB(Ind)-'91#	16/7*
34	†Walker, Herschel	RB	6-1	225	3/3/62	6	Georgia	Wrightsville, Ga.	T(Dall)-'89	16/16
89	Walker, Wayne	WR	5-8	162	12/27/66	2	Texas Tech	Waco, Tex.	PB(SD)-'91#	0*
41	Wilcots, Solomon	S	5-11	195	10/3/64	5	Colorado	Compton, Calif.	PB(Cin)-'91#	16/12*
58	†Williams, Jimmy	LB	6-3	225	11/15/60	10	Nebraska	Washington, D.C.	FA-'90	4/0
11	Wilson, Wade	QB	6-3	210	2/1/59	11	East Texas State	Greenville, Tex.	D8-'81	6/4
73	†Wolfley, Craig	G	6-1	277	5/19/58	12	Syracuse	Buffalo, N.Y.	FA-'90	8/2
22	Wright, Felix	S	6-2	195	6/22/59	7	Drake	Carthage, Mo.	PB(Clev)-'91#	16/16*
65	Zimmerman, Gary	T	6-6	283	12/13/61	6	Oregon	Walnut, Calif.	T(NYG)-'86	16/16

* Hammerstein played 16 games with Cincinnati in '90; Manusky played 16 games with Washington; Morris played 5 games with New England; Pruitt played 6 games with Miami; Salisbury active for 14 games but did not play; Vanderbeek played 16 games with Indianapolis; W. Walker missed '90 season due to injury; Wilcots played 16 games with Cincinnati; Wright played 16 games with Cleveland.

† Option playout; subject to developments.

Plan B unconditional free agent.

Retired—Scott Studwell, 15-year linebacker, 16 games in '90.

Players lost through Plan B (3): CB Mike Brim (NYJ; 16 games in '90), WR Pat Newman (NO; 0), RB Allen Rice (GB; 15).

Also played with Vikings in '90—LB Walker Lee Ashley (4 games), T Paul Blair (2), LB David Braxton (1), RB Jessie Clark (5), DE Willie Fears (2), K Jim Gallery (2), WR Ira Hillary (3), G David Huffman (1), S Ken Johnson (4), QB Gilbert Renfroe (1).

COACHING STAFF

Head Coach, Jerry Burns

Pro Career: Named fourth head coach in Vikings' history on January 6, 1986. Served as Vikings' assistant head coach and offensive coordinator under Bud Grant in 1985. Since his arrival in Minnesota as offensive coordinator in 1968, he became known as an innovator and was credited with popularizing such changes as the one-back offense and short passing game. Has coached in six Super Bowls. Directed Vikings' offense in Super Bowls IV, VIII, IX, and XI, and coached defensive backs for Vince Lombardi on Green Bay's Super Bowl I and II champions. He coached with the Packers in 1966-67 before joining the Vikings in 1968. No pro playing experience. Career record: 47-38.

Background: Quarterback at Michigan 1949-50. Began coaching career at Hawaii in 1951 as backfield coach for football team and head baseball coach. Moved to Whittier (Calif.) College in 1952 as backfield coach before returning to native Detroit in 1953 as head football coach at St. Mary's of Redford High School. Assistant coach at Iowa from 1954-60 before being named Hawkeyes head coach in 1961. Iowa was 16-27-2 in five seasons under Burns.

Personal: Born January 24, 1927, in Detroit, Mich. Graduated from Michigan with bachelor of science degree in physical education. Jerry and his wife, Marlyn, live in Eden Prairie, Minn., and have five children—Michael, Erin, Kelly, Kathy, and Kerry.

Assistant Coaches

Tom Batta, tight ends-special teams; born October 6, 1942, Youngstown, Ohio, lives in Bloomington, Minn. Offensive-defensive lineman Kent State 1961-63. No pro playing experience. College coach: Akron 1973, Colorado 1974-78, Kansas 1979-82, North Carolina State 1983. Pro coach: Joined Vikings in 1984.

Maxie Baughan, linebackers; born August 3, 1938, Forkland, Ala., lives in Eden Prairie, Minn. Center-linebacker Georgia Tech 1956-60. Pro linebacker Philadelphia Eagles 1960-65, Los Angeles Rams 1966-70, Washington Redskins 1971, 1974. College coach: Georgia Tech 1972-73; Cornell 1983-88 (head coach). Pro coach: Baltimore Colts 1975-79, Detroit Lions 1980-82, joined Vikings in 1990.

Jerry Brown, defensive backs; born September 28, 1949, Kent, Ohio, lives in Eden Prairie, Minn. Defensive back Northwestern 1969-72. No pro playing experience. College coach: Eastern Illinois 1977-79, Cal State-Fullerton 1980-87. Pro coach: Joined Vikings in 1988.

John Brunner, running backs; born September 6, 1937, Perkasie, Pa., lives in Eden Prairie, Minn. Running back Maryland 1955-56, East Stroudsburg State 1958-59. No pro playing experience. College coach: Villanova 1967-69, Temple 1970-73, 1976-79, Princeton 1974-75. Pro coach: Detroit Lions 1980-82, Green Bay Packers 1983, Tampa Bay Buccaneers 1984, New England Patriots 1985-86 (scout), joined Vikings in 1987.

Monte Kiffin, defensive coordinator; born February 29, 1940, Lexington, Ky., lives in Bloomington, Minn. Offensive-defensive tackle Nebraska 1958-63. Pro defensive end Winnipeg Blue Bombers (CFL) 1965-66. College coach: Nebraska 1966-76, Arkansas 1977-79, North Carolina State 1980-82 (head coach). Pro coach: Green Bay Packers 1983, Buffalo Bills 1984-85, Minnesota Vikings 1985-89, New York Jets 1990, rejoined Vikings in 1991.

John Michels, offensive line; born February 15, 1931, Philadelphia, Pa., lives in Bloomington, Minn. Guard Tennessee 1949-52. Pro guard Philadelphia Eagles 1953, 1956, Winnipeg Blue Bombers (CFL) 1957. College coach: Texas A&M 1958. Pro coach: Winnipeg Blue Bombers (CFL) 1959-66, joined Vikings in 1967.

Tom Moore, assistant head coach/offense; born November 7, 1938, Owatanna, Minn., lives in Bloomington, Minn. Quarterback Iowa 1957-60. No pro playing experience. College coach: Iowa 1961-62, Dayton 1965-68, Wake Forest 1969, Georgia Tech 1970-71, Minnesota 1972-73, 1975-76. Pro coach: New York Stars (WFL) 1974, Pittsburgh Steelers 1977-89, joined Vikings in 1990.

Dick Rehbein, wide receivers; born November 22, 1955, Green Bay, Wis., lives in Edina, Minn. Center Ripon 1973-77. No pro playing experience. Pro coach: Green Bay Packers 1979-83, Los Angeles Express (USFL) 1984, joined Vikings in 1984.

Marc Trestman, quarterbacks; born January 15, 1956, Minneapolis, Minn., lives in Eden Prairie, Minn. Quarterback Minnesota 1975-77, Moorhead (Minn.) State 1978. Pro quarterback Minnesota Vikings 1979. College coach: Miami 1981-84. Pro coach: Minnesota Vikings 1985-86, Tampa Bay Buccaneers 1987, Cleveland Browns 1988-89, rejoined Vikings in 1990.

Paul Wiggin, defensive line; born November 18, 1934, Modesto, Calif., lives in Eden Prairie, Minn. Offensive-defensive tackle Stanford 1953-56. Pro defensive end Cleveland Browns 1957-67. College coach: Stanford 1980-83 (head coach). Pro coach: San Francisco 49ers 1968-74, Kansas City Chiefs 1975-77 (head coach), New Orleans Saints 1978-79, joined Vikings in 1985.

Minnesota Vikings 1991 First-Year Roster

Name	Pos.	Ht.	Wt.	Birth-date	College	Hometown	How Acq.
Baldwin, Randy	RB	5-10	216	8/19/67	Mississippi	Griffin, Ga.	D4
Caesar, Ivan	LB	6-1	241	1/7/67	Boston College	St. Thomas, Virgin Is.	D11
Cochrane, Chris	QB	6-2	217	6/6/69	Cornell	Scarsdale, N.Y.	FA
Daniels, Greg	T	6-5	263	2/3/69	Wisconsin-LaCrosse	Burlington, Wis.	FA
Fair, David	RB	6-1	212	7/12/67	Mississippi State	Starkville, Miss.	FA
Griffin, Frank	TE	6-4	232	2/5/70	Southern California	Rancho Cordova, Calif.	FA
Hudson, Gerald	RB	6-4	199	5/13/68	Oklahoma State	Ennis, Tex.	FA
Hughes, Darren	WR	5-10	172	6/3/67	Carson-Newman	Harbor City, Tenn.	D12
Jenkins, Carlos	LB	6-3	222	7/12/68	Michigan State	Boynton Beach, Fla.	D3
Johnson, Reggie	DE	6-2	274	12/11/67	Arizona	Dolton, Ill.	D8
Mims, Carl	CB	5-10	180	10/28/65	Sam Houston State	Gainesville, Tex.	FA
Neely, Glen	G	6-4	287	1/3/67	Florida	Olive Branch, Miss.	FA
Obee, Terry (1)	WR	5-10	182	6/15/68	Oregon	Vallejo, Calif.	FA-'90
Owens, Anthony	WR	6-1	189	8/3/67	Tennessee State	Nashville, Tenn.	FA
Pierce, Brady	T	6-6	291	9/2/67	Wisconsin	Menomonie, Wis.	D10
Reagan, Scott	DT	6-4	274	7/29/67	Humboldt State	Panorama City, Calif.	D7
Reed, Jake	WR	6-3	216	9/28/67	Grambling	Oxford, Fla.	D3
Scott, Todd	CB	5-10	204	1/23/68	S.W. Louisiana	Galveston, Tex.	D6
Thome, Chris	C	6-4	285	1/15/69	Minnesota	St. Paul, Minn.	D5
Welborne, Tripp	S	6-0	205	11/20/68	Michigan	Reidsville, N.C.	D7
Westbrooks, David	DT	6-4	252	3/23/68	Howard	Miami, Fla.	FA-'90

The term NFL Rookie is defined as a player who is in his first season of professional football and has not been on the roster of another professional football team for any regular-season or postseason games. A Rookie is designated by an "R" on NFL rosters. Players who have been active in another professional football league or players who have NFL experience, including either preseason training camp or being on an active roster for fewer than three regular-season or postseason games, are termed NFL First-Year Players. An NFL First-Year Player is designated by a "1" on NFL rosters. Thereafter, a player on an NFL active roster for at least three regular-season or postseason games is credited with an additional year of NFL playing experience.

NOTES

National Football Conference Western Division

Team Colors: Old Gold, Black, and White

1500 Poydras Street
New Orleans, Louisiana 70112
Telephone: (504) 733-0255

Club Officials

Owner/General Partner: Tom Benson
President/General Manager: Jim Finks
Vice President/Administration: Jim Miller
Business Manager/Controller: Bruce Broussard
Director of Player Personnel: Bill Kuharich
Director of Marketing: Greg Suit
Assistant Director of Marketing: Bill Ferrante
Director of Media Relations: Rusty Kasmiersky
Assistant Director of Media Relations: Neal Gulkis
Director of Travel/Entertainment: Barra Birrcher
Director of Community Relations: Chanel Lagarde
Player Personnel Scouts: Bill Baker, Hamp Cook, Hokie Gajan, Tom Marino, Carmen Piccone
Ticket Manager: Sandy King
Trainer: Dean Kleinschmidt
Equipment Manager: Dan Simmons
Video Director: Albert Aucoin

Stadium: Louisiana Superdome • **Capacity:** 69,065
1500 Poydras Street
New Orleans, Louisiana 70112

Playing Surface: AstroTurf

Training Camp: University of Wisconsin-LaCrosse
LaCrosse, Wisconsin 54601

1991 Schedule

Preseason

Aug. 3	**Minnesota**	7:00
Aug. 10	**Green Bay**	7:00
Aug. 17	at Indianapolis	7:30
Aug. 24	at Miami	8:00

Regular Season

Sept. 1	**Seattle**	12:00
Sept. 8	at Kansas City	12:00
Sept. 15	**Los Angeles Rams**	7:00
Sept. 22	**Minnesota**	12:00
Sept. 29	at Atlanta	1:00
Oct. 6	**Open Date**	
Oct. 13	at Philadelphia	1:00
Oct. 20	**Tampa Bay**	12:00
Oct. 27	**Chicago**	12:00
Nov. 3	at Los Angeles Rams	1:00
Nov. 10	**San Francisco**	12:00
Nov. 17	at San Diego	1:00
Nov. 24	**Atlanta**	7:00
Dec. 1	at San Francisco	1:00
Dec. 8	at Dallas	12:00
Dec. 16	**L.A. Raiders** (Monday)	8:00
Dec. 22	at Phoenix	2:00

Saints Coaching History

(129-222-5)

1967-70	Tom Fears*	13-34-2
1970-72	J.D. Roberts	7-25-3
1973-75	John North**	11-23-0
1975	Ernie Hefferle	1-7-0
1976-77	Hank Stram	7-21-0
1978-80	Dick Nolan***	15-29-0
1980	Dick Stanfel	1-3-0
1981-85	O.A. (Bum) Phillips****	27-42-0
1985	Wade Phillips	1-3-0
1986-90	Jim Mora	46-35-0

*Released after seven games in 1970
**Released after six games in 1975
***Released after 12 games in 1980
****Resigned after 12 games in 1985

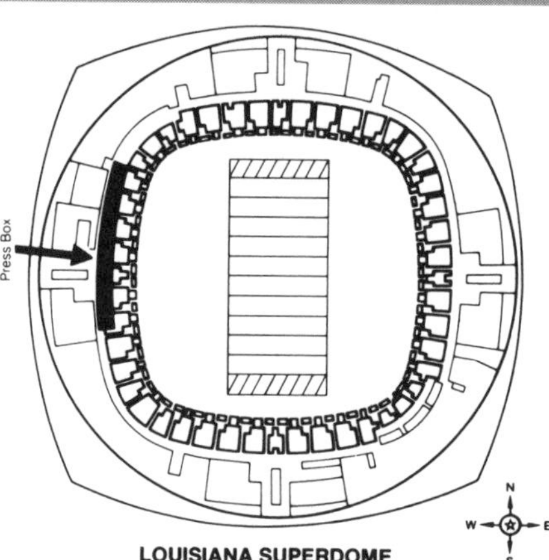

LOUISIANA SUPERDOME

Record Holders

Individual Records—Career

Category	Name	Performance
Rushing (Yds.)	George Rogers, 1981-84	4,267
Passing (Yds.)	Archie Manning, 1971-1982	21,734
Passing (TDs)	Archie Manning, 1971-1982	115
Receiving (No.)	Eric Martin, 1985-1990	332
Receiving (Yds.)	Eric Martin, 1985-1990	5,060
Interceptions	Dave Waymer, 1980-89	37
Punting (Avg.)	Tom McNeill, 1967-69	42.3
Punt Return (Avg.)	Mel Gray, 1986-88	13.4
Kickoff Return (Avg.)	Walter Roberts, 1967	26.3
Field Goals	Morten Andersen, 1982-1990	192
Touchdowns (Tot.)	Dalton Hilliard, 1986-1990	38
Points	Morten Andersen, 1982-1990	852

Individual Records—Single Season

Category	Name	Performance
Rushing (Yds.)	George Rogers, 1981	1,674
Passing (Yds.)	Archie Manning, 1980	3,716
Passing (TDs)	Archie Manning, 1980	23
Receiving (No.)	Eric Martin, 1988	85
Receiving (Yds.)	Eric Martin, 1989	1,090
Interceptions	Dave Whitsell, 1967	10
Punting (Avg.)	Brian Hansen, 1984	43.8
Punt Return (Avg.)	Mel Gray, 1987	14.7
Kickoff Return (Avg.)	Don Shy, 1969	27.9
Field Goals	Morten Andersen, 1985	31
Touchdowns (Tot.)	Dalton Hilliard, 1989	18
Points	Morten Andersen, 1987	121

Individual Records—Single Game

Category	Name	Performance
Rushing (Yds.)	George Rogers, 9-4-83	206
Passing (Yds.)	Archie Manning, 12-7-80	377
Passing (TDs)	Billy Kilmer, 11-2-69	6
Receiving (No.)	Tony Galbreath, 9-10-78	14
Receiving (Yds.)	Wes Chandler, 9-2-79	205
Interceptions	Tommy Myers, 9-3-78	3
	Dave Waymer, 10-6-85	3
	Reggie Sutton, 10-18-87	3
Field Goals	Morten Andersen, 12-1-85	5
	Morten Andersen, 11-15-87	5
Touchdowns (Tot.)	Many times	3
	Last time by Rueben Mayes, 9-23-90	
Points	Many times	18
	Last time by Rueben Mayes, 9-23-90	

1990 Team Record

Preseason (4-1)

Date	Result		Opponents
8/5	W	17-10	vs. L.A. Raiders at London
8/11	W	13-10	at Minnesota
8/18	L	13-27	vs. Green Bay at Madison, Wis.
8/25	W	28-23	Buffalo
8/31	W	17-14	Indianapolis
		88-84	

Regular Season (8-8)

Date	Result		Opponents	Att.
9/10	L	12-13	San Francisco	68,629
9/16	L	3-32	at Minnesota	56,272
9/23	W	28- 7	Phoenix	61,110
10/7	L	27-28	at Atlanta	57,401
10/14	W	25-20	Cleveland	68,608
10/21	L	10-23	at Houston	57,908
10/28	L	10-27	Detroit	64,368
11/4	W	21- 7	at Cincinnati	60,067
11/11	W	35- 7	Tampa Bay	67,865
11/18	L	17-31	at Washington	52,573
11/25	W	10- 7	Atlanta	68,629
12/2	L	13-17	at Dallas	60,087
12/9	W	24-20	at L.A. Rams	56,864
12/16	L	6- 9	Pittsburgh	68,582
12/23	W	13-10	at San Francisco	60,112
12/31	W	20-17	L.A. Rams	68,647

Postseason (0-1)

Date	Result		Opponent	Att.
1/6	L	6-16	at Chicago	60,767

Score by Periods

Saints	54	82	48	90	0	—	274
Opponents	30	82	76	87	0	—	275

Attendance

Home 536,438 Away 461,294 Total 997,732
Single-game home record, 70,940 (11-4-79)
Single-season home record, 536,438 (1990)

1990 Team Statistics

	Saints	Opp.
Total First Downs	254	279
Rushing	107	91
Passing	134	167
Penalty	13	21
Third Down: Made/Att.	84/209	85/217
Third Down: Pct.	40.2	39.2
Fourth Down: Made/Att.	5/9	9/17
Fourth Down: Pct.	55.6	52.9
Total Net Yards	4476	4878
Avg. Per Game	279.8	304.9
Total Plays	931	986
Avg. Per Play	4.8	4.9
Net Yards Rushing	1850	1559
Avg. Per Game	115.6	97.4
Total Rushes	464	410
Net Yards Passing	2626	3319
Avg. Per Game	164.1	207.4
Sacked/Yards Lost	20/131	42/265
Gross Yards	2757	3584
Att./Completions	447/226	534/316
Completion Pct.	50.6	59.2
Had Intercepted	23	8
Punts/Avg.	71/42.1	74/40.9
Net Punting Avg.	36.2	34.9
Penalties/Yards Lost	108/829	87/655
Fumbles/Ball Lost	29/16	35/19
Touchdowns	30	30
Rushing	14	8
Passing	15	21
Returns	1	1
Avg. Time of Possession	29:59	30:01

1990 Individual Statistics

Scoring	TD R	TD P	TD Rt	PAT	FG	Saf	TP
Andersen	0	0	0	29/29	21/27	0	92
Mayes	7	0	0	0/0	0/0	0	42
E. Martin	0	5	0	0/0	0/0	0	30
Heyward	4	0	0	0/0	0/0	0	24
Turner	0	4	0	0/0	0/0	0	24
Brenner	0	2	0	0/0	0/0	0	12
Fenerty	2	0	0	0/0	0/0	0	12
Perriman	0	2	0	0/0	0/0	0	12
Fourcade	1	0	0	0/0	0/0	0	6
Hilliard	0	1	0	0/0	0/0	0	6
Maxie	0	0	1	0/0	0/0	0	6
Scales	0	1	0	0/0	0/0	0	6
Saints	14	15	1	29/29	21/27	1	274
Opponents	8	21	1	30/30	21/35	1	275

Passing	Att.	Comp.	Yds.	Pct.	TD	Int.	Tkld.	Rate
Walsh, Dall.-N.O.	336	179	2010	53.3	12	13	10/76	67.2
Walsh, N.O.	327	175	1970	53.5	12	13	10/76	67.5
Fourcade	116	50	785	43.1	3	8	8/44	46.1
Kramer	3	1	2	33.3	0	1	2/11	2.8
Heyward	1	0	0	0.0	0	1	0/0	0.0
Saints	447	226	2757	50.6	15	23	20/131	59.7
Opponents	534	316	3584	59.2	21	8	42/265	86.2

Rushing	Att.	Yds.	Avg.	LG	TD
Heyward	129	599	4.6	47t	4
Mayes	138	510	3.7	18	7
Fenerty	73	355	4.9	60t	2
Hilliard	90	284	3.2	17	0
Fourcade	15	77	5.1	12	1
Walsh, Dall.-N.O.	20	25	1.3	18	0
Walsh, N.O.	19	25	1.3	18	0
Saints	464	1850	4.0	60t	14
Opponents	410	1559	3.8	35	8

Receiving	No.	Yds.	Avg.	LG	TD
E. Martin	63	912	14.5	58	5
Perriman	36	382	10.6	29	2
Turner	21	396	18.9	68t	4
Fenerty	18	209	11.6	28	0
Heyward	18	121	6.7	12	0
Brenner	17	213	12.5	31t	2
Hilliard	14	125	8.9	20	1
Mayes	12	121	10.1	66	0
Tice	11	113	10.3	19	0
Scales	8	64	8.0	20	1
Alphin	4	57	14.3	17	0
Hill	3	35	11.7	13	0
Hilgenberg	1	9	9.0	9	0
Saints	226	2757	12.2	68t	15
Opponents	316	3584	11.3	51t	21

Interceptions	No.	Yds.	Avg.	LG	TD
Maxie	2	88	44.0	50t	1
Cook	2	55	27.5	50	0
Atkins	2	15	7.5	15	0
Thompson	2	0	0.0	0	0
Saints	8	158	19.8	50t	1
Opponents	23	283	12.3	73	0

Punting	No.	Yds.	Avg.	In 20	LG
Barnhardt	70	2990	42.7	20	65
Saints	71	2990	42.1	20	65
Opponents	74	3024	40.9	18	57

Punt Returns	No.	FC	Yds.	Avg.	LG	TD
V. Buck	37	8	305	8.2	33	0
Morse	8	1	95	11.9	18	0
Saints	45	9	400	8.9	33	0
Opponents	43	12	302	7.0	24	0

Kickoff Returns	No.	Yds.	Avg.	LG	TD
Fenerty	28	572	20.4	58	0
Atkins	19	471	24.8	50	0
Morse	4	56	14.0	18	0
V. Buck	3	38	12.7	17	0
Mayes	2	39	19.5	21	0
Heyward	1	12	12.0	12	0
Mack	1	17	17.0	17	0
Saints	58	1205	20.8	58	0
Opponents	36	583	16.2	56	0

Sacks	No.
Swilling	11.0
Turnbull	9.0
Jackson	6.0
Wilks	5.5
W. Martin	4.0
Atkins	3.0
Cook	1.0
Johnson	1.0
Simmons	1.0
Mills	0.5
Saints	42.0
Opponents	20.0

1991 Draft Choices

Round	Name	Pos.	College
2.	Wesley Carroll	WR	Miami
5.	Reginald Jones	DB	Memphis State
6.	Fred McAfee	RB	Mississippi College
7.	Hayward Haynes	G	Florida State
8.	Frank Wainright	TE	Northern Colorado
9.	Anthony Wallace	RB	California
11.	Scott Ross	LB	Southern California
12.	Mark Drabczak	G	Minnesota

New Orleans Saints 1991 Veteran Roster

No.	Name	Pos.	Ht.	Wt.	Birth-date	NFL Exp.	College	Hometown	How Acq.	'90 Games/ Starts
86	Alphin, Gerald	WR	6-3	220	5/21/64	2	Kansas State	St. Louis, Mo.	FA-'90	11/0
7	Andersen, Morten	K	6-2	221	8/19/60	10	Michigan State	Indianapolis, Ind.	D4-'82	16/0
28	Atkins, Gene	S	6-1	200	11/22/64	5	Florida A&M	Tallahassee, Fla.	D7-'87	16/16
6	Barnhardt, Tommy	P	6-2	207	6/11/63	5	North Carolina	China Grove, N.C.	FA-'89	16/0
85	†Brenner, Hoby	TE	6-5	245	6/2/59	11	Southern California	Fullerton, Calif.	D3b-'81	16/16
67	Brock, Stan	T	6-6	278	6/8/58	12	Colorado	Beaverton, Ore.	D1-'80	16/16
26	Buck, Vince	CB	6-0	198	1/12/68	2	Central State, Ohio	Owensboro, Ky.	D2-'90	16/1
41	Cook, Toi	CB	5-11	188	12/3/64	5	Stanford	Van Nuys, Calif.	D8-'87	16/16
71	Cooper, Richard	T	6-4	285	11/1/64	2	Tennessee	Memphis, Tenn.	FA-'89	2/1
72	Dombrowski, Jim	T	6-5	298	10/19/63	6	Virginia	Williamsville, N.Y.	D1-'86	16/16
89	Early, Quinn	WR	6-0	188	4/13/65	4	Iowa	Great Neck, N.Y.	PB(SD)-'91#	14/4*
22	Fenerty, Gill	RB	6-0	205	8/24/63	2	Holy Cross	New Orleans, La.	D7-'86	15/0
52	Forde, Brian	LB	6-3	225	11/1/63	4	Washington State	Montreal, Canada	D7-'88	16/1
11	Fourcade, John	QB	6-1	215	10/11/60	5	Mississippi	Marrero, La.	FA-'87	7/5
91	†Goff, Robert	NT	6-3	270	10/2/65	4	Auburn	Bradenton, Fla.	FA-'90	15/10
74	†Haverdink, Kevin	T	6-5	285	10/20/65	3	Western Michigan	Hamilton, Mich.	D5-'89	15/15
3	Hebert, Bobby	QB	6-4	215	8/19/60	6	Northwestern Louisiana	Cut Off, La.	FA-'85	0*
34	†Heyward, Craig	RB	5-11	260	9/26/66	4	Pittsburgh	Passaic, N.J.	D1-'88	16/15
61	Hilgenberg, Joel	C-G	6-2	252	7/10/62	8	Iowa	Iowa City, Iowa	D4-'84	16/16
87	†Hill, Lonzell	WR	5-11	189	9/25/65	5	Washington	Stockton, Calif.	D2-'87	13/0
21	Hilliard, Dalton	RB	5-8	204	1/21/64	6	Louisiana State	Patterson, La.	D2-'86	6/6
57	Jackson, Rickey	LB	6-2	243	3/20/58	11	Pittsburgh	Pahokee, Fla.	D2-'81	16/16
53	†Johnson, Vaughan	LB	6-3	235	3/24/62	6	North Carolina State	Morehead City, N.C.	SD1-'84	16/16
23	†Jordan, Buford	RB	6-0	223	6/26/62	6	McNeese State	Iota, La.	FA-'90	6/0
24	Mack, Milton	CB	5-11	182	9/20/63	5	Alcorn State	Jackson, Miss.	D5-'87	16/2
42	Manoa, Tim	RB	6-1	245	9/9/64	4	Penn State	Pittsburgh, Pa.	PB(Clev)-'91#	0*
84	Martin, Eric	WR	6-1	207	11/8/61	7	Louisiana State	Van Vleck, Tex.	D7-'85	16/16
93	Martin, Wayne	DE	6-5	275	10/26/65	3	Arkansas	Cherry Valley, Ark.	D1-'89	11/11
40	†Massey, Robert	CB	5-10	182	2/17/67	3	North Carolina Central	Charlotte, N.C.	D2-'89	16/16
39	Maxie, Brett	S	6-2	194	1/13/62	7	Texas Southern	Dallas, Tex.	FA-'85	16/16
36	Mayes, Rueben	RB	5-11	200	6/6/63	5	Washington State	N. Battleford, Saskatchewan	D3a-'86	15/8
69	Miller, Les	NT	6-7	300	3/1/65	5	Fort Hays State	Arkansas City, Kan.	PB(SD)-'91#	14/9*
51	Mills, Sam	LB	5-9	225	6/3/59	6	Montclair State	Long Branch, N.J.	FA-'86	16/14
35	†Morse, Bobby	RB	5-10	213	10/3/65	4	Michigan State	Muskegon, Mich.	FA-'89	10/0
80	†Perriman, Brett	WR	5-9	180	10/10/65	4	Miami	Miami, Fla.	D2-'88	16/15
83	Scales, Greg	TE	6-4	253	5/9/66	4	Wake Forest	Winston-Salem, N.C.	D5a-'88	16/0
96	Simmons, Michael	DE	6-4	269	11/14/65	2	Mississippi State	Eupora, Miss.	FA-'89	16/3
99	Smeenge, Joel	DE	6-5	250	4/1/68	2	Western Michigan	Grand Rapids, Mich.	D3-'90	15/0
33	Spears, Ernest	S	5-11	192	11/6/67	2	Southern California	Oceanside, Calif.	D10b-'90	16/0
56	Swilling, Pat	LB	6-3	242	10/25/64	6	Georgia Tech	Toccoa, Ga.	D3b-'86	16/16
82	†Tice, John	TE	6-5	249	6/22/60	9	Maryland	Central Islip, N.Y.	D3a-'83	16/4
65	Trapilo, Steve	G	6-5	281	9/20/64	5	Boston College	Dorchester, Mass.	D4-'87	16/16
97	Turnbull, Renaldo	DE	6-4	248	1/5/66	2	West Virginia	St. Thomas, Virgin Islands	D1-'90	16/6
88	†Turner, Floyd	WR	5-11	188	5/29/66	3	Northwestern Louisiana	Mansfield, La.	D6-'89	16/0
4	Walsh, Steve	QB	6-2	200	12/1/66	3	Miami	St. Paul, Minn.	T(Dall)-'90	13/11*
94	†Wilks, Jim	NT	6-5	275	3/12/58	11	San Diego State	Pasadena, Calif.	D12-'81	15/15
90	Williams, James	LB	6-0	230	10/10/68	2	Mississippi State	North Natchez, Miss.	D6b-'90	14/0
92	Winston, DeMond	LB	6-2	239	9/14/68	2	Vanderbilt	Lansing, Mich.	D4-'90	16/0

* Early played 14 games with San Diego in '90; Hebert last active with Saints in '89; Manoa missed '90 season due to injury; Miller played 14 games with San Diego; Walsh played 1 game with Dallas, 12 with New Orleans.

† Option playout; subject to developments.

\# Plan B unconditional free agent.

Players lost through Plan B (3): TE Charles Arbuckle (Clev; 0 games in '90), NT Travis Davis (Ind; 2), T Glenn Derby (GB; 4).

Also played with Saints in '90—QB Tommy Kramer (1 game).

COACHING STAFF

Head Coach, Jim Mora

Pro Career: Begins sixth year as an NFL head coach, after leading Saints to second playoff appearance in club history in 1990 with an 8-8 mark. Was named 1987 NFL coach of the year after leading Saints to a 12-4 record and the team's first playoff appearance. Came to New Orleans following a three-year career as the winningest coach in USFL history as head coach of the Philadelphia/Baltimore Stars. Directed Stars to championship game in each of his three seasons and won league championship in 1984 and 1985. He won USFL coach of the year honors following the 1984 season. Mora began his pro coaching career in 1978 as defensive line coach of the Seattle Seahawks. In 1982, he became defensive coordinator of the New England Patriots and played a vital role in the Patriots' march to the playoffs that year. No pro playing experience. Career record: 46-35.

Background: Played tight end and defensive end at Occidental College. Assistant coach at Occidental 1960-63 and head coach 1964-66. Linebacker coach at Stanford (1967) on a staff that included former Eagles head coach Dick Vermeil. Defensive assistant at Colorado 1968-73. Linebacker coach under Vermeil at UCLA 1974. Defensive coordinator at Washington 1975-77. Received bachelor's degree in physical education from Occidental in 1957. Also holds master's degree in education from Southern California.

Personal: Born May 24, 1935, in Glendale, Calif. Jim and his wife, Connie, live in Metairie, La., and have three sons—Michael, Stephen, and Jim (defensive backs coach for the San Diego Chargers).

Assistant Coaches

Paul Boudreau, offensive line; born December 30, 1949, Somerville, Mass., lives in Destrehan, La. Guard Boston College 1971-73. No pro playing experience. College coach: Boston College 1974-76, Maine 1977-78, Dartmouth 1979-81, Navy 1983. Pro coach: Edmonton Eskimos (CFL) 1983-86, joined Saints in 1987.

Dom Capers, defensive backs; born August 7, 1950, Cambridge, Ohio, lives in Destrehan, La. Defensive back Mount Union College 1968-71. No pro playing experience. College coach: Hawaii 1975-76, San Jose State 1977, California 1978-79, Tennessee 1980-81, Ohio State 1982-83. Pro coach: Philadelphia/Baltimore Stars (USFL) 1984-85, joined Saints in 1986.

Vic Fangio, outside linebackers; born August 22, 1958, Dunmore, Pa., lives in Destrehan, La. Defensive back East Stroudsburg 1976-78. No pro playing experience. College coach: North Carolina 1983. Pro coach: Philadelphia/Baltimore Stars (USFL) 1984-85, joined Saints in 1986.

Joe Marciano, tight ends-special teams; born February 10, 1954, Scranton, Pa., lives in Kenner, La. Quarterback Temple 1972-75. No pro playing experience. College coach: East Stroudsburg 1977, Rhode Island 1978-79, Villanova 1980, Penn State 1981, Temple 1982. Pro coach: Philadelphia/Baltimore Stars (USFL) 1983-85, joined Saints in 1986.

Russell Paternostro, strength and conditioning; born July 21, 1940, New Orleans, La., lives in Covington, La. San Diego State. No college or pro playing experience. Pro coach: Joined Saints in 1981.

John Pease, defensive line; born October 14, 1943, Pittsburgh, Pa., lives in Kenner, La. Wingback Utah 1963-64. No pro playing experience. College coach: Fullerton, Calif., J.C. 1970-73, Long Beach State 1974-76, Utah 1977, Washington 1978-83. Pro coach: Philadelphia/Baltimore Stars (USFL) 1983-85, joined Saints in 1986.

New Orleans Saints 1991 First-Year Roster

Name	Pos.	Ht.	Wt.	Birth-date	College	Hometown	How Acq.
Aeilts, Rick (1)	TE	6-4	245	12/13/65	Southeastern Missouri	Champaign, Ill.	FA
Brockman, Lonnie (1)	LB	6-3	230	3/14/68	West Virginia	Pittsburgh, Pa.	FA
Callahan, Craig	LB	6-1	227	5/25/69	Holy Cross	Newark, Del.	FA
Carroll, Wesley	WR	6-0	183	9/6/67	Miami	Cleveland, Ohio	D2
Cole, Leon (1)	DE	6-4	285	11/8/65	Texas A&M	East Orange, N.J.	FA
Dodd, Robert	T	6-4	297	4/8/69	Portland State	Aurora, Ore.	FA
Drabczak, Mark	G	6-4	278	10/19/63	Minnesota	Minneapolis, Minn.	D12
Griffith, Brent (1)	T	6-6	300	12/14/65	Minnesota-Duluth	Little Falls, Minn.	FA
Hammond, Spencer	LB	6-1	223	8/6/67	Alabama	Rome, Ga.	FA
Haynes, Hayward	G	6-2	280	6/29/67	Florida State	Bartow, Fla.	D7
Jones, Reggie	CB	6-1	202	1/11/69	Memphis State	West Memphis, Ark.	D5
Keim, Mike	T	6-7	285	11/12/65	Brigham Young	Eagar, Ariz.	FA
Leggett, Brad (1)	C	6-4	270	1/16/66	Southern California	Fountain Valley, Calif.	FA-'90
McAfee, Fred	RB	5-10	193	6/20/68	Mississippi College	Philadelphia, Miss.	D6
Newman, Patrick (1)	WR	5-11	189	9/10/68	Utah State	San Diego, Calif.	FA
Nicholson, Calvin (1)	CB	5-9	183	7/9/67	Oregon State	Inglewood, Calif.	D11-'89
Pope, Bobby	CB	5-10	191	1/9/67	Western Oregon	Oakland, Calif.	FA
Port, Chris (1)	G	6-5	290	11/2/67	Duke	Wanaque, N.J.	D12-'90
Ross, Scott	LB	6-1	235	12/7/68	Southern California	El Toro, Calif.	D11
Sign, Bobby (1)	C	6-2	285	5/23/66	Baylor	Arlington, Tex.	FA
Simien, Kerry (1)	WR	5-10	185	12/14/66	Texas A&I	Houston, Tex.	FA-'90
Stant, Pat	LB	6-4	227	2/13/69	Tulane	New Orleans, La.	FA
Thornton, John	DE	6-3	303	6/28/69	Cincinnati	Flint, Mich.	FA
Tingelhoff, Pat	WR	5-10	192	1/1/68	Minnesota	Prior Lake, Minn.	FA
Vines, Kenny (1)	G	6-4	285	5/3/67	Central State, Ohio	Baltimore, Md.	FA
Wainright, Frank	TE	6-3	236	10/10/67	Northern Colorado	Arvada, Colo.	D8
Wallace, Anthony	RB	6-0	191	7/8/69	California	Altadena, Calif.	D9
Ward, Lorenzo	S	6-3	212	4/26/67	Alabama	Greensboro, Ala.	FA
Wheeler, Todd (1)	C	6-4	269	7/25/67	Georgia	Lindale, Ga.	FA-'89
Williams, Reggie (1)	WR	6-1	194	2/8/66	Pittsburgh	Beaver Falls, Pa.	FA

The term NFL Rookie is defined as a player who is in his first season of professional football and has not been on the roster of another professional football team for any regular-season or postseason games. A Rookie is designated by an "R" on NFL rosters. Players who have been active in another professional football league or players who have NFL experience, including either preseason training camp or being on an active roster for fewer than three regular-season or postseason games, are termed NFL First-Year Players. An NFL First-Year Player is designated by a "1" on NFL rosters. Thereafter, a player on an NFL active roster for at least three regular-season or postseason games is credited with an additional year of NFL playing experience.

NOTES

Steve Sidwell, defensive coordinator-inside linebackers; born August 30, 1944, Winfield, Kan., lives in Destrehan, La. Linebacker Colorado 1962-65. No pro playing experience. College coach: Colorado 1966-73, Nevada-Las Vegas 1974-75, Southern Methodist 1976-81. Pro coach: New England Patriots 1982-84, Indianapolis Colts 1985, joined Saints in 1986.

Jim Skipper, running backs; born January 23, 1949, Breaux Bridge, La., lives in Kenner, La. Defensive back Whittier College 1971-72. No pro playing experience. College coach: Cal Poly-Pomona 1974-76, San Jose State 1977-78, Pacific 1979, Oregon 1980-82. Pro coach: Philadelphia/Baltimore Stars (USFL) 1983-85, joined Saints in 1986.

Carl Smith, offensive coordinator-quarterbacks; born April 26, 1948, Wasco, Calif., lives in Kenner, La. Defensive back Cal Poly-SLO 1968-70. No pro playing experience. College coach: Cal Poly-SLO 1971, Colorado 1972-73, Southwestern Louisiana 1974-78, Lamar 1979-81, North Carolina State 1982. Pro coach: Philadelphia/Baltimore Stars (USFL) 1983-85, joined Saints in 1986.

Steve Walters, wide receivers; born June 16, 1948, Jonesboro, Ark., lives in Destrehan, La. Quarterback-defensive back Arkansas 1967-70. No pro playing experience. College coach: Tampa 1973, Northeast Louisiana 1974-75, Morehead State 1976, Tulsa 1977-78, Memphis State 1979, Southern Methodist 1980-81, Alabama 1985. Pro coach: New England Patriots 1982-84, joined Saints in 1986.

National Football Conference Eastern Division

Team Colors: Blue, Red, and White

Giants Stadium
East Rutherford, New Jersey 07073
Telephone: (201) 935-8111

Club Officials

President/Co-CEO: Wellington T. Mara
Chairman/Co-CEO: Preston Robert Tisch
Executive Vice President/General Counsel: John K. Mara, Esq.
Vice President-Secretary: Raymond J. Walsh
Vice President-General Manager: George Young
Assistant General Manager: Harry Hulmes
Controller: John Pasquali
Director of Player Personnel: Tom Boisture
Director of Pro Personnel: Tim Rooney
Director of Media Services: Ed Croke
Director of Promotions: Tom Power
Director of Special Projects: Victor Del Guercio
Ticket Manager: John Gorman
Head Trainer: Ronnie Barnes
Assistant Trainers: John Johnson, Mike Ryan
Equipment Manager: Ed Wagner, Jr.

Stadium: Giants Stadium • **Capacity:** 77,311
East Rutherford, New Jersey 07073

Playing Surface: AstroTurf

Training Camp: Fairleigh Dickinson-Madison
Florham Park, N.J. 07932

1991 Schedule

Preseason

Aug. 5	**Buffalo**	6:00
Aug. 10	at Cleveland	9:00
Aug. 17	**New York Jets**	8:00
Aug. 24	at New England	4:00

Regular Season

Sept. 2	**San Francisco** (Monday)	9:00
Sept. 8	**Los Angeles Rams**	1:00
Sept. 15	at Chicago	12:00
Sept. 22	**Cleveland**	1:00
Sept. 29	at Dallas	12:00
Oct. 6	**Phoenix**	4:00
Oct. 14	at Pittsburgh (Monday)	9:00
Oct. 20	**Open Date**	
Oct. 27	**Washington**	7:30
Nov. 4	at Philadelphia (Monday)	9:00
Nov. 10	at Phoenix	2:00
Nov. 17	**Dallas**	4:00
Nov. 24	at Tampa Bay	1:00
Dec. 1	at Cincinnati	4:00
Dec. 8	**Philadelphia**	1:00
Dec. 15	at Washington	4:00
Dec. 21	**Houston** (Saturday)	12:30

Giants Coaching History

(480-390-32)

1925	Bob Folwell	8-4-0
1926	Joe Alexander	8-4-1
1927-28	Earl Potteiger	15-8-3
1929-30	LeRoy Andrews*	24-5-1
1930	Benny Friedman	2-0-0
1931-53	Steve Owen	153-108-17
1954-60	Jim Lee Howell	54-29-4
1961-68	Allie Sherman	57-54-4
1969-73	Alex Webster	29-40-1
1974-76	Bill Arnsparger**	7-28-0
1976-78	John McVay	14-23-0
1979-82	Ray Perkins	24-35-0
1983-90	Bill Parcells	85-52-1

*Released after 15 games in 1930
**Released after seven games in 1976

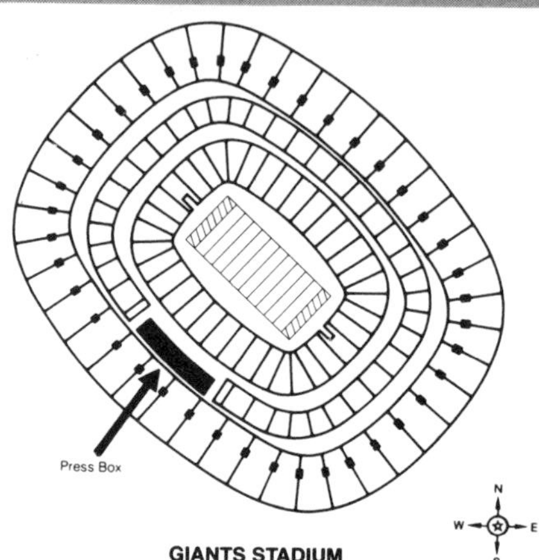

GIANTS STADIUM

Record Holders

Individual Records—Career

Category	Name	Performance
Rushing (Yds.)	Joe Morris, 1982-88	5,296
Passing (Yds.)	Phil Simms, 1979-1990	28,519
Passing (TDs)	Charlie Conerly, 1948-1961	173
Receiving (No.)	Joe Morrison, 1959-1972	395
Receiving (Yds.)	Frank Gifford, 1952-1960, 1962-64	5,434
Interceptions	Emlen Tunnell, 1948-1958	74
Punting (Avg.)	Don Chandler, 1956-1964	43.8
Punt Return (Avg.)	David Meggett, 1989-1990	11.8
Kickoff Return (Avg.)	Rocky Thompson, 1971-72	27.2
Field Goals	Pete Gogolak, 1966-1974	126
Touchdowns (Tot.)	Frank Gifford, 1952-1960, 1962-64	78
Points	Pete Gogolak, 1966-1974	646

Individual Records—Single Season

Category	Name	Performance
Rushing (Yds.)	Joe Morris, 1986	1,516
Passing (Yds.)	Phil Simms, 1984	4,044
Passing (TDs)	Y.A. Tittle, 1963	36
Receiving (No.)	Earnest Gray, 1983	78
Receiving (Yds.)	Homer Jones, 1967	1,209
Interceptions	Otto Schnellbacher, 1951	11
	Jim Patton, 1958	11
Punting (Avg.)	Don Chandler, 1959	46.6
Punt Return (Avg.)	Merle Hapes, 1942	15.5
Kickoff Return (Avg.)	John Salscheider, 1949	31.6
Field Goals	Ali Haji-Sheikh, 1983	*35
Touchdowns (Tot.)	Joe Morris, 1985	21
Points	Ali Haji-Sheikh, 1983	127

Individual Records—Single Game

Category	Name	Performance
Rushing (Yds.)	Gene Roberts, 11-12-50	218
Passing (Yds.)	Phil Simms, 10-13-85	513
Passing (TDs)	Y.A. Tittle, 10-28-62	*7
Receiving (No.)	Mark Bavaro, 10-13-85	12
Receiving (Yds.)	Del Shofner, 10-28-62	269
Interceptions	Many times	3
	Last time by Terry Kinard, 9-27-87	
Field Goals	Joe Danelo, 10-18-81	6
Touchdowns (Tot.)	Ron Johnson, 10-2-72	4
	Earnest Gray, 9-7-80	4
Points	Ron Johnson, 10-2-72	24
	Earnest Gray, 9-7-80	24

*NFL Record

1990 Team Record

Preseason (4-0)

Date	Result		Opponents
8/13	W	20- 6	at Buffalo
8/18	W	13-10	at Houston
8/25	W	17- 7	N.Y. Jets
9/1	W	28-10	Cleveland
		78-33	

Regular Season (13-3)

Date	Result		Opponents	Att.
9/9	W	27-20	Philadelphia	76,202
9/16	W	28- 7	at Dallas	61,090
9/23	W	20- 3	Miami	76,483
9/30	W	31-17	Dallas	75,923
10/14	W	24-20	at Washington	54,737
10/21	W	20-19	Phoenix	76,518
10/28	W	21-10	Washington	75,321
11/5	W	24- 7	at Indianapolis	58,688
11/11	W	31- 7	at L.A. Rams	64,632
11/18	W	20- 0	Detroit	76,109
11/25	L	13-31	at Philadelphia	66,706
12/3	L	3- 7	at San Francisco	66,092
12/9	W	23-15	Minnesota	76,121
12/15	L	13-17	Buffalo	66,893
12/23	W	24-21	at Phoenix	41,212
12/30	W	13-10	at New England	60,410

Postseason (3-0)

Date	Result		Opponent	Att.
1/13	W	31- 3	Chicago	77,025
1/20	W	15-13	at San Francisco	66,334
1/27	W	20-19	Buffalo	73,813

Score by Periods

Giants	66	118	52	99	0	—	335
Opponents	28	72	60	51	0	—	211

Attendance

Home 599,570 Away 473,569 Total 1,073,139
Single-game home record, 77,025 (1-13-91)
Single-season home record, 599,570 (1990)

1990 Team Statistics

	Giants	Opp.
Total First Downs	273	245
Rushing	120	90
Passing	135	139
Penalty	18	16
Third Down: Made/Att.	81/209	72/199
Third Down: Pct.	38.8	36.2
Fourth Down: Made/Att.	8/17	7/17
Fourth Down: Pct.	47.1	41.2
Total Net Yards	4805	4206
Avg. Per Game	300.3	262.9
Total Plays	968	914
Avg. Per Play	5.0	4.6
Net Yards Rushing	2049	1459
Avg. Per Game	128.1	91.2
Total Rushes	541	388
Net Yards Passing	2756	2747
Avg. Per Game	172.3	171.7
Sacked/Yards Lost	29/142	30/186
Gross Yards	2898	2933
Att./Completions	398/231	496/278
Completion Pct.	58.0	56.0
Had Intercepted	5	23
Punts/Avg.	75/44.1	76/41.3
Net Punting Avg.	37.3	34.1
Penalties/Yards Lost	83/655	83/569
Fumbles/Ball Lost	21/9	28/11
Touchdowns	39	23
Rushing	17	9
Passing	18	12
Returns	4	2
Avg. Time of Possession	32:15	27:45

1990 Individual Statistics

Scoring	TD R	TD P	TD Rt	PAT	FG	Saf	TP
Bahr	0	0	0	29/30	17/23	0	80
Anderson	11	0	0	0/0	0/0	0	66
Bavaro	0	5	0	0/0	0/0	0	30
Ingram	0	5	0	0/0	0/0	0	30
Baker	0	4	0	0/0	0/0	0	24
Hampton	2	2	0	0/0	0/0	0	24
Allegre	0	0	0	9/9	4/5	0	21
Hostetler	2	0	0	0/0	0/0	0	12
Meggett	0	1	1	0/0	0/0	0	12
Duerson	0	0	1	0/0	0/0	0	6
Mrosko	0	1	0	0/0	0/0	0	6
Simms	1	0	0	0/0	0/0	0	6
Taylor	0	0	1	0/0	0/0	0	6
Tillman	1	0	0	0/0	0/0	0	6
Walls	0	0	1	0/0	0/0	0	6
Giants	17	18	4	38/39	21/28	0	335
Opponents	9	12	2	23/23	16/22	1	211

Passing	Att.	Comp.	Yds.	Pct.	TD	Int.	Tkld.	Rate
Simms	311	184	2284	59.2	15	4	20/104	92.7
Hostetler	87	47	614	54.0	3	1	9/38	83.2
Giants	398	231	2898	58.0	18	5	29/142	90.6
Opponents	496	278	2933	56.0	12	23	30/186	62.2

Rushing	Att.	Yds.	Avg.	LG	TD
Anderson	225	784	3.5	28	11
Hampton	109	455	4.2	41	2
Tillman	84	231	2.8	17	1
Hostetler	39	190	4.9	30	2
Meggett	22	164	7.5	51	0
Carthon	36	143	4.0	12	0
Simms	21	61	2.9	20	1
Rouson	3	14	4.7	6	0
Ingram	1	4	4.0	4	0
Baker	1	3	3.0	3	0
Giants	541	2049	3.8	51	17
Opponents	388	1459	3.8	31	9

Receiving	No.	Yds.	Avg.	LG	TD
Meggett	39	410	10.5	38	1
Bavaro	33	393	11.9	61	5
Hampton	32	274	8.6	27t	2
Baker	26	541	20.8	80t	4
Ingram	26	499	19.2	57t	5
Anderson	18	139	7.7	18	0
Carthon	14	151	10.8	63	0
Manuel	11	169	15.4	19	0
Cross	8	106	13.3	21	0
Tillman	8	18	2.3	16	0
Turner	6	69	11.5	18	0
Kyles	4	77	19.3	35	0
Mrosko	3	27	9.0	16	1
Robinson	2	13	6.5	7	0
Rouson	1	12	12.0	12	0
Giants	231	2898	12.5	80t	18
Opponents	278	2933	10.6	68t	12

Interceptions	No.	Yds.	Avg.	LG	TD
Walls	6	80	13.3	40	1
Jackson	5	8	1.6	5	0
Reasons	3	13	4.3	10	0
P. Williams	3	4	1.3	4	0
Collins	2	0	0.0	0	0
Taylor	1	11	11.0	11t	1
Duerson	1	0	0.0	0	0
Guyton	1	0	0.0	0	0
Johnson	1	0	0.0	0	0
Giants	23	116	5.0	40	2
Opponents	5	54	10.8	22t	1

Punting	No.	Yds.	Avg.	In 20	LG
Landeta	75	3306	44.1	24	67
Giants	75	3306	44.1	24	67
Opponents	76	3140	41.3	12	57

Punt Returns	No.	FC	Yds.	Avg.	LG	TD
Meggett	43	12	467	10.9	68t	1
Giants	43	12	467	10.9	68t	1
Opponents	41	6	291	7.1	32	0

Kickoff Returns	No.	Yds.	Avg.	LG	TD
Meggett	21	492	23.4	58	0
Hampton	20	340	17.0	33	0
Ingram	3	42	14.0	26	0
Cross	1	10	10.0	10	0
Whitmore	1	0	0.0	0	0
Guyton	0	0	—	0	0
Giants	46	884	19.2	58	0
Opponents	65	1245	19.2	90t	1

Sacks	No.
Taylor	10.5
Marshall	4.5
Jackson	4.0
Johnson	3.5
Howard	3.0
Fox	1.5
Banks	1.0
Cooks	1.0
Thompson	1.0
Giants	30.0
Opponents	29.0

1991 Draft Choices

Round	Name	Pos.	College
1.	Jarrod Bunch	RB	Michigan
2.	Kanavis McGhee	LB	Colorado
3.	Ed McCaffrey	WR	Stanford
4.	Clarence Jones	T	Maryland
5.	Anthony Moss	LB	Florida State
6.	Corey Miller	LB	South Carolina
7.	Simmie Carter	DB	So. Mississippi
8.	Lamar McGriggs	DB	Western Illinois
9.	Jerry Bouldin	WR	Mississippi State
10.	Luis Cristobal	G	Miami
11.	Ted Popson	TE	Portland State
12.	Larry Wanke	QB	John Carroll

New York Giants 1991 Veteran Roster

No.	Name	Pos.	Ht.	Wt.	Birth-date	NFL Exp.	College	Hometown	How Acq.	'90 Games/ Starts
51	Abrams, Bobby	LB	6-3	230	4/12/67	2	Michigan	Detroit, Mich.	FA-'90	16/0
24	†Anderson, Ottis	RB	6-2	225	11/19/57	13	Miami	West Palm Beach, Fla.	T(StL)-'86	16/11
9	†Bahr, Matt	K	5-10	175	7/6/56	13	Penn State	Langhorne, Pa.	FA-'90	13/0
85	†Baker, Stephen	WR	5-8	160	8/30/64	5	Fresno State	San Antonio, Tex.	D3-'87	16/8
58	Banks, Carl	LB	6-4	235	8/29/62	8	Michigan State	Flint, Mich.	D1-'84	9/8
89	Bavaro, Mark	TE	6-4	245	4/28/63	7	Notre Dame	Danvers, Mass.	D4-'85	15/15
46	Brown, Roger	CB	6-0	196	12/16/66	2	Virginia Tech	Baltimore, Md.	FA-'90	5/0
44	Carthon, Maurice	RB	6-1	225	4/24/61	7	Arkansas State	Osceola, Ark.	FA-'85	16/13
6	†Cavanaugh, Matt	QB	6-2	210	10/27/56	14	Pittsburgh	Youngstown, Ohio	FA-'90	0*
25	Collins, Mark	CB	5-10	190	1/16/64	6	Cal State-Fullerton	San Bernardino, Calif.	D2-'86	13/12
98	Cooks, Johnie	LB	6-4	251	11/23/58	10	Mississippi State	Leland, Miss.	FA-'88	14/6
87	†Cross, Howard	TE	6-5	245	8/8/67	3	Alabama	Huntsville, Ala.	D6-'89	16/8
99	DeOssie, Steve	LB	6-2	248	11/22/62	8	Boston College	Tacoma, Wash.	FA-'89	16/13
77	Dorsey, Eric	DE	6-5	280	8/5/64	6	Notre Dame	McLean, Va.	D1-'86	16/11
26	†Duerson, Dave	S	6-1	208	11/28/60	9	Notre Dame	Muncie, Ind.	FA-'90	16/2
76	†Elliott, John	T	6-7	305	4/1/65	4	Michigan	Lake Ronkonkoma, N.Y.	D2-'88	8/8
93	Fox, Mike	DE	6-6	275	8/5/67	2	West Virginia	Akron, Ohio	D2-'90	16/0
29	†Guyton, Myron	S	6-1	205	8/26/67	3	Eastern Kentucky	Metcalf, Ga.	D8-'89	16/16
27	Hampton, Rodney	RB	5-11	215	4/3/69	2	Georgia	Houston, Tex.	D1-'90	15/2
15	†Hostetler, Jeff	QB	6-3	212	4/22/61	7	West Virginia	Johnstown, Pa.	D3-'84	16/2
74	Howard, Erik	NT	6-4	268	11/12/64	6	Washington State	San Jose, Calif.	D2a-'86	16/16
82	†Ingram, Mark	WR	5-10	188	8/23/65	5	Michigan State	Rockford, Ill.	D1-'87	16/14
47	Jackson, Greg	S	6-1	200	8/20/66	3	Louisiana State	Hialeah, Fla.	D3a-'89	14/14
52	†Johnson, Pepper	LB	6-3	248	6/29/64	6	Ohio State	Detroit, Mich.	D2b-'86	16/16
49	Kaumeyer, Thom	S	5-11	190	3/17/67	2	Oregon	La Jolla, Calif.	PB(Sea)-'91#	13/0*
61	Kratch, Bob	G	6-3	288	1/6/66	3	Iowa	Mahwah, N.J.	D3-'89	14/10
5	Landeta, Sean	P	6-0	200	1/6/62	6	Towson State	Baltimore, Md.	FA-'85	16/0
70	Marshall, Leonard	DE	6-3	285	10/22/61	9	Louisiana State	Franklin, La.	D2-'83	16/6
57	†McGrew, Lawrence	LB	6-6	250	7/23/57	11	Southern California	Berkeley, Calif.	FA-'90	11/1
30	†Meggett, David	RB-KR	5-7	180	4/30/66	3	Towson State	Charleston, S.C.	D5-'89	16/1
86	Milling, James	WR	5-9	156	2/14/65	3	Maryland	Winnsboro, S.C.	PB(Atl)-'91#	7/0*
60	Moore, Eric	T	6-5	290	1/21/65	4	Indiana	Berkeley, Mo.	D1-'88	15/14
80	Mrosko, Bob	TE	6-5	270	11/13/65	3	Penn State	Cleveland, Ohio	FA-'90	16/2
65	Oates, Bart	C	6-3	265	12/16/58	7	Brigham Young	Albany, Ga.	FA-'85	16/16
55	Reasons, Gary	LB	6-4	234	2/18/62	8	Northwestern Louisiana	Crowley, Tex.	D4a-'84	16/3
64	Rehder, Tom	G-T	6-7	290	1/27/65	4	Notre Dame	Sacramento, Calif.	FA-'90	8/0
72	Riesenberg, Doug	T	6-5	275	7/22/65	5	California	Moscow, Idaho	D6a-'87	16/16
66	†Roberts, William	T	6-5	280	8/5/62	7	Ohio State	Miami, Fla.	D1a-'84	16/16
81	†Robinson, Stacy	WR	5-11	186	2/19/62	7	North Dakota State	St. Paul, Minn.	FA-'90	5/0
11	Simms, Phil	QB	6-3	214	11/3/55	12	Morehead State	Louisville, Ky.	D1-'79	14/14
56	Taylor, Lawrence	LB	6-3	243	2/4/59	11	North Carolina	Williamsburg, Va.	D1-'81	16/16
21	†Thompson, Reyna	CB	6-0	193	8/28/63	6	Baylor	Dallas, Tex.	FA-'89	16/4
34	Tillman, Lewis	RB	6-0	195	4/16/66	3	Jackson State	Oklahoma City, Okla.	D4-'89	16/3
28	Walls, Everson	CB	6-1	194	12/28/59	11	Grambling	Dallas, Tex.	FA-'90	16/16
73	†Washington, John	DE	6-4	275	2/20/63	6	Oklahoma State	Houston, Tex.	D3-'86	16/13
36	White, Adrian	S	6-0	200	4/6/64	4	Florida	Orange Park, Fla.	D2-'87	0*
59	Williams, Brian	C-G	6-5	300	6/8/66	3	Minnesota	Mt. Lebanon, Pa.	D1-'89	16/1
23	Williams, Perry	CB	6-2	203	5/12/61	8	North Carolina State	Hamlet, N.C.	D7-'83	16/2

* Cavanaugh active for 7 games but did not play in '90; Kaumeyer played 13 games with Seattle in '90; Milling played 7 games with Atlanta; White missed '90 season due to injury.

† Option playout; subject to developments.

Plan B unconditional free agent.

Players lost through Plan B (4): WR Troy Kyles (SD; 9 games in '90), RB Lee Rouson (Clev; 16), K Matt Stover (Clev; 0), S David Whitmore (SF; 16).

Also played with Giants in '90—K Raul Allegre (3 games), WR Odessa Turner (4), DT Kent Wells (6).

COACHING STAFF

Head Coach, Ray Handley

Pro Career: Became thirteenth head coach in New York Giants history on May 15, 1991. Had served as running backs coach with Giants since 1984, and was then named offensive coordinator in February, 1991, before replacing Bill Parcells, who resigned as head coach on May 15, 1991.

Background: Running back at Stanford 1963-65. No pro playing experience. College assistant at Stanford 1967, 1971-74, 1979-83, Army 1968-69, Air Force 1975-78.

Personal: Born October 8, 1944, Artesia, N.M. Ray and his wife, JoAnne, live in West Orange, N.J., and have a son, Donnie, and a daughter, Cami.

Assistant Coaches

Fred Bruney, defensive backs; born December 30, 1931, Martins Ferry, Ohio, lives in Chatham, N.J. Running back Ohio State 1950-52. Pro defensive back San Francisco 49ers 1953-56, Pittsburgh Steelers 1957, Los Angeles Rams 1958, Boston Patriots 1960-62. College coach: Ohio State 1959. Pro coach: Boston Patriots 1963; Philadelphia Eagles 1964-68, 1977-85, Atlanta Falcons 1969-76, 1986-89, Tampa Bay Buccaneers 1990, joined Giants in 1991.

Romeo Crennell, defensive line; born June 18, 1947, Lynchburg, Va., lives in Montvale, N.J. Defensive lineman Western Kentucky 1966-69. No pro playing experience. College coach: Western Kentucky 1970-74, Texas Tech 1975-77, Mississippi 1978-79, Georgia Tech 1980. Pro coach: Joined Giants in 1981.

Ron Erhardt, assistant head coach; born February 27, 1932, Mandan, N.D., lives in Wykoff, N.J. Quarterback Jamestown (N.D.) College 1951-54. No pro playing experience. College coach: North Dakota State 1963-72 (head coach 1966-72). Pro coach: New England Patriots 1973-81 (head coach 1979-81), joined Giants in 1982.

Jim Fassel, quarterbacks; born August 31, 1949, Anaheim, Calif., lives in East Rutherford, N.J. Quarterback Southern California 1969-70, Long Beach State 1971. Pro quarterback Chicago Bears 1972, Houston Oilers 1972, San Diego Chargers 1972. College coach: Fullerton (Calif.) J.C. 1973, Utah 1976, 1985-89 (head coach), Weber State 1977-78, Stanford 1979-83. Pro coach: Hawaii (WFL) 1974, Portland Breakers (USFL) 1984, joined Giants in 1991.

Al Groh, defensive coordinator; born July 13, 1944, New York City, lives in Randolph, N.J. Defensive end Virginia 1964-67. No pro playing experience. College coach: Army 1968-69, Virginia 1970-72, North Carolina 1973-77, Air Force 1978-79, Texas Tech 1980, Wake Forest 1981-86 (head coach), South Carolina 1988. Pro coach: Atlanta Falcons 1987, joined Giants in 1989.

Fred Hoaglin, offensive line; born January 28, 1944, Alliance, Ohio, lives in Sparta, N.J. Center Pittsburgh 1962-65. Pro center Cleveland Browns 1966-72, Baltimore Colts 1973, Houston Oilers 1974-75, Seattle Seahawks 1976. Pro coach: Detroit Lions 1978-84, joined Giants in 1985.

Johnny Parker, strength and conditioning; born February 1, 1947, Greenville, S.C., lives in Montvale, N.J. Graduate of Mississippi, master's degree from Delta State University. No college or pro playing experience. College coach: South Carolina 1974-76, Indiana 1977-79, Louisiana State 1980, Mississippi 1981-83. Pro coach: Joined Giants in 1984.

Mike Pope, tight ends; born March 15, 1942, Monroe, N.C., lives in River Vale, N.J. Quarterback Lenoir Rhyne 1962-64. No pro playing experience. College coach: Florida State 1970-74, Texas Tech 1975-77, Mississippi 1978-82. Pro coach: Joined Giants in 1983.

New York Giants 1991 First-Year Roster

Name	Pos.	Ht.	Wt.	Birth-date	College	Hometown	How Acq.
Ashe, Richard (1)	TE	6-5	252	3/14/67	Humboldt State	Moreno Valley, Calif.	FA
Boler, Chuck	T-G	6-4	295	10/25/67	Memphis State	Tuscaloosa, Ala.	FA
Bouldin, Jerry	WR	6-0	190	1/7/69	Mississippi State	Madison, Miss.	D9
Butler, Jay	T	6-7	306	9/10/69	Bucknell	New Brunswick, N.J.	FA
Bunch, Jarrod	RB	6-2	248	8/9/68	Michigan	Ashtabula, Ohio	D1
Carter, Simmie	CB-S	5-11	185	4/19/67	Southern Mississippi	Harvey, La.	D7
Clair, Kiernan	QB	6-3	222	3/5/69	Hamilton	Teaneck, N.J.	FA
Cristobal, Luis	G	6-3	290	1/4/68	Miami	Miami, Fla.	D10
Fann, Albert	RB	6-1	218	5/27/69	Cal State-Northridge	Los Angeles, Calif.	FA
Gale, Chris	DT-DE	6-4	268	10/14/68	Jackson State	Vicksburg, Miss.	FA
Hill, Demetrius	DT-DE	6-2	270	3/27/67	Mississippi State	Houston, Tex.	FA
Jones, Clarence	T	6-6	280	5/6/68	Maryland	Brooklyn, N.Y.	D4
Jones, Stanley	DT-DE	6-3	284	7/1/68	Hampton Institute	Newark, N.J.	FA
Kelley, Matt	LB	6-2	230	1/30/67	Boston College	Stamford, Conn.	FA
Kelner, Daniel	WR	6-0	180	7/29/68	Wisconsin-Eau Claire	Minneapolis, Minn.	FA
Kinnon, Duane	RB	6-1	223	12/22/68	Syracuse	Brooklyn, N.Y.	FA
McCaffery, Ed	WR	6-5	215	8/17/68	Stanford	Allentown, Pa.	D3
McCummings, Gary	G	6-3	280	9/2/68	Syracuse	Philadelphia, Pa.	FA
McGhee, Kanavis	LB	6-4	257	10/4/68	Colorado	Houston, Tex.	D2
McGriggs, Lamar	CB-S	6-3	210	5/9/68	Western Illinois	Chicago, Ill.	D8
Medice, Larry	G	6-4	295	7/31/68	Oklahoma	New Orleans, La.	FA
Miller, Corey	LB	6-2	255	10/25/68	South Carolina	Pageland, S.C.	D6
Moss, Anthony	LB	6-4	240	10/12/67	Florida State	Miami, Fla.	D5
Peoples, Mark	CB-S	5-9	185	1/23/68	Central Missouri St.	East St. Louis, Ill.	FA
Popson, Ted	TE	6-4	245	9/10/66	Portland State	Granada Hills, Calif.	D11
Richardson, Mike	RB	5-10	195	10/13/69	Louisiana Tech	Natchez, Miss.	FA
Rolen, Chad	DT	6-2	273	3/2/68	Arkansas	Mt. Pleasant, Tex.	FA
Rouen, Tom	P	6-3	218	6/9/68	Colorado	Hindsdale, Ill.	FA
Satter, Tony	RB	5-11	205	4/11/69	North Dakota State	Louisville, Ky.	FA
Segina, Richard	G	6-3	275	11/10/68	Rice	Mission, Tex.	FA
Shell, Alex	WR	6-4	200	2/24/68	Arkansas State	Carrollton, Ga.	FA
Taylor, Greg	WR	5-8	168	1/27/68	Auburn	Lee County, Ala.	FA
Tripp, Dennis	DT	6-3	266	2/13/67	North Carolina	Farmville, N.C.	FA
Wanke, Larry	QB	6-3	220	4/2/68	John Carroll	South Euclid, Ohio	D12
Washington, Ben	CB-S	5-9	189	5/18/67	Southern Mississippi	Yazoo City, Miss.	FA
Williams, Jerry	DT-DE	6-0	277	10/26/68	Arkansas-Pine Bluff	Greenwood, Miss.	FA

The term NFL Rookie is defined as a player who is in his first season of professional football and has not been on the roster of another professional football team for any regular-season or postseason games. A Rookie is designated by an "R" on NFL rosters. Players who have been active in another professional football league or players who have NFL experience, including either preseason training camp or being on an active roster for fewer than three regular-season or postseason games, are termed NFL First-Year Players. An NFL First-Year Player is designated by a "1" on NFL rosters. Thereafter, a player on an NFL active roster for at least three regular-season or postseason games is credited with an additional year of NFL playing experience.

NOTES

George Sefcik, wide receivers; born December 27, 1939, Cleveland, Ohio, lives in East Rutherford, N.J. Halfback Notre Dame 1959-61. No pro playing experience. College coach: Notre Dame 1963-68, Kentucky 1969-72. Pro coach: Baltimore Colts 1973-74, Cleveland Browns 1975-77, 1989-90, Cincinnati Bengals 1979-83, Green Bay Packers 1984-87, Kansas City Chiefs 1988, joined Giants in 1991.

Mike Sweatman, special teams; born October 23, 1946, Kansas City, Mo., lives in Wayne, N.J. Linebacker Kansas 1964-67. No pro playing experience. College coach: Kansas 1973-74, 1979-82, Tulsa 1977-78, Tennessee 1983. Pro coach: Minnesota Vikings 1984, joined Giants in 1985.

Bob Trott, defensive assistant; born March 19, 1954, Kannapolis, N.C., lives in East Rutherford, N.J. Defensive back North Carolina 1973-75. No pro playing experience. College coach: North Carolina 1976-77, Air Force 1978-83, Arkansas 1984-89, Clemson 1990. Pro coach: Joined Giants in 1991.

Charlie Weis, running backs, born March 30, 1956, Trenton, N.J., lives in Middlesex, N.J. No college or pro playing experience. College coach: South Carolina 1985-88. Pro coach: Joined Giants in 1990.

National Football Conference Eastern Division

Team Colors: Kelly Green, Silver, and White

Veterans Stadium
Broad Street and Pattison Avenue
Philadelphia, Pennsylvania 19148
Telephone: (215) 463-2500

Club Officials
Owner: Norman Braman
President-Chief Operating Officer: Harry Gamble
Vice President: Suzi Braman
V.P.-Chief Financial Officer: Mimi Box
V.P.-Marketing and Development: Decker Uhlhorn
Asst. to the President: George Azar
Asst. to the President-General Counsel: Bob Wallace
Director of Player Personnel: Joe Woolley
Asst. to Dir. of Player Personnel: Tom Gamble
Director of Public Relations: Ron Howard
Assoc. Dir. of Sales and Marketing: Leslie Stephenson
Dir. of Alumni Relations/Traveling Sec.: Jim Gallagher
Director of Administration: Vicki Chatley
Ticket Manager: Leo Carlin
Director of Sales: Lou Scheinfeld
Asst. Director of Penthouse Sales: Ken Iman
Trainer: Otho Davis
Asst. Trainer: David Price
Player Relations Consultant: Lem Burnham, Ph.D.
Equipment Manager: Rusty Sweeney
Video Director: Mike Dougherty

Stadium: Veterans Stadium •
Capacity: 65,356
Broad Street and Pattison Avenue
Philadelphia, Pennsylvania 19148

Playing Surface: AstroTurf-8

Training Camp: West Chester University
West Chester, Pennsylvania 19382

1991 Schedule

Preseason

July 28	vs. Buffalo at London	1:00*
Aug. 3	at New York Jets	8:00
Aug. 10	at Cincinnati	7:30
Aug. 17	**Pittsburgh**	7:30
Aug. 23	**Indianapolis**	7:30

*P.M. Eastern Time

Regular Season

Sept. 1	at Green Bay	12:00
Sept. 8	**Phoenix**	1:00
Sept. 15	at Dallas	12:00
Sept. 22	**Pittsburgh**	1:00
Sept. 30	at Washington (Monday)	9:00
Oct. 6	at Tampa Bay	1:00
Oct. 13	**New Orleans**	1:00
Oct. 20	**Open Date**	
Oct. 27	**San Francisco**	1:00
Nov. 4	**N.Y. Giants** (Monday)	9:00
Nov. 10	at Cleveland	1:00
Nov. 17	**Cincinnati**	1:00
Nov. 24	at Phoenix	2:00
Dec. 2	at Houston (Monday)	8:00
Dec. 8	at New York Giants	1:00
Dec. 15	**Dallas**	1:00
Dec. 22	**Washington**	4:00

Eagles Coaching History

(333-414-24)

1933-35	Lud Wray	9-21-1
1936-40	Bert Bell	10-44-2
1941-50	Earle (Greasy) Neale*	66-44-5
1951	Alvin (Bo) McMillin**	2-0-0
1951	Wayne Millner	2-8-0
1952-55	Jim Trimble	25-20-3
1956-57	Hugh Devore	7-16-1
1958-60	Lawrence (Buck) Shaw	20-16-1
1961-63	Nick Skorich	15-24-3
1964-68	Joe Kuharich	28-41-1
1969-71	Jerry Williams***	7-22-2
1971-72	Ed Khayat	8-15-2
1973-75	Mike McCormack	16-25-1
1976-82	Dick Vermeil	57-51-0
1983-85	Marion Campbell****	17-29-1
1985	Fred Bruney	1-0-0
1986-90	Buddy Ryan	43-38-1

*Co-coach with Walt Kiesling in Philadelphia-Pittsburgh merger in 1943
**Retired after two games in 1951
***Released after three games in 1971
****Released after 15 games in 1985

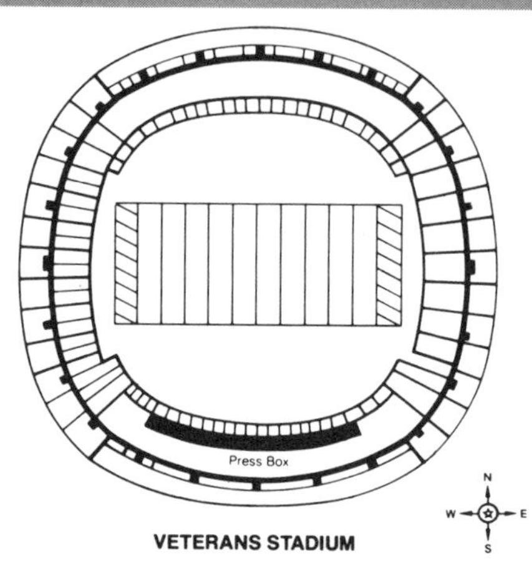

VETERANS STADIUM

Record Holders

Individual Records—Career

Category	Name	Performance
Rushing (Yds.)	Wilbert Montgomery, 1977-1984	6,538
Passing (Yds.)	Ron Jaworski, 1977-1986	26,963
Passing (TDs)	Ron Jaworski, 1977-1986	175
Receiving (No.)	Harold Carmichael, 1971-1983	589
Receiving (Yds.)	Harold Carmichael, 1971-1983	8,978
Interceptions	Bill Bradley, 1969-1976	34
Punting (Avg.)	Joe Muha, 1946-1950	42.9
Punt Return (Avg.)	Steve Van Buren, 1944-1951	13.9
Kickoff Return (Avg.)	Steve Van Buren, 1944-1951	26.7
Field Goals	Paul McFadden, 1984-87	91
Touchdowns (Tot.)	Harold Carmichael, 1971-1983	79
Points	Bobby Walston, 1951-1962	881

Individual Records—Single Season

Category	Name	Performance
Rushing (Yds.)	Wilbert Montgomery, 1979	1,512
Passing (Yds.)	Randall Cunningham, 1988	3,808
Passing (TDs)	Sonny Jurgensen, 1961	32
Receiving (No.)	Keith Jackson, 1988	81
	Keith Byars, 1990	81
Receiving (Yds.)	Mike Quick, 1983	1,409
Interceptions	Bill Bradley, 1971	11
Punting (Avg.)	Joe Muha, 1948	47.2
Punt Return (Avg.)	Steve Van Buren, 1944	15.3
Kickoff Return (Avg.)	Al Nelson, 1972	29.1
Field Goals	Paul McFadden, 1984	30
Touchdowns (Tot.)	Steve Van Buren, 1945	18
Points	Paul McFadden, 1984	116

Individual Records—Single Game

Category	Name	Performance
Rushing (Yds.)	Steve Van Buren, 11-27-49	205
Passing (Yds.)	Bobby Thomason, 11-18-53	437
Passing (TDs)	Adrian Burk, 10-17-54	*7
Receiving (No.)	Don Looney, 12-1-40	14
Receiving (Yds.)	Tommy McDonald, 12-10-60	237
Interceptions	Russ Craft, 9-24-50	*4
Field Goals	Tom Dempsey, 11-12-72	6
Touchdowns (Tot.)	Many times	4
	Last time by Wilbert Montgomery, 10-7-79	
Points	Bobby Walston, 10-17-54	25

*NFL Record

1990 Team Record

Preseason (2-2)

Date	Result		Opponents
8/11	L	6-17	N.Y. Jets
8/18	W	23-14	Miami
8/27	W	17-16	at Indianapolis
9/1	L	10-20	at Pittsburgh
		56-67	

Regular Season (10-6)

Date	Result		Opponents	Att.
9/9	L	20-27	at N.Y. Giants	76,202
9/16	L	21-23	Phoenix	64,396
9/23	W	27-21	at L.A. Rams	63,644
9/30	L	23-24	Indianapolis	62,067
10/15	W	32-24	Minnesota	66,296
10/21	L	7-13	at Washington	53,567
10/28	W	21-20	at Dallas	62,605
11/4	W	48-20	New England	65,514
11/12	W	28-14	Washington	65,857
11/18	W	24-23	at Atlanta	53,755
11/25	W	31-13	N.Y. Giants	66,706
12/2	L	23-30	at Buffalo	79,320
12/9	L	20-23	at Miami (OT)	67,034
12/16	W	31- 0	Green Bay	65,627
12/23	W	17- 3	Dallas	63,895
12/29	W	23-21	at Phoenix	31,796

(OT) Overtime

Postseason (0-1)

Date	Result		Opponent	Att.
1/5	L	6-20	Washington	65,287

Score by Periods

Eagles	84	104	67	141	0	—	396
Opponents	71	81	40	104	3	—	299

Attendance

Home 520,360 Away 487,523 Total 1,007,883
Single-game home record, 72,111 (11-1-81)
Single-season home record, 557,325 (1980)

1990 Team Statistics

	Eagles	Opp.
Total First Downs	325	251
Rushing	132	59
Passing	170	169
Penalty	23	23
Third Down: Made/Att.	90/218	68/217
Third Down: Pct.	41.3	31.3
Fourth Down: Made/Att.	9/12	8/18
Fourth Down: Pct.	75.0	44.4
Total Net Yards	5700	4660
Avg. Per Game	356.3	291.3
Total Plays	1069	948
Avg. Per Play	5.3	4.9
Net Yards Rushing	2556	1172
Avg. Per Game	159.8	73.3
Total Rushes	540	336
Net Yards Passing	3144	3488
Avg. Per Game	196.5	218.0
Sacked/Yards Lost	50/438	46/283
Gross Yards	3582	3771
Att./Completions	479/281	566/273
Completion Pct.	58.7	48.2
Had Intercepted	13	19
Punts/Avg.	74/40.9	86/40.3
Net Punting Avg.	35.5	34.4
Penalties/Yards Lost	120/981	94/706
Fumbles/Ball Lost	32/15	32/11
Touchdowns	48	33
Rushing	10	9
Passing	34	23
Returns	4	1
Avg. Time of Possession	33:19	26:41

1990 Individual Statistics

Scoring	TD R	TD P	TD Rt	PAT	FG	Saf	TP
Ruzek	0	0	0	45/48	21/29	0	108
Williams	0	9	0	0/0	0/0	0	54
Barnett	0	8	0	0/0	0/0	0	48
Kei. Jackson	0	6	0	0/0	0/0	0	36
Cunningham	5	0	0	0/0	0/0	0	30
Sherman	1	3	0	0/0	0/0	0	24
Toney	1	3	0	0/0	0/0	0	24
Byars	0	3	0	0/0	0/0	0	18
Allen	0	0	1	0/0	0/0	0	6
Drummond	1	0	0	0/0	0/0	0	6
Evans	0	0	1	0/0	0/0	0	6
Frizzell	0	0	1	0/0	0/0	0	6
Hargrove	0	1	0	0/0	0/0	0	6
Quick	0	1	0	0/0	0/0	0	6
Sanders	1	0	0	0/0	0/0	0	6
Simmons	0	0	1	0/0	0/0	0	6
Vick	1	0	0	0/0	0/0	0	6
Eagles	10	34	4	45/48	21/29	0	396
Opponents	9	23	1	32/33	23/32	0	299

Passing	Att.	Comp.	Yds.	Pct.	TD	Int.	Tkld.	Rate
Cunning-ham	465	271	3466	58.3	30	13	49/431	91.6
McMahon	9	6	63	66.7	0	0	1/7	86.8
Byars	4	4	53	100.0	4	0	0/0	158.3
Feagles	1	0	0	0.0	0	0	0/0	39.6
Eagles	479	281	3582	58.7	34	13	50/438	94.5
Opponents	566	273	3771	48.2	23	19	46/283	69.6

Rushing	Att.	Yds.	Avg.	LG	TD
Cunningham	118	942	8.0	52t	5
Sherman	164	685	4.2	36	1
Toney	132	452	3.4	20	1
Sanders	56	208	3.7	39	1
Byars	37	141	3.8	23	0
Vick	16	58	3.6	17	1
Drummond	8	33	4.1	9	1
Williams	2	20	10.0	18	0
Barnett	2	13	6.5	12	0
Feagles	2	3	1.5	3	0
McMahon	3	1	0.3	3	0
Eagles	540	2556	4.7	52t	10
Opponents	336	1172	3.5	51	9

Receiving	No.	Yds.	Avg.	LG	TD
Byars	81	819	10.1	54	3
Kei. Jackson	50	670	13.4	37t	6
Williams	37	602	16.3	45t	9
Barnett	36	721	20.0	95t	8
Sherman	23	167	7.3	26	3
Shuler	18	190	10.6	25	0
Toney	17	133	7.8	32	3
Quick	9	135	15.0	39	1
Drummond	5	39	7.8	29	0
Sanders	2	20	10.0	12	0
Ken. Jackson	1	43	43.0	43	0
Hargrove	1	34	34.0	34t	1
Le Bel	1	9	9.0	9	0
Eagles	281	3582	12.7	95t	34
Opponents	273	3771	13.8	78t	23

Interceptions	No.	Yds.	Avg.	LG	TD
Hopkins	5	45	9.0	21	0
Frizzell	3	91	30.3	37	1
Allen	3	37	12.3	35t	1
B. Smith	3	1	0.3	1	0
Evans	1	43	43.0	22t	1
White	1	33	33.0	33	0
Golic	1	12	12.0	12	0
Joyner	1	9	9.0	9	0
Hoage	1	0	0.0	0	0
Eagles	19	271	14.3	42	3
Opponents	13	88	6.8	38	0

Punting	No.	Yds.	Avg.	In 20	LG
Feagles	72	3026	42.0	20	60
Eagles	74	3026	40.9	20	60
Opponents	86	3470	40.3	22	59

Punt Returns	No.	FC	Yds.	Avg.	LG	TD
R. Harris, Dall.-Phil.	28	8	214	7.6	30	0
R. Harris, Phil.	16	2	151	9.4	30	0
Hargrove	12	2	83	6.9	13	0
Edwards	8	7	60	7.5	13	0
Bellamy	2	0	22	11.0	22	0
Williams	2	0	−1	−0.5	0	0
Eagles	40	11	315	7.9	30	0
Opponents	37	19	338	9.1	68t	1

Kickoff Returns	No.	Yds.	Avg.	LG	TD
Hargrove	19	341	17.9	30	0
Sanders	15	299	19.9	37	0
Ken. Jackson	6	125	20.8	30	0
Barnett	4	65	16.3	22	0
Edwards	3	36	12.0	14	0
R. Harris, Dall.-Phil.	2	44	22.0	44	0
R. Harris, Phil.	1	44	44.0	44	0
Vick	2	22	11.0	13	0
Allen	1	2	2.0	2	0
Bellamy	1	17	17.0	17	0
Hager	1	0	0.0	0	0
Jenkins	1	14	14.0	14	0
Eagles	54	965	17.9	44	0
Opponents	74	1408	19.0	40	0

Sacks	No.
White	15.0
Joyner	7.5
Simmons	7.5
Small	3.5
Pitts	3.0
Golic	2.0
Hopkins	2.0
Frizzell	1.5
J. Brown	1.0
Chapura	1.0
Evans	1.0
Hoage	1.0
Eagles	46.0
Opponents	50.0

1991 Draft Choices

Round	Name	Pos.	College
1.	Antone Davis	T	Tennessee
2.	Jesse Campbell	DB	North Carolina St.
3.	Rob Selby	T	Auburn
4.	William Thomas	LB	Texas A&M
5.	Craig Erickson	QB	Miami
6.	Andy Harmon	DE	Kent State
7.	James Joseph	RB	Auburn
8.	Scott Kowalkowski	LB	Notre Dame
9.	C. Weatherspoon	RB	Houston
10.	Eric Harmon	G	Clemson
11.	Mike Flores	DE	Louisville
12.	Darrell Beavers	DB	Morehead State

Philadelphia Eagles 1991 Veteran Roster

No.	Name	Pos.	Ht.	Wt.	Birth-date	NFL Exp.	College	Hometown	How Acq.	'90 Games/ Starts
72	Alexander, David	C	6-3	275	7/28/64	5	Tulsa	Broken Arrow, Okla.	D5-'87	16/16
21	Allen, Eric	CB	5-10	180	11/22/65	4	Arizona State	San Diego, Calif.	D2-'88	16/15
86	Barnett, Fred	WR	6-0	199	6/17/66	2	Arkansas State	Gunnison, Miss.	D3-'90	16/11
81	Bellamy, Mike	WR	6-0	195	6/28/66	2	Illinois	Chicago, Ill.	D2-'90	6/0
42	Booty, John	CB	6-0	180	10/9/65	4	Texas Christian	Carthage, Tex.	PB(NYJ)-'91#	13/1*
99	†Brown, Jerome	DT	6-2	295	2/4/65	5	Miami	Brooksville, Fla.	D1-'87	16/15
41	Byars, Keith	RB	6-1	238	10/14/63	6	Ohio State	Dayton, Ohio	D1-'86	16/15
97	Chapura, Dick	DT	6-3	277	6/15/64	5	Missouri	Sarasota, Fla.	FA-'90	10/0*
69	†Collie, Bruce	G	6-6	270	6/27/62	7	Texas-Arlington	San Antonio, Tex.	W(SF)-'90	12/2
12	Cunningham, Randall	QB	6-4	205	3/27/63	7	Nevada-Las Vegas	Santa Barbara, Calif.	D2-'85	16/16
78	†Darwin, Matt	T	6-4	275	3/11/63	5	Texas A&M	Spring, Tex.	D4-'86	2/2
36	Drummond, Robert	RB	6-1	205	6/21/67	3	Syracuse	Jamesville, N.Y.	D3a-'89	4/0
56	Evans, Byron	LB	6-2	235	2/23/64	5	Arizona	Phoenix, Ariz.	D4-'87	16/16
5	Feagles, Jeff	P	6-1	205	3/7/66	4	Miami	Phoenix, Ariz.	W(NE)-'90	16/0
90	†Golic, Mike	DT	6-5	275	12/12/62	6	Notre Dame	Cleveland, Ohio	FA-'87	16/13
71	Gray, Cecil	G	6-4	275	2/16/68	2	North Carolina	Norfolk, Va.	D9-'90	12/1
54	Hager, Britt	LB	6-1	225	2/20/66	3	Texas	Odessa, Tex.	D3-'89	16/1
80	Harris, Rod	WR	5-10	185	11/14/66	3	Texas A&M	Dallas, Tex.	W(Dall)-'90	11/0*
73	Heller, Ron	T	6-6	280	8/25/62	8	Penn State	Farmingdale, N.Y.	T(Sea)-'88	16/14
48	†Hopkins, Wes	S	6-1	215	9/26/61	8	Southern Methodist	Birmingham, Ala.	D2a-'83	15/12
88	Jackson, Keith	TE	6-2	250	4/19/65	4	Oklahoma	Little Rock, Ark.	D1-'88	14/14
83	Jackson, Kenny	WR	6-0	180	2/15/62	8	Penn State	Camden, N.J.	FA-'90	14/0
46	Jenkins, Izel	CB	5-10	190	5/27/64	4	North Carolina State	Wilson, N.C.	D11-'88	15/4
59	†Joyner, Seth	LB	6-2	235	11/18/64	6	Texas-El Paso	Spring Valley, N.Y.	D8-'86	16/16
94	Kaufusi, Steve	DE	6-4	257	10/17/63	3	Brigham Young	Salt Lake City, Utah	D12-'88	16/0
62	McKnight, Dennis	C-G	6-3	280	9/31/59	9	Drake	Staten Island, N.Y.	PB(Det)-'91#	14/0*
9	†McMahon, Jim	QB	6-1	195	8/21/59	10	Brigham Young	Northbrook, Ill.	FA-'90	5/0
74	†Pitts, Mike	DT	6-5	280	9/25/60	9	Alabama	Baltimore, Md.	T(Atl)-'87	4/3
82	Quick, Mike	WR	6-2	195	5/14/59	10	North Carolina State	Hamlet, N.C.	D1-'82	4/4
55	Rose, Ken	LB	6-1	215	6/9/62	5	Nevada-Las Vegas	Sacramento, Calif.	FA-'90	15/0*
7	Ruzek, Roger	K	6-1	200	12/17/60	5	Weber State	San Francisco, Calif.	FA-'89	16/0
45	†Sanders, Thomas	RB	5-11	202	1/4/62	7	Texas A&M	Giddings, Tex.	FA-'90	10/0
79	†Schad, Mike	G	6-5	290	10/2/63	4	Queens College, Canada	Bellville, Ontario	PB(Rams)-'89#	12/12
23	†Sherman, Heath	RB	6-0	205	3/27/67	3	Texas A&I	El Campo, Tex.	D6-'89	14/5
85	†Shuler, Mickey	TE	6-3	230	8/21/56	14	Penn State	Enola, Pa.	FA-'90	16/6
96	†Simmons, Clyde	DE	6-6	280	8/4/64	6	Western Carolina	Wilmington, N.C.	D9-'86	16/16
68	†Singletary, Reggie	T	6-3	285	1/17/64	5	North Carolina State	Whiteville, N.C.	FA-'89	16/16
52	Small, Jessie	LB	6-3	240	11/30/66	3	Eastern Kentucky	Boston, Ga.	D2-'89	15/14
26	Smith, Ben	CB-S	5-11	185	5/14/67	2	Georgia	Warner Robins, Ga.	D1-'90	16/13
63	Smith, Daryle	T	6-5	276	1/18/64	5	Tennessee	Powell, Tenn.	FA-'90	3/0
66	Solt, Ron	G	6-3	275	5/19/62	7	Maryland	Wilkes-Barre, Pa.	T(Ind)-'88	15/15
61	Tamburello, Ben	C-G	6-3	270	9/9/64	4	Auburn	Birmingham, Ala.	D3-'87	16/2
10	Teltschik, John	P	6-2	215	3/8/64	5	Texas	Kerrville, Tex.	W(Chi)-'86	0*
25	Toney, Anthony	RB	6-0	230	9/23/62	6	Texas A&M	Salinas, Calif.	D2a-'86	15/11
43	†Vick, Roger	RB	6-3	235	8/11/64	5	Texas A&M	Tomball, Tex.	T(NYJ)-'90	14/0
20	Waters, Andre	S	5-11	200	3/10/62	8	Cheyney State	Pahokee, Fla.	FA-'84	14/13
92	White, Reggie	DE	6-5	285	12/19/61	7	Tennessee	Chattanooga, Tenn.	SD1-'84	16/16
89	Williams, Calvin	WR	5-11	190	3/3/67	2	Purdue	Baltimore, Md.	D5-'90	16/14

* Booty played 13 games with N.Y. Jets in '90; Chapura played 3 games with Phoenix, 7 with Philadelphia; Harris played 7 games with Dallas, 4 with Philadelphia; McKnight played 14 games with Detroit; Rose played 7 games with Cleveland; Teltschik missed '90 season due to injury.

† Option playout; subject to developments.

Plan B unconditional free agent.

Players lost through Plan B (6): T Louis Cheek (GB; 1 game in '90), CB-S William Frizzell (TB; 16), CB-S Terry Hoage (Wash; 16), TE Harper Le Bel (Atl; 16), LB Ricky Shaw (KC; 8), CB-S Kevin Thompson (Sea; 0).

Also played with Eagles in '90—DE David Bailey (13 games), WR-KR Anthony Edwards (5), WR Marvin Hargrove (7), LB Al Harris (16), CB Sammy Lilly (8), DE Greg Mark (2).

COACHING STAFF

Head Coach, Rich Kotite

Pro Career: Became the eighteenth head coach in Eagles' history on January 8, 1991, succeeding Buddy Ryan, after serving as offensive coordinator for one season. In 1990, Kotite's offense led the NFL in rushing and time of possession, and also led the NFC in scoring and touchdown passes. Under Kotite, quarterback Randall Cunningham flourished. The sixth-year pro had his best season when he was the NFC's second highest-rated passer and also was the conference's fourth leading rusher. Kotite had previously served as the New York Jets' offensive coordinator and receivers coach from 1985-89 after originally joining the club as receivers coach in 1983. In each of Kotite's years at the helm of the New York offense, the Jets finished near the top in the AFC in total offense, including a third-place ranking in 1985. Kotite began his pro coaching career with New Orleans in 1977 before joining Cleveland the following year. Kotite was the Browns' receivers coach, aiding in the development of perennial all-pro tight end Ozzie Newsome from 1978-82 before joining the Jets. During his playing career, he was known as a scrappy tight end and outstanding special teams performer with the New York Giants (1967, 1969-72) and Steelers (1968).

Background: Attended Poly Prep in Brooklyn, N.Y. After a brief boxing career at the University of Miami where he was the school's heavyweight champ, he served as a sparring partner for Cassius Clay, later known as Muhammad Ali. Kotite became a Little All-America tight end at Wagner College in Staten Island, N.Y.

Personal: Born in Brooklyn on October 13, 1942. He and his wife, Elizabeth, live in Mt. Laurel, N.J. and have one daughter—Alexandra.

Assistant Coaches

Dave Atkins, special teams; born May 18, 1949, Victoria, Tex., lives in Marlton, N.J. Running back Texas-El Paso 1970-72. Pro running back San Francisco 49ers 1973, Honolulu (WFL) 1974, San Diego Chargers 1975. College coach: Texas-El Paso 1979-80, San Diego State 1981-85. Pro coach: Joined Eagles in 1986.

Zeke Bratkowski, quarterbacks; born October 20, 1931, Danville, Ill., lives in Mt. Laurel, N.J. Quarterback Georgia 1951-53. Pro quarterback: Chicago Bears 1954, 1957-60, Los Angeles Rams 1961-63, Green Bay Packers 1963-68, 1971. Pro Coach: Green Bay Packers 1969-70, 1975-81, Chicago Bears 1972-74, Baltimore-Indianapolis Colts 1982-84, New York Jets 1985-89, Cleveland Browns 1990, joined Eagles in 1991.

Lew Carpenter, receivers; born January 12, 1932, Hayti, Mo., lives in Mt. Laurel, N.J. Running back, end Arkansas 1950-52. Pro running back-defensive back-end: Detroit Lions 1953-55, Cleveland Browns 1957-58, Green Bay Packers 1959-63. College coach: Southwest Texas State 1989. Pro coach: Minnesota Vikings 1964-66, Atlanta Falcons 1967-68, Washington Redskins 1969-70, St. Louis Cardinals 1971-72, Houston Oilers 1973-74, Green Bay Packers 1975-85, Detroit Lions 1986-88, joined Eagles in 1990.

Bud Carson, defensive coordinator, secondary; born April 28, 1931, Freeport, Pa., lives in Mt. Laurel, N.J. Defensive back North Carolina 1950-52. No pro playing experience. College coach: North Carolina 1957-64, South Carolina 1965, Georgia Tech 1966-71 (head coach 1967-71), Kansas 1984. Pro coach: Pittsburgh Steelers 1972-77, Los Angeles Rams 1978-81, Baltimore Colts 1982, Kansas City Chiefs 1983, New York Jets 1985-88, Cleveland Browns 1989-90 (head coach), joined Eagles in 1991.

Peter Giunta, defensive assistant; born August 11, 1956, Salem, Mass., lives in Bensalem, Pa. Running back-defensive back Northeastern 1974-77. No pro playing experience. College coach: Penn State 1981-83, Brown 1984-87, Lehigh 1988-90. Pro coach: Joined Eagles in 1991.

Philadelphia Eagles 1991 First-Year Roster

Name	Pos.	Ht.	Wt.	Birth-date	College	Hometown	How Acq.
Baird, Dave	WR	6-1	200	10/22/68	Lafayette	Imperial, N.J.	FA
Beavers, Darrell	LB-S	6-2	222	1/24/68	Morehead State	Joliet, Ill.	D12
Bell, David	CB-S	5-10	180	11/15/67	Widener	Lindenwold, N.J.	FA
Benson, Ken	LB	6-1	215	3/4/69	Arkansas	Manhattan, Kan.	FA
Boozer, Brad	P	6-2	185	12/31/68	Louisiana Tech	Waco, Tex.	FA
Campbell, Jesse	S	6-1	215	4/11/69	North Carolina State	Vanceboro, N.C.	D2
Constantatos, Mike	DT	6-3	260	5/26/68	Temple	Commack, N.J.	FA
Curry, Ron	LB	6-2	238	5/7/67	Cheyney State	Pittsburgh, Pa.	FA
Davis, Antone	T	6-4	325	2/28/67	Tennessee	Ft. Valley, Ga.	D1
Erickson, Craig	QB	6-1	197	5/17/69	Miami	West Palm Beach, Fla.	D5
Flores, Mike	DE	6-3	256	12/1/66	Louisville	Youngstown, Ohio	D11
Goebel, Brad	QB	6-3	198	10/13/67	Baylor	Cuero, Tex.	FA
Grant, Steven	WR	6-1	190	8/15/68	Grambling	Charleston, S.C.	FA
Harmon, Andy	DE	6-4	265	4/6/69	Kent State	Centerville, Ohio	D6
Harmon, Eric	G	6-1	285	3/3/67	Clemson	Camden, N.J.	D10
Hollis, Mike	CB	6-1	172	3/22/68	Maryland	Rockville, Md.	FA
Hudson, John (1)	G-C	6-2	275	1/29/68	Auburn	Memphis, Tenn.	D11a
Johnson, David	CB-S	6-0	195	11/19/67	Boston College	Voorhees, N.J.	FA
Johnson, Maurice (1)	TE	6-2	243	1/9/67	Temple	Washington, D.C.	FA
Joseph, James	RB	6-0	222	10/28/67	Auburn	Phenix City, Ala.	D7
Kowalkowski, Scott	LB	6-2	228	8/23/68	Notre Dame	Orchard Lake, Mich.	D8
Kovell, Paul	TE	6-2	233	4/28/68	Indiana, Pa.	Uniontown, Pa.	FA
McPherson, Don (1)	QB	6-1	190	4/2/65	Syracuse	Lakeview, N.Y.	FA
Moten, Ron (1)	LB	6-1	232	9/15/64	Florida	Clearwater, Fla.	FA
Pepper, Cam	G	6-5	277	10/25/68	Illinois	Victoria, Tex.	FA
Russell, Lamonde	WR	6-1	204	12/31/67	Alabama	Oneata, Ala.	FA
Scaife, Rodney	CB	5-9	185	8/16/66	Delta State	Clarendon, Ark.	FA
Selby, Rob	G-T	6-3	286	10/11/67	Auburn	Birmingham, Ala.	D3
Smith, Otis (1)	CB	5-11	184	10/22/65	Missouri	Metairie, La.	FA
Sweeley, Joe	WR	6-0	181	5/19/69	Widener	Broomall, Pa.	FA
Taltoan, Brian	DT	6-2	282	8/10/68	Howard	Harrisburg, Pa.	FA
Thomas, William	LB	6-2	218	8/13/68	Texas A&M	Amarillo, Tex.	D4
Weatherspoon, Chuck	RB	5-7	229	7/31/68	Houston	La Habra, Calif.	D9

The term NFL Rookie is defined as a player who is in his first season of professional football and has not been on the roster of another professional football team for any regular-season or postseason games. A Rookie is designated by an "R" on NFL rosters. Players who have been active in another professional football league or players who have NFL experience, including either preseason training camp or being on an active roster for fewer than three regular-season or postseason games, are termed NFL First-Year Players. An NFL First-Year Player is designated by a "1" on NFL rosters. Thereafter, a player on an NFL active roster for at least three regular-season or postseason games is credited with an additional year of NFL playing experience.

NOTES

Dale Haupt, defensive line; born April 12, 1929, Manitowoc, Wis., lives in Cherry Hill, N.J. Defensive lineman-linebacker Wyoming 1950-53. No pro playing experience. College coach: Tennessee 1960-63, Iowa State 1964-65, Richmond 1966-71, North Carolina State 1972-76, Duke 1977. Pro coach: Chicago Bears 1978-85, joined Eagles in 1986.

Dan Neal, offensive line; born August 30, 1949, Corbin, Ky., lives in Cherry Hill, N.J. Center Kentucky 1970-72. Pro center Baltimore Colts 1973-74, Chicago Bears 1975-83. Pro coach: Joined Eagles in 1986.

Jim Vechiarella, linebackers; born February 20, 1937, Youngstown, Ohio, lives in Mt. Laurel, N.J. Linebacker Youngstown State 1955-57. No pro playing experience. College coach: Youngstown State 1964-74, Southern Illinois 1976-77, Tulane 1978-80. Pro coach: Charlotte (WFL) 1975, Los Angeles Rams 1981-82, Kansas City Chiefs 1983-85, New York Jets 1986-89, Cleveland Browns 1990, joined Eagles in 1991.

Bill Walsh, offensive line; born September 8, 1927, Phillipsburg, N.J., lives in Marlton, N.J. Center Notre Dame 1945-48. Pro center Pittsburgh Steelers 1949-54. College coach: Notre Dame 1955-58, Kansas State 1959. Pro coach: Dallas Texans-Kansas City Chiefs 1960-74, Atlanta Falcons 1975-82, Houston Oilers 1983-86, joined Eagles in 1987.

Jim Williams, strength and conditioning; born March 29, 1948, Kingston, Pa., lives in Mt. Laurel, N.J. No college or pro playing experience. College coach: Nebraska 1972-74, Arkansas 1974-77, Wyoming 1977-79. Pro coach: New York Giants 1979-81, New York Jets 1982-89, joined Eagles in 1991.

Richard Wood, running backs; born February 2, 1936, Lanett, Ala., lives in Mt. Laurel, N.J. Quarterback Auburn 1956-59. Pro quarterback Baltimore Colts 1960-61, San Diego Chargers 1962, Denver Broncos 1962, New York Jets 1963-64, Oakland Raiders 1965, Miami Dolphins 1966. College coach: Georgia 1967-68, Mississippi 1971-73, Auburn 1986. Pro coach: Oakland Raiders 1969-70, Cleveland Browns 1974, New Orleans Saints 1976-77, Atlanta Falcons 1978-82, Philadelphia Eagles 1983, Kansas City Chiefs 1987-88, New England Patriots 1989-90, rejoined Eagles in 1991.

PHOENIX CARDINALS

National Football Conference Eastern Division

Team Colors: Cardinal Red, Black, and White

P.O. Box 888
Phoenix, Arizona 85001-0888
Telephone: (602) 379-0101

Club Officials

President: William V. Bidwill
Executive Vice President: Joe Rhein
Vice President/General Manager: Larry Wilson
Secretary and General Counsel: Thomas J. Guilfoil
Treasurer: Charley Schlegel
Director of Pro Personnel: Erik Widmark
Director of Player Personnel: George Boone
Public Relations Director: Paul Jensen
Media Coordinator: Greg Gladysiewski
Director of Community Relations: Adele Harris
Director of Marketing: Joe Castor
Ticket Manager: Steve Walsh
Trainer: John Omohundro
Assistant Trainers: Jim Shearer, Jeff Herndon
Equipment Manager: Mark Ahlemeier
Assistant Equipment Manager: Steve Christensen

Stadium: Sun Devil Stadium • **Capacity:** 72,608
Fifth Street
Tempe, Arizona 85287

Playing Surface: Grass

Training Camp: Northern Arizona University
Flagstaff, Arizona 86011

1991 Schedule

Preseason

Aug. 3	at Seattle	7:30
Aug. 11	at Chicago	7:00
Aug. 17	**New England**	7:30
Aug. 23	**Denver**	7:30

Regular Season

Sept. 1	at Los Angeles Rams	1:00
Sept. 8	at Philadelphia	1:00
Sept. 15	at Washington	1:00
Sept. 22	**Dallas**	5:00
Sept. 29	**New England**	1:00
Oct. 6	at New York Giants	4:00
Oct. 13	at Minnesota	12:00
Oct. 20	**Atlanta**	1:00
Oct. 27	**Minnesota**	2:00
Nov. 3	at Dallas	12:00
Nov. 10	**New York Giants**	2:00
Nov. 17	at San Francisco	1:00
Nov. 24	**Philadelphia**	2:00
Dec. 1	**Open Date**	
Dec. 8	**Washington**	2:00
Dec. 15	at Denver	2:00
Dec. 22	**New Orleans**	2:00

Cardinals Coaching History

Chicago 1920-59
St. Louis 1960-87
(371-493-39)

1920-22	John (Paddy) Driscoll	17-8-4
1923-24	Arnold Horween	13-8-1
1925-26	Norman Barry	16-8-2
1927	Guy Chamberlin	3-7-1
1928	Fred Gillies	1-5-0
1929	Dewey Scanlon	6-6-1
1930	Ernie Nevers	5-6-2
1931	LeRoy Andrews*	0-1-0
1931	Ernie Nevers	5-3-0
1932	Jack Chevigny	2-6-2
1933-34	Paul Schissler	6-15-1
1935-38	Milan Creighton	16-26-4
1939	Ernie Nevers	1-10-0
1940-42	Jimmy Conzelman	8-22-3
1943-45	Phil Handler**	1-29-0
1946-48	Jimmy Conzelman	27-10-0
1949	Phil Handler-Buddy Parker***	2-4-0
1949	Raymond (Buddy) Parker	4-1-1
1950-51	Earl (Curly) Lambeau****	7-15-0
1951	Phil Handler-Cecil Isbell#	1-1-0
1952	Joe Kuharich	4-8-0
1953-54	Joe Stydahar	3-20-1
1955-57	Ray Richards	14-21-1
1958-61	Frank (Pop) Ivy##	17-29-2
1961	Chuck Drulis-Ray Prochaska-Ray Willsey###	2-0-0
1962-65	Wally Lemm	27-26-3
1966-70	Charley Winner	35-30-5
1971-72	Bob Hollway	8-18-2
1973-77	Don Coryell	42-29-1
1978-79	Bud Wilkinson####	9-20-0
1979	Larry Wilson	2-1-0
1980-85	Jim Hanifan	39-50-1
1986-89	Gene Stallings@	23-34-1
1989	Hank Kuhlmann	0-5-0
1990	Joe Bugel	5-11-0

*Resigned after one game in 1931
**Co-coach with Walt Kiesling in Chicago Cardinals-Pittsburgh merger in 1944
***Co-coaches for first six games in 1949
****Resigned after 10 games in 1951
#Co-coaches
##Resigned after 12 games in 1961
###Co-coaches
####Released after 13 games in 1979
@Released after 11 games in 1989

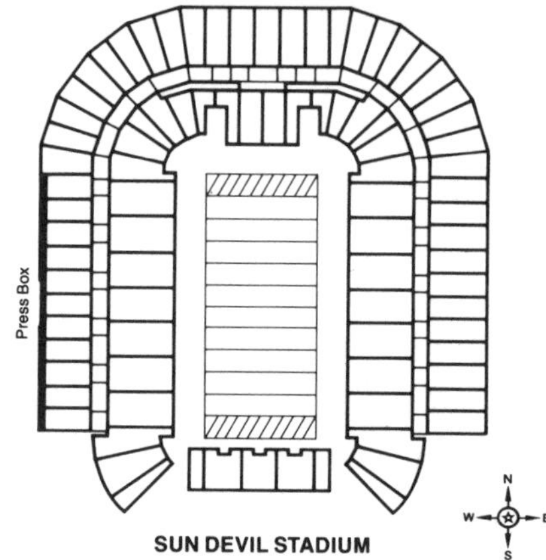

SUN DEVIL STADIUM

Record Holders

Individual Records—Career

Category	Name	Performance
Rushing (Yds.)	Ottis Anderson, 1979-1986	7,999
Passing (Yds.)	Jim Hart, 1966-1983	34,639
Passing (TDs)	Jim Hart, 1966-1983	209
Receiving (No.)	Roy Green, 1979-1990	522
Receiving (Yds.)	Roy Green, 1979-1990	8,497
Interceptions	Larry Wilson, 1960-1972	52
Punting (Avg.)	Jerry Norton, 1959-1961	44.9
Punt Return (Avg.)	Charley Trippi, 1947-1955	13.7
Kickoff Return (Avg.)	Ollie Matson, 1952, 1954-58	28.5
Field Goals	Jim Bakken, 1962-1978	282
Touchdowns (Tot.)	Roy Green, 1979-1990	70
Points	Jim Bakken, 1962-1978	1,380

Individual Records—Single Season

Category	Name	Performance
Rushing (Yds.)	Ottis Anderson, 1979	1,605
Passing (Yds.)	Neil Lomax, 1984	4,614
Passing (TDs)	Charley Johnson, 1963	28
	Neil Lomax, 1984	28
Receiving (No.)	J.T. Smith, 1987	91
Receiving (Yds.)	Roy Green, 1984	1,555
Interceptions	Bob Nussbaumer, 1949	12
Punting (Avg.)	Jerry Norton, 1960	45.6
Punt Return (Avg.)	John (Red) Cochran, 1949	20.9
Kickoff Return (Avg.)	Ollie Matson, 1958	35.5
Field Goals	Jim Bakken, 1967	27
Touchdowns (Tot.)	John David Crow, 1962	17
Points	Jim Bakken, 1967	117
	Neil O'Donoghue, 1984	117

Individual Records—Single Game

Category	Name	Performance
Rushing (Yds.)	John David Crow, 12-18-60	203
Passing (Yds.)	Neil Lomax, 12-16-84	468
Passing (TDs)	Jim Hardy, 10-2-50	6
	Charley Johnson, 9-26-65	6
	Charley Johnson, 11-2-69	6
Receiving (No.)	Sonny Randle, 11-4-62	16
Receiving (Yds.)	Sonny Randle, 11-4-62	256
Interceptions	Bob Nussbaumer, 11-13-49	*4
	Jerry Norton, 11-20-60	*4
Field Goals	Jim Bakken, 9-24-67	*7
Touchdowns (Tot.)	Ernie Nevers, 11-28-29	*6
Points	Ernie Nevers, 11-28-29	*40

*NFL Record

1990 Team Record

Preseason (0-4)

Date	Result		Opponents
8/11	L	9-34	Seattle
8/18	L	9-17	Chicago
8/25	L	7-27	at L.A. Rams
8/31	L	14-25	at Denver
		39-103	

Regular Season (5-11)

Date	Result		Opponents	Att.
9/9	L	0-31	at Washington	52,649
9/16	W	23-21	at Philadelphia	64,396
9/23	L	7-28	at New Orleans	61,110
9/30	L	10-38	Washington	49,303
10/14	W	20- 3	Dallas	45,235
10/21	L	19-20	at N.Y. Giants	76,518
10/28	L	21-31	Chicago	71,233
11/4	L	3-23	at Miami	54,924
11/11	L	14-45	at Buffalo	74,904
11/18	L	21-24	Green Bay	46,878
11/25	W	34-14	New England	30,110
12/2	W	20-17	Indianapolis	31,885
12/9	W	24-13	at Atlanta	36,222
12/16	L	10-41	at Dallas	60,190
12/23	L	21-24	N.Y. Giants	41,212
12/29	L	21-23	Philadelphia	31,796

Score by Periods

Cardinals	27	81	65	95	0	—	268
Opponents	88	113	79	116	0	—	396

Attendance

Home 347,652 Away 480,913 Total 828,565
Single-game home record, 67,139 (9-12-88)
Single-season home record, 472,937 (1988)

1990 Team Statistics

	Cardinals	Opp.
Total First Downs	270	306
Rushing	115	140
Passing	135	146
Penalty	20	20
Third Down: Made/Att.	77/194	90/198
Third Down: Pct.	39.7	45.5
Fourth Down: Made/Att.	7/16	8/16
Fourth Down: Pct.	43.8	50.0
Total Net Yards	4745	5216
Avg. Per Game	296.6	326.0
Total Plays	934	959
Avg. Per Play	5.1	5.4
Net Yards Rushing	1915	2318
Avg. Per Game	119.7	144.9
Total Rushes	451	521
Net Yards Passing	2830	2898
Avg. Per Game	176.9	181.1
Sacked/Yards Lost	44/288	36/232
Gross Yards	3118	3130
Att./Completions	439/238	402/233
Completion Pct.	54.2	58.0
Had Intercepted	18	16
Punts/Avg.	67/42.8	63/43.6
Net Punting Avg.	37.4	36.3
Penalties/Yards Lost	96/883	96/834
Fumbles/Ball Lost	25/14	28/11
Touchdowns	31	50
Rushing	13	20
Passing	16	29
Returns	2	1
Avg. Time of Possession	28:38	31:22

1990 Individual Statistics

Scoring	TD R	TD P	TD Rt	PAT	FG	Saf	TP
Del Greco	0	0	0	31/31	17/27	0	82
Johnson	5	0	0	0/0	0/0	0	30
Green	0	4	0	0/0	0/0	0	24
Jones	0	4	0	0/0	0/0	0	24
Proehl	0	4	0	0/0	0/0	0	24
Thompson	4	0	0	0/0	0/0	0	24
Rosenbach	3	0	0	0/0	0/0	0	18
Flagler	1	1	0	0/0	0/0	0	12
J. Smith	0	2	0	0/0	0/0	0	12
Turner	0	0	2	0/0	0/0	0	12
Sharpe	0	1	0	0/0	0/0	0	6
Cardinals	13	16	2	31/31	17/27	0	268
Opponents	20	29	1	48/50	16/20	0	396

Passing	Att.	Comp.	Yds.	Pct.	TD	Int.	Tkld.	Rate
Rosenbach	437	237	3098	54.2	16	17	44/288	72.8
Green	1	1	20	100.0	0	0	0/0	118.8
Johnson	1	0	0	0.0	0	1	0/0	0.0
Cardinals	439	238	3118	54.2	16	18	44/288	71.9
Opponents	402	233	3130	58.0	29	16	36/232	90.3

Rushing	Att.	Yds.	Avg.	LG	TD
Johnson	234	926	4.0	41	5
Rosenbach	85	473	5.6	25	3
Thompson	106	390	3.7	40	4
Flagler	13	85	6.5	29t	1
Jones	4	33	8.3	15	0
Sikahema	3	8	2.7	4	0
Proehl	1	4	4.0	4	0
J. Smith	1	4	4.0	4	0
Wolfley	2	3	1.5	2	0
Tupa	1	0	0.0	0	0
Camarillo	1	−11	−11.0	−11	0
Cardinals	451	1915	4.2	41	13
Opponents	521	2318	4.4	43	20

Receiving	No.	Yds.	Avg.	LG	TD
Proehl	56	802	14.3	45t	4
Green	53	797	15.0	54	4
Jones	43	724	16.8	68t	4
Johnson	25	241	9.6	35	0
J. Smith	18	225	12.5	45t	2
Reeves	18	126	7.0	16	0
Flagler	13	130	10.0	21	1
Sikahema	7	51	7.3	13	0
Thompson	2	11	5.5	6	0
Jorden	2	10	5.0	6	0
Sharpe	1	1	1.0	1t	1
Cardinals	238	3118	13.1	68t	16
Opponents	233	3130	13.4	67t	29

Interceptions	No.	Yds.	Avg.	LG	TD
McDonald	4	63	15.8	38	0
Taylor	3	50	16.7	34	0
Mack	2	53	26.5	39	0
Young	2	8	4.0	5	0
Jax	2	5	2.5	4	0
Turner	1	70	70.0	47t	2
Zordich	1	25	25.0	25	0
Bell	1	0	0.0	0	0
Cardinals	16	274	17.1	47t	2
Opponents	18	201	11.2	57t	1

Punting	No.	Yds.	Avg.	In 20	LG
Camarillo	67	2865	42.8	16	63
Cardinals	67	2865	42.8	16	63
Opponents	63	2747	43.6	16	60

Punt Returns	No.	FC	Yds.	Avg.	LG	TD
Sikahema	36	6	306	8.5	20	0
J. Smith	3	0	34	11.3	16	0
Proehl	1	1	2	2.0	2	0
Cardinals	40	7	342	8.6	20	0
Opponents	41	11	258	6.3	27	0

Kickoff Returns	No.	Yds.	Avg.	LG	TD
Sikahema	27	544	20.1	32	0
Centers	16	272	17.0	26	0
Flagler	10	167	16.7	27	0
Proehl	4	53	13.3	15	0
Jax	2	17	8.5	9	0
Green	1	15	15.0	15	0
Cardinals	60	1068	17.8	32	0
Opponents	56	1060	18.9	39	0

Sacks	No.
Harvey	10.0
Nunn	9.0
Saddler	4.0
Bell	3.0
Jax	3.0
Wahler	2.5
Hill	1.5
Hairston	1.0
Mack	1.0
Osborne	1.0
Cardinals	36.0
Opponents	44.0

1991 Draft Choices

Round	Name	Pos.	College
1.	Eric Swann	DE	No College
2.	Mike Jones	DE	North Carolina St.
3.	Aeneas Williams	DB	Southern University
4.	Dexter Davis	DB	Clemson
5.	Vance Hammond	DT	Clemson
6.	Eduardo Vega	T	Memphis State
7.	Ivory Lee Brown	RB	Ark.-Pine Bluff
8.	Greg Amsler	RB	Tennessee
	Jerry Evans	TE	Toledo
	Scott Evans	DT	Oklahoma
10.	Herbie Anderson	DB	Texas A&I
11.	Nathan LaDuke	DB	Arizona State
12.	Jeff Bridewell	QB	Cal-Davis

Phoenix Cardinals 1991 Veteran Roster

No.	Name	Pos.	Ht.	Wt.	Birth-date	NFL Exp.	College	Hometown	How Acq.	'90 Games/ Starts
55	Bell, Anthony	LB	6-3	235	7/2/64	6	Michigan State	Ft. Lauderdale, Fla.	D1-'86	16/16
54	†Braxton, David	LB	6-1	232	5/26/65	3	Wake Forest	Jacksonville, N.C.	FA-'90	11/0
16	Camarillo, Rich	P	5-11	193	11/29/59	11	Washington	Pico Rivera, Calif.	FA-'89	16/0
37	Centers, Larry	RB	5-10	203	6/1/68	2	Stephen F. Austin	Tatum, Tex.	D5-'90	6/0
79	Clasby, Bob	NT	6-5	276	9/28/60	5	Notre Dame	Milton, Mass.	FA-'86	1/1
93	Coleman, Sidney	LB	6-2	250	1/14/64	4	Southern Mississippi	Gulfport, Miss.	PB(TB)-'91#	16/0*
5	Davis, Greg	K	5-11	197	10/29/65	5	Citadel	Atlanta, Ga.	PB(Atl)-'91#	16/0*
17	Del Greco, Al	K	5-10	195	3/2/62	8	Auburn	Key Biscayne, Fla.	FA-'87	16/0
94	Faulkner, Jeff	DE	6-3	305	4/4/64	3	Southern	Miami, Fla.	PB(Ind)-'91#	7/0*
32	†Flagler, Terrence	RB	6-0	200	9/24/64	5	Clemson	Fernandia Beach, Fla.	FA-'90	13/0
20	Flutie, Darren	WR	5-10	187	11/18/66	2	Boston College	Natick, Mass.	FA-'90	0*
81	Green, Roy	WR	6-0	197	6/30/57	13	Henderson State	Magnolia, Ark.	D4-'79	16/16
56	Harvey, Ken	LB	6-2	228	5/6/65	4	California	Austin, Tex.	D1-'88	16/16
18	Hill, Derek	WR	6-1	193	11/4/67	3	Arizona	Los Angeles, Calif.	PB(Pitt)-'91#	16/12*
58	Hill, Eric	LB	6-1	251	11/14/66	3	Louisiana State	Galveston, Tex.	D1-'89	16/16
83	Holmes, Don	WR	5-10	182	4/1/61	6	Mesa, Colo.	Miami, Fla.	W(Ind)-'86	6/0
80	Jackson, John	WR	5-10	175	1/2/67	2	Southern California	Diamond Bar, Calif.	FA-'90	9/0
53	†Jax, Garth	LB	6-2	236	9/16/63	6	Florida State	Houston, Tex.	PB(Dall)-'89#	16/12
39	Johnson, Johnny	RB	6-2	216	6/11/68	2	San Jose State	Santa Cruz, Calif.	D7-'90	14/14
86	Jones, Ernie	WR	5-11	196	12/15/64	4	Indiana	Elkhart, Ind.	D7-'88	15/8
85	Jorden, Tim	TE	6-2	220	10/30/66	2	Indiana	Westchester, Ohio	FA-'89	16/11
57	Kauahi, Kani	C	6-2	274	9/6/59	9	Hawaii	Kekaha, Hawaii	PB(GB)-'89#	15/0
70	Kennard, Derek	G	6-3	319	9/9/62	6	Nevada-Reno	Stockton, Calif.	SD2-'84	16/16
51	Lewis, Bill	C	6-7	278	7/12/63	6	Nebraska	Sioux City, Iowa	PB(Raid)-'90#	16/16
30	Little, David	RB	6-2	226	4/18/61	8	Middle Tennessee State	Fresno, Calif.	FA-'90	11/0
22	Lomack, Tony	WR	5-8	180	4/27/68	2	Florida	Tallahassee, Fla.	FA-'91	0*
29	Lynch, Lorenzo	CB	5-9	200	4/6/63	4	Cal State-Sacramento	Oakland, Calif.	PB(Chi)-'90#	16/0
47	Mack, Cedric	CB	6-0	185	9/14/60	9	Baylor	Freeport, Tex.	D2-'83	16/16
92	†Manley, Dexter	DE	6-3	257	2/2/59	11	Oklahoma State	Houston, Tex.	W(Wash)-'90#	4/0
46	McDonald, Tim	S	6-2	209	1/6/65	5	Southern California	Fresno, Calif.	D2-'87	16/16
78	†Nunn, Freddie Joe	LB	6-4	250	4/9/62	7	Mississippi	Louisville, Miss.	D1-'85	16/16
90	Osborne, Eldonta	LB	6-0	226	8/12/67	2	Louisiana Tech	Quitman, La.	FA-'90	12/0
87	Proehl, Ricky	WR	5-10	185	3/7/68	2	Wake Forest	Hillsborough, N.J.	D3-'90	16/2
89	Reeves, Walter	TE	6-3	262	12/15/65	3	Auburn	Eufala, Ala.	D2-'89	16/16
63	†Robbins, Tootie	T	6-5	322	6/2/58	10	East Carolina	Merry Hill, N.C.	D4-'82	16/16
3	Rosenbach, Timm	QB	6-2	215	10/27/66	3	Washington State	Pullman, Wash.	SD1-'89	16/16
72	Saddler, Rod	DE	6-5	280	9/26/65	5	Texas A&M	Decatur, Ga.	D4-'87	16/15
67	†Sharpe, Luis	T	6-4	290	6/16/60	10	UCLA	Detroit, Mich.	D1-'82	16/16
61	†Smith, Lance	G	6-2	285	11/1/63	7	Louisiana State	Kannapolis, N.C.	D3-'85	16/16
69	Smith, Vernice	G-T	6-2	289	10/24/65	2	Florida A&M	Orlando, Fla.	FA-'89	11/0
91	Stowe, Tyronne	LB	6-1	236	5/30/65	5	Rutgers	Passaic, N.J.	PB(Pitt)-'91#	15/0*
27	†Taylor, Jay	CB	5-9	175	11/8/67	3	San Jose State	San Diego, Calif.	D6-'89	16/16
34	Thompson, Anthony	RB	5-11	207	4/8/67	2	Indiana	Terre Haute, Ind.	D2-'90	13/3
19	†Tupa, Tom	QB-P	6-4	225	2/6/66	4	Ohio State	Brecksville, Ohio	D3-'88	15/0
23	†Turner, Marcus	CB-S	6-0	187	1/13/66	3	UCLA	Lakewood, Calif.	W(Den)-'89	16/1
66	Wahler, Jim	NT	6-3	276	7/29/66	3	UCLA	San Jose, Calif.	D4-'89	16/16
60	Walker, Jeff	G-T	6-4	286	1/22/63	3	Memphis State	Olive Branch, Miss.	PB(NO)-'90#	0*
68	Wolf, Joe	T	6-5	283	12/28/66	3	Boston College	Allentown, Pa.	D1b-'89	15/0
24	Wolfley, Ron	RB	6-0	222	10/14/62	7	West Virginia	Orchard Park, N.Y.	D4-'85	13/2
43	Young, Lonnie	S	6-1	192	7/18/63	7	Michigan State	Flint, Mich.	D12-'85	16/16
38	†Zordich, Michael	S	5-11	200	10/12/63	5	Penn State	Youngstown, Ohio	PB(NYJ)-'89#	16/0

* Coleman played 16 games with Tampa Bay in '90; Davis played 16 games with Atlanta; Faulkner played 7 games with Indianapolis; Flutie, Lomack, and Walker missed '90 season due to injury; D. Hill played 16 games with Pittsburgh; Stowe played 15 games with Pittsburgh.

† Option playout; subject to developments.

\# Plan B unconditional free agent.

Retired: Carl Hairston, 16-year defensive lineman, 16 games in '90.

Players lost through Plan B (7): LB David Bavaro (Buff; 14 games in '90), CB Stanley Blair (SF; 5), S Tracey Eaton (Atl; 11), T Mike Graybill (Det; 0), LB Jeroy Robinson (SF; 3), RB-KR Vai Sikahema (GB; 16), LB Chris Washington (SF; 8).

Also played with Cardinals in '90: DT Dick Chapura (3 games), DE Elston Ridgle (10), RB Dennis Smith (4), WR J.T. Smith (13).

Coaching Staff

Head Coach, Joe Bugel

Pro Career: Named head coach on February 7, 1990. Became thirty-first head coach in the history of the franchise dating back to 1920. Assistant head coach-offense under Joe Gibbs with Washington Redskins from 1981-89. Tutored the famous "Hogs" as Redskins' offensive line coach during his tenure with Washington. The Redskins reached the playoffs five times in nine seasons, posting an 11-3 (.786) postseason record. Washington won three NFL championships and four division titles in that span. Four Redskin offensive linemen earned Pro Bowl recognition under Bugel's tutelage—Jeff Bostic, Russ Grimm, Joe Jacoby, and Mark May. He coached Houston Oilers' offensive line from 1977-80 when team set rushing and passing records (1980). He began his professional coaching career with the Detroit Lions in 1975-76. Career record: 5-11.

Background: Offensive guard at Western Kentucky (1960-62). He served as an assistant coach at Western Kentucky (1964-68), Navy (1969), Iowa State (1973), and Ohio State (1974).

Personal: Born March 10, 1940, in Pittsburgh, Pa. Joe and wife Brenda, live in Phoenix, and have three daughters—Angie, Holly, and Jennifer.

Assistant Coaches

Ted Cottrell, defensive line; born June 13, 1947, Chester, Pa., lives in Phoenix. Linebacker Delaware Valley College 1966-68. Pro linebacker Atlanta Falcons 1969-70, Winnipeg Blue Bombers (CFL) 1971. College coach: Rutgers 1973-80, 1983. Pro coach: Kansas City Chiefs 1981-82, New Jersey Generals (USFL) 1983-84, Buffalo Bills 1986-89, joined Cardinals in 1990.

Bobby Hammond, running backs; born February 20, 1952, Orangeburg, S.C., lives in Phoenix. Running back Morgan State 1973-75. Pro running back New York Giants 1976-79, Washington Redskins 1979-80. Pro coach: New York Jets 1983-89, joined Cardinals in 1990.

Jim Johnson, defensive secondary; born May 26, 1941, Maywood, Ill., lives in Phoenix. Quarterback Missouri 1959-62. Pro tight end Buffalo Bills 1963-64. College coach: Missouri Southern 1967-68 (head coach), Drake 1969-72, Indiana 1973-76, Notre Dame 1977-80. Pro coach: Oklahoma Outlaws (USFL) 1984, Jacksonville Bulls (USFL) 1985, joined Cardinals in 1986.

Tom Lovat, offensive line; born December 28, 1938, Bingham, Utah, lives in Phoenix. Guard-linebacker Utah 1958-60. No pro playing experience. College coach: Utah 1967, 1972-76 (head coach 1974-76), Idaho State 1968-70, Stanford 1977-79, Wyoming 1989. Pro coach: Saskatchewan Roughriders (CFL) 1971, Green Bay Packers 1980, St. Louis Cardinals 1981-84, Indianapolis Colts 1985-88, rejoined Cardinals in 1990.

Mike Murphy, defensive assistant/quality control; born September 25, 1944, New York, N.Y., lives in Phoenix. Guard-linebacker Huron, S.D., College 1962-65. No pro playing experience. College coach: Vermont 1970-73, Idaho State 1974-76, Western Illinois 1977-78. Pro coach: Saskatchewan Roughriders (CFL) 1979-83, Chicago Blitz (USFL) 1984, Detroit Lions 1985-89, joined Cardinals in 1990.

Joe Pascale, outside linebackers; born April 4, 1946, New York, N.Y., lives in Phoenix. Linebacker Connecticut 1963-66. No pro playing experience. College coach: Connecticut 1967-68, Rhode Island 1969-73, Idaho State 1974-76 (head coach 1976), Princeton 1977-79. Pro coach: Montreal Alouettes (CFL) 1980-81, Ottawa Rough Riders (CFL) 1982-83, New Jersey Generals (USFL) 1984-85, joined Cardinals in 1986.

Ted Plumb, receivers; born August 20, 1939, Reno, Nev., lives in Phoenix. Wide receiver Baylor 1960-61. Pro wide receiver Buffalo Bills 1962. College coach: Cerritos, Calif., J.C. 1966-67, Texas Christian 1968-70, Tulsa 1971, Kansas 1972-73. Pro coach: New York Giants 1974-76, Atlanta Falcons 1977-79, Chicago Bears 1980-85, Philadelphia Eagles 1986-89, joined Cardinals in 1990.

Phoenix Cardinals 1991 First-Year Roster

Name	Pos.	Ht.	Wt.	Birth-date	College	Hometown	How Acq.
Amsler, Greg	RB	6-2	236	12/19/67	Tennessee	Chatham, N.J.	D8a
Anderson, Herbie	CB	5-10	183	11/19/68	Texas A&I	Port Arthur, Tex.	D10
Bridewell, Jeff	QB	6-4	214	5/13/67	California-Davis	Napa, Calif.	D12
Brown, Eddie	WR	5-11	192	10/2/69	Louisiana Tech	Miami, Fla.	FA
Brown, Ivory Lee	RB	6-1	243	8/17/69	Arkansas-Pine Bluff	Palestine, Tex.	D7
Davis, Dexter	CB	5-9	175	3/20/70	Clemson	Brooklyn, N.Y.	D4
Evans, Jerry	TE	6-4	255	9/28/68	Toledo	Lorain, Ohio	D8b
Evans, Scott	DE	6-3	261	3/29/68	Oklahoma	Cincinnati, Ohio	D8c
Field, Amod (1)	WR	5-11	181	10/11/67	Montclair State	Passaic, N.J.	FA-'90
Grimm, Donn	LB	6-2	241	4/4/69	Notre Dame	Scottsdale, Pa.	FA
Hammond, Vance	DT	6-6	300	12/4/67	Clemson	Spartanburg, S.C.	D5
Hazard, Manny	WR	5-8	175	7/22/69	Houston	Daly City, Calif.	FA
Jacevicius, Al	T	6-5	320	1/19/68	Eastern Kentucky	Worcester, Mass.	FA
Jones, Mike	DT-DE	6-3	274	8/25/69	North Carolina State	Columbia, S.C.	D2
Jones, Richard	P	6-2	189	3/26/65	Arizona State	Scottsdale, Ariz.	FA
Kupp, Craig (1)	QB	6-4	215	4/14/67	Pacific Lutheran	Selah, Wash.	FA
LaDuke, Nathan	S	5-9	192	10/8/68	Arizona State	Phoenix, Ariz.	D11
Nord, Mike	T	6-7	290	11/23/67	North Alabama	Lexington, Ky.	FA
Nyberg, Brent	WR	6-2	195	11/13/68	Brigham Young	Provo, Utah	FA
Rush, Kenyatta	DE	6-3	249	12/17/68	Temple	Philadelphia, Pa.	FA
Swann, Eric	DE-DT	6-4	311	8/16/70	No College	Lillington, N.C.	D1
Vega, Ed	T	6-5	340	11/5/67	Memphis State	Inglewood, Calif.	D6
Williams, Aeneas	CB	5-10	187	1/29/69	Southern	New Orleans, La.	D3
Williams, Willie (1)	T	6-5	296	8/6/67	Louisiana State	Houston, Tex.	SD9-'90
Wright, Willie	LB	6-4	239	3/9/68	Wyoming	Riverton, Wyo.	FA

The term NFL Rookie is defined as a player who is in his first season of professional football and has not been on the roster of another professional football team for any regular-season or postseason games. A Rookie is designated by an "R" on NFL rosters. Players who have been active in another professional football league or players who have NFL experience, including either preseason training camp or being on an active roster for fewer than three regular-season or postseason games, are termed NFL First-Year Players. An NFL First-Year Player is designated by a "1" on NFL rosters. Thereafter, a player on an NFL active roster for at least three regular-season or postseason games is credited with an additional year of NFL playing experience.

NOTES

Jerry Rhome, offensive coordinator; born March 6, 1942, Dallas, Tex., lives in Phoenix. Quarterback Southern Methodist 1960-61, Tulsa 1963-64. Pro quarterback Dallas Cowboys 1965-68, Cleveland Browns 1969, Houston Oilers 1970, Los Angeles Rams 1971-72. College coach: Tulsa 1973-75. Pro coach: Seattle Seahawks 1976-82, Washington Redskins 1983-87, San Diego Chargers 1988, Dallas Cowboys 1989, joined Cardinals in 1990.

Pete Rodriguez, special teams; born July 25, 1940, Chicago, Ill., lives in Phoenix. Guard-linebacker Denver University 1959-60, Western State, Colo. 1961-63. No pro playing experience. College coach: Western State, Colo. 1964, Arizona 1968-69, Western Illinois 1970-73, 1979-82 (head coach), Florida State 1974-75, Iowa State 1976-78, Northern Iowa 1986. Pro coach: Michigan Panthers (USFL) 1983-84, Denver Gold (USFL) 1985, Jacksonville Bulls (USFL) 1986, Ottawa Rough Riders (CFL) 1987, Los Angeles Raiders 1988-89, joined Cardinals in 1990.

Bob Rogucki, strength and conditioning; born September 27, 1953, Clarksburg, W. Va., lives in Phoenix. No college or pro playing experience. College coach: Penn State 1981, Weber State 1982, Army 1983-89, joined Cardinals in 1990.

Fritz Shurmur, defensive coordinator; born July 15, 1932, Riverview, Mich., lives in Phoenix. Center Albion 1951-53. No pro playing experience. College coach: Albion 1956-61, Wyoming 1962-74 (head coach 1971-74). Pro coach: Detroit Lions 1975-77, New England Patriots 1978-81, L.A. Rams 1982-90, joined Cardinals in 1991.

National Football Conference Western Division

Team Colors: Forty Niners Gold and Scarlet

4949 Centennial Boulevard
Santa Clara, California 95054
Telephone: (408) 562-4949

Club Officials

Owner: Edward J. DeBartolo, Jr.
President: Carmen Policy
Vice President-Football Administration: John McVay
Vice President-Business Operations & C.F.O: Keith Simon
Administrative Assistant: Dwight Clark
Director of Pro Scouting: Allan Webb
Director of College Scouting: Tony Razzano
Director of Public Relations: Jerry Walker
Director of Planning/Community Involvement: Rodney Knox
Director of Marketing/Promotions: Laurie Albrecht
Coordinator of Football Operations: Neal Dahlen
Ticket Manager: Lynn Carrozzi
Director of Stadium Operations: Murlan (Mo) Fowell
Video Director: Robert Yanagi
Trainer: Lindsy McLean
Equipment Manager: Bronco Hinek

Stadium: Candlestick Park • **Capacity:** 66,455
San Francisco, California 94124

Playing Surface: Grass

Training Camp: Sierra Community College
Rocklin, California 95677

1991 Schedule

Preseason

July 27	at Los Angeles Raiders	1:00
Aug. 3	vs. Chicago at Berlin	7:30*
Aug. 7	**Denver**	6:00
Aug. 19	**San Diego**	6:00
Aug. 23	at Seattle	5:00

*P.M. Eastern Time

Regular Season

Sept. 2	at N.Y. Giants (Monday)	9:00
Sept. 8	**San Diego**	1:00
Sept. 15	at Minnesota	12:00
Sept. 22	**Los Angeles Rams**	1:00
Sept. 29	at Los Angeles Raiders	1:00
Oct. 6	**Open Date**	
Oct. 13	at Atlanta	1:00
Oct. 20	**Detroit**	1:00
Oct. 27	at Philadelphia	1:00
Nov. 3	**Atlanta**	1:00
Nov. 10	at New Orleans	12:00
Nov. 17	**Phoenix**	1:00
Nov. 25	at L.A. Rams (Monday)	6:00
Dec. 1	**New Orleans**	1:00
Dec. 8	at Seattle	1:00
Dec. 14	**Kansas City** (Saturday)	1:00
Dec. 23	**Chicago** (Monday)	6:00

49ers Coaching History

(314-268-13)

1950-54	Lawrence (Buck) Shaw	33-25-2
1955	Norman (Red) Strader	4-8-0
1956-58	Frankie Albert	19-17-1
1959-63	Howard (Red) Hickey*	27-27-1
1963-67	Jack Christiansen	26-38-3
1968-75	Dick Nolan	56-56-5
1976	Monte Clark	8-6-0
1977	Ken Meyer	5-9-0
1978	Pete McCulley**	1-8-0
1978	Fred O'Connor	1-6-0
1979-88	Bill Walsh	102-63-1
1989-90	George Seifert	32-5-0

*Resigned after three games in 1963
**Released after nine games in 1978

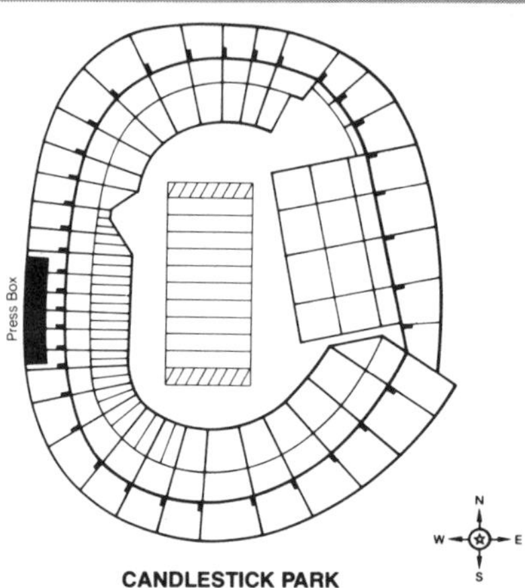

CANDLESTICK PARK

Record Holders

Individual Records—Career

Category	Name	Performance
Rushing (Yds.)	Joe Perry, 1950-1960, 1963	7,344
Passing (Yds.)	Joe Montana, 1979-1990	34,998
Passing (TDs)	Joe Montana, 1979-1990	242
Receiving (No.)	Roger Craig, 1983-1990	508
Receiving (Yds.)	Jerry Rice, 1985-1990	7,866
Interceptions	Ronnie Lott, 1981-1990	51
Punting (Avg.)	Tommy Davis, 1959-1969	44.7
Punt Return (Avg.)	Manfred Moore, 1974-75	14.7
Kickoff Return (Avg.)	Abe Woodson, 1958-1964	29.4
Field Goals	Ray Wersching, 1977-1987	190
Touchdowns (Tot.)	Jerry Rice, 1985-1990	83
Points	Ray Wersching, 1977-1987	979

Individual Records—Single Season

Category	Name	Performance
Rushing (Yds.)	Roger Craig, 1988	1,502
Passing (Yds.)	Joe Montana, 1990	3,944
Passing (TDs)	Joe Montana, 1987	31
Receiving (No.)	Jerry Rice, 1990	100
Receiving (Yds.)	Jerry Rice, 1986	1,570
Interceptions	Dave Baker, 1960	10
	Ronnie Lott, 1986	10
Punting (Avg.)	Tommy Davis, 1965	45.8
Punt Return (Avg.)	Dana McLemore, 1982	22.3
Kickoff Return (Avg.)	Joe Arenas, 1953	34.4
Field Goals	Mike Cofer, 1989	29
Touchdowns (Tot.)	Jerry Rice, 1987	23
Points	Jerry Rice, 1987	138

Individual Records—Single Game

Category	Name	Performance
Rushing (Yds.)	Delvin Williams, 10-31-76	194
Passing (Yds.)	Joe Montana, 10-14-90	476
Passing (TDs)	Joe Montana, 10-14-90	6
Receiving (No.)	Jerry Rice, 10-14-90	13
Receiving (Yds.)	John Taylor, 12-11-89	286
Interceptions	Dave Baker, 12-4-60	*4
Field Goals	Ray Wersching, 10-16-83	6
Touchdowns (Tot.)	Jerry Rice, 10-14-90	5
Points	Jerry Rice, 10-14-90	30

*NFL Record

1990 Team Record

Preseason (1-3)

Date	Result		Opponents
8/11	L	13-23	L.A. Raiders
8/20	W	27-24	at Denver
8/25	L	28-29	at San Diego
8/31	L	10-30	Seattle
		78-106	

Regular Season (14-2)

Date	Result		Opponents	Att.
9/10	W	13-12	at New Orleans	68,629
9/16	W	26-13	Washington	64,287
9/23	W	19-13	Atlanta	62,858
10/7	W	24-21	at Houston	59,931
10/14	W	45-35	at Atlanta	57,921
10/21	W	27- 7	Pittsburgh	64,301
10/28	W	20-17	Cleveland	63,672
11/4	W	24-20	at Green Bay	58,835
11/11	W	24- 6	at Dallas	62,966
11/18	W	31- 7	Tampa Bay	62,221
11/25	L	17-28	L.A. Rams	62,633
12/3	W	7- 3	N.Y. Giants	66,092
12/9	W	20-17	at Cincinnati (OT)	60,084
12/17	W	26-10	at L.A. Rams	65,619
12/23	L	10-13	New Orleans	60,112
12/30	W	20-17	at Minnesota	51,590

(OT) Overtime

Postseason (1-1)

Date	Result		Opponent	Att.
1/12	W	28-10	Washington	65,292
1/20	L	13-15	N.Y. Giants	66,334

Score by Periods

49ers	44	131	84	91	3	—	353
Opponents	64	74	33	68	0	—	239

Attendance

Home 506,186 Away 485,605 Total 991,791
Single-game home record, 66,334 (1-20-91)
Single-season home record, 506,186 (1990)

1990 Team Statistics

	49ers	Opp.
Total First Downs	324	250
Rushing	107	77
Passing	201	157
Penalty	16	16
Third Down: Made/Att.	113/233	71/199
Third Down: Pct.	48.5	35.7
Fourth Down: Made/Att.	7/9	4/15
Fourth Down: Pct.	77.8	26.7
Total Net Yards	5895	4273
Avg. Per Game	368.4	267.1
Total Plays	1074	919
Avg. Per Play	5.5	4.6
Net Yards Rushing	1718	1258
Avg. Per Game	107.4	78.6
Total Rushes	454	353
Net Yards Passing	4177	3015
Avg. Per Game	261.1	188.4
Sacked/Yards Lost	37/194	44/263
Gross Yards	4371	3278
Att./Completions	583/360	522/265
Completion Pct.	61.7	50.8
Had Intercepted	16	17
Punts/Avg.	70/36.2	82/40.0
Net Punting Avg.	30.9	34.2
Penalties/Yards Lost	104/828	85/641
Fumbles/Ball Lost	24/14	21/14
Touchdowns	40	26
Rushing	12	7
Passing	28	17
Returns	0	2
Avg. Time of Possession	32:49	27:11

1990 Individual Statistics

Scoring	TD R	TD P	TD Rt	PAT	FG	Saf	TP
Cofer	0	0	0	39/39	24/36	0	111
Rice	0	13	0	0/0	0/0	0	78
Rathman	7	0	0	0/0	0/0	0	42
Taylor	0	7	0	0/0	0/0	0	42
Jones	0	5	0	0/0	0/0	0	30
Sydney	2	1	0	0/0	0/0	0	18
Sherrard	0	2	0	0/0	0/0	0	12
Craig	1	0	0	0/0	0/0	0	6
D. Carter	1	0	0	0/0	0/0	0	6
Montana	1	0	0	0/0	0/0	0	6
Turner	0	0	0	0/0	0/0	1	2
49ers	12	28	0	39/39	24/36	1	353
Opponents	7	17	2	26/26	19/23	0	239

Passing	Att.	Comp.	Yds.	Pct.	TD	Int.	Tkld.	Rate
Montana	520	321	3944	61.7	26	16	29/153	89.0
Young	62	38	427	61.3	2	0	8/41	92.6
Helton	1	1	0	100.0	0	0	0/0	79.2
49ers	583	360	4371	61.7	28	16	37/194	89.4
Opponents	522	265	3278	50.8	17	17	44/263	67.8

Rushing	Att.	Yds.	Avg.	LG	TD
D. Carter	114	460	4.0	74t	1
Craig	141	439	3.1	26	1
Rathman	101	318	3.1	22	7
Sydney	35	166	4.7	19	2
Montana	40	162	4.1	20	1
Young	15	159	10.6	31	0
Henderson	6	14	2.3	9	0
Rice	2	0	0.0	2	0
49ers	454	1718	3.8	74t	12
Opponents	353	1258	3.6	27	7

Receiving	No.	Yds.	Avg.	LG	TD
Rice	100	1502	15.0	64t	13
Jones	56	747	13.3	67t	5
Taylor	49	748	15.3	78t	7
Rathman	48	327	6.8	28	0
D. Carter	25	217	8.7	26	0
Craig	25	201	8.0	31	0
Sherrard	17	264	15.5	43	2
Sydney	10	116	11.6	23t	1
Williams	9	54	6.0	9	0
Wilson	7	89	12.7	34	0
R. Lewis	5	44	8.8	14	0
Walls	5	27	5.4	11	0
Henderson	4	35	8.8	9	0
49ers	360	4371	12.1	78t	28
Opponents	265	3278	12.4	75t	17

Interceptions	No.	Yds.	Avg.	LG	TD
Waymer	7	64	9.1	24	0
Griffin	3	32	10.7	23	0
Lott	3	26	8.7	15	0
K. Lewis	1	28	28.0	28	0
Plummer, Den.-S.F.	1	16	16.0	16	0
Davis	1	13	13.0	13	0
Millen	1	8	8.0	8	0
Pollard	1	0	0.0	0	0
49ers	17	171	10.1	28	0
Opponents	16	176	11.0	65t	1

Punting	No.	Yds.	Avg.	In 20	LG
Helton	69	2537	36.8	15	56
49ers	70	2537	36.2	15	56
Opponents	82	3280	40.0	15	59

Punt Returns	No.	FC	Yds.	Avg.	LG	TD
Taylor	26	5	212	8.2	30	0
Griffin	16	8	105	6.6	20	0
Davis	5	3	38	7.6	24	0
Wilson	1	0	1	1.0	1	0
49ers	48	16	356	7.4	30	0
Opponents	30	13	215	7.2	20	0

Kickoff Returns	No.	Yds.	Avg.	LG	TD
D. Carter	41	783	19.1	35	0
Tillman	6	111	18.5	30	0
Sydney	2	33	16.5	19	0
Williams	2	7	3.5	7	0
Griffin	1	15	15.0	15	0
Walls	1	16	16.0	16	0
49ers	53	965	18.2	35	0
Opponents	66	1284	19.5	50	0

Sacks	No.
Haley	16.0
Fagan	9.0
Brown	6.0
Holt	6.0
Burt	2.0
M. Carter	1.0
Jackson	1.0
Roberts	1.0
Romanowski	1.0
Turner	1.0
49ers	44.0
Opponents	37.0

1991 Draft Choices

Round	Name	Pos.	College
1.	Ted Washington	DT	Louisville
2.	Ricky Watters	RB	Notre Dame
	John Johnson	LB	Clemson
4.	Mitch Donahue	LB	Wyoming
5.	Merton Hanks	DB	Iowa
	Harry Boatswain	T	New Haven
6.	Scott Bowles	T	North Texas State
7.	Sheldon Canley	RB	San Jose State
8.	Tony Hargain	WR	Oregon
9.	Louis Riddick	DB	Pittsburgh
10.	Byron Holdbrooks	NT	Alabama
11.	Bobby Slaughter	WR	Louisiana Tech
12.	Cliff Confer	DE	Michigan State

San Francisco 49ers 1991 Veteran Roster

No.	Name	Pos.	Ht.	Wt.	Birth-date	NFL Exp.	College	Hometown	How Acq.	'90 Games/ Starts
79	Barton, Harris	G	6-4	280	4/19/64	5	North Carolina	Atlanta, Ga.	D1a-'87	16/16
13	†Bono, Steve	QB	6-4	215	5/11/62	7	UCLA	Norristown, Pa.	FA-'89	0*
22	Bowles, Todd	S	6-2	205	11/18/63	6	Temple	Elizabeth, N.J.	PB(Wash)-'91#	16/16*
96	Brown, Dennis	DE	6-4	290	11/6/67	2	Washington	Long Beach, Calif.	D2a-'90	15/0
46	Brown, Steve	CB	6-0	187	3/20/60	9	Oregon	Sacramento, Calif.	PB(Hou)-'91#	16/0*
64	Burt, Jim	NT	6-1	270	6/7/59	11	Miami	Waldwick, N.J.	FA-'89	11/3
35	Carter, Dexter	RB	5-9	170	9/15/67	2	Florida State	Appling County, Ga.	D1-'90	16/5
95	Carter, Michael	NT	6-2	285	10/29/60	8	Southern Methodist	Dallas, Tex.	D5a-'84	15/13
6	Cofer, Mike	K	6-1	190	2/19/62	4	North Carolina State	Charlotte, N.C.	FA-'88	16/0
38	Cox, Greg	S	6-0	217	1/6/65	4	San Jose State	San Jose, Calif.	PB(NYG)-'90#	13/0
25	Davis, Eric	CB	5-11	178	1/26/68	2	Jacksonville State	Anniston, Ala.	D2b-'90	16/0
59	DeLong, Keith	LB	6-2	235	8/14/67	3	Tennessee	Knoxville, Tenn.	D1-'89	16/13
50	Etienne, LeRoy	LB	6-2	245	7/25/66	2	Nebraska	New Iberia, La.	FA-'90	10/0
75	Fagan, Kevin	DE	6-4	265	4/25/63	5	Miami	Lake Worth, Fla.	D4c-'86	16/16
67	Foster, Roy	G	6-4	290	5/24/60	10	Southern California	Shawnee Mission, Kan.	PB(Mia)-'91#	16/3*
98	Goss, Antonio	LB	6-4	228	8/11/66	3	North Carolina	Pelham, Ga.	D6-'86	0*
29	†Griffin, Don	CB	6-0	176	3/17/64	6	Middle Tennessee State	Randleman, N.C.	D6-'86	16/16
94	Haley, Charles	LB-DE	6-5	230	1/6/64	6	James Madison	Campbell County, Va.	D4a-'86	16/16
60	Harvey, Stacy	LB	6-3	250	3/8/65	2	Arizona State	Pasadena, Calif.	FA-'91	0*
9	Helton, Barry	P	6-3	205	1/2/66	4	Colorado	Simia, Colo.	D4-'88	16/0
30	Henderson, Keith	RB	6-1	220	8/4/66	3	Georgia	Cartersville, Ga.	D3-'89	2/0
76	Hodge, Milford	DE	6-3	278	3/11/61	5	Washington State	San Francisco, Calif.	FA-'91	0*
78	Holt, Pierce	DE	6-4	280	1/1/62	4	Angelo State	Houston, Tex.	D2b-'88	16/16
90	Ingram, Darryl	TE	6-3	240	5/2/66	2	California	Lubbock, Tex.	FA-'91	0*
40	†Jackson, Johnny	S	6-1	204	1/11/67	3	Houston	Harlingen, Tex.	D5a-'89	16/4
84	Jones, Brent	TE	6-4	230	2/12/63	5	Santa Clara	San Jose, Calif.	FA-'87	16/16
90	Jordan, Darin	LB	6-2	245	12/4/64	2	Northeastern	Stroughton, Mass.	PB(Raid)-'91#	0*
45	Lewis, Kevin	CB	5-11	173	11/14/66	2	Northwestern Louisiana	New Orleans, La.	FA-'90	10/0
83	Lewis, Ronald	WR	5-11	173	3/25/68	2	Florida State	Jacksonville, Fla.	D3a-'90	8/0
27	Mandley, Pete	WR	5-10	192	7/29/61	7	Northern Arizona	Mesa, Ariz.	FA-'91	5/2*
62	McIntyre, Guy	G	6-3	265	2/17/61	8	Georgia	Thomasville, Ga.	D3-'84	16/16
71	Mitz, Alonzo	DE	6-4	278	6/5/63	5	Florida	Ft. Pierce, Fla.	FA-'91	0*
2	Mojsiejenko, Ralf	P	6-3	212	1/28/63	7	Michigan State	Bridgman, Mich.	FA-'91	12/0*
16	Montana, Joe	QB	6-2	195	6/11/56	13	Notre Dame	New Eagle, Pa.	D3-'79	15/15
69	Neville, Tom	G	6-5	298	9/4/61	4	Fresno State	Fairbanks, Alaska	FA-'91	0*
77	†Paris, Bubba	T	6-6	306	10/6/60	9	Michigan	Louisville, Ky.	D2-'82	16/16
28	Plummer, Bruce	CB	6-0	198	9/1/64	5	Mississippi State	Bogalusa, La.	FA-'91	8/0*
72	Pollack, Frank	T-G	6-5	285	11/5/67	2	Northern Arizona	Phoenix, Ariz.	D6-'90	15/0
26	†Pollard, Darryl	CB	5-11	187	5/11/65	5	Weber State	Colorado Springs, Colo.	FA-'88	16/16
57	Radloff, Wayne	C	6-5	277	5/17/61	6	Georgia	Lawrenceville, Ga.	PB(Atl)-'90#	0*
44	Rathman, Tom	RB	6-1	232	10/7/62	6	Nebraska	Grand Island, Neb.	D3a-'86	16/16
80	Rice, Jerry	WR	6-2	200	10/13/62	7	Mississippi Valley State	Crawford, Miss.	D1-'85	16/16
91	†Roberts, Larry	DE	6-3	275	6/2/63	6	Alabama	Dothan, Ala.	D2-'86	6/0
57	Robinson, Jeroy	LB	6-2	245	6/14/68	2	Texas A&M	Bryan, Tex.	PB(Phx)-'91#	3/0*
53	†Romanowski, Bill	LB	6-4	231	4/2/66	4	Boston College	Vernon, Conn.	D3-'88	16/16
61	Sapolu, Jessie	C	6-4	260	3/10/61	6	Hawaii	Honolulu, Hawaii	D11-'83	16/16
88	Sherrard, Mike	WR	6-2	187	6/21/63	4	UCLA	Los Angeles, Calif.	PB(Dall)-'89#	7/2
92	Siglar, Ricky	T	6-7	296	6/14/66	2	San Jose State	Albuquerque, N.M.	FA-'89	16/0
72	Smith, Sean	DE	6-4	272	3/27/65	4	Grambling	Bogalusa, La.	FA-'91	0*
24	Sydney, Harry	RB	6-0	217	6/26/59	5	Kansas	Fayetteville, N.C.	FA-'87	16/0
82	Taylor, John	WR	6-1	185	3/31/62	5	Delaware State	Pennsauken, N.J.	D3c-'86	14/14
60	†Thomas, Chuck	C	6-3	280	12/24/60	6	Oklahoma	Houston, Tex.	FA-'87	16/0
23	†Tillman, Spencer	RB	5-11	206	4/21/64	5	Oklahoma	Houston, Tex.	PB(Hou)-'89#	16/0
74	Wallace, Steve	T	6-5	276	12/27/64	6	Auburn	Atlanta, Ga.	D4b-'86	16/16
89	Walls, Wesley	TE	6-5	246	2/26/66	3	Mississippi	Pontotoc, Miss.	D2-'89	16/0
99	Walter, Michael	LB	6-3	238	11/30/60	9	Oregon	Eugene, Ore.	FA-'84	3/3
51	Washington, Chris	LB	6-4	240	3/6/62	7	Iowa State	Tampa, Fla.	PB(Phx)-'91#	8/0*
43	Waymer, Dave	S	6-1	188	7/1/58	12	Notre Dame	Mooresville, N.C.	PB(NO)-'90#	16/9
93	Wells, Kent	NT	6-4	295	7/25/67	2	Nebraska	Lincoln, Neb.	FA-'91	6/0*
41	Whitmore, David	S	6-0	235	7/6/67	2	Stephen F. Austin	Daingerfield, Tex.	PB(NYG)-'91#	16/0*
81	Williams, Jamie	TE	6-4	245	2/25/60	9	Nebraska	Houston, Tex.	PB(Hou)-'89#	16/0
8	Young, Steve	QB	6-2	200	10/11/61	7	Brigham Young	Greenwich, Conn.	T(TB)-'87	6/1

* Bono active for 7 games but did not play; Bowles played 16 games with Washington in '90; S. Brown played 16 games with Houston; Foster played 16 games with Miami; Goss active for 2 games with San Diego but did not play; Harvey last active with Kansas City in '89; Hodge last active with New England in '89; Ingram last active with Minnesota in '89; Jordan and Radloff missed '90 season due to injury; Mandley played 5 games with Kansas City; Mitz last active with Seattle in '89; Mojsiejenko played 12 games with Washington; Neville last active with Detroit in '89; Plummer played 7 games with Denver, 1 with San Francisco; Robinson played 3 games with Phoenix; Smith last active with Rams in '89; Washington played 8 games with Phoenix; Wells played 6 games with New York Giants; Whitmore played 16 games with New York Giants.

† Option playout; subject to developments.

Plan B unconditional free agent.

Players lost through Plan B (3): RB Roger Craig (Raid; 11 games in '90), S Ronnie Lott (Raid; 11), LB Matt Millen (Wash; 16).

Also played with 49ers in '90—S Chet Brooks (8 games), LB Jim Fahnhorst (3), NT Pete Kugler (10), LB Keena Turner (16), CB Eric Wright (9).

COACHING STAFF

Head Coach, George Seifert

Pro Career: Named 49ers' head coach on January 26, 1989, after serving as the team's defensive coordinator since 1983. Immediately earned a place in league history, winning a record 17 games his first year and becoming only the second rookie head coach to lead his team to a Super Bowl title (Don McCafferty of Baltimore in 1970 was the first). Recorded the NFL's best won-loss mark in 1990, posting a 14-2 record and guided San Francisco to its fifth consecutive NFC West title. Joined 49ers as secondary coach in 1980. In only his second season in the pro ranks, San Francisco had the second best defense in the league and won a Super Bowl (XVI) title, despite starting three rookies in the defensive backfield. Appointed the team's defensive coordinator in 1983. Finished 1987 with the top defense in the NFL and a 13-2 record. In 1988, San Francisco's defense ranked third en route to the Super Bowl XXIII title. No pro playing experience. Career record: 32-5.

Background: Linebacker at University of Utah (1960-62). Served a six-month tour of duty with the U.S. Army following graduation. Returned to Utah as a graduate assistant in 1964. Named head coach at Westminster College in Salt Lake City in 1965. Assistant at Iowa (1966), Oregon (1967-71), and Stanford (1972-74). Left Stanford to become head coach at Cornell (1975-76). Joined Bill Walsh's staff at Stanford in 1977 and helped the Cardinal to a two-year mark of 17-7, including victories in the Sun and Bluebonnet Bowls. Received bachelor's degree in zoology (1963) and master's degree in physical education (1966) from Utah.

Personal: Born January 22, 1940, in San Francisco. He and his wife, Linda, have two children—Eve and Jason—and live in Sunnyvale, Calif.

Assistant Coaches

Jerry Attaway, conditioning; born January 3, 1946, Susanville, Calif., lives in San Jose, Calif. Defensive back Yuba, Calif., J.C. 1964-65, Cal-Davis 1967. No pro playing experience. College coach: Cal-Davis 1970-71, Idaho 1972-74, Utah State 1975-77, Southern California 1978-82. Pro coach: Joined 49ers in 1983.

Tommy Hart, defensive assistant; born November 11, 1944, Macon, Ga., lives in Redwood City, Calif. Offensive guard/defensive end Morris Brown 1964-68. Pro defensive end San Francisco 49ers 1968-77, Chicago Bears 1978-79, New Orleans Saints 1980. Pro coach: Joined 49ers in 1982.

Mike Holmgren, offensive coordinator/quarterbacks; born June 15, 1948, San Francisco, Calif., lives in San Jose, Calif. Quarterback Southern California 1966-69. No pro playing experience. College coach: San Francisco State 1981, Brigham Young 1982-85. Pro coach: Joined 49ers in 1986.

Sherman Lewis, receivers; born June 29, 1942, Louisville, Ky., lives in Sunnyvale, Calif. Running back Michigan State 1961-63. Pro running back Toronto Argonauts (CFL) 1964-65, New York Jets 1966. College coach: Michigan State 1969-82. Pro coach: Joined 49ers in 1983.

John Marshall, defensive line; born October 2, 1945, Arroyo Grande, Calif., lives in Pleasanton, Calif. Linebacker Washington State 1964. No pro playing experience. College coach: Oregon 1970-76, Southern California 1977-79. Pro coach: Green Bay Packers 1980-82, Atlanta Falcons 1983-85, Indianapolis Colts 1986-88, joined 49ers in 1989.

Bobb McKittrick, offensive line; born December 29, 1935, Baker, Ore., lives in San Mateo, Calif. Guard Oregon State 1955-57. No pro playing experience. College coach: Oregon State 1961-64, UCLA 1965-70. Pro coach: Los Angeles Rams 1971-72, San Diego Chargers 1974-78, joined 49ers in 1979.

Bill McPherson, defensive coordinator; born October 24, 1931, Santa Clara, Calif., lives in San Jose, Calif. Tackle Santa Clara 1950-52. No pro playing experience. College coach: Santa Clara 1963-74, UCLA 1975-77. Pro coach: Philadelphia Eagles 1978, joined 49ers in 1979.

San Francisco 49ers 1991 First-Year Roster

Name	Pos.	Ht.	Wt.	Birth-date	College	Hometown	How Acq.
Barnes, Randy	NT	6-4	305	6/16/66	Texas A&M	St. Albans, W.Va.	FA
Beach, Sanjay (1)	WR	6-1	190	2/21/66	Colorado State	Freeport, N.Y.	FA-'90
Boatswain, Harry	T	6-4	295	6/26/69	New Haven	Brooklyn, N.Y.	D5b
Bowles, Scott	T	6-5	280	12/20/67	North Texas State	Wichita Falls, Tex.	D6
Caliguire, Dean (1)	C	6-2	282	3/2/67	Pittsburgh	Pittsburgh, Pa.	D4a-'90
Canley, Sheldon	RB	5-9	195	4/19/68	San Jose State	Lompoc, Calif.	D7
Compton, Gary	WR	6-3	191	5/9/68	East Texas State	Irving, Tex.	FA
Confer, Cliff	DE	6-3	270	8/13/68	Michigan State	New Lothrup, Mich.	D12
Donahue, Mitch	LB	6-2	254	2/4/68	Wyoming	Billings, Mont.	D4a
Gray, James (1)	RB	5-11	205	3/2/67	Texas Tech	Ft. Worth, Tex.	FA
Grayson, Dan (1)	LB	6-3	245	7/27/67	Washington State	Woodland, Wash.	FA
Green, Anthony (1)	WR	6-0	188	6/12/67	Western Kentucky	Dallas, Tex.	FA
Hanks, Merton	CB	6-2	185	3/12/68	Iowa	Lake Highlands, Tex.	D5a
Hargain, Tony	WR	6-0	188	12/26/67	Oregon	North Highlands, Calif.	D8
Harrison, Martin (1)	LB-DE	6-5	240	9/20/67	Washington	Bellevue, Wash.	D10-'90
Holdbrooks, Byron	NT	6-5	280	11/8/67	Alabama	Haleyville, Ala.	D10
Joelson, Greg (1)	DE	6-3	270	8/22/66	Arizona State	Coos Bay, Ore.	FA
Johnson, John	LB	6-3	230	5/8/68	Clemson	LaGrange, Ga.	D2c
Martini, Ralph	QB	6-2	217	8/7/67	San Jose State	Roseville, Calif.	FA
Proctor, Basil (1)	LB	6-3	235	10/6/66	West Virginia	Miami, Fla.	FA
Riddick, Louis	S	6-2	217	3/15/69	Pittsburgh	Pennridge, Pa.	D9
Sanfratello, Mike	DE	6-4	265	5/28/68	Northern Arizona	Scottsdale, Ariz.	FA
Slaughter, Bobby	WR	5-11	171	4/24/68	Louisiana Tech	Ruston, La.	D11
Smith, Tony (1)	G	6-3	285	3/17/67	California	Placerville, Calif.	FA
Walker, Adam (1)	RB	6-1	210	6/7/68	Pittsburgh	Munhall, Pa.	FA
Washington, Ted	NT-DE	6-4	299	4/13/68	Louisville	Tampa, Fla.	D1
Watters, Ricky	RB	6-1	212	4/7/69	Notre Dame	Harrisburg, Pa.	D2a
Wiese, Brett (1)	G-C	6-4	280	8/6/66	Washington	Issaquah, Wash.	FA-'90

The term NFL Rookie is defined as a player who is in his first season of professional football and has not been on the roster of another professional football team for any regular-season or postseason games. A Rookie is designated by an "R" on NFL rosters. Players who have been active in another professional football league or players who have NFL experience, including either preseason training camp or being on an active roster for fewer than three regular-season or postseason games, are termed NFL First-Year Players. An NFL First-Year Player is designated by a "1" on NFL rosters. Thereafter, a player on an NFL active roster for at least three regular-season or postseason games is credited with an additional year of NFL playing experience.

NOTES

Ray Rhodes, defensive backfield; born October 20, 1950, Mexia, Tex., lives in Fremont, Calif. Running back-wide receiver Texas Christian 1969-70, Tulsa 1972-73. Pro defensive back New York Giants 1974-79, San Francisco 49ers 1980. Pro coach: Joined 49ers in 1981.

Ray Sherman, running backs; born November 27, 1951, Berkeley, Calif., lives in Santa Clara, Calif. Wide receiver Laney, Calif., J.C. 1969-70, Fresno State 1971-72. Pro defensive back Green Bay Packers 1973. College coach: San Jose State 1974, California 1975, 1981, Michigan State 1976-77, Wake Forest 1978-80, Purdue 1982-85, Georgia 1986-87. Pro coach: Houston Oilers 1988-89, Atlanta Falcons 1990, joined 49ers in 1991.

Lynn Stiles, special teams/tight ends; born April 12, 1941, Kermit, Tex., lives in Sunnyvale, Calif. Guard Utah 1961-62. No pro playing experience. College coach: Utah 1963-65, Iowa 1966-70, UCLA 1971-75, San Jose State 1976-78 (head coach). Pro coach: Philadelphia Eagles 1979-85, joined 49ers in 1987.

Bob Zeman, linebackers; born February 22, 1937, Wheaton, Ill., lives in Boulder Creek, Calif. Fullback/halfback Wisconsin 1957-59. Pro defensive back Los Angeles/San Diego Chargers 1960-61, 1965-66, Denver Broncos 1962-63. College coach: Northwestern 1968-69, Wisconsin 1970. Pro coach: Oakland Raiders 1971-77, 1984-86, Denver Broncos 1978-82, Buffalo Bills 1983, joined 49ers in 1989.

National Football Conference Central Division

Team Colors: Florida Orange, White, and Red

One Buccaneer Place
Tampa, Florida 33607
Telephone: (813) 870-2700

Club Officials

Owner: Hugh F. Culverhouse
President: Gay Culverhouse
General Manager: Phil Krueger
General Counsel: Richard McKay
Director of Ticket Operations: Terry Wooten
Director of Public Relations: Rick Odioso
Director of Corporate Sales & Community Relations: Jane Acton
Director of Player Personnel: Jerry Angelo
Director of Pro Personnel: Ruston Webster
College Scouts: James Harris, Tim Ruskell
Controller: Patrick Smith
Manager of Advertising & Sales: Paul Sickmon
Manager of Operations: Paul Royak
Assistant Director-Ticket Operations: Lori Grimm
Asst. Director-Public Relations: Cheryl Harden
Media Relations Assistant: Mark Schiefelbein
Trainer: Chris Smith
Assistant Trainer: Joe Joe Petrone
Equipment Manager: Frank Pupello
Assistant Equipment Manager: Carl Melchior
Video Director: Dave Levy
Assistant Video Director: Pat Brazil
Computer Services Coordinator: Terri Kimbell
Administrative Assistant: John Ross

Stadium: Tampa Stadium • **Capacity:** 74,315
North Dale Mabry
Tampa, Florida 33607

Playing Surface: Grass

Training Camp: University of Tampa
401 W. Kennedy Boulevard
Tampa, Florida 33606

1991 Schedule

Preseason

Aug. 5	at Cleveland	8:30
Aug. 10	**Miami**	7:00
Aug. 17	at Atlanta	7:00
Aug. 23	**Kansas City**	8:00

Regular Season

Sept. 1	at New York Jets	1:00
Sept. 8	**Chicago**	1:00
Sept. 15	at Green Bay	12:00
Sept. 22	**Buffalo**	4:00
Sept. 29	at Detroit	1:00
Oct. 6	**Philadelphia**	1:00
Oct. 13	**Open Date**	
Oct. 20	at New Orleans	12:00
Oct. 27	**Green Bay**	1:00
Nov. 3	at Minnesota	12:00
Nov. 10	**Detroit**	1:00
Nov. 17	at Atlanta	1:00
Nov. 24	**New York Giants**	1:00
Dec. 1	at Miami	1:00
Dec. 8	**Minnesota**	8:00
Dec. 14	at Chicago (Saturday)	11:30
Dec. 22	**Indianapolis**	1:00

Buccaneers Coaching History

(69-162-1)

1976-84	John McKay	45-91-1
1985-86	Leeman Bennett	4-28-0
1987-90	Ray Perkins*	19-41-0
1990	Richard Williamson	1-2-0

*Released after 13 games in 1990

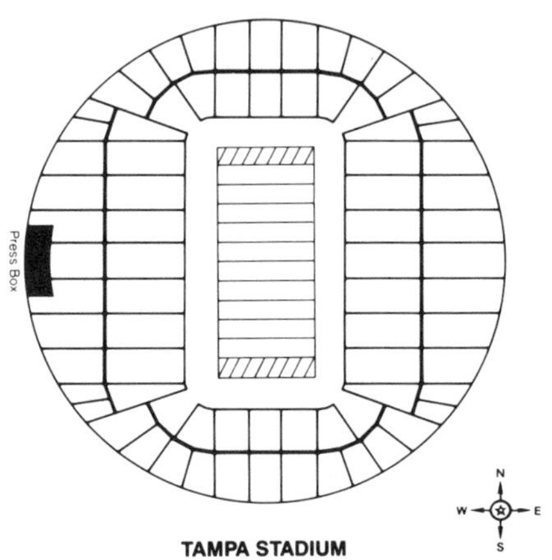

TAMPA STADIUM

Record Holders

Individual Records—Career

Category	Name	Performance
Rushing (Yds.)	James Wilder, 1981-89	5,957
Passing (Yds.)	Doug Williams, 1978-1982	12,648
Passing (TDs)	Doug Williams, 1978-1982	73
Receiving (No.)	James Wilder, 1981-89	430
Receiving (Yds.)	Kevin House, 1980-86	4,928
Interceptions	Cedric Brown, 1977-1984	29
Punting (Avg.)	Frank Garcia, 1983-87	41.1
Punt Return (Avg.)	Bobby Futrell, 1986-89	8.3
Kickoff Return (Avg.)	Isaac Hagins, 1976-1980	21.9
Field Goals	Donald Igwebuike, 1985-89	94
Touchdowns (Tot.)	James Wilder, 1981-89	46
Points	Donald Igwebuike, 1985-89	416

Individual Records—Single Season

Category	Name	Performance
Rushing (Yds.)	James Wilder, 1984	1,544
Passing (Yds.)	Doug Williams, 1981	3,563
Passing (TDs)	Doug Williams, 1980	20
	Vinny Testaverde, 1989	20
Receiving (No.)	James Wilder, 1984	85
Receiving (Yds.)	Kevin House, 1981	1,176
Interceptions	Cedric Brown, 1981	9
Punting (Avg.)	Larry Swider, 1981	42.7
Punt Return (Avg.)	Willie Drewrey, 1989	11.0
Kickoff Return (Avg.)	Isaac Hagins, 1977	23.5
Field Goals	Steve Christie, 1990	23
Touchdowns (Tot.)	James Wilder, 1984	13
Points	Donald Igwebuike, 1989	99

Individual Records—Single Game

Category	Name	Performance
Rushing (Yds.)	James Wilder, 11-6-83	219
Passing (Yds.)	Doug Williams, 11-16-80	486
Passing (TDs)	Steve DeBerg, 9-13-87	5
Receiving (No.)	James Wilder, 9-15-85	13
Receiving (Yds.)	Mark Carrier, 12-6-87	212
Interceptions	Many times	2
	Last time by Harry Hamilton, 12-23-90	
Field Goals	Many times	4
	Last time by Steve Christie, 12-16-90	4
Touchdowns (Tot.)	Jimmie Giles, 10-20-85	4
Points	Jimmie Giles, 10-20-85	24

1990 Team Record

Preseason (3-1)

Date	Result		Opponents
8/11	W	30-17	Cincinnati
8/18	W	44-10	vs. New England at Jacksonville
8/24	L	3-10	at Seattle
8/30	W	23-14	N.Y. Jets
		100-51	

Regular Season (6-10)

Date	Result		Opponents	Att.
9/9	W	38-21	at Detroit	56,692
9/16	L	14-35	L.A. Rams	59,705
9/23	W	23-20	Detroit	55,075
9/30	W	23-20	at Minnesota (OT)	54,462
10/7	L	10-14	at Dallas	60,076
10/14	W	26-14	Green Bay	67,472
10/21	L	13-17	Dallas	68,315
10/28	L	10-41	at San Diego	40,653
11/4	L	6-26	Chicago	68,555
11/11	L	7-35	at New Orleans	67,865
11/18	L	7-31	at San Francisco	62,221
11/25	L	10-20	at Green Bay	53,677
12/2	W	23-17	Atlanta	42,839
12/16	W	26-13	Minnesota	47,272
12/23	L	14-27	at Chicago	46,456
12/30	L	14-16	N.Y. Jets	46,543

(OT) Overtime

Score by Periods

Buccaneers	41	99	50	71	3	—	264
Opponents	59	112	100	96	0	—	367

Attendance

Home 455,686 Away 442,102 Total 897,788
Single-game home record, 72,077 (10-8-89)
Single-season home record, 545,980 (1979)

1990 Team Statistics

	Buccaneers	Opp.
Total First Downs	238	313
Rushing	83	129
Passing	142	168
Penalty	13	16
Third Down: Made/Att.	76/204	93/205
Third Down: Pct.	37.3	45.4
Fourth Down: Made/Att.	9/19	7/13
Fourth Down: Pct.	47.4	53.8
Total Net Yards	4475	5479
Avg. Per Game	279.7	342.4
Total Plays	911	1001
Avg. Per Play	4.9	5.5
Net Yards Rushing	1626	2223
Avg. Per Game	101.6	138.9
Total Rushes	410	496
Net Yards Passing	2849	3256
Avg. Per Game	178.1	203.5
Sacked/Yards Lost	53/433	34/204
Gross Yards	3282	3460
Att./Completions	448/245	471/263
Completion Pct.	54.7	55.8
Had Intercepted	24	25
Punts/Avg.	72/40.3	55/40.5
Net Punting Avg.	34.0	35.7
Penalties/Yards Lost	77/651	78/617
Fumbles/Ball Lost	38/19	33/17
Touchdowns	28	45
Rushing	7	20
Passing	18	22
Returns	3	3
Avg. Time of Possession	28:11	31:49

1990 Individual Statistics

Scoring	TD R	TD P	TD Rt	PAT	FG	Saf	TP
Christie	0	0	0	27/27	23/27	0	96
G. Anderson	3	2	0	0/0	0/0	0	30
Hill	0	5	0	0/0	0/0	0	30
Carrier	0	4	0	0/0	0/0	0	24
Haddix	0	0	3	0/0	0/0	0	18
Cobb	2	0	0	0/0	0/0	0	12
Hall	0	2	0	0/0	0/0	0	12
Perkins	0	2	0	0/0	0/0	0	12
Chandler	1	0	0	0/0	0/0	0	6
Drewrey	0	1	0	0/0	0/0	0	6
Harvey	0	1	0	0/0	0/0	0	6
Peebles	0	1	0	0/0	0/0	0	6
Testaverde	1	0	0	0/0	0/0	0	6
Buccaneers	7	18	3	27/27	23/27	0	264
Opponents	20	22	3	43/45	18/27	0	367

Passing	Att.	Comp.	Yds.	Pct.	TD	Int.	Tkld.	Rate
Testaverde	365	203	2818	55.6	17	18	38/330	75.6
Chandler	83	42	464	50.6	1	6	15/103	41.4
Buccaneers	448	245	3282	54.7	18	24	53/433	69.3
Opponents	471	263	3460	55.8	22	25	34/204	72.7

Rushing	Att.	Yds.	Avg.	LG	TD
G. Anderson	166	646	3.9	22	3
Cobb	151	480	3.2	17	2
Testaverde	38	280	7.4	48t	1
Harvey	27	113	4.2	14	0
Chandler	13	71	5.5	18	1
Perkins	13	36	2.8	9	0
Carlson	1	0	0.0	0	0
Hill	1	0	0.0	0	0
Buccaneers	410	1626	4.0	48t	7
Opponents	496	2223	4.5	47t	20

Receiving	No.	Yds.	Avg.	LG	TD
Carrier	49	813	16.6	68t	4
Hill	42	641	15.3	48t	5
Cobb	39	299	7.7	17	0
G. Anderson	38	464	12.2	74	2
Hall	31	464	15.0	54t	2
Harvey	11	86	7.8	18	1
Pillow	8	118	14.8	23	0
Perkins	8	85	10.6	34	2
Drewrey	7	182	26.0	89t	1
Peebles	6	50	8.3	18	1
J. Anderson	5	77	15.4	52	0
Testaverde	1	3	3.0	3	0
Buccaneers	245	3282	13.4	89t	18
Opponents	263	3460	13.2	75t	22

Interceptions	No.	Yds.	Avg.	LG	TD
Haddix	7	231	33.0	65t	3
Hamilton	5	39	7.8	27	0
Robinson	4	81	20.3	27	0
Reynolds	3	70	23.3	46	0
Everett	3	28	9.3	23	0
Rice	2	7	3.5	4	0
Moss	1	31	31.0	31	0
Buccaneers	25	487	19.5	65t	3
Opponents	24	346	14.4	64t	2

Punting	No.	Yds.	Avg.	In 20	LG
Royals	72	2902	40.3	8	62
Buccaneers	72	2902	40.3	8	62
Opponents	55	2230	40.5	16	54

Punt Returns	No.	FC	Yds.	Avg.	LG	TD
Drewrey	23	15	184	8.0	16	0
Buccaneers	23	15	184	8.0	16	0
Opponents	39	16	352	9.0	36	0

Kickoff Returns	No.	Yds.	Avg.	LG	TD
Peebles	18	369	20.5	55	0
Drewrey	14	244	17.4	29	0
Harvey	12	207	17.3	27	0
Cobb	11	223	20.3	45	0
G. Anderson	6	123	20.5	37	0
Coleman	1	9	9.0	9	0
Hall	1	0	0.0	0	0
Buccaneers	63	1175	18.7	55	0
Opponents	43	1036	24.1	65	0

Sacks	No.
B. Thomas	7.5
Randle	5.5
Murphy	4.0
Moss	3.5
Newton	3.0
White	2.5
Marve	2.0
McCants	2.0
Skow	2.0
Cannon	1.0
Davis	1.0
Buccaneers	34.0
Opponents	53.0

1991 Draft Choices

Round	Name	Pos.	College
1.	Charles McRae	T	Tennessee
3.	Lawrence Dawsey	WR	Florida State
	Robert Wilson	RB	Texas A&M
4.	Tony Covington	DB	Virginia
5.	Terry Bagsby	LB	East Texas State
	Tim Ryan	G	Notre Dame
6.	Rhett Hall	DT	California
7.	Calvin Tiggle	LB	Georgia Tech
8.	Marty Carter	DB	Middle Tenn. St.
9.	Treamelle Taylor	WR	Nevada-Reno
10.	Pat O'Hara	QB	Southern California
	Hyland Hickson	RB	Michigan State
11.	Mike Sunvold	DT	Minnesota
12.	Al Chamblee	LB	Virginia Tech

Tampa Bay Buccaneers 1991 Veteran Roster

No.	Name	Pos.	Ht.	Wt.	Birth-date	NFL Exp.	College	Hometown	How Acq.	'90 Games/ Starts
40	Anderson, Gary	RB	6-1	190	4/18/61	6	Arkansas	Columbia, Mo.	T(SD)-'90	16/13
89	Anderson, Jesse	TE	6-2	245	7/26/66	2	Mississippi State	West Point, Miss.	D4a-'90	16/2
56	†Anno, Sam	LB	6-2	235	1/26/65	5	Southern California	Santa Monica, Calif.	PB(Minn)-'89#	16/0
75	Bax, Carl	G	6-4	290	1/5/66	3	Missouri	St. Charles, Mo.	D8-'89	9/6
62	Beckles, Ian	G	6-1	295	7/20/67	2	Indiana	Montreal, Canada	D5-'90	16/16
69	†Bruhin, John	G	6-3	285	12/9/64	4	Tennessee	Knoxville, Tenn.	D4b-'88	14/1
78	Cannon, John	DE	6-5	265	7/30/60	10	William & Mary	Long Branch, N.J.	D3-'82	15/5
7	Carlson, Jeff	QB	6-3	215	5/23/66	2	Weber State	Cypress, Calif.	FA-'90	1/0
88	Carrier, Mark	WR	6-0	185	10/28/65	5	Nicholls State	Church Point, La.	D3-'87	16/16
17	Chandler, Chris	QB	6-4	220	10/12/65	4	Washington	Everett, Wash.	T(Ind)-'90	7/3
2	Christie, Steve	K	6-0	185	11/13/67	2	William & Mary	Oakville, Ohio	FA-'90	16/0
33	Cobb, Reggie	RB	6-0	225	7/7/68	2	Tennessee	Knoxville, Tenn.	D2-'90	16/13
79	Davis, Reuben	DE	6-4	285	5/7/65	4	North Carolina	Greensboro, N.C.	D8-'88	16/16
76	Dill, Scott	G	6-5	285	4/5/66	4	Memphis State	Birmingham, Ala.	PB(Phx)-'90#	3/2
87	†Drewrey, Willie	WR	5-7	170	4/28/63	7	West Virginia	Columbus, N.J.	PB(Hou)-'89#	16/1
42	Everett, Eric	CB-S	5-10	170	7/13/66	4	Texas Tech	Daingerfield, Tex.	PB(Phil)-'90#	16/0
81	Ford, Chris	WR	6-1	185	5/20/67	2	Lamar	Houston, Tex.	FA-'90	1/0
21	Frizzell, William	CB-S	6-3	205	9/8/62	8	North Carolina Central	Greenville, N.C.	PB(Phil)-'91#	16/1*
60	Grimes, Randy	C	6-4	275	7/20/60	9	Baylor	Tyler, Tex.	D2-'83	16/15
74	Gruber, Paul	T	6-5	290	2/24/65	4	Wisconsin	Prairie du Sac, Wis.	D1-'89	16/16
45	†Haddix, Wayne	CB	6-1	205	7/23/63	4	Liberty	Middleton, Tenn.	FA-'90	16/16
82	Hall, Ron	TE	6-4	245	3/15/64	5	Hawaii	Escondido, Calif.	D4b-'87	16/16
39	Hamilton, Harry	S	6-0	195	11/29/62	8	Penn State	Nanticoke, Pa.	FA-'88	16/16
26	Harvey, John	RB	5-11	185	12/28/66	2	Texas-El Paso	Spring Valley, N.Y.	FA-'90	16/1
84	Hill, Bruce	WR	6-0	180	2/29/64	5	Arizona State	Lancaster, Calif.	D4c-'87	13/13
97	Jones, Marlon	DE	6-4	270	7/1/64	4	Central State, Ohio	Baltimore, Md.	PB(Clev)-'91#	0*
38	Lawson, Jamie	RB	5-10	240	10/2/65	3	Nicholls State	Raceland, La.	PB(NE)-'91#	6/0*
99	Marve, Eugene	LB	6-2	240	8/14/60	10	Saginaw Valley	Flint, Mich.	T(Buff)-'88	16/16
61	Mayberry, Tony	C	6-4	285	12/8/67	2	Wake Forest	Springfield, Va.	D4b-'90	16/1
52	McCants, Keith	LB	6-3	255	4/19/68	2	Alabama	Mobile, Ala.	D1-'90	15/4
73	McHale, Tom	G	6-4	280	2/25/63	5	Cornell	Gaithersburg, Md.	FA-'87	7/7
59	Murphy, Kevin	LB	6-2	235	9/8/63	6	Oklahoma	Plano, Tex.	D2b-'86	15/7
96	Newton, Tim	NT	6-0	275	3/23/63	7	Florida	Orlando, Fla.	FA-'90	14/5
83	Peebles, Danny	WR	5-11	180	4/30/66	3	North Carolina State	Raleigh, N.C.	D2-'89	10/0
32	Perkins, Bruce	RB	6-2	230	8/14/67	2	Arizona State	Waterloo, Iowa	FA-'90	16/3
54	†Randle, Ervin	LB	6-1	250	10/12/62	7	Baylor	Hearne, Tex.	D3-'85	16/7
29	Reynolds, Ricky	CB	5-11	190	1/19/65	5	Washington State	Sacramento, Calif.	D2a-'87	15/15
31	Rice, Rodney	CB	5-8	180	6/18/66	3	Brigham Young	Atwater, Calif.	PB(NE)-'90#	16/1
30	Robinson, Mark	S	5-11	200	9/13/62	8	Penn State	Silver Spring, Md.	T(KC)-'88	16/16
3	Royals, Mark	P	6-5	215	6/22/64	2	Appalachian State	Mathews, Va.	FA-'90	16/0
98	Seals, Ray	DE	6-3	270	6/17/65	2	No College	Syracuse, N.Y.	FA-'91	8/0*
71	Skow, Jim	DE	6-3	250	6/29/63	6	Nebraska	Omaha, Neb.	T(Cin)-'90	12/10
72	Taylor, Rob	T	6-6	290	11/14/60	6	Northwestern	Fairmont, Ohio	FA-'86	16/16
14	Testaverde, Vinny	QB	6-5	215	11/13/63	5	Miami	Elmont, N.Y.	D1-'87	15/13
51	Thomas, Broderick	LB	6-4	245	2/20/67	3	Nebraska	Houston, Tex.	D1-'89	16/15
86	Thomas, Ed	TE	6-3	235	5/4/66	2	Houston	Houston, Tex.	FA-'91	7/0
91	White, Robb	DE	6-5	280	5/25/65	3	South Dakota	Aberdeen, S.D.	FA-'90	7/1

* Frizzell played 16 games with Philadelphia in '90; Jones last active with Cleveland in '89; Lawson played 6 games with Tampa Bay, 1 game with New England; Seals played 8 games with Tampa Bay.

† Option playout; subject to developments.

Plan B unconditional free agent.

Traded—LB Winston Moss to Los Angeles Raiders.

Players lost through Plan B (7): LB Sidney Coleman (Phx; 16 games in '90), RB Derrick Douglas (GB; 0), S Odie Harris (Dall; 16), WR Frank Pillow (Det; 16), DE Benji Roland (Atl; 3), T Harry Swayne (SD; 10), DE Willie Wyatt (Pitt; 7).

Also played with Buccaneers in '90—WR Terry Anthony (1 game), CB-S Bobby Futrell (1), NT Curt Jarvis (7).

COACHING STAFF

Head Coach, Richard Williamson

Pro Career: Named fourth coach in Tampa Bay Buccaneers' history on February 4, 1991, after serving as the team's interim head coach for final three games of 1990 season. Coached the receivers for four seasons with the Buccaneers (1987-90) after serving in the same capacity with the Kansas City Chiefs (1983-86). Developed Pro Bowl players Carlos Carson (Chiefs) and Mark Carrier (Buccaneers). As a player, he spent the 1963 preseason with the Boston Patriots. Career record: 1-2.

Background: Head coach at Memphis State for six seasons (1975-80) where he compiled a 31-35 record. Named Southern Independent coach of the year in 1976. Coached in the Blue-Gray All-Star game twice. College assistant at Alabama (1963-67, 1970-71) and Arkansas (1968-69, 1972-74). College receiver at Alabama 1961-62.

Personal: Born April 13, 1941, in Ft. Deposit, Ala. Richard and his wife, Norma, live in Tampa and have two children—Rich and Caroline.

Assistant Coaches

Jeff Fitzgerald, defensive assistant; born April 18, 1960, Burbank, Calif., lives in Tampa. No college or pro playing experience. College coach: Cincinnati 1985, Alabama 1986-89. Pro coach: Joined Buccaneers in 1990.

Ray Hamilton, defensive line assistant; born January 20, 1951, Oklahoma City, Okla., lives in Tampa. Defensive tackle Oklahoma 1970-72. Pro defensive tackle New England Patriots 1973-81. Pro coach: New England Patriots 1985-89, joined Buccaneers in 1991.

Tim Harkness, receivers; born April 2, 1955, Fort Jackson, S.C., lives in Tampa. Guard Johnson C. Smith 1973-77. No pro playing experience. College coach: Georgia Tech 1982-84, Alabama 1985-86, Illinois 1987-90. Pro coach: Joined Buccaneers in 1991.

Kent Johnston, strength and conditioning; born February 21, 1956, Mexia, Tex., lives in Tampa. Defensive back Stephen F. Austin 1974-77. No pro playing experience. College coach: Northeast Louisiana 1979, Northwestern State (La.) 1980-81, Alabama 1983-86. Pro coach: Joined Buccaneers in 1987.

Hank Kuhlmann, offensive coordinator; born October 6, 1937, Webster Groves, Mo., lives in Tampa. Running back Missouri 1956-59. No pro playing experience. College coach: Missouri 1962-71, Notre Dame 1975-77. Pro coach: Green Bay Packers 1972-74, Chicago Bears 1978-82, Birmingham Stallions (USFL) 1983-85. Phoenix Cardinals 1986-90 (scout, 1990), joined Buccaneers in 1991.

Dale Lindsey, linebackers; born January 18, 1943, Bedford, Ind., lives in Tampa. Linebacker Western Kentucky 1961-64. Pro linebacker Cleveland Browns 1965-73. College coach: Southern Methodist 1988-89. Pro coach: Cleveland Browns 1974, Portland Storm (WFL) 1975-76, Toronto Argonauts (CFL) 1979-82, Boston Breakers (USFL) 1983, New Jersey Generals (USFL) 1984-85, Green Bay Packers 1986-87, New England Patriots 1990, joined Buccaneers in 1991.

Alan Lowry, special teams, tight ends; born November 21, 1950, Irving, Tex., lives in Tampa. Defensive back-quarterback Texas 1970-72. No pro playing experience. College coach: Virginia Tech 1974, Wyoming 1975, Texas 1976-81. Pro coach: Dallas Cowboys 1982-90, joined Buccaneers in 1991.

Carl Mauck, offensive line; born July 7, 1947, McLeansboro, Ill., lives in Tampa. Linebacker-center Southern Illinois 1966-68. Pro center Baltimore Colts 1969, Miami Dolphins 1970, San Diego Chargers 1971-74, Houston Oilers 1975-81. Pro coach: New Orleans Saints 1982-85, Kansas City Chiefs 1986-88, joined Buccaneers in 1991.

Tampa Bay Buccaneers 1991 First-Year Roster

Name	Pos.	Ht.	Wt.	Birth-date	College	Hometown	How Acq.
Bagsby, Terry	LB	6-0	235	1/20/69	East Texas State	New Boston, Tex.	D5a
Carter, Marty	S	6-1	200	12/17/69	Middle Tennessee St.	La Grange, Ga.	D8
Chamblee, Al	LB	6-1	240	11/17/68	Virginia Tech	Virginia Beach, Va.	D12
Clark, Irvin	DT-DE	6-3	260	11/11/65	Florida A&M	Greensboro, Fla.	FA
Covington, Tony	S	5-11	190	12/26/67	Virginia	Winston-Salem, N.C.	D4
Crum, Maurice	LB	6-0	220	4/19/69	Miami	Tampa, Fla.	FA
Dawsey, Lawrence	WR	6-0	195	11/16/67	Florida State	Dothan, Ala.	D3a
Dudley, Tim	RB	5-10	195	9/6/68	Hampton Institute	Roanoke, Va.	FA
Gindorf, Mike	DT-DE	6-5	270	6/29/69	Concordia	Crosby, Mich.	FA
Godfrey, Eddie	CB-S	6-2	175	3/3/68	Western Kentucky	Lakeland, Fla.	FA
Hall, Rhett	DE	6-2	260	12/5/68	California	San Jose, Calif.	D6
Hardy, Robert	RB	5-10	210	9/16/67	Carson-Newman	Gaffney, S.C.	FA
Hickson, Hyland	RB	5-9	220	2/25/69	Michigan State	Ft. Lauderdale, Fla.	D10b
Hinton, Pat	LB	6-2	230	11/2/68	South Carolina	Atlanta, Ga.	FA
Hunter, Malvin	LB	6-2	235	11/20/69	Wisconsin	Harvey, Ill.	FA
Jennings, Bennie	TE	6-4	250	7/18/67	North Alabama	Fayetteville, Tenn.	FA
Joseph, Dale	CB-S	6-2	175	3/8/67	Howard Payne	Channelview, Tex.	FA
McRae, Charles	T	6-7	290	9/16/68	Tennessee	Clinton, Tenn.	D1
Nitkowski, Chip	T-G	6-5	280	11/28/68	Duke	Brackenridge, Pa.	FA
O'Hara, Pat	QB	6-3	205	9/27/68	Southern California	Santa Monica, Calif.	D10a
Polczinski, Nick	G-T	6-4	325	11/28/68	Wisconsin	Oconton Falls, Wis.	FA
Reed, Darryl	CB-S	6-1	185	10/27/67	Oregon	Harbor City, Calif.	FA
Robertson, Derrell	DE	6-7	245	9/22/67	Mississippi State	Winona, Tex.	FA
Rogers, Glenn	CB-S	6-0	185	6/8/69	Memphis State	Memphis, Tenn.	FA
Ryan, Tim	G	6-2	280	9/2/68	Notre Dame	Kansas City, Mo.	D5b
Sunvold, Mike	DT	6-3	260	9/21/67	Minnesota	Brooklyn Center, Minn.	D11
Taylor, Treamelle	WR-KR	5-10	175	11/8/69	Nevada-Reno	Gardena, Calif.	D9
Tiggle, Calvin	LB	6-1	235	11/10/68	Georgia Tech	Ft. Washington, Md.	D7
Watson, Ken	RB	6-2	230	9/14/68	South Carolina	Deland, Fla.	FA
Wilson, Robert	RB	6-0	240	1/13/69	Texas A&M	Houston, Tex.	D3b
Windon, Calvin	RB	5-11	202	3/17/68	Louisiana State	Orlando, Fla.	FA

The term NFL Rookie is defined as a player who is in his first season of professional football and has not been on the roster of another professional football team for any regular-season or postseason games. A Rookie is designated by an "R" on NFL rosters. Players who have been active in another professional football league or players who have NFL experience, including either preseason training camp or being on an active roster for fewer than three regular-season or postseason games, are termed NFL First-Year Players. An NFL First-Year Player is designated by a "1" on NFL rosters. Thereafter, a player on an NFL active roster for at least three regular-season or postseason games is credited with an additional year of NFL playing experience.

NOTES

Floyd Peters, defensive coordinator; born May 21, 1936, Council Bluffs, Iowa, lives in Tampa. Defensive tackle-guard San Francisco State 1954-57. Pro defensive tackle Baltimore Colts 1958, Cleveland Browns 1959-62, Detroit Lions 1963, Philadelphia Eagles 1964-69, Washington Redskins 1970. Pro coach: Washington Redskins 1970, Miami Dolphins 1971-73 (scout), New York Giants 1974-75, San Francisco 49ers 1976-77, Detroit Lions 1978-81, St. Louis Cardinals 1982-85, Minnesota Vikings 1986-90, joined Buccaneers in 1991.

Tom Schertz, offensive assistant; born August 7, 1965, Tiskilwa, Ill., lives in Tampa. Tight end-tackle Illinois 1983-87. No pro playing experience. College coach: Southern Illinois 1990. Pro coach: Joined Buccaneers in 1991.

Steve Shafer, defensive backs; born December 8, 1940, Glendale, Calif., lives in Tampa. Quarterback-defensive back Utah State 1961-62. Pro defensive back British Columbia Lions (CFL) 1963-67. College coach: San Mateo, Calif., J.C. 1968-74, (head coach 1973-74), San Diego State 1975-82. Pro coach: Los Angeles Rams 1983-90, joined Buccaneers in 1991.

Morris Watts, quarterbacks; born January 26, 1938, Seneca, Mo., lives in Tampa. Running back Tulsa 1958-61. No pro playing experience. College coach: Drake 1965-71, Louisville 1972, Indiana 1973-81, Kansas 1982, Louisiana State 1983, Michigan State 1986-90. Pro coach: Birmingham Stallions 1984-85 (USFL), joined Buccaneers in 1991.

Richard Wood, defensive assistant; born May 31, 1953, Elizabeth, N.J., lives in Tampa. Linebacker Southern California 1972-74. Pro linebacker New York Jets 1975, Tampa Bay Buccaneers 1976-84. Pro coach: Joined Buccaneers in 1991.

National Football Conference Eastern Division

Team Colors: Burgundy and Gold

Redskin Park, P.O. Box 17247
Dulles International Airport
Washington, D.C. 20041
Telephone: (703) 471-9100

Club Officials

Chairman of the Board-CEO: Jack Kent Cooke
Executive Vice President: John Kent Cooke
Secretary: Stuart Haney
Controller: Gregory Dillon
Board of Directors: Jack Kent Cooke, John Kent Cooke, James Lacher, William A. Shea
General Manager: Charley Casserly
Assistant General Manager: Bobby Mitchell
Director of Pro Player Personnel: Kirk Mee
Director of Pro Scouting: Joe Mack
Director of College Scouting: George Saimes
Scouts: Mel Kaufman, Chuck Banker, Gene Bates, Mike Hagen, Miller McCalmon, Larry Boynn
V.P./Communications: Charlie Dayton
Director of Media Relations: Mike McCall
Asst. Dir. of Marketing/Stadium Operations: John Kent Cooke, Jr.
Video Director: Donnie Schoenmann
Assistant Video Director: Hugh McPhillips
Ticket Manager: Sue Barton
Asst. Ticket Mgrs.: Larry Desautels, Tony Lyman
Head Trainer: Bubba Tyer
Assistant Trainers: Al Bellamy, Kevin Bastin
Equipment Manager: Jay Brunetti
Asst. Equipment Manager: Jeff Parsons

Stadium: RFK Stadium • **Capacity:** 55,683
East Capitol Street
Washington, D.C. 20003

Playing Surface: Grass

Training Camp: Dickinson College
Carlisle, Pennsylvania 17013

1991 Schedule

Preseason

Aug. 4	at Pittsburgh	8:00
Aug. 10	at New England	7:00
Aug. 16	**Cleveland**	8:00
Aug. 24	vs. New York Jets at Columbia, S.C.	7:00

Regular Season

Sept. 1	**Detroit**	8:00
Sept. 9	at Dallas (Monday)	8:00
Sept. 15	**Phoenix**	1:00
Sept. 22	at Cincinnati	1:00
Sept. 30	**Philadelphia** (Monday)	9:00
Oct. 6	at Chicago	12:00
Oct. 13	**Cleveland**	1:00
Oct. 20	**Open Date**	
Oct. 27	at New York Giants	7:30
Nov. 3	**Houston**	1:00
Nov. 10	**Atlanta**	1:00
Nov. 17	at Pittsburgh	1:00
Nov. 24	**Dallas**	1:00
Dec. 1	at Los Angeles Rams	1:00
Dec. 8	at Phoenix	2:00
Dec. 15	**New York Giants**	4:00
Dec. 22	at Philadelphia	4:00

Redskins Coaching History

Boston 1932-36
(419-355-26)

1932	Lud Wray	4-4-2
1933-34	William (Lone Star) Dietz	11-11-2
1935	Eddie Casey	2-8-1
1936-42	Ray Flaherty	56-23-3
1943	Arthur (Dutch) Bergman	7-4-1
1944-45	Dudley DeGroot	14-6-1
1946-48	Glen (Turk) Edwards	16-18-1
1949	John Whelchel*	3-3-1
1949-51	Herman Ball**	4-16-0
1951	Dick Todd	5-4-0
1952-53	Earl (Curly) Lambeau	10-13-1
1954-58	Joe Kuharich	26-32-2
1959-60	Mike Nixon	4-18-2
1961-65	Bill McPeak	21-46-3
1966-68	Otto Graham	17-22-3
1969	Vince Lombardi	7-5-2
1970	Bill Austin	6-8-0
1971-77	George Allen	69-35-1
1978-80	Jack Pardee	24-24-0
1981-90	Joe Gibbs	113-55-0

*Released after seven games in 1949
**Released after three games in 1951

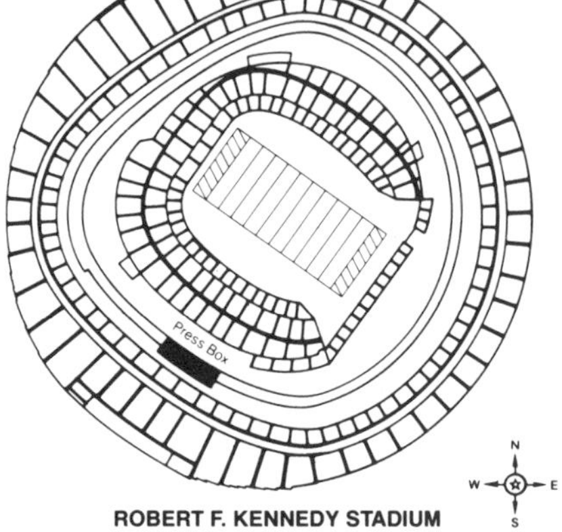

ROBERT F. KENNEDY STADIUM

Record Holders

Individual Records—Career

Category	Name	Performance
Rushing (Yds.)	John Riggins, 1976-79, 1981-85	7,472
Passing (Yds.)	Joe Theismann, 1974-1985	25,206
Passing (TDs)	Sonny Jurgensen, 1964-1974	209
Receiving (No.)	Art Monk, 1980-1990	730
Receiving (Yds.)	Art Monk, 1980-1990	9,935
Interceptions	Brig Owens, 1966-1977	36
Punting (Avg.)	Sammy Baugh, 1937-1952	*45.1
Punt Return (Avg.)	Johnny Williams, 1952-53	12.8
Kickoff Return (Avg.)	Bobby Mitchell, 1962-68	28.5
Field Goals	Mark Moseley, 1974-1986	263
Touchdowns (Tot.)	Charley Taylor, 1964-1977	90
Points	Mark Moseley, 1974-1986	1,206

Individual Records—Single Season

Category	Name	Performance
Rushing (Yds.)	John Riggins, 1983	1,347
Passing (Yds.)	Jay Schroeder, 1986	4,109
Passing (TDs)	Sonny Jurgensen, 1967	31
Receiving (No.)	Art Monk, 1984	*106
Receiving (Yds.)	Bobby Mitchell, 1963	1,436
Interceptions	Dan Sandifer, 1948	13
Punting (Avg.)	Sammy Baugh, 1940	*51.4
Punt Return (Avg.)	Johnny Williams, 1952	15.3
Kickoff Return (Avg.)	Mike Nelms, 1981	29.7
Field Goals	Mark Moseley, 1983	33
Touchdowns (Tot.)	John Riggins, 1983	*24
Points	Mark Moseley, 1983	161

Individual Records—Single Game

Category	Name	Performance
Rushing (Yds.)	Gerald Riggs, 9-17-89	221
Passing (Yds.)	Sammy Baugh, 10-31-43	446
Passing (TDs)	Sammy Baugh, 10-31-43	6
	Sammy Baugh, 11-23-47	6
Receiving (No.)	Art Monk, 12-15-85	13
	Kelvin Bryant, 12-7-86	13
	Art Monk, 11-4-90	13
Receiving (Yds.)	Anthony Allen, 10-4-87	255
Interceptions	Sammy Baugh, 11-14-43	*4
	Dan Sandifer, 10-31-48	*4
Field Goals	Many times	5
	Last time by Chip Lohmiller, 12-30-90	
Touchdowns (Tot.)	Dick James, 12-17-61	4
	Larry Brown, 12-4-73	4
Points	Dick James, 12-17-61	24
	Larry Brown, 12-4-73	24

*NFL Record

1990 Team Record

Preseason (3-1)

Date	Result		Opponents
8/11	L	27-31	vs. Atlanta at Chapel Hill, N.C.
8/17	W	27-24	Pittsburgh
8/25	W	31-13	at Cleveland
8/31	W	37-10	L.A. Rams
		122-78	

Regular Season (10-6)

Date	Result		Opponents	Att.
9/9	W	31- 0	Phoenix	52,649
9/16	L	13-26	at San Francisco	64,287
9/23	W	19-15	Dallas	53,804
9/30	W	38-10	at Phoenix	49,303
10/14	L	20-24	N.Y. Giants	54,737
10/21	W	13- 7	Philadelphia	53,567
10/28	L	10-21	at N.Y. Giants	75,321
11/4	W	41-38	at Detroit (OT)	69,326
11/12	L	14-28	at Philadelphia	65,857
11/18	W	31-17	New Orleans	52,573
11/22	L	17-27	at Dallas	60,355
12/2	W	42-20	Miami	53,599
12/9	W	10- 9	Chicago	53,920
12/15	W	25-10	at New England	22,286
12/22	L	28-35	at Indianapolis	58,173
12/30	W	29-14	Buffalo	52,397

(OT) Overtime

Postseason (1-1)

Date	Result		Opponent	Att.
1/5	W	20- 6	at Philadelphia	65,287
1/12	L	10-28	at San Francisco	65,292

Score by Periods

Redskins	49	108	103	118	3	—	381
Opponents	37	98	75	91	0	—	301

Attendance

Home 427,246 Away 464,908 Total 892,154
Single-game home record, 55,750 (11-10-85)
Single-season home record, 434,854 (1986)

1990 Team Statistics

	Redskins	Opp.
Total First Downs	327	267
Rushing	117	77
Passing	193	166
Penalty	17	24
Third Down: Made/Att.	103/221	77/201
Third Down: Pct.	46.6	38.3
Fourth Down: Made/Att.	6/15	7/16
Fourth Down: Pct.	40.0	43.8
Total Net Yards	5562	4730
Avg. Per Game	347.6	295.6
Total Plays	1073	941
Avg. Per Play	5.2	5.0
Net Yards Rushing	2083	1587
Avg. Per Game	130.2	99.2
Total Rushes	515	382
Net Yards Passing	3479	3143
Avg. Per Game	217.4	196.4
Sacked/Yards Lost	22/132	45/340
Gross Yards	3611	3483
Att./Completions	536/301	514/281
Completion Pct.	56.2	54.7
Had Intercepted	22	21
Punts/Avg.	55/37.5	76/43.3
Net Punting Avg.	33.4	36.9
Penalties/Yards Lost	102/824	89/712
Fumbles/Ball Lost	14/6	24/12
Touchdowns	41	35
Rushing	16	8
Passing	22	21
Returns	3	6
Avg. Time of Possession	32:19	27:41

1990 Individual Statistics

Scoring	TD R	TD P	TD Rt	PAT	FG	Saf	TP
Lohmiller	0	0	0	41/41	30/40	0	131
Clark	0	8	0	0/0	0/0	0	48
Byner	6	1	0	0/0	0/0	0	42
Riggs	6	0	0	0/0	0/0	0	36
Monk	0	5	0	0/0	0/0	0	30
Sanders	0	3	0	0/0	0/0	0	18
Humphries	2	0	0	0/0	0/0	0	12
J. Johnson	0	2	0	0/0	0/0	0	12
Bryant	0	1	0	0/0	0/0	0	6
Gouveia	0	0	1	0/0	0/0	0	6
Green	0	0	1	0/0	0/0	0	6
Hobbs	0	1	0	0/0	0/0	0	6
Mitchell	1	0	0	0/0	0/0	0	6
Rutledge	1	0	0	0/0	0/0	0	6
Walton	0	0	1	0/0	0/0	0	6
Warren	0	1	0	0/0	0/0	0	6
Redskins	16	22	3	41/41	30/40	2	381
Opponents	8	21	6	35/35	18/23	1	301

Passing	Att.	Comp.	Yds.	Pct.	TD	Int.	Tkld.	Rate
Rypien	304	166	2070	54.6	16	11	6/33	78.4
Humphries	156	91	1015	58.3	3	10	9/62	57.5
Rutledge	68	40	455	58.8	2	1	6/34	82.7
Mitchell	6	3	40	50.0	0	0	1/3	71.5
Byner	2	1	31	50.0	1	0	0/0	135.4
Redskins	536	301	3611	56.2	22	22	22/132	73.5
Opponents	514	281	3483	54.7	21	21	45/340	72.5

Rushing	Att.	Yds.	Avg.	LG	TD
Byner	297	1219	4.1	22	6
Riggs	123	475	3.9	20	6
Humphries	23	106	4.6	17	2
Dupard	19	85	4.5	11	0
Mitchell	15	81	5.4	21	1
Monk	7	59	8.4	26	0
Bryant	6	24	4.0	12	0
Sanders	4	17	4.3	12	0
Rutledge	4	12	3.0	12t	1
Goodburn, K.C.-Wash.	1	5	5.0	5	0
Rypien	15	4	0.3	8	0
Clark	1	1	1.0	1	0
Mojsiejenko	1	0	0.0	0	0
Redskins	515	2083	4.0	26	16
Opponents	382	1587	4.2	48t	8

Receiving	No.	Yds.	Avg.	LG	TD
Clark	75	1112	14.8	53t	8
Monk	68	770	11.3	44	5
Sanders	56	727	13.0	38	3
Byner	31	279	9.0	19	1
Bryant	26	248	9.5	37	1
J. Johnson	15	218	14.5	35	2
Warren	15	123	8.2	18	1
Riggs	7	60	8.6	18	0
Howard	3	36	12.0	17	0
Stanley	2	15	7.5	12	0
Mitchell	2	5	2.5	5	0
Hobbs	1	18	18.0	18t	1
Redskins	301	3611	12.0	53t	22
Opponents	281	3483	12.4	80t	21

Interceptions	No.	Yds.	Avg.	LG	TD
Mayhew	7	20	2.9	15	0
Green	4	20	5.0	18t	1
Bowles	3	74	24.7	43	0
Walton	2	118	59.0	61	1
Edwards	2	33	16.5	33	0
Marshall	1	6	6.0	6	0
A. Johnson	1	0	0.0	0	0
Coleman	1	0	0.0	0	0
Redskins	21	271	12.9	61	2
Opponents	22	271	12.3	42t	5

Punting	No.	Yds.	Avg.	In 20	LG
Mojsiejenko	43	1687	39.2	17	53
Goodburn, K.C.-Wash.	28	1030	36.8	12	58
Goodburn, Wash.	11	377	34.3	6	48
Redskins	55	2064	37.5	23	53
Opponents	76	3290	43.3	21	59

Punt Returns	No.	FC	Yds.	Avg.	LG	TD
Stanley	24	8	176	7.3	32	0
Mitchell	12	4	107	8.9	26	0
Howard	10	4	99	9.9	21	0
Green	1	1	6	6.0	6	0
Thomas	1	0	0	0.0	0	0
Redskins	48	17	388	8.1	32	0
Opponents	30	10	205	6.8	30	0

Kickoff Returns	No.	Yds.	Avg.	LG	TD
Howard	22	427	19.4	35	0
Mitchell	18	365	20.3	37	0
Stanley	9	177	19.7	37	0
Hobbs	6	92	15.3	21	0
Dupard	2	0	0.0	0	0
Gouveia	2	23	11.5	15	0
Middleton	1	7	7.0	7	0
Sanders	1	22	22.0	22	0
Bowles	0	0	—	0	0
Redskins	61	1113	18.2	37	0
Opponents	58	1008	17.4	47	0

Sacks	No.
Stokes	7.5
Collins	6.0
Mann	5.5
Marshall	5.0
Coleman	3.0
Geathers	3.0
T. Johnson	3.0
Rocker	3.0
Williams	3.0
Koch	2.0
Bowles	1.0
Caldwell	1.0
Gouveia	1.0
Grant	1.0
Redskins	45.0
Opponents	22.0

1991 Draft Choices

Round	Name	Pos.	College
1.	Bobby Wilson	DT	Michigan State
3.	Ricky Ervins	RB	Southern California
6.	Dennis Ramson	TE	Texas A&M
7.	Keith Cash	WR	Texas
8.	Jimmy Spencer	DB	Florida
9.	Charles Bell	DB	Baylor
10.	Cris Shale	P	Bowling Green
11.	David Gulledge	DB	Jacksonville State
12.	Keenan McCardell	WR	Nevada-Las Vegas

Washington Redskins 1991 Veteran Roster

No.	Name	Pos.	Ht.	Wt.	Birth-date	NFL Exp.	College	Hometown	How Acq.	'90 Games/ Starts
61	Adickes, Mark	G	6-4	275	4/22/61	6	Baylor	Richardson, Tex.	PB(KC)-'90#	8/1
53	Bostic, Jeff	C	6-2	260	9/18/58	12	Clemson	Greensboro, N.C.	FA-'80	16/16
82	Brandes, John	TE	6-2	250	4/2/64	5	Cameron University	Arlington, Tex.	PB(Ind)-'90#	16/0
67	Brown, Ray	T	6-5	280	12/12/62	5	Arkansas State	Marion, Ark.	PB(Phx)-'89#	0*
38	Brown, Tom	RB	6-1	228	11/20/64	2	Pittsburgh	Ridgeway, Pa.	PB(Mia)-'90#	0*
21	Byner, Earnest	RB	5-10	215	9/15/62	8	East Carolina	Milledgeville, Ga.	T(Clev)-'89	16/16
50	Caldwell, Ravin	LB	6-3	229	8/4/63	5	Arkansas	Ft. Smith, Ark.	D5-'86	16/0
84	Clark, Gary	WR	5-9	173	5/1/62	7	James Madison	Dublin, Va.	FA-'85	16/16
51	Coleman, Monte	LB	6-2	230	11/4/57	13	Central Arkansas	Pine Bluff, Ark.	D11-'79	15/0
55	Collins, Andre	LB	6-1	230	5/4/68	2	Penn State	Cinnaminson, N.J.	D2-'90	16/16
26	Copeland, Danny	S	6-2	210	1/24/66	3	Eastern Kentucky	Thomasville, Ga.	PB(KC)-'91#	14/0*
25	†Dupard, Reggie	RB	5-11	205	10/30/63	6	Southern Methodist	River Ridge, La.	FA-'90	7/0
27	Edwards, Brad	S	6-2	196	3/22/66	4	South Carolina	Fayetteville, N.C.	PB(Minn)-'90#	16/1
97	Geathers, James	DT	6-7	290	6/26/60	7	Wichita State	Georgetown, S.C.	PB(NO)-'90#	9/1
2	†Goodburn, Kelly	P	6-2	202	4/14/62	5	Emporia State	Correctionville, Iowa	FA-'90	4/0
54	Gouveia, Kurt	LB	6-1	227	9/14/64	5	Brigham Young	Honolulu, Hawaii	D8-'86	16/7
77	Grant, Darryl	DT	6-1	275	11/22/59	11	Rice	San Antonio, Tex.	D9-'81	16/15
28	Green, Darrell	CB	5-8	170	2/15/60	9	Texas A&I	Houston, Tex.	D1-'83	16/16
68	†Grimm, Russ	G	6-3	275	5/2/59	11	Pittsburgh	Southmoreland, Pa.	D3-'81	15/11
34	Hoage, Terry	S	6-3	201	4/11/62	8	Georgia	Huntsville, Tex.	PB(Phil)-'91#	16/3*
86	†Hobbs, Stephen	WR	5-11	195	11/14/65	2	North Alabama	Mendenhall, Miss.	PB(KC)-'89#	7/0
80	Howard, Joe	WR	5-8	170	12/21/62	3	Notre Dame	Washington, D.C.	FA-'89	15/0
16	Humphries, Stan	QB	6-2	223	4/14/65	3	Northeastern Louisiana	Shreveport, La.	D6-'88	7/5
66	†Jacoby, Joe	G-T	6-7	310	7/6/59	11	Louisville	Louisville, Ky.	FA-'81	16/6
47	Johnson, A.J.	CB	5-8	176	6/22/67	3	Southwest Texas State	San Antonio, Tex.	D6-'89	5/0
88	Johnson, Jimmie	TE	6-2	246	10/6/66	3	Howard	Augusta, Ga.	D12a-'89	16/5
45	Johnson, Sidney	CB	5-9	175	3/7/65	3	California	Cerritos, Calif.	FA-'90	10/1
78	Johnson, Tim	DT	6-3	261	1/29/65	5	Penn State	Sarasota, Fla.	T(Pitt)-'90	16/2
74	Koch, Markus	DE	6-5	275	2/13/63	6	Boise State	Ontario, Canada	D2a-'85	13/13
79	Lachey, Jim	T	6-6	290	6/4/63	7	Ohio State	St. Henry, Ohio	T(Raid)-'88	16/16
8	Lohmiller, Chip	K	6-3	213	7/16/66	4	Minnesota	Minneapolis, Minn.	D2-'88	16/0
71	Mann, Charles	DE	6-6	270	4/12/61	9	Nevada-Reno	Sacramento, Calif.	D3-'83	15/15
58	Marshall, Wilber	LB	6-1	230	4/18/62	8	Florida	Titusville, Fla.	FA-'88	16/15
35	†Mayhew, Martin	CB	5-8	172	10/8/65	3	Florida State	Tallahassee, Fla.	PB(Buff)-'89#	16/15
20	Mays, Alvoid	CB	5-9	180	7/10/66	2	West Virginia	Bradenton, Fla.	FA-'90	15/1
63	McKenzie, Raleigh	C-G	6-2	270	2/8/63	7	Tennessee	Knoxville, Tenn.	D11-'85	16/12
87	Middleton, Ron	TE	6-2	255	7/17/65	5	Auburn	Atmore, Ala.	PB(Clev)-'90#	16/5
52	Millen, Matt	LB	6-2	245	3/12/58	12	Penn State	Whitehall, Pa.	PB(SF)-'91#	16/16*
30	Mitchell, Brian	RB	5-10	195	8/18/68	2	Southwestern Louisiana	Plaquemine, La.	D5-'90	15/0
81	Monk, Art	WR	6-3	209	12/5/57	12	Syracuse	White Plains, N.Y.	D1-'80	16/16
37	Riggs, Gerald	RB	6-1	232	11/6/60	10	Arizona State	Las Vegas, Nev.	T(Atl)-'89	10/0
99	Rocker, Tracy	DT	6-3	288	4/9/66	3	Auburn	Atlanta, Ga.	D3-'89	8/7
10	Rutledge, Jeff	QB	6-1	195	1/22/57	13	Alabama	Birmingham, Ala.	PB(NYG)-'90#	10/1
11	†Rypien, Mark	QB	6-4	234	10/2/62	4	Washington State	Spokane, Wash.	D6-'86	10/10
83	Sanders, Ricky	WR	5-11	180	8/30/62	6	Southwest Texas State	Temple, Tex.	T(NE)-'86	16/6
69	Schlereth, Mark	G	6-3	285	1/25/66	3	Idaho	Anchorage, Alaska	D10-'89	12/7
23	Settle, John	RB	5-9	210	6/2/65	5	Appalachian State	Ruffin, N.C.	PB(Atl)-'91#	6/0*
76	Simmons, Ed	T	6-5	300	12/31/63	5	Eastern Washington	Stockton, Calif.	D6b-'87	13/11
89	Stanley, Walter	WR	5-9	180	11/5/62	7	Mesa, Colo.	Chicago, Ill.	PB(Det)-'90#	9/1
60	Stokes, Fred	DE	6-3	262	3/14/64	5	Georgia Southern	Vidalia, Ga.	PB(Rams)-'89#	16/3
31	Vaughn, Clarence	S	6-0	202	7/17/64	4	Northern Illinois	Chicago, Ill.	D8-'87	0*
40	Walton, Alvin	S	6-0	180	3/14/64	6	Kansas	Banning, Calif.	D3-'86	16/16
85	Warren, Don	TE	6-4	242	5/5/56	13	San Diego State	Covina, Calif.	D4-'79	16/15
48	†Whisenhunt, Ken	TE	6-3	240	2/28/62	5	Georgia Tech	Augusta, Ga.	PB(Atl)-'89#	2/0
75	†Williams, Eric	DT	6-4	286	2/24/62	8	Washington State	Stockton, Calif.	T(Det)-'90	13/8

* R. Brown and Vaughn missed '90 season due to injury; T. Brown last active with Miami in '89; Copeland played 14 games with Kansas City in '90; Hoage played 16 games with Philadelphia; Millen played 16 games with San Francisco; Settle played 6 games with Atlanta.

† Option playout; subject to developments.

Plan B unconditional free agent.

Players lost through Plan B (3): S Todd Bowles (SF; 16 games in '90), LB Greg Manusky (Minn; 16), G-T Mark May (SD; 0).

Also played with Redskins in '90—RB Kelvin Bryant (15 games), CB Brian Davis (7), CB Wayne Davis (1), LB Randy Kirk (1), P Ralf Mojsiejenko (12), TE Terry Orr (2), CB Johnny Thomas (4), RB James Wilder (1).

COACHING STAFF

Head Coach, Joe Gibbs

Pro Career: Enters eleventh season as Redskins' all-time leader in wins. He is the fourth-winningest coach among active NFL coaches with 113 career wins. Has led Redskins to two Super Bowl titles and three Super Bowl appearances. Washington has appeared in postseason play six of last nine seasons under Gibbs. Named head coach on January 13, 1981, after spending eight years as an NFL assistant coach and nine seasons on the collegiate level. Came to Redskins from San Diego Chargers, where he was offensive coordinator in 1979 and 1980. Prior to that, he was offensive coordinator for the Tampa Bay Buccaneers in 1978 and offensive backfield coach for the St. Louis Cardinals from 1973-77. While he was with San Diego, the Chargers won the AFC West title and led the NFL in passing two consecutive years. No pro playing experience. Career record: 113-55.

College: Played tight end, linebacker, and guard under Don Coryell at San Diego State in 1961 and 1962 after spending two years at Cerritos, Calif., J.C. 1959-60. Started college coaching career at San Diego State 1964-66, followed by Florida State 1967-68, Southern California 1969-70, and Arkansas 1971-72.

Personal: Born November 25, 1940, in Mocksville, N.C. Graduated from Santa Fe Springs, Calif., High School. Two-time national racquetball champion and ranked second in the over-35 category in 1978. He and his wife, Pat, live in Vienna, Va., and have two sons—J. D. and Coy.

Assistant Coaches

Don Breaux, running backs; born August 3, 1940, Jennings, La., lives in Centreville, Va. Quarterback McNeese State 1959-61. Pro quarterback Denver Broncos 1963, San Diego Chargers 1964-65. College coach: Florida State 1966-67, Arkansas 1968-71, 1977-80, Florida 1973-74, Texas 1975-76. Pro coach: joined Redskins in 1981.

Jack Burns, quarterbacks; born January 3, 1949, Tampa, Fla., lives in Ashburn, Va. Safety Florida 1967-71. No pro playing experience. College coach: Florida 1971-73, 1975, Louisville 1974, 1985-88, Texas 1976, Vanderbilt 1977-78, Auburn 1979-80. Pro scout: Tampa Bay Bandits (USFL) 1981-83. Pro coach: Joined Redskins in 1989.

Bobby DePaul, administrative assistant, defensive assistant; born January 29, 1963, Cheverly, Md., lives in Bowie, Md. Linebacker Maryland 1982-83. No pro playing experience. College coach: Catholic University 1986-88. Pro coach: Joined Redskins in 1989.

Rod Dowhower, offensive assistant, passing game; born April 15, 1943, Ord, Neb., lives in Ashburn, Va. Quarterback San Diego State 1963-65. No pro playing experience. College coach: San Diego State 1966-72. UCLA 1974-75, Boise State 1976, Stanford 1977-79 (head coach 1979). Pro coach: St. Louis Cardinals 1973, 1982-84, Denver Broncos 1980-81, Indianapolis Colts 1985-86 (head coach), Atlanta Falcons 1987-89, joined Redskins in 1990.

Jim Hanifan, offensive line; born September 21, 1933, Compton, Calif., lives in Reston, Va. Tight end California 1952-54. Pro tight end Toronto Argonauts (CFL) 1955. College coach: Glendale, Calif., J.C. 1964-66, Utah 1967-70, California 1971-72, San Diego State 1972-73. Pro coach: St. Louis Cardinals 1974-85 (head coach 1980-85), Atlanta Falcons 1987-89 (interim head coach last four games of 1989), joined Redskins in 1990.

Larry Peccatiello, defensive coordinator; born December 21, 1935, Newark, N.J., lives in Warrenton, Va. Receiver William & Mary 1955-58. No pro playing experience. College coach: William & Mary 1961-68, Navy 1969-70, Rice 1971. Pro coach: Houston Oilers 1972-75, Seattle Seahawks 1976-80, joined Redskins in 1981.

Washington Redskins 1991 First-Year Roster

Name	Pos.	Ht.	Wt.	Birth-date	College	Hometown	How Acq.
Batson, Walter	WR	5-10	175	3/17/69	Stanford	Miami, Fla.	FA
Beatty, Dan	C	6-3	270	9/18/67	Ohio State	East Liverpool, Ohio	FA
Bell, Charles	CB	5-10	170	5/15/68	Baylor	Waco, Tex.	D9
Bradford, Jack	LB	6-3	226	5/8/68	Maryland	Columbia, Md.	FA
Cahoon, Victor	WR	5-9	180	12/20/68	Arizona State	Manassas, Va.	FA
Cash, Keith	TE	6-4	214	8/7/69	Texas	San Antonio, Tex.	D7
Elliott, Shane	T	6-3	290	12/26/68	Weber State	Provo, Utah	FA
Ervins, Ricky	RB	5-7	200	12/7/68	Southern California	Pasadena, Calif.	D3
Fruge, Gene	DT	6-3	275	9/6/67	Southern California	San Jose, Calif.	FA
Gulledge, David	CB-S	6-1	203	10/26/67	Jacksonville State	Pell City, Ala.	D11
Howard, Reggie	DE	6-3	270	1/21/68	Baylor	Plano, Tex.	FA
Jenkins, James	TE	6-2	235	8/17/67	Rutgers	Staten Island, N.Y.	FA
Johnson, Brian	LB	6-2	225	10/1/67	Mesa, Colo.	Colorado Springs, Colo.	FA
McCardell, Kennan	WR	6-1	185	1/6/70	Nevada-Las Vegas	Houston, Tex.	D12
McCartin, Matt	T	6-5	275	1/26/68	Penn State	Highland Park, Tex.	FA
Pearson, Jeff	C	6-3	270	12/11/67	Michigan State	Chicago, Ill.	FA
Ransom, Dennis	TE	6-3	248	10/14/67	Texas A&M	Italy, Tex.	D6
Rayam, Thomas (1)	DE	6-6	285	1/3/68	Alabama	Orlando, Fla.	FA
Rogers, Ted	LB	6-2	240	11/10/69	Williams	Bethesda, Md.	FA
Shale, Cris	P	6-0	170	6/27/68	Bowling Green	Beaver Creek, Ohio	D10
Spencer, Jimmy	CB	5-9	180	3/29/69	Florida	South Bay, Fla.	D8
Stearns, Chris	G	6-5	280	5/13/68	Virginia	Fairfax, Va.	FA
Willingham, Gary	DE	6-2	260	9/15/68	Howard	Atlanta, Ga.	FA
Wilson, Bobby	DT	6-2	276	3/4/68	Michigan State	Chicago, Ill.	D1

The term NFL Rookie is defined as a player who is in his first season of professional football and has not been on the roster of another professional football team for any regular-season or postseason games. A Rookie is designated by an "R" on NFL rosters. Players who have been active in another professional football league or players who have NFL experience, including either preseason training camp or being on an active roster for fewer than three regular-season or postseason games, are termed NFL First-Year Players. An NFL First-Year Player is designated by a "1" on NFL rosters. Thereafter, a player on an NFL active roster for at least three regular-season or postseason games is credited with an additional year of NFL playing experience.

NOTES

Richie Petitbon, assistant head coach-defense; born April 18, 1938, New Orleans, La., lives in Vienna, Va. Quarterback-defensive back Tulane 1955-58. Pro defensive back Chicago Bears 1959-67, Los Angeles Rams 1969-70, Washington Redskins 1971-73. Pro coach: Houston Oilers 1974-77, joined Redskins in 1978.

Dan Riley, conditioning; born October 19, 1949, Syracuse, N.Y., lives in Herndon, Va. No college or pro playing experience. College coach: Army 1973-76, Penn State 1977-81. Pro coach: Joined Redskins in 1982.

Wayne Sevier, special teams; born July 3, 1941, San Diego, Calif., lives in Broad Run, Va. Quarterback Chaffey, Calif., J.C. 1960, San Diego State 1961-62. No pro playing experience. College coach: California Western 1968-69. Pro coach: St. Louis Cardinals 1974-75, Atlanta Falcons 1976, San Diego Chargers 1979-80, 1987-88, Washington Redskins 1981-86, rejoined Redskins in 1989.

Warren Simmons, tight ends; born February 25, 1942, Poughkeepsie, N.Y., lives in Ashburn, Va. Center San Diego State 1963-65. No pro playing experience. College coach: Cal State-Fullerton 1972-75, Cerritos, Calif., J.C. 1976-80. Pro coach: Joined Redskins in 1981.

Charley Taylor, wide receivers; born September 28, 1942, Grand Prairie, Tex., lives in Reston, Va. Running back Arizona State 1961-63. Pro running back-wide receiver Washington Redskins 1964-76. Pro coach: Joined Redskins in 1982.

Emmitt Thomas, defensive backs; born June 4, 1943, Angleton,Tex., lives in Reston, Va. Quarteback-wide receiver Bishop (Tex.) College 1963-65. Pro defensive back Kansas City Chiefs 1966-78. College coach: Central Missouri State 1979-80. Pro coach: St. Louis Cardinals 1981-85, joined Redskins in 1986.

LaVern Torgeson, defensive line; born February 28, 1929, LaCrosse, Wash., lives in Fairfax, Va. Center-linebacker Washington State 1948-50. Pro linebacker Detroit Lions 1951-54, Washington Redskins 1955-58. Pro coach: Washington Reskins 1959-61, 1971-77, Pittsburgh Steelers 1962-68, Los Angeles Rams 1969-70, 1978-80, rejoined Redskins in 1981.

Steve Wetzel, assistant strength; born May 11, 1963, Washington, D.C., lives in Fairfax, Va. No college or pro playing experience. College coach: Maryland 1985-89, George Mason 1990. Pro coach: Joined Redskins in 1990.

1990 SEASON IN REVIEW

Trades

1990 Interconference Trades

Running back **Greg Bell** from the Los Angeles Rams to the Los Angeles Raiders for a draft choice (6/20).

Running back **Lorenzo Hampton** from Denver to Dallas for a draft choice (7/28).

Quarterback **Chris Chandler** from Indianapolis to Tampa Bay for a draft choice (7/31).

Quarterback **Don McPherson** from Philadelphia to Houston for a draft choice (8/3).

Tackle **Ken Reeves** from Philadelphia to Cleveland for a draft choice (8/7).

Tight end **David Little** from Denver to Phoenix for a draft choice (8/15).

Center **Dale Hellestrae** from the Los Angeles Raiders to Dallas for a draft choice (8/20).

Defensive back **Carl Carter** from Phoenix to Cincinnati for linebacker **Chris Chenault** (8/21).

Defensive tackle **Tim Johnson** from Pittsburgh to Washington for a draft choice (8/23).

Guard **Dave Widell** from Dallas to Denver for a draft choice (8/24).

Wide receiver **John Ford** from Detroit to Seattle for a draft choice (8/27).

Punter **Keith English** from San Diego to the Los Angeles Rams for a draft choice (8/28).

Tackle **Ronnie Lee** from Atlanta to Seattle for a draft choice (8/28).

Guard **Mike Zandofsky** from Phoenix to San Diego for a draft choice (8/29).

Defensive end **Jim Skow** from Cincinnati to Tampa Bay for defensive back **Roderick Jones** (9/1).

Running back **Alonzo Highsmith** from Houston to Dallas for a draft choice (9/3).

Nose tackle **Shawn Lee** from Atlanta to Miami for a draft choice (9/3).

Guard **John Gesek** from the Los Angeles Raiders to Dallas for a draft choice (9/3).

Running back **Roger Vick** from the New York Jets to Philadelphia for a draft choice (9/3).

Running back **Brent Fullwood** from Green Bay to Cleveland for a draft choice (10/9).

Defensive end **David Galloway** from Phoenix to Denver for a draft choice (10/16).

1991 Interconference Trades

Cornerback **Vestee Jackson** from Chicago to Miami for defensive end **Eric Kumerow** (1/31).

Linebacker **Winston Moss** from Tampa Bay to the Los Angeles Raiders for the Raiders' third- and fifth-round choices in 1991. Tampa Bay selected running back **Robert Wilson** (Texas A&M) and guard **Tim Ryan** (Notre Dame) (4/22).

Linebacker **John Levelis** from San Francisco to the New York Jets for past considerations (4/16).

New England's first-round choice in 1991 to Dallas for Minnesota's first-round choice and Dallas's second-round choice in 1991 plus undisclosed considerations. Dallas selected nose tackle **Russell Maryland** (Miami). New England selected tackle **Pat Harlow** (Southern California) and defensive back **Jerome Henderson** (Clemson) (4/20).

Cornerback **Tim McKyer** from Miami to Atlanta for the Falcons' third-round choice and Miami's twelfth-round choice (previously obtained by Atlanta) in 1991. Miami selected running back **Aaron Craver** (Fresno State) and defensive tackle **Joe Brunson** (Tennessee-Chattanooga) (4/22).

New Orleans's first-round choice in 1991 from Dallas to New England for Houston's first-round choice and Buffalo's fourth-round choice in 1991. New England selected running back **Leonard Russell** (Arizona State). Dallas subsequently traded Houston's first-round choice in 1991 to Washington and selected defensive end **Kevin Harris** (Texas Southern) (4/21).

Cincinnati's second-round choice in 1991 to San Francisco for Miami's second-round choice and the 49ers' fourth-round choice in 1991. San Francisco selected running back **Ricky Watters** (Notre Dame). Cincinnati selected defensive tackle **Lamar Rogers** (Auburn) and wide receiver **Rob Carpenter** (Syracuse) (4/21).

Washington's second-round choice in 1991 and fifth-round choice in 1992 to San Diego for the Chargers' first-round choice in 1992. San Diego selected guard **Eric Moten** (Michigan State) (4/21).

Green Bay's third-round choice in 1991 to the New York Jets for the Jets' third- and fifth-round choices in 1991. New York selected linebacker **Morris Lewis** (Georgia). Green Bay selected defensive end **Don Davey** (Wisconsin) and traded the Jets' fifth-round choice to Miami (4/22).

Running back **Gaston Green** and the Los Angeles Rams' fourth-round choice in 1991 to Denver for tackle **Gerald Perry** and the Broncos' twelfth-round choice in 1991. Denver selected wide receiver **Derrick Russell** (Arkansas). Los Angeles selected tackle **Jeff Pahukoa** (Washington) (4/22).

The New York Jets' fifth-round choice in 1991 from Green Bay to Miami for the Dolphins' fifth- and sixth-round choices in 1991. Miami selected guard **Eugene Williams** (Iowa State). Green Bay selected punter **Jeff Fite** (Memphis State) and center **Joe Garten** (Colorado) (4/22).

Minnesota's sixth-round choice in 1991 to the Los Angeles Raiders for the Raiders' sixth-round choice and Dallas's seventh-round choice (previously obtained from Minnesota) in 1991. The Raiders selected defensive tackle **Nolan Harrison** (Indiana). Minnesota selected defensive back **Todd Scott** (Southwestern Louisiana) and defensive back **Tripp Welborne** (Michigan) (4/22).

1990 AFC Trades

Running back **Napoleon McCallum** from San Diego to the Los Angeles Raiders for a draft choice (4/27).

Wide receiver **Jamie Holland** from San Diego to the Los Angeles Raiders for a draft choice (5/4).

Linebacker **Willie Walker** from Seattle to the New York Jets for a draft choice (7/27).

Linebacker **Joe Kelly** and tackle **Scott James** from Cincinnati to the New York Jets for wide receiver **Reggie Rembert** (8/27).

Guard **Eric Still** from Houston to New England for a draft choice (8/27).

Linebacker **Alex Gordon** from the New York Jets to the Los Angeles Raiders for defensive back **Dennis Price** (10/15).

Defensive back **Vann McElroy** from the Los Angeles Raiders to Seattle for a draft choice (10/16).

1991 AFC Trades

Tackle **Ron Mattes** from Seattle to the New York Jets for a future draft choice (1/31).

Tackle **Irv Eatman** from Kansas City to the New York Jets for defensive end **Ron Stallworth** (2/1).

Linebacker **John Grimsley** from Houston to Miami for the Dolphins' third-round choice in 1991. Houston selected tackle **Kevin Donnalley** (North Carolina) (4/21).

Houston's first-round choice in 1991 to New England for the Patriots' second-round choice in 1991 and Seattle's fourth-round choice in 1991. New England subsequently traded Houston's first-round choice in 1991 to Dallas. Houston selected defensive back **Mike Dumas** (Indiana) and defensive tackle **David Rocker** (Auburn) (4/21).

Seattle's second-round choice in 1991 to the Los Angeles Raiders for the Raiders' second-round choice and New Orleans's fourth-round choice in 1991. Los Angeles selected running back **Nick Bell** (Iowa). Seattle selected wide receiver **Doug Thomas** (Clemson) and kicker **John Kasay** (Georgia) (4/21).

Denver's fourth-round choice in 1991 from New England to Pittsburgh for the Steelers' fourth- and fifth-round choices in 1991. Pittsburgh selected defensive back **Sammy Walker** (Texas Tech). New England traded Pittsburgh's fourth-round choice in 1991 to the Los Angeles Raiders and traded Pittsburgh's fifth-round choice in 1991 to San Diego (4/22).

Pittsburgh's fourth-round choice in 1991 from New England to the Los Angeles Raiders for Dallas's fifth-round choice in 1991 and the Raiders' fourth-round choice in 1992. Los Angeles selected wide receiver **Raghib Ismail** (Notre Dame). New England selected tight end **Ben Coates** (Livingstone) (4/22).

New England's fifth-round choice in 1991 from Pittsburgh to San Diego for the Los Angeles Raiders' eleventh-round choice in 1991 and fourth-round choice in 1992. San Diego selected defensive back **Floyd Fields** (Arizona State). New England selected punter **Paul Alsbury** (Southwest Texas State) (4/22).

Defensive end **Bob Buczkowski** from Cleveland to Seattle for the Seahawks' ninth-round choice in 1991. Cleveland selected wide receiver **Shawn Wiggins** (Wyoming) (4/22).

1990 NFC Trades

Quarterback **Chuck Long** from Detroit to the Los Angeles Rams for a draft choice (5/2).

Running back **Greg Paterra** from Atlanta to Detroit for a draft choice (8/21).

Tight end **Robert Awalt** from Phoenix to Dallas for a draft choice (8/29).

Defensive end **Robert Goff** from Tampa Bay to New Orleans for a draft choice (9/3).

Defensive tackle **Eric Williams** from Detroit to Washington for running back **James Wilder** and a draft choice (9/13).

Quarterback **Steve Walsh** from Dallas to New Orleans for a draft choice (9/25).

1991 NFC Trades

Green Bay's first-round choice in 1991 to Philadelphia for the Eagles' first-round choice in 1991 and first-round choice in 1992. Philadelphia selected tackle **Antone Davis** (Tennessee). Green Bay selected defensive back **Vinnie Carr** (Ohio State) (4/21).

Houston's first-round choice in 1991 from Dallas to Washington for the Redskins' first- and fifth-round choices in 1991. Washington selected defensive tackle **Bobby Wilson** (Michigan State). Dallas selected defensive tackle **Kelvin Pritchett** (Mississippi) and linebacker **Darrick Brownlow** (Illinois) (4/22).

The rights to defensive tackle **Kelvin Pritchett** (Mississippi) from Dallas to Detroit for the Lions' second- and third-round choices in 1991 and Miami's fourth-round choice in 1991. Dallas selected linebacker **Dixon Edwards** (Michigan State), guard **James Richards** (California), and defensive end **Tony Hill** (Tennessee-Chattanooga) (4/21).

San Francisco's third-round choice in 1991 to Green Bay for the Packers' fourth- and fifth-round choices in 1991. Green Bay selected running back **Chuck Webb** (Tennessee). San Francisco selected linebacker **Mitch Donahue** (Wyoming) and defensive back **Merton Hanks** (Iowa) (4/22).

1990 PRESEASON STANDINGS

American Football Conference

Eastern Division

	W	L	T	Pct.	Pts.	OP
N.Y. Jets	2	2	0	.500	58	46
Miami	1	3	0	.250	54	69
Buffalo	0	4	0	.000	49	107
Indianapolis	0	4	0	.000	47	63
New Eng.†	0	4	0	.000	48	132

Central Division

	W	L	T	Pct.	Pts.	OP
Pittsburgh†	2	2	0	.500	83	71
Cincinnati	1	3	0	.250	71	100
Houston	1	3	0	.250	68	75
Cleveland*	1	4	0	.200	68	105

Western Division

	W	L	T	Pct.	Pts.	OP
L.A. Rdrs.***	4	1	0	.800	103	54
Seattle**	4	1	0	.800	94	42
San Diego	3	1	0	.750	94	105
Denver**	3	2	0	.600	91	72
K.C.††	1	3	0	.250	51	88

**Includes Hall of Fame Game*
***Includes American Bowl '90 in Tokyo*
****Includes American Bowl '90 in London*
†Includes American Bowl '90 in Montreal
††Includes American Bowl '90 in Berlin

National Football Conference

Eastern Division

	W	L	T	Pct.	Pts.	OP
N.Y. Giants	4	0	0	1.000	78	33
Washington	3	1	0	.750	122	78
Philadelphia	2	2	0	.500	56	67
Dallas	1	3	0	.250	56	80
Phoenix	0	4	0	.000	39	103

Central Division

	W	L	T	Pct.	Pts.	OP
Detroit	4	0	0	1.000	119	68
Chicago*	4	1	0	.800	78	42
Minnesota	3	1	0	.750	75	61
Tampa Bay	3	1	0	.750	100	51
Green Bay	1	3	0	.250	65	82

Western Division

	W	L	T	Pct.	Pts.	OP
Atlanta	4	0	0	1.000	127	72
N.O.***	4	1	0	.800	88	84
L.A. Rams††	2	2	0	.500	83	77
San Fran.	1	3	0	.250	78	106

AFC Preseason Results—Team By Team

Eastern Division

BUFFALO (0-4)

6	*N.Y. Giants	20
13	Detroit	24
23	New Orleans	28
7	Chicago	35
49		107

INDIANAPOLIS (0-4)

7	*Denver	16
10	Seattle	13
16	*Philadelphia	17
14	New Orleans	17
47		63

MIAMI (1-3)

6	Chicago	10
14	Philadelphia	23
17	*Denver	16
17	*Minnesota	20
54		69

NEW ENGLAND (0-4)

14	Pittsburgh (ABM)	30
10	Tampa Bay	44
10	*Cincinnati (OT)	13
14	*Atlanta	45
48		132

N.Y. JETS (2-2)

17	Philadelphia	6
20	Kansas City	0
7	N.Y. Giants	17
14	Tampa Bay	23
58		46

Central Division

CINCINNATI (1-3)

17	Tampa Bay	30
17	Atlanta	34
13	New Eng. (OT)	10
24	*Detroit	26
71		100

CLEVELAND (1-4)

0	Chicago (HOF)	13
25	Green Bay	10
20	*Minnesota	23
13	*Washington	31
10	N.Y. Giants	28
68		105

HOUSTON (1-3)

10	*Detroit	34
10	*N.Y. Giants	13
21	Minnesota	22
27	Dallas	6
68		75

PITTSBURGH (2-2)

30	New Eng. (ABM)	14
24	Washington	27
9	Dallas	20
20	*Philadelphia	10
83		71

Western Division

DENVER (3-2)

10	Seattle (ABT)	7
16	Indianapolis	7
24	*San Francisco	27
16	Miami	17
25	*Phoenix	14
91		72

KANSAS CITY (1-3)

3	L.A. Rams (ABB)	19
0	*N.Y. Jets	20
21	Detroit	35
27	*Green Bay	14
51		88

L.A. RAIDERS (4-1)

10	New Orl. (ABL)	17
23	San Francisco	13
16	*Dallas	14
20	Chicago	3
34	*San Diego	7
103		54

SAN DIEGO (3-1)

28	*Dallas	16
30	L.A. Rams	27
29	*San Francisco	28
7	L.A. Raiders	34
94		105

SEATTLE (4-1)

7	Denver (ABT)	10
34	Phoenix	9
13	*Indianapolis	10
10	*Tampa Bay	3
30	San Francisco	10
94		42

NFC Preseason Results—Team By Team

Eastern Division

DALLAS (1-3)

16	San Diego	28
14	L.A. Raiders	16
20	*Pittsburgh	9
6	*Houston	27
56		80

N.Y. GIANTS (4-0)

20	Buffalo	6
13	Houston	10
17	*N.Y. Jets	7
28	*Cleveland	10
78		33

PHILADELPHIA (2-2)

6	*N.Y. Jets	17
23	*Miami	14
17	Indianapolis	16
10	Pittsburgh	20
56		67

PHOENIX (0-4)

9	*Seattle	34
9	*Chicago	17
7	L.A. Rams	27
14	Denver	25
39		103

WASHINGTON (3-1)

27	Atlanta	31
27	*Pittsburgh	24
31	Cleveland	13
37	*L.A. Rams	10
122		78

Central Division

CHICAGO (4-1)

13	Cleveland (HOF)	0
10	*Miami	6
17	Phoenix	9
3	*L.A. Raiders	20
35	Buffalo	7
78		42

DETROIT (4-0)

34	Houston	10
24	*Buffalo	13
35	*Kansas City	21
26	Cincinnati	24
119		68

GREEN BAY (1-3)

10	*Cleveland	25
27	New Orleans	13
14	Atlanta	17
14	Kansas City	27
65		82

MINNESOTA (3-1)

10	*New Orleans	13
23	Cleveland	20
22	*Houston	21
20	Miami	17
75		71

TAMPA BAY (3-1)

30	*Cincinnati	17
44	New England	10
3	Seattle	10
23	*N.Y. Jets	14
100		51

Western Division

ATLANTA (4-0)

31	Washington	27
34	*Cincinnati	17
17	Green Bay	14
45	New England	14
127		72

L.A. RAMS (2-2)

19	Kansas City (ABB)	3
27	*San Diego	30
27	*Phoenix	7
10	Washington	37
83		77

NEW ORLEANS (4-1)

17	L.A. Raid. (ABL)	10
13	Minnesota	10
13	Green Bay	27
28	*Buffalo	23
17	*Indianapolis	14
88		84

SAN FRANCISCO (1-3)

13	*L.A. Raiders	23
27	Denver	24
28	San Diego	29
10	Seattle	30
78		106

**denotes home game*
(OT) denotes overtime
(HOF) denotes Hall of Fame Game
(ABT) denotes American Bowl '90 in Tokyo
(ABL) denotes American Bowl '90 in London
(ABM) denotes American Bowl '90 in Montreal
(ABB) denotes American Bowl '90 in Berlin

1990 NFL STANDINGS

American Football Conference

Eastern Division

	W	L	T	Pct.	Pts.	OP
Buffalo	13	3	0	.813	428	263
Miami*	12	4	0	.750	336	242
Indianapolis	7	9	0	.438	281	353
N.Y. Jets	6	10	0	.375	295	345
New England	1	15	0	.063	181	446

Central Division

	W	L	T	Pct.	Pts.	OP
Cincinnati	9	7	0	.563	360	352
Houston*	9	7	0	.563	405	307
Pittsburgh	9	7	0	.563	292	240
Cleveland	3	13	0	.188	228	462

Western Division

	W	L	T	Pct.	Pts.	OP
L.A. Raiders	12	4	0	.750	337	268
Kansas City*	11	5	0	.688	369	257
Seattle	9	7	0	.563	306	286
San Diego	6	10	0	.375	315	281
Denver	5	11	0	.313	331	374

National Football Conference

Eastern Division

	W	L	T	Pct.	Pts.	OP
N.Y. Giants	13	3	0	.813	335	211
Philadelphia*	10	6	0	.625	396	299
Washington*	10	6	0	.625	381	301
Dallas	7	9	0	.438	244	308
Phoenix	5	11	0	.313	268	396

Central Division

	W	L	T	Pct.	Pts.	OP
Chicago	11	5	0	.688	348	280
Tampa Bay	6	10	0	.375	264	367
Detroit	6	10	0	.375	373	413
Green Bay	6	10	0	.375	271	347
Minnesota	6	10	0	.375	351	326

Western Division

	W	L	T	Pct.	Pts.	OP
San Francisco	14	2	0	.875	353	239
New Orleans*	8	8	0	.500	274	275
L.A. Rams	5	11	0	.313	345	412
Atlanta	5	11	0	.313	348	365

**Wild Card qualifiers for playoffs*

Cincinnati won AFC Central title based on best head-to-head record (3-1) vs. Houston (2-2) and Pittsburgh (1-3). Houston was Wild Card based on better conference record (8-4) than Seattle (7-5) and Pittsburgh (6-6). Philadelphia finished second in the NFC East based on better division record (5-3) than Washington (4-4). Tampa Bay was second in NFC Central based on 5-1 record vs. Detroit, Green Bay, and Minnesota. Detroit finished third based on best net division points (minus 8) vs. Green Bay (minus 40) in fourth. Minnesota was fifth based on 4-8 conference record. The Los Angeles Rams finished third in NFC West based on net points in division (plus 1) vs. Atlanta (minus 31).

First-Round Playoffs

AFC ..... Miami 17, Kansas City 16, January 5, at Miami
Cincinnati 41, Houston 14, January 6, at Cincinnati

NFC ..... Washington 20, Philadelphia 6, January 5, at Philadelphia
Chicago 16, New Orleans 6, January 6, at Chicago

Divisional Playoffs

AFC ..... Buffalo 44, Miami 34, January 12, at Buffalo
L.A. Raiders 20, Cincinnati 10, January 13, at Los Angeles

NFC ..... San Francisco 28, Washington 10, January 12, at San Francisco
N.Y. Giants 31, Chicago 3, January 13, at New York

Championship Games

AFC ..... Buffalo 51, L.A. Raiders 3, January 20, at Buffalo

NFC ..... N.Y. Giants 15, San Francisco 13, January 20, at San Francisco

SUPER BOWL XXV ..... N.Y. Giants 20, Buffalo 19, January 27, at Tampa Stadium, Tampa, Florida

AFC-NFC PRO BOWL ..... AFC 23, NFC 21, February 3, at Aloha Stadium, Honolulu, Hawaii

AFC Season Records—Team by Team

BUFFALO (13-3)		
26	*Indianapolis	10
7	at Miami	30
30	at N.Y. Jets	7
29	*Denver	28
38	*L.A. Raiders	24
	OPEN DATE	
30	*N.Y. Jets	27
27	at New England	10
42	at Cleveland	0
45	*Phoenix	14
14	*New England	0
24	at Houston	27
30	*Philadelphia	23
31	at Indianapolis	7
17	at N.Y. Giants	13
24	*Miami	14
14	at Washington	29
428		263

CINCINNATI (9-7)		
25	*N.Y. Jets	20
21	at San Diego	16
41	*New England	7
16	at Seattle	31
34	at L.A. Rams (OT)	31
17	at Houston	48
34	at Cleveland	13
17	at Atlanta	38
7	*New Orleans	21
	OPEN DATE	
27	*Pittsburgh	3
20	*Indianapolis	34
16	at Pittsburgh	12
17	*San Fran. (OT)	20
7	at L.A. Raiders	24
40	*Houston	20
21	*Cleveland	14
360		352

CLEVELAND (3-13)		
13	*Pittsburgh	3
21	at N.Y. Jets	24
14	*San Diego	24
0	at Kansas City	34
30	at Denver	29
20	at New Orleans	25
13	*Cincinnati	34
17	at San Francisco	20
0	*Buffalo	42
	OPEN DATE	
23	*Houston	35
13	*Miami	30
23	*L.A. Rams	38
14	at Houston	58
13	*Atlanta	10
0	at Pittsburgh	35
14	at Cincinnati	21
228		462

DENVER (5-11)		
9	at L.A. Raiders	14
24	*Kansas City	23
34	*Seattle (OT)	31
28	at Buffalo	29
29	*Cleveland	30
17	*Pittsburgh	34
27	at Indianapolis	17
	OPEN DATE	
22	at Minnesota	27
7	at San Diego	19
13	*Chicago (OT)	16
27	at Detroit	40
20	*L.A. Raiders	23
20	at Kansas City	31
20	*San Diego	10
12	at Seattle	17
22	*Green Bay	13
331		374

HOUSTON (9-7)		
27	at Atlanta	47
9	at Pittsburgh	20
24	*Indianapolis	10
17	at San Diego	7
21	*San Francisco	24
48	*Cincinnati	17
23	*New Orleans	10
12	*N.Y. Jets	17
13	at L.A. Rams	17
	OPEN DATE	
35	at Cleveland	23
27	*Buffalo	24
10	at Seattle (OT)	13
58	*Cleveland	14
27	at Kansas City	10
20	at Cincinnati	40
34	*Pittsburgh	14
405		307

INDIANAPOLIS (7-9)		
10	at Buffalo	26
14	*New England	16
10	at Houston	24
24	at Philadelphia	23
23	*Kansas City	19
	OPEN DATE	
17	*Denver	27
7	*Miami	27
7	*N.Y. Giants	24
13	at New England	10
17	*N.Y. Jets	14
34	at Cincinnati	20
17	at Phoenix	20
7	*Buffalo	31
29	at N.Y. Jets	21
35	*Washington	28
17	at Miami	23
281		353

KANSAS CITY (11-5)		
24	*Minnesota	21
23	at Denver	24
17	at Green Bay	3
34	*Cleveland	0
19	at Indianapolis	23
43	*Detroit	24
7	at Seattle	19
	OPEN DATE	
9	*L.A. Raiders	7
16	*Seattle	17
27	*San Diego	10
27	at L.A. Raiders	24
37	at New England	7
31	*Denver	20
10	*Houston	27
24	at San Diego	21
21	at Chicago	10
369		257

L.A. RAIDERS (12-4)		
14	*Denver	9
17	at Seattle	13
20	*Pittsburgh	3
24	*Chicago	10
24	at Buffalo	38
24	*Seattle	17
24	at San Diego	9
	OPEN DATE	
7	at Kansas City	9
16	*Green Bay	29
13	at Miami	10
24	*Kansas City	27
23	at Denver	20
38	at Detroit	31
24	*Cincinnati	7
28	at Minnesota	24
17	*San Diego	12
337		268

MIAMI (12-4)		
27	at New England	24
30	*Buffalo	7
3	at N.Y. Giants	20
28	at Pittsburgh	6
20	*N.Y. Jets	16
	OPEN DATE	
17	*New England	10
27	at Indianapolis	7
23	*Phoenix	3
17	at N.Y. Jets	3
10	*L.A. Raiders	13
30	at Cleveland	13
20	at Washington	42
23	*Philadelphia (OT)	20
24	*Seattle	17
14	at Buffalo	24
23	*Indianapolis	17
336		242

NEW ENGLAND (1-15)		
24	*Miami	27
16	at Indianapolis	14
7	at Cincinnati	41
13	*N.Y. Jets	37
20	*Seattle	33
	OPEN DATE	
10	at Miami	17
10	*Buffalo	27
20	at Philadelphia	48
10	*Indianapolis	13
0	at Buffalo	14
14	at Phoenix	34
7	*Kansas City	37
3	at Pittsburgh	24
10	*Washington	25
7	at N.Y. Jets	42
10	*N.Y. Giants	13
181		446

N.Y. JETS (6-10)		
20	at Cincinnati	25
24	*Cleveland	21
7	*Buffalo	30
37	at New England	13
16	at Miami	20
3	*San Diego	39
27	at Buffalo	30
17	at Houston	12
24	*Dallas	9
3	*Miami	17
14	at Indianapolis	17
7	*Pittsburgh	24
17	at San Diego	38
	OPEN DATE	
21	*Indianapolis	29
42	*New England	7
16	at Tampa Bay	14
295		345

PITTSBURGH (9-7)		
3	at Cleveland	13
20	*Houston	9
3	at L.A. Raiders	20
6	*Miami	28
36	*San Diego	14
34	at Denver	17
7	at San Francisco	27
41	*L.A. Rams	10
21	*Atlanta	9
	OPEN DATE	
3	at Cincinnati	27
24	at N.Y. Jets	7
12	*Cincinnati	16
24	*New England	3
9	at New Orleans	6
35	*Cleveland	0
14	at Houston	34
292		240

SAN DIEGO (6-10)		
14	at Dallas	17
16	*Cincinnati	21
24	at Cleveland	14
7	*Houston	17
14	at Pittsburgh	36
39	at N.Y. Jets	3
9	*L.A. Raiders	24
41	*Tampa Bay	10
31	at Seattle	14
19	*Denver	7
10	at Kansas City	27
10	*Seattle (OT)	13
38	*N.Y. Jets	17
	OPEN DATE	
10	at Denver	20
21	*Kansas City	24
12	at L.A. Raiders	17
315		281

SEATTLE (9-7)		
0	at Chicago	17
13	*L.A. Raiders	17
31	at Denver (OT)	34
31	*Cincinnati	16
33	at New England	20
17	at L.A. Raiders	24
19	*Kansas City	7
	OPEN DATE	
14	*San Diego	31
17	at Kansas City	16
21	*Minnesota	24
13	at San Diego (OT)	10
13	*Houston (OT)	10
20	at Green Bay	14
17	at Miami	24
17	*Denver	12
30	*Detroit	10
306		286

NFC Season Records—Team by Team

ATLANTA (5-11)

47	*Houston	27
14	at Detroit	21
13	at San Francisco	19
	OPEN DATE	
28	*New Orleans	27
35	*San Francisco	45
24	at L.A. Rams	44
38	*Cincinnati	17
9	at Pittsburgh	21
24	at Chicago	30
23	*Philadelphia	24
7	at New Orleans	10
17	at Tampa Bay	23
13	*Phoenix	24
10	at Cleveland	13
20	*L.A. Rams	13
26	*Dallas	7
348		365

CHICAGO (11-5)

17	*Seattle	0
31	at Green Bay	13
19	*Minnesota	16
10	at L.A. Raiders	24
27	*Green Bay	13
38	*L.A. Rams	9
	OPEN DATE	
31	at Phoenix	21
26	at Tampa Bay	6
30	*Atlanta	24
16	at Denver (OT)	13
13	at Minnesota	41
23	*Detroit (OT)	17
9	at Washington	10
21	at Detroit	38
27	*Tampa Bay	14
10	*Kansas City	21
348		280

DALLAS (7-9)

17	*San Diego	14
7	*N.Y. Giants	28
15	at Washington	19
17	at N.Y. Giants	31
14	*Tampa Bay	10
3	at Phoenix	20
17	at Tampa Bay	13
20	*Philadelphia	21
9	at N.Y. Jets	24
6	*San Francisco	24
24	at L.A. Rams	21
27	*Washington	17
17	*New Orleans	13
	OPEN DATE	
41	*Phoenix	10
3	at Philadelphia	17
7	at Atlanta	26
244		308

DETROIT (6-10)

21	*Tampa Bay	38
21	*Atlanta	14
20	at Tampa Bay	23
21	*Green Bay	24
34	at Minnesota	27
24	at Kansas City	43
	OPEN DATE	
27	at New Orleans	10
38	*Washington (OT)	41
7	*Minnesota	17
0	at N.Y. Giants	20
40	*Denver	27
17	at Chicago (OT)	23
31	*L.A. Raiders	38
38	*Chicago	21
24	at Green Bay	17
10	at Seattle	30
373		413

GREEN BAY (6-10)

36	*L.A. Rams	24
13	*Chicago	31
3	*Kansas City	17
24	at Detroit	21
13	at Chicago	27
14	at Tampa Bay	26
	OPEN DATE	
24	*Minnesota	10
20	*San Francisco	24
29	at L.A. Raiders	16
24	at Phoenix	21
20	*Tampa Bay	10
7	at Minnesota	23
14	*Seattle	20
0	at Philadelphia	31
17	*Detroit	24
13	at Denver	22
271		347

L.A. RAMS (5-11)

24	at Green Bay	36
35	at Tampa Bay	14
21	*Philadelphia	27
	OPEN DATE	
31	*Cincinnati (OT)	34
9	at Chicago	38
44	*Atlanta	24
10	at Pittsburgh	41
17	*Houston	13
7	*N.Y. Giants	31
21	*Dallas	24
28	at San Francisco	17
38	at Cleveland	23
20	*New Orleans	24
10	*San Francisco	26
13	at Atlanta	20
17	at New Orleans	20
345		412

MINNESOTA (6-10)

21	at Kansas City	24
32	*New Orleans	3
16	at Chicago	19
20	*Tampa Bay (OT)	23
27	*Detroit	34
24	at Philadelphia	32
	OPEN DATE	
10	at Green Bay	24
27	*Denver	22
17	at Detroit	7
24	at Seattle	21
41	*Chicago	13
23	*Green Bay	7
15	at N.Y. Giants	23
13	at Tampa Bay	26
24	*L.A. Raiders	28
17	*San Francisco	20
351		326

NEW ORLEANS (8-8)

12	*San Francisco	13
3	at Minnesota	32
28	*Phoenix	7
	OPEN DATE	
27	at Atlanta	28
25	*Cleveland	20
10	at Houston	23
10	*Detroit	27
21	at Cincinnati	7
35	*Tampa Bay	7
17	at Washington	31
10	*Atlanta	7
13	at Dallas	17
24	at L.A. Rams	20
6	*Pittsburgh	9
13	at San Francisco	10
20	*L.A. Rams	17
274		275

N.Y. GIANTS (13-3)

27	*Philadelphia	20
28	at Dallas	7
20	*Miami	3
31	*Dallas	17
	OPEN DATE	
24	at Washington	20
20	*Phoenix	19
21	*Washington	10
24	at Indianapolis	7
31	at L.A. Rams	7
20	*Detroit	0
13	at Philadelphia	31
3	at San Francisco	7
23	*Minnesota	15
13	*Buffalo	17
24	at Phoenix	21
13	at New England	10
335		211

PHILADELPHIA (10-6)

20	at N.Y. Giants	27
21	*Phoenix	23
27	at L.A. Rams	21
23	*Indianapolis	24
	OPEN DATE	
32	*Minnesota	24
7	at Washington	13
21	at Dallas	20
48	*New England	20
28	*Washington	14
24	at Atlanta	23
31	*N.Y. Giants	13
23	at Buffalo	30
20	at Miami (OT)	23
31	*Green Bay	0
17	*Dallas	3
23	at Phoenix	21
396		299

PHOENIX (5-11)

0	at Washington	31
23	at Philadelphia	21
7	at New Orleans	28
10	*Washington	38
	OPEN DATE	
20	*Dallas	3
19	at N.Y. Giants	20
21	*Chicago	31
3	at Miami	23
14	at Buffalo	45
21	*Green Bay	24
34	*New England	14
20	*Indianapolis	17
24	at Atlanta	13
10	at Dallas	41
21	*N.Y. Giants	24
21	*Philadelphia	23
268		396

SAN FRANCISCO (14-2)

13	at New Orleans	12
26	*Washington	13
19	*Atlanta	13
	OPEN DATE	
24	at Houston	21
45	at Atlanta	35
27	*Pittsburgh	7
20	*Cleveland	17
24	at Green Bay	20
24	at Dallas	6
31	*Tampa Bay	7
17	*L.A. Rams	28
7	*N.Y. Giants	3
20	at Cincinnati (OT)	17
26	at L.A. Rams	10
10	*New Orleans	13
20	at Minnesota	17
353		239

TAMPA BAY (6-10)

38	at Detroit	21
14	*L.A. Rams	35
23	*Detroit	20
23	at Minnesota (OT)	20
10	at Dallas	14
26	*Green Bay	14
13	*Dallas	17
10	at San Diego	41
6	*Chicago	26
7	at New Orleans	35
7	at San Francisco	31
10	at Green Bay	20
23	*Atlanta	17
	OPEN DATE	
26	*Minnesota	13
14	at Chicago	27
14	*N.Y. Jets	16
264		367

WASHINGTON (10-6)

31	*Phoenix	0
13	at San Francisco	26
19	*Dallas	15
38	at Phoenix	10
	OPEN DATE	
20	*N.Y. Giants	24
13	*Philadelphia	7
10	at N.Y. Giants	21
41	at Detroit (OT)	38
14	at Philadelphia	28
31	*New Orleans	17
17	at Dallas	27
42	*Miami	20
10	*Chicago	9
25	at New England	10
28	at Indianapolis	35
29	*Buffalo	14
381		301

** denotes home game*
(OT) denotes overtime

Attendance figures as they appear in the following, and in the club-by-club sections starting on page 26, are turnstile counts and not paid attendance. Paid attendance totals are on page 203.

First Week Summaries

Standings

American Football Conference

Eastern Division

	W	L	T	Pct.	Pts.	OP
Buffalo	1	0	0	1.000	26	10
Miami	1	0	0	1.000	27	24
Indianapolis	0	1	0	.000	10	26
New England	0	1	0	.000	24	27
N.Y. Jets	0	1	0	.000	20	25

Central Division

	W	L	T	Pct.	Pts.	OP
Cincinnati	1	0	0	1.000	25	20
Cleveland	1	0	0	1.000	13	3
Houston	0	1	0	.000	27	47
Pittsburgh	0	1	0	.000	3	13

Western Division

	W	L	T	Pct.	Pts.	OP
Kansas City	1	0	0	1.000	24	21
L.A. Raiders	1	0	0	1.000	14	9
Denver	0	1	0	.000	9	14
San Diego	0	1	0	.000	14	17
Seattle	0	1	0	.000	0	17

National Football Conference

Eastern Division

	W	L	T	Pct.	Pts.	OP
Dallas	1	0	0	1.000	17	14
N.Y. Giants	1	0	0	1.000	27	20
Washington	1	0	0	1.000	31	0
Philadelphia	0	1	0	.000	20	27
Phoenix	0	1	0	.000	0	31

Central Division

	W	L	T	Pct.	Pts.	OP
Chicago	1	0	0	1.000	17	0
Green Bay	1	0	0	1.000	36	24
Tampa Bay	1	0	0	1.000	38	21
Detroit	0	1	0	.000	21	38
Minnesota	0	1	0	.000	21	24

Western Division

	W	L	T	Pct.	Pts.	OP
Atlanta	1	0	0	1.000	47	27
San Francisco	1	0	0	1.000	13	12
L.A. Rams	0	1	0	.000	24	36
New Orleans	0	1	0	.000	12	13

Sunday, September 9

Los Angeles Raiders 14, Denver 9—at Memorial Coliseum, attendance 54,206. Jerry Robinson and Terry McDaniel each had defensive scores as the Raiders defeated the Broncos. Trailing 6-0 in the third quarter, Robinson picked off John Elway's pass and ran five yards for a touchdown. McDaniel then returned a fumble 42 yards for a score late in the third quarter to give Los Angeles a 14-6 advantage. David Treadwell's three field goals provided the Broncos' only scoring.

Denver	3	3	0	3	— 9
L.A. Raiders	0	0	14	0	— 14

Den —FG Treadwell 42
Den —FG Treadwell 44
Raiders—Robinson 5 interception return (Jaeger kick)
Raiders—McDaniel 42 fumble recovery return (Jaeger kick)
Den —FG Treadwell 24

Atlanta 47, Houston 27—at Atlanta-Fulton County Stadium, attendance 56,222. Atlanta turned four turnovers into 24 points to overcome the Oilers. Former Houston head coach Jerry Glanville, making his debut as coach of the Falcons, defeated his former team. The Falcons took a 21-0 first-quarter lead on rookie running back Steve Broussard's six-yard run, Bobby Butler's fumble recovery in the end zone, and Jessie Tuggle's 65-yard fumble recovery return. Greg Davis added field goals for the Falcons from 39, 39, 36, and 51 yards, Andre Rison scored on a 26-yard pass from Chris Miller and Deion Sanders returned an interception 82 yards to complete Atlanta's scoring.

Houston	0	7	0	20	— 27
Atlanta	21	6	7	13	— 47

Atl —Broussard 6 run (Davis kick)
Atl —Butler recovered fumble in end zone (Davis kick)
Atl —Tuggle 65 fumble recovery return (Davis kick)
Atl —FG Davis 39
Atl —FG Davis 39
Hou—T. Jones 15 pass from Moon (Zendejas kick)
Atl —Rison 26 pass from Miller (Davis kick)
Atl —FG Davis 36
Hou—Givins 80 pass from Moon (Zendejas kick)
Hou—Givins 6 pass from Moon (Zendejas kick)
Hou—Ford 3 pass from Moon (kick failed)
Atl —FG Davis 51
Atl —Sanders 82 interception return (Davis kick)

Buffalo 26, Indianapolis 10—at Rich Stadium, attendance 78,899. Scott Norwood kicked four field goals, including three in the first half, as the Bills downed the Colts. Jim Kelly's three-yard touchdown pass to Butch Rolle and Norwood's field goals from 31 and 37 yards gave Buffalo a 16-3 halftime advantage. Colts rookie quarterback Jeff George completed a 25-yard scoring pass to Stanley Morgan midway through the third period to narrow the score to 16-10, but Norwood's 47-yard field goal and Thurman Thomas' six-yard touchdown run put the game away for Buffalo in the fourth quarter.

Indianapolis	3	0	7	0	— 10
Buffalo	3	13	0	10	— 26

Buff—FG Norwood 29
Ind —FG Biasucci 24
Buff—Rolle 3 pass from Kelly (Norwood kick)
Buff—FG Norwood 31
Buff—FG Norwood 37
Ind —Morgan 25 pass from George (Biasucci kick)
Buff—FG Norwood 47
Buff—Thomas 6 run (Norwood kick)

Green Bay 36, Los Angeles Rams 24—at Lambeau Field, attendance 57,685. Anthony Dilweg threw for three touchdowns, including two to tight end Ed West, as the Packers defeated the Rams. Dilweg, making his first NFL start, completed scoring passes to West (four yards) and Jeff Query (47) in the first half. Dilweg also found West early in the fourth quarter with a seven-yard touchdown pass. Chris Jacke added field goals of 26, 53, and 40 yards for Green Bay. Dilweg, who completed 20 of 32 passes for 248 yards, was named NFC Offensive Player of the Week.

L.A. Rams	7	7	3	7	— 24
Green Bay	0	17	3	16	— 36

Rams—Warner 6 run (Lansford kick)
GB —West 4 pass from Dilweg (Jacke kick)
GB —FG Jacke 26
Rams—Anderson 40 pass from Everett (Lansford kick)
GB —Query 47 pass from Dilweg (Jacke kick)
GB —FG Jacke 53
Rams—FG Lansford 41
GB —West 7 pass from Dilweg (Jacke kick)
GB —Fullwood 2 run (kick failed)
Rams—Holohan 2 pass from Everett (Lansford kick)
GB —FG Jacke 40

Miami 27, New England 24—at Foxboro Stadium, attendance 45,305. Dan Marino's seven-yard touchdown pass to Tony Paige with 1:46 remaining lifted the Dolphins over the Patriots. Miami running back Sammie Smith, who carried 23 times for a career-high 159 yards and a touchdown, earned AFC Offensive Player of the Week honors. The victory ended the Dolphins' five-game opening-day losing streak.

Miami	3	10	7	7	— 27
New England	7	14	3	0	— 24

Mia—FG Stoyanovich 31
NE —Fryar 22 pass from Grogan (Staurovsky kick)
Mia—FG Stoyanovich 37
NE —Stephens 1 run (Staurovsky kick)
NE —Cook 35 pass from Grogan (Staurovsky kick)
Mia—Martin 35 pass from Marino (Stoyanovich kick)
Mia—Smith 3 run (Stoyanovich kick)
NE —FG Staurovsky 42
Mia—Paige 7 pass from Marino (Stoyanovich kick)

Kansas City 24, Minnesota 21—at Arrowhead Stadium, attendance 68,363. Steve DeBerg passed for two touchdowns and Christian Okoye ran for another as the Chiefs defeated the Vikings. DeBerg connected on scoring passes to Bill Jones (four yards) and Todd McNair (22) in the first quarter. Wade Wilson threw an eight-yard touchdown pass to Herschel Walker to put Minnesota ahead 21-17, but Okoye ran two yards for a touchdown midway through the fourth quarter to give Kansas City the victory.

Minnesota	7	7	7	0	— 21
Kansas City	14	3	0	7	— 24

KC —B. Jones 4 pass from DeBerg (Lowery kick)
KC —McNair 22 pass from DeBerg (Lowery kick)
Minn—Walker 6 pass from Wilson (Igwebuike kick)
Minn—Jordan 26 pass from Wilson (Igwebuike kick)
KC —FG Lowery 43
Minn—Walker 8 pass from Wilson (Igwebuike kick)
KC —Okoye 2 run (Lowery kick)

Cincinnati 25, New York Jets 20—at Riverfront Stadium, attendance 56,167. The Bengals scored 15 points in the fourth quarter as they rallied to defeat the Jets. Trailing 20-10 midway through the final period, Cincinnati quarterback Boomer Esiason threw a three-yard touchdown pass to James Brooks and David Fulcher tackled New York quarterback Ken O'Brien for a safety to cut the Jets' lead to 20-19. Jim Breech then added two field goals from 44 and 37 yards for the game-winning points. Fulcher's interception with 24 seconds remaining secured the victory.

N.Y. Jets	0	10	7	3	— 20
Cincinnati	0	3	7	15	— 25

Cin —FG Breech 43
NYJ—Toon 46 pass from O'Brien (Leahy kick)
NYJ—FG Leahy 33
Cin —Brown 10 pass from Esiason (Breech kick)
NYJ—Toon 9 pass from O'Brien (Leahy kick)
NYJ—FG Leahy 26
Cin —Brooks 3 pass from Esiason (Breech kick)
Cin —Safety, Fulcher tackled O'Brien in end zone
Cin —FG Breech 44
Cin —FG Breech 37

Washington 31, Phoenix 0—at Robert F. Kennedy Stadium, attendance 52,649. Mark Rypien completed three touchdown passes as the Redskins shut out the Cardinals. Washington took a 14-0 halftime lead on Rypien's 37-yard touchdown pass to Ricky Sanders (set up by Darrell Green's interception) and his four-yard scoring pass to Earnest Byner (set up by Martin Mayhew's interception). Gary Clark scored on a 43-yard reception from Rypien and Alvin Walton returned an interception 57 yards for a touchdown in the third quarter to put the game out of reach. Chip Lohmiller's 29-yard field goal completed the scoring. Phoenix head coach Joe Bugel made his debut against his former team.

Phoenix	0	0	0	0	— 0
Washington	7	7	14	3	— 31

Wash—Sanders 37 pass from Rypien (Lohmiller kick)
Wash—Byner 4 pass from Rypien (Lohmiller kick)
Wash—Clark 43 pass from Rypien (Lohmiller kick)
Wash—Walton 57 interception return (Lohmiller kick)
Wash—FG Lohmiller 29

Cleveland 13, Pittsburgh 3—at Cleveland Stadium, attendance 78,298. Anthony Blaylock returned a fumble for a touchdown to highlight the Browns' win over the Steelers. Pittsburgh led 3-0 at halftime but Blaylock's 30-yard scoring return and Jerry Kauric's field goals from 28 and 47 yards put the game out of reach. The Steelers' defense registered seven sacks. The Browns' victory was their first season-opening win at home since 1978.

Pittsburgh	0	3	0	0	— 3
Cleveland	0	0	10	3	— 13

Pitt —FG Anderson 19
Clev—Blaylock 30 fumble recovery return (Kauric kick)
Clev—FG Kauric 28
Clev—FG Kauric 47

Dallas 17, San Diego 14—at Texas Stadium, attendance 48,063. Troy Aikman scored on a one-yard run late in fourth quarter to lead the Cowboys over the Chargers. Aikman connected with Dennis McKinnon for a 28-yard touchdown pass to give Dallas a 7-0 lead in the first period, but Mark Vlasic hit Craig McEwen with a 14-yard scoring pass and Marion Butts ran one yard for a score to put San Diego ahead 14-7 at halftime. Aikman directed a 53-yard drive to set up his game-winning touchdown run.

San Diego	7	7	0	0	— 14
Dallas	7	0	0	10	— 17

Dall—McKinnon 28 pass from Aikman (Willis kick)
SD —McEwen 14 pass from Vlasic (Reveiz kick)
SD —Butts 1 run (Reveiz kick)
Dall—FG Willis 31
Dall—Aikman 1 run (Willis kick)

Chicago 17, Seattle 0—at Soldier Field, attendance 64,400. Neal Anderson scored on a pair of touchdown runs as the Bears shut out the Seahawks. Anderson, who rushed 20 times for 101 yards, scored on runs of 17 and four yards. Chicago's defense recorded three sacks and had two interceptions while limiting Seattle to 132 total yards. The victory was Chicago's seventh consecutive opening-day win.

Seattle	0	0	0	0	— 0
Chicago	3	7	0	7	— 17

Chi—FG Butler 47
Chi—Anderson 17 run (Butler kick)
Chi—Anderson 4 run (Butler kick)

Tampa Bay 38, Detroit 21—at Pontiac Silverdome, attendance 56,692. Vinny Testaverde completed three touchdown passes and the Buccaneers' defense had six sacks to lead Tampa Bay past the Lions. Testaverde completed scoring passes to Ron Hall (54 yards), Bruce Perkins (eight), and Gary Anderson (19) to give Tampa Bay a 21-14 halftime lead. Reggie Cobb ran two yards for a touchdown and Steve Christie kicked a 22-yard field goal to increase the Buccaneers lead to 31-14 in the fourth quarter. Wayne Haddix's 62-yard interception return for a touchdown late in the fourth quarter finished Tampa Bay's scoring.

Tampa Bay	7	14	7	10	— 38
Detroit	14	0	0	7	— 21

TB —Hall 54 pass from Testaverde (Christie kick)
Det—Clark 26 pass from Peete (Murray kick)
Det—Sanders 1 run (Murray kick)
TB —Perkins 8 pass from Testaverde (Christie kick)
TB —Anderson 19 pass from Testaverde (Christie kick)

TB — Cobb 2 run (Christie kick)
TB — FG Christie 22
Det — Clark 16 pass from Gagliano (Murray kick)
TB — Haddix 62 interception return (Christie kick)

Sunday Night, September 9

New York Giants 27, Philadelphia 20—at Giants Stadium, attendance 76,202. David Meggett returned a punt 68 yards for a touchdown to lead the Giants past the Eagles. Trailing 10-6 in the third quarter, New York took a 13-10 lead on Phil Simms's 12-yard scoring pass to Rodney Hampton. Simms's 41-yard touchdown pass to Mark Ingram increased the Giants' lead to 27-10. Philadelphia scored 10 unanswered points in the fourth quarter, but could get no closer.

Philadelphia	3	7	0	10	—	20
N.Y. Giants	6	0	14	7	—	27

NYG — FG Allegre 38
NYG — FG Allegre 46
Phil — FG Ruzek 37
Phil — Toney 18 pass from Byars (Ruzek kick)
NYG — Hampton 12 pass from Simms (Allegre kick)
NYG — Meggett 68 punt return (Allegre kick)
NYG — Ingram 41 pass from Simms (Allegre kick)
Phil — Cunningham 1 run (Ruzek kick)
Phil — FG Ruzek 29

Monday, September 10

San Francisco 13, New Orleans 12—at Louisiana Superdome, attendance 68,629. Mike Cofer kicked a 38-yard field goal with nine seconds remaining to help the 49ers edge the Saints. Morten Andersen kicked three field goals (41, 39, and 28 yards) to give New Orleans a 9-3 advantage, but Joe Montana hit Brent Jones with a four-yard scoring pass to put San Francisco ahead 10-9 in the third quarter. Andersen then kicked a 32-yard field goal as the Saints regained the lead 12-10, but Montana drove the 49ers 60 yards to Cofer's game-winning kick.

San Francisco	3	0	7	3	—	13
New Orleans	3	6	0	3	—	12

SF — FG Cofer 52
NO — FG Andersen 41
NO — FG Andersen 39
NO — FG Andersen 28
SF — Jones 4 pass from Montana (Cofer kick)
NO — FG Andersen 32
SF — FG Cofer 38

Second Week Summaries

Standings

American Football Conference

Eastern Division

	W	L	T	Pct.	Pts.	OP
Miami	2	0	0	1.000	57	31
Buffalo	1	1	0	.500	33	40
New England	1	1	0	.500	40	41
N.Y. Jets	1	1	0	.500	44	46
Indianapolis	0	2	0	.000	24	42

Central Division

	W	L	T	Pct.	Pts.	OP
Cincinnati	2	0	0	1.000	46	36
Cleveland	1	1	0	.500	34	27
Pittsburgh	1	1	0	.500	23	22
Houston	0	2	0	.000	36	67

Western Division

	W	L	T	Pct.	Pts.	OP
L.A. Raiders	2	0	0	1.000	31	22
Denver	1	1	0	.500	33	37
Kansas City	1	1	0	.500	47	45
San Diego	0	2	0	.000	30	38
Seattle	0	2	0	.000	13	34

National Football Conference

Eastern Division

	W	L	T	Pct.	Pts.	OP
N.Y. Giants	2	0	0	1.000	55	27
Dallas	1	1	0	.500	24	42
Phoenix	1	1	0	.500	23	52
Washington	1	1	0	.500	44	26
Philadelphia	0	2	0	.000	41	50

Central Division

	W	L	T	Pct.	Pts.	OP
Chicago	2	0	0	1.000	48	13
Detroit	1	1	0	.500	42	52
Green Bay	1	1	0	.500	49	55
Minnesota	1	1	0	.500	53	27
Tampa Bay	1	1	0	.500	52	56

Western Division

	W	L	T	Pct.	Pts.	OP
San Francisco	2	0	0	1.000	39	25
Atlanta	1	1	0	.500	61	48
L.A. Rams	1	1	0	.500	59	50
New Orleans	0	2	0	.000	15	45

Sunday, September 16

Detroit 21, Atlanta 14—at Pontiac Silverdome, attendance 48,961. Rodney Peete threw two touchdown passes to lead the Lions past the Falcons. Detroit jumped to a 21-7 halftime lead on Peete's scoring passes of 12 yards to Terry Greer and five yards to Richard Johnson, and Barry Sanders's 17-yard run. Atlanta rookie running back Steve Broussard ran three yards for a touchdown to provide the game's only scoring in the second half.

Atlanta	7	0	7	0	—	14
Detroit	7	14	0	0	—	21

Det — Greer 12 pass from Peete (Murray kick)
Atl — Rison 10 pass from Miller (Davis kick)
Det — R. Johnson 5 pass from Peete (Murray kick)
Det — B. Sanders 17 run (Murray kick)
Atl — Broussard 3 run (Davis kick)

Miami 30, Buffalo 7—at Joe Robbie Stadium, attendance 68,490. Sammie Smith ran for two touchdowns as the Dolphins downed the Bills to break a six-game losing streak to Buffalo. Miami took a 16-0 halftime lead on Smith's two-yard run and Pete Stoyanovich's three field goals (23, 29, and 48 yards). Dan Marino's 17-yard scoring pass to Tony Paige early in the fourth quarter finished the Dolphins' scoring and put Miami ahead 30-0. Buffalo's Larry Kinnebrew ran one yard for a touchdown to prevent the shutout.

Buffalo	0	0	0	7	—	7
Miami	0	16	7	7	—	30

Mia — S. Smith 2 run (Stoyanovich kick)
Mia — FG Stoyanovich 23
Mia — FG Stoyanovich 29
Mia — FG Stoyanovich 48
Mia — S. Smith 1 run (Stoyanovich kick)
Mia — Paige 17 pass from Marino (Stoyanovich kick)
Buff — Kinnebrew 1 run (Norwood kick)

Chicago 31, Green Bay 13—at Lambeau Field, attendance 58,938. Jim Harbaugh passed for two touchdowns and ran for another to help the Bears overcome the Packers. Chicago led 17-10 in the first half on scoring runs by Neal Anderson (one yard) and Harbaugh (two), and Kevin Butler's 41-yard field goal. Chicago's defense recorded six sacks, including two each by Richard Dent and Trace Armstrong. Jim Morrissey's fumble recovery set up Harbaugh's 40-yard touchdown pass to Ron Morris in the third quarter. Harbaugh then hit Anderson for a 16-yard scoring pass in the fourth quarter to complete the scoring.

Chicago	0	17	7	7	—	31
Green Bay	7	3	3	0	—	13

GB — Woodside 10 run (Jacke kick)
Chi — FG Butler 41
Chi — Anderson 1 run (Butler kick)
Chi — Harbaugh 2 run (Butler kick)
GB — FG Jacke 37
Chi — Morris 40 pass from Harbaugh (Butler kick)
GB — FG Jacke 37
Chi — Anderson 16 pass from Harbaugh (Butler kick)

Cincinnati 21, San Diego 16—at San Diego Jack Murphy Stadium, attendance 48,098. Boomer Esiason threw three touchdown passes, including two to Eddie Brown, as the Bengals defeated the Chargers. Esiason connected with James Brooks (10 yards) and Brown (30) in the second quarter, and hit Brown with a 23-yard scoring pass to put the Bengals ahead 21-16 in the fourth quarter. Brown, who finished with 10 receptions for 178 yards, was named AFC Offensive Player of the Week.

Cincinnati	0	14	0	7	—	21
San Diego	13	3	0	0	—	16

SD — Harmon 36 pass from Tolliver (Reveiz kick)
SD — Caravello 17 pass from Tolliver (kick failed)
Cin — Brooks 10 pass from Esiason (Breech kick)
SD — FG Reveiz 19
Cin — Brown 30 pass from Esiason (Breech kick)
Cin — Brown 23 pass from Esiason (Breech kick)

New York Jets 24, Cleveland 21—at Giants Stadium, attendance 67,354. Freeman McNeil and Johnny Hector each ran for touchdowns to help the Jets overcome the Browns. McNeil (two yards) and Hector (six) had scoring runs in the first quarter to put New York ahead 14-7. The Jets then took a 24-7 halftime advantage on Pat Leahy's 47-yard field goal and Brad Baxter's one-yard run for a touchdown. The Browns narrowed the score to 24-21 on Bernie Kosar's four-yard pass to Reggie Langhorne and Leroy Hoard's nine-yard run, but could get no closer. Cleveland's Eric Metcalf returned the opening kickoff 98 yards for a touchdown to account for the Browns' other points.

Cleveland	7	0	7	7	—	21
N.Y. Jets	14	10	0	0	—	24

Clev — Metcalf 98 kickoff return (Kauric kick)
NYJ — McNeil 2 run (Leahy kick)
NYJ — Hector 6 run (Leahy kick)
NYJ — FG Leahy 47
NYJ — Baxter 1 run (Leahy kick)
Clev — Langhorne 4 pass from Kosar (Kauric kick)
Clev — Hoard 9 run (Kauric kick)

Los Angeles Raiders 17, Seattle 13—at Kingdome, attendance 61,889. Greg Bell's one-yard touchdown run with 1:26 remaining led the Raiders over the Seahawks. Bell's touchdown plunge capped a 65-yard drive. Jay Schroeder's 12-yard scoring pass to Mervyn Fernandez tied the game 10-10 in the fourth quarter. Seattle went ahead 13-10 with 6:07 left in the game on Norm Johnson's 19-yard field goal.

L.A. Raiders	3	0	0	14	—	17
Seattle	0	3	7	3	—	13

Raiders — FG Jaeger 47
Sea — FG Johnson 22
Sea — J.L. Williams 2 run (Johnson kick)
Raiders — Fernandez 12 pass from Schroeder (Jaeger kick)
Sea — FG Johnson 19
Raiders — Bell 1 run (Jaeger kick)

Los Angeles Rams 35, Tampa Bay 14—at Tampa Stadium, attendance 59,705. Jim Everett threw for 269 yards and four touchdowns as the Rams easily beat the Buccaneers. Los Angeles took a 28-7 halftime lead behind Everett's scoring passes to Buford McGee (six yards) and Henry Ellard (14) in the first period, and Robert Delpino (10) in the second quarter, along with Bobby Humphery's 44-yard interception return for a score. Everett and Delpino completed the Rams' scoring with a 42-yard touchdown pass in the third quarter.

L.A. Rams	14	14	7	0	—	35
Tampa Bay	0	7	0	7	—	14

Rams — McGee 6 pass from Everett (Lansford kick)
Rams — Ellard 14 pass from Everett (Lansford kick)
Rams — Delpino 10 pass from Everett (Lansford kick)
TB — Hill 48 pass from Testaverde (Christie kick)
Rams — Humphery 44 interception return (Lansford kick)
Rams — Delpino 42 pass from Everett (Lansford kick)
TB — G. Anderson 1 run (Christie kick)

New England 16, Indianapolis 14—at Hoosier Dome, attendance 49,256. Jason Staurovsky kicked three field goals to lift the Patriots over the Colts. Steve Grogan opened New England's scoring with a 27-yard touchdown pass to Hart Lee Dykes in the second quarter. Staurovsky kicked field goals from 39, 27, and 25 yards in the second half to complete the Patriots' scoring. New England's defense recorded two sacks and four interceptions. The victory was the Patriots' fourth straight over the Colts and their eleventh in 13 meetings.

New England	0	7	3	6	—	16
Indianapolis	7	0	0	7	—	14

Ind — Bentley 1 run (Biasucci kick)
NE — Dykes 27 pass from Grogan (Staurovsky kick)
NE — FG Staurovsky 39
NE — FG Staurovsky 27
NE — FG Staurovsky 25
Ind — Brooks 68 pass from George (Biasucci kick)

Minnesota 32, New Orleans 3—at Metrodome, attendance 56,272. Wade Wilson completed three touchdown passes as the Vikings rolled over the Saints to record their thirteenth consecutive victory at the Metrodome. Minnesota took an 18-3 halftime lead on Donald Igwebuike's three field goals (30, 48, and 38 yards), Wilson's 15-yard scoring pass to Anthony Carter, and Mark Dusbabek's safety. Wilson also threw scoring passes to Herschel Walker (five yards) and Steve Jordan (15) in the third quarter. The Vikings' defense forced five turnovers and had three sacks.

New Orleans	0	3	0	0	—	3
Minnesota	3	15	14	0	—	32

Minn — FG Igwebuike 30
Minn — Safety, Dusbabek tackled Hilliard in end zone
Minn — FG Igwebuike 48
NO — FG Andersen 37
Minn — A. Carter 15 pass from Wilson (Igwebuike kick)
Minn — FG Igwebuike 38
Minn — Walker 5 pass from Wilson (Igwebuike kick)
Minn — Jordan 15 pass from Wilson (Igwebuike kick)

New York Giants 28, Dallas 7—at Texas Stadium, attendance 61,090. Lawrence Taylor returned an interception for a score to highlight the Giants' win over the Cowboys. After a scoreless first quarter, Phil Simms scrambled for a four-yard score and Ottis Anderson ran one yard for a touchdown to put New York ahead 14-7 at halftime. In the second half, Simms connected with Mark Bavaro on a four-yard touchdown pass and Taylor returned an interception 11 yards for a score to put the game away. The Giants limited the Cowboys to nine first downs and held a 41:40 to 18:20 time-of-possession advantage.

N.Y. Giants	0	14	7	7	—	28
Dallas	0	7	0	0	—	7

NYG — Simms 4 run (Allegre kick)
NYG — Anderson 1 run (Allegre kick)
Dall — Wright 90 kickoff return (Willis kick)
NYG — Bavaro 4 pass from Simms (Allegre kick)
NYG — Taylor 11 interception return (Allegre kick)

Phoenix 23, Philadelphia 21—at Veterans Stadium, attendance 64,396. Al Del Greco's 42-yard field goal with 25 seconds remaining gave the Cardinals a come-from-behind win over the Eagles. Philadelphia led 21-14 midway through the fourth quarter, but Phoenix narrowed the score to 21-20 on two Del Greco field goals (25 and 50 yards). Timm Rosenbach led a 58-yard drive to set up Del Greco's decisive kick. The victory was Joe Bugel's first as Cardinals' head coach.

Phoenix	0	7	7	9	—	23
Philadelphia	14	0	7	0	—	21

Phil — Hargrove 34 pass from Cunningham (Ruzek kick)
Phil — Cunningham 1 run (Ruzek kick)
Phx — Johnson 22 run (Del Greco kick)
Phx — Thompson 1 run (Del Greco kick)
Phil — Sherman 2 pass from Cunningham (Ruzek kick)
Phx — FG Del Greco 25
Phx — FG Del Greco 50
Phx — FG Del Greco 42

San Francisco 26, Washington 13—at Candlestick Park, attendance 64,287. Joe Montana passed for two touchdowns and Mike Cofer kicked four field goals as the 49ers defeated the Redskins. San Francisco jumped to a 20-10 halftime lead on Montana's scoring passes of 12 yards to Jerry Rice and 49 yards to John Taylor, and Cofer's field goals of 31 and 30 yards. Cofer also added two field goals (26 and 34 yards) in the second half. Montana's 390 yards passing gave him 31,654 career yards, surpassing John Brodie's club record of 31,548.

Washington 0 10 3 0 — 13
San Francisco 3 17 3 3 — 26

SF —FG Cofer 31
SF —Rice 12 pass from Montana (Cofer kick)
Wash—FG Lohmiller 37
SF —Taylor 49 pass from Montana (Cofer kick)
Wash—Monk 35 pass from Rypien (Lohmiller kick)
SF —FG Cofer 30
Wash—FG Lohmiller 20
SF —FG Cofer 26
SF —FG Cofer 34

Sunday Night, September 16

Pittsburgh 20, Houston 9—at Three Rivers Stadium, attendance 54,814. David Johnson returned an interception 26 yards for a score and Rod Woodson returned a punt 52 yards for a touchdown to lift the Steelers over the Oilers. Johnson's return and Gary Anderson's 31-yard field goal put Pittsburgh ahead 10-7 at halftime. Houston scored a safety in the third quarter to narrow the score to 10-9, but Anderson's 27-yard field goal and Woodson's punt return in the fourth quarter put the game out of reach.

Houston 0 7 2 0 — 9
Pittsburgh 7 3 0 10 — 20

Pitt —D. Johnson 26 interception return (Anderson kick)
Hou—White 1 run (Zendejas kick)
Pitt —FG Anderson 31
Hou—Safety, Childress tackled Brister in end zone
Pitt —FG Anderson 27
Pitt —Woodson 52 punt return (Anderson kick)

Monday, September 17

Denver 24, Kansas City 23—at Mile High Stadium, attendance 75,277. David Treadwell's 22-yard field goal as time expired lifted the Broncos over the Chiefs. Denver took a 14-9 halftime lead on a pair of Bobby Humphrey touchdown runs (37 and six yards). The Broncos added another touchdown in the third quarter on John Elway's two-yard keeper. Steve DeBerg and Stephone Paige combined for two touchdowns for the Chiefs in the fourth quarter, including an 83-yard scoring completion with less than two minutes remaining to put the Chiefs ahead 23-21.

Kansas City 3 6 0 14 — 23
Denver 7 7 7 3 — 24

KC —FG Lowery 39
Den—Humphrey 37 run (Treadwell kick)
KC —FG Lowery 29
Den—Humphrey 6 run (Treadwell kick)
KC —FG Lowery 31
Den—Elway 2 run (Treadwell kick)
KC —Paige 16 pass from DeBerg (Lowery kick)
KC —Paige 83 pass from DeBerg (Lowery kick)
Den—FG Treadwell 22

Third Week Summaries

Standings

American Football Conference

Eastern Division	W	L	T	Pct.	Pts.	OP
Buffalo	2	1	0	.667	63	47
Miami	2	1	0	.667	60	51
New England	1	2	0	.333	47	82
N.Y. Jets	1	2	0	.333	51	76
Indianapolis	0	3	0	.000	34	66
Central Division						
Cincinnati	3	0	0	1.000	87	43
Cleveland	1	2	0	.333	48	51
Houston	1	2	0	.333	60	77
Pittsburgh	1	2	0	.333	26	42
Western Division						
L.A. Raiders	3	0	0	1.000	51	25
Denver	2	1	0	.667	67	68
Kansas City	2	1	0	.667	64	48
San Diego	1	2	0	.333	54	52
Seattle	0	3	0	.000	44	68

National Football Conference

Eastern Division	W	L	T	Pct.	Pts.	OP
N.Y. Giants	3	0	0	1.000	75	30
Washington	2	1	0	.667	63	41
Dallas	1	2	0	.333	39	61
Philadelphia	1	2	0	.333	68	71
Phoenix	1	2	0	.333	30	80
Central Division						
Chicago	3	0	0	1.000	67	29
Tampa Bay	2	1	0	.667	75	76
Detroit	1	2	0	.333	62	75
Green Bay	1	2	0	.333	52	72
Minnesota	1	2	0	.333	69	46
Western Division						
San Francisco	3	0	0	1.000	58	38
Atlanta	1	2	0	.333	74	67
L.A. Rams	1	2	0	.333	80	77
New Orleans	1	2	0	.333	43	52

Sunday, September 23

San Francisco 19, Atlanta 13—at Candlestick Park, attendance 62,858. Joe Montana threw for 398 yards and two touchdowns as the 49ers defeated the Falcons. Montana hit Jerry Rice with a 35-yard scoring pass and connected with Brent Jones with a 67-yard touchdown strike in the third quarter to put San Francisco ahead 19-10. Rice had eight receptions for 171 yards, while Jones had five for 125. Falcons wide receiver Andre Rison had 11 receptions for 128 yards.

Atlanta 3 0 7 3 — 13
San Francisco 0 5 14 0 — 19

Atl —FG Davis 37
SF—Safety, Miller forced out of end zone
SF—FG Cofer 47
SF—Rice 35 pass from Montana (Cofer kick)
Atl —Collins 7 pass from Miller (Davis kick)
SF—Jones 67 pass from Montana (Cofer kick)
Atl —FG Davis 35

Washington 19, Dallas 15—at Robert F. Kennedy Stadium, attendance 53,804. Chip Lohmiller kicked four field goals to help the Redskins over the Cowboys. Lohmiller, whose first two field goals (37 and 23 yards) gave Washington a 6-3 halftime lead, added two others in the third quarter (24 and 55). Early in the fourth quarter, Darrell Green returned an interception 18 yards for the Redskins' only touchdown. Washington's defense recorded eight sacks, had one fumble recovery, and two interceptions.

Dallas 0 3 3 9 — 15
Washington 3 3 6 7 — 19

Wash—FG Lohmiller 37
Dall —FG Willis 33
Wash—FG Lohmiller 23
Dall —FG Willis 41
Wash—FG Lohmiller 24
Wash—FG Lohmiller 55
Wash—Green 18 interception return (Lohmiller kick)
Dall —Smith 2 run (Willis kick)
Dall —Safety, Mojsiejenko ran out of end zone

Houston 24, Indianapolis 10—at Astrodome, attendance 50,093. Lorenzo White scored two touchdowns as the Oilers beat the Colts. White caught two scoring passes from Warren Moon (13 and 7 yards) to give Houston a 14-0 halftime lead. Tony Zendejas kicked a 30-yard field goal and Moon completed a six-yard touchdown strike to Ernest Givins in the second half to finish the Oilers' scoring. Moon, who completed 29 of 39 for 308 yards, improved his career passing yardage to 19,289, breaking George Blanda's club record (19,149).

Indianapolis 0 0 10 0 — 10
Houston 0 14 3 7 — 24

Hou—White 13 pass from Moon (Zendejas kick)
Hou—White 7 pass from Moon (Zendejas kick)
Ind —FG Biasucci 33
Hou—FG Zendejas 30
Ind —Beach 16 pass from Trudeau (Biasucci kick)
Hou—Givins 6 pass from Moon (Zendejas kick)

Kansas City 17, Green Bay 3—at Lambeau Field, attendance 58,817. Christian Okoye ran for a score and Stan Petry returned an interception for a touchdown to lead the Chiefs past the Packers. Okoye scored on a five-yard touchdown run in the second quarter to put Kansas City ahead 7-3 at halftime. The Chiefs put the game away on Nick Lowery's 20-yard field goal and Petry's 33-yard interception return for a touchdown in the fourth quarter. Kansas City's defense had six sacks and two fumble recoveries. Chris Jacke's 46-yard field goal in the second quarter provided the Packers' only score.

Kansas City 0 7 0 10 — 17
Green Bay 0 3 0 0 — 3

GB—FG Jacke 46
KC—Okoye 5 run (Lowery kick)
KC—FG Lowery 20
KC—Petry 33 interception return (Lowery kick)

New York Giants 20, Miami 3—at Giants Stadium, attendance 76,483. Ottis Anderson rushed for two touchdowns as the Giants defeated the Dolphins. Anderson scored on a pair of touchdown runs (one and two yards) and Raul Allegre kicked two field goals (22 and 45 yards) to finish the Giants' scoring. New York held Miami to 39 yards rushing and had a commanding 40:18 to 19:42 time-of-possession advantage. Anderson rushed for 72 yards to move into eighth place on the NFL's all-time rushing list with 9,433 yards.

Miami 0 0 3 0 — 3
N.Y. Giants 3 7 0 10 — 20

NYG—FG Allegre 22
NYG—Anderson 1 run (Allegre kick)
Mia —FG Stoyanovich 51
NYG—Anderson 2 run (Allegre kick)
NYG—FG Allegre 45

Chicago 19, Minnesota 16—at Soldier Field, attendance 65,420. Kevin Butler's fourth field goal of the game, a 52-yarder with four seconds remaining, lifted the Bears over the Vikings. Neal Anderson ran eight yards for a touchdown and Butler kicked two field goals (23 and 51 yards) to put Chicago ahead 13-6 at halftime. Butler's 32-yard field goal gave the Bears a 16-9 lead, but Wade Wilson's 17-yard touchdown pass to Hassan Jones tied the game 16-16 with 1:55 remaining. Minnesota mishandled a snap on a punt to set up Butler's decisive kick.

Minnesota 0 6 3 7 — 16
Chicago 3 10 3 3 — 19

Chi —FG Butler 23
Chi —FG Butler 51
Minn—FG Igwebuike 26
Chi —Anderson 8 run (Butler kick)
Minn—FG Igwebuike 24
Minn—FG Igwebuike 22
Chi —FG Butler 32
Minn—Jones 17 pass from Wilson (Igwebuike kick)
Chi —FG Butler 52

Cincinnati 41, New England 7—at Riverfront Stadium, attendance 56,470. Boomer Esiason completed two touchdown passes and Jim Breech set an NFL record as the Bengals crushed the Patriots. Cincinnati jumped to a commanding 31-7 halftime lead on Esiason's 42-yard scoring pass to Eddie Brown, Lee Johnson's four-yard pass to Rodney Holman on a fake field-goal attempt, scoring runs by Harold Green (three yards) and James Brooks (six), and Breech's 46-yard field goal. Breech's field goals and extra points gave him 152 consecutive games with a score, overtaking the NFL record of 151, held by former Vikings kicker Fred Cox (1963-1973).

New England 0 7 0 0 — 7
Cincinnati 17 14 3 7 — 41

Cin—FG Breech 46
Cin—Brown 42 pass from Esiason (Breech kick)
Cin—Holman 4 pass from Johnson (Breech kick)
Cin—Green 3 run (Breech kick)
Cin—Brooks 6 run (Breech kick)
NE —Cook 7 pass from Wilson (Staurovsky kick)
Cin—FG Breech 23
Cin—Holman 3 pass from Esiason (Breech kick)

Philadelphia 27, Los Angeles Rams 21—at Anaheim Stadium, attendance 63,644. Randall Cunningham's two touchdown passes and Anthony Toney's 103 yards rushing helped the Eagles win their first game of the season. Philadelphia took a 17-14 halftime lead on Cunningham's scoring strikes to Mike Quick (15 yards) and rookie Calvin Williams (14). Roger Ruzek kicked an 18-yard field goal and Robert Drummond ran two yards for a touchdown in the second half to finish the Eagles' scoring.

Philadelphia 3 14 3 7 — 27
L.A. Rams 7 7 0 7 — 21

Phil —FG Ruzek 43
Rams—Ellard 50 pass from Everett (Lansford kick)
Phil —Quick 15 pass from Cunningham (Ruzek kick)
Rams—McGee 10 pass from Everett (Lansford kick)
Phil —Williams 14 pass from Cunningham (Ruzek kick)
Phil —FG Ruzek 18
Phil —Drummond 2 run (Ruzek kick)
Rams—Gary 1 run (Lansford kick)

New Orleans 28, Phoenix 7—at Louisiana Superdome, attendance 61,110. Rueben Mayes ran for three scores to lead the Saints over the Cardinals. Mayes, who missed the entire 1989 season because of injury, scored on runs of 10, four, and 14 yards to help New Orleans score 21 unanswered points in the second half. The Saints scored their first touchdown of the season on John Fourcade's 14-yard pass to Eric Martin in the second quarter.

Phoenix 0 0 7 0 — 7
New Orleans 0 7 7 14 — 28

NO —Martin 14 pass from Fourcade (Andersen kick)
Phx—Proehl 37 pass from Rosenbach (Del Greco kick)
NO —Mayes 10 run (Andersen kick)
NO —Mayes 4 run (Andersen kick)
NO —Mayes 14 run (Andersen kick)

Los Angeles Raiders 20, Pittsburgh 3—at Memorial Coliseum, attendance 50,657. Marcus Allen and Mervyn Fernandez each scored touchdowns as the Raiders defeated the Steelers. Jeff Jaeger kicked two field goals (40 and 45 yards) and Allen ran one yard for a touchdown to put the Raiders ahead 13-3 in the fourth quarter. Jay Schroeder then fired a 66-yard scoring strike to Fernandez to cap the scoring. The Raiders won their eighth consecutive game at home while the Steelers' offense failed to score a touchdown for the third straight game.

Pittsburgh 3 0 0 0 — 3
L.A. Raiders 0 3 3 14 — 20

Pitt —FG Anderson 31
Raiders—FG Jaeger 40
Raiders—FG Jaeger 45
Raiders—Allen 1 run (Jaeger kick)
Raiders—Fernandez 66 pass from Schroeder (Jaeger kick)

San Diego 24, Cleveland 14—at Cleveland Stadium, attendance 77,429. Billy Joe Tolliver and Anthony Miller combined for two touchdown passes as the Chargers downed the Browns. Trailing 14-10 in the third quarter, San

Diego went ahead on Tolliver's 23-yard scoring pass to Miller. Rod Bernstine then ran one yard for a touchdown in the fourth quarter to put the game out of reach. San Diego's defense had three sacks while holding the Browns to just 44 yards rushing.

San Diego	3	7	7	7	—	24
Cleveland	7	7	0	0	—	14

SD —FG Reveiz 42
Clev—M. Johnson 64 interception return (Kauric kick)
SD —A. Miller 19 pass from Tolliver (Reveiz kick)
Clev—Hoard 1 run (Kauric kick)
SD —A. Miller 23 pass from Tolliver (Reveiz kick)
SD —Bernstine 1 run (Reveiz kick)

Denver 34, Seattle 31—at Mile High Stadium, attendance 75,290. David Treadwell's 25-yard field goal with 9:14 elapsed in overtime lifted the Broncos over the Seahawks. Denver took a 28-14 halftime lead on John Elway's scoring strikes to Mark Jackson (6 and 29 yards) and Melvin Bratton (one), and Karl Mecklenburg's two-yard fumble recovery return for a score. Seattle tied the game on Derrick Fenner's four-yard scoring run in the fourth quarter. The Seahawks' Norm Johnson missed a 39-yard field goal at the end of regulation and a 44-yard attempt in overtime that could have won the game. Fenner rushed for 144 yards on 22 carries for Seattle.

Seattle	7	7	10	7	0	—	31
Denver	14	14	0	3	3	—	34

Sea—Fenner 4 run (Johnson kick)
Den—Jackson 6 pass from Elway (Treadwell kick)
Den—Mecklenburg 2 fumble recovery return (Treadwell kick)
Sea—Fenner 2 run (Johnson kick)
Den—Jackson 29 pass from Elway (Treadwell kick)
Den—Bratton 1 pass from Elway (Treadwell kick)
Sea—FG Johnson 39
Sea—Heller 2 pass from Krieg (Johnson kick)
Den—FG Treadwell 27
Sea—Fenner 4 run (Johnson kick)
Den—FG Treadwell 25

Sunday Night, September 23

Tampa Bay 23, Detroit 20—at Tampa Stadium, attendance 55,075. Vinny Testaverde's fourth-quarter touchdown pass to John Harvey helped the Buccaneers overcome the Lions. Detroit took a 20-16 lead midway through the final period on Rodney Peete's five-yard touchdown pass to Robert Clark. Tampa Bay countered when Testaverde completed a pair of 26-yard passes to Bruce Hill and Ron Hall in the game-winning drive to set up his three-yard touchdown pass to Harvey.

Detroit	3	3	7	7	—	20
Tampa Bay	0	6	3	14	—	23

Det—FG Murray 25
TB —FG Christie 55
TB —FG Christie 28
Det—FG Murray 33
Det—Peete 1 run (Murray kick)
TB —FG Christie 21
TB —Anderson 10 run (Christie kick)
Det—Clark 5 pass from Peete (Murray kick)
TB —Harvey 3 pass from Testaverde (Christie kick)

Monday, September 24

Buffalo 30, New York Jets 7—at Giants Stadium, attendance 69,927. Thurman Thomas carried 18 times for 214 yards as the Bills easily beat the Jets. Trailing 7-0, Buffalo scored 30 unanswered points on Kenneth Davis's one-yard touchdown run, Butch Rolle's two-yard touchdown catch, Scott Norwood's three field goals (48, 42, and 27 yards), and Jim Kelly's six-yard touchdown pass to Keith McKeller.

Buffalo	7	13	3	7	—	30
N.Y. Jets	7	0	0	0	—	7

NYJ—Baxter 1 run (Leahy kick)
Buff—K. Davis 1 run (Norwood kick)
Buff—Rolle 2 pass from Kelly (Norwood kick)
Buff—FG Norwood 48
Buff—FG Norwood 42
Buff—FG Norwood 27
Buff—McKeller 6 pass from Kelly (Norwood kick)

Fourth Week Summaries

Standings

American Football Conference

Eastern Division	W	L	T	Pct.	Pts.	OP
Buffalo	3	1	0	.750	92	75
Miami	3	1	0	.750	88	57
N.Y. Jets	2	2	0	.500	88	89
Indianapolis	1	3	0	.250	58	89
New England	1	3	0	.250	60	119
Central Division						
Cincinnati	3	1	0	.750	103	74
Houston	2	2	0	.500	77	84
Cleveland	1	3	0	.250	48	85
Pittsburgh	1	3	0	.250	32	70
Western Division						
L.A. Raiders	4	0	0	1.000	75	35
Kansas City	3	1	0	.750	98	48
Denver	2	2	0	.500	95	97
San Diego	1	3	0	.250	61	69
Seattle	1	3	0	.250	75	84

National Football Conference

Eastern Division	W	L	T	Pct.	Pts.	OP
N.Y. Giants	4	0	0	1.000	106	47
Washington	3	1	0	.750	101	51
Dallas	1	3	0	.250	56	92
Philadelphia	1	3	0	.250	91	95
Phoenix	1	3	0	.250	40	118
Central Division						
Chicago	3	1	0	.750	77	53
Tampa Bay	3	1	0	.750	98	96
Green Bay	2	2	0	.500	76	93
Detroit	1	3	0	.250	83	99
Minnesota	1	3	0	.250	89	69
Western Division						
San Francisco	3	0	0	1.000	58	38
Atlanta	1	2	0	.333	74	67
L.A. Rams	1	2	0	.333	80	77
New Orleans	1	2	0	.333	43	52

Sunday, September 30

Los Angeles Raiders 24, Chicago 10—at Memorial Coliseum, attendance 80,156. Marcus Allen ran for two touchdowns and Greg Townsend returned a fumble for a score to highlight the Raiders' win over the Bears. Los Angeles opened a 10-7 advantage on Allen's one-yard run for a touchdown and Jeff Jaeger's 27-yard field goal. Aaron Wallace forced a fumble that was recovered and returned one yard for a touchdown by Townsend in the second quarter to put Los Angeles ahead 17-10 at halftime. Allen then completed the scoring with a three-yard touchdown run in the fourth quarter. The Raiders' defense had six sacks, while the team improved its record to 4-0, Los Angeles's best start since 1984.

Chicago	7	3	0	0	—	10
L.A. Raiders	10	7	0	7	—	24

Raiders—Allen 1 run (Jaeger kick)
Chi —Gentry 80 pass from Harbaugh (Butler kick)
Raiders—FG Jaeger 27
Raiders—Townsend 1 fumble recovery return (Jaeger kick)
Chi —FG Butler 22
Raiders—Allen 3 run (Jaeger kick)

Kansas City 34, Cleveland 0—at Arrowhead Stadium, attendance 75,462. Steve DeBerg passed for two touchdowns and Kansas City's special teams blocked and returned two punts for scores as the Chiefs blanked the Browns. Kansas City took a 24-0 halftime lead on Chris Martin's 31-yard blocked punt return for a touchdown, DeBerg's scoring passes to Robb Thomas (47 yards) and Emile Harry (six), and Nick Lowery's 39-yard field goal. Lowery added a 34-yard field goal and Kevin Ross returned a blocked punt four yards for a score in the third period to finish the scoring.

Cleveland	0	0	0	0	—	0
Kansas City	7	17	10	0	—	34

KC—R. Thomas 47 pass from DeBerg (Lowery kick)
KC—FG Lowery 39
KC—Martin 31 blocked punt return (Lowery kick)
KC—Harry 6 pass from DeBerg (Lowery kick)
KC—FG Lowery 34
KC—Ross 4 blocked punt return (Lowery kick)

New York Giants 31, Dallas 17—at Giants Stadium, attendance 75,923. Phil Simms completed three touchdown passes to help the Giants record their sixth consecutive win over the Cowboys. New York took a 17-3 halftime advantage on Simms's scoring passes to Mark Ingram (12 yards) and Bob Mrosko (seven), and Matt Bahr's 34-yard field goal. Simms's final touchdown pass, a 27-yarder to Rodney Hampton, capped a 75-yard drive and gave the Giants an insurmountable 24-10 lead early in the fourth quarter. The Giants' defense held the Cowboys to only 51 yards rushing.

Dallas	0	3	7	7	—	17
N.Y. Giants	7	10	0	14	—	31

NYG—Ingram 12 pass from Simms (Bahr kick)
Dall —FG Willis 22
NYG—FG Bahr 34
NYG—Mrosko 7 pass from Simms (Bahr kick)
Dall —Smith 4 run (Willis kick)
NYG—Hampton 27 pass from Simms (Bahr kick)
NYG—Hostetler 12 run (Bahr kick)
Dall —Novacek 7 pass from Aikman (Willis kick)

Buffalo 29, Denver 28—at Rich Stadium, attendance 74,393. The Bills scored 20 points within a 1:33 span of the fourth quarter to rally and defeat the Broncos. Trailing 21-9 in the final period, Nate Odomes blocked a Broncos' field-goal attempt which was recovered by Cornelius Bennett, who returned the ball 80 yards for a touchdown. One minute later, Leonard Smith returned an interception 39 yards for a touchdown to put Buffalo ahead 22-21. Bennett's fumble recovery set up Kenneth Davis's two-yard touchdown run to put Buffalo ahead 29-21. The Broncos' Bobby Humphrey rushed 34 times for 177 yards.

Denver	7	7	7	7	—	28
Buffalo	0	3	6	20	—	29

Den—Humphrey 1 run (Treadwell kick)
Den—Sewell 3 run (Treadwell kick)
Buff—FG Norwood 37
Buff—D. Smith 12 run (kick failed)
Den—Winder 3 run (Treadwell kick)
Buff—Bennett 80 blocked field goal return (Norwood kick)
Buff—L. Smith 39 interception return (kick failed)
Buff—K. Davis 2 run (Norwood kick)
Den—Nattiel 7 pass from Elway (Treadwell kick)

Green Bay 24, Detroit 21—at Pontiac Silverdome, attendance 64,509. Don Majkowski threw for 289 yards and three touchdowns to lead the Packers over the Lions. Trailing 21-10 in the fourth quarter, Majkowski completed a four-yard touchdown pass to Michael Haddix to narrow the score to 21-17. Majkowski then led the Packers to the game-winning score on a 66-yard, nine-play drive capped by his 26-yard touchdown pass to Jeff Query with 55 seconds remaining.

Green Bay	0	10	0	14	—	24
Detroit	7	7	7	0	—	21

Det—Clark 4 pass from Peete (Murray kick)
GB —FG Jacke 34
GB —West 3 pass from Majkowski (Jacke kick)
Det—Sanders 3 run (Murray kick)
Det—Peete 7 run (Murray kick)
GB —Haddix 4 pass from Majkowski (Jacke kick)
GB —Query 26 pass from Majkowski (Jacke kick)

Houston 17, San Diego 7—at San Diego Jack Murphy Stadium, attendance 48,762. Warren Moon completed 27 of 46 passes for 355 yards and two touchdowns to lead the Oilers over the Chargers. Houston took a 14-7 halftime lead on Moon's scoring passes to Drew Hill (nine yards) and Ernest Givins (22). Bubba McDowell intercepted a pass to set up Tony Zendejas's 34-yard field goal in the fourth quarter.

Houston	7	7	0	3	—	17
San Diego	0	7	0	0	—	7

Hou—Hill 9 pass from Moon (Zendejas kick)
SD —A. Miller 27 pass from Tolliver (Reveiz kick)
Hou—Givins 22 pass from Moon (Zendejas kick)
Hou—FG Zendejas 34

Indianapolis 24, Philadelphia 23—at Veterans Stadium, attendance 62,067. Jack Trudeau threw a touchdown pass to Bill Brooks on the game's final play to give the Colts a victory over the Eagles. Trailing 20-10 in the third quarter, the Colts' Albert Bentley ran 26 yards for a touchdown to narrow the score to 20-17. Roger Ruzek increased Philadelphia's lead to 23-17 with a 31-yard field goal. Trudeau then led the 14-play, 83-yard game-winning drive. Trudeau also completed a five-yard touchdown pass to Jessie Hester in the first quarter.

Indianapolis	7	3	7	7	—	24
Philadelphia	3	14	3	3	—	23

Phil—FG Ruzek 22
Ind —Hester 5 pass from Trudeau (Biasucci kick)
Phil—Keith Jackson 35 pass from Cunningham (Ruzek kick)
Phil—Barnett 21 pass from Cunningham (Ruzek kick)
Ind —FG Biasucci 41
Phil—FG Ruzek 44
Ind —Bentley 26 run (Biasucci kick)
Phil—FG Ruzek 31
Ind —Brooks 6 pass from Trudeau (Biasucci kick)

Miami 28, Pittsburgh 6—at Three Rivers Stadium, attendance 54,691. Sammie Smith ran for two touchdowns and the Dolphins' defense recorded five sacks in their win over the Steelers. Miami jumped to a 21-3 halftime lead on Smith's touchdown runs of one and seven yards and Dan Marino's 35-yard scoring pass to Mark Clayton. Tony Paige ran one yard for the Dolphins' only points in the second half.

Miami	7	14	0	7	—	28
Pittsburgh	0	3	3	0	—	6

Mia—S. Smith 1 run (Stoyanovich kick)
Mia—S. Smith 7 run (Stoyanovich kick)
Mia—Clayton 35 pass from Marino (Stoyanovich kick)
Pitt—FG Anderson 46
Pitt—FG Anderson 35
Mia—Paige 1 run (Stoyanovich kick)

New York Jets 37, New England 13—at Foxboro Stadium, attendance 36,724. Brad Baxter ran for two touchdowns and Pat Leahy kicked three field goals as the Jets routed the Patriots. New York took a 34-6 third-period lead on scoring runs by Baxter (1 and 28 yards) and Freeman McNeil (4), rookie Rob Moore's 69-yard reception from Ken O'Brien, and two Leahy field goals (24 and 18 yards). Moore had nine catches for 175 yards.

N.Y. Jets	7	17	10	3	—	37
New England	3	3	0	7	—	13

NYJ—Baxter 1 run (Leahy kick)
NE —FG Staurovsky 46
NYJ—Moore 69 pass from O'Brien (Leahy kick)
NE —FG Staurovsky 40
NYJ—FG Leahy 24
NYJ—McNeil 4 run (Leahy kick)
NYJ—Baxter 28 run (Leahy kick)
NYJ—FG Leahy 18

NE —Perryman 4 run (Staurovsky kick)
NYJ—FG Leahy 46

Tampa Bay 23, Minnesota 20—at Metrodome, attendance 54,462. Steve Christie's 36-yard field goal with 5:49 remaining in overtime lifted the Buccaneers over the Vikings. Gary Anderson ran two yards for a touchdown and Christie kicked field goals of 39 and 22 yards to give Tampa Bay a 13-6 lead entering the fourth quarter. Minnesota took a 20-13 lead behind Rich Gannon's touchdown passes to Anthony Carter (seven yards) and Hassan Jones (41). Vinny Testaverde completed an 11-yard touchdown pass to Bruce Hill to force the extra period. Wayne Haddix's interception set up Christie's winning kick.

Tampa Bay	7	3	3	7	3	— 23
Minnesota	0	3	3	14	0	— 20

TB —Anderson 2 run (Christie kick)
Minn—FG Igwebuike 28
TB —FG Christie 39
TB —FG Christie 22
Minn—FG Igwebuike 32
Minn—A. Carter 7 pass from Gannon (Igwebuike kick)
Minn—Jones 41 pass from Gannon (Igwebuike kick)
TB —Hill 11 pass from Testaverde (Christie kick)
TB —FG Christie 36

Sunday Night, September 30

Washington 38, Phoenix 10—at Sun Devil Stadium, attendance 49,303. Stan Humphries completed two touchdown passes and scrambled for a third to help the Redskins defeat the Cardinals. Humphries, making his first NFL start in place of injured Mark Rypien, connected with Gary Clark on a pair of 42-yard scoring passes and ran one yard for a touchdown. Gerald Riggs and Earnest Byner each scored on one-yard runs and Chip Lohmiller added a 26-yard field goal to complete Washington's scoring. Clark finished the day with eight receptions for 162 yards.

Washington	0	7	10	21	— 38
Phoenix	0	10	0	0	— 10

Phx —FG Del Greco 32
Wash—Riggs 1 run (Lohmiller kick)
Phx —R. Green 12 pass from Rosenbach (Del Greco kick)
Wash—FG Lohmiller 26
Wash—Clark 42 pass from Humphries (Lohmiller kick)
Wash—Humphries 1 run (Lohmiller kick)
Wash—Clark 42 pass from Humphries (Lohmiller kick)
Wash—Byner 1 run (Lohmiller kick)

Monday, October 1

Seattle 31, Cincinnati 16—at Kingdome, attendance 60,135. Derrick Fenner scored three touchdowns as the Seahawks notched their first victory of the year while handing the Bengals their first loss of the season. Fenner scored on runs of four and three yards and caught a two-yard touchdown reception from Dave Krieg. Krieg also completed a 63-yard touchdown pass to Tommy Kane and Norm Johnson kicked a 51-yard field goal for Seattle. Rufus Porter had two of the Seahawks' three sacks.

Cincinnati	0	6	3	7	— 16
Seattle	3	7	7	14	— 31

Sea—FG Johnson 51
Cin —FG Breech 34
Sea—Fenner 4 run (Johnson kick)
Cin —FG Breech 26
Sea—Fenner 3 run (Johnson kick)
Cin —FG Breech 43
Sea—Kane 63 pass from Krieg (Johnson kick)
Cin —Price 66 punt return (Breech kick)
Sea—Fenner 2 pass from Krieg (Johnson kick)

Fifth Week Summaries

Standings

American Football Conference

Eastern Division

	W	L	T	Pct.	Pts.	OP
Buffalo	4	1	0	.800	130	99
Miami	4	1	0	.800	108	73
Indianapolis	2	3	0	.400	81	108
N.Y. Jets	2	3	0	.400	104	109
New England	1	4	0	.200	80	152

Central Division

	W	L	T	Pct.	Pts.	OP
Cincinnati	4	1	0	.800	137	105
Cleveland	2	3	0	.400	78	114
Houston	2	3	0	.400	98	108
Pittsburgh	2	3	0	.400	68	84

Western Division

	W	L	T	Pct.	Pts.	OP
L.A. Raiders	4	1	0	.800	99	73
Kansas City	3	2	0	.600	117	71
Denver	2	3	0	.400	124	127
Seattle	2	3	0	.400	108	104
San Diego	1	4	0	.200	75	105

National Football Conference

Eastern Division

	W	L	T	Pct.	Pts.	OP
N.Y. Giants	4	0	0	1.000	106	47
Washington	3	1	0	.750	101	51
Dallas	2	3	0	.400	70	102
Philadelphia	1	3	0	.250	91	95
Phoenix	1	3	0	.250	40	118

Central Division

	W	L	T	Pct.	Pts.	OP
Chicago	4	1	0	.800	104	66
Tampa Bay	3	2	0	.600	108	110
Detroit	2	3	0	.400	117	126
Green Bay	2	3	0	.400	89	120
Minnesota	1	4	0	.200	116	103

Western Division

	W	L	T	Pct.	Pts.	OP
San Francisco	4	0	0	1.000	82	59
Atlanta	2	2	0	.500	102	94
L.A. Rams	1	3	0	.250	111	111
New Orleans	1	3	0	.250	70	80

Sunday, October 7

Cincinnati 34, Los Angeles Rams 31—at Anaheim Stadium, attendance 62,619. Jim Breech's 44-yard field goal with 3:04 remaining in overtime gave the Bengals a victory over the Rams. Cincinnati jumped to a 21-7 halftime lead on Boomer Esiason's scoring passes to James Brooks (27 and 9 yards) and Eric Ball's one-yard touchdown run. Esiason, who finished the day completing 30 of 44 pass attempts for 471 yards, hit Harold Green with a 14-yard touchdown pass in the third quarter to give the Bengals a 28-14 lead. Los Angeles tied the game 28-28 in the fourth quarter on Cleveland Gary's one-yard run. Breech and Lansford each kicked 40-yard field goals to force the overtime. Breech's game-winning kick came at the end of a 63-yard, eight-play drive. Three Bengals' receivers amassed more than 100 yards receiving: Rodney Holman (10 for 161), Tim McGee (eight for 142), and James Brooks (seven for 109).

Cincinnati	14	7	7	3	3	— 34
L.A. Rams	0	7	14	10	0	— 31

Cin —Brooks 27 pass from Esiason (Breech kick)
Cin —Brooks 9 pass from Esiason (Breech kick)
Cin —Ball 1 run (Breech kick)
Rams—Gary 2 run (Lansford kick)
Rams—Anderson 55 pass from Everett (Lansford kick)
Cin —H. Green 14 pass from Esiason (Breech kick)
Rams—Johnson 9 pass from Everett (Lansford kick)
Rams—Gary 1 run (Lansford kick)
Cin —FG Breech 40
Rams—FG Lansford 40
Cin —FG Breech 44

Detroit 34, Minnesota 27—at Metrodome, attendance 57,586. Bob Gagliano completed three touchdown passes as the Lions rallied to defeat the Vikings. Minnesota led 20-10 in the first half on two Donald Igwebuike field goals (36 and 48 yards) and Rich Gannon's scoring passes of 11 yards to Hassan Jones and eight yards to Anthony Carter. Detroit took a 34-20 lead by scoring 24 consecutive points on Gagliano's touchdown passes to Richard Johnson (five yards) and Terry Greer (16), Eddie Murray's 23-yard field goal, and Barry Sanders's one-yard run. Minnesota closed the margin to 34-27 on Herschel Walker's two-yard run for a score with less than three minutes remaining, but the Lions held on for the win.

Detroit	3	7	7	17	— 34
Minnesota	6	14	0	7	— 27

Minn—FG Igwebuike 36
Det —FG Murray 32
Minn—FG Igwebuike 48
Det —B. Sanders 22 pass from Gagliano (Murray kick)
Minn—H. Jones 11 pass from Gannon (Igwebuike kick)
Minn—A. Carter 8 pass from Gannon (Igwebuike kick)
Det —R. Johnson 5 pass from Gagliano (Murray kick)
Det —FG Murray 23
Det —Greer 16 pass from Gagliano (Murray kick)
Det —B. Sanders 1 run (Murray kick)
Minn—Walker 2 run (Igwebuike kick)

Chicago 27, Green Bay 13—at Soldier Field, attendance 59,929. Mike Tomczak threw for one touchdown and ran for another as the Bears downed the Packers. Tomczak ran six yards for a touchdown in the third quarter to give Chicago a 17-6 lead. Neal Anderson, who rushed 21 times for 141 yards and scored on a three-yard run, ran 52 yards to set up Tomczak's two-yard scoring pass to Cap Boso with 2:56 remaining. Kevin Butler kicked field goals of 50 and 51 yards for the Bears.

Green Bay	3	3	0	7	— 13
Chicago	7	3	7	10	— 27

GB—FG Jacke 38
Chi—Anderson 3 run (Butler kick)
GB—FG Jacke 27
Chi—FG Butler 50
Chi—Tomczak 6 run (Butler kick)
GB—Sharpe 76 pass from Majkowski (Jacke kick)
Chi—FG Butler 51
Chi—Boso 2 pass from Tomczak (Butler kick)

Indianapolis 23, Kansas City 19—at Hoosier Dome, attendance 54,950. Albert Bentley ran 10 yards for a touchdown midway through the fourth quarter as the Colts rallied to defeat the Chiefs. Trailing 19-13 in the fourth quarter, Indianapolis safety Mike Prior recovered a fumble at the Kansas City 21-yard line to set up Bentley's scoring run. Dean Biassuci kicked his third field goal of the day (18 yards) to complete the Colts' scoring.

Kansas City	10	6	3	0	— 19
Indianapolis	0	10	0	13	— 23

KC—FG Lowery 37
KC—R. Thomas 21 pass from DeBerg (Lowery kick)
KC—FG Lowery 39
Ind—FG Biasucci 38
Ind—Bentley 9 pass from Trudeau (Biasucci kick)
KC—FG Lowery 44
KC—FG Lowery 35
Ind—FG Biasucci 21
Ind—Bentley 10 run (Biasucci kick)
Ind—FG Biasucci 18

Atlanta 28, New Orleans 27—at Atlanta-Fulton County Stadium, attendance 57,401. Chris Miller completed a three-yard touchdown pass to Andre Rison with 1:33 remaining in the game as the Falcons edged the Saints. Trailing 17-14 in the third quarter, Miller hit Rison with a 20-yard scoring pass to go ahead 21-17. John Fourcade's three-yard touchdown pass to Hoby Brenner and Morten Andersen's 23-yard field goal put New Orleans back on top 27-21. Miller, who completed 23 of 44 passes for 366 yards and three touchdowns, led an 80-yard drive to the winning score. The Falcons' victory snapped their six-game losing streak against the Saints.

New Orleans	7	10	7	3	— 27
Atlanta	7	7	7	7	— 28

Atl —Miller 1 run (Davis kick)
NO—Turner 68 pass from Fourcade (Andersen kick)
Atl —Collins 9 pass from Miller (Davis kick)
NO—Fourcade 5 run (Andersen kick)
NO—FG Andersen 46
Atl —Rison 20 pass from Miller (Davis kick)
NO—Brenner 3 pass from Fourcade (Andersen kick)
NO—FG Andersen 23
Atl —Rison 3 pass from Miller (Davis kick)

Miami 20, New York Jets 16—at Joe Robbie Stadium, attendance 69,678. Dan Marino completed a 13-yard touchdown pass to Mark Duper with 1:03 remaining as the Dolphins rallied to defeat the Jets. New York took a 13-0 halftime lead on Ken O'Brien's nine-yard touchdown pass to Rob Moore and a pair of Pat Leahy field goals from 25 and 19 yards. Miami tied the game in the third quarter on Marc Logan's 11-yard touchdown run and Marino's 69-yard scoring strike to Duper. Leahy's third field goal (30 yards) put the Jets ahead 16-13, but Marino led an 80-yard drive in 14 plays that culminated the game-winning score. Duper had five receptions for 125 yards.

N.Y. Jets	3	10	0	3	— 16
Miami	0	0	13	7	— 20

NYJ—FG Leahy 25
NYJ—Moore 9 pass from O'Brien (Leahy kick)
NYJ—FG Leahy 19
Mia —Logan 11 run (kick failed)
Mia —Duper 69 pass from Marino (Stoyanovich kick)
NYJ—FG Leahy 30
Mia —Duper 13 pass from Marino (Stoyanovich kick)

Pittsburgh 36, San Diego 14—at Three Rivers Stadium, attendance 53,486. Bubby Brister completed two second-quarter touchdown passes to rookie tight end Eric Green as the Steelers defeated the Chargers. Brister hit Green with touchdown passes of eight and one yard to mark the Steelers' first offensive touchdowns of the 1990 season. Pittsburgh took a 24-7 third-quarter lead when Dwayne Woodruff returned an interception 23 yards to set up Warren Williams's two-yard touchdown run in the third quarter. Dwight Stone blocked a punt out of the end zone for a safety and Barry Foster scored on a two-yard run in the fourth quarter.

San Diego	7	0	7	0	— 14
Pittsburgh	3	14	7	12	— 36

Pitt—FG Anderson 45
SD —Plummer 2 pass from Tolliver (Carney kick)
Pitt—Green 8 pass from Brister (Anderson kick)
Pitt—Green 1 pass from Brister (Anderson kick)
Pitt—W. Williams 2 run (Anderson kick)
SD —L. Miller fumble recovery in end zone (Carney kick)
Pitt—Safety, Stone blocked punt out of end zone
Pitt—FG Anderson 45
Pitt—Foster 2 run (Anderson kick)

San Francisco 24, Houston 21—at Astrodome, attendance 59,931. Joe Montana's 46-yard scoring strike to John Taylor midway through the fourth quarter rallied the 49ers past the Oilers. Houston led 14-7 at halftime, but San Francisco tied the score on Montana's 78-yard touchdown pass to Taylor. Houston moved back in front 21-14 on Warren Moon's 18-yard scoring pass to Haywood Jeffires. Mike Cofer kicked a 23-yard field goal to narrow the score to 21-17 before Montana found Taylor with the game-winning pass. Taylor led all receivers with 132 yards on four catches.

San Francisco	0	7	7	10	— 24
Houston	14	0	7	0	— 21

Hou—Moon 1 run (Zendejas kick)
Hou—Hill 30 pass from Moon (Zendejas kick)
SF —Rice 6 pass from Montana (Cofer kick)
SF —Taylor 78 pass from Montana (Cofer kick)
Hou—Jeffires 18 pass from Moon (Zendejas kick)

SF —FG Cofer 23
SF —Taylor 46 pass from Montana (Cofer kick)

Seattle 33, New England 20—at Foxboro Stadium, attendance 39,735. The Seahawks scored two touchdowns late in the fourth quarter to give Seattle a come-from-behind victory over the Patriots. Dave Krieg's 45-yard touchdown pass to Jeff Chadwick put the Seahawks on top 26-20 with 2:37 remaining in the game. Melvin Jenkins's fumble recovery set up Derrick Fenner's five-yard scoring run 24 seconds later to put the game away. Krieg also completed a 20-yard touchdown pass to Tommy Kane and Fenner added a five-yard run in the first quarter. Norm Johnson kicked field goals of 31 and 19 yards.

Seattle	13	6	0	14	— 33
New England	3	7	7	3	— 20

Sea—Fenner 5 run (kick failed)
Sea—Kane 20 pass from Krieg (Johnson kick)
NE —FG Staurovsky 53
Sea—FG Johnson 31
Sea—FG Johnson 19
NE —B. Williams 45 fumble recovery return (Staurovsky kick)
NE —Dykes 35 pass from Wilson (Staurovsky kick)
NE —FG Staurovsky 48
Sea—Chadwick 45 pass from Krieg (Johnson kick)
Sea—Fenner 5 run (Johnson kick)

Dallas 14, Tampa Bay 10—at Texas Stadium, attendance 60,076. Rookie Emmitt Smith's 14-yard touchdown run early in the fourth quarter proved to be the decisive score as the Cowboys held on to defeat the Buccaneers. Dallas took a 7-3 halftime lead on Troy Aikman's 12-yard scoring pass to Jay Novacek. Tampa Bay went ahead 10-7 in the third quarter on Vinny Testaverde's 58-yard touchdown pass to Gary Anderson. Smith carried 23 times for 121 yards, the most by a Dallas running back since Herschel Walker gained 134 yards on December 4, 1988.

Tampa Bay	0	3	7	0	— 10
Dallas	7	0	0	7	— 14

Dall—Novacek 12 pass from Aikman (Willis kick)
TB —FG Christie 33
TB —Anderson 58 pass from Testaverde (Christie kick)
Dall—E. Smith 14 run (Willis kick)

Sunday Night, October 7

Buffalo 38, Los Angeles Raiders 24—at Rich Stadium, attendance 80,076. The Bills scored 24 unanswered points in the fourth quarter to highlight their victory over the Raiders. Despite Jim Kelly's completed touchdown passes to Andre Reed (13 yards), Keith McKeller (15), and James Lofton (42), Buffalo trailed 24-21 in the fourth quarter. Buffalo went ahead 28-24 on Steve Tasker's blocked punt which James Williams returned 38 yards for a touchdown. Cornelius Bennett then sacked quarterback Jay Schroeder, causing a fumble which he recovered to set up Scott Norwood's 23-yard field goal. Nate Odomes then returned a fumble 49 yards for a touchdown to complete the Bills' scoring.

L.A. Raiders	7	3	7	7	— 24
Buffalo	0	7	7	24	— 38

Raiders—Gault 11 pass from Schroeder (Jaeger kick)
Buff —Reed 13 pass from Kelly (Norwood kick)
Raiders—FG Jaeger 19
Raiders—Allen 1 run (Jaeger kick)
Buff —McKeller 15 pass from Kelly (Norwood kick)
Raiders—S. Smith 4 pass from Schroeder (Jaeger kick)
Buff —Lofton 42 pass from Kelly (Norwood kick)
Buff —J. Williams 38 blocked punt return (Norwood kick)
Buff —FG Norwood 23
Buff —Odomes 49 fumble recovery return (Norwood kick)

Monday, October 8

Cleveland 30, Denver 29—at Mile High Stadium, attendance 74,814. Jerry Kauric kicked a 30-yard field goal as time expired to lead the Browns past the Broncos. Bernie Kosar, who completed 24 of 38 passes for 318 yards, led the comeback by throwing a third-quarter touchdown pass to Kevin Mack (11 yards) and a 24-yarder to Brian Brennan with 3:21 remaining. Webster Slaughter led all receivers with seven catches for 123 yards, which included a 43-yard scoring reception from Kosar in the first half.

Cleveland	6	7	7	10	— 30
Denver	7	12	0	10	— 29

Den —Elway 13 run (Treadwell kick)
Clev—Metcalf 5 run (kick failed)
Den —FG Treadwell 20
Clev—Slaughter 43 pass from Kosar (Kauric kick)
Den —Humphrey 19 run (Treadwell kick)
Den —Safety, Fletcher blocked punt out of end zone
Clev—Mack 11 pass from Kosar (Kauric kick)
Den —Jackson 16 run (Treadwell kick)
Den —FG Treadwell 25
Clev—Brennan 24 pass from Kosar (Kauric kick)
Clev—FG Kauric 30

Sixth Week Summaries

Standings

American Football Conference

Eastern Division	W	L	T	Pct.	Pts.	OP
Buffalo	4	1	0	.800	130	99
Miami	4	1	0	.800	108	73
Indianapolis	2	3	0	.400	81	108
N.Y. Jets	2	4	0	.333	107	148
New England	1	4	0	.200	80	152
Central Division						
Cincinnati	4	2	0	.667	154	153
Houston	3	3	0	.500	146	125
Pittsburgh	3	3	0	.500	102	101
Cleveland	2	4	0	.333	98	139
Western Division						
L.A. Raiders	5	1	0	.833	123	90
Kansas City	4	2	0	.667	160	95
Denver	2	4	0	.333	141	161
San Diego	2	4	0	.333	114	108
Seattle	2	4	0	.333	125	128

National Football Conference

Eastern Division	W	L	T	Pct.	Pts.	OP
N.Y. Giants	5	0	0	1.000	130	67
Washington	3	2	0	.600	121	75
Philadelphia	2	3	0	.400	123	119
Phoenix	2	3	0	.400	60	121
Dallas	2	4	0	.333	73	122
Central Division						
Chicago	5	1	0	.833	142	75
Tampa Bay	4	2	0	.667	134	124
Detroit	2	4	0	.333	141	169
Green Bay	2	4	0	.333	103	146
Minnesota	1	5	0	.167	140	135
Western Division						
San Francisco	5	0	0	1.000	127	94
Atlanta	2	3	0	.400	137	139
New Orleans	2	3	0	.400	95	100
L.A. Rams	1	4	0	.200	120	149

Sunday, October 14

New Orleans 25, Cleveland 20—at Louisiana Superdome, attendance 68,608. Steve Walsh, playing his first game at quarterback for the Saints since being traded from the Cowboys, completed three touchdown passes as New Orleans overcame Cleveland. Walsh replaced John Fourcade in the second quarter and threw a four-yard touchdown pass to Dalton Hilliard to help the Saints to a 9-6 halftime advantage. Walsh connected on scoring strikes of 49 yards to Floyd Turner and 13 yards to Eric Martin in the second half. Saints cornerback Robert Massey blocked a punt out of the end zone for a safety to complete New Orleans's scoring. The victory was the Saints' thirteenth consecutive over an AFC opponent, tying the Miami Dolphins' NFL record set in 1978-1981.

Cleveland	0	6	0	14	— 20
New Orleans	3	6	7	9	— 25

NO —FG Andersen 52
Clev—FG Kauric 37
NO —Hilliard 4 pass from Walsh (kick failed)
Clev—FG Kauric 39
NO —Turner 49 pass from Walsh (Andersen kick)
NO —Martin 13 pass from Walsh (Andersen kick)
NO —Safety, Massey blocked punt out of end zone
Clev—Slaughter 13 pass from Kosar (Kauric kick)
Clev—Mack 1 run (Kauric kick)

Phoenix 20, Dallas 3—at Sun Devil Stadium, attendance 45,235. Rookies Anthony Thompson and Johnny Johnson each ran for touchdowns to help the Cardinals defeat the Cowboys. Phoenix jumped to a 10-0 halftime advantage on Thompson's one-yard run and Al Del Greco's 28-yard field goal. Jay Taylor's 34-yard interception return set up Del Greco's second field goal of the day (28 yards) early in the fourth quarter to give the Cardinals a 13-3 lead. Johnson ran nine yards for a score in the fourth quarter to finish Phoenix's scoring. Johnson's 120-yard rushing performance made him the first Cardinal to rush for more than 100 yards since Earl Ferrell gained 110 yards on October 30, 1988. It also marked the first time in 15 games that the Cowboys allowed an opponent to rush for 100 yards.

Dallas	0	0	3	0	— 3
Phoenix	7	3	0	10	— 20

Phx—Thompson 1 run (Del Greco kick)
Phx—FG Del Greco 28
Dall—FG Willis 37
Phx—FG Del Greco 28
Phx—J. Johnson 9 run (Del Greco kick)

Kansas City 43, Detroit 24—at Arrowhead Stadium, attendance 74,312. Barry Word and Christian Okoye both ran for a pair of touchdowns to lead the Chiefs past the Lions. Kansas City took a 17-14 halftime advantage on Okoye's four-yard run for a touchdown, Nick Lowery's 21-yard field goal, and Steve DeBerg's one-yard pass to Jonathan Hayes. Okoye added a one-yard run in the third quarter and Word scored on runs of 53 and one yard in the fourth quarter. Word's 200 yards rushing set a Chiefs' club record, breaking Joe Delaney's 193-yard rushing effort against Houston on November 15, 1981.

Detroit	14	0	0	10	— 24
Kansas City	3	14	12	14	— 43

KC —FG Lowery 21
Det—Sanders 47 pass from Gagliano (Karlis kick)
Det—Sanders 13 run (Karlis kick)
KC —Hayes 1 pass from DeBerg (Lowery kick)
KC —Okoye 4 run (Lowery kick)
KC —FG Lowery 32
KC —Safety, Maas tackled Gagliano in end zone
KC —Okoye 1 run (Lowery kick)
Det—FG Karlis 21
KC —Word 53 run (Lowery kick)
Det—Wilder 8 pass from Ware (Karlis kick)
KC —Word 1 run (Lowery kick)

Tampa Bay 26, Green Bay 14—at Tampa Stadium, attendance 67,472. Vinny Testaverde threw for a touchdown and Tampa Bay's defense had five interceptions as the Buccaneers defeated the Packers. Tampa Bay jumped to a 16-0 halftime lead on Steve Christie's three field goals (24, 32, and 39 yards) and Testaverde's 14-yard scoring pass to Ron Hall. Wayne Haddix had two interceptions, including one returned 29 yards for a touchdown in the third quarter.

Green Bay	0	0	14	0	— 14
Tampa Bay	3	13	10	0	— 26

TB —FG Christie 24
TB —FG Christie 32
TB —FG Christie 39
TB —Hall 14 pass from Testaverde (Christie kick)
TB —FG Christie 32
GB—Query recovered fumble in end zone (Jacke kick)
TB —Haddix 29 interception return (Christie kick)
GB—Fontenot 8 pass from Majkowski (Jacke kick)

Houston 48, Cincinnati 17—at Astrodome, attendance 53,501. Warren Moon completed 21 of 33 passes for 369 yards and a career-high five touchdowns as the Oilers easily beat the Bengals. The Oilers jumped to a 31-10 halftime lead on Moon's scoring passes to Tony Jones (33 yards), Drew Hill (33), and Leonard Harris (42), Tony Zendejas's 22-yard field goal, and Richard Johnson's 30-yard interception returned for a touchdown. Cris Dishman's interception set up Moon's 11-yard touchdown pass to Ernest Givins in the third quarter. Moon's three-yard scoring pass to Haywood Jeffires and Zendejas's 23-yard field goal finished Houston's scoring. Moon was named AFC Offensive Player of the Week for his performance.

Cincinnati	7	3	7	0	— 17
Houston	7	24	7	10	— 48

Cin —Taylor 2 run (Breech kick)
Hou—T. Jones 33 pass from Moon (Zendejas kick)
Cin —FG Breech 29
Hou—D. Hill 33 pass from Moon (Zendejas kick)
Hou—R. Johnson 30 interception return (Zendejas kick)
Hou—Harris 42 pass from Moon (Zendejas kick)
Hou—FG Zendejas 22
Hou—Givins 11 pass from Moon (Zendejas kick)
Cin —Holman 5 pass from Esiason (Breech kick)
Hou—Jeffires 3 pass from Moon (Zendejas kick)
Hou—FG Zendejas 23

New York Giants 24, Washington 20—at Robert F. Kennedy Stadium, attendance 54,737. Phil Simms completed two touchdown passes as the Giants downed the Redskins to remain undefeated. Simms connected with Stephen Baker on an 80-yard scoring strike to give New York a 7-3 halftime lead. The Giants took a 21-13 advantage in the third quarter on Ottis Anderson's five-yard touchdown run and Simms's two-yard scoring pass to Mark Bavaro. Gerald Riggs's one-yard touchdown run narrowed the score to 21-20, but Matt Bahr kicked a 19-yard field goal late in the fourth quarter to put the game away. The Giants' 5-0 start matched the team record for wins to start a season set in 1941.

N.Y. Giants	0	7	14	3	— 24
Washington	3	0	10	7	— 20

Wash—FG Lohmiller 42
NYG —Baker 80 pass from Simms (Bahr kick)
Wash—FG Lohmiller 35
NYG —Anderson 5 run (Bahr kick)
Wash—Sanders 31 pass from Byner (Lohmiller kick)
NYG —Bavaro 2 pass from Simms (Bahr kick)
Wash—Riggs 1 run (Lohmiller kick)
NYG —FG Bahr 19

Pittsburgh 34, Denver 17—at Mile High Stadium, attendance 74,285. Bubby Brister threw four touchdown passes, including three to rookie tight end Eric Green, to help the Steelers overcome the Broncos. Brister's first two scoring passes were to Louis Lipps (six yards) and Green (three) in the second quarter. Pittsburgh went ahead 21-17 in the third quarter on Merril Hoge's six-yard scoring run. Brister finished the day with two touchdown passes to Green (10 and 3 yards) in the fourth quarter.

Pittsburgh	0	14	7	13	— 34
Denver	10	7	0	0	— 17

Den—Winder 1 run (Treadwell kick)
Den—FG Treadwell 24
Pitt —Lipps 6 pass from Brister (Anderson kick)
Den—Sewell 2 run (Treadwell kick)
Pitt —Green 3 pass from Brister (Anderson kick)
Pitt —Hoge 6 run (Anderson kick)

Pitt —Green 10 pass from Brister (kick failed)
Pitt —Green 3 pass from Brister (Anderson kick)

San Diego 39, New York Jets 3—at Giants Stadium, attendance 63,311. Marion Butts carried 26 times for 121 yards and two touchdowns to lead the Chargers past the Jets. San Diego scored 22 first-half points on Burt Grossman's tackling of Ken O'Brien in the end zone for a safety, Billy Joe Tolliver's 29-yard touchdown pass to Anthony Miller, Butts's five-yard scoring run, and a pair of John Carney field goals (34 and 42 yards). Butts (six yards) and Rod Bernstine (40) ran for scores in the second half. The Chargers held a 35:37 to 24:23 time-of-possession advantage and limited the Jets to nine first downs and 53 yards passing.

San Diego	2	20	10	7 —	39
N.Y. Jets	3	0	0	0 —	3

SD —Safety, Grossman tackled O'Brien in end zone
NYJ—FG Leahy 22
SD —Miller 29 pass from Tolliver (Carney kick)
SD —Butts 5 run (Carney kick)
SD —FG Carney 34
SD —FG Carney 42
SD —Butts 6 run (Carney kick)
SD —FG Carney 37
SD —Bernstine 40 run (Carney kick)

San Francisco 45, Atlanta 35—at Atlanta-Fulton County Stadium, attendance 57,921. Joe Montana threw for a career-high 476 yards and six touchdowns as the 49ers downed the Falcons to remain undefeated. Montana completed five of his scoring passes to Jerry Rice, including three in the first half (24, 25, and 19 yards), to help San Francisco take a 31-21 halftime lead. Montana also connected with Mike Sherrard on a 43-yard scoring pass and found Rice for touchdown passes of 13 and 15 yards in the second half. Rice set a club record with 13 catches for 225 yards. Montana's six scoring passes also broke the club record. The two were named co-NFC Offensive Players of the Week.

San Francisco	14	17	7	7 —	45
Atlanta	7	14	0	14 —	35

SF—Rice 24 pass from Montana (Cofer kick)
Atl—Rison 75 pass from Miller (Davis kick)
SF—Rice 25 pass from Montana (Cofer kick)
Atl—Butler 62 blocked punt return (Davis kick)
SF—Sherrard 43 pass from Montana (Cofer kick)
SF—Rice 19 pass from Montana (Cofer kick)
Atl—Milling 5 pass from Miller (Davis kick)
SF—FG Cofer 56
SF—Rice 13 pass from Montana (Cofer kick)
SF—Rice 15 pass from Montana (Cofer kick)
Atl—Wilkins 3 pass from Miller (Davis kick)
Atl—Rison 13 pass from Campbell (Davis kick)

Los Angeles Raiders 24, Seattle 17—at Memorial Coliseum, attendance 50,624. Jay Schroeder completed three touchdown passes as the Raiders defeated the Seahawks for their tenth consecutive home victory. Schroeder threw scoring passes to Steve Smith (one yard), Mervyn Fernandez (three), and Ethan Horton (three) on the Raiders' first three possessions of the game to give Los Angeles a 21-0 second-quarter advantage. Seattle countered with a pair of Dave Krieg touchdown passes to Paul Skansi (five yards) and Tommy Kane (31) late in the second quarter to narrow the margin to 21-14. Norm Johnson's 34-yard field goal closed the score to 21-17, but Jeff Jaeger's 22-yard kick sealed the victory.

Seattle	0	14	3	0 —	17
L.A. Raiders	7	14	0	3 —	24

Raiders—S. Smith 1 pass from Schroeder (Jaeger kick)
Raiders—Fernandez 3 pass from Schroeder (Jaeger kick)
Raiders—Horton 3 pass from Schroeder (Jaeger kick)
Sea —Skansi 5 pass from Krieg (Johnson kick)
Sea —Kane 31 pass from Krieg (Johnson kick)
Sea —FG Johnson 34
Raiders—FG Jaeger 22

Sunday Night, October 14

Chicago 38, Los Angeles Rams 9—at Soldier Field, attendance 59,383. Jim Harbaugh completed two touchdown passes and ran for another as the Bears rolled over the Rams. Chicago scored 28 unanswered points on its first four possessions in the first half on Harbaugh's touchdown passes to Neal Anderson (12 yards) and Ron Morris (18), and scoring runs by Harbaugh (12 yards) and Brad Muster (13). Kevin Butler kicked a 27-yard field goal and Anderson added a 15-yard touchdown run in the second half for the Bears.

L.A. Rams	0	0	6	3 —	9
Chicago	14	14	3	7 —	38

Chi —Anderson 12 pass from Harbaugh (Butler kick)
Chi —Harbaugh 12 run (Butler kick)
Chi —Morris 18 pass from Harbaugh (Butler kick)
Chi —Muster 13 run (Butler kick)
Chi —FG Butler 27
Rams—McGee 11 pass from Everett (kick failed)
Rams—FG Lansford 35
Chi —Anderson 15 run (Butler kick)

Monday, October 15

Philadelphia 32, Minnesota 24—at Veterans Stadium, attendance 66,296. Anthony Toney's touchdown run and Roger Ruzek's 19-yard field goal late in the fourth quarter rallied the Eagles past the Vikings. Minnesota jumped to a 21-9 lead in the first half on Rich Gannon's touchdown passes to former Eagle Cris Carter (42 and 78 yards) and Rick Fenney's one-yard scoring run. Ruzek kicked a pair of third-quarter field goals (30 and 29 yards) to close the margin to 21-15. Randall Cunningham fired a 40-yard scoring strike to Fred Barnett and Clyde Simmons's fumble recovery set up Toney's game-winning touchdown run.

Minnesota	7	14	0	3 —	24
Philadelphia	9	0	6	17 —	32

Phil —FG Ruzek 38
Phil —Williams 19 pass from Cunningham (Ruzek kick)
Minn—C. Carter 42 pass from Gannon (Igwebuike kick)
Minn—Fenney 1 run (Igwebuike kick)
Minn—C. Carter 78 pass from Gannon (Igwebuike kick)
Phil —FG Ruzek 30
Phil —FG Ruzek 29
Minn—FG Igwebuike 33
Phil —Barnett 40 pass from Cunningham (Ruzek kick)
Phil —Toney 6 run (Ruzek kick)
Phil —FG Ruzek 19

Seventh Week Summaries

Standings

American Football Conference

Eastern Division

	W	L	T	Pct.	Pts.	OP
Buffalo	5	1	0	.833	160	126
Miami	5	1	0	.833	125	83
Indianapolis	2	4	0	.333	98	135
N.Y. Jets	2	5	0	.286	134	178
New England	1	5	0	.167	90	169

Central Division

	W	L	T	Pct.	Pts.	OP
Cincinnati	5	2	0	.714	188	166
Houston	4	3	0	.571	169	135
Pittsburgh	3	4	0	.429	109	128
Cleveland	2	5	0	.286	101	173

Western Division

	W	L	T	Pct.	Pts.	OP
L.A. Raiders	6	1	0	.857	147	99
Kansas City	4	3	0	.571	167	114
Denver	3	4	0	.429	168	178
Seattle	3	4	0	.429	144	135
San Diego	2	5	0	.286	123	132

National Football Conference

Eastern Division

	W	L	T	Pct.	Pts.	OP
N.Y. Giants	6	0	0	1.000	150	86
Washington	4	2	0	.667	134	82
Dallas	3	4	0	.429	90	135
Philadelphia	2	4	0	.333	130	132
Phoenix	2	4	0	.333	79	141

Central Division

	W	L	T	Pct.	Pts.	OP
Chicago	5	1	0	.833	142	75
Tampa Bay	4	3	0	.571	147	141
Detroit	2	4	0	.333	141	169
Green Bay	2	4	0	.333	103	146
Minnesota	1	5	0	.167	140	135

Western Division

	W	L	T	Pct.	Pts.	OP
San Francisco	6	0	0	1.000	154	101
Atlanta	2	4	0	.333	161	183
L.A. Rams	2	4	0	.333	164	173
New Orleans	2	4	0	.333	105	123

Thursday, October 18

Miami 17, New England 10—at Joe Robbie Stadium, attendance 62,630. Mark Higgs returned a blocked punt for a touchdown to highlight the Dolphins' win over the Patriots. Pete Stoyanovich's 41-yard field goal and Higgs's blocked punt return put Miami ahead 10-3 at halftime. Dan Marino directed a 64-yard drive to set up Sammie Smith's two-yard touchdown run in the third quarter. Midway through the fourth quarter, the Patriots narrowed the score to 17-10 on Marc Wilson's four-yard scoring pass to George Adams, but the Dolphins held on for the win. The victory put Miami at 5-1, its best start since 1984.

New England	0	3	0	7 —	10
Miami	0	10	7	0 —	17

NE —FG Staurovsky 41
Mia—FG Stoyanovich 47
Mia—Higgs 19 blocked punt return (Stoyanovich kick)
Mia—S. Smith 2 run (Stoyanovich kick)
NE —Adams 4 pass from Wilson (Staurovsky kick)

Sunday, October 21

Los Angeles Rams 44, Atlanta 24—at Anaheim Stadium, attendance 54,761. Jim Everett completed 24 of 38 passes for 302 yards and three touchdowns as the Rams overcame the Falcons. Los Angeles scored 20 unanswered points in the second quarter on Cleveland Gary's 23-yard run, Everett's one-yard pass to Damone Johnson, and a pair of Mike Lansford field goals (46 and 24 yards). Everett then hit Henry Ellard with a 35-yard scoring pass and added a 37-yard touchdown strike to Flipper Anderson in the third quarter to put the Rams ahead 34-17. Gary, who had 19 carries for 102 yards, finished Los Angeles's scoring with a one-yard run in the fourth quarter. Ellard, who had six receptions for 109 yards, became the Rams' all-time leading receiver with 6,311 yards, surpassing Elroy (Crazylegs) Hirsch (6,289).

Atlanta	10	0	7	7 —	24
L.A. Rams	0	20	14	10 —	44

Atl —FG Davis 41
Atl —Dixon 5 pass from Miller (Davis kick)
Rams—Gary 23 run (Lansford kick)
Rams—FG Lansford 46
Rams—D. Johnson 1 pass from Everett (Lansford kick)
Rams—FG Lansford 24
Atl —Rison 71 pass from Miller (Davis kick)
Rams—Ellard 35 pass from Everett (Lansford kick)
Rams—Anderson 37 pass from Everett (Lansford kick)
Rams—Gary 1 run (Lansford kick)
Rams—FG Lansford 32
Atl —Rison 14 pass from Campbell (Davis kick)

Dallas 17, Tampa Bay 13—at Tampa Stadium, attendance 68,315. Troy Aikman's 28-yard touchdown pass to Michael Irvin with 23 seconds remaining in the game gave the Cowboys a win over the Buccaneers. Dallas, trailing 10-0 in the third quarter, tied the score on Ken Willis's 24-yard field goal and Issiac Holt's 64-yard interception return for a touchdown. Tampa Bay kicker Steve Christie kicked a 32-yard field goal for the go-ahead score with less than two minutes left, but Aikman then directed his 80-yard game-winning drive.

Dallas	0	0	3	14 —	17
Tampa Bay	3	7	0	3 —	13

TB —FG Christie 23
TB —Peebles 3 pass from Testaverde (Christie kick)
Dall—FG Willis 24
Dall—Holt 64 interception return (Willis kick)
TB —FG Christie 32
Dall—Irvin 28 pass from Aikman (Willis kick)

Denver 27, Indianapolis 17—at Hoosier Dome, attendance 59,850. John Elway completed 21 of 30 passes for 317 yards and two touchdowns to lead the Broncos over the Colts. Denver took a 17-10 halftime advantage on Elway's scoring passes to Ricky Nattiel (52 yards) and Mark Jackson (five), and David Treadwell's 39-yard field goal. Indianapolis tied the game in the fourth quarter on Jack Trudeau's five-yard scoring pass to Jessie Hester, but the Broncos went ahead on Treadwell's 42-yard field goal and Steve Sewell's two-yard run. Jackson had six receptions for 127 yards.

Denver	7	10	0	10 —	27
Indianapolis	3	7	0	7 —	17

Den—Nattiel 52 pass from Elway (Treadwell kick)
Ind —FG Biasucci 32
Den—Jackson 5 pass from Elway (Treadwell kick)
Den—FG Treadwell 39
Ind —A. Johnson 1 pass from Trudeau (Biasucci kick)
Ind —Hester 5 pass from Trudeau (Biasucci kick)
Den—FG Treadwell 42
Den—Sewell 2 run (Treadwell kick)

Seattle 19, Kansas City 7—at Kingdome, attendance 60,358. Norm Johnson kicked four field goals and Seattle's defense had three fumble recoveries to help the Seahawks defeat Kansas City. The Chiefs scored first on a 33-yard pass from Steve DeBerg to J.J. Birden late in the first half. Johnson then scored 12 unanswered points on field goals of 39, 27, 39, and 43 yards to put Seattle ahead 12-7. Rufus Porter's fumble recovery set up a four-yard touchdown run by John L. Williams late in the fourth quarter for the Seahawks' final score.

Kansas City	0	7	0	0 —	7
Seattle	0	3	3	13 —	19

KC —Birden 33 pass from DeBerg (Lowery kick)
Sea—FG Johnson 39
Sea—FG Johnson 27
Sea—FG Johnson 39
Sea—FG Johnson 43
Sea—Williams 4 run (Johnson kick)

Los Angeles Raiders 24, San Diego 9—at San Diego Jack Murphy Stadium, attendance 60,569. Bo Jackson ran for two touchdowns as the Raiders downed the Chargers to improve their record to 6-1. Jackson, making his season debut, ran for scores of five and seven yards, and Jeff Jaeger added a 24-yard field goal to give Los Angeles a 17-6 lead midway through the third quarter. Jay Schroeder's eight-yard touchdown pass to Willie Gault completed the Raiders' scoring.

L.A. Raiders	0	10	7	7 —	24
San Diego	3	3	3	0 —	9

SD —FG Carney 27
Raiders—FG Jaeger 24
Raiders—Jackson 5 run (Jaeger kick)
SD —FG Carney 37
Raiders—Jackson 7 run (Jaeger kick)
SD —FG Carney 37
Raiders—Gault 8 pass from Schroeder (Jaeger kick)

Houston 23, New Orleans 10—at Astrodome, attendance 57,908. Lorenzo White ran for one touchdown and caught another to lead the Oilers over the Saints. Houston took a 10-3 halftime advantage on Warren Moon's six-yard scoring pass to White and Tony Zendejas's 43-yard field goal. White added a one-yard touchdown run and Zendejas kicked a pair of field goals (45 and 33 yards) in the second half to put the game away. The loss ended the Saints' NFL-record-tying streak of 13 consecutive interconference victories.

New Orleans	3	0	0	7	—	10
Houston	0	10	10	3	—	23

NO — FG Andersen 20
Hou — White 6 pass from Moon (Zendejas kick)
Hou — FG Zendejas 43
Hou — White 1 run (Zendejas kick)
Hou — FG Zendejas 45
NO — Brenner 31 pass from Walsh (Andersen kick)
Hou — FG Zendejas 33

Buffalo 30, New York Jets 27—at Rich Stadium, attendance 79,002. Jim Kelly completed a scoring pass to Jamie Mueller with 19 seconds remaining in the game to rally the Bills over the Jets. New York jumped to a 21-7 lead midway through the second quarter, but Kelly threw a touchdown strike to Andre Reed (14 yards) and Scott Norwood kicked a 29-yard field goal to tighten the score to 21-17 at halftime. Kelly then connected on a 60-yard touchdown bomb to James Lofton to tie the game 24-24 in the third quarter. The Jets went ahead 27-24 on Pat Leahy's 24-yard field goal, but Kelly topped off a 71-yard, 11-play drive with his game-winning 14-yard pass to Mueller.

N.Y. Jets	7	14	3	3	—	27
Buffalo	0	17	7	6	—	30

NYJ — McNeil 5 run (Leahy kick)
NYJ — Boyer 1 pass from O'Brien (Leahy kick)
Buff — Reed 19 pass from Kelly (Norwood kick)
NYJ — Toon 19 pass from O'Brien (Leahy kick)
Buff — Reed 14 pass from Kelly (Norwood kick)
Buff — FG Norwood 29
NYJ — FG Leahy 28
Buff — Lofton 60 pass from Kelly (Norwood kick)
NYJ — FG Leahy 25
Buff — Mueller 14 pass from Kelly (kick failed)

Washington 13, Philadelphia 7—at Robert F. Kennedy Stadium, attendance 53,567. Gerald Riggs ran for a touchdown and Chip Lohmiller kicked two field goals to provide the only scoring the Redskins needed to defeat the Eagles. Riggs's one-yard touchdown run was the only score in the first half. Washington took a 10-0 lead in the fourth quarter on Lohmiller's 33-yard field goal. Lohmiller added a 39-yard kick midway through the final period to finish the Redskins' scoring. The Eagles averted being shut out when quarterback Randall Cunningham threw a nine-yard touchdown pass to Fred Barnett with 43 seconds left in the game.

Philadelphia	0	0	0	7	—	7
Washington	0	7	0	6	—	13

Wash — Riggs 1 run (Lohmiller kick)
Wash — FG Lohmiller 33
Wash — FG Lohmiller 39
Phil — Barnett 9 pass from Cunningham (Ruzek kick)

New York Giants 20, Phoenix 19—at Giants Stadium, attendance 76,518. Matt Bahr kicked a 40-yard field goal as time expired to lead the Giants to victory over the Cardinals. With the score tied 10-10 in the third quarter, Al Del Greco kicked three field goals (18, 34, and 45 yards) to put Phoenix ahead 19-10. Jeff Hostetler, who replaced the injured Phil Simms at quarterback for the Giants, then completed a 38-yard scoring pass to Stephen Baker with 3:21 remaining and led the 76-yard march that set up Bahr's winning kick. The victory put New York at 6-0, its best start ever.

Phoenix	3	7	6	3	—	19
N.Y. Giants	7	3	0	10	—	20

NYG — Anderson 4 run (Bahr kick)
Phx — FG Del Greco 39
NYG — FG Bahr 34
Phx — Sharpe 1 pass from Rosenbach (Del Greco kick)
Phx — FG Del Greco 18
Phx — FG Del Greco 34
Phx — FG Del Greco 45
NYG — Baker 38 pass from Hostetler (Bahr kick)
NYG — FG Bahr 40

San Francisco 27, Pittsburgh 7—at Candlestick Park, attendance 64,301. Tom Rathman ran for a pair of touchdowns as the 49ers defeated the Steelers to remain unbeaten. San Francisco took a 10-7 lead in the first half on Mike Cofer's 39-yard field goal and Mike Sherrard's five-yard scoring pass from Joe Montana. Cofer added a 20-yard field goal and Rathman ran for two one-yard scores in the second half to put the game away. Montana passed for 197 yards, ending his streak of 300-yard passing games at four.

Pittsburgh	7	0	0	0	—	7
San Francisco	0	10	10	7	—	27

Pitt — Bell 2 pass from Brister (Anderson kick)
SF — FG Cofer 39
SF — Sherrard 5 pass from Montana (Cofer kick)
SF — FG Cofer 20
SF — Rathman 1 run (Cofer kick)
SF — Rathman 1 run (Cofer kick)

Monday, October 22

Cincinnati 34, Cleveland 13—at Cleveland Stadium, attendance 78,567. Boomer Esiason completed two touchdown passes as the Bengals improved their record to 5-2 by beating the Browns. Cincinnati took a 17-10 halftime advantage on Esiason's 19-yard touchdown pass to Rodney Holman, James Brooks's 28-yard run for a score, and Jim Breech's 20-yard field goal. The Bengals increased their lead by scoring 17 unanswered points in the second half on Esiason's two-yard scoring pass to Mike Barber, Breech's 21-yard field goal, and Ickey Woods's one-yard run.

Cincinnati	7	10	3	14	—	34
Cleveland	3	10	0	0	—	13

Cin — Holman 19 pass from Esiason (Breech kick)
Clev — FG Kauric 21
Cin — Brooks 28 run (Breech kick)
Cin — FG Breech 20
Clev — FG Kauric 30
Clev — Hoard 1 run (Kauric kick)
Cin — FG Breech 21
Cin — Barber 2 pass from Esiason (Breech kick)
Cin — Woods 1 run (Breech kick)

Eighth Week Summaries

Standings

American Football Conference

Eastern Division	W	L	T	Pct.	Pts.	OP
Buffalo	6	1	0	.857	187	136
Miami	6	1	0	.857	152	90
N.Y. Jets	3	5	0	.375	151	190
Indianapolis	2	5	0	.286	105	162
New England	1	6	0	.143	100	196
Central Division						
Cincinnati	5	3	0	.625	205	204
Houston	4	4	0	.500	181	152
Pittsburgh	4	4	0	.500	150	138
Cleveland	2	6	0	.250	128	193
Western Division						
L.A. Raiders	6	1	0	.857	147	99
Kansas City	4	3	0	.571	167	114
Denver	3	4	0	.429	168	178
Seattle	3	4	0	.429	144	135
San Diego	3	5	0	.375	164	142

National Football Conference

Eastern Division	W	L	T	Pct.	Pts.	OP
N.Y. Giants	7	0	0	1.000	171	96
Washington	4	3	0	.571	144	103
Philadelphia	3	4	0	.429	151	152
Dallas	3	5	0	.375	110	156
Phoenix	2	5	0	.286	100	172
Central Division						
Chicago	6	1	0	.857	173	96
Tampa Bay	4	4	0	.500	157	182
Detroit	3	4	0	.429	168	179
Green Bay	3	4	0	.429	127	156
Minnesota	1	6	0	.143	150	159
Western Division						
San Francisco	7	0	0	1.000	174	118
Atlanta	3	4	0	.429	199	200
L.A. Rams	2	5	0	.286	174	214
New Orleans	2	5	0	.286	115	150

Sunday, October 28

Buffalo 27, New England 10—at Foxboro Stadium, attendance 51,959. Thurman Thomas carried 22 times for 136 yards and a touchdown as the Bills marched past the Patriots. Buffalo jumped to a 14-3 halftime lead on scoring runs by Don Smith (one yard) and Thomas (three). Scott Norwood kicked a pair of 35-yard field goals and Jim Kelly hit Keith McKeller with a 20-yard scoring strike in the third quarter to put the game away. The Bills improved their record to 6-1 while the Patriots fell to 1-6.

Buffalo	7	7	13	0	—	27
New England	0	3	0	7	—	10

Buff — D. Smith 1 run (Norwood kick)
Buff — Thomas 3 run (Norwood kick)
NE — FG Staurovsky 32
Buff — FG Norwood 35
Buff — FG Norwood 35
Buff — McKeller 20 pass from Kelly (Norwood kick)
NE — Martin 19 pass from Grogan (Staurovsky kick)

Chicago 31, Phoenix 21—at Sun Devil Stadium, attendance 71,233. Jim Harbaugh passed and ran for a touchdown, and Neal Anderson ran for two others, to help the Bears over the Cardinals. Chicago took an overwhelming 28-0 halftime lead on Anderson's pair of two-yard touchdown runs, Harbaugh's 67-yard scoring pass to Ron Morris, and Harbaugh's one-yard run for a score. Kevin Butler added a 33-yard field goal in the second half. The Bears amassed 382 yards of total offense.

Chicago	7	21	0	3	—	31
Phoenix	0	7	7	7	—	21

Chi — Anderson 2 run (Butler kick)
Chi — Harbaugh 1 run (Butler kick)
Chi — Morris 67 pass from Harbaugh (Butler kick)
Chi — Anderson 2 run (Butler kick)
Phx — J. T. Smith 3 pass from Rosenbach (Del Greco kick)
Phx — J. Johnson 21 run (Del Greco kick)
Chi — FG Butler 33
Phx — Green 40 pass from Rosenbach (Del Greco kick)

San Francisco 20, Cleveland 17—at Candlestick Park, attendance 63,672. Mike Cofer's 45-yard field goal with five seconds left helped the 49ers beat the Browns to remain undefeated. San Francisco built a 14-0 halftime lead on Joe Montana's 14-yard touchdown pass to Jerry Rice and Tom Rathman's one-yard scoring run. The 49ers took a 17-3 lead on Cofer's 40-yard field goal in the third quarter, but Mike Pagel's scoring passes to Webster Slaughter (11 yards) and Ozzie Newsome (four) tied the game 17-17 with 1:10 remaining. The 49ers' defense registered four sacks and had three turnovers.

Cleveland	0	0	3	14	—	17
San Francisco	0	14	3	3	—	20

SF — Rice 14 pass from Montana (Cofer kick)
SF — Rathman 1 run (Cofer kick)
Clev — FG Kauric 45
SF — FG Cofer 40
Clev — Slaughter 11 pass from Pagel (Kauric kick)
Clev — Newsome 4 pass from Pagel (Kauric kick)
SF — FG Cofer 45

Detroit 27, New Orleans 10—at Louisiana Superdome, attendance 64,368. Jimmie Williams returned a fumble 53 yards for a touchdown to highlight the Lions' win over the Saints. Trailing 10-7, Detroit's Rich Karlis kicked a 25-yard field goal to tie the game in the third quarter. The Lions then scored 17 unanswered points on Williams's fumble recovery return, Karlis's 39-yard field goal, and Barry Sanders's two-yard run. Robert Clark, who had six catches for 127 yards, had Detroit's first touchdown—a five-yard reception from Rodney Peete in the second quarter.

Detroit	0	7	10	10	—	27
New Orleans	7	3	0	0	—	10

NO — Martin 6 pass from Walsh (Andersen kick)
Det — Clark 5 pass from Peete (Karlis kick)
NO — FG Andersen 47
Det — FG Karlis 25
Det — Williams 53 fumble recovery return (Karlis kick)
Det — FG Karlis 39
Det — Sanders 2 run (Karlis kick)

Miami 27, Indianapolis 7—at Hoosier Dome, attendance 59,213. Cliff Odom recovered a fumble in the end zone to lead the Dolphins past the Colts. Odom's touchdown came on Indianapolis's first series of the game. Miami increased its lead to 17-0 at halftime on Pete Stoyanovich's 34-yard field goal and Dan Marino's five-yard pass to Jim Jensen. Stoyanovich's 53-yard field goal and Tony Paige's two-yard run for a score in the second half finished the Dolphins' scoring. Miami's defense had three sacks and limited the Colts to only 31 yards rushing. The Dolphins earned their fourth consecutive victory, the team's longest streak in five years.

Miami	10	7	3	7	—	27
Indianapolis	0	7	0	0	—	7

Mia — Odom fumble recovery in end zone (Stoyanovich kick)
Mia — FG Stoyanovich 34
Ind — Goode 54 fumble recovery return (Biasucci kick)
Mia — Jensen 5 pass from Marino (Stoyanovich kick)
Mia — FG Stoyanovich 53
Mia — Paige 2 run (Stoyanovich kick)

Green Bay 24, Minnesota 10—at Milwaukee County Stadium, attendance 55,125. Darrell Thompson and Don Majkowski each ran for touchdowns to help the Packers past the Vikings. Green Bay took a 10-3 halftime lead on Chris Jacke's 35-yard field goal and Thompson's 12-yard run for a score. The Packers put the game away in the second half by scoring 14 unanswered points on Shawn Patterson's nine-yard interception return for a touchdown and Majkowski's six-yard run. Green Bay's defense had five interceptions. Vikings wide receiver Anthony Carter had nine catches for 141 yards.

Minnesota	0	3	0	7	—	10
Green Bay	3	7	7	7	—	24

GB — FG Jacke 35
Minn — FG Igwebuike 20
GB — Thompson 12 run (Jacke kick)
GB — Patterson 9 interception return (Jacke kick)
GB — Majkowski 6 run (Jacke kick)
Minn — A. Carter 49 pass from Gannon (Igwebuike kick)

New York Jets 17, Houston 12—at Astrodome, attendance 56,337. Darrell Davis recovered a fumble in the end zone early in the fourth quarter to give the Jets a win over the Oilers. New York held a 7-6 advantage at halftime on Ken O'Brien's 42-yard scoring pass to Al Toon. Houston jumped ahead 12-7 in the third quarter on Warren Moon's nine-yard strike to Haywood Jeffires, but Davis's fumble recovery moved the Jets back in front 14-13. Pat Leahy's 32-yard field goal late in the fourth period assured the Jets' victory.

N.Y. Jets	0	7	0	10	—	17
Houston	3	3	6	0	—	12

Hou — FG Garcia 42
NYJ — Toon 42 pass from O'Brien (Leahy kick)
Hou — FG Garcia 49
Hou — Jeffires 9 pass from Moon (kick failed)
NYJ — Davis recovered fumble in end zone (Leahy kick)
NYJ — FG Leahy 32

Philadelphia 21, Dallas 20—at Texas Stadium, attendance 62,605. Randall Cunningham completed a touchdown pass to Calvin Williams late in the fourth quarter as the Eagles rallied to defeat the Cowboys. Cunningham threw a 10-yard scoring pass to Anthony Toney in the opening period to give Philadelphia a 7-3 halftime lead. Troy Aikman connected on a 29-yard scoring pass to Jay Novacek and Emmitt Smith ran three yards for a score to put Dallas ahead 20-14 with 4:02 remaining in the game. Williams's scoring reception with 33 seconds left in the game capped an 85-yard, 13-play drive.

Philadelphia	7	0	0	14	—	21
Dallas	0	3	3	14	—	20

Phil — Toney 10 pass from Cunningham (Ruzek kick)
Dall — FG Willis 43
Dall — FG Willis 43
Phil — Sherman 19 run (Ruzek kick)
Dall — Novacek 29 pass from Aikman (Willis kick)
Dall — E. Smith 3 run (Willis kick)
Phil — Williams 10 pass from Cunningham (Ruzek kick)

San Diego 41, Tampa Bay 10—at San Diego Jack Murphy Stadium, attendance 40,653. Marion Butts ran for three touchdowns as the Chargers easily defeated the Buccaneers. San Diego jumped to a 24-7 halftime lead on Butts's scoring runs (one and two yards), Anthony Miller's 31-yard scoring reception from Billy Joe Tolliver, and John Carney's 28-yard field goal. The Chargers increased their lead in the fourth quarter to 41-7 by scoring 17 unanswered points on rushing scores by Rod Bernstine (20 yards) and Butts (five), and a 27-yard field goal by Carney. Gill Byrd had two of San Diego's four interceptions.

Tampa Bay	0	7	3	0	—	10
San Diego	7	17	0	17	—	41

SD — Butts 1 run (Carney kick)
SD — A. Miller 31 pass from Tolliver (Carney kick)
TB — Carrier 68 pass from Chandler (Christie kick)
SD — FG Carney 28
SD — Butts 2 run (Carney kick)
TB — FG Christie 48
SD — Bernstine 20 run (Carney kick)
SD — FG Carney 27
SD — Butts 5 run (Carney kick)

New York Giants 21, Washington 10—at Giants Stadium, attendance 75,321. Phil Simms completed two touchdown passes as the Giants downed the Redskins for the sixth consecutive time. After a scoreless first period, Simms hit Stephen Baker with a four-yard scoring strike and then found Mark Bavaro with a 13-yard touchdown pass to put New York ahead 14-3 at halftime. Washington narrowed the score to 14-10 on Stan Humphries's five-yard run in the third quarter. Everson Walls then returned an interception 28 yards for a score in the final period to assure the Giants' victory. Walls's interception was the forty-eighth of his career and his first NFL touchdown.

Washington	0	3	7	0	—	10
N.Y. Giants	0	14	0	7	—	21

NYG — Baker 4 pass from Simms (Bahr kick)
NYG — Bavaro 13 pass from Simms (Bahr kick)
Wash — FG Lohmiller 45
Wash — Humphries 5 run (Lohmiller kick)
NYG — Walls 28 interception return (Bahr kick)

Sunday Night, October 28

Atlanta 38, Cincinnati 17—at Atlanta-Fulton County Stadium, attendance 53,214. Chris Miller passed for two touchdowns and Deion Sanders returned a punt for a score to help the Falcons roll over the Bengals. Scott Case's interception set up Mike Rozier's one-yard touchdown run and Case's fumble recovery set up another score, a three-yard touchdown pass from Miller to Floyd Dixon to help Atlanta to a 17-7 halftime lead. Miller and Dixon combined for an 11-yard score and Steve Broussard ran 50 yards for a touchdown in the second half to put the game away. Sanders's 79-yard punt return for a touchdown was the longest in Falcons' history.

Cincinnati	0	7	3	7	—	17
Atlanta	10	7	14	7	—	38

Atl — FG Davis 27
Atl — Rozier 1 run (Davis kick)
Cin — Brooks 6 run (Breech kick)
Atl — Dixon 3 pass from Miller (Davis kick)
Atl — Sanders 79 punt return (Davis kick)
Cin — FG Breech 35
Atl — Dixon 11 pass from Miller (Davis kick)
Cin — Brown 4 pass from Esiason (Breech kick)
Atl — Broussard 50 run (Davis kick)

Monday, October 29

Pittsburgh 41, Los Angeles Rams 10—at Three Rivers Stadium, attendance 56,466. Bubby Brister threw four touchdown passes and Merril Hoge had three scores as the Steelers overcame the Rams. Pittsburgh took a 17-10 lead at halftime on Brister's touchdown passes to Hoge (six yards) and Eric Green (17), and Gary Anderson's 42-yard field goal. The Steelers put the game away in the second half as they blanked the Rams while scoring 24 points on Hoge's one-yard run, Anderson's 30-yard field goal, and Brister's touchdown passes to Dwight Stone (eight yards) and Hoge (two). The margin of victory was Pittsburgh's largest since its opening game of the 1985 season, a 45-3 win over Indianapolis.

L.A. Rams	7	3	0	0	—	10
Pittsburgh	14	3	10	14	—	41

Rams — Green 100 kickoff return (Lansford kick)
Pitt — Hoge 6 pass from Brister (Anderson kick)
Pitt — Green 17 pass from Brister (Anderson kick)
Rams — FG Lansford 32
Pitt — FG Anderson 42
Pitt — FG Anderson 30
Pitt — Hoge 1 run (Anderson kick)
Pitt — Stone 8 pass from Brister (Anderson kick)
Pitt — Hoge 2 pass from Brister (Anderson kick)

Ninth Week Summaries

Standings

American Football Conference

Eastern Division	W	L	T	Pct.	Pts.	OP
Buffalo	7	1	0	.875	229	136
Miami	7	1	0	.875	175	93
N.Y. Jets	4	5	0	.444	175	199
Indianapolis	2	6	0	.250	112	186
New England	1	7	0	.125	120	244
Central Division						
Cincinnati	5	4	0	.556	212	225
Pittsburgh	5	4	0	.556	171	147
Houston	4	5	0	.444	194	169
Cleveland	2	7	0	.222	128	235
Western Division						
L.A. Raiders	6	2	0	.750	154	108
Kansas City	5	3	0	.625	176	121
San Diego	4	5	0	.444	195	156
Denver	3	5	0	.375	190	205
Seattle	3	5	0	.375	158	166

National Football Conference

Eastern Division	W	L	T	Pct.	Pts.	OP
N.Y. Giants	8	0	0	1.000	195	103
Washington	5	3	0	.625	185	141
Philadelphia	4	4	0	.500	199	172
Dallas	3	6	0	.333	119	180
Phoenix	2	6	0	.250	103	195
Central Division						
Chicago	7	1	0	.875	199	102
Tampa Bay	4	5	0	.444	163	208
Detroit	3	5	0	.375	206	220
Green Bay	3	5	0	.375	147	180
Minnesota	2	6	0	.250	177	181
Western Division						
San Francisco	8	0	0	1.000	198	138
Atlanta	3	5	0	.375	208	221
L.A. Rams	3	5	0	.375	191	227
New Orleans	3	5	0	.375	136	157

Sunday, November 4

Pittsburgh 21, Atlanta 9—at Three Rivers Stadium, attendance 57,093. Bubby Brister threw two second-half touchdown passes to lift the Steelers over the Falcons. The Falcons led 9-0 midway through the third quarter on three Greg Davis field goals (41, 43, and 38 yards), but Brister's 11-yard scoring pass to Louis Lipps cut Atlanta's lead to 9-7. Larry Griffin's interception set up Brister's 19-yard touchdown pass to Mike Mularkey to give Pittsburgh a 14-9 lead. The Steelers increased their advantage to 21-9 when Warren Williams ran 70 yards for a score with less than three minutes remaining.

Atlanta	6	3	0	0	—	9
Pittsburgh	0	0	7	14	—	21

Atl — FG Davis 41
Atl — FG Davis 43
Atl — FG Davis 38
Pitt — Lipps 11 pass from Brister (Anderson kick)
Pitt — Mularkey 19 pass from Brister (Anderson kick)
Pitt — Williams 70 run (Anderson kick)

Buffalo 42, Cleveland 0—at Cleveland Stadium, attendance 78,331. Thurman Thomas ran for two touchdowns and caught another as the Bills blanked the Browns for their sixth consecutive victory. Thomas ran for two touchdowns (3 and 11 yards) to provide the only scoring in the first half. Buffalo scored 28 second-half points on touchdown runs by Jamie Mueller (one yard) and Kenneth Davis (three), Jim Kelly's 11-yard scoring pass to Thomas, and Darryl Talley's 60-yard interception return for a touchdown. The win was the largest margin of victory in Bills' history.

Buffalo	7	7	7	21	—	42
Cleveland	0	0	0	0	—	0

Buff — Thomas 3 run (Norwood kick)
Buff — Thomas 11 run (Norwood kick)
Buff — Mueller 1 run (Norwood kick)
Buff — Thomas 11 pass from Kelly (Norwood kick)
Buff — Davis 3 run (Norwood kick)
Buff — D. Talley 60 interception return (Norwood kick)

Chicago 26, Tampa Bay 6—at Tampa Stadium, attendance 68,575. Mark Carrier had two of Chicago's five interceptions as the Bears overcame the Buccaneers. Brad Muster's 12-yard touchdown run opened the scoring and gave Chicago a 7-0 lead. Carrier's interceptions set up Neal Anderson's one-yard scoring run and Kevin Butler's 30-yard field goal within a 2:35 span in the first quarter. The Bears increased their lead to 26-0 in the third quarter on Jim Harbaugh's 19-yard touchdown completion to Dennis Gentry and Butler's 22-yard field goal. Vinny Testaverde's five-yard scoring pass to Bruce Perkins in the fourth quarter prevented the shutout.

Chicago	0	17	9	0	—	26
Tampa Bay	0	0	0	6	—	6

Chi — Muster 12 run (Butler kick)
Chi — Anderson 1 run (Butler kick)
Chi — FG Butler 30
Chi — Gentry 19 pass from Harbaugh (kick failed)
Chi — FG Butler 22
TB — Perkins 5 pass from Testaverde (run failed)

New York Jets 24, Dallas 9—at Giants Stadium, attendance 68,086. Rookie Terance Mathis returned a punt 98 yards for a touchdown to highlight the Jets' win over the Cowboys. Mathis's punt return for a score gave New York a 7-6 halftime edge. The Jets scored 17 points in the second half to put the game away on Pat Leahy's 24-yard field goal and touchdown runs by Brad Baxter (two yards) and Freeman McNeil (one). Mathis's punt return tied an NFL record held by three others; most recently by the Dallas Cowboys' Dennis Morgan against St. Louis in 1974.

Dallas	3	3	0	3	—	9
N.Y. Jets	0	7	3	14	—	24

Dall — FG Willis 37
NYJ — Mathis 98 punt return (Leahy kick)
Dall — FG Willis 35
NYJ — FG Leahy 24
Dall — FG Willis 32
NYJ — Baxter 2 run (Leahy kick)
NYJ — McNeil 1 run (Leahy kick)

Los Angeles Rams 17, Houston 13—at Anaheim Stadium, attendance 52,628. Jim Everett threw a touchdown pass and Cleveland Gary ran for another as the Rams defeated the Oilers. Trailing 10-3 in the second quarter, Gary scored on a one-yard plunge and Everett connected with Damone Johnson on a two-yard scoring pass to put Los Angeles ahead 17-10 at halftime. Bobby Humphery batted down Warren Moon's fourth-down pass with 40 seconds remaining to secure the Rams' victory.

Houston	10	0	0	3	—	13
L.A. Rams	3	14	0	0	—	17

Hou — Hill 40 pass from Moon (Garcia kick)
Rams — FG Lansford 19
Hou — FG Garcia 27
Rams — Gary 1 run (Lansford kick)
Rams — D. Johnson 2 pass from Everett (Lansford kick)
Hou — FG Garcia 31

Kansas City 9, Los Angeles Raiders 7—at Arrowhead Stadium, attendance 70,951. Nick Lowery's three field goals provided all the points the Chiefs needed in their win over the Raiders. Kevin Porter's recovery of a blocked punt at the Raiders' 17-yard line set up Lowery's first field goal (36 yards). Lowery added a 48-yard field goal in the first quarter to put Kansas City ahead 6-0 until the fourth period when the Raiders' Steve Smith ran two yards for a touchdown to put Los Angeles ahead 7-6. Lowery's 41-yard field goal in the fourth quarter gave Kansas City the victory.

L.A. Raiders	0	0	0	7	—	7
Kansas City	6	0	0	3	—	9

KC — FG Lowery 36
KC — FG Lowery 48
Raiders — Smith 2 run (Jaeger kick)
KC — FG Lowery 41

Philadelphia 48, New England 20—at Veterans Stadium, attendance 65,514. Randall Cunningham completed four touchdown passes and also ran for 124 yards as the Eagles rolled over the Patriots. Cunningham, who completed 15 of 24 passes for 240 yards, connected on scoring passes to Keith Jackson (37 and 3 yards), Fred Barnett (37), and Calvin Williams (23). Cunningham's touchdown pass to Jackson capped an 80-yard drive to put Philadelphia ahead 27-10 at halftime. Heath Sherman carried 24 times for 113 yards to mark the first time since December 17, 1978, that two Philadelphia rushers gained more than 100 yards each.

New England	3	7	3	7	—	20
Philadelphia	10	10	7	21	—	48

Phil — FG Ruzek 27
NE — FG Staurovsky 39
Phil — Barnett 37 pass from Cunningham (Ruzek kick)
Phil — FG Ruzek 34
NE — Fryar 36 pass from Wilson (Staurovsky kick)
Phil — Keith Jackson 37 pass from Cunningham (Ruzek kick)
Phil — Williams 23 pass from Cunningham (Ruzek kick)
NE — FG Staurovsky 44
Phil — Keith Jackson 3 pass from Cunningham (Ruzek kick)
NE — Cook 14 pass from Wilson (Staurovsky kick)
Phil — Cunningham 52 run (Ruzek kick)
Phil — Vick 1 run (Ruzek kick)

New Orleans 21, Cincinnati 7—at Riverfront Stadium, attendance 60,067. Craig Heyward carried 19 times for 122 yards and a touchdown as the Saints defeated the Bengals. New Orleans took a 14-7 halftime lead on Steve Walsh's five-yard scoring pass to Gill Fenerty and Rueben Mayes's six-yard run for a score. Boomer Esiason hit Eddie Brown with a nine-yard touchdown pass in the second quarter for the Bengals' only score of the game. Heyward's one-yard run provided the only points in the second half. Mayes rushed for 115 yards on 30 carries.

New Orleans	7	7	0	7	—	21
Cincinnati	0	7	0	0	—	7

NO—Fenerty 5 pass from Walsh (Andersen kick)
NO—Mayes 6 run (Andersen kick)
Cin—Brown 9 pass from Esiason (Breech kick)
NO—Heyward 1 run (Andersen kick)

Miami 23, Phoenix 3—at Joe Robbie Stadium, attendance 54,924. Dan Marino threw two touchdown passes and the Dolphins' defense registered five sacks in their victory over the Cardinals. Marino completed touchdown passes of 17 yards to Tony Paige and seven yards to Mark Clayton. Pete Stoyanovich added field goals of 19, 21, and 19 yards. The victory was Miami's fifth consecutive and improved the Dolphins' record to 5-0 against the Cardinals.

Phoenix	0	3	0	0	—	3
Miami	3	10	10	0	—	23

Mia—FG Stoyanovich 19
Mia—Paige 17 pass from Marino (Stoyanovich kick)
Mia—FG Stoyanovich 21
Phx—FG Del Greco 44
Mia—Clayton 7 pass from Marino (Stoyanovich kick)
Mia—FG Stoyanovich 19

San Diego 31, Seattle 14—at Kingdome, attendance 59,646. Billy Joe Tolliver completed two touchdown passes and Nate Lewis returned a punt 63 yards for a score to help the Chargers beat the Seahawks. Tolliver threw scoring strikes of 11 yards to Ronnie Harmon and 45 yards to Quinn Early to give San Diego a 14-7 halftime advantage. Les Miller recovered a fumble in the end zone for a touchdown late in the third quarter for the Chargers. San Diego's defense recorded four sacks. The victory was the Chargers' first at the Kingdome since September 7, 1980.

San Diego	7	7	17	0	—	31
Seattle	0	7	0	7	—	14

SD—Harmon 11 pass from Tolliver (Carney kick)
Sea—J. L. Williams 21 run (Johnson kick)
SD—Early 45 pass from Tolliver (Carney kick)
SD—FG Carney 20
SD—Lewis 63 punt return (Carney kick)
SD—L. Miller fumble recovery in end zone (Carney kick)
Sea—Blades 18 pass from Krieg (Johnson kick)

San Francisco 24, Green Bay 20—at Lambeau Field, attendance 58,835. Joe Montana completed three touchdown passes as the 49ers rallied past the Packers. Green Bay led 10-7 at halftime, but San Francisco tied the game in the third quarter on Mike Cofer's 22-yard field goal. Montana then connected on scoring strikes to Brent Jones (six yards) and Jerry Rice (64) for the victory. Montana, who completed 25 of 40 passes for 411 yards and no interceptions, moved past John Hadl (33,513) into fifth place on the NFL's career passing-yardage list with 33,599 yards.

San Francisco	0	7	3	14	—	24
Green Bay	3	7	0	10	—	20

GB—FG Jacke 30
GB—Sharpe 20 pass from Majkowski (Jacke kick)
SF—Taylor 23 pass from Montana (Cofer kick)
SF—FG Cofer 22
SF—Jones 6 pass from Montana (Cofer kick)
GB—FG Jacke 37
SF—Rice 64 pass from Montana (Cofer kick)
GB—Sharpe 17 pass from Majkowski (Jacke kick)

Washington 41, Detroit 38—at Pontiac Silverdome, attendance 69,326. Chip Lohmiller's 34-yard field goal with 5:50 remaining in overtime lifted the Redskins over the Lions. Trailing 38-24 in the fourth quarter, Washington's third-string quarterback Jeff Rutledge replaced injured starter Stan Humphries and completed a 34-yard touchdown pass to Gary Clark. Rutledge then capped an 85-yard, 15-play drive with a 12-yard touchdown run with 18 seconds left to send the game into overtime. Rutledge, who directed a 12-play, 69-yard drive to set up Lohmiller's game-winning kick, was named NFC Offensive Player of the Week.

Washington	7	7	7	17	3	—	41
Detroit	7	21	10	0	0	—	38

Det—Clark 33 pass from Peete (Karlis kick)
Wash—Green 8 run (Lohmiller kick)
Det—Peete 10 run (Karlis kick)
Det—White 34 interception return (Karlis kick)
Wash—Johnson 40 pass from Humphries (Lohmiller kick)
Det—Matthews 24 pass from Peete (Karlis kick)
Det—Sanders 45 run (Karlis kick)
Wash—Riggs 3 run (Lohmiller kick)
Det—FG Karlis 26
Wash—FG Lohmiller 38
Wash—Clark 34 pass from Rutledge (Lohmiller kick)
Wash—Rutledge 12 run (Lohmiller kick)
Wash—FG Lohmiller 34

Sunday Night, November 4

Minnesota 27, Denver 22—at Metrodome, attendance 57,331. Anthony Carter had five receptions for 146 yards and a touchdown as the Vikings came back to defeat the Broncos. Minnesota, which trailed 16-7 at halftime, gained a 17-16 edge in the third quarter on Donald Igwebuike's 38-yard field goal and Joey Browner's 26-yard interception return for a score. Denver then took the lead on a pair of 46-yard field goals by David Treadwell. The Vikings opened the fourth quarter on Rich Gannon's 56-yard scoring pass to Carter to take a 24-22 lead. Igwebuike added a 41-yard field goal late in the game to finish Minnesota's scoring.

Denver	6	10	6	0	—	22
Minnesota	0	7	10	10	—	27

Den—Johnson 3 pass from Elway (kick blocked)
Den—Bratton 1 run (Treadwell kick)
Den—FG Treadwell 31
Minn—Fenney 4 run (Igwebuike kick)
Minn—FG Igwebuike 38
Minn—Browner 26 interception return (Igwebuike kick)
Den—FG Treadwell 46
Den—FG Treadwell 46
Minn—A. Carter 56 pass from Gannon (Igwebuike kick)
Minn—FG Igwebuike 41

Monday, November 5

New York Giants 24, Indianapolis 7—at Hoosier Dome, attendance 58,688. Ottis Anderson ran for a pair of touchdowns and Dave Duerson returned a fumble for a score as the Giants downed the Colts to remain undefeated. New York took a 17-0 halftime lead on Matt Bahr's 23-yard field goal and Anderson's two- and three-yard scoring runs. Indianapolis narrowed the margin to 17-7 midway through the third quarter on Albert Bentley's one-yard touchdown plunge, but Duerson's 31-yard fumble recovery return for a score put the game away.

N.Y. Giants	3	14	0	7	—	24
Indianapolis	0	0	7	0	—	7

NYG—FG Bahr 23
NYG—Anderson 2 run (Bahr kick)
NYG—Anderson 3 run (Bahr kick)
Ind—Bentley 1 run (Biasucci kick)
NYG—Duerson 31 fumble recovery return (Bahr kick)

Tenth Week Summaries

Standings

American Football Conference

Eastern Division

	W	L	T	Pct.	Pts.	OP
Buffalo	8	1	0	.889	274	150
Miami	8	1	0	.889	192	96
N.Y. Jets	4	6	0	.400	178	216
Indianapolis	3	6	0	.333	125	196
New England	1	8	0	.111	130	257

Central Division

	W	L	T	Pct.	Pts.	OP
Cincinnati	5	4	0	.556	212	225
Pittsburgh	5	4	0	.556	171	147
Houston	4	5	0	.444	194	169
Cleveland	2	7	0	.222	128	235

Western Division

	W	L	T	Pct.	Pts.	OP
L.A. Raiders	6	3	0	.667	170	137
Kansas City	5	4	0	.556	192	138
San Diego	5	5	0	.500	214	163
Seattle	4	5	0	.444	175	182
Denver	3	6	0	.333	197	224

National Football Conference

Eastern Division

	W	L	T	Pct.	Pts.	OP
N.Y. Giants	9	0	0	1.000	226	110
Philadelphia	5	4	0	.556	227	186
Washington	5	4	0	.556	199	169
Dallas	3	7	0	.300	125	204
Phoenix	2	7	0	.222	117	240

Central Division

	W	L	T	Pct.	Pts.	OP
Chicago	8	1	0	.889	229	126
Green Bay	4	5	0	.444	176	196
Tampa Bay	4	6	0	.400	170	243
Detroit	3	6	0	.333	213	237
Minnesota	3	6	0	.333	194	188

Western Division

	W	L	T	Pct.	Pts.	OP
San Francisco	9	0	0	1.000	222	144
New Orleans	4	5	0	.444	171	164
Atlanta	3	6	0	.333	232	251
L.A. Rams	3	6	0	.333	198	258

Sunday, November 11

Chicago 30, Atlanta 24—at Soldier Field, attendance 62,855. Wendell Davis had five receptions for 105 yards and a touchdown in the Bears' win over the Falcons. Chicago took a 17-3 halftime advantage on Kevin Butler's 21-yard field goal, Neal Anderson's eight-yard run for a score, and Jim Harbaugh's eight-yard touchdown pass to Davis. Brad Muster ran one yard for a touchdown and Vestee Jackson returned an interception 45 yards for a score in the second half to complete Chicago's scoring.

Atlanta	3	0	7	14	—	24
Chicago	0	17	7	6	—	30

Atl—FG Davis 36
Chi—FG Butler 21
Chi—Anderson 8 run (Butler kick)
Chi—Davis 8 pass from Harbaugh (Butler kick)
Chi—Muster 1 run (Butler kick)
Atl—Johnson 5 pass from Miller (Davis kick)
Atl—Broussard 1 run (Davis kick)
Chi—Jackson 45 interception return (kick failed)
Atl—Rison 11 pass from Miller (Davis kick)

San Diego 19, Denver 7—at San Diego Jack Murphy Stadium, attendance 59,557. John Carney kicked four field goals and San Diego linebacker Gary Plummer ran for a score as the Chargers downed the Broncos for their third consecutive win. Denver scored first to take a 7-0 lead on John Elway's 22-yard touchdown strike to Vance Johnson. Carney gave San Diego a 9-7 advantage with three field goals (19, 23, and 43 yards). Plummer's one-yard scoring plunge was set up by Gill Byrd's interception midway through the final period. The Chargers' Marion Butts led all rushers with 114 yards on 16 carries.

Denver	7	0	0	0	—	7
San Diego	0	9	3	7	—	19

Den—Johnson 22 pass from Elway (Treadwell kick)
SD—FG Carney 19
SD—FG Carney 23
SD—FG Carney 43
SD—FG Carney 32
SD—Plummer 1 run (Carney kick)

Green Bay 29, Los Angeles Raiders 16—at Los Angeles Coliseum, attendance 50,855. Don Majkowski passed for two touchdowns and Chris Jacke kicked a club-record five field goals to lift the Packers over the Raiders. Jacke's fourth field goal of the game (23 yards) broke a 16-16 tie in the third quarter. Majkowski, who connected with Vince Workman for a five-yard scoring pass in the second quarter, then hit Perry Kemp with a 28-yard touchdown strike to increase Green Bay's lead to 26-16. Jerry Holmes's interception set up Jacke's final field goal (20 yards) with 17 seconds remaining. The loss snapped a 10-game home winning streak for the Raiders.

Green Bay	3	13	3	10	—	29
L.A. Raiders	13	3	0	0	—	16

Raiders—Allen 5 run (Jaeger kick)
GB—FG Jacke 39
Raiders—Allen 2 run (kick failed)
GB—FG Jacke 51
GB—FG Jacke 32
GB—Workman 5 pass from Majkowski (Jacke kick)
Raiders—FG Jaeger 24
GB—FG Jacke 23
GB—Kemp 28 pass from Majkowski (Jacke kick)
GB—FG Jacke 20

Indianapolis 13, New England 10—at Foxboro Stadium, attendance 28,924. Jeff George hit Bill Brooks with a 26-yard touchdown pass with 2:05 left in the game to help the Colts defeat the Patriots and snap a three-game losing streak. New England led 10-3 at halftime on Marvin Allen's one-yard touchdown run and Jason Staurovsky's 29-yard field goal. Indianapolis got back into the game by scoring 10 unanswered points in the second half on Dean Biasucci's 38-yard field goal and George's game-winning pass to Brooks.

Indianapolis	0	3	3	7	—	13
New England	7	3	0	0	—	10

NE—Allen 1 run (Staurovsky kick)
Ind—FG Biasucci 54
NE—FG Staurovsky 29
Ind—FG Biasucci 38
Ind—Brooks 26 pass from George (Biasucci kick)

Miami 17, New York Jets 3—at Giants Stadium, attendance 68,362. The Dolphins' defense recorded four sacks, two interceptions, and held the Jets to just 154 total yards en route to their sixth consecutive victory. Field goals by Pete Stoyanovich (23 yards) and Pat Leahy (24) provided the only scoring in the first half. Greg Baty's fumble recovery set up Dan Marino's four-yard touchdown pass to Tony Paige that gave Miami a 10-3 lead in the third quarter. The Dolphins put the game away in the fourth quarter when Tim McKyer intercepted a pass to set up Marc Logan's one-yard scoring run. The win moved the 8-1 Dolphins into a tie for the AFC East lead with the Buffalo Bills.

Miami	3	0	7	7	—	17
N.Y. Jets	0	3	0	0	—	3

Mia—FG Stoyanovich 23
NYJ—FG Leahy 24
Mia—Paige 4 pass form Marino (Stoyanovich kick)
Mia—Logan 1 run (Stoyanovich kick)

Minnesota 17, Detroit 7—at Pontiac Silverdome, attendance 68,264. The Vikings capitalized on turnovers by the Lions to score 17 points in their win over Detroit. Minnesota took a 7-0 halftime lead when Michael Brim's interception set up Rich Gannon's one-yard touchdown run. Pat Eilers's fumble recovery on the opening kickoff of the second half set up Fuad Reveiz's 27-yard field goal. Detroit narrowed the score midway through the third period to 10-7 on Bob Gagliano's 18-yard touchdown pass to Jeff Campbell. Al Noga returned an interception 26 yards for a score with 1:21 remaining to clinch the Vikings' victory.

Minnesota	0	7	3	7	— 17
Detroit	0	0	7	0	— 7

Minn — Gannon 1 run (Reveiz kick)
Minn — FG Reveiz 27
Det — Campbell 18 pass from Gagliano (Karlis kick)
Minn — Noga 26 interception return (Reveiz kick)

New York Giants 31, Los Angeles Rams 7—at Anaheim Stadium, attendance 64,632. Ottis Anderson, Rodney Hampton, and Lewis Tillman each ran for touchdowns as the Giants defeated the Rams to improve their record to 8-0. New York jumped to a 10-0 halftime advantage on Matt Bahr's 44-yard field goal and Phil Simms's nine-yard touchdown pass to Mark Bavaro. Hampton's 19-yard scoring run capped an 85-yard drive in the third quarter. Anderson (three yards) and Tillman (one) had touchdown runs in the fourth quarter to put the game away.

N.Y. Giants	3	7	7	14	— 31
L.A. Rams	0	0	7	0	— 7

NYG — FG Bahr 44
NYG — Bavaro 9 pass from Simms (Bahr kick)
Rams — Gary 3 run (Lansford kick)
NYG — Hampton 19 run (Bahr kick)
NYG — Anderson 3 run (Bahr kick)
NYG — Tillman 1 run (Bahr kick)

Buffalo 45, Phoenix 14—at Rich Stadium, attendance 74,904. Jim Kelly completed four scoring passes to four different receivers as the Bills upended the Cardinals. Kelly had three of his touchdown passes in the second quarter on completions to Keith McKeller (18 yards), Butch Rolle (1), and Steve Tasker (24) to give Buffalo a 21-7 half-time lead. The Bills added 24 points in the fourth quarter on Scott Norwood's 25-yard field goal, Kelly's 11-yard pass to Don Beebe, and scoring runs by Jamie Mueller (one yard) and Kenneth Davis (13). Thurman Thomas rushed 26 times for 112 yards for Buffalo.

Phoenix	7	0	7	0	— 14
Buffalo	0	21	0	24	— 45

Phx — Johnson 1 run (Del Greco kick)
Buff — McKeller 18 pass from Kelly (Norwood kick)
Buff — Rolle 1 pass from Kelly (Norwood kick)
Buff — Tasker 24 pass from Kelly (Norwood kick)
Phx — Jones 29 pass from Rosenbach (Del Greco kick)
Buff — FG Norwood 25
Buff — Beebe 11 pass from Kelly (Norwood kick)
Buff — Mueller 1 run (Norwood kick)
Buff — K. Davis 13 run (Norwood kick)

Seattle 17, Kansas City 16—at Arrowhead Stadium, attendance 71,285. Dave Krieg's 25-yard touchdown pass to Paul Skansi as time expired rallied the Seahawks past the Chiefs for their first Arrowhead Stadium victory since 1980. Seattle took a 10-6 third-quarter lead on a 43-yard field goal by Norm Johnson and Krieg's 54-yard scoring strike to Jeff Chadwick. Nick Lowery's 24-yard field goal and Dan Saleaumua's fumble recovery in the end zone put Kansas City ahead 16-10 in the fourth quarter. Krieg directed a 66-yard, four-play drive to set up his game-winning scoring pass to Skansi. The Chiefs' Derrick Thomas had seven sacks, breaking the NFL record of six set by San Francisco's Fred Dean against New Orleans in 1983.

Seattle	0	3	7	7	— 17
Kansas City	0	6	10	0	— 16

KC — FG Lowery 25
Sea — FG Johnson 43
KC — FG Lowery 30
Sea — Chadwick 54 pass from Krieg (Johnson kick)
KC — FG Lowery 24
KC — Saleaumua recovered fumble in end zone (Lowery kick)
Sea — Skansi 25 pass from Krieg (Johnson kick)

New Orleans 35, Tampa Bay 7—at Louisiana Superdome, attendance 67,865. Craig Heyward carried 20 times for 155 yards and two touchdowns to lead the Saints over the Buccaneers. Heyward scored on touchdown runs of 47 and 2 yards, while teammate Rueben Mayes also ran for two scores (4 and 1 yards). Mayes's second touchdown run was set up by Toi Cook's 50-yard interception return. Heyward, who turned in his second consecutive 100-yard performance, was named NFC Offensive Player of the Week.

Tampa Bay	7	0	0	0	— 7
New Orleans	0	14	14	7	— 35

TB — Chandler 12 run (Christie kick)
NO — Perriman 26 pass from Walsh (Andersen kick)
NO — Heyward 47 run (Andersen kick)
NO — Mayes 4 run (Andersen kick)
NO — Heyward 2 run (Andersen kick)
NO — Mayes 1 run (Andersen kick)

Sunday Night, November 11

San Francisco 24, Dallas 6—at Texas Stadium, attendance 62,966. Joe Montana, making his Texas Stadium debut, passed for one touchdown and ran for another as the 49ers beat the Cowboys. San Francisco took a 17-6 halftime lead on Montana's seven-yard scoring pass to Jerry Rice, Tom Rathman's one-yard run for a touchdown, and Mike Cofer's 42-yard field goal. Montana's four-yard scoring run provided the game's only second-half scoring. The 49ers limited the Cowboys to just 156 total yards and held a 40:39 to 19:21 time-of-possession advantage.

San Francisco	0	17	0	7	— 24
Dallas	3	3	0	0	— 6

Dall — FG Willis 23
SF — Rathman 1 run (Cofer kick)
SF — Rice 7 pass from Montana (Cofer kick)
Dall — FG Willis 37
SF — FG Cofer 42
SF — Montana 4 run (Cofer kick)

Monday, November 12

Philadelphia 28, Washington 14—at Veterans Stadium, attendance 65,857. Heath Sherman rushed for 124 yards on 35 carries and scored two touchdowns as the Eagles marched past the Redskins. Sherman scored on a pair of touchdown receptions (nine and two yards) in the third quarter to extend Philadelphia's lead to 28-7. The Eagles' two other touchdowns came on defensive plays when William Frizzell returned an interception 30 yards for a score and Clyde Simmons recovered a fumble and returned it 18 yards for a touchdown. Redskins running back Brian Mitchell, who took over at quarterback replacing the injured Jeff Rutledge and Stan Humphries, scored Washington's last points on a one-yard run.

Washington	0	7	0	7	— 14
Philadelphia	7	0	21	0	— 28

Phil — Frizzell 30 interception return (Ruzek kick)
Wash — Warren 8 pass from Rutledge (Lohmiller kick)
Phil — Sherman 9 pass from Byars (Ruzek kick)
Phil — Simmons 18 fumble recovery return (Ruzek kick)
Phil — Sherman 2 pass from Cunningham (Ruzek kick)
Wash — Mitchell 1 run (Lohmiller kick)

Eleventh Week Summaries

Standings

American Football Conference

Eastern Division	W	L	T	Pct.	Pts.	OP
Buffalo	9	1	0	.900	288	150
Miami	8	2	0	.800	202	109
Indianapolis	4	6	0	.400	142	210
N.Y. Jets	4	7	0	.364	192	233
New England	1	9	0	.100	130	271
Central Division						
Cincinnati	6	4	0	.600	239	228
Houston	5	5	0	.500	229	192
Pittsburgh	5	5	0	.500	174	174
Cleveland	2	8	0	.200	151	270
Western Division						
L.A. Raiders	7	3	0	.700	183	147
Kansas City	6	4	0	.600	219	148
San Diego	5	6	0	.455	224	190
Seattle	4	6	0	.400	196	206
Denver	3	7	0	.300	210	240

National Football Conference

Eastern Division	W	L	T	Pct.	Pts.	OP
N.Y. Giants	10	0	0	1.000	246	110
Philadelphia	6	4	0	.600	251	209
Washington	6	4	0	.600	230	186
Dallas	4	7	0	.364	149	225
Phoenix	2	8	0	.200	138	264
Central Division						
Chicago	9	1	0	.900	245	139
Green Bay	5	5	0	.500	200	217
Minnesota	4	6	0	.400	218	209
Tampa Bay	4	7	0	.364	177	274
Detroit	3	7	0	.300	213	257
Western Division						
San Francisco	10	0	0	1.000	253	151
New Orleans	4	6	0	.400	188	195
Atlanta	3	7	0	.300	255	275
L.A. Rams	3	7	0	.300	219	282

Sunday, November 18

Chicago 16, Denver 13—at Mile High Stadium, attendance 75,013. Kevin Butler's 44-yard field goal with 1:46 remaining in overtime gave the Bears a win over the Broncos. Chicago took a 13-6 third-quarter lead on Mike Singletary's fumble recovery to set up Butler's 32-yard field goal and Jim Morrissey's interception led to Brad Muster's 10-yard scoring run. John Elway's nine-yard touchdown run tied the game 13-13 with 1:14 remaining. The Bears registered six sacks en route to their sixth consecutive victory.

Chicago	0	3	10	0	3	— 16
Denver	3	3	0	7	0	— 13

Den — FG Treadwell 27
Chi — FG Butler 37
Den — FG Treadwell 24
Chi — FG Butler 32
Chi — Muster 10 run (Butler kick)
Den — Elway 9 run (Treadwell kick)
Chi — FG Butler 44

Dallas 24, Los Angeles Rams 21—at Anaheim Stadium, attendance 58,589. Troy Aikman completed 17 of 32 passes for 303 yards and three touchdowns to lead the Cowboys over the Rams. Aikman threw scoring passes to Michael Irvin (10 and 61 yards) and Tommie Agee (six) in the first half to give Dallas a 21-14 halftime lead. Cleveland Gary had three touchdown runs for the Rams, including a one-yard plunge in the third quarter to tie the game 21-21, but Ken Willis connected on a 23-yard field goal for the win.

Dallas	7	14	0	3	— 24
L.A. Rams	7	7	7	0	— 21

Rams — Gary 16 run (Lansford kick)
Dall — Irvin 10 pass from Aikman (Willis kick)
Rams — Gary 4 run (Lansford kick)
Dall — Agee 6 pass fom Aikman (Willis kick)
Dall — Irvin 61 pass from Aikman (Willis kick)
Rams — Gary 1 run (Lansford kick)
Dall — FG Willis 23

New York Giants 20, Detroit 0—at Giants Stadium, attendance 76,109. Phil Simms passed for two touchdowns and Matt Bahr kicked two field goals as the Giants blanked the Lions for their tenth consecutive victory. New York scored all its points in the first half as Simms connected on touchdown passes to Stephen Baker (33 yards) and Mark Ingram (57), and Bahr added field goals from 24 and 49 yards.

Detroit	0	0	0	0	— 0
N.Y. Giants	7	13	0	0	— 20

NYG — Baker 33 pass from Simms (Bahr kick)
NYG — FG Bahr 24
NYG — Ingram 57 pass from Simms (Bahr kick)
NYG — FG Bahr 49

Green Bay 24, Phoenix 21—at Sun Devil Stadium, attendance 46,878. Anthony Dilweg's one-yard touchdown pass to Ed West with 16 seconds left in the game helped the Packers defeat the Cardinals. Green Bay took a 10-0 lead in the second quarter, but Phoenix came back and scored 21 consecutive points on Timm Rosenbach's touchdown passes to Ernie Jones (22 and 25 yards) and Roy Green (27). Dilweg, who replaced the injured Don Majkowski in the second quarter, completed a 15-yard scoring pass to Clarence Weathers to cut the Cardinals' lead to 21-17 in the fourth quarter.

Green Bay	7	3	0	14	— 24
Phoenix	0	7	7	7	— 21

GB — Sharpe 54 pass from Majkowski (Jacke kick)
GB — FG Jacke 21
Phx — E. Jones 22 pass from Rosenbach (Del Greco kick)
Phx — Green 27 pass from Rosenbach (Del Greco kick)
Phx — E. Jones 25 pass from Rosenbach (Del Greco kick)
GB — Weathers 15 pass from Dilweg (Jacke kick)
GB — West 1 pass from Dilweg (Jacke kick)

Houston 35, Cleveland 23—at Cleveland Stadium, attendance 76,726. Warren Moon completed 24 of 32 passes for 322 yards and five touchdowns as the Oilers beat the Browns. Houston led 14-13 at halftime on Moon's scoring passes to Lorenzo White (three yards) and Haywood Jeffires (46). Cleveland took a 16-14 lead in the third quarter, but Moon's scoring strikes to Curtis Duncan (37 yards), Tony Jones (23), and Ernest Givins (seven) put the game away. Duncan finished the day with seven receptions for 130 yards.

Houston	7	7	0	21	— 35
Cleveland	6	7	3	7	— 23

Clev — Newsome 13 pass from Kosar (kick failed)
Hou — White 3 pass from Moon (Garcia kick)
Clev — Gainer 1 run (Kauric kick)
Hou — Jeffires 46 pass from Moon (Garcia kick)
Clev — FG Kauric 22
Hou — Duncan 37 pass from Moon (Garcia kick)
Hou — Jones 23 pass from Moon (Garica kick)
Hou — Givins 7 pass from Moon (Garcia kick)
Clev — Langhorne 4 pass from Kosar (Kauric kick)

Minnesota 24, Seattle 21—at Kingdome, attendance 59,735. Fuad Reveiz's 24-yard field goal as time expired lifted the Vikings over the Seahawks. Minnesota took a 14-7 second-quarter lead on Rich Gannon's touchdown passes to Hassan Jones (eight yards) and Anthony Carter (11). Brian Blades's five-yard scoring reception from Dave Krieg and Derrick Fenner's one-yard touchdown run gave Seattle a 21-14 advantage midway through the fourth quarter. The Vikings tied the game 21-21 on Herschel Walker's 58-yard scoring run with 2:28 remaining. Joey Browner's interception set up Reveiz's winning kick.

Minnesota	7	7	0	10	— 24
Seattle	7	7	0	7	— 21

Sea — Blades 9 pass from Krieg (Johnson kick)
Minn — Jones 8 pass from Gannon (Reveiz kick)
Minn — A. Carter 11 pass from Gannon (Reveiz kick)
Sea — Blades 5 pass from Krieg (Johnson kick)
Sea — Fenner 1 run (Johnson kick)
Minn — Walker 58 run (Reveiz kick)
Minn — FG Reveiz 24

Buffalo 14, New England 0—at Rich Stadium, attendance 74,720. Thurman Thomas's two touchdown runs provided the game's only scoring as the Bills defeated the Patriots. Thomas, who rushed for 165 yards on 22 carries, scored on a five-yard run in the first quarter. James Williams's interception set up Thomas's 80-yard touchdown run with 1:38 remaining in the game. The victory gave the Bills their eighth consecutive win.

New England	0	0	0	0 —	0
Buffalo	7	0	0	7 —	14

Buff — Thomas 5 run (Norwood kick)
Buff — Thomas 80 run (Norwood kick)

Washington 31, New Orleans 17—at Robert F. Kennedy Stadium, attendance 52,573. Mark Rypien completed 26 of 38 passes for 311 yards and four touchdowns to lead the Redskins past the Saints. Rypien completed scoring passes to Gary Clark (eight and 19 yards), Art Monk (seven), and Kelvin Bryant (three). He also led a 15-play, 58-yard drive to set up Chip Lohmiller's 39-yard field goal for Washington's initial score in the first quarter. Clark led all receivers with eight catches for 131 yards. Earnest Byner had 26 carries for 116 yards. Monk's four catches gave him 702 career receptions, making him only the third player in NFL history with more than 700 receptions, joining Steve Largent and Charlie Joiner.

New Orleans	7	3	0	7 —	17
Washington	3	14	14	0 —	31

NO — Perriman 16 pass from Walsh (Andersen kick)
Wash — FG Lohmiller 39
Wash — Clark 8 pass from Rypien (Lohmiller kick)
NO — FG Andersen 38
Wash — Monk 7 pass from Rypien (Lohmiller kick)
Wash — Clark 19 pass from Rypien (Lohmiller kick)
Wash — Bryant 3 pass from Rypien (Lohmiller kick)
NO — Turner 8 pass from Walsh (Andersen kick)

Indianapolis 17, New York Jets 14—at Hoosier Dome, attendance 47,283. Jeff George completed 14 of 22 passes for a career-high 249 yards and two touchdowns as the Colts rallied to defeat the Jets. Pat Leahy kicked four field goals (32, 21, 29, and 40) and Dennis Byrd tackled George in the end zone for a safety as New York jumped to a 14-0 lead. The Colts' first score was set up when George recovered a fumble following Erik McMillan's interception in the third quarter. George then fired a 43-yard scoring pass to Jessie Hester for Indianapolis's initial points. George hit Stanley Morgan with a three-yard touchdown strike to tie the score 14-14. Dean Biasucci's 38-yard field goal proved to be the game-winning points.

N.Y. Jets	3	5	6	0 —	14
Indianapolis	0	0	7	10 —	17

NYJ — FG Leahy 32
NYJ — Safety, Byrd tackled George in end zone
NYJ — FG Leahy 21
NYJ — FG Leahy 29
NYJ — FG Leahy 40
Ind — Hester 43 pass from George (Biasucci kick)
Ind — Morgan 3 pass from George (Biasucci kick)
Ind — FG Biasucci 38

Philadelphia 24, Atlanta 23—at Atlanta-Fulton County Stadium, attendance 53,755. Roger Ruzek kicked a 46-yard field goal with less than two minutes remaining in the game to lead the Eagles over the Falcons. Atlanta led 16-7 in the fourth quarter, but Cunningham threw touchdown passes of 17 yards to Keith Jackson and 30 yards to Calvin Williams within a 58-second span to put Philadelphia ahead 21-16. Jerome Brown's fumble recovery set up Cunningham's scoring throw to Williams. The Falcons recaptured the lead on Chris Miller's 23-yard touchdown pass to Andre Rison.

Philadelphia	0	7	0	17 —	24
Atlanta	0	10	3	10 —	23

Atl — Johnson 1 run (Davis kick)
Phil — Jackson 1 pass from Cunningham (Ruzek kick)
Atl — FG Davis 53
Atl — FG Davis 46
Atl — FG Davis 28
Phil — Jackson 17 pass from Cunningham (Ruzek kick)
Phil — Williams 30 pass from Cunningham (Ruzek kick)
Atl — Rison 23 pass from Miller (Davis kick)
Phil — FG Ruzek 46

Kansas City 27, San Diego 10—at Arrowhead Stadium, attendance 63,717. Steve DeBerg completed three touchdown passes, including a pair to Bill Jones, as the Chiefs rolled over the Chargers. Kansas City jumped to a 17-3 halftime lead on DeBerg's touchdown passes to J.J. Birden (90 yards) and Jones (two), and Nick Lowery's 36-yard field goal. Kevin Ross's interception set up Lowery's second field goal (37 yards) in the third quarter. DeBerg threw a six-yard touchdown pass to Jones in the fourth quarter to complete the Chiefs' scoring.

San Diego	3	0	7	0 —	10
Kansas City	10	7	3	7 —	27

KC — Birden 90 pass from DeBerg (Lowery kick)
KC — FG Lowery 36
SD — FG Carney 42
KC — B. Jones 2 pass from DeBerg (Lowery kick)
SD — Walker 2 pass from Tolliver (Carney kick)
KC — FG Lowery 37
KC — B. Jones 6 pass from DeBerg (Lowery kick)

San Francisco 31, Tampa Bay 7—at Candlestick Park, attendance 62,221. Joe Montana connected with Brent Jones for two touchdown passes as the 49ers tied an NFL record with their eighteenth consecutive victory. San Francisco jumped to a 17-0 halftime advantage on Montana's scoring passes to Jones (11 and four yards) and Mike Cofer's 24-yard field goal. Roger Craig (10 yards) and Harry Sydney (one) had touchdown runs in the second half to put the game away. Montana, who threw for 230 yards to lift his season total to 3,065, became the first NFL player to eclipse the 3,000-yard passing mark in seven seasons.

Tampa Bay	0	0	7	0 —	7
San Francisco	7	10	7	7 —	31

SF — Jones 11 pass from Montana (Cofer kick)
SF — FG Cofer 24
SF — Jones 4 pass from Montana (Cofer kick)
TB — Haddix 65 interception return (Christie kick)
SF — Craig 10 run (Cofer kick)
SF — Sydney 1 run (Cofer kick)

Sunday Night, November 18

Cincinnati 27, Pittsburgh 3—at Riverfront Stadium, attendance 60,064. Barney Bussey returned a fumble 70 yards for a touchdown and Jim Breech kicked a pair of field goals to help the Bengals record their fifth consecutive win over the Steelers. Cincinnati took an insurmountable 24-0 third-quarter lead on Ickey Woods's scoring run (five yards), Breech's 21-yard field goal, Bussey's fumble recovery, and Craig Taylor's one-yard run. Breech's 33-yard field goal capped the Bengals' scoring. James Brooks carried 20 times for 105 yards.

Pittsburgh	0	0	0	3 —	3
Cincinnati	7	3	14	3 —	27

Cin — Woods 5 run (Breech kick)
Cin — FG Breech 21
Cin — Taylor 1 run (Breech kick)
Cin — Bussey 70 fumble recovery return (Breech kick)
Pitt — FG Anderson 31
Cin — FG Breech 33

Monday, November 19

Los Angeles Raiders 13, Miami 10—at Joe Robbie Stadium, attendance 75,553. Marcus Allen carried 19 times for 79 yards and a touchdown to lead the Raiders past the Dolphins. Los Angeles took a 10-7 halftime lead on Allen's two-yard touchdown run after Jeff Jaeger's 23-yard field goal. Jaeger added a 43-yard kick in the second half to complete the scoring. The Raiders held Miami to just 14 yards rushing, the lowest in Dolphins' history.

L.A. Raiders	0	10	3	0 —	13
Miami	0	7	0	3 —	10

Raiders — FG Jaeger 23
Raiders — Allen 2 run (Jaeger kick)
Mia — Schwedes 14 pass from Marino (Stoyanovich kick)
Raiders — FG Jaeger 43
Mia — FG Stoyanovich 26

Twelfth Week Summaries

Standings

American Football Conference

Eastern Division

	W	L	T	Pct.	Pts.	OP
Buffalo	9	2	0	.818	312	177
Miami	9	2	0	.818	232	122
Indianapolis	5	6	0	.455	176	230
N.Y. Jets	4	8	0	.333	199	257
New England	1	10	0	.091	144	305

Central Division

	W	L	T	Pct.	Pts.	OP
Cincinnati	6	5	0	.545	259	262
Houston	6	5	0	.545	256	216
Pittsburgh	6	5	0	.545	198	181
Cleveland	2	9	0	.182	164	300

Western Division

	W	L	T	Pct.	Pts.	OP
Kansas City	7	4	0	.636	246	172
L.A. Raiders	7	4	0	.636	207	174
Seattle	5	6	0	.455	209	216
San Diego	5	7	0	.417	234	203
Denver	3	8	0	.273	237	280

National Football Conference

Eastern Division

	W	L	T	Pct.	Pts.	OP
N.Y. Giants	10	1	0	.909	259	141
Philadelphia	7	4	0	.636	282	222
Washington	6	5	0	.545	247	213
Dallas	5	7	0	.417	176	242
Phoenix	3	8	0	.273	172	278

Central Division

	W	L	T	Pct.	Pts.	OP
Chicago	9	2	0	.818	258	180
Green Bay	6	5	0	.545	220	227
Minnesota	5	6	0	.455	259	222
Detroit	4	7	0	.364	253	284
Tampa Bay	4	8	0	.333	187	294

Western Division

	W	L	T	Pct.	Pts.	OP
San Francisco	10	1	0	.909	270	179
New Orleans	5	6	0	.455	198	202
L.A. Rams	4	7	0	.364	247	299
Atlanta	3	8	0	.273	262	285

Thursday, November 22

Detroit 40, Denver 27—at Pontiac Silverdome, attendance 73,896. Barry Sanders carried 23 times for 147 yards and scored two touchdowns to lead the Lions past the Broncos. Detroit jumped to a 27-17 halftime lead on a pair of Bob Gagliano scoring passes to Richard Johnson (11 and 43 yards), Sanders's seven-yard run, and two Eddie Murray field goals (24 and 32 yards). Gagliano hit Sanders with a 35-yard touchdown pass in the third quarter and Murray added field goals from 43 and 45 yards to complete the scoring. It was the most points scored by the Lions since a 44-40 loss to Green Bay on Thanksgiving Day in 1986.

Denver	7	10	3	7 —	27
Detroit	21	6	7	6 —	40

Det — Johnson 11 pass from Gagliano (Murray kick)
Den — Bratton 1 run (Treadwell kick)
Det — Sanders 7 run (Murray kick)
Det — Johnson 43 pass from Gagliano (Murray kick)
Det — FG Murray 24
Den — FG Treadwell 24
Den — Henderson 49 interception return (Treadwell kick)
Det — FG Murray 32
Den — FG Treadwell 32
Det — Sanders 35 pass from Gagliano (Murray kick)
Den — Bratton 1 run (Treadwell kick)
Det — FG Murray 43
Det — FG Murray 45

Dallas 27, Washington 17—at Texas Stadium, attendance 60,355. Emmitt Smith ran for two touchdowns and Ken Willis kicked two field goals to help the Cowboys beat the Redskins. Dallas built a 10-0 first-quarter lead on Willis's 49-yard field goal and Troy Aikman's 12-yard touchdown pass to Michael Irvin. Washington came back to take the lead 17-10 in the third quarter on Earnest Byner's five-yard run, Chip Lohmiller's 25-yard field goal, and Mark Rypien's six-yard scoring strike to Ricky Sanders. Smith, who ran 23 times for 132 yards, had a pair of scoring runs (1 and 48 yards) in the second half to bring Dallas back. The win gave the Cowboys a 4-0 advantage over the Redskins in Thanksgiving Day games.

Washington	0	7	10	0 —	17
Dallas	10	0	7	10 —	27

Dall — FG Willis 49
Dall — Irvin 12 pass from Aikman (Willis kick)
Wash — Byner 5 run (Lohmiller kick)
Wash — FG Lohmiller 25
Wash — Sanders 6 pass from Rypien (Lohmiller kick)
Dall — Smith 1 run (Willis kick)
Dall — FG Willis 41
Dall — Smith 48 run (Willis kick)

Sunday, November 25

New Orleans 10, Atlanta 7—at Louisiana Superdome, attendance 68,229. Steve Walsh's six-yard scoring pass to Eric Martin with 2:10 remaining in the game lifted the Saints over the Falcons. New Orleans took a 3-0 lead on Morten Andersen's 20-yard field goal as time expired at the end of the first half. Chris Miller completed a 51-yard touchdown pass to George Thomas midway through the fourth quarter to put Atlanta ahead 7-3, but Walsh directed an 86-yard drive to set up his winning touchdown pass.

Atlanta	0	0	0	7 —	7
New Orleans	0	3	0	7 —	10

NO — FG Andersen 20
Atl — Thomas 51 pass from Miller (Davis kick)
NO — Martin 6 pass from Walsh (Andersen kick)

Minnesota 41, Chicago 13—at Metrodome, attendance 58,666. Rich Gannon threw three touchdown passes and Herschel Walker accumulated 176 total yards as the Vikings notched their fourth consecutive victory. Walker returned the opening kickoff 64 yards, setting up Fuad Reveiz's 41-yard field goal, and scored touchdowns on a two-yard run and a 17-yard reception from Gannon. Gannon also completed scoring passes to Hassan Jones (five yards) and Anthony Carter (22) to give Minnesota a 34-3 lead at halftime. Mike Merriweather, who recorded 1.5 of the Vikings' seven sacks, returned a fumble recovery 33 yards for a score and was named NFC Defensive Player of the Week.

Chicago	0	3	7	3 —	13
Minnesota	13	21	7	0 —	41

Minn — FG Reveiz 41
Minn — FG Reveiz 45
Minn — Walker 2 run (Reveiz kick)
Minn — Walker 17 pass from Gannon (Reveiz kick)
Minn — H. Jones 5 pass from Gannon (Reveiz kick)
Chi — FG Butler 41
Minn — A. Carter 22 pass from Gannon (Reveiz kick)
Minn — Merriweather 33 fumble recovery return (Reveiz kick)
Chi — Green 10 pass from Harbaugh (Butler kick)
Chi — FG Butler 43

Indianapolis 34, Cincinnati 20—at Riverfront Stadium, attendance 60,051. Eric Dickerson carried 22 times for 143 yards and a touchdown to help the Colts past the Bengals. Indianapolis jumped to a 17-6 halftime lead on Jeff George's 19-yard touchdown pass to Jessie Hester, Dickerson's one-yard run for a touchdown, and Dean Biasucci's 22-yard field goal. George hit Bill Brooks with a five-yard touchdown pass and Stanley Morgan with a six-yard strike to put Indianapolis ahead 31-6 in the third quarter. Biasucci's 26-yard field goal completed the Colts' scoring.

Indianapolis 7 10 14 3 — 34
Cincinnati 6 0 14 0 — 20

Cin — Woods 1 run (kick failed)
Ind — Hester 19 pass from George (Biasucci kick)
Ind — Dickerson 1 run (Biasucci kick)
Ind — FG Biasucci 22
Ind — B. Brooks 5 pass from George (Biasucci kick)
Ind — Morgan 6 pass from George (Biasucci kick)
Cin — Brown 21 pass from Esiason (Breech kick)
Cin — Brown 20 pass from Esiason (Breech kick)
Ind — FG Biasucci 26

Kansas City 27, Los Angeles Raiders 24—at Los Angeles Coliseum, attendance 65,170. Steve DeBerg completed three touchdown passes as the Chiefs defeated the Raiders for the second time in three weeks. DeBerg hit Emile Harry with a 19-yard scoring pass in the second quarter and Nick Lowery kicked a 35-yard field goal to help Kansas City to a 10-10 halftime tie. DeBerg also connected on a pair of 11-yard touchdown passes to Bill Jones and Lowery added a 36-yard field goal in the second half to give the Chiefs the lead for good. The victory marked the first time Kansas City had swept the season series over the Raiders since 1981.

Kansas City 0 10 10 7 — 27
L.A. Raiders 0 10 7 7 — 24

KC — FG Lowery 35
Raiders — Allen 3 run (Jaeger kick)
KC — Harry 19 pass from DeBerg (Lowery kick)
Raiders — FG Jaeger 50
KC — B. Jones 11 pass from DeBerg (Lowery kick)
Raiders — Allen 10 run (Jaeger kick)
KC — FG Lowery 36
KC — B. Jones 11 pass from DeBerg (Lowery kick)
Raiders — Allen 5 run (Jaeger kick)

Los Angeles Rams 28, San Francisco 17—at Candlestick Park, attendance 62,633. Cleveland Gary had two touchdown runs and one scoring reception to help the Rams knock the 49ers from the undefeated ranks. Los Angeles jumped to a 21-7 halftime lead on Buford McGee's 22-yard scoring pass to Gary and scoring runs by both Gary (10 yards) and McGee (six). San Francisco narrowed the score to 21-17 on Joe Montana's 23-yard touchdown pass to Harry Sydney and Mike Cofer's 42-yard field goal. Vince Newsome's interception set up a 90-yard drive capped by Gary's one-yard touchdown run to put the game away in the fourth quarter. The loss ended the 49ers' bid to become the first NFL team to win 19 consecutive games.

L.A. Rams 7 14 0 7 — 28
San Francisco 0 7 10 0 — 17

Rams — Gary 22 pass from McGee (Lansford kick)
Rams — Gary 10 run (Lansford kick)
SF — Taylor 5 pass from Montana (Cofer kick)
Rams — McGee 6 run (Lansford kick)
SF — Sydney 23 pass from Montana (Cofer kick)
SF — FG Cofer 42
Rams — Gary 1 run (Lansford kick)

Miami 30, Cleveland 13—at Cleveland Stadium, attendance 70,225. Dan Marino passed for two touchdowns and Kerry Glenn returned an interception for a score in the Dolphins' victory over the Browns. Miami opened a 27-0 lead on Marino's touchdown passes to Mark Duper (five yards) and James Pruitt (35), Sammie Smith's four-yard scoring run, and Glenn's 31-yard interception return. Pete Stoyanovich added a 40-yard field goal in the third quarter to complete the Dolphins' scoring. Marino, who threw for 245 yards to give him 30,099 career passing yards, became the eleventh NFL player to throw for more than 30,000 career yards. Marino achieved this in 114 games, the shortest span in NFL history, bettering Dan Fouts's mark of 131 games.

Miami 14 13 3 0 — 30
Cleveland 0 3 3 7 — 13

Mia — Duper 5 pass from Marino (Stoyanovich kick)
Mia — Pruitt 35 pass from Marino (Stoyanovich kick)
Mia — Smith 4 run (kick failed)
Mia — Glenn 31 interception return (Stoyanovich kick)
Clev — FG Kauric 36
Clev — FG Kauric 42
Mia — FG Stoyanovich 40
Clev — Mack 2 run (Kauric kick)

Phoenix 34, New England 14—at Sun Devil Stadium, attendance 30,110. Anthony Thompson carried 28 times for 136 yards and a touchdown as the Cardinals defeated the Patriots. Thompson ran for a five-yard touchdown and Timm Rosenbach, who led an 80-yard drive, scored on a two-yard run for a 14-14 halftime tie. The Cardinals scored 20 unanswered points in the second half on scoring runs by Rosenbach (six yards) and Terrence Flagler (29), and a pair of Al Del Greco field goals (29 and 50 yards).

New England 7 7 0 0 — 14
Phoenix 7 7 10 10 — 34

Phx — Thompson 5 run (Del Greco kick)
NE — Stephens 18 pass from Hodson (Staurovsky kick)
Phx — Rosenbach 2 run (Del Greco kick)
NE — Cook 22 pass from Hodson (Staurovsky kick)
Phx — FG Del Greco 29
Phx — Rosenbach 6 run (Del Greco kick)
Phx — Flagler 29 run (Del Greco kick)
Phx — FG Del Greco 50

Philadelphia 31, New York Giants 13—at Veterans Stadium, attendance 66,706. Randall Cunningham completed two touchdown passes and ran for a third as the Eagles downed the previously unbeaten Giants. Cunningham fired a 49-yard touchdown pass to Fred Barnett and capped an 80-yard drive with a one-yard scoring run in the first half. Philadelphia took a commanding 31-13 lead in the second half on Roger Ruzek's 39-yard field goal, Cunningham's six-yard touchdown pass to Calvin Williams, and Byron Evans's 23-yard interception return for a score. Cunningham, who passed for 229 yards and rushed for 66 more, was named NFC Offensive Player of the Week.

N.Y. Giants 7 6 0 0 — 13
Philadelphia 7 7 3 14 — 31

NYG — Ingram 15 pass from Simms (Bahr kick)
Phil — Barnett 49 pass from Cunningham (Ruzek kick)
Phil — Cunningham 1 run (Ruzek kick)
NYG — Bavaro 4 pass from Simms (kick failed)
Phil — FG Ruzek 39
Phil — Williams 6 pass from Cunningham (Ruzek kick)
Phil — Evans 23 interception return (Ruzek kick)

Pittsburgh 24, New York Jets 7—at Giants Stadium, attendance 57,806. Bubby Brister threw two touchdown passes as the Steelers defeated the Jets for the eleventh time in 12 meetings. Pittsburgh broke a 7-7 tie in the third quarter on Gary Anderson's 33-yard field goal. The Steelers put the game away in the fourth quarter on Merril Hoge's one-yard scoring run and Brister's three-yard touchdown pass to Louis Lipps. Pittsburgh held the Jets to eight first downs and maintained a 39:25 to 20:35 time-of-possession advantage.

Pittsburgh 0 7 3 14 — 24
N.Y. Jets 0 7 0 0 — 7

NYJ — Moore 53 pass from O'Brien (Leahy kick)
Pitt — W. Williams 5 pass from Brister (Anderson kick)
Pitt — FG Anderson 33
Pitt — Hoge 1 run (Anderson kick)
Pitt — Lipps 3 pass from Brister (Anderson kick)

Green Bay 20, Tampa Bay 10—at Milwaukee County Stadium, attendance 53,677. Anthony Dilweg, replacing injured Don Majkowski, passed for two touchdowns as the Packers handed the Buccaneers their sixth consecutive loss. Dilweg completed a four-yard touchdown pass to Sterling Sharpe in the first quarter. Scott Stephens's fumble recovery set up Dilweg's second touchdown pass, a two-yard completion to Michael Haddix, in the third quarter. Chris Jacke added two field goals of 25 yards.

Tampa Bay 0 3 7 0 — 10
Green Bay 0 7 10 3 — 20

GB — Sharpe 4 pass from Dilweg (Jacke kick)
TB — FG Christie 33
GB — M. Haddix 2 pass from Dilweg (Jacke kick)
GB — FG Jacke 25
TB — Hill 11 pass from Testaverde (Christie kick)
GB — FG Jacke 25

Sunday Night, November 25

Seattle 13, San Diego 10—at San Diego Jack Murphy Stadium, attendance 50,096. Norm Johnson's 40-yard field goal with 11:59 remaining in overtime gave the Seahawks a win over the Chargers. Eugene Robinson's 30-yard interception return set up Derrick Fenner's one-yard touchdown run to tie the game 10-10 late in fourth quarter. Rufus Porter's fumble recovery on the Chargers' 23-yard line set up the winning kick. John L. Williams led all receivers with nine catches for 110 yards.

Seattle 0 3 0 7 3 — 13
San Diego 0 3 7 0 0 — 10

SD — FG Carney 20
Sea — FG Johnson 26
SD — Cox 8 pass from Tolliver (Carney kick)
Sea — Fenner 1 run (Johnson kick)
Sea — FG Johnson 40

Monday, November 26

Houston 27, Buffalo 24—at Astrodome, attendance 60,130. Warren Moon completed 16 of 22 passes for 300 yards and two touchdowns as the Oilers downed the Bills. Moon fired a 37-yard pass to Haywood Jeffires early in the first quarter to open the scoring. Teddy Garcia kicked two field goals from 25 and 36 yards to give Houston a 14-13 halftime edge. Lorenzo White ran one yard for a touchdown and Moon hit Leonard Harris with a three-yard scoring pass in the second half. White, who rushed 18 times for 125 yards and had five receptions for 89 yards, was named AFC Offensive Player of the Week.

Buffalo 7 7 3 7 — 24
Houston 7 6 7 7 — 27

Hou — Jeffires 37 pass from Moon (Garcia kick)
Buff — Metzelaars 1 pass from Kelly (Norwood kick)
Hou — FG Garcia 25
Hou — FG Garcia 36
Buff — McKeller 12 pass from Kelly (Norwood kick)
Buff — FG Norwood 43
Hou — White 1 run (Garcia kick)
Hou — Harris 3 pass from Moon (Garcia kick)
Buff — Thomas 2 run (Norwood kick)

Thirteenth Week Summaries

Standings

American Football Conference

Eastern Division	W	L	T	Pct.	Pts.	OP
Buffalo	10	2	0	.833	342	200
Miami	9	3	0	.750	252	164
Indianapolis	5	7	0	.417	193	250
N.Y. Jets	4	9	0	.308	216	295
New England	1	11	0	.083	151	342
Central Division						
Cincinnati	7	5	0	.583	275	274
Houston	6	6	0	.500	266	229
Pittsburgh	6	6	0	.500	210	197
Cleveland	2	10	0	.167	187	338
Western Division						
Kansas City	8	4	0	.667	283	179
L.A. Raiders	8	4	0	.667	230	194
Seattle	6	6	0	.500	222	226
San Diego	6	7	0	.462	272	220
Denver	3	9	0	.250	257	303

National Football Conference

Eastern Division	W	L	T	Pct.	Pts.	OP
N.Y. Giants**	10	2	0	.833	262	148
Philadelphia	7	5	0	.583	305	252
Washington	7	5	0	.583	289	233
Dallas	6	7	0	.462	193	255
Phoenix	4	8	0	.333	192	295
Central Division						
Chicago*	10	2	0	.833	281	197
Green Bay	6	6	0	.500	227	250
Minnesota	6	6	0	.500	282	229
Tampa Bay	5	8	0	.385	210	311
Detroit	4	8	0	.333	270	307
Western Division						
San Francisco*	11	1	0	.917	277	182
L.A. Rams	5	7	0	.417	285	322
New Orleans	5	7	0	.417	211	219
Atlanta	3	9	0	.250	279	308

**Clinched Division Title*
***Clinched Playoff Position*

Sunday, December 2

Tampa Bay 23, Atlanta 17—at Tampa Stadium, attendance 42,839. Vinny Testaverde passed for two touchdowns and Steve Christie kicked three field goals to lead the Buccaneers over the Falcons. Tampa Bay took a 13-7 halftime lead on Testaverde's 89-yard touchdown pass to Willie Drewrey and Christie's field goals from 39 and 44 yards. Atlanta took a 17-16 fourth-quarter lead but Testaverde's 35-yard touchdown pass to Mark Carrier secured the victory.

Atlanta 7 0 0 10 — 17
Tampa Bay 0 13 0 10 — 23

Atl — Johnson 3 run (Davis kick)
TB — Drewrey 89 pass from Testaverde (Christie kick)
TB — FG Christie 39
TB — FG Christie 44
Atl — Rozier 9 run (Davis kick)
TB — FG Christie 21
Atl — FG Davis 46
TB — Carrier 35 pass from Testaverde (Christie kick)

Cincinnati 16, Pittsburgh 12—at Three Rivers Stadium, attendance 58,200. Eddie Brown and James Brooks each scored touchdowns as the Bengals defeated the Steelers to give them a one-game lead over Pittsburgh and Houston in the AFC Central. Cincinnati scored all its points in the first half on Brown's 50-yard scoring reception from Boomer Esiason, James Francis's safety, and Brooks' seven-yard touchdown run. Cincinnati's victory was its third consecutive win at Three Rivers Stadium.

Cincinnati 7 9 0 0 — 16
Pittsburgh 6 0 3 3 — 12

Pitt — FG Anderson 32
Cin — Brown 50 pass from Esiason (Breech kick)
Pitt — FG Anderson 36
Cin — Safety, Francis tackled Brister in end zone
Cin — Brooks 7 run (Breech kick)
Pitt — FG Anderson 29
Pitt — FG Anderson 48

Chicago 23, Detroit 17—at Soldier Field, attendance 66,946. Jim Harbaugh hit Neal Anderson with a 50-yard touchdown pass with 4:03 remaining in overtime to lead the Bears past the Lions. Chicago built a 14-10 halftime lead on scoring runs by Brad Muster (six yards) and Harbaugh (two). Detroit went ahead early in the fourth quarter 17-14 on Bob Gagliano's 22-yard touchdown pass to Richard Johnson. Ron Rivera's interception set up Kevin Butler's 19-yard field goal with 33 seconds remaining to send the game into overtime.

Detroit 7 3 0 7 0 — 17
Chicago 0 14 0 3 6 — 23

Det — Peete 1 run (Murray kick)
Chi — Muster 6 run (Butler kick)

Det—FG Murray 34
Chi—Harbaugh 2 run (Butler kick)
Det—Johnson 22 pass from Gagliano (Murray kick)
Chi—FG Butler 19
Chi—Anderson 50 pass from Harbaugh

Seattle 13, Houston 10—at Kingdome, attendance 57,692. Norm Johnson's 42-yard field goal with 4:25 elapsed in overtime gave the Seahawks a win over the Oilers. Chris Warren ran one yard for a touchdown and Johnson kicked a 39-yard field goal to give Seattle a 10-3 lead entering the fourth quarter. Warren Moon then completed a two-yard scoring pass to Ernest Givins to tie the game 10-10. Dave Wyman's fumble recovery in overtime set up Johnson's winning kick. It was the second consecutive week the Seahawks were victorious in overtime.

Houston	0	3	0	7	0	— 10
Seattle	0	7	3	0	3	— 13

Hou—FG Garcia 29
Sea—Warren 1 run (Johnson kick)
Sea—FG Johnson 39
Hou—Givins 2 pass from Moon (Garcia kick)
Sea—FG Johnson 42

Phoenix 20, Indianapolis 17—at Sun Devil Stadium, attendance 31,885. Marcus Turner and Cedric Mack combined to turn an interception into a touchdown as the Cardinals downed the Colts. Phoenix trailed 17-6 entering the fourth quarter, but Timm Rosenbach's one-yard run closed the margin to 17-13. Mack then intercepted Jeff George's pass and lateraled the ball to Turner, who ran 21 yards for the go-ahead points.

Indianapolis	10	0	7	0	— 17
Phoenix	0	6	0	14	— 20

Ind —FG Biasucci 49
Ind —A. Johnson 15 pass from George (Biasucci kick)
Phx—FG Del Greco 32
Phx—FG Del Greco 39
Ind —Hester 6 pass from George (Biasucci kick)
Phx—Rosenbach 1 run (Del Greco kick)
Phx—Turner 21 lateral from Mack interception (Del Greco kick)

Kansas City 37, New England 7—at Foxboro Stadium, attendance 26,280. Steve DeBerg completed 15 of 21 passes for 331 yards and two touchdowns as the Chiefs rolled over the Patriots. Kansas City jumped to a 23-0 halftime lead on DeBerg's scoring passes to Stephone Paige (86 yards) and Robb Thomas (11), and Nick Lowery's three field goals (19, 32, and 45 yards). Christian Okoye scored on a pair of one-yard touchdown runs in the second half to put the game away. Paige had seven receptions for 151 yards.

Kansas City	13	10	7	7	— 37
New England	0	0	7	0	— 7

KC—Paige 86 pass from DeBerg (Lowery kick)
KC—FG Lowery 19
KC—FG Lowery 32
KC—FG Lowery 45
KC—R. Thomas 11 pass from DeBerg (Lowery kick)
KC—Okoye 1 run (Lowery kick)
NE—Cook 2 pass from Hodson (Staurovsky kick)
KC—Okoye 1 run (Lowery kick)

Los Angeles Raiders 23, Denver 20—at Mile High Stadium, attendance 74,162. Bo Jackson carried 13 times for 117 yards and two touchdowns as the Raiders handed the Broncos their fifth consecutive loss. Jackson ran 11 yards for a touchdown in the third quarter to give Los Angeles a 14-10 lead. Jackson's 62-yard scoring run and Jeff Jaeger's 46-yard field goal increased the Raiders' lead to 23-13. John Elway completed an eight-yard touchdown pass to Michael Young late in the fourth quarter, but the Raiders held on for the win.

L.A. Raiders	7	0	7	9	— 23
Denver	3	7	0	10	— 20

Den —FG Treadwell 45
Raiders—Smith 4 run (Jaeger kick)
Den —Johnson 21 pass from Elway (Treadwell kick)
Raiders—Jackson 11 run (Jaeger kick)
Den —FG Treadwell 21
Raiders—Jackson 62 run (kick failed)
Raiders—FG Jaeger 46
Den —Young 8 pass from Elway (Treadwell kick)

Los Angeles Rams 38, Cleveland 23—at Cleveland Stadium, attendance 61,981. Jim Everett passed for four touchdowns to four different receivers as the Rams downed the Browns. Los Angeles went ahead 17-3 on Everett's scoring passes of one yard to Pete Holohan and 16 yards to Gaston Green, and Mike Lansford's 30-yard field goal. Cleveland Gary ran one yard for a touchdown and Everett hit Robert Delpino (21 yards) and Buford McGee (nine) for scoring strikes in the second half. Henry Ellard caught six passes to give him 402 career receptions, breaking the Rams' record of 400, set by Tom Fears.

L.A. Rams	3	14	14	7	— 38
Cleveland	3	0	14	6	— 23

Rams—FG Lansford 30
Clev —FG Kauric 37
Rams—Holohan 1 pass from Everett (Lansford kick)
Rams—Green 16 pass from Everett (Lansford kick)
Rams—Gary 1 run (Lansford kick)
Clev —Slaughter 17 pass from Kosar (Kauric kick)
Rams—Delpino 21 pass from Everett (Lansford kick)
Clev —Mack 3 pass from Kosar (Kauric kick)
Rams—McGee 9 pass from Everett (Lansford kick)
Clev —Mack 1 run (kick failed)

Washington 42, Miami 20—at Robert F. Kennedy Stadium, attendance 53,599. Earnest Byner rushed for 157 yards and three touchdowns as the Redskins crushed the Dolphins. Byner scored on runs of two, seven, and 13 yards. Mark Rypien completed touchdown passes to Art Monk (six and seven yards) and Jimmie Johnson (three). Washington gained 467 yards in total offense, held a 40:09 to 19:51 time-of-possession advantage, and had 29 first downs compared to Miami's 13.

Miami	0	3	3	14	— 20
Washington	7	14	14	7	— 42

Wash—Byner 2 run (Lohmiller kick)
Wash—Monk 6 pass from Rypien (Lohmiller kick)
Wash—Byner 7 run (Lohmiller kick)
Mia —FG Stoyanovich 21
Mia —FG Stoyanovich 44
Wash—Johnson 3 pass from Rypien (Lohmiller kick)
Wash—Byner 13 run (Lohmiller kick)
Mia —Pruitt 24 pass from Marino (Stoyanovich kick)
Mia —Williams 42 interception return (Stoyanovich kick)
Wash—Monk 7 pass from Rypien (Lohmiller kick)

Dallas 17, New Orleans 13—at Texas Stadium, attendance 60,087. Troy Aikman completed a touchdown pass to Darryl Johnston as the Cowboys rallied to defeat the Saints. New Orleans held a 10-0 halftime lead, but Dallas cut the deficit to 10-7 in the third quarter on Emmitt Smith's one-yard run for a touchdown. Aikman's five-yard touchdown pass to Johnston early in the fourth quarter put Dallas ahead 14-13. Ken Willis kicked a 47-yard field goal to cap the Cowboys' scoring. Dallas's win increased their record to 8-0 against the Saints at Texas Stadium.

New Orleans	3	7	3	0	— 13
Dallas	0	0	7	10	— 17

NO —FG Andersen 43
NO —Mayes 15 run (Andersen kick)
Dall—E. Smith 1 run (Willis kick)
NO —FG Andersen 50
Dall—Johnston 5 pass from Aikman (Willis kick)
Dall—FG Willis 47

San Diego 38, New York Jets 17—at San Diego Jack Murphy Stadium, attendance 40,877. Marion Butts ran for two touchdowns and Billy Joe Tolliver passed for two more to lead the Chargers over the Jets. Butts, who carried 26 times for 159 yards, scored on runs of one and four yards in the first half. Tolliver threw scoring strikes to Anthony Miller (24 yards) and Nate Lewis (19) in the second half. Butts raised his season rushing total to 1,154 yards to become the seventh Chargers' player to rush for more than 1,000 yards in a season.

N.Y. Jets	3	7	0	7	— 17
San Diego	7	10	7	14	— 38

NYJ—FG Leahy 38
SD —Butts 1 run (Carney kick)
SD —Butts 4 run (Carney kick)
NYJ—Toon 21 pass from O'Brien (Leahy kick)
SD —FG Carney 22
SD —A. Miller 24 pass from Tolliver (Carney kick)
NYJ—Toon 8 pass from O'Brien (Leahy kick)
SD —Lewis 19 pass from Tolliver (Carney kick)
SD —Lewis 10 run (Carney kick)

Buffalo 30, Philadelphia 23—at Rich Stadium, attendance 79,320. Jim Kelly completed 19 of 32 passes for 334 yards and three touchdowns as the Bills held on to defeat the Eagles. Kelly connected on all three of his scoring passes in the first half on completions to James Lofton (63 yards), Andre Reed (56), and Thurman Thomas (four). Scott Norwood added a 43-yard field goal as Buffalo built a 24-0 first-quarter lead. Philadelphia scored 23 unanswered points to narrow the score to 24-23 on three Randall Cunningham touchdown passes to Keith Jackson (18 yards), Fred Barnett (95), and Keith Byars (one), and Roger Ruzek's 32-yard field goal. Norwood connected on a pair of field goals (21 and 45 yards) to assure the win. Lofton caught five passes for 174 yards to move into third place on the NFL's all-time receiving yardage list.

Philadelphia	0	16	7	0	— 23
Buffalo	24	0	3	3	— 30

Buff—Lofton 63 pass from Kelly (Norwood kick)
Buff—FG Norwood 43
Buff—Reed 56 pass from Kelly (Norwood kick)
Buff—Thomas 4 pass from Kelly (Norwood kick)
Phil —Keith Jackson 18 pass from Cunningham (kick failed)
Phil —FG Ruzek 32
Phil —Barnett 95 pass from Cunningham (Ruzek kick)
Phil —Byars 1 pass from Cunningham (Ruzek kick)
Buff—FG Norwood 21
Buff—FG Norwood 45

Sunday Night, December 2

Minnesota 23, Green Bay 7—at Metrodome, attendance 62,058. Rich Gannon and Anthony Carter connected on a 56-yard touchdown pass to lead the Vikings past the Packers for their fifth consecutive victory. Fuad Reveiz kicked three field goals (29, 32, and 41 yards) to put Minnesota ahead 9-7 in the third quarter. Minnesota put the game away on Gannon's scoring pass to Carter and Al Noga's sacking of Anthony Dilweg and recovering the ball in the end zone for a touchdown.

Green Bay	0	0	7	0	— 7
Minnesota	3	3	17	0	— 23

Minn—FG Reveiz 29
Minn—FG Reveiz 32
GB —Green 36 blocked punt return (Jacke kick)
Minn—FG Reveiz 41
Minn—A. Carter 56 pass from Gannon (Reveiz kick)
Minn—Noga recovered fumble in end zone (Reveiz kick)

Monday, December 3

San Francisco 7, New York Giants 3—at Candlestick Park, attendance 66,413. Joe Montana completed a touchdown pass to John Taylor to lead the 49ers over the Giants. All 10 points were scored in the first half. Matt Bahr kicked a 20-yard field goal to put New York ahead 3-0. Montana then found Roger Craig with a 31-yard pass to set up his 23-yard scoring throw to Taylor to go ahead 7-3. The 49ers' defense recorded four sacks and a fumble recovery.

N.Y. Giants	0	3	0	0	— 3
San Francisco	0	7	0	0	— 7

NYG—FG Bahr 20
SF —J. Taylor 23 pass from Montana (Cofer kick)

Fourteenth Week Summaries

Standings

American Football Conference

Eastern Division	W	L	T	Pct.	Pts.	OP
Buffalo**	11	2	0	.846	373	207
Miami**	10	3	0	.769	275	184
Indianapolis	5	8	0	.385	200	281
N.Y. Jets	4	9	0	.308	216	295
New England	1	12	0	.077	154	366
Central Division						
Cincinnati	7	6	0	.538	292	294
Houston	7	6	0	.538	324	243
Pittsburgh	7	6	0	.538	243	200
Cleveland	2	11	0	.154	201	396
Western Division						
Kansas City	9	4	0	.692	314	199
L.A. Raiders	9	4	0	.692	268	225
Seattle	7	6	0	.538	242	240
San Diego	6	7	0	.462	272	220
Denver	3	10	0	.231	277	334

National Football Conference

Eastern Division	W	L	T	Pct.	Pts.	OP
N.Y. Giants*	11	2	0	.846	285	163
Washington	8	5	0	.615	299	242
Philadelphia	7	6	0	.538	325	275
Dallas	6	7	0	.462	193	255
Phoenix	5	8	0	.385	216	308
Central Division						
Chicago*	10	3	0	.769	290	207
Green Bay	6	7	0	.462	241	270
Minnesota	6	7	0	.462	297	252
Tampa Bay	5	8	0	.385	210	311
Detroit	4	9	0	.308	301	345
Western Division						
San Francisco*	12	1	0	.923	297	199
New Orleans	6	7	0	.462	235	239
L.A. Rams	5	8	0	.385	305	346
Atlanta	3	10	0	.231	292	332

**Clinched Division Title*
***Clinched Playoff Position*

Sunday, December 9

Buffalo 31, Indianapolis 7—at Hoosier Dome, attendance 53,268. Thurman Thomas ran for two scores and Buffalo's defense recorded five sacks and three interceptions as the Bills routed the Colts to earn a playoff berth. Jim Kelly hit Andre Reed with two scoring passes (34 and seven yards) in the first quarter and Thomas ran five yards for a score as Buffalo built a 21-0 halftime lead. Thomas's second scoring run from 23 yards was set up by defensive end Leon Seals's interception in the fourth quarter. Reed's two scoring receptions gave him 37 career touchdowns, surpassing Elbert Dubenion's club-record 35.

Buffalo	14	7	3	7	— 31
Indianapolis	0	0	7	0	— 7

Buff—Reed 34 pass from Kelly (Norwood kick)
Buff—Reed 7 pass from Kelly (Norwood kick)
Buff—Thomas 5 run (Norwood kick)
Ind —George 1 run (Biasucci kick)
Buff—FG Norwood 25
Buff—Thomas 23 run (Norwood kick)

Washington 10, Chicago 9—at Robert F. Kennedy Stadium, attendance 53,920. Chip Lohmiller's 35-yard field goal with 2:14 left in the game gave the Redskins a come-from-behind victory over the Bears. Kevin Butler's three field goals from 29, 23, and 46 yards gave Chicago a 9-0 halftime lead. Mark Rypien narrowed the score to 9-7 in the third quarter on an eight-yard touchdown pass to Gary

Clark. Earnest Byner rushed for 121 yards on 28 carries for the Redskins. Butler's three field goals raised his career total to a Bears' record 131.

Chicago	3	6	0	0	— 9
Washington	0	0	7	3	— 10

Chi —FG Butler 29
Chi —FG Butler 23
Chi —FG Butler 46
Wash—Clark 8 pass from Rypien (Lohmiller kick)
Wash—FG Lohmiller 35

Houston 58, Cleveland 14—at Astrodome, attendance 54,469. Lorenzo White ran for four touchdowns and Warren Moon completed two scoring passes as the Oilers handed the Browns their eighth consecutive loss. Houston took an insurmountable 45-7 halftime lead on three touchdown runs by White (10, one, and seven yards), a pair of Warren Moon scoring passes to Ernest Givins (six yards) and Leonard Harris (17), Terry Kinard's 72-yard fumble recovery return, and Teddy Garcia's 45-yard field goal. White, who rushed 18 times for 116 yards, added a five-yard touchdown run in the third quarter. The Oilers' 58 points set a club record and their 45 first-half points were the third highest in NFL history.

Cleveland	0	7	7	0	— 14
Houston	14	31	7	6	— 58

Hou —White 10 run (Garcia kick)
Hou —White 1 run (Garcia kick)
Hou —Kinard 72 fumble recovery return (Garcia kick)
Hou —Givins 6 pass from Moon (Garcia kick)
Clev—Metcalf 101 kickoff return (Kauric kick)
Hou —FG Garcia 45
Hou —White 7 run (Garcia kick)
Hou —Harris 17 pass from Moon (Garcia kick)
Hou —White 5 run (Garcia kick)
Clev—Metcalf 31 pass from Kosar (Kauric kick)
Hou —T. Jones 9 pass from Carlson (kick failed)

Kansas City 31, Denver 20—at Arrowhead Stadium, attendance 74,347. Steve DeBerg completed three touchdown passes as the Chiefs beat the Broncos to remain in a first-place tie with the Raiders in the AFC Western Division. Kansas City trailed 13-10 at halftime on DeBerg's 49-yard scoring pass to Stephone Paige and Nick Lowery's 33-yard field goal. Dino Hackett's fumble recovery set up Barry Word's one-yard touchdown run for the go-ahead score in the third quarter. DeBerg then hit Danta Whitaker with a one-yard touchdown pass and Robb Thomas with a 27-yard scoring reception.

Denver	0	13	0	7	— 20
Kansas City	7	3	7	14	— 31

KC —Paige 49 pass from DeBerg (Lowery kick)
Den—Sharpe 5 pass from Elway (kick failed)
Den—Young 16 pass from Elway (Treadwell kick)
KC —FG Lowery 33
KC —Word 1 run (Lowery kick)
KC —Whitaker 1 pass from DeBerg (Lowery kick)
Den—Humphrey 2 run (Treadwell kick)
KC —R. Thomas 27 pass from DeBerg (Lowery kick)

New York Giants 23, Minnesota 15—at Giants Stadium, attendance 76,121. Ottis Anderson ran for two touchdowns as the Giants downed the Vikings to clinch their second consecutive NFC Eastern Division title. Trailing 15-10 in the fourth quarter, Bahr kicked a 48-yard field goal and Anderson ran two yards for a touchdown to put New York ahead 20-15. Anderson also scored on a one-yard run in the second quarter. Lawrence Taylor, who had two-and-a-half sacks and forced an interception to set up Bahr's decisive fourth-quarter field goal, was named NFC Defensive Player of the Week.

Minnesota	5	7	3	0	— 15
N.Y. Giants	3	7	0	13	— 23

Minn—Safety, Doleman sacked Simms in end zone
Minn—FG Reveiz 22
NYG—FG Bahr 36
Minn—A. Anderson 1 run (Reveiz kick)
NYG—O. Anderson 1 run (Bahr kick)
Minn—FG Reveiz 37
NYG—FG Bahr 48
NYG—O. Anderson 2 run (Bahr kick)
NYG—FG Bahr 18

Pittsburgh 24, New England 3—at Three Rivers Stadium, attendance 48,354. Merril Hoge ran for two touchdowns as the Steelers defeated the Patriots to give head coach Chuck Noll his 200th career victory. Gary Anderson's 42-yard field goal opened the scoring and Hoge's eight-yard run gave Pittsburgh a 10-3 halftime advantage. The Steelers increased their lead to 24-3 in the second half on Bubby Brister's 14-yard touchdown pass to Eric Green and Hoge's 41-yard scoring run. Hoge finished the day with 19 carries for 117 yards. Noll joined George Halas, Tom Landry, Don Shula, and Curly Lambeau as the only coaches in NFL history to win 200 games.

New England	0	3	0	0	— 3
Pittsburgh	3	7	7	7	— 24

Pitt—FG Anderson 42
Pitt—Hoge 8 run (Anderson kick)
NE —FG Staurovsky 49
Pitt—Green 14 pass from Brister (Anderson kick)
Pitt—Hoge 41 run (Anderson kick)

New Orleans 24, Los Angeles Rams 20—at Anaheim Stadium, attendance 65,844. Steve Walsh's four-yard scoring pass to Eric Martin in the fourth quarter helped the Saints come back to defeat the Rams. New Orleans trailed 20-10 in the fourth quarter on Brett Maxie's 50-yard interception return for a touchdown and Morten Andersen's 48-yard field goal. Gill Fenerty, who carried 10 times for 104 yards, scored on a 60-yard run early in the fourth quarter to narrow the deficit to 20-17. Rickey Jackson's fumble recovery set up Walsh's game-winning touchdown strike.

New Orleans	0	3	7	14	— 24
L.A. Rams	0	10	7	3	— 20

Rams—FG Lansford 38
NO —FG Andersen 48
Rams—Everett 2 run (Lansford kick)
NO —Maxie 50 interception return (Andersen kick)
Rams—Ellard 42 pass from Everett (Lansford kick)
Rams—FG Lansford 18
NO —Fenerty 60 run (Andersen kick)
NO —Martin 4 pass from Walsh (Andersen kick)

Phoenix 24, Atlanta 13—at Atlanta-Fulton County Stadium, attendance 36,222. Cedric Mack, Jay Taylor, and Marcus Turner turned an interception into a score as the Cardinals downed the Falcons. Phoenix broke a 10-10 halftime tie on Anthony Thompson's one-yard touchdown run in the third quarter. With less than five minutes left in the game, Scott Campbell's pass was intercepted by Mack, who lateraled to Taylor, who then lateraled to Turner to cover 47 yards for a touchdown. Ricky Proehl, who had six receptions for 102 yards, scored on a 45-yard catch for the Cardinals in the first half.

Phoenix	0	10	7	7	— 24
Atlanta	3	7	0	3	— 13

Atl —FG Davis 41
Phx—Proehl 45 pass from Rosenbach (Del Greco kick)
Atl —Wilkins 20 pass from Campbell (Davis kick)
Phx—FG Del Greco 37
Phx—Thompson 1 run (Del Greco kick)
Atl —FG Davis 24
Phx—Turner 47 interception return (Del Greco kick)

San Francisco 20, Cincinnati 17—at Riverfront Stadium, attendance 60,084. Mike Cofer's 23-yard field goal 6:12 into overtime gave the 49ers the victory over the Bengals. Trailing 17-14 in the fourth quarter, Montana led a 55-yard, seven-play drive capped by Cofer's 23-yard field goal with 57 seconds remaining in regulation. San Francisco won the coin toss for the extra period and drove for the winning field goal in its opening series. San Francisco increased its road victory streak to an NFL-record 17 games.

San Francisco	7	0	7	3	3	— 20
Cincinnati	7	0	10	0	0	— 17

Cin—C. Taylor 2 pass from Esiason (Breech kick)
SF —Rathman 1 run (Cofer kick)
Cin—FG Breech 38
SF —Sydney 3 run (Cofer kick)
Cin—Woods 1 run (Breech kick)
SF —FG Cofer 23
SF —FG Cofer 23

Seattle 20, Green Bay 14—at Milwaukee County Stadium, attendance 52,015. Derrick Fenner rushed for 112 yards on 20 carries and a touchdown to lead the Seahawks past the Packers. Fenner's 14-yard scoring run, combined with Dave Krieg's eight-yard touchdown pass to Jeff Chadwick, and Norm Johnson's 37-yard field goal, gave Seattle a 17-0 halftime advantage. Johnson kicked a 22-yard field goal in the third quarter to complete the Seahawks' scoring. Packers backup quarterback Blair Kiel completed fourth-quarter touchdown passes to Perry Kemp (13 yards) and Ed West (one) to get back in the game with 3:32 left, but Green Bay could get no closer.

Seattle	7	10	3	0	— 20
Green Bay	0	0	0	14	— 14

Sea—Chadwick 8 pass from Krieg (Johnson kick)
Sea—FG Johnson 37
Sea—Fenner 14 run (Johnson kick)
Sea—FG Johnson 22
GB —P. Kemp 13 pass from Kiel (Jacke kick)
GB —West 1 pass from Kiel (Jacke kick)

Sunday Night, December 9

Miami 23, Philadelphia 20—at Joe Robbie Stadium, attendance 67,034. Pete Stoyanovich kicked a 34-yard field goal with 2:28 left in overtime to give the Dolphins a victory over the Eagles. Dan Marino, who completed 27 of 54 passes for 365 yards, opened the scoring by hitting Tony Martin with a 28-yard touchdown in the first quarter. Trailing 20-10 in the fourth quarter, Marino found Mark Duper with a six-yard touchdown pass to narrow the score to 20-17. Stoyanovich then kicked a 34-yard field goal with three seconds remaining in regulation to force the extra period.

Philadelphia	0	10	3	7	0	— 20
Miami	10	0	0	10	3	— 23

Mia—Martin 28 pass from Marino (Stoyanovich kick)
Mia—FG Stoyanovich 24
Phil—Byars 3 pass from Cunningham (Ruzek kick)
Phil—FG Ruzek 53
Phil—FG Ruzek 33
Phil—Williams 45 pass from Cunningham (Ruzek kick)
Mia—Duper 6 pass from Marino (Stoyanovich kick)
Mia—FG Stoyanovich 34
Mia—FG Stoyanovich 34

Monday, December 10

Los Angeles Raiders 38, Detroit 31—at Pontiac Silverdome, attendance 72,190. Jay Schroeder passed for three touchdowns as the Raiders downed the Lions to improve their record to 9-4. Los Angeles scored 21 first-half points on Schroeder's 68-yard scoring strike to Willie Gault, and touchdown runs by Marcus Allen (two yards) and Bo Jackson (55). Los Angeles went ahead 35-24 on Schroeder's touchdown passes to Mervyn Fernandez (10 yards) and Tim Brown (three) in the third quarter. Barry Sanders rushed for 176 yards on 25 carries to become only the tenth player in NFL history to have 1,000-yard rushing efforts in his first two seasons.

L.A. Raiders	14	7	14	3	— 38
Detroit	21	3	0	7	— 31

Det —Sanders 35 run (Murray kick)
Raiders—Gault 68 pass from Schroeder (Jaeger kick)
Det —Sanders 5 run (Murray kick)
Raiders—Allen 2 run (Jaeger kick)
Det —Campbell 11 pass from Peete (Murray kick)
Det —FG Murray 47
Raiders—Jackson 55 run (Jaeger kick)
Raiders—Fernandez 10 pass from Schroeder (Jaeger kick)
Raiders—Brown 3 pass from Schroeder (Jaeger kick)
Det —Peete 6 run (Murray kick)
Raiders—FG Jaeger 37

Fifteenth Week Summaries

Standings

American Football Conference

Eastern Division	W	L	T	Pct.	Pts.	OP
Buffalo**	12	2	0	.857	390	220
Miami**	11	3	0	.786	299	201
Indianapolis	6	8	0	.429	229	302
N.Y. Jets	4	10	0	.286	237	324
New England	1	13	0	.071	164	391
Central Division						
Houston	8	6	0	.571	351	253
Pittsburgh	8	6	0	.571	243	206
Cincinnati	7	7	0	.500	299	318
Cleveland	3	11	0	.214	214	406
Western Division						
L.A. Raiders**	10	4	0	.714	292	232
Kansas City	9	5	0	.643	324	226
Seattle	7	7	0	.500	259	264
San Diego	6	8	0	.429	282	240
Denver	4	10	0	.286	297	344

National Football Conference

Eastern Division	W	L	T	Pct.	Pts.	OP
N.Y. Giants*	11	3	0	.786	298	180
Washington**	9	5	0	.643	324	252
Philadelphia**	8	6	0	.571	356	275
Dallas	7	7	0	.500	234	265
Phoenix	5	9	0	.357	226	349
Central Division						
Chicago*	10	4	0	.714	311	245
Green Bay	6	8	0	.429	241	301
Minnesota	6	8	0	.429	310	278
Tampa Bay	6	8	0	.429	236	324
Detroit	5	9	0	.357	339	366
Western Division						
San Francisco*	13	1	0	.929	323	209
New Orleans	6	8	0	.429	241	248
L.A. Rams	5	9	0	.357	315	372
Atlanta	3	11	0	.214	302	345

**Clinched Division Title*
***Clinched Playoff Position*

Saturday, December 15

Buffalo 17, New York Giants 13—at Giants Stadium, attendance 66,893. Jim Kelly passed for one touchdown and Thurman Thomas ran for another as the Bills downed the Giants. New York scored first on Ottis Anderson's one-yard run, but Kelly's six-yard pass to Andre Reed and Thomas's two-yard scoring run put Buffalo ahead 14-10 at halftime. Frank Reich, who replaced the injured Kelly in the second half, completed a 43-yard pass to Don Beebe to set up Scott Norwood's 29-yard field goal in the fourth quarter.

Buffalo	7	7	0	3	— 17
N.Y. Giants	7	3	3	0	— 13

NYG—Anderson 1 run (Bahr kick)
Buff —Reed 6 pass from Kelly (Norwood kick)
Buff —Thomas 2 run (Norwood kick)
NYG—FG Bahr 23
NYG—FG Bahr 22
Buff —FG Norwood 29

Washington 25, New England 10—at Foxboro Stadium, attendance 22,286. Earnest Byner ran 39 times for 149 yards to help put the Redskins in the playoffs for the first time since 1987. Washington jumped to a 19-0 first-half lead on Kurt Gouveia's 39-yard fumble recovery return, a safety when the Patriots snapped the ball out of the end zone, Byner's five-yard touchdown run, and Chip Lohmiller's 19-yard field goal. Lohmiller added two more field goals in the second half from 38 and 26 yards. Byner, who gained more than 100 yards for the third consecutive week, lifted his season rushing total to 1,031 yards. The Patriots fell to 1-13.

Washington	9	10	0	6	—	25
New England	0	0	7	3	—	10

Wash—Gouveia 39 fumble recovery return (Lohmiller kick)
Wash—Safety, ball snapped out of end zone
Wash—Byner 5 run (Lohmiller kick)
Wash—FG Lohmiller 19
NE —Stephens 4 run (Staurovsky kick)
NE —FG Staurovsky 42
Wash—FG Lohmiller 38
Wash—FG Lohmiller 26

Sunday, December 16

Cleveland 13, Atlanta 10—at Cleveland Stadium, attendance 46,536. Kevin Mack ran five yards for a touchdown as the Browns defeated the Falcons to end an eight-game losing streak. Mack's touchdown run and Jerry Kauric's 23-yard field goal put Cleveland ahead 10-3 at halftime. Kauric added a 41-yard field goal in the third quarter for the Browns' final points. Atlanta's Hugh Millen replaced starting quarterback Scott Campbell and threw an 11-yard scoring pass to Floyd Dixon on the last play of the game.

Atlanta	0	3	0	7	—	10
Cleveland	0	10	3	0	—	13

Atl —FG Davis 30
Clev—Mack 5 run (Kauric kick)
Clev—FG Kauric 23
Clev—FG Kauric 41
Atl —Dixon 11 pass from Millen (Davis kick)

Los Angeles Raiders 24, Cincinnati 7—at Los Angeles Coliseum, attendance 54,132. Jay Schroeder passed for three touchdowns as the Raiders downed the Bengals to clinch their first playoff berth since 1985. Riki Ellison's interception set up Schroeder's first touchdown pass, of five yards to Tim Brown. Los Angeles took a 17-7 halftime lead as Schroeder and Brown hooked up again on a 44-yard touchdown reception and Terry McDaniel picked off a pass to set up Jeff Jaeger's 39-yard field goal. Schroeder completed a one-yard pass to Ethan Horton to provide the game's only points in the second half. Ellison was named AFC Defensive Player of the Week.

Cincinnati	7	0	0	0	—	7
L.A. Raiders	7	10	7	0	—	24

Cin —McGee 41 pass from Esiason (Breech kick)
Raiders—T. Brown 5 pass from Schroeder (Jaeger kick)
Raiders—T. Brown 44 pass from Schroeder (Jaeger kick)
Raiders—FG Jaeger 39
Raiders—Horton 1 pass from Schroeder (Jaeger kick)

Philadelphia 31, Green Bay 0—at Veterans Stadium, attendance 65,627. Randall Cunningham completed one touchdown pass and ran for another as the Eagles blanked the Packers to earn an NFC Wild Card spot. Philadelphia jumped to a 17-0 halftime lead on running back Keith Byars's eight-yard scoring pass to Anthony Toney, Roger Ruzek's 34-yard field goal, and Cunningham's 12-yard touchdown pass to Byars. Cunningham added a 17-yard run and Thomas Sanders ran one yard for a score in the fourth quarter to complete the Eagles' scoring. Philadelphia's defense had five sacks and held Green Bay to 158 yards total offense. Rookie wide receiver Fred Barnett had five receptions for 108 yards.

Green Bay	0	0	0	0	—	0
Philadelphia	7	10	0	14	—	31

Phil—Toney 8 pass from Byars (Ruzek kick)
Phil—FG Ruzek 34
Phil—Byars 12 pass from Cunningham (Ruzek kick)
Phil—Cunningham 17 run (Ruzek kick)
Phil—Sanders 1 run (Ruzek kick)

Houston 27, Kansas City 10—at Arrowhead Stadium, attendance 61,756. Warren Moon completed 27 of 45 passes for 527 yards and three touchdowns as the Oilers marched over the Chiefs. Moon's passing yardage was the second highest in NFL history, falling just 27 yards short of the record (554), set by Rams quarterback Norm Van Brocklin in 1951. Haywood Jeffires caught nine passes for 245 yards, including an 87-yard scoring strike from Moon. Moon also hit Tony Jones for a pair of touchdown passes (24 and 2 yards). Teddy Garcia kicked field goals of 32 and 26 yards. Moon was named AFC Offensive Player of the Week for his performance.

Houston	7	3	7	10	—	27
Kansas City	0	7	3	0	—	10

Hou—T. Jones 24 pass from Moon (Garcia kick)
Hou—FG Garcia 32
KC —Birden 62 pass from DeBerg (Lowery kick)
Hou—Jeffires 87 pass from Moon (Garcia kick)
KC —FG Lowery 35
Hou—FG Garcia 26
Hou—T. Jones 2 pass from Moon (Garcia kick)

Indianapolis 29, New York Jets 21—at Giants Stadium, attendance 41,423. Eric Dickerson ran for 117 yards and two touchdowns as the Colts rallied to post their fourth consecutive victory. Trailing 14-10 in the third quarter, Dickerson scored on a pair of one-yard runs to give Indianapolis a 23-14 lead. Dean Biasucci then kicked two field goals in the fourth quarter (20 and 37 yards) to put the game away. Dickerson, who also had five catches for 45 yards, notched his sixtieth career 100-yard rushing performance.

Indianapolis	3	7	13	6	—	29
N.Y. Jets	7	7	0	7	—	21

Ind —FG Biasucci 35
NYJ—Moore 6 pass from O'Brien (Leahy kick)
NYJ—Baxter 1 run (Leahy kick)
Ind —Verdin 23 pass from George (Biasucci kick)
Ind —Dickerson 1 run (Biasucci kick)
Ind —Dickerson 1 run (kick failed)
Ind —FG Biasucci 20
Ind —FG Biasucci 37
NYJ—Moore 10 pass from Taylor (Leahy kick)

Tampa Bay 26, Minnesota 13—at Tampa Stadium, attendance 47,272. Vinny Testaverde ran for one score and threw for another to lead the Buccaneers over the Vikings in interim coach Richard Williamson's debut. Testaverde's 105 yards rushing included a 48-yard scoring run in the first quarter. Tampa Bay broke the game open in the second quarter by scoring 16 points to take a 23-0 halftime advantage on Testaverde's 25-yard touchdown strike to Mark Carrier and Steve Christie's three field goals (50, 43, and 42 yards). Testaverde's rushing yardage was the most ever by a Buccaneers' quarterback.

Minnesota	0	0	13	0	—	13
Tampa Bay	7	16	3	0	—	26

TB —Testaverde 48 run (Christie kick)
TB —FG Christie 50
TB —FG Christie 43
TB —FG Christie 42
TB —Carrier 25 pass from Testaverde (Christie kick)
Minn—H. Jones 75 pass from Wilson (Reveiz kick)
TB —FG Christie 30
Minn—Walker 1 run (kick failed)

Dallas 41, Phoenix 10—at Texas Stadium, attendance 60,190. Rookie Emmitt Smith tied a club record with four touchdown runs as the Cowboys remained in contention for a playoff spot by defeating the Cardinals. Smith ran for scores of one and 11 yards in the first quarter and added one- and six-yard touchdown runs in the second half. Troy Aikman completed an eight-yard scoring pass to Michael Irvin and Darryl Johnston ran six yards for a touchdown to complete Dallas's scoring. The victory marked the first time the Cowboys had won four consecutive games since 1985.

Phoenix	3	0	0	7	—	10
Dallas	13	7	7	14	—	41

Phx—FG Del Greco 38
Dall—Smith 1 run (kick failed)
Dall—Smith 11 run (Willis kick)
Dall—Irvin 8 pass from Aikman (Willis kick)
Dall—Smith 1 run (Willis kick)
Dall—Smith 6 run (Willis kick)
Phx—J. Johnson 1 run (Del Greco kick)
Dall—Johnston 6 run (Willis kick)

Pittsburgh 9, New Orleans 6—at Louisiana Superdome, attendance 68,582. Gary Anderson's 43-yard field goal with 1:44 remaining gave the Steelers a win over the Saints. In a battle between two of the top-three most accurate kickers in NFL history, Anderson scored first on a 29-yard field goal to give Pittsburgh a 3-0 halftime lead. Morten Andersen responded in the second half by kicking field goals of 50 and 43 yards to put New Orleans on top 6-3 in the fourth quarter. Anderson's 42-yard field goal tied the game with 5:24 remaining.

Pittsburgh	0	3	0	6	—	9
New Orleans	0	0	3	3	—	6

Pitt—FG Anderson 29
NO—FG Andersen 50
NO—FG Andersen 43
Pitt—FG Anderson 42
Pitt—FG Anderson 43

Denver 20, San Diego 10—at Mile High Stadium, attendance 64,919. John Elway completed two touchdown passes as the Broncos defeated the Chargers to break a six-game losing streak. Denver led 14-3 after three quarters on scoring passes from Elway to Michael Young (25 and 3 yards). David Treadwell kicked a career-long 49-yard field goal, but Billy Joe Tolliver's 22-yard touchdown pass to Craig McEwen narrowed the score to 17-10 in the fourth quarter. Treadwell's final field goal from 26 yards secured the victory.

San Diego	0	3	0	7	—	10
Denver	0	7	7	6	—	20

SD —FG Carney 30
Den—Young 25 pass from Elway (Treadwell kick)
Den—Young 3 pass from Elway (Treadwell kick)
Den—FG Treadwell 49
SD —McEwen 22 pass from Tolliver (Carney kick)
Den—FG Treadwell 26

Miami 24, Seattle 17—at Joe Robbie Stadium, attendance 57,851. Dan Marino completed two touchdown passes and Miami's defense held Seattle to 83 yards rushing en route to victory. Marino threw a four-yard scoring pass to James Pruitt and Troy Stradford ran six yards for a touchdown to put the Dolphins ahead 17-10 at halftime. Miami increased its lead to 24-10 in the third quarter on Marino's 11-yard scoring strike to Ferrell Edmunds. Seattle's Dave Krieg connected with Jeff Chadwick for a 13-yard touchdown pass to narrow the score to 24-17. John Offerdahl and Tim McKyer each had fourth-quarter interceptions to halt two Seahawks' scoring drives.

Seattle	3	7	0	7	—	17
Miami	3	14	7	0	—	24

Sea—FG Johnson 24
Mia—FG Stoyanovich 32
Sea—Fenner 2 run (Johnson kick)
Mia —Pruitt 4 pass from Marino (Stoyanovich kick)
Mia —Stradford 6 run (Stoyanovich kick)
Mia —Edmunds 11 pass from Marino (Stoyanovich kick)
Sea—Chadwick 13 pass from Krieg (Johnson kick)

Sunday Night, December 16

Detroit 38, Chicago 21—at Pontiac Silverdome, attendance 67,559. Rodney Peete passed for 316 yards and four touchdowns as the Lions overcame the Bears. Peete completed three scoring passes in the first half on a pair of touchdowns to Robert Clark (20 and 1 yards) and Richard Johnson (44) to give Detroit a 21-7 halftime lead. Peete connected with Terry Greer for a 68-yard scoring pass in the third quarter. Barry Sanders ran one yard for a touchdown in the fourth quarter to finish the Lions' scoring. Bears rookie Mark Carrier had his ninth interception, tying the Bears' season record set by Roosevelt Taylor in 1963.

Chicago	7	0	7	7	—	21
Detroit	0	21	7	10	—	38

Chi—Muster 1 run (Butler kick)
Det—Clark 20 pass from Peete (Murray kick)
Det—Johnson 44 pass from Peete (Murray kick)
Det—Clark 1 pass from Peete (Murray kick)
Chi—Dent 45 fumble recovery return (Butler kick)
Det—Greer 68 pass from Peete (Murray kick)
Det—Sanders 1 run (Murray kick)
Det—FG Murray 26
Chi—Davis 8 pass from Willis (Butler kick)

Monday, December 17

San Francisco 26, Los Angeles Rams 10—at Anaheim Stadium, attendance 65,619. Rookie Dexter Carter carried 13 times for 124 yards and a touchdown to help the 49ers past the Rams. The victory gave San Francisco the home-field advantage throughout the playoffs. The 49ers took a 16-7 halftime lead on Joe Montana's 60-yard touchdown pass to Jerry Rice, Mike Cofer's 23-yard field goal, and Tom Rathman's one-yard run for a touchdown. Cofer added a 31-yard field goal in the third quarter and Carter exploded for a 74-yard scoring run in the fourth period to cap the scoring. San Francisco extended its NFL record to 18 consecutive road victories.

San Francisco	3	13	3	7	—	26
L.A. Rams	0	7	3	0	—	10

SF —FG Cofer 23
SF —Rathman 1 run (pass failed)
SF —Rice 60 pass from Montana (Cofer kick)
Rams—Faison 8 pass from Everett (Lansford kick)
SF —FG Cofer 31
Rams—FG Lansford 21
SF —Carter 74 run (Cofer kick)

Sixteenth Week Summaries

Standings

American Football Conference

Eastern Division

	W	L	T	Pct.	Pts.	OP
Buffalo*	13	2	0	.867	414	234
Miami**	11	4	0	.733	313	225
Indianapolis	7	8	0	.467	264	330
N.Y. Jets	5	10	0	.333	279	331
New England	1	14	0	.067	171	433
Central Division						
Pittsburgh	9	6	0	.600	278	206
Cincinnati	8	7	0	.533	339	338
Houston	8	7	0	.533	371	293
Cleveland	3	12	0	.200	214	441
Western Division						
L.A. Raiders**	11	4	0	.733	320	256
Kansas City**	10	5	0	.667	348	247
Seattle	8	7	0	.533	276	276
San Diego	6	9	0	.400	303	264
Denver	4	11	0	.267	309	361

National Football Conference

Eastern Division

	W	L	T	Pct.	Pts.	OP
N.Y. Giants*	12	3	0	.800	322	201
Philadelphia**	9	6	0	.600	373	278
Washington**	9	6	0	.600	352	287
Dallas	7	8	0	.467	237	282
Phoenix	5	10	0	.333	247	373

Central Division

Chicago*	11	4	0	.733	338	259
Detroit	6	9	0	.400	363	383
Green Bay	6	9	0	.400	258	325
Minnesota	6	9	0	.400	334	306
Tampa Bay	6	9	0	.400	250	351

Western Division

San Francisco*	13	2	0	.867	333	222
New Orleans	7	8	0	.467	254	258
L.A. Rams	5	10	0	.333	328	392
Atlanta	4	11	0	.267	322	358

**Clinched Division Title*
***Clinched Playoff Berth*

Saturday, December 22

Detroit 24, Green Bay 17—at Lambeau Field, attendance 46,700. The Lions scored two touchdowns in the fourth quarter to defeat the Packers. Green Bay jumped to a 17-10 third-quarter lead, but Detroit's Ray Crockett returned a fumble 22 yards for a touchdown to tie the game in the fourth quarter. Barry Sanders, who carried 19 times for 133 yards, then ran six yards for the go-ahead score with less than four minutes to play. The game, which was played in a 28-degree-below-zero wind chill, eliminated the Packers from playoff contention.

Detroit	7	0	3	14	— 24
Green Bay	7	0	10	0	— 17

GB — Kiel 3 run (Jacke kick)
Det — Peete 26 run (Murray kick)
GB — Thompson 76 kickoff return (Jacke kick)
Det — FG Murray 22
GB — FG Jacke 25
Det — Crockett 22 fumble recovery return (Murray kick)
Det — Sanders 6 run (Murray kick)

Los Angeles Raiders 28, Minnesota 17—at Metrodome, attendance 63,314. Jay Schroeder passed for four touchdowns as the Raiders defeated the Vikings to move within one game of clinching the AFC Western Division title. Los Angeles went ahead 28-10 in the fourth quarter on Schroeder's three-yard scoring pass to Ethan Horton, which was set up by his 61-yard completion to Willie Gault. Schroeder's earlier touchdown passes went to Mervyn Fernandez (17 yards), Sam Graddy (47), and Marcus Allen (19). The loss eliminated the Vikings from playoff contention.

L.A. Raiders	14	0	7	7	— 28
Minnesota	0	10	0	7	— 17

Raiders — Fernandez 17 pass from Schroeder (Jaeger kick)
Raiders — Graddy 47 pass from Schroeder (Jaeger kick)
Minn — FG Reveiz 28
Minn — C. Carter 27 pass from Wilson (Reveiz kick)
Raiders — Allen 19 pass from Schroeder (Jaeger kick)
Raiders — Horton 3 pass from Schroeder (Jaeger kick)
Minn — H. Jones 4 pass from Gannon (Reveiz kick)

Saturday Night, December 22

Indianapolis 35, Washington 28—at Hoosier Dome, attendance 58,173. The Colts scored 21 points in the fourth quarter to come from behind and beat the Redskins. Washington led 25-14 in the final period, but Jeff George completed an eight-yard touchdown pass to Stanley Morgan to narrow the score to 25-21. Chip Lohmiller added a 27-yard field goal to help Washington increase its lead to 28-21. George then fired a 12-yard scoring pass to Bill Brooks to tie the game with 1:21 remaining. Rookie Alan Grant's 25-yard interception return for a touchdown with 50 seconds left gave the Colts the victory.

Washington	7	6	5	10	— 28
Indianapolis	0	14	0	21	— 35

Wash — Monk 12 pass from Rypien (Lohmiller kick)
Ind — Dickerson 4 run (Biasucci kick)
Ind — Morgan 42 pass from George (Biasucci kick)
Wash — FG Lohmiller 53
Wash — FG Lohmiller 56
Wash — Safety, George intentional grounding in end zone
Wash — FG Lohmiller 29
Wash — Clark 53 pass from Rypien (Lohmiller kick)
Ind — Morgan 8 pass from George (Biasucci kick)
Wash — FG Lohmiller 27
Ind — Brooks 12 pass from George (Biasucci kick)
Ind — Grant 25 interception return (Biasucci kick)

Sunday, December 23

Cincinnati 40, Houston 20—at Riverfront Stadium, attendance 60,044. Boomer Esiason completed two touchdown passes and Ickey Woods ran for two others as the Bengals downed the Oilers. James Brooks led Cincinnati by rushing for a club-record 201 yards, including a 56-yard touchdown dash late in the second quarter. Esiason completed two fourth-quarter touchdown passes to Eric Kattus (16 and 22 yards) to put the game away. Houston and Cincinnati moved into a second-place tie in the AFC Central Division, one game behind the first-place Steelers. The game, which was played in 20-degree temperature, helped the Bengals improve their record to 16-6 against the Oilers at Cincinnati's Riverfront Stadium.

Houston	0	13	7	0	— 20
Cincinnati	0	13	14	13	— 40

Hou — FG Garcia 29
Hou — Jeffires 21 pass from Moon (Garcia kick)
Cin — Woods 1 run (kick blocked)
Hou — FG Garcia 36
Cin — Brooks 56 run (Breech kick)
Hou — Moon 1 run (Garcia kick)
Cin — Jennings 1 run (Breech kick)
Cin — Woods 1 run (Breech kick)
Cin — Kattus 16 pass from Esiason (Breech kick)
Cin — Kattus 22 pass from Esiason (kick blocked)

Pittsburgh 35, Cleveland 0—at Three Rivers Stadium, attendance 51,665. Bubby Brister completed four touchdown passes as the Steelers blanked the Browns and gained sole possession of the AFC Central Division lead with a 9-6 record. Pittsburgh scored all of its points in the first half on Brister's scoring passes to Mike Mularkey (20 and 2 yards), Chris Calloway (20), and Merril Hoge (12), and Warren Williams's one-yard run. The Steelers held a 39:19 to 20:41 time-of-possession advantage. The Browns lost eight fumbles to tie a team record. The 35-point margin of victory was Pittsburgh's largest against Cleveland since a 42-6 win in 1975.

Cleveland	0	0	0	0	— 0
Pittsburgh	21	14	0	0	— 35

Pitt — Mularkey 20 pass from Brister (Anderson kick)
Pitt — Calloway 20 pass from Brister (Anderson kick)
Pitt — Mularkey 2 pass from Brister (Anderson kick)
Pitt — Hoge 12 pass from Brister (Anderson kick)
Pitt — W. Williams 1 run (Anderson kick)

Philadelphia 17, Dallas 3—at Veterans Stadium, attendance 63,895. Eagles running back Keith Byars threw a touchdown pass to Calvin Williams to help lead the Eagles over the Cowboys. Philadelphia took a 10-3 halftime lead on Byars's 18-yard pass to Williams and Roger Ruzek's 29-yard field goal. Eric Allen returned an interception 35 yards for a score midway through the fourth quarter to put the game away. The Eagles' defense had four interceptions and two sacks and held the Cowboys to 199 total yards.

Dallas	0	3	0	0	— 3
Philadelphia	7	3	0	7	— 17

Phil — C. Williams 18 pass from Byars (Ruzek kick)
Dall — FG Willis 46
Phil — FG Ruzek 29
Phil — Allen 35 interception return (Ruzek kick)

Kansas City 24, San Diego 21—at San Diego Jack Murphy Stadium, attendance 45,135. Nick Lowery kicked a 32-yard field goal with 2:46 remaining to lead the Chiefs over the Chargers and into the playoffs. Kansas City took a 21-7 halftime lead on Steve DeBerg's touchdown passes to Stephone Paige (eight yards) and Todd McNair (40), and Barry Word's 11-yard run. San Diego tied the game 21-21 early in the fourth quarter on Rod Bernstine's three-yard run and Kitrick Taylor's 55-yard punt return. The victory gave the Chiefs their first playoff spot since 1986.

Kansas City	7	14	0	3	— 24
San Diego	7	0	7	7	— 21

KC — Paige 8 pass from DeBerg (Lowery kick)
SD — A. Miller 5 pass from Tolliver (Carney kick)
KC — Word 11 run (Lowery kick)
KC — McNair 40 pass from DeBerg (Lowery kick)
SD — Bernstine 3 run (Carney kick)
SD — Taylor 55 punt return (Carney kick)
KC — FG Lowery 32

Atlanta 20, Los Angeles Rams 13—at Atlanta-Fulton County Stadium, attendance 30,021. Scott Case returned an interception 36 yards for a touchdown as the Falcons defeated the Rams to snap a seven-game losing streak. Atlanta put the game away in the first half by taking a 20-10 halftime advantage on Case's interception return, Greg Davis's two field goals (21 and 23 yards), and Mike Rozier's 11-yard run.

L.A. Rams	7	3	3	0	— 13
Atlanta	10	10	0	0	— 20

Atl — Case 36 interception return (Davis kick)
Atl — FG Davis 21
Rams — Gary 7 run (Lansford kick)
Atl — Rozier 11 run (Davis kick)
Rams — FG Lansford 19
Atl — FG Davis 23
Rams — FG Lansford 25

Buffalo 24, Miami 14—at Rich Stadium, attendance 80,235. Frank Reich passed for two touchdowns as the Bills clinched the AFC Eastern Division by defeating the Dolphins. Reich, who started in place of injured quarterback Jim Kelly, completed scoring passes to James Lofton (seven yards) and Andre Reed (11). Thurman Thomas rushed for 154 yards on 30 carries and had a 13-yard touchdown run in the fourth quarter. The win gave Buffalo home-field advantage throughout the playoffs.

Miami	0	0	7	7	— 14
Buffalo	0	7	10	7	— 24

Buff — Lofton 7 pass from Reich (Norwood kick)
Buff — Reed 11 pass from Reich (Norwood kick)
Mia — Duper 30 pass from Marino (Stoyanovich kick)
Buff — FG Norwood 21
Buff — Thomas 13 run (Norwood kick)
Mia — Clayton 11 pass from Marino (Stoyanovich kick)

New York Jets 42, New England 7—at Giants Stadium, attendance 46,641. Freeman McNeil ran for two touchdowns and Ken O'Brien passed for two others as the Jets ended a five-game losing streak by beating the Patriots. New York took a 21-7 lead on touchdown runs by Johnny Hector (seven yards) and McNeil (one), and O'Brien's two-yard touchdown pass to Rob Moore. New York put the game away in the second half on McNeil's second scoring run of the game (one yard), O'Brien's six-yard scoring pass to Blair Thomas, and rookie quarterback Troy Taylor's five-yard run for a touchdown. The loss was New England's club-record thirteenth straight.

New England	0	7	0	0	— 7
N.Y. Jets	7	14	14	7	— 42

NYJ — Hector 7 run (Leahy kick)
NE — Fryar 24 pass from Wilson (Staurovsky kick)
NYJ — Moore 2 pass from O'Brien (Leahy kick)
NYJ — McNeil 9 run (Leahy kick)
NYJ — McNeil 1 run (Leahy kick)
NYJ — Thomas 6 pass from O'Brien (Leahy kick)
NYJ — Taylor 5 run (Leahy kick)

New Orleans 13, San Francisco 10—at Candlestick Park, attendance 60,112. Morten Andersen kicked a 40-yard field goal with 4:43 remaining to help the Saints beat the 49ers. Tom Rathman ran one yard for a touchdown to open the scoring for the 49ers. Steve Walsh threw a five-yard touchdown pass to Greg Scales to tie the game 7-7. Anderson kicked a 30-yard field goal to give the Saints a 10-7 halftime lead. Mike Cofer's 30-yard field goal re-tied the game 10-10 midway through the fourth quarter. Rickey Jackson recovered a fumble with 47 seconds remaining to secure the win.

New Orleans	7	3	0	3	— 13
San Francisco	7	0	0	3	— 10

SF — Rathman 1 run (Cofer kick)
NO — Scales 5 pass from Walsh (Andersen kick)
NO — FG Andersen 30
SF — FG Cofer 30
NO — FG Andersen 40

New York Giants 24, Phoenix 21—at Sun Devil Stadium, attendance 41,212. Jeff Hostetler, starting in place of injured Phil Simms, scored on a four-yard run as the Giants earned a bye in the first week of the playoffs by defeating the Cardinals. New York built a 10-0 lead on Matt Bahr's 27-yard field goal and Rodney Hampton's two-yard touchdown run. Hostetler hit Mark Ingram with a 44-yard scoring pass and ran for a four-yard touchdown in the second half to put the game away. Everson Walls recorded his fiftieth career interception to end a key Cardinals' drive in the second half.

N.Y. Giants	3	7	7	7	— 24
Phoenix	0	7	7	7	— 21

NYG — FG Bahr 27
NYG — Hampton 2 run (Bahr kick)
Phx — Flagler 11 pass from Rosenbach (Del Greco kick)
NYG — Ingram 44 pass from Hostetler (Bahr kick)
Phx — E. Jones 68 pass from Rosenbach (Del Greco kick)
NYG — Hostetler 4 run (Bahr kick)
Phx — Proehl 3 pass from Rosenbach (Del Greco kick)

Chicago 27, Tampa Bay 14—at Soldier Field, attendance 46,456. Mike Tomczak, making his first start of the season, completed two touchdown passes and ran for a third as the Bears beat the Buccaneers. Tomczak, replacing injured Jim Harbaugh, threw scoring passes to Wendell Davis (18 yards) and James Thornton (12). Tomczak also scored on a one-yard run in the second quarter. Kevin Butler added field goals of 46 and 43 yards for the Bears. The temperature at game time was 11 degrees with a minus-three degree wind chill.

Tampa Bay	7	0	0	7	— 14
Chicago	0	14	10	3	— 27

TB — Carrier 5 pass from Testaverde (Christie kick)
Chi — Tomczak 1 run (Butler kick)
Chi — Davis 18 pass from Tomczak (Butler kick)
Chi — Thornton 12 pass from Tomczak (Butler kick)
Chi — FG Butler 46
Chi — FG Butler 43
TB — Hill 4 pass from Testaverde (Christie kick)

Sunday Night, December 23

Seattle 17, Denver 12—at Kingdome, attendance 55,845. Dave Krieg passed for one touchdown and Derrick Fenner ran for another as the Seahawks kept their playoff hopes alive by defeating the Broncos. Krieg threw a five-yard touchdown pass to Tommy Kane and Norm Johnson kicked a 21-yard field goal to help Seattle to a 10-10 tie at halftime. Denver went ahead 12-10 when Dave Krieg was called for a safety for intentional grounding in the end zone. Eugene Robinson returned an interception 39 yards in the third quarter to set up Fenner's winning run.

Denver	3	7	2	0	— 12
Seattle	3	7	7	0	— 17

Den — FG Treadwell 49
Sea — FG Johnson 21
Den — Humphrey 1 run (Treadwell kick)
Sea — Kane 5 pass from Krieg (Johnson kick)
Den — Safety, Krieg intentional grounding in end zone
Sea — Fenner 1 run (Johnson kick)

Seventeenth Week Summaries

Standings

American Football Conference

Eastern Division

	W	L	T	Pct.	Pts.	OP
Buffalo*	13	3	0	.813	428	263
Miami**	12	4	0	.750	336	242
Indianapolis	7	9	0	.438	281	353
N.Y. Jets	6	10	0	.375	295	345
New England	1	15	0	.063	181	446

Central Division

	W	L	T	Pct.	Pts.	OP
Cincinnati*	9	7	0	.563	360	352
Houston**	9	7	0	.563	405	307
Pittsburgh	9	7	0	.563	292	240
Cleveland	3	13	0	.188	228	462

Western Division

	W	L	T	Pct.	Pts.	OP
L.A. Raiders*	12	4	0	.750	337	268
Kansas City**	11	5	0	.688	369	257
Seattle	9	7	0	.563	306	286
San Diego	6	10	0	.375	315	281
Denver	5	11	0	.313	331	374

National Football Conference

Eastern Division

	W	L	T	Pct.	Pts.	OP
N.Y. Giants*	13	3	0	.813	335	211
Philadelphia**	10	6	0	.625	396	299
Washington**	10	6	0	.625	381	301
Dallas	7	9	0	.438	244	308
Phoenix	5	11	0	.313	268	396

Central Division

	W	L	T	Pct.	Pts.	OP
Chicago*	11	5	0	.688	348	280
Tampa Bay	6	10	0	.375	264	367
Detroit	6	10	0	.375	373	413
Green Bay	6	10	0	.375	271	347
Minnesota	6	10	0	.375	351	326

Western Division

	W	L	T	Pct.	Pts.	OP
San Francisco*	14	2	0	.875	353	239
New Orleans**	8	8	0	.500	274	275
L.A. Rams	5	11	0	.313	345	412
Atlanta	5	11	0	.313	348	365

**Division Champion*
***Wild Card Team*

Note: Cincinnati won AFC Central title based on best head-to-head record (3-1) vs. Houston (2-2) and Pittsburgh (1-3). Houston was Wild Card based on better conference record (8-4) than Seattle (7-5) and Pittsburgh (6-6). Philadelphia finished second in the NFC East based on better division record (5-3) than Washington (4-4). Tampa Bay was second in NFC Central based on 5-1 record vs. Detroit, Green Bay, and Minnesota. Detroit is third based on best net division points (minus 8) vs. Green Bay (minus 40) in fourth. Minnesota was fifth based on 4-8 conference record. Los Angeles Rams were third in NFC West based on net points in division (plus 1) vs. Atlanta (minus 31).

Saturday, December 29

Kansas City 21, Chicago 10—at Soldier Field, attendance 60,262. Nick Lowery kicked five field goals to help the Chiefs defeat the Bears. Kansas City led 12-10 at halftime on Lowery's four field goals (19, 30, 43, and 32 yards). Christian Okoye capped a 66-yard, 12-play drive with a three-yard scoring run in the third quarter for the Chiefs' only touchdown. Lowery's five field goals gave him 21 straight, breaking Jan Stenerud's club record of 16. He finished the regular season with 33 field goals and 139 points, both team season records.

Kansas City	6	6	6	3	— 21
Chicago	3	7	0	0	— 10

KC —FG Lowery 19
Chi—FG Butler 24
KC —FG Lowery 30
KC —FG Lowery 43
Chi—Bailey 95 punt return (Butler kick)
KC —FG Lowery 32
KC —Okoye 3 run (kick failed)
KC —FG Lowery 38

Philadelphia 23, Phoenix 21—at Sun Devil Stadium, attendance 31,796. Randall Cunningham passed for three touchdowns, including two to Fred Barnett, as the Eagles defeated the Cardinals. Eric Allen's interception set up Cunningham's first touchdown pass, a 16-yard completion to Barnett in the first quarter. Cunningham then hit Calvin Williams with a 12-yard scoring strike in the second quarter and found Barnett again in the third quarter for a three-yard touchdown pass. Roger Ruzek added a 44-yard field goal for Philadelphia. Reggie White had three of the Eagles' six sacks. The victory gave Philadelphia the home-field advantage in the NFC Wild Card Game.

Philadelphia	7	6	7	3	— 23
Phoenix	0	7	0	14	— 21

Phil—Barnett 16 pass from Cunningham (Ruzek kick)
Phil—Williams 27 pass from Cunningham (kick failed)
Phx—Green 12 pass from Rosenbach (Del Greco kick)
Phil—Barnett 3 pass from Cunningham (Ruzek kick)
Phil—FG Ruzek 44
Phx—Proehl 38 pass from Rosenbach (Del Greco kick)
Phx—J.T. Smith 45 pass from Rosenbach (Del Greco kick)

Sunday, December 30

Washington 29, Buffalo 14—at Robert F. Kennedy Stadium, attendance 52,397. Chip Lohmiller kicked five field goals and Gerald Riggs ran for a touchdown to lead the Redskins over the Bills. Lohmiller kicked field goals of 37, 24, and 19 yards to provide the only scoring in the first half. Washington put the game away in the second half on Lohmiller's 43- and 32-yard field goals, Riggs's three-yard run which was set up by Alvin Walton's 61-yard interception return, and Mark Rypien's 18-yard touchdown pass to Steve Hobbs.

Buffalo	0	0	7	7	— 14
Washington	3	6	3	17	— 29

Wash—FG Lohmiller 37
Wash—FG Lohmiller 24
Wash—FG Lohmiller 19
Buff —Davis 13 pass from Gilbert (Norwood kick)
Wash—FG Lohmiller 43
Wash—FG Lohmiller 32
Wash—Riggs 3 run (Lohmiller kick)
Wash—Hobbs 18 pass from Rypien (Lohmiller kick)
Buff —Tasker 20 pass from Gilbert (Norwood kick)

Cincinnati 21, Cleveland 14—at Riverfront Stadium, attendance 60,041. Boomer Esiason's fourth-quarter touchdown pass to Eric Ball helped the Bengals defeat the Browns. After a scoreless first quarter, James Francis returned an interception 17 yards for a touchdown and Esiason hit Rodney Holman with a 22-yard scoring strike to put Cincinnati ahead 14-0 at halftime. Cleveland tied the game 14-14 in the third quarter on Kevin Mack's two-yard run and Mike Pagel's 16-yard pass to Brian Brennan. Esiason found Ball with a four-yard touchdown pass for the go-ahead score.

Cleveland	0	0	14	0	— 14
Cincinnati	0	14	0	7	— 21

Cin —Francis 17 interception return (Breech kick)
Cin —Holman 22 pass from Esiason (Breech kick)
Clev—Mack 2 run (Kauric kick)
Clev—Brennan 16 pass from Pagel (Kauric kick)
Cin —Ball 4 pass from Esiason (Breech kick)

Atlanta 26, Dallas 7—at Atlanta-Fulton County Stadium, attendance 50,097. Keith Jones returned a kickoff for a score and Deion Sanders brought back an interception for a touchdown to highlight the Falcons' win over the Cowboys. Atlanta's Tracy Johnson ran one yard for a touchdown to produce the only points in the first half. The Falcons increased their lead to 16-0 as Jones returned the second-half kickoff 76 yards for a touchdown and Tim Green tackled Emmitt Smith in the end zone for a safety. Greg Davis kicked a 23-yard field goal and Sanders returned an interception 61 yards for a score in the fourth quarter to complete Atlanta's scoring. Babe Laufenberg, who started in place of injured Troy Aikman, threw a 27-yard touchdown pass to Jay Novacek late in the fourth quarter to avert the shutout.

Dallas	0	0	0	7	— 7
Atlanta	0	7	9	10	— 26

Atl —Johnson 1 run (Davis kick)
Atl —Jones 76 kickoff return (Davis kick)
Atl —Safety, Green tackled Smith in end zone
Atl —FG Davis 23
Atl —Sanders 61 interception return (Davis kick)
Dall—Novacek 27 pass from Laufenberg (Willis kick)

Seattle 30, Detroit 10—at Kingdome, attendance 50,681. Derrick Fenner rushed for two touchdowns as the Seahawks kept their playoff hopes alive by beating the Lions. Fenner scored on a one-yard run in the first quarter and Norm Johnson kicked a 43-yard field goal to help Seattle to a 10-10 halftime tie. Eugene Robinson returned a fumble 16 yards for a touchdown in the third quarter for the go-ahead score. The Seahawks increased their lead on Johnson's two field goals (25 and 37 yards) and Fenner's nine-yard touchdown run. Detroit's Barry Sanders finished the year with 1,304 rushing yards to capture the NFL title and become the first Lions' player to earn the top spot since Byron "Whizzer" White in 1940.

Detroit	0	10	0	0	— 10
Seattle	7	3	10	10	— 30

Sea—Fenner 1 run (Johnson kick)
Det —FG Murray 24
Det —Sanders 16 run (Murray kick)
Sea—FG Johnson 43
Sea—Robinson 16 fumble recovery return (Johnson kick)
Sea—FG Johnson 25
Sea—FG Johnson 37
Sea—Fenner 9 run (Johnson kick)

Denver 22, Green Bay 13—at Mile High Stadium, attendance 46,943. John Elway completed a touchdown pass and Bobby Humphrey ran for another to lead the Broncos over the Packers. Humphrey ran five yards for a touchdown to break a 6-6 halftime tie. Elway then hit Mark Jackson with a 15-yard scoring pass to increase Denver's lead to 20-6 in the third quarter. Karl Mecklenburg capped the Broncos' scoring by sacking Anthony Dilweg in the end zone for a safety.

Green Bay	3	3	0	7	— 13
Denver	3	3	14	2	— 22

Den—FG Treadwell 22
GB —FG Jacke 37
Den—FG Treadwell 31
GB —FG Jacke 24
Den—Humphrey 5 run (Treadwell kick)
Den—Jackson 15 pass from Elway (Treadwell kick)
GB —Sharpe 9 pass from Dilweg (Jacke kick)
Den—Safety, Mecklenburg tackled Dilweg in end zone

Miami 23, Indianapolis 17—at Joe Robbie Stadium, attendance 59,547. Sammie Smith rushed 29 times for 108 yards and scored two touchdowns to help the Dolphins past the Colts. Miami took a 16-7 halftime lead on Dan Marino's 53-yard touchdown pass to Smith in the first quarter, Smith's one-yard scoring run, and a safety as Colts quarterback Jeff George was called for intentional grounding in the end zone. Jeff Cross forced a fumble which was returned 13 yards for a touchdown by Brian Sochia in the fourth quarter. The victory gave Miami home-field advantage for the AFC Wild Card Game.

Indianapolis	7	7	0	3	— 17
Miami	7	9	0	7	— 23

Ind —Bentley 15 pass from George (Biasucci kick)
Mia—Smith 53 pass from Marino (Stoyanovich kick)
Mia—Smith 1 run (Stoyanovich kick)
Ind —Hester 64 pass from George (Biasucci kick)
Mia—Safety, George intentional grounding in end zone
Mia—Sochia 13 fumble recovery return (Stoyanovich kick)
Ind —FG Biasucci 55

N.Y. Giants 13, New England 10—at Foxboro Stadium, attendance 60,410. Jeff Hostetler completed a touchdown pass and Matt Bahr kicked two field goals as the Giants narrowly defeated the Patriots. New York jumped to a 10-0 first-quarter lead on David Meggett's 17-yard scoring reception from Hostetler and Bahr's 33-yard field goal. New England tied the game 10-10 on Tommy Hodson's 40-yard touchdown pass to Irving Fryar and Jason Staurovsky's 19-yard field goal, but Bahr's 27-yard field goal with six seconds remaining in the first half proved to be the game-winner. The Patriots suffered their club-record fourteenth consecutive loss and were winless at home for the first time in their 31-year history.

N.Y. Giants	10	3	0	0	— 13
New England	0	10	0	0	— 10

NYG—Meggett 17 pass from Hostetler (Bahr kick)
NYG—FG Bahr 44
NE —Fryar 40 pass from Hodson (Staurovsky kick)
NE —FG Staurovsky 19
NYG—FG Bahr 27

New York Jets 16, Tampa Bay 14—at Tampa Stadium, attendance 46,543. Blair Thomas ran for a touchdown and Pat Leahy kicked three field goals as the Jets edged the Buccaneers. New York took a 13-7 halftime advantage on two field goals (21 and 32 yards) and Thomas's five-yard scoring run. Leahy added a 25-yard field goal in the third quarter to finish the Jets' scoring. Bruce Hill caught a seven-yard scoring pass from Vinny Testaverde to close the margin to 16-14, but Tampa Bay could get no closer.

N.Y. Jets	0	13	3	0	— 16
Tampa Bay	0	7	0	7	— 14

NYJ—FG Leahy 21
TB —Cobb 1 run (Christie kick)
NYJ—FG Leahy 32
NYJ—Thomas 5 run (Leahy kick)
NYJ—FG Leahy 25
TB —Hill 7 pass from Testaverde (Christie kick)

Los Angeles Raiders 17, San Diego 12—at Los Angeles Coliseum, attendance 62,593. Jay Schroeder connected with Steve Smith for a touchdown pass late in the fourth quarter as the Raiders rallied to defeat the Chargers and win the AFC Western Division title. Trailing 9-7 going into the fourth quarter, Jeff Jaeger kicked a 45-yard field goal to put Los Angeles ahead 10-9. John Carney's 21-yard field goal put San Diego back on top 12-10 early in the fourth period. Smith's 17-yard scoring reception with 3:53 remaining capped an 80-yard, 11-play drive.

San Diego	3	6	0	3	— 12
L.A. Raiders	0	7	0	10	— 17

SD —FG Carney 19
Raiders—Allen 1 run (Jaeger kick)
SD —McEwen 7 pass from Friesz (kick blocked)
Raiders—FG Jaeger 45
SD —FG Carney 21
Raiders—Smith 17 pass from Schroeder (Jaeger kick)

San Francisco 20, Minnesota 17—at Metrodome, attendance 51,590. Steve Young's 34-yard touchdown pass to John Taylor with 29 seconds remaining lifted the 49ers over the Vikings. Trailing 10-0 at halftime, Mike Cofer kicked two field goals (29 and 35 yards) to narrow the score to 10-6 in the fourth quarter. Young then completed a 14-yard touchdown pass to Jerry Rice to put San Francisco ahead 13-10. Alfred Anderson's one-yard run for a touchdown gave Minnesota a 17-13 lead with 3:14 remaining in the game. Young completed six of seven passes for

88 yards in the winning drive. San Francisco extended its NFL record to 19 consecutive road victories.

San Francisco	0	0	3	17 —	20
Minnesota	3	7	0	7 —	17

Minn—FG Reveiz 34
Minn—Walker 9 run (Reveiz kick)
SF —FG Cofer 29
SF —FG Cofer 35
SF —Rice 14 pass from Young (Cofer kick)
Minn—Anderson 1 run (Reveiz kick)
SF —Taylor 34 pass to Young (Cofer kick)

Sunday Night, December 30

Houston 34, Pittsburgh 14—at Astrodome, attendance 56,906. Cody Carlson completed three touchdown passes to help the Oilers secure an AFC Wild Card spot. Carlson, making his first NFL start since 1988 in place of injured Warren Moon, led Houston to a 24-0 halftime lead on Lorenzo White's one-yard scoring run, scoring strikes to Ernest Givins (14 yards) and Drew Hill (three), and Teddy Garcia's 47-yard field goal. Carlson hit Haywood Jeffires with a 53-yard touchdown pass in the second half, and Garcia connected on a 45-yard field goal to complete the Oilers' scoring. The loss eliminated the Steelers from the playoffs.

Pittsburgh	0	0	7	7 —	14
Houston	7	17	7	3 —	34

Hou—White 1 run (Garcia kick)
Hou—Givins 14 pass from Carlson (Garcia kick)
Hou—Hill 3 pass from Carlson (Garcia kick)
Hou—FG Garcia 47
Pitt —Hoge 4 run (Anderson kick)
Hou—Jeffires 53 pass from Carlson (Garcia kick)
Pitt —Hoge 3 run (Anderson kick)
Hou—FG Garcia 45

Monday, December 31

New Orleans 20, Los Angeles Rams 17—at Louisiana Superdome, attendance 68,647. Morten Andersen's 24-yard field goal with two seconds remaining lifted the Saints over the Rams and into the playoffs. New Orleans led 14-7 at halftime on Steve Walsh's 26-yard scoring pass to Floyd Turner and Craig Heyward's one-yard run. Following a scoreless third period, Jim Everett completed touchdown passes to Willie Anderson (47 yards) and Robert Delpino (one) to tie the game 17-17 with 1:19 remaining.

L.A. Rams	0	3	0	14 —	17
New Orleans	7	7	0	6 —	20

NO —Turner 26 pass from Walsh (Andersen kick)
Rams—FG Lansford 24
NO —Heyward 1 run (Andersen kick)
Rams—Anderson 47 pass from Everett (Lansford kick)
NO —FG Andersen 41
Rams—Delpino 1 pass from Everett (Lansford kick)
NO —FG Andersen 24

Eighteenth Week Summaries

Saturday, January 5, 1991
AFC First-Round Playoff Game

Miami 17, Kansas City 16—at Joe Robbie Stadium, attendance 67,276. Dan Marino led two fourth-quarter scoring drives in the Dolphins' 17-16 comeback win over the Chiefs. Kansas City jumped to a 10-3 halftime lead on Nick Lowery's 27-yard field goal and Steve DeBerg's 26-yard scoring strike to Stephone Paige. Dolphins kicker Pete Stoyanovich kicked an NFL-playoff record 58-yard field goal for Miami's only score in the first half. The Chiefs increased their lead to 16-3 when Nick Lowery added field goals of 25 and 38 yards in the third quarter. In the fourth quarter, Marino led a 10-play, 66-yard drive capped by his one-yard touchdown pass to Tony Paige to narrow the score to 16-10. Marino directed a second march of 85 yards which was topped off by his 12-yard touchdown pass to Mark Clayton to put Miami ahead 17-16 with 2:28 left in the game. A 52-yard field goal attempt by Lowery with 49 seconds remaining fell short.

Kansas City	3	7	6	0 —	16
Miami	0	3	0	14 —	17

KC —FG Lowery 27
Mia—FG Stoyanovich 58
KC —Paige 26 pass from DeBerg (Lowery kick)
KC —FG Lowery 25
KC —FG Lowery 38
Mia—Paige 1 pass from Marino (Stoyanovich kick)
Mia—Clayton 12 pass from Marino (Stoyanovich kick)

Saturday, January 5, 1991
NFC First-Round Playoff Game

Washington 20, Philadelphia 6—at Veterans Stadium, attendance 65,287. The Washington Redskins captured an NFC First-Round Playoff victory over division-rival Philadelphia. Roger Ruzek connected on field goals from 37 and 28 yards to give Philadelphia a 6-0 lead. Redskins quarterback Mark Rypien ignited his club's offensive attack with a 16-yard scoring strike to wide receiver Art Monk that gave Washington a 7-6 lead. Redskins kicker Chip Lohmiller's 20-yard field goal with eight seconds remaining before halftime gave the Redskins a 10-6 lead at intermission. The Redskins added 10 more points in the second half as Lohmiller converted his second field goal of the game (19 yards). Rypien completed the scoring with a three-yard touchdown pass to wide receiver Gary Clark. Rypien completed 15 of 31 passes for 206 yards and two touchdowns, while running back Earnest Byner totaled 126 scrimmage yards.

Washington	0	10	10	0 —	20
Philadelphia	3	3	0	0 —	6

Phil —FG Ruzek 37
Phil —FG Ruzek 28
Wash—Monk 16 pass from Rypien (Lohmiller kick)
Wash—FG Lohmiller 20
Wash—FG Lohmiller 19
Wash—Clark 2 pass from Rypien (Lohmiller kick)

Sunday, January 6, 1991
AFC First-Round Playoff Game

Cincinnati 41, Houston 14—at Riverfront Stadium, attendance 60,012. Boomer Esiason completed two touchdown passes and ran for a third in the Bengals' victory over the Oilers. Cincinnati built a 20-0 halftime lead as Ickey Woods ran one yard for a touchdown, Esiason flipped a two-yard scoring pass to Harold Green, and Jim Breech kicked two field goals (27 and 30 yards), while outgaining the Oilers 222 yards to 36 in the first half. Cincinnati increased its lead to 34-0 in the third quarter when Eric Ball ran three yards for a touchdown and Esiason scored on a 10-yard keeper following James Francis's fumble recovery at Houston's 10-yard line. The Oilers scored on two touchdown passes from Cody Carlson to Ernest Givins (16 and 5 yards). Cincinnati held a 39:45 to 20:15 time-of-possession advantage and had 24 first downs to Houston's 13.

Houston	0	0	7	7 —	14
Cincinnati	10	10	14	7 —	41

Cin —Woods 1 run (Breech kick)
Cin —FG Breech 27
Cin —Green 2 pass from Esiason (Breech kick)
Cin —FG Breech 30
Cin —Ball 3 run (Breech kick)
Cin —Esiason 10 run (Breech kick)
Hou—Givins 16 pass from Carlson (Garcia kick)
Cin —Kattus 9 pass from Esiason (Breech kick)
Hou—Givins 5 pass from Carlson (Breech kick)

Sunday, January 6, 1991
NFC First-Round Playoff Game

Chicago 16, New Orleans 6—at Soldier Field, attendance 60,767. The NFC Central Division champion Bears advanced to the divisional playoffs with a victory over the Saints. Quarterback Mike Tomczak completed 12 of 25 passes for 166 yards, including an 18-yard touchdown pass to tight end James Thornton. Bears running back Neal Anderson totaled 166 yards and tied Walter Payton's team postseason record for 27 carries in a game, set January 5, 1986, against the New York Giants. Anderson also caught four passes for 42 yards and had a 22-yard completion to wide receiver Ron Morris. Bears kicker Kevin Butler kicked three field goals (19, 22, and 21 yards). The Bears held a 16-6 advantage in first downs and a 365-193 advantage in total yards. Tomczak's 38-yard completion to wide receiver Dennis Gentry with less than three minutes remaining clinched Chicago's victory. The Bears' defense held New Orleans to 65 yards rushing.

New Orleans	0	3	0	3 —	6
Chicago	3	7	3	3 —	16

Chi—FG Butler 19
Chi—Thornton 18 pass from Tomczak (Butler kick)
NO—FG Andersen 47
Chi—FG Butler 22
NO—FG Andersen 38
Chi—FG Butler 21

Nineteenth Week Summaries

Saturday, January 12, 1991
AFC Divisional Playoff Game

Buffalo 44, Miami 34—at Rich Stadium, attendance 77,087. Thurman Thomas ran for two touchdowns and Andre Reed caught two others as the Bills defeated the Dolphins to advance to the AFC Championship Game. Thomas rushed for 117 yards on 32 carries, which included a pair of five-yard scoring runs. Quarterback Jim Kelly, who returned to the starting lineup for Buffalo after being sidelined with an injury, completed three touchdown passes, including first-half strikes to Andre Reed (40 yards) and James Lofton (13). Scott Norwood's two field goals (24 and 22 yards) and Thomas's touchdown run gave the Bills a 27-17 halftime advantage. Dan Marino completed a two-yard touchdown pass to Roy Foster in the opening minute of the fourth quarter to narrow the score to 30-27, but Buffalo countered with Thomas's second scoring run of the day and Kelly's 26-yard touchdown throw to Reed. Kelly completed 19 of 29 pass attempts for 339 yards. The Bills' 44 points shattered the club playoff record of 31, set against the New York Jets in the 1981 AFC Wild Card contest. Their 493 total yards also set a club playoff mark.

Miami	3	14	3	14 —	34
Buffalo	13	14	3	14 —	44

Buff—Reed 40 pass from Kelly (Norwood kick)
Mia —FG Stoyanovich 49
Buff—FG Norwood 24
Buff—FG Norwood 22
Buff—Thomas 5 run (Norwood kick)
Mia —Duper 64 pass from Marino (Stoyanovich kick)
Buff—Lofton 13 pass from Kelly (Norwood kick)
Mia —Marino 2 run (Stoyanovich kick)
Mia —FG Stoyanovich 22
Buff—FG Norwood 28
Mia —Foster 2 pass from Marino (Stoyanovich kick)
Buff—Thomas 5 run (Norwood kick)
Buff—Reed 26 pass from Kelly (Norwood kick)
Mia —Martin 8 pass from Marino (Stoyanovich kick)

Saturday, January 12, 1991
NFC Divisional Playoff Game

San Francisco 28, Washington 10—at Candlestick Park, attendance 65,292. Joe Montana, who completed 22 of 31 passes for 274 yards and two touchdowns with one interception, passed for 200 yards in the first half as the 49ers advanced to their third consecutive NFC Championship Game. Washington, which defeated Philadelphia 20-6 in the first round of the NFC playoffs, outgained the 49ers 441-338 in total offense and took an early 7-0 lead. Quarterback Mark Rypien hit wide receiver Art Monk with a 31-yard touchdown pass, but San Francisco tied the game 7-7 on Tom Rathman's one-yard run. Washington regained the lead 10-7 on Chip Lohmiller's 44-yard field goal with 36 seconds remaining in the opening period before Montana helped his club to a 21-10 halftime advantage with a 10-yard touchdown pass to Jerry Rice, who caught six passes for 68 yards. Montana also threw an eight-yard scoring strike to wide receiver Mike Sherrard. Neither club scored an offensive touchdown in the second half, but the 49ers' Michael Carter returned a deflected pass 61 yards for a touchdown.

Washington	10	0	0	0 —	10
San Francisco	7	14	0	7 —	28

Wash—Monk 31 pass from Rypien (Lohmiller kick)
SF —Rathman 1 run (Cofer kick)
Wash—FG Lohmiller 44
SF —Rice 10 pass from Montana (Cofer kick)
SF —Sherrard 8 pass from Montana (Cofer kick)
SF —Carter 61 interception return (Cofer kick)

Sunday, January 13, 1991
AFC Divisional Playoff Game

Los Angeles Raiders 20, Cincinnati 10—at Los Angeles Coliseum, attendance 92,045. Jay Schroeder completed two scoring passes to help the Raiders defeat the Bengals to earn a spot in the AFC Championship Game. Cincinnati scored first on Jim Breech's 27-yard field goal in the second quarter. Schroeder hit Mervyn Fernandez with a 13-yard scoring strike to give Los Angeles a 7-3 halftime lead. The Raiders increased their lead to 10-3 on Jeff Jaeger's 49-yard field goal in the third quarter. Los Angeles broke a 10-10 tie by scoring 10 unanswered fourth-quarter points on Schroeder's 41-yard pass to Ethan Horton and Jaeger's 25-yard field goal. The Raiders rushed for 235 yards, including 140 yards by Marcus Allen on 21 carries. Bo Jackson added 77 yards on six carries. Greg Townsend recorded three of the Raiders' four sacks.

Cincinnati	0	3	0	7 —	10
L.A. Raiders	0	7	3	10 —	20

Cin —FG Breech 27
Raiders—Fernandez 13 pass from Schroeder (Jaeger kick)
Raiders—FG Jaeger 49
Cin —Jennings 8 pass from Esiason (Breech kick)
Raiders—Horton 41 pass from Schroeder (Jaeger kick)
Raiders—FG Jaeger 25

Sunday, January 13, 1991
NFC Divisional Playoff Game

New York Giants 31, Chicago 3—at Giants Stadium, attendance 77,025. Giants quarterback Jeff Hostetler completed 10 of 17 passes for 112 yards and two touchdowns, and rushed six times for 43 yards, including a three-yard touchdown, as the Giants rolled over Chicago and earned a spot in the NFC Championship Game. New York scored first to take a 3-0 lead on Matt Bahr's 46-yard field goal. Hostetler then completed the first of his two touchdown passes—a 21-yarder to Stephen Baker, who caught three passes for 58 yards. Chicago closed to 10-3 when Kevin Butler kicked a 33-yard field goal. New York extended its lead to 17-3 at halftime on Hostetler's five-yard touchdown pass to tight end Howard Cross. The Giants added touchdowns in the third and fourth periods as Hostetler scored on a three-yard run in the third quarter and running back Maurice Carthon on a one-yard run with seven seconds remaining. Chicago running back Neal Anderson was held to 19 yards on 12 carries. New York held a 194-27 rushing advantage. Giants cornerbacks Everson Walls and Mark Collins each had interceptions.

Chicago	0	3	0	0 —	3
N.Y. Giants	10	7	7	7 —	31

NYG—FG Bahr 46
NYG—Baker 21 pass from Hostetler (Bahr kick)
Chi —FG Butler 33
NYG—Cross 5 pass from Hostetler (Bahr kick)
NYG—Hostetler 3 run (Bahr kick)
NYG—Carthon 1 run (Bahr kick)

Twentieth Week Summaries

Sunday, January 20, 1991
AFC Championship Game

Buffalo 51, Los Angeles Raiders 3—at Rich Stadium, attendance 80,325. Kenneth Davis ran for three touchdowns and Jim Kelly threw for 300 yards as the Bills gained their first Super Bowl berth by defeating the Raiders. Buffalo set an NFL playoff record by scoring 41 first-half points on Jim Kelly's touchdown passes to James Lofton (13 and 8 yards), a pair of scoring runs by Davis (one and three yards), Thurman Thomas's 12-yard touchdown run, and Darryl Talley's 27-yard interception return for a score. Davis added a one-yard scoring run and Scott Norwood kicked a 39-yard field goal in the second half. The Raiders managed just one score, a 41-yard field goal by Jeff Jaeger in the first quarter. Thomas finished with 138 yards rushing and 61 yards receiving. Lofton had five receptions for 113 yards. The Bills' 51 points tied an AFC playoff record as did Davis's three touchdown runs.

L.A. Raiders	3	0	0	0 —	3
Buffalo	21	20	0	10 —	51

Buffalo — Lofton 13 pass from Kelly (Norwood kick)
Raiders — FG Jaeger 41
Buff — Thomas 12 run (Norwood kick)
Buff — Talley 27 interception return (Norwood kick)
Buff — Davis 1 run (kick blocked)
Buff — Davis 3 run (Norwood kick)
Buff — Lofton 8 pass from Kelly (Norwood kick)
Buff — Davis 1 run (Norwood kick)
Buff — FG Norwood 39

Sunday, January 20, 1991
NFC Championship Game

New York Giants 15, San Francisco 13—at Candlestick Park, attendance 65,750. The NFC Eastern Division champion New York Giants advanced to the Super Bowl for the first time since 1986 by defeating NFC West titlist and two-time defending Super Bowl champion San Francisco. Giants backup quarterback Jeff Hostetler completed 15 of 27 passes for 176 yards and executed the final drive to set up Matt Bahr's game-winning 42-yard field goal as time expired. The Giants controlled the ball for 39 minutes and outgained San Francisco 152 to 39 yards rushing. The teams fought to a 6-6 halftime tie on two field goals by both Bahr and 49ers kicker Mike Cofer. Quarterback Joe Montana and wide receiver John Taylor hooked up on a 61-yard scoring play for the game's only touchdown, to give San Francisco a 13-6 advantage. Bahr, who accounted for all of New York's scoring via five field goals, scored the next nine points by converting field goals from 46, 38, and 42 yards. His game-winning attempt was set up when linebacker Lawrence Taylor recovered a fumble forced by nose tackle Erik Howard. Hostetler drove the Giants 33 yards in six plays before Bahr's decisive kick. New York running back Ottis Anderson led all rushers with 67 yards on 20 carries and wide receiver Mark Ingram caught five passes for 82 yards.

N.Y. Giants	3	3	3	6 —	15
San Francisco	3	3	7	0 —	13

SF — FG Cofer 47
NYG — FG Bahr 28
NYG — FG Bahr 42
SF — FG Cofer 35
SF — Taylor 61 pass from Montana (Cofer kick)
NYG — FG Bahr 46
NYG — FG Bahr 38
NYG — FG Bahr 42

Twenty-First Week Summaries

Sunday, January 27, 1991
Super Bowl XXV
Tampa, Florida

New York Giants 20, Buffalo 19—at Tampa Stadium, Tampa, Florida, attendance 73,813. The NFC champion New York Giants won their first Super Bowl title since 1986 with a 20-19 victory over AFC titlist Buffalo. New York, employing its ball-control offense, had possession for 40:33, a Super Bowl record. The Bills, who scored 95 points in their previous two playoff games, had the ball for less than eight minutes in the second half and just 19:27 for the game. Fourteen of New York's 73 plays came on its initial drive of the third quarter that covered 75 yards and consumed a Super Bowl-record 9:29 before running back Ottis Anderson ran one yard for a touchdown. Giants quarterback Jeff Hostetler kept the long drive going by converting three third-down plays—an 11-yard pass to running back David Meggett on third-and-eight, a 14-yard completion to wide receiver Mark Ingram on third-and-13, and a nine-yard pass to tight end Howard Cross on third-and-four. Buffalo took a 12-3 lead midway through the second quarter before Hostetler's 14-yard scoring strike to wide receiver Stephen Baker closed the margin to 12-10 at halftime. New York's record drive capped by Anderson's touchdown gave the Giants a 17-12 lead, but Buffalo's Thurman Thomas ran 31 yards for a touchdown on the opening play of the fourth quarter to help Buffalo recapture the lead 19-17. Giants kicker Matt Bahr's 21-yard field goal gave New York a 20-19 lead, but Buffalo's Scott Norwood had a chance to win the game with seconds remaining before his 47-yard field goal attempt sailed wide right. Hostetler completed 20 of 32 passes for 222 yards and one touchdown. Ingram caught five passes for 74 yards; tight end Mark Bavaro five for 50. Anderson rushed 21 times for 102 yards and one touchdown to capture the most valuable player award.

Buffalo	3	9	0	7 —	19
N.Y. Giants	3	7	7	3 —	20

NYG — FG Bahr 28
Buff — FG Norwood 23
Buff — D. Smith 1 run (Norwood kick)
Buff — Safety, Smith tackled Hostetler in the end zone
NYG — Baker 14 pass from Hostetler (Bahr kick)
NYG — Anderson 1 run (Bahr kick)
Buff — Thomas 31 run (Norwood kick)
NYG — FG Bahr 21

Twenty-Second Week Summaries

Sunday, February 3, 1991
AFC-NFC Pro Bowl
Honolulu, Hawaii

AFC 23, NFC 21—at Aloha Stadium, attendance 50,345. Buffalo's Jim Kelly and Houston's Ernest Givins combined on a 13-yard scoring pass late in the fourth quarter to rally the AFC over the NFC. Phoenix rookie Johnny Johnson scored on runs of one and nine yards to put the NFC ahead 14-3 in the third quarter. Buffalo's Andre Reed, who led all receivers with four catches for 80 yards, caught a 20-yard scoring reception from Kelly early in the fourth quarter to move the AFC within one point. Barry Sanders ran 22 yards for a touchdown to increase the NFC's lead to 21-13. Miami's Jeff Cross blocked a 46-yard field-goal attempt by New Orleans's Morten Andersen with seven seconds remaining to preserve the win. Buffalo's Bruce Smith had three sacks and a blocked field goal. Kelly, who completed 13 of 19 passes for 210 yards and two touchdowns, was voted the Dan McGuire Award as player of the game. The AFC's victory narrowed the NFC's Pro Bowl series lead to 12-9.

AFC	3	0	3	17 —	23
NFC	0	7	7	7 —	21

AFC — FG Lowery 26
NFC — J. Johnson 1 run (Andersen kick)
AFC — FG Lowery 43
NFC — J. Johnson 9 run (Andersen kick)
AFC — Reed 20 pass from Kelly (Lowery kick)
NFC — Sanders 22 run (Andersen kick)
AFC — FG Lowery 34
AFC — Givins 13 pass from Kelly (Lowery kick)

1990 PFWA All-Pro Team

Selected by the Professional Football Writers of America

Offense

Jerry Rice, San Francisco ... Wide Receiver
Andre Rison, Atlanta ... Wide Receiver
Keith Jackson, Philadelphia ... Tight End
Anthony Muñoz, Cincinnati ... Tackle
Jim Lachey, Washington ... Tackle
Bruce Matthews, Houston ... Guard
Steve Wisniewski, Los Angeles Raiders ... Guard
Kent Hull, Buffalo ... Center
Randall Cunningham, Philadelphia ... Quarterback
Barry Sanders, Detroit ... Running Back
Thurman Thomas, Buffalo ... Running Back
Nick Lowery, Kansas City ... Kicker
Mel Gray, Detroit ... Kick Returner

Defense

Bruce Smith, Buffalo ... Defensive End
Reggie White, Philadelphia ... Defensive End
Michael Dean Perry, Cleveland ... Defensive Tackle
Ray Childress, Houston ... Defensive Tackle
Derrick Thomas, Kansas City ... Outside Linebacker
Charles Haley, San Francisco ... Outside Linebacker
Pepper Johnson, New York Giants ... Inside Linebacker
John Offerdahl, Miami ... Inside Linebacker
Rod Woodson, Pittsburgh ... Cornerback
Albert Lewis, Kansas City ... Cornerback
Joey Browner, Minnesota ... Safety
Ronnie Lott, San Francisco ... Safety
Sean Landeta, New York Giants ... Punter
David Meggett, New York Giants ... Punt Returner

1990 Associated Press All-Pro Team

Offense

Jerry Rice, San Francisco ... Wide Receiver
Andre Rison, Atlanta ... Wide Receiver
Keith Jackson, Philadelphia ... Tight End
Anthony Muñoz, Cincinnati ... Tackle
Jim Lachey, Washington ... Tackle
Bruce Matthews, Houston ... Guard
Randall McDaniel, Minnesota ... Guard
Kent Hull, Buffalo ... Center
Joe Montana, San Francisco ... Quarterback
Thurman Thomas, Buffalo ... Running Back
Barry Sanders, Detroit ... Running Back
Nick Lowery, Kansas City ... Kicker

Defense

Reggie White, Philadelphia ... Defensive End
Bruce Smith, Buffalo ... Defensive End
Jerome Brown, Philadelphia ... Defensive Tackle
Michael Dean Perry, Cleveland ... Defensive Tackle
Derrick Thomas, Kansas City ... Outside Linebacker
Charles Haley, San Francisco ... Outside Linebacker
Pepper Johnson, New York Giants ... Inside Linebacker
John Offerdahl, Miami ... Inside Linebacker
Rod Woodson, Pittsburgh ... Cornerback
Albert Lewis, Kansas City ... Cornerback
Ronnie Lott, San Francisco ... Safety
Joey Browner, Minnesota ... Safety
Sean Landeta, New York Giants ... Punter
Mel Gray, Detroit ... Kick Returner

1990 All-NFL Team

Selected by the Associated Press and Professional Football Writers of America

Offense

Jerry Rice, San Francisco (AP, PFWA) ... Wide Receiver
Andre Rison, Atlanta (AP, PFWA) ... Wide Receiver
Keith Jackson, Philadelphia (AP, PFWA) ... Tight End
Anthony Muñoz, Cincinnati (AP, PFWA) ... Tackle
Jim Lachey, Washington (AP, PFWA) ... Tackle
Bruce Matthews, Houston (AP, PFWA) ... Guard
Randall McDaniel, Minnesota (AP) ... Guard
Steve Wisniewski, Los Angeles Raiders (PFWA) ... Guard
Kent Hull, Buffalo (AP, PFWA) ... Center
Joe Montana, San Francisco (AP) ... Quarterback
Randall Cunningham, Philadelphia (PFWA) ... Quarterback
Thurman Thomas, Buffalo (AP, PFWA) ... Running Back
Barry Sanders, Detroit (AP, PFWA) ... Running Back

Defense

Reggie White, Philadelphia (AP, PFWA) ... Defensive End
Bruce Smith, Buffalo (AP, PFWA) ... Defensive End
Michael Dean Perry, Cleveland (AP, PFWA) ... Defensive Tackle
Jerome Brown, Philadelphia (AP) ... Defensive Tackle
Ray Childress, Houston (PFWA) ... Defensive Tackle
Derrick Thomas, Kansas City (AP, PFWA) ... Outside Linebacker
Charles Haley, San Francisco (AP, PFWA) ... Outside Linebacker
Pepper Johnson, New York Giants (AP, PFWA) ... Inside Linebacker
John Offerdahl, Miami (AP, PFWA) ... Inside Linebacker
Rod Woodson, Pittsburgh (AP, PFWA) ... Cornerback
Albert Lewis, Kansas City (AP, PFWA) ... Cornerback
Ronnie Lott, San Francisco (AP, PFWA) ... Safety
Joey Browner, Minnesota (AP, PFWA) ... Safety

Specialists

Nick Lowery, Kansas City (AP, PFWA) ... Kicker
Sean Landeta, New York Giants (AP, PFWA) ... Punter
Mel Gray, Detroit (AP, PFWA) ... Kick Returner
David Meggett, New York Giants (PFWA) ... Punt Returner

1990 UPI All-AFC Team

Selected by United Press International

Offense

Andre Reed, Buffalo	Wide Receiver
Ernest Givins, Houston	Wide Receiver
Rodney Holman, Cincinnati	Tight End
Anthony Muñoz, Cincinnati	Tackle
John Alt, Kansas City	Tackle
Steve Wisniewski, Los Angeles Raiders	Guard
Bruce Matthews, Houston	Guard
Kent Hull, Buffalo	Center
Warren Moon, Houston	Quarterback
Thurman Thomas, Buffalo	Running Back
Marion Butts, San Diego	Running Back
Nick Lowery, Kansas City	Kicker

Defense

Bruce Smith, Buffalo	Defensive End
Greg Townsend, Los Angeles Raiders	Defensive End
Michael Dean Perry, Cleveland	Defensive Tackle
Derrick Thomas, Kansas City	Outside Linebacker
Cornelius Bennett, Buffalo	Outside Linebacker
John Offerdahl, Miami	Inside Linebacker
David Little, Pittsburgh	Inside Linebacker
Rod Woodson, Pittsburgh	Cornerback
Albert Lewis, Kansas City	Cornerback
David Fulcher, Cincinnati	Safety
Steve Atwater, Denver	Safety
Rohn Stark, Indianapolis	Punter
Rod Woodson, Pittsburgh	Kick Returner
Clarence Verdin, Indianapolis	Punt Returner

1990 UPI All-NFC Team

Selected by United Press International

Offense

Jerry Rice, San Francisco	Wide Receiver
Andre Rison, Atlanta	Wide Receiver
Keith Jackson, Philadelphia	Tight End
Jim Lachey, Washington	Tackle
Lomas Brown, Detroit	Tackle
Randall McDaniel, Minnesota	Guard
Guy McIntyre, San Francisco	Guard
Jay Hilgenberg, Chicago	Center
Randall Cunningham, Philadelphia	Quarterback
Barry Sanders, Detroit	Running Back
Neal Anderson, Chicago	Running Back
Steve Christie, Tampa Bay	Kicker

Defense

Reggie White, Philadelphia	Defensive End
Richard Dent, Chicago	Defensive End
Jerome Brown, Philadelphia	Defensive Tackle
Charles Haley, San Francisco	Outside Linebacker
Lawrence Taylor, New York Giants	Outside Linebacker
Pepper Johnson, New York Giants	Inside Linebacker
Mike Singletary, Chicago	Inside Linebacker
Darrell Green, Washington	Cornerback
Mark Collins, New York Giants	Cornerback
Mark Carrier, Chicago	Safety
Joey Browner, Minnesota	Safety
Sean Landeta, New York Giants	Punter
Mel Gray, Detroit	Kick Returner
David Meggett, New York Giants	Punt Returner

1990 PFWA All-Rookie Team

Selected by Professional Football Writers of America

Offense

Fred Barnett, Philadelphia	Wide Receiver
Ricky Proehl, Phoenix (tie)	Wide Receiver
Rob Moore, New York Jets (tie)	Wide Receiver
Eric Green, Pittsburgh	Tight End
Richmond Webb, Miami	Tackle
Leo Goeas, San Diego	Tackle
Keith Sims, Miami	Guard
Dave Szott, Kansas City	Guard
Tim Grunhard, Kansas City	Center
Jeff George, Indianapolis	Quarterback
Johnny Johnson, Phoenix	Running Back
Emmitt Smith, Dallas	Running Back
Steve Christie, Tampa Bay	Kicker

Defense

Renaldo Turnbull, New Orleans	Defensive End
Ray Agnew, New England	Defensive End
Cortez Kennedy, Seattle	Defensive Tackle
Jimmie Jones, Dallas	Defensive Tackle
James Francis, Cincinnati	Outside Linebacker
Aaron Wallace, Los Angeles Raiders	Outside Linebacker
Percy Snow, Kansas City	Inside Linebacker
Ben Smith, Philadelphia	Cornerback
James Williams, Buffalo	Cornerback
Robert Blackmon, Seattle	Safety
Mark Carrier, Chicago	Safety

1990 UPI All-Rookie Team

Selected by United Press International

Offense

Ricky Proehl, Phoenix	Wide Receiver
Rob Moore, New York Jets	Wide Receiver
Eric Green, Pittsburgh	Tight End
Richmond Webb, Miami	Tackle
Leo Goeas, San Diego	Tackle
Keith Sims, Miami	Guard
Dave Szott, Kansas City	Guard
Tim Grunhard, Kansas City	Center
Jeff George, Indianapolis	Quarterback
Emmitt Smith, Dallas	Running Back
Johnny Johnson, Phoenix	Running Back
Steve Christie, Tampa Bay	Kicker
Johnny Bailey, Chicago	Kick Returner

Defense

Renaldo Turnbull, New Orleans	Defensive End
Jimmie Jones, Dallas	Defensive End
Tory Epps, Atlanta	Defensive Tackle
James Francis, Cincinnati	Outside Linebacker
Aaron Wallace, Los Angeles Raiders	Outside Linebacker
Percy Snow, Kansas City	Inside Linebacker
Junior Seau, San Diego	Inside Linebacker
James Williams, Buffalo	Cornerback
Ben Smith, Philadelphia	Cornerback
Mark Carrier, Chicago	Safety
Robert Blackmon, Seattle	Safety
Bryan Barker, Kansas City	Punter

1990 Professional Football Awards

	NFL	AFC	NFC
Professional Football Writers of America			
Most Valuable Player	Randall Cunningham		
Rookie of the Year	Mark Carrier		
Coach of the Year	Art Shell		
Associated Press			
Most Valuable Player	Joe Montana		
Offensive Player of the Year	Warren Moon		
Defensive Player of the Year	Bruce Smith		
Rookie of the Year—Offensive	Emmitt Smith		
Rookie of the Year—Defensive	Mark Carrier		
Coach of the Year	Jimmy Johnson		
United Press International			
Offensive Player of the Year		Warren Moon	Randall Cunningham
Defensive Player of the Year		Bruce Smith	Charles Haley
Coach of the Year		Art Shell	Jimmy Johnson
Rookie of the Year		Richmond Webb	Mark Carrier
The Sporting News			
Player of the Year	Jerry Rice		
Rookie of the Year	Richmond Webb		
Football News			
Player of the Year		Bruce Smith	Randall Cunningham
Coach of the Year		Art Shell	George Seifert
Pro Football Weekly			
Offensive Player of the Year	Randall Cunningham		
Defensive Player of the Year	Bruce Smith		
Rookie of the Year—Offensive	Emmitt Smith		
Rookie of the Year—Defensive	Mark Carrier		
Coach of the Year	Art Shell		
Football Digest			
Player of the Year	Randall Cunningham		
Rookie of the Year—Offensive	Johnny Johnson		
Rookie of the Year—Defensive	Mark Carrier		
Coach of the Year	Don Shula		
Maxwell Club			
Player of the Year (Bert Bell Trophy)	Randall Cunningham		
Super Bowl XXV Most Valuable Player			
(Pete Rozelle Trophy)	Ottis Anderson		
AFC-NFC Pro Bowl			
Player of the Game (Dan McGuire Award)	Jim Kelly		

AFC-NFC Players of the Week:

	AFC Offense	AFC Defense	NFC Offense	NFC Defense
Week 1	RB Sammie Smith, Mia.	S David Fulcher, Cin.	QB Anthony Dilweg, G.B.	LB Lawrence Taylor, NYG
Week 2	WR Eddie Brown, Cin.	CB Rod Woodson, Pitt.	QB Joe Montana, S.F.	LB Chris Spielman, Det.
Week 3	RB Thurman Thomas, Buff.	CB Kevin Ross, K.C.	WR Jerry Rice, S.F.	DE Richard Dent, Chi.
Week 4	QB Jack Trudeau, Ind.	LB Cornelius Bennett, Buff.	QB Don Majkowski, G.B.	S Mark Robinson, T.B.
Week 5	QB Boomer Esiason, Cin.	LB Cornelius Bennett, Buff.	QB Chris Miller, Atl.	LB Charles Haley, S.F.
Week 6	QB Warren Moon, Hou.	DE Bill Maas, K.C.	QB Joe Montana, S.F. & WR Jerry Rice, S.F.	S Greg Jackson, NYG
Week 7	WR Andre Reed, Buff.	LB Johnny Meads, Hou.	QB Jim Everett, Rams	CB Issiac Holt, Dall.
Week 8	WR Al Toon, NYJ	CB Gill Byrd, S.D.	Chicago Offensive Line	CB Everson Walls, NYG
Week 9	QB Bubby Brister, Pitt.	CB Albert Lewis, K.C.	QB Jeff Rutledge, Wash.	S Mark Carrier, Chi.
Week 10	QB Dave Krieg, Sea.	LB Derrick Thomas, K.C.	RB Craig Heyward, N.O.	DE Richard Dent, Chi.
Week 11	QB Warren Moon, Hou.	S Barney Bussey, Cin.	QB Mark Rypien, Wash.	LB Mike Singletary, Chi.
Week 12	RB Lorenzo White, Hou.	S Nesby Glasgow, Sea.	QB Randall Cunningham, Phil.	LB Mike Merriweather, Chi.
Week 13	RB Marion Butts, S.D.	DE Bruce Smith, Buff.	T Jim Lachey, Wash.	DE Al Noga, Minn.
Week 14	QB Dan Marino, Mia.	DE Bruce Smith, Buff.	RB Barry Sanders, Det.	LB Lawrence Taylor, NYG
Week 15	QB Warren Moon, Hou.	LB Riki Ellison, Raiders	QB Rodney Peete, Det.	S James Washington, Dall.
Week 16	RB James Brooks, Cin.	LB Darryl Talley, Buff.	QB Jeff Hostetler, NYG	S Scott Case, Atl.
Week 17	QB Cody Carlson, Hou.	DE Jacob Green, Sea.	QB Steve Young, S.F.	LB Wilber Marshall, Wash.

AFC-NFC Players of the Month:

	AFC Offense	AFC Defense	NFC Offense	NFC Defense
Sept.	QB Steve DeBerg, K.C.	DE Greg Townsend, Raiders	QB Vinny Testaverde, T.B.	DE Trace Armstrong, Chi.
Oct.	QB Bubby Brister, Pitt.	LB John Offerdahl, Mia. & DE Jeff Cross, Mia.	WR Andre Rison, Atl.	LB Charles Haley, S.F.
Nov.	QB Warren Moon, Hou.	LB Derrick Thomas, K.C.	QB Randall Cunningham, Phil.	S Joey Browner, Minn.
Dec.	QB Jay Schroeder, Raiders	DE Bruce Smith, Buff.	RB Earnest Byner, Wash.	LB Rickey Jackson, N.O.

Ten Best Rushing Performances, 1990

	Attempts	Yards	TD
1. Thurman Thomas Buffalo vs. N.Y. Jets, September 24	18	214	0
2. James Brooks Cincinnati vs. Houston, December 23	20	201	1
3. Barry Word Kansas City vs. Detroit, October 14	18	200	2
4. Bobby Humphrey Denver vs. Buffalo, September 30	34	177	1
5. Barry Sanders Detroit vs. L.A. Raiders, December 10	25	176	2
6. Thurman Thomas Buffalo vs. New England, November 18	22	165	2
7. Sammie Smith Miami vs. New England, September 9	23	159	1
Marion Butts San Diego vs. N.Y. Jets, December 2	26	159	2
9. Earnest Byner Washington vs. Miami, December 2	32	157	3
10. Craig Heyward New Orleans vs. Tampa Bay, November 11	20	155	2
Mike Rozier Atlanta vs. Dallas, December 30	21	155	0

100-Yard Rushing Performances, 1990

First Week
Sammie Smith, Miami — 159 yards vs. New England
Neal Anderson, Chicago — 101 yards vs. Seattle

Second Week
Bobby Humphrey, Denver — 132 yards vs. Kansas City
Marion Butts, San Diego — 103 yards vs. Cincinnati

Third Week
Thurman Thomas, Buffalo — 214 yards vs. N.Y. Jets
Derrick Fenner, Seattle — 144 yards vs. Denver
Bobby Humphrey, Denver — 129 yards vs. Seattle
Christian Okoye, Kansas City — 122 yards vs. Green Bay
Anthony Toney, Philadelphia — 103 yards vs. L.A. Rams

Fourth Week
Bobby Humphrey, Denver — 177 yards vs. Buffalo
Gary Anderson, Tampa Bay — 108 yards vs. Minnesota
Blair Thomas, N.Y. Jets — 100 yards vs. New England

Fifth Week
Neal Anderson, Chicago — 141 yards vs. Green Bay
Emmitt Smith, Dallas — 121 yards vs. Tampa Bay
Bobby Humphrey, Denver — 106 yards vs. Cleveland

Sixth Week
Barry Word, Kansas City — 200 yards vs. Detroit
Marion Butts, San Diego — 121 yards vs. N.Y. Jets
Johnny Johnson, Phoenix — 120 yards vs. Dallas

Seventh Week
Johnny Johnson, Phoenix — 108 yards vs. N.Y. Giants
Cleveland Gary, L.A. Rams — 102 yards vs. Atlanta

Eighth Week
Thurman Thomas, Buffalo — 136 yards vs. New England

Ninth Week
Randall Cunningham, Phil. — 124 yards vs. New England
Craig Heyward, New Orleans — 122 yards vs. Cincinnati
Rueben Mayes, New Orleans — 115 yards vs. Cincinnati
Heath Sherman, Philadelphia — 113 yards vs. New England
Barry Sanders, Detroit — 104 yards vs. Washington

Tenth Week
Craig Heyward, New Orleans — 155 yards vs. Tampa Bay
Heath Sherman, Philadelphia — 124 yards vs. Washington
Marion Butts, San Diego — 114 yards vs. Denver
Thurman Thomas, Buffalo — 112 yards vs. Phoenix

Eleventh Week
Thurman Thomas, Buffalo — 165 yards vs. New England
Earnest Byner, Washington — 116 yards vs. New Orleans
Neal Anderson, Chicago — 110 yards vs. Denver
James Brooks, Cincinnati — 105 yards vs. Pittsburgh
Cleveland Gary, L.A. Rams — 103 yards vs. Dallas
Johnny Johnson, Phoenix — 103 yards vs. Green Bay

Twelfth Week
Barry Sanders, Detroit — 147 yards vs. Denver
Eric Dickerson, Indianapolis — 143 yards vs. Cincinnati
Anthony Thompson, Phoenix — 136 yards vs. New England
Emmitt Smith, Dallas — 132 yards vs. Washington
Marion Butts, San Diego — 128 yards vs. Seattle
Lorenzo White, Houston — 125 yards vs. Buffalo

Thirteenth Week
Marion Butts, San Diego — 159 yards vs. N.Y. Jets
Earnest Byner, Washington — 157 yards vs. Miami
Bo Jackson, L.A. Raiders — 117 yards vs. Denver
Mike Rozier, Atlanta — 115 yards vs. Tampa Bay
Barry Word, Kansas City — 112 yards vs. New England

Fourteenth Week
Barry Sanders, Detroit — 176 yards vs. L.A. Raiders
Bo Jackson, L.A. Raiders — 129 yards vs. Detroit
Earnest Byner, Washington — 121 yards vs. Chicago
Merril Hoge, Pittsburgh — 117 yards vs. New England
Lorenzo White, Houston — 116 yards vs. Cleveland
Derrick Fenner, Seattle — 112 yards vs. Green Bay
Gill Fenerty, New Orleans — 104 yards vs. L.A. Rams

Fifteenth Week
Earnest Byner, Washington — 149 yards vs. New England
Dexter Carter, San Francisco — 124 yards vs. L.A. Rams
Eric Dickerson, Indianapolis — 117 yards vs. N.Y. Jets
Bo Jackson, L.A. Raiders — 117 yards vs. Cincinnati
Rodney Hampton, N.Y. Giants — 105 yards vs. Buffalo
Vinny Testaverde, Tampa Bay — 105 yards vs. Minnesota
Emmitt Smith, Dallas — 103 yards vs. Phoenix
Neal Anderson, Chicago — 100 yards vs. Detroit

Sixteenth Week
James Brooks, Cincinnati — 201 yards vs. Houston
Earnest Byner, Washington — 154 yards vs. Indianapolis
Thurman Thomas, Buffalo — 154 yards vs. Miami
Barry Sanders, Detroit — 133 yards vs. Green Bay
Barry Word, Kansas City — 106 yards vs. San Diego
Mike Rozier, Atlanta — 102 yards vs. L.A. Rams
Steve Young, San Francisco — 102 yards vs. New Orleans
Barry Foster, Pittsburgh — 100 yards vs. Cleveland

Seventeenth Week
Mike Rozier, Atlanta — 155 yards vs. Dallas
Rod Bernstine, San Diego — 114 yards vs. L.A. Raiders
Eric Dickerson, Indianapolis — 110 yards vs. Miami
Sammie Smith, Miami — 108 yards vs. Indianapolis

Times 100 or More (74)
Butts, Byner, Thomas, 5; N. Anderson, Humphrey, Sanders, 4; Dickerson, Jackson, J. Johnson, Rozier, E. Smith, Word, 3; Fenner, Gary, Heyward, Rozier, Sherman, S. Smith, L. White, 2.

Ten Best Passing Performances, 1990

		Att.	Comp.	Yards	TD
1.	Warren Moon Houston vs. Kansas City, December 16	45	27	527	3
2.	Boomer Esiason Cincinnati vs. L.A. Rams, October 7	45	31	490	3
3.	Joe Montana San Francisco vs. Atlanta, October 14	49	32	476	6
4.	Joe Montana San Francisco vs. Green Bay, November 4	40	25	411	3
5.	Joe Montana San Francisco vs. Atlanta, September 23	35	24	398	2
6.	Warren Moon Houston vs. Atlanta, September 9	52	31	397	4
7.	Steve DeBerg Kansas City vs. Denver, September 17	45	26	395	2
8.	Joe Montana San Francisco vs. Washington, September 16	44	29	390	2
9.	Warren Moon Houston vs. N.Y. Jets, October 28	43	30	381	1
	Timm Rosenbach Phoenix vs. N.Y. Giants, December 23	41	23	381	3

300-Yard Passing Performances, 1990

First Week	
Warren Moon, Houston	397 yards vs. Atlanta
Jim Everett, L.A. Rams	340 yards vs. Green Bay
Ken O'Brien, N.Y. Jets	300 yards vs. Cincinnati
Second Week	
Steve DeBerg, Kansas City	395 yards vs. Denver
Joe Montana, San Francisco	390 yards vs. Washington
Third Week	
Joe Montana, San Francisco	398 yards vs. Atlanta
Chris Miller, Atlanta	337 yards vs. San Francisco
Warren Moon, Houston	308 yards vs. Indianapolis
Fourth Week	
Warren Moon, Houston	355 yards vs. San Diego
Jack Trudeau, Indianapolis	329 yards vs. Philadelphia
Fifth Week	
Boomer Esiason, Cincinnati	490 yards vs. L.A. Rams
Jim Everett, L.A. Rams	372 yards vs. Cincinnati
Chris Miller, Atlanta	366 yards vs. New Orleans
Bernie Kosar, Cleveland	318 yards vs. Denver
Joe Montana, San Francisco	318 yards vs. Houston
Sixth Week	
Joe Montana, San Francisco	476 yards vs. Atlanta
Warren Moon, Houston	369 yards vs. Cincinnati
Don Majkowski, Green Bay	355 yards vs. Tampa Bay
Bubby Brister, Pittsburgh	353 yards vs. Denver
Seventh Week	
John Elway, Denver	317 yards vs. Indianapolis
Jack Trudeau, Indianapolis	312 yards vs. Denver
Jim Everett, L.A. Rams	302 yards vs. Atlanta
Eighth Week	
Warren Moon, Houston	381 yards vs. N.Y. Jets
Ninth Week	
Joe Montana, San Francisco	411 yards vs. Green Bay
Jeff Rutledge, Washington	363 yards vs. Detroit
Warren Moon, Houston	343 yards vs. L.A. Rams
Tenth Week	
Dave Krieg, Seattle	306 yards vs. Kansas City
Eleventh Week	
Warren Moon, Houston	322 yards vs. Cleveland
Mark Rypien, Washington	311 yards vs. New Orleans
Troy Aikman, Dallas	303 yards vs. L.A. Rams
Twelfth Week	
Warren Moon, Houston	300 yards vs. Buffalo
Thirteenth Week	
Vinny Testaverde, Tampa Bay	351 yards vs. Atlanta
Jim Kelly, Buffalo	334 yards vs. Philadelphia
Steve DeBerg, Kansas City	331 yards vs. New England
Fourteenth Week	
Jim Everett, L.A. Rams	365 yards vs. New Orleans
Dan Marino, Miami	365 yards vs. Philadelphia
John Elway, Denver	328 yards vs. Kansas City
Fifteenth Week	
Warren Moon, Houston	527 yards vs. Kansas City
Wade Wilson, Minnesota	374 yards vs. Tampa Bay
Rodney Peete, Detroit	316 yards vs. Chicago
Billy Joe Tolliver, San Diego	308 yards vs. Denver
Sixteenth Week	
Timm Rosenbach, Phoenix	381 yards vs. N.Y. Giants
Seventeenth Week	
Timm Rosenbach, Phoenix	301 yards vs. Philadelphia

Times 300 or More (43)
Moon, 9; Montana, 5; Everett, 4; DeBerg, Elway, Miller, Trudeau, Rosenbach, 2.

Ten Best Receiving Performances, 1990

	Yards	No.	TD
1. Haywood Jeffries Houston vs. Kansas City, December 16	245	9	1
2. Jerry Rice San Francisco vs. Atlanta, October 14	225	13	5
3. Stephone Paige Kansas City vs. Denver, September 17	206	10	2
4. Jerry Rice San Francisco vs. Green Bay, November 4	187	6	1
5. Eddie Brown Cincinnati vs. San Diego, September 16	178	10	2
6. Rob Moore N.Y. Jets vs. New England, September 30	175	9	1
7. James Lofton Buffalo vs. Philadelphia, December 2	174	5	1
8. Andre Rison Atlanta vs. San Francisco, October 14	172	9	2
9. Jerry Rice San Francisco vs. Atlanta, September 23	171	8	1
10. Art Monk Washington vs. Detroit, November 4	168	13	0

100-Yard Receiving Performances, 1990

(Number in parentheses is receptions.)

First Week	
Willie Anderson, L.A. Rams	128 yards (5) vs. Green Bay
Mark Jackson, Denver	121 yards (7) vs. L.A. Raiders
Al Toon, N.Y. Jets	118 yards (8) vs. Cincinnati
Richard Clark, Detroit	117 yards (6) vs. Tampa Bay
Ernest Givins, Houston	109 yards (4) vs. Atlanta
Henry Ellard, L.A. Rams	106 yards (6) vs. Green Bay
Second Week	
Stephone Paige, Kansas City	206 yards (10) vs. Denver
Eddie Brown, Cincinnati	178 yards (10) vs. San Diego
John Taylor, San Francisco	160 yards (8) vs. Washington
Vance Johnson, Denver	150 yards (6) vs. Kansas City
Anthony Miller, San Diego	137 yards (9) vs. Cincinnati
Gary Clark, Washington	106 yards (7) vs. San Francisco
Hassan Jones, Minnesota	103 yards (4) vs. New Orleans
Third Week	
Jerry Rice, San Francisco	171 yards (8) vs. Atlanta
Tim McGee, Cincinnati	163 yards (6) vs. New England
Henry Ellard, L.A. Rams	145 yards (7) vs. Philadelphia
Mervyn Fernandez, L.A. Raiders	130 yards (5) vs. Pittsburgh
Andre Rison, Atlanta	128 yards (11) vs. San Francisco
Brent Jones, San Francisco	125 yards (5) vs. Atlanta
Drew Hill, Houston	123 yards (10) vs. Indianapolis
Vance Johnson, Denver	120 yards (9) vs. Seattle
Fourth Week	
Rob Moore, N.Y. Jets	175 yards (9) vs. New England
Gary Clark, Washington	162 yards (8) vs. Phoenix
Keith Byars, Philadelphia	133 yards (12) vs. Indianapolis
Albert Bentley, Indianapolis	104 yards (3) vs. Philadelphia
Bruce Hill, Tampa Bay	104 yards (5) vs. Minnesota
Willie Gault, L.A. Raiders	103 yards (4) vs. Chicago
Hassan Jones, Minnesota	101 yards (5) vs. Tampa Bay
Fifth Week	
Rodney Holman, Cincinnati	161 yards (10) vs. L.A. Rams
Andre Rison, Atlanta	154 yards (10) vs. New Orleans
Willie Anderson, L.A. Rams	144 yards (7) vs. Cincinnati
Tim McGee, Cincinnati	142 yards (8) vs. L.A. Rams
Mervyn Fernandez, L.A. Raiders	134 yards (8) vs. Buffalo
John Taylor, San Francisco	132 yards (4) vs. Houston
Sterling Sharpe, Green Bay	129 yards (5) vs. Chicago
Mark Duper, Miami	125 yards (5) vs. N.Y. Jets
Webster Slaughter, Cleveland	123 yards (7) vs. Denver
James Brooks, Cincinnati	109 yards (7) vs. L.A. Rams
Hart Lee Dykes, New England	103 yards (5) vs. Seattle
Henry Ellard, L.A. Rams	100 yards (7) vs. Cincinnati
Sixth Week	
Jerry Rice, San Francisco	225 yards (13) vs. Atlanta
Andre Rison, Atlanta	172 yards (9) vs. San Francisco
Eric Martin, New Orleans	153 yards (8) vs. Cleveland
Cris Carter, Minnesota	151 yards (6) vs. Philadelphia
Louis Lipps, Pittsburgh	141 yards (9) vs. Denver
Sterling Sharpe, Green Bay	139 yards (7) vs. Tampa Bay
Barry Sanders, Detroit	135 yards (5) vs. Kansas City
Fred Barnett, Philadelphia	114 yards (4) vs. Minnesota
Stephen Baker, N.Y. Giants	109 yards (3) vs. Washington
Ernest Givins, Houston	101 yards (6) vs. Cincinnati
Anthony Miller, San Diego	100 yards (5) vs. N.Y. Jets
Seventh Week	
Andre Rison, Atlanta	161 yards (5) vs. L.A. Rams
Jessie Hester, Indianapolis	152 yards (8) vs. Denver
Mark Jackson, Denver	127 yards (6) vs. Indianapolis
Andre Reed, Buffalo	116 yards (8) vs. N.Y. Jets
Mark Carrier, Tampa Bay	113 yards (6) vs. Dallas
Henry Ellard, L.A. Rams	109 yards (6) vs. Atlanta
Eighth Week	
Anthony Carter, Minnesota	141 yards (9) vs. Green Bay
Robert Clark, Detroit	127 yards (6) vs. New Orleans
Al Toon, N.Y. Jets	119 yards (7) vs. Houston
Jay Novacek, Dallas	105 yards (7) vs. Philadelphia
Ninth Week	
Jerry Rice, San Francisco	187 yards (6) vs. Green Bay
Art Monk, Washington	168 yards (13) vs. Detroit
Anthony Carter, Minnesota	146 yards (5) vs. Denver
Gary Clark, Washington	132 yards (8) vs. Detroit
Ricky Sanders, Washington	132 yards (11) vs. Detroit
Andre Reed, Buffalo	122 yards (7) vs. Cleveland
Irving Fryar, New England	115 yards (4) vs. Philadelphia
Tenth Week	
Jerry Rice, San Francisco	147 yards (12) vs. Dallas
Wendell Davis, Chicago	105 yards (5) vs. Atlanta
Eleventh Week	
Sterling Sharpe, Green Bay	157 yards (10) vs. Phoenix
Gary Clark, Washington	131 yards (8) vs. New Orleans
Eric Martin, New Orleans	131 yards (10) vs. Washington
Curtis Duncan, Houston	130 yards (7) vs. Cleveland
Ernie Jones, Phoenix	117 yards (7) vs. Green Bay
Emmitt Smith, Dallas	117 yards (4) vs. L.A. Rams
Webster Slaughter, Cleveland	104 yards (6) vs. Houston
Roy Green, Phoenix	102 yards (4) vs. Green Bay
Al Toon, N.Y. Jets	100 yards (7) vs. Indianapolis
Twelfth Week	
Willie Anderson, L.A. Rams	149 yards (8) vs. San Francisco
Keith Byars, Philadelphia	128 yards (8) vs. N.Y. Giants
John L. Williams, Seattle	110 yards (9) vs. San Diego
Drew Hill, Houston	102 yards (6) vs. Buffalo
Thirteenth Week	
James Lofton, Buffalo	174 yards (5) vs. Philadelphia
Stephone Paige, Kansas City	151 yards (7) vs. New England
Willie Drewrey, Tampa Bay	119 yards (2) vs. Atlanta
Fred Barnett, Philadelphia	112 yards (2) vs. Buffalo
Fourteenth Week	
Willie Anderson, L.A. Rams	123 yards (5) vs. New Orleans
Henry Ellard, L.A. Rams	107 yards (5) vs. New Orleans
Ricky Proehl, Phoenix	102 yards (6) vs. Atlanta
Willie Gault, L.A. Raiders	101 yards (3) vs. Detroit
Jerry Rice, San Francisco	101 yards (8) vs. Cincinnati
Fifteenth Week	
Haywood Jeffires, Houston	245 yards (9) vs. Kansas City
Hassan Jones, Minnesota	162 yards (7) vs. Tampa Bay
Tommy Kane, Seattle	162 yards (10) vs. Miami
Ronnie Harmon, San Diego	116 yards (8) vs. Denver
Fred Barnett, Philadelphia	108 yards (5) vs. Green Bay
Anthony Carter, Minnesota	106 yards (8) vs. Tampa Bay
Jerry Rice, San Francisco	104 yards (5) vs. L.A. Rams
Andre Rison, Atlanta	100 yards (6) vs. Cleveland

Sixteenth Week

Roy Green, Phoenix	147 yards (8) vs. N.Y. Giants
Ernie Jones, Phoenix	130 yards (4) vs. N.Y. Giants
Cris Carter, Minnesota	127 yards (8) vs. L.A. Raiders
Willie Gault, L.A. Raiders	117 yards (2) vs. Minnesota
Todd McNair, Kansas City	111 yards (3) vs. San Diego
Ed West, Green Bay	103 yards (7) vs. Detroit

Seventeenth Week

Ricky Proehl, Phoenix	132 yards (7) vs. Philadelphia
Henry Ellard, L.A. Rams	130 yards (5) vs. New Orleans
Jerry Rice, San Francisco	118 yards (9) vs. Minnesota
Webster Slaughter, Cleveland	115 yards (6) vs. Cincinnati
Eric Green, Pittsburgh	105 yards (7) vs. Houston

Times 100 or More (111)
Rice, 7; Ellard, 6; Rison, 5; W. Anderson, G. Clark, 4; Barnett, A. Carter, Gault, H. Jones, Slaughter, Toon, 3; Byars, C. Carter, R. Clark, Fernandez, R. Green, Hill, M. Jackson, V. Johnson, E. Jones, E. Martin, McGee, A. Miller, Paige, Proehl, Reed, B. Sanders, J. Taylor, 2.

Top Quarterback Sack Performances, 1990

(2.5 or More Sacks Per Game Needed to Qualify)

First Week

Ervin Randle, Tampa Bay	3.0 vs. Detroit
Greg Townsend, L.A. Raiders	3.0 vs. Denver

Second Week

Ray Childress, Houston	2.5 vs. Pittsburgh

Third Week

Jeff Cross, Miami	3.0 vs. Pittsburgh
Reggie White, Philadelphia	3.0 vs. Indianapolis

Fourth Week
None

Fifth Week

Derrick Thomas, Kansas City	3.0 vs. Indianapolis
Jimmie Jones, Dallas	2.5 vs. Tampa Bay

Sixth Week
None

Seventh Week

Ken Harvey, Phoenix	3.0 vs. N.Y. Giants

Eighth Week
None

Ninth Week

Simon Fletcher, Denver	4.0 vs. Minnesota

Tenth Week

*Derrick Thomas, Kansas City	7.0 vs. Seattle
Pat Swilling, New Orleans	4.0 vs. Tampa Bay
Scott Davis, L.A. Raiders	3.0 vs. Green Bay

Eleventh Week
None

Twelfth Week

Chris Doleman, Minnesota	2.5 vs. Chicago
Fred Stokes, Washington	2.5 vs. Dallas

Thirteenth Week

Kevin Greene, L.A. Rams	3.0 vs. Cleveland

Fourteenth Week

Bruce Smith, Buffalo	4.0 vs. Indianapolis
Lawrence Taylor, N.Y. Giants	2.5 vs. Minnesota

Fifteenth Week

Michael Dean Perry, Cleveland	2.5 vs. Atlanta

Sixteenth Week

Dennis Byrd, N.Y. Jets	3.0 vs. New England

Seventeenth Week

Ken Clarke, Minnesota	3.0 vs. San Francisco
Jacob Green, Seattle	3.0 vs. Detroit

*NFL Record

American Football Conference Offense

	Buff.	Cin.	Clev.	Den.	Hou.	Ind.	K.C.	Raid.	Mia.	N.E.	N.Y.J.	Pitt.	S.D.	Sea.
First Downs	302	277	259	323	376	245	280	258	303	239	295	263	272	284
Rushing	123	107	74	126	97	81	104	110	90	65	128	93	112	112
Passing	161	151	167	170	251	142	153	133	190	156	143	150	142	154
Penalty	18	19	18	27	28	22	23	15	23	18	24	20	18	18
Rushes	479	484	345	462	328	335	504	496	420	383	476	456	484	457
Net Yds. Gained	2080	2120	1220	1872	1417	1282	1948	2028	1535	1398	2127	1880	2257	1749
Avg. Gain	4.3	4.4	3.5	4.1	4.3	3.8	3.9	4.1	3.7	3.7	4.5	4.1	4.7	3.8
Avg. Yds. per Game	130.0	132.5	76.3	117.0	88.6	80.1	121.8	126.8	95.9	87.4	132.9	117.5	141.1	109.3
Passes Attempted	425	425	573	527	639	488	449	336	539	514	451	408	472	448
Completed	263	237	301	305	399	269	260	183	310	274	246	237	246	265
% Completed	61.9	55.8	52.5	57.9	62.4	55.1	57.9	54.5	57.5	53.3	54.5	58.1	52.1	59.2
Total Yds. Gained	3404	3152	3407	3671	5072	3297	3458	2885	3611	3208	3059	2887	2840	3194
Times Sacked	27	34	42	46	39	51	22	29	16	58	40	33	20	40
Yds. Lost	208	209	260	330	267	424	191	197	99	443	300	242	157	360
Net Yds. Gained	3196	2943	3147	3341	4805	2873	3267	2688	3512	2765	2759	2645	2683	2834
Avg. Yds. per Game	199.8	183.9	196.7	208.8	300.3	179.6	204.2	168.0	219.5	172.8	172.4	165.3	167.7	177.1
Net Yds. per Pass Play	7.07	6.41	5.12	5.83	7.09	5.33	6.94	7.36	6.33	4.83	5.62	6.00	5.45	5.81
Yds. per Comp.	12.94	13.30	11.32	12.04	12.71	12.26	13.30	15.77	11.65	11.71	12.43	12.18	11.54	12.05
Combined Net Yds. Gained	5276	5063	4367	5213	6222	4155	5215	4716	5047	4163	4886	4525	4940	4583
% Total Yds. Rushing	39.4	41.9	27.9	35.9	22.8	30.9	37.4	43.0	30.4	33.6	43.5	41.5	45.7	38.2
% Total Yds. Passing	60.6	58.1	72.1	64.1	77.2	69.1	62.6	57.0	69.6	66.4	56.5	58.5	54.3	61.8
Avg. Yds. per Game	329.8	316.4	272.9	325.8	388.9	259.7	325.9	294.8	315.4	260.2	305.4	282.8	308.8	286.4
Ball Control Plays	931	943	960	1035	1006	874	975	861	975	955	967	897	976	945
Avg. Yds. per Play	5.7	5.4	4.5	5.0	6.2	4.8	5.3	5.5	5.2	4.4	5.1	5.0	5.1	4.8
Avg. Time of Poss.	28:39	29:21	27:12	30:50	31:35	26:27	31:30	29:28	30:10	28:21	30:05	30:06	30:19	30:47
Third Down Efficiency	44.1	40.3	38.9	41.5	52.2	30.3	41.0	47.8	42.7	37.9	38.3	40.2	45.3	43.5
Had Intercepted	11	23	23	18	15	21	5	10	12	20	11	15	19	20
Yds. Opp. Returned	156	233	422	169	237	221	86	100	184	143	186	124	310	252
Ret. by Opp. for TD	0	1	3	3	2	1	0	0	0	0	0	0	1	0
Punts	58	65	78	60	34	72	81	62	72	92	61	66	62	67
Yds. Punted	2281	2739	2879	2612	1530	3084	3132	2315	3022	3752	2398	2454	2442	2722
Avg. Yds. per Punt	39.3	42.1	36.9	43.5	45.0	42.8	38.7	37.3	42.0	40.8	39.3	37.2	39.4	40.6
Punt Returns	25	30	31	33	30	36	37	34	39	29	30	39	35	36
Yds. Returned	177	255	209	256	172	402	254	295	233	134	319	398	336	337
Avg. Yds. per Return	7.1	8.5	6.7	7.8	5.7	11.2	6.9	8.7	6.0	4.6	10.6	10.2	9.6	9.4
Returned for TD	0	1	0	0	0	0	0	0	0	0	1	1	2	0
Kickoff Returns	51	62	71	66	47	65	46	64	43	77	61	50	55	50
Yds. Returned	1040	1266	1276	1260	861	1189	784	1237	780	1395	1129	956	1188	985
Avg. Yds. per Return	20.4	20.4	18.0	19.1	18.3	18.3	17.0	19.3	18.1	18.1	18.5	19.1	21.6	19.7
Returned for TD	0	0	2	0	0	0	0	0	0	0	0	0	0	0
Fumbles	17	25	37	30	34	23	30	24	33	33	28	40	24	32
Lost	10	12	23	14	21	10	14	14	15	16	13	17	13	16
Out of Bounds	0	3	1	2	0	0	2	1	1	3	2	6	1	1
Own Rec. for TD	0	0	0	0	0	0	0	0	0	0	0	0	0	0
Opp. Rec. by	17	16	9	15	12	15	25	9	8	18	11	18	11	18
Opp. Rec. for TD	1	1	1	1	1	1	1	2	2	1	1	0	2	1
Penalties	92	83	122	108	135	79	111	97	64	99	101	110	103	89
Yds. Penalized	683	627	922	775	1009	590	886	682	486	744	848	928	886	746
Total Points Scored	428	360	228	331	405	281	369	337	336	181	295	292	315	306
Total TDs	53	44	27	36	49	33	38	42	39	19	32	33	36	34
TDs Rushing	20	16	10	19	10	9	11	20	13	4	16	11	14	18
TDs Passing	28	25	13	15	37	22	23	19	21	14	14	20	18	15
TDs on Ret. and Rec.	5	3	4	2	2	2	4	3	5	1	2	2	4	1
Extra Points	50	41	24	34	46	32	37	40	37	19	32	32	34	33
Safeties	0	2	0	3	1	0	1	0	1	0	1	1	1	0
Field Goals Made	20	17	14	25	21	17	34	15	21	16	23	20	21	23
Field Goals Attempted	29	22	20	34	32	24	37	20	25	22	26	25	28	32
% Successful	69.0	77.3	70.0	73.5	65.6	70.8	91.9	75.0	84.0	72.7	88.5	80.0	75.0	71.9

American Football Conference Defense

	Buff.	Cin.	Clev.	Den.	Hou.	Ind.	K.C.	Raid.	Mia.	N.E.	N.Y.J.	Pitt.	S.D.	Sea.
First Downs	288	308	314	306	279	320	268	266	268	307	318	257	268	280
Rushing	105	116	117	110	88	130	85	95	110	151	112	102	92	86
Passing	159	180	169	181	160	176	164	152	145	139	186	130	152	171
Penalty	24	12	28	15	31	14	19	19	13	17	20	25	24	23
Rushes	483	442	511	456	392	513	373	439	461	565	423	446	424	413
Net Yds. Gained	1808	2085	2105	1963	1575	2212	1640	1716	1831	2676	2018	1615	1515	1605
Avg. Gain	3.7	4.7	4.1	4.3	4.0	4.3	4.4	3.9	4.0	4.7	4.8	3.6	3.6	3.9
Avg. Yds. per Game	113.0	130.3	131.6	122.7	98.4	138.3	102.5	107.3	114.4	167.3	126.1	100.9	94.7	100.3
Passes Attempted	455	543	444	479	460	492	512	437	462	374	516	460	462	504
Completed	254	300	253	284	267	301	267	246	257	218	311	236	254	300
% Completed	55.8	55.2	57.0	59.3	58.0	61.2	52.1	56.3	55.6	58.3	60.3	51.3	55.0	59.5
Total Yds. Gained	3125	3725	3296	3671	3332	3605	3662	3032	3064	3245	3745	2728	3255	3256
Times Sacked	43	25	32	34	38	29	60	48	45	33	38	34	45	33
Yds. Lost	326	205	211	289	272	203	421	335	348	224	308	228	345	252
Net Yds. Gained	2799	3520	3085	3382	3060	3402	3241	2697	2716	3021	3437	2500	2910	3004
Avg. Yds. per Game	174.9	220.0	192.8	211.4	191.3	212.6	202.6	168.6	169.8	188.8	214.8	156.3	181.9	187.8
Net Yds. per Pass Play	5.62	6.20	6.48	6.59	6.14	6.53	5.67	5.56	5.36	7.42	6.20	5.06	5.74	5.59
Yds. Gained per Comp.	12.30	12.42	13.03	12.93	12.48	11.98	13.72	12.33	11.92	14.89	12.04	11.56	12.81	10.85
Combined Net Yds. Gained	4607	5605	5190	5345	4635	5614	4881	4413	4547	5697	5455	4115	4425	4609
% Total Yds. Rushing	39.2	37.2	40.6	36.7	34.0	39.4	33.6	38.9	40.3	47.0	37.0	39.2	34.2	34.8
% Total Yds. Passing	60.8	62.8	59.4	63.3	66.0	60.6	66.4	61.1	59.7	53.0	63.0	60.8	65.8	65.2
Avg. Yds. per Game	287.9	350.3	324.4	334.1	289.7	350.9	305.1	275.8	284.2	356.1	340.9	257.2	276.6	288.1
Ball Control Plays	981	1010	987	969	890	1034	945	924	968	972	977	940	931	950
Avg. Yds. per Play	4.7	5.5	5.3	5.5	5.2	5.4	5.2	4.8	4.7	5.9	5.6	4.4	4.8	4.9
Avg. Time of Poss.	31:21	30:39	32:49	29:10	28:25	33:33	28:30	30:32	29:50	31:39	29:55	29:54	29:41	29:13
Third Down Efficiency	42.8	43.5	49.3	43.1	39.0	42.6	39.7	37.3	38.2	43.8	44.2	39.7	42.4	40.1
Intercepted by	18	15	13	10	21	9	20	13	19	14	18	24	19	12
Yds. Returned by	151	146	212	190	295	173	250	102	288	194	205	385	188	182
Returned for TD	2	1	1	1	1	1	1	1	2	0	0	1	0	0
Punts	66	63	68	62	62	58	72	64	75	56	56	64	70	77
Yds. Punted	2523	2634	2589	2565	2402	2435	2662	2447	3001	2282	2321	2616	2886	3225
Avg. Yds. per Punt	38.2	41.8	38.1	41.4	38.7	42.0	37.0	38.2	40.0	40.8	41.4	40.9	41.2	41.9
Punt Returns	31	36	41	22	23	42	44	24	40	50	35	16	28	29
Yds. Returned	251	352	425	159	186	334	411	153	397	503	269	105	131	254
Avg. Yds. per Return	8.1	9.8	10.4	7.2	8.1	8.0	9.3	6.4	9.9	10.1	7.7	6.6	4.7	8.8
Returned for TD	0	1	0	0	1	0	2	0	0	0	0	0	0	2
Kickoff Returns	73	43	45	69	71	49	81	49	53	38	61	56	62	51
Yds. Returned	1129	945	805	1319	1329	961	1391	1026	1092	665	1185	1245	1048	910
Avg. Yds. per Return	15.5	22.0	17.9	19.1	18.7	19.6	17.2	20.9	20.6	17.5	19.4	22.2	16.9	17.8
Returned for TD	0	0	0	0	1	0	0	0	0	0	1	1	0	0
Fumbles	33	32	24	36	22	25	38	21	23	25	29	33	26	32
Lost	17	16	9	15	12	15	25	9	8	18	11	18	11	18
Out of Bounds	0	5	2	1	1	1	1	0	0	1	5	3	1	2
Own Rec. for TD	0	0	0	0	0	0	0	0	0	0	0	0	0	0
Opp. Rec. by	10	12	23	14	21	10	14	14	15	16	13	17	13	16
Opp. Rec. for TD	0	0	1	1	3	3	0	1	1	1	0	3	0	4
Penalties	107	101	95	105	134	104	122	86	95	73	106	89	87	108
Yds. Penalized	839	824	684	819	1015	781	859	710	759	488	876	719	720	766
Total Points Scored	263	352	462	374	307	353	257	268	242	446	345	240	281	286
Total TDs	30	41	59	43	37	36	30	26	26	52	39	26	33	32
TDs Rushing	13	15	21	16	12	12	12	4	11	29	15	13	10	7
TDs Passing	17	24	32	22	18	20	16	20	14	21	23	9	22	19
TDs on Ret. and Rec.	0	2	6	5	7	4	2	2	1	2	1	4	1	6
Extra Points	29	40	56	38	34	35	29	25	26	51	35	26	33	32
Safeties	0	0	2	0	0	3	0	0	0	1	2	2	1	1
Field Goals Made	18	22	16	26	17	32	16	29	20	27	24	18	16	20
Field Goals Attempted	24	29	27	33	21	43	20	33	29	31	32	28	21	27
% Successful	75.0	75.9	59.3	78.8	81.0	74.4	80.0	87.9	69.0	87.1	75.0	64.3	76.2	74.1

National Football Conference Offense

	Atl.	Chi.	Dall.	Det.	G.B.	Rams	Minn.	N.O.	N.Y.G.	Phil.	Phx.	S.F.	T.B.	Wash.
First Downs	273	295	250	278	276	311	288	253	273	325	270	324	238	327
Rushing	84	142	88	112	72	89	106	107	120	132	115	107	83	117
Passing	168	134	135	152	183	191	164	133	135	170	135	201	142	193
Penalty	21	19	27	14	21	31	18	13	18	23	20	16	13	17
Rushes	420	551	393	366	350	422	455	464	541	540	452	454	410	515
Net Yds. Gained	1594	2436	1500	1927	1369	1612	1867	1850	2049	2556	1912	1718	1626	2083
Avg. Gain	3.8	4.4	3.8	5.3	3.9	3.8	4.1	4.0	3.8	4.7	4.2	3.8	4.0	4.0
Avg. Yds. per Game	99.6	152.3	93.8	120.4	85.6	100.8	116.7	115.6	128.1	159.8	119.5	107.4	101.6	130.2
Passes Attempted	528	430	475	460	541	561	497	447	398	479	439	583	448	536
Completed	293	229	254	242	302	310	265	226	231	281	238	360	245	301
% Completed	55.5	53.3	53.5	52.6	55.8	55.3	53.3	50.6	58.0	58.7	54.2	61.7	54.7	56.2
Total Yds. Gained	3726	2827	2898	3328	3696	4016	3445	2757	2898	3582	3118	4371	3282	3611
Times Sacked	46	43	43	44	62	30	49	20	29	50	43	37	53	22
Yds. Lost	265	283	317	278	390	198	278	131	142	438	285	194	433	132
Net Yds. Gained	3461	2544	2581	3050	3306	3818	3167	2626	2756	3144	2833	4177	2849	3479
Avg. Yds. per Game	216.3	159.0	161.3	190.6	206.6	238.6	197.9	164.1	172.3	196.5	177.1	261.1	178.1	217.4
Net Yds. per Pass Play	6.03	5.38	4.98	6.05	5.48	6.46	5.80	5.62	6.45	5.94	5.88	6.74	5.69	6.23
Yds. Gained per Comp.	12.72	12.34	11.41	13.75	12.24	12.95	13.00	12.20	12.55	12.75	13.10	12.14	13.40	12.00
Combined Net Yds. Gained	5055	4980	4081	4977	4675	5430	5034	4476	4805	5700	4745	5895	4475	5562
% Total Yds. Rushing	31.5	48.9	36.8	38.7	29.3	29.7	37.1	41.3	42.6	44.8	40.3	29.1	36.3	37.5
% Total Yds. Passing	68.5	51.1	63.2	61.3	70.7	70.3	62.9	58.7	57.4	55.2	59.7	70.9	63.7	62.5
Avg. Yds. per Game	315.9	311.3	255.1	311.1	292.2	339.4	314.6	279.8	300.3	356.3	296.6	368.4	279.7	347.6
Ball Control Plays	994	1024	911	870	953	1013	1001	931	968	1069	934	1074	911	1073
Avg. Yds. per Play	5.1	4.9	4.5	5.7	4.9	5.4	5.0	4.8	5.0	5.3	5.1	5.5	4.9	5.2
Avg. Time of Poss.	31:05	33:06	28:44	25:33	29:34	29:59	29:34	29:59	32:15	33:19	28:38	32:49	28:11	32:19
Third Down Efficiency	36.8	36.7	33.8	33.5	38.8	38.2	37.7	40.2	38.8	41.3	39.7	48.5	37.3	46.6
Had Intercepted	18	12	24	20	21	17	24	23	5	13	18	16	24	22
Yds. Opp. Returned	368	164	353	346	293	204	260	283	54	88	201	176	346	271
Ret. by Opp. for TD	2	0	4	3	2	2	1	0	1	0	1	1	2	5
Punts	70	78	79	63	65	69	79	71	75	74	67	70	72	55
Yds. Punted	2913	3073	3413	2560	2431	2663	3299	2990	3306	3026	2865	2537	2902	2064
Avg. Yds. per Punt	41.6	39.4	43.2	40.6	37.4	38.6	41.8	42.1	44.1	40.9	42.8	36.2	40.3	37.5
Punt Returns	35	36	39	35	32	35	33	45	43	40	40	48	23	48
Yds. Returned	279	399	250	361	308	346	225	400	467	315	342	356	184	388
Avg. Yds. per Return	8.0	11.1	6.4	10.3	9.6	9.9	6.8	8.9	10.9	7.9	8.6	7.4	8.0	8.1
Returned for TD	1	1	0	0	0	0	0	0	1	0	0	0	0	0
Kickoff Returns	58	54	54	70	63	63	66	58	46	54	60	53	63	62
Yds. Returned	1229	879	1102	1466	1303	1279	1249	1205	884	965	1068	965	1175	1113
Avg. Yds. per Return	21.2	16.3	20.4	20.9	20.7	20.3	18.9	20.8	19.2	17.9	17.8	18.2	18.7	18.0
Returned for TD	1	0	1	0	1	1	0	0	0	0	0	0	0	0
Fumbles	40	29	27	29	37	25	30	29	21	32	25	24	38	14
Lost	21	14	9	16	22	14	13	16	9	15	14	14	19	6
Out of Bounds	4	1	4	2	3	3	2	2	0	2	2	3	4	2
Own Rec. for TD	0	0	0	0	0	0	0	0	0	0	0	0	0	0
Opp. Rec. by	18	14	19	18	14	19	11	19	11	11	11	14	17	12
Opp. Rec. for TD	2	1	0	2	1	0	2	0	1	1	0	0	0	1
Penalties	125	75	98	88	84	87	83	108	83	120	96	104	77	102
Yds. Penalized	1004	615	729	711	669	632	565	829	655	981	883	828	651	824
Total Points Scored	348	348	244	373	271	345	351	274	335	396	268	353	264	381
Total TDs	40	39	27	46	29	43	39	30	39	48	31	40	28	41
TDs Rushing	11	22	13	19	5	17	10	14	17	10	13	12	7	16
TDs Passing	21	14	12	24	20	24	25	15	18	34	16	28	18	22
TDs on Ret. and Rec.	8	3	2	3	4	2	4	1	4	4	2	0	3	3
Extra Points	40	36	26	46	28	42	38	29	38	45	31	39	27	41
Safeties	1	0	1	0	0	0	2	1	0	0	0	1	0	2
Field Goals Made	22	26	18	17	23	15	25	21	21	21	17	24	23	30
Field Goals Attempted	33	37	25	26	30	24	28	27	28	29	27	36	27	40
% Successful	66.7	70.3	72.0	65.4	76.7	62.5	89.3	77.8	75.0	72.4	63.0	66.7	85.2	75.0

National Football Conference Defense

	Atl.	Chi.	Dall.	Det.	G.B.	Rams	Minn.	N.O.	N.Y.G.	Phil.	Phx.	S.F.	T.B.	Wash.
First Downs	300	256	280	334	286	286	257	279	245	251	306	250	313	267
Rushing	79	91	109	142	113	93	107	91	90	59	140	77	129	77
Passing	179	147	153	173	160	175	136	167	139	169	146	157	168	166
Penalty	42	18	18	19	13	18	14	21	16	23	20	16	16	24
Rushes	413	391	482	532	475	418	503	410	388	337	521	353	496	382
Net Yds. Gained	1357	1572	1976	2388	2059	1649	2074	1559	1459	1169	2318	1258	2223	1587
Avg. Gain	3.3	4.0	4.1	4.5	4.3	3.9	4.1	3.8	3.8	3.5	4.4	3.6	4.5	4.2
Avg. Yds. per Game	84.8	98.3	123.5	149.3	128.7	103.1	129.6	97.4	91.2	73.1	144.9	78.6	138.9	99.2
Passes Attempted	537	495	470	507	479	501	422	534	496	566	402	522	471	514
Completed	297	258	271	319	256	296	218	316	278	273	233	265	263	281
% Completed	55.3	52.1	57.7	62.9	53.4	59.1	51.7	59.2	56.0	48.2	58.0	50.8	55.8	54.7
Total Yds. Gained	4127	3220	2931	3625	3555	3942	2920	3584	2933	3771	3130	3278	3460	3483
Times Sacked	33	41	36	41	27	30	47	42	30	45	36	44	34	45
Yds. Lost	214	300	292	279	172	180	277	265	186	280	232	263	204	340
Net Yds. Gained	3913	2920	2639	3346	3383	3762	2643	3319	2747	3491	2898	3015	3256	3143
Avg. Yds. per Game	244.6	182.5	164.9	209.1	211.4	235.1	165.2	207.4	171.7	218.2	181.1	188.4	203.5	196.4
Net Yds. per Pass Play	6.86	5.45	5.22	6.11	6.69	7.08	5.64	5.76	5.22	5.71	6.62	5.33	6.45	5.62
Yds. Gained per Comp.	13.90	12.48	10.82	11.36	13.89	13.32	13.39	11.34	10.55	13.81	13.43	12.37	13.16	12.40
Combined Net Yds. Gained	5270	4492	4615	5734	5442	5411	4717	4878	4206	4660	5216	4273	5479	4730
% Total Yds. Rushing	25.7	35.0	42.8	41.6	37.8	30.5	44.0	32.0	34.7	25.1	44.4	29.4	40.6	33.6
% Total Yds. Passing	74.3	65.0	57.2	58.4	62.2	69.5	56.0	68.0	65.3	74.9	55.6	70.6	59.4	66.4
Avg. Yds. per Game	329.4	280.8	288.4	358.4	340.1	338.2	294.8	304.9	262.9	291.3	326.0	267.1	342.4	295.6
Ball Control Plays	983	927	988	1080	981	949	972	986	914	948	959	919	1001	941
Avg. Yds. per Play	5.4	4.8	4.7	5.3	5.5	5.7	4.9	4.9	4.6	4.9	5.4	4.6	5.5	5.0
Avg. Time of Poss.	28:55	26:54	31:16	34:27	30:26	30:01	30:26	30:01	27:45	26:41	31:22	27:11	31:49	27:41
Third Down Efficiency	34.5	34.6	40.9	47.7	40.5	42.8	34.3	39.2	36.2	31.3	45.5	35.7	45.4	38.4
Intercepted by	17	31	11	17	16	12	22	8	23	19	16	17	25	21
Yds. Returned by	237	268	126	273	154	105	358	158	116	271	274	171	487	271
Returned for TD	3	1	1	1	1	1	2	1	2	3	2	0	3	2
Punts	74	74	70	62	69	66	77	74	76	86	63	82	55	76
Yds. Punted	2974	2804	2866	2530	2698	2733	3030	3024	3140	3470	2747	3280	2230	3290
Avg. Yds. per Punt	40.2	37.9	40.9	40.8	39.1	41.4	39.4	40.9	41.3	40.3	43.6	40.0	40.5	43.3
Punt Returns	39	39	43	29	34	46	44	43	41	37	41	30	39	30
Yds. Returned	314	322	438	233	266	420	513	302	291	338	258	215	352	205
Avg. Yds. per Return	8.1	8.3	10.2	8.0	7.8	9.1	11.7	7.0	7.1	9.1	6.3	7.2	9.0	6.8
Returned for TD	0	0	1	0	0	0	0	0	0	1	0	0	0	0
Kickoff Returns	49	73	55	70	56	68	62	36	65	74	56	66	43	58
Yds. Returned	814	1494	1136	1229	1125	1406	1350	583	1245	1408	1060	1284	1036	1008
Avg. Yds. per Return	16.6	20.5	20.7	17.6	20.1	20.7	21.8	16.2	19.2	19.0	18.9	19.5	24.1	17.4
Returned for TD	0	0	1	1	0	0	0	0	1	0	0	0	0	0
Fumbles	26	38	32	31	26	32	25	35	28	32	28	21	33	24
Lost	18	14	19	18	14	19	11	19	11	11	11	14	17	12
Out of Bounds	1	2	4	3	1	2	3	2	6	2	2	0	2	4
Own Rec. for TD	0	0	0	0	0	0	0	0	0	0	0	0	0	0
Opp. Rec. by	21	14	9	16	22	14	13	16	9	15	14	14	19	6
Opp. Rec. for TD	0	2	0	2	2	0	0	1	0	0	0	0	1	1
Penalties	95	84	104	97	109	109	100	87	83	94	96	85	78	90
Yds. Penalized	811	676	911	788	854	968	787	655	569	706	834	641	617	712
Total Points Scored	365	280	308	413	347	412	326	275	211	299	396	239	367	301
Total TDs	44	31	36	49	40	49	34	30	23	33	50	26	45	35
TDs Rushing	11	10	18	22	16	17	12	8	9	9	20	7	20	8
TDs Passing	31	19	12	21	20	30	20	21	12	23	29	17	22	21
TDs on Ret. and Rec.	2	2	6	6	4	2	2	1	2	1	1	2	3	6
Extra Points	42	28	36	48	39	46	32	30	23	32	48	26	43	35
Safeties	1	0	1	1	1	0	0	1	1	0	0	0	0	1
Field Goals Made	19	22	18	23	22	24	30	21	16	23	16	19	18	18
Field Goals Attempted	28	28	26	30	34	31	36	35	22	32	20	23	27	23
% Successful	67.9	78.6	69.2	76.7	64.7	77.4	83.3	60.0	72.7	71.9	80.0	82.6	66.7	78.3

AFC, NFC, and NFL Summary

	AFC Offense Total	AFC Offense Average	AFC Defense Total	AFC Defense Average	NFC Offense Total	NFC Offense Average	NFC Defense Total	NFC Defense Average	NFL Total	NFL Average
First Downs	3976	284.0	4047	289.1	3981	284.4	3910	279.3	7957	284.2
Rushing	1422	101.6	1499	107.1	1474	105.3	1397	99.8	2896	103.4
Passing	2263	161.6	2264	161.7	2236	159.7	2235	159.6	4499	160.7
Penalty	291	20.8	284	20.3	271	19.4	278	19.9	562	20.1
Rushes	6109	436.4	6341	452.9	6333	452.4	6101	435.8	12442	444.4
Net Yds. Gained	24913	1779.5	26364	1883.1	26099	1864.2	24648	1760.6	51012	1821.9
Avg. Gain	—	4.1	—	4.2	—	4.1	—	4.0	—	4.1
Avg. Yds. per Game	—	111.2	—	117.7	—	116.5	—	110.0	—	113.9
Passes Attempted	6694	478.1	6600	471.4	6822	487.3	6916	494.0	13516	482.7
Completed	3795	271.1	3748	267.7	3777	269.8	3824	273.1	7572	270.4
% Completed	—	56.7	—	56.8	—	55.4	—	55.3	—	56.0
Total Yds. Gained	47145	3367.5	46741	3338.6	47555	3396.8	47959	3425.6	94700	3382.1
Times Sacked	497	35.5	537	38.4	571	40.8	531	37.9	1068	38.1
Yds. Lost	3687	263.4	3967	283.4	3764	268.9	3484	248.9	7451	266.1
Net Yds. Gained	43458	3104.1	42774	3055.3	43791	3127.9	44475	3176.8	87249	3116.0
Avg. Yds. per Game	—	194.0	—	191.0	—	195.5	—	198.6	—	194.8
Net Yds. per Pass Play	—	6.04	—	5.99	—	5.92	—	5.97	—	5.98
Yds. Gained per Comp.	—	12.42	—	12.47	—	12.59	—	12.54	—	12.51
Combined Net Yds. Gained	68371	4883.6	69138	4938.4	69890	4992.1	69123	4937.4	138261	4937.9
% Total Yds. Rushing	—	36.4	—	38.1	—	37.3	—	35.7	—	36.9
% Total Yds. Passing	—	63.6	—	61.9	—	62.7	—	64.3	—	63.1
Avg. Yds. per Game	—	305.2	—	308.7	—	312.0	—	308.6	—	308.6
Ball Control Plays	13300	950.0	13478	962.7	13726	980.4	13548	967.7	27026	965.2
Avg. Yds. per Play	—	5.1	—	5.1	—	5.1	—	5.1	—	5.1
Third Down Efficiency	—	41.7	—	41.9	—	39.3	—	39.1	—	40.5
Interceptions	223	15.9	225	16.1	257	18.4	255	18.2	480	17.1
Yds. Returned	2823	201.6	2961	211.5	3407	243.4	3269	233.5	6230	222.5
Returned for TD	11	0.8	12	0.9	24	1.7	23	1.6	35	1.3
Punts	930	66.4	913	65.2	987	70.5	1004	71.7	1917	68.5
Yds. Punted	37362	2668.7	36588	2613.4	40042	2860.1	40816	2915.4	77404	2764.4
Avg. Yds. per Punt	—	40.2	—	40.1	—	40.6	—	40.7	—	40.4
Punt returns	464	33.1	461	32.9	532	38.0	535	38.2	996	35.6
Yds. Returned	3777	269.8	3930	280.7	4620	330.0	4467	319.1	8397	299.9
Avg. Yds. per Return	—	8.1	—	8.5	—	8.7	—	8.4	—	8.4
Returned for TD	5	0.4	6	0.4	3	0.2	2	0.1	8	0.3
Kickoff Returns	808	57.7	801	57.2	824	58.9	831	59.4	1632	58.3
Yds. Returned	15346	1096.1	15050	1075.0	15882	1134.4	16178	1155.6	31228	1115.3
Avg. Yds. per Return	—	19.0	—	18.8	—	19.3	—	19.5	—	19.1
Returned for TD	2	0.1	3	0.2	4	0.3	3	0.2	6	0.2
Fumbles	410	29.3	399	28.5	400	28.6	411	29.4	810	28.9
Lost	208	14.9	202	14.4	202	14.4	208	14.9	410	14.6
Out of Bounds	23	1.6	23	1.6	34	2.4	34	2.4	57	2.0
Own Rec. for TD	0	0.0	0	0.0	0	0.0	0	0.0	0	0.0
Opp. Rec.	202	14.4	208	14.9	208	14.9	202	14.4	410	14.6
Opp. Rec. for TD	16	1.1	18	1.3	11	0.8	9	0.6	27	1.0
Penalties	1393	99.5	1412	100.9	1330	95.0	1311	93.6	2723	97.3
Yds. Penalized	10812	772.3	10859	775.6	10576	755.4	10529	752.1	21388	763.9
Total Points Scored	4464	318.9	4476	319.7	4551	325.1	4539	324.2	9015	322.0
Total TDs	515	36.8	510	36.4	520	37.1	525	37.5	1035	37.0
TDs Rushing	191	13.6	190	13.6	186	13.3	187	13.4	377	13.5
TDs Passing	284	20.3	277	19.8	291	20.8	298	21.3	575	20.5
TDs on Ret. and Rec.	40	2.9	43	3.1	43	3.1	40	2.9	83	3.0
Extra Points	491	35.1	489	34.9	506	36.1	508	36.3	997	35.6
Safeties	11	0.8	12	0.9	8	0.6	7	0.5	19	0.7
Field Goals Made	287	20.5	301	21.5	303	21.6	289	20.6	590	21.1
Field Goals Attempted	376	26.9	398	28.4	417	29.8	395	28.2	793	28.3
% Successful	—	76.3	—	75.6	—	72.7	—	73.2	—	74.4

Club Leaders

	Offense	Defense
First Downs	Hou. 376	N.Y.G. 245
Rushing	Chi. 142	Phil. 59
Passing	Hou. 251	Pitt. 130
Penalty	Rams 31	Cin. 12
Rushes	Chi. 551	Phil. 337
Net Yds. Gained	Phil. 2556	Phil. 1169
Avg. Gain	Det. 5.3	Atl. 3.3
Passes Attempted	Hou. 639	N.E. 374
Completed	Hou. 399	Minn. & N.E. 218
% Completed	Hou. 62.4	Phil. 48.2
Total Yds. Gained	Hou. 5072	Pitt. 2728
Times Sacked	Mia. 16	K.C. 60
Yds. Lost	Mia. 99	K.C. 421
Net Yds. Gained	Hou. 4805	Pitt. 2500
Net Yds. per Pass Play	Raiders 7.36	Pitt. 5.06
Yds. Gained per Comp.	Raiders 15.77	N.Y.G. 10.55
Combined Net Yds. Gained	Hou. 6222	Pitt. 4115
% Total Yds. Rushing	Chi. 48.9	Phil. 25.1
% Total Yds. Passing	Hou. 77.2	N.E. 53.0
Ball Control Plays	S.F. 1074	Hou. 890
Avg. Yds. per Play	Hou. 6.18	Pitt. 4.38
Avg. Time of Poss.	Phil. 33:19	—
Third Down Efficiency	Hou. 52.2	Phil. 31.3
Interceptions	—	Chi. 31
Yds. Returned	—	T.B. 487
Returned for TD	—	Atl., Phil & T.B. 3
Punts	N.E. 92	—
Yds. Punted	N.E. 3752	—
Avg. Yds. per Punt	Hou. 45.0	—
Punt Returns	S.F. & Wash. 48	Pitt. 16
Yds. Returned	N.Y.G. 467	Pitt. 105
Avg. Yds. per Return	Ind. 11.2	S.D. 4.7
Returned for TD	S.D. 2	—
Kickoff Returns	N.E. 77	N.O. 36
Yds. Returned	Det. 1466	N.O. 583
Avg. Yds. per Return	S.D. 21.6	Buff. 15.5
Returned for TD	Clev. 2	—
Total Points Scored	Buff. 428	N.Y.G. 211
Total TDs	Buff. 53	N.Y.G. 23
TDs Rushing	Chi. 22	Raiders 4
TDs Passing	Hou. 37	Pitt. 9
TDs on Ret. and Rec.	Atl. 8	Buff. 0
Extra Points	Buff. 50	N.Y.G. 23
Safeties	Den. 3	—
Field Goals Made	K.C. 34	Five with 16
Field Goals Attempted	Wash. 40	K.C. & Phx. 20
% Successful	K.C. 91.9	Clev. 59.3

National Football League Club Rankings By Yards

	Offense			Defense		
Team	Total	Rush	Pass	Total	Rush	Pass
Atlanta	10	21	6	19	3	28
Buffalo	6	7	10	8	15	7
Chicago	13	2	28	6	7	10
Cincinnati	9	5	15	25	22	26
Cleveland	25	28	12	17	23	15
Dallas	28	23	27	10	18	2
Denver	8	14	7	20	17	21
Detroit	14	11	14	28	27	20
Green Bay	20	26	8	22	20	22
Houston	*1	24	*1	11	8	14
Indianapolis	27	27	16	26	24	23
Kansas City	7	10	9	16	12	17
L.A. Raiders	19	9	23	4	14	4
L.A. Rams	5	20	3	21	13	27
Miami	11	22	4	7	16	5
Minnesota	12	15	11	13	21	3
New England	26	25	20	27	28	13
New Orleans	23	16	26	15	6	19
N.Y. Giants	17	8	22	2	4	6
N.Y. Jets	16	4	21	23	19	24
Philadelphia	3	*1	13	12	*1	25
Phoenix	18	12	19	18	26	8
Pittsburgh	22	13	25	*1	11	*1
San Diego	15	3	24	5	5	9
San Francisco	2	18	2	3	2	12
Seattle	21	17	18	9	10	11
Tampa Bay	24	19	17	24	25	18
Washington	4	6	5	14	9	16

* = League leader

AFC Takeaways/Giveaways

	Takeaways			Giveaways			
	Int.	Fum.	Total	Int.	Fum.	Total	Net Diff.
Kansas City	20	25	45	5	14	19	26
Buffalo	18	17	35	11	10	21	14
Pittsburgh	24	18	42	15	17	32	10
N.Y. Jets	18	11	29	11	13	24	5
Miami	19	8	27	12	15	27	0
L.A. Raiders	13	9	22	10	14	24	-2
San Diego	19	11	30	19	13	32	-2
Houston	21	12	33	15	21	36	-3
Cincinnati	15	16	31	23	12	35	-4
New England	14	18	32	20	16	36	-4
Seattle	12	18	30	20	16	36	-6
Denver	10	15	25	18	14	32	-7
Indianapolis	9	15	24	21	10	31	-7
Cleveland	13	9	22	23	23	46	-24

NFC Takeaways/Giveaways

	Takeaways			Giveaways			
	Int.	Fum.	Total	Int.	Fum.	Total	Net Diff.
N.Y. Giants	23	11	34	5	9	14	20
Chicago	31	14	45	12	14	26	19
Washington	21	12	33	22	6	28	5
Philadelphia	19	11	30	13	15	28	2
San Francisco	17	14	31	16	14	30	1
L.A. Rams	12	19	31	17	14	31	0
Detroit	17	18	35	20	16	36	-1
Tampa Bay	25	17	42	24	19	43	-1
Dallas	11	19	30	24	9	33	-3
Atlanta	17	18	35	18	21	39	-4
Minnesota	22	11	33	24	13	37	-4
Phoenix	16	11	27	18	14	32	-5
New Orleans	8	19	27	23	16	39	-12
Green Bay	16	14	30	21	22	43	-13

Scoring

Points
AFC: 139—Nick Lowery, Kansas City
NFC: 131—Chip Lohmiller, Washington

Touchdowns
NFC: 16—Barry Sanders, Detroit
AFC: 15—Derrick Fenner, Seattle

Extra Points
AFC: 50—Scott Norwood, Buffalo
NFC: 45—Roger Ruzek, Philadelphia

Field Goals
AFC: 34—Nick Lowery, Kansas City
NFC: 30—Chip Lohmiller, Washington

Field Goal Attempts
NFC: 40—Chip Lohmiller, Washington
AFC: 37—Nick Lowery, Kansas City

Longest Field Goal
NFC: 56—Mike Cofer, San Francisco at Atlanta, October 14
Chip Lohmiller, Washington at Indianapolis, December 22
AFC: 55—Dean Biasucci, Indianapolis at Miami, December 30

Most Points, Game
NFC: 30—Jerry Rice, San Francisco at Atlanta, October 14 (5 TD)
AFC: 24—Lorenzo White, Houston vs. Cleveland, December 9 (4 TD)

Team Leaders, Points
AFC: BUFFALO: 110, Scott Norwood; CINCINNATI: 92, Jim Breech; CLEVELAND: 66, Jerry Kauric; DENVER: 109, David Treadwell; HOUSTON: 72, Lorenzo White; INDIANAPOLIS: 83, Dean Biasucci; KANSAS CITY: 139, Nick Lowery; L.A. RAIDERS: 85, Jeff Jaeger; MIAMI: 100, Pete Stoyanovich; NEW ENGLAND: 67, Jason Staurovsky; N.Y. JETS: 101, Pat Leahy; PITTSBURGH: 92, Gary Anderson; SAN DIEGO: 84, John Carney; SEATTLE: 102, Norm Johnson.
NFC: ATLANTA: 106, Greg Davis; CHICAGO: 114, Kevin Butler; DALLAS: 80, Ken Willis; DETROIT: 96, Barry Sanders; GREEN BAY: 97, Chris Jacke ; L.A. RAMS: 90, Cleveland Gary; MINNESOTA: 61, Donald Igwebuike; N.Y. GIANTS: 80, Matt Bahr; PHILADELPHIA: 108, Roger Ruzek; PHOENIX: 82, Al Del Greco; SAN FRANCISCO: 111, Mike Cofer; TAMPA BAY: 96, Steve Christie; WASHINGTON: 131, Chip Lohmiller.

Team Champion
AFC: 428—Buffalo
NFC: 396—Philadelphia

AFC Scoring—Team

	TD	TDR	TDP	TD Misc.	PAT	PAT Att.	FG	FG Att.	SAF	TP
Buffalo	53	20	28	5	50	53	20	29	0	428
Houston	49	10	37	2	46	49	21	32	1	405
Kansas City	38	11	23	4	37	38	34	37	1	369
Cincinnati	44	16	25	3	41	44	17	22	2	360
L.A. Raiders	42	20	19	3	40	42	15	20	0	337
Miami	39	13	21	5	37	39	21	25	1	336
Denver	36	19	15	2	34	36	25	34	3	331
San Diego	36	14	18	4	34	36	21	28	1	315
Seattle	34	18	15	1	33	34	23	32	0	306
N.Y. Jets	32	16	14	2	32	32	23	26	1	295
Pittsburgh	33	11	20	2	32	33	20	25	1	292
Indianapolis	33	9	22	2	32	33	17	24	0	281
Cleveland	27	10	13	4	24	27	14	20	0	228
New England	19	4	14	1	19	19	16	22	0	181
AFC Total	515	191	284	40	491	515	287	376	11	4464
AFC Average	36.8	13.6	20.3	2.9	35.1	36.8	20.5	26.9	0.8	318.9

NFC Scoring—Team

	TD	TDR	TDP	TD Misc.	PAT	PAT Att.	FG	FG Att.	SAF	TP
Philadelphia	48	10	34	4	45	48	21	29	0	396
Washington	41	16	22	3	41	41	30	40	2	381
Detroit	46	19	24	3	46	46	17	26	0	373
San Francisco	40	12	28	0	39	40	24	36	1	353
Minnesota	39	10	25	4	38	39	25	28	2	351
Atlanta	40	11	21	8	40	40	22	33	1	348
Chicago	39	22	14	3	36	38	26	37	0	348
L.A. Rams	43	17	24	2	42	43	15	24	0	345
N.Y. Giants	39	17	18	4	38	39	21	28	0	335
New Orleans	30	14	15	1	29	30	21	27	1	274
Green Bay	29	5	20	4	28	29	23	30	0	271
Phoenix	31	13	16	2	31	31	17	27	0	268
Tampa Bay	28	7	18	3	27	28	23	27	0	264
Dallas	27	13	12	2	26	27	18	25	1	244
NFC Total	520	186	291	43	506	519	303	417	8	4551
NFC Average	37.1	13.3	20.8	3.1	36.1	37.1	21.6	29.8	0.6	325.1
League Total	1035	377	575	83	997	1034	590	793	19	9015
League Average	37.0	13.5	20.5	3.0	35.6	36.9	21.1	28.3	0.7	322.0

NFL Top 10 Scorers—Touchdowns

	TD	TDR	TDP	TD Misc.	TP
Sanders, Barry, Det.	16	13	3	0	96
Fenner, Derrick, Sea.	15	14	1	0	90
Gary, Cleveland, L.A. Rams	15	14	1	0	90
Allen, Marcus, L.A.Raiders	13	12	1	0	78
Anderson, Neal, Chi.	13	10	3	0	78
Rice, Jerry, S.F.	13	0	13	0	78
Thomas, Thurman, Buff.	13	11	2	0	78
White, Lorenzo, Hou.	12	8	4	0	72
Anderson, Ottis, N.Y. Giants	11	11	0	0	66
Smith, Emmitt, Dall.	11	11	0	0	66

NFL Top 10 Scorers—Kicking

	PAT	PAT Att.	FG	FG Att.	TP
Lowery, Nick, K.C.	37	38	34	37	139
Lohmiller, Chip, Wash.	41	41	30	40	131
Butler, Kevin, Chi.	36	37	26	37	114
Cofer, Mike, S.F.	39	39	24	36	111
Norwood, Scott, Buff.	50	52	20	29	110
Treadwell, David, Den.	34	36	25	34	109
Ruzek, Roger, Phil.	45	48	21	29	108
Davis, Greg, Atl.	40	40	22	33	106
Johnson, Norm, Sea.	33	34	23	32	102
Leahy, Pat, N.Y. Jets	32	32	23	26	101

AFC Scoring—Individual

Kickers	PAT	PAT Att.	FG	FG Att.	TP
Lowery, Nick, K.C.	37	38	34	37	139
Norwood, Scott, Buff.	50	52	20	29	110
Treadwell, David, Den.	34	36	25	34	109
Johnson, Norm, Sea.	33	34	23	32	102
Leahy, Pat, N.Y. Jets	32	32	23	26	101
Stoyanovich, Pete, Mia.	37	37	21	25	100
Anderson, Gary, Pitt.	32	32	20	25	92
Breech, Jim, Cin.	41	44	17	21	92
Jaeger, Jeff, L.A. Raiders	40	42	15	20	85
Carney, John, S.D.	27	28	19	21	84
Biasucci, Dean, Ind.	32	33	17	24	83
Garcia, Teddy, Hou.	26	28	14	20	68
Staurovsky, Jason, N.E.	19	19	16	22	67
Kauric, Jerry, Clev.	24	27	14	20	66
Zendejas, Tony, Hou.	20	21	7	12	41

Non-Kickers	TD	TDR	TDP	TD Misc.	TP
Fenner, Derrick, Sea.	15	14	1	0	90
Allen, Marcus, L.A. Raiders	13	12	1	0	78
Thomas, Thurman, Buff.	13	11	2	0	78
White, Lorenzo, Hou.	12	8	4	0	72
Hoge, Merril, Pitt.	10	7	3	0	60
Brooks, James, Cin.	9	5	4	0	54
Brown, Eddie, Cin.	9	0	9	0	54
Givins, Ernest, Hou.	9	0	9	0	54
Smith, Sammie, Mia.	9	8	1	0	54
Butts, Marion, S.D.	8	8	0	0	48
Jeffires, Haywood, Hou.	8	0	8	0	48
Reed, Andre, Buff.	8	0	8	0	48
Green, Eric, Pitt.	7	0	7	0	42
Humphrey, Bobby, Den.	7	7	0	0	42
Mack, Kevin, Clev.	7	5	2	0	42
Miller, Anthony, S.D.	7	0	7	0	42
Okoye, Christian, K.C.	7	7	0	0	42
Baxter, Brad, N.Y. Jets	6	6	0	0	36
Bentley, Albert, Ind.	6	4	2	0	36
Hester, Jessie, Ind.	6	0	6	0	36
Jones, Tony, Hou.	6	0	6	0	36
McNeil, Freeman, N.Y. Jets	6	6	0	0	36
Moore, Rob, N.Y. Jets	6	0	6	0	36
Paige, Tony, Mia.	6	2	4	0	36
Toon, Al, N.Y. Jets	6	0	6	0	36
Woods, Ickey, Cin.	6	6	0	0	36
Brooks, Bill, Ind.	5	0	5	0	30
Cook, Marv, N.E.	5	0	5	0	30
Davis, Kenneth, Buff.	5	4	1	0	30
Duper, Mark, Mia.	5	0	5	0	30
Fernandez, Mervyn, Raiders	5	0	5	0	30
Hill, Drew, Hou.	5	0	5	0	30
Holman, Rodney, Cin.	5	0	5	0	30
Jackson, Bo, L.A. Raiders	5	5	0	0	30
Jackson, Mark, Den.	5	1	4	0	30
Jones, Bill, K.C.	5	0	5	0	30
McKeller, Keith, Buff.	5	0	5	0	30
Morgan, Stanley, Ind.	5	0	5	0	30

	TD	TDR	TDP	TD Misc.	TP
Paige, Stephone, K.C.	5	0	5	0	30
Smith, Steve, L.A. Raiders	5	2	3	0	30
Bernstine, Rod, S.D.	4	4	0	0	24
Bratton, Mel, Den.	4	3	1	0	24
Chadwick, Jeff, Sea.	4	0	4	0	24
Dickerson, Eric, Ind.	4	4	0	0	24
Fryar, Irving, N.E.	4	0	4	0	24
Kane, Tommy, Sea.	4	0	4	0	24
Lofton, James, Buff.	4	0	4	0	24
Metcalf, Eric, Clev.	4	1	1	2	24
Slaughter, Webster, Clev.	4	0	4	0	24
Thomas, Robb, K.C.	4	0	4	0	24
Williams, Warren, Pitt.	4	3	1	0	24
Word, Barry, K.C.	4	4	0	0	24
Young, Mike, Den.	4	0	4	0	24
Birden, J.J., K.C.	3	0	3	0	18
Blades, Brian, Sea.	3	0	3	0	18
Brown, Tim, L.A. Raiders	3	0	3	0	18
Clayton, Mark, Mia.	3	0	3	0	18
Elway, John, Den.	3	3	0	0	18
Gault, Willie, L.A. Raiders	3	0	3	0	18
Harris, Leonard, Hou.	3	0	3	0	18
Hoard, Leroy, Clev.	3	3	0	0	18
Horton, Ethan, L.A. Raiders	3	0	3	0	18
Johnson, Vance, Den.	3	0	3	0	18
Lewis, Nate, S.D.	3	1	1	1	18
Lipps, Louis, Pitt.	3	0	3	0	18
McEwen, Craig, S.D.	3	0	3	0	18
Mueller, Jamie, Buff.	3	2	1	0	18
Mularkey, Mike, Pitt.	3	0	3	0	18
Pruitt, James, Mia.	3	0	3	0	18
Rolle, Butch, Buff.	3	0	3	0	18
Sewell, Steve, Den.	3	3	0	0	18
Stephens, John, N.E.	3	2	1	0	18
Taylor, Craig, Cin.	3	2	1	0	18
Williams, John L., Sea.	3	3	0	0	18
Ball, Eric, Cin.	2	1	1	0	12
Brennan, Brian, Clev.	2	0	2	0	12
Dykes, Hart Lee, N.E.	2	0	2	0	12
Green, Harold, Cin.	2	1	1	0	12
Harmon, Ronnie, S.D.	2	0	2	0	12
Harry, Emile, K.C.	2	0	2	0	12
Hector, Johnny, N.Y. Jets	2	2	0	0	12
Johnson, Anthony, Ind.	2	0	2	0	12
Kattus, Eric, Cin.	2	0	2	0	12
Langhorne, Reggie, Clev.	2	0	2	0	12
Logan, Marc, Mia.	2	2	0	0	12
Martin, Tony, Mia.	2	0	2	0	12
McNair, Todd, K.C.	2	0	2	0	12
Miller, Les, S.D.	2	0	0	2	12
Moon, Warren, Hou.	2	2	0	0	12
Nattiel, Ricky, Den.	2	0	2	0	12
Newsome, Ozzie, Clev.	2	0	2	0	12
Plummer, Gary, S.D.	2	1	1	0	12
Skansi, Paul, Sea.	2	0	2	0	12
Smith, Don, Buff.	2	2	0	0	12
Tasker, Steve, Buff.	2	0	2	0	12
Thomas, Blair, N.Y. Jets	2	1	1	0	12
Winder, Sammy, Den.	2	2	0	0	12
Francis, James, Cin.	1	0	0	1	*8
Mecklenburg, Karl, Den.	1	0	0	1	*8
Adams, George, N.E.	1	0	1	0	6
Allen, Marvin, N.E.	1	1	0	0	6
Barber, Mike, Cin.	1	0	1	0	6
Beach, Pat, Ind.	1	0	1	0	6
Beebe, Don, Buff.	1	0	1	0	6
Bell, Greg, L.A. Raiders	1	1	0	0	6
Bell, Richard, Pitt.	1	0	1	0	6
Bennett, Cornelius, Buff.	1	0	0	1	6
Blaylock, Anthony, Clev.	1	0	0	1	6
Boyer, Mark, N.Y. Jets	1	0	1	0	6
Bussey, Barney, Cin.	1	0	0	1	6
Calloway, Chris, Pitt.	1	0	1	0	6
Caravello, Joe, S.D.	1	0	1	0	6
Cox, Arthur, S.D.	1	0	1	0	6
Davis, Darrell, N.Y. Jets	1	0	0	1	6
Duncan, Curtis, Hou.	1	0	1	0	6
Early, Quinn, S.D.	1	0	1	0	6
Edmunds, Ferrell, Mia.	1	0	1	0	6
Ford, Bernard, Hou.	1	0	1	0	6
Foster, Barry, Pitt.	1	1	0	0	6
Gainer, Derrick, Clev.	1	1	0	0	6
George, Jeff, Ind.	1	1	0	0	6
Glenn, Kerry, Mia.	1	0	0	1	6
Goode, Chris, Ind.	1	0	0	1	6
Graddy, Sam, L.A. Raiders	1	0	1	0	6
Grant, Alan, Ind.	1	0	0	1	6
Hayes, Jonathan, K.C.	1	0	1	0	6
Heller, Ron, Sea.	1	0	1	0	6
Henderson, Wymon, Den.	1	0	0	1	6
Higgs, Mark, Mia.	1	0	0	1	6
Jennings, Stanford, Cin.	1	1	0	0	6
Jensen, Jim, Mia.	1	0	1	0	6
Johnson, David, Pitt.	1	0	0	1	6
Johnson, Mike, Clev.	1	0	0	1	6
Johnson, Richard, Hou.	1	0	0	1	6
Kinard, Terry, Hou.	1	0	0	1	6
Kinnebrew, Larry, Buff.	1	1	0	0	6
Martin, Chris, K.C.	1	0	0	1	6
Martin, Sammy, N.E.	1	0	1	0	6
Mathis, Terance, N.Y. Jets	1	0	0	1	6
McDaniel, Terry, L.A. Raiders	1	0	0	1	6
McGee, Tim, Cin.	1	0	1	0	6
Metzelaars, Pete, Buff.	1	0	1	0	6
Odom, Cliff, Mia.	1	0	0	1	6
Odomes, Nate, Buff.	1	0	0	1	6
Perryman, Bob, N.E.	1	1	0	0	6
Petry, Stan, K.C.	1	0	0	1	6
Price, Mitchell, Cin.	1	0	0	1	6
Robinson, Eugene, Sea.	1	0	0	1	6
Robinson, Jerry, L.A. Raiders	1	0	0	1	6
Ross, Kevin, K.C.	1	0	0	1	6
Saleaumua, Dan, K.C.	1	0	0	1	6
Schwedes, Scott, Mia.	1	0	1	0	6
Sharpe, Shannon, Den.	1	0	1	0	6
Smith, Leonard, Buff.	1	0	0	1	6
Sochia, Brian, Mia.	1	0	0	1	6
Stone, Dwight, Pitt.	1	0	1	0	6
Stradford, Troy, Mia.	1	1	0	0	6
Talley, Darryl, Buff.	1	0	0	1	6
Taylor, Kitrick, S.D.	1	0	0	1	6
Taylor, Troy, N.Y. Jets	1	1	0	0	6
Townsend, Greg, L.A. Raiders	1	0	0	1	6
Verdin, Clarence, Ind.	1	0	1	0	6
Walker, Derrick, S.D.	1	0	1	0	6
Warren, Chris, Sea.	1	1	0	0	6
Whitaker, Danta, K.C.	1	0	1	0	6
Williams, Brent, N.E.	1	0	0	1	6
Williams, James, Buff.	1	0	0	1	6
Williams, Jarvis, Mia.	1	0	0	1	6
Woodson, Rod, Pitt.	1	0	0	1	6
Byrd, Dennis, N.Y. Jets	0	0	0	0	*2
Childress, Ray, Hou.	0	0	0	0	*2
Fletcher, Simon, Den.	0	0	0	0	*2
Fulcher, David, Cin.	0	0	0	0	*2
Grossman, Burt, S.D.	0	0	0	0	*2
Maas, Bill, K.C.	0	0	0	0	*2
Stowe, Tyronne, Pitt.	0	0	0	0	*2

** Indicates safety scored.*

NFC Scoring—Individual

Kickers	PAT	PAT Att.	FG	FG Att.	TP
Lohmiller, Chip, Wash.	41	41	30	40	131
Butler, Kevin, Chi.	36	37	26	37	114
Cofer, Mike, S.F.	39	39	24	36	111
Ruzek, Roger, Phil.	45	48	21	29	108
Davis, Greg, Atl.	40	40	22	33	106
Jacke, Chris, G.B.	28	29	23	30	97
Christie, Steve, T.B.	27	27	23	27	96
Andersen, Morten, N.O.	29	29	21	27	92
Lansford, Mike, L.A. Rams	42	43	15	24	87
Del Greco, Al, Phx.	31	31	17	27	82
Bahr, Matt, N.Y. Giants	29	30	17	23	80
Willis, Ken, Dall.	26	26	18	25	80
Murray, Eddie, Det.	34	34	13	19	73
Reveiz, Fuad, S.D.-Minn.	26	27	13	19	65
Igwebuike, Donald, Minn.	19	19	14	16	61
Karlis, Rich, Det.	12	12	4	7	24
Allegre, Raul, N.Y. Giants	9	9	4	5	21

Non-Kickers	TD	TDR	TDP	TD Misc.	TP
Sanders, Barry, Det.	16	13	3	0	96
Gary, Cleveland, L.A. Rams	15	14	1	0	90
Anderson, Neal, Chi.	13	10	3	0	78
Rice, Jerry, S.F.	13	0	13	0	78
Anderson, Ottis, N.Y. Giants	11	11	0	0	66
Smith, Emmitt, Dall.	11	11	0	0	66
Rison, Andre, Atl.	10	0	10	0	60
Walker, Herschel, Minn.	9	5	4	0	54
Williams, Calvin, Phil.	9	0	9	0	54
Barnett, Fred, Phil.	8	0	8	0	48
Carter, Anthony, Minn.	8	0	8	0	48
Clark, Gary, Wash.	8	0	8	0	48

	TD	TDR	TDP	TD Misc.	TP
Clark, Robert, Det.	8	0	8	0	48
Byner, Earnest, Wash.	7	6	1	0	42
Jones, Hassan, Minn.	7	0	7	0	42
Mayes, Rueben, N.O.	7	7	0	0	42
Rathman, Tom, S.F.	7	7	0	0	42
Taylor, John, S.F.	7	0	7	0	42
Jackson, Keith, Phil.	6	0	6	0	36
Johnson, Richard, Det.	6	0	6	0	36
Muster, Brad, Chi.	6	6	0	0	36
Peete, Rodney, Det.	6	6	0	0	36
Riggs, Gerald, Wash.	6	6	0	0	36
Sharpe, Sterling, G.B.	6	0	6	0	36
Anderson, Gary, T.B.	5	3	2	0	30
Bavaro, Mark, N.Y. Giants	5	0	5	0	30
Cunningham, Randall, Phil.	5	5	0	0	30
Hill, Bruce, T.B.	5	0	5	0	30
Ingram, Mark, N.Y. Giants	5	0	5	0	30
Irvin, Michael, Dall.	5	0	5	0	30
Johnson, Johnny, Phx.	5	5	0	0	30
Jones, Brent, S.F.	5	0	5	0	30
Martin, Eric, N.O.	5	0	5	0	30
McGee, Buford, L.A. Rams	5	1	4	0	30
Monk, Art, Wash.	5	0	5	0	30
West, Ed, G.B.	5	0	5	0	30
Anderson, Willie, L.A. Rams	4	0	4	0	24
Baker, Stephen, N.Y. Giants	4	0	4	0	24
Broussard, Steve, Atl.	4	4	0	0	24
Carrier, Mark, T.B.	4	0	4	0	24
Delpino, Robert, L.A. Rams	4	0	4	0	24
Dixon, Floyd, Atl.	4	0	4	0	24
Ellard, Henry, L.A. Rams	4	0	4	0	24
Green, Roy, Phx.	4	0	4	0	24
Hampton, Rodney, N.Y. Giants	4	2	2	0	24
Harbaugh, Jim, Chi.	4	4	0	0	24
Heyward, Craig, N.O.	4	4	0	0	24
Johnson, Tracy, Atl.	4	3	1	0	24
Jones, Ernie, Phx.	4	0	4	0	24
Novacek, Jay, Dall.	4	0	4	0	24
Proehl, Ricky, Phx.	4	0	4	0	24
Sherman, Heath, Phil.	4	1	3	0	24
Thompson, Anthony, Phx.	4	4	0	0	24
Toney, Anthony, Phil.	4	1	3	0	24
Turner, Floyd, N.O.	4	0	4	0	24
Byars, Keith, Phil.	3	0	3	0	18
Carter, Cris, Minn.	3	0	3	0	18
Davis, Wendell, Chi.	3	0	3	0	18
Greer, Terry, Det.	3	0	3	0	18
Haddix, Wayne, T.B.	3	0	0	3	18
Johnson, Damone, L.A. Rams	3	0	3	0	18
Jordan, Steve, Minn.	3	0	3	0	18
Morris, Ron, Chi.	3	0	3	0	18
Query, Jeff, G.B.	3	0	2	1	18
Rosenbach, Timm, Phx.	3	3	0	0	18
Rozier, Mike, Atl.	3	3	0	0	18
Sanders, Deion, Atl.	3	0	0	3	18
Sanders, Ricky, Wash.	3	0	3	0	18
Sydney, Harry, S.F.	3	2	1	0	18
Anderson, Alfred, Minn.	2	2	0	0	12
Brenner, Hoby, N.O.	2	0	2	0	12
Butler, Bobby, Atl.	2	0	0	2	12
Campbell, Jeff, Det.	2	0	2	0	12
Cobb, Reggie, T.B.	2	2	0	0	12
Collins, Shawn, Atl.	2	0	2	0	12
Fenerty, Gill, N.O.	2	2	0	0	12
Fenney, Rick, Minn.	2	2	0	0	12
Flagler, Terrence, Phx.	2	1	1	0	12
Gentry, Dennis, Chi.	2	0	2	0	12
Green, Gaston, L.A. Rams	2	0	1	1	12
Haddix, Michael, G.B.	2	0	2	0	12
Hall, Ron, T.B.	2	0	2	0	12
Holohan, Pete, L.A. Rams	2	0	2	0	12
Hostetler, Jeff, N.Y. Giants	2	2	0	0	12
Humphries, Stan, Wash.	2	2	0	0	12
Johnson, Jimmie, Wash.	2	0	2	0	12
Johnston, Daryl, Dall.	2	1	1	0	12
Kemp, Perry, G.B.	2	0	2	0	12
Meggett, David, N.Y. Giants	2	0	1	1	12
Noga, Al, Minn.	2	0	0	2	12
Perkins, Bruce, T.B.	2	0	2	0	12
Perriman, Brett, N.O.	2	0	2	0	12
Sherrard, Mike, S.F.	2	0	2	0	12
Smith, J.T., Phx.	2	0	2	0	12
Thompson, Darrell, G.B.	2	1	0	1	12
Tomczak, Mike, Chi.	2	2	0	0	12
Turner, Marcus, Phx.	2	0	0	2	12
Wilkins, Gary, Atl.	2	0	2	0	12
Agee, Tommie, Dall.	1	0	1	0	6
Aikman, Troy, Dall.	1	1	0	0	6

	TD	TDR	TDP	TD Misc.	TP
Allen, Eric, Phil.	1	0	0	1	6
Bailey, Johnny, Chi.	1	0	0	1	6
Boso, Cap, Chi.	1	0	1	0	6
Browner, Joey, Minn.	1	0	0	1	6
Bryant, Kelvin, Wash.	1	0	1	0	6
Carter, Dexter, S.F.	1	1	0	0	6
Case, Scott, Atl.	1	0	0	1	6
Chandler, Chris, T.B.	1	1	0	0	6
Craig, Roger, S.F.	1	1	0	0	6
Crockett, Ray, Det.	1	0	0	1	6
Dent, Richard, Chi.	1	0	0	1	6
Drewrey, Willie, T.B.	1	0	1	0	6
Drummond, Robert, Phil.	1	1	0	0	6
Duerson, Dave, N.Y. Giants	1	0	0	1	6
Evans, Byron, Phil.	1	0	0	1	6
Everett, Jim, L.A. Rams	1	1	0	0	6
Faison, Derrick, L.A. Rams	1	0	1	0	6
Fontenot, Herman, G.B.	1	0	1	0	6
Fourcade, John, N.O.	1	1	0	0	6
Frizzell, William, Phil.	1	0	0	1	6
Fullwood, Brent, G.B.	1	1	0	0	6
Gannon, Rich, Minn.	1	1	0	0	6
Gouveia, Kurt, Wash.	1	0	0	1	6
Green, Darrell, Wash.	1	0	0	1	6
Green, Mark, Chi.	1	0	1	0	6
Greene, Tiger, G.B.	1	0	0	1	6
Hargrove, Marvin, Phil.	1	0	1	0	6
Harvey, John, T.B.	1	0	1	0	6
Hilliard, Dalton, N.O.	1	0	1	0	6
Hobbs, Stevie, Wash.	1	0	1	0	6
Holt, Issiac, Dall.	1	0	0	1	6
Humphery, Bobby, L.A. Rams	1	0	0	1	6
Jackson, Vestee, Chi.	1	0	0	1	6
Jones, Keith, Atl.	1	0	0	1	6
Kiel, Blair, G.B.	1	1	0	0	6
Majkowski, Don, G.B.	1	1	0	0	6
Matthews, Aubrey, Det.	1	0	1	0	6
Maxie, Brett, N.O.	1	0	0	1	6
McKinnon, Dennis, Dall.	1	0	1	0	6
Merriweather, Mike, Minn.	1	0	0	1	6
Miller, Chris, Atl.	1	1	0	0	6
Milling, James, Atl.	1	0	1	0	6
Mitchell, Brian, Wash.	1	1	0	0	6
Montana, Joe, S.F.	1	1	0	0	6
Mrosko, Bob, N.Y. Giants	1	0	1	0	6
Patterson, Shawn, G.B.	1	0	0	1	6
Peebles, Danny, T.B.	1	0	1	0	6
Quick, Mike, Phil.	1	0	1	0	6
Rutledge, Jeff, Wash.	1	1	0	0	6
Sanders, Thomas, Phil.	1	1	0	0	6
Scales, Greg, N.O.	1	0	1	0	6
Sharpe, Luis, Phx.	1	0	1	0	6
Simmons, Clyde, Phil.	1	0	0	1	6
Simms, Phil, N.Y. Giants	1	1	0	0	6
Taylor, Lawrence, N.Y. Giants	1	0	0	1	6
Testaverde, Vinny, T.B.	1	1	0	0	6
Thomas, George, Atl.	1	0	1	0	6
Thornton, James, Chi.	1	0	1	0	6
Tillman, Lewis, N.Y. Giants	1	1	0	0	6
Tuggle, Jessie, Atl.	1	0	0	1	6
Vick, Roger, Phil.	1	1	0	0	6
Walls, Everson, N.Y. Giants	1	0	0	1	6
Walton, Alvin, Wash.	1	0	0	1	6
Warner, Curt, L.A. Rams	1	1	0	0	6
Warren, Don, Wash.	1	0	1	0	6
Weathers, Clarence, G.B.	1	0	1	0	6
White, William, Det.	1	0	0	1	6
Wilder, James, Det.	1	0	1	0	6
Williams, Jimmy, Det.	1	0	0	1	6
Woodside, Keith, G.B.	1	1	0	0	6
Workman, Vince, G.B.	1	0	1	0	6
Wright, Alexander, Dall.	1	0	0	1	6
Doleman, Chris, Minn.	0	0	0	0	*2
Dusbabek, Mark, Minn.	0	0	0	0	*2
Green, Tim, Atl.	0	0	0	0	*2
Turner, Keena, S.F.	0	0	0	0	*2

** indicates safety scored.*

Field Goals

Best Percentage
- **AFC:** .919—Nick Lowery, Kansas City
- **NFC:** .875—Donald Igwebuike, Minnesota

Made
- **AFC:** 34—Nick Lowery, Kansas City
- **NFC:** 30—Chip Lohmiller, Washington

Attempts
- **NFC:** 40—Chip Lohmiller, Washington
- **AFC:** 37—Nick Lowery, Kansas City

Longest
- **NFC:** 56—Mike Cofer, San Francisco; Chip Lohmiller, Washington
- **AFC:** 55—Dean Biasucci, Indianapolis

Average Yards Made
- **AFC:** 38.4—Jason Staurovsky, New England
- **NFC:** 37.7—Morten Andersen, New Orleans

AFC Field Goals—Team

	FG	FG Att.	Pct.	Long
Kansas City	34	37	919	48
N.Y. Jets	23	26	885	47
Miami	21	25	840	53
Pittsburgh	20	25	800	48
Cincinnati	17	22	773	46
L.A. Raiders	15	20	750	50
San Diego	21	28	750	43
Denver	25	34	735	49
New England	16	22	727	53
Seattle	23	32	719	51
Indianapolis	17	24	708	55
Cleveland	14	20	700	47
Buffalo	20	29	690	48
Houston	21	32	656	49
AFC Total	287	376	—	55
AFC Average	20.5	26.9	763	—

NFC Field Goals—Team

	FG	FG Att.	Pct.	Long
Minnesota	25	28	893	48
Tampa Bay	23	27	852	54
New Orleans	21	27	778	52
Green Bay	23	30	767	53
N.Y. Giants	21	28	750	49
Washington	30	40	750	56
Philadelphia	21	29	724	53
Dallas	18	25	720	49
Chicago	26	37	703	52
Atlanta	22	33	667	53
San Francisco	24	36	667	56
Detroit	17	26	654	47
Phoenix	17	27	630	50
L.A. Rams	15	24	625	46
NFC Total	303	417	—	56
NFC Average	21.6	29.8	727	—
League Totals	590	793	—	56
League Average	21.1	28.3	744	—

AFC Field Goals—Individual

	1-19	20-29	30-39	40-49	50 & Over	Totals	Avg. Yds. Att.	Avg. Yds. Made	Avg. Yds. Miss	Long
Lowery, Nick, K.C.	2-2	5-5	21-22	6-7	0-1	34-37	34.4	33.8	41.7	48
	1.000	1.000	.955	.857	.000	.919				
Carney, John, S.D.	2-2	8-8	6-7	3-3	0-1	19-21	31.0	29.5	45.0	43
	1.000	1.000	.857	1.000	.000	.905				
Leahy, Pat, N.Y. Jets	2-2	12-12	6-7	3-5	0-0	23-26	30.2	28.7	41.0	47
	1.000	1.000	.857	.600	—	.885				
Stoyanovich, Pete, Mia.	2-2	7-8	6-7	4-5	2-3	21-25	34.2	33.1	40.3	53
	1.000	.875	.857	.800	.667	.840				
Breech, Jim, Cin.	0-0	6-6	5-6	6-9	0-0	17-21	35.2	33.8	41.3	46
	—	1.000	.833	.667	—	.810				
Anderson, Gary, Pitt.	1-1	3-3	8-8	8-11	0-2	20-25	38.2	35.8	48.0	48
	1.000	1.000	1.000	.727	.000	.800				
Jaeger, Jeff, L.A. Raiders	1-1	5-5	2-3	6-9	1-2	15-20	37.9	35.5	44.8	50
	1.000	1.000	.667	.667	.500	.750				
Treadwell, David, Den.	0-0	13-14	4-6	8-13	0-1	25-34	34.7	32.3	41.6	49
	—	.929	.667	.615	.000	.735				
Staurovsky, Jason, N.E.	1-1	3-3	3-3	8-11	1-4	16-22	41.5	38.4	49.8	53
	1.000	1.000	1.000	.727	.250	.727				
Johnson, Norm, Sea.	2-2	7-7	8-14	5-6	1-3	23-32	35.1	33.1	40.2	51
	1.000	1.000	.571	.833	.333	.719				
Biasucci, Dean, Ind.	1-1	5-6	7-8	2-4	2-5	17-24	37.0	34.2	44.0	55
	1.000	.833	.875	.500	.400	.708				
Garcia, Teddy, Hou.	0-0	5-5	4-5	5-7	0-3	14-20	38.4	35.3	45.7	49
	—	1.000	.800	.714	.000	.700				
Kauric, Jerry, Clev.	0-0	5-5	5-8	4-7	0-0	14-20	35.3	33.4	39.7	47
	—	1.000	.625	.571	—	.700				
Norwood, Scott, Buff.	0-0	9-11	5-8	6-10	0-0	20-29	34.5	33.6	36.4	48
	—	.818	.625	.600	—	.690				
Non-Qualifiers (Less than 15 attempts)										
Zendejas, Tony, Hou.	0-0	2-3	3-5	2-4	0-0	7-12	35.0	32.9	38.0	45
	—	.667	.600	.500	—	.583				
Johnson, Lee, Cin.	0-0	0-0	0-0	0-0	0-1	0-1	52.0	—	52.0	—
	—	—	—	—	.000	.000				
AFC Total	15-15	95-102	93-118	77-115	7-26	287-376	35.4	33.4	42.1	55
	1.000	.931	.788	.670	.269	.763				
League Total	26-27	194-203	196-250	146-235	28-78	590-793	36.1	33.7	42.9	56
	.963	.956	.784	.621	.359	.744				

Leader based on percentage, minimum 16 field-goal attempts

NFC Field Goals—Individual

	1-19	20-29	30-39	40-49	50 & Over	Totals	Avg. Yds. Att.	Avg. Yds. Made	Avg. Yds. Miss	Long
Igwebuike, Donald, Minn.	0-0	5-5	6-6	3-5	0-0	14-16	34.6	33.1	45.0	48
	—	1.000	1.000	.600	—	.875				
Christie, Steve, T.B.	0-0	7-7	10-13	4-5	2-2	23-27	34.9	34.2	39.0	54
	—	1.000	.769	.800	1.00	.852				
Andersen, Morten, N.O.	0-0	5-5	5-6	8-12	3-4	21-27	39.3	37.7	44.8	52
	—	1.000	.833	.667	.750	.778				
Jacke, Chris, G.B.	0-0	9-9	10-13	2-4	2-4	23-30	35.5	33.1	43.1	53
	—	1.000	.769	.500	.500	.767				
Lohmiller, Chip, Wash.	2-2	10-10	12-14	3-6	3-8	30-40	36.8	34.0	45.4	56
	1.000	1.000	.857	.500	.375	.750				
Bahr, Matt, N.Y. Giants	2-2	7-7	3-3	5-9	0-2	17-23	35.6	31.3	47.8	49
	1.000	1.000	1.000	.556	.000	.739				
Ruzek, Roger, Phil.	2-2	5-7	9-12	4-7	1-1	21-29	34.8	33.9	37.3	53
	1.000	.714	.750	.571	1.000	.724				
Willis, Ken, Dall.	0-0	4-4	7-9	7-8	0-4	18-25	38.6	35.8	45.9	49
	—	1.000	.778	.875	.000	.720				
Butler, Kevin, Chi.	1-1	8-8	5-8	8-13	4-7	26-37	37.8	35.7	42.8	52
	1.000	1.000	.625	.615	.571	.703				
Murray, Eddie, Det.	0-0	6-6	4-6	3-5	0-2	13-19	35.0	31.5	42.5	47
	—	1.000	.667	.600	.000	.684				
Reveiz, Fuad, S.D.-Minn.	1-1	5-6	3-4	4-8	0-0	13-19	34.3	32.4	38.5	45
	1.000	.833	.750	.500	—	.684				
Cofer, Mike, S.F.	0-0	10-10	7-9	5-11	2-6	24-36	37.9	33.5	46.7	56
	—	1.000	.778	.455	.333	.667				
Davis, Greg, Atl.	0-0	6-6	8-9	6-13	2-5	22-33	39.2	36.3	44.9	53
	—	1.000	.889	.462	.400	.667				
Del Greco, Al, Phx.	1-1	4-4	7-10	3-6	2-6	17-27	39.3	35.9	45.0	50
	1.000	1.000	.700	.500	.333	.630				
Lansford, Mike, L.A. Rams	3-4	4-4	5-7	3-9	0-0	15-24	33.2	29.6	39.2	46
	.750	1.000	.714	.333	—	.625				
Non-Qualifiers (Less than 15 attempts)										
Allegre, Raul, Giants	0-0	1-1	1-1	2-3	0-0	4-5	38.2	37.8	40.0	46
	—	1.000	1.000	.667	—	.800				
Karlis, Rich, Det.	0-0	3-3	1-3	0-0	0-1	4-7	34.1	27.8	42.7	39
	—	1.000	.333	—	.000	.571				
NFC Total	11-12	99-101	103-132	69-120	21-52	303-417	36.7	34.1	43.6	56
	.917	.980	.780	.575	.404	.727				
League Total	26-27	194-203	196-250	146-235	28-78	590-793	36.1	33.7	42.9	56
	.963	.956	.784	.621	.359	.744				

Leader based on percentage, minimum 16 field goal attempts

Rushing

Individual Champions
- **NFC:** 1304—Barry Sanders, Detroit
- **AFC:** 1297—Thurman Thomas, Buffalo

Most Yards, Game
- **AFC:** 214—Thurman Thomas, Buffalo at N.Y. Jets, September 24 (18 attempts)
- **NFC:** 176—Barry Sanders, Detroit vs. L.A. Raiders, December 10 (25 attempts, 2 TD)

Longest
- **AFC:** 88—Bo Jackson, L.A. Raiders vs. Cincinnati, December 16
- **NFC:** 74—Dexter Carter, San Francisco at L.A. Rams, December 17 - TD

Attempts
- **NFC:** 297—Earnest Byner, Washington
- **AFC:** 288—Bobby Humphrey, Denver

Most Attempts, Game
- **NFC:** 39—Earnest Byner, Washington at New England, December 15 (149 yards)
- **AFC:** 34—Bobby Humphrey, Denver at Buffalo, September 30 (177 yards)

Yards Per Attempt
- **NFC:** 8.0—Randall Cunningham, Philadelphia
- **AFC:** 5.6—Bo Jackson, L.A. Raiders

Touchdowns
- **AFC:** 14—Derrick Fenner, Seattle
- **NFC:** 14—Cleveland Gary, L.A. Rams

Team Leaders, Yards

AFC: BUFFALO: 1297, Thurman Thomas; CINCINNATI: 1004, James Brooks; CLEVELAND: 702, Kevin Mack; DENVER: 1202, Bobby Humphrey; HOUSTON: 702, Lorenzo White; INDIANAPOLIS: 677, Eric Dickerson; KANSAS CITY: 1015, Barry Word; L.A. RAIDERS: 698, Bo Jackson; MIAMI: 831, Sammie Smith,; NEW ENGLAND: 808, John Stephens; N.Y. JETS: 620, Blair Thomas; PITTSBURGH: 772, Merril Hoge; SAN DIEGO: 1225, Marion Butts; SEATTLE: 859, Derrick Fenner.

NFC: ATLANTA: 675, Mike Rozier; CHICAGO: 1078, Neal Anderson; DALLAS: 937, Emmitt Smith; DETROIT: 1304, Barry Sanders; GREEN BAY: 311, Michael Haddix; L.A. RAMS: 808, Cleveland Gary; MINNESOTA: 770, Herschel Walker; NEW ORLEANS: 599, Craig Heyward; N.Y. GIANTS: 784, Ottis Anderson; PHILADELPHIA: 942, Randall Cunningham; PHOENIX: 926, Johnny Johnson; SAN FRANCISCO: 460, Dexter Carter; TAMPA BAY: 646, Gary Anderson; WASHINGTON: 1219, Earnest Byner.

Team Champions
- **NFC:** 2556—Philadelphia
- **AFC:** 2257—San Diego

AFC Rushing—Team

	Att.	Yards	Avg.	Long	TD
San Diego	484	2257	4.7	52	14
N.Y. Jets	476	2127	4.5	41	16
Cincinnati	484	2120	4.4	t56	16
Buffalo	479	2080	4.3	t80	20
L.A. Raiders	496	2028	4.1	88	20
Kansas City	504	1948	3.9	t53	11
Pittsburgh	456	1880	4.1	t70	11
Denver	462	1872	4.1	t37	19
Seattle	457	1749	3.8	36	18
Miami	420	1535	3.7	33	13
Houston	328	1417	4.3	31	10
Cleveland	345	1120	3.5	42	10
Indianapolis	335	1282	3.8	43	9
New England	383	1398	3.313/	29	4

NFC Rushing—Team

	Att.	Yards	Avg.	Long	TD
Philadelphia	540	2556	4.7	t52	10
Chicago	551	2436	4.4	52	22
Washington	515	2083	4.0	26	16
N.Y. Giants	541	2049	3.8	51	17
Detroit	366	1927	5.3	t45	19
Phoenix	452	1912	4.2	41	13
Minnesota	455	1867	4.1	t58	10
New Orleans	464	1850	4.0	t60	14
San Francisco	454	1718	3.8	t74	12
Tampa Bay	410	1626	4.0	t48	7
L.A. Rams	422	1612	3.8	48	17
Atlanta	420	1594	3.8	67	11
Dallas	393	1500	3.8	t48	13
Green Bay	350	1369	3.9	37	5

NFL Top 10 Rushers

	Att	Yards	Avg	Long	TD
Sanders, Barry, Det.	255	1304	5.1	t45	13
Thomas, Thurman, Buff.	271	1297	4.8	t80	11
Butts, Marion, S.D.	265	1225	4.6	52	8
Byner, Earnest, Wash.	297	1219	4.1	22	6
Humphrey, Bobby, Den.	288	1202	4.2	t37	7
Anderson, Neal, Chi.	260	1078	4.1	52	10
Word, Barry, K.C.	204	1015	5.0	t53	4
Brooks, James, Cin.	195	1004	5.1	t56	5
Cunningham, Randall, Phil.	118	942	8.0	t52	5
Smith, Emmitt, Dall.	241	937	3.9	t48	11

AFC Rushing—Individual

	Att.	Yards	Avg.	Long	TD
Thomas, Thurman, Buff.	271	1297	4.8	t80	11
Butts, Marion, S.D.	265	1225	4.6	52	8
Humphrey, Bobby, Den.	288	1202	4.2	t37	7
Word, Barry, K.C.	204	1015	5.0	t53	4
Brooks, James, Cin.	195	1004	5.1	t56	5
Fenner, Derrick, Sea.	215	859	4.0	36	14
Smith, Sammie, Mia.	226	831	3.7	33	8
Stephens, John, N.E.	212	808	3.8	26	2
Okoye, Christian, K.C.	245	805	3.3	32	7
Hoge, Merril, Pitt.	203	772	3.8	t41	7
Williams, John L., Sea.	187	714	3.8	25	3
Mack, Kevin, Clev.	158	702	4.4	26	5
White, Lorenzo, Hou.	168	702	4.2	22	8
Jackson, Bo, L.A. Raiders	125	698	5.6	88	5
Allen, Marcus, L.A. Raiders	179	682	3.8	28	12
Dickerson, Eric, Ind.	166	677	4.1	43	4
Thomas, Blair, N.Y. Jets	123	620	5.0	41	1
Bernstine, Rod, S.D.	124	589	4.8	t40	4
Bentley, Albert, Ind.	137	556	4.1	t26	4
Baxter, Brad, N.Y. Jets	124	539	4.3	t28	6
McNeil, Freeman, N.Y. Jets	99	458	4.6	29	6
Worley, Tim, Pitt.	109	418	3.8	38	0
Williams, Warren, Pitt.	68	389	5.7	t70	3
Hector, Johnny, N.Y. Jets	91	377	4.1	22	2
Harmon, Ronnie, S.D.	66	363	5.5	41	0
Green, Harold, Cin.	83	353	4.3	39	1
Smith, Steve, L.A. Raiders	81	327	4.0	17	2
Logan, Marc, Mia.	79	317	4.0	17	2
Davis, Kenneth, Buff.	64	302	4.7	47	4
Pinkett, Allen, Hou.	66	268	4.1	19	0
Woods, Ickey, Cin.	64	268	4.2	32	6
Elway, John, Den.	50	258	5.2	21	3
Metcalf, Eric, Clev.	80	248	3.1	17	1
Allen, Marvin, N.E.	63	237	3.8	29	1
Taylor, Craig, Cin.	51	216	4.2	24	2
Moon, Warren, Hou.	55	215	3.9	17	2
Mueller, Jamie, Buff.	59	207	3.5	20	2
Foster, Barry, Pitt.	36	203	5.6	38	1
Bell, Greg, L.A. Raiders	47	164	3.5	21	1
Esiason, Boomer, Cin.	49	157	3.2	21	0
Hoard, Leroy, Clev.	58	149	2.6	42	3
Stradford, Troy, Mia.	37	138	3.7	15	1
Winder, Sammy, Den.	42	120	2.9	19	2
Krieg, Dave, Sea.	32	115	3.6	25	0
Adams, George, N.E.	28	111	4.0	13	0
Perryman, Bob, N.E.	32	97	3.0	13	1
Paige, Tony, Mia.	32	95	3.0	11	2
Bratton, Mel, Den.	27	82	3.0	10	3
Smith, Don, Buff.	20	82	4.1	13	2
Ezor, Blake, Den.	23	81	3.5	15	0
Gainer, Derrick, Clev.	30	81	2.7	9	1
Schroeder, Jay, L.A. Raiders	37	81	2.2	17	0
Hodson, Tom, N.E.	12	79	6.6	23	0
Jones, Victor, Hou.	14	75	5.4	14	0
Ball, Eric, Cin.	22	72	3.3	15	1
O'Brien, Ken, N.Y. Jets	21	72	3.4	15	0
Higgs, Mark, Mia.	10	67	6.7	27	0
Givins, Ernest, Hou.	3	65	21.7	31	0
Brister, Bubby, Pitt.	25	64	2.6	11	0
Kelly, Jim, Buff.	22	63	2.9	15	0
McNair, Todd, K.C.	14	61	4.4	13	0
Tatupu, Mosi, N.E.	16	56	3.5	15	0
Carlson, Cody, Hou.	11	52	4.7	16	0
Kubiak, Gary, Den.	9	52	5.8	18	0
Jones, Bill, K.C.	10	47	4.7	14	0
Jennings, Stanford, Cin.	12	46	3.8	13	1
Sewell, Steve, Den.	17	46	2.7	8	3
Mueller, Vance, L.A. Raiders	13	43	3.3	12	0
Gardner, Carwell, Buff.	15	41	2.7	14	0
Secules, Scott, Mia.	8	34	4.3	17	0
Eason, Tony, N.Y. Jets	7	29	4.1	24	0
Marino, Dan, Mia.	16	29	1.8	15	0
Slaughter, Webster, Clev.	5	29	5.8	17	0
Jackson, Mark, Den.	5	28	5.6	t16	1
Trudeau, Jack, Ind.	10	28	2.8	9	0
Lewis, Nate, S.D.	4	25	6.3	t10	1
McCallum, Napoleon, Raiders	10	25	2.5	6	0
Reich, Frank, Buff.	15	24	1.6	9	0
Beebe, Don, Buff.	1	23	23.0	23	0
Reed, Andre, Buff.	3	23	7.7	26	0
Tolliver, Billy Joe, S.D.	14	22	1.6	14	0
Jones, James, Sea.	5	20	4.0	5	0
Taylor, Troy, N.Y. Jets	2	20	10.0	15	1
Blades, Brian, Sea.	3	19	6.3	12	0
Bell, Richard, Pitt.	5	18	3.6	12	0
Kinnebrew, Larry, Buff.	9	18	2.0	4	1
Stryzinski, Dan, Pitt.	3	17	5.7	9	0
Saxon, James, K.C.	3	15	5.0	8	0
Limbrick, Garrett, Mia.	5	14	2.8	5	0
Nelson, Darrin, S.D.	3	14	4.7	5	0
Kosar, Bernie, Clev.	10	13	1.3	5	0
Miller, Anthony, S.D.	3	13	4.3	10	0
Loville, Derek, Sea.	7	12	1.7	4	0
James, Lynn, Cin.	1	11	11.0	11	0
Warren, Chris, Sea.	6	11	1.8	4	1
Clark, Ken, Ind.	7	10	1.4	11	0
Fernandez, Mervyn, L.A. Raiders	3	10	3.3	9	0
Strom, Rick, Pitt.	4	10	2.5	10	0
Hester, Jessie, Ind.	4	9	2.3	10	0
Mathis, Terance, N.Y. Jets	2	9	4.5	10	0
Brown, A.B., N.Y. Jets	1	8	8.0	8	0
Martin, Tony, Mia.	1	8	8.0	8	0
Overton, Don, N.E.	5	8	1.6	6	0
Wilson, Marc, N.E.	5	7	1.4	6	0
Jensen, Jim, Mia.	4	6	1.5	2	0
Pelluer, Steve, K.C.	5	6	1.2	5	0
Wilhelm, Erik, Cin.	6	6	1.0	4	0
Morris, Jamie, N.E.	2	4	2.0	3	0
Goodburn, Kelly, K.C.	1	5	5.0	5	0
Banks, Fred, Mia.	1	3	3.0	3	0
Friesz, John, S.D.	1	3	3.0	3	0
Plummer, Gary, S.D.	2	3	1.5	2	1
Porter, Kerry, Den.	1	3	3.0	3	0
George, Jeff, Ind.	11	2	0.2	6	1
McNeal, Travis, Sea.	1	2	2.0	2	0
Prokop, Joe, N.Y. Jets	3	2	0.7	8	0
Gannon, Chris, N.E.	1	0	0.0	0	0
Hansen, Brian, N.E.	1	0	0.0	0	0
Vlasic, Mark, S.D.	1	0	0.0	0	0
Wilson, Walter, S.D.	1	0	0.0	0	0
Jones, Fred, K.C.	1	-1	-1.0	-1	0
Pagel, Mike, Clev.	3	-1	-0.3	0	0
Redden, Barry, Clev.	1	-1	-1.0	-1	0
Evans, Vince, L.A. Raiders	1	-2	-2.0	-2	0
Jones, Tony, Hou.	1	-2	-2.0	-2	0
Chadwick, Jeff, Sea.	1	-3	-3.0	-3	0
Wellsandt, Doug, N.Y. Jets	1	-3	-3.0	-3	0
Fryar, Irving, N.E.	2	-4	-2.0	-1	0
Moore, Rob, N.Y. Jets	2	-4	-2.0	4	0
DeBerg, Steve, K.C.	21	-5	-0.2	6	0
Grogan, Steve, N.E.	4	-5	-1.3	0	0
Lipps, Louis, Pitt.	1	-5	-5.0	-5	0
Stone, Dwight, Pitt.	2	-6	-3.0	10	0
Edmunds, Ferrell, Mia.	1	-7	-7.0	-7	0
Barber, Mike, Cin.	1	-13	-13.0	-13	0

t indicates touchdown.
Leader based on most yards gained.

NFC Rushing—Individual

	Att.	Yards	Avg.	Long	TD
Sanders, Barry, Det.	255	1304	5.1	t45	13
Byner, Earnest, Wash.	297	1219	4.1	22	6
Anderson, Neal, Chi.	260	1078	4.1	52	10
Cunningham, Randall, Phil.	118	942	8.0	t52	5
Smith, Emmitt, Dall.	241	937	3.9	t48	11
Johnson, Johnny, Phx.	234	926	4.0	41	5
Gary, Cleveland, L.A. Rams	204	808	4.0	48	14
Anderson, Ottis, N.Y. Giants	225	784	3.5	28	11
Walker, Herschel, Minn.	184	770	4.2	t58	5
Rozier, Mike, Hou.-Atl.	163	717	4.4	67	3
Sherman, Heath, Phil.	164	685	4.2	36	1
Muster, Brad, Chi.	141	664	4.7	28	6
Anderson, Gary, T.B.	166	646	3.9	22	3
Heyward, Craig, N.O.	129	599	4.6	t47	4
Mayes, Rueben, N.O.	138	510	3.7	18	7
Cobb, Reggie, T.B.	151	480	3.2	17	2
Riggs, Gerald, Wash.	123	475	3.9	20	6
Rosenbach, Timm, Phx.	86	470	5.5	25	3
Carter, Dexter, S.F.	114	460	4.0	t74	1
Hampton, Rodney, N.Y. Giants	109	455	4.2	41	2
Broussard, Steve, Atl.	126	454	3.6	t50	4

	Att.	Yards	Avg.	Long	TD
Toney, Anthony, Phil.	132	452	3.4	20	1
Craig, Roger, S.F.	141	439	3.1	26	1
Thompson, Anthony, Phx.	106	390	3.7	40	4
Fenney, Rick, Minn.	87	376	4.3	27	2
Peete, Rodney, Det.	47	363	7.7	37	6
Fenerty, Gill, N.O.	73	355	4.9	t60	2
Harbaugh, Jim, Chi.	51	321	6.3	17	4
Rathman, Tom, S.F.	101	318	3.1	22	7
Haddix, Michael, G.B.	98	311	3.2	13	0
Hilliard, Dalton, N.O.	90	284	3.2	17	0
Testaverde, Vinny, T.B.	38	280	7.4	t48	1
Gannon, Rich, Minn.	52	268	5.2	27	1
Thompson, Darrell, G.B.	76	264	3.5	37	1
Green, Gaston, L.A. Rams	68	261	3.8	31	0
McGee, Buford, L.A. Rams	44	234	5.3	19	1
Tillman, Lewis, N.Y. Giants	84	231	2.8	17	1
Agee, Tommie, Dall.	53	213	4.0	28	0
Sanders, Thomas, Phil.	56	208	3.7	39	1
Anderson, Alfred, Minn.	59	207	3.5	14	2
Hostetler, Jeff, N.Y. Giants	39	190	4.9	30	2
Majkowski, Don, G.B.	29	186	6.4	24	1
Jones, Keith, Atl.	49	185	3.8	22	0
Woodside, Keith, G.B.	46	182	4.0	21	1
Aikman, Troy, Dall.	40	172	4.3	20	1
Sydney, Harry, S.F.	35	166	4.7	19	2
Meggett, David, N.Y. Giants	22	164	7.5	51	0
Montana, Joe, S.F.	40	162	4.1	20	1
Young, Steve, S.F.	15	159	10.6	31	0
Gagliano, Bob, Det.	46	145	3.2	22	0
Carthon, Maurice, N.Y. Giants	36	143	4.0	12	0
Byars, Keith, Phil.	37	141	3.8	23	0
Warner, Curt, L.A. Rams	49	139	2.8	9	1
Green, Mark, Chi.	27	126	4.7	14	0
Fullwood, Brent, G.B.	44	124	2.8	16	1
Dilweg, Anthony, G.B.	21	114	5.4	22	0
Harvey, John, T.B.	27	113	4.2	14	0
Humphries, Stan, Wash.	23	106	4.6	17	2
Johnson, Tracy, Atl.	30	106	3.5	12	3
Miller, Chris, Atl.	26	99	3.8	18	1
Bailey, Johnny, Chi.	26	86	3.3	9	0
Dupard, Reggie, Wash.	19	85	4.5	11	0
Flagler, Terrence, Phx.	13	85	6.5	t29	1
Mitchell, Brian, Wash.	15	81	5.4	21	1
Wilson, Wade, Minn.	12	79	6.6	24	0
Fourcade, John, N.O.	15	77	5.1	12	1
Fontenot, Herman, G.B.	17	76	4.5	18	0
Rice, Allen, Minn.	22	74	3.4	13	0
Dupree, Marcus, L.A. Rams	19	72	3.8	13	0
Chandler, Chris, T.B.	13	71	5.5	18	1
Ware, Andre, Det.	7	64	9.1	30	0
Simms, Phil, N.Y. Giants	21	61	2.9	20	1
Monk, Art, Wash.	7	59	8.4	26	0
Vick, Roger, Phil.	16	58	3.6	17	1
Rouse, James, Chi.	16	56	3.5	10	0
Delpino, Robert, L.A. Rams	13	52	4.0	13	0
Wilder, James, Det.	11	51	4.6	13	0
Workman, Vince, G.B.	8	51	6.4	31	0
Clark, Jessie, Minn.	16	49	3.1	11	0
Highsmith, Alonzo, Dall.	19	48	2.5	7	0
Dixon, James, Dall.	11	43	3.9	18	0
Gentry, Dennis, Chi.	11	43	3.9	11	0
Tomczak, Mike, Chi.	12	41	3.4	14	2
Query, Jeff, G.B.	3	39	13.0	18	0
Campbell, Scott, Atl.	9	38	4.2	20	0
Perkins, Bruce, T.B.	13	36	2.8	9	0
Johnston, Daryl, Dall.	10	35	3.5	8	1
Drummond, Robert, Phil.	8	33	4.1	9	1
Jones, Ernie, Phx.	4	33	8.3	15	0
Everett, Jim, L.A. Rams	20	31	1.6	15	1
Morris, Ron, Chi.	2	26	13.0	16	0
Wright, Alexander, Dall.	3	26	8.7	14	0
Walsh, Steve, Dall.-N.O.	20	25	1.3	18	0
Bryant, Kelvin, Wash.	6	24	4.0	12	0
Lang, Gene, Atl.	9	24	2.7	9	0
Ellard, Henry, L.A. Rams	2	21	10.5	13	0
Saxon, Mike, Dall.	1	20	20.0	20	0
Williams, Calvin, Phil.	2	20	10.0	18	0
Smith, Cedric, Minn.	9	19	2.1	7	0
Sanders, Ricky, Wash.	4	17	4.3	12	0
Carter, Anthony, Minn.	3	16	5.3	11	0
Settle, John, Atl.	9	16	1.8	4	0
Henderson, Keith, S.F.	6	14	2.3	9	0
Rouson, Lee, N.Y. Giants	3	14	4.7	6	0
Sharpe, Sterling, G.B.	2	14	7.0	10	0
Anderson, Willie, L.A. Rams	1	13	13.0	13	0
Barnett, Fred, Phil.	2	13	6.5	12	0
Dozier, D.J., Minn.	6	12	2.0	4	0
Rutledge, Jeff, Wash.	4	12	3.0	t12	1
Kiel, Blair, G.B.	5	9	1.8	4	1
Pringle, Mike, Atl.	2	9	4.5	9	0
Sikahema, Vai, Phx.	3	8	2.7	4	0
Carter, Cris, Minn.	2	6	3.0	8	0
Laufenberg, Babe, Dall.	2	6	3.0	5	0
Smith, Timmy, Dall.	6	6	1.0	3	0
Tate, Lars, Chi.	3	5	1.7	4	0
Bates, Bill, Dall.	1	4	4.0	4	0
Ingram, Mark, N.Y. Giants	1	4	4.0	4	0
Proehl, Ricky, Phx.	1	4	4.0	4	0
Rypien, Mark, Wash.	15	4	0.3	8	0
Smith, J.T., Phx.	1	4	4.0	4	0
Baker, Stephen, N.Y. Giants	1	3	3.0	3	0
Feagles, Jeff, Phil.	2	3	1.5	3	0
Wolfley, Ron, Phx.	2	3	1.5	2	0
Clark, Gary, Wash.	1	1	1.0	1	0
McMahon, Jim, Phil.	3	1	0.3	3	0
Carlson, Jeff, T.B.	1	0	0.0	0	0
Hill, Bruce, T.B.	1	0	0.0	0	0
Mojsiejenko, Ralf, Wash.	1	0	0.0	0	0
Rice, Jerry, S.F.	2	0	0.0	2	0
Tupa, Tom, Phx.	1	0	0.0	0	0
Kemp, Perry, G.B.	1	-1	-1.0	-1	0
Perry, William, Chi.	1	-1	-1.0	-1	0
Martin, Kelvin, Dall.	4	-2	-0.5	3	0
Newsome, Harry, Minn.	2	-2	-1.0	0	0
Jones, Hassan, Minn.	1	-7	-7.0	-7	0
McKinnon, Dennis, Dall.	1	-8	-8.0	-8	0
Buford, Maury, Chi.	1	-9	-9.0	-9	0
Camarillo, Rich, Phx.	1	-11	-11.0	-11	0
Millen, Hugh, Atl.	7	-12	-1.7	2	0
English, Keith, L.A. Rams	2	-19	-9.5	-8	0

t indicates touchdown.
Leader based on mosts yards gained.

Passing

Individual Champions (Rating Points)
AFC: 101.2—Jim Kelly, Buffalo
NFC: 92.7—Phil Simms, N.Y. Giants

Completion Percentage
AFC: 63.3—Jim Kelly, Buffalo
NFC: 61.7—Joe Montana, San Francisco

Attempts
AFC: 584—Warren Moon, Houston
NFC: 554—Jim Everett, L.A. Rams

Completions
AFC: 362—Warren Moon, Houston
NFC: 321—Joe Montana, San Francisco

Yards
AFC: 4689—Warren Moon, Houston
NFC: 3989—Jim Everett, L.A. Rams

Most Yards, Game
AFC: 527—Warren Moon, Houston at Kansas City, December 16 (27-45, 3 TD)
NFC: 476—Joe Montana, San Francisco at Atlanta, October 14 (32-49, 6 TD)

Longest
NFC: 95—Randall Cunningham (to Fred Barnett), Philadelphia at Buffalo, December 2 - TD
AFC: 90—Bubby Brister (to Dwight Stone), Pittsburgh at Denver, October 14
Steve DeBerg (to J.J. Birden), Kansas City vs. San Diego, November 18 - TD

Yards Per Attempt
AFC: 8.53—Jay Schroeder, L.A. Raiders
NFC: 7.72—Vinny Testaverde, Tampa Bay

Touchdown Passes
AFC: 33—Warren Moon, Houston
NFC: 30—Randall Cunningham, Philadelphia

Most Touchdown Passes, Game
NFC: 6—Joe Montana, San Francisco at Atlanta, October 14 (32-49, 476 yards)
AFC: 5—Warren Moon, Houston vs. Cincinnati, October 14 (21-33, 369 yards)
Warren Moon, Houston at Cleveland, November 18 (24-32, 322 yards)

Lowest Interception Percentage
AFC: 0.9—Steve DeBerg, Kansas City
NFC: 1.3—Phil Simms, N.Y. Giants

Team Champions
AFC: 4805—Houston
NFC: 4177—San Francisco

AFC Passing—Team

	Att.	Comp.	Pct. Comp.	Gross Yards	Tkd.	Yards Lost	Net Yards	TD	Pct. TD	Long	Int.	Pct. Int.	Avg. Yds. Att.	Att. Yds. Comp.
Houston	639	399	62.4	5072	39	267	4805	37	5.8	t87	15	2.3	7.94	12.71
Miami	539	310	57.5	3611	16	99	3512	21	3.9	t69	12	2.2	6.70	11.65
Denver	527	305	57.9	3671	46	330	3341	15	2.8	66	18	3.4	6.97	12.04
Kansas City	449	260	57.9	3458	22	191	3267	23	5.1	t90	5	1.1	7.70	13.30
Buffalo	425	263	61.9	3404	27	208	3196	28	6.6	71	11	2.6	8.01	12.94
Cleveland	573	301	52.5	3407	42	260	3147	13	2.3	50	23	2.0	5.95	11.32
Cincinnati	425	237	55.8	3152	34	209	2943	25	5.9	53	23	5.4	7.42	13.30
Indianapolis	488	269	55.1	3297	51	424	2873	22	4.5	75	21	4.3	6.76	12.26
Seattle	448	265	59.2	3194	40	360	2834	15	3.3	t63	20	4.5	7.13	12.05
New England	514	274	53.3	3208	58	443	2765	14	2.7	56	20	3.9	6.24	11.71
N.Y. Jets	451	246	54.5	3059	40	300	2759	14	3.1	t69	11	2.4	6.78	12.43
L.A. Raiders	336	183	54.5	2885	29	197	2688	19	5.7	t68	10	3.0	8.59	15.77
San Diego	472	246	52.1	2840	20	157	2683	18	3.8	t45	19	4.0	6.02	11.54
Pittsburgh	408	237	58.1	2887	33	242	2645	20	4.9	90	15	3.0	7.08	12.18
AFC Total	6694	3795	—	47145	497	3687	43458	284	—	t90	223	—	—	—
AFC Average	478.1	271.1	56.7	3367.5	35.5	263.4	3104.1	20.3	4.2	—	15.9	3.3	7.04	12.42

NFC Passing—Team

	Att.	Comp.	Pct. Comp.	Gross Yards	Tkd.	Yards Lost	Net Yards	TD	Pct. TD	Long	Int.	Pct. Int.	Avg. Yds. Att.	Att. Yds. Comp.
San Francisco	583	360	61.7	4371	37	194	4177	28	4.8	t78	16	2.7	7.50	12.14
L.A. Rams	561	310	55.3	4016	30	198	3818	24	4.3	t55	17	3.0	7.16	12.95
Washington	536	301	56.2	3611	22	132	3479	22	4.1	t53	22	4.1	6.74	12.00
Atlanta	528	293	55.5	3726	46	265	3461	21	4.0	t75	18	3.4	7.06	12.72
Green Bay	541	302	55.8	3696	62	390	3306	20	3.7	t76	21	3.9	6.83	12.24
Minnesota	497	265	53.3	3445	49	278	3167	25	5.0	t78	24	4.8	6.93	13.00
Philadelphia	479	281	58.7	3582	50	438	3144	34	7.1	t95	13	2.7	7.48	12.75
Detroit	460	242	52.6	3328	44	278	3050	24	5.2	t68	20	4.3	7.23	13.75
Tampa Bay	448	245	54.7	3282	53	433	2849	18	4.0	t89	24	5.4	7.33	13.40
Phoenix	439	238	54.2	3118	43	285	2833	16	3.6	t68	18	4.1	7.10	13.10
N.Y. Giants	398	231	58.0	2898	29	142	2756	18	4.5	t80	5	1.3	7.28	12.55
New Orleans	447	226	50.6	2757	20	131	2626	15	3.4	t68	23	5.1	6.17	12.20
Dallas	475	254	53.5	2898	43	317	2581	12	2.5	t61	24	5.1	6.10	11.41
Chicago	430	229	53.3	2827	43	283	2544	14	3.3	t80	12	2.8	6.57	12.34
NFC Total	6822	3777	—	47555	571	3764	43791	291	—	t95	257	—	—	—
NFC Average	487.3	269.8	55.4	3396.8	40.8	268.9	3127.9	20.8	4.3	—	18.4	3.8	6.97	12.59
League Total	13516	7572	—	94700	1068	7451	87249	575	—	t95	480	—	—	—
League Average	482.7	270.4	56.0	3382.1	38.1	266.1	3116.0	20.5	4.3	—	17.1	3.6	7.01	12.51

Leader based on net yards.

NFL Top 10 Individual Qualifiers

	Att.	Comp.	Pct. Comp.	Yards	Avg. Gain	TD	Pct. TD	Long	Int.	Pct. Int.	Tkd.	Yards Lost	Rating Points
Kelly, Jim, Buff.	346	219	63.3	2829	8.18	24	6.9	71	9	2.6	20	158	101.2
Moon, Warren, Hou.	584	362	62.0	4689	8.03	33	5.7	t87	13	2.2	36	252	96.8
DeBerg, Steve, K.C.	444	258	58.1	3444	7.76	23	5.2	t90	4	0.9	22	191	96.3
Simms, Phil, N.Y. Giants	311	184	59.2	2284	7.34	15	4.8	t80	4	1.3	20	104	92.7
Cunningham, Randall, Phil.	465	271	58.3	3466	7.45	30	6.5	t95	13	2.8	49	431	91.6
Schroeder, Jay, L.A. Raiders	334	182	54.5	2849	8.53	19	5.7	t68	9	2.7	29	197	90.8
Montana, Joe, S.F.	520	321	61.7	3944	7.58	26	5.0	t78	16	3.1	29	153	89.0
Marino, Dan, Mia.	531	306	57.6	3563	6.71	21	4.0	t69	11	2.1	15	90	82.6
Harbaugh, Jim, Chi.	312	180	57.7	2178	6.98	10	3.2	t80	6	1.9	31	206	81.9
Brister, Bubby, Pitt.	387	223	57.6	2725	7.04	20	5.2	90	14	3.6	28	213	81.6

AFC Passing—Individual Qualifiers

	Att.	Comp.	Pct. Comp.	Yards	Avg. Gain	TD	Pct. TD	Long	Int.	Pct. Int.	Tkd.	Yards Lost	Rating Points
Kelly, Jim, Buff.	346	219	63.3	2829	8.18	24	6.9	71	9	2.6	20	158	101.2
Moon, Warren, Hou.	584	362	62.0	4689	8.03	33	5.7	t87	13	2.2	36	252	96.8
DeBerg, Steve, K.C.	444	258	58.1	3444	7.76	23	5.2	t90	4	0.9	22	191	96.3
Schroeder, Jay, L.A. Raiders	334	182	54.5	2849	8.53	19	5.7	t68	9	2.7	29	197	90.8
Marino, Dan, Mia.	531	306	57.6	3563	6.71	21	4.0	t69	11	2.1	15	90	82.6
Brister, Bubby, Pitt.	387	223	57.6	2725	7.04	20	5.2	90	14	3.6	28	213	81.6
Elway, John, Den.	502	294	58.6	3526	7.02	15	3.0	66	14	2.8	43	311	78.5
O'Brien, Ken, N.Y. Jets	411	226	55.0	2855	6.95	13	3.2	t69	10	2.4	34	262	77.3
Esiason, Boomer, Cin.	402	224	55.7	3031	7.54	24	6.0	53	22	5.5	31	198	77.0
George, Jeff, Ind.	334	181	54.2	2152	6.44	16	4.8	75	13	3.9	37	320	73.8
Krieg, Dave, Sea.	448	265	59.2	3194	7.13	15	3.3	t63	20	4.5	40	360	73.6
Tolliver, Billy Joe, S.D.	410	216	52.7	2574	6.28	16	3.9	t45	16	3.9	19	150	68.9
Kosar, Bernie, Clev.	423	230	54.4	2562	6.06	10	2.4	50	15	3.5	37	220	65.7

	Att.	Comp.	Pct. Comp.	Yards	Avg. Gain	TD	Pct. TD	Long	Int.	Pct. Int.	Tkd.	Yards Lost	Rating Points
Wilson, Marc, N.E.	265	139	52.5	1625	6.13	6	2.3	t36	11	4.2	29	228	61.6
Non-qualifiers													
Taylor, Troy, N.Y. Jets	10	7	70.0	49	4.90	1	10.0	15	0	0.0	2	3	114.2
Carlson, Cody, Hou.	55	37	67.3	383	6.96	4	7.3	t53	2	3.6	3	15	96.3
Reich, Frank, Buff.	63	36	57.1	469	7.44	2	3.2	43	0	0.0	6	41	91.3
Wilhelm, Erik, Cin.	19	12	63.2	117	6.16	0	0.0	19	0	0.0	1	2	80.4
Trudeau, Jack, Ind.	144	84	58.3	1078	7.49	6	4.2	73	6	4.2	14	104	78.4
Grogan, Steve, N.E.	92	50	54.3	615	6.68	4	4.3	48	3	3.3	9	68	76.1
Gilbert, Gale, Buff.	15	8	53.3	106	7.07	2	13.3	23	2	13.3	1	9	76.0
Strom, Rick, Pitt.	21	14	66.7	162	7.71	0	0.0	22	1	4.8	5	29	69.9
Hodson, Tom, N.E.	156	85	54.5	968	6.21	4	2.6	56	5	3.2	20	147	68.5
Friesz, John, S.D.	22	11	50.0	98	4.45	1	4.5	17	1	4.5	1	7	58.5
Eason, Tony, N.Y. Jets	28	13	46.4	155	5.54	0	0.0	31	1	3.6	4	35	49.0
Pagel, Mike, Clev.	148	69	46.6	819	5.53	3	2.0	32	8	5.4	5	40	48.2
Vlasic, Mark, S.D.	40	19	47.5	168	4.20	1	2.5	27	2	5.0	0	0	46.7
Kubiak, Gary, Den.	22	11	50.0	145	6.59	0	0.0	36	4	18.2	3	19	31.6
Less than 10 attempts													
Allen, Marcus, L.A. Raiders	1	0	0.0	0	0.00	0	0.0	0	1	100.0	0	0	0.0
Evans, Vince, L.A.Raiders	1	1	100.0	36	36.00	0	0.0	36	0	0.0	0	0	118.8
Ferguson, Joe, Ind.	8	2	25.0	21	2.63	0	0.0	13	2	25.0	0	0	0.0
Francis, Jeff, Clev.	2	2	100.0	26	13.00	0	0.0	17	0	0.0	0	0	118.8
Herrmann, Mark, Ind.	1	1	100.0	6	6.00	0	0.0	6	0	0.0	0	0	91.7
Humphrey, Bobby, Den.	2	0	0.0	0	0.00	0	0.0	0	0	0.0	0	0	39.6
James, Lynn, Cin.	1	0	0.0	0	0.00	0	0.0	0	0	0.0	0	0	39.6
Jensen, Jim, Mia.	1	1	100.0	31	31.00	0	0.0	31	0	0.0	0	0	118.8
Johnson, Lee, Cin.	1	1	100.0	4	4.00	1	100.0	t4	0	0.0	0	0	122.9
Pelluer, Steve, K.C.	5	2	40.0	14	2.80	0	0.0	11	1	20.0	0	0	8.3
Philcox, Todd, Cin.	2	0	0.0	0	0.00	0	0.0	0	1	50.0	2	9	0.0
Secules, Scott, Mia.	7	3	42.9	17	2.43	0	0.0	8	1	14.3	1	9	10.7
Sewell, Steve, Den.	1	0	0.0	0	0.00	0	0.0	0	0	0.0	0	0	39.6
Smith, Don, Buff.	1	0	0.0	0	0.00	0	0.0	0	0	0.0	0	0	39.6
Stark, Rohn, Ind.	1	1	100.0	40	40.00	0	0.0	40	0	0.0	0	0	118.8
Stephens, John, N.E.	1	0	0.0	0	0.00	0	0.0	0	1	100.0	0	0	0.0
Toon, Al, N.Y. Jets	2	0	0.0	0	0.00	0	0.0	0	0	0.0	0	0	39.6

t indicates touchdown.
Leader based on rating points, minimum 224 attempts.

NFC Passing—Individual Qualifiers

	Att.	Comp.	Pct. Comp.	Yards	Avg. Gain	TD	Pct. TD	Long	Int.	Pct. Int.	Tkd.	Yards Lost	Rating Points
Simms, Phil, N.Y. Giants	311	184	59.2	2284	7.34	15	4.8	t80	4	1.3	20	104	92.7
Cunningham, Randall, Phil.	465	271	58.3	3466	7.45	30	6.5	t95	13	2.8	49	431	91.6
Montana, Joe, S.F.	520	321	61.7	3944	7.58	26	5.0	t78	16	3.1	29	153	89.0
Harbaugh, Jim, Chi.	312	180	57.7	2178	6.98	10	3.2	t80	6	1.9	31	206	81.9
Peete, Rodney, Det.	271	142	52.4	1974	7.28	13	4.8	t68	8	3.0	27	173	79.8
Everett, Jim, L.A. Rams	554	307	55.4	3989	7.20	23	4.2	t55	17	3.1	30	198	79.3
Miller, Chris, Atl.	388	222	57.2	2735	7.05	17	4.4	t75	14	3.6	26	167	78.7
Rypien, Mark, Wash.	304	166	54.6	2070	6.81	16	5.3	t53	11	3.6	6	33	78.4
Testaverde, Vinny, T.B.	365	203	55.6	2818	7.72	17	4.7	t89	18	4.9	38	330	75.6
Majkowski, Don, G.B.	264	150	56.8	1925	7.29	10	3.8	t76	12	4.5	32	178	73.5
Rosenbach, Timm, Phx.	437	237	54.2	3098	7.09	16	3.7	t68	17	3.9	43	285	72.8
Gannon, Rich, Minn.	349	182	52.1	2278	6.53	16	4.6	t78	16	4.6	34	188	68.9
Walsh, Steve, Dall.-N.O.	336	179	53.3	2010	5.98	12	3.6	58	13	3.9	10	76	67.2
Aikman, Troy, Dall.	399	226	56.6	2579	6.46	11	2.8	t61	18	4.5	39	288	66.6
Non-Qualifiers													
Young, Steve, S.F.	62	38	61.3	427	6.89	2	3.2	t34	0	0.0	8	41	92.6
Willis, Peter Tom, Chi.	13	9	69.2	106	8.15	1	7.7	18	1	7.7	1	7	87.3
Hostetler, Jeff, N.Y. Giants	87	47	54.0	614	7.06	3	3.4	t44	1	1.1	9	38	83.2
Rutledge, Jeff, Wash.	68	40	58.8	455	6.69	2	2.9	40	1	1.5	6	34	82.7
Millen, Hugh, Atl.	63	34	54.0	427	6.78	1	1.6	53	0	0.0	11	43	80.6
Wilson, Wade, Minn.	146	82	56.2	1155	7.91	9	6.2	t75	8	5.5	15	90	79.6
Kiel, Blair, G.B.	85	51	60.0	504	5.93	2	2.4	22	2	2.4	8	62	74.8
Gagliano, Bob, Det.	159	87	54.7	1190	7.48	10	6.3	t47	10	6.3	13	83	73.6
Dilweg, Anthony, G.B.	192	101	52.6	1267	6.60	8	4.2	59	7	3.6	22	150	72.1
Campbell, Scott, Atl.	76	36	47.4	527	6.93	3	3.9	70	4	5.3	9	55	61.7
Humphries, Stan, Wash.	156	91	58.3	1015	6.51	3	1.9	44	10	6.4	9	62	57.5
Fourcade, John, N.O.	116	50	43.1	785	6.77	3	2.6	t68	8	6.9	8	44	46.1
Ware, Andre, Det.	30	13	43.3	164	5.47	1	3.3	33	2	6.7	4	22	44.3
Tomczak, Mike, Chi.	104	39	37.5	521	5.01	3	2.9	48	5	4.8	11	70	43.8
Chandler, Chris, T.B.	83	42	50.6	464	5.59	1	1.2	t68	6	7.2	15	103	41.4
Laufenberg, Babe, Dall.	67	24	35.8	279	4.16	1	1.5	t27	6	9.0	4	29	16.9
Less than 10 attempts													
Bailey, Johnny, Chi.	1	1	100.0	22	22.00	0	0.0	22	0	0.0	0	0	118.8
Byars, Keith, Phil.	4	4	100.0	53	13.25	4	100.0	t18	0	0.0	0	0	158.3
Byner, Earnest, Wash.	2	1	50.0	31	15.50	1	50.0	t31	0	0.0	0	0	135.4
Feagles, Jeff, Phil.	1	0	0.0	0	0.00	0	0.0	0	0	0.0	0	0	39.6
Green, Roy, Phx.	1	1	100.0	20	20.00	0	0.0	20	0	0.0	0	0	118.8
Helton, Barry, S.F.	1	1	100.0	0	0.00	0	0.0	0	0	0.0	0	0	79.2
Heyward, Craig, N.O.	1	0	0.0	0	0.00	0	0.0	0	1	100.0	0	0	0.0
Johnson, Johnny, Phx.	1	0	0.0	0	0.00	0	0.0	0	1	100.0	0	0	0.0

Jones, Keith, Atl.	1	1	100.0	37	37.00	0	0.0	37	0	0.0	0	0	118.8
Kramer, Tommy, N.O.	3	1	33.3	2	0.67	0	0.0	2	1	33.3	2	11	2.8
Long, Chuck, L.A. Rams	5	1	20.0	4	0.80	0	0.0	4	0	0.0	0	0	39.6
McGee, Buford, L.A. Rams	2	2	100.0	23	11.50	1	50.0	t22	0	0.0	0	0	154.2
McMahon, Jim, Phil.	9	6	66.7	63	7.00	0	0.0	21	0	0.0	1	7	86.8
Mitchell, Brian, Wash.	6	3	50.0	40	6.67	0	0.0	18	0	0.0	1	3	71.5
Walker, Herschel, Minn.	2	1	50.0	12	6.00	0	0.0	12	0	0.0	0	0	68.8

t indicates touchdown.
Leader based on rating points, minimum 224 attempts.

Pass Receiving

Individual Champions

NFC: 100—Jerry Rice, San Francisco
AFC: 74—Drew Hill, Houston
Haywood Jeffires, Houston

Most Receptions, Game

NFC: 13—Jerry Rice, San Francisco at Atlanta, October 14 (225 yards, 5 TD)
Art Monk, Washington at Detroit, November 4 (168 yards) (OT)
AFC: 10—Eddie Brown, Cincinnati at San Diego, September 16 (178 yards, 2 TD)
Stephone Paige, Kansas City at Denver, September 17 (206 yards, 2 TD)
Drew Hill, Houston vs. Indianapolis, September 23 (123 yards)
Rodney Holman, Cincinnati at L.A. Rams, October 7 (161 yards) (OT)
Tommy Kane, Seattle at Miami, December 16 (162 yards)

Yards

NFC: 1502—Jerry Rice, San Francisco
AFC: 1048—Haywood Jeffires, Houston

Most Yards, Game

AFC: 245—Haywood Jeffires, Houston at Kansas City, December 16 (9 receptions - 1 TD)
NFC: 225—Jerry Rice, San Francisco at Atlanta, October 14 (13 receptions - 5 TD)

Longest

NFC: 95—Fred Barnett (from Randall Cunningham) Philadelphia at Buffalo, December 2 - TD
AFC: 90—Dwight Stone (from Bubby Brister) Pittsburgh at Denver, October 14
J.J. Birden (from Steve DeBerg) Kansas City vs. San Diego, November 18 - TD

Yards Per Reception

NFC: 21.5—Willie Anderson, L.A. Rams
AFC: 20.3—James Lofton, Buffalo

Touchdowns

NFC: 13—Jerry Rice, San Francisco
AFC: 9—Eddie Brown, Cincinnati
Ernest Givins, Houston

Team Leaders, Receptions

AFC: BUFFALO: 71, Andre Reed; CINCINNATI: 44, Eddie Brown; CLEVELAND: 59, Webster Slaughter; DENVER: 57, Mark Jackson; HOUSTON: 74: Drew Hill; Haywood Jeffries; INDIANAPOLIS: 71, Albert Bentley; KANSAS CITY: 65, Stephone Paige; L.A. RAIDERS: 52, Mervyn Fernandez; MIAMI: 52, Mark Duper; NEW ENGLAND: 54, Irving Fryar; N.Y. JETS: 57, Al Toon; PITTSBURGH: 50, Louis Lipps; SAN DIEGO: 63, Anthony Miller; SEATTLE: 73, John L. Williams.

NFC: ATLANTA: 82, Andre Rison; CHICAGO: 47, Brad Muster; DALLAS: 64, Kelvin Martin; DETROIT: 64, Richard Johnson; GREEN BAY: 67, Sterling Sharpe; L.A. RAMS: 76, Henry Ellard; MINNESOTA: 70, Anthony Carter; NEW ORLEANS: 63, Eric Martin; N.Y. GIANTS: 39, David Meggett; PHILADELPHIA: 81, Keith Byars; PHOENIX: 56, Ricky Proehl; SAN FRANCISCO: 100, Jerry Rice; TAMPA BAY: 49, Mark Carrier; WASHINGTON: 75, Gary Clark.

NFL Top 10 Pass Receivers

	No.	Yards	Avg.	Long	TD
Rice, Jerry, S.F.	100	1502	15.0	t64	13
Rison, Andre, Atl.	82	1208	14.7	t75	10
Byars, Keith, Phil.	81	819	10.1	54	3
Ellard, Henry, L.A. Rams	76	1294	17.0	t50	4
Clark, Gary, Wash.	75	1112	14.8	t53	8
Jeffires, Haywood, Hou.	74	1048	14.2	t87	8
Hill, Drew, Hou.	74	1019	13.8	57	5
Williams, John L., Sea.	73	699	9.6	60	0
Givins, Ernest, Hou.	72	979	13.6	t80	9
Reed, Andre, Buff.	71	945	13.3	t56	8
Bentley, Albert, Ind.	71	664	9.4	73	2

NFL Top 10 Pass Receivers By Yards

	Yards	No.	Avg.	Long	TD
Rice, Jerry, S.F.	1502	100	15.0	t64	13
Ellard, Henry, L.A. Rams	1294	76	17.0	t50	4
Rison, Andre, Atl.	1208	82	14.7	t75	10
Clark, Gary, Wash.	1112	75	14.8	t53	8
Sharpe, Sterling, G.B.	1105	67	16.5	t76	6
Anderson, Willie, L.A. Rams	1097	51	21.5	t55	4
Jeffires, Haywood, Hou.	1048	74	14.2	t87	8
Paige, Stephone, K.C.	1021	65	15.7	t86	5
Hill, Drew, Hou.	1019	74	13.8	57	5
Carter, Anthony, Minn.	1008	70	14.4	t56	8

AFC Pass Receiving—Individual

	No.	Yards	Avg.	Long	TD
Jeffires, Haywood, Hou.	74	1048	14.2	t87	8
Hill, Drew, Hou.	74	1019	13.8	57	5
Williams, John L., Sea.	73	699	9.6	60	0
Givins, Ernest, Hou.	72	979	13.6	t80	9
Reed, Andre, Buff.	71	945	13.3	t56	8
Bentley, Albert, Ind.	71	664	9.4	73	2
Duncan, Curtis, Hou.	66	785	11.9	t37	1
Paige, Stephone, K.C.	65	1021	15.7	t86	5
Miller, Anthony, S.D.	63	933	14.8	t31	7
Brooks, Bill, Ind.	62	823	13.3	75	5
Slaughter, Webster, Clev.	59	847	14.4	50	4
Jackson, Mark, Den.	57	926	16.2	66	4
Toon, Al, N.Y. Jets	57	757	13.3	t46	6
Metcalf, Eric, Clev.	57	452	7.9	35	1
Hester, Jessie, Ind.	54	924	17.1	t64	6
Fryar, Irving, N.E.	54	856	15.9	56	4
Johnson, Vance, Den.	54	747	13.8	49	3
Fernandez, Mervyn, L.A. Raiders	52	839	16.1	t66	5
Duper, Mark, Mia.	52	810	15.6	t69	5
Kane, Tommy, Sea.	52	776	14.9	t63	4
Cook, Marv, N.E.	51	455	8.9	t35	5
Gault, Willie, L.A. Raiders	50	985	19.7	t68	3
Lipps, Louis, Pitt.	50	682	13.6	37	3
Thomas, Thurman, Buff.	49	532	10.9	63	2
Blades, Brian, Sea.	49	525	10.7	24	3
Harmon, Ronnie, S.D.	46	511	11.1	t36	2
Langhorne, Reggie, Clev.	45	585	13.0	39	2
Brennan, Brian, Clev.	45	568	12.6	28	2
Brown, Eddie, Cin.	44	706	16.0	t50	9
Moore, Rob, N.Y. Jets	44	692	15.7	t69	6
Jensen, Jim, Mia.	44	365	8.3	18	1
McGee, Tim, Cin.	43	737	17.1	52	1
Mack, Kevin, Clev.	42	360	8.6	30	2
Thomas, Robb, K.C.	41	545	13.3	t47	4
Harry, Emile, K.C.	41	519	12.7	60	2
Holman, Rodney, Cin.	40	596	14.9	53	5
McNair, Todd, K.C.	40	507	12.7	65	2
Hoge, Merril, Pitt.	40	342	8.6	27	3
Boyer, Mark, N.Y. Jets	40	334	8.4	25	1
White, Lorenzo, Hou.	39	368	9.4	29	4
Lofton, James, Buff.	35	712	20.3	71	4
Paige, Tony, Mia.	35	247	7.1	t17	4
Dykes, Hart Lee, N.E.	34	549	16.1	t35	2
McKeller, Keith, Buff.	34	464	13.6	43	5
Green, Eric, Pitt.	34	387	11.4	46	7
Horton, Ethan, L.A. Raiders	33	404	12.2	36	3
Clayton, Mark, Mia.	32	406	12.7	43	3
Mularkey, Mike, Pitt.	32	365	11.4	28	3
Edmunds, Ferrell, Mia.	31	446	14.4	35	1
Jones, Tony, Hou.	30	409	13.6	47	6
Stradford, Troy, Mia.	30	257	8.6	23	0
Martin, Tony, Mia.	29	388	13.4	45	2
McEwen, Craig, S.D.	29	325	11.2	32	3
Kay, Clarence, Den.	29	282	9.7	22	0
Bratton, Mel, Den.	29	276	9.5	63	1
Young, Mike, Den.	28	385	13.8	42	4
Stephens, John, N.E.	28	196	7.0	43	1
Chadwick, Jeff, Sea.	27	478	17.7	t54	4
Brooks, James, Cin.	26	269	10.3	35	4
Sewell, Steve, Den.	26	268	10.3	36	0
Hill, Derek, Pitt.	25	391	15.6	66	0
Humphrey, Bobby, Den.	24	152	6.3	26	0
Morgan, Stanley, Ind.	23	364	15.8	t42	5
Newsome, Ozzie, Clev.	23	240	10.4	38	2
Walker, Derrick, S.D.	23	240	10.4	23	1
Skansi, Paul, Sea.	22	257	11.7	t25	2
McMurtry, Greg, N.E.	22	240	10.9	26	0
Jones, Cedric, N.E.	21	301	14.3	26	0
Smith, Don, Buff.	21	225	10.7	39	0
Thomas, Blair, N.Y. Jets	20	204	10.2	55	1

	No.	Yards	Avg.	Long	TD
Woods, Ickey, Cin.	20	162	8.1	22	0
Stone, Dwight, Pitt.	19	332	17.5	90	1
Mathis, Terance, N.Y. Jets	19	245	12.9	23	0
Jones, Bill, K.C.	19	137	7.2	19	5
Nattiel, Ricky, Den.	18	297	16.5	t52	2
Brown, Tim, L.A. Raiders	18	265	14.7	51	3
Dickerson, Eric, Ind.	18	92	5.1	17	0
Winder, Sammy, Den.	17	145	8.5	17	0
Fenner, Derrick, Sea.	17	143	8.4	50	1
McNeil, Freeman, N.Y. Jets	16	230	14.4	59	0
Adams, George, N.E.	16	146	9.1	28	1
Butts, Marion, S.D.	16	117	7.3	26	0
Mueller, Jamie, Buff.	16	106	6.6	30	1
Birden, J.J., K.C.	15	352	23.5	t90	3
Early, Quinn, S.D.	15	238	15.9	t45	1
Allen, Marcus, L.A. Raiders	15	189	12.6	30	1
Perryman, Bob, N.E.	15	88	5.9	15	0
Burkett, Chris, N.Y. Jets	14	204	14.6	46	0
Barber, Mike, Cin.	14	196	14.0	28	1
Lewis, Nate, S.D.	14	192	13.7	40	1
Verdin, Clarence, Ind.	14	178	12.7	45	1
Cox, Arthur, S.D.	14	93	6.6	12	1
Pruitt, James, Mia.	13	235	18.1	t35	3
Harris, Leonard, Hou.	13	172	13.2	t42	3
Heller, Ron, Sea.	13	157	12.1	23	1
Banks, Fred, Mia.	13	131	10.1	23	0
Bell, Richard, Pitt.	12	137	11.4	43	1
Beach, Pat, Ind.	12	124	10.3	21	1
Green, Harold, Cin.	12	90	7.5	22	1
Beebe, Don, Buff.	11	221	20.1	49	1
Kattus, Eric, Cin.	11	145	13.2	31	2
Smith, Sammie, Mia.	11	134	12.2	t53	1
Roberts, Alfredo, K.C.	11	119	10.8	27	0
Pinkett, Allen, Hou.	11	85	7.7	38	0
McNeal, Travis, Sea.	10	143	14.3	30	0
Calloway, Chris, Pitt.	10	124	12.4	t20	1
Ford, Bernard, Hou.	10	98	9.8	24	1
Wilson, Walter, S.D.	10	87	8.7	20	0
Hoard, Leroy, Clev.	10	73	7.3	17	0
Metzelaars, Pete, Buff.	10	60	6.0	12	1
Hayes, Jonathan, K.C.	9	83	9.2	21	1
Davis, Kenneth, Buff.	9	78	8.7	16	1
Riggs, Jim, Cin.	8	79	9.9	21	0
Sievers, Eric, N.E.	8	77	9.6	25	0
Baxter, Brad, N.Y. Jets	8	73	9.1	22	0
Hector, Johnny, N.Y. Jets	8	72	9.0	25	0
Worley, Tim, Pitt.	8	70	8.8	27	0
Mobley, Orson, Den.	8	41	5.1	9	0
Bernstine, Rod, S.D.	8	40	5.0	11	0
Sharpe, Shannon, Den.	7	99	14.1	33	1
Mandley, Pete, K.C.	7	97	13.9	24	0
Gainer, Derrick, Clev.	7	85	12.1	20	0
Logan, Marc, Mia.	7	54	7.7	12	0
Smith, Kendal, Cin.	7	45	6.4	11	0
Joines, Vernon, Clev.	6	86	14.3	24	0
Jackson, Bo, L.A. Raiders	6	68	11.3	18	0
Mowatt, Zeke, N.E.	6	67	11.2	16	0
Dressel, Chris, N.Y. Jets	6	66	11.0	21	0
Schwedes, Scott, Mia.	6	66	11.0	19	1
Allen, Marvin, N.E.	6	48	8.0	19	0
Timpson, Michael, N.E.	5	91	18.2	42	0
Dawkins, Dale, N.Y. Jets	5	68	13.6	31	0
McNeil, Gerald, Hou.	5	63	12.6	16	0
Wellsandt, Doug, N.Y. Jets	5	57	11.4	20	0
Williams, Warren, Pitt.	5	42	8.4	13	1
Johnson, Anthony, Ind.	5	32	6.4	t15	2
Clark, Ken, Ind.	5	23	4.6	11	0
Martin, Sammy, N.E.	4	65	16.3	t19	1
Galbraith, Scott, Clev.	4	62	15.5	28	0
Townsell, JoJo, N.Y. Jets	4	57	14.3	18	0
Porter, Kerry, Den.	4	44	11.0	16	0
Simmons, Stacy, Ind.	4	33	8.3	12	0
Smith, Steve, L.A. Raiders	4	30	7.5	t17	3
Nelson, Darrin, S.D.	4	29	7.3	10	0
Word, Barry, K.C.	4	28	7.0	10	0
Jennings, Stanford, Cin.	4	23	5.8	13	0
Limbrick, Garrett, Mia.	4	23	5.8	9	0
Okoye, Christian, K.C.	4	23	5.8	8	0
Dyal, Mike, L.A. Raiders	3	51	17.0	29	0
Brown, Andre, Mia.	3	49	16.3	24	0
James, Lynn, Cin.	3	36	12.0	16	0
Taylor, Craig, Cin.	3	22	7.3	20	1
Verhulst, Chris, Den.	3	13	4.3	6	0
Rolle, Butch, Buff.	3	6	2.0	t3	3
Ball, Eric, Cin.	2	46	23.0	t48	1
Tasker, Steve, Buff.	2	44	22.0	t24	2
Talley, John, Clev.	2	28	14.0	19	0
Caravello, Joe, S.D.	2	21	10.5	t17	1
Overton, Don, N.E.	2	19	9.5	15	0
Whitaker, Danta, K.C.	2	17	8.5	16	1
Edwards, Al, Buff.	2	11	5.5	6	0
Tatupu, Mosi, N.E.	2	10	5.0	6	0
Graddy, Sam, L.A. Raiders	1	47	47.0	t47	1
Prior, Mike, Ind.	1	40	40.0	40	0
Jones, James, Sea.	1	22	22.0	22	0
Kauric, Jerry, Clev.	1	21	21.0	21	0
O'Shea, Terry, Pitt.	1	13	13.0	13	0
Hendrickson, Steve, S.D.	1	12	12.0	12	0
Bell, Greg, L.A. Raiders	1	7	7.0	7	0
Jones, Fred, K.C.	1	5	5.0	5	0
Saxon, James, K.C.	1	5	5.0	5	0
Foster, Barry, Pitt.	1	2	2.0	2	0
Plummer, Gary, S.D.	1	2	2.0	t2	1
Lanier, Ken, Den.	1	-4	-4.0	-4	0
Krieg, Dave, Sea.	1	-6	-6.0	-6	0

t indicates touchdown.
Leader based on most passes caught.

NFC Pass Receiving—Individual

	No.	Yards	Avg.	Long	TD
Rice, Jerry, S.F.	100	1502	15.0	t64	13
Rison, Andre, Atl.	82	1208	14.7	t75	10
Byars, Keith, Phil.	81	819	10.1	54	3
Ellard, Henry, L.A. Rams	76	1294	17.0	t50	4
Clark, Gary, Wash.	75	1112	14.8	t53	8
Carter, Anthony, Minn.	70	1008	14.4	t56	8
Monk, Art, Wash.	68	770	11.3	44	5
Sharpe, Sterling, G.B.	67	1105	16.5	t76	6
Martin, Kelvin, Dall.	64	732	11.4	45	0
Johnson, Richard, Det.	64	727	11.4	t44	6
Martin, Eric, N.O.	63	912	14.5	58	5
Novacek, Jay, Dall.	59	657	11.1	41	4
Proehl, Ricky, Phx.	56	802	14.3	t45	4
Jones, Brent, S.F.	56	747	13.3	t67	5
Sanders, Ricky, Wash.	56	727	13.0	38	3
Green, Roy, Phx.	53	797	15.0	54	4
Clark, Robert, Det.	52	914	17.6	57	8
Anderson, Willie, L.A. Rams	51	1097	21.5	t55	4
Jones, Hassan, Minn.	51	810	15.9	t75	7
Jackson, Keith, Phil.	50	670	13.4	t37	6
Carrier, Mark, T.B.	49	813	16.6	t68	4
Taylor, John, S.F.	49	748	15.3	t78	7
Holohan, Pete, L.A. Rams	49	475	9.7	28	2
Rathman, Tom, S.F.	48	327	6.8	28	0
Muster, Brad, Chi.	47	452	9.6	48	0
McGee, Buford, L.A. Rams	47	388	8.3	25	4
Jordan, Steve, Minn.	45	636	14.1	38	3
Kemp, Perry, G.B.	44	527	12.0	29	2
Jones, Ernie, Phx.	43	724	16.8	t68	4
Hill, Bruce, T.B.	42	641	15.3	t48	5
Anderson, Neal, Chi.	42	484	11.5	t50	3
Davis, Wendell, Chi.	39	572	14.7	51	3
Meggett, David, N.Y. Giants	39	410	10.5	38	1
Cobb, Reggie, T.B.	39	299	7.7	17	0
Anderson, Gary, T.B.	38	464	12.2	74	2
Dixon, Floyd, Atl.	38	399	10.5	34	4
Williams, Calvin, Phil.	37	602	16.3	t45	9
Barnett, Fred, Phil.	36	721	20.0	t95	8
Sanders, Barry, Det.	36	480	13.3	t47	3
Perriman, Brett, N.O.	36	382	10.6	29	2
Walker, Herschel, Minn.	35	315	9.0	32	4
Collins, Shawn, Atl.	34	503	14.8	61	2
Query, Jeff, G.B.	34	458	13.5	t47	2
Bavaro, Mark, N.Y. Giants	33	393	11.9	61	5
Weathers, Clarence, G.B.	33	390	11.8	29	1
Hampton, Rodney, N.Y. Giants	32	274	8.6	t27	2
Hall, Ron, T.B.	31	464	15.0	t54	2
Haynes, Michael, Atl.	31	445	14.4	60	0
Morris, Ron, Chi.	31	437	14.1	t67	3
Fontenot, Herman, G.B.	31	293	9.5	59	1
Byner, Earnest, Wash.	31	279	9.0	19	1
Matthews, Aubrey, Det.	30	349	11.6	52	1
Agee, Tommie, Dall.	30	272	9.1	30	1
Gary, Cleveland, L.A. Rams	30	150	5.0	t22	1
Carter, Cris, Minn.	27	413	15.3	t78	3
West, Ed, G.B.	27	356	13.2	50	5
Baker, Stephen, N.Y. Giants	26	541	20.8	t80	4
Ingram, Mark, N.Y. Giants	26	499	19.2	t57	5
Bryant, Kelvin, Wash.	26	248	9.5	37	1
Johnson, Johnny, Phx.	25	241	9.6	35	0
Carter, Dexter, S.F.	25	217	8.7	26	0
Craig, Roger, S.F.	25	201	8.0	31	0
Smith, Emmitt, Dall.	24	228	9.5	57	0
Woodside, Keith, G.B.	24	184	7.7	25	0
Broussard, Steve, Atl.	24	160	6.7	18	0

	No.	Yards	Avg.	Long	TD
Gentry, Dennis, Chi.	23	320	13.9	t80	2
Sherman, Heath, Phil.	23	167	7.3	26	3
Turner, Floyd, N.O.	21	396	18.9	t68	4
Irvin, Michael, Dall.	20	413	20.7	t61	5
Greer, Terry, Det.	20	332	16.6	t68	3
Thornton, James, Chi.	19	254	13.4	32	1
Campbell, Jeff, Det.	19	236	12.4	51	2
Thomas, George, Atl.	18	383	21.3	72	1
Smith, J.T., Phx.	18	225	12.5	t45	2
Fenerty, Gill, N.O.	18	209	11.6	28	0
Shuler, Mickey, Phil.	18	190	10.6	25	0
Milling, James, Atl.	18	161	8.9	24	1
Anderson, Ottis, N.Y. Giants	18	139	7.7	18	0
Reeves, Walter, Phx.	18	126	7.0	16	0
Heyward, Craig, N.O.	18	121	6.7	12	0
Cox, Aaron, L.A. Rams	17	266	15.6	32	0
Sherrard, Mike, S.F.	17	264	15.5	43	2
Brenner, Hoby, N.O.	17	213	12.5	t31	2
Toney, Anthony, Phil.	17	133	7.8	32	3
Fenney, Rick, Minn.	17	112	6.6	17	0
Johnson, Jimmie, Wash.	15	218	14.5	35	2
Delpino, Robert, L.A. Rams	15	172	11.5	t42	4
Warren, Don, Wash.	15	123	8.2	18	1
McKinnon, Dennis, Dall.	14	172	12.3	t28	1
Carthon, Maurice, N.Y. Giants	14	151	10.8	63	0
Johnston, Daryl, Dall.	14	148	10.6	26	1
Hilliard, Dalton, N.O.	14	125	8.9	20	1
Awalt, Robert, Dall.	13	133	10.2	25	0
Flagler, Terrence, Phx.	13	130	10.0	21	1
Rozier, Mike, Hou.-Atl.	13	105	8.1	24	0
Jones, Keith, Atl.	13	103	7.9	16	0
Haddix, Michael, G.B.	13	94	7.2	28	2
Anderson, Alfred, Minn.	13	80	6.2	17	0
Wilkins, Gary, Atl.	12	175	14.6	37	2
Farr, Mike, Det.	12	170	14.2	44	0
Harris, Jackie, G.B.	12	157	13.1	26	0
Mayes, Rueben, N.O.	12	121	10.1	66	0
Johnson, Damone, L.A. Rams	12	66	5.5	11	3
Manuel, Lionel, N.Y. Giants	11	169	15.4	19	0
Boso, Cap, Chi.	11	135	12.3	25	1
Tice, John, N.O.	11	113	10.3	19	0
Wright, Alexander, Dall.	11	104	9.5	20	0
Harvey, John, T.B.	11	86	7.8	18	1
Sydney, Harry, S.F.	10	116	11.6	t23	1
Johnson, Tracy, Atl.	10	79	7.9	16	1
Quick, Mike, Phil.	9	135	15.0	39	1
Williams, Jamie, S.F.	9	54	6.0	9	0
Pillow, Frank, T.B.	8	118	14.8	23	0
Phillips, Jason, Det.	8	112	14.0	29	0
Cross, Howard, N.Y. Giants	8	106	13.3	21	0
Perkins, Bruce, T.B.	8	85	10.6	34	2
Scales, Greg, N.O.	8	64	8.0	20	1
Carter, Pat, L.A. Rams	8	58	7.3	16	0
Tillman, Lewis, N.Y. Giants	8	18	2.3	16	0
Drewrey, Willie, T.B.	7	182	26.0	t89	1
Wilson, Mike, S.F.	7	89	12.7	34	0
Wilson, Charles, G.B.	7	84	12.0	18	0
Kozlowski, Glen, Chi.	7	83	11.9	32	0
Riggs, Gerald, Wash.	7	60	8.6	18	0
Sikahema, Vai, Phx.	7	51	7.3	13	0
Turner, Odessa, N.Y. Giants	6	69	11.5	18	0
Peebles, Danny, T.B.	6	50	8.3	18	1
Anderson, Jesse, T.B.	5	77	15.4	52	0
Lewis, Ronald, S.F.	5	44	8.8	14	0
Drummond, Robert, Phil.	5	39	7.8	29	0
Walls, Wesley, S.F.	5	27	5.4	11	0
Kyles, Troy, N.Y. Giants	4	77	19.3	35	0
Alphin, Gerald, N.O.	4	57	14.3	17	0
Rice, Allen, Minn.	4	46	11.5	24	0
Bailey, Stacey, Atl.	4	44	11.0	13	0
Henderson, Keith, S.F.	4	35	8.8	9	0
Workman, Vince, G.B.	4	30	7.5	9	1
Green, Mark, Chi.	4	26	6.5	t10	1
Howard, Joe, Wash.	3	36	12.0	17	0
Hill, Lonzell, N.O.	3	35	11.7	13	0
Faison, Derrick, L.A. Rams	3	27	9.0	12	1
Mrosko, Bob, N.Y. Giants	3	27	9.0	16	1
Fullwood, Brent, G.B.	3	17	5.7	10	0
Highsmith, Alonzo, Dall.	3	13	4.3	7	0
Thompson, Darrell, G.B.	3	1	0.3	1	0
Waddle, Tom, Chi.	2	32	16.0	23	0
Dixon, James, Dall.	2	26	13.0	21	0
Green, Gaston, L.A. Rams	2	23	11.5	t16	1
Sanders, Thomas, Phil.	2	20	10.0	12	0
Smith, Quintin, Chi.	2	20	10.0	12	0
Stanley, Walter, Wash.	2	15	7.5	12	0
Robinson, Stacy, N.Y. Giants	2	13	6.5	7	0
Thompson, Anthony, Phx.	2	11	5.5	6	0
Jorden, Tim, Phx.	2	10	5.0	6	0
Mitchell, Brian, Wash.	2	5	2.5	5	0
Jackson, Kenny, Phil.	1	43	43.0	43	0
Hargrove, Marvin, Phil.	1	34	34.0	t34	1
Hobbs, Stevie, Wash.	1	18	18.0	t18	1
Dozier, D.J., Minn.	1	12	12.0	12	0
Rouson, Lee, N.Y. Giants	1	12	12.0	12	0
Hilgenberg, Joel, N.O.	1	9	9.0	9	0
LeBel, Harper, Phil.	1	9	9.0	9	0
Lewis, Leo, Minn.	1	9	9.0	9	0
Wilder, James, Det.	1	8	8.0	t8	1
Coley, James, Chi.	1	7	7.0	7	0
Lang, Gene, Atl.	1	7	7.0	7	0
Tomczak, Mike, Chi.	1	5	5.0	5	0
Clark, Jessie, Minn.	1	4	4.0	4	0
Testaverde, Vinny, T.B.	1	3	3.0	3	0
Sharpe, Luis, Phx.	1	1	1.0	t1	1

t indicates touchdown.
Leader based on most passes caught.

Interceptions

Individual Champions
NFC:10—Mark Carrier, Chicago
AFC: 8—Richard Johnson, Houston
Most Interceptions, Game
NFC: 3—Mark Carrier, Chicago at Washington, December 9 (3 yards)
AFC: 2—By 14 players
Yards
NFC: 231—Wayne Haddix, Tampa Bay
AFC: 110—Dwayne Woodruff, Pittsburgh
Longest
NFC: 82—Deion Sanders, Atlanta vs. Houston, September 9 - TD
AFC: 73—Ronnie Lippett, New England vs. Miami, September 9
Touchdowns
NFC: 3—Wayne Haddix, Tampa Bay
AFC: 1—By 12 players
Team Leaders, Interceptions
AFC: BUFFALO: 3, Kirby Jackson; CINCINNATI; 4, Barney Bussey, David Fulcher; CLEVELAND: 3, Felix Wright; DENVER: 2, Steve Atwater, Wymon Henderson, Alton Montgomery; HOUSTON: 8, Richard Johnson; INDIANAPOLIS: 3, Mike Prior; KANSAS CITY: 5, Kevin Ross; L.A. RAIDERS: 3, Eddie Anderson, Mike Harden, Terry McDaniel; MIAMI: 5, Louis Oliver, Jarvis Williams; NEW ENGLAND: 4, Maurice Hurst, Ronnie Lippett, Fred Marion; N.Y. JETS: 5, Erik McMillan; PITTSBURGH: 5, Rod Woodson; SAN DIEGO: 7, Gill Byrd; SEATTLE: 3, Dwayne Harper, Eugene Robinson.
NFC: ATLANTA: 3, Bobby Butler, Scott Case, Charles Dimry, Brian Jordan, Deion Sanders; CHICAGO: 10, Mark Carrier; DALLAS: 3, Issiac Holt, James Washington; DETROIT: 5 ,William White; GREEN BAY: 3, LeRoy Butler, Jerry Holmes, Mark Murphy; L.A. RAMS: 4, Bobby Humphery, Vince Newsome; MINNESOTA: 7, Joey Browner; NEW ORLEANS: 2, Gene Atkins, Toi Cook, Brett Maxie, Bennie Thompson; N.Y. GIANTS: 6, Everson Walls; PHILADELPHIA: 5, Wes Hopkins; PHOENIX: 4, Tim McDonald; SAN FRANCISCO: 7, Dave Waymer; TAMPA BAY: 7, Wayne Haddix ; WASHINGTON: 7, Martin Mayhew

Team Champions
NFC: 31—Chicago
AFC: 24—Pittsburgh

AFC Interceptions—Team

	No.	Yards	Avg.	Long	TD
Pittsburgh	24	385	16.0	59	1
Houston	21	295	14.0	47	1
Kansas City	20	250	12.5	40	1
Miami	19	288	15.2	t42	2
San Diego	19	188	9.9	67	0
N.Y. Jets	18	205	11.4	39	0
Buffalo	18	151	8.4	t60	2
Cincinnati	15	146	9.7	29	1
New England	14	194	13.9	73	0
Cleveland	13	212	16.3	t64	1
L.A. Raiders	13	102	7.8	31	1
Seattle	12	182	15.2	47	0
Denver	10	190	19.0	t49	1
Indianapolis	9	173	19.2	40	1
AFC Total	225	2961	—	73	12
AFC Average	16.1	211.5	13.2	—	.09

NFC Interceptions—Team

	No.	Yards	Avg.	Long	TD
Chicago	31	268	8.6	t45	1
Tampa Bay	25	487	19.5	t65	3
N.Y. Giants	23	116	5.0	40	2

Minnesota	22	358	16.3	73	2
Washington	21	271	12.9	61	2
Philadelphia	19	271	14.3	42	3
Detroit	17	273	16.1	48	1
Atlanta	17	237	13.9	t82	3
San Francisco	17	171	10.1	28	0
Phoenix	16	274	17.1	t47	2
Green Bay	16	154	9.6	32	1
L.A. Rams	12	105	8.8	t44	1
Dallas	11	126	11.5	t64	1
New Orleans	8	158	19.8	t50	1
NFC Total	255	3269	——	t82	23
NFC Average	18.2	233.5	12.8	—	1.6
League Total	480	6230	——	t82	35
League Average	17.1	222.5	13.0	—	1.3

NFL Top 10 Interceptors

	No.	Yards	Avg.	Long	TD
Carrier, Mark, Chi.	10	39	3.9	14	0
Johnson, Richard, Hou.	8	100	12.5	35	1
Haddix, Wayne, T.B.	7	231	33.0	t65	3
Browner, Joey, Minn.	7	103	14.7	31	1
Waymer, Dave, S.F.	7	64	9.1	24	0
Byrd, Gill, S.D.	7	63	9.0	24	0
Mayhew, Martin, Wash.	7	20	2.9	15	0
Walls, Everson, N.Y. Giants	6	80	13.3	40	1
Stinson, Lemuel, Chi.	6	66	11.0	30	0
White, William, Det.	5	120	24.0	48	1
Ross, Kevin, K.C.	5	97	19.4	40	0
McMillan, Erik, N.Y. Jets	5	92	18.4	25	0
Oliver, Louis, Mia.	5	87	17.4	35	0
Williams, Jarvis, Mia.	5	82	16.4	t42	1
Woodson, Rod, Pitt.	5	67	13.4	34	0
Hopkins, Wes, Phil.	5	45	9.0	21	0
Hamilton, Harry, T.B.	5	39	7.8	27	0
Jackson, Greg, N.Y. Giants	5	8	1.6	5	0

AFC Interceptions—Individual

	No.	Yards	Avg.	Long	TD
Johnson, Richard, Hou.	8	100	12.5	35	1
Byrd, Gill, S.D.	7	63	9.0	24	0
Ross, Kevin, K.C.	5	97	19.4	40	0
McMillan, Erik, N.Y. Jets	5	92	18.4	25	0
Oliver, Louis, Mia.	5	87	17.4	35	0
Williams, Jarvis, Mia.	5	82	16.4	t42	1
Woodson, Rod, Pitt.	5	67	13.4	34	0
Lippett, Ronnie, N.E.	4	94	23.5	73	0
Griffin, Larry, Pitt.	4	75	18.8	36	0
Kinard, Terry, Hou.	4	75	18.8	47	0
Hurst, Maurice, N.E.	4	61	15.3	36	0
Dishman, Cris, Hou.	4	50	12.5	42	0
McKyer, Tim, Mia.	4	40	10.0	21	0
Bussey, Barney, Cin.	4	37	9.3	18	0
Fulcher, David, Cin.	4	20	5.0	18	0
Marion, Fred, N.E.	4	17	4.3	16	0
Woodruff, Dwayne, Pitt.	3	110	36.7	59	0
Robinson, Eugene, Sea.	3	89	29.7	39	0
Harper, Dwayne, Sea.	3	69	23.0	47	0
Prior, Mike, Ind.	3	66	22.0	36	0
Wright, Felix, Clev.	3	56	18.7	36	0
Anderson, Eddie, L.A. Raiders	3	49	16.3	31	0
Clifton, Kyle, N.Y. Jets	3	49	16.3	39	0
Cherry, Deron, K.C.	3	40	13.3	21	0
Billups, Lewis, Cin.	3	39	13.0	29	0
Petry, Stan, K.C.	3	33	11.0	t33	1
Donaldson, Jeff, K.C.	3	28	9.3	14	0
Washington, Brian, N.Y. Jets	3	22	7.3	13	0
McDaniel, Terry, L.A. Raiders	3	20	6.7	15	0
Harden, Mike, L.A. Raiders	3	19	6.3	15	0
Jackson, Kirby, Buff.	3	16	5.3	14	0
Everett, Thomas, Pitt.	3	2	0.7	2	0
Henderson, Wymon, Den.	2	71	35.5	t49	1
Johnson, David, Pitt.	2	60	30.0	34	1
Talley, Darryl, Buff.	2	60	30.0	t60	1
Taylor, Keith, Ind.	2	51	25.5	40	0
Blaylock, Anthony, Clev.	2	45	22.5	45	0
Curtis, Travis, N.Y. Jets	2	45	22.5	23	0
Montgomery, Alton, Den.	2	43	21.5	24	0
Smith, Leonard, Buff.	2	39	19.5	t39	1
Atwater, Steve, Den.	2	32	16.0	27	0
Glenn, Kerry, Mia.	2	31	15.5	t31	1
Wyman, David, Sea.	2	24	12.0	22	0
Hagy, John, Buff.	2	23	11.5	23	0
Rembert, Johnny, N.E.	2	22	11.0	11	0
Lewis, Albert, K.C.	2	15	7.5	15	0
Seale, Sam, S.D.	2	14	7.0	14	0
Braggs, Stephen, Clev.	2	13	6.5	11	0
Smith, Billy Ray, S.D.	2	12	6.0	12	0
McDowell, Bubba, Hou.	2	11	5.5	11	0
Frank, Donald, S.D.	2	8	4.0	4	0
Hasty, James, N.Y. Jets	2	0	0.0	0	0
Kelso, Mark, Buff.	2	0	0.0	0	0
Minnifield, Frank, Clev.	2	0	0.0	0	0
Williams, James, Buff.	2	0	0.0	0	0
Stargell, Tony, N.Y. Jets	2	-3	-1.5	0	0
Rolling, Henry, S.D.	1	67	67.0	67	0
Johnson, Mike, Clev.	1	64	64.0	t64	1
Little, David, Pitt.	1	35	35.0	35	0
Meads, Johnny, Hou.	1	32	32.0	32	0
Offerdahl, John, Mia.	1	28	28.0	28	0
Allen, Patrick, Hou.	1	27	27.0	27	0
Grant, Alan, Ind.	1	25	25.0	t25	1
White, Leon, Cin.	1	21	21.0	21	0
Hinkle, Bryan, Pitt.	1	19	19.0	19	0
Lyles, Lester, S.D.	1	19	19.0	19	0
Francis, James, Cin.	1	17	17.0	t17	1
Gash, Thane, Clev.	1	16	16.0	16	0
Plummer, Bruce, Den.	1	16	16.0	16	0
Hobley, Liffort, Mia.	1	15	15.0	15	0
Waiters, Van, Clev.	1	15	15.0	15	0
Burruss, Lloyd, K.C.	1	14	14.0	14	0
Bentley, Ray, Buff.	1	13	13.0	13	0
Porter, Kevin, K.C.	1	13	13.0	13	0
Smith, Dennis, Den.	1	13	13.0	13	0
Herrod, Jeff, Ind.	1	12	12.0	12	0
Zander, Carl, Cin.	1	12	12.0	12	0
Braxton, Tyrone, Den.	1	10	10.0	10	0
Goode, Chris, Ind.	1	10	10.0	10	0
Pearson, J.C., K.C.	1	10	10.0	10	0
Bickett, Duane, Ind.	1	9	9.0	9	0
Lloyd, Greg, Pitt.	1	9	9.0	9	0
Ellison, Riki, L.A. Raiders	1	7	7.0	7	0
Fuller, Joe, S.D.	1	5	5.0	5	0
Kumerow, Eric, Mia.	1	5	5.0	5	0
Lang, Le-Lo, Den.	1	5	5.0	5	0
Robinson, Jerry, L.A. Raiders	1	5	5.0	t5	1
Willis, Keith, Pitt.	1	5	5.0	5	0
Grayson, Dave, Clev.	1	3	3.0	3	0
Jones, Aaron, Pitt.	1	3	3.0	3	0
Washington, Lionel, L.A. Raiders	1	2	2.0	2	0
Bayless, Martin, S.D.	1	0	0.0	0	0
Bolcar, Ned, Sea.	1	0	0.0	0	0
Elder, Donnie, S.D.	1	0	0.0	0	0
Glenn, Vencie, S.D.	1	0	0.0	0	0
Hall, Delton, Pitt.	1	0	0.0	0	0
Hicks, Cliff, Buff.	1	0	0.0	0	0
Hunter, Patrick, Sea.	1	0	0.0	0	0
Jefferson, James, Sea.	1	0	0.0	0	0
Jenkins, Mel, Sea.	1	0	0.0	0	0
Knight, Leander, Hou.	1	0	0.0	0	0
Lake, Carnell, Pitt.	1	0	0.0	0	0
Mayes, Michael, N.Y. Jets	1	0	0.0	0	0
Odomes, Nate, Buff.	1	0	0.0	0	0
Pool, David, Buff.	1	0	0.0	0	0
Price, Mitchell, Cin.	1	0	0.0	0	0
Seals, Leon, Buff.	1	0	0.0	0	0
Snow, Percy, K.C.	1	0	0.0	0	0
Townsend, Greg, L.A. Raiders	1	0	0.0	0	0

t indicates touchdown.
Leader based on most interceptions.

NFC Interceptions—Individual

	No.	Yards	Avg.	Long	TD
Carrier, Mark, Chi.	10	39	3.9	14	0
Haddix, Wayne, T.B.	7	231	33.0	t65	3
Browner, Joey, Minn.	7	103	14.7	31	1
Waymer, Dave, S.F.	7	64	9.1	24	0
Mayhew, Martin, Wash.	7	20	2.9	15	0
Walls, Everson, N.Y. Giants	6	80	13.3	40	1
Stinson, Lemuel, Chi.	6	66	11.0	30	0
White, William, Det.	5	120	24.0	48	1
Hopkins, Wes, Phil.	5	45	9.0	21	0
Hamilton, Harry, T.B.	5	39	7.8	27	0
Jackson, Greg, N.Y. Giants	5	8	1.6	5	0
Robinson, Mark, T.B.	4	81	20.3	27	0
McDonald, Tim, Phx.	4	63	15.8	38	0
Humphery, Bobby, L.A. Rams	4	52	13.0	t44	1
Newsome, Vince, L.A. Rams	4	47	11.8	22	0
Green, Darrell, Wash.	4	20	5.0	t18	1
Sanders, Deion, Atl.	3	153	51.0	t82	2
Merriweather, Mike, Minn.	3	108	36.0	73	0

	No.	Yards	Avg.	Long	TD
Frizzell, William, Phil.	3	91	30.3	37	1
Bowles, Todd, Wash.	3	74	24.7	43	0
Holt, Issiac, Dall.	3	72	24.0	t64	1
Reynolds, Ricky, T.B.	3	70	23.3	46	0
Taylor, Jay, Phx.	3	50	16.7	34	0
Butler, LeRoy, G.B.	3	42	14.0	28	0
Holmes, Jerry, G.B.	3	39	13.0	24	0
Case, Scott, Atl.	3	38	12.7	t36	1
Allen, Eric, Phil.	3	37	12.3	t35	1
Griffin, Don, S.F.	3	32	10.7	23	0
Everett, Eric, T.B.	3	28	9.3	23	0
Lott, Ronnie, S.F.	3	26	8.7	15	0
Washington, James, Dall.	3	24	8.0	13	0
Dent, Richard, Chi.	3	21	7.0	15	0
McMillian, Audrey, Minn.	3	20	6.7	20	0
Woolford, Donnell, Chi.	3	18	6.0	9	0
Crockett, Ray, Det.	3	17	5.7	9	0
Dimry, Charles, Atl.	3	16	5.3	13	0
Jordan, Brian, Atl.	3	14	4.7	14	0
Reasons, Gary, N.Y. Giants	3	13	4.3	10	0
Murphy, Mark, G.B.	3	6	2.0	4	0
Williams, Perry, N.Y. Giants	3	4	1.3	4	0
Smith, Ben, Phil.	3	1	0.3	1	0
Butler, Bobby, Atl.	3	0	0.0	0	0
Walton, Alvin, Wash.	2	118	59.0	61	1
Maxie, Brett, N.O.	2	88	44.0	t50	1
Cook, Toi, N.O.	2	55	27.5	50	0
Mack, Cedric, Phx.	2	53	26.5	39	0
Paul, Markus, Chi.	2	49	24.5	26	0
Edwards, Brad, Wash.	2	33	16.5	33	0
Lee, Carl, Minn.	2	29	14.5	25	0
Stephen, Scott, G.B.	2	26	13.0	26	0
Blades, Bennie, Det.	2	25	12.5	21	0
Rutland, Reggie, Minn.	2	21	10.5	16	0
Mitchell, Roland, Atl.	2	16	8.0	16	0
Atkins, Gene, N.O.	2	15	7.5	15	0
Rivera, Ron, Chi.	2	13	6.5	13	0
Morrissey, Jim, Chi.	2	12	6.0	12	0
Brim, Michael, Minn.	2	11	5.5	11	0
Young, Lonnie, Phx.	2	8	4.0	5	0
Rice, Rodney, T.B.	2	7	3.5	4	0
Gayle, Shaun, Chi.	2	5	2.5	5	0
Jax, Garth, Phx.	2	5	2.5	4	0
Collins, Mark, N.Y. Giants	2	0	0.0	0	0
Newman, Anthony, L.A. Rams	2	0	0.0	0	0
Thompson, Bennie, N.O.	2	0	0.0	0	0
Turner, Marcus, Phx.	1	70	70.0	t47	2
Jackson, Vestee, Chi.	1	45	45.0	t45	1
Evans, Byron, Phil.	1	43	43.0	t22	1
McNorton, Bruce, Det.	1	33	33.0	33	0
White, Reggie, Phil.	1	33	33.0	33	0
Holland, Johnny, G.B.	1	32	32.0	32	0
Moss, Winston, T.B.	1	31	31.0	31	0
Doleman, Chris, Minn.	1	30	30.0	30	0
Lewis, Kevin, S.F.	1	28	28.0	28	0
Oldham, Chris, Det.	1	28	28.0	28	0
Gant, Kenneth, Dall.	1	26	26.0	26	0
Noga, Al, Minn.	1	26	26.0	t26	1
Zordich, Mike, Phx.	1	25	25.0	25	0
Irvin, LeRoy, Det.	1	22	22.0	22	0
Welch, Herb, Det.	1	16	16.0	16	0
Davis, Eric, S.F.	1	13	13.0	13	0
Golic, Mike, Phil.	1	12	12.0	12	0
Spielman, Chris, Det.	1	12	12.0	12	0
Taylor, Lawrence, N.Y. Giants	1	11	11.0	t11	1
Fullington, Darrell, Minn.	1	10	10.0	10	0
Joyner, Seth, Phil.	1	9	9.0	9	0
Patterson, Shawn, G.B.	1	9	9.0	t9	1
Millen, Matt, S.F.	1	8	8.0	8	0
Marshall, Wilber, Wash.	1	6	6.0	6	0
Terrell, Pat, L.A. Rams	1	6	6.0	6	0
Bates, Bill, Dall.	1	4	4.0	4	0
Bell, Anthony, Phx.	1	0	0.0	0	0
Cecil, Chuck, G.B.	1	0	0.0	0	0
Cofer, Mike, Det.	1	0	0.0	0	0
Coleman, Monte, Wash.	1	0	0.0	0	0
Duerson, Dave, N.Y. Giants	1	0	0.0	0	0
Guyton, Myron, N.Y. Giants	1	0	0.0	0	0
Hendrix, Manuel, Dall.	1	0	0.0	0	0
Henley, Darryl, L.A. Rams	1	0	0.0	0	0
Hoage, Terry, Phil.	1	0	0.0	0	0
Horton, Ray, Dall.	1	0	0.0	0	0
Johnson, A.J., Wash.	1	0	0.0	0	0
Johnson, Pepper, N.Y. Giants	1	0	0.0	0	0
Jones, Victor, Det.	1	0	0.0	0	0
Lee, Mark, G.B.	1	0	0.0	0	0
Pitts, Ron, G.B.	1	0	0.0	0	0
Pollard, Darryl, S.F.	1	0	0.0	0	0
Williams, Robert, Dall.	1	0	0.0	0	0

t indicates touchdown.
Leader based on most interceptions

Punting

Average Yards Per Punt
AFC: 44.4—Mike Horan, Denver
NFC: 44.1—Sean Landeta, N.Y. Giants
Net Average Yards Per Punt
AFC: 38.9—Mike Horan, Denver
NFC: 37.4—Rich Camarillo, Phoenix
Longest
AFC: 70—Lee Johnson, Cincinnati vs. New England, September 23
Lee Johnson, Cincinnati at Cleveland, October 22
NFC: 67—Sean Landeta, N.Y. Giants vs. Minnesota, December 9
Punts
AFC: 90—Brian Hansen, New England
NFC: 79—Mike Saxon, Dallas
Punts, Game
AFC: 10—Brian Hansen, New England vs. Indianapolis, November 11 (385 yards)
NFC: 9—Barry Helton, San Francisco vs. Giants, December 3 (357 yards)
Don Bracken, Green Bay at Philadelphia, December 16 (320 yards)
Team Champions
AFC: 45.0—Houston
NFC: 44.1—N.Y. Giants

AFC Punting—Team

	Net Punts	Gross Yards	Long	Gross Avg.	TB	Blk.	Opp. Ret.	Ret. Yards	In 20	Net Avg.
Houston	34	1530	60	45.0	5	0	23	186	7	36.6
Denver	60	2612	67	43.5	7	1	22	159	14	38.5
Indianapolis	72	3084	61	42.8	3	1	42	334	24	37.4
Cincinnati	65	2739	70	42.1	9	0	36	352	12	34.0
Miami	72	3022	62	42.0	3	0	40	397	20	35.6
New England	92	3752	69	40.8	8	2	50	503	18	33.6
Seattle	67	2722	54	40.6	8	0	29	254	18	34.4
San Diego	62	2442	59	39.4	2	1	28	131	14	36.6
Buffalo	58	2281	55	39.3	4	0	31	251	12	33.6
N.Y. Jets	61	2398	58	39.3	3	0	35	269	18	33.9
Kansas City	81	3132	58	38.7	3	0	44	411	22	32.9
L.A. Raiders	62	2315	57	37.3	4	2	24	153	19	33.6
Pittsburgh	66	2454	51	37.2	5	1	16	105	18	34.1
Cleveland	78	2879	65	36.9	2	4	41	425	13	30.9
AFC Total	930	37362	70	—	66	12	461	3930	229	—
AFC Average	66.4	2668.7	—	40.2	4.7	0.9	32.9	280.7	16.4	34.5

NFC Punting—Team

	Net Punts	Gross Yards	Long	Gross Avg.	TB	Blk.	Opp. Ret.	Ret. Yards	In 20	Net Avg.
N.Y. Giants	75	3306	67	44.1	11	0	41	291	24	37.3
Dallas	79	3413	62	43.2	8	0	43	438	20	35.6
Phoenix	67	2865	63	42.8	5	0	41	258	16	37.4
New Orleans	71	2990	65	42.1	6	1	43	302	20	36.2
Minnesota	79	3299	61	41.8	8	1	44	513	19	33.2
Atlanta	70	2913	59	41.6	4	0	39	314	15	36.0
Philadelphia	74	3026	60	40.9	3	2	37	338	20	35.5
Detroit	63	2560	59	40.6	5	0	29	233	10	35.3
Tampa Bay	72	2902	62	40.3	5	0	39	352	8	34.0
Chicago	78	3073	59	39.4	7	2	39	322	22	33.5
L.A. Rams	69	2663	58	38.6	2	1	46	420	8	31.9
Washington	55	2064	53	37.5	1	1	30	205	23	33.4
Green Bay	65	2431	59	37.4	2	1	34	266	17	32.7
San Francisco	70	2537	56	36.2	8	1	30	215	15	30.9
NFC Total	987	40042	67	—	75	10	535	4467	237	—
NFC Average	70.5	2860.1	—	40.6	5.4	0.7	38.2	319.1	16.9	34.5
League Total	1917	77404	70	—	141	22	996	8397	466	—
League Avg.	68.5	2764.4	—	40.4	5.0	0.8	35.6	299.9	16.6	34.5

NFL Top 10 Punters

	Net Punts	Gross Yards	Long	Gross Avg.	Total Punts	TB	Blk.	Opp. Ret.	Ret. Yards	In 20	Net Avg.
Horan, Mike, Den.	58	2575	67	44.4	59	6	1	22	159	14	38.9
Landeta, Sean, N.Y. Giants	75	3306	67	44.1	75	11	0	41	291	24	37.3
Stark, Rohn, Ind.	71	3084	61	43.4	72	3	1	42	334	24	37.4
Saxon, Mike, Dall.	79	3413	62	43.2	79	8	0	43	438	20	35.6
Camarillo, Rich, Phx.	67	2865	63	42.8	67	5	0	41	258	16	37.4
Barnhardt, Tommy, N.O.	70	2990	65	42.7	71	6	1	43	302	20	36.2
Newsome, Harry, Minn.	78	3299	61	42.3	79	8	1	44	513	19	33.2
Johnson, Lee, Cin.	64	2705	70	42.3	64	8	0	36	352	12	34.3
Feagles, Jeff, Phil.	72	3026	60	42.0	74	3	2	37	338	20	35.5
Roby, Reggie, Mia.	72	3022	62	42.0	72	3	0	40	397	20	35.6

AFC Punting—Individual

	Net Punts	Gross Yards	Long	Gross Avg.	Total Punts	TB	Blk.	Opp. Ret.	Ret. Yards	In 20	Net Avg.
Horan, Mike, Den.	58	2575	67	44.4	59	6	1	22	159	14	38.9
Stark, Rohn, Ind.	71	3084	61	43.4	72	3	1	42	334	24	37.4
Johnson, Lee, Cin.	64	2705	70	42.3	64	8	0	36	352	12	34.3
Roby, Reggie, Mia.	72	3022	62	42.0	72	3	0	40	397	20	35.6
Hansen, Brian, N.E.	90	3752	69	41.7	92	8	2	50	503	18	33.6
Donnelly, Rick, Sea.	67	2722	54	40.6	67	8	0	29	254	18	34.4
Prokop, Joe, N.Y. Jets	59	2363	58	40.1	59	3	0	33	257	18	34.7
Kidd, John, S.D.	61	2442	59	40.0	62	2	1	28	131	14	36.6
Tuten, Rick, Buff.	53	2107	55	39.8	53	4	0	26	214	12	34.2
Wagner, Bryan, Clev.	74	2879	65	38.9	78	2	4	41	425	13	30.9
Barker, Bryan, K.C.	64	2479	56	38.7	64	1	0	38	324	16	33.4
Gossett, Jeff, L.A. Raiders	60	2315	57	38.6	62	4	2	24	153	19	33.6
Stryzinski, Dan, Pitt.	65	2454	51	37.8	66	5	1	16	105	18	34.1
Non-Qualifiers											
Montgomery, Greg, Hou.	34	1530	60	45.0	34	5	0	23	186	7	36.6
Nies, John, Buff.	5	174	39	34.8	5	0	0	5	37	0	27.4
Breech, Jim, Cin.	1	34	34	34.0	1	1	0	0	0	0	14.0
Elway, John, Den.	1	37	37	37.0	1	1	0	0	0	0	17.0
Leahy, Pat, N.Y. Jets	1	12	12	12.0	1	0	0	1	0	0	12.0
O'Brien, Ken, N.Y. Jets	1	23	23	23.0	1	0	0	1	12	0	11.0

Leader based on gross average, minimum 40 punts.

NFC Punting—Individual

	Net Punts	Gross Yards	Long	Gross Avg.	Total Punts	TB	Blk.	Opp. Ret.	Ret. Yards	In 20	Net Avg.
Landeta, Sean, N.Y. Giants	75	3306	67	44.1	75	11	0	41	291	24	37.3
Saxon, Mike, Dall.	79	3413	62	43.2	79	8	0	43	438	20	35.6
Camarillo, Rich, Phx.	67	2865	63	42.8	67	5	0	41	258	16	37.4
Barnhardt, Tommy, N.O.	70	2990	65	42.7	71	6	1	43	302	20	36.2
Newsome, Harry, Minn.	78	3299	61	42.3	79	8	1	44	513	19	33.2
Feagles, Jeff, Phil.	72	3026	60	42.0	74	3	2	37	338	20	35.5
Fulhage, Scott, Atl.	70	2913	59	41.6	70	4	0	39	314	15	36.0
Arnold, Jim, Det.	63	2560	59	40.6	63	5	0	29	233	10	35.3
Buford, Maury, Chi.	76	3073	59	40.4	78	7	2	39	322	22	33.5
Royals, Mark, T.B.	72	2902	62	40.3	72	5	0	39	352	8	34.0
Mojsiejenko, Ralf, Wash.	43	1687	53	39.2	44	0	1	25	182	17	34.2
English, Keith, L.A. Rams	68	2663	58	39.2	69	2	1	46	420	8	31.9
Bracken, Don, G.B.	64	2431	59	38.0	65	2	1	34	266	17	32.7
Helton, Barry, S.F.	69	2537	56	36.8	70	8	1	30	215	15	30.9
Non-Qualifiers											
Goodburn, Kelly, K.C.-Wash.	28	1030	58	36.8	28	3	0	11	110	12	30.7

Leader based on gross average, minimum 40 punts.

Punt Returns

Yards Per Return
AFC: 12.8—Clarence Verdin, Indianapolis
NFC: 11.1—Johnny Bailey, Chicago

Yards
NFC: 467—David Meggett, N.Y. Giants
AFC: 398—Rod Woodson, Pittsburgh

Yards, Game
AFC: 124—Clarence Verdin, Indianapolis at New England, November 11 (6 returns)
NFC: 95—Johnny Bailey, Chicago vs. Kansas City, December 29 (1 return)

Longest
AFC: 98—Terance Mathis, N.Y. Jets vs. Dallas, November 4 - TD
NFC: 95—Johnny Bailey, Chicago vs. Kansas City, December 29 - TD

Returns
NFC: 43—David Meggett, N.Y. Giants
AFC: 38—Rod Woodson, Pittsburgh

Returns, Game
AFC: 6—Tim Brown, L.A. Raiders at Kansas City, November 4 (27 yards)
Clarence Verdin, Indianapolis at New England, November 11 (124 yards)
Irving Fryar, New England vs. Indianapolis, November 11 (39 yards)
NFC: 6—Mel Gray, Detroit vs. Atlanta, September 16 (32 yards)
Walter Stanley, Washington at Phoenix, September 30 (42 yards)
Deion Sanders, Atlanta at New Orleans, November 25 (50 yards)
Rod Harris, Philadelphia vs. Green Bay, December 16 (91 yards)

Fair Catches
AFC: 20—Gerald McNeil, Houston
NFC: 15—Willie Drewrey, Tampa Bay
Leo Lewis, Minnesota

Touchdowns
AFC: 1—Nate Lewis, San Diego
Terance Mathis, N.Y. Jets
Mitchell Price, Cincinnati
Kitrick Taylor, San Diego
Rod Woodson, Pittsburgh
NFC: 1—Johnny Bailey, Chicago
David Meggett, N.Y. Giants
Deion Sanders, Atlanta

Team Champion
AFC: 11.2—Indianapolis
NFC: 11.1—Chicago

AFC Punt Returns—Team

	No.	FC	Yards	Avg.	Long	TD
Indianapolis	36	9	402	11.2	36	0
N.Y. Jets	30	11	319	10.6	t98	1
Pittsburgh	39	8	398	10.2	t52	1
San Diego	35	16	336	9.6	t63	2
Seattle	36	16	337	9.4	39	0
L.A. Raiders	34	8	295	8.7	39	0
Cincinnati	30	14	255	8.5	t66	1
Denver	33	12	256	7.8	32	0
Buffalo	25	9	177	7.1	25	0
Kansas City	37	6	254	6.9	37	0
Cleveland	31	15	209	6.7	25	0
Miami	39	18	233	6.0	35	0
Houston	30	21	172	5.7	26	0
New England	29	10	134	4.6	17	0
AFC Total	464	173	3777	—	t98	5
AFC Average	33.1	12.4	269.8	8.1	—	0.4

NFC Punt Returns—Team

	No.	FC	Yards	Avg.	Long	TD
Chicago	36	13	399	11.1	t95	1
N.Y. Giants	43	12	467	10.9	t68	1
Detroit	35	7	361	10.3	39	0
L.A. Rams	35	7	346	9.9	26	0
Green Bay	32	9	308	9.6	25	0
New Orleans	45	9	400	8.9	33	0
Phoenix	40	7	342	8.6	20	0
Washington	48	17	388	8.1	32	0
Tampa Bay	23	15	184	8.0	16	0
Atlanta	35	17	279	8.0	t79	1
Philadelphia	40	11	315	7.9	30	0
San Francisco	48	16	356	7.4	30	0
Minnesota	33	24	225	6.8	30	0
Dallas	39	11	250	6.4	20	0
NFC Total	532	175	4620	—	t95	3
NFC Average	38.0	12.5	330.0	8.7	—	0.2
League Total	996	348	8397	—	t98	8
League Average	35.6	12.4	299.9	8.4	—	0.3

NFL Top 10 Punt Returners

	No.	FC	Yards	Avg.	Long	TD
Verdin, Clarence, Ind.	31	3	396	12.8	36	0
Bailey, Johnny, Chi.	36	13	399	11.1	t95	1
Meggett, David, Giants	43	12	467	10.9	t68	1
Gray, Mel, Det.	34	7	361	10.6	39	0
Woodson, Rod, Pitt.	38	8	398	10.5	t52	1
Query, Jeff, G.B.	32	7	308	9.6	25	0
Warren, Chris, Sea.	28	16	269	9.6	39	0
Brown, Tim, L.A. Raiders	34	8	295	8.7	39	0
Price, Mitchell, Cin.	29	14	251	8.7	t66	1
Sanders, Deion, Atl.	29	13	250	8.6	t79	1

AFC Punt Returns—Individual

	No.	FC	Yards	Avg.	Long	TD
Verdin, Clarence, Ind.	31	3	396	12.8	36	0
Woodson, Rod, Pitt.	38	8	398	10.5	t52	1
Warren, Chris, Sea.	28	16	269	9.6	39	0
Brown, Tim, L.A. Raiders	34	8	295	8.7	39	0
Price, Mitchell, Cin.	29	14	251	8.7	t66	1
Clark, Kevin, Den.	21	1	159	7.6	32	0
Worthen, Naz, K.C.	25	3	180	7.2	37	0
McNeil, Gerald, Hou.	30	20	172	5.7	26	0
Martin, Tony, Mia.	26	9	140	5.4	35	0
Fryar, Irving, N.E.	28	10	133	4.8	17	0
Non-Qualifiers						
Townsell, JoJo, N.Y. Jets	17	4	154	9.1	20	0
Schwedes, Scott, S.D.-Mia.	14	3	122	8.7	23	0
Edwards, Al, Buff.	14	5	92	6.6	16	0
Lewis, Nate, S.D.	13	8	117	9.0	t63	1
Adams, Stefon, Clev.	13	4	81	6.2	25	0
Mathis, Terance, N.Y. Jets	11	7	165	15.0	t98	1
Johnson, Vance, Den.	11	11	92	8.4	29	0
Hale, Chris, Buff.	10	4	76	7.6	25	0
Birden, J.J., K.C.	10	3	72	7.2	22	0
Brennan, Brian, Clev.	9	4	72	8.0	15	0
Jefferson, James, Sea.	8	0	68	8.5	14	0
Mays, Jerry, S.D.	7	4	30	4.3	17	0
Taylor, Kitrick, S.D.	6	3	112	18.7	t55	1
Nelson, Darrin, S.D.	3	0	44	14.7	33	0
Stradford, Troy, Mia.	3	2	4	1.3	4	0
Grant, Alan, Ind.	2	0	6	3.0	6	0
Prior, Mike, Ind.	2	6	0	0.0	0	0
Odomes, Nate, Buff.	1	0	9	9.0	9	0
Nattiel, Ricky, Den.	1	0	5	5.0	5	0
Smith, Kendal, Cin.	1	0	4	4.0	4	0
Harry, Emile, K.C.	1	0	2	2.0	2	0
Martin, Sammy, N.E.	1	0	1	1.0	1	0
Daniel, Eugene, Ind.	1	0	0	0.0	0	0
Hasty, James, N.Y. Jets	1	0	0	0.0	0	0
Hill, Derek, Pitt.	1	0	0	0.0	0	0
Lyles, Lester, S.D.	1	0	0	0.0	0	0
Odegard, Don, N.Y. Jets	1	0	0	0.0	0	0
Waiters, Van, Clev.	1	0	0	0.0	0	0
Whitaker, Danta, K.C.	1	0	0	0.0	0	0
Williams, Jarvis, Mia.	1	5	0	0.0	0	0
Duncan, Curtis, Hou.	0	1	0	—	0	0

t indicates touchdown.
Leader based on average return, minimum 20 returns.

NFC Punt Returns—Individual

	No.	FC	Yards	Avg.	Long	TD
Bailey, Johnny, Chi.	36	13	399	11.1	t95	1
Meggett, David, Giants	43	12	467	10.9	t68	1
Gray, Mel, Det.	34	7	361	10.6	39	0
Query, Jeff, G.B.	32	7	308	9.6	25	0
Sanders, Deion, Atl.	29	13	250	8.6	t79	1
Sikahema, Vai, Phx.	36	6	306	8.5	20	0
Buck, Vince, N.O.	37	8	305	8.2	33	0
Taylor, John, S.F.	26	5	212	8.2	30	0
Drewrey, Willie, T.B.	23	15	184	8.0	16	0
Harris, Rod, Dall.-Phil.	28	8	214	7.6	30	0
Stanley, Walter, Wash.	24	8	176	7.3	32	0
Lewis, Leo, Clev.-Minn.	33	22	236	7.2	30	0
Shepard, Derrick, Dall.	20	1	121	6.1	13	0
Non-Qualifiers						
Henley, Darryl, L.A. Rams	19	4	195	10.3	26	0
Griffin, Don, S.F.	16	8	105	6.6	20	0
Sutton, Mickey, L.A. Rams	14	3	136	9.7	22	0
Mitchell, Brian, Wash.	12	4	107	8.9	26	0
Hargrove, Marvin, Phil.	12	2	83	6.9	13	0
Howard, Joe, Wash.	10	4	99	9.9	21	0
Morse, Bobby, N.O.	8	1	95	11.9	18	0
Edwards, Anthony, Phil.	8	7	60	7.5	13	0
Hillary, Ira, Minn.	8	4	45	5.6	12	0
Martin, Kelvin, Dall.	5	3	46	9.2	17	0
Davis, Eric, S.F.	5	3	38	7.6	24	0
Smith, J.T., Phx.	3	0	34	11.3	16	0
Bellamy, Mike, Phil.	2	0	22	11.0	22	0
McKinnon, Dennis, Dall.	2	1	20	10.0	20	0
Jordan, Brian, Atl.	2	4	19	9.5	10	0
Ellard, Henry, L.A. Rams	2	0	15	7.5	8	0
Rison, Andre, Atl.	2	0	10	5.0	8	0
Williams, Calvin, Phil.	2	0	-1	-0.5	0	0
Green, Darrell, Wash.	1	1	6	6.0	6	0
Proehl, Ricky, Phx.	1	1	2	2.0	2	0
Wilson, Mike, S.F.	1	0	1	1.0	1	0
Campbell, Jeff, Det.	1	0	0	0.0	0	0
Mitchell, Roland, Atl.	1	0	0	0.0	0	0
Reid, Michael, Atl.	1	0	0	0.0	0	0
Thomas, Johnny, Wash.	1	0	0	0.0	0	0
Carter, Anthony, Minn.	0	5	0	—	0	0
Pitts, Ron, G.B.	0	2	0	—	0	0

t indicates touchdown
Leader based on average return, minimum 20 returns.

Kickoff Returns

Yards Per Return
AFC: 25.3—Kevin Clark, Denver
NFC: 23.4—David Meggett, N.Y. Giants

Yards
AFC: 1052—Eric Metcalf, Cleveland
NFC: 966—Herschel Walker, Minnesota

Yards, Game
AFC: 165—Eric Metcalf, Cleveland at Houston, December 9 (4 returns)
NFC: 145—Danny Peebles, Tampa Bay vs. Chicago, November 4 (6 returns)

Longest
AFC: 101—Eric Metcalf, Cleveland at Houston, December 9 - TD
NFC: 99—Gaston Green, L.A. Rams at Pittsburgh, October 29 - TD

Returns
AFC: 52—Eric Metcalf, Cleveland
NFC: 44—Herschel Walker, Minnesota

Returns, Game
NFC: 7—Herschel Walker, Minnesota at Philadelphia, October 15 (122 yards)
Larry Centers, Phoenix at Dallas, December 16 (123 yards)
AFC: 6—Terance Mathis, N.Y. Jets vs. Buffalo, September 24 (116 yards)
Eric Metcalf, Cleveland at Kansas City, September 30 (84 yards)

Stacey Simmons, Indianapolis at Philadelphia, September 30 (125 yards)
Ron Brown, L.A. Raiders vs. Green Bay, November 11 (113 yards)
Brent Fullwood, Cleveland vs. Miami, November 25 (119 yards)
Terance Mathis, N.Y. Jets vs. Indianapolis, December 16 (99 yards)
Eric Metcalf, Cleveland at Pittsburgh, December 23 (111 yards)

Touchdowns
AFC: 2—Eric Metcalf, Cleveland
NFC: 1—Gaston Green, L.A. Rams
Keith Jones, Atlanta
Darrell Thompson, Green Bay
Alexander Wright, Dallas

Team Champions
AFC: 21.6—San Diego
NFC: 21.2—Atlanta

AFC Kickoff Returns—Team

	No.	Yards	Avg.	Long	TD
San Diego	55	1188	21.6	90	0
Cincinnati	62	1266	20.4	43	0
Buffalo	51	1040	20.4	54	0
Seattle	50	985	19.7	71	0
L.A. Raiders	64	1237	19.3	87	0
Pittsburgh	50	956	19.1	49	0
Denver	66	1260	19.1	75	0
N.Y. Jets	61	1129	18.5	63	0
Houston	47	861	18.3	64	0
Indianapolis	65	1189	18.3	44	0
Miami	43	780	18.1	35	0
New England	77	1395	18.1	38	0
Cleveland	71	1276	18.0	t101	2
Kansas City	46	784	17.0	46	0
AFC Total	808	15346	—	t101	2
AFC Average	57.7	1096.1	19.0	—	0.1

NFC Kickoff Returns—Team

	No.	Yards	Avg.	Long	TD
Atlanta	58	1229	21.2	t76	1
Detroit	70	1466	20.9	65	0
New Orleans	58	1205	20.8	58	0
Green Bay	63	1303	20.7	t76	1
Dallas	54	1102	20.4	t90	1
L.A. Rams	63	1279	20.3	t99	1
N.Y. Giants	46	884	19.2	58	0
Minnesota	66	1249	18.9	64	0
Tampa Bay	63	1175	18.7	55	0
San Francisco	53	965	18.2	35	0
Washington	62	1113	18.0	37	0
Philadelphia	54	965	17.9	44	0
Phoenix	60	1068	17.8	32	0
Chicago	54	879	16.3	59	0
NFC Total	824	15882	—	t99	4
NFC Average	58.9	1134.4	19.3	—	0.3
League Total	1632	31228	—	t101	6
League Average	58.3	1115.3	19.1	—	0.2

NFL Top 10 Kickoff Returners

	No.	Yards	Avg.	Long	TD
Clark, Kevin, Den.	20	505	25.3	75	0
Elder, Donnie, S.D.	24	571	23.8	90	0
Meggett, David, N.Y. Giants	21	492	23.4	58	0
Gray, Mel, Det.	41	939	22.9	65	0
Wilson, Charles, G.B.	35	798	22.8	36	0
Green, Gaston, L.A. Rams	25	560	22.4	t99	1
Walker, Herschel, Minn.	44	966	22.0	64	0
Woodson, Rod, Pitt.	35	764	21.8	49	0
Sanders, Deion, Atl.	39	851	21.8	50	0
Warren, Chris, Sea.	23	478	20.8	71	0

AFC Kickoff Returns—Individual

	No.	Yards	Avg.	Long	TD
Clark, Kevin, Den.	20	505	25.3	75	0
Elder, Donnie, S.D.	24	571	23.8	90	0
Woodson, Rod, Pitt.	*35	764	21.8	49	0
Warren, Chris, Sea.	23	478	20.8	71	0
Martin, Sammy, N.E.	25	515	20.6	38	0
Holland, Jamie, L.A. Raiders	32	655	20.5	87	0
McNeil, Gerald, Hou.	27	551	20.4	64	0
Metcalf, Eric, Clev.	52	1052	20.2	t101	2
Jennings, Stanford, Cin.	29	584	20.1	33	0
Smith, Don, Buff.	32	643	20.1	38	0
Brown, Ron, L.A. Raiders	30	575	19.2	34	0
Logan, Marc, Mia.	20	367	18.4	35	0
Mathis, Terance, N.Y. Jets	43	787	18.3	35	0
Non-Qualifiers					
Simmons, Stacey, Ind.	19	348	18.3	34	0
Loville, Derek, Sea.	18	359	19.9	29	0
Verdin, Clarence, Ind.	18	350	19.4	44	0
Lewis, Nate, S.D.	17	383	22.5	39	0
Ball, Eric, Cin.	16	366	22.9	38	0
Grant, Alan, Ind.	15	280	18.7	29	0
Montgomery, Alton, Den.	14	286	20.4	59	0
McNair, Todd, K.C.	14	227	16.2	23	0
Ford, Bernard, Hou.	14	219	15.6	23	0
Ezor, Blake, Den.	13	214	16.5	50	0
Edwards, Al, Buff.	11	256	23.3	54	0
Worthen, Naz, K.C.	11	226	20.5	32	0
Bentley, Albert, Ind.	11	211	19.2	36	0
Robinson, Junior, N.E.	11	211	19.2	27	0
Morris, Jamie, N.E.	11	202	18.4	22	0
Allen, Marvin, N.E.	11	168	15.3	34	0
Higgs, Mark, Mia.	10	210	21.0	30	0
Price, Mitchell, Cin.	*10	191	19.1	33	0
Overton, Don, N.E.	10	188	18.8	23	0
Jones, Fred, K.C.	9	175	19.4	46	0
Frank, Donald, S.D.	8	172	21.5	31	0
Townsell, JoJo, N.Y. Jets	7	158	22.6	38	0
Johnson, Vance, Den.	6	126	21.0	39	0
Beebe, Don, Buff.	6	119	19.8	27	0
Fullwood, Brent, Clev.	6	119	19.8	27	0
Stone, Dwight, Pitt.	5	91	18.2	24	0
Odegard, Don, N.Y. Jets	5	89	17.8	25	0
Saxon, James, K.C.	5	81	16.2	23	0
Adams, Stefon, Clev.-Mia.	5	49	9.8	15	0
Jefferson, James, Sea.	4	96	24.0	26	0
Pinkett, Allen, Hou.	4	91	22.8	28	0
Winder, Sammy, Den.	4	55	13.8	24	0
Mandley, Pete, K.C.	4	51	12.8	23	0
Nelson, Darrin, S.D.	4	36	9.0	26	0
Timpson, Michael, N.E.	3	62	20.7	26	0
Stradford, Troy, Mia.	3	56	18.7	21	0
Bratton, Mel, Den.	3	37	12.3	18	0
Williams, Jerrol, Pitt.	3	31	10.3	20	0
Foster, Barry, Pitt.	3	29	9.7	13	0
Galbraith, Scott, Clev.	3	16	5.3	10	0
Schwedes, Scott, Mia.	2	52	26.0	30	0
Smith, Kendal, Cin.	2	35	17.5	20	0
Collins, Tony, Mia.	2	30	15.0	30	0
McNeal, Travis, Sea.	2	29	14.5	17	0
Jones, Cedric, N.E.	2	24	12.0	13	0
Rolle, Butch, Buff.	2	22	11.0	11	0
Jones, James, Sea.	2	21	10.5	13	0
Coleman, Pat, N.E.	2	18	9.0	12	0
Hoard, Leroy, Clev.	2	18	9.0	10	0
Johnson, Eddie, Clev.	2	17	8.5	11	0
Griffin, Larry, Pitt.	2	16	8.0	14	0
Kay, Clarence, Den.	2	10	5.0	7	0
Nichols, Gerald, N.Y. Jets	2	3	1.5	3	0
Norgard, Erik, Hou.	2	0	0.0	0	0
Brown, A.B., N.Y. Jets	1	63	63.0	63	0
James, Lynn, Cin.	1	43	43.0	43	0
Jackson, Mark, Den.	1	18	18.0	18	0
Paige, Tony, Mia.	1	18	18.0	18	0
Green, Eric, Pitt.	1	16	16.0	16	0
Kinchen, Brian, Mia.	1	16	16.0	16	0
Taylor, Craig, Cin.	1	16	16.0	16	0
Barnett, Harlon, Clev.	1	15	15.0	15	0
Barber, Mike, Cin.	1	14	14.0	14	0
Birden, J.J., K.C.	1	14	14.0	14	0
Boyer, Mark, N.Y. Jets	1	14	14.0	14	0
Miller, Anthony, S.D.	1	13	13.0	13	0
Orr, Terry, S.D.	1	13	13.0	13	0
Kattus, Eric, Cin.	1	10	10.0	10	0
Word, Barry, K.C.	1	10	10.0	10	0
Lipps, Louis, Pitt.	1	9	9.0	9	0
Mobley, Orson, Den.	1	9	9.0	9	0
Sims, Keith, Mia.	1	9	9.0	9	0
Duffy, Roger, N.Y. Jets	1	8	8.0	8	0
Adams, George, N.E.	1	7	7.0	7	0
Dressel, Chris, N.Y. Jets	1	7	7.0	7	0
Riggs, Jim, Cin.	1	7	7.0	7	0
Turk, Dan, L.A. Raiders	1	7	7.0	7	0
Graf, Rick, Mia.	1	6	6.0	6	0
Talley, John, Clev.	1	6	6.0	6	0
Glasgow, Nesby, Sea.	1	2	2.0	2	0
Atwater, Steve, Den.	1	0	0.0	0	0
Ball, Michael, Ind.	1	0	0.0	0	0

	No.	Yards	Avg.	Long	TD
Gainer, Derrick, Clev.	1	0	0.0	0	0
Jarvis, Ralph, Ind.	1	0	0.0	0	0
McCallum, Napoleon, Raiders	1	0	0.0	0	0
McSwain, Rod, N.E.	1	0	0.0	0	0
Nattiel, Ricky, Den.	1	0	0.0	0	0
Roberts, Alfredo, K.C.	1	0	0.0	0	0
Martin, Tony, Mia.	*0	0	—	0	0
Olsavsky, Jerry, Pitt.	*0	0	—	0	0

t indicates touchdown
** indicates fair catch.*
Leader based on average return, minimum 20 returns.

NFC Kickoff Returns—Individual

	No.	Yards	Avg.	Long	TD
Meggett, David, N.Y. Giants	21	492	23.4	58	0
Gray, Mel, Det.	41	939	22.9	65	0
Wilson, Charles, G.B.	35	798	22.8	36	0
Green, Gaston, L.A. Rams	25	560	22.4	t99	1
Walker, Herschel, Minn.	44	966	22.0	64	0
Sanders, Deion, Atl.	39	851	21.8	50	0
Dixon, James, Dall.	36	736	20.4	47	0
Fenerty, Gill, N.O.	28	572	20.4	58	0
Sikahema, Vai, Phx.	27	544	20.1	32	0
Delpino, Robert, L.A. Rams	*20	389	19.5	38	0
Howard, Joe, Wash.	22	427	19.4	35	0
Carter, Dexter, S.F.	41	783	19.1	35	0
Hampton, Rodney, N.Y. Giants	20	340	17.0	33	0
Bailey, Johnny, Chi.	23	363	15.8	30	0
Non-Qualifiers					
Atkins, Gene, N.O.	19	471	24.8	50	0
Hargrove, Marvin, Phil.	19	341	17.9	30	0
Gentry, Dennis, Chi.	18	388	21.6	59	0
Peebles, Danny, T.B.	18	369	20.5	55	0
Mitchell, Brian, Wash.	18	365	20.3	37	0
Berry, Latin, L.A. Rams	17	315	18.5	29	0
Centers, Larry, Phx.	16	272	17.0	26	0
Sanders, Thomas, Phil.	*15	299	19.9	37	0
Drewrey, Willie, T.B.	14	244	17.4	29	0
Workman, Vince, G.B.	14	210	15.0	26	0
Oldham, Chris, Det.	13	234	18.0	42	0
Wright, Alexander, Dall.	12	276	23.0	t90	1
Campbell, Jeff, Det.	12	238	19.8	38	0
Harvey, John, T.B.	12	207	17.3	27	0
Rice, Allen, Minn.	*12	176	14.7	24	0
Cobb, Reggie, T.B.	11	223	20.3	45	0
Flagler, Terrence, Phx.	10	167	16.7	27	0
Stanley, Walter, Wash.	9	177	19.7	37	0
Jones, Keith, Atl.	8	236	29.5	t76	1
Green, Mark, Chi.	7	112	16.0	20	0
Bland, Carl, G.B.	7	104	14.9	24	0
Jackson, Kenny, Phil.	6	125	20.8	30	0
Anderson, Gary, T.B.	6	123	20.5	37	0
Tillman, Spencer, S.F.	6	111	18.5	30	0
Hobbs, Stevie, Wash.	6	92	15.3	21	0
Shepard, Derrick, Dall.	4	75	18.8	22	0
Barnett, Fred, Phil.	4	65	16.3	22	0
Morse, Bobby, N.O.	4	56	14.0	18	0
Proehl, Ricky, Phx.	4	53	13.3	15	0
Thompson, Darrell, G.B.	3	103	34.3	t76	1
Fontenot, Herman, G.B.	3	88	29.3	50	0
Broussard, Steve, Atl.	3	45	15.0	23	0
Anderson, Alfred, Minn.	3	44	14.7	24	0
Ingram, Mark, N.Y. Giants	3	42	14.0	26	0
Lewis, Leo, Minn.	3	39	13.0	15	0
Buck, Vince, N.O.	3	38	12.7	17	0
Edwards, Anthony, Phil.	*3	36	12.0	14	0
Rouse, James, Chi.	3	17	5.7	10	0
Harris, Rod, Dall.-Phil.	2	44	22.0	44	0
Phillips, Jason, Det.	2	43	21.5	23	0
Mayes, Rueben, N.O.	2	39	19.5	21	0
Sydney, Harry, S.F.	2	33	16.5	19	0
Gouveia, Kurt, Wash.	2	23	11.5	15	0
Vick, Roger, Phil.	2	22	11.0	13	0
Jax, Garth, Phx.	2	17	8.5	9	0
Williams, Jamie, S.F.	2	7	3.5	7	0
Johnson, Tracy, Atl.	2	2	1.0	6	0
Dupard, Reggie, Wash.	2	0	0.0	0	0
Gordon, Tim, Atl.	1	43	43.0	43	0
Sanders, Ricky, Wash.	1	22	22.0	22	0
Lang, Gene, Atl.	1	18	18.0	18	0
Bellamy, Mike, Phil.	1	17	17.0	17	0
Mack, Milton, N.O.	1	17	17.0	17	0
Smith, Cedric, Minn.	1	16	16.0	16	0
Walls, Wesley, S.F.	1	16	16.0	16	0
Green, Roy, Phx.	1	15	15.0	15	0
Griffin, Don, S.F.	1	15	15.0	15	0
McDonald, Mike, L.A. Rams	1	15	15.0	15	0
Stepnoski, Mark, Dall.	1	15	15.0	15	0
Jenkins, Izel, Phil.	1	14	14.0	14	0
Pringle, Mike, Atl.	1	14	14.0	14	0
Case, Scott, Atl.	1	13	13.0	13	0
Andolsek, Eric, Det.	1	12	12.0	12	0
Heyward, Craig, N.O.	1	12	12.0	12	0
Cross, Howard, N.Y. Giants	1	10	10.0	10	0
Coleman, Sidney, T.B.	1	9	9.0	9	0
Middleton, Ron, Wash.	1	7	7.0	7	0
Wilkins, Gary, Atl.	1	7	7.0	7	0
Hillary, Ira, Minn.	1	6	6.0	6	0
Schreiber, Adam, Minn.	1	5	5.0	5	0
Allen, Eric, Phil.	1	2	2.0	2	0
Bowles, Todd, Wash.	1	0	0.0	0	0
Dixon, Floyd, Atl.	1	0	0.0	0	0
Hager, Britt, Phil.	1	0	0.0	0	0
Hall, Ron, T.B.	1	0	0.0	0	0
McKnight, Dennis, Det.	*1	0	0.0	0	0
Roper, John, Chi.	1	0	0.0	0	0
Tate, Lars, Chi.	1	0	0.0	0	0
West, Ed, G.B.	1	0	0.0	0	0
Whitmore, Dave, N.Y. Giants	1	0	0.0	0	0
Ryan, Tim, Chi.	*1	-1	-1.0	-1	0
Jordan, Steve, Minn.	1	-3	-3.0	-3	0
Guyton, Myron, N.Y. Giants	*0	0	—	0	0

t indicates touchdown
** indicates fair catch.*
Leader based on average return, minimum 20 returns.

Fumbles

Most Fumbles
AFC: 18—Warren Moon, Houston
NFC: 12—Cleveland Gary, L.A. Rams

Most Fumbles, Game
AFC: 5—Dave Krieg, Seattle at San Diego, November 25 (OT)
NFC: 3—By 9 players

Own Fumbles Recovered
NFC: 6—Reggie Cobb, Tampa Bay
Rich Gannon, Minnesota
AFC: 5—Kevin Mack, Cleveland

Most Own Fumbles Recovered, Game
NFC: 3—Jeff Hostetler, N.Y. Giants vs. Phoenix, October 21
Rich Gannon, Minnesota at Detroit, November 11
AFC: 2—Jack Trudeau, Indianapolis at Philadelphia, September 30
Harold Green, Cincinnati at Seattle, October 1
Kevin Mack, Cleveland vs. Buffalo, November 4
Gary Kubiak, Denver at Minnesota, November 4
Rod Woodson, Pittsburgh at N.Y. Jets, November 25
Bubby Brister, Pittsburgh at N.Y. Jets, November 25
Melvin Bratton, Denver vs. Green Bay, December 30

Opponents' Fumbles Recovered
NFC: 7—Rickey Jackson, New Orleans
AFC: 6—Dan Saleaumua, Kansas City

Most Opponents' Fumbles Recovered, Game
AFC: 2—James Hasty, N.Y. Jets vs. Cleveland, September 16
Bob Golic, L.A. Raiders vs. Pittsburgh, September 23
Fred Marion, New England at Miami, October 18
Ronnie Lippett, New England at Miami, October 18
Steve Tasker, Buffalo vs. Phoenix, November 11
Donald Evans, Pittsburgh vs. Cleveland, December 23
NFC: 2—Jerry Holmes, Green Bay vs. L.A. Rams, September 9
Kevin Greene, L.A. Rams at San Francisco, November 25

Yards
AFC: 72—Terry Kinard, Houston
NFC: 65—Jessie Tuggle, Atlanta

Longest
AFC: 72—Terry Kinard, Houston vs. Cleveland, December 9 - TD
NFC: 65—Jessie Tuggle, Atlanta vs. Houston, September 9 - TD

AFC Fumbles—Team

	Fum.	Own Rec.	Fum. OB	TD	Opp. Rec.	TD	Yds	Tot. Rec.
Buffalo	17	7	0	0	17	1	68	24
Indianapolis	23	13	0	0	15	1	86	28
L.A. Raiders	24	9	1	0	9	2	27	18
San Diego	24	10	1	0	11	2	10	21
Cincinnati	25	10	3	0	16	1	95	26
N.Y. Jets	28	13	2	0	11	1	-17	24
Denver	30	14	2	0	15	1	30	29
Kansas City	30	14	2	0	25	1	-11	39
Seattle	32	15	1	0	18	1	49	33
Miami	33	17	1	0	8	2	17	25
New England	33	14	3	0	18	1	24	32
Houston	34	13	0	0	12	1	72	25
Cleveland	37	13	1	0	9	1	15	22
Pittsburgh	40	17	6	0	18	0	58	35
AFC Total	410	179	23	0	202	16	523	381
AFC Average	29.3	12.8	1.6	0.0	14.4	1.1	37.4	27.2

NFC Fumbles—Team

	Fum.	Own Rec.	Fum. OB	TD	Opp. Rec.	TD	Yds	Tot. Rec.
Washington	14	6	2	0	12	1	47	18
N.Y. Giants	21	12	0	0	11	1	25	23
San Francisco	24	7	3	0	14	0	37	21
Phoenix	25	9	2	0	11	0	10	20
L.A. Rams	25	8	3	0	19	0	-5	27
Dallas	27	14	4	0	19	0	39	33
Chicago	29	14	1	0	14	1	58	28
Detroit	29	11	2	0	18	2	65	29
New Orleans	29	11	2	0	19	0	15	30
Minnesota	30	15	2	0	11	2	28	26
Philadelphia	32	15	2	0	11	1	34	26
Green Bay	37	12	3	0	14	1	47	26
Tampa Bay	38	15	4	0	17	0	-8	32
Atlanta	40	15	4	0	18	2	50	33
NFC Total	400	164	34	0	208	11	442	372
NFC Average	28.6	11.7	2.4	0.0	14.9	0.8	31.6	26.6
League Total	810	343	57	0	410	27	965	753
League Average	28.9	12.3	2.0	0.0	14.6	1.0	34.5	26.9

Fumbled though the end zone, ball awarded to opponents: None.
Fum OB = Fumbled out of bounds.
Yards includes aborted plays, own recoveries, and opponents' recoveries.

AFC Fumbles—Individual

	Fum.	Own Rec.	Opp. Rec.	Yds	Tot. Rec.
Adams, George, N.E.	1	0	0	0	0
Adams, Stefon, Clev.	2	0	0	0	0
Agnew, Ray, N.E.	0	0	1	0	1
Allen, Marcus, L.A. Raiders	1	1	0	0	1
Allen, Marvin, N.E.	1	2	1	0	3
Anderson, Eddie, L.A. Raiders	0	0	1	0	1
Armstrong, Bruce, N.E.	0	2	0	4	2
Bailey, Carlton, Buff.	0	0	1	0	1
Bailey, Edwin, Sea.	0	2	0	3	2
Baldinger, Rich, K.C.	0	1	0	0	1
Ball, Eric, Cin.	1	0	0	0	0
Banks, Chip, Ind.	0	0	1	0	1
Banks, Fred, Mia.	0	2	0	0	2
Barker, Leo, Cin.	0	0	1	0	1
Baty, Greg, Mia.	0	0	1	0	1
Baxter, Brad, N.Y. Jets	4	1	0	0	1
Bayless, Martin, S.D.	0	0	1	0	1
Bell, Mike, K.C.	0	0	1	0	1
Bennett, Cornelius, Buff.	0	0	2	0	2
Bentley, Albert, Ind.	2	1	0	11	1
Bentley, Ray, Buff.	0	0	1	10	1
Bernstine, Rod, S.D.	1	0	0	0	0
Bickett, Duane, Ind.	0	0	2	0	2
Billups, Lewis, Cin.	0	0	2	4	2
Birden, J.J., K.C.	1	0	0	0	0
Blackmon, Robert, Sea.	0	0	1	0	1
Blankenship, Brian, Pitt.	1	0	0	0	0
Blaylock, Anthony, Clev.	0	0	1	30	1
Boyer, Mark, N.Y. Jets	1	0	0	0	0
Brady, Ed, Cin.	0	0	1	0	1
Braggs, Stephen, Clev.	0	1	1	16	2
Bratton, Mel, Den.	3	3	0	0	3
Brennan, Brian, Clev.	1	0	0	0	0
Brister, Bubby, Pitt.	9	4	0	-28	4
Brooks, James, Cin.	3	1	0	0	1
Brown, Richard, S.D.	0	0	1	0	1
Brown, Ron, L.A. Raiders	1	0	0	0	0
Brown, Tim, L.A. Raiders	3	0	0	0	0
Burkett, Chris, N.Y. Jets	0	0	1	0	1
Burruss, Lloyd, K.C.	0	0	1	2	1
Bussey, Barney, Cin.	0	0	1	70	1
Butts, Marion, S.D.	0	1	0	0	1
Carter, Carl, Cin.	0	1	2	0	3
Chadwick, Jeff, Sea.	1	1	1	0	2
Childress, Ray, Hou.	0	0	1	0	1
Clayton, Mark, Mia.	1	0	0	0	0
Clifton, Kyle, N.Y. Jets	0	0	1	0	1
Cook, Marv, N.E.	2	0	0	0	0
Corrington, Kip, Den.	0	0	1	0	1
Cox, Arthur, S.D.	2	0	0	0	0
Criswell, Jeff, N.Y. Jets	0	1	0	0	1
Cross, Jeff, Mia.	0	0	2	0	2
Curtis, Travis, N.Y. Jets	0	1	0	0	1
Davis, Darrell, N.Y. Jets	0	0	1	0	1
Davis, Kenneth, Buff.	1	1	0	0	1
DeBerg, Steve, K.C.	9	3	0	-31	3
Dressel, Chris, N.Y. Jets	1	0	0	0	0
Duncan, Curtis, Hou.	1	0	0	0	0
Duper, Mark, Mia.	1	0	0	0	0
Eason, Tony, N.Y. Jets	2	1	0	0	1
Edmunds, Ferrell, Mia.	2	2	0	0	2
Elder, Donnie, S.D.	2	2	0	0	2
Elway, John, Den.	8	1	0	-3	1
Esiason, Boomer, Cin.	11	2	0	-23	2
Evans, Donald, Pitt.	0	0	3	59	3
Ezor, Blake, Den.	1	0	0	0	0
Fairs, Eric, Hou.	0	0	1	0	1
Farren, Paul, Clev.	0	1	0	0	1
Feasel, Grant, Sea.	0	1	0	0	1
Fenner, Derrick, Sea.	3	1	0	0	1
Fletcher, Simon, Den.	0	0	1	0	1
Ford, Bernard, Hou.	2	0	0	0	0
Foster, Barry, Pitt.	2	1	0	0	1
Francis, Jeff, Clev.	0	1	0	0	1
Freeman, Lorenzo, Pitt.	0	0	1	0	1
Fryar, Irving, N.E.	1	1	0	0	1
Fuller, William, Hou.	0	0	1	0	1
Galbraith, Scott, Clev.	0	0	1	0	1
Gannon, Chris, N.E.	1	0	0	-25	0
Gash, Thane, Clev.	0	0	2	0	2
Gault, Willie, L.A. Raiders	1	0	0	0	0
George, Jeff, Ind.	4	1	1	0	2
Givins, Ernest, Hou.	1	0	0	0	0
Glasgow, Nesby, Sea.	1	0	1	6	1
Goad, Tim, N.E.	0	0	1	0	1
Goeas Leo, S.D.	0	1	0	0	1
Golic, Bob, L.A. Raiders	0	0	2	0	2
Goode, Chris, Ind.	0	0	2	63	2
Graf, Rick, Mia.	0	1	0	3	1
Grant, Alan, Ind.	1	1	1	5	2
Grant, David, Cin.	0	0	1	0	1
Grayson, Dave, Clev.	0	0	1	0	1
Green, Eric, Pitt.	1	1	0	0	1
Green, Harold, Cin.	2	2	0	0	2
Green, Jacob, Sea.	0	0	1	0	1
Griffin, Larry, Pitt.	1	1	0	1	1
Griggs, David, Mia.	0	0	1	0	1
Grimsley, John, Hou.	0	0	3	0	3
Grogan, Steve, N.E.	1	0	0	0	0
Hackett, Dino, K.C.	0	0	2	0	2
Hale, Chris, Buff.	0	0	3	0	3
Hand, Jon, Ind.	0	0	1	0	1
Hansen, Brian, N.E.	1	1	1	-18	2
Harmon, Ronnie, S.D.	1	0	0	0	0
Hasty, James, N.Y. Jets	1	0	3	0	3
Heck, Andy, Sea.	0	1	0	0	1
Hector, Johnny, N.Y. Jets	2	0	0	0	0
Henderson, Wymon, Den.	0	0	1	-2	1
Hester, Jessie, Ind.	0	2	0	0	2
Higgs, Mark, Mia.	1	0	0	0	0
Hill, Derek, Pitt.	1	1	0	0	1
Hinkle, Bryan, Pitt.	0	0	2	0	2
Hoard, Leroy, Clev.	6	0	0	0	0
Hobley, Liffort, Mia.	1	0	0	0	0
Hodson, Tom, N.E.	5	0	0	0	0
Hoge, Merril, Pitt.	6	2	0	0	2
Holman, Rodney, Cin.	1	0	0	0	0
Holmes, Ron, Den.	0	0	1	2	1
Horton, Ethan, L.A. Raiders	1	0	0	0	0
Humphrey, Bobby, Den.	8	2	0	0	2
Hunter, Ivy Joe, Ind.	0	1	0	0	1
Hunter, Patrick, Sea.	0	0	1	13	1
Hurst, Maurice, N.E.	1	0	0	0	0
Ilkin, Tunch, Pitt.	0	1	0	0	1
Jackson, Bo, L.A. Raiders	3	0	0	0	0
Jackson, Mark, Den.	1	0	0	0	0
Jarvis, Ralph, Ind.	1	0	1	1	1
Jefferson, James, Sea.	1	1	0	0	1
Jenkins, Mel, Sea.	0	0	2	0	2
Jennings, Stanford, Cin.	2	0	0	0	0
Jensen, Jim, Mia.	1	0	0	0	0
Johnson, David, Pitt.	0	0	1	9	1
Johnson, Vance, Den.	1	0	0	0	0
Joines, Vernon, Clev.	0	1	0	0	1
Jones, Aaron, Pitt.	0	0	1	0	1
Jones, Fred, K.C.	1	1	0	0	1
Jones, Rod, Cin.	0	0	1	1	1
Jones, Sean, Hou.	0	0	1	0	1
Jones, Victor, Hou.	1	0	0	0	0
Kane, Tommy, Sea.	1	0	0	0	0
Kartz, Keith, Den.	1	1	0	0	1
Kay, Clarence, Den.	0	1	0	0	1
Kelly, Jim, Buff.	4	2	0	-8	2
Kelly, Joe, N.Y. Jets	0	0	1	0	1
Kennedy, Cortez, Sea.	0	0	1	0	1

	Fum.	Own Rec.	Opp. Rec.	Yds.	Tot. Rec.
Kidd, John, S.D.	1	0	1	0	1
Kinard, Terry, Hou.	0	0	1	72	1
Knight, Leander, Hou.	0	0	1	0	1
Kosar, Bernie, Clev.	6	1	0	-9	1
Kozak, Scott, Hou.	0	1	0	0	1
Kragen, Greg, Den.	0	0	2	0	2
Krieg, Dave, Sea.	16	2	0	0	2
Krumrie, Tim, Cin.	0	0	1	0	1
Kubiak, Gary, Den.	2	2	0	-8	2
Lake, Carnell, Pitt.	0	0	1	0	1
Langhorne, Reggie, Clev.	2	1	0	0	1
Lanier, Ken, Den.	0	1	0	0	1
Larson, Kurt, Ind.	0	1	1	0	2
Lathon, Lamar, Hou.	0	1	0	0	1
Lee Ronnie, Sea.	0	2	0	0	2
Lewis, Albert, K.C.	0	0	3	1	3
Lewis, Nate, S.D.	3	2	0	0	2
Limbrick, Garrett, Mia.	1	1	0	0	1
Lippett, Ronnie, N.E.	0	0	4	16	4
Lipps, Louis, Pitt.	1	0	0	0	0
Little, David, Pitt.	0	0	2	6	2
Lofton, James, Buff.	0	0	1	0	1
Logan, Marc, Mia.	4	1	0	0	1
Long, Howie, L.A. Raiders	0	0	1	1	1
Loville, Derek, Sea.	1	0	0	0	0
Lucas, Tim, Den.	0	0	1	0	1
Maas, Bill, K.C.	0	0	1	0	1
Mack, Kevin, Clev.	6	5	0	1	5
Mandley, Pete, K.C.	1	0	0	0	0
Marino, Dan, Mia.	3	2	0	0	2
Marion, Fred, N.E.	0	0	4	0	4
Martin, Chris, K.C.	0	0	4	3	4
Martin, Tony, Mia.	4	2	0	0	2
Mathis, Terance, N.Y. Jets	1	0	0	0	0
Matich, Trevor, N.Y. Jets	0	1	0	0	1
Matthews, Bruce, Hou.	0	1	0	0	1
Mayes, Michael, N.Y. Jets	0	0	1	3	1
Mays, Jerry, S.D.	1	0	0	0	0
McDaniel, Terry, L.A. Raiders	0	0	2	44	2
McDowell, Bubba, Hou.	0	0	1	0	1
McEwen, Craig, S.D.	1	0	0	0	0
McGee, Tim, Cin.	1	0	0	0	0
McKeller, Keith, Buff.	1	0	0	0	0
McMillan, Erik, N.Y. Jets	3	0	1	1	1
McMurtry, Greg, N.E.	1	0	0	0	0
McNair, Todd, K.C.	1	1	0	0	1
McNeil, Freeman, N.Y. Jets	1	0	0	0	0
McNeil, Gerald, Hou.	4	0	0	0	0
McSwain, Rod, N.E.	0	0	1	0	1
Mecklenburg, Karl, Den.	0	0	2	24	2
Metcalf, Eric, Clev.	8	1	0	0	1
Metzelaars, Pete, Buff.	1	0	0	0	0
Millard, Bryan, Sea.	0	1	0	0	1
Miller, Anthony, S.D.	2	1	0	0	1
Miller, Les, S.D.	0	0	3	1	3
Mobley, Orson, Den.	1	1	0	0	1
Montgomery, Alton, Den.	1	1	1	0	2
Montoya, Max, L.A. Raiders	0	1	0	0	1
Moon, Warren, Hou.	18	4	0	0	4
Moore, Rob, N.Y. Jets	1	0	0	0	0
Moore, Stevon, Mia.	0	0	1	0	1
Morgan, Stanley, Ind.	1	0	0	0	0
Morris, Jamie, N.E.	1	0	0	0	0
Morris, Mike, Clev.	1	0	0	-23	0
Mosebar, Don, L.A. Raiders	0	1	0	0	1
Mott, Joe, N.Y. Jets	0	0	1	0	1
Mowatt, Zeke, N.E.	1	0	0	0	0
Mueller, Jamie, Buff.	1	0	0	0	0
Mueller, Vance, L.A. Raiders	0	1	0	0	1
Mularkey, Mike, Pitt.	1	0	0	0	0
Nash, Joe, Sea.	0	0	1	0	1
Nelson, Darrin, S.D.	1	0	0	0	0
Nichols, Gerald, N.Y. Jets	0	1	0	0	1
O'Brien, Ken, N.Y. Jets	5	4	0	-4	4
Odom, Cliff, Mia.	0	0	1	1	1
Odomes, Nate, Buff.	0	0	3	49	3
Oglesby, Alfred, Mia.	0	0	1	0	1
Okoye, Christian, K.C.	6	1	0	0	1
O'Neal, Leslie, S.D.	1	0	2	10	2
Orr, Terry, S.D.	0	0	1	0	1
Pagel, Mike, Clev.	3	1	0	0	1
Paige, Stephone, K.C.	3	1	0	0	1
Paige, Tony, Mia.	1	2	0	0	2
Patterson, Elvis, L.A. Raiders	0	0	1	0	1
Pearson, J.C., K.C.	0	0	1	0	1
Perry, Michael Dean, Clev.	0	0	1	0	1
Perryman, Bob, N.E.	2	0	0	0	0

	Fum.	Own Rec.	Opp. Rec.	Yds.	Tot. Rec.
Pickel, Bill, L.A. Raiders	0	0	1	0	1
Pike, Chris, Clev.	0	0	1	0	1
Pinkett, Allen, Hou.	0	2	0	0	2
Porter, Kevin, K.C.	1	0	0	0	0
Porter, Rufus, Sea.	0	0	4	11	4
Price, Mitchell, Cin.	2	1	1	0	2
Prior, Mike, Ind.	1	0	2	6	2
Prokop, Joe, N.Y. Jets	1	0	0	-17	0
Reed, Andre, Buff.	1	1	0	0	1
Reich, Frank, Buff.	1	0	0	0	0
Riggs, Jim, Cin.	0	1	0	0	1
Ritcher, Jim, Buff.	0	1	0	0	1
Robbins, Randy, Den.	0	0	2	26	2
Robinson, Eugene, Sea.	0	0	4	16	4
Robinson, Gerald, S.D.	0	0	1	0	1
Robinson, Junior, N.E.	2	0	0	0	0
Rolling, Henry, S.D.	0	1	0	0	1
Ross, Kevin, K.C.	0	0	3	0	3
Saleaumua, Dan, K.C.	0	0	6	0	6
Saxon, James, K.C.	1	0	0	0	0
Schroeder, Jay, L.A. Raiders	11	2	0	-19	2
Seale, Sam, S.D.	0	1	0	0	1
Seals, Leon, Buff.	0	0	2	8	2
Sharpe, Shannon, Den.	1	0	0	0	0
Sievers, Eric, N.E.	1	0	0	0	0
Simmons, Stacy, Ind.	1	1	0	0	1
Sims, Keith, Mia.	0	1	0	0	1
Siragusa, Tony, Ind.	0	0	1	0	1
Slaughter, Webster, Clev.	2	0	0	0	0
Smith, Al, Hou.	0	0	1	0	1
Smith, Dennis, Den.	0	0	2	0	2
Smith, Don, Buff.	1	0	0	0	0
Smith, Doug, Hou.	0	0	1	0	1
Smith, Elliot, Den.	0	0	1	0	1
Smith, Kendal, Cin.	0	1	0	0	1
Smith, Leonard, Buff.	0	0	1	0	1
Smith, Neil, K.C.	0	0	1	0	1
Smith, Sammie, Mia.	8	2	0	0	2
Smith, Steve, L.A. Raiders	3	1	0	0	1
Sochia, Brian, Mia.	0	0	1	13	1
Stallworth, Ron, N.Y. Jets	0	0	1	0	1
Stargell, Tony, N.Y. Jets	0	1	0	0	1
Stephens, John, N.E.	5	3	0	0	3
Stone, Dwight, Pitt.	1	1	1	0	2
Stowe, Tyronne, Pitt.	0	0	1	0	1
Stradford, Troy, Mia.	5	0	0	0	0
Strom, Rick, Pitt.	1	1	0	-3	1
Stryzinski, Dan, Pitt.	0	1	0	0	1
Sweeney, Jim, N.Y. Jets	0	1	0	0	1
Szott, David, K.C.	0	1	0	0	1
Talley, Darryl, Buff.	0	0	1	4	1
Tasker, Steve, Buff.	0	0	2	5	2
Taylor, Keith, Ind.	0	0	1	0	1
Thomas, Blair, N.Y. Jets	3	0	0	0	0
Thomas, Derrick, K.C.	0	0	2	14	2
Thomas, Thurman, Buff.	6	2	0	0	2
Tippett, Andre, N.E.	0	0	2	7	2
Tolliver, Billy Joe, S.D.	6	1	1	0	2
Townsell, JoJo, N.Y. Jets	2	0	0	0	0
Townsend, Greg, L.A. Raiders	0	0	1	1	1
Trudeau, Jack, Ind.	11	4	0	0	4
Tuatagaloa, Natu, Cin.	0	0	2	0	2
Veasey, Craig, Pitt.	0	0	1	0	1
Verdin, Clarence, Ind.	1	0	0	0	0
Villa, Danny, N.E.	0	1	0	0	1
Vlasic, Mark, S.D.	1	0	0	-1	0
Walker, Derrick, S.D.	1	0	0	0	0
Walker, Tony, Ind.	0	1	0	0	1
Warren, Chris, Sea.	3	1	0	0	1
Washington, Brian, N.Y. Jets	0	1	0	0	1
Webster, Mike, K.C.	0	1	0	0	1
Whitaker, Danta, K.C.	1	0	0	0	0
White, Lorenzo, Hou.	7	3	0	0	3
Widell, Doug, Den.	0	1	0	0	1
Wilcots, Solomon, Cin.	0	0	1	3	1
Wilhelm, Erik, Cin.	1	1	0	0	1
Williams, Brent, N.E.	0	0	2	45	2
Williams, David, Hou.	0	1	0	0	1
Williams, Ed, N.E.	0	0	1	0	1
Williams, Jarvis, Mia.	0	1	0	0	1
Williams, Jerrol, Pitt.	1	0	2	1	2
Williams, John L., Sea.	5	2	0	0	2
Williams, Warren, Pitt.	5	0	0	0	0
Willis, Keith, Pitt.	0	0	1	0	1
Wilson, Marc, N.E.	6	4	0	-5	4
Winder, Sammy, Den.	2	0	0	-9	0
Winters, Frank, K.C.	0	2	0	0	2

	Fum.	Own Rec.	Opp. Rec.	Yds.	Tot. Rec.
Woodruff, Dwayne, Pitt.	0	0	1	13	1
Woods, Ickey, Cin.	1	0	0	0	0
Woodson, Rod, Pitt.	3	3	0	0	3
Word, Barry, K.C.	4	1	0	0	1
Worley, Tim, Pitt.	6	0	0	0	0
Worthen, Naz, K.C.	1	1	0	0	1
Wright, Felix, Clev.	0	0	1	0	1
Wright, Steve, L.A. Raiders	0	2	0	0	2
Wyman, David, Sea.	0	0	1	0	1
Young, Fredd, Ind.	0	0	1	0	1
Zander, Carl, Cin.	0	0	2	40	2

Yards includes aborted plays, own recoveries, and opponents' recoveries.

NFC Fumbles—Individual

	Fum.	Own Rec.	Opp. Rec.	Yds.	Tot. Rec.
Aikman, Troy, Dall.	5	1	0	0	1
Albritton, Vince, Dall.	0	0	2	0	2
Allen, Eric, Phil.	0	0	1	0	1
Anderson, Alfred, Minn.	1	0	0	0	0
Anderson, Gary, T.B.	7	0	0	0	0
Anderson, Neal, Chi.	2	0	0	0	0
Anderson, Ottis, N.Y. Giants	1	2	0	22	2
Anderson, Willie, L.A. Rams	0	1	0	0	1
Andolsek, Eric, Det.	0	1	0	0	1
Armstrong, Trace, Chi.	0	1	1	0	2
Atkins, Gene, N.O.	1	0	3	0	3
Awalt, Robert, Dall.	1	0	0	0	0
Bailey, Johnny, Chi.	8	4	0	0	4
Banks, Carl, N.Y. Giants	0	0	1	0	1
Bellamy, Mike, Phil.	1	0	1	0	1
Bennett, Tony, G.B.	0	0	1	0	1
Blades, Bennie, Det.	0	0	1	0	1
Bland, Carl, G.B.	0	0	1	0	1
Bowles, Todd, Wash.	0	0	1	0	1
Brock, Stan, N.O.	0	1	0	0	1
Brooks, Chet, S.F.	0	0	1	0	1
Broussard, Steve, Atl.	6	0	0	0	0
Brown, Jerome, Phil.	0	0	5	10	5
Brown, Robert, G.B.	0	0	1	0	1
Bryan, Rick, Atl.	0	0	1	0	1
Buck, Vince, N.O.	2	1	1	0	2
Buford, Maury, Chi.	1	0	0	0	0
Butler, Bobby, Atl.	0	0	2	0	2
Byars, Keith, Phil.	4	1	0	0	1
Byner, Earnest, Wash.	2	1	0	0	1
Caldwell, Ravin, Wash.	0	0	1	0	1
Camarillo, Rich, Phx.	1	0	0	0	0
Campbell, Jeff, Det.	1	0	0	0	0
Campbell, Scott, Atl.	1	0	0	0	0
Campen, James, G.B.	2	0	0	-21	0
Cannon, John, T.B.	0	0	2	0	2
Carlson, Jeff, T.B.	1	0	0	0	0
Carrier, Mark, Chi.	0	0	2	16	2
Carrington, Darren, Det.	0	0	1	0	1
Carter, Anthony, Minn.	2	0	0	0	0
Carter, Dexter, S.F.	8	2	0	0	2
Carthon, Maurice, N.Y. Giants	1	0	0	0	0
Case, Scott, Atl.	0	0	2	0	2
Caston, Toby, Det.	0	0	1	0	1
Centers, Larry, Phx.	1	0	0	0	0
Chandler, Chris, T.B.	5	1	0	-2	1
Chapura, Dick, Phil.	0	1	0	0	1
Clarke, Ken, Minn.	0	0	1	0	1
Cline, Jackie, Det.	0	0	1	0	1
Cobb, Reggie, T.B.	8	6	0	0	6
Cofer, Mike, Det.	0	0	2	0	2
Collins, Shawn, Atl.	1	2	0	0	2
Craig, Roger, S.F.	2	0	0	0	0
Crockett, Ray, Det.	0	0	2	22	2
Cunningham, Randall, Phil.	9	3	0	-4	3
Dallafior, Ken, Det.	0	1	0	0	1
Davis, Eric, S.F.	0	0	1	34	1
Davis, Reuben, T.B.	0	0	1	0	1
Davis, Wendell, Chi.	1	0	0	0	0
DeLong, Keith, S.F.	0	1	2	0	3
DeOssie, Steve, N.Y. Giants	0	0	1	0	1
Del Greco, Al, Phx.	0	1	0	0	1
Delpino, Robert, L.A. Rams	1	0	0	0	0
Dent, Richard, Chi.	0	0	3	45	3
Dilweg, Anthony, G.B.	10	4	0	-9	4
Dixon, James, Dall.	2	0	0	0	0
Douglass, Maurice, Chi.	0	0	1	1	1
Drewrey, Willie, T.B.	1	0	0	0	0
Duckens, Mark, Det.	0	0	1	0	1
Duerson, Dave, N.Y. Giants	0	0	1	31	1
Dukes, Jamie, Atl.	1	1	0	-6	1
Dusbabek, Mark, Minn.	0	0	1	0	1

	Fum.	Own Rec.	Opp. Rec.	Yds.	Tot. Rec.
Edwards, Anthony, Phil.	2	0	0	0	0
Eilers, Pat, Minn.	0	0	1	0	1
Ellard, Henry, L.A. Rams	4	0	0	0	0
Everett, Eric, T.B.	0	0	1	0	1
Everett, Jim, L.A. Rams	4	0	0	-12	0
Fenerty, Gill, N.O.	4	0	0	0	0
Fenney, Rick, Minn.	3	1	0	0	1
Fontenot, Herman, G.B.	1	0	1	0	1
Fontenot, Jerry, Chi.	1	0	0	0	0
Forde, Brian, N.O.	0	0	1	0	1
Fourcade, John, N.O.	4	1	0	0	1
Francis, Ron, Dall.	0	0	2	0	2
Fullington, Darrell, Minn.	0	0	1	0	1
Fullwood, Brent, G.B.	1	0	0	0	0
Gagliano, Bob, Det.	5	0	0	-10	0
Gann, Mike, Atl.	0	0	3	0	3
Gannon, Rich, Minn.	10	6	0	-3	6
Gary, Cleveland, L.A. Rams	12	0	0	0	0
Gayle, Shaun, Chi.	0	2	1	2	3
Gentry, Dennis, Chi.	1	0	0	0	0
Gesek, John, Dall.	0	2	0	0	2
Gibson, Dennis, Det.	0	0	1	0	1
Glover, Kevin, Det.	0	1	0	0	1
Goff, Robert, N.O.	0	0	1	13	1
Gogan, Kevin, Dall.	0	1	0	0	1
Gouveia, Kurt, Wash.	0	0	1	39	1
Grant, Darryl, Wash.	0	0	2	2	2
Gray, Jerry, L.A. Rams	0	0	1	0	1
Gray, Mel, Det.	4	3	0	0	3
Green, Gaston, L.A. Rams	1	2	0	0	2
Green, Roy, Phx.	1	0	0	0	0
Green, Tim, Atl.	0	0	1	0	1
Greene, Kevin, L.A. Rams	0	0	4	0	4
Greer, Terry, Det.	0	1	0	0	1
Griffin, Don, S.F.	1	1	1	0	2
Grimes, Randy, T.B.	1	0	0	-14	0
Gruber, Paul, T.B.	0	1	0	0	1
Guyton, Myron, N.Y. Giants	0	0	2	0	2
Haddix, Michael, G.B.	3	0	0	0	0
Haddix, Wayne, T.B.	1	0	0	0	0
Haley, Charles, S.F.	0	0	1	0	1
Hamel, Dean, Dall.	0	0	1	0	1
Hamilton, Harry, T.B.	1	0	2	0	2
Hampton, Rodney, N.Y. Giants	2	0	0	0	0
Harbaugh, Jim, Chi.	8	3	0	-4	3
Hargrove, Marvin, Phil.	2	0	0	0	0
Harris, Rod, Dall.-Phil.	3	1	0	0	1
Harris, Tim, G.B.	0	0	2	28	2
Harvey, John, T.B.	2	1	0	0	1
Harvey, Ken, Phx.	0	0	1	0	1
Hayworth, Tracy, Det.	0	0	1	0	1
Hendrix, Manuel, Dall.	0	1	0	0	1
Heyward, Craig, N.O.	3	0	0	0	0
Highsmith, Alonzo, Dall.	1	0	0	0	0
Hilgenberg, Joel, N.O.	0	1	0	0	1
Hilliard, Dalton, N.O.	2	1	0	0	1
Hinton, Chris, Atl.	0	1	0	0	1
Holland, Johnny, G.B.	0	0	1	0	1
Holmes, Jerry, G.B.	0	0	3	44	3
Holohan, Pete, L.A. Rams	2	0	0	0	0
Holt, Pierce, S.F.	0	0	2	0	2
Hoover, Houston, Atl.	0	1	1	0	2
Hopkins, Wes, Phil.	0	0	1	0	1
Horton, Ray, Dall.	0	0	4	11	4
Hostetler, Jeff, N.Y. Giants	4	5	0	-4	5
Howard, Joe, Wash.	0	1	0	0	1
Humphery, Bobby, L.A. Rams	0	0	2	5	2
Ingram, Mark, N.Y. Giants	1	0	0	0	0
Irwin, Tim, Minn.	1	2	0	2	2
Jackson, John, Phx.	0	0	1	0	1
Jackson, Keith, Phil.	1	0	0	0	0
Jackson, Rickey, N.O.	0	0	7	0	7
Jamison, George, Det.	0	0	1	0	1
Jarvis, Curt, T.B.	0	0	1	6	1
Jeffcoat, Jim, Dall.	0	0	1	28	1
Johnson, Jimmie, Wash.	1	0	0	0	0
Johnson, Johnny, Phx.	7	1	0	0	1
Johnson, Pepper, N.Y. Giants	0	0	1	0	1
Johnson, Richard, Det.	2	1	0	0	1
Johnson, Tim, Wash.	0	0	1	0	1
Johnson, Tracy, Atl.	1	0	0	0	0
Johnson, Vaughan, N.O.	0	0	1	0	1
Johnston, Daryl, Dall.	1	1	0	0	1
Jones, Brent, S.F.	2	2	0	0	2
Jones, Keith, Atl.	2	0	0	0	0
Jordan, Brian, Atl.	0	0	1	0	1
Jordan, Steve, Minn.	3	0	0	0	0
Joyner, Seth, Phil.	1	0	0	0	0

	Fum.	Own Rec.	Opp. Rec.	Yds.	Tot. Rec.
Kemp, Perry, G.B.	2	0	0	0	0
Kenn, Mike, Atl.	0	1	0	0	1
Ker, Crawford, Dall.	0	1	0	0	1
Kiel, Blair, G.B.	2	1	0	0	1
Koch, Markus, Wash.	0	0	1	0	1
Lachey, Jim, Wash.	0	1	0	0	1
Laufenberg, Babe, Dall.	1	1	0	0	1
LeBel, Harper, Phil.	1	0	0	0	0
Lewis, Leo, Minn.	1	0	0	0	0
Lockhart, Eugene, Dall.	0	0	1	0	1
Lott, Ronnie, S.F.	0	0	1	3	1
Love, Duval, L.A. Rams	0	2	0	0	2
Lowdermilk, Kirk, Minn.	0	1	0	0	1
Lyles, Robert, Atl.	0	0	1	0	1
Mack, Cedric, Phx.	0	0	1	17	1
Majkowski, Don, G.B.	6	3	0	-10	3
Mandarich, Tony, G.B.	0	1	0	0	1
Mangum, John, Chi.	0	1	0	0	1
Marshall, Wilber, Wash.	0	0	1	4	1
Martin, Eric, N.O.	3	1	0	2	1
Martin, Kelvin, Dall.	2	1	0	0	1
Massey, Robert, N.O.	0	0	2	0	2
Matthews, Aubrey, Det.	2	0	0	0	0
Mayes, Rueben, N.O.	1	0	0	0	0
Mays, Alvoid, Wash.	0	1	0	0	1
McCants, Keith, T.B.	0	0	1	0	1
McDonald, Tim, Phx.	0	0	1	0	1
McGee, Buford, L.A. Rams	0	1	0	0	1
McKinnon, Dennis, Dall.	1	0	0	0	0
Meggett, Dave, N.Y. Giants	3	2	0	0	2
Merriweather, Mike, Minn.	0	0	4	44	4
Millen, Hugh, Atl.	3	0	0	0	0
Millen, Matt, S.F.	0	0	1	0	1
Miller, Chris, Atl.	11	4	0	-9	4
Mills, Sam, N.O.	0	0	1	0	1
Mitchell, Brian, Wash.	2	0	0	0	0
Mitchell, Roland, Atl.	1	0	2	0	2
Monk, Art, Wash.	0	1	0	0	1
Montana, Joe, S.F.	4	0	0	0	0
Morrissey, Jim, Chi.	0	1	2	0	3
Morse, Bobby, N.O.	1	0	0	0	0
Moss, Winston, T.B.	0	0	1	0	1
Mrosko, Bob, N.Y. Giants	0	1	0	0	1
Muster, Brad, Chi.	3	1	0	0	1
Newman, Anthony, L.A. Rams	0	0	1	0	1
Newsome, Harry, Minn.	1	1	0	-13	1
Newsome, Vince, L.A. Rams	0	0	1	0	1
Newton, Nate, Dall.	0	2	0	0	2
Noga, Al, Minn.	0	0	1	0	1
Norton, Ken, Dall.	0	0	2	0	2
Novacek, Jay, Dall.	1	0	0	0	0
Novoselsky, Brent, Minn.	0	1	0	0	1
Nunn, Freddie Joe, Phx.	0	0	1	0	1
Oates, Bart, N.Y. Giants	1	0	0	-19	0
Oldham, Chris, Det.	2	0	0	0	0
Paul, Markus, Chi.	1	0	0	0	0
Peebles, Danny, T.B.	1	1	0	3	1
Peete, Rodney, Det.	9	1	0	0	1
Perkins, Bruce, T.B.	0	1	0	0	1
Perriman, Brett, N.O.	2	1	0	0	1
Piel, Mike, L.A. Rams	0	0	2	0	2
Pillow, Frank, T.B.	0	0	1	0	1
Pitts, Ron, G.B.	0	0	1	0	1
Pollard, Darryl, S.F.	0	0	1	0	1
Pruitt, Mickey, Chi.	0	0	1	0	1
Query, Jeff, G.B.	3	2	1	0	3
Rade, John, Atl.	0	0	1	0	1
Rathman, Tom, S.F.	2	0	1	0	1
Reasons, Gary, N.Y. Giants	0	0	3	0	3
Reeves, Walter, Phx.	1	1	0	0	1
Reid, Michael, Atl.	1	0	0	0	0
Reynolds, Ricky, T.B.	0	0	2	0	2
Rice, Allen, Minn.	1	1	0	0	1
Rice, Jerry, S.F.	1	0	0	0	0
Riggs, Gerald, Wash.	2	1	0	0	1
Rison, Andre, Atl.	2	0	0	0	0
Rivera, Ron, Chi.	0	0	2	0	2
Robbins, Tootie, Phx.	0	1	0	0	1
Rosenbach, Timm, Phx.	10	4	0	0	4
Rozier, Mike, Atl.	6	3	0	0	3
Ruettgers, Ken, G.B.	0	1	0	0	1
Rutledge, Jeff, Wash.	1	0	0	0	0
Rypien, Mark, Wash.	2	0	0	-3	0
Saddler, Rod, Phx.	0	0	2	0	2
Sanders, Barry, Det.	4	2	0	0	2
Sanders, Deion, Atl.	4	2	0	0	2
Schad, Mike, Phil.	0	1	0	0	1
Shelley, Elbert, Atl.	0	0	1	0	1
Shepard, Derrick, Dall.	1	1	0	0	1
Sherman, Heath, Phil.	4	3	0	0	3
Shuler, Mickey, Phil.	1	0	0	0	0
Sikahema, Vai, Phx.	2	1	0	0	1
Simmons, Clyde, Phil.	0	0	2	28	2
Simmons, Michael, N.O.	0	0	1	0	1
Simms, Phil, N.Y. Giants	7	2	0	-5	2
Singletary, Mike, Chi.	0	0	1	0	1
Skow, Jim, T.B.	0	0	1	0	1
Smith, Doug, L.A. Rams	0	2	0	0	2
Smith, Emmitt, Dall.	7	0	0	0	0
Smith, Vinson, Dall.	0	0	2	0	2
Spielman, Chris, Det.	0	0	2	0	2
Stanley, Walter, Wash.	3	0	0	0	0
Stephen, Scott, G.B.	1	0	2	15	2
Stewart, Michael, L.A. Rams	0	0	2	0	2
Stokes, Fred, Wash.	0	0	4	5	4
Strauthers, Tom, Minn.	0	0	1	0	1
Stubbs, Danny, Dall.	0	0	2	0	2
Sydney, Harry, S.F.	1	0	0	0	0
Taylor, John, S.F.	2	0	0	0	0
Taylor, Lawrence, N.Y. Giants	0	0	1	0	1
Taylor, Rob, T.B.	0	1	0	-1	1
Terrell, Pat, L.A. Rams	1	0	1	0	1
Testaverde, Vinny, T.B.	10	3	0	0	3
Thayer, Tom, Chi.	0	1	0	0	1
Thomas, Broderick, T.B.	0	0	2	0	2
Thomas, Henry, Minn.	0	0	1	0	1
Thomas, Johnny, Wash.	1	0	0	0	0
Thompson, Anthony, Phx.	1	0	0	0	0
Thompson, Darrell, G.B.	1	0	0	0	0
Thompson, Reyna, N.Y. Giants	0	0	1	0	1
Thornton, James, Chi.	1	0	0	0	0
Tice, John, N.O.	1	1	0	0	1
Tomczak, Mike, Chi.	2	0	0	-2	0
Toney, Anthony, Phil.	3	3	0	0	3
Trapilo, Steve, N.O.	0	1	0	0	1
Tuggle, Jessie, Atl.	0	0	2	65	2
Tupa, Tom, Phx.	1	0	0	-7	0
Turnbull, Renaldo, N.O.	0	0	1	0	1
Turner, Marcus, Phx.	0	0	1	0	1
Walker, Herschel, Minn.	4	0	0	0	0
Walsh, Steve, Dall.-N.O.	6	2	0	0	2
Warner, Curt, L.A. Rams	1	0	0	0	0
Washington, James, Dall.	0	1	2	0	3
Waymer, Dave, S.F.	0	0	1	0	1
Welch, Herb, Det.	0	0	1	0	1
West, Ed, G.B.	3	0	0	0	0
White, Reggie, Phil.	0	0	1	0	1
Whitmore, Dave, N.Y. Giants	1	0	0	0	0
Wilcher, Mike, L.A. Rams	0	0	4	2	4
Williams, Calvin, Phil.	2	2	0	0	2
Williams, Jimmy, Det.	0	0	3	53	3
Wilson, Mike, S.F.	0	1	0	0	1
Wilson, Wade, Minn.	3	1	0	-2	1
Wolfley, Craig, Minn.	0	1	0	0	1
Woodside, Keith, G.B.	2	0	0	0	0
Wright, Alexander, Dall.	1	1	0	0	1
Wright, Alvin, L.A. Rams	0	0	1	0	1
Wright, Eric, S.F.	0	0	1	0	1
Wyatt, Willie, T.B.	0	0	1	0	1
Young, Lonnie, Phx.	0	0	2	0	2
Young, Steve, S.F.	1	0	0	0	0
Zordich, Mike, Phx.	0	0	1	0	1

Yards includes aborted plays, own recoveries, and opponents' recoveries.

Sacks

Individual Champions

AFC: 20.0—Derrick Thomas, Kansas City
NFC: 16.0—Charles Haley, San Francisco

Most Sacks, Game

AFC: 7.0—Derrick Thomas, Kansas City vs. Seattle, November 11
NFC: 4.0—Pat Swilling, New Orleans vs. Tampa Bay, November 11

Team Champions

AFC: 60—Kansas City
NFC: 47—Minnesota

AFC Sacks—Team

	Sacks	Yards
Kansas City	60	421
L.A. Raiders	48	335
Miami	45	348
San Diego	45	345
Buffalo	43	326
Houston	38	272
N.Y. Jets	38	308
Denver	34	289
Pittsburgh	34	228
New England	33	224
Seattle	33	252
Cleveland	32	211
Indianapolis	29	203
Cincinnati	25	205
AFC Total	537	3967
AFC Average	38.4	283.4

NFC Sacks—Team

	Sacks	Yards
Minnesota	47	277
Philadelphia	45	280
Washington	45	340
San Francisco	44	263
New Orleans	42	265
Chicago	41	300
Detroit	41	279
Dallas	36	292
Phoenix	36	232
Tampa Bay	34	204
Atlanta	33	214
N.Y. Giants	30	186
L.A. Rams	30	180
Green Bay	27	172
NFC Total	531	3484
NFC Average	37.9	248.9
League Total	1068	7451
League Average	38.1	266.1

NFL Top 10 Individual Leaders in Sacks

	Total		Total
Thomas, Derrick, K.C.	20.0	Byrd, Dennis, N.Y. Jets	13.0
Smith, Bruce, Buff.	19.0	Greene, Kevin, L.A. Rams	13.0
Haley, Charles, S.F.	16.0	Green, Jacob, Sea.	12.5
White, Reggie, Phil.	14.0	Jones, Sean, Hou.	12.5
O'Neal, Leslie, S.D.	13.5	Townsend, Greg, L.A. Raiders	12.5

AFC Sacks—Individual

Thomas, Derrick, K.C.	20.0
Smith, Bruce, Buff.	19.0
O'Neal, Leslie, S.D.	13.5
Byrd, Dennis, N.Y. Jets	13.0
Green, Jacob, Sea.	12.5
Jones, Sean, Hou.	12.5
Townsend, Greg, L.A. Raiders	12.5
Cross, Jeff, Mia.	11.5
Perry, Michael Dean, Clev.	11.5
Fletcher, Simon, Den.	11.0
Davis, Scott, L.A. Raiders	10.0
Grossman, Burt, S.D.	10.0
Smith, Neil, K.C.	9.5
Wallace, Aaron, L.A. Raiders	9.0
Childress, Ray, Hou.	8.0
Francis, James, Cin.	8.0
Fuller, William, Hou.	8.0
Clancy, Sam, Ind.	7.5
Williams, Lee, S.D.	7.5
Saleaumua, Dan, K.C.	7.0
Junior, E.J., Mia.	6.0
Long, Howie, L.A. Raiders	6.0
Williams, Brent, N.E.	6.0
Williams, Gerald, Pitt.	6.0
Bryant, Jeff, Sea.	5.5
Griggs, David, Mia.	5.5
Maas, Bill, K.C.	5.5
Martin, Chris, K.C.	5.5
Davis, Darrell, N.Y. Jets	5.0
Mecklenburg, Karl, Den.	5.0
Porter, Rufus, Sea.	5.0
Willis, Keith, Pitt.	5.0
Wright, Jeff, Buff.	5.0
Banks, Chip, Ind.	4.5
Bickett, Duane, Ind.	4.5
Lloyd, Greg, Pitt.	4.5
Mersereau, Scott, N.Y. Jets	4.5
Tuatagaloa, Natu, Cin.	4.5
Washington, Marvin, N.Y. Jets	4.5
Bennett, Cornelius, Buff.	4.0
Golic, Bob, L.A. Raiders	4.0
Herrod, Jeff, Ind.	4.0
Lageman, Jeff, N.Y. Jets	4.0
Powers, Warren, Den.	4.0
Seals, Leon, Buff.	4.0
Talley, Darryl, Buff.	4.0
Wilson, Karl, Mia.	4.0
Davidson, Kenny, Pitt.	3.5
Griffin, Leonard, K.C.	3.5
Matthews, Clay, Clev.	3.5
Nichols, Gerald, N.Y. Jets	3.5
Pleasant, Anthony, Clev.	3.5
Rolling, Henry, S.D.	3.5
Tippett, Andre, N.E.	3.5
Baker, Al, Clev.	3.0
Bayless, Martin, S.D.	3.0
Evans, Donald, Pitt.	3.0
Hackett, Dino, K.C.	3.0
Hand, Jon, Ind.	3.0
Hobby, Marion, N.E.	3.0
Hobley, Liffort, Mia.	3.0
Holmes, Ron, Den.	3.0
Singleton, Chris, N.E.	3.0
Woods, Tony, Sea.	3.0
Agnew, Ray, N.E.	2.5
Braggs, Stephen, Clev.	2.5
Brown, Vincent, N.E.	2.5
Goad, Tim, N.E.	2.5
Johnson, Ezra, Hou.	2.5
Meads, Johnny, Hou.	2.5
Oglesby, Alfred, Mia.	2.5
Bailey, Carlton, Buff.	2.0
Brooks, Michael, Den.	2.0
Burnett, Rob, Clev.	2.0
Bussey, Barney, Cin.	2.0
Cooper, Louis, K.C.	2.0
Faulkner, Jeff, Ind.	2.0
Freeman, Lorenzo, Pitt.	2.0
Galloway, David, Den.	2.0
Glasgow, Nesby, Sea.	2.0
Green, Hugh, Mia.	2.0
Hammerstein, Mike, Cin.	2.0
Hinkle, Bryan, Pitt.	2.0
Jenkins, A.J., Pitt.	2.0
Johnson, Mike, Clev.	2.0
Jones, Aaron, Pitt.	2.0
Kragen, Greg, Den.	2.0
Krumrie, Tim, Cin.	2.0
Lodish, Mike, Buff.	2.0
McClendon, Skip, Cin.	2.0
McDaniel, Terry, L.A. Raiders	2.0
McSwain, Rod, N.E.	2.0
Nickerson, Hardy, Pitt.	2.0
Robinson, Gerald, S.D.	2.0
Robinson, Jerry, L.A. Raiders	2.0
Smith, Doug, Hou.	2.0
Snow, Percy, K.C.	2.0
Veris, Garin, N.E.	2.0
Williams, Ed, N.E.	2.0
Williams, Jarvis, Mia.	2.0
Lee, Shawn, Mia.	1.5
Pickel, Bill, L.A. Raiders	1.5
Smith, Sean, N.E.	1.5
Thompson, Donnell, Ind.	1.5
Atwater, Steve, Den.	1.0
Bell, Mike, K.C.	1.0
Blaylock, Anthony, Clev.	1.0
Brown, J.B., Mia.	1.0
Comeaux, Darren, Sea.	1.0
Conlan, Shane, Buff.	1.0
Dennison, Rick, Den.	1.0
Fulcher, David, Cin.	1.0
Gibson, Tom, Clev.	1.0
Glenn, Kerry, Mia.	1.0
Grant, David, Cin.	1.0
Grayson, Dave, Clev.	1.0
Hicks, Cliff, Buff.	1.0
Johnson, Troy, N.Y. Jets	1.0
Kennedy, Cortez, Sea.	1.0
Lake, Carnell, Pitt.	1.0
Lucas, Tim, Den.	1.0
McElroy, Vann, Sea.	1.0
Meisner, Greg, K.C.	1.0
Miller, Les, S.D.	1.0
Nash, Joe, Sea.	1.0
Odom, Cliff, Mia.	1.0
Offerdahl, John, Mia.	1.0
Oliver, Louis, Mia.	1.0
Rembert, Johnny, N.E.	1.0
Reynolds, Ed, N.E.	1.0
Seau, Junior, S.D.	1.0
Siragusa, Tony, Ind.	1.0
Smith, Al, Hou.	1.0
Smith, Billy Ray, S.D.	1.0
Sochia, Brian, Mia.	1.0
Stallworth, Ron, N.Y. Jets	1.0
Townsend, Andre, Den.	1.0
Turner, T.J., Mia.	1.0
Walker, Kevin, Cin.	1.0
Washington, Brian, N.Y. Jets	1.0
White, Leon, Cin.	1.0
Williams, Jerrol, Pitt.	1.0
Wise, Mike, L.A. Raiders	1.0
Wyman, David, Sea.	1.0
Alm, Jeff, Hou.	0.5
Buck, Jason, Cin.	0.5
Buczkowski, Bob, Clev.	0.5
Clifton, Kyle, N.Y. Jets	0.5
Elder, Donnie, S.D.	0.5
Gannon, Chris, N.E.	0.5
Garner, Hal, Buff.	0.5
Hinkle, George, S.D.	0.5
McDowell, Bubba, Hou.	0.5
Montgomery, Glenn, Hou.	0.5
Patton, Marvcus, Buff.	0.5
Phillips, Joe, S.D.	0.5
Waiters, Van, Clev.	0.5

NFC Sacks—Individual

Haley, Charles, S.F.	16.0
White, Reggie, Phil.	14.0
Greene, Kevin, L.A. Rams	13.0
Dent, Richard, Chi.	12.0
Doleman, Chris, Minn.	11.0
Swilling, Pat, N.O.	11.0
Taylor, Lawrence, N.Y. Giants	10.5
Armstrong, Trace, Chi.	10.0
Cofer, Mike, Det.	10.0
Harvey, Ken, Phx.	10.0
Fagan, Kevin, S.F.	9.5
Nunn, Freddie Joe, Phx.	9.0
Turnbull, Renaldo, N.O.	9.0
Thomas, Henry, Minn.	8.5
Jones, Jimmie, Dall.	7.5
Joyner, Seth, Phil.	7.5
Simmons, Clyde, Phil.	7.5
Stokes, Fred, Wash.	7.5
Stubbs, Danny, Dall.	7.5

Thomas, Broderick, T.B.	7.5
Clarke, Ken, Minn.	7.0
Harris, Tim, G.B.	7.0
Brown, Dennis, S.F.	6.0
Collins, Andre, Wash.	6.0
Green, Tim, Atl.	6.0
Jackson, Rickey, N.O.	6.0
Noga, Al, Minn.	6.0
Tolbert, Tony, Dall.	6.0
Holt, Pierce, S.F.	5.5
Mann, Charles, Wash.	5.5
Randle, Ervin, T.B.	5.5
Wilks, Jim, N.O.	5.5
Marshall, Wilber, Wash.	5.0
Piel, Mike, L.A. Rams	5.0
Tuggle, Jessie, Atl.	5.0
Marshall, Leonard, N.Y. Giants	4.5
Noonan, Danny, Dall.	4.5
Brock, Matt, G.B.	4.0
Bruce, Aundray, Atl.	4.0
Hayworth, Tracy, Det.	4.0
Jackson, Greg, N.Y. Giants	4.0
Martin, Wayne, N.O.	4.0
McMichael, Steve, Chi.	4.0
Murphy, Kevin, T.B.	4.0
Patterson, Shawn, G.B.	4.0
Perry, William, Chi.	4.0
Saddler, Rod, Phx.	4.0
Strauthers, Tom, Minn.	4.0
Gann, Mike, Atl.	3.5
Jeffcoat, Jim, Dall.	3.5
Johnson, Pepper, N.Y. Giants	3.5
Moss, Winston, T.B.	3.5
Small, Jessie, Phil.	3.5
Atkins, Gene, N.O.	3.0
Bell, Anthony, Phx.	3.0
Bennett, Tony, G.B.	3.0
Brown, Robert, G.B.	3.0
Browner, Joey, Minn.	3.0
Case, Scott, Atl.	3.0
Coleman, Monte, Wash.	3.0
Cox, Ron, Chi.	3.0
Duckens, Mark, Det.	3.0
Epps, Tory, Atl.	3.0
Ferguson, Keith, Det.	3.0
Geathers, James, Wash.	3.0
Hawkins, Bill, L.A. Rams	3.0
Howard, Erik, N.Y. Giants	3.0
Hunter, Jeff, Det.	3.0
Jax, Garth, Phx.	3.0
Johnson, Tim, Wash.	3.0
Newton, Tim, T.B.	3.0
Owens, Dan, Det.	3.0
Pitts, Mike, Phil.	3.0
Reid, Michael, Atl.	3.0
Rocker, Tracy, Wash.	3.0
Williams, Eric, Wash.	3.0
Williams, Jimmy, Det.	3.0
Merriweather, Mike, Minn.	2.5
Norton, Ken, Dall.	2.5
Wahler, Jim, Phx.	2.5
White, Robb, T.B.	2.5
Ball, Jerry, Det.	2.0
Bethune, George, L.A. Rams	2.0
Burt, Jim, S.F.	2.0
Conner, Darion, Atl.	2.0
Faryniarz, Brett, L.A. Rams	2.0
Golic, Mike, Phil.	2.0
Hopkins, Wes, Phil.	2.0
Jamison, George, Det.	2.0
Jones, Dante, Chi.	2.0
Koch, Markus, Wash.	2.0
Marve, Eugene, T.B.	2.0
McCants, Keith, T.B.	2.0
Millard, Keith, Minn.	2.0
Reed, Doug, L.A. Rams	2.0
Skow, Jim, T.B.	2.0
Spielman, Chris, Det.	2.0
Woolford, Donnell, Chi.	2.0
Del Rio, Jack, Dall.	1.5
Fox, Mike, N.Y. Giants	1.5
Frizzell, William, Phil.	1.5
Hill, Eric, Phx.	1.5
Lyles, Robert, Atl.	1.5
Banks, Carl, N.Y. Giants	1.0
Blades, Bennie, Det.	1.0
Bowles, Todd, Wash.	1.0
Brooks, Kevin, Det.	1.0
Brown, Jerome, Phil.	1.0
Bryan, Rick, Atl.	1.0
Caldwell, Ravin, Wash.	1.0
Cannon, John, T.B.	1.0
Carter, Michael, S.F.	1.0
Casillas, Tony, Atl.	1.0
Chapura, Dick, Phil.	1.0
Cline, Jackie, Det.	1.0
Cook, Toi, N.O.	1.0
Cooks, Johnie, N.Y. Giants	1.0
Crockett, Ray, Det.	1.0
Davis, Reuben, T.B.	1.0
Dent, Burnell, G.B.	1.0
Evans, Byron, Phil.	1.0
Fullington, Darrell, Minn.	1.0
Gayle, Shaun, Chi.	1.0
Gouveia, Kurt, Wash.	1.0
Grant, Darryl, Wash.	1.0
Hairston, Carl, Phx.	1.0
Hamel, Dean, Dall.	1.0
Hoage, Terry, Phil.	1.0
Holmes, Jerry, G.B.	1.0
Jackson, Johnny, S.F.	1.0
Johnson, Vaughan, N.O.	1.0
Jones, Victor, Det.	1.0
Lockhart, Eugene, Dall.	1.0
Mack, Cedric, Phx.	1.0
Murphy, Mark, G.B.	1.0
Nelson, Bob, G.B.	1.0
Noble, Brian, G.B.	1.0
Osborne, Eldonta, Phx.	1.0
Pruitt, Mickey, Chi.	1.0
Randle, John, Minn.	1.0
Roberts, Larry, S.F.	1.0
Romanowski, Bill, S.F.	1.0
Roper, John, Chi.	1.0
Simmons, Michael, N.O.	1.0
Singletary, Mike, Chi.	1.0
Smith, Brian, L.A. Rams	1.0
Solomon, Jesse, Dall.	1.0
Spindler, Marc, Det.	1.0
Stephen, Scott, G.B.	1.0
Thompson, Reyna, N.Y. Giants	1.0
Turner, Keena, S.F.	1.0
Wilcher, Mike, L.A. Rams	1.0
Wright, Alvin, L.A. Rams	1.0
Mills, Sam, N.O.	0.5

1990 NFL Paid Attendance Breakdown

	Games	Attendance	Average
AFC Preseason	8	325,291	40,661
NFC Preseason	7	340,168	48,595
AFC-NFC Preseason, Interconference	44	2,192,843	49,837
NFL Preseason Total	**59**	**2,858,302**	**48,455**
AFC Regular Season	86	5,410,441	62,912
NFC Regular Season	86	5,331,930	61,999
AFC-NFC Regular Season, Interconference	52	3,217,525	61,875
NFL Regular Season Total	**224**	**13,959,896**	**62,321**
AFC First-Round Playoffs	2		
(Houston at Cincinnati)		59,428	
(Kansas City at Miami)		72,259	
AFC Divisional Playoffs	2		
(Cincinnati at Los Angeles Raiders)		91,003	
(Miami at Buffalo)		79,752	
AFC Championship Game	1		
(Los Angeles Raiders at Buffalo)		80,362	
NFC First-Round Playoffs	2		
(New Orleans at Chicago)		66,268	
(Washington at Philadelphia)		65,757	
NFC Divisional Playoffs	2		
(Washington at San Francisco)		65,559	
(Chicago at New York Giants)		76,663	
NFC Championship Game	1		
(New York Giants at San Francisco)		66,334	
Super Bowl XXV at Tampa, Florida	1		
(Buffalo vs. New York Giants)		73,813	
AFC-NFC Pro Bowl at Honolulu, Hawaii	1	50,345	
NFL Postseason Total	**12**	**847,543**	**70,629**
NFL All Games	**295**	**17,665,671**	**59,884**

One Million Plus Club

During the 1990 season, 15 clubs drew a combined home and away paid attendance of more than one million. The Buffalo Bills drew an NFL-leading 1,143,883 fans in 1990.

Team	Total Paid Home Attendance	Total Paid Visiting Attendance	Total Paid Attendance
Buffalo	621,528	522,355	1,143,883
Denver	598,766	528,807	1,127,573
Cleveland	582,988	538,045	1,121,033
N.Y. Giants	608,150	477,600	1,085,750
Chicago	528,539	546,742	1,075,281
Detroit	539,718	522,216	1,061,934
N.Y. Jets	603,647	444,043	1,047,690
Miami	522,941	520,878	1,043,819
Kansas City	578,958	453,825	1,032,783
Philadelphia	525,425	505,850	1,031,275
L.A. Raiders	459,125	564,407	1,023,532
San Francisco	523,013	495,633	1,018,646
Minnesota	494,803	520,282	1,015,085
New Orleans	528,674	483,255	1,011,929
Pittsburgh	473,286	530,848	1,004,134

INSIDE THE NUMBERS

Seventy-Two Notes on the NFL's Seventy-Second Season

1 Father-son combination serve as active on-field officials in the NFL: Jerry Bergman, a head linesman in his twenty-sixth season, and son Jeff, a line judge in his first year in the league.

2 Number of victories needed by Miami Dolphins coach Don Shula to join George Halas (325) as the only NFL coaches to achieve 300 career wins.

3 Consecutive AFC East division titles (1988-90) by the Buffalo Bills, matching the team record set from 1964 to 1966.

4 Consecutive road wins needed by the San Francisco 49ers (18 consecutive road wins entering 1991) to break the all-time team sports record of 21 set by baseball's Detroit Tigers in 1983 and 1984.

5 Fumbles needed by Seattle Seahawks quarterback Dave Krieg (102 fumbles entering 1991) to break the NFL career record of 106 fumbles held by Dan Fouts.

6 Rushing touchdowns needed by Indianapolis Colts running back Eric Dickerson (86 entering 1991) to move past Franco Harris into fourth place in NFL history.

7 Consecutive opening-day wins by the Chicago Bears, the longest current streak in the NFL.

8 Seasons in which Kansas City Chiefs kicker Nick Lowery has scored 100-or-more points, an NFL record.

9 Number of times both teams had at least one possession in the 10 overtime games in 1990.

10 Touchdown receptions needed by San Francisco 49ers wide receiver Jerry Rice (79 entering 1991) to move up to third place in NFL history, behind Steve Largent (100) and Don Hutson (99).

11 Number of consecutive Pro Bowls appearances by New York Giants linebacker Lawrence Taylor if he is voted to the NFC Pro Bowl roster following the 1991 season. Taylor currently holds the Pro Bowl record with 10 appearances.

12 Number of years the AFC has won the AFC-NFC interconference series since the 1970 merger. The AFC holds 12-4-5 lead over the NFC.

13 Regular-season tie games which have been played in the NFL since the overtime rule was adopted in 1974.

14 Wins needed by Pittsburgh Steelers coach Chuck Noll to become the fifth coach in NFL history to win 200 games.

15 Number of teams which drew a combined home and away paid attendance of more than one million in 1990.

16 Touchdown passes needed by Seattle Seahawks quarterback Dave Krieg to become the fifteenth quarterback in NFL history to throw 200 scoring passes.

17 Weeks during which each NFL team will complete its 16-game regular-season schedule in 1991.

18 Equals the most players ever selected from one school in an NFL Draft. Frank Dancewicz was the first pick of the draft and also the first of the 18 players selected from Notre Dame in 1946.

19 Years of Public Service Announcements during NFL telecasts. Since 1971, more than 500 NFL owners, players, coaches, and wives have participated in these public service spots.

20 Number of points New York Giants scored in victory over the Buffalo Bills in Super Bowl XXV. The one-point win (20-19) was the slimmest margin of victory in Super Bowl history.

21 Receptions needed by Washington Redskins wide receiver Art Monk (730 entering 1991) to move past Charlie Joiner (750) into second place in NFL history, behind Steve Largent (819).

22 Number of postseason appearances by season by the Cleveland Browns, Los Angeles Rams, and New York Giants, most in NFL history.

23 Equals the number of years the Dallas Cowboys have won their season opener. Dallas's 23-7-1 record on opening day tops the NFL.

24 Jersey number of New York Giants running back Ottis Anderson, who was the first recipient of the Pete Rozelle Award as the Super Bowl MVP for his performance in Super Bowl XXV.

25 Points needed by New York Giants kicker Matt Bahr to become the eighteenth player in NFL history to score 1,000 points.

26 Of January, 1992, the date of Super Bowl XXVI at the Hubert H. Humphrey Metrodome in Minneapolis.

27 Years as an NFL official for referee Pat Haggerty, the longest tenure of any active on-field official.

28 Years as an NFL head coach for the Miami Dolphins' Don Shula, the longest total for any active head coach. He spent seven years (1963-69) with the Colts (73-26-4) and begins his twenty-second season with the Dolphins (225-111-2) in 1991.

29 Number of victories by the Los Angeles Raiders on ABC-TV's Monday Night Football, most of any NFL team.

30 Number of years ago that Canton, Ohio, was selected as the site of the Pro Football Hall of Fame. This year's class of five inductees brings the total to 160 of NFL greats named to the Hall of Fame.

31 Year anniversary of the Shotgun formation, created by Red Hickey of the San Francisco 49ers for their *fleet* rookie quarterback Billy Kilmer.

32 Wins for Don Shula vs. the Buffalo Bills, the most against any single team among his 298 career victories.

33 Receptions needed by Indianapolis Colts wide receiver Stanley Morgan (557 entering 1991) to move into top 10 in receptions in NFL history.

34 Jersey number of running back Earl Campbell, one of five Hall of Fame inductees in 1991. The other inductees are John Hannah, Stan Jones, Tex Schramm, and Jan Stenerud.

35 Year anniversary of CBS becoming the first network to broadcast NFL games to selected TV markets across the country.

36 Year anniversary—August 28, 1955—of the first sudden-death overtime game. The Los Angeles Rams defeated the New York Giants 23-17 three minutes into overtime in a preseason game in Portland, Oregon. Three years later—December 28, 1958—the first sudden-death overtime in an NFL Championship Game was played when the Baltimore Colts defeated the Giants 23-17 after 8:15 of overtime.

37 Number of yards Buffalo Bills wide receiver James Lofton needs to become the third player to gain 12,000 receiving yards. Steve Largent (13,089) and Charlie Joiner (12,146) are the others.

38 Points needed by New York Jets kicker Pat Leahy to become the fourth player in NFL history to score 1,400 points. The others are George Blanda (2,002), Jan Stenerud (1,699), and Jim Turner (1,439).

39 According to a 1990 survey, 39.1 percent of people 18 or older chose the NFL as the number-one spectator sport.

40 Rushing attempts needed by Los Angeles Raiders running back Marcus Allen to become tenth player in NFL history with 2,000 career rushes.

41 Completions needed by Denver Broncos quarterback John Elway to become the twenty-fifth quarterback in NFL history to amass 2,000 completions.

42 Seasons in the NFL for the Cleveland Browns and San Francisco 49ers, teams that entered the league from the All-America Conference in 1950.

43 Percent of games won by seven points or less in 1990 (97 of 224).

44 Yards per punt (44.4) by Denver Broncos punter Mike Horan, the NFL's punting champion last season. It marked the seventh time in 31 years that Denver has produced the league's punting champion.

45 Number of takeaways by the Chicago Bears and Kansas City Chiefs last season, most in the NFL.

46 Jersey number of former Oakland/Los Angeles Raiders tight end Todd Christensen, who was waived by the Dallas Cowboys and New York Giants before signing with the Raiders in 1979. After retiring in 1989, Christensen used his NFL playing career to move into a second career in broadcasting with NBC-TV.

47 Represents the number of players on a team's regular-season roster. At least two players must be designated inactive each week to drop to the game time limit of 45. Beginning with the 1991 season, if a team has only two quarterbacks on its 45-player Active List, a third quarterback from its Inactive List is permitted to dress for the game, but if he participates in the game, the other two quarterbacks are thereafter prohibited from playing.

48 Points needed by Kansas City Chiefs kicker Nick Lowery to become the tenth player in NFL history to score 1,200 points.

49 Years ago, the 1942 Chicago Bears finished the season 11-0 and averaged outscoring the opposition 34-8. They lost the NFL Championship Game to the Washington Redskins, 14-6.

50 Or more receptions by Miami Dolphins wide receiver Mark Clayton would make him the seventeenth player in NFL history to have registered six-or-more seasons with 50-plus receptions.

51 Career interceptions by Los Angeles Raiders safety Ronnie Lott, the most by any active player.

52 Year anniversary of NBC-TV showing the first-ever broadcast of an NFL game. The game between the Brooklyn Dodgers and the Philadelphia Eagles was seen on approximately 1,000 television sets on October 22, 1939.

53 Year that 1991 Hall of Fame inductee Stan Jones was drafted out of Maryland by the Chicago Bears. Jones went on to play 12 seasons with the Bears and finished his career with the Redskins in 1966. Jones and 26 former Bears are enshrined in the Pro Football Hall of Fame, most of any NFL team.

54 Year of birth of Kansas City Chiefs quarterback Steve DeBerg—oldest starting player during the 1990 season.

55 Victories over NFC teams by the Miami Dolphins for most interconference wins among all NFL teams.

56 This year's NFL Pro Bowl on February 2, 1992, will mark the fifty-sixth time the game has been played. Last year's game was won by the AFC 23-21 in front of 50,345 fans, the twelfth consecutive sellout in Honolulu's Aloha Stadium.

57 Year anniversary of the Chicago Bears-Detroit Lions game which was the first game ever broadcast nationally. The game was broadcast on Thanksgiving Day, November 29, 1934. Graham McNamee was the announcer for CBS Radio.

58 Completions needed by Kansas City Chiefs quarterback Steve DeBerg (2,376 entering 1991) to move past Sonny Jurgensen into ninth place in NFL history.

59 Defensive backs selected in the 1991 NFL draft, the most players chosen from any position. The first defensive back chosen was UCLA's Eric Turner, selected by the Cleveland Browns as the second pick overall in the draft.

60 Approximate number of countries that viewed the Super Bowl XXV broadcast in 1991.

61 Year that the first million dollar gate in the history of professional football was achieved when the Green Bay Packers defeated the New York Giants 37-0 in Green Bay on December 31, 1961. Gross receipts, including radio and TV, were $1,013,792.

62 Year anniversary of Chicago Cardinals' Ernie Nevers scoring 40 points in one game, the oldest individual single game record. Nevers scored six rushing touchdowns and four extra points as the Cardinals defeated the Bears 40-6 on November 28, 1929.

63 Percent (63.3) of passes completed last season by Buffalo Bills quarterback Jim Kelly, who led the NFL in 1990 with a 101.2 quarterback rating.

64 Points are the most scored in a shutout victory (Philadelphia Eagles vs. Cincinnati Bengals on November 6, 1934).

65 Yards on receptions needed by Washington Redskins wide receiver Art Monk to make him the eighth receiver in NFL history to accumulate 10,000 career yards.

66 Points needed by Pittsburgh Steelers kicker Gary Anderson to move into nineteenth place in NFL history ahead of Sam Baker (975).

67 Jersey number of Dallas Cowboys defensive tackle Russell Maryland, the number-one pick in the 1991 draft.

68 Rushing yards needed by Denver Broncos quarterback John Elway to reach 2,000 for his career. Fran Tarkenton is the NFL's all-time quarterback rushing leader with 3,674 yards.

69 Year anniversary—June 24, 1922—of the American Professional Football Association changing its name to the National Football League.

70 Jerry Seeman's jersey number before he retired after the 1990 season to become the NFL's Director of Officiating.

71 Seasons in the NFL for the Green Bay Packers, who finished 3-2-1 in their initial season of 1921.

72 NFL's seventy-second season begins weekend of September 1–2, 1991.

Comparison of Joe Montana's Career Statistics With Hall of Fame Quarterbacks Whose Careers Ended Since 1945

Passing

	Att.	Comp.	Pct.	Yds.	Avg.	Lng.	TD	Pct.	Int.	Pct.	Rating
Joe Montana	4579	2914	63.6	34,998	7.64	96t	242	5.3	123	2.7	93.4
Sammy Baugh	2995	1693	56.5	21,886	7.31	86t	187	6.2	203	6.8	72.0
George Blanda	4007	1911	47.7	26,920	6.72	95t	236	5.9	277	6.9	60.8
Terry Bradshaw	3901	2025	51.9	27,989	7.17	90t	212	5.4	210	5.4	70.9
Len Dawson	3741	2136	57.1	28,711	7.67	92t	239	6.4	183	4.9	82.6
Otto Graham	1565	872	55.7	13,499	8.63	81t	88	5.6	94	6.0	78.1
Bob Griese	3429	1926	56.2	25,092	7.32	86t	192	5.6	172	5.0	77.1
Arnie Herber*	1175	481	40.9	8,041	6.84	92t	78	6.6	106	9.0	49.3
Sonny Jurgensen	4262	2433	57.1	32,224	7.56	99t	255	6.0	189	4.4	82.8
Bobby Layne	3700	1814	49.0	26,768	7.23	97t	196	5.3	243	6.6	63.4
Sid Luckman	1744	904	51.8	14,686	8.42	86t	137	7.9	132	7.6	75.0
Joe Namath	3762	1886	50.1	27,663	7.35	91	173	4.6	220	5.8	65.6
Bart Starr	3149	1808	57.4	24,718	7.85	91t	152	4.8	138	4.4	80.5
Roger Staubach	2958	1685	57.0	22,700	7.67	91t	153	5.2	109	3.7	83.4
Fran Tarkenton	6467	3686	57.0	47,003	7.27	89t	342	5.3	266	4.1	80.4
Y.A. Tittle	3817	2118	55.5	28,339	7.42	78t	212	5.6	221	5.8	73.8
Johnny Unitas	5186	2830	54.6	40,239	7.76	89t	290	5.6	253	4.9	78.2
Norm Van Brocklin	2895	1553	53.6	23,611	8.16	91t	173	6.0	178	6.1	75.3
Bob Waterfield	1617	814	50.3	11,849	7.33	91t	97	6.0	128	7.9	61.6

Rushing

	Yrs.	Last Year	G	Att.	Yds.	Avg.	Lng.	TD
Joe Montana	12	1990	166	411	1567	3.8	21	20
Sammy Baugh	16	1952	165	324	325	1.0	41t	9
George Blanda	26	1975	340	135	344	2.5	19	9
Terry Bradshaw	14	1983	168	444	2257	5.1	39	32
Len Dawson	19	1975	211	294	1293	4.4	43	9
Otto Graham	6	1955	72	306	682	2.2	36	33
Bob Griese	14	1980	161	261	994	3.8	35	7
Arnie Herber*	13	1945	x	250	116	0.5	x	2
Sonny Jurgensen	18	1974	218	181	492	2.7	33	15
Bobby Layne	15	1962	175	611	2451	4.0	36	25
Sid Luckman	12	1950	128	204	−239	1.2	40t	4
Joe Namath	13	1977	140	71	140	2.0	39	7
Bart Starr	16	1971	196	247	1308	5.3	39	15
Roger Staubach	11	1979	131	410	2264	5.5	33	20
Fran Tarkenton	18	1978	246	675	3674	5.4	52t	32
Y.A. Tittle	15	1964	178	291	999	3.4	45	33
Johnny Unitas	18	1973	211	450	1777	3.9	34	13
Norm Van Brocklin	12	1960	140	102	40	0.4	16	11
Bob Waterfield	8	1952	91	75	21	0.3	25	13

*statistics do not include 1930-31 seasons. xUnavailable.

Joe Montana's Game-by-Game Postseason Career

Date	Game	Opponent	Att.	Comp.	Pct.	Yds.	Avg.	TD	Int.	Rating
Jan. 3, 1982	NFC Divisional Playoff	N.Y. Giants	31	20	64.5	304	9.81	2	1	104.8
Jan. 10, 1982	NFC Championship Game	Dallas	35	22	62.9	286	8.17	3	3	81.4
Jan. 24, 1982	Super Bowl XVI	Cincinnati	22	14	63.6	157	7.14	1	0	100.0
Dec. 31, 1983	NFC Divisional Playoff	Detroit	31	18	58.1	201	6.48	1	1	74.8
Jan. 8, 1984	NFC Championship Game	Washington	48	27	56.3	347	7.23	3	1	91.2
Dec. 29, 1984	NFC Divisional Playoff	N.Y. Giants	39	25	64.1	309	7.92	3	3	82.1
Jan. 6, 1985	NFC Championship Game	Chicago	34	18	52.9	233	6.85	1	2	60.0

Date	Game	Opponent	Att.	Comp.	Pct.	Yds.	Avg.	TD	Int.	Rating
Jan. 20, 1985	Super Bowl XIX	Miami	35	24	68.6	331	9.46	3	0	127.2
Dec. 29, 1985	NFC First-Round Game	N.Y. Giants	47	26	55.3	296	6.30	0	1	65.6
Jan. 4, 1987	NFC Divisional Playoff	N.Y. Giants	15	8	53.3	98	6.53	0	2	34.2
Jan. 9, 1988	NFC Divisional Playoff	Minnesota	26	12	46.2	109	4.19	0	1	42.0
Jan. 1, 1989	NFC Divisional Playoff	Minnesota	27	16	59.3	178	6.59	3	1	100.5
Jan. 8, 1989	NFC Championship Game	Chicago	27	17	63.0	288	10.67	3	0	136.0
Jan. 22, 1989	Super Bowl XXIII	Cincinnati	36	23	63.9	357	9.92	2	0	115.2
Jan. 6, 1990	NFC Divisional Playoff	Minnesota	24	17	70.8	241	10.04	4	0	142.5
Jan. 14, 1990	NFC Championship Game	L.A. Rams	30	26	86.7	262	8.73	2	0	125.3
Jan. 28, 1990	Super Bowl XXIV	Denver	29	22	75.9	297	10.24	5	0	147.6
Jan. 12, 1991	NFC Divisional Playoff	Washington	31	22	71.0	274	8.84	2	1	106.1
Jan. 20, 1991	NFC Championship Game	N.Y. Giants	26	18	69.2	190	7.31	1	0	103.0
Totals (19 games)			593	375	63.2	4758	8.02	39	17	98.2

Highest NFL Postseason Pass Ratings (Minimum: 100 Attempts)

	Games	Att.	Comp.	Pct.	Yds.	Avg. Gain	TD	Int.	Rating
Bart Starr	10	213	130	61.0	1753	8.23	15	3	104.8
Joe Montana	19	593	375	63.2	4758	8.02	39	17	98.2
Ken Anderson	6	166	110	66.3	1321	7.96	9	6	93.5
Joe Theismann	10	211	128	60.7	1782	8.45	11	7	91.4
Jim Kelly	6	199	115	57.8	1663	8.36	10	8	85.1
Ken Stabler	13	351	203	57.8	2641	7.52	19	13	84.2
Terry Bradshaw	19	456	261	57.2	3833	8.41	30	26	83.0
Phil Simms	8	228	128	56.1	1461	6.41	10	4	82.9
Jim Plunkett	10	272	162	59.6	2293	8.43	11	12	81.9
Bernie Kosar	7	260	146	56.2	1860	7.15	15	10	81.9

Highest NFL Postseason Pass Ratings, Active Players (Minimum: 100 Attempts)

	Games	Att.	Comp.	Pct.	Yds.	Avg. Gain	TD	Int.	Rating
Joe Montana	19	593	375	63.2	4758	8.02	39	17	98.2
Jim Kelly	6	199	115	57.8	1663	8.36	10	8	85.1
Phil Simms	8	228	128	56.1	1461	6.41	10	4	82.9
Bernie Kosar	7	260	146	56.2	1860	7.15	15	10	81.9
Dan Marino	8	313	173	55.3	2224	7.11	18	12	80.9
Dave Krieg	7	183	94	51.4	1242	6.79	9	6	75.9
Wade Wilson	6	185	99	53.5	1322	7.15	7	6	75.6
Jim McMahon	7	130	70	53.8	967	7.44	4	4	75.4
John Elway	11	330	170	51.5	2641	8.00	15	15	74.6
Warren Moon	5	182	107	58.8	1305	7.17	5	7	74.1

All-Time Rankings of Players in Four Categories That Determine NFL Passer Rating

Minimum: 1500 Attempts

Completion Percentage

	Pct.	Att.	Comp.
Joe Montana	63.64	4579	2914
Jim Kelly	59.91	2088	1251
Ken Stabler	59.85	3793	2270
Danny White	59.69	2950	1761
Dan Marino	59.32	4181	2480
Ken Anderson	59.31	4475	2654
Ken O'Brien	58.96	2878	1697
Dan Fouts	58.83	5604	3297
Tony Eason	58.25	1564	911
Dave Krieg	58.01	3291	1909

Touchdown Percentage

	Pct.	Att.	TD
Sid Luckman	7.86	1744	137
Frank Ryan	6.99	2133	149
Len Dawson	6.39	3741	239
Daryle Lamonica	6.31	2601	164
Sammy Baugh	6.24	2995	187
Charley Conerly	6.11	2833	173
Bob Waterfield	6.00	1617	97
Earl Morrall	5.99	2689	161
Sonny Jurgensen	5.98	4262	255
Norm Van Brocklin	5.98	2895	173

Average Yards Per Pass

	Avg.	Att.	Yards
Otto Graham	8.63	1565	13,499
Sid Luckman	8.42	1744	14,686
Norm Van Brocklin	8.16	2895	23,611
Boomer Esiason	7.96	2687	21,381
Ed Brown	7.85	1987	15,600
Bart Starr	7.85	3149	24,718
Johnny Unitas	7.76	5186	40,239
Earl Morrall	7.74	2689	20,809
Dan Fouts	7.68	5604	43,040
Len Dawson	7.67	3741	28,711

Interception Percentage

	Pct.	Att.	Int.
Bernie Kosar	2.62	2363	62
Joe Montana	2.69	4579	123
Ken O'Brien	2.71	2878	78
Neil Lomax	2.85	3153	90
Randall Cunningham	3.15	2253	71
Dan Marino	3.25	4181	136
Tony Eason	3.26	1564	51
Roman Gabriel	3.31	4498	149
Jim Kelly	3.45	2088	72
Bill Kenney	3.54	2430	86

Teams That Finished In First Place In Their Division the Season After Finishing in Last Place

Season	Team	Record	Previous Season
1967	Houston	9-4-1	*3-11
1968	Minnesota	8-6	3-8-3
1970	Cincinnati	8-6	4-9-1
1970	San Francisco	10-3-1	4-8-2
1972	Green Bay	10-4	4-8-2
1975	Baltimore	10-4	2-12
1979	Tampa Bay	10-6	5-11
1981	Cincinnati	12-4	6-10
1987	Indianapolis	9-6	3-13
1988	Cincinnati	12-4	4-11
1990	Cincinnati	9-7	8-8

*tied for last place

Records of NFL Teams, 1981-90

AFC	W - L - T	Pct.	Division Titles	Playoff Berths	Postseason Record	Super Bowl Record
Miami	98-53-1	.648	4	6	7-6	0-2
Denver	90-61-1	.595	4	5	6-5	0-3
L.A. Raiders	90-62-0	.592	3	5	5-4	1-0
Cincinnati	84-68-0	.553	3	4	5-4	0-2
Seattle	83-69-0	.546	1	4	3-4	0-0
Pittsburgh	77-75-0	.507	2	4	2-4	0-0
N.Y. Jets	75-75-2	.500	0	4	3-4	0-0
Cleveland	75-76-1	.497	4	6	3-6	0-0
Buffalo	71-81-0	.467	3	4	4-4	0-1
Kansas City	69-81-2	.461	0	2	0-2	0-0
New England	69-83-0	.454	1	3	3-3	0-1
San Diego	67-85-0	.441	1	2	2-2	0-0
Houston	60-92-0	.395	0	4	2-4	0-0
Indianapolis	54-97-1	.359	1	1	0-1	0-0

NFC	W - L - T	Pct.	Division Titles	Playoff Berths	Postseason Record	Super Bowl Record
San Francisco	112-39-1	.740	8	9	14-5	4-0
Washington	101-51-0	.664	3	6	12-4	2-1
Chicago	96-56-0	.632	6	6	6-5	1-0
N.Y. Giants	90-61-1	.595	3	6	9-4	2-0
L.A. Rams	80-72-0	.526	1	6	4-6	0-0
Philadelphia	74-76-2	.493	1	4	0-4	0-0
Dallas	74-78-0	.487	2	4	3-4	0-0
Minnesota	74-78-0	.487	1	4	4-4	0-0
New Orleans	74-78-0	.487	0	2	0-2	0-0
Green Bay	66-84-2	.441	0	1	1-1	0-0
Phoenix	62-88-2	.414	0	1	0-1	0-0
Detroit	58-93-1	.385	1	2	0-2	0-0
Atlanta	50-101-1	.332	0	1	0-1	0-0
Tampa Bay	46-106-0	.303	1	2	0-2	0-0

Indianapolis totals include Baltimore, 1981-83
L.A. Raiders totals include Oakland, 1981
Phoenix totals include St. Louis, 1981-87

In 1982, due to players' strike, the divisional format was abandoned. (L.A. Raiders and Washington won regular-season conference titles, not included in "Division Titles" totals listed above. Sixteen teams were awarded playoff berths, included in totals listed above.)

Home Records, 1981-90

AFC	W - L - T	Pct.
Denver	58-19-0	.753
Miami	55-19-1	.740
Seattle	51-26-0	.662
Cincinnati	49-27-0	.645
L.A. Raiders	49-27-0	.645
Kansas City	46-29-0	.613
Pittsburgh	46-29-0	.613
Buffalo	47-30-0	.610
Cleveland	42-32-1	.567
Houston	42-34-0	.553
New England	41-35-0	.539
N.Y. Jets	39-36-1	.520
San Diego	38-37-0	.507
Indianapolis	30-45-1	.401

NFC	W - L - T	Pct.
Chicago	56-20-0	.737
Washington	55-20-0	.733
San Francisco	51-25-0	.671
N.Y. Giants	51-26-0	.662
Minnesota	47-30-0	.610
L.A. Rams	42-34-0	.553
Dallas	41-35-0	.539
New Orleans	40-36-0	.526
Philadelphia	40-36-1	.526
Green Bay	36-39-1	.480
Phoenix	35-39-1	.473
Detroit	34-41-1	.454
Tampa Bay	31-45-0	.408
Atlanta	29-47-1	.396

Road Records, 1981-90

AFC	W - L - T	Pct.
Miami	43-34-0	.558
L.A. Raiders	41-35-0	.539
N.Y. Jets	36-39-1	.480
Cincinnati	35-41-0	.461
Denver	32-42-1	.433
Cleveland	33-44-0	.429
Seattle	32-43-0	.427
Pittsburgh	31-46-0	.403
San Diego	29-48-0	.377
New England	28-48-0	.368
Buffalo	24-51-0	.320
Indianapolis	24-52-0	.316
Kansas City	23-52-2	.312
Houston	18-58-0	.237

NFC	W - L - T	Pct.
San Francisco	61-14-1	.809
Washington	46-31-0	.597
N.Y. Giants	39-35-1	.527
Chicago	40-36-0	.526
L.A. Rams	38-38-0	.500
Philadelphia	34-40-1	.460
New Orleans	34-42-0	.447
Dallas	33-43-0	.434
Green Bay	30-45-1	.401
Minnesota	27-48-0	.360
Phoenix	27-49-1	.357
Detroit	24-52-0	.316
Atlanta	21-54-0	.280
Tampa Bay	15-61-0	.197

Records by Months, 1981-90

AFC	Sept. W - L - T	Oct. W - L - T	Nov. W - L - T	*Dec. W - L - T	Total W - L - T	Pct.
Miami	24-12	23-14-1	25-16	26-11	98-53-1	.648
Denver	23-12-1	26-12	23-18	18-19	90-61-1	.595
L.A. Raiders	24-12	22-16	21-20	23-14	90-62-0	.592
Cincinnati	18-16	21-20	22-18	23-14	84-68-0	.553
Seattle	16-19	23-16	21-20	23-14	83-69-0	.546
Pittsburgh	15-20	23-17	20-20	19-18	77-75-0	.507
N.Y. Jets	21-15	18-19-2	22-20	14-21	75-75-2	.500
Cleveland	17-19	20-19	21-18-1	17-20	75-76-1	.497
Buffalo	18-18	21-17	20-21	12-25	71-81-0	.467
Kansas City	20-16	13-24-1	14-26-1	22-15	69-81-2	.461
New England	14-22	20-18	19-22	16-21	69-83-0	.454
San Diego	16-20	13-26	21-20	17-19	67-85-0	.441
Houston	12-24	15-24	18-22	15-22	60-92-0	.395
Indianapolis	9-27	16-22	13-28	16-20-1	54-97-1	.359

NFC	Sept. W - L - T	Oct. W - L - T	Nov. W - L - T	*Dec. W - L - T	Total W - L - T	Pct.
San Francisco	25-10	29-9-1	27-13	31-7	112-39-1	.740
Washington	20-16	24-14	29-13	28-8	101-51-0	.664
Chicago	24-12	25-13	28-13	19-18	96-56-0	.632
N.Y. Giants	22-14	22-15-1	22-18	24-14	90-61-1	.595
L.A. Rams	22-13	20-19	21-20	17-20	80-72-0	.526
Philadelphia	15-21	23-15	19-21-1	17-19-1	74-76-2	.493
Dallas	23-13	18-21	20-22	13-22	74-78-0	.487
Minnesota	21-15	16-22	22-20	15-21	74-78-0	.487
New Orleans	16-19	18-21	24-17	16-21	74-78-0	.487
Green Bay	10-25-1	16-22	21-20	19-17-1	66-84-2	.441
Phoenix	14-22	16-21-1	17-25	15-20-1	62-88-2	.414
Detroit	12-24	16-22	16-25-1	14-22	58-93-1	.385
Atlanta	16-19	11-27-1	12-29	11-26	50-101-1	.332
Tampa Bay	12-24	8-31	14-27	12-24	46-106-0	.303

Indianapolis totals include Baltimore, 1981-83
L.A. Raiders totals include Oakland, 1981
Phoenix totals include St. Louis, 1981-87

*Includes for each team one game played during January.

Takeaways/Giveaways in 1981-90

	Takeaways			Giveaways			
AFC	Int.	Fum.	Total	Int.	Fum.	Total	Net Diff.
Kansas City	220	168	388	178	158	336	52
Seattle	204	193	397	193	157	350	47
Denver	210	172	382	197	147	344	38
Pittsburgh	238	148	386	203	153	356	30
Cincinnati	189	143	332	164	139	303	29
N.Y. Jets	192	141	333	162	160	322	11
New England	177	164	341	203	141	344	− 3
Miami	189	131	320	187	140	327	− 7
Indianapolis	156	160	316	197	132	329	−13
Cleveland	193	128	321	185	167	352	−31
Houston	166	151	317	207	162	369	−52
San Diego	185	151	336	228	166	394	−58
L.A. Raiders	175	144	319	214	164	378	−59
Buffalo	164	148	312	212	165	377	−65

	Takeaways			Giveaways			
NFC	Int.	Fum.	Total	Int.	Fum.	Total	Net Diff.
San Francisco	227	142	369	135	134	269	100
Philadelphia	212	162	374	177	142	319	55
Washington	217	143	360	180	143	323	37
Minnesota	212	166	378	216	133	349	29
Chicago	234	141	375	188	162	350	25
N.Y. Giants	199	142	341	177	146	323	18
L.A. Rams	197	157	354	186	166	352	2
Atlanta	182	153	335	183	160	343	− 8
Dallas	208	154	362	227	153	380	−18
Tampa Bay	198	164	362	228	156	384	−22
New Orleans	185	159	344	212	156	368	−24
Green Bay	202	173	375	237	168	405	−30
Detroit	185	154	339	215	161	376	−37
Phoenix	161	138	299	186	159	345	−46

Indianapolis totals include Baltimore, 1981-83
L.A. Raiders totals include Oakland, 1981
Phoenix totals include St. Louis, 1981-87

High and Low Single-Game Yardage Totals, 1981-90

Most Total Yards, Game

676 Washington vs. Detroit, Nov. 4, 1990 (OT)
661 San Diego vs. Cincinnati, Dec. 20, 1982
621 Cincinnati vs. N.Y. Jets, Dec. 21, 1986
597 N.Y. Jets vs. Miami, Nov. 27, 1988
594 Chicago vs. Green Bay, Dec. 7, 1980

Fewest Total Yards, Game

24 Chicago vs. Detroit, Nov. 22, 1981
53 Pittsburgh vs. Cleveland, Sept. 10, 1989
57 New England vs. N.Y. Jets, Sept. 19, 1982
60 Detroit vs. Minnesota, Nov. 24, 1988
65 Tampa Bay vs. Green Bay, Dec. 1, 1985
65 Seattle vs. New England, Dec. 4, 1988

Most Yards Rushing, Game

356 L.A. Raiders vs. Seattle, Nov. 30, 1987
354 Dallas vs. Baltimore, Dec. 6, 1981
343 Pittsburgh vs. N.Y. Jets, Sept. 20, 1981
328 New England vs. N.Y. Jets, Sept. 18, 1983
310 Kansas City vs. Detroit, Oct. 14, 1990

Fewest Yards Rushing, Game

0 Buffalo vs. Chicago, Oct. 2, 1988
1 Tampa Bay vs. Washington, Oct. 22, 1989
2 New England vs. New Orleans, Nov. 30, 1986
6 N.Y. Giants vs. L.A. Rams, Nov. 12, 1989
8 N.Y. Giants vs. L.A. Rams, Sept. 30, 1984

Most Yards Passing, Game

521 Miami vs. N.Y. Jets, Oct. 23, 1988
506 L.A. Rams vs. Chicago, Dec. 26, 1982
499 Houston vs. Kansas City, Dec. 16, 1990
494 San Diego vs. Seattle, Sept. 15, 1985
486 San Diego vs. Cincinnati, Dec. 20, 1982

Fewest Yards Passing, Game

−22 Atlanta vs. Chicago, Nov. 24, 1985
−20 Chicago vs. Detroit, Nov. 22, 1981
−13 Cincinnati vs. San Diego, Oct. 4, 1987
−4 Houston vs. Cincinnati, Oct. 4, 1981
−4 New England vs. N.Y. Jets, Sept. 19, 1982

NFL Individual Leaders, 1981-90

Points
1048, Nick Lowery
944, Jim Breech
927, Pat Leahy
910, Gary Anderson
900, Eddie Murray

Touchdowns
93, Marcus Allen
90, Eric Dickerson
83, Jerry Rice
75, James Brooks
67, Mark Clayton
67, Roy Green

Field Goals
239, Nick Lowery
206, Gary Anderson
198, Eddie Murray
192, Morten Andersen
189, Pat Leahy

Rushes
2616, Eric Dickerson
1973, Walter Payton
1960, Marcus Allen
1911, Gerald Riggs
1910, Tony Dorsett

Rushing Yards
11,903, Eric Dickerson
8340, Walter Payton
8115, Tony Dorsett
7957, Marcus Allen
7940, Gerald Riggs

Rushing TDs
86, Eric Dickerson
75, Marcus Allen
63, Ottis Anderson
62, John Riggins
58, Gerald Riggs

Passes
4283, Joe Montana
4181, Dan Marino
3572, John Elway
3302, Phil Simms
3289, Dave Krieg

TD Passes
241, Dan Marino
226, Joe Montana
184, Dave Krieg
150, Boomer Esiason
143, Phil Simms

Receiving TDs
79, Jerry Rice
66, Mark Clayton
66, Roy Green
63, Steve Largent
61, Mike Quick

Completions
2725, Joe Montana
2480, Dan Marino
1959, John Elway
1909, Dave Krieg
1837, Phil Simms

Receptions
672, Art Monk
529, Steve Largent
521, Roy Green
518, Ozzie Newsome
508, Roger Craig

Interceptions
51, Ronnie Lott
50, Everson Walls
46, Deron Cherry
44, Dave Waymer
40, Dave Brown

Passing Yards
33,107, Joe Montana
31,416, Dan Marino
24,721, John Elway
24,455, Phil Simms
24,052, Dave Krieg

Reception Yards
9138, Art Monk
8951, James Lofton
8481, Roy Green
8272, Steve Largent
7866, Jerry Rice

Sacks (since 1982)
114.5, Lawrence Taylor
95, Reggie White
93, Richard Dent
91.5, Jacob Green
91, Dexter Manley

Records for Each Current NFL Team for Most Points in a Game (Regular Season Only)

Note: When the record has been achieved more than once, only the most recent game is shown; summaries are listed in alphabetical order by conference. Bold face indicates team holding record.

BUFFALO BILLS
September 18, 1966, at Buffalo
Miami .... 3 7 0 14 — 24
Buffalo .... 21 27 3 7 — 58
TDs: Buff—Bobby Burnett 2, Butch Byrd 2, Jack Spikes 2, Bobby Crockett, Jack Kemp; Mia—Dave Kocourek, Bo Roberson, John Roderick. TD Passes: Buff—Jack Kemp, Daryle Lamonica; Mia—George Wilson 3. FGs: Buff—Booth Lusteg; Mia—Gene Mingo.

CINCINNATI BENGALS
December 17, 1989, at Cincinnati
Houston .... 0 0 0 7 — 7
Cincinnati .... 21 10 21 9 — 61
TDs: Cin—Eddie Brown 2, Eric Ball, James Brooks, Ira Hillary, Rodney Holman, Tim McGee, Craig Taylor; Hou—Lorenzo White. TD Passes: Cin—Boomer Esiason 4, Erik Wilhelm. FGs: Cin—Jim Breech 2.

CLEVELAND BROWNS
November 7, 1954, at Cleveland
Washington .... 0 3 0 0 — 3
Cleveland .... 13 14 21 14 — 62
TDs: Clev—Darrell Brewster 2, Mo Bassett, Ken Gorgal, Otto Graham, Dub Jones, Dante Lavelli, Curley Morrison. TD Passes: Clev—George Ratterman 3, Otto Graham. FGs: Clev—Lou Groza 2; Wash—Vic Janowicz.

DENVER BRONCOS
October 6, 1963, at Denver
San Diego .... 13 7 0 14 — 34
Denver .... 3 14 9 24 — 50
TDs: Den—Lionel Taylor 2, Goose Gonsoulin, Gene Prebola, Donnie Stone; SD—Keith Lincoln 2, Lance Alworth, Paul Lowe, Jacque MacKinnon. TD Passes: Den—John McCormick 3; SD—Tobin Rote 3, John Hadl 2. FGs: Den—Gene Mingo 5.

HOUSTON OILERS
December 9, 1990, at Houston
Cleveland .... 0 7 7 0 — 14
Houston .... 14 31 7 6 — 58
TDs: Hou—Lorenzo White 4, Ernest Givins, Leonard Harris, Tony Jones, Terry Kinard; Clev—Eric Metcalf 2. TD Passes: Hou—Warren Moon 2, Cody Carlson; Clev—Bernie Kosar. FG: Hou—Teddy Garcia.

INDIANAPOLIS COLTS
December 12, 1976, at Baltimore
Buffalo .... 3 3 7 7 — 20
Baltimore Colts .... 7 13 28 10 — 58
TDs: Balt—Roger Carr, Raymond Chester, Glenn Doughty, Roosevelt Leaks, Derrel Luce, Lydell Mitchell, Howard Stevens; Buff—Bob Chandler, O.J. Simpson. TD Passes: Balt—Bert Jones 3; Buff—Gary Marangi. FGs: Balt—Toni Linhart 3; Buff—George Jakowenko 2.

KANSAS CITY CHIEFS
September 7, 1963, at Denver
Kansas City .... 14 14 21 10 — 59
Denver .... 0 7 0 0 — 7
TDs: KC—Chris Burford 2, Frank Jackson 2, Dave Grayson, Abner Haynes, Sherrill Headrick, Curtis McClinton; Den—Lionel Taylor. TD Passes: KC—Len Dawson 4, Curtis McClinton; Den—Mickey Slaughter. FG: KC—Tommy Brooker.

LOS ANGELES RAIDERS
December 22, 1963, at Oakland
Houston .... 14 21 14 0 — 49
Oakland Raiders .... 7 28 7 10 — 52
TDs: Oak—Art Powell 4, Clem Daniels, Claude Gibson, Ken Herock; Hou—Willard Dewveall 2, Dave Smith 2, Charley Hennigan, Bob McLeod, Charley Tolar. TD Passes: Oak—Tom Flores 6; Hou—George Blanda 5. FG: Oak—Mike Mercer.

MIAMI DOLPHINS
November 24, 1977, at St. Louis
Miami .... 14 14 20 7 — 55
St. Louis .... 7 0 0 7 — 14
TDs: Mia—Nat Moore 3, Gary Davis, Duriel Harris, Leroy Harris, Benny Malone, Andre Tillman; StL—Ike Harris, Terry Metcalf. TD Passes: Mia—Bob Griese 6; StL—Jim Hart.

NEW ENGLAND PATRIOTS
September 9, 1979, at New England
New York Jets .... 3 0 0 0 — 3
New England .... 14 21 7 14 — 56
TDs: NE—Harold Jackson 3, Stanley Morgan 2, Allan Clark, Andy Johnson, Don Westbrook. TD Passes: NE—Steve Grogan 5, Tom Owen. FG: NYJ—Pat Leahy.

NEW YORK JETS
November 17, 1985, at New York
Tampa Bay .... 14 7 7 0 — 28
New York Jets .... 17 24 14 7 — 62
TDs: NYJ—Mickey Shuler 3, Johnny Hector 2, Tony Paige, Al Toon, Wesley Walker; TB—James Wilder 2, Kevin House, Calvin Magee. TD Passes: NYJ—Ken O'Brien 5; TB—Steve DeBerg 2. FGs: NYJ—Pat Leahy 2.

PITTSBURGH STEELERS
November 30, 1952, at Pittsburgh
New York Giants .... 0 0 7 0 — 7
Pittsburgh .... 14 14 7 28 — 63
TDs: Pitt—Lynn Chandnois 2, Dick Hensley 2, Jack Butler, George Hays, Ray Mathews, Ed Modzelewski, Elbie Nickel; NYG—Bill Stribling. TD Passes: Pitt—Jim Finks 4, Gary Kerkorian; NYG—Tom Landry.

SAN DIEGO CHARGERS
December 22, 1963, at San Diego
Denver .... 7 10 3 0 — 20
San Diego .... 10 16 10 22 — 58
TDs: SD—Paul Lowe 2, Chuck Allen, Bobby Jackson, Dave Kocourek, Keith Lincoln, Jacque MacKinnon; Den—Billy Joe, Donnie Stone. TD Passes: SD—John Hadl, Tobin Rote; Den—Don Breaux. FGs: SD—George Blair 3; Den—Gene Mingo 2.

SEATTLE SEAHAWKS
October 30, 1977, at Seattle
Buffalo .... 3 0 7 7 — 17
Seattle .... 14 28 7 7 — 56
TDs: Sea—Steve Largent 2, Duke Fergerson, Al Hunter, David Sims, Sherman Smith, Don Testerman, Jim Zorn; Buff—Joe Ferguson, John Kimbrough. TD Passes: Sea—Jim Zorn 4; Buff—Joe Ferguson. FG: Buff—Carson Long.

ATLANTA FALCONS
September 16, 1973, at New Orleans
Atlanta .... 0 24 21 17 — 62
New Orleans .... 0 0 7 0 — 7
TDs: Atl—Ken Burrow 2, Eddie Ray 2, Wes Chesson, Tom Hayes, Art Malone, Joe Profit; NO—Bill Butler. TD Passes: Atl—Dick Shiner 3, Bob Lee; NO—Archie Manning. FGs: Atl—Nick Mike-Mayer.

CHICAGO BEARS
December 7, 1980, at Chicago
Green Bay .... 0 7 0 0 — 7
Chicago .... 0 28 13 20 — 61
TDs: Chi—Walter Payton 3, Brian Baschnagel, Robin Earl, Roland Harper, Willie McClendon, Len Walterscheid, Rickey Watts; GB—James Lofton. TD Passes: Chi—Vince Evans 3; GB—Lynn Dickey.

DALLAS COWBOYS
October 12, 1980, at Dallas
San Francisco .... 0 7 0 7 — 14
Dallas .... 14 24 14 7 — 59
TDs: Dall—Drew Pearson 3, Ron Springs 2, Tony Dorsett, Billy Joe DuPree, Robert Newhouse; SF—Dwight Clark 2. TD Passes: Dall—Danny White 4; SF—Steve DeBerg 2. FG: Dall—Rafael Septien.

DETROIT LIONS
October 26, 1952, at Green Bay
Detroit .... 14 14 14 10 — 52
Green Bay .... 7 3 7 0 — 17
TDs: Det—Jug Girard 2, Bob Hoernschemeyer 2, Jack Christiansen, Jim Smith, Bill Swiacki; GB—Billy Howton, Jim Keane. TD Passes: Det—Bobby Layne 3; GB—Babe Parilli, Tobin Rote. FGs: Det—Pat Harder; GB—Bill Reichardt.

GREEN BAY PACKERS
October 7, 1945, at Milwaukee
Detroit .... 0 7 7 7 — 21
Green Bay .... 0 41 9 7 — 57
TDs: GB—Don Hutson 4, Charley Brock, Irv Comp, Ted Fritsch, Clyde Goodnight; Det—Chuck Fenenbock, John Greene, Bob Westfall. TD Passes: GB—Tex McKay 4, Lou Brock, Irv Comp; Det—Dave Ryan.

LOS ANGELES RAMS
October 22, 1950, at Los Angeles
Baltimore .... 13 0 7 7 — 27
Los Angeles .... 21 14 14 21 — 70
TDs: LA—Bob Boyd 2, Vitamin T. Smith 2, Tom Fears, Elroy (Crazylegs) Hirsch, Dick Hoerner, Ralph Pasquariello, Dan Towler, Bob Waterfield; Balt—Chet Mutryn 2, Adrian Burk, Billy Stone. TD Passes: LA—Norm Van Brocklin 2, Bob Waterfield 2, Glenn Davis; Balt—Adrian Burk 3.

MINNESOTA VIKINGS
October 18, 1970, at Minnesota
Dallas .... 3 3 0 7 — 13
Minnesota .... 14 20 17 3 — 54
TDs: Minn—Clint Jones 2, Ed Sharockman 2, John Beasley, Dave Osborn; Dall—Calvin Hill. TD Pass: Minn—Gary Cuozzo. FGs: Minn—Fred Cox 4; Dall—Mike Clark 2.

NEW ORLEANS SAINTS
November 21, 1976, at Seattle

New Orleans .... 3 17 28 3 — 51
Seattle .... 6 0 7 14 — 27

TDs: NO—Bobby Douglass 2, Tony Galbreath, Chuck Muncie, Tom Myers, Elex Price; Sea—Sherman Smith 2, Steve Largent, Jim Zorn. TD Pass: Sea—Bill Munson. FGs: NO—Rich Szaro 3.

NEW YORK GIANTS
November 26, 1972, at New York

Philadelphia .... 3 7 0 0 — 10
New York Giants .... 14 24 10 14 — 62

TDs: NYG—Don Herrmann 2, Ron Johnson 2, Bob Tucker 2, Randy Johnson; Phil—Harold Jackson. TD Passes: NYG—Norm Snead 3, Randy Johnson 2; Phil—John Reaves. FGs: NYG—Pete Gogolak 2; Phil—Tom Dempsey.

PHILADELPHIA EAGLES
November 6, 1934, at Philadelphia

Cincinnati Reds .... 0 0 0 0 — 0
Philadelphia .... 26 6 12 20 — 64

TDs: Phil—Joe Carter 3, Swede Hanson 3, Marvin Ellstrom, Roger Kirkman, Ed Matesic, Ed Storm. TD Passes: Phil—Ed Matesic 2, Albert Weiner 2, Marvin Elstrom.

PHOENIX CARDINALS
November 13, 1949, at New York

Chicago Cardinals ..... 7 31 14 13 — 65
New York Bulldogs ...... 7 0 6 7 — 20

TDs: Chi—Red Cochran 2, Pat Harder 2, Bill Dewell, Mel Kutner, Bob Ravensburg, Vic Schwall, Charlie Trippi; NY—Joe Golding, Frank Muehlheuser, Johnny Rauch. TD Passes: Chi—Paul Christman 3, Jim Hardy 3; NY—Bobby Layne. FG: Chi—Pat Harder.

SAN FRANCISCO 49ERS
September 19, 1965, at San Francisco

Chicago .... 3 0 0 21 — 24
San Francisco .... 0 24 21 7 — 52

TDs: SF—Bernie Casey 2, John David Crow, Charlie Krueger, Gary Lewis, Dave Parks, Ken Willard; Chi—Charlie Bivins 2, Andy Livingston. TD Passes: SF—John Brodie 4; Chi—Rudy Bukich 2. FGs: SF—Tommy Davis; Chi—Roger LeClerc.

TAMPA BAY BUCCANEERS
September 13, 1987, at Tampa Bay

Atlanta .... 0 3 0 7 — 10
Tampa Bay .... 14 13 7 14 — 48

TDs: TB—Gerald Carter 2, Cliff Austin, Steve Bartalo, Mark Carrier, Phil Freeman, Calvin Magee; Atl—Stacey Bailey. TD Passes: TB—Steve DeBerg 5; Atl—Scott Campbell. FG: Atl—Mick Luckhurst.

WASHINGTON REDSKINS
November 27, 1966, at Washington

New York Giants .... 0 14 14 13 — 41
Washington .... 13 21 14 24 — 72

TDs: Wash—A. D. Whitfield 3, Brig Owens 2, Charley Taylor 2, Rickie Harris, Joe Don Looney, Bobby Mitchell; NYG—Allen Jacobs, Homer Jones, Dan Lewis, Joe Morrison, Aaron Thomas, Gary Wood. TD Passes: Wash—Sonny Jurgensen 3; NYG—Gary Wood 2, Tom Kennedy. FG: Wash—Charlie Gogolak.

NFL Games In Which a Team Has Scored 60 or More Points

(Home team in capitals)

Regular Season

WASHINGTON 72, New York Giants 41 .... November 27, 1966
LOS ANGELES RAMS 70, Baltimore 27 .... October 22, 1950
Chicago Cardinals 65, NEW YORK BULLDOGS 20 ... November 13, 1949
LOS ANGELES RAMS 65, Detroit 24 .... October 29, 1950
PHILADELPHIA 64, Cincinnati 0 .... November 6, 1934
CHICAGO CARDINALS 63, New York Giants 35 ..... October 17, 1948
AKRON 62, Oorang 0 .... October 29,1922
PITTSBURGH 62, New York Giants 7 .... November 30, 1952
CLEVELAND 62, New York Giants 14 .... December 6, 1953
CLEVELAND 62, Washington 3 .... November 7, 1954
NEW YORK GIANTS 62, Philadelphia 10 .... November 26, 1972
Atlanta 62, NEW ORLEANS 7 .... September 16, 1973
NEW YORK JETS 62, Tampa Bay 28 .... November 17, 1985
CHICAGO 61, San Francisco 20 .... December 12, 1965
Cincinnati 61, HOUSTON 17 .... December 17, 1972
CHICAGO 61, Green Bay 7 .... December 7, 1980
CINCINNATI 61, Houston 7 .... December 17, 1989
ROCK ISLAND 60, Evansville 0 .... October 15, 1922
CHICAGO CARDINALS 60, Rochester 0 .... October 7, 1923

Postseason

Chicago Bears 73, WASHINGTON 0 .... December 8, 1940

Youngest and Oldest Regular Starters in NFL in 1990

Minimum: 8 Games Started

Five Youngest Regular Starters

	Birthdate	Starts	Position
Emmitt Smith, Dallas	5/15/69	15	RB
Junior Seau, San Diego	1/19/69	15	LB
Rob Moore, Jets	9/27/68	13	WR
Courtney Hall, San Diego	8/26/68	16	C
James Francis, Cincinnati	8/4/68	16	LB

Five Oldest Regular Starters

	Birthdate	Starts	Position
Steve DeBerg, Kansas City	1/19/54	16	QB
Jackie Slater, Rams	5/27/54	15	T
Scott Studwell, Minnesota	8/27/54	15	LB
Raymond Clayborn, Cleveland	1/2/55	16	DB
J. T. Smith, Phoenix	10/29/55	8	WR

Youngest and Oldest Regular Starters By Position

Minimum: 8 Games Started

	Youngest	Oldest
QB	12/8/67 Jeff George, Ind.	1/19/54 Steve DeBerg, K.C.
RB	5/15/69 Emmitt Smith, Dall.	1/19/57 Ottis Anderson, Giants
WR	9/27/68 Rob Moore, Jets	10/29/55 J. T. Smith, Phx.
TE	8/8/67 Howard Cross, Giants	3/16/56 Ozzie Newsome, Clev.
C	8/26/68 Courtney Hall, S.D.	11/25/56 Doug Smith, Rams
G	12/12/67 David Szott, K.C.	5/12/56 Max Montoya, Raiders
T	1/11/67 Richmond Webb, Mia.	5/27/54 Jackie Slater, Rams
DE	12/9/67 Ray Agnew, N.E.	12/9/56 Al Baker, Clev.
DT	5/28/67 Tory Epps, Atl.	8/26/56 Ken Clarke, Minn.
LB	1/19/69 Junior Seau, S.D.	8/27/54 Scott Studwell, Minn.
CB	11/8/67 Jay Taylor, Phx.	1/2/55 Raymond Clayborn, Clev.
S	4/28/68 Mark Carrier, Chi.	4/15/57 Nesby Glasgow, Sea.

Eric Dickerson's Career Rushing vs. Each Opponent

Opponent	Games	Rushes	Yards	Yards Per Rush	Yards Per Game	TD
Atlanta	9	179	852	4.8	94.7	9
Buffalo	7	150	580	3.9	82.9	3
Chicago	4	115	482	4.2	120.5	5
Cincinnati	3	75	384	5.1	128.0	3
Cleveland	5	109	492	4.5	98.4	2
Dallas	2	49	244	5.0	122.0	1
Denver	3	43	249	5.8	83.0	4
Detroit	2	54	329	6.1	164.5	4
Green Bay	4	95	426	4.5	106.5	2
Houston	4	105	609	5.8	152.3	4
Indianapolis	1	25	121	4.8	121.0	1
Kansas City	1	26	68	2.6	68.0	1
L.A. Raiders	1	25	98	3.9	98.0	0
L.A. Rams	1	21	116	5.5	116.0	1
Miami	8	184	917	5.0	114.6	6
Minnesota	3	73	217	3.0	72.3	1
New England	8	179	641	3.6	80.1	3
New Orleans	9	192	907	4.7	100.8	6
N.Y. Giants	4	86	338	3.9	84.5	1
N.Y. Jets	9	196	787	4.0	87.4	8
Philadelphia	2	45	161	3.6	80.5	0
Phoenix	4	96	585	6.1	146.3	4
Pittsburgh	1	23	49	2.1	49.0	0
San Diego	4	105	452	4.3	113.0	0
San Francisco	9	170	832	4.9	92.4	3
Seattle	1	31	150	4.8	150.0	3
Tampa Bay	5	143	749	5.2	149.8	10
Washington	2	22	68	3.1	34.0	1
Totals	116	2616	11,903	4.6	102.6	86

Phoenix totals include three games vs. St. Louis

Roger Craig's Career Rushing vs. Each Opponent

Opponent	Games	Rushes	Yards	Yards Per Rush	Yards Per Game	TD
Atlanta	15	200	988	4.9	65.9	6
Buffalo	2	40	152	3.8	76.0	1
Chicago	5	46	176	3.8	35.2	0
Cincinnati	3	45	166	3.7	55.3	0
Cleveland	2	22	71	3.2	35.5	2
Dallas	4	57	235	4.1	58.8	2
Denver	2	48	260	5.4	130.0	0
Detroit	3	42	185	4.4	61.7	1
Green Bay	4	39	136	3.5	34.0	0
Houston	3	33	136	4.1	45.3	1
Indianapolis	2	26	153	5.9	76.5	2
Kansas City	1	15	55	3.7	55.0	1
L.A. Raiders	2	27	92	3.4	46.0	0
L.A. Rams	16	243	1001	4.1	62.6	9
Miami	2	29	154	5.3	77.0	2
Minnesota	5	71	247	3.5	49.4	3
New England	3	56	206	3.7	68.7	2
New Orleans	15	198	788	4.0	52.5	5
N.Y. Giants	5	66	256	3.9	51.2	0
N.Y. Jets	3	42	190	4.5	63.3	2
Philadelphia	4	50	186	3.7	46.5	0
Phoenix	4	51	277	5.4	69.3	2
Pittsburgh	2	16	45	2.8	22.5	0
San Diego	1	17	87	5.1	87.0	2
Seattle	2	36	161	4.5	80.5	0
Tampa Bay	6	84	339	4.0	56.5	7
Washington	5	87	322	3.7	64.4	0
Totals	121	1686	7064	4.2	58.4	50

Phoenix totals include three games vs. St. Louis

Joe Montana's Career Passing vs. Each Opponent

Opponent	Games	Att.	Cmp.	Pct.	Yards	Avg. Gain	TD	Int.	Sacked
Atlanta	21	567	370	65.3	4436	7.82	36	17	33/235
Buffalo	2	64	43	67.2	381	5.95	2	0	6/46
Chicago	7	162	90	55.6	1023	6.31	5	4	20/144
Cincinnati	4	141	90	63.8	923	6.55	7	6	9/75
Cleveland	4	140	88	62.9	1003	7.16	7	6	6/48
Dallas	5	126	84	66.7	1114	8.84	9	3	7/48
Denver	4	106	58	54.7	779	7.35	4	3	6/50
Detroit	5	120	74	61.7	713	5.94	2	2	9/55
Green Bay	5	149	104	69.8	1264	8.48	7	2	8/50
Houston	4	135	95	70.4	1164	8.62	10	4	5/31
Indianapolis	1	26	15	57.7	233	8.96	1	0	3/29
Kansas City	2	69	43	62.3	488	7.07	2	2	3/16
L.A. Raiders	4	96	51	53.1	659	6.86	4	1	11/92
L.A. Rams	23	693	446	64.4	5632	8.13	37	15	47/297
Miami	2	30	19	63.3	267	8.90	1	0	3/22
Minnesota	5	104	66	63.5	829	7.97	9	3	7/28
New England	4	108	69	63.9	791	7.32	6	2	6/39
New Orleans	20	508	314	61.8	3704	7.29	31	14	38/225
N.Y. Giants	8	210	132	62.9	1435	6.83	10	3	7/38
N.Y. Jets	3	79	48	60.8	538	6.81	3	3	3/17
Philadelphia	3	54	35	64.8	546	10.11	5	2	9/52
Phoenix	6	141	95	67.4	1389	9.85	13	5	7/53
Pittsburgh	4	150	100	66.7	919	6.13	4	8	3/20
San Diego	3	68	45	66.2	627	9.22	6	2	2/13
Seattle	3	62	37	59.7	539	8.69	6	4	3/17
Tampa Bay	8	254	176	69.3	1860	7.32	8	6	11/70
Washington	6	217	127	58.5	1742	8.03	7	6	9/84
Totals	166	4579	2914	63.6	34,998	7.64	242	123	281/1894

L.A. Raiders totals include one game vs. Oakland
Phoenix totals include six games vs. St. Louis

Phil Simms's Career Passing vs. Each Opponent

Opponent	Games	Att.	Cmp.	Pct.	Yards	Avg. Gain	TD	Int.	Sacked
Atlanta	4	116	66	56.9	910	7.84	4	3	12/81
Buffalo	1	10	6	60.0	59	5.90	0	0	1/0
Chicago	1	28	15	53.6	181	6.46	1	0	8/53
Cincinnati	1	62	40	64.5	513	8.27	1	2	7/70
Cleveland	1	37	23	62.2	289	7.81	1	2	4/22
Dallas	20	516	269	52.1	4169	8.08	33	30	50/376
Denver	3	78	43	55.1	519	6.65	1	1	8/64
Detroit	4	112	78	69.6	935	8.35	6	0	11/73
Green Bay	5	156	97	62.2	1302	8.35	11	4	16/111
Houston	1	24	13	54.2	234	9.75	2	1	0/0
Indianapolis	2	35	24	68.6	239	6.83	1	5	5/33
Kansas City	3	82	42	51.2	587	7.16	5	5	7/52
L.A. Raiders	2	55	31	56.4	408	7.42	2	2	5/39
L.A. Rams	7	235	131	55.7	1565	6.66	7	6	27/224
Miami	1	25	13	52.0	182	7.28	0	0	1/3
Minnesota	3	58	33	56.9	428	7.38	1	2	4/27
New Orleans	5	155	90	58.1	1011	6.52	5	7	13/88
N.Y. Jets	4	135	78	57.8	928	6.87	5	2	21/167
Philadelphia	17	526	264	50.2	3667	6.97	20	18	51/365
Phoenix	16	438	220	50.2	2853	6.51	28	10	44/275
Pittsburgh	1	16	10	62.5	106	6.63	1	1	3/24
San Diego	3	99	54	54.5	667	6.74	1	4	8/72
San Francisco	7	258	143	55.4	1802	6.98	8	8	31/185
Seattle	3	78	43	55.1	487	6.24	3	5	9/59
Tampa Bay	6	177	101	57.1	960	5.42	5	5	17/189
Washington	17	458	237	51.7	3518	7.68	21	20	53/403
Totals	138	3969	2164	54.5	28,519	7.19	171	141	416/3055

Indianapolis totals include one game vs. Baltimore
Phoenix totals include 12 games vs. St. Louis

Dan Marino's Career Passing vs. Each Opponent

Opponent	Games	Att.	Cmp.	Pct.	Yards	Avg. Gain	TD	Int.	Sacked
Atlanta	1	40	20	50.0	303	7.58	2	4	0/0
Buffalo	15	513	329	64.1	3897	7.60	28	22	17/142
Cincinnati	3	103	60	58.3	745	7.23	4	1	4/30
Cleveland	4	151	87	57.6	1178	7.80	9	5	0/0
Dallas	3	115	66	57.4	860	7.48	6	3	4/36
Denver	1	43	25	58.1	390	9.07	3	0	3/25
Detroit	1	44	23	52.3	247	5.61	2	2	1/8
Green Bay	3	114	76	66.7	939	8.24	9	5	1/5
Houston	5	140	78	55.7	998	7.13	8	7	2/9
Indianapolis	16	512	308	59.7	3894	7.61	28	6	12/86
Kansas City	3	119	69	58.0	815	6.85	6	3	2/20
L.A. Raiders	5	178	100	56.2	1235	6.94	11	5	7/64
L.A. Rams	2	84	54	64.3	682	8.12	7	2	1/4
Minnesota	1	37	20	54.1	264	7.14	2	3	0/0
New England	15	513	290	56.5	3449	6.72	21	26	9/80
New Orleans	2	63	39	61.9	391	6.21	4	1	1/6
N.Y. Giants	1	30	14	46.7	115	3.83	0	2	1/7
N.Y. Jets	14	548	325	59.3	4480	8.18	40	18	14/87
Philadelphia	3	127	72	56.7	987	7.77	6	2	5/45
Phoenix	2	61	42	68.9	634	10.39	5	0	1/9
Pittsburgh	6	175	110	62.9	1333	7.62	9	9	1/4
San Diego	3	122	77	63.1	957	7.84	6	1	4/29
San Francisco	2	75	42	56.0	495	6.60	3	4	3/29
Seattle	1	29	17	58.6	250	8.62	2	1	1/8
Tampa Bay	2	85	54	63.5	568	6.68	5	1	0/0
Washington	3	111	60	54.1	927	8.35	9	2	1/2
Totals	119	4181	2480	59.3	31,416	7.51	241	136	98/760

Indianapolis totals include two games vs. Baltimore
Phoenix totals include one game vs. St. Louis

John Elway's Career Passing vs. Each Opponent

Opponent	Games	Att.	Cmp.	Pct.	Yards	Avg. Gain	TD	Int.	Sacked
Atlanta	2	64	35	54.7	526	8.22	4	2	4/26
Buffalo	4	109	55	50.5	739	6.78	5	4	8/70
Chicago	4	94	51	54.3	650	6.91	3	4	9/65
Cincinnati	2	47	30	63.8	355	7.55	4	1	2/13
Cleveland	5	141	74	52.5	1034	7.33	7	5	5/43
Dallas	1	24	12	50.0	200	8.33	3	0	1/2
Detroit	3	88	56	63.6	699	7.94	2	2	7/72
Green Bay	3	94	55	58.5	546	5.81	1	4	1/4
Houston	1	35	17	48.6	256	7.31	3	3	2/15
Indianapolis	6	183	98	53.6	1315	7.19	6	2	16/127
Kansas City	14	434	231	53.2	2864	6.60	8	24	28/195
L.A. Raiders	14	410	227	55.4	2660	6.49	15	19	34/298
L.A. Rams	2	74	39	52.7	501	6.77	5	2	3/24
Miami	1	37	18	48.6	250	6.76	0	1	3/24
Minnesota	3	68	46	67.6	551	8.10	8	1	6/41
New England	4	140	75	53.6	917	6.55	6	4	6/35
New Orleans	2	79	46	58.2	519	6.57	4	2	4/35
N.Y. Giants	2	94	52	55.3	628	6.68	1	2	3/19
N.Y. Jets	1	28	13	46.4	145	5.18	0	1	5/27
Philadelphia	3	84	44	52.4	567	6.75	4	5	13/104
Phoenix	1	29	20	69.0	247	8.52	2	2	2/14
Pittsburgh	5	144	77	53.5	950	6.60	5	4	11/80
San Diego	15	457	253	55.4	3002	6.57	11	18	36/240
San Francisco	2	81	41	50.6	425	5.25	3	3	5/43
Seattle	15	499	274	54.9	3893	7.80	24	13	33/261
Washington	1	35	20	57.1	282	8.06	1	0	3/23
Totals	116	3572	1959	54.8	24,721	6.92	135	128	250/1900

Boomer Esiason's Career Passing vs. Each Opponent

Opponent	Games	Att.	Cmp.	Pct.	Yards	Avg. Gain	TD	Int.	Sacked
Atlanta	3	67	34	50.7	367	5.48	1	2	3/3
Buffalo	5	106	60	56.6	840	7.92	5	3	5/42
Chicago	2	66	32	48.5	396	6.00	2	4	6/56
Cleveland	13	289	152	52.6	2044	7.07	12	12	18/128
Dallas	2	54	31	57.4	470	8.70	6	0	2/9
Denver	1	30	21	70.0	306	10.20	2	1	1/4
Detroit	2	66	43	65.2	566	8.58	3	2	2/3
Green Bay	1	24	15	62.5	207	8.63	3	0	3/24
Houston	13	363	213	58.7	3115	8.58	21	16	24/172
Indianapolis	3	92	51	55.4	658	7.15	4	3	9/72
Kansas City	4	121	67	55.4	940	7.77	5	3	7/71
L.A. Raiders	4	80	44	55.0	659	8.24	4	2	5/44
L.A. Rams	1	45	31	68.9	490	10.89	3	0	1/7
Miami	2	61	34	55.7	422	6.16	2	1	4/52
Minnesota	2	79	48	60.8	619	7.84	4	4	7/62
New England	5	150	81	54.0	1238	8.25	9	7	9/66
New Orleans	3	75	33	44.0	309	4.12	3	2	9/71
N.Y. Giants	1	24	15	62.5	193	8.04	3	0	4/36
N.Y. Jets	6	147	82	55.8	1301	8.85	12	6	13/93
Philadelphia	1	32	20	62.5	363	11.34	4	1	1/10
Phoenix	2	38	24	63.2	356	9.37	4	1	3/22
Pittsburgh	13	346	204	59.0	3017	8.72	17	14	22/196
San Diego	3	97	56	57.7	748	7.71	8	5	10/84
San Francisco	2	49	26	53.1	294	6.00	2	2	5/28
Seattle	4	100	54	54.0	722	7.22	2	3	10/80
Tampa Bay	1	28	17	60.7	197	7.04	5	0	1/1
Washington	2	58	32	55.2	544	9.38	4	2	4/39
Totals	101	2687	1520	56.6	21,381	7.96	150	98	186/1475

Phoenix totals include one game vs. St. Louis

Warren Moon's Career Passing vs. Each Opponent

Opponent	Games	Att.	Cmp.	Pct.	Yards	Avg. Gain	TD	Int.	Sacked
Atlanta	3	114	63	55.3	847	7.43	8	5	7/37
Buffalo	5	134	74	55.2	1010	7.54	5	6	9/73
Chicago	2	55	28	50.9	521	9.47	3	3	5/49
Cincinnati	13	395	216	54.7	2968	7.51	18	15	31/274
Cleveland	13	384	215	56.0	2987	7.78	16	16	34/270

Opponent	Games	Att.	Cmp.	Pct.	Yards	Avg. Gain	TD	Int.	Sacked
Dallas	2	55	26	47.3	441	8.02	2	4	14/98
Denver	1	17	8	47.1	122	7.18	1	0	4/36
Detroit	2	76	51	67.1	743	9.78	3	4	0/0
Green Bay	1	21	14	66.7	218	10.38	2	1	0/0
Indianapolis	6	216	131	60.6	1795	8.31	11	7	12/86
Kansas City	5	166	96	57.8	1290	7.77	6	4	21/146
L.A. Raiders	3	105	50	47.6	754	7.18	4	5	11/96
L.A. Rams	3	115	66	57.4	853	7.42	3	5	6/49
Miami	4	76	55	72.4	739	9.72	4	3	8/88
Minnesota	2	57	30	52.6	349	6.12	1	1	9/65
New England	1	29	14	48.3	227	7.83	1	2	3/25
New Orleans	3	81	42	51.9	496	6.12	2	2	5/37
N.Y. Giants	1	47	26	55.3	330	7.02	2	2	3/32
N.Y. Jets	2	71	50	70.4	588	8.28	4	0	6/46
Phoenix	2	61	31	50.8	453	7.43	4	2	3/21
Pittsburgh	13	371	204	55.0	2633	7.10	15	15	31/236
San Diego	4	136	72	52.9	988	7.27	5	2	7/53
San Francisco	3	102	60	58.8	745	7.30	6	5	6/39
Seattle	2	60	37	61.7	414	6.90	2	2	2/12
Tampa Bay	1	23	14	60.9	149	6.48	2	0	0/0
Washington	2	58	28	48.3	329	5.67	4	1	5/38
Totals	99	3025	1701	56.2	22,989	7.60	134	112	242/1906

Phoenix totals include one game vs. St. Louis

Jim Kelly's Career Passing vs. Each Opponent

Opponent	Games	Att.	Cmp.	Pct.	Yards	Avg. Gain	TD	Int.	Sacked
Atlanta	1	22	17	77.3	231	10.50	2	1	3/18
Chicago	1	37	20	54.1	273	7.38	0	1	6/56
Cincinnati	3	72	47	65.3	616	8.56	5	4	5/49
Cleveland	3	93	56	60.2	737	7.93	5	0	6/31
Denver	3	101	58	57.4	600	5.94	2	5	7/55
Green Bay	1	14	10	71.4	80	5.71	1	2	3/14
Houston	4	145	90	62.1	1141	7.87	11	5	16/128
Indianapolis	9	277	167	60.3	2058	7.43	17	7	10/84
Kansas City	2	72	41	56.9	481	6.68	3	4	4/39
L.A. Raiders	3	81	46	56.8	625	7.72	5	2	4/28
Miami	8	234	153	65.4	1830	7.82	9	4	15/126
Minnesota	1	31	17	54.8	204	6.58	0	1	1/8
New England	9	233	133	57.1	1797	7.71	8	10	31/256
New Orleans	1	35	17	48.6	211	6.03	2	3	2/7
N.Y. Giants	1	11	7	63.6	115	10.46	1	0	0/0
N.Y. Jets	9	267	156	58.4	2118	7.93	19	8	15/97
Philadelphia	2	71	39	54.9	488	6.87	4	3	2/20
Phoenix	2	26	17	65.4	270	10.39	4	1	5/34
Pittsburgh	2	54	31	57.4	383	7.09	2	1	5/25
San Francisco	1	42	26	61.9	265	6.31	0	3	2/10
Seattle	2	48	26	54.2	324	6.75	1	2	2/21
Tampa Bay	2	79	52	65.8	591	7.48	3	2	3/33
Washington	1	43	25	58.1	292	6.79	1	3	3/33
Totals	71	2088	1251	59.9	15,730	7.53	105	72	150/1172

Phoenix totals include one game vs. St. Louis

Jerry Rice's Career Receiving vs. Each Opponent

Opponent	Games	Rec.	Yards	Yards Per Rec.	Yards Per Game	TD
Atlanta	11	56	975	17.4	88.6	13
Buffalo	1	3	46	15.3	46.0	1
Chicago	4	19	299	15.7	74.8	5
Cincinnati	2	12	187	15.6	93.5	2
Cleveland	2	13	193	14.8	96.5	4
Dallas	3	21	286	13.6	95.3	2
Denver	2	7	145	20.7	72.5	0
Detroit	2	3	38	12.7	19.0	0
Green Bay	4	23	432	18.8	108.0	4
Houston	2	13	155	11.9	77.5	2
Indianapolis	2	12	335	27.9	167.5	4
Kansas City	1	1	19	19.0	19.0	0
L.A. Raiders	2	8	155	19.4	77.5	0
L.A. Rams	12	52	990	19.0	82.5	7
Miami	1	3	76	25.3	76.0	2
Minnesota	4	21	351	16.7	87.8	3
New England	2	10	147	14.7	73.5	2
New Orleans	12	52	872	16.8	72.7	6
N.Y. Giants	4	21	325	15.5	81.3	3
N.Y. Jets	2	10	192	19.2	96.0	1
Philadelphia	2	9	234	26.0	117.0	3
Phoenix	2	7	193	27.6	96.5	3
Pittsburgh	2	11	137	12.5	68.5	1
San Diego	1	6	171	28.5	171.0	2
Seattle	2	8	205	25.6	102.5	3
Tampa Bay	4	24	325	13.5	81.3	4
Washington	4	21	383	18.2	95.8	2
Totals	92	446	7866	17.6	85.5	79

Phoenix totals include one game vs. St. Louis

Starting Records of Active NFL Quarterbacks Minimum: 10 starts

	W-L-T	Pct.
Joe Montana	100-39	.719
Jim McMahon	50-22	.694
Jay Schroeder	44-20	.688
Mike Tomczak	21-10	.677
John Fourcade	7-4	.636
Mark Rypien	19-11	.633
Dan Marino	74-43	.632
Jeff Kemp	13-8-1	.614
John Elway	69-44-1	.610
Phil Simms	82-53	.607
Dave Krieg	66-44	.600
Randall Cunningham	40-28-1	.587
Bob Gagliano	7-5	.583
Wade Wilson	25-18	.581
Jim Harbaugh	12-9	.571
Jim Kelly	40-31	.563
Bernie Kosar	42-33-1	.559
Steve Grogan	75-60	.556
Boomer Esiason	51-42	.548
Tony Eason	29-24	.547
Steve Beuerlein	8-7	.533
Jim Everett	34-30	.531
Chris Chandler	10-9	.526
Don Majkowski	19-18-1	.513
Ken O'Brien	41-45-1	.477
Bubby Brister	21-24	.467
Cliff Stoudt	9-11	.450
Steve Walsh	7-9	.438
Warren Moon	43-56	.434
Billy Joe Tolliver	8-11	.421
Rich Gannon	5-7	.417
Jeff George	5-7	.417
Jack Trudeau	14-23	.378
Rodney Peete	7-12	.368
Steve DeBerg	41-75-1	.355
Vinny Testaverde	16-30	.348
Steve Young	10-19	.345
Steve Pelluer	9-19-1	.328
Mike Pagel	17-36-1	.324
Timm Rosenbach	5-12	.294
Troy Aikman	7-19	.269
Chris Miller	11-31	.262
Jeff Rutledge	2-7-1	.250
Chuck Long	4-17	.190
Mark Herrmann	2-9	.182
Scott Campbell	2-11	.154

Individual NFL Leaders Over Last 2 Seasons, Last 3 Seasons, Last 4 Seasons

Last 2 Seasons	Last 3 Seasons	Last 4 Seasons
Points		
259 Chip Lohmiller	368 Mike Cofer	432 Nick Lowery
247 Mike Cofer	356 Chip Lohmiller	427 Morten Andersen
245 Nick Lowery	354 Scott Norwood	415 Scott Norwood
229 David Treadwell	349 Nick Lowery	411 Mike Lansford
225 Scott Norwood	324 Mike Lansford	388 Gary Anderson
Touchdowns		
30 Jerry Rice	40 Neal Anderson	63 Jerry Rice
30 Barry Sanders	40 Jerry Rice	46 Neal Anderson
28 Neal Anderson	34 Greg Bell	35 Greg Bell
25 Ottis Anderson	33 Ottis Anderson	35 James Brooks
25 Thurman Thomas	32 James Brooks	34 Herschel Walker
Field Goals		
59 Chip Lohmiller	85 Nick Lowery	104 Nick Lowery
58 Nick Lowery	80 Mike Cofer	95 Morten Andersen
53 Mike Cofer	78 Chip Lohmiller	91 Gary Anderson
52 David Treadwell	75 Scott Norwood	87 Dean Biasucci
45 Greg Davis	69 Gary Anderson	85 Scott Norwood
45 Chris Jacke		
Rushes		
615 Christian Okoye	868 Eric Dickerson	1151 Eric Dickerson
582 Bobby Humphrey	795 Herschel Walker	1004 Herschel Walker
569 Thurman Thomas	783 Neal Anderson	937 Roger Craig
550 Ottis Anderson	776 Thurman Thomas	912 Neal Anderson
535 Barry Sanders	753 John Stephens	877 Christian Okoye
Rushing Yards		
2774 Barry Sanders	3647 Eric Dickerson	4935 Eric Dickerson
2541 Thurman Thomas	3459 Neal Anderson	4090 Herschel Walker
2353 Neal Anderson	3422 Thurman Thomas	4045 Neal Anderson
2353 Bobby Humphrey	3199 Herschel Walker	3810 Roger Craig
2285 Christian Okoye	3174 James Brooks	3464 James Brooks

Last 2 Seasons	Last 3 Seasons	Last 4 Seasons
Rushing TDs		
27 Barry Sanders	33 Neal Anderson	36 Neal Anderson
25 Ottis Anderson	33 Ottis Anderson	33 Ottis Anderson
21 Neal Anderson	32 Greg Bell	32 Greg Bell
19 Christian Okoye	27 Barry Sanders	31 Eric Dickerson
17 Marion Butts	25 Eric Dickerson	27 Barry Sanders
17 Thurman Thomas		
Passes		
1081 Dan Marino	1687 Dan Marino	2131 Dan Marino
1072 Jim Everett	1589 Jim Everett	1963 Randall Cunningham
1048 Warren Moon	1557 Randall Cunningham	1891 Jim Everett
997 Randall Cunningham	1414 John Elway	1824 John Elway
947 Dave Krieg	1342 Warren Moon	1710 Warren Moon
Completions		
642 Warren Moon	968 Dan Marino	1231 Dan Marino
614 Dan Marino	919 Jim Everett	1096 Joe Montana
611 Jim Everett	862 Randall Cunningham	1085 Randall Cunningham
592 Joe Montana	830 Joe Montana	1081 Jim Everett
561 Randall Cunningham	802 Warren Moon	1015 John Elway
Passing Yards		
8320 Warren Moon	12,263 Jim Everett	15,239 Dan Marino
8299 Jim Everett	11,994 Dan Marino	14,327 Jim Everett
7560 Dan Marino	10,674 Randall Cunningham	13,500 Joe Montana
7465 Joe Montana	10,647 Warren Moon	13,460 Randall Cunningham
6866 Randall Cunningham	10,446 Joe Montana	13,453 Warren Moon
TD Passes		
56 Warren Moon	83 Jim Everett	101 Joe Montana
52 Boomer Esiason	80 Boomer Esiason	99 Dan Marino
52 Jim Everett	75 Randall Cunningham	98 Randall Cunningham
52 Joe Montana	73 Dan Marino	96 Boomer Esiason
51 Randall Cunningham	73 Warren Moon	94 Warren Moon
Receptions		
182 Jerry Rice	246 Jerry Rice	311 Jerry Rice
159 Andre Reed	232 Henry Ellard	287 Andre Reed
157 Sterling Sharpe	230 Andre Reed	283 Henry Ellard
154 Gary Clark	226 Art Monk	281 Al Toon
154 Art Monk	221 Keith Byars	269 Gary Clark
Reception Yards		
2985 Jerry Rice	4291 Jerry Rice	5369 Jerry Rice
2676 Henry Ellard	4090 Henry Ellard	4889 Henry Ellard
2528 Sterling Sharpe	3319 Sterling Sharpe	4299 Gary Clark
2341 Gary Clark	3299 Anthony Carter	4221 Anthony Carter
2257 Andre Reed	3233 Gary Clark	4087 Drew Hill
Receiving TDs		
30 Jerry Rice	39 Jerry Rice	61 Jerry Rice
18 Sterling Sharpe	26 Mark Clayton	33 Mark Clayton
17 Gary Clark	24 Eddie Brown	31 Gary Clark
17 Anthony Miller	24 Gary Clark	29 Drew Hill
17 Andre Reed	23 Drew Hill	28 Andre Reed
17 John Taylor	23 Andre Reed	
Interceptions		
14 Gill Byrd	21 Gill Byrd	23 Joey Browner
13 Dave Waymer	19 Erik McMillan	21 Gill Byrd
12 Joey Browner	17 Joey Browner	21 Mark Kelso
12 David Fulcher	17 David Fulcher	21 Dave Waymer
12 Felix Wright	17 Harry Hamilton	21 Felix Wright
	17 Felix Wright	
Sacks		
32 Chris Doleman	46 Kevin Greene	64 Reggie White
32 Bruce Smith	43 Bruce Smith	55 Bruce Smith
30 Derrick Thomas	43 Reggie White	53 Lawrence Taylor
29.5 Kevin Greene	41 Lawrence Taylor	52.5 Kevin Greene
27.5 Pat Swilling	40 Chris Doleman	51 Chris Doleman
	40 Tim Harris	

NFL Team Leaders Over Last 2 Seasons, Last 3 Seasons, Last 4 Seasons

Last 2 Seasons	Last 3 Seasons	Last 4 Seasons
Highest Won-Lost Percentage		
.875 San Francisco	.792 San Francisco	.810 San Francisco
.781 N.Y. Giants	.729 N.Y. Giants	.651 Buffalo
.688 Buffalo	.708 Buffalo	.651 N.Y. Giants
.656 Philadelphia	.646 Philadelphia	.635 Chicago
.625 three teams	.604 Chicago	.619 New Orleans
	.604 Cincinnati	
Most Points		
837 Buffalo	1212 Cincinnati	1623 San Francisco
795 San Francisco	1194 Houston	1539 Houston
771 L.A. Rams	1178 L.A. Rams	1497 Cincinnati
770 Houston	1166 Buffalo	1495 L.A. Rams
767 Washington	1164 San Francisco	1491 Washington
Most Total Yards		
12,163 San Francisco	18,063 San Francisco	24,050 San Francisco
11,815 Washington	17,494 Washington	23,091 Washington
11,649 Houston	17,280 L.A. Rams	22,598 Cincinnati
11,472 L.A. Rams	17,221 Cincinnati	22,077 Houston
11,164 Cincinnati	16,854 Houston	21,931 L.A. Rams
Most Rushing Yards		
4764 Philadelphia	7313 Cincinnati	9477 Cincinnati
4723 Chicago	7042 Chicago	8996 Chicago
4603 Cincinnati	6709 Philadelphia	8736 Philadelphia
4344 Buffalo	6477 Buffalo	8444 San Francisco
4175 Kansas City	6207 San Francisco	8317 Buffalo
Most Passing Yards		
8479 San Francisco	12,244 Miami	16,120 Miami
8304 Houston	11,964 Washington	15,606 San Francisco
7951 L.A. Rams	11,856 San Francisco	15,459 Washington
7828 Washington	11,756 L.A. Rams	14,560 Houston
7728 Miami	11,260 Houston	14,310 L.A. Rams
Fewest Turnovers		
44 N.Y. Giants	71 N.Y. Giants	107 San Francisco
55 San Francisco	81 San Francisco	113 N.Y. Giants
58 Indianapolis	86 Philadelphia	121 Philadelphia
58 L.A. Raiders	88 Indianapolis	122 Indianapolis
60 three teams	91 L.A. Raiders	122 L.A. Raiders
Fewest Points Allowed		
463 N.Y. Giants	767 N.Y. Giants	1039 San Francisco
492 San Francisco	786 San Francisco	1079 N.Y. Giants
543 Kansas City	817 Buffalo	1122 Buffalo
565 L.A. Raiders	834 Minnesota	1142 New Orleans
566 Pittsburgh	859 New Orleans	1154 Chicago
Fewest Total Yards Allowed		
8870 N.Y. Giants	12,992 Minnesota	17,561 San Francisco
8891 San Francisco	13,466 San Francisco	17,816 Minnesota
8901 Minnesota	13,956 N.Y. Giants	18,614 N.Y. Giants
9174 Kansas City	14,200 Kansas City	18,796 Chicago
9189 San Diego	14,231 Buffalo	19,052 Cleveland
Fewest Rushing Yards Allowed		
2641 San Francisco	4229 San Francisco	5840 San Francisco
2774 Philadelphia	4426 Philadelphia	6069 Philadelphia
2885 New Orleans	4664 New Orleans	6208 Chicago
2931 Washington	4676 Washington	6214 New Orleans
2998 N.Y. Giants	4757 N.Y. Giants	6355 Washington
Fewest Passing Yards Allowed		
5144 Minnesota	7633 Minnesota	10,733 Minnesota
5760 L.A. Raiders	8202 Kansas City	11,508 Kansas City
5768 Kansas City	8729 Buffalo	11,583 Buffalo
5861 San Diego	8931 L.A. Raiders	11,658 L.A. Raiders
5872 N.Y. Giants	9093 Cleveland	11,721 San Francisco
Most Opponents' Turnovers		
86 Philadelphia	130 Philadelphia	178 Philadelphia
84 Pittsburgh	122 Minnesota	161 Pittsburgh
83 Chicago	118 Chicago	159 Minnesota
81 Tampa Bay	117 Pittsburgh	153 Green Bay
78 Kansas City	114 Tampa Bay	150 Tampa Bay

Longest Streaks in NFL History

Games Played		
282	Jim Marshall	1960-79
240	Mick Tingelhoff	1962-78
234	Jim Bakken	1962-78
Games Scoring		
165	Jim Breech	1980-90 (current)
151	Fred Cox	1963-73
133	Garo Yepremian	1970-79
Games Scoring Touchdowns		
18	Lenny Moore	1963-65
14	O.J. Simpson	1975
13	John Riggins	1982-83
	Jerry Rice	1986-87
Extra Points		
234	Tommy Davis	1959-65
221	Jim Turner	1967-74
202	Gary Anderson	1983-88
Games Scoring Field Goals		
31	Fred Cox	1968-70
28	Jim Turner	1970-72
	Chip Lohmiller	1988-90
23	Morten Andersen	1986-88
Field Goals		
24	Kevin Butler	1988-89
23	Mark Moseley	1981-82
22	Pat Leahy	1985-86
100-Yard Rushing Games		
11	Marcus Allen	1985-86
9	Walter Payton	1985
7	O.J. Simpson	1972-73
	Earl Campbell	1979

Games Rushing For Touchdowns

13	John Riggins	1982-83
	George Rogers	1985-86
11	Lenny Moore	1963-64
10	Greg Bell	1988-89

Passes Completed

22	Joe Montana	1987
20	Ken Anderson	1983
18	Steve DeBerg	1982
	Lynn Dickey	1983
	Joe Montana	1984
	Don Majkowski	1989

300-Yard Passing Games

5	Joe Montana	1982
4	Dan Fouts	1979
	Bill Kenney	1983
	Joe Montana	1990
	Warren Moon	1990

Games Passing For Touchdowns

47	Johnny Unitas	1956-60
30	Dan Marino	1985-87
28	Dave Krieg	1983-85

Passes Without Interception

294	Bart Starr	1964-65
214	Fran Tarkenton	1968-69
211	Ken O'Brien	1987-88

Games With Receptions

177	Steve Largent	1977-89
150	Ozzie Newsome	1979-89
127	Harold Carmichael	1972-80

100-Yard Receiving Games

7	Charley Hennigan	1961
	Bill Groman	1961
6	Raymond Berry	1960
	Pat Studstill	1966
5	Elroy (Crazylegs) Hirsch	1951
	Bob Boyd	1954
	Terry Barr	1963
	Lance Alworth	1966

Games With Touchdown Receptions

13	Jerry Rice	1986-87
11	Elroy (Crazylegs) Hirsch	1950-51
	Buddy Dial	1959-60
9	Lance Alworth	1963

Games With Interceptions

8	Tom Morrow	1962-63
7	Paul Krause	1964
	Larry Wilson	1966
	Ben Davis	1968

Punts Without A Block

623	Dave Jennings	1976-83
619	Ray Guy	1979-86
578	Bobby Walden	1964-72

Records of Teams on Opening Day, 1933-90

AFC	W	L	T	Pct.	Longest W Strk.	Longest L Strk.	Current Streak
L.A. Raiders	19	12	0	.613	5	5	W-4
Denver	18	12	1	.600	3	4	L-1
Cleveland	24	17	0	.585	5	5	W-3
San Diego	18	13	0	.581	6	4	L-4
Indianapolis	20	18	0	.526	8	7	L-7
Cincinnati	12	11	0	.522	4	4	W-1
Pittsburgh	27	25	4	.519	4	3	L-2
Houston	16	15	0	.516	4	3	L-2
Kansas City	16	15	0	.516	5	4	W-1
New England	15	16	0	.484	6	3	L-1
Miami	11	13	1	.458	4	5	W-1
N.Y. Jets	13	18	0	.419	3	5	L-3
Buffalo	12	19	0	.387	3	5	W-3
Seattle	4	11	0	.267	3	8	L-2

NFC	W	L	T	Pct.	Longest W Strk.	Longest L Strk.	Current Streak
Dallas	23	7	1	.767	17	3	W-1
N.Y. Giants	32	22	4	.593	3	3	W-3
Minnesota	17	12	1	.586	4	2	L-1
Chicago	33	24	1	.579	7	6	W-7
Atlanta	14	11	0	.560	5	3	W-1
L.A. Rams	29	24	0	.547	5	6	L-1
Detroit	30	26	2	.536	7	4	L-2
Green Bay	29	26	3	.527	5	6	W-1
Washington	28	26	4	.519	6	5	W-1
San Francisco	19	21	1	.475	4	3	W-3
Phoenix	25	31	1	.446	6	6	L-1
Tampa Bay	6	9	0	.400	3	5	W-2
Philadelphia	22	34	1	.393	5	9	L-1
New Orleans	5	19	0	.208	1	6	L-1

Note: All tied games occurred prior to 1972, when calculation of ties in percentages as half-win, half-loss was begun.

Records of NFL Teams in 1990 Maintaining Leads and Coming From Behind

	Status at Halftime			Status After 3 Quarters		
AFC	Leading	Tied	Trailing	Leading	Tied	Trailing
Buffalo	10-1	0-0	3-2	10-0	1-0	2-3
Cincinnati	6-0	1-1	2-6	6-0	1-0	2-7
Cleveland	1-1	0-0	2-12	3-1	0-1	0-11
Denver	4-8	1-1	0-2	5-2	0-0	0-9
Houston	8-1	0-1	1-5	8-2	0-0	1-5
Indianapolis	2-1	0-1	5-7	2-1	0-0	5-8
Kansas City	9-3	1-0	1-2	10-3	0-0	1-2
L.A. Raiders	6-1	2-2	4-1	10-1	0-0	2-3
Miami	8-0	2-0	2-4	9-0	1-0	2-4
New England	0-2	1-1	0-12	1-2	0-0	0-13
N.Y. Jets	6-5	0-2	0-3	5-2	0-2	1-6
Pittsburgh	6-1	1-1	2-5	7-0	1-0	1-7
San Diego	5-3	0-1	1-6	6-4	0-0	0-6
Seattle	4-0	3-2	2-5	6-1	0-1	3-5

	Status at Halftime			Status After 3 Quarters		
NFC	Leading	Tied	Trailing	Leading	Tied	Trailing
Atlanta	4-2	0-1	1-8	4-2	0-0	1-9
Chicago	10-1	0-0	1-4	11-1	0-0	0-4
Dallas	4-0	0-0	3-9	1-0	2-0	4-9
Detroit	3-3	1-2	2-5	4-3	0-0	2-7
Green Bay	4-1	1-2	1-7	4-1	0-1	2-8
L.A. Rams	5-1	0-0	0-10	5-1	0-1	0-9
Minnesota	4-4	1-0	1-6	4-5	1-0	1-5
New Orleans	7-4	0-0	1-4	7-2	0-1	1-5
N.Y. Giants	10-0	1-0	2-3	11-0	0-0	2-3
Philadelphia	7-3	1-1	2-2	8-3	0-0	2-3
Phoenix	1-1	2-1	2-9	3-2	0-0	2-9
San Francisco	9-0	1-0	4-2	11-0	1-0	2-2
Tampa Bay	5-1	1-0	0-9	5-2	0-0	1-8
Washington	7-0	0-1	3-4	8-1	0-1	2-4
Totals	155-48	21-21	48-155	174-42	8-8	42-174

Trailing at Halftime

	1981-90	1990 ONLY
Home Teams	220-606-3 (.267)	23-57-0 (.288)
Road Teams	208-890-4 (.191)	25-98-0 (.203)
All Teams	428-1496-7 (.223)	48-155-0 (.236)

Trailing After Three Quarters

	1981-90	1990 ONLY
Home Teams	186-675-2 (.217)	22-69-0 (.242)
Road Teams	170-975-5 (.150)	20-105-0 (.160)
All Teams	356-1650-7 (.179)	42-174-0 (.194)

Oldest Individual Single-Season or Single-Game Records in NFL Record & Fact Book

Regular-Season Records That Have Not Been Surpassed or Tied

Most Points, Game—40, Ernie Nevers, Chi. Cardinals vs. Chi. Bears, Nov. 28, 1929 (6-td, 4-pat)

Most Touchdowns Rushing, Game—6, Ernie Nevers, Chi. Cardinals vs. Chi. Bears, Nov. 28, 1929

Highest Punting Average, Season (Qualifiers)—51.40, Sammy Baugh, Washington, 1940 (35-1,799)

Highest Punting Average, Game (minimum: 4 punts)—61.75, Bob Cifers, Detroit vs. Chi. Bears, Nov. 24, 1946 (4-247)

Highest Average Gain, Pass Receptions, Season (minimum: 24 receptions)—32.58, Don Currivan, Boston, 1947 (24-782)

Highest Average Gain, Passing, Game (minimum: 20 passes)—18.58, Sammy Baugh, Washington vs. Boston, Oct. 31, 1948 (24-446)

Most Touchdowns, Fumble Recoveries, Game—2, Fred (Dippy) Evans, Chi. Bears vs. Washington, Nov. 28, 1948

Most Yards Gained, Intercepted Passes, Rookie, Season—301, Don Doll, Detroit, 1949

Most Passes Had Intercepted, Game—8, Jim Hardy, Chi. Cardinals vs. Philadelphia, Sept. 24, 1950

Highest Average Gain, Rushing, Game (minimum: 10 attempts)—17.09, Marion Motley, Cleveland vs. Pittsburgh, Oct. 29, 1950 (11-188)

Most Yards Gained, Kickoff Returns, Game—294, Wally Triplett, Detroit vs. Los Angeles, Oct. 29, 1950

Highest Kickoff Return Average, Game (minimum: 3 returns)—73.50, Wally Triplett, Detroit vs. Los Angeles, Oct. 29, 1950 (4-294)

Most Pass Receptions, Game—18, Tom Fears, Los Angeles vs. Green Bay, Dec. 3, 1950

Highest Punt Return Average, Season (Qualifiers)—23.00, Herb Rich, Baltimore, 1950 (12-276)

Highest Punt Return Average, Rookie, Season (Qualifiers)—23.00, Herb Rich, Baltimore, 1950 (12-276)

Most Yards Passing, Game—554, Norm Van Brocklin, Los Angeles vs. N.Y. Yanks, Sept. 28, 1951

Most Touchdowns, Punt Returns, Rookie, Season—4, Jack Christiansen, Detroit, 1951

Most Interceptions By, Season—14, Dick (Night Train) Lane, Los Angeles, 1952

Most Interceptions By, Rookie, Season—14, Dick (Night Train) Lane, Los Angeles, 1952

Highest Average Gain, Passing, Season (Qualifiers)—11.17, Tommy O'Connell, Cleveland, 1957 (110-1,229)

Most Points, Season—176, Paul Hornung, Green Bay, 1960 (15-td, 41-pat, 15-fg)

Most Yards Gained, Pass Receptions, Rookie, Season—1,473, Bill Groman, Houston, 1960

Largest Trades in NFL History

(Based on number of players or draft choices involved)

15—March 26, 1953—T Mike McCormack, DT Don Colo, LB Tom Catlin, DB John Petitbon, and G Herschell Forester from Baltimore to Cleveland for DB Don Shula, DB Bert Rechichar, DB Carl Taseff, LB Ed Sharkey, E Gern Nagler, QB Harry Agganis, T Dick Batten, T Stu Sheets, G Art Spinney, and G Elmer Willhoite.

15—January 28, 1971—LB Marlin McKeever, first- and third-round choices in 1971, and third-, fourth-, fifth-, sixth-, and seventh-round choices in 1972 from Washington to the Los Angeles Rams for LB Maxie Baughan, LB Jack Pardee, LB Myron Pottios, RB Jeff Jordan, G John Wilbur, DT Diron Talbert, and a fifth-round choice in 1971.

12—June 13, 1952—Selection rights to Les Richter from the Dallas Texans to the Los Angeles Rams for RB Dick Hoerner, DB Tom Keane, DB George Sims, C Joe Reid, HB Billy Baggett, T Jack Halliday, FB Dick McKissack, LB Vic Vasicek, E Richard Wilkins, C Aubrey Phillips, and RB Dave Anderson.

10—March 23, 1959—Ollie Matson from the Chicago Cardinals to the Los Angeles Rams for T Frank Fuller, DE Glenn Holtzman, T Ken Panfil, DT Art Hauser, E John Tracey, FB Larry Hickman, HB Don Brown, the Rams second-round choice in 1960, and a player to be delivered during the 1959 training camp.

10—October 31, 1987—RB Eric Dickerson from the Los Angeles Rams to Indianapolis. The rights to LB Cornelius Bennett from Indianapolis to Buffalo. Indianapolis running back Owen Gill and the Colts' first- and second-round choices in 1988 and second-round choice in 1989, plus Bills running back Greg Bell and Buffalo's first-round choice in 1988 and first- and second-round choices in 1989 to the Rams.

Retired Uniform Numbers in NFL

AFC

Buffalo:	None	
Cincinnati:	Bob Johnson	54
Cleveland:	Otto Graham	14
	Jim Brown	32
	Ernie Davis	45
	Don Fleming	46
	Lou Groza	76
Denver:	Frank Tripucka	18
	Floyd Little	44
Houston:	Earl Campbell	34
	Jim Norton	43
	Elvin Bethea	65
Indianapolis:	Johnny Unitas	19
	Buddy Young	22
	Lenny Moore	24
	Art Donovan	70
	Jim Parker	77
	Raymond Berry	82
	Gino Marchetti	89
Kansas City:	Len Dawson	16
	Abner Haynes	28
	Stone Johnson	33
	Mack Lee Hill	36
	Bobby Bell	78
Los Angeles Raiders:	None	
Miami:	Bob Griese	12
New England:	Gino Cappelletti	20
	Steve Nelson	57
	John Hannah	73
	Jim Hunt	79
	Bob Dee	89
New York Jets:	Joe Namath	12
	Don Maynard	13
Pittsburgh:	None	
San Diego:	Dan Fouts	14
Seattle:	"Fans/the twelfth man"	12

NFC

Atlanta:	William Andrews	31
	Jeff Van Note	57
	Tommy Nobis	60
Chicago:	Bronko Nagurski	3
	George McAfee	5
	Willie Galimore	28
	Walter Payton	34
	Brian Piccolo	41
	Sid Luckman	42
	Bill Hewitt	56
	Bill George	61
	Bulldog Turner	66
	Red Grange	77
Dallas:	None	
Detroit:	Dutch Clark	7
	Bobby Layne	22
	Doak Walker	37
	Joe Schmidt	56
	Chuck Hughes	85
	Charlie Sanders	88
Green Bay:	Tony Canadeo	3
	Don Hutson	14
	Bart Starr	15
	Ray Nitschke	66
Los Angeles Rams:	Bob Waterfield	7
	Merlin Olsen	74
Minnesota:	Fran Tarkenton	10
	Alan Page	88
New Orleans:	Jim Taylor	31
	Doug Atkins	81
New York Giants:	Ray Flaherty	1
	Mel Hein	7
	Y.A. Tittle	14
	Al Blozis	32
	Joe Morrison	40
	Charlie Conerly	42
	Ken Strong	50
Philadelphia:	Steve Van Buren	15
	Tom Brookshier	40
	Pete Retzlaff	44
	Chuck Bednarik	60
	Al Wistert	70
Phoenix:	Larry Wilson	8
	Stan Mauldin	77
	J.V. Cain	88
	Marshall Goldberg	99
San Francisco:	John Brodie	12
	Joe Perry	34
	Jimmy Johnson	37
	Hugh McElhenny	39
	Charlie Krueger	70
	Leo Nomellini	73
	Dwight Clark	87
Tampa Bay:	Lee Roy Selmon	63
Washington:	Sammy Baugh	33

1990 NFL Score by Quarters

AFC Offense	1	2	3	4	OT	PTS
Buffalo	83	116	69	160	0	428
Houston	83	152	70	100	0	405
Kansas City	86	123	71	89	0	369
Cincinnati	79	110	78	90	3	360
L.A. Raiders	82	84	76	95	0	337
Miami	60	113	77	83	3	336
Denver	87	120	46	75	3	331
San Diego	69	102	75	69	0	315
Seattle	50	94	60	96	6	306
N.Y. Jets	61	131	46	57	0	295
Pittsburgh	64	71	54	103	0	292
Indianapolis	47	68	85	81	0	281
Cleveland	32	57	71	68	0	228
New England	30	81	30	40	0	181

NFC Offense	1	2	3	4	OT	PTS
Philadelphia	84	104	67	141	0	396
Washington	49	108	103	118	3	381
Detroit	111	102	65	95	0	373
San Francisco	44	131	84	91	3	353
Minnesota	54	131	80	86	0	351
Atlanta	94	74	68	112	0	348
Chicago	54	156	70	59	9	348
L.A. Rams	62	130	85	68	0	345
N.Y. Giants	66	118	52	99	0	335
New Orleans	54	82	48	90	0	274
Green Bay	36	76	57	102	0	271
Phoenix	27	81	65	95	0	268
Tampa Bay	41	99	50	71	3	264
Dallas	50	46	40	108	0	244

AFC Defense	1	2	3	4	OT	PTS
Pittsburgh	58	86	56	40	0	240
Miami	30	108	39	65	0	242
Kansas City	48	66	62	81	0	257
Buffalo	55	74	72	62	0	263
L.A. Raiders	59	89	33	87	0	268
San Diego	54	111	27	86	3	281
Seattle	50	112	53	68	3	286
Houston	54	95	71	84	3	307
N.Y. Jets	38	100	90	117	0	345
Cincinnati	70	115	101	63	3	352
Indianapolis	87	128	43	95	0	353
Denver	60	85	95	131	3	374
New England	120	128	88	110	0	446
Cleveland	107	182	61	112	0	462

NFC Defense	1	2	3	4	OT	PTS
N.Y. Giants	28	72	60	51	0	211
San Francisco	64	74	33	68	0	239
New Orleans	30	82	76	87	0	275
Chicago	59	80	53	88	0	280
Philadelphia	71	81	40	104	3	299
Washington	37	98	75	91	0	301
Dallas	54	102	52	100	0	308
Minnesota	76	76	66	105	3	326
Green Bay	64	103	88	92	0	347
Atlanta	35	143	72	115	0	365
Tampa Bay	59	112	100	96	0	367
Phoenix	88	113	79	116	0	396
L.A. Rams	98	123	74	114	3	412
Detroit	86	122	83	113	9	413

NFL TOTALS	1	2	3	4	OT	PTS
	1739	2860	1842	2541	33	9015

Team Leaders

Offense	Most Scored	Fewest Scored
1st Quarter	111, Detroit	27, Phoenix
2nd Quarter	156, Chicago	46, Dallas
3rd Quarter	103, Washington	30, New England
4th Quarter	160, Buffalo	40, New England

Defense	Most Allowed	Fewest Allowed
1st Quarter	120, New England	28, N.Y. Giants
2nd Quarter	182, Cleveland	66, Kansas City
3rd Quarter	101, Cincinnati	27, San Diego
4th Quarter	131, Denver	40, Pittsburgh

Greatest Comebacks in NFL History (Most Points Overcome To Win Game)

Regular-Season Games

From 28 points behind to win:
December 7, 1980, at San Francisco

New Orleans	14	21	0	0	0 — 35
San Francisco	0	7	14	14	3 — 38

NO —Harris 33 pass from Manning (Ricardo kick)
NO —Childs 21 pass from Manning (Ricardo kick)
NO —Holmes 1 run (Ricardo kick)
SF —Solomon 57 punt return (Wersching kick)
NO —Holmes 1 run (Ricardo kick)
NO —Harris 41 pass from Manning (Ricardo kick)
SF —Montana 1 run (Wersching kick)
SF —Clark 71 pass from Montana (Wersching kick)
SF —Solomon 14 pass from Montana (Wersching kick)
SF —Elliott 7 run (Wersching kick)
SF —FG Wersching 36

	N.O.	S.F.
First Downs	27	24
Total Yards	519	430
Yards Rushing	143	176
Yards Passing	376	254
Turnovers	3	0

From 25 points behind to win:
November 8, 1987, at St. Louis

Tampa Bay	7	7	14	0 — 28
St. Louis	0	3	0	28 — 31

TB —Carrier 5 pass from DeBerg (Igwebuike kick)
TB —Carter 3 pass from DeBerg (Igwebuike kick)
StL —FG Gallery 31
TB —Smith 34 pass from DeBerg (Igwebuike kick)
TB —Smith 3 run (Igwebuike kick)
StL —Awalt 4 pass from Lomax (Gallery kick)
StL —Noga 23 fumble recovery (Gallery kick)
StL —J. Smith 11 pass from Lomax (Gallery kick)
StL —J. Smith 17 pass from Lomax (Gallery kick)

	T.B.	St.L.
First Downs	26	26
Total Yards	377	415
Yards Rushing	83	137
Yards Passing	294	278
Turnovers	1	2

From 24 points behind to win:
October 27, 1946, at Washington

Philadelphia	0	0	14	14 — 28
Washington	10	14	0	0 — 24

Wash — Rosato 2 run (Poillon kick)
Wash — FG Poillon 28
Wash — Rosato 4 run (Poillon kick)
Wash — Lapka recovered fumble in end zone (Poillon kick)
Phil — Steele 1 run (Lio kick)
Phil — Pritchard 45 pass from Thompson (Lio kick)
Phil — Steinke 7 pass from Thompson (Lio kick)
Phil — Ferrante 30 pass from Thompson (Lio kick)

	Phil.	Wash.
First Downs	14	8
Total Yards	262	127
Yards Rushing	34	66
Yards Passing	228	61
Turnovers	6	3

From 24 points behind to win:
October 20, 1957, at Detroit

Baltimore	7	14	6	0 — 27
Detroit	0	3	7	21 — 31

Balt —Mutscheller 15 pass from Unitas (Rechichar kick)
Det —FG Martin 47
Balt —Moore 72 pass from Unitas (Rechichar kick)
Balt —Mutscheller 52 pass from Unitas (Rechichar kick)
Balt —Moore 4 pass from Unitas (kick failed)
Det —Junker 14 pass from Rote (Layne kick)
Det —Cassady 26 pass from Layne (Layne kick)
Det —Johnson 1 run (Layne kick)
Det —Cassady 29 pass from Layne (Layne kick)

	Balt.	Det.
First Downs	15	20
Total Yards	322	369
Yards Rushing	117	178
Yards Passing	205	191
Turnovers	6	4

From 24 points behind to win:
October 25, 1959, at Chicago

Philadelphia	0	0	21	7 — 28
Chi. Cardinals	7	10	7	0 — 24

Chi —Crow 10 pass from Roach (Conrad kick)
Chi —J. Hill 77 blocked field goal return (Conrad kick)
Chi —FG Conrad 15
Chi —Lane 37 interception return (Conrad kick)
Phil —Barnes 1 run (Walston kick)
Phil —McDonald 29 pass from Van Brocklin (Walston kick)
Phil —Barnes 2 run (Walston kick)
Phil —McDonald 22 pass from Van Brocklin (Walston kick)

	Phil.	Chi.
First Downs	22	14
Total Yards	399	313
Yards Rushing	168	163
Yards Passing	231	150
Turnovers	2	6

From 24 points behind to win:
October 23, 1960, at Denver

Boston	10	7	7	0 — 24
Denver	0	0	14	17 — 31

Bos — FG Cappelletti 12
Bos — Colclough 10 pass from Songin (Cappelletti kick)
Bos — Wells 6 pass from Songin (Cappelletti kick)
Bos — Miller 47 pass from Songin (Cappelletti kick)
Den — Carmichael 21 pass from Tripucka (Mingo kick)
Den — Jessup 19 pass from Tripucka (Mingo kick)
Den — Carmichael 35 lateral from Taylor, pass from Tripucka (Mingo kick)
Den — Taylor 8 pass from Tripucka (Mingo kick)
Den — FG Mingo 9

	Bos.	Den.
First Downs	19	16
Total Yards	434	326
Yards Rushing	211	65
Yards Passing	223	261
Turnovers	7	4

From 24 points behind to win:
December 15, 1974, at Miami

New England	21	3	0	3 — 27
Miami	0	17	7	10 — 34

NE —Hannah recovered fumble in end zone (J. Smith kick)
NE —Sanders 23 interception return (J. Smith kick)

NE —Herron 4 pass from Plunkett (J. Smith kick)
NE —FG J. Smith 46
Mia—Nottingham 1 run (Yepremian kick)
Mia—Baker 37 pass from Morrall (Yepremian kick)
Mia—FG Yepremian 28
Mia—Baker 46 pass from Morrall (Yepremian kick)
NE —FG J. Smith 34
Mia—Nottingham 2 run (Yepremian kick)
Mia—FG Yepremian 40

	N.E.	Mia.
First Downs	18	18
Total Yards	333	333
Yards Rushing	114	61
Yards Passing	219	272
Turnovers	3	4

From 24 points behind to win:
December 4, 1977, at Minnesota

San Francisco	0	10	14	3	— 27
Minnesota	0	0	7	21	— 28

SF —Delvin Williams 2 run (Wersching kick)
SF —FG Wersching 31
SF —Dave Williams 80 kickoff return (Wersching kick)
SF —Delvin Williams 5 run (Wersching kick)
Minn—McClanahan 15 pass from Lee (Cox kick)
Minn—Rashad 8 pass from Kramer (Cox kick)
Minn—Tucker 9 pass from Kramer (Cox kick)
SF —FG Wersching 31
Minn—S. White 69 pass from Kramer (Cox kick)

	S.F.	Minn.
First Downs	19	18
Total Yards	243	309
Yards Rushing	196	52
Yards Passing	47	257
Turnovers	2	5

From 24 points behind to win:
September 23, 1979, at Denver

Seattle	10	10	14	0	— 34
Denver	0	10	21	6	— 37

Sea—FG Herrera 28
Sea—Doornink 5 run (Herrera kick)
Den—FG Turner 27
Sea—Doornink 5 run (Herrera kick)
Den—Armstrong 2 run (Turner kick)
Sea—FG Herrera 22
Sea—McCullum 13 pass from Zorn (Herrera kick)
Sea—Smith 1 run (Herrera kick)
Den—Studdard 2 pass from Morton (Turner kick)
Den—Moses 11 pass from Morton (Turner kick)
Den—Upchurch 35 pass from Morton (Turner kick)
Den—Lytle 1 run (kick failed)

	Sea.	Den.
First Downs	22	23
Total Yards	350	344
Yards Rushing	153	90
Yards Passing	197	254
Turnovers	4	3

From 24 points behind to win:
September 23, 1979, at Cincinnati

Houston	0	10	17	0	3	— 30
Cincinnati	14	10	0	3	0	— 27

Cin —Johnson 1 run (Bahr kick)
Cin —Alexander 2 run (Bahr kick)
Cin —Johnson 1 run (Bahr kick)
Cin —FG Bahr 52
Hou—Burrough 35 pass from Pastorini (Fritsch kick)
Hou—FG Fritsch 33
Hou—Campbell 8 run (Fritsch kick)
Hou—Caster 22 pass from Pastorini (Fritsch kick)
Hou—FG Fritsch 47
Cin —FG Bahr 55
Hou—FG Fritsch 29

	Hou.	Cin.
First Downs	19	21
Total Yards	361	265
Yards Rushing	177	165
Yards Passing	184	100
Turnovers	3	2

From 24 points behind to win:
November 22, 1982, at Los Angeles

San Diego	10	14	0	0	— 24
L.A. Raiders	0	7	14	7	— 28

SD —FG Benirschke 19
SD —Scales 29 pass from Fouts (Benirschke kick)
SD —Muncie 2 run (Benirschke kick)
SD —Muncie 1 run (Benirschke kick)
Raiders—Christensen 1 pass from Plunkett (Bahr kick)
Raiders—Allen 3 run (Bahr kick)
Raiders—Allen 6 run (Bahr kick)
Raiders—Hawkins 1 run (Bahr kick)

	S.D.	Raiders
First Downs	26	23
Total Yards	411	326
Yards Rushing	72	181
Yards Passing	339	145
Turnovers	4	2

From 24 points behind to win:
September 26, 1988, at Denver

L.A. Raiders	0	0	14	13	3	— 30
Denver	7	17	0	3	0	— 27

Den —Dorsett 1 run (Karlis kick)
Den —Dorsett 1 run (Karlis kick)
Den —Sewell 7 pass from Elway (Karlis kick)
Den —FG Karlis 39
Raiders—Smith 40 pass from Schroeder (Bahr kick)
Raiders—Smith 42 pass from Schroeder (Bahr kick)
Raiders—FG Bahr 28
Raiders—Allen 4 run (Bahr kick)
Den —FG Karlis 25
Raiders—FG Bahr 44
Raiders—FG Bahr 35

	Raiders	Den.
First Downs	20	23
Total Yards	363	398
Yards Rushing	128	189
Yards Passing	235	209
Turnovers	1	5

Postseason Games

From 20 points behind to win:
Western Conference Playoff Game
December 22, 1957, at San Francisco

Detroit	0	7	14	10	— 31
San Francisco	14	10	3	0	— 27

SF —Owens 34 pass from Tittle (Soltau kick)
SF —McElhenny 47 pass from Tittle (Soltau kick)
Det—Junker 4 pass from Rote (Martin kick)
SF —Wilson 12 pass from Tittle (Soltau kick)
SF —FG Soltau 25
SF —FG Soltau 10
Det—Tracy 2 run (Martin kick)
Det—Tracy 58 run (Martin kick)
Det—Gedman 3 run (Martin kick)
Det—FG Martin 14

	Det.	S.F.
First Downs	22	20
Total Yards	324	351
Yards Rushing	129	127
Yards Passing	195	224
Turnovers	5	4

From 18 points behind to win:
NFC Divisional Playoff Game
December 23, 1972, at San Francisco

Dallas	3	10	0	17	— 30
San Francisco	7	14	7	0	— 28

SF —Washington 97 kickoff return (Gossett kick)
Dall—FG Fritsch 37
SF —Schreiber 1 run (Gossett kick)
SF —Schreiber 1 run (Gossett kick)
Dall—FG Fritsch 45
Dall—Alworth 28 pass from Morton (Fritsch kick)
SF —Schreiber 1 run (Gossett kick)
Dall—FG Fritsch 27
Dall—Parks 20 pass from Staubach (Fritsch kick)
Dall—Sellers 10 pass from Staubach (Fritsch kick)

	Dall.	S.F.
First Downs	22	13
Total Yards	402	255
Yards Rushing	165	105
Yards Passing	237	150
Turnovers	5	3

From 18 points behind to win:
AFC Divisional Playoff Game
January 4, 1986, at Miami

Cleveland	7	7	7	0	— 21
Miami	3	0	14	7	— 24

Mia —FG Reveiz 51
Clev—Newsome 16 pass from Kosar (Bahr kick)
Clev—Byner 21 run (Bahr kick)
Clev—Byner 66 run (Bahr kick)

Mia —Moore 6 pass from Marino (Reveiz kick)
Mia —Davenport 31 run (Reveiz kick)
Mia —Davenport 1 run (Reveiz kick)

	Clev.	Mia.
First Downs	17	20
Total Yards	313	330
Yards Rushing	251	92
Yards Passing	62	238
Turnovers	1	1

From 14 points behind to win:
NFC Divisional Playoff Game
January 3, 1981, at Philadelphia

Minnesota	7	7	2	0	— 16
Philadelphia	0	7	14	10	— 31

Minn —S. White 30 pass from Kramer (Danmeier kick)
Minn —Brown 1 run (Danmeier kick)
Phil —Carmichael 9 pass from Jaworski (Franklin kick)
Phil —Montgomery 8 run (Franklin kick)
Minn —Safety, Jaworski tackled in end zone by Martin and Blair
Phil —Montgomery 5 run (Franklin kick)
Phil —FG Franklin 33
Phil —Harrington 2 run (Franklin kick)

	Minn.	Phil.
First Downs	14	24
Total Yards	215	305
Yards Rushing	36	126
Yards Passing	179	179
Turnovers	8	3

From 14 points behind to win:
NFC Divisional Playoff Game
January 4, 1981, at Atlanta

Dallas	3	7	0	20	— 30
Atlanta	10	7	7	3	— 27

Atl —FG Mazzetti 38
Atl —Jenkins 60 pass from Bartkowski (Mazzetti kick)
Dall —FG Septien 38
Dall —DuPree 5 pass from D. White (Mazzetti kick)
Atl —Cain 1 run (Mazzetti kick)
Atl —Andrews 5 pass from Bartkowski (Mazzetti kick)
Dall —Newhouse 1 run (Septien kick)
Atl —FG Mazzetti 34
Dall —D. Pearson 14 pass from D. White (Septien kick)
Dall —D. Pearson 23 pass from D. White (pass failed)

	Dall.	Atl.
First Downs	22	18
Total Yards	422	371
Yards Rushing	112	86
Yards Passing	310	283
Turnovers	2	2

From 14 points behind to win:
NFC Divisional Playoff Game
January 10, 1988, at Chicago

Washington	0	14	7	0	— 21
Chicago	7	7	3	0	— 17

Chi —Thomas 2 run (Butler kick)
Chi —Morris 14 pass from McMahon (Butler kick)
Wash —Rogers 3 run (Haji-Sheikh kick)
Wash —Didier 18 pass from Williams (Haji-Sheikh kick)
Wash —Green 52 punt return (Haji-Sheikh kick)
Chi —FG Butler 25

	Wash.	Chi.
First Downs	17	15
Total Yards	272	280
Yards Rushing	72	110
Yards Passing	200	170
Turnovers	2	3

Records of NFL Teams Since 1970 AFL-NFL Merger

AFC	W - L - T	Pct.	Division Titles	Playoff Berths	Post-season Record	Super Bowl Record
Miami	210-100-2	.677	9	13	15-11	2-3
L.A. Raiders	201-105-6	.656	9	13	17-10	3-0
Pittsburgh	185-126-1	.595	9	12	16-8	4-0
Denver	173-133-6	.565	6	8	8-8	0-4
Cincinnati	164-148-0	.526	5	7	5-7	0-2
Cleveland	158-151-3	.511	6	9	3-9	0-0
Seattle*	112-116-0	.491	1	4	3-4	0-0
New England	145-167-0	.465	2	5	3-5	0-1
Kansas City	137-168-7	.450	1	3	0-3	0-0
San Diego	136-171-5	.443	3	4	3-4	0-0
Indianapolis	134-176-2	.432	5	6	4-5	1-0
Buffalo	133-177-2	.429	4	6	4-6	0-1
N.Y. Jets	132-178-2	.426	0	4	3-4	0-0
Houston	131-179-2	.423	0	7	6-7	0-0

NFC	W - L - T	Pct.	Division Titles	Playoff Berths	Post-season Record	Super Bowl Record
Washington	198-113-1	.637	4	11	14-9	2-2
L.A. Rams	189-119-4	.613	8	14	10-14	0-1
Dallas	191-121-0	.612	9	14	19-12	2-3
Minnesota	182-128-2	.587	10	13	11-13	0-3
San Francisco	178-131-3	.576	11	12	16-8	4-0
Chicago	163-148-1	.524	6	8	6-7	1-0
N.Y. Giants	144-166-2	.465	3	6	9-4	2-0
Philadelphia	142-164-6	.465	2	7	3-7	0-1
Phoenix	136-170-6	.445	2	3	0-3	0-0
Detroit	133-175-4	.432	1	3	0-3	0-0
Green Bay	128-176-8	.423	1	2	1-2	0-0
Atlanta	122-186-4	.396	1	3	1-3	0-0
New Orleans	117-191-4	.380	0	2	0-2	0-0
Tampa Bay*	68-159-1	.300	2	3	1-3	0-0

*entered NFL in 1976.
Indianapolis totals include Baltimore, 1970-83.
L.A. Raiders totals include Oakland, 1970-81.
Phoenix totals include St. Louis, 1970-87.

Tie games before 1972 are not calculated in won-lost percentage.

In 1982, due to players' strike, the divisional format was abandoned. (L.A. Raiders and Washington won regular-season conference titles, not included in "Division Titles" totals listed above. Sixteen teams were awarded playoff berths, included in totals listed above.)

Longest Winning Streaks Since 1970

Regular-season games

16	Miami, 1971-73	(1 in 1971, 14 in 1972, 1 in 1973)
16	Miami, 1983-84	(5 in 1983, 11 in 1984)
15	San Francisco, 1989-90	(5 in 1989, 10 in 1990)
14	Oakland, 1976-77	(10 in 1976, 4 in 1977)
13	Chicago, 1984-85	(1 in 1984, 12 in 1985)
13	Minnesota, 1974-75	(3 in 1974, 10 in 1975)
13	N.Y. Giants, 1989-90	(3 in 1989, 10 in 1990)
11	Pittsburgh, 1975	
11	Baltimore, 1975-76	(9 in 1975, 2 in 1976)
10	Miami, 1973	
10	Pittsburgh, 1976-77	(9 in 1976, 1 in 1977)
10	Denver, 1984	

NFL Playoff Appearances by Seasons

Team	Number of Seasons in Playoffs
Cleveland	22
Los Angeles Rams	22
New York Giants	22
Chicago	19
Dallas	18
Washington	17
Los Angeles Raiders	16
Minnesota	15
Green Bay	13
Miami	13
Pittsburgh	13
San Francisco	13
Houston	12
Indianapolis	11
Philadelphia	11
Buffalo	10
San Diego	9
Denver	8
Detroit	8
Cincinnati	7
Kansas City	7
New England	6
New York Jets	6
Phoenix	5
Seattle	4
Atlanta	3
Tampa Bay	3
New Orleans	2

Teams in Super Bowl Contention, 1978-90

	With 3 Weeks to Play	With 2 Weeks to Play	With 1 Week to Play
1990	23	20	15
1989	21	18	17
1988	21	18	15
1987	19	19	15
1986	19	17	14
1985	21	18	13
1984	18	14	13
1983	24	19	15

1982	20	17	12
1981	21	20	16
1980	20	14	12
1979	19	15	13
1978	20	17	12

Games Decided by 7 Points or Less and 3 Points or Less (1970-90)

	Games Decided by 7 Points or Less	Games Decided by 3 Points or Less
1970	59 of 182 (32.4%)	34 of 182 (18.7%)
1971	76 of 182 (41.8%)	35 of 182 (19.2%)
1972	71 of 182 (39.0%)	38 of 182 (20.9%)
1973	60 of 182 (32.9%)	28 of 182 (15.4%)
1974	91 of 182 (50.0%)	37 of 182 (20.3%)
1975	62 of 182 (34.1%)	35 of 182 (19.2%)
1976	73 of 196 (37.2%)	38 of 196 (19.4%)
1977	85 of 196 (43.4%)	36 of 196 (18.4%)
1978	108 of 224 (48.2%)	49 of 224 (21.9%)
1979	104 of 224 (46.4%)	51 of 224 (22.8%)
1980	108 of 224 (48.2%)	58 of 224 (25.9%)
1981	91 of 224 (40.6%)	60 of 224 (26.8%)
1982	61 of 126 (48.4%)	33 of 126 (26.2%)
1983	106 of 224 (47.3%)	54 of 224 (24.1%)
1984	95 of 224 (42.4%)	58 of 224 (25.9%)
1985	87 of 224 (38.8%)	38 of 224 (17.0%)
1986	106 of 224 (47.3%)	48 of 224 (21.4%)
1987	99 of 210 (47.1%)	40 of 210 (19.0%)
1988	113 of 224 (50.4%)	62 of 224 (27.7%)
1989	107 of 224 (47.8%)	55 of 224 (24.6%)
1990	97 of 224 (43.3%)	54 of 224 (24.1%)

1990 Records of Teams in Close Games

AFC	Overall Record	Decided by 7 Pts. or Less	Decided By 3 Pts. or Less
Buffalo	13-3	4-1	2-1
Cincinnati	9-7	5-1	1-1
Cleveland	3-13	2-4	2-2
Denver	5-11	2-7	2-4
Houston	9-7	1-4	1-2
Indianapolis	7-9	5-3	3-2
Kansas City	11-5	4-3	4-2
L.A. Raiders	12-4	8-2	2-2
Miami	12-4	6-1	2-1
New England	1-15	1-4	1-3
N.Y. Jets	6-10	3-4	2-2
Pittsburgh	9-7	1-1	1-0
San Diego	6-10	0-5	0-3
Seattle	9-7	5-5	3-2
NFC	**Overall Record**	**Decided by 7 Pts. or Less**	**Decided By 3 Pts. or Less**
Atlanta	5-11	2-7	1-3
Chicago	11-5	4-1	2-1
Dallas	7-9	5-2	2-1
Detroit	6-10	3-5	0-3
Green Bay	6-10	2-3	2-0
L.A. Rams	5-11	1-6	0-3
Minnesota	6-10	2-6	1-4
New Orleans	8-8	5-4	3-3
N.Y. Giants	13-3	5-2	3-0
Philadelphia	10-6	4-6	3-3
Phoenix	5-11	2-4	2-4
San Francisco	14-2	8-1	5-1
Tampa Bay	6-10	3-3	2-1
Washington	10-6	4-2	2-0

Super Bowl Champions Who Did Not Make Playoffs The Following Year

Washington—Super Bowl XXII champions did not make playoffs in the 1988 season.
N.Y. Giants—Super Bowl XXI champions did not make playoffs in the 1987 season.
San Francisco—Super Bowl XVI champions did not make playoffs in the 1982 season.
Oakland—Super Bowl XV champions did not make playoffs in the 1981 season.
Pittsburgh—Super Bowl XIV champions did not make playoffs in the 1980 season.
Kansas City—Super Bowl IV champions did not make playoffs in the 1970 season.
Green Bay—Super Bowl II champions did not make playoffs in the 1968 season.

HISTORY

PRO FOOTBALL HALL OF FAME

The Professional Football Hall of Fame is located in Canton, Ohio, site of the organizational meeting on September 17, 1920, from which the National Football League evolved. The NFL recognized Canton as the Hall of Fame site on April 27, 1961. Canton area individuals, foundations, and companies donated almost $400,000 in cash and services to provide funds for the construction of the original two-building complex, which was dedicated on September 7, 1963. The original Hall of Fame complex was almost doubled in size with the completion of a $620,000 expansion project that was dedicated on May 10, 1971. A second expansion project was completed on November 20, 1978. It now features four exhibition areas and a theater twice the size of the original one.

The Hall represents the sport of pro football in many ways—through four large and colorful exhibition galleries, in the twin enshrinement halls, with numerous fan-participation electronic devices, a research library, and a museum store.

In recent years, the Pro Football Hall of Fame has become an extremely popular tourist attraction. At the end of 1990, a total of 4,861,871 fans had visited the Hall of Fame.

New members of the Pro Football Hall of Fame are elected annually by a 31-member National Board of Selectors, made up of media representatives from every league city, two at-large representatives, and a representative of the Pro Football Writers of America. Between four and seven new members are elected each year. An affirmative vote of approximately 80 percent is needed for election.

Any fan may nominate any eligible player or contributor simply by writing to the Pro Football Hall of Fame. Players must be retired five years to be eligible, while a coach need only to be retired with no time limit specified. Contributors (administrators, owners, *et al.*) may be elected while they are still active.

The charter class of 17 enshrinees was elected in 1963 and the honor roll now stands at 160 with the election of a five-man class in 1991. That class consists of Earl Campbell, John Hannah, Stan Jones, Tex Schramm, and Jan Stenerud.

Roster of Members

HERB ADDERLEY
Defensive back. 6-1, 200. Born in Philadelphia, Pennsylvania, June 8, 1939. Michigan State. Inducted in 1980. 1961-69 Green Bay Packers, 1970-72 Dallas Cowboys.

LANCE ALWORTH
Wide receiver. 6-0, 184. Born in Houston, Texas, August 3, 1940. Arkansas. Inducted in 1978. 1962-70 San Diego Chargers, 1971-72 Dallas Cowboys.

DOUG ATKINS
Defensive end. 6-8, 275. Born in Humboldt, Tennessee, May 8, 1930. Tennessee. Inducted in 1982. 1953-54 Cleveland Browns, 1955-66 Chicago Bears, 1967-69 New Orleans Saints.

MORRIS (RED) BADGRO
End. 6-0, 190. Born in Orilla, Washington, December 1, 1902. Southern California. Inducted in 1981. 1927 New York Yankees, 1930-35 New York Giants, 1936 Brooklyn Dodgers.

CLIFF BATTLES
Halfback. 6-1, 201. Born in Akron, Ohio, May 1, 1910. Died April 28, 1981. West Virginia Wesleyan. Inducted in 1968. 1932 Boston Braves, 1933-36 Boston Redskins, 1937 Washington Redskins.

SAMMY BAUGH
Quarterback. 6-2, 180. Born in Temple, Texas, March 17, 1914. Texas Christian. Inducted in 1963. 1937-52 Washington Redskins.

CHUCK BEDNARIK
Center-linebacker. 6-3, 230. Born in Bethlehem, Pennsylvania, May 1, 1925. Pennsylvania. Inducted in 1967. 1949-62 Philadelphia Eagles.

BERT BELL
Team owner. Commissioner. Born in Philadelphia, Pennsylvania, February 25, 1895. Died October 11, 1959. Pennsylvania. Inducted in 1963. 1933-40 Philadelphia Eagles, 1941-42 Pittsburgh Steelers, 1943 Phil-Pitt, 1944-46 Pittsburgh Steelers. Commissioner, 1946-59.

BOBBY BELL
Linebacker. 6-4, 225. Born in Shelby, North Carolina, June 17, 1940. Minnesota. Inducted in 1983. 1963-74 Kansas City Chiefs.

RAYMOND BERRY
End. 6-2, 187. Born in Corpus Christi, Texas, February 27, 1933. Southern Methodist. Inducted in 1973. 1955-67 Baltimore Colts.

CHARLES W. BIDWILL, SR.
Team owner. Born in Chicago, Illinois, September 16, 1895. Died April 19, 1947. Loyola of Chicago. Inducted in 1967. 1933-43 Chicago Cardinals, 1944 Card-Pitt, 1945-47 Chicago Cardinals.

FRED BILETNIKOFF
Wide receiver. 6-1, 190. Born in Erie, Pennsylvania, February 23, 1943. Florida State. Inducted in 1988. 1965-78 Oakland Raiders.

GEORGE BLANDA
Quarterback-kicker. 6-2, 215. Born in Youngwood, Pennsylvania, September 17, 1927. Kentucky. Inducted in 1981. 1949-58 Chicago Bears, 1950 Baltimore Colts, 1960-66 Houston Oilers, 1967-75 Oakland Raiders.

MEL BLOUNT
Cornerback. 6-3, 205. Born in Vidalia, Georgia, April 10, 1948. Southern University. Inducted in 1989. 1970-83 Pittsburgh Steelers.

TERRY BRADSHAW
Quarterback. 6-3, 210. Born in Shreveport, Louisiana, September 2, 1948. Louisiana Tech. Inducted in 1989. 1970-83 Pittsburgh Steelers.

JIM BROWN
Fullback. 6-2, 232. Born in St. Simons, Georgia, February 17, 1936. Syracuse. Inducted in 1971. 1957-65 Cleveland Browns.

PAUL BROWN
Coach. Born in Norwalk, Ohio, September 7, 1908. Miami, Ohio. Inducted in 1967. 1946-49 Cleveland Browns (AAFC), 1950-62 Cleveland Browns, 1968-75 Cincinnati Bengals.

ROOSEVELT BROWN
Tackle. 6-3, 255. Born in Charlottesville, Virginia, October 20, 1932. Morgan State. Inducted in 1975. 1953-65 New York Giants.

WILLIE BROWN
Defensive back. 6-1, 210. Born in Yazoo City, Mississippi, December 2, 1940. Grambling. Inducted in 1984. 1963-66 Denver Broncos, 1967-78 Oakland Raiders.

BUCK BUCHANAN
Defensive tackle. 6-7, 274. Born in Gainesville, Alabama, September 10, 1940. Grambling. Inducted in 1990. 1963-75 Kansas City Chiefs.

DICK BUTKUS
Linebacker. 6-3, 245. Born in Chicago, Illinois, December 9, 1942. Illinois. Inducted in 1979. 1965-73 Chicago Bears.

EARL CAMPBELL
Running back. 5-11, 233. Born in Tyler, Texas, March 29, 1955. Texas. Inducted in 1991. 1978-84 Houston Oilers, 1984-85 New Orleans Saints.

TONY CANADEO
Halfback. 5-11, 195. Born in Chicago, Illinois, May 5, 1919. Gonzaga. Inducted in 1974. 1941-44, 1946-52 Green Bay Packers.

JOE CARR
NFL president. Born in Columbus, Ohio, October 22, 1880. Died May 20, 1939. Did not attend college. Inducted in 1963. President, 1921-39 National Football League.

GUY CHAMBERLIN
End. Coach. 6-2, 210. Born in Blue Springs, Nebraska, January 16, 1894. Died April 4, 1967. Nebraska. Inducted in 1965. 1920 Decatur Staleys, 1921 Chicago Staleys, player-coach 1922-23 Canton Bulldogs, 1924 Cleveland Bulldogs, 1925-26 Frankford Yellow Jackets, 1927 Chicago Cardinals.

JACK CHRISTIANSEN
Defensive back. 6-1, 185. Born in Sublette, Kansas, December 20, 1928. Died June 29, 1986. Colorado State. Inducted in 1970. 1951-58 Detroit Lions.

EARL (DUTCH) CLARK
Quarterback. 6-0, 185. Born in Fowler, Colorado, October 11, 1906. Died August 5, 1978. Colorado College. Inducted in 1963. 1931-32 Portsmouth Spartans, 1934-38 Detroit Lions.

GEORGE CONNOR
Tackle-linebacker. 6-3, 240. Born in Chicago, Illinois, January 21, 1925. Holy Cross, Notre Dame. Inducted in 1975. 1948-55 Chicago Bears.

JIMMY CONZELMAN
Quarterback. Coach. Team owner. 6-0, 180. Born in St. Louis, Missouri, March 6, 1898. Died July 31, 1970. Washington, Missouri. Inducted in 1964. 1920 Decatur Staleys, 1921-22 Rock Island, Ill., Independents, 1923-24 Milwaukee Badgers; owner-coach, 1925-26 Detroit Panthers; player-coach 1927-29, coach 1930 Providence Steam Roller; coach, 1940-42 Chicago Cardinals, 1946-48 Chicago Cardinals.

LARRY CSONKA
Running back. 6-3, 235. Born in Stow, Ohio, December 25, 1946. Syracuse. Inducted in 1987. Miami Dolphins 1968-74, 1979, New York Giants 1976-78.

WILLIE DAVIS
Defensive end. 6-3, 245. Born in Lisbon, Louisiana, July 24, 1934. Grambling. Inducted in 1981. 1958-59 Cleveland Browns, 1960-69 Green Bay Packers.

LEN DAWSON
Quarterback. 6-0, 190. Born in Alliance, Ohio, June 20, 1935. Purdue. Inducted in 1987. Pittsburgh Steelers 1957-59, Cleveland Browns 1960-61, Dallas Texans 1962, Kansas City Chiefs 1963-75.

MIKE DITKA
Tight end. 6-3, 225. Born in Carnegie, Pennsylvania, October 18, 1939. Pittsburgh. Inducted in 1988. 1961-66 Chicago Bears, 1967-68 Philadelphia Eagles, 1969-72 Dallas Cowboys.

ART DONOVAN
Defensive tackle. 6-3, 265. Born in Bronx, New York, June 5, 1925. Boston College. Inducted in 1968. 1950 Baltimore Colts, 1951 New York Yanks, 1952 Dallas Texans, 1953-61 Baltimore Colts.

JOHN (PADDY) DRISCOLL
Quarterback. 5-11, 160. Born in Evanston, Illinois, January 11, 1896. Died June 29, 1968. Northwestern. Inducted in 1965. 1920 Decatur Staleys, 1920-25 Chicago Cardinals, 1926-29 Chicago Bears. Coach, 1956-57 Chicago Bears.

BILL DUDLEY
Halfback. 5-10, 176. Born in Bluefield, Virginia, December 24, 1921. Virginia. Inducted in 1966. 1942, 1945-46 Pittsburgh Steelers, 1947-49 Detroit Lions, 1950-51, 1953 Washington Redskins.

GLEN (TURK) EDWARDS
Tackle. 6-2, 260. Born in Mold, Washington, September 28, 1907. Died January 12, 1973. Washington State. Inducted in 1969. 1932 Boston Braves, 1933-36 Boston Redskins, 1937-40 Washington Redskins.

WEEB EWBANK
Coach. Born in Richmond, Indiana, May 6, 1907. Miami, Ohio. Inducted in 1978. 1954-62 Baltimore Colts, 1963-73 New York Jets.

TOM FEARS
End. 6-2, 215. Born in Los Angeles, California, December 3, 1923. Santa Clara, UCLA. Inducted in 1970. 1948-56 Los Angeles Rams.

RAY FLAHERTY
End. Coach. Born in Spokane, Washington, September 1, 1904. Gonzaga. Inducted in 1976. 1926 Los Angeles

Wildcats (AFL), 1927-28 New York Yankees, 1928-29, 1931-35 New York Giants. Coach, 1936 Boston Redskins, 1937-42 Washington Redskins, 1946-48 New York Yankees (AAFC), 1949 Chicago Hornets (AAFC).

LEN FORD
End. 6-5, 260. Born in Washington, D.C., February 18, 1926. Died March 14, 1972. Michigan. Inducted in 1976. 1948-49 Los Angeles Dons (AAFC), 1950-57 Cleveland Browns, 1958 Green Bay Packers.

DAN FORTMANN
Guard. 6-0, 207. Born in Pearl River, New York, April 11, 1916. Colgate. Inducted in 1965. 1936-43 Chicago Bears.

FRANK GATSKI
Center. 6-3, 240. Born in Farmington, West Virginia, March 18, 1922. Marshall, Auburn. Inducted in 1985. 1946-49 Cleveland Browns (AAFC), 1950-56 Cleveland Browns, 1957 Detroit Lions.

BILL GEORGE
Linebacker. 6-2, 230. Born in Waynesburg, Pennsylvania, October 27, 1930. Died September 30, 1982. Wake Forest. Inducted in 1974. 1952-65 Chicago Bears, 1966 Los Angeles Rams.

FRANK GIFFORD
Halfback. 6-1, 195. Born in Santa Monica, California, August 16, 1930. Southern California. Inducted in 1977. 1952-60, 1962-64 New York Giants.

SID GILLMAN
Coach. Born in Minneapolis, Minnesota, October 26, 1911. Ohio State. Inducted in 1983. 1955-59 Los Angeles Rams, 1960 Los Angeles Chargers, 1961-69 San Diego Chargers, 1973-74 Houston Oilers.

OTTO GRAHAM
Quarterback. 6-1, 195. Born in Waukegan, Illinois, December 6, 1921. Northwestern. Inducted in 1965. 1946-49 Cleveland Browns (AAFC), 1950-55 Cleveland Browns.

HAROLD (RED) GRANGE
Halfback. 6-0, 185. Born in Forksville, Pennsylvania, June 13, 1903. Died January 28, 1991. Illinois. Inducted in 1963. 1925 Chicago Bears, 1926 New York Yankees (AFL), 1927 New York Yankees, 1929-34 Chicago Bears.

JOE GREENE
Defensive tackle. 6-4, 260. Born in Temple, Texas, September 24, 1946. North Texas State. Inducted in 1987. 1969-81 Pittsburgh Steelers.

FORREST GREGG
Tackle. 6-4, 250. Born in Birthright, Texas, October 18, 1933. Southern Methodist. Inducted in 1977. 1956, 1958-70 Green Bay Packers, 1971 Dallas Cowboys.

BOB GRIESE
Quarterback. 6-1, 190. Born in Evansville, Indiana, February 3, 1945. Purdue. Inducted in 1990. 1967-80 Miami Dolphins.

LOU GROZA
Tackle-kicker. 6-3, 250. Born in Martin's Ferry, Ohio, January 25, 1924. Ohio State. Inducted in 1974. 1946-49 Cleveland Browns (AAFC), 1950-59, 1961-67 Cleveland Browns.

JOE GUYON
Halfback. 6-1, 180. Born in Mahnomen, Minnesota, November 26, 1892. Died November 27, 1971. Carlisle, Georgia Tech. Inducted in 1966. 1920 Canton Bulldogs, 1921 Cleveland Indians, 1922-23 Oorang Indians, 1924 Rock Island, Ill., Independents, 1924-25 Kansas City Cowboys, 1927 New York Giants.

GEORGE HALAS
End. Coach. Team owner. Born in Chicago, Illinois, February 2, 1895. Died October 31, 1983. Illinois. Inducted in 1963. 1920 Decatur Staleys, 1921 Chicago Staleys, 1922-29 Chicago Bears; coach, 1933-42, 1946-55, 1958-67 Chicago Bears.

JACK HAM
Linebacker. 6-1, 225. Born in Johnstown, Pennsylvania, December 23, 1948. Penn State. Inducted in 1988. 1971-82 Pittsburgh Steelers.

JOHN HANNAH
Guard. 6-3, 265. Born in Canton, Georgia, April 4, 1951. Alabama. Inducted in 1991. 1973-85 New England Patriots.

FRANCO HARRIS
Running back. 6-2, 225. Born in Fort Dix, New Jersey, March 7, 1950. Penn State. Inducted in 1990. 1972-83 Pittsburgh Steelers, 1984 Seattle Seahawks.

ED HEALEY
Tackle. 6-3, 220. Born in Indian Orchard, Massachusetts, December 28, 1894. Died December 9, 1978. Dartmouth. Inducted in 1964. 1920-22 Rock Island, Ill., Independents, 1922-27 Chicago Bears.

MEL HEIN
Center. 6-2, 225. Born in Redding, California, August 22, 1909. Washington State. Inducted in 1963. 1931-45 New York Giants.

TED HENDRICKS
Linebacker. 6-7, 235. Born in Guatemala City, Guatemala, November 1, 1947. Miami. Inducted in 1990. 1969-73 Baltimore Colts, 1974 Green Bay Packers, 1975-81 Oakland Raiders, 1982-83 Los Angeles Raiders.

WILBUR (PETE) HENRY
Tackle. 6-0, 250. Born in Mansfield, Ohio, October 31, 1897. Died February 7, 1952. Washington & Jefferson. Inducted in 1963. 1920-23, 1925-26 Canton Bulldogs, 1927 New York Giants, 1927-28 Pottsville Maroons.

ARNIE HERBER
Quarterback. 6-1, 200. Born in Green Bay, Wisconsin, April 2, 1910. Died October 14, 1969. Wisconsin, Regis College. Inducted in 1966. 1930-40 Green Bay Packers, 1944-45 New York Giants.

BILL HEWITT
End. 5-11, 191. Born in Bay City, Michigan, October 8, 1909. Died January 14, 1947. Michigan. Inducted in 1971. 1932-36 Chicago Bears, 1937-39 Philadelphia Eagles, 1943 Phil-Pitt.

CLARKE HINKLE
Fullback. 5-11, 201. Born in Toronto, Ohio, April 10, 1909. Died November 9, 1988. Bucknell. Inducted in 1964. 1932-41 Green Bay Packers.

ELROY (CRAZYLEGS) HIRSCH
Halfback-end. 6-2, 190. Born in Wausau, Wisconsin, June 17, 1923. Wisconsin, Michigan. Inducted in 1968. 1946-48 Chicago Rockets (AAFC), 1949-57 Los Angeles Rams.

PAUL HORNUNG
Halfback. 6-2, 220. Born in Louisville, Kentucky, December 23, 1935. Notre Dame. Inducted in 1986. 1957-62, 1964-66 Green Bay Packers.

KEN HOUSTON
Safety. 6-3, 198. Born in Lufkin, Texas, November 12, 1944. Prairie View A&M. Inducted in 1986. 1967-72 Houston Oilers, 1973-80 Washington Redskins.

CAL HUBBARD
Tackle. 6-5, 250. Born in Keytesville, Missouri, October 31, 1900. Died October 17, 1977. Centenary, Geneva. Inducted in 1963. 1927-28 New York Giants, 1929-33, 1935 Green Bay Packers, 1936 New York Giants, 1936 Pittsburgh Pirates.

SAM HUFF
Linebacker. 6-1, 230. Born in Morgantown, West Virginia, October 4, 1934. West Virginia. Inducted in 1982. 1956-63 New York Giants, 1964-67, 1969 Washington Redskins.

LAMAR HUNT
Team owner. Born in El Dorado, Arkansas, August 2, 1932. Southern Methodist. Inducted in 1972. 1960-62 Dallas Texans, 1963-90 Kansas City Chiefs.

DON HUTSON
End. 6-1, 180. Born in Pine Bluff, Arkansas, January 31, 1913. Alabama. Inducted in 1963. 1935-45 Green Bay Packers.

JOHN HENRY JOHNSON
Fullback. 6-2, 225. Born in Waterproof, Louisiana, November 24, 1929. St. Mary's, Arizona State. Inducted in 1987. San Francisco 49ers 1954-56, Detroit Lions 1957-59, Pittsburgh Steelers 1960-65, Houston Oilers 1966.

DAVID (DEACON) JONES
Defensive end. 6-5, 250. Born in Eatonville, Florida, December 9, 1938. Mississippi Vocational. Inducted in 1980. 1961-71 Los Angeles Rams, 1972-73 San Diego Chargers, 1974 Washington Redskins.

STAN JONES
Guard-defensive tackle. 6-1, 250. Born in Altoona, Pennsylvania, November 24, 1931. Maryland. Inducted in 1991. 1954-65 Chicago Bears, 1966 Washington Redskins.

SONNY JURGENSEN
Quarterback. 6-0, 203. Born in Wilmington, North Carolina, August 23, 1934. Duke. Inducted in 1983. 1957-63 Philadelphia Eagles, 1964-74 Washington Redskins.

WALT KIESLING
Guard. Coach. 6-2, 245. Born in St. Paul, Minnesota, March 27, 1903. Died March 2, 1962. St. Thomas (Minnesota). Inducted in 1966. 1926-27 Duluth Eskimos, 1928 Pottsville Maroons, 1929-33 Chicago Cardinals, 1934 Chicago Bears, 1935-36 Green Bay Packers, 1937-38 Pittsburgh Pirates; coach, 1939-42 Pittsburgh Steelers; co-coach, 1943 Phil-Pitt, 1944 Card-Pitt; coach, 1954-56 Pittsburgh Steelers.

FRANK (BRUISER) KINARD
Tackle. 6-1, 210. Born in Pelahatchie, Mississippi, October 23, 1914. Died September 7, 1985. Mississippi. Inducted in 1971. 1938-44 Brooklyn Dodgers-Tigers, 1946-47 New York Yankees (AAFC).

EARL (CURLY) LAMBEAU
Coach. Born in Green Bay, Wisconsin, April 9, 1898. Died June 1, 1965. Notre Dame. Inducted in 1963. 1919-49 Green Bay Packers, 1950-51 Chicago Cardinals, 1952-53 Washington Redskins.

JACK LAMBERT
Linebacker. 6-4, 220. Born in Mantua, Ohio, July 8, 1952. Kent State. Inducted in 1990. 1974-84 Pittsburgh Steelers.

TOM LANDRY
Coach. Born in Mission, Texas, September 11, 1924. Texas. Inducted in 1990. 1960-88 Dallas Cowboys.

DICK (NIGHT TRAIN) LANE
Defensive back. 6-2, 210. Born in Austin, Texas, April 16, 1928. Scottsbluff Junior College. Inducted in 1974. 1952-53 Los Angeles Rams, 1954-59 Chicago Cardinals, 1960-65 Detroit Lions.

JIM LANGER
Center. 6-2, 255. Born in Little Falls, Minnesota, May 16, 1948. South Dakota State. Inducted in 1987. Miami Dolphins 1970-79, Minnesota Vikings 1980-81.

WILLIE LANIER
Linebacker. 6-1, 245. Born in Clover, Virginia, August 21, 1945. Morgan State. Inducted in 1986. 1967-77 Kansas City Chiefs.

YALE LARY
Defensive back-punter. 5-11, 189. Born in Fort Worth, Texas, November 24, 1930. Texas A&M. Inducted in 1979. 1952-53, 1956-64 Detroit Lions.

DANTE LAVELLI
End. 6-0, 199. Born in Hudson, Ohio, February 23, 1923. Ohio State. Inducted in 1975. 1946-49 Cleveland Browns (AAFC), 1950-56 Cleveland Browns.

BOBBY LAYNE
Quarterback. 6-2, 190. Born in Santa Anna, Texas, December 19, 1926. Died December 1, 1986. Texas. Inducted in 1967. 1948 Chicago Bears, 1949 New York Bulldogs, 1950-58 Detroit Lions, 1958-62 Pittsburgh Steelers.

ALPHONSE (TUFFY) LEEMANS
Fullback. 6-0, 200. Born in Superior, Wisconsin, November 12, 1912. Died January 19, 1979. George Washington. Inducted in 1978. 1936-43 New York Giants.

BOB LILLY
Defensive tackle. 6-5, 260. Born in Olney, Texas, July 26, 1939. Texas Christian. Inducted in 1980. 1961-74 Dallas Cowboys.

VINCE LOMBARDI
Coach. Born in Brooklyn, New York, June 11, 1913. Died September 3, 1970. Fordham. Inducted in 1971. 1959-67 Green Bay Packers, 1969 Washington Redskins.

SID LUCKMAN
Quarterback. 6-0, 195. Born in Brooklyn, New York, November 21, 1916. Columbia. Inducted in 1965. 1939-50 Chicago Bears.

ROY (LINK) LYMAN
Tackle. 6-2, 252. Born in Table Rock, Nebraska, November 30, 1898. Died December 16, 1972. Nebraska. Inducted in 1964. 1922-23, 1925 Canton Bulldogs, 1924 Cleveland Bulldogs, 1925 Frankford Yellow Jackets, 1926-28, 1930-31, 1933-34 Chicago Bears.

TIM MARA
Team owner. Born in New York, New York, July 29, 1887. Died February 17, 1959. Did not attend college. Inducted in 1963. 1925-59 New York Giants.

GINO MARCHETTI
Defensive end. 6-4, 245. Born in Smithers, West Virginia, January 2, 1927. San Francisco. Inducted in 1972. 1952 Dallas Texans, 1953-64, 1966 Baltimore Colts.

GEORGE PRESTON MARSHALL
Team owner. Born in Grafton, West Virginia, October 11, 1897. Died August 9, 1969. Randolph-Macon. Inducted in 1963. 1932 Boston Braves, 1933-36 Boston Redskins, 1937-69 Washington Redskins.

OLLIE MATSON
Halfback. 6-2, 220. Born in Trinity, Texas, May 1, 1930. San Francisco. Inducted in 1972. 1952, 1954-58 Chicago Cardinals, 1959-62 Los Angeles Rams, 1963 Detroit Lions, 1964-66 Philadelphia Eagles.

DON MAYNARD
Wide receiver. 6-1, 175. Born in Crosbyton, Texas, January 25, 1935. Texas Western. Inducted in 1987. New York Giants 1958, New York Titans 1960-62, New York Jets 1963-72, St. Louis Cardinals 1973.

GEORGE McAFEE
Halfback. 6-0, 177. Born in Ironton, Ohio, March 13, 1918. Duke. Inducted in 1966. 1940-41, 1945-50 Chicago Bears.

MIKE McCORMACK
Tackle. 6-4, 248. Born in Chicago, Illinois, June 21, 1930. Kansas. Inducted in 1984. 1951 New York Yanks, 1954-62 Cleveland Browns.

HUGH McELHENNY
Halfback. 6-1, 198. Born in Los Angeles, California, December 31, 1928. Washington. Inducted in 1970. 1952-60 San Francisco 49ers, 1961-62 Minnesota Vikings, 1963 New York Giants, 1964 Detroit Lions.

JOHNNY BLOOD (McNALLY)
Halfback. 6-0, 185. Born in New Richmond, Wisconsin, November 27, 1903. Died November 28, 1985. St. John's (Minnesota). Inducted in 1963. 1925-26 Milwaukee Badgers, 1926-27 Duluth Eskimos, 1928 Pottsville Maroons, 1929-33, 1935-36 Green Bay Packers, 1934 Pittsburgh Pirates; player-coach, 1937-39 Pittsburgh Pirates.

MIKE MICHALSKE
Guard. 6-0, 209. Born in Cleveland, Ohio, April 24, 1903. Died October 26, 1983. Penn State. Inducted in 1964. 1926 New York Yankees (AFL), 1927-28 New York Yankees, 1929-35, 1937 Green Bay Packers.

WAYNE MILLNER
End. 6-0, 191. Born in Roxbury, Massachusetts, January 31, 1913. Died November 19, 1976. Notre Dame. Inducted in 1968. 1936 Boston Redskins, 1937-41, 1945 Washington Redskins.

BOBBY MITCHELL
Running back-wide receiver. 6-0, 195. Born in Hot Springs, Arkansas, June 6, 1935. Illinois. Inducted in 1983. 1958-61 Cleveland Browns, 1962-68 Washington Redskins.

RON MIX
Tackle. 6-4, 250. Born in Los Angeles, California, March 10, 1938. Southern California. Inducted in 1979. 1960 Los Angeles Chargers, 1961-69 San Diego Chargers, 1971 Oakland Raiders.

LENNY MOORE
Back. 6-1, 198. Born in Reading, Pennsylvania, November 25, 1933. Penn State. Inducted in 1975. 1956-67 Baltimore Colts.

MARION MOTLEY
Fullback. 6-1, 238. Born in Leesburg, Georgia, June 5, 1920. South Carolina State, Nevada. Inducted in 1968. 1946-49 Cleveland Browns (AAFC), 1950-53 Cleveland Browns, 1955 Pittsburgh Steelers.

GEORGE MUSSO
Guard-tackle. 6-2, 270. Born in Collinsville, Illinois. April 8, 1910. Millikin. Inducted in 1982. 1933-44 Chicago Bears.

BRONKO NAGURSKI
Fullback. 6-2, 225. Born in Rainy River, Ontario, Canada, November 3, 1908. Died January 7, 1990. Minnesota. Inducted in 1963. 1930-37, 1943 Chicago Bears.

JOE NAMATH
Quarterback. 6-2, 200. Born in Beaver Falls, Pennsylvania, May 31, 1943. Alabama. Inducted in 1985. 1965-76 New York Jets, 1977 Los Angeles Rams.

EARLE (GREASY) NEALE
Coach. Born in Parkersburg, West Virginia, November 5, 1891. Died November 2, 1973. West Virginia Wesleyan. Inducted in 1969. 1941-42, 1944-50 Philadelphia Eagles; co-coach, Phil-Pitt 1943.

ERNIE NEVERS
Fullback. 6-1, 205. Born in Willow River, Minnesota, June 11, 1903. Died May 3, 1976. Stanford. Inducted in 1963. 1926-27 Duluth Eskimos, 1929-31 Chicago Cardinals.

RAY NITSCHKE
Linebacker. 6-3, 235. Born in Elmwood Park, Illinois, December 29, 1936. Illinois. Inducted in 1978. 1958-72 Green Bay Packers.

LEO NOMELLINI
Defensive tackle. 6-3, 250. Born in Lucca, Italy, June 19, 1924. Minnesota. Inducted in 1969. 1950-63 San Francisco 49ers.

MERLIN OLSEN
Defensive tackle. 6-5, 270. Born in Logan, Utah, September 15, 1940. Utah State. Inducted in 1982. 1962-76 Los Angeles Rams.

JIM OTTO
Center. 6-2, 255. Born in Wausau, Wisconsin, January 5, 1938. Miami. Inducted in 1980. 1960-74 Oakland Raiders.

STEVE OWEN
Tackle. Coach. 6-0, 235. Born in Cleo Springs, Oklahoma, April 21, 1898. Died May 17, 1964. Phillips. Inducted in 1966. 1924-25 Kansas City Cowboys, 1926-30 New York Giants; coach, 1931-53 New York Giants.

ALAN PAGE
Defensive tackle. 6-4, 225. Born in Canton, Ohio, August 7, 1945. Notre Dame. Inducted in 1988. 1967-78 Minnesota Vikings, 1978-81 Chicago Bears.

CLARENCE (ACE) PARKER
Quarterback. 5-11, 168. Born in Portsmouth, Virginia, May 17, 1912. Duke. Inducted in 1972. 1937-41 Brooklyn Dodgers, 1945 Boston Yanks, 1946 New York Yankees (AAFC).

JIM PARKER
Guard-tackle. 6-3, 273. Born in Macon, Georgia, April 3, 1934. Ohio State. Inducted in 1973. 1957-67 Baltimore Colts.

JOE PERRY
Fullback. 6-0, 200. Born in Stevens, Arkansas, January 22, 1927. Compton Junior College. Inducted in 1969. 1948-49 San Francisco 49ers (AAFC), 1950-60, 1963 San Francisco 49ers, 1961-62 Baltimore Colts.

PETE PIHOS
End. 6-1, 210. Born in Orlando, Florida, October 22, 1923. Indiana. Inducted in 1970. 1947-55 Philadelphia Eagles.

HUGH (SHORTY) RAY
Supervisor of officials 1938-56. Born in Highland Park, Illinois, September 21, 1884. Died September 16, 1956. Illinois. Inducted in 1966.

DAN REEVES
Team owner. Born in New York, New York, June 30, 1912. Died April 15, 1971. Georgetown. Inducted in 1967. 1941-45 Cleveland Rams, 1946-71 Los Angeles Rams.

JIM RINGO
Center. 6-1, 235. Born in Orange, New Jersey, November 21, 1931. Syracuse. Inducted in 1981. 1953-63 Green Bay Packers, 1964-67 Philadelphia Eagles.

ANDY ROBUSTELLI
Defensive end. 6-0, 230. Born in Stamford, Connecticut, December 6, 1925. Arnold College. Inducted in 1971. 1951-55 Los Angeles Rams, 1956-64 New York Giants.

ART ROONEY
Team owner. Born in Coulterville, Pennsylvania, January 27, 1901. Died August 25, 1988. Georgetown, Duquesne. Inducted in 1964. 1933-40 Pittsburgh Pirates, 1941-42, 1945-88 Pittsburgh Steelers, 1943 Phil-Pitt, 1944 Card-Pitt.

PETE ROZELLE
Commissioner. Born in South Gate, California, March 1, 1926. San Francisco. Inducted in 1985. Commissioner, 1960-89.

BOB ST. CLAIR
Tackle. 6-9, 265. Born in San Francisco, California, February 18, 1931. San Francisco, Tulsa. Inducted in 1990. 1953-63 San Francisco 49ers.

GALE SAYERS
Running back. 6-0, 200. Born in Wichita, Kansas, May 30, 1943. Kansas. Inducted in 1977. 1965-71 Chicago Bears.

JOE SCHMIDT
Linebacker. 6-0, 222. Born in Pittsburgh, Pennsylvania, January 19, 1932. Pittsburgh. Inducted in 1973. 1953-65 Detroit Lions.

TEX SCHRAMM
Team president-general manager. Born in San Gabriel, California, June 2, 1920. Texas. Inducted in 1991. 1947-57 Los Angeles Rams. 1960-88 Dallas Cowboys.

ART SHELL
Tackle. 6-5, 285. Born in Charleston, South Carolina, November 25, 1946. Maryland State-Eastern Shore. Inducted in 1989. 1968-81 Oakland Raiders, 1982 Los Angeles Raiders.

O.J. SIMPSON
Running back. 6-1, 212. Born in San Francisco, California, July 9, 1947. Southern California. Inducted in 1985. 1969-77 Buffalo Bills, 1978-79 San Francisco 49ers.

BART STARR
Quarterback. 6-1, 200. Born in Montgomery, Alabama, January 9, 1934. Alabama. Inducted in 1977. 1956-71 Green Bay Packers.

ROGER STAUBACH
Quarterback. 6-3, 202. Born in Cincinnati, Ohio, February 5, 1942. Navy. Inducted in 1985. 1969-79 Dallas Cowboys.

ERNIE STAUTNER
Defensive tackle. 6-2, 235. Born in Prinzing-by-Cham, Bavaria, Germany, April 20, 1925. Boston College. Inducted in 1969. 1950-63 Pittsburgh Steelers.

JAN STENERUD
Kicker. 6-2, 190. Born in Fetsund, Norway, November 26, 1942. Montana State. Inducted in 1991. 1967-79 Kansas City Chiefs, 1980-83 Green Bay Packers, 1984-85 Minnesota Vikings.

KEN STRONG
Halfback. 5-11, 210. Born in New Haven, Connecticut, August 6, 1906. Died October 5, 1979. New York University. Inducted in 1967. 1929-32 Staten Island Stapletons, 1933-35, 1939, 1944-47 New York Giants, 1936-37 New York Yanks (AFL).

JOE STYDAHAR
Tackle. 6-4, 230. Born in Kaylor, Pennsylvania, March 3, 1912. Died

March 23, 1977. West Virginia. Inducted in 1967. 1936-42, 1945-46 Chicago Bears.

FRAN TARKENTON
Quarterback. 6-0, 185. Born in Richmond, Virginia, February 3, 1940. Georgia. Inducted in 1986. 1961-66, 1972-78 Minnesota Vikings, 1967-71 New York Giants.

CHARLEY TAYLOR
Running back-wide receiver. 6-3, 210. Born in Grand Prairie, Texas, September 28, 1941. Arizona State. Inducted in 1984. 1964-75, 1977 Washington Redskins.

JIM TAYLOR
Fullback. 6-0, 216. Born in Baton Rouge, Louisiana, September 20, 1935. Louisiana State. Inducted in 1976. 1958-66 Green Bay Packers, 1967 New Orleans Saints.

JIM THORPE
Halfback. 6-1, 190. Born in Prague, Oklahoma, May 28, 1888. Died March 28, 1953. Carlisle. Inducted in 1963. 1915-17, 1919-20, 1926 Canton Bulldogs, 1921 Cleveland Indians, 1922-23 Oorang Indians, 1924 Rock Island, Ill., Independents, 1925 New York Giants, 1928 Chicago Cardinals.

Y. A. TITTLE
Quarterback. 6-0, 200. Born in Marshall, Texas, October 24, 1926. Louisiana State. Inducted in 1971. 1948-49 Baltimore Colts (AAFC), 1950 Baltimore Colts, 1951-60 San Francisco 49ers, 1961-64 New York Giants.

GEORGE TRAFTON
Center. 6-2, 235. Born in Chicago, Illinois, December 6, 1896. Died September 5, 1971. Notre Dame. Inducted in 1964. 1920 Decatur Staleys, 1921 Chicago Staleys, 1922-32 Chicago Bears.

CHARLEY TRIPPI
Halfback. 6-0, 185. Born in Pittston, Pennsylvania, December 14, 1922. Georgia. Inducted in 1968. 1947-55 Chicago Cardinals.

EMLEN TUNNELL
Safety. 6-1, 200. Born in Bryn Mawr, Pennsylvania, March 29, 1925. Died July 23, 1975. Toledo, Iowa. Inducted in 1967. 1948-58 New York Giants, 1959-61 Green Bay Packers.

CLYDE (BULLDOG) TURNER
Center. 6-2, 235. Born in Sweetwater, Texas, November 10, 1919. Hardin-Simmons. Inducted in 1966. 1940-52 Chicago Bears.

JOHNNY UNITAS
Quarterback. 6-1, 195. Born in Pittsburgh, Pennsylvania, May 7, 1933. Louisville. Inducted in 1979. 1956-72 Baltimore Colts, 1973 San Diego Chargers.

GENE UPSHAW
Guard. 6-5, 255. Born in Robstown, Texas, August 15, 1945. Texas A & I. Inducted in 1987. Oakland Raiders 1967-81.

NORM VAN BROCKLIN
Quarterback. 6-1, 190. Born in Eagle Butte, South Dakota, March 15, 1926. Died May 2, 1983. Oregon. Inducted in 1971. 1949-57 Los Angeles Rams, 1958-60 Philadelphia Eagles.

STEVE VAN BUREN
Halfback. 6-1, 200. Born in La Ceiba, Honduras, December 28, 1920. Louisiana State. Inducted in 1965. 1944-51 Philadelphia Eagles.

DOAK WALKER
Halfback. 5-10, 172. Born in Dallas, Texas, January 1, 1927. Southern Methodist. Inducted in 1986. 1950-55 Detroit Lions.

PAUL WARFIELD
Wide receiver. 6-0, 188. Born in Warren, Ohio, November 28, 1942. Ohio State. Inducted in 1983. 1964-69, 1976-77 Cleveland Browns, 1970-74 Miami Dolphins.

BOB WATERFIELD
Quarterback. 6-2, 200. Born in Elmira, New York, July 26, 1920. Died March 25, 1983. UCLA. Inducted in 1965. 1945 Cleveland Rams, 1946-52 Los Angeles Rams.

ARNIE WEINMEISTER
Defensive tackle. 6-4, 235. Born in Rhein, Saskatchewan, Canada, March 23, 1923. Washington. Inducted in 1984. 1948-49 New York Yankees (AAFC), 1950-53 New York Giants.

BILL WILLIS
Guard. 6-2, 215. Born in Columbus, Ohio, October 5, 1921. Ohio State. Inducted in 1977. 1946-49 Cleveland Browns (AAFC), 1950-53 Cleveland Browns.

LARRY WILSON
Safety. 6-0, 190. Born in Rigby, Idaho, March 24, 1938. Utah. Inducted in 1978. 1960-72 St. Louis Cardinals.

ALEX WOJCIECHOWICZ
Center. 6-0, 235. Born in South River, New Jersey, August 12, 1915. Fordham. Inducted in 1968. 1938-46 Detroit Lions, 1946-50 Philadelphia Eagles.

WILLIE WOOD
Safety. 5-10, 190. Born in Washington, D.C., December 23, 1936. Southern California. Inducted in 1989. 1960-71 Green Bay Packers.

A CHRONOLOGY OF PROFESSIONAL FOOTBALL

1869 Rutgers and Princeton played a college soccer football game, the first ever, November 6. The game used modified London Football Association rules. During the next seven years, rugby gained favor with the major eastern schools over soccer, and modern football began to develop from rugby.

1876 At the Massasoit convention, the first rules for American football were written. Walter Camp, who would become known as the father of American football, first became involved with the game.

1892 In an era in which football was a major attraction of local athletic clubs, an intense competition between two Pittsburgh-area clubs, the Allegheny Athletic Association (AAA) and the Pittsburgh Athletic Club (PAC), led to the making of the first professional football player. Former Yale All-America guard William (Pudge) Heffelfinger was paid $500 by the AAA to play in a game against the PAC, becoming the first person to be paid to play football, November 12. The AAA won the game 4-0 when Heffelfinger picked up a PAC fumble and ran 35 yards for a touchdown.

1893 The Pittsburgh Athletic Club signed one of its players, probably halfback Grant Dibert, to the first known pro football contract, which covered all of the PAC's games for the year.

1895 John Brallier became the first football player to openly turn pro, accepting $10 and expenses to play for the Latrobe YMCA against the Jeannette Athletic Club.

1896 The Allegheny Athletic Association team fielded the first completely professional team for its abbreviated two-game season.

1897 The Latrobe Athletic Association football team went entirely professional, becoming the first team to play a full season with only professionals.

1898 A touchdown was changed from four points to five.

1899 Chris O'Brien formed a neighborhood team, which played under the name the Morgan Athletic Club, on the south side of Chicago. The team later became known as the Normals, then the Racine (for a street in Chicago) Cardinals, the Chicago Cardinals, the St. Louis Cardinals, and, in 1988, the Phoenix Cardinals. The team remains the oldest continuing operation in pro football.

1900 William C. Temple took over the team payments for the Duquesne Country and Athletic Club, becoming the first known individual club owner.

1902 Baseball's Philadelphia Athletics, managed by Connie Mack, and the Philadelphia Phillies formed professional football teams, joining the Pittsburgh Stars in the first attempt at a pro football league, named the National Football League. The Athletics won the first night football game ever played, 39-0 over Kanaweola AC at Elmira, New York, November 21.

All three teams claimed the pro championship for the year, but the league president, Dave Berry, named the Stars the champions. Pitcher Rube Waddell was with the Athletics, and pitcher Christy Mathewson a fullback for Pittsburgh.

The first World Series of pro football, actually a five-team tournament, was played among a team made up of players from both the Athletics and the Phillies, but simply named New York; the New York Knickerbockers; the Syracuse AC; the Warlow AC; and the Orange (New Jersey) AC at New York's original Madison Square Garden. New York and Syracuse played the first indoor football game before 3,000, December 28. Syracuse, with Glen (Pop) Warner at guard, won 6-0 and went on to win the tournament.

1903 The Franklin (Pa.) Athletic Club won the second and last World Series of pro football over the Oreos AC of Asbury Park, New Jersey; the Watertown Red and Blacks; and the Orange AC.

Pro football was popularized in Ohio when the Massillon Tigers, a strong amateur team, hired four Pittsburgh pros to play in the season-ending game against Akron. At the same time, pro football declined in the Pittsburgh area, and the emphasis on the pro game moved west from Pennsylvania to Ohio.

1904 A field goal was changed from five points to four.

Ohio had at least seven pro teams, with Massillon winning the Ohio Independent Championship, that is, the pro title. Talk surfaced about forming a state-wide league to end spiraling salaries brought about by constant bidding for players and to write universal rules for the game. The feeble attempt to start the league failed.

Halfback Charles Follis signed a contract with the Shelby AC, making him the first-known black pro football player.

1905 The Canton AC, later to become known as the Bulldogs, became a professional team. Massillon again won the Ohio League championship.

1906 The forward pass was legalized. The first authenticated pass completion in a pro game came on October 27, when George (Peggy) Parratt of Massillon threw a completion to Dan (Bullet) Riley in a victory over a combined Benwood-Moundsville team.

Archrivals Canton and Massillon, the two best pro teams in America, played twice, with Canton winning the first game but Massillon winning the second and the Ohio League championship. A betting scandal and the financial disaster wrought upon the two clubs by paying huge salaries caused a temporary decline in interest in pro football in the two cities and, somewhat, through Ohio.

1909 A field goal dropped from four points to three.

1912 A touchdown was increased from five points to six.

Jack Cusack revived a strong pro team in Canton.

1913 Jim Thorpe, a former football and track star at the Carlisle Indian School (Pa.) and a double gold medal winner at the 1912 Olympics in Stockholm, played for the Pine Village Pros in Indiana.

1915 Massillon again fielded a major team, reviving the old rivalry with Canton. Cusack signed Thorpe to play for Canton for $250 a game.

1916 With Thorpe and former Carlisle teammate Pete Calac starring, Canton went 9-0-1, won the Ohio League championship, and was acclaimed the pro football champion.

1917 Despite an upset by Massillon, Canton again won the Ohio League championship.

1919 Canton again won the Ohio League championship, despite the team having been turned over from Cusack to Ralph Hay. Thorpe and Calac were joined in the backfield by Joe Guyon.

Earl (Curly) Lambeau and George Calhoun organized the Green Bay Packers. Lambeau's employer at the Indian Packing Company provided $500 for equipment and allowed the team to use the company field for practices. The Packers went 10-1.

1920 Pro football was in a state of confusion due to three major problems: dramatically rising salaries; players continually jumping from one team to another following the highest offer; and the use of college players still enrolled in school. A league in which all the members would follow the same rules seemed the answer. An organizational meeting, at which the Akron Pros, Canton Bulldogs, Cleveland Indians, and Dayton Triangles were represented, was held in Canton, Ohio, August 20. This meeting resulted in the formation of the American Professional Football Conference.

A second organizational meeting was held in Canton, September 17. The teams were from four states—Akron, Canton, Cleveland, and Dayton from Ohio; the Hammond Pros and Muncie Flyers from Indiana; the Rochester Jeffersons from New York; and the Rock Island Independents, Decatur Staleys, and Racine Cardinals from Illinois. The name of the league was changed to the American Professional Football Association. Hoping to capitalize on his fame, the members elected Thorpe president; Stanley Cofall of Cleveland was elected vice president. A membership fee of $100 per team was charged to give an appearance of respectability, but no team ever paid it. Scheduling was left up to the teams, and there were wide variations, both in the overall number of games played and in the number played against APFA member teams.

Four other teams—the Buffalo All-Americans, Chicago Tigers, Columbus Panhandles, and Detroit Heralds—joined the league sometime during the year. On September 26, the first game featuring an APFA team was played at Rock Island's Douglas Park. A crowd of 800 watched the Independents defeat the St. Paul Ideals 48-0. A week later, October 3, the first game matching two APFA teams was held. At Triangle Park, Dayton defeated Columbus 14-0, with Lou Partlow of Dayton scoring the first touchdown in a game between Association teams. The same day, Rock Island defeated Muncie 45-0.

By the beginning of December, most of the teams in the APFA had abandoned their hopes for a championship, and some of them, including the Chicago Tigers and the Detroit Heralds, had finished their seasons, disbanded, and had their franchises canceled by the Association. Four teams—Akron, Buffalo, Canton, and Decatur—still had championship aspirations, but a series of late-season games among them left Akron as the only undefeated team in the Association. At one of these games, Akron sold tackle Bob Nash to Buffalo for $300 and five percent of the gate receipts—the first APFA player deal.

1921 At the league meeting in Akron, April 30, the championship of the 1920 season was awarded to the Akron Pros. The APFA was reorganized, with Joe Carr of the Columbus Panhandles named president and Carl Storck of Dayton secretary-treasurer. Carr moved the Association's headquarters to Columbus, drafted a league constitution and by-laws, gave teams territorial rights, restricted player movements, developed membership criteria for the franchises, and issued standings for the first time, so that the APFA would have a clear champion.

The Association's membership increased to 22 teams, including the Green Bay Packers, who were awarded to John Clair of the Acme Packing Company.

Thorpe moved from Canton to the Cleveland Indians, but he was hurt early in the season and played very little.

A.E. Staley turned the Decatur Staleys over to player-coach George Halas, who moved the team to Cubs Park in Chicago. Staley paid Halas $5,000 to keep the name Staleys for one more year. Halas made halfback Ed (Dutch) Sternaman his partner.

The Staleys claimed the APFA championship with a 9-1-1 record, as did Buffalo at 9-1-2. Carr ruled in favor of the Staleys, giving Halas his first championship.

1922 After admitting the use of players who had college eligibility remaining during the 1921 season, Clair and the Green Bay management withdrew from the APFA, January 28. Curly Lambeau promised to obey league rules and then used $50 of his own money to buy back the franchise. Bad weather and low attendance plagued the Packers, and Lambeau went broke, but local merchants arranged a $2,500 loan for the club. A public non-profit corporation was set up to operate the team, with Lambeau as head coach and manager.

The American Professional Football Association changed its name to the National Football League, June 24. The Chicago Staleys became the Chicago Bears.

The NFL fielded 18 teams, including the new Oorang Indians of Marion, Ohio, an all-Indian team featuring Thorpe, Joe Guyon, and Pete Calac, and sponsored by the Oorang dog kennels.

Canton, led by player-coach Guy Chamberlin and tackles Link Lyman and Wilbur (Pete) Henry, emerged as the league's first true powerhouse, going 10-0-2.

1923 For the first time, all of the franchises considered to be part of the NFL fielded teams. Thorpe played first for Oorang, then for the Toledo Maroons. Against the Bears, Thorpe fumbled, and Halas picked up the ball and returned it 98 yards for a touchdown, a record that would last until 1972.

Canton had its second consecutive undefeated season, going 11-0-1 for the NFL title.

1924 The league had 18 franchises, including new ones in Kansas City, Kenosha, and Frankford, a section of Philadelphia. League champion Canton, successful on the field but not at the box office, was purchased by the owner of the Cleveland franchise, who kept the Canton franchise inactive, while using the best players for his Cleveland team, which he renamed the Bulldogs. Cleveland won the title with a 7-1-1 record.

1925 Five new franchises were admitted to the NFL—the New York Giants, who were awarded to Tim Mara and Billy Gibson for $500; the Detroit Panthers, featuring Jimmy Conzelman as owner, coach, and tailback; the Providence Steam Roller; a new Canton Bulldogs team; and the Pottsville Maroons, who had been perhaps the most successful independent pro team. The NFL established its first player limit, at 16 players.

Late in the season, the NFL made its greatest coup in gaining national recognition. Shortly after the University of Illinois season ended in November, All-America halfback Harold (Red) Grange signed a contract to play with the Chicago Bears. On Thanksgiving Day, a crowd of 36,000—the largest in pro football history—watched Grange and the Bears play the Chicago Cardinals to a scoreless tie at Wrigley Field. At the beginning of December, the Bears left on a barnstorming tour that saw them play eight games in 12 days, in St. Louis, Philadelphia, New York City, Washington, Boston, Pittsburgh, Detroit, and Chicago. A crowd of 73,000 watched the game against the Giants at the Polo Grounds, helping assure the future of the troubled NFL franchise in New York. The Bears then played nine more games in the South and West, including a game in Los Angeles, in which 75,000 fans watched them defeat the Los Angeles Tigers in the Los Angeles Memorial Coliseum.

Pottsville and the Chicago Cardinals were the top contenders for the league title, with Pottsville winning a late-season meeting 21-7. Pottsville scheduled a game against a team of former Notre Dame players for Shibe Park in Philadelphia. Frankford lodged a protest not only because the game was in Frankford's protected territory, but because it was being played the same day as a Yellow Jackets home game. Carr gave three different notices forbidding Pottsville to play the game, but Pottsville played anyway, December 12. That day, Carr fined the club, suspended it from all rights and privileges (including the right to play for the NFL championship), and returned its franchise to the league. The Cardinals, who ended the season with the best record in the league, were named the 1925 champions.

1926 Grange's manager, C.C. Pyle, told the Bears that Grange wouldn't play for them unless he was paid a five-figure salary and given one-third ownership of the team. The Bears refused. Pyle leased Yankee Stadium in New York City, then petitioned for an NFL franchise. After he was refused, he started the first American Football League. It lasted one season and included Grange's New York Yankees and eight other teams. The AFL champion Philadelphia Quakers played a December game against the New York Giants, seventh in the NFL, and the Giants won 31-0. At the end of the season, the AFL folded.

Halas pushed through a rule that prohibited any team from signing a player whose college class had not graduated.

The NFL grew to 22 teams, including the Duluth Eskimos, who signed All-America fullback Ernie Nevers of Stanford, giving the league a gate attraction to rival Grange. The 15-member Eskimos, dubbed the Iron Men of the North, played 29 exhibition and league games, 28 on the road, and Nevers played in all but 29 minutes of them.

Frankford edged the Bears for the championship, despite Halas having obtained John (Paddy) Driscoll from the Cardinals. On December 4, the Yellow Jackets scored in the final two minutes to defeat the Bears 7-6 and move ahead of them in the standings.

1927 At a special meeting in Cleveland, April 23, Carr decided to secure the NFL's future by eliminating the financially weaker teams and consolidating the quality players onto a limited number of more successful teams. The new-look NFL dropped to 12 teams, and the center of gravity of the league left the Midwest, where the NFL had started, and began to emerge in the large cities of the East. One of the new teams was Grange's New York Yankees, but Grange suffered a knee injury and the Yankees finished in the middle of the pack. The NFL championship was won by the cross-town rival New York Giants, who posted 10 shutouts in 13 games.

1928 Grange and Nevers both retired from pro football, and Duluth disbanded, as the NFL was reduced to only 10 teams. The Providence Steam Roller of Jimmy Conzelman and Pearce Johnson won the championship, playing in the Cycledrome, a 10,000-seat oval that had been built for bicycle races.

1929 Chris O'Brien sold the Chicago Cardinals to David Jones, July 27.

The NFL added a fourth official, the field judge, July 28.

Grange and Nevers returned to the NFL. Nevers scored six rushing touchdowns and four extra points as the Cardinals beat Grange's Bears 40-6, November 28. The 40 points set a record that remains the NFL's oldest.

Providence became the first NFL team to host a game at night under floodlights, against the Cardinals, November 3.

The Packers added back Johnny Blood (McNally), tackle Cal Hubbard, and guard Mike Michalske, and won their first NFL championship, edging the Giants, who featured quarterback Benny Friedman.

1930 Dayton, the last of the NFL's original franchises, was purchased by John Dwyer, moved to Brooklyn, and renamed the Dodgers. The Portsmouth, Ohio, Spartans entered the league.

The Packers edged the Giants for the title, but the most improved team was the Bears. Halas retired as a player and replaced himself as coach of the Bears with Ralph Jones, who refined the T-formation by introducing wide ends and a halfback in motion. Jones also introduced rookie All-America fullback-tackle Bronko Nagurski.

The Giants defeated a team of former Notre Dame players coached by Knute Rockne 22-0 before 55,000 at the Polo Grounds, December 14. The proceeds went to the New York Unemployment Fund to help those suffering because of the Great Depression, and the easy victory helped give the NFL credibility with the press and the public.

1931 The NFL decreased to 10 teams, and halfway through the season the Frankford franchise folded. Carr fined the Bears, Packers, and Portsmouth $1,000 each for using players whose college classes had not graduated.

The Packers won an unprecedented third consecutive title, beating out the Spartans, who were led by rookie backs Earl (Dutch) Clark and Glenn Presnell.

1932 George Preston Marshall, Vincent Bendix, Jay O'Brien, and M. Dorland Doyle were awarded a franchise for Boston, July 9. Despite the presence of two rookies—halfback Cliff Battles and tackle Glen (Turk) Edwards—the new team, named the Braves, lost money and Marshall was left as the sole owner at the end of the year.

NFL membership dropped to eight teams, the lowest in history. Official statistics were kept for the first time. The Bears and the Spartans finished the season in the first-ever tie for first place. After the season finale, the league office arranged for the first playoff game in NFL history. The game was moved indoors to Chicago Stadium because of bitter cold and heavy snow. The arena allowed only an 80-yard field that came right to the walls. The goal posts were moved from the end lines to the goal lines and, for safety, inbounds lines or hashmarks where the ball would be put in play were drawn 10 yards from the walls that butted against the sidelines. The Bears won 9-0, December 18, scoring the winning touchdown on a two-yard pass from Nagurski to Grange. The Spartans claimed Nagurski's pass was thrown from less than five yards behind the line of scrimmage, violating the existing passing rule, but the play stood.

1933 The NFL, which long had followed the rules of college football, made a number of significant changes from the college game for the first time and began to independently develop rules serving its needs and the style of play it preferred. The innovations from the 1932 championship game—inbounds line or hashmarks and goal posts on the goal lines—were adopted. Also the forward pass was legalized from anywhere behind the line of scrimmage, February 25.

Marshall and Halas pushed through a proposal that divided the NFL into two divisions, with the winners to meet in an annual championship game, July 8.

Three new franchises joined the league—the Pittsburgh Pirates of Art Rooney, the Philadelphia Eagles of Bert Bell and Lud Wray, and the Cincinnati Reds. The Staten Island Stapletons suspended operations for a year, but never returned to the league.

Halas bought out Sternaman, became sole owner of the Bears, and reinstated himself as head coach. Marshall changed the name of the Boston Braves to the Redskins. David Jones sold the Chicago Cardinals to Charles W. Bidwill.

In the first NFL Championship Game scheduled before the season, the Western Division champion Bears defeated the Eastern Division champion Giants 23-21 at Wrigley Field, December 17.

1934 G.A. (Dick) Richards purchased the Portsmouth Spartans, moved them to Detroit, and renamed them the Lions.

Professional football gained new prestige when the Bears were matched against the best college football players in the first Chicago College All-Star Game, August 31. The game ended in a scoreless tie before 79,432 at Soldier Field.

The Cincinnati Reds lost their first eight games, then were suspended from the league for defaulting on payments. The St. Louis Gunners, an independent team, joined the NFL by buying the Cincinnati franchise and went 1-2 the last three weeks.

Rookie Beattie Feathers of the Bears became the NFL's first 1,000-yard rusher, gaining 1,004 on 101 carries. The Thanksgiving Day game between the Bears and the Lions became the first NFL game broadcast nationally, with Graham McNamee the announcer for CBS radio.

In the championship game, on an extremely cold and icy day at the Polo Grounds, the Giants trailed the Bears 13-3 in the third quarter before changing to basketball shoes for better footing. The Giants won 30-13 in what has come to be known as the Sneakers Game, December 9.

The player waiver rule was adopted, December 10.

1935 The NFL adopted Bert Bell's proposal to hold an annual draft of college players, to begin in 1936, with teams selecting in an inverse order of finish, May 19. The inbounds line or hashmarks were moved nearer the center of the field, 15 yards from the sidelines.

All-America end Don Hutson of Alabama joined Green Bay. The Lions defeated the Giants 26-7 in the NFL Championship Game, December 15.

1936 There were no franchise transactions for the first year since the formation of the NFL. It also was the first year in which all member teams played the same number of games.

The Eagles made University of Chicago halfback and Heisman Trophy winner Jay Berwanger the first player ever selected in the NFL draft, February 8. The Eagles traded his rights to the Bears, but Berwanger never played pro football. The first player selected to actually sign was the number-two pick, Riley Smith of Alabama, who was selected by Boston.

A rival league was formed, and it became the second to call itself the American Football League. The Boston Shamrocks were its champions.

Due to poor attendance, Marshall, the owner of the host team, moved the Championship Game from Boston to the Polo Grounds in New York. Green Bay defeated the Redskins 21-6, December 13.

1937 Homer Marshman was granted a Cleveland franchise, named the Rams, February 12. Marshall moved the Redskins to Washington, D.C., February 13. The Redskins signed

TCU All-America tailback Sammy Baugh, who led them to a 28-21 victory over the Bears in the NFL Championship Game, December 12.

The Los Angeles Bulldogs had an 8-0 record to win the AFL title, but then the two-year-old league folded.

1938 At the suggestion of Halas, Hugh (Shorty) Ray became a technical advisor on rules and officiating to the NFL. A new rule called for a 15-yard penalty for roughing the passer.

Rookie Byron (Whizzer) White of the Pittsburgh Pirates led the NFL in rushing. The Giants defeated the Packers 23-17 for the NFL title, December 11.

Marshall, *Los Angeles Times* sports editor Bill Henry, and promoter Tom Gallery established the Pro Bowl game between the NFL champion and a team of pro all-stars.

1939 The New York Giants defeated the Pro All-Stars 13-10 in the first Pro Bowl, at Wrigley Field, Los Angeles, January 15.

Carr, NFL president since 1921, died in Columbus, May 20. Carl Storck was named acting president, May 25.

An NFL game was televised for the first time when NBC broadcast the Brooklyn Dodgers-Philadelphia Eagles game from Ebbets Field to the approximately 1,000 sets then in New York.

Green Bay defeated New York 27-0 in the NFL Championship Game, December 10 at Milwaukee. NFL attendance exceeded one million in a season for the first time, reaching 1,071,200.

1940 A six-team rival league, the third to call itself the American Football League, was formed, and the Columbus Bullies won its championship.

Halas's Bears, with additional coaching by Clark Shaughnessy of Stanford, defeated the Redskins 73-0 in the NFL Championship Game, December 8. The game, which was the most decisive victory in NFL history, popularized the Bears' T-formation with a man-in-motion. It was the first championship carried on network radio, broadcast by Red Barber to 120 stations of the Mutual Broadcasting System, which paid $2,500 for the rights.

Art Rooney sold the Pittsburgh franchise to Alexis Thompson, December 9, then bought part interest in the Philadelphia Eagles.

1941 Elmer Layden was named the first Commissioner of the NFL, March 1; Storck, the acting president, resigned, April 5. NFL headquarters were moved to Chicago.

Bell and Rooney traded the Eagles to Thompson for the Pirates, then renamed their new team the Steelers. Homer Marshman sold the Rams to Daniel F. Reeves and Fred Levy, Jr.

The league by-laws were revised to provide for playoffs in case there were ties in division races, and sudden-death overtimes in case a playoff game was tied after four quarters. An official *NFL Record Manual* was published for the first time.

Columbus again won the championship of the AFL, but the two-year-old league then folded.

The Bears and the Packers finished in a tie for the Western Division championship, setting up the first divisional playoff game in league history. The Bears won 33-14, then defeated the Giants 37-9 for the NFL championship, December 21.

1942 Players departing for service in World War II depleted the rosters of NFL teams. Halas left the Bears in midseason to join the Navy, and Luke Johnsos and Heartley (Hunk) Anderson served as co-coaches as the Bears went 11-0 in the regular season. The Redskins defeated the Bears 14-6 in the NFL Championship Game, December 13.

1943 The Cleveland Rams, with co-owners Reeves and Levy in the service, were granted permission to suspend operations for one season, April 6. Levy transferred his stock in the team to Reeves, April 16.

The NFL adopted free substitution, April 7. The league also made the wearing of helmets mandatory and approved a 10-game schedule for all teams.

Philadelphia and Pittsburgh were granted permission to merge for one season, June 19. The team, known as Phil-Pitt (and called the Steagles by fans), divided home games between the two cities, and Earle (Greasy) Neale of Philadelphia and Walt Kiesling of Pittsburgh served as co-coaches. The merger automatically dissolved the last day of the season, December 5.

Ted Collins was granted a franchise for Boston, to become active in 1944.

Sammy Baugh led the league in passing, punting, and interceptions. He led the Redskins to a tie with the Giants for the Eastern Division title, and then to a 28-0 victory in a divisional playoff game. The Bears beat the Redskins 41-21 in the NFL Championship Game, December 26.

1944 Collins, who had wanted a franchise in Yankee Stadium in New York, named his new team in Boston the Yanks. Cleveland resumed operations. The Brooklyn Dodgers changed their name to the Tigers.

Coaching from the bench was legalized, April 20.

The Cardinals and the Steelers were granted permission to merge for one year under the name Card-Pitt, April 21. Phil Handler of the Cardinals and Walt Kiesling of the Steelers served as co-coaches. The merger automatically dissolved the last day of the season, December 3.

In the NFL Championship Game, Green Bay defeated the New York Giants 14-7, December 17.

1945 The inbounds lines or hashmarks were moved from 15 yards away from the sidelines to nearer the center of the field—20 yards from the sidelines.

Brooklyn and Boston merged into a team that played home games in both cities and was known simply as The Yanks. The team was coached by former Boston head coach Herb Kopf. In December, the Brooklyn franchise withdrew from the NFL to join the new All-America Football Conference; all the players on its active and reserve lists were assigned to The Yanks, who once again became the Boston Yanks.

Halas rejoined the Bears late in the season after service with the U.S. Navy. Although Halas took over much of the coaching duties, Anderson and Johnsos remained the coaches of record throughout the season.

Steve Van Buren of Philadelphia led the NFL in rushing, kickoff returns, and scoring.

After the Japanese surrendered ending World War II, a count showed that the NFL service roster, limited to men who had played in league games, totaled 638, 21 of whom had died in action.

Rookie quarterback Bob Waterfield led Cleveland to a 15-14 victory over Washington in the NFL Championship Game, December 16.

1946 The contract of Commissioner Layden was not renewed, and Bert Bell, the co-owner of the Steelers, replaced him, January 11. Bell moved the league headquarters from Chicago to the Philadelphia suburb of Bala-Cynwyd.

Free substitution was withdrawn and substitutions were limited to no more than three men at a time. Forward passes were made automatically incomplete upon striking the goal posts, January 11.

The NFL took on a truly national appearance for the first time when Reeves was granted permission by the league to move his NFL champion Rams to Los Angeles.

The rival All-America Football Conference began play with eight teams. The Cleveland Browns, coached by Paul Brown, won the AAFC's first championship, defeating the New York Yankees 14-9.

Bill Dudley of the Steelers led the NFL in rushing, interceptions, and punt returns, and won the league's most valuable player award.

Backs Frank Filchock and Merle Hapes of the Giants were questioned about an attempt by a New York man to fix the championship game with the Bears. Bell suspended Hapes but allowed Filchock to play; he played well, but Chicago won 24-14, December 15.

1947 The NFL added a fifth official, the back judge.

A bonus choice was made for the first time in the NFL draft. One team each year would select the special choice before the first round began. The Chicago Bears won a lottery and the rights to the first choice and drafted back Bob Fenimore of Oklahoma A&M.

The Cleveland Browns again won the AAFC title, defeating the New York Yankees 14-3.

Charles Bidwill, Sr., owner of the Cardinals, died April 19, but his wife and sons retained ownership of the team. On December 28, the Cardinals won the NFL Championship Game 28-21 over the Philadelphia Eagles, who had beaten Pittsburgh 21-0 in a playoff.

1948 Plastic helmets were prohibited. A flexible artificial tee was permitted at the kickoff. Officials other than the referee were equipped with whistles, not horns, January 14.

Fred Mandel sold the Detroit Lions to a syndicate headed by D. Lyle Fife, January 15.

Halfback Fred Gehrke of the Los Angeles Rams painted horns on the Rams' helmets, the first modern helmet emblems in pro football.

The Cleveland Browns won their third straight championship in the AAFC, going 14-0 and then defeating the Buffalo Bills 49-7.

In a blizzard, the Eagles defeated the Cardinals 7-0 in the NFL Championship Game, December 19.

1949 Alexis Thompson sold the champion Eagles to a syndicate headed by James P. Clark, January 15. The Boston Yanks became the New York Bulldogs, sharing the Polo Grounds with the Giants.

Free substitution was adopted for one year, January 20.

The NFL had two 1,000-yard rushers in the same season for the first time—Steve Van Buren of Philadelphia and Tony Canadeo of Green Bay.

The AAFC played its season with a one-division, seven-team format. On December 9, Bell announced a merger agreement in which three AAFC franchises—Cleveland, San Francisco, and Baltimore—would join the NFL in 1950. The Browns won their fourth consecutive AAFC title, defeating the 49ers 21-7, December 11.

In a heavy rain, the Eagles defeated the Rams 14-0 in the NFL Championship Game, December 18.

1950 Unlimited free substitution was restored, opening the way for the era of two platoons and specialization in pro football, January 20.

Curly Lambeau, founder of the franchise and Green Bay's head coach since 1921, resigned under fire, February 1.

The name National Football League was restored after about three months as the National-American Football League. The American and National conferences were created to replace the Eastern and Western divisions, March 3.

The New York Bulldogs became the Yanks and divided the players of the former AAFC Yankees with the Giants. A special allocation draft was held in which the 13 teams drafted the remaining AAFC players, with special consideration for Baltimore, which received 15 choices compared to 10 for other teams.

The Los Angeles Rams became the first NFL team to have all of its games—both home and away—televised. The Washington Redskins followed the Rams in arranging to televise their games; other teams made deals to put selected games on television.

In the first game of the season, former AAFC champion Cleveland defeated NFL champion Philadelphia 35-10. For the first time, deadlocks occurred in both conferences and playoffs were necessary. The Browns defeated the Giants in the American and the Rams defeated the Bears in the National. Cleveland defeated Los Angeles 30-28 in the NFL Championship Game, December 24.

1951 The Pro Bowl game, dormant since 1942, was revived under a new format matching the all-stars of each conference at the Los Angeles Memorial Coliseum. The American Conference defeated the National Conference 28-27, January 14.

Abraham Watner returned the Baltimore franchise and its player contracts back to the NFL for $50,000. Baltimore's former players were made available for drafting at the same time as college players, January 18.

A rule was passed that no tackle, guard, or center would be eligible to catch a forward pass, January 18.

The Rams reversed their television policy and televised only road games.

The NFL Championship Game was televised coast-to-coast for the first time, December 23. The DuMont Network paid $75,000 for the rights to the game, in which the Rams defeated the Browns 24-17.

1952 Ted Collins sold the New York Yanks' franchise back to the NFL, January 19. A new franchise was awarded to a group in Dallas after it purchased the assets of the Yanks, January 24. The new Texans went 1-11, with the owners turning the franchise back to the league in midseason. For the last five games of the season, the commissioner's office operated the Texans as a road team, using Hershey, Pennsylvania, as a home base. At the end of the season the franchise was cancelled, the last time an NFL team failed.

The Pittsburgh Steelers abandoned the Single-Wing for the T-formation, the last pro team to do so.

The Detroit Lions won their first NFL championship in 17 years, defeating the Browns 17-7 in the title game, December 28.

1953 A Baltimore group headed by Carroll Rosenbloom was granted a franchise and was awarded the holdings of the defunct Dallas organization, January 23. The team, named the Colts, put together the largest trade in league history, acquiring 10 players from Cleveland in exchange for five.

The names of the American and National conferences were changed to the Eastern and Western conferences, January 24.

Jim Thorpe died, March 28.

Mickey McBride, founder of the Cleveland Browns, sold the franchise to a syndicate headed by Dave R. Jones, June 10.

The NFL policy of blacking out home games was upheld by Judge Allan K. Grim of the U.S. District Court in Philadelphia, November 12.

The Lions again defeated the Browns in the NFL Championship Game, winning 17-16, December 27.

1954 The Canadian Football League began a series of raids on NFL teams, signing quarterback Eddie LeBaron and defensive end Gene Brito of Washington and defensive tackle Arnie Weinmeister of the Giants, among others.

Fullback Joe Perry of the 49ers became the first player in league history to gain 1,000 yards rushing in consecutive seasons.

Cleveland defeated Detroit 56-10 in the NFL Championship Game, December 26.

1955 The sudden-death overtime rule was used for the first time in a preseason game between the Rams and Giants at Portland, Oregon, August 28. The Rams won 23-17 three minutes into overtime.

A rule change declared the ball dead immediately if the ball carrier touched the ground with any part of his body except his hands or feet while in the grasp of an opponent.

The NFL Players Association was founded.

The Baltimore Colts made an 80-cent phone call to Johnny Unitas and signed him as a free agent. Another quarterback, Otto Graham, played his last game as the Browns defeated the Rams 38-14 in the NFL Championship Game, December 26. Graham had quarterbacked the Browns to 10 championship-game appearances in 10 years.

NBC replaced DuMont as the network for the title game, paying a rights fee of $100,000.

1956 Grabbing an opponent's facemask (other than the ball carrier) was made illegal. Using radio receivers to communicate with players on the field was prohibited. A natural leather ball with white end stripes replaced the white ball with black stripes for night games.

The Giants moved from the Polo Grounds to Yankee Stadium.

Halas retired as coach of the Bears, and was replaced by Paddy Driscoll.

CBS became the first network to broadcast some NFL regular-season games to selected television markets across the nation.

The Giants routed the Bears 47-7 in the NFL Championship Game, December 30.

1957 Pete Rozelle was named general manager of the Rams. Anthony J. Morabito, founder and co-owner of the 49ers, died of a heart attack during a game against the Bears at Kezar Stadium, October 28. An NFL-record crowd of 102,368 saw the 49ers-Rams game at the Los Angeles Memorial Coliseum, November 10.

The Lions came from 20 points down to post a 31-27 playoff victory over the 49ers, December 22. Detroit defeated Cleveland 59-14 in the NFL Championship Game, December 29.

1958 The bonus selection in the draft was eliminated, January 29. The last selection was quarterback King Hill of Rice by the Chicago Cardinals.

Halas reinstated himself as coach of the Bears.

Jim Brown of Cleveland gained an NFL-record 1,527 yards rushing. In a divisional playoff game, the Giants held Brown to eight yards and defeated Cleveland 10-0.

Baltimore, coached by Weeb Ewbank, defeated the Giants 23-17 in the first sudden-death overtime in an NFL Championship Game, December 28. The game ended when Colts fullback Alan Ameche scored on a one-yard touchdown run after 8:15 of overtime.

1959 Vince Lombardi was named head coach of the Green Bay Packers, January 28. Tim Mara, the co-founder of the Giants, died, February 17.

Lamar Hunt of Dallas announced his intentions to form a second pro football league. The first meeting was held in Chicago, August 14, and consisted of Hunt representing Dallas; Bob Howsam, Denver; K.S. (Bud) Adams, Houston; Barron Hilton, Los Angeles; Max Winter and Bill Boyer, Minneapolis; and Harry Wismer, New York City. They made plans to begin play in 1960.

The new league was named the American Football League, August 22. Buffalo, owned by Ralph Wilson, became the seventh franchise, October 28. Boston, owned by William H. Sullivan, became the eighth team, November 22. The first AFL draft, lasting 33 rounds, was held, November 22. Joe Foss was named AFL Commissioner, November 30. An additional draft of 20 rounds was held by the AFL, December 2.

NFL Commissioner Bert Bell died of a heart attack suffered at Franklin Field, Philadelphia, during the last two minutes of a game between the Eagles and the Steelers, October 11. Treasurer Austin Gunsel was named president in the office of the commissioner, October 14.

The Colts again defeated the Giants in the NFL Championship Game, 31-16, December 27.

1960 Pete Rozelle was elected NFL Commissioner as a compromise choice on the twenty-third ballot, January 26. Rozelle moved the league offices to New York City.

Hunt was elected AFL president for 1960, January 26. Minneapolis withdrew from the AFL, January 27, and the same ownership was given an NFL franchise for Minnesota (to start in 1961), January 28. Dallas received an NFL franchise for 1960, January 28. Oakland received an AFL franchise, January 30.

The AFL adopted the two-point option on points after touchdown, January 28. A no-tampering verbal pact, relative to players' contracts, was agreed to between the NFL and AFL, February 9.

The NFL owners voted to allow the transfer of the Chicago Cardinals to St. Louis, March 13.

The AFL signed a five-year television contract with ABC, June 9.

The Boston Patriots defeated the Buffalo Bills 28-7 before 16,000 at Buffalo in the first AFL preseason game, July 30. The Denver Broncos defeated the Patriots 13-10 before 21,597 at Boston in the first AFL regular-season game, September 9.

Philadelphia defeated Green Bay 17-13 in the NFL Championship Game, December 26.

1961 The Houston Oilers defeated the Los Angeles Chargers 24-16 before 32,183 in the first AFL Championship Game, January 1.

Detroit defeated Cleveland 17-16 in the first Playoff Bowl, or Bert Bell Benefit Bowl, between second-place teams in each conference in Miami, January 7.

End Willard Dewveall of the Bears played out his option and joined the Oilers, becoming the first player to deliberately move from one league to the other, January 14.

Ed McGah, Wayne Valley, and Robert Osborne bought out their partners in the ownership of the Raiders, January 17. The Chargers were transferred to San Diego, February 10. Dave R. Jones sold the Browns to a group headed by Arthur B. Modell, March 22. The Howsam brothers sold the Broncos to a group headed by Calvin Kunz and Gerry Phipps, May 26.

NBC was awarded a two-year contract for radio and television rights to the NFL Championship Game for $615,000 annually, $300,000 of which was to go directly into the NFL Player Benefit Plan, April 5.

Canton, Ohio, where the league that became the NFL was formed in 1920, was chosen as the site of the Pro Football Hall of Fame, April 27. Dick McCann, a former Redskins executive, was named executive director.

A bill legalizing single-network television contracts by professional sports leagues was introduced in Congress by Representative Emanuel Celler. It passed the House and Senate and was signed into law by President John F. Kennedy, September 30.

Houston defeated San Diego 10-3 for the AFL championship, December 24. Green Bay won its first NFL championship since 1944, defeating the New York Giants 37-0, December 31.

1962 The Western Division defeated the Eastern Division 47-27 in the first AFL All-Star Game, played before 20,973 in San Diego, January 7.

Both leagues prohibited grabbing any player's facemask. The AFL voted to make the scoreboard clock the official timer of the game.

The NFL entered into a single-network agreement with CBS for telecasting all regular-season games for $4,650,000 annually, January 10.

Judge Roszel Thompson of the U.S. District Court in Baltimore ruled against the AFL in its antitrust suit against the NFL, May 21. The AFL had charged the NFL with monopoly and conspiracy in areas of expansion, television, and player signings. The case lasted two and a half years, the trial two months.

McGah and Valley acquired controlling interest in the Raiders, May 24. The AFL assumed financial responsibility for the New York Titans, November 8. With Commissioner Rozelle as referee, Daniel F. Reeves regained the ownership of the Rams, outbidding his partners in sealed-envelope bidding for the team, November 27.

The Dallas Texans defeated the Oilers 20-17 for the AFL championship at Houston after 17 minutes, 54 seconds of overtime on a 25-yard field goal by Tommy Brooker, December 23. The game lasted a record 77 minutes, 54 seconds.

Judge Edward Weinfeld of the U.S. District Court in New York City upheld the legality of the NFL's television blackout within a 75-mile radius of home games and denied an injunction that would have forced the championship game between the Giants and the Packers to be televised in the New York City area, December 28. The Packers beat the Giants 16-7 for the NFL title, December 30.

1963 The Dallas Texans transferred to Kansas City, becoming the Chiefs, February 8. The New York Titans were sold to a five-man syndicate headed by David (Sonny) Werblin, March 28. Weeb Ewbank became the Titans' new head coach and the team's name was changed to the Jets, April 15. They began play in Shea Stadium.

NFL Properties, Inc., was founded to serve as the licensing arm of the NFL.

Rozelle indefinitely suspended Green Bay halfback Paul Hornung and Detroit defensive tackle Alex Karras for placing bets on their own teams and on other NFL games; he also fined five other Detroit players $2,000 each for betting on one game in which they did not participate, and the Detroit Lions Football Company $2,000 on each of two counts for failure to report information promptly and for lack of sideline supervision.

Paul Brown, head coach of the Browns since their inception, was fired and replaced by Blanton Collier. Don Shula replaced Weeb Ewbank as head coach of the Colts.

The AFL allowed the Jets and Raiders to select players from other franchises in hopes of giving the league more competitive balance, May 11.

NBC was awarded exclusive network broadcasting rights for the 1963 AFL Championship Game for $926,000, May 23.

The Pro Football Hall of Fame was dedicated at Canton, Ohio, September 7.

The U.S. Fourth Circuit Court of Appeals reaffirmed the lower court's finding for the NFL in the $10-million suit brought by the AFL, ending three and a half years of litigation, November 21.

Jim Brown of Cleveland rushed for an NFL single-season record 1,863 yards.

Boston defeated Buffalo 26-8 in the first divisional playoff game in AFL history, December 28.

The Bears defeated the Giants 14-10 in the NFL Championship Game, a record sixth and last title for Halas in his thirty-sixth season as the Bears' coach, December 29.

1964 The Chargers defeated the Patriots in the AFL Championship Game, January 5.

William Clay Ford, the Lions' president since 1961, purchased the team, January 10. A group representing the late James P. Clark sold the Eagles to a group headed by Jerry Wolman, January 21. Carroll Rosenbloom, the majority owner of the Colts since 1953, acquired complete ownership of the team, January 23.

CBS submitted the winning bid of $14.1 million per year for the NFL regular-season television rights for 1964 and 1965, January 24. CBS acquired the rights to the championship games for 1964 and 1965 for $1.8 million per game, April 17.

The AFL signed a five-year, $36-million television contract with NBC to begin with the 1965 season, January 29.

Hornung and Karras were reinstated by Rozelle, March 16.

Pete Gogolak of Cornell signed a contract with Buffalo, becoming the first soccer-style kicker in pro football.

Buffalo defeated San Diego 20-7 in the AFL Championship Game, December 26. Cleveland defeated Baltimore 27-0 in the NFL Championship Game, December 27.

1965 The NFL teams pledged not to sign college seniors until completion of all their games, including bowl games, and empowered the Commissioner to discipline the clubs up to as much as the loss of an entire draft list for a violation of the pledge, February 15.

The NFL added a sixth official, the line judge, February 19. The color of the officials' penalty flags was changed from white to bright gold, April 5.

Atlanta was awarded an NFL franchise for 1966, with Rankin Smith, Sr., as owner, June 30. Miami was awarded an AFL franchise for 1966, with Joe Robbie and Danny Thomas as owners, August 16.

Green Bay defeated Baltimore 13-10 in sudden-death overtime in a Western Conference playoff game. Don Chandler kicked a 25-yard field goal for the Packers after 13 minutes, 39 seconds of overtime, December 26. The Packers then defeated the Browns 23-12 in the NFL Championship Game, January 2.

In the AFL Championship Game, the Bills again defeated the Chargers, 23-0, December 26.

CBS acquired the rights to the NFL regular-season games in 1966 and 1967, with an option for 1968, for $18.8 million per year, December 29.

1966 The AFL-NFL war reached its peak, as the leagues spent a combined $7 million to sign their 1966 draft choices. The NFL signed 75 percent of its 232 draftees, the AFL 46 percent of its 181. Of the 111 common draft choices, 79 signed with the NFL, 28 with the AFL, and 4 went unsigned.

The rights to the 1966 and 1967 NFL Championship Games were sold to CBS for $2 million per game, February 14.

Foss resigned as AFL Commissioner, April 7. Al Davis, the head coach and general manager of the Raiders, was named to replace him, April 8.

Goal posts offset from the goal line, painted bright yellow, and with uprights 20 feet above the crossbar were made standard in the NFL, May 16.

A series of secret meetings regarding a possible AFL-NFL merger were held in the spring between Hunt of Kansas City and Tex Schramm of Dallas. Rozelle announced the merger, June 8. Under the agreement, the two leagues would combine to form an expanded league with 24 teams, to be increased to 26 in 1968 and to 28 by 1970 or soon thereafter. All existing franchises would be retained, and no franchises would be transferred outside their metropolitan areas. While maintaining separate schedules through 1969, the leagues agreed to play an annual AFL-NFL World Championship Game beginning in January, 1967, and to hold a combined draft, also beginning in 1967. Preseason games would be held between teams of each league starting in 1967. Official regular-season play would start in 1970 when the two leagues would officially merge to form one league with two conferences. Rozelle was named Commissioner of the expanded league setup.

Davis rejoined the Raiders, and Milt Woodard was named president of the AFL, July 25.

The St. Louis Cardinals moved into newly constructed Busch Memorial Stadium.

Barron Hilton sold the Chargers to a group headed by Eugene Klein and Sam Schulman, August 25.

Congress approved the AFL-NFL merger, passing legislation exempting the agreement itself from antitrust action, October 21.

New Orleans was awarded an NFL franchise to begin play in 1967, November 1. John Mecom, Jr., of Houston was designated majority stockholder and president of the franchise, December 15.

The NFL was realigned for the 1967-69 seasons into the Capitol and Century Divisions in the Eastern Conference and the Central and Coastal Divisions in the Western Conference, December 2. New Orleans and the New York Giants agreed to switch divisions in 1968 and return to the 1967 alignment in 1969.

The rights to the Super Bowl for four years were sold to CBS and NBC for $9.5 million, December 13.

1967 Green Bay earned the right to represent the NFL in the first AFL-NFL World Championship Game by defeating Dallas 34-27, January 1. The same day, Kansas City defeated Buffalo 31-7 to represent the AFL. The Packers defeated the Chiefs 35-10 before 61,946 fans at the Los Angeles Memorial Coliseum in the first game between AFL and NFL teams, January 15. The winning players' share for the Packers was $15,000 each, and the losing players' share for the Chiefs was $7,500 each. The game was televised by both CBS and NBC.

The "sling-shot" goal post and a six-foot-wide border around the field were made standard in the NFL, February 22.

Baltimore made Bubba Smith, a Michigan State defensive lineman, the first choice in the first combined AFL-NFL draft, March 14.

The AFL awarded a franchise to begin play in 1968 to Cincinnati, May 24. A group with Paul Brown as part owner, general manager, and head coach, was awarded the Cincinnati franchise, September 27.

Arthur B. Modell, the president of the Cleveland Browns, was elected president of the NFL, May 28.

An AFL team defeated an NFL team for the first time, when Denver beat Detroit 13-7 in a preseason game, August 5.

Green Bay defeated Dallas 21-17 for the NFL championship on a last-minute one-yard quarterback sneak by Bart Starr in 13-below-zero temperature at Green Bay, December 31. The same day, Oakland defeated Houston 40-7 for the AFL championship.

1968 Green Bay defeated Oakland 33-14 in Super Bowl II at Miami, January 14. The game had the first $3-million gate in pro football history.

Vince Lombardi resigned as head coach of the Packers, but remained as general manager, January 28.

Werblin sold his shares in the Jets to his partners Don Lillis, Leon Hess, Townsend Martin, and Phil Iselin, May 21. Lillis assumed the presidency of the club, but then died July 23. Iselin was appointed president, August 6.

Halas retired for the fourth and last time as head coach of the Bears, May 27.

The Oilers left Rice Stadium for the Astrodome and became the first NFL team to play its home games in a domed stadium.

The movie "Heidi" became a footnote in sports history when NBC didn't show the last 1:05 of the Jets-Raiders game in order to permit the children's special to begin on time. The Raiders scored two touchdowns in the last 42 seconds to win 43-32, November 17.

Ewbank became the first coach to win titles in both the NFL and AFL when his Jets defeated the Raiders 27-23 for the AFL championship, December 29. The same day, Baltimore defeated Cleveland 34-0.

1969 The AFL established a playoff format for the 1969 season, with the winner in one division playing the runner-up in the other, January 11.

An AFL team won the Super Bowl for the first time, as the Jets defeated the Colts 16-7 at Miami, January 12 in Super Bowl III. The title Super Bowl was recognized by the NFL for the first time.

Vince Lombardi became part owner, executive vice-president, and head coach of the Washington Redskins, Feb. 7.

Wolman sold the Eagles to Leonard Tose, May 1.

Baltimore, Cleveland, and Pittsburgh agreed to join the AFL teams to form the 13-team American Football Conference of the NFL in 1970, May 17. The NFL also agreed on a playoff format that would include one "wild-card" team per conference—the second-place team with the best record.

Monday Night Football was signed for 1970. ABC acquired the rights to televise 13 NFL regular-season Monday night games in 1970, 1971, and 1972.

George Preston Marshall, president emeritus of the Redskins, died at 72, August 9.

The NFL marked its fiftieth year by the wearing of a special patch by each of the 16 teams.

1970 Kansas City defeated Minnesota 23-7 in Super Bowl IV at New Orleans, January 11. The gross receipts of approximately $3.8 million were the largest ever for a one-day sports event.

Four-year television contracts, under which CBS would televise all NFC games and NBC all AFC games (except Monday night games) and the two would divide televising the Super Bowl and AFC-NFC Pro Bowl games, were announced, January 26.

Art Modell resigned as president of the NFL, March 12. Milt Woodard resigned as president of the AFL, March 13. Lamar Hunt was elected president of the AFC and George Halas was elected president of the NFC, March 19.

The merged 26-team league adopted rules changes putting names on the backs of players' jerseys, making a point after touchdown worth only one point, and making the scoreboard clock the official timing device of the game, March 18.

The Players Negotiating Committee and the NFL Players Association announced a four-year agreement guaranteeing approximately $4,535,000 annually to player pension and insurance benefits, August 3. The owners also agreed to contribute $250,000 annually to improve or implement items such as disability payments, widows' benefits, maternity benefits, and dental benefits. The agreement also provided for increased preseason game and per diem payments, averaging approximately $2.6 million annually.

The Pittsburgh Steelers moved into Three Rivers Stadium. The Cincinnati Bengals moved to Riverfront Stadium.

Lombardi died of cancer at 57, September 3.

Tom Dempsey of New Orleans kicked a game-winning NFL-record 63-yard field goal against Detroit, November 8.

1971 Baltimore defeated Dallas 16-13 on Jim O'Brien's 32-yard field goal with five seconds to go in Super Bowl V at Miami, January 17. The NBC telecast was viewed in an estimated 23,980,000 homes, the largest audience ever for a one-day sports event.

The NFC defeated the AFC 27-6 in the first AFC-NFC Pro Bowl at Los Angeles, January 24.

The Boston Patriots changed their name to the New England Patriots, March 25. Their new stadium, Schaefer Stadium, was dedicated in a 20-14 preseason victory over the Giants.

The Philadelphia Eagles left Franklin Field and played their games at the new Veterans Stadium.

The San Francisco 49ers left Kezar Stadium and moved their games to Candlestick Park.

Daniel F. Reeves, the president

and general manager of the Rams, died at 58, April 15.

The Dallas Cowboys moved from the Cotton Bowl into their new home, Texas Stadium, October 24.

Miami defeated Kansas City 27-24 in sudden-death overtime in an AFC Divisional Playoff Game, December 25. Garo Yepremian kicked a 37-yard field goal for the Dolphins after 22 minutes, 40 seconds of overtime, as the game lasted 82 minutes, 40 seconds overall, making it the longest game in history.

1972 Dallas defeated Miami 24-3 in Super Bowl VI at New Orleans, January 16. The CBS telecast was viewed in an estimated 27,450,000 homes, the top-rated one-day telecast ever.

The inbounds lines or hashmarks were moved nearer the center of the field, 23 yards, 1 foot, 9 inches from the sidelines, March 23. The method of determining won-lost percentage in standings changed. Tie games, previously not counted in the standings, were made equal to a half-game won and a half-game lost, May 24.

Robert Irsay purchased the Los Angeles Rams and transferred ownership of the club to Carroll Rosenbloom in exchange for the Baltimore Colts, July 13.

William V. Bidwill purchased the stock of his brother Charles (Stormy) Bidwill to become the sole owner of the St. Louis Cardinals, September 2.

The National District Attorneys Association endorsed the position of professional leagues in opposing proposed legalization of gambling on professional team sports, September 28.

Franco Harris's "Immaculate Reception" gave the Steelers their first postseason win ever, 13-7 over the Raiders, December 23.

1973 Rozelle announced that all Super Bowl VII tickets were sold and that the game would be telecast in Los Angeles, the site of the game, on an experimental basis, January 3.

Miami defeated Washington 14-7 in Super Bowl VII at Los Angeles, completing a 17-0 season, the first perfect-record regular-season and postseason mark in NFL history, January 14. The NBC telecast was viewed by approximately 75 million people.

The AFC defeated the NFC 33-28 in the Pro Bowl in Dallas, the first time since 1942 that the game was played outside Los Angeles, January 21.

A jersey numbering system was adopted, April 5: 1-19 for quarterbacks and specialists, 20-49 for running backs and defensive backs, 50-59 for centers and linebackers, 60-79 for defensive linemen and interior offensive linemen other than centers, and 80-89 for wide receivers and tight ends. Players who had been in the NFL in 1972 could continue to use old numbers.

NFL Charities, a non-profit organization, was created to derive an income from monies generated from NFL Properties' licensing of NFL trademarks and team names, June 26. NFL Charities was set up to support education and charitable activities and to supply economic support to persons formerly associated with professional football who were no longer able to support themselves.

Congress adopted experimental legislation (for three years) requiring any NFL game that had been declared a sellout 72 hours prior to kickoff to be made available for local televising, September 14. The legislation provided for an annual review to be made by the Federal Communications Commission.

The Buffalo Bills moved their home games from War Memorial Stadium to Rich Stadium in nearby Orchard Park. The Giants tied the Eagles 23-23 in the final game in Yankee Stadium, September 23. The Giants played the rest of their home games at the Yale Bowl in New Haven, Connecticut.

A rival league, the World Football League, was formed and was reported in operation, October 2. It had plans to start play in 1974.

O.J. Simpson of Buffalo became the first player to rush for more than 2,000 yards in a season, gaining 2,003.

1974 Miami defeated Minnesota 24-7 in Super Bowl VIII at Houston, the second consecutive Super Bowl championship for the Dolphins, January 13. The CBS telecast was viewed by approximately 75 million people.

Rozelle was given a 10-year contract effective January 1, 1973, February 27.

Tampa Bay was awarded a franchise to begin operation in 1976, April 24.

Sweeping rules changes were adopted to add action and tempo to games: one sudden-death overtime period was added for preseason and regular-season games; the goal posts were moved from the goal line to the end lines; kickoffs were moved from the 40- to the 35-yard line; after missed field goals from beyond the 20, the ball was to be returned to the line of scrimmage; restrictions were placed on members of the punting team to open up return possibilities; roll-blocking and cutting of wide receivers was eliminated; the extent of downfield contact a defender could have with an eligible receiver was restricted; the penalties for offensive holding, illegal use of the hands, and tripping were reduced from 15 to 10 yards; wide receivers blocking back toward the ball within three yards of the line of scrimmage were prevented from blocking below the waist, April 25.

The Toronto Northmen of the WFL signed Larry Csonka, Jim Kiick, and Paul Warfield of Miami, March 31.

Seattle was awarded an NFL franchise to begin play in 1976, June 4. Lloyd W. Nordstrom, president of the Seattle Seahawks, and Hugh Culverhouse, president of the Tampa Bay Buccaneers, signed franchise agreements, December 5.

The Birmingham Americans defeated the Florida Blazers 22-21 in the WFL World Bowl, winning the league championship, December 5.

1975 Pittsburgh defeated Minnesota 16-6 in Super Bowl IX at New Orleans, the Steelers' first championship since entering the NFL in 1933. The NBC telecast was viewed by approximately 78 million people.

The divisional winners with the highest won-loss percentage were made the home team for the divisional playoffs, and the surviving winners with the highest percentage made home teams for the championship games, June 26.

Referees were equipped with wireless microphones for all preseason, regular-season, and playoff games.

The Lions moved to the new Pontiac Silverdome. The Giants played their home games in Shea Stadium. The Saints moved into the Louisiana Superdome.

The World Football League folded, October 22.

1976 Pittsburgh defeated Dallas 21-17 in Super Bowl X in Miami. The Steelers joined Green Bay and Miami as the only teams to win two Super Bowls; the Cowboys became the first wild-card team to play in the Super Bowl. The CBS telecast was viewed by an estimated 80 million people, the largest television audience in history.

Lloyd Nordstrom, the president of the Seahawks, died at 66, January 20. His brother Elmer succeeded him as majority representative of the team.

The owners awarded Super Bowl XII, to be played on January 15, 1978, to New Orleans. They also adopted the use of two 30-second clocks for all games, visible to both players and fans to note the official time between the ready-for-play signal and snap of the ball, March 16.

A veteran player allocation was held to stock the Seattle and Tampa Bay franchises with 39 players each, March 30-31. In the college draft, Seattle and Tampa Bay each received eight extra choices, April 8-9.

The Giants moved into new Giants Stadium in East Rutherford, New Jersey.

The Steelers defeated the College All-Stars in a storm-shortened Chicago College All-Star Game, the last of the series, July 23. St. Louis defeated San Diego 20-10 in a preseason game before 38,000 in Korakuen Stadium, Tokyo, in the first NFL game outside of North America, August 16.

1977 Oakland defeated Minnesota 32-14 before a record crowd of 100,421 in Super Bowl XI at Pasadena, January 9. The paid attendance was a pro record 103,438. The NBC telecast was viewed by 81.9 million people, the largest ever to view a sports event. The victory was the fifth consecutive for the AFC in the Super Bowl.

The NFL Players Association and the NFL Management Council ratified a collective bargaining agreement extending until 1982, covering five football seasons while continuing the pension plan—including years 1974, 1975, and 1976—with contributions totaling more than $55 million. The total cost of the agreement was estimated at $107 million. The agreement called for a college draft at least through 1986; contained a no-strike, no-suit clause; established a 43-man active player limit; reduced pension vesting to four years; provided for increases in minimum salaries and preseason and postseason pay; improved insurance, medical, and dental benefits; modified previous practices in player movement and control; and reaffirmed the NFL Commissioner's disciplinary authority. Additionally, the agreement called for the NFL member clubs to make payments totaling $16 million the next 10 years to settle various legal disputes, February 25.

The San Francisco 49ers were sold to Edward J. DeBartolo, Jr., March 28.

A 16-game regular season, 4-game preseason was adopted to begin in 1978, March 29. A second wild card team was adopted for the playoffs beginning in 1978, with the wild card teams to play each other and the winners advancing to a round of eight postseason series.

The Seahawks were permanently aligned in the AFC Western Division and the Buccaneers in the NFC Central Division, March 31.

The owners awarded Super Bowl XIII, to be played on January 21, 1979, to Miami, to be played in the Orange Bowl; Super Bowl XIV, to be played January 20, 1980, was awarded to Pasadena, to be played in the Rose Bowl, June 14.

Rules changes were adopted to open up the passing game and to cut down on injuries. Defenders were permitted to make contact with eligible receivers only once; the head slap was outlawed; offensive linemen were prohibited from thrusting their hands to an opponent's neck, face, or head; and wide receivers were prohibited from clipping, even in the legal clipping zone.

Rozelle negotiated contracts with the three television networks to televise all NFL regular-season and postseason games, plus selected preseason games, for four years beginning with the 1978 season. ABC was awarded yearly rights to 16 Monday night games, four prime-time games, the AFC-NFC Pro Bowl, and the Hall of Fame games. CBS received the rights to all NFC regular-season and postseason games (except those in the ABC package) and to Super Bowls XIV and XVI. NBC received the rights to all AFC regular-season and postseason games (except those in the ABC package) and to Super Bowls XIII and XV. Industry sources considered it the largest single television package ever negotiated, October.

Chicago's Walter Payton set a single-game rushing record with 275 yards (40 carries) against Minnesota, November 20.

1978 Dallas defeated Denver 27-10 in Super Bowl XII, held indoors for the first time, at the Louisiana Superdome in New Orleans, January 15. The CBS telecast was viewed by more than 102 million people, meaning the game was watched by more viewers than any other show of any kind in the history of television. Dallas's victory was the first for the NFC in six years.

According to a Louis Harris Sports Survey, 70 percent of the nation's sports fans said they followed football, compared to 54 percent who followed baseball. Football increased its lead as the country's favorite, 26 percent to 16 percent for baseball, January 19.

A seventh official, the side judge, was added to the officiating crew, March 14.

The NFL continued a trend toward opening up the game. Rules changes permitted a defender to maintain contact with a receiver within five yards of the line of scrimmage, but restricted contact beyond that point. The pass-blocking rule was interpreted to permit the extending of arms and open hands, March 17.

A study on the use of instant replay as an officiating aid was made during seven nationally televised preseason games.

The NFL played for the first time in

Mexico City, with the Saints defeating the Eagles 14-7 in a preseason game, August 5.

Bolstered by the expansion of the regular-season schedule from 14 to 16 weeks, NFL paid attendance exceeded 12 million (12,771,800) for the first time. The per-game average of 57,017 was the third-highest in league history and the most since 1973.

1979 Pittsburgh defeated Dallas 35-31 in Super Bowl XIII at Miami to become the first team ever to win three Super Bowls, January 21. The NBC telecast was viewed in 35,090,000 homes, by an estimated 96.6 million fans.

The owners awarded three future Super Bowl sites: Super Bowl XV to the Louisiana Superdome in New Orleans, to be played on January 25, 1981; Super Bowl XVI to the Pontiac Silverdome in Pontiac, Michigan, to be played on January 24, 1982; and Super Bowl XVII to Pasadena's Rose Bowl, to be played on January 30, 1983, March 13.

NFL rules changes emphasized additional player safety. The changes prohibited players on the receiving team from blocking below the waist during kickoffs, punts, and field-goal attempts; prohibited the wearing of torn or altered equipment and exposed pads that could be hazardous; extended the zone in which there could be no crackback blocks; and instructed officials to quickly whistle a play dead when a quarterback was clearly in the grasp of a tackler, March 16.

Rosenbloom, the president of the Rams, drowned at 72, April 2. His widow, Georgia, assumed control of the club.

1980 Pittsburgh defeated the Los Angeles Rams 31-19 in Super Bowl XIV at Pasadena to become the first team to win four Super Bowls, January 20. The game was viewed in a record 35,330,000 homes.

The AFC-NFC Pro Bowl, won 37-27 by the NFC, was played before 48,060 fans at Aloha Stadium in Honolulu, Hawaii. It was the first time in the 30-year history of the Pro Bowl that the game was played in a non-NFL city.

Rules changes placed greater restrictions on contact in the area of the head, neck, and face. Under the heading of "personal foul," players were prohibited from directly striking, swinging, or clubbing on the head, neck, or face. Starting in 1980, a penalty could be called for such contact whether or not the initial contact was made below the neck area.

CBS, with a record bid of $12 million, won the national radio rights to 26 NFL regular-season games and all 10 postseason games for the 1980-83 seasons.

The Los Angeles Rams moved their home games to Anaheim Stadium in nearby Orange County, California.

The Oakland Raiders joined the Los Angeles Coliseum Commission's antitrust suit against the NFL. The suit contended the league violated antitrust laws in declining to approve a proposed move by the Raiders from Oakland to Los Angeles.

NFL regular-season attendance of nearly 13.4 million set a record for the third year in a row. The average paid attendance for the 224-game 1980 regular season was 59,787, the highest in the league's 61-year history. NFL games in 1980 were played before 92.4 percent of total stadium capacity.

Television ratings in 1980 were the second-best in NFL history, trailing only the combined ratings of the 1976 season. All three networks posted gains, and NBC's 15.0 rating was its best ever. CBS and ABC had their best ratings since 1977, with 15.3 and 20.8 ratings, respectively. CBS Radio reported a record audience of 7 million for Monday night and special games.

1981 Oakland defeated Philadelphia 27-10 in Super Bowl XV at the Louisiana Superdome in New Orleans, to become the first wild-card team to win a Super Bowl, January 25.

Edgar F. Kaiser, Jr., purchased the Denver Broncos from Gerald and Allan Phipps, February 26.

The owners adopted a disaster plan for re-stocking a team should the club be involved in a fatal accident, March 20.

The owners awarded Super Bowl XVIII to Tampa, to be played in Tampa Stadium on January 22, 1984, June 3.

A CBS-New York Times poll showed that 48 percent of sports fans preferred football to 31 percent for baseball.

The NFL teams hosted 167 representatives from 44 predominantly black colleges during training camps for a total of 289 days. The program was adopted for renewal during each training camp period.

NFL regular-season attendance—13.6 million for an average of 60,745—set a record for the fourth year in a row. It also was the first time the per-game average exceeded 60,000. NFL games in 1981 were played before 93.8 percent of total stadium capacity.

ABC and CBS set all-time rating highs. ABC finished with a 21.7 rating and CBS with a 17.5 rating. NBC was down slightly to 13.9.

1982 San Francisco defeated Cincinnati 26-21 in Super Bowl XVI at the Pontiac Silverdome, in the first Super Bowl held in the North, January 24. The CBS telecast achieved the highest rating of any televised sports event ever, 49.1 with a 73.0 share. The game was viewed by a record 110.2 million fans. CBS Radio reported a record 14 million listeners for the game.

The NFL signed a five-year contract with the three television networks (ABC, CBS, and NBC) to televise all NFL regular-season and postseason games starting with the 1982 season.

The owners awarded the 1983, 1984, and 1985 AFC-NFC Pro Bowls to Honolulu's Aloha Stadium.

A jury ruled against the NFL in the antitrust trial brought by the Los Angeles Coliseum Commission and the Oakland Raiders, May 7. The verdict cleared the way for the Raiders to move to Los Angeles, where they defeated Green Bay 24-3 in their first preseason game, August 29.

The 1982 season was reduced from a 16-game schedule to nine as the result of a 57-day players' strike. The strike was called by the NFLPA at midnight on Monday, September 20, following the Green Bay at New York Giants game. Play resumed November 21-22 following ratification of the Collective Bargaining Agreement by NFL owners, November 17 in New York.

Under the Collective Bargaining Agreement, which was to run through the 1986 season, the NFL draft was extended through 1992 and the veteran free-agent system was left basically unchanged. A minimum salary schedule for years of experience was established; training camp and postseason pay were increased; players' medical, insurance, and retirement benefits were increased; and a severance-pay system was introduced to aid in career transition, a first in professional sports.

Despite the players' strike, the average paid attendance in 1982 was 58,472, the fifth-highest in league history.

The owners awarded the sites of two Super Bowls, December 14: Super Bowl XIX, to be played on January 20, 1985, to Stanford University Stadium in Stanford, California, with San Francisco as host team; and Super Bowl XX, to be played on January 26, 1986, to the Louisiana Superdome in New Orleans.

1983 Because of the shortened season, the NFL adopted a format of 16 teams competing in a Super Bowl Tournament for the 1982 playoffs. The NFC's number-one seed, Washington, defeated the AFC's number-two seed, Miami, 27-17 in Super Bowl XVII at the Rose Bowl in Pasadena, January 30.

Super Bowl XVII was the second-highest rated live television program of all time, giving the NFL a sweep of the top 10 live programs in television history. The game was viewed in more than 40 million homes, the largest ever for a live telecast.

Halas, the owner of the Bears and the last surviving member of the NFL's second organizational meeting, died at 88, October 31.

1984 The Los Angeles Raiders defeated Washington 38-9 in Super Bowl XVIII at Tampa Stadium, January 22. The game achieved a 46.4 rating and 71.0 share.

An 11-man group headed by H.R. (Bum) Bright purchased the Dallas Cowboys from Clint Murchison, Jr., March 20. Club president Tex Schramm was designated as managing general partner.

Patrick Bowlen purchased a majority interest in the Denver Broncos from Edgar Kaiser, Jr., March 21.

The Colts relocated to Indianapolis, March 28. Their new home became the Hoosier Dome.

The owners awarded two Super Bowl sites at their May 23-25 meetings: Super Bowl XXI, to be played on January 25, 1987, to the Rose Bowl in Pasadena; and Super Bowl XXII, to be played on January 31, 1988, to San Diego Jack Murphy Stadium.

The New York Jets moved their home games to Giants Stadium in East Rutherford, New Jersey.

Alex G. Spanos purchased a majority interest in the San Diego Chargers from Eugene V. Klein, August 28.

Houston defeated Pittsburgh 23-20 to mark the one-hundredth overtime game in regular-season play since overtime was adopted in 1974, December 2.

On the field, many all-time records were set: Dan Marino of Miami passed for 5,084 yards and 48 touchdowns; Eric Dickerson of the Los Angeles Rams rushed for 2,105 yards; Art Monk of Washington caught 106 passes; and Walter Payton of Chicago broke Jim Brown's career rushing mark, finishing the season with 13,309 yards.

According to a CBS Sports/New York Times survey, 53 percent of the nation's sports fans said they most enjoyed watching football, compared to 18 percent for baseball, December 2-4.

NFL paid attendance exceeded 13 million for the fifth consecutive complete regular season when 13,398,112, an average of 59,813, attended games. The figure was the second-highest in league history. Teams averaged 42.4 points per game, the second-highest total since the 1970 merger.

1985 San Francisco defeated Miami 38-16 in Super Bowl XIX at Stanford Stadium in Stanford, California, January 20. The game was viewed on television by more people than any other live event in history. President Ronald Reagan, who took his second oath of office before tossing the coin for the game, was one of 115,936,000 viewers. The game drew a 46.4 rating and a 63.0 share. In addition, 6 million people watched the Super Bowl in the United Kingdom and a similar number in Italy. Super Bowl XIX had a direct economic impact of $113.5 million on the San Francisco Bay area.

NBC Radio and the NFL entered into a two-year agreement granting NBC the radio rights to a 37-game package in each of the 1985-86 seasons, March 6. The package included 27 regular-season games and 10 postseason games.

The owners awarded two Super Bowl sites at their annual meeting, March 10-15: Super Bowl XXIII, to be played on January 22, 1989, to the proposed Dolphins Stadium in Miami; and Super Bowl XXIV, to be played on January 28, 1990, to the Louisiana Superdome in New Orleans.

Norman Braman, in partnership with Edward Leibowitz, bought the Philadelphia Eagles from Leonard Tose, April 29.

Bruce Smith, a Virginia Tech defensive lineman selected by Buffalo, was the first player chosen in the fiftieth NFL draft, April 30.

A group headed by Tom Benson, Jr., was approved to purchase the New Orleans Saints from John W. Mecom, Jr., June 3.

The NFL owners adopted a resolution calling for a series of overseas preseason games, beginning in 1986, with one game to be played in England/Europe and/or one game in Japan each year. The game would be a fifth preseason game for the clubs involved and all arrangements and selection of the clubs would be under the control of the Commissioner, May 23.

The league-wide conversion to videotape from movie film for coaching study was approved.

Commissioner Rozelle was authorized to extend the commitment to Honolulu's Aloha Stadium for the AFC-NFC Pro Bowl for 1988, 1989, and 1990, October 15.

The NFL set a single-weekend paid attendance record when 902,657 tickets were sold for the weekend of October 27-28.

A Louis Harris poll in December revealed that pro football remained the sport most followed by Americans. Fifty-nine percent of those surveyed followed pro football, compared with 54 percent who followed baseball.

The Chicago-Miami Monday game had the highest rating, 29.6, and share, 46.0, of any prime-time game in NFL history, December 2. The game was viewed in more than 25 million homes.

The NFL showed a ratings increase on all three networks for the season, gaining 4 percent on NBC, 10 on CBS, and 16 on ABC.

1986 Chicago defeated New England 46-10 in Super Bowl XX at the Louisiana Superdome, January 26. The Patriots had earned the right to play the Bears by becoming the first wild-card team to win three consecutive games on the road. The NBC telecast replaced the final episode of M*A*S*H as the most-viewed television program in history, with an audience of 127 million viewers, according to A.C. Nielsen figures. In addition to drawing a 48.3 rating and a 70 percent share in the United States, Super Bowl XX was televised to 59 foreign countries and beamed via satellite to the QE II. An estimated 300 million Chinese viewed a tape delay of the game in March. NBC Radio figures indicated an audience of 10 million for the game.

Super Bowl XX injected more than $100 million into the New Orleans-area economy, and fans spent $250 per day and a record $17.69 per person on game day.

The owners adopted limited use of instant replay as an officiating aid, prohibited players from wearing or otherwise displaying equipment, apparel, or other items that carry commercial names, names of organizations, or personal messages of any type, March 11.

After an 11-week trial, a jury in U.S. District Court in New York awarded the United States Football League one dollar in its $1.7 billion antitrust suit against the NFL. The jury rejected all of the USFL's television-related claims, which were the self-proclaimed heart of the USFL's case, July 29.

Chicago defeated Dallas 17-6 at Wembley Stadium in London in the first American Bowl. The game drew a sellout crowd of 82,699 and the NBC national telecast in this country produced a 12.4 rating and 36 percent share, making it the second-highest-rated daytime preseason game and highest daytime preseason television audience ever with 10,650,000 viewers, August 3.

Monday Night Football became the longest-running prime-time series in the history of the ABC network.

Instant replay was used to reverse two plays in 31 preseason games. During the regular season, 374 plays were closely reviewed by replay officials, leading to 38 reversals in 224 games. Eighteen plays were closely reviewed by instant replay in 10 postseason games with three reversals.

1987 The New York Giants defeated Denver 39-20 in Super Bowl XXI and captured their first NFL title since 1956. The game, played in Pasadena's Rose Bowl, drew a sellout crowd of 101,063. According to A.C. Nielsen figures, the CBS broadcast of the game was viewed in the U.S. on television by 122,640,000 people, making the telecast the second most-watched television show of all-time behind Super Bowl XX. The game was watched live or on tape in 55 foreign countries and NBC Radio's broadcast of the game was heard by a record 10.1 million people.

The NFL set an all-time paid attendance mark of 17,304,463 for all games, including preseason, regular-season, and postseason. Average regular-season game attendance (60,663) exceeded the 60,000 figure for only the second time in league history.

New three-year TV contracts with ABC, CBS, and NBC were announced for 1987-89 at the NFL annual meeting in Maui, Hawaii, March 15. Commissioner Rozelle and Broadcast Committee Chairman Art Modell also announced a three-year contract with ESPN to televise a mini-series of 13 prime-time games each season. The ESPN contract was the first with a cable network. However, NFL games on ESPN also were scheduled for regular television in the city of the visiting team and in the home city if the game was sold out 72 hours in advance.

Owners also voted to continue in effect for one year the instant replay system used during the 1986 season.

A special payment program was adopted to benefit nearly 1,000 former NFL players who participated in the League before the current Bert Bell NFL Pension Plan was created and made retroactive to the 1959 season. Players covered by the new program spent at least five years in the League and played all or part of their career prior to 1959. Each vested player would receive $60 per month for each year of service in the League for life.

Possible sites for Super Bowl XXV were reduced to five locations by the NFL Super Bowl XXV Site Selection Committee: Anaheim Stadium, Los Angeles Memorial Coliseum, Joe Robbie Stadium, San Diego Jack Murphy Stadium, and Tampa Stadium.

NFL and CBS Radio jointly announced agreement granting CBS the radio rights to a 40-game package in each of the next three NFL seasons, 1987-89, April 7.

NFL owners awarded Super Bowl XXV, to be played on January 27, 1991, to Tampa Stadium, May 20.

Over 400 former NFL players from the pre-1959 era received first payments from NFL owners, July 1.

The NFL's debut on ESPN produced the two highest-rated and most-watched sports programs in basic cable history. The Chicago at Miami game on August 16 drew an 8.9 rating in 3.81 million homes. Those records fell two weeks later when the Los Angeles Raiders at Dallas game achieved a 10.2 cable rating in 4.36 million homes.

Fifty-eight preseason games drew a record paid attendance of 3,116,870.

The 1987 season was reduced from a 16-game season to 15 as the result of a 24-day players' strike. The strike was called by the NFLPA on Tuesday, September 22, following the New England at New York Jets game. Games scheduled for the third weekend were cancelled but the games of weeks four, five, and six were played with replacement teams. Striking players returned for the seventh week of the season, October 25.

In a three-team deal involving 10 players and/or draft choices, the Los Angeles Rams traded running back Eric Dickerson to the Indianapolis Colts for six draft choices and two players. Buffalo obtained the rights to linebacker Cornelius Bennett from Indianapolis, sending Greg Bell and three draft choices to the Rams. The Colts added Owen Gill and three draft choices of their own to complete the deal with the Rams, October 31.

The Chicago at Minnesota game became the highest rated and most-watched sports program in basic cable history when it drew a 14.4 cable rating in 6.5 million homes, December 6.

Instant replay was used to reverse eight plays in 52 preseason games. During the strike-shortened 210-game regular season, 490 plays were closely reviewed by replay officials, leading to 57 reversals. Eighteen plays were closely reviewed by instant replay in 10 postseason games, with three reversals.

1988 Washington defeated Denver 42-10 in Super Bowl XXII to earn a second victory this decade in the NFL Championship Game. The game, played for the first time in San Diego Jack Murphy Stadium, drew a sellout crowd of 73,302. According to A.C. Nielsen figures, the ABC broadcast of the game was viewed in the U.S. on television by 115,000,000 people. The game was seen live or on tape in 60 foreign countries, including the People's Republic of China, and CBS's radio broadcast of the game was heard by 13.7 million people.

A total of 811 players shared in the postseason pool of $16.9 million, the most ever distributed in a single season.

In a unanimous 3-0 decision, the 2nd Circuit Court of Appeals in New York upheld the verdict of the jury that in July, 1986, had awarded the United States Football League one dollar in its $1.7 billion antitrust suit against the NFL. In a 91-page opinion, Judge Ralph K. Winter said the USFL sought through court decree the success it failed to gain among football fans, March 10.

By a 23-5 margin, owners voted to continue the instant replay system for the third consecutive season with the Instant Replay Official to be assigned to a regular seven-man, on-the-field crew. At the NFL annual meeting in Phoenix, Arizona, a 45-second clock was also approved to replace the 30-second clock. For a normal sequence of plays, the interval between plays was changed to 45 seconds from the time the ball is signaled dead until it is snapped on the succeeding play.

NFL owners approved the transfer of the Cardinals' franchise from St. Louis to Phoenix; approved two Supplemental Drafts each year—one prior to training camp and one prior to the regular season; and voted to initiate an annual series of games in Japan/Asia as early as the 1989 preseason, March 14-18.

The NFL Annual Selection Meeting returned to a separate two-day format and for the first time originated on a Sunday. ESPN drew a 3.6 rating during their seven-hour coverage of the draft, which was viewed in 1.6 million homes, April 24-25.

Art Rooney, founder and owner of the Steelers, died at 87, August 25.

Paid and average attendance of 934,271 and 66,734 at 14 games on October 16-17 set single weekend records.

Commissioner Rozelle announced that two teams would play a preseason game as part of the American Bowl series on August 6, 1989, in the Korakuen Tokyo Dome in Japan, December 16.

NFL regular-season paid attendance of 13,535,335 and the average of 60,427 was the third highest all-time. Buffalo set an NFL team single-season, in-house attendance mark of 622,793.

1989 San Francisco defeated Cincinnati 20-16 in Super Bowl XXIII. The game, played for the first time at Joe Robbie Stadium in Miami, was attended by a sellout crowd of 75,129. NBC's telecast of the game was watched by an estimated 110,780,000 viewers, according to A.C. Nielsen, making it the sixth most-watched program in television history. The game was seen live or on tape in 60 foreign countries, including an estimated 300 million in China. The CBS Radio broadcast of the game was heard by 11.2 million people.

Commissioner Rozelle announced his retirement, pending the naming of a successor, March 22 at the NFL annual meeting in Palm Desert, California.

Following the announcement, AFC president Lamar Hunt and NFC president Wellington Mara announced the formation of a six-man search committee composed of Art Modell, Robert Parins, Dan Rooney, and Ralph Wilson. Hunt and Mara served as co-chairmen.

By a 24-4 margin, owners voted to continue the instant replay system for the fourth straight season. A strengthened policy regarding anabolic steroids and masking agents was announced by Commissioner Rozelle. NFL clubs called for strong disciplinary measures in cases of feigned injuries and adopted a joint proposal by the Long-Range Planning and Finance committees regarding player personnel rules, March 19-23.

Two hundred twenty-nine unconditional free agents signed with new teams under management's Plan B system, April 1.

Jerry Jones purchased a majority interest in the Dallas Cowboys from H.R. (Bum) Bright, April 18.

Tex Schramm was named president of the new World League of American Football to work with a six-man committee of Dan Rooney, chairman; Norman Braman, Lamar Hunt, Victor Kiam, Mike Lynn, and Bill Walsh, April 18.

NFL and CBS Radio jointly announced agreement extending CBS's radio rights to an annual 40-game package through the 1994 season, April 18.

NFL owners awarded Super Bowl XXVI, to be played on January 26, 1992, to Minneapolis, May 24.

As of opening day, September 10, of the 229 Plan B free agents, 111 were active and 23 others were on teams' reserve lists. Ninety-two others were waived and three retired.

Art Shell was named head coach

of the Los Angeles Raiders making him the NFL's first black head coach since Fritz Pollard coached the Akron Pros in 1921, October 3.

The site of the New England Patriots at San Francisco 49ers game scheduled for Candlestick Park on October 22 was switched to Stanford Stadium in the aftermath of the Bay Area Earthquake of October 17. The change was announced on October 19.

Paul Tagliabue became the seventh chief executive of the NFL on October 26 when he was chosen to succeed Commissioner Pete Rozelle on the sixth ballot of a three-day meeting in Cleveland, Ohio.

In all, 12 ballots were required to select Tagliabue. Two were conducted at a meeting in Chicago on July 6, and four at a meeting in Dallas on October 10-11. On the twelfth ballot, with Seattle absent, Tagliabue received more than the 19 affirmative votes required for election from among the 27 clubs present.

The transfer from Commissioner Rozelle to Commissioner Tagliabue took place at 12:01 A.M. on Sunday, November 5.

NFL Charities donated $1 million through United Way to benefit Bay Area earthquake victims, November 6.

NFL paid attendance of 17,399,538 was the highest total in league history. This included a total of 13,625,662 for an average of 60,829—both NFL records—for the 224-game regular season.

1990 San Francisco defeated Denver 55-10 in Super Bowl XXIV at the Louisiana Superdome, January 28. San Francisco joined Pittsburgh as the NFL's only teams to win four Super Bowls.

The NFL announced revisions in its 1990 Draft eligibility rules. College juniors became eligible but must renounce their collegiate football eligibility before applying for the NFL Draft, February 16.

Commissioner Tagliabue announced NFL teams will play their 16-game schedule over 17 weeks in 1990 and 1991 and 16 games over 18 weeks in 1992 and 1993, February 27.

The NFL revised its playoff format to include two additional wild card teams (one per conference).

Commissioner Tagliabue and Broadcast Committee Chairman Art Modell announced a four-year contract with Turner Broadcasting to televise nine Sunday-night games.

New four-year TV agreements were ratified for 1990-93 for ABC, CBS, NBC, ESPN, and TNT at the NFL annual meeting in Orlando, Florida, March 12. The contracts totaled $3.6 billion, the largest in TV history.

The NFL announced plans to expand its American Bowl series of preseason games. In addition to games in London and Tokyo, American Bowl games were scheduled for Berlin, Germany, and Montreal, Canada, in 1990.

For the fifth straight year, NFL owners voted to continue a limited system of Instant Replay. Beginning in 1990, the replay official will have a two-minute time limit to make a decision. The vote was 21-7, March 12.

Commissioner Tagliabue announced the formation of a Committee on Expansion and Realignment, March 13. He also named a Player Advisory Council, comprised of 12 former NFL players, March 14.

One-hundred eighty-four Plan B unconditional free agents signed with new teams, April 2.

Commissioner Tagliabue appointed Dr. John Lombardo as the League's Drug Advisor for anabolic steroids, April 25 and named Dr. Lawrence Brown as the League's Advisor for Drugs of Abuse, May 17.

NFL owners awarded Super Bowl XXVIII, to be played in 1994, to the proposed Georgia Dome, May 23.

Commissioner Tagliabue named NFL referee Jerry Seeman as NFL Director of Officiating, replacing Art McNally, who announced his retirement, July 12.

NFL International Week was celebrated with four preseason games in seven days in Tokyo, London, Berlin, and Montreal. More than 200,000 fans on three continents attended the four games, August 4-11.

Commissioner Tagliabue announced the NFL Teacher of the Month program in which the League furnishes grants and scholarships in recognition of teachers who provided a positive influence upon NFL players in elementary and secondary schools, Sept. 20.

For the first time since 1957, every NFL club won at least one of its first four games, Oct. 1.

NFL total paid attendance of 17,665,671 was the highest total in League history. The regular-season total paid attendance of 13,959,896 and average of 62,321 for 224 games were the highest ever, surpassing the previous records set in the 1989 season.

1991 The New York Giants defeated Buffalo 20-19 in Super Bowl XXV to capture their second title in five years. The game was played before a sellout crowd of 73,813 at Tampa Stadium and became the first Super Bowl decided by one point, January 27. The ABC broadcast of the game was seen by more than 112,000,000 people in the United States and was seen live or taped in 60 other countries.

NFL playoff games earned the top television rating spot of the week for each week of the month-long playoffs, January 29.

A total of 693 players shared in the postseason pool of $14.9 million.

New York businessman Robert Tisch purchased a 50 percent interest in the New York Giants from Mrs. Helen Mara Nugent and her children, Tim Mara and Maura Mara Concannon, February 2.

Commissioner Tagliabue named Neil Austrian to the newly created position of President of the NFL to be chief operating officer for League-wide business and financial operations, February 27.

NFL owners voted to continue a limited system of Instant Replay for the sixth consecutive year. The vote was 21-7, March 19.

The NFL launched the World League of American Football, the first sports league to operate on a weekly basis on two separate continents, March 23.

One-hundred thirty-nine Plan B unconditional free agents signed with new teams, April 1.

NFL Charities presented a $250,000 donation to the United Service Organization. The donation was the second largest single grant ever by NFL Charities, April 5.

Commissioner Tagliabue named Harold Henderson as Executive Vice President for Labor Relations and Chairman of the NFL Management Council Executive Committee, April 8.

Russell Maryland, a University of Miami defensive lineman, was selected by Dallas, becoming the first player chosen in the 1991 NFL Draft, April 21.

NFL owners approved a recommendation from the Expansion and Realignment Committee to add two teams for the 1994 season, resulting in six divisions of five teams each, May 22.

NFL owners awarded Super Bowl XXIX, to be played on January 29, 1995, to Miami, May 23.

NFL COMMISSIONERS AND PRESIDENTS*

1920 . . . . Jim Thorpe, President
1921-39 . . . . Joe Carr, President
1939-41 . . . . . Carl Storck, President
1941-46 . . . . Elmer Layden, Commissioner
1946-59 . . . Bert Bell, Commissioner
1960-89 . . . . Pete Rozelle, Commissioner
1989-present . . . . . . Paul Tagliabue, Commissioner

*NFL treasurer Austin Gunsel served as president in the office of the commissioner following the death of Bert Bell (Oct. 11, 1959) until the election of Pete Rozelle (Jan. 26, 1960).

1990

American Conference

Eastern Division

	W	L	T	Pct.	Pts.	OP
Buffalo	13	3	0	.813	428	263
Miami*	12	4	0	.750	336	242
Indianapolis	7	9	0	.438	281	353
N.Y. Jets	6	10	0	.375	295	345
New England	1	15	0	.063	181	446

Central Division

	W	L	T	Pct.	Pts.	OP
Cincinnati	9	7	0	.563	360	352
Houston*	9	7	0	.563	405	307
Pittsburgh	9	7	0	.563	292	240
Cleveland	3	13	0	.188	228	462

Western Division

	W	L	T	Pct.	Pts.	OP
L.A. Raiders	12	4	0	.750	337	268
Kansas City*	11	5	0	.688	369	257
Seattle	9	7	0	.563	306	286
San Diego	6	10	0	.375	315	281
Denver	5	11	0	.313	331	374

National Conference

Eastern Division

	W	L	T	Pct.	Pts.	OP
N.Y. Giants	13	3	0	.813	335	211
Philadelphia*	10	6	0	.625	396	299
Washington*	10	6	0	.625	381	301
Dallas	7	9	0	.438	244	308
Phoenix	5	11	0	.313	268	396

Central Division

	W	L	T	Pct.	Pts.	OP
Chicago	11	5	0	.688	348	280
Tampa Bay	6	10	0	.375	264	367
Detroit	6	10	0	.375	373	413
Green Bay	6	10	0	.375	271	347
Minnesota	6	10	0	.375	351	326

Western Division

	W	L	T	Pct.	Pts.	OP
San Francisco	14	2	0	.875	353	239
New Orleans*	8	8	0	.500	274	275
L.A. Rams	5	11	0	.313	345	412
Atlanta	5	11	0	.313	348	365

**Wild Card qualifiers for playoffs*

Cincinnati won AFC Central title based on best head-to-head record (3-1) vs. Houston (2-2) and Pittsburgh (1-3). Houston was Wild Card based on better conference record (8-4) than Seattle (7-5) and Pittsburgh (6-6). Philadelphia finished second in the NFC East based on better division record (5-3) than Washington (4-4). Tampa Bay was second in NFC Central based on 5-1 record vs. Detroit, Green Bay, and Minnesota. Detroit finished third based on best net division points (minus 8) vs. Green Bay (minus 40) in fourth. Minnesota was fifth based on 4-8 conference record. The Los Angeles Rams finished third in NFC West based on net points in division (plus 1) vs. Atlanta (minus 31).

First round playoffs: MIAMI 17, Kansas City 16; CINCINNATI 41, Houston 14

Divisional playoffs: BUFFALO 44, Miami 34; L.A. RAIDERS 20, Cincinnati 10

AFC championship: BUFFALO 51, L.A. Raiders 3

First round playoffs: Washington 20, PHILADELPHIA 6; CHICAGO 16, New Orleans 6

Divisional playoffs: SAN FRANCISCO 28, Washington 10; N.Y. GIANTS 31, Chicago 3

NFC championship: N.Y. Giants 15, SAN FRANCISCO 13

Super Bowl XXV: N.Y. Giants (NFC) 20, Buffalo (AFC) 19 at Tampa Stadium, Tampa, Florida

In the Past Standings section, home teams in playoff games are indicated by capital letters.

1989

American Conference

Eastern Division

	W	L	T	Pct.	Pts.	OP
Buffalo	9	7	0	.563	409	317
Indianapolis	8	8	0	.500	298	301
Miami	8	8	0	.500	331	379
New England	5	11	0	.313	297	391
N.Y. Jets	4	12	0	.250	253	411

Central Division

	W	L	T	Pct.	Pts.	OP
Cleveland	9	6	1	.594	334	254
Houston*	9	7	0	.563	365	412
Pittsburgh*	9	7	0	.563	265	326
Cincinnati	8	8	0	.500	404	285

Western Division

	W	L	T	Pct.	Pts.	OP
Denver	11	5	0	.688	362	226
Kansas City	8	7	1	.531	318	286
L.A. Raiders	8	8	0	.500	315	297
Seattle	7	9	0	.438	241	327
San Diego	6	10	0	.375	266	290

National Conference

Eastern Division

	W	L	T	Pct.	Pts.	OP
N.Y. Giants	12	4	0	.750	348	252
Philadelphia*	11	5	0	.688	342	274
Washington	10	6	0	.625	386	308
Phoenix	5	11	0	.313	258	377
Dallas	1	15	0	.063	204	393

Central Division

	W	L	T	Pct.	Pts.	OP
Minnesota	10	6	0	.625	351	275
Green Bay	10	6	0	.625	362	356
Detroit	7	9	0	.438	312	364
Chicago	6	10	0	.375	358	377
Tampa Bay	5	11	0	.313	320	419

Western Division

	W	L	T	Pct.	Pts.	OP
San Francisco	14	2	0	.875	442	253
L.A. Rams*	11	5	0	.688	426	344
New Orleans	9	7	0	.563	386	301
Atlanta	3	13	0	.188	279	437

**Wild Card qualifiers for playoffs*

Indianapolis finished ahead of Miami in AFC East because of better conference record (7-5 vs. 6-8). Houston finished ahead of Pittsburgh in AFC Central because of head-to-head sweep (2-0). Minnesota finished ahead of Green Bay in NFC Central because of better division record (6-2 vs. 5-3).

First round playoff: Pittsburgh 26, HOUSTON 23 (OT)

Divisional playoffs: CLEVELAND 34, Buffalo 30; DENVER 24, Pittsburgh 23

AFC championship: DENVER 37, Cleveland 21

First round playoff: L.A. Rams 21, PHILADELPHIA 7

Divisional playoffs: L.A. Rams 19, N.Y. GIANTS 13 (OT); SAN FRANCISCO 41, Minnesota 13

NFC championship: SAN FRANCISCO 30, L.A. Rams 3

Super Bowl XXIV: San Francisco (NFC) 55, Denver (AFC) 10 at Louisiana Superdome, New Orleans, Louisiana

1988

American Conference

Eastern Division

	W	L	T	Pct.	Pts.	OP
Buffalo	12	4	0	.750	329	237
Indianapolis	9	7	0	.563	354	315
New England	9	7	0	.563	250	284
N.Y. Jets	8	7	1	.531	372	354
Miami	6	10	0	.375	319	380

Central Division

	W	L	T	Pct.	Pts.	OP
Cincinnati	12	4	0	.750	448	329
Cleveland*	10	6	0	.625	304	288
Houston*	10	6	0	.625	424	365
Pittsburgh	5	11	0	.313	336	421

Western Division

	W	L	T	Pct.	Pts.	OP
Seattle	9	7	0	.563	339	329
Denver	8	8	0	.500	327	352
L.A. Raiders	7	9	0	.438	325	369
San Diego	6	10	0	.375	231	332
Kansas City	4	11	1	.281	254	320

National Conference

Eastern Division

	W	L	T	Pct.	Pts.	OP
Philadelphia	10	6	0	.625	379	319
N.Y. Giants	10	6	0	.625	359	304
Washington	7	9	0	.438	345	387
Phoenix	7	9	0	.438	344	398
Dallas	3	13	0	.188	265	381

Central Division

	W	L	T	Pct.	Pts.	OP
Chicago	12	4	0	.750	312	215
Minnesota*	11	5	0	.688	406	233
Tampa Bay	5	11	0	.313	261	350
Detroit	4	12	0	.250	220	313
Green Bay	4	12	0	.250	240	315

Western Division

	W	L	T	Pct.	Pts.	OP
San Francisco	10	6	0	.625	369	294
L.A. Rams*	10	6	0	.625	407	293
New Orleans	10	6	0	.625	312	283
Atlanta	5	11	0	.313	244	315

**Wild Card qualifiers for playoffs*

Indianapolis finished second in AFC East on basis of better record versus common opponents (7-5) over New England (6-6). Cleveland gained first AFC Wild Card position based on better division record (4-2) over Houston (3-3). Philadelphia finished first in NFC East on basis of head-to-head sweep over New York Giants. Washington finished third in NFC East on basis of better division record (4-4) over Phoenix (3-5). Detroit finished fourth in NFC Central on basis of head-to-head sweep over Green Bay. San Francisco finished first in NFC West based on better head-to-head record (3-1) over Los Angeles Rams (2-2) and New Orleans (1-3). Los Angeles Rams finished second in NFC West on basis of better division record (4-2) over New Orleans (3-3) and earned Wild Card position based on better conference record (8-4) over New York Giants (9-5) and New Orleans (6-6).

First round playoff: Houston 24, CLEVELAND 23

Divisional playoffs: CINCINNATI 21, Seattle 13; BUFFALO 17, Houston 10

AFC championship: CINCINNATI 21, Buffalo 10

First round playoff: MINNESOTA 28, Los Angeles Rams 17

Divisional playoffs: CHICAGO 20, Philadelphia 12; SAN FRANCISCO 34, Minnesota 9

NFC championship: San Francisco 28, CHICAGO 3

Super Bowl XXIII: San Francisco (NFC) 20, Cincinnati (AFC) 16 at Joe Robbie Stadium, Miami, Florida

1987

American Conference

Eastern Division

	W	L	T	Pct.	Pts.	OP
Indianapolis	9	6	0	.600	300	238
New England	8	7	0	.533	320	293
Miami	8	7	0	.533	362	335
Buffalo	7	8	0	.467	270	305
N.Y. Jets	6	9	0	.400	334	360

Central Division

	W	L	T	Pct.	Pts.	OP
Cleveland	10	5	0	.667	390	239
Houston*	9	6	0	.600	345	349
Pittsburgh	8	7	0	.533	285	299
Cincinnati	4	11	0	.267	285	370

Western Division

	W	L	T	Pct.	Pts.	OP
Denver	10	4	1	.700	379	288
Seattle*	9	6	0	.600	371	314
San Diego	8	7	0	.533	253	317
L.A. Raiders	5	10	0	.333	301	289
Kansas City	4	11	0	.267	273	388

National Conference

Eastern Division

	W	L	T	Pct.	Pts.	OP
Washington	11	4	0	.733	379	285
Dallas	7	8	0	.467	340	348
St. Louis	7	8	0	.467	362	368
Philadelphia	7	8	0	.467	337	380
N.Y. Giants	6	9	0	.400	280	312

Central Division

	W	L	T	Pct.	Pts.	OP
Chicago	11	4	0	.733	356	282
Minnesota*	8	7	0	.533	336	335
Green Bay	5	9	1	.367	255	300
Tampa Bay	4	11	0	.267	286	360
Detroit	4	11	0	.267	269	384

Western Division

	W	L	T	Pct.	Pts.	OP
San Francisco	13	2	0	.867	459	253
New Orleans*	12	3	0	.800	422	283
L.A. Rams	6	9	0	.400	317	361
Atlanta	3	12	0	.200	205	436

**Wild Card qualifiers for playoffs*

Houston gained first AFC Wild Card position on better conference record (7-4) over Seattle (5-6).

First round playoff: HOUSTON 23, Seattle 20 (OT)

Divisional playoffs: CLEVELAND 38, Indianapolis 21; DENVER 34, Houston 10

AFC championship: DENVER 38, Cleveland 33

First round playoff: Minnesota 44, NEW ORLEANS 10

Divisional playoffs: Minnesota 36, SAN FRANCISCO 24; Washington 21, CHICAGO 17

NFC championship: WASHINGTON 17, Minnesota 10

Super Bowl XXII: Washington (NFC) 42, Denver (AFC) 10, at San Diego Jack Murphy Stadium, San Diego, Calif.

Note: 1987 regular season was reduced from 16 to 15 games for each team due to players' strike.

1986

American Conference

Eastern Division

	W	L	T	Pct.	Pts.	OP
New England	11	5	0	.688	412	307
N.Y. Jets*	10	6	0	.625	364	386
Miami	8	8	0	.500	430	405
Buffalo	4	12	0	.250	287	348
Indianapolis	3	13	0	.188	229	400

Central Division

	W	L	T	Pct.	Pts.	OP
Cleveland	12	4	0	.750	391	310
Cincinnati	10	6	0	.625	409	394
Pittsburgh	6	10	0	.375	307	336
Houston	5	11	0	.313	274	329

Western Division

	W	L	T	Pct.	Pts.	OP
Denver	11	5	0	.688	378	327
Kansas City*	10	6	0	.625	358	326
Seattle	10	6	0	.625	366	293
L.A. Raiders	8	8	0	.500	323	346
San Diego	4	12	0	.250	335	396

National Conference

Eastern Division

	W	L	T	Pct.	Pts.	OP
N.Y. Giants	14	2	0	.875	371	236
Washington*	12	4	0	.750	368	296
Dallas	7	9	0	.438	346	337
Philadelphia	5	10	1	.344	256	312
St. Louis	4	11	1	.281	218	351

Central Division

	W	L	T	Pct.	Pts.	OP
Chicago	14	2	0	.875	352	187
Minnesota	9	7	0	.563	398	273
Detroit	5	11	0	.313	277	326
Green Bay	4	12	0	.250	254	418
Tampa Bay	2	14	0	.125	239	473

Western Division

	W	L	T	Pct.	Pts.	OP
San Francisco	10	5	1	.656	374	247
L.A. Rams*	10	6	0	.625	309	267
Atlanta	7	8	1	.469	280	280
New Orleans	7	9	0	.438	288	287

**Wild Card qualifiers for playoffs*

New York Jets gained first AFC Wild Card position on better conference record (8-4) over Kansas City (9-5), Seattle (7-5), and Cincinnati (7-5). Kansas City gained second Wild Card based on better conference record (9-5) over Seattle (7-5) and Cincinnati (7-5).

First round playoff: NEW YORK JETS 35, Kansas City 15
Divisional playoffs: CLEVELAND 23, New York Jets 20 (OT)
DENVER 22, New England 17
AFC championship: Denver 23, CLEVELAND 20 (OT)
First round playoff: WASHINGTON 19, Los Angeles Rams 7
Divisional playoffs: Washington 27, CHICAGO 13
NEW YORK GIANTS 49, San Francisco 3
NFC championship: NEW YORK GIANTS 17, Washington 0
Super Bowl XXI: New York Giants (NFC) 39, Denver (AFC) 20, at Rose Bowl, Pasadena, Calif.

1985

American Conference

Eastern Division

	W	L	T	Pct.	Pts.	OP
Miami	12	4	0	.750	428	320
N.Y. Jets*	11	5	0	.688	393	264
New England*	11	5	0	.688	362	290
Indianapolis	5	11	0	.313	320	386
Buffalo	2	14	0	.125	200	381

Central Division

	W	L	T	Pct.	Pts.	OP
Cleveland	8	8	0	.500	287	294
Cincinnati	7	9	0	.438	441	437
Pittsburgh	7	9	0	.438	379	355
Houston	5	11	0	.313	284	412

Western Division

	W	L	T	Pct.	Pts.	OP
L.A. Raiders	12	4	0	.750	354	308
Denver	11	5	0	.688	380	329
Seattle	8	8	0	.500	349	303
San Diego	8	8	0	.500	467	435
Kansas City	6	10	0	.375	317	360

National Conference

Eastern Division

	W	L	T	Pct.	Pts.	OP
Dallas	10	6	0	.625	357	333
N.Y. Giants*	10	6	0	.625	399	283
Washington	10	6	0	.625	297	312
Philadelphia	7	9	0	.438	286	310
St. Louis	5	11	0	.313	278	414

Central Division

	W	L	T	Pct.	Pts.	OP
Chicago	15	1	0	.938	456	198
Green Bay	8	8	0	.500	337	355
Minnesota	7	9	0	.438	346	359
Detroit	7	9	0	.438	307	366
Tampa Bay	2	14	0	.125	294	448

Western Division

	W	L	T	Pct.	Pts.	OP
L.A. Rams	11	5	0	.688	340	277
San Francisco*	10	6	0	.625	411	263
New Orleans	5	11	0	.313	294	401
Atlanta	4	12	0	.250	282	452

**Wild Card qualifiers for playoffs*

New York Jets gained first AFC Wild Card position on better conference record (9-3) over New England (8-4) and Denver (8-4). New England gained second AFC Wild Card position based on better record vs. common opponents (4-2) than Denver (3-3). Dallas won NFC Eastern Division title based on better record (4-0) vs. New York Giants (1-3) and Washington (1-3). New York Giants gained first NFC Wild Card position based on better conference record (8-4) over San Francisco (7-5) and Washington (6-6). San Francisco gained second NFC Wild Card position based on head-to-head victory over Washington.

First round playoff: New England 26, NEW YORK JETS 14
Divisional playoffs: MIAMI 24, Cleveland 21;
New England 27, LOS ANGELES RAIDERS 20
AFC championship: New England 31, MIAMI 14
First round playoff: NEW YORK GIANTS 17, San Francisco 3
Divisional playoffs: LOS ANGELES RAMS 20, Dallas 0;
CHICAGO 21, New York Giants 0
NFC championship: CHICAGO 24, Los Angeles Rams 0
Super Bowl XX: Chicago (NFC) 46, New England (AFC) 10, at Louisiana Superdome, New Orleans, La.

1984

American Conference

Eastern Division

	W	L	T	Pct.	Pts.	OP
Miami	14	2	0	.875	513	298
New England	9	7	0	.563	362	352
N.Y. Jets	7	9	0	.438	332	364
Indianapolis	4	12	0	.250	239	414
Buffalo	2	14	0	.125	250	454

Central Division

	W	L	T	Pct.	Pts.	OP
Pittsburgh	9	7	0	.563	387	310
Cincinnati	8	8	0	.500	339	339
Cleveland	5	11	0	.313	250	297
Houston	3	13	0	.188	240	437

Western Division

	W	L	T	Pct.	Pts.	OP
Denver	13	3	0	.813	353	241
Seattle*	12	4	0	.750	418	282
L.A. Raiders*	11	5	0	.688	368	278
Kansas City	8	8	0	.500	314	324
San Diego	7	9	0	.438	394	413

National Conference

Eastern Division

	W	L	T	Pct.	Pts.	OP
Washington	11	5	0	.688	426	310
N.Y. Giants*	9	7	0	.563	299	301
St. Louis	9	7	0	.563	423	345
Dallas	9	7	0	.563	308	308
Philadelphia	6	9	1	.406	278	320

Central Division

	W	L	T	Pct.	Pts.	OP
Chicago	10	6	0	.625	325	248
Green Bay	8	8	0	.500	390	309
Tampa Bay	6	10	0	.375	335	380
Detroit	4	11	1	.281	283	408
Minnesota	3	13	0	.188	276	484

Western Division

	W	L	T	Pct.	Pts.	OP
San Francisco	15	1	0	.938	475	227
L.A. Rams*	10	6	0	.625	346	316
New Orleans	7	9	0	.438	298	361
Atlanta	4	12	0	.250	281	382

**Wild Card qualifiers for playoffs*

New York Giants clinched Wild Card berth based on 3-1 record vs. St. Louis's 2-2 and Dallas's 1-3. St. Louis finished ahead of Dallas based on better division record (5-3 to 3-5).

First round playoff: SEATTLE 13, Los Angeles Raiders 7
Divisional playoffs: MIAMI 31, Seattle 10; Pittsburgh 24, DENVER 17
AFC championship: MIAMI 45, Pittsburgh 28
First round playoff: New York Giants 16, LOS ANGELES RAMS 13
Divisional playoffs: SAN FRANCISCO 21, New York Giants 10;
Chicago 23, WASHINGTON 19
NFC championship: SAN FRANCISCO 23, Chicago 0
Super Bowl XIX: San Francisco (NFC) 38, Miami (AFC) 16, at Stanford Stadium, Stanford, Calif.

1983

American Conference

Eastern Division

	W	L	T	Pct.	Pts.	OP
Miami	12	4	0	.750	389	250
New England	8	8	0	.500	274	289
Buffalo	8	8	0	.500	283	351
Baltimore	7	9	0	.438	264	354
N.Y. Jets	7	9	0	.438	313	331

Central Division

	W	L	T	Pct.	Pts.	OP
Pittsburgh	10	6	0	.625	355	303
Cleveland	9	7	0	.563	356	342
Cincinnati	7	9	0	.438	346	302
Houston	2	14	0	.125	288	460

Western Division

	W	L	T	Pct.	Pts.	OP
L.A. Raiders	12	4	0	.750	442	338
Seattle*	9	7	0	.563	403	397
Denver*	9	7	0	.563	302	327
San Diego	6	10	0	.375	358	462
Kansas City	6	10	0	.375	386	367

National Conference

Eastern Division

	W	L	T	Pct.	Pts.	OP
Washington	14	2	0	.875	541	332
Dallas*	12	4	0	.750	479	360
St. Louis	8	7	1	.531	374	428
Philadelphia	5	11	0	.313	233	322
N.Y. Giants	3	12	1	.219	267	347

Central Division

	W	L	T	Pct.	Pts.	OP
Detroit	9	7	0	.563	347	286
Green Bay	8	8	0	.500	429	439
Chicago	8	8	0	.500	311	301
Minnesota	8	8	0	.500	316	348
Tampa Bay	2	14	0	.125	241	380

Western Division

	W	L	T	Pct.	Pts.	OP
San Francisco	10	6	0	.625	432	293
L.A. Rams*	9	7	0	.563	361	344
New Orleans	8	8	0	.500	319	337
Atlanta	7	9	0	.438	370	389

**Wild Card qualifiers for playoffs*

Seattle and Denver gained Wild Card berths over Cleveland because of their victories over the Browns.

First round playoff: SEATTLE 31, Denver 7
Divisional playoffs: Seattle 27, MIAMI 20; LOS ANGELES RAIDERS 38, Pittsburgh 10
AFC championship: LOS ANGELES RAIDERS 30, Seattle 14
First round playoff: Los Angeles Rams 24, DALLAS 17
Divisional playoffs: SAN FRANCISCO 24, Detroit 23; WASHINGTON 51, L.A. Rams 7
NFC championship: WASHINGTON 24, San Francisco 21
Super Bowl XVIII: Los Angeles Raiders (AFC) 38, Washington (NFC) 9, at Tampa Stadium, Tampa, Fla.

1982

American Conference

	W	L	T	Pct.	Pts.	OP
L.A. Raiders	8	1	0	.889	260	200
Miami	7	2	0	.778	198	131
Cincinnati	7	2	0	.778	232	177
Pittsburgh	6	3	0	.667	204	146
San Diego	6	3	0	.667	288	221
N.Y. Jets	6	3	0	.667	245	166
New England	5	4	0	.556	143	157
Cleveland	4	5	0	.444	140	182
Buffalo	4	5	0	.444	150	154
Seattle	4	5	0	.444	127	147
Kansas City	3	6	0	.333	176	184
Denver	2	7	0	.222	148	226
Houston	1	8	0	.111	136	245
Baltimore	0	8	1	.056	113	236

National Conference

	W	L	T	Pct.	Pts.	OP
Washington	8	1	0	.889	190	128
Dallas	6	3	0	.667	226	145
Green Bay	5	3	1	.611	226	169
Minnesota	5	4	0	.556	187	198
Atlanta	5	4	0	.556	183	199
St. Louis	5	4	0	.556	135	170
Tampa Bay	5	4	0	.556	158	178
Detroit	4	5	0	.444	181	176
New Orleans	4	5	0	.444	129	160
N.Y. Giants	4	5	0	.444	164	160
San Francisco	3	6	0	.333	209	206
Chicago	3	6	0	.333	141	174
Philadelphia	3	6	0	.333	191	195
L.A. Rams	2	7	0	.222	200	250

As the result of a 57-day players' strike, the 1982 NFL regular season schedule was reduced from 16 weeks to 9. At the conclusion of the regular season, the NFL conducted a 16-team postseason Super Bowl Tournament. Eight teams from each conference were seeded 1-8 based on their records during the season.

Miami finished ahead of Cincinnati based on better conference record (6-1 to 6-2). Pittsburgh won common games tie-breaker with San Diego (3-1 to 2-1) after New York Jets were eliminated from three-way tie based on conference record (Pittsburgh and San Diego 5-3 vs. Jets 2-3). Cleveland finished ahead of Buffalo and Seattle based on better conference record (4-3 to 3-3 to 3-5). Minnesota (4-1), Atlanta (4-3), St. Louis (5-4), Tampa Bay (3-3) seeds were determined by best won-lost record in conference games. Detroit finished ahead of New Orleans and the New York Giants based on better conference record (4-4 to 3-5 to 3-5).

First round playoff: MIAMI 28, New England 13
LOS ANGELES RAIDERS 27, Cleveland 10
New York Jets 44, CINCINNATI 17
San Diego 31, PITTSBURGH 28
Second round playoff: New York Jets 17, LOS ANGELES RAIDERS 14
MIAMI 34, San Diego 13
AFC championship: MIAMI 14, New York Jets 0
First round playoff: WASHINGTON 31, Detroit 7
GREEN BAY 41, St. Louis 16
MINNESOTA 30, Atlanta 24
DALLAS 30, Tampa Bay 17
Second round playoff: WASHINGTON 21, Minnesota 7
DALLAS 37, Green Bay 26
NFC championship: WASHINGTON 31, Dallas 17
Super Bowl XVII: Washington (NFC) 27, Miami (AFC) 17, at Rose Bowl, Pasadena, Calif.

1981

American Conference

Eastern Division

	W	L	T	Pct.	Pts.	OP
Miami	11	4	1	.719	345	275
N.Y. Jets*	10	5	1	.656	355	287
Buffalo*	10	6	0	.625	311	276
Baltimore	2	14	0	.125	259	533
New England	2	14	0	.125	322	370

Central Division

	W	L	T	Pct.	Pts.	OP
Cincinnati	12	4	0	.750	421	304
Pittsburgh	8	8	0	.500	356	297
Houston	7	9	0	.438	281	355
Cleveland	5	11	0	.313	276	375

Western Division

	W	L	T	Pct.	Pts.	OP
San Diego	10	6	0	.625	478	390
Denver	10	6	0	.625	321	289
Kansas City	9	7	0	.563	343	290
Oakland	7	9	0	.438	273	343
Seattle	6	10	0	.375	322	388

National Conference

Eastern Division

	W	L	T	Pct.	Pts.	OP
Dallas	12	4	0	.750	367	277
Philadelphia*	10	6	0	.625	368	221
N.Y. Giants*	9	7	0	.563	295	257
Washington	8	8	0	.500	347	349
St. Louis	7	9	0	.438	315	408

Central Division

	W	L	T	Pct.	Pts.	OP
Tampa Bay	9	7	0	.563	315	268
Detroit	8	8	0	.500	397	322
Green Bay	8	8	0	.500	324	361
Minnesota	7	9	0	.438	325	369
Chicago	6	10	0	.375	253	324

Western Division

	W	L	T	Pct.	Pts.	OP
San Francisco	13	3	0	.813	357	250
Atlanta	7	9	0	.438	426	355
Los Angeles	6	10	0	.375	303	351
New Orleans	4	12	0	.250	207	378

**Wild Card qualifiers for playoffs*

San Diego won AFC Western title over Denver on the basis of a better division record (6-2 to 5-3). Buffalo won a Wild Card playoff berth over Denver as the result of a 9-7 victory in head-to-head competition.

First round playoff: Buffalo 31, NEW YORK JETS 27
Divisional playoffs: San Diego 41, MIAMI 38 (OT); CINCINNATI 28, Buffalo 21
AFC championship: CINCINNATI 27, San Diego 7
First round playoff: New York Giants 27, PHILADELPHIA 21
Divisional playoffs: DALLAS 38, Tampa Bay 0; SAN FRANCISCO 38, New York Giants 24
NFC championship: SAN FRANCISCO 28, Dallas 27
Super Bowl XVI: San Francisco (NFC) 26, Cincinnati (AFC) 21, at Silverdome, Pontiac, Mich.

1980

American Conference

Eastern Division

	W	L	T	Pct.	Pts.	OP
Buffalo	11	5	0	.688	320	260
New England	10	6	0	.625	441	325
Miami	8	8	0	.500	266	305
Baltimore	7	9	0	.438	355	387
N.Y. Jets	4	12	0	.250	302	395

Central Division

	W	L	T	Pct.	Pts.	OP
Cleveland	11	5	0	.688	357	310
Houston*	11	5	0	.688	295	251
Pittsburgh	9	7	0	.563	352	313
Cincinnati	6	10	0	.375	244	312

Western Division

	W	L	T	Pct.	Pts.	OP
San Diego	11	5	0	.688	418	327
Oakland*	11	5	0	.688	364	306
Kansas City	8	8	0	.500	319	336
Denver	8	8	0	.500	310	323
Seattle	4	12	0	.250	291	408

National Conference

Eastern Division

	W	L	T	Pct.	Pts.	OP
Philadelphia	12	4	0	.750	384	222
Dallas*	12	4	0	.750	454	311
Washington	6	10	0	.375	261	293
St. Louis	5	11	0	.313	299	350
N.Y. Giants	4	12	0	.250	249	425

Central Division

	W	L	T	Pct.	Pts.	OP
Minnesota	9	7	0	.563	317	308
Detroit	9	7	0	.563	334	272
Chicago	7	9	0	.438	304	264
Tampa Bay	5	10	1	.344	271	341
Green Bay	5	10	1	.344	231	371

Western Division

	W	L	T	Pct.	Pts.	OP
Atlanta	12	4	0	.750	405	272
Los Angeles*	11	5	0	.688	424	289
San Francisco	6	10	0	.375	320	415
New Orleans	1	15	0	.063	291	487

**Wild Card qualifiers for playoffs*

Philadelphia won division title over Dallas on the basis of best net points in division games (plus 84 net points to plus 50). Minnesota won division title because of a better conference record than Detroit (8-4 to 9-5). Cleveland won division title because of a better conference record than Houston (8-4 to 7-5). San Diego won division title over Oakland on the basis of best net points in division games (plus 60 net points to plus 37).

First round playoff: OAKLAND 27, Houston 7
Divisional playoffs: SAN DIEGO 20, Buffalo 14; Oakland 14, CLEVELAND 12
AFC championship: Oakland 34, SAN DIEGO 27
First round playoff: DALLAS 34, Los Angeles 13
Divisional playoffs: PHILADELPHIA 31, Minnesota 16; Dallas 30, ATLANTA 27
NFC championship: PHILADELPHIA 20, Dallas 7
Super Bowl XV: Oakland (AFC) 27, Philadelphia (NFC) 10, at Louisiana Superdome, New Orleans, La.

1979

American Conference

Eastern Division

	W	L	T	Pct.	Pts.	OP
Miami	10	6	0	.625	341	257
New England	9	7	0	.563	411	326
N.Y. Jets	8	8	0	.500	337	383
Buffalo	7	9	0	.438	268	279
Baltimore	5	11	0	.313	271	351

Central Division

	W	L	T	Pct.	Pts.	OP
Pittsburgh	12	4	0	.750	416	262
Houston*	11	5	0	.688	362	331
Cleveland	9	7	0	.563	359	352
Cincinnati	4	12	0	.250	337	421

Western Division

	W	L	T	Pct.	Pts.	OP
San Diego	12	4	0	.750	411	246
Denver*	10	6	0	.625	289	262
Seattle	9	7	0	.563	378	372
Oakland	9	7	0	.563	365	337
Kansas City	7	9	0	.438	238	262

National Conference

Eastern Division

	W	L	T	Pct.	Pts.	OP
Dallas	11	5	0	.688	371	313
Philadelphia*	11	5	0	.688	339	282
Washington	10	6	0	.625	348	295
N.Y. Giants	6	10	0	.375	237	323
St. Louis	5	11	0	.313	307	358

Central Division

	W	L	T	Pct.	Pts.	OP
Tampa Bay	10	6	0	.625	273	237
Chicago*	10	6	0	.625	306	249
Minnesota	7	9	0	.438	259	337
Green Bay	5	11	0	.313	246	316
Detroit	2	14	0	.125	219	365

Western Division

	W	L	T	Pct.	Pts.	OP
Los Angeles	9	7	0	.563	323	309
New Orleans	8	8	0	.500	370	360
Atlanta	6	10	0	.375	300	388
San Francisco	2	14	0	.125	308	416

**Wild Card qualifiers for playoffs*

Dallas won division title because of a better conference record than Philadelphia (10-2 to 9-3). Tampa Bay won division title because of a better division record than Chicago (6-2 to 5-3). Chicago won a Wild Card berth over Washington on the basis of best net points in all games (plus 57 net points to plus 53).

First round playoff: HOUSTON 13, Denver 7
Divisional playoffs: Houston 17, SAN DIEGO 14; PITTSBURGH 34, Miami 14
AFC championship: PITTSBURGH 27, Houston 13
First round playoff: PHILADELPHIA 27, Chicago 17
Divisional playoffs: TAMPA BAY 24, Philadelphia 17; Los Angeles 21, DALLAS 19
NFC championship: Los Angeles 9, TAMPA BAY 0
Super Bowl XIV: Pittsburgh (AFC) 31, Los Angeles (NFC) 19, at Rose Bowl, Pasadena, Calif.

1978

American Conference

Eastern Division

	W	L	T	Pct.	Pts.	OP
New England	11	5	0	.688	358	286
Miami*	11	5	0	.688	372	254
N.Y. Jets	8	8	0	.500	359	364
Buffalo	5	11	0	.313	302	354
Baltimore	5	11	0	.313	239	421

Central Division

	W	L	T	Pct.	Pts.	OP
Pittsburgh	14	2	0	.875	356	195
Houston*	10	6	0	.625	283	298
Cleveland	8	8	0	.500	334	356
Cincinnati	4	12	0	.250	252	284

Western Division

	W	L	T	Pct.	Pts.	OP
Denver	10	6	0	.625	282	198
Oakland	9	7	0	.563	311	283
Seattle	9	7	0	.563	345	358
San Diego	9	7	0	.563	355	309
Kansas City	4	12	0	.250	243	327

National Conference

Eastern Division

	W	L	T	Pct.	Pts.	OP
Dallas	12	4	0	.750	384	208
Philadelphia*	9	7	0	.563	270	250
Washington	8	8	0	.500	273	283
St. Louis	6	10	0	.375	248	296
N.Y. Giants	6	10	0	.375	264	298

Central Division

	W	L	T	Pct.	Pts.	OP
Minnesota	8	7	1	.531	294	306
Green Bay	8	7	1	.531	249	269
Detroit	7	9	0	.438	290	300
Chicago	7	9	0	.438	253	274
Tampa Bay	5	11	0	.313	241	259

Western Division

	W	L	T	Pct.	Pts.	OP
Los Angeles	12	4	0	.750	316	245
Atlanta*	9	7	0	.563	240	290
New Orleans	7	9	0	.438	281	298
San Francisco	2	14	0	.125	219	350

**Wild Card qualifiers for playoffs*

New England won division title on the basis of a better division record than Miami (6-2 to 5-3). Minnesota won division title because of a better head-to-head record against Green Bay (1-0-1).

First round playoff: Houston 17, MIAMI 9
Divisional playoffs: Houston 31, NEW ENGLAND 14; PITTSBURGH 33, Denver 10
AFC championship: PITTSBURGH 34, Houston 5
First round playoff: ATLANTA 14, Philadelphia 13
Divisional playoffs: DALLAS 27, Atlanta 20; LOS ANGELES 34, Minnesota 10
NFC championship: Dallas 28, LOS ANGELES 0
Super Bowl XIII: Pittsburgh (AFC) 35, Dallas (NFC) 31, at Orange Bowl, Miami, Fla.

1977

American Conference

Eastern Division

	W	L	T	Pct.	Pts.	OP
Baltimore	10	4	0	.714	295	221
Miami	10	4	0	.714	313	197
New England	9	5	0	.643	278	217
N.Y. Jets	3	11	0	.214	191	300
Buffalo	3	11	0	.214	160	313

Central Division

	W	L	T	Pct.	Pts.	OP
Pittsburgh	9	5	0	.643	283	243
Houston	8	6	0	.571	299	230
Cincinnati	8	6	0	.571	238	235
Cleveland	6	8	0	.429	269	267

Western Division

	W	L	T	Pct.	Pts.	OP
Denver	12	2	0	.857	274	148
Oakland*	11	3	0	.786	351	230
San Diego	7	7	0	.500	222	205
Seattle	5	9	0	.357	282	373
Kansas City	2	12	0	.143	225	349

National Conference

Eastern Division

	W	L	T	Pct.	Pts.	OP
Dallas	12	2	0	.857	345	212
Washington	9	5	0	.643	196	189
St. Louis	7	7	0	.500	272	287
Philadelphia	5	9	0	.357	220	207
N.Y. Giants	5	9	0	.357	181	265

Central Division

	W	L	T	Pct.	Pts.	OP
Minnesota	9	5	0	.643	231	227
Chicago*	9	5	0	.643	255	253
Detroit	6	8	0	.429	183	252
Green Bay	4	10	0	.286	134	219
Tampa Bay	2	12	0	.143	103	223

Western Division

	W	L	T	Pct.	Pts.	OP
Los Angeles	10	4	0	.714	302	146
Atlanta	7	7	0	.500	179	129
San Francisco	5	9	0	.357	220	260
New Orleans	3	11	0	.214	232	336

**Wild Card qualifier for playoffs*

Baltimore won division title on the basis of a better conference record than Miami (9-3 to 8-4). Chicago won a Wild Card berth over Washington on the basis of best net points in conference games (plus 48 net points to plus 4).

Divisional playoffs: DENVER 34, Pittsburgh 21; Oakland 37, BALTIMORE 31 (OT)
AFC championship: DENVER 20, Oakland 17
Divisional playoffs: DALLAS 37, Chicago 7; Minnesota 14, LOS ANGELES 7
NFC championship: DALLAS 23, Minnesota 6
Super Bowl XII: Dallas (NFC) 27, Denver (AFC) 10, at Louisiana Superdome, New Orleans, La.

1976

American Conference

Eastern Division

	W	L	T	Pct.	Pts.	OP
Baltimore	11	3	0	.786	417	246
New England*	11	3	0	.786	376	236
Miami	6	8	0	.429	263	264
N.Y. Jets	3	11	0	.214	169	383
Buffalo	2	12	0	.143	245	363

Central Division

	W	L	T	Pct.	Pts.	OP
Pittsburgh	10	4	0	.714	342	138
Cincinnati	10	4	0	.714	335	210
Cleveland	9	5	0	.643	267	287
Houston	5	9	0	.357	222	273

Western Division

	W	L	T	Pct.	Pts.	OP
Oakland	13	1	0	.929	350	237
Denver	9	5	0	.643	315	206
San Diego	6	8	0	.429	248	285
Kansas City	5	9	0	.357	290	376
Tampa Bay	0	14	0	.000	125	412

National Conference

Eastern Division

	W	L	T	Pct.	Pts.	OP
Dallas	11	3	0	.786	296	194
Washington*	10	4	0	.714	291	217
St. Louis	10	4	0	.714	309	267
Philadelphia	4	10	0	.286	165	286
N.Y. Giants	3	11	0	.214	170	250

Central Division

	W	L	T	Pct.	Pts.	OP
Minnesota	11	2	1	.821	305	176
Chicago	7	7	0	.500	253	216
Detroit	6	8	0	.429	262	220
Green Bay	5	9	0	.357	218	299

Western Division

	W	L	T	Pct.	Pts.	OP
Los Angeles	10	3	1	.750	351	190
San Francisco	8	6	0	.571	270	190
Atlanta	4	10	0	.286	172	312
New Orleans	4	10	0	.286	253	346
Seattle	2	12	0	.143	229	429

**Wild Card qualifier for playoffs*

Baltimore won division title on the basis of a better division record than New England (7-1 to 6-2). Pittsburgh won division title because of a two-game sweep over Cincinnati. Washington won Wild Card berth over St. Louis because of a two-game sweep over Cardinals.

Divisional playoffs: OAKLAND 24, New England 21; Pittsburgh 40, BALTIMORE 14
AFC championship: OAKLAND 24, Pittsburgh 7
Divisional playoffs: MINNESOTA 35, Washington 20; Los Angeles 14, DALLAS 12
NFC championship: MINNESOTA 24, Los Angeles 13
Super Bowl XI: Oakland (AFC) 32, Minnesota (NFC) 14, at Rose Bowl, Pasadena, Calif.

1975

American Conference

Eastern Division

	W	L	T	Pct.	Pts.	OP
Baltimore	10	4	0	.714	395	269
Miami	10	4	0	.714	357	222
Buffalo	8	6	0	.571	420	355
New England	3	11	0	.214	258	358
N.Y. Jets	3	11	0	.214	258	433

Central Division

	W	L	T	Pct.	Pts.	OP
Pittsburgh	12	2	0	.857	373	162
Cincinnati*	11	3	0	.786	340	246
Houston	10	4	0	.714	293	226
Cleveland	3	11	0	.214	218	372

Western Division

	W	L	T	Pct.	Pts.	OP
Oakland	11	3	0	.786	375	255
Denver	6	8	0	.429	254	307
Kansas City	5	9	0	.357	282	341
San Diego	2	12	0	.143	189	345

National Conference

Eastern Division

	W	L	T	Pct.	Pts.	OP
St. Louis	11	3	0	.786	356	276
Dallas*	10	4	0	.714	350	268
Washington	8	6	0	.571	325	276
N.Y. Giants	5	9	0	.357	216	306
Philadelphia	4	10	0	.286	225	302

Central Division

	W	L	T	Pct.	Pts.	OP
Minnesota	12	2	0	.857	377	180
Detroit	7	7	0	.500	245	262
Chicago	4	10	0	.286	191	379
Green Bay	4	10	0	.286	226	285

Western Division

	W	L	T	Pct.	Pts.	OP
Los Angeles	12	2	0	.857	312	135
San Francisco	5	9	0	.357	255	286
Atlanta	4	10	0	.286	240	289
New Orleans	2	12	0	.143	165	360

**Wild Card qualifier for playoffs*

Baltimore won division title on the basis of a two-game sweep over Miami.

Divisional playoffs: PITTSBURGH 28, Baltimore 10; OAKLAND 31, Cincinnati 28
AFC championship: PITTSBURGH 16, Oakland 10
Divisional playoffs: LOS ANGELES 35, St. Louis 23; Dallas 17, MINNESOTA 14
NFC championship: Dallas 37, LOS ANGELES 7
Super Bowl X: Pittsburgh (AFC) 21, Dallas (NFC) 17, at Orange Bowl, Miami, Fla.

1974

American Conference

Eastern Division

	W	L	T	Pct.	Pts.	OP
Miami	11	3	0	.786	327	216
Buffalo*	9	5	0	.643	264	244
New England	7	7	0	.500	348	289
N.Y. Jets	7	7	0	.500	279	300
Baltimore	2	12	0	.143	190	329

Central Division

	W	L	T	Pct.	Pts.	OP
Pittsburgh	10	3	1	.750	305	189
Cincinnati	7	7	0	.500	283	259
Houston	7	7	0	.500	236	282
Cleveland	4	10	0	.286	251	344

Western Division

	W	L	T	Pct.	Pts.	OP
Oakland	12	2	0	.857	355	228
Denver	7	6	1	.536	302	294
Kansas City	5	9	0	.357	233	293
San Diego	5	9	0	.357	212	285

National Conference

Eastern Division

	W	L	T	Pct.	Pts.	OP
St. Louis	10	4	0	.714	285	218
Washington*	10	4	0	.714	320	196
Dallas	8	6	0	.571	297	235
Philadelphia	7	7	0	.500	242	217
N.Y. Giants	2	12	0	.143	195	299

Central Division

	W	L	T	Pct.	Pts.	OP
Minnesota	10	4	0	.714	310	195
Detroit	7	7	0	.500	256	270
Green Bay	6	8	0	.429	210	206
Chicago	4	10	0	.286	152	279

Western Division

	W	L	T	Pct.	Pts.	OP
Los Angeles	10	4	0	.714	263	181
San Francisco	6	8	0	.429	226	236
New Orleans	5	9	0	.357	166	263
Atlanta	3	11	0	.214	111	271

**Wild Card qualifier for playoffs*

St. Louis won division title because of a two-game sweep over Washington.

Divisional playoffs: OAKLAND 28, Miami 26; PITTSBURGH 32, Buffalo 14
AFC championship: Pittsburgh 24, OAKLAND 13
Divisional playoffs: MINNESOTA 30, St. Louis 14; LOS ANGELES 19, Washington 10
NFC championship: MINNESOTA 14, Los Angeles 10
Super Bowl IX: Pittsburgh (AFC) 16, Minnesota (NFC) 6, at Tulane Stadium, New Orleans, La.

1973

American Conference

Eastern Division

	W	L	T	Pct.	Pts.	OP
Miami	12	2	0	.857	343	150
Buffalo	9	5	0	.643	259	230
New England	5	9	0	.357	258	300
Baltimore	4	10	0	.286	226	341
N.Y. Jets	4	10	0	.286	240	306

Central Division

	W	L	T	Pct.	Pts.	OP
Cincinnati	10	4	0	.714	286	231
Pittsburgh*	10	4	0	.714	347	210
Cleveland	7	5	2	.571	234	255
Houston	1	13	0	.071	199	447

Western Division

	W	L	T	Pct.	Pts.	OP
Oakland	9	4	1	.679	292	175
Denver	7	5	2	.571	354	296
Kansas City	7	5	2	.571	231	192
San Diego	2	11	1	.179	188	386

National Conference

Eastern Division

	W	L	T	Pct.	Pts.	OP
Dallas	10	4	0	.714	382	203
Washington*	10	4	0	.714	325	198
Philadelphia	5	8	1	.393	310	393
St. Louis	4	9	1	.321	286	365
N.Y. Giants	2	11	1	.179	226	362

Central Division

	W	L	T	Pct.	Pts.	OP
Minnesota	12	2	0	.857	296	168
Detroit	6	7	1	.464	271	247
Green Bay	5	7	2	.429	202	259
Chicago	3	11	0	.214	195	334

Western Division

	W	L	T	Pct.	Pts.	OP
Los Angeles	12	2	0	.857	388	178
Atlanta	9	5	0	.643	318	224
New Orleans	5	9	0	.357	163	312
San Francisco	5	9	0	.357	262	319

**Wild Card qualifier for playoffs*

Cincinnati won division title on the basis of a better conference record than Pittsburgh (8-3 to 7-4). Dallas won division title on the basis of a better point differential vs. Washington (net 13 points).

Divisional playoffs: OAKLAND 33, Pittsburgh 14; MIAMI 34, Cincinnati 16
AFC championship: MIAMI 27, Oakland 10
Divisional playoffs: MINNESOTA 27, Washington 20; DALLAS 27, Los Angeles 16
NFC championship: Minnesota 27, DALLAS 10
Super Bowl VIII: Miami (AFC) 24, Minnesota (NFC) 7, at Rice Stadium, Houston, Tex.

1972

American Conference

Eastern Division

	W	L	T	Pct.	Pts.	OP
Miami	14	0	0	1.000	385	171
N.Y. Jets	7	7	0	.500	367	324
Baltimore	5	9	0	.357	235	252
Buffalo	4	9	1	.321	257	377
New England	3	11	0	.214	192	446

Central Division

	W	L	T	Pct.	Pts.	OP
Pittsburgh	11	3	0	.786	343	175
Cleveland*	10	4	0	.714	268	249
Cincinnati	8	6	0	.571	299	229
Houston	1	13	0	.071	164	380

Western Division

	W	L	T	Pct.	Pts.	OP
Oakland	10	3	1	.750	365	248
Kansas City	8	6	0	.571	287	254
Denver	5	9	0	.357	325	350
San Diego	4	9	1	.321	264	344

National Conference

Eastern Division

	W	L	T	Pct.	Pts.	OP
Washington	11	3	0	.786	336	218
Dallas*	10	4	0	.714	319	240
N.Y. Giants	8	6	0	.571	331	247
St. Louis	4	9	1	.321	193	303
Philadelphia	2	11	1	.179	145	352

Central Division

	W	L	T	Pct.	Pts.	OP
Green Bay	10	4	0	.714	304	226
Detroit	8	5	1	.607	339	290
Minnesota	7	7	0	.500	301	252
Chicago	4	9	1	.321	225	275

Western Division

	W	L	T	Pct.	Pts.	OP
San Francisco	8	5	1	.607	353	249
Atlanta	7	7	0	.500	269	274
Los Angeles	6	7	1	.464	291	286
New Orleans	2	11	1	.179	215	361

**Wild Card qualifier for playoffs*

Divisional playoffs: PITTSBURGH 13, Oakland 7; MIAMI 20, Cleveland 14
AFC championship: Miami 21, PITTSBURGH 17
Divisional playoffs: Dallas 30, SAN FRANCISCO 28; WASHINGTON 16, Green Bay 3
NFC championship: WASHINGTON 26, Dallas 3
Super Bowl VII: Miami (AFC) 14, Washington (NFC) 7, at Memorial Coliseum, Los Angeles, Calif.

1971

American Conference

Eastern Division

	W	L	T	Pct.	Pts.	OP
Miami	10	3	1	.769	315	174
Baltimore*	10	4	0	.714	313	140
New England	6	8	0	.429	238	325
N.Y. Jets	6	8	0	.429	212	299
Buffalo	1	13	0	.071	184	394

Central Division

	W	L	T	Pct.	Pts.	OP
Cleveland	9	5	0	.643	285	273
Pittsburgh	6	8	0	.429	246	292
Houston	4	9	1	.308	251	330
Cincinnati	4	10	0	.286	284	265

Western Division

	W	L	T	Pct.	Pts.	OP
Kansas City	10	3	1	.769	302	208
Oakland	8	4	2	.667	344	278
San Diego	6	8	0	.429	311	341
Denver	4	9	1	.308	203	275

National Conference

Eastern Division

	W	L	T	Pct.	Pts.	OP
Dallas	11	3	0	.786	406	222
Washington*	9	4	1	.692	276	190
Philadelphia	6	7	1	.462	221	302
St. Louis	4	9	1	.308	231	279
N.Y. Giants	4	10	0	.286	228	362

Central Division

	W	L	T	Pct.	Pts.	OP
Minnesota	11	3	0	.786	245	139
Detroit	7	6	1	.538	341	286
Chicago	6	8	0	.429	185	276
Green Bay	4	8	2	.333	274	298

Western Division

	W	L	T	Pct.	Pts.	OP
San Francisco	9	5	0	.643	300	216
Los Angeles	8	5	1	.615	313	260
Atlanta	7	6	1	.538	274	277
New Orleans	4	8	2	.333	266	347

**Wild Card qualifier for playoffs*

Divisional playoffs: Miami 27, KANSAS CITY 24 (OT); Baltimore 20, CLEVELAND 3
AFC championship: MIAMI 21, Baltimore 0
Divisional playoffs: Dallas 20, MINNESOTA 12; SAN FRANCISCO 24, Washington 20
NFC championship: DALLAS 14, San Francisco 3
Super Bowl VI: Dallas (NFC) 24, Miami (AFC) 3, at Tulane Stadium, New Orleans, La.

1970

American Conference

Eastern Division

	W	L	T	Pct.	Pts.	OP
Baltimore	11	2	1	.846	321	234
Miami*	10	4	0	.714	297	228
N.Y. Jets	4	10	0	.286	255	286
Buffalo	3	10	1	.231	204	337
Boston Patriots	2	12	0	.143	149	361

Central Division

	W	L	T	Pct.	Pts.	OP
Cincinnati	8	6	0	.571	312	255
Cleveland	7	7	0	.500	286	265
Pittsburgh	5	9	0	.357	210	272
Houston	3	10	1	.231	217	352

Western Division

	W	L	T	Pct.	Pts.	OP
Oakland	8	4	2	.667	300	293
Kansas City	7	5	2	.583	272	244
San Diego	5	6	3	.455	282	278
Denver	5	8	1	.385	253	264

National Conference

Eastern Division

	W	L	T	Pct.	Pts.	OP
Dallas	10	4	0	.714	299	221
N.Y. Giants	9	5	0	.643	301	270
St. Louis	8	5	1	.615	325	228
Washington	6	8	0	.429	297	314
Philadelphia	3	10	1	.231	241	332

Central Division

	W	L	T	Pct.	Pts.	OP
Minnesota	12	2	0	.857	335	143
Detroit*	10	4	0	.714	347	202
Chicago	6	8	0	.429	256	261
Green Bay	6	8	0	.429	196	293

Western Division

	W	L	T	Pct.	Pts.	OP
San Francisco	10	3	1	.769	352	267
Los Angeles	9	4	1	.692	325	202
Atlanta	4	8	2	.333	206	261
New Orleans	2	11	1	.154	172	347

**Wild Card qualifier for playoffs*

Divisional playoffs: BALTIMORE 17, Cincinnati 0; OAKLAND 21, Miami 14
AFC championship: BALTIMORE 27, Oakland 17
Divisional playoffs: DALLAS 5, Detroit 0; San Francisco 17, MINNESOTA 14
NFC championship: Dallas 17, SAN FRANCISCO 10
Super Bowl V: Baltimore (AFC) 16, Dallas (NFC) 13, at Orange Bowl, Miami, Fla.

1969 NFL

Eastern Conference

Capitol Division

	W	L	T	Pct.	Pts.	OP
Dallas	11	2	1	.846	369	223
Washington	7	5	2	.583	307	319
New Orleans	5	9	0	.357	311	393
Philadelphia	4	9	1	.308	279	377

Century Division

	W	L	T	Pct.	Pts.	OP
Cleveland	10	3	1	.769	351	300
N.Y. Giants	6	8	0	.429	264	298
St. Louis	4	9	1	.308	314	389
Pittsburgh	1	13	0	.071	218	404

Western Conference

Coastal Division

	W	L	T	Pct.	Pts.	OP
Los Angeles	11	3	0	.786	320	243
Baltimore	8	5	1	.615	279	268
Atlanta	6	8	0	.429	276	268
San Francisco	4	8	2	.333	277	319

Central Division

	W	L	T	Pct.	Pts.	OP
Minnesota	12	2	0	.857	379	133
Detroit	9	4	1	.692	259	188
Green Bay	8	6	0	.571	269	221
Chicago	1	13	0	.071	210	339

Conference championships: Cleveland 38, DALLAS 14; MINNESOTA 23, Los Angeles 20
NFL championship: MINNESOTA 27, Cleveland 7
Super Bowl IV: Kansas City (AFL) 23, Minnesota (NFL) 7, at Tulane Stadium, New Orleans, La.

1969 AFL

Eastern Division

	W	L	T	Pct.	Pts.	OP
N.Y. Jets	10	4	0	.714	353	269
Houston	6	6	2	.500	278	279
Boston Patriots	4	10	0	.286	266	316
Buffalo	4	10	0	.286	230	359
Miami	3	10	1	.231	233	332

Western Division

	W	L	T	Pct.	Pts.	OP
Oakland	12	1	1	.923	377	242
Kansas City	11	3	0	.786	359	177
San Diego	8	6	0	.571	288	276
Denver	5	8	1	.385	297	344
Cincinnati	4	9	1	.308	280	367

Divisional Playoffs: Kansas City 13, N.Y. JETS 6; OAKLAND 56, Houston 7
AFL championship: Kansas City 17, OAKLAND 7

1968 NFL

Eastern Conference

Capitol Division

	W	L	T	Pct.	Pts.	OP
Dallas	12	2	0	.857	431	186
N.Y. Giants	7	7	0	.500	294	325
Washington	5	9	0	.357	249	358
Philadelphia	2	12	0	.143	202	351

Century Division

	W	L	T	Pct.	Pts.	OP
Cleveland	10	4	0	.714	394	273
St. Louis	9	4	1	.692	325	289
New Orleans	4	9	1	.308	246	327
Pittsburgh	2	11	1	.154	244	397

Western Conference

Coastal Division

	W	L	T	Pct.	Pts.	OP
Baltimore	13	1	0	.929	402	144
Los Angeles	10	3	1	.769	312	200
San Francisco	7	6	1	.538	303	310
Atlanta	2	12	0	.143	170	389

Central Division

	W	L	T	Pct.	Pts.	OP
Minnesota	8	6	0	.571	282	242
Chicago	7	7	0	.500	250	333
Green Bay	6	7	1	.462	281	227
Detroit	4	8	2	.333	207	241

Conference championships: CLEVELAND 31, Dallas 20; BALTIMORE 24, Minnesota 14
NFL championship: Baltimore 34, CLEVELAND 0
Super Bowl III: N.Y. Jets (AFL) 16, Baltimore (NFL) 7, at Orange Bowl, Miami, Fla.

1968 AFL

Eastern Division

	W	L	T	Pct.	Pts.	OP
N.Y. Jets	11	3	0	.786	419	280
Houston	7	7	0	.500	303	248
Miami	5	8	1	.385	276	355
Boston Patriots	4	10	0	.286	229	406
Buffalo	1	12	1	.077	199	367

Western Division

	W	L	T	Pct.	Pts.	OP
Oakland	12	2	0	.857	453	233
Kansas City	12	2	0	.857	371	170
San Diego	9	5	0	.643	382	310
Denver	5	9	0	.357	255	404
Cincinnati	3	11	0	.214	215	329

Western Division playoff: OAKLAND 41, Kansas City 6
AFL championship: N.Y. JETS 27, Oakland 23

1967 NFL

Eastern Conference

Capitol Division

	W	L	T	Pct.	Pts.	OP
Dallas	9	5	0	.643	342	268
Philadelphia	6	7	1	.462	351	409
Washington	5	6	3	.455	347	353
New Orleans	3	11	0	.214	233	379

Century Division

	W	L	T	Pct.	Pts.	OP
Cleveland	9	5	0	.643	334	297
N.Y. Giants	7	7	0	.500	369	379
St. Louis	6	7	1	.462	333	356
Pittsburgh	4	9	1	.308	281	320

Western Conference

Coastal Division

	W	L	T	Pct.	Pts.	OP
Los Angeles	11	1	2	.917	398	196
Baltimore	11	1	2	.917	394	198
San Francisco	7	7	0	.500	273	337
Atlanta	1	12	1	.077	175	422

Central Division

	W	L	T	Pct.	Pts.	OP
Green Bay	9	4	1	.692	332	209
Chicago	7	6	1	.538	239	218
Detroit	5	7	2	.417	260	259
Minnesota	3	8	3	.273	233	294

Los Angeles won division title on the basis of advantage in points (58-34) in two games vs. Baltimore.

Conference championships: DALLAS 52, Cleveland 14; GREEN BAY 28, Los Angeles 7

NFL championship: GREEN BAY 21, Dallas 17

Super Bowl II: Green Bay (NFL) 33, Oakland (AFL) 14, at Orange Bowl, Miami, Fla.

1967 AFL

Eastern Division

	W	L	T	Pct.	Pts.	OP
Houston	9	4	1	.692	258	199
N.Y. Jets	8	5	1	.615	371	329
Buffalo	4	10	0	.286	237	285
Miami	4	10	0	.286	219	407
Boston Patriots	3	10	1	.231	280	389

Western Division

	W	L	T	Pct.	Pts.	OP
Oakland	13	1	0	.929	468	233
Kansas City	9	5	0	.643	408	254
San Diego	8	5	1	.615	360	352
Denver	3	11	0	.214	256	409

AFL championship: OAKLAND 40, Houston 7

1966 NFL

Eastern Conference

	W	L	T	Pct.	Pts.	OP
Dallas	10	3	1	.769	445	239
Cleveland	9	5	0	.643	403	259
Philadelphia	9	5	0	.643	326	340
St. Louis	8	5	1	.615	264	265
Washington	7	7	0	.500	351	355
Pittsburgh	5	8	1	.385	316	347
Atlanta	3	11	0	.214	204	437
N.Y. Giants	1	12	1	.077	263	501

Western Conference

	W	L	T	Pct.	Pts.	OP
Green Bay	12	2	0	.857	335	163
Baltimore	9	5	0	.643	314	226
Los Angeles	8	6	0	.571	289	212
San Francisco	6	6	2	.500	320	325
Chicago	5	7	2	.417	234	272
Detroit	4	9	1	.308	206	317
Minnesota	4	9	1	.308	292	304

NFL championship: Green Bay 34, DALLAS 27

Super Bowl I: Green Bay (NFL) 35, Kansas City (AFL) 10, at Memorial Coliseum, Los Angeles, Calif.

1966 AFL

Eastern Division

	W	L	T	Pct.	Pts.	OP
Buffalo	9	4	1	.692	358	255
Boston Patriots	8	4	2	.677	315	283
N.Y. Jets	6	6	2	.500	322	312
Houston	3	11	0	.214	335	396
Miami	3	11	0	.214	213	362

Western Division

	W	L	T	Pct.	Pts.	OP
Kansas City	11	2	1	.846	448	276
Oakland	8	5	1	.615	315	288
San Diego	7	6	1	.538	335	284
Denver	4	10	0	.286	196	381

AFL championship: Kansas City 31, BUFFALO 7

1965 NFL

Eastern Conference

	W	L	T	Pct.	Pts.	OP
Cleveland	11	3	0	.786	363	325
Dallas	7	7	0	.500	325	280
N.Y. Giants	7	7	0	.500	270	338
Washington	6	8	0	.429	257	301
Philadelphia	5	9	0	.357	363	359
St. Louis	5	9	0	.357	296	309
Pittsburgh	2	12	0	.143	202	397

Western Conference

	W	L	T	Pct.	Pts.	OP
Green Bay	10	3	1	.769	316	224
Baltimore	10	3	1	.769	389	284
Chicago	9	5	0	.643	409	275
San Francisco	7	6	1	.538	421	402
Minnesota	7	7	0	.500	383	403
Detroit	6	7	1	.462	257	295
Los Angeles	4	10	0	.286	269	328

Western Conference playoff: GREEN BAY 13, Baltimore 10 (OT)

NFL championship: GREEN BAY 23, Cleveland 12

1965 AFL

Eastern Division

	W	L	T	Pct.	Pts.	OP
Buffalo	10	3	1	.769	313	226
N.Y. Jets	5	8	1	.385	285	303
Boston Patriots	4	8	2	.333	244	302
Houston	4	10	0	.286	298	429

Western Division

	W	L	T	Pct.	Pts.	OP
San Diego	9	2	3	.818	340	227
Oakland	8	5	1	.615	298	239
Kansas City	7	5	2	.583	322	285
Denver	4	10	0	.286	303	392

AFL championship: Buffalo 23, SAN DIEGO 0

1964 NFL

Eastern Conference

	W	L	T	Pct.	Pts.	OP
Cleveland	10	3	1	.769	415	293
St. Louis	9	3	2	.750	357	331
Philadelphia	6	8	0	.429	312	313
Washington	6	8	0	.429	307	305
Dallas	5	8	1	.385	250	289
Pittsburgh	5	9	0	.357	253	315
N.Y. Giants	2	10	2	.167	241	399

Western Conference

	W	L	T	Pct.	Pts.	OP
Baltimore	12	2	0	.857	428	225
Green Bay	8	5	1	.615	342	245
Minnesota	8	5	1	.615	355	296
Detroit	7	5	2	.583	280	260
Los Angeles	5	7	2	.417	283	339
Chicago	5	9	0	.357	260	379
San Francisco	4	10	0	.286	236	330

NFL championship: CLEVELAND 27, Baltimore 0

1964 AFL

Eastern Division

	W	L	T	Pct.	Pts.	OP
Buffalo	12	2	0	.857	400	242
Boston Patriots	10	3	1	.769	365	297
N.Y. Jets	5	8	1	.385	278	315
Houston	4	10	0	.286	310	355

Western Division

	W	L	T	Pct.	Pts.	OP
San Diego	8	5	1	.615	341	300
Kansas City	7	7	0	.500	366	306
Oakland	5	7	2	.417	303	350
Denver	2	11	1	.154	240	438

AFL championship: BUFFALO 20, San Diego 7

1963 NFL

Eastern Conference

	W	L	T	Pct.	Pts.	OP
N.Y. Giants	11	3	0	.786	448	280
Cleveland	10	4	0	.714	343	262
St. Louis	9	5	0	.643	341	283
Pittsburgh	7	4	3	.636	321	295
Dallas	4	10	0	.286	305	378
Washington	3	11	0	.214	279	398
Philadelphia	2	10	2	.167	242	381

Western Conference

	W	L	T	Pct.	Pts.	OP
Chicago	11	1	2	.917	301	144
Green Bay	11	2	1	.846	369	206
Baltimore	8	6	0	.571	316	285
Detroit	5	8	1	.385	326	265
Minnesota	5	8	1	.385	309	390
Los Angeles	5	9	0	.357	210	350
San Francisco	2	12	0	.143	198	391

NFL championship: CHICAGO 14, N.Y. Giants 10

1963 AFL

Eastern Division

	W	L	T	Pct.	Pts.	OP
Boston Patriots	7	6	1	.538	327	257
Buffalo	7	6	1	.538	304	291
Houston	6	8	0	.429	302	372
N.Y. Jets	5	8	1	.385	249	399

Western Division

	W	L	T	Pct.	Pts.	OP
San Diego	11	3	0	.786	399	256
Oakland	10	4	0	.714	363	288
Kansas City	5	7	2	.417	347	263
Denver	2	11	1	.154	301	473

Eastern Division playoff: Boston 26, BUFFALO 8

AFL championship: SAN DIEGO 51, Boston 10

1962 NFL

Eastern Conference

	W	L	T	Pct.	Pts.	OP
N.Y. Giants	12	2	0	.857	398	283
Pittsburgh	9	5	0	.643	312	363
Cleveland	7	6	1	.538	291	257
Washington	5	7	2	.417	305	376
Dallas Cowboys	5	8	1	.385	398	402
St. Louis	4	9	1	.308	287	361
Philadelphia	3	10	1	.231	282	356

Western Conference

	W	L	T	Pct.	Pts.	OP
Green Bay	13	1	0	.929	415	148
Detroit	11	3	0	.786	315	177
Chicago	9	5	0	.643	321	287
Baltimore	7	7	0	.500	293	288
San Francisco	6	8	0	.429	282	331
Minnesota	2	11	1	.154	254	410
Los Angeles	1	12	1	.077	220	334

NFL championship: Green Bay 16, N.Y. GIANTS 7

1962 AFL

Eastern Division

	W	L	T	Pct.	Pts.	OP
Houston	11	3	0	.786	387	270
Boston Patriots	9	4	1	.692	346	295
Buffalo	7	6	1	.538	309	272
N.Y. Titans	5	9	0	.357	278	423

Western Division

	W	L	T	Pct.	Pts.	OP
Dallas Texans	11	3	0	.786	389	233
Denver	7	7	0	.500	353	334
San Diego	4	10	0	.286	314	392
Oakland	1	13	0	.071	213	370

AFL championship: Dallas Texans 20, HOUSTON 17 (OT)

1961 NFL

Eastern Conference

	W	L	T	Pct.	Pts.	OP
N.Y. Giants	10	3	1	.769	368	220
Philadelphia	10	4	0	.714	361	297
Cleveland	8	5	1	.615	319	270
St. Louis	7	7	0	.500	279	267
Pittsburgh	6	8	0	.429	295	287
Dallas Cowboys	4	9	1	.308	236	380
Washington	1	12	1	.077	174	392

Western Conference

	W	L	T	Pct.	Pts.	OP
Green Bay	11	3	0	.786	391	223
Detroit	8	5	1	.615	270	258
Baltimore	8	6	0	.571	302	307
Chicago	8	6	0	.571	326	302
San Francisco	7	6	1	.538	346	272
Los Angeles	4	10	0	.286	263	333
Minnesota	3	11	0	.214	285	407

NFL championship: GREEN BAY 37, N.Y. Giants 0

1961 AFL

Eastern Division

	W	L	T	Pct.	Pts.	OP
Houston	10	3	1	.769	513	242
Boston Patriots	9	4	1	.692	413	313
N.Y. Titans	7	7	0	.500	301	390
Buffalo	6	8	0	.429	294	342

Western Division

	W	L	T	Pct.	Pts.	OP
San Diego	12	2	0	.857	396	219
Dallas Texans	6	8	0	.429	334	343
Denver	3	11	0	.214	251	432
Oakland	2	12	0	.143	237	458

AFL championship: Houston 10, SAN DIEGO 3

1960 NFL

Eastern Conference

	W	L	T	Pct.	Pts.	OP
Philadelphia	10	2	0	.833	321	246
Cleveland	8	3	1	.727	362	217
N.Y. Giants	6	4	2	.600	271	261
St. Louis	6	5	1	.545	288	230
Pittsburgh	5	6	1	.455	240	275
Washington	1	9	2	.100	178	309

Western Conference

	W	L	T	Pct.	Pts.	OP
Green Bay	8	4	0	.667	332	209
Detroit	7	5	0	.583	239	212
San Francisco	7	5	0	.583	208	205
Baltimore	6	6	0	.500	288	234
Chicago	5	6	1	.455	194	299
L.A. Rams	4	7	1	.364	265	297
Dallas Cowboys	0	11	1	.000	177	369

NFL championship: PHILADELPHIA 17, Green Bay 13

1960 AFL

Eastern Conference

	W	L	T	Pct.	Pts.	OP
Houston	10	4	0	.714	379	285
N.Y. Titans	7	7	0	.500	382	399
Buffalo	5	8	1	.385	296	303
Boston	5	9	0	.357	286	349

Western Conference

	W	L	T	Pct.	Pts.	OP
L.A. Chargers	10	4	0	.714	373	336
Dallas Texans	8	6	0	.571	362	253
Oakland	6	8	0	.429	319	388
Denver	4	9	1	.308	309	393

AFL championship: HOUSTON 24, L.A. Chargers 16

1959

Eastern Conference

	W	L	T	Pct.	Pts.	OP
N.Y. Giants	10	2	0	.833	284	170
Cleveland	7	5	0	.583	270	214
Philadelphia	7	5	0	.583	268	278
Pittsburgh	6	5	1	.545	257	216
Washington	3	9	0	.250	185	350
Chi. Cardinals	2	10	0	.167	234	324

Western Conference

	W	L	T	Pct.	Pts.	OP
Baltimore	9	3	0	.750	374	251
Chi. Bears	8	4	0	.667	252	196
Green Bay	7	5	0	.583	248	246
San Francisco	7	5	0	.583	255	237
Detroit	3	8	1	.273	203	275
Los Angeles	2	10	0	.167	242	315

NFL championship: BALTIMORE 31, N.Y. Giants 16

1958

Eastern Conference

	W	L	T	Pct.	Pts.	OP
N.Y. Giants	9	3	0	.750	246	183
Cleveland	9	3	0	.750	302	217
Pittsburgh	7	4	1	.636	261	230
Washington	4	7	1	.364	214	268
Chi. Cardinals	2	9	1	.182	261	356
Philadelphia	2	9	1	.182	235	306

Western Conference

	W	L	T	Pct.	Pts.	OP
Baltimore	9	3	0	.750	381	203
Chi. Bears	8	4	0	.667	298	230
Los Angeles	8	4	0	.667	344	278
San Francisco	6	6	0	.500	257	324
Detroit	4	7	1	.364	261	276
Green Bay	1	10	1	.091	193	382

Eastern Conference playoff: N.Y. GIANTS 10, Cleveland 0
NFL championship: Baltimore 23, N.Y. GIANTS 17 (OT)

1957

Eastern Conference

	W	L	T	Pct.	Pts.	OP
Cleveland	9	2	1	.818	269	172
N.Y. Giants	7	5	0	.583	254	211
Pittsburgh	6	6	0	.500	161	178
Washington	5	6	1	.455	251	230
Philadelphia	4	8	0	.333	173	230
Chi. Cardinals	3	9	0	.250	200	299

Western Conference

	W	L	T	Pct.	Pts.	OP
Detroit	8	4	0	.667	251	231
San Francisco	8	4	0	.667	260	264
Baltimore	7	5	0	.583	303	235
Los Angeles	6	6	0	.500	307	278
Chi. Bears	5	7	0	.417	203	211
Green Bay	3	9	0	.250	218	311

Western Conference playoff: Detroit 31, SAN FRANCISCO 27
NFL championship: DETROIT 59, Cleveland 14

1956

Eastern Conference

	W	L	T	Pct.	Pts.	OP
N.Y. Giants	8	3	1	.727	264	197
Chi. Cardinals	7	5	0	.583	240	182
Washington	6	6	0	.500	183	225
Cleveland	5	7	0	.417	167	177
Pittsburgh	5	7	0	.417	217	250
Philadelphia	3	8	1	.273	143	215

Western Conference

	W	L	T	Pct.	Pts.	OP
Chi. Bears	9	2	1	.818	363	246
Detroit	9	3	0	.750	300	188
San Francisco	5	6	1	.455	233	284
Baltimore	5	7	0	.417	270	322
Green Bay	4	8	0	.333	264	342
Los Angeles	4	8	0	.333	291	307

NFL championship: N.Y. GIANTS 47, Chi. Bears 7

1955

Eastern Conference

	W	L	T	Pct.	Pts.	OP
Cleveland	9	2	1	.818	349	218
Washington	8	4	0	.667	246	222
N.Y. Giants	6	5	1	.545	267	223
Chi. Cardinals	4	7	1	.364	224	252
Philadelphia	4	7	1	.364	248	231
Pittsburgh	4	8	0	.333	195	285

Western Conference

	W	L	T	Pct.	Pts.	OP
Los Angeles	8	3	1	.727	260	231
Chi. Bears	8	4	0	.667	294	251
Green Bay	6	6	0	.500	258	276
Baltimore	5	6	1	.455	214	239
San Francisco	4	8	0	.333	216	298
Detroit	3	9	0	.250	230	275

NFL championship: Cleveland 38, LOS ANGELES 14

1954

Eastern Conference

	W	L	T	Pct.	Pts.	OP
Cleveland	9	3	0	.750	336	162
Philadelphia	7	4	1	.636	284	230
N.Y. Giants	7	5	0	.583	293	184
Pittsburgh	5	7	0	.417	219	263
Washington	3	9	0	.250	207	432
Chi. Cardinals	2	10	0	.167	183	347

Western Conference

	W	L	T	Pct.	Pts.	OP
Detroit	9	2	1	.818	337	189
Chi. Bears	8	4	0	.667	301	279
San Francisco	7	4	1	.636	313	251
Los Angeles	6	5	1	.545	314	285
Green Bay	4	8	0	.333	234	251
Baltimore	3	9	0	.250	131	279

NFL championship: CLEVELAND 56, Detroit 10

1953

Eastern Conference

	W	L	T	Pct.	Pts.	OP
Cleveland	11	1	0	.917	348	162
Philadelphia	7	4	1	.636	352	215
Washington	6	5	1	.545	208	215
Pittsburgh	6	6	0	.500	211	263
N.Y. Giants	3	9	0	.250	179	277
Chi. Cardinals	1	10	1	.091	190	337

Western Conference

	W	L	T	Pct.	Pts.	OP
Detroit	10	2	0	.833	271	205
San Francisco	9	3	0	.750	372	237
Los Angeles	8	3	1	.727	366	236
Chi. Bears	3	8	1	.273	218	262
Baltimore	3	9	0	.250	182	350
Green Bay	2	9	1	.182	200	338

NFL championship: DETROIT 17, Cleveland 16

1952

American Conference

	W	L	T	Pct.	Pts.	OP
Cleveland	8	4	0	.667	310	213
N.Y. Giants	7	5	0	.583	234	231
Philadelphia	7	5	0	.583	252	271
Pittsburgh	5	7	0	.417	300	273
Chi. Cardinals	4	8	0	.333	172	221
Washington	4	8	0	.333	240	287

National Conference

	W	L	T	Pct.	Pts.	OP
Detroit	9	3	0	.750	344	192
Los Angeles	9	3	0	.750	349	234
San Francisco	7	5	0	.583	285	221
Green Bay	6	6	0	.500	295	312
Chi. Bears	5	7	0	.417	245	326
Dallas Texans	1	11	0	.083	182	427

National Conference playoff: DETROIT 31, Los Angeles 21
NFL championship: Detroit 17, CLEVELAND 7

1951

American Conference

	W	L	T	Pct.	Pts.	OP
Cleveland	11	1	0	.917	331	152
N.Y. Giants	9	2	1	.818	254	161
Washington	5	7	0	.417	183	296
Pittsburgh	4	7	1	.364	183	235
Philadelphia	4	8	0	.333	234	264
Chi. Cardinals	3	9	0	.250	210	287

National Conference

	W	L	T	Pct.	Pts.	OP
Los Angeles	8	4	0	.667	392	261
Detroit	7	4	1	.636	336	259
San Francisco	7	4	1	.636	255	205
Chi. Bears	7	5	0	.583	286	282
Green Bay	3	9	0	.250	254	375
N.Y. Yanks	1	9	2	.100	241	382

NFL championship: LOS ANGELES 24, Cleveland 17

1950

American Conference

	W	L	T	Pct.	Pts.	OP
Cleveland	10	2	0	.833	310	144
N.Y. Giants	10	2	0	.833	268	150
Philadelphia	6	6	0	.500	254	141
Pittsburgh	6	6	0	.500	180	195
Chi. Cardinals	5	7	0	.417	233	287
Washington	3	9	0	.250	232	326

National Conference

	W	L	T	Pct.	Pts.	OP
Los Angeles	9	3	0	.750	466	309
Chi. Bears	9	3	0	.750	279	207
N.Y. Yanks	7	5	0	.583	366	367
Detroit	6	6	0	.500	321	285
Green Bay	3	9	0	.250	244	406
San Francisco	3	9	0	.250	213	300
Baltimore	1	11	0	.083	213	462

American Conference playoff: CLEVELAND 8, N.Y. Giants 3
National Conference playoff: LOS ANGELES 24, Chi. Bears 14
NFL championship: CLEVELAND 30, Los Angeles 28

1949

Eastern Division

	W	L	T	Pct.	Pts.	OP
Philadelphia	11	1	0	.917	364	134
Pittsburgh	6	5	1	.545	224	214
N.Y. Giants	6	6	0	.500	287	298
Washington	4	7	1	.364	268	339
N.Y. Bulldogs	1	10	1	.091	153	365

Western Division

	W	L	T	Pct.	Pts.	OP
Los Angeles	8	2	2	.800	360	239
Chi. Bears	9	3	0	.750	332	218
Chi. Cardinals	6	5	1	.545	360	301
Detroit	4	8	0	.333	237	259
Green Bay	2	10	0	.167	114	329

NFL championship: Philadelphia 14, LOS ANGELES 0

1948

Eastern Division

	W	L	T	Pct.	Pts.	OP
Philadelphia	9	2	1	.818	376	156
Washington	7	5	0	.583	291	287
N.Y. Giants	4	8	0	.333	297	388
Pittsburgh	4	8	0	.333	200	243
Boston	3	9	0	.250	174	372

Western Division

	W	L	T	Pct.	Pts.	OP
Chi. Cardinals	11	1	0	.917	395	226
Chi. Bears	10	2	0	.833	375	151
Los Angeles	6	5	1	.545	327	269
Green Bay	3	9	0	.250	154	290
Detroit	2	10	0	.167	200	407

NFL championship: PHILADELPHIA 7, Chi. Cardinals 0

1947

Eastern Division

	W	L	T	Pct.	Pts.	OP
Philadelphia	8	4	0	.667	308	242
Pittsburgh	8	4	0	.667	240	259
Boston	4	7	1	.364	168	256
Washington	4	8	0	.333	295	367
N.Y. Giants	2	8	2	.200	190	309

Western Division

	W	L	T	Pct.	Pts.	OP
Chi. Cardinals	9	3	0	.750	306	231
Chi. Bears	8	4	0	.667	363	241
Green Bay	6	5	1	.545	274	210
Los Angeles	6	6	0	.500	259	214
Detroit	3	9	0	.250	231	305

Eastern Division playoff: Philadelphia 21, PITTSBURGH 0
NFL championship: CHI. CARDINALS 28, Philadelphia 21

1946

Eastern Division

	W	L	T	Pct.	Pts.	OP
N.Y. Giants	7	3	1	.700	236	162
Philadelphia	6	5	0	.545	231	220
Washington	5	5	1	.500	171	191
Pittsburgh	5	5	1	.500	136	117
Boston	2	8	1	.200	189	273

Western Division

	W	L	T	Pct.	Pts.	OP
Chi. Bears	8	2	1	.800	289	193
Los Angeles	6	4	1	.600	277	257
Green Bay	6	5	0	.545	148	158
Chi. Cardinals	6	5	0	.545	260	198
Detroit	1	10	0	.091	142	310

NFL championship: Chi. Bears 24, N.Y. GIANTS 14

1945

Eastern Division

	W	L	T	Pct.	Pts.	OP
Washington	8	2	0	.800	209	121
Philadelphia	7	3	0	.700	272	133
N.Y. Giants	3	6	1	.333	179	198
Boston	3	6	1	.333	123	211
Pittsburgh	2	8	0	.200	79	220

Western Division

	W	L	T	Pct.	Pts.	OP
Cleveland	9	1	0	.900	244	136
Detroit	7	3	0	.700	195	194
Green Bay	6	4	0	.600	258	173
Chi. Bears	3	7	0	.300	192	235
Chi. Cardinals	1	9	0	.100	98	228

NFL championship: CLEVELAND 15, Washington 14

1944

Eastern Division

	W	L	T	Pct.	Pts.	OP
N.Y. Giants	8	1	1	.889	206	75
Philadelphia	7	1	2	.875	267	131
Washington	6	3	1	.667	169	180
Boston	2	8	0	.200	82	233
Brooklyn	0	10	0	.000	69	166

Western Division

	W	L	T	Pct.	Pts.	OP
Green Bay	8	2	0	.800	238	141
Chi. Bears	6	3	1	.667	258	172
Detroit	6	3	1	.667	216	151
Cleveland	4	6	0	.400	188	224
Card-Pitt	0	10	0	.000	108	328

NFL championship: Green Bay 14, N.Y. GIANTS 7

1943

Eastern Division

	W	L	T	Pct.	Pts.	OP
Washington	6	3	1	.667	229	137
N.Y. Giants	6	3	1	.667	197	170
Phil-Pitt	5	4	1	.556	225	230
Brooklyn	2	8	0	.200	65	234

Western Division

	W	L	T	Pct.	Pts.	OP
Chi. Bears	8	1	1	.889	303	157
Green Bay	7	2	1	.778	264	172
Detroit	3	6	1	.333	178	218
Chi. Cardinals	0	10	0	.000	95	238

Eastern Division playoff: Washington 28, N.Y. GIANTS 0
NFL championship: CHI. BEARS 41, Washington 21

1942

Eastern Division

	W	L	T	Pct.	Pts.	OP
Washington	10	1	0	.909	227	102
Pittsburgh	7	4	0	.636	167	119
N.Y. Giants	5	5	1	.500	155	139
Brooklyn	3	8	0	.273	100	168
Philadelphia	2	9	0	.182	134	239

Western Division

	W	L	T	Pct.	Pts.	OP
Chi. Bears	11	0	0	1.000	376	84
Green Bay	8	2	1	.800	300	215
Cleveland	5	6	0	.455	150	207
Chi. Cardinals	3	8	0	.273	98	209
Detroit	0	11	0	.000	38	263

NFL championship: WASHINGTON 14, Chi. Bears 6

1941

Eastern Division

	W	L	T	Pct.	Pts.	OP
N.Y. Giants	8	3	0	.727	238	114
Brooklyn	7	4	0	.636	158	127
Washington	6	5	0	.545	176	174
Philadelphia	2	8	1	.200	119	218
Pittsburgh	1	9	1	.100	103	276

Western Division

	W	L	T	Pct.	Pts.	OP
Chi. Bears	10	1	0	.909	396	147
Green Bay	10	1	0	.909	258	120
Detroit	4	6	1	.400	121	195
Chi. Cardinals	3	7	1	.300	127	197
Cleveland	2	9	0	.182	116	244

Western Division playoff: CHI. BEARS 33, Green Bay 14
NFL championship: CHI. BEARS 37, N.Y. Giants 9

1940

Eastern Division

	W	L	T	Pct.	Pts.	OP
Washington	9	2	0	.818	245	142
Brooklyn	8	3	0	.727	186	120
N.Y. Giants	6	4	1	.600	131	133
Pittsburgh	2	7	2	.222	60	178
Philadelphia	1	10	0	.091	111	211

Western Division

	W	L	T	Pct.	Pts.	OP
Chi. Bears	8	3	0	.727	238	152
Green Bay	6	4	1	.600	238	155
Detroit	5	5	1	.500	138	153
Cleveland	4	6	1	.400	171	191
Chi. Cardinals	2	7	2	.222	139	222

NFL championship: Chi. Bears 73, WASHINGTON 0

1939

Eastern Division

	W	L	T	Pct.	Pts.	OP
N.Y. Giants	9	1	1	.900	168	85
Washington	8	2	1	.800	242	94
Brooklyn	4	6	1	.400	108	219
Philadelphia	1	9	1	.100	105	200
Pittsburgh	1	9	1	.100	114	216

Western Division

	W	L	T	Pct.	Pts.	OP
Green Bay	9	2	0	.818	233	153
Chi. Bears	8	3	0	.727	298	157
Detroit	6	5	0	.545	145	150
Cleveland	5	5	1	.500	195	164
Chi. Cardinals	1	10	0	.091	84	254

NFL championship: GREEN BAY 27, N.Y. Giants 0

1938

Eastern Division

	W	L	T	Pct.	Pts.	OP
N.Y. Giants	8	2	1	.800	194	79
Washington	6	3	2	.667	148	154
Brooklyn	4	4	3	.500	131	161
Philadelphia	5	6	0	.455	154	164
Pittsburgh	2	9	0	.182	79	169

Western Division

	W	L	T	Pct.	Pts.	OP
Green Bay	8	3	0	.727	223	118
Detroit	7	4	0	.636	119	108
Chi. Bears	6	5	0	.545	194	148
Cleveland	4	7	0	.364	131	215
Chi. Cardinals	2	9	0	.182	111	168

NFL championship: N.Y. GIANTS 23, Green Bay 17

1937

Eastern Division

	W	L	T	Pct.	Pts.	OP
Washington	8	3	0	.727	195	120
N.Y. Giants	6	3	2	.667	128	109
Pittsburgh	4	7	0	.364	122	145
Brooklyn	3	7	1	.300	82	174
Philadelphia	2	8	1	.200	86	177

Western Division

	W	L	T	Pct.	Pts.	OP
Chi. Bears	9	1	1	.900	201	100
Green Bay	7	4	0	.636	220	122
Detroit	7	4	0	.636	180	105
Chi. Cardinals	5	5	1	.500	135	165
Cleveland	1	10	0	.091	75	207

NFL championship: Washington 28, CHI. BEARS 21

1936

Eastern Division

	W	L	T	Pct.	Pts.	OP
Boston	7	5	0	.583	149	110
Pittsburgh	6	6	0	.500	98	187
N.Y. Giants	5	6	1	.455	115	163
Brooklyn	3	8	1	.273	92	161
Philadelphia	1	11	0	.083	51	206

Western Division

	W	L	T	Pct.	Pts.	OP
Green Bay	10	1	1	.909	248	118
Chi. Bears	9	3	0	.750	222	94
Detroit	8	4	0	.667	235	102
Chi. Cardinals	3	8	1	.273	74	143

NFL championship: Green Bay 21, Boston 6, at Polo Grounds, N.Y.

1935

Eastern Division

	W	L	T	Pct.	Pts.	OP
N. Y. Giants	9	3	0	.750	180	96
Brooklyn	5	6	1	.455	90	141
Pittsburgh	4	8	0	.333	100	209
Boston	2	8	1	.200	65	123
Philadelphia	2	9	0	.182	60	179

Western Division

	W	L	T	Pct.	Pts.	OP
Detroit	7	3	2	.700	191	111
Green Bay	8	4	0	.667	181	96
Chi. Bears	6	4	2	.600	192	106
Chi. Cardinals	6	4	2	.600	99	97

NFL championship: DETROIT 26, N.Y. Giants 7
One game between Boston and Philadelphia was canceled.

1934

Eastern Division

	W	L	T	Pct.	Pts.	OP
N.Y. Giants	8	5	0	.615	147	107
Boston	6	6	0	.500	107	94
Brooklyn	4	7	0	.364	61	153
Philadelphia	4	7	0	.364	127	85
Pittsburgh	2	10	0	.167	51	206

Western Division

	W	L	T	Pct.	Pts.	OP
Chi. Bears	13	0	0	1.000	286	86
Detroit	10	3	0	.769	238	59
Green Bay	7	6	0	.538	156	112
Chi. Cardinals	5	6	0	.455	80	84
St. Louis	1	2	0	.333	27	61
Cincinnati	0	8	0	.000	10	243

NFL championship: N.Y. GIANTS 30, Chi. Bears 13

1933

Eastern Division

	W	L	T	Pct.	Pts.	OP
N.Y. Giants	11	3	0	.786	244	101
Brooklyn	5	4	1	.556	93	54
Boston	5	5	2	.500	103	97
Philadelphia	3	5	1	.375	77	158
Pittsburgh	3	6	2	.333	67	208

Western Division

	W	L	T	Pct.	Pts.	OP
Chi. Bears	10	2	1	.833	133	82
Portsmouth	6	5	0	.545	128	87
Green Bay	5	7	1	.417	170	107
Cincinnati	3	6	1	.333	38	110
Chi. Cardinals	1	9	1	.100	52	101

NFL championship: CHI. BEARS 23, N.Y. Giants 21

1932

	W	L	T	Pct.
Chicago Bears	7	1	6	.875
Green Bay Packers	10	3	1	.769
Portsmouth Spartans	6	2	4	.750
Boston Braves	4	4	2	.500
New York Giants	4	6	2	.400
Brooklyn Dodgers	3	9	0	.250
Chicago Cardinals	2	6	2	.250
Staten Island Stapletons	2	7	3	.222

Chicago Bears and Portsmouth finished regularly scheduled games tied for first place. Bears won playoff game, which counted in standings, 9-0.

1931

	W	L	T	Pct.
Green Bay Packers	12	2	0	.857
Portsmouth Spartans	11	3	0	.786
Chicago Bears	8	5	0	.615
Chicago Cardinals	5	4	0	.556
New York Giants	7	6	1	.538
Providence Steam Roller	4	4	3	.500
Staten Island Stapletons	4	6	1	.400
Cleveland Indians	2	8	0	.200
Brooklyn Dodgers	2	12	0	.143
Frankford Yellow Jackets	1	6	1	.143

1930

	W	L	T	Pct.
Green Bay Packers	10	3	1	.769
New York Giants	13	4	0	.765
Chicago Bears	9	4	1	.692
Brooklyn Dodgers	7	4	1	.636
Providence Steam Roller	6	4	1	.600
Staten Island Stapletons	5	5	2	.500
Chicago Cardinals	5	6	2	.455
Portsmouth Spartans	5	6	3	.455
Frankford Yellow Jackets	4	13	1	.222
Minneapolis Red Jackets	1	7	1	.125
Newark Tornadoes	1	10	1	.091

1929

	W	L	T	Pct.
Green Bay Packers	12	0	1	1.000
New York Giants	13	1	1	.929
Frankford Yellow Jackets	9	4	5	.692
Chicago Cardinals	6	6	1	.500
Boston Bulldogs	4	4	0	.500
Orange Tornadoes	3	4	4	.429
Staten Island Stapletons	3	4	3	.429
Providence Steam Roller	4	6	2	.400
Chicago Bears	4	9	2	.308
Buffalo Bisons	1	7	1	.125
Minneapolis Red Jackets	1	9	0	.100
Dayton Triangles	0	6	0	.000

1928

	W	L	T	Pct.
Providence Steam Roller	8	1	2	.889
Frankford Yellow Jackets	11	3	2	.786
Detroit Wolverines	7	2	1	.778
Green Bay Packers	6	4	3	.600
Chicago Bears	7	5	1	.583
New York Giants	4	7	2	.364
New York Yankees	4	8	1	.333
Pottsville Maroons	2	8	0	.200
Chicago Cardinals	1	5	0	.167
Dayton Triangles	0	7	0	.000

1927

	W	L	T	Pct.
New York Giants	11	1	1	.917
Green Bay Packers	7	2	1	.778
Chicago Bears	9	3	2	.750
Cleveland Bulldogs	8	4	1	.667
Providence Steam Roller	8	5	1	.615
New York Yankees	7	8	1	.467
Frankford Yellow Jackets	6	9	3	.400
Pottsville Maroons	5	8	0	.385
Chicago Cardinals	3	7	1	.300
Dayton Triangles	1	6	1	.143
Duluth Eskimos	1	8	0	.111
Buffalo Bisons	0	5	0	.000

1926

	W	L	T	Pct.
Frankford Yellow Jackets	14	1	1	.933
Chicago Bears	12	1	3	.923
Pottsville Maroons	10	2	1	.833
Kansas City Cowboys	8	3	0	.727
Green Bay Packers	7	3	3	.700
Los Angeles Buccaneers	6	3	1	.667
New York Giants	8	4	1	.667
Duluth Eskimos	6	5	3	.545
Buffalo Rangers	4	4	2	.500
Chicago Cardinals	5	6	1	.455
Providence Steam Roller	5	7	1	.417
Detroit Panthers	4	6	2	.400
Hartford Blues	3	7	0	.300
Brooklyn Lions	3	8	0	.273
Milwaukee Badgers	2	7	0	.222
Akron Pros	1	4	3	.200
Dayton Triangles	1	4	1	.200
Racine Tornadoes	1	4	0	.200
Columbus Tigers	1	6	0	.143
Canton Bulldogs	1	9	3	.100
Hammond Pros	0	4	0	.000
Louisville Colonels	0	4	0	.000

1925

	W	L	T	Pct.
Chicago Cardinals	11	2	1	.846
Pottsville Maroons	10	2	0	.833
Detroit Panthers	8	2	2	.800
New York Giants	8	4	0	.667
Akron Indians	4	2	2	.667
Frankford Yellow Jackets	13	7	0	.650
Chicago Bears	9	5	3	.643
Rock Island Independents	5	3	3	.625
Green Bay Packers	8	5	0	.615
Providence Steam Roller	6	5	1	.545
Canton Bulldogs	4	4	0	.500
Cleveland Bulldogs	5	8	1	.385
Kansas City Cowboys	2	5	1	.286
Hammond Pros	1	4	0	.250
Buffalo Bisons	1	6	2	.143
Duluth Kelleys	0	3	0	.000
Rochester Jeffersons	0	6	1	.000
Milwaukee Badgers	0	6	0	.000
Dayton Triangles	0	7	1	.000
Columbus Tigers	0	9	0	.000

1924

	W	L	T	Pct.
Cleveland Bulldogs	7	1	1	.875
Chicago Bears	6	1	4	.857
Frankford Yellow Jackets	11	2	1	.846
Duluth Kelleys	5	1	0	.833
Rock Island Independents	6	2	2	.750
Green Bay Packers	7	4	0	.636
Racine Legion	4	3	3	.571
Chicago Cardinals	5	4	1	.556
Buffalo Bisons	6	5	0	.545
Columbus Tigers	4	4	0	.500
Hammond Pros	2	2	1	.500
Milwaukee Badgers	5	8	0	.385
Akron Indians	2	6	0	.333
Dayton Triangles	2	6	0	.333
Kansas City Blues	2	7	0	.222
Kenosha Maroons	0	5	1	.000
Minneapolis Marines	0	6	0	.000
Rochester Jeffersons	0	7	0	.000

1923

	W	L	T	Pct.
Canton Bulldogs	11	0	1	1.000
Chicago Bears	9	2	1	.818
Green Bay Packers	7	2	1	.778
Milwaukee Badgers	7	2	3	.778
Cleveland Indians	3	1	3	.750
Chicago Cardinals	8	4	0	.667
Duluth Kelleys	4	3	0	.571
Columbus Tigers	5	4	1	.556
Buffalo All-Americans	4	4	3	.500
Racine Legion	4	4	2	.500
Toledo Maroons	2	3	2	.400
Rock Island Independents	2	3	3	.400
Minneapolis Marines	2	5	2	.286
St. Louis All-Stars	1	4	2	.200
Hammond Pros	1	5	1	.167
Dayton Triangles	1	6	1	.143
Akron Indians	1	6	0	.143
Oorang Indians	1	10	0	.091
Rochester Jeffersons	0	2	0	.000
Louisville Brecks	0	3	0	.000

1922

	W	L	T	Pct.
Canton Bulldogs	10	0	2	1.000
Chicago Bears	9	3	0	.750
Chicago Cardinals	8	3	0	.727
Toledo Maroons	5	2	2	.714
Rock Island Independents	4	2	1	.667
Racine Legion	6	4	1	.600
Dayton Triangles	4	3	1	.571
Green Bay Packers	4	3	3	.571
Buffalo All-Americans	5	4	1	.556
Akron Pros	3	5	2	.375
Milwaukee Badgers	2	4	3	.333
Oorang Indians	2	6	0	.250
Minneapolis Marines	1	3	0	.250
Louisville Brecks	1	3	0	.250
Evansville Crimson Giants	0	3	0	.000
Rochester Jeffersons	0	4	1	.000
Hammond Pros	0	5	1	.000
Columbus Panhandles	0	7	0	.000

1921

	W	L	T	Pct.
Chicago Staleys	9	1	1	.900
Buffalo All-Americans	9	1	2	.900
Akron Pros	8	3	1	.727
Canton Bulldogs	5	2	3	.714
Rock Island Independents	4	2	1	.667
Evansville Crimson Giants	3	2	0	.600
Green Bay Packers	3	2	1	.600
Dayton Triangles	4	4	1	.500
Chicago Cardinals	3	3	2	.500
Rochester Jeffersons	2	3	0	.400
Cleveland Indians	3	5	0	.375
Washington Senators	1	2	0	.333
Cincinnati Celts	1	3	0	.250
Hammond Pros	1	3	1	.250
Minneapolis Marines	1	3	1	.250
Detroit Heralds	1	5	1	.167
Columbus Panhandles	1	8	0	.111
Tonawanda Kardex	0	1	0	.000
Muncie Flyers	0	2	0	.000
Louisville Brecks	0	2	0	.000
New York Giants	0	2	0	.000

1920

	W	L	T	Pct.
Akron Pros	8	0	3	1.000
Decatur Staleys	10	1	2	.909
Buffalo All-Americans	9	1	1	.900
Chicago Cardinals	6	2	2	.750
Rock Island Independents	6	2	2	.750
Dayton Triangles	5	2	2	.714
Rochester Jeffersons	6	3	2	.667
Canton Bulldogs	7	4	2	.636
Detroit Heralds	2	3	3	.400
Cleveland Tigers	2	4	2	.333
Chicago Tigers	2	5	1	.286
Hammond Pros	2	5	0	.286
Columbus Panhandles	2	6	2	.250
Muncie Flyers	0	1	0	.000

ALL-TIME TEAM VS. TEAM RESULTS

RS = REGULAR SEASON
PS = POSTSEASON

ATLANTA vs. BUFFALO
RS: Falcons lead series, 3-2
1973—Bills, 17-6 (A)
1977—Bills, 3-0 (B)
1980—Falcons, 30-14 (B)
1983—Falcons, 31-14 (A)
1989—Falcons, 30-28 (A)
(RS Pts.—Falcons 97, Bills 76)

ATLANTA vs. CHICAGO
RS: Falcons lead series, 9-7
1966—Bears, 23-6 (C)
1967—Bears, 23-14 (A)
1968—Falcons, 16-13 (C)
1969—Falcons, 48-31 (A)
1970—Bears, 23-14 (A)
1972—Falcons, 37-21 (C)
1973—Falcons, 46-6 (A)
1974—Falcons, 13-10 (A)
1976—Falcons, 10-0 (C)
1977—Falcons, 16-10 (C)
1978—Bears, 13-7 (C)
1980—Falcons, 28-17 (A)
1983—Falcons, 20-17 (C)
1985—Bears, 36-0 (C)
1986—Bears, 13-10 (A)
1990—Bears, 30-24 (C)
(RS Pts.—Falcons 309, Bears 286)

ATLANTA vs. CINCINNATI
RS: Bengals lead series, 5-2
1971—Falcons, 9-6 (C)
1975—Bengals, 21-14 (A)
1978—Bengals, 37-7 (C)
1981—Bengals, 30-28 (A)
1984—Bengals, 35-14 (C)
1987—Bengals, 16-10 (A)
1990—Falcons, 38-17 (A)
(RS Pts.—Bengals 162, Falcons 120)

ATLANTA vs. CLEVELAND
RS: Browns lead series, 8-1
1966—Browns, 49-17 (A)
1968—Browns, 30-7 (C)
1971—Falcons, 31-14 (C)
1976—Browns, 20-17 (A)
1978—Browns, 24-16 (A)
1981—Browns, 28-17 (C)
1984—Browns, 23-7 (A)
1987—Browns, 38-3 (C)
1990—Browns, 13-10 (C)
(RS Pts.—Browns 239, Falcons 125)

ATLANTA vs. DALLAS
RS: Cowboys lead series, 7-5
PS: Cowboys lead series, 2-0
1966—Cowboys, 47-14 (A)
1967—Cowboys, 37-7 (D)
1969—Cowboys, 24-17 (A)
1970—Cowboys, 13-0 (D)
1974—Cowboys, 24-0 (A)
1976—Falcons, 17-10 (A)
1978—*Cowboys, 27-20 (D)
1980—*Cowboys, 30-27 (A)
1985—Cowboys, 24-10 (D)
1986—Falcons, 37-35 (D)
1987—Falcons, 21-10 (D)
1988—Cowboys, 26-20 (D)
1989—Falcons 27-21 (A)
1990—Falcons, 26-7 (A)
(RS Pts.—Cowboys 278, Falcons 196)
(PS Pts.—Cowboys 57, Falcons 47)
**NFC Divisional Playoff*

ATLANTA vs. DENVER
RS: Broncos lead series, 4-3
1970—Broncos, 24-10 (D)
1972—Falcons, 23-20 (A)
1975—Falcons, 35-21 (A)
1979—Broncos, 20-17 (A) OT
1982—Falcons, 34-27 (D)
1985—Broncos, 44-28 (A)
1988—Broncos, 30-14 (D)
(RS Pts.—Broncos 186, Falcons 161)

ATLANTA vs. DETROIT
RS: Lions lead series, 16-5
1966—Lions, 28-10 (D)
1967—Lions, 24-3 (D)
1968—Lions, 24-7 (A)
1969—Lions, 27-21 (D)
1971—Lions, 41-38 (D)
1972—Lions, 26-23 (A)
1973—Lions, 31-6 (D)
1975—Lions, 17-14 (A)
1976—Lions, 24-10 (D)
1977—Falcons, 17-6 (A)
1978—Falcons, 14-0 (A)
1979—Lions, 24-23 (D)
1980—Falcons, 43-28 (A)
1983—Falcons, 30-14 (D)
1984—Lions, 27-24 (A) OT
1985—Lions, 28-27 (A)
1986—Falcons, 20-6 (D)
1987—Lions, 30-13 (A)
1988—Lions, 31-17 (D)
1989—Lions, 31-24 (A)
1990—Lions, 21-14 (D)
(RS Pts.—Lions 488, Falcons 398)

ATLANTA vs. GREEN BAY
RS: Packers lead series, 9-7
1966—Packers, 56-3 (Mil)
1967—Packers, 23-0 (Mil)
1968—Packers, 38-7 (A)
1969—Packers, 28-10 (GB)
1970—Packers, 27-24 (GB)
1971—Falcons, 28-21 (A)
1972—Falcons, 10-9 (Mil)
1974—Falcons, 10-3 (A)
1975—Packers, 22-13 (GB)
1976—Packers, 24-20 (A)
1979—Falcons, 25-7 (A)
1981—Falcons, 31-17 (GB)
1982—Packers, 38-7 (A)
1983—Falcons, 47-41 (A) OT
1988—Falcons, 20-0 (A)
1989—Packers, 23-21 (Mil)
(RS Pts.—Packers 377, Falcons 276)

ATLANTA vs. HOUSTON
RS: Falcons lead series, 5-2
1972—Falcons, 20-10 (A)
1976—Oilers, 20-14 (H)
1978—Falcons, 20-14 (A)
1981—Falcons, 31-27 (H)
1984—Falcons, 42-10 (A)
1987—Oilers, 37-33 (H)
1990—Falcons, 47-27 (A)
(RS Pts.—Falcons 207, Oilers 145)

ATLANTA vs. *INDIANAPOLIS
RS: Colts lead series, 10-0
1966—Colts, 19-7 (A)
1967—Colts, 38-31 (B)
Colts, 49-7 (A)
1968—Colts, 28-20 (A)
Colts, 44-0 (B)
1969—Colts, 21-14 (A)
Colts, 13-6 (B)
1974—Colts, 17-7 (A)
1986—Colts, 28-23 (A)
1989—Colts, 13-9 (I)
(RS Pts.—Colts 270, Falcons 124)
**Franchise in Baltimore prior to 1984*

ATLANTA vs. KANSAS CITY
RS: Chiefs lead series, 2-0
1972—Chiefs, 17-14 (A)
1985—Chiefs, 38-10 (KC)
(RS Pts.—Chiefs 55, Falcons 24)

ATLANTA vs. *L.A. RAIDERS
RS: Raiders lead series, 4-2
1971—Falcons, 24-13 (A)
1975—Raiders, 37-34 (O) OT
1979—Raiders, 50-19 (O)
1982—Raiders, 38-14 (A)
1985—Raiders, 34-24 (A)
1988—Falcons, 12-6 (LA)
(RS Pts.—Raiders 178, Falcons 127)
**Franchise in Oakland prior to 1982*

ATLANTA vs. L.A. RAMS
RS: Rams lead series, 35-11-2
1966—Rams, 19-14 (A)
1967—Rams, 31-3 (A)
Rams, 20-3 (LA)
1968—Rams, 27-14 (LA)
Rams, 17-10 (A)
1969—Rams, 17-7 (LA)
Rams, 38-6 (A)
1970—Tie, 10-10 (LA)
Rams, 17-7 (A)
1971—Tie, 20-20 (LA)
Rams, 24-16 (A)
1972—Falcons, 31-3 (A)
Rams, 20-7 (LA)
1973—Rams, 31-0 (LA)
Falcons, 15-13 (A)
1974—Rams, 21-0 (LA)
Rams, 30-7 (A)
1975—Rams, 22-7 (LA)
Rams, 16-7 (A)
1976—Rams, 30-14 (A)
Rams, 59-0 (LA)
1977—Falcons, 17-6 (A)
Rams, 23-7 (LA)
1978—Rams, 10-0 (LA)
Falcons, 15-7 (A)
1979—Rams, 20-14 (LA)
Rams, 34-13 (A)
1980—Falcons, 13-10 (A)
Rams, 20-17 (LA) OT
1981—Rams, 37-35 (A)
Rams, 21-16 (LA)
1982—Falcons, 34-17 (A)
1983—Rams, 27-21 (LA)
Rams, 36-13 (A)
1984—Falcons, 30-28 (LA)
Rams, 24-10 (A)
1985—Rams, 17-6 (LA)
Falcons, 30-14 (A)
1986—Falcons, 26-14 (A)
Rams, 14-7 (LA)
1987—Falcons, 24-20 (A)
Rams, 33-0 (LA)
1988—Rams, 33-0 (A)
Rams, 22-7 (LA)
1989—Rams, 31-21 (A)
Rams, 26-14 (LA)
1990—Rams, 44-24 (LA)
Falcons, 20-13 (A)
(RS Pts.—Rams 1,086, Falcons 632)

ATLANTA vs. MIAMI
RS: Dolphins lead series, 4-1
1970—Dolphins, 20-7 (A)
1974—Dolphins, 42-7 (M)
1980—Dolphins, 20-17 (A)
1983—Dolphins, 31-24 (M)
1986—Falcons, 20-14 (M)
(RS Pts.—Dolphins 127, Falcons 75)

ATLANTA vs. MINNESOTA
RS: Vikings lead series, 10-6
PS: Vikings lead series, 1-0
1966—Falcons, 20-13 (M)
1967—Falcons, 21-20 (A)
1968—Vikings, 47-7 (M)
1969—Falcons, 10-3 (A)
1970—Vikings, 37-7 (A)
1971—Vikings, 24-7 (M)
1973—Falcons, 20-14 (A)
1974—Vikings, 23-10 (M)
1975—Vikings, 38-0 (M)
1977—Vikings, 14-7 (A)
1980—Vikings, 24-23 (M)
1981—Falcons, 31-30 (A)
1982—*Vikings, 30-24 (M)
1984—Vikings, 27-20 (M)
1985—Falcons, 14-13 (A)
1987—Vikings, 24-13 (M)
1989—Vikings, 43-17 (M)
(RS Pts.—Vikings 394, Falcons 227)
(PS Pts.—Vikings 30, Falcons 24)
**NFC First Round Playoff*

ATLANTA vs. NEW ENGLAND
RS: Series tied, 3-3
1972—Patriots, 21-20 (NE)
1977—Patriots, 16-10 (A)
1980—Falcons, 37-21 (NE)
1983—Falcons, 24-13 (A)
1986—Patriots, 25-17 (NE)
1989—Falcons, 16-15 (A)
(RS Pts.—Falcons 124, Patriots 111)

ATLANTA vs. NEW ORLEANS
RS: Falcons lead series, 25-18
1967—Saints, 27-24 (NO)
1969—Falcons, 45-17 (A)
1970—Falcons, 14-3 (NO)
Falcons, 32-14 (A)
1971—Falcons, 28-6 (A)
Falcons, 24-20 (NO)
1972—Falcons, 21-14 (NO)
Falcons, 36-20 (A)
1973—Falcons, 62-7 (NO)
Falcons, 14-10 (A)
1974—Saints, 14-13 (NO)
Saints, 13-3 (A)
1975—Falcons, 14-7 (A)
Saints, 23-7 (NO)
1976—Saints, 30-0 (NO)
Falcons, 23-20 (A)
1977—Saints, 21-20 (NO)
Falcons, 35-7 (A)
1978—Falcons, 20-17 (NO)
Falcons, 20-17 (A)
1979—Falcons, 40-34 (NO) OT
Saints, 37-6 (A)
1980—Falcons, 41-14 (NO)
Falcons, 31-13 (A)
1981—Falcons, 27-0 (A)
Falcons, 41-10 (NO)
1982—Falcons, 35-0 (A)
Saints, 35-6 (NO)
1983—Saints, 19-17 (A)
Saints, 27-10 (NO)
1984—Falcons, 36-28 (NO)
Saints, 17-13 (A)
1985—Falcons, 31-24 (A)
Falcons, 16-10 (NO)
1986—Falcons, 31-10 (NO)
Saints, 14-9 (A)
1987—Saints, 38-0 (A)
1988—Saints, 29-21 (A)
Saints, 10-9 (NO)
1989—Saints, 20-13 (NO)
Saints, 26-17 (A)
1990—Falcons, 28-27 (A)
Saints, 10-7 (NO)
(RS Pts.—Falcons 940, Saints 759)

ATLANTA vs. N.Y. GIANTS
RS: Series tied, 6-6
1966—Falcons, 27-16 (NY)
1968—Falcons, 24-21 (A)
1971—Giants, 21-17 (A)
1974—Falcons, 14-7 (New Haven)
1977—Falcons, 17-3 (A)
1978—Falcons, 23-20 (A)
1979—Giants, 24-3 (NY)
1981—Giants, 27-24 (A) OT
1982—Falcons, 16-14 (NY)
1983—Giants, 16-13 (A) OT
1984—Giants, 19-7 (A)
1988—Giants, 23-16 (A)
(RS Pts.—Giants 211, Falcons 201)

ATLANTA vs. N.Y. JETS
RS: Jets lead series, 3-2
1973—Falcons, 28-20 (NY)
1980—Jets, 14-7 (A)
1983—Falcons, 27-21 (NY)
1986—Jets, 28-14 (A)
1989—Jets, 27-7 (NY)
(RS Pts.—Jets 110, Falcons 83)

ATLANTA vs. PHILADELPHIA
RS: Eagles lead series, 8-6-1
PS: Falcons lead series, 1-0
1966—Eagles, 23-10 (P)
1967—Eagles, 38-7 (A)
1969—Falcons, 27-3 (P)
1970—Tie, 13-13 (P)
1973—Falcons, 44-27 (P)
1976—Eagles, 14-13 (A)
1978—*Falcons, 14-13 (A)
1979—Falcons, 14-10 (P)
1980—Falcons, 20-17 (P)
1981—Eagles, 16-13 (P)
1983—Eagles, 28-24 (A)
1984—Falcons, 26-10 (A)
1985—Eagles, 23-17 (P) OT
1986—Eagles, 16-0 (A)
1988—Falcons, 27-24 (P)
1990—Eagles, 24-23 (A)
(RS Pts.—Eagles 286, Falcons 278)
(PS Pts.—Falcons 14, Eagles 13)
**NFC First Round Playoff*

ATLANTA vs. *PHOENIX
RS: Cardinals lead series, 9-4
1966—Falcons, 16-10 (A)
1968—Cardinals, 17-12 (StL)
1971—Cardinals, 26-9 (A)
1973—Cardinals, 32-10 (A)
1975—Cardinals, 23-20 (StL)
1978—Cardinals, 42-21 (StL)
1980—Falcons, 33-27 (StL) OT
1981—Falcons, 41-20 (A)
1982—Cardinals, 23-20 (A)
1986—Falcons, 33-13 (A)
1987—Cardinals, 34-21 (A)
1989—Cardinals, 34-20 (P)
1990—Cardinals, 24-13 (A)
(RS Pts.—Cardinals 325, Falcons 269)
**Franchise in St. Louis prior to 1988*

ATLANTA vs. PITTSBURGH
RS: Steelers lead series, 8-1
1966—Steelers, 57-33 (A)
1968—Steelers, 41-21 (A)
1970—Falcons, 27-16 (A)
1974—Steelers, 24-17 (P)
1978—Steelers, 31-7 (P)
1981—Steelers, 34-20 (A)
1984—Steelers, 35-10 (P)
1987—Steelers, 28-12 (A)
1990—Steelers, 21-9 (P)
(RS Pts.—Steelers 287, Falcons 156)

ATLANTA vs. SAN DIEGO
RS: Falcons lead series, 2-1
1973—Falcons, 41-0 (SD)
1979—Falcons, 28-26 (SD)
1988—Chargers, 10-7 (A)
(RS Pts.—Falcons 76, Chargers 36)

ATLANTA vs. SAN FRANCISCO
RS: 49ers lead series, 29-18-1
1966—49ers, 44-7 (A)
1967—49ers, 38-7 (SF)
49ers, 34-28 (A)
1968—49ers, 28-13 (SF)
49ers, 14-12 (A)
1969—Falcons, 24-12 (A)
Falcons, 21-7 (SF)
1970—Falcons, 21-20 (A)
49ers, 24-20 (SF)
1971—Falcons, 20-17 (A)
49ers, 24-3 (SF)
1972—49ers, 49-14 (A)
49ers, 20-0 (SF)
1973—49ers, 13-9 (A)

Falcons, 17-3 (SF)
1974—49ers, 16-10 (A)
49ers, 27-0 (SF)
1975—Falcons, 17-3 (SF)
Falcons, 31-9 (A)
1976—49ers, 15-0 (SF)
Falcons, 21-16 (A)
1977—Falcons, 7-0 (SF)
49ers, 10-3 (A)
1978—Falcons, 20-17 (SF)
Falcons, 21-10 (A)
1979—49ers, 20-15 (SF)
Falcons, 31-21 (A)
1980—Falcons, 20-17 (SF)
Falcons, 35-10 (A)
1981—Falcons, 34-17 (A)
49ers, 17-14 (SF)
1982—Falcons, 17-7 (SF)
1983—49ers, 24-20 (SF)
Falcons, 28-24 (A)
1984—49ers, 14-5 (SF)
49ers, 35-17 (A)
1985—49ers, 35-16 (SF)
49ers, 38-17 (A)
1986—Tie, 10-10 (A) OT
49ers, 20-0 (SF)
1987—49ers, 25-17 (A)
49ers, 35-7 (SF)
1988—Falcons, 34-17 (SF)
49ers, 13-3 (A)
1989—49ers, 45-3 (SF)
49ers, 23-10 (A)
1990—49ers, 19-13 (SF)
49ers, 45-35 (A)
(RS Pts.—49ers 1,001, Falcons 747)

ATLANTA vs. SEATTLE
RS: Seahawks lead series, 4-0
1976—Seahawks, 30-13 (S)
1979—Seahawks, 31-28 (A)
1985—Seahawks, 30-26 (S)
1988—Seahawks, 31-20 (A)
(RS Pts.—Seahawks 122, Falcons 87)

ATLANTA vs. TAMPA BAY
RS: Buccaneers lead series, 5-4
1977—Falcons, 17-0 (TB)
1978—Buccaneers, 14-9 (TB)
1979—Falcons, 17-14 (A)
1981—Buccaneers, 24-23 (TB)
1984—Buccaneers, 23-6 (TB)
1986—Falcons, 23-20 (TB) OT
1987—Buccaneers, 48-10 (TB)
1988—Falcons, 17-10 (A)
1990—Buccaneers, 23-17 (TB)
(RS Pts.—Buccaneers 176, Falcons 139)

ATLANTA vs. WASHINGTON
RS: Redskins lead series, 10-3-1
1966—Redskins, 33-20 (W)
1967—Tie, 20-20 (A)
1969—Redskins, 27-20 (W)
1972—Redskins, 24-13 (W)
1975—Redskins, 30-27 (A)
1977—Redskins, 10-6 (W)
1978—Falcons, 20-17 (A)
1979—Redskins, 16-7 (A)
1980—Falcons, 10-6 (A)
1983—Redskins, 37-21 (W)
1984—Redskins, 27-14 (W)
1985—Redskins, 44-10 (A)
1987—Falcons, 21-20 (A)
1989—Redskins, 31-30 (A)
(RS Pts.—Redskins 342, Falcons 239)

BUFFALO vs. ATLANTA
RS: Falcons lead series, 3-2;
See Atlanta vs. Buffalo

BUFFALO vs. CHICAGO
RS: Bears lead series, 3-1
1970—Bears, 31-13 (C)
1974—Bills, 16-6 (B)
1979—Bears, 7-0 (B)
1988—Bears, 24-3 (C)
(RS Pts.—Bears 68, Bills 32)

BUFFALO vs. CINCINNATI
RS: Bengals lead series, 9-6
PS: Bengals lead series, 2-0
1968—Bengals, 34-23 (C)
1969—Bills, 16-13 (B)
1970—Bengals, 43-14 (B)
1973—Bengals, 16-13 (B)
1975—Bengals, 33-24 (C)
1978—Bills, 5-0 (B)
1979—Bills, 51-24 (B)
1980—Bills, 14-0 (C)
1981—Bengals, 27-24 (C) OT
*Bengals, 28-21 (C)
1983—Bills, 10-6 (C)
1984—Bengals, 52-21 (C)
1985—Bengals, 23-17 (B)
1986—Bengals, 36-33 (C) OT
1988—Bengals, 35-21 (C)
**Bengals, 21-10 (C)
1989—Bills, 24-7 (B)
(RS Pts.—Bengals 349, Bills 310)
(PS Pts.—Bengals 49, Bills 31)
**AFC Divisional Playoff*
***AFC Championship*

BUFFALO vs. CLEVELAND
RS: Browns lead series, 7-3
PS: Browns lead series, 1-0
1972—Browns, 27-10 (C)
1974—Bills, 15-10 (C)
1977—Browns, 27-16 (B)
1978—Browns, 41-20 (C)
1981—Bills, 22-13 (B)
1984—Browns, 13-10 (B)
1985—Browns, 17-7 (C)
1986—Browns, 21-17 (B)
1987—Browns, 27-21 (C)
1989—*Browns, 34-30 (C)
1990—Bills, 42-0 (C)
(RS Pts.—Browns 196, Bills 180)
(PS Pts.—Browns 34, Bills 30)
**AFC Divisional Playoff*

BUFFALO vs. DALLAS
RS: Cowboys lead series, 3-1
1971—Cowboys, 49-37 (B)
1976—Cowboys, 17-10 (D)
1981—Cowboys, 27-14 (D)
1984—Bills, 14-3 (B)
(RS Pts.—Cowboys 96, Bills 75)

BUFFALO vs. DENVER
RS: Bills lead series, 15-10-1
1960—Broncos, 27-21 (B)
Tie, 38-38 (D)
1961—Broncos, 22-10 (B)
Bills, 23-10 (D)
1962—Broncos, 23-20 (B)
Bills, 45-38 (D)
1963—Bills, 30-28 (D)
Bills, 27-17 (B)
1964—Bills, 30-13 (B)
Bills, 30-19 (D)
1965—Bills, 30-15 (D)
Bills, 31-13 (B)
1966—Bills, 38-21 (B)
1967—Bills, 17-16 (D)
Broncos, 21-20 (B)
1968—Broncos, 34-32 (D)
1969—Bills, 41-28 (B)
1970—Broncos, 25-10 (B)
1975—Bills, 38-14 (B)
1977—Broncos, 26-6 (D)
1979—Broncos, 19-16 (B)
1981—Bills, 9-7 (B)
1984—Broncos, 37-7 (B)
1987—Bills, 21-14 (B)
1989—Broncos, 28-14 (B)
1990—Bills, 29-28 (B)
(RS Pts.—Bills 633, Broncos 581)

BUFFALO vs. DETROIT
RS: Series tied, 1-1-1
1972—Tie, 21-21 (B)
1976—Lions, 27-14 (D)
1979—Bills, 20-17 (D)
(RS Pts.—Lions 65, Bills 55)

BUFFALO vs. GREEN BAY
RS: Bills lead series, 3-1
1974—Bills, 27-7 (GB)
1979—Bills, 19-12 (B)
1982—Packers, 33-21 (Mil)
1988—Bills, 28-0 (B)
(RS Pts.—Bills 95, Packers 52)

BUFFALO vs. HOUSTON
RS: Oilers lead series, 19-11
PS: Bills lead series, 1-0
1960—Bills, 25-24 (B)
Oilers, 31-23 (H)
1961—Bills, 22-12 (H)
Oilers, 28-16 (B)
1962—Oilers, 28-23 (B)
Oilers, 17-14 (H)
1963—Oilers, 31-20 (B)
Oilers, 28-14 (H)
1964—Bills, 48-17 (H)
Bills, 24-10 (B)
1965—Oilers, 19-17 (B)
Bills, 29-18 (H)
1966—Bills, 27-20 (B)
Bills, 42-20 (H)
1967—Oilers, 20-3 (B)
Oilers, 10-3 (H)
1968—Oilers, 30-7 (B)
Oilers, 35-6 (H)
1969—Oilers, 17-3 (B)
Oilers, 28-14 (H)
1971—Oilers, 20-14 (B)
1974—Oilers, 21-9 (B)
1976—Oilers, 13-3 (B)
1978—Oilers, 17-10 (H)
1983—Bills, 30-13 (B)
1985—Bills, 20-0 (B)
1986—Oilers, 16-7 (H)
1987—Bills, 34-30 (B)
1988—*Bills, 17-10 (B)
1989—Bills, 47-41 (H) OT
1990—Oilers, 27-24 (H)
(RS Pts.—Oilers 641, Bills 578)
(PS Pts.—Bills 17, Oilers 10)
**AFC Divisional Playoff*

BUFFALO vs. *INDIANAPOLIS
RS: Bills lead series, 21-19-1
1970—Tie, 17-17 (Balt)
Colts, 20-14 (Buff)
1971—Colts, 43-0 (Buff)
Colts, 24-0 (Balt)
1972—Colts, 17-0 (Buff)
Colts, 35-7 (Balt)
1973—Bills, 31-13 (Buff)
Bills, 24-17 (Balt)
1974—Bills, 27-14 (Balt)
Bills, 6-0 (Buff)
1975—Bills, 38-31 (Balt)
Colts, 42-35 (Buff)
1976—Colts, 31-13 (Buff)
Colts, 58-20 (Balt)
1977—Colts, 17-14 (Balt)
Colts, 31-13 (Buff)
1978—Bills, 24-17 (Buff)
Bills, 21-14 (Balt)
1979—Bills, 31-13 (Balt)
Colts, 14-13 (Buff)
1980—Colts, 17-12 (Buff)
Colts, 28-24 (Balt)
1981—Bills, 35-3 (Balt)
Bills, 23-17 (Buff)
1982—Bills, 20-0 (Buff)
1983—Bills, 28-23 (Buff)
Bills, 30-7 (Balt)
1984—Colts, 31-17 (I)
Bills, 21-15 (Buff)
1985—Colts, 49-17 (I)
Bills, 21-9 (Buff)
1986—Bills, 24-13 (Buff)
Colts, 24-14 (I)
1987—Colts, 47-6 (Buff)
Bills, 27-3 (I)
1988—Bills, 34-23 (Buff)
Colts, 17-14 (I)
1989—Colts, 37-14 (I)
Bills, 30-7 (Buff)
1990—Bills, 26-10 (Buff)
Bills, 31-7 (I)
(RS Pts.—Colts 855, Bills 816)
**Franchise in Baltimore prior to 1984*

BUFFALO vs. *KANSAS CITY
RS: Bills lead series, 15-11-1
PS: Chiefs lead series, 1-0
1960—Texans, 45-28 (B)
Texans, 24-7 (D)
1961—Bills, 27-24 (B)
Bills, 30-20 (D)
1962—Texans, 41-21 (D)
Bills, 23-14 (B)
1963—Tie, 27-27 (B)
Bills, 35-26 (KC)
1964—Bills, 34-17 (B)
Bills, 35-22 (KC)
1965—Bills, 23-7 (KC)
Bills, 34-25 (B)
1966—Chiefs, 42-20 (B)
Bills, 29-14 (KC)*
**Chiefs, 31-7 (B)
1967—Chiefs, 23-13 (KC)
1968—Chiefs, 18-7 (B)
1969—Chiefs, 29-7 (B)
Chiefs, 22-19 (KC)
1971—Chiefs, 22-9 (KC)
1973—Bills, 23-14 (B)
1976—Bills, 50-17 (B)
1978—Bills, 28-13 (B)
Chiefs, 14-10 (KC)
1982—Bills, 14-9 (B)
1983—Bills, 14-9 (KC)
1986—Chiefs, 20-17 (B)
Bills, 17-14 (KC)
(RS Pts.—Bills 596, Chiefs 577)
(PS Pts.—Chiefs 31, Bills 7)
**Franchise in Dallas prior to 1963 and known as Texans*
***AFL Championship*

BUFFALO vs. *L.A. RAIDERS
RS: Series tied, 13-13
PS: Bills lead series, 1-0
1960—Bills, 38-9 (B)
Raiders, 20-7 (O)
1961—Raiders, 31-22 (B)
Bills, 26-21 (O)
1962—Bills, 14-6 (B)
Bills, 10-6 (O)
1963—Raiders, 35-17 (O)
Bills, 12-0 (B)
1964—Bills, 23-20 (B)
Raiders, 16-13 (O)
1965—Bills, 17-12 (B)
Bills, 17-14 (O)
1966—Bills, 31-10 (O)
1967—Raiders, 24-20 (B)
Raiders, 28-21 (O)
1968—Raiders, 48-6 (B)
Raiders, 13-10 (O)
1969—Raiders, 50-21 (O)
1972—Raiders, 28-16 (O)
1974—Bills, 21-20 (B)
1977—Raiders, 34-13 (O)
1980—Bills, 24-7 (B)
1983—Raiders, 27-24 (B)
1987—Raiders, 34-21 (LA)
1988—Bills, 37-21 (B)
1990—Bills, 38-24 (B)
**Bills, 51-3 (B)
(RS Pts.—Raiders 558, Bills 519)
(PS Pts.—Bills 51, Raiders 3)
**Franchise in Oakland prior to 1982*
***AFC Championship*

BUFFALO vs. L.A. RAMS
RS: Rams lead series, 3-2
1970—Rams, 19-0 (B)
1974—Rams, 19-14 (LA)
1980—Bills, 10-7 (B) OT
1983—Rams, 41-17 (LA)
1989—Bills, 23-20 (B)
(RS Pts.—Rams 106, Bills 64)

BUFFALO vs. MIAMI
RS: Dolphins lead series, 35-14-1
PS: Bills lead series, 1-0
1966—Bills, 58-24 (B)
Bills, 29-0 (M)
1967—Bills, 35-13 (B)
Dolphins, 17-14 (M)
1968—Tie, 14-14 (M)
Dolphins, 21-17 (B)
1969—Dolphins, 24-6 (M)
Bills, 28-3 (B)
1970—Dolphins, 33-14 (B)
Dolphins, 45-7 (M)
1971—Dolphins, 29-14 (B)
Dolphins, 34-0 (M)
1972—Dolphins, 24-23 (M)
Dolphins, 30-16 (B)
1973—Dolphins, 27-6 (M)
Dolphins, 17-0 (B)
1974—Dolphins, 24-16 (B)
Dolphins, 35-28 (M)
1975—Dolphins, 35-30 (B)
Dolphins, 31-21 (M)
1976—Dolphins, 30-21 (B)
Dolphins, 45-27 (M)
1977—Dolphins, 13-0 (B)
Dolphins, 31-14 (M)
1978—Dolphins, 31-24 (M)
Dolphins, 25-24 (B)
1979—Dolphins, 9-7 (B)
Dolphins, 17-7 (M)
1980—Bills, 17-7 (B)
Dolphins, 17-14 (M)
1981—Bills, 31-21 (B)
Dolphins, 16-6 (M)
1982—Dolphins, 9-7 (B)
Dolphins, 27-10 (M)
1983—Dolphins, 12-0 (B)
Bills, 38-35 (M) OT
1984—Dolphins, 21-17 (B)
Dolphins, 38-7 (M)
1985—Dolphins, 23-14 (B)
Dolphins, 28-0 (M)
1986—Dolphins, 27-14 (M)
Dolphins, 34-24 (B)
1987—Bills, 34-31 (M) OT
Bills, 27-0 (B)
1988—Bills, 9-6 (B)
Bills, 31-6 (M)
1989—Bills, 27-24 (M)
Bills, 31-17 (B)
1990—Dolphins, 30-7 (M)
Bills, 24-14 (B)
*Bills, 44-34 (B)
(RS Pts.—Dolphins 1,124, Bills 889)
(PS Pts.—Bills 44, Dolphins 34)
**AFC Divisional Playoff*

BUFFALO vs. MINNESOTA
RS: Vikings lead series, 4-2
1971—Vikings, 19-0 (M)
1975—Vikings, 35-13 (B)
1979—Vikings, 10-3 (M)
1982—Bills, 23-22 (B)
1985—Vikings, 27-20 (B)
1988—Bills, 13-10 (B)
(RS Pts.—Vikings 123, Bills 72)

BUFFALO vs. *NEW ENGLAND
RS: Patriots lead series, 32-28-1
PS: Patriots lead series, 1-0
1960—Bills, 13-0 (Bos)
Bills, 38-14 (Buff)
1961—Patriots, 23-21 (Buff)
Patriots, 52-21 (Bos)
1962—Tie, 28-28 (Buff)
Patriots, 21-10 (Bos)
1963—Bills, 28-21 (Buff)
Patriots, 17-7 (Bos)
**Patriots, 26-8 (Buff)
1964—Patriots, 36-28 (Buff)
Bills, 24-14 (Bos)

1965—Bills, 24-7 (Buff)
Bills, 23-7 (Bos)
1966—Patriots, 20-10 (Buff)
Patriots, 14-3 (Bos)
1967—Patriots, 23-0 (Buff)
Bills, 44-16 (Bos)
1968—Patriots, 16-7 (Buff)
Patriots, 23-6 (Bos)
1969—Bills, 23-16 (Buff)
Patriots, 35-21 (Bos)
1970—Bills, 45-10 (Bos)
Patriots, 14-10 (Buff)
1971—Patriots, 38-33 (NE)
Bills, 27-20 (Buff)
1972—Bills, 38-14 (Buff)
Bills, 27-24 (NE)
1973—Bills, 31-13 (NE)
Bills, 37-13 (Buff)
1974—Bills, 30-28 (Buff)
Bills, 29-28 (NE)
1975—Bills, 45-31 (Buff)
Bills, 34-14 (NE)
1976—Patriots, 26-22 (Buff)
Patriots, 20-10 (NE)
1977—Bills, 24-14 (NE)
Patriots, 20-7 (Buff)
1978—Patriots, 14-10 (Buff)
Patriots, 26-24 (NE)
1979—Patriots, 26-6 (Buff)
Bills, 16-13 (NE) OT
1980—Bills, 31-13 (Buff)
Patriots, 24-2 (NE)
1981—Bills, 20-17 (Buff)
Bills, 19-10 (NE)
1982—Patriots, 30-19 (NE)
1983—Patriots, 31-0 (Buff)
Patriots, 21-7 (NE)
1984—Patriots, 21-17 (Buff)
Patriots, 38-10 (NE)
1985—Patriots, 17-14 (Buff)
Patriots, 14-3 (NE)
1986—Patriots, 23-3 (Buff)
Patriots, 22-19 (NE)
1987—Patriots, 14-7 (NE)
Patriots, 13-7 (Buff)
1988—Bills, 16-14 (NE)
Bills, 23-20 (Buff)
1989—Bills, 31-10 (Buff)
Patriots, 33-24 (NE)
1990—Bills, 27-10 (NE)
Bills, 14-0 (Buff)
(RS Pts.—Patriots 1,204, Bills 1,197)
(PS Pts.—Patriots 26, Bills 8)
Franchise in Boston prior to 1971
**Division Playoff*

BUFFALO vs. NEW ORLEANS
RS: Series tied, 2-2
1973—Saints, 13-0 (NO)
1980—Bills, 35-26 (NO)
1983—Bills, 27-21 (B)
1989—Saints, 22-19 (B)
(RS Pts.—Saints 82, Bills 81)

BUFFALO vs. N.Y. GIANTS
RS: Bills lead series, 3-2
PS: Giants lead series, 1-0
1970—Giants, 20-6 (NY)
1975—Giants, 17-14 (B)
1978—Bills, 41-17 (B)
1987—Bills, 6-3 (B) OT
1990—Bills, 17-13 (NY)
*Giants, 20-19 (Tampa)
(RS Pts.—Bills 84, Giants 70)
(PS Pts.—Giants 20, Bills 19)
Super Bowl XXV

BUFFALO vs. *N.Y. JETS
RS: Bills lead series, 32-28
PS: Bills lead series, 1-0
1960—Titans, 27-3 (NY)
Titans, 17-13 (B)
1961—Bills, 41-31 (B)
Titans, 21-14 (NY)
1962—Titans, 17-6 (B)
Bills, 20-3 (NY)
1963—Bills, 45-14 (B)
Bills, 19-10 (NY)
1964—Bills, 34-24 (B)
Bills, 20-7 (NY)
1965—Bills, 33-21 (B)
Jets, 14-12 (NY)
1966—Bills, 33-23 (NY)
Bills, 14-3 (B)
1967—Bills, 20-17 (B)
Jets, 20-10 (NY)
1968—Bills, 37-35 (B)
Jets, 25-21 (NY)
1969—Jets, 33-19 (B)
Jets, 16-6 (NY)
1970—Bills, 34-31 (B)
Bills, 10-6 (NY)
1971—Jets, 28-17 (NY)
Jets, 20-7 (B)
1972—Jets, 41-24 (B)
Jets, 41-3 (NY)
1973—Bills, 9-7 (B)
Bills, 34-14 (NY)
1974—Bills, 16-12 (B)
Jets, 20-10 (NY)
1975—Bills, 42-14 (B)
Bills, 24-23 (NY)
1976—Jets, 17-14 (NY)
Jets, 19-14 (B)
1977—Jets, 24-19 (B)
Bills, 14-10 (NY)
1978—Jets, 21-20 (B)
Jets, 45-14 (NY)
1979—Bills, 46-31 (B)
Bills, 14-12 (NY)
1980—Bills, 20-10 (B)
Bills, 31-24 (NY)
1981—Bills, 31-0 (B)
Jets, 33-14 (NY)
**Bills, 31-27 (NY)
1983—Jets, 34-10 (B)
Bills, 24-17 (NY)
1984—Jets, 28-26 (B)
Jets, 21-17 (NY)
1985—Jets, 42-3 (NY)
Jets, 27-7 (B)
1986—Jets, 28-24 (B)
Jets, 14-13 (NY)
1987—Jets, 31-28 (B)
Bills, 17-14 (NY)
1988—Bills, 37-14 (NY)
Bills, 9-6 (B) OT
1989—Bills, 34-3 (B)
Bills, 37-0 (NY)
1990—Bills, 30-7 (NY)
Bills, 30-27 (B)
(RS Pts.—Bills 1,247, Jets 1,194)
(PS Pts.—Bills 31, Jets 27)
Jets known as Titans prior to 1963
**AFC First Round Playoff*

BUFFALO vs. PHILADELPHIA
RS: Eagles lead series, 4-2
1973—Bills, 27-26 (B)
1981—Eagles, 20-14 (B)
1984—Eagles, 27-17 (B)
1985—Eagles, 21-17 (P)
1987—Eagles, 17-7 (P)
1990—Bills, 30-23 (B)
(RS Pts.—Eagles 134, Bills 112)

BUFFALO vs. *PHOENIX
RS: Series tied, 3-3
1971—Cardinals, 28-23 (B)
1975—Bills, 32-14 (StL)
1981—Cardinals, 24-0 (StL)
1984—Cardinals, 37-7 (StL)
1986—Bills, 17-10 (B)
1990—Bills, 45-14 (B)
(RS Pts.—Cardinals 127, Bills 124)
Franchise in St. Louis prior to 1988

BUFFALO vs. PITTSBURGH
RS: Series tied, 5-5
PS: Steelers lead series, 1-0
1970—Steelers, 23-10 (P)
1972—Steelers, 38-21 (B)
1974—*Steelers, 32-14 (P)
1975—Bills, 30-21 (P)
1978—Steelers, 28-17 (B)
1979—Steelers, 28-0 (P)
1980—Bills, 28-13 (B)
1982—Bills, 13-0 (B)
1985—Steelers, 30-24 (P)
1986—Bills, 16-12 (B)
1988—Bills, 36-28 (B)
(RS Pts.—Steelers 221, Bills 195)
(PS Pts.—Steelers 32, Bills 14)
AFC Divisional Playoff

BUFFALO vs. *SAN DIEGO
RS: Chargers lead series, 16-7-2
PS: Bills lead series, 2-1
1960—Chargers, 24-10 (B)
Bills, 32-3 (LA)
1961—Chargers, 19-11 (B)
Chargers, 28-10 (SD)
1962—Bills, 35-10 (B)
Bills, 40-20 (SD)
1963—Chargers, 14-10 (SD)
Chargers, 23-13 (B)
1964—Bills, 30-3 (B)
Bills, 27-24 (SD)
**Bills, 20-7 (B)
1965—Chargers, 34-3 (B)
Tie, 20-20 (SD)
**Bills, 23-0 (SD)
1966—Chargers, 27-7 (SD)
Tie, 17-17 (B)
1967—Chargers, 37-17 (B)
1968—Chargers, 21-6 (B)
1969—Chargers, 45-6 (SD)
1971—Chargers, 20-3 (SD)
1973—Chargers, 34-7 (SD)
1976—Chargers, 34-13 (B)
1979—Chargers, 27-19 (SD)
1980—Bills, 26-24 (SD)
***Chargers, 20-14 (SD)
1981—Bills, 28-27 (SD)
1985—Chargers, 14-9 (B)
Chargers, 40-7 (SD)
(RS Pts.—Chargers 589, Bills 406)
(PS Pts.—Bills 57, Chargers 27)
Franchise in Los Angeles prior to 1961
**AFL Championship*
***AFC Divisional Playoff*

BUFFALO vs. SAN FRANCISCO
RS: Series tied, 2-2
1972—Bills, 27-20 (B)
1980—Bills, 18-13 (SF)
1983—49ers, 23-10 (B)
1989—49ers, 21-10 (SF)
(RS Pts.—49ers 77, Bills 65)

BUFFALO vs. SEATTLE
RS: Seahawks lead series, 3-1
1977—Seahawks, 56-17 (S)
1984—Seahawks, 31-28 (S)
1988—Bills, 13-3 (S)
1989—Seahawks, 17-16 (S)
(RS Pts.—Seahawks 107, Bills 74)

BUFFALO vs. TAMPA BAY
RS: Buccaneers lead series, 4-1
1976—Bills, 14-9 (TB)
1978—Buccaneers, 31-10 (TB)
1982—Buccaneers, 24-23 (TB)
1986—Buccaneers, 34-28 (TB)
1988—Buccaneers, 10-5 (TB)
(RS Pts.—Buccaneers 108, Bills 80)

BUFFALO vs. WASHINGTON
RS: Redskins lead series, 4-2
1972—Bills, 24-17 (W)
1977—Redskins, 10-0 (B)
1981—Bills, 21-14 (B)
1984—Redskins, 41-14 (W)
1987—Redskins, 27-7 (B)
1990—Redskins, 29-14 (W)
(RS Pts.—Redskins 138, Bills 80)

CHICAGO vs. ATLANTA
RS: Falcons lead series, 9-7;
See Atlanta vs. Chicago

CHICAGO vs. BUFFALO
RS: Bears lead series, 3-1;
See Buffalo vs. Chicago

CHICAGO vs. CINCINNATI
RS: Series tied, 2-2
1972—Bengals, 13-3 (Chi)
1980—Bengals, 17-14 (Chi) OT
1986—Bears, 44-7 (Cin)
1989—Bears, 17-14 (Chi)
(RS Pts.—Bears 78, Bengals 51)

CHICAGO vs. CLEVELAND
RS: Browns lead series, 7-3
1951—Browns, 42-21 (Cle)
1954—Browns, 39-10 (Chi)
1960—Browns, 42-0 (Cle)
1961—Bears, 17-14 (Chi)
1967—Browns, 24-0 (Cle)
1969—Browns, 28-24 (Chi)
1972—Bears, 17-0 (Cle)
1980—Browns, 27-21 (Cle)
1986—Bears, 41-31 (Chi)
1989—Browns, 27-7 (Cle)
(RS Pts.—Browns 274, Bears 158)

CHICAGO vs. DALLAS
RS: Cowboys lead series, 7-6
PS: Cowboys lead series, 1-0
1960—Bears, 17-7 (C)
1962—Bears, 34-33 (D)
1964—Cowboys, 24-10 (C)
1968—Cowboys, 34-3 (C)
1971—Bears, 23-19 (C)
1973—Cowboys, 20-17 (C)
1976—Cowboys, 31-21 (D)
1977—*Cowboys, 37-7 (D)
1979—Cowboys, 24-20 (D)
1981—Cowboys, 10-9 (D)
1984—Cowboys, 23-14 (C)
1985—Bears, 44-0 (D)
1986—Bears, 24-10 (D)
1988—Bears, 17-7 (C)
(RS Pts.—Bears 253, Cowboys 242)
(PS Pts.—Cowboys 37, Bears 7)
NFC Divisional Playoff

CHICAGO vs. DENVER
RS: Bears lead series, 5-4
1971—Broncos, 6-3 (D)
1973—Bears, 33-14 (D)
1976—Broncos, 28-14 (C)
1978—Broncos, 16-7 (D)
1981—Bears, 35-24 (C)
1983—Bears, 31-14 (C)
1984—Bears, 27-0 (C)
1987—Broncos, 31-29 (D)
1990—Bears, 16-13 (D) OT
(RS Pts.—Bears 195, Broncos 146)

CHICAGO vs. *DETROIT
RS: Bears lead series, 71-46-5
1930—Spartans, 7-6 (P)
Bears, 14-6 (C)
1931—Bears, 9-6 (C)
Spartans, 3-0 (P)
1932—Tie, 13-13 (C)
Tie, 7-7 (P)
Bears, 9-0 (C)
1933—Bears, 17-14 (C)
Bears, 17-7 (P)
1934—Bears, 19-16 (D)
Bears, 10-7 (C)
1935—Tie, 20-20 (C)
Lions, 14-2 (D)
1936—Bears, 12-10 (C)
Lions, 13-7 (D)
1937—Bears, 28-20 (C)
Bears, 13-0 (D)
1938—Lions, 13-7 (C)
Lions, 14-7 (D)
1939—Lions, 10-0 (C)
Bears, 23-13 (D)
1940—Bears, 7-0 (C)
Lions, 17-14 (D)
1941—Bears, 49-0 (C)
Bears, 24-7 (D)
1942—Bears, 16-0 (C)
Bears, 42-0 (D)
1943—Bears, 27-21 (D)
Bears, 35-14 (C)
1944—Tie, 21-21 (C)
Lions, 41-21 (D)
1945—Lions, 16-10 (D)
Lions, 35-28 (C)
1946—Bears, 42-6 (C)
Bears, 45-24 (D)
1947—Bears, 33-24 (C)
Bears, 34-14 (D)
1948—Bears, 28-0 (C)
Bears, 42-14 (D)
1949—Bears, 27-24 (C)
Bears, 28-7 (D)
1950—Bears, 35-21 (D)
Bears, 6-3 (C)
1951—Bears, 28-23 (D)
Lions, 41-28 (C)
1952—Bears, 24-23 (C)
Lions, 45-21 (D)
1953—Lions, 20-16 (C)
Lions, 13-7 (D)
1954—Lions, 48-23 (D)
Bears, 28-24 (C)
1955—Bears, 24-14 (D)
Bears, 21-20 (C)
1956—Lions, 42-10 (D)
Bears, 38-21 (C)
1957—Bears, 27-7 (D)
Lions, 21-13 (C)
1958—Bears, 20-7 (D)
Bears, 21-16 (C)
1959—Bears, 24-14 (D)
Bears, 25-14 (C)
1960—Bears, 28-7 (C)
Lions, 36-0 (D)
1961—Bears, 31-17 (D)
Lions, 16-15 (C)
1962—Lions, 11-3 (D)
Bears, 3-0 (C)
1963—Bears, 37-21 (D)
Bears, 24-14 (C)
1964—Lions, 10-0 (C)
Bears, 27-24 (D)
1965—Bears, 38-10 (C)
Bears, 17-10 (D)
1966—Lions, 14-3 (D)
Tie, 10-10 (C)
1967—Bears, 14-3 (C)
Bears, 27-13 (D)
1968—Lions, 42-0 (D)
Lions, 28-10 (C)
1969—Lions, 13-7 (D)
Lions, 20-3 (C)
1970—Lions, 28-14 (D)
Lions, 16-10 (C)
1971—Bears, 28-23 (D)
Lions, 28-3 (C)
1972—Lions, 38-24 (C)
Lions, 14-0 (D)
1973—Lions, 30-7 (C)
Lions, 40-7 (D)
1974—Bears, 17-9 (C)
Lions, 34-17 (D)
1975—Lions, 27-7 (D)
Bears, 25-21 (C)
1976—Bears, 10-3 (C)
Lions, 14-10 (D)
1977—Bears, 30-20 (C)
Bears, 31-14 (D)
1978—Bears, 19-0 (D)
Lions, 21-17 (C)
1979—Bears, 35-7 (C)
Lions, 20-0 (D)
1980—Bears, 24-7 (C)
Bears, 23-17 (D) OT
1981—Lions, 48-17 (D)
Lions, 23-7 (C)
1982—Lions, 17-10 (D)

Bears, 20-17 (C)
1983—Lions, 31-17 (D)
Lions, 38-17 (C)
1984—Bears, 16-14 (C)
Bears, 30-13 (D)
1985—Bears, 24-3 (C)
Bears, 37-17 (D)
1986—Bears, 13-7 (C)
Bears, 16-13 (D)
1987—Bears, 30-10 (C)
1988—Bears, 24-7 (D)
Bears, 13-12 (C)
1989—Bears, 47-27 (D)
Lions, 27-17 (C)
1990—Bears, 23-17 (C) OT
Lions, 38-21 (D)
(RS Pts.—Bears 2,306, Lions 2,064)
Franchise in Portsmouth prior to 1934 and known as the Spartans

***CHICAGO vs. GREEN BAY**
RS: Bears lead series, 77-57-6
PS: Bears lead series, 1-0
1921—Staleys, 20-0 (C)
1923—Bears, 3-0 (GB)
1924—Bears, 3-0 (C)
1925—Packers, 14-10 (GB)
Bears, 21-0 (C)
1926—Tie, 6-6 (GB)
Bears, 19-13 (C)
Tie, 3-3 (C)
1927—Bears, 7-6 (GB)
Bears, 14-6 (C)
1928—Tie, 12-12 (GB)
Packers, 16-6 (C)
Packers, 6-0 (C)
1929—Packers, 23-0 (GB)
Packers, 14-0 (C)
Packers, 25-0 (C)
1930—Packers, 7-0 (GB)
Packers, 13-12 (C)
Bears, 21-0 (C)
1931—Packers, 7-0 (GB)
Packers, 6-2 (C)
Bears, 7-6 (C)
1932—Tie, 0-0 (GB)
Packers, 2-0 (C)
Bears, 9-0 (C)
1933—Bears, 14-7 (GB)
Bears, 10-7 (C)
Bears, 7-6 (C)
1934—Bears, 24-10 (GB)
Bears, 27-14 (C)
1935—Packers, 7-0 (GB)
Packers, 17-14 (C)
1936—Bears, 30-3 (GB)
Packers, 21-10 (C)
1937—Bears, 14-2 (GB)
Packers, 24-14 (C)
1938—Bears, 2-0 (GB)
Packers, 24-17 (C)
1939—Packers, 21-16 (GB)
Bears, 30-27 (C)
1940—Bears, 41-10 (GB)
Bears, 14-7 (C)
1941—Bears, 25-17 (GB)
Packers, 16-14 (C)
**Bears, 33-14 (C)
1942—Bears, 44-28 (GB)
Bears, 38-7 (C)
1943—Tie, 21-21 (GB)
Bears, 21-7 (C)
1944—Packers, 42-28 (GB)
Bears, 21-0 (C)
1945—Packers, 31-21 (GB)
Bears, 28-24 (C)
1946—Bears, 30-7 (GB)
Bears, 10-7 (C)
1947—Packers, 29-20 (GB)
Bears, 20-17 (C)
1948—Bears, 45-7 (GB)
Bears, 7-6 (C)
1949—Bears, 17-0 (GB)
Bears, 24-3 (C)
1950—Packers, 31-21 (GB)
Bears, 28-14 (C)
1951—Bears, 31-20 (GB)
Bears, 24-13 (C)
1952—Bears, 24-14 (GB)
Packers, 41-28 (C)
1953—Bears, 17-13 (GB)
Tie, 21-21 (C)
1954—Bears, 10-3 (GB)
Bears, 28-23 (C)
1955—Packers, 24-3 (GB)
Bears, 52-31 (C)
1956—Bears, 37-21 (GB)
Bears, 38-14 (C)
1957—Packers, 21-17 (GB)
Bears, 21-14 (C)
1958—Bears, 34-20 (GB)
Bears, 24-10 (C)
1959—Packers, 9-6 (GB)
Bears, 28-17 (C)
1960—Bears, 17-14 (GB)
Packers, 41-13 (C)
1961—Packers, 24-0 (GB)
Packers, 31-28 (C)
1962—Packers, 49-0 (GB)
Packers, 38-7 (C)
1963—Bears, 10-3 (GB)
Bears, 26-7 (C)
1964—Packers, 23-12 (GB)
Packers, 17-3 (C)
1965—Packers, 23-14 (GB)
Bears, 31-10 (C)
1966—Packers, 17-0 (C)
Packers, 13-6 (GB)
1967—Packers, 13-10 (GB)
Packers, 17-13 (C)
1968—Bears, 13-10 (GB)
Packers, 28-27 (C)
1969—Packers, 17-0 (GB)
Packers, 21-3 (C)
1970—Packers, 20-19 (GB)
Bears, 35-17 (C)
1971—Packers, 17-14 (C)
Packers, 31-10 (GB)
1972—Packers, 20-17 (GB)
Packers, 23-17 (C)
1973—Bears, 31-17 (GB)
Packers, 21-0 (C)
1974—Bears, 10-9 (C)
Packers, 20-3 (Mil)
1975—Bears, 27-14 (C)
Packers, 28-7 (GB)
1976—Bears, 24-13 (C)
Bears, 16-10 (GB)
1977—Bears, 26-0 (GB)
Bears, 21-10 (C)
1978—Packers, 24-14 (GB)
Bears, 14-0 (C)
1979—Bears, 6-3 (C)
Bears, 15-14 (GB)
1980—Packers, 12-6 (GB) OT
Bears, 61-7 (C)
1981—Packers, 16-9 (C)
Packers, 21-17 (GB)
1983—Packers, 31-28 (GB)
Bears, 23-21 (C)
1984—Bears, 9-7 (GB)
Packers, 20-14 (C)
1985—Bears, 23-7 (C)
Bears, 16-10 (GB)
1986—Bears, 25-12 (GB)
Bears, 12-10 (C)
1987—Bears, 26-24 (GB)
Bears, 23-10 (C)
1988—Bears, 24-6 (GB)
Bears, 16-0 (C)
1989—Packers, 14-13 (GB)
Packers, 40-28 (C)
1990—Bears, 31-13 (GB)
Bears, 27-13 (C)
(RS Pts.—Bears 2,375, Packers 2,056)
(PS Pts.—Bears 33, Packers 14)
**Bears known as Staleys prior to 1922*
***Division Playoff*

CHICAGO vs. HOUSTON
RS: Oilers lead series, 3-2
1973—Bears, 35-14 (C)
1977—Oilers, 47-0 (H)
1980—Oilers, 10-6 (C)
1986—Bears, 20-7 (H)
1989—Oilers, 33-28 (C)
(RS Pts.—Oilers 111, Bears 89)

CHICAGO vs. *INDIANAPOLIS
RS: Colts lead series, 21-15
1953—Colts, 13-9 (B)
Colts, 16-14 (C)
1954—Bears, 28-9 (C)
Bears, 28-13 (B)
1955—Colts, 23-17 (B)
Bears, 38-10 (C)
1956—Colts, 28-21 (B)
Bears, 58-27 (C)
1957—Colts, 21-10 (B)
Colts, 29-14 (C)
1958—Colts, 51-38 (B)
Colts, 17-0 (C)
1959—Bears, 26-21 (B)
Colts, 21-7 (C)
1960—Colts, 42-7 (B)
Colts, 24-20 (C)
1961—Bears, 24-10 (C)
Bears, 21-20 (B)
1962—Bears, 35-15 (C)
Bears, 57-0 (B)
1963—Bears, 10-3 (C)
Bears, 17-7 (B)
1964—Colts, 52-0 (B)
Colts, 40-24 (C)
1965—Colts, 26-21 (C)
Bears, 13-0 (B)
1966—Bears, 27-17 (C)
Colts, 21-16 (B)
1967—Colts, 24-3 (C)
1968—Colts, 28-7 (B)
1969—Colts, 24-21 (C)
1970—Colts, 21-20 (B)
1975—Colts, 35-7 (C)
1983—Colts, 22-19 (B) OT
1985—Bears, 17-10 (C)
1988—Bears, 17-13 (I)
(RS Pts.—Colts 753, Bears 711)
**Franchise in Baltimore prior to 1984*

CHICAGO vs. KANSAS CITY
RS: Bears lead series, 3-2
1973—Chiefs, 19-7 (KC)
1977—Bears, 28-27 (C)
1981—Bears, 16-13 (KC) OT
1987—Bears, 31-28 (C)
1990—Chiefs, 21-10 (C)
(RS Pts.—Chiefs 108, Bears 92)

CHICAGO vs. *L.A. RAIDERS
RS: Raiders lead series, 4-3
1972—Raiders, 28-21 (O)
1976—Raiders, 28-27 (C)
1978—Raiders, 25-19 (C) OT
1981—Bears, 23-6 (O)
1984—Bears, 17-6 (C)
1987—Bears, 6-3 (LA)
1990—Raiders, 24-10 (LA)
(RS Pts.—Bears 123, Raiders 120)
**Franchise in Oakland prior to 1982*

CHICAGO vs. *L.A. RAMS
RS: Bears lead series, 44-28-3
PS: Series tied, 1-1
1937—Bears, 20-2 (Clev)
Bears, 15-7 (C)
1938—Rams, 14-7 (C)
Rams, 23-21 (Clev)
1939—Bears, 30-21 (Clev)
Bears, 35-21 (C)
1940—Bears, 21-14 (Clev)
Bears, 47-25 (C)
1941—Bears, 48-21 (Clev)
Bears, 31-13 (C)
1942—Bears, 21-7 (Clev)
Bears, 47-0 (C)
1944—Rams, 19-7 (Clev)
Bears, 28-21 (C)
1945—Rams, 17-0 (Clev)
Rams, 41-21 (C)
1946—Tie, 28-28 (C)
Bears, 27-21 (LA)
1947—Bears, 41-21 (LA)
Rams, 17-14 (C)
1948—Bears, 42-21 (C)
Bears, 21-6 (LA)
1949—Rams, 31-16 (C)
Rams, 27-24 (LA)
1950—Bears, 24-20 (LA)
Bears, 24-14 (C)
**Rams, 24-14 (LA)
1951—Rams, 42-17 (C)
1952—Rams, 31-7 (LA)
Rams, 40-24 (C)
1953—Rams, 38-24 (LA)
Bears, 24-21 (C)
1954—Rams, 42-38 (LA)
Bears, 24-13 (C)
1955—Bears, 31-20 (LA)
Bears, 24-3 (C)
1956—Bears, 35-24 (LA)
Bears, 30-21 (C)
1957—Bears, 34-26 (C)
Bears, 16-10 (LA)
1958—Bears, 31-10 (C)
Rams, 41-35 (LA)
1959—Rams, 28-21 (C)
Bears, 26-21 (LA)
1960—Bears, 34-27 (C)
Tie, 24-24 (LA)
1961—Bears, 21-17 (LA)
Bears, 28-24 (C)
1962—Bears, 27-23 (LA)
Bears, 30-14 (C)
1963—Bears, 52-14 (LA)
Bears, 6-0 (C)
1964—Bears, 38-17 (C)
Bears, 34-24 (LA)
1965—Rams, 30-28 (LA)
Bears, 31-6 (C)
1966—Rams, 31-17 (LA)
Bears, 17-10 (C)
1967—Rams, 28-17 (C)
1968—Bears, 17-16 (LA)
1969—Rams, 9-7 (C)
1971—Rams, 17-3 (LA)
1972—Tie, 13-13 (C)
1973—Rams, 26-0 (C)
1975—Rams, 38-10 (LA)
1976—Rams, 20-12 (LA)
1977—Bears, 24-23 (C)
1979—Bears, 27-23 (C)
1981—Rams, 24-7 (C)
1982—Bears, 34-26 (LA)
1983—Rams, 21-14 (LA)
1984—Rams, 29-13 (LA)
1985—***Bears, 24-0 (C)
1986—Rams, 20-17 (C)
1988—Rams, 23-3 (LA)
1989—Bears, 20-10 (C)
1990—Bears, 38-9 (C)
(RS Pts.—Bears 1,764, Rams 1,539)
(PS Pts.—Bears 38, Rams 24)
**Franchise in Cleveland prior to 1946*
***Conference Playoff*
****NFC Championship*

CHICAGO vs. MIAMI
RS: Dolphins lead series, 4-1
1971—Dolphins, 34-3 (M)
1975—Dolphins, 46-13 (C)
1979—Dolphins, 31-16 (M)
1985—Dolphins, 38-24 (M)
1988—Bears, 34-7 (C)
(RS Pts.—Dolphins 156, Bears 90)

CHICAGO vs. MINNESOTA
RS: Vikings lead series, 30-27-2
1961—Vikings, 37-13 (M)
Bears, 52-35 (C)
1962—Bears, 13-0 (M)
Bears, 31-30 (C)
1963—Bears, 28-7 (M)
Tie, 17-17 (C)
1964—Bears, 34-28 (M)
Vikings, 41-14 (C)
1965—Bears, 45-37 (M)
Vikings, 24-17 (C)
1966—Bears, 13-10 (M)
Bears, 41-28 (C)
1967—Bears, 17-7 (M)
Tie, 10-10 (C)
1968—Bears, 27-17 (M)
Bears, 26-24 (C)
1969—Vikings, 31-0 (C)
Vikings, 31-14 (M)
1970—Vikings, 24-0 (C)
Vikings, 16-13 (M)
1971—Bears, 20-17 (M)
Vikings, 27-10 (C)
1972—Bears, 13-10 (C)
Vikings, 23-10 (M)
1973—Vikings, 22-13 (C)
Vikings, 31-13 (M)
1974—Vikings, 11-7 (M)
Vikings, 17-0 (C)
1975—Vikings, 28-3 (M)
Vikings, 13-9 (C)
1976—Vikings, 20-19 (M)
Bears, 14-13 (C)
1977—Vikings, 22-16 (M) OT
Bears, 10-7 (C)
1978—Vikings, 24-20 (C)
Vikings, 17-14 (M)
1979—Bears, 26-7 (C)
Vikings, 30-27 (M)
1980—Vikings, 34-14 (C)
Vikings, 13-7 (M)
1981—Vikings, 24-21 (M)
Bears, 10-9 (C)
1982—Vikings, 35-7 (M)
1983—Vikings, 23-14 (C)
Bears, 19-13 (M)
1984—Bears, 16-7 (C)
Bears, 34-3 (M)
1985—Bears, 33-24 (M)
Bears, 27-9 (C)
1986—Bears, 23-0 (C)
Vikings, 23-7 (M)
1987—Bears, 27-7 (C)
Bears, 30-24 (M)
1988—Vikings, 31-7 (C)
Vikings, 28-27 (M)
1989—Bears, 38-7 (C)
Vikings, 27-16 (M)
1990—Bears, 19-16 (C)
Vikings, 41-13 (M)
(RS Pts.—Vikings 1,191, Bears 1,078)

CHICAGO vs. NEW ENGLAND
RS: Patriots lead series, 3-2
PS: Bears lead series, 1-0
1973—Patriots, 13-10 (C)
1979—Patriots, 27-7 (C)
1982—Bears, 26-13 (C)
1985—Bears, 20-7 (C)
*Bears, 46-10 (New Orleans)
1988—Patriots, 30-7 (NE)
(RS Pts.—Patriots 100, Bears 70)
(PS Pts.—Bears 46, Patriots 10)
**Super Bowl XX*

CHICAGO vs. NEW ORLEANS
RS: Bears lead series, 7-5
PS: Bears lead series, 1-0
1968—Bears, 23-17 (NO)
1970—Bears, 24-3 (NO)
1971—Bears, 35-14 (C)
1973—Saints, 21-16 (NO)
1974—Bears, 24-10 (C)
1975—Bears, 42-17 (NO)
1977—Saints, 42-24 (C)
1980—Bears, 22-3 (C)

1982—Saints, 10-0 (C)
1983—Saints, 34-31 (NO) OT
1984—Bears, 20-7 (C)
1987—Saints, 19-17 (C)
1990—*Bears, 16-6 (C)
(RS Pts.—Bears 278, Saints 197)
(PS Pts.—Bears 16, Saints 6)
*NFC First Round Playoff

CHICAGO vs. N.Y. GIANTS
RS: Bears lead series, 23-14-2
PS: Bears lead series, 5-3
1925—Bears, 19-7 (NY)
Giants, 9-0 (C)
1926—Bears, 7-0 (C)
1927—Giants, 13-7 (NY)
1928—Bears, 13-0 (C)
1929—Giants, 26-14 (C)
Giants, 34-0 (NY)
Giants, 14-9 (C)
1930—Giants, 12-0 (C)
Bears, 12-0 (NY)
1931—Bears, 6-0 (C)
Bears, 12-6 (NY)
Giants, 25-6 (C)
1932—Bears, 28-8 (NY)
Bears, 6-0 (C)
1933—Bears, 14-10 (C)
Giants, 3-0 (NY)
*Bears, 23-21 (C)
1934—Bears, 27-7 (C)
Bears, 10-9 (NY)
*Giants, 30-13 (NY)
1935—Bears, 20-3 (NY)
Giants, 3-0 (C)
1936—Bears, 25-7 (NY)
1937—Tie, 3-3 (NY)
1939—Giants, 16-13 (NY)
1940—Bears, 37-21 (NY)
1941—*Bears, 37-9 (C)
1942—Bears, 26-7 (NY)
1943—Bears, 56-7 (NY)
1946—Giants, 14-0 (NY)
*Bears, 24-14 (NY)
1948—Bears, 35-14 (C)
1949—Giants, 35-28 (NY)
1956—Tie, 17-17 (NY)
*Giants, 47-7 (NY)
1962—Giants, 26-24 (C)
1963—*Bears, 14-10 (C)
1965—Bears, 35-14 (NY)
1967—Bears, 34-7 (C)
1969—Giants, 28-24 (NY)
1970—Bears, 24-16 (NY)
1974—Bears, 16-13 (C)
1977—Bears, 12-9 (NY) OT
1985—**Bears, 21-0 (C)
1987—Bears, 34-19 (C)
1990—**Giants, 31-3 (NY)
(RS Pts.—Bears 653, Giants 462)
(PS Pts.—Giants 162, Bears 142)
*NFL Championship
**NFC Divisional Playoff

CHICAGO vs. N.Y. JETS
RS: Bears lead series, 2-1
1974—Jets, 23-21 (C)
1979—Bears, 23-13 (C)
1985—Bears, 19-6 (NY)
(RS Pts.—Bears 63, Jets 42)

CHICAGO vs. PHILADELPHIA
RS: Bears lead series, 22-3-1
PS: Series tied, 1-1
1933—Tie, 3-3 (P)
1935—Bears, 39-0 (P)
1936—Bears, 17-0 (P)
Bears, 28-7 (P)
1938—Bears, 28-6 (P)
1939—Bears, 27-14 (C)
1941—Bears, 49-14 (P)
1942—Bears, 45-14 (C)
1944—Bears, 28-7 (P)
1946—Bears, 21-14 (C)
1947—Bears, 40-7 (C)
1948—Eagles, 12-7 (P)
1949—Bears, 38-21 (C)
1955—Bears, 17-10 (C)
1961—Eagles, 16-14 (P)
1963—Bears, 16-7 (C)
1968—Bears, 29-16 (P)
1970—Bears, 20-16 (C)
1972—Bears, 21-12 (P)
1975—Bears, 15-13 (C)
1979—*Eagles, 27-17 (P)
1980—Eagles, 17-14 (P)
1983—Bears, 7-6 (P)
Bears, 17-14 (C)
1986—Bears, 13-10 (C) OT
1987—Bears, 35-3 (P)
1988—**Bears, 20-12 (C)
1989—Bears, 27-13 (C)
(RS Pts.—Bears 615, Eagles 272)
(PS Pts.—Eagles 39, Bears 37)
*NFC First Round Playoff
**NFC Divisional Playoff

***CHICAGO vs. **PHOENIX**
RS: Bears lead series, 51-25-6
(NP denotes Normal Park;
Wr denotes Wrigley Field;
Co denotes Comiskey Park;
So denotes Soldier Field;
all Chicago)
1920—Cardinals, 7-6 (NP)
Staleys, 10-0 (Wr)
1921—Tie, 0-0 (Wr)
1922—Cardinals, 6-0 (Co)
Cardinals, 9-0 (Co)
1923—Bears, 3-0 (Wr)
1924—Bears, 6-0 (Wr)
Bears, 21-0 (Co)
1925—Cardinals, 9-0 (Co)
Tie, 0-0 (Wr)
1926—Bears, 16-0 (Wr)
Bears, 10-0 (So)
Tie, 0-0 (Wr)
1927—Bears, 9-0 (NP)
Cardinals, 3-0 (Wr)
1928—Bears, 15-0 (NP)
Bears, 34-0 (Wr)
1929—Tie, 0-0 (Wr)
Cardinals, 40-6 (Co)
1930—Bears, 32-6 (Co)
Bears, 6-0 (Wr)
1931—Bears, 26-13 (Wr)
Bears, 18-7 (Wr)
1932—Tie, 0-0 (Wr)
Bears, 34-0 (Wr)
1933—Bears, 12-9 (Wr)
Bears, 22-6 (Wr)
1934—Bears, 20-0 (Wr)
Bears, 17-6 (Wr)
1935—Tie, 7-7 (Wr)
Bears, 13-0 (Wr)
1936—Bears, 7-3 (Wr)
Cardinals, 14-7 (Wr)
1937—Bears, 16-7 (Wr)
Bears, 42-28 (Wr)
1938—Bears, 16-13 (So)
Bears, 34-28 (Wr)
1939—Bears, 44-7 (Wr)
Bears, 48-7 (Co)
1940—Cardinals, 21-7 (Co)
Bears, 31-23 (Wr)
1941—Bears, 53-7 (Wr)
Bears, 34-24 (Co)
1942—Bears, 41-14 (Wr)
Bears, 21-7 (Co)
1943—Bears, 20-0 (Wr)
Bears, 35-24 (Co)
1945—Cardinals, 16-7 (Wr)
Bears, 28-20 (Co)
1946—Bears, 34-17 (Co)
Cardinals, 35-28 (Wr)
1947—Cardinals, 31-7 (Co)
Cardinals, 30-21 (Wr)
1948—Bears, 28-17 (Co)
Cardinals, 24-21 (Wr)
1949—Bears, 17-7 (Co)
Bears, 52-21 (Wr)
1950—Bears, 27-6 (Wr)
Cardinals, 20-10 (Co)
1951—Cardinals, 28-14 (Co)
Cardinals, 24-14 (Wr)
1952—Cardinals, 21-10 (Co)
Bears, 10-7 (Wr)
1953—Cardinals, 24-17 (Wr)
1954—Bears, 29-7 (Co)
1955—Cardinals, 53-14 (Co)
1956—Bears, 10-3 (Wr)
1957—Bears, 14-6 (Co)
1958—Bears, 30-14 (Wr)
1959—Bears, 31-7 (So)
1965—Bears, 34-13 (Wr)
1966—Cardinals, 24-17 (StL)
1967—Bears, 30-3 (Wr)
1969—Cardinals, 20-17 (StL)
1972—Bears, 27-10 (StL)
1975—Cardinals, 34-20 (So)
1977—Cardinals, 16-13 (StL)
1978—Bears, 17-10 (So)
1979—Bears, 42-6 (So)
1982—Cardinals, 10-7 (So)
1984—Cardinals, 38-21 (StL)
1990—Bears, 31-21 (P)
(RS Pts.—Bears 1,548, Cardinals 998)
*Franchise in Decatur prior to 1921; Bears known as Staleys prior to 1922
**Franchise in St. Louis prior to 1988 and in Chicago prior to 1960

CHICAGO vs. *PITTSBURGH
RS: Bears lead series, 15-4-1
1934—Bears, 28-0 (P)
1935—Bears, 23-7 (P)
1936—Bears, 27-9 (P)
Bears, 26-6 (C)
1937—Bears, 7-0 (P)
1939—Bears, 32-0 (P)
1941—Bears, 34-7 (C)
1945—Bears, 28-7 (P)
1947—Bears, 49-7 (C)
1949—Bears, 30-21 (C)
1958—Steelers, 24-10 (P)
1959—Bears, 27-21 (C)
1963—Tie, 17-17 (P)
1967—Steelers, 41-13 (P)
1969—Bears, 38-7 (C)
1971—Bears, 17-15 (C)
1975—Steelers, 34-3 (P)
1980—Steelers, 38-3 (P)
1986—Bears, 13-10 (C) OT
1989—Bears, 20-0 (P)
(RS Pts.—Bears 445, Steelers 271)
*Steelers known as Pirates prior to 1941

CHICAGO vs. SAN DIEGO
RS: Chargers lead series, 4-1
1970—Chargers, 20-7 (C)
1974—Chargers, 28-21 (SD)
1978—Chargers, 40-7 (SD)
1981—Bears, 20-17 (C) OT
1984—Chargers, 20-7 (SD)
(RS Pts.—Chargers 125, Bears 62)

CHICAGO vs. SAN FRANCISCO
RS: Bears lead series, 25-24-1
PS: 49ers lead series, 2-0
1950—Bears, 32-20 (SF)
Bears, 17-0 (C)
1951—Bears, 13-7 (C)
1952—49ers, 40-16 (C)
Bears, 20-17 (SF)
1953—49ers, 35-28 (C)
49ers, 24-14 (SF)
1954—49ers, 31-24 (C)
Bears, 31-27 (SF)
1955—49ers, 20-19 (C)
Bears, 34-23 (SF)
1956—Bears, 31-7 (C)
Bears, 38-21 (SF)
1957—49ers, 21-17 (C)
49ers, 21-17 (SF)
1958—Bears, 28-6 (C)
Bears, 27-14 (SF)
1959—49ers, 20-17 (SF)
Bears, 14-3 (C)
1960—Bears, 27-10 (C)
49ers, 25-7 (SF)
1961—Bears, 31-0 (C)
49ers, 41-31 (SF)
1962—Bears, 30-14 (SF)
49ers, 34-27 (C)
1963—49ers, 20-14 (SF)
Bears, 27-7 (C)
1964—49ers, 31-21 (SF)
Bears, 23-21 (C)
1965—49ers, 52-24 (SF)
Bears, 61-20 (C)
1966—Tie, 30-30 (C)
49ers, 41-14 (SF)
1967—Bears, 28-14 (SF)
1968—Bears, 27-19 (C)
1969—49ers, 42-21 (SF)
1970—49ers, 37-16 (C)
1971—49ers, 13-0 (SF)
1972—49ers, 34-21 (C)
1974—49ers, 34-0 (C)
1975—49ers, 31-3 (SF)
1976—Bears, 19-12 (SF)
1978—Bears, 16-13 (SF)
1979—Bears, 28-27 (SF)
1981—49ers, 28-17 (SF)
1983—Bears, 13-3 (C)
1984—*49ers, 23-0 (SF)
1985—Bears, 26-10 (SF)
1987—49ers, 41-0 (SF)
1988—Bears, 10-9 (C)
*49ers, 28-3 (C)
1989—49ers, 26-0 (SF)
(RS Pts.—49ers 1,096, Bears 1,049)
(PS Pts.—49ers 51, Bears 3)
*NFC Championship

CHICAGO vs. SEATTLE
RS: Seahawks lead series, 4-2
1976—Bears, 34-7 (S)
1978—Seahawks, 31-29 (C)
1982—Seahawks, 20-14 (S)
1984—Seahawks, 38-9 (S)
1987—Seahawks, 34-21 (C)
1990—Bears, 17-0 (C)
(RS Pts.—Seahawks 130, Bears 124)

CHICAGO vs. TAMPA BAY
RS: Bears lead series, 20-6
1977—Bears, 10-0 (TB)
1978—Buccaneers, 33-19 (TB)
Bears, 14-3 (C)
1979—Buccaneers, 17-13 (C)
Bears, 14-0 (TB)
1980—Bears, 23-0 (C)
Bears, 14-13 (TB)
1981—Bears, 28-17 (C)
Buccaneers, 20-10 (TB)
1982—Buccaneers, 26-23 (TB) OT
1983—Bears, 17-10 (C)
Bears, 27-0 (TB)
1984—Bears, 34-14 (C)
Bears, 44-9 (TB)
1985—Bears, 38-28 (C)
Bears, 27-19 (TB)
1986—Bears, 23-3 (TB)
Bears, 48-14 (C)
1987—Bears, 20-3 (C)
Bears, 27-26 (TB)
1988—Bears, 28-10 (C)
Bears, 27-15 (TB)
1989—Buccaneers, 42-35 (TB)
Buccaneers, 32-31 (C)
1990—Bears, 26-6 (TB)
Bears, 27-14 (C)
(RS Pts.—Bears 647, Buccaneers 374)

CHICAGO vs. *WASHINGTON
RS: Bears lead series, 18-11-1
PS: Redskins lead series, 4-3
1932—Tie, 7-7 (B)
1933—Bears, 7-0 (C)
Redskins, 10-0 (B)
1934—Bears, 21-0 (B)
1935—Bears, 30-14 (B)
1936—Bears, 26-0 (B)
1937—**Redskins, 28-21 (C)
1938—Bears, 31-7 (C)
1940—Redskins, 7-3 (W)
**Bears, 73-0 (W)
1941—Bears, 35-21 (C)
1942—**Redskins, 14-6 (W)
1943—Redskins, 21-7 (W)
**Bears, 41-21 (C)
1945—Redskins, 28-21 (W)
1946—Bears, 24-20 (C)
1947—Bears, 56-20 (W)
1948—Bears, 48-13 (C)
1949—Bears, 31-21 (W)
1951—Bears, 27-0 (W)
1953—Bears, 27-24 (W)
1957—Redskins, 14-3 (C)
1964—Redskins, 27-20 (W)
1968—Redskins, 38-28 (C)
1971—Bears, 16-15 (C)
1974—Redskins, 42-0 (W)
1976—Bears, 33-7 (C)
1978—Bears, 14-10 (W)
1980—Bears, 35-21 (C)
1981—Redskins, 24-7 (C)
1984—***Bears, 23-19 (W)
1985—Bears, 45-10 (C)
1986—***Redskins, 27-13 (C)
1987—***Redskins, 21-17 (C)
1988—Bears, 34-14 (W)
1989—Redskins, 38-14 (W)
1990—Redskins, 10-9 (W)
(RS Pts.—Bears 659, Redskins 483)
(PS Pts.—Bears 194, Redskins 130)
*Franchise in Boston prior to 1937 and known as Braves prior to 1933
**NFL Championship
***NFC Divisional Playoff

CINCINNATI vs. ATLANTA
RS: Bengals lead series, 5-2;
See Atlanta vs. Cincinnati

CINCINNATI vs. BUFFALO
RS: Bengals lead series, 9-6
PS: Bengals lead series, 2-0;
See Buffalo vs. Cincinnati

CINCINNATI vs. CHICAGO
RS: Series tied, 2-2;
See Chicago vs. Cincinnati

CINCINNATI vs. CLEVELAND
RS: Bengals lead series, 22-19
1970—Browns, 30-27 (Cle)
Bengals, 14-10 (Cin)
1971—Browns, 27-24 (Cin)
Browns, 31-27 (Cle)
1972—Browns, 27-6 (Cle)
Browns, 27-24 (Cin)
1973—Browns, 17-10 (Cle)
Bengals, 34-17 (Cin)
1974—Bengals, 33-7 (Cin)
Bengals, 34-24 (Cle)
1975—Bengals, 24-17 (Cin)
Browns, 35-23 (Cle)
1976—Bengals, 45-24 (Cle)
Bengals, 21-6 (Cin)
1977—Browns, 13-3 (Cin)
Bengals, 10-7 (Cle)
1978—Browns, 13-10 (Cle) OT
Bengals, 48-16 (Cin)
1979—Browns, 28-27 (Cle)
Bengals, 16-12 (Cin)
1980—Browns, 31-7 (Cle)
Browns, 27-24 (Cin)
1981—Browns, 20-17 (Cin)
Bengals, 41-21 (Cle)
1982—Bengals, 23-10 (Cin)
1983—Browns, 17-7 (Cle)
Bengals, 28-21 (Cin)
1984—Bengals, 12-9 (Cin)

Bengals, 20-17 (Cle) OT
1985—Bengals, 27-10 (Cin)
Browns, 24-6 (Cle)
1986—Bengals, 30-13 (Cle)
Browns, 34-3 (Cin)
1987—Browns, 34-0 (Cin)
Browns, 38-24 (Cle)
1988—Bengals, 24-17 (Cin)
Browns, 23-16 (Cle)
1989—Bengals, 21-14 (Cin)
Bengals, 21-0 (Cle)
1990—Bengals, 34-13 (Cle)
Bengals, 21-14 (Cin)
(RS Pts.—Bengals 866, Browns 795)

CINCINNATI vs. DALLAS
RS: Series tied, 2-2
1973—Cowboys, 38-10 (D)
1979—Cowboys, 38-13 (D)
1985—Bengals, 50-24 (C)
1988—Bengals, 38-24 (D)
(RS Pts.—Cowboys 124, Bengals 111)

CINCINNATI vs. DENVER
RS: Broncos lead series, 9-6
1968—Bengals, 24-10 (C)
Broncos, 10-7 (D)
1969—Broncos, 30-23 (C)
Broncos, 27-16 (D)
1971—Bengals, 24-10 (D)
1972—Bengals, 21-10 (C)
1973—Broncos, 28-10 (D)
1975—Bengals, 17-16 (D)
1976—Bengals, 17-7 (C)
1977—Broncos, 24-13 (C)
1979—Broncos, 10-0 (D)
1981—Bengals, 38-21 (C)
1983—Broncos, 24-17 (D)
1984—Broncos, 20-17 (D)
1986—Broncos, 34-28 (D)
(RS Pts.—Broncos 281, Bengals 272)

CINCINNATI vs. DETROIT
RS: Bengals lead series, 3-2
1970—Lions, 38-3 (D)
1974—Lions, 23-19 (C)
1983—Bengals, 17-9 (C)
1986—Bengals, 24-17 (D)
1989—Bengals, 42-7 (C)
(RS Pts.—Bengals 105, Lions 94)

CINCINNATI vs. GREEN BAY
RS: Bengals lead series, 4-2
1971—Packers, 20-17 (GB)
1976—Bengals, 28-7 (C)
1977—Bengals, 17-7 (Mil)
1980—Packers, 14-9 (GB)
1983—Bengals, 34-14 (C)
1986—Bengals, 34-28 (Mil)
(RS Pts.—Bengals 139, Packers 90)

CINCINNATI vs. HOUSTON
RS: Bengals lead series, 24-19-1
PS: Bengals lead series, 1-0
1968—Oilers, 27-17 (C)
1969—Tie, 31-31 (H)
1970—Oilers, 20-13 (C)
Bengals, 30-20 (H)
1971—Oilers, 10-6 (H)
Bengals, 28-13 (C)
1972—Bengals, 30-7 (C)
Bengals, 61-17 (H)
1973—Bengals, 24-10 (C)
Bengals, 27-24 (H)
1974—Oilers, 34-21 (C)
Oilers, 20-3 (H)
1975—Bengals, 21-19 (H)
Bengals, 23-19 (C)
1976—Bengals, 27-7 (H)
Bengals, 31-27 (C)
1977—Bengals, 13-10 (C) OT
Oilers, 21-16 (H)
1978—Bengals, 28-13 (C)
Oilers, 17-10 (H)
1979—Oilers, 30-27 (C) OT
Oilers, 42-21 (H)
1980—Oilers, 13-10 (C)
Oilers, 23-3 (H)
1981—Oilers, 17-10 (H)
Bengals, 34-21 (C)
1982—Bengals, 27-6 (C)
Bengals, 35-27 (H)
1983—Bengals, 55-14 (H)
Bengals, 38-10 (C)
1984—Bengals, 13-3 (C)
Bengals, 31-13 (H)
1985—Oilers, 44-27 (H)
Bengals, 45-27 (C)
1986—Bengals, 31-28 (C)
Oilers, 32-28 (H)
1987—Oilers, 31-29 (C)
Oilers, 21-17 (H)
1988—Bengals, 44-21 (C)
Oilers, 41-6 (H)
1989—Oilers, 26-24 (H)
Bengals, 61-7 (C)
1990—Oilers, 48-17 (H)
Bengals, 40-20 (C)
*Bengals, 41-14 (C)
(RS Pts.—Bengals 1,133, Oilers 931)
(PS Pts.—Bengals 41, Oilers 14)
**AFC First Round Playoff*

CINCINNATI vs. *INDIANAPOLIS
RS: Colts lead series, 6-5
PS: Colts lead series, 1-0
1970—**Colts, 17-0 (B)
1972—Colts, 20-19 (C)
1974—Bengals, 24-14 (B)
1976—Colts, 28-27 (B)
1979—Colts, 38-28 (B)
1980—Bengals, 34-33 (C)
1981—Bengals, 41-19 (B)
1982—Bengals, 20-17 (B)
1983—Colts, 34-31 (C)
1987—Bengals, 23-21 (I)
1989—Colts, 23-12 (C)
1990—Colts, 34-20 (C)
(RS Pts.—Colts 281, Bengals 279)
(PS Pts.—Colts 17, Bengals 0)
**Franchise in Baltimore prior to 1984*
***AFC Divisional Playoff*

CINCINNATI vs. KANSAS CITY
RS: Chiefs lead series, 10-9
1968—Chiefs, 13-3 (KC)
Chiefs, 16-9 (C)
1969—Bengals, 24-19 (C)
Chiefs, 42-22 (KC)
1970—Chiefs, 27-19 (C)
1972—Bengals, 23-16 (KC)
1973—Bengals, 14-6 (C)
1974—Bengals, 33-6 (C)
1976—Bengals, 27-24 (KC)
1977—Bengals, 27-7 (KC)
1978—Chiefs, 24-23 (C)
1979—Chiefs, 10-7 (C)
1980—Bengals, 20-6 (KC)
1983—Chiefs, 20-15 (KC)
1984—Chiefs, 27-22 (C)
1986—Chiefs, 24-14 (KC)
1987—Bengals, 30-27 (C) OT
1988—Chiefs, 31-28 (KC)
1989—Bengals, 21-17 (KC)
(RS Pts.—Bengals 381, Chiefs 362)

CINCINNATI vs. *L.A. RAIDERS
RS: Raiders lead series, 13-5
PS: Raiders lead series, 2-0
1968—Raiders, 31-10 (O)
Raiders, 34-0 (C)
1969—Bengals, 31-17 (C)
Raiders, 37-17 (O)
1970—Bengals, 31-21 (C)
1971—Raiders, 31-27 (O)
1972—Raiders, 20-14 (C)
1974—Raiders, 30-27 (O)
1975—Bengals, 14-10 (C)
**Raiders, 31-28 (O)
1976—Raiders, 35-20 (O)
1978—Raiders, 34-21 (C)
1980—Raiders, 28-17 (O)
1982—Bengals, 31-17 (C)
1983—Raiders, 20-10 (C)
1985—Raiders, 13-6 (LA)
1988—Bengals, 45-21 (LA)
1989—Raiders, 28-7 (LA)
1990—Raiders, 24-7 (LA)
**Raiders, 20-10 (LA)
(RS Pts.—Raiders 451, Bengals 335)
(PS Pts.—Raiders 51, Bengals 38)
**Franchise in Oakland prior to 1982*
***AFC Divisional Playoff*

CINCINNATI vs. L.A. RAMS
RS: Bengals lead series, 4-2
1972—Rams, 15-12 (LA)
1976—Bengals, 20-12 (C)
1978—Bengals, 20-19 (LA)
1981—Bengals, 24-10 (C)
1984—Rams, 24-14 (C)
1990—Bengals, 34-31 (LA) OT
(RS Pts.—Bengals 124, Rams 111)

CINCINNATI vs. MIAMI
RS: Dolphins lead series, 8-3
PS: Dolphins lead series, 1-0
1968—Dolphins, 24-22 (C)
Bengals, 38-21 (M)
1969—Bengals, 27-21 (C)
1971—Dolphins, 23-13 (C)
1973—*Dolphins, 34-16 (M)
1974—Dolphins, 24-3 (M)
1977—Bengals, 23-17 (C)
1978—Dolphins, 21-0 (M)
1980—Dolphins, 17-16 (M)
1983—Dolphins, 38-14 (M)
1987—Dolphins, 20-14 (C)
1989—Dolphins, 20-13 (C)
(RS Pts.—Dolphins 280, Bengals 199)
(PS Pts.—Dolphins 34, Bengals 16)
**AFC Divisional Playoff*

CINCINNATI vs. MINNESOTA
RS: Series tied, 3-3
1973—Bengals, 27-0 (C)
1977—Vikings, 42-10 (M)
1980—Bengals, 14-0 (C)
1983—Vikings, 20-14 (M)
1986—Bengals, 24-20 (C)
1989—Vikings, 29-21 (M)
(RS Pts.—Vikings 111, Bengals 110)

CINCINNATI vs. *NEW ENGLAND
RS: Patriots lead series, 7-5
1968—Patriots, 33-14 (B)
1969—Patriots, 25-14 (C)
1970—Bengals, 45-7 (C)
1972—Bengals, 31-7 (NE)
1975—Bengals, 27-10 (C)
1978—Patriots, 10-3 (C)
1979—Patriots, 20-14 (C)
1984—Patriots, 20-14 (NE)
1985—Patriots, 34-23 (NE)
1986—Bengals, 31-7 (NE)
1988—Patriots, 27-21 (NE)
1990—Bengals, 41-7 (C)
(RS Pts.—Bengals 278, Patriots 207)
**Franchise in Boston prior to 1971*

CINCINNATI vs. NEW ORLEANS
RS: Saints lead series, 4-3
1970—Bengals, 26-6 (C)
1975—Bengals, 21-0 (NO)
1978—Saints, 20-18 (C)
1981—Saints, 17-7 (NO)
1984—Bengals, 24-21 (NO)
1987—Saints, 41-24 (C)
1990—Saints, 21-7 (C)
(RS Pts.—Bengals 127, Saints 126)

CINCINNATI vs. N.Y. GIANTS
RS: Bengals lead series, 3-0
1972—Bengals, 13-10 (C)
1977—Bengals, 30-13 (C)
1985—Bengals, 35-30 (C)
(RS Pts.—Bengals 78, Giants 53)

CINCINNATI vs. N.Y. JETS
RS: Jets lead series, 7-6
PS: Jets lead series, 1-0
1968—Jets, 27-14 (NY)
1969—Jets, 21-7 (C)
Jets, 40-7 (NY)
1971—Jets, 35-21 (NY)
1973—Bengals, 20-14 (C)
1976—Bengals, 42-3 (NY)
1981—Bengals, 31-30 (NY)
1982—*Jets, 44-17 (C)
1984—Jets, 43-23 (NY)
1985—Jets, 29-20 (C)
1986—Bengals, 52-21 (C)
1987—Jets, 27-20 (NY)
1988—Bengals, 36-19 (C)
1990—Bengals, 25-20 (C)
(RS Pts.—Jets 329, Bengals 318)
(PS Pts.—Jets 44, Bengals 17)
**AFC First Round Playoff*

CINCINNATI vs. PHILADELPHIA
RS: Bengals lead series, 5-0
1971—Bengals, 37-14 (C)
1975—Bengals, 31-0 (P)
1979—Bengals, 37-13 (C)
1982—Bengals, 18-14 (P)
1988—Bengals, 28-24 (P)
(RS Pts.—Bengals 151, Eagles 65)

CINCINNATI vs. *PHOENIX
RS: Bengals lead series, 3-1
1973—Bengals, 42-24 (C)
1979—Bengals, 34-28 (C)
1985—Cardinals, 41-27 (StL)
1988—Bengals, 21-14 (C)
(RS Pts.—Bengals 124, Cardinals 107)
**Franchise in St. Louis prior to 1988*

CINCINNATI vs. PITTSBURGH
RS: Bengals lead series, 21-20
1970—Steelers, 21-10 (P)
Bengals, 34-7 (C)
1971—Steelers, 21-10 (P)
Steelers, 21-13 (C)
1972—Bengals, 15-10 (C)
Steelers, 40-17 (P)
1973—Bengals, 19-7 (C)
Steelers, 20-13 (P)
1974—Bengals, 17-10 (C)
Steelers, 27-3 (P)
1975—Steelers, 30-24 (C)
Steelers, 35-14 (P)
1976—Steelers, 23-6 (P)
Steelers, 7-3 (C)
1977—Steelers, 20-14 (P)
Bengals, 17-10 (C)
1978—Steelers, 28-3 (C)
Steelers, 7-6 (P)
1979—Bengals, 34-10 (C)
Steelers, 37-17 (P)
1980—Bengals, 30-28 (C)
Bengals, 17-16 (P)
1981—Bengals, 34-7 (C)
Bengals, 17-10 (P)
1982—Steelers, 26-20 (P) OT
1983—Steelers, 24-14 (C)
Bengals, 23-10 (P)
1984—Steelers, 38-17 (P)
Bengals, 22-20 (C)
1985—Bengals, 37-24 (P)
Bengals, 26-21 (C)
1986—Bengals, 24-22 (C)
Steelers, 30-9 (P)
1987—Steelers, 23-20 (P)
Steelers, 30-16 (C)
1988—Bengals, 17-12 (P)
Bengals, 42-7 (C)
1989—Bengals, 41-10 (C)
Bengals, 26-16 (P)
1990—Bengals, 27-3 (C)
Bengals, 16-12 (P)
(RS Pts.—Bengals 784, Steelers 780)

CINCINNATI vs. SAN DIEGO
RS: Chargers lead series, 11-8
PS: Bengals lead series, 1-0
1968—Chargers, 29-13 (SD)
Chargers, 31-10 (C)
1969—Bengals, 34-20 (C)
Chargers, 21-14 (SD)
1970—Bengals, 17-14 (SD)
1971—Bengals, 31-0 (C)
1973—Bengals, 20-13 (SD)
1974—Chargers, 20-17 (C)
1975—Bengals, 47-17 (C)
1977—Chargers, 24-3 (SD)
1978—Chargers, 22-13 (SD)
1979—Chargers, 26-24 (C)
1980—Chargers, 31-14 (C)
1981—Bengals, 40-17 (SD)
*Bengals, 27-7 (C)
1982—Chargers, 50-34 (SD)
1985—Chargers, 44-41 (C)
1987—Chargers, 10-9 (C)
1988—Bengals, 27-10 (C)
1990—Bengals, 21-16 (SD)
(RS Pts.—Bengals 429, Chargers 415)
(PS Pts.—Bengals 27, Chargers 7)
**AFC Championship*

CINCINNATI vs. SAN FRANCISCO
RS: 49ers lead series, 5-1
PS: 49ers lead series, 2-0
1974—Bengals, 21-3 (SF)
1978—49ers, 28-12 (SF)
1981—49ers, 21-3 (C)
*49ers, 26-21 (Detroit)
1984—49ers, 23-17 (SF)
1987—49ers, 27-26 (C)
1988—**49ers, 20-16 (Miami)
1990—49ers, 20-17 (C)
(RS Pts.—49ers 122, Bengals 96)
(PS Pts.—49ers 46, Bengals 37)
**Super Bowl XVI*
***Super Bowl XXIII*

CINCINNATI vs. SEATTLE
RS: Bengals lead series, 5-4
PS: Bengals lead series, 1-0
1977—Bengals, 42-20 (C)
1981—Bengals, 27-21 (C)
1982—Bengals, 24-10 (C)
1984—Seahawks, 26-6 (C)
1985—Seahawks, 28-24 (C)
1986—Bengals, 34-7 (C)
1987—Bengals, 17-10 (S)
1988—*Bengals, 21-13 (C)
1989—Seahawks, 24-17 (C)
1990—Seahawks, 31-16 (S)
(RS Pts.—Bengals 207, Seahawks 177)
(PS Pts.—Bengals 21, Seahawks 13)
**AFC Divisional Playoff*

CINCINNATI vs. TAMPA BAY
RS: Bengals lead series, 3-1
1976—Bengals, 21-0 (C)
1980—Buccaneers, 17-12 (C)
1983—Bengals, 23-17 (TB)
1989—Bengals, 56-23 (C)
(RS Pts.—Bengals 112, Buccaneers 57)

CINCINNATI vs. WASHINGTON
RS: Redskins lead series, 3-2
1970—Redskins, 20-0 (W)
1974—Bengals, 28-17 (C)
1979—Redskins, 28-14 (W)
1985—Redskins, 27-24 (W)
1988—Bengals, 20-17 (C) OT
(RS Pts.—Redskins 109, Bengals 86)

CLEVELAND vs. ATLANTA
RS: Browns lead series, 8-1;
See Atlanta vs. Cleveland

CLEVELAND vs. BUFFALO
RS: Browns lead series, 7-3
PS: Browns lead series, 1-0;
See Buffalo vs. Cleveland

CLEVELAND vs. CHICAGO
RS: Browns lead series, 7-3;
See Chicago vs. Cleveland

CLEVELAND vs. CINCINNATI
RS: Bengals lead series, 22-19;
See Cincinnati vs. Cleveland

CLEVELAND vs. DALLAS
RS: Browns lead series, 14-8
PS: Browns lead series, 2-1

1960—Browns, 48-7 (D)
1961—Browns, 25-7 (C)
Browns, 38-17 (D)
1962—Browns, 19-10 (C)
Cowboys, 45-21 (D)
1963—Browns, 41-24 (D)
Browns, 27-17 (C)
1964—Browns, 27-6 (C)
Browns, 20-16 (D)
1965—Browns, 23-17 (C)
Browns, 24-17 (D)
1966—Browns, 30-21 (C)
Cowboys, 26-14 (D)
1967—Cowboys, 21-14 (C)
*Cowboys, 52-14 (D)
1968—Cowboys, 28-7 (C)
*Browns, 31-20 (C)
1969—Browns, 42-10 (C)
*Browns, 38-14 (D)
1970—Cowboys, 6-2 (C)
1974—Cowboys, 41-17 (D)
1979—Browns, 26-7 (C)
1982—Cowboys, 31-14 (D)
1985—Cowboys, 20-7 (D)
1988—Browns, 24-21 (C)
(RS Pts.—Browns 510, Cowboys 415)
(PS Pts.—Cowboys 86, Browns 83)
Conference Championship

CLEVELAND vs. DENVER
RS: Broncos lead series, 9-5
PS: Broncos lead series, 3-0
1970—Browns, 27-13 (D)
1971—Broncos, 27-0 (C)
1972—Browns, 27-20 (D)
1974—Browns, 23-21 (C)
1975—Broncos, 16-15 (D)
1976—Broncos, 44-13 (D)
1978—Broncos, 19-7 (C)
1980—Broncos, 19-16 (C)
1981—Broncos, 23-20 (D) OT
1983—Broncos, 27-6 (D)
1984—Broncos, 24-14 (C)
1986—*Broncos, 23-20 (C) OT
1987—*Broncos, 38-33 (D)
1988—Broncos, 30-7 (D)
1989—Browns, 16-13 (C)
*Broncos, 37-21 (D)
1990—Browns, 30-29 (D)
(RS Pts.—Broncos 325, Browns 221)
(PS Pts.—Broncos 98, Browns 74)
AFC Championship

CLEVELAND vs. DETROIT
RS: Lions lead series, 10-3
PS: Lions lead series, 3-1
1952—Lions, 17-6 (D)
*Lions, 17-7 (C)
1953—*Lions, 17-16 (D)
1954—Lions, 14-10 (C)
*Browns, 56-10 (C)
1957—Lions, 20-7 (D)
*Lions, 59-14 (D)
1958—Lions, 30-10 (C)
1963—Lions, 38-10 (D)
1964—Browns, 37-21 (C)
1967—Lions, 31-14 (D)
1969—Lions, 28-21 (C)
1970—Lions, 41-24 (C)
1975—Lions, 21-10 (D)
1983—Browns, 31-26 (D)
1986—Browns, 24-21 (C)
1989—Lions, 13-10 (D)
(RS Pts.—Lions 321, Browns 214)
(PS Pts.—Lions 103, Browns 93)
NFL Championship

CLEVELAND vs. GREEN BAY
RS: Packers lead series, 7-5
PS: Packers lead series, 1-0
1953—Browns, 27-0 (Mil)
1955—Browns, 41-10 (C)
1956—Browns, 24-7 (Mil)
1961—Packers, 49-17 (C)
1964—Packers, 28-21 (Mil)
1965—*Packers, 23-12 (GB)
1966—Packers, 21-20 (C)
1967—Packers, 55-7 (Mil)
1969—Browns, 20-7 (C)
1972—Packers, 26-10 (C)
1980—Browns, 26-21 (C)
1983—Packers, 35-21 (Mil)
1986—Packers, 17-14 (C)
(RS Pts.—Packers 276, Browns 248)
(PS Pts.—Packers 23, Browns 12)
NFL Championship

CLEVELAND vs. HOUSTON
RS: Browns lead series, 26-15
PS: Oilers lead series, 1-0
1970—Browns, 28-14 (C)
Browns, 21-10 (H)
1971—Browns, 31-0 (C)
Browns, 37-24 (H)
1972—Browns, 23-17 (H)
Browns, 20-0 (C)
1973—Browns, 42-13 (C)
Browns, 23-13 (H)
1974—Browns, 20-7 (C)
Oilers, 28-24 (H)
1975—Oilers, 40-10 (C)
Oilers, 21-10 (H)
1976—Browns, 21-7 (H)
Browns, 13-10 (C)
1977—Browns, 24-23 (H)
Oilers, 19-15 (C)
1978—Oilers, 16-13 (C)
Oilers, 14-10 (H)
1979—Oilers, 31-10 (H)
Browns, 14-7 (C)
1980—Oilers, 16-7 (C)
Browns, 17-14 (H)
1981—Oilers, 9-3 (C)
Oilers, 17-13 (H)
1982—Browns, 20-14 (H)
1983—Browns, 25-19 (C) OT
Oilers, 34-27 (H)
1984—Browns, 27-10 (C)
Browns, 27-20 (H)
1985—Browns, 21-6 (H)
Browns, 28-21 (C)
1986—Browns, 23-20 (H)
Browns, 13-10 (C) OT
1987—Oilers, 15-10 (C)
Browns, 40-7 (H)
1988—Oilers, 24-17 (H)
Browns, 28-23 (C)
*Oilers, 24-23 (C)
1989—Browns, 28-17 (C)
Browns, 24-20 (H)
1990—Oilers 35-23 (C)
Oilers 58-14 (H)
(RS Pts.—Browns 844, Oilers 723)
(PS Pts.—Oilers 24, Browns 23)
AFC First Round Playoff

CLEVELAND vs. *INDIANAPOLIS
RS: Browns lead series, 11-5
PS: Series tied, 2-2
1956—Colts, 21-7 (C)
1959—Browns, 38-31 (B)
1962—Colts, 36-14 (C)
1964—**Browns, 27-0 (C)
1968—Browns, 30-20 (B)
**Colts, 34-0 (C)
1971—Browns, 14-13 (B)
***Colts, 20-3 (C)
1973—Browns, 24-14 (C)
1975—Colts, 21-7 (B)
1978—Browns, 45-24 (B)
1979—Browns, 13-10 (C)
1980—Browns, 28-27 (B)
1981—Browns, 42-28 (C)
1983—Browns, 41-23 (C)
1986—Browns, 24-9 (I)
1987—Colts, 9-7 (C)
***Browns, 38-21 (C)
1988—Browns, 23-17 (C)
1989—Colts, 23-17 (I) OT
(RS Pts.—Browns 374, Colts 326)
(PS Pts.—Colts 75, Browns 68)
Franchise in Baltimore prior to 1984
***NFL Championship*
****AFC Divisional Playoff*

CLEVELAND vs. KANSAS CITY
RS: Series tied, 6-6-2
1971—Chiefs, 13-7 (KC)
1972—Chiefs, 31-7 (C)
1973—Tie, 20-20 (KC)
1975—Browns, 40-14 (C)
1976—Chiefs, 39-14 (KC)
1977—Browns, 44-7 (C)
1978—Chiefs, 17-3 (KC)
1979—Browns, 27-24 (KC)
1980—Browns, 20-13 (C)
1984—Chiefs, 10-6 (KC)
1986—Browns, 20-7 (C)
1988—Browns, 6-3 (KC)
1989—Tie, 10-10 (C) OT
1990—Chiefs, 34-0 (KC)
(RS Pts.—Chiefs 242, Browns 224)

CLEVELAND vs. *L.A.RAIDERS
RS: Raiders lead series, 8-2
PS: Raiders lead series, 2-0
1970—Raiders, 23-20 (O)
1971—Raiders, 34-20 (C)
1973—Browns, 7-3 (O)
1974—Raiders, 40-24 (C)
1975—Raiders, 38-17 (O)
1977—Raiders, 26-10 (C)
1979—Raiders, 19-14 (O)
1980—**Raiders, 14-12 (C)
1982—***Raiders, 27-10 (LA)
1985—Raiders, 21-20 (C)
1986—Raiders, 27-14 (LA)
1987—Browns, 24-17 (LA)
(RS Pts.—Raiders 248, Browns 170)
(PS Pts.—Raiders 41, Browns 22)
Franchise in Oakland prior to 1982
***AFC Divisional Playoff*
****AFC First Round Playoff*

CLEVELAND vs. L.A. RAMS
RS: Series tied, 7-7
PS: Browns lead series, 2-1
1950—*Browns, 30-28 (C)
1951—Browns, 38-23 (LA)
*Rams, 24-17 (LA)
1952—Browns, 37-7 (C)
1955—*Browns, 38-14 (LA)
1957—Browns, 45-31 (C)
1958—Browns, 30-27 (LA)
1963—Browns, 20-6 (C)
1965—Rams, 42-7 (LA)
1968—Rams, 24-6 (C)
1973—Rams, 30-17 (LA)
1977—Rams, 9-0 (C)
1978—Browns, 30-19 (C)
1981—Rams, 27-16 (LA)
1984—Rams, 20-17 (LA)
1987—Browns, 30-17 (C)
1990—Rams, 38-23 (C)
(RS Pts.—Rams 320, Browns 316)
(PS Pts.—Browns 85, Rams 66)
NFL Championship

CLEVELAND vs. MIAMI
RS: Series tied, 4-4
PS: Dolphins lead series, 2-0
1970—Browns, 28-0 (M)
1972—*Dolphins, 20-14 (M)
1973—Dolphins, 17-9 (C)
1976—Browns, 17-13 (C)
1979—Browns, 30-24 (C) OT
1985—*Dolphins, 24-21 (M)
1986—Browns, 26-16 (C)
1988—Dolphins, 38-31 (M)
1989—Dolphins, 13-10 (M) OT
1990—Dolphins, 30-13 (C)
(RS Pts.—Browns 164, Dolphins 151)
(PS Pts.—Dolphins 44, Browns 35)
AFC Divisional Playoff

CLEVELAND vs. MINNESOTA
RS: Vikings lead series, 6-3
PS: Vikings lead series, 1-0
1965—Vikings, 27-17 (C)
1967—Browns, 14-10 (C)
1969—Vikings, 51-3 (M)
*Vikings, 27-7 (M)
1973—Vikings, 26-3 (M)
1975—Vikings, 42-10 (C)
1980—Vikings, 28-23 (M)
1983—Vikings, 27-21 (C)
1986—Browns, 23-20 (M)
1989—Browns, 23-17 (C) OT
(RS Pts.—Vikings 248, Browns 137)
(PS Pts.—Vikings 27, Browns 7)
NFL Championship

CLEVELAND vs. NEW ENGLAND
RS: Browns lead series, 7-2
1971—Browns, 27-7 (C)
1974—Browns, 21-14 (NE)
1977—Browns, 30-27 (C) OT
1980—Patriots, 34-17 (NE)
1982—Browns, 10-7 (C)
1983—Browns, 30-0 (NE)
1984—Patriots, 17-16 (C)
1985—Browns, 24-20 (C)
1987—Browns, 20-10 (NE)
(RS Pts.—Browns 195, Patriots 136)

CLEVELAND vs. NEW ORLEANS
RS: Browns lead series, 8-3
1967—Browns, 42-7 (NO)
1968—Browns, 24-10 (NO)
Browns, 35-17 (C)
1969—Browns, 27-17 (NO)
1971—Browns, 21-17 (NO)
1975—Browns, 17-16 (C)
1978—Browns, 24-16 (NO)
1981—Browns, 20-17 (C)
1984—Saints, 16-14 (C)
1987—Saints, 28-21 (NO)
1990—Saints, 25-20 (NO)
(RS Pts.—Browns 265, Saints 186)

CLEVELAND vs. N.Y. GIANTS
RS: Browns lead series, 25-15-2
PS: Series tied, 1-1
1950—Giants, 6-0 (C)
Giants, 17-13 (NY)
*Browns, 8-3 (C)
1951—Browns, 14-13 (C)
Browns, 10-0 (NY)
1952—Giants, 17-9 (C)
Giants, 37-34 (NY)
1953—Browns, 7-0 (NY)
Browns, 62-14 (C)
1954—Browns, 24-14 (C)
Browns, 16-7 (NY)
1955—Browns, 24-14 (C)
Tie, 35-35 (NY)
1956—Giants, 21-9 (C)
Browns, 24-7 (NY)
1957—Browns, 6-3 (C)
Browns, 34-28 (NY)
1958—Giants, 21-17 (C)
Giants, 13-10 (NY)
*Giants, 10-0 (NY)
1959—Giants, 10-6 (C)
Giants, 48-7 (NY)
1960—Giants, 17-13 (C)
Browns, 48-34 (NY)
1961—Giants, 37-21 (C)
Tie, 7-7 (NY)
1962—Browns, 17-7 (C)
Giants, 17-13 (NY)
1963—Browns, 35-24 (NY)
Giants, 33-6 (C)
1964—Browns, 42-20 (C)
Browns, 52-20 (NY)
1965—Browns, 38-14 (NY)
Browns, 34-21 (C)
1966—Browns, 28-7 (NY)
Browns, 49-40 (C)
1967—Giants, 38-34 (NY)
Browns, 24-14 (C)
1968—Browns, 45-10 (C)
1969—Browns, 28-17 (C)
Giants, 27-14 (NY)
1973—Browns, 12-10 (C)
1977—Browns, 21-7 (NY)
1985—Browns, 35-33 (NY)
(RS Pts.—Browns 977, Giants 779)
(PS Pts.—Giants 13, Browns 8)
Conference Playoff

CLEVELAND vs. N.Y. JETS
RS: Browns lead series, 8-5
PS: Browns lead series, 1-0
1970—Browns, 31-21 (C)
1972—Browns, 26-10 (NY)
1976—Browns, 38-17 (C)
1978—Browns, 37-34 (C) OT
1979—Browns, 25-22 (NY) OT
1980—Browns, 17-14 (C)
1981—Jets, 14-13 (C)
1983—Browns, 10-7 (C)
1984—Jets, 24-20 (C)
1985—Jets, 37-10 (NY)
1986—*Browns, 23-20 (C) OT
1988—Jets, 23-3 (C)
1989—Browns, 38-24 (C)
1990—Jets, 24-21 (NY)
(RS Pts.—Browns 289, Jets 271)
(PS Pts.—Browns 23, Jets 20)
AFC Divisional Playoff

CLEVELAND vs. PHILADELPHIA
RS: Browns lead series, 30-11-1
1950—Browns, 35-10 (P)
Browns, 13-7 (C)
1951—Browns, 20-17 (C)
Browns, 24-9 (NY)
1952—Browns, 49-7 (P)
Eagles, 28-20 (C)
1953—Browns, 37-13 (C)
Eagles, 42-27 (P)
1954—Eagles, 28-10 (P)
Browns, 6-0 (C)
1955—Browns, 21-17 (C)
Eagles, 33-17 (P)
1956—Browns, 16-0 (P)
Browns, 17-14 (C)
1957—Browns, 24-7 (C)
Eagles, 17-7 (P)
1958—Browns, 28-14 (C)
Browns, 21-14 (P)
1959—Browns, 28-7 (C)
Browns, 28-21 (P)
1960—Browns, 41-24 (P)
Eagles, 31-29 (C)
1961—Eagles, 27-20 (P)
Browns, 45-24 (C)
1962—Eagles, 35-7 (P)
Tie, 14-14 (C)
1963—Browns, 37-7 (C)
Browns, 23-17 (P)
1964—Browns, 28-20 (P)
Browns, 38-24 (C)
1965—Browns, 35-17 (P)
Browns, 38-34 (C)
1966—Browns, 27-7 (C)
Eagles, 33-21 (P)
1967—Eagles, 28-24 (P)
1968—Browns, 47-13 (C)
1969—Browns, 27-20 (P)
1972—Browns, 27-17 (P)
1976—Browns, 24-3 (C)
1979—Browns, 24-19 (P)
1982—Eagles, 24-21 (C)
1988—Browns, 19-3 (C)
(RS Pts.—Browns 1,064, Eagles 746)

CLEVELAND vs. *PHOENIX
RS: Browns lead series, 31-10-3
1950—Browns, 34-24 (Cle)
Browns, 10-7 (Chi)
1951—Browns, 34-17 (Chi)
Browns, 49-28 (Cle)
1952—Browns, 28-13 (Cle)
Browns, 10-0 (Chi)
1953—Browns, 27-7 (Chi)
Browns, 27-16 (Cle)

1954—Browns, 31-7 (Cle)
Browns, 35-3 (Chi)
1955—Browns, 26-20 (Chi)
Browns, 35-24 (Cle)
1956—Cardinals, 9-7 (Chi)
Cardinals, 24-7 (Cle)
1957—Browns, 17-7 (Chi)
Browns, 31-0 (Cle)
1958—Browns, 35-28 (Cle)
Browns, 38-24 (Chi)
1959—Browns, 34-7 (Chi)
Browns, 17-7 (Cle)
1960—Browns, 28-27 (Cle)
Tie, 17-17 (StL)
1961—Browns, 20-17 (Cle)
Browns, 21-10 (StL)
1962—Browns, 34-7 (StL)
Browns, 38-14 (Cle)
1963—Cardinals, 20-14 (Cle)
Browns, 24-10 (StL)
1964—Tie, 33-33 (Cle)
Cardinals, 28-19 (StL)
1965—Cardinals, 49-13 (Cle)
Browns, 27-24 (StL)
1966—Cardinals, 34-28 (Cle)
Browns, 38-10 (StL)
1967—Browns, 20-16 (Cle)
Browns, 20-16 (StL)
1968—Cardinals, 27-21 (Cle)
Cardinals, 27-16 (StL)
1969—Tie, 21-21 (Cle)
Browns, 27-21 (StL)
1974—Cardinals, 29-7 (StL)
1979—Browns, 38-20 (StL)
1985—Cardinals, 27-24 (Cle) OT
1988—Browns, 29-21 (P)
(RS Pts.—Browns 1,109, Cardinals 797)
**Franchise in St. Louis prior to 1988, and in Chicago prior to 1960*

CLEVELAND vs. PITTSBURGH
RS: Browns lead series, 49-33
1950—Browns, 30-17 (P)
Browns, 45-7 (C)
1951—Browns, 17-0 (C)
Browns, 28-0 (P)
1952—Browns, 21-20 (P)
Browns, 29-28 (C)
1953—Browns, 34-16 (C)
Browns, 20-16 (P)
1954—Steelers, 55-27 (P)
Browns, 42-7 (C)
1955—Browns, 41-14 (C)
Browns, 30-7 (P)
1956—Browns, 14-10 (P)
Steelers, 24-16 (C)
1957—Browns, 23-12 (P)
Browns, 24-0 (C)
1958—Browns, 45-12 (P)
Browns, 27-10 (C)
1959—Steelers, 17-7 (P)
Steelers, 21-20 (C)
1960—Browns, 28-20 (C)
Steelers, 14-10 (P)
1961—Browns, 30-28 (P)
Steelers, 17-13 (C)
1962—Browns, 41-14 (P)
Browns, 35-14 (C)
1963—Browns, 35-23 (C)
Steelers, 9-7 (P)
1964—Steelers, 23-7 (C)
Browns, 30-17 (P)
1965—Browns, 24-19 (C)
Browns, 42-21 (P)
1966—Browns, 41-10 (C)
Steelers, 16-6 (P)
1967—Browns, 21-10 (C)
Browns, 34-14 (P)
1968—Browns, 31-24 (C)
Browns, 45-24 (P)
1969—Browns, 42-31 (C)
Browns, 24-3 (P)
1970—Browns, 15-7 (C)
Steelers, 28-9 (P)
1971—Browns, 27-17 (C)
Steelers, 26-9 (P)
1972—Browns, 26-24 (C)
Steelers, 30-0 (P)
1973—Steelers, 33-6 (P)
Browns, 21-16 (C)
1974—Steelers, 20-16 (P)
Steelers, 26-16 (C)
1975—Steelers, 42-6 (C)
Steelers, 31-17 (P)
1976—Steelers, 31-14 (P)
Browns, 18-16 (C)
1977—Steelers, 28-14 (C)
Steelers, 35-31 (P)
1978—Steelers, 15-9 (P) OT
Steelers, 34-14 (C)
1979—Steelers, 51-35 (C)
Steelers, 33-30 (P) OT
1980—Browns, 27-26 (C)
Steelers, 16-13 (P)
1981—Steelers, 13-7 (P)
Steelers, 32-10 (C)
1982—Browns, 10-9 (C)
Steelers, 37-21 (P)
1983—Steelers, 44-17 (P)
Browns, 30-17 (C)
1984—Browns, 20-10 (C)
Steelers, 23-20 (P)
1985—Browns, 17-7 (C)
Steelers, 10-9 (P)
1986—Browns, 27-24 (P)
Browns, 37-31 (C) OT
1987—Browns, 34-10 (C)
Browns, 19-13 (P)
1988—Browns, 23-9 (P)
Browns, 27-7 (C)
1989—Browns, 51-0 (P)
Steelers, 17-7 (C)
1990—Browns, 13-3 (C)
Steelers, 35-0 (P)
(RS Pts.—Browns 1,858, Steelers 1,580)

CLEVELAND vs. SAN DIEGO
RS: Chargers lead series, 7-5-1
1970—Chargers, 27-10 (C)
1972—Browns, 21-17 (SD)
1973—Tie, 16-16 (C)
1974—Chargers, 36-35 (SD)
1976—Browns, 21-17 (C)
1977—Chargers, 37-14 (SD)
1981—Chargers, 44-14 (C)
1982—Chargers, 30-13 (C)
1983—Browns, 30-24 (SD) OT
1985—Browns, 21-7 (SD)
1986—Browns, 47-17 (C)
1987—Chargers, 27-24 (SD) OT
1990—Chargers, 24-14 (C)
(RS Pts.—Chargers 323, Browns 280)

CLEVELAND vs. SAN FRANCISCO
RS: Browns lead series, 8-6
1950—Browns, 34-14 (C)
1951—49ers, 24-10 (SF)
1953—Browns, 23-21 (C)
1955—Browns, 38-3 (SF)
1959—49ers, 21-20 (C)
1962—Browns, 13-10 (SF)
1968—Browns, 33-21 (SF)
1970—49ers, 34-31 (SF)
1974—Browns, 7-0 (C)
1978—Browns, 24-7 (C)
1981—Browns, 15-12 (SF)
1984—49ers, 41-7 (C)
1987—49ers, 38-24 (SF)
1990—49ers, 20-17 (SF)
(RS Pts.—Browns 296, 49ers 266)

CLEVELAND vs. SEATTLE
RS: Seahawks lead series, 8-3
1977—Seahawks, 20-19 (S)
1978—Seahawks, 47-24 (S)
1979—Seahawks, 29-24 (C)
1980—Browns, 27-3 (S)
1981—Seahawks, 42-21 (S)
1982—Browns, 21-7 (S)
1983—Seahawks, 24-9 (C)
1984—Seahawks, 33-0 (S)
1985—Seahawks, 31-13 (S)
1988—Seahawks, 16-10 (C)
1989—Browns, 17-7 (S)
(RS Pts.—Seahawks 259, Browns 185)

CLEVELAND vs. TAMPA BAY
RS: Browns lead series, 4-0
1976—Browns, 24-7 (TB)
1980—Browns, 34-27 (TB)
1983—Browns, 20-0 (C)
1989—Browns, 42-31 (TB)
(RS Pts.—Browns 120, Buccaneers 65)

CLEVELAND vs. WASHINGTON
RS: Browns lead series, 32-8-1
1950—Browns, 20-14 (C)
Browns, 45-21 (W)
1951—Browns, 45-0 (C)
1952—Browns, 19-15 (C)
Browns, 48-24 (W)
1953—Browns, 30-14 (W)
Browns, 27-3 (C)
1954—Browns, 62-3 (C)
Browns, 34-14 (W)
1955—Redskins, 27-17 (C)
Browns, 24-14 (W)
1956—Redskins, 20-9 (W)
Redskins, 20-17 (C)
1957—Browns, 21-17 (C)
Tie, 30-30 (W)
1958—Browns, 20-10 (W)
Browns, 21-14 (C)
1959—Browns, 34-7 (C)
Browns, 31-17 (W)
1960—Browns, 31-10 (W)
Browns, 27-16 (C)
1961—Browns, 31-7 (C)
Browns, 17-6 (W)
1962—Redskins, 17-16 (C)
Redskins, 17-9 (W)
1963—Browns, 37-14 (C)
Browns, 27-20 (W)
1964—Browns, 27-13 (W)
Browns, 34-24 (C)
1965—Browns, 17-7 (W)
Browns, 24-16 (C)
1966—Browns, 38-14 (W)
Browns, 14-3 (C)
1967—Browns, 42-37 (C)
1968—Browns, 24-21 (W)
1969—Browns, 27-23 (C)
1971—Browns, 20-13 (W)
1975—Redskins, 23-7 (C)
1979—Redskins, 13-9 (C)
1985—Redskins, 14-7 (C)
1988—Browns, 17-13 (W)
(RS Pts.—Browns 1,056, Redskins 625)

DALLAS vs. ATLANTA
RS: Cowboys lead series, 7-5
PS: Cowboys lead series, 2-0;
See Atlanta vs. Dallas

DALLAS vs. BUFFALO
RS: Cowboys lead series, 3-1;
See Buffalo vs. Dallas

DALLAS vs. CHICAGO
RS: Cowboys lead series, 7-6
PS: Cowboys lead series, 1-0;
See Chicago vs. Dallas

DALLAS vs. CINCINNATI
RS: Series tied, 2-2;
See Cincinnati vs. Dallas

DALLAS vs. CLEVELAND
RS: Browns lead series, 14-8
PS: Browns lead series, 2-1;
See Cleveland vs. Dallas

DALLAS vs. DENVER
RS: Series tied, 2-2
PS: Cowboys lead series, 1-0
1973—-Cowboys, 22-10 (Den)
1977—Cowboys, 14-6 (Dal)
*Cowboys, 27-10 (New Orleans)
1980—Broncos, 41-20 (Den)
1986—Broncos, 29-14 (Den)
(RS Pts.—Broncos 86, Cowboys 70)
(PS Pts.—Cowboys 27, Broncos 10)
**Super Bowl XII*

DALLAS vs. DETROIT
RS: Cowboys lead series, 6-4
PS: Cowboys lead series, 1-0
1960—Lions, 23-14 (Det)
1963—Cowboys, 17-14 (Dal)
1968—Cowboys, 59-13 (Dal)
1970—*Cowboys, 5-0 (Dal)
1972—Cowboys, 28-24 (Dal)
1975—Cowboys, 36-10 (Det)
1977—Cowboys, 37-0 (Dal)
1981—Lions, 27-24 (Det)
1985—Lions, 26-21 (Det)
1986—Cowboys, 31-7 (Det)
1987—Lions, 27-17 (Det)
(RS Pts.—Cowboys 284, Lions 171)
(PS Pts.—Cowboys 5, Lions 0)
**NFC Divisional Playoff*

DALLAS vs. GREEN BAY
RS: Packers lead series, 8-4
PS: Packers lead series, 2-1
1960—Packers, 41-7 (GB)
1964—Packers, 45-21 (D)
1965—Packers, 13-3 (Mil)
1966—*Packers, 34-27 (D)
1967—*Packers, 21-17 (GB)
1968—Packers, 28-17 (D)
1970—Cowboys, 16-3 (D)
1972—Packers, 16-13 (Mil)
1975—Packers, 19-17 (D)
1978—Cowboys, 42-14 (Mil)
1980—Cowboys, 28-7 (Mil)
1982—**Cowboys, 37-26 (D)
1984—Cowboys, 20-6 (D)
1989—Packers, 31-13 (GB)
Packers, 20-10 (D)
(RS Pts.—Packers 243, Cowboys 207)
(PS Pts.—Cowboys 81, Packers 81)
**NFL Championship*
***NFC Second Round Playoff*

DALLAS vs. HOUSTON
RS: Cowboys lead series, 4-2
1970—Cowboys, 52-10 (D)
1974—Cowboys, 10-0 (H)
1979—Oilers, 30-24 (D)
1982—Cowboys, 37-7 (H)
1985—Cowboys, 17-10 (H)
1988—Oilers, 25-17 (D)
(RS Pts.—Cowboys 157, Oilers 82)

DALLAS vs. *INDIANAPOLIS
RS: Cowboys lead series, 6-2
PS: Colts lead series, 1-0
1960—Colts, 45-7 (D)
1967—Colts, 23-17 (B)
1969—Cowboys, 27-10 (D)
1970—**Colts, 16-13 (Miami)
1972—Cowboys, 21-0 (B)
1976—Cowboys, 30-27 (D)
1978—Cowboys, 38-0 (D)
1981—Cowboys, 37-13 (B)
1984—Cowboys, 22-3 (D)
(RS Pts.—Cowboys 199, Colts 121)
(PS Pts.—Colts 16, Cowboys 13)
**Franchise in Baltimore prior to 1984*
***Super Bowl V*

DALLAS vs. KANSAS CITY
RS: Series tied, 2-2
1970—Cowboys, 27-16 (KC)
1975—Chiefs, 34-31 (D)
1983—Cowboys, 41-21 (D)
1989—Chiefs, 36-28 (KC)
(RS Pts.—Cowboys 127, Chiefs 107)

DALLAS vs. *L.A. RAIDERS
RS: Raiders lead series, 3-1
1974—Raiders, 27-23 (O)
1980—Cowboys, 19-13 (O)
1983—Raiders, 40-38 (D)
1986—Raiders, 17-13 (D)
(RS Pts.—Raiders 97, Cowboys 93)
**Franchise in Oakland prior to 1982*

DALLAS vs. L.A. RAMS
RS: Series tied, 8-8
PS: Series tied, 4-4
1960—Rams, 38-13 (D)
1962—Cowboys, 27-17 (LA)
1967—Rams, 35-13 (D)
1969—Rams, 24-23 (LA)
1971—Cowboys, 28-21 (D)
1973—Rams, 37-31 (LA)
*Cowboys, 27-16 (D)
1975—Cowboys, 18-7 (D)
**Cowboys, 37-7 (LA)
1976—*Rams, 14-12 (D)
1978—Rams, 27-14 (LA)
**Cowboys, 28-0 (LA)
1979—Cowboys, 30-6 (D)
*Rams, 21-19 (D)
1980—Rams, 38-14 (LA)
***Cowboys, 34-13 (D)
1981—Cowboys, 29-17 (D)
1983—***Rams, 24-17 (D)
1984—Cowboys, 20-13 (LA)
1985—*Rams, 20-0 (LA)
1986—Rams, 29-10 (LA)
1987—Cowboys, 29-21 (LA)
1989—Rams, 35-31 (D)
1990—Cowboys, 24-21 (LA)
(RS Pts.—Rams 386, Cowboys 354)
(PS Pts.—Cowboys 174, Rams 115)
**NFC Divisional Playoff*
***NFC Championship*
****NFC First Round Playoff*

DALLAS vs. MIAMI
RS: Dolphins lead series, 5-1
PS: Cowboys lead series, 1-0
1971—*Cowboys, 24-3 (New Orleans)
1973—Dolphins, 14-7 (D)
1978—Dolphins, 23-16 (M)
1981—Cowboys, 28-27 (D)
1984—Dolphins, 28-21 (M)
1987—Dolphins, 20-14 (D)
1989—Dolphins, 17-14 (D)
(RS Pts.—Dolphins 129, Cowboys 100)
(PS Pts.—Cowboys 24, Dolphins 3)
**Super Bowl VI*

DALLAS vs. MINNESOTA
RS: Cowboys lead series, 7-6
PS: Cowboys lead series, 3-1
1961—Cowboys, 21-7 (D)
Cowboys, 28-0 (M)
1966—Cowboys, 28-17 (D)
1968—Cowboys, 20-7 (M)
1970—Vikings, 54-13 (M)
1971—*Cowboys, 20-12 (M)
1973—**Vikings, 27-10 (D)
1974—Vikings, 23-21 (D)
1975—*Cowboys, 17-14 (M)
1977—Cowboys, 16-10 (M) OT
**Cowboys, 23-6 (D)
1978—Vikings, 21-10 (D)
1979—Cowboys, 36-20 (M)
1982—Vikings, 31-27 (M)
1983—Cowboys, 37-24 (M)
1987—Vikings, 44-38 (D) OT
1988—Vikings, 43-3 (D)
(RS Pts.—Vikings 301, Cowboys 298)
(PS Pts.—Cowboys 70, Vikings 59)
**NFC Divisional Playoff*
***NFC Championship*

DALLAS vs. NEW ENGLAND
RS: Cowboys lead series, 6-0
1971—Cowboys, 44-21 (D)
1975—Cowboys, 34-31 (NE)
1978—Cowboys, 17-10 (D)
1981—Cowboys, 35-21 (NE)
1984—Cowboys, 20-17 (D)
1987—Cowboys, 23-17 (NE) OT
(RS Pts.—Cowboys 173, Patriots 117)

DALLAS vs. NEW ORLEANS
RS: Cowboys lead series, 12-3
1967—Cowboys, 14-10 (D)

Cowboys, 27-10 (NO)
1968—Cowboys, 17-3 (NO)
1969—Cowboys, 21-17 (NO)
Cowboys, 33-17 (D)
1971—Saints, 24-14 (NO)
1973—Cowboys, 40-3 (D)
1976—Cowboys, 24-6 (NO)
1978—Cowboys, 27-7 (D)
1982—Cowboys, 21-7 (D)
1983—Cowboys, 21-20 (D)
1984—Cowboys, 30-27 (D) OT
1988—Saints, 20-17 (NO)
1989—Saints, 28-0 (NO)
1990—Cowboys, 17-13 (D)
(RS Pts.—Cowboys 323, Saints 212)

DALLAS vs. N.Y. GIANTS
RS: Cowboys lead series, 35-20-2
1960—Tie, 31-31 (NY)
1961—Giants, 31-10 (D)
Cowboys, 17-16 (NY)
1962—Giants, 41-10 (D)
Giants, 41-31 (NY)
1963—Giants, 37-21 (NY)
Giants, 34-27 (D)
1964—Tie, 13-13 (D)
Cowboys, 31-21 (NY)
1965—Cowboys, 31-2 (D)
Cowboys, 38-20 (NY)
1966—Cowboys, 52-7 (D)
Cowboys, 17-7 (NY)
1967—Cowboys, 38-24 (D)
1968—Giants, 27-21 (D)
Cowboys, 28-10 (NY)
1969—Cowboys, 25-3 (D)
1970—Cowboys, 28-10 (D)
Giants, 23-20 (NY)
1971—Cowboys, 20-13 (D)
Cowboys, 42-14 (NY)
1972—Cowboys, 23-14 (NY)
Giants, 23-3 (D)
1973—Cowboys, 45-28 (D)
Cowboys, 23-10 (New Haven)
1974—Giants, 14-6 (D)
Cowboys, 21-7 (New Haven)
1975—Cowboys, 13-7 (NY)
Cowboys, 14-3 (D)
1976—Cowboys, 24-14 (NY)
Cowboys, 9-3 (D)
1977—Cowboys, 41-21 (D)
Cowboys, 24-10 (NY)
1978—Cowboys, 34-24 (NY)
Cowboys, 24-3 (D)
1979—Cowboys, 16-14 (NY)
Cowboys, 28-7 (D)
1980—Cowboys, 24-3 (D)
Giants, 38-35 (NY)
1981—Cowboys, 18-10 (D)
Giants, 13-10 (NY) OT
1983—Cowboys, 28-13 (D)
Cowboys, 38-20 (NY)
1984—Giants, 28-7 (NY)
Giants, 19-7 (D)
1985—Cowboys, 30-29 (NY)
Cowboys, 28-21 (D)
1986—Cowboys, 31-28 (D)
Giants, 17-14 (NY)
1987—Cowboys, 16-14 (NY)
Cowboys, 33-24 (D)
1988—Giants, 12-10 (D)
Giants, 29-21 (NY)
1989—Giants, 30-13 (D)
Giants, 15-0 (NY)
1990—Giants, 28-7 (D)
Giants, 31-17 (NY)
(RS Pts.—Cowboys 1,286, Giants 1,049)

DALLAS vs. N.Y. JETS
RS: Cowboys lead series, 4-1
1971—Cowboys, 52-10 (D)
1975—Cowboys, 31-21 (NY)
1978—Cowboys, 30-7 (NY)
1987—Cowboys, 38-24 (NY)
1990—Jets, 24-9 (NY)
(RS Pts.—Cowboys 160, Jets 86)

DALLAS vs. PHILADELPHIA
RS: Cowboys lead series, 36-24
PS: Eagles lead series, 1-0
1960—Eagles, 27-25 (D)
1961—Eagles, 43-7 (D)
Eagles, 35-13 (P)
1962—Cowboys, 41-19 (D)
Eagles, 28-14 (P)
1963—Eagles, 24-21 (P)
Cowboys, 27-20 (D)
1964—Eagles, 17-14 (D)
Eagles, 24-14 (P)
1965—Eagles, 35-24 (D)
Cowboys, 21-19 (P)
1966—Cowboys, 56-7 (D)
Eagles, 24-23 (P)
1967—Eagles, 21-14 (P)
Cowboys, 38-17 (D)
1968—Cowboys, 45-13 (P)
Cowboys, 34-14 (D)
1969—Cowboys, 38-7 (P)
Cowboys, 49-14 (D)
1970—Cowboys, 17-7 (P)
Cowboys, 21-17 (D)
1971—Cowboys, 42-7 (P)
Cowboys, 20-7 (D)
1972—Cowboys, 28-6 (D)
Cowboys, 28-7 (P)
1973—Eagles, 30-16 (P)
Cowboys, 31-10 (D)
1974—Eagles, 13-10 (P)
Cowboys, 31-24 (D)
1975—Cowboys, 20-17 (P)
Cowboys, 27-17 (D)
1976—Cowboys, 27-7 (D)
Cowboys, 26-7 (P)
1977—Cowboys, 16-10 (P)
Cowboys, 24-14 (D)
1978—Cowboys, 14-7 (D)
Cowboys, 31-13 (P)
1979—Eagles, 31-21 (D)
Cowboys, 24-17 (P)
1980—Eagles, 17-10 (P)
Cowboys, 35-27 (D)
*Eagles, 20-7 (P)
1981—Cowboys, 17-14 (P)
Cowboys, 21-10 (D)
1982—Eagles, 24-20 (D)
1983—Cowboys, 37-7 (D)
Cowboys, 27-20 (P)
1984—Cowboys, 23-17 (D)
Cowboys, 26-10 (P)
1985—Eagles, 16-14 (P)
Cowboys, 34-17 (D)
1986—Cowboys, 17-14 (P)
Eagles, 23-21 (D)
1987—Cowboys, 41-22 (D)
Eagles, 37-20 (P)
1988—Eagles, 24-23 (P)
Eagles, 23-7 (D)
1989—Eagles, 27-0 (D)
Eagles, 20-10 (P)
1990—Eagles, 21-20 (D)
Eagles, 17-3 (P)
(RS Pts.—Cowboys 1,418, Eagles 1,083)
(PS Pts.—Eagles 20, Cowboys 7)
**NFC Championship*

DALLAS vs. *PHOENIX
RS: Cowboys lead series, 34-22-1
1960—Cardinals, 12-10 (StL)
1961—Cardinals, 31-17 (D)
Cardinals, 31-13 (StL)
1962—Cardinals, 28-24 (D)
Cardinals, 52-20 (StL)
1963—Cardinals, 34-7 (D)
Cowboys, 28-24 (StL)
1964—Cardinals, 16-6 (D)
Cowboys, 31-13 (StL)
1965—Cardinals, 20-13 (StL)
Cowboys, 27-13 (D)
1966—Tie, 10-10 (StL)
Cowboys, 31-17 (D)
1967—Cowboys, 46-21 (D)
1968—Cowboys, 27-10 (StL)
1969—Cowboys, 24-3 (D)
1970—Cardinals, 20-7 (StL)
Cardinals, 38-0 (D)
1971—Cowboys, 16-13 (StL)
Cowboys, 31-12 (D)
1972—Cowboys, 33-24 (D)
Cowboys, 27-6 (StL)
1973—Cowboys, 45-10 (D)
Cowboys, 30-3 (StL)
1974—Cardinals, 31-28 (StL)
Cowboys, 17-14 (D)
1975—Cowboys, 37-31 (D) OT
Cardinals, 31-17 (StL)
1976—Cardinals, 21-17 (StL)
Cowboys, 19-14 (D)
1977—Cowboys, 30-24 (StL)
Cardinals, 24-17 (D)
1978—Cowboys, 21-12 (D)
Cowboys, 24-21 (StL) OT
1979—Cowboys, 22-21 (StL)
Cowboys, 22-13 (D)
1980—Cowboys, 27-24 (StL)
Cowboys, 31-21 (D)
1981—Cowboys, 30-17 (D)
Cardinals, 20-17 (StL)
1982—Cowboys, 24-7 (StL)
1983—Cowboys, 34-17 (StL)
Cowboys, 35-17 (D)
1984—Cardinals, 31-20 (D)
Cowboys, 24-17 (StL)
1985—Cardinals, 21-10 (StL)
Cowboys, 35-17 (D)
1986—Cowboys, 31-7 (StL)
Cowboys, 37-6 (D)
1987—Cardinals, 24-13 (StL)
Cowboys, 21-16 (D)
1988—Cowboys, 17-14 (P)
Cardinals, 16-10 (D)
1989—Cardinals, 19-10 (D)
Cardinals, 24-20 (P)
1990—Cardinals, 20-3 (P)
Cowboys, 41-10 (D)
(RS Pts.—Cowboys 1,284, Cardinals 1,083)
**Franchise in St. Louis prior to 1988*

DALLAS vs. PITTSBURGH
RS: Series tied, 11-11
PS: Steelers lead series, 2-0
1960—Steelers, 35-28 (D)
1961—Cowboys, 27-24 (D)
Steelers, 37-7 (P)
1962—Steelers, 30-28 (D)
Cowboys, 42-27 (P)
1963—Steelers, 27-21 (P)
Steelers, 24-19 (D)
1964—Steelers, 23-17 (P)
Cowboys, 17-14 (D)
1965—Steelers, 22-13 (P)
Cowboys, 24-17 (D)
1966—Cowboys, 52-21 (D)
Cowboys, 20-7 (P)
1967—Cowboys, 24-21 (P)
1968—Cowboys, 28-7 (D)
1969—Cowboys, 10-7 (P)
1972—Cowboys, 17-13 (D)
1975—*Steelers, 21-17 (Miami)
1977—Steelers, 28-13 (P)
1978—**Steelers, 35-31 (Miami)
1979—Steelers, 14-3 (P)
1982—Steelers, 36-28 (D)
1985—Cowboys, 27-13 (D)
1988—Steelers, 24-21 (P)
(RS Pts.—Cowboys 486, Steelers 471)
(PS Pts.—Steelers 56, Cowboys 48)
**Super Bowl X*
***Super Bowl XIII*

DALLAS vs. SAN DIEGO
RS: Cowboys lead series, 4-1
1972—Cowboys, 34-28 (SD)
1980—Cowboys, 42-31 (D)
1983—Chargers, 24-23 (SD)
1986—Cowboys, 24-21 (SD)
1990—Cowboys, 17-14 (D)
(RS Pts.—Cowboys 140, Chargers 118)

DALLAS vs. SAN FRANCISCO
RS: 49ers lead series, 9-5-1
PS: Cowboys lead series, 3-1
1960—49ers, 26-14 (D)
1963—49ers, 31-24 (SF)
1965—Cowboys, 39-31 (D)
1967—49ers, 24-16 (SF)
1969—Tie, 24-24 (D)
1970—*Cowboys, 17-10 (SF)
1971—*Cowboys, 14-3 (D)
1972—49ers, 31-10 (D)
**Cowboys, 30-28 (SF)
1974—Cowboys, 20-14 (D)
1977—Cowboys, 42-35 (SF)
1979—Cowboys, 21-13 (SF)
1980—Cowboys, 59-14 (D)
1981—49ers, 45-14 (SF)
*49ers, 28-27 (SF)
1983—49ers, 42-17 (SF)
1985—49ers, 31-16 (SF)
1989—49ers, 31-14 (D)
1990—49ers, 24-6 (D)
(RS Pts.—49ers 416, Cowboys 336)
(PS Pts.—Cowboys 88, 49ers 69)
**NFC Championship*
***NFC Divisional Playoff*

DALLAS vs. SEATTLE
RS: Cowboys lead series, 3-1
1976—Cowboys, 28-13 (S)
1980—Cowboys, 51-7 (D)
1983—Cowboys, 35-10 (S)
1986—Seahawks, 31-14 (D)
(RS Pts.—Cowboys 128, Seahawks 61)

DALLAS vs. TAMPA BAY
RS: Cowboys lead series, 6-0
PS: Cowboys lead series, 2-0
1977—Cowboys, 23-7 (D)
1980—Cowboys, 28-17 (D)
1981—*Cowboys, 38-0 (D)
1982—Cowboys, 14-9 (D)
**Cowboys, 30-17 (D)
1983—Cowboys, 27-24 (D) OT
1990—Cowboys, 14-10 (D)
Cowboys 17-13 (TB)
(RS Pts.—Cowboys 123, Buccaneers 80)
(PS Pts.—Cowboys 68, Buccaneers 17)
**NFC Divisional Playoff*
***NFC First Round Playoff*

DALLAS vs. WASHINGTON
RS: Cowboys lead series, 34-24-2
PS: Redskins lead series, 2-0
1960—Redskins, 26-14 (W)
1961—Tie, 28-28 (D)
Redskins, 34-24 (W)
1962—Tie, 35-35 (D)
Cowboys, 38-10 (W)
1963—Redskins, 21-17 (W)
Cowboys, 35-20 (D)
1964—Cowboys, 24-18 (D)
Redskins, 28-16 (W)
1965—Cowboys, 27-7 (D)
Redskins, 34-31 (W)
1966—Cowboys, 31-30 (W)
Redskins, 34-31 (D)
1967—Cowboys, 17-14 (W)
Redskins, 27-20 (D)
1968—Cowboys, 44-24 (W)
Cowboys, 29-20 (D)
1969—Cowboys, 41-28 (W)
Cowboys, 20-10 (D)
1970—Cowboys, 45-21 (W)
Cowboys, 34-0 (D)
1971—Redskins, 20-16 (D)
Cowboys, 13-0 (W)
1972—Redskins, 24-20 (W)
Cowboys, 34-24 (D)
*Redskins, 26-3 (W)
1973—Redskins, 14-7 (W)
Cowboys, 27-7 (D)
1974—Redskins, 28-21 (W)
Cowboys, 24-23 (D)
1975—Redskins, 30-24 (W) OT
Cowboys, 31-10 (D)
1976—Cowboys, 20-7 (W)
Redskins, 27-14 (D)
1977—Cowboys, 34-16 (D)
Cowboys, 14-7 (W)
1978—Redskins, 9-5 (W)
Cowboys, 37-10 (D)
1979—Redskins, 34-20 (W)
Cowboys, 35-34 (D)
1980—Cowboys, 17-3 (W)
Cowboys, 14-10 (D)
1981—Cowboys, 26-10 (W)
Cowboys, 24-10 (D)
1982—Cowboys, 24-10 (W)
*Redskins, 31-17 (W)
1983—Cowboys, 31-30 (W)
Redskins, 31-10 (D)
1984—Redskins, 34-14 (W)
Redskins, 30-28 (D)
1985—Cowboys, 44-14 (D)
Cowboys, 13-7 (W)
1986—Cowboys, 30-6 (D)
Redskins, 41-14 (W)
1987—Redskins, 13-7 (D)
Redskins, 24-20 (W)
1988—Redskins, 35-17 (D)
Cowboys, 24-17 (W)
1989—Redskins, 30-7 (D)
Cowboys, 13-3 (W)
1990—Redskins, 19-15 (W)
Cowboys, 27-17 (D)
(RS Pts.—Cowboys, 1,416, Redskins 1,187)
(PS Pts.—Redskins 57, Cowboys 20)
**NFC Championship*

DENVER vs. ATLANTA
RS: Broncos lead series, 4-3;
See Atlanta vs. Denver

DENVER vs. BUFFALO
RS: Bills lead series, 15-10-1;
See Buffalo vs. Denver

DENVER vs. CHICAGO
RS: Bears lead series, 5-4;
See Chicago vs. Denver

DENVER vs. CINCINNATI
RS: Broncos lead series, 9-6;
See Cincinnati vs. Denver

DENVER vs. CLEVELAND
RS: Broncos lead series, 9-5
PS: Broncos lead series, 3-0;
See Cleveland vs. Denver

DENVER vs. DALLAS
RS: Series tied, 2-2
PS: Cowboys lead series, 1-0;
See Dallas vs. Denver

DENVER vs. DETROIT
RS: Broncos lead series, 4-3
1971—Lions, 24-20 (Den)
1974—Broncos, 31-27 (Det)
1978—Lions, 17-14 (Det)
1981—Broncos, 27-21 (Den)
1984—Broncos, 28-7 (Det)
1987—Broncos, 34-0 (Den)
1990—Lions, 40-27 (Det)
(RS Pts.—Broncos 181, Lions 136)

DENVER vs. GREEN BAY
RS: Broncos lead series, 4-1-1
1971—Packers, 34-13 (Mil)
1975—Broncos, 23-13 (D)
1978—Broncos, 16-3 (D)
1984—Broncos, 17-14 (D)
1987—Tie, 17-17 (Mil) OT
1990—Broncos, 22-13 (D)
(RS Pts.—Broncos 108, Packers 94)

DENVER vs. HOUSTON
RS: Oilers lead series, 18-10-1
PS: Series tied, 1-1
1960—Oilers, 45-25 (D)
Oilers, 20-10 (H)
1961—Oilers, 55-14 (D)

Oilers, 45-14 (H)
1962—Broncos, 20-10 (D)
Oilers, 34-17 (H)
1963—Oilers, 20-14 (H)
Oilers, 33-24 (D)
1964—Oilers, 38-17 (D)
Oilers, 34-15 (H)
1965—Broncos, 28-17 (D)
Broncos, 31-21 (H)
1966—Oilers, 45-7 (H)
Broncos, 40-38 (D)
1967—Oilers, 10-6 (H)
Oilers, 20-18 (D)
1968—Oilers, 38-17 (H)
1969—Oilers, 24-21 (H)
Tie, 20-20 (D)
1970—Oilers, 31-21 (H)
1972—Broncos, 30-17 (D)
1973—Broncos, 48-20 (H)
1974—Broncos, 37-14 (D)
1976—Oilers, 17-3 (H)
1977—Broncos, 24-14 (H)
1979—*Oilers, 13-7 (H)
1980—Oilers, 20-16 (D)
1983—Broncos, 26-14 (H)
1985—Broncos, 31-20 (D)
1987—Oilers, 40-10 (D)
**Broncos, 34-10 (D)
(RS Pts.—Oilers 774, Broncos 604)
(PS Pts.—Broncos 41, Oilers 23)
AFC First Round Playoff
**AFC Divisional Playoff*

DENVER vs. *INDIANAPOLIS
RS: Broncos lead series, 8-2
1974—Broncos, 17-6 (B)
1977—Broncos, 27-13 (D)
1978—Colts, 7-6 (B)
1981—Broncos, 28-10 (D)
1983—Broncos, 17-10 (B)
Broncos, 21-19 (D)
1985—Broncos, 15-10 (I)
1988—Colts, 55-23 (I)
1989—Broncos, 14-3 (D)
1990—Broncos, 27-17 (I)
(RS Pts.—Broncos 195, Colts 150)
Franchise in Baltimore prior to 1984

DENVER vs. *KANSAS CITY
RS: Chiefs lead series, 36-25
1960—Texans, 17-14 (D)
Texans, 34-7 (Da)
1961—Texans, 19-12 (D)
Texans, 49-21 (Da)
1962—Texans, 24-3 (D)
Texans, 17-10 (Da)
1963—Chiefs, 59-7 (D)
Chiefs, 52-21 (KC)
1964—Broncos, 33-27 (D)
Chiefs, 49-39 (KC)
1965—Chiefs, 31-23 (D)
Chiefs, 45-35 (KC)
1966—Chiefs, 37-10 (KC)
Chiefs, 56-10 (D)
1967—Chiefs, 52-9 (KC)
Chiefs, 38-24 (D)
1968—Chiefs, 34-2 (KC)
Chiefs, 30-7 (D)
1969—Chiefs, 26-13 (D)
Chiefs, 31-17 (KC)
1970—Broncos, 26-13 (D)
Chiefs, 16-0 (KC)
1971—Chiefs, 16-3 (D)
Chiefs, 28-10 (KC)
1972—Chiefs, 45-24 (D)
Chiefs, 24-21 (KC)
1973—Chiefs, 16-14 (KC)
Broncos, 14-10 (D)
1974—Broncos, 17-14 (KC)
Chiefs, 42-34 (D)
1975—Broncos, 37-33 (D)
Chiefs, 26-13 (KC)
1976—Broncos, 35-26 (KC)
Broncos, 17-16 (D)
1977—Broncos, 23-7 (D)
Broncos, 14-7 (KC)
1978—Broncos, 23-17 (KC) OT
Broncos, 24-3 (D)
1979—Broncos, 24-10 (KC)
Broncos, 20-3 (D)
1980—Chiefs, 23-17 (D)
Chiefs, 31-14 (KC)
1981—Chiefs, 28-14 (KC)
Broncos, 16-13 (D)
1982—Chiefs, 37-16 (D)
1983—Broncos, 27-24 (D)
Chiefs, 48-17 (KC)
1984—Broncos, 21-0 (D)
Chiefs, 16-13 (KC)
1985—Broncos, 30-10 (KC)
Broncos, 14-13 (D)
1986—Broncos, 38-17 (D)
Chiefs, 37-10 (KC)
1987—Broncos, 26-17 (KC)
Broncos, 20-17 (D)
1988—Chiefs, 20-13 (KC)
Broncos, 17-11 (D)
1989—Broncos, 34-20 (D)
Broncos, 16-13 (KC)
1990—Broncos, 24-23 (D)
Chiefs, 31-20 (KC)
(RS Pts.—Chiefs 1,548, Broncos 1,127)
Franchise in Dallas prior to 1963 and known as Texans

DENVER vs. *L.A. RAIDERS
RS: Raiders lead series, 41-18-2
PS: Broncos lead series, 1-0
1960—Broncos, 31-14 (D)
Raiders, 48-10 (O)
1961—Raiders, 33-19 (O)
Broncos, 27-24 (D)
1962—Broncos, 44-7 (D)
Broncos, 23-6 (O)
1963—Raiders, 26-10 (D)
Raiders, 35-31 (O)
1964—Raiders, 40-7 (O)
Tie, 20-20 (D)
1965—Raiders, 28-20 (D)
Raiders, 24-13 (O)
1966—Raiders, 17-3 (D)
Raiders, 28-10 (O)
1967—Raiders, 51-0 (O)
Raiders, 21-17 (D)
1968—Raiders, 43-7 (D)
Raiders, 33-27 (O)
1969—Raiders, 24-14 (D)
Raiders, 41-10 (O)
1970—Raiders, 35-23 (O)
Raiders, 24-19 (D)
1971—Raiders, 27-16 (D)
Raiders, 21-13 (O)
1972—Broncos, 30-23 (O)
Raiders, 37-20 (D)
1973—Tie, 23-23 (D)
Raiders, 21-17 (O)
1974—Raiders, 28-17 (D)
Broncos, 20-17 (O)
1975—Raiders, 42-17 (D)
Raiders, 17-10 (O)
1976—Raiders, 17-10 (D)
Raiders, 19-6 (O)
1977—Broncos, 30-7 (O)
Raiders, 24-14 (D)
**Broncos, 20-17 (D)
1978—Broncos, 14-6 (D)
Broncos, 21-6 (O)
1979—Raiders, 27-3 (O)
Raiders, 14-10 (D)
1980—Raiders, 9-3 (O)
Raiders, 24-21 (D)
1981—Broncos, 9-7 (D)
Broncos, 17-0 (O)
1982—Raiders, 27-10 (LA)
1983—Raiders, 22-7 (D)
Raiders, 22-20 (LA)
1984—Broncos, 16-13 (D)
Broncos, 22-19 (LA) OT
1985—Raiders, 31-28 (LA) OT
Raiders, 17-14 (D) OT
1986—Broncos, 38-36 (D)
Broncos, 21-10 (LA)
1987—Broncos, 30-14 (D)
Broncos, 23-17 (LA)
1988—Raiders, 30-27 (D) OT
Raiders, 21-20 (LA)
1989—Broncos, 31-21 (D)
Raiders, 16-13 (LA) OT
1990—Raiders, 14-9 (LA)
Raiders, 23-20 (D)
(RS Pts.—Raiders 1,391, Broncos 1,075)
(PS Pts.—Broncos 20, Raiders 17)
Franchise in Oakland prior to 1982
**AFC Championship*

DENVER vs. L.A. RAMS
RS: Series tied, 3-3
1972—Broncos, 16-10 (LA)
1974—Rams, 17-10 (D)
1979—Rams, 13-9 (D)
1982—Broncos, 27-24 (LA)
1985—Rams, 20-16 (LA)
1988—Broncos, 35-24 (D)
(RS Pts.—Broncos 113, Rams 108)

DENVER vs. MIAMI
RS: Dolphins lead series, 5-2-1
1966—Dolphins, 24-7 (M)
Broncos, 17-7 (D)
1967—Dolphins, 35-21 (M)
1968—Broncos, 21-14 (D)
1969—Dolphins, 27-24 (M)
1971—Tie, 10-10 (D)
1975—Dolphins, 14-13 (M)
1985—Dolphins, 30-26 (D)
(RS Pts.—Dolphins 161, Broncos 139)

DENVER vs. MINNESOTA
RS: Vikings lead series, 4-2
1972—Vikings, 23-20 (D)
1978—Vikings, 12-9 (M) OT
1981—Broncos, 19-17 (D)
1984—Broncos, 42-21 (D)
1987—Vikings, 34-27 (M)
1990—Vikings, 27-22 (M)
(RS Pts.—Broncos 139, Vikings 134)

DENVER vs. *NEW ENGLAND
RS: Broncos lead series, 14-12
PS: Broncos lead series, 1-0
1960—Broncos, 13-10 (B)
Broncos, 31-24 (D)
1961—Patriots, 45-17 (B)
Patriots, 28-24 (D)
1962—Patriots, 41-16 (B)
Patriots, 33-29 (D)
1963—Broncos, 14-10 (D)
Patriots, 40-21 (B)
1964—Patriots, 39-10 (D)
Patriots, 12-7 (B)
1965—Broncos, 27-10 (B)
Patriots, 28-20 (D)
1966—Patriots, 24-10 (D)
Broncos, 17-10 (B)
1967—Broncos, 26-21 (D)
1968—Patriots, 20-17 (D)
Broncos, 35-14 (B)
1969—Broncos, 35-7 (D)
1972—Broncos, 45-21 (D)
1976—Patriots, 38-14 (NE)
1979—Broncos, 45-10 (D)
1980—Patriots, 23-14 (NE)
1984—Broncos, 26-19 (D)
1986—Broncos, 27-20 (D)
**Broncos, 22-17 (D)
1987—Broncos, 31-20 (D)
1988—Broncos, 21-10 (D)
(RS Pts.—Broncos 592, Patriots 577)
(PS Pts.—Broncos 22, Patriots 17)
Franchise in Boston prior to 1971
**AFC Divisional Playoff*

DENVER vs. NEW ORLEANS
RS: Broncos lead series, 4-1
1970—Broncos, 31-6 (NO)
1974—Broncos, 33-17 (D)
1979—Broncos, 10-3 (D)
1985—Broncos, 34-23 (D)
1988—Saints, 42-0 (NO)
(RS Pts.—Broncos 108, Saints 91)

DENVER vs. N.Y. GIANTS
RS: Giants lead series, 3-2
PS: Giants lead series, 1-0
1972—Giants, 29-17 (NY)
1976—Broncos, 14-13 (D)
1980—Broncos, 14-9 (NY)
1986—Giants, 19-16 (NY)
*Giants, 39-20 (Pasadena)
1989—Giants, 14-7 (D)
(RS Pts.—Giants 84, Broncos 68)
(PS Pts.—Giants 39, Broncos 20)
Super Bowl XXI

DENVER vs. *N.Y. JETS
RS: Jets lead series, 11-10-1
1960—Titans, 28-24 (NY)
Titans, 30-27 (D)
1961—Titans, 35-28 (NY)
Broncos, 27-10 (D)
1962—Broncos, 32-10 (NY)
Titans, 46-45 (D)
1963—Tie, 35-35 (NY)
Jets, 14-9 (D)
1964—Jets, 30-6 (NY)
Broncos, 20-16 (D)
1965—Broncos, 16-13 (D)
Jets, 45-10 (NY)
1966—Jets, 16-7 (D)
1967—Jets, 38-24 (D)
Broncos, 33-24 (NY)
1968—Broncos, 21-13 (NY)
1969—Broncos, 21-19 (D)
1973—Broncos, 40-28 (NY)
1976—Broncos, 46-3 (D)
1978—Jets, 31-28 (D)
1980—Broncos, 31-24 (D)
1986—Jets, 22-10 (NY)
(RS Pts.—Broncos 540, Jets 530)
Jets known as Titans prior to 1963

DENVER vs. PHILADELPHIA
RS: Eagles lead series, 4-2
1971—Eagles, 17-16 (P)
1975—Broncos, 25-10 (D)
1980—Eagles, 27-6 (P)
1983—Eagles, 13-10 (D)
1986—Broncos, 33-7 (P)
1989—Eagles, 28-24 (D)
(RS Pts.—Broncos 114, Eagles 102)

DENVER vs. *PHOENIX
RS: Broncos lead series, 2-0-1
1973—Tie, 17-17 (StL)
1977—Broncos, 7-0 (D)
1989—Broncos, 37-0 (P)
(RS Pts.—Broncos 61, Cardinals 17)
Franchise in St. Louis prior to 1988

DENVER vs. PITTSBURGH
RS: Broncos lead series, 8-5-1
PS: Series tied, 2-2
1970—Broncos, 16-13 (D)
1971—Broncos, 22-10 (P)
1973—Broncos, 23-13 (P)
1974—Tie, 35-35 (D) OT
1975—Steelers, 20-9 (P)
1977—Broncos, 21-7 (D)
*Broncos, 34-21 (D)
1978—Steelers, 21-17 (D)
*Steelers, 33-10 (P)
1979—Steelers, 42-7 (P)
1983—Broncos, 14-10 (P)
1984—*Steelers, 24-17 (D)
1985—Broncos, 31-23 (P)
1986—Broncos, 21-10 (P)
1988—Steelers, 39-21 (P)
1989—Broncos, 34-7 (D)
*Broncos, 24-23 (D)
1990—Steelers, 34-17 (D)
(RS Pts.—Broncos 288, Steelers 284)
(PS Pts.—Steelers 101, Broncos 85)
AFC Divisional Playoff

DENVER vs. *SAN DIEGO
RS: Broncos lead series, 31-30-1
1960—Chargers, 23-19 (D)
Chargers, 41-33 (LA)
1961—Chargers, 37-0 (SD)
Chargers, 19-16 (D)
1962—Broncos, 30-21 (D)
Broncos, 23-20 (SD)
1963—Broncos, 50-34 (D)
Chargers, 58-20 (SD)
1964—Chargers, 42-14 (SD)
Chargers, 31-20 (D)
1965—Chargers, 34-31 (SD)
Chargers, 33-21 (D)
1966—Chargers, 24-17 (SD)
Broncos, 20-17 (D)
1967—Chargers, 38-21 (D)
Chargers, 24-20 (SD)
1968—Chargers, 55-24 (SD)
Chargers, 47-23 (D)
1969—Broncos, 13-0 (D)
Chargers, 45-24 (SD)
1970—Chargers, 24-21 (SD)
Tie, 17-17 (D)
1971—Broncos, 20-16 (D)
Chargers, 45-17 (SD)
1972—Chargers, 37-14 (SD)
Broncos, 38-13 (D)
1973—Broncos, 30-19 (D)
Broncos, 42-28 (SD)
1974—Broncos, 27-7 (D)
Chargers, 17-0 (SD)
1975—Broncos, 27-17 (SD)
Broncos, 13-10 (D) OT
1976—Broncos, 26-0 (D)
Broncos, 17-0 (SD)
1977—Broncos, 17-14 (SD)
Broncos, 17-9 (D)
1978—Broncos, 27-14 (D)
Chargers, 23-0 (SD)
1979—Broncos, 7-0 (D)
Chargers, 17-7 (SD)
1980—Chargers, 30-13 (D)
Broncos, 20-13 (SD)
1981—Broncos, 42-24 (D)
Chargers, 34-17 (SD)
1982—Chargers, 23-3 (D)
Chargers, 30-20 (SD)
1983—Broncos, 14-6 (D)
Chargers, 31-7 (SD)
1984—Broncos, 16-13 (SD)
Broncos, 16-13 (D)
1985—Chargers, 30-10 (SD)
Broncos, 30-24 (D) OT
1986—Broncos, 31-14 (SD)
Chargers, 9-3 (D)
1987—Broncos, 31-17 (SD)
Broncos, 24-0 (D)
1988—Broncos, 34-3 (D)
Broncos, 12-0 (SD)
1989—Broncos, 16-10 (D)
Chargers, 19-16 (SD)
1990—Chargers, 19-7 (SD)
Broncos, 20-10 (D)
(RS Pts.—Chargers 1,342, Broncos 1,225)
Franchise in Los Angeles prior to 1961

DENVER vs. SAN FRANCISCO
RS: Broncos lead series, 4-2
PS: 49ers lead series, 1-0
1970—49ers, 19-14 (SF)
1973—49ers, 36-34 (D)
1979—Broncos, 38-28 (SF)
1982—Broncos, 24-21 (D)
1985—Broncos, 17-16 (D)
1988—Broncos, 16-13 (SF) OT
1989—*49ers, 55-10 (New Orleans)
(RS Pts.—Broncos 143, 49ers 133)
(PS Pts.—49ers 55, Broncos 10)
Super Bowl XXIV

DENVER vs. SEATTLE
RS: Broncos lead series, 16-11
PS: Seahawks lead series, 1-0

1977—Broncos, 24-13 (S)
1978—Broncos, 28-7 (D)
Broncos, 20-17 (S) OT
1979—Broncos, 37-34 (D)
Seahawks, 28-23 (S)
1980—Broncos, 36-20 (D)
Broncos, 25-17 (S)
1981—Seahawks, 13-10 (S)
Broncos, 23-13 (D)
1982—Seahawks, 17-10 (D)
Seahawks, 13-11 (S)
1983—Seahawks, 27-19 (S)
Broncos, 38-27 (D)
*Seahawks, 31-7 (S)
1984—Seahawks, 27-24 (D)
Broncos, 31-14 (S)
1985—Broncos, 13-10 (D) OT
Broncos, 27-24 (S)
1986—Broncos, 20-13 (D)
Seahawks, 41-16 (S)
1987—Broncos, 40-17 (D)
Seahawks, 28-21 (S)
1988—Seahawks, 21-14 (D)
Seahawks, 42-14 (S)
1989—Broncos, 24-21 (S) OT
Broncos, 41-14 (D)
1990—Broncos, 34-31 (D) OT
Seahawks, 17-12 (S)
(RS Pts.—Broncos 635, Seahawks 566)
(PS Pts.—Seahawks 31, Broncos 7)
AFC First Round Playoff

DENVER vs. TAMPA BAY
RS: Broncos lead series, 2-0
1976—Broncos, 48-13 (D)
1981—Broncos, 24-7 (TB)
(RS Pts.—Broncos 72, Buccaneers 20)

DENVER vs. WASHINGTON
RS: Broncos lead series, 3-2
PS: Redskins lead series, 1-0
1970—Redskins, 19-3 (D)
1974—Redskins, 30-3 (W)
1980—Broncos, 20-17 (D)
1986—Broncos, 31-30 (D)
1987—*Redskins, 42-10 (San Diego)
1989—Broncos, 14-10 (W)
(RS Pts.—Redskins 106, Broncos 71)
(PS Pts.—Redskins 42, Broncos 10)
Super Bowl XXII

DETROIT vs. ATLANTA
RS: Lions lead series, 16-5;
See Atlanta vs. Detroit

DETROIT vs. BUFFALO
RS: Series tied, 1-1-1;
See Buffalo vs. Detroit

DETROIT vs. CHICAGO
RS: Bears lead series, 71-46-5;
See Chicago vs. Detroit

DETROIT vs. CINCINNATI
RS: Bengals lead series, 3-2;
See Cincinnati vs. Detroit

DETROIT vs. CLEVELAND
RS: Lions lead series, 10-3
PS: Lions lead series, 3-1;
See Cleveland vs. Detroit

DETROIT vs. DALLAS
RS: Cowboys lead series, 6-4
PS: Cowboys lead series, 1-0;
See Dallas vs. Detroit

DETROIT vs. DENVER
RS: Broncos lead series, 4-3;
See Denver vs. Detroit

***DETROIT vs. GREEN BAY**
RS: Packers lead series, 61-53-7
1930—Packers, 47-13 (GB)
Tie, 6-6 (P)
1932—Packers, 15-10 (GB)
Spartans, 19-0 (P)
1933—Packers, 17-0 (GB)
Spartans, 7-0 (P)
1934—Lions, 3-0 (GB)
Packers, 3-0 (D)
1935—Packers, 13-9 (GB)
Packers, 31-7 (GB)
Lions, 20-10 (D)
1936—Packers, 20-18 (GB)
Packers, 26-17 (D)
1937—Packers, 26-6 (GB)
Packers, 14-13 (D)
1938—Lions, 17-7 (GB)
Packers, 28-7 (D)
1939—Packers, 26-7 (GB)
Packers, 12-7 (D)
1940—Lions, 23-14 (GB)
Packers, 50-7 (D)
1941—Packers, 23-0 (GB)
Packers, 24-7 (D)
1942—Packers, 38-7 (Mil)
Packers, 28-7 (D)
1943—Packers, 35-14 (GB)
Packers, 27-6 (D)
1944—Packers, 27-6 (GB)
Packers, 14-0 (D)
1945—Packers, 57-21 (Mil)
Lions, 14-3 (D)
1946—Packers, 10-7 (Mil)
Packers, 9-0 (D)
1947—Packers, 34-17 (GB)
Packers, 35-14 (D)
1948—Packers, 33-21 (GB)
Lions, 24-20 (D)
1949—Packers, 16-14 (GB)
Lions, 21-7 (D)
1950—Lions, 45-7 (GB)
Lions, 24-21 (D)
1951—Lions, 24-17 (GB)
Lions, 52-35 (D)
1952—Lions, 52-17 (GB)
Lions, 48-24 (D)
1953—Lions, 14-7 (GB)
Lions, 34-15 (D)
1954—Lions, 21-17 (GB)
Lions, 28-24 (D)
1955—Packers, 20-17 (GB)
Lions, 24-10 (D)
1956—Lions, 20-16 (GB)
Packers, 24-20 (D)
1957—Lions, 24-14 (GB)
Lions, 18-6 (D)
1958—Tie, 13-13 (GB)
Lions, 24-14 (D)
1959—Packers, 28-10 (GB)
Packers, 24-17 (D)
1960—Packers, 28-9 (GB)
Lions, 23-10 (D)
1961—Lions, 17-13 (Mil)
Packers, 17-9 (D)
1962—Packers, 9-7 (GB)
Lions, 26-14 (D)
1963—Packers, 31-10 (Mil)
Tie, 13-13 (D)
1964—Packers, 14-10 (D)
Packers, 30-7 (GB)
1965—Packers, 31-21 (D)
Lions, 12-7 (GB)
1966—Packers, 23-14 (GB)
Packers, 31-7 (D)
1967—Tie, 17-17 (GB)
Packers, 27-17 (D)
1968—Lions, 23-17 (GB)
Tie, 14-14 (D)
1969—Packers, 28-17 (D)
Lions, 16-10 (GB)
1970—Lions, 40-0 (GB)
Lions, 20-0 (D)
1971—Lions, 31-28 (D)
Tie, 14-14 (Mil)
1972—Packers, 24-23 (D)
Packers, 33-7 (GB)
1973—Tie, 13-13 (GB)
Lions, 34-0 (D)
1974—Packers, 21-19 (Mil)
Lions, 19-17 (D)
1975—Lions, 30-16 (Mil)
Lions, 13-10 (D)
1976—Packers, 24-14 (GB)
Lions, 27-6 (D)
1977—Lions, 10-6 (D)
Packers, 10-9 (GB)
1978—Packers, 13-7 (D)
Packers, 35-14 (Mil)
1979—Packers, 24-16 (Mil)
Packers, 18-13 (D)
1980—Lions, 29-7 (Mil)
Lions, 24-3 (D)
1981—Lions, 31-27 (D)
Packers, 31-17 (GB)
1982—Lions, 30-10 (GB)
Lions, 27-24 (D)
1983—Lions, 38-14 (D)
Lions, 23-20 (Mil) OT
1984—Packers, 41-9 (GB)
Lions, 31-28 (D)
1985—Packers, 43-10 (GB)
Packers, 26-23 (D)
1986—Lions, 21-14 (GB)
Packers, 44-40 (D)
1987—Lions, 19-16 (GB) OT
Packers, 34-33 (D)
1988—Lions, 19-9 (Mil)
Lions, 30-14 (D)
1989—Packers, 23-20 (Mil) OT
Lions, 31-22 (D)
1990—Packers, 24-21 (D)
Lions, 24-17 (GB)
(RS Pts.—Packers 2,345, Lions 2,157)
**Franchise in Portsmouth prior to 1934 and known as the Spartans*

DETROIT vs. HOUSTON
RS: Oilers lead series, 3-2
1971—Lions, 31-7 (H)
1975—Oilers, 24-8 (H)
1983—Oilers, 27-17 (H)
1986—Lions, 24-13 (D)
1989—Oilers, 35-31 (H)
(RS Pts.—Lions 111, Oilers 106)

DETROIT vs. *INDIANAPOLIS
RS: Colts lead series, 17-16-2
1953—Lions, 27-17 (B)
Lions, 17-7 (D)
1954—Lions, 35-0 (D)
Lions, 27-3 (B)
1955—Colts, 28-13 (B)
Lions, 24-14 (D)
1956—Lions, 31-14 (B)
Lions, 27-3 (D)
1957—Colts, 34-14 (B)
Lions, 31-27 (D)
1958—Colts, 28-15 (B)
Colts, 40-14 (D)
1959—Colts, 21-9 (B)
Colts, 31-24 (D)
1960—Lions, 30-17 (D)
Lions, 20-15 (B)
1961—Lions, 16-15 (B)
Colts, 17-14 (D)
1962—Lions, 29-20 (B)
Lions, 21-14 (D)
1963—Colts, 25-21 (D)
Colts, 24-21 (B)
1964—Colts, 34-0 (D)
Lions, 31-14 (B)
1965—Colts, 31-7 (B)
Tie, 24-24 (D)
1966—Colts, 45-14 (B)
Lions, 20-14 (D)
1967—Colts, 41-7 (B)
1968—Colts, 27-10 (D)
1969—Tie, 17-17 (B)
1973—Colts, 29-27 (D)
1977—Lions, 13-10 (B)
1980—Colts, 10-9 (D)
1985—Colts, 14-6 (I)
(RS Pts.—Colts 724, Lions 665)
**Franchise in Baltimore prior to 1984*

DETROIT vs. KANSAS CITY
RS: Chiefs lead series, 4-3
1971—Lions, 32-21 (D)
1975—Chiefs, 24-21 (KC) OT
1980—Chiefs, 20-17 (KC)
1981—Lions, 27-10 (D)
1987—Chiefs, 27-20 (D)
1988—Lions, 7-6 (KC)
1990—Chiefs, 43-24 (KC)
(RS Pts.—Chiefs 151, Lions 148)

DETROIT vs. *L.A. RAIDERS
RS: Raiders lead series, 5-2
1970—Lions, 28-14 (D)
1974—Raiders, 35-13 (O)
1978—Raiders, 29-17 (O)
1981—Lions, 16-0 (D)
1984—Raiders, 24-3 (D)
1987—Raiders, 27-7 (LA)
1990—Raiders, 38-31 (D)
(RS Pts.—Raiders 167, Lions 115)
**Franchise in Oakland prior to 1982*

DETROIT vs. *L.A. RAMS
RS: Rams lead series, 39-33-1
PS: Lions lead series, 1-0
1937—Lions, 28-0 (C)
Lions, 27-7 (D)
1938—Rams, 21-17 (C)
Lions, 6-0 (D)
1939—Lions, 15-7 (D)
Rams, 14-3 (C)
1940—Lions, 6-0 (D)
Rams, 24-0 (C)
1941—Lions, 17-7 (D)
Lions, 14-0 (C)
1942—Rams, 14-0 (D)
Rams, 27-7 (C)
1944—Rams, 20-17 (D)
Lions, 26-14 (C)
1945—Rams, 28-21 (D)
1946—Rams, 35-14 (LA)
Rams, 41-20 (D)
1947—Rams, 27-13 (D)
Rams, 28-17 (LA)
1948—Rams, 44-7 (LA)
Rams, 34-27 (D)
1949—Rams, 27-24 (LA)
Rams, 21-10 (D)
1950—Rams, 30-28 (D)
Rams, 65-24 (LA)
1951—Rams, 27-21 (D)
Lions, 24-22 (LA)
1952—Lions, 17-14 (LA)
Lions, 24-16 (D)
**Lions, 31-21 (D)
1953—Rams, 31-19 (D)
Rams, 37-24 (LA)
1954—Lions, 21-3 (D)
Lions, 27-24 (LA)
1955—Rams, 17-10 (D)
Rams, 24-13 (LA)
1956—Lions, 24-21 (D)
Lions, 16-7 (LA)
1957—Lions, 10-7 (D)
Rams, 35-17 (LA)
1958—Rams, 42-28 (D)
Lions, 41-24 (LA)
1959—Lions, 17-7 (LA)
Lions, 23-17 (D)
1960—Rams, 48-35 (LA)
Lions, 12-10 (D)
1961—Lions, 14-13 (D)
Lions, 28-10 (LA)
1962—Lions, 13-10 (D)
Lions, 12-3 (LA)
1963—Lions, 23-2 (LA)
Rams, 28-21 (D)
1964—Tie, 17-17 (LA)
Lions, 37-17 (D)
1965—Lions, 20-0 (D)
Lions, 31-7 (LA)
1966—Rams, 14-7 (D)
Rams, 23-3 (LA)
1967—Rams, 31-7 (D)
1968—Rams, 10-7 (LA)
1969—Lions, 28-0 (D)
1970—Lions, 28-23 (LA)
1971—Rams, 21-13 (D)
1972—Lions, 34-17 (LA)
1974—Rams, 16-13 (LA)
1975—Rams, 20-0 (D)
1976—Rams, 20-17 (D)
1980—Lions, 41-20 (LA)
1981—Rams, 20-13 (LA)
1982—Lions, 19-14 (LA)
1983—Rams, 21-10 (LA)
1986—Rams, 14-10 (LA)
1987—Rams, 37-16 (D)
1988—Rams, 17-10 (LA)
(RS Pts.—Rams 1,413, Lions 1,303)
(PS Pts.—Lions 31, Rams 21)
**Franchise in Cleveland prior to 1946*
***Conference Playoff*

DETROIT vs. MIAMI
RS: Dolphins lead series, 2-1
1973—Dolphins, 34-7 (M)
1979—Dolphins, 28-10 (D)
1985—Lions, 31-21 (D)
(RS Pts.—Dolphins 83, Lions 48)

DETROIT vs. MINNESOTA
RS: Vikings lead series, 38-19-2
1961—Lions, 37-10 (M)
Lions, 13-7 (D)
1962—Lions, 17-6 (M)
Lions, 37-23 (D)
1963—Lions, 28-10 (D)
Vikings, 34-31 (M)
1964—Lions, 24-20 (M)
Tie, 23-23 (D)
1965—Lions, 31-29 (M)
Vikings, 29-7 (D)
1966—Lions, 32-31 (M)
Vikings, 28-16 (D)
1967—Tie, 10-10 (M)
Lions, 14-3 (D)
1968—Vikings, 24-10 (M)
Vikings, 13-6 (D)
1969—Vikings, 24-10 (M)
Vikings, 27-0 (D)
1970—Vikings, 30-17 (D)
Vikings, 24-20 (M)
1971—Vikings, 16-13 (D)
Vikings, 29-10 (M)
1972—Vikings, 34-10 (D)
Vikings, 16-14 (M)
1973—Vikings, 23-9 (D)
Vikings, 28-7 (M)
1974—Vikings, 7-6 (D)
Lions, 20-16 (M)
1975—Vikings, 25-19 (M)
Lions, 17-10 (D)
1976—Vikings, 10-9 (D)
Vikings, 31-23 (M)
1977—Vikings, 14-7 (M)
Vikings, 30-21 (D)
1978—Vikings, 17-7 (M)
Lions, 45-14 (D)
1979—Vikings, 13-10 (D)
Vikings, 14-7 (M)
1980—Lions, 27-7 (D)
Vikings, 34-0 (M)
1981—Vikings, 26-24 (M)
Lions, 45-7 (D)
1982—Vikings, 34-31 (D)
1983—Vikings, 20-17 (M)
Lions, 13-2 (D)
1984—Vikings, 29-28 (D)
Lions, 16-14 (M)
1985—Vikings, 16-13 (M)
Lions, 41-21 (D)
1986—Lions, 13-10 (M)
Vikings, 24-10 (D)
1987—Vikings, 34-19 (M)
Vikings, 17-14 (D)
1988—Vikings, 44-17 (M)
Vikings, 23-0 (D)
1989—Vikings, 24-17 (M)
Vikings, 20-7 (D)

1990—Lions, 34-27 (M)
Vikings, 17-7 (D)
(RS Pts.—Vikings 1,205, Lions 1,030)
DETROIT vs. NEW ENGLAND
RS: Series tied, 2-2
1971—Lions, 34-7 (NE)
1976—Lions, 30-10 (D)
1979—Patriots, 24-17 (NE)
1985—Patriots, 23-6 (NE)
(RS Pts.—Lions 87, Patriots 64)
DETROIT vs. NEW ORLEANS
RS: Lions lead series, 6-5-1
1968—Tie, 20-20 (D)
1970—Saints, 19-17 (NO)
1972—Lions, 27-14 (D)
1973—Saints, 20-13 (NO)
1974—Lions, 19-14 (D)
1976—Saints, 17-16 (NO)
1977—Lions, 23-19 (D)
1979—Saints, 17-7 (NO)
1980—Lions, 24-13 (D)
1988—Saints, 22-14 (D)
1989—Lions, 21-14 (D)
1990—Lions, 27-10 (NO)
(RS Pts.—Lions 228, Saints 199)
***DETROIT vs. N.Y. GIANTS**
RS: Lions lead series, 17-15-1
PS: Lions lead series, 1-0
1930—Giants, 19-6 (P)
1931—Spartans, 14-6 (P)
Giants, 14-0 (NY)
1932—Spartans, 7-0 (P)
Spartans, 6-0 (NY)
1933—Spartans, 17-7 (P)
Giants, 13-10 (NY)
1934—Lions, 9-0 (D)
1935—**Lions, 26-7 (D)
1936—Giants, 14-7 (NY)
Lions, 38-0 (D)
1937—Lions, 17-0 (NY)
1939—Lions, 18-14 (D)
1941—Giants, 20-13 (NY)
1943—Tie, 0-0 (D)
1945—Giants, 35-14 (NY)
1947—Lions, 35-7 (D)
1949—Lions, 45-21 (NY)
1953—Lions, 27-16 (NY)
1955—Giants, 24-19 (D)
1958—Giants, 19-17 (D)
1962—Giants, 17-14 (NY)
1964—Lions, 26-3 (D)
1967—Lions, 30-7 (NY)
1969—Lions, 24-0 (D)
1972—Lions, 30-16 (D)
1974—Lions, 20-19 (D)
1976—Giants, 24-10 (NY)
1982—Giants, 13-6 (D)
1983—Lions, 15-9 (D)
1988—Giants, 30-10 (NY)
Giants, 13-10 (D) OT
1989—Giants, 24-14 (NY)
1990—Giants, 20-0 (NY)
(RS Pts.—Lions, 528, Giants 424)
(PS Pts.—Lions 26, Giants 7)
**Franchise in Portsmouth prior to 1934 and known as the Spartans*
***NFL Championship*
DETROIT vs. N.Y. JETS
RS: Jets lead series, 3-2
1972—Lions, 37-20 (D)
1979—Jets, 31-10 (NY)
1982—Jets, 28-13 (D)
1985—Lions, 31-20 (D)
1988—Jets, 17-10 (D)
(RS Pts.—Jets 116, Lions 101)
***DETROIT vs. PHILADELPHIA**
RS: Lions lead series, 12-9-2
1933—Spartans, 25-0 (P)
1934—Lions, 10-0 (P)
1935—Lions, 35-0 (D)
1936—Lions, 23-0 (P)
1938—Eagles, 21-7 (D)
1940—Lions, 21-0 (P)
1941—Lions, 21-17 (D)
1945—Lions, 28-24 (D)
1948—Eagles, 45-21 (P)
1949—Eagles, 22-14 (D)
1951—Lions, 28-10 (P)
1954—Tie, 13-13 (D)
1957—Lions, 27-16 (P)
1960—Eagles, 28-10 (P)
1961—Eagles, 27-24 (D)
1965—Lions, 35-28 (P)
1968—Eagles, 12-0 (D)
1971—Eagles, 23-20 (D)
1974—Eagles, 28-17 (P)
1977—Lions, 17-13 (D)
1979—Eagles, 44-7 (P)
1984—Tie, 23-23 (D) OT
1986—Lions, 13-11 (P)
(RS Pts.—Lions 439, Eagles 405)
**Franchise in Portsmouth prior to 1934 and known as the Spartans*

***DETROIT vs. **PHOENIX**
RS: Lions lead series, 25-16-5
1930—Tie, 0-0 (P)
Cardinals, 23-0 (C)
1931—Cardinals, 20-19 (C)
1932—Tie, 7-7 (P)
1933—Spartans, 7-6 (P)
1934—Lions, 6-0 (D)
Lions, 17-13 (C)
1935—Tie, 10-10 (D)
Lions, 7-6 (C)
1936—Lions, 39-0 (D)
Lions, 14-7 (C)
1937—Lions, 16-7 (C)
Lions, 16-7 (D)
1938—Lions, 10-0 (D)
Lions, 7-3 (C)
1939—Lions, 21-3 (D)
Lions, 17-3 (C)
1940—Tie, 0-0 (Buffalo)
Lions, 43-14 (C)
1941—Tie, 14-14 (C)
Lions, 21-3 (D)
1942—Cardinals, 13-0 (C)
Cardinals, 7-0 (D)
1943—Lions, 35-17 (D)
Lions, 7-0 (C)
1945—Lions, 10-0 (C)
Lions, 26-0 (D)
1946—Cardinals, 34-14 (C)
Cardinals, 36-14 (D)
1947—Cardinals, 45-21 (C)
Cardinals, 17-7 (D)
1948—Cardinals, 56-20 (C)
Cardinals, 28-14 (D)
1949—Lions, 24-7 (C)
Cardinals, 42-19 (D)
1959—Lions, 45-21 (D)
1961—Lions, 45-14 (StL)
1967—Cardinals, 38-28 (StL)
1969—Lions, 20-0 (D)
1970—Lions, 16-3 (D)
1973—Lions, 20-16 (StL)
1975—Cardinals, 24-13 (D)
1978—Cardinals, 21-14 (StL)
1980—Lions, 20-7 (D)
Cardinals, 24-23 (StL)
1989—Cardinals, 16-13 (D)
(RS Pts.—Lions 759, Cardinals 642)
**Franchise in Portsmouth prior to 1934 and known as the Spartans*
***Franchise in St. Louis prior to 1988 and in Chicago prior to 1960*
DETROIT vs. *PITTSBURGH
RS: Lions lead series, 13-10-1
1934—Lions, 40-7 (D)
1936—Lions, 28-3 (D)
1937—Lions, 7-3 (D)
1938—Lions, 16-7 (D)
1940—Pirates, 10-7 (D)
1942—Steelers, 35-7 (D)
1946—Lions, 17-7 (D)
1947—Steelers, 17-10 (P)
1948—Lions, 17-14 (D)
1949—Steelers, 14-7 (P)
1950—Lions, 10-7 (D)
1952—Lions, 31-6 (P)
1953—Lions, 38-21 (D)
1955—Lions, 31-28 (P)
1956—Lions, 45-7 (D)
1959—Tie, 10-10 (P)
1962—Lions, 45-7 (D)
1966—Steelers, 17-3 (P)
1967—Steelers, 24-14 (D)
1969—Steelers, 16-13 (P)
1973—Steelers, 24-10 (P)
1983—Lions, 45-3 (D)
1986—Steelers, 27-17 (P)
1989—Steelers, 23-3 (D)
(RS Pts.—Lions 471, Steelers 337)
**Steelers known as Pirates prior to 1941*
DETROIT vs. SAN DIEGO
RS: Lions lead series, 3-2
1972—Lions, 34-20 (D)
1977—Lions, 20-0 (D)
1978—Lions, 31-14 (D)
1981—Chargers, 28-23 (SD)
1984—Chargers, 27-24 (SD)
(RS Pts.—Lions 132, Chargers 89)
DETROIT vs. SAN FRANCISCO
RS: Lions lead series, 25-23-1
PS: Series tied, 1-1
1950—Lions, 24-7 (D)
49ers, 28-27 (SF)
1951—49ers, 20-10 (D)
49ers, 21-17 (SF)
1952—49ers, 17-3 (SF)
49ers, 28-0 (D)
1953—Lions, 24-21 (D)
Lions, 14-10 (SF)
1954—49ers, 37-31 (SF)
Lions, 48-7 (D)
1955—49ers, 27-24 (D)
49ers, 38-21 (SF)
1956—Lions, 20-17 (D)
Lions, 17-13 (SF)
1957—49ers, 35-31 (SF)
Lions, 31-10 (D)
*Lions, 31-27 (SF)
1958—49ers, 24-21 (SF)
Lions, 35-21 (D)
1959—49ers, 34-13 (D)
49ers, 33-7 (SF)
1960—49ers, 14-10 (D)
Lions, 24-0 (SF)
1961—49ers, 49-0 (D)
Tie, 20-20 (SF)
1962—Lions, 45-24 (D)
Lions, 38-24 (SF)
1963—Lions, 26-3 (D)
Lions, 45-7 (SF)
1964—Lions, 26-17 (SF)
Lions, 24-7 (D)
1965—49ers, 27-21 (D)
49ers, 17-14 (SF)
1966—49ers, 27-24 (SF)
49ers, 41-14 (D)
1967—Lions, 45-3 (SF)
1968—49ers, 14-7 (D)
1969—Lions, 26-14 (SF)
1970—Lions, 28-7 (D)
1971—49ers, 31-27 (SF)
1973—Lions, 30-20 (D)
1974—Lions, 17-13 (D)
1975—Lions, 28-17 (SF)
1977—49ers, 28-7 (SF)
1978—Lions, 33-14 (D)
1980—Lions, 17-13 (D)
1981—Lions, 24-17 (D)
1983—**49ers, 24-23 (SF)
1984—49ers, 30-27 (D)
1985—Lions, 23-21 (D)
1988—49ers, 20-13 (SF)
(RS Pts.—Lions 1,101, 49ers 987)
(PS Pts.—Lions 54, 49ers 51)
**Conference Playoff*
***NFC Divisional Playoff*
DETROIT vs. SEATTLE
RS: Seahawks lead series, 4-1
1976—Lions, 41-14 (S)
1978—Seahawks, 28-16 (S)
1984—Seahawks, 38-17 (S)
1987—Seahawks, 37-14 (D)
1990—Seahawks, 30-10 (S)
(RS Pts.—Seahawks 147, Lions 98)
DETROIT vs. TAMPA BAY
RS: Series tied, 13-13
1977—Lions, 16-7 (D)
1978—Lions, 15-7 (TB)
Lions, 34-23 (D)
1979—Buccaneers, 31-16 (TB)
Buccaneers, 16-14 (D)
1980—Lions, 24-10 (TB)
Lions, 27-14 (D)
1981—Buccaneers, 28-10 (TB)
Buccaneers, 20-17 (D)
1982—Buccaneers, 23-21 (TB)
1983—Lions, 11-0 (TB)
Lions, 23-20 (D)
1984—Buccaneers, 21-17 (TB)
Lions, 13-7 (D) OT
1985—Lions, 30-9 (D)
Buccaneers, 19-16 (TB) OT
1986—Buccaneers, 24-20 (D)
Lions, 38-17 (TB)
1987—Buccaneers, 31-27 (D)
Lions, 20-10 (TB)
1988—Buccaneers, 23-20 (D)
Buccaneers, 21-10 (TB)
1989—Lions, 17-16 (TB)
Lions, 33-7 (D)
1990—Buccaneers, 38-21 (D)
Buccaneers, 23-20 (TB)
(RS Pts.—Lions 530, Buccaneers 465)
***DETROIT vs. **WASHINGTON**
RS: Redskins lead series, 20-8
PS: Redskins lead series, 1-0
1932—Spartans, 10-0 (P)
1933—Spartans, 13-0 (B)
1934—Lions, 24-0 (D)
1935—Lions, 17-7 (B)
Lions, 14-0 (D)
1938—Redskins, 7-5 (D)
1939—Redskins, 31-7 (W)
1940—Redskins, 20-14 (D)
1942—Redskins, 15-3 (D)
1943—Redskins, 42-20 (W)
1946—Redskins, 17-16 (W)
1947—Lions, 38-21 (D)
1948—Redskins, 46-21 (W)
1951—Lions, 35-17 (D)
1956—Redskins, 18-17 (W)
1965—Lions, 14-10 (D)
1968—Redskins, 14-3 (W)
1970—Redskins, 31-10 (W)
1973—Redskins, 20-0 (D)
1976—Redskins, 20-7 (W)
1978—Redskins, 21-19 (D)
1979—Redskins, 27-24 (D)
1981—Redskins, 33-31 (W)
1982—***Redskins, 31-7 (W)
1983—Redskins, 38-17 (W)
1984—Redskins, 28-14 (W)
1985—Redskins, 24-3 (W)
1987—Redskins, 20-13 (W)
1990—Redskins, 41-38 (D)
(RS Pts.—Redskins 568, Lions 447)
(PS Pts.—Redskins 31, Lions 7)
**Franchise in Portsmouth prior to 1934 and known as the Spartans.*
***Franchise in Boston prior to 1937*
****NFC First Round Playoff*

GREEN BAY vs. ATLANTA
RS: Packers lead series, 9-7;
See Atlanta vs. Green Bay
GREEN BAY vs. BUFFALO
RS: Bills lead series, 3-1;
See Buffalo vs. Green Bay
GREEN BAY vs. CHICAGO
RS: Bears lead series, 77-57-6
PS: Bears lead series, 1-0;
See Chicago vs. Green Bay
GREEN BAY vs. CINCINNATI
RS: Bengals lead series, 4-2;
See Cincinnati vs. Green Bay
GREEN BAY vs. CLEVELAND
RS: Packers lead series, 7-5
PS: Packers lead series, 1-0;
See Cleveland vs. Green Bay
GREEN BAY vs. DALLAS
RS: Packers lead series, 8-4
PS: Packers lead series, 2-1;
See Dallas vs. Green Bay
GREEN BAY vs. DENVER
RS: Broncos lead series, 4-1-1;
See Denver vs. Green Bay
GREEN BAY vs. DETROIT
RS: Packers lead series, 61-53-7;
See Detroit vs. Green Bay
GREEN BAY vs. HOUSTON
RS: Oilers lead series, 3-2
1972—Packers, 23-10 (H)
1977—Oilers, 16-10 (GB)
1980—Oilers, 22-3 (GB)
1983—Packers, 41-38 (H) OT
1986—Oilers, 31-3 (GB)
(RS Pts.—Oilers 117, Packers 80)
GREEN BAY vs. *INDIANAPOLIS
RS: Colts lead series, 18-17-1
PS: Packers lead series, 1-0
1953—Packers, 37-14 (GB)
Packers, 35-24 (B)
1954—Packers, 7-6 (B)
Packers, 24-13 (Mil)
1955—Colts, 24-20 (Mil)
Colts, 14-10 (B)
1956—Packers, 38-33 (Mil)
Colts, 28-21 (B)
1957—Colts, 45-17 (Mil)
Packers, 24-21 (B)
1958—Colts, 24-17 (Mil)
Colts, 56-0 (B)
1959—Colts, 38-21 (B)
Colts, 28-24 (Mil)
1960—Packers, 35-21 (GB)
Colts, 38-24 (B)
1961—Packers, 45-7 (GB)
Colts, 45-21 (B)
1962—Packers, 17-6 (B)
Packers, 17-13 (GB)
1963—Packers, 31-20 (GB)
Packers, 34-20 (B)
1964—Colts, 21-20 (GB)
Colts, 24-21 (B)
1965—Packers, 20-17 (Mil)
Packers, 42-27 (B)
**Packers, 13-10 (GB) OT
1966—Packers, 24-3 (Mil)
Packers, 14-10 (B)
1967—Colts, 13-10 (B)
1968—Colts, 16-3 (GB)
1969—Colts, 14-6 (B)
1970—Colts, 13-10 (Mil)
1974—Packers, 20-13 (B)
1982—Tie, 20-20 (B) OT
1985—Colts, 37-10 (I)
1988—Colts, 20-13 (GB)
(RS Pts.—Colts 786, Packers 752)
(PS Pts.—Packers 13, Colts 10)
**Franchise in Baltimore prior to 1984*
***Conference Playoff*
GREEN BAY vs. KANSAS CITY
RS: Chiefs lead series, 3-1-1
PS: Packers lead series, 1-0
1966—*Packers, 35-10 (Los Angeles)
1973—Tie, 10-10 (Mil)
1977—Chiefs, 20-10 (KC)
1987—Packers, 23-3 (KC)

1989—Chiefs, 21-3 (GB)
1990—Chiefs, 17-3 (GB)
(RS Pts.—Chiefs 71, Packers 49)
(PS Pts.—Packers 35, Chiefs 10)
**Super Bowl I*

GREEN BAY vs. *L.A. RAIDERS
RS: Raiders lead series, 5-1
PS: Packers lead series, 1-0
1967—**Packers, 33-14 (Miami)
1972—Raiders, 20-14 (GB)
1976—Raiders, 18-14 (O)
1978—Raiders, 28-3 (GB)
1984—Raiders, 28-7 (LA)
1987—Raiders, 20-0 (GB)
1990—Packers, 29-16 (LA)
(RS Pts.—Raiders 130, Packers 67)
(PS Pts.—Packers 33, Raiders 14)
**Franchise in Oakland prior to 1982*
***Super Bowl II*

GREEN BAY vs. *L.A. RAMS
RS: Rams lead series, 41-34-2
PS: Packers lead series, 1-0
1937—Packers, 35-10 (C)
Packers, 35-7 (GB)
1938—Packers, 26-17 (GB)
Packers, 28-7 (C)
1939—Rams, 27-24 (GB)
Packers, 7-6 (C)
1940—Packers, 31-14 (GB)
Tie, 13-13 (C)
1941—Packers, 24-7 (Mil)
Packers, 17-14 (C)
1942—Packers, 45-28 (GB)
Packers, 30-12 (C)
1944—Packers, 30-21 (GB)
Packers, 42-7 (C)
1945—Rams, 27-14 (GB)
Rams, 20-7 (C)
1946—Rams, 21-17 (Mil)
Rams, 38-17 (LA)
1947—Packers, 17-14 (Mil)
Packers, 30-10 (LA)
1948—Packers, 16-0 (GB)
Rams, 24-10 (LA)
1949—Rams, 48-7 (GB)
Rams, 35-7 (LA)
1950—Rams, 45-14 (Mil)
Rams, 51-14 (LA)
1951—Rams, 28-0 (Mil)
Rams, 42-14 (LA)
1952—Rams, 30-28 (Mil)
Rams, 45-27 (LA)
1953—Rams, 38-20 (Mil)
Rams, 33-17 (LA)
1954—Packers, 35-17 (Mil)
Rams, 35-27 (LA)
1955—Packers, 30-28 (Mil)
Rams, 31-17 (LA)
1956—Packers, 42-17 (Mil)
Rams, 49-21 (LA)
1957—Rams, 31-27 (Mil)
Rams, 42-17 (LA)
1958—Rams, 20-7 (GB)
Rams, 34-20 (LA)
1959—Rams, 45-6 (Mil)
Packers, 38-20 (LA)
1960—Rams, 33-31 (Mil)
Packers, 35-2 (LA)
1961—Packers, 35-17 (GB)
Packers, 24-17 (LA)
1962—Packers, 41-10 (Mil)
Packers, 20-17 (LA)
1963—Packers, 42-10 (GB)
Packers, 31-14 (LA)
1964—Rams, 27-17 (Mil)
Tie, 24-24 (LA)
1965—Packers, 6-3 (Mil)
Rams, 21-10 (LA)
1966—Packers, 24-13 (GB)
Packers, 27-23 (LA)
1967—Rams, 27-24 (LA)
**Packers, 28-7 (Mil)
1968—Rams, 16-14 (Mil)
1969—Rams, 34-21 (LA)
1970—Rams, 31-21 (GB)
1971—Rams, 30-13 (LA)
1973—Rams, 24-7 (LA)
1974—Packers, 17-6 (Mil)
1975—Rams, 22-5 (LA)
1977—Rams, 24-6 (Mil)
1978—Rams, 31-14 (LA)
1980—Rams, 51-21 (LA)
1981—Rams, 35-23 (LA)
1982—Packers, 35-23 (Mil)
1983—Packers, 27-24 (Mil)
1984—Packers, 31-6 (Mil)
1985—Rams, 34-17 (LA)
1988—Rams, 34-7 (GB)
1989—Rams, 41-38 (LA)
1990—Packers, 36-24 (GB)
(RS Pts.—Rams 1,875, Packers 1,694)
(PS Pts.—Packers 28, Rams 7)
**Franchise in Cleveland prior to 1946*
***Conference Championship*

GREEN BAY vs. MIAMI
RS: Dolphins lead series, 6-0
1971—Dolphins, 27-6 (Mia)
1975—Dolphins, 31-7 (GB)
1979—Dolphins, 27-7 (Mia)
1985—Dolphins, 34-24 (GB)
1988—Dolphins, 24-17 (Mia)
1989—Dolphins, 23-20 (Mil)
(RS Pts.—Dolphins 166, Packers 81)

GREEN BAY vs. MINNESOTA
RS: Packers lead series, 30-28-1
1961—Packers, 33-7 (Minn)
Packers, 28-10 (Mil)
1962—Packers, 34-7 (GB)
Packers, 48-21 (Minn)
1963—Packers, 37-28 (Minn)
Packers, 28-7 (GB)
1964—Vikings, 24-23 (GB)
Packers, 42-13 (Minn)
1965—Packers, 38-13 (Minn)
Packers, 24-19 (GB)
1966—Vikings, 20-17 (GB)
Packers, 28-16 (Minn)
1967—Vikings, 10-7 (Mil)
Packers, 30-27 (Minn)
1968—Vikings, 26-13 (Mil)
Vikings, 14-10 (Minn)
1969—Vikings, 19-7 (Minn)
Vikings, 9-7 (Mil)
1970—Packers, 13-10 (Mil)
Vikings, 10-3 (Minn)
1971—Vikings, 24-13 (GB)
Vikings, 3-0 (Minn)
1972—Vikings, 27-13 (GB)
Packers, 23-7 (Minn)
1973—Vikings, 11-3 (Minn)
Vikings, 31-7 (GB)
1974—Vikings, 32-17 (GB)
Packers, 19-7 (Minn)
1975—Vikings, 28-17 (GB)
Vikings, 24-3 (Minn)
1976—Vikings, 17-10 (Mil)
Vikings, 20-9 (Minn)
1977—Vikings, 19-7 (Minn)
Vikings, 13-6 (GB)
1978—Vikings, 21-7 (Minn)
Tie, 10-10 (GB) OT
1979—Vikings, 27-21 (Minn) OT
Packers, 19-7 (Mil)
1980—Packers, 16-3 (GB)
Packers, 25-13 (Minn)
1981—Vikings, 30-13 (Mil)
Packers, 35-23 (Minn)
1982—Packers, 26-7 (Mil)
1983—Vikings, 20-17 (GB) OT
Packers, 29-21 (Minn)
1984—Packers, 45-17 (Mil)
Packers, 38-14 (Minn)
1985—Packers, 20-17 (Mil)
Packers, 27-17 (Minn)
1986—Vikings, 42-7 (Minn)
Vikings, 32-6 (GB)
1987—Packers, 23-16 (Minn)
Packers, 16-10 (Mil)
1988—Packers, 34-14 (Minn)
Packers, 18-6 (GB)
1989—Vikings, 26-14 (Minn)
Packers, 20-19 (Mil)
1990—Packers, 24-10 (Mil)
Vikings, 23-7 (Minn)
(RS Pts.—Packers 1,134, Vikings 1,018)

GREEN BAY vs. NEW ENGLAND
RS: Series tied, 2-2
1973—Patriots, 33-24 (NE)
1979—Packers, 27-14 (GB)
1985—Patriots, 26-20 (NE)
1988—Packers, 45-3 (Mil)
(RS Pts.—Packers 116, Patriots 76)

GREEN BAY vs. NEW ORLEANS
RS: Packers lead series, 11-4
1968—Packers, 29-7 (Mil)
1971—Saints, 29-21 (Mil)
1972—Packers, 30-20 (NO)
1973—Packers, 30-10 (Mil)
1975—Saints, 20-19 (NO)
1976—Packers, 32-27 (Mil)
1977—Packers, 24-20 (NO)
1978—Packers, 28-17 (Mil)
1979—Packers, 28-19 (Mil)
1981—Packers, 35-7 (NO)
1984—Packers, 23-13 (NO)
1985—Packers, 38-14 (Mil)
1986—Saints, 24-10 (NO)
1987—Saints, 33-24 (NO)
1989—Packers, 35-34 (GB)
(RS Pts.—Packers 406, Saints 294)

GREEN BAY vs. N.Y. GIANTS
RS: Packers lead series, 21-19-2
PS: Packers lead series, 4-1
1928—Giants, 6-0 (GB)
Packers, 7-0 (NY)
1929—Packers, 20-6 (NY)
1930—Packers, 14-7 (GB)
Giants, 13-6 (NY)
1931—Packers, 27-7 (GB)
Packers, 14-10 (NY)
1932—Packers, 13-0 (GB)
Giants, 6-0 (NY)
1933—Giants, 10-7 (Mil)
Giants, 17-6 (NY)
1934—Packers, 20-6 (Mil)
Giants, 17-3 (NY)
1935—Packers, 16-7 (GB)
1936—Packers, 26-14 (NY)
1937—Giants, 10-0 (NY)
1938—Giants, 15-3 (NY)
*Giants, 23-17 (NY)
1939—*Packers, 27-0 (Mil)
1940—Giants, 7-3 (NY)
1942—Tie, 21-21 (NY)
1943—Packers, 35-21 (NY)
1944—Giants, 24-0 (NY)
*Packers, 14-7 (NY)
1945—Packers, 23-14 (NY)
1947—Tie, 24-24 (NY)
1948—Giants, 49-3 (Mil)
1949—Giants, 30-10 (GB)
1952—Packers, 17-3 (NY)
1957—Giants, 31-17 (GB)
1959—Giants, 20-3 (NY)
1961—Packers, 20-17 (Mil)
*Packers, 37-0 (GB)
1962—*Packers, 16-7 (NY)
1967—Packers, 48-21 (NY)
1969—Packers, 20-10 (Mil)
1971—Giants, 42-40 (GB)
1973—Packers, 16-14 (New Haven)
1975—Packers, 40-14 (Mil)
1980—Giants, 27-21 (NY)
1981—Packers, 27-14 (NY)
Packers, 26-24 (Mil)
1982—Packers, 27-19 (NY)
1983—Giants, 27-3 (NY)
1985—Packers, 23-20 (GB)
1986—Giants, 55-24 (NY)
1987—Giants, 20-10 (NY)
(RS Pts.—Giants 719, Packers 683)
(PS Pts.—Packers 111, Giants 37)
**NFL Championship*

GREEN BAY vs. N.Y. JETS
RS: Jets lead series, 4-1
1973—Packers, 23-7 (Mil)
1979—Jets, 27-22 (GB)
1981—Jets, 28-3 (NY)
1982—Jets, 15-13 (NY)
1985—Jets, 24-3 (Mil)
(RS Pts.—Jets 101, Packers 64)

GREEN BAY vs. PHILADELPHIA
RS: Packers lead series, 18-5
PS: Eagles lead series, 1-0
1933—Packers, 35-9 (GB)
Packers, 10-0 (P)
1934—Packers, 19-6 (GB)
1935—Packers, 13-6 (P)
1937—Packers, 37-7 (Mil)
1939—Packers, 23-16 (P)
1940—Packers, 27-20 (GB)
1942—Packers, 7-0 (P)
1946—Packers, 19-7 (P)
1947—Eagles, 28-14 (P)
1951—Packers, 37-24 (GB)
1952—Packers, 12-10 (Mil)
1954—Packers, 37-14 (P)
1958—Packers, 38-35 (GB)
1960—*Eagles, 17-13 (P)
1962—Packers, 49-0 (P)
1968—Packers, 30-13 (GB)
1970—Packers, 30-17 (Mil)
1974—Eagles, 36-14 (P)
1976—Packers, 28-13 (GB)
1978—Eagles, 10-3 (P)
1979—Eagles, 21-10 (GB)
1987—Packers, 16-10 (GB) OT
1990—Eagles, 31-0 (P)
(RS Pts.—Packers 508, Eagles 333)
(PS Pts.—Eagles 17, Packers 13)
**NFL Championship*

GREEN BAY vs. *PHOENIX
RS: Packers lead series, 39-21-4
PS: Packers lead series, 1-0
1921—Tie, 3-3 (C)
1922—Cardinals, 16-3 (C)
1924—Cardinals, 3-0 (C)
1925—Cardinals, 9-6 (C)
1926—Cardinals, 13-7 (GB)
Packers, 3-0 (C)
1927—Packers, 13-0 (GB)
Tie, 6-6 (C)
1928—Packers, 20-0 (GB)
1929—Packers, 9-2 (GB)
Packers, 7-6 (C)
Packers, 12-0 (C)
1930—Packers, 14-0 (GB)
Cardinals, 13-6 (C)
1931—Packers, 26-7 (GB)
Cardinals, 21-13 (C)
1932—Packers, 15-7 (GB)
Packers, 19-9 (C)
1933—Packers, 14-6 (C)
1934—Packers, 15-0 (GB)
Cardinals, 9-0 (Mil)
Cardinals, 6-0 (C)
1935—Cardinals, 7-6 (GB)
Cardinals, 3-0 (Mil)
Cardinals, 9-7 (C)
1936—Packers, 10-7 (GB)
Packers, 24-0 (Mil)
Tie, 0-0 (C)
1937—Cardinals, 14-7 (GB)
Packers, 34-13 (Mil)
1938—Packers, 28-7 (Mil)
Packers, 24-22 (Buffalo)
1939—Packers, 14-10 (GB)
Packers, 27-20 (Mil)
1940—Packers, 31-6 (Mil)
Packers, 28-7 (C)
1941—Packers, 14-13 (Mil)
Packers, 17-9 (GB)
1942—Packers, 17-13 (C)
Packers, 55-24 (GB)
1943—Packers, 28-7 (C)
Packers, 35-14 (Mil)
1945—Packers, 33-14 (GB)
1946—Packers, 19-7 (C)
Cardinals, 24-6 (GB)
1947—Cardinals, 14-10 (GB)
Cardinals, 21-20 (C)
1948—Cardinals, 17-7 (Mil)
Cardinals, 42-7 (C)
1949—Cardinals, 39-17 (Mil)
Cardinals, 41-21 (C)
1955—Packers, 31-14 (GB)
1956—Packers, 24-21 (C)
1962—Packers, 17-0 (Mil)
1963—Packers, 30-7 (StL)
1967—Packers, 31-23 (StL)
1969—Packers, 45-28 (GB)
1971—Tie, 16-16 (StL)
1973—Packers, 25-21 (GB)
1976—Cardinals, 29-0 (StL)
1982—**Packers, 41-16 (GB)
1984—Packers, 24-23 (GB)
1985—Cardinals, 43-28 (StL)
1988—Packers, 26-17 (P)
1990—Packers, 24-21 (P)
(RS Pts.—Packers 1,082, Cardinals 823)
(PS Pts.—Packers 41, Cardinals 16)
**Franchise in St. Louis prior to 1988, and in Chicago prior to 1960*
***NFC First Round Playoff*

GREEN BAY vs. *PITTSBURGH
RS: Packers lead series, 16-11
1933—Packers, 47-0 (GB)
1935—Packers, 27-0 (GB)
Packers, 34-14 (P)
1936—Packers, 42-10 (Mil)
1938—Packers, 20-0 (GB)
1940—Packers, 24-3 (Mil)
1941—Packers, 54-7 (P)
1942—Packers, 24-21 (Mil)
1946—Packers, 17-7 (GB)
1947—Steelers, 18-17 (Mil)
1948—Steelers, 38-7 (P)
1949—Steelers, 30-7 (Mil)
1951—Packers, 35-33 (Mil)
Steelers, 28-7 (P)
1953—Steelers, 31-14 (P)
1954—Steelers, 21-20 (GB)
1957—Packers, 27-10 (P)
1960—Packers, 19-13 (P)
1963—Packers, 33-14 (Mil)
1965—Packers, 41-9 (P)
1967—Steelers, 24-17 (GB)
1969—Packers, 38-34 (P)
1970—Packers, 20-12 (P)
1975—Steelers, 16-13 (Mil)
1980—Steelers, 22-20 (P)
1983—Steelers, 25-21 (GB)
1986—Steelers, 27-3 (P)
(RS Pts.—Packers 648, Steelers 467)
**Steelers known as Pirates prior to 1941*

GREEN BAY vs. SAN DIEGO
RS: Packers lead series, 3-1
1970—Packers, 22-20 (SD)
1974—Packers, 34-0 (GB)
1978—Packers, 24-3 (SD)
1984—Chargers, 34-28 (GB)
(RS Pts.—Packers 108, Chargers 57)

GREEN BAY vs. SAN FRANCISCO
RS: 49ers lead series, 25-21-1
1950—Packers, 25-21 (GB)
49ers, 30-14 (SF)
1951—49ers, 31-19 (SF)
1952—49ers, 24-14 (SF)
1953—49ers, 37-7 (Mil)
49ers, 48-14 (SF)
1954—49ers, 23-17 (Mil)
49ers, 35-0 (SF)

1955—Packers, 27-21 (Mil)
Packers, 28-7 (SF)
1956—49ers, 17-16 (GB)
49ers, 38-20 (SF)
1957—49ers, 24-14 (Mil)
49ers, 27-20 (SF)
1958—49ers, 33-12 (Mil)
49ers, 48-21 (SF)
1959—Packers, 21-20 (GB)
Packers, 36-14 (SF)
1960—Packers, 41-14 (Mil)
Packers, 13-0 (SF)
1961—Packers, 30-10 (GB)
49ers, 22-21 (SF)
1962—Packers, 31-13 (Mil)
Packers, 31-21 (SF)
1963—Packers, 28-10 (Mil)
Packers, 21-17 (SF)
1964—Packers, 24-14 (Mil)
49ers, 24-14 (SF)
1965—Packers, 27-10 (GB)
Tie, 24-24 (SF)
1966—49ers, 21-20 (SF)
Packers, 20-7 (Mil)
1967—Packers, 13-0 (GB)
1968—49ers, 27-20 (SF)
1969—Packers, 14-7 (Mil)
1970—49ers, 26-10 (SF)
1972—Packers, 34-24 (Mil)
1973—49ers, 20-6 (SF)
1974—49ers, 7-6 (SF)
1976—49ers, 26-14 (GB)
1977—Packers, 16-14 (Mil)
1980—Packers, 23-16 (Mil)
1981—49ers, 13-3 (Mil)
1986—49ers, 31-17 (Mil)
1987—49ers, 23-12 (GB)
1989—Packers, 21-17 (SF)
1990—49ers, 24-20 (GB)
(RS Pts.—49ers 980, Packers 899)

GREEN BAY vs. SEATTLE
RS: Series tied, 3-3
1976—Packers, 27-20 (Mil)
1978—Packers, 45-28 (Mil)
1981—Packers, 34-24 (GB)
1984—Seahawks, 30-24 (Mil)
1987—Seahawks, 24-13 (S)
1990—Seahawks, 20-14 (Mil)
(RS Pts.—Packers 157, Seahawks 146)

GREEN BAY vs. TAMPA BAY
RS: Packers lead series, 12-11-1
1977—Packers, 13-0 (TB)
1978—Packers, 9-7 (GB)
Packers, 17-7 (TB)
1979—Buccaneers, 21-10 (GB)
Buccaneers, 21-3 (TB)
1980—Tie, 14-14 (TB) OT
Buccaneers, 20-17 (Mil)
1981—Buccaneers, 21-10 (GB)
Buccaneers, 37-3 (TB)
1983—Packers, 55-14 (GB)
Packers, 12-9 (TB) OT
1984—Buccaneers, 30-27 (TB) OT
Packers, 27-14 (GB)
1985—Packers, 21-0 (GB)
Packers, 20-17 (TB)
1986—Packers, 31-7 (Mil)
Packers, 21-7 (TB)
1987—Buccaneers, 23-17 (Mil)
1988—Buccaneers, 13-10 (GB)
Buccaneers, 27-24 (TB)
1989—Buccaneers, 23-21 (GB)
Packers, 17-16 (TB)
1990—Buccaneers, 26-14 (TB)
Packers, 20-10 (Mil)
(RS Pts.—Packers 433, Buccaneers 383)

GREEN BAY vs. *WASHINGTON
RS: Packers lead series, 13-12-1
PS: Series tied, 1-1
1932—Packers, 21-0 (B)
1933—Tie, 7-7 (GB)
Redskins, 20-7 (B)
1934—Packers, 10-0 (B)
1936—Packers, 31-2 (GB)
Packers, 7-3 (B)
**Packers, 21-6 (New York)
1937—Redskins, 14-6 (W)
1939—Packers, 24-14 (Mil)
1941—Packers, 22-17 (W)
1943—Redskins, 33-7 (Mil)
1946—Packers, 20-7 (W)
1947—Packers, 27-10 (Mil)
1948—Redskins, 23-7 (Mil)
1949—Redskins, 30-0 (W)
1950—Packers, 35-21 (Mil)
1952—Packers, 35-20 (Mil)
1958—Redskins, 37-21 (W)
1959—Packers, 21-0 (GB)
1968—Packers, 27-7 (W)
1972—Redskins, 21-16 (W)
***Redskins, 16-3 (W)
1974—Redskins, 17-6 (GB)
1977—Redskins, 10-9 (W)
1979—Redskins, 38-21 (W)
1983—Packers, 48-47 (GB)
1986—Redskins, 16-7 (GB)
1988—Redskins, 20-17 (Mil)
(RS Pts.—Packers 459, Redskins 434)
(PS Pts.—Packers 24, Redskins 22)
**Franchise in Boston prior to 1937 and known as Braves prior to 1933*
***NFL Championship*
****NFC Divisional Playoff*

HOUSTON vs. ATLANTA
RS: Falcons lead series, 5-2;
See Atlanta vs. Houston

HOUSTON vs. BUFFALO
RS: Oilers lead series, 19-11
PS: Bills lead series, 1-0;
See Buffalo vs. Houston

HOUSTON vs. CHICAGO
RS: Oilers lead series, 3-2;
See Chicago vs. Houston

HOUSTON vs. CINCINNATI
RS: Bengals lead series, 24-19-1
PS: Bengals lead series, 1-0;
See Cincinnati vs. Houston

HOUSTON vs. CLEVELAND
RS: Browns lead series, 26-15
PS: Oilers lead series, 1-0;
See Cleveland vs. Houston

HOUSTON vs. DALLAS
RS: Cowboys lead series, 4-2;
See Dallas vs. Houston

HOUSTON vs. DENVER
RS: Oilers lead series, 18-10-1
PS: Series tied, 1-1;
See Denver vs. Houston

HOUSTON vs. DETROIT
RS: Oilers lead series, 3-2;
See Detroit vs. Houston

HOUSTON vs. GREEN BAY
RS: Oilers lead series, 3-2;
See Green Bay vs. Houston

HOUSTON vs. *INDIANAPOLIS
RS: Series tied, 6-6
1970—Colts, 24-20 (H)
1973—Oilers, 31-27 (B)
1976—Colts, 38-14 (B)
1979—Oilers, 28-16 (B)
1980—Oilers, 21-16 (H)
1983—Colts, 20-10 (B)
1984—Colts, 35-21 (H)
1985—Colts, 34-16 (I)
1986—Oilers, 31-17 (H)
1987—Colts, 51-27 (I)
1988—Oilers, 17-14 (I) OT
1990—Oilers 24-10 (H)
(RS Pts.—Colts 302, Oilers 260)
**Franchise in Baltimore prior to 1984*

HOUSTON vs. *KANSAS CITY
RS: Chiefs lead series, 21-14
PS: Chiefs lead series, 1-0
1960—Oilers, 20-10 (H)
Texans, 24-0 (D)
1961—Texans, 26-21 (D)
Oilers, 38-7 (H)
1962—Texans, 31-7 (H)
Oilers, 14-6 (D)
**Texans, 20-17 (H) OT
1963—Chiefs, 28-7 (KC)
Oilers, 28-7 (H)
1964—Chiefs, 28-7 (KC)
Chiefs, 28-19 (H)
1965—Chiefs, 52-21 (KC)
Oilers, 38-36 (H)
1966—Chiefs, 48-23 (KC)
1967—Chiefs, 25-20 (H)
Oilers, 24-19 (KC)
1968—Chiefs, 26-21 (H)
Chiefs, 24-10 (KC)
1969—Chiefs, 24-0 (KC)
1970—Chiefs, 24-9 (KC)
1971—Chiefs, 20-16 (H)
1973—Chiefs, 38-14 (KC)
1974—Chiefs, 17-7 (H)
1975—Oilers, 17-13 (KC)
1977—Oilers, 34-20 (H)
1978—Oilers, 20-17 (KC)
1979—Oilers, 20-6 (H)
1980—Chiefs, 21-20 (KC)
1981—Chiefs, 23-10 (KC)
1983—Chiefs, 13-10 (H) OT
1984—Oilers, 17-16 (KC)
1985—Oilers, 23-20 (H)
1986—Chiefs, 27-13 (KC)
1988—Oilers, 7-6 (H)
1989—Chiefs, 34-0 (KC)
1990—Oilers 27-10 (KC)
(RS Pts.—Chiefs 774, Oilers 582)
(PS Pts.—Chiefs 20, Oilers 17)
**Franchise in Dallas prior to 1963 and known as Texans*
***AFL Championship*

HOUSTON vs. *L.A. RAIDERS
RS: Raiders lead series, 19-12
PS: Raiders lead series, 3-0
1960—Oilers, 37-22 (O)
Raiders, 14-13 (H)
1961—Oilers, 55-0 (H)
Oilers, 47-16 (O)
1962—Oilers, 28-20 (O)
Oilers, 32-17 (H)
1963—Raiders, 24-13 (H)
Raiders, 52-49 (O)
1964—Oilers, 42-28 (H)
Raiders, 20-10 (O)
1965—Raiders, 21-17 (O)
Raiders, 33-21 (H)
1966—Oilers, 31-0 (H)
Raiders, 38-23 (O)
1967—Raiders, 19-7 (H)
**Raiders, 40-7 (O)
1968—Raiders, 24-15 (H)
1969—Raiders, 21-17 (O)
***Raiders, 56-7 (O)
1971—Raiders, 41-21 (O)
1972—Raiders, 34-0 (H)
1973—Raiders, 17-6 (H)
1975—Oilers, 27-26 (O)
1976—Raiders, 14-13 (H)
1977—Raiders, 34-29 (O)
1978—Raiders, 21-17 (O)
1979—Oilers, 31-17 (H)
1980—****Raiders, 27-7 (O)
1981—Oilers, 17-16 (H)
1983—Raiders, 20-6 (LA)
1984—Raiders, 24-14 (H)
1986—Raiders, 28-17 (H)
1988—Oilers, 38-35 (H)
1989—Oilers, 23-7 (H)
(RS Pts.—Oilers 716, Raiders 703)
(PS Pts.—Raiders 123, Oilers 21)
**Franchise in Oakland prior to 1982*
***AFL Championship*
****Inter-Divisional Playoff*
*****AFC First Round Playoff*

HOUSTON vs. L.A. RAMS
RS: Rams lead series, 4-2
1973—Rams, 31-26 (H)
1978—Rams, 10-6 (H)
1981—Oilers, 27-20 (LA)
1984—Rams, 27-16 (LA)
1987—Oilers, 20-16 (H)
1990—Rams, 17-13 (LA)
(RS Pts.—Rams 121, Oilers 108)

HOUSTON vs. MIAMI
RS: Series tied, 10-10
PS: Oilers lead series, 1-0
1966—Dolphins, 20-13 (H)
Dolphins, 29-28 (M)
1967—Oilers, 17-14 (H)
Oilers, 41-10 (M)
1968—Oilers, 24-10 (M)
Dolphins, 24-7 (H)
1969—Oilers, 22-10 (H)
Oilers, 32-7 (M)
1970—Dolphins, 20-10 (H)
1972—Dolphins, 34-13 (M)
1975—Oilers, 20-19 (H)
1977—Dolphins, 27-7 (M)
1978—Oilers, 35-30 (H)
*Oilers, 17-9 (M)
1979—Oilers, 9-6 (M)
1981—Dolphins, 16-10 (H)
1983—Dolphins, 24-17 (H)
1984—Dolphins, 28-10 (M)
1985—Oilers, 26-23 (H)
1986—Dolphins, 28-7 (M)
1989—Oilers, 39-7 (H)
(RS Pts.—Oilers 387, Dolphins 386)
(PS Pts.—Oilers 17, Dolphins 9)
**AFC First Round Playoff*

HOUSTON vs. MINNESOTA
RS: Vikings lead series, 3-2
1974—Vikings, 51-10 (M)
1980—Oilers, 20-16 (H)
1983—Vikings, 34-14 (M)
1986—Oilers, 23-10 (H)
1989—Vikings, 38-7 (M)
(RS Pts.—Vikings 149, Oilers 74)

HOUSTON vs. *NEW ENGLAND
RS: Patriots lead series, 16-13-1
PS: Oilers lead series, 1-0
1960—Oilers, 24-10 (B)
Oilers, 37-21 (H)
1961—Tie, 31-31 (B)
Oilers, 27-15 (H)
1962—Patriots, 34-21 (B)
Oilers, 21-17 (H)
1963—Patriots, 45-3 (B)
Patriots, 46-28 (H)
1964—Patriots, 25-24 (B)
Patriots, 34-17 (H)
1965—Oilers, 31-10 (H)
Patriots, 42-14 (B)
1966—Patriots, 27-21 (B)
Patriots, 38-14 (H)
1967—Patriots, 18-7 (B)
Oilers, 27-6 (H)
1968—Oilers, 16-0 (B)
Oilers, 45-17 (H)
1969—Patriots, 24-0 (B)
Oilers, 27-23 (H)
1971—Patriots, 28-20 (NE)
1973—Patriots, 32-0 (H)
1975—Oilers, 7-0 (NE)
1978—Oilers, 26-23 (NE)
**Oilers, 31-14 (NE)
1980—Oilers, 38-34 (H)
1981—Patriots, 38-10 (NE)
1982—Patriots, 29-21 (NE)
1987—Patriots, 21-7 (H)
1988—Oilers, 31-6 (H)
1989—Patriots, 23-13 (NE)
(RS Pts.—Patriots 717, Oilers 608)
(PS Pts.—Oilers 31, Patriots 14)
**Franchise in Boston prior to 1971*
***AFC Divisional Playoff*

HOUSTON vs. NEW ORLEANS
RS: Series tied, 3-3-1
1971—Tie, 13-13 (H)
1976—Oilers, 31-26 (NO)
1978—Oilers, 17-12 (NO)
1981—Saints, 27-24 (H)
1984—Saints, 27-10 (H)
1987—Saints, 24-10 (NO)
1990—Oilers 23-10 (H)
(RS Pts.—Saints 139, Oilers 128)

HOUSTON vs. N.Y. GIANTS
RS: Giants lead series, 3-0
1973—Giants, 34-14 (NY)
1982—Giants, 17-14 (NY)
1985—Giants, 35-14 (H)
(RS Pts.—Giants 86, Oilers 42)

HOUSTON vs. *N.Y. JETS
RS: Oilers lead series, 15-12-1
1960—Oilers, 27-21 (H)
Oilers, 42-28 (NY)
1961—Oilers, 49-13 (H)
Oilers, 48-21 (NY)
1962—Oilers, 56-17 (H)
Oilers, 44-10 (NY)
1963—Jets, 24-17 (NY)
Oilers, 31-27 (H)
1964—Jets, 24-21 (NY)
Oilers, 33-17 (H)
1965—Oilers, 27-21 (H)
Jets, 41-14 (NY)
1966—Jets, 52-13 (NY)
Oilers, 24-0 (H)
1967—Tie, 28-28 (NY)
1968—Jets, 20-14 (H)
Jets, 26-7 (NY)
1969—Jets, 26-17 (NY)
Jets, 34-26 (H)
1972—Oilers, 26-20 (H)
1974—Oilers, 27-22 (NY)
1977—Oilers, 20-0 (H)
1979—Oilers, 27-24 (H) OT
1980—Jets, 31-28 (NY) OT
1981—Jets, 33-17 (NY)
1984—Oilers, 31-20 (H)
1988—Jets, 45-3 (NY)
1990—Jets, 17-12 (H)
(RS Pts.—Oilers 729, Jets 662)
**Jets known as Titans prior to 1963*

HOUSTON vs. PHILADELPHIA
RS: Eagles lead series, 4-0
1972—Eagles, 18-17 (H)
1979—Eagles, 26-20 (H)
1982—Eagles, 35-14 (P)
1988—Eagles, 32-23 (P)
(RS Pts.—Eagles 111, Oilers 74)

HOUSTON vs. *PHOENIX
RS: Cardinals lead series, 3-2
1970—Cardinals, 44-0 (StL)
1974—Cardinals, 31-27 (H)
1979—Cardinals, 24-17 (H)
1985—Oilers, 20-10 (StL)
1988—Oilers, 38-20 (H)
(RS Pts.—Cardinals 129, Oilers 102)
**Franchise in St. Louis prior to 1988*

HOUSTON vs. PITTSBURGH
RS: Steelers lead series, 26-15
PS: Steelers lead series, 3-0
1970—Oilers, 19-7 (P)
Steelers, 7-3 (H)
1971—Steelers, 23-16 (P)
Oilers, 29-3 (H)
1972—Steelers, 24-7 (P)
Steelers, 9-3 (H)
1973—Steelers, 36-7 (H)
Steelers, 33-7 (P)
1974—Steelers, 13-7 (H)
Oilers, 13-10 (P)
1975—Steelers, 24-17 (P)
Steelers, 32-9 (H)
1976—Steelers, 32-16 (P)
Steelers, 21-0 (H)

1977—Oilers, 27-10 (H)
Steelers, 27-10 (P)
1978—Oilers, 24-17 (P)
Steelers, 13-3 (H)
*Steelers, 34-5 (P)
1979—Steelers, 38-7 (P)
Oilers, 20-17 (H)
*Steelers, 27-13 (P)
1980—Steelers, 31-17 (P)
Oilers, 6-0 (H)
1981—Steelers, 26-13 (P)
Oilers, 21-20 (H)
1982—Steelers, 24-10 (H)
1983—Steelers, 40-28 (H)
Steelers, 17-10 (P)
1984—Steelers, 35-7 (P)
Oilers, 23-20 (H) OT
1985—Steelers, 20-0 (P)
Steelers, 30-7 (H)
1986—Steelers, 22-16 (H) OT
Steelers, 21-10 (P)
1987—Oilers, 23-3 (P)
Oilers, 24-16 (H)
1988—Oilers, 34-14 (P)
Steelers, 37-34 (H)
1989—Oilers, 27-0 (H)
Oilers, 23-16 (P)
**Steelers, 26-23 (H)
1990—Steelers, 20-9 (P)
Oilers 34-14 (H)
(RS Pts.—Steelers 822, Oilers 620)
(PS Pts.—Steelers 87, Oilers 41)
AFC Championship
***AFC First Round Playoff*

HOUSTON vs. *SAN DIEGO
RS: Chargers lead series, 17-12-1
PS: Oilers lead series, 3-0
1960—Oilers, 38-28 (H)
Chargers, 24-21 (LA)
**Oilers, 24-16 (H)
1961—Chargers, 34-24 (SD)
Oilers, 33-13 (H)
**Oilers, 10-3 (SD)
1962—Oilers, 42-17 (SD)
Oilers, 33-27 (H)
1963—Chargers, 27-0 (SD)
Chargers 20-14 (H)
1964—Chargers, 27-21 (SD)
Chargers, 20-17 (H)
1965—Chargers, 31-14 (SD)
Chargers, 37-26 (H)
1966—Chargers, 28-22 (H)
1967—Chargers, 13-3 (SD)
Oilers, 24-17 (H)
1968—Chargers, 30-14 (SD)
1969—Chargers, 21-17 (H)
1970—Tie, 31-31 (SD)
1971—Oilers, 49-33 (H)
1972—Chargers, 34-20 (SD)
1974—Oilers, 21-14 (H)
1975—Oilers, 33-17 (H)
1976—Chargers, 30-27 (SD)
1978—Chargers, 45-24 (H)
1979—***Oilers, 17-14 (SD)
1984—Chargers, 31-14 (SD)
1985—Oilers, 37-35 (H)
1986—Chargers, 27-0 (SD)
1987—Oilers, 33-18 (H)
1989—Oilers, 34-27 (SD)
1990—Oilers 17-7 (SD)
(RS Pts.—Chargers 763, Oilers 703)
(PS Pts.—Oilers 51, Chargers 33)
Franchise in Los Angeles prior to 1961
***AFL Championship*
****AFC Divisional Playoff*

HOUSTON vs. SAN FRANCISCO
RS: 49ers lead series, 5-2
1970—49ers, 30-20 (H)
1975—Oilers, 27-13 (SF)
1978—Oilers, 20-19 (H)
1981—49ers, 28-6 (SF)
1984—49ers, 34-21 (H)
1987—49ers, 27-20 (SF)
1990—49ers, 24-21 (H)
(RS Pts.—49ers 175, Oilers 135)

HOUSTON vs. SEATTLE
RS: Seahawks lead series, 4-3
PS: Oilers lead series, 1-0
1977—Oilers, 22-10 (S)
1979—Seahawks, 34-14 (S)
1980—Seahawks, 26-7 (H)
1981—Oilers, 35-17 (H)
1982—Oilers, 23-21 (H)
1987—*Oilers, 23-20 (H) OT
1988—Seahawks, 27-24 (S)
1990—Seahawks, 13-10 (S) OT
(RS Pts.—Seahawks 148, Oilers 135)
(PS Pts.—Oilers 23, Seahawks 20)
AFC First Round Playoff

HOUSTON vs. TAMPA BAY
RS: Oilers lead series, 3-1
1976—Oilers, 20-0 (H)
1980—Oilers, 20-14 (H)
1983—Buccaneers, 33-24 (TB)
1989—Oilers, 20-17 (H)
(RS Pts.—Oilers 84, Buccaneers 64)

HOUSTON vs. WASHINGTON
RS: Oilers lead series, 3-2
1971—Redskins, 22-13 (W)
1975—Oilers, 13-10 (H)
1979—Oilers, 29-27 (W)
1985—Redskins, 16-13 (W)
1988—Oilers, 41-17 (H)
(RS Pts.—Oilers 109, Redskins 92)

INDIANAPOLIS vs. ATLANTA
RS: Colts lead series, 10-0;
See Atlanta vs. Indianapolis

INDIANAPOLIS vs. BUFFALO
RS: Bills lead series, 21-19-1;
See Buffalo vs. Indianapolis

INDIANAPOLIS vs. CHICAGO
RS: Colts lead series, 21-15;
See Chicago vs. Indianapolis

INDIANAPOLIS vs. CINCINNATI
RS: Colts lead series, 6-5
PS: Colts lead series, 1-0;
See Cincinnati vs. Indianapolis

INDIANAPOLIS vs. CLEVELAND
RS: Browns lead series, 11-5
PS: Series tied, 2-2;
See Cleveland vs. Indianapolis

INDIANAPOLIS vs. DALLAS
RS: Cowboys lead series, 6-2
PS: Colts lead series, 1-0;
See Dallas vs. Indianapolis

INDIANAPOLIS vs. DENVER
RS: Broncos lead series, 8-2;
See Denver vs. Indianapolis

INDIANAPOLIS vs. DETROIT
RS: Colts lead series, 17-16-2;
See Detroit vs. Indianapolis

INDIANAPOLIS vs. GREEN BAY
RS: Colts lead series, 18-17-1
PS: Packers lead series, 1-0;
See Green Bay vs. Indianapolis

INDIANAPOLIS vs. HOUSTON
RS: Series tied, 6-6;
See Houston vs. Indianapolis

***INDIANAPOLIS vs. KANSAS CITY**
RS: Chiefs lead series, 6-4
1970—Chiefs, 44-24 (B)
1972—Chiefs, 24-10 (KC)
1975—Colts, 28-14 (B)
1977—Colts, 17-6 (KC)
1979—Chiefs, 14-0 (KC)
Chiefs, 10-7 (B)
1980—Colts, 31-24 (KC)
Chiefs, 38-28 (B)
1985—Chiefs, 20-7 (KC)
1990—Colts, 23-19 (I)
(RS Pts.—Chiefs 213, Colts 175)
Franchise in Baltimore prior to 1984

***INDIANAPOLIS vs **L.A. RAIDERS**
RS: Raiders lead series, 3-2
PS: Series tied, 1-1
1970—***Colts, 27-17 (B)
1971—Colts, 37-14 (O)
1973—Raiders, 34-21 (B)
1975—Raiders, 31-20 (B)
1977—****Raiders, 37-31 (B) OT
1984—Raiders, 21-7 (LA)
1986—Colts, 30-24 (LA)
(RS Pts.—Raiders 124, Colts 115)
(PS Pts.—Colts 58, Raiders 54)
Franchise in Baltimore prior to 1984
***Franchise in Oakland prior to 1982*
****AFC Championship*
*****AFC Divisional Playoff*

***INDIANAPOLIS vs. L.A. RAMS**
RS: Colts lead series, 20-16-2
1953—Rams, 21-13 (B)
Rams, 45-2 (LA)
1954—Rams, 48-0 (B)
Colts, 22-21 (LA)
1955—Tie, 17-17 (B)
Rams, 20-14 (LA)
1956—Colts, 56-21 (B)
Rams, 31-7 (LA)
1957—Colts, 31-14 (B)
Rams, 37-21 (LA)
1958—Colts, 34-7 (B)
Rams, 30-28 (LA)
1959—Colts, 35-21 (B)
Colts, 45-26 (LA)
1960—Colts, 31-17 (B)
Rams, 10-3 (LA)
1961—Colts, 27-24 (B)
Rams, 34-17 (LA)
1962—Colts, 30-27 (B)
Colts, 14-2 (LA)
1963—Rams, 17-16 (LA)
Colts, 19-16 (B)
1964—Colts, 35-20 (B)
Colts, 24-7 (LA)
1965—Colts, 35-20 (B)
Colts, 20-17 (LA)
1966—Colts, 17-3 (LA)
Rams, 23-7 (B)
1967—Tie, 24-24 (B)
Rams, 34-10 (LA)
1968—Colts, 27-10 (B)
Colts, 28-24 (LA)
1969—Rams, 27-20 (B)
Colts, 13-7 (LA)
1971—Colts, 24-17 (B)
1975—Rams, 24-13 (LA)
1986—Rams, 24-7 (I)
1989—Rams, 31-17 (LA)
(RS Pts.—Rams 818, Colts 803)
Franchise in Baltimore prior to 1984

***INDIANAPOLIS vs. MIAMI**
RS: Dolphins lead series, 29-13
PS: Dolphins lead series, 1-0
1970—Colts, 35-0 (B)
Dolphins, 34-17 (M)
1971—Dolphins, 17-14 (M)
Colts, 14-3 (B)
**Dolphins, 21-0 (M)
1972—Dolphins, 23-0 (B)
Dolphins, 16-0 (M)
1973—Dolphins, 44-0 (M)
Colts, 16-3 (B)
1974—Dolphins, 17-7 (M)
Dolphins, 17-16 (B)
1975—Colts, 33-17 (M)
Colts, 10-7 (B) OT
1976—Colts, 28-14 (B)
Colts, 17-16 (M)
1977—Colts, 45-28 (B)
Dolphins, 17-6 (M)
1978—Dolphins, 42-0 (B)
Dolphins, 26-8 (M)
1979—Dolphins, 19-0 (M)
Dolphins, 28-24 (B)
1980—Colts, 30-17 (M)
Dolphins, 24-14 (B)
1981—Dolphins, 31-28 (B)
Dolphins, 27-10 (M)
1982—Dolphins, 24-20 (M)
Dolphins, 34-7 (B)
1983—Dolphins, 21-7 (B)
Dolphins, 37-0 (M)
1984—Dolphins, 44-7 (M)
Dolphins, 35-17 (I)
1985—Dolphins, 30-13 (M)
Dolphins, 34-20 (I)
1986—Dolphins, 30-10 (M)
Dolphins, 17-13 (I)
1987—Dolphins, 23-10 (I)
Colts, 40-21 (M)
1988—Colts, 15-13 (I)
Colts, 31-28 (M)
1989—Dolphins, 19-13 (M)
Colts, 42-13 (I)
1990—Dolphins, 27-7 (I)
Dolphins, 23-17 (M)
(RS Pts.—Dolphins 960, Colts 661)
(PS Pts.—Dolphins 21, Colts 0)
Franchise in Baltimore prior to 1984
***AFC Championship*

***INDIANAPOLIS vs. MINNESOTA**
RS: Colts lead series, 11-6-1
PS: Colts lead series, 1-0
1961—Colts, 34-33 (B)
Vikings, 28-20 (M)
1962—Colts, 34-7 (M)
Colts, 42-17 (B)
1963—Colts, 37-34 (M)
Colts, 41-10 (B)
1964—Vikings, 34-24 (M)
Colts, 17-14 (B)
1965—Colts, 35-16 (B)
Colts, 41-21 (M)
1966—Colts, 38-23 (M)
Colts, 20-17 (B)
1967—Tie, 20-20 (M)
1968—Colts, 21-9 (B)
**Colts, 24-14 (B)
1969—Vikings, 52-14 (M)
1971—Vikings, 10-3 (M)
1982—Vikings, 13-10 (M)
1988—Vikings, 12-3 (M)
(RS Pts.—Colts 454, Vikings 370)
(PS Pts.—Colts 24, Vikings 14)
Franchise in Baltimore prior to 1984
***Conference Championship*

***INDIANAPOLIS vs. **NEW ENGLAND**
RS: Patriots lead series, 23-18
1970—Colts, 14-6 (Bos)
Colts, 27-3 (Balt)
1971—Colts, 23-3 (NE)
Patriots, 21-17 (Balt)
1972—Colts, 24-17 (NE)
Colts, 31-0 (Balt)
1973—Patriots, 24-16 (NE)
Colts, 18-13 (Balt)
1974—Patriots, 42-3 (NE)
Patriots, 27-17 (Balt)
1975—Patriots, 21-10 (NE)
Colts, 34-21 (Balt)
1976—Colts, 27-13 (NE)
Patriots, 21-14 (Balt)
1977—Patriots, 17-3 (NE)
Colts, 30-24 (Balt)
1978—Colts, 34-27 (NE)
Patriots, 35-14 (Balt)
1979—Colts, 31-26 (Balt)
Patriots, 50-21 (NE)
1980—Patriots, 37-21 (Balt)
Patriots, 47-21 (NE)
1981—Colts, 29-28 (NE)
Colts, 23-21 (Balt)
1982—Patriots, 24-13 (Balt)
1983—Colts, 29-23 (NE) OT
Colts, 12-7 (B)
1984—Patriots, 50-17 (I)
Patriots, 16-10 (NE)
1985—Patriots, 34-15 (NE)
Patriots, 38-31 (I)
1986—Patriots, 33-3 (NE)
Patriots, 30-21 (I)
1987—Colts, 30-16 (I)
Patriots, 24-0 (NE)
1988—Patriots, 21-17 (NE)
Colts, 24-21 (I)
1989—Patriots, 23-20 (I) OT
Patriots, 22-16 (NE)
1990—Patriots, 16-14 (I)
Colts, 13-10 (NE)
(RS Pts.—Patriots 952, Colts 787)
Franchise in Baltimore prior to 1984
***Franchise in Boston prior to 1971*

***INDIANAPOLIS vs. NEW ORLEANS**
RS: Colts lead series, 3-2
1967—Colts, 30-10 (B)
1969—Colts, 30-10 (NO)
1973—Colts, 14-10 (B)
1986—Saints, 17-14 (I)
1989—Saints, 41-6 (NO)
(RS Pts.—Colts 94, Saints 88)
Franchise in Baltimore prior to 1984

***INDIANAPOLIS vs. N.Y. GIANTS**
RS: Colts lead series, 5-4
PS: Colts lead series, 2-0
1954—Colts, 20-14 (B)
1955—Giants, 17-7 (NY)
1958—Giants, 24-21 (NY)
**Colts, 23-17 (NY) OT
1959—**Colts, 31-16 (B)
1963—Giants, 37-28 (B)
1968—Colts, 26-0 (NY)
1971—Colts, 31-7 (NY)
1975—Colts, 21-0 (NY)
1979—Colts, 31-7 (NY)
1990—Giants, 24-7 (I)
(RS Pts.—Colts 192, Giants 130)
(PS Pts.—Colts 54, Giants 33)
Franchise in Baltimore prior to 1984
***NFL Championship*

***INDIANAPOLIS vs. N.Y. JETS**
RS: Colts lead series, 23-18
PS: Jets lead series, 1-0
1968—**Jets 16-7 (Miami)
1970—Colts, 29-22 (NY)
Colts, 35-20 (B)
1971—Colts, 22-0 (B)
Colts, 14-13 (NY)
1972—Jets, 44-34 (B)
Jets, 24-20 (NY)
1973—Jets, 34-10 (B)
Jets, 20-17 (NY)
1974—Colts, 35-20 (NY)
Jets, 45-38 (B)
1975—Colts, 45-28 (NY)
Colts, 52-19 (B)
1976—Colts, 20-0 (NY)
Colts, 33-16 (B)
1977—Colts, 20-12 (NY)
Colts, 33-12 (B)
1978—Jets, 33-10 (B)
Jets, 24-16 (NY)
1979—Colts, 10-8 (B)
Jets, 30-17 (NY)
1980—Colts, 17-14 (NY)
Colts, 35-21 (B)
1981—Jets, 41-14 (B)
Jets, 25-0 (NY)
1982—Jets, 37-0 (NY)
1983—Colts, 17-14 (NY)
Jets, 10-6 (B)
1984—Jets, 23-14 (I)
Colts, 9-5 (NY)
1985—Jets, 25-20 (NY)
Jets, 35-17 (I)
1986—Jets, 26-7 (I)
Jets, 31-16 (NY)
1987—Colts, 6-0 (I)
Colts, 19-14 (NY)
1988—Colts, 38-14 (I)
Jets, 34-16 (NY)
1989—Colts, 17-10 (NY)

Colts, 27-10 (I)
1990—Colts, 17-14 (I)
Colts, 29-21 (NY)
(RS Pts.—Colts 851, Jets 848)
(PS Pts.—Jets 16, Colts 7)
*Franchise in Baltimore prior to 1984
**Super Bowl III

***INDIANAPOLIS vs. PHILADELPHIA**
RS: Colts lead series, 6-5
1953—Eagles, 45-14 (P)
1965—Colts, 34-24 (B)
1967—Colts, 38-6 (P)
1969—Colts, 24-20 (B)
1970—Colts, 29-10 (B)
1974—Eagles, 30-10 (P)
1978—Eagles, 17-14 (B)
1981—Eagles, 38-13 (P)
1983—Colts, 22-21 (P)
1984—Eagles, 16-7 (P)
1990—Colts, 24-23 (P)
(RS Pts.—Eagles 250, Colts 229)
*Franchise in Baltimore prior to 1984

***INDIANAPOLIS vs. **PHOENIX**
RS: Cardinals lead series, 6-4
1961—Colts, 16-0 (B)
1964—Colts, 47-27 (B)
1968—Colts, 27-0 (B)
1972—Cardinals, 10-3 (B)
1976—Cardinals, 24-17 (StL)
1978—Colts, 30-17 (StL)
1980—Cardinals, 17-10 (B)
1981—Cardinals, 35-24 (B)
1984—Cardinals, 34-33 (I)
1990—Cardinals, 20-17 (P)
(RS Pts.—Colts 224, Cardinals 184)
*Franchise in Baltimore prior to 1984
**Franchise in St. Louis prior to 1988

***INDIANAPOLIS vs. PITTSBURGH**
RS: Steelers lead series, 8-4
PS: Steelers lead series, 2-0
1957—Steelers, 19-13 (B)
1968—Colts, 41-7 (P)
1971—Colts, 34-21 (B)
1974—Steelers, 30-0 (B)
1975—**Steelers, 28-10 (P)
1976—**Steelers, 40-14 (B)
1977—Colts, 31-21 (B)
1978—Steelers, 35-13 (P)
1979—Steelers, 17-13 (P)
1980—Steelers, 20-17 (B)
1983—Steelers, 24-13 (B)
1984—Colts, 17-16 (I)
1985—Steelers, 45-3 (P)
1987—Steelers, 21-7 (P)
(RS Pts.—Steelers 276, Colts 202)
(PS Pts.—Steelers 68, Colts 24)
*Franchise in Baltimore prior to 1984
**AFC Divisional Playoff

***INDIANAPOLIS vs. SAN DIEGO**
RS: Chargers lead series, 6-5
1970—Colts, 16-14 (SD)
1972—Chargers, 23-20 (B)
1976—Colts, 37-21 (SD)
1981—Chargers, 43-14 (B)
1982—Chargers, 44-26 (SD)
1984—Chargers, 38-10 (I)
1986—Chargers, 17-3 (I)
1987—Chargers, 16-13 (I)
Colts, 20-7 (SD)
1988—Colts, 16-0 (SD)
1989—Colts, 10-6 (I)
(RS Pts.—Chargers 229, Colts 185)
*Franchise in Baltimore prior to 1984

***INDIANAPOLIS vs. SAN FRANCISCO**
RS: Colts lead series, 21-16
1953—49ers, 38-21 (B)
49ers, 45-14 (SF)
1954—Colts, 17-13 (B)
49ers, 10-7 (SF)
1955—Colts, 26-14 (B)
49ers, 35-24 (SF)
1956—49ers, 20-17 (B)
49ers, 30-17 (SF)
1957—Colts, 27-21 (B)
49ers, 17-13 (SF)
1958—Colts, 35-27 (B)
49ers, 21-12 (SF)
1959—Colts, 45-14 (B)
Colts, 34-14 (SF)
1960—49ers, 30-22 (B)
49ers, 34-10 (SF)
1961—Colts, 20-17 (B)
Colts, 27-24 (SF)
1962—49ers, 21-13 (B)
Colts, 22-3 (SF)
1963—Colts, 20-14 (SF)
Colts, 20-3 (B)
1964—Colts, 37-7 (B)
Colts, 14-3 (SF)
1965—Colts, 27-24 (B)
Colts, 34-28 (SF)
1966—Colts, 36-14 (B)
Colts, 30-14 (SF)
1967—Colts, 41-7 (B)
Colts, 26-9 (SF)
1968—Colts, 27-10 (B)
Colts, 42-14 (SF)
1969—49ers, 24-21 (B)
49ers, 20-17 (SF)
1972—49ers, 24-21 (SF)
1986—49ers, 35-14 (SF)
1989—49ers, 30-24 (I)
(RS Pts.—Colts 874, 49ers 728)
*Franchise in Baltimore prior to 1984

***INDIANAPOLIS vs. SEATTLE**
RS: Colts lead series, 2-0
1977—Colts, 29-14 (S)
1978—Colts, 17-14 (S)
(RS Pts.—Colts 46, Seahawks 28)
*Franchise in Baltimore prior to 1984

***INDIANAPOLIS vs. TAMPA BAY**
RS: Colts lead series, 4-1
1976—Colts, 42-17 (B)
1979—Buccaneers, 29-26 (B) OT
1985—Colts, 31-23 (TB)
1987—Colts, 24-6 (I)
1988—Colts, 35-31 (I)
(RS Pts.—Colts 158, Buccaneers 106)
*Franchise in Baltimore prior to 1984

***INDIANAPOLIS vs. WASHINGTON**
RS: Colts lead series, 16-6
1953—Colts, 27-17 (B)
1954—Redskins, 24-21 (W)
1955—Redskins, 14-13 (B)
1956—Colts, 19-17 (B)
1957—Colts, 21-17 (W)
1958—Colts, 35-10 (B)
1959—Redskins, 27-24 (W)
1960—Colts, 20-0 (B)
1961—Colts, 27-6 (W)
1962—Colts, 34-21 (B)
1963—Colts, 36-20 (W)
1964—Colts, 45-17 (B)
1965—Colts, 38-7 (W)
1966—Colts, 37-10 (B)
1967—Colts, 17-13 (W)
1969—Colts, 41-17 (B)
1973—Redskins, 22-14 (W)
1977—Colts, 10-3 (B)
1978—Colts, 21-17 (B)
1981—Redskins, 38-14 (W)
1984—Redskins, 35-7 (I)
1990—Colts, 35-28 (I)
(RS Pts.—Colts 556, Redskins 380)
*Franchise in Baltimore prior to 1984

KANSAS CITY vs. ATLANTA
RS: Chiefs lead series, 2-0;
See Atlanta vs. Kansas City

KANSAS CITY vs. BUFFALO
RS: Bills lead series, 15-11-1
PS: Chiefs lead series, 1-0;
See Buffalo vs. Kansas City

KANSAS CITY vs. CHICAGO
RS: Bears lead series, 3-2;
See Chicago vs. Kansas City

KANSAS CITY vs. CINCINNATI
RS: Chiefs lead series, 10-9;
See Cincinnati vs. Kansas City

KANSAS CITY vs. CLEVELAND
RS: Series tied, 6-6-2;
See Cleveland vs. Kansas City

KANSAS CITY vs. DALLAS
RS: Series tied, 2-2;
See Dallas vs. Kansas City

KANSAS CITY vs. DENVER
RS: Chiefs lead series, 36-25;
See Denver vs. Kansas City

KANSAS CITY vs. DETROIT
RS: Chiefs lead series, 4-3;
See Detroit vs. Kansas City

KANSAS CITY vs. GREEN BAY
RS: Chiefs lead series, 3-1-1
PS: Packers lead series, 1-0;
See Green Bay vs. Kansas City

KANSAS CITY vs. HOUSTON
RS: Chiefs lead series, 21-14
PS: Chiefs lead series, 1-0;
See Houston vs. Kansas City

KANSAS CITY vs. INDIANAPOLIS
RS: Chiefs lead series, 6-4;
See Indianapolis vs. Kansas City

***KANSAS CITY vs. **L.A. RAIDERS**
RS: Raiders lead series, 34-25-2
PS: Series tied, 1-1
1960—Texans, 34-16 (O)
Raiders, 20-19 (D)
1961—Texans, 42-35 (O)
Texans, 43-11 (D)
1962—Texans, 26-16 (O)
Texans, 35-7 (D)
1963—Raiders, 10-7 (O)
Raiders, 22-7 (KC)
1964—Chiefs, 21-9 (O)
Chiefs, 42-7 (KC)
1965—Raiders, 37-10 (O)
Chiefs, 14-7 (KC)
1966—Chiefs, 32-10 (O)
Raiders, 34-13 (KC)
1967—Raiders, 23-21 (O)
Raiders, 44-22 (KC)
1968—Chiefs, 24-10 (KC)
Raiders, 38-21 (O)
***Raiders, 41-6 (O)
1969—Raiders, 27-24 (KC)
Raiders, 10-6 (O)
****Chiefs, 17-7 (O)
1970—Tie, 17-17 (KC)
Raiders, 20-6 (O)
1971—Tie, 20-20 (O)
Chiefs, 16-14 (KC)
1972—Chiefs, 27-14 (KC)
Raiders, 26-3 (O)
1973—Chiefs, 16-3 (KC)
Raiders, 37-7 (O)
1974—Raiders, 27-7 (O)
Raiders, 7-6 (KC)
1975—Chiefs, 42-10 (KC)
Raiders, 28-20 (O)
1976—Raiders, 24-21 (KC)
Raiders, 21-10 (O)
1977—Raiders, 37-28 (KC)
Raiders, 21-20 (O)
1978—Raiders, 28-6 (O)
Raiders, 20-10 (KC)
1979—Chiefs, 35-7 (KC)
Chiefs, 24-21 (O)
1980—Raiders, 27-14 (KC)
Chiefs, 31-17 (O)
1981—Chiefs, 27-0 (KC)
Chiefs, 28-17 (O)
1982—Raiders, 21-16 (KC)
1983—Raiders, 21-20 (LA)
Raiders, 28-20 (KC)
1984—Raiders, 22-20 (KC)
Raiders, 17-7 (LA)
1985—Chiefs, 36-20 (KC)
Raiders, 19-10 (LA)
1986—Raiders, 24-17 (KC)
Chiefs, 20-17 (LA)
1987—Raiders, 35-17 (LA)
Chiefs, 16-10 (KC)
1988—Raiders, 27-17 (KC)
Raiders, 17-10 (LA)
1989—Chiefs, 24-19 (KC)
Raiders, 20-14 (LA)
1990—Chiefs, 9-7 (KC)
Chiefs, 27-24 (LA)
(RS Pts.—Chiefs 1,204, Raiders 1,204)
(PS Pts.—Raiders 48, Chiefs 23)
*Franchise in Dallas prior to 1963 and known as Texans
**Franchise in Oakland prior to 1982
***Division Playoff
****AFL Championship

KANSAS CITY vs. L.A. RAMS
RS: Rams lead series, 3-0
1973—Rams, 23-13 (KC)
1982—Rams, 20-14 (LA)
1985—Rams, 16-0 (KC)
(RS Pts.—Rams 59, Chiefs 27)

KANSAS CITY vs. MIAMI
RS: Chiefs lead series, 9-6
PS: Dolphins lead series, 2-0
1966—Chiefs, 34-16 (KC)
Chiefs, 19-18 (M)
1967—Chiefs, 24-0 (M)
Chiefs, 41-0 (KC)
1968—Chiefs, 48-3 (M)
1969—Chiefs, 17-10 (KC)
1971—*Dolphins, 27-24 (KC) OT
1972—Dolphins, 20-10 (KC)
1974—Dolphins, 9-3 (M)
1976—Chiefs, 20-17 (M) OT
1981—Dolphins, 17-7 (KC)
1983—Dolphins, 14-6 (M)
1985—Dolphins, 31-0 (M)
1987—Dolphins, 42-0 (M)
1989—Chiefs, 26-21 (KC)
Chiefs, 27-24 (M)
1990—**Dolphins, 17-16 (M)
(RS Pts.—Chiefs 282, Dolphins 242)
(PS Pts.—Dolphins 44, Chiefs 40)
*AFC Divisional Playoff
**AFC First Round Playoff

KANSAS CITY vs. MINNESOTA
RS: Series tied, 2-2
PS: Chiefs lead series, 1-0
1969—*Chiefs, 23-7 (New Orleans)
1970—Vikings, 27-10 (M)
1974—Vikings, 35-15 (KC)
1981—Chiefs, 10-6 (M)
1990—Chiefs, 24-21 (KC)
(RS Pts.—Vikings 89, Chiefs 59)
(PS Pts.—Chiefs 23, Vikings 7)
*Super Bowl IV

***KANSAS CITY vs. **NEW ENGLAND**
RS: Chiefs lead series, 12-7-3
1960—Patriots, 42-14 (B)
Texans, 34-0 (D)
1961—Patriots, 18-17 (D)
Patriots, 28-21 (B)
1962—Texans, 42-28 (D)
Texans, 27-7 (B)
1963—Tie, 24-24 (B)
Chiefs, 35-3 (KC)
1964—Patriots, 24-7 (B)
Patriots, 31-24 (KC)
1965—Chiefs, 27-17 (KC)
Tie, 10-10 (B)
1966—Chiefs, 43-24 (B)
Tie, 27-27 (KC)
1967—Chiefs, 33-10 (B)
1968—Chiefs, 31-17 (KC)
1969—Chiefs, 31-0 (B)
1970—Chiefs, 23-10 (KC)
1973—Chiefs, 10-7 (NE)
1977—Patriots, 21-17 (NE)
1981—Patriots, 33-17 (NE)
1990—Chiefs, 37-7 (NE)
(RS Pts.—Chiefs 551, Patriots 388)
*Franchise located in Dallas prior to 1963 and known as Texans
**Franchise in Boston prior to 1971

KANSAS CITY vs. NEW ORLEANS
RS: Series tied, 2-2
1972—Chiefs, 20-17 (NO)
1976—Saints, 27-17 (KC)
1982—Saints, 27-17 (NO)
1985—Chiefs, 47-27 (NO)
(RS Pts.—Chiefs 101, Saints 98)

KANSAS CITY vs. N.Y. GIANTS
RS: Giants lead series, 5-1
1974—Giants, 33-27 (KC)
1978—Giants, 26-10 (NY)
1979—Giants, 21-17 (KC)
1983—Chiefs, 38-17 (KC)
1984—Giants, 28-27 (NY)
1988—Giants, 28-12 (NY)
(RS Pts.—Giants 153, Chiefs 131)

***KANSAS CITY vs. **N.Y. JETS**
RS: Chiefs lead series, 13-12-1
PS: Series tied, 1-1
1960—Titans, 37-35 (D)
Titans, 41-35 (NY)
1961—Titans, 28-7 (NY)
Texans, 35-24 (D)
1962—Texans, 20-17 (D)
Texans, 52-31 (NY)
1963—Jets, 17-0 (NY)
Chiefs, 48-0 (KC)
1964—Jets, 27-14 (NY)
Chiefs, 24-7 (KC)
1965—Chiefs, 14-10 (NY)
Jets, 13-10 (KC)
1966—Chiefs, 32-24 (NY)
1967—Chiefs, 42-18 (KC)
Chiefs, 21-7 (NY)
1968—Jets, 20-19 (KC)
1969—Chiefs, 34-16 (NY)
***Chiefs, 13-6 (NY)
1971—Jets, 13-10 (NY)
1974—Chiefs, 24-16 (KC)
1975—Jets, 30-24 (KC)
1982—Chiefs, 37-13 (KC)
1984—Jets, 17-16 (KC)
Jets, 28-7 (NY)
1986—****Jets, 35-15 (NY)
1987—Jets, 16-9 (KC)
1988—Tie, 17-17 (NY)
Chiefs, 38-34 (KC)
(RS Pts.—Chiefs 624, Jets 521)
(PS Pts.—Jets 41, Chiefs 28)
*Franchise in Dallas prior to 1963 and known as Texans
**Jets known as Titans prior to 1963
***Inter-Divisional Playoff
****AFC First Round Playoff

KANSAS CITY vs. PHILADELPHIA
RS: Eagles lead series, 1-0
1972—Eagles, 21-20 (KC)

KANSAS CITY vs. *PHOENIX
RS: Chiefs lead series, 3-1-1
1970—Tie, 6-6 (KC)
1974—Chiefs, 17-13 (StL)
1980—Chiefs, 21-13 (StL)
1983—Chiefs, 38-14 (KC)
1986—Cardinals, 23-14 (StL)
(RS Pts.—Chiefs 96, Cardinals 69)
*Franchise in St. Louis prior to 1988

KANSAS CITY vs. PITTSBURGH
RS: Steelers lead series, 12-5
1970—Chiefs, 31-14 (P)
1971—Chiefs, 38-16 (KC)
1972—Steelers, 16-7 (P)
1974—Steelers, 34-24 (KC)
1975—Steelers, 28-3 (P)
1976—Steelers, 45-0 (KC)
1978—Steelers, 27-24 (P)
1979—Steelers, 30-3 (KC)
1980—Steelers, 21-16 (P)
1981—Chiefs, 37-33 (P)

1982—Steelers, 35-14 (P)
1984—Chiefs, 37-27 (P)
1985—Steelers, 36-28 (KC)
1986—Chiefs, 24-19 (P)
1987—Steelers, 17-16 (KC)
1988—Steelers, 16-10 (P)
1989—Steelers, 23-17 (P)
(RS Pts.—Steelers 437, Chiefs 329)

***KANSAS CITY vs. **SAN DIEGO**
RS: Chargers lead series, 31-29-1
1960—Chargers, 21-20 (LA)
Texans, 17-0 (D)
1961—Chargers, 26-10 (D)
Chargers, 24-14 (SD)
1962—Chargers, 32-28 (SD)
Texans, 26-17 (D)
1963—Chargers, 24-10 (SD)
Chargers, 38-17 (KC)
1964—Chargers, 28-14 (KC)
Chiefs, 49-6 (SD)
1965—Tie, 10-10 (SD)
Chiefs, 31-7 (KC)
1966—Chiefs, 24-14 (KC)
Chiefs, 27-17 (SD)
1967—Chargers, 45-31 (SD)
Chargers, 17-16 (KC)
1968—Chiefs, 27-20 (KC)
Chiefs, 40-3 (SD)
1969—Chiefs, 27-9 (SD)
Chiefs, 27-3 (KC)
1970—Chiefs, 26-14 (KC)
Chargers, 31-13 (SD)
1971—Chargers, 21-14 (SD)
Chiefs, 31-10 (KC)
1972—Chiefs, 26-14 (SD)
Chargers, 27-17 (KC)
1973—Chiefs, 19-0 (SD)
Chiefs, 33-6 (KC)
1974—Chiefs, 24-14 (SD)
Chargers, 14-7 (KC)
1975—Chiefs, 12-10 (SD)
Chargers, 28-20 (KC)
1976—Chargers, 30-16 (KC)
Chiefs, 23-20 (SD)
1977—Chargers, 23-7 (KC)
Chiefs, 21-16 (SD)
1978—Chargers, 29-23 (SD) OT
Chiefs, 23-0 (KC)
1979—Chargers, 20-14 (KC)
Chargers, 28-7 (SD)
1980—Chargers, 24-7 (KC)
Chargers, 20-7 (SD)
1981—Chargers, 42-31 (KC)
Chargers, 22-20 (SD)
1982—Chiefs, 19-12 (KC)
1983—Chargers, 17-14 (KC)
Chargers, 41-38 (SD)
1984—Chiefs, 31-13 (KC)
Chiefs, 42-21 (SD)
1985—Chargers, 31-20 (SD)
Chiefs, 38-34 (KC)
1986—Chiefs, 42-41 (KC)
Chiefs, 24-23 (SD)
1987—Chiefs, 20-13 (KC)
Chargers, 42-21 (SD)
1988—Chargers, 24-23 (KC)
Chargers, 24-13 (SD)
1989—Chargers, 21-6 (SD)
Chargers, 20-13 (KC)
1990—Chiefs, 27-10 (KC)
Chiefs, 24-21 (SD)
(RS Pts.—Chiefs 1,321, Chargers 1,232)
**Franchise in Dallas prior to 1963 and known as Texans*
***Franchise in Los Angeles prior to 1961*

KANSAS CITY vs. SAN FRANCISCO
RS: 49ers lead series, 3-1
1971—Chiefs, 26-17 (SF)
1975—49ers, 20-3 (KC)
1982—49ers, 26-13 (KC)
1985—49ers, 31-3 (SF)
(RS Pts.—49ers 94, Chiefs 45)

KANSAS CITY vs. SEATTLE
RS: Chiefs lead series, 13-12
1977—Seahawks, 34-31 (KC)
1978—Seahawks, 13-10 (KC)
Seahawks, 23-19 (S)
1979—Chiefs, 24-6 (S)
Chiefs, 37-21 (KC)
1980—Seahawks, 17-16 (KC)
Chiefs, 31-30 (S)
1981—Chiefs, 20-14 (S)
Chiefs, 40-13 (KC)
1983—Chiefs, 17-13 (KC)
Seahawks, 51-48 (S) OT
1984—Seahawks, 45-0 (S)
Chiefs, 34-7 (KC)
1985—Chiefs, 28-7 (KC)
Seahawks, 24-6 (S)
1986—Seahawks, 23-17 (S)
Chiefs, 27-7 (KC)
1987—Seahawks, 43-14 (S)
Chiefs, 41-20 (KC)
1988—Seahawks, 31-10 (S)
Chiefs, 27-24 (KC)
1989—Chiefs, 20-16 (S)
Chiefs, 20-10 (KC)
1990—Seahawks, 19-7 (S)
Seahawks, 17-16 (KC)
(RS Pts.—Chiefs 560, Seahawks 528)

KANSAS CITY vs. TAMPA BAY
RS: Chiefs lead series, 4-2
1976—Chiefs, 28-19 (TB)
1978—Buccaneers, 30-13 (KC)
1979—Buccaneers, 3-0 (TB)
1981—Chiefs, 19-10 (KC)
1984—Chiefs, 24-20 (KC)
1986—Chiefs, 27-20 (KC)
(RS Pts.—Chiefs 111, Buccaneers 102)

KANSAS CITY vs. WASHINGTON
RS: Chiefs lead series, 2-1
1971—Chiefs, 27-20 (KC)
1976—Chiefs, 33-30 (W)
1983—Redskins, 27-12 (W)
(RS Pts.—Redskins 77, Chiefs 72)

L.A. RAIDERS vs. ATLANTA
RS: Raiders lead series, 4-2;
See Atlanta vs. L.A. Raiders

L.A. RAIDERS vs. BUFFALO
RS: Series tied, 13-13
PS: Bills lead series, 1-0;
See Buffalo vs. L.A. Raiders

L.A. RAIDERS vs. CHICAGO
RS: Raiders lead series, 4-3;
See Chicago vs. L.A. Raiders

L.A. RAIDERS vs. CINCINNATI
RS: Raiders lead series, 13-5
PS: Raiders lead series, 2-0;
See Cincinnati vs. L.A. Raiders

L.A. RAIDERS vs. CLEVELAND
RS: Raiders lead series, 8-2
PS: Raiders lead series, 2-0;
See Cleveland vs. L.A. Raiders

L.A. RAIDERS vs. DALLAS
RS: Raiders lead series, 3-1;
See Dallas vs. L.A. Raiders

L.A. RAIDERS vs. DENVER
RS: Raiders lead series, 41-18-2
PS: Broncos lead series, 1-0;
See Denver vs. L.A. Raiders

L.A. RAIDERS vs. DETROIT
RS: Raiders lead series, 5-2;
See Detroit vs. L.A. Raiders

L.A. RAIDERS vs. GREEN BAY
RS: Raiders lead series, 5-1
PS: Packers lead series, 1-0;
See Green Bay vs. L.A. Raiders

L.A. RAIDERS vs. HOUSTON
RS: Raiders lead series, 19-12
PS: Raiders lead series, 3-0;
See Houston vs. L.A. Raiders

L.A. RAIDERS vs. INDIANAPOLIS
RS: Raiders lead series, 3-2
PS: Series tied, 1-1;
See Indianapolis vs. L.A. Raiders

L.A. RAIDERS vs. KANSAS CITY
RS: Raiders lead series, 34-25-2
PS: Series tied, 1-1;
See Kansas City vs. L.A. Raiders

***L.A. RAIDERS vs. L.A. RAMS**
RS: Raiders lead series, 4-2
1972—Raiders, 45-17 (O)
1977—Rams, 20-14 (LA)
1979—Raiders, 24-17 (LA)
1982—Raiders, 37-31 (LA Raiders)
1985—Raiders, 16-6 (LA Rams)
1988—Rams, 22-17 (LA Raiders)
(RS Pts.—Raiders 153, Rams 113)
**Franchise in Oakland prior to 1982*

***L.A. RAIDERS vs. MIAMI**
RS: Raiders lead series, 14-3-1
PS: Raiders lead series, 2-1
1966—Raiders, 23-14 (M)
Raiders, 21-10 (O)
1967—Raiders, 31-17 (O)
1968—Raiders, 47-21 (M)
1969—Raiders, 20-17 (O)
Tie, 20-20 (M)
1970—Dolphins, 20-13 (M)
**Raiders, 21-14 (O)
1973—Raiders, 12-7 (O)
***Dolphins, 27-10 (M)
1974—**Raiders, 28-26 (O)
1975—Raiders, 31-21 (M)
1978—Dolphins, 23-6 (M)
1979—Raiders, 13-3 (O)
1980—Raiders, 16-10 (O)
1981—Raiders, 33-17 (M)
1983—Raiders, 27-14 (LA)
1984—Raiders, 45-34 (M)
1986—Raiders, 30-28 (M)
1988—Dolphins, 24-14 (LA)
1990—Raiders, 13-10 (M)
(RS Pts.—Raiders 415, Dolphins 310)
(PS Pts.—Dolphins 67, Raiders 59)
**Franchise in Oakland prior to 1982*
***AFC Divisional Playoff*
****AFC Championship*

***L.A. RAIDERS vs. MINNESOTA**
RS: Raiders lead series, 5-2
PS: Raiders lead series, 1-0
1973—Vikings, 24-16 (M)
1976—**Raiders, 32-14 (Pasadena)
1977—Raiders, 35-13 (O)
1978—Raiders, 27-20 (O)
1981—Raiders, 36-10 (M)
1984—Raiders, 23-20 (LA)
1987—Vikings, 31-20 (M)
1990—Raiders, 28-24 (M)
(RS Pts.—Raiders 185, Vikings 142)
(PS Pts.—Raiders 32, Vikings 14)
**Franchise in Oakland prior to 1982*
***Super Bowl XI*

***L.A. RAIDERS vs. **NEW ENGLAND**
RS: Series tied, 12-12-1
PS: Series tied, 1-1
1960—Raiders, 27-14 (O)
Patriots, 34-28 (B)
1961—Patriots, 20-17 (B)
Patriots, 35-21 (O)
1962—Patriots, 26-16 (B)
Raiders, 20-0 (O)
1963—Patriots, 20-14 (O)
Patriots, 20-14 (B)
1964—Patriots, 17-14 (O)
Tie, 43-43 (B)
1965—Raiders, 24-10 (B)
Raiders, 30-21 (O)
1966—Patriots, 24-21 (B)
1967—Raiders, 35-7 (O)
Raiders, 48-14 (B)
1968—Raiders, 41-10 (O)
1969—Raiders, 38-23 (B)
1971—Patriots, 20-6 (NE)
1974—Raiders, 41-26 (O)
1976—Patriots, 48-17 (NE)
***Raiders, 24-21 (O)
1978—Patriots, 21-14 (O)
1981—Raiders, 27-17 (O)
1985—Raiders, 35-20 (NE)
***Patriots, 27-20 (LA)
1987—Patriots, 26-23 (NE)
1989—Raiders, 24-21 (LA)
(RS Pts.—Raiders 638, Patriots 537)
(PS Pts.—Patriots 48, Raiders 44)
**Franchise in Oakland prior to 1982*
***Franchise in Boston prior to 1971*
****AFC Divisional Playoff*

***L.A. RAIDERS vs. NEW ORLEANS**
RS: Raiders lead series, 3-1-1
1971—Tie, 21-21 (NO)
1975—Raiders, 48-10 (O)
1979—Raiders, 42-35 (NO)
1985—Raiders, 23-13 (LA)
1988—Saints, 20-6 (NO)
(RS Pts.—Raiders 140, Saints 99)
**Franchise in Oakland prior to 1982*

***L.A. RAIDERS vs. N.Y. GIANTS**
RS: Raiders lead series, 3-2
1973—Raiders, 42-0 (O)
1980—Raiders, 33-17 (NY)
1983—Raiders, 27-12 (LA)
1986—Giants, 14-9 (LA)
1989—Giants, 34-17 (NY)
(RS Pts.—Raiders 128, Giants 77)
**Franchise in Oakland prior to 1982*

***L.A. RAIDERS vs. **N.Y. JETS**
RS: Raiders lead series, 13-9-2
PS: Jets lead series, 2-0
1960—Raiders, 28-27 (NY)
Titans, 31-28 (O)
1961—Titans, 14-6 (O)
Titans, 23-12 (NY)
1962—Titans, 28-17 (O)
Titans, 31-21 (NY)
1963—Jets, 10-7 (NY)
Raiders, 49-26 (O)
1964—Jets, 35-13 (NY)
Raiders, 35-26 (O)
1965—Tie, 24-24 (NY)
Raiders, 24-14 (O)
1966—Raiders, 24-21 (NY)
Tie, 28-28 (O)
1967—Jets, 27-14 (NY)
Raiders, 38-29 (O)
1968—Raiders, 43-32 (O)
***Jets, 27-23 (NY)
1969—Raiders, 27-14 (NY)
1970—Raiders, 14-13 (NY)
1972—Raiders, 24-16 (O)
1977—Raiders, 28-27 (NY)
1979—Jets, 28-19 (NY)
1982—****Jets, 17-14 (LA)
1985—Raiders, 31-0 (LA)
1989—Raiders, 14-7 (NY)
(RS Pts.—Raiders 568, Jets 531)
(PS Pts.—Jets 44, Raiders 37)
**Franchise in Oakland prior to 1982*
***Jets known as Titans prior to 1963*
****AFL Championship*
*****AFC Second Round Playoff*

***L.A. RAIDERS vs. PHILADELPHIA**
RS: Eagles lead series, 3-2
PS: Raiders lead series, 1-0
1971—Raiders, 34-10 (O)
1976—Raiders, 26-7 (P)
1980—Eagles, 10-7 (P)
**Raiders, 27-10 (NO)
1986—Eagles, 33-27 (LA) OT
1989—Eagles, 10-7 (P)
(RS Pts.—Raiders 101, Eagles 70)
(PS Pts.—Raiders 27, Eagles 10)
**Franchise in Oakland prior to 1982*
***Super Bowl XV*

***L.A. RAIDERS vs. **PHOENIX**
RS: Raiders lead series, 2-1
1973—Raiders, 17-10 (StL)
1983—Cardinals, 34-24 (LA)
1989—Raiders, 16-14 (LA)
(RS Pts.—Cardinals 58, Raiders 57)
**Franchise in Oakland prior to 1982*
***Franchise in St. Louis prior to 1988*

***L.A. RAIDERS vs. PITTSBURGH**
RS: Raiders lead series, 7-3
PS: Series tied, 3-3
1970—Raiders, 31-14 (O)
1972—Steelers, 34-28 (P)
**Steelers, 13-7 (P)
1973—Steelers, 17-9 (O)
**Raiders, 33-14 (O)
1974—Raiders, 17-0 (P)
***Steelers, 24-13 (O)
1975—***Steelers, 16-10 (P)
1976—Raiders, 31-28 (O)
***Raiders, 24-7 (O)
1977—Raiders, 16-7 (P)
1980—Raiders, 45-34 (P)
1981—Raiders, 30-27 (O)
1983—**Raiders, 38-10 (LA)
1984—Steelers, 13-7 (LA)
1990—Raiders, 20-3 (LA)
(RS Pts.—Raiders 234, Steelers 177)
(PS Pts.—Raiders 125, Steelers 84)
**Franchise in Oakland prior to 1982*
***AFC Divisional Playoff*
****AFC Championship*

***L.A. RAIDERS vs. **SAN DIEGO**
RS: Raiders lead series, 39-21-2
PS: Raiders lead series, 1-0
1960—Chargers, 52-28 (LA)
Chargers, 41-17 (O)
1961—Chargers, 44-0 (SD)
Chargers, 41-10 (O)
1962—Chargers, 42-33 (O)
Chargers, 31-21 (SD)
1963—Raiders, 34-33 (SD)
Raiders, 41-27 (O)
1964—Chargers, 31-17 (O)
Raiders, 21-20 (SD)
1965—Chargers, 17-6 (O)
Chargers, 24-14 (SD)
1966—Chargers, 29-20 (O)
Raiders, 41-19 (SD)
1967—Raiders, 51-10 (O)
Raiders, 41-21 (SD)
1968—Chargers, 23-14 (O)
Raiders, 34-27 (SD)
1969—Raiders, 24-12 (SD)
Raiders, 21-16 (O)
1970—Tie, 27-27 (SD)
Raiders, 20-17 (O)
1971—Raiders, 34-0 (SD)
Raiders, 34-33 (O)
1972—Tie, 17-17 (O)
Raiders, 21-19 (SD)
1973—Raiders, 27-17 (SD)
Raiders, 31-3 (O)
1974—Raiders, 14-10 (SD)
Raiders, 17-10 (O)
1975—Raiders, 6-0 (SD)
Raiders, 25-0 (O)
1976—Raiders, 27-17 (SD)
Raiders, 24-0 (O)
1977—Raiders, 24-0 (O)
Chargers, 12-7 (SD)
1978—Raiders, 21-20 (SD)
Chargers, 27-23 (O)
1979—Chargers, 30-10 (SD)
Raiders, 45-22 (O)
1980—Chargers, 30-24 (SD) OT
Raiders, 38-24 (O)
***Raiders, 34-27 (SD)
1981—Chargers, 55-21 (O)
Chargers, 23-10 (SD)
1982—Raiders, 28-24 (LA)
Raiders, 41-34 (SD)
1983—Raiders, 42-10 (SD)
Raiders, 30-14 (LA)
1984—Raiders, 33-30 (LA)
Raiders, 44-37 (SD)
1985—Raiders, 34-21 (LA)

Chargers, 40-34 (SD) OT
1986—Raiders, 17-13 (LA)
Raiders, 37-31 (SD) OT
1987—Chargers, 23-17 (LA)
Chargers, 16-14 (SD)
1988—Raiders, 24-13 (LA)
Raiders, 13-3 (SD)
1989—Raiders, 40-14 (LA)
Chargers, 14-12 (SD)
1990—Raiders, 24-9 (SD)
Raiders, 17-12 (LA)
(RS Pts.—Raiders 1,536, Chargers 1,331)
(PS Pts.—Raiders 34, Chargers 27)
Franchise in Oakland prior to 1982
***Franchise in Los Angeles prior to 1961*
****AFC Championship*

***L.A. RAIDERS vs. SAN FRANCISCO**
RS: Raiders lead series, 4-2
1970—49ers, 38-7 (O)
1974—Raiders, 35-24 (SF)
1979—Raiders, 23-10 (O)
1982—Raiders, 23-17 (SF)
1985—49ers, 34-10 (LA)
1988—Raiders, 9-3 (SF)
(RS Pts.—49ers 126, Raiders 107)
**Franchise in Oakland prior to 1982*

***L.A. RAIDERS vs. SEATTLE**
RS: Seahawks lead series, 14-12
PS: Series tied, 1-1
1977—Raiders, 44-7 (O)
1978—Seahawks, 27-7 (S)
Seahawks, 17-16 (O)
1979—Seahawks, 27-10 (S)
Seahawks, 29-24 (O)
1980—Raiders, 33-14 (O)
Raiders, 19-17 (S)
1981—Raiders, 20-10 (O)
Raiders, 32-31 (S)
1982—Raiders, 28-23 (LA)
1983—Seahawks, 38-36 (S)
Seahawks, 34-21 (LA)
**Raiders, 30-14 (LA)
1984—Raiders, 28-14 (LA)
Seahawks, 17-14 (S)
***Seahawks, 13-7 (S)
1985—Seahawks, 33-3 (S)
Raiders, 13-3 (LA)
1986—Raiders, 14-10 (LA)
Seahawks, 37-0 (S)
1987—Seahawks, 35-13 (LA)
Raiders, 37-14 (S)
1988—Seahawks, 35-27 (S)
Seahawks, 43-37 (LA)
1989—Seahawks, 24-20 (LA)
Seahawks, 23-17 (S)
1990—Raiders, 17-13 (S)
Raiders, 24-17 (LA)
(RS Pts.—Seahawks 592, Raiders 554)
(PS Pts.—Raiders 37, Seahawks 27)
**Franchise in Oakland prior to 1982*
***AFC Championship*
****AFC First Round Playoff*

***L.A. RAIDERS vs. TAMPA BAY**
RS: Raiders lead series, 2-0
1976—Raiders, 49-16 (O)
1981—Raiders, 18-16 (O)
(RS Pts.—Raiders 67, Buccaneers 32)
**Franchise in Oakland prior to 1982*

***L.A. RAIDERS vs. WASHINGTON**
RS: Raiders lead series, 4-2
PS: Raiders lead series, 1-0
1970—Raiders, 34-20 (O)
1975—Raiders, 26-23 (W) OT
1980—Raiders, 24-21 (O)
1983—Redskins, 37-35 (W)
**Raiders, 38-9 (Tampa)
1986—Redskins, 10-6 (W)
1989—Raiders, 37-24 (LA)
(RS Pts.—Raiders 162, Redskins 135)
(PS Pts.—Raiders 38, Redskins 9)
**Franchise in Oakland prior to 1982*
***Super Bowl XVIII*

L.A. RAMS vs. ATLANTA
RS: Rams lead series, 35-11-2;
See Atlanta vs. L.A. Rams

L.A. RAMS vs. BUFFALO
RS: Rams lead series, 3-2;
See Buffalo vs. L.A. Rams

L.A. RAMS vs. CHICAGO
RS: Bears lead series, 44-28-3
PS: Series tied, 1-1;
See Chicago vs. L.A. Rams

L.A. RAMS vs. CINCINNATI
RS: Bengals lead series, 4-2;
See Cincinnati vs. L.A. Rams

L.A. RAMS vs. CLEVELAND
RS: Series tied, 7-7
PS: Browns lead series, 2-1;
See Cleveland vs. L.A. Rams

L.A. RAMS vs. DALLAS
RS: Series tied, 8-8
PS: Series tied, 4-4;
See Dallas vs. L.A. Rams

L.A. RAMS vs. DENVER
RS: Series tied, 3-3;
See Denver vs. L.A. Rams

L.A. RAMS vs. DETROIT
RS: Rams lead series, 39-33-1
PS: Lions lead series, 1-0;
See Detroit vs. L.A. Rams

L.A. RAMS vs. GREEN BAY
RS: Rams lead series, 41-34-2
PS: Packers lead series, 1-0;
See Green Bay vs. L.A. Rams

L.A. RAMS vs. HOUSTON
RS: Rams lead series, 4-2;
See Houston vs. L.A. Rams

L.A. RAMS vs. INDIANAPOLIS
RS: Colts lead series, 20-16-2;
See Indianapolis vs. L.A. Rams

L.A. RAMS vs. KANSAS CITY
RS: Rams lead series, 3-0;
See Kansas City vs. L.A. Rams

L.A. RAMS VS. L.A. RAIDERS
RS: Raiders lead series, 4-2;
See L.A. Raiders vs. L.A. Rams

L.A. RAMS vs. MIAMI
RS: Dolphins lead series, 4-1
1971—Dolphins, 20-14 (LA)
1976—Rams, 31-28 (M)
1980—Dolphins, 35-14 (LA)
1983—Dolphins, 30-14 (M)
1986—Dolphins 37-31 (LA) OT
(RS Pts.—Dolphins 150, Rams 104)

L.A. RAMS vs. MINNESOTA
RS: Vikings lead series, 13-11-2
PS: Vikings lead series, 5-1
1961—Rams, 31-17 (LA)
Vikings, 42-21 (M)
1962—Vikings, 38-14 (LA)
Tie, 24-24 (M)
1963—Rams, 27-24 (LA)
Vikings, 21-13 (M)
1964—Rams, 22-13 (LA)
Vikings, 34-13 (M)
1965—Vikings, 38-35 (LA)
Vikings, 24-13 (M)
1966—Vikings, 35-7 (M)
Rams, 21-6 (LA)
1967—Rams, 39-3 (LA)
1968—Rams, 31-3 (M)
1969—Vikings, 20-13 (LA)
*Vikings, 23-20 (M)
1970—Vikings, 13-3 (M)
1972—Vikings, 45-41 (LA)
1973—Vikings, 10-9 (M)
1974—Rams, 20-17 (LA)
**Vikings, 14-10 (M)
1976—Tie, 10-10 (M) OT
**Vikings, 24-13 (M)
1977—Rams, 35-3 (LA)
***Vikings, 14-7 (LA)
1978—Rams, 34-17 (M)
***Rams, 34-10 (LA)
1979—Rams, 27-21 (LA) OT
1985—Rams, 13-10 (LA)
1987—Vikings, 21-16 (LA)
1988—****Vikings, 28-17 (M)
1989—Vikings, 23-21 (M) OT
(RS Pts.—Rams 553, Vikings 532)
(PS Pts.—Vikings 113, Rams 101)
**Conference Championship*
***NFC Championship*
****NFC Divisional Playoff*
*****NFC First Round Playoff*

L.A. RAMS vs. NEW ENGLAND
RS: Patriots lead series, 3-2
1974—Patriots, 20-14 (NE)
1980—Rams, 17-14 (NE)
1983—Patriots, 21-7 (LA)
1986—Patriots, 30-28 (LA)
1989—Rams, 24-20 (NE)
(RS Pts.—Patriots 105, Rams 90)

L.A. RAMS vs. NEW ORLEANS
RS: Rams lead series, 26-16
1967—Rams, 27-13 (NO)
1969—Rams, 36-17 (LA)
1970—Rams, 30-17 (NO)
Rams, 34-16 (LA)
1971—Saints, 24-20 (NO)
Rams, 45-28 (LA)
1972—Rams, 34-14 (LA)
Saints, 19-16 (NO)
1973—Rams, 29-7 (LA)
Rams, 24-13 (NO)
1974—Rams, 24-0 (LA)
Saints, 20-7 (NO)
1975—Rams, 38-14 (LA)
Rams, 14-7 (NO)
1976—Rams, 16-10 (NO)
Rams, 33-14 (LA)
1977—Rams, 14-7 (LA)
Saints, 27-26 (NO)
1978—Rams, 26-20 (NO)
Saints, 10-3 (LA)
1979—Rams, 35-17 (NO)
Saints, 29-14 (LA)
1980—Rams, 45-31 (LA)
Rams, 27-7 (NO)
1981—Saints, 23-17 (NO)
Saints, 21-13 (LA)
1983—Rams, 30-27 (LA)
Rams, 26-24 (NO)
1984—Rams, 28-10 (NO)
Rams, 34-21 (LA)
1985—Rams, 28-10 (LA)
Saints, 29-3 (NO)
1986—Saints, 6-0 (NO)
Rams, 26-13 (LA)
1987—Saints, 37-10 (NO)
Saints, 31-14 (LA)
1988—Rams, 12-10 (NO)
Saints, 14-10 (LA)
1989—Saints, 40-21 (LA)
Rams, 20-17 (NO) OT
1990—Saints, 24-20 (LA)
Saints, 20-17 (NO)
(RS Pts.—Rams 946, Saints 758)

***L.A. RAMS vs. N.Y. GIANTS**
RS: Rams lead series, 18-8
PS: Series tied, 1-1
1938—Giants, 28-0 (NY)
1940—Rams, 13-0 (NY)
1941—Giants, 49-14 (NY)
1945—Rams, 21-17 (NY)
1946—Rams, 31-21 (NY)
1947—Rams, 34-10 (LA)
1948—Rams, 52-37 (NY)
1953—Rams, 21-7 (LA)
1954—Rams, 17-16 (NY)
1959—Giants, 23-21 (LA)
1961—Giants, 24-14 (NY)
1966—Rams, 55-14 (LA)
1968—Rams, 24-21 (LA)
1970—Rams, 31-3 (NY)
1973—Rams, 40-6 (LA)
1976—Rams, 24-10 (LA)
1978—Rams, 20-17 (NY)
1979—Giants, 20-14 (LA)
1980—Rams, 28-7 (NY)
1981—Giants, 10-7 (NY)
1983—Rams, 16-6 (NY)
1984—Rams, 33-12 (LA)
**Giants, 16-13 (LA)
1985—Giants, 24-19 (NY)
1988—Rams, 45-31 (NY)
1989—Rams, 31-10 (LA)
***Rams, 19-13 (NY) OT
1990—Giants, 31-7 (LA)
(RS Pts.—Rams 632, Giants 454)
(PS Pts.—Rams 32, Giants 29)
**Franchise in Cleveland prior to 1946*
***NFC First Round Playoff*
****NFC Divisional Playoff*

L.A. RAMS vs. N.Y. JETS
RS: Rams lead series, 4-2
1970—Jets, 31-20 (LA)
1974—Rams, 20-13 (NY)
1980—Rams, 38-13 (LA)
1983—Jets, 27-24 (NY) OT
1986—Rams, 17-3 (NY)
1989—Rams, 38-14 (LA)
(RS Pts.—Rams 157, Jets 101)

***L.A. RAMS vs. PHILADELPHIA**
RS: Rams lead series, 15-11-1
PS: Series tied, 1-1
1937—Rams, 21-3 (P)
1939—Rams, 35-13 (Colorado Springs)
1940—Rams, 21-13 (C)
1942—Rams, 24-14 (Akron)
1944—Eagles, 26-13 (P)
1945—Eagles, 28-14 (P)
1946—Eagles, 25-14 (LA)
1947—Eagles, 14-7 (P)
1948—Tie, 28-28 (LA)
1949—Eagles, 38-14 (P)
**Eagles, 14-0 (LA)
1950—Eagles, 56-20 (P)
1955—Rams, 23-21 (P)
1956—Rams, 27-7 (LA)
1957—Rams, 17-13 (LA)
1959—Eagles, 23-20 (P)
1964—Rams, 20-10 (LA)
1967—Rams, 33-17 (LA)
1969—Rams, 23-17 (P)
1972—Rams, 34-3 (P)
1975—Rams, 42-3 (P)
1977—Rams, 20-0 (LA)
1978—Rams, 16-14 (P)
1983—Eagles, 13-9 (P)
1985—Rams, 17-6 (P)
1986—Eagles, 34-20 (P)
1988—Eagles, 30-24 (P)
1989—***Rams, 21-7 (P)
1990—Eagles, 27-21 (LA)
(RS Pts.—Rams 577, Eagles 496)
(PS Pts.—Rams 21, Eagles 21)
**Franchise in Cleveland prior to 1946*
***NFL Championship*
****NFC First Round Playoff*

***L.A. RAMS vs. **PHOENIX**
RS: Rams lead series, 22-16-2
PS: Rams lead series, 1-0
1937—Cardinals, 6-0 (Clev)
Cardinals, 13-7 (Chi)
1938—Cardinals, 7-6 (Clev)
Cardinals, 31-17 (Chi)
1939—Rams, 24-0 (Chi)
Rams, 14-0 (Clev)
1940—Rams, 26-14 (Clev)
Cardinals, 17-7 (Chi)
1941—Rams, 10-6 (Clev)
Cardinals, 7-0 (Chi)
1942—Cardinals, 7-0 (Chi)
Rams, 7-3 (Clev)
1945—Rams, 21-0 (Clev)
Rams, 35-21 (Chi)
1946—Cardinals, 34-10 (Chi)
Rams, 17-14 (LA)
1947—Rams, 27-7 (LA)
Cardinals, 17-10 (Chi)
1948—Cardinals, 27-22 (LA)
Cardinals, 27-24 (Chi)
1949—Tie, 28-28 (Chi)
Cardinals, 31-27 (LA)
1951—Rams, 45-21 (LA)
1953—Tie, 24-24 (Chi)
1954—Rams, 28-17 (LA)
1958—Rams, 20-14 (Chi)
1960—Cardinals, 43-21 (LA)
1965—Rams, 27-3 (StL)
1968—Rams, 24-13 (StL)
1970—Rams, 34-13 (LA)
1972—Cardinals, 24-14 (StL)
1975—***Rams, 35-23 (LA)
1976—Cardinals, 30-28 (LA)
1979—Rams, 21-0 (LA)
1980—Rams, 21-13 (StL)
1984—Rams, 16-13 (StL)
1985—Rams, 46-14 (LA)
1986—Rams, 16-10 (StL)
1987—Rams, 27-24 (StL)
1988—Cardinals, 41-27 (LA)
1989—Rams, 37-14 (LA)
(RS Pts.—Rams 815, Cardinals 648)
(PS Pts.—Rams 35, Cardinals 23)
**Franchise in Cleveland prior to 1946*
***Franchise in St. Louis prior to 1988 and in Chicago prior to 1960*
****NFC Divisional Playoff*

***L.A. RAMS vs. **PITTSBURGH**
RS: Rams lead series, 13-4-2
PS: Steelers lead series, 1-0
1938—Rams, 13-7 (New Orleans)
1939—Tie, 14-14 (C)
1941—Rams, 17-14 (Akron)
1947—Rams, 48-7 (P)
1948—Rams, 31-14 (LA)
1949—Tie, 7-7 (P)
1952—Rams, 28-14 (LA)
1955—Rams, 27-26 (LA)
1956—Steelers, 30-13 (P)
1961—Rams, 24-14 (LA)
1964—Rams, 26-14 (P)
1968—Rams, 45-10 (LA)
1971—Rams, 23-14 (P)
1975—Rams, 10-3 (LA)
1978—Rams, 10-7 (LA)
1979—***Steelers, 31-19 (Pasadena)
1981—Steelers, 24-0 (P)
1984—Steelers, 24-14 (P)
1987—Rams, 31-21 (LA)
1990—Steelers, 41-10 (P)
(RS Pts.—Rams 391, Steelers 305)
(PS Pts.—Steelers 31, Rams 19)
**Franchise in Cleveland prior to 1946*
***Steelers known as Pirates prior to 1941*
****Super Bowl XIV*

L.A. RAMS vs. SAN DIEGO
RS: Series tied, 2-2
1970—Rams, 37-10 (LA)
1975—Rams, 13-10 (SD) OT
1979—Chargers, 40-16 (LA)
1988—Chargers, 38-24 (LA)
(RS Pts.—Chargers 98, Rams 90)

L.A. RAMS vs. SAN FRANCISCO
RS: Rams lead series, 48-32-2
PS: 49ers lead series, 1-0
1950—Rams, 35-14 (SF)
Rams, 28-21 (LA)
1951—49ers, 44-17 (SF)
Rams, 23-16 (LA)
1952—Rams, 35-9 (LA)
Rams, 34-21 (SF)
1953—49ers, 31-30 (SF)
49ers, 31-27 (LA)
1954—Tie, 24-24 (LA)
Rams, 42-34 (SF)
1955—Rams, 23-14 (SF)
Rams, 27-14 (LA)
1956—49ers, 33-30 (SF)

Rams, 30-6 (LA)
1957—49ers, 23-20 (SF)
Rams, 37-24 (LA)
1958—Rams, 33-3 (SF)
Rams, 56-7 (LA)
1959—49ers, 34-0 (SF)
49ers, 24-16 (LA)
1960—49ers, 13-9 (SF)
49ers, 23-7 (LA)
1961—49ers, 35-0 (SF)
Rams, 17-7 (LA)
1962—Rams, 28-14 (SF)
49ers, 24-17 (LA)
1963—Rams, 28-21 (LA)
Rams, 21-17 (SF)
1964—Rams, 42-14 (LA)
49ers, 28-7 (SF)
1965—49ers, 45-21 (LA)
49ers, 30-27 (SF)
1966—Rams, 34-3 (LA)
49ers, 21-13 (SF)
1967—49ers, 27-24 (LA)
Rams, 17-7 (SF)
1968—Rams, 24-10 (LA)
Tie, 20-20 (SF)
1969—Rams, 27-21 (SF)
Rams, 41-30 (LA)
1970—49ers, 20-6 (LA)
Rams, 30-13 (SF)
1971—Rams, 20-13 (SF)
Rams, 17-6 (LA)
1972—Rams, 31-7 (LA)
Rams, 26-16 (SF)
1973—Rams, 40-20 (SF)
Rams, 31-13 (LA)
1974—Rams, 37-14 (LA)
Rams, 15-13 (SF)
1975—Rams, 23-14 (SF)
49ers, 24-23 (LA)
1976—49ers, 16-0 (LA)
Rams, 23-3 (SF)
1977—Rams, 34-14 (LA)
Rams, 23-10 (SF)
1978—Rams, 27-10 (LA)
Rams, 31-28 (SF)
1979—Rams, 27-24 (LA)
Rams, 26-20 (SF)
1980—Rams, 48-26 (LA)
Rams, 31-17 (SF)
1981—49ers, 20-17 (SF)
49ers, 33-31 (LA)
1982—49ers, 30-24 (LA)
Rams, 21-20 (SF)
1983—Rams, 10-7 (SF)
49ers, 45-35 (LA)
1984—49ers, 33-0 (LA)
49ers, 19-16 (SF)
1985—49ers, 28-14 (LA)
Rams, 27-20 (SF)
1986—Rams, 16-13 (LA)
49ers, 24-14 (SF)
1987—49ers, 31-10 (LA)
49ers, 48-0 (SF)
1988—49ers, 24-21 (LA)
Rams, 38-16 (SF)
1989—Rams, 13-12 (SF)
49ers, 30-27 (LA)
*49ers, 30-3 (SF)
1990—Rams, 28-17 (SF)
49ers, 26-10 (LA)
(RS Pts.—Rams 1,932, 49ers 1,674)
(PS Pts.—49ers 30, Rams 3)
NFC Championship

L.A. RAMS vs. SEATTLE
RS: Rams lead series, 4-0
1976—Rams, 45-6 (LA)
1979—Rams, 24-0 (S)
1985—Rams, 35-24 (S)
1988—Rams, 31-10 (LA)
(RS Pts.—Rams 135, Seahawks 40)

L.A. RAMS vs. TAMPA BAY
RS: Rams lead series, 7-2
PS: Rams lead series, 1-0
1977—Rams, 31-0 (LA)
1978—Rams, 26-23 (LA)
1979—Buccaneers, 21-6 (TB)
*Rams, 9-0 (TB)
1980—Buccaneers, 10-9 (TB)
1984—Rams, 34-33 (TB)
1985—Rams, 31-27 (TB)
1986—Rams, 26-20 (LA) OT
1987—Rams, 35-3 (LA)
1990—Rams, 35-14 (TB)
(RS Pts.—Rams 233, Buccaneers 151)
(PS Pts.—Rams 9, Buccaneers 0)
NFC Championship

***L.A. RAMS vs. WASHINGTON**
RS: Redskins lead series, 13-4-1
PS: Series tied, 2-2
1937—Redskins, 16-7 (C)
1938—Redskins, 37-13 (W)
1941—Redskins, 17-13 (W)
1942—Redskins, 33-14 (W)
1944—Redskins, 14-10 (W)
1945—**Rams, 15-14 (C)
1948—Rams, 41-13 (W)
1949—Rams, 53-27 (LA)
1951—Redskins, 31-21 (W)
1962—Redskins, 20-14 (W)
1963—Redskins, 37-14 (LA)
1967—Tie, 28-28 (LA)
1969—Rams, 24-13 (W)
1971—Redskins, 38-24 (LA)
1974—Redskins, 23-17 (LA)
***Rams, 19-10 (LA)
1977—Redskins, 17-14 (W)
1981—Redskins, 30-7 (LA)
1983—Redskins, 42-20 (LA)
***Redskins, 51-7 (W)
1986—****Redskins, 19-7 (W)
1987—Rams, 30-26 (W)
(RS Pts.—Redskins 462, Rams 364)
(PS Pts.—Redskins 94, Rams 48)
**Franchise in Cleveland prior to 1946*
***NFL Championship*
****NFC Divisional Playoff*
*****NFC First Round Playoff*

MIAMI vs. ATLANTA
RS: Dolphins lead series, 4-1;
See Atlanta vs. Miami

MIAMI vs. BUFFALO
RS: Dolphins lead series, 35-14-1
PS: Bills lead series, 1-0;
See Buffalo vs. Miami

MIAMI vs. CHICAGO
RS: Dolphins lead series, 4-1;
See Chicago vs. Miami

MIAMI vs. CINCINNATI
RS: Dolphins lead series, 8-3
PS: Dolphins lead series, 1-0;
See Cincinnati vs. Miami

MIAMI vs. CLEVELAND
RS: Series tied, 4-4
PS: Dolphins lead series, 2-0;
See Cleveland vs. Miami

MIAMI vs. DALLAS
RS: Dolphins lead series, 5-1
PS: Cowboys lead series, 1-0;
See Dallas vs. Miami

MIAMI vs. DENVER
RS: Dolphins lead series, 5-2-1;
See Denver vs. Miami

MIAMI vs. DETROIT
RS: Dolphins lead series, 2-1;
See Detroit vs. Miami

MIAMI vs. GREEN BAY
RS: Dolphins lead series, 6-0;
See Green Bay vs. Miami

MIAMI vs. HOUSTON
RS: Series tied, 10-10
PS: Oilers lead series, 1-0;
See Houston vs. Miami

MIAMI vs. INDIANAPOLIS
RS: Dolphins lead series, 29-13
PS: Dolphins lead series, 1-0;
See Indianapolis vs. Miami

MIAMI vs. KANSAS CITY
RS: Chiefs lead series, 9-6
PS: Dolphins lead series, 2-0;
See Kansas City vs. Miami

MIAMI vs. L.A. RAIDERS
RS: Raiders lead series, 14-3-1
PS: Raiders lead series, 2-1;
See L.A. Raiders vs. Miami

MIAMI vs. L.A. RAMS
RS: Dolphins lead series, 4-1;
See L.A. Rams vs. Miami

MIAMI vs. MINNESOTA
RS: Dolphins lead series, 4-1
PS: Dolphins lead series, 1-0
1972—Dolphins, 16-14 (Minn)
1973—*Dolphins, 24-7 (Houston)
1976—Vikings, 29-7 (Mia)
1979—Dolphins, 27-12 (Minn)
1982—Dolphins, 22-14 (Mia)
1988—Dolphins, 24-7 (Mia)
(RS Pts.—Dolphins 96, Vikings 76)
(PS Pts.—Dolphins 24, Vikings 7)
**Super Bowl VIII*

MIAMI vs. *NEW ENGLAND
RS: Dolphins lead series, 28-20
PS: Series tied, 1-1
1966—Patriots, 20-14 (M)
1967—Patriots, 41-10 (B)
Dolphins, 41-32 (M)
1968—Dolphins, 34-10 (B)
Dolphins, 38-7 (M)
1969—Dolphins, 17-16 (B)
Patriots, 38-23 (Tampa)
1970—Patriots, 27-14 (B)
Dolphins, 37-20 (M)
1971—Dolphins, 41-3 (M)
Patriots, 34-13 (NE)
1972—Dolphins, 52-0 (M)
Dolphins, 37-21 (NE)
1973—Dolphins, 44-23 (M)
Dolphins, 30-14 (NE)
1974—Patriots, 34-24 (NE)
Dolphins, 34-27 (M)
1975—Dolphins, 22-14 (NE)
Dolphins, 20-7 (M)
1976—Patriots, 30-14 (NE)
Dolphins, 10-3 (M)
1977—Dolphins, 17-5 (M)
Patriots, 14-10 (NE)
1978—Patriots, 33-24 (NE)
Dolphins, 23-3 (M)
1979—Patriots, 28-13 (NE)
Dolphins, 39-24 (M)
1980—Patriots, 34-0 (NE)
Dolphins, 16-13 (M) OT
1981—Dolphins, 30-27 (NE) OT
Dolphins, 24-14 (M)
1982—Patriots, 3-0 (NE)
**Dolphins, 28-13 (M)
1983—Dolphins, 34-24 (M)
Patriots, 17-6 (NE)
1984—Dolphins, 28-7 (M)
Dolphins, 44-24 (NE)
1985—Patriots, 17-13 (NE)
Dolphins, 30-27 (M)
***Patriots, 31-14 (M)
1986—Patriots, 34-7 (NE)
Patriots, 34-27 (M)
1987—Patriots, 28-21 (NE)
Patriots, 24-10 (M)
1988—Patriots, 21-10 (NE)
Patriots, 6-3 (M)
1989—Dolphins, 24-10 (NE)
Dolphins, 31-10 (M)
1990—Dolphins, 27-24 (NE)
Dolphins, 17-10 (M)
(RS Pts.—Dolphins 1,097, Patriots 936)
(PS Pts.—Patriots 44, Dolphins 42)
**Franchise in Boston prior to 1971*
***AFC First Round Playoff*
****AFC Championship*

MIAMI vs. NEW ORLEANS
RS: Dolphins lead series, 4-1
1970—Dolphins, 21-10 (M)
1974—Dolphins, 21-0 (NO)
1980—Dolphins, 21-16 (M)
1983—Saints, 17-7 (NO)
1986—Dolphins, 31-27 (NO)
(RS Pts.—Dolphins 101, Saints 70)

MIAMI vs. N.Y. GIANTS
RS: Series tied, 1-1
1972—Dolphins, 23-13 (NY)
1990—Giants, 20-3 (NY)
(RS Pts.—Giants 33, Dolphins 26)

MIAMI vs. N.Y. JETS
RS: Dolphins lead series, 26-23-1
PS: Dolphins lead series, 1-0
1966—Jets, 19-14 (M)
Jets, 30-13 (NY)
1967—Jets, 29-7 (NY)
Jets, 33-14 (M)
1968—Jets, 35-17 (NY)
Jets, 31-7 (M)
1969—Jets, 34-31 (NY)
Jets, 27-9 (M)
1970—Dolphins, 20-6 (NY)
Dolphins, 16-10 (M)
1971—Jets, 14-10 (M)
Dolphins, 30-14 (NY)
1972—Dolphins, 27-17 (NY)
Dolphins, 28-24 (M)
1973—Dolphins, 31-3 (M)
Dolphins, 24-14 (NY)
1974—Dolphins, 21-17 (M)
Jets, 17-14 (NY)
1975—Dolphins, 43-0 (NY)
Dolphins, 27-7 (M)
1976—Dolphins, 16-0 (M)
Dolphins, 27-7 (NY)
1977—Dolphins, 21-17 (M)
Dolphins, 14-10 (NY)
1978—Jets, 33-20 (NY)
Jets, 24-13 (M)
1979—Jets, 33-27 (NY)
Jets, 27-24 (M)
1980—Jets, 17-14 (NY)
Jets, 24-17 (M)
1981—Tie, 28-28 (M) OT
Jets, 16-15 (NY)
1982—Dolphins, 45-28 (NY)
Dolphins, 20-19 (M)
*Dolphins, 14-0 (M)
1983—Dolphins, 32-14 (NY)
Dolphins, 34-14 (M)
1984—Dolphins, 31-17 (NY)
Dolphins, 28-17 (M)
1985—Jets, 23-7 (NY)
Dolphins, 21-17 (M)
1986—Jets, 51-45 (NY) OT
Dolphins, 45-3 (M)
1987—Jets, 37-31 (NY) OT
Dolphins, 37-28 (M)
1988—Jets, 44-30 (M)
Jets, 38-34 (NY)
1989—Jets, 40-33 (M)
Dolphins, 31-23 (NY)
1990—Dolphins, 20-16 (M)
Dolphins, 17-3 (NY)
(RS Pts.—Dolphins 1,180, Jets 1,049)
(PS Pts.—Dolphins 14, Jets 0)
**AFC Championship*

MIAMI vs. PHILADELPHIA
RS: Dolphins lead series, 5-2
1970—Eagles, 24-17 (P)
1975—Dolphins, 24-16 (M)
1978—Eagles, 17-3 (P)
1981—Dolphins, 13-10 (M)
1984—Dolphins, 24-23 (M)
1987—Dolphins, 28-10 (P)
1990—Dolphins, 23-20 (M) OT
(RS Pts.—Dolphins 132, Eagles 120)

MIAMI vs. *PHOENIX
RS: Dolphins lead series, 6-0
1972—Dolphins, 31-10 (M)
1977—Dolphins, 55-14 (StL)
1978—Dolphins, 24-10 (M)
1981—Dolphins, 20-7 (StL)
1984—Dolphins, 36-28 (StL)
1990—Dolphins, 23-3 (M)
(RS Pts.—Dolphins 189, Cardinals 72)
**Franchise in St. Louis prior to 1988*

MIAMI vs. PITTSBURGH
RS: Dolphins lead series, 7-4
PS: Dolphins lead series, 2-1
1971—Dolphins, 24-21 (M)
1972—*Dolphins, 21-17 (P)
1973—Dolphins, 30-26 (M)
1976—Steelers, 14-3 (P)
1979—**Steelers, 34-14 (P)
1980—Steelers, 23-10 (P)
1981—Dolphins, 30-10 (M)
1984—Dolphins, 31-7 (P)
*Dolphins, 45-28 (M)
1985—Dolphins, 24-20 (M)
1987—Dolphins, 35-24 (M)
1988—Steelers, 40-24 (P)
1989—Steelers, 34-14 (M)
1990—Dolphins, 28-6 (P)
(RS Pts.—Dolphins 253, Steelers 225)
(PS Pts.—Dolphins 80, Steelers 79)
**AFC Championship*
***AFC Divisional Playoff*

MIAMI vs. SAN DIEGO
RS: Chargers lead series, 8-5
PS: Series tied, 1-1
1966—Chargers, 44-10 (SD)
1967—Chargers, 24-0 (SD)
Dolphins, 41-24 (M)
1968—Chargers, 34-28 (SD)
1969—Chargers, 21-14 (M)
1972—Dolphins, 24-10 (M)
1974—Dolphins, 28-21 (SD)
1977—Chargers, 14-13 (M)
1978—Dolphins, 28-21 (SD)
1980—Chargers, 27-24 (M) OT
1981—*Chargers, 41-38 (M) OT
1982—**Dolphins, 34-13 (M)
1984—Chargers, 34-28 (SD) OT
1986—Chargers, 50-28 (SD)
1988—Dolphins, 31-28 (M)
(RS Pts.—Chargers 352, Dolphins 297)
(PS Pts.—Dolphins 72, Chargers 54)
**AFC Divisional Playoff*
***AFC Second Round Playoff*

MIAMI vs. SAN FRANCISCO
RS: Dolphins lead series, 4-1
PS: 49ers lead series, 1-0
1973—Dolphins, 21-13 (M)
1977—Dolphins, 19-15 (SF)
1980—Dolphins, 17-13 (M)
1983—Dolphins, 20-17 (SF)
1984—*49ers, 38-16 (Stanford)
1986—49ers, 31-16 (M)
(RS Pts.—Dolphins 93, 49ers 89)
(PS Pts.—49ers 38, Dolphins 16)
**Super Bowl XIX*

MIAMI vs. SEATTLE
RS: Dolphins lead series, 3-1
PS: Series tied, 1-1
1977—Dolphins, 31-13 (M)
1979—Dolphins, 19-10 (M)
1983—*Seahawks, 27-20 (M)
1984—*Dolphins, 31-10 (M)
1987—Seahawks, 24-20 (S)
1990—Dolphins, 24-17 (M)
(RS Pts.—Dolphins 94, Seahawks 64)
(PS Pts.—Dolphins 51, Seahawks 37)
**AFC Divisional Playoff*

MIAMI vs. TAMPA BAY
RS: Dolphins lead series, 3-1
1976—Dolphins, 23-20 (TB)
1982—Buccaneers, 23-17 (TB)
1985—Dolphins, 41-38 (M)
1988—Dolphins, 17-14 (TB)
(RS Pts.—Dolphins 98, Buccaneers 95)

MIAMI vs. WASHINGTON
RS: Dolphins lead series, 4-2
PS: Series tied, 1-1
1972—*Dolphins, 14-7 (Los Angeles)
1974—Redskins, 20-17 (W)
1978—Dolphins, 16-0 (W)
1981—Dolphins, 13-10 (M)
1982—**Redskins, 27-17 (Pasadena)
1984—Dolphins, 35-17 (W)
1987—Dolphins, 23-21 (M)
1990—Redskins, 42-20 (W)
(RS Pts.—Dolphins 124, Redskins 110)
(PS Pts.—Redskins 34, Dolphins 31)
Super Bowl VII
**Super Bowl XVII*

MINNESOTA vs. ATLANTA
RS: Vikings lead series, 10-6
PS: Vikings lead series, 1-0;
See Atlanta vs. Minnesota
MINNESOTA vs. BUFFALO
RS: Vikings lead series, 4-2;
See Buffalo vs. Minnesota
MINNESOTA vs. CHICAGO
RS: Vikings lead series, 30-27-2;
See Chicago vs. Minnesota
MINNESOTA vs. CINCINNATI
RS: Series tied, 3-3;
See Cincinnati vs. Minnesota
MINNESOTA vs. CLEVELAND
RS: Vikings lead series, 6-3
PS: Vikings lead series, 1-0;
See Cleveland vs. Minnesota
MINNESOTA vs. DALLAS
RS: Cowboys lead series, 7-6
PS: Cowboys lead series, 3-1;
See Dallas vs. Minnesota
MINNESOTA vs. DENVER
RS: Vikings lead series, 4-2;
See Denver vs. Minnesota
MINNESOTA vs. DETROIT
RS: Vikings lead series, 38-19-2;
See Detroit vs. Minnesota
MINNESOTA vs. GREEN BAY
RS: Packers lead series, 30-28-1;
See Green Bay vs. Minnesota
MINNESOTA vs. HOUSTON
RS: Vikings lead series, 3-2;
See Houston vs. Minnesota
MINNESOTA vs. INDIANAPOLIS
RS: Colts lead series, 11-6-1
PS: Colts lead series, 1-0;
See Indianapolis vs. Minnesota
MINNESOTA vs. KANSAS CITY
RS: Series tied, 2-2
PS: Chiefs lead series, 1-0;
See Kansas City vs. Minnesota
MINNESOTA vs. L.A. RAIDERS
RS: Raiders lead series, 5-2
PS: Raiders lead series, 1-0;
See L.A. Raiders vs. Minnesota
MINNESOTA vs. L.A. RAMS
RS: Vikings lead series, 13-11-2
PS: Vikings lead series, 5-1;
See L.A. Rams vs. Minnesota
MINNESOTA vs. MIAMI
RS: Dolphins lead series, 4-1
PS: Dolphins lead series, 1-0;
See Miami vs. Minnesota
MINNESOTA vs. *NEW ENGLAND
RS: Series tied, 2-2
1970—Vikings, 35-14 (B)
1974—Patriots, 17-14 (M)
1979—Patriots, 27-23 (NE)
1988—Vikings, 36-6 (M)
(RS Pts.—Vikings 108, Patriots 64)
Franchise in Boston prior to 1971
MINNESOTA vs. NEW ORLEANS
RS: Vikings lead series, 11-4
PS: Vikings lead series, 1-0
1968—Saints, 20-17 (NO)
1970—Vikings, 26-0 (M)
1971—Vikings, 23-10 (NO)
1972—Vikings, 37-6 (M)
1974—Vikings, 29-9 (M)
1975—Vikings, 20-7 (NO)
1976—Vikings, 40-9 (NO)
1978—Saints, 31-24 (NO)
1980—Vikings, 23-20 (NO)
1981—Vikings, 20-10 (M)
1983—Saints, 17-16 (NO)
1985—Saints, 30-23 (M)
1986—Vikings, 33-17 (M)
1987—*Vikings, 44-10 (NO)
1988—Vikings, 45-3 (M)
1990—Vikings, 32-3 (M)
(RS Pts.—Vikings 408, Saints 192)
(PS Pts.—Vikings 44, Saints 10)
NFC First Round Playoff
MINNESOTA vs. N.Y. GIANTS
RS: Vikings lead series, 6-4
1964—Vikings, 30-21 (NY)
1965—Vikings, 40-14 (M)
1967—Vikings, 27-24 (M)
1969—Giants, 24-23 (NY)
1971—Vikings, 17-10 (NY)
1973—Vikings, 31-7 (New Haven)
1976—Vikings, 24-7 (M)
1986—Giants, 22-20 (M)
1989—Giants, 24-14 (NY)
1990—Giants, 23-15 (NY)
(RS Pts.—Vikings 241, Giants 176)
MINNESOTA vs. N.Y. JETS
RS: Jets lead series, 3-1
1970—Jets, 20-10 (NY)
1975—Vikings, 29-21 (M)
1979—Jets, 14-7 (NY)
1982—Jets 42-14 (M)
(RS Pts.—Jets 97, Vikings 60)
MINNESOTA vs. PHILADELPHIA
RS: Vikings lead series, 10-5
PS: Eagles lead series, 1-0
1962—Vikings, 31-21 (M)
1963—Vikings, 34-13 (P)
1968—Vikings, 24-17 (P)
1971—Vikings, 13-0 (P)
1973—Vikings, 28-21 (M)
1976—Vikings, 31-12 (P)
1978—Vikings, 28-27 (M)
1980—Eagles, 42-7 (M)
*Eagles, 31-16 (P)
1981—Vikings, 35-23 (M)
1984—Eagles, 19-17 (P)
1985—Vikings, 28-23 (P)
Eagles, 37-35 (M)
1988—Vikings, 23-21 (M)
1989—Eagles, 10-9 (P)
1990—Eagles, 32-24 (P)
(RS Pts.—Vikings 367, Eagles 318)
(PS Pts.—Eagles 31, Vikings 16)
NFC Divisional Playoff
MINNESOTA vs. *PHOENIX
RS: Cardinals lead series, 7-2
PS: Vikings lead series, 1-0
1963—Cardinals, 56-14 (M)
1967—Cardinals, 34-24 (M)
1969—Vikings, 27-10 (StL)
1972—Cardinals, 19-17 (M)
1974—Vikings, 28-24 (StL)
**Vikings, 30-14 (M)
1977—Cardinals, 27-7 (M)
1979—Cardinals, 37-7 (StL)
1981—Cardinals, 30-17 (StL)
1983—Cardinals, 41-31 (StL)
(RS Pts.—Cardinals 278, Vikings 172)
(PS Pts.—Vikings 30, Cardinals 14)
Franchise in St. Louis prior to 1988
**NFC Divisional Playoff*
MINNESOTA vs. PITTSBURGH
RS: Vikings lead series, 6-4
PS: Steelers lead series, 1-0
1962—Steelers, 39-31 (P)
1964—Vikings, 30-10 (M)
1967—Vikings, 41-27 (P)
1969—Vikings, 52-14 (M)
1972—Steelers, 23-10 (P)
1974—*Steelers, 16-6 (New Orleans)
1976—Vikings, 17-6 (M)
1980—Steelers, 23-17 (M)
1983—Vikings, 17-14 (P)
1986—Vikings, 31-7 (M)
1989—Steelers, 27-14 (P)
(RS Pts.—Vikings 260, Steelers 190)
(PS Pts.—Steelers 16, Vikings 6)
Super Bowl IX
MINNESOTA vs. SAN DIEGO
RS: Series tied, 3-3
1971—Chargers, 30-14 (SD)
1975—Vikings, 28-13 (M)
1978—Chargers, 13-7 (M)
1981—Vikings, 33-31 (SD)
1984—Chargers, 42-13 (M)
1985—Vikings, 21-17 (M)
(RS Pts.—Chargers 146, Vikings 116)
MINNESOTA vs. SAN FRANCISCO
RS: Vikings lead series, 14-13-1
PS: 49ers lead series, 3-1
1961—49ers, 38-24 (M)
49ers, 38-28 (SF)
1962—49ers, 21-7 (SF)
49ers, 35-12 (M)
1963—Vikings, 24-20 (SF)
Vikings, 45-14 (M)
1964—Vikings, 27-22 (SF)
Vikings, 24-7 (M)
1965—Vikings, 42-41 (SF)
49ers, 45-24 (M)
1966—Tie, 20-20 (SF)
Vikings, 28-3 (SF)
1967—49ers, 27-21 (M)
1968—Vikings, 30-20 (SF)
1969—Vikings, 10-7 (M)
1970—*49ers, 17-14 (M)
1971—49ers, 13-9 (M)
1972—49ers, 20-17 (SF)
1973—Vikings, 17-13 (SF)
1975—Vikings, 27-17 (M)
1976—49ers, 20-16 (SF)
1977—Vikings, 28-27 (M)
1979—Vikings, 28-22 (M)
1983—49ers, 48-17 (M)
1984—49ers, 51-7 (SF)
1985—Vikings, 28-21 (M)
1986—Vikings, 27-24 (SF) OT
1987—*Vikings, 36-24 (SF)
1988—49ers, 24-21 (SF)
*49ers, 34-9 (SF)
1989—*49ers, 41-13 (SF)
1990—49ers, 20-17 (M)
(RS Pts.—49ers 678, Vikings 625)
(PS Pts.—49ers 116, Vikings 72)
NFC Divisional Playoff
MINNESOTA vs. SEATTLE
RS: Seahawks lead series, 3-2
1976—Vikings, 27-21 (M)
1978—Seahawks, 29-28 (S)
1984—Seahawks, 20-12 (M)
1987—Seahawks, 28-17 (S)
1990—Vikings, 24-21 (S)
(RS Pts.—Seahawks 119, Vikings 108)
MINNESOTA vs. TAMPA BAY
RS: Vikings lead series, 18-8
1977—Vikings, 9-3 (TB)
1978—Buccaneers, 16-10 (M)
Vikings, 24-7 (TB)
1979—Buccaneers, 12-10 (M)
Vikings, 23-22 (TB)
1980—Vikings, 38-30 (M)
Vikings, 21-10 (TB)
1981—Buccaneers, 21-13 (TB)
Vikings, 25-10 (M)
1982—Vikings, 17-10 (M)
1983—Vikings, 19-16 (TB) OT
Buccaneers, 17-12 (M)
1984—Buccaneers, 35-31 (TB)
Vikings, 27-24 (M)
1985—Vikings, 31-16 (TB)
Vikings, 26-7 (M)
1986—Vikings, 23-10 (TB)
Vikings, 45-13 (M)
1987—Buccaneers, 20-10 (TB)
Vikings, 23-17 (M)
1988—Vikings, 14-13 (M)
Vikings, 49-20 (TB)
1989—Vikings, 17-3 (M)
Vikings, 24-10 (TB)
1990—Buccaneers, 23-20 (M) OT
Buccaneers, 26-13 (TB)
(RS Pts.—Vikings 574, Buccaneers 411)
MINNESOTA vs. WASHINGTON
RS: Redskins lead series, 5-3
PS: Series tied, 2-2
1968—Vikings, 27-14 (M)
1970—Vikings, 19-10 (W)
1972—Redskins, 24-21 (M)
1973—*Vikings, 27-20 (M)
1975—Redskins, 31-30 (W)
1976—*Vikings, 35-20 (M)
1980—Vikings, 39-14 (W)
1982—**Redskins, 21-7 (W)
1984—Redskins, 31-17 (M)
1986—Redskins, 44-38 (W) OT
1987—Redskins, 27-24 (M) OT
***Redskins, 17-10 (W)
(RS Pts.—Vikings 215, Redskins 195)
(PS Pts.—Vikings 79, Redskins 78)
NFC Divisional Playoff
**NFC Second Round Playoff*
***NFC Championship*

NEW ENGLAND vs. ATLANTA
RS: Series tied, 3-3;
See Atlanta vs. New England
NEW ENGLAND vs. BUFFALO
RS: Patriots lead series, 32-28-1
PS: Patriots lead series, 1-0;
See Buffalo vs. New England
NEW ENGLAND vs. CHICAGO
RS: Patriots lead series, 3-2
PS: Bears lead series, 1-0;
See Chicago vs. New England
NEW ENGLAND vs. CINCINNATI
RS: Patriots lead series, 7-5;
See Cincinnati vs. New England
NEW ENGLAND vs. CLEVELAND
RS: Browns lead series, 7-2;
See Cleveland vs. New England
NEW ENGLAND vs. DALLAS
RS: Cowboys lead series, 6-0;
See Dallas vs. New England
NEW ENGLAND vs. DENVER
RS: Broncos lead series, 14-12
PS: Broncos lead series, 1-0;
See Denver vs. New England
NEW ENGLAND vs. DETROIT
RS: Series tied, 2-2;
See Detroit vs. New England
NEW ENGLAND vs. GREEN BAY
RS: Series tied, 2-2;
See Green Bay vs. New England
NEW ENGLAND vs. HOUSTON
RS: Patriots lead series, 16-13-1
PS: Oilers lead series, 1-0;
See Houston vs. New England
NEW ENGLAND vs. INDIANAPOLIS
RS: Patriots lead series, 23-18;
See Indianapolis vs. New England
NEW ENGLAND vs. KANSAS CITY
RS: Chiefs lead series, 12-7-3;
See Kansas City vs. New England
NEW ENGLAND vs. L.A. RAIDERS
RS: Series tied, 12-12-1
PS: Series tied, 1-1;
See L.A. Raiders vs. New England
NEW ENGLAND vs. L.A. RAMS
RS: Patriots lead series, 3-2;
See L.A. Rams vs. New England
NEW ENGLAND vs. MIAMI
RS: Dolphins lead series, 28-20
PS: Series tied, 1-1;
See Miami vs. New England
NEW ENGLAND vs. MINNESOTA
RS: Series tied, 2-2;
See Minnesota vs. New England
NEW ENGLAND vs. NEW ORLEANS
RS: Patriots lead series, 5-1
1972—Patriots, 17-10 (NO)
1976—Patriots, 27-6 (NE)
1980—Patriots, 38-27 (NO)
1983—Patriots, 7-0 (NE)
1986—Patriots, 21-20 (NO)
1989—Saints, 28-24 (NE)
(RS Pts.—Patriots 134, Saints 91)
***NEW ENGLAND vs. N.Y. GIANTS**
RS: Giants lead series, 3-1
1970—Giants, 16-0 (B)
1974—Patriots, 28-20 (New Haven)
1987—Giants, 17-10 (NY)
1990—Giants, 13-10 (NE)
(RS Pts.—Giants 66, Patriots 48)
Franchise in Boston prior to 1971
***NEW ENGLAND vs. **N.Y. JETS**
RS: Jets lead series, 34-26-1
PS: Patriots lead series, 1-0
1960—Patriots, 28-24 (NY)
Patriots, 38-21 (B)
1961—Titans, 21-20 (B)
Titans, 37-30 (NY)
1962—Patriots, 43-14 (NY)
Patriots, 24-17 (B)
1963—Patriots, 38-14 (B)
Jets, 31-24 (NY)
1964—Patriots, 26-10 (B)
Jets, 35-14 (NY)
1965—Jets, 30-20 (B)
Patriots, 27-23 (NY)
1966—Tie, 24-24 (B)
Jets, 38-28 (NY)
1967—Jets, 30-23 (NY)
Jets, 29-24 (B)
1968—Jets, 47-31 (Birmingham)
Jets, 48-14 (NY)
1969—Jets, 23-14 (B)
Jets, 23-17 (NY)
1970—Jets, 31-21 (B)
Jets, 17-3 (NY)
1971—Patriots, 20-0 (NE)
Jets, 13-6 (NY)
1972—Jets, 41-13 (NE)
Jets, 34-10 (NY)
1973—Jets, 9-7 (NE)
Jets, 33-13 (NY)
1974—Patriots, 24-0 (NY)
Jets, 21-16 (NE)
1975—Jets, 36-7 (NY)
Jets, 30-28 (NE)
1976—Patriots, 41-7 (NE)
Patriots, 38-24 (NY)
1977—Jets, 30-27 (NY)
Patriots, 24-13 (NE)
1978—Patriots, 55-21 (NE)
Patriots, 19-17 (NY)
1979—Patriots, 56-3 (NE)
Jets, 27-26 (NY)
1980—Patriots, 21-11 (NY)
Patriots, 34-21 (NE)
1981—Jets, 28-24 (NY)
Jets, 17-6 (NE)
1982—Jets, 31-7 (NE)
1983—Patriots, 23-13 (NE)
Jets, 26-3 (NY)
1984—Patriots, 28-21 (NY)
Patriots, 30-20 (NE)
1985—Patriots, 20-13 (NE)
Jets, 16-13 (NY) OT
***Patriots, 26-14 (NY)
1986—Patriots, 20-6 (NY)
Jets, 31-24 (NE)
1987—Jets, 43-24 (NY)
Patriots, 42-20 (NE)
1988—Patriots, 28-3 (NE)
Patriots, 14-13 (NY)

1989—Patriots, 27-24 (NY)
Jets, 27-26 (NE)
1990—Jets, 37-13 (NE)
Jets, 42-7 (NY)
(RS Pts.—Jets 1,409, Patriots 1,395)
(PS Pts.—Patriots 26, Jets 14)
Franchise in Boston prior to 1971
**Jets known as Titans prior to 1963*
***AFC First Round Playoff*

NEW ENGLAND vs. PHILADELPHIA
RS: Eagles lead series, 5-2
1973—Eagles, 24-23 (P)
1977—Patriots, 14-6 (NE)
1978—Patriots, 24-14 (NE)
1981—Eagles, 13-3 (P)
1984—Eagles, 27-17 (P)
1987—Eagles, 34-31 (NE) OT
1990—Eagles, 48-20 (P)
(RS Pts.—Eagles 166, Patriots 132)

***NEW ENGLAND vs. **PHOENIX**
RS: Cardinals lead series, 5-1
1970—Cardinals, 31-0 (StL)
1975—Cardinals, 24-17 (StL)
1978—Patriots, 16-6 (StL)
1981—Cardinals, 27-20 (NE)
1984—Cardinals, 33-10 (NE)
1990—Cardinals, 34-14 (P)
(RS Pts.—Cardinals 155, Patriots 77)
Franchise in Boston prior to 1971
**Franchise in St. Louis prior to 1988*

NEW ENGLAND vs. PITTSBURGH
RS: Steelers lead series, 7-3
1972—Steelers, 33-3 (P)
1974—Steelers, 21-17 (NE)
1976—Patriots, 30-27 (P)
1979—Steelers, 16-13 (NE) OT
1981—Steelers, 27-21 (P) OT
1982—Steelers, 37-14 (P)
1983—Patriots, 28-23 (P)
1986—Patriots, 34-0 (P)
1989—Steelers, 28-10 (P)
1990—Steelers, 24-3 (P)
(RS Pts.—Steelers 236, Patriots 173)

***NEW ENGLAND vs. **SAN DIEGO**
RS: Patriots lead series, 13-11-2
PS: Chargers lead series, 1-0
1960—Patriots, 35-0 (LA)
Chargers, 45-16 (B)
1961—Chargers, 38-27 (B)
Patriots, 41-0 (SD)
1962—Patriots, 24-20 (B)
Patriots, 20-14 (SD)
1963—Chargers, 17-13 (SD)
Chargers, 7-6 (B)
***Chargers, 51-10 (SD)
1964—Patriots, 33-28 (SD)
Chargers, 26-17 (B)
1965—Tie, 10-10 (B)
Patriots, 22-6 (SD)
1966—Chargers, 24-0 (SD)
Patriots, 35-17 (B)
1967—Chargers, 28-14 (SD)
Tie, 31-31 (SD)
1968—Chargers, 27-17 (B)
1969—Chargers, 13-10 (B)
Chargers, 28-18 (SD)
1970—Chargers, 16-14 (B)
1973—Patriots, 30-14 (NE)
1975—Patriots, 33-19 (SD)
1977—Patriots, 24-20 (SD)
1978—Patriots, 28-23 (NE)
1979—Patriots, 27-21 (NE)
1983—Patriots, 37-21 (NE)
(RS Pts.—Patriots 582, Chargers 513)
(PS Pts.—Chargers 51, Patriots 10)
Franchise in Boston prior to 1971
**Franchise in Los Angeles prior to 1961*
***AFL Championship*

NEW ENGLAND vs. SAN FRANCISCO
RS: 49ers lead series, 5-1
1971—49ers, 27-10 (SF)
1975—Patriots, 24-16 (NE)
1980—49ers, 21-17 (SF)
1983—49ers, 33-13 (NE)
1986—49ers, 29-24 (NE)
1989—49ers, 37-20 (SF)
(RS Pts.—49ers 163, Patriots 108)

NEW ENGLAND vs. SEATTLE
RS: Patriots lead series, 6-4
1977—Patriots, 31-0 (NE)
1980—Patriots, 37-31 (S)
1982—Patriots, 16-0 (S)
1983—Seahawks, 24-6 (S)
1984—Patriots, 38-23 (NE)
1985—Patriots, 20-13 (S)
1986—Seahawks, 38-31 (NE)
1988—Patriots, 13-7 (NE)
1989—Seahawks, 24-3 (NE)
1990—Seahawks, 33-20 (NE)
(RS Pts.—Patriots 215, Seahawks 193)

NEW ENGLAND vs. TAMPA BAY
RS: Patriots lead series, 3-0
1976—Patriots, 31-14 (TB)
1985—Patriots, 32-14 (TB)
1988—Patriots, 10-7 (NE) OT
(RS Pts.—Patriots 73, Buccaneers 35)

NEW ENGLAND vs. WASHINGTON
RS: Redskins lead series, 4-1
1972—Patriots, 24-23 (NE)
1978—Redskins, 16-14 (NE)
1981—Redskins, 24-22 (W)
1984—Redskins, 26-10 (NE)
1990—Redskins, 25-10 (NE)
(RS Pts.—Redskins 114, Patriots 80)

NEW ORLEANS vs. ATLANTA
RS: Falcons lead series, 25-18;
See Atlanta vs. New Orleans

NEW ORLEANS vs. BUFFALO
RS: Series tied, 2-2;
See Buffalo vs. New Orleans

NEW ORLEANS vs. CHICAGO
RS: Bears lead series, 7-5
PS: Bears lead series, 1-0;
See Chicago vs. New Orleans

NEW ORLEANS vs. CINCINNATI
RS: Saints lead series, 4-3;
See Cincinnati vs. New Orleans

NEW ORLEANS vs. CLEVELAND
RS: Browns lead series, 8-3;
See Cleveland vs. New Orleans

NEW ORLEANS vs. DALLAS
RS: Cowboys lead series, 12-3;
See Dallas vs. New Orleans

NEW ORLEANS vs. DENVER
RS: Broncos lead series, 4-1;
See Denver vs. New Orleans

NEW ORLEANS vs. DETROIT
RS: Lions lead series, 6-5-1;
See Detroit vs. New Orleans

NEW ORLEANS vs. GREEN BAY
RS: Packers lead series, 11-4;
See Green Bay vs. New Orleans

NEW ORLEANS vs. HOUSTON
RS: Series tied, 3-3-1;
See Houston vs. New Orleans

NEW ORLEANS vs. INDIANAPOLIS
RS: Colts lead series, 3-2;
See Indianapolis vs. New Orleans

NEW ORLEANS vs. KANSAS CITY
RS: Series tied, 2-2;
See Kansas City vs. New Orleans

NEW ORLEANS vs. L.A. RAIDERS
RS: Raiders lead series, 3-1-1;
See L.A. Raiders vs. New Orleans

NEW ORLEANS vs. L.A. RAMS
RS: Rams lead series, 26-16;
See L.A. Rams vs. New Orleans

NEW ORLEANS vs. MIAMI
RS: Dolphins lead series, 4-1;
See Miami vs. New Orleans

NEW ORLEANS vs. MINNESOTA
RS: Vikings lead series, 11-4
PS: Vikings lead series, 1-0;
See Minnesota vs. New Orleans

NEW ORLEANS vs. NEW ENGLAND
RS: Patriots lead series, 5-1;
See New England vs. New Orleans

NEW ORLEANS vs. N.Y. GIANTS
RS: Giants lead series, 8-6
1967—Giants, 27-21 (NY)
1968—Giants, 38-21 (NY)
1969—Saints, 25-24 (NY)
1970—Saints, 14-10 (NO)
1972—Giants, 45-21 (NY)
1975—Giants, 28-14 (NY)
1978—Saints, 28-17 (NO)
1979—Saints, 24-14 (NO)
1981—Giants, 20-7 (NY)
1984—Saints, 10-3 (NY)
1985—Giants, 21-13 (NO)
1986—Giants, 20-17 (NY)
1987—Saints, 23-14 (NO)
1988—Giants, 13-12 (NO)
(RS Pts.—Giants 294, Saints 250)

NEW ORLEANS vs. N.Y. JETS
RS: Jets lead series, 4-2
1972—Jets, 18-17 (NY)
1977—Jets, 16-13 (NO)
1980—Saints, 21-20 (NY)
1983—Jets, 31-28 (NO)
1986—Jets, 28-23 (NY)
1989—Saints, 29-14 (NO)
(RS Pts.—Saints 131, Jets 127)

NEW ORLEANS vs. PHILADELPHIA
RS: Eagles lead series, 9-7
1967—Saints, 31-24 (NO)
Eagles, 48-21 (P)
1968—Eagles, 29-17 (P)
1969—Eagles, 13-10 (P)
Saints, 26-17 (NO)
1972—Saints, 21-3 (NO)
1974—Saints, 14-10 (NO)
1977—Eagles, 28-7 (P)
1978—Eagles, 24-17 (NO)
1979—Eagles, 26-14 (NO)
1980—Eagles, 34-21 (NO)
1981—Eagles, 31-14 (NO)
1983—Saints, 20-17 (P) OT
1985—Saints, 23-21 (NO)
1987—Eagles, 27-17 (P)
1989—Saints, 30-20 (NO)
(RS Pts.—Eagles 372, Saints 303)

NEW ORLEANS vs. *PHOENIX
RS: Cardinals lead series, 10-6
1967—Cardinals, 31-20 (StL)
1968—Cardinals, 21-20 (NO)
Cardinals, 31-17 (StL)
1969—Saints, 51-42 (StL)
1970—Cardinals, 24-17 (StL)
1974—Saints, 14-0 (NO)
1977—Cardinals, 49-31 (StL)
1980—Cardinals, 40-7 (NO)
1981—Cardinals, 30-3 (StL)
1982—Cardinals, 21-7 (NO)
1983—Saints, 28-17 (NO)
1984—Saints, 34-24 (NO)
1985—Cardinals, 28-16 (StL)
1986—Saints, 16-7 (StL)
1987—Cardinals, 24-19 (StL)
1990—Saints, 28-7 (NO)
(RS Pts.—Cardinals 396, Saints 328)
Franchise in St. Louis prior to 1988

NEW ORLEANS vs. PITTSBURGH
RS: Series tied, 5-5
1967—Steelers, 14-10 (NO)
1968—Saints, 16-12 (P)
Saints, 24-14 (NO)
1969—Saints, 27-24 (NO)
1974—Steelers, 28-7 (NO)
1978—Steelers, 20-14 (P)
1981—Steelers, 20-6 (NO)
1984—Saints, 27-24 (NO)
1987—Saints, 20-16 (P)
1990—Steelers, 9-6 (NO)
(RS Pts.—Steelers 181, Saints 157)

NEW ORLEANS vs. SAN DIEGO
RS: Chargers lead series, 3-1
1973—Chargers, 17-14 (SD)
1977—Chargers, 14-0 (NO)
1979—Chargers, 35-0 (NO)
1988—Saints, 23-17 (SD)
(RS Pts.—Chargers 83, Saints 37)

NEW ORLEANS vs. SAN FRANCISCO
RS: 49ers lead series, 29-12-2
1967—49ers, 27-13 (SF)
1969—Saints, 43-38 (NO)
1970—Tie, 20-20 (SF)
49ers, 38-27 (NO)
1971—49ers, 38-20 (NO)
Saints, 26-20 (SF)
1972—49ers, 37-2 (NO)
Tie, 20-20 (SF)
1973—49ers, 40-0 (SF)
Saints, 16-10 (NO)
1974—49ers, 17-13 (NO)
49ers, 35-21 (SF)
1975—49ers, 35-21 (SF)
49ers, 16-6 (NO)
1976—49ers, 33-3 (SF)
49ers, 27-7 (NO)
1977—49ers, 10-7 (NO) OT
49ers, 20-17 (SF)
1978—Saints, 14-7 (SF)
Saints, 24-13 (NO)
1979—Saints, 30-21 (SF)
Saints, 31-20 (NO)
1980—49ers, 26-23 (NO)
49ers, 38-35 (SF) OT
1981—49ers, 21-14 (SF)
49ers, 21-17 (NO)
1982—Saints, 23-20 (SF)
1983—49ers, 32-13 (NO)
49ers, 27-0 (SF)
1984—49ers, 30-20 (SF)
49ers, 35-3 (NO)
1985—Saints, 20-17 (SF)
49ers, 31-19 (NO)
1986—49ers, 26-17 (SF)
Saints, 23-10 (NO)
1987—49ers, 24-22 (NO)
Saints, 26-24 (SF)
1988—49ers, 34-33 (NO)
49ers, 30-17 (SF)
1989—49ers, 24-20 (NO)
49ers, 31-13 (SF)
1990—49ers, 13-12 (NO)
Saints, 13-10 (SF)
(RS Pts.—49ers 1,066, Saints 764)

NEW ORLEANS vs. SEATTLE
RS: Series tied, 2-2
1976—Saints, 51-27 (S)
1979—Seahawks, 38-24 (S)
1985—Seahawks, 27-3 (NO)
1988—Saints, 20-19 (S)
(RS Pts.—Seahawks 111, Saints 98)

NEW ORLEANS vs. TAMPA BAY
RS: Saints lead series, 9-4
1977—Buccaneers, 33-14 (NO)
1978—Saints, 17-10 (TB)
1979—Saints, 42-14 (TB)
1981—Buccaneers, 31-14 (NO)
1982—Buccaneers, 13-10 (NO)
1983—Saints, 24-21 (TB)
1984—Saints, 17-13 (NO)
1985—Saints, 20-13 (NO)
1986—Saints, 38-7 (NO)
1987—Saints, 44-34 (NO)
1988—Saints, 13-9 (NO)
1989—Buccaneers, 20-10 (TB)
1990—Saints, 35-7 (NO)
(RS Pts.—Saints 298, Buccaneers 225)

NEW ORLEANS vs. WASHINGTON
RS: Redskins lead series, 11-4
1967—Redskins, 30-10 (NO)
Saints, 30-14 (W)
1968—Saints, 37-17 (NO)
1969—Redskins, 26-20 (NO)
Redskins, 17-14 (W)
1971—Redskins, 24-14 (W)
1973—Saints, 19-3 (NO)
1975—Redskins, 41-3 (W)
1979—Saints, 14-10 (W)
1980—Redskins, 22-14 (W)
1982—Redskins, 27-10 (NO)
1986—Redskins, 14-6 (NO)
1988—Redskins, 27-24 (W)
1989—Redskins, 16-14 (NO)
1990—Redskins, 31-17 (W)
(RS Pts.—Redskins 319, Saints 246)

N.Y. GIANTS vs. ATLANTA
RS: Series tied, 6-6;
See Atlanta vs. N.Y. Giants

N.Y. GIANTS vs. BUFFALO
RS: Bills lead series, 3-2
PS: Giants lead series, 1-0;
See Buffalo vs. N.Y. Giants

N.Y. GIANTS vs. CHICAGO
RS: Bears lead series, 23-14-2
PS: Bears lead series, 5-3;
See Chicago vs. N.Y. Giants

N.Y. GIANTS vs. CINCINNATI
RS: Bengals lead series, 3-0;
See Cincinnati vs. N.Y. Giants

N.Y. GIANTS vs. CLEVELAND
RS: Browns lead series, 25-15-2
PS: Series tied, 1-1;
See Cleveland vs. N.Y. Giants

N.Y. GIANTS vs. DALLAS
RS: Cowboys lead series, 35-20-2;
See Dallas vs. N.Y. Giants

N.Y. GIANTS vs. DENVER
RS: Giants lead series, 3-2
PS: Giants lead series, 1-0;
See Denver vs. N.Y. Giants

N.Y. GIANTS vs. DETROIT
RS: Lions lead series, 17-15-1
PS: Lions lead series, 1-0;
See Detroit vs. N.Y. Giants

N.Y. GIANTS vs. GREEN BAY
RS: Packers lead series, 21-19-2
PS: Packers lead series, 4-1;
See Green Bay vs. N.Y. Giants

N.Y. GIANTS vs. HOUSTON
RS: Giants lead series, 3-0;
See Houston vs. N.Y. Giants

N.Y. GIANTS vs. INDIANAPOLIS
RS: Colts lead series, 5-4
PS: Colts lead series, 2-0;
See Indianapolis vs. N.Y. Giants

N.Y. GIANTS vs. KANSAS CITY
RS: Giants lead series, 5-1;
See Kansas City vs. N.Y. Giants

N.Y. GIANTS vs. L.A. RAIDERS
RS: Raiders lead series, 3-2;
See L.A. Raiders vs. N.Y. Giants

N.Y. GIANTS vs. L.A. RAMS
RS: Rams lead series, 18-8
PS: Series tied, 1-1;
See L.A. Rams vs. N.Y. Giants

N.Y. GIANTS vs. MIAMI
RS: Series tied, 1-1;
See Miami vs. N.Y. Giants

N.Y. GIANTS vs. MINNESOTA
RS: Vikings lead series, 6-4;
See Minnesota vs. N.Y. Giants

N.Y. GIANTS vs. NEW ENGLAND
RS: Giants lead series, 3-1;
See New England vs. N.Y. Giants

N.Y. GIANTS vs. NEW ORLEANS
RS: Giants lead series, 8-6;
See New Orleans vs. N.Y. Giants

N.Y. GIANTS vs. N.Y. JETS
RS: Series tied, 3-3
1970—Giants, 22-10 (NYJ)
1974—Jets, 26-20 (New Haven) OT
1981—Jets, 26-7 (NYG)
1984—Giants, 20-10 (NYJ)
1987—Giants, 20-7 (NYG)
1988—Jets, 27-21 (NYJ)
(RS Pts.—Giants 110, Jets 106)

N.Y. GIANTS vs. PHILADELPHIA
RS: Giants lead series, 60-50-2
PS: Giants lead series, 1-0
1933—Giants, 56-0 (NY)
Giants, 20-14 (P)
1934—Giants, 17-0 (NY)
Eagles, 6-0 (P)
1935—Giants, 10-0 (NY)
Giants, 21-14 (P)
1936—Eagles, 10-7 (P)
Giants, 21-17 (NY)
1937—Giants, 16-7 (P)
Giants, 21-0 (NY)
1938—Eagles, 14-10 (P)
Giants, 17-7 (NY)
1939—Giants, 13-3 (P)
Giants, 27-10 (NY)
1940—Giants, 20-14 (P)
Giants, 17-7 (NY)
1941—Giants, 24-0 (P)
Giants, 16-0 (NY)
1942—Giants, 35-17 (NY)
Giants, 14-0 (P)
1944—Eagles, 24-17 (NY)
Tie, 21-21 (P)
1945—Eagles, 38-17 (P)
Giants, 28-21 (NY)
1946—Eagles, 24-14 (P)
Giants, 45-17 (NY)
1947—Eagles, 23-0 (P)
Eagles, 41-24 (NY)
1948—Eagles, 45-0 (P)
Eagles, 35-14 (NY)
1949—Eagles, 24-3 (NY)
Eagles, 17-3 (P)
1950—Giants, 7-3 (NY)
Giants, 9-7 (P)
1951—Giants, 26-24 (NY)
Giants, 23-7 (P)
1952—Giants, 31-7 (P)
Eagles, 14-10 (NY)
1953—Eagles, 30-7 (P)
Giants, 37-28 (NY)
1954—Giants, 27-14 (NY)
Eagles, 29-14 (P)
1955—Eagles, 27-17 (P)
Giants, 31-7 (NY)
1956—Giants, 20-3 (NY)
Giants, 21-7 (P)
1957—Giants, 24-20 (P)
Giants, 13-0 (NY)
1958—Eagles, 27-24 (P)
Giants, 24-10 (NY)
1959—Eagles, 49-21 (P)
Giants, 24-7 (NY)
1960—Eagles, 17-10 (NY)
Eagles, 31-23 (P)
1961—Giants, 38-21 (NY)
Giants, 28-24 (P)
1962—Giants, 29-13 (P)
Giants, 19-14 (NY)
1963—Giants, 37-14 (P)
Giants, 42-14 (NY)
1964—Eagles, 38-7 (P)
Eagles, 23-17 (NY)
1965—Giants, 16-14 (P)
Giants, 35-27 (NY)
1966—Eagles, 35-17 (P)
Eagles, 31-3 (NY)
1967—Giants, 44-7 (NY)
1968—Giants, 34-25 (P)
Giants, 7-6 (NY)
1969—Eagles, 23-20 (NY)
1970—Giants, 30-23 (NY)
Eagles, 23-20 (P)
1971—Eagles, 23-7 (P)
Eagles, 41-28 (NY)
1972—Giants, 27-12 (P)
Giants, 62-10 (NY)
1973—Tie, 23-23 (NY)
Eagles, 20-16 (P)
1974—Eagles, 35-7 (P)
Eagles, 20-7 (New Haven)
1975—Giants, 23-14 (P)
Eagles, 13-10 (NY)
1976—Eagles, 20-7 (P)
Eagles, 10-0 (NY)
1977—Eagles, 28-10 (NY)
Eagles, 17-14 (P)
1978—Eagles, 19-17 (NY)
Eagles, 20-3 (P)
1979—Eagles, 23-17 (P)
Eagles, 17-13 (NY)
1980—Eagles, 35-3 (P)
Eagles, 31-16 (NY)
1981—Eagles, 24-10 (NY)
Giants, 20-10 (P)
*Giants, 27-21 (P)
1982—Giants, 23-7 (NY)
Giants, 26-24 (P)
1983—Eagles, 17-13 (NY)
Giants, 23-0 (P)
1984—Giants, 28-27 (NY)
Eagles, 24-10 (P)
1985—Giants, 21-0 (NY)
Giants, 16-10 (P) OT
1986—Giants, 35-3 (NY)
Giants, 17-14 (P)
1987—Giants, 20-17 (P)
Giants, 23-20 (NY) OT
1988—Eagles, 24-13 (P)
Eagles, 23-17 (NY) OT
1989—Eagles, 21-19 (P)
Eagles, 24-17 (NY)
1990—Giants, 27-20 (NY)
Eagles, 31-13 (P)
(RS Pts.—Giants 2,155, Eagles 1,984)
(PS Pts.—Giants 27, Eagles 21)
NFC First Round Playoff

N.Y. GIANTS vs. *PHOENIX
RS: Giants lead series, 61-33-2
1926—Giants, 20-0 (NY)
1927—Giants, 28-7 (NY)
1929—Giants, 24-21 (NY)
1930—Giants, 25-12 (NY)
Giants, 13-7 (C)
1935—Cardinals, 14-13 (NY)
1936—Giants, 14-6 (NY)
1938—Giants, 6-0 (NY)
1939—Giants, 17-7 (NY)
1941—Cardinals, 10-7 (NY)
1942—Giants, 21-7 (NY)
1943—Giants, 24-13 (NY)
1946—Giants, 28-24 (NY)
1947—Giants, 35-31 (NY)
1948—Cardinals, 63-35 (NY)
1949—Giants, 41-38 (C)
1950—Cardinals, 17-3 (C)
Giants, 51-21 (NY)
1951—Giants, 28-17 (NY)
Giants, 10-0 (C)
1952—Cardinals, 24-23 (NY)
Giants, 28-6 (C)
1953—Giants, 21-7 (NY)
Giants, 23-20 (C)
1954—Giants, 41-10 (C)
Giants, 31-17 (NY)
1955—Cardinals, 28-17 (C)
Giants, 10-0 (NY)
1956—Cardinals, 35-27 (C)
Giants, 23-10 (NY)
1957—Giants, 27-14 (NY)
Giants, 28-21 (C)
1958—Giants, 37-7 (Buffalo)
Cardinals, 23-6 (NY)
1959—Giants, 9-3 (NY)
Giants, 30-20 (Minn)
1960—Giants, 35-14 (StL)
Cardinals, 20-13 (NY)
1961—Cardinals, 21-10 (NY)
Giants, 24-9 (StL)
1962—Giants, 31-14 (StL)
Giants, 31-28 (NY)
1963—Giants, 38-21 (StL)
Cardinals, 24-17 (NY)
1964—Giants, 34-17 (NY)
Tie, 10-10 (StL)
1965—Giants, 14-10 (NY)
Giants, 28-15 (StL)
1966—Cardinals, 24-19 (StL)
Cardinals, 20-17 (NY)
1967—Giants, 37-20 (StL)
Giants, 37-14 (NY)
1968—Cardinals, 28-21 (NY)
1969—Cardinals, 42-17 (StL)
Giants, 49-6 (NY)
1970—Giants, 35-17 (NY)
Giants, 34-17 (StL)
1971—Giants, 21-20 (StL)
Cardinals, 24-7 (NY)
1972—Giants, 27-21 (NY)
Giants, 13-7 (StL)
1973—Cardinals, 35-27 (StL)
Giants, 24-13 (New Haven)
1974—Cardinals, 23-21 (New Haven)
Cardinals, 26-14 (StL)
1975—Cardinals, 26-14 (StL)
Cardinals, 20-13 (NY)
1976—Cardinals, 27-21 (StL)
Cardinals, 17-14 (NY)
1977—Cardinals, 28-0 (StL)
Giants, 27-7 (NY)
1978—Cardinals, 20-10 (StL)
Giants, 17-0 (NY)
1979—Cardinals, 27-14 (NY)
Cardinals, 29-20 (StL)
1980—Giants, 41-35 (StL)
Cardinals, 23-7 (NY)
1981—Giants, 34-14 (NY)
Giants, 20-10 (StL)
1982—Cardinals, 24-21 (StL)
1983—Tie, 20-20 (StL) OT
Cardinals, 10-6 (NY)
1984—Giants, 16-10 (NY)
Cardinals, 31-21 (StL)
1985—Giants, 27-17 (NY)
Giants, 34-3 (StL)
1986—Giants, 13-6 (StL)
Giants, 27-7 (NY)
1987—Giants, 30-7 (NY)
Cardinals, 27-24 (StL)
1988—Cardinals, 24-17 (P)
Giants, 44-7 (NY)
1989—Giants, 35-7 (NY)
Giants, 20-13 (P)
1990—Giants, 20-19 (NY)
Giants, 24-21 (P)
(RS Pts.—Giants 2,180, Cardinals 1,656)
Franchise in St. Louis prior to 1988 and in Chicago prior to 1960

N.Y. GIANTS vs. *PITTSBURGH
RS: Giants lead series, 41-26-3
1933—Giants, 23-2 (P)
Giants, 27-3 (NY)
1934—Giants, 14-12 (P)
Giants, 17-7 (NY)
1935—Giants, 42-7 (P)
Giants, 13-0 (NY)
1936—Pirates, 10-7 (P)
1937—Giants, 10-7 (P)
Giants, 17-0 (NY)
1938—Giants, 27-14 (P)
Pirates, 13-10 (NY)
1939—Giants, 14-7 (P)
Giants, 23-7 (NY)
1940—Tie, 10-10 (P)
Giants, 12-0 (NY)
1941—Giants, 37-10 (P)
Giants, 28-7 (NY)
1942—Steelers, 13-10 (P)
Steelers, 17-9 (NY)
1945—Giants, 34-6 (P)
Steelers, 21-7 (NY)
1946—Giants, 17-14 (P)
Giants, 7-0 (NY)
1947—Steelers, 38-21 (NY)
Steelers, 24-7 (P)
1948—Giants, 34-27 (NY)
Steelers, 38-28 (P)
1949—Steelers, 28-7 (P)
Steelers, 21-17 (NY)
1950—Giants, 18-7 (P)
Steelers, 17-6 (NY)
1951—Tie, 13-13 (P)
Giants, 14-0 (NY)
1952—Steelers, 63-7 (P)
1953—Steelers, 24-14 (P)
Steelers, 14-10 (NY)
1954—Giants, 30-6 (P)
Giants, 24-3 (NY)
1955—Steelers, 30-23 (P)
1956—Steelers, 19-17 (NY)
1956—Giants, 38-10 (NY)
Giants, 17-14 (P)
1957—Giants, 35-0 (NY)
Steelers, 21-10 (P)
1958—Giants, 17-6 (NY)
Steelers, 31-10 (P)
1959—Giants, 21-16 (P)
Steelers, 14-9 (NY)
1960—Giants, 19-17 (P)
Giants, 27-24 (NY)
1961—Giants, 17-14 (P)
Giants, 42-21 (NY)
1962—Giants, 31-27 (P)
Steelers, 20-17 (NY)
1963—Steelers, 31-0 (P)
Giants, 33-17 (NY)
1964—Steelers, 27-24 (P)
Steelers, 44-17 (NY)
1965—Giants, 23-13 (P)
Giants, 35-10 (NY)
1966—Tie, 34-34 (P)
Steelers, 47-28 (NY)
1967—Giants, 27-24 (P)
Giants, 28-20 (NY)
1968—Giants, 34-20 (P)
1969—Giants, 10-7 (NY)
Giants, 21-17 (P)
1971—Steelers, 17-13 (P)
1976—Steelers, 27-0 (NY)
1985—Giants, 28-10 (NY)
(RS Pts.—Giants 1,370, Steelers 1,159)
Steelers known as Pirates prior to 1941

N.Y. GIANTS vs. SAN DIEGO
RS: Giants lead series, 4-2
1971—Giants, 35-17 (NY)
1975—Giants, 35-24 (NY)
1980—Chargers, 44-7 (SD)
1983—Chargers, 41-34 (NY)
1986—Giants, 20-7 (NY)
1989—Giants, 20-13 (SD)
(RS Pts.—Giants 151, Chargers 146)

N.Y. GIANTS vs. SAN FRANCISCO
RS: Giants lead series, 10-9
PS: Giants lead series, 3-2
1952—Giants, 23-14 (NY)
1956—Giants, 38-21 (SF)
1957—49ers, 27-17 (NY)
1960—Giants, 21-19 (SF)
1963—Giants, 48-14 (NY)
1968—49ers, 26-10 (NY)
1972—Giants, 23-17 (SF)
1975—Giants, 26-23 (SF)
1977—Giants, 20-17 (NY)
1978—Giants, 27-10 (NY)
1979—Giants, 32-16 (NY)
1980—49ers, 12-0 (SF)
1981—49ers, 17-10 (SF)
*49ers, 38-24 (SF)
1984—49ers, 31-10 (NY)
*49ers, 21-10 (SF)
1985—**Giants, 17-3 (NY)
1986—Giants, 21-17 (SF)
*Giants, 49-3 (NY)
1987—49ers, 41-21 (NY)
1988—49ers, 20-17 (NY)
1989—49ers, 34-24 (SF)
1990—49ers, 7-3 (SF)
***Giants, 15-13 (SF)
(RS Pts.—Giants 391, 49ers 386)
(PS Pts.—Giants 115, 49ers 75)
NFC Divisional Playoff
***NFC First Round Playoff*
****NFC Championship*

N.Y. GIANTS vs. SEATTLE
RS: Giants lead series, 4-2
1976—Giants, 28-16 (NY)
1980—Giants, 27-21 (S)
1981—Giants, 32-0 (S)
1983—Seahawks, 17-12 (NY)
1986—Seahawks, 17-12 (S)
1989—Giants, 15-3 (NY)
(RS Pts.—Giants 126, Seahawks 74)

N.Y. GIANTS vs. TAMPA BAY
RS: Giants lead series, 6-3
1977—Giants, 10-0 (TB)
1978—Giants, 19-13 (TB)
Giants, 17-14 (NY)
1979—Giants, 17-14 (NY)
Buccaneers, 31-3 (TB)
1980—Buccaneers, 30-13 (TB)
1984—Giants, 17-14 (NY)
Buccaneers, 20-17 (TB)
1985—Giants, 22-20 (NY)
(RS Pts.—Buccaneers 156, Giants 135)

N.Y. GIANTS vs. *WASHINGTON
RS: Giants lead series, 66-47-3
PS: Series tied, 1-1
1932—Braves, 14-6 (B)
Tie, 0-0 (NY)
1933—Redskins, 21-20 (B)
Giants, 7-0 (NY)
1934—Giants, 16-13 (B)
Giants, 3-0 (NY)
1935—Giants, 20-12 (B)
Giants, 17-6 (NY)
1936—Giants, 7-0 (B)
Redskins, 14-0 (NY)
1937—Redskins, 13-3 (W)
Redskins, 49-14 (NY)
1938—Giants, 10-7 (W)
Giants, 36-0 (NY)
1939—Tie, 0-0 (W)
Giants, 9-7 (NY)
1940—Redskins, 21-7 (W)
Giants, 21-7 (NY)
1941—Giants, 17-10 (W)
Giants, 20-13 (NY)
1942—Giants, 14-7 (W)
Redskins, 14-7 (NY)
1943—Giants, 14-10 (NY)
Giants, 31-7 (W)
**Redskins, 28-0 (NY)
1944—Giants, 16-13 (NY)
Giants, 31-0 (W)
1945—Redskins, 24-14 (NY)
Redskins, 17-0 (W)
1946—Redskins, 24-14 (W)
Giants, 31-0 (NY)
1947—Redskins, 28-20 (W)
Giants, 35-10 (NY)
1948—Redskins, 41-10 (W)
Redskins, 28-21 (NY)
1949—Giants, 45-35 (W)
Giants, 23-7 (NY)
1950—Giants, 21-17 (W)
Giants, 24-21 (NY)
1951—Giants, 35-14 (W)
Giants, 28-14 (NY)
1952—Giants, 14-10 (W)
Redskins, 27-17 (NY)
1953—Redskins, 13-9 (W)
Redskins, 24-21 (NY)
1954—Giants, 51-21 (W)
Giants, 24-7 (NY)
1955—Giants, 35-7 (NY)
Giants, 27-20 (W)
1956—Redskins, 33-7 (W)
Giants, 28-14 (NY)
1957—Giants, 24-20 (W)
Redskins, 31-14 (NY)

1958—Giants, 21-14 (W)
Giants, 30-0 (NY)
1959—Giants, 45-14 (NY)
Giants, 24-10 (W)
1960—Tie, 24-24 (NY)
Giants, 17-3 (W)
1961—Giants, 24-21 (W)
Giants, 53-0 (NY)
1962—Giants, 49-34 (NY)
Giants, 42-24 (W)
1963—Giants, 24-14 (W)
Giants, 44-14 (NY)
1964—Giants, 13-10 (NY)
Redskins, 36-21 (W)
1965—Redskins, 23-7 (NY)
Giants, 27-10 (W)
1966—Giants, 13-10 (NY)
Redskins, 72-41 (W)
1967—Redskins, 38-34 (W)
1968—Giants, 48-21 (NY)
Giants, 13-10 (W)
1969—Redskins, 20-14 (W)
1970—Giants, 35-33 (NY)
Giants, 27-24 (W)
1971—Redskins, 30-3 (NY)
Redskins, 23-7 (W)
1972—Redskins, 23-16 (NY)
Redskins, 27-13 (W)
1973—Redskins, 21-3 (New Haven)
Redskins, 27-24 (W)
1974—Redskins, 13-10 (New Haven)
Redskins, 24-3 (W)
1975—Redskins, 49-13 (W)
Redskins, 21-13 (NY)
1976—Redskins, 19-17 (W)
Giants, 12-9 (NY)
1977—Giants, 20-17 (NY)
Giants, 17-6 (W)
1978—Giants, 17-6 (NY)
Redskins, 16-13 (W) OT
1979—Redskins, 27-0 (W)
Giants, 14-6 (NY)
1980—Redskins, 23-21 (NY)
Redskins, 16-13 (W)
1981—Giants, 17-7 (W)
Redskins, 30-27 (NY) OT
1982—Redskins, 27-17 (NY)
Redskins, 15-14 (W)
1983—Redskins, 33-17 (NY)
Redskins, 31-22 (W)
1984—Redskins, 30-14 (W)
Giants, 37-13 (NY)
1985—Giants, 17-3 (NY)
Redskins, 23-21 (W)
1986—Giants, 27-20 (NY)
Giants, 24-14 (W)
***Giants, 17-0 (NY)
1987—Redskins, 38-12 (NY)
Redskins, 23-19 (W)
1988—Giants, 27-20 (NY)
Giants, 24-23 (W)
1989—Giants, 27-24 (W)
Giants, 20-17 (NY)
1990—Giants, 24-20 (W)
Giants, 21-10 (NY)
(RS Pts.—Giants 2,305, Redskins 2,068)
(PS Pts.—Redskins 28, Giants 17)
Franchise in Boston prior to 1937 and known as Braves prior to 1933
**Division Playoff*
***NFC Championship*

N.Y. JETS vs. ATLANTA
RS: Jets lead series, 3-2;
See Atlanta vs. N.Y. Jets
N.Y. JETS vs. BUFFALO
RS: Bills lead series, 32-28
PS: Bills lead series, 1-0;
See Buffalo vs. N.Y. Jets
N.Y. JETS vs. CHICAGO
RS: Bears lead series, 2-1;
See Chicago vs. N.Y. Jets
N.Y. JETS vs. CINCINNATI
RS: Jets lead series, 7-6
PS: Jets lead series, 1-0;
See Cincinnati vs. N.Y. Jets
N.Y. JETS vs. CLEVELAND
RS: Browns lead series, 8-5
PS: Browns lead series, 1-0;
See Cleveland vs. N.Y. Jets
N.Y. JETS vs. DALLAS
RS: Cowboys lead series, 4-1;
See Dallas vs. N.Y. Jets
N.Y. JETS vs. DENVER
RS: Jets lead series, 11-10-1;
See Denver vs. N.Y. Jets
N.Y. JETS vs. DETROIT
RS: Jets lead series, 3-2;
See Detroit vs. N.Y. Jets
N.Y. JETS vs. GREEN BAY
RS: Jets lead series, 4-1;
See Green Bay vs. N.Y. Jets

N.Y. JETS vs. HOUSTON
RS: Oilers lead series, 15-12-1;
See Houston vs. N.Y. Jets
N.Y. JETS vs. INDIANAPOLIS
RS: Colts lead series, 23-18
PS: Jets lead series, 1-0;
See Indianapolis vs. N.Y. Jets
N.Y. JETS vs. KANSAS CITY
RS: Chiefs lead series, 13-12-1
PS: Series tied, 1-1;
See Kansas City vs. N.Y. Jets
N.Y. JETS vs. L.A. RAIDERS
RS: Raiders lead series, 13-9-2
PS: Jets lead series, 2-0;
See L.A. Raiders vs. N.Y. Jets
N.Y. JETS vs. L.A. RAMS
RS: Rams lead series, 4-2;
See L.A. Rams vs. N.Y. Jets
N.Y. JETS vs. MIAMI
RS: Dolphins lead series, 26-23-1
PS: Dolphins lead series, 1-0;
See Miami vs. N.Y. Jets
N.Y. JETS vs. MINNESOTA
RS: Jets lead series, 3-1;
See Minnesota vs. N.Y. Jets
N.Y. JETS vs. NEW ENGLAND
RS: Jets lead series, 34-26-1
PS: Patriots lead series, 1-0;
See New England vs. N.Y. Jets
N.Y. JETS vs. NEW ORLEANS
RS: Jets lead series, 4-2;
See New Orleans vs. N.Y. Jets
N.Y. JETS vs. N.Y. GIANTS
RS: Series tied, 3-3;
See N.Y. Giants vs. N.Y. Jets
N.Y. JETS vs. PHILADELPHIA
RS: Eagles lead series, 4-0
1973—Eagles, 24-23 (P)
1977—Eagles, 27-0 (P)
1978—Eagles, 17-9 (P)
1987—Eagles, 38-27 (NY)
(RS Pts.—Eagles 106, Jets 59)
N.Y. JETS vs. *PHOENIX
RS: Cardinals lead series, 2-1
1971—Cardinals, 17-10 (StL)
1975—Cardinals 37-6 (NY)
1978—Jets, 23-10 (NY)
(RS Pts.—Cardinals 64, Jets 39)
Franchise in St. Louis prior to 1988
N.Y. JETS vs. PITTSBURGH
RS: Steelers lead series, 11-1
1970—Steelers, 21-17 (P)
1973—Steelers, 26-14 (P)
1975—Steelers, 20-7 (NY)
1977—Steelers, 23-20 (NY)
1978—Steelers, 28-17 (NY)
1981—Steelers, 38-10 (P)
1983—Steelers, 34-7 (NY)
1984—Steelers, 23-17 (NY)
1986—Steelers, 45-24 (NY)
1988—Jets, 24-20 (NY)
1989—Steelers, 13-0 (NY)
1990—Steelers, 24-7 (NY)
(RS Pts.—Steelers 315, Jets 164)
***N.Y. JETS vs. **SAN DIEGO**
RS: Chargers lead series, 16-8-1
1960—Chargers, 21-7 (NY)
Chargers, 50-43 (LA)
1961—Chargers, 25-10 (NY)
Chargers, 48-13 (SD)
1962—Chargers, 40-14 (SD)
Titans, 23-3 (NY)
1963—Chargers, 24-20 (SD)
Chargers, 53-7 (NY)
1964—Tie, 17-17 (NY)
Chargers, 38-3 (SD)
1965—Chargers, 34-9 (NY)
Chargers, 38-7 (SD)
1966—Jets, 17-16 (NY)
Chargers, 42-27 (SD)
1967—Jets, 42-31 (SD)
1968—Jets, 23-20 (NY)
Jets, 37-15 (SD)
1969—Chargers, 34-27 (SD)
1971—Chargers, 49-21 (SD)
1974—Jets, 27-14 (NY)
1975—Chargers, 24-16 (SD)
1983—Jets, 41-29 (SD)
1989—Jets, 20-17 (SD)
1990—Chargers, 39-3 (NY)
Chargers, 38-17 (SD)
(RS Pts.—Chargers 759, Jets 491)
Jets known as Titans prior to 1963
**Franchise in Los Angeles prior to 1961*
N.Y. JETS vs. SAN FRANCISCO
RS: 49ers lead series, 5-1
1971—49ers, 24-21 (NY)
1976—49ers, 17-6 (SF)
1980—49ers, 37-27 (NY)
1983—Jets, 27-13 (SF)
1986—49ers, 24-10 (SF)
1989—49ers, 23-10 (NY)
(RS Pts.—49ers 138, Jets 101)

N.Y. JETS vs. SEATTLE
RS: Seahawks lead series, 7-3
1977—Seahawks, 17-0 (NY)
1978—Seahawks, 24-17 (NY)
1979—Seahawks, 30-7 (S)
1980—Seahawks, 27-17 (NY)
1981—Seahawks, 19-3 (NY)
Seahawks, 27-23 (S)
1983—Seahawks, 17-10 (NY)
1985—Jets, 17-14 (NY)
1986—Jets, 38-7 (S)
1987—Jets, 30-14 (NY)
(RS Pts.—Seahawks 196, Jets 162)
N.Y. JETS vs. TAMPA BAY
RS: Jets lead series, 4-1
1976—Jets, 34-0 (NY)
1982—Jets, 32-17 (NY)
1984—Buccaneers, 41-21 (TB)
1985—Jets, 62-28 (NY)
1990—Jets, 16-14 (TB)
(RS Pts.—Jets 165, Buccaneers 100)
N.Y. JETS vs. WASHINGTON
RS: Redskins lead series, 4-0
1972—Redskins, 35-17 (NY)
1976—Redskins, 37-16 (NY)
1978—Redskins, 23-3 (W)
1987—Redskins, 17-16 (W)
(RS Pts.—Redskins 112, Jets 52)

PHILADELPHIA vs. ATLANTA
RS: Eagles lead series, 8-6-1
PS: Falcons lead series, 1-0;
See Atlanta vs. Philadelphia
PHILADELPHIA vs. BUFFALO
RS: Eagles lead series, 4-2;
See Buffalo vs. Philadelphia
PHILADELPHIA vs. CHICAGO
RS: Bears lead series, 22-3-1
PS: Series tied, 1-1;
See Chicago vs. Philadelphia
PHILADELPHIA vs. CINCINNATI
RS: Bengals lead series, 5-0;
See Cincinnati vs. Philadelphia
PHILADELPHIA vs. CLEVELAND
RS: Browns lead series, 30-11-1;
See Cleveland vs. Philadelphia
PHILADELPHIA vs. DALLAS
RS: Cowboys lead series, 36-24
PS: Eagles lead series, 1-0;
See Dallas vs. Philadelphia
PHILADELPHIA vs. DENVER
RS: Eagles lead series, 4-2;
See Denver vs. Philadelphia
PHILADELPHIA vs. DETROIT
RS: Lions lead series, 12-9-2;
See Detroit vs. Philadelphia
PHILADELPHIA vs. GREEN BAY
RS: Packers lead series, 18-5
PS: Eagles lead series, 1-0;
See Green Bay vs. Philadelphia
PHILADELPHIA vs. HOUSTON
RS: Eagles lead series, 4-0;
See Houston vs. Philadelphia
PHILADELPHIA vs. INDIANAPOLIS
RS: Colts lead series, 6-5;
See Indianapolis vs. Philadelphia
PHILADELPHIA vs. KANSAS CITY
RS: Eagles lead series, 1-0;
See Kansas City vs. Philadelphia
PHILADELPHIA vs. L.A. RAIDERS
RS: Eagles lead series, 3-2
PS: Raiders lead series, 1-0;
See L.A. Raiders vs. Philadelphia
PHILADELPHIA vs. L.A. RAMS
RS: Rams lead series, 15-11-1
PS: Series tied, 1-1;
See L.A. Rams vs. Philadelphia
PHILADELPHIA vs. MIAMI
RS: Dolphins lead series, 5-2;
See Miami vs. Philadelphia
PHILADELPHIA vs. MINNESOTA
RS: Vikings lead series, 10-5
PS: Eagles lead series, 1-0;
See Minnesota vs. Philadelphia
PHILADELPHIA vs. NEW ENGLAND
RS: Eagles lead series, 5-2;
See New England vs. Philadelphia
PHILADELPHIA vs. NEW ORLEANS
RS: Eagles lead series, 9-7;
See New Orleans vs. Philadelphia
PHILADELPHIA vs. N.Y. GIANTS
RS: Giants lead series, 60-50-2
PS: Giants lead series, 1-0;
See N.Y. Giants vs. Philadelphia
PHILADELPHIA vs. N.Y. JETS
RS: Eagles lead series, 4-0;
See N.Y. Jets vs. Philadelphia
PHILADELPHIA vs. *PHOENIX
RS: Cardinals lead series, 42-39-5
PS: Series tied, 1-1
1935—Cardinals, 12-3 (C)
1936—Cardinals, 13-0 (C)
1937—Tie, 6-6 (P)
1938—Eagles, 7-0 (Erie, Pa.)
1941—Eagles, 21-14 (P)
1945—Eagles, 21-6 (P)
1947—Cardinals, 45-21 (P)
**Cardinals, 28-21 (C)
1948—Cardinals, 21-14 (C)
**Eagles, 7-0 (P)
1949—Eagles, 28-3 (P)
1950—Eagles, 45-7 (C)
Cardinals, 14-10 (P)
1951—Eagles, 17-14 (C)
1952—Eagles, 10-7 (P)
Cardinals, 28-22 (C)
1953—Eagles, 56-17 (C)
Eagles, 38-0 (P)
1954—Eagles, 35-16 (C)
Eagles, 30-14 (P)
1955—Tie, 24-24 (C)
Eagles, 27-3 (P)
1956—Cardinals, 20-6 (P)
Cardinals, 28-17 (C)
1957—Eagles, 38-21 (C)
Cardinals, 31-27 (P)
1958—Tie, 21-21 (C)
Eagles, 49-21 (P)
1959—Eagles, 28-24 (Minn)
Eagles, 27-17 (P)
1960—Eagles, 31-27 (P)
Eagles, 20-6 (StL)
1961—Cardinals, 30-27 (P)
Eagles, 20-7 (StL)
1962—Cardinals, 27-21 (P)
Cardinals, 45-35 (StL)
1963—Cardinals, 28-24 (P)
Cardinals, 38-14 (StL)
1964—Cardinals, 38-13 (P)
Cardinals, 36-34 (StL)
1965—Eagles, 34-27 (P)
Eagles, 28-24 (StL)
1966—Cardinals, 16-13 (StL)
Cardinals, 41-10 (P)
1967—Cardinals, 48-14 (StL)
1968—Cardinals, 45-17 (P)
1969—Eagles, 34-30 (StL)
1970—Cardinals, 35-20 (P)
Cardinals, 23-14 (StL)
1971—Eagles, 37-20 (StL)
Eagles, 19-7 (P)
1972—Tie, 6-6 (P)
Cardinals, 24-23 (StL)
1973—Cardinals, 34-23 (P)
Eagles, 27-24 (StL)
1974—Cardinals, 7-3 (StL)
Cardinals, 13-3 (P)
1975—Cardinals, 31-20 (StL)
Cardinals, 24-23 (P)
1976—Cardinals, 33-14 (StL)
Cardinals, 17-14 (P)
1977—Cardinals, 21-17 (P)
Cardinals, 21-16 (StL)
1978—Cardinals, 16-10 (P)
Eagles, 14-10 (StL)
1979—Eagles, 24-20 (StL)
Eagles, 16-13 (P)
1980—Cardinals, 24-14 (StL)
Eagles, 17-3 (P)
1981—Eagles, 52-10 (StL)
Eagles, 38-0 (P)
1982—Cardinals, 23-20 (P)
1983—Cardinals, 14-11 (P)
Cardinals, 31-7 (StL)
1984—Cardinals, 34-14 (P)
Cardinals, 17-16 (StL)
1985—Eagles, 30-7 (P)
Eagles, 24-14 (StL)
1986—Cardinals, 13-10 (StL)
Tie, 10-10 (P) OT
1987—Eagles, 28-23 (StL)
Cardinals, 31-19 (P)
1988—Eagles, 31-21 (P)
Eagles, 23-17 (Phx)
1989—Eagles, 17-5 (Phx)
Eagles, 31-14 (P)
1990—Cardinals, 23-21 (P)
Eagles, 23-21 (Phx)
(RS Pts.—Eagles 1,864, Cardinals 1,742)
Franchise in St. Louis prior to 1988 and in Chicago prior to 1960
**NFL Championship*
PHILADELPHIA vs. *PITTSBURGH
RS: Eagles lead series, 42-25-3
PS: Eagles lead series, 1-0
1933—Eagles, 25-6 (Phila)
1934—Eagles, 17-0 (Pitt)
Pirates, 9-7 (Phila)
1935—Pirates, 17-7 (Phila)
Eagles, 17-6 (Pitt)
1936—Pirates, 17-0 (Pitt)
Pirates, 6-0 (Johnstown, Pa.)
1937—Pirates, 27-14 (Pitt)
Pirates, 16-7 (Pitt)
1938—Eagles, 27-7 (Buffalo)
Eagles, 14-7 (Charleston, W. Va.)

1939—Eagles, 17-14 (Phila)
Pirates, 24-12 (Pitt)
1940—Pirates, 7-3 (Pitt)
Eagles, 7-0 (Phila)
1941—Eagles, 10-7 (Pitt)
Tie, 7-7 (Phila)
1942—Eagles, 24-14 (Pitt)
Steelers, 14-0 (Phila)
1945—Eagles, 45-3 (Pitt)
Eagles, 30-6 (Phila)
1946—Steelers, 10-7 (Pitt)
Eagles, 10-7 (Phila)
1947—Steelers, 35-24 (Pitt)
Eagles, 21-0 (Phila)
**Eagles, 21-0 (Pitt)
1948—Eagles, 34-7 (Pitt)
Eagles, 17-0 (Phila)
1949—Eagles, 38-7 (Pitt)
Eagles, 34-17 (Phila)
1950—Eagles, 17-10 (Pitt)
Steelers, 9-7 (Phila)
1951—Eagles, 34-13 (Pitt)
Steelers, 17-13 (Phila)
1952—Eagles, 31-25 (Pitt)
Eagles, 26-21 (Phila)
1953—Eagles, 23-17 (Phila)
Eagles, 35-7 (Pitt)
1954—Eagles, 24-22 (Phila)
Steelers, 17-7 (Pitt)
1955—Steelers, 13-7 (Pitt)
Eagles, 24-0 (Phila)
1956—Eagles, 35-21 (Pitt)
Eagles, 14-7 (Phila)
1957—Steelers, 6-0 (Pitt)
Eagles, 7-6 (Phila)
1958—Steelers, 24-3 (Pitt)
Steelers, 31-24 (Phila)
1959—Eagles, 28-24 (Phila)
Steelers, 31-0 (Pitt)
1960—Eagles, 34-7 (Phila)
Steelers, 27-21 (Pitt)
1961—Eagles, 21-16 (Phila)
Eagles, 35-24 (Pitt)
1962—Steelers, 13-7 (Pitt)
Steelers, 26-17 (Phila)
1963—Tie, 21-21 (Phila)
Tie, 20-20 (Pitt)
1964—Eagles, 21-7 (Phila)
Eagles, 34-10 (Pitt)
1965—Steelers, 20-14 (Phila)
Eagles, 47-13 (Pitt)
1966—Eagles, 31-14 (Pitt)
Eagles, 27-23 (Phila)
1967—Eagles, 34-24 (Phila)
1968—Steelers, 6-3 (Pitt)
1969—Eagles, 41-27 (Phila)
1970—Eagles, 30-20 (Phila)
1974—Steelers, 27-0 (Pitt)
1979—Eagles, 17-14 (Phila)
1988—Eagles, 27-26 (Pitt)
(RS Pts.—Eagles 1,336, Steelers 993)
(PS Pts.—Eagles 21, Steelers 0)
Steelers known as Pirates prior to 1941
***Division Playoff*

PHILADELPHIA vs. SAN DIEGO
RS: Chargers lead series, 3-2
1974—Eagles, 13-7 (SD)
1980—Chargers, 22-21 (SD)
1985—Chargers, 20-14 (SD)
1986—Eagles, 23-7 (P)
1989—Chargers, 20-17 (SD)
(RS Pts.—Eagles 88, Chargers 76)

PHILADELPHIA vs. SAN FRANCISCO
RS: 49ers lead series, 11-4-1
1951—Eagles, 21-14 (P)
1953—49ers, 31-21 (SF)
1956—Tie, 10-10 (P)
1958—49ers, 30-24 (P)
1959—49ers, 24-14 (SF)
1964—49ers, 28-24 (P)
1966—Eagles, 35-34 (SF)
1967—49ers, 28-27 (P)
1969—49ers, 14-13 (SF)
1971—49ers, 31-3 (P)
1973—49ers, 38-28 (SF)
1975—Eagles, 27-17 (P)
1983—Eagles, 22-17 (SF)
1984—49ers, 21-9 (P)
1985—49ers, 24-13 (SF)
1989—49ers, 38-28 (P)
(RS Pts.—49ers 399, Eagles 319)

PHILADELPHIA vs. SEATTLE
RS: Eagles lead series, 3-1
1976—Eagles, 27-10 (P)
1980—Eagles, 27-20 (S)
1986—Seahawks, 24-20 (S)
1989—Eagles, 31-7 (P)
(RS Pts.—Eagles 105, Seahawks 61)

PHILADELPHIA vs. TAMPA BAY
RS: Eagles lead series, 3-0
PS: Buccaneers lead series, 1-0
1977—Eagles, 13-3 (P)
1979—*Buccaneers, 24-17 (TB)
1981—Eagles, 20-10 (P)
1988—Eagles, 41-14 (TB)
(RS Pts.—Eagles 74, Buccaneers 27)
(PS Pts.—Buccaneers 24, Eagles 17)
**NFC Divisional Playoff*

PHILADELPHIA vs. *WASHINGTON
RS: Redskins lead series, 64-42-5
PS: Redskins lead series, 1-0
1934—Redskins, 6-0 (B)
Redskins, 14-7 (P)
1935—Eagles, 7-6 (B)
1936—Redskins, 26-3 (P)
Redskins, 17-7 (B)
1937—Eagles, 14-0 (W)
Redskins, 10-7 (P)
1938—Redskins, 26-23 (P)
Redskins, 20-14 (W)
1939—Redskins, 7-0 (P)
Redskins, 7-6 (W)
1940—Redskins, 34-17 (P)
Redskins, 13-6 (W)
1941—Redskins, 21-17 (P)
Redskins, 20-14 (W)
1942—Redskins, 14-10 (P)
Redskins, 30-27 (W)
1944—Tie, 31-31 (P)
Eagles, 37-7 (W)
1945—Redskins, 24-14 (W)
Eagles, 16-0 (P)
1946—Eagles, 28-24 (W)
Redskins, 27-10 (P)
1947—Eagles, 45-42 (P)
Eagles, 38-14 (W)
1948—Eagles, 45-0 (W)
Eagles, 42-21 (P)
1949—Eagles, 49-14 (P)
Eagles, 44-21 (W)
1950—Eagles, 35-3 (P)
Eagles, 33-0 (W)
1951—Redskins, 27-23 (P)
Eagles, 35-21 (W)
1952—Eagles, 38-20 (P)
Redskins, 27-21 (W)
1953—Tie, 21-21 (P)
Redskins, 10-0 (W)
1954—Eagles, 49-21 (W)
Eagles, 41-33 (P)
1955—Redskins, 31-30 (P)
Redskins, 34-21 (W)
1956—Eagles, 13-9 (P)
Redskins, 19-17 (W)
1957—Eagles, 21-12 (P)
Redskins, 42-7 (W)
1958—Redskins, 24-14 (P)
Redskins, 20-0 (W)
1959—Eagles, 30-23 (P)
Eagles, 34-14 (W)
1960—Eagles, 19-13 (P)
Eagles, 38-28 (W)
1961—Eagles, 14-7 (P)
Eagles, 27-24 (W)
1962—Redskins, 27-21 (P)
Eagles, 37-14 (W)
1963—Eagles, 37-24 (W)
Redskins, 13-10 (P)
1964—Redskins, 35-20 (W)
Redskins, 21-10 (P)
1965—Redskins, 23-21 (W)
Eagles, 21-14 (P)
1966—Redskins, 27-13 (P)
Eagles, 37-28 (W)
1967—Eagles, 35-24 (P)
Tie, 35-35 (W)
1968—Redskins, 17-14 (W)
Redskins, 16-10 (P)
1969—Tie, 28-28 (W)
Redskins, 34-29 (P)
1970—Redskins, 33-21 (P)
Redskins, 24-6 (W)
1971—Tie, 7-7 (W)
Redskins, 20-13 (P)
1972—Redskins, 14-0 (W)
Redskins, 23-7 (P)
1973—Redskins, 28-7 (P)
Redskins, 38-20 (W)
1974—Redskins, 27-20 (P)
Redskins, 26-7 (W)
1975—Eagles, 26-10 (P)
Eagles, 26-3 (W)
1976—Redskins, 20-17 (P) OT
Redskins, 24-0 (W)
1977—Redskins, 23-17 (W)
Redskins, 17-14 (P)
1978—Redskins, 35-30 (W)
Eagles, 17-10 (P)
1979—Eagles, 28-17 (P)
Redskins, 17-7 (W)
1980—Eagles, 24-14 (P)
Eagles, 24-0 (W)
1981—Eagles, 36-13 (P)
Redskins, 15-13 (W)
1982—Redskins, 37-34 (P) OT
Redskins, 13-9 (W)
1983—Redskins, 23-13 (P)
Redskins, 28-24 (W)
1984—Redskins, 20-0 (W)
Eagles, 16-10 (P)
1985—Eagles, 19-6 (W)
Redskins, 17-12 (P)
1986—Redskins, 41-14 (W)
Redskins, 21-14 (P)
1987—Redskins, 34-24 (W)
Eagles, 31-27 (P)
1988—Redskins, 17-10 (W)
Redskins, 20-19 (P)
1989—Eagles, 42-37 (W)
Redskins, 10-3 (P)
1990—Redskins, 13-7 (W)
Eagles, 28-14 (P)
**Redskins, 20-6 (P)
(RS Pts.—Eagles 2,243, Redskins 2,205)
(PS Pts.—Redskins 20, Eagles 6)
**Franchise in Boston prior to 1937*
***NFC First Round Playoff*

PHOENIX vs. ATLANTA
RS: Cardinals lead series, 9-4;
See Atlanta vs. Phoenix

PHOENIX vs. BUFFALO
RS: Series tied, 3-3;
See Buffalo vs. Phoenix

PHOENIX vs. CHICAGO
RS: Bears lead series, 51-25-6;
See Chicago vs. Phoenix

PHOENIX vs. CINCINNATI
RS: Bengals lead series, 3-1;
See Cincinnati vs. Phoenix

PHOENIX vs. CLEVELAND
RS: Browns lead series, 31-10-3;
See Cleveland vs. Phoenix

PHOENIX vs. DALLAS
RS: Cowboys lead series, 34-22-1;
See Dallas vs. Phoenix

PHOENIX vs. DENVER
RS: Broncos lead series, 2-0-1;
See Denver vs. Phoenix

PHOENIX vs. DETROIT
RS: Lions lead series, 25-16-5;
See Detroit vs. Phoenix

PHOENIX vs. GREEN BAY
RS: Packers lead series, 39-21-4
PS: Packers lead series, 1-0;
See Green Bay vs. Phoenix

PHOENIX vs. HOUSTON
RS: Cardinals lead series, 3-2;
See Houston vs. Phoenix

PHOENIX vs. INDIANAPOLIS
RS: Cardinals lead series, 6-4;
See Indianapolis vs. Phoenix

PHOENIX vs. KANSAS CITY
RS: Chiefs lead series, 3-1-1;
See Kansas City vs. Phoenix

PHOENIX vs. L.A. RAIDERS
RS: Raiders lead series, 2-1;
See L.A. Raiders vs. Phoenix

PHOENIX vs. L.A. RAMS
RS: Rams lead series, 22-16-2
PS: Rams lead series, 1-0;
See L.A. Rams vs. Phoenix

PHOENIX vs. MIAMI
RS: Dolphins lead series, 6-0;
See Miami vs. Phoenix

PHOENIX vs. MINNESOTA
RS: Cardinals lead series, 7-2
PS: Vikings lead series, 1-0;
See Minnesota vs. Phoenix

PHOENIX vs. NEW ENGLAND
RS: Cardinals lead series, 5-1;
See New England vs. Phoenix

PHOENIX vs. NEW ORLEANS
RS: Cardinals lead series, 10-6;
See New Orleans vs. Phoenix

PHOENIX vs. N.Y. GIANTS
RS: Giants lead series, 61-33-2;
See N.Y. Giants vs. Phoenix

PHOENIX vs. N.Y. JETS
RS: Cardinals lead series, 2-1;
See N.Y. Jets vs. Phoenix

PHOENIX vs. PHILADELPHIA
RS: Cardinals lead series, 42-39-5
PS: Series tied, 1-1;
See Philadelphia vs. Phoenix

***PHOENIX vs. **PITTSBURGH**
RS: Steelers lead series, 29-21-3
1933—Pirates, 14-13 (C)
1935—Pirates, 17-13 (P)
1936—Cardinals, 14-6 (C)
1937—Cardinals, 13-7 (P)
1939—Cardinals, 10-0 (P)
1940—Tie, 7-7 (P)
1942—Steelers, 19-3 (P)
1945—Steelers, 23-0 (P)
1946—Steelers, 14-7 (P)
1948—Cardinals, 24-7 (P)
1950—Steelers, 28-17 (C)
Steelers, 28-7 (P)
1951—Steelers, 28-14 (C)
1952—Steelers, 34-28 (C)
Steelers, 17-14 (P)
1953—Steelers, 31-28 (P)
Steelers, 21-17 (C)
1954—Cardinals, 17-14 (C)
Steelers, 20-17 (P)
1955—Steelers, 14-7 (P)
Cardinals, 27-13 (C)
1956—Steelers, 14-7 (P)
Cardinals, 38-27 (C)
1957—Steelers, 29-20 (P)
Steelers, 27-2 (C)
1958—Steelers, 27-20 (C)
Steelers, 38-21 (P)
1959—Cardinals, 45-24 (C)
Steelers, 35-20 (P)
1960—Steelers, 27-14 (P)
Cardinals, 38-7 (StL)
1961—Steelers, 30-27 (P)
Cardinals, 20-0 (StL)
1962—Steelers, 26-17 (StL)
Steelers, 19-7 (P)
1963—Steelers, 23-10 (P)
Cardinals, 24-23 (StL)
1964—Cardinals, 34-30 (StL)
Cardinals, 21-20 (P)
1965—Cardinals, 20-7 (P)
Cardinals, 21-17 (P)
1966—Steelers, 30-9 (P)
Cardinals, 6-3 (StL)
1967—Cardinals, 28-14 (P)
Tie, 14-14 (StL)
1968—Tie, 28-28 (StL)
Cardinals, 20-10 (P)
1969—Cardinals, 27-14 (P)
Cardinals, 47-10 (StL)
1972—Steelers, 25-19 (StL)
1979—Steelers, 24-21 (StL)
1985—Steelers, 23-10 (P)
1988—Cardinals, 31-14 (Phx)
(RS Pts.—Steelers 1,021, Cardinals 983)
**Franchise in St. Louis prior to 1988 and in Chicago prior to 1960*
***Steelers known as Pirates prior to 1941*

***PHOENIX vs. SAN DIEGO**
RS: Chargers lead series, 4-1
1971—Chargers, 20-17 (SD)
1976—Chargers, 43-24 (SD)
1983—Cardinals, 44-14 (StL)
1987—Chargers, 28-24 (SD)
1989—Chargers, 24-13 (P)
(RS Pts.—Chargers 129, Cardinals 122)
**Franchise in St. Louis prior to 1988*

***PHOENIX vs. SAN FRANCISCO**
RS: Series tied, 8-8
1951—Cardinals, 27-21 (SF)
1957—Cardinals, 20-10 (SF)
1962—49ers, 24-17 (StL)
1964—Cardinals, 23-13 (SF)
1968—49ers, 35-17 (SF)
1971—49ers, 26-14 (StL)
1974—Cardinals, 34-9 (SF)
1976—Cardinals, 23-20 (StL) OT
1978—Cardinals, 16-10 (SF)
1979—Cardinals, 13-10 (StL)
1980—49ers, 24-21 (SF) OT
1982—49ers, 31-20 (StL)
1983—49ers, 42-27 (StL)
1986—49ers, 43-17 (SF)
1987—49ers, 34-28 (SF)
1988—Cardinals, 24-23 (P)
(RS Pts.—49ers 375, Cardinals 341)
**Franchise in St. Louis prior to 1988 and in Chicago prior to 1960*

***PHOENIX vs. SEATTLE**
RS: Cardinals lead series, 3-0
1976—Cardinals, 30-24 (S)
1983—Cardinals, 33-28 (StL)
1989—Cardinals, 34-24 (S)
(RS Pts.—Cardinals 97, Seahawks 76)
**Franchise in St. Louis prior to 1988*

***PHOENIX vs. TAMPA BAY**
RS: Cardinals lead series, 6-4
1977—Buccaneers, 17-7 (TB)
1981—Buccaneers, 20-10 (TB)
1983—Cardinals, 34-27 (TB)
1985—Buccaneers, 16-0 (TB)
1986—Cardinals, 30-19 (TB)
Cardinals, 21-17 (StL)
1987—Cardinals, 31-28 (StL)
Cardinals, 31-14 (TB)
1988—Cardinals, 30-24 (TB)
1989—Buccaneers, 14-13 (P)
(RS Pts.—Cardinals 207, Buccaneers 196)
**Franchise in St. Louis prior to 1988*

***PHOENIX vs. **WASHINGTON**
RS: Redskins lead series, 58-33-2;
1932—Cardinals, 9-0 (B)
Braves, 8-6 (C)
1933—Redskins, 10-0 (C)
Tie, 0-0 (B)
1934—Redskins, 9-0 (B)

1935—Cardinals, 6-0 (B)
1936—Redskins, 13-10 (B)
1937—Cardinals, 21-14 (W)
1939—Redskins, 28-7 (W)
1940—Redskins, 28-21 (W)
1942—Redskins, 28-0 (W)
1943—Redskins, 13-7 (W)
1945—Redskins, 24-21 (W)
1947—Redskins, 45-21 (W)
1949—Cardinals, 38-7 (C)
1950—Cardinals, 38-28 (W)
1951—Redskins, 7-3 (C)
Redskins, 20-17 (W)
1952—Redskins, 23-7 (C)
Cardinals, 17-6 (W)
1953—Redskins, 24-13 (C)
Redskins, 28-17 (W)
1954—Cardinals, 38-16 (C)
Redskins, 37-20 (W)
1955—Cardinals, 24-10 (W)
Redskins, 31-0 (C)
1956—Cardinals, 31-3 (W)
Redskins, 17-14 (C)
1957—Redskins, 37-14 (C)
Cardinals, 44-14 (W)
1958—Cardinals, 37-10 (C)
Redskins, 45-31 (W)
1959—Cardinals, 49-21 (C)
Redskins, 23-14 (W)
1960—Cardinals, 44-7 (StL)
Cardinals, 26-14 (W)
1961—Cardinals, 24-0 (W)
Cardinals, 38-24 (StL)
1962—Redskins, 24-14 (W)
Tie, 17-17 (StL)
1963—Cardinals, 21-7 (W)
Cardinals, 24-20 (StL)
1964—Cardinals, 23-17 (W)
Cardinals, 38-24 (StL)
1965—Cardinals, 37-16 (W)
Redskins, 24-20 (StL)
1966—Cardinals, 23-7 (StL)
Redskins, 26-20 (W)
1967—Cardinals, 27-21 (W)
1968—Cardinals, 41-14 (StL)
1969—Redskins, 33-17 (W)
1970—Cardinals, 27-17 (StL)
Redskins, 28-27 (W)
1971—Redskins, 24-17 (StL)
Redskins, 20-0 (W)
1972—Redskins, 24-10 (W)
Redskins, 33-3 (StL)
1973—Cardinals, 34-27 (StL)
Redskins, 31-13 (W)
1974—Cardinals, 17-10 (W)
Cardinals, 23-20 (StL)
1975—Redskins, 27-17 (W)
Cardinals, 20-17 (StL) OT
1976—Redskins, 20-10 (W)
Redskins, 16-10 (StL)
1977—Redskins, 24-14 (W)
Redskins, 26-20 (StL)
1978—Redskins, 28-10 (StL)
Cardinals, 27-17 (W)
1979—Redskins, 17-7 (StL)
Redskins, 30-28 (W)
1980—Redskins, 23-0 (W)
Redskins, 31-7 (StL)
1981—Cardinals, 40-30 (StL)
Redskins, 42-21 (W)
1982—Redskins, 12-7 (StL)
Redskins, 28-0 (W)
1983—Redskins, 38-14 (StL)
Redskins, 45-7 (W)
1984—Cardinals, 26-24 (StL)
Redskins, 29-27 (W)
1985—Redskins, 27-10 (W)
Redskins, 27-16 (StL)
1986—Redskins, 28-21 (W)
Redskins, 20-17 (StL)
1987—Redskins, 28-21 (W)
Redskins, 34-17 (StL)
1988—Cardinals, 30-21 (P)
Redskins, 33-17 (W)
1989—Redskins, 30-28 (W)
Redskins, 29-10 (P)
1990—Redskins, 31-0 (W)
Redskins, 38-10 (P)
(RS Pts.—Redskins 2,026, Cardinals 1,729)
Franchise in St. Louis prior to 1988 and in Chicago prior to 1960
***Franchise in Boston prior to 1937 and known as Braves prior to 1933*

PITTSBURGH vs. ATLANTA
RS: Steelers lead series, 8-1;
See Atlanta vs. Pittsburgh
PITTSBURGH vs. BUFFALO
RS: Series tied, 5-5
PS: Steelers lead series, 1-0;
See Buffalo vs. Pittsburgh
PITTSBURGH vs. CHICAGO
RS: Bears lead series, 15-4-1;
See Chicago vs. Pittsburgh
PITTSBURGH vs. CINCINNATI
RS: Bengals lead series, 21-20;
See Cincinnati vs. Pittsburgh
PITTSBURGH vs. CLEVELAND
RS: Browns lead series, 49-33;
See Cleveland vs. Pittsburgh
PITTSBURGH vs. DALLAS
RS: Series tied, 11-11
PS: Steelers lead series, 2-0;
See Dallas vs. Pittsburgh
PITTSBURGH vs. DENVER
RS: Broncos lead series, 8-5-1
PS: Series tied, 2-2;
See Denver vs. Pittsburgh
PITTSBURGH vs. DETROIT
RS: Lions lead series, 13-10-1;
See Detroit vs. Pittsburgh
PITTSBURGH vs. GREEN BAY
RS: Packers lead series, 16-11;
See Green Bay vs. Pittsburgh
PITTSBURGH vs. HOUSTON
RS: Steelers lead series, 26-15
PS: Steelers lead series, 3-0;
See Houston vs. Pittsburgh
PITTSBURGH vs. INDIANAPOLIS
RS: Steelers lead series, 8-4
PS: Steelers lead series, 2-0;
See Indianapolis vs. Pittsburgh
PITTSBURGH vs. KANSAS CITY
RS: Steelers lead series, 12-5;
See Kansas City vs. Pittsburgh
PITTSBURGH vs. L.A. RAIDERS
RS: Raiders lead series, 7-3
PS: Series tied, 3-3;
See L.A. Raiders vs. Pittsburgh
PITTSBURGH vs. L.A. RAMS
RS: Rams lead series, 13-4-2
PS: Steelers lead series, 1-0;
See L.A. Rams vs. Pittsburgh
PITTSBURGH vs. MIAMI
RS: Dolphins lead series, 7-4
PS: Dolphins lead series, 2-1;
See Miami vs. Pittsburgh
PITTSBURGH vs. MINNESOTA
RS: Vikings lead series, 6-4
PS: Steelers lead series, 1-0;
See Minnesota vs. Pittsburgh
PITTSBURGH vs. NEW ENGLAND
RS: Steelers lead series, 7-3;
See New England vs. Pittsburgh
PITTSBURGH vs. NEW ORLEANS
RS: Series tied, 5-5;
See New Orleans vs. Pittsburgh
PITTSBURGH vs. N.Y. GIANTS
RS: Giants lead series, 41-26-3;
See N.Y. Giants vs. Pittsburgh
PITTSBURGH vs. N.Y. JETS
RS: Steelers lead series, 11-1;
See N.Y. Jets vs. Pittsburgh
PITTSBURGH vs. PHILADELPHIA
RS: Eagles lead series, 42-25-3
PS: Eagles lead series, 1-0;
See Philadelphia vs. Pittsburgh
PITTSBURGH vs. PHOENIX
RS: Steelers lead series, 29-21-3;
See Phoenix vs. Pittsburgh
PITTSBURGH vs. SAN DIEGO
RS: Steelers lead series, 11-4
PS: Chargers lead series, 1-0
1971—Steelers, 21-17 (P)
1972—Steelers, 24-2 (SD)
1973—Steelers, 38-21 (P)
1975—Steelers, 37-0 (SD)
1976—Steelers, 23-0 (P)
1977—Steelers, 10-9 (SD)
1979—Chargers, 35-7 (SD)
1980—Chargers, 26-17 (SD)
1982—*Chargers, 31-28 (P)
1983—Steelers, 26-3 (P)
1984—Steelers, 52-24 (P)
1985—Chargers, 54-44 (SD)
1987—Steelers, 20-16 (SD)
1988—Chargers, 20-14 (SD)
1989—Steelers, 20-17 (P)
1990—Steelers, 36-14 (P)
(RS Pts.—Steelers 389, Chargers 258)
(PS Pts.—Chargers 31, Steelers 28)
AFC First Round Playoff
PITTSBURGH vs. SAN FRANCISCO
RS: Series tied, 7-7
1951—49ers, 28-24 (P)
1952—Steelers, 24-7 (SF)
1954—49ers, 31-3 (SF)
1958—49ers, 23-20 (SF)
1961—Steelers, 20-10 (P)
1965—49ers, 27-17 (SF)
1968—49ers, 45-28 (P)
1973—Steelers, 37-14 (SF)
1977—Steelers, 27-0 (P)
1978—Steelers, 24-7 (SF)
1981—49ers, 17-14 (P)
1984—Steelers, 20-17 (SF)
1987—Steelers, 30-17 (P)
1990—49ers, 27-7 (SF)
(RS Pts.—Steelers 295, 49ers 270)
PITTSBURGH vs. SEATTLE
RS: Steelers lead series, 4-3
1977—Steelers, 30-20 (P)
1978—Steelers, 21-10 (P)
1981—Seahawks, 24-21 (S)
1982—Seahawks, 16-0 (S)
1983—Steelers, 27-21 (S)
1986—Seahawks, 30-0 (S)
1987—Steelers, 13-9 (P)
(RS Pts.—Seahawks 130, Steelers 112)
PITTSBURGH vs. TAMPA BAY
RS: Steelers lead series, 4-0
1976—Steelers, 42-0 (P)
1980—Steelers, 24-21 (TB)
1983—Steelers, 17-12 (P)
1989—Steelers, 31-22 (TB)
(RS Pts.—Steelers 114, Buccaneers 55)
***PITTSBURGH vs. **WASHINGTON**
RS: Redskins lead series, 41-27-3
1933—Redskins, 21-6 (P)
Pirates, 16-14 (B)
1934—Redskins, 7-0 (P)
Redskins, 39-0 (B)
1935—Pirates, 6-0 (P)
Redskins, 13-3 (B)
1936—Pirates, 10-0 (P)
Redskins, 30-0 (B)
1937—Redskins, 34-20 (W)
Pirates, 21-13 (P)
1938—Redskins, 7-0 (P)
Redskins, 15-0 (W)
1939—Redskins, 44-14 (W)
Redskins, 21-14 (P)
1940—Redskins, 40-10 (P)
Redskins, 37-10 (W)
1941—Redskins, 24-20 (P)
Redskins, 23-3 (W)
1942—Redskins, 28-14 (W)
Redskins, 14-0 (P)
1945—Redskins, 14-0 (P)
Redskins, 24-0 (W)
1946—Tie, 14-14 (W)
Steelers, 14-7 (P)
1947—Redskins, 27-26 (W)
Steelers, 21-14 (P)
1948—Redskins, 17-14 (W)
Steelers, 10-7 (P)
1949—Redskins, 27-14 (P)
Redskins, 27-14 (W)
1950—Steelers, 26-7 (W)
Redskins, 24-7 (P)
1951—Redskins, 22-7 (P)
Steelers, 20-10 (W)
1952—Redskins, 28-24 (P)
Steelers, 24-23 (W)
1953—Redskins, 17-9 (P)
Steelers, 14-13 (W)
1954—Steelers, 37-7 (P)
Redskins, 17-14 (W)
1955—Redskins, 23-14 (P)
Redskins, 28-17 (W)
1956—Steelers, 30-13 (P)
Steelers, 23-0 (W)
1957—Steelers, 28-7 (P)
Redskins, 10-3 (W)
1958—Steelers, 24-16 (P)
Tie, 14-14 (W)
1959—Redskins, 23-17 (P)
Steelers, 27-6 (W)
1960—Tie, 27-27 (W)
Steelers, 22-10 (P)
1961—Steelers, 20-0 (P)
Steelers, 30-14 (P)
1962—Steelers, 23-21 (P)
Steelers, 27-24 (W)
1963—Steelers, 38-27 (P)
Steelers, 34-28 (W)
1964—Redskins, 30-0 (P)
Steelers, 14-7 (W)
1965—Redskins, 31-3 (P)
Redskins, 35-14 (W)
1966—Redskins, 33-27 (P)
Redskins, 24-10 (W)
1967—Redskins, 15-10 (P)
1968—Redskins, 16-13 (W)
1969—Redskins, 14-7 (P)
1973—Steelers, 21-16 (P)
1979—Steelers, 38-7 (P)
1985—Redskins, 30-23 (P)
1988—Redskins, 30-29 (W)
(RS Pts.—Redskins 1,349, Steelers 1,103)
Steelers known as Pirates prior to 1941
***Franchise in Boston prior to 1937*

SAN DIEGO vs. ATLANTA
RS: Falcons lead series, 2-1;
See Atlanta vs. San Diego
SAN DIEGO vs. BUFFALO
RS: Chargers lead series, 16-7-2
PS: Bills lead series, 2-1;
See Buffalo vs. San Diego
SAN DIEGO vs. CHICAGO
RS: Chargers lead series, 4-1;
See Chicago vs. San Diego
SAN DIEGO vs. CINCINNATI
RS: Chargers lead series, 11-8
PS: Bengals lead series, 1-0;
See Cincinnati vs. San Diego
SAN DIEGO vs. CLEVELAND
RS: Chargers lead series, 7-5-1;
See Cleveland vs. San Diego
SAN DIEGO vs. DALLAS
RS: Cowboys lead series, 4-1;
See Dallas vs. San Diego
SAN DIEGO vs. DENVER
RS: Broncos lead series, 31-30-1;
See Denver vs. San Diego
SAN DIEGO vs. DETROIT
RS: Lions lead series, 3-2;
See Detroit vs. San Diego
SAN DIEGO vs. GREEN BAY
RS: Packers lead series, 3-1;
See Green Bay vs. San Diego
SAN DIEGO vs. HOUSTON
RS: Chargers lead series, 17-12-1
PS: Oilers lead series, 3-0;
See Houston vs. San Diego
SAN DIEGO vs. INDIANAPOLIS
RS: Chargers lead series, 6-5;
See Indianapolis vs. San Diego
SAN DIEGO vs. KANSAS CITY
RS: Chargers lead series, 31-29-1;
See Kansas City vs. San Diego
SAN DIEGO vs. L.A. RAIDERS
RS: Raiders lead series, 39-21-2
PS: Raiders lead series, 1-0;
See L.A. Raiders vs. San Diego
SAN DIEGO vs. L.A. RAMS
RS: Series tied, 2-2;
See L.A. Rams vs. San Diego
SAN DIEGO vs. MIAMI
RS: Chargers lead series, 8-5
PS: Series tied, 1-1;
See Miami vs. San Diego
SAN DIEGO vs. MINNESOTA
RS: Series tied, 3-3;
See Minnesota vs. San Diego
SAN DIEGO vs. NEW ENGLAND
RS: Patriots lead series, 13-11-2
PS: Chargers lead series, 1-0;
See New England vs. San Diego
SAN DIEGO vs. NEW ORLEANS
RS: Chargers lead series, 3-1;
See New Orleans vs. San Diego
SAN DIEGO vs. N.Y. GIANTS
RS: Giants lead series, 4-2;
See N.Y. Giants vs. San Diego
SAN DIEGO vs. N.Y. JETS
RS: Chargers lead series, 16-8-1;
See N.Y. Jets vs. San Diego
SAN DIEGO vs. PHILADELPHIA
RS: Chargers lead series, 3-2;
See Philadelphia vs. San Diego
SAN DIEGO vs. PHOENIX
RS: Chargers lead series, 4-1;
See Phoenix vs. San Diego
SAN DIEGO vs. PITTSBURGH
RS: Steelers lead series, 11-4
PS: Chargers lead series, 1-0;
See Pittsburgh vs. San Diego
SAN DIEGO vs. SAN FRANCISCO
RS: Chargers lead series, 3-2
1972—49ers, 34-3 (SF)
1976—Chargers, 13-7 (SD) OT
1979—Chargers, 31-9 (SD)
1982—Chargers, 41-37 (SF)
1988—49ers, 48-10 (SD)
(RS Pts.—49ers 135, Chargers 98)
SAN DIEGO vs. SEATTLE
RS: Seahawks lead series, 13-11
1977—Chargers, 30-28 (S)
1978—Chargers, 24-20 (S)
Chargers, 37-10 (SD)
1979—Chargers, 33-16 (S)
Chargers, 20-10 (SD)
1980—Chargers, 34-13 (S)
Chargers, 21-14 (SD)
1981—Chargers, 24-10 (SD)
Seahawks, 44-23 (S)
1983—Seahawks, 34-31 (S)
Chargers, 28-21 (SD)
1984—Seahawks, 31-17 (S)
Seahawks, 24-0 (SD)
1985—Seahawks, 49-35 (SD)
Seahawks, 26-21 (S)
1986—Seahawks, 33-7 (S)
Seahawks, 34-24 (SD)
1987—Seahawks, 34-3 (S)
1988—Chargers, 17-6 (SD)
Seahawks, 17-14 (S)
1989—Seahawks, 17-16 (SD)
Seahawks, 10-7 (S)
1990—Chargers, 31-14 (S)

Seahawks, 13-10 (SD) OT
(RS Pts.—Seahawks 528, Chargers 507)
SAN DIEGO vs. TAMPA BAY
RS: Chargers lead series, 4-0
1976—Chargers, 23-0 (TB)
1981—Chargers, 24-23 (TB)
1987—Chargers, 17-13 (TB)
1990—Chargers, 41-10 (SD)
(RS Pts.—Chargers 105, Buccaneers 46)
SAN DIEGO vs. WASHINGTON
RS: Redskins lead series, 5-0
1973—Redskins, 38-0 (W)
1980—Redskins, 40-17 (W)
1983—Redskins, 27-24 (SD)
1986—Redskins, 30-27 (SD)
1989—Redskins, 26-21 (W)
(RS Pts.—Redskins 161, Chargers 89)

SAN FRANCISCO vs. ATLANTA
RS: 49ers lead series, 29-18-1;
See Atlanta vs. San Francisco
SAN FRANCISCO vs. BUFFALO
RS: Series tied, 2-2;
See Buffalo vs. San Francisco
SAN FRANCISCO vs. CHICAGO
RS: Bears lead series, 25-24-1
PS: 49ers lead series, 2-0;
See Chicago vs. San Francisco
SAN FRANCISCO vs. CINCINNATI
RS: 49ers lead series, 5-1
PS: 49ers lead series, 2-0;
See Cincinnati vs. San Francisco
SAN FRANCISCO vs. CLEVELAND
RS: Browns lead series, 8-6;
See Cleveland vs. San Francisco
SAN FRANCISCO vs. DALLAS
RS: 49ers lead series, 9-5-1
PS: Cowboys lead series, 3-1;
See Dallas vs. San Francisco
SAN FRANCISCO vs. DENVER
RS: Broncos lead series, 4-2;
PS: 49ers lead series, 1-0;
See Denver vs. San Francisco
SAN FRANCISCO vs. DETROIT
RS: Lions lead series, 25-23-1
PS: Series tied, 1-1;
See Detroit vs. San Francisco
SAN FRANCISCO vs. GREEN BAY
RS: 49ers lead series, 21-21-1;
See Green Bay vs. San Francisco
SAN FRANCISCO vs. HOUSTON
RS: 49ers lead series, 5-2;
See Houston vs. San Francisco
SAN FRANCISCO vs. INDIANAPOLIS
RS: Colts lead series, 21-16;
See Indianapolis vs. San Francisco
SAN FRANCISCO vs. KANSAS CITY
RS: 49ers lead series, 3-1;
See Kansas City vs. San Francisco
SAN FRANCISCO vs. L.A RAIDERS
RS: Raiders lead series, 4-2;
See L.A. Raiders vs. San Francisco
SAN FRANCISCO vs. L.A. RAMS
RS: Rams lead series, 48-32-2
PS: 49ers lead series, 1-0;
See L.A. Rams vs. San Francisco
SAN FRANCISCO vs. MIAMI
RS: Dolphins lead series, 4-1
PS: 49ers lead series, 1-0;
See Miami vs. San Francisco
SAN FRANCISCO vs. MINNESOTA
RS: Vikings lead series, 14-13-1
PS: 49ers lead series, 3-1;
See Minnesota vs. San Francisco
SAN FRANCISCO vs. NEW ENGLAND
RS: 49ers lead series, 5-1;
See New England vs. San Francisco
SAN FRANCISCO vs. NEW ORLEANS
RS: 49ers lead series, 29-12-2;
See New Orleans vs. San Francisco
SAN FRANCISCO vs. N.Y. GIANTS
RS: Giants lead series, 10-9
PS: Giants lead series, 3-2;
See N.Y. Giants vs. San Francisco
SAN FRANCISCO vs. N.Y. JETS
RS: 49ers lead series, 5-1;
See N.Y. Jets vs. San Francisco
SAN FRANCISCO vs. PHILADELPHIA
RS: 49ers lead series, 11-4-1;
See Philadelphia vs. San Francisco
SAN FRANCISCO vs. PHOENIX
RS: Series tied, 8-8;
See Phoenix vs. San Francisco
SAN FRANCISCO vs. PITTSBURGH
RS: Series tied, 7-7;
See Pittsburgh vs. San Francisco
SAN FRANCISCO vs. SAN DIEGO
RS: Chargers lead series, 3-2;
See San Diego vs. San Francisco
SAN FRANCISCO vs. SEATTLE
RS: 49ers lead series, 3-1
1976—49ers, 37-21 (S)
1979—Seahawks, 35-24 (SF)
1985—49ers, 19-6 (SF)
1988—49ers, 38-7 (S)
(RS Pts.—49ers 118, Seahawks 69)
SAN FRANCISCO vs. TAMPA BAY
RS: 49ers lead series, 9-1
1977—49ers, 20-10 (SF)
1978—49ers, 6-3 (SF)
1979—49ers, 23-7 (SF)
1980—Buccaneers, 24-23 (SF)
1983—49ers, 35-21 (SF)
1984—49ers, 24-17 (SF)
1986—49ers, 31-7 (TB)
1987—49ers, 24-10 (TB)
1989—49ers, 20-16 (TB)
1990—49ers, 31-7 (SF)
(RS. Pts.—49ers 237, Buccaneers 122)
SAN FRANCISCO vs. WASHINGTON
RS: 49ers lead series, 9-6-1
PS: 49ers lead series, 2-1
1952—49ers, 23-17 (W)
1954—49ers, 41-7 (SF)
1955—Redskins, 7-0 (W)
1961—49ers, 35-3 (SF)
1967—Redskins, 31-28 (W)
1969—Tie, 17-17 (SF)
1970—49ers, 26-17 (SF)
1971—*49ers, 24-20 (SF)
1973—Redskins, 33-9 (W)
1976—Redskins, 24-21 (SF)
1978—Redskins, 38-20 (W)
1981—49ers, 30-17 (W)
1983—**Redskins, 24-21 (W)
1984—49ers, 37-31 (SF)
1985—49ers, 35-8 (W)
1986—Redskins, 14-6 (W)
1988—49ers, 37-21 (SF)
1990—49ers, 26-13 (SF)
*49ers, 28-10 (SF)
(RS Pts.—49ers 391, Redskins 298)
(PS Pts.—49ers 73, Redskins 54)
**NFC Divisional Playoff*
***NFC Championship*

SEATTLE vs. ATLANTA
RS: Seahawks lead series, 4-0;
See Atlanta vs. Seattle
SEATTLE vs. BUFFALO
RS: Seahawks lead series, 3-1;
See Buffalo vs. Seattle
SEATTLE vs. CHICAGO
RS: Seahawks lead series, 4-2;
See Chicago vs. Seattle
SEATTLE vs. CINCINNATI
RS: Bengals lead series, 5-4
PS: Bengals lead series, 1-0;
See Cincinnati vs. Seattle
SEATTLE vs. CLEVELAND
RS: Seahawks lead series, 8-3;
See Cleveland vs. Seattle
SEATTLE vs. DALLAS
RS: Cowboys lead series, 3-1;
See Dallas vs. Seattle
SEATTLE vs. DENVER
RS: Broncos lead series, 16-11
PS: Seahawks lead series, 1-0;
See Denver vs. Seattle
SEATTLE vs. DETROIT
RS: Seahawks lead series, 4-1;
See Detroit vs. Seattle
SEATTLE vs. GREEN BAY
RS: Series tied, 3-3;
See Green Bay vs. Seattle
SEATTLE vs. HOUSTON
RS: Seahawks lead series, 4-3;
PS: Oilers lead series, 1-0;
See Houston vs. Seattle
SEATTLE vs. INDIANAPOLIS
RS: Colts lead series, 2-0;
See Indianapolis vs. Seattle
SEATTLE vs. KANSAS CITY
RS: Chiefs lead series, 13-12;
See Kansas City vs. Seattle
SEATTLE vs. L.A. RAIDERS
RS: Seahawks lead series, 14-12
PS: Series tied, 1-1;
See L.A. Raiders vs. Seattle
SEATTLE vs. L.A. RAMS
RS: Rams lead series, 4-0;
See L.A. Rams vs. Seattle
SEATTLE vs. MIAMI
RS: Dolphins lead series, 3-1
PS: Series tied, 1-1;
See Miami vs. Seattle
SEATTLE vs. MINNESOTA
RS: Seahawks lead series, 3-2;
See Minnesota vs. Seattle
SEATTLE vs. NEW ENGLAND
RS: Patriots lead series, 6-4;
See New England vs. Seattle
SEATTLE vs. NEW ORLEANS
RS: Series tied, 2-2;
See New Orleans vs. Seattle
SEATTLE vs. N.Y. GIANTS
RS: Giants lead series, 4-2;
See N.Y. Giants vs. Seattle
SEATTLE vs. N.Y. JETS
RS: Seahawks lead series, 7-3;
See N.Y. Jets vs. Seattle
SEATTLE vs. PHILADELPHIA
RS: Eagles lead series, 3-1;
See Philadelphia vs. Seattle
SEATTLE vs. PHOENIX
Cardinals lead series, 3-0;
See Phoenix vs. Seattle
SEATTLE vs. PITTSBURGH
RS: Steelers lead series, 4-3;
See Pittsburgh vs. Seattle
SEATTLE vs. SAN DIEGO
RS: Seahawks lead series, 13-11;
See San Diego vs. Seattle
SEATTLE vs. SAN FRANCISCO
RS: 49ers lead series, 3-1;
See San Francisco vs. Seattle
SEATTLE vs. TAMPA BAY
RS: Seahawks lead series, 2-0
1976—Seahawks, 13-10 (TB)
1977—Seahawks, 30-23 (S)
(RS Pts.—Seahawks 43, Buccaneers 33)
SEATTLE vs. WASHINGTON
RS: Redskins lead series, 4-1
1976—Redskins, 31-7 (W)
1980—Seahawks, 14-0 (W)
1983—Redskins, 27-17 (S)
1986—Redskins, 19-14 (W)
1989—Redskins, 29-0 (S)
(RS Pts.—Redskins 106, Seahawks 52)

TAMPA BAY vs. ATLANTA
RS: Buccaneers lead series, 5-4;
See Atlanta vs. Tampa Bay
TAMPA BAY vs. BUFFALO
RS: Buccaneers lead series, 4-1;
See Buffalo vs. Tampa Bay
TAMPA BAY vs. CHICAGO
RS: Bears lead series, 20-6;
See Chicago vs. Tampa Bay
TAMPA BAY vs. CINCINNATI
RS: Bengals lead series, 3-1;
See Cincinnati vs. Tampa Bay
TAMPA BAY vs. CLEVELAND
RS: Browns lead series, 4-0;
See Cleveland vs. Tampa Bay
TAMPA BAY vs. DALLAS
RS: Cowboys lead series, 6-0
PS: Cowboys lead series, 2-0;
See Dallas vs. Tampa Bay
TAMPA BAY vs. DENVER
RS: Broncos lead series, 2-0;
See Denver vs. Tampa Bay
TAMPA BAY vs. DETROIT
RS: Series tied 13-13;
See Detroit vs. Tampa Bay
TAMPA BAY vs. GREEN BAY
RS: Packers lead series, 12-11-1;
See Green Bay vs. Tampa Bay
TAMPA BAY vs. HOUSTON
RS: Oilers lead series, 3-1;
See Houston vs. Tampa Bay
TAMPA BAY vs. INDIANAPOLIS
RS: Colts lead series, 4-1;
See Indianapolis vs. Tampa Bay
TAMPA BAY vs. KANSAS CITY
RS: Chiefs lead series, 4-2;
See Kansas City vs. Tampa Bay
TAMPA BAY vs. L.A RAIDERS
RS: Raiders lead series, 2-0;
See L.A. Raiders vs. Tampa Bay
TAMPA BAY vs. L.A. RAMS
RS: Rams lead series, 7-2
PS: Rams lead series, 1-0;
See L.A. Rams vs. Tampa Bay
TAMPA BAY vs. MIAMI
RS: Dolphins lead series, 3-1;
See Miami vs. Tampa Bay
TAMPA BAY vs. MINNESOTA
RS: Vikings lead series, 18-8;
See Minnesota vs. Tampa Bay
TAMPA BAY vs. NEW ENGLAND
RS: Patriots lead series, 3-0;
See New England vs. Tampa Bay
TAMPA BAY vs. NEW ORLEANS
RS: Saints lead series, 9-4;
See New Orleans vs. Tampa Bay
TAMPA BAY vs. N.Y. GIANTS
RS: Giants lead series, 6-3;
See N.Y. Giants vs. Tampa Bay
TAMPA BAY vs. N.Y. JETS
RS: Jets lead series, 4-1;
See N.Y. Jets vs. Tampa Bay
TAMPA BAY vs. PHILADELPHIA
RS: Eagles lead series, 3-0
PS: Buccaneers lead series, 1-0;
See Philadelphia vs. Tampa Bay
TAMPA BAY vs. PHOENIX
RS: Cardinals lead series, 6-4;
See Phoenix vs. Tampa Bay
TAMPA BAY vs. PITTSBURGH
RS: Steelers lead series, 4-0;
See Pittsburgh vs. Tampa Bay
TAMPA BAY vs. SAN DIEGO
RS: Chargers lead series, 4-0;
See San Diego vs. Tampa Bay
TAMPA BAY vs. SAN FRANCISCO
RS: 49ers lead series, 9-1;
See San Francisco vs. Tampa Bay
TAMPA BAY vs. SEATTLE
RS: Seahawks lead series, 2-0;
See Seattle vs. Tampa Bay
TAMPA BAY vs. WASHINGTON
RS: Redskins lead series, 3-0
1977—Redskins, 10-0 (TB)
1982—Redskins, 21-13 (TB)
1989—Redskins, 32-28 (W)
(RS Pts.—Redskins 63, Buccaneers 41)

WASHINGTON vs. ATLANTA
RS: Redskins lead series, 10-3-1;
See Atlanta vs. Washington
WASHINGTON vs. BUFFALO
RS: Redskins lead series, 4-2;
See Buffalo vs. Washington
WASHINGTON vs. CHICAGO
RS: Bears lead series, 18-11-1
PS: Redskins lead series, 4-3;
See Chicago vs. Washington
WASHINGTON vs. CINCINNATI
RS: Redskins lead series, 3-2;
See Cincinnati vs. Washington
WASHINGTON vs. CLEVELAND
RS: Browns lead series, 32-8-1;
See Cleveland vs. Washington
WASHINGTON vs. DALLAS
RS: Cowboys lead series, 34-24-2
PS: Redskins lead series, 2-0;
See Dallas vs. Washington
WASHINGTON vs. DENVER
RS: Broncos lead series, 3-2
PS: Redskins lead series, 1-0;
See Denver vs. Washington
WASHINGTON vs. DETROIT
RS: Redskins lead series, 20-8
PS: Redskins lead series, 1-0;
See Detroit vs. Washington
WASHINGTON vs. GREEN BAY
RS: Packers lead series, 13-12-1
PS: Series tied, 1-1;
See Green Bay vs. Washington
WASHINGTON vs. HOUSTON
RS: Oilers lead series, 3-2;
See Houston vs. Washington
WASHINGTON vs. INDIANAPOLIS
RS: Colts lead series, 16-6;
See Indianapolis vs. Washington
WASHINGTON vs. KANSAS CITY
RS: Chiefs lead series, 2-1;
See Kansas City vs. Washington
WASHINGTON vs. L.A. RAIDERS
RS: Raiders lead series, 4-2
PS: Raiders lead series, 1-0;
See L.A. Raiders vs. Washington
WASHINGTON vs. L.A. RAMS
RS: Redskins lead series, 13-4-1
PS: Series tied, 2-2;
See L.A. Rams vs. Washington
WASHINGTON vs. MIAMI
RS: Dolphins lead series, 4-2
PS: Series tied, 1-1;
See Miami vs. Washington
WASHINGTON vs. MINNESOTA
RS: Redskins lead series, 5-3
PS: Series tied, 2-2;
See Minnesota vs. Washington
WASHINGTON vs. NEW ENGLAND
RS: Redskins lead series, 4-1;
See New England vs. Washington
WASHINGTON vs. NEW ORLEANS
RS: Redskins lead series, 11-4;
See New Orleans vs. Washington
WASHINGTON vs. N.Y. GIANTS
RS: Giants lead series, 66-47-3
PS: Series tied, 1-1;
See N.Y. Giants vs. Washington
WASHINGTON vs. N.Y. JETS
RS: Redskins lead series, 4-0;
See N.Y. Jets vs. Washington
WASHINGTON vs. PHILADELPHIA
RS: Redskins lead series, 64-42-5
PS: Redskins lead series, 1-0;
See Philadelphia vs. Washington
WASHINGTON vs. PHOENIX
RS: Redskins lead series, 58-33-2;
See Phoenix vs. Washington
WASHINGTON vs. PITTSBURGH
RS: Redskins lead series, 41-27-3;
See Pittsburgh vs. Washington
WASHINGTON vs. SAN DIEGO
RS: Redskins lead series, 5-0;
See San Diego vs. Washington

WASHINGTON vs. SAN FRANCISCO
RS: 49ers lead series, 9-6-1
PS: 49ers lead series, 2-1;
See San Francisco vs. Washington
WASHINGTON vs. SEATTLE
RS: Redskins lead series, 4-1;
See Seattle vs. Washington
WASHINGTON vs. TAMPA BAY
RS: Redskins lead series, 3-0;
See Tampa Bay vs. Washington

SUPER BOWL SUMMARIES

Results

Season	Date	Winner (Share)	Loser (Share)	Score	Site	Attendance
XXV	1-27-91	N.Y. Giants ($36,000)	Buffalo ($18,000)	20-19	Tampa	73,813
XXIV	1-28-90	San Francisco ($36,000)	Denver ($18,000)	55-10	New Orleans	72,919
XXIII	1-22-89	San Francisco ($36,000)	Cincinnati ($18,000)	20-16	Miami	75,129
XXII	1-31-88	Washington ($36,000)	Denver ($18,000)	42-10	San Diego	73,302
XXI	1-25-87	N.Y. Giants ($36,000)	Denver ($18,000)	39-20	Pasadena	101,063
XX	1-26-86	Chicago ($36,000)	New England ($18,000)	46-10	New Orleans	73,818
XIX	1-20-85	San Francisco ($36,000)	Miami ($18,000)	38-16	Stanford	84,059
XVIII	1-22-84	L.A. Raiders ($36,000)	Washington ($18,000)	38-9	Tampa	72,920
XVII	1-30-83	Washington ($36,000)	Miami ($18,000)	27-17	Pasadena	103,667
XVI	1-24-82	San Francisco ($18,000)	Cincinnati ($9,000)	26-21	Pontiac	81,270
XV	1-25-81	Oakland ($18,000)	Philadelphia ($9,000)	27-10	New Orleans	76,135
XIV	1-20-80	Pittsburgh ($18,000)	Los Angeles ($9,000)	31-19	Pasadena	103,985
XIII	1-21-79	Pittsburgh ($18,000)	Dallas ($9,000)	35-31	Miami	79,484
XII	1-15-78	Dallas ($18,000)	Denver ($9,000)	27-10	New Orleans	75,583
XI	1-9-77	Oakland ($15,000)	Minnesota ($7,500)	32-14	Pasadena	103,438
X	1-18-76	Pittsburgh ($15,000)	Dallas ($7,500)	21-17	Miami	80,187
IX	1-12-75	Pittsburgh ($15,000)	Minnesota ($7,500)	16-6	New Orleans	80,997
VIII	1-13-74	Miami ($15,000)	Minnesota ($7,500)	24-7	Houston	71,882
VII	1-14-73	Miami ($15,000)	Washington ($7,500)	14-7	Los Angeles	90,182
VI	1-16-72	Dallas ($15,000)	Miami ($7,500)	24-3	New Orleans	81,023
V	1-17-71	Baltimore ($15,000)	Dallas ($7,500)	16-13	Miami	79,204
IV	1-11-70	Kansas City ($15,000)	Minnesota ($7,500)	23-7	New Orleans	80,562
III	1-12-69	N.Y. Jets ($15,000)	Baltimore ($7,500)	16-7	Miami	75,389
II	1-14-68	Green Bay ($15,000)	Oakland ($7,500)	33-14	Miami	75,546
I	1-15-67	Green Bay ($15,000)	Kansas City ($7,500)	35-10	Los Angeles	61,946

Super Bowl Composite Standings

	W	L	Pct.	Pts.	OP
Pittsburgh Steelers	4	0	1.000	103	73
San Francisco 49ers	4	0	1.000	163	63
Green Bay Packers	2	0	1.000	68	24
New York Giants	2	0	1.000	59	39
Chicago Bears	1	0	1.000	46	10
New York Jets	1	0	1.000	16	7
Oakland/L.A. Raiders	3	1	.750	111	66
Washington Redskins	2	2	.500	85	79
Baltimore Colts	1	1	.500	23	29
Kansas City Chiefs	1	1	.500	33	42
Dallas Cowboys	2	3	.400	112	85
Miami Dolphins	2	3	.400	74	103
Buffalo Bills	0	1	.000	19	20
Los Angeles Rams	0	1	.000	19	31
New England Patriots	0	1	.000	10	46
Philadelphia Eagles	0	1	.000	10	27
Cincinnati Bengals	0	2	.000	37	46
Denver Broncos	0	4	.000	50	163
Minnesota Vikings	0	4	.000	34	95

Past Super Bowl Most Valuable Players

Super Bowl I — QB Bart Starr, Green Bay
Super Bowl II — QB Bart Starr, Green Bay
Super Bowl III — QB Joe Namath, New York Jets
Super Bowl IV — QB Len Dawson, Kansas City
Super Bowl V — LB Chuck Howley, Dallas
Super Bowl VI — QB Roger Staubach, Dallas
Super Bowl VII — S Jake Scott, Miami
Super Bowl VIII — RB Larry Csonka, Miami
Super Bowl IX — RB Franco Harris, Pittsburgh
Super Bowl X — WR Lynn Swann, Pittsburgh
Super Bowl XI — WR Fred Biletnikoff, Oakland
Super Bowl XII — DT Randy White and DE Harvey Martin, Dallas
Super Bowl XIII — QB Terry Bradshaw, Pittsburgh
Super Bowl XIV — QB Terry Bradshaw, Pittsburgh
Super Bowl XV — QB Jim Plunkett, Oakland
Super Bowl XVI — QB Joe Montana, San Francisco
Super Bowl XVII — RB John Riggins, Washington
Super Bowl XVIII — RB Marcus Allen, Los Angeles Raiders
Super Bowl XIX — QB Joe Montana, San Francisco
Super Bowl XX — DE Richard Dent, Chicago
Super Bowl XXI — QB Phil Simms, New York Giants
Super Bowl XXII — QB Doug Williams, Washington
Super Bowl XXIII — WR Jerry Rice, San Francisco
Super Bowl XXIV — QB Joe Montana, San Francisco
Super Bowl XXV — RB Ottis Anderson, New York Giants

Super Bowl XXV

Tampa Stadium, Tampa, Florida — January 27, 1991

Attendance: 73,813

NEW YORK GIANTS 20, BUFFALO 19—The NFC champion New York Giants won their first Super Bowl title since 1986 with a 20-19 victory over AFC titlist Buffalo. New York, employing its ball-control offense, had possession for 40 minutes, 33 seconds, a Super Bowl record. The Bills, who scored 95 points in their previous two playoff games leading to Super Bowl XXV, had the ball for less than eight minutes in the second half and just 19:27 for the game. Fourteen of New York's 73 plays came on its initial drive of the third quarter which covered 75 yards and consumed a Super Bowl-record 9:29 before running back Ottis Anderson ran one yard for a touchdown. Giants quarterback Jeff Hostetler kept the long drive going by converting three third-down plays—an 11-yard pass to running back David Meggett on third-and-eight, a 14-yard toss to wide receiver Mark Ingram on third-and-13, and a nine-yard pass to Howard Cross on third-and-four—to give New York a 17-12 lead in the third quarter. Buffalo jumped to a 12-3 lead midway through the second quarter before Hostetler completed a 14-yard scoring strike to wide receiver Stephen Baker to close the score to 12-10 at halftime. Buffalo's Thurman Thomas ran 31 yards for a touchdown on the opening play of the fourth quarter to help Buffalo recapture the lead 19-17. Giants kicker Matt Bahr's 21-yard field goal gave the Giants a 20-19 lead, but Buffalo's Scott Norwood had a chance to win the game with seconds remaining before his 47-yard field-goal attempt sailed wide right. Hostetler completed 20 of 32 passes for 222 yards and one touchdown for the game. Wide receiver Mark Ingram caught five passes for 74 yards; tight end Mark Bavaro five for 50. Anderson rushed 21 times for 102 yards and one touchdown to capture the most-valuable-player honors. Thomas totaled 190 scrimmage yards, rushing 15 times for 135 yards and catching five passes for 55 yards.

Buffalo (19)	Offense	N.Y. Giants (20)
James Lofton	WR	Mark Ingram
Will Wolford	LT	John Elliott
Jim Ritcher	LG	William Roberts
Kent Hull	C	Bart Oates
John Davis	RG	Eric Moore
Howard Ballard	RT	Doug Riesenberg
Keith McKeller	TE	Mark Bavaro
Andre Reed	WR/TE	Howard Cross
Jim Kelly	QB	Jeff Hostetler
Al Edwards	WR/TE	Bob Mrosko
Thurman Thomas	RB	Ottis Anderson
	Defense	
Leon Seals	LE/DL	Erik Howard
Jeff Wright	NT/DL	Leonard Marshall
Bruce Smith	RE/LLB	Carl Banks
Cornelius Bennett	LOLB/MLB	Pepper Johnson
Shane Conlan	LILB/RLB	Lawrence Taylor
Ray Bentley	RILB/CB	Reyna Thompson
Darryl Talley	ROLB/CB	Perry Williams
Kirby Jackson	LCB	Mark Collins
Nate Odomes	RCB	Everson Walls
Leonard Smith	SS	Greg Jackson
Mark Kelso	FS	Myron Guyton

Substitutions

Buffalo—Offense: K—Scott Norwood. P—Rick Tuten. QB—Frank Reich. RB—Kenneth Davis, Carwell Gardner, Jamie Mueller, Don Smith. WR—Steve Tasker. TE—Pete Metzelaars, Butch Rolle. C—Adam Lingner. G—Mitch Frerotte, Glenn Parker. Defense: E—Mike Lodish, Mark Pike. NT—Gary Baldinger. LB—Carlton Bailey, Hal Garner. CB—Clifford Hicks, James Williams. S—Dwight Drane, John Hagy. DNP: QB—Gale Gilbert.

N.Y. Giants—Offense: K—Matt Bahr. P—Sean Landeta. RB—Maurice Carthon, David Meggett, Lee Rouson, Lewis Tillman. WR—Stephen Baker, Troy Kyles, Stacy Robinson. C—Brian Williams. G—Bob Kratch. Defense: E—Eric Dorsey, Mike Fox, John Washington. LB—Bobby Abrams, Johnie Cooks, Steve DeOssie, Lawrence McGrew, Gary Reasons. CB—Roger Brown. S—Dave Duerson, David Whitmore. DNP: QB—Matt Cavanaugh.

Officials

Referee—Jerry Seeman. Umpire—Art Demmas. Line Judge: Dick McKenzie. Head Linesman—Sid Semon. Back Judge—Banks Williams. Field Judge—Jack Vaughan. Side Judge—Larry Nemmers. Replay Official—Mark Burns.

Scoring

Buffalo (AFC)	3	9	0	7 — 19
N.Y. Giants (NFC)	3	7	7	3 — 20

NYG—FG Bahr 28
Buff —FG Norwood 23
Buff —D. Smith 1 run (Norwood kick)
Buff —Safety, B. Smith tackled Hostetler in end zone
NYG—Baker 14 pass from Hostetler (Bahr kick)
NYG—Anderson 1 run (Bahr kick)
Buff —Thomas 31 run (Norwood kick)
NYG—FG Bahr 21

Team Statistics

	Buffalo	N.Y. Giants
Total First Downs	18	24
First Downs Rushing	8	10
First Downs Passing	9	13
First Downs Penalty	1	1
Total Net Yardage	371	386
Total Offensive Plays	56	73
Average Gain per Offensive Play	6.6	5.3
Rushes	25	39
Yards Gained Rushing (net)	166	172
Average Yards per Rush	6.6	4.4
Passes Attempted	30	32
Passes Completed	18	20
Had Intercepted	0	0
Tackled Attempting to Pass	1	2
Yards Lost Attempting to Pass	7	8
Yards Gained Passing (net)	205	214
Punts	6	4
Average Distance	38.8	43.8
Punt Returns	0	2
Punt Return Yardage	0	37
Kickoff Returns	6	3
Kickoff Return Yardage	114	48
Interception Return Yardage	0	0
Total Return Yardage	114	85
Fumbles	1	0
Own Fumbles Recovered	1	0
Opponents Fumbles Recovered	0	0
Penalties	6	5
Yards Penalized	35	31
Total Points Scored	19	20
Touchdowns Rushing	2	1
Touchdowns Passing	0	1
Touchdowns Returns	0	0
Extra Points	2	2
Field Goals	1	2
Field Goals Attempted	2	2
Safeties	1	0
Third Down Efficiency	1/8	9/16
Fourth Down Efficiency	0/0	0/1
Time of Possession	19:27	40:33

Individual Statistics

Rushing

Buffalo	No.	Yds.	LG	TD
Thomas	15	135	31t	1
Kelly	6	23	9	0
K. Davis	2	4	3	0
Mueller	1	3	3	0
D. Smith	1	1	1t	1
N.Y. Giants	**No.**	**Yds.**	**LG**	**TD**
Anderson	21	102	24	1
Meggett	9	48	17	0
Carthon	3	12	5	0
Hostetler	6	10	5	0

Passing

Buffalo	Att.	Comp.	Yds.	TD	Int.
Kelly	30	18	212	0	0
Giants	**Att.**	**Comp.**	**Yds.**	**TD**	**Int.**
Hostetler	32	20	222	1	0

Receiving

Buffalo	No.	Yds.	LG	TD
Reed	8	62	20	0
Thomas	5	55	15	0
K. Davis	2	23	19	0
McKeller	2	11	6	0
Lofton	1	61	61	0
N.Y. Giants	**No.**	**Yds.**	**LG**	**TD**
Ingram	5	74	22	0
Bavaro	5	50	19	0
Cross	4	39	13	0
Baker	2	31	17	1
Meggett	2	18	11	0
Anderson	1	7	7	0
Carthon	1	3	3	0

Interceptions

Buffalo	No.	Yds.	LG	TD
None				
N.Y. Giants	**No.**	**Yds.**	**LG**	**TD**
None				

Punting

Buffalo	No.	Avg.	LG	Blk.
Tuten	6	38.8	47	0
N.Y. Giants	**No.**	**Avg.**	**LG**	**Blk.**
Landeta	4	43.8	54	0

Punt Returns

Buffalo	No.	FC	Yds.	LG	TD
Edwards	0	3	0	0	0
N.Y. Giants	**No.**	**FC**	**Yds.**	**LG**	**TD**
Meggett	2	3	37	20	0

Kickoff Returns

Buffalo	No.	Yds.	LG	TD
D. Smith	4	66	24	0
Edwards	2	48	33	0
N.Y. Giants	**No.**	**Yds.**	**LG**	**TD**
Meggett	2	26	16	0
Duerson	1	22	22	0

Super Bowl XXIV

Louisiana Superdome, New Orleans, Louisiana — January 28, 1990
Attendance: 72,919

SAN FRANCISCO 55, DENVER 10—NFC titlist San Francisco won its fourth Super Bowl championship with a 55-10 victory over AFC champion Denver. The 49ers, who also won Super Bowls XVI, XIX, and XXIII, tied the Pittsburgh Steelers for most Super Bowl victories. The Steelers captured Super Bowls IX, X, XIII, and XIV. San Francisco's 55 points broke the previous Super Bowl scoring mark of 46 points by Chicago in Super Bowl XX. San Francisco scored touchdowns on four of its six first-half possessons to hold a 27-3 lead at halftime. The 49ers' first-half scoring drives were lengthy and time-consuming (10 plays for 66 yards, 10 for 54, 14 for 69, and 5 for 59). Interceptions by Michael Walter and Chet Brooks ended the Broncos' first two possessions of the second half. San Francisco quarterback Joe Montana was named the Super Bowl most valuable player for a record third time. Montana completed 22 of 29 passes for 297 yards and a Super Bowl-record five touchdowns (old record: four, Terry Bradshaw, Pittsburgh, Super Bowl XIII, and Doug Williams, Washington, Super Bowl XXII). Jerry Rice, Super Bowl XXIII most valuable player, caught seven passes for 148 yards and three touchdowns. The 49ers' domination included first downs (28 to 12), net yards (461 to 167), and time of possession (39:31 to 20:29).

Scoring

San Francisco (NFC)	13	14	14	14 — 55
Denver (AFC)	3	0	7	0 — 10

SF —Rice 20 pass from Montana (Cofer kick)
Den—FG Treadwell 42
SF —Jones 7 pass from Montana (kick failed)
SF —Rathman 1 run (Cofer kick)
SF —Rice 38 pass from Montana (Cofer kick)
SF —Rice 28 pass from Montana (Cofer kick)
SF —Taylor 35 pass from Montana (Cofer kick)
Den—Elway 3 run (Treadwell kick)
SF —Rathman 3 run (Cofer kick)
SF —Craig 1 run (Cofer kick)

Super Bowl XXIII

Joe Robbie Stadium, Miami, Florida — January 22, 1989
Attendance: 75,129

SAN FRANCISCO 20, CINCINNATI 16—NFC champion San Francisco captured its third Super Bowl of the 1980s by defeating AFC champion Cincinnati 20-16. The 49ers, who also won Super Bowls XVI and XIX, are the first NFC team to win three Super Bowls. Pittsburgh with four Super Bowl titles (IX, X, XIII, and XIV) and the Oakland/Los Angeles Raiders with three (XI, XV, and XVIII) lead AFC franchises. Even though San Francisco held an advantage in total net yards (453 to 229), the 49ers found themselves trailing the Bengals late in the game. With the score tied 13-13, Cincinnati took a 16-13 lead on Jim Breech's 40-yard field goal with 3:20 remaining. It was Breech's third field goal of the day and came after successful earlier attempts of 34 and 43 yards. The 49ers started their winning drive at their own 8-yard line. Over the next 11 plays, San Francisco covered 92 yards with the decisive score coming on a 10-yard pass from quarterback Joe Montana to wide receiver John Taylor with 34 seconds remaining. At halftime, the score was 3-3, which represented the first time in Super Bowl history the game was tied at intermission. After the teams traded third-period field goals, the Bengals jumped ahead 13-6 on Stanford Jennings's 93-yard kickoff return for a touchdown with 34 seconds remaining in the quarter. The 49ers didn't waste any time coming back as they covered 85 yards in four plays, concluding with Montana's 14-yard scoring pass to Rice 57 seconds into the final stanza. Rice was named the game's most valuable player after compiling 11 catches for a Super Bowl-record 215 yards. Montana completed 23 of 36 passes for a Super Bowl-record 357 yards and two touchdowns.

Scoring

Cincinnati (AFC)	0	3	10	3 — 16
San Francisco (NFC)	3	0	3	14 — 20

SF —FG Cofer 41
Cin—FG Breech 34
Cin—FG Breech 43
SF —FG Cofer 32
Cin—Jennings 93 kickoff return (Breech kick)
SF —Rice 14 pass from Montana (Cofer kick)
Cin—FG Breech 40
SF —Taylor 10 pass from Montana (Cofer kick)

Super Bowl XXII

San Diego Jack Murphy Stadium, San Diego, California January 31, 1988
Attendance: 73,302

WASHINGTON 42, DENVER 10—NFC champion Washington won Super Bowl XXII and its second NFL championship of the 1980s with a 42-10 decision over AFC champion Denver. The Redskins, who also won Super Bowl XVII, enjoyed a record-setting second quarter en route to the victory. The Broncos broke in front 10-0 when quarterback John Elway threw a 56-yard touchdown pass to wide receiver Ricky Nattiel on the Broncos' first play from scrimmage. Following a Washington punt, Denver's Rich Karlis kicked a 24-yard field goal to cap a seven-play, 61-yard scoring drive. The Redskins then erupted for 35 points on five straight possessions in the second period and coasted thereafter. The 35 points established an NFL postseason mark for most points scored in a period, bettering the previous total of 21 by San Francisco in Super Bowl XIX and Chicago in Super Bowl XX. Redskins quarterback Doug Williams led the second-period explosion by throwing a Super Bowl record-tying four touchdown passes, including 80- and 50-yarders to wide receiver Ricky Sanders, a 27-yarder to wide receiver Gary Clark, and an 8-yarder to tight end Clint Didier. Washington scored five touchdowns in 18 plays with total time of possession of only 5:47. Overall, Williams completed 18 of 29 passes for 340 yards and was named the game's most valuable player. His pass-yardage total eclipsed the previous Super Bowl record of 331 yards by Joe Montana of San Francisco in Super Bowl XIX. Sanders ended with 193 yards on eight catches, breaking the previous Super Bowl yardage record of 161 yards by Lynn Swann of Pittsburgh in Game X. Rookie running back Timmy Smith was the game's leading rusher with 22 carries for a Super Bowl-record 204 yards, breaking the previous mark of 191 yards by Marcus Allen of the Raiders in Game XVIII. Smith also scored twice on runs of 58 and four yards. Washington's six touchdowns and 602 total yards gained also set Super Bowl records. Redskins cornerback Barry Wilburn had two of the team's three interceptions, and strong safety Alvin Walton had two of Washington's five sacks.

Washington (NFC)	0	35	0	7	— 42
Denver (AFC)	10	0	0	0	— 10

Den —Nattiel 56 pass from Elway (Karlis kick)
Den —FG Karlis 24
Wash—Sanders 80 pass from Williams (Haji-Sheikh kick)
Wash—Clark 27 pass from Williams (Haji-Sheikh kick)
Wash—Smith 58 run (Haji-Sheikh kick)
Wash—Sanders 50 pass from Williams (Haji-Sheikh kick)
Wash—Didier 8 pass from Williams (Haji-Sheikh kick)
Wash—Smith 4 run (Haji-Sheikh kick)

Super Bowl XXI

Rose Bowl, Pasadena, California January 25, 1987
Attendance: 101,063

NEW YORK GIANTS 39, DENVER 20—The NFC champion New York Giants captured their first NFL title since 1956 when they downed the AFC champion Denver Broncos 39-20, in Super Bowl XXI. The victory marked the NFC's fifth NFL title in the past six seasons. The Broncos, behind the passing of quarterback John Elway, who was 13 of 20 for 187 yards in the first half, held a 10-9 lead at intermission, the narrowest halftime margin in Super Bowl history. Denver's Rich Karlis opened the scoring with a Super Bowl record-tying 48-yard field goal. New York drove 78 yards in nine plays on the next series to take a 7-3 lead on quarterback Phil Simms's six-yard touchdown pass to tight end Zeke Mowatt. The Broncos came right back with a 58-yard scoring drive on six plays capped by Elway's four-yard touchdown run. The only scoring in the second period was the sack of Elway in the end zone by defensive end George Martin for a New York safety. The Giants produced a key defensive stand early in the second quarter when the Broncos had a first down at the New York one-yard line, but failed to score on three running plays and Karlis's 23-yard missed field-goal attempt. The Giants took command of the game in the third period en route to a 30-point second half, the most ever scored in one half of Super Bowl play. New York took the lead for good on tight end Mark Bavaro's 13-yard touchdown catch 4:52 into the third period. The nine-play, 63-yard scoring drive included the successful conversion of a fourth down and one play on the New York 46-yard line. Denver was limited to only two net yards on 10 offensive plays in the third period. Simms set Super Bowl records for most consecutive completions (10) and highest completion percentage (88 percent on 22 completions in 25 attempts). He also passed for 268 yards and three touchdowns and was named the game's most valuable player. New York running back Joe Morris was the game's leading rusher with 20 carries for 67 yards. Denver wide receiver Vance Johnson led all receivers with five catches for 121 yards. The Giants defeated their three playoff opponents by a cumulative total of 82 points (New York 105, opponents 23), the largest such margin by a Super Bowl winner.

Denver (AFC)	10	0	0	10	— 20
N.Y. Giants (NFC)	7	2	17	13	— 39

Den —FG Karlis 48
NYG—Mowatt 6 pass from Simms (Allegre kick)
Den —Elway 4 run (Karlis kick)
NYG—Safety, Martin tackled Elway in end zone
NYG—Bavaro 13 pass from Simms (Allegre kick)
NYG—FG Allegre 21
NYG—Morris 1 run (Allegre kick)
NYG—McConkey 6 pass from Simms (Allegre kick)
Den —FG Karlis 28
NYG—Anderson 2 run (kick failed)
Den —V. Johnson 47 pass from Elway (Karlis kick)

Super Bowl XX

Louisiana Superdome, New Orleans, Louisiana January 26, 1986
Attendance: 73,818

CHICAGO 46, NEW ENGLAND 10—The NFC champion Chicago Bears, seeking their first NFL title since 1963, scored a Super Bowl-record 46 points in downing AFC champion New England 46-10 in Super Bowl XX. The previous record for most points in a Super Bowl was 38, shared by San Francisco in XIX and the Los Angeles Raiders in XVIII. The Bears' league-leading defense tied the Super Bowl record for sacks (seven) and limited the Patriots to a record-low seven yards rushing. New England took the quickest lead in Super Bowl history when Tony Franklin kicked a 36-yard field goal with 1:19 elapsed in the first period. The score came about because of Larry McGrew's fumble recovery at the Chicago 19-yard line. However, the Bears rebounded for a 23-3 first-half lead, while building a yardage advantage of 236 total yards to New England's minus 19. Running back Matt Suhey rushed eight times for 37 yards, including an 11-yard touchdown run, and caught one pass for 24 yards in the first half. After the Patriots first drive of the second half ended with a punt to the Bears' 4-yard line, Chicago marched 96 yards in nine plays with quarterback Jim McMahon's one-yard scoring run capping the drive. McMahon became the first quarterback in Super Bowl history to rush for a pair of touchdowns. The Bears completed their scoring via a 28-yard interception return by reserve cornerback Reggie Phillips, a one-yard run by defensive tackle/fullback William Perry, and a safety when defensive end Henry Waechter tackled Patriots quarterback Steve Grogan in the end zone. Bears defensive end Richard Dent became the fourth defender to be named the game's most valuable player after contributing 1½ sacks. The Bears' victory margin of 36 points was the largest in Super Bowl history, bettering the previous mark of 29 by the Los Angeles Raiders when they topped Washington 38-9 in Game XVIII. McMahon completed 12 of 20 passes for 256 yards before leaving the game in the fourth period with a wrist injury. The NFL's all-time leading rusher, Bears running back Walter Payton, carried 22 times for 61 yards. Wide receiver Willie Gault caught four passes for 129 yards, the fourth-most receiving yards in a Super Bowl. Chicago coach Mike Ditka became the second man (Tom Flores of Raiders was the other) who played in a Super Bowl and coached a team to a victory in the game.

Chicago (NFC)	13	10	21	2	— 46
New England (AFC)	3	0	0	7	— 10

NE—FG Franklin 36
Chi—FG Butler 28
Chi—FG Butler 24
Chi—Suhey 11 run (Butler kick)
Chi—McMahon 2 run (Butler kick)
Chi—FG Butler 24
Chi—McMahon 1 run (Butler kick)
Chi—Phillips 28 interception return (Butler kick)
Chi—Perry 1 run (Butler kick)
NE—Fryar 8 pass from Grogan (Franklin kick)
Chi—Safety, Waechter tackled Grogan in end zone

Super Bowl XIX

Stanford Stadium, Stanford, California January 20, 1985
Attendance: 84,059

SAN FRANCISCO 38, MIAMI 16—The San Francisco 49ers captured their second Super Bowl title with a dominating offense and a defense that tamed Miami's explosive passing attack. The Dolphins held a 10-7 lead at the end of the first period, which represented the most points scored by two teams in an opening quarter of a Super Bowl. However, the 49ers used excellent field position in the second period to build a 28-16 halftime lead. Running back Roger Craig set a Super Bowl record by scoring three touchdowns on pass receptions of 8 and 16 yards and a run of 2 yards. San Francisco's Joe Montana was voted the game's most valuable player. He joined Green Bay's Bart Starr and Pittsburgh's Terry Bradshaw as the only two-time Super Bowl most valuable players. Montana completed 24 of 35 passes for a Super Bowl-record 331 yards and three touchdowns, and rushed five times for 59 yards, including a six-yard touchdown. Craig had 58 yards on 15 carries and caught seven passes for 77 yards. Wendell Tyler rushed 13 times for 65 yards and had four catches for 70 yards. Dwight Clark had six receptions for 77 yards, while Russ Francis had five for 60. San Francisco's 537 total net yards bettered the previous Super Bowl record of 429 yards by Oakland in Super Bowl XI. The 49ers also held a time of possession advantage over the Dolphins of 37:11 to 22:49.

Miami (AFC)	10	6	0	0	— 16
San Francisco (NFC)	7	21	10	0	— 38

Mia—FG von Schamann 37
SF —Monroe 33 pass from Montana (Wersching kick)
Mia—D. Johnson 2 pass from Marino (von Schamann kick)
SF —Craig 8 pass from Montana (Wersching kick)
SF —Montana 6 run (Wersching kick)
SF —Craig 2 run (Wersching kick)
Mia—FG von Schamann 31
Mia—FG von Schamann 30
SF —FG Wersching 27
SF —Craig 16 pass from Montana (Wersching kick)

Super Bowl XVIII

Tampa Stadium, Tampa, Florida January 22, 1984
Attendance: 72,920

LOS ANGELES RAIDERS 38, WASHINGTON 9—The Los Angeles Raiders dominated the Washington Redskins from the beginning in Super Bowl XVIII and achieved the most lopsided victory in Super Bowl history, surpassing Green Bay's 35-10 win over Kansas City in Super Bowl I. The Raiders took a 7-0 lead 4:52 into the game when Derrick Jensen blocked a Jeff Hayes punt and recovered it in the end zone for a touchdown. With 9:14 remaining in the first half, Raiders quarterback Jim Plunkett threw a 12-yard touchdown pass to wide receiver Cliff Branch to complete a three-play, 65-yard drive. Washington cut the Raiders' lead to 14-3 on a 24-yard field goal by Mark Moseley. With seven seconds left in the first half, Raiders linebacker Jack Squirek intercepted a Joe Theismann pass at the Redskins' 5-yard line and ran it in for a touchdown to give Los Angeles a 21-3 halftime lead. In the third period, running back Marcus Allen, who rushed for a Super Bowl record 191 yards on 20 carries, increased the Raiders' lead to 35-3 on touchdown runs of five and 74 yards, the latter erasing the previous Super Bowl record of 58 yards set by Baltimore's Tom Matte in Game III. Allen was named the game's most valuable player. The victory over Washington raised Raiders coach Tom Flores' playoff record to 8-1, including a 27-10 win against Philadelphia in Super Bowl XV. The 38 points scored by the Raiders were the highest total by a Super Bowl team. The previous high was 35 points by Green Bay in Game I.

Washington (NFC)	0	3	6	0	— 9
L.A. Raiders (AFC)	7	14	14	3	— 38

Raiders—Jensen recovered blocked punt in end zone (Bahr kick)
Raiders—Branch 12 pass from Plunkett (Bahr kick)
Wash —FG Moseley 24
Raiders—Squirek 5 interception return (Bahr kick)
Wash —Riggins 1 run (kick blocked)
Raiders—Allen 5 run (Bahr kick)
Raiders—Allen 74 run (Bahr kick)
Raiders—FG Bahr 21

Super Bowl XVII

Rose Bowl, Pasadena, California January 30, 1983
Attendance: 103,667

WASHINGTON 27, MIAMI 17—Fullback John Riggins's Super Bowl-record 166 yards on 38 carries sparked Washington to a 27-17 victory over AFC champion Miami. It was Riggins's fourth straight 100-yard rushing game during the playoffs, also a record. The win marked Washington's first NFL title since 1942, and was only the second time in Super Bowl history NFL/NFC teams scored consecutive victories (Green Bay did it in Super Bowls I and II and San Francisco won Super Bowl XVI). The Redskins, under second-year head coach Joe Gibbs, used a balanced offense that accounted for 400 total yards (a Super Bowl-record 276 yards rushing and 124 passing), second in Super Bowl history to 429 yards by Oakland in Super Bowl XI. The Dolphins built a 17-10 halftime lead on a 76-yard touchdown pass from quarterback David Woodley to wide receiver Jimmy Cefalo 6:49 into the first period, a 20-yard field goal by Uwe von Schamann with 6:00 left in the half, and a Super Bowl-record 98-yard kickoff return by Fulton Walker with 1:38 remaining. Washington had tied the score at 10-10 with 1:51 left on a four-yard touchdown pass from Joe Theismann to wide receiver Alvin Garrett. Mark Moseley started the Redskins' scoring with a 31-yard field goal late in the first period, and added a 20-yarder midway through the third period to cut the Dolphins' lead to 17-13. Riggins, who was voted the game's most valuable player, gave Washington its first lead of the game with 10:01 left when he ran 43 yards off left tackle for a touchdown on a fourth-and-one situation. Wide receiver Charlie Brown caught a six-yard scoring pass from Theismann with 1:55 left to complete the scoring. The Dolphins managed only 176 yards (142 in first half). Theismann completed 15 of 23 passes for 143 yards, with two touchdowns and two interceptions. For Miami, Woodley was 4 of 14 for 97 yards, with one touchdown, and one interception. Don Strock was 0 for 3 in relief.

Miami (AFC)	7	10	0	0	— 17
Washington (NFC)	0	10	3	14	— 27

Mia —Cefalo 76 pass from Woodley (von Schamann kick)
Wash—FG Moseley 31
Mia —FG von Schamann 20
Wash—Garrett 4 pass from Theismann (Moseley kick)
Mia —Walker 98 kickoff return (von Schamann kick)
Wash—FG Moseley 20
Wash—Riggins 43 run (Moseley kick)
Wash—Brown 6 pass from Theismann (Moseley kick)

Super Bowl XVI

Pontiac Silverdome, Pontiac, Michigan January 24, 1982
Attendance: 81,270

SAN FRANCISCO 26, CINCINNATI 21—Ray Wersching's Super Bowl record-tying four field goals and Joe Montana's controlled passing helped lift the San Francisco 49ers to their first NFL championship with a 26-21 victory over Cincinnati. The 49ers built a game-record 20-0 halftime lead via Montana's one-yard touchdown run, which capped an 11-play, 68-yard drive; fullback Earl Cooper's 11-yard scoring pass from Montana, which climaxed a Super Bowl record 92-yard drive on 12 plays; and Wersching's 22- and 26-yard field goals. The Bengals rebounded in the second half, closing the gap to 20-14 on quarterback Ken Anderson's five-yard run and Dan Ross's four-yard reception from Anderson, who established Super Bowl passing records for completions (25) and completion percentage (73.5 percent on 25 of 34). Wersching added early fourth-period field goals of 40 and 23 yards to increase the 49ers' lead to 26-14. The Bengals managed to score on an Anderson-to-Ross three-yard pass with only 16 seconds remaining. Ross set a Super Bowl record with 11 receptions for 104 yards. Montana, the game's most valuable player, completed 14 of 22 passes for 157 yards. Cincinnati compiled 356 yards to San Francisco's 275, which marked the first time in Super Bowl history that the team that gained the most yards from scrimmage lost the game.

San Francisco (NFC)	7	13	0	6	— 26
Cincinnati (AFC)	0	0	7	14	— 21

SF —Montana 1 run (Wersching kick)
SF —Cooper 11 pass from Montana (Wersching kick)
SF —FG Wersching 22
SF —FG Wersching 26
Cin—Anderson 5 run (Breech kick)
Cin—Ross 4 pass from Anderson (Breech kick)
SF —FG Wersching 40
SF —FG Wersching 23
Cin—Ross 3 pass from Anderson (Breech kick)

Super Bowl XV

Louisiana Superdome, New Orleans, Louisiana January 25, 1981
Attendance: 76,135

OAKLAND 27, PHILADELPHIA 10—Jim Plunkett threw three touchdown passes, including an 80-yarder to Kenny King, as the Raiders became the first wild-card team to win the Super Bowl. Plunkett's touchdown bomb to King—the longest play in Super Bowl history—gave Oakland a decisive 14-0 lead with nine seconds left in the first period. Linebacker Rod Martin had set up Oakland's first touchdown, a two-yard reception by Cliff Branch, with a 16-yard interception return to the Eagles' 32 yard line. The Eagles never recovered from that early deficit, managing only a Tony Franklin field goal (30 yards) and an eight-yard touchdown pass from Ron Jaworski to Keith Krepfle the rest of the game. Plunkett, who became a starter in the sixth game of the season, completed 13 of 21 for 261 yards and was named the game's most valuable player. Oakland won nine of 11 games with Plunkett starting, but that was good enough only for second place in the AFC West, although they tied division winner San Diego with an 11-5 record. The Raiders, who had previously won Super Bowl XI over Minnesota, had to win three playoff games to get to the championship game. Oakland defeated Houston 27-7 at home followed by road victories over Cleveland, 14-12 and San Diego, 34-27. Oakland's Mark van Eeghen was the game's leading rusher with 75 yards on 18 carries. Philadelphia's Wilbert Montgomery led all receivers with six receptions for 91 yards. Branch had five for 67 and Harold Carmichael of Philadelphia five for 83. Martin finished the game with three interceptions, a Super Bowl record.

Oakland (AFC)	14	0	10	3	— 27
Philadelphia (NFC)	0	3	0	7	— 10

Oak—Branch 2 pass from Plunkett (Bahr kick)
Oak—King 80 pass from Plunkett (Bahr kick)
Phil —FG Franklin 30
Oak—Branch 29 pass from Plunkett (Bahr kick)
Oak—FG Bahr 46
Phil —Krepfle 8 pass from Jaworski (Franklin kick)
Oak—FG Bahr 35

Super Bowl XIV

Rose Bowl, Pasadena, California January 20, 1980
Attendance: 103,985

PITTSBURGH 31, LOS ANGELES 19—Terry Bradshaw completed 14 of 21 passes for 309 yards and set two passing records as the Steelers became the first team to win four Super Bowls. Despite three interceptions by the Rams, Bradshaw kept his poise and brought the Steelers from behind twice in the second half. Trailing 13-10 at halftime, Pittsburgh went ahead 17-13 when Bradshaw hit Lynn Swann with a 47-yard touchdown pass after 2:48 of the third quarter. On the Rams' next possession Vince Ferragamo, who completed 15 of 25 passes for 212 yards, responded with a 50-yard pass to Billy Waddy that moved Los Angeles from its own 26 to the Steelers' 24. On the following play, Lawrence McCutcheon connected with Ron Smith on a halfback option pass that gave the Rams a 19-17 lead. On Pittsburgh's initial possession of the final period, Bradshaw lofted a 73-yard scoring pass to John Stallworth to put the Steelers in front to stay, 24-19. Franco Harris scored on a one-yard run later in the quarter to seal the verdict. A 45-yard pass from Bradshaw to Stallworth was the key play in the drive to Harris's score. Bradshaw, the game's most valuable player for the second straight year, set career Super Bowl records for most touchdown passes (nine) and most passing yards (932). Larry Anderson gave the Steelers excellent field position throughout the game with five kickoff returns for a record 162 yards.

Los Angeles (NFC)	7	6	6	0	— 19
Pittsburgh (AFC)	3	7	7	14	— 31

Pitt—FG Bahr 41
LA—Bryant 1 run (Corral kick)
Pitt—Harris 1 run (Bahr kick)
LA—FG Corral 31
LA—FG Corral 45
Pitt—Swann 47 pass from Bradshaw (Bahr kick)
LA—Smith 24 pass from McCutcheon (kick failed)
Pitt—Stallworth 73 pass from Bradshaw (Bahr kick)
Pitt—Harris 1 run (Bahr kick)

Super Bowl XIII

Orange Bowl, Miami, Florida January 21, 1979
Attendance: 79,484

PITTSBURGH 35, DALLAS 31—Terry Bradshaw threw a record four touchdown passes to lead the Steelers to victory. The Steelers became the first team to win three Super Bowls, mostly because of Bradshaw's accurate arm. Bradshaw, voted the game's most valuable player, completed 17 of 30 passes for 318 yards, a personal high. Four of those passes went for touchdowns—two to John Stallworth and the third, with 26 seconds remaining in the second period, to Rocky Bleier for a 21-14 halftime lead. The Cowboys scored twice before intermission on Roger Staubach's 39-yard pass to Tony Hill and a 37-yard fumble return by linebacker Mike Hegman, who stole the ball from Bradshaw. The Steelers broke open the contest with two touchdowns in a span of 19 seconds midway through the final period. Franco Harris rambled 22 yards up the middle to give the Steelers a 28-17 lead with 7:10 left. Pittsburgh got the ball right back when Randy White fumbled the kickoff and Dennis Winston recovered for the Steelers. On first down, Bradshaw fired his fourth touchdown pass, an 18-yarder to Lynn Swann to boost the Steelers' lead to 35-17 with 6:51 to play. The Cowboys refused to let the Steelers run away with the contest. Staubach connected with Billy Joe DuPree on a seven-yard scoring pass with 2:23 left. Then the Cowboys recovered an onside kick and Staubach took them in for another score, passing four yards to Butch Johnson with 22 seconds remaining. Bleier recovered another onside kick with 17 seconds left to seal the victory for the Steelers.

Pittsburgh (AFC)	7	14	0	14	— 35
Dallas (NFC)	7	7	3	14	— 31

Pitt —Stallworth 28 pass from Bradshaw (Gerela kick)
Dall—Hill 39 pass from Staubach (Septien kick)
Dall—Hegman 37 fumble recovery return (Septien kick)
Pitt —Stallworth 75 pass from Bradshaw (Gerela kick)
Pitt —Bleier 7 pass from Bradshaw (Gerela kick)
Dall—FG Septien 27
Pitt —Harris 22 run (Gerela kick)
Pitt —Swann 18 pass from Bradshaw (Gerela kick)
Dall—DuPree 7 pass from Staubach (Septien kick)
Dall—B. Johnson 4 pass from Staubach (Septien kick)

Super Bowl XII

Louisiana Superdome, New Orleans, Louisiana — January 15, 1978
Attendance: 75,583

DALLAS 27, DENVER 10—The Cowboys evened their Super Bowl record at 2-2 by defeating Denver before a sellout crowd of 75,583, plus 102,010,000 television viewers, the largest audience ever to watch a sporting event. Dallas converted two interceptions into 10 points and Efren Herrera added a 35-yard field goal for a 13-0 halftime advantage. In the third period Craig Morton engineered a drive to the Cowboys' 30 and Jim Turner's 47-yard field goal made the score 13-3. After an exchange of punts, Butch Johnson made a spectacular diving catch in the end zone to complete a 45-yard pass from Roger Staubach and put the Cowboys ahead 20-3. Following Rick Upchurch's 67-yard kickoff return, Norris Weese guided the Broncos to a touchdown to cut the Dallas lead to 20-10. Dallas clinched the victory when running back Robert Newhouse threw a 29-yard touchdown pass to Golden Richards with 7:04 remaining in the game. It was the first pass thrown by Newhouse since 1975. Harvey Martin and Randy White, who were named co-most valuable players, led the Cowboys' defense, which recovered four fumbles and intercepted four passes.

Dallas (NFC)	10	3	7	7	— 27
Denver (AFC)	0	0	10	0	— 10

Dall—Dorsett 3 run (Herrera kick)
Dall—FG Herrera 35
Dall—FG Herrera 43
Den—FG Turner 47
Dall—Johnson 45 pass from Staubach (Herrera kick)
Den—Lytle 1 run (Turner kick)
Dall—Richards 29 pass from Newhouse (Herrera kick)

Super Bowl XI

Rose Bowl, Pasadena, California — January 9, 1977
Attendance: 103,438

OAKLAND 32, MINNESOTA 14—The Raiders won their first NFL championship before a record Super Bowl crowd plus 81 million television viewers, the largest audience ever to watch a sporting event. The Raiders gained a record-breaking 429 yards, including running back Clarence Davis's 137 yards rushing. Wide receiver Fred Biletnikoff made four key receptions, which earned him the game's most valuable player trophy. Oakland scored on three successive possessions in the second quarter to build a 16-0 halftime lead. Errol Mann's 24-yard field goal opened the scoring, then the AFC champions put together drives of 64 and 35 yards, scoring on a one-yard pass from Ken Stabler to Dave Casper and a one-yard run by Pete Banaszak. The Raiders increased their lead to 19-0 on a 40-yard field goal in the third quarter, but Minnesota responded with a 12-play, 58-yard drive late in the period, with Fran Tarkenton passing eight yards to wide receiver Sammy White to cut the deficit to 19-7. Two fourth-quarter interceptions clinched the title for the Raiders. One set up Banaszak's second touchdown run, the other resulted in cornerback Willie Brown's Super Bowl-record 75-yard interception return.

Oakland (AFC)	0	16	3	13	— 32
Minnesota (NFC)	0	0	7	7	— 14

Oak —FG Mann 24
Oak —Casper 1 pass from Stabler (Mann kick)
Oak —Banaszak 1 run (kick failed)
Oak —FG Mann 40
Minn—S. White 8 pass from Tarkenton (Cox kick)
Oak —Banaszak 2 run (Mann kick)
Oak —Brown 75 interception return (kick failed)
Minn—Voigt 13 pass from Lee (Cox kick)

Super Bowl X

Orange Bowl, Miami, Florida — January 18, 1976
Attendance: 80,187

PITTSBURGH 21, DALLAS 17—The Steelers won the Super Bowl for the second year in a row on Terry Bradshaw's 64-yard touchdown pass to Lynn Swann and an aggressive defense that snuffed out a late rally by the Cowboys with an end-zone interception on the final play of the game. In the fourth quarter, Pittsburgh ran on fourth down and gave up the ball on the Cowboys' 39 with 1:22 to play. Roger Staubach ran and passed for two first downs but his last desperation pass was picked off by Glen Edwards. Dallas's scoring was the result of two touchdown passes by Staubach, one to Drew Pearson for 29 yards and the other to Percy Howard for 34 yards. Toni Fritsch had a 36-yard field goal. The Steelers scored on two touchdown passes by Bradshaw, one to Randy Grossman for seven yards and the long bomb to Swann. Roy Gerela had 36- and 18-yard field goals. Reggie Harrison blocked a punt through the end zone for a safety. Swann set a Super Bowl record by gaining 161 yards on his four receptions.

Dallas (NFC)	7	3	0	7	— 17
Pittsburgh (AFC)	7	0	0	14	— 21

Dall—D. Pearson 29 pass from Staubach (Fritsch kick)
Pitt —Grossman 7 pass from Bradshaw (Gerela kick)
Dall—FG Fritsch 36
Pitt —Safety, Harrison blocked Hoopes's punt through end zone
Pitt —FG Gerela 36
Pitt —FG Gerela 18
Pitt —Swann 64 pass from Bradshaw (kick failed)
Dall—P. Howard 34 pass from Staubach (Fritsch kick)

Super Bowl IX

Tulane Stadium, New Orleans, Louisiana — January 12, 1975
Attendance: 80,997

PITTSBURGH 16, MINNESOTA 6—AFC champion Pittsburgh, in its initial Super Bowl appearance, and NFC champion Minnesota, making a third bid for its first Super Bowl title, struggled through a first half in which the only score was produced by the Steelers' defense when Dwight White downed Vikings' quarterback Fran Tarkenton in the end zone for a safety 7:49 into the second period. The Steelers forced another break and took advantage on the second-half kickoff when Minnesota's Bill Brown fumbled and Marv Kellum recovered for Pittsburgh on the Vikings' 30. After Rocky Bleier failed to gain on first down, Franco Harris carried three consecutive times for 24 yards, a loss of 3, and a 12-yard touchdown and a 9-0 lead. Though its offense was completely stymied by Pittsburgh's defense, Minnesota managed to move into a threatening position after 4:27 of the final period when Matt Blair blocked Bobby Walden's punt and Terry Brown recovered the ball in the end zone for a touchdown. Fred Cox's kick failed and the Steelers led 9-6. Pittsburgh wasted no time putting the victory away. The Steelers took the ensuing kickoff and marched 66 yards in 11 plays, climaxed by Terry Bradshaw's four-yard scoring pass to Larry Brown with 3:31 left. Pittsburgh's defense permitted Minnesota only 119 yards total offense, including a Super Bowl low of 17 yards rushing. The Steelers, meanwhile, gained 333 yards, including Harris's record 158 yards on 34 carries.

Pittsburgh (AFC)	0	2	7	7	— 16
Minnesota (NFC)	0	0	0	6	— 6

Pitt —Safety, White downed Tarkenton in end zone
Pitt —Harris 12 run (Gerela kick)
Minn—T. Brown recovered blocked punt in end zone (kick failed)
Pitt —L. Brown 4 pass from Bradshaw (Gerela kick)

Super Bowl VIII

Rice Stadium, Houston, Texas — January 13, 1974
Attendance: 71,882

MIAMI 24, MINNESOTA 7—The defending NFL champion Dolphins, representing the AFC for the third straight year, scored the first two times they had possession on marches of 62 and 56 yards while the Miami defense limited the Vikings to only seven plays in the first period. Larry Csonka climaxed the initial 10-play drive with a five-yard touchdown bolt through right guard after 5:27 had elapsed. Four plays later, Miami began another 10-play scoring drive, which ended with Jim Kiick bursting one yard through the middle for another touchdown after 13:38 of the period. Garo Yepremian added a 28-yard field goal midway in the second period for a 17-0 Miami lead. Minnesota then drove from its 20 to a second-and-two situation on the Miami 7 yard line with 1:18 left in the half. But on two plays, Miami limited Oscar Reed to one yard. On fourth-and-one from the 6, Reed went over right tackle, but Dolphins middle linebacker Nick Buoniconti jarred the ball loose and Jake Scott recovered for Miami to halt the Minnesota threat. The Vikings were unable to muster enough offense in the second half to threaten the Dolphins. Csonka rushed 33 times for a Super Bowl-record 145 yards. Bob Griese of Miami completed six of seven passes for 73 yards.

Minnesota (NFC)	0	0	0	7	— 7
Miami (AFC)	14	3	7	0	— 24

Mia —Csonka 5 run (Yepremian kick)
Mia —Kiick 1 run (Yepremian kick)
Mia —FG Yepremian 28
Mia —Csonka 2 run (Yepremian kick)
Minn—Tarkenton 4 run (Cox kick)

Super Bowl VII

Memorial Coliseum, Los Angeles, California — January 14, 1973
Attendance: 90,182

MIAMI 14, WASHINGTON 7—The Dolphins played virtually perfect football in the first half as their defense permitted the Redskins to cross midfield only once and their offense turned good field position into two touchdowns. On its third possession, Miami opened its first scoring drive from the Dolphins' 37 yard line. An 18-yard pass from Bob Griese to Paul Warfield preceded by three plays Griese's 28-yard touchdown pass to Howard Twilley. After Washington moved from its 17 to the Miami 48 with two minutes remaining in the first half, Dolphins linebacker Nick Buoniconti intercepted a Billy Kilmer pass at the Miami 41 and returned it to the Washington 27. Jim Kiick ran for three yards, Larry Csonka for three, Griese passed to Jim Mandich for 19, and Kiick gained one to the 1-yard line. With 18 seconds left until intermission, Kiick scored from the 1. Washington's only touchdown came with 7:07 left in the game and resulted from a misplayed field-goal attempt and fumble by Garo Yepremian, with the Redskins' Mike Bass picking the ball out of the air and running 49 yards for the score. Jake Scott returned his second interception from three yards deep in the end zone to the Redskins' 48-yard line with just over five minutes to play, ending Washington's best scoring opportunity of the second half. Scott was voted the game's most valuable player.

Miami (AFC)	7	7	0	0	— 14
Washington (NFC)	0	0	0	7	— 7

Mia —Twilley 28 pass from Griese (Yepremian kick)
Mia —Kiick 1 run (Yepremian kick)
Wash—Bass 49 fumble recovery return (Knight kick)

Super Bowl VI

Tulane Stadium, New Orleans, Louisiana — January 16, 1972
Attendance: 81,023

DALLAS 24, MIAMI 3—The Cowboys rushed for a record 252 yards and their defense limited the Dolphins to a low of 185 yards while not permitting a touchdown for the first time in Super Bowl history. Dallas converted Chuck Howley's recovery of Larry Csonka's first fumble of the season into a 3-0 advantage and led at halftime 10-3. After Dallas received the second-half kickoff, Duane Thomas led a 71-yard march in eight plays for a 17-3 margin. Howley intercepted Bob Griese's pass at the 50 and returned it to the Miami 9 early in the fourth period, and three plays later Roger Staubach passed seven yards to Mike Ditka for the final touchdown. Thomas rushed for 95 yards and Walt Garrison gained 74. Staubach, voted the game's most valuable player, completed 12 of 19 passes for 119 yards and two touchdowns.

Dallas (NFC)	3	7	7	7	— 24
Miami (AFC)	0	3	0	0	— 3

Dall—FG Clark 9
Dall—Alworth 7 pass from Staubach (Clark kick)
Mia—FG Yepremian 31
Dall—D. Thomas 3 run (Clark kick)
Dall—Ditka 7 pass from Staubach (Clark kick)

Super Bowl V

Orange Bowl, Miami, Florida — January 17, 1971
Attendance: 79,204

BALTIMORE 16, DALLAS 13—A 32-yard field goal by first-year kicker Jim O'Brien brought the Baltimore Colts a victory over the Dallas Cowboys in the final five seconds of Super Bowl V. The game between the champions of the AFC and NFC was played on artificial turf for the first time. Dallas led 13-6 at the half but interceptions by Rick Volk and Mike Curtis set up a Baltimore touchdown and O'Brien's decisive kick in the fourth period. Earl Morrall relieved an injured Johnny Unitas late in the first half, although Unitas completed the Colts' only scoring pass. It caromed off receiver Eddie Hinton's fingertips, off Dallas defensive back Mel Renfro, and finally settled into the grasp of John Mackey, who went 45 yards to score on a 75-yard play.

Baltimore (AFC)	0	6	0	10	— 16
Dallas (NFC)	3	10	0	0	— 13

Dall—FG Clark 14
Dall—FG Clark 30
Balt—Mackey 75 pass from Unitas (kick blocked)
Dall—Thomas 7 pass from Morton (Clark kick)
Balt—Nowatzke 2 run (O'Brien kick)
Balt—FG O'Brien 32

Super Bowl IV

Tulane Stadium, New Orleans, Louisiana — January 11, 1970
Attendance: 80,562

KANSAS CITY 23, MINNESOTA 7—The AFL squared the Super Bowl at two games apiece with the NFL, building a 16-0 halftime lead behind Len Dawson's superb quarterbacking and a powerful defense. Dawson, the fourth consecutive quarterback to be chosen the Super Bowl's top player, called an almost flawless game, completing 12 of 17 passes and hitting Otis Taylor on a 46-yard play for the final Chiefs touchdown. The Kansas City defense limited Minnesota's strong rushing game to 67 yards and had three interceptions and two fumble recoveries. The crowd of 80,562 set a Super Bowl record, as did the gross receipts of $3,817,872.69.

Minnesota (NFL)	0	0	7	0	— 7
Kansas City (AFL)	3	13	7	0	— 23

KC —FG Stenerud 48
KC —FG Stenerud 32
KC —FG Stenerud 25
KC —Garrett 5 run (Stenerud kick)
Minn—Osborn 4 run (Cox kick)
KC —Taylor 46 pass from Dawson (Stenerud kick)

Super Bowl III

Orange Bowl, Miami, Florida — January 12, 1969
Attendance: 75,389

NEW YORK JETS 16, BALTIMORE 7—Jets quarterback Joe Namath "guaranteed" victory on the Thursday before the game, then went out and led the AFL to its first Super Bowl victory over a Baltimore team that had lost only once in 16 games all season. Namath, chosen the outstanding player, completed 17 of 28 passes for 206 yards and directed a steady attack that dominated the NFL champions after the Jets' defense had intercepted Colts quarterback Earl Morrall three times in the first half. The Jets had 337 total yards, including 121 yards rushing by Matt Snell. Johnny Unitas, who had missed most of the season with a sore elbow, came off the bench and led Baltimore to its only touchdown late in the fourth quarter after New York led 16-0.

New York Jets (AFL)	0	7	6	3	— 16
Baltimore (NFL)	0	0	0	7	— 7

NYJ—Snell 4 run (Turner kick)
NYJ—FG Turner 32
NYJ—FG Turner 30
NYJ—FG Turner 9
Balt—Hill 1 run (Michaels kick)

Super Bowl II

Orange Bowl, Miami, Florida — January 14, 1968
Attendance: 75,546

GREEN BAY 33, OAKLAND 14—Green Bay, after winning its third consecutive NFL championship, won the Super Bowl title for the second straight year 33-14 over the AFL champion Raiders in a game that drew the first $3-million gate in football history. Bart Starr again was chosen the game's most valuable player as he completed 13 of 24 passes for 202 yards and one touchdown and directed a Packers attack that was in control all the way after building a 16-7 halftime lead. Don Chandler kicked four field goals and all-pro cornerback Herb Adderley capped the Green Bay scoring with a 60-yard run with an interception. The game marked the last for Vince Lombardi as Packers coach, ending nine years at Green Bay in which he won six Western Conference championships, five NFL championships, and two Super Bowls.

Green Bay (NFL)	3	13	10	7	— 33
Oakland (AFL)	0	7	0	7	— 14

GB —FG Chandler 39
GB —FG Chandler 20
GB —Dowler 62 pass from Starr (Chandler kick)
Oak—Miller 23 pass from Lamonica (Blanda kick)
GB —FG Chandler 43
GB —Anderson 2 run (Chandler kick)
GB —FG Chandler 31
GB —Adderley 60 interception return (Chandler kick)
Oak—Miller 23 pass from Lamonica (Blanda kick)

Super Bowl I

Memorial Coliseum, Los Angeles, California — January 15, 1967
Attendance: 61,946

GREEN BAY 35, KANSAS CITY 10—The Green Bay Packers opened the Super Bowl series by defeating Kansas City's American Football League champions 35-10 behind the passing of Bart Starr, the receiving of Max McGee, and a key interception by all-pro safety Willie Wood. Green Bay broke open the game with three second-half touchdowns, the first of which was set up by Wood's 50-yard return of an interception to the Chiefs' 5 yard line. McGee, filling in for ailing Boyd Dowler after having caught only four passes all season, caught seven from Starr for 138 yards and two touchdowns. Elijah Pitts ran for two other scores. The Chiefs' 10 points came in the second quarter, the only touchdown on a seven-yard pass from Len Dawson to Curtis McClinton. Starr completed 16 of 23 passes for 250 yards and two touchdowns and was chosen the most valuable player. The Packers collected $15,000 per man and the Chiefs $7,500—the largest single-game shares in the history of team sports.

Kansas City (AFL)	0	10	0	0	— 10
Green Bay (NFL)	7	7	14	7	— 35

GB—McGee 37 pass from Starr (Chandler kick)
KC—McClinton 7 pass from Dawson (Mercer kick)
GB—Taylor 14 run (Chandler kick)
KC—FG Mercer 31
GB—Pitts 5 run (Chandler kick)
GB—McGee 13 pass from Starr (Chandler kick)
GB—Pitts 1 run (Chandler kick)

AFC Championship Game

Includes AFL Championship Games (1960-69)

Results

Season	Date	Winner (Share)	Loser (Share)	Score	Site	Attendance
1990	Jan. 20	Buffalo ($18,000)	L.A. Raiders ($18,000)	51-3	Buffalo	80,325
1989	Jan. 14	Denver ($18,000)	Cleveland ($18,000)	37-21	Denver	76,046
1988	Jan. 8	Cincinnati ($18,000)	Buffalo ($18,000)	21-10	Cincinnati	59,747
1987	Jan. 17	Denver ($18,000)	Cleveland ($18,000)	38-33	Denver	76,197
1986	Jan. 11	Denver ($18,000)	Cleveland ($18,000)	23-20*	Cleveland	79,973
1985	Jan. 12	New England ($18,000)	Miami ($18,000)	31-14	Miami	75,662
1984	Jan. 6	Miami ($18,000)	Pittsburgh ($18,000)	45-28	Miami	76,029
1983	Jan. 8	L.A. Raiders ($18,000)	Seattle ($18,000)	30-14	Los Angeles	91,445
1982	Jan. 23	Miami ($18,000)	N.Y. Jets ($18,000)	14-0	Miami	67,396
1981	Jan. 10	Cincinnati ($9,000)	San Diego ($9,000)	27-7	Cincinnati	46,302
1980	Jan. 11	Oakland ($9,000)	San Diego ($9,000)	34-27	San Diego	52,675
1979	Jan. 6	Pittsburgh ($9,000)	Houston ($9,000)	27-13	Pittsburgh	50,475
1978	Jan. 7	Pittsburgh ($9,000)	Houston ($9,000)	34-5	Pittsburgh	50,725
1977	Jan. 1	Denver ($9,000)	Oakland ($9,000)	20-17	Denver	75,044
1976	Dec. 26	Oakland ($8,500)	Pittsburgh ($5,500)	24-7	Oakland	53,821
1975	Jan. 4	Pittsburgh ($8,500)	Oakland ($5,500)	16-10	Pittsburgh	50,609
1974	Dec. 29	Pittsburgh ($8,500)	Oakland ($5,500)	24-13	Oakland	53,800
1973	Dec. 30	Miami ($8,500)	Oakland ($5,500)	27-10	Miami	79,325
1972	Dec. 31	Miami ($8,500)	Pittsburgh ($5,500)	21-17	Pittsburgh	50,845
1971	Jan. 2	Miami ($8,500)	Baltimore ($5,500)	21-0	Miami	76,622
1970	Jan. 3	Baltimore ($8,500)	Oakland ($5,500)	27-17	Baltimore	54,799
1969	Jan. 4	Kansas City ($7,755)	Oakland ($6,252)	17-7	Oakland	53,564
1968	Dec. 29	N.Y. Jets ($7,007)	Oakland ($5,349)	27-23	New York	62,627
1967	Dec. 31	Oakland ($6,321)	Houston ($4,996)	40-7	Oakland	53,330
1966	Jan. 1	Kansas City ($5,309)	Buffalo ($3,799)	31-7	Buffalo	42,080
1965	Dec. 26	Buffalo ($5,189)	San Diego ($3,447)	23-0	San Diego	30,361
1964	Dec. 26	Buffalo ($2,668)	San Diego ($1,738)	20-7	Buffalo	40,242
1963	Jan. 5	San Diego ($2,498)	Boston ($1,596)	51-10	San Diego	30,127
1962	Dec. 23	Dallas ($2,206)	Houston ($1,471)	20-17*	Houston	37,981
1961	Dec. 24	Houston ($1,792)	San Diego ($1,111)	10-3	San Diego	29,556
1960	Jan. 1	Houston ($1,025)	L.A. Chargers ($718)	24-16	Houston	32,183

Sudden death overtime.

AFC Championship Game Composite Standings

	W	L	Pct.	Pts.	OP
Denver Broncos	4	0	1.000	118	91
Kansas City Chiefs*	3	0	1.000	68	31
Cincinnati Bengals	2	0	1.000	48	17
Miami Dolphins	5	1	.833	142	86
Buffalo Bills	3	2	.600	111	62
Pittsburgh Steelers	4	3	.571	153	131
Baltimore Colts	1	1	.500	27	38
New England Patriots**	1	1	.500	41	65
New York Jets	1	1	.500	27	37
Houston Oilers	2	4	.333	76	140
Oakland/L.A. Raiders	4	8	.333	228	264
San Diego Chargers***	1	6	.143	111	148
Seattle Seahawks	0	1	.000	14	30
Cleveland Browns	0	3	.000	74	98

**One game played when franchise was in Dallas (Texans). (Won 20-17)*
***One game played when franchise was in Boston. (Lost 51-10)*
****One game played when franchise was in Los Angeles. (Lost 24-16)*

1990 American Football Conference Championship Game

Rich Stadium, Orchard Park, New York — January 20, 1991

Attendance: 80,325

BUFFALO 51, LOS ANGELES RAIDERS 3—Kenneth Davis ran for three touchdowns and Jim Kelly passed for 300 yards as the Bills gained their first Super Bowl berth by defeating the Raiders. Buffalo set an NFL playoff record by scoring 41 first-half points on Kelly's touchdown passes to James Lofton (13 yards), a pair of scoring runs by Davis (one and three yards), Thurman Thomas's 12-yard touchdown run, and linebacker Darryl Talley's 27-yard interception return for a score. Davis added a one-yard scoring run and Scott Norwood kicked a 39-yard field goal in the second half. The Raiders managed just one score, a 41-yard field goal by Jeff Jaeger in the first quarter. Thomas finished with 138 yards rushing and 61 yards receiving. Lofton had five receptions for 113 yards. The Bills' 51 points tied an AFC playoff record as did Davis's three touchdown runs.

L.A. Raiders (3)	Offense	Buffalo (51)
Willie Gault	WR	James Lofton
Rory Graves	LT	Will Wolford
Steve Wisniewski	LG	Jim Ritcher
Don Mosebar	C	Kent Hull
Max Montoya	RG	John Davis
Steve Wright	RT	Howard Ballard
Ethan Horton	TE	Keith McKeller
Mervyn Fernandez	WR	Andre Reed
Jay Schroeder	QB	Jim Kelly
Steve Smith	RB	Thurman Thomas
Marcus Allen	RB-WR	Al Edwards
	Defense	
Howie Long	LE	Leon Seals
Bob Golic	LT-NT	Jeff Wright
Scott Davis	RT-RE	Bruce Smith
Greg Townsend	RE-LOLB	Cornelius Bennett
Jerry Robinson	LLB-LILB	Shane Conlan
Riki Ellison	MLB-RILB	Ray Bentley
Tom Benson	RLB-ROLB	Darryl Talley
Terry McDaniel	LCB	Kirby Jackson
Lionel Washington	RCB	Nate Odomes
Mike Harden	SS	Leonard Smith
Eddie Anderson	FS	Mark Kelso

Substitutions

L.A. Raiders—Offense: K—Jeff Jaeger. P—Jeff Gossett. QB—Vince Evans. RB—Greg Bell, Napoleon McCallum, Vance Mueller. WR—Tim Brown, Sam Graddy, Jamie Holland. TE—Mike Dyal. C—Dan Turk. G—Todd Peat. T—Bruce Wilkerson. Defense: E—Mike Wise. T—Bill Pickel. LB—Alex Gordon, Darin Jordan, Aaron Wallace. CB—Ron Brown, Torin Dorn, Garry Lewis. S—Dan Land, Elvis Patterson. DNP: None.

Buffalo—Offense: K—Scott Norwood. P—Rick Tuten. QB—Frank Reich. RB—Kenneth Davis, Carwell Gardner, Jamie Mueller, Don Smith. WR—Steve Tasker. TE—Pete Metzelaars, Butch Rolle. C—Adam Lingner. G—Mitch Frerotte, Glenn Parker. Defense: E—Mike Lodish, Mark Pike. NT—Gary Baldinger. LB—Carlton Bailey, Hal Garner. CB—Clifford Hicks, James Williams. S—Dwight Drane, John Hagy. DNP: QB—Gale Gilbert.

Officials

Referee—Jim Tunney. Umpire—Ron Botchan. Line Judge—Ron Blum. Head Linesman—Paul Weidner. Back Judge—Bob Moore. Field Judge—Bernie Kukar. Side Judge—Stan Kemp. Replay Official—George Sladky.

Scoring

L.A. Raiders	3	0	0	0	— 3
Buffalo	21	20	0	10	— 51

Buff —Lofton 13 pass from Kelly (Norwood kick)
Raiders—FG Jaeger 41
Buff —Thomas 12 run (Norwood kick)
Buff —Talley 27 interception return (Norwood kick)
Buff —K. Davis 1 run (kick blocked)
Buff —K. Davis 3 run (Norwood kick)
Buff —Lofton 8 pass from Kelly (Norwood kick)
Buff —K. Davis 1 run (Norwood kick)
Buff —FG Norwood 39

Team Statistics

	L.A. Raiders	Buffalo
Total First Downs	21	30
First Downs Rushing	12	14
First Downs Passing	8	15
First Downs Penalty	1	1
Total Net Yardage	320	502
Total Offensive Plays	68	69
Average Gain per Offensive Play	4.7	7.3
Rushes	28	46
Yards Gained Rushing (net)	151	202
Average Yards per Rush	5.4	4.4
Passes Attempted	39	23
Passes Completed	15	17
Had Intercepted	6	1
Tackled Attempting to Pass	1	0
Yards Lost Attempting to Pass	7	0
Yards Gained Passing (net)	169	300
Punts	3	2
Average Distance	40.3	37.5
Punt Returns	2	2
Punt Return Yardage	22	30
Kickoff Returns	9	2
Kickoff Return Yardage	119	30
Interception Return Yardage	0	113
Total Return Yardage	141	173
Fumbles	1	3
Own Fumbles Recovered	0	3
Opponents Fumbles Recovered	0	1
Penalties	2	6
Yards Penalized	28	32
Total Points Scored	3	51
Touchdowns Rushing	0	4
Touchdowns Passing	0	2
Touchdowns Returns	0	1
Extra Points	0	6
Field Goals	1	1
Field Goals Attempted	1	2
Safeties	0	0
Third Down Efficiency	4/12	5/11
Fourth Down Efficiency	0/1	1/1
Time of Possession	28:25	31:35

Individual Statistics

Rushing

L.A. Raiders	No.	Yds.	LG	TD
Bell	5	36	11	0
Evans	4	33	15	0
Schroeder	4	33	12	0
Allen	10	26	5	0
Smith	4	19	7	0
McCallum	1	4	4	0
Buffalo	**No.**	**Yds.**	**LG**	**TD**
Thomas	25	138	15	1
Gardner	1	23	23	0
K. Davis	10	21	6	3
Kelly	2	12	11	0
Mueller	3	6	6	0
D. Smith	3	3	4	0
Reich	2	−1	0	0

Passing

Raiders	Att.	Comp.	Yds.	TD	Int.
Schroeder	31	13	150	0	5
Evans	8	2	26	0	1
Buffalo	**Att.**	**Comp.**	**Yds.**	**TD**	**Int.**
Kelly	23	17	300	2	1

Receiving

L.A. Raiders	No.	Yds.	LG	TD
Fernandez	4	57	26	0
Horton	3	25	11	0
Gault	2	32	26	0
Bell	2	26	21	0
Allen	2	19	16	0
T. Brown	2	17	9	0
Buffalo	**No.**	**Yds.**	**LG**	**TD**
Lofton	5	113	41	2
Thomas	5	61	17	0
McKeller	3	44	23	0
Tasker	2	53	44	0
Reed	2	29	15	0

Interceptions

L.A. Raiders	No.	Yds.	LG	TD
Lewis	1	0	0	0
Buffalo	**No.**	**Yds.**	**LG**	**TD**
Talley	2	48	27t	1
Bentley	1	32	32	0
L. Smith	1	24	24	0
Odomes	1	9	9	0
Kelso	1	0	0	0

Punting

L.A. Raiders	No.	Avg.	LG	Blk.
Gossett	3	40.3	46	0
Buffalo	**No.**	**Avg.**	**LG**	**Blk.**
Tuten	2	37.5	41	0

Punt Returns

L.A. Raiders	No.	FC	Yds.	LG	TD
Patterson	1	0	17	17	0
T. Brown	1	0	5	5	0
Buffalo	**No.**	**FC**	**Yds.**	**LG**	**TD**
Odomes	1	0	18	18	0
Edwards	1	0	12	12	0

Kickoff Returns

L.A. Raiders	No.	Yds.	LG	TD
Holland	6	60	17	0
R. Brown	3	59	30	0
Buffalo	**No.**	**Yds.**	**LG**	**TD**
Edwards	1	19	19	0
D. Smith	1	11	11	0

NFC Championship Game

Includes NFL Championship Games (1933-69)

Results

Season	Date	Winner (Share)	Loser (Share)	Score	Site	Attendance
1990	Jan. 20	N.Y. Giants ($18,000)	San Francisco ($18,000)	15-13	San Francisco	65,750
1989	Jan. 14	San Francisco ($18,000)	L.A. Rams ($18,000)	30-3	San Francisco	65,634
1988	Jan. 8	San Francisco ($18,000)	Chicago ($18,000)	28-3	Chicago	66,946
1987	Jan. 17	Washington ($18,000)	Minnesota ($18,000)	17-10	Washington	55,212
1986	Jan. 11	New York Giants ($18,000)	Washington ($18,000)	17-0	New York	76,891
1985	Jan. 12	Chicago ($18,000)	L.A. Rams ($18,000)	24-0	Chicago	66,030
1984	Jan. 6	San Francisco ($18,000)	Chicago ($18,000)	23-0	San Francisco	61,336
1983	Jan. 8	Washington ($18,000)	San Francisco ($18,000)	24-21	Washington	55,363
1982	Jan. 22	Washington ($18,000)	Dallas ($18,000)	31-17	Washington	55,045
1981	Jan. 10	San Francisco ($9,000)	Dallas ($9,000)	28-27	San Francisco	60,525
1980	Jan. 11	Philadelphia ($9,000)	Dallas ($9,000)	20-7	Philadelphia	71,522
1979	Jan. 6	Los Angeles ($9,000)	Tampa Bay ($9,000)	9-0	Tampa Bay	72,033
1978	Jan. 7	Dallas ($9,000)	Los Angeles ($9,000)	28-0	Los Angeles	71,086
1977	Jan. 1	Dallas ($9,000)	Minnesota ($9,000)	23-6	Dallas	64,293
1976	Dec. 26	Minnesota ($8,500)	Los Angeles ($5,500)	24-13	Minnesota	48,379
1975	Jan. 4	Dallas ($8,500)	Los Angeles ($5,500)	37-7	Los Angeles	88,919
1974	Dec. 29	Minnesota ($8,500)	Los Angeles ($5,500)	14-10	Minnesota	48,444
1973	Dec. 30	Minnesota ($8,500)	Dallas ($5,500)	27-10	Dallas	64,422
1972	Dec. 31	Washington ($8,500)	Dallas ($5,500)	26-3	Washington	53,129
1971	Jan. 2	Dallas ($8,500)	San Francisco ($5,500)	14-3	Dallas	63,409
1970	Jan. 3	Dallas ($8,500)	San Francisco ($5,500)	17-10	San Francisco	59,364
1969	Jan. 4	Minnesota ($7,930)	Cleveland ($5,118)	27-7	Minnesota	46,503
1968	Dec. 29	Baltimore ($9,306)	Cleveland ($5,963)	34-0	Cleveland	78,410
1967	Dec. 31	Green Bay ($7,950)	Dallas ($5,299)	21-17	Green Bay	50,861
1966	Jan. 1	Green Bay ($9,813)	Dallas ($6,527)	34-27	Dallas	74,152
1965	Jan. 2	Green Bay ($7,819)	Cleveland ($5,288)	23-12	Green Bay	50,777
1964	Dec. 27	Cleveland ($8,052)	Baltimore ($5,571)	27-0	Cleveland	79,544
1963	Dec. 29	Chicago ($5,899)	New York ($4,218)	14-10	Chicago	45,801
1962	Dec. 30	Green Bay ($5,888)	New York ($4,166)	16-7	New York	64,892
1961	Dec. 31	Green Bay ($5,195)	New York ($3,339)	37-0	Green Bay	39,029
1960	Dec. 26	Philadelphia ($5,116)	Green Bay ($3,105)	17-13	Philadelphia	67,325
1959	Dec. 27	Baltimore ($4,674)	New York ($3,083)	31-16	Baltimore	57,545
1958	Dec. 28	Baltimore ($4,718)	New York ($3,111)	23-17*	New York	64,185
1957	Dec. 29	Detroit ($4,295)	Cleveland ($2,750)	59-14	Detroit	55,263
1956	Dec. 30	New York ($3,779)	Chi. Bears ($2,485)	47-7	New York	56,836
1955	Dec. 26	Cleveland ($3,508)	Los Angeles ($2,316)	38-14	Los Angeles	85,693
1954	Dec. 26	Cleveland ($2,478)	Detroit ($1,585)	56-10	Cleveland	43,827
1953	Dec. 27	Detroit ($2,424)	Cleveland ($1,654)	17-16	Detroit	54,577
1952	Dec. 28	Detroit ($2,274)	Cleveland ($1,712)	17-7	Cleveland	50,934
1951	Dec. 23	Los Angeles ($2,108)	Cleveland ($1,483)	24-17	Los Angeles	57,522
1950	Dec. 24	Cleveland ($1,113)	Los Angeles ($686)	30-28	Cleveland	29,751
1949	Dec. 18	Philadelphia ($1,094)	Los Angeles ($739)	14-0	Los Angeles	27,980
1948	Dec. 19	Philadelphia ($1,540)	Chi. Cardinals ($874)	7-0	Philadelphia	36,309

Season	Date	Winner (Share)	Loser (Share)	Score	Site	Attendance
1947	Dec. 28	Chi. Cardinals ($1,132)	Philadelphia ($754)	28-21	Chicago	30,759
1946	Dec. 15	Chi. Bears ($1,975)	New York ($1,295)	24-14	New York	58,346
1945	Dec. 16	Cleveland ($1,469)	Washington ($902)	15-14	Cleveland	32,178
1944	Dec. 17	Green Bay ($1,449)	New York ($814)	14-7	New York	46,016
1943	Dec. 26	Chi. Bears ($1,146)	Washington ($765)	41-21	Chicago	34,320
1942	Dec. 13	Washington ($965)	Chi. Bears ($637)	14-6	Washington	36,006
1941	Dec. 21	Chi. Bears ($430)	New York ($288)	37-9	Chicago	13,341
1940	Dec. 8	Chi. Bears ($873)	Washington ($606)	73-0	Washington	36,034
1939	Dec. 10	Green Bay ($703.97)	New York ($455.57)	27-0	Milwaukee	32,279
1938	Dec. 11	New York ($504.45)	Green Bay ($368.81)	23-17	New York	48,120
1937	Dec. 12	Washington ($225.90)	Chi. Bears ($127.78)	28-21	Chicago	15,870
1936	Dec. 13	Green Bay ($250)	Boston ($180)	21-6	New York	29,545
1935	Dec. 15	Detroit ($313.35)	New York ($200.20)	26-7	Detroit	15,000
1934	Dec. 9	New York ($621)	Chi. Bears ($414.02)	30-13	New York	35,059
1933	Dec. 17	Chi. Bears ($210.34)	New York ($140.22)	23-21	Chicago	26,000

**Sudden death overtime.*

NFC Championship Game Composite Standings

	W	L	Pct.	Pts.	OP
Green Bay Packers	8	2	.800	223	116
Philadelphia Eagles	4	1	.800	79	48
Baltimore Colts	3	1	.750	88	60
Detroit Lions*	4	2	.667	129	109
Minnesota Vikings	4	2	.667	108	80
Washington Redskins**	6	5	.545	181	245
Chicago Bears	7	6	.536	286	245
Phoenix Cardinals***	1	1	.500	28	28
San Francisco 49ers	4	4	.500	156	103
Dallas Cowboys	5	7	.417	227	213
Cleveland Browns	4	7	.364	224	253
New York Giants	5	11	.313	240	322
Los Angeles Rams****	3	9	.250	123	270
Tampa Bay Buccaneers	0	1	.000	0	9

**One game played when franchise was in Portsmouth. (Lost 9-0)*
***One game played when franchise was in Boston. (Lost 21-6)*
****Both games played when franchise was in Chicago. (Won 28-21, lost 7-0)*
*****One game played when franchise was in Cleveland. (Won 15-14)*

1990 National Football Conference Championship Game

Candlestick Park, San Francisco, California — January 20, 1991

Attendance: 65,750

NEW YORK GIANTS 15, SAN FRANCISCO 13—The NFC East champion New York Giants advanced to the Super Bowl for the first time since 1986 by defeating NFC West titlist and defending Super Bowl champion San Francisco. Giants backup quarterback Jeff Hostetler completed 15 of 27 passes for 176 yards and executed the final drive to set up Matt Bahr's game-winning 42-yard field goal as time expired. The Giants controlled the ball for 39 minutes and outgained San Francisco 152 to 39 yards rushing. The teams fought to a 6-6 halftime tie on two field goals apiece by both Bahr and 49ers kicker Mike Cofer. Quarterback Joe Montana and wide receiver John Taylor hooked up on a 61-yard scoring play for the game's only touchdown, to give San Francisco a 13-6 advantage. Bahr, who accounted for all of New York's scoring via five field goals, scored the next nine points by converting field goals from 46, 38, and 42 yards. His game-winning attempt was set up when linebacker Lawrence Taylor recovered a fumble forced by nose tackle Erik Howard. Hostetler drove the Giants 33 yards in six plays before Bahr's kick. New York running back Ottis Anderson led all rushers with 67 yards on 20 carries and wide receiver Mark Ingram caught five passes for 82 yards.

N.Y. Giants (15)	Offense	San Francisco (13)
Mark Ingram	WR	John Taylor
John Elliott	LT	Bubba Paris
William Roberts	LG	Guy McIntyre
Bart Oates	C	Jesse Sapolu
Eric Moore	RG	Harris Barton
Doug Riesenberg	RT	Steve Wallace
Mark Bavaro	TE	Brent Jones
Stephen Baker	WR	Jerry Rice
Jeff Hostetler	QB	Joe Montana
Ottis Anderson	RB	Roger Craig
Maurice Carthon	RB	Tom Rathman
	Defense	
Mike Fox	LE	Pierce Holt
Erik Howard	NT	Michael Carter
Leonard Marshall	RE	Kevin Fagan
Carl Banks	LOLB	Charles Haley
Gary Reasons	LILB	Matt Millen
Pepper Johnson	RILB	Keith DeLong
Lawrence Taylor	ROLB	Bill Romanowski
Mark Collins	LCB	Darryl Pollard
Everson Walls	RCB	Don Griffin
Greg Jackson	SS	Dave Waymer
Myron Guyton	FS	Ronnie Lott

Substitutions

N.Y. Giants—Offense: K—Matt Bahr. P—Sean Landeta. QB—Matt Cavanaugh. RB—David Meggett, Lee Rouson, Lewis Tillman. WR—Stacy Robinson. TE—Howard Cross, Bob Mrosko. G—Brian Williams, Bob Kratch. Defense: E—Eric Dorsey. NT—John Washington. LB—Bobby Abrams, Steve DeOssie, Lawrence McGrew. CB—Roger Brown, Reyna Thompson, Perry Williams. S—Dave Duerson, David Whitmore. DNP: WR—Troy Kyles. LB—Johnie Cooks.

San Francisco—Offense: K—Mike Cofer. P—Barry Helton. QB—Steve Young. RB—Dexter Carter, Keith Henderson, Harry Sydney, Spencer Tillman. WR—Mike Sherrard, Mike Wilson. TE—Wesley Walls, Jamie Williams. C—Chuck Thomas. G—Ricky Siglar. T—Frank Pollack. Defense: E—Dennis Brown, Larry Roberts. NT—Jim Burt, Pete Kugler. LB—Keena Turner, Michael Walter. CB—Eric Davis, Kevin Lewis. S—Johnny Jackson. DNP—None.

Officials

Referee—Jerry Markbreit. Umpire—Bob Boylston. Line Judge—Ron Baynes. Head Linesman—Jerry Bergman. Back Judge—Doug Toole. Field Judge—Donnie Hampton. Side Judge—Bill Quinby. Replay Official—Tom Kelleher.

Scoring

N.Y. Giants	3	3	3	6	— 15
San Francisco	3	3	7	0	— 13

SF —FG Cofer 47
Giants—FG Bahr 28
Giants—FG Bahr 42
SF —FG Cofer 35
SF —Taylor 61 pass from Montana (Cofer kick)
Giants—FG Bahr 46
Giants—FG Bahr 38
Giants—FG Bahr 42

Team Statistics

	N.Y. Giants	San Francisco
Total First Downs	20	13
First Downs Rushing	8	1
First Downs Passing	8	11
First Downs Penalty	4	1
Total Net Yardage	311	240
Total Offensive Plays	68	41
Average Gain per Offensive Play	4.6	5.9
Rushes	36	11
Yards Gained Rushing (net)	152	39
Average Yards per Rush	4.2	3.5
Passes Attempted	29	27
Passes Completed	15	19
Had Intercepted	0	0
Tackled Attempting to Pass	3	3
Yards Lost Attempting to Pass	17	14
Yards Gained Passing (net)	159	201
Punts	3	5
Average Distance	41.3	40.0
Punt Returns	5	2
Punt Return Yardage	42	40
Kickoff Returns	3	4
Kickoff Return Yardage	39	85
Interception Return Yardage	0	0
Total Return Yardage	81	125
Fumbles	0	3
Own Fumbles Recovered	0	2
Opponents Fumbles Recovered	1	0
Penalties	5	9
Yards Penalized	45	63
Total Points Scored	15	13
Touchdowns Rushing	0	0
Touchdowns Passing	0	1
Touchdowns Returns	0	0

	N.Y. Giants	San Francisco
Extra Points	0	1
Field Goals	5	2
Field Goals Attempted	6	2
Safeties	0	0
Third Down Efficiency	6/15	1/8
Fourth Down Efficiency	1/1	0/0
Time of Possession	38:59	21:01

Individual Statistics

Rushing

N.Y. Giants	No.	Yds.	LG	TD
Anderson	20	67	27	0
Meggett	10	36	8	0
Reasons	1	30	30	0
Hostetler	3	11	6	0
Carthon	2	8	6	0
San Fran.	**No.**	**Yds.**	**LG**	**TD**
Craig	8	26	7	0
Montana	2	9	6	0
Rathman	1	4	4	0

Passing

N.Y. Giants	Att.	Comp.	Yds.	TD	Int.
Hostetler	27	15	176	0	0
Cavanaugh	1	0	0	0	0
Meggett	1	0	0	0	0
San Fran.	**Att.**	**Comp.**	**Yds.**	**TD**	**Int.**
Montana	26	18	190	1	0
Young	1	1	25	0	0

Receiving

N.Y. Giants	No.	Yds.	LG	TD
Ingram	5	82	21	0
Bavaro	5	54	13	0
Baker	2	22	13	0
Meggett	2	15	15	0
Anderson	1	3	3	0
San Fran.	**No.**	**Yds.**	**LG**	**TD**
Rice	5	54	19	0
Rathman	4	16	12	0
Jones	3	46	25	0
Craig	3	16	8	0
Taylor	2	75	61t	1
Sherrard	2	8	5	0

Interceptions

N.Y. Giants	No.	Yds.	LG	TD
None				
San Fran.	**No.**	**Yds.**	**LG**	**TD**
None				

Punting

N.Y. Giants	No.	Avg.	LG	Blk.
Landeta	3	41.3	55	0
San Fran.	**No.**	**Avg.**	**LG**	**Blk.**
Helton	5	40.0	53	0

Punt Returns

N.Y. Giants	No.	FC	Yds.	LG	TD
Meggett	5	0	42	18	0
San Fran.	**No.**	**FC**	**Yds.**	**LG**	**TD**
Taylor	2	1	40	31	0

Kickoff Returns

N.Y. Giants	No.	Yds.	LG	TD
Meggett	2	36	18	0
Cross	1	3	3	0
San Fran.	**No.**	**Yds.**	**LG**	**TD**
Carter	3	74	28	0
Tillman	1	11	11	0

AFC Divisional Playoffs

Includes Second-Round Playoff Games (1982), AFC Inter-Divisional Games (1969), and special playoff games to break ties for AFL Division Championships (1963, 1968)

Results

Season	Date	Winner (Share)	Loser (Share)	Score	Site	Attendance
1990	Jan. 13	L.A. Raiders ($10,000)	Cincinnati ($10,000)	20-10	Los Angeles	92,045
	Jan. 12	Buffalo ($10,000)	Miami ($10,000)	44-34	Buffalo	77,087
1989	Jan. 7	Denver ($10,000)	Pittsburgh ($10,000)	24-23	Denver	75,477
	Jan. 6	Cleveland ($10,000)	Buffalo ($10,000)	34-30	Cleveland	78,921
1988	Jan. 1	Buffalo ($10,000)	Houston ($10,000)	17-10	Buffalo	79,532
	Dec. 31	Cincinnati ($10,000)	Seattle ($10,000)	21-13	Cincinnati	58,560
1987	Jan. 10	Denver ($10,000)	Houston ($10,000)	34-10	Denver	75,440
	Jan. 9	Cleveland ($10,000)	Indianapolis ($10,000)	38-21	Cleveland	79,372
1986	Jan. 4	Denver ($10,000)	New England ($10,000)	22-17	Denver	75,262
	Jan. 3	Cleveland ($10,000)	N.Y. Jets ($10,000)	23-20*	Cleveland	79,720
1985	Jan. 5	New England ($10,000)	L.A. Raiders ($10,000)	27-20	Los Angeles	87,163
	Jan. 4	Miami ($10,000)	Cleveland ($10,000)	24-21	Miami	74,667
1984	Dec. 30	Pittsburgh ($10,000)	Denver ($10,000)	24-17	Denver	74,981
	Dec. 29	Miami ($10,000)	Seattle ($10,000)	31-10	Miami	73,469
1983	Jan. 1	L.A. Raiders ($10,000)	Pittsburgh ($10,000)	38-10	Los Angeles	90,380
	Dec. 31	Seattle ($10,000)	Miami ($10,000)	27-20	Miami	74,136
1982	Jan. 16	Miami ($10,000)	San Diego ($10,000)	34-13	Miami	71,383
	Jan. 15	N.Y. Jets ($10,000)	L.A. Raiders ($10,000)	17-14	Los Angeles	90,038
1981	Jan. 3	Cincinnati ($5,000)	Buffalo ($5,000)	28-21	Cincinnati	55,420
	Jan. 2	San Diego ($5,000)	Miami ($5,000)	41-38*	Miami	73,735
1980	Jan. 4	Oakland ($5,000)	Cleveland ($5,000)	14-12	Cleveland	78,245
	Jan. 3	San Diego ($5,000)	Buffalo ($5,000)	20-14	San Diego	52,253
1979	Dec. 30	Pittsburgh ($5,000)	Miami ($5,000)	34-14	Pittsburgh	50,214
	Dec. 29	Houston ($5,000)	San Diego ($5,000)	17-14	San Diego	51,192
1978	Dec. 31	Houston ($5,000)	New England ($5,000)	31-14	New England	60,735
	Dec. 30	Pittsburgh ($5,000)	Denver ($5,000)	33-10	Pittsburgh	50,230
1977	Dec. 24	Oakland ($5,000)	Baltimore ($5,000)	37-31	Baltimore	59,925
	Dec. 24	Denver ($5,000)	Pittsburgh ($5,000)	34-21	Denver	75,059
1976	Dec. 19	Pittsburgh ($)	Baltimore ($)	40-14	Baltimore	59,296
	Dec. 18	Oakland ($)	New England ($)	24-21	Oakland	53,050
1975	Dec. 28	Oakland ($)	Cincinnati ($)	31-28	Oakland	53,030
	Dec. 27	Pittsburgh ($)	Baltimore ($)	28-10	Pittsburgh	49,557
1974	Dec. 22	Pittsburgh ($)	Buffalo ($)	32-14	Pittsburgh	49,841
	Dec. 21	Oakland ($)	Miami ($)	28-26	Oakland	53,023
1973	Dec. 23	Miami ($)	Cincinnati ($)	34-16	Miami	78,928
	Dec. 22	Oakland ($)	Pittsburgh ($)	33-14	Oakland	52,646
1972	Dec. 24	Miami ($)	Cleveland ($)	20-14	Miami	78,916
	Dec. 23	Pittsburgh ($)	Oakland ($)	13-7	Pittsburgh	50,327
1971	Dec. 26	Baltimore ($)	Cleveland ($)	20-3	Cleveland	70,734
	Dec. 25	Miami ($)	Kansas City ($)	27-24*	Kansas City	45,822
1970	Dec. 27	Oakland ($)	Miami ($)	21-14	Oakland	52,594
	Dec. 26	Baltimore ($)	Cincinnati ($)	17-0	Baltimore	49,694
1969	Dec. 21	Oakland ($)	Houston ($)	56-7	Oakland	53,539
	Dec. 20	Kansas City ($)	N.Y. Jets ($)	13-6	New York	62,977
1968	Dec. 22	Oakland ($)	Kansas City ($)	41-6	Oakland	53,605
1963	Dec. 28	Boston ($)	Buffalo ($)	26-8	Buffalo	33,044

**Sudden Death Overtime.*

$ Players received 1/14 of annual salary for playoff appearances.

1990 AFC Divisional Playoff Games

Rich Stadium, Orchard Park, New York — January 12, 1991

Attendance: 77,087

BUFFALO 44, MIAMI 34—Thurman Thomas ran for two touchdowns and Andre Reed caught two as the Bills defeated the Dolphins to advance to the AFC Championship Game. Quarterback Jim Kelly returned to the starting lineup after being sidelined with an injury and completed three touchdown passes, including first-half strikes to Reed (40 yards) and James Lofton (13). Scott Norwood's two field goals (24 and 22 yards) and Thomas's first five-yard touchdown run gave the Bills a 27-17 halftime advantage. Dan Marino completed a two-yard touchdown pass to guard Roy Foster in the opening minute of the fourth quarter to narrow the score to 30-27, but Buffalo countered with Thomas's second five-yard scoring run of the day and Kelly's 26-yard touchdown pass to Reed. Kelly completed 19 of 29 passes for 339 yards. Thomas rushed for 117 yards on 32 carries. The Bills' 44 points shattered the club playoff record of 31, set against the New York Jets in the 1981 AFC Wild Card game. Buffalo's 493 total yards also set a club playoff mark.

Miami	3	14	3	14	— 34
Buffalo	13	14	3	14	— 44

Buff—Reed 40 pass from Kelly (Norwood kick)
Mia—FG Stoyanovich 49
Buff—FG Norwood 24
Buff—FG Norwood 22
Buff—Thomas 5 run (Norwood kick)
Mia—Duper 64 pass from Marino (Stoyanovich kick)
Buff—Lofton 13 pass from Kelly (Norwood kick)
Mia—Marino 2 run (Stoyanovich kick)
Mia—FG Stoyanovich 22
Buff—FG Norwood 28
Mia—Foster 2 pass from Marino (Stoyanovich kick)
Buff—Thomas 5 run (Norwood kick)
Buff—Reed 26 pass from Kelly (Norwood kick)
Mia—Martin 8 pass from Marino (Stoyanovich kick)

Memorial Coliseum, Los Angeles, California — January 13, 1991

Attendance: 92,045

LOS ANGELES RAIDERS 20, CINCINNATI 10—Jay Schroeder connected on two scoring passes to help the Raiders defeat the Bengals and gain entry into the AFC Championship Game. Cincinnati scored first on Jim Breech's 27-yard field goal in the second quarter. Schroeder hit Mervyn Fernandez with a 13-yard scoring strike to give Los Angeles a 7-3 halftime lead. The Raiders increased their lead to 10-3 on Jeff Jaeger's 49-yard field goal in the third quarter. Los Angeles put the game away by scoring 10 unanswered fourth-quarter points on Schroeder's 41-yard pass to Ethan Horton and Jaeger's 25-yard field goal. The Raiders rushed for 235 yards, including 140 by Marcus Allen on 21 carries. Bo Jackson added 77 yards on six carries. Greg Townsend recorded three of the Raiders' four sacks.

Cincinnati	0	3	0	7	— 10
L.A. Raiders	0	7	3	10	— 20

Cin —FG Breech 27
Raiders—Fernandez 13 pass from Schroeder (Jaeger kick)
Raiders—FG Jaeger 49
Cin —Jennings 8 pass from Esiason (Breech kick)
Raiders—Horton 41 pass from Schroeder (Jaeger kick)
Raiders—FG Jaeger 25

NFC Divisional Playoffs

Includes Second-Round Playoff Games (1982), NFL Conference Championship Games (1967-69), and special playoff games to break ties for NFL Division or Conference Championships (1941, 1943, 1947, 1950, 1952, 1957, 1958, 1965)

Results

Season	Date	Winner (Share)	Loser (Share)	Score	Site	Attendance
1990	Jan. 13	N.Y. Giants ($10,000)	Chicago ($10,000)	31-3	East Rutherford	77,025
	Jan. 12	San Francisco ($10,000)	Washington ($10,000)	28-10	San Francisco	65,292
1989	Jan. 7	L.A. Rams ($10,000)	N.Y. Giants ($10,000)	19-13*	East Rutherford	76,526
	Jan. 6	San Francisco ($10,000)	Minnesota ($10,000)	41-13	San Francisco	64,918
1988	Jan. 1	San Francisco ($10,000)	Minnesota ($10,000)	34-9	San Francisco	61,848
	Dec. 31	Chicago ($10,000)	Philadelphia ($10,000)	20-12	Chicago	65,534
1987	Jan. 10	Washington ($10,000)	Chicago ($10,000)	21-17	Chicago	65,268
	Jan. 9	Minnesota ($10,000)	San Francisco ($10,000)	36-24	San Francisco	63,008
1986	Jan. 4	N.Y. Giants ($10,000)	San Francisco ($10,000)	49-3	East Rutherford	75,691
	Jan. 3	Washington ($10,000)	Chicago ($10,000)	27-13	Chicago	65,524
1985	Jan. 5	Chicago ($10,000)	N.Y. Giants ($10,000)	21-0	Chicago	65,670
	Jan. 4	L.A. Rams ($10,000)	Dallas ($10,000)	20-0	Anaheim	66,581
1984	Dec. 30	Chicago ($10,000)	Washington ($10,000)	23-19	Washington	55,431
	Dec. 29	San Francisco ($10,000)	N.Y. Giants ($10,000)	21-10	San Francisco	60,303
1983	Jan. 1	Washington ($10,000)	L.A. Rams ($10,000)	51-7	Washington	54,440
	Dec. 31	San Francisco ($10,000)	Detroit ($10,000)	24-23	San Francisco	59,979
1982	Jan. 16	Dallas ($10,000)	Green Bay ($10,000)	37-26	Dallas	63,972
	Jan. 15	Washington ($10,000)	Minnesota ($10,000)	21-7	Washington	54,593
1981	Jan. 3	San Francisco ($5,000)	N.Y. Giants ($5,000)	38-24	San Francisco	58,360
	Jan. 2	Dallas ($5,000)	Tampa Bay ($5,000)	38-0	Dallas	64,848
1980	Jan. 4	Dallas ($5,000)	Atlanta ($5,000)	30-27	Atlanta	59,793
	Jan. 3	Philadelphia ($5,000)	Minnesota ($5,000)	31-16	Philadelphia	70,178
1979	Dec. 30	Los Angeles ($5,000)	Dallas ($5,000)	21-19	Dallas	64,792
	Dec. 29	Tampa Bay ($5,000)	Philadelphia ($5,000)	24-17	Tampa Bay	71,402
1978	Dec. 31	Los Angeles ($5,000)	Minnesota ($5,000)	34-10	Los Angeles	70,436
	Dec. 30	Dallas ($5,000)	Atlanta ($5,000)	27-20	Dallas	63,406
1977	Dec. 26	Dallas ($5,000)	Chicago ($5,000)	37-7	Dallas	63,260
	Dec. 26	Minnesota ($5,000)	Los Angeles ($5,000)	14-7	Los Angeles	70,203
1976	Dec. 19	Los Angeles ($)	Dallas ($)	14-12	Dallas	63,283
	Dec. 18	Minnesota ($)	Washington ($)	35-20	Minnesota	47,466
1975	Dec. 28	Dallas ($)	Minnesota ($)	17-14	Minnesota	48,050
	Dec. 27	Los Angeles ($)	St. Louis ($)	35-23	Los Angeles	73,459
1974	Dec. 22	Los Angeles ($)	Washington ($)	19-10	Los Angeles	77,925
	Dec. 21	Minnesota ($)	St. Louis ($)	30-14	Minnesota	48,150
1973	Dec. 23	Dallas ($)	Los Angeles ($)	27-16	Dallas	63,272
	Dec. 22	Minnesota ($)	Washington ($)	27-20	Minnesota	48,040
1972	Dec. 24	Washington ($)	Green Bay ($)	16-3	Washington	52,321
	Dec. 23	Dallas ($)	San Francisco ($)	30-28	San Francisco	59,746
1971	Dec. 26	San Francisco ($)	Washington ($)	24-20	San Francisco	45,327
	Dec. 25	Dallas ($)	Minnesota ($)	20-12	Minnesota	47,307
1970	Dec. 27	San Francisco ($)	Minnesota ($)	17-14	Minnesota	45,103
	Dec. 26	Dallas ($)	Detroit ($)	5-0	Dallas	69,613
1969	Dec. 28	Cleveland ($)	Dallas ($)	38-14	Dallas	69,321
	Dec. 27	Minnesota ($)	Los Angeles ($)	23-20	Minnesota	47,900
1968	Dec. 22	Baltimore ($)	Minnesota ($)	24-14	Baltimore	60,238
	Dec. 21	Cleveland ($)	Dallas ($)	31-20	Cleveland	81,497
1967	Dec. 24	Dallas ($)	Cleveland ($)	52-14	Dallas	70,786
	Dec. 23	Green Bay ($)	Los Angeles ($)	28-7	Milwaukee	49,861
1965	Dec. 26	Green Bay ($)	Baltimore ($)	13-10*	Green Bay	50,484
1958	Dec. 21	N.Y. Giants (#)	Cleveland (#)	10-0	New York	61,274
1957	Dec. 22	Detroit (#)	San Francisco (#)	31-27	San Francisco	60,118
1952	Dec. 21	Detroit (#)	Los Angeles (#)	31-21	Detroit	47,645
1950	Dec. 17	Los Angeles (#)	Chicago Bears (#)	24-14	Los Angeles	83,501
	Dec. 17	Cleveland (#)	N.Y. Giants (#)	8-3	Cleveland	33,054

Season	Date	Winner (Share)	Loser (Share)	Score	Site	Attendance
1947	Dec. 21	Philadelphia (#)	Pittsburgh (#)	21-0	Pittsburgh	35,729
1943	Dec. 19	Washington (¢)	N.Y. Giants (¢)	28-0	New York	42,800
1941	Dec. 14	Chicago Bears (¢)	Green Bay (¢)	33-14	Chicago	43,425

**Sudden Death Overtime.*
$ Players received 1/14 of annual salary for playoff appearances.
 # Players received 1/12 of annual salary for playoff appearances.
¢ Players received 1/10 of annual salary for playoff appearances.

1990 NFC Divisional Playoff Games

Candlestick Park, San Francisco, California January 12, 1991
Attendance: 65,292

SAN FRANCISCO 28, WASHINGTON 10—Joe Montana, who completed 22 of 31 passes for 274 yards and two touchdowns, passed for 200 yards in the first half as the 49ers advanced to their third straight NFC Championship Game. Washington, which had defeated Philadelphia 20-6 in an NFC Wild Card Game, outgained the 49ers 441-338 in total offense and took an early 7-0 lead on quarterback Mark Rypien's 31-yard touchdown pass to Art Monk. San Francisco tied the game at 7-7 on Tom Rathman's one-yard run. Washington regained the lead 10-7 on Chip Lohmiller's 44-yard field goal with 36 seconds remaining in the first period. Montana helped his club to a 21-10 halftime advantage with a 10-yard touchdown pass to Jerry Rice. Montana also completed an eight-yard scoring strike to wide receiver Mike Sherrard. Neither club scored an offensive touchdown in the second half, but 49ers' nose tackle Michael Carter returned a deflected pass 61 yards for a touchdown.

Washington	10	0	0	0 — 10
San Francisco	7	14	0	7 — 28

Wash—Monk 31 pass from Rypien (Lohmiller kick)
SF —Rathman 1 run (Cofer kick)
Wash—FG Lohmiller 44
SF —Rice 10 pass from Montana (Cofer kick)
SF —Sherrard 8 pass from Montana (Cofer kick)
SF —Carter 61 interception return (Cofer kick)

Giants Stadium, East Rutherford, New Jersey January 13, 1991
Attendance: 77,025

NEW YORK GIANTS 31, CHICAGO 3—Giants quarterback Jeff Hostetler completed 10 of 17 passes for 112 yards and two touchdowns and rushed six times for 43 yards as the Giants rolled over Chicago and earned a spot in the NFC Championship Game. New York scored first to take a 3-0 lead on Matt Bahr's 46-yard field goal. Hostetler then completed a 21-yard touchdown pass to Stephen Baker to give the Giants a 10-0 first-quarter advantage. Chicago closed to 10-3 on Kevin Butler's 33-yard field goal, but New York extended its lead to 17-3 at halftime on Hostetler's five-yard touchdown pass to tight end Howard Cross. The Giants added touchdowns in the third and fourth periods on Hostetler's three-yard run and Maurice Carthon's one-yard run. Chicago running back Neal Anderson was held to 19 yards on 12 carries. New York held a 194-27 rushing advantage. Giants cornerbacks Everson Walls and Mark Collins each had interceptions.

Chicago	0	3	0	0 — 3
N.Y. Giants	10	7	7	7 — 31

NYG—FG Bahr 46
NYG—Baker 21 pass from Hostetler (Bahr kick)
Chi —FG Butler 33
NYG—Cross 5 pass from Hostetler (Bahr kick)
NYG—Hostetler 3 run (Bahr kick)
NYG—Carthon 1 run (Bahr kick)

AFC Wild Card Playoff Games

Results

Season	Date	Winner (Share)	Loser (Share)	Score	Site	Attendance
1990	Jan. 6	Cincinnati ($6,000)	Houston ($6,000)	41-14	Cincinnati	60,012
	Jan. 5	Miami ($6,000)	Kansas City ($6,000)	17-16	Miami	67,276
1989	Dec. 31	Pittsburgh ($6,000)	Houston ($6,000)	26-23*	Houston	59,406
1988	Dec. 26	Houston ($6,000)	Cleveland ($6,000)	24-23	Cleveland	75,896
1987	Jan. 3	Houston ($6,000)	Seattle ($6,000)	23-20*	Houston	50,519
1986	Dec. 28	N.Y. Jets ($6,000)	Kansas City ($6,000)	35-15	East Rutherford	75,210
1985	Dec. 28	New England ($6,000)	N.Y. Jets ($6,000)	26-14	East Rutherford	75,945
1984	Dec. 22	Seattle ($6,000)	L.A. Raiders ($6,000)	13-7	Seattle	62,049
1983	Dec. 24	Seattle ($6,000)	Denver ($6,000)	31-7	Seattle	64,275
1982	Jan. 9	N.Y. Jets ($6,000)	Cincinnati ($6,000)	44-17	Cincinnati	57,560
	Jan. 9	San Diego ($6,000)	Pittsburgh ($6,000)	31-28	Pittsburgh	53,546
	Jan. 8	L.A. Raiders ($6,000)	Cleveland ($6,000)	27-10	Los Angeles	56,555
	Jan. 8	Miami ($6,000)	New England ($6,000)	28-13	Miami	68,842
1981	Dec. 27	Buffalo ($3,000)	N.Y. Jets ($3,000)	31-27	New York	57,050
1980	Dec. 28	Oakland ($3,000)	Houston ($3,000)	27-7	Oakland	53,333
1979	Dec. 23	Houston ($3,000)	Denver ($3,000)	13-7	Houston	48,776
1978	Dec. 24	Houston ($3,000)	Miami ($3,000)	17-9	Miami	72,445

**Sudden death overtime.*

1990 AFC Wild Card Playoff Games

Joe Robbie Stadium, Miami, Florida January 5, 1991
Attendance: 67,276

MIAMI 17, KANSAS CITY 16—Dan Marino led two fourth-quarter scoring drives in the Dolphins' 17-16 comeback win over the Chiefs. Kansas City jumped to a 10-3 halftime lead on Nick Lowery's 27-yard field goal and Steve DeBerg's 26-yard scoring strike to Stephone Paige. Dolphins kicker Pete Stoyanovich kicked an NFL-playoff record 58-yard field goal for Miami's only score in the first half. The Chiefs increased their lead to 16-3 when Nick Lowery added field goals of 25 and 38 yards in the third quarter. In the fourth quarter, Marino completed a one-yard touchdown pass to Tony Paige to narrow the score to 16-10. Marino then directed the game-winning drive of 85 yards which was finished off by his 12-yard touchdown pass to Mark Clayton to put Miami ahead 17-16 with 2:28 left in the game. A 52-yard field-goal attempt by Lowery with 49 seconds remaining fell short.

Kansas City	3	7	6	0 — 16
Miami	0	3	0	14 — 17

KC —FG Lowery 27
Mia—FG Stoyanovich 58
KC —Paige 26 pass from DeBerg (Lowery kick)
KC —FG Lowery 25
KC —FG Lowery 38
Mia—Paige 1 pass from Marino (Stoyanovich kick)
Mia—Clayton 12 pass from Marino (Stoyanovich kick)

Riverfront Stadium, Cincinnati, Ohio January 6, 1991
Attendance: 60,012

CINCINNATI 41, HOUSTON 14—Boomer Esiason completed two touchdown passes and ran for a third in the Bengals' victory over the Oilers. Cincinnati built a 20-0 halftime lead as Ickey Woods ran one yard for a touchdown, Esiason completed a two-yard scoring pass to Harold Green, and Jim Breech kicked two field goals (27 and 30 yards). Cincinnati increased its lead to 34-0 in the third quarter when Eric Ball ran three yards for a touchdown and Esiason scored on a 10-yard keeper following James Francis's fumble recovery at Houston's 10-yard line. The Bengals finished their scoring on a nine-yard pass from Esiason to Eric Kattus. The Oilers got on the board on two scoring passes from Cody Carlson to Ernest Givins (16 and 5 yards). Cincinnati held a 39:45 to 20:15 time-of-possession advantage and had 24 first downs to Houston's 13.

Houston	0	0	7	7 — 14
Cincinnati	10	10	14	7 — 41

Cin —Woods 1 run (Breech kick)
Cin —FG Breech 27
Cin —Green 2 pass from Esiason (Breech kick)
Cin —FG Breech 30
Cin —Ball 3 run (Breech kick)
Cin —Esiason 10 run (Breech kick)
Hou—Givins 16 pass from Carlson (Garcia kick)
Cin —Kattus 9 pass from Esiason (Breech kick)
Hou—Givins 5 pass from Carlson (Garcia kick)

NFC Wild Card Playoff Games

Results

Season	Date	Winner (Share)	Loser (Share)	Score	Site	Attendance
1990	Jan. 6	Chicago ($6,000)	New Orleans ($6,000)	16-6	Chicago	60,767
	Jan. 5	Washington ($6,000)	Philadelphia ($6,000)	20-6	Philadelphia	65,287
1989	Dec. 31	L.A. Rams ($6,000)	Philadelphia ($6,000)	21-7	Philadelphia	65,479
1988	Dec. 26	Minnesota ($6,000)	L.A. Rams ($6,000)	28-17	Minnesota	61,204
1987	Jan. 3	Minnesota ($6,000)	New Orleans ($6,000)	44-10	New Orleans	68,546
1986	Dec. 28	Washington ($6,000)	L.A. Rams ($6,000)	19-7	Washington	54,567
1985	Dec. 29	N.Y. Giants ($6,000)	San Francisco ($6,000)	17-3	East Rutherford	75,131
1984	Dec. 23	N.Y. Giants ($6,000)	L.A. Rams ($6,000)	16-3	Anaheim	67,037
1983	Dec. 26	L.A. Rams ($6,000)	Dallas ($6,000)	24-17	Dallas	62,118
1982	Jan. 9	Dallas ($6,000)	Tampa Bay ($6,000)	30-17	Dallas	65,042
	Jan. 9	Minnesota ($6,000)	Atlanta ($6,000)	30-24	Minnesota	60,560
	Jan. 8	Green Bay ($6,000)	St. Louis ($6,000)	41-16	Green Bay	54,282
	Jan. 8	Washington ($6,000)	Detroit ($6,000)	31-7	Washington	55,045
1981	Dec. 27	N.Y. Giants ($3,000)	Philadelphia ($3,000)	27-21	Philadelphia	71,611
1980	Dec. 28	Dallas ($3,000)	Los Angeles ($3,000)	34-13	Dallas	63,052
1979	Dec. 23	Philadelphia ($3,000)	Chicago ($3,000)	27-17	Philadelphia	69,397
1978	Dec. 24	Atlanta ($3,000)	Philadelphia ($3,000)	14-13	Atlanta	59,403

1990 NFC Wild Card Playoff Games

Veterans Stadium, Philadelphia, Pennsylvania — January 5, 1991
Attendance: 65,287

WASHINGTON 20, PHILADELPHIA 6—The Washington Redskins captured an NFC Wild Card playoff victory over division-rival Philadelphia by scoring 20 unanswered points after falling behind 6-0. The Eagles, who failed to convert two early turnovers into touchdowns, led 6-0 in the second quarter on Roger Ruzek's field goals from 37 and 28 yards. Redskins quarterback Mark Rypien ignited his club's offensive attack with a 16-yard scoring strike to wide receiver Art Monk that gave Washington a lead it would not relinquish. Redskins kicker Chip Lohmiller's 20-yard field goal with eight seconds remaining before halftime gave the Redskins a 10-6 lead. The Redskins added 10 points in the second half as Lohmiller converted his second field goal (19 yards) and Rypien completed a three-yard touchdown pass to wide receiver Gary Clark. Rypien completed 15 of 31 passes for 206 yards and two touchdowns, while running back Earnest Byner gained 126 total yards.

Washington	0	10	10	0	— 20
Philadelphia	3	3	0	0	— 6

Phil —FG Ruzek 37
Phil —FG Ruzek 28
Wash—Monk 16 pass from Rypien (Lohmiller kick)
Wash—FG Lohmiller 20
Wash—FG Lohmiller 19
Wash—Clark 3 pass from Rypien (Lohmiller kick)

Soldier Field, Chicago, Illinois — January 6, 1991
Attendance: 60,767

CHICAGO 16, NEW ORLEANS 6—The NFC Central Division champion Bears advanced to the divisional playoffs with a victory over the Saints. Quarterback Mike Tomczak completed 12 of 25 passes for 166 yards, including an 18-yard touchdown pass to tight end James Thornton. Bears running back Neal Anderson totaled 166 yards and tied Walter Payton's team postseason record for carries in a game (27), set January 5, 1986, against the New York Giants. Anderson also caught four passes for 42 yards and had a 22-yard completion to wide receiver Ron Morris. Bears kicker Kevin Butler kicked three field goals (19, 22 and 21 yards). Chicago totaled 365 yards on offense, held a 16-6 advantage in first downs, and a 365-193 advantage in total yards. Tomczak's 38-yard completion to wide receiver Dennis Gentry with less than three minutes remaining clinched Chicago's victory. The Bears' defense held New Orleans to 65 yards rushing.

New Orleans	0	3	0	3	— 6
Chicago	3	7	3	3	— 16

Chi—FG Butler 19
Chi—Thornton 18 pass from Tomczak (Butler kick)
NO—FG Andersen 47
Chi—FG Butler 22
NO—FG Andersen 38
Chi—FG Butler 21

AFC-NFC Pro Bowl At A Glance (1971-1991)

NFC leads series, 12-9

Results

Year	Date	Winner (Share)	Loser (Share)	Score	Site	Attendance
1991	Feb. 3	AFC ($10,000)	NFC ($5,000)	23-21	Honolulu	50,345
1990	Feb. 4	NFC ($10,000)	AFC ($5,000)	27-21	Honolulu	50,445
1989	Jan. 29	NFC ($10,000)	AFC ($5,000)	34-3	Honolulu	50,113
1988	Feb. 7	AFC ($10,000)	NFC ($5,000)	15-6	Honolulu	50,113
1987	Feb. 1	AFC ($10,000)	NFC ($5,000)	10-6	Honolulu	50,101
1986	Feb. 2	NFC ($10,000)	AFC ($5,000)	28-24	Honolulu	50,101
1985	Jan. 27	AFC ($10,000)	NFC ($5,000)	22-14	Honolulu	50,385
1984	Jan. 29	NFC ($10,000)	AFC ($5,000)	45-3	Honolulu	50,445
1983	Feb. 6	NFC ($10,000)	AFC ($5,000)	20-19	Honolulu	49,883
1982	Jan. 31	AFC ($5,000)	NFC ($2,500)	16-13	Honolulu	50,402
1981	Feb. 1	NFC ($5,000)	AFC ($2,500)	21-7	Honolulu	50,360
1980	Jan. 27	NFC ($5,000)	AFC ($2,500)	37-27	Honolulu	49,800
1979	Jan. 29	NFC ($5,000)	AFC ($2,500)	13-7	Los Angeles	46,281
1978	Jan. 23	NFC ($5,000)	AFC ($2,500)	14-13	Tampa	51,337
1977	Jan. 17	AFC ($2,000)	NFC ($1,500)	24-14	Seattle	64,752
1976	Jan. 26	NFC ($2,000)	AFC ($1,500)	23-20	New Orleans	30,546
1975	Jan. 20	NFC ($2,000)	AFC ($1,500)	17-10	Miami	26,484
1974	Jan. 20	AFC ($2,000)	NFC ($1,500)	15-13	Kansas City	66,918
1973	Jan. 21	AFC ($2,000)	NFC ($1,500)	33-28	Irving	37,091
1972	Jan. 23	AFC ($2,000)	NFC ($1,500)	26-13	Los Angeles	53,647
1971	Jan. 24	NFC ($2,000)	AFC ($1,500)	27-6	Los Angeles	48,222

1991 AFC-NFC Pro Bowl

Aloha Stadium, Honolulu, Hawaii — February 3, 1991

Attendance: 50,345

AFC 23, NFC 21—Buffalo's Jim Kelly and Houston's Ernest Givins combined for a 13-yard scoring pass late in the fourth quarter to rally the AFC over the NFC. Phoenix rookie Johnny Johnson scored on runs of one and nine yards to put the NFC ahead 14-3 in the third quarter. Buffalo's Andre Reed, who led all receivers with four catches for 80 yards, caught a 20-yard scoring reception from Kelly early in the fourth quarter to move the AFC to within one point. Barry Sanders ran 22 yards for touchdown to increase the NFC's lead to 21-13. Miami's Jeff Cross blocked a 46-yard field-goal attempt by New Orleans's Morten Andersen with seven seconds remaining to preserve the win. Buffalo's Bruce Smith recorded three sacks and also had a blocked field goal. Kelly, who completed 13 of 19 passes for 210 yards and two touchdowns, was voted the Dan McGuire Award as player of the game. The AFC's victory narrowed the NFC's Pro Bowl series lead to 12-9.

AFC (23)	Offense	NFC (21)
Anthony Miller (San Diego)	WR	Jerry Rice (San Francisco)
Richmond Webb (Miami)	LT	Jim Lachey (Washington)
Mike Munchak (Houston)	LG	Randall McDaniel (Minnesota)
Kent Hull (Buffalo)	C	Jay Hilgenberg (Chicago)
Bruce Matthews (Houston)	RG	Guy McIntyre (San Francisco)
Bruce Armstrong (New England)	RT	Jackie Slater (L.A. Rams)
Rodney Holman (Cincinnati)	TE	Keith Jackson (Philadelphia)
Andre Reed (Buffalo)	WR	Andre Rison (Atlanta)
Warren Moon (Houston)	QB	Randall Cunningham (Philadelphia)
Bobby Humphrey (Denver)	RB	Barry Sanders (Detroit)
Thurman Thomas (Buffalo)	RB	Earnest Byner (Washington)
	Defense	
Bruce Smith (Buffalo)	LE	Reggie White (Philadelphia)
Michael Dean Perry (Cleveland)	NT	Jerry Ball (Detroit)
Greg Townsend (L.A. Raiders)	RE	Chris Doleman (Minnesota)
Derrick Thomas (Kansas City)	LOLB	Charles Haley (San Francisco)
David Little (Pittsburgh)	LILB	Pepper Johnson (N.Y. Giants)
Shane Conlan (Buffalo)	RILB	Mike Singletary (Chicago)
Leslie O'Neal (San Diego)	ROLB	Lawrence Taylor (N.Y. Giants)
Albert Lewis (Kansas City)	LCB	Darrell Green (Washington)
Rod Woodson (Pittsburgh)	RCB	Carl Lee (Minnesota)
David Fulcher (Cincinnati)	SS	Joey Browner (Minnesota)
Steve Atwater (Denver)	FS	Ronnie Lott (San Francisco)

Substitutions

AFC—Offense: K—Nick Lowery (Kansas City). P—Rohn Stark (Indianapolis). QB—Jim Kelly (Buffalo). RB—James Brooks (Cincinnati), John L. Williams (Seattle). WR—Ernest Givins (Houston), Drew Hill (Houston). TE—Ferrell Edmunds (Miami). KR—Clarence Verdin (Indianapolis). C—Don Mosebar (L.A. Raiders). G—Steve Wisniewski (L.A. Raiders). T—Will Wolford (Buffalo). ST—Steve Tasker (Buffalo). Defense: E—Jeff Cross (Miami). NT—Ray Childress (Houston). LB—Cornelius Bennett (Buffalo), Mike Johnson (Cleveland), Darryl Talley (Buffalo). CB—Kevin Ross (Kansas City). S—Dennis Smith (Denver). DNP—None.

NFC—Offense: K—Morten Andersen (New Orleans). P—Sean Landeta (N.Y. Giants). QB—Jim Everett (L.A. Rams). RB—Johnny Johnson (Phoenix), Emmitt Smith (Dallas). WR—Gary Clark (Washington), Sterling Sharpe (Green Bay). TE—Steve Jordan (Minnesota). KR—Mel Gray (Detroit). C—Bart Oates (N.Y. Giants). G—William Roberts (N.Y. Giants). T—Lomas Brown (Detroit). Defense: E—Richard Dent (Chicago). NT—Erik Howard (N.Y. Giants). LB—Vaughan Johnson (New Orleans), Chris Spielman (Detroit), Pat Swilling (New Orleans). CB—Wayne Haddix (Tampa Bay). S—Mark Carrier (Chicago). ST—Reyna Thompson (N.Y. Giants). DNP—None.

Head Coaches

AFC—Art Shell (L.A. Raiders)
NFC—George Seifert (San Francisco)

Officials

Referee—Gordon McCarter. Umpire—Neil Gereb. Line Judge—Tom Barnes. Head Linesman—Aaron Pointer. Back Judge—Paul Baetz. Field Judge—Bob Wortman. Side Judge—Tom Fincken.

Scoring

AFC	3	0	3	17	— 23
NFC	0	7	7	7	— 21

AFC—FG Lowery 26
NFC—J. Johnson 1 run (Andersen kick)
AFC—FG Lowery 43
NFC—J. Johnson 9 run (Andersen kick)
AFC—Reed 20 pass from Kelly (Lowery kick)
NFC—Sanders 22 run (Andersen kick)
AFC—FG Lowery 34
AFC—Givins 13 pass from Kelly (Lowery kick)

Team Statistics

	AFC	NFC
Total First Downs	17	22
First Downs Rushing	5	8
First Downs Passing	10	13
First Downs Penalty	2	1
Total Net Yardage	358	368
Total Offensive Plays	52	61
Average Gain per Offensive Play	6.9	6.0
Rushes	20	28
Yards Gained Rushing (net)	90	90
Average Yards per Rush	4.5	3.2
Passes Attempted	30	29
Passes Completed	19	19
Had Intercepted	0	0
Tackled Attempting to Pass	2	4
Yards Lost Attempting to Pass	14	28
Yards Gained Passing (net)	268	278
Punts	2	3
Average Distance	50.5	43.3
Punt Returns	2	1
Punt Return Yardage	28	−1
Kickoff Returns	1	6
Kickoff Return Yardage	23	109
Interception Return Yardage	0	0
Total Return Yardage	51	108
Fumbles	2	0
Own Fumbles Recovered	2	0
Opponents Fumbles Recovered	0	0
Penalties	6	4
Yards Penalized	30	20

Total Points Scored	23	21
Touchdowns	2	3
Touchdowns Rushing	0	3
Touchdowns Passing	2	0
Touchdowns Returns	0	0
Extra Points	2	3
Field Goals	3	0
Field Goals Attempted	4	3
Safeties	0	0
Third Down Efficiency	3/10	7/12
Fourth Down Efficiency	0/0	0/0
Time of Possession	26:32	33:28

Individual Statistics

Rushing

AFC	No.	Yds.	LG	TD
Thomas	7	38	17	0
Brooks	5	36	19	0
Williams	3	8	8	0
Humphrey	2	7	4	0
Kelly	3	1	2	0
NFC	**No.**	**Yds.**	**LG**	**TD**
Sanders	7	35	22t	1
J. Johnson	10	32	9t	2
Cunningham	3	11	5	0
Smith	5	7	4	0
Byner	2	6	3	0
Everett	1	−1	−1	0

Passing

AFC	Att.	Comp.	Yds.	TD	Int.
Kelly	19	13	210	2	0
Moon	11	6	72	0	0
NFC	**Att.**	**Comp.**	**Yds.**	**TD**	**Int.**
Everett	18	13	138	0	0
Cunning-ham	11	6	168	0	0

Receiving

AFC	No.	Yds.	LG	TD
Reed	4	80	38	1
Thomas	4	36	16	0
Miller	3	49	33	0
Brooks	3	47	49	0
Edmunds	1	27	27	0
Givins	1	13	13t	1
Hill	1	12	12	0
Holman	1	12	12	0
Humphrey	1	6	6	0
NFC	**No.**	**Yds.**	**LG**	**TD**
Clark	6	65	19	0
Rice	3	62	49	0
Jordan	3	45	29	0
Jackson	2	47	28	0
Sanders	2	24	19	0
Byner	1	43	43	0
J. Johnson	1	10	10	0
Sharpe	1	10	10	0

Interceptions

AFC	No.	Yds.	LG	TD
None				
NFC	**No.**	**Yds.**	**LG**	**TD**
None				

Punting

AFC	No.	Avg.	LG	Blk.
Stark	2	50.5	51	0
NFC	**No.**	**Avg.**	**LG**	**Blk.**
Landeta	3	43.3	56	0

Punt Returns

AFC	No.	FC	Yds.	LG	TD
Verdin	2	0	28	20	0
NFC	**No.**	**FC**	**Yds.**	**LG**	**TD**
Gray	1	0	−1	−1	0

Kickoff Returns

AFC	No.	Yds.	LG	TD
Miller	1	23	23	0
NFC	**No.**	**Yds.**	**LG**	**TD**
Gray	5	96	33	0
Smith	1	13	13	0

1990 AFC-NFC Pro Bowl

Aloha Stadium, Honolulu, Hawaii — February 4, 1990

Attendance: 50,445

NFC 27, AFC 21—The NFC captured its second straight Pro Bowl as the defense accounted for a pair of touchdowns and forced five turnovers before the eleventh consecutive sellout crowd at Aloha Stadium. The AFC held a 7-6 halftime edge on a one-yard scoring run by Christian Okoye of the Chiefs. The NFC then rallied with 21 unanswered points in the third quarter. David Meggett of the Giants began the comeback with an 11-yard touchdown reception from Philadelphia's Randall Cunningham. The Rams' Jerry Gray followed with a 51-yard interception return for a score and the Vikings' Keith Millard added an eight-yard fumble return for a touchdown four minutes later to give the NFC a commanding 27-7 lead. Seattle's Dave Krieg rallied the AFC with a five-yard touchdown pass to Miami's Ferrell Edmunds. Cleveland's Mike Johnson then returned an interception 22 yards for a score to pull the AFC to within six points 27-21. Gray, who was credited with seven tackles, was voted the Dan McGuire Award as player of the game. Krieg led all quarterbacks by completing 15 of 23 for 148 yards and one touchdown. Buffalo's Thurman Thomas topped all receivers with five catches for 47 yards, while Indianapolis's Eric Dickerson led all rushers with 46 yards on 15 carries. The win gave the NFC a 12-8 advantage in Pro Bowl games since 1971.

NFC	3	3	21	0	— 27
AFC	0	7	0	14	— 21

NFC—FG Murray 23
NFC—FG Murray 41
AFC—Okoye 1 run (Treadwell kick)
NFC—Meggett 11 pass from Cunningham (Murray kick)
NFC—Gray 51 interception return (Murray kick)
NFC—Millard 8 fumble recovery return (Murray kick)
AFC—Edmunds 5 pass from Krieg (Treadwell kick)
AFC—M. Johnson 22 interception return (Treadwell kick)

1989 AFC-NFC Pro Bowl

Aloha Stadium, Honolulu, Hawaii — January 29, 1989

Attendance: 50,113

NFC 34, AFC 3—The NFC scored 34 unanswered points to snap a two-game losing streak to the AFC before the tenth straight sellout crowd in Honolulu's Aloha Stadium. Bills kicker Scott Norwood provided the AFC's only points on a 38-yard field goal 6:23 into the game. Touchdown runs by Dallas's Herschel Walker (four yards) and Atlanta's John Settle (one) brought the NFC a 14-3 half-time lead. Walker added a seven-yard scoring run, the Saints' Morten Andersen kicked field goals of 27 and 51 yards, and Los Angeles Rams' wide receiver Henry Ellard caught an eight-yard scoring pass from Minnesota quarterback Wade Wilson in the second half to complete the scoring. Chicago running back Neal Anderson and Philadelphia quarterback Randall Cunningham, who were both appearing in their first Pro Bowl, also played major roles in the NFC's victory. Anderson rushed 13 times for 85 yards and had two receptions for 17. Cunningham, who was voted the game's outstanding player, completed 10 of 14 passes for 63 yards and rushed for 49 yards. The NFC, which had five takeaways, outgained the AFC 355 yards to 167 and held a time-of-possession advantage of 35:18 to 24:42. Houston quarterback Warren Moon completed 13 of 20 passes for 134 yards for the AFC. The win gave the NFC an 11-8 advantage in Pro Bowl games.

AFC	3	0	0	0	— 3
NFC	7	7	10	10	— 34

AFC—FG Norwood 38
NFC—Walker 4 run (Andersen kick)
NFC—Settle 1 run (Andersen kick)
NFC—FG Andersen 27
NFC—Walker 7 run (Andersen kick)
NFC—FG Andersen 51
NFC—Ellard 8 pass from Wilson (Andersen kick)

1988 AFC-NFC Pro Bowl

Aloha Stadium, Honolulu, Hawaii — February 7, 1988

Attendance: 50,113

AFC 15, NFC 6—Led by a tenacious pass rush, the AFC defeated the NFC for the second consecutive year, 15-6, before the ninth straight sellout crowd in Honolulu's Aloha Stadium. Buffalo quarterback Jim Kelly scored the game's lone touchdown on a one-yard run for a 7-6 halftime lead. Colts kicker Dean Biasucci added field goals from 37 and 30 yards to complete the AFC's scoring. Saints kicker Morten Andersen had 25- and 36-yard field goals to account for the NFC's points. AFC defenders held the NFC to 213 yards and recorded eight sacks. Bills defensive end Bruce Smith, who had five tackles and two sacks, was voted the game's outstanding player. Oilers running back Mike Rozier led all rushers with 49 yards on nine carries. Jets wide receiver Al Toon had five receptions for 75 yards. The AFC generated 341 yards total offense and held a time-of-possession advantage of 34:14 to 25:46. By winning, the AFC cut the NFC's lead in the Pro Bowl series to 10-8.

NFC	0	6	0	0	— 6
AFC	0	7	6	2	— 15

NFC—FG Andersen 25
AFC—Kelly 1 run (Biasucci kick)
NFC—FG Andersen 36
AFC—FG Biasucci 37
AFC—FG Biasucci 30
AFC—Safety, Montana forced out of end zone

1987 AFC-NFC Pro Bowl

Aloha Stadium, Honolulu, Hawaii — February 1, 1987

Attendance: 50,101

AFC 10, NFC 6—The AFC defeated the NFC, 10-6, in the lowest-scoring game in AFC-NFC Pro Bowl history. The AFC took a 10-0 halftime lead on Broncos quarterback John Elway's 10-yard touchdown pass to Raiders tight end Todd Christensen and Patriots kicker Tony Franklin's 26-yard field goal. The AFC defense made the lead stand up by forcing the NFC to settle for a pair of field goals from 38 and 19 yards by Saints kicker Morten Andersen after the NFC had first downs at the AFC 31-, 7-, 16-, 15-, 5-, and 7-yard lines. Both AFC scores were set up by fumble recoveries by Seahawks linebacker Fredd Young and Dolphins linebacker John Offerdahl, respectively. Eagles defensive end Reggie White, who tied a Pro Bowl record with four sacks and also contributed seven solo tackles, was voted the game's outstanding player. The AFC victory cut the NFC's lead in the Pro Bowl series to 10-7.

AFC	7	3	0	0	— 10
NFC	0	0	3	3	— 6

AFC—Christensen 10 pass from Elway (Franklin kick)
AFC—FG Franklin 26
NFC—FG Andersen 38
NFC—FG Andersen 19

1986 AFC-NFC Pro Bowl

Aloha Stadium, Honolulu, Hawaii — February 2, 1986

Attendance: 50,101

NFC 28, AFC 24—New York Giants quarterback Phil Simms brought the NFC back from a 24-7 halftime deficit to a 28-24 win over the AFC. Simms, who completed 15 of 27 passes for 212 yards and three touchdowns, was named the most valuable player of the game. The AFC had taken its first-half lead behind a two-yard run by Los Angeles Raiders running back Marcus Allen, who also threw a 51-yard scoring pass to San Diego wide receiver Wes Chandler, an 11-yard touchdown catch by Pittsburgh wide receiver Louis Lipps, and a 34-yard field goal by Steelers kicker Gary Anderson. Minnesota's Joey Browner accounted for the NFC's only score before halftime with a 48-yard touchdown interception return. After intermission, the NFC blanked the AFC while scoring three touchdowns via a 15-yard catch by Washington wide receiver Art Monk, a 2-yard reception by Dallas tight end Doug Cosbie, and a 15-yard catch by Tampa Bay tight end Jimmie Giles with 2:47 remaining in the game. The victory gave the NFC a 10-6 Pro Bowl record vs. the AFC.

NFC	0	7	7	14	— 28
AFC	7	17	0	0	— 24

AFC—Allen 2 run (Anderson kick)
NFC—Browner 48 interception return (Andersen kick)

AFC—Chandler 51 pass from Allen (Anderson kick)
AFC—FG Anderson 34
AFC—Lipps 11 pass from O'Brien (Anderson kick)
NFC—Monk 15 pass from Simms (Andersen kick)
NFC—Cosbie 2 pass from Simms (Andersen kick)
NFC—Giles 15 pass from Simms (Andersen kick)

1985 AFC-NFC Pro Bowl

Aloha Stadium, Honolulu, Hawaii — January 27, 1985
Attendance: 50,385

AFC 22, NFC 14—Defensive end Art Still of the Kansas City Chiefs recovered a fumble and returned it 83 yards for a touchdown to clinch the AFC's victory over the NFC. Still's touchdown came in the fourth period with the AFC trailing 14-12 and was one of several outstanding defensive plays in a Pro Bowl dominated by two record-breaking defenses. Both teams combined for a Pro Bowl-record 17 sacks, including four by New York Jets defensive end Mark Gastineau, who was named the game's outstanding player. The AFC's first score came on a safety when Gastineau tackled running back Eric Dickerson of the Los Angeles Rams in the end zone. The AFC's second score, a six-yard pass from Miami's Dan Marino to Los Angeles Raiders running back Marcus Allen, was set up by a partial block of a punt by Seahawks linebacker Fredd Young. The NFC leads the series 9-6.

AFC	0	9	0	13	— 22
NFC	0	0	7	7	— 14

AFC—Safety, Gastineau tackled Dickerson in end zone
AFC—Allen 6 pass from Marino (Johnson kick)
NFC—Lofton 13 pass from Montana (Stenerud kick)
NFC—Payton 1 run (Stenerud kick)
AFC—FG Johnson 33
AFC—Still 83 fumble recovery return (Johnson kick)
AFC—FG Johnson 22

1984 AFC-NFC Pro Bowl

Aloha Stadium, Honolulu, Hawaii — January 29, 1984
Attendance: 50,445

NFC 45, AFC 3—The NFC won its sixth Pro Bowl in the last seven seasons, 45-3 over the AFC. The NFC was led by the passing of most valuable player Joe Theismann of Washington, who completed 21 of 27 passes for 242 yards and three touchdowns. Theismann set Pro Bowl records for completions and touchdown passes. The NFC established Pro Bowl marks for most points scored and fewest points allowed. Running back William Andrews of Atlanta had six carries for 43 yards and caught four passes for 49 yards, including scoring receptions of 16 and 2 yards. Los Angeles Rams rookie Eric Dickerson gained 46 yards on 11 carries, including a 14-yard touchdown run, and had 45 yards on five catches. Rams safety Nolan Cromwell had a 44-yard interception return for a touchdown early in the third period to give the NFC a commanding 24-3 lead. Green Bay wide receiver James Lofton caught an eight-yard touchdown pass, while tight end teammate Paul Coffman had a six-yard scoring catch.

NFC	3	14	14	14	— 45
AFC	0	3	0	0	— 3

NFC—FG Haji-Sheikh 23
NFC—Andrews 16 pass from Theismann (Haji-Sheikh kick)
NFC—Andrews 2 pass from Montana (Haji-Sheikh kick)
AFC—FG Anderson 43
NFC—Cromwell 44 interception return (Haji-Sheikh kick)
NFC—Lofton 8 pass from Theismann (Haji-Sheikh kick)
NFC—Coffman 6 pass from Theismann (Haji-Sheikh kick)
NFC—Dickerson 14 run (Haji-Sheikh kick)

1983 AFC-NFC Pro Bowl

Aloha Stadium, Honolulu, Hawaii — February 6, 1983
Attendance: 49,883

NFC 20, AFC 19—Danny White threw an 11-yard touchdown pass to John Jefferson with 35 seconds remaining to give the NFC a 20-19 victory over the AFC. White, who completed 14 of 26 passes for 162 yards, kept the winning 65-yard drive alive with a 14-yard completion to Jefferson on a fourth-and-seven play at the AFC 25. The AFC was ahead 12-10 at halftime and increased the lead to 19-10 in the third period, when Marcus Allen scored on a one-yard run. Dan Fouts, who attempted 30 passes, set Pro Bowl records for most completions (17) and yards (274). John Stallworth was the AFC's leading receiver with seven catches for 67 yards. William Andrews topped the NFC with five receptions for 48 yards. Fouts and Jefferson were voted co-winners of the player of the game award.

AFC	9	3	7	0	— 19
NFC	0	10	0	10	— 20

AFC—Walker 34 pass from Fouts (Benirschke kick)
AFC—Safety, Still tackled Theismann in end zone
NFC—Andrews 3 run (Moseley kick)
NFC—FG Moseley 35
AFC—FG Benirschke 29
AFC—Allen 1 run (Benirschke kick)
NFC—FG Moseley 41
NFC—Jefferson 11 pass from D. White (Moseley kick)

1982 AFC-NFC Pro Bowl

Aloha Stadium, Honolulu, Hawaii — January 31, 1982
Attendance: 50,402

AFC 16, NFC 13—Nick Lowery kicked a 23-yard field goal with three seconds remaining to give the AFC a 16-13 victory over the NFC. Lowery's kick climaxed a 69-yard drive directed by quarterback Dan Fouts. The NFC gained a 13-13 tie with 2:43 to go when Tony Dorsett ran four yards for a touchdown. In the drive to the game-winning field goal, Fouts completed three passes, including a 23-yarder to San Diego teammate Kellen Winslow that put the ball on the NFC's 5-yard line. Two plays later, Lowery kicked the field goal. Winslow, who caught six passes for 86 yards, was named co-player of the game along with NFC defensive end Lee Roy Selmon.

NFC	0	6	0	7	— 13
AFC	0	0	13	3	— 16

NFC—Giles 4 pass from Montana (kick blocked)
AFC—Muncie 2 run (kick failed)
AFC—Campbell 1 run (Lowery kick)
NFC—Dorsett 4 run (Septien kick)
AFC—FG Lowery 23

1981 AFC-NFC Pro Bowl

Aloha Stadium, Honolulu, Hawaii — February 1, 1981
Attendance: 50,360

NFC 21, AFC 7—Ed Murray kicked four field goals and Steve Bartkowski fired a 55-yard scoring pass to Alfred Jenkins to lead the NFC to its fourth straight victory over the AFC and a 7-4 edge in the series. Murray was named the game's most valuable player and missed tying Garo Yepremian's Pro Bowl record of five field goals when a 37-yard attempt hit the crossbar with 22 seconds remaining. The AFC's only score came on a nine-yard pass from Brian Sipe to Stanley Morgan in the second period. Bartkowski completed 9 of 21 passes for 173 yards, while Sipe connected on 10 of 15 for 142 yards. Ottis Anderson led all rushers with 70 yards on 10 carries. Earl Campbell, the NFL's leading rusher in 1980, was limited to 24 yards on eight attempts.

AFC	0	7	0	0	— 7
NFC	3	6	0	12	— 21

NFC—FG Murray 31
AFC—Morgan 9 pass from Sipe (J. Smith kick)
NFC—FG Murray 31
NFC—FG Murray 34
NFC—Jenkins 55 pass from Bartkowski (Murray kick)
NFC—FG Murray 36
NFC—Safety, Shell called for holding in end zone

1980 AFC-NFC Pro Bowl

Aloha Stadium, Honolulu, Hawaii — January 27, 1980
Attendance: 49,800

NFC 37, AFC 27—Running back Chuck Muncie ran for two touchdowns and threw a 25-yard option pass for another score to give the NFC its third consecutive victory over the AFC. Muncie, who was selected the game's most valuable player, snapped a 3-3 tie on a one-yard touchdown run at 1:41 of the second quarter, then scored on an 11-yard run in the fourth quarter for the NFC's final touchdown. Two scoring records were set in the game—37 points by the NFC, eclipsing the 33 by the AFC in 1973, and the 64 points by both teams, surpassing the 61 scored in 1973.

NFC	3	20	7	7	— 37
AFC	3	7	10	7	— 27

NFC—FG Moseley 37
AFC—FG Fritsch 19
NFC—Muncie 1 run (Moseley kick)
AFC—Pruitt 1 pass from Bradshaw (Fritsch kick)
NFC—D. Hill 13 pass from Manning (kick failed)
NFC—T. Hill 25 pass from Muncie (Moseley kick)
NFC—Henry 86 punt return (Moseley kick)
AFC—Campbell 2 run (Fritsch kick)
AFC—FG Fritsch 29
NFC—Muncie 11 run (Moseley kick)
AFC—Campbell 1 run (Fritsch kick)

1979 AFC-NFC Pro Bowl

Memorial Coliseum, Los Angeles, California — January 29, 1979
Attendance: 46,281

NFC 13, AFC 7—Roger Staubach completed 9 of 15 passes for 125 yards, including the winning touchdown on a 19-yard strike to Dallas Cowboys teammate Tony Hill in the third period. The winning drive began at the AFC's 45 yard line after a shanked punt. Staubach hit Ahmad Rashad with passes of 15 and 17 yards to set up Hill's decisive catch. The victory gave the NFC a 5-4 advantage in Pro Bowl games. Rashad, who accounted for 89 yards on five receptions, was named the player of the game. The AFC led 7-6 at halftime on Bob Griese's eight-yard scoring toss to Steve Largent late in the second quarter. Largent finished the game with five receptions for 75 yards. The NFC scored first as Archie Manning marched his team 70 yards in 11 plays, capped by Wilbert Montgomery's two-yard touchdown run. The AFC's Earl Campbell was the game's leading rusher with 66 yards on 12 carries.

AFC	0	7	0	0	— 7
NFC	0	6	7	0	— 13

NFC—Montgomery 2 run (kick failed)
AFC—Largent 8 pass from Griese (Yepremian kick)
NFC—T. Hill 19 pass from Staubach (Corral kick)

1978 AFC-NFC Pro Bowl

Tampa Stadium, Tampa, Florida — January 23, 1978
Attendance: 51,337

NFC 14, AFC 13—Walter Payton, the NFL's leading rusher in 1977, sparked a second-half comeback to give the NFC a 14-13 win and tie the series between the two conferences at four victories each. Payton, who was the game's most valuable player, gained 77 yards on 13 carries and scored the tying touchdown on a one-yard burst with 7:37 left in the game. Efren Herrera kicked the winning extra point. The AFC dominated the first half of the game, taking a 13-0 lead on field goals of 21 and 39 yards by Toni Linhart and a 10-yard touchdown pass from Ken Stabler to Oakland teammate Cliff Branch. On the NFC's first possession of the second half, Pat Haden put together the first touchdown drive after Eddie Brown returned Ray Guy's punt to the AFC 46-yard line. Haden connected on all four of his passes on that drive, finally hitting Terry Metcalf with a four-yard scoring toss. The NFC continued to rally and, with Jim Hart at quarterback, moved 63 yards in 12 plays for the go-ahead score. During the winning drive, Hart completed five of six passes for 38 yards and Payton picked up 20 more on the ground.

AFC	3	10	0	0	— 13
NFC	0	0	7	7	— 14

AFC—FG Linhart 21
AFC—Branch 10 pass from Stabler (Linhart kick)
AFC—FG Linhart 39
NFC—Metcalf 4 pass from Haden (Herrera kick)
NFC—Payton 1 run (Herrera kick)

1977 AFC-NFC Pro Bowl

Kingdome, Seattle, Washington — January 17, 1977
Attendance: 64,752

AFC 24, NFC 14—O.J. Simpson's three-yard touchdown burst at 7:03 of the first quarter gave the AFC a lead it would not surrender, the victory breaking a two-game NFC win streak and giving the American Conference stars a 4-3 series lead. The AFC took a 17-7 lead midway through the second period on the first of two Ken Anderson touchdown passes, a 12-yarder to Charlie Joiner. But the NFC mounted a 73-yard drive capped by Lawrence McCutcheon's one-yard touchdown plunge to pull within three of the AFC, 17-14, at the half. Following a scoreless third quarter, player of the game Mel Blount thwarted a possible NFC score when he intercepted Jim Hart's pass in the end zone. Less than three minutes later, Blount again picked off a Hart pass, returning it 16 yards to the NFC 27. That set up Anderson's 27-yard touchdown strike to Cliff Branch for the final score.

NFC	0	14	0	0	— 14
AFC	10	7	0	7	— 24

AFC—Simpson 3 run (Linhart kick)
AFC—FG Linhart 31
NFC—Thomas 15 run (Bakken kick)
AFC—Joiner 12 pass from Anderson (Linhart kick)
NFC—McCutcheon 1 run (Bakken kick)
AFC—Branch 27 pass from Anderson (Linhart kick)

1976 AFC-NFC Pro Bowl

Superdome, New Orleans, Louisiana — January 26, 1976
Attendance: 30,546

NFC 23, AFC 20—Mike Boryla, a late substitute who did not enter the game until 5:39 remained, lifted the National Football Conference to a 23-20 victory over the American Football Conference with two touchdown passes in the final minutes. It was the second straight NFC win, squaring the series at 3-3. Until Boryla started firing the ball the AFC was in control, leading 13-0 at the half. Boryla entered the game after Billy Johnson had raced 90 yards with a punt to make the score 20-9 in favor of the AFC. He floated a 14-yard pass to Terry Metcalf and later fired an eight-yarder to Mel Gray for the winner.

AFC	0	13	0	7	— 20
NFC	0	0	9	14	— 23

AFC—FG Stenerud 20
AFC—FG Stenerud 35
AFC—Burrough 64 pass from Pastorini (Stenerud kick)
NFC—FG Bakken 42
NFC—Foreman 4 pass from Hart (kick blocked)
AFC—Johnson 90 punt return (Stenerud kick)
NFC—Metcalf 14 pass from Boryla (Bakken kick)
NFC—Gray 8 pass from Boryla (Bakken kick)

1975 AFC-NFC Pro Bowl

Orange Bowl, Miami, Florida — January 20, 1975
Attendance: 26,484

NFC 17, AFC 10—Los Angeles quarterback James Harris, who took over the NFC offense after Jim Hart of St. Louis suffered a laceration above his right eye in the second period, threw a pair of touchdown passes early in the fourth period to pace the NFC to its second victory in the five-game Pro Bowl series. The NFC win snapped a three-game AFC victory string. Harris, who was named the player of the game, connected with St. Louis's Mel Gray for an eight-yard touchdown 2:03 into the final period. One minute and 24 seconds later, following a recovery by Washington's Ken Houston of a fumble by Franco Harris of Pittsburgh, Harris tossed another eight-yard scoring pass to Washington's Charley Taylor for the decisive points.

NFC	0	3	0	14	— 17
AFC	0	0	10	0	— 10

NFC—FG Marcol 33
AFC—Warfield 32 pass from Griese (Gerela kick)
AFC—FG Gerela 33
NFC—Gray 8 pass from J. Harris (Marcol kick)
NFC—Taylor 8 pass from J. Harris (Marcol kick)

1974 AFC-NFC Pro Bowl

Arrowhead Stadium, Kansas City, Missouri — January 20, 1974
Attendance: 66,918

AFC 15, NFC 13—Miami's Garo Yepremian kicked his fifth consecutive field goal without a miss from the 42-yard line with 21 seconds remaining to give the AFC its third straight victory since the NFC won the inaugural game following the 1970 season. The field goal by Yepremian, who was voted the game's outstanding player, offset a 21-yard field goal by Atlanta's Nick Mike-Mayer that had given the NFC a 13-12 advantage with 1:41 remaining. The only touchdown in the game was scored by the NFC on a 14-yard pass from Philadelphia's Roman Gabriel to Lawrence McCutcheon of the Los Angeles Rams.

NFC	0	10	0	3	— 13
AFC	3	3	3	6	— 15

AFC—FG Yepremian 16
NFC—FG Mike-Mayer 27
NFC—McCutcheon 14 pass from Gabriel (Mike-Mayer kick)
AFC—FG Yepremian 37
AFC—FG Yepremian 27
AFC—FG Yepremian 41
NFC—FG Mike-Mayer 21
AFC—FG Yepremian 42

1973 AFC-NFC Pro Bowl

Texas Stadium, Irving, Texas — January 21, 1973
Attendance: 37,091

AFC 33, NFC 28—Paced by the rushing and receiving of player of the game O.J. Simpson, the AFC erased a 14-0 first period deficit and built a commanding 33-14 lead midway through the fourth period before the NFC managed two touchdowns in the final minute of play. Simpson rushed for 112 yards and caught three passes for 58 more to gain unanimous recognition in the balloting for player of the game. John Brockington scored three touchdowns for the NFC.

AFC	0	10	10	13	— 33
NFC	14	0	0	14	— 28

NFC—Brockington 1 run (Marcol kick)
NFC—Brockington 3 pass from Kilmer (Marcol kick)
AFC—Simpson 7 run (Gerela kick)
AFC—FG Gerela 18
AFC—FG Gerela 22
AFC—Hubbard 11 run (Gerela kick)
AFC—O. Taylor 5 pass from Lamonica (kick failed)
AFC—Bell 12 interception return (Gerela kick)
NFC—Brockington 1 run (Marcol kick)
NFC—Kwalick 12 pass from Snead (Marcol kick)

1972 AFC-NFC Pro Bowl

Memorial Coliseum, Los Angeles, California — January 23, 1972
Attendance: 53,647

AFC 26, NFC 13—Four field goals by Jan Stenerud of Kansas City, including a 6-6 tie-breaker from 48 yards, helped lift the AFC from a 6-0 deficit to a 19-6 advantage early in the fourth period. The AFC defense picked off three interceptions. Stenerud was selected as the outstanding offensive player and his Kansas City teammate, linebacker Willie Lanier, was the game's outstanding defensive player.

AFC	0	3	13	10	— 26
NFC	0	6	0	7	— 13

NFC—Grim 50 pass from Landry (kick failed)
AFC—FG Stenerud 25
AFC—FG Stenerud 23
AFC—FG Stenerud 48
AFC—Morin 5 pass from Dawson (Stenerud kick)
AFC—FG Stenerud 42
NFC—V. Washington 2 run (Knight kick)
AFC—F. Little 6 run (Stenerud kick)

1971 AFC-NFC Pro Bowl

Memorial Coliseum, Los Angeles, California — January 24, 1971
Attendance: 48,222

NFC 27, AFC 6—Mel Renfro of Dallas broke open the first meeting between the American Football Conference and National Football Conference all-star teams as he returned a pair of punts 82 and 56 yards for touchdowns in the final period to provide the NFC with a 27-6 victory over the AFC. Renfro was voted the game's outstanding back and linebacker Fred Carr of Green Bay the outstanding lineman.

AFC	0	3	3	0	— 6
NFC	0	3	10	14	— 27

AFC—FG Stenerud 37
NFC—FG Cox 13
NFC—Osborn 23 pass from Brodie (Cox kick)
NFC—FG Cox 35
AFC—FG Stenerud 16
NFC—Renfro 82 punt return (Cox kick)
NFC—Renfro 56 punt return (Cox kick)

Pro Bowl All-Time Results

Date	Result	Site (attendance)	Honored players
Jan. 15, 1939	New York Giants 13, Pro All-Stars 10	Wrigley Field, Los Angeles (20,000)	
Jan. 14, 1940	Green Bay 16, NFL All-Stars 7	Gilmore Stadium, Los Angeles (18,000)	
Dec. 29, 1940	Chicago Bears 28, NFL All-Stars 14	Gilmore Stadium, Los Angeles (21,624)	
Jan. 4, 1942	Chicago Bears 35, NFL All-Stars 24	Polo Grounds, New York (17,725)	
Dec. 27, 1942	NFL All-Stars 17, Washington 14	Shibe Park, Philadelphia (18,671)	
Jan. 14, 1951	American Conf. 28, National Conf. 27	Los Angeles Memorial Coliseum (53,676)	Otto Graham, Cleveland, player of the game
Jan. 12, 1952	National Conf. 30, American Conf. 13	Los Angeles Memorial Coliseum (19,400)	Dan Towler, Los Angeles, player of the game
Jan. 10, 1953	National Conf. 27, American Conf. 7	Los Angeles Memorial Coliseum (34,208)	Don Doll, Detroit, player of the game
Jan. 17, 1954	East 20, West 9	Los Angeles Memorial Coliseum (44,214)	Chuck Bednarik, Philadelphia, player of the game
Jan. 16, 1955	West 26, East 19	Los Angeles Memorial Coliseum (43,972)	Billy Wilson, San Francisco, player of the game
Jan. 15, 1956	East 31, West 30	Los Angeles Memorial Coliseum (37,867)	Ollie Matson, Chi. Cardinals, player of the game
Jan. 13, 1957	West 19, East 10	Los Angeles Memorial Coliseum (44,177)	Bert Rechichar, Baltimore, outstanding back Ernie Stautner, Pittsburgh, outstanding lineman
Jan. 12, 1958	West 26, East 7	Los Angeles Memorial Coliseum (66,634)	Hugh McElhenny, San Francisco, outstanding back Gene Brito, Washington, outstanding lineman
Jan. 11, 1959	East 28, West 21	Los Angeles Memorial Coliseum (72,250)	Frank Gifford, N.Y. Giants, outstanding back Doug Atkins, Chi. Bears, outstanding lineman
Jan. 17, 1960	West 38, East 21	Los Angeles Memorial Coliseum (56,876)	Johnny Unitas, Baltimore, outstanding back Gene (Big Daddy) Lipscomb, Baltimore, outstanding lineman
Jan. 15, 1961	West 35, East 31	Los Angeles Memorial Coliseum (62,971)	Johnny Unitas, Baltimore, outstanding back Sam Huff, N.Y. Giants, outstanding lineman
Jan. 7, 1962	AFL West 47, East 27	Balboa Stadium, San Diego (20,973)	Cotton Davidson, Dallas Texans, player of the game
Jan. 14, 1962	NFL West 31, East 30	Los Angeles Memorial Coliseum (57,409)	Jim Brown, Cleveland, outstanding back Henry Jordan, Green Bay, outstanding lineman
Jan. 13, 1963	AFL West 21, East 14	Balboa Stadium, San Diego (27,641)	Curtis McClinton, Dallas Texans, outstanding offensive player Earl Faison, San Diego, outstanding defensive player
Jan. 13, 1963	NFL East 30, West 20	Los Angeles Memorial Coliseum (61,374)	Jim Brown, Cleveland, outstanding back Gene (Big Daddy) Lipscomb, Pittsburgh, outstanding lineman
Jan. 12, 1964	NFL West 31, East 17	Los Angeles Memorial Coliseum (67,242)	Johnny Unitas, Baltimore, player of the game Gino Marchetti, Baltimore, outstanding lineman
Jan. 19, 1964	AFL West 27, East 24	Balboa Stadium, San Diego (20,016)	Keith Lincoln, San Diego, outstanding offensive player Archie Matsos, Oakland, outstanding defensive player
Jan. 10, 1965	NFL West 34, East 14	Los Angeles Memorial Coliseum (60,598)	Fran Tarkenton, Minnesota, outstanding back Terry Barr, Detroit, outstanding lineman
Jan. 16, 1965	AFL West 38, East 14	Jeppesen Stadium, Houston (15,446)	Keith Lincoln, San Diego, outstanding offensive player Willie Brown, Denver, outstanding defensive player
Jan. 15, 1966	AFL All-Stars 30, Buffalo 19	Rice Stadium, Houston (35,572)	Joe Namath, N.Y. Jets, most valuable player, offense Frank Buncom, San Diego, most valuable player, defense
Jan. 15, 1966	NFL East 36, West 7	Los Angeles Memorial Coliseum (60,124)	Jim Brown, Cleveland, outstanding back Dale Meinert, St. Louis, outstanding lineman
Jan. 21, 1967	AFL East 30, West 23	Oakland-Alameda County Coliseum (18,876)	Babe Parilli, Boston, outstanding offensive player Verlon Biggs, N.Y. Jets, outstanding defensive player
Jan. 22, 1967	NFL East 20, West 10	Los Angeles Memorial Coliseum (15,062)	Gale Sayers, Chicago, outstanding back Floyd Peters, Philadelphia, outstanding lineman
Jan. 21, 1968	AFL East 25, West 24	Gator Bowl, Jacksonville, Fla. (40,103)	Joe Namath and Don Maynard, N.Y. Jets, out. off. players Leslie (Speedy) Duncan, San Diego, out. def. player
Jan. 21, 1968	NFL West 38, East 20	Los Angeles Memorial Coliseum (53,289)	Gale Sayers, Chicago, outstanding back Dave Robinson, Green Bay, outstanding lineman
Jan. 19, 1969	AFL West 38, East 25	Gator Bowl, Jacksonville, Fla. (41,058)	Len Dawson, Kansas City, outstanding offensive player George Webster, Houston, outstanding defensive player
Jan. 19, 1969	NFL West 10, East 7	Los Angeles Memorial Coliseum (32,050)	Roman Gabriel, Los Angeles, outstanding back Merlin Olsen, Los Angeles, outstanding lineman
Jan. 17, 1970	AFL West 26, East 3	Astrodome, Houston (30,170)	John Hadl, San Diego, player of the game
Jan. 18, 1970	NFL West 16, East 13	Los Angeles Memorial Coliseum (57,786)	Gale Sayers, Chicago, outstanding back George Andrie, Dallas, outstanding lineman
Jan. 24, 1971	NFC 27, AFC 6	Los Angeles Memorial Coliseum (48,222)	Mel Renfro, Dallas, outstanding back Fred Carr, Green Bay, outstanding lineman
Jan. 23, 1972	AFC 26, NFC 13	Los Angeles Memorial Coliseum (53,647)	Jan Stenerud, Kansas City, outstanding offensive player Willie Lanier, Kansas City, outstanding defensive player
Jan. 21, 1973	AFC 33, NFC 28	Texas Stadium, Irving (37,091)	O.J. Simpson, Buffalo, player of the game
Jan. 20, 1974	AFC 15, NFC 13	Arrowhead Stadium, Kansas City (66,918)	Garo Yepremian, Miami, player of the game
Jan. 20, 1975	NFC 17, AFC 10	Orange Bowl, Miami (26,484)	James Harris, Los Angeles, player of the game
Jan. 26, 1976	NFC 23, AFC 20	Louisiana Superdome, New Orleans (30,546)	Billy Johnson, Houston, player of the game
Jan. 17, 1977	AFC 24, NFC 14	Kingdome, Seattle (64,752)	Mel Blount, Pittsburgh, player of the game
Jan. 23, 1978	NFC 14, AFC 13	Tampa Stadium (51,337)	Walter Payton, Chicago, player of the game
Jan. 29, 1979	NFC 13, AFC 7	Los Angeles Memorial Coliseum (46,281)	Ahmad Rashad, Minnesota, player of the game
Jan. 27, 1980	NFC 37, AFC 27	Aloha Stadium, Honolulu (49,800)	Chuck Muncie, New Orleans, player of the game
Feb. 1, 1981	NFC 21, AFC 7	Aloha Stadium, Honolulu (50,360)	Eddie Murray, Detroit, player of the game
Jan. 31, 1982	AFC 16, NFC 13	Aloha Stadium, Honolulu (50,402)	Kellen Winslow, San Diego, and Lee Roy Selmon, Tampa Bay, players of the game
Feb. 6, 1983	NFC 20, AFC 19	Aloha Stadium, Honolulu (49,883)	Dan Fouts, San Diego, and John Jefferson, Green Bay, players of the game
Jan. 29, 1984	NFC 45, AFC 3	Aloha Stadium, Honolulu (50,445)	Joe Theismann, Washington, player of the game
Jan. 27, 1985	AFC 22, NFC 14	Aloha Stadium, Honolulu (50,385)	Mark Gastineau, N.Y. Jets, player of the game
Feb. 2, 1986	NFC 28, AFC 24	Aloha Stadium, Honolulu (50,101)	Phil Simms, N.Y. Giants, player of the game
Feb. 1, 1987	AFC 10, NFC 6	Aloha Stadium, Honolulu (50,101)	Reggie White, Philadelphia, player of the game
Feb. 7, 1988	AFC 15, NFC 6	Aloha Stadium, Honolulu (50,113)	Bruce Smith, Buffalo, player of the game
Jan. 29, 1989	NFC 34, AFC 3	Aloha Stadium, Honolulu (50,113)	Randall Cunningham, Philadelphia, player of the game
Feb. 4, 1990	NFC 27, AFC 21	Aloha Stadium, Honolulu (50,445)	Jerry Gray, L.A. Rams, player of the game
Feb. 3, 1991	AFC 23, NFC 21	Aloha Stadium, Honolulu (50,345)	Jim Kelly, Buffalo, player of the game

Pro Football Hall of Fame Game

1962	New York Giants 21, St. Louis Cardinals 21
1963	Pittsburgh Steelers 16, Cleveland Browns 7
1964	Baltimore Colts 48, Pittsburgh Steelers 17
1965	Washington Redskins 20, Detroit Lions 3
1966	No game
1967	Philadelphia Eagles 28, Cleveland Browns 13
1968	Chicago Bears 30, Dallas Cowboys 24
1969	Green Bay Packers 38, Atlanta Falcons 24
1970	New Orleans Saints 14, Minnesota Vikings 13
1971	Los Angeles Rams (NFC) 17, Houston Oilers (AFC) 6
1972	Kansas City Chiefs (AFC) 23, New York Giants (NFC) 17
1973	San Francisco 49ers (NFC) 20, New England Patriots (AFC) 7
1974	St. Louis Cardinals (NFC) 21, Buffalo Bills (AFC) 13
1975	Washington Redskins (NFC) 17, Cincinnati Bengals (AFC) 9
1976	Denver Broncos (AFC) 10, Detroit Lions (NFC) 7
1977	Chicago Bears (NFC) 20, New York Jets (AFC) 6
1978	Philadelphia Eagles (NFC) 17, Miami Dolphins (AFC) 3
1979	Oakland Raiders (AFC) 20, Dallas Cowboys (NFC) 13
1980*	San Diego Chargers (AFC) 0, Green Bay Packers (NFC) 0
1981	Cleveland Browns (AFC) 24, Atlanta Falcons (NFC) 10
1982	Minnesota Vikings (NFC) 30, Baltimore Colts (AFC) 14
1983	Pittsburgh Steelers (AFC) 27, New Orleans Saints (NFC) 14
1984	Seattle Seahawks (AFC) 38, Tampa Bay Buccaneers (NFC) 0
1985	New York Giants (NFC) 21, Houston Oilers (AFC) 20
1986	New England Patriots (AFC) 21, St. Louis Cardinals (NFC) 16
1987	San Francisco 49ers (NFC) 20, Kansas City Chiefs (AFC) 7
1988	Cincinnati Bengals (AFC) 14, Los Angeles Rams (NFC) 7
1989	Washington Redskins (NFC) 31, Buffalo Bills (AFC) 6
1990	Chicago Bears (NFC) 13, Cleveland Browns (AFC) 0

*Game called with 5:29 remaining due to severe thunder & lightning.

NFL International Games

Date	Site	Teams
Aug. 12, 1950	Ottawa, Canada	N.Y. Giants 20, Ottawa Roughriders 6
Aug. 11, 1951	Ottawa, Canada	N.Y. Giants 38, Ottawa Roughriders 6
Aug. 5, 1959	Toronto, Canada	Chi. Cardinals 55, Tor. Argonauts 26
Aug. 6, 1960	Toronto, Canada	Pittsburgh 43, Toronto Argonauts 16
Aug. 15, 1960	Toronto, Canada	Chicago Bears 16, N.Y. Giants 7
Aug. 2, 1961	Toronto, Canada	St. Louis 36, Toronto Argonauts 7
Aug. 5, 1961	Montreal, Canada	Chi. Bears 34, Montreal Allouettes 16
Aug. 8, 1961	Hamilton, Canada	Hamilton Tiger-Cats 38, Buffalo 21
Aug. 11, 1969	Montreal, Canada	Pittsburgh 17, N.Y. Giants 13
Aug. 25, 1969	Montreal, Canada	Detroit 22, Boston Patriots 9
Aug. 16, 1976	Tokyo, Japan	St. Louis 20, San Diego 10
Aug. 5, 1978	Mexico City, Mexico	New Orleans 14, Philadelphia 7
Aug. 6, 1983	London, England	Minnesota 28, St. Louis 10
Aug. 3, 1986	London, England	Chicago Bears 17, Dallas 6
Aug. 9, 1987	London, England	L.A. Rams 28, Denver 27
July 31, 1988	London, England	Miami 27, San Francisco 21
Aug. 14, 1988	Goteborg, Sweden	Minnesota 28, Chicago 21
Aug. 18, 1988	Montreal, Canada	N.Y. Jets 11, Cleveland 7
Aug. 5, 1989	Tokyo, Japan	L.A. Rams 16, San Francisco 13 (OT)
Aug. 6, 1989	London, England	Philadelphia 17, Cleveland 13
Aug. 4, 1990	Tokyo, Japan	Denver 10, Seattle 7
Aug. 5, 1990	London, England	New Orleans 17, L.A. Raiders 10
Aug. 9, 1990	Montreal, Canada	New England 30, Pittsburgh 14
Aug. 11, 1990	Berlin, Germany	L.A. Rams 19, Kansas City 3

Chicago All-Star Game

Pro teams won 31, lost 9, and tied 2. The game was discontinued after 1976.

Year	Date	Winner	Loser	Attendance
1976*	July 23	Pittsburgh 24	All-Stars 0	52,895
1975	Aug. 1	Pittsburgh 21	All-Stars 14	54,103
1974		No game was played		
1973	July 27	Miami 14	All-Stars 3	54,103
1972	July 28	Dallas 20	All-Stars 7	54,162
1971	July 30	Baltimore 24	All-Stars 17	52,289
1970	July 31	Kansas City 24	All-Stars 3	69,940
1969	Aug. 1	N.Y. Jets 26	All-Stars 24	74,208
1968	Aug. 2	Green Bay 34	All-Stars 17	69,917
1967	Aug. 4	Green Bay 27	All-Stars 0	70,934
1966	Aug. 5	Green Bay 38	All-Stars 0	72,000
1965	Aug. 6	Cleveland 24	All-Stars 16	68,000
1964	Aug. 7	Chicago 28	All-Stars 17	65,000
1963	Aug. 2	All-Stars 20	Green Bay 17	65,000
1962	Aug. 3	Green Bay 42	All-Stars 20	65,000
1961	Aug. 4	Philadelphia 28	All-Stars 14	66,000
1960	Aug. 12	Baltimore 32	All-Stars 7	70,000
1959	Aug. 14	Baltimore 29	All-Stars 0	70,000
1958	Aug. 15	All-Stars 35	Detroit 19	70,000
1957	Aug. 9	N.Y. Giants 22	All-Stars 12	75,000
1956	Aug. 10	Cleveland 26	All-Stars 0	75,000
1955	Aug. 12	All-Stars 30	Cleveland 27	75,000
1954	Aug. 13	Detroit 31	All-Stars 6	93,470
1953	Aug. 14	Detroit 24	All-Stars 10	93,818
1952	Aug. 15	Los Angeles 10	All-Stars 7	88,316
1951	Aug. 17	Cleveland 33	All-Stars 0	92,180
1950	Aug. 11	All-Stars 17	Philadelphia 7	88,885
1949	Aug. 12	Philadelphia 38	All-Stars 0	93,780
1948	Aug. 20	Chi. Cardinals 28	All-Stars 0	101,220
1947	Aug. 22	All-Stars 16	Chi. Bears 0	105,840
1946	Aug. 23	All-Stars 16	Los Angeles 0	97,380
1945	Aug. 30	Green Bay 19	All-Stars 7	92,753
1944	Aug. 30	Chi. Bears 24	All-Stars 21	48,769
1943	Aug. 25	All-Stars 27	Washington 7	48,471
1942	Aug. 28	Chi. Bears 21	All-Stars 0	101,100
1941	Aug. 28	Chi. Bears 37	All-Stars 13	98,203
1940	Aug. 29	Green Bay 45	All-Stars 28	84,567
1939	Aug. 30	N.Y. Giants 9	All-Stars 0	81,456
1938	Aug. 31	All-Stars 28	Washington 16	74,250
1937	Sept. 1	All-Stars 6	Green Bay 0	84,560
1936	Sept. 3	All-Stars 7	Detroit 7 (tie)	76,000
1935	Aug. 29	Chi. Bears 5	All-Stars 0	77,450
1934	Aug. 31	Chi. Bears 0	All-Stars 0 (tie)	79,432

*Game shortened due to thunderstorms.

NFL Playoff Bowl

Western Conference won 8, Eastern Conference won 2.
All games played at Miami's Orange Bowl.

1970	Los Angeles Rams 31, Dallas Cowboys 0
1969	Dallas Cowboys 17, Minnesota Vikings 13
1968	Los Angeles Rams 30, Cleveland Browns 6
1967	Baltimore Colts 20, Philadelphia Eagles 14
1966	Baltimore Colts 35, Dallas Cowboys 3
1965	St. Louis Cardinals 24, Green Bay Packers 17
1964	Green Bay Packers 40, Cleveland Browns 23
1963	Detroit Lions 17, Pittsburgh Steelers 10
1962	Detroit Lions 28, Philadelphia Eagles 10
1961	Detroit Lions 17, Cleveland Browns 16

AFC VS. NFC (REGULAR SEASON), 1970-1990

	1970	1971	1972	1973	1974	1975	1976	1977	1978	1979	1980	1981	1982	1983	1984	1985	1986	1987	1988	1989	1990	Totals
Miami	2-1	3-0	3-0	3-0	2-1	3-0	0-2	2-0	3-1	4-0	4-0	3-1	1-1	3-1	4-0	3-1	2-2	3-0	3-1	2-0	2-2	55-14
L.A. Raiders	1-2	1-1-1	3-0	2-1	3-0	3-0	3-0	1-1	4-0	4-0	2-2	2-2	3-0	2-2	3-1	3-1	1-3	2-2	1-3	2-2	3-1	49-24-1
Pittsburgh	0-3	1-2	2-1	3-0	3-0	2-1	1-1	2-0	3-1	3-1	4-0	3-1	1-0	2-2	3-1	1-3	2-2	2-2	1-3	3-1	3-1	45-26
Cincinnati	1-2	1-2	2-1	2-1	2-1	3-0	2-0	2-1	2-2	2-2	2-2	2-2	1-0	3-1	2-2	2-2	3-1	1-2	4-0	2-2	1-3	42-29
Denver	2-2	1-3	1-3	0-3-1	2-2	2-1	2-0	1-1	2-2	3-1	3-1	3-1	2-1	0-2	3-1	3-1	3-1	2-1-1	3-1	2-2	1-3	41-33-2
Seattle								1-0	3-1	3-1	1-3	0-2	1-0	1-3	4-0	2-2	3-1	4-0	1-3	0-4	2-2	26-22
Cleveland	0-3	2-1	1-2	1-2	1-2	1-3	2-0	1-1	4-0	3-1	3-1	3-1	0-2	2-2	1-3	1-3	2-2	2-2	4-0	3-1	1-3	38-35
San Diego	1-2	2-1	0-3	1-2	1-2	0-3	2-0	1-1	2-2	3-1	2-2	2-2	1-0	2-2	4-0	1-1	0-4	2-0	2-2	2-2	1-1	32-33
Kansas City	0-2-1	2-1	2-1	1-1-1	1-2	2-1	1-1	1-1	0-2	0-2	2-0	2-2	0-3	2-2	1-1	2-2	1-1	1-2	0-2	2-0	4-0	27-29-2
N.Y. Jets	2-1	0-3	1-2	0-3	2-1	0-3	0-2	1-1	1-3	3-1	1-3	2-0	4-0	3-1	0-2	2-2	2-2	0-4	2-0	1-3	2-0	29-37
Indianapolis	3-0	2-1	0-3	2-1	1-2	2-1	0-2	1-1	2-2	1-1	1-1	0-4	0-1-1	2-0	0-4	3-1	1-3	1-0	2-2	1-3	2-2	27-35-1
Houston	0-3	0-2-1	0-3	0-3	0-3	3-0	2-0	2-0	2-2	2-2	4-0	1-3	0-3	1-3	0-4	1-3	2-2	2-2	3-1	3-1	1-3	29-43-1
Buffalo	0-3	0-3	2-0-1	2-1	2-1	1-2	0-2	1-1	1-1	2-2	3-1	1-3	1-2	1-3	1-3	0-2	1-1	1-2	2-2	1-3	3-1	26-39-1
New England	0-3	0-3	3-0	2-1	3-0	1-2	1-1	2-0	2-2	3-1	1-3	0-4	0-1	2-2	0-4	3-1	3-1	0-3	2-2	0-4	0-4	28-42-0
Tampa Bay							0-1															0-1
TOTALS	12-27-1	15-23-2	20-19-1	19-19-2	23-17	23-17	16-12	19-9	31-21	36-16	33-19	24-28	15-14-1	26-26	26-26	27-25	26-26	23-22-1	30-22	24-28	26-26	494-442-8

NFC VS. AFC (REGULAR SEASON), 1970-1990

	1970	1971	1972	1973	1974	1975	1976	1977	1978	1979	1980	1981	1982	1983	1984	1985	1986	1987	1988	1989	1990	Totals
Dallas	3-0	3-0	3-0	2-1	2-1	2-1	2-0	1-1	3-1	1-3	3-1	4-0	2-1	2-2	2-2	3-1	1-3	2-1	0-4	0-2	1-1	42-26
Washington	2-1	1-2	1-2	2-1	2-1	1-2	1-1	1-1	2-2	2-2	1-3	2-2		4-0	3-1	4-0	3-1	2-1	1-3	2-2	3-1	40-29
San Francisco	4-0	2-1	2-1	1-2	0-3	1-2	1-1	0-2	1-3	0-4	2-2	3-1	1-3	2-2	3-1	3-1	4-0	3-1	2-2	4-0	4-0	43-32
Philadelphia	2-1	1-2	2-1	2-1	2-1	0-3	0-2	1-1	3-1	2-2	3-1	3-1	2-1	1-1	3-1	1-1	2-2	3-1	2-2	3-1	1-3	39-30
L.A. Rams	2-1	1-2	1-2	3-0	3-1	3-0	1-1	2-0	2-2	2-2	2-2	1-3	1-2	1-3	3-1	3-1	2-2	1-2	2-2	3-1	2-2	41-32
N.Y. Giants	3-0	1-2	1-2	1-2	1-2	2-1	0-2	0-2	1-1	1-1	1-3	1-1	1-0	0-4	2-0	2-2	3-1	2-1	1-1	4-0	3-1	31-29
Minnesota	2-1	2-1	1-2	2-1	2-1	4-0	2-0	1-1	1-3	1-3	1-3	1-3	1-3	4-0	0-4	2-0	1-3	2-1	2-2	2-2	2-2	36-36
Phoenix	2-0-1	2-1	1-2	0-2-1	2-1	2-1	1-1	0-2	0-4	1-3	1-1	3-1		3-1	3-1	2-2	1-1	0-1	1-3	1-3	2-2	28-33-2
Chicago	1-2	1-2	1-2	2-2	0-3	0-3	0-2	1-1	0-4	2-2	0-4	4-0	1-1	1-1	2-2	3-1	4-0	2-2	3-1	2-2	2-2	32-39
Detroit	3-0	4-0	2-0-1	0-3	1-2	1-2	2-0	2-0	2-2	0-4	0-2	2-2	0-1	1-3	0-4	2-2	1-3	0-4	1-1	1-3	1-3	26-41-1
New Orleans	0-3	0-1-2	0-3	1-2	0-3	0-3	1-2	0-2	1-3	0-4	1-3	2-2	1-0	1-3	3-1	0-4	1-3	4-0	4-0	4-0	2-2	26-44-2
Atlanta	1-2	3-0	2-2	2-1	0-3	1-2	0-2	0-2	1-3	1-3	2-2	1-3	1-1	3-1	1-3	0-4	1-3	0-4	1-3	2-2	2-2	25-48
Green Bay	2-1	2-1	2-1	1-1-1	2-1	0-3	0-2	0-3	2-2	1-3	1-3	1-1	1-1-1	2-2	0-4	0-4	1-3	1-2-1	1-3	0-2	1-3	21-46-3
Tampa Bay								0-1	2-0	2-0	1-3	0-4	2-1	1-3	1-1	0-4	1-1	0-2	1-3	0-4	0-2	11-29
Seattle							1-0															1-0
TOTALS	27-12-1	23-15-2	19-20-1	19-19-2	17-23	17-23	12-16	9-19	21-31	16-36	19-33	28-24	14-15-1	26-26	26-26	25-27	26-26	22-23-1	22-30	28-24	26-26	442-494-8

1990 Interconference Games
(Home Team in capital letters)

AFC 26, NFC 26

AFC Victories

KANSAS CITY 24, Minnesota 21
Kansas City 17, GREEN BAY 3
LOS ANGELES RAIDERS 24, Chicago 10
Indianapolis 24, PHILADELPHIA 23
Cincinnati 34, LOS ANGELES RAMS 31
KANSAS CITY 43, Detroit 24
HOUSTON 23, New Orleans 10
SAN DIEGO 41, Tampa Bay 10
PITTSBURGH 41, Los Angeles Rams 10
PITTSBURGH 21, Atlanta 9
NEW YORK JETS 24, Dallas 9
MIAMI 27, Phoenix 3
BUFFALO 45, Phoenix 14
BUFFALO 30, Philadelphia 23
Seattle 20, GREEN BAY 14
MIAMI 23, Philadelphia 20
Los Angeles Raiders 38, DETROIT 31
Buffalo 17, NEW YORK GIANTS 13
CLEVELAND 13, Atlanta 10
Pittsburgh 9, NEW ORLEANS 6
Los Angeles Raiders 28, MINNESOTA 24
INDIANAPOLIS 35, Washington 28
Kansas City 21, CHICAGO 10
SEATTLE 30, Detroit 10
DENVER 22, Green Bay 13
New York Jets 16, TAMPA BAY 14

NFC Victories

ATLANTA 47, Houston 27
DALLAS 17, San Diego 14
CHICAGO 17, Seattle 0
NEW YORK GIANTS 20, Miami 3
San Francisco 24, HOUSTON 21
NEW ORLEANS 25, Cleveland 20
SAN FRANCISCO 27, Pittsburgh 7
SAN FRANCISCO 20, Cleveland 17
ATLANTA 38, Cincinnati 17
LOS ANGELES RAMS 17, Houston 13
PHILADELPHIA 48, New England 20
New Orleans 21, CINCINNATI 7
MINNESOTA 27, Denver 22
New York Giants 24, INDIANAPOLIS 7
Green Bay 29, LOS ANGELES RAIDERS 16
Chicago 16, DENVER 13
Minnesota 24, SEATTLE 21
DETROIT 40, Denver 27
PHOENIX 34, New England 14
PHOENIX 20, Indianapolis 17
WASHINGTON 42, Miami 20
Los Angeles Rams 38, CLEVELAND 24
San Francisco 20, CINCINNATI 17
Washington 25, NEW ENGLAND 10
WASHINGTON 29, Buffalo 14
New York Giants 13, NEW ENGLAND 10

Regular Season Interconference Records, 1970-1990

American Football Conference

Eastern Division	W	L	T	Pct.
Miami	55	14	0	.797
New York Jets	29	37	0	.439
Indianapolis	27	35	1	.437
Buffalo	26	39	1	.402
New England	28	42	0	.400
Central Division				
Pittsburgh	45	26	0	.634
Cincinnati	42	29	0	.592
Cleveland	38	35	0	.521
Houston	29	43	1	.404
Western Division				
Los Angeles Raiders	49	24	1	.669
Denver	41	33	2	.553
Seattle	26	22	0	.542
San Diego	32	33	0	.492
Kansas City	27	29	2	.483

National Football Conference

Eastern Division	W	L	T	Pct.
Dallas	42	26	0	.618
Washington	40	29	0	.580
Philadelphia	39	30	0	.565
New York Giants	31	29	0	.517
Phoenix	28	33	2	.460
Central Division				
Minnesota	36	36	0	.500
Chicago	32	39	0	.451
Detroit	26	41	1	.390
Green Bay	21	46	3	.321
Tampa Bay	11	29	0	.275
Western Division				
San Francisco	43	32	0	.573
Los Angeles Rams	41	32	0	.562
New Orleans	26	44	2	.375
Atlanta	25	48	0	.342

Interconference Victories, 1970-1990

Regular Season

	AFC	NFC	Tie
1970	12	27	1
1971	15	23	2
1972	20	19	1
1973	19	19	2
1974	23	17	0
1975	23	17	0
1976	16	12	0
1977	19	9	0
1978	31	21	0
1979	36	16	0
1980	33	19	0
1981	24	28	0
1982	15	14	1
1983	26	26	0
1984	26	26	0
1985	27	25	0
1986	26	26	0
1987	23	22	1
1988	30	22	0
1989	24	28	0
1990	26	26	0
Total	494	442	8

Preseason

	AFC	NFC	Tie
1970	21	28	1
1971	28	28	3
1972	27	25	4
1973	23	35	2
1974	35	25	0
1975	30	26	1
1976	30	31	0
1977	38	25	0
1978	20	19	0
1979	25	18	0
1980	22	20	1
1981	18	19	0
1982	25	16	0
1983	15	24	0
1984	16	19	0
1985	10	22	1
1986	22	17	0
1987	22	22	0
1988	23	16	1
1989	16	27	0
1990	15	29	0
Total	481	491	14

Monday Night Football, 1970-1990

(Home Team in capitals, games listed in chronological order.)

1990
San Francisco 13, NEW ORLEANS 12
DENVER 24, Kansas City 23
Buffalo 30, NEW YORK JETS 7
SEATTLE 31, Cincinnati 16
Cleveland 30, DENVER 29
PHILADELPHIA 32, Minnesota 24
Cincinnati 34, CLEVELAND 13
PITTSBURGH 41, Los Angeles Rams 10
New York Giants 24, INDIANAPOLIS 7
PHILADELPHIA 28, Washington 14
Los Angeles Raiders 13, MIAMI 10
HOUSTON 27, Buffalo 24
SAN FRANCISCO 7, New York Giants 3
Los Angeles Raiders 38, DETROIT 31
San Francisco 26, LOS ANGELES RAMS 10
NEW ORLEANS 20, Los Angeles Rams 17

1989
New York Giants 27, WASHINGTON 24
Denver 28, BUFFALO 14
CINCINNATI 21, Cleveland 14
CHICAGO 27, Philadelphia 13
Los Angeles Raiders 14, NEW YORK JETS 7
BUFFALO 23, Los Angeles Rams 20
CLEVELAND 27, Chicago 7
NEW YORK GIANTS 24, Minnesota 14
SAN FRANCISCO 31, New Orleans 13
HOUSTON 26, Cincinnati 24
Denver 14, WASHINGTON 10
SAN FRANCISCO 34, New York Giants 24
SEATTLE 17, Buffalo 16
San Francisco 30, LOS ANGELES RAMS 27
NEW ORLEANS 30, Philadelphia 20
MINNESOTA 29, Cincinnati 21

1988
NEW YORK GIANTS 27, Washington 20
Dallas 17, PHOENIX 14
CLEVELAND 23, Indianapolis 17
Los Angeles Raiders 30, DENVER 27 (OT)
NEW ORLEANS 20, Dallas 17
PHILADELPHIA 24, New York Giants 13
Buffalo 37, NEW YORK JETS 14
CHICAGO 10, San Francisco 9
INDIANAPOLIS 55, Denver 23
HOUSTON 24, Cleveland 17
Buffalo 31, MIAMI 6
SAN FRANCISCO 37, Washington 21
SEATTLE 35, Los Angeles Raiders 27
LOS ANGELES RAMS 23, Chicago 3
MIAMI 38, Cleveland 31
MINNESOTA 28, Chicago 27

1987
CHICAGO 34, New York Giants 19
NEW YORK JETS 43, New England 24
San Francisco 41, NEW YORK GIANTS 21
DENVER 30, Los Angeles Raiders 14
Washington 13, DALLAS 7
CLEVELAND 30, Los Angeles Rams 17
MINNESOTA 34, Denver 27
DALLAS 33, New York Giants 24
NEW YORK JETS 30, Seattle 14
DENVER 31, Chicago 29
Los Angeles Rams 30, WASHINGTON 26
Los Angeles Raiders 37, SEATTLE 14
MIAMI 37, New York Jets 28
SAN FRANCISCO 41, Chicago 0
Dallas 29, LOS ANGELES RAMS 21
New England 24, MIAMI 10

1986
DALLAS 31, New York Giants 28
Denver 21, PITTSBURGH 10
Chicago 25, GREEN BAY 12
Dallas 31, ST. LOUIS 7
SEATTLE 33, San Diego 7
CINCINNATI 24, Pittsburgh 22
NEW YORK JETS 22, Denver 10
NEW YORK GIANTS 27, Washington 20
Los Angeles Rams 20, CHICAGO 17
CLEVELAND 26, Miami 16
WASHINGTON 14, San Francisco 6
MIAMI 45, New York Jets 3
New York Giants 21, SAN FRANCISCO 17
SEATTLE 37, Los Angeles Raiders 0
Chicago 16, DETROIT 13
New England 34, MIAMI 27

1985
DALLAS 44, Washington 14
CLEVELAND 17, Pittsburgh 7
Los Angeles Rams 35, SEATTLE 24
Cincinnati 37, PITTSBURGH 24
WASHINGTON 27, St. Louis 10
NEW YORK JETS 23, Miami 7
CHICAGO 23, Green Bay 7
LOS ANGELES RAIDERS 34, San Diego 21
ST. LOUIS 21, Dallas 10
DENVER 17, San Francisco 16
WASHINGTON 23, New York Giants 21
SAN FRANCISCO 19, Seattle 6
MIAMI 30, Chicago 24
Los Angeles Rams 27, SAN FRANCISCO 20
MIAMI 30, New England 27
L.A. Raiders 16, L.A. RAMS 6

1984
Dallas 20, LOS ANGELES RAMS 13
SAN FRANCISCO 37, Washington 31
Miami 21, BUFFALO 17
LOS ANGELES RAIDERS 33, San Diego 30
PITTSBURGH 38, Cincinnati 17
San Francisco 31, NEW YORK GIANTS 10
DENVER 17, Green Bay 14
Los Angeles Rams 24, ATLANTA 10
Seattle 24, SAN DIEGO 0
WASHINGTON 27, Atlanta 14
SEATTLE 17, Los Angeles Raiders 14
NEW ORLEANS 27, Pittsburgh 24
MIAMI 28, New York Jets 17
SAN DIEGO 20, Chicago 7
Los Angeles Raiders 24, DETROIT 3
MIAMI 28, Dallas 21

1983
Dallas 31, WASHINGTON 30
San Diego 17, KANSAS CITY 14
LOS ANGELES RAIDERS 27, Miami 14
NEW YORK GIANTS 27, Green Bay 3
New York Jets 34, BUFFALO 10
Pittsburgh 24, CINCINNATI 14
GREEN BAY 48, Washington 47
ST. LOUIS 20, New York Giants 20 (OT)
Washington 27, SAN DIEGO 24
DETROIT 15, New York Giants 9
Los Angeles Rams 36, ATLANTA 13
New York Jets 31, NEW ORLEANS 28
MIAMI 38, Cincinnati 14
DETROIT 13, Minnesota 2
Green Bay 12, TAMPA BAY 9 (OT)
SAN FRANCISCO 42, Dallas 17

1982
Pittsburgh 36, DALLAS 28
Green Bay 27, NEW YORK GIANTS 19
LOS ANGELES RAIDERS 28, San Diego 24
TAMPA BAY 23, Miami 17
New York Jets 28, DETROIT 13
Dallas 37, HOUSTON 7
SAN DIEGO 50, Cincinnati 34
MIAMI 27, Buffalo 10
MINNESOTA 31, Dallas 27

1981
San Diego 44, CLEVELAND 14
Oakland 36, MINNESOTA 10
Dallas 35, NEW ENGLAND 21
Los Angeles 24, CHICAGO 7
PHILADELPHIA 16, Atlanta 13
BUFFALO 31, Miami 21
DETROIT 48, Chicago 17
PITTSBURGH 26, Houston 13
DENVER 19, Minnesota 17
DALLAS 27, Buffalo 14
SEATTLE 44, San Diego 23
ATLANTA 31, Minnesota 30
MIAMI 13, Philadelphia 10
OAKLAND 30, Pittsburgh 27
LOS ANGELES 21, Atlanta 16
SAN DIEGO 23, Oakland 10

1980
Dallas 17, WASHINGTON 3
Houston 16, CLEVELAND 7
PHILADELPHIA 35, New York Giants 3
NEW ENGLAND 23, Denver 14
CHICAGO 23, Tampa Bay 0
DENVER 20, Washington 17
Oakland 45, PITTSBURGH 34
NEW YORK JETS 17, Miami 14
CLEVELAND 27, Chicago 21
HOUSTON 38, New England 34
Oakland 19, SEATTLE 17
Los Angeles 27, NEW ORLEANS 7
OAKLAND 9, Denver 3
MIAMI 16, New England 13 (OT)
LOS ANGELES 38, Dallas 14
SAN DIEGO 26, Pittsburgh 17

1979
Pittsburgh 16, NEW ENGLAND 13 (OT)
Atlanta 14, PHILADELPHIA 10
WASHINGTON 27, New York Giants 0
CLEVELAND 26, Dallas 7
GREEN BAY 27, New England 14
OAKLAND 13, Miami 3
NEW YORK JETS 14, Minnesota 7
PITTSBURGH 42, Denver 7
Seattle 31, ATLANTA 28
Houston 9, MIAMI 6
Philadelphia 31, DALLAS 21
LOS ANGELES 20, Atlanta 14
SEATTLE 30, New York Jets 7
Oakland 42, NEW ORLEANS 35
HOUSTON 20, Pittsburgh 17
SAN DIEGO 17, Denver 7

1978
DALLAS 38, Baltimore 0
MINNESOTA 12, Denver 9 (OT)
Baltimore 34, NEW ENGLAND 27
Minnesota 24, CHICAGO 20
WASHINGTON 9, Dallas 5
MIAMI 21, Cincinnati 0
DENVER 16, Chicago 7
Houston 24, PITTSBURGH 17
ATLANTA 15, Los Angeles 7
BALTIMORE 21, Washington 17
Oakland 34, CINCINNATI 21
HOUSTON 35, Miami 30
Pittsburgh 24, SAN FRANCISCO 7
SAN DIEGO 40, Chicago 7
Cincinnati 20, LOS ANGELES 19
MIAMI 23, New England 3

1977
PITTSBURGH 27, San Francisco 0
CLEVELAND 30, New England 27 (OT)
Oakland 37, KANSAS CITY 28
CHICAGO 24, Los Angeles 23
PITTSBURGH 20, Cincinnati 14
LOS ANGELES 35, Minnesota 3
ST. LOUIS 28, New York Giants 0
BALTIMORE 10, Washington 3
St. Louis 24, DALLAS 17
WASHINGTON 10, Green Bay 9
OAKLAND 34, Buffalo 13
MIAMI 17, Baltimore 6
Dallas 42, SAN FRANCISCO 35

1976
Miami 30, BUFFALO 21
Oakland 24, KANSAS CITY 21
Washington 20, PHILADELPHIA 17 (OT)
MINNESOTA 17, Pittsburgh 6
San Francisco 16, LOS ANGELES 0
NEW ENGLAND 41, New York Jets 7
WASHINGTON 20, St. Louis 10
BALTIMORE 38, Houston 14
CINCINNATI 20, Los Angeles 12
DALLAS 17, Buffalo 10
Baltimore 17, MIAMI 16
SAN FRANCISCO 20, Minnesota 16
OAKLAND 35, Cincinnati 20

1975
Oakland 31, MIAMI 21
DENVER 23, Green Bay 13
Dallas 36, DETROIT 10
WASHINGTON 27, St. Louis 17
New York Giants 17, BUFFALO 14

Minnesota 13, CHICAGO 9
Los Angeles 42, PHILADELPHIA 3
Kansas City 34, DALLAS 31
CINCINNATI 33, Buffalo 24
Pittsburgh 32, HOUSTON 9
MIAMI 20, New England 7
OAKLAND 17, Denver 10
SAN DIEGO 24, New York Jets 16

1974
BUFFALO 21, Oakland 20
PHILADELPHIA 13, Dallas 10
WASHINGTON 30, Denver 3
MIAMI 21, New York Jets 17
DETROIT 17, San Francisco 13
CHICAGO 10, Green Bay 9
PITTSBURGH 24, Atlanta 17
Los Angeles 15, SAN FRANCISCO 13
Minnesota 28, ST. LOUIS 24
Kansas City 42, DENVER 34
Pittsburgh 28, NEW ORLEANS 7
MIAMI 24, Cincinnati 3
Washington 23, LOS ANGELES 17

1973
GREEN BAY 23, New York Jets 7
DALLAS 40, New Orleans 3
DETROIT 31, Atlanta 6
WASHINGTON 14, Dallas 7
Miami 17, CLEVELAND 9
DENVER 23, Oakland 23
BUFFALO 23, Kansas City 14
PITTSBURGH 21, Washington 16
KANSAS CITY 19, Chicago 7
ATLANTA 20, Minnesota 14
SAN FRANCISCO 20, Green Bay 6
MIAMI 30, Pittsburgh 26
LOS ANGELES 40, New York Giants 6

1972
Washington 24, MINNESOTA 21
Kansas City 20, NEW ORLEANS 17
New York Giants 27, PHILADELPHIA 12
Oakland 34, HOUSTON 0
Green Bay 24, DETROIT 23
CHICAGO 13, Minnesota 10
DALLAS 28, Detroit 24
Baltimore 24, NEW ENGLAND 17
Cleveland 21, SAN DIEGO 17
WASHINGTON 24, Atlanta 13
MIAMI 31, St. Louis 10
Los Angeles 26, SAN FRANCISCO 16
OAKLAND 24, New York Jets 16

1971
Minnesota 16, DETROIT 13
ST. LOUIS 17, New York Jets 10
Oakland 34, CLEVELAND 20
DALLAS 20, New York Giants 13
KANSAS CITY 38, Pittsburgh 16
MINNESOTA 10, Baltimore 3
GREEN BAY 14, Detroit 14
BALTIMORE 24, Los Angeles 17
SAN DIEGO 20, St. Louis 17
ATLANTA 28, Green Bay 21
MIAMI 34, Chicago 3
Kansas City 26, SAN FRANCISCO 17
Washington 38, LOS ANGELES 24

1970
CLEVELAND 31, New York Jets 21
Kansas City 44, BALTIMORE 24
DETROIT 28, Chicago 14
Green Bay 22, SAN DIEGO 20
OAKLAND 34, Washington 20
MINNESOTA 13, Los Angeles 3
PITTSBURGH 21, Cincinnati 10
Baltimore 13, GREEN BAY 10
St. Louis 38, DALLAS 0
PHILADELPHIA 23, New York Giants 20
Miami 20, ATLANTA 7
Cleveland 21, HOUSTON 10
Detroit 28, LOS ANGELES 23

Monday Night Won-Lost Records, 1970-1990

	Total	1990	1989	1988	1987	1986	1985	1984	1983	1982	1981	1980	1979	1978	1977	1976	1975	1974	1973	1972	1971	1970
Buffalo	7-12	1-1	1-2	2-0				0-1	0-1	0-1	1-1				0-1	0-2	0-2	1-0	1-0			
Cincinnati	7-13	1-1	1-2			1-0	1-0	0-1	0-2	0-1				1-2	0-1	1-1	1-0	0-1				0-1
Cleveland	12-8	1-1	1-1	1-2	1-0	1-0	1-0				0-1	1-1	1-0		1-0				0-1	1-0	0-1	2-0
Denver	12-13-1	1-1	2-0	0-2	2-1	1-1	1-0	1-0			1-0	1-2	0-2	1-1			1-1	0-2	0-0-1			
Houston	9-6	1-0	1-0	1-0						0-1	0-1	2-0	2-0	2-0		0-1	0-1			0-1		0-1
Indianapolis	9-6	0-1		1-1										2-1	1-1	2-0				1-0	1-1	1-1
Kansas City	7-5	0-1							0-1						0-1	0-1	1-0	1-0	1-1	1-0	2-0	1-0
L.A. Raiders	29-6-1	2-0	1-0	1-1	1-1	0-1	2-0	2-1	1-0	1-0	2-1	3-0	2-0	1-0	2-0	2-0	2-0	0-1	0-0-1	2-0	1-0	1-0
Miami	24-15	0-1		1-1	1-1	1-2	2-1	3-0	1-1	1-1	1-1	1-1	0-2	2-1	1-0	1-1	1-1	2-0	2-0	1-0	1-0	1-0
New England	4-12				1-1	1-0	0-1				0-1	1-2	0-2	0-2	0-1	1-0	0-1			0-1		
N.Y. Jets	9-14	0-1	0-1	0-1	2-1	1-1	1-0	0-1	2-0	1-0		1-0	1-1			0-1	0-1	0-1	0-1	0-1	0-1	0-1
Pittsburgh	15-13	1-0				0-2	0-2	1-1	1-0	1-0	1-1	0-2	2-1	1-1	2-0	0-1	1-0	2-0	1-1		0-1	1-0
San Diego	10-9					0-1	0-1	1-2	1-1	1-1	2-1	1-0	1-0	1-0			1-0			0-1	1-0	0-1
Seattle	10-5	1-0	1-0	1-0	0-2	2-0	0-2	2-0			1-0	0-1	2-0									
Atlanta	5-11							0-2	0-1		1-2		1-2	1-0				0-1	1-1	0-1	1-0	0-1
Chicago	10-18		1-1	1-2	1-2	2-1	1-1	0-1			0-2	1-1		0-3	1-0		0-1	1-0	0-1	1-0	0-1	0-1
Dallas	19-16			1-1	2-1	2-0	1-1	1-1	1-1	1-2	2-0	1-1	0-2	1-1	1-1	1-0	1-1	0-1	1-1	1-0	1-0	0-1
Detroit	7-8-1	0-1				0-1		0-1	2-0	0-1	1-0						0-1	1-0	1-0	0-2	0-1-1	2-0
Green Bay	7-10-1					0-1	0-1	0-1	2-1	1-0			1-0		0-1		0-1	0-1	1-1	1-0	0-1-1	1-1
L.A. Rams	17-19	0-3	0-2	1-0	1-2	1-0	2-1	1-1	1-0		2-0	2-0	1-0	0-2	1-1	0-2	1-0	1-1	1-0	1-0	0-2	0-2
Minnesota	12-12	0-1	1-1	1-0	1-0				0-1	1-0	0-3		0-1	2-0	0-1	1-1	1-0	1-0	0-1	0-2	2-0	1-0
New Orleans	4-8	1-1	1-1	1-0				1-0	0-1			0-1	0-1					0-1	0-1	0-1		
N.Y. Giants	9-17-1	1-1	2-1	1-1	0-3	2-1	0-1	0-1	1-1-1	0-1		0-1	0-1		0-1		1-0		0-1	1-0	0-1	0-1
Philadelphia	8-7	2-0	0-2	1-0							1-1	1-0	1-1			0-1	0-1	1-0		0-1		1-0
Phoenix	5-8-1			0-1		0-1	1-1		0-0-1					2-0	0-1	0-1	0-1		0-1	1-1	1-0	
San Francisco	16-12	3-0	3-0	1-1	2-0	0-2	1-2	2-0	1-0					0-1	0-2	2-0		0-2	1-0	0-1	0-1	
Tampa Bay	1-2								0-1	1-0		0-1										
Washington	17-16	0-1	0-2	0-2	1-1	1-1	2-1	1-1	1-2			0-2	1-0	1-1	1-1	2-0	1-0	2-0	1-1	2-0	1-0	0-1

Monday Night Syndrome

1990

Of the 15 winning teams:
9 won the next week
6 lost the next week
0 tied the next week

Of the 15 losing teams:
10 won the next week
4 lost the next week
0 tied the next week
1 had Open Date the next week

Of the 30 NFL teams:
19 won the next week
10 lost the next week
0 tied the next week
1 had Open Date the next week

1970-1989

Of the 289 winning teams:
168 won the next week
118 lost the next week
3 tied the next week

Of the 289 losing teams:
157 won the next week
130 lost the next week
1 tied the next week
1 had Open Date the next week

Of the 6 tying teams:
5 won the next week
1 lost the next week
0 tied the next week

Of the 584 NFL teams:
330 won the next week
249 lost the next week
4 tied the next week
1 had Open Date the next week

Thursday-Sunday Night Football, 1974-1990

(Home Team in capitals, games listed in chronological order.)

1990
NEW YORK GIANTS 27, Philadelphia 20 (Sun.)
PITTSBURGH 20, Houston 9 (Sun.)
TAMPA BAY 23, Detroit 20 (Sun.)
Washington 38, PHOENIX 10 (Sun.)
BUFFALO 38, Los Angeles Raiders 24 (Sun.)
CHICAGO 38, Los Angeles Rams 9 (Sun.)
MIAMI 17, New England 10 (Thurs.)
ATLANTA 38, Cincinnati 17 (Sun.)
MINNESOTA 27, Denver 22 (Sun.)
San Francisco 24, DALLAS 6 (Sun.)
CINCINNATI 27, Pittsburgh 3 (Sun.)
Seattle 13, SAN DIEGO 10 (Sun.)
MINNESOTA 23, Green Bay 7 (Sun.)
MIAMI 23, Philadelphia 20 (Sun.)
DETROIT 38, Chicago 21 (Sun.)
INDIANAPOLIS 35, Washington 28 (Sat.)
SEATTLE 17, Denver 12 (Sun.)
HOUSTON 34, Pittsburgh 14 (Sun.)

1989
Dallas 13, WASHINGTON 3 (Sun.)
SAN DIEGO 14, Los Angeles Raiders 12 (Sun.)
INDIANAPOLIS 27, New York Jets 10 (Sun.)
Los Angeles Rams 20, NEW ORLEANS 17 (Sun.)
MINNESOTA 27, Chicago 16 (Sun.)
MIAMI 31, New England 10 (Sun.)
SEATTLE 23, Los Angeles Raiders 17 (Sun.)
Cleveland 24, HOUSTON 20 (Sat.)

1988
HOUSTON 41, Washington 17 (Sun.)
Los Angeles Raiders 13, SAN DIEGO 3 (Sun.)
Minnesota 34, DALLAS 3 (Sun.)
New England 6, MIAMI 3 (Sun.)
New York Giants 13, NEW ORLEANS 12 (Sun.)
Pittsburgh 37, HOUSTON 34 (Sun.)
SEATTLE 42, Denver 14 (Sun.)
Los Angeles Rams 38, SAN FRANCISCO 16 (Sun.)

1987
NEW YORK GIANTS 17, New England 10 (Sun.)
SAN DIEGO 16, Los Angeles Raiders 14 (Sun.)
Miami 20, DALLAS 14 (Sun.)
SAN FRANCISCO 38, Cleveland 24 (Sun.)
Chicago 30, MINNESOTA 24 (Sun.)
SEATTLE 28, Denver 21 (Sun.)
MIAMI 23, Washington 21 (Sun.)
SAN FRANCISCO 48, Los Angeles Rams 0 (Sun.)

1986
New England 20, NEW YORK JETS 6 (Thurs.)
Cincinnati 30, CLEVELAND 13 (Thurs.)
Los Angeles Raiders 37, SAN DIEGO 31 (OT) (Thurs.)
LOS ANGELES RAMS 29, Dallas 10 (Sun.)
SAN FRANCISCO 24, Los Angeles Rams 14 (Fri.)

1985
KANSAS CITY 36, Los Angeles Raiders 20 (Thurs.)
Chicago 33, MINNESOTA 24 (Thurs.)
Dallas 30, NEW YORK GIANTS 29 (Sun.)
SAN DIEGO 54, Pittsburgh 44 (Sun.)
Denver 27, SEATTLE 24 (Fri.)

1984
Pittsburgh 23, NEW YORK JETS 17 (Thurs.)
Denver 24, CLEVELAND 14 (Sun.)
DALLAS 30, New Orleans 27 (Sun.)
Washington 31, MINNESOTA 17 (Thurs.)
SAN FRANCISCO 19, Los Angeles Rams 16 (Fri.)

1983
San Francisco 48, MINNESOTA 17 (Thurs.)
CLEVELAND 17, Cincinnati 7 (Thurs.)
Los Angeles Raiders 40, DALLAS 38 (Sun.)
Los Angeles Raiders 42, SAN DIEGO 10 (Thurs.)
MIAMI 34, New York Jets 14 (Fri.)

1982
BUFFALO 23, Minnesota 22 (Thurs.)
SAN FRANCISCO 30, Los Angeles Rams 24 (Thurs.)
ATLANTA 17, San Francisco 7 (Sun.)

1981
MIAMI 30, Pittsburgh 10 (Thurs.)
Philadelphia 20, BUFFALO 14 (Thurs.)
DALLAS 29, Los Angeles 17 (Sun.)
HOUSTON 17, Cleveland 13 (Thurs.)

1980
TAMPA BAY 10, Los Angeles 9 (Thurs.)
DALLAS 42, San Diego 31 (Sun.)
San Diego 27, MIAMI 24 (OT) (Thurs.)
HOUSTON 6, Pittsburgh 0 (Thurs.)

1979
Los Angeles 13, DENVER 9 (Thurs.)
DALLAS 30, Los Angeles 6 (Sun.)
OAKLAND 45, San Diego 22 (Thurs.)
MIAMI 39, New England 24 (Thurs.)

1978
New England 21, OAKLAND 14 (Sun.)
Minnesota 21, DALLAS 10 (Thurs.)
LOS ANGELES 10, Pittsburgh 7 (Sun.)
Denver 21, OAKLAND 6 (Sun.)

1977
Minnesota 30, DETROIT 21 (Sat.)

1976
Los Angeles 20, DETROIT 17 (Sat.)

1975
LOS ANGELES 10, Pittsburgh 3 (Sat.)

1974
OAKLAND 27, Dallas 23 (Sat.)

History of Overtime Games

Preseason

Aug. 28, 1955	Los Angeles 23, New York Giants 17, at Portland, Oregon
Aug. 24, 1962	Denver 27, Dallas Texans 24, at Fort Worth, Texas
Aug. 10, 1974	San Diego 20, New York Jets 14, at San Diego
Aug. 17, 1974	Pittsburgh 33, Philadelphia 30, at Philadelphia
Aug. 17, 1974	Dallas 19, Houston 13, at Dallas
Aug. 17, 1974	Cincinnati 13, Atlanta 7, at Atlanta
Sept. 6, 1974	Buffalo 23, New York Giants 17, at Buffalo
Aug. 9, 1975	Baltimore 23, Denver 20, at Denver
Aug. 30, 1975	New England 20, Green Bay 17, at Milwaukee
Sept. 13, 1975	Minnesota 14, San Diego 14, at San Diego
Aug. 1, 1976	New England 13, New York Giants 7, at New England
Aug. 2, 1976	Kansas City 9, Houston 3, at Kansas City
Aug. 20, 1976	New Orleans 26, Baltimore 20, at Baltimore
Sept. 4, 1976	Dallas 26, Houston 20, at Dallas
Aug. 13, 1977	Seattle 23, Dallas 17, at Seattle
Aug. 28, 1977	New England 13, Pittsburgh 10, at New England
Aug. 28, 1977	New York Giants 24, Buffalo 21, at East Rutherford, N.J.
Aug. 2, 1979	Seattle 12, Minnesota 9, at Minnesota
Aug. 4, 1979	Los Angeles 20, Oakland 14, at Los Angeles
Aug. 24, 1979	Denver 20, New England 17, at Denver
Aug. 23, 1980	Tampa Bay 20, Cincinnati 14, at Tampa Bay
Aug. 5, 1981	San Francisco 27, Seattle 24, at Seattle
Aug. 29, 1981	New Orleans 20, Detroit 17, at New Orleans
Aug. 28, 1982	Miami 17, Kansas City 17, at Kansas City
Sept. 3, 1982	Miami 16, New York Giants 13, at Miami
Aug. 6, 1983	L.A. Raiders 26, San Francisco 23, at Los Angeles
Aug. 6, 1983	Atlanta 13, Washington 10, at Atlanta
Aug. 13, 1983	St. Louis 27, Chicago 24, at St. Louis
Aug. 18, 1983	New York Jets 20, Cincinnati 17, at Cincinnati
Aug. 27, 1983	Chicago 20, Kansas City 17, at Chicago
Aug. 11, 1984	Pittsburgh 20, Philadelphia 17, at Pittsburgh
Aug. 9, 1985	Buffalo 10, Detroit 10, at Pontiac, Mich.
Aug. 10, 1985	Minnesota 16, Miami 13, at Miami
Aug. 17, 1985	Dallas 27, San Diego 24, at San Diego
Aug. 24, 1985	N.Y. Giants 34, N.Y. Jets 31, at East Rutherford, N.J.
Aug. 15, 1986	Washington 27, Pittsburgh 24, at Washington
Aug. 15, 1986	Detroit 30, Seattle 27, at Detroit
Aug. 23, 1986	Los Angeles Rams 20, San Diego 17, at Anaheim
Aug. 30, 1986	Minnesota 23, Indianapolis 20, at Indianapolis
Aug. 23, 1987	Philadelphia 19, New England 13, at New England
Sept. 5, 1987	Cleveland 30, Green Bay 24, at Milwaukee
Sept. 6, 1987	Kansas City 13, St. Louis 10, at Memphis, Tenn.
Aug. 11, 1988	Seattle 16, Detroit 13, at Detroit
Aug. 19, 1988	Miami 16, Denver 13, at Miami
Aug. 20, 1988	Houston 20, Los Angeles Rams 17, at Anaheim
Aug. 21, 1988	Minnesota 19, Phoenix 16, at Phoenix
Aug. 5, 1989	Los Angeles Rams 16, San Francisco 13, at Tokyo, Japan
Aug. 26, 1989	Denver 24, Dallas 21, at Denver
Sept. 1, 1989	N.Y. Jets 15, Kansas City 13, at Kansas City
Aug. 24, 1990	Cincinnati 13, New England 10, at New England

Regular Season

Sept. 22, 1974—Pittsburgh 35, Denver 35, at Denver; Steelers win toss. Gilliam's pass intercepted and returned by Rowser to Denver's 42. Turner misses 41-yard field goal. Walden punts and Greer returns to Broncos' 39. Van Heusen punts and Edwards returns to Steelers' 16. Game ends with Steelers on own 26.

Nov. 10, 1974—New York Jets 26, New York Giants 20, at New Haven, Conn.; Giants win toss. Gogolak misses 42-yard field goal. Namath passes to Boozer for five yards and touchdown at 6:53.

Sept. 28, 1975—Dallas 37, St. Louis 31, at Dallas; Cardinals win toss. Hart's pass intercepted and returned by Jordan to Cardinals' 37. Staubach passes to DuPree for three yards and touchdown at 7:53.

Oct. 12, 1975—Los Angeles 13, San Diego 10, at San Diego; Chargers win toss. Partee punts to Rams' 14. Dempsey kicks 22-yard field goal at 9:27.

Nov. 2, 1975—Washington 30, Dallas 24, at Washington; Cowboys win toss. Staubach's pass intercepted and returned by Houston to Cowboys' 35. Kilmer runs one yard for touchdown at 6:34.

Nov. 16, 1975—St. Louis 20, Washington 17, at St. Louis; Cardinals win toss. Bakken kicks 37-yard field goal at 7:00.

Nov. 23, 1975—Kansas City 24, Detroit 21, at Kansas City; Lions win toss. Chiefs take over on downs at own 38. Stenerud kicks 26-yard field goal at 6:44.

Nov. 23, 1975—Oakland 26, Washington 23, at Washington; Redskins win toss. Bragg punts to Raiders' 42. Blanda kicks 27-yard field goal at 7:13.

Nov. 30, 1975—Denver 13, San Diego 10, at Denver; Broncos win toss. Turner kicks 25-yard field goal at 4:13.

Nov. 30, 1975—Oakland 37, Atlanta 34, at Oakland; Falcons win toss. James punts to Raiders' 16. Guy punts and Herron returns to Falcons' 41. Nick Mike-Mayer misses 45-yard field goal. Guy punts into Falcons' end zone. James punts to Raiders' 39. Blanda kicks 36-yard field goal at 15:00.

Dec. 14, 1975—Baltimore 10, Miami 7, at Baltimore; Dolphins win toss. Seiple punts to Colts' 4. Linhart kicks 31-yard field goal at 12:44.

Sept. 19, 1976—Minnesota 10, Los Angeles 10, at Minnesota; Vikings win toss. Tarkenton's pass intercepted by Monte Jackson and returned to Minnesota 16. Allen blocks Dempsey's 30-yard field goal attempt, ball rolls into end zone for touchback. Clabo punts and Scribner returns to Rams' 20. Rusty Jackson punts to Vikings' 35. Tarkenton's pass intercepted by Kay at Rams' 1, no return. Game ends with Rams on own 3.

***Sept. 27, 1976—Washington 20, Philadelphia 17,** at Philadelphia; Eagles win toss. Jones punts and E. Brown loses one yard on return to Redskins' 40. Bragg punts 51 yards into end zone for touchback. Jones punts and E. Brown returns to Redskins' 42. Bragg punts and Marshall returns to Eagles' 41. Boryla's pass intercepted by Dusek at Redskins' 37, no return. Bragg punts and Bradley returns. Philadelphia holding penalty moves ball back to Eagles' 8. Boryla pass intercepted by E. Brown and returned to Eagles' 22. Moseley kicks 29-yard field goal at 12:49.

Oct. 17, 1976—Kansas City 20, Miami 17, at Miami; Chiefs win toss. Wilson punts into end zone for touchback. Bulaich fumbles into Kansas City end zone, Collier recovers for touchback. Stenerud kicks 34-yard field goal at 14:48.

Oct. 31, 1976—St. Louis 23, San Francisco 20, at St. Louis; Cardinals win toss. Joyce punts and Leonard fumbles on return, Jones recovers at 49ers' 43. Bakken kicks 21-yard field goal at 6:42.

Dec. 5, 1976—San Diego 13, San Francisco 7, at San Diego; Chargers win toss. Morris runs 13 yards for touchdown at 5:12.

Sept. 18, 1977—Dallas 16, Minnesota 10, at Minnesota; Vikings win toss. Dallas starts on Vikings' 47 after a punt early in the overtime period. Staubach scores seven plays later on a four-yard run in 6:14.

***Sept. 26, 1977—Cleveland 30, New England 27,** at Cleveland; Browns win toss. Sipe throws a 22-yard pass to Logan at Patriots' 19. Cockroft kicks 35-yard field goal at 4:45.

Oct. 16, 1977—Minnesota 22, Chicago 16, at Minnesota; Bears win toss. Parsons punts 53 yards to Vikings' 18. Minnesota drives to Bears' 11. On a first-and-10, Vikings fake a field goal and holder Krause hits Voigt with a touchdown pass at 6:45.

Oct. 30, 1977—Cincinnati 13, Houston 10, at Cincinnati; Bengals win toss. Bahr kicks a 22-yard field goal at 5:51.

Nov. 13, 1977—San Francisco 10, New Orleans 7, at New Orleans; Saints win toss. Saints fail to move ball and Blanchard punts to 49ers' 41. Wersching kicks a 33-yard field goal at 6:33.

Dec. 18, 1977—Chicago 12, New York Giants 9, at East Rutherford, N.J.; Giants win toss. The ball changes hands eight times before Thomas kicks a 28-yard field goal at 14:51.

Sept. 10, 1978—Cleveland 13, Cincinnati 10, at Cleveland; Browns win toss. Collins returns kickoff 41 yards to Browns' 47. Cockroft kicks 27-yard field goal at 4:30.

***Sept. 11, 1978—Minnesota 12, Denver 9,** at Minnesota; Vikings win toss. Danmeier kicks 44-yard field goal at 2:56.

Sept. 24, 1978—Pittsburgh 15, Cleveland 9, at Pittsburgh; Steelers win toss. Cunningham scores on a 37-yard "gadget" pass from Bradshaw at 3:43. Steelers start winning drive on their 21.

Sept. 24, 1978—Denver 23, Kansas City 17, at Kansas City; Broncos win toss. Dilts punts to Kansas City. Chiefs advance to Broncos' 40 where Reed fails to make first down on fourth-and-one situation. Broncos march downfield. Preston scores two-yard touchdown at 10:28.

Oct. 1, 1978—Oakland 25, Chicago 19, at Chicago; Bears win toss. Both teams punt on first possession. On Chicago's second offensive series, Colzie intercepts Avellini's pass and returns it to Bears' 3. Three plays later, Whittington runs two yards for a touchdown at 5:19.

Oct. 15, 1978—Dallas 24, St. Louis 21, at St. Louis; Cowboys win toss. Dallas drives from its 23 into field goal range. Septien kicks 27-yard field goal at 3:28.

Oct. 29, 1978—Denver 20, Seattle 17, at Seattle; Broncos win toss. Ball changes hands four times before Turner kicks 18-yard field goal at 12:59.

Nov. 12, 1978—San Diego 29, Kansas City 23, at San Diego; Chiefs win toss. Fouts hits Jefferson for decisive 14-yard touchdown pass on the last play (15:00) of overtime period.

Nov. 12, 1978—Washington 16, New York Giants 13, at Washington; Redskins win toss. Moseley kicks winning 45-yard field goal at 8:32 after missing first down field goal attempt of 35 yards at 4:50.

Nov. 26, 1978—Green Bay 10, Minnesota 10, at Green Bay; Packers win toss. Both teams have possession of the ball four times.

Dec. 9, 1978—Cleveland 37, New York Jets 34, at Cleveland; Browns win toss. Cockroft kicks 22-yard field goal at 3:07.

Sept. 2, 1979—Atlanta 40, New Orleans 34, at New Orleans; Falcons win toss. Bartkowski's pass intercepted by Myers and returned to Falcons' 46. Erxleben punts to Falcons' 4. James punts to Chandler on Saints' 43. Erxleben punts and Ryckman returns to Falcons' 28. James punts and Chandler returns to Saints' 36. Erxleben retrieves punt snap on Saints' 1 and attempts pass. Mayberry intercepts and returns six yards for touchdown at 8:22.

Sept. 2, 1979—Cleveland 25, New York Jets 22, at New York; Jets win toss. Leahy's 43-yard field goal attempt goes wide right at 4:41. Evans's punt blocked by Dykes is recovered by Newton. Ramsey punts into end zone for touchback. Evans punts and Harper returns to Jets' 24. Robinson's pass intercepted by Davis and returned 33 yards to Jets' 31. Cockroft kicks 27-yard field goal at 14:45.

***Sept. 3, 1979—Pittsburgh 16, New England 13,** at Foxboro; Patriots win toss. Hare punts to Swann at Steelers' 31. Bahr kicks 41-yard field goal at 5:10.

Sept. 9, 1979—Tampa Bay 29, Baltimore 26, at Baltimore; Colts win toss. Landry fumbles, recovered by Kollar at Colts' 14. O'Donoghue kicks 31-yard, first-down field goal at 1:41.

Sept. 16, 1979—Denver 20, Atlanta 17, at Atlanta; Broncos win toss. Broncos march 65 yards to Falcons' 7. Turner kicks 24-yard field goal at 6:15.

Sept. 23, 1979—Houston 30, Cincinnati 27, at Cincinnati; Oilers win toss. Parsley punts and Lusby returns to Bengals' 33. Bahr's 32-yard field goal attempt is wide right at 8:05. Parsley's punt downed on Bengals' 5. McInally punts and Ellender returns to Bengals' 42. Fritsch's third down, 29-yard field goal attempt hits left upright and bounces through at 14:28.

Sept. 23, 1979—Minnesota 27, Green Bay 21, at Minnesota; Vikings win toss. Kramer throws 50-yard touchdown pass to Rashad at 3:18.

Oct. 28, 1979—Houston 27, New York Jets 24, at Houston; Oilers win toss. Oilers march 58 yards to Jets' 18. Fritsch kicks 35-yard field goal at 5:10.

Nov. 18, 1979—Cleveland 30, Miami 24, at Cleveland; Browns win toss. Sipe passes 39 yards to Rucker for touchdown at 1:59.

Nov. 25, 1979—Pittsburgh 33, Cleveland 30, at Pittsburgh; Browns win toss. Sipe's pass intercepted by Blount on Steelers' 4. Bradshaw pass intercepted by Bolton on Browns' 12. Evans punts and Bell returns to Steelers' 17. Bahr kicks 37-yard field goal at 14:51.

Nov. 25, 1979—Buffalo 16, New England 13, at Foxboro; Patriots win toss. Hare's punt downed on Bills' 38. Jackson punts and Morgan returns to Patriots' 20. Grogan's pass intercepted by Haslett and returned to Bills' 42. Ferguson's 51-yard pass to Butler sets up N. Mike-Mayer's 29-yard field goal at 9:15.

Dec. 2, 1979—Los Angeles 27, Minnesota 21, at Los Angeles; Rams win toss. Clark punts and Miller returns to Vikings' 25. Kramer's pass intercepted by Brown and returned to Rams' 40. Cromwell, holding for 22-yard field goal attempt, runs around left end untouched for winning score at 6:53.

Sept. 7, 1980—Green Bay 12, Chicago 6, at Green Bay; Bears win toss. Parsons punts and Nixon returns 16 yards. Five plays later, Marcol returns own blocked field goal attempt 24 yards for touchdown at 6:00.

Sept. 14, 1980—San Diego 30, Oakland 24, at San Diego; Raiders win toss. Pastorini's first-down pass intercepted by Edwards. Millen intercepts Fouts' first-down pass and returns to San Diego 46. Bahr's 50-yard field goal attempt partially blocked by Williams and recovered on Chargers' 32. Eight plays later, Fouts throws 24-yard touchdown pass to Jefferson at 8:09.

Sept. 14, 1980—San Francisco 24, St. Louis 21, at San Francisco; Cardinals win toss. Swider punts and Robinson returns to 49ers' 32. San Francisco drives 52 yards to St. Louis 16, where Wersching kicks 33-yard field goal at 4:12.

Oct. 12, 1980—Green Bay 14, Tampa Bay 14, at Tampa Bay; Packers win toss. Teams trade punts twice. Lee returns second Tampa Bay punt to Green Bay 42. Dickey completes three passes to Buccaneers' 18, where Birney's 36-yard field goal attempt is wide right as time expires.

Nov. 9, 1980—Atlanta 33, St. Louis 27, at St. Louis; Falcons win toss. Strong runs 21 yards for touchdown at 4:20.

#Nov. 20, 1980—San Diego 27, Miami 24, at Miami; Chargers win toss. Partridge punts into end zone, Dolphins take over on their own 20. Woodley's pass for Nathan intercepted by Lowe and returned 28 yards to Dolphins' 12. Benirschke kicks 28-yard field goal at 7:14.

Nov. 23, 1980—New York Jets 31, Houston 28, at New York; Jets win toss. Leahy kicks 38-yard field goal at 3:58.

Nov. 27, 1980—Chicago 23, Detroit 17, at Detroit; Bears win toss. Williams returns kickoff 95 yards for touchdown at 0:21.

Dec. 7, 1980—Buffalo 10, Los Angeles 7, at Buffalo; Rams win toss. Corral punts and Hooks returns to Bills' 34. Ferguson's 30-yard pass to Lewis sets up N. Mike-Mayer's 30-yard field goal at 5:14.

Dec. 7, 1980—San Francisco 38, New Orleans 35, at San Francisco; Saints win toss. Erxleben's punt downed by Hardy on 49ers' 27. Wersching kicks 36-yard field goal at 7:40.

***Dec. 8, 1980—Miami 16, New England 13,** at Miami; Dolphins win toss. Von Schamann kicks 23-yard field goal at 3:20.

Dec. 14, 1980—Cincinnati 17, Chicago 14, at Chicago; Bengals win toss. Breech kicks 28-yard field goal at 4:23.

Dec. 21, 1980—Los Angeles 20, Atlanta 17, at Los Angeles; Rams win toss. Corral's punt downed at Rams' 37. James punts into end zone for touchback. Corral's punt downed on Falcons' 17. Bartkowski fumbles when hit by Harris, recovered by Delaney. Corral kicks 23-yard field goal on first play of possession at 7:00.

Sept. 27, 1981—Cincinnati 27, Buffalo 24, at Cincinnati; Bills win toss. Cater punts into end zone for touchback. Bengals drive to the Bills' 10 where Breech kicks 28-yard field goal at 9:33.

Sept. 27, 1981—Pittsburgh 27, New England 21, at Pittsburgh; Patriots win toss. Hubach punts and Smith returns five yards to midfield. Four plays later Bradshaw throws 24-yard touchdown pass to Swann at 3:19.

Oct. 4, 1981—Miami 28, New York Jets 28, at Miami; Jets win toss. Teams trade punts twice. Leahy's 48-yard field goal attempt is wide right as time expires.

Oct. 25, 1981—New York Giants 27, Atlanta 24, at Atlanta; Giants win toss. Jennings' punt goes out of bounds at New York 47. Bright returns Atlanta punt to Giants' 14. Woerner fair catches punt at own 28. Andrews fumbles on first play, recovered by Van Pelt. Danelo kicks 40-yard field goal four plays later at 9:20.

Oct. 25, 1981—Chicago 20, San Diego 17, at Chicago; Bears win toss. Teams trade punts. Bears' second punt returned by Brooks to Chargers' 33. Fouts pass intercepted by Fencik and returned 32 yards to San Diego 27. Roveto kicks 27-yard field goal seven plays later at 9:30.

Nov. 8, 1981—Chicago 16, Kansas City 13, at Kansas City; Bears win toss. Teams trade punts. Kansas City takes over on downs on its own 38. Fuller's fumble recovered by Harris on Chicago 36. Roveto's 37-yard field goal wide, but Chiefs penalized for leverage. Roveto's 22-yard field goal attempt three plays later is good at 13:07.

Nov. 8, 1981—Denver 23, Cleveland 20, at Denver; Browns win toss. D. Smith recovers Hill's fumble at Denver 48. Morton's 33-yard pass to Upchurch and six-yard run by Preston set up Steinfort's 30-yard field goal at 4:10.

Nov. 8, 1981—Miami 30, New England 27, at New England; Dolphins win toss. Orosz punts and Morgan returns six yards to New England 26. Grogan's pass intercepted by Brudzinski who returns 19 yards to Patriots' 26. Von Schamann kicks 30-yard field goal on first down at 7:09.

Nov. 15, 1981—Washington 30, New York Giants 27, at New York; Giants win toss. Nelms returns Giants' punt 26 yards to New York 47. Five plays later Moseley kicks 48-yard field goal at 3:44.

Dec. 20, 1981—New York Giants 13, Dallas 10, at New York; Cowboys win toss and kick off. Jennings punts to Dallas 40. Taylor recovers Dorsett's fumble on second down. Danelo's 33-yard field goal attempt hits right upright and bounces back. White's pass for Pearson intercepted by Hunt and returned seven yards to Dallas 24. Four plays later Danelo kicks 35-yard field goal at 6:19.

Sept. 12, 1982—Washington 37, Philadelphia 34, at Philadelphia; Redskins win toss. Theismann completes five passes for 63 yards to set up Moseley's 26-yard field goal at 4:47.

Sept. 19, 1982—Pittsburgh 26, Cincinnati 20, at Pittsburgh; Bengals win toss. Anderson's pass intended for Kreider intercepted by Woodruff and returned 30 yards to Cincinnati 2. Bradshaw completes two-yard touchdown pass to Stallworth on first down at 1:08.

Dec. 19, 1982—Baltimore 20, Green Bay 20, at Baltimore; Packers win toss. K. Anderson intercepts Dickey's first-down pass and returns to Packers' 42. Miller's 44-yard field goal attempt blocked by G. Lewis. Teams trade punts before Stenerud's 47-yard field goal attempt is wide right. Teams trade punts again before time expires in Colts possession.

Jan. 2, 1983—Tampa Bay 26, Chicago 23, at Tampa Bay; Bears win toss. Parsons punts to T. Bell at Buccaneers' 40. Capece kicks 33-yard field goal at 3:14.

Sept. 4, 1983—Baltimore 29, New England 23, at New England; Patriots win toss. Cooks runs 52 yards with fumble recovery three plays into overtime at 0:30.

Sept. 4, 1983—Green Bay 41, Houston 38, at Houston; Packers win toss. Stenerud kicks 42-yard field goal at 5:55.

Sept. 11, 1983—New York Giants 16, Atlanta 13, at Atlanta; Giants win toss. Dennis returns kickoff 54 yards to Atlanta 41. Haji-Sheikh kicks 30-yard field goal at 3:38.

Sept. 18, 1983—New Orleans 34, Chicago 31, at New Orleans; Bears win toss. Parsons punts and Groth returns five yards to New Orleans 34. Stabler pass intercepted by Schmidt at Chicago 47. Parsons punt downed by Gentry at New Orleans 2. Stabler gains 36 yards in four passes; Wilson 38 in six carries. Andersen kicks 41-yard field goal at 10:57.

Sept. 18, 1983—Minnesota 19, Tampa Bay 16, at Tampa; Vikings win toss. Coleman punts and Bell returns eight yards to Tampa Bay 47. Capece's 33-yard field goal attempt sails wide at 7:26. Dils and Young combine for 48-yard gain to Tampa Bay 27. Ricardo kicks 42-yard field goal at 9:27.

Sept. 25, 1983—Baltimore 22, Chicago 19, at Baltimore; Colts win toss. Allegre kicks 33-yard field goal nine plays later at 4:51.

Sept. 25, 1983—Cleveland 30, San Diego 24, at San Diego; Browns win toss. Walker returns kickoff 33 yards to Cleveland 37. Sipe completes 48-yard touchdown pass to Holt four plays later at 1:53.

Sept. 25, 1983—New York Jets 27, Los Angeles Rams 24, at New York; Jets win toss. Ramsey punts to Irvin who returns to 25 but penalty puts Rams on own 13. Holmes 30-yard interception return sets up Leahy's 26-yard field goal at 3:22.

Oct. 9, 1983—Buffalo 38, Miami 35, at Miami; Dolphins win toss. Von Schamann's 52-yard field goal attempt goes wide at 12:36. Cater punts to Clayton who loses 11 to own 13. Von Schamann's 43-yard field goal attempt sails wide at 5:15. Danelo kicks 36-yard field goal nine plays later at 13:58.

Oct. 9, 1983—Dallas 27, Tampa Bay 24, at Dallas; Cowboys win toss. Septien's 51-yard field goal attempt goes wide but Buccaneers penalized for roughing kicker. Septien kicks 42-yard field goal at 4:38.

Oct. 23, 1983—Kansas City 13, Houston 10, at Houston; Chiefs win toss. Lowery kicks 41-yard field goal 13 plays later at 7:41.

Oct. 23, 1983—Minnesota 20, Green Bay 17, at Green Bay; Packers win toss. Scribner's punt downed on Vikings' 42. Ricardo kicks 32-yard field goal eight plays later at 5:05.

***Oct. 24, 1983—New York Giants 20, St. Louis 20,** at St. Louis; Cardinals win toss. Teams trade punts before O'Donoghue's 44-yard field goal attempt is wide left. Jennings' punt returned by Bird to St. Louis 21. Lomax pass intercepted by Haynes who loses six yards to New York 33. Jennings' punt downed on St. Louis 17. O'Donoghue's 19-yard field goal attempt is wide right. Rutledge's pass intercepted by L. Washington who returns 25 yards to New York 25. O'Donoghue's 42-yard field goal attempt is wide right. Rutledge's pass intercepted by W. Smith at St. Louis 33 to end game.

Oct. 30, 1983—Cleveland 25, Houston 19, at Cleveland; Oilers win toss. Teams trade punts. Nielsen's pass intercepted by Whitwell who returns to Houston 20. Green runs 20 yards for touchdown on first down at 6:34.

Nov. 20, 1983—Detroit 23, Green Bay 20, at Milwaukee; Packers win toss. Scribner punts and Jenkins returns 14 yards to Green Bay 45. Murray's 33-yard field goal attempt is wide left at 9:32. Whitehurst's pass intercepted by Watkins and returned to Green Bay 27. Murray kicks 37-yard field goal four plays later at 8:30.

Nov. 27, 1983—Atlanta 47, Green Bay 41, at Atlanta; Packers win toss. K. Johnson returns interception 31 yards for touchdown at 2:13.

Nov. 27, 1983—Seattle 51, Kansas City 48, at Seattle; Seahawks win toss. Dixon's 47-yard kickoff return sets up N. Johnson's 42-yard field goal at 1:36.

Dec. 11, 1983—New Orleans 20, Philadelphia 17, at Philadelphia; Eagles win toss. Runager punts to Groth who fair catches on New Orleans 32. Stabler completes two passes for 36 yards to Goodlow to set up Andersen's 50-yard field goal at 5:30.

***Dec. 12, 1983—Green Bay 12, Tampa Bay 9,** at Tampa; Packers win toss. Stenerud kicks 23-yard field goal 11 plays later at 4:07.

Sept. 9, 1984—Detroit 27, Atlanta 24, at Atlanta; Lions win toss. Murray kicks 48-yard field goal nine plays later at 5:06.

Sept. 30, 1984—Tampa Bay 30, Green Bay 27, at Tampa; Packers win toss. Scribner punts 44 yards to Tampa Bay 2. Epps returns Garcia's punt three yards to Green Bay 27. Scribner's punt downed on Buccaneers' 33. Ariri kicks 46-yard field goal 11 plays later at 10:32.

Oct. 14, 1984—Detroit 13, Tampa Bay 7, at Detroit; Buccaneers win toss. Tampa Bay drives to Lions' 39 before Wilder fumbles. Five plays later Danielson hits Thompson with 37-yard touchdown pass at 4:34.

Oct. 21, 1984—Dallas 30, New Orleans 27, at Dallas; Cowboys win toss. Septien kicks 41-yard field goal eight plays later at 3:42.

Oct. 28, 1984—Denver 22, Los Angeles Raiders 19, at Los Angeles; Raiders win toss. Hawkins fumble recovered by Foley at Denver 7. Teams trade punts. Karlis' 42-yard field goal attempt is wide left. Teams trade punts. Wilson pass intercepted by R. Jackson at Los Angeles 45, returned 23 yards to Los Angeles 22. Karlis kicks 35-yard field goal two plays later at 15:00.

Nov. 4, 1984—Philadelphia 23, Detroit 23, at Detroit; Lions win toss. Lions drive to Eagles' 3 in eight plays. Murray's 21-yard field goal attempt hits right upright and bounces back. Jaworski's pass intercepted by Watkins at Detroit 5. Teams trade punts. Cooper returns Black's punt five yards to Eagles' 14. Time expires four plays later with Eagles on own 21.

Nov. 18, 1984—San Diego 34, Miami 28, at San Diego; Chargers win toss. McGee scores eight plays later on a 25-yard run at 3:17.

Dec. 2, 1984—Cincinnati 20, Cleveland 17, at Cleveland; Browns win toss. Simmons returns Cox's punt 30 yards to Cleveland 35. Breech kicks 35-yard field goal seven plays later at 4:34.

Dec. 2, 1984—Houston 23, Pittsburgh 20, at Houston; Oilers win toss. Cooper kicks 30-yard field goal 16 plays later at 5:53.

Sept. 8, 1985—St. Louis 27, Cleveland 24, at Cleveland; Cardinals win toss. O'Donoghue kicks 35-yard field goal nine plays later at 5:27.

Sept. 29, 1985—New York Giants 16, Philadelphia 10, at Philadelphia; Eagles win toss. Jaworski's pass tipped by Quick and intercepted by Patterson who returns 29 yards for touchdown at 0:55.

Oct. 20, 1985—Denver 13, Seattle 10, at Denver; Seahawks win toss. Teams trade punts twice. Krieg's pass intercepted by Hunter and returned to Seahawks' 15. Karlis kicks 24-yard field goal four plays later at 9:19.

Nov. 10, 1985—Philadelphia 23, Atlanta 17, at Philadelphia; Falcons win toss. Donnelly's 62-yard punt goes out of bounds at Eagles' 1. Jaworski completes 99-yard touchdown pass to Quick two plays later at 1:49.

Nov. 10, 1985—San Diego 40, Los Angeles Raiders 34, at San Diego; Chargers win toss. James scores on 17-yard run seven plays later at 3:44.

Nov. 17, 1985—Denver 30, San Diego 24, at Denver; Chargers win toss. Thomas' 40-yard field goal attempt blocked by Smith and returned 60 yards by Wright for touchdown at 4:45.

Nov. 24, 1985—New York Jets 16, New England 13, at New York; Jets win toss. Teams trade punts twice. Patriots' second punt returned 46 yards by Sohn to Patriots' 15. Leahy kicks 32-yard field goal one play later at 10:05.

Nov. 24, 1985—Tampa Bay 19, Detroit 16, at Tampa; Lions win toss. Teams trade punts. Lions' punt downed on Buccaneers' 38. Igwebuike kicks 24-yard field goal 11 plays later at 12:31.

Nov. 24, 1985—Los Angeles Raiders 31, Denver 28, at Los Angeles; Raiders win toss. Bahr kicks 32-yard field goal six plays later at 2:42.

Dec. 8, 1985—Los Angeles Raiders 17, Denver 14, at Denver; Broncos win toss. Teams trade punts twice. Elway's fumble recovered by Townsend at Broncos' 8. Bahr kicks 26-yard field goal one play later at 4:55.

Sept. 14, 1986—Chicago 13, Philadelphia 10, at Chicago; Eagles win toss. Crawford's fumble of kickoff recovered by Jackson at Eagles' 35. Butler kicks 23-yard field goal 10 plays later at 5:56.

Sept. 14, 1986—Cincinnati 36, Buffalo 33, at Cincinnati; Bills win toss. Zander intercepts Kelly's first-down pass and returns it to Bills' 17. Breech kicks 20-yard field goal two plays later at 0:56.

Sept. 21, 1986—New York Jets 51, Miami 45, at New York; Jets win toss. O'Brien completes 43-yard touchdown pass to Walker five plays later at 2:35.

Sept. 28, 1986—Pittsburgh 22, Houston 16, at Houston; Oilers win toss. Johnson's punt returned 41 yards by Woods to Oilers' 15. Abercrombie scores on three-yard run three plays later at 2:35.

Sept. 28, 1986—Atlanta 23, Tampa Bay 20, at Tampa; Falcons win toss. Teams trade punts. Luckhurst kicks 34-yard field goal 10 plays later at 12:35.

Oct. 5, 1986—Los Angeles Rams 26, Tampa Bay 20, at Anaheim; Rams win toss. Dickerson scores four plays later on 42-yard run at 2:16.

Oct. 12, 1986—Minnesota 27, San Francisco 24, at San Francisco; Vikings win toss. C. Nelson kicks 28-yard field goal nine plays later at 4:27.

Oct. 19, 1986—San Francisco 10, Atlanta 10, at Atlanta; Falcons win toss. Teams trade punts twice. Donnelly punts to 49ers' 27. The following play Wilson recovers Rice's fumble at 49ers' 46 as time expires.

Nov. 2, 1986—Washington 44, Minnesota 38, at Washington; Redskins win toss. Schroeder completes 38-yard touchdown pass to Clark four plays later at 1:46.

Nov. 20, 1986—Los Angeles Raiders 37, San Diego 31, at San Diego; Raiders win toss. Teams trade punts. Allen scores five plays later on 28-yard run at 8:33.

Nov. 23, 1986—Cleveland 37, Pittsburgh 31, at Cleveland; Browns win toss. Teams trade punts. Six plays later Kosar hits Slaughter with 36-yard touchdown pass at 6:37.

Nov. 30, 1986—Chicago 13, Pittsburgh 10, at Chicago; Bears win toss and kick off. Newsome's punt returned by Barnes to Chicago 49. Butler kicks 42-yard field goal five plays later at 3:55.

Nov. 30, 1986—Philadelphia 33, Los Angeles Raiders 27, at Los Angeles; Eagles win toss. Teams trade punts. Long recovers Cunningham's fumble at Philadelphia 42. Waters returns Allen's fumble 81 yards to Los Angeles 4. Cunningham scores on one-yard run two plays later at 6:53.

Nov. 30, 1986—Cleveland 13, Houston 10, at Cleveland; Oilers win toss and kick off. Gossett punts to Houston 39. Luck's pass intercepted by Minnifield at Cleveland 21. Gossett punts to Houston 34. Luck's pass intercepted by Minnifield at Cleveland 43 who returns 20 yards to Houston 37. Moseley kicks 29-yard field goal nine plays later at 14:44.

Dec. 7, 1986—St. Louis 10, Philadelphia 10, at Philadelphia; Cardinals win toss. White blocks Schubert's 40-yard field goal attempt. Teams trade punts. McFadden's 43-yard field goal attempt is wide left. Schubert's 37-yard field goal attempt is wide right. Cavanaugh's pass intercepted by Carter and returned to Eagles' 48 to end game.

Dec. 14, 1986—Miami 37, Los Angeles Rams 31, at Anaheim; Dolphins win toss. Marino completes 20-yard touchdown pass to Duper six plays later at 3:04.

Sept. 20, 1987—Denver 17, Green Bay 17, at Green Bay; Packers win toss. Del Greco's 47-yard field goal attempt is short. Teams trade punts. Elway intercepted by Noble who returns 10 yards to Green Bay 34. Davis fumbles on next play and Smith recovers. Two plays later, Karlis's 40-yard field goal attempt is wide left. Time expires two plays later with Packers on own 23.

Oct. 11, 1987—Detroit 19, Green Bay 16, at Green Bay; Lions win toss. Prindle's 42-yard field goal attempt is wide left. Packers punt downed on Detroit 17. Prindle kicks 31-yard field goal 16 plays later at 12:26.

Oct. 18, 1987—New York Jets 37, Miami 31, at New York; Jets win toss. Teams trade punts. Ryan intercepted by Hooper at Jets' 47 who returns 11 yards. Mackey intercepted by Haslett at Jets' 37 who returns 9 yards. Jets punt. Mackey intercepted by Radachowsky who returns 45 yards to Miami 24. Ryan completes eight-yard touchdown pass to Hunter five plays later at 14:26.

Oct. 18, 1987—Green Bay 16, Philadelphia 10, at Green Bay; Packers win toss. Hargrove scores on seven-yard run 10 plays later at 5:04.

Oct. 18, 1987—Buffalo 6, New York Giants 3, at Buffalo; Bills win toss. Schlopy's 28-yard field goal attempt is wide left. Teams trade punts. Rutledge intercepted by Clark who returns 23 yards to Buffalo 40. Schlopy kicks 27-yard field goal nine plays later at 14:41.

Oct. 25, 1987—Buffalo 34, Miami 31, at Miami; Bills win toss. Norwood kicks 27-yard field goal seven plays later at 4:12.

Nov. 1, 1987—San Diego 27, Cleveland 24, at San Diego; Browns win toss. Kosar intercepted by Glenn who returns 20 yards to Browns' 25. Abbott kicks 33-yard field goal three plays later at 2:16.

Nov. 15, 1987—Dallas 23, New England 17, at New England; Cowboys win toss. Walker scores on 60-yard run four plays later at 1:50.

Nov. 26, 1987—Minnesota 44, Dallas 38, at Dallas; Vikings win toss. Coleman's punt downed by Hilton at Cowboys' 37. White intercepted by Studwell who returns 12 yards to Vikings' 37. D. Nelson scores on 24-yard run seven plays later at 7:51.

Nov. 29, 1987—Philadelphia 34, New England 31, at New England; Patriots win toss. Ramsey intercepted by Joyner who returns 29 yards to Eagles' 32. Fryar fair catches Teltschik's punt at Patriots' 13. Franklin's 46-yard field goal attempt is short. McFadden's 39-yard field goal attempt is wide left. Tatupu fumbles on next play and Cobb recovers. McFadden kicks 38-yard field goal four plays later at 12:16.

Dec. 6, 1987—New York Giants 23, Philadelphia 20, at New York; Giants win toss and kick off. Teams trade punts twice. Teltschik's punt is returned 16 yards by McConkey to Eagles' 33. Three plays later, Allegre's 50-yard field goal attempt is blocked by Joyner and returned 25 yards by Hoage to Eagles' 30. McConkey returns Teltschik's punt four yards to Giants' 44. Allegre kicks 28-yard field goal four plays later at 10:42.

Dec. 6, 1987—Cincinnati 30, Kansas City 27, at Cincinnati; Bengals win toss. Teams trade punts. Breech kicks 32-yard field goal 16 plays later at 9:44.

Dec. 26, 1987—Washington 27, Minnesota 24, at Minnesota; Redskins win toss. Haji-Sheikh kicks 26-yard field goal six plays later at 2:09.

Sept. 4, 1988—Houston 17, Indianapolis 14, at Indianapolis; Colts win toss. Dickerson fumble recovered by Odom who returns six yards to Colts' 42. Zendejas kicks 35-yard field goal six plays later at 3:51.

***Sept. 26, 1988—Los Angeles Raiders 30, Denver 27,** at Denver; Broncos win toss. Teams trade punts twice. Elway intercepted by Lee who returns 20 yards to Broncos' 31. Bahr kicks 35-yard field goal four plays later at 12:35.

Oct. 2, 1988—New York Jets 17, Kansas City 17, at New York; Chiefs win toss. Chiefs punt goes into end zone for touchback. Leahy's 44-yard field goal attempt is wide right. Chiefs punt is returned by Townsell to Jets' 26. Burruss recovers McNeil's fumble at Chiefs' 11. DeBerg intercepted by Humphery at Jets' 49. Three plays later, time expires.

Oct. 9, 1988—Denver 16, San Francisco 13, at San Francisco; Broncos win toss and kick off. Young intercepted by Haynes at Broncos' 32. Denver punt downed at 49ers' 5. Young intercepted by Wilson who returns seven yards to 49ers' 5. Karlis kicks 22-yard field goal two plays later at 8:11.

Oct. 30, 1988—New York Giants 13, Detroit 10, at Detroit; Lions win toss. James's fumble recovered by Taylor at Lions' 22. Three plays later, McFadden kicks 33-yard field goal at 1:13.

Nov. 20, 1988—Buffalo 9, New York Jets 6, at Buffalo; Jets win toss. Vick's fumble recovered by Bennett at Bills' 32. Norwood kicks 30-yard field goal five plays later at 3:47.

Nov. 20, 1988—Philadelphia 23, New York Giants 17, at New York; Eagles win toss. Philadelphia's punt goes into end zone for touchback. Hostetler intercepted by Hoage who returns 11 yards to Giants' 41. Six plays later, Zendejas's 30-yard field-goal attempt is blocked and ball is recovered behind line of scrimmage by Eagles' Simmons, who runs 15 yards for touchdown at 3:09.

Dec. 11, 1988—New England 10, Tampa Bay 7, at New England; Buccaneers win toss and kick off. Staurovsky kicks 27-yard field goal six plays later at 3:08.

Dec. 17, 1988—Cincinnati 20, Washington 17, at Cincinnati; Bengals win toss. Cincinnati's punt returned by Oliphant to Redskins' 16. Grant recovers Williams's fumble at Redskins' 17. Breech kicks 20-yard field goal three plays later at 7:01.

Sept. 24, 1989—Buffalo 47, Houston 41, at Houston; Oilers win toss. Johnson returns Brady's kickoff 17 yards to Oilers' 19. Oilers drive to Buffalo 25, Zendejas's 37-yard field goal blocked, but Bills offsides and Zendejas's second attempt is wide left. Bills' ball and Kelly completes series of passes, including 28-yard game-winner to Andre Reed, at 8:42.

Oct. 8, 1989—Miami 13, Cleveland 10, at Miami; Browns win toss. Metcalf returns Stoyanovich's kickoff 20 yards to Browns' 28. Browns drive ball 46 yards in eight plays; Bahr wide left on 44-yard field goal attempt. Dolphins ball. Browns called for pass interference on Marino pass to Banks at Cleveland 47. Two plays later, Banks's 20-yard reception at Browns' 23 sets up winning 35-yard field goal by Stoyanovich at 6:23.

Oct. 22, 1989—Denver 24, Seattle 21, at Seattle; Seahawks win toss. Treadwell's 56-yard kickoff returned 18 yards by Jefferson to Seahawks' 27. Seahawks drive to Broncos' 22 in 10 plays, but Johnson's 40-yard field goal attempt wide left. Smith intercepts a Krieg pass and returns it 28 yards to Seahawks' 10. Treadwell kicks winning 27-yard field goal at 7:46.

Oct. 29, 1989—New England 23, Indianapolis 20, at Indianapolis; Patriots win toss. Biasucci kickoff returned 13 yards to Patriots' 23 by Martin. Holding penalty brings ball back to Patriots' 13. After six plays, Feagles punt returned 11 yards by Verdin to Colts' 28. Six plays later, Colts punt to Martin at Patriots' 12. Grogan completes three straight passes to Patriots' 44. Five consecutive runs put New England on Colts' 33. Davis kicks a 51-yard winning field goal for Patriots at 9:46.

Oct. 29, 1989—Green Bay 23, Detroit 20, at Milwaukee; Lions win toss. Sanders touchback on Jacke kickoff. On first play, Murphy intercepts Lions' Peete and returns it three yards to Packers' 26. Fullwood gains five yards on three plays to set up Jacke's 38-yard field goal at 2:14.

Nov. 5, 1989—Minnesota 23, Los Angeles Rams 21, at Minneapolis; Rams win toss. Karlis's kick returned 18 yards by Delpino to Rams' 19. Drive stops at Rams' 28. Merriweather blocks Hatcher's punt at 12. Ball rolls out of end zone for safety.

Nov. 19, 1989—Cleveland 10, Kansas City 10, at Cleveland; Browns win toss. Browns punt three times; Chiefs twice; before Kansas City's Lowery misses 47-yard field goal with 17 seconds remaining in overtime. Kosar's pass intercepted as time expired.

Nov. 26, 1989—Los Angeles Rams 20, New Orleans 17, at New Orleans; Saints win toss. Lansford's kickoff returned 27 yards to Saints' 30. After four plays, Barnhardt punts to Rams' 15. Saints penalized 35 yards for interference to Rams' 43. Three plays later, Everett hits Anderson with 14-yard pass to Saints' 40, then 26-yarder to put Rams in field goal position. Lansford kicks 31-yard field goal at 6:38.

Dec. 3, 1989—Los Angeles Raiders 16, Denver 13, at Los Angeles; Broncos win toss. Bell returns Jaeger kickoff 14 yards to Broncos' 18. Broncos' penalized for illegal block to Broncos' 9. Elway completes three passes for two first downs. On third and eight Elway sacked for 10-yard loss. Horan punts, Adams calls for fair catch at Raiders' 29. Dyal's 26-yard reception moves Raiders to Denver 43. Raiders move ball 34 yards in three plays to set up Jaeger's 26-yard field goal at 7:02.

Dec. 10, 1989—Indianapolis 23, Cleveland 17, at Indianapolis; Browns win toss. Teams trade punts. McNeil returns Colts' punt 42 yards to 42. Seven plays later, Bahr misses 35-yard field goal attempt. Three plays later, Stark punts and McNeil returns ball to 50-yard line. Two plays later, Prior intercepts Kosar's pass at Colts' 42 and returns it 58 yards for touchdown at 10:54.

Dec. 17, 1989—Cleveland 23, Minnesota 17, at Cleveland; Browns win toss. Browns punt to Vikings' 18. Six plays later, Vikings punt to Browns' 22. Nine plays later, Bahr lines up to attempt 31-yard field goal. Holder Pagel takes snap and passes 14 yards to Waiters for touchdown at 9:30.

Sept. 23, 1990—Denver 34, Seattle 31, at Denver; Seahawks win toss. Loville returns kickoff 19 yards to Seahawks' 27. Seahawks drive to Broncos' 26, where Johnson misses 44-yard field goal wide right. Broncos take over and Elway completes series of passes to set up Treadwell's 25-yard field goal at 9:14.

Sept. 30, 1990—Tampa Bay 23, Minnesota 20, at Minnesota; Vikings win toss. Vikings drive to Buccaneers' 31; Igwebuike's 48-yard field goal attempt wide left. Buccaneers drive to Vikings' 43 and punt. Gannon's pass is intercepted at Vikings' 26 by Wayne Haddix. Buccaneers drive to Vikings' 19 to set up Christie's 36-yard field goal at 9:11.

Oct. 7, 1990—Cincinnati 34, Los Angeles Rams 31, at Anaheim; Rams win toss. Berry returns kickoff to Rams' 21. After 3 plays, English punts and Green downs ball at Bengals' 25. After 3 plays, Johnson punts and Sutton downs ball at Rams' 29-yard line. After 3 plays, English punts and Price signals fair catch at Bengals' 47. Esiason completes series of passes to 26-yard line to set up Breech's 44-yard field goal at 11:56.

Nov. 4, 1990—Washington 41, Detroit 38, at Detroit; Redskins win toss. Howard downs kickoff on Redskins' 15. After 3 plays, Mojsiejenko punts to Redskins' 45. After 3 plays, Arnold punts to Redskins' 10. Rutledge completes series of passes to set up Lohmiller's 34-yard field goal at 9:10.

Nov. 18, 1990—Chicago 16, Denver 13, at Denver; Broncos win toss. Ezor returns kickoff to Broncos' 12. Both teams have ball twice and have to punt after each possession. Broncos punt after third possession of overtime and Bailey returns 20 yards to Broncos' 34. Harbaugh completes 10-yard pass to Thornton to set up Butler's 44-yard field goal at 13:14.

Nov. 25, 1990—Seattle 13, San Diego 10, at San Diego; Chargers win toss. Lewis returns kickoff to Chargers' 22. After 2 plays, Cox fumbles and ball is recovered by Porter at Chargers' 23. After two plays, Johnson kicks 40-yard field goal at 3:01.

Dec. 2, 1990—Chicago 23, Detroit 17, at Chicago; Lions win toss. Gray returns kickoff to Lions' 35. After 10 plays, Murray misses 35-yard field goal. Bears take possession at Chicago 20. Harbaugh completes 50-yard game-winning pass to Anderson at 10:57.

Dec. 2, 1990—Seattle 13, Houston 10, at Seattle; Seahawks win toss. Warren returns kickoff to Seahawks' 13. After 5 plays, Donnelly punts to Oilers' 23-yard line. Ford's fumble recovered by Wyman. Seahawks take possession at Oilers' 27. After 2 plays, Johnson kicks 42-yard field goal at 4:25.

Dec. 9, 1990—Miami 23, Philadelphia 20, at Miami; Eagles win toss. After 11 plays, Feagles punts to Dolphins' 26. After 6 plays, Roby punts to Eagles' 14 and Harris returns to 25. After 3 plays, Feagles punts to Dolphins' 43. Marino completes series of passes to Eagles' 22. Stoyanovich kicks 39-yard field goal at 12:32.

Dec. 9, 1990—San Francisco 20, Cincinnati 17, at Cincinnati; 49ers win toss. Carter returns kickoff to 49ers' 19. After 10 plays, Cofer kicks 23-yard field goal at 6:12.

*indicates Monday night game
#indicates Thursday night game

Postseason

Dec. 28, 1958—Baltimore 23, New York Giants 17, at New York; Giants win toss. Maynard returns kickoff to Giants' 20. Chandler punts and Taseff returns one yard to Colts' 20. Colts win at 8:15 on a one-yard run by Ameche.

Dec. 23, 1962—Dallas Texans 20, Houston Oilers 17, at Houston; Texans win toss and kick off. Jancik returns kickoff to Oilers' 33. Norton punts and Jackson makes fair catch on Texans' 22. Wilson punts and Jancik makes fair catch on Oilers' 45. Robinson intercepts Blanda's pass and returns 13 yards to Oilers' 47. Wilson's punt rolls dead at Oilers' 12. Hull intercepts Blanda's pass and returns 23 yards to midfield. Texans win at 17:54 on a 25-yard field goal by Brooker.

Dec. 26, 1965—Green Bay 13, Baltimore 10, at Green Bay; Packers win toss. Moore returns kickoff to Packers' 22. Chandler punts and Haymond returns nine yards to Colts' 41. Gilburg punts and Wood makes fair catch at Packers' 21. Chandler punts and Haymond returns one yard to Colts' 41. Michaels misses 47-yard field goal. Packers win at 13:39 on 25-yard field goal by Chandler.

Dec. 25, 1971—Miami 27, Kansas City 24, at Kansas City; Chiefs win toss. Podolak, after a lateral from Buchanan, returns kickoff to Chiefs' 46. Stenerud's 42-yard field goal is blocked. Seiple punts and Podolak makes fair catch at Chiefs' 17. Wilson punts and Scott returns 18 yards to Dolphins' 39. Yepremian misses 62-yard field goal. Scott intercepts Dawson's pass and returns 13 yards to Dolphins' 46. Seiple punts and Podolak loses one yard to Chiefs' 15. Wilson punts and Scott makes fair catch on Dolphins' 30. Dolphins win at 22:40 on a 37-yard field goal by Yepremian.

Dec. 24, 1977—Oakland 37, Baltimore 31, at Baltimore; Colts win toss. Raiders start on own 42 following a punt late in the first overtime. Oakland works way into field goal range on Stabler's 19-yard pass to Branch at Colts' 26. Four plays later, on the second play of the second overtime, Stabler hits Casper with a 10-yard touchdown pass at 15:43.

Jan. 2, 1982—San Diego 41, Miami 38, at Miami; Chargers win toss. San Diego drives from its 13 to Miami 8. On second-and-goal, Benirschke misses 27-yard field goal attempt wide left at 9:15. Miami has the ball twice and San Diego twice more before the Dolphins get their third possession. Miami drives from the San Diego 46 to Chargers' 17 and on fourth-and-two, von Schamann's 34-yard field goal attempt is blocked by San Diego's Winslow after 11:27. Fouts then completes four of five passes, including a 39-yarder to Joiner that puts the ball on Dolphins' 10. On first down, Benirschke kicks a 29-yard field goal at 13:52. San Diego's winning drive covered 74 yards in six plays.

Jan. 3, 1987—Cleveland 23, New York Jets 20, at Cleveland; Jets win toss. Jets' punt downed at Browns' 26. Moseley's 23-yard field goal attempt is wide right. Teams trade punts. Jets' second punt downed at Browns' 31. First overtime period expires eight plays later with Browns in possession at Jets' 42. Moseley kicks 27-yard field goal four plays into second overtime at 17:02.

Jan. 11, 1987—Denver 23, Cleveland 20, at Cleveland; Browns win toss. Broncos hold Browns on four downs. Browns' punt returned four yards to Denver's 25. Elway completes 22- and 28-yard passes to set up Karlis's 33-yard field goal nine plays into drive at 5:38.

Jan. 3, 1988—Houston 23, Seattle 20, at Houston; Seahawks win toss. Rodriguez punts to K. Johnson who returns one yard to Houston 15. Zendejas kicks 32-yard field goal 12 plays later at 8:05.

Dec. 31, 1989—Pittsburgh 26, Houston 23, at Houston; Steelers win toss. Steelers punt to Oilers. Oilers' fumble recovered by Woodson and returned three yards. Four plays and 13 yards later, Anderson kicks a 50-yard field goal at 3:26.

Jan. 7, 1990—Los Angeles Rams 19, New York Giants 13, at New York; Rams win toss. Everett completes two passes to move ball to Giants' 48. White called for pass interference; ball spotted on Giants' 25. Everett hits Anderson with a 30-yard touchdown pass at 1:06.

NFL Postseason Overtime Games (By Length of Game)

Dec. 25, 1971	Miami 27, KANSAS CITY 24	82:40
Dec. 23, 1962	Dallas Texans 20, HOUSTON 17	77:54
Jan. 3, 1987	CLEVELAND 23, New York Jets 20	77:02
Dec. 24, 1977	Oakland 37, BALTIMORE 31	75:43
Jan. 2, 1982	San Diego 41, MIAMI 38	73:52
Dec. 26, 1965	GREEN BAY 13, Baltimore 10	73:39
Dec. 28, 1958	Baltimore 23, N.Y. GIANTS 17	68:15
Jan. 3, 1988	HOUSTON 23, Seattle 20	68:05
Jan. 11, 1987	Denver 23, CLEVELAND 20	65:38
Dec. 31, 1989	Pittsburgh 26, HOUSTON 23	63:26
Jan. 7, 1990	Los Angeles Rams 19, N.Y. GIANTS 13	61:06

Home team in CAPS

Overtime Won-Lost Records, 1974-1990 (Regular Season)

AFC	W	L	T
Buffalo	7	2	0
Cincinnati	8	4	0
Cleveland	10	8	1
Denver	11	6	2
Houston	4	9	0
Indianapolis	4	3	1
Kansas City	3	5	2
Los Angeles Raiders	8	4	0
Miami	5	9	1
New England	2	10	0
New York Jets	6	4	2
Pittsburgh	6	3	1
San Diego	7	7	0
Seattle	3	4	0

NFC	W	L	T
Atlanta	4	7	1
Chicago	8	7	0
Dallas	6	3	0
Detroit	4	7	1
Green Bay	5	6	4
Los Angeles Rams	5	5	1
Minnesota	8	6	2
New Orleans	2	5	0
New York Giants	6	6	1
Philadelphia	4	8	2
Phoenix	3	4	2
San Francisco	4	4	1
Tampa Bay	5	7	1
Washington	8	3	0

Overtime Games By Year (Regular Season)

1990-10	1981-10
1989-11	1980-13
1988- 9	1979-12
1987-13	1978-11
1986-16	1977- 6
1985-10	1976- 5
1984- 9	1975- 9
1983-19	1974- 2
1982- 4	

Overtime Game Summary—1974-1990

There have been 169 overtime games in regular-season play since the rule was adopted in 1974 (10 in 1990). Breakdown follows:

123 (9) times both teams had at least one possession (73%)

46 (1) times the team which won the coin toss drove for winning score (31 FG, 15 TD) (27%)

80 (3) times the team which won the coin toss won the game (47%)

76 (7) times the team which lost the coin toss won the game (45%)

108 (9) games were decided by a field goal (64%)

47 (1) games were decided by a touchdown (28%)

1 (0) game was decided by a safety (.6%)

13 (0) games ended tied (8%). Last time: Nov. 19, 1989, Cleveland 10, Kansas City 10, at Cleveland

Note: The number in parentheses represents the 1990 season total in each category.

Most Overtime Games, Season

5 Green Bay Packers, 1983
4 Denver Broncos, 1985
4 Cleveland Browns, 1989
3 By many teams, last time: Seattle Seahawks, 1990

Longest Consecutive Game Streaks Without Overtime (current)

72 games Atlanta Falcons (last OT game, 10/19/86 vs. San Francisco)
66 games Pittsburgh Steelers (last OT game, 11/30/86 vs. Chicago)
65 games Phoenix Cardinals (last OT game, 12/7/86 vs. Philadelphia)

Shortest Overtime Games

0:21 (Chicago 23, Detroit 17; 11/27/80)—only kickoff return for TD
0:30 (Baltimore 29, New England 23; 9/4/83)
0:55 (New York Giants 16, Philadelphia 10; 9/29/85)

There have been 11 overtime postseason games dating back to 1958. In 10 cases, both teams had at least one possession. Last time: 1/7/90; Los Angeles Rams 19, New York Giants 13.

Longest Overtime Games (All Postseason Games)

22:40 Miami 27, Kansas City 24; 12/25/71
17:54 Dallas Texans 20, Houston 17; 12/23/62
17:02 Cleveland 23, New York Jets 20; 1/3/87

There have been 11 postseason overtime games dating back to 1958. Ten times, both teams had at least one possession. Last postseason overtime: Los Angeles Rams 19, New York Giants 13, 1/7/90.

Overtime Scoring Summary

108 were decided by a field goal

20 were decided by a touchdown pass

16 were decided by a touchdown run

4 were decided by interceptions (Atlanta 40, New Orleans 34, 9/2/79; Atlanta 47, Green Bay 41, 11/27/83; New York Giants 16, Philadelphia 10, 9/29/85; Indianapolis 23, Cleveland 17, 12/10/89)

2 were decided on a fake field goal/touchdown pass (Minnesota 22, Chicago 16, 10/16/77; Cleveland 23, Minnesota 17, 12/17/89)

1 was decided by a kickoff return (Chicago 23, Detroit 17, 11/27/80)

1 was decided by a fumble recovery (Baltimore 29, New England 23, 9/4/83)

1 was decided on a fake field goal/touchdown run (Los Angeles Rams 27, Minnesota 21, 12/2/79)

1 was decided on a blocked field goal (Denver 30, San Diego 24, 11/17/85)

1 was decided on a blocked field goal/recovery by kicker (Green Bay 12, Chicago 6, 9/7/80)

1 was decided on a blocked field goal/recovery by kicking team (Philadelphia 23, New York Giants 17, 11/20/88)

1 was decided by a safety (Minnesota 23, Los Angeles Rams 21, 11/5/89)

13 ended tied

Overtime Records

Longest Touchdown Pass
99 Yards—Ron Jaworski to Mike Quick, Philadelphia 23, Atlanta 17 (11/10/85)
50 Yards—Tommy Kramer to Ahmad Rashad, Minnesota 27, Green Bay 21 (9/23/79)
50 Yards—Jim Harbaugh to Neal Anderson, Chicago 23, Detroit 17 (12/2/90)

Longest Touchdown Run
60 Yards—Herschel Walker, Dallas 23, New England 17 (11/15/87)
42 Yards—Eric Dickerson, Los Angeles Rams 26, Tampa Bay 20 (10/5/86)
28 Yards—Marcus Allen, Los Angeles Raiders 37, San Diego 31 (11/20/86)

Longest Field Goal
51 Yards—Greg Davis, New England 23, Indianapolis 20 (10/29/89)
50 Yards—Morten Andersen, New Orleans 20, Philadelphia 17 (12/11/83)
48 Yards—Eddie Murray, Detroit 27, Atlanta 24 (9/9/84);
Mark Moseley, Washington 30, New York Giants 27 (11/15/81)

Longest Touchdown Plays
99 Yards—(Pass) Ron Jaworski to Mike Quick, Philadelphia 23, Atlanta 17 (11/10/85)
60 Yards—(Blocked field goal return) Louis Wright, Denver 30, San Diego 24 (11/17/85)
(Run) Herschel Walker, Dallas 23, New England 17 (11/15/87)
58 Yards—(Interception return) Mike Prior, Indianapolis 23, Cleveland 17 (12/10/89)

NFL Paid Attendance

Year	Regular Season	Average	Postseason	Super Bowl
1990#	13,959,896 (224 games)	#62,321	847,543 (12)	73,813
1989	13,625,662 (224 games)	60,829	685,771 (10)	72,919
1988	13,539,848 (224 games)	60,446	658,317 (10)	75,129
1987*	11,406,166 (210 games)	54,315	656,977 (10)	73,302
1986	13,588,551 (224 games)	60,663	734,002 (10)	101,063
1985	13,345,047 (224 games)	59,567	710,768 (10)	73,818
1984	13,398,112 (224 games)	59,813	665,194 (10)	84,059
1983	13,277,222 (224 games)	59,273	675,513 (10)	72,932
1982**	7,367,438 (126 games)	58,472	1,033,153 (16)	103,667
1981	13,606,990 (224 games)	60,745	637,763 (10)	81,270
1980	13,392,230 (224 games)	59,787	624,430 (10)	75,500
1979	13,182,039 (224 games)	58,848	630,326 (10)	103,985
1978	12,771,800 (224 games)	57,017	624,388 (10)	79,641
1977	11,018,632 (196 games)	56,218	534,925 (8)	75,804
1976	11,070,543 (196 games)	56,482	492,884 (8)	103,438
1975	10,213,193 (182 games)	56,116	475,919 (8)	80,187
1974	10,236,322 (182 games)	56,244	438,664 (8)	80,997
1973	10,730,933 (182 games)	58,961	525,433 (8)	71,882
1972	10,445,827 (182 games)	57,395	483,345 (8)	90,182
1971	10,076,035 (182 games)	55,363	483,891 (8)	81,023
1970	9,533,333 (182 games)	52,381	458,493 (8)	79,204
1969	6,096,127 (112 games) NFL	54,430	162,279 (3)	80,562
	2,843,373 (70 games) AFL	40,620	167,088 (3)	
1968	5,882,313 (112 games) NFL	52,521	215,902 (3)	75,377
	2,635,004 (70 games) AFL	37,643	114,438 (2)	
1967	5,938,924 (112 games) NFL	53,026	166,208 (3)	75,546
	2,295,697 (63 games) AFL	36,439	53,330 (1)	
1966	5,337,044 (105 games) NFL	50,829	74,152 (1)	†61,946
	2,160,369 (63 games) AFL	34,291	42,080 (1)	
1965	4,634,021 (98 games) NFL	47,286	100,304 (2)	
	1,782,384 (56 games) AFL	31,828	30,361 (1)	
1964	4,563,049 (98 games) NFL	46,562	79,544 (1)	
	1,447,875 (56 games) AFL	25,855	40,242 (1)	
1963	4,163,643 (98 games) NFL	42,486	45,801 (1)	
	1,208,697 (56 games) AFL	21,584	63,171 (2)	
1962	4,003,421 (98 games) NFL	40,851	64,892 (1)	
	1,147,302 (56 games) AFL	20,487	37,981 (1)	
1961	3,986,159 (98 games) NFL	40,675	39,029 (1)	
	1,002,657 (56 games) AFL	17,904	29,556 (1)	
1960	3,128,296 (78 games) NFL	40,106	67,325 (1)	
	926,156 (56 games) AFL	16,538	32,183 (1)	
1959	3,140,000 (72 games)	43,617	57,545 (1)	
1958	3,006,124 (72 games)	41,752	123,659 (2)	
1957	2,836,318 (72 games)	39,393	119,579 (2)	
1956	2,551,263 (72 games)	35,434	56,836 (1)	
1955	2,521,836 (72 games)	35,026	85,693 (1)	
1954	2,190,571 (72 games)	30,425	43,827 (1)	
1953	2,164,585 (72 games)	30,064	54,577 (1)	
1952	2,052,126 (72 games)	28,502	97,507 (2)	
1951	1,913,019 (72 games)	26,570	57,522 (1)	
1950	1,977,753 (78 games)	25,356	136,647 (3)	
1949	1,391,735 (60 games)	23,196	27,980 (1)	
1948	1,525,243 (60 games)	25,421	36,309 (1)	
1947	1,837,437 (60 games)	30,624	66,268 (2)	
1946	1,732,135 (55 games)	31,493	58,346 (1)	
1945	1,270,401 (50 games)	25,408	32,178 (1)	
1944	1,019,649 (50 games)	20,393	46,016 (1)	
1943	969,128 (40 games)	24,228	71,315 (2)	
1942	887,920 (55 games)	16,144	36,006 (1)	
1941	1,108,615 (55 games)	20,157	55,870 (2)	
1940	1,063,025 (55 games)	19,328	36,034 (1)	
1939	1,071,200 (55 games)	19,476	32,279 (1)	
1938	937,197 (55 games)	17,040	48,120 (1)	
1937	963,039 (55 games)	17,510	15,878 (1)	
1936	816,007 (54 games)	15,111	29,545 (1)	
1935	638,178 (53 games)	12,041	15,000 (1)	
1934	492,684 (60 games)	8,211	35,059 (1)	

Record

*Players' 24-day strike reduced 224-game schedule to 210 games.

**Players' 57-day strike reduced 224-game schedule to 126 games.

†Only Super Bowl that did not sell out.

NFL's 10 Biggest Attendance Weekends

(Paid Count)

Weekend	Games	Attendance
October 16-17, 1988	14	934,211
November 3-4, 1990	14	916,127
October 29-30, 1989	14	915,401
November 17-18, 1990	14	905,486
October 27-28, 1985	14	902,128
October 12-13, 1980	14	898,223
September 23-24, 1984	14	894,402
November 11-12, 1979	14	890,972
October 8-9, 1989	14	888,271
September 17-18, 1989	14	888,264

NFL's 10 Highest Scoring Weekends

Point Total	Date	Weekend
761	October 16-17, 1983	7th
736	October 25-26, 1987	7th
732	November 9-10, 1980	10th
725	November 24, 27-28, 1983	13th
714	September 17-18, 1989	2nd
711	November 26, 29-30, 1987	12th
710	November 28, December 1-2, 1985	13th
696	October 2-3, 1983	5th
693	September 24-25, 1989	3rd
676	September 21-22, 1980	3rd

Top 10 Televised Sports Events

(Based on A.C. Nielsen Figures)

Program	Date	Network	Share	Rating
Super Bowl XVI	1/24/82	CBS	73.0	49.1
Super Bowl XVII	1/30/83	NBC	69.0	48.6
Super Bowl XX	1/26/86	NBC	70.0	48.3
Super Bowl XII	1/15/78	CBS	67.0	47.2
Super Bowl XIII	1/21/79	NBC	74.0	47.1
Super Bowl XVIII	1/22/84	CBS	71.0	46.4
Super Bowl XIX	1/20/85	ABC	63.0	46.4
Super Bowl XIV	1/20/80	CBS	67.0	46.3
Super Bowl XXI	1/25/87	CBS	66.0	45.8
Super Bowl XI	1/9/77	NBC	73.0	44.4

Ten Most Watched TV Programs & Estimated Total Number of Viewers

(Based on A.C. Nielsen Figures)

Program	Date	Network	*Total Viewers
Super Bowl XX	Jan. 26, 1986	NBC	127,000,000
Super Bowl XXI	Jan. 25, 1987	CBS	122,640,000
M*A*S*H (Special)	Feb. 28, 1983	CBS	121,624,000
Super Bowl XIX	Jan. 20, 1985	ABC	115,936,000
Super Bowl XXII	Jan. 31, 1988	ABC	115,000,000
Super Bowl XXV	Jan. 27, 1991	ABC	112,140,000
Super Bowl XXIII	Jan. 22, 1989	NBC	110,800,000
Super Bowl XVI	Jan. 24, 1982	CBS	110,230,000
Super Bowl XVII	Jan. 30, 1983	NBC	109,040,000
Super Bowl XXIV	Jan. 28, 1990	CBS	109,000,000

*Watched some portion of the broadcast

NUMBER-ONE DRAFT CHOICES

Season	Team	Player	Position	College
1991	Dallas	Russell Maryland	DT	Miami
1990	Indianapolis	Jeff George	QB	Illinois
1989	Dallas	Troy Aikman	QB	UCLA
1988	Atlanta	Aundray Bruce	LB	Auburn
1987	Tampa Bay	Vinny Testaverde	QB	Miami
1986	Tampa Bay	Bo Jackson	RB	Auburn
1985	Buffalo	Bruce Smith	DE	Virginia Tech
1984	New England	Irving Fryar	WR	Nebraska
1983	Baltimore	John Elway	QB	Stanford
1982	New England	Kenneth Sims	DT	Texas
1981	New Orleans	George Rogers	RB	South Carolina
1980	Detroit	Billy Sims	RB	Oklahoma
1979	Buffalo	Tom Cousineau	LB	Ohio State
1978	Houston	Earl Campbell	RB	Texas
1977	Tampa Bay	Ricky Bell	RB	Southern California
1976	Tampa Bay	Lee Roy Selmon	DE	Oklahoma
1975	Atlanta	Steve Bartkowski	QB	California
1974	Dallas	Ed Jones	DE	Tennessee State
1973	Houston	John Matuszak	DE	Tampa
1972	Buffalo	Walt Patulski	DE	Notre Dame
1971	New England	Jim Plunkett	QB	Stanford
1970	Pittsburgh	Terry Bradshaw	QB	Louisiana Tech
1969	Buffalo (AFL)	O.J. Simpson	RB	Southern California
1968	Minnesota	Ron Yary	T	Southern California
1967	Baltimore	Bubba Smith	DT	Michigan State
1966	Atlanta	Tommy Nobis	LB	Texas
	Miami (AFL)	Jim Grabowski	RB	Illinois
1965	New York Giants	Tucker Frederickson	RB	Auburn
	Houston (AFL)	Lawrence Elkins	E	Baylor
1964	San Francisco	Dave Parks	E	Texas Tech
	Boston (AFL)	Jack Concannon	QB	Boston College
1963	Los Angeles	Terry Baker	QB	Oregon State
	Kansas City (AFL)	Buck Buchanan	DT	Grambling
1962	Washington	Ernie Davis	RB	Syracuse
	Oakland (AFL)	Roman Gabriel	QB	North Carolina State
1961	Minnesota	Tommy Mason	RB	Tulane
	Buffalo (AFL)	Ken Rice	G	Auburn
1960	Los Angeles	Billy Cannon	RB	Louisiana State
	(AFL had no formal first pick)			
1959	Green Bay	Randy Duncan	QB	Iowa
1958	Chicago Cardinals	King Hill	QB	Rice
1957	Green Bay	Paul Hornung	HB	Notre Dame
1956	Pittsburgh	Gary Glick	DB	Colorado A&M
1955	Baltimore	George Shaw	QB	Oregon
1954	Cleveland	Bobby Garrett	QB	Stanford
1953	San Francisco	Harry Babcock	E	Georgia
1952	Los Angeles	Bill Wade	QB	Vanderbilt
1951	New York Giants	Kyle Rote	HB	Southern Methodist
1950	Detroit	Leon Hart	E	Notre Dame
1949	Philadelphia	Chuck Bednarik	C	Pennsylvania
1948	Washington	Harry Gilmer	QB	Alabama
1947	Chicago Bears	Bob Fenimore	HB	Oklahoma A&M
1946	Boston	Frank Dancewicz	QB	Notre Dame
1945	Chicago Cardinals	Charley Trippi	HB	Georgia
1944	Boston	Angelo Bertelli	QB	Notre Dame
1943	Detroit	Frank Sinkwich	HB	Georgia
1942	Pittsburgh	Bill Dudley	HB	Virginia
1941	Chicago Bears	Tom Harmon	HB	Michigan
1940	Chicago Cardinals	George Cafego	HB	Tennessee
1939	Chicago Cardinals	Ki Aldrich	C	Texas Christian
1938	Cleveland	Corbett Davis	FB	Indiana
1937	Philadelphia	Sam Francis	FB	Nebraska
1936	Philadelphia	Jay Berwanger	HB	Chicago

Note: From 1947 through 1958, the first selection in the draft was a Bonus pick, awarded to the winner of a random draw. That club, in turn, forfeited its last-round draft choice. The winner of the Bonus choice was eliminated from future draws. The system was abolished after 1958, by which time all clubs had received a Bonus choice.

FIRST-ROUND SELECTIONS

If club had no first-round selection, first player drafted is listed with round in parentheses.

Atlanta Falcons

Year	Player, College, Position
1966	Tommy Nobis, Texas, LB
	Randy Johnson, Texas A&I, QB
1967	Leo Carroll, San Diego State, DE (2)
1968	Claude Humphrey, Tennessee State, DE
1969	George Kunz, Notre Dame, T
1970	John Small, Citadel, LB
1971	Joe Profit, Northeast Louisiana, RB
1972	Clarence Ellis, Notre Dame, DB
1973	Greg Marx, Notre Dame, DT (2)
1974	Gerald Tinker, Kent State, WR (2)
1975	Steve Bartkowski, California, QB
1976	Bubba Bean, Texas A&M, RB
1977	Warren Bryant, Kentucky, T
	Wilson Faumuina, San Jose State, DT
1978	Mike Kenn, Michigan, T
1979	Don Smith, Miami, DE
1980	Junior Miller, Nebraska, TE
1981	Bobby Butler, Florida State, DB
1982	Gerald Riggs, Arizona State, RB
1983	Mike Pitts, Alabama, DE
1984	Rick Bryan, Oklahoma, DT
1985	Bill Fralic, Pittsburgh, T
1986	Tony Casillas, Oklahoma, NT
	Tim Green, Syracuse, LB
1987	Chris Miller, Oregon, QB
1988	Aundray Bruce, Auburn, LB
1989	Deion Sanders, Florida State, DB
	Shawn Collins, Northern Arizona, WR
1990	Steve Broussard, Washington State, RB
1991	Bruce Pickens, Nebraska, DB
	Mike Pritchard, Colorado, WR

Buffalo Bills

Year	Player, College, Position
1960	Richie Lucas, Penn State, QB
1961	Ken Rice, Auburn, T
1962	Ernie Davis, Syracuse, RB
1963	Dave Behrman, Michigan State, C
1964	Carl Eller, Minnesota, DE
1965	Jim Davidson, Ohio State, T
1966	Mike Dennis, Mississippi, RB
1967	John Pitts, Arizona State, S
1968	Haven Moses, San Diego State, WR
1969	O.J. Simpson, Southern California, RB
1970	Al Cowlings, Southern California, DE
1971	J. D. Hill, Arizona State, WR
1972	Walt Patulski, Notre Dame, DE
1973	Paul Seymour, Michigan, TE
	Joe DeLamielleure, Michigan State, G
1974	Reuben Gant, Oklahoma State, TE
1975	Tom Ruud, Nebraska, LB
1976	Mario Clark, Oregon, DB
1977	Phil Dokes, Oklahoma State, DT
1978	Terry Miller, Oklahoma State, RB
1979	Tom Cousineau, Ohio State, LB
	Jerry Butler, Clemson, WR
1980	Jim Ritcher, North Carolina State, C
1981	Booker Moore, Penn State, RB
1982	Perry Tuttle, Clemson, WR
1983	Tony Hunter, Notre Dame, TE
	Jim Kelly, Miami, QB
1984	Greg Bell, Notre Dame, RB
1985	Bruce Smith, Virginia Tech, DE
	Derrick Burroughs, Memphis State, DB
1986	Ronnie Harmon, Iowa, RB
	Will Wolford, Vanderbilt, T
1987	Shane Conlan, Penn State, LB
1988	Thurman Thomas, Oklahoma State, RB (2)
1989	Don Beebe, Chadron, Neb., WR (3)
1990	James Williams, Fresno State, DB
1991	Henry Jones, Illinois, DB

Chicago Bears

Year	Player, College, Position
1936	Joe Stydahar, West Virginia, T
1937	Les McDonald, Nebraska, E
1938	Joe Gray, Oregon State, B
1939	Sid Luckman, Columbia, QB
	Bill Osmanski, Holy Cross, B
1940	Clyde (Bulldog) Turner, Hardin-Simmons, C
1941	Tom Harmon, Michigan, B
	Norm Standlee, Stanford, B
	Don Scott, Ohio State, B
1942	Frankie Albert, Stanford, B
1943	Bob Steber, Missouri, B
1944	Ray Evans, Kansas, B
1945	Don Lund, Michigan, B
1946	Johnny Lujack, Notre Dame, QB
1947	Bob Fenimore, Oklahoma State, B
	Don Kindt, Wisconsin, B
1948	Bobby Layne, Texas, QB
	Max Bumgardner, Texas, E
1949	Dick Harris, Texas, C
1950	Chuck Hunsinger, Florida, B
	Fred Morrison, Ohio State, B
1951	Bob Williams, Notre Dame, B
	Billy Stone, Bradley, B
	Gene Schroeder, Virginia, E
1952	Jim Dooley, Miami, B
1953	Billy Anderson, Compton (Calif.) J.C., B
1954	Stan Wallace, Illinois, B
1955	Ron Drzewiecki, Marquette, B
1956	Menan (Tex) Schriewer, Texas, E
1957	Earl Leggett, Louisiana State, T
1958	Chuck Howley, West Virginia, G
1959	Don Clark, Ohio State, B
1960	Roger Davis, Syracuse, G
1961	Mike Ditka, Pittsburgh, E
1962	Ronnie Bull, Baylor, RB
1963	Dave Behrman, Michigan State, C
1964	Dick Evey, Tennessee, DT
1965	Dick Butkus, Illinois, LB
	Gale Sayers, Kansas, RB
	Steve DeLong, Tennessee, T
1966	George Rice, Louisiana State, DT
1967	Loyd Phillips, Arkansas, DE
1968	Mike Hull, Southern California, RB
1969	Rufus Mayes, Ohio State, T
1970	George Farmer, UCLA, WR (3)
1971	Joe Moore, Missouri, RB
1972	Lionel Antoine, Southern Illinois, T
	Craig Clemons, Iowa, DB
1973	Wally Chambers, Eastern Kentucky, DE
1974	Waymond Bryant, Tennessee State, LB
	Dave Gallagher, Michigan, DT
1975	Walter Payton, Jackson State, RB
1976	Dennis Lick, Wisconsin, T
1977	Ted Albrecht, California, T
1978	Brad Shearer, Texas, DT (3)
1979	Dan Hampton, Arkansas, DT
	Al Harris, Arizona State, DE
1980	Otis Wilson, Louisville, LB
1981	Keith Van Horne, Southern California, T
1982	Jim McMahon, Brigham Young, QB
1983	Jim Covert, Pittsburgh, T
	Willie Gault, Tennessee, WR
1984	Wilber Marshall, Florida, LB
1985	William Perry, Clemson, DT
1986	Neal Anderson, Florida, RB
1987	Jim Harbaugh, Michigan, QB
1988	Brad Muster, Stanford, RB
	Wendell Davis, Louisiana State, WR
1989	Donnell Woolford, Clemson, DB
	Trace Armstrong, Florida, DE
1990	Mark Carrier, Southern California, DB
1991	Stan Thomas, Texas, T

Cincinnati Bengals

Year	Player, College, Position
1968	Bob Johnson, Tennessee, C
1969	Greg Cook, Cincinnati, QB
1970	Mike Reid, Penn State, DT
1971	Vernon Holland, Tennessee State, T
1972	Sherman White, California, DE
1973	Isaac Curtis, San Diego State, WR
1974	Bill Kollar, Montana State, DT
1975	Glenn Cameron, Florida, LB
1976	Billy Brooks, Oklahoma, WR
	Archie Griffin, Ohio State, RB
1977	Eddie Edwards, Miami, DT
	Wilson Whitley, Houston, DT
	Mike Cobb, Michigan State, TE
1978	Ross Browner, Notre Dame, DT
	Blair Bush, Washington, C
1979	Jack Thompson, Washington State, QB
	Charles Alexander, Louisiana State, RB
1980	Anthony Muñoz, Southern California, T
1981	David Verser, Kansas, WR
1982	Glen Collins, Mississippi State, DE
1983	Dave Rimington, Nebraska, C
1984	Ricky Hunley, Arizona, LB
	Pete Koch, Maryland, DE
	Brian Blados, North Carolina, T
1985	Eddie Brown, Miami, WR
	Emanuel King, Alabama, LB
1986	Joe Kelly, Washington, LB
	Tim McGee, Tennessee, WR
1987	Jason Buck, Brigham Young, DE
1988	Rickey Dixon, Oklahoma, DB
1989	Eric Ball, UCLA, RB (2)
1990	James Francis, Baylor, LB
1991	Alfred Williams, Colorado, LB

Cleveland Browns

Year	Player, College, Position
1950	Ken Carpenter, Oregon State, B
1951	Ken Konz, Louisiana State, B
1952	Bert Rechichar, Tennessee, DB
	Harry Agganis, Boston U., QB
1953	Doug Atkins, Tennessee, DE
1954	Bobby Garrett, Stanford, QB
	John Bauer, Illinois, G
1955	Kurt Burris, Oklahoma, C
1956	Preston Carpenter, Arkansas, B
1957	Jim Brown, Syracuse, RB
1958	Jim Shofner, Texas Christian, DB
1959	Rich Kreitling, Illinois, DE
1960	Jim Houston, Ohio State, DE
1961	Bobby Crespino, Mississippi, TE
1962	Gary Collins, Maryland, WR
	Leroy Jackson, Western Illinois, RB
1963	Tom Hutchinson, Kentucky, WR
1964	Paul Warfield, Ohio State, WR
1965	James Garcia, Purdue, T (2)
1966	Milt Morin, Massachusetts, TE
1967	Bob Matheson, Duke, LB
1968	Marvin Upshaw, Trinity, Tex., DT-DE
1969	Ron Johnson, Michigan, RB
1970	Mike Phipps, Purdue, QB
	Bob McKay, Texas, T
1971	Clarence Scott, Kansas State, CB
1972	Thom Darden, Michigan, DB
1973	Steve Holden, Arizona State, WR
	Pete Adams, Southern California, T
1974	Billy Corbett, Johnson C. Smith, T (2)
1975	Mack Mitchell, Houston, DE
1976	Mike Pruitt, Purdue, RB
1977	Robert Jackson, Texas A&M, LB
1978	Clay Matthews, Southern California, LB
	Ozzie Newsome, Alabama, TE
1979	Willis Adams, Houston, WR
1980	Charles White, Southern California, RB
1981	Hanford Dixon, Southern Mississippi, DB
1982	Chip Banks, Southern California, LB
1983	Ron Brown, Arizona State, WR (2)
1984	Don Rogers, UCLA, DB
1985	Greg Allen, Florida State, RB (2)
1986	Webster Slaughter, San Diego State, WR (2)
1987	Mike Junkin, Duke, LB
1988	Clifford Charlton, Florida, LB
1989	Eric Metcalf, Texas, RB
1990	Leroy Hoard, Michigan, RB (2)
1991	Eric Turner, UCLA, DB

Dallas Cowboys

Year	Player, College, Position
1960	None
1961	Bob Lilly, Texas Christian, DT
1962	Sonny Gibbs, Texas Christian, QB (2)
1963	Lee Roy Jordan, Alabama, LB
1964	Scott Appleton, Texas, DT
1965	Craig Morton, California, QB
1966	John Niland, Iowa, G
1967	Phil Clark, Northwestern, DB (3)
1968	Dennis Homan, Alabama, WR
1969	Calvin Hill, Yale, RB

1970 Duane Thomas, West Texas State, RB
1971 Tody Smith, Southern California, DE
1972 Bill Thomas, Boston College, RB
1973 Billy Joe DuPree, Michigan State, TE
1974 Ed (Too Tall) Jones, Tennessee State, DE
Charley Young, North Carolina State, RB
1975 Randy White, Maryland, LB
Thomas Henderson, Langston, LB
1976 Aaron Kyle, Wyoming, DB
1977 Tony Dorsett, Pittsburgh, RB
1978 Larry Bethea, Michigan State, DE
1979 Robert Shaw, Tennessee, C
1980 Bill Roe, Colorado, LB (3)
1981 Howard Richards, Missouri, T
1982 Rod Hill, Kentucky State, DB
1983 Jim Jeffcoat, Arizona State, DE
1984 Billy Cannon, Jr., Texas A&M, LB
1985 Kevin Brooks, Michigan, DE
1986 Mike Sherrard, UCLA, WR
1987 Danny Noonan, Nebraska, DT
1988 Michael Irvin, Miami, WR
1989 Troy Aikman, UCLA, QB
1990 Emmitt Smith, Florida, RB
1991 Russell Maryland, Miami, DT
Alvin Harper, Tennessee, WR
Kelvin Pritchett, Mississippi, DT

Denver Broncos

Year	Player, College, Position
1960	Roger LeClerc, Trinity, Conn., C
1961	Bob Gaiters, New Mexico State, RB
1962	Merlin Olsen, Utah State, DT
1963	Kermit Alexander, UCLA, CB
1964	Bob Brown, Nebraska, T
1965	Dick Butkus, Illinois, LB (2)
1966	Jerry Shay, Purdue, DT
1967	Floyd Little, Syracuse, RB
1968	Curley Culp, Arizona State, DE (2)
1969	Grady Cavness, Texas-El Paso, DB (2)
1970	Bob Anderson, Colorado, RB
1971	Marv Montgomery, Southern California, T
1972	Riley Odoms, Houston, TE
1973	Otis Armstrong, Purdue, RB
1974	Randy Gradishar, Ohio State, LB
1975	Louis Wright, San Jose State, DB
1976	Tom Glassic, Virginia, G
1977	Steve Schindler, Boston College, G
1978	Don Latimer, Miami, DT
1979	Kelvin Clark, Nebraska, T
1980	Rulon Jones, Utah State, DE (2)
1981	Dennis Smith, Southern California, DB
1982	Gerald Willhite, San Jose State, RB
1983	Chris Hinton, Northwestern, G
1984	Andre Townsend, Mississippi, DE (2)
1985	Steve Sewell, Oklahoma, RB
1986	Jim Juriga, Illinois, T (4)
1987	Ricky Nattiel, Florida, WR
1988	Ted Gregory, Syracuse, NT
1989	Steve Atwater, Arkansas, DB
1990	Alton Montgomery, Houston, DB (2)
1991	Mike Croel, Nebraska, LB

Detroit Lions

Year	Player, College, Position
1936	Sid Wagner, Michigan State, G
1937	Lloyd Cardwell, Nebraska, B
1938	Alex Wojciechowicz, Fordham, C
1939	John Pingel, Michigan State, B
1940	Doyle Nave, Southern California, B
1941	Jim Thomason, Texas A&M, B
1942	Bob Westfall, Michigan, B
1943	Frank Sinkwich, Georgia, B
1944	Otto Graham, Northwestern, B
1945	Frank Szymanski, Notre Dame, C
1946	Bill Dellastatious, Missouri, B
1947	Glenn Davis, Army, B
1948	Y.A. Tittle, Louisiana State, B
1949	John Rauch, Georgia, B
1950	Leon Hart, Notre Dame, E
	Joe Watson, Rice, C
1951	Dick Stanfel, San Francisco, G (2)
1952	Yale Lary, Texas A&M, B (3)
1953	Harley Sewell, Texas, G
1954	Dick Chapman, Rice, T
1955	Dave Middleton, Auburn, B
1956	Hopalong Cassady, Ohio State, B
1957	Bill Glass, Baylor, G
1958	Alex Karras, Iowa, T
1959	Nick Pietrosante, Notre Dame, B
1960	John Robinson, Louisiana State, S
1961	Danny LaRose, Missouri, T (2)
1962	John Hadl, Kansas, QB
1963	Daryl Sanders, Ohio State, T
1964	Pete Beathard, Southern California, QB
1965	Tom Nowatzke, Indiana, RB
1966	Nick Eddy, Notre Dame, RB (2)
1967	Mel Farr, UCLA, RB
1968	Greg Landry, Massachusetts, QB
	Earl McCullouch, Southern California, WR
1969	Altie Taylor, Utah State, RB (2)
1970	Steve Owens, Oklahoma, RB
1971	Bob Bell, Cincinnati, DT
1972	Herb Orvis, Colorado, DE
1973	Ernie Price, Texas A&I, DE
1974	Ed O'Neil, Penn State, LB
1975	Lynn Boden, South Dakota State, G
1976	James Hunter, Grambling, DB
	Lawrence Gaines, Wyoming, RB
1977	Walt Williams, New Mexico State, DB (2)
1978	Luther Bradley, Notre Dame, DB
1979	Keith Dorney, Penn State, T
1980	Billy Sims, Oklahoma, RB
1981	Mark Nichols, San Jose State, WR
1982	Jimmy Williams, Nebraska, LB
1983	James Jones, Florida, RB
1984	David Lewis, California, TE
1985	Lomas Brown, Florida, T
1986	Chuck Long, Iowa, QB
1987	Reggie Rogers, Washington, DE
1988	Bennie Blades, Miami, DB
1989	Barry Sanders, Oklahoma State, RB
1990	Andre Ware, Houston, QB
1991	Herman Moore, Virginia, WR

Green Bay Packers

Year	Player, College, Position
1936	Russ Letlow, San Francisco, G
1937	Eddie Jankowski, Wisconsin, B
1938	Cecil Isbell, Purdue, B
1939	Larry Buhler, Minnesota, B
1940	Harold Van Every, Minnesota, B
1941	George Paskvan, Wisconsin, B
1942	Urban Odson, Minnesota, T
1943	Dick Wildung, Minnesota, T
1944	Merv Pregulman, Michigan, G
1945	Walt Schlinkman, Texas Tech, B
1946	Johnny (Strike) Strzykalski, Marquette, B
1947	Ernie Case, UCLA, B
1948	Earl (Jug) Girard, Wisconsin, B
1949	Stan Heath, Nevada, B
1950	Clayton Tonnemaker, Minnesota, C
1951	Bob Gain, Kentucky, T
1952	Babe Parilli, Kentucky, QB
1953	Al Carmichael, Southern California, B
1954	Art Hunter, Notre Dame, T
	Veryl Switzer, Kansas State, B
1955	Tom Bettis, Purdue, G
1956	Jack Losch, Miami, B
1957	Paul Hornung, Notre Dame, B
	Ron Kramer, Michigan, E
1958	Dan Currie, Michigan State, C
1959	Randy Duncan, Iowa, B
1960	Tom Moore, Vanderbilt, RB
1961	Herb Adderley, Michigan State, CB
1962	Earl Gros, Louisiana State, RB
1963	Dave Robinson, Penn State, LB
1964	Lloyd Voss, Nebraska, DT
1965	Donny Anderson, Texas Tech, RB
	Lawrence Elkins, Baylor, E
1966	Jim Grabowski, Illinois, RB
	Gale Gillingham, Minnesota, T
1967	Bob Hyland, Boston College, C
	Don Horn, San Diego State, QB
1968	Fred Carr, Texas-El Paso, LB
	Bill Lueck, Arizona, G
1969	Rich Moore, Villanova, DT
1970	Mike McCoy, Notre Dame, DT
	Rich McGeorge, Elon, TE
1971	John Brockington, Ohio State, RB
1972	Willie Buchanon, San Diego State, DB
	Jerry Tagge, Nebraska, QB
1973	Barry Smith, Florida State, WR
1974	Barty Smith, Richmond, RB
1975	Bill Bain, Southern California, G (2)
1976	Mark Koncar, Colorado, T
1977	Mike Butler, Kansas, DE
	Ezra Johnson, Morris Brown, DE
1978	James Lofton, Stanford, WR
	John Anderson, Michigan, LB
1979	Eddie Lee Ivery, Georgia Tech, RB
1980	Bruce Clark, Penn State, DE
	George Cumby, Oklahoma, LB
1981	Rich Campbell, California, QB
1982	Ron Hallstrom, Iowa, G
1983	Tim Lewis, Pittsburgh, DB
1984	Alphonso Carreker, Florida State, DE
1985	Ken Ruettgers, Southern California, T
1986	Kenneth Davis, Texas Christian, RB (2)
1987	Brent Fullwood, Auburn, RB
1988	Sterling Sharpe, South Carolina, WR
1989	Tony Mandarich, Michigan State, T
1990	Tony Bennett, Mississippi, LB
	Darrell Thompson, Minnesota, RB
1991	Vinnie Clark, Ohio State, DB

Houston Oilers

Year	Player, College, Position
1960	Billy Cannon, Louisiana State, RB
1961	Mike Ditka, Pittsburgh, E
1962	Ray Jacobs, Howard Payne, DT
1963	Danny Brabham, Arkansas, LB
1964	Scott Appleton, Texas, DT
1965	Lawrence Elkins, Baylor, WR
1966	Tommy Nobis, Texas, LB
1967	George Webster, Michigan State, LB
	Tom Regner, Notre Dame, G
1968	Mac Haik, Mississippi, WR (2)
1969	Ron Pritchard, Arizona State, LB
1970	Doug Wilkerson, N. Carolina Central, G
1971	Dan Pastorini, Santa Clara, QB
1972	Greg Sampson, Stanford, DE
1973	John Matuszak, Tampa, DE
	George Amundson, Iowa State, RB
1974	Steve Manstedt, Nebraska, LB (4)
1975	Robert Brazile, Jackson State, LB
	Don Hardeman, Texas A&I, RB
1976	Mike Barber, Louisiana Tech, TE (2)
1977	Morris Towns, Missouri, T
1978	Earl Campbell, Texas, RB
1979	Mike Stensrud, Iowa State, DE (2)
1980	Angelo Fields, Michigan State, T (2)
1981	Michael Holston, Morgan State, WR (3)
1982	Mike Munchak, Penn State, G
1983	Bruce Matthews, Southern California, T
1984	Dean Steinkuhler, Nebraska, T
1985	Ray Childress, Texas A&M, DE
	Richard Johnson, Wisconsin, DB
1986	Jim Everett, Purdue, QB
1987	Alonzo Highsmith, Miami, RB
	Haywood Jeffires, North Carolina St., WR
1988	Lorenzo White, Michigan State, RB
1989	David Williams, Florida, T
1990	Lamar Lathon, Houston, LB
1991	Mike Dumas, Indiana, DB (2)

Indianapolis Colts

Year	Player, College, Position
1953	Billy Vessels, Oklahoma, B
1954	Cotton Davidson, Baylor, B
1955	George Shaw, Oregon, B
	Alan Ameche, Wisconsin, FB
1956	Lenny Moore, Penn State, B
1957	Jim Parker, Ohio State, G
1958	Lenny Lyles, Louisville, B
1959	Jackie Burkett, Auburn, C
1960	Ron Mix, Southern California, T
1961	Tom Matte, Ohio State, RB
1962	Wendell Harris, Louisiana State, S
1963	Bob Vogel, Ohio State, T
1964	Marv Woodson, Indiana, CB
1965	Mike Curtis, Duke, LB
1966	Sam Ball, Kentucky, T
1967	Bubba Smith, Michigan State, DT
	Jim Detwiler, Michigan, RB
1968	John Williams, Minnesota, G
1969	Eddie Hinton, Oklahoma, WR
1970	Norman Bulaich, Texas Christian, RB
1971	Don McCauley, North Carolina, RB
	Leonard Dunlap, North Texas State, DB
1972	Tom Drougas, Oregon, T
1973	Bert Jones, Louisiana State, QB
	Joe Ehrmann, Syracuse, DT
1974	John Dutton, Nebraska, DE
	Roger Carr, Louisiana Tech, WR
1975	Ken Huff, North Carolina, G

1976	Ken Novak, Purdue, DT
1977	Randy Burke, Kentucky, WR
1978	Reese McCall, Auburn, TE
1979	Barry Krauss, Alabama, LB
1980	Curtis Dickey, Texas A&M, RB
	Derrick Hatchett, Texas, DB
1981	Randy McMillan, Pittsburgh, RB
	Donnell Thompson, North Carolina, DT
1982	Johnie Cooks, Mississippi State, LB
	Art Schlichter, Ohio State, QB
1983	John Elway, Stanford, QB
1984	Leonard Coleman, Vanderbilt, DB
	Ron Solt, Maryland, G
1985	Duane Bickett, Southern California, LB
1986	Jon Hand, Alabama, DE
1987	Cornelius Bennett, Alabama, LB
1988	Chris Chandler, Washington, QB (3)
1989	Andre Rison, Michigan State, WR
1990	Jeff George, Illinois, QB
1991	Shane Curry, Miami, DE (2)

Kansas City Chiefs

Year	Player, College, Position
1960	Don Meredith, Southern Methodist, QB
1961	E.J. Holub, Texas Tech, C
1962	Ronnie Bull, Baylor, RB
1963	Buck Buchanan, Grambling, DT
	Ed Budde, Michigan State, G
1964	Pete Beathard, Southern California, QB
1965	Gale Sayers, Kansas, RB
1966	Aaron Brown, Minnesota, DE
1967	Gene Trosch, Miami, DE-DT
1968	Mo Moorman, Texas A&M, G
	George Daney, Texas-El Paso, G
1969	Jim Marsalis, Tennessee State, CB
1970	Sid Smith, Southern California, T
1971	Elmo Wright, Houston, WR
1972	Jeff Kinney, Nebraska, RB
1973	Gary Butler, Rice, TE (2)
1974	Woody Green, Arizona State, RB
1975	Elmore Stephens, Kentucky, TE (2)
1976	Rod Walters, Iowa, G
1977	Gary Green, Baylor, DB
1978	Art Still, Kentucky, DE
1979	Mike Bell, Colorado State, DE
	Steve Fuller, Clemson, QB
1980	Brad Budde, Southern California, G
1981	Willie Scott, South Carolina, TE
1982	Anthony Hancock, Tennessee, WR
1983	Todd Blackledge, Penn State, QB
1984	Bill Maas, Pittsburgh, DT
	John Alt, Iowa, T
1985	Ethan Horton, North Carolina, RB
1986	Brian Jozwiak, West Virginia, T
1987	Paul Palmer, Temple, RB
1988	Neil Smith, Nebraska, DE
1989	Derrick Thomas, Alabama, LB
1990	Percy Snow, Michigan State, LB
1991	Harvey Williams, Louisiana State, RB

Los Angeles Raiders

Year	Player, College, Position
1960	Dale Hackbart, Wisconsin, CB
1961	Joe Rutgens, Illinois, DT
1962	Roman Gabriel, North Carolina State, QB
1963	George Wilson, Alabama, RB (6)
1964	Tony Lorick, Arizona State, RB
1965	Harry Schuh, Memphis State, T
1966	Rodger Bird, Kentucky, S
1967	Gene Upshaw, Texas A&I, G
1968	Eldridge Dickey, Tennessee State, QB
1969	Art Thoms, Syracuse, DT
1970	Raymond Chester, Morgan State, TE
1971	Jack Tatum, Ohio State, S
1972	Mike Siani, Villanova, WR
1973	Ray Guy, Southern Mississippi, P
1974	Henry Lawrence, Florida A&M, T
1975	Neal Colzie, Ohio State, DB
1976	Charles Philyaw, Texas Southern, DT (2)
1977	Mike Davis, Colorado, DB (2)
1978	Dave Browning, Washington, DE (2)
1979	Willie Jones, Florida State, DE (2)
1980	Marc Wilson, Brigham Young, QB
1981	Ted Watts, Texas Tech, DB
	Curt Marsh, Washington, T
1982	Marcus Allen, Southern California, RB
1983	Don Mosebar, Southern California, T
1984	Sean Jones, Northeastern, DE (2)
1985	Jessie Hester, Florida State, WR
1986	Bob Buczkowski, Pittsburgh, DE
1987	John Clay, Missouri, T
1988	Tim Brown, Notre Dame, WR
	Terry McDaniel, Tennessee, DB
	Scott Davis, Illinois, DE
1989	Jeff Francis, Tennessee, QB (6)
1990	Anthony Smith, Arizona, DE
1991	Todd Marinovich, Southern California, QB

Los Angeles Rams

Year	Player, College, Position
1937	Johnny Drake, Purdue, B
1938	Corbett Davis, Indiana, B
1939	Parker Hall, Mississippi, B
1940	Ollie Cordill, Rice, B
1941	Rudy Mucha, Washington, C
1942	Jack Wilson, Baylor, B
1943	Mike Holovak, Boston College, B
1944	Tony Butkovich, Illinois, B
1945	Elroy (Crazylegs) Hirsch, Wisconsin, B
1946	Emil Sitko, Notre Dame, B
1947	Herman Wedemeyer, St. Mary's, Calif., B
1948	Tom Keane, West Virginia, B (2)
1949	Bobby Thomason, Virginia Military, B
1950	Ralph Pasquariello, Villanova, B
	Stan West, Oklahoma, G
1951	Bud McFadin, Texas, G
1952	Bill Wade, Vanderbilt, QB
	Bob Carey, Michigan State, E
1953	Donn Moomaw, UCLA, C
	Ed Barker, Washington State, E
1954	Ed Beatty, Cincinnati, C
1955	Larry Morris, Georgia Tech, C
1956	Joe Marconi, West Virginia, B
	Charles Horton, Vanderbilt, B
1957	Jon Arnett, Southern California, B
	Del Shofner, Baylor, E
1958	Lou Michaels, Kentucky, T
	Jim Phillips, Auburn, E
1959	Dick Bass, Pacific, B
	Paul Dickson, Baylor, T
1960	Billy Cannon, Louisiana State, RB
1961	Marlin McKeever, So. California, E-LB
1962	Roman Gabriel, North Carolina State, QB
	Merlin Olsen, Utah State, DT
1963	Terry Baker, Oregon State, QB
	Rufus Guthrie, Georgia Tech, G
1964	Bill Munson, Utah State, QB
1965	Clancy Williams, Washington State, CB
1966	Tom Mack, Michigan, G
1967	Willie Ellison, Texas Southern, RB (2)
1968	Gary Beban, UCLA, QB (2)
1969	Larry Smith, Florida, RB
	Jim Seymour, Notre Dame, WR
	Bob Klein, Southern California, TE
1970	Jack Reynolds, Tennessee, LB
1971	Isiah Robertson, Southern, LB
	Jack Youngblood, Florida, DE
1972	Jim Bertelsen, Texas, RB (2)
1973	Cullen Bryant, Colorado, DB (2)
1974	John Cappelletti, Penn State, RB
1975	Mike Fanning, Notre Dame, DT
	Dennis Harrah, Miami, T
	Doug France, Ohio State, T
1976	Kevin McLain, Colorado State, LB
1977	Bob Brudzinski, Ohio State, LB
1978	Elvis Peacock, Oklahoma, RB
1979	George Andrews, Nebraska, LB
	Kent Hill, Georgia Tech, T
1980	Johnnie Johnson, Texas, DB
1981	Mel Owens, Michigan, LB
1982	Barry Redden, Richmond, RB
1983	Eric Dickerson, Southern Methodist, RB
1984	Hal Stephens, East Carolina, DE (5)
1985	Jerry Gray, Texas, DB
1986	Mike Schad, Queen's University, Canada, T
1987	Donald Evans, Winston-Salem, DE (2)
1988	Gaston Green, UCLA, RB
	Aaron Cox, Arizona State, WR
1989	Bill Hawkins, Miami, DE
	Cleveland Gary, Miami, RB
1990	Bern Brostek, Washington, C
1991	Todd Lyght, Notre Dame, DB

Miami Dolphins

Year	Player, College, Position
1966	Jim Grabowski, Illinois, RB
	Rick Norton, Kentucky, QB
1967	Bob Griese, Purdue, QB
1968	Larry Csonka, Syracuse, RB
	Doug Crusan, Indiana, T
1969	Bill Stanfill, Georgia, DE
1970	Jim Mandich, Michigan, TE (2)
1971	Otto Stowe, Iowa State, WR (2)
1972	Mike Kadish, Notre Dame, DT
1973	Chuck Bradley, Oregon, C (2)
1974	Donald Reese, Jackson State, DE
1975	Darryl Carlton, Tampa, T
1976	Larry Gordon, Arizona State, LB
	Kim Bokamper, San Jose State, LB
1977	A.J. Duhe, Louisiana State, DT
1978	Guy Benjamin, Stanford, QB (2)
1979	Jon Giesler, Michigan, T
1980	Don McNeal, Alabama, DB
1981	David Overstreet, Oklahoma, RB
1982	Roy Foster, Southern California, G
1983	Dan Marino, Pittsburgh, QB
1984	Jackie Shipp, Oklahoma, LB
1985	Lorenzo Hampton, Florida, RB
1986	John Offerdahl, Western Michigan, LB (2)
1987	John Bosa, Boston College, DE
1988	Eric Kumerow, Ohio State, DE
1989	Sammie Smith, Florida State, RB
	Louis Oliver, Florida, DB
1990	Richmond Webb, Texas A&M, T
1991	Randal Hill, Miami, WR

Minnesota Vikings

Year	Player, College, Position
1961	Tommy Mason, Tulane, RB
1962	Bill Miller, Miami, WR (3)
1963	Jim Dunaway, Mississippi, T
1964	Carl Eller, Minnesota, DE
1965	Jack Snow, Notre Dame, WR
1966	Jerry Shay, Purdue, DT
1967	Clint Jones, Michigan State, RB
	Gene Washington, Michigan State, WR
	Alan Page, Notre Dame, DT
1968	Ron Yary, Southern California, T
1969	Ed White, California, G (2)
1970	John Ward, Oklahoma State, DT
1971	Leo Hayden, Ohio State, RB
1972	Jeff Siemon, Stanford, LB
1973	Chuck Foreman, Miami, RB
1974	Fred McNeill, UCLA, LB
	Steve Riley, Southern California, T
1975	Mark Mullaney, Colorado State, DE
1976	James White, Oklahoma State, DT
1977	Tommy Kramer, Rice, QB
1978	Randy Holloway, Pittsburgh, DE
1979	Ted Brown, North Carolina State, RB
1980	Doug Martin, Washington, DT
1981	Mardye McDole, Mississippi State, WR (2)
1982	Darrin Nelson, Stanford, RB
1983	Joey Browner, Southern California, DB
1984	Keith Millard, Washington State, DE
1985	Chris Doleman, Pittsburgh, LB
1986	Gerald Robinson, Auburn, DE
1987	D.J. Dozier, Penn State, RB
1988	Randall McDaniel, Arizona State, G
1989	David Braxton, Wake Forest, LB (2)
1990	Mike Jones, Texas A&M, TE (3)
1991	Carlos Jenkins, Michigan State, LB (3)

New England Patriots

Year	Player, College, Position
1960	Ron Burton, Northwestern, RB
1961	Tommy Mason, Tulane, RB
1962	Gary Collins, Maryland, WR
1963	Art Graham, Boston College, WR
1964	Jack Concannon, Boston College, QB
1965	Jerry Rush, Michigan State, DE
1966	Karl Singer, Purdue, T
1967	John Charles, Purdue, S
1968	Dennis Byrd, North Carolina State, DE
1969	Ron Sellers, Florida State, WR
1970	Phil Olsen, Utah State, DE
1971	Jim Plunkett, Stanford, QB
1972	Tom Reynolds, San Diego State, WR (2)
1973	John Hannah, Alabama, G
	Sam Cunningham, So. California, RB
	Darryl Stingley, Purdue, WR
1974	Steve Corbett, Boston College, G (2)
1975	Russ Francis, Oregon, TE

1976 Mike Haynes, Arizona State, DB
Pete Brock, Colorado, C
Tim Fox, Ohio State, DB
1977 Raymond Clayborn, Texas, DB
Stanley Morgan, Tennessee, WR
1978 Bob Cryder, Alabama, G
1979 Rick Sanford, South Carolina, DB
1980 Roland James, Tennessee, DB
Vagas Ferguson, Notre Dame, RB
1981 Brian Holloway, Stanford, T
1982 Kenneth Sims, Texas, DT
Lester Williams, Miami, DT
1983 Tony Eason, Illinois, QB
1984 Irving Fryar, Nebraska, WR
1985 Trevor Matich, Brigham Young, C
1986 Reggie Dupard, Southern Methodist, RB
1987 Bruce Armstrong, Louisville, T
1988 John Stephens, Northwestern St., La., RB
1989 Hart Lee Dykes, Oklahoma State, WR
1990 Chris Singleton, Arizona, LB
Ray Agnew, North Carolina State, DE
1991 Pat Harlow, Southern California, T
Leonard Russell, Arizona State, RB

New Orleans Saints

Year	Player, College, Position
1967	Les Kelley, Alabama, RB
1968	Kevin Hardy, Notre Dame, DE
1969	John Shinners, Xavier, G
1970	Ken Burrough, Texas Southern, WR
1971	Archie Manning, Mississippi, QB
1972	Royce Smith, Georgia, G
1973	Derland Moore, Oklahoma, DE (2)
1974	Rick Middleton, Ohio State, LB
1975	Larry Burton, Purdue, WR
	Kurt Schumacher, Ohio State, T
1976	Chuck Muncie, California, RB
1977	Joe Campbell, Maryland, DE
1978	Wes Chandler, Florida, WR
1979	Russell Erxleben, Texas, P-K
1980	Stan Brock, Colorado, T
1981	George Rogers, South Carolina, RB
1982	Lindsay Scott, Georgia, WR
1983	Steve Korte, Arkansas, G (2)
1984	James Geathers, Wichita State, DE
1985	Alvin Toles, Tennessee, LB
1986	Jim Dombrowski, Virginia, T
1987	Shawn Knight, Brigham Young, DT
1988	Craig Heyward, Pittsburgh, RB
1989	Wayne Martin, Arkansas, DE
1990	Renaldo Turnbull, West Virginia, DE
1991	Wesley Carroll, Miami, WR (2)

New York Giants

Year	Player, College, Position
1936	Art Lewis, Ohio U., T
1937	Ed Widseth, Minnesota, T
1938	George Karamatic, Gonzaga, B
1939	Walt Neilson, Arizona, B
1940	Grenville Lansdell, Southern California, B
1941	George Franck, Minnesota, B
1942	Merle Hapes, Mississippi, B
1943	Steve Filipowicz, Fordham, B
1944	Billy Hillenbrand, Indiana, B
1945	Elmer Barbour, Wake Forest, B
1946	George Connor, Notre Dame, T
1947	Vic Schwall, Northwestern, B
1948	Tony Minisi, Pennsylvania, B
1949	Paul Page, Southern Methodist, B
1950	Travis Tidwell, Auburn, B
1951	Kyle Rote, Southern Methodist, B
	Jim Spavital, Oklahoma A&M, B
1952	Frank Gifford, Southern California, B
1953	Bobby Marlow, Alabama, B
1954	Ken Buck, Pacific, C (2)
1955	Joe Heap, Notre Dame, B
1956	Henry Moore, Arkansas, B (2)
1957	Sam DeLuca, South Carolina, T (2)
1958	Phil King, Vanderbilt, B
1959	Lee Grosscup, Utah, B
1960	Lou Cordileone, Clemson, G
1961	Bruce Tarbox, Syracuse, G (2)
1962	Jerry Hillebrand, Colorado, LB
1963	Frank Lasky, Florida, T (2)
1964	Joe Don Looney, Oklahoma, RB
1965	Tucker Frederickson, Auburn, RB
1966	Francis Peay, Missouri, T
1967	Louis Thompson, Alabama, DT (4)
1968	Dick Buzin, Penn State, T (2)
1969	Fred Dryer, San Diego State, DE
1970	Jim Files, Oklahoma, LB
1971	Rocky Thompson, West Texas State, WR
1972	Eldridge Small, Texas A&I, DB
	Larry Jacobson, Nebraska, DE
1973	Brad Van Pelt, Michigan State, LB (2)
1974	John Hicks, Ohio State, G
1975	Al Simpson, Colorado State, T (2)
1976	Troy Archer, Colorado, DE
1977	Gary Jeter, Southern California, DT
1978	Gordon King, Stanford, T
1979	Phil Simms, Morehead State, QB
1980	Mark Haynes, Colorado, DB
1981	Lawrence Taylor, North Carolina, LB
1982	Butch Woolfolk, Michigan, RB
1983	Terry Kinard, Clemson, DB
1984	Carl Banks, Michigan State, LB
	William Roberts, Ohio State, T
1985	George Adams, Kentucky, RB
1986	Eric Dorsey, Notre Dame, DE
1987	Mark Ingram, Michigan State, WR
1988	Eric Moore, Indiana, T
1989	Brian Williams, Minnesota, C-G
1990	Rodney Hampton, Georgia, RB
1991	Jarrod Bunch, Michigan, RB

New York Jets

Year	Player, College, Position
1960	George Izo, Notre Dame, QB
1961	Tom Brown, Minnesota, G
1962	Sandy Stephens, Minnesota, QB
1963	Jerry Stovall, Louisiana State, S
1964	Matt Snell, Ohio State, RB
1965	Joe Namath, Alabama, QB
	Tom Nowatzke, Indiana, RB
1966	Bill Yearby, Michigan, DT
1967	Paul Seiler, Notre Dame, T
1968	Lee White, Weber State, RB
1969	Dave Foley, Ohio State, T
1970	Steve Tannen, Florida, CB
1971	John Riggins, Kansas, RB
1972	Jerome Barkum, Jackson State, WR
	Mike Taylor, Michigan, LB
1973	Burgess Owens, Miami, DB
1974	Carl Barzilauskas, Indiana, DT
1975	Anthony Davis, Southern California, RB (2)
1976	Richard Todd, Alabama, QB
1977	Marvin Powell, Southern California, T
1978	Chris Ward, Ohio State, T
1979	Marty Lyons, Alabama, DE
1980	Johnny (Lam) Jones, Texas, WR
1981	Freeman McNeil, UCLA, RB
1982	Bob Crable, Notre Dame, LB
1983	Ken O'Brien, Cal-Davis, QB
1984	Russell Carter, Southern Methodist, DB
	Ron Faurot, Arkansas, DE
1985	Al Toon, Wisconsin, WR
1986	Mike Haight, Iowa, T
1987	Roger Vick, Texas A&M, RB
1988	Dave Cadigan, Southern California, T
1989	Jeff Lageman, Virginia, LB
1990	Blair Thomas, Penn State, RB
1991	Browning Nagle, Louisville, QB (2)

Philadelphia Eagles

Year	Player, College, Position
1936	Jay Berwanger, Chicago, B
1937	Sam Francis, Nebraska, B
1938	Jim McDonald, Ohio State, B
1939	Davey O'Brien, Texas Christian, B
1940	George McAfee, Duke, B
1941	Art Jones, Richmond, B (2)
1942	Pete Kmetovic, Stanford, B
1943	Joe Muha, Virginia Military, B
1944	Steve Van Buren, Louisiana State, B
1945	John Yonaker, Notre Dame, E
1946	Leo Riggs, Southern California, B
1947	Neill Armstrong, Oklahoma A&M, E
1948	Clyde (Smackover) Scott, Arkansas, B
1949	Chuck Bednarik, Pennsylvania, C
	Frank Tripucka, Notre Dame, B
1950	Harry (Bud) Grant, Minnesota, E
1951	Ebert Van Buren, Louisiana State, B
	Chet Mutryn, Xavier, B
1952	Johnny Bright, Drake, B
1953	Al Conway, Army, B (2)
1954	Neil Worden, Notre Dame, B
1955	Dick Bielski, Maryland, B
1956	Bob Pellegrini, Maryland, C
1957	Clarence Peaks, Michigan State, B
1958	Walt Kowalczyk, Michigan State, B
1959	J.D. Smith, Rice, T (2)
1960	Ron Burton, Northwestern, RB
1961	Art Baker, Syracuse, RB
1962	Pete Case, Georgia, G (2)
1963	Ed Budde, Michigan State, G
1964	Bob Brown, Nebraska, T
1965	Ray Rissmiller, Georgia, T (2)
1966	Randy Beisler, Indiana, DE
1967	Harry Jones, Arkansas, RB
1968	Tim Rossovich, Southern California, DE
1969	Leroy Keyes, Purdue, RB
1970	Steve Zabel, Oklahoma, TE
1971	Richard Harris, Grambling, DE
1972	John Reaves, Florida, QB
1973	Jerry Sisemore, Texas, T
	Charle Young, Southern California, TE
1974	Mitch Sutton, Kansas, DT (3)
1975	Bill Capraun, Miami, T (7)
1976	Mike Smith, Florida, DE (4)
1977	Skip Sharp, Kansas, DB (5)
1978	Reggie Wilkes, Georgia Tech, LB (3)
1979	Jerry Robinson, UCLA, LB
1980	Roynell Young, Alcorn State, DB
1981	Leonard Mitchell, Houston, DE
1982	Mike Quick, North Carolina State, WR
1983	Michael Haddix, Mississippi State, RB
1984	Kenny Jackson, Penn State, WR
1985	Kevin Allen, Indiana, T
1986	Keith Byars, Ohio State, RB
1987	Jerome Brown, Miami, DT
1988	Keith Jackson, Oklahoma, TE
1989	Jessie Small, Eastern Kentucky, LB (2)
1990	Ben Smith, Georgia, DB
1991	Antone Davis, Tennessee, T

Phoenix Cardinals

Year	Player, College, Position
1936	Jim Lawrence, Texas Christian, B
1937	Ray Buivid, Marquette, B
1938	Jack Robbins, Arkansas, B
1939	Charles (Ki) Aldrich, Texas Christian, C
1940	George Cafego, Tennessee, B
1941	John Kimbrough, Texas A&M, B
1942	Steve Lach, Duke, B
1943	Glenn Dobbs, Tulsa, B
1944	Pat Harder, Wisconsin, B
1945	Charley Trippi, Georgia, B
1946	Dub Jones, Louisiana State, B
1947	DeWitt (Tex) Coulter, Army, T
1948	Jim Spavital, Oklahoma A&M, B
1949	Bill Fischer, Notre Dame, G
1950	Jack Jennings, Ohio State, T (2)
1951	Jerry Groom, Notre Dame, C
1952	Ollie Matson, San Francisco, B
1953	Johnny Olszewski, California, B
1954	Lamar McHan, Arkansas, B
1955	Max Boydston, Oklahoma, E
1956	Joe Childress, Auburn, B
1957	Jerry Tubbs, Oklahoma, C
1958	King Hill, Rice, B
	John David Crow, Texas A&M, B
1959	Bill Stacy, Mississippi State, B
1960	George Izo, Notre Dame, QB
1961	Ken Rice, Auburn, T
1962	Fate Echols, Northwestern, DT
	Irv Goode, Kentucky, C
1963	Jerry Stovall, Louisiana State, S
	Don Brumm, Purdue, DE
1964	Ken Kortas, Louisville, DT
1965	Joe Namath, Alabama, QB
1966	Carl McAdams, Oklahoma, LB
1967	Dave Williams, Washington, WR
1968	MacArthur Lane, Utah State, RB
1969	Roger Wehrli, Missouri, DB
1970	Larry Stegent, Texas A&M, RB
1971	Norm Thompson, Utah, CB
1972	Bobby Moore, Oregon, RB-WR
1973	Dave Butz, Purdue, DT
1974	J.V. Cain, Colorado, TE
1975	Tim Gray, Texas A&M, DB
1976	Mike Dawson, Arizona, DT
1977	Steve Pisarkiewicz, Missouri, QB
1978	Steve Little, Arkansas, K
	Ken Greene, Washington State, DB
1979	Ottis Anderson, Miami, RB

1980 Curtis Greer, Michigan, DE
1981 E. J. Junior, Alabama, LB
1982 Luis Sharpe, UCLA, T
1983 Leonard Smith, McNeese State, DB
1984 Clyde Duncan, Tennessee, WR
1985 Freddie Joe Nunn, Mississippi, LB
1986 Anthony Bell, Michigan State, LB
1987 Kelly Stouffer, Colorado State, QB
1988 Ken Harvey, California, LB
1989 Eric Hill, Louisiana State, LB
Joe Wolf, Boston College, G
1990 Anthony Thompson, Indiana, RB (2)
1991 Eric Swann, No College, DE

Pittsburgh Steelers

Year	Player, College, Position
1936	Bill Shakespeare, Notre Dame, B
1937	Mike Basrak, Duquesne, C
1938	Byron (Whizzer) White, Colorado, B
1939	Bill Patterson, Baylor, B (3)
1940	Kay Eakin, Arkansas, B
1941	Chet Gladchuk, Boston College, C (2)
1942	Bill Dudley, Virginia, B
1943	Bill Daley, Minnesota, B
1944	Johnny Podesto, St. Mary's, Calif., B
1945	Paul Duhart, Florida, B
1946	Felix (Doc) Blanchard, Army, B
1947	Hub Bechtol, Texas, E
1948	Dan Edwards, Georgia, E
1949	Bobby Gage, Clemson, B
1950	Lynn Chandnois, Michigan State, B
1951	Butch Avinger, Alabama, B
1952	Ed Modzelewski, Maryland, B
1953	Ted Marchibroda, St. Bonaventure, B
1954	Johnny Lattner, Notre Dame, B
1955	Frank Varrichione, Notre Dame, T
1956	Gary Glick, Colorado A&M, B
	Art Davis, Mississippi State, B
1957	Len Dawson, Purdue, B
1958	Larry Krutko, West Virginia, B (2)
1959	Tom Barnett, Purdue, B (8)
1960	Jack Spikes, Texas Christian, RB
1961	Myron Pottios, Notre Dame, LB (2)
1962	Bob Ferguson, Ohio State, RB
1963	Frank Atkinson, Stanford, T (8)
1964	Paul Martha, Pittsburgh, S
1965	Roy Jefferson, Utah, WR (2)
1966	Dick Leftridge, West Virginia, RB
1967	Don Shy, San Diego State, RB (2)
1968	Mike Taylor, Southern California, T
1969	Joe Greene, North Texas State, DT
1970	Terry Bradshaw, Louisiana Tech, QB
1971	Frank Lewis, Grambling, WR
1972	Franco Harris, Penn State, RB
1973	J.T. Thomas, Florida State, DB
1974	Lynn Swann, Southern California, WR
1975	Dave Brown, Michigan, DB
1976	Bennie Cunningham, Clemson, TE
1977	Robin Cole, New Mexico, LB
1978	Ron Johnson, Eastern Michigan, DB
1979	Greg Hawthorne, Baylor, RB
1980	Mark Malone, Arizona State, QB
1981	Keith Gary, Oklahoma, DE
1982	Walter Abercrombie, Baylor, RB
1983	Gabriel Rivera, Texas Tech, DT
1984	Louis Lipps, Southern Mississippi, WR
1985	Darryl Sims, Wisconsin, DE
1986	John Rienstra, Temple, G
1987	Rod Woodson, Purdue, DB
1988	Aaron Jones, Eastern Kentucky, DE
1989	Tim Worley, Georgia, RB
	Tom Ricketts, Pittsburgh, T
1990	Eric Green, Liberty, TE
1991	Huey Richardson, Florida, DE

San Diego Chargers

Year	Player, College, Position
1960	Monty Stickles, Notre Dame, E
1961	Earl Faison, Indiana, DE
1962	Bob Ferguson, Ohio State, RB
1963	Walt Sweeney, Syracuse, G
1964	Ted Davis, Georgia Tech, LB
1965	Steve DeLong, Tennessee, DE
1966	Don Davis, Cal State-Los Angeles, DT
1967	Ron Billingsley, Wyoming, DE
1968	Russ Washington, Missouri, DT
	Jimmy Hill, Texas A&I, DB
1969	Marty Domres, Columbia, QB
	Bob Babich, Miami, Ohio, LB
1970	Walker Gillette, Richmond, WR
1971	Leon Burns, Long Beach State, RB
1972	Pete Lazetich, Stanford, DE (2)
1973	Johnny Rodgers, Nebraska, WR
1974	Bo Matthews, Colorado, RB
	Don Goode, Kansas, LB
1975	Gary Johnson, Grambling, DT
	Mike Williams, Louisiana State, DB
1976	Joe Washington, Oklahoma, RB
1977	Bob Rush, Memphis State, C
1978	John Jefferson, Arizona State, WR
1979	Kellen Winslow, Missouri, TE
1980	Ed Luther, San Jose State, QB (4)
1981	James Brooks, Auburn, RB
1982	Hollis Hall, Clemson, DB (7)
1983	Billy Ray Smith, Arkansas, LB
	Gary Anderson, Arkansas, WR
	Gill Byrd, San Jose State, DB
1984	Mossy Cade, Texas, DB
1985	Jim Lachey, Ohio State, G
1986	Leslie O'Neal, Oklahoma State, DE
	James FitzPatrick, Southern California, T
1987	Rod Bernstine, Texas A&M, TE
1988	Anthony Miller, Tennessee, WR
1989	Burt Grossman, Pittsburgh, DE
1990	Junior Seau, Southern California, LB
1991	Stanley Richard, Texas, DB

San Francisco 49ers

Year	Player, College, Position
1950	Leo Nomellini, Minnesota, T
1951	Y.A. Tittle, Louisiana State, B
1952	Hugh McElhenny, Washington, B
1953	Harry Babcock, Georgia, E
	Tom Stolhandske, Texas, E
1954	Bernie Faloney, Maryland, B
1955	Dickie Moegle, Rice, B
1956	Earl Morrall, Michigan State, B
1957	John Brodie, Stanford, B
1958	Jim Pace, Michigan, B
	Charlie Krueger, Texas A&M, T
1959	Dave Baker, Oklahoma, B
	Dan James, Ohio State, C
1960	Monty Stickles, Notre Dame, E
1961	Jimmy Johnson, UCLA, CB
	Bernie Casey, Bowling Green, WR
	Bill Kilmer, UCLA, QB
1962	Lance Alworth, Arkansas, WR
1963	Kermit Alexander, UCLA, CB
1964	Dave Parks, Texas Tech, WR
1965	Ken Willard, North Carolina, RB
	George Donnelly, Illinois, DB
1966	Stan Hindman, Mississippi, DE
1967	Steve Spurrier, Florida, QB
	Cas Banaszek, Northwestern, T
1968	Forrest Blue, Auburn, C
1969	Ted Kwalick, Penn State, TE
	Gene Washington, Stanford, WR
1970	Cedrick Hardman, North Texas State, DE
	Bruce Taylor, Boston U., DB
1971	Tim Anderson, Ohio State, DB
1972	Terry Beasley, Auburn, WR
1973	Mike Holmes, Texas Southern, DB
1974	Wilbur Jackson, Alabama, RB
	Bill Sandifer, UCLA, DT
1975	Jimmy Webb, Mississippi State, DT
1976	Randy Cross, UCLA, C (2)
1977	Elmo Boyd, Eastern Kentucky, WR (3)
1978	Ken MacAfee, Notre Dame, TE
	Dan Bunz, Cal State-Long Beach, LB
1979	James Owens, UCLA, WR (2)
1980	Earl Cooper, Rice, RB
	Jim Stuckey, Clemson, DT
1981	Ronnie Lott, Southern California, DB
1982	Bubba Paris, Michigan, T (2)
1983	Roger Craig, Nebraska, RB (2)
1984	Todd Shell, Brigham Young, LB
1985	Jerry Rice, Mississippi Valley State, WR
1986	Larry Roberts, Alabama, DE (2)
1987	Harris Barton, North Carolina, T
	Terrence Flagler, Clemson, RB
1988	Danny Stubbs, Miami, DE (2)
1989	Keith DeLong, Tennessee, LB
1990	Dexter Carter, Florida State, RB
1991	Ted Washington, Louisville, DT

Seattle Seahawks

Year	Player, College, Position
1976	Steve Niehaus, Notre Dame, DT
1977	Steve August, Tulsa, G
1978	Keith Simpson, Memphis State, DB
1979	Manu Tuiasosopo, UCLA, DT
1980	Jacob Green, Texas A&M, DE
1981	Ken Easley, UCLA, DB
1982	Jeff Bryant, Clemson, DE
1983	Curt Warner, Penn State, RB
1984	Terry Taylor, Southern Illinois, DB
1985	Owen Gill, Iowa, RB (2)
1986	John L. Williams, Florida, RB
1987	Tony Woods, Pittsburgh, LB
1988	Brian Blades, Miami, WR (2)
1989	Andy Heck, Notre Dame, T
1990	Cortez Kennedy, Miami, DT
1991	Dan McGwire, San Diego State, QB

Tampa Bay Buccaneers

Year	Player, College, Position
1976	Lee Roy Selmon, Oklahoma, DT
1977	Ricky Bell, Southern California, RB
1978	Doug Williams, Grambling, QB
1979	Greg Roberts, Oklahoma, G (2)
1980	Ray Snell, Wisconsin, G
1981	Hugh Green, Pittsburgh, LB
1982	Sean Farrell, Penn State, G
1983	Randy Grimes, Baylor, C (2)
1984	Keith Browner, Southern California, LB (2)
1985	Ron Holmes, Washington, DE
1986	Bo Jackson, Auburn, RB
	Roderick Jones, Southern Methodist, DB
1987	Vinny Testaverde, Miami, QB
1988	Paul Gruber, Wisconsin, T
1989	Broderick Thomas, Nebraska, LB
1990	Keith McCants, Alabama, LB
1991	Charles McRae, Tennessee, T

Washington Redskins

Year	Player, College, Position
1936	Riley Smith, Alabama, B
1937	Sammy Baugh, Texas Christian, B
1938	Andy Farkas, Detroit, B
1939	I.B. Hale, Texas Christian, T
1940	Ed Boell, New York U., B
1941	Forest Evashevski, Michigan, B
1942	Orban (Spec) Sanders, Texas, B
1943	Jack Jenkins, Missouri, B
1944	Mike Micka, Colgate, B
1945	Jim Hardy, Southern California, B
1946	Cal Rossi, UCLA, B*
1947	Cal Rossi, UCLA, B
1948	Harry Gilmer, Alabama, B
	Lowell Tew, Alabama, B
1949	Rob Goode, Texas A&M, B
1950	George Thomas, Oklahoma, B
1951	Leon Heath, Oklahoma, B
1952	Larry Isbell, Baylor, B
1953	Jack Scarbath, Maryland, B
1954	Steve Meilinger, Kentucky, E
1955	Ralph Guglielmi, Notre Dame, B
1956	Ed Vereb, Maryland, B
1957	Don Bosseler, Miami, B
1958	Mike Sommer, George Washington, B (2)
1959	Don Allard, Boston College, B
1960	Richie Lucas, Penn State, QB
1961	Norman Snead, Wake Forest, QB
	Joe Rutgens, Illinois, DT
1962	Ernie Davis, Syracuse, RB
1963	Pat Richter, Wisconsin, TE
1964	Charley Taylor, Arizona State, RB-WR
1965	Bob Breitenstein, Tulsa, T (2)
1966	Charlie Gogolak, Princeton, K
1967	Ray McDonald, Idaho, RB
1968	Jim Smith, Oregon, DB
1969	Eugene Epps, Texas-El Paso, DB (2)
1970	Bill Brundige, Colorado, DT (2)
1971	Cotton Speyrer, Texas, WR (2)
1972	Moses Denson, Maryland State, RB (8)
1973	Charles Cantrell, Lamar, G (5)
1974	Jon Keyworth, Colorado, TE (6)
1975	Mike Thomas, Nevada-Las Vegas, RB (6)
1976	Mike Hughes, Baylor, G (5)
1977	Duncan McColl, Stanford, DE (4)
1978	Tony Green, Florida, RB (6)
1979	Don Warren, San Diego State, TE (4)

1980 Art Monk, Syracuse, WR
1981 Mark May, Pittsburgh, T
1982 Vernon Dean, San Diego State, DB (2)
1983 Darrell Green, Texas A&I, DB
1984 Bob Slater, Oklahoma, DT (2)
1985 Tory Nixon, San Diego State, DB (2)
1986 Markus Koch, Boise State, DE (2)
1987 Brian Davis, Nebraska, DB (2)
1988 Chip Lohmiller, Minnesota, K (2)
1989 Tracy Rocker, Auburn, DT (3)
1990 Andre Collins, Penn State, LB (2)
1991 Bobby Wilson, Michigan State, DT

RECORDS

Compiled by Elias Sports Bureau

The following records reflect all available official information on the National Football League from its formation in 1920 to date. Also included are all applicable records from the American Football League, 1960-69.

Individual Records

Service

Most Seasons

26 George Blanda, Chi. Bears, 1949, 1950-58; Baltimore, 1950; Houston, 1960-66; Oakland, 1967-75
21 Earl Morrall, San Francisco, 1956; Pittsburgh, 1957-58; Detroit, 1958-64; N.Y. Giants, 1965-67; Baltimore, 1968-71; Miami, 1972-76
20 Jim Marshall, Cleveland, 1960; Minnesota, 1961-79

Most Seasons, One Club

19 Jim Marshall, Minnesota, 1961-79
18 Jim Hart, St. Louis, 1966-83
Jeff Van Note, Atlanta, 1969-86
17 Lou Groza, Cleveland, 1950-59, 1961-67
Johnny Unitas, Baltimore, 1956-72
John Brodie, San Francisco, 1957-73
Jim Bakken, St. Louis, 1962-78
Mick Tingelhoff, Minnesota, 1962-78
Pat Leahy, N.Y. Jets, 1974-90

Most Games Played, Career

340 George Blanda, Chi. Bears, 1949, 1950-58; Baltimore, 1950; Houston, 1960-66; Oakland, 1967-75
282 Jim Marshall, Cleveland, 1960; Minnesota, 1961-79
263 Jan Stenerud, Kansas City, 1967-79; Green Bay, 1980-83; Minnesota, 1984-85

Most Consecutive Games Played, Career

282 Jim Marshall, Cleveland, 1960; Minnesota, 1961-79
240 Mick Tingelhoff, Minnesota, 1962-78
234 Jim Bakken, St. Louis, 1962-78

Head Coach

Most Seasons, Head Coach

40 George Halas, Chi. Bears, 1920-29, 1933-42, 1946-55, 1958-67
33 Earl (Curly) Lambeau, Green Bay, 1921-49; Chi. Cardinals, 1950-51; Washington, 1952-53
29 Tom Landry, Dallas, 1960-88

Most Games Won, Head Coach

319 George Halas, Chi. Bears, 1920-29, 1933-42, 1946-55, 1958-67
281 Don Shula, Baltimore, 1963-69; Miami, 1970-90
250 Tom Landry, Dallas, 1960-88

Most Games Lost, Head Coach

162 Tom Landry, Dallas, 1960-88
148 George Halas, Chi. Bears, 1920-29, 1933-42, 1946-55, 1958-67
139 Chuck Noll, Pittsburgh, 1969-90

Scoring

Most Seasons Leading League

5 Don Hutson, Green Bay, 1940-44
Gino Cappelletti, Boston, 1961, 1963-66
3 Earl (Dutch) Clark, Portsmouth, 1932; Detroit, 1935-36
Pat Harder, Chi. Cardinals, 1947-49
Paul Hornung, Green Bay, 1959-61
2 Jack Manders, Chi. Bears, 1934, 1937
Gordy Soltau, San Francisco, 1952-53
Doak Walker, Detroit, 1950, 1955
Gene Mingo, Denver, 1960, 1962
Jim Turner, N.Y. Jets, 1968-69
Fred Cox, Minnesota, 1969-70
Chester Marcol, Green Bay, 1972, 1974
John Smith, New England, 1979-80

Most Consecutive Seasons Leading League

5 Don Hutson, Green Bay, 1940-44
4 Gino Cappelletti, Boston, 1963-66
3 Pat Harder, Chi. Cardinals, 1947-49
Paul Hornung, Green Bay, 1959-61

Points

Most Points, Career

2,002 George Blanda, Chi. Bears, 1949, 1950-58; Baltimore, 1950; Houston, 1960-66; Oakland, 1967-75 (9-td, 943-pat, 335-fg)
1,699 Jan Stenerud, Kansas City, 1967-79; Green Bay, 1980-83; Minnesota, 1984-85 (580-pat, 373-fg)
1,439 Jim Turner, N.Y. Jets, 1964-70; Denver, 1971-79 (1-td, 521-pat, 304-fg)

Most Points, Season

176 Paul Hornung, Green Bay, 1960 (15-td, 41-pat, 15-fg)
161 Mark Moseley, Washington, 1983 (62-pat, 33-fg)
155 Gino Cappelletti, Boston, 1964 (7-td, 38-pat, 25-fg)

Most Points, No Touchdowns, Season

161 Mark Moseley, Washington, 1983 (62-pat, 33-fg)
145 Jim Turner, N.Y. Jets, 1968 (43-pat, 34-fg)
144 Kevin Butler, Chicago, 1985 (51-pat, 31-fg)

Most Seasons, 100 or More Points

8 Nick Lowery, Kansas City, 1981, 1983-86, 1988-90
7 Jan Stenerud, Kansas City, 1967-71; Green Bay, 1981, 1983
6 Gino Cappelletti, Boston, 1961-66
George Blanda, Houston, 1960-61; Oakland, 1967-69, 1973
Bruce Gossett, Los Angeles, 1966-67, 1969; San Francisco, 1970-71, 1973

Most Points, Rookie, Season

144 Kevin Butler, Chicago, 1985 (51-pat, 31-fg)
132 Gale Sayers, Chicago, 1965 (22-td)
128 Doak Walker, Detroit, 1950 (11-td, 38-pat, 8-fg)
Cookie Gilchrist, Buffalo, 1962 (15-td, 14-pat, 8-fg)
Chester Marcol, Green Bay, 1972 (29-pat, 33-fg)

Most Points, Game

40 Ernie Nevers, Chi. Cardinals vs. Chi. Bears, Nov. 28, 1929 (6-td, 4-pat)
36 Dub Jones, Cleveland vs. Chi. Bears, Nov. 25, 1951 (6-td)
Gale Sayers, Chicago vs. San Francisco, Dec. 12, 1965 (6-td)
33 Paul Hornung, Green Bay vs. Baltimore, Oct. 8, 1961 (4-td, 6-pat, 1-fg)

Most Consecutive Games Scoring

165 Jim Breech, Oakland, 1979; Cincinnati, 1980-90 (current)
151 Fred Cox, Minnesota, 1963-73
133 Garo Yepremian, Miami, 1970-78; New Orleans, 1979

Touchdowns

Most Seasons Leading League

8 Don Hutson, Green Bay, 1935-38, 1941-44
3 Jim Brown, Cleveland, 1958-59, 1963
Lance Alworth, San Diego, 1964-66
2 By many players

Most Consecutive Seasons Leading League

4 Don Hutson, Green Bay, 1935-38, 1941-44
3 Lance Alworth, San Diego, 1964-66
2 By many players

Most Touchdowns, Career

126 Jim Brown, Cleveland, 1957-65 (106-r, 20-p)
125 Walter Payton, Chicago, 1975-87 (110-r, 15-p)
116 John Riggins, N.Y. Jets, 1971-75; Washington, 1976-79, 1981-85 (104-r, 12-p)

Most Touchdowns, Season

24 John Riggins, Washington, 1983 (24-r)
23 O.J. Simpson, Buffalo, 1975 (16-r, 7-p)
Jerry Rice, San Francisco, 1987 (1-r, 22-p)
22 Gale Sayers, Chicago, 1965 (14-r, 6-p, 2-ret)
Chuck Foreman, Minnesota, 1975 (13-r, 9-p)

Most Touchdowns, Rookie, Season

22 Gale Sayers, Chicago, 1965 (14-r, 6-p, 2-ret)
20 Eric Dickerson, L.A. Rams, 1983 (18-r, 2-p)
16 Billy Sims, Detroit, 1980 (13-r, 3-p)

Most Touchdowns, Game

6 Ernie Nevers, Chi. Cardinals vs. Chi. Bears, Nov. 28, 1929 (6-r)
Dub Jones, Cleveland vs. Chi. Bears, Nov. 25, 1951 (4-r, 2-p)
Gale Sayers, Chicago vs. San Francisco, Dec. 12, 1965 (4-r, 1-p, 1-ret)
5 Bob Shaw, Chi. Cardinals vs. Baltimore, Oct. 2, 1950 (5-p)
Jim Brown, Cleveland vs. Baltimore, Nov. 1, 1959 (5-r)
Abner Haynes, Dall. Texans vs. Oakland, Nov. 26, 1961 (4-r, 1-p)
Billy Cannon, Houston vs. N.Y. Titans, Dec. 10, 1961 (3-r, 2-p)
Cookie Gilchrist, Buffalo vs. N.Y. Jets, Dec. 8, 1963 (5-r)
Paul Hornung, Green Bay vs. Baltimore, Dec. 12, 1965 (3-r, 2-p)
Kellen Winslow, San Diego vs. Oakland, Nov. 22, 1981 (5-p)
Jerry Rice, San Francisco vs. Atlanta, Oct. 14, 1990 (5-p)
4 By many players

Most Consecutive Games Scoring Touchdowns

18 Lenny Moore, Baltimore, 1963-65
14 O.J. Simpson, Buffalo, 1975
13 John Riggins, Washington, 1982-83
Jerry Rice, San Francisco, 1986-87

Points After Touchdown

Most Seasons Leading League

8 George Blanda, Chi. Bears, 1956; Houston, 1961-62; Oakland, 1967-69, 1972, 1974
4 Bob Waterfield, Cleveland, 1945; Los Angeles, 1946, 1950, 1952
3 Earl (Dutch) Clark, Portsmouth, 1932; Detroit, 1935-36
Jack Manders, Chi. Bears, 1933-35
Don Hutson, Green Bay, 1941-42, 1945

Most Points After Touchdown Attempted, Career

959 George Blanda, Chi. Bears, 1949, 1950-58; Baltimore, 1950; Houston, 1960-66; Oakland, 1967-75
657 Lou Groza, Cleveland, 1950-59, 1961-67
601 Jan Stenerud, Kansas City, 1967-79; Green Bay, 1980-83; Minnesota, 1984-85

Most Points After Touchdown Attempted, Season

70 Uwe von Schamann, Miami, 1984
65 George Blanda, Houston, 1961
63 Mark Moseley, Washington, 1983

Most Points After Touchdown Attempted, Game

10 Charlie Gogolak, Washington vs. N.Y. Giants, Nov. 27, 1966
9 Pat Harder, Chi. Cardinals vs. N.Y. Giants, Oct. 17, 1948; vs. N.Y. Bulldogs, Nov. 13, 1949
Bob Waterfield, Los Angeles vs. Baltimore, Oct. 22, 1950
Bob Thomas, Chicago vs. Green Bay, Dec. 7, 1980
8 By many players

Most Points After Touchdown, Career

943 George Blanda, Chi. Bears, 1949, 1950-58; Baltimore, 1950; Houston, 1960-66; Oakland, 1967-75
641 Lou Groza, Cleveland, 1950-59, 1961-67
580 Jan Stenerud, Kansas City, 1967-79; Green Bay, 1980-83; Minnesota, 1984-85

Most Points After Touchdown, Season

66 Uwe von Schamann, Miami, 1984
64 George Blanda, Houston, 1961
62 Mark Moseley, Washington, 1983

Most Points After Touchdown, Game

9 Pat Harder, Chi. Cardinals vs. N.Y. Giants, Oct. 17, 1948
Bob Waterfield, Los Angeles vs. Baltimore, Oct. 22, 1950
Charlie Gogolak, Washington vs. N.Y. Giants, Nov. 27, 1966
8 By many players

Most Consecutive Points After Touchdown

234 Tommy Davis, San Francisco, 1959-65
221 Jim Turner, N.Y. Jets, 1967-70; Denver, 1971-74
202 Gary Anderson, Pittsburgh, 1983-88

Highest Points After Touchdown Percentage, Career (200 points after touchdown)

99.43 Tommy Davis, San Francisco, 1959-69 (350-348)
99.32 Gary Anderson, Pittsburgh, 1982-90 (294-292)

98.94 Nick Lowery, New England, 1978; Kansas City, 1980-90 (379-375)

Most Points After Touchdown, No Misses, Season

56 Danny Villanueva, Dallas, 1966
Ray Wersching, San Francisco, 1984
54 Mike Clark, Dallas, 1968
George Blanda, Oakland, 1968
53 Pat Harder, Chi. Cardinals, 1948

Most Points After Touchdown, No Misses, Game

9 Pat Harder, Chi. Cardinals vs. N.Y. Giants, Oct. 17, 1948
Bob Waterfield, Los Angeles vs. Baltimore, Oct. 22, 1950
8 By many players

Field Goals

Most Seasons Leading League

5 Lou Groza, Cleveland, 1950, 1952-54, 1957
4 Jack Manders, Chi. Bears, 1933-34, 1936-37
Ward Cuff, N.Y. Giants, 1938-39, 1943; Green Bay, 1947
Mark Moseley, Washington, 1976-77, 1979, 1982
3 Bob Waterfield, Los Angeles, 1947, 1949, 1951
Gino Cappelletti, Boston, 1961, 1963-64
Fred Cox, Minnesota, 1965, 1969-70
Jan Stenerud, Kansas City, 1967, 1970, 1975

Most Consecutive Seasons Leading League

3 Lou Groza, Cleveland, 1952-54
2 By many players

Most Field Goals Attempted, Career

638 George Blanda, Chi. Bears, 1949, 1950-58; Baltimore, 1950; Houston, 1960-66; Oakland, 1967-75
558 Jan Stenerud, Kansas City, 1967-79; Green Bay, 1980-83; Minnesota, 1984-85
488 Jim Turner, N.Y. Jets, 1964-70; Denver, 1971-79

Most Field Goals Attempted, Season

49 Bruce Gossett, Los Angeles, 1966
Curt Knight, Washington, 1971
48 Chester Marcol, Green Bay, 1972
47 Jim Turner, N.Y. Jets, 1969
David Ray, Los Angeles, 1973
Mark Moseley, Washington, 1983

Most Field Goals Attempted, Game

9 Jim Bakken, St. Louis vs. Pittsburgh, Sept. 24, 1967
8 Lou Michaels, Pittsburgh vs. St. Louis, Dec. 2, 1962
Garo Yepremian, Detroit vs. Minnesota, Nov. 13, 1966
Jim Turner, N.Y. Jets vs. Buffalo, Nov. 3, 1968
7 By many players

Most Field Goals, Career

373 Jan Stenerud, Kansas City, 1967-79; Green Bay, 1980-83; Minnesota, 1984-85
335 George Blanda, Chi. Bears, 1949, 1950-58; Baltimore, 1950; Houston, 1960-66; Oakland, 1967-75
304 Jim Turner, N.Y. Jets, 1964-70; Denver, 1971-79

Most Field Goals, Season

35 Ali Haji-Sheikh, N.Y. Giants, 1983
34 Jim Turner, N.Y. Jets, 1968
Nick Lowery, Kansas City, 1990
33 Chester Marcol, Green Bay, 1972
Mark Moseley, Washington, 1983
Gary Anderson, Pittsburgh, 1985

Most Field Goals, Rookie, Season

35 Ali Haji-Sheikh, N.Y. Giants, 1983
33 Chester Marcol, Green Bay, 1972
31 Kevin Butler, Chicago, 1985

Most Field Goals, Game

7 Jim Bakken, St. Louis vs. Pittsburgh, Sept. 24, 1967
Rich Karlis, Minnesota vs. L.A. Rams, Nov. 5, 1989 (OT)
6 Gino Cappelletti, Boston vs. Denver, Oct. 4, 1964
Garo Yepremian, Detroit vs. Minnesota, Nov. 13, 1966
Jim Turner, N.Y. Jets vs. Buffalo, Nov. 3, 1968
Tom Dempsey, Philadelphia vs. Houston, Nov. 12, 1972
Bobby Howfield, N.Y. Jets vs. New Orleans, Dec. 3, 1972
Jim Bakken, St. Louis vs. Atlanta, Dec. 9, 1973
Joe Danelo, N.Y. Giants vs. Seattle, Oct. 18, 1981
Ray Wersching, San Francisco vs. New Orleans, Oct. 16, 1983
Gary Anderson, Pittsburgh vs. Denver, Oct. 23, 1988
5 By many players

Most Field Goals, One Quarter

4 Garo Yepremian, Detroit vs. Minnesota, Nov. 13, 1966 (second quarter)
Curt Knight, Washington vs. N.Y. Giants, Nov. 15, 1970 (second quarter)
Roger Ruzek, Dallas vs. N.Y. Giants, Nov. 2, 1987 (fourth quarter)
3 By many players

Most Consecutive Games Scoring Field Goals

31 Fred Cox, Minnesota, 1968-70
28 Jim Turner, N.Y. Jets, 1970; Denver, 1971-72
Chip Lohmiller, Washington, 1988-90
23 Morten Andersen, New Orleans, 1986-88

Most Consecutive Field Goals

24 Kevin Butler, Chicago, 1988-89
23 Mark Moseley, Washington, 1981-82
22 Pat Leahy, N.Y. Jets, 1985-86

Longest Field Goal

63 Tom Dempsey, New Orleans vs. Detroit, Nov. 8, 1970
60 Steve Cox, Cleveland vs. Cincinnati, Oct. 21, 1984
59 Tony Franklin, Philadelphia vs. Dallas, Nov. 12, 1979
Pete Stoyanovich, Miami vs. N.Y. Jets, Nov. 12, 1989

Highest Field Goal Percentage, Career (100 field goals)

78.96 Nick Lowery, New England, 1978; Kansas City, 1980-90 (328-259)
77.15 Gary Anderson, Pittsburgh, 1982-90 (267-206)
77.11 Morten Andersen, New Orleans, 1982-90 (249-192)

Highest Field Goal Percentage, Season (Qualifiers)

95.24 Mark Moseley, Washington, 1982 (21-20)
Ed Murray, Detroit, 1988 (21-20)
Ed Murray, Detroit, 1989 (21-20)
91.89 Nick Lowery, Kansas City, 1990 (37-34)
91.67 Jan Stenerud, Green Bay, 1981 (24-22)

Most Field Goals, No Misses, Game

7 Rich Karlis, Minnesota vs. L.A. Rams, Nov. 5, 1989 (OT)
6 Gino Cappelletti, Boston vs. Denver, Oct. 4, 1964
Joe Danelo, N.Y. Giants vs. Seattle, Oct. 18, 1981
Ray Wersching, San Francisco vs. New Orleans, Oct. 16, 1983
Gary Anderson, Pittsburgh vs. Denver, Oct. 23, 1988
5 By many players

Most Field Goals, 50 or More Yards, Career

18 Nick Lowery, New England, 1978; Kansas City, 1980-90
17 Jan Stenerud, Kansas City, 1967-79; Green Bay, 1980-83; Minnesota, 1984-85
16 Morten Andersen, New Orleans, 1982-90

Most Field Goals, 50 or More Yards, Season

6 Dean Biasucci, Indianapolis, 1988
5 Fred Steinfort, Denver, 1980
Norm Johnson, Seattle, 1986
4 Horst Muhlmann, Cincinnati, 1970
Mark Moseley, Washington, 1977
Nick Lowery, Kansas City, 1980
Raul Allegre, Baltimore, 1983
Kevin Butler, Chicago, 1990

Most Field Goals, 50 or More Yards, Game

2 Jim Martin, Detroit vs. Baltimore, Oct. 23, 1960
Tom Dempsey, New Orleans vs. Los Angeles, Dec. 6, 1970
Chris Bahr, Cincinnati vs. Houston, Sept. 23, 1979
Nick Lowery, Kansas City vs. Seattle, Sept. 14, 1980
Mark Moseley, Washington vs. New Orleans, Oct. 26, 1980
Fred Steinfort, Denver vs. Seattle, Dec. 21, 1980
Mick Luckhurst, Atlanta vs. Denver, Dec. 5, 1982
Morten Andersen, New Orleans vs. Philadelphia, Dec. 11, 1983
Mick Luckhurst, Atlanta vs. L.A. Rams, Oct. 7, 1984
Paul McFadden, Philadelphia vs. Detroit, Nov. 4, 1984
Chip Lohmiller, Washington vs. Indianapolis, Dec. 22, 1990
Nick Lowery, Kansas City vs. New Orleans, Sept. 8, 1985
Pat Leahy, N.Y. Jets vs. New England, Oct. 20, 1985
Tony Zendejas, Houston vs. San Diego, Nov. 24, 1985
Norm Johnson, Seattle vs. L.A. Raiders, Dec. 8, 1986
Raul Allegre, N.Y. Giants vs. Philadelphia, Nov. 15, 1987
Nick Lowery, Kansas City vs. Detroit, Nov. 26, 1987
Dean Biasucci, Indianapolis vs. Miami, Sept. 25, 1988
Paul McFadden, Atlanta vs. Buffalo, Nov. 5, 1989
Kevin Butler, Chicago vs. Minnesota, Sept. 23, 1990
Kevin Butler, Chicago vs. Green Bay, Oct. 7, 1990
Chip Lohmiller, Washington vs. Indianapolis, Dec. 22, 1990

Safeties

Most Safeties, Career

4 Ted Hendricks, Baltimore, 1969-73; Green Bay, 1974; Oakland, 1975-81; L.A. Raiders, 1982-83
Doug English, Detroit, 1975-79, 1981-85
3 Bill McPeak, Pittsburgh, 1949-57
Charlie Krueger, San Francisco, 1959-73
Ernie Stautner, Pittsburgh, 1950-63
Jim Katcavage, N.Y. Giants, 1956-68
Roger Brown, Detroit, 1960-66; Los Angeles, 1967-69
Bruce Maher, Detroit, 1960-67; N.Y. Giants, 1968-69
Ron McDole, St. Louis, 1961; Houston, 1962; Buffalo, 1963-70; Washington, 1971-78
Alan Page, Minnesota, 1967-78; Chicago, 1979-81
Lyle Alzado, Denver, 1971-78; Cleveland, 1979-81; L.A. Raiders, 1982-85
Rulon Jones, Denver, 1980-88
Steve McMichael, New England, 1980; Chicago, 1981-90
2 By many players

Most Safeties, Season

2 Tom Nash, Green Bay, 1932
Roger Brown, Detroit, 1962
Ron McDole, Buffalo, 1964
Alan Page, Minnesota, 1971
Fred Dryer, Los Angeles, 1973
Benny Barnes, Dallas, 1973
James Young, Houston, 1977
Tom Hannon, Minnesota, 1981
Doug English, Detroit, 1983
Don Blackmon, New England, 1985
Tim Harris, Green Bay, 1988

Most Safeties, Game

2 Fred Dryer, Los Angeles vs. Green Bay, Oct. 21, 1973

Rushing

Most Seasons Leading League

8 Jim Brown, Cleveland, 1957-61, 1963-65
4 Steve Van Buren, Philadelphia, 1945, 1947-49
O.J. Simpson, Buffalo, 1972-73, 1975-76
Eric Dickerson, L.A. Rams, 1983-84, 1986; Indianapolis, 1988
3 Earl Campbell, Houston, 1978-80

Most Consecutive Seasons Leading League

5 Jim Brown, Cleveland, 1957-61
3 Steve Van Buren, Philadelphia, 1947-49
Jim Brown, Cleveland, 1963-65
Earl Campbell, Houston, 1978-80
2 Bill Paschal, N.Y. Giants, 1943-44
Joe Perry, San Francisco, 1953-54
Jim Nance, Boston, 1966-67
Leroy Kelly, Cleveland, 1967-68
O.J. Simpson, Buffalo, 1972-73; 1975-76
Eric Dickerson, L.A. Rams, 1983-84

Attempts

Most Seasons Leading League

6 Jim Brown, Cleveland, 1958-59, 1961, 1963-65
4 Steve Van Buren, Philadelphia, 1947-50
Walter Payton, Chicago, 1976-79
3 Cookie Gilchrist, Buffalo, 1963-64; Denver, 1965
Jim Nance, Boston, 1966-67, 1969
O. J. Simpson, Buffalo, 1973-75

Eric Dickerson, L.A. Rams, 1983, 1986; Indianapolis, 1988

Most Consecutive Seasons Leading League
4 Steve Van Buren, Philadelphia, 1947-50
Walter Payton, Chicago, 1976-79
3 Jim Brown, Cleveland, 1963-65
Cookie Gilchrist, Buffalo, 1963-64; Denver, 1965
O.J. Simpson, Buffalo, 1973-75
2 By many players

Most Attempts, Career
3,838 Walter Payton, Chicago, 1975-87
2,949 Franco Harris, Pittsburgh, 1972-83; Seattle, 1984
2,936 Tony Dorsett, Dallas, 1977-87; Denver, 1988

Most Attempts, Season
407 James Wilder, Tampa Bay, 1984
404 Eric Dickerson, L.A. Rams, 1986
397 Gerald Riggs, Atlanta, 1985

Most Attempts, Rookie, Season
390 Eric Dickerson, L.A. Rams, 1983
378 George Rogers, New Orleans, 1981
335 Curt Warner, Seattle, 1983

Most Attempts, Game
45 Jamie Morris, Washington vs. Cincinnati, Dec. 17, 1988 (OT)
43 Butch Woolfolk, N.Y. Giants vs. Philadelphia, Nov. 20, 1983
James Wilder, Tampa Bay vs. Green Bay, Sept. 30, 1984 (OT)
42 James Wilder, Tampa Bay vs. Pittsburgh, Oct. 30, 1983

Yards Gained

Most Yards Gained, Career
16,726 Walter Payton, Chicago, 1975-87
12,739 Tony Dorsett, Dallas, 1977-87; Denver, 1988
12,312 Jim Brown, Cleveland, 1957-65

Most Seasons, 1,000 or More Yards Rushing
10 Walter Payton, Chicago, 1976-81, 1983-86
8 Franco Harris, Pittsburgh, 1972, 1974-79, 1983
Tony Dorsett, Dallas, 1977-81, 1983-85
7 Jim Brown, Cleveland, 1958-61, 1963-65
Eric Dickerson, L.A. Rams, 1983-86; L.A. Rams-Indianapolis, 1987; Indianapolis, 1988-89

Most Consecutive Seasons, 1,000 or More Yards Rushing
7 Eric Dickerson, L.A. Rams, 1983-86; L.A. Rams-Indianapolis, 1987; Indianapolis, 1988-89
6 Franco Harris, Pittsburgh, 1974-79
Walter Payton, Chicago, 1976-81
5 Jim Taylor, Green Bay, 1960-64
O.J. Simpson, Buffalo, 1972-76
Tony Dorsett, Dallas, 1977-81

Most Yards Gained, Season
2,105 Eric Dickerson, L.A. Rams, 1984
2,003 O.J. Simpson, Buffalo, 1973
1,934 Earl Campbell, Houston, 1980

Most Yards Gained, Rookie, Season
1,808 Eric Dickerson, L.A. Rams, 1983
1,674 George Rogers, New Orleans, 1981
1,605 Ottis Anderson, St. Louis, 1979

Most Yards Gained, Game
275 Walter Payton, Chicago vs. Minnesota, Nov. 20, 1977
273 O.J. Simpson, Buffalo vs. Detroit, Nov. 25, 1976
250 O.J. Simpson, Buffalo vs. New England, Sept. 16, 1973

Most Games, 200 or More Yards Rushing, Career
6 O.J. Simpson, Buffalo, 1969-77; San Francisco, 1978-79
4 Jim Brown, Cleveland, 1957-65
Earl Campbell, Houston, 1978-84; New Orleans, 1984-85
3 Eric Dickerson, L.A. Rams, 1983-87; Indianapolis, 1987-90

Most Games, 200 or More Yards Rushing, Season
4 Earl Campbell, Houston, 1980
3 O.J. Simpson, Buffalo, 1973
2 Jim Brown, Cleveland, 1963
O.J. Simpson, Buffalo, 1976
Walter Payton, Chicago, 1977
Eric Dickerson, L.A. Rams, 1984
Greg Bell, L.A. Rams, 1989

Most Consecutive Games, 200 or More Yards Rushing
2 O.J. Simpson, Buffalo, 1973, 1976
Earl Campbell, Houston, 1980

Most Games, 100 or More Yards Rushing, Career
77 Walter Payton, Chicago, 1975-87
61 Eric Dickerson, L.A. Rams, 1983-87; Indianapolis, 1987-90
58 Jim Brown, Cleveland, 1957-65

Most Games, 100 or More Yards Rushing, Season
12 Eric Dickerson, L.A. Rams, 1984
11 O.J. Simpson, Buffalo, 1973
Earl Campbell, Houston, 1979
Marcus Allen, L.A. Raiders, 1985
Eric Dickerson, L.A. Rams, 1986
10 Walter Payton, Chicago, 1977, 1985
Earl Campbell, Houston, 1980

Most Consecutive Games, 100 or More Yards Rushing
11 Marcus Allen, L.A. Raiders, 1985-86
9 Walter Payton, Chicago, 1985
7 O.J. Simpson, Buffalo, 1972-73
Earl Campbell, Houston, 1979

Longest Run From Scrimmage
99 Tony Dorsett, Dallas vs. Minnesota, Jan. 3, 1983 (TD)
97 Andy Uram, Green Bay vs. Chi. Cardinals, Oct. 8, 1939 (TD)
Bob Gage, Pittsburgh vs. Chi. Bears, Dec. 4, 1949 (TD)
96 Jim Spavital, Baltimore vs. Green Bay, Nov. 5, 1950 (TD)
Bob Hoernschemeyer, Detroit vs. N.Y. Yanks, Nov. 23, 1950 (TD)

Average Gain

Highest Average Gain, Career (700 attempts)
5.22 Jim Brown, Cleveland, 1957-65 (2,359-12,312)
5.14 Eugene (Mercury) Morris, Miami, 1969-75; San Diego, 1976 (804-4,133)
5.00 Gale Sayers, Chicago, 1965-71 (991-4,956)

Highest Average Gain, Season (Qualifiers)
9.94 Beattie Feathers, Chi. Bears, 1934 (101-1,004)
7.98 Randall Cunningham, Philadelphia 1990 (118-942)
6.87 Bobby Douglass, Chicago, 1972 (141-968)

Highest Average Gain, Game (10 attempts)
17.09 Marion Motley, Cleveland vs. Pittsburgh, Oct. 29, 1950 (11-188)
16.70 Bill Grimes, Green Bay vs. N.Y. Yanks, Oct. 8, 1950 (10-167)
16.57 Bobby Mitchell, Cleveland vs. Washington, Nov. 15, 1959 (14-232)

Touchdowns

Most Seasons Leading League
5 Jim Brown, Cleveland, 1957-59, 1963, 1965
4 Steve Van Buren, Philadelphia, 1945, 1947-49
3 Abner Haynes, Dall. Texans, 1960-62
Cookie Gilchrist, Buffalo, 1962-64
Paul Lowe, L.A. Chargers, 1960; San Diego, 1961, 1965
Leroy Kelly, Cleveland, 1966-68

Most Consecutive Seasons Leading League
3 Steve Van Buren, Philadelphia, 1947-49
Jim Brown, Cleveland, 1957-59
Abner Haynes, Dall. Texans, 1960-62
Cookie Gilchrist, Buffalo, 1962-64
Leroy Kelly, Cleveland, 1966-68

Most Touchdowns, Career
110 Walter Payton, Chicago, 1975-87
106 Jim Brown, Cleveland, 1957-65
104 John Riggins, N.Y. Jets, 1971-75; Washington, 1976-79, 1981-85

Most Touchdowns, Season
24 John Riggins, Washington, 1983
21 Joe Morris, N.Y. Giants, 1985
19 Jim Taylor, Green Bay, 1962
Earl Campbell, Houston, 1979
Chuck Muncie, San Diego, 1981

Most Touchdowns, Rookie, Season
18 Eric Dickerson, L.A. Rams, 1983
15 Ickey Woods, Cincinnati, 1988
14 Gale Sayers, Chicago, 1965
Barry Sanders, Detroit, 1989

Most Touchdowns, Game
6 Ernie Nevers, Chi. Cardinals vs. Chi. Bears, Nov. 28, 1929
5 Jim Brown, Cleveland vs. Baltimore, Nov. 1, 1959
Cookie Gilchrist, Buffalo vs. N.Y. Jets, Dec. 8, 1963
4 By many players

Most Consecutive Games Rushing for Touchdowns
13 John Riggins, Washington, 1982-83
George Rogers, Washington, 1985-86
11 Lenny Moore, Baltimore, 1963-64
10 Greg Bell, L.A. Rams, 1988-89

Passing

Most Seasons Leading League
6 Sammy Baugh, Washington, 1937, 1940, 1943, 1945, 1947, 1949
4 Len Dawson, Dall. Texans; 1962; Kansas City, 1964, 1966, 1968
Roger Staubach, Dallas, 1971, 1973, 1978-79
Ken Anderson, Cincinnati, 1974-75, 1981-82
3 Arnie Herber, Green Bay, 1932, 1934, 1936
Norm Van Brocklin, Los Angeles, 1950, 1952, 1954
Bart Starr, Green Bay, 1962, 1964, 1966

Most Consecutive Seasons Leading League
2 Cecil Isbell, Green Bay, 1941-42
Milt Plum, Cleveland, 1960-61
Ken Anderson, Cincinnati, 1974-75, 1981-82
Roger Staubach, Dallas, 1978-79

Pass Rating

Highest Pass Rating, Career (1,500 attempts)
93.4 Joe Montana, San Francisco, 1979-90
88.5 Dan Marino, Miami, 1983-90
85.8 Jim Kelly, Buffalo, 1986-90

Highest Pass Rating, Season (Qualifiers)
112.4 Joe Montana, San Francisco, 1989
110.4 Milt Plum, Cleveland, 1960
109.9 Sammy Baugh, Washington, 1945

Highest Pass Rating, Rookie, Season (Qualifiers)
96.0 Dan Marino, Miami, 1983
88.2 Greg Cook, Cincinnati, 1969
84.0 Charlie Conerly, N.Y. Giants, 1948

Attempts

Most Seasons Leading League
4 Sammy Baugh, Washington, 1937, 1943, 1947-48
Johnny Unitas, Baltimore, 1957, 1959-61
George Blanda, Chi. Bears, 1953; Houston, 1963-65
3 Arnie Herber, Green Bay, 1932, 1934, 1936
Sonny Jurgensen, Washington, 1966-67, 1969
Dan Marino, Miami, 1984, 1986, 1988
2 By many players

Most Consecutive Seasons Leading League
3 Johnny Unitas, Baltimore, 1959-61
George Blanda, Houston, 1963-65
2 By many players

Most Passes Attempted, Career
6,467 Fran Tarkenton, Minnesota, 1961-66, 1972-78; N.Y. Giants, 1967-71
5,604 Dan Fouts, San Diego, 1973-87
5,186 Johnny Unitas, Baltimore, 1956-72; San Diego, 1973

Most Passes Attempted, Season
623 Dan Marino, Miami, 1986
609 Dan Fouts, San Diego, 1981
606 Dan Marino, Miami, 1988

Most Passes Attempted, Rookie, Season
439 Jim Zorn, Seattle, 1976
417 Jack Trudeau, Indianapolis, 1986
375 Norm Snead, Washington, 1961

Most Passes Attempted, Game
68 George Blanda, Houston vs. Buffalo, Nov. 1, 1964
66 Chris Miller, Atlanta vs. Detroit, Dec. 24, 1989
62 Joe Namath, N.Y. Jets vs. Baltimore, Oct. 18, 1970
Steve Dils, Minnesota vs. Tampa Bay, Sept. 5, 1981
Phil Simms, N.Y. Giants vs. Cincinnati, Oct. 13, 1985
Randall Cunningham, Philadelphia vs. Chicago, Oct. 2, 1989

Completions

Most Seasons Leading League
5 Sammy Baugh, Washington, 1937, 1943, 1945, 1947-48
4 George Blanda, Chi. Bears, 1953; Houston, 1963-65
Sonny Jurgensen, Philadelphia, 1961; Washington, 1966-67, 1969
Dan Marino, Miami, 1984-86, 1988
3 Arnie Herber, Green Bay, 1932, 1934, 1936
Johnny Unitas, Baltimore, 1959-60, 1963
John Brodie, San Francisco, 1965, 1968, 1970
Fran Tarkenton, Minnesota, 1975-76, 1978
Most Consecutive Seasons Leading League
3 George Blanda, Houston, 1963-65
Dan Marino, Miami, 1984-86
2 By many players
Most Passes Completed, Career
3,686 Fran Tarkenton, Minnesota, 1961-66, 1972-78; N.Y. Giants, 1967-71
3,297 Dan Fouts, San Diego, 1973-87
2,914 Joe Montana, San Francisco, 1979-90
Most Passes Completed, Season
378 Dan Marino, Miami, 1986
362 Dan Marino, Miami, 1984
Warren Moon, Houston, 1990
360 Dan Fouts, San Diego, 1981
Most Passes Completed, Rookie, Season
208 Jim Zorn, Seattle, 1976
204 Jack Trudeau, Indianapolis, 1986
183 Jeff Komlo, Detroit, 1979
Most Passes Completed, Game
42 Richard Todd, N.Y. Jets vs. San Francisco, Sept. 21, 1980
40 Ken Anderson, Cincinnati vs. San Diego, Dec. 20, 1982
Phil Simms, N.Y. Giants vs. Cincinnati, Oct. 13, 1985
39 Dan Marino, Miami vs. Buffalo, Nov. 16, 1986
Most Consecutive Passes Completed
22 Joe Montana, San Francisco vs. Cleveland (5), Nov. 29, 1987; vs. Green Bay (17), Dec. 6, 1987
20 Ken Anderson, Cincinnati vs. Houston, Jan. 2, 1983
18 Steve DeBerg, Denver vs. L.A. Rams (17), Dec. 12, 1982; vs. Kansas City (1), Dec. 19, 1982
Lynn Dickey, Green Bay vs. Houston, Sept. 4, 1983
Joe Montana, San Francisco vs. L.A. Rams (13), Oct. 28, 1984; vs. Cincinnati (5), Nov. 4, 1984
Dan Majkowski, Green Bay vs. New Orleans, Sept. 18, 1989

Completion Percentage

Most Seasons Leading League
8 Len Dawson, Dall. Texans, 1962; Kansas City, 1964-69, 1975
7 Sammy Baugh, Washington, 1940, 1942-43, 1945, 1947-49
5 Joe Montana, San Francisco, 1980-81, 1985, 1987, 1989
Most Consecutive Seasons Leading League
6 Len Dawson, Kansas City, 1964-69
3 Sammy Baugh, Washington, 1947-49
Otto Graham, Cleveland, 1953-55
Milt Plum, Cleveland, 1959-61
2 By many players
Highest Completion Percentage, Career (1,500 attempts)
63.64 Joe Montana, San Francisco, 1979-90 (4,579-2,914)
59.91 Jim Kelly, Buffalo, 1986-90 (2,088-1,251)
59.85 Ken Stabler, Oakland, 1970-79; Houston, 1980-81; New Orleans, 1982-84 (3,793-2,270)
Highest Completion Percentage, Season (Qualifiers)
70.55 Ken Anderson, Cincinnati, 1982 (309-218)
70.33 Sammy Baugh, Washington, 1945 (182-128)
70.21 Joe Montana, San Francisco, 1989 (386-271)
Highest Completion Percentage, Rookie, Season (Qualifiers)
58.45 Dan Marino, Miami, 1983 (296-173)
57.14 Jim McMahon, Chicago, 1982 (269-181)
56.07 Fran Tarkenton, Minnesota, 1961 (280-157)
Highest Completion Percentage, Game (20 attempts)
90.91 Ken Anderson, Cincinnati vs. Pittsburgh, Nov. 10, 1974 (22-20)
90.48 Lynn Dickey, Green Bay vs. New Orleans, Dec. 13, 1981 (21-19)
87.50 Danny White, Dallas vs. Philadelphia, Nov. 6, 1983 (24-21)

Yards Gained

Most Seasons Leading League
5 Sonny Jurgensen, Philadelphia, 1961-62; Washington, 1966-67, 1969
4 Sammy Baugh, Washington, 1937, 1940, 1947-48
Johnny Unitas, Baltimore, 1957, 1959-60, 1963
Dan Fouts, San Diego, 1979-82
Dan Marino, Miami, 1984-86, 1988
3 Arnie Herber, Green Bay, 1932, 1934, 1936
Sid Luckman, Chi. Bears, 1943, 1945-46
John Brodie, San Francisco, 1965, 1968, 1970
John Hadl, San Diego, 1965, 1968, 1971
Joe Namath, N.Y. Jets, 1966-67, 1972
Most Consecutive Seasons Leading League
4 Dan Fouts, San Diego, 1979-82
3 Dan Marino, Miami, 1984-86
2 By many players
Most Yards Gained, Career
47,003 Fran Tarkenton, Minnesota, 1961-66, 1972-78; N.Y. Giants, 1967-71
43,040 Dan Fouts, San Diego, 1973-87
40,239 Johnny Unitas, Baltimore, 1956-72; San Diego, 1973
Most Seasons, 3,000 or More Yards Passing
7 Dan Marino, Miami, 1984-90
Joe Montana, San Francisco, 1981, 1983-85, 1987, 1989-90
6 Dan Fouts, San Diego, 1979-81, 1984-86
John Elway, Denver, 1985-90
Boomer Esiason, Cincinnati, 1985-90
5 Sonny Jurgensen, Philadelphia, 1961-62; Washington, 1966-67, 1969
Tommy Kramer, Minnesota, 1979-81, 1985-86
Phil Simms, N.Y. Giants, 1984-86, 1988-89
Most Yards Gained, Season
5,084 Dan Marino, Miami, 1984
4,802 Dan Fouts, San Diego, 1981
4,746 Dan Marino, Miami, 1986
Most Yards Gained, Rookie, Season
2,571 Jim Zorn, Seattle, 1976
2,507 Dennis Shaw, Buffalo, 1970
2,337 Norm Snead, Washington, 1961
Most Yards Gained, Game
554 Norm Van Brocklin, Los Angeles vs. N.Y. Yanks, Sept. 28, 1951
527 Warren Moon, Houston vs. Kansas City, Dec. 16, 1990
521 Dan Marino, Miami vs. N.Y. Jets, Oct. 23, 1988
Most Games, 400 or More Yards Passing, Career
10 Dan Marino, Miami, 1983-90
7 Joe Montana, San Francisco, 1979-90
6 Dan Fouts, San Diego, 1973-87
Most Games, 400 or More Yards Passing, Season
4 Dan Marino, Miami, 1984
3 Dan Marino, Miami, 1986
2 George Blanda, Houston, 1961
Sonny Jurgensen, Philadelphia, 1961
Joe Namath, N.Y. Jets, 1972
Dan Fouts, San Diego, 1982
Dan Fouts, San Diego, 1985
Phil Simms, N.Y. Giants, 1985
Ken O'Brien, N.Y. Jets, 1986
Bernie Kosar, Cleveland, 1986
Dan Marino, Miami, 1988
Randall Cunningham, Philadelphia, 1989
Joe Montana, San Francisco, 1989
Joe Montana, San Francisco, 1990
Most Consecutive Games, 400 or More Yards Passing
2 Dan Fouts, San Diego, 1982
Dan Marino, Miami, 1984
Phil Simms, N.Y. Giants, 1985
Most Games, 300 or More Yards Passing, Career
51 Dan Fouts, San Diego, 1973-87
38 Dan Marino, Miami, 1983-90
35 Joe Montana, San Francisco, 1979-90
Most Games, 300 or More Yards Passing, Season
9 Dan Marino, Miami, 1984
Warren Moon, Houston, 1990
8 Dan Fouts, San Diego, 1980
7 Dan Fouts, San Diego, 1981, 1985
Bill Kenney, Kansas City, 1983
Neil Lomax, St. Louis, 1984
Most Consecutive Games, 300 or More Yards Passing, Season
5 Joe Montana, San Francisco, 1982
4 Dan Fouts, San Diego, 1979
Bill Kenney, Kansas City, 1983
Joe Montana, San Francisco, 1990
Warren Moon, Houston, 1990
3 By many players
Longest Pass Completion (All TDs except as noted)
99 Frank Filchock (to Farkas), Washington vs. Pittsburgh, Oct. 15, 1939
George Izo (to Mitchell), Washington vs. Cleveland, Sept. 15, 1963
Karl Sweetan (to Studstill), Detroit vs. Baltimore, Oct. 16, 1966
Sonny Jurgensen (to Allen), Washington vs. Chicago, Sept. 15, 1968
Jim Plunkett (to Branch), L.A. Raiders vs. Washington, Oct. 2, 1983
Ron Jaworski (to Quick), Philadelphia vs. Atlanta, Nov. 10, 1985
98 Doug Russell (to Tinsley), Chi. Cardinals vs. Cleveland, Nov. 27, 1938
Ogden Compton (to Lane), Chi. Cardinals vs. Green Bay, Nov. 13, 1955
Bill Wade (to Farrington), Chicago Bears vs. Detroit, Oct. 8, 1961
Jacky Lee (to Dewveall), Houston vs. San Diego, Nov. 25, 1962
Earl Morrall (to Jones), N.Y. Giants vs. Pittsburgh, Sept. 11, 1966
Jim Hart (to Moore), St. Louis vs. Los Angeles, Dec. 10, 1972 (no TD)
97 Pat Coffee (to Tinsley), Chi. Cardinals vs. Chi. Bears, Dec. 5, 1937
Bobby Layne (to Box), Detroit vs. Green Bay, Nov. 26, 1953
George Shaw (to Tarr), Denver vs. Boston, Sept. 21, 1962
Bernie Kosar (to Slaughter), Cleveland vs. Chicago, Oct. 23, 1989

Average Gain

Most Seasons Leading League
7 Sid Luckman, Chi. Bears, 1939-43, 1946-47
3 Arnie Herber, Green Bay, 1932, 1934, 1936
Norm Van Brocklin, Los Angeles, 1950, 1952, 1954
Len Dawson, Dall. Texans, 1962; Kansas City, 1966, 1968
Bart Starr, Green Bay, 1966-68
Most Consecutive Seasons Leading League
5 Sid Luckman, Chi. Bears, 1939-43
3 Bart Starr, Green Bay, 1966-68
2 Bernie Masterson, Chi. Bears, 1937-38
Sid Luckman, Chi. Bears, 1946-47
Johnny Unitas, Baltimore, 1964-65
Terry Bradshaw, Pittsburgh, 1977-78
Steve Grogan, New England, 1980-81
Highest Average Gain, Career (1,500 attempts)
8.63 Otto Graham, Cleveland, 1950-55 (1,565-13,499)
8.42 Sid Luckman, Chi. Bears, 1939-50 (1,744-14,686)
8.16 Norm Van Brocklin, Los Angeles, 1949-57; Philadelphia, 1958-60 (2,895-23,611)
Highest Average Gain, Season (Qualifiers)
11.17 Tommy O'Connell, Cleveland, 1957 (110-1,229)
10.86 Sid Luckman, Chi. Bears, 1943 (202-2,194)
10.55 Otto Graham, Cleveland, 1953 (258-2,722)
Highest Average Gain, Rookie, Season (Qualifiers)
9.411 Greg Cook, Cincinnati, 1969 (197-1,854)

9.409 Bob Waterfield, Cleveland, 1945 (171-1,609)
8.36 Zeke Bratkowski, Chi. Bears, 1954 (130-1,087)

Highest Average Gain, Game (20 attempts)
18.58 Sammy Baugh, Washington vs. Boston, Oct. 31, 1948 (24-446)
18.50 Johnny Unitas, Baltimore vs. Atlanta, Nov. 12, 1967 (20-370)
17.71 Joe Namath, N.Y. Jets vs. Baltimore, Sept. 24, 1972 (28-496)

Touchdowns

Most Seasons Leading League
4 Johnny Unitas, Baltimore, 1957-60
Len Dawson, Dall. Texans, 1962; Kansas City, 1963, 1965-66
3 Arnie Herber, Green Bay, 1932, 1934, 1936
Sid Luckman, Chi. Bears, 1943, 1945-46
Y.A. Tittle, San Francisco, 1955; N.Y. Giants, 1962-63
Dan Marino, Miami, 1984-86
2 By many players

Most Consecutive Seasons Leading League
4 Johnny Unitas, Baltimore, 1957-60
3 Dan Marino, Miami, 1984-86
2 By many players

Most Touchdown Passes, Career
342 Fran Tarkenton, Minnesota, 1961-66, 1972-78; N.Y. Giants, 1967-71
290 Johnny Unitas, Baltimore, 1956-72: San Diego, 1973
255 Sonny Jurgensen, Philadelphia, 1957-63; Washington, 1964-74

Most Touchdown Passes, Season
48 Dan Marino, Miami, 1984
44 Dan Marino, Miami, 1986
36 George Blanda, Houston, 1961
Y.A. Tittle, N.Y. Giants, 1963

Most Touchdown Passes, Rookie, Season
22 Charlie Conerly, N.Y. Giants, 1948
20 Dan Marino, Miami, 1983
19 Jim Plunkett, New England, 1971

Most Touchdown Passes, Game
7 Sid Luckman, Chi. Bears vs. N.Y. Giants, Nov. 14, 1943
Adrian Burk, Philadelphia vs. Washington, Oct. 17, 1954
George Blanda, Houston vs. N.Y. Titans, Nov. 19, 1961
Y.A. Tittle, N.Y. Giants vs. Washington, Oct. 28, 1962
Joe Kapp, Minnesota vs. Baltimore, Sept. 28, 1969
6 By many players. Last time: Joe Montana, San Francisco vs. Atlanta, Oct. 14, 1990

Most Games, Four or More Touchdown Passes, Career
17 Johnny Unitas, Baltimore, 1956-72; San Diego, 1973
16 Dan Marino, Miami, 1983-90
13 George Blanda, Chi. Bears, 1949, 1950-58; Baltimore, 1950; Houston, 1960-66; Oakland, 1967-75

Most Games, Four or More Touchdown Passes, Season
6 Dan Marino, Miami, 1984
5 Dan Marino, Miami, 1986
4 George Blanda, Houston, 1961
Vince Ferragamo, Los Angeles, 1980

Most Consecutive Games, Four or More Touchdown Passes
4 Dan Marino, Miami, 1984
2 By many players

Most Consecutive Games, Touchdown Passes
47 Johnny Unitas, Baltimore, 1956-60
30 Dan Marino, Miami, 1985-87
28 Dave Krieg, Seattle, 1983-85

Had Intercepted

Most Consecutive Passes Attempted, None Intercepted
294 Bart Starr, Green Bay, 1964-65
233 Steve DeBerg, Kansas City, 1990
214 Fran Tarkenton, N.Y. Giants, 1968-69

Most Passes Had Intercepted, Career
277 George Blanda, Chi. Bears, 1949, 1950-58; Baltimore, 1950; Houston, 1960-66; Oakland, 1967-75
268 John Hadl, San Diego, 1962-72; Los Angeles, 1973-74; Green Bay, 1974-75; Houston, 1976-77
266 Fran Tarkenton, Minnesota, 1961-66, 1972-78; N.Y. Giants, 1967-71

Most Passes Had Intercepted, Season
42 George Blanda, Houston, 1962
35 Vinny Testaverde, Tampa Bay, 1988
34 Frank Tripucka, Denver, 1960

Most Passes Had Intercepted, Game
8 Jim Hardy, Chi. Cardinals vs. Philadelphia, Sept. 24, 1950
7 Parker Hall, Cleveland vs. Green Bay, Nov. 8, 1942
Frank Sinkwich, Detroit vs. Green Bay, Oct. 24, 1943
Bob Waterfield, Los Angeles vs. Green Bay, Oct. 17, 1948
Zeke Bratkowski, Chicago vs. Baltimore, Oct. 2, 1960
Tommy Wade, Pittsburgh vs. Philadelphia, Dec. 12, 1965
Ken Stabler, Oakland vs. Denver, Oct. 16, 1977
Steve DeBerg, Tampa Bay vs. San Francisco, Sept. 7, 1986
6 By many players

Most Attempts, No Interceptions, Game
60 Davey O'Brien, Philadelphia vs. Washington, Dec. 1, 1940
57 Joe Montana, San Francisco vs. Atlanta, Oct. 6, 1985
54 Dan Marino, Miami vs. Buffalo, Nov. 16, 1986
Dan Marino, Miami vs. Philadelphia, Dec. 9, 1990 (OT)

Lowest Percentage, Passes Had Intercepted

Most Seasons Leading League, Lowest Percentage, Passes Had Intercepted
5 Sammy Baugh, Washington, 1940, 1942, 1944-45, 1947
3 Charlie Conerly, N.Y. Giants, 1950, 1956, 1959
Bart Starr, Green Bay, 1962, 1964, 1966
Roger Staubach, Dallas, 1971, 1977, 1979
Ken Anderson, Cincinnati, 1972, 1981-82
Ken O'Brien, N.Y. Jets, 1985, 1987-88
2 By many players

Lowest Percentage, Passes Had Intercepted, Career (1,500 attempts)
2.62 Bernie Kosar, Cleveland, 1985-90 (2,363-62)
2.69 Joe Montana, San Francisco, 1979-90 (4,579-123)
2.71 Ken O'Brien, N.Y. Jets, 1984-90 (2,878-78)

Lowest Percentage, Passes Had Intercepted, Season (Qualifiers)
0.66 Joe Ferguson, Buffalo, 1976 (151-1)
0.90 Steve DeBerg, Kansas City, 1990 (444-4)
1.16 Steve Bartkowski, Atlanta, 1983 (432-5)

Lowest Percentage, Passes Had Intercepted, Rookie, Season (Qualifiers)
2.03 Dan Marino, Miami, 1983 (296-6)
2.10 Gary Wood, N.Y. Giants, 1964 (143-3)
2.82 Bernie Kosar, Cleveland, 1985 (248-7)

Times Sacked

Times Sacked has been compiled since 1963.

Most Times Sacked, Career
483 Fran Tarkenton, Minnesota, 1961-66, 1972-78; N.Y. Giants, 1967-71
416 Phil Simms, N.Y. Giants, 1979-81, 1983-90
405 Craig Morton, Dallas, 1965-74; N.Y. Giants, 1974-76; Denver, 1977-82

Most Times Sacked, Season
72 Randall Cunningham, Philadelphia, 1986
62 Ken O'Brien, N.Y. Jets, 1985
61 Neil Lomax, St. Louis, 1985

Most Times Sacked, Game
12 Bert Jones, Baltimore vs. St. Louis, Oct. 26, 1980
Warren Moon, Houston vs. Dallas, Sept. 29, 1985
11 Charley Johnson, St. Louis vs. N.Y. Giants, Nov. 1, 1964
Bart Starr, Green Bay vs. Detroit, Nov. 7, 1965
Jack Kemp, Buffalo vs. Oakland, Oct. 15, 1967
Bob Berry, Atlanta vs. St. Louis, Nov. 24, 1968
Greg Landry, Detroit vs. Dallas, Oct. 6, 1975
Ron Jaworski, Philadelphia vs. St. Louis, Dec. 18, 1983
Paul McDonald, Cleveland vs. Kansas City, Sept. 30, 1984
Archie Manning, Minnesota vs. Chicago, Oct. 28, 1984
Steve Pelluer, Dallas vs. San Diego, Nov. 16, 1986
Randall Cunningham, Philadelphia vs. L.A. Raiders, Nov. 30, 1986 (OT)
David Norrie, N.Y. Jets vs. Dallas, Oct. 4, 1987
10 By many players

Pass Receiving

Most Seasons Leading League
8 Don Hutson, Green Bay, 1936-37, 1939, 1941-45
5 Lionel Taylor, Denver, 1960-63, 1965
3 Tom Fears, Los Angeles, 1948-50
Pete Pihos, Philadelphia, 1953-55
Billy Wilson, San Francisco, 1954, 1956-57
Raymond Berry, Baltimore, 1958-60
Lance Alworth, San Diego, 1966, 1968-69

Most Consecutive Seasons Leading League
5 Don Hutson, Green Bay, 1941-45
4 Lionel Taylor, Denver, 1960-63
3 Tom Fears, Los Angeles, 1948-50
Pete Pihos, Philadelphia, 1953-55
Raymond Berry, Baltimore, 1958-60

Most Pass Receptions, Career
819 Steve Largent, Seattle, 1976-89
750 Charlie Joiner, Houston, 1969-72; Cincinnati, 1972-75; San Diego, 1976-86
730 Art Monk, Washington, 1980-90

Most Seasons, 50 or More Pass Receptions
10 Steve Largent, Seattle, 1976, 1978-81, 1983-87
8 Art Monk, Washington, 1980-81, 1984-86, 1988-90
7 Raymond Berry, Baltimore, 1958-62, 1965-66
Art Powell, N.Y. Titans, 1960-62; Oakland, 1963-66
Lance Alworth, San Diego, 1963-69
Charley Taylor, Washington, 1964, 1966-67, 1969, 1973-75
Charlie Joiner, San Diego, 1976, 1979-81, 1983-85
Wes Chandler, New Orleans, 1979-80; New Orleans-San Diego, 1981; San Diego, 1983-86
Dwight Clark, San Francisco, 1980-86
James Lofton, Green Bay, 1979-81, 1983-86
Kellen Winslow, San Diego, 1980-84, 1986-87

Most Pass Receptions, Season
106 Art Monk, Washington, 1984
101 Charley Hennigan, Houston, 1964
100 Lionel Taylor, Denver, 1961
Jerry Rice, San Francisco, 1990

Most Pass Receptions, Rookie, Season
83 Earl Cooper, San Francisco, 1980
81 Keith Jackson, Philadelphia, 1988
72 Bill Groman, Houston, 1960

Most Pass Receptions, Game
18 Tom Fears, Los Angeles vs. Green Bay, Dec. 3, 1950
17 Clark Gaines, N.Y. Jets vs. San Francisco, Sept. 21, 1980
16 Sonny Randle, St. Louis vs. N.Y. Giants, Nov. 4, 1962

Most Consecutive Games, Pass Receptions
177 Steve Largent, Seattle, 1977-89
150 Ozzie Newsome, Cleveland, 1979-89
127 Harold Carmichael, Philadelphia, 1972-80

Yards Gained

Most Seasons Leading League
7 Don Hutson, Green Bay, 1936, 1938-39, 1941-44
3 Raymond Berry, Baltimore, 1957, 1959-60
Lance Alworth, San Diego, 1965-66, 1968
Jerry Rice, San Francisco, 1986, 1989-90
2 By many players

Most Consecutive Seasons Leading League
4 Don Hutson, Green Bay, 1941-44
2 By many players

Most Yards Gained, Career
13,089 Steve Largent, Seattle, 1976-89
12,146 Charlie Joiner, Houston, 1969-72; Cincinnati, 1972-75; San Diego, 1976-86
11,963 James Lofton, Green Bay, 1978-86; L.A. Raiders, 1987-88; Buffalo, 1989-90

Most Seasons, 1,000 or More Yards, Pass Receiving
8 Steve Largent, Seattle, 1978-81, 1983-86
7 Lance Alworth, San Diego, 1963-69

5 Art Powell, N.Y. Titans, 1960, 1962; Oakland, 1963-64, 1966
Don Maynard, N.Y. Jets, 1960, 1962, 1965, 1967-68
James Lofton, Green Bay, 1980-81, 1983-85
Jerry Rice, San Francisco, 1986-90

Most Yards Gained, Season
1,746 Charley Hennigan, Houston, 1961
1,602 Lance Alworth, San Diego, 1965
1,570 Jerry Rice, San Francisco, 1986

Most Yards Gained, Rookie, Season
1,473 Bill Groman, Houston, 1960
1,231 Bill Howton, Green Bay, 1952
1,131 Bill Brooks, Indianapolis, 1986

Most Yards Gained, Game
336 Willie Anderson, L.A. Rams vs. New Orleans, Nov. 26, 1989 (OT)
309 Stephone Paige, Kansas City vs. San Diego, Dec. 22, 1985
303 Jim Benton, Cleveland vs. Detroit, Nov. 22, 1945

Most Games, 200 or More Yards Pass Receiving, Career
5 Lance Alworth, San Diego, 1962-70; Dallas, 1971-72
4 Don Hutson, Green Bay, 1935-45
Charley Hennigan, Houston, 1960-66
3 Don Maynard, N.Y. Giants, 1958; N.Y. Jets, 1960-72; St. Louis, 1973
Wes Chandler, New Orleans, 1978-81; San Diego, 1981-87; San Francisco, 1988
Jerry Rice, San Francisco, 1985-90

Most Games, 200 or More Yards Pass Receiving, Season
3 Charley Hennigan, Houston, 1961
2 Don Hutson, Green Bay, 1942
Gene Roberts, N.Y. Giants, 1949
Lance Alworth, San Diego, 1963
Don Maynard, N.Y. Jets, 1968

Most Games, 100 or More Yards Pass Receiving, Career
50 Don Maynard, N.Y. Giants, 1958; N.Y. Jets, 1960-72; St. Louis, 1973
41 Lance Alworth, San Diego, 1962-70; Dallas, 1971-72
40 Steve Largent, Seattle, 1976-89

Most Games, 100 or More Yards Pass Receiving, Season
10 Charley Hennigan, Houston, 1961
9 Elroy (Crazylegs) Hirsch, Los Angeles, 1951
Bill Groman, Houston, 1960
Lance Alworth, San Diego, 1965
Don Maynard, N.Y. Jets, 1967
Stanley Morgan, New England, 1986
Mark Carrier, Tampa Bay, 1989
8 Charley Hennigan, Houston, 1964
Lance Alworth, San Diego, 1967
Mark Duper, Miami, 1986
Jerry Rice, San Francisco, 1989

Most Consecutive Games, 100 or More Yards Pass Receiving
7 Charley Hennigan, Houston, 1961
Bill Groman, Houston, 1961
6 Raymond Berry, Baltimore, 1960
Pat Studstill, Detroit, 1966
5 Elroy (Crazylegs) Hirsch, Los Angeles, 1951
Bob Boyd, Los Angeles, 1954
Terry Barr, Detroit, 1963
Lance Alworth, San Diego, 1966

Longest Pass Reception (All TDs except as noted)
99 Andy Farkas (from Filchock), Washington vs. Pittsburgh, Oct. 15, 1939
Bobby Mitchell (from Izo), Washington vs. Cleveland, Sept. 15, 1963
Pat Studstill (from Sweetan), Detroit vs. Baltimore, Oct. 16, 1966
Gerry Allen (from Jurgensen), Washington vs. Chicago, Sept. 15, 1968
Cliff Branch (from Plunkett), L.A. Raiders vs. Washington, Oct. 2, 1983
Mike Quick (from Jaworski), Philadelphia vs. Atlanta, Nov. 10, 1985
98 Gaynell Tinsley (from Russell), Chi. Cardinals vs. Cleveland, Nov. 17, 1938
Dick (Night Train) Lane (from Compton), Chi. Cardinals vs. Green Bay, Nov. 13, 1955
John Farrington (from Wade), Chicago vs. Detroit, Oct. 8, 1961
Willard Dewveall (from Lee), Houston vs. San Diego, Nov. 25, 1962
Homer Jones (from Morrall), N.Y. Giants vs. Pittsburgh, Sept. 11, 1966
Bobby Moore (from Hart), St. Louis vs. Los Angeles, Dec. 10, 1972 (no TD)
97 Gaynell Tinsley (from Coffee), Chi. Cardinals vs. Chi. Bears, Dec. 5, 1937
Cloyce Box (from Layne), Detroit vs. Green Bay, Nov. 26, 1953
Jerry Tarr (from Shaw), Denver vs. Boston, Sept. 21, 1962
Webster Slaughter (from Kosar), Cleveland vs. Chicago, Oct. 23, 1989

Average Gain

Highest Average Gain, Career (200 receptions)
22.26 Homer Jones, N.Y. Giants, 1964-69; Cleveland, 1970 (224-4,986)
20.83 Buddy Dial, Pittsburgh, 1959-63; Dallas, 1964-66 (261-5,436)
20.56 Willie Gault, Chicago, 1983-87; L.A. Raiders, 1988-90 (278-5,717)

Highest Average Gain, Season (24 receptions)
32.58 Don Currivan, Boston, 1947 (24-782)
31.44 Bucky Pope, Los Angeles, 1964 (25-786)
28.60 Bobby Duckworth, San Diego, 1984 (25-715)

Highest Average Gain, Game (3 receptions)
60.67 Bill Groman, Houston vs. Denver, Nov. 20, 1960 (3-182)
Homer Jones, N.Y. Giants vs. Washington, Dec. 12, 1965 (3-182)
60.33 Don Currivan, Boston vs. Washington, Nov. 30, 1947 (3-181)
59.67 Bobby Duckworth, San Diego vs. Chicago, Dec. 3, 1984 (3-179)

Touchdowns

Most Seasons Leading League
9 Don Hutson, Green Bay, 1935-38, 1940-44
4 Jerry Rice, San Francisco, 1986-87, 1989-90
3 Lance Alworth, San Diego, 1964-66

Most Consecutive Seasons Leading League
5 Don Hutson, Green Bay, 1940-44
4 Don Hutson, Green Bay, 1935-38
3 Lance Alworth, San Diego, 1964-66

Most Touchdowns, Career
100 Steve Largent, Seattle, 1976-89
99 Don Hutson, Green Bay, 1935-45
88 Don Maynard, N.Y. Giants, 1958; N.Y. Jets, 1960-72; St. Louis, 1973

Most Touchdowns, Season
22 Jerry Rice, San Francisco, 1987
18 Mark Clayton, Miami, 1984
17 Don Hutson, Green Bay, 1942
Elroy (Crazylegs) Hirsch, Los Angeles, 1951
Bill Groman, Houston, 1961
Jerry Rice, San Francisco, 1989

Most Touchdowns, Rookie, Season
13 Bill Howton, Green Bay, 1952
John Jefferson, San Diego, 1979
12 Harlon Hill, Chi. Bears, 1954
Bill Groman, Houston, 1960
Mike Ditka, Chicago, 1961
Bob Hayes, Dallas, 1965
10 Bill Swiacki, N.Y. Giants, 1948
Bucky Pope, Los Angeles, 1964
Sammy White, Minnesota, 1976
Daryl Turner, Seattle, 1984

Most Touchdowns, Game
5 Bob Shaw, Chi. Cardinals vs. Baltimore, Oct. 2, 1950
Kellen Winslow, San Diego vs. Oakland, Nov. 22, 1981
Jerry Rice, San Francisco vs. Atlanta, Oct. 14, 1990
4 By many players

Most Consecutive Games, Touchdowns
13 Jerry Rice, San Francisco, 1986-87
11 Elroy (Crazylegs) Hirsch, Los Angeles, 1950-51
Buddy Dial, Pittsburgh, 1959-60
9 Lance Alworth, San Diego, 1963

Interceptions By

Most Seasons Leading League
3 Everson Walls, Dallas, 1981-82, 1985
2 Dick (Night Train) Lane, Los Angeles, 1952; Chi. Cardinals, 1954
Jack Christiansen, Detroit, 1953, 1957
Milt Davis, Baltimore, 1957, 1959
Dick Lynch, N.Y. Giants, 1961, 1963
Johnny Robinson, Kansas City, 1966, 1970
Bill Bradley, Philadelphia, 1971-72
Emmitt Thomas, Kansas City, 1969, 1974

Most Interceptions By, Career
81 Paul Krause, Washington, 1964-67; Minnesota, 1968-79
79 Emlen Tunnell, N.Y. Giants, 1948-58; Green Bay, 1959-61
68 Dick (Night Train) Lane, Los Angeles, 1952-53; Chi. Cardinals, 1954-59; Detroit, 1960-65

Most Interceptions By, Season
14 Dick (Night Train) Lane, Los Angeles, 1952
13 Dan Sandifer, Washington, 1948
Orban (Spec) Sanders, N.Y. Yanks, 1950
Lester Hayes, Oakland, 1980
12 By nine players

Most Interceptions By, Rookie, Season
14 Dick (Night Train) Lane, Los Angeles, 1952
13 Dan Sandifer, Washington, 1948
12 Woodley Lewis, Los Angeles, 1950
Paul Krause, Washington, 1964

Most Interceptions By, Game
4 Sammy Baugh, Washington vs. Detroit, Nov. 14, 1943
Dan Sandifer, Washington vs. Boston, Oct. 31, 1948
Don Doll, Detroit vs. Chi. Cardinals, Oct. 23, 1949
Bob Nussbaumer, Chi. Cardinals vs. N.Y. Bulldogs, Nov. 13, 1949
Russ Craft, Philadelphia vs. Chi. Cardinals, Sept. 24, 1950
Bobby Dillon, Green Bay vs. Detroit, Nov. 26, 1953
Jack Butler, Pittsburgh vs. Washington, Dec. 13, 1953
Austin (Goose) Gonsoulin, Denver vs. Buffalo, Sept. 18, 1960
Jerry Norton, St. Louis vs. Washington, Nov. 20, 1960; vs. Pittsburgh, Nov. 26, 1961
Dave Baker, San Francisco vs. L.A. Rams, Dec. 4, 1960
Bobby Ply, Dall. Texans vs. San Diego, Dec. 16, 1962
Bobby Hunt, Kansas City vs. Houston, Oct. 4, 1964
Willie Brown, Denver vs. N.Y. Jets, Nov. 15, 1964
Dick Anderson, Miami vs. Pittsburgh, Dec. 3, 1973
Willie Buchanon, Green Bay vs. San Diego, Sept. 24, 1978
Deron Cherry, Kansas City vs. Seattle, Sept. 29, 1985

Most Consecutive Games, Passes Intercepted By
8 Tom Morrow, Oakland, 1962-63
7 Paul Krause, Washington, 1964
Larry Wilson, St. Louis, 1966
Ben Davis, Cleveland, 1968
6 Dick (Night Train) Lane, Chi. Cardinals, 1954-55
Will Sherman, Los Angeles, 1954-55
Jim Shofner, Cleveland, 1960
Paul Krause, Minnesota, 1968
Willie Williams, N.Y. Giants, 1968
Kermit Alexander, San Francisco, 1968-69
Mel Blount, Pittsburgh, 1975
Eric Harris, Kansas City, 1980
Lester Hayes, Oakland, 1980
Barry Wilburn, Washington, 1987

Yards Gained

Most Seasons Leading League
2 Dick (Night Train) Lane, Los Angeles, 1952; Chi. Cardinals, 1954
Herb Adderley, Green Bay, 1965, 1969
Dick Anderson, Miami, 1968, 1970

Most Yards Gained, Career
1,282 Emlen Tunnell, N.Y. Giants, 1948-58; Green Bay, 1959-61
1,207 Dick (Night Train) Lane, Los Angeles, 1952-53; Chi. Cardinals, 1954-59; Detroit, 1960-65
1,185 Paul Krause, Washington, 1964-67; Minnesota, 1968-79

Most Yards Gained, Season
349 Charlie McNeil, San Diego, 1961
301 Don Doll, Detroit, 1949
298 Dick (Night Train) Lane, Los Angeles, 1952

Most Yards Gained, Rookie, Season
301 Don Doll, Detroit, 1949
298 Dick (Night Train) Lane, Los Angeles, 1952
275 Woodley Lewis, Los Angeles, 1950

Most Yards Gained, Game
177 Charlie McNeil, San Diego vs. Houston, Sept. 24, 1961
167 Dick Jauron, Detroit vs. Chicago, Nov. 18, 1973
151 Tom Myers, New Orleans vs. Minnesota, Sept. 3, 1978
Mike Haynes, L.A. Raiders vs. Miami, Dec. 2, 1984

Longest Return (All TDs)
103 Vencie Glenn, San Diego vs. Denver, Nov. 29, 1987
102 Bob Smith, Detroit vs. Chi. Bears, Nov. 24, 1949
Erich Barnes, N.Y. Giants vs. Dall. Cowboys, Oct. 15, 1961
Gary Barbaro, Kansas City vs. Seattle, Dec. 11, 1977
Louis Breeden, Cincinnati vs. San Diego, Nov. 8, 1981
101 Richie Petitbon, Chicago vs Los Angeles, Dec. 9, 1962
Henry Carr, N.Y. Giants vs. Los Angeles, Nov. 13, 1966
Tony Greene, Buffalo vs. Kansas City, Oct. 3, 1976
Tom Pridemore, Atlanta vs. San Francisco, Sept. 20, 1981

Touchdowns

Most Touchdowns, Career
9 Ken Houston, Houston, 1967-72; Washington, 1973-80
7 Herb Adderley, Green Bay, 1961-69; Dallas, 1970-72
Erich Barnes, Chi. Bears, 1958-60; N.Y. Giants, 1961-64; Cleveland, 1965-70
Lem Barney, Detroit, 1967-77
6 Tom Janik, Denver, 1963-64; Buffalo, 1965-68; Boston, 1969-70; New England, 1971
Miller Farr, Denver, 1965; San Diego, 1965-66; Houston, 1967-69; St. Louis, 1970-72; Detroit, 1973
Bobby Bell, Kansas City, 1963-74

Most Touchdowns, Season
4 Ken Houston, Houston, 1971
Jim Kearney, Kansas City, 1972
3 Dick Harris, San Diego, 1961
Dick Lynch, N.Y. Giants, 1963
Herb Adderley, Green Bay, 1965
Lem Barney, Detroit, 1967
Miller Farr, Houston, 1967
Monte Jackson, Los Angeles, 1976
Rod Perry, Los Angeles, 1978
Ronnie Lott, San Francisco, 1981
Lloyd Burruss, Kansas City, 1986
Wayne Haddix, Tampa Bay, 1990
2 By many players

Most Touchdowns, Rookie, Season
3 Lem Barney, Detroit, 1967
Ronnie Lott, San Francisco, 1981
2 By many players

Most Touchdowns, Game
2 Bill Blackburn, Chi. Cardinals vs. Boston, Oct. 24, 1948
Dan Sandifer, Washington vs. Boston, Oct. 31, 1948
Bob Franklin, Cleveland vs. Chicago, Dec. 11, 1960
Bill Stacy, St. Louis vs. Dall. Cowboys, Nov. 5, 1961
Jerry Norton, St. Louis vs. Pittsburgh, Nov. 26, 1961
Miller Farr, Houston vs. Buffalo, Dec. 7, 1968
Ken Houston, Houston vs. San Diego, Dec. 19, 1971
Jim Kearney, Kansas City vs. Denver, Oct. 1, 1972
Lemar Parrish, Cincinnati vs. Houston, Dec. 17, 1972
Dick Anderson, Miami vs. Pittsburgh, Dec. 3, 1973
Prentice McCray, New England vs. N.Y. Jets, Nov. 21, 1976
Kenny Johnson, Atlanta vs. Green Bay, Nov. 27, 1983 (OT)
Mike Kozlowski, Miami vs. N.Y. Jets, Dec. 16, 1983
Dave Brown, Seattle vs. Kansas City, Nov. 4, 1984
Lloyd Burruss, Kansas City vs. San Diego, Oct. 19, 1986

Punting

Most Seasons Leading League
4 Sammy Baugh, Washington, 1940-43
Jerrel Wilson, Kansas City, 1965, 1968, 1972-73
3 Yale Lary, Detroit, 1959, 1961, 1963
Jim Fraser, Denver, 1962-64
Ray Guy, Oakland, 1974-75, 1977
Rohn Stark, Baltimore, 1983; Indianapolis, 1985-86
2 By many players

Most Consecutive Seasons Leading League
4 Sammy Baugh, Washington, 1940-43
3 Jim Fraser, Denver, 1962-64
2 By many players

Punts

Most Punts, Career
1,154 Dave Jennings, N.Y. Giants, 1974-84; N.Y. Jets, 1985-87
1,083 John James, Atlanta, 1972-81; Detroit, 1982, Houston, 1982-84
1,072 Jerrel Wilson, Kansas City, 1963-77; New England, 1978

Most Punts, Season
114 Bob Parsons, Chicago, 1981
109 John James, Atlanta, 1978
108 John Teltschik, Philadelphia, 1986

Most Punts, Rookie, Season
108 John Teltschik, Philadelphia, 1986
99 Lewis Colbert, Kansas City, 1986
96 Mike Connell, San Francisco, 1978
Chris Norman, Denver, 1984

Most Punts, Game
15 John Teltschik, Philadelphia vs. N.Y. Giants, Dec. 6, 1987 (OT)
14 Dick Nesbitt, Chi. Cardinals vs. Chi. Bears, Nov. 30, 1933
Keith Molesworth, Chi. Bears vs. Green Bay, Dec. 10, 1933
Sammy Baugh, Washington vs. Philadelphia, Nov. 5, 1939
Carl Kinscherf, N.Y. Giants vs. Detroit, Nov. 7, 1943
George Taliaferro, N.Y. Yanks vs. Los Angeles, Sept. 28, 1951
12 By many players. Last time: Bryan Wagner, Cleveland vs. Kansas City, Nov. 19, 1989 (OT)

Longest Punt
98 Steve O'Neal, N.Y. Jets vs. Denver, Sept. 21, 1969
94 Joe Lintzenich, Chi. Bears vs. N.Y. Giants, Nov. 16, 1931
91 Randall Cunningham, Philadelphia vs. N.Y. Giants, Dec. 3, 1989

Average Yardage

Highest Average, Punting, Career (300 punts)
45.10 Sammy Baugh, Washington, 1937-52 (338-15,245)
44.68 Tommy Davis, San Francisco, 1959-69 (511-22,833)
44.29 Yale Lary, Detroit, 1952-53, 1956-64 (503-22,279)

Highest Average, Punting, Season (Qualifiers)
51.40 Sammy Baugh, Washington, 1940 (35-1,799)
48.94 Yale Lary, Detroit, 1963 (35-1,713)
48.73 Sammy Baugh, Washington, 1941 (30-1,462)

Highest Average, Punting, Rookie, Season (Qualifiers)
46.40 Bobby Walden, Minnesota, 1964 (72-3,341)
46.22 Dave Lewis, Cincinnati, 1970 (79-3,651)
45.92 Frank Sinkwich, Detroit, 1943 (12-551)

Highest Average, Punting, Game (4 punts)
61.75 Bob Cifers, Detroit vs. Chi. Bears, Nov. 24, 1946 (4-247)
61.60 Roy McKay, Green Bay vs. Chi. Cardinals, Oct. 28, 1945 (5-308)
59.40 Sammy Baugh, Washington vs. Detroit, Oct. 27, 1940 (5-297)

Punts Had Blocked

Most Consecutive Punts, None Blocked
623 Dave Jennings, N.Y. Giants, 1976-83
619 Ray Guy, Oakland, 1979-81; L.A. Raiders, 1982-86
578 Bobby Walden, Minnesota, 1964-67; Pittsburgh, 1968-72

Most Punts Had Blocked, Career
14 Herman Weaver, Detroit, 1970-76; Seattle, 1977-80
13 Harry Newsome, Pittsburgh, 1985-89; Minnesota, 1990
12 Jerrel Wilson, Kansas City, 1963-77; New England, 1978
Tom Blanchard, N.Y. Giants, 1971-73; New Orleans, 1974-78; Tampa Bay, 1979-81

Most Punts Had Blocked, Season
6 Harry Newsome, Pittsburgh, 1988
4 Bryan Wagner, Cleveland, 1990
3 By many players

Punt Returns

Most Seasons Leading League
3 Les (Speedy) Duncan, San Diego, 1965-66; Washington, 1971
Rick Upchurch, Denver, 1976, 1978, 1982
2 Dick Christy, N.Y. Titans, 1961-62
Claude Gibson, Oakland, 1963-64
Billy Johnson, Houston, 1975, 1977

Punt Returns

Most Punt Returns, Career
282 Billy Johnson, Houston, 1974-80; Atlanta, 1982-87; Washington, 1988
267 J.T. Smith, Washington, 1978; Kansas City, 1978-84; St. Louis, 1985-87; Phoenix, 1988-90
258 Emlen Tunnell, N.Y. Giants, 1948-58; Green Bay, 1959-61

Most Punt Returns, Season
70 Danny Reece, Tampa Bay, 1979
62 Fulton Walker, Miami-L.A. Raiders, 1985
58 J. T. Smith, Kansas City, 1979
Greg Pruitt, L.A. Raiders, 1983
Leo Lewis, Minnesota, 1988

Most Punt Returns, Rookie, Season
57 Lew Barnes, Chicago, 1986
54 James Jones, Dallas, 1980
53 Louis Lipps, Pittsburgh, 1984

Most Punt Returns, Game
11 Eddie Brown, Washington vs. Tampa Bay, Oct. 9, 1977
10 Theo Bell, Pittsburgh vs. Buffalo, Dec. 16, 1979
Mike Nelms, Washington vs. New Orleans, Dec. 26, 1982
9 Rodger Bird, Oakland vs. Denver, Sept. 10, 1967
Ralph McGill, San Francisco vs. Atlanta, Oct. 29, 1972
Ed Podolak, Kansas City vs. San Diego, Nov. 10, 1974
Anthony Leonard, San Francisco vs. New Orleans, Oct. 17, 1976
Butch Johnson, Dallas vs. Buffalo, Nov. 15, 1976
Larry Marshall, Philadelphia vs. Tampa Bay, Sept. 18, 1977
Nesby Glasgow, Baltimore vs. Kansas City, Sept. 2, 1979
Mike Nelms, Washington vs. St. Louis, Dec. 21, 1980
Leon Bright, N.Y. Giants vs. Philadelphia, Dec. 11, 1982
Pete Shaw, N.Y. Giants vs. Philadelphia, Nov. 20, 1983
Cleotha Montgomery, L.A. Raiders vs. Detroit, Dec. 10, 1984
Phil McConkey, N.Y. Giants vs. Philadelphia, Dec. 6, 1987 (OT)

Fair Catches

Most Fair Catches, Career
102 Willie Wood, Green Bay, 1960-71
99 Phil McConkey, N.Y. Giants, 1984-88; Green Bay, 1986; San Diego, 1989
83 Leo Lewis, Minnesota, 1981-90; Cleveland 1990

Most Fair Catches, Season
27 Leo Lewis, Minnesota, 1989
25 Mark Konecny, Philadelphia, 1988
Phil McConkey, N.Y. Giants, 1988
24 Ken Graham, San Diego, 1969

Most Fair Catches, Game
7 Lem Barney, Detroit vs. Chicago, Nov. 21, 1976
Bobby Morse, Philadelphia vs. Buffalo, Dec. 27, 1987
6 Jake Scott, Miami vs. Buffalo, Dec. 20, 1970
Greg Pruitt, L.A. Raiders vs. Seattle, Oct. 7, 1984
Phil McConkey, San Diego vs. Kansas City, Dec. 17, 1989
Gerald McNeil, Houston vs. Pittsburgh, Sept. 16, 1990
5 By many players

Yards Gained

Most Seasons Leading League
3 Alvin Haymond, Baltimore, 1965-66; Los Angeles, 1969
2 Bill Dudley, Pittsburgh, 1942, 1946

Emlen Tunnell, N.Y. Giants, 1951-52
Dick Christy, N.Y. Titans, 1961-62
Claude Gibson, Oakland, 1963-64
Rodger Bird, Oakland, 1966-67
J. T. Smith, Kansas City, 1979-80
Vai Sikahema, St. Louis, 1986-87
David Meggett, N.Y. Giants, 1989-90

Most Yards Gained, Career
3,317 Billy Johnson, Houston, 1974-80; Atlanta, 1982-87; Washington, 1988
3,008 Rick Upchurch, Denver, 1975-83
2,764 J.T. Smith, Washington, 1978; Kansas City, 1978-84; St. Louis, 1985-87; Phoenix, 1988-90

Most Yards Gained, Season
692 Fulton Walker, Miami-L.A. Raiders, 1985
666 Greg Pruitt, L.A. Raiders, 1983
656 Louis Lipps, Pittsburgh, 1984

Most Yards Gained, Rookie, Season
656 Louis Lipps, Pittsburgh, 1984
655 Neal Colzie, Oakland, 1975
608 Mike Haynes, New England, 1976

Most Yards Gained, Game
207 LeRoy Irvin, Los Angeles vs. Atlanta, Oct. 11, 1981
205 George Atkinson, Oakland vs. Buffalo, Sept. 15, 1968
184 Tom Watkins, Detroit vs. San Francisco, Oct. 6, 1963

Longest Punt Return (All TDs)
98 Gil LeFebvre, Cincinnati vs. Brooklyn, Dec. 3, 1933
Charlie West, Minnesota vs. Washington, Nov. 3, 1968
Dennis Morgan, Dallas vs. St. Louis, Oct. 13, 1974
Terance Mathis, N.Y. Jets vs. Dallas, Nov. 4, 1990
97 Greg Pruitt, L.A. Raiders vs. Washington, Oct. 2, 1983
96 Bill Dudley, Washington vs. Pittsburgh, Dec. 3, 1950

Average Yardage

Highest Average, Career (75 returns)
12.78 George McAfee, Chi. Bears, 1940-41, 1945-50 (112-1,431)
12.75 Jack Christiansen, Detroit, 1951-58 (85-1,084)
12.55 Claude Gibson, San Diego, 1961-62; Oakland, 1963-65 (110-1,381)

Highest Average, Season (Qualifiers)
23.00 Herb Rich, Baltimore, 1950 (12-276)
21.47 Jack Christiansen, Detroit, 1952 (15-322)
21.28 Dick Christy, N.Y. Titans, 1961 (18-383)

Highest Average, Rookie, Season (Qualifiers)
23.00 Herb Rich, Baltimore, 1950 (12-276)
20.88 Jerry Davis, Chi. Cardinals, 1948 (16-334)
20.73 Frank Sinkwich, Detroit, 1943 (11-228)

Highest Average, Game (3 returns)
47.67 Chuck Latourette, St. Louis vs. New Orleans, Sept. 29, 1968 (3-143)
47.33 Johnny Roland, St. Louis vs. Philadelphia, Oct. 2, 1966 (3-142)
45.67 Dick Christy, N.Y. Titans vs. Denver, Sept. 24, 1961 (3-137)

Touchdowns

Most Touchdowns, Career
8 Jack Christiansen, Detroit, 1951-58
Rick Upchurch, Denver, 1975-83
6 Billy Johnson, Houston, 1974-80; Atlanta, 1982-87; Washington, 1988
5 Emlen Tunnell, N.Y. Giants, 1948-58; Green Bay, 1959-61

Most Touchdowns, Season
4 Jack Christiansen, Detroit, 1951
Rick Upchurch, Denver, 1976
3 Emlen Tunnell, N.Y. Giants, 1951
Billy Johnson, Houston, 1975
LeRoy Irvin, Los Angeles, 1981
2 By many players

Most Touchdowns, Rookie, Season
4 Jack Christiansen, Detroit, 1951
2 By six players

Most Touchdowns, Game
2 Jack Christiansen, Detroit vs. Los Angeles, Oct. 14, 1951; vs. Green Bay, Nov. 22, 1951
Dick Christy, N.Y. Titans vs. Denver, Sept. 24, 1961
Rick Upchurch, Denver vs. Cleveland, Sept. 26, 1976
LeRoy Irvin, Los Angeles vs. Atlanta, Oct. 11, 1981
Vai Sikahema, St. Louis vs. Tampa Bay, Dec. 21, 1986

Kickoff Returns

Most Seasons Leading League
3 Abe Woodson, San Francisco, 1959, 1962-63
2 Lynn Chandnois, Pittsburgh, 1951-52
Bobby Jancik, Houston, 1962-63
Travis Williams, Green Bay, 1967; Los Angeles, 1971

Kickoff Returns

Most Kickoff Returns, Career
275 Ron Smith, Chicago, 1965, 1970-72; Atlanta, 1966-67; Los Angeles, 1968-69; San Diego, 1973; Oakland, 1974
243 Bruce Harper, N.Y. Jets, 1977-84
194 Steve Odom, Green Bay, 1974-79; N.Y. Giants, 1979

Most Kickoff Returns, Season
60 Drew Hill, Los Angeles, 1981
55 Bruce Harper, N.Y. Jets, 1978, 1979
David Turner, Cincinnati, 1979
Stump Mitchell, St. Louis, 1981
53 Eddie Payton, Minnesota, 1980
Buster Rhymes, Minnesota, 1985

Most Kickoff Returns, Rookie, Season
55 Stump Mitchell, St. Louis, 1981
53 Buster Rhymes, Minnesota, 1985
50 Nesby Glasgow, Baltimore, 1979
Dino Hall, Cleveland, 1979

Most Kickoff Returns, Game
9 Noland Smith, Kansas City vs. Oakland, Nov. 23, 1967
Dino Hall, Cleveland vs. Pittsburgh, Oct. 7, 1979
Paul Palmer, Kansas City vs. Seattle, Sept. 20, 1987
8 George Taliaferro, N.Y. Yanks vs. N.Y. Giants, Dec. 3, 1950
Bobby Jancik, Houston vs. Boston, Dec. 8, 1963; vs. Oakland, Dec. 22, 1963
Mel Renfro, Dallas vs. Green Bay, Nov. 29, 1964
Willie Porter, Boston vs. N.Y. Jets, Sept. 22, 1968
Keith Moody, Buffalo vs. Seattle, Oct. 30, 1977
Brian Baschnagel, Chicago vs. Houston, Nov. 6, 1977
Bruce Harper, N.Y. Jets vs. New England, Oct. 29, 1978; vs. New England, Sept. 9, 1979
Dino Hall, Cleveland vs. Pittsburgh, Nov. 25, 1979
Terry Metcalf, Washington vs. St. Louis, Sept. 20, 1981
Harlan Huckleby, Green Bay vs. Washington, Oct. 17, 1983
Gary Ellerson, Green Bay vs. St. Louis, Sept. 29, 1985
Bobby Humphery, N.Y. Jets vs. Cincinnati, Dec. 21, 1986
Bobby Joe Edmonds, Seattle vs. L.A. Raiders, Nov. 30, 1987
Joe Cribbs, Miami vs. Pittsburgh, Dec. 18, 1988
7 By many players

Yards Gained

Most Seasons Leading League
3 Bruce Harper, N.Y. Jets, 1977-79
2 Marshall Goldberg, Chi. Cardinals, 1941-42
Woodley Lewis, Los Angeles, 1953-54
Al Carmichael, Green Bay, 1956-57
Timmy Brown, Philadelphia, 1961, 1963
Bobby Jancik, Houston, 1963, 1966
Ron Smith, Atlanta, 1966-67

Most Yards Gained, Career
6,922 Ron Smith, Chicago, 1965, 1970-72; Atlanta, 1966-67; Los Angeles, 1968-69; San Diego, 1973; Oakland, 1974
5,538 Abe Woodson, San Francisco, 1958-64; St. Louis, 1965-66
5,407 Bruce Harper, N.Y. Jets, 1977-84

Most Yards Gained, Season
1,345 Buster Rhymes, Minnesota, 1985
1,317 Bobby Jancik, Houston, 1963
1,314 Dave Hampton, Green Bay, 1971

Most Yards Gained, Rookie, Season
1,345 Buster Rhymes, Minnesota, 1985
1,292 Stump Mitchell, St. Louis, 1981
1,245 Odell Barry, Denver, 1964

Most Yards Gained, Game
294 Wally Triplett, Detroit vs. Los Angeles, Oct. 29, 1950
247 Timmy Brown, Philadelphia vs. Dallas, Nov. 6, 1966
244 Noland Smith, Kansas City vs. San Diego, Oct. 15, 1967

Longest Kickoff Return (All TDs)
106 Al Carmichael, Green Bay vs. Chi. Bears, Oct. 7, 1956
Noland Smith, Kansas City vs. Denver, Dec. 17, 1967
Roy Green, St. Louis vs. Dallas, Oct. 21, 1979
105 Frank Seno, Chi. Cardinals vs. N.Y. Giants, Oct. 20, 1946
Ollie Matson, Chi. Cardinals vs. Washington, Oct. 14, 1956
Abe Woodson, San Francisco vs. Los Angeles, Nov. 8, 1959
Timmy Brown, Philadelphia vs. Cleveland, Sept. 17, 1961
Jon Arnett, Los Angeles vs. Detroit, Oct. 29, 1961
Eugene (Mercury) Morris, Miami vs. Cincinnati, Sept. 14, 1969
Travis Williams, Los Angeles vs. New Orleans, Dec. 5, 1971
104 By many players

Average Yardage

Highest Average, Career (75 returns)
30.56 Gale Sayers, Chicago, 1965-71 (91-2,781)
29.57 Lynn Chandnois, Pittsburgh, 1950-56 (92-2,720)
28.69 Abe Woodson, San Francisco, 1958-64; St. Louis, 1965-66 (193-5,538)

Highest Average, Season (Qualifiers)
41.06 Travis Williams, Green Bay, 1967 (18-739)
37.69 Gale Sayers, Chicago, 1967 (16-603)
35.50 Ollie Matson, Chi. Cardinals, 1958 (14-497)

Highest Average, Rookie, Season (Qualifiers)
41.06 Travis Williams, Green Bay, 1967 (18-739)
33.08 Tom Moore, Green Bay, 1960 (12-397)
32.88 Duriel Harris, Miami, 1976 (17-559)

Highest Average, Game (3 returns)
73.50 Wally Triplett, Detroit vs. Los Angeles, Oct. 29, 1950 (4-294)
67.33 Lenny Lyles, San Francisco vs. Baltimore, Dec. 18, 1960 (3-202)
65.33 Ken Hall, Houston vs. N.Y. Titans, Oct. 23, 1960 (3-196)

Touchdowns

Most Touchdowns, Career
6 Ollie Matson, Chi. Cardinals, 1952, 1954-58; L.A. Rams, 1959-62; Detroit, 1963; Philadelphia, 1964
Gale Sayers, Chicago, 1965-71
Travis Williams, Green Bay, 1967-70; Los Angeles, 1971
5 Bobby Mitchell, Cleveland, 1958-61; Washington, 1962-68
Abe Woodson, San Francisco, 1958-64; St. Louis, 1965-66
Timmy Brown, Green Bay, 1959; Philadelphia, 1960-67; Baltimore, 1968
4 Cecil Turner, Chicago, 1968-73
Ron Brown, L.A. Rams, 1984-89; L.A. Raiders, 1990

Most Touchdowns, Season
4 Travis Williams, Green Bay, 1967
Cecil Turner, Chicago, 1970
3 Verda (Vitamin T) Smith, Los Angeles, 1950
Abe Woodson, San Francisco, 1963
Gale Sayers, Chicago, 1967
Raymond Clayborn, New England, 1977
Ron Brown, L.A. Rams, 1985
2 By many players

Most Touchdowns, Rookie, Season
4 Travis Williams, Green Bay, 1967
3 Raymond Clayborn, New England, 1977
2 By seven players

Most Touchdowns, Game
2 Timmy Brown, Philadelphia vs. Dallas, Nov. 6, 1966
Travis Williams, Green Bay vs. Cleveland, Nov. 12, 1967
Ron Brown, L.A. Rams vs. Green Bay, Nov. 24, 1985

Combined Kick Returns

Most Combined Kick Returns, Career

510 Ron Smith, Chicago, 1965, 1970-72; Atlanta, 1966-67; Los Angeles, 1968-69; San Diego, 1973; Oakland, 1974 (p-235, k-275)
426 Bruce Harper, N.Y. Jets, 1977-84 (p-183, k-243)
423 Alvin Haymond, Baltimore, 1964-67; Philadelphia, 1968; Los Angeles, 1969-71; Washington, 1972; Houston, 1973 (p-253, k-170)

Most Combined Kick Returns, Season

100 Larry Jones, Washington, 1975 (p-53, k-47)
97 Stump Mitchell, St. Louis, 1981 (p-42, k-55)
94 Nesby Glasgow, Baltimore, 1979 (p-44, k-50)

Most Combined Kick Returns, Game

13 Stump Mitchell, St. Louis vs. Atlanta, Oct. 18, 1981 (p-6, k-7)
12 Mel Renfro, Dallas vs. Green Bay, Nov. 29, 1964 (p-4, k-8)
Larry Jones, Washington vs. Dallas, Dec. 13, 1975 (p-6, k-6)
Eddie Brown, Washington vs. Tampa Bay, Oct. 9, 1977 (p-11, k-1)
Nesby Glasgow, Baltimore vs. Denver, Sept. 2, 1979 (p-9, k-3)
11 By many players

Yards Gained

Most Yards Returned, Career

8,710 Ron Smith, Chicago, 1965, 1970-72; Atlanta, 1966-67; Los Angeles, 1968-69; San Diego, 1973; Oakland, 1974 (p-1,788, k-6,922)
7,191 Bruce Harper, N.Y. Jets, 1977-84 (p-1,784, k-5,407)
6,740 Les (Speedy) Duncan, San Diego, 1964-70; Washington, 1971-74 (p-2,201, k-4,539)

Most Yards Returned, Season

1,737 Stump Mitchell, St. Louis, 1981 (p-445, k-1,292)
1,658 Bruce Harper, N.Y. Jets, 1978 (p-378, k-1,280)
1,591 Mike Nelms, Washington, 1981 (p-492, k-1,099)

Most Yards Returned, Game

294 Wally Triplett, Detroit vs. Los Angeles, Oct. 29, 1950 (k-294)
Woodley Lewis, Los Angeles vs. Detroit, Oct. 18, 1953 (p-120, k-174)
289 Eddie Payton, Detroit vs. Minnesota, Dec. 17, 1977 (p-105, k-184)
282 Les (Speedy) Duncan, San Diego vs. N.Y. Jets, Nov. 24, 1968 (p-102, k-180)

Touchdowns

Most Touchdowns, Career

9 Ollie Matson, Chi. Cardinals, 1952, 1954-58; Los Angeles, 1959-62; Detroit, 1963; Philadelphia, 1964-66 (p-3, k-6)
8 Jack Christiansen, Detroit, 1951-58 (p-8)
Bobby Mitchell, Cleveland, 1958-61; Washington, 1962-68 (p-3, k-5)
Gale Sayers, Chicago, 1965-71 (p-2, k-6)
Rick Upchurch, Denver, 1975-83 (p-8)
Billy Johnson, Houston, 1974-80; Atlanta, 1982-87; Washington, 1988 (p-6, k-2)
7 Abe Woodson, San Francisco, 1958-64; St. Louis, 1965-66 (p-2, k-5)

Most Touchdowns, Season

4 Jack Christiansen, Detroit, 1951 (p-4)
Emlen Tunnell, N.Y. Giants, 1951 (p-3, k-1)
Gale Sayers, Chicago, 1967 (p-1, k-3)
Travis Williams, Green Bay, 1967 (k-4)
Cecil Turner, Chicago, 1970 (k-4)
Billy Johnson, Houston, 1975 (p-3, k-1)
Rick Upchurch, Denver, 1976 (p-4)
3 Verda (Vitamin T) Smith, Los Angeles, 1950 (k-3)
Abe Woodson, San Francisco, 1963 (k-3)
Raymond Clayborn, New England, 1977 (k-3)
Billy Johnson, Houston, 1977 (p-2, k-1)
LeRoy Irvin, Los Angeles, 1981 (p-3)
Ron Brown, L.A. Rams, 1985 (k-3)
2 By many players

Most Touchdowns, Game

2 Jack Christiansen, Detroit vs. Los Angeles, Oct. 14, 1951 (p-2); vs. Green Bay, Nov. 22, 1951 (p-2)
Jim Patton, N.Y. Giants vs. Washington, Oct. 30, 1955 (p-1, k-1)
Bobby Mitchell, Cleveland vs. Philadelphia, Nov. 23, 1958 (p-1, k-1)
Dick Christy, N.Y. Titans vs. Denver, Sept. 24, 1961 (p-2)
Al Frazier, Denver vs. Boston, Dec. 3, 1961 (p-1, k-1)
Timmy Brown, Philadelphia vs. Dallas, Nov. 6, 1966 (k-2)
Travis Williams, Green Bay vs. Cleveland, Nov. 12, 1967 (k-2); vs. Pittsburgh, Nov. 2, 1969 (p-1, k-1)
Gale Sayers, Chicago vs. San Francisco, Dec. 3, 1967 (p-1, k-1)
Rick Upchurch, Denver vs. Cleveland, Sept. 26, 1976 (p-2)
Eddie Payton, Detroit vs. Minnesota, Dec. 17, 1977 (p-1, k-1)
LeRoy Irvin, Los Angeles vs. Atlanta, Oct. 11, 1981 (p-2)
Ron Brown, L.A. Rams vs. Green Bay, Nov. 24, 1985 (k-2)
Vai Sikahema, St. Louis vs. Tampa Bay, Dec. 21, 1986 (p-2)

Fumbles

Most Fumbles, Career

106 Dan Fouts, San Diego, 1973-87
105 Roman Gabriel, Los Angeles, 1962-72; Philadelphia, 1973-77
102 Dave Krieg, Seattle, 1980-90

Most Fumbles, Season

18 Dave Krieg, Seattle, 1989
Warren Moon, Houston, 1990
17 Dan Pastorini, Houston, 1973
Warren Moon, Houston, 1984
Randall Cunningham, Philadelphia, 1989
16 Don Meredith, Dallas, 1964
Joe Cribbs, Buffalo, 1980
Steve Fuller, Kansas City, 1980
Paul McDonald, Cleveland, 1984
Phil Simms, N.Y. Giants, 1985

Most Fumbles, Game

7 Len Dawson, Kansas City vs. San Diego, Nov. 15, 1964
6 Sam Etcheverry, St. Louis vs. N.Y. Giants, Sept. 17, 1961
Dave Krieg, Seattle vs. Kansas City, Nov. 5, 1989
5 Paul Christman, Chi. Cardinals vs. Green Bay, Nov. 10, 1946
Charlie Conerly, N.Y. Giants vs. San Francisco, Dec. 1, 1957
Jack Kemp, Buffalo vs. Houston, Oct. 29, 1967
Roman Gabriel, Philadelphia vs. Oakland, Nov. 21, 1976
Randall Cunningham, Philadelphia vs. L.A. Raiders, Nov. 30, 1986 (OT)
Willie Totten, Buffalo vs. Indianapolis, Oct. 4, 1987
Dave Walter, Cincinnati vs. Seattle, Oct. 11, 1987
Dave Krieg, Seattle vs. San Diego, Nov. 25, 1990 (OT)

Fumbles Recovered

Most Fumbles Recovered, Career, Own and Opponents'

43 Fran Tarkenton, Minnesota, 1961-66, 1972-78; N.Y. Giants, 1967-71 (43 own)
38 Jack Kemp, Pittsburgh, 1957; L.A. Chargers, 1960; San Diego, 1961-62; Buffalo, 1962-67, 1969 (38 own)
Dan Fouts, San Diego, 1973-87 (37 own, 1 opp)
37 Roman Gabriel, Los Angeles, 1962-72; Philadelphia, 1973-77 (37 own)

Most Fumbles Recovered, Season, Own and Opponents'

9 Don Hultz, Minnesota, 1963 (9 opp)
Dave Krieg, Seattle, 1989 (9 own)
8 Paul Christman, Chi. Cardinals, 1945 (8 own)
Joe Schmidt, Detroit, 1955 (8 opp)
Bill Butler, Minnesota, 1963 (8 own)
Kermit Alexander, San Francisco, 1965 (4 own, 4 opp)
Jack Lambert, Pittsburgh, 1976 (1 own, 7 opp)
Danny White, Dallas, 1981 (8 own)
Dan Marino, Miami, 1988 (7 own, 1 opp)
7 By many players

Most Fumbles Recovered, Game, Own and Opponents'

4 Otto Graham, Cleveland vs. N.Y. Giants, Oct. 25, 1953 (4 own)
Sam Etcheverry, St. Louis vs. N.Y. Giants, Sept. 17, 1961 (4 own)
Roman Gabriel, Los Angeles vs. San Francisco, Oct. 12, 1969 (4 own)
Joe Ferguson, Buffalo vs. Miami, Sept. 18, 1977 (4 own)
Randall Cunningham, Philadelphia vs. L.A. Raiders, Nov. 30, 1986 (OT) (4 own)
3 By many players

Own Fumbles Recovered

Most Own Fumbles Recovered, Career

43 Fran Tarkenton, Minnesota, 1961-66, 1972-78; N.Y. Giants, 1967-71
38 Jack Kemp, Pittsburgh, 1957; L.A. Chargers, 1960; San Diego, 1961-62; Buffalo, 1962-67, 1969
37 Roman Gabriel, Los Angeles, 1962-72; Philadelphia, 1973-77
Dan Fouts, San Diego, 1973-87

Most Own Fumbles Recovered, Season

9 Dave Krieg, Seattle, 1989
8 Paul Christman, Chi. Cardinals, 1945
Bill Butler, Minnesota, 1963
Danny White, Dallas, 1981
7 By many players

Most Own Fumbles Recovered, Game

4 Otto Graham, Cleveland vs. N.Y. Giants, Oct. 25, 1953
Sam Etcheverry, St. Louis vs. N.Y. Giants, Sept. 17, 1961
Roman Gabriel, Los Angeles vs. San Francisco, Oct. 12, 1969
Joe Ferguson, Buffalo vs. Miami, Sept. 18, 1977
Randall Cunningham, Philadelphia vs. L.A. Raiders, Nov. 30, 1986 (OT)
3 By many players

Opponents' Fumbles Recovered

Most Opponents' Fumbles Recovered, Career

29 Jim Marshall, Cleveland, 1960; Minnesota, 1961-79
25 Dick Butkus, Chicago, 1965-73
23 Carl Eller, Minnesota, 1964-78; Seattle, 1979
Reggie Williams, Cincinnati, 1976-89

Most Opponents' Fumbles Recovered, Season

9 Don Hultz, Minnesota, 1963
8 Joe Schmidt, Detroit, 1955
7 Alan Page, Minnesota, 1970
Jack Lambert, Pittsburgh, 1976
Ray Childress, Houston, 1988
Rickey Jackson, New Orleans, 1990

Most Opponents' Fumbles Recovered, Game

3 Corwin Clatt, Chi. Cardinals vs. Detroit, Nov. 6, 1949
Vic Sears, Philadelphia vs. Green Bay, Nov. 2, 1952
Ed Beatty, San Francisco vs. Los Angeles, Oct. 7, 1956
Ron Carroll, Houston vs. Cincinnati, Oct. 27, 1974
Maurice Spencer, New Orleans vs. Atlanta, Oct. 10, 1976
Steve Nelson, New England vs. Philadelphia, Oct. 8, 1978
Charles Jackson, Kansas City vs. Pittsburgh, Sept. 6, 1981
Willie Buchanon, San Diego vs. Denver, Sept. 27, 1981
Joey Browner, Minnesota vs. San Francisco, Sept. 8, 1985
Ray Childress, Houston vs. Washington, Oct. 30, 1988
2 By many players

Yards Returning Fumbles

Longest Fumble Run (All TDs)

104 Jack Tatum, Oakland vs. Green Bay, Sept. 24, 1972 (opp)
98 George Halas, Chi. Bears vs. Oorang Indians, Marion, Ohio, Nov. 4, 1923 (opp)
97 Chuck Howley, Dallas vs. Atlanta, Oct. 2, 1966 (opp)

Touchdowns

Most Touchdowns, Career (Total)

4 Bill Thompson, Denver, 1969-81
3 Ralph Heywood, Detroit, 1947-48; Boston, 1948; N.Y. Bulldogs, 1949
Leo Sugar, Chi. Cardinals, 1954-59; St. Louis, 1960; Philadelphia, 1961; Detroit, 1962
Bud McFadin, Los Angeles, 1952-56; Denver, 1960-63; Houston, 1964-65
Doug Cline, Houston, 1960-66; San Diego, 1966
Bob Lilly, Dall. Cowboys, 1961-74
Chris Hanburger, Washington, 1965-78
Lemar Parrish, Cincinnati, 1970-77; Washington, 1978-81; Buffalo, 1982
Paul Krause, Washington, 1964-67; Minnesota, 1968-79
Brad Dusek, Washington, 1974-81
David Logan, Tampa Bay, 1979-86; Green Bay, 1987
Thomas Howard, Kansas City, 1977-83; St. Louis, 1984-85
Greg Townsend, L.A. Raiders, 1983-90
Les Miller, San Diego, 1987-90
2 By many players

Most Touchdowns, Season (Total)
2 Harold McPhail, Boston, 1934
Harry Ebding, Detroit, 1937
John Morelli, Boston, 1944
Frank Maznicki, Boston, 1947
Fred (Dippy) Evans, Chi. Bears, 1948
Ralph Heywood, Boston, 1948
Art Tait, N.Y. Yanks, 1951
John Dwyer, Los Angeles, 1952
Leo Sugar, Chi. Cardinals, 1957
Doug Cline, Houston, 1961
Jim Bradshaw, Pittsburgh, 1964
Royce Berry, Cincinnati, 1970
Ahmad Rashad, Buffalo, 1974
Tim Gray, Kansas City, 1977
Charles Phillips, Oakland, 1978
Kenny Johnson, Atlanta, 1981
George Martin, N.Y. Giants, 1981
Del Rodgers, Green Bay, 1982
Mike Douglass, Green Bay, 1983
Shelton Robinson, Seattle, 1983
Erik McMillan, N.Y. Jets, 1989
Les Miller, San Diego, 1990

Most Touchdowns, Career (Own recovered)
2 Ken Kavanaugh, Chi. Bears, 1940-41, 1945-50
Mike Ditka, Chicago, 1961-66; Philadelphia, 1967-68; Dallas, 1969-72
Gail Cogdill, Detroit, 1960-68; Baltimore, 1968; Atlanta, 1969-70
Ahmad Rashad, St. Louis, 1972-73; Buffalo, 1974; Minnesota, 1976-82
Jim Mitchell, Atlanta, 1969-79
Drew Pearson, Dallas, 1973-83
Del Rodgers, Green Bay, 1982, 1984; San Francisco, 1987-88

Most Touchdowns, Season (Own recovered)
2 Ahmad Rashad, Buffalo, 1974
Del Rodgers, Green Bay, 1982
1 By many players

Most Touchdowns, Career (Opponents' recovered)
3 Leo Sugar, Chi. Cardinals, 1954-59; St. Louis, 1960; Philadelphia, 1961; Detroit, 1962
Doug Cline, Houston, 1960-66; San Diego, 1966
Bud McFadin, Los Angeles, 1952-56; Denver, 1960-63; Houston, 1964-65
Bob Lilly, Dall. Cowboys, 1961-74
Chris Hanburger, Washington, 1965-78
Paul Krause, Washington, 1964-67; Minnesota, 1968-79
Lemar Parrish, Cincinnati, 1970-77; Washington, 1978-81; Buffalo, 1982
Bill Thompson, Denver, 1969-81
Brad Dusek, Washington, 1974-81
David Logan, Tampa Bay, 1979-86; Green Bay, 1987
Thomas Howard, Kansas City, 1977-83; St. Louis, 1984-85
Greg Townsend, L.A. Raiders, 1983-90
Les Miller, San Diego, 1987-90
2 By many players

Most Touchdowns, Season (Opponents' recovered)
2 Harold McPhail, Boston, 1934
Harry Ebding, Detroit, 1937
John Morelli, Boston, 1944
Frank Maznicki, Boston, 1947
Fred (Dippy) Evans, Chi. Bears, 1948
Ralph Heywood, Boston, 1948
Art Tait, N.Y. Yanks, 1951
John Dwyer, Los Angeles, 1952
Leo Sugar, Chi. Cardinals, 1957
Doug Cline, Houston, 1961
Jim Bradshaw, Pittsburgh, 1964
Royce Berry, Cincinnati, 1970
Tim Gray, Kansas City, 1977
Charles Phillips, Oakland, 1978
Kenny Johnson, Atlanta, 1981
George Martin, N.Y. Giants, 1981
Mike Douglass, Green Bay, 1983
Shelton Robinson, Seattle, 1983
Erik McMillan, N.Y. Jets, 1989
Les Miller, San Diego, 1990

Most Touchdowns, Game (Opponents' recovered)
2 Fred (Dippy) Evans, Chi. Bears vs. Washington, Nov. 28, 1948

Combined Net Yards Gained
Rushing, receiving, interception returns, punt returns, kickoff returns, and fumble returns

Most Seasons Leading League
5 Jim Brown, Cleveland, 1958-61, 1964
3 Cliff Battles, Boston, 1932-33; Washington, 1937
Gale Sayers, Chicago, 1965-67
Eric Dickerson, L.A. Rams, 1983-84, 1986
2 By many players

Most Consecutive Seasons Leading League
4 Jim Brown, Cleveland, 1958-61
3 Gale Sayers, Chicago, 1965-67
2 Cliff Battles, Boston, 1932-33
Charley Trippi, Chi. Cardinals, 1948-49
Timmy Brown, Philadelphia, 1962-63
Floyd Little, Denver, 1967-68
James Brooks, San Diego, 1981-82
Eric Dickerson, L.A. Rams, 1983-84

Attempts
Most Attempts, Career
4,368 Walter Payton, Chicago, 1975-87
3,351 Tony Dorsett, Dallas, 1977-87; Denver, 1988
3,281 Franco Harris, Pittsburgh, 1972-83; Seattle, 1984

Most Attempts, Season
496 James Wilder, Tampa Bay, 1984
449 Marcus Allen, L.A. Raiders, 1985
442 Eric Dickerson, L.A. Rams, 1983

Most Attempts, Rookie, Season
442 Eric Dickerson, L.A. Rams, 1983
395 George Rogers, New Orleans, 1981
390 Joe Cribbs, Buffalo, 1980

Most Attempts, Game
48 James Wilder, Tampa Bay vs. Pittsburgh, Oct. 30, 1983
47 James Wilder, Tampa Bay vs. Green Bay, Sept. 30, 1984 (OT)
46 Gerald Riggs, Atlanta vs. L.A. Rams, Nov. 17, 1985

Yards Gained
Most Yards Gained, Career
21,803 Walter Payton, Chicago, 1975-87
16,326 Tony Dorsett, Dallas, 1977-87; Denver, 1988
15,459 Jim Brown, Cleveland, 1957-65

Most Yards Gained, Season
2,535 Lionel James, San Diego, 1985
2,462 Terry Metcalf, St. Louis, 1975
2,444 Mack Herron, New England, 1974

Most Yards Gained, Rookie, Season
2,317 Tim Brown, L.A. Raiders, 1988
2,272 Gale Sayers, Chicago, 1965
2,212 Eric Dickerson, L.A. Rams, 1983

Most Yards Gained, Game
373 Billy Cannon, Houston vs. N.Y. Titans, Dec. 10, 1961
345 Lionel James, San Diego vs. L.A. Raiders, Nov. 10, 1985 (OT)
341 Timmy Brown, Philadelphia vs. St. Louis, Dec. 16, 1962

Sacks
Sacks have been compiled since 1982.

Most Sacks, Career
114.5 Lawrence Taylor, N.Y. Giants, 1982-90
95 Reggie White, Philadelphia, 1985-90
93 Richard Dent, Chicago, 1983-90

Most Sacks, Season
22 Mark Gastineau, N.Y. Jets, 1984
21 Reggie White, Philadelphia, 1987
Chris Doleman, Minnesota, 1989
20.5 Lawrence Taylor, N.Y. Giants, 1986

Most Sacks, Rookie, Season
12.5 Leslie O'Neal, San Diego, 1986
12 Charles Haley, San Francisco, 1986
11 Vernon Maxwell, Baltimore, 1983

Most Sacks, Game
7 Derrick Thomas, Kansas City vs. Seattle, Nov. 11, 1990
6 Fred Dean, San Francisco vs. New Orleans, Nov. 13, 1983
5.5 William Gay, Detroit vs. Tampa Bay, Sept. 4, 1983

Miscellaneous
Longest Return of Missed Field Goal (All TDs)
101 Al Nelson, Philadelphia vs. Dallas, Sept. 26, 1971
100 Al Nelson, Philadelphia vs. Cleveland, Dec. 11, 1966
Ken Ellis, Green Bay vs. N.Y. Giants, Sept. 19, 1971
99 Jerry Williams, Los Angeles vs. Green Bay, Dec. 16, 1951
Carl Taseff, Baltimore vs. Los Angeles, Dec. 12, 1959
Timmy Brown, Philadelphia vs. St. Louis, Sept. 16, 1962

Team Records

Championships
Most Seasons League Champion
11 Green Bay, 1929-31, 1936, 1939, 1944, 1961-62, 1965-67
9 Chi. Bears, 1921, 1932-33, 1940-41, 1943, 1946, 1963, 1985
6 N.Y. Giants, 1927, 1934, 1938, 1956, 1986, 1990

Most Consecutive Seasons League Champion
3 Green Bay, 1929-31
Green Bay, 1965-67
2 Canton, 1922-23
Chi. Bears, 1932-33
Chi. Bears, 1940-41
Philadelphia, 1948-49
Detroit, 1952-53
Cleveland, 1954-55
Baltimore, 1958-59
Houston, 1960-61
Green Bay, 1961-62
Buffalo, 1964-65
Miami, 1972-73
Pittsburgh, 1974-75
Pittsburgh, 1978-79
San Francisco, 1988-89

Most Times Finishing First, Regular Season (Since 1933)
18 Clev. Browns, 1950-55, 1957, 1964-65, 1967-69, 1971, 1980, 1985-87, 1989
17 N.Y. Giants, 1933-35, 1938-39, 1941, 1944, 1946, 1956, 1958-59, 1961-63, 1986, 1989-90
16 Chi. Bears, 1933-34, 1937, 1940-43, 1946, 1956, 1963, 1984-88, 1990

Most Consecutive Times Finishing First, Regular Season (Since 1933)
7 Los Angeles, 1973-79
6 Cleveland, 1950-55
Dallas, 1966-71
Minnesota, 1973-78
Pittsburgh, 1974-79
5 Oakland, 1972-76
Chicago, 1984-88
San Francisco, 1986-90

Games Won
Most Consecutive Games Won
17 Chi. Bears, 1933-34
16 Chi. Bears, 1941-42
Miami, 1971-73
Miami, 1983-84

15 L.A. Chargers/San Diego, 1960-61
San Francisco, 1989-90

Most Consecutive Games Without Defeat
25 Canton, 1921-23 (won 22, tied 3)
24 Chi. Bears, 1941-43 (won 23, tied 1)
23 Green Bay, 1928-30 (won 21, tied 2)

Most Games Won, Season
15 San Francisco, 1984
Chicago, 1985
14 Miami, 1972
Pittsburgh, 1978
Washington, 1983
Miami, 1984
Chicago, 1986
N.Y. Giants, 1986
San Francisco, 1989
San Francisco, 1990
13 By many teams

Most Consecutive Games Won, Season
14 Miami, 1972
13 Chi. Bears, 1934
12 Minnesota, 1969
Chicago, 1985

Most Consecutive Games Won, Start of Season
14 Miami, 1972, entire season
13 Chi. Bears, 1934, entire season
12 Chicago, 1985

Most Consecutive Games Won, End of Season
14 Miami, 1972, entire season
13 Chi. Bears, 1934, entire season
11 Chi. Bears, 1942, entire season
Cleveland, 1951

Most Consecutive Games Without Defeat, Season
14 Miami, 1972 (won 14)
13 Chi. Bears, 1926 (won 11, tied 2)
Green Bay, 1929 (won 12, tied 1)
Chi. Bears, 1934 (won 13)
Baltimore, 1967 (won 11, tied 2)
12 Canton, 1922 (won 10, tied 2)
Canton, 1923 (won 11, tied 1)
Minnesota, 1969 (won 12)
Chicago, 1985 (won 12)

Most Consecutive Games Without Defeat, Start of Season
14 Miami, 1972 (won 14), entire season
13 Chi. Bears, 1926 (won 11, tied 2)
Green Bay, 1929 (won 12, tied 1), entire season
Chi. Bears, 1934 (won 13), entire season
Baltimore, 1967 (won 11, tied 2)
12 Canton, 1922 (won 10, tied 2), entire season
Canton, 1923 (won 11, tied 1), entire season
Chicago, 1985 (won 12)

Most Consecutive Games Without Defeat, End of Season
14 Miami, 1972 (won 14), entire season
13 Green Bay, 1929 (won 12, tied 1), entire season
Chi. Bears, 1934 (won 13), entire season
12 Canton, 1922 (won 10, tied 2), entire season
Canton, 1923 (won 11, tied 1), entire season

Most Consecutive Home Games Won
27 Miami, 1971-74
20 Green Bay, 1929-32
18 Oakland, 1968-70
Dallas, 1979-81

Most Consecutive Home Games Without Defeat
30 Green Bay, 1928-33 (won 27, tied 3)
27 Miami, 1971-74 (won 27)
23 Chi. Bears, 1923-25 (won 19, tied 6)

Most Consecutive Road Games Won
18 San Francisco, 1988-90 (current)
11 L.A. Chargers/San Diego, 1960-61
San Francisco, 1987-88
10 Chi. Bears, 1941-42
Dallas, 1968-69
New Orleans, 1987-88

Most Consecutive Road Games Without Defeat
18 San Francisco, 1988-90 (won 18, current)
13 Chi. Bears, 1941-43 (won 12, tied 1)
12 Green Bay, 1928-30 (won 10, tied 2)

Most Shutout Games Won or Tied, Season (Since 1932)
7 Chi. Bears, 1932 (won 4, tied 3)
Green Bay, 1932 (won 6, tied 1)
Detroit, 1934 (won 7)
5 Chi. Cardinals, 1934 (won 5)
N.Y. Giants, 1944 (won 5)
Pittsburgh, 1976 (won 5)
4 By many teams

Most Consecutive Shutout Games Won or Tied (Since 1932)
7 Detroit, 1934 (won 7)
3 Chi. Bears, 1932 (tied 3)
Green Bay, 1932 (won 3)
New York, 1935 (won 3)
St. Louis, 1970 (won 3)
Pittsburgh, 1976 (won 3)
2 By many teams

Games Lost

Most Consecutive Games Lost
26 Tampa Bay, 1976-77
19 Chi. Cardinals, 1942-43, 1945
Oakland, 1961-62
18 Houston, 1972-73

Most Consecutive Games Without Victory
26 Tampa Bay, 1976-77 (lost 26)
23 Rochester, 1922-25 (lost 21, tied 2)
Washington, 1960-61 (lost 20, tied 3)
19 Dayton, 1927-29 (lost 18, tied 1)
Chi. Cardinals, 1942-43, 1945 (lost 19)
Oakland, 1961-62 (lost 19)

Most Games Lost, Season
15 New Orleans, 1980
Dallas, 1989
New England, 1990
14 Tampa Bay, 1976
San Francisco, 1978
Detroit, 1979
San Francisco, 1979
Baltimore, 1981
New England, 1981
Houston, 1983
Tampa Bay, 1983
Buffalo, 1984
Buffalo, 1985
Tampa Bay, 1985
Tampa Bay, 1986
13 By many teams

Most Consecutive Games Lost, Season
14 Tampa Bay, 1976
New Orleans, 1980
Baltimore, 1981
New England, 1990
13 Oakland, 1962
Pittsburgh, 1969
Indianapolis, 1986
12 Tampa Bay, 1977

Most Consecutive Games Lost, Start of Season
14 Tampa Bay, 1976, entire season
New Orleans, 1980
13 Oakland, 1962
Indianapolis, 1986
12 Tampa Bay, 1977

Most Consecutive Games Lost, End of Season
14 Tampa Bay, 1976, entire season
New England, 1990
13 Pittsburgh, 1969
11 Philadelphia, 1936
Detroit, 1942, entire season
Houston, 1972

Most Consecutive Games Without Victory, Season
14 Tampa Bay, 1976 (lost 14), entire season
New Orleans, 1980 (lost 14)
Baltimore, 1981 (lost 14)
New England, 1990 (lost 14)
13 Washington, 1961 (lost 12, tied 1)
Oakland, 1962 (lost 13)
Pittsburgh, 1969 (lost 13)
Indianapolis, 1986 (lost 13)
12 Dall. Cowboys, 1960 (lost 11, tied 1) entire season
Tampa Bay, 1977 (lost 12)

Most Consecutive Games Without Victory, Start of Season
14 Tampa Bay, 1976 (lost 14), entire season
New Orleans, 1980 (lost 14)
13 Washington, 1961 (lost 12, tied 1)
Oakland, 1962 (lost 13)
Indianapolis, 1986 (lost 13)
12 Dall. Cowboys, 1960 (lost 11, tied 1), entire season
Tampa Bay, 1977 (lost 12)

Most Consecutive Games Without Victory, End of Season
14 Tampa Bay, 1976, (lost 14) entire season
New England, 1990 (lost 14)
13 Pittsburgh, 1969 (lost 13)
12 Dall. Cowboys, 1960 (lost 11, tied 1) entire season

Most Consecutive Home Games Lost
14 Dallas, 1988-89
13 Houston, 1972-73
Tampa Bay, 1976-77
11 Oakland, 1961-62
Los Angeles, 1961-63

Most Consecutive Home Games Without Victory
14 Dallas, 1988-89 (lost 14)
13 Houston, 1972-73 (lost 13)
Tampa Bay, 1976-77 (lost 13)
12 Philadelphia, 1936-38 (lost 11, tied 1)

Most Consecutive Road Games Lost
23 Houston, 1981-84
22 Buffalo, 1983-86
19 Tampa Bay, 1983-85

Most Consecutive Road Games Without Victory
23 Houston, 1981-84 (lost 23)
22 Buffalo, 1983-86 (lost 22)
19 Tampa Bay, 1983-85 (lost 19)

Most Shutout Games Lost or Tied, Season (Since 1932)
6 Cincinnati, 1934 (lost 6)
Pittsburgh, 1934 (lost 6)
Philadelphia, 1936 (lost 6)
Tampa Bay, 1977 (lost 6)
5 Boston, 1932 (lost 4, tied 1)
N.Y. Giants, 1932 (lost 4, tied 1)
Boston, 1933 (lost 4, tied 1)
Cincinnati, 1933 (lost 4, tied 1)
Brooklyn, 1934 (lost 5)
Brooklyn, 1942 (lost 5)
Detroit, 1942 (lost 5)
Tampa Bay, 1976 (lost 5)
4 By many teams

Most Consecutive Shutout Games Lost or Tied (Since 1932)
6 Brooklyn, 1942-43 (lost 6)
4 Chi. Bears, 1932 (lost 1, tied 3)

Philadelphia, 1936 (lost 4)
3 Chi. Cardinals, 1934 (lost 3), 1938 (lost 3)
Brooklyn, 1935 (lost 3), 1937 (lost 3)
Oakland, 1981 (lost 3)

Tie Games

Most Tie Games, Season
6 Chi. Bears, 1932
5 Frankford, 1929
4 Chi. Bears, 1924
Orange, 1929
Portsmouth, 1932

Most Consecutive Tie Games
3 Chi. Bears, 1932
2 By many teams

Scoring

Most Seasons Leading League
9 Chi. Bears, 1934-35, 1939, 1941-43, 1946-47, 1956
6 Green Bay, 1932, 1936-38, 1961-62
L.A. Rams, 1950-52, 1957, 1967, 1973
5 Oakland, 1967-69, 1974, 1977
Dallas, 1966, 1968, 1971, 1978, 1980
San Diego, 1963, 1965, 1981-82, 1985
San Francisco, 1953, 1965, 1970, 1987, 1989

Most Consecutive Seasons Leading League
3 Green Bay, 1936-38
Chi. Bears, 1941-43
Los Angeles, 1950-52
Oakland, 1967-69

Points

Most Points, Season
541 Washington, 1983
513 Houston, 1961
Miami, 1984
479 Dallas, 1983

Fewest Points, Season (Since 1932)
37 Cincinnati/St. Louis, 1934
38 Cincinnati, 1933
Detroit, 1942
51 Pittsburgh, 1934
Philadelphia, 1936

Most Points, Game
72 Washington vs. N.Y. Giants, Nov. 27, 1966
70 Los Angeles vs. Baltimore, Oct. 22, 1950
65 Chi. Cardinals vs. N.Y. Bulldogs, Nov. 13, 1949
Los Angeles vs. Detroit, Oct. 29, 1950

Most Points, Both Teams, Game
113 Washington (72) vs. N.Y. Giants (41), Nov. 27, 1966
101 Oakland (52) vs. Houston (49), Dec. 22, 1963
99 Seattle (51) vs. Kansas City (48), Nov. 27, 1983 (OT)

Fewest Points, Both Teams, Game
0 In many games. Last time: N.Y. Giants vs. Detroit, Nov. 7, 1943

Most Points, Shutout Victory, Game
64 Philadelphia vs. Cincinnati, Nov. 6, 1934
62 Akron vs. Oorang, Oct. 29, 1922
60 Rock Island vs. Evansville, Oct. 15, 1922
Chi. Cardinals vs. Rochester, Oct. 7, 1923

Fewest Points, Shutout Victory, Game
2 Green Bay vs. Chi. Bears, Oct. 16, 1932
Chi. Bears vs. Green Bay, Sept. 18, 1938

Most Points Overcome to Win Game
28 San Francisco vs. New Orleans, Dec. 7, 1980 (OT) (trailed 7-35, won 38-35)
25 St. Louis vs. Tampa Bay, Nov. 8, 1987 (trailed 3-28, won 31-28)
24 Philadelphia vs. Washington, Oct. 27, 1946 (trailed 0-24, won 28-24)
Detroit vs. Baltimore, Oct. 20, 1957 (trailed 3-27, won 31-27)
Philadelphia vs. Chi. Cardinals, Oct. 25, 1959 (trailed 0-24, won 28-24)
Denver vs. Boston, Oct. 23, 1960 (trailed 0-24, won 31-24)
Miami vs. New England, Dec. 15, 1974 (trailed 0-24, won 34-27)
Minnesota vs. San Francisco, Dec. 4, 1977 (trailed 0-24, won 28-27)
Denver vs. Seattle, Sept. 23, 1979 (trailed 10-34, won 37-34)
Houston vs. Cincinnati, Sept. 23, 1979 (OT) (trailed 0-24, won 30-27)
L.A. Raiders vs. San Diego, Nov. 22, 1982 (trailed 0-24, won 28-24)
L.A. Raiders vs. Denver, Sept. 26, 1988 (OT) (trailed 0-24, won 30-27)

Most Points Overcome to Tie Game
31 Denver vs. Buffalo, Nov. 27, 1960 (trailed 7-38, tied 38-38)
28 Los Angeles vs. Philadelphia, Oct. 3, 1948 (trailed 0-28, tied 28-28)

Most Points, Each Half
1st: 49 Green Bay vs. Tampa Bay, Oct. 2, 1983
48 Buffalo vs. Miami, Sept. 18, 1966
45 Green Bay vs. Cleveland, Nov. 12, 1967
Indianapolis vs. Denver, Oct. 31, 1988
Houston vs. Cleveland, Dec. 9, 1990
2nd: 49 Chi. Bears vs. Philadelphia, Nov. 30, 1941
48 Chi. Cardinals vs. Baltimore, Oct. 2, 1950
N.Y. Giants vs. Baltimore, Nov. 19, 1950
45 Cincinnati vs. Houston, Dec. 17, 1972

Most Points, Both Teams, Each Half
1st: 70 Houston (35) vs. Oakland (35), Dec. 22, 1963
62 N.Y. Jets (41) vs. Tampa Bay (21), Nov. 17, 1985
59 St. Louis (31) vs. Philadelphia (28), Dec. 16, 1962
2nd: 65 Washington (38) vs. N.Y. Giants (27), Nov. 27, 1966
62 L.A. Raiders (31) vs. San Diego (31), Jan. 2, 1983
58 New England (37) vs. Baltimore (21), Nov. 23, 1980
N.Y. Jets (37) vs. New England (21), Sept. 21, 1987

Most Points, One Quarter
41 Green Bay vs. Detroit, Oct. 7, 1945 (second quarter)
Los Angeles vs. Detroit, Oct. 29, 1950 (third quarter)
37 Los Angeles vs. Green Bay, Sept. 21, 1980 (second quarter)
35 Chi. Cardinals vs. Boston, Oct. 24, 1948 (third quarter)
Green Bay vs. Cleveland, Nov. 12, 1967 (first quarter)
Green Bay vs. Tampa Bay, Oct. 2, 1983 (second quarter)

Most Points, Both Teams, One Quarter
49 Oakland (28) vs. Houston (21), Dec. 22, 1963 (second quarter)
48 Green Bay (41) vs. Detroit (7), Oct. 7, 1945 (second quarter)
Los Angeles (41) vs. Detroit (7), Oct. 29, 1950 (third quarter)
47 St. Louis (27) vs. Philadelphia (20), Dec. 13, 1964 (second quarter)

Most Points, Each Quarter
1st: 35 Green Bay vs. Cleveland, Nov. 12, 1967
31 Buffalo vs. Kansas City, Sept. 13, 1964
28 By six teams
2nd: 41 Green Bay vs. Detroit, Oct. 7, 1945
37 Los Angeles vs. Green Bay, Sept. 21, 1980
35 Green Bay vs. Tampa Bay, Oct. 2, 1983
3rd: 41 Los Angeles vs. Detroit, Oct. 29, 1950
35 Chi. Cardinals vs. Boston, Oct. 24, 1948
28 By nine teams
4th: 31 Oakland vs. Denver, Dec. 17, 1960
Oakland vs. San Diego, Dec. 8, 1963
Atlanta vs. Green Bay, Sept. 13, 1981
28 By many teams

Most Points, Both Teams, Each Quarter
1st: 42 Green Bay (35) vs. Cleveland (7), Nov. 12, 1967
35 Dall. Texans (21) vs. N.Y. Titans (14), Nov. 11, 1962
Dallas (28) vs. Philadelphia (7), Oct. 19, 1969
Kansas City (21) vs. Seattle (14), Dec. 11, 1977
Detroit (21) vs. L.A. Raiders (14), Dec. 10, 1990
34 Los Angeles (21) vs. Baltimore (13), Oct. 22, 1950
Oakland (21) vs. Atlanta (13), Nov. 30, 1975
2nd: 49 Oakland (28) vs. Houston (21), Dec. 22, 1963
48 Green Bay (41) vs. Detroit (7), Oct. 7, 1945
47 St. Louis (27) vs. Philadelphia (20), Dec. 13, 1964
3rd: 48 Los Angeles (41) vs. Detroit (7), Oct. 29, 1950
42 Washington (28) vs. Philadelphia (14), Oct. 1, 1955
41 Green Bay (21) vs. N.Y. Yanks (20), Oct. 8, 1950
4th: 42 Chi. Cardinals (28) vs. Philadelphia (14), Dec. 7, 1947
Green Bay (28) vs. Chi. Bears (14), Nov. 6, 1955
N.Y. Jets (28) vs. Boston (14), Oct. 27, 1968
Pittsburgh (21) vs. Cleveland (21), Oct. 18, 1969
41 Baltimore (27) vs. New England (14), Sept. 18, 1978
New England (27) vs. Baltimore (14), Nov. 23, 1980
40 Chicago (21) vs. Tampa Bay (19), Nov. 19, 1989

Most Consecutive Games Scoring
274 Cleveland, 1950-71
218 Dallas, 1970-85
217 Oakland, 1966-81

Touchdowns

Most Seasons Leading League, Touchdowns
13 Chi. Bears, 1932, 1934-35, 1939, 1941-44, 1946-48, 1956, 1965
7 Dallas, 1966, 1968, 1971, 1973, 1977-78, 1980
6 Oakland, 1967-69, 1972, 1974, 1977
San Diego, 1963, 1965, 1979, 1981-82, 1985

Most Consecutive Seasons Leading League, Touchdowns
4 Chi. Bears, 1941-44
Los Angeles, 1949-52
3 Chi. Bears, 1946-48
Baltimore, 1957-59
Oakland, 1967-69
2 By many teams

Most Touchdowns, Season
70 Miami, 1984
66 Houston, 1961
64 Los Angeles, 1950

Fewest Touchdowns, Season (Since 1932)
3 Cincinnati, 1933
4 Cincinnati/St. Louis, 1934
5 Detroit, 1942

Most Touchdowns, Game
10 Philadelphia vs. Cincinnati, Nov. 6, 1934
Los Angeles vs. Baltimore, Oct. 22, 1950
Washington vs. N.Y. Giants, Nov. 27, 1966
9 Chi. Cardinals vs. Rochester, Oct. 7, 1923
Chi. Cardinals vs. N.Y. Giants, Oct. 17, 1948
Chi. Cardinals vs. N.Y. Bulldogs, Nov. 13, 1949
Los Angeles vs. Detroit, Oct. 29, 1950
Pittsburgh vs. N.Y. Giants, Nov. 30, 1952
Chicago vs. San Francisco, Dec. 12, 1965
Chicago vs. Green Bay, Dec. 7, 1980
8 By many teams.

Most Touchdowns, Both Teams, Game
16 Washington (10) vs. N.Y. Giants (6), Nov. 27, 1966
14 Chi. Cardinals (9) vs. N.Y. Giants (5), Oct. 17, 1948
Los Angeles (10) vs. Baltimore (4), Oct. 22, 1950
Houston (7) vs. Oakland (7), Dec. 22, 1963
13 New Orleans (7) vs. St. Louis (6), Nov. 2, 1969
Kansas City (7) vs. Seattle (6), Nov. 27, 1983 (OT)
San Diego (8) vs. Pittsburgh (5), Dec. 8, 1985
N.Y. Jets (7) vs. Miami (6), Sept. 21, 1986 (OT)

Most Consecutive Games Scoring Touchdowns
166 Cleveland, 1957-69
97 Oakland, 1966-73
96 Kansas City, 1963-70

Points After Touchdown

Most Points After Touchdown, Season
66 Miami, 1984
65 Houston, 1961
62 Washington, 1983

Fewest Points After Touchdown, Season
2 Chi. Cardinals, 1933
3 Cincinnati, 1933
Pittsburgh, 1934
4 Cincinnati/St. Louis, 1934

Most Points After Touchdown, Game
10 Los Angeles vs. Baltimore, Oct. 22, 1950
9 Chi. Cardinals vs. N.Y. Giants, Oct. 17, 1948
Pittsburgh vs. N.Y. Giants, Nov. 30, 1952
Washington vs. N.Y. Giants, Nov. 27, 1966
8 By many teams

Most Points After Touchdown, Both Teams, Game
14 Chi. Cardinals (9) vs. N.Y. Giants (5), Oct. 17, 1948
Houston (7) vs. Oakland (7), Dec. 22, 1963
Washington (9) vs. N.Y. Giants (5), Nov. 27, 1966
13 Los Angeles (10) vs. Baltimore (3), Oct. 22, 1950
12 In many games

Field Goals

Most Seasons Leading League, Field Goals
11 Green Bay, 1935-36, 1940-43, 1946-47, 1955, 1972, 1974
7 Washington, 1945, 1956, 1971, 1976-77, 1979, 1982
N.Y. Giants, 1933, 1937, 1939, 1941, 1944, 1959, 1983
5 Portsmouth/Detroit, 1932-33, 1937-38, 1980
Kansas City, 1966-67, 1970, 1975, 1990

Most Consecutive Seasons Leading League, Field Goals
4 Green Bay, 1940-43
3 Cleveland, 1952-54
2 By many teams

Most Field Goals Attempted, Season
49 Los Angeles, 1966
Washington, 1971
48 Green Bay, 1972
47 N.Y. Jets, 1969
Los Angeles, 1973
Washington, 1983

Fewest Field Goals Attempted, Season (Since 1938)
0 Chi. Bears, 1944
2 Cleveland, 1939
Card-Pitt, 1944
Boston, 1946
Chi. Bears, 1947
3 Chi. Bears, 1945
Cleveland, 1945

Most Field Goals Attempted, Game
9 St. Louis vs. Pittsburgh, Sept. 24, 1967
8 Pittsburgh vs. St. Louis, Dec. 2, 1962
Detroit vs. Minnesota, Nov. 13, 1966
N.Y. Jets vs. Buffalo, Nov. 3, 1968
7 By many teams

Most Field Goals Attempted, Both Teams, Game
11 St. Louis (6) vs. Pittsburgh (5), Nov. 13, 1966
Washington (6) vs. Chicago (5), Nov. 14, 1971
Green Bay (6) vs. Detroit (5), Sept. 29, 1974
Washington (6) vs. N.Y. Giants (5), Nov. 14, 1976
10 Denver (5) vs. Boston (5), Nov. 11, 1962
Boston (7) vs. San Diego (3), Sept. 20, 1964
Buffalo (7) vs. Houston (3), Dec. 5, 1965
St. Louis (7) vs. Atlanta (3), Dec. 11, 1966
Boston (7) vs. Buffalo (3), Sept. 24, 1967
Detroit (7) vs. Minnesota (3), Sept. 20, 1971
Washington (7) vs. Houston (3), Oct. 10, 1971
Green Bay (5) vs. St. Louis (5), Dec. 5, 1971
Kansas City (7) vs. Buffalo (3), Dec. 19, 1971
Kansas City (5) vs. San Diego (5), Oct. 29, 1972
Minnesota (6) vs. Chicago (4), Sept. 23, 1973
Cleveland (7) vs. Denver (3), Oct. 19, 1975
Cleveland (5) vs. Denver (5), Oct. 5, 1980
9 In many games

Most Field Goals, Season
35 N.Y. Giants, 1983
34 N.Y. Jets, 1968
Kansas City, 1990
33 Green Bay, 1972
Washington, 1983
Pittsburgh, 1985
New Orleans, 1987

Fewest Field Goals, Season (Since 1932)
0 Boston, 1932, 1935
Chi. Cardinals, 1932, 1945
Green Bay, 1932, 1944
N.Y. Giants, 1932
Brooklyn, 1944
Card-Pitt, 1944
Chi. Bears, 1944, 1947
Boston, 1946
Baltimore, 1950
Dallas, 1952

Most Field Goals, Game
7 St. Louis vs. Pittsburgh, Sept. 24, 1967
Minnesota vs. L.A. Rams, Nov. 5, 1989 (OT)
6 Boston vs. Denver, Oct. 4, 1964
Detroit vs. Minnesota, Nov. 13, 1966
N.Y. Jets vs. Buffalo, Nov. 3, 1968
Philadelphia vs. Houston, Nov. 12, 1972
N.Y. Jets vs. New Orleans, Dec. 3, 1972
St. Louis vs. Atlanta, Dec. 9, 1973
N.Y. Giants vs. Seattle, Oct. 18, 1981
San Francisco vs. New Orleans, Oct. 16, 1983
Pittsburgh vs. Denver, Oct. 23, 1988
5 By many teams

Most Field Goals, Both Teams, Game
8 Cleveland (4) vs. St. Louis (4), Sept. 20, 1964
Chicago (5) vs. Philadelphia (3), Oct. 20, 1968
Washington (5) vs. Chicago (3), Nov. 14, 1971
Kansas City (5) vs. Buffalo (3), Dec. 19, 1971
Detroit (4) vs. Green Bay (4), Sept. 29, 1974
Cleveland (5) vs. Denver (3), Oct. 19, 1975
New England (4) vs. San Diego (4), Nov. 9, 1975
San Francisco (6) vs. New Orleans (2), Oct. 16, 1983
Seattle (5) vs. L.A. Raiders (3), Dec. 18, 1988
7 In many games

Most Consecutive Games Scoring Field Goals
31 Minnesota, 1968-70
28 Washington, 1988-90
22 San Francisco, 1988-89

Safeties

Most Safeties, Season
4 Cleveland, 1927
Detroit, 1962
3 By many teams

Most Safeties, Game
3 L.A. Rams vs. N.Y. Giants, Sept. 30, 1984
2 N.Y. Giants vs. Pottsville, Oct. 30, 1927
Chi. Bears vs. Pottsville, Nov. 13, 1927
Detroit vs. Brooklyn, Dec. 1, 1935
N.Y. Giants vs. Pittsburgh, Sept. 17, 1950
N.Y. Giants vs. Washington, Nov. 5, 1961
Chicago vs. Pittsburgh, Nov. 9, 1969
Dallas vs. Philadelphia, Nov. 19, 1972
Los Angeles vs. Green Bay, Oct. 21, 1973
Oakland vs. San Diego, Oct. 26, 1975
Denver vs. Seattle, Jan. 2, 1983
New Orleans vs. Cleveland, Sept. 13, 1987
Buffalo vs. Denver, Nov. 8, 1987

Most Safeties, Both Teams, Game
3 L.A. Rams (3) vs. N.Y. Giants (0), Sept. 30, 1984
2 Chi. Cardinals (1) vs. Frankford (1), Nov. 19, 1927
Chi. Cardinals (1) vs. Cincinnati (1), Nov. 12, 1933
Chi. Bears (1) vs. San Francisco (1), Oct. 19, 1952
Cincinnati (1) vs. Los Angeles (1), Oct. 22, 1972
Chi. Bears (1) vs. San Francisco (1), Sept. 19, 1976
Baltimore (1) vs. Miami (1), Oct. 29, 1978
Atlanta (1) vs. Detroit (1), Oct. 5, 1980
Houston (1) vs. Philadelphia (1), Oct. 2, 1988
(Also see previous record)

First Downs

Most Seasons Leading League
9 Chi. Bears, 1935, 1939, 1941, 1943, 1945, 1947-49, 1955
7 San Diego, 1965, 1969, 1980-83, 1985
6 L.A. Rams, 1946, 1950-51, 1954, 1957, 1973

Most Consecutive Seasons Leading League
4 San Diego, 1980-83
3 Chi. Bears, 1947-49
2 By many teams

Most First Downs, Season
387 Miami, 1984
380 San Diego, 1985
379 San Diego, 1981

Fewest First Downs, Season
51 Cincinnati, 1933
64 Pittsburgh, 1935
67 Philadelphia, 1937

Most First Downs, Game
39 N.Y. Jets vs. Miami, Nov. 27, 1988
Washington vs. Detroit, Nov. 4, 1990 (OT)
38 Los Angeles vs. N.Y. Giants, Nov. 13, 1966
37 Green Bay vs. Philadelphia, Nov. 11, 1962

Fewest First Downs, Game
0 N.Y. Giants vs. Green Bay, Oct. 1, 1933
Pittsburgh vs. Boston, Oct. 29, 1933
Philadelphia vs. Detroit, Sept. 20, 1935
N.Y. Giants vs. Washington, Sept. 27, 1942
Denver vs. Houston, Sept. 3, 1966

Most First Downs, Both Teams, Game
62 San Diego (32) vs. Seattle (30), Sept. 15, 1985
59 Miami (31) vs. Buffalo (28), Oct. 9, 1983 (OT)
Seattle (33) vs. Kansas City (26), Nov. 27, 1983 (OT)
N.Y. Jets (32) vs. Miami (27), Sept. 21, 1986 (OT)
N.Y. Jets (39) vs. Miami (20), Nov. 27, 1988
58 Los Angeles (30) vs. Chi. Bears (28), Oct. 24, 1954
Denver (34) vs. Kansas City (24), Nov. 18, 1974
Atlanta (35) vs. New Orleans (23), Sept. 2, 1979 (OT)
Pittsburgh (36) vs. Cleveland (22), Nov. 25, 1979 (OT)
San Diego (34) vs. Miami (24), Nov. 18, 1984 (OT)
Cincinnati (32) vs. San Diego (26), Sept. 22, 1985

Fewest First Downs, Both Teams, Game
7 Chi. Cardinals (2) vs. Detroit (5), Sept. 15, 1940
9 Pittsburgh (1) vs. Boston (8), Oct. 27, 1935
Boston (4) vs. Brooklyn (5), Nov. 24, 1935
N.Y. Giants (3) vs. Detroit (6), Nov. 7, 1943
Pittsburgh (4) vs. Chi. Cardinals (5), Nov. 11, 1945
N.Y. Bulldogs (1) vs. Philadelphia (8), Sept. 22, 1949
10 N.Y. Giants (4) vs. Washington (6), Dec. 11, 1960

Most First Downs, Rushing, Season
181 New England, 1978
177 Los Angeles, 1973
176 Chicago, 1985

Fewest First Downs, Rushing, Season
36 Cleveland, 1942
Boston, 1944
39 Brooklyn, 1943
40 Philadelphia, 1940
Detroit, 1945

Most First Downs, Rushing, Game
25 Philadelphia vs. Washington, Dec. 2, 1951
23 St. Louis vs. New Orleans, Oct. 5, 1980
21 Cleveland vs. Philadelphia, Dec. 13, 1959
Green Bay vs. Philadelphia, Nov. 11, 1962

Los Angeles vs. New Orleans, Nov. 25, 1973
Pittsburgh vs. Kansas City, Nov. 7, 1976
New England vs. Denver, Nov. 28, 1976
Oakland vs. Green Bay, Sept. 17, 1978

Fewest First Downs, Rushing, Game
0 By many teams. Last time: Green Bay vs. Seattle, Dec. 9, 1990

Most First Downs, Rushing, Both Teams, Game
36 Philadelphia (25) vs. Washington (11), Dec. 2, 1951
31 Detroit (18) vs. Washington (13), Sept. 30, 1951
30 Los Angeles (17) vs. Minnesota (13), Nov. 5, 1961
New Orleans (17) vs. Green Bay (13), Sept. 9, 1979
New Orleans (16) vs. San Francisco (14), Nov. 11, 1979
New England (16) vs. Kansas City (14), Oct. 4, 1981

Fewest First Downs, Rushing, Both Teams, Game
2 Houston (0) vs. Denver (2), Dec. 2, 1962
3 Philadelphia (1) vs. Pittsburgh (2), Oct. 27, 1957
Boston (1) vs. Buffalo (2), Nov. 15, 1964
Los Angeles (0) vs. San Francisco (3), Dec. 6, 1964
Pittsburgh (1) vs. St. Louis (2), Nov. 13, 1966
4 In many games

Most First Downs, Passing, Season
259 San Diego, 1985
251 Houston, 1990
250 Miami, 1986

Fewest First Downs, Passing, Season
18 Pittsburgh, 1941
23 Brooklyn, 1942
N.Y. Giants, 1944
24 N.Y. Giants, 1943

Most First Downs, Passing, Game
29 N.Y. Giants vs. Cincinnati, Oct. 13, 1985
27 San Diego vs. Seattle, Sept. 15, 1985
26 Miami vs. Cleveland, Dec. 12, 1988

Fewest First Downs, Passing, Game
0 By many teams. Last time: Houston vs. Kansas City, Oct. 9, 1988

Most First Downs, Passing, Both Teams, Game
43 San Diego (23) vs. Cincinnati (20), Dec. 20, 1982
Miami (24) vs. N.Y. Jets (19), Sept. 21, 1986 (OT)
42 San Francisco (22) vs. San Diego (20), Dec. 11, 1982
41 San Diego (27) vs. Seattle (14), Sept. 15, 1985
Miami (26) vs. Cleveland (15), Dec. 12, 1988

Fewest First Downs, Passing, Both Teams, Game
0 Brooklyn vs. Pittsburgh, Nov. 29, 1942
1 Green Bay (0) vs. Cleveland (1), Sept. 21, 1941
Pittsburgh (0) vs. Brooklyn (1), Oct. 11, 1942
N.Y. Giants (0) vs. Detroit (1), Nov. 7, 1943
Pittsburgh (0) vs. Chi. Cardinals (1), Nov. 11, 1945
N.Y. Bulldogs (0) vs. Philadelphia (1), Sept. 22, 1949
Chicago (0) vs. Buffalo (1), Oct. 7, 1979
2 In many games

Most First Downs, Penalty, Season
42 Chicago, 1987
41 Denver, 1986
39 Seattle, 1978

Fewest First Downs, Penalty, Season
2 Brooklyn, 1940
4 Chi. Cardinals, 1940
N.Y. Giants, 1942, 1944
Washington, 1944
Cleveland, 1952
Kansas City, 1969
5 Brooklyn, 1939
Chi. Bears, 1939
Detroit, 1953
Los Angeles, 1953
Houston, 1982

Most First Downs, Penalty, Game
11 Denver vs. Houston, Oct. 6, 1985
9 Chi. Bears vs. Cleveland, Nov. 25, 1951
Baltimore vs. Pittsburgh, Oct. 30, 1977
N.Y. Jets vs. Houston, Sept. 18, 1988
8 Philadelphia vs. Detroit, Dec. 2, 1979
Cincinnati vs. N.Y. Jets, Oct. 6, 1985
Buffalo vs. Houston, Sept. 20, 1987
Houston vs. Atlanta, Sept. 9, 1990

Fewest First Downs, Penalty, Game
0 By many teams

Most First Downs, Penalty, Both Teams, Game
11 Chi. Bears (9) vs. Cleveland (2), Nov. 25, 1951
Cincinnati (8) vs. N.Y. Jets (3), Oct. 6, 1985
Denver (11) vs. Houston (0), Oct. 6, 1985
Detroit (6) vs. Dallas (5), Nov. 8, 1987
N.Y. Jets (9) vs. Houston (2), Sept. 18, 1988
10 In many games

Net Yards Gained Rushing and Passing

Most Seasons Leading League
12 Chi. Bears, 1932, 1934-35, 1939, 1941-44, 1947, 1949, 1955-56
7 San Diego, 1963, 1965, 1980-83, 1985
6 L.A. Rams, 1946, 1950-51, 1954, 1957, 1973
Baltimore, 1958-60, 1964, 1967, 1976
Dall. Cowboys, 1966, 1968-69, 1971, 1974, 1977

Most Consecutive Seasons Leading League
4 Chi. Bears, 1941-44
San Diego, 1980-83
3 Baltimore, 1958-60
Houston, 1960-62
Oakland, 1968-70
2 By many teams

Most Yards Gained, Season
6,936 Miami, 1984
6,744 San Diego, 1981
6,535 San Diego, 1985

Fewest Yards Gained, Season
1,150 Cincinnati, 1933
1,443 Chi. Cardinals, 1934
1,486 Chi. Cardinals, 1933

Most Yards Gained, Game
735 Los Angeles vs. N.Y. Yanks, Sept. 28, 1951
683 Pittsburgh vs. Chi. Cardinals, Dec. 13, 1958
682 Chi. Bears vs. N.Y. Giants, Nov. 14, 1943

Fewest Yards Gained, Game
−7 Seattle vs. Los Angeles, Nov. 4, 1979
−5 Denver vs. Oakland, Sept. 10, 1967
14 Chi. Cardinals vs. Detroit, Sept. 15, 1940

Most Yards Gained, Both Teams, Game
1,133 Los Angeles (636) vs. N.Y. Yanks (497), Nov. 19, 1950
1,102 San Diego (661) vs. Cincinnati (441), Dec. 20, 1982
1,087 St. Louis (589) vs. Philadelphia (498), Dec. 16, 1962

Fewest Yards Gained, Both Teams, Game
30 Chi. Cardinals (14) vs. Detroit (16), Sept. 15, 1940
136 Chi. Cardinals (50) vs. Green Bay (86), Nov. 18, 1934
154 N.Y. Giants (51) vs. Washington (103), Dec. 11, 1960

Most Consecutive Games, 400 or More Yards Gained
11 San Diego, 1982-83
6 Houston, 1961-62
San Diego, 1981
San Francisco, 1987
5 Chi. Bears, 1947
Philadelphia, 1953
Chi. Bears, 1955
Oakland, 1968
New England, 1981
Cincinnati, 1986

Most Consecutive Games, 300 or More Yards Gained
29 Los Angeles, 1949-51
26 Miami, 1983-85
19 Cleveland, 1978-79
San Diego, 1980-82
San Francisco, 1988-89

Rushing

Most Seasons Leading League
16 Chi. Bears, 1932, 1934-35, 1939-42, 1951, 1955-56, 1968, 1977, 1983-86
6 Cleveland, 1958-59, 1963, 1965-67
5 Buffalo, 1962, 1964, 1973, 1975, 1982

Most Consecutive Seasons Leading League
4 Chi. Bears, 1939-42, 1983-86
3 Detroit, 1936-38
San Francisco, 1952-54
Cleveland, 1965-67
2 By many teams

Most Rushing Attempts, Season
681 Oakland, 1977
674 Chicago, 1984
671 New England, 1978

Fewest Rushing Attempts, Season
211 Philadelphia, 1982
219 San Francisco, 1982
225 Houston, 1982

Most Rushing Attempts, Game
72 Chi. Bears vs. Brooklyn, Oct. 20, 1935
70 Chi. Cardinals vs. Green Bay, Dec. 5, 1948
69 Chi. Cardinals vs. Green Bay, Dec. 6, 1936
Kansas City vs. Cincinnati, Sept. 3, 1978

Fewest Rushing Attempts, Game
6 Chi. Cardinals vs. Boston, Oct. 29, 1933
7 Oakland vs. Buffalo, Oct. 15, 1963
Houston vs. N.Y. Giants, Dec. 8, 1985
8 Denver vs. Oakland, Dec. 17, 1960
Buffalo vs. St. Louis, Sept. 9, 1984

Most Rushing Attempts, Both Teams, Game
108 Chi. Cardinals (70) vs. Green Bay (38), Dec. 5, 1948
105 Oakland (62) vs. Atlanta (43), Nov. 30, 1975 (OT)
104 Chi. Bears (64) vs. Pittsburgh (40), Oct. 18, 1936

Fewest Rushing Attempts, Both Teams, Game
36 Cincinnati (16) vs. Chi. Bears (20), Sept. 30, 1934
37 Atlanta (18) vs. San Francisco (19), Oct. 6, 1985
38 N.Y. Jets (13) vs. Buffalo (25), Nov. 8, 1964
Indianapolis (18) vs. Houston (20), Sept. 23, 1990
Atlanta (14) vs. San Francisco (24), Oct. 14, 1990
Houston (17) vs. Kansas City (21), Dec. 16, 1990

Yards Gained

Most Yards Gained Rushing, Season
3,165 New England, 1978
3,088 Buffalo, 1973
2,986 Kansas City, 1978

Fewest Yards Gained Rushing, Season
298 Philadelphia, 1940
467 Detroit, 1946
471 Boston, 1944

Most Yards Gained Rushing, Game
426 Detroit vs. Pittsburgh, Nov. 4, 1934
423 N.Y. Giants vs. Baltimore, Nov. 19, 1950
420 Boston vs. N.Y. Giants, Oct. 8, 1933

Fewest Yards Gained Rushing, Game
−53 Detroit vs. Chi. Cardinals, Oct. 17, 1943
−36 Philadelphia vs. Chi. Bears, Nov. 19, 1939
−33 Phil-Pitt vs. Brooklyn, Oct. 2, 1943

Most Yards Gained Rushing, Both Teams, Game
595 Los Angeles (371) vs. N.Y. Yanks (224), Nov. 18, 1951
574 Chi. Bears (396) vs. Pittsburgh (178), Oct. 10, 1934
558 Boston (420) vs. N.Y. Giants (138), Oct. 8, 1933

Fewest Yards Gained Rushing, Both Teams, Game
−15 Detroit (−53) vs. Chi. Cardinals (38), Oct. 17, 1943

4 Detroit (−10) vs. Chi. Cardinals (14), Sept. 15, 1940
62 L.A. Rams (15) vs. San Francisco (47), Dec. 6, 1964

Average Gain
Highest Average Gain, Rushing, Season
5.74 Cleveland, 1963
5.65 San Francisco, 1954
5.56 San Diego, 1963
Lowest Average Gain, Rushing, Season
0.94 Philadelphia, 1940
1.45 Boston, 1944
1.55 Pittsburgh, 1935

Touchdowns
Most Touchdowns, Rushing, Season
36 Green Bay, 1962
33 Pittsburgh, 1976
30 Chi. Bears, 1941
New England, 1978
Washington, 1983
Fewest Touchdowns, Rushing, Season
1 Brooklyn, 1934
2 Chi. Cardinals, 1933
Cincinnati, 1933
Pittsburgh, 1934
Philadelphia, 1935
Philadelphia, 1936
Philadelphia, 1937
Philadelphia, 1938
Pittsburgh, 1940
Philadelphia, 1972
3 By many teams
Most Touchdowns, Rushing, Game
7 Los Angeles vs. Atlanta, Dec. 4, 1976
6 By many teams
Most Touchdowns, Rushing, Both Teams, Game
8 Los Angeles (6) vs. N.Y. Yanks (2), Nov. 18, 1951
Chi. Bears (5) vs. Green Bay (3), Nov. 6, 1955
Cleveland (6) vs. Los Angeles (2), Nov. 24, 1957
7 In many games

Passing
Attempts
Most Passes Attempted, Season
709 Minnesota, 1981
662 San Diego, 1984
645 Miami, 1986
Fewest Passes Attempted, Season
102 Cincinnati, 1933
106 Boston, 1933
120 Detroit, 1937
Most Passes Attempted, Game
68 Houston vs. Buffalo, Nov 1, 1964
66 Atlanta vs. Detroit, Dec. 24, 1989
65 San Diego vs. Kansas City, Oct. 19, 1986
Fewest Passes Attempted, Game
0 Green Bay vs. Portsmouth, Oct. 8, 1933
Detroit vs. Cleveland, Sept. 10, 1937
Pittsburgh vs. Brooklyn, Nov. 16, 1941
Pittsburgh vs. Los Angeles, Nov. 13, 1949
Cleveland vs. Philadelphia, Dec. 3, 1950
Most Passes Attempted, Both Teams, Game
104 Miami (55) vs. N.Y. Jets (49), Oct. 18, 1987 (OT)
102 San Francisco (57) vs. Atlanta (45), Oct. 6, 1985
100 Tampa Bay (54) vs. Kansas City (46), Oct. 28, 1984
San Francisco (60) vs. Washington (40), Nov. 17, 1986
Philadelphia (62) vs. Chicago (38), Oct. 2, 1989
Fewest Passes Attempted, Both Teams, Game
4 Chi. Cardinals (1) vs. Detroit (3), Nov. 3, 1935
Detroit (0) vs. Cleveland (4), Sept. 10, 1937
6 Chi. Cardinals (2) vs. Detroit (4), Sept. 15, 1940
8 Brooklyn (2) vs. Philadelphia (6), Oct. 1, 1939

Completions
Most Passes Completed, Season
401 San Diego, 1984
399 Houston, 1990
392 Miami, 1986
Fewest Passes Completed, Season
25 Cincinnati, 1933
33 Boston, 1933
34 Chi. Cardinals, 1934
Detroit, 1934
Most Passes Completed, Game
42 N.Y. Jets vs. San Francisco, Sept. 21, 1980
40 Cincinnati vs. San Diego, Dec. 20, 1982
Dallas vs. Detroit, Sept. 15, 1985
N.Y. Giants vs. Cincinnati, Oct. 13, 1985
39 Miami vs. Buffalo, Nov. 16, 1986
Fewest Passes Completed, Game
0 By many teams. Last time: Buffalo vs. N.Y. Jets, Sept. 29, 1974
Most Passes Completed, Both Teams, Game
68 San Francisco (37) vs. Atlanta (31), Oct. 6, 1985
66 Cincinnati (40) vs. San Diego (26), Dec. 20, 1982
65 San Diego (33) vs. San Francisco (32), Dec. 11, 1982
San Diego (37) vs. Miami (28), Nov. 18, 1984 (OT)
Fewest Passes Completed, Both Teams, Game
1 Chi. Cardinals (0) vs. Philadelphia (1), Nov. 8, 1936
Detroit (0) vs. Cleveland (1), Sept. 10, 1937
Chi. Cardinals (0) vs. Detroit (1), Sept. 15, 1940
Brooklyn (0) vs. Pittsburgh (1), Nov. 29, 1942
2 Chi. Cardinals (0) vs. Detroit (2), Nov. 3, 1935
Buffalo (0) vs. N.Y. Jets (2), Sept. 29, 1974
Chi. Cardinals (0) vs. Green Bay (2), Nov. 18, 1934
3 In seven games

Yards Gained
Most Seasons Leading League, Passing Yardage
10 San Diego, 1965, 1968, 1971, 1978-83, 1985
8 Chi. Bears, 1932, 1939, 1941, 1943, 1945, 1949, 1954, 1964
Washington, 1938, 1940, 1944, 1947-48, 1967, 1974, 1989
6 Clev. Browns, 1951, 1953-55, 1959-60
Dall. Texans/Kansas City, 1962, 1964, 1966-69
San Francisco, 1952, 1957-58, 1965, 1981, 1983
Most Consecutive Seasons Leading League, Passing Yardage
6 San Diego, 1978-83
4 Green Bay, 1934-37
3 Miami, 1986-88
Most Yards Gained, Passing, Season
5,018 Miami, 1984
4,870 San Diego, 1985
4,805 Houston, 1990
Fewest Yards Gained, Passing, Season
302 Chi. Cardinals, 1934
357 Cincinnati, 1933
459 Boston, 1934
Most Yards Gained, Passing, Game
554 Los Angeles vs. N.Y. Yanks, Sept. 28, 1951
530 Minnesota vs. Baltimore, Sept. 28, 1969
521 Miami vs. N.Y. Jets, Oct. 23, 1988
Fewest Yards Gained, Passing, Game
−53 Denver vs. Oakland, Sept. 10, 1967
−52 Cincinnati vs. Houston, Oct. 31, 1971
−39 Atlanta vs. San Francisco, Oct. 23, 1976
Most Yards Gained, Passing, Both Teams, Game
884 N.Y. Jets (449) vs. Miami (435), Sept. 21, 1986 (OT)
883 San Diego (486) vs. Cincinnati (397), Dec. 20, 1982
849 Minnesota (471) vs. Washington (378), Nov. 2, 1986 (OT)
Fewest Yards Gained, Passing, Both Teams, Game
−11 Green Bay (−10) vs. Dallas (−1), Oct. 24, 1965
1 Chi. Cardinals (0) vs. Philadelphia (1), Nov. 8, 1936
7 Brooklyn (0) vs. Pittsburgh (7), Nov. 29, 1942

Times Sacked
Most Seasons Leading League, Fewest Times Sacked
10 Miami, 1973, 1982-90
4 San Diego, 1963-64, 1967-68
San Francisco, 1964-65, 1970-71
3 N.Y. Jets, 1965-66, 1968
Houston, 1961-62, 1978
St. Louis, 1974-76
Most Consecutive Seasons Leading League, Fewest Times Sacked
9 Miami, 1982-90
3 St. Louis, 1974-76
2 By many teams
Most Times Sacked, Season
104 Philadelphia, 1986
72 Philadelphia, 1987
70 Atlanta, 1968
Fewest Times Sacked, Season
7 Miami, 1988
8 San Francisco, 1970
St. Louis, 1975
9 N.Y. Jets, 1966
Most Times Sacked, Game
12 Pittsburgh vs. Dallas, Nov. 20, 1966
Baltimore vs. St. Louis, Oct. 26, 1980
Detroit vs. Chicago, Dec. 16, 1984
Houston vs. Dallas, Sept. 29, 1985
11 St. Louis vs. N.Y. Giants, Nov. 1, 1964
Los Angeles vs. Baltimore, Nov. 22, 1964
Denver vs. Buffalo, Dec. 13, 1964
Green Bay vs. Detroit, Nov. 7, 1965
Buffalo vs. Oakland, Oct. 15, 1967
Denver vs. Oakland, Nov. 5, 1967
Atlanta vs. St. Louis, Nov. 24, 1968
Detroit vs. Dallas, Oct. 6, 1975
Philadelphia vs. St. Louis, Dec. 18, 1983
Cleveland vs. Kansas City, Sept. 30, 1984
Minnesota vs. Chicago, Oct. 28, 1984
Atlanta vs. Cleveland, Nov. 18, 1984
Dallas vs. San Diego, Nov. 16, 1986
Philadelphia vs. Detroit, Nov. 16, 1986
Philadelphia vs. L.A. Raiders, Nov. 30, 1986 (OT)
L.A. Raiders vs. Seattle, Dec. 8, 1986
N.Y. Jets vs. Dallas, Oct. 4, 1987
Philadelphia vs. Chicago, Oct. 4, 1987
10 By many teams
Most Times Sacked, Both Teams, Game
18 Green Bay (10) vs. San Diego (8), Sept. 24, 1978
17 Buffalo (10) vs. N.Y. Titans (7), Nov. 23, 1961
Pittsburgh (12) vs. Dallas (5), Nov. 20, 1966
Atlanta (9) vs. Philadelphia (8), Dec. 16, 1984
Philadelphia (11) vs. L.A. Raiders (6), Nov. 30, 1986 (OT)
16 Los Angeles (11) vs. Baltimore (5), Nov. 22, 1964
Buffalo (11) vs. Oakland (5), Oct. 15, 1967

Completion Percentage
Most Seasons Leading League, Completion Percentage
11 Washington, 1937, 1939-40, 1942-45, 1947-48, 1969-70
8 San Francisco, 1952, 1957-58, 1965, 1981, 1983, 1987, 1989
7 Green Bay, 1936, 1941, 1961-62, 1964, 1966, 1968
Most Consecutive Seasons Leading League, Completion Percentage
4 Washington, 1942-45
Kansas City, 1966-69
3 Cleveland, 1953-55

2 By many teams

Highest Completion Percentage, Season

70.65 Cincinnati, 1982 (310-219)
70.19 San Francisco, 1989 (483-339)
64.27 San Francisco, 1987 (501-322)

Lowest Completion Percentage, Season

22.9 Philadelphia, 1936 (170-39)
24.5 Cincinnati, 1933 (102-25)
25.0 Pittsburgh, 1941 (168-42)

Touchdowns

Most Touchdowns, Passing, Season

49 Miami, 1984
48 Houston, 1961
46 Miami, 1986

Fewest Touchdowns, Passing, Season

0 Cincinnati, 1933
Pittsburgh, 1945
1 Boston, 1932
Boston, 1933
Chi. Cardinals, 1934
Cincinnati/St. Louis, 1934
Detroit, 1942
2 Chi. Cardinals, 1932
Stapleton, 1932
Chi. Cardinals, 1935
Brooklyn, 1936
Pittsburgh, 1942

Most Touchdowns, Passing, Game

7 Chi. Bears vs. N.Y. Giants, Nov. 14, 1943
Philadelphia vs. Washington, Oct. 17, 1954
Houston vs. N.Y. Titans, Nov. 19, 1961
Houston vs. N.Y. Titans, Oct. 14, 1962
N.Y. Giants vs. Washington, Oct. 28, 1962
Minnesota vs. Baltimore, Sept. 28, 1969
San Diego vs. Oakland, Nov. 22, 1981
6 By many teams.

Most Touchdowns, Passing, Both Teams, Game

12 New Orleans (6) vs. St. Louis (6), Nov. 2, 1969
11 N.Y. Giants (7) vs. Washington (4), Oct. 28, 1962
Oakland (6) vs. Houston (5), Dec. 22, 1963
10 San Diego (5) vs. Seattle (5), Sept. 15, 1985
Miami (6) vs. N.Y. Jets (4), Sept. 21, 1986 (OT)

Passes Had Intercepted

Most Passes Had Intercepted, Season

48 Houston, 1962
45 Denver, 1961
41 Card-Pitt, 1944

Fewest Passes Had Intercepted, Season

5 Cleveland, 1960
Green Bay, 1966
Kansas City, 1990
N.Y. Giants, 1990
6 Green Bay, 1964
St. Louis, 1982
7 Los Angeles, 1969

Most Passes Had Intercepted, Game

9 Detroit vs. Green Bay, Oct. 24, 1943
Pittsburgh vs. Philadelphia, Dec. 12, 1965
8 Green Bay vs. N.Y. Giants, Nov. 21, 1948
Chi. Cardinals vs. Philadelphia, Sept. 24, 1950
N.Y. Yanks vs. N.Y. Giants, Dec. 16, 1951
Denver vs. Houston, Dec. 2, 1962
Chi. Bears vs. Detroit, Sept. 22, 1968
Baltimore vs. N.Y. Jets, Sept. 23, 1973
7 By many teams. Last time: Green Bay vs. New Orleans, Sept. 14, 1986

Most Passes Had Intercepted, Both Teams, Game

13 Denver (8) vs. Houston (5), Dec. 2, 1962
11 Philadelphia (7) vs. Boston (4), Nov. 3, 1935
Boston (6) vs. Pittsburgh (5), Dec. 1, 1935
Cleveland (7) vs. Green Bay (4), Oct. 30, 1938
Green Bay (7) vs. Detroit (4), Oct. 20, 1940
Detroit (7) vs. Chi. Bears (4), Nov. 22, 1942
Detroit (7) vs. Cleveland (4), Nov. 26, 1944
Chi. Cardinals (8) vs. Philadelphia (3), Sept. 24, 1950
Washington (7) vs. N.Y. Giants (4), Dec. 8, 1963
Pittsburgh (9) vs. Philadelphia (2), Dec 12, 1965
10 In many games

Punting

Most Seasons Leading League (Average Distance)

7 Denver, 1962-64, 1966-67, 1982, 1988
6 Washington, 1940-43, 1945, 1958
Kansas City, 1968, 1971-73, 1979, 1984
4 L.A. Rams, 1946, 1949, 1955-56
Baltimore/Indianapolis, 1966, 1969, 1983, 1985

Most Consecutive Seasons Leading League (Average Distance)

4 Washington, 1940-43
3 Cleveland, 1950-52
Denver, 1962-64
Kansas City, 1971-73

Most Punts, Season

114 Chicago, 1981
113 Boston, 1934
Brooklyn, 1934
112 Boston, 1935

Fewest Punts, Season

23 San Diego, 1982
31 Cincinnati, 1982
32 Chi. Bears, 1941

Most Punts, Game

17 Chi. Bears vs. Green Bay, Oct. 22, 1933
Cincinnati vs. Pittsburgh, Oct. 22, 1933
16 Cincinnati vs. Portsmouth, Sept. 17, 1933
Chi. Cardinals vs. Chi. Bears, Nov. 30, 1933
Chi. Cardinals vs. Detroit, Sept. 15, 1940

Fewest Punts, Game

0 By many teams. Last time: Green Bay vs. Chicago, Dec. 17, 1989

Most Punts, Both Teams, Game

31 Chi. Bears (17) vs. Green Bay (14), Oct. 22, 1933
Cincinnati (17), vs. Pittsburgh (14), Oct. 22, 1933
29 Chi. Cardinals (15) vs. Cincinnati (14), Nov. 12, 1933
Chi. Cardinals (16) vs. Chi. Bears (13), Nov. 30, 1933
Chi. Cardinals (16) vs. Detroit (13), Sept. 15, 1940

Fewest Punts, Both Teams, Game

1 Baltimore (0) vs. Cleveland (1), Nov. 1, 1959
Dall. Cowboys (0) vs. Cleveland (1), Dec. 3, 1961
Chicago (0) vs. Detroit (1), Oct. 1, 1972
San Francisco (0) vs. N.Y. Giants (1), Oct. 15, 1972
Green Bay (0) vs. Buffalo (1), Dec. 5, 1982
Miami (0) vs. Buffalo (1), Oct. 12, 1986
Green Bay (0) vs. Chicago (1), Dec. 17, 1989
2 In many games

Average Yardage

Highest Average Distance, Punting, Season

47.6 Detroit, 1961 (56-2,664)
47.0 Pittsburgh, 1961 (73-3,431)
46.9 Pittsburgh, 1953 (80-3,752)

Lowest Average Distance, Punting, Season

32.7 Card-Pitt, 1944 (60-1,964)
33.8 Cincinnati, 1986 (59-1,996)
33.9 Detroit, 1969 (74-2,510)

Punt Returns

Most Seasons Leading League (Average Return)

8 Detroit, 1943-45, 1951-52, 1962, 1966, 1969
7 Chi. Cardinals/St. Louis, 1948-49, 1955-56, 1959, 1986-87
5 Cleveland, 1958, 1960, 1964-65, 1967
Green Bay, 1950, 1953-54, 1961, 1972
Dall. Texans/Kansas City, 1960, 1968, 1970, 1979-80

Most Consecutive Seasons Leading League (Average Return)

3 Detroit, 1943-45
2 By many teams

Most Punt Returns, Season

71 Pittsburgh, 1976
Tampa Bay, 1979
L.A. Raiders, 1985
67 Pittsburgh, 1974
Los Angeles, 1978
L.A. Raiders, 1984
65 San Francisco, 1976

Fewest Punt Returns, Season

12 Baltimore, 1981
San Diego, 1982
14 Los Angeles, 1961
Philadelphia, 1962
Baltimore, 1982
15 Houston, 1960
Washington, 1960
Oakland, 1961
N.Y. Giants, 1969
Philadelphia, 1973
Kansas City, 1982

Most Punt Returns, Game

12 Philadelphia vs. Cleveland, Dec. 3, 1950
11 Chi. Bears vs. Chi. Cardinals, Oct. 8, 1950
Washington vs. Tampa Bay, Oct. 9, 1977
10 Philadelphia vs. N.Y. Giants, Nov. 26, 1950
Philadelphia vs. Tampa Bay, Sept. 18, 1977
Pittsburgh vs. Buffalo, Dec. 16, 1979
Washington vs. New Orleans, Dec. 26, 1982

Most Punt Returns, Both Teams, Game

17 Philadelphia (12) vs. Cleveland (5), Dec. 3, 1950
16 N.Y. Giants (9) vs. Philadelphia (7), Dec. 12, 1954
Washington (11) vs. Tampa Bay (5), Oct. 9, 1977
15 Detroit (8) vs. Cleveland (7), Sept. 27, 1942
Los Angeles (8) vs. Baltimore (7), Nov. 27, 1966
Pittsburgh (8) vs. Houston (7), Dec. 1, 1974
Philadelphia (10) vs. Tampa Bay (5), Sept. 18, 1977
Baltimore (9) vs. Kansas City (6), Sept. 2, 1979
Washington (10) vs. New Orleans (5), Dec. 26, 1982
L.A. Raiders (8) vs. Cleveland (7), Nov. 16, 1986

Fair Catches

Most Fair Catches, Season

34 Baltimore, 1971
32 San Diego, 1969
30 St. Louis, 1967
Minnesota, 1971

Fewest Fair Catches, Season

0 San Diego, 1975
New England, 1976
Tampa Bay, 1976
Pittsburgh, 1977
Dallas, 1982
1 Cleveland, 1974
San Francisco, 1975
Kansas City, 1976
St. Louis, 1976
San Diego, 1976
L.A. Rams, 1982
St. Louis, 1982
Tampa Bay, 1982
2 By many teams

Most Fair Catches, Game
7 Minnesota vs. Dallas, Sept. 25, 1966
Detroit vs. Chicago, Nov. 21, 1976
Philadelphia vs. Buffalo, Dec. 27, 1987
6 By many teams

Yards Gained

Most Yards, Punt Returns, Season
785 L.A. Raiders, 1985
781 Chi. Bears, 1948
774 Pittsburgh, 1974
Fewest Yards, Punt Returns, Season
27 St. Louis, 1965
35 N.Y. Giants, 1965
37 New England, 1972
Most Yards, Punt Returns, Game
231 Detroit vs. San Francisco, Oct. 6, 1963
225 Oakland vs. Buffalo, Sept. 15, 1968
219 Los Angeles vs. Atlanta, Oct. 11, 1981
Most Yards, Punt Returns, Both Teams, Game
282 Los Angeles (219) vs. Atlanta (63), Oct. 11, 1981
245 Detroit (231) vs. San Francisco (14), Oct. 6, 1963
244 Oakland (225) vs. Buffalo (19), Sept. 15, 1968

Average Yards Returning Punts

Highest Average, Punt Returns, Season
20.2 Chi. Bears, 1941 (27-546)
19.1 Chi. Cardinals, 1948 (35-669)
18.2 Chi. Cardinals, 1949 (30-546)
Lowest Average, Punt Returns, Season
1.2 St. Louis, 1965 (23-27)
1.5 N.Y. Giants, 1965 (24-35)
1.7 Washington, 1970 (27-45)

Touchdowns Returning Punts

Most Touchdowns, Punt Returns, Season
5 Chi. Cardinals, 1959
4 Chi. Cardinals, 1948
Detroit, 1951
N.Y. Giants, 1951
Denver, 1976
3 Washington, 1941
Detroit, 1952
Pittsburgh, 1952
Houston, 1975
Los Angeles, 1981
Most Touchdowns, Punt Returns, Game
2 Detroit vs. Los Angeles, Oct. 14, 1951
Detroit vs. Green Bay, Nov. 22, 1951
Chi. Cardinals vs. Pittsburgh, Nov. 1, 1959
Chi. Cardinals vs. N.Y. Giants, Nov. 22, 1959
N.Y. Titans vs. Denver, Sept. 24, 1961
Denver vs. Cleveland, Sept. 26, 1976
Los Angeles vs. Atlanta, Oct. 11, 1981
St. Louis vs. Tampa Bay, Dec. 21, 1986
Most Touchdowns, Punt Returns, Both Teams, Game
2 Philadelphia (1) vs. Washington (1), Nov. 9, 1952
Kansas City (1) vs. Buffalo (1), Sept. 11, 1966
Baltimore (1) vs. New England (1), Nov. 18, 1979
L.A. Raiders (1) vs. Philadelphia (1), Nov. 30, 1986 (OT)
(Also see previous record)

Kickoff Returns

Most Seasons Leading League (Average Return)
7 Washington, 1942, 1947, 1962-63, 1973-74, 1981
6 Chicago Bears, 1943, 1948, 1958, 1966, 1972, 1985
5 N.Y. Giants, 1944, 1946, 1949, 1951, 1953
Most Consecutive Seasons Leading League (Average Return)
3 Denver, 1965-67
2 By many teams
Most Kickoff Returns, Season
88 New Orleans, 1980
86 Minnesota, 1984
84 Baltimore, 1981
Fewest Kickoff Returns, Season
17 N.Y. Giants, 1944
20 N.Y. Giants, 1941, 1943
Chi. Bears, 1942
23 Washington, 1942
Most Kickoff Returns, Game
12 N.Y. Giants vs. Washington, Nov. 27, 1966
10 By many teams
Most Kickoff Returns, Both Teams, Game
19 N.Y. Giants (12) vs. Washington (7), Nov. 27, 1966
18 Houston (10) vs. Oakland (8), Dec. 22, 1963
17 Washington (9) vs. Green Bay (8), Oct. 17, 1983
San Diego (9) vs. Pittsburgh (8), Dec. 8, 1985
Detroit (9) vs. Green Bay (8), Nov. 27, 1986
L.A. Raiders (9) vs. Seattle (8), Dec. 18, 1988

Yards Gained

Most Yards, Kickoff Returns, Season
1,973 New Orleans, 1980
1,824 Houston, 1963
1,801 Denver, 1963
Fewest Yards, Kickoff Returns, Season
282 N.Y. Giants, 1940
381 Green Bay, 1940
424 Chicago, 1963
Most Yards, Kickoff Returns, Game
362 Detroit vs. Los Angeles, Oct. 29, 1950
304 Chi. Bears vs. Green Bay, Nov. 9, 1952
295 Denver vs. Boston, Oct. 4, 1964
Most Yards, Kickoff Returns, Both Teams, Game
560 Detroit (362) vs. Los Angeles (198), Oct. 29, 1950
453 Washington (236) vs. Philadelphia (217), Sept. 28, 1947
447 N.Y. Giants (236) vs. Cleveland (211), Dec. 4, 1966

Average Yardage

Highest Average, Kickoff Returns, Season
29.4 Chicago, 1972 (52-1,528)
28.9 Pittsburgh, 1952 (39-1,128)
28.2 Washington, 1962 (61-1,720)
Lowest Average, Kickoff Returns, Season
16.27 Chicago, 1990 (54-879)
16.31 Chicago, 1963 (26-424)
16.4 Chicago, 1983 (58-953)

Touchdowns

Most Touchdowns, Kickoff Returns, Season
4 Green Bay, 1967
Chicago, 1970
3 Los Angeles, 1950
Chi. Cardinals, 1954
San Francisco, 1963
Denver, 1966
Chicago, 1967
New England, 1977
L.A. Rams, 1985
2 By many teams
Most Touchdowns, Kickoff Returns, Game
2 Chi. Bears vs. Green Bay, Sept. 22, 1940
Chi. Bears vs. Green Bay, Nov. 9, 1952
Philadelphia vs. Dallas, Nov. 6, 1966
Green Bay vs. Cleveland, Nov. 12, 1967
L.A. Rams vs. Green Bay, Nov. 24, 1985
Most Touchdowns, Kickoff Returns, Both Teams, Game
2 Washington (1) vs. Philadelphia (1), Nov. 1, 1942
Washington (1) vs. Philadelphia (1), Sept. 28, 1947
Los Angeles (1) vs. Detroit (1), Oct. 29, 1950
N.Y. Yanks (1) vs. N.Y. Giants (1), Nov. 4, 1951 (consecutive)
Baltimore (1) vs. Chi. Bears (1), Oct. 4, 1958
Buffalo (1) vs. Boston (1), Nov. 3, 1962
Pittsburgh (1) vs. Dallas (1), Oct. 30, 1966
St. Louis (1) vs. Washington (1), Sept. 23, 1973 (consecutive)
Atlanta (1) vs. San Francisco (1), Dec. 20, 1987 (consecutive)
Houston (1) vs. Pittsburgh (1), Dec. 4, 1988
(Also see previous record)

Fumbles

Most Fumbles, Season
56 Chi. Bears, 1938
San Francisco, 1978
54 Philadelphia, 1946
51 New England, 1973
Fewest Fumbles, Season
8 Cleveland, 1959
11 Green Bay, 1944
12 Brooklyn, 1934
Detroit, 1943
Cincinnati, 1982
Minnesota, 1982
Most Fumbles, Game
10 Phil-Pitt vs. New York, Oct. 9, 1943
Detroit vs. Minnesota, Nov. 12, 1967
Kansas City vs. Houston, Oct. 12, 1969
San Francisco vs. Detroit, Dec. 17, 1978
9 Philadelphia vs. Green Bay, Oct. 13, 1946
Kansas City vs. San Diego, Nov. 15, 1964
N.Y. Giants vs. Buffalo, Oct. 20, 1975
St. Louis vs. Washington, Oct. 25, 1976
San Diego vs. Green Bay, Sept. 24, 1978
Pittsburgh vs. Cincinnati, Oct. 14, 1979
Cleveland vs. Seattle, Dec. 20, 1981
Cleveland vs. Pittsburgh, Dec. 23, 1990
8 By many teams
Most Fumbles, Both Teams, Game
14 Washington (8) vs. Pittsburgh (6), Nov. 14, 1937
Chi. Bears (7) vs. Cleveland (7), Nov. 24, 1940
St. Louis (8) vs. N.Y. Giants (6), Sept. 17, 1961
Kansas City (10) vs. Houston (4), Oct. 12, 1969
13 Washington (8) vs. Pittsburgh (5), Nov. 14, 1937
Philadelphia (7) vs. Boston (6), Dec. 8, 1946
N.Y. Giants (7) vs. Washington (6), Nov. 5, 1950
Kansas City (9) vs. San Diego (4), Nov. 15, 1964
Buffalo (7) vs. Denver (6), Dec. 13, 1964
N.Y. Jets (7) vs. Houston (6), Sept. 12, 1965
Houston (8) vs. Pittsburgh (5), Dec. 9, 1973
St. Louis (9) vs. Washington (4), Oct. 25, 1976
Cleveland (9) vs. Seattle (4), Dec. 20, 1981
Green Bay (7) vs. Detroit (6), Oct. 6, 1985
12 In many games

Fumbles Lost

Most Fumbles Lost, Season
36 Chi. Cardinals, 1959
31 Green Bay, 1952
29 Chi. Cardinals, 1946
Pittsburgh, 1950
Fewest Fumbles Lost, Season
3 Philadelphia, 1938
Minnesota, 1980
4 San Francisco, 1960
Kansas City, 1982
5 Chi. Cardinals, 1943
Detroit, 1943

N.Y. Giants, 1943
Cleveland, 1959
Minnesota, 1982

Most Fumbles Lost, Game

8 St. Louis vs. Washington, Oct. 25, 1976
Cleveland vs. Pittsburgh, Dec. 23, 1990
7 Cincinnati vs. Buffalo, Nov. 30, 1969
Pittsburgh vs. Cincinnati, Oct. 14, 1979
Cleveland vs. Seattle, Dec. 20, 1981
6 By many teams

Fumbles Recovered

Most Fumbles Recovered, Season, Own and Opponents'

58 Minnesota, 1963 (27 own, 31 opp)
51 Chi. Bears, 1938 (37 own, 14 opp)
San Francisco, 1978 (24 own, 27 opp)
50 Philadelphia, 1987 (23 own, 27 opp)

Fewest Fumbles Recovered, Season, Own and Opponents'

9 San Francisco, 1982 (5 own, 4 opp)
11 Cincinnati, 1982 (5 own, 6 opp)
13 Baltimore, 1967 (5 own, 8 opp)
N.Y. Jets, 1967 (7 own, 6 opp)
Philadelphia, 1968 (6 own, 7 opp)
Miami, 1973 (5 own, 8 opp)
Chicago, 1982 (6 own, 7 opp)
Denver, 1982 (6 own, 7 opp)
Miami, 1982 (5 own, 8 opp)
N.Y. Giants, 1982 (7 own, 6 opp)

Most Fumbles Recovered, Game, Own and Opponents'

10 Denver vs. Buffalo, Dec. 13, 1964 (5 own, 5 opp)
Pittsburgh vs. Houston, Dec. 9, 1973 (5 own, 5 opp)
Washington vs. St. Louis, Oct. 25, 1976 (2 own, 8 opp)
9 St. Louis vs. N.Y. Giants, Sept. 17, 1961 (6 own, 3 opp)
Houston vs. Cincinnati, Oct. 27, 1974 (4 own, 5 opp)
Kansas City vs. Dallas, Nov. 10, 1975 (4 own, 5 opp)
Green Bay vs. Detroit, Oct. 6, 1985 (5 own, 4 opp)
8 By many teams

Most Own Fumbles Recovered, Season

37 Chi. Bears, 1938
28 Pittsburgh, 1987
27 Philadelphia, 1946
Minnesota, 1963

Fewest Own Fumbles Recovered, Season

2 Washington, 1958
3 Detroit, 1956
Cleveland, 1959
Houston, 1982
4 By many teams

Most Opponents' Fumbles Recovered, Season

31 Minnesota, 1963
29 Cleveland, 1951
28 Green Bay, 1946
Houston, 1977
Seattle, 1983

Fewest Opponents' Fumbles Recovered, Season

3 Los Angeles, 1974
4 Philadelphia, 1944
San Francisco, 1982
5 Baltimore, 1982

Most Opponents' Fumbles Recovered, Game

8 Washington vs. St. Louis, Oct. 25, 1976
7 Buffalo vs. Cincinnati, Nov. 30, 1969
Seattle vs. Cleveland, Dec. 20, 1981
6 By many teams. Last time: New England vs. L.A. Rams, Dec. 11, 1983

Touchdowns

Most Touchdowns, Fumbles Recovered, Season, Own and Opponents'

5 Chi. Bears, 1942 (1 own, 4 opp)
Los Angeles, 1952 (1 own, 4 opp)
San Francisco, 1965 (1 own, 4 opp)
Oakland, 1978 (2 own, 3 opp)
4 Chi. Bears, 1948 (1 own, 3 opp)
Boston, 1948 (4 opp)
Denver, 1979 (1 own, 3 opp)
Atlanta, 1981 (1 own, 3 opp)
Denver, 1984 (4 opp)
St. Louis, 1987 (4 opp)
Minnesota, 1989 (4 opp)
3 By many teams

Most Touchdowns, Own Fumbles Recovered, Season

2 Chi. Bears, 1953
New England, 1973
Buffalo, 1974
Denver, 1975
Oakland, 1978
Green Bay, 1982
New Orleans, 1983
Cleveland, 1986
Green Bay, 1989

Most Touchdowns, Opponents' Fumbles Recovered, Season

4 Detroit, 1937
Chi. Bears, 1942
Boston, 1948
Los Angeles, 1952
San Francisco, 1965
Denver, 1984
St. Louis, 1987
Minnesota, 1989
3 By many teams

Most Touchdowns, Fumbles Recovered, Game, Own and Opponents'

2 By many teams

Most Touchdowns, Own Fumbles Recovered, Game

1 By many teams

Most Touchdowns, Opponents' Fumbles Recovered, Game

2 Detroit vs. Cleveland, Nov. 7, 1937
Philadelphia vs. N.Y. Giants, Sept. 25, 1938
Chi. Bears vs. Washington, Nov. 28, 1948
N.Y. Giants vs. Pittsburgh, Sept. 17, 1950
Cleveland vs. Dall. Cowboys, Dec. 3, 1961
Cleveland vs. N.Y. Giants, Oct. 25, 1964
Green Bay vs. Dallas, Nov. 26, 1964
San Francisco vs. Detroit, Nov. 14, 1965
Oakland vs. Buffalo, Dec. 24, 1967
N.Y. Giants vs. Green Bay, Sept. 19, 1971
Washington vs. San Diego, Sept. 16, 1973
New Orleans vs. San Francisco, Oct. 19, 1975
Cincinnati vs. Pittsburgh, Oct. 14, 1979
Atlanta vs. Detroit, Oct. 5, 1980
Kansas City vs. Oakland, Oct. 5, 1980
New England vs. Baltimore, Nov. 23, 1980
Denver vs. Green Bay, Oct. 15, 1984
Miami vs. Kansas City, Oct. 11, 1987
St. Louis vs. New Orleans, Oct. 11, 1987
Minnesota vs. Atlanta, Dec. 10, 1989

Turnovers

(Number of times losing the ball on interceptions and fumbles.)

Most Turnovers, Season

63 San Francisco, 1978
58 Chi. Bears, 1947
Pittsburgh, 1950
N.Y. Giants, 1983
57 Green Bay, 1950
Houston, 1962, 1963
Pittsburgh, 1965

Fewest Turnovers, Season

12 Kansas City, 1982
14 N.Y. Giants, 1943
Cleveland, 1959
N.Y. Giants, 1990
16 San Francisco, 1960
Cincinnati, 1982
St. Louis, 1982
Washington, 1982

Most Turnovers, Game

12 Detroit vs. Chi. Bears, Nov. 22, 1942
Chi. Cardinals vs. Philadelphia, Sept. 24, 1950
Pittsburgh vs. Philadelphia, Dec. 12, 1965
11 San Diego vs. Green Bay, Sept. 24, 1978
10 Washington vs. N.Y. Giants, Dec. 4, 1938
Pittsburgh vs. Green Bay, Nov. 23, 1941
Detroit vs. Green Bay, Oct. 24, 1943
Chi. Cardinals vs. Green Bay, Nov. 10, 1946
Chi. Cardinals vs. N.Y. Giants, Nov. 2, 1952
Minnesota vs. Detroit, Dec. 9, 1962
Houston vs. Oakland, Sept. 7, 1963
Washington vs. N.Y. Giants, Dec. 8, 1963
Chicago vs. Detroit, Sept. 22, 1968
St. Louis vs. Washington, Oct. 25, 1976
N.Y. Jets vs. New England, Nov. 21, 1976
San Francisco vs. Dallas, Oct. 12, 1980
Cleveland vs. Seattle, Dec. 20, 1981
Detroit vs. Denver, Oct. 7, 1984

Most Turnovers, Both Teams, Game

17 Detroit (12) vs. Chi. Bears (5), Nov. 22, 1942
Boston (9) vs. Philadelphia (8), Dec. 8, 1946
16 Chi. Cardinals (12) vs. Philadelphia (4), Sept. 24, 1950
Chi. Cardinals (8) vs. Chi. Bears (8), Dec. 7, 1958
Minnesota (10) vs. Detroit (6), Dec. 9, 1962
Houston (9) vs. Kansas City (7), Oct. 12, 1969
15 Philadelphia (8) vs. Chi. Cardinals (7), Oct. 3, 1954
Denver (9) vs. Houston (6), Dec. 2, 1962
Washington (10) vs. N.Y. Giants (5), Dec. 8, 1963
St. Louis (9) vs. Kansas City (6), Oct. 2, 1983

Penalties

Most Seasons Leading League, Fewest Penalties

12 Miami, 1968, 1976-84, 1986, 1990
9 Pittsburgh, 1946-47, 1950-52, 1954, 1963, 1965, 1968
6 Boston/New England, 1962, 1964-65, 1973, 1987, 1989

Most Consecutive Seasons Leading League, Fewest Penalties

9 Miami, 1976-84
3 Pittsburgh, 1950-52
2 By many teams

Most Seasons Leading League, Most Penalties

16 Chi. Bears, 1941-44, 1946-49, 1951, 1959-61, 1963, 1965, 1968, 1976
7 Oakland/L.A. Raiders, 1963, 1966, 1968-69, 1975, 1982, 1984
6 L.A. Rams, 1950, 1952, 1962, 1969, 1978, 1980

Most Consecutive Seasons Leading League, Most Penalties

4 Chi. Bears, 1941-44, 1946-49
3 Chi. Cardinals, 1954-56
Chi. Bears, 1959-61
Houston, 1988-90

Fewest Penalties, Season

19 Detroit, 1937
21 Boston, 1935
24 Philadelphia, 1936

Most Penalties, Season

149 Houston, 1989
144 Buffalo, 1983
143 L.A. Raiders, 1984

Fewest Penalties, Game

0 By many teams. Last time: Dallas vs. Washington, Nov. 5, 1989

Most Penalties, Game

22 Brooklyn vs. Green Bay, Sept. 17, 1944

Chi. Bears vs. Philadelphia, Nov. 26, 1944
21 Cleveland vs. Chi. Bears, Nov. 25, 1951
20 Tampa Bay vs. Seattle, Oct. 17, 1976

Fewest Penalties, Both Teams, Game
0 Brooklyn vs. Pittsburgh, Oct. 28, 1934
Brooklyn vs. Boston, Sept. 28, 1936
Cleveland vs. Chi. Bears, Oct. 9, 1938
Pittsburgh vs. Philadelphia, Nov. 10, 1940

Most Penalties, Both Teams, Game
37 Cleveland (21) vs. Chi. Bears (16), Nov. 25, 1951
35 Tampa Bay (20) vs. Seattle (15), Oct. 17, 1976
33 Brooklyn (22) vs. Green Bay (11), Sept. 17, 1944

Yards Penalized

Most Seasons Leading League, Fewest Yards Penalized
12 Miami, 1967-68, 1973, 1977-84, 1990
8 Boston/Washington, 1935, 1953-54, 1956-58, 1970, 1985
7 Pittsburgh, 1946-47, 1950, 1952, 1962, 1965, 1968

Most Consecutive Seasons Leading League, Fewest Yards Penalized
8 Miami, 1977-84
3 Washington, 1956-58
Boston, 1964-66
2 By many teams

Most Seasons Leading League, Most Yards Penalized
15 Chi. Bears, 1935, 1937, 1939-44, 1946-47, 1949, 1951, 1961-62, 1968
7 Oakland/L.A. Raiders, 1963-64, 1968-69, 1975, 1982, 1984
6 Buffalo, 1962, 1967, 1970, 1972, 1981, 1983
Houston, 1961, 1985-86, 1988-90

Most Consecutive Seasons Leading League, Most Yards Penalized
6 Chi. Bears, 1939-44
3 Cleveland, 1976-78
Houston, 1988-90
2 By many teams

Fewest Yards Penalized, Season
139 Detroit, 1937
146 Philadelphia, 1937
159 Philadelphia, 1936

Most Yards Penalized, Season
1,274 Oakland, 1969
1,239 Baltimore, 1979
1,209 L.A. Raiders, 1984

Fewest Yards Penalized, Game
0 By many teams. Last time: Dallas vs. Washington, Nov. 5, 1989

Most Yards Penalized, Game
209 Cleveland vs. Chi. Bears, Nov. 25, 1951
190 Tampa Bay vs. Seattle, Oct. 17, 1976
189 Houston vs. Buffalo, Oct. 31, 1965

Fewest Yards Penalized, Both Teams, Game
0 Brooklyn vs. Pittsburgh, Oct. 28, 1934
Brooklyn vs. Boston, Sept. 28, 1936
Cleveland vs. Chi. Bears, Oct. 9, 1938
Pittsburgh vs. Philadelphia, Nov. 10, 1940

Most Yards Penalized, Both Teams, Game
374 Cleveland (209) vs. Chi. Bears (165), Nov. 25, 1951
310 Tampa Bay (190) vs. Seattle (120), Oct. 17, 1976
309 Green Bay (184) vs. Boston (125), Oct. 21, 1945

Defense

Scoring

Most Seasons Leading League, Fewest Points Allowed
9 Chi. Bears, 1932, 1936-37, 1942, 1948, 1963, 1985-86, 1988
N.Y. Giants, 1935, 1938-39, 1941, 1944, 1958-59, 1961, 1990
6 Cleveland, 1951, 1953-57
5 Green Bay, 1935, 1947, 1962, 1965-66

Most Consecutive Seasons Leading League, Fewest Points Allowed
5 Cleveland, 1953-57
3 Buffalo, 1964-66
Minnesota, 1969-71
2 By many teams

Fewest Points Allowed, Season (Since 1932)
44 Chi. Bears, 1932
54 Brooklyn, 1933
59 Detroit, 1934

Most Points Allowed, Season
533 Baltimore, 1981
501 N.Y. Giants, 1966
487 New Orleans, 1980

Fewest Touchdowns Allowed, Season (Since 1932)
6 Chi. Bears, 1932
Brooklyn, 1933
7 Detroit, 1934
8 Green Bay, 1932

Most Touchdowns Allowed, Season
68 Baltimore, 1981
66 N.Y. Giants, 1966
63 Baltimore, 1950

First Downs

Fewest First Downs Allowed Season
77 Detroit, 1935
79 Boston, 1935
82 Washington, 1937

Most First Downs Allowed, Season
406 Baltimore, 1981
371 Seattle, 1981
366 Green Bay, 1983

Fewest First Downs Allowed, Rushing, Season
35 Chi. Bears, 1942
40 Green Bay, 1939
41 Brooklyn, 1944

Most First Downs Allowed, Rushing, Season
179 Detroit, 1985
178 New Orleans, 1980
175 Seattle, 1981

Fewest First Downs Allowed, Passing, Season
33 Chi. Bears, 1943
34 Pittsburgh, 1941
Washington, 1943
35 Detroit, 1940
Philadelphia, 1940, 1944

Most First Downs Allowed, Passing, Season
218 San Diego, 1985
216 San Diego, 1981
N.Y. Jets, 1986
214 Baltimore, 1981

Fewest First Downs Allowed, Penalty, Season
1 Boston, 1944
3 Philadelphia, 1940
Pittsburgh, 1945
Washington, 1957
4 Cleveland, 1940
Green Bay, 1943
N.Y. Giants, 1943

Most First Downs Allowed, Penalty, Season
48 Houston, 1985
46 Houston, 1986
43 L.A. Raiders, 1984

Net Yards Allowed Rushing and Passing

Most Seasons Leading League, Fewest Yards Allowed
8 Chi. Bears, 1942-43, 1948, 1958, 1963, 1984-86
6 N.Y. Giants, 1938, 1940-41, 1951, 1956, 1959
5 Boston/Washington, 1935-37, 1939, 1946
Philadelphia, 1944-45, 1949, 1953, 1981
Minnesota, 1969-70, 1975, 1988-89

Most Consecutive Seasons Leading League, Fewest Yards Allowed
3 Boston/Washington, 1935-37
Chicago, 1984-86
2 By many teams

Fewest Yards Allowed, Season
1,539 Chi. Cardinals, 1934
1,703 Chi. Bears, 1942
1,789 Brooklyn, 1933

Most Yards Allowed, Season
6,793 Baltimore, 1981
6,403 Green Bay, 1983
6,352 Minnesota, 1984

Rushing

Most Seasons Leading League, Fewest Yards Allowed
10 Chi. Bears, 1937, 1939, 1942, 1946, 1949, 1963, 1984-85, 1987-88
7 Detroit, 1938, 1950, 1952, 1962, 1970, 1980-81
6 Dallas, 1966-69, 1972, 1978
Philadelphia, 1944-45, 1947-48, 1953, 1990

Most Consecutive Seasons Leading League, Fewest Yards Allowed
4 Dallas, 1966-69
2 By many teams

Fewest Yards Allowed, Rushing, Season
519 Chi. Bears, 1942
558 Philadelphia, 1944
762 Pittsburgh, 1982

Most Yards Allowed, Rushing, Season
3,228 Buffalo, 1978
3,106 New Orleans, 1980
3,010 Baltimore, 1978

Fewest Touchdowns Allowed, Rushing, Season
2 Detroit, 1934
Dallas, 1968
Minnesota, 1971
3 By many teams

Most Touchdowns Allowed, Rushing, Season
36 Oakland, 1961
31 N.Y. Giants, 1980
Tampa Bay, 1986
30 Baltimore, 1981

Passing

Most Seasons Leading League, Fewest Yards Allowed
8 Green Bay, 1947-48, 1962, 1964-68
7 Washington, 1939, 1942, 1945, 1952-53, 1980, 1985
6 Chi. Bears, 1938, 1943-44, 1958, 1960, 1963
Minnesota, 1969-70, 1972, 1975-76, 1989
Pittsburgh, 1941, 1946, 1951, 1955, 1974, 1990

Most Consecutive Seasons Leading League, Fewest Yards Allowed
5 Green Bay, 1964-68
2 By many teams

Fewest Yards Allowed, Passing, Season
545 Philadelphia, 1934
558 Portsmouth, 1933
585 Chi. Cardinals, 1934

Most Yards Allowed, Passing, Season
4,389 N.Y. Jets, 1986
4,311 San Diego, 1981
4,293 San Diego, 1985

Fewest Touchdowns Allowed, Passing, Season
1 Portsmouth, 1932
Philadelphia, 1934
2 Brooklyn, 1933
Chi. Bears, 1934
3 Chi. Bears, 1932
Green Bay, 1932
Green Bay, 1934
Chi. Bears, 1936
New York, 1939

New York, 1944

Most Touchdowns Allowed, Passing, Season

40 Denver, 1963
38 St. Louis, 1969
37 Washington, 1961
Baltimore, 1981

Sacks

Most Seasons Leading League

5 Oakland/L.A. Raiders, 1966-68, 1982, 1986
4 Boston/New England, 1961, 1963, 1977, 1979
Dallas, 1966, 1968-69, 1978
Dallas/Kansas City, 1960, 1965, 1969, 1990
3 San Francisco, 1967, 1972, 1976
L.A. Rams, 1968, 1970, 1988

Most Consecutive Seasons Leading League

3 Oakland, 1966-68
2 Dallas, 1968-69

Most Sacks, Season

72 Chicago, 1984
71 Minnesota, 1989
70 Chicago, 1987

Fewest Sacks, Season

11 Baltimore, 1982
12 Buffalo, 1982
13 Baltimore, 1981

Most Sacks, Game

12 Dallas vs. Pittsburgh, Nov. 20, 1966
St. Louis vs. Baltimore, Oct. 26, 1980
Chicago vs. Detroit, Dec. 16, 1984
Dallas vs. Houston, Sept. 29, 1985
11 N.Y. Giants vs. St. Louis, Nov. 1, 1964
Baltimore vs. Los Angeles, Nov. 22, 1964
Buffalo vs. Denver, Dec. 13, 1964
Detroit vs. Green Bay, Nov. 7, 1965
Oakland vs. Buffalo, Oct. 15, 1967
Oakland vs. Denver, Nov. 5, 1967
St. Louis vs. Atlanta, Nov. 24, 1968
Dallas vs. Detroit, Oct. 6, 1975
St. Louis vs. Philadelphia, Dec. 18, 1983
Kansas City vs. Cleveland, Sept. 30, 1984
Chicago vs. Minnesota, Oct. 28, 1984
Cleveland vs. Atlanta, Nov. 18, 1984
Detroit vs. Philadelphia, Nov. 16, 1986
San Diego vs. Dallas, Nov. 16, 1986
L.A. Raiders vs. Philadelphia, Nov. 30, 1986 (OT)
Seattle vs. L.A. Raiders, Dec. 8, 1986
Chicago vs. Philadelphia, Oct. 4, 1987
Dallas vs. N.Y. Jets, Oct. 4, 1987
10 By many teams

Most Opponents Yards Lost Attempting to Pass, Season

666 Oakland, 1967
583 Chicago, 1984
573 San Francisco, 1976

Fewest Opponents Yards Lost Attempting to Pass, Season

75 Green Bay, 1956
77 N.Y. Bulldogs, 1949
78 Green Bay, 1958

Interceptions By

Most Seasons Leading League

9 N.Y. Giants, 1933, 1937-39, 1944, 1948, 1951, 1954, 1961
8 Green Bay, 1940, 1942-43, 1947, 1955, 1957, 1962, 1965
Chi. Bears, 1935-36, 1941-42, 1946, 1963, 1985, 1990
6 Kansas City, 1966-70, 1974

Most Consecutive Seasons Leading League

5 Kansas City, 1966-70
3 N.Y. Giants, 1937-39
2 By many teams

Most Passes Intercepted By, Season

49 San Diego, 1961
42 Green Bay, 1943
41 N.Y. Giants, 1951

Fewest Passes Intercepted By, Season

3 Houston, 1982
5 Baltimore, 1982
6 Houston, 1972
St. Louis, 1982

Most Passes Intercepted By, Game

9 Green Bay vs. Detroit, Oct. 24, 1943
Philadelphia vs. Pittsburgh, Dec. 12, 1965
8 N.Y. Giants vs. Green Bay, Nov. 21, 1948
Philadelphia vs. Chi. Cardinals, Sept. 24, 1950
N.Y. Giants vs. N.Y. Yanks, Dec. 16, 1951
Houston vs. Denver, Dec. 2, 1962
Detroit vs. Chicago, Sept. 22, 1968
N.Y. Jets vs. Baltimore, Sept. 23, 1973
7 By many teams. Last time: New Orleans vs. Green Bay, Sept. 14, 1986

Most Consecutive Games, One or More Interceptions By

46 L.A. Chargers/San Diego, 1960-63
37 Detroit, 1960-63
36 Boston, 1944-47

Most Yards Returning Interceptions, Season

929 San Diego, 1961
712 Los Angeles, 1952
697 Seattle, 1984

Fewest Yards Returning Interceptions, Season

5 Los Angeles, 1959
37 Dallas, 1989
42 Philadelphia, 1982

Most Yards Returning Interceptions, Game

325 Seattle vs. Kansas City, Nov. 4, 1984
314 Los Angeles vs. San Francisco, Oct. 18, 1964
245 Houston vs. N.Y. Jets, Oct. 15, 1967

Most Touchdowns, Returning Interceptions, Season

9 San Diego, 1961
7 Seattle, 1984
6 Cleveland, 1960
Green Bay, 1966
Detroit, 1967
Houston, 1967

Most Touchdowns Returning Interceptions, Game

4 Seattle vs. Kansas City, Nov. 4, 1984
3 Baltimore vs. Green Bay, Nov. 5, 1950
Cleveland vs. Chicago, Dec. 11, 1960
Philadelphia vs. Pittsburgh, Dec. 12, 1965
Baltimore vs. Pittsburgh, Sept. 29, 1968
Buffalo vs. N.Y. Jets, Sept. 29, 1968
Houston vs. San Diego, Dec. 19, 1971
Cincinnati vs. Houston, Dec. 17, 1972
Tampa Bay vs. New Orleans, Dec. 11, 1977
2 By many teams

Most Touchdowns Returning Interceptions, Both Teams, Game

4 Philadelphia (3) vs. Pittsburgh (1), Dec. 12, 1965
Seattle (4) vs. Kansas City (0), Nov. 4, 1984
3 Los Angeles (2) vs. Detroit (1), Nov. 1, 1953
Cleveland (2) vs. N.Y. Giants (1), Dec. 18, 1960
Pittsburgh (2) vs. Cincinnati (1), Oct. 10, 1983
Kansas City (2) vs. San Diego (1), Oct. 19, 1986
(Also see previous record)

Punt Returns

Fewest Opponents Punt Returns, Season

7 Washington, 1962
San Diego, 1982
10 Buffalo, 1982
11 Boston, 1962

Most Opponents Punt Returns, Season

71 Tampa Bay, 1976, 1977
69 N.Y. Giants, 1953
68 Cleveland, 1974

Fewest Yards Allowed, Punt Returns, Season

22 Green Bay, 1967
34 Washington, 1962
39 Cleveland, 1959
Washington, 1972

Most Yards Allowed, Punt Returns, Season

932 Green Bay, 1949
913 Boston, 1947
906 New Orleans, 1974

Lowest Average Allowed, Punt Returns, Season

1.20 Chi. Cardinals, 1954 (46-55)
1.22 Cleveland, 1959 (32-39)
1.55 Chi. Cardinals, 1953 (44-68)

Highest Average Allowed, Punt Returns, Season

18.6 Green Bay, 1949 (50-932)
18.0 Cleveland, 1977 (31-558)
17.9 Boston, 1960 (20-357)

Most Touchdowns Allowed, Punt Returns, Season

4 New York, 1959
3 Green Bay, 1949
Chi. Cardinals, 1951
Los Angeles, 1951
Washington, 1952
Dallas, 1952
Pittsburgh, 1959
N.Y. Jets, 1968
Cleveland, 1977
Atlanta, 1986
Tampa Bay, 1986
2 By many teams

Kickoff Returns

Fewest Opponents Kickoff Returns, Season

10 Brooklyn, 1943
15 Detroit, 1942
Brooklyn, 1944
18 Cleveland, 1941
Boston, 1944

Most Opponents Kickoff Returns, Season

91 Washington, 1983
89 New England, 1980
88 San Diego, 1981

Fewest Yards Allowed, Kickoff Returns, Season

225 Brooklyn, 1943
293 Brooklyn, 1944
361 Seattle, 1982

Most Yards Allowed, Kickoff Returns, Season

2,045 Kansas City, 1966
1,827 Chicago, 1985
1,816 N.Y. Giants, 1963

Lowest Average Allowed, Kickoff Returns, Season

14.3 Cleveland, 1980 (71-1,018)
15.0 Seattle, 1982 (24-361)
15.5 Buffalo, 1990 (73-1,129)

Highest Average Allowed, Kickoff Returns, Season

29.5 N.Y. Jets, 1972 (47-1,386)
29.4 Los Angeles, 1950 (48-1,411)
29.1 New England, 1971 (49-1,427)

Most Touchdowns Allowed, Kickoff Returns, Season

3 Minnesota, 1963, 1970
Dallas, 1966
Detroit, 1980
Pittsburgh, 1986
2 By many teams

Fumbles

Fewest Opponents Fumbles, Season

11 Cleveland, 1956
Baltimore, 1982
13 Los Angeles, 1956
Chicago, 1960
Cleveland, 1963
Cleveland, 1965
Detroit, 1967
San Diego, 1969
14 Baltimore, 1970
Oakland, 1975
Buffalo, 1982
St. Louis, 1982
San Francisco, 1982

Most Opponents Fumbles, Season

50 Minnesota, 1963
San Francisco, 1978
48 N.Y. Giants, 1980
N.Y. Jets, 1986
47 N.Y. Giants, 1977
Seattle, 1984

Turnovers

(Number of times losing the ball on interceptions and fumbles.)

Fewest Opponents Turnovers, Season

11 Baltimore, 1982
13 San Francisco, 1982
15 St. Louis, 1982

Most Opponents Turnovers, Season

66 San Diego, 1961
63 Seattle, 1984
61 Washington, 1983

Most Opponents Turnovers, Game

12 Chi. Bears vs. Detroit, Nov. 22, 1942
Philadelphia vs. Chi. Cardinals, Sept. 24, 1950
Philadelphia vs. Pittsburgh, Dec. 12, 1965
11 Green Bay vs. San Diego, Sept. 24, 1978
10 N.Y. Giants vs. Washington, Dec. 4, 1938
Green Bay vs. Pittsburgh, Nov. 23, 1941
Green Bay vs. Detroit, Oct. 24, 1943
Green Bay vs. Chi. Cardinals, Nov. 10, 1946
N.Y. Giants vs. Chi. Cardinals, Nov. 2, 1952
Detroit vs. Minnesota, Dec. 9, 1962
Oakland vs. Houston, Sept. 7, 1963
N.Y. Giants vs. Washington, Dec. 8, 1963
Detroit vs. Chicago, Sept. 22, 1968
Washington vs. St. Louis, Oct. 25, 1976
New England vs. N.Y. Jets, Nov. 21, 1976
Dallas vs. San Francisco, Oct. 12, 1980
Seattle vs. Cleveland, Dec. 20, 1981
Denver vs. Detroit, Oct. 7, 1984

NOTES

OUTSTANDING PERFORMERS

1,000 Yards Rushing in a Season

Year	Player, Team	Att.	Yards	Avg.	Long	TD
1990	Barry Sanders, Detroit[2]	255	1,304	5.1	45	13
	Thurman Thomas, Buffalo[2]	271	1,297	4.8	80	11
	Marion Butts, San Diego	265	1,225	4.6	52	8
	Earnest Byner, Washington[2]	297	1,219	4.1	22	6
	Bobby Humphrey, Denver[2]	288	1,202	4.2	37	7
	Neal Anderson, Chicago[3]	260	1,078	4.1	52	10
	Barry Word, Kansas City	204	1,015	5.0	53	4
	James Brooks, Cincinnati[3]	195	1,004	5.1	56	5
1989	Christian Okoye, Kansas City	370	1,480	4.0	59	12
	*Barry Sanders, Detroit	280	1,470	5.3	34	14
	Eric Dickerson, Indianapolis[7]	314	1,311	4.2	21	7
	Neal Anderson, Chicago[2]	274	1,275	4.7	73	11
	Dalton Hilliard, New Orleans	344	1,262	3.7	40	13
	Thurman Thomas, Buffalo	298	1,244	4.2	38	6
	James Brooks, Cincinnati[2]	221	1,239	5.6	65	7
	*Bobby Humphrey, Denver	294	1,151	3.9	40	7
	Greg Bell, L.A. Rams[3]	272	1,137	4.2	47	15
	Roger Craig, San Francisco[3]	271	1,054	3.9	27	6
	Ottis Anderson, N.Y. Giants[6]	325	1,023	3.1	36	14
1988	Eric Dickerson, Indianapolis[6]	388	1,659	4.3	41	14
	Herschel Walker, Dallas	361	1,514	4.2	38	5
	Roger Craig, San Francisco[2]	310	1,502	4.8	46	9
	Greg Bell, L.A. Rams[2]	288	1,212	4.2	44	16
	*John Stephens, New England	297	1,168	3.9	52	4
	Gary Anderson, San Diego	225	1,119	5.0	36	3
	Neal Anderson, Chicago	249	1,106	4.4	80	12
	Joe Morris, N.Y. Giants[3]	307	1,083	3.5	27	5
	*Ickey Woods, Cincinnati	203	1,066	5.3	56	15
	Curt Warner, Seattle[4]	266	1,025	3.9	29	10
	John Settle, Atlanta	232	1,024	4.4	62	7
	Mike Rozier, Houston	251	1,002	4.0	28	10
1987	Charles White, L.A. Rams	324	1,374	4.2	58	11
	Eric Dickerson, L.A. Rams-Indianapolis[5]	283	1,288	4.6	57	6
1986	Eric Dickerson, L.A. Rams[4]	404	1,821	4.5	42	11
	Joe Morris, N.Y. Giants[2]	341	1,516	4.4	54	14
	Curt Warner, Seattle[3]	319	1,481	4.6	60	13
	*Rueben Mayes, New Orleans	286	1,353	4.7	50	8
	Walter Payton, Chicago[10]	321	1,333	4.2	41	8
	Gerald Riggs, Atlanta[3]	343	1,327	3.9	31	9
	George Rogers, Washington[4]	303	1,203	4.0	42	18
	James Brooks, Cincinnati	205	1,087	5.3	56	5
1985	Marcus Allen, L.A. Raiders[3]	390	1,759	4.6	61	11
	Gerald Riggs, Atlanta[2]	397	1,719	4.3	50	10
	Walter Payton, Chicago[9]	324	1,551	4.8	40	9
	Joe Morris, N.Y. Giants	294	1,336	4.5	65	21
	Freeman McNeil, N.Y. Jets[2]	294	1,331	4.5	69	3
	Tony Dorsett, Dallas[8]	305	1,307	4.3	60	7
	James Wilder, Tampa Bay[2]	365	1,300	3.6	28	10
	Eric Dickerson, L.A. Rams[3]	292	1,234	4.2	43	12
	Craig James, New England	263	1,227	4.7	65	5
	*Kevin Mack, Cleveland	222	1,104	5.0	61	7
	Curt Warner, Seattle[2]	291	1,094	3.8	38	8
	George Rogers, Washington[3]	231	1,093	4.7	35	7
	Roger Craig, San Francisco	214	1,050	4.9	62	9
	Earnest Jackson, Philadelphia[2]	282	1,028	3.6	59	5
	Stump Mitchell, St. Louis	183	1,006	5.5	64	7
	Earnest Byner, Cleveland	244	1,002	4.1	36	8
1984	Eric Dickerson, L.A. Rams[2]	379	2,105	5.6	66	14
	Walter Payton, Chicago[8]	381	1,684	4.4	72	11
	James Wilder, Tampa Bay	407	1,544	3.8	37	13
	Gerald Riggs, Atlanta	353	1,486	4.2	57	13
	Wendell Tyler, San Francisco[3]	246	1,262	5.1	40	7
	John Riggins, Washington[5]	327	1,239	3.8	24	14
	Tony Dorsett, Dallas[7]	302	1,189	3.9	31	6
	Earnest Jackson, San Diego	296	1,179	4.0	32	8
	Ottis Anderson, St. Louis[5]	289	1,174	4.1	24	6
	Marcus Allen, L.A. Raiders[2]	275	1,168	4.2	52	13
	Sammy Winder, Denver	296	1,153	3.9	24	4
	*Greg Bell, Buffalo	262	1,100	4.2	85	7
	Freeman McNeil, N.Y. Jets	229	1,070	4.7	53	5
1983	*Eric Dickerson, L.A. Rams	390	1,808	4.6	85	18
	William Andrews, Atlanta[4]	331	1,567	4.7	27	7
	*Curt Warner, Seattle	335	1,449	4.3	60	13
	Walter Payton, Chicago[7]	314	1,421	4.5	49	6
	John Riggins, Washington[4]	375	1,347	3.6	44	24
	Tony Dorsett, Dallas[6]	289	1,321	4.6	77	8
	Earl Campbell, Houston[5]	322	1,301	4.0	42	12
	Ottis Anderson, St. Louis[4]	296	1,270	4.3	43	5
	Mike Pruitt, Cleveland[4]	293	1,184	4.0	27	10
	George Rogers, New Orleans[2]	256	1,144	4.5	76	5
	Joe Cribbs, Buffalo[3]	263	1,131	4.3	45	3
	Curtis Dickey, Baltimore	254	1,122	4.4	56	4
	Tony Collins, New England	219	1,049	4.8	50	10
	Billy Sims, Detroit[3]	220	1,040	4.7	41	7
	Marcus Allen, L.A. Raiders	266	1,014	3.8	19	9
	Franco Harris, Pittsburgh[8]	279	1,007	3.6	19	5
1981	*George Rogers, New Orleans	378	1,674	4.4	79	13
	Tony Dorsett, Dallas[5]	342	1,646	4.8	75	4
	Billy Sims, Detroit[2]	296	1,437	4.9	51	13
	Wilbert Montgomery, Philadelphia[3]	286	1,402	4.9	41	8
	Ottis Anderson, St. Louis[3]	328	1,376	4.2	28	9
	Earl Campbell, Houston[4]	361	1,376	3.8	43	10
	William Andrews, Atlanta[3]	289	1,301	4.5	29	10
	Walter Payton, Chicago[6]	339	1,222	3.6	39	6
	Chuck Muncie, San Diego[2]	251	1,144	4.6	73	19
	*Joe Delaney, Kansas City	234	1,121	4.8	82	3
	Mike Pruitt, Cleveland[3]	247	1,103	4.5	21	7
	Joe Cribbs, Buffalo[2]	257	1,097	4.3	35	3
	Pete Johnson, Cincinnati	274	1,077	3.9	39	12
	Wendell Tyler, Los Angeles[2]	260	1,074	4.1	69	12
	Ted Brown, Minnesota	274	1,063	3.9	34	6
1980	Earl Campbell, Houston[3]	373	1,934	5.2	55	13
	Walter Payton, Chicago[5]	317	1,460	4.6	69	6
	Ottis Anderson, St. Louis[2]	301	1,352	4.5	52	9
	William Andrews, Atlanta[2]	265	1,308	4.9	33	4
	*Billy Sims, Detroit	313	1,303	4.2	52	13
	Tony Dorsett, Dallas[4]	278	1,185	4.3	56	11
	*Joe Cribbs, Buffalo	306	1,185	3.9	48	11
	Mike Pruitt, Cleveland[2]	249	1,034	4.2	56	6
1979	Earl Campbell, Houston[2]	368	1,697	4.6	61	19
	Walter Payton, Chicago[4]	369	1,610	4.4	43	14
	*Ottis Anderson, St. Louis	331	1,605	4.8	76	8
	Wilbert Montgomery, Philadelphia[2]	338	1,512	4.5	62	9
	Mike Pruitt, Cleveland	264	1,294	4.9	77	9
	Ricky Bell, Tampa Bay	283	1,263	4.5	49	7
	Chuck Muncie, New Orleans	238	1,198	5.0	69	11
	Franco Harris, Pittsburgh[7]	267	1,186	4.4	71	11
	John Riggins, Washington[3]	260	1,153	4.4	66	9
	Wendell Tyler, Los Angeles	218	1,109	5.1	63	9
	Tony Dorsett, Dallas[3]	250	1,107	4.4	41	6
	*William Andrews, Atlanta	239	1,023	4.3	23	3
1978	*Earl Campbell, Houston	302	1,450	4.8	81	13
	Walter Payton, Chicago[3]	333	1,395	4.2	76	11
	Tony Dorsett, Dallas[2]	290	1,325	4.6	63	7
	Delvin Williams, Miami[2]	272	1,258	4.6	58	8
	Wilbert Montgomery, Philadelphia	259	1,220	4.7	47	9
	Terdell Middleton, Green Bay	284	1,116	3.9	76	11
	Franco Harris, Pittsburgh[6]	310	1,082	3.5	37	8
	Mark van Eeghen, Oakland[3]	270	1,080	4.0	34	9
	*Terry Miller, Buffalo	238	1,060	4.5	60	7
	Tony Reed, Kansas City	206	1,053	5.1	62	5
	John Riggins, Washington[2]	248	1,014	4.1	31	5
1977	Walter Payton, Chicago[2]	339	1,852	5.5	73	14
	Mark van Eeghen, Oakland[2]	324	1,273	3.9	27	7
	Lawrence McCutcheon, Los Angeles[4]	294	1,238	4.2	48	7
	Franco Harris, Pittsburgh[5]	300	1,162	3.9	61	11
	Lydell Mitchell, Baltimore[3]	301	1,159	3.9	64	3
	Chuck Foreman, Minnesota[3]	270	1,112	4.1	51	6
	Greg Pruitt, Cleveland[3]	236	1,086	4.6	78	3
	Sam Cunningham, New England	270	1,015	3.8	31	4
	*Tony Dorsett, Dallas	208	1,007	4.8	84	12
1976	O.J. Simpson, Buffalo[5]	290	1,503	5.2	75	8
	Walter Payton, Chicago	311	1,390	4.5	60	13
	Delvin Williams, San Francisco	248	1,203	4.9	80	7
	Lydell Mitchell, Baltimore[2]	289	1,200	4.2	43	5
	Lawrence McCutcheon, Los Angeles[3]	291	1,168	4.0	40	9
	Chuck Foreman, Minnesota[2]	278	1,155	4.2	46	13
	Franco Harris, Pittsburgh[4]	289	1,128	3.9	30	14
	Mike Thomas, Washington	254	1,101	4.3	28	5
	Rocky Bleier, Pittsburgh	220	1,036	4.7	28	5
	Mark van Eeghen, Oakland	233	1,012	4.3	21	3
	Otis Armstrong, Denver[2]	247	1,008	4.1	31	5
	Greg Pruitt, Cleveland[2]	209	1,000	4.8	64	4
1975	O.J. Simpson, Buffalo[4]	329	1,817	5.5	88	16
	Franco Harris, Pittsburgh[3]	262	1,246	4.8	36	10
	Lydell Mitchell, Baltimore	289	1,193	4.1	70	11
	Jim Otis, St. Louis	269	1,076	4.0	30	5
	Chuck Foreman, Minnesota	280	1,070	3.8	31	13
	Greg Pruitt, Cleveland	217	1,067	4.9	50	8
	John Riggins, N.Y. Jets	238	1,005	4.2	42	8
	Dave Hampton, Atlanta	250	1,002	4.0	22	5
1974	Otis Armstrong, Denver	263	1,407	5.3	43	9
	*Don Woods, San Diego	227	1,162	5.1	56	7
	O.J. Simpson, Buffalo[3]	270	1,125	4.2	41	3
	Lawrence McCutcheon, Los Angeles[2]	236	1,109	4.7	23	3
	Franco Harris, Pittsburgh[2]	208	1,006	4.8	54	5
1973	O.J. Simpson, Buffalo[2]	332	2,003	6.0	80	12
	John Brockington, Green Bay[3]	265	1,144	4.3	53	3
	Calvin Hill, Dallas[2]	273	1,142	4.2	21	6
	Lawrence McCutcheon, Los Angeles	210	1,097	5.2	37	2
	Larry Csonka, Miami[3]	219	1,003	4.6	25	5
1972	O.J. Simpson, Buffalo	292	1,251	4.3	94	6
	Larry Brown, Washington[2]	285	1,216	4.3	38	8
	Ron Johnson, N.Y. Giants[2]	298	1,182	4.0	35	9
	Larry Csonka, Miami[2]	213	1,117	5.2	45	6
	Marv Hubbard, Oakland	219	1,100	5.0	39	4
	*Franco Harris, Pittsburgh	188	1,055	5.6	75	10
	Calvin Hill, Dallas	245	1,036	4.2	26	6
	Mike Garrett, San Diego[2]	272	1,031	3.8	41	6
	John Brockington, Green Bay[2]	274	1,027	3.7	30	8
	Eugene (Mercury) Morris, Miami	190	1,000	5.3	33	12
1971	Floyd Little, Denver	284	1,133	4.0	40	6
	*John Brockington, Green Bay	216	1,105	5.1	52	4
	Larry Csonka, Miami	195	1,051	5.4	28	7
	Steve Owens, Detroit	246	1,035	4.2	23	8
	Willie Ellison, Los Angeles	211	1,000	4.7	80	4
1970	Larry Brown, Washington	237	1,125	4.7	75	5
	Ron Johnson, N.Y. Giants	263	1,027	3.9	68	8
1969	Gale Sayers, Chicago[2]	236	1,032	4.4	28	8
1968	Leroy Kelly, Cleveland[3]	248	1,239	5.0	65	16
	*Paul Robinson, Cincinnati	238	1,023	4.3	87	8
1967	Jim Nance, Boston[2]	269	1,216	4.5	53	7
	Leroy Kelly, Cleveland[2]	235	1,205	5.1	42	11
	Hoyle Granger, Houston	236	1,194	5.1	67	6
	Mike Garrett, Kansas City	236	1,087	4.6	58	9

1966	Jim Nance, Boston	299	1,458	4.9	65	11
	Gale Sayers, Chicago	229	1,231	5.4	58	8
	Leroy Kelly, Cleveland	209	1,141	5.5	70	15
	Dick Bass, Los Angeles[2]	248	1,090	4.4	50	8
1965	Jim Brown, Cleveland[7]	289	1,544	5.3	67	17
	Paul Lowe, San Diego[2]	222	1,121	5.0	59	7
1964	Jim Brown, Cleveland[6]	280	1,446	5.2	71	7
	Jim Taylor, Green Bay[5]	235	1,169	5.0	84	12
	John Henry Johnson, Pittsburgh[2]	235	1,048	4.5	45	7
1963	Jim Brown, Cleveland[5]	291	1,863	6.4	80	12
	Clem Daniels, Oakland	215	1,099	5.1	74	3
	Jim Taylor, Green Bay[4]	248	1,018	4.1	40	9
	Paul Lowe, San Diego	177	1,010	5.7	66	8
1962	Jim Taylor, Green Bay[3]	272	1,474	5.4	51	19
	John Henry Johnson, Pittsburgh	251	1,141	4.5	40	7
	*Cookie Gilchrist, Buffalo	214	1,096	5.1	44	13
	Abner Haynes, Dall. Texans	221	1,049	4.7	71	13
	Dick Bass, Los Angeles	196	1,033	5.3	57	6
	Charlie Tolar, Houston	244	1,012	4.1	25	7
1961	Jim Brown, Cleveland[4]	305	1,408	4.6	38	8
	Jim Taylor, Green Bay[2]	243	1,307	5.4	53	15
1960	Jim Brown, Cleveland[3]	215	1,257	5.8	71	9
	Jim Taylor, Green Bay	230	1,101	4.8	32	11
	John David Crow, St. Louis	183	1,071	5.9	57	6
1959	Jim Brown, Cleveland[2]	290	1,329	4.6	70	14
	J. D. Smith, San Francisco	207	1,036	5.0	73	10
1958	Jim Brown, Cleveland	257	1,527	5.9	65	17
1956	Rick Casares, Chi. Bears	234	1,126	4.8	68	12
1954	Joe Perry, San Francisco[2]	173	1,049	6.1	58	8
1953	Joe Perry, San Francisco	192	1,018	5.3	51	10
1949	Steve Van Buren, Philadelphia[2]	263	1,146	4.4	41	11
	Tony Canadeo, Green Bay	208	1,052	5.1	54	4
1947	Steve Van Buren, Philadelphia	217	1,008	4.6	45	13
1934	*Beattie Feathers, Chi. Bears	101	1,004	9.9	82	8

First year in the league.

200 Yards Rushing in a Game

Date	Player, Team, Opponent	Att.	Yards	TD
Dec. 23, 1990	James Brooks, Cincinnati vs. Houston	20	201	1
Oct. 14, 1990	Barry Word, Kansas City vs. Detroit	18	200	2
Sept. 24, 1990	Thurman Thomas, Buffalo vs. N.Y. Jets	18	214	0
Dec. 24, 1989	Greg Bell, L.A. Rams vs. New England	26	210	1
Sept. 24, 1989	Greg Bell, L.A. Rams vs. Green Bay	28	221	2
Sept. 17, 1989	Gerald Riggs, Washington vs. Philadelphia	29	221	1
Dec. 18, 1988	Gary Anderson, San Diego vs. Kansas City	34	217	1
Nov. 30, 1987	*Bo Jackson, L.A. Raiders vs. Seattle	18	221	2
Nov. 15, 1987	Charles White, L.A. Rams vs. St. Louis	34	213	1
Dec. 7, 1986	Rueben Mayes, New Orleans vs. Miami	28	203	2
Oct. 5, 1986	Eric Dickerson, L.A. Rams vs. Tampa Bay (OT)	30	207	2
Dec. 21, 1985	George Rogers, Washington vs. St. Louis	34	206	1
Dec. 21, 1985	Joe Morris, N.Y. Giants vs. Pittsburgh	36	202	3
Dec. 9, 1984	Eric Dickerson, L.A. Rams vs. Houston	27	215	2
Nov. 18, 1984	*Greg Bell, Buffalo vs. Dallas	27	206	1
Nov. 4, 1984	Eric Dickerson, L.A. Rams vs. St. Louis	21	208	0
Sept. 2, 1984	Gerald Riggs, Atlanta vs. New Orleans	35	202	2
Nov. 27, 1983	*Curt Warner, Seattle vs. Kansas City (OT)	32	207	3
Nov. 6, 1983	James Wilder, Tampa Bay vs. Minnesota	31	219	1
Sept. 18, 1983	Tony Collins, New England vs. N.Y. Jets	23	212	3
Sept. 4, 1983	George Rogers, New Orleans vs. St. Louis	24	206	2
Dec. 21, 1980	Earl Campbell, Houston vs. Minnesota	29	203	1
Nov. 16, 1980	Earl Campbell, Houston vs. Chicago	31	206	0
Oct. 26, 1980	Earl Campbell, Houston vs. Cincinnati	27	202	2
Oct. 19, 1980	Earl Campbell, Houston vs. Tampa Bay	33	203	0
Nov. 26, 1978	*Terry Miller, Buffalo vs. N.Y. Giants	21	208	2
Dec. 4, 1977	*Tony Dorsett, Dallas vs. Philadelphia	23	206	2
Nov. 20, 1977	Walter Payton, Chicago vs. Minnesota	40	275	1
Oct. 30, 1977	Walter Payton, Chicago vs. Green Bay	23	205	2
Dec. 5, 1976	O.J. Simpson, Buffalo vs. Miami	24	203	1
Nov. 25, 1976	O.J. Simpson, Buffalo vs. Detroit	29	273	2
Oct. 24, 1976	Chuck Foreman, Minnesota vs. Philadelphia	28	200	2
Dec. 14, 1975	Greg Pruitt, Cleveland vs. Kansas City	26	214	3
Sept. 28, 1975	O.J. Simpson, Buffalo vs. Pittsburgh	28	227	1
Dec. 16, 1973	O.J. Simpson, Buffalo vs. N.Y. Jets	34	200	1
Dec. 9, 1973	O.J. Simpson, Buffalo vs. New England	22	219	1
Sept. 16, 1973	O.J. Simpson, Buffalo vs. New England	29	250	2
Dec. 5, 1971	Willie Ellison, Los Angeles vs. New Orleans	26	247	1
Dec. 20, 1970	John (Frenchy) Fuqua, Pittsburgh vs. Philadelphia	20	218	2
Nov. 3, 1968	Gale Sayers, Chicago vs. Green Bay	24	205	0
Oct. 30, 1966	Jim Nance, Boston vs. Oakland	38	208	2
Oct. 10, 1964	John Henry Johnson, Pittsburgh vs. Cleveland	30	200	3
Dec. 8, 1963	Cookie Gilchrist, Buffalo vs. N.Y. Jets	36	243	5
Nov. 3, 1963	Jim Brown, Cleveland vs. Philadelphia	28	223	1
Oct. 20, 1963	Clem Daniels, Oakland vs. N.Y. Jets	27	200	2
Sept. 22, 1963	Jim Brown, Cleveland vs. Dallas	20	232	2
Dec. 10, 1961	Billy Cannon, Houston vs. N.Y. Titans	25	216	3
Nov. 19, 1961	Jim Brown, Cleveland vs. Philadelphia	34	237	4
Dec. 18, 1960	John David Crow, St. Louis vs. Pittsburgh	24	203	0
Nov. 15, 1959	Bobby Mitchell, Cleveland vs. Washington	14	232	3
Nov. 24, 1957	*Jim Brown, Cleveland vs. Los Angeles	31	237	4
Dec. 16, 1956	*Tom Wilson, Los Angeles vs. Green Bay	23	223	0
Nov. 22, 1953	Dan Towler, Los Angeles vs. Baltimore	14	205	1
Nov. 12, 1950	Gene Roberts, N.Y. Giants vs. Chi. Cardinals	26	218	2
Nov. 27, 1949	Steve Van Buren, Philadelphia vs. Pittsburgh	27	205	0
Oct. 8, 1933	Cliff Battles, Boston vs. N.Y. Giants	16	215	1

First year in the league.

Times 200 or More

56 times by 38 players . . . Simpson 6; Brown, Campbell 4; Bell, Dickerson 3; Payton, Riggs, Rogers 2.

4,000 Yards Passing in a Season

Year	Player, Team	Att.	Comp.	Pct.	Yards	TD	Int.
1990	Warren Moon, Houston	584	362	62.0	4,689	33	13
1989	Don Majkowski, Green Bay	599	353	58.9	4,318	27	20
	Jim Everett, L.A. Rams	518	304	58.7	4,310	29	17
1988	Dan Marino, Miami[4]	606	354	58.4	4,434	28	23
1986	Dan Marino, Miami[3]	623	378	60.7	4,746	44	23
	Jay Schroeder, Washington	541	276	51.0	4,109	22	22
1985	Dan Marino, Miami[2]	567	336	59.3	4,137	30	21
1984	Dan Marino, Miami	564	362	64.2	5,084	48	17
	Neil Lomax, St. Louis	560	345	61.6	4,614	28	16
	Phil Simms, N.Y. Giants	533	286	53.7	4,044	22	18
1983	Lynn Dickey, Green Bay	484	289	59.7	4,458	32	29
	Bill Kenney, Kansas City	603	346	57.4	4,348	24	18
1981	Dan Fouts, San Diego[3]	609	360	59.1	4,802	33	17
1980	Dan Fouts, San Diego[2]	589	348	59.1	4,715	30	24
	Brian Sipe, Cleveland	554	337	60.8	4,132	30	14
1979	Dan Fouts, San Diego	530	332	62.6	4,082	24	24
1967	Joe Namath, N.Y. Jets	491	258	52.5	4,007	26	28

400 Yards Passing in a Game

Date	Player, Team, Opponent	Att.	Comp.	Yards	TD
Dec. 16, 1990	Warren Moon, Houston vs. Kansas City	45	27	527	3
Nov. 4, 1990	Joe Montana, San Francisco vs. Green Bay	40	25	411	3
Oct. 14, 1990	Joe Montana, San Francisco vs. Atlanta	49	32	476	6
Oct. 7, 1990	Boomer Esiason, Cincinnati vs. L.A. Rams (OT)	45	31	490	3
Dec. 23, 1989	Warren Moon, Houston vs. Cleveland	51	32	414	2
Dec. 11, 1989	Joe Montana, San Francisco vs. L.A. Rams	42	30	458	3
Nov. 26, 1989	Jim Everett, L.A. Rams vs. New Orleans (OT)	51	29	454	1
Nov. 26, 1989	Mark Rypien, Washington vs. Chicago	47	30	401	4
Oct. 2, 1989	Randall Cunningham, Philadelphia vs. Chicago	62	32	401	1
Sept. 24, 1989	Joe Montana, San Francisco vs. Philadelphia	34	25	428	5
Sept. 24, 1989	Dan Marino, Miami vs. N.Y. Jets	55	33	427	3
Sept. 17, 1989	Randall Cunningham, Phil. vs. Washington	46	34	447	5
Dec. 18, 1988	Dave Krieg, Seattle at L.A. Raiders	32	19	410	4
Dec. 12, 1988	Dan Marino, Miami vs. Cleveland	50	30	404	4
Oct. 23, 1988	Dan Marino, Miami vs. N.Y. Jets	60	35	521	3
Oct. 16, 1988	Vinny Testaverde, Tampa Bay at Indianapolis	42	25	469	2
Sept. 11, 1988	Doug Williams, Washington vs. Pittsburgh	52	30	430	2
Nov. 29, 1987	Tom Ramsey, New England vs. Philadelphia	53	34	402	3
Nov. 22, 1987	Boomer Esiason, Cincinnati vs. Pittsburgh	53	30	409	0
Sept. 20, 1987	Neil Lomax, St. Louis vs. San Diego	61	32	457	3
Dec. 21, 1986	Boomer Esiason, Cincinnati vs. N.Y. Jets	30	23	425	5
Dec. 14, 1986	Dan Marino, Miami vs. L.A. Rams (OT)	46	29	403	5
Nov. 23, 1986	Bernie Kosar, Cleveland vs. Pittsburgh (OT)	46	28	414	2
Nov. 17, 1986	Joe Montana, San Francisco vs. Washington	60	33	441	0
Nov. 16, 1986	Dan Marino, Miami vs. Buffalo	54	39	404	4
Nov. 10, 1986	Bernie Kosar, Cleveland vs. Miami	50	32	401	0
Nov. 2, 1986	Tommy Kramer, Minnesota vs. Washington (OT)	35	20	490	4
Nov. 2, 1986	Ken O'Brien, N.Y. Jets vs. Seattle	32	26	431	4
Oct. 27, 1986	Jay Schroeder, Washington vs. N.Y. Giants	40	22	420	1
Oct. 12, 1986	Steve Grogan, New England vs. N.Y. Jets	42	23	401	3
Sept. 21, 1986	Ken O'Brien, N.Y. Jets vs. Miami (OT)	43	29	479	4
Sept. 21, 1986	Dan Marino, Miami vs. N.Y. Jets (OT)	50	30	448	6
Sept. 21, 1986	Tony Eason, New England vs. Seattle	45	26	414	3
Dec. 20, 1985	John Elway, Denver vs. Seattle	42	24	432	1
Nov. 10, 1985	Dan Fouts, San Diego vs. L.A. Raiders (OT)	41	26	436	4
Oct. 13, 1985	Phil Simms, N.Y. Giants vs. Cincinnati	62	40	513	1
Oct. 13, 1985	Dave Krieg, Seattle vs. Atlanta	51	33	405	4
Oct. 6, 1985	Phil Simms, N.Y. Giants vs. Dallas	36	18	432	3
Oct. 6, 1985	Joe Montana, San Francisco vs. Atlanta	57	37	429	5
Sept. 19, 1985	Tommy Kramer, Minnesota vs. Chicago	55	28	436	3
Sept. 15, 1985	Dan Fouts, San Diego vs. Seattle	43	29	440	4
Dec. 16, 1984	Neil Lomax, St. Louis vs. Washington	46	37	468	2
Dec. 9, 1984	Dan Marino, Miami vs. Indianapolis	41	29	404	4
Dec. 2, 1984	Dan Marino, Miami vs. L.A. Raiders	57	35	470	4
Nov. 25, 1984	Dave Krieg, Seattle vs. Denver	44	30	406	3
Nov. 4, 1984	Dan Marino, Miami vs. N.Y. Jets	42	23	422	2
Oct. 21, 1984	Dan Fouts, San Diego vs. L.A. Raiders	45	24	410	3
Sept. 30, 1984	Dan Marino, Miami vs. St. Louis	36	24	429	3
Sept. 2, 1984	Phil Simms, N.Y. Giants vs. Philadelphia	30	23	409	4
Dec. 11, 1983	Bill Kenney, Kansas City vs. San Diego	41	31	411	4
Nov. 20, 1983	Dave Krieg, Seattle vs. Denver	42	31	418	3
Oct. 9, 1983	Joe Ferguson, Buffalo vs. Miami (OT)	55	38	419	5
Oct. 2, 1983	Joe Theismann, Washington vs. L.A. Raiders	39	23	417	3
Sept. 25, 1983	Richard Todd, N.Y. Jets vs. L.A. Rams (OT)	50	37	446	2
Dec. 26, 1982	Vince Ferragamo, L.A. Rams vs. Chicago	46	30	509	3
Dec. 20, 1982	Dan Fouts, San Diego vs. Cincinnati	40	25	435	1
Dec. 20, 1982	Ken Anderson, Cincinnati vs. San Diego	56	40	416	2
Dec. 11, 1982	Dan Fouts, San Diego vs. San Francisco	48	33	444	5
Nov. 21, 1982	Joe Montana, San Francisco vs. St. Louis	39	26	408	3
Nov. 15, 1981	Steve Bartkowski, Atlanta vs. Pittsburgh	50	33	416	2
Oct. 25, 1981	Brian Sipe, Cleveland vs. Baltimore	41	30	444	4
Oct. 25, 1981	David Woodley, Miami vs. Dallas	37	21	408	3
Oct. 11, 1981	Tommy Kramer, Minnesota vs. San Diego	43	27	444	4
Dec. 14, 1980	Tommy Kramer, Minnesota vs. Cleveland	49	38	456	4
Nov. 16, 1980	Doug Williams, Tampa Bay vs. Minnesota	55	30	486	4
Oct. 19, 1980	Dan Fouts, San Diego vs. N.Y. Giants	41	26	444	3
Oct. 12, 1980	Lynn Dickey, Green Bay vs. Tampa Bay (OT)	51	35	418	1
Sept. 21, 1980	Richard Todd, N.Y. Jets vs. San Francisco	60	42	447	3
Oct. 3, 1976	James Harris, Los Angeles vs. Miami	29	17	436	2
Nov. 17, 1975	Ken Anderson, Cincinnati vs. Buffalo	46	30	447	2
Nov. 18, 1974	Charley Johnson, Denver vs. Kansas City	42	28	445	2
Dec. 11, 1972	Joe Namath, N.Y. Jets vs. Oakland	46	25	403	1
Sept. 24, 1972	Joe Namath, N.Y. Jets vs. Baltimore	28	15	496	6
Dec. 21, 1969	Don Horn, Green Bay vs. St. Louis	31	22	410	5
Sept. 28, 1969	Joe Kapp, Minnesota vs. Baltimore	43	28	449	7
Sept. 9, 1968	Pete Beathard, Houston vs. Kansas City	48	23	413	2
Nov. 26, 1967	Sonny Jurgensen, Washington vs. Cleveland	50	32	418	3
Oct. 1, 1967	Joe Namath, N.Y. Jets vs. Miami	39	23	415	3
Sept. 17, 1967	Johnny Unitas, Baltimore vs. Atlanta	32	22	401	2

Nov. 13, 1966	Don Meredith, Dallas vs. Washington	29	21	406	2
Nov. 28, 1965	Sonny Jurgensen, Washington vs. Dallas	43	26	411	3
Oct. 24, 1965	Fran Tarkenton, Minnesota vs. San Francisco	35	21	407	3
Nov. 1, 1964	Len Dawson, Kansas City vs. Denver	38	23	435	6
Oct. 25, 1964	Cotton Davidson, Oakland vs. Denver	36	23	427	5
Oct. 16, 1964	Babe Parilli, Boston vs. Oakland	47	25	422	4
Dec. 22, 1963	Tom Flores, Oakland vs. Houston	29	17	407	6
Nov. 17, 1963	Norm Snead, Washington vs. Pittsburgh	40	23	424	2
Nov. 10, 1963	Don Meredith, Dallas vs. San Francisco	48	30	460	3
Oct. 13, 1963	Charley Johnson, St. Louis vs. Pittsburgh	41	20	428	2
Dec. 16, 1962	Sonny Jurgensen, Philadelphia vs. St. Louis	34	15	419	5
Nov. 18, 1962	Bill Wade, Chicago vs. Dall. Cowboys	46	28	466	2
Oct. 28, 1962	Y.A. Tittle, N.Y. Giants vs. Washington	39	27	505	7
Sept. 15, 1962	Frank Tripucka, Denver vs. Buffalo	56	29	447	2
Dec. 17, 1961	Sonny Jurgensen, Philadelphia vs. Detroit	42	27	403	3
Nov. 19, 1961	George Blanda, Houston vs. N.Y. Titans	32	20	418	7
Oct. 29, 1961	George Blanda, Houston vs. Buffalo	32	18	464	4
Oct. 29, 1961	Sonny Jurgensen, Philadelphia vs. Washington	41	27	436	3
Oct. 13, 1961	Jacky Lee, Houston vs. Boston	41	27	457	2
Dec. 13, 1958	Bobby Layne, Pittsburgh vs. Chi. Cardinals	49	23	409	2
Nov. 8, 1953	Bobby Thomason, Philadelphia vs. N.Y. Giants	44	22	437	4
Oct. 4, 1952	Otto Graham, Cleveland vs. Pittsburgh	49	21	401	3
Sept. 28, 1951	Norm Van Brocklin, Los Angeles vs. N.Y. Yanks	41	27	554	5
Dec. 11, 1949	Johnny Lujack, Chi. Bears vs. Chi. Cardinals	39	24	468	6
Oct. 31, 1948	Sammy Baugh, Washington vs. Boston	24	17	446	4
Oct. 31, 1948	Jim Hardy, Los Angeles vs. Chi. Cardinals	53	28	406	3
Nov. 14, 1943	Sid Luckman, Chi. Bears vs. N.Y. Giants	32	21	433	7

Times 400 or More

106 times by 59 players...Marino 10; Montana 7; Fouts 6; Jurgensen 5; Kramer, Krieg 4; Esiason, Namath, Simms 3; Anderson, Blanda, Cunningham, Johnson, Kosar, Lomax, Meredith, Moon, O'Brien, Todd, Williams 2.

1,000 Yards Pass Receiving in a Season

Year	Player, Team	No.	Yards	Avg.	Long	TD
1990	Jerry Rice, San Francisco[5]	100	1,502	15.0	64	13
	Henry Ellard, L.A. Rams[3]	76	1,294	17.0	50	4
	Andre Rison, Atlanta	82	1,208	14.7	75	10
	Gary Clark, Washington[4]	75	1,112	14.8	53	8
	Sterling Sharpe, Green Bay[2]	67	1,105	16.5	76	6
	Willie Anderson, L.A. Rams[2]	51	1,097	21.5	55	4
	Haywood Jeffires, Houston	74	1,048	14.2	87	8
	Stephone Paige, Kansas City	65	1,021	15.7	86	5
	Drew Hill, Houston[4]	74	1,019	13.8	57	5
	Anthony Carter, Minnesota[3]	70	1,008	14.4	56	8
1989	Jerry Rice, San Francisco[4]	82	1,483	18.1	68	17
	Sterling Sharpe, Green Bay	90	1,423	15.8	79	12
	Mark Carrier, Tampa Bay	86	1,422	16.5	78	9
	Henry Ellard, L.A. Rams[2]	70	1,382	19.7	53	8
	Andre Reed, Buffalo	88	1,312	14.9	78	9
	Anthony Miller, San Diego	75	1,252	16.7	69	10
	Webster Slaughter, Cleveland	65	1,236	19.0	97	6
	Gary Clark, Washington[3]	79	1,229	15.6	80	9
	Tim McGee, Cincinnati	65	1,211	18.6	74	8
	Art Monk, Washington[4]	86	1,186	13.8	60	8
	Willie Anderson, L.A. Rams	44	1,146	26.0	78	5
	Ricky Sanders, Washington[2]	80	1,138	14.2	68	4
	Vance Johnson, Denver	76	1,095	14.4	69	7
	Richard Johnson, Detroit	70	1,091	15.6	75	8
	Eric Martin, New Orleans[2]	68	1,090	16.0	53	8
	John Taylor, San Francisco	60	1,077	18.0	95	10
	Mervyn Fernandez, L.A. Raiders	57	1,069	18.8	75	9
	Anthony Carter, Minnesota[2]	65	1,066	16.4	50	4
	Brian Blades, Seattle	77	1,063	13.8	60	5
	Mark Clayton, Miami[4]	64	1,011	15.8	78	9
1988	Henry Ellard, L.A. Rams	86	1,414	16.4	68	10
	Jerry Rice, San Francisco[3]	64	1,306	20.4	96	9
	Eddie Brown, Cincinnati	53	1,273	24.0	86	9
	Anthony Carter, Minnesota	72	1,225	17.0	67	6
	Ricky Sanders, Washington	73	1,148	15.7	55	12
	Drew Hill, Houston[3]	72	1,141	15.8	57	10
	Mark Clayton, Miami[3]	86	1,129	13.1	45	14
	Roy Green, Phoenix[3]	68	1,097	16.1	52	7
	Eric Martin, New Orleans	85	1,083	12.7	40	7
	Al Toon, N.Y. Jets[2]	93	1,067	11.5	42	5
	Bruce Hill, Tampa Bay	58	1,040	17.9	42	9
	Lionel Manuel, N.Y. Giants	65	1,029	15.8	46	4
1987	J.T. Smith, St. Louis[2]	91	1,117	12.3	38	8
	Jerry Rice, San Francisco[2]	65	1,078	16.6	57	22
	Gary Clark, Washington[2]	56	1,066	19.0	84	7
	Carlos Carson, Kansas City[3]	55	1,044	19.0	81	7
1986	Jerry Rice, San Francisco	86	1,570	18.3	66	15
	Stanley Morgan, New England[3]	84	1,491	17.8	44	10
	Mark Duper, Miami[3]	67	1,313	19.6	85	11
	Gary Clark, Washington	74	1,265	17.1	55	7
	Al Toon, N.Y. Jets	85	1,176	13.8	62	8
	Todd Christensen, L.A. Raiders[3]	95	1,153	12.1	35	8
	Mark Clayton, Miami[2]	60	1,150	19.2	68	10
	*Bill Brooks, Indianapolis	65	1,131	17.4	84	8
	Drew Hill, Houston[2]	65	1,112	17.1	81	5
	Steve Largent, Seattle[8]	70	1,070	15.3	38	9
	Art Monk, Washington[3]	73	1,068	14.6	69	4
	*Earnest Givins, Houston	61	1,062	17.4	60	3
	Cris Collinsworth, Cincinnati[4]	62	1,024	16.5	46	10
	Wesley Walker, N.Y. Jets[2]	49	1,016	20.7	83	12
	J.T. Smith, St. Louis	80	1,014	12.7	45	6
	Mark Bavaro, N.Y. Giants	66	1,001	15.2	41	4
1985	Steve Largent, Seattle[7]	79	1,287	16.3	43	6
	Mike Quick, Philadelphia[3]	73	1,247	17.1	99	11
	Art Monk, Washington[2]	91	1,226	13.5	53	2
	Wes Chandler, San Diego[4]	67	1,199	17.9	75	10
	Drew Hill, Houston	64	1,169	18.3	57	9
	James Lofton, Green Bay[5]	69	1,153	16.7	56	4
	Louis Lipps, Pittsburgh	59	1,134	19.2	51	12
	Cris Collinsworth, Cincinnati[3]	65	1,125	17.3	71	5
	Tony Hill, Dallas[3]	74	1,113	15.0	53	7
	Lionel James, San Diego	86	1,027	11.9	67	6
	Roger Craig, San Francisco	92	1,016	11.0	73	6
1984	Roy Green, St. Louis[2]	78	1,555	19.9	83	12
	John Stallworth, Pittsburgh[3]	80	1,395	17.4	51	11
	Mark Clayton, Miami	73	1,389	19.0	65	18
	Art Monk, Washington	106	1,372	12.9	72	7
	James Lofton, Green Bay[4]	62	1,361	22.0	79	7
	Mark Duper, Miami[2]	71	1,306	18.4	80	8
	Steve Watson, Denver[3]	69	1,170	17.0	73	7
	Steve Largent, Seattle[6]	74	1,164	15.7	65	12
	Tim Smith, Houston[2]	69	1,141	16.5	75	4
	Stacey Bailey, Atlanta	67	1,138	17.0	61	6
	Carlos Carson, Kansas City[2]	57	1,078	18.9	57	4
	Mike Quick, Philadelphia[2]	61	1,052	17.2	90	9
	Todd Christensen, L.A. Raiders[2]	80	1,007	12.6	38	7
	Kevin House, Tampa Bay[2]	76	1,005	13.2	55	5
	Ozzie Newsome, Cleveland[2]	89	1,001	11.2	52	5
1983	Mike Quick, Philadelphia	69	1,409	20.4	83	13
	Carlos Carson, Kansas City	80	1,351	16.9	50	7
	James Lofton, Green Bay[3]	58	1,300	22.4	74	8
	Todd Christensen, L.A. Raiders	92	1,247	13.6	45	12
	Roy Green, St. Louis	78	1,227	15.7	71	14
	Charlie Brown, Washington	78	1,225	15.7	75	8
	Tim Smith, Houston	83	1,176	14.2	47	6
	Kellen Winslow, San Diego[3]	88	1,172	13.3	46	8
	Earnest Gray, N.Y. Giants	78	1,139	14.6	62	5
	Steve Watson, Denver[2]	59	1,133	19.2	78	5
	Cris Collinsworth, Cincinnati[2]	66	1,130	17.1	63	5
	Steve Largent, Seattle[5]	72	1,074	14.9	46	11
	Mark Duper, Miami	51	1,003	19.7	85	10
1982	Wes Chandler, San Diego[3]	49	1,032	21.1	66	9
1981	Alfred Jenkins, Atlanta[2]	70	1,358	19.4	67	13
	James Lofton, Green Bay[2]	71	1,294	18.2	75	8
	Frank Lewis, Buffalo[2]	70	1,244	17.8	33	4
	Steve Watson, Denver	60	1,244	20.7	95	13
	Steve Largent, Seattle[4]	75	1,224	16.3	57	9
	Charlie Joiner, San Diego[4]	70	1,188	17.0	57	7
	Kevin House, Tampa Bay	56	1,176	21.0	84	9
	Wes Chandler, N.O.-San Diego[2]	69	1,142	16.6	51	6
	Dwight Clark, San Francisco	85	1,105	13.0	78	4
	John Stallworth, Pittsburgh[2]	63	1,098	17.4	55	5
	Kellen Winslow, San Diego[2]	88	1,075	12.2	67	10
	Pat Tilley, St. Louis	66	1,040	15.8	75	3
	Stanley Morgan, New England[2]	44	1,029	23.4	76	6
	Harold Carmichael, Philadelphia[3]	61	1,028	16.9	85	6
	Freddie Scott, Detroit	53	1,022	19.3	48	5
	*Cris Collinsworth, Cincinnati	67	1,009	15.1	74	8
	Joe Senser, Minnesota	79	1,004	12.7	53	8
	Ozzie Newsome, Cleveland	69	1,002	14.5	62	6
	Sammy White, Minnesota	66	1,001	15.2	53	3
1980	John Jefferson, San Diego[3]	82	1,340	16.3	58	13
	Kellen Winslow, San Diego	89	1,290	14.5	65	9
	James Lofton, Green Bay	71	1,226	17.3	47	4
	Charlie Joiner, San Diego[3]	71	1,132	15.9	51	4
	Ahmad Rashad, Minnesota[2]	69	1,095	15.9	76	5
	Steve Largent, Seattle[3]	66	1,064	16.1	67	6
	Tony Hill, Dallas[2]	60	1,055	17.6	58	8
	Alfred Jenkins, Atlanta	57	1,026	18.0	57	6
1979	Steve Largent, Seattle[2]	66	1,237	18.7	55	9
	John Stallworth, Pittsburgh	70	1,183	16.9	65	8
	Ahmad Rashad, Minnesota	80	1,156	14.5	52	9
	John Jefferson, San Diego[2]	61	1,090	17.9	65	10
	Frank Lewis, Buffalo	54	1,082	20.0	55	2
	Wes Chandler, New Orleans	65	1,069	16.4	85	6
	Tony Hill, Dallas	60	1,062	17.7	75	10
	Drew Pearson, Dallas[2]	55	1,026	18.7	56	8
	Wallace Francis, Atlanta	74	1,013	13.7	42	8
	Harold Jackson, New England[3]	45	1,013	22.5	59	7
	Charlie Joiner, San Diego[2]	72	1,008	14.0	39	4
	Stanley Morgan, New England	44	1,002	22.8	63	12
1978	Wesley Walker, N.Y. Jets	48	1,169	24.4	77	8
	Steve Largent, Seattle	71	1,168	16.5	57	8
	Harold Carmichael, Philadelphia[2]	55	1,072	19.5	56	8
	*John Jefferson, San Diego	56	1,001	17.9	46	13
1976	Roger Carr, Baltimore	43	1,112	25.9	79	11
	Cliff Branch, Oakland[2]	46	1,111	24.2	88	12
	Charlie Joiner, San Diego	50	1,056	21.1	81	7
1975	Ken Burrough, Houston	53	1,063	20.1	77	8
1974	Cliff Branch, Oakland	60	1,092	18.2	67	13
	Drew Pearson, Dallas	62	1,087	17.5	50	2
1973	Harold Carmichael, Philadelphia	67	1,116	16.7	73	9
1972	Harold Jackson, Philadelphia[2]	62	1,048	16.9	77	4
	John Gilliam, Minnesota	47	1,035	22.0	66	7
1971	Otis Taylor, Kansas City[2]	57	1,110	19.5	82	7
1970	Gene Washington, San Francisco	53	1,100	20.8	79	12
	Marlin Briscoe, Buffalo	57	1,036	18.2	48	8
	Dick Gordon, Chicago	71	1,026	14.5	69	13
	Gary Garrison, San Diego[2]	44	1,006	22.9	67	12
1969	Warren Wells, Oakland[2]	47	1,260	26.8	80	14
	Harold Jackson, Philadelphia	65	1,116	17.2	65	9
	Roy Jefferson, Pittsburgh[2]	67	1,079	16.1	63	9
	Dan Abramowicz, New Orleans	73	1,015	13.9	49	7
	Lance Alworth, San Diego[7]	64	1,003	15.7	76	4

Year	Player, Team	No.	Yards	Avg.	Long	TD
1968	Lance Alworth, San Diego[6]	68	1,312	19.3	80	10
	Don Maynard, N.Y. Jets[5]	57	1,297	22.8	87	10
	George Sauer, N.Y. Jets[3]	66	1,141	17.3	43	3
	Warren Wells, Oakland	53	1,137	21.5	94	11
	Gary Garrison, San Diego	52	1,103	21.2	84	10
	Roy Jefferson, Pittsburgh	58	1,074	18.5	62	11
	Paul Warfield, Cleveland	50	1,067	21.3	65	12
	Homer Jones, N.Y. Giants[3]	45	1,057	23.5	84	7
	Fred Biletnikoff, Oakland	61	1,037	17.0	82	6
	Lance Rentzel, Dallas	54	1,009	18.7	65	6
1967	Don Maynard, N.Y. Jets[4]	71	1,434	20.2	75	10
	Ben Hawkins, Philadelphia	59	1,265	21.4	87	10
	Homer Jones, N.Y. Giants[2]	49	1,209	24.7	70	13
	Jackie Smith, St. Louis	56	1,205	21.5	76	9
	George Sauer, N.Y. Jets[2]	75	1,189	15.9	61	6
	Lance Alworth, San Diego[5]	52	1,010	19.4	71	9
1966	Lance Alworth, San Diego[4]	73	1,383	18.9	78	13
	Otis Taylor, Kansas City	58	1,297	22.4	89	8
	Pat Studstill, Detroit	67	1,266	18.9	99	5
	Bob Hayes, Dallas[2]	64	1,232	19.3	95	13
	Charlie Frazier, Houston	57	1,129	19.8	79	12
	Charley Taylor, Washington	72	1,119	15.5	86	12
	George Sauer, N.Y. Jets	63	1,081	17.2	77	5
	Homer Jones, N.Y. Giants	48	1,044	21.8	98	8
	Art Powell, Oakland[5]	53	1,026	19.4	46	11
1965	Lance Alworth, San Diego[3]	69	1,602	23.2	85	14
	Dave Parks, San Francisco	80	1,344	16.8	53	12
	Don Maynard, N.Y. Jets[3]	68	1,218	17.9	56	14
	Pete Retzlaff, Philadelphia	66	1,190	18.0	78	10
	Lionel Taylor, Denver[4]	85	1,131	13.3	63	6
	Tommy McDonald, Los Angeles[3]	67	1,036	15.5	51	9
	*Bob Hayes, Dallas	46	1,003	21.8	82	12
1964	Charley Hennigan, Houston[3]	101	1,546	15.3	53	8
	Art Powell, Oakland[4]	76	1,361	17.9	77	11
	Lance Alworth, San Diego[2]	61	1,235	20.2	82	13
	Johnny Morris, Chicago	93	1,200	12.9	63	10
	Elbert Dubenion, Buffalo	42	1,139	27.1	72	10
	Terry Barr, Detroit[2]	57	1,030	18.1	58	9
1963	Bobby Mitchell, Washington[2]	69	1,436	20.8	99	7
	Art Powell, Oakland[3]	73	1,304	17.9	85	16
	Buddy Dial, Pittsburgh[2]	60	1,295	21.6	83	9
	Lance Alworth, San Diego	61	1,205	19.8	85	11
	Del Shofner, N.Y. Giants[4]	64	1,181	18.5	70	9
	Lionel Taylor, Denver[3]	78	1,101	14.1	72	10
	Terry Barr, Detroit	66	1,086	16.5	75	13
	Charley Hennigan, Houston[2]	61	1,051	17.2	83	10
	Sonny Randle, St. Louis[2]	51	1,014	19.9	68	12
	Bake Turner, N.Y. Jets	71	1,009	14.2	53	6
1962	Bobby Mitchell, Washington	72	1,384	19.2	81	11
	Sonny Randle, St. Louis	63	1,158	18.4	86	7
	Tommy McDonald, Philadelphia[2]	58	1,146	19.8	60	10
	Del Shofner, N.Y. Giants[3]	53	1,133	21.4	69	12
	Art Powell, N.Y. Titans[2]	64	1,130	17.7	80	8
	Frank Clarke, Dall. Cowboys	47	1,043	22.2	66	14
	Don Maynard, N.Y. Titans[2]	56	1,041	18.6	86	8
1961	Charley Hennigan, Houston	82	1,746	21.3	80	12
	Lionel Taylor, Denver[2]	100	1,176	11.8	52	4
	Bill Groman, Houston[2]	50	1,175	23.5	80	17
	Tommy McDonald, Philadelphia	64	1,144	17.9	66	13
	Del Shofner, N.Y. Giants[2]	68	1,125	16.5	46	11
	Jim Phillips, Los Angeles	78	1,092	14.0	69	5
	*Mike Ditka, Chicago	56	1,076	19.2	76	12
	Dave Kocourek, San Diego	55	1,055	19.2	76	4
	Buddy Dial, Pittsburgh	53	1,047	19.8	88	12
	R.C. Owens, San Francisco	55	1,032	18.8	54	5
1960	*Bill Groman, Houston	72	1,473	20.5	92	12
	Raymond Berry, Baltimore	74	1,298	17.5	70	10
	Don Maynard, N.Y. Titans	72	1,265	17.6	65	6
	Lionel Taylor, Denver	92	1,235	13.4	80	12
	Art Powell, N.Y. Titans	69	1,167	16.9	76	14
1958	Del Shofner, Los Angeles	51	1,097	21.5	92	8
1956	Bill Howton, Green Bay[2]	55	1,188	21.6	66	12
	Harlon Hill, Chi. Bears[2]	47	1,128	24.0	79	11
1954	Bob Boyd, Los Angeles	53	1,212	22.9	80	6
	*Harlon Hill, Chi. Bears	45	1,124	25.0	76	12
1953	Pete Pihos, Philadelphia	63	1,049	16.7	59	10
1952	*Bill Howton, Green Bay	53	1,231	23.2	90	13
1951	Elroy (Crazylegs) Hirsch, Los Angeles	66	1,495	22.7	91	17
1950	Tom Fears, Los Angeles[2]	84	1,116	13.3	53	7
	Cloyce Box, Detroit	50	1,009	20.2	82	11
1949	Bob Mann, Detroit	66	1,014	15.4	64	4
	Tom Fears, Los Angeles	77	1,013	13.2	51	9
1945	Jim Benton, Cleveland	45	1,067	23.7	84	8
1942	Don Hutson, Green Bay	74	1,211	16.4	73	17

First year in the league.

250 Yards Pass Receiving in a Game

Date	Player, Team, Opponent	No.	Yards	TD
Dec. 11, 1989	John Taylor, San Francisco vs. L.A. Rams	11	286	2
Nov. 26, 1989	Willie Anderson, L.A. Rams vs. New Orleans (OT)	15	336	1
Oct. 18, 1987	Steve Largent, Seattle vs. Detroit	15	261	3
Oct. 4, 1987	*Anthony Allen, Washington vs. St. Louis	7	255	3
Dec. 22, 1985	Stephone Paige, Kansas City vs. San Diego	8	309	2
Dec. 20, 1982	Wes Chandler, San Diego vs. Cincinnati	10	260	2
Sept. 23, 1979	*Jerry Butler, Buffalo vs. N.Y. Jets	10	255	4
Nov. 4, 1962	Sonny Randle, St. Louis vs. N.Y. Giants	16	256	1
Oct. 28, 1962	Del Shofner, N.Y. Giants vs. Washington	11	269	1
Oct. 13, 1961	Charley Hennigan, Houston vs. Boston	13	272	1
Oct. 21, 1956	Billy Howton, Green Bay vs. Los Angeles	7	257	2
Dec. 3, 1950	Cloyce Box, Detroit vs. Baltimore	12	302	4
Nov. 22, 1945	Jim Benton, Cleveland vs. Detroit	10	303	1

First year in the league.

2,000 Combined Net Yards Gained in a Season

Year	Player, Team	Rushing Att.-Yds.	Pass Rec.	Punt Ret.	Kickoff Ret.	Fum. Runs	Total Yds.
1990	Herschel Walker, Minnesota	184-770	35-315	0-0	44-966	4-0	267-2,051
1988	*Tim Brown, L.A. Raiders	14-50	43-725	49-444	41-1,098	7-0	154-2,317
	Roger Craig, San Fran.	310-1,502	76-534	0-0	2-32	2-0	390-2,068
	Eric Dickerson, Indianapolis	388-1,659	36-377	0-0	0-0	1-0	425-2,036
	Herschel Walker, Dallas	361-1,514	53-505	0-0	0-0	3-0	417-2,019
1986	Eric Dickerson, L.A. Rams	404-1,821	26-205	0-0	0-0	2-0	432-2,026
	Gary Anderson, San Diego	127-442	80-871	25-227	24-482	2-0	258-2,022
1985	Lionel James, San Diego	105-516	86-1,027	25-213	36-779	1-0	253-2,535
	Marcus Allen, L.A. Raiders	380-1,759	67-555	0-0	0-0	2-(−6)	449-2,308
	Roger Craig, San Fran.	214-1,050	92-1,016	0-0	0-0	0-0	306-2,066
	Walter Payton, Chicago	324-1,551	49-483	0-0	0-0	1-0	374-2,034
1984	Eric Dickerson, L.A. Rams	379-2,105	21-139	0-0	0-0	4-15	404-2,259
	James Wilder, Tampa Bay	407-1,544	85-685	0-0	0-0	4-0	496-2,229
	Walter Payton, Chicago	381-1,684	45-368	0-0	0-0	1-0	427-2,052
1983	*Eric Dickerson, L.A. Rams	390-1,808	51-404	0-0	0-0	1-0	442-2,212
	William Andrews, Atlanta	331-1,567	59-609	0-0	0-0	2-0	392-2,176
	Walter Payton, Chicago	314-1,421	53-607	0-0	0-0	2-0	369-2,028
1981	*James Brooks, San Diego	109-525	46-329	22-290	40-949	2-0	219-2,093
	William Andrews, Atlanta	289-1,301	81-735	0-0	0-0	0-0	370-2,036
1980	Bruce Harper, N.Y. Jets	45-126	50-634	28-242	49-1,070	3-0	175-2,072
1979	Wilbert Montgomery, Phil.	338-1,512	41-494	0-0	1-6	2-0	382-2,012
1978	Bruce Harper, N.Y. Jets	58-303	13-196	30-378	55-1,280	1-0	157-2,157
1977	Walter Payton, Chicago	339-1,852	27-269	0-0	2-95	5-0	373-2,216
	Terry Metcalf, St. Louis	149-739	34-403	14-108	32-772	1-0	230-2,022
1975	Terry Metcalf, St. Louis	165-816	43-378	23-285	35-960	2-23	268-2,462
	O.J. Simpson, Buffalo	329-1,817	28-426	0-0	0-0	1-0	358-2,243
1974	Mack Herron, New England	231-824	38-474	35-517	28-629	3-0	335-2,444
	Otis Armstrong, Denver	263-1,407	38-405	0-0	16-386	1-0	318-2,198
	Terry Metcalf, St. Louis	152-718	50-377	26-340	20-623	7-0	255-2,058
1973	O.J. Simpson, Buffalo	332-2,003	6-70	0-0	0-0	0-0	338-2,073
1966	Gale Sayers, Chicago	229-1,231	34-447	6-44	23-718	3-0	295-2,440
	Leroy Kelly, Cleveland	209-1,141	32-366	13-104	19-403	0-0	273-2,014
1965	*Gale Sayers, Chicago	166-867	29-507	16-238	21-660	4-0	236-2,272
1963	Timmy Brown, Philadelphia	192-841	36-487	16-152	33-945	2-3	279-2,428
	Jim Brown, Cleveland	291-1,863	24-268	0-0	0-0	0-0	315-2,131
1962	Timmy Brown, Philadelphia	137-545	52-849	6-81	30-831	4-0	229-2,306
	Dick Christy, N.Y. Titans	114-535	62-538	15-250	38-824	2-0	231-2,147
1961	Billy Cannon, Houston	200-948	43-586	9-70	18-439	2-0	272-2,043
1960	*Abner Haynes, Dall. Texans	156-875	55-576	14-215	19-434	4-0	248-2,100

First year in the league.

300 Combined Net Yards Gained in a Game

Date	Player, Team, Opponent	No.	Yards	TD
Dec. 11, 1989	John Taylor, San Francisco vs. L.A. Rams	14	321	2
Nov. 26, 1989	Willie Anderson, L.A. Rams vs. New Orleans (OT)	15	336	1
Nov. 28, 1988	Tim Brown, L.A. Raiders vs. San Diego	12	306	1
Dec. 22, 1985	Stephone Paige, Kansas City vs. San Diego	8	309	2
Nov. 10, 1985	Lionel James, San Diego vs. L.A. Raiders (OT)	23	345	0
Sept. 22, 1985	Lionel James, San Diego vs. Cincinnati	20	316	2
Dec. 21, 1975	Walter Payton, Chicago vs. New Orleans	32	300	1
Nov. 23, 1975	Greg Pruitt, Cleveland vs. Cincinnati	28	304	2
Nov. 1, 1970	Eugene (Mercury) Morris, Miami vs. Baltimore	17	302	0
Oct. 4, 1970	O. J. Simpson, Buffalo vs. N.Y. Jets	26	303	2
Dec. 6, 1969	Jerry LeVias, Houston vs. N.Y. Jets	18	329	1
Nov. 2, 1969	Travis Williams, Green Bay vs. Pittsburgh	11	314	3
Dec. 18, 1966	Gale Sayers, Chicago vs. Minnesota	20	339	2
Dec. 12, 1965	Gale Sayers, Chicago vs. San Francisco	17	336	6
Nov. 17, 1963	Gary Ballman, Pittsburgh vs. Washington	12	320	2
Dec. 16, 1962	Timmy Brown, Philadelphia vs. St. Louis	19	341	2
Dec. 10, 1961	Billy Cannon, Houston vs. N.Y. Titans	32	373	5
Nov 19, 1961	Jim Brown, Cleveland vs. Philadelphia	38	313	4
Dec. 3, 1950	Cloyce Box, Detroit vs. Baltimore	13	302	4
Oct. 29, 1950	Wally Triplett, Detroit vs. Los Angeles	11	331	1
Nov. 22, 1945	Jim Benton, Cleveland vs. Detroit	10	303	1

Top 20 Scorers

Player	Years	TD	FG	PAT	TP
George Blanda	26	9	335	943	2,002
Jan Stenerud	19	0	373	580	1,699
Jim Turner	16	1	304	521	1,439
Mark Moseley	16	0	300	482	1,382
Jim Bakken	17	0	282	534	1,380
Fred Cox	15	0	282	519	1,365
Pat Leahy	17	0	278	528	1,362
Lou Groza	17	1	234	641	1,349
Chris Bahr	14	0	241	490	1,213
Nick Lowery	12	0	259	375	1,152
Gino Cappelletti	11	42	176	350	1,130
Ray Wersching	15	0	222	456	1,122
Don Cockroft	13	0	216	432	1,080
Garo Yepremian	14	0	210	444	1,074
Jim Breech	12	0	201	459	1,062
Bruce Gossett	11	0	219	374	1,031
Eddie Murray	11	0	225	341	1,016
Sam Baker	15	2	179	428	977
Matt Bahr	12	0	199	378	975
Rafael Septien	10	0	180	420	960

Cappelletti's total includes four two-point conversions.

Top 20 Touchdown Scorers

Player	Years	Rush	Rec.	Returns	Total TD
Jim Brown	9	106	20	0	126
Walter Payton	13	110	15	0	125
John Riggins	14	104	12	0	116
Lenny Moore	12	63	48	2	113
Don Hutson	11	3	99	3	105
Steve Largent	14	1	100	0	101
Franco Harris	13	91	9	0	100
Marcus Allen	9	75	17	1	93

Jim Taylor	10	83	10	0	93
Tony Dorsett	12	77	13	1	91
Bobby Mitchell	11	18	65	8	91
Eric Dickerson	8	86	4	0	90
Leroy Kelly	10	74	13	3	90
Charley Taylor	13	11	79	0	90
Don Maynard	15	0	88	0	88
Lance Alworth	11	2	85	0	87
Paul Warfield	13	1	85	0	86
Ottis Anderson	12	80	5	0	85
Tommy McDonald	12	0	84	1	85
Jerry Rice	6	4	79	0	83

Top 20 Rushers

Player	Years	Att.	Yards	Avg.	Long	TD
Walter Payton	13	3,838	16,726	4.4	76	110
Tony Dorsett	12	2,936	12,739	4.3	99	77
Jim Brown	9	2,359	12,312	5.2	80	106
Franco Harris	13	2,949	12,120	4.1	75	91
Eric Dickerson	8	2,616	11,903	4.6	85	86
John Riggins	14	2,916	11,352	3.9	66	104
O.J. Simpson	11	2,404	11,236	4.7	94	61
Ottis Anderson	12	2,499	10,101	4.0	76	80
Earl Campbell	8	2,187	9,407	4.3	81	74
Jim Taylor	10	1,941	8,597	4.4	84	83
Joe Perry	14	1,737	8,378	4.8	78	53
Larry Csonka	11	1,891	8,081	4.3	54	64
Marcus Allen	9	1,960	7,957	4.1	61	75
Gerald Riggs	9	1,911	7,940	4.2	58	58
Freeman McNeil	10	1,704	7,604	4.5	69	36
Mike Pruitt	11	1,844	7,378	4.0	77	51
James Brooks	10	1,515	7,347	4.8	65	47
Leroy Kelly	10	1,727	7,274	4.2	70	74
George Rogers	7	1,692	7,176	4.2	79	54
Roger Craig	8	1,686	7,064	4.2	71	50

Top 20 Combined Yards Gained

	Years	Tot.	Rush.	Rec.	Int. Ret.	Punt Ret.	Kickoff Ret.	Fumble Ret.
Walter Payton	13	21,803	16,726	4,538	0	0	539	0
Tony Dorsett	12	16,326	12,739	3,554	0	0	0	33
Jim Brown	9	15,459	12,312	2,499	0	0	648	0
Franco Harris	13	14,622	12,120	2,287	0	0	233	−18
O.J. Simpson	11	14,368	11,236	2,142	0	0	990	0
Bobby Mitchell	11	14,078	2,735	7,954	0	699	2,690	0
James Brooks	10	13,709	7,347	3,274	0	565	2,523	0
Eric Dickerson	8	13,643	11,903	1,725	0	0	0	15
John Riggins	14	13,435	11,352	2,090	0	0	0	−7
Steve Largent	14	13,396	83	13,089	0	68	156	0
Greg Pruitt	12	13,262	5,672	3,069	0	2,007	2,514	0
Ottis Anderson	12	13,151	10,101	3,021	0	0	0	29
Ollie Matson	14	12,884	5,173	3,285	51	595	3,746	34
Tim Brown	10	12,684	3,862	3,399	0	639	4,781	3
Lenny Moore	12	12,451	5,174	6,039	0	56	1,180	2
Don Maynard	15	12,379	70	11,834	0	132	343	0
Charlie Joiner	18	12,367	22	12,146	0	0	194	5
Leroy Kelly	10	12,330	7,274	2,281	0	990	1,784	1
James Lofton	13	12,236	246	11,963	0	0	0	27
Floyd Little	9	12,173	6,323	2,418	0	893	2,523	16

Top 20 Passers

Player	Years	Att.	Comp.	Pct. Comp.	Yards	TD	Pct. TD	Int.	Pct. Int.	Avg. Gain	Rating
Joe Montana	12	4,579	2,914	63.6	34,998	242	5.3	123	2.7	7.64	93.4
Dan Marino	8	4,181	2,480	59.3	31,416	241	5.8	136	3.3	7.51	88.5
Jim Kelly	5	2,088	1,251	59.9	15,730	105	5.0	72	3.4	7.53	85.8
Boomer Esiason	7	2,687	1,520	56.6	21,381	150	5.6	98	3.6	7.96	85.8
Roger Staubach	11	2,958	1,685	57.0	22,700	153	5.2	109	3.7	7.67	83.4
Neil Lomax	8	3,153	1,817	57.6	22,771	136	4.3	90	2.9	7.22	82.7
Sonny Jurgensen	18	4,262	2,433	57.1	32,224	255	6.0	189	4.4	7.56	82.6
Len Dawson	19	3,741	2,136	57.1	28,711	239	6.4	183	4.9	7.67	82.6
Dave Krieg	11	3,291	1,909	58.0	24,052	184	5.6	136	4.1	7.31	82.3
Jim Everett	5	2,038	1,154	56.6	15,345	101	5.0	73	3.6	7.53	82.2
Ken O'Brien	8	2,878	1,697	59.0	20,444	109	3.8	78	2.7	7.10	82.2
Ken Anderson	16	4,475	2,654	59.3	32,838	197	4.4	160	3.6	7.34	81.9
Danny White	13	2,950	1,761	59.7	21,959	155	5.3	132	4.5	7.44	81.7
Bart Starr	16	3,149	1,808	57.4	24,718	152	4.8	138	4.4	7.85	80.5
Fran Tarkenton	18	6,467	3,686	57.0	47,003	342	5.3	266	4.1	7.27	80.4
Bernie Kosar	6	2,363	1,364	57.7	16,450	85	3.6	62	2.6	6.96	80.3
Dan Fouts	15	5,604	3,297	58.8	43,040	254	4.5	242	4.3	7.68	80.2
Warren Moon	7	3,025	1,701	56.2	22,989	134	4.4	112	3.7	7.60	79.9
Tony Eason	8	1,564	911	58.2	11,142	61	3.9	51	3.3	7.12	79.7
Jim McMahon	9	1,840	1,056	57.4	13,398	77	4.2	66	3.6	7.28	79.3

1,500 or more attempts. The passing ratings are based on performance standards established for completion percentage, interception percentage, touchdown percentage, and average gain. Passers are allocated points according to how their marks compare with those standards.

Top 20 Pass Receivers

Player	Years	No.	Yards	Avg.	Long	TD
Steve Largent	14	819	13,089	16.0	74	100
Charlie Joiner	18	750	12,146	16.2	87	65
Art Monk	11	730	9,935	13.6	79	52
Ozzie Newsome	13	662	7,980	12.1	74	47
Charley Taylor	13	649	9,110	14.0	88	79
James Lofton	13	642	11,963	18.6	80	61
Don Maynard	15	633	11,834	18.7	87	88
Raymond Berry	13	631	9,275	14.7	70	68
Harold Carmichael	14	590	8,985	15.2	85	79
Fred Biletnikoff	14	589	8,974	15.2	82	76
Harold Jackson	16	579	10,372	17.9	79	76
Lionel Taylor	10	567	7,195	12.7	80	45
Wes Chandler	11	559	8,966	16.0	85	56
Stanley Morgan	14	557	10,716	19.2	76	72

Player	Years	No.	Yards	Avg.	Long	TD
J.T. Smith	13	544	6,974	12.8	77	35
Lance Alworth	11	542	10,266	18.9	85	85
Kellen Winslow	9	541	6,741	12.5	67	45
John Stallworth	14	537	8,723	16.2	74	63
Roy Green	12	522	8,496	16.3	83	66
Bobby Mitchell	11	521	7,954	15.3	99	65

Top 20 Interceptors

Player	Years	No.	Yards	Avg.	Long	TD
Paul Krause	16	81	1,185	14.6	81	3
Emlen Tunnell	14	79	1,282	16.2	55	4
Dick (Night Train) Lane	14	68	1,207	17.8	80	5
Ken Riley	15	65	596	9.2	66	5
Dick LeBeau	13	62	762	12.3	70	3
Dave Brown	15	62	698	11.3	90	5
Emmitt Thomas	13	58	937	16.2	73	5
Bobby Boyd	9	57	994	17.4	74	4
Johnny Robinson	12	57	741	13.0	57	1
Mel Blount	14	57	736	12.9	52	2
Lem Barney	11	56	1,077	19.2	71	7
Pat Fischer	17	56	941	16.8	69	4
Willie Brown	16	54	472	8.7	45	2
Bobby Dillon	8	52	976	18.8	61	5
Jack Butler	9	52	826	15.9	52	4
Larry Wilson	13	52	800	15.4	96	5
Jim Patton	12	52	712	13.7	51	2
Mel Renfro	14	52	626	12.0	90	3
Bobby Bryant	13	51	749	14.7	56	3
Ronnie Lott	10	51	643	12.6	83	5
Donnie Shell	14	51	490	9.6	67	2

Top 20 Punters

Player	Years	No.	Yards	Avg.	Long	Blk.
Sammy Baugh	16	338	15,245	45.1	85	9
Tommy Davis	11	511	22,833	44.7	82	2
Yale Lary	11	503	22,279	44.3	74	4
Rohn Stark	9	664	29,267	44.1	72	6
Horace Gillom	7	385	16,872	43.8	80	5
Jerry Norton	11	358	15,671	43.8	78	2
Don Chandler	12	660	28,678	43.5	90	4
Sean Landeta	6	376	16,331	43.4	71	1
Reggie Roby	8	466	20,127	43.2	77	2
Jerrel Wilson	16	1,072	46,139	43.0	72	12
Norm Van Brocklin	12	523	22,413	42.9	72	3
Danny Villanueva	8	488	20,862	42.8	68	2
Bobby Joe Green	14	970	41,317	42.6	75	3
Sam Baker	15	703	29,938	42.6	72	2
Ralf Mojsiejenko	6	397	16,877	42.5	74	5
Rich Camarillo	10	651	27,664	42.5	76	4
Bob Waterfield	8	315	13,367	42.4	88	5
Ray Guy	14	1,049	44,493	42.4	74	3
Curley Johnson	10	559	23,651	42.3	73	6
Jim Arnold	8	608	25,682	42.2	69	4

300 or more punts.

Top 20 Punt Returners

Player	Years	No.	Yards	Avg.	Long	TD
George McAfee	8	112	1,431	12.8	74	2
Jack Christiansen	8	85	1,084	12.8	89	8
Claude Gibson	5	110	1,381	12.6	85	3
Clarence Verdin	5	76	931	12.3	73	2
Bill Dudley	9	124	1,515	12.2	96	3
Rick Upchurch	9	248	3,008	12.1	92	8
David Meggett	2	89	1,049	11.8	76	2
Billy Johnson	14	282	3,317	11.8	87	6
Mack Herron	3	84	982	11.7	66	0
Mel Gray	5	94	1,094	11.6	80	1
Billy Thompson	13	157	1,814	11.6	60	0
Henry Ellard	8	133	1,509	11.3	83	4
Louis Lipps	7	107	1,212	11.3	76	3
Rodger Bird	3	94	1,063	11.3	78	0
Bosh Pritchard	6	95	1,072	11.3	81	2
Bobby Joe Edmonds	4	105	1,178	11.2	75	1
John Taylor	4	107	1,194	11.2	95	2
Vai Sikahema	5	193	2,152	11.2	76	3
Terry Metcalf	6	84	936	11.1	69	1
Bob Hayes	11	104	1,158	11.1	90	3

75 or more returns.

Top 20 Kickoff Returners

Player	Years	No.	Yards	Avg.	Long	TD
Gale Sayers	7	91	2,781	30.6	103	6
Lynn Chandnois	7	92	2,720	29.6	93	3
Abe Woodson	9	193	5,538	28.7	105	5
Claude (Buddy) Young	6	90	2,514	27.9	104	2
Travis Williams	5	102	2,801	27.5	105	6
Joe Arenas	7	139	3,798	27.3	96	1
Clarence Davis	8	79	2,140	27.1	76	0
Steve Van Buren	8	76	2,030	26.7	98	3
Lenny Lyles	12	81	2,161	26.7	103	3
Eugene (Mercury) Morris	8	111	2,947	26.5	105	3
Bobby Jancik	6	158	4,185	26.5	61	0
Mel Renfro	14	85	2,246	26.4	100	2
Bobby Mitchell	11	102	2,690	26.4	98	5
Ollie Matson	14	143	3,746	26.2	105	6
Alvin Haymond	10	170	4,438	26.1	98	2
Noland Smith	3	82	2,137	26.1	106	1
Al Nelson	9	101	2,625	26.0	78	0
Tim Brown	10	184	4,781	26.0	105	5
Vic Washington	6	129	3,341	25.9	98	1
Dave Hampton	8	113	2,923	25.9	101	3

75 or more returns.

YEARLY STATISTICAL LEADERS

Annual Scoring Leaders

Year	Player, Team	TD	FG	PAT	TP
1990	Nick Lowery, Kansas City, AFC	0	34	37	139
	Chip Lohmiller, Washington, NFC	0	30	41	131
1989	Mike Cofer, San Francisco, NFC	0	29	49	136
	*David Treadwell, Denver, AFC	0	27	39	120
1988	Scott Norwood, Buffalo, AFC	0	32	33	129
	*Mike Cofer, San Francisco, NFC	0	27	40	121
1987	Jerry Rice, San Francisco, NFC	23	0	0	138
	Jim Breech, Cincinnati, AFC	0	24	25	97
1986	Tony Franklin, New England, AFC	0	32	44	140
	Kevin Butler, Chicago, NFC	0	28	36	120
1985	*Kevin Butler, Chicago, NFC	0	31	51	144
	Gary Anderson, Pittsburgh, AFC	0	33	40	139
1984	Ray Wersching, San Francisco, NFC	0	25	56	131
	Gary Anderson, Pittsburgh, AFC	0	24	45	117
1983	Mark Moseley, Washington, NFC	0	33	62	161
	Gary Anderson, Pittsburgh, AFC	0	27	38	119
1982	*Marcus Allen, L.A. Raiders, AFC	14	0	0	84
	Wendell Tyler, L.A. Rams, NFC	13	0	0	78
1981	Ed Murray, Detroit, NFC	0	25	46	121
	Rafael Septien, Dallas, NFC	0	27	40	121
	Jim Breech, Cincinnati, AFC	0	22	49	115
	Nick Lowery, Kansas City, AFC	0	26	37	115
1980	John Smith, New England, AFC	0	26	51	129
	*Ed Murray, Detroit, NFC	0	27	35	116
1979	John Smith, New England, AFC	0	23	46	115
	Mark Moseley, Washington, NFC	0	25	39	114
1978	*Frank Corral, Los Angeles, NFC	0	29	31	118
	Pat Leahy, N.Y. Jets, AFC	0	22	41	107
1977	Errol Mann, Oakland, AFC	0	20	39	99
	Walter Payton, Chicago, NFC	16	0	0	96
1976	Toni Linhart, Baltimore, AFC	0	20	49	109
	Mark Moseley, Washington, NFC	0	22	31	97
1975	O.J. Simpson, Buffalo, AFC	23	0	0	138
	Chuck Foreman, Minnesota, NFC	22	0	0	132
1974	Chester Marcol, Green Bay, NFC	0	25	19	94
	Roy Gerela, Pittsburgh, AFC	0	20	33	93
1973	David Ray, Los Angeles, NFC	0	30	40	130
	Roy Gerela, Pittsburgh, AFC	0	29	36	123
1972	*Chester Marcol, Green Bay, NFC	0	33	29	128
	Bobby Howfield, N.Y. Jets, AFC	0	27	40	121
1971	Garo Yepremian, Miami, AFC	0	28	33	117
	Curt Knight, Washington, NFC	0	29	27	114
1970	Fred Cox, Minnesota, NFC	0	30	35	125
	Jan Stenerud, Kansas City, AFC	0	30	26	116
1969	Jim Turner, N.Y. Jets, AFL	0	32	33	129
	Fred Cox, Minnesota, NFL	0	26	43	121
1968	Jim Turner, N.Y. Jets, AFL	0	34	43	145
	Leroy Kelly, Cleveland, NFL	20	0	0	120
1967	Jim Bakken, St. Louis, NFL	0	27	36	117
	George Blanda, Oakland, AFL	0	20	56	116
1966	Gino Cappelletti, Boston, AFL	6	16	35	119
	Bruce Gossett, Los Angeles, NFL	0	28	29	113
1965	*Gale Sayers, Chicago, NFL	22	0	0	132
	Gino Cappelletti, Boston, AFL	9	17	27	132
1964	Gino Cappelletti, Boston, AFL	7	25	36	#155
	Lenny Moore, Baltimore, NFL	20	0	0	120
1963	Gino Cappelletti, Boston, AFL	2	22	35	113
	Don Chandler, N.Y. Giants, NFL	0	18	52	106
1962	Gene Mingo, Denver, AFL	4	27	32	137
	Jim Taylor, Green Bay, NFL	19	0	0	114
1961	Gino Cappelletti, Boston, AFL	8	17	48	147
	Paul Hornung, Green Bay, NFL	10	15	41	146
1960	Paul Hornung, Green Bay, NFL	15	15	41	176
	*Gene Mingo, Denver, AFL	6	18	33	123
1959	Paul Hornung, Green Bay	7	7	31	94
1958	Jim Brown, Cleveland	18	0	0	108
1957	Sam Baker, Washington	1	14	29	77
	Lou Groza, Cleveland	0	15	32	77
1956	Bobby Layne, Detroit	5	12	33	99
1955	Doak Walker, Detroit	7	9	27	96
1954	Bobby Walston, Philadelphia	11	4	36	114
1953	Gordy Soltau, San Francisco	6	10	48	114
1952	Gordy Soltau, San Francisco	7	6	34	94
1951	Elroy (Crazylegs) Hirsch, Los Angeles	17	0	0	102
1950	*Doak Walker, Detroit	11	8	38	128
1949	Pat Harder, Chi. Cardinals	8	3	45	102
	Gene Roberts, N.Y. Giants	17	0	0	102
1948	Pat Harder, Chi. Cardinals	6	7	53	110
1947	Pat Harder, Chi. Cardinals	7	7	39	102
1946	Ted Fritsch, Green Bay	10	9	13	100
1945	Steve Van Buren, Philadelphia	18	0	2	110
1944	Don Hutson, Green Bay	9	0	31	85
1943	Don Hutson, Green Bay	12	3	36	117
1942	Don Hutson, Green Bay	17	1	33	138
1941	Don Hutson, Green Bay	12	1	20	95
1940	Don Hutson, Green Bay	7	0	15	57
1939	Andy Farkas, Washington	11	0	2	68
1938	Clarke Hinkle, Green Bay	7	3	7	58
1937	Jack Manders, Chi. Bears	5	8	15	69
1936	Earl (Dutch) Clark, Detroit	7	4	19	73
1935	Earl (Dutch) Clark, Detroit	6	1	16	55
1934	Jack Manders, Chi. Bears	3	10	31	79
1933	Ken Strong, N.Y. Giants	6	5	13	64
	Glenn Presnell, Portsmouth	6	6	10	64
1932	Earl (Dutch) Clark, Portsmouth	6	3	10	55

**First year in the league.*
#Cappelletti's total includes a two-point conversion.

Annual Leaders—Most Field Goals Made

Year	Player, Team	Att.	Made	Pct.
1990	Nick Lowery, Kansas City, AFC	34	37	91.9
	Chip Lohmiller, Washington, NFC	30	40	75.0
1989	Rich Karlis, Minnesota, NFC	39	31	79.5
	*David Treadwell, Denver, AFC	33	27	81.8
1988	Scott Norwood, Buffalo, AFC	37	32	86.5
	*Mike Cofer, San Francisco, NFC	38	27	71.1
1987	Morten Andersen, New Orleans, NFC	36	28	77.8
	Dean Biasucci, Indianapolis, AFC	27	24	88.9
	Jim Breech, Cincinnati, AFC	30	24	80.0
1986	Tony Franklin, New England, AFC	41	32	78.0
	Kevin Butler, Chicago, NFC	41	28	68.3
1985	Gary Anderson, Pittsburgh, AFC	42	33	78.6
	Morten Andersen, New Orleans, NFC	35	31	88.6
	*Kevin Butler, Chicago, NFC	37	31	83.8
1984	*Paul McFadden, Philadelphia, NFC	37	30	81.1
	Gary Anderson, Pittsburgh, AFC	32	24	75.0
	Matt Bahr, Cleveland, AFC	32	24	75.0
1983	*Ali Haji-Sheikh, N.Y. Giants, NFC	42	35	83.3
	*Raul Allegre, Baltimore, AFC	35	30	85.7
1982	Mark Moseley, Washington, NFC	21	20	95.2
	Nick Lowery, Kansas City, AFC	24	19	79.2
1981	Rafael Septien, Dallas, NFC	35	27	77.1
	Nick Lowery, Kansas City, AFC	36	26	72.2
1980	*Ed Murray, Detroit, NFC	42	27	64.3
	John Smith, New England, AFC	34	26	76.5
	Fred Steinfort, Denver, AFC	34	26	76.5
1979	Mark Moseley, Washington, NFC	33	25	75.8
	John Smith, New England, AFC	33	23	69.7
1978	*Frank Corral, Los Angeles, NFC	43	29	67.4
	Pat Leahy, N.Y. Jets, AFC	30	22	73.3
1977	Mark Moseley, Washington, NFC	37	21	56.8
	Errol Mann, Oakland, AFC	28	20	71.4
1976	Mark Moseley, Washington, NFC	34	22	64.7
	Jan Stenerud, Kansas City, AFC	38	21	55.3
1975	Jan Stenerud, Kansas City, AFC	32	22	68.8
	Toni Fritsch, Dallas, NFC	35	22	62.9
1974	Chester Marcol, Green Bay, NFC	39	25	64.1
	Roy Gerela, Pittsburgh, AFC	29	20	69.0
1973	David Ray, Los Angeles, NFC	47	30	63.8
	Roy Gerela, Pittsburgh, AFC	43	29	67.4
1972	*Chester Marcol, Green Bay, NFC	48	33	68.8
	Roy Gerela, Pittsburgh, AFC	41	28	68.3
1971	Curt Knight, Washington, NFC	49	29	59.2
	Garo Yepremian, Miami, AFC	40	28	70.0
1970	Jan Stenerud, Kansas City, AFC	42	30	71.4
	Fred Cox, Minnesota, NFC	46	30	65.2
1969	Jim Turner, N.Y. Jets, AFL	47	32	68.1
	Fred Cox, Minnesota, NFL	37	26	70.3
1968	Jim Turner, N.Y. Jets, AFL	46	34	73.9
	Mac Percival, Chicago, NFL	36	25	69.4
1967	Jim Bakken, St. Louis, NFL	39	27	69.2
	Jan Stenerud, Kansas City, AFL	36	21	58.3
1966	Bruce Gossett, Los Angeles, NFL	49	28	57.1
	Mike Mercer, Oakland-Kansas City, AFL	30	21	70.0
1965	Pete Gogolak, Buffalo, AFL	46	28	60.9
	Fred Cox, Minnesota, NFL	35	23	65.7
1964	Jim Bakken, St. Louis, NFL	38	25	65.8
	Gino Cappelletti, Boston, AFL	39	25	64.1
1963	Jim Martin, Baltimore, NFL	39	24	61.5
	Gino Cappelletti, Boston, AFL	38	22	57.9
1962	Gene Mingo, Denver, AFL	39	27	69.2
	Lou Michaels, Pittsburgh, NFL	42	26	61.9
1961	Steve Myhra, Baltimore, NFL	39	21	53.8
	Gino Cappelletti, Boston, AFL	32	17	53.1
1960	Tommy Davis, San Francisco, NFL	32	19	59.4
	*Gene Mingo, Denver, AFL	28	18	64.3
1959	Pat Summerall, New York Giants	29	20	69.0
1958	Paige Cothren, Los Angeles	25	14	56.0
	*Tom Miner, Pittsburgh	28	14	50.0
1957	Lou Groza, Cleveland	22	15	68.2
1956	Sam Baker, Washington	25	17	68.0
1955	Fred Cone, Green Bay	24	16	66.7
1954	Lou Groza, Cleveland	24	16	66.7
1953	Lou Groza, Cleveland	26	23	88.5
1952	Lou Groza, Cleveland	33	19	57.6
1951	Bob Waterfield, Los Angeles	23	13	56.5
1950	*Lou Groza, Cleveland	19	13	68.4
1949	Cliff Patton, Philadelphia	18	9	50.0
	Bob Waterfield, Los Angeles	16	9	56.3
1948	Cliff Patton, Philadelphia	12	8	66.7
1947	Ward Cuff, Green Bay	16	7	43.8
	Pat Harder, Chi. Cardinals	10	7	70.0
	Bob Waterfield, Los Angeles	16	7	43.8
1946	Ted Fritsch, Green Bay	17	9	52.9
1945	Joe Aguirre, Washington	13	7	53.8
1944	Ken Strong, N.Y. Giants	12	6	50.0
1943	Ward Cuff, N.Y. Giants	9	3	33.3
	Don Hutson, Green Bay	5	3	60.0
1942	Bill Daddio, Chi. Cardinals	10	5	50.0
1941	Clarke Hinkle, Green Bay	14	6	42.9
1940	Clarke Hinkle, Green Bay	14	9	64.3
1939	Ward Cuff, N.Y. Giants	16	7	43.8
1938	Ward Cuff, N.Y. Giants	9	5	55.6
	Ralph Kercheval, Brooklyn	13	5	38.5
1937	Jack Manders, Chi. Bears		8	
1936	Jack Manders, Chi. Bears		7	

Year	Player, Team	
	Armand Niccolai, Pittsburgh	7
1935	Armand Niccolai, Pittsburgh	6
	Bill Smith, Chi. Cardinals	6
1934	Jack Manders, Chi. Bears	10
1933	*Jack Manders, Chi. Bears	6
	Glenn Presnell, Portsmouth	6
1932	Earl (Dutch) Clark, Portsmouth	3

*First year in the league.

Annual Rushing Leaders

Year	Player, Team	Att.	Yards	Avg.	TD
1990	Barry Sanders, Detroit, NFC	255	1,304	5.1	13
	Thurman Thomas, Buffalo, AFC	271	1,297	4.8	11
1989	Christian Okoye, Kansas City, AFC	370	1,480	4.0	12
	*Barry Sanders, Detroit, NFC	280	1,470	5.3	14
1988	Eric Dickerson, Indianapolis, AFC	388	1,659	4.3	14
	Herschel Walker, Dallas, NFC	361	1,514	4.2	5
1987	Charles White, L.A. Rams, NFC	324	1,374	4.2	11
	Eric Dickerson, Indianapolis, AFC	223	1,011	4.5	5
1986	Eric Dickerson, L.A. Rams, NFC	404	1,821	4.5	11
	Curt Warner, Seattle, AFC	319	1,481	4.6	13
1985	Marcus Allen, L.A. Raiders, AFC	380	1,759	4.6	11
	Gerald Riggs, Atlanta, NFC	397	1,719	4.3	10
1984	Eric Dickerson, L.A. Rams, NFC	379	2,105	5.6	14
	Earnest Jackson, San Diego, AFC	296	1,179	4.0	8
1983	*Eric Dickerson, L.A. Rams, NFC	390	1,808	4.6	18
	*Curt Warner, Seattle, AFC	335	1,449	4.3	13
1982	Freeman McNeil, N.Y. Jets, AFC	151	786	5.2	6
	Tony Dorsett, Dallas, NFC	177	745	4.2	5
1981	*George Rogers, New Orleans, NFC	378	1,674	4.4	13
	Earl Campbell, Houston, AFC	361	1,376	3.8	10
1980	Earl Campbell, Houston, AFC	373	1,934	5.2	13
	Walter Payton, Chicago, NFC	317	1,460	4.6	6
1979	Earl Campbell, Houston, AFC	368	1,697	4.6	19
	Walter Payton, Chicago, NFC	369	1,610	4.4	14
1978	*Earl Campbell, Houston, AFC	302	1,450	4.8	13
	Walter Payton, Chicago, NFC	333	1,395	4.2	11
1977	Walter Payton, Chicago, NFC	339	1,852	5.5	14
	Mark van Eeghen, Oakland, AFC	324	1,273	3.9	7
1976	O.J. Simpson, Buffalo, AFC	290	1,503	5.2	8
	Walter Payton, Chicago, NFC	311	1,390	4.5	13
1975	O.J. Simpson, Buffalo, AFC	329	1,817	5.5	16
	Jim Otis, St. Louis, NFC	269	1,076	4.0	5
1974	Otis Armstrong, Denver, AFC	263	1,407	5.3	9
	Lawrence McCutcheon, Los Angeles, NFC	236	1,109	4.7	3
1973	O.J. Simpson, Buffalo, AFC	332	2,003	6.0	12
	John Brockington, Green Bay, NFC	265	1,144	4.3	3
1972	O.J. Simpson, Buffalo, AFC	292	1,251	4.3	6
	Larry Brown, Washington, NFC	285	1,216	4.3	8
1971	Floyd Little, Denver, AFC	284	1,133	4.0	6
	*John Brockington, Green Bay, NFC	216	1,105	5.1	4
1970	Larry Brown, Washington, NFC	237	1,125	4.7	5
	Floyd Little, Denver, AFC	209	901	4.3	3
1969	Gale Sayers, Chicago, NFL	236	1,032	4.4	8
	Dickie Post, San Diego, AFL	182	873	4.8	6
1968	Leroy Kelly, Cleveland, NFL	248	1,239	5.0	16
	*Paul Robinson, Cincinnati, AFL	238	1,023	4.3	8
1967	Jim Nance, Boston, AFL	269	1,216	4.5	7
	Leroy Kelly, Cleveland, NFL	235	1,205	5.1	11
1966	Jim Nance, Boston, AFL	299	1,458	4.9	11
	Gale Sayers, Chicago, NFL	229	1,231	5.4	8
1965	Jim Brown, Cleveland, NFL	289	1,544	5.3	17
	Paul Lowe, San Diego, AFL	222	1,121	5.0	7
1964	Jim Brown, Cleveland, NFL	280	1,446	5.2	7
	Cookie Gilchrist, Buffalo, AFL	230	981	4.3	6
1963	Jim Brown, Cleveland, NFL	291	1,863	6.4	12
	Clem Daniels, Oakland, AFL	215	1,099	5.1	3
1962	Jim Taylor, Green Bay, NFL	272	1,474	5.4	19
	*Cookie Gilchrist, Buffalo, AFL	214	1,096	5.1	13
1961	Jim Brown, Cleveland, NFL	305	1,408	4.6	8
	Billy Cannon, Houston, AFL	200	948	4.7	6
1960	Jim Brown, Cleveland, NFL	215	1,257	5.8	9
	*Abner Haynes, Dall. Texans, AFL	156	875	5.6	9
1959	Jim Brown, Cleveland	290	1,329	4.6	14
1958	Jim Brown, Cleveland	257	1,527	5.9	17
1957	*Jim Brown, Cleveland	202	942	4.7	9
1956	Rick Casares, Chi. Bears	234	1,126	4.8	12
1955	*Alan Ameche, Baltimore	213	961	4.5	9
1954	Joe Perry, San Francisco	173	1,049	6.1	8
1953	Joe Perry, San Francisco	192	1,018	5.3	10
1952	Dan Towler, Los Angeles	156	894	5.7	10
1951	Eddie Price, N.Y. Giants	271	971	3.6	7
1950	*Marion Motley, Cleveland	140	810	5.8	3
1949	Steve Van Buren, Philadelphia	263	1,146	4.4	11
1948	Steve Van Buren, Philadelphia	201	945	4.7	10
1947	Steve Van Buren, Philadelphia	217	1,008	4.6	13
1946	Bill Dudley, Pittsburgh	146	604	4.1	3
1945	Steve Van Buren, Philadelphia	143	832	5.8	15
1944	Bill Paschal, N.Y. Giants	196	737	3.8	9
1943	*Bill Paschal, N.Y. Giants	147	572	3.9	10
1942	*Bill Dudley, Pittsburgh	162	696	4.3	5
1941	Clarence (Pug) Manders, Brooklyn	111	486	4.4	5
1940	Byron (Whizzer) White, Detroit	146	514	3.5	5
1939	*Bill Osmanski, Chicago	121	699	5.8	7
1938	*Byron (Whizzer) White, Pittsburgh	152	567	3.7	4
1937	Cliff Battles, Washington	216	874	4.0	5
1936	*Alphonse (Tuffy) Leemans, N.Y. Giants	206	830	4.0	2
1935	Doug Russell, Chi. Cardinals	140	499	3.6	0
1934	*Beattie Feathers, Chi. Bears	101	1,004	9.9	8
1933	Jim Musick, Boston	173	809	4.7	5
1932	*Cliff Battles, Boston	148	576	3.9	3

*First year in the league.

Annual Passing Leaders

Year	Player, Team	Att.	Comp.	Yards	TD	Int.
1990	Jim Kelly, Buffalo, AFC	346	219	2,829	24	9
	Phil Simms, N.Y. Giants, NFC	311	184	2,284	15	4
1989	Joe Montana, San Francisco, NFC	386	271	3,521	26	8
	Boomer Esiason, Cincinnati, AFC	455	258	3,525	28	11
1988	Boomer Esiason, Cincinnati, AFC	388	223	3,572	28	14
	Wade Wilson, Minnesota, NFC	332	204	2,746	15	9
1987	Joe Montana, San Francisco, NFC	398	266	3,054	31	13
	Bernie Kosar, Cleveland, AFC	389	241	3,033	22	9
1986	Tommy Kramer, Minnesota, NFC	372	208	3,000	24	10
	Dan Marino, Miami, AFC	623	378	4,746	44	23
1985	Ken O'Brien, N.Y. Jets, AFC	488	297	3,888	25	8
	Joe Montana, San Francisco, NFC	494	303	3,653	27	13
1984	Dan Marino, Miami, AFC	564	362	5,084	48	17
	Joe Montana, San Francisco, NFC	432	279	3,630	28	10
1983	Steve Bartkowski, Atlanta, NFC	432	274	3,167	22	5
	*Dan Marino, Miami, AFC	296	173	2,210	20	6
1982	Ken Anderson, Cincinnati, AFC	309	218	2,495	12	9
	Joe Theismann, Washington, NFC	252	161	2,033	13	9
1981	Ken Anderson, Cincinnati, AFC	479	300	3,754	29	10
	Joe Montana, San Francisco, NFC	488	311	3,565	19	12
1980	Brian Sipe, Cleveland, AFC	554	337	4,132	30	14
	Ron Jaworski, Philadelphia, NFC	451	257	3,529	27	12
1979	Roger Staubach, Dallas, NFC	461	267	3,586	27	11
	Dan Fouts, San Diego, AFC	530	332	4,082	24	24
1978	Roger Staubach, Dallas, NFC	413	231	3,190	25	16
	Terry Bradshaw, Pittsburgh, AFC	368	207	2,915	28	20
1977	Bob Griese, Miami, AFC	307	180	2,252	22	13
	Roger Staubach, Dallas, NFC	361	210	2,620	18	9
1976	Ken Stabler, Oakland, AFC	291	194	2,737	27	17
	James Harris, Los Angeles, NFC	158	91	1,460	8	6
1975	Ken Anderson, Cincinnati, AFC	377	228	3,169	21	11
	Fran Tarkenton, Minnesota, NFC	425	273	2,994	25	13
1974	Ken Anderson, Cincinnati, AFC	328	213	2,667	18	10
	Sonny Jurgensen, Washington, NFC	167	107	1,185	11	5
1973	Roger Staubach, Dallas, NFC	286	179	2,428	23	15
	Ken Stabler, Oakland, AFC	260	163	1,997	14	10
1972	Norm Snead, N.Y. Giants, NFC	325	196	2,307	17	12
	Earl Morrall, Miami, AFC	150	83	1,360	11	7
1971	Roger Staubach, Dallas, NFC	211	126	1,882	15	4
	Bob Griese, Miami, AFC	263	145	2,089	19	9
1970	John Brodie, San Francisco, NFC	378	223	2,941	24	10
	Daryle Lamonica, Oakland, AFC	356	179	2,516	22	15
1969	Sonny Jurgensen, Washington, NFL	442	274	3,102	22	15
	*Greg Cook, Cincinnati, AFL	197	106	1,854	15	11
1968	Len Dawson, Kansas City, AFL	224	131	2,109	17	9
	Earl Morrall, Baltimore, NFL	317	182	2,909	26	17
1967	Sonny Jurgensen, Washington, NFL	508	288	3,747	31	16
	Daryle Lamonica, Oakland, AFL	425	220	3,228	30	20
1966	Bart Starr, Green Bay, NFL	251	156	2,257	14	3
	Len Dawson, Kansas City, AFL	284	159	2,527	26	10
1965	Rudy Bukich, Chicago, NFL	312	176	2,641	20	9
	John Hadl, San Diego, AFL	348	174	2,798	20	21
1964	Len Dawson, Kansas City, AFL	354	199	2,879	30	18
	Bart Starr, Green Bay, NFL	272	163	2,144	15	4
1963	Y.A. Tittle, N.Y. Giants, NFL	367	221	3,145	36	14
	Tobin Rote, San Diego, AFL	286	170	2,510	20	17
1962	Len Dawson, Dall. Texans, AFL	310	189	2,759	29	17
	Bart Starr, Green Bay, NFL	285	178	2,438	12	9
1961	George Blanda, Houston, AFL	362	187	3,330	36	22
	Milt Plum, Cleveland, NFL	302	177	2,416	18	10
1960	Milt Plum, Cleveland, NFL	250	151	2,297	21	5
	Jack Kemp, L.A. Chargers, AFL	406	211	3,018	20	25
1959	Charlie Conerly, N.Y. Giants	194	113	1,706	14	4
1958	Eddie LeBaron, Washington	145	79	1,365	11	10
1957	Tommy O'Connell, Cleveland	110	63	1,229	9	8
1956	Ed Brown, Chi. Bears	168	96	1,667	11	12
1955	Otto Graham, Cleveland	185	98	1,721	15	8
1954	Norm Van Brocklin, Los Angeles	260	139	2,637	13	21
1953	Otto Graham, Cleveland	258	167	2,722	11	9
1952	Norm Van Brocklin, Los Angeles	205	113	1,736	14	17
1951	Bob Waterfield, Los Angeles	176	88	1,566	13	10
1950	Norm Van Brocklin, Los Angeles	233	127	2,061	18	14
1949	Sammy Baugh, Washington	255	145	1,903	18	14
1948	Tommy Thompson, Philadelphia	246	141	1,965	25	11
1947	Sammy Baugh, Washington	354	210	2,938	25	15
1946	Bob Waterfield, Los Angeles	251	127	1,747	18	17
1945	Sammy Baugh, Washington	182	128	1,669	11	4
	Sid Luckman, Chi. Bears	217	117	1,725	14	10
1944	Frank Filchock, Washington	147	84	1,139	13	9
1943	Sammy Baugh, Washington	239	133	1,754	23	19
1942	Cecil Isbell, Green Bay	268	146	2,021	24	14
1941	Cecil Isbell, Green Bay	206	117	1,479	15	11
1940	Sammy Baugh, Washington	177	111	1,367	12	10
1939	*Parker Hall, Cleveland	208	106	1,227	9	13
1938	Ed Danowski, N.Y. Giants	129	70	848	7	8
1937	*Sammy Baugh, Washington	171	81	1,127	8	14
1936	Arnie Herber, Green Bay	173	77	1,239	11	13
1935	Ed Danowski, N.Y. Giants	113	57	794	10	9
1934	Arnie Herber, Green Bay	115	42	799	8	12
1933	*Harry Newman, N.Y. Giants	136	53	973	11	17
1932	Arnie Herber, Green Bay	101	37	639	9	9

*First year in the league.

Annual Pass Receiving Leaders

Year	Player, Team	No.	Yards	Avg.	TD
1990	Jerry Rice, San Francisco, NFC	100	1,502	15.0	13
	Haywood Jeffires, Houston, AFC	74	1,048	14.2	8
	Drew Hill, Houston, AFC	74	1,019	13.8	5
1989	Sterling Sharpe, Green Bay, NFC	90	1,423	15.8	12
	Andre Reed, Buffalo, AFC	88	1,312	14.9	9

1988	Al Toon, N.Y. Jets, AFC	93	1,067	11.5	5
	Henry Ellard, L.A. Rams, NFC	86	1,414	16.4	10
1987	J.T. Smith, St. Louis, NFC	91	1,117	12.3	8
	Al Toon, N.Y. Jets, AFC	68	976	14.4	5
1986	Todd Christensen, L.A. Raiders, AFC	95	1,153	12.1	8
	Jerry Rice, San Francisco, NFC	86	1,570	18.3	15
1985	Roger Craig, San Francisco, NFC	92	1,016	11.0	6
	Lionel James, San Diego, AFC	86	1,027	11.9	6
1984	Art Monk, Washington, NFC	106	1,372	12.9	7
	Ozzie Newsome, Cleveland, AFC	89	1,001	11.2	5
1983	Todd Christensen, L.A. Raiders, AFC	92	1,247	13.6	12
	Roy Green, St. Louis, NFC	78	1,227	15.7	14
	Charlie Brown, Washington, NFC	78	1,225	15.7	8
	Earnest Gray, N.Y. Giants, NFC	78	1,139	14.6	5
1982	Dwight Clark, San Francisco, NFC	60	913	15.2	5
	Kellen Winslow, San Diego, AFC	54	721	13.4	6
1981	Kellen Winslow, San Diego, AFC	88	1,075	12.2	10
	Dwight Clark, San Francisco, NFC	85	1,105	13.0	4
1980	Kellen Winslow, San Diego, AFC	89	1,290	14.5	9
	*Earl Cooper, San Francisco, NFC	83	567	6.8	4
1979	Joe Washington, Baltimore, AFC	82	750	9.1	3
	Ahmad Rashad, Minnesota, NFC	80	1,156	14.5	9
1978	Rickey Young, Minnesota, NFC	88	704	8.0	5
	Steve Largent, Seattle, AFC	71	1,168	16.5	8
1977	Lydell Mitchell, Baltimore, AFC	71	620	8.7	4
	Ahmad Rashad, Minnesota, NFC	51	681	13.4	2
1976	MacArthur Lane, Kansas City, AFC	66	686	10.4	1
	Drew Pearson, Dallas, NFC	58	806	13.9	6
1975	Chuck Foreman, Minnesota, NFC	73	691	9.5	9
	Reggie Rucker, Cleveland, AFC	60	770	12.8	3
	Lydell Mitchell, Baltimore, AFC	60	544	9.1	4
1974	Lydell Mitchell, Baltimore, AFC	72	544	7.6	2
	Charles Young, Philadelphia, NFC	63	696	11.0	3
1973	Harold Carmichael, Philadelphia, NFC	67	1,116	16.7	9
	Fred Willis, Houston, AFC	57	371	6.5	1
1972	Harold Jackson, Philadelphia, NFC	62	1,048	16.9	4
	Fred Biletnikoff, Oakland, AFC	58	802	13.8	7
1971	Fred Biletnikoff, Oakland, AFC	61	929	15.2	9
	Bob Tucker, N.Y. Giants, NFC	59	791	13.4	4
1970	Dick Gordon, Chicago, NFC	71	1,026	14.5	13
	Marlin Briscoe, Buffalo, AFC	57	1,036	18.2	8
1969	Dan Abramowicz, New Orleans, NFL	73	1,015	13.9	7
	Lance Alworth, San Diego, AFL	64	1,003	15.7	4
1968	Clifton McNeil, San Francisco, NFL	71	994	14.0	7
	Lance Alworth, San Diego, AFL	68	1,312	19.3	10
1967	George Sauer, N.Y. Jets, AFL	75	1,189	15.9	6
	Charley Taylor, Washington, NFL	70	990	14.1	9
1966	Lance Alworth, San Diego, AFL	73	1,383	18.9	13
	Charley Taylor, Washington, NFL	72	1,119	15.5	12
1965	Lionel Taylor, Denver, AFL	85	1,131	13.3	6
	Dave Parks, San Francisco, NFL	80	1,344	16.8	12
1964	Charley Hennigan, Houston, AFL	101	1,546	15.3	8
	Johnny Morris, Chicago, NFL	93	1,200	12.9	10
1963	Lionel Taylor, Denver, AFL	78	1,101	14.1	10
	Bobby Joe Conrad, St. Louis, NFL	73	967	13.2	10
1962	Lionel Taylor, Denver, AFL	77	908	11.8	4
	Bobby Mitchell, Washington, NFL	72	1,384	19.2	11
1961	Lionel Taylor, Denver, AFL	100	1,176	11.8	4
	Jim (Red) Phillips, Los Angeles, NFL	78	1,092	14.0	5
1960	Lionel Taylor, Denver, AFL	92	1,235	13.4	12
	Raymond Berry, Baltimore, NFL	74	1,298	17.5	10
1959	Raymond Berry, Baltimore	66	959	14.5	14
1958	Raymond Berry, Baltimore	56	794	14.2	9
	Pete Retzlaff, Philadelphia	56	766	13.7	2
1957	Billy Wilson, San Francisco	52	757	14.6	6
1956	Billy Wilson, San Francisco	60	889	14.8	5
1955	Pete Pihos, Philadelphia	62	864	13.9	7
1954	Pete Pihos, Philadelphia	60	872	14.5	10
	Billy Wilson, San Francisco	60	830	13.8	5
1953	Pete Pihos, Philadelphia	63	1,049	16.7	10
1952	Mac Speedie, Cleveland	62	911	14.7	5
1951	Elroy (Crazylegs) Hirsch, Los Angeles	66	1,495	22.7	17
1950	Tom Fears, Los Angeles	84	1,116	13.3	7
1949	Tom Fears, Los Angeles	77	1,013	13.2	9
1948	*Tom Fears, Los Angeles	51	698	13.7	4
1947	Jim Keane, Chi. Bears	64	910	14.2	10
1946	Jim Benton, Los Angeles	63	981	15.6	6
1945	Don Hutson, Green Bay	47	834	17.7	9
1944	Don Hutson, Green Bay	58	866	14.9	9
1943	Don Hutson, Green Bay	47	776	16.5	11
1942	Don Hutson, Green Bay	74	1,211	16.4	17
1941	Don Hutson, Green Bay	58	738	12.7	10
1940	*Don Looney, Philadelphia	58	707	12.2	4
1939	Don Hutson, Green Bay	34	846	24.9	6
1938	Gaynell Tinsley, Chi. Cardinals	41	516	12.6	1
1937	Don Hutson, Green Bay	41	552	13.5	7
1936	Don Hutson, Green Bay	34	536	15.8	8
1935	*Tod Goodwin, N.Y. Giants	26	432	16.6	4
1934	Joe Carter, Philadelphia	16	238	14.9	4
	Morris (Red) Badgro, N.Y. Giants	16	206	12.9	1
1933	John (Shipwreck) Kelly, Brooklyn	22	246	11.2	3
1932	Ray Flaherty, N.Y. Giants	21	350	16.7	3

**First year in the league.*

Annual Interception Leaders

Year	Player, Team	No.	Yards	TD
1990	*Mark Carrier, Chicago, NFC	10	39	0
	Richard Johnson, Houston, AFC	8	100	1
1989	Felix Wright, Cleveland, AFC	9	91	1
	Eric Allen, Philadelphia, NFC	8	38	0
1988	Scott Case, Atlanta, NFC	10	47	0
	Erik McMillan, N.Y. Jets, AFC	8	168	2
1987	Barry Wilburn, Washington, NFC	9	135	1
	Mike Prior, Indianapolis, AFC	6	57	0
	Mark Kelso, Buffalo, AFC	6	25	0
	Keith Bostic, Houston, AFC	6	−14	0
1986	Ronnie Lott, San Francisco, NFC	10	134	1
	Deron Cherry, Kansas City, AFC	9	150	0
1985	Everson Walls, Dallas, NFC	9	31	0
	Albert Lewis, Kansas City, AFC	8	59	0
	Eugene Daniel, Indianapolis, AFC	8	53	0
1984	Ken Easley, Seattle, AFC	10	126	2
	*Tom Flynn, Green Bay, NFC	9	106	0
1983	Mark Murphy, Washington, NFC	9	127	0
	Ken Riley, Cincinnati, AFC	8	89	2
	Vann McElroy, L.A. Raiders, AFC	8	68	0
1982	Everson Walls, Dallas, NFC	7	61	0
	Ken Riley, Cincinnati, AFC	5	88	1
	Bobby Jackson, N.Y. Jets, AFC	5	84	1
	Dwayne Woodruff, Pittsburgh, AFC	5	53	0
	Donnie Shell, Pittsburgh, AFC	5	27	0
1981	*Everson Walls, Dallas, NFC	11	133	0
	John Harris, Seattle, AFC	10	155	2
1980	Lester Hayes, Oakland, AFC	13	273	1
	Nolan Cromwell, Los Angeles, NFC	8	140	1
1979	Mike Reinfeldt, Houston, AFC	12	205	0
	Lemar Parrish, Washington, NFC	9	65	0
1978	Thom Darden, Cleveland, AFC	10	200	0
	Ken Stone, St. Louis, NFC	9	139	0
	Willie Buchanon, Green Bay, NFC	9	93	1
1977	Lyle Blackwood, Baltimore, AFC	10	163	0
	Rolland Lawrence, Atlanta, NFC	7	138	0
1976	Monte Jackson, Los Angeles, NFC	10	173	3
	Ken Riley, Cincinnati, AFC	9	141	1
1975	Mel Blount, Pittsburgh, AFC	11	121	0
	Paul Krause, Minnesota, NFC	10	201	0
1974	Emmitt Thomas, Kansas City, AFC	12	214	2
	Ray Brown, Atlanta, NFC	8	164	1
1973	Dick Anderson, Miami, AFC	8	163	2
	Mike Wagner, Pittsburgh, AFC	8	134	0
	Bobby Bryant, Minnesota, NFC	7	105	1
1972	Bill Bradley, Philadelphia, NFC	9	73	0
	Mike Sensibaugh, Kansas City, AFC	8	65	0
1971	Bill Bradley, Philadelphia, NFC	11	248	0
	Ken Houston, Houston, AFC	9	220	4
1970	Johnny Robinson, Kansas City, AFC	10	155	0
	Dick LeBeau, Detroit, NFC	9	96	0
1969	Mel Renfro, Dallas, NFL	10	118	0
	Emmitt Thomas, Kansas City, AFL	9	146	1
1968	Dave Grayson, Oakland, AFL	10	195	1
	Willie Williams, N.Y. Giants, NFL	10	103	0
1967	Miller Farr, Houston, AFL	10	264	3
	*Lem Barney, Detroit, NFL	10	232	3
	Tom Janik, Buffalo, AFL	10	222	2
	Dave Whitsell, New Orleans, NFL	10	178	2
	Dick Westmoreland, Miami, AFL	10	127	1
1966	Larry Wilson, St. Louis, NFL	10	180	2
	Johnny Robinson, Kansas City, AFL	10	136	1
	Bobby Hunt, Kansas City, AFL	10	113	0
1965	W.K. Hicks, Houston, AFL	9	156	0
	Bobby Boyd, Baltimore, NFL	9	78	1
1964	Dainard Paulson, N.Y. Jets, AFL	12	157	1
	*Paul Krause, Washington, NFL	12	140	1
1963	Fred Glick, Houston, AFL	12	180	1
	Dick Lynch, N.Y. Giants, NFL	9	251	3
	Roosevelt Taylor, Chicago, NFL	9	172	1
1962	Lee Riley, N.Y. Titans, AFL	11	122	0
	Willie Wood, Green Bay, NFL	9	132	0
1961	Billy Atkins, Buffalo, AFL	10	158	0
	Dick Lynch, N.Y. Giants, NFL	9	60	0
1960	*Austin (Goose) Gonsoulin, Denver, AFL	11	98	0
	Dave Baker, San Francisco, NFL	10	96	0
	Jerry Norton, St. Louis, NFL	10	96	0
1959	Dean Derby, Pittsburgh	7	127	0
	Milt Davis, Baltimore	7	119	1
	Don Shinnick, Baltimore	7	70	0
1958	Jim Patton, N.Y. Giants	11	183	0
1957	*Milt Davis, Baltimore	10	219	2
	Jack Christiansen, Detroit	10	137	1
	Jack Butler, Pittsburgh	10	85	0
1956	Lindon Crow, Chi. Cardinals	11	170	0
1955	Will Sherman, Los Angeles	11	101	0
1954	Dick (Night Train) Lane, Chi. Cardinals	10	181	0
1953	Jack Christiansen, Detroit	12	238	1
1952	*Dick (Night Train) Lane, Los Angeles	14	298	2
1951	Otto Schnellbacher, N.Y. Giants	11	194	2
1950	*Orban (Spec) Sanders, N.Y. Yanks	13	199	0
1949	Bob Nussbaumer, Chi. Cardinals	12	157	0
1948	*Dan Sandifer, Washington	13	258	2
1947	Frank Reagan, N.Y. Giants	10	203	0
	Frank Seno, Boston	10	100	0
1946	Bill Dudley, Pittsburgh	10	242	1
1945	Roy Zimmerman, Philadelphia	7	90	0
1944	*Howard Livingston, N.Y. Giants	9	172	1
1943	Sammy Baugh, Washington	11	112	0
1942	Clyde (Bulldog) Turner, Chi. Bears	8	96	1
1941	Marshall Goldberg, Chi. Cardinals	7	54	0
	*Art Jones, Pittsburgh	7	35	0
1940	Clarence (Ace) Parker, Brooklyn	6	146	1
	Kent Ryan, Detroit	6	65	0
	Don Hutson, Green Bay	6	24	0

**First year in the league.*

Annual Punting Leaders

Year	Player, Team	No.	Avg.	Long
1990	Mike Horan, Denver, AFC	58	44.4	67
	Sean Landeta, N.Y. Giants, NFC	75	44.1	67
1989	Rich Camarillo, Phoenix, NFC	76	43.4	58
	Greg Montgomery, Houston, AFC	56	43.3	63
1988	Harry Newsome, Pittsburgh, AFC	65	45.4	62
	Jim Arnold, Detroit, NFC	97	42.4	69
1987	Rick Donnelly, Atlanta, NFC	61	44.0	62
	Ralf Mojsiejenko, San Diego, AFC	67	42.9	57
1986	Rohn Stark, Indianapolis, AFC	76	45.2	63
	Sean Landeta, N.Y. Giants, NFC	79	44.8	61
1985	Rohn Stark, Indianapolis, AFC	78	45.9	68
	*Rick Donnelly, Atlanta, NFC	59	43.6	68
1984	Jim Arnold, Kansas City, AFC	98	44.9	63
	*Brian Hansen, New Orleans, NFC	69	43.8	66
1983	Rohn Stark, Baltimore, AFC	91	45.3	68
	*Frank Garcia, Tampa Bay, NFC	95	42.2	64
1982	Luke Prestridge, Denver, AFC	45	45.0	65
	Carl Birdsong, St. Louis, NFC	54	43.8	65
1981	Pat McInally, Cincinnati, AFC	72	45.4	62
	Tom Skladany, Detroit, NFC	64	43.5	74
1980	Dave Jennings, N.Y. Giants, NFC	94	44.8	63
	Luke Prestridge, Denver, AFC	70	43.9	57
1979	*Bob Grupp, Kansas City, AFC	89	43.6	74
	Dave Jennings, N.Y. Giants, NFC	104	42.7	72
1978	Pat McInally, Cincinnati, AFC	91	43.1	65
	*Tom Skladany, Detroit, NFC	86	42.5	63
1977	Ray Guy, Oakland, AFC	59	43.3	74
	Tom Blanchard, New Orleans, NFC	82	42.4	66
1976	Marv Bateman, Buffalo, AFC	86	42.8	78
	John James, Atlanta, NFC	101	42.1	67
1975	Ray Guy, Oakland, AFC	68	43.8	64
	Herman Weaver, Detroit, NFC	80	42.0	61
1974	Ray Guy, Oakland, AFC	74	42.2	66
	Tom Blanchard, New Orleans, NFC	88	42.1	71
1973	Jerrel Wilson, Kansas City, AFC	80	45.5	68
	*Tom Wittum, San Francisco, NFC	79	43.7	62
1972	Jerrel Wilson, Kansas City, AFC	66	44.8	69
	Dave Chapple, Los Angeles, NFC	53	44.2	70
1971	Dave Lewis, Cincinnati, AFC	72	44.8	56
	Tom McNeill, Philadelphia, NFC	73	42.0	64
1970	*Dave Lewis, Cincinnati, AFC	79	46.2	63
	*Julian Fagan, New Orleans, NFC	77	42.5	64
1969	David Lee, Baltimore, NFL	57	45.3	66
	Dennis Partee, San Diego, AFL	71	44.6	62
1968	Jerrel Wilson, Kansas City, AFL	63	45.1	70
	Billy Lothridge, Atlanta, NFL	75	44.3	70
1967	Bob Scarpitto, Denver, AFL	105	44.9	73
	Billy Lothridge, Atlanta, NFL	87	43.7	62
1966	Bob Scarpitto, Denver, AFL	76	45.8	70
	*David Lee, Baltimore, NFL	49	45.6	64
1965	Gary Collins, Cleveland, NFL	65	46.7	71
	Jerrel Wilson, Kansas City, AFL	69	45.4	64
1964	*Bobby Walden, Minnesota, NFL	72	46.4	73
	Jim Fraser, Denver, AFL	73	44.2	67
1963	Yale Lary, Detroit, NFL	35	48.9	73
	Jim Fraser, Denver, AFL	81	44.4	66
1962	Tommy Davis, San Francisco, NFL	48	45.6	82
	Jim Fraser, Denver, AFL	55	43.6	75
1961	Yale Lary, Detroit, NFL	52	48.4	71
	Billy Atkins, Buffalo, AFL	85	44.5	70
1960	Jerry Norton, St. Louis, NFL	39	45.6	62
	*Paul Maguire, L.A. Chargers, AFL	43	40.5	61
1959	Yale Lary, Detroit	45	47.1	67
1958	Sam Baker, Washington	48	45.4	64
1957	Don Chandler, N.Y. Giants	60	44.6	61
1956	Norm Van Brocklin, Los Angeles	48	43.1	72
1955	Norm Van Brocklin, Los Angeles	60	44.6	61
1954	Pat Brady, Pittsburgh	66	43.2	72
1953	Pat Brady, Pittsburgh	80	46.9	64
1952	Horace Gillom, Cleveland	61	45.7	73
1951	Horace Gillom, Cleveland	73	45.5	66
1950	*Fred (Curly) Morrison, Chi. Bears	57	43.3	65
1949	*Mike Boyda, N.Y. Bulldogs	56	44.2	61
1948	Joe Muha, Philadelphia	57	47.3	82
1947	Jack Jacobs, Green Bay	57	43.5	74
1946	Roy McKay, Green Bay	64	42.7	64
1945	Roy McKay, Green Bay	44	41.2	73
1944	Frank Sinkwich, Detroit	45	41.0	73
1943	Sammy Baugh, Washington	50	45.9	81
1942	Sammy Baugh, Washington	37	48.2	74
1941	Sammy Baugh, Washington	30	48.7	75
1940	Sammy Baugh, Washington	35	51.4	85
1939	*Parker Hall, Cleveland	58	40.8	80

**First year in the league.*

Annual Punt Return Leaders

Year	Player, Team	No.	Yards	Avg.	Long	TD
1990	Clarence Verdin, Indianapolis, AFC	31	396	12.8	36	0
	*Johnny Bailey, Chicago, NFC	36	399	11.1	95	1
1989	Walter Stanley, Detroit, NFC	36	496	13.8	74	0
	Clarence Verdin, Indianapolis, AFC	23	296	12.9	49	1
1988	John Taylor, San Francisco, NFC	44	556	12.6	95	2
	JoJo Townsell, N.Y. Jets, AFC	35	409	11.7	59	1
1987	Mel Gray, New Orleans, NFC	24	352	14.7	80	0
	Bobby Joe Edmonds, Seattle, AFC	20	251	12.6	40	0
1986	*Bobby Joe Edmonds, Seattle, AFC	34	419	12.3	75	1
	*Vai Sikahema, St. Louis, NFC	43	522	12.1	71	2
1985	Irving Fryar, New England, AFC	37	520	14.1	85	2
	Henry Ellard, L.A. Rams, NFC	37	501	13.5	80	1
1984	Mike Martin, Cincinnati, AFC	24	376	15.7	55	0
	Henry Ellard, L.A. Rams, NFC	30	403	13.4	83	2
1983	*Henry Ellard, L.A. Rams, NFC	16	217	13.6	72	1
	Kirk Springs, N.Y. Jets, AFC	23	287	12.5	76	1
1982	Rick Upchurch, Denver, AFC	15	242	16.1	78	2
	Billy Johnson, Atlanta, NFC	24	273	11.4	71	0
1981	LeRoy Irvin, Los Angeles, NFC	46	615	13.4	84	3
	*James Brooks, San Diego, AFC	22	290	13.2	42	0
1980	J. T. Smith, Kansas City, AFC	40	581	14.5	75	2
	*Kenny Johnson, Atlanta, NFC	23	281	12.2	56	0
1979	John Sciarra, Philadelphia, NFC	16	182	11.4	38	0
	*Tony Nathan, Miami, AFC	28	306	10.9	86	1
1978	Rick Upchurch, Denver, AFC	36	493	13.7	75	1
	Jackie Wallace, Los Angeles, NFC	52	618	11.9	58	0
1977	Billy Johnson, Houston, AFC	35	539	15.4	87	2
	Larry Marshall, Philadelphia, NFC	46	489	10.6	48	0
1976	Rick Upchurch, Denver, AFC	39	536	13.7	92	4
	Eddie Brown, Washington, NFC	48	646	13.5	71	1
1975	Billy Johnson, Houston, AFC	40	612	15.3	83	3
	Terry Metcalf, St. Louis, NFC	23	285	12.4	69	1
1974	Lemar Parrish, Cincinnati, AFC	18	338	18.8	90	2
	Dick Jauron, Detroit, NFC	17	286	16.8	58	0
1973	Bruce Taylor, San Francisco, NFC	15	207	13.8	61	0
	Ron Smith, San Diego, AFC	27	352	13.0	84	2
1972	*Ken Ellis, Green Bay, NFC	14	215	15.4	80	1
	Chris Farasopoulos, N.Y. Jets, AFC	17	179	10.5	65	1
1971	Les (Speedy) Duncan, Washington, NFC	22	233	10.6	33	0
	Leroy Kelly, Cleveland, AFC	30	292	9.7	74	0
1970	Ed Podolak, Kansas City, AFC	23	311	13.5	60	0
	*Bruce Taylor, San Francisco, NFC	43	516	12.0	76	0
1969	Alvin Haymond, Los Angeles, NFL	33	435	13.2	52	0
	*Bill Thompson, Denver, AFL	25	288	11.5	40	0
1968	Bob Hayes, Dallas, NFL	15	312	20.8	90	2
	Noland Smith, Kansas City, AFL	18	270	15.0	80	1
1967	Floyd Little, Denver, AFL	16	270	16.9	72	1
	Ben Davis, Cleveland, NFL	18	229	12.7	52	1
1966	Les (Speedy) Duncan, San Diego, AFL	18	238	13.2	81	1
	Johnny Roland, St. Louis, NFL	20	221	11.1	86	1
1965	Leroy Kelly, Cleveland, NFL	17	265	15.6	67	2
	Les (Speedy) Duncan, San Diego, AFL	30	464	15.5	66	2
1964	Bobby Jancik, Houston, AFL	12	220	18.3	82	1
	Tommy Watkins, Detroit, NFL	16	238	14.9	68	2
1963	Dick James, Washington, NFL	16	214	13.4	39	0
	Claude (Hoot) Gibson, Oakland, AFL	26	307	11.8	85	2
1962	Dick Christy, N.Y. Titans, AFL	15	250	16.7	73	2
	Pat Studstill, Detroit, NFL	29	457	15.8	44	0
1961	Dick Christy, N.Y. Titans, AFL	18	383	21.3	70	2
	Willie Wood, Green Bay, NFL	14	225	16.1	72	2
1960	*Abner Haynes, Dall. Texans, AFL	14	215	15.4	46	0
	Abe Woodson, San Francisco, NFL	13	174	13.4	48	0
1959	Johnny Morris, Chi. Bears	14	171	12.2	78	1
1958	Jon Arnett, Los Angeles	18	223	12.4	58	0
1957	Bert Zagers, Washington	14	217	15.5	76	2
1956	Ken Konz, Cleveland	13	187	14.4	65	1
1955	Ollie Matson, Chi. Cardinals	13	245	18.8	78	2
1954	*Veryl Switzer, Green Bay	24	306	12.8	93	1
1953	Charley Trippi, Chi. Cardinals	21	239	11.4	38	0
1952	Jack Christiansen, Detroit	15	322	21.5	79	2
1951	Claude (Buddy) Young, N.Y. Yanks	12	231	19.3	79	1
1950	*Herb Rich, Baltimore	12	276	23.0	86	1
1949	Verda (Vitamin T) Smith, Los Angeles	27	427	15.8	85	1
1948	George McAfee, Chi. Bears	30	417	13.9	60	1
1947	*Walt Slater, Pittsburgh	28	435	15.5	33	0
1946	Bill Dudley, Pittsburgh	27	385	14.3	52	0
1945	*Dave Ryan, Detroit	15	220	14.7	56	0
1944	*Steve Van Buren, Philadelphia	15	230	15.3	55	1
1943	Andy Farkas, Washington	15	168	11.2	33	0
1942	Merlyn Condit, Brooklyn	21	210	10.0	23	0
1941	Byron (Whizzer) White, Detroit	19	262	13.8	64	0

**First year in the league.*

Annual Kickoff Return Leaders

Year	Player, Team	No.	Yards	Avg.	Long	TD
1990	Kevin Clark, Denver, AFC	20	505	25.3	75	0
	David Meggett, N.Y. Giants, NFC	21	492	23.4	58	0
1989	Rod Woodson, Pittsburgh, AFC	36	982	27.3	84	1
	Mel Gray, Detroit, NFC	24	640	26.7	57	0
1988	*Tim Brown, L.A. Raiders, AFC	41	1,098	26.8	97	1
	Donnie Elder, Tampa Bay, NFC	34	772	22.7	51	0
1987	Sylvester Stamps, Atlanta, NFC	24	660	27.5	97	1
	Paul Palmer, Kansas City, AFC	38	923	24.3	95	2
1986	Dennis Gentry, Chicago, NFC	20	576	28.8	91	1
	*Lupe Sanchez, Pittsburgh, AFC	25	591	23.6	64	0
1985	Ron Brown, L.A. Rams, NFC	28	918	32.8	98	3
	Glen Young, Cleveland, AFC	35	898	25.7	63	0
1984	*Bobby Humphery, N.Y. Jets, AFC	22	675	30.7	97	1
	Barry Redden, L.A. Rams, NFC	23	530	23.0	40	0
1983	Fulton Walker, Miami, AFC	36	962	26.7	78	0
	Darrin Nelson, Minnesota, NFC	18	445	24.7	50	0
1982	*Mike Mosley, Buffalo, AFC	18	487	27.1	66	0
	Alvin Hall, Detroit, NFC	16	426	26.6	96	1
1981	Mike Nelms, Washington, NFC	37	1,099	29.7	84	0
	Carl Roaches, Houston, AFC	28	769	27.5	96	1
1980	Horace Ivory, New England, AFC	36	992	27.6	98	1
	Rich Mauti, New Orleans, NFC	31	798	25.7	52	0
1979	Larry Brunson, Oakland, AFC	17	441	25.9	89	0
	*Jimmy Edwards, Minnesota, NFC	44	1,103	25.1	83	0
1978	Steve Odom, Green Bay, NFC	25	677	27.1	95	1
	*Keith Wright, Cleveland, AFC	30	789	26.3	86	0
1977	*Raymond Clayborn, New England, AFC	28	869	31.0	101	3
	*Wilbert Montgomery, Philadelphia, NFC	23	619	26.9	99	1
1976	*Duriel Harris, Miami, AFC	17	559	32.9	69	0
	Cullen Bryant, Los Angeles, NFC	16	459	28.7	90	1

1975	*Walter Payton, Chicago, NFC	14	444	31.7	70	0
	Harold Hart, Oakland, AFC	17	518	30.5	102	1
1974	Terry Metcalf, St. Louis, NFC	20	623	31.2	94	1
	Greg Pruitt, Cleveland, AFC	22	606	27.5	88	1
1973	Carl Garrett, Chicago, NFC	16	486	30.4	67	0
	*Wallace Francis, Buffalo, AFC	23	687	29.9	101	2
1972	Ron Smith, Chicago, NFC	30	924	30.8	94	1
	*Bruce Laird, Baltimore, AFC	29	843	29.1	73	0
1971	Travis Williams, Los Angeles, NFC	25	743	29.7	105	1
	Eugene (Mercury) Morris, Miami, AFC	15	423	28.2	94	1
1970	Jim Duncan, Baltimore, AFC	20	707	35.4	99	1
	Cecil Turner, Chicago, NFC	23	752	32.7	96	4
1969	Bobby Williams, Detroit, NFL	17	563	33.1	96	1
	*Bill Thompson, Denver, AFL	18	513	28.5	63	0
1968	Preston Pearson, Baltimore, NFL	15	527	35.1	102	2
	*George Atkinson, Oakland, AFL	32	802	25.1	60	0
1967	*Travis Williams, Green Bay, NFL	18	739	41.1	104	4
	*Zeke Moore, Houston, AFL	14	405	28.9	92	1
1966	Gale Sayers, Chicago, NFL	23	718	31.2	93	2
	*Goldie Sellers, Denver, AFL	19	541	28.5	100	2
1965	Tommy Watkins, Detroit, NFL	17	584	34.4	94	0
	Abner Haynes, Denver, AFL	34	901	26.5	60	0
1964	*Clarence Childs, N.Y. Giants, NFL	34	987	29.0	100	1
	Bo Roberson, Oakland, AFL	36	975	27.1	59	0
1963	Abe Woodson, San Francisco, NFL	29	935	32.2	103	3
	Bobby Jancik, Houston, AFL	45	1,317	29.3	53	0
1962	Abe Woodson, San Francisco, NFL	37	1,157	31.3	79	0
	*Bobby Jancik, Houston, AFL	24	826	30.3	61	0
1961	Dick Bass, Los Angeles, NFL	23	698	30.3	64	0
	*Dave Grayson, Dall. Texans, AFL	16	453	28.3	73	0
1960	*Tom Moore, Green Bay, NFL	12	397	33.1	84	0
	Ken Hall, Houston, AFL	19	594	31.3	104	1
1959	Abe Woodson, San Francisco	13	382	29.4	105	1
1958	Ollie Matson, Chi. Cardinals	14	497	35.5	101	2
1957	*Jon Arnett, Los Angeles	18	504	28.0	98	1
1956	*Tom Wilson, Los Angeles	15	477	31.8	103	1
1955	Al Carmichael, Green Bay	14	418	29.9	100	1
1954	Billy Reynolds, Cleveland	14	413	29.5	51	0
1953	Joe Arenas, San Francisco	16	551	34.4	82	0
1952	Lynn Chandnois, Pittsburgh	17	599	35.2	93	2
1951	Lynn Chandnois, Pittsburgh	12	390	32.5	55	0
1950	Verda (Vitamin T) Smith, Los Angeles	22	742	33.7	97	3
1949	*Don Doll, Detroit	21	536	25.5	56	0
1948	*Joe Scott, N.Y. Giants	20	569	28.5	99	1
1947	Eddie Saenz, Washington	29	797	27.5	94	2
1946	Abe Karnofsky, Boston	21	599	28.5	97	1
1945	Steve Van Buren, Philadelphia	13	373	28.7	98	1
1944	Bob Thurbon, Card.-Pitt.	12	291	24.3	55	0
1943	Ken Heineman, Brooklyn	16	444	27.8	69	0
1942	Marshall Goldberg, Chi. Cardinals	15	393	26.2	95	1
1941	Marshall Goldberg, Chi. Cardinals	12	290	24.2	41	0

First year in the league.

Points Scored

Year	Team	Points
1990	Buffalo, AFC	428
	Philadelphia, NFC	396
1989	San Francisco, NFC	442
	Buffalo, AFC	409
1988	Cincinnati, AFC	448
	L.A. Rams, NFC	407
1987	San Francisco, NFC	459
	Cleveland, AFC	390
1986	Miami, AFC	430
	Minnesota, NFC	398
1985	San Diego, AFC	467
	Chicago, NFC	456
1984	Miami, AFC	513
	San Francisco, NFC	475
1983	Washington, NFC	541
	L.A. Raiders, AFC	442
1982	San Diego, AFC	288
	Dallas, NFC	226
	Green Bay, NFC	226
1981	San Diego, AFC	478
	Atlanta, NFC	426
1980	Dallas, NFC	454
	New England, AFC	441
1979	Pittsburgh, AFC	416
	Dallas, NFC	371
1978	Dallas, NFC	384
	Miami, AFC	372
1977	Oakland, AFC	351
	Dallas, NFC	345
1976	Baltimore, AFC	417
	Los Angeles, NFC	351
1975	Buffalo, AFC	420
	Minnesota, NFC	377
1974	Oakland, AFC	355
	Washington, NFC	320
1973	Los Angeles, NFC	388
	Denver, AFC	354
1972	Miami, AFC	385
	San Francisco, NFC	353
1971	Dallas, NFC	406
	Oakland, AFC	344
1970	San Francisco, NFC	352
	Baltimore, AFC	321
1969	Minnesota, NFL	379
	Oakland, AFL	377
1968	Oakland, AFL	453
	Dallas, NFL	431
1967	Oakland, AFL	468
	Los Angeles, NFL	398
1966	Kansas City, AFL	448
	Dallas, NFL	445
1965	San Francisco, NFL	421
	San Diego, AFL	340
1964	Baltimore, NFL	428
	Buffalo, AFL	400
1963	N.Y. Giants, NFL	448
	San Diego, AFL	399
1962	Green Bay, NFL	415
	Dall. Texans, AFL	389
1961	Houston, AFL	513
	Green Bay, NFL	391
1960	N.Y. Titans, AFL	382
	Cleveland, NFL	362
1959	Baltimore	374
1958	Baltimore	381
1957	Los Angeles	307
1956	Chi. Bears	363
1955	Cleveland	349
1954	Detroit	337
1953	San Francisco	372
1952	Los Angeles	349
1951	Los Angeles	392
1950	Los Angeles	466
1949	Philadelphia	364
1948	Chi. Cardinals	395
1947	Chi. Bears	363
1946	Chi. Bears	289
1945	Philadelphia	272
1944	Philadelphia	267
1943	Chi. Bears	303
1942	Chi. Bears	376
1941	Chi. Bears	396
1940	Washington	245
1939	Chi. Bears	298
1938	Green Bay	223
1937	Green Bay	220
1936	Green Bay	248
1935	Chi. Bears	192
1934	Chi. Bears	286
1933	N.Y. Giants	244
1932	Green Bay	152

Total Yards Gained

Year	Team	Yards
1990	Houston, AFC	6,222
	San Francisco, NFC	5,895
1989	San Francisco, NFC	6,268
	Cincinnati, AFC	6,101
1988	Cincinnati, AFC	6,057
	San Francisco, NFC	5,900
1987	San Francisco, NFC	5,987
	Denver, AFC	5,624
1986	Cincinnati, AFC	6,490
	San Francisco, NFC	6,082
1985	San Diego, AFC	6,535
	San Francisco, NFC	5,920
1984	Miami, AFC	6,936
	San Francisco, NFC	6,366
1983	San Diego, AFC	6,197
	Green Bay, NFC	6,172
1982	San Diego, AFC	4,048
	San Francisco, NFC	3,242
1981	San Diego, AFC	6,744
	Detroit, NFC	5,933
1980	San Diego, AFC	6,410
	Los Angeles, NFC	6,006
1979	Pittsburgh, AFC	6,258
	Dallas, NFC	5,968
1978	New England, AFC	5,965
	Dallas, NFC	5,959
1977	Dallas, NFC	4,812
	Oakland, AFC	4,736
1976	Baltimore, AFC	5,236
	St. Louis, NFC	5,136
1975	Buffalo, AFC	5,467
	Dallas, NFC	5,025
1974	Dallas, NFC	4,983
	Oakland, AFC	4,718
1973	Los Angeles, NFC	4,906
	Oakland, AFC	4,773
1972	Miami, AFC	5,036
	N.Y. Giants, NFC	4,483
1971	Dallas, NFC	5,035
	San Diego, AFC	4,738
1970	Oakland, AFC	4,829
	San Francisco, NFC	4,503
1969	Dallas, NFL	5,122
	Oakland, AFL	5,036
1968	Oakland, AFL	5,696
	Dallas, NFL	5,117
1967	N.Y. Jets, AFL	5,152
	Baltimore, NFL	5,008
1966	Dallas, NFL	5,145
	Kansas City, AFL	5,114
1965	San Francisco, NFL	5,270
	San Diego, AFL	5,188
1964	Buffalo, AFL	5,206
	Baltimore, NFL	4,779
1963	San Diego, AFL	5,153
	N.Y. Giants, NFL	5,024
1962	N.Y. Giants, NFL	5,005
	Houston, AFL	4,971
1961	Houston, AFL	6,288
	Philadelphia, NFL	5,112
1960	Houston, AFL	4,936
	Baltimore, NFL	4,245
1959	Baltimore	4,458
1958	Baltimore	4,539
1957	Los Angeles	4,143
1956	Chi. Bears	4,537
1955	Chi. Bears	4,316
1954	Los Angeles	5,187
1953	Philadelphia	4,811
1952	Cleveland	4,352
1951	Los Angeles	5,506
1950	Los Angeles	5,420
1949	Chi. Bears	4,873
1948	Chi. Cardinals	4,705
1947	Chi. Bears	5,053
1946	Los Angeles	3,793
1945	Washington	3,549
1944	Chi. Bears	3,239
1943	Chi. Bears	4,045
1942	Chi. Bears	3,900
1941	Chi. Bears	4,265
1940	Green Bay	3,400
1939	Chi. Bears	3,988
1938	Green Bay	3,037
1937	Green Bay	3,201
1936	Detroit	3,703
1935	Chi. Bears	3,454
1934	Chi. Bears	3,900
1933	N.Y. Giants	2,973
1932	Chi. Bears	2,755

Yards Rushing

Year	Team	Yards
1990	Philadelphia, NFC	2,556
	San Diego, AFC	2,257
1989	Cincinnati, AFC	2,483
	Chicago, NFC	2,287
1988	Cincinnati, AFC	2,710
	San Francisco, NFC	2,523
1987	San Francisco, NFC	2,237
	L.A. Raiders, AFC	2,197
1986	Chicago, NFC	2,700
	Cincinnati, AFC	2,533
1985	Chicago, NFC	2,761
	Indianapolis, AFC	2,439
1984	Chicago, NFC	2,974
	N.Y. Jets, AFC	2,189
1983	Chicago, NFC	2,727
	Baltimore, AFC	2,695
1982	Buffalo, AFC	1,371
	Dallas, NFC	1,313
1981	Detroit, NFC	2,795
	Kansas City, AFC	2,633
1980	Los Angeles, NFC	2,799
	Houston, AFC	2,635
1979	N.Y. Jets, AFC	2,646
	St. Louis, NFC	2,582
1978	New England, AFC	3,165
	Dallas, NFC	2,783
1977	Chicago, NFC	2,811
	Oakland, AFC	2,627
1976	Pittsburgh, AFC	2,971
	Los Angeles, NFC	2,528
1975	Buffalo, AFC	2,974
	Dallas, NFC	2,432
1974	Dallas, NFC	2,454
	Pittsburgh, AFC	2,417
1973	Buffalo, AFC	3,088
	Los Angeles, NFC	2,925
1972	Miami, AFC	2,960
	Chicago, NFC	2,360
1971	Miami, AFC	2,429
	Detroit, NFC	2,376
1970	Dallas, NFC	2,300
	Miami, AFC	2,082
1969	Dallas, NFL	2,276
	Kansas City, AFL	2,220
1968	Chicago, NFL	2,377
	Kansas City, AFL	2,227
1967	Cleveland, NFL	2,139
	Houston, AFL	2,122
1966	Kansas City, AFL	2,274
	Cleveland, NFL	2,166
1965	Cleveland, NFL	2,331
	San Diego, AFL	2,085
1964	Green Bay, NFL	2,276
	Buffalo, AFL	2,040
1963	Cleveland, NFL	2,639
	San Diego, AFL	2,203
1962	Buffalo, AFL	2,480
	Green Bay, NFL	2,460
1961	Green Bay, NFL	2,350
	Dall. Texans, AFL	2,189
1960	St. Louis, NFL	2,356
	Oakland, AFL	2,056
1959	Cleveland	2,149
1958	Cleveland	2,526
1957	Los Angeles	2,142
1956	Chi. Bears	2,468
1955	Chi. Bears	2,388
1954	San Francisco	2,498
1953	San Francisco	2,230
1952	San Francisco	1,905
1951	Chi. Bears	2,408
1950	N.Y. Giants	2,336
1949	Philadelphia	2,607
1948	Chi. Cardinals	2,560
1947	Los Angeles	2,171
1946	Green Bay	1,765
1945	Cleveland	1,714
1944	Philadelphia	1,661
1943	Phil-Pitt	1,730
1942	Chi. Bears	1,881
1941	Chi. Bears	2,263
1940	Chi. Bears	1,818
1939	Chi. Bears	2,043
1938	Detroit	1,893
1937	Detroit	2,074
1936	Detroit	2,885
1935	Chi. Bears	2,096
1934	Chi. Bears	2,847
1933	Boston	2,260
1932	Chi. Bears	1,770

Yards Passing

Leadership in this category has been based on net yards since 1952.

Year	Team	Yards
1990	Houston, AFC	4,805
	San Francisco, NFC	4,177
1989	Washington, NFC	4,349
	Miami, AFC	4,216
1988	Miami, AFC	4,516
	Washington, NFC	4,136
1987	Miami, AFC	3,876
	San Francisco, NFC	3,750
1986	Miami, AFC	4,779
	San Francisco, NFC	4,096
1985	San Diego, AFC	4,870
	Dallas, NFC	3,861
1984	Miami, AFC	5,018
	St. Louis, NFC	4,257
1983	San Diego, AFC	4,661
	Green Bay, NFC	4,365
1982	San Diego, AFC	2,927
	San Francisco, NFC	2,502
1981	San Diego, AFC	4,739
	Minnesota, NFC	4,333
1980	San Diego, AFC	4,531
	Minnesota, NFC	3,688

Year	Team	Yards
1979	San Diego, AFC	3,915
	San Francisco, NFC	3,641
1978	San Diego, AFC	3,375
	Minnesota, NFC	3,243
1977	Buffalo, AFC	2,530
	St. Louis, NFC	2,499
1976	Baltimore, AFC	2,933
	Minnesota, NFC	2,855
1975	Cincinnati, AFC	3,241
	Washington, NFC	2,917
1974	Washington, NFC	2,978
	Cincinnati, AFC	2,804
1973	Philadelphia, NFC	2,998
	Denver, AFC	2,519
1972	N.Y. Jets, AFC	2,777
	San Francisco, NFC	2,735
1971	San Diego, AFC	3,134
	Dallas, NFC	2,786
1970	San Francisco, NFC	2,923
	Oakland, AFC	2,865
1969	Oakland, AFL	3,271
	San Francisco, NFL	3,158
1968	San Diego, AFL	3,623
	Dallas, NFL	3,026
1967	N.Y. Jets, AFL	3,845
	Washington, NFL	3,730
1966	N.Y. Jets, AFL	3,464
	Dallas, NFL	3,023
1965	San Francisco, NFL	3,487
	San Diego, AFL	3,103
1964	Houston, AFL	3,527
	Chicago, NFL	2,841
1963	Baltimore, NFL	3,296
	Houston, AFL	3,222
1962	Denver, AFL	3,404
	Philadelphia, NFL	3,385
1961	Houston, AFL	4,392
	Philadelphia, NFL	3,605
1960	Houston, AFL	3,203
	Baltimore, NFL	2,956
1959	Baltimore	2,753
1958	Pittsburgh	2,752
1957	Baltimore	2,388
1956	Los Angeles	2,419
1955	Philadelphia	2,472
1954	Chi. Bears	3,104
1953	Philadelphia	3,089
1952	Cleveland	2,566
1951	Los Angeles	3,296
1950	Los Angeles	3,709
1949	Chi. Bears	3,055
1948	Washington	2,861
1947	Washington	3,336
1946	Los Angeles	2,080
1945	Chi. Bears	1,857
1944	Washington	2,021
1943	Chi. Bears	2,310
1942	Green Bay	2,407
1941	Chi. Bears	2,002
1940	Washington	1,887
1939	Chi. Bears	1,965
1938	Washington	1,536
1937	Green Bay	1,398
1936	Green Bay	1,629
1935	Green Bay	1,449
1934	Green Bay	1,165
1933	N.Y. Giants	1,348
1932	Chi. Bears	1,013

Fewest Points Allowed

Year	Team	Points
1990	N.Y. Giants, NFC	211
	Pittsburgh, AFC	240
1989	Denver, AFC	226
	N.Y. Giants, NFC	252
1988	Chicago, NFC	215
	Buffalo, AFC	237
1987	Indianapolis, AFC	238
	San Francisco, NFC	253
1986	Chicago, NFC	187
	Seattle, AFC	293
1985	Chicago, NFC	198
	N.Y. Jets, AFC	264
1984	San Francisco, NFC	227
	Denver, AFC	241
1983	Miami, AFC	250
	Detroit, NFC	286
1982	Washington, NFC	128
	Miami, AFC	131
1981	Philadelphia, NFC	221
	Miami, AFC	275
1980	Philadelphia, NFC	222
	Houston, AFC	251
1979	Tampa Bay, NFC	237
	San Diego, AFC	246
1978	Pittsburgh, AFC	195
	Dallas, NFC	208
1977	Atlanta, NFC	129
	Denver, AFC	148
1976	Pittsburgh, AFC	138
	Minnesota, NFC	176
1975	Los Angeles, NFC	135
	Pittsburgh, AFC	162
1974	Los Angeles, NFC	181
	Pittsburgh, AFC	189
1973	Miami, AFC	150
	Minnesota, NFC	168
1972	Miami, AFC	171
	Washington, NFC	218
1971	Minnesota, NFC	139
	Baltimore, AFC	140
1970	Minnesota, NFC	143
	Miami, AFC	228
1969	Minnesota, NFL	133
	Kansas City, AFL	177
1968	Baltimore, NFL	144
	Kansas City, AFL	170
1967	Los Angeles, NFL	196
	Houston, AFL	199
1966	Green Bay, NFL	163
	Buffalo, AFL	255
1965	Green Bay, NFL	224
	Buffalo, AFL	226
1964	Baltimore, NFL	225
	Buffalo, AFL	242
1963	Chicago, NFL	144
	San Diego, AFL	255
1962	Green Bay, NFL	148
	Dall. Texans, AFL	233
1961	San Diego, AFL	219
	N.Y. Giants, NFL	220
1960	San Francisco, NFL	205
	Dall. Texans, AFL	253
1959	N.Y. Giants	170
1958	N.Y. Giants	183
1957	Cleveland	172
1956	Cleveland	177
1955	Cleveland	218
1954	Cleveland	162
1953	Cleveland	162
1952	Detroit	192
1951	Cleveland	152
1950	Philadelphia	141
1949	Philadelphia	134
1948	Chi. Bears	151
1947	Green Bay	210
1946	Pittsburgh	117
1945	Washington	121
1944	N.Y. Giants	75
1943	Washington	137
1942	Chi. Bears	84
1941	N.Y. Giants	114
1940	Brooklyn	120
1939	N.Y. Giants	85
1938	N.Y. Giants	79
1937	Chi. Bears	100
1936	Chi. Bears	94
1935	Green Bay	96
	N.Y. Giants	96
1934	Detroit	59
1933	Brooklyn	54
1932	Chi. Bears	44

Fewest Total Yards Allowed

Year	Team	Yards
1990	Pittsburgh, AFC	4,115
	N.Y. Giants, NFC	4,206
1989	Minnesota, NFC	4,184
	Kansas City, AFC	4,293
1988	Minnesota, NFC	4,091
	Buffalo, AFC	4,578
1987	San Francisco, NFC	4,095
	Cleveland, AFC	4,264
1986	Chicago, NFC	4,130
	L.A. Raiders, AFC	4,804
1985	Chicago, NFC	4,135
	L.A. Raiders, AFC	4,603
1984	Chicago, NFC	3,863
	Cleveland, AFC	4,641
1983	Cincinnati, AFC	4,327
	New Orleans, NFC	4,691
1982	Miami, AFC	2,312
	Tampa Bay, NFC	2,442
1981	Philadelphia, NFC	4,447
	N.Y. Jets, AFC	4,871
1980	Buffalo, AFC	4,101
	Philadelphia, NFC	4,443
1979	Tampa Bay, NFC	3,949
	Pittsburgh, AFC	4,270
1978	Los Angeles, NFC	3,893
	Pittsburgh, AFC	4,168
1977	Dallas, NFC	3,213
	New England, AFC	3,638
1976	Pittsburgh, AFC	3,323
	San Francisco, NFC	3,562
1975	Minnesota, NFC	3,153
	Oakland, AFC	3,629
1974	Pittsburgh, AFC	3,074
	Washington, NFC	3,285
1973	Los Angeles, NFC	2,951
	Oakland, AFC	3,160
1972	Miami, AFC	3,297
	Green Bay, NFC	3,474
1971	Baltimore, AFC	2,852
	Minnesota, NFC	3,406
1970	Minnesota, NFC	2,803
	N.Y. Jets, AFC	3,655
1969	Minnesota, NFL	2,720
	Kansas City, AFL	3,163
1968	Los Angeles, NFL	3,118
	N.Y. Jets, AFL	3,363
1967	Oakland, AFL	3,294
	Green Bay, NFL	3,300
1966	St. Louis, NFL	3,492
	Oakland, AFL	3,910
1965	San Diego, AFL	3,262
	Detroit, NFL	3,557
1964	Green Bay, NFL	3,179
	Buffalo, AFL	3,878
1963	Chicago, NFL	3,176
	Boston, AFL	3,834
1962	Detroit, NFL	3,217
	Dall. Texans, AFL	3,951
1961	San Diego, AFL	3,726
	Baltimore, NFL	3,782
1960	St. Louis, NFL	3,029
	Buffalo, AFL	3,866
1959	N.Y. Giants	2,843
1958	Chi. Bears	3,066
1957	Pittsburgh	2,791
1956	N.Y. Giants	3,081
1955	Cleveland	2,841
1954	Cleveland	2,658
1953	Philadelphia	2,998
1952	Cleveland	3,075
1951	N.Y. Giants	3,250
1950	Cleveland	3,154
1949	Philadelphia	2,831
1948	Chi. Bears	2,931
1947	Green Bay	3,396
1946	Washington	2,451
1945	Philadelphia	2,073
1944	Philadelphia	1,943
1943	Chi. Bears	2,262
1942	Chi. Bears	1,703
1941	N.Y. Giants	2,368
1940	N.Y. Giants	2,219
1939	Washington	2,116
1938	N.Y. Giants	2,029
1937	Washington	2,123
1936	Boston	2,181
1935	Boston	1,996
1934	Chi. Cardinals	1,539
1933	Brooklyn	1,789

Fewest Yards Rushing Allowed

Year	Team	Yards
1990	Philadelphia, NFC	1,169
	San Diego, AFC	1,515
1989	New Orleans, NFC	1,326
	Denver, AFC	1,580
1988	Chicago, NFC	1,326
	Houston, AFC	1,592
1987	Chicago, NFC	1,413
	Cleveland, AFC	1,433
1986	N.Y. Giants, NFC	1,284
	Denver, AFC	1,651
1985	Chicago, NFC	1,319
	N.Y. Jets, AFC	1,516
1984	Chicago, NFC	1,377
	Pittsburgh, AFC	1,617
1983	Washington, NFC	1,289
	Cincinnati, AFC	1,499
1982	Pittsburgh, AFC	762
	Detroit, NFC	854
1981	Detroit, NFC	1,623
	Kansas City, AFC	1,747
1980	Detroit, NFC	1,599
	Cincinnati, AFC	1,680
1979	Denver, AFC	1,693
	Tampa Bay, NFC	1,873
1978	Dallas, NFC	1,721
	Pittsburgh, AFC	1,774
1977	Denver, AFC	1,531
	Dallas, NFC	1,651
1976	Pittsburgh, AFC	1,457
	Los Angeles, NFC	1,564
1975	Minnesota, NFC	1,532
	Houston, AFC	1,680
1974	Los Angeles, NFC	1,302
	New England, AFC	1,587
1973	Los Angeles, NFC	1,270
	Oakland, AFC	1,470
1972	Dallas, NFC	1,515
	Miami, AFC	1,548
1971	Baltimore, AFC	1,113
	Dallas, NFC	1,144
1970	Detroit, NFC	1,152
	N.Y. Jets, AFC	1,283
1969	Dallas, NFL	1,050
	Kansas City, AFL	1,091
1968	Dallas, NFL	1,195
	N.Y. Jets, AFL	1,195
1967	Dallas, NFL	1,081
	Oakland, AFL	1,129
1966	Buffalo, AFL	1,051
	Dallas, NFL	1,176
1965	San Diego, AFL	1,094
	Los Angeles, NFL	1,409
964	Buffalo, AFL	913
	Los Angeles, NFL	1,501
1963	Boston, AFL	1,107
	Chicago, NFL	1,442
1962	Detroit, NFL	1,231
	Dall. Texans, AFL	1,250
1961	Boston, AFL	1,041
	Pittsburgh, NFL	1,463
1960	St. Louis, NFL	1,212
	Dall. Texans, AFL	1,338
1959	N.Y. Giants	1,261
1958	Baltimore	1,291
1957	Baltimore	1,174
1956	N.Y. Giants	1,443
1955	Cleveland	1,189
1954	Cleveland	1,050
1953	Philadelphia	1,117
1952	Detroit	1,145
1951	N.Y. Giants	913
1950	Detroit	1,367
1949	Chi. Bears	1,196
1948	Philadelphia	1,209
1947	Philadelphia	1,329
1946	Chi. Bears	1,060
1945	Philadelphia	817
1944	Philadelphia	558
1943	Phil-Pitt	793
1942	Chi. Bears	519
1941	Washington	1,042
1940	N.Y. Giants	977
1939	Chi. Bears	812
1938	Detroit	1,081
1937	Chi. Bears	933
1936	Boston	1,148
1935	Boston	998
1934	Chi. Cardinals	954
1933	Brooklyn	964

Fewest Yards Passing Allowed

Leadership in this category has been based on net yards since 1952.

Year	Team	Yards
1990	Pittsburgh, AFC	2,500
	Dallas, NFC	2,639
1989	Minnesota, NFC	2,501
	Kansas City, AFC	2,527
1988	Kansas City, AFC	2,434
	Minnesota, NFC	2,489
1987	San Francisco, NFC	2,484
	L.A. Raiders, AFC	2,727
1986	St. Louis, NFC	2,637
	New England, AFC	2,978
1985	Washington, NFC	2,746
	Pittsburgh, AFC	2,783
1984	New Orleans, NFC	2,453
	Cleveland, AFC	2,696
1983	New Orleans, NFC	2,691
	Cincinnati, AFC	2,828
1982	Miami, AFC	1,027
	Tampa Bay, NFC	1,384
1981	Philadelphia, NFC	2,696
	Buffalo, AFC	2,870
1980	Washington, NFC	2,171
	Buffalo, AFC	2,282
1979	Tampa Bay, NFC	2,076
	Buffalo, AFC	2,530
1978	Buffalo, AFC	1,960
	Los Angeles, NFC	2,048
1977	Atlanta, NFC	1,384
	San Diego, AFC	1,725
1976	Minnesota, NFC	1,575
	Cincinnati, AFC	1,758
1975	Minnesota, NFC	1,621
	Cincinnati, AFC	1,729
1974	Pittsburgh, AFC	1,466
	Atlanta, NFC	1,572
1973	Miami, AFC	1,290
	Atlanta, NFC	1,430
1972	Minnesota, NFC	1,699
	Cleveland, AFC	1,736
1971	Atlanta, NFC	1,638
	Baltimore, AFC	1,739
1970	Minnesota, NFC	1,438
	Kansas City, AFC	2,010
1969	Minnesota, NFL	1,631
	Kansas City, AFL	2,072
1968	Houston, AFL	1,671
	Green Bay, NFL	1,796
1967	Green Bay, NFL	1,377
	Buffalo, AFL	1,825
1966	Green Bay, NFL	1,959
	Oakland, AFL	2,118
1965	Green Bay, NFL	1,981
	San Diego, AFL	2,168
1964	Green Bay, NFL	1,647
	San Diego, AFL	2,518
1963	Chicago, NFL	1,734
	Oakland, AFL	2,589
1962	Green Bay, NFL	1,746
	Oakland, AFL	2,306

1961	Baltimore, NFL	1,913
	San Diego, AFL	2,363
1960	Chicago, NFL	1,388
	Buffalo, AFL	2,124
1959	N.Y. Giants	1,582
1958	Chi. Bears	1,769
1957	Cleveland	1,300
1956	Cleveland	1,103
1955	Pittsburgh	1,295
1954	Cleveland	1,608
1953	Washington	1,751
1952	Washington	1,580
1951	Pittsburgh	1,687
1950	Cleveland	1,581
1949	Philadelphia	1,607
1948	Green Bay	1,626
1947	Green Bay	1,790
1946	Pittsburgh	939
1945	Washington	1,121
1944	Chi. Bears	1,052
1943	Chi. Bears	980
1942	Washington	1,093
1941	Pittsburgh	1,168
1940	Philadelphia	1,012
1939	Washington	1,116
1938	Chi. Bears	897
1937	Detroit	804
1936	Philadelphia	853
1935	Chi. Cardinals	793
1934	Philadelphia	545
1933	Portsmouth	558

Compiled by Elias Sports Bureau

1967: Super Bowl I
1968: Super Bowl II
1969: Super Bowl III
1970: Super Bowl IV
1971: Super Bowl V
1972: Super Bowl VI
1973: Super Bowl VII
1974: Super Bowl VIII
1975: Super Bowl IX
1976: Super Bowl X
1977: Super Bowl XI
1978: Super Bowl XII
1979: Super Bowl XIII
1980: Super Bowl XIV
1981: Super Bowl XV
1982: Super Bowl XVI
1983: Super Bowl XVII
1984: Super Bowl XVIII
1985: Super Bowl XIX
1986: Super Bowl XX
1987: Super Bowl XXI
1988: Super Bowl XXII
1989: Super Bowl XXIII
1990: Super Bowl XXIV
1991: Super Bowl XXV

Individual Records

Service

Most Games
5 Marv Fleming, Green Bay, 1967-68; Miami, 1972-74
Larry Cole, Dallas, 1971-72, 1976, 1978-79
Cliff Harris, Dallas, 1971-72, 1976, 1978-79
D.D. Lewis, Dallas, 1971-72, 1976, 1978-79
Preston Pearson, Baltimore, 1969; Pittsburgh, 1975; Dallas, 1976, 1978-79
Charlie Waters, Dallas, 1971-72, 1976, 1978-79
Rayfield Wright, Dallas, 1971-72, 1976, 1978-79
4 By many players

Most Games, Winning Team
4 By many players

Most Games, Coach
6 Don Shula, Baltimore, 1969; Miami, 1972-74, 1983, 1985
5 Tom Landry, Dallas, 1971-72, 1976, 1978-79
4 Bud Grant, Minnesota, 1970, 1974-75, 1977
Chuck Noll, Pittsburgh, 1975-76, 1979-80

Most Games, Winning Team, Coach
4 Chuck Noll, Pittsburgh, 1975-76, 1979-80
3 Bill Walsh, San Francisco, 1982, 1985, 1989
2 Vince Lombardi, Green Bay, 1967-68
Tom Landry, Dallas, 1972, 1978
Don Shula, Miami, 1973-74
Tom Flores, Oakland, 1981; L.A. Raiders, 1984
Joe Gibbs, Washington, 1983, 1988
Bill Parcells, N.Y. Giants, 1987, 1991

Most Games, Losing Team, Coach
4 Bud Grant, Minnesota, 1970, 1974-75, 1977
Don Shula, Baltimore, 1969; Miami, 1972, 1983, 1985
3 Tom Landry, Dallas, 1971, 1976, 1979
Dan Reeves, Denver, 1987-88, 1990

Scoring

Points

Most Points, Career
24 Franco Harris, Pittsburgh, 4 games (4-td)
Roger Craig, San Francisco, 3 games (4-td)
Jerry Rice, San Francisco, 2 games (4-td)
22 Ray Wersching, San Francisco, 2 games (7-pat, 5-fg)
20 Don Chandler, Green Bay, 2 games (8-pat, 4-fg)

Most Points, Game
18 Roger Craig, San Francisco vs. Miami, 1985 (3-td)
Jerry Rice, San Francisco vs. Denver, 1990 (3-td)
15 Don Chandler, Green Bay vs. Oakland, 1968 (3-pat, 4-fg)
14 Ray Wersching, San Francisco vs. Cincinnati, 1982 (2-pat, 4-fg)
Kevin Butler, Chicago vs. New England, 1986 (5-pat, 3-fg)

Touchdowns

Most Touchdowns, Career
4 Franco Harris, Pittsburgh, 4 games (4-r)
Roger Craig, San Francisco, 3 games (2-r, 2-p)
Jerry Rice, San Francisco, 2 games (4-p)
3 John Stallworth, Pittsburgh, 4 games (3-p)
Lynn Swann, Pittsburgh, 4 games (3-p)
Cliff Branch, Oakland-L.A. Raiders, 3 games (3-p)

Most Touchdowns, Game
3 Roger Craig, San Francisco vs. Miami, 1985 (1-r, 2-p)
Jerry Rice, San Francisco vs. Denver, 1990 (3-p)
2 Max McGee, Green Bay vs. Kansas City, 1967 (2-p)
Elijah Pitts, Green Bay vs. Kansas City, 1967 (2-r)
Bill Miller, Oakland vs. Green Bay, 1968 (2-p)
Larry Csonka, Miami vs. Minnesota, 1974 (2-r)
Pete Banaszak, Oakland vs. Minnesota, 1977 (2-r)
John Stallworth, Pittsburgh vs. Dallas, 1979 (2-p)
Franco Harris, Pittsburgh vs. Los Angeles, 1980 (2-r)
Cliff Branch, Oakland vs. Philadelphia, 1981 (2-p)
Dan Ross, Cincinnati vs. San Francisco, 1982 (2-p)
Marcus Allen, L.A. Raiders vs. Washington, 1984 (2-r)
Jim McMahon, Chicago vs. New England, 1986 (2-r)
Ricky Sanders, Washington vs. Denver, 1988 (2-p)
Timmy Smith, Washington vs. Denver, 1988 (2-r)
Tom Rathman, San Francisco vs. Denver, 1990 (2-r)

Points After Touchdown

Most Points After Touchdown, Career
9 Mike Cofer, San Francisco, 2 games (10 att)
8 Don Chandler, Green Bay, 2 games (8 att)
Roy Gerela, Pittsburgh, 3 games (9 att)
Chris Bahr, Oakland-L.A. Raiders, 2 games (8 att)
7 Ray Wersching, San Francisco, 2 games (7 att)

Most Points After Touchdown, Game
7 Mike Cofer, San Francisco vs. Denver, 1990 (8 att)
6 Ali Haji-Sheikh, Washington vs. Denver, 1988 (6 att)
5 Don Chandler, Green Bay vs. Kansas City, 1967 (5 att)
Roy Gerela, Pittsburgh vs. Dallas, 1979 (5 att)
Chris Bahr, L.A. Raiders vs. Washington, 1984 (5 att)
Ray Wersching, San Francisco vs. Miami, 1985 (5 att)
Kevin Butler, Chicago vs. New England, 1986 (5 att)

Field Goals

Field Goals Attempted, Career
7 Roy Gerela, Pittsburgh, 3 games
6 Jim Turner, N.Y. Jets-Denver, 2 games
Rich Karlis, Denver, 2 games
5 Efren Herrera, Dallas, 1 game
Ray Wersching, San Francisco, 2 games

Most Field Goals Attempted, Game
5 Jim Turner, N.Y. Jets vs. Baltimore, 1969
Efren Herrera, Dallas vs. Denver, 1978
4 Don Chandler, Green Bay vs. Oakland, 1968
Roy Gerela, Pittsburgh vs. Dallas, 1976
Ray Wersching, San Francisco vs. Cincinnati, 1982
Rich Karlis, Denver vs. N.Y. Giants, 1987
Mike Cofer, San Francisco vs. Cincinnati, 1989

Most Field Goals, Career
5 Ray Wersching, San Francisco, 2 games (5 att)
4 Don Chandler, Green Bay, 2 games (4 att)
Jim Turner, N.Y. Jets-Denver, 2 games (6 att)
Uwe von Schamann, Miami, 2 games (4 att)
3 Mike Clark, Dallas, 2 games (3 att)
Jan Stenerud, Kansas City, 1 game (3 att)
Chris Bahr, Oakland-L.A. Raiders, 2 games (4 att)
Mark Moseley, Washington, 2 games (4 att)
Kevin Butler, Chicago, 1 game (3 att)
Rich Karlis, Denver, 2 games (6 att)
Jim Breech, Cincinnati, 2 games (3 att)
Matt Bahr, Pittsburgh-N.Y. Giants, 2 games (3 att)

Most Field Goals, Game
4 Don Chandler, Green Bay vs. Oakland, 1968
Ray Wersching, San Francisco vs. Cincinnati, 1982
3 Jim Turner, N.Y. Jets vs. Baltimore, 1969
Jan Stenerud, Kansas City vs. Minnesota, 1970
Uwe von Schamann, Miami vs. San Francisco, 1985
Kevin Butler, Chicago vs. New England, 1986
Jim Breech, Cincinnati vs. San Francisco, 1989

Longest Field Goal
48 Jan Stenerud, Kansas City vs. Minnesota, 1970
Rich Karlis, Denver vs. N.Y. Giants, 1987
47 Jim Turner, Denver vs. Dallas, 1978
46 Chris Bahr, Oakland vs. Philadelphia, 1981

Safeties

Most Safeties, Game
1 Dwight White, Pittsburgh vs. Minnesota, 1975
Reggie Harrison, Pittsburgh vs. Dallas, 1976
Henry Waechter, Chicago vs. New England, 1986
George Martin, N.Y. Giants vs. Denver, 1987
Bruce Smith, Buffalo vs. N.Y. Giants, 1991

Rushing

Attempts

Most Attempts, Career
101 Franco Harris, Pittsburgh, 4 games
64 John Riggins, Washington, 2 games
57 Larry Csonka, Miami, 3 games

Most Attempts, Game
38 John Riggins, Washington vs. Miami, 1983
34 Franco Harris, Pittsburgh vs. Minnesota, 1975
33 Larry Csonka, Miami vs. Minnesota, 1974

Yards Gained

Most Yards Gained, Career
354 Franco Harris, Pittsburgh, 4 games
297 Larry Csonka, Miami, 3 games
230 John Riggins, Washington, 2 games

Most Yards Gained, Game
204 Timmy Smith, Washington vs. Denver, 1988
191 Marcus Allen, L.A. Raiders vs. Washington, 1984
166 John Riggins, Washington vs. Miami, 1983

Longest Run From Scrimmage
74 Marcus Allen, L.A. Raiders vs. Washington, 1984 (TD)
58 Tom Matte, Baltimore vs. N.Y. Jets, 1969
Timmy Smith, Washington vs. Denver, 1988 (TD)
49 Larry Csonka, Miami vs. Washington, 1973

Average Gain

Highest Average Gain, Career (20 attempts)
9.6 Marcus Allen, L.A. Raiders, 1 game (20-191)
9.3 Timmy Smith, Washington, 1 game (22-204)
5.3 Walt Garrison, Dallas, 2 games (26-139)

Highest Average Gain, Game (10 attempts)
10.5 Tom Matte, Baltimore vs. N.Y. Jets, 1969 (11-116)
9.6 Marcus Allen, L.A. Raiders vs. Washington, 1984 (20-191)
9.3 Timmy Smith, Washington vs. Denver, 1988 (22-204)

Touchdowns

Most Touchdowns, Career
4 Franco Harris, Pittsburgh, 4 games
2 Elijah Pitts, Green Bay, 1 game
Jim Kiick, Miami, 3 games
Larry Csonka, Miami, 3 games
Pete Banaszak, Oakland, 2 games
Marcus Allen, L.A. Raiders, 1 game
John Riggins, Washington, 2 games
Jim McMahon, Chicago, 1 game
Timmy Smith, Washington, 1 game
Roger Craig, San Francisco, 3 games

Tom Rathman, San Francisco, 2 games
Ottis Anderson, N.Y. Giants, 2 games

Most Touchdowns, Game

2 Elijah Pitts, Green Bay vs. Kansas City, 1967
Larry Csonka, Miami vs. Minnesota, 1974
Pete Banaszak, Oakland vs. Minnesota, 1977
Franco Harris, Pittsburgh vs. Los Angeles, 1980
Marcus Allen, L.A. Raiders vs. Washington, 1984
Jim McMahon, Chicago vs. New England, 1986
Timmy Smith, Washington vs. Denver, 1988
Tom Rathman, San Francisco vs. Denver, 1990

Passing

Attempts

Most Passes Attempted, Career

122 Joe Montana, San Francisco, 4 games
101 John Elway, Denver, 3 games
98 Roger Staubach, Dallas, 4 games

Most Passes Attempted, Game

50 Dan Marino, Miami vs. San Francisco, 1985
38 Ron Jaworski, Philadelphia vs. Oakland, 1981
John Elway, Denver vs. Washington, 1988
37 John Elway, Denver vs. N.Y. Giants, 1987

Completions

Most Passes Completed, Career

83 Joe Montana, San Francisco, 4 games
61 Roger Staubach, Dallas, 4 games
49 Terry Bradshaw, Pittsburgh, 4 games

Most Passes Completed, Game

29 Dan Marino, Miami vs. San Francisco, 1985
25 Ken Anderson, Cincinnati vs. San Francisco, 1982
24 Joe Montana, San Francisco vs. Miami, 1985

Most Consecutive Completions, Game

13 Joe Montana, San Francisco vs. Denver, 1990
10 Phil Simms, N.Y. Giants vs. Denver, 1987
8 Len Dawson, Kansas City vs. Green Bay, 1967
Joe Theismann, Washington vs. Miami, 1983

Completion Percentage

Highest Completion Percentage, Career (40 attempts)

68.0 Joe Montana, San Francisco, 4 games (122-83)
63.6 Len Dawson, Kansas City, 2 games (44-28)
63.4 Bob Griese, Miami, 3 games (41-26)

Highest Completion Percentage, Game (20 attempts)

88.0 Phil Simms, N.Y. Giants vs. Denver, 1987 (25-22)
75.9 Joe Montana, San Francisco vs. Denver, 1990 (29-22)
73.5 Ken Anderson, Cincinnati vs. San Francisco, 1982 (34-25)

Yards Gained

Most Yards Gained, Career

1,142 Joe Montana, San Francisco, 4 games
932 Terry Bradshaw, Pittsburgh, 4 games
734 Roger Staubach, Dallas, 4 games

Most Yards Gained, Game

357 Joe Montana, San Francisco vs. Cincinnati, 1989
340 Doug Williams, Washington vs. Denver, 1988
331 Joe Montana, San Francisco vs. Miami, 1985

Longest Pass Completion

80 Jim Plunkett (to King), Oakland vs. Philadelphia, 1981 (TD)
Doug Williams (to Sanders), Washington vs. Denver, 1988 (TD)
76 David Woodley (to Cefalo), Miami vs. Washington, 1983 (TD)
75 Johnny Unitas (to Mackey), Baltimore vs. Dallas, 1971 (TD)
Terry Bradshaw (to Stallworth), Pittsburgh vs. Dallas, 1979 (TD)

Average Gain

Highest Average Gain, Career (40 attempts)

11.10 Terry Bradshaw, Pittsburgh, 4 games (84-932)
9.62 Bart Starr, Green Bay, 2 games (47-452)
9.41 Jim Plunkett, Oakland-L.A. Raiders, 2 games (46-433)

Highest Average Gain, Game (20 attempts)

14.71 Terry Bradshaw, Pittsburgh vs. Los Angeles, 1980 (21-309)
12.80 Jim McMahon, Chicago vs. New England, 1986 (20-256)
12.43 Jim Plunkett, Oakland vs. Philadelphia, 1981 (21-261)

Touchdowns

Most Touchdown Passes, Career

11 Joe Montana, San Francisco, 4 games
9 Terry Bradshaw, Pittsburgh, 4 games
8 Roger Staubach, Dallas, 4 games

Most Touchdown Passes, Game

5 Joe Montana, San Francisco vs. Denver, 1990
4 Terry Bradshaw, Pittsburgh vs. Dallas, 1979
Doug Williams, Washington vs. Denver, 1988
3 Roger Staubach, Dallas vs. Pittsburgh, 1979
Jim Plunkett, Oakland vs. Philadelphia, 1981
Joe Montana, San Francisco vs. Miami, 1985
Phil Simms, N.Y. Giants vs. Denver, 1987

Had Intercepted

Lowest Percentage, Passes Had Intercepted, Career (40 attempts)

0.00 Jim Plunkett, Oakland-L.A. Raiders, 2 games (46-0)
Joe Montana, San Francisco, 4 games (122-0)
2.13 Bart Starr, Green Bay, 2 games (47-1)
4.00 Dan Marino, Miami, 1 game (50-2)

Most Attempts, Without Interception, Game

36 Joe Montana, San Francisco vs. Cincinnati, 1989
35 Joe Montana, San Francisco vs. Miami, 1985
32 Jeff Hostetler, N.Y. Giants vs. Buffalo, 1991

Most Passes Had Intercepted, Career

7 Craig Morton, Dallas-Denver, 2 games
6 Fran Tarkenton, Minnesota, 3 games
John Elway, Denver, 3 games
4 Earl Morrall, Baltimore-Miami, 4 games
Roger Staubach, Dallas, 4 games
Terry Bradshaw, Pittsburgh, 4 games
Joe Theismann, Washington, 2 games

Most Passes Had Intercepted, Game

4 Craig Morton, Denver vs. Dallas, 1978
3 By eight players

Pass Receiving

Receptions

Most Receptions, Career

20 Roger Craig, San Francisco, 3 games
18 Jerry Rice, San Francisco, 2 games
16 Lynn Swann, Pittsburgh, 4 games

Most Receptions, Game

11 Dan Ross, Cincinnati vs. San Francisco, 1982
Jerry Rice, San Francisco vs. Cincinnati, 1989
10 Tony Nathan, Miami vs. San Francisco, 1985
9 Ricky Sanders, Washington vs. Denver, 1988

Yards Gained

Most Yards Gained, Career

364 Lynn Swann, Pittsburgh, 4 games
363 Jerry Rice, San Francisco, 2 games
268 John Stallworth, Pittsburgh, 4 games

Most Yards Gained, Game

215 Jerry Rice, San Francisco vs. Cincinnati, 1989
193 Ricky Sanders, Washington vs. Denver, 1988
161 Lynn Swann, Pittsburgh vs. Dallas, 1976

Longest Reception

80 Kenny King (from Plunkett), Oakland vs. Philadelphia, 1981 (TD)
Ricky Sanders (from Williams), Washington vs. Denver, 1988 (TD)
76 Jimmy Cefalo (from Woodley), Miami vs. Washington, 1983 (TD)
75 John Mackey (from Unitas), Baltimore vs. Dallas, 1971 (TD)
John Stallworth (from Bradshaw), Pittsburgh vs. Dallas, 1979 (TD)

Average Gain

Highest Average Gain, Career (8 receptions)

24.4 John Stallworth, Pittsburgh, 4 games (11-268)
22.8 Lynn Swann, Pittsburgh, 4 games (16-364)
21.4 Ricky Sanders, Washington, 1 game (9-193)

Highest Average Gain, Game (3 receptions)

40.33 John Stallworth, Pittsburgh vs. Los Angeles, 1980 (3-121)
40.25 Lynn Swann, Pittsburgh vs. Dallas, 1979 (4-161)
38.33 John Stallworth, Pittsburgh vs. Dallas, 1979 (3-115)

Touchdowns

Most Touchdowns, Career

4 Jerry Rice, San Francisco, 2 games
3 John Stallworth, Pittsburgh, 4 games
Lynn Swann, Pittsburgh, 4 games
Cliff Branch, Oakland-L.A. Raiders, 3 games
2 Max McGee, Green Bay, 2 games
Bill Miller, Oakland, 1 game
Butch Johnson, Dallas, 2 games
Dan Ross, Cincinnati, 1 game
Roger Craig, San Francisco, 3 games
Ricky Sanders, Washington, 1 game
John Taylor, San Francisco, 2 games

Most Touchdowns, Game

3 Jerry Rice, San Francisco vs. Denver, 1990
2 Max McGee, Green Bay vs. Kansas City, 1967
Bill Miller, Oakland vs. Green Bay, 1968
John Stallworth, Pittsburgh vs. Dallas, 1979
Cliff Branch, Oakland vs. Philadelphia, 1981
Dan Ross, Cincinnati vs. San Francisco, 1982
Roger Craig, San Francisco vs. Miami, 1985
Ricky Sanders, Washington vs. Denver, 1988

Interceptions By

Most Interceptions By, Career

3 Chuck Howley, Dallas, 2 games
Rod Martin, Oakland-L.A. Raiders, 2 games
2 Randy Beverly, N.Y. Jets, 1 game
Jake Scott, Miami, 3 games
Mike Wagner, Pittsburgh, 3 games
Mel Blount, Pittsburgh, 4 games
Eric Wright, San Francisco, 4 games
Barry Wilburn, Washington, 1 game

Most Interceptions By, Game

3 Rod Martin, Oakland vs. Philadelphia, 1981
2 Randy Beverly, N.Y. Jets vs. Baltimore, 1969
Chuck Howley, Dallas vs. Baltimore, 1971
Jake Scott, Miami vs. Washington, 1973
Barry Wilburn, Washington vs. Denver, 1988

Yards Gained

Most Yards Gained, Career

75 Willie Brown, Oakland, 2 games
63 Chuck Howley, Dallas, 2 games
Jake Scott, Miami, 3 games
60 Herb Adderley, Green Bay-Dallas, 4 games

Most Yards Gained, Game

75 Willie Brown, Oakland vs. Minnesota, 1977
63 Jake Scott, Miami vs. Washington, 1973
60 Herb Adderley, Green Bay vs. Oakland, 1968

Longest Return

75 Willie Brown, Oakland vs. Minnesota, 1977 (TD)
60 Herb Adderley, Green Bay vs. Oakland, 1968 (TD)
55 Jake Scott, Miami vs. Washington, 1973

Touchdowns
Most Touchdowns, Game
1 Herb Adderley, Green Bay vs. Oakland, 1968
Willie Brown, Oakland vs. Minnesota, 1977
Jack Squirek, L.A. Raiders vs. Washington, 1984
Reggie Phillips, Chicago vs. New England, 1986

Punting
Most Punts, Career
17 Mike Eischeid, Oakland-Minnesota, 3 games
15 Larry Seiple, Miami, 3 games
Mike Horan, Denver, 3 games
14 Ron Widby, Dallas, 2 games
Ray Guy, Oakland-L.A. Raiders, 3 games
Most Punts, Game
9 Ron Widby, Dallas vs. Baltimore, 1971
7 By eight players
Longest Punt
63 Lee Johnson, Cincinnati vs. San Francisco, 1989
62 Rich Camarillo, New England vs. Chicago, 1986
61 Jerrel Wilson, Kansas City vs. Green Bay, 1967

Average Yardage
Highest Average, Punting, Career (10 punts)
46.5 Jerrel Wilson, Kansas City, 2 games (11-511)
41.9 Ray Guy, Oakland-L.A. Raiders, 3 games (14-587)
41.3 Larry Seiple, Miami, 3 games (15-620)
Highest Average, Punting, Game (4 punts)
48.5 Jerrel Wilson, Kansas City vs. Minnesota, 1970 (4-194)
46.3 Jim Miller, San Francisco vs. Cincinnati, 1982 (4-185)
45.3 Jerrel Wilson, Kansas City vs. Green Bay, 1967 (7-317)

Punt Returns
Most Punt Returns, Career
6 Willie Wood, Green Bay, 2 games
Jake Scott, Miami, 3 games
Theo Bell, Pittsburgh, 2 games
Mike Nelms, Washington, 1 game
John Taylor, San Francisco, 2 games
5 Dana McLemore, San Francisco, 1 game
4 By seven players
Most Punt Returns, Game
6 Mike Nelms, Washington vs. Miami, 1983
5 Willie Wood, Green Bay vs. Oakland, 1968
Dana McLemore, San Francisco vs. Miami, 1985
4 By six players
Most Fair Catches, Game
3 Ron Gardin, Baltimore vs. Dallas, 1971
Golden Richards, Dallas vs. Pittsburgh, 1976
Greg Pruitt, L.A. Raiders vs. Washington, 1984
Al Edwards, Buffalo vs. N.Y. Giants, 1991
David Meggett, N.Y. Giants vs. Buffalo, 1991

Yards Gained
Most Yards Gained, Career
94 John Taylor, San Francisco, 2 games
52 Mike Nelms, Washington, 1 game
51 Dana McLemore, San Francisco, 1 game
Most Yards Gained, Game
56 John Taylor, San Francisco vs. Cincinnati, 1989
52 Mike Nelms, Washington vs. Miami, 1983
51 Dana McLemore, San Francisco vs. Miami, 1985
Longest Return
45 John Taylor, San Francisco vs. Cincinnati, 1989
34 Darrell Green, Washington vs. L.A. Raiders, 1984
31 Willie Wood, Green Bay vs. Oakland, 1968

Average Yardage
Highest Average, Career (4 returns)
15.7 John Taylor, San Francisco, 2 games (6-94)
10.8 Neal Colzie, Oakland, 1 game (4-43)
10.2 Dana McLemore, San Francisco, 1 game (5-51)
Highest Average, Game (3 returns)
18.7 John Taylor, San Francisco vs. Cincinnati, 1989 (3-56)
12.7 John Taylor, San Francisco vs. Denver, 1990 (3-38)
11.3 Lynn Swann, Pittsburgh vs. Minnesota, 1975 (3-34)

Touchdowns
Most Touchdowns, Game
None

Kickoff Returns
Most Kickoff Returns, Career
10 Ken Bell, Denver, 3 games
8 Larry Anderson, Pittsburgh, 2 games
Fulton Walker, Miami, 2 games
7 Preston Pearson, Baltimore-Pittsburgh-Dallas, 5 games
Stephen Starring, New England, 1 game
Most Kickoff Returns, Game
7 Stephen Starring, New England vs. Chicago, 1986
6 Darren Carrington, Denver vs. San Francisco, 1990
5 Larry Anderson, Pittsburgh vs. Los Angeles, 1980
Billy Campfield, Philadelphia vs. Oakland, 1981
David Verser, Cincinnati vs. San Francisco, 1982
Alvin Garrett, Washington vs. L.A. Raiders, 1984
Ken Bell, Denver vs. Washington, 1988

Yards Gained
Most Yards Gained, Career
283 Fulton Walker, Miami, 2 games
207 Larry Anderson, Pittsburgh, 2 games
177 Ken Bell, Denver, 3 games
Most Yards Gained, Game
190 Fulton Walker, Miami vs. Washington, 1983
162 Larry Anderson, Pittsburgh vs. Los Angeles, 1980
153 Stephen Starring, New England vs. Chicago, 1986
Longest Return
98 Fulton Walker, Miami vs. Washington, 1983 (TD)
93 Stanford Jennings, Cincinnati vs. San Francisco, 1989 (TD)
67 Rick Upchurch, Denver vs. Dallas, 1978

Average Yardage
Highest Average, Career (4 returns)
35.4 Fulton Walker, Miami, 2 games (8-283)
25.9 Larry Anderson, Pittsburgh, 2 games (8-207)
24.3 Darren Carrington, Denver, 1 game (6-146)
Highest Average, Game (3 returns)
47.5 Fulton Walker, Miami vs. Washington, 1983 (4-190)
32.4 Larry Anderson, Pittsburgh vs. Los Angeles, 1980 (5-162)
31.3 Rick Upchurch, Denver vs. Dallas, 1978 (3-94)

Touchdowns
Most Touchdowns, Game
1 Fulton Walker, Miami vs. Washington, 1983
Stanford Jennings, Cincinnati vs. San Francisco, 1989

Fumbles
Most Fumbles, Career
5 Roger Staubach, Dallas, 4 games
3 Franco Harris, Pittsburgh, 4 games
Terry Bradshaw, Pittsburgh, 4 games
John Elway, Denver, 3 games
2 By six players
Most Fumbles, Game
3 Roger Staubach, Dallas vs. Pittsburgh, 1976
2 Franco Harris, Pittsburgh vs. Minnesota, 1975
Butch Johnson, Dallas vs. Denver, 1978
Terry Bradshaw, Pittsburgh vs. Dallas, 1979
Joe Montana, San Francisco vs. Cincinnati, 1989
John Elway, Denver vs. San Francisco, 1990

Recoveries
Most Fumbles Recovered, Career
2 Jake Scott, Miami, 3 games (1 own, 1 opp)
Fran Tarkenton, Minnesota, 3 games (2 own)
Franco Harris, Pittsburgh, 4 games (2 own)
Roger Staubach, Dallas, 4 games (2 own)
Bobby Walden, Pittsburgh, 2 games (2 own)
John Fitzgerald, Dallas, 4 games (2 own)
Randy Hughes, Dallas, 3 games (2 opp)
Butch Johnson, Dallas, 2 games (2 own)
Mike Singletary, Chicago, 1 game (2 opp)
John Elway, Denver, 3 games (2 own)
Most Fumbles Recovered, Game
2 Jake Scott, Miami vs. Minnesota, 1974 (1 own, 1 opp)
Roger Staubach, Dallas vs. Pittsburgh, 1976 (2 own)
Randy Hughes, Dallas vs. Denver, 1978 (2 opp)
Butch Johnson, Dallas vs. Denver, 1978 (2 own)
Mike Singletary, Chicago vs. New England, 1986 (2 opp)

Yards Gained
Most Yards Gained, Game
49 Mike Bass, Washington vs. Miami, 1973 (opp)
37 Mike Hegman, Dallas vs. Pittsburgh, 1979 (opp)
21 Randy Hughes, Dallas vs. Denver, 1978 (opp)
Longest Return
49 Mike Bass, Washington vs. Miami, 1973 (TD)
37 Mike Hegman, Dallas vs. Pittsburgh, 1979 (TD)
19 Randy Hughes, Dallas vs. Denver, 1978

Touchdowns
Most Touchdowns, Game
1 Mike Bass, Washington vs. Miami, 1973 (opp 49 yds)
Mike Hegman, Dallas vs. Pittsburgh, 1979 (opp 37 yds)

Combined Net Yards Gained
(Rushing, receiving, interception returns, punt returns, kickoff returns, and fumble returns)
Attempts
Most Attempts, Career
108 Franco Harris, Pittsburgh, 4 games
73 Roger Craig, San Francisco, 3 games
66 John Riggins, Washington, 2 games
Most Attempts, Game
39 John Riggins, Washington vs. Miami, 1983
35 Franco Harris, Pittsburgh vs. Minnesota, 1975
34 Matt Snell, N.Y. Jets vs. Baltimore, 1969

Yards Gained
Most Yards Gained, Career
468 Franco Harris, Pittsburgh, 4 games
410 Roger Craig, San Francisco, 3 games
391 Lynn Swann, Pittsburgh, 4 games
Most Yards Gained, Game
239 Ricky Sanders, Washington vs. Denver, 1988
220 Jerry Rice, San Francisco vs. Cincinnati, 1989
213 Timmy Smith, Washington vs. Denver, 1988

Sacks
Sacks have been compiled since 1983.
Most Sacks, Game
2 Dwaine Board, San Francisco vs. Miami, 1985
Dennis Owens, New England vs. Chicago, 1986
Otis Wilson, Chicago vs. New England, 1986

Leonard Marshall, N.Y. Giants vs. Denver, 1987
Alvin Walton, Washington vs. Denver, 1988
Charles Haley, San Francisco vs. Cincinnati, 1989
Danny Stubbs, San Francisco, 1990

Team Records

Games, Victories, Defeats

Most Games
5 Dallas, 1971-72, 1976, 1978-79
Miami, 1972-74, 1983, 1985
4 Minnesota, 1970, 1974-75, 1977
Pittsburgh, 1975-76, 1979-80
Oakland/L.A. Raiders, 1968, 1977, 1981, 1984
Washington, 1973, 1983-84, 1988
Denver, 1978, 1987-88, 1990
San Francisco, 1982, 1985, 1989-90

Most Consecutive Games
3 Miami, 1972-74
2 Green Bay, 1967-68
Dallas, 1971-72
Minnesota, 1974-75
Pittsburgh, 1975-76, 1979-80
Washington, 1983-84
Denver, 1987-88
San Francisco 1989-90

Most Games Won
4 Pittsburgh, 1975-76, 1979-80
San Francisco, 1982, 1985, 1989-90
3 Oakland/L.A. Raiders, 1977, 1981, 1984
2 Green Bay, 1967-68
Miami, 1973-74
Dallas, 1972, 1978
Washington, 1983, 1988
N.Y. Giants, 1987, 1991

Most Consecutive Games Won
2 Green Bay, 1967-68
Miami, 1973-74
Pittsburgh, 1975-76, 1979-80
San Francisco, 1989-90

Most Games Lost
4 Minnesota, 1970, 1974-75, 1977
Denver, 1978, 1987-88, 1990
3 Dallas, 1971, 1976, 1979
Miami, 1972, 1983, 1985
2 Washington, 1973, 1984
Cincinnati, 1982, 1989

Most Consecutive Games Lost
2 Minnesota, 1974-75
Denver, 1987-88

Scoring

Most Points, Game
55 San Francisco vs. Denver, 1990
46 Chicago vs. New England, 1986
42 Washington vs. Denver, 1988

Fewest Points, Game
3 Miami vs. Dallas, 1972
6 Minnesota vs. Pittsburgh, 1975
7 By four teams

Most Points, Both Teams, Game
66 Pittsburgh (35) vs. Dallas (31), 1979
65 San Francisco (55) vs. Denver (10), 1990
59 N.Y. Giants (39) vs. Denver (20), 1987

Fewest Points, Both Teams, Game
21 Washington (7) vs. Miami (14), 1973
22 Minnesota (6) vs. Pittsburgh (16), 1975
23 Baltimore (7) vs. N.Y. Jets (16), 1969

Largest Margin of Victory, Game
45 San Francisco vs. Denver, 1990 (55-10)
36 Chicago vs. New England, 1986 (46-10)
32 Washington vs. Denver, 1988 (42-10)

Most Points, Each Half
1st: 35 Washington vs. Denver, 1988
2nd: 30 N.Y. Giants vs. Denver, 1987

Most Points, Each Quarter
1st: 14 Miami vs. Minnesota, 1974
Oakland vs. Philadelphia, 1981
2nd: 35 Washington vs. Denver, 1988
3rd: 21 Chicago vs. New England, 1986
4th: 14 Pittsburgh vs. Dallas, 1976; vs. Dallas, 1979; vs. Los Angeles, 1980
Dallas vs. Pittsburgh, 1979
Cincinnati vs. San Francisco, 1982
Washington vs. Miami, 1983
San Francisco vs. Cincinnati, 1989; vs. Denver, 1990

Most Points, Both Teams, Each Half
1st: 45 Washington (35) vs. Denver (10), 1988
2nd: 40 N.Y. Giants (30) vs. Denver (10), 1987

Fewest Points, Both Teams, Each Half
1st: 2 Minnesota (0) vs. Pittsburgh (2), 1975
2nd: 7 Miami (0) vs. Washington (7), 1973
Denver (0) vs. Washington (7), 1988

Most Points, Both Teams, Each Quarter
1st: 17 Miami (10) vs. San Francisco (7), 1985
Denver (10) vs. N.Y. Giants (7), 1987
2nd: 35 Washington (35) vs. Denver (0), 1988
3rd: 21 Chicago (21) vs. New England (0), 1986
San Francisco (14) vs. Denver (7), 1990
4th: 28 Dallas (14) vs. Pittsburgh (14), 1979

Touchdowns

Most Touchdowns, Game
8 San Francisco vs. Denver, 1990
6 Washington vs. Denver, 1988
5 Green Bay vs. Kansas City, 1967
Pittsburgh vs. Dallas, 1979
L.A. Raiders vs. Washington, 1984
San Francisco vs. Miami, 1985
Chicago vs. New England, 1986
N.Y. Giants vs. Denver, 1987

Fewest Touchdowns, Game
0 Miami vs. Dallas, 1972
1 By 16 teams

Most Touchdowns, Both Teams, Game
9 Pittsburgh (5) vs. Dallas (4), 1979
San Francisco (8) vs. Denver (1), 1990
7 N.Y. Giants (5) vs. Denver (2), 1987
Washington (6) vs. Denver (1), 1988
6 Green Bay (5) vs. Kansas City (1), 1967
Oakland (4) vs. Minnesota (2), 1977
Pittsburgh (4) vs. Los Angeles (2), 1980
L.A. Raiders (5) vs. Washington (1), 1984
San Francisco (5) vs. Miami (1), 1985
Chicago (5) vs. New England (1), 1986

Fewest Touchdowns, Both Teams, Game
2 Baltimore (1) vs. N.Y. Jets (1), 1969
3 In six games

Points After Touchdown

Most Points After Touchdown, Game
7 San Francisco vs. Denver, 1990
6 Washington vs. Denver, 1988
5 Green Bay vs. Kansas City, 1967
Pittsburgh vs. Dallas, 1979
L.A. Raiders vs. Washington, 1984
San Francisco vs. Miami, 1985
Chicago vs. New England, 1986

Most Points After Touchdown, Both Teams, Game
9 Pittsburgh (5) vs. Dallas (4), 1979
8 San Francisco (7) vs. Denver (1), 1990
7 Washington (6) vs. Denver (1), 1988

Fewest Points After Touchdown, Both Teams, Game
2 Baltimore (1) vs. N.Y. Jets (1), 1969
Baltimore (1) vs. Dallas (1), 1971
Minnesota (0) vs. Pittsburgh (2), 1975

Field Goals

Most Field Goals Attempted, Game
5 N.Y. Jets vs. Baltimore, 1969
Dallas vs. Denver, 1978
4 Green Bay vs. Oakland, 1968
Pittsburgh vs. Dallas, 1976
San Francisco vs. Cincinnati, 1982; 1989
Denver vs. N.Y. Giants, 1987

Most Field Goals Attempted, Both Teams, Game
7 N.Y. Jets (5) vs. Baltimore (2), 1969
San Francisco (4) vs. Cincinnati (3), 1989
6 Dallas (5) vs. Denver (1), 1978
5 Green Bay (4) vs. Oakland (1), 1968
Pittsburgh (4) vs. Dallas (1), 1976
Oakland (3) vs. Philadelphia (2), 1981
Denver (4) vs. N.Y. Giants (1), 1987

Fewest Field Goals Attempted, Both Teams, Game
1 Minnesota (0) vs. Miami (1), 1974
San Francisco (0) vs. Denver (1), 1990
2 Green Bay (0) vs. Kansas City (2), 1967
Miami (1) vs. Washington (1), 1973
Dallas (1) vs. Pittsburgh (1), 1979

Most Field Goals, Game
4 Green Bay vs. Oakland, 1968
San Francisco vs. Cincinnati, 1982
3 N.Y. Jets vs. Baltimore, 1969
Kansas City vs. Minnesota, 1970
Miami vs. San Francisco, 1985
Chicago vs. New England, 1986
Cincinnati vs. San Francisco, 1989

Most Field Goals, Both Teams, Game
5 Cincinnati (3) vs. San Francisco (2), 1989
4 Green Bay (4) vs. Oakland (0), 1968
San Francisco (4) vs. Cincinnati (0), 1982
Miami (3) vs. San Francisco (1), 1985
Chicago (3) vs. New England (1), 1986
Buffalo (2) vs. N.Y. Giants (2), 1991
3 In eight games

Fewest Field Goals, Both Teams, Game
0 Miami vs. Washington, 1973
Pittsburgh vs. Minnesota, 1975
1 Green Bay (0) vs. Kansas City (1), 1967
Minnesota (0) vs. Miami (1), 1974
Pittsburgh (0) vs. Dallas (1), 1979
Washington (0) vs. Denver (1), 1988
San Francisco (0) vs. Denver (1), 1990

Safeties

Most Safeties, Game
1 Pittsburgh vs. Minnesota, 1975; vs. Dallas, 1976
Chicago vs. New England, 1986
N.Y. Giants vs. Denver, 1987
Buffalo vs. N.Y. Giants, 1991

First Downs

Most First Downs, Game
31 San Francisco vs. Miami, 1985
28 San Francisco vs. Denver, 1990
25 Washington vs. Denver, 1988

Fewest First Downs, Game
9 Minnesota vs. Pittsburgh, 1975
Miami vs. Washington, 1983
10 Dallas vs. Baltimore, 1971
Miami vs. Dallas, 1972
11 Denver vs. Dallas, 1978

Most First Downs, Both Teams, Game
50 San Francisco (31) vs. Miami (19), 1985
47 N.Y. Giants (24) vs. Denver (23), 1987
44 Cincinnati (24) vs. San Francisco (20), 1982

Fewest First Downs, Both Teams, Game
24 Dallas (10) vs. Baltimore (14), 1971
26 Minnesota (9) vs. Pittsburgh (17), 1975
27 Pittsburgh (13) vs. Dallas (14), 1976

Rushing

Most First Downs, Rushing, Game
16 San Francisco vs. Miami, 1985
15 Dallas vs. Miami, 1972
14 Washington vs. Miami, 1983
San Francisco vs. Denver, 1990

Fewest First Downs, Rushing, Game
1 New England vs. Chicago, 1986
2 Minnesota vs. Kansas City, 1970; vs. Pittsburgh, 1975; vs. Oakland, 1977
Pittsburgh vs. Dallas, 1979
Miami vs. San Francisco, 1985
3 Miami vs. Dallas, 1972
Philadelphia vs. Oakland, 1981

Most First Downs, Rushing, Both Teams, Game
21 Washington (14) vs. Miami (7), 1983
19 Washington (13) vs. Denver (6), 1988
San Francisco (14) vs. Denver (5), 1990
18 Dallas (15) vs. Miami (3), 1972
Miami (13) vs. Minnesota (5), 1974
San Francisco (16) vs. Miami (2), 1985
N.Y. Giants (10) vs. Buffalo (8), 1991

Fewest First Downs, Rushing, Both Teams, Game
8 Baltimore (4) vs. Dallas (4), 1971
Pittsburgh (2) vs. Dallas (6), 1979
9 Philadelphia (3) vs. Oakland (6), 1981
10 Minnesota (2) vs. Kansas City (8), 1970

Passing

Most First Downs, Passing, Game
17 Miami vs. San Francisco, 1985
16 Denver vs. N.Y. Giants, 1987
San Francisco vs. Cincinnati, 1989
15 Minnesota vs. Oakland, 1977
Pittsburgh vs. Dallas, 1979
San Francisco vs. Miami, 1985

Fewest First Downs, Passing, Game
1 Denver vs. Dallas, 1978
2 Miami vs. Washington, 1983
4 Miami vs. Minnesota, 1974

Most First Downs, Passing, Both Teams, Game
32 Miami (17) vs. San Francisco (15), 1985
29 Denver (16) vs. N.Y. Giants (13), 1987
28 Pittsburgh (15) vs. Dallas (13), 1979

Fewest First Downs, Passing, Both Teams, Game
9 Denver (1) vs. Dallas (8), 1978
10 Minnesota (5) vs. Pittsburgh (5), 1975
11 Dallas (5) vs. Baltimore (6), 1971
Miami (2) vs. Washington (9), 1983

Penalty

Most First Downs, Penalty, Game
4 Baltimore vs. Dallas, 1971
Miami vs. Minnesota, 1974
Cincinnati vs. San Francisco, 1982
3 Kansas City vs. Minnesota, 1970
Minnesota vs. Oakland, 1977

Most First Downs, Penalty, Both Teams, Game
6 Cincinnati (4) vs. San Francisco (2), 1982
5 Baltimore (4) vs. Dallas (1), 1971
Miami (4) vs. Minnesota (1), 1974
4 Kansas City (3) vs. Minnesota (1), 1970

Fewest First Downs, Penalty, Both Teams, Game
0 Dallas vs. Miami, 1972
Miami vs. Washington, 1973
Dallas vs. Pittsburgh, 1976
Miami vs. San Francisco, 1985
1 Green Bay (0) vs. Kansas City (1), 1967
Miami (0) vs. Washington (1), 1983
Cincinnati (0) vs. San Francisco (1), 1989
San Francisco (0) vs. Denver (1), 1990

Net Yards Gained Rushing and Passing

Most Yards Gained, Game
602 Washington vs. Denver, 1988
537 San Francisco vs. Miami, 1985
461 San Francisco vs. Denver, 1990

Fewest Yards Gained, Game
119 Minnesota vs. Pittsburgh, 1975
123 New England vs. Chicago, 1986
156 Denver vs. Dallas, 1978

Most Yards Gained, Both Teams, Game
929 Washington (602) vs. Denver (327), 1988
851 San Francisco (537) vs. Miami (314), 1985
782 Oakland (429) vs. Minnesota (353), 1977

Fewest Yards Gained, Both Teams, Game
452 Minnesota (119) vs. Pittsburgh (333), 1975
481 Washington (228) vs. Miami (253), 1973
Denver (156) vs. Dallas (325), 1978
497 Minnesota (238) vs. Miami (259), 1974

Rushing

Attempts

Most Attempts, Game
57 Pittsburgh vs. Minnesota, 1975
53 Miami vs. Minnesota, 1974
52 Oakland vs. Minnesota, 1977
Washington vs. Miami, 1983

Fewest Attempts, Game
9 Miami vs. San Francisco, 1985
11 New England vs. Chicago, 1986
17 Denver vs. Washington, 1988; vs. San Francisco, 1990

Most Attempts, Both Teams, Game
81 Washington (52) vs. Miami (29), 1983
78 Pittsburgh (57) vs. Minnesota (21), 1975
Oakland (52) vs. Minnesota (26), 1977
77 Miami (53) vs. Minnesota (24), 1974
Pittsburgh (46) vs. Dallas (31), 1976

Fewest Attempts, Both Teams, Game
49 Miami (9) vs. San Francisco (40), 1985
53 Kansas City (19) vs. Green Bay (34), 1967
55 San Francisco (27) vs. Cincinnati (28), 1989

Yards Gained

Most Yards Gained, Game
280 Washington vs. Denver, 1988
276 Washington vs. Miami, 1983
266 Oakland vs. Minnesota, 1977

Fewest Yards Gained, Game
7 New England vs. Chicago, 1986
17 Minnesota vs. Pittsburgh, 1975
25 Miami vs. San Francisco, 1985

Most Yards Gained, Both Teams, Game
377 Washington (280) vs. Denver (97), 1988
372 Washington (276) vs. Miami (96), 1983
338 N.Y. Giants (172) vs. Buffalo (166), 1991

Fewest Yards Gained, Both Teams, Game
171 Baltimore (69) vs. Dallas (102), 1971
174 New England (7) vs. Chicago (167), 1986
186 Philadelphia (69) vs. Oakland (117), 1981

Average Gain

Highest Average Gain, Game
7.00 L.A. Raiders vs. Washington, 1984 (33-231)
Washington vs. Denver, 1988 (40-280)
6.64 Buffalo vs. N.Y. Giants, 1991 (25-166)
6.22 Baltimore vs. N.Y. Jets, 1969 (23-143)

Lowest Average Gain, Game
0.64 New England vs. Chicago, 1986 (11-7)
0.81 Minnesota vs. Pittsburgh, 1975 (21-17)
2.23 Baltimore vs. Dallas, 1971 (31-69)

Touchdowns

Most Touchdowns, Game
4 Chicago vs. New England, 1986
3 Green Bay vs. Kansas City, 1967
Miami vs. Minnesota, 1974
San Francisco vs. Denver, 1990
2 Oakland vs. Minnesota, 1977
Pittsburgh vs. Los Angeles, 1980
L.A. Raiders vs. Washington, 1984
San Francisco vs. Miami, 1985
N.Y. Giants vs. Denver, 1987
Washington vs. Denver, 1988
Buffalo vs. N.Y. Giants, 1991

Fewest Touchdowns, Game
0 By 17 teams

Most Touchdowns, Both Teams, Game
4 Miami (3) vs. Minnesota (1), 1974
Chicago (4) vs. New England (0), 1986
San Francisco (3) vs. Denver (1), 1990
3 Green Bay (3) vs. Kansas City (0), 1967
Pittsburgh (2) vs. Los Angeles (1), 1980
L.A. Raiders (2) vs. Washington (1), 1984
N.Y. Giants (2) vs. Denver (1), 1987
Buffalo (2) vs. N.Y. Giants (1), 1991

Fewest Touchdowns, Both Teams, Game
0 Pittsburgh vs. Dallas, 1976
Oakland vs. Philadelphia, 1981
Cincinnati vs. San Francisco, 1989
1 In seven games

Passing

Attempts

Most Passes Attempted, Game
50 Miami vs. San Francisco, 1985
44 Minnesota vs. Oakland, 1977
41 Baltimore vs. N.Y. Jets, 1969
Denver vs. N.Y. Giants, 1987

Fewest Passes Attempted, Game
7 Miami vs. Minnesota, 1974
11 Miami vs. Washington, 1973
14 Pittsburgh vs. Minnesota, 1975

Most Passes Attempted, Both Teams, Game
85 Miami (50) vs. San Francisco (35), 1985
70 Baltimore (41) vs. N.Y. Jets (29), 1969
69 Denver (39) vs. Washington (30), 1988
Fewest Passes Attempted, Both Teams, Game
35 Miami (7) vs. Minnesota (28), 1974
39 Miami (11) vs. Washington (28), 1973
40 Pittsburgh (14) vs. Minnesota (26), 1975
Miami (17) vs. Washington (23), 1983

Completions
Most Passes Completed, Game
29 Miami vs. San Francisco, 1985
26 Denver vs. N.Y. Giants, 1987
25 Cincinnati vs. San Francisco, 1982
Fewest Passes Completed, Game
4 Miami vs. Washington, 1983
6 Miami vs. Minnesota, 1974
8 Miami vs. Washington, 1973
Denver vs. Dallas, 1978
Most Passes Completed, Both Teams, Game
53 Miami (29) vs. San Francisco (24), 1985
48 Denver (26) vs. N.Y. Giants (22), 1987
39 Cincinnati (25) vs. San Francisco (14), 1982
Fewest Passes Completed, Both Teams, Game
19 Miami (4) vs. Washington (15), 1983
20 Pittsburgh (9) vs. Minnesota (11), 1975
22 Miami (8) vs. Washington (14), 1973

Completion Percentage
Highest Completion Percentage, Game (20 attempts)
88.0 N.Y. Giants vs. Denver, 1987 (25-22)
75.0 San Francisco vs. Denver, 1990 (32-24)
73.5 Cincinnati vs. San Francisco, 1982 (34-25)
Lowest Completion Percentage, Game (20 attempts)
32.0 Denver vs. Dallas, 1978 (25-8)
37.9 Denver vs. San Francisco, 1990 (29-11)
38.5 Denver vs. Washington, 1988 (39-15)

Yards Gained
Most Yards Gained, Game
341 San Francisco vs. Cincinnati, 1989
326 San Francisco vs. Miami, 1985
322 Washington vs. Denver, 1988
Fewest Yards Gained, Game
35 Denver vs. Dallas, 1978
63 Miami vs. Minnesota, 1974
69 Miami vs. Washington, 1973
Most Yards Gained, Both Teams, Game
615 San Francisco (326) vs. Miami (289), 1985
583 Denver (320) vs. N.Y. Giants (263), 1987
552 Washington (322) vs. Denver (230), 1988
Fewest Yards Gained, Both Teams, Game
156 Miami (69) vs. Washington (87), 1973
186 Pittsburgh (84) vs. Minnesota (102), 1975
205 Dallas (100) vs. Miami (105), 1972

Times Sacked
Most Times Sacked, Game
7 Dallas vs. Pittsburgh, 1976
New England vs. Chicago, 1986
6 Kansas City vs. Green Bay, 1967
Washington vs. L.A. Raiders, 1984
Denver vs. San Francisco, 1990
5 Dallas vs. Denver, 1978; vs. Pittsburgh, 1979
Cincinnati vs. San Francisco, 1982; 1989
Denver vs. Washington, 1988
Fewest Times Sacked, Game
0 Baltimore vs. N.Y. Jets, 1969; vs. Dallas, 1971
Minnesota vs. Pittsburgh, 1975
Pittsburgh vs. Los Angeles, 1980
Philadelphia vs. Oakland, 1981
1 By 10 teams
Most Times Sacked, Both Teams, Game
10 New England (7) vs. Chicago (3), 1986
9 Kansas City (6) vs. Green Bay (3), 1967
Dallas (7) vs. Pittsburgh (2), 1976
Dallas (5) vs. Denver (4), 1978
Dallas (5) vs. Pittsburgh (4), 1979
Cincinnati (5) vs. San Francisco (4), 1989
8 Washington (6) vs. L.A. Raiders (2), 1984
Fewest Times Sacked, Both Teams, Game
1 Philadelphia (0) vs. Oakland (1), 1981
2 Baltimore (0) vs. N.Y. Jets (2), 1969
Baltimore (0) vs. Dallas (2), 1971
Minnesota (0) vs. Pittsburgh (2), 1975
3 In four games

Touchdowns
Most Touchdowns, Game
5 San Francisco vs. Denver, 1990
4 Pittsburgh vs. Dallas, 1979
Washington vs. Denver, 1988
3 Dallas vs. Pittsburgh, 1979
Oakland vs. Philadelphia, 1981
San Francisco vs. Miami, 1985
N.Y. Giants vs. Denver, 1987
Fewest Touchdowns, Game
0 By 14 teams
Most Touchdowns, Both Teams, Game
7 Pittsburgh (4) vs. Dallas (3), 1979
5 Washington (4) vs. Denver (1), 1988
San Francisco (5) vs. Denver (0), 1990
4 Dallas (2) vs. Pittsburgh (2), 1976
Oakland (3) vs. Philadelphia (1), 1981
San Francisco (3) vs. Miami (1), 1985
N.Y. Giants (3) vs. Denver (1), 1987
Fewest Touchdowns, Both Teams, Game
0 N.Y. Jets vs. Baltimore, 1969
Miami vs. Minnesota, 1974
1 In six games

Interceptions By
Most Interceptions By, Game
4 N.Y. Jets vs. Baltimore, 1969
Dallas vs. Denver, 1978
3 By nine teams
Most Interceptions By, Both Teams, Game
6 Baltimore (3) vs. Dallas (3), 1971
4 In six games
Fewest Interceptions By, Both Teams, Game
0 Buffalo vs. N.Y. Giants, 1991
1 Oakland (0) vs. Green Bay (1), 1968
Miami (0) vs. Dallas (1), 1972
Minnesota (0) vs. Miami (1), 1974
N.Y. Giants (0) vs. Denver (1), 1987
San Francisco (1) vs. Cincinnati (0), 1989

Yards Gained
Most Yards Gained, Game
95 Miami vs. Washington, 1973
91 Oakland vs. Minnesota, 1977
89 Pittsburgh vs. Dallas, 1976
Most Yards Gained, Both Teams, Game
95 Miami (95) vs. Washington (0), 1973
91 Oakland (91) vs. Minnesota (0), 1977
89 Pittsburgh (89) vs. Dallas (0), 1976

Touchdowns
Most Touchdowns, Game
1 Green Bay vs. Oakland, 1968
Oakland vs. Minnesota, 1977
L.A. Raiders vs. Washington, 1984
Chicago vs. New England, 1986

Punting
Most Punts, Game
9 Dallas vs. Baltimore, 1971
8 Washington vs. L.A. Raiders, 1984
7 By seven teams
Fewest Punts, Game
2 Pittsburgh vs. Los Angeles, 1980
Denver vs. N.Y. Giants, 1987
3 By nine teams
Most Punts, Both Teams, Game
15 Washington (8) vs. L.A. Raiders (7), 1984
13 Dallas (9) vs. Baltimore (4), 1971
Pittsburgh (7) vs. Minnesota (6), 1975
12 In three games
Fewest Punts, Both Teams, Game
5 Denver (2) vs. N.Y. Giants (3), 1987
6 Oakland (3) vs. Philadelphia (3), 1981
7 In four games

Average Yardage
Highest Average, Game (4 punts)
48.50 Kansas City vs. Minnesota, 1970 (4-194)
46.25 San Francisco vs. Cincinnati, 1982 (4-185)
45.29 Kansas City vs. Green Bay, 1967 (7-317)
Lowest Average, Game (4 punts)
31.20 Washington vs. Miami, 1973 (5-156)
32.38 Washington vs. L.A. Raiders, 1984 (8-259)
32.40 Oakland vs. Minnesota, 1977 (5-162)

Punt Returns
Most Punt Returns, Game
6 Washington vs. Miami, 1983
5 By five teams
Fewest Punt Returns, Game
0 Minnesota vs. Miami, 1974
Buffalo vs. N.Y. Giants, 1991
1 By 11 teams
Most Punt Returns, Both Teams, Game
9 Pittsburgh (5) vs. Minnesota (4), 1975
8 Green Bay (5) vs. Oakland (3), 1968
Baltimore (5) vs. Dallas (3), 1971
Washington (6) vs. Miami (2), 1983
7 Green Bay (4) vs. Kansas City (3), 1967
Oakland (4) vs. Minnesota (3), 1977
San Francisco (5) vs. Miami (2), 1985
Fewest Punt Returns, Both Teams, Game
2 Dallas (1) vs. Miami (1), 1972
Denver (1) vs. N.Y. Giants (1), 1987
Buffalo (0) vs. N.Y. Giants (2), 1991
3 Kansas City (1) vs. Minnesota (2), 1970
Minnesota (0) vs. Miami (3), 1974
Washington (1) vs. Denver (2), 1988
4 L.A. Raiders (2) vs. Washington (2), 1984
Chicago (2) vs. New England (2), 1986

Yards Gained
Most Yards Gained, Game
56 San Francisco vs. Cincinnati, 1989
52 Washington vs. Miami, 1983
51 San Francisco vs. Miami, 1985

Fewest Yards Gained, Game
−1 Dallas vs. Miami, 1972
0 By six teams

Most Yards Gained, Both Teams, Game
74 Washington (52) vs. Miami (22), 1983
66 San Francisco (51) vs. Miami (15), 1985
61 San Francisco (56) vs. Cincinnati (5), 1989

Fewest Yards Gained, Both Teams, Game
13 Miami (4) vs. Washington (9), 1973
18 Kansas City (0) vs. Minnesota (18), 1970
Washington (0) vs. Denver (18), 1988
20 Dallas (−1) vs. Miami (21), 1972
Minnesota (0) vs. Miami (20), 1974

Average Return

Highest Average, Game (3 returns)
18.7 San Francisco vs. Cincinnati, 1989 (3-56)
12.7 San Francisco vs. Denver, 1990 (3-38)
10.8 Oakland vs. Minnesota, 1977 (4-43)

Touchdowns

Most Touchdowns, Game
None

Kickoff Returns

Most Kickoff Returns, Game
9 Denver vs. San Francisco, 1990
7 Oakland vs. Green Bay, 1968
Minnesota vs. Oakland, 1977
Cincinnati vs. San Francisco, 1982
Washington vs. L.A. Raiders, 1984
Miami vs. San Francisco, 1985
New England vs. Chicago, 1986
6 By seven teams

Fewest Kickoff Returns, Game
1 N.Y. Jets vs. Baltimore, 1969
L.A. Raiders vs. Washington, 1984
2 By six teams

Most Kickoff Returns, Both Teams, Game
12 Denver (9) vs. San Francisco (3), 1990
11 Los Angeles (6) vs. Pittsburgh (5), 1980
Miami (7) vs. San Francisco (4), 1985
New England (7) vs. Chicago (4), 1986
10 Oakland (7) vs. Green Bay (3), 1968

Fewest Kickoff Returns, Both Teams, Game
5 N.Y. Jets (1) vs. Baltimore (4), 1969
Miami (2) vs. Washington (3), 1973
6 In three games

Yards Gained

Most Yards Gained, Game
222 Miami vs. Washington, 1983
196 Denver vs. San Francisco, 1990
173 Denver vs. Dallas, 1978

Fewest Yards Gained, Game
17 L.A. Raiders vs. Washington, 1984
25 N.Y. Jets vs. Baltimore, 1969
32 Pittsburgh vs. Minnesota, 1975

Most Yards Gained, Both Teams, Game
279 Miami (222) vs. Washington (57), 1983
245 Denver (196) vs. San Francisco (49), 1990
231 Pittsburgh (162) vs. Los Angeles (79), 1980

Fewest Yards Gained, Both Teams, Game
78 Miami (33) vs. Washington (45), 1973
82 Pittsburgh (32) vs. Minnesota (50), 1975
92 San Francisco (40) vs. Cincinnati (52), 1982

Average Gain

Highest Average, Game (3 returns)
44.0 Cincinnati vs. San Francisco, 1989 (3-132)
37.0 Miami vs. Washington, 1983 (6-222)
32.4 Pittsburgh vs. Los Angeles, 1980 (5-162)

Touchdowns

Most Touchdowns, Game
1 Miami vs. Washington, 1983
Cincinnati vs. San Francisco, 1989

Penalties

Most Penalties, Game
12 Dallas vs. Denver, 1978
10 Dallas vs. Baltimore, 1971
9 Dallas vs. Pittsburgh, 1979

Fewest Penalties, Game
0 Miami vs. Dallas, 1972
Pittsburgh vs. Dallas, 1976
Denver vs. San Francisco, 1990
1 Green Bay vs. Oakland, 1968
Miami vs. Minnesota, 1974; vs. San Francisco, 1985
2 By four teams

Most Penalties, Both Teams, Game
20 Dallas (12) vs. Denver (8), 1978
16 Cincinnati (8) vs. San Francisco (8), 1982
14 Dallas (10) vs. Baltimore (4), 1971
Dallas (9) vs. Pittsburgh (5), 1979

Fewest Penalties, Both Teams, Game
2 Pittsburgh (0) vs. Dallas (2), 1976
3 Miami (0) vs. Dallas (3), 1972
Miami (1) vs. San Francisco (2), 1985
4 Denver (0) vs. San Francisco (4), 1990

Yards Penalized

Most Yards Penalized, Game
133 Dallas vs. Baltimore, 1971
122 Pittsburgh vs. Minnesota, 1975
94 Dallas vs. Denver, 1978

Fewest Yards Penalized, Game
0 Miami vs. Dallas, 1972
Pittsburgh vs. Dallas, 1976
Denver vs. San Francisco, 1990
4 Miami vs. Minnesota, 1974
10 Miami vs. San Francisco, 1985
San Francisco vs. Miami, 1985

Most Yards Penalized, Both Teams, Game
164 Dallas (133) vs. Baltimore (31), 1971
154 Dallas (94) vs. Denver (60), 1978
140 Pittsburgh (122) vs. Minnesota (18), 1975

Fewest Yards Penalized, Both Teams, Game
15 Miami (0) vs. Dallas (15), 1972
20 Pittsburgh (0) vs. Dallas (20), 1976
Miami (10) vs. San Francisco (10), 1985
38 Denver (0) vs. San Francisco (38), 1990

Fumbles

Most Fumbles, Game
6 Dallas vs. Denver, 1978
5 Baltimore vs. Dallas, 1971
4 By five teams

Fewest Fumbles, Game
0 By 10 teams

Most Fumbles, Both Teams, Game
10 Dallas (6) vs. Denver (4), 1978
8 Dallas (4) vs. Pittsburgh (4), 1976
7 Pittsburgh (4) vs. Minnesota (3), 1975
New England (4) vs. Chicago (3), 1986

Fewest Fumbles, Both Teams, Game
0 Los Angeles vs. Pittsburgh, 1980
1 Oakland (0) vs. Minnesota (1), 1977
Oakland (0) vs. Philadelphia (1), 1981
Denver (0) vs. Washington (1), 1988
N.Y. Giants (0) vs. Buffalo (1), 1991
2 In four games

Most Fumbles Lost, Game
4 Baltimore vs. Dallas, 1971
Denver vs. Dallas, 1978
New England vs. Chicago, 1986
2 In many games

Most Fumbles Lost, Both Teams, Game
6 Denver (4) vs. Dallas (2), 1978
New England (4) vs. Chicago (2), 1986
5 Baltimore (4) vs. Dallas (1), 1971
4 Minnesota (2) vs. Pittsburgh (2), 1975
Dallas (2) vs. Pittsburgh (2), 1979

Fewest Fumbles Lost, Both Teams, Game
0 Green Bay vs. Kansas City, 1967
Dallas vs. Pittsburgh, 1976
Los Angeles vs. Pittsburgh, 1980
Denver vs. N.Y. Giants, 1987
Denver vs. Washington, 1988
Buffalo vs. N.Y. Giants, 1991
1 Washington (0) vs. Miami (1), 1973
Miami (0) vs. Minnesota (1), 1974
Oakland (0) vs. Minnesota (1), 1977
Oakland (0) vs. Philadelphia (1), 1981
Washington (0) vs. Miami (1), 1983
Cincinnati (0) vs. San Francisco (1), 1989
2 In five games

Most Fumbles Recovered, Game
8 Dallas vs. Denver, 1978 (4 own, 4 opp)
5 Chicago vs. New England, 1986 (1 own, 4 opp)
4 Pittsburgh vs. Minnesota, 1975 (2 own, 2 opp)
Dallas vs. Pittsburgh, 1976 (4 own)

Turnovers

(Number of times losing the ball on interceptions and fumbles.)

Most Turnovers, Game
8 Denver vs. Dallas, 1978
7 Baltimore vs. Dallas, 1971
6 New England vs. Chicago, 1986

Fewest Turnovers, Game
0 Green Bay vs. Oakland, 1968
Miami vs. Minnesota, 1974
Pittsburgh vs. Dallas, 1976
Oakland vs. Minnesota, 1977; vs. Philadelphia, 1981
N.Y. Giants vs. Denver, 1987; vs. Buffalo, 1991
San Francisco vs. Denver, 1990
Buffalo vs. N.Y. Giants, 1991
1 By many teams

Most Turnovers, Both Teams, Game
11 Baltimore (7) vs. Dallas (4), 1971
10 Denver (8) vs. Dallas (2), 1978
8 New England (6) vs. Chicago (2), 1986

Fewest Turnovers, Both Teams, Game
0 Buffalo vs. N.Y. Giants, 1991
1 N.Y. Giants (0) vs. Denver (1), 1987
2 Green Bay (1) vs. Kansas City (1), 1967
Miami (0) vs. Minnesota (2), 1974
Cincinnati (1) vs. San Francisco (1), 1989

POSTSEASON GAME RECORDS

Compiled by Elias Sports Bureau

Throughout this all-time postseason record section, the following abbreviations are used to indicate various levels of postseason games:

SB Super Bowl (1966 to date)
AFC AFC Championship Game (1970 to date) or AFL Championship Game (1960-69)
NFC NFC Championship Game (1970 to date) or NFL Championship Game (1933-69)
AFC-D AFC Divisional Playoff Game (1970 to date), AFC Second-Round Playoff Game (1982), AFL Inter-Divisional Playoff Game (1969), or special playoff game to break tie for AFL Division Championship (1963, 1968)
NFC-D NFC Divisional Playoff Game (1970 to date), NFC Second-Round Playoff Game (1982), NFL Conference Championship Game (1967-69), or special playoff game to break tie for NFL Division or Conference Championship (1941, 1943, 1947, 1950, 1952, 1957, 1958, 1965)
AFC-FR AFC First-Round Playoff Game (1978 to date)
NFC-FR NFC First-Round Playoff Game (1978 to date)

Year references are to the season following which the postseason game occurred, even if the game was played in the next calendar year.

Postseason Game Composite Standings

	W	L	Pct.	Pts.	OP
Green Bay Packers	13	5	.722	416	259
Pittsburgh Steelers	16	9	.640	582	494
San Francisco 49ers	16	9	.640	607	452
Los Angeles Raiders*	20	13	.606	784	596
Detroit Lions	6	4	.600	221	208
Miami Dolphins	15	11	.577	586	528
Washington Redskins**	17	13	.567	599	557
Dallas Cowboys	20	16	.556	805	640
Chicago Bears	13	12	.520	516	473
Denver Broncos	8	8	.500	323	426
Indianapolis Colts***	8	8	.500	285	300
Kansas City Chiefs****	5	5	.500	175	199
New York Jets	5	5	.500	206	183
Philadelphia Eagles	7	8	.467	244	234
Minnesota Vikings	13	15	.464	518	570
Houston Oilers	8	10	.444	272	428
New York Giants	13	17	.433	509	539
Buffalo Bills	6	8	.429	309	293
Seattle Seahawks	3	4	.429	128	139
Cincinnati Bengals	5	7	.417	246	257
New England Patriots†	4	6	.400	195	258
Los Angeles Rams††	13	20	.394	501	697
Cleveland Browns	10	18	.357	567	650
San Diego Chargers†††	4	8	.333	230	279
Atlanta Falcons	1	3	.250	85	100
Tampa Bay Buccaneers	1	3	.250	41	94
Phoenix Cardinals††††	1	4	.200	81	134
New Orleans Saints	0	2	.000	16	60

** 24 games played when franchise was in Oakland (won 15, lost 9, 587 points scored, 435 points allowed).*
*** One game played when franchise was in Boston (lost 21-6).*
**** 15 games played when franchise was in Baltimore (won 8, lost 7, 264 points scored, 262 points allowed).*
***** One game played when franchise was Dallas Texans (won 20-17).*
†Two games played when franchise was in Boston (won 26-8, lost 51-10).
††One game played when franchise was in Cleveland (won 15-14).
†††One game played when franchise was in Los Angeles (lost 24-16).
††††Two games played when franchise was in Chicago (won 28-21, lost 7-0), three games played when franchise was in St. Louis (lost 30-14, lost 35-23, lost 41-16).

Individual Records

Service

Most Games, Career
27 D. D. Lewis, Dallas (SB-5, NFC-9, NFC-D 12, NFC-FR 1)
26 Larry Cole, Dallas (SB-5, NFC-8, NFC-D-12, NFC-FR 1)
25 Charlie Waters, Dallas (SB-5, NFC-9, NFC-D 10, NFC-FR 1)

Scoring

Points

Most Points, Career
115 George Blanda, Chi. Bears-Houston-Oakland, 19 games (49-pat, 22-fg)
102 Franco Harris, Pittsburgh, 19 games (17-td)
96 Matt Bahr, Pittsburgh-Cleveland-N.Y. Giants, 13 games (39-pat, 19-fg)

Most Points, Game
19 Pat Harder, NFC-D: Detroit vs. Los Angeles, 1952 (2-td, 4-pat, 1-fg)
Paul Hornung, NFC: Green Bay vs. N.Y. Giants, 1961 (1-td, 4-pat, 3-fg)
18 By 18 players

Touchdowns

Most Touchdowns, Career
17 Franco Harris, Pittsburgh, 19 games (16-r, 1-p)
12 John Riggins, Washington, 9 games (12-r)
John Stallworth, Pittsburgh, 18 games (12-p)
Jerry Rice, San Francisco, 11 games (12-p)
10 Fred Biletnikoff, Oakland, 19 games (10-p)
Larry Csonka, Miami, 12 games (9-r, 1-p)
Tony Dorsett, Dallas, 17 games (9-r, 1-p)
Marcus Allen, L.A. Raiders, 9 games (8-r, 2-p)

Most Touchdowns, Game
3 Andy Farkas, NFC-D: Washington vs. N.Y. Giants, 1943 (3-r)
Tom Fears, NFC-D: Los Angeles vs. Chi. Bears, 1950 (3-p)
Otto Graham, NFC: Cleveland vs. Detroit, 1954 (3-r)
Gary Collins, NFC: Cleveland vs. Baltimore, 1964 (3-p)
Craig Baynham, NFC-D: Dallas vs. Cleveland, 1967 (2-r, 1-p)
Fred Biletnikoff, AFC-D: Oakland vs. Kansas City, 1968 (3-p)
Tom Matte, NFC: Baltimore vs. Cleveland, 1968 (3-r)
Larry Schreiber, NFC-D: San Francisco vs. Dallas, 1972 (3-r)
Larry Csonka, AFC: Miami vs. Oakland, 1973 (3-r)
Franco Harris, AFC-D: Pittsburgh vs. Buffalo, 1974 (3-r)
Preston Pearson, NFC: Dallas vs. Los Angeles, 1975 (3-p)
Dave Casper, AFC-D: Oakland vs. Baltimore, 1977 (OT) (3-p)
Alvin Garrett, NFC-FR: Washington vs. Detroit, 1982 (3-p)
John Riggins, NFC-D: Washington vs. L.A. Rams, 1983 (3-r)
Roger Craig, SB: San Francisco vs. Miami, 1984 (1-r, 2-p)
Jerry Rice, NFC-D: San Francisco vs. Minnesota, 1988 (3-p)
Jerry Rice, SB: San Francisco vs. Denver, 1989 (3-p)
Kenneth Davis, AFC: Buffalo vs. L.A. Raiders, 1990 (3-r)

Most Consecutive Games Scoring Touchdowns
8 John Stallworth, Pittsburgh, 1978-83
7 John Riggins, Washington, 1982-84
Marcus Allen, L.A. Raiders, 1982-85
5 Duane Thomas, Dallas, 1970-71
Franco Harris, Pittsburgh, 1974-75
Franco Harris, Pittsburgh, 1977-79
James Lofton, Green Bay-Buffalo, 1982-90

Points After Touchdown

Most Points After Touchdown, Career
49 George Blanda, Chi. Bears-Houston-Oakland, 19 games (49 att)
41 Rafael Septien, L.A. Rams-Dallas, 15 games (41 att)
39 Matt Bahr, Pittsburgh-Cleveland-N.Y. Giants, 13 games (39 att)

Most Points After Touchdown, Game
8 Lou Groza, NFC: Cleveland vs. Detroit, 1954 (8 att)
Jim Martin, NFC: Detroit vs. Cleveland, 1957 (8 att)
George Blanda, AFC-D: Oakland vs. Houston, 1969 (8 att)
7 Danny Villanueva, NFC-D: Dallas vs. Cleveland, 1967 (7 att)
Raul Allegre, NFC-D: N.Y. Giants vs. San Francisco, 1986
Mike Cofer, SB: San Francisco vs. Denver, 1989 (8 att)
6 George Blair, AFC: San Diego vs. Boston, 1963 (6 att)
Mark Moseley, NFC-D: Washington vs. L.A. Rams, 1983 (6 att)
Uwe von Schamann, AFC: Miami vs. Pittsburgh, 1984 (6 att)
Ali Haji-Sheikh, SB: Washington vs. Denver, 1987 (6 att)
Scott Norwood, AFC: Buffalo vs. L.A. Raiders, 1990 (7 att)

Most Points After Touchdown, No Misses, Career
49 George Blanda, Chi. Bears-Houston-Oakland, 19 games
41 Rafael Septien, L.A. Rams-Dallas, 14 games
39 Matt Bahr, Pittsburgh-Cleveland-N.Y. Giants, 13 games

Field Goals

Most Field Goals Attempted, Career
39 George Blanda, Chi. Bears-Houston-Oakland, 19 games
31 Mark Moseley, Washington-Cleveland, 11 games
27 Roy Gerela, Houston-Pittsburgh, 15 games

Most Field Goals Attempted, Game
6 George Blanda, AFC: Oakland vs. Houston, 1967
David Ray, NFC-D: Los Angeles vs. Dallas, 1973
Mark Moseley, AFC-D: Cleveland vs. N.Y. Jets, 1986 (OT)
Matt Bahr, NFC: N.Y. Giants vs. San Francisco, 1990
5 Jerry Kramer, NFC: Green Bay vs. N.Y. Giants, 1962
Gino Cappelletti, AFC-D: Boston vs. Buffalo, 1963
Pete Gogolak, AFC: Buffalo vs. San Diego, 1965
Jan Stenerud, AFC-D: Kansas City vs. N.Y. Jets, 1969
George Blanda, AFC-D: Oakland vs. Pittsburgh, 1973
Ed Murray, NFC-D: Detroit vs. San Francisco, 1983
Mark Moseley, NFC: Washington vs. San Francisco, 1983
Tony Franklin, AFC-FR: New England vs. N.Y. Jets, 1985
Tony Zendejas, AFC-FR: Houston vs. Seattle, 1987 (OT)
Chuck Nelson, NFC-D: Minnesota vs. San Francisco, 1987
Luis Zendejas, NFC-D: Philadelphia vs. Chicago, 1988
4 By many players

Most Field Goals, Career
22 George Blanda, Chi. Bears-Houston-Oakland, 19 games
20 Toni Fritsch, Dallas-Houston, 14 games
19 Matt Bahr, Pittsburgh-Cleveland-N.Y. Giants, 13 games

Most Field Goals, Game
5 Chuck Nelson, NFC-D: Minnesota vs. San Francisco, 1987
Matt Bahr, NFC: N.Y. Giants vs. San Francisco, 1990
4 Gino Cappelletti, AFC-D: Boston vs. Buffalo, 1963
George Blanda, AFC: Oakland vs. Houston, 1967
Don Chandler, SB: Green Bay vs. Oakland, 1967
Curt Knight, NFC: Washington vs. Dallas, 1972
George Blanda, AFC-D: Oakland vs. Pittsburgh, 1973
Ray Wersching, SB: San Francisco vs. Cincinnati, 1981
Tony Franklin, AFC-FR: New England vs. N.Y. Jets, 1985
Jess Atkinson, NFC-FR: Washington vs. L.A. Rams, 1986
Luis Zendejas, NFC-D: Philadelphia vs. Chicago, 1988
Gary Anderson, AFC-FR: Pittsburgh vs. Houston, 1989 (OT)
3 By many players

Most Consecutive Field Goals
15 Rafael Septien, Dallas, 1978-82
9 Chuck Nelson, Minnesota, 1987
8 Tony Fritsch, Houston, 1978-79

Longest Field Goal
58 Pete Stoyanovich, AFC-FR: Miami vs. Kansas City, 1990
54 Ed Murray, NFC-D: Detroit vs. San Francisco, 1983
52 Lou Groza, NFC: Cleveland vs. Los Angeles, 1951
Curt Knight, NFC-D: Washington vs. Minnesota, 1973
Matt Bahr, AFC-FR: Cleveland vs. L.A. Raiders, 1982

Safeties
Most Safeties, Game
1 Bill Willis, NFC-D: Cleveland vs. N.Y. Giants, 1950
Carl Eller, NFC-D: Minnesota vs. Los Angeles, 1969
George Andrie, NFC-D: Dallas vs. Detroit, 1970
Alan Page, NFC-D: Minnesota vs. Dallas, 1971
Dwight White, SB: Pittsburgh vs. Minnesota, 1974
Reggie Harrison, SB: Pittsburgh vs. Dallas, 1975
Jim Jensen, NFC-D: Dallas vs. Los Angeles, 1976
Ted Washington, AFC: Houston vs. Pittsburgh, 1978
Randy White, NFC-D: Dallas vs. Los Angeles, 1979
Henry Waechter, SB: Chicago vs. New England, 1985
Rulon Jones, AFC-FR: Denver vs. New England, 1986
George Martin, SB: N.Y. Giants vs. Denver, 1986
D.D. Hoggard, AFC: Cleveland vs. Denver, 1987
Bruce Smith, SB: Buffalo vs. N.Y. Giants, 1990

Rushing
Attempts
Most Attempts, Career
400 Franco Harris, Pittsburgh, 19 games
302 Tony Dorsett, Dallas, 17 games
251 John Riggins, Washington, 9 games
Most Attempts, Game
38 Ricky Bell, NFC-D: Tampa Bay vs. Philadelphia, 1979
John Riggins, SB: Washington vs. Miami, 1982
37 Lawrence McCutcheon, NFC-D: Los Angeles vs. St. Louis, 1975
John Riggins, NFC-D: Washington vs. Minnesota, 1982
36 John Riggins, NFC: Washington vs. Dallas, 1982
John Riggins, NFC: Washington vs. San Francisco, 1983

Yards Gained
Most Yards Gained, Career
1,556 Franco Harris, Pittsburgh, 19 games
1,383 Tony Dorsett, Dallas, 17 games
996 John Riggins, Washington, 9 games
Most Yards Gained, Game
248 Eric Dickerson, NFC-D: L.A. Rams vs. Dallas, 1985
206 Keith Lincoln, AFC: San Diego vs. Boston, 1963
204 Timmy Smith, SB: Washington vs. Denver, 1987
Most Games, 100 or More Yards Rushing, Career
6 John Riggins, Washington, 9 games
5 Franco Harris, Pittsburgh, 19 games
Marcus Allen, L.A. Raiders, 9 games
4 Larry Csonka, Miami, 12 games
Chuck Foreman, Minnesota, 13 games
Most Consecutive Games, 100 or More Yards Rushing
6 John Riggins, Washington, 1982-83
3 Larry Csonka, Miami, 1973-74
Franco Harris, Pittsburgh, 1974-75
Marcus Allen, L.A. Raiders, 1983
Thurman Thomas, Buffalo, 1990 (current)
2 By many players
Longest Run From Scrimmage
80 Roger Craig, NFC-D: San Francisco vs. Minnesota, 1988 (TD)
74 Marcus Allen, SB: L.A. Raiders vs. Washington, 1983 (TD)
71 Hugh McElhenny, NFC-D: San Francisco vs. Detroit, 1957
James Lofton, NFC-D: Green Bay vs. Dallas, 1982 (TD)

Average Gain
Highest Average Gain, Career (50 attempts)
6.71 Timmy Smith, Washington, 3 games (51-342)
6.67 Paul Lowe, L.A. Chargers-San Diego, 5 games (57-380)
5.76 Marcus Allen, L.A. Raiders, 9 games (160-922)
Highest Average Gain, Game (10 attempts)
15.90 Elmer Angsman, NFC: Chi. Cardinals vs. Philadelphia, 1947 (10-159)
15.85 Keith Lincoln, AFC: San Diego vs. Boston, 1963 (13-206)
10.90 Bill Osmanski, NFC: Chi. Bears vs. Washington, 1940 (10-109)

Touchdowns
Most Touchdowns, Career
16 Franco Harris, Pittsburgh, 19 games
12 John Riggins, Washington, 9 games
9 Larry Csonka, Miami, 12 games
Tony Dorsett, Dallas, 17 games
Most Touchdowns, Game
3 Andy Farkas, NFC-D: Washington vs. N.Y. Giants, 1943
Otto Graham, NFC: Cleveland vs. Detroit, 1954
Tom Matte, NFC: Baltimore vs. Cleveland, 1968
Larry Schreiber, NFC-D: San Francisco vs. Dallas, 1972
Larry Csonka, AFC: Miami vs. Oakland, 1973
Franco Harris, AFC-D: Pittsburgh vs. Buffalo, 1974
John Riggins, NFC-D: Washington vs. L.A. Rams, 1983
Kenneth Davis, AFC: Buffalo vs. L.A. Raiders, 1990
Most Consecutive Games Rushing for Touchdowns
7 John Riggins, Washington, 1982-84
5 Franco Harris, Pittsburgh, 1974-75
Franco Harris, Pittsburgh, 1977-79
3 By many players

Passing
Pass Rating
Highest Pass Rating, Career (100 attempts)
104.8 Bart Starr, Green Bay, 10 games
98.2 Joe Montana, San Francisco, 19 games
93.3 Ken Anderson, Cincinnati, 6 games

Attempts
Most Passes Attempted, Career
593 Joe Montana, San Francisco, 19 games
456 Terry Bradshaw, Pittsburgh, 19 games
410 Roger Staubach, Dallas, 20 games
Most Passes Attempted, Game
64 Bernie Kosar, AFC-D: Cleveland vs. N.Y. Jets, 1986 (OT)
54 Randall Cunningham, NFC-D: Philadelphia vs. Chicago, 1988
Jim Kelly, AFC-D: Buffalo vs. Cleveland, 1989
53 Dan Fouts, AFC-D: San Diego vs. Miami, 1981 (OT)
Danny White, NFC-FR: Dallas vs. L.A. Rams, 1983

Completions
Most Passes Completed, Career
375 Joe Montana, San Francisco, 19 games
261 Terry Bradshaw, Pittsburgh, 19 games
223 Roger Staubach, Dallas, 20 games
Most Passes Completed, Game
33 Dan Fouts, AFC-D: San Diego vs. Miami, 1981 (OT)
Bernie Kosar, AFC-D: Cleveland vs. N.Y. Jets, 1986 (OT)
32 Neil Lomax, NFC-FR: St. Louis vs. Green Bay, 1982
Danny White, NFC-FR: Dallas vs. L.A. Rams, 1983
29 Don Strock, AFC-D: Miami vs. San Diego, 1981 (OT)
Dan Marino, SB: Miami vs. San Francisco, 1984
Warren Moon, AFC-FR: Houston vs. Pittsburgh, 1989 (OT)

Completion Percentage
Highest Completion Percentage, Career (100 attempts)
66.3 Ken Anderson, Cincinnati, 6 games (166-110)
63.2 Joe Montana, San Francisco, 19 games (593-375)
61.2 Dan Pastorini, Houston, 5 games (116-71)
Highest Completion Percentage, Game (15 completions)
88.0 Phil Simms, SB: N.Y. Giants vs. Denver, 1986 (25-22)
86.7 Joe Montana, NFC: San Francisco vs. L.A. Rams, 1989 (30-26)
84.2 David Woodley, AFC-FR: Miami vs. New England, 1982 (19-16)

Yards Gained
Most Yards Gained, Career
4,758 Joe Montana, San Francisco, 19 games
3,833 Terry Bradshaw, Pittsburgh, 19 games
2,791 Roger Staubach, Dallas, 20 games
Most Yards Gained, Game
489 Bernie Kosar, AFC-D: Cleveland vs. N.Y. Jets, 1986 (OT)
433 Dan Fouts, AFC-D: San Diego vs. Miami, 1981 (OT)
421 Dan Marino, AFC: Miami vs. Pittsburgh, 1984
Most Games, 300 or More Yards Passing, Career
5 Dan Fouts, San Diego, 7 games
Joe Montana, San Francisco, 19 games
4 Dan Marino, Miami, 6 games
3 Terry Bradshaw, Pittsburgh, 19 games
Danny White, Dallas, 17 games
Most Consecutive Games, 300 or More Yards Passing
4 Dan Fouts, San Diego, 1979-81
3 Jim Kelly, Buffalo 1989-90
2 Daryle Lamonica, Oakland, 1968
Ken Anderson, Cincinnati, 1981-82
Terry Bradshaw, Pittsburgh, 1979-82
Joe Montana, San Francisco, 1983-84
Dan Marino, Miami, 1984
Longest Pass Completion
93 Daryle Lamonica (to Dubenion), AFC-D: Buffalo vs. Boston, 1963 (TD)
88 George Blanda (to Cannon), AFC: Houston vs. L.A. Chargers, 1960 (TD)
86 Don Meredith (to Hayes), NFC-D: Dallas vs. Cleveland, 1967 (TD)

Average Gain
Highest Average Gain, Career (100 attempts)
8.45 Joe Theismann, Washington, 10 games (211-1,782)
8.43 Jim Plunkett, Oakland-L.A. Raiders, 10 games (272-2,293)
8.41 Terry Bradshaw, Pittsburgh, 19 games (456-3,833)
Highest Average Gain, Game (20 attempts)
14.71 Terry Bradshaw, SB: Pittsburgh vs. Los Angeles, 1979 (21-309)
13.33 Bob Waterfield, NFC-D: Los Angeles vs. Chi. Bears, 1950 (21-280)
13.16 Dan Marino, AFC: Miami vs. Pittsburgh, 1984 (32-421)

Touchdowns
Most Touchdown Passes, Career
39 Joe Montana, San Francisco, 19 games
30 Terry Bradshaw, Pittsburgh, 19 games
24 Roger Staubach, Dallas, 20 games
Most Touchdown Passes, Game
6 Daryle Lamonica, AFC-D: Oakland vs. Houston, 1969
5 Sid Luckman, NFC: Chi. Bears vs. Washington, 1943
Daryle Lamonica, AFC-D: Oakland vs. Kansas City, 1968
Joe Montana, SB: San Francisco vs. Denver, 1989
4 Otto Graham, NFC: Cleveland vs. Los Angeles, 1950
Tobin Rote, NFC: Detroit vs. Cleveland, 1957
Bart Starr, NFC: Green Bay vs. Dallas, 1966
Ken Stabler, AFC-D: Oakland vs. Miami, 1974
Roger Staubach, NFC: Dallas vs. Los Angeles, 1975
Terry Bradshaw, SB: Pittsburgh vs. Dallas, 1978
Don Strock, AFC-D: Miami vs. San Diego, 1981 (OT)
Lynn Dickey, NFC-FR: Green Bay vs. St. Louis, 1982
Dan Marino, AFC: Miami vs. Pittsburgh, 1984
Doug Williams, SB: Washington vs. Denver, 1987
Jim Kelly, AFC-D: Buffalo vs. Cleveland, 1989
Joe Montana, NFC-D: San Francisco vs. Minnesota, 1989
Most Consecutive Games, Touchdown Passes
10 Ken Stabler, Oakland, 1973-77
9 John Elway, Denver, 1984-89
8 Terry Bradshaw, Pittsburgh, 1977-82
Joe Montana, San Francisco, 1981-84
Joe Montana, San Francisco, 1988-90 (current)

Had Intercepted
Lowest Percentage, Passes Had Intercepted, Career (100 attempts)
1.41 Bart Starr, Green Bay, 10 games (213-3)
1.75 Phil Simms, N.Y. Giants, 8 games (228-4)
3.07 Jim McMahon, Chicago-Philadelphia, 7 games (130-4)
Most Attempts Without Interception, Game
48 Warren Moon, AFC-FR: Houston vs. Pittsburgh, 1989 (OT)
47 Daryle Lamonica, AFC: Oakland vs. N.Y. Jets, 1968
42 Dan Fouts, AFC-FR: San Diego vs. Pittsburgh, 1982
Most Passes Had Intercepted, Career
26 Terry Bradshaw, Pittsburgh, 19 games
19 Roger Staubach, Dallas, 20 games
17 George Blanda, Chi. Bears-Houston-Oakland, 19 games
Fran Tarkenton, Minnesota, 11 games
Joe Montana, San Francisco, 19 games
Most Passes Had Intercepted, Game
6 Frank Filchock, NFC: N.Y. Giants vs. Chi. Bears, 1946
Bobby Layne, NFC: Detroit vs. Cleveland, 1954
Norm Van Brocklin, NFC: Los Angeles vs. Cleveland, 1955
5 Frank Filchock, NFC: Washington vs. Chi. Bears, 1940
George Blanda, AFC: Houston vs. San Diego, 1961
George Blanda, AFC: Houston vs. Dall. Texans, 1962 (OT)
Y.A. Tittle, NFC: N.Y. Giants vs. Chicago, 1963
Mike Phipps, AFC-D: Cleveland vs. Miami, 1972
Dan Pastorini, AFC: Houston vs. Pittsburgh, 1978
Dan Fouts, AFC-D: San Diego vs. Houston, 1979
Tommy Kramer, NFC-D: Minnesota vs. Philadelphia, 1980
Dan Fouts, AFC-D: San Diego vs. Miami, 1982
Richard Todd, AFC: N.Y. Jets vs Miami, 1982
Gary Danielson, NFC-D: Detroit vs. San Francisco, 1983
Jay Schroeder, AFC: L.A. Raiders vs. Buffalo, 1990
4 By many players

Pass Receiving
Receptions
Most Receptions, Career
73 Cliff Branch, Oakland-L.A. Raiders, 22 games
70 Fred Biletnikoff, Oakland, 19 games
67 Drew Pearson, Dallas, 22 games
Most Receptions, Game
13 Kellen Winslow, AFC-D: San Diego vs. Miami, 1981 (OT)
Thurman Thomas, AFC-D: Buffalo vs. Cleveland, 1989
12 Raymond Berry, NFC: Baltimore vs. N.Y. Giants, 1958
11 Dante Lavelli, NFC: Cleveland vs. Los Angeles, 1950
Dan Ross, SB: Cincinnati vs. San Francisco, 1981
Franco Harris, AFC-FR: Pittsburgh vs. San Diego, 1982
Steve Watson, AFC-D: Denver vs. Pittsburgh, 1984
John L. Williams, AFC-D: Seattle vs. Cincinnati, 1988
Jerry Rice, SB: San Francisco vs. Cincinnati, 1988
Ernest Givins, AFC-FR: Houston vs. Pittsburgh, 1989 (OT)
Most Consecutive Games, Pass Receptions
22 Drew Pearson, Dallas, 1973-83
18 Paul Warfield, Cleveland-Miami, 1964-74
Cliff Branch, Oakland-L.A. Raiders, 1974-83
17 John Stallworth, Pittsburgh, 1974-84

Yards Gained
Most Yards Gained, Career
1,289 Cliff Branch, Oakland-L.A. Raiders, 22 games
1,167 Fred Biletnikoff, Oakland, 19 games
1,121 Paul Warfield, Cleveland-Miami, 18 games
Most Yards Gained, Game
227 Anthony Carter, NFC-D: Minnesota vs. San Francisco, 1987
215 Jerry Rice, SB: San Francisco vs. Cincinnati, 1988
198 Tom Fears, NFC-D: Los Angeles vs. Chi. Bears, 1950
Most Games, 100 or More Yards Receiving, Career
5 John Stallworth, Pittsburgh, 18 games
4 Fred Biletnikoff, Oakland, 19 games
Dwight Clark, San Francisco, 7 games
Jerry Rice, San Francisco, 11 games
3 Tom Fears, L.A. Rams, 6 games
Cliff Branch, Oakland-L.A. Raiders, 22 games
Tony Nathan, Miami, 10 games
Mark Duper, Miami, 8 games
Art Monk, Washington, 10 games
James Lofton, Green Bay-Buffalo, 6 games
Most Consecutive Games, 100 or More Yards Receiving, Career
3 Tom Fears, Los Angeles, 1950-51
Jerry Rice, San Francisco, 1988-89
2 Lenny Moore, Baltimore, 1958-59
Fred Biletnikoff, Oakland, 1968
Paul Warfield, Miami, 1971
Charlie Joiner, San Diego, 1981
Dwight Clark, San Francisco, 1981
Cris Collinsworth, Cincinnati, 1981-82
John Stallworth, Pittsburgh, 1979-82
Wesley Walker, N.Y. Jets, 1982
Charlie Brown, Washington, 1983
Steve Largent, Seattle, 1984-87
Andre Reed, Buffalo, 1989-90
James Lofton, Buffalo, 1990
Longest Reception
93 Elbert Dubenion (from Lamonica), AFC-D: Buffalo vs. Boston, 1963 (TD)
88 Billy Cannon (from Blanda), AFC: Houston vs. L.A. Chargers, 1960 (TD)
86 Bob Hayes (from Meredith), NFC: Dallas vs. Cleveland, 1967 (TD)

Average Gain
Highest Average Gain, Career (20 receptions)
24.3 Willie Gault, Chicago-L.A. Raiders, 9 games (20-486)
22.9 James Lofton, Green Bay-Buffalo, 6 games (24-550)
22.8 Harold Jackson, L.A. Rams-New England-Minnesota-Seattle, 14 games (24-548)
Highest Average Gain, Game (3 receptions)
46.3 Harold Jackson, NFC: Los Angeles vs. Minnesota, 1974 (3-139)
42.7 Billy Cannon, AFC: Houston vs. L.A. Chargers, 1960 (3-128)
42.0 Lenny Moore, NFC: Baltimore vs. N.Y. Giants, 1959 (3-126)

Touchdowns
Most Touchdowns, Career
12 John Stallworth, Pittsburgh, 18 games
Jerry Rice, San Francisco, 11 games
10 Fred Biletnikoff, Oakland, 19 games
9 Lynn Swann, Pittsburgh, 16 games
Most Touchdowns, Game
3 Tom Fears, NFC-D: Los Angeles vs. Chi. Bears, 1950
Gary Collins, NFC: Cleveland vs. Baltimore, 1964
Fred Biletnikoff, AFC-D: Oakland vs. Kansas City, 1968
Preston Pearson, NFC: Dallas vs. Los Angeles, 1975
Dave Casper, AFC-D: Oakland vs. Baltimore, 1977 (OT)
Alvin Garrett, NFC-FR: Washington vs. Detroit, 1982
Jerry Rice, NFC-D: San Francisco vs. Minnesota, 1988
Jerry Rice, SB: San Francisco vs. Denver, 1989
Most Consecutive Games, Touchdown Passes Caught
8 John Stallworth, Pittsburgh, 1978-83
5 James Lofton, Green Bay-Buffalo, 1982-90
4 Lynn Swann, Pittsburgh, 1978-79
Harold Carmichael, Philadelphia, 1978-80
Fred Solomon, San Francisco, 1983-84
Jerry Rice, San Francisco, 1988-89
John Taylor, San Francisco, 1988-89

Interceptions By
Most Interceptions, Career
9 Charlie Waters, Dallas, 25 games
Bill Simpson, Los Angeles-Buffalo, 11 games
8 Lester Hayes, Oakland-L.A. Raiders, 13 games
Ronnie Lott, San Francisco, 19 games
7 Willie Brown, Oakland, 17 games
Dennis Thurman, Dallas, 14 games
Most Interceptions, Game
4 Vernon Perry, AFC-D: Houston vs. San Diego, 1979
3 Joe Laws, NFC: Green Bay vs. N.Y. Giants, 1944
Charlie Waters, NFC-D: Dallas vs. Chicago, 1977
Rod Martin, SB: Oakland vs. Philadelphia, 1980
Dennis Thurman, NFC-D: Dallas vs. Green Bay, 1982
A.J. Duhe, AFC: Miami vs. N.Y. Jets, 1982
2 By many players
Most Consecutive Games, Interceptions
3 Warren Lahr, Cleveland, 1950-51
Ken Gorgal, Cleveland, 1950-53
Joe Schmidt, Detroit, 1954-57
Emmitt Thomas, Kansas City, 1969
Mel Renfro, Dallas, 1970
Rick Volk, Baltimore, 1970-71
Mike Wagner, Pittsburgh, 1975-76
Randy Hughes, Dallas, 1977-78
Vernon Perry, Houston, 1979-80
Lester Hayes, Oakland, 1980
Gerald Small, Miami, 1982
Lester Hayes, L.A. Raiders, 1982-83
Fred Marion, New England, 1985
John Harris, Seattle-Minnesota, 1984-87
Felix Wright, Cleveland, 1987-88

Yards Gained
Most Yards Gained, Career
196 Willie Brown, Oakland, 17 games
152 Ronnie Lott, San Francisco, 19 games
151 Glen Edwards, Pittsburgh-San Diego, 17 games
Most Yards Gained, Game
98 Darrol Ray, AFC-FR: N.Y. Jets vs. Cincinnati, 1982
94 LeRoy Irvin, NFC-FR: L.A. Rams vs. Dallas, 1983
88 Walt Sumner, NFC-D: Cleveland vs. Dallas, 1969
Longest Return
98 Darrol Ray, AFC-FR: N.Y. Jets vs. Cincinnati, 1982 (TD)
94 LeRoy Irvin, NFC-FR: L.A. Rams vs. Dallas, 1983
88 Walt Sumner, NFC-D: Cleveland vs. Dallas, 1969 (TD)

Touchdowns
Most Touchdowns, Career
3 Willie Brown, Oakland, 17 games
2 Lester Hayes, Oakland-L.A. Raiders, 13 games
Ronnie Lott, San Francisco, 19 games
Most Touchdowns, Game
1 By 46 players

Punting
Most Punts, Career
111 Ray Guy, Oakland-L.A. Raiders, 22 games
84 Danny White, Dallas, 18 games
73 Mike Eischeid, Oakland-Minnesota, 14 games
Most Punts, Game
14 Dave Jennings, AFC-D: N.Y. Jets vs. Cleveland, 1986 (OT)
12 David Lee, AFC-D: Baltimore vs. Oakland, 1977 (OT)
11 Ken Strong, NFC: N.Y. Giants vs. Chi. Bears, 1933
Jim Norton, AFC: Houston vs. Oakland, 1967
Dale Hatcher, NFC: L.A. Rams vs. Chicago, 1985
Longest Punt
76 Ed Danowski, NFC: N.Y. Giants vs. Detroit, 1935
72 Charlie Conerly, NFC-D: N.Y. Giants vs. Cleveland, 1950
71 Ray Guy, AFC: Oakland vs. San Diego, 1980

Average Yardage
Highest Average, Career (20 punts)
44.5 Rich Camarillo, New England, 6 games (35-1,559)

44.4 Lee Johnson, Cleveland-Cincinnati, 7 games (28-1,244)
43.4 Jerrel Wilson, Kansas City-New England, 8 games (43-1,866)

Highest Average, Game (4 punts)
56.0 Ray Guy, AFC: Oakland vs. San Diego, 1980 (4-224)
52.5 Sammy Baugh, NFC: Washington vs. Chi. Bears, 1942 (6-315)
51.6 Lee Johnson, AFC-D: Cincinnati vs. L.A. Raiders, 1990 (5-258)

Punt Returns

Most Punt Returns, Career
25 Theo Bell, Pittsburgh-Tampa Bay, 10 games
21 Gerald McNeil, Cleveland-Houston, 8 games
19 Willie Wood, Green Bay, 10 games
Butch Johnson, Dallas-Denver, 18 games
Phil McConkey, N.Y. Giants, 5 games

Most Punt Returns, Game
7 Ron Gardin, AFC-D: Baltimore vs. Cincinnati, 1970
Carl Roaches, AFC-FR: Houston vs. Oakland, 1980
Gerald McNeil, AFC-D: Cleveland vs. N.Y. Jets, 1986 (OT)
Phil McConkey, NFC-D: N.Y. Giants vs. San Francisco, 1986
6 George McAfee, NFC-D: Chi. Bears vs. Los Angeles, 1950
Eddie Brown, NFC-D: Washington vs. Minnesota, 1976
Theo Bell, AFC: Pittsburgh vs. Houston, 1978
Eddie Brown, NFC: Los Angeles vs. Tampa Bay, 1979
John Sciarra, NFC: Philadelphia vs. Dallas, 1980
Kurt Sohn, AFC: N.Y. Jets vs. Miami, 1982
Mike Nelms, SB: Washington vs. Miami, 1982
Anthony Carter, NFC-FR: Minnesota vs. New Orleans, 1987
5 By many players

Yards Gained

Most Yards Gained, Career
237 Anthony Carter, Minnesota, 6 games
221 Neal Colzie, Oakland-Miami-Tampa Bay, 10 games
211 Gerald McNeil, Cleveland-Houston, 8 games

Most Yards Gained, Game
143 Anthony Carter, NFC-FR: Minnesota vs. New Orleans, 1987
141 Bob Hayes, NFC-D: Dallas vs. Cleveland, 1967
102 Charley Trippi, NFC: Chi. Cardinals vs. Philadelphia, 1947

Longest Return
84 Anthony Carter, NFC-FR: Minnesota vs. New Orleans, 1987 (TD)
81 Hugh Gallarneau, NFC-D: Chi. Bears vs. Green Bay, 1941 (TD)
79 Bosh Pritchard, NFC-D: Philadelphia vs. Pittsburgh, 1947 (TD)

Average Yardage

Highest Average, Career (10 returns)
15.8 Anthony Carter, Minnesota, 6 games (15-237)
12.6 Bob Hayes, Dallas, 15 games (12-151)
12.4 Mike Fuller, San Diego-Cincinnati, 7 games (13-161)

Highest Average Gain, Game (3 returns)
47.0 Bob Hayes, NFC-D: Dallas vs. Cleveland, 1967 (3-141)
29.0 George (Butch) Byrd, AFC: Buffalo vs. San Diego, 1965 (3-87)
25.3 Bosh Pritchard, NFC-D: Philadelphia vs. Pittsburgh, 1947 (4-101)

Touchdowns

Most Touchdowns
1 Hugh Gallarneau, NFC-D: Chicago Bears vs. Green Bay, 1941
Bosh Pritchard, NFC-D: Philadelphia vs. Pittsburgh, 1947
Charley Trippi, NFC: Chicago Cardinals vs. Philadelphia, 1947
Verda (Vitamin T) Smith, NFC-D: Los Angeles vs. Detroit, 1952
George (Butch) Byrd, AFC: Buffalo vs. San Diego, 1965
Golden Richards, NFC: Dallas vs. Minnesota, 1973
Wes Chandler, AFC-D: San Diego vs. Miami, 1981 (OT)
Shaun Gayle, NFC-D: Chicago vs. N.Y. Giants, 1985
Anthony Carter, NFC-FR: Minnesota vs. New Orleans, 1987
Darrell Green, NFC-D: Washington vs. Chicago, 1987

Kickoff Returns

Most Kickoff Returns, Career
29 Fulton Walker, Miami-L.A. Raiders, 10 games
21 Ken Bell, Denver, 9 games
19 Preston Pearson, Baltimore-Pittsburgh-Dallas, 22 games

Most Kickoff Returns, Game
8 Marc Logan, AFC-D: Miami vs. Buffalo, 1990
7 Don Bingham, NFC: Chi. Bears vs. N.Y. Giants, 1956
Reggie Brown, NFC-FR: Atlanta vs. Minnesota, 1982
David Verser, AFC-FR: Cincinnati vs. N.Y. Jets, 1982
Del Rodgers, NFC-D: Green Bay vs. Dallas, 1982
Henry Ellard, NFC-D: L.A. Rams vs. Washington, 1983
Stephen Starring, SB: New England vs. Chicago, 1985
6 By many players

Yards Gained

Most Yards Gained, Career
677 Fulton Walker, Miami-L.A. Raiders, 10 games
481 Carl Garrett, Oakland, 5 games
458 Cullen Bryant, L.A. Rams-Seattle, 19 games

Most Yards Gained, Game
190 Fulton Walker, SB: Miami vs. Washington, 1982
170 Les (Speedy) Duncan, NFC-D: Washington vs. San Francisco, 1971
169 Carl Garrett, AFC-D: Oakland vs. Baltimore, 1977 (OT)

Longest Return
98 Fulton Walker, SB: Miami vs. Washington, 1982 (TD)
97 Vic Washington, NFC-D: San Francisco vs. Dallas, 1972 (TD)
93 Stanford Jennings, SB: Cincinnati vs. San Francisco, 1988 (TD)

Average Yardage

Highest Average, Career (10 returns)
30.1 Carl Garrett, Oakland, 5 games (16-481)
27.9 George Atkinson, Oakland, 16 games (12-335)
27.7 Eric Metcalf, Cleveland, 2 games (10-277)

Highest Average, Game (3 returns)
56.7 Les (Speedy) Duncan, NFC-D: Washington vs. San Francisco, 1971 (3-170)
51.3 Ed Podolak, AFC-D: Kansas City vs. Miami, 1971 (OT) (3-154)
49.0 Les (Speedy) Duncan, AFC: San Diego vs. Buffalo, 1964 (3-147)

Touchdowns

Most Touchdowns
1 Vic Washington, NFC-D: San Francisco vs. Dallas, 1972
Nat Moore, AFC-D: Miami vs. Oakland, 1974
Marshall Johnson, AFC-D: Baltimore vs. Oakland, 1977 (OT)
Fulton Walker, SB: Miami vs. Washington, 1982
Stanford Jennings, SB: Cincinnati vs. San Francisco, 1988
Eric Metcalf, AFC-D: Cleveland vs. Buffalo, 1989

Fumbles

Most Fumbles, Career
13 Tony Dorsett, Dallas, 17 games
10 Franco Harris, Pittsburgh, 19 games
Terry Bradshaw, Pittsburgh, 19 games
Roger Staubach, Dallas, 20 games
9 Chuck Foreman, Minnesota, 13 games

Most Fumbles, Game
4 Brian Sipe, AFC-D: Cleveland vs. Oakland, 1980
3 Y.A. Tittle, NFC-D: San Francisco vs. Detroit, 1957
Bill Nelsen, AFC-D: Cleveland vs. Baltimore, 1972
Chuck Foreman, NFC: Minnesota vs. Los Angeles, 1974
Lawrence McCutcheon, NFC-D: Los Angeles vs. St. Louis, 1975
Roger Staubach, SB: Dallas vs. Pittsburgh, 1975
Terry Bradshaw, AFC: Pittsburgh vs. Houston, 1978
Earl Campbell, AFC: Houston vs. Pittsburgh, 1978
Franco Harris, AFC: Pittsburgh vs. Houston, 1978
Chuck Muncie, AFC: San Diego vs. Cincinnati, 1981
Andra Franklin, AFC-FR: Miami vs. New England, 1982
Eric Dickerson, NFC-FR: L.A. Rams vs. Washington, 1986
2 By many players

Recoveries

Most Own Fumbles Recovered, Career
5 Roger Staubach, Dallas, 20 games
4 Fran Tarkenton, Minnesota, 11 games
3 Alex Webster, N.Y. Giants, 7 games
Don Meredith, Dallas, 4 games
Franco Harris, Pittsburgh, 19 games
Gerry Mullins, Pittsburgh, 18 games
Ron Jaworski, Los Angeles-Philadelphia, 10 games
Lyle Blackwood, Cincinnati-Baltimore-Miami, 14 games
Joe Montana, San Francisco, 19 games
Warren Moon, Houston, 5 games
Bernie Kosar, Cleveland, 7 games

Most Opponents' Fumbles Recovered, Career
4 Cliff Harris, Dallas, 21 games
Harvey Martin, Dallas, 22 games
Ted Hendricks, Baltimore-Oakland-L.A. Raiders, 21 games
Alvin Walton, Washington, 8 games
3 Paul Krause, Minnesota, 19 games
Jack Lambert, Pittsburgh, 18 games
Fred Dryer, Los Angeles, 14 games
Charlie Waters, Dallas, 25 games
Jack Ham, Pittsburgh, 16 games
Mike Hegman, Dallas, 16 games
Tom Jackson, Denver, 10 games
Mike Singletary, Chicago, 11 games
Monte Coleman, Washington, 16 games
Darryl Grant, Washington, 16 games
Wes Hopkins, Philadelphia, 3 games
2 By many players

Most Fumbles Recovered, Game, Own and Opponents'
3 Jack Lambert, AFC: Pittsburgh vs. Oakland, 1975 (3 opp)
Ron Jaworski, NFC-FR: Philadelphia vs. N.Y. Giants, 1981 (3 own)
2 By many players

Yards Gained

Longest Return
93 Andy Russell, AFC-D: Pittsburgh vs. Baltimore, 1975 (opp, TD)
60 Mike Curtis, NFC-D: Baltimore vs. Minnesota, 1968 (opp, TD)
Hugh Green, NFC-FR: Tampa Bay vs. Dallas, 1982 (opp, TD)
52 Wilber Marshall, NFC: Chicago vs. L.A. Rams, 1985 (opp, TD)

Touchdowns

Most Touchdowns
1 By 22 players

Combined Net Yards Gained

Rushing, receiving, interception returns, punt returns, kickoff returns, and fumble returns.

Attempts

Most Attempts, Career
454 Franco Harris, Pittsburgh, 19 games
350 Tony Dorsett, Dallas, 17 games
275 Chuck Foreman, Minnesota, 13 games

Most Attempts, Game
40 Lawrence McCutcheon, NFC-D: Los Angeles vs. St. Louis, 1975
39 John Riggins, SB: Washington vs. Miami, 1982
38 Ricky Bell, NFC-D: Tampa Bay vs. Philadelphia, 1979
Rob Carpenter, NFC-FR: N.Y. Giants vs. Philadelphia, 1981

Yards Gained

Most Yards Gained, Career
2,060 Franco Harris, Pittsburgh, 19 games
1,786 Tony Dorsett, Dallas, 17 games
1,471 Roger Craig, San Francisco, 16 games

Most Yards Gained, Game
350 Ed Podolak, AFC-D: Kansas City vs. Miami, 1971 (OT)
329 Keith Lincoln, AFC: San Diego vs. Boston, 1963
285 Bob Hayes, NFC-D: Dallas vs. Cleveland, 1967

Sacks

Sacks have been compiled since 1982

Most Sacks, Career

10.5 Richard Dent, Chicago, 9 games
9 Charles Mann, Washington, 12 games
8 Dexter Manley, Washington, 14 games

Most Sacks, Game

3.5 Rich Milot, NFC-D: Washington vs. Chicago, 1984
Richard Dent, NFC-D: Chicago vs. N.Y. Giants, 1985
3 Richard Dent, NFC-D: Chicago vs. Washington, 1984
Garin Veris, AFC-FR: New England vs. N.Y. Jets, 1985
Gary Jeter, NFC-D: L.A. Rams vs. Dallas, 1985
Carl Hairston, AFC-D: Cleveland vs. N.Y. Jets, 1986 (OT)
Charles Mann, NFC-D: Washington vs. Chicago, 1987
Kevin Greene, NFC-FR: L.A. Rams vs. Minnesota, 1988
Greg Townsend, AFC-D: L.A. Raiders vs. Cincinnati, 1990
2.5 Lyle Alzado, AFC-D: L.A. Raiders vs. Pittsburgh, 1983
Jacob Green, AFC-FR: Seattle vs. L.A. Raiders, 1984
Larry Roberts, NFC-D: San Francisco vs. Minnesota, 1988

Team Records

Games, Victories, Defeats

Most Seasons Participating in Postseason Games

22 Cleveland/L.A. Rams, 1945, 1949-52, 1955, 1967, 1969, 1973-80, 1983-86, 1988-89
Cleveland, 1950-55, 1957-58, 1964-65, 1967-69, 1971-72, 1980, 1982, 1985-89
N.Y. Giants, 1933-35, 1938-39, 1941, 1943-44, 1946, 1950, 1956, 1958-59, 1961-63, 1981, 1984-86, 1989-90
19 Chicago, 1933-34, 1937, 1940-43, 1946, 1950, 1956, 1963, 1977, 1979, 1984-88, 1990
18 Dallas, 1966-73, 1975-83, 1985

Most Consecutive Seasons Participating in Postseason Games

9 Dallas, 1975-83
8 Dallas, 1966-73
Pittsburgh, 1972-79
Los Angeles, 1973-80
San Francisco, 1983-90
6 Cleveland, 1950-55
Oakland, 1972-77
Minnesota, 1973-78

Most Games

36 Dallas, 1966-73, 1975-83, 1985
33 Cleveland/L.A. Rams, 1945, 1949-52, 1955, 1967, 1969, 1973-80, 1983-86, 1988-89
Oakland/L.A. Raiders, 1967-70, 1973-77, 1980, 1982-85, 1990
30 Boston/Washington, 1936-37, 1940, 1942-43, 1945, 1971-74, 1976-77, 1982-84, 1986-87, 1990
N.Y. Giants, 1933-35, 1938-39, 1941, 1943-44, 1946, 1950, 1956, 1958-59, 1961-63, 1981, 1984-86, 1989-90

Most Games Won

20 Dallas, 1967, 1970-73, 1975, 1977-78, 1980-82
Oakland/L.A. Raiders, 1967-70, 1973-77, 1980, 1982-83, 1990
17 Washington, 1937, 1942-43, 1972, 1982-83, 1986-87, 1990
16 Pittsburgh, 1972, 1974-76, 1978-79, 1984, 1989
San Francisco, 1970-71, 1981, 1983-84, 1988-90

Most Consecutive Games Won

9 Green Bay, 1961-62, 1965-67
7 Pittsburgh, 1974-76
San Francisco, 1988-90
6 Miami, 1972-73
Pittsburgh, 1978-79
Washington, 1982-83

Most Games Lost

20 L.A. Rams, 1949-50, 1952, 1955, 1967, 1969, 1973-80, 1983-86, 1988-89
18 Cleveland, 1951-53, 1957-58, 1965, 1967-69, 1971-72, 1980, 1982, 1985-89
17 N.Y. Giants, 1933, 1935, 1939, 1941, 1943-44, 1946, 1950, 1958-59, 1961-63, 1981, 1984-85, 1989

Most Consecutive Games Lost

6 N.Y. Giants, 1939, 1941, 1943-44, 1946, 1950
Cleveland, 1969, 1971-72, 1980, 1982, 1985
5 N.Y. Giants, 1958-59, 1961-63
Los Angeles, 1952, 1955, 1967, 1969, 1973
Denver, 1977-79, 1983-84
Baltimore/Indianapolis, 1971, 1975-77, 1987 (current)
Philadelphia, 1980-81, 1988-90 (current)
4 Washington, 1972-74, 1976
Miami, 1974, 1978-79, 1981
Chi. Cardinals/St. Louis, 1948, 1974-75, 1982 (current)
Boston/New England, 1963, 1976, 1978, 1982

Scoring

Most Points, Game

73 NFC: Chi. Bears vs. Washington, 1940
59 NFC: Detroit vs. Cleveland, 1957
56 NFC: Cleveland vs. Detroit, 1954
AFC-D: Oakland vs. Houston, 1969

Most Points, Both Teams, Game

79 AFC-D: San Diego (41) vs. Miami (38), 1981 (OT)
78 AFC-D: Buffalo (44) vs. Miami (34), 1990
73 NFC: Chi. Bears (73) vs. Washington (0), 1940
NFC: Detroit (59) vs. Cleveland (14), 1957
AFC: Miami (45) vs. Pittsburgh (28), 1984

Fewest Points, Both Teams, Game

5 NFC-D: Detroit (0) vs. Dallas (5), 1970
7 NFC: Chi. Cardinals (0) vs. Philadelphia (7), 1948
9 NFC: Tampa Bay (0) vs. Los Angeles (9), 1979

Largest Margin of Victory, Game

73 NFC: Chi. Bears vs. Washington, 1940 (73-0)
49 AFC-D: Oakland vs. Houston, 1969 (56-7)
48 AFC: Buffalo vs. L.A. Raiders, 1990 (51-3)

Most Points, Shutout Victory, Game

73 NFC: Chi. Bears vs. Washington, 1940
38 NFC-D: Dallas vs. Tampa Bay, 1981
37 NFC: Green Bay vs. N.Y. Giants, 1961

Most Points Overcome to Win Game

20 NFC-D: Detroit vs. San Francisco, 1957 (trailed 7-27, won 31-27)
18 NFC-D: Dallas vs. San Francisco, 1972 (trailed 3-21, won 30-28)
AFC-D: Miami vs. Cleveland, 1985 (trailed 3-21, won 24-21)
14 NFC-D: Philadelphia vs. Minnesota, 1980 (trailed 0-14, won 31-16)
NFC-D: Dallas vs. Atlanta, 1980 (trailed 10-24, won 30-27)
NFC-D: Washington vs. Chicago, 1987 (trailed 0-14, won 21-17)

Most Points, Each Half

1st: 41 AFC: Buffalo vs. L.A. Raiders, 1990
38 NFC-D: Washington vs. L.A. Rams, 1983
35 NFC: Cleveland vs. Detroit, 1954
AFC-D: Oakland vs. Houston, 1969
SB: Washington vs. Denver, 1987
2nd: 45 NFC: Chi. Bears vs. Washington, 1940
30 SB: N.Y. Giants vs. Denver, 1986
AFC: Cleveland vs. Denver, 1987
28 NFC: Chi. Bears vs. N. Y. Giants, 1941
NFC: Detroit vs. Cleveland, 1957
NFC-D: Dallas vs. Cleveland, 1967
NFC-D: Dallas vs. Tampa Bay, 1981
SB: San Francisco vs. Denver, 1989

Most Points, Each Quarter

1st: 28 AFC-D: Oakland vs. Houston, 1969
24 AFC-D: San Diego vs. Miami, 1981
21 NFC: Chi. Bears vs. Washington, 1940
AFC: San Diego vs. Boston, 1963
AFC-D: Oakland vs. Kansas City, 1968
AFC: Oakland vs. San Diego, 1980
AFC: Buffalo vs. L.A. Raiders, 1990
2nd: 35 SB: Washington vs. Denver, 1987
26 AFC-D: Pittsburgh vs. Buffalo, 1974
24 NFC-D: Chi. Bears vs. Green Bay, 1941
NFC: Green Bay vs. N. Y. Giants, 1961
3rd: 26 NFC: Chi. Bears vs. Washington, 1940
21 NFC-D: Dallas vs. Cleveland, 1967
NFC-D: Dallas vs. Tampa Bay, 1981
AFC-D: L.A. Raiders vs. Pittsburgh, 1983
SB: Chicago vs. New England, 1985
NFC-D: N.Y. Giants vs. San Francisco, 1986
AFC: Cleveland vs. Denver, 1987
AFC: Cleveland vs. Denver, 1989
17 NFC: Cleveland vs. Baltimore, 1964
NFC-D: Dallas vs. Chicago, 1977
SB: N.Y. Giants vs. Denver, 1986
4th 27 NFC: N.Y. Giants vs. Chi. Bears, 1934
24 NFC: Baltimore vs. N. Y. Giants, 1959
21 AFC: Pittsburgh vs. Oakland, 1974
NFC: Dallas vs. Los Angeles, 1978
AFC-FR: N. Y. Jets vs. Cincinnati, 1982
NFC: San Francisco vs. Washington, 1983
OT: 6 NFC: Baltimore vs. N.Y. Giants, 1958
AFC-D: Oakland vs. Baltimore, 1977
NFC-D: L.A. Rams vs. N.Y. Giants, 1989

Touchdowns

Most Touchdowns, Game

11 NFC: Chi. Bears vs. Washington, 1940
8 NFC: Cleveland vs. Detroit, 1954
NFC: Detroit vs. Cleveland, 1957
AFC-D: Oakland vs. Houston, 1969
SB: San Francisco vs. Denver, 1989
7 AFC: San Diego vs. Boston, 1963
NFC-D: Dallas vs. Cleveland, 1967
NFC-D: N.Y. Giants vs. San Francisco, 1986
AFC: Buffalo vs. L.A. Raiders, 1990

Most Touchdowns, Both Teams, Game

11 NFC: Chi. Bears (11) vs. Washington (0), 1940
10 NFC: Detroit (8) vs. Cleveland (2), 1957
AFC-D: Miami (5) vs. San Diego (5), 1981 (OT)
AFC: Miami (6) vs. Pittsburgh (4), 1984
9 NFC: Chi. Bears (6) vs. Washington (3), 1943
NFC: Cleveland (8) vs. Detroit (1), 1954
NFC-D: Dallas (7) vs. Cleveland (2), 1967
AFC-D: Oakland (8) vs. Houston (1), 1969
AFC-D: Oakland (5) vs. Baltimore (4), 1977 (OT)
SB: Pittsburgh (5) vs. Dallas (4), 1978
AFC: Denver (5) vs. Cleveland (4), 1987
SB: San Francisco (8) vs. Denver (1), 1989
AFC-D: Buffalo (5) vs. Miami (4), 1990

Fewest Touchdowns, Both Teams, Game

0 NFC-D: N.Y. Giants vs. Cleveland, 1950
NFC-D: Dallas vs. Detroit, 1970
NFC: Los Angeles vs. Tampa Bay, 1979
1 NFC: Chi. Cardinals (0) vs. Philadelphia (1), 1948
AFC: San Diego (0) vs. Houston (1), 1961
AFC-D: N. Y. Jets (0) vs. Kansas City (1), 1969
NFC-D: Green Bay (0) vs. Washington (1), 1972
NFC-FR: New Orleans (0) vs. Chicago (1), 1990
NFC: N.Y. Giants (0) vs. San Francisco (1), 1990
2 In many games

Points After Touchdown

Most Points After Touchdown, Game

8 NFC: Cleveland vs. Detroit, 1954
NFC: Detroit vs. Cleveland, 1957
AFC-D: Oakland vs. Houston, 1969
7 NFC: Chi. Bears vs. Washington, 1940
NFC-D: Dallas vs. Cleveland, 1967
NFC-D: N.Y. Giants vs. San Francisco, 1986

SB: San Francisco vs. Denver, 1989
6 AFC: San Diego vs. Boston, 1963
NFC-D: Washington vs. L.A. Rams, 1983
AFC: Miami vs. Pittsburgh, 1984
AFC: Buffalo vs. L.A. Raiders, 1990

Most Points After Touchdown, Both Teams, Game
10 NFC: Detroit (8) vs. Cleveland (2), 1957
AFC-D: Miami (5) vs. San Diego (5), 1981 (OT)
AFC: Miami (6) vs. Pittsburgh (4), 1984
9 NFC: Cleveland (8) vs. Detroit (1), 1954
NFC-D: Dallas (7) vs. Cleveland (2), 1967
AFC-D: Oakland (8) vs. Houston (1), 1969
AFC: Denver (5) vs. Cleveland (4), 1987
AFC-D: Buffalo (5) vs. Miami (4), 1990
8 In many games

Fewest Points After Touchdown, Both Teams, Game
0 NFC-D: N.Y. Giants vs. Cleveland, 1950
NFC-D: Dallas vs. Detroit, 1970
NFC: Los Angeles vs. Tampa Bay, 1979

Field Goals

Most Field Goals, Game
5 NFC-D: Minnesota vs. San Francisco, 1987
NFC: N.Y. Giants vs. San Francisco, 1990
4 AFC-D: Boston vs. Buffalo, 1963
AFC: Oakland vs. Houston, 1967
SB: Green Bay vs. Oakland, 1967
NFC: Washington vs. Dallas, 1972
AFC-D: Oakland vs. Pittsburgh, 1973
SB: San Francisco vs. Cincinnati, 1981
AFC-FR: New England vs. N.Y. Jets, 1985
NFC-FR: Washington vs. L.A. Rams, 1986
NFC-D: Philadelphia vs. Chicago, 1988
AFC-FR: Pittsburgh vs. Houston, 1989 (OT)
3 By many teams

Most Field Goals, Both Teams, Game
7 AFC-FR: Pittsburgh (4) vs. Houston (3), 1989 (OT)
NFC: N.Y. Giants (5) vs. San Francisco (2), 1990
6 NFC-D: Minnesota (5) vs. San Francisco (1), 1987
NFC-D: Philadelphia (4) vs. Chicago (2), 1988
5 In many games

Most Field Goals Attempted, Game
6 AFC: Oakland vs. Houston, 1967
NFC-D: Los Angeles vs. Dallas, 1973
AFC-D: Cleveland vs. N.Y. Jets, 1986 (OT)
NFC: N.Y. Giants vs. San Francisco, 1990
5 By many teams

Most Field Goals Attempted, Both Teams, Game
9 NFC-D: Philadelphia (5) vs. Chicago (4), 1988
8 NFC-D: Los Angeles (6) vs. Dallas (2), 1973
NFC-D: Detroit (5) vs. San Francisco (3), 1983
AFC-D: Cleveland (6) vs. N.Y. Jets (2), 1986 (OT)
NFC-D: Minnesota (5) vs. San Francisco (3), 1987
AFC-FR: Houston (4) vs. Pittsburgh (4), 1989 (OT)
NFC-FR: Chicago (4) vs. New Orleans (4), 1990
NFC: N.Y. Giants (6) vs. San Francisco (2), 1990
7 In many games

Safeties

Most Safeties, Game
1 By 18 teams

First Downs

Most First Downs, Game
34 AFC-D: San Diego vs. Miami, 1981 (OT)
33 AFC-D: Cleveland vs. N.Y. Jets, 1986 (OT)
31 SB: San Francisco vs. Miami, 1984

Fewest First Downs, Game
6 NFC: N.Y. Giants vs. Green Bay, 1961
7 NFC: Green Bay vs. Boston, 1936
NFC-D: Pittsburgh vs. Philadelphia, 1947
NFC: Chi. Cardinals vs. Philadelphia, 1948
NFC: Los Angeles vs. Philadelphia, 1949
NFC-D: Cleveland vs. N. Y. Giants, 1958
AFC-D: Cincinnati vs. Baltimore, 1970
NFC-D: Detroit vs. Dallas, 1970
8 By many teams

Most First Downs, Both Teams, Game
59 AFC-D: San Diego (34) vs. Miami (25), 1981 (OT)
55 AFC-FR: San Diego (29) vs. Pittsburgh (26), 1982
51 AFC: Buffalo (30) vs. L.A. Raiders (21), 1990

Fewest First Downs, Both Teams, Game
15 NFC: Green Bay (7) vs. Boston (8), 1936
19 NFC: N. Y. Giants (9) vs. Green Bay (10), 1939
NFC: Washington (9) vs. Chi. Bears (10), 1942
20 NFC-D: Cleveland (9) vs. N. Y. Giants (11), 1950

Rushing

Most First Downs, Rushing, Game
19 NFC-FR: Dallas vs. Los Angeles, 1980
18 AFC-D: Miami vs. Cincinnati, 1973
AFC-D: Pittsburgh vs. Buffalo, 1974
17 AFC-D: Cincinnati vs. Seattle, 1988

Fewest First Downs, Rushing, Game
0 NFC: Los Angeles vs. Philadelphia, 1949
AFC-D: Buffalo vs. Boston, 1963
AFC: Oakland vs. Pittsburgh, 1974
NFC-FR: New Orleans vs. Minnesota, 1987
NFC: L.A. Rams vs. San Francisco, 1989
NFC-D: Chicago vs. N.Y. Giants, 1990
1 NFC: N. Y. Giants vs. Green Bay, 1961
AFC-D: Houston vs. Oakland, 1969
NFC: Los Angeles vs. Dallas, 1975
AFC-FR: Cleveland vs. L. A. Raiders, 1982
NFC-D: N.Y. Giants vs. Chicago, 1985
SB: New England vs. Chicago, 1985
AFC-FR: Seattle vs. Houston, 1987 (OT)
NFC-D: Philadelphia vs. Chicago, 1988
AFC-D: Seattle vs. Cincinnati, 1988
NFC: San Francisco vs. N.Y. Giants, 1990
2 By many teams

Most First Downs, Rushing, Both Teams, Game
26 AFC: Buffalo (14) vs. L.A. Raiders (12), 1990
25 NFC-FR: Dallas (19) vs. Los Angeles (6), 1980
23 NFC: Cleveland (15) vs. Detroit (8), 1952
AFC-D: Miami (18) vs. Cincinnati (5), 1973
AFC-D: Pittsburgh (18) vs. Buffalo (5), 1974

Fewest First Downs, Rushing, Both Teams, Game
5 AFC-D: Buffalo (0) vs. Boston (5), 1963
6 NFC: Green Bay (2) vs. Boston (4), 1936
NFC-D: Baltimore (2) vs. Minnesota (4), 1968
AFC-D: Houston (1) vs. Oakland (5), 1969
7 NFC-D: Washington (2) vs. N. Y. Giants (5), 1943
NFC: Baltimore (3) vs. N. Y. Giants (4), 1959
NFC: Washington (3) vs. Dallas (4), 1972
AFC-FR: N. Y. Jets (3) vs. Buffalo (4), 1981

Passing

Most First Downs, Passing, Game
21 AFC-D: Miami vs. San Diego, 1981 (OT)
AFC-D: San Diego vs. Miami, 1981 (OT)
AFC-D: Cleveland vs. N.Y. Jets, 1986 (OT)
NFC-D: Philadelphia vs. Chicago, 1988
20 NFC-FR: Dallas vs. L.A. Rams, 1983
AFC-D: Buffalo vs. Cleveland, 1989
19 NFC-FR: St. Louis vs. Green Bay, 1982
NFC-FR: Dallas vs. Tampa Bay, 1982
AFC-FR: Pittsburgh vs. San Diego, 1982
AFC-FR: San Diego vs. Pittsburgh, 1982
NFC: Dallas vs. Washington, 1982

Fewest First Downs, Passing, Game
0 NFC: Philadelphia vs. Chi. Cardinals, 1948
1 NFC-D: N. Y. Giants vs. Washington, 1943
NFC: Cleveland vs. Detroit, 1953
SB: Denver vs. Dallas, 1977
2 By many teams

Most First Downs, Passing, Both Teams, Game
42 AFC-D: Miami (21) vs. San Diego (21), 1981 (OT)
38 AFC-FR: Pittsburgh (19) vs. San Diego (19), 1982
34 NFC-FR: Washington (18) vs. San Francisco (16), 1990

Fewest First Downs, Passing, Both Teams, Game
2 NFC: Philadelphia (0) vs. Chi. Cardinals (2), 1948
4 NFC-D: Cleveland (2) vs. N. Y. Giants (2), 1950
5 NFC: Detroit (2) vs. N. Y. Giants (3), 1935
NFC: Green Bay (2) vs. N. Y. Giants (3), 1939

Penalty

Most First Downs, Penalty, Game
7 AFC-D: New England vs. Oakland, 1976
6 AFC-D: Cleveland vs. N.Y. Jets, 1986 (OT)
5 AFC-FR: Cleveland vs. L. A. Raiders, 1982

Most First Downs, Penalty, Both Teams, Game
9 AFC-D: New England (7) vs. Oakland (2), 1976
8 NFC-FR: Atlanta (4) vs. Minnesota (4), 1982
7 AFC-D: Baltimore (4) vs. Oakland (3), 1977 (OT)

Net Yards Gained Rushing and Passing

Most Yards Gained, Game
610 AFC: San Diego vs. Boston, 1963
602 SB: Washington vs. Denver, 1987
569 AFC: Miami vs. Pittsburgh, 1984

Fewest Yards Gained, Game
86 NFC-D: Cleveland vs. N.Y. Giants, 1958
99 NFC: Chi. Cardinals vs. Philadelphia, 1948
114 NFC-D: N.Y. Giants vs. Washington, 1943

Most Yards Gained, Both Teams, Game
1,036 AFC-D: San Diego (564) vs. Miami (472), 1981 (OT)
1,024 AFC: Miami (569) vs. Pittsburgh (455), 1984
929 SB: Washington (602) vs. Denver (327), 1987

Fewest Yards Gained, Both Teams, Game
331 NFC: Chi. Cardinals (99) vs. Philadelphia (232), 1948
332 NFC-D: N.Y. Giants (150) vs. Cleveland (182), 1950
336 NFC: Boston (116) vs. Green Bay (220), 1936

Rushing

Attempts

Most Attempts, Game
65 NFC: Detroit vs. N.Y. Giants, 1935
61 NFC: Philadelphia vs. Los Angeles, 1949
59 AFC: New England vs. Miami, 1985

Fewest Attempts, Game
9 SB: Miami vs. San Francisco, 1984
10 NFC: L.A. Rams vs. San Francisco, 1989
11 SB: New England vs. Chicago, 1985
AFC-FR: Seattle vs. Houston, 1987 (OT)
NFC: San Francisco vs. N.Y. Giants, 1990

Most Attempts, Both Teams, Game
109 NFC: Detroit (65) vs. N.Y. Giants (44), 1935
97 AFC-D: Baltimore (50) vs. Oakland (47), 1977 (OT)
91 NFC: Philadelphia (57) vs. Chi. Cardinals (34), 1948

Fewest Attempts, Both Teams, Game
45 AFC-FR: N.Y. Jets (22) vs. Buffalo (23), 1981
46 AFC: Buffalo (13) vs. Kansas City (33), 1966
47 NFC: San Francisco (11) vs. N.Y. Giants (36), 1990

Yards Gained

Most Yards Gained, Game

382 NFC: Chi. Bears vs. Washington, 1940
338 NFC-FR: Dallas vs. Los Angeles, 1980
318 AFC: San Diego vs. Boston, 1963

Fewest Yards Gained, Game

7 AFC-D: Buffalo vs. Boston, 1963
SB: New England vs. Chicago, 1985
17 SB: Minnesota vs. Pittsburgh, 1974
18 AFC-D: Seattle vs. Cincinnati, 1988

Most Yards Gained, Both Teams, Game

430 NFC-FR: Dallas (338) vs. Los Angeles (92), 1980
426 NFC: Cleveland (227) vs. Detroit (199), 1952
404 NFC: Chi. Bears (382) vs. Washington (22), 1940

Fewest Yards Gained, Both Teams, Game

90 AFC-D: Buffalo (7) vs. Boston (83), 1963
106 NFC: Boston (39) vs. Green Bay (67), 1936
128 NFC-FR: Philadelphia (53) vs. Atlanta (75), 1978

Average Gain

Highest Average Gain, Game

9.94 AFC: San Diego vs. Boston, 1963 (32-318)
9.29 NFC-D: Green Bay vs. Dallas, 1982 (17-158)
7.35 NFC-FR: Dallas vs. Los Angeles, 1980 (46-338)

Lowest Average Gain, Game

0.58 AFC-D: Buffalo vs. Boston, 1963 (12-7)
0.64 SB: New England vs. Chicago, 1985 (11-7)
0.81 SB: Minnesota vs. Pittsburgh, 1974 (21-17)

Touchdowns

Most Touchdowns, Game

7 NFC: Chi. Bears vs. Washington, 1940
5 NFC: Cleveland vs. Detroit, 1954
4 NFC: Detroit vs. N.Y. Giants, 1935
AFC: San Diego vs. Boston, 1963
NFC-D: Dallas vs. Cleveland, 1967
NFC: Baltimore vs. Cleveland, 1968
NFC-FR: Dallas vs. Los Angeles, 1980
AFC-D: L.A. Raiders vs. Pittsburgh, 1983
SB: Chicago vs. New England, 1985
AFC: Buffalo vs. L.A. Raiders, 1990

Most Touchdowns, Both Teams, Game

7 NFC: Chi. Bears (7) vs. Washington (0), 1940
6 NFC: Cleveland (5) vs. Detroit (1), 1954
5 NFC: Chi. Cardinals (3) vs. Philadelphia (2), 1947
AFC: San Diego (4) vs. Boston (1), 1963
AFC-D: Cincinnati (3) vs. Buffalo (2), 1981

Passing

Attempts

Most Attempts, Game

65 AFC-D: Cleveland vs. N.Y. Jets, 1986 (OT)
55 NFC-D: Philadelphia vs. Chicago, 1988
54 AFC-D: San Diego vs. Miami, 1981 (OT)
AFC-D: Buffalo vs. Cleveland, 1989
NFC-D: Minnesota vs. San Francisco, 1989

Fewest Attempts, Game

5 NFC: Detroit vs. N.Y. Giants, 1935
6 AFC: Miami vs. Oakland, 1973
7 SB: Miami vs. Minnesota, 1973

Most Attempts, Both Teams, Game

102 AFC-D: San Diego (54) vs. Miami (48), 1981 (OT)
96 AFC: N.Y. Jets (49) vs. Oakland (47), 1968
95 AFC-D: Cleveland (65) vs. N.Y. Jets (30), 1986 (OT)

Fewest Attempts, Both Teams, Game

18 NFC: Detroit (5) vs. N.Y. Giants (13), 1935
21 NFC: Chi. Bears (7) vs. N.Y. Giants (14), 1933
23 NFC: Chi. Cardinals (11) vs. Philadelphia (12), 1948

Completions

Most Completions, Game

34 AFC-D: Cleveland vs. N.Y. Jets, 1986 (OT)
33 AFC-D: San Diego vs. Miami, 1981 (OT)
32 NFC-FR: St. Louis vs. Green Bay, 1982
NFC-FR: Dallas vs. L.A. Rams, 1983

Fewest Completions, Game

2 NFC: Detroit vs. N.Y. Giants, 1935
NFC: Philadelphia vs. Chi. Cardinals, 1948
3 NFC: N.Y. Giants vs. Chi. Bears, 1941
NFC: Green Bay vs. N.Y. Giants, 1944
NFC: Chi. Cardinals vs. Philadelphia, 1947
NFC: Chi. Cardinals vs. Philadelphia, 1948
NFC-D: Cleveland vs. N.Y. Giants, 1950
NFC-D: N.Y. Giants vs. Cleveland, 1950
NFC: Cleveland vs. Detroit, 1953
AFC: Miami vs. Oakland, 1973
4 NFC-D: Dallas vs. Detroit, 1970
AFC: Miami vs. Baltimore, 1971
SB: Miami vs. Washington, 1982
AFC-FR: Seattle vs. L.A. Raiders, 1984

Most Completions, Both Teams, Game

64 AFC-D: San Diego (33) vs. Miami (31), 1981 (OT)
55 AFC-FR: Pittsburgh (28) vs. San Diego (27), 1982
53 SB: Miami (29) vs. San Francisco (24), 1984

Fewest Completions, Both Teams, Game

5 NFC: Philadelphia (2) vs. Chi. Cardinals (3), 1948
6 NFC: Detroit (2) vs. N.Y. Giants (4), 1935
NFC-D: Cleveland (3) vs. N.Y. Giants (3), 1950
11 NFC: Green Bay (3) vs. N.Y. Giants (8), 1944
NFC-D: Dallas (4) vs. Detroit (7), 1970

Completion Percentage

Highest Completion Percentage, Game (20 attempts)

88.0 SB: N.Y. Giants vs. Denver, 1986 (25-22)
87.1 NFC: San Francisco vs. L.A. Rams, 1989 (31-27)
80.0 NFC-D: Washington vs. L.A. Rams, 1983 (25-20)

Lowest Completion Percentage, Game (20 attempts)

18.5 NFC: Tampa Bay vs. Los Angeles, 1979 (27-5)
20.0 NFC-D: N.Y. Giants vs. Washington, 1943 (20-4)
25.8 NFC: Chi. Bears vs. Washington, 1937 (31-8)

Yards Gained

Most Yards Gained, Game

483 AFC-D: Cleveland vs. N.Y. Jets, 1986 (OT)
435 AFC: Miami vs. Pittsburgh, 1984
415 AFC-D: San Diego vs. Miami, 1981 (OT)

Fewest Yards Gained, Game

3 NFC: Chi. Cardinals vs. Philadelphia, 1948
7 NFC: Philadelphia vs. Chi. Cardinals, 1948
9 NFC-D: N.Y. Giants vs. Cleveland, 1950
NFC: Cleveland vs. Detroit, 1953

Most Yards Gained, Both Teams, Game

809 AFC-D: San Diego (415) vs. Miami (394), 1981 (OT)
747 AFC: Miami (435) vs. Pittsburgh (312), 1984
666 AFC-D: Cleveland (483) vs. N.Y. Jets (183), 1986 (OT)

Fewest Yards Gained, Both Teams, Game

10 NFC: Chi. Cardinals (3) vs. Philadelphia (7), 1948
38 NFC-D: N.Y. Giants (9) vs. Cleveland (29), 1950
102 NFC-D: Dallas (22) vs. Detroit (80), 1970

Times Sacked

Most Times Sacked, Game

9 AFC: Kansas City vs. Buffalo, 1966
NFC: Chicago vs. San Francisco, 1984
AFC-D: N.Y. Jets vs. Cleveland, 1986 (OT)
8 NFC: Green Bay vs. Dallas, 1967
NFC: Minnesota vs. Washington, 1987
7 NFC-D: Dallas vs. Los Angeles, 1973
SB: Dallas vs. Pittsburgh, 1975
AFC-FR: Houston vs. Oakland, 1980
NFC-D: Washington vs. Chicago, 1984
SB: New England vs. Chicago, 1985

Most Times Sacked, Both Teams, Game

13 AFC: Kansas City (9) vs. Buffalo (4), 1966
AFC-D: N.Y. Jets (9) vs. Cleveland (4), 1986 (OT)
12 NFC-D: Dallas (7) vs. Los Angeles (5), 1973
NFC-D: Washington (7) vs. Chicago (5), 1984
NFC: Chicago (9) vs. San Francisco (3), 1984
10 AFC-FR: Houston (7) vs. Oakland (3), 1980
NFC-D: N.Y. Giants (6) vs. San Francisco (4), 1984
SB: New England (7) vs. Chicago (3), 1985

Fewest Times Sacked, Both Teams, Game

0 AFC-D: Buffalo vs. Pittsburgh, 1974
AFC-FR: Pittsburgh vs. San Diego, 1982
AFC-D: Buffalo vs. Miami, 1990
1 In many games

Touchdowns

Most Touchdowns, Game

6 AFC-D: Oakland vs. Houston, 1969
5 NFC: Chi. Bears vs. Washington, 1943
NFC: Detroit vs. Cleveland, 1957
AFC-D: Oakland vs. Kansas City, 1968
SB: San Francisco vs. Denver, 1989
4 By many teams

Most Touchdowns, Both Teams, Game

7 NFC: Chi. Bears (5) vs. Washington (2), 1943
AFC-D: Oakland (6) vs. Houston (1), 1969
SB: Pittsburgh (4) vs. Dallas (3), 1978
AFC-D: Miami (4) vs. San Diego (3), 1981 (OT)
AFC: Miami (4) vs. Pittsburgh (3), 1984
AFC-D: Buffalo (4) vs. Cleveland (3), 1989
6 NFC-FR: Green Bay (4) vs. St. Louis (2), 1982
AFC: Cleveland (3) vs. Denver (3), 1987
5 In many games

Interceptions By

Most Interceptions By, Game

8 NFC: Chi. Bears vs. Washington, 1940
7 NFC: Cleveland vs. Los Angeles, 1955
6 NFC: Green Bay vs. N.Y. Giants, 1939
NFC: Chi. Bears vs. N.Y. Giants, 1946
NFC: Cleveland vs. Detroit, 1954
AFC: San Diego vs. Houston, 1961
AFC: Buffalo vs. L.A. Raiders, 1990

Most Interceptions By, Both Teams, Game

10 NFC: Cleveland (7) vs. Los Angeles (3), 1955
AFC: San Diego (6) vs. Houston (4), 1961
9 NFC: Green Bay (6) vs. N.Y. Giants (3), 1939
8 NFC: Chi. Bears (8) vs. Washington (0), 1940
NFC: Chi. Bears (6) vs. N.Y. Giants (2), 1946
NFC: Cleveland (6) vs. Detroit (2), 1954
AFC-FR: Buffalo (4) vs. N.Y. Jets (4), 1981
AFC: Miami (5) vs. N.Y. Jets (3), 1982

Yards Gained

Most Yards Gained, Game

138 AFC-FR: N.Y. Jets vs. Cincinnati, 1982
136 AFC: Dall. Texans vs. Houston, 1962 (OT)
130 NFC-D: Los Angeles vs. St. Louis, 1975

Most Yards Gained, Both Teams, Game

156 NFC: Green Bay (123) vs. N.Y. Giants (33), 1939
149 NFC: Cleveland (103) vs. Los Angeles (46), 1955

141 AFC-FR: Buffalo (79) vs. N.Y. Jets (62), 1981

Touchdowns
Most Touchdowns, Game
3 NFC: Chi. Bears vs. Washington, 1940
2 NFC-D: Los Angeles vs. St. Louis, 1975
1 In many games

Punting
Most Punts, Game
14 AFC-D: N.Y. Jets vs. Cleveland, 1986 (OT)
13 NFC: N.Y. Giants vs. Chi. Bears, 1933
AFC-D: Baltimore vs. Oakland, 1977 (OT)
11 AFC: Houston vs. Oakland, 1967
AFC-D: Houston vs. Oakland, 1969
NFC: L.A. Rams vs. Chicago, 1985
Fewest Punts, Game
0 NFC-FR: St. Louis vs. Green Bay, 1982
AFC-FR: N.Y. Jets vs. Cincinnati, 1982
1 NFC-D: Cleveland vs. Dallas, 1969
AFC: Miami vs. Oakland, 1973
AFC-D: Oakland vs. Cincinnati, 1975
AFC-D: Pittsburgh vs. Baltimore, 1976
AFC: Pittsburgh vs. Houston, 1978
NFC-FR: Green Bay vs. St. Louis, 1982
AFC-FR: Miami vs. New England, 1982
AFC-FR: San Diego vs. Pittsburgh, 1982
AFC-D: Cleveland vs. Indianapolis, 1987
AFC-D: Buffalo vs. Miami, 1990
2 In many games
Most Punts, Both Teams, Game
23 NFC: N.Y. Giants (13) vs. Chi. Bears (10), 1933
22 AFC-D: N.Y. Jets (14) vs. Cleveland (8), 1986 (OT)
21 AFC-D: Baltimore (13) vs. Oakland (8), 1977 (OT)
NFC: L.A. Rams (11) vs. Chicago (10), 1985
Fewest Punts, Both Teams, Game
1 NFC-FR: St. Louis (0) vs. Green Bay (1), 1982
2 AFC-FR: N.Y. Jets (0) vs. Cincinnati (2), 1982
3 AFC: Miami (1) vs. Oakland (2), 1973
AFC-FR: San Diego (1) vs. Pittsburgh (2), 1982
AFC-D: Buffalo (1) vs. Miami (2), 1990

Average Yardage
Highest Average, Punting, Game (4 punts)
56.0 AFC: Oakland vs. San Diego, 1980
52.5 NFC: Washington vs. Chi. Bears, 1942
51.6 AFC-D: Cincinnati vs. L.A. Raiders, 1990
Lowest Average, Punting, Game (4 punts)
24.9 NFC: Washington vs. Chi. Bears, 1937
25.3 AFC-FR: Pittsburgh vs. Houston, 1989
25.5 NFC: Green Bay vs. N.Y. Giants, 1962

Punt Returns
Most Punt Returns, Game
8 NFC: Green Bay vs. N.Y. Giants, 1944
7 By eight teams
Most Punt Returns, Both Teams, Game
13 AFC-FR: Houston (7) vs. Oakland (6), 1980
11 NFC: Green Bay (8) vs. N.Y. Giants (3), 1944
NFC-D: Green Bay (6) vs. Baltimore (5), 1965
10 In many games
Fewest Punt Returns, Both Teams, Game
0 NFC: Chi. Bears vs. N.Y. Giants, 1941
AFC: Boston vs. San Diego, 1963
NFC-FR: Green Bay vs. St. Louis, 1982
1 AFC: Miami (0) vs. Pittsburgh (1), 1972
AFC: Cincinnati (0) vs. San Diego (1), 1981
AFC-FR: Cincinnati (0) vs. N.Y. Jets (1), 1982
AFC-FR: San Diego (0) vs. Pittsburgh (1), 1982
NFC-D: Minnesota (0) vs. Washington (1), 1982
AFC: Seattle (0) vs. L.A. Raiders (1), 1983
AFC-D: Pittsburgh (0) vs. Denver (1), 1989
2 In many games

Yards Gained
Most Yards Gained, Game
155 NFC-D: Dallas vs. Cleveland, 1967
150 NFC: Chi. Cardinals vs. Philadelphia, 1947
143 NFC-FR: Minnesota vs. New Orleans, 1987
Fewest Yards Gained, Game
−10 NFC: Green Bay vs. Cleveland, 1965
−9 NFC: Dallas vs. Green Bay, 1966
AFC-D: Kansas City vs. Oakland, 1968
−5 AFC-D: Miami vs. Oakland, 1970
NFC-D: San Francisco vs. Dallas, 1972
NFC: Dallas vs. Washington, 1972
Most Yards Gained, Both Teams, Game
166 NFC-D: Dallas (155) vs. Cleveland (11), 1967
160 NFC: Chi. Cardinals (150) vs. Philadelphia (10), 1947
146 NFC-D: Philadelphia (112) vs. Pittsburgh (34), 1947
Fewest Yards Gained, Both Teams, Game
−9 NFC: Dallas (−9) vs. Green Bay (0), 1966
−6 AFC-D: Miami (−5) vs. Oakland (−1), 1970
−3 NFC-D: San Francisco (−5) vs. Dallas (2), 1972

Touchdowns
Most Touchdowns, Game
1 By 10 teams

Kickoff Returns
Most Kickoff Returns, Game
10 NFC-D: L.A. Rams vs. Washington, 1983
9 NFC: Chi. Bears vs. N.Y. Giants, 1956
AFC: Boston vs. San Diego, 1963
AFC: Houston vs. Oakland, 1967
SB: Denver vs. San Francisco, 1989
AFC-D: Miami vs. Buffalo, 1990
AFC: L.A. Raiders vs. Buffalo, 1990
8 By many teams
Most Kickoff Returns, Both Teams, Game
15 AFC-D: Miami (9) vs. Buffalo (6), 1990
13 NFC-D: Green Bay (7) vs. Dallas (6), 1982
12 In many games
Fewest Kickoff Returns, Both Teams, Game
1 NFC: Green Bay (0) vs. Boston (1), 1936
2 NFC-D: Los Angeles (0) vs. Chi. Bears (2), 1950
AFC: Houston (0) vs. San Diego (2), 1961
AFC-D: Oakland (1) vs. Pittsburgh (1), 1972
AFC-D: N.Y. Jets (0) vs. L.A. Raiders (2), 1982
AFC: Miami (1) vs. N.Y. Jets (1), 1982
NFC: N.Y. Giants (0) vs. Washington (2), 1986
3 In many games

Yards Gained
Most Yards Gained, Game
225 NFC: Washington vs. Chi. Bears, 1940
222 SB: Miami vs. Washington, 1982
215 AFC: Houston vs. Oakland, 1967
Most Yards Gained, Both Teams, Game
379 AFC-D: Baltimore (193) vs. Oakland (186), 1977 (OT)
321 NFC-D: Dallas (173) vs. Green Bay (148), 1982
318 AFC-D: Miami (183) vs. Oakland (135), 1974
Fewest Yards Gained, Both Teams, Game
15 NFC: N.Y. Giants (0) vs. Washington (15), 1986
31 NFC-D: Los Angeles (0) vs. Chi. Bears (31), 1950
32 NFC: Green Bay (0) vs. Boston (32), 1936

Touchdowns
Most Touchdowns, Game
1 NFC-D: San Francisco vs. Dallas, 1972
AFC-D: Miami vs. Oakland, 1974
AFC-D: Baltimore vs. Oakland, 1977 (OT)
SB: Miami vs. Washington, 1982
SB: Cincinnati vs. San Francisco, 1988
AFC-D: Cleveland vs. Buffalo, 1989

Penalties
Most Penalties, Game
14 AFC-FR: Oakland vs. Houston, 1980
NFC-D: San Francisco vs. N.Y. Giants, 1981
13 AFC-FR: Houston vs. Cleveland, 1988
12 NFC-D: Chi. Bears vs. Green Bay, 1941
AFC-D: Pittsburgh vs. Baltimore, 1976
SB: Dallas vs. Denver, 1977
AFC-FR: N.Y. Jets vs. Cincinnati, 1982
Fewest Penalties, Game
0 NFC: Philadelphia vs. Green Bay, 1960
NFC-D: Detroit vs. Dallas, 1970
AFC-D: Miami vs. Oakland, 1970
SB: Miami vs. Dallas, 1971
NFC-D: Washington vs. Minnesota, 1973
SB: Pittsburgh vs. Dallas, 1975
NFC: San Francisco vs. Chicago, 1988
SB: Denver vs. San Francisco, 1989
AFC-D: L.A. Raiders vs. Cincinnati, 1990
1 By many teams
Most Penalties, Both Teams, Game
22 AFC-FR: Oakland (14) vs. Houston (8), 1980
NFC-D: San Francisco (14) vs. N.Y. Giants (8), 1981
AFC-FR: Houston (13) vs. Cleveland (9), 1988
21 AFC-D: Oakland (11) vs. New England (10), 1976
20 SB: Dallas (12) vs. Denver (8), 1977
Fewest Penalties, Both Teams, Game
1 AFC-D: L.A. Raiders (0) vs. Cincinnati (1), 1990
2 NFC: Washington (1) vs. Chi. Bears (1), 1937
NFC-D: Washington (0) vs. Minnesota (2), 1973
SB: Pittsburgh (0) vs. Dallas (2), 1975
3 AFC: Miami (1) vs. Baltimore (2), 1971
NFC: San Francisco (1) vs. Dallas (2), 1971
SB: Miami (0) vs. Dallas (3), 1971
AFC-D: Pittsburgh (1) vs. Oakland (2), 1972
AFC-D: Miami (1) vs. Cincinnati (2), 1973
SB: Miami (1) vs. San Francisco (2), 1984
NFC: San Francisco (0) vs. Chicago (3), 1988

Yards Penalized
Most Yards Penalized, Game
145 NFC-D: San Francisco vs. N.Y. Giants, 1981
133 SB: Dallas vs. Baltimore, 1970
128 NFC-D: Chi. Bears vs. Green Bay, 1941
Fewest Yards Penalized, Game
0 By nine teams
Most Yards Penalized, Both Teams, Game
206 NFC-D: San Francisco (145) vs. N.Y. Giants (61), 1981
193 AFC-FR: Houston (118) vs. Cleveland (75), 1988
192 AFC-D: Denver (104) vs. Pittsburgh (88), 1978
Fewest Yards Penalized, Both Teams, Game
5 AFC-D: L.A. Raiders (0) vs. Cincinnati (5), 1990
9 NFC-D: Washington (0) vs. Minnesota (9), 1973
15 SB: Miami (0) vs. Dallas (15), 1971

Fumbles
Most Fumbles, Game
6 By 10 teams

Most Fumbles, Both Teams, Game

12 AFC: Houston (6) vs. Pittsburgh (6), 1978
10 NFC: Chi. Bears (5) vs. N.Y. Giants (5), 1934
SB: Dallas (6) vs. Denver (4), 1977
9 NFC-D: San Francisco (6) vs. Detroit (3), 1957
NFC-D: San Francisco (5) vs. Dallas (4), 1972
NFC: Dallas (5) vs. Philadelphia (4), 1980

Most Fumbles Lost, Game

4 NFC: N.Y. Giants vs. Baltimore, 1958 (OT)
AFC: Kansas City vs. Oakland, 1969
SB: Baltimore vs. Dallas, 1970
AFC: Pittsburgh vs. Oakland, 1975
SB: Denver vs. Dallas, 1977
AFC: Houston vs. Pittsburgh, 1978
AFC: Miami vs. New England, 1985
SB: New England vs. Chicago, 1985
NFC-FR: L.A. Rams vs. Washington, 1986
3 By many teams

Fewest Fumbles, Both Teams, Game

0 NFC: Green Bay vs. Cleveland, 1965
AFC: Buffalo vs. San Diego, 1965
AFC-D: Oakland vs. Miami, 1974
AFC-D: Houston vs. San Diego, 1979
NFC-D: Dallas vs. Los Angeles, 1979
SB: Los Angeles vs. Pittsburgh, 1979
AFC-D: Buffalo vs. Cincinnati, 1981
AFC-D: Cleveland vs. N.Y. Jets, 1986 (OT)
AFC-D: Denver vs. New England, 1986
NFC-D: San Francisco vs. Washington, 1990
1 In many games

Recoveries

Most Total Fumbles Recovered, Game

8 SB: Dallas vs. Denver, 1977 (4 own, 4 opp)
7 NFC: Chi. Bears vs. N.Y. Giants, 1934 (5 own, 2 opp)
NFC-D: San Francisco vs. Detroit, 1957 (4 own, 3 opp)
NFC-D: San Francisco vs. Dallas, 1972 (4 own, 3 opp)
AFC: Pittsburgh vs. Houston, 1978 (3 own, 4 opp)
6 AFC: Houston vs. San Diego, 1961 (4 own, 2 opp)
AFC-D: Cleveland vs. Baltimore, 1971 (4 own, 2 opp)
AFC-D: Cleveland vs. Oakland, 1980 (5 own, 1 opp)
NFC: Philadelphia vs. Dallas, 1980 (3 own, 3 opp)

Most Own Fumbles Recovered, Game

5 NFC: Chi. Bears vs. N.Y. Giants, 1934
AFC-D: Cleveland vs. Oakland, 1980
4 By many teams

Turnovers

(Numbers of times losing the ball on interceptions and fumbles.)

Most Turnovers, Game

9 NFC: Washington vs. Chi. Bears, 1940
NFC: Detroit vs. Cleveland, 1954
AFC: Houston vs. Pittsburgh, 1978
8 NFC: N.Y. Giants vs. Chi. Bears, 1946
NFC: Los Angeles vs. Cleveland, 1955
NFC: Cleveland vs. Detroit, 1957
SB: Denver vs. Dallas, 1977
NFC-D: Minnesota vs. Philadelphia, 1980
7 AFC: Houston vs. San Diego, 1961
SB: Baltimore vs. Dallas, 1970
AFC: Pittsburgh vs. Oakland, 1975
NFC-D: Chicago vs. Dallas, 1977
NFC: Los Angeles vs. Dallas, 1978
AFC-D: San Diego vs. Miami, 1982
AFC: Buffalo vs. L.A. Raiders, 1990

Fewest Turnovers, Game

0 By many teams

Most Turnovers, Both Teams, Game

14 AFC: Houston (9) vs. Pittsburgh (5), 1978
13 NFC: Detroit (9) vs. Cleveland (4), 1954
AFC: Houston (7) vs. San Diego (6), 1961
12 AFC: Pittsburgh (7) vs. Oakland (5), 1975

Fewest Turnovers, Both Teams, Game

0 SB: Buffalo vs. N.Y. Giants, 1990
1 AFC-D: Baltimore (0) vs. Cincinnati (1), 1970
AFC-D: Pittsburgh (0) vs. Buffalo (1), 1974
AFC: Oakland (0) vs. Pittsburgh (1), 1976
NFC-D: Minnesota (0) vs. Washington (1), 1982
NFC-D: Chicago (0) vs. N.Y. Giants (1), 1985
SB: N.Y. Giants (0) vs. Denver (1), 1986
NFC: Washington (0) vs. Minnesota (1), 1987
AFC-D: Cincinnati (0) vs. L.A. Raiders (1), 1990
NFC: N.Y. Giants (0) vs. San Francisco (1), 1990
2 In many games

AFC-NFC PRO BOWL RECORDS

Compiled by Elias Sports Bureau

Individual Records

Service
Most Games

10 Lawrence Taylor, N.Y. Giants, 1982-91
9 *Ken Houston, Houston, 1971-73; Washington, 1974-79
Joe Greene, Pittsburgh, 1971-77, 1979-80
Jack Lambert, Pittsburgh, 1976-84
Walter Payton, Chicago, 1977-81, 1984-87
Harry Carson, N.Y. Giants, 1979-80, 1982-88
Mike Webster, Pittsburgh, 1979-86, 1988
Ronnie Lott, San Francisco, 1982-85, 1987-91
8 Tom Mack, Los Angeles, 1971-76, 1978-79
*Franco Harris, Pittsburgh, 1973-76, 1978-81
Lemar Parrish, Cincinnati, 1971-72, 1975-77; Washington, 1978, 1980-81
Art Shell, Oakland, 1973-79, 1981
Ted Hendricks, Baltimore, 1972-74; Green Bay, 1975; Oakland, 1981-82; L.A. Raiders, 1983-84
*John Hannah, New England, 1977, 1979-83, 1985-86
*Randy White, Dallas, 1978, 1980-86
*Mike Haynes, New England, 1978-81, 1983; L.A. Raiders, 1985-87
**Anthony Muñoz, Cincinnati, 1982-87, 1989-90
Mike Singletary, Chicago, 1984-91
*Also selected, but did not play, in one additional game
**Also selected, but did not play, in two additional games

Scoring
Points

Most Points, Career

30 Jan Stenerud, Kansas City, 1971-72, 1976; Green Bay, 1985 (6-pat, 8-fg)
29 Morten Andersen, New Orleans, 1986-89, 1991 (11-pat, 6-fg)
22 Eddie Murray, Detroit, 1981, 1990 (4-pat, 6 fg)

Most Points, Game

18 John Brockington, Green Bay, 1973 (3-td)
15 Garo Yepremian, Miami, 1974 (5-fg)
14 Jan Stenerud, Kansas City, 1972 (2-pat, 4-fg)

Touchdowns
Most Touchdowns, Career

3 John Brockington, Green Bay, 1972-74 (2-r, 1-p)
Earl Campbell, Houston, 1979-82, 1984 (3-r)
Chuck Muncie, New Orleans, 1980; San Diego, 1982-83 (3-r)
William Andrews, Atlanta, 1981-84 (1-r, 2-p)
Marcus Allen, L.A. Raiders, 1983, 1985-86, 1988 (2-r, 1-p)
2 By 12 players

Most Touchdowns, Game

3 John Brockington, Green Bay, 1973 (2-r, 1-p)
2 Mel Renfro, Dallas, 1971 (2-ret)
Earl Campbell, Houston, 1980 (2-r)
Chuck Muncie, New Orleans, 1980 (2-r)
William Andrews, Atlanta, 1984 (2-p)
Herschel Walker, Dallas, 1989 (2-r)
Johnny Johnson, Phoenix, 1991 (2-r)

Points After Touchdown
Most Points After Touchdown, Career

11 Morten Andersen, New Orleans, 1986-89, 1991 (11 att)
6 Chester Marcol, Green Bay, 1973, 1975 (6 att)
Mark Moseley, Washington, 1980, 1983 (7 att)
Ali Haji-Sheikh, N.Y. Giants, 1984 (6 att)
Jan Stenerud, Kansas City, 1971-72, 1976; Green Bay, 1985 (6 att)

Most Points After Touchdown, Game

6 Ali Haji-Sheikh, N.Y. Giants, 1984 (6 att)
4 Chester Marcol, Green Bay, 1973 (4 att)
Mark Moseley, Washington, 1980 (5 att)
Morten Andersen, New Orleans, 1986 (4 att), 1989 (4 att)

Field Goals
Most Field Goals Attempted, Career

15 Jan Stenerud, Kansas City, 1971-72, 1976; Green Bay, 1985
11 Morten Andersen, New Orleans, 1986-89, 1991
9 Eddie Murray, Detroit, 1981, 1990

Most Field Goals Attempted, Game

6 Jan Stenerud, Kansas City, 1972
Ed Murray, Detroit, 1981
Mark Moseley, Washington, 1983
5 Garo Yepremian, Miami, 1974
4 Jan Stenerud, Kansas City, 1976
Nick Lowery, Kansas City, 1991

Most Field Goals, Career

8 Jan Stenerud, Kansas City, 1971-72, 1976; Green Bay, 1985
6 Morten Andersen, New Orleans, 1986-89, 1991
Ed Murray, Detroit, 1981, 1990
5 Garo Yepremian, Miami, 1974, 1979

Most Field Goals, Game

5 Garo Yepremian, Miami, 1974 (5 att)
4 Jan Stenerud, Kansas City, 1972 (6 att)
Ed Murray, Detroit, 1981 (6 att)
3 Nick Lowery, Kansas City, 1991 (4 att)

Longest Field Goal

51 Morten Andersen, New Orleans, 1989
48 Jan Stenerud, Kansas City, 1972
43 Gary Anderson, Pittsburgh, 1984
Nick Lowery, Kansas City, 1991

Safeties
Most Safeties, Game

1 Art Still, Kansas City, 1983
Mark Gastineau, N.Y. Jets, 1985

Rushing
Attempts

Most Attempts, Career

81 Walter Payton, Chicago, 1977-81, 1984-87
68 O.J. Simpson, Buffalo, 1973-77
63 Eric Dickerson, L.A. Rams, 1984-85, 1987; Indianapolis, 1988-90

Most Attempts, Game

19 O.J. Simpson, Buffalo, 1974
17 Marv Hubbard, Oakland, 1974
16 O.J. Simpson, Buffalo, 1973
Marcus Allen, L.A. Raiders, 1986

Yards Gained
Most Yards Gained, Career

368 Walter Payton, Chicago, 1977-81, 1984-87
356 O.J. Simpson, Buffalo, 1973-77
220 Earl Campbell, Houston, 1979-82, 1984

Most Yards Gained, Game

112 O. J. Simpson, Buffalo, 1973
104 Marv Hubbard, Oakland, 1974
85 Neal Anderson, Chicago, 1989

Longest Run From Scrimmage

41 Lawrence McCutcheon, Los Angeles, 1976
32 Randall Cunningham, Philadelphia, 1989
30 O.J. Simpson, Buffalo, 1975

Average Gain
Highest Average Gain, Career (20 attempts)

5.81 Marv Hubbard, Oakland, 1972-74 (36-209)
5.71 Wilbert Montgomery, Philadelphia, 1979-80 (21-120)
5.36 Larry Csonka, Miami, 1971-72, 1975 (22-118)

Highest Average Gain, Game (10 attempts)

7.00 O.J. Simpson, Buffalo, 1973 (16-112)
Ottis Anderson, St. Louis, 1981 (10-70)
6.91 Walter Payton, Chicago, 1985 (11-76)
6.90 Earl Campbell, Houston, 1980 (10-69)

Touchdowns
Most Touchdowns, Career

3 Earl Campbell, Houston, 1979-82, 1984
Chuck Muncie, New Orleans, 1980; San Diego, 1982-83
2 John Brockington, Green Bay, 1972-74
O.J. Simpson, Buffalo, 1973-77
Walter Payton, Chicago, 1977-81, 1984-87
Marcus Allen, L.A. Raiders, 1983, 1985-86, 1988
Herschel Walker, Dallas, 1988-89
Johnny Johnson, Phoenix, 1991

Most Touchdowns, Game

2 John Brockington, Green Bay, 1973
Earl Campbell, Houston, 1980
Chuck Muncie, New Orleans, 1980
Herschel Walker, Dallas, 1989
Johnny Johnson, Phoenix, 1991

Passing
Attempts

Most Attempts, Career

120 Dan Fouts, San Diego, 1980-84, 1986
88 Bob Griese, Miami, 1971-72, 1974-75, 1977, 1979
57 Joe Montana, San Francisco, 1982, 1984-85, 1988

Most Attempts, Game

32 Bill Kenney, Kansas City, 1984
30 Dan Fouts, San Diego, 1983
28 Jim Hart, St. Louis, 1976

Completions
Most Completions, Career

63 Dan Fouts, San Diego, 1980-84, 1986
44 Bob Griese, Miami, 1971-72, 1974-75, 1977, 1979
33 Ken Anderson, Cincinnati, 1976-77, 1982-83

Most Completions, Game

21 Joe Theismann, Washington, 1984
17 Dan Fouts, San Diego, 1983
16 Dan Fouts, San Diego, 1986

Completion Percentage
Highest Completion Percentage, Career (40 attempts)

68.9 Joe Theismann, Washington, 1983-84 (45-31)
58.9 Ken Anderson, Cincinnati, 1976-77, 1982-83 (56-33)
55.8 Warren Moon, Houston, 1989-91 (43-24)

Highest Completion Percentage, Game (10 attempts)

90.0 Archie Manning, New Orleans, 1980 (10-9)
77.8 Joe Theismann, Washington, 1984 (27-21)
72.2 Jim Everett, L.A. Rams, 1991 (18-13)

Yards Gained
Most Yards Gained, Career

890 Dan Fouts, San Diego, 1980-84, 1986
554 Bob Griese, Miami, 1971-72, 1974-75, 1977, 1979
398 Ken Anderson, Cincinnati, 1976-77, 1982-83

Most Yards Gained, Game

274 Dan Fouts, San Diego, 1983

242 Joe Theismann, Washington, 1984
212 Phil Simms, N.Y. Giants, 1986

Longest Completion

64 Dan Pastorini, Houston (to Burrough, Houston), 1976 (TD)
59 Randall Cunningham, Philadelphia (to Jackson, Philadelphia [19 yards] lateral to Byner, Washington [40 yards]), 1991
57 James Harris, Los Angeles (to Gray, St. Louis), 1975
Ken Anderson, Cincinnati (to G. Pruitt, Cleveland), 1977

Average Gain

Highest Average Gain, Career (40 attempts)

7.91 Randall Cunningham, Philadelphia, 1989-91 (44-348)
7.64 Joe Theismann, Washington, 1983-84 (45-344)
7.42 Dan Fouts, San Diego, 1980-84, 1986 (120-890)

Highest Average Gain, Game (10 attempts)

15.27 Randall Cunningham, Philadelphia, 1991 (11-168)
11.40 Ken Anderson, Cincinnati, 1977 (10-114)
11.20 Archie Manning, New Orleans, 1980 (10-112)

Touchdowns

Most Touchdowns, Career

3 Joe Theismann, Washington, 1983-84
Joe Montana, San Francisco, 1982, 1984-85, 1988
Phil Simms, N.Y. Giants, 1986
2 James Harris, Los Angeles, 1975
Mike Boryla, Philadelphia, 1976
Ken Anderson, Cincinnati, 1976-77, 1982-83
Jim Kelly, Buffalo, 1988, 1991

Most Touchdowns, Game

3 Joe Theismann, Washington, 1984
Phil Simms, N.Y. Giants, 1986
2 James Harris, Los Angeles, 1975
Mike Boryla, Philadelphia, 1976
Ken Anderson, Cincinnati, 1977
Jim Kelly, Buffalo, 1991

Had Intercepted

Most Passes Had Intercepted, Career

8 Dan Fouts, San Diego, 1980-84, 1986
6 Jim Hart, St. Louis, 1975-78
5 Ken Stabler, Oakland, 1974-75, 1978

Most Passes Had Intercepted, Game

5 Jim Hart, St. Louis, 1977
4 Ken Stabler, Oakland, 1974
3 Dan Fouts, San Diego, 1986
Mark Rypien, Washington, 1990

Most Attempts, Without Interception, Game

27 Joe Theismann, Washington, 1984
Phil Simms, N.Y. Giants, 1986
26 John Brodie, San Francisco, 1971
Danny White, Dallas, 1983
21 Roman Gabriel, Philadelphia, 1974
Dan Marino, Miami, 1985

Percentage, Passes Had Intercepted

Lowest Percentage, Passes Had Intercepted, Career (40 attempts)

0.00 Joe Theismann, Washington, 1983-84 (45-0)
2.13 Dave Krieg, Seattle, 1985, 1989-90 (47-1)
2.27 Randall Cunningham, Philadelphia, 1989-91 (44-1)

Pass Receiving

Receptions

Most Receptions, Career

18 Walter Payton, Chicago, 1977-81, 1984-87
17 Steve Largent, Seattle, 1979, 1982, 1985-88
14 John Stallworth, Pittsburgh, 1980, 1983, 1985
James Lofton, Green Bay, 1979, 1981-86
Marcus Allen, L.A. Raiders, 1983, 1985-86, 1988

Most Receptions, Game

8 Steve Largent, Seattle, 1986
7 John Stallworth, Pittsburgh, 1983
6 John Stallworth, Pittsburgh, 1980
Kellen Winslow, San Diego, 1982
Gary Clark, Washington, 1991

Yards Gained

Most Yards Gained, Career

236 Steve Largent, Seattle, 1979, 1982, 1985-88
226 Wes Chandler, New Orleans, 1980; San Diego, 1983-84, 1986
206 James Lofton, Green Bay, 1979, 1981-86

Most Yards Gained, Game

114 Wes Chandler, San Diego, 1986
96 Ken Burrough, Houston, 1976
91 Alfred Jenkins, Atlanta, 1981

Longest Reception

64 Ken Burrough, Houston (from Pastorini, Houston), 1976 (TD)
59 Keith Jackson, Philadelphia (19 yards) lateral to Earnest Byner, Washington (40 yards) (from Cunningham, Philadelphia), 1991
57 Mel Gray, St. Louis (from Harris, Los Angeles), 1975
Greg Pruitt, Cleveland (from Anderson, Cincinnati), 1977

Touchdowns

Most Touchdowns, Career

2 Mel Gray, St. Louis, 1975-78
Cliff Branch, Oakland, 1975-78
Terry Metcalf, St. Louis, 1975-76, 1978
Tony Hill, Dallas, 1979-80, 1986
William Andrews, Atlanta, 1981-84
James Lofton, Green Bay, 1979, 1981-86
Jimmie Giles, Tampa Bay, 1981-83, 1986

Most Touchdowns, Game

2 William Andrews, Atlanta, 1984

Interceptions By

Most Interceptions By, Career

4 Everson Walls, Dallas, 1982-84, 1986
3 Ken Houston, Houston, 1971-73; Washington, 1974-79
Jack Lambert, Pittsburgh, 1976-84
Ted Hendricks, Baltimore, 1972-74; Green Bay, 1975; Oakland, 1981-82; L.A. Raiders, 1983-84
Mike Haynes, New England, 1978-81, 1983; L.A. Raiders, 1985-87
2 By seven players

Most Interceptions By, Game

2 Mel Blount, Pittsburgh, 1977
Everson Walls, Dallas, 1982, 1983
LeRoy Irvin, L.A. Rams, 1986
David Fulcher, Cincinnati, 1990

Yards Gained

Most Yards Gained, Career

77 Ted Hendricks, Baltimore, 1972-74; Green Bay, 1975; Oakland, 1981-82; L.A. Raiders, 1983-84
51 Jerry Gray, L.A. Rams, 1987-90
48 Joey Browner, Minnesota, 1986-90

Most Yards Gained, Game

65 Ted Hendricks, Baltimore, 1973
51 Jerry Gray, L.A. Rams, 1990
48 Joey Browner, Minnesota, 1986

Longest Gain

65 Ted Hendricks, Baltimore, 1973
51 Jerry Gray, L.A. Rams, 1990 (TD)
48 Joey Browner, Minnesota, 1986 (TD)

Touchdowns

Most Touchdowns, Game

1 Bobby Bell, Kansas City, 1973
Nolan Cromwell, L.A. Rams, 1984
Joey Browner, Minnesota, 1986
Jerry Gray, L.A. Rams, 1990
Mike Johnson, Cleveland, 1990

Punting

Most Punts, Career

33 Ray Guy, Oakland, 1974-79, 1981
19 Dave Jennings, N.Y. Giants, 1979-81, 1983
16 Jerrel Wilson, Kansas City, 1971-73
Tom Wittum, San Francisco, 1974-75
Rohn Stark, Indianapolis, 1986-87, 1991

Most Punts, Game

10 Reggie Roby, Miami, 1985
9 Tom Wittum, San Francisco, 1974
Rohn Stark, Indianapolis, 1987
8 Jerrel Wilson, Kansas City, 1971
Tom Skladany, Detroit, 1982

Longest Punt

64 Tom Wittum, San Francisco, 1974
61 Reggie Roby, Miami, 1985
60 Ron Widby, Dallas, 1972

Average Yardage

Highest Average, Career (10 punts)

45.25 Jerrel Wilson, Kansas City, 1971-73 (16-724)
44.79 Reggie Roby, Miami, 1985, 1990 (14-627)
44.64 Ray Guy, Oakland, 1974-79, 1981 (33-1,473)

Highest Average, Game (4 punts)

49.57 Jim Arnold, Detroit, 1988 (7-347)
49.00 Ray Guy, Oakland, 1974 (4-196)
47.75 Bob Grupp, Kansas City, 1980 (4-191)

Punt Returns

Most Punt Returns, Career

13 Rick Upchurch, Denver, 1977, 1979-80, 1983
11 Vai Sikahema, St. Louis, 1987-88
10 Mike Nelms, Washington, 1981-83

Most Punt Returns, Game

7 Vai Sikahema, St. Louis, 1987
6 Henry Ellard, L.A. Rams, 1985
Gerald McNeil, Cleveland, 1988
5 Rick Upchurch, Denver, 1980
Mike Nelms, Washington, 1981
Carl Roaches, Houston, 1982

Most Fair Catches, Game

2 Jerry Logan, Baltimore, 1971
Dick Anderson, Miami, 1974
Henry Ellard, L.A. Rams, 1985

Yards Gained

Most Yards Gained, Career

183 Billy Johnson, Houston, 1976, 1978; Atlanta, 1984
138 Rick Upchurch, Denver, 1977, 1979-80, 1983
119 Mike Nelms, Washington, 1981-83

Most Yards Gained, Game

159 Billy Johnson, Houston, 1976
138 Mel Renfro, Dallas, 1971
117 Wally Henry, Philadelphia, 1980

Longest Punt Return

90 Billy Johnson, Houston, 1976 (TD)
86 Wally Henry, Philadelphia, 1980 (TD)
82 Mel Renfro, Dallas, 1971 (TD)

Touchdowns

Most Touchdowns, Game

2 Mel Renfro, Dallas, 1971
1 Billy Johnson, Houston, 1976
Wally Henry, Philadelphia, 1980

Kickoff Returns

Most Kickoff Returns, Career

10 Rick Upchurch, Denver, 1977, 1979-80, 1983
Greg Pruitt, Cleveland, 1974-75, 1977-78; L.A. Raiders, 1984
8 Mike Nelms, Washington, 1981-83
6 Terry Metcalf, St. Louis, 1975-76, 1978
Vai Sikahema, St. Louis, 1987-88

Most Kickoff Returns, Game

6 Greg Pruitt, L.A. Raiders, 1984
5 Les (Speedy) Duncan, Washington, 1972
Ron Smith, Chicago, 1973
Herb Mul-Key, Washington, 1974
Mel Gray, Detroit, 1991
4 By six players

Yards Gained

Most Yards Gained, Career

309 Greg Pruitt, Cleveland, 1974-75, 1977-78; L.A. Raiders, 1984
222 Rick Upchurch, Denver, 1977, 1979-80, 1983
175 Les (Speedy) Duncan, Washington, 1972

Most Yards Gained, Game

192 Greg Pruitt, L.A. Raiders, 1984
175 Les (Speedy) Duncan, Washington, 1972
152 Ron Smith, Chicago, 1973

Longest Kickoff Return

62 Greg Pruitt, L.A. Raiders, 1984
61 Eugene (Mercury) Morris, Miami, 1972
55 Ron Smith, Chicago, 1973

Touchdowns

Most Touchdowns, Game

None

Fumbles

Most Fumbles, Career

6 Dan Fouts, San Diego, 1980-84, 1986
4 Lawrence McCutcheon, Los Angeles, 1974-78
Franco Harris, Pittsburgh, 1973-76, 1978-81
Jay Schroeder, Washington, 1987
Vai Sikahema, St. Louis, 1987-88
3 O.J. Simpson, Buffalo, 1973-77
William Andrews, Atlanta, 1981-84
Joe Montana, San Francisco, 1982, 1984-85, 1988
Walter Payton, Chicago, 1977-81, 1984-87
Neil Lomax, St. Louis, 1985, 1988

Most Fumbles, Game

4 Jay Schroeder, Washington, 1987
3 Dan Fouts, San Diego, 1982
Vai Sikahema, St. Louis, 1987
2 By 11 players

Recoveries

Most Fumbles Recovered, Career

3 Harold Jackson, Philadelphia, 1973; Los Angeles, 1974, 1976, 1978 (3-own)
Dan Fouts, San Diego, 1980-84, 1986 (3-own)
Randy White, Dallas, 1978, 1980-86 (3-opp)
2 By many players

Most Fumbles Recovered, Game

2 Dick Anderson, Miami, 1974 (1-own, 1-opp)
Harold Jackson, Los Angeles, 1974 (2-own)
Dan Fouts, San Diego, 1982 (2-own)
Joey Browner, Minnesota, 1990 (2-opp)

Yardage

Longest Fumble Return

83 Art Still, Kansas City, 1985 (TD, opp)
51 Phil Villapiano, Oakland, 1974 (opp)
37 Sam Mills, New Orleans, 1988 (opp)

Touchdowns

Most Touchdowns, Game

1 Art Still, Kansas City, 1985
Keith Millard, Minnesota, 1990

Sacks

Sacks have been compiled since 1983.

Most Sacks, Career

7 Mark Gastineau, N.Y. Jets, 1983-86
Reggie White, Philadelphia, 1987-91
Howie Long, L.A. Raiders, 1984-88, 1990

Most Sacks, Game

4 Mark Gastineau, N.Y. Jets, 1985
Reggie White, Philadelphia, 1987
3 Richard Dent, Chicago, 1985
Bruce Smith, Buffalo, 1991
2 By many players

Team Records

Scoring

Most Points, Game

45 NFC, 1984

Fewest Points, Game

3 AFC, 1984, 1989

Most Points, Both Teams, Game

64 NFC (37) vs. AFC (27), 1980

Fewest Points, Both Teams, Game

16 NFC (6) vs. AFC (10), 1987

Touchdowns

Most Touchdowns, Game

6 NFC, 1984

Fewest Touchdowns, Game

0 AFC, 1971, 1974, 1984, 1989
NFC, 1987, 1988

Most Touchdowns, Both Teams, Game

8 AFC (4) vs. NFC (4), 1973
NFC (5) vs. AFC (3), 1980

Fewest Touchdowns, Both Teams, Game

1 AFC (0) vs. NFC (1), 1974
NFC (0) vs. AFC (1), 1987
NFC (0) vs. AFC (1), 1988

Points After Touchdown

Most Points After Touchdown, Game

6 NFC, 1984

Most Points After Touchdown, Both Teams, Game

7 NFC (4) vs. AFC (3), 1973
NFC (4) vs. AFC (3), 1980
NFC (4) vs. AFC (3), 1986

Field Goals

Most Field Goals Attempted, Game

6 AFC, 1972
NFC, 1981, 1983

Most Field Goals Attempted, Both Teams, Game

9 NFC (6) vs. AFC (3), 1983

Most Field Goals, Game

5 AFC, 1974

Most Field Goals, Both Teams, Game

7 AFC (5) vs. NFC (2), 1974

Net Yards Gained Rushing And Passing

Most Yards Gained, Game

466 AFC, 1983

Fewest Yards Gained, Game

146 AFC, 1971

Most Yards Gained, Both Teams, Game

811 AFC (466) vs. NFC (345), 1983

Fewest Yards Gained, Both Teams, Game

424 AFC (202) vs. NFC (222), 1987

Rushing

Attempts

Most Attempts, Game

50 AFC, 1974

Fewest Attempts, Game

15 AFC, 1989

Most Attempts, Both Teams, Game

80 AFC (50) vs. NFC (30), 1974

Fewest Attempts, Both Teams, Game

48 AFC (20) vs. NFC (28), 1991

Yards Gained

Most Yards Gained, Game

224 NFC, 1976

Fewest Yards Gained, Game

64 NFC, 1974

Most Yards Gained, Both Teams, Game

425 NFC (224) vs. AFC (201), 1976

Fewest Yards Gained, Both Teams, Game

178 AFC (66) vs. NFC (112), 1971

Touchdowns

Most Touchdowns, Game

3 NFC, 1989, 1991

Most Touchdowns, Both Teams, Game

4 AFC (2) vs. NFC (2), 1973
AFC (2) vs. NFC (2), 1980

Passing

Attempts

Most Attempts, Game

50 AFC, 1983

Fewest Attempts, Game

17 NFC, 1972

Most Attempts, Both Teams, Game

94 AFC (50) vs. NFC (44), 1983

Fewest Attempts, Both Teams, Game

42 NFC (17) vs. AFC (25), 1972

Completions

Most Completions, Game

31 AFC, 1983

Fewest Completions, Game

7 NFC, 1972, 1982

Most Completions, Both Teams, Game

55 AFC (31) vs. NFC (24), 1983

Fewest Completions, Both Teams, Game

18 NFC (7) vs. AFC (11), 1972

Yards Gained

Most Yards Gained, Game

387 AFC, 1983

Fewest Yards Gained, Game

42 NFC, 1982

Most Yards Gained, Both Teams, Game

608 AFC (387) vs. NFC (221), 1983

Fewest Yards Gained, Both Teams, Game

215 NFC (89) vs. AFC (126), 1972

Times Sacked
Most Times Sacked, Game
9 NFC, 1985
Fewest Times Sacked, Game
0 NFC, 1971
Most Times Sacked, Both Teams, Game
17 NFC (9) vs. AFC (8), 1985
Fewest Times Sacked, Both Teams, Game
4 AFC (2) vs. NFC (2), 1978

Touchdowns
Most Touchdowns, Game
4 NFC, 1984
Most Touchdowns, Both Teams, Game
5 NFC (3) vs. AFC (2), 1986

Interceptions By
Most Interceptions By, Game
6 AFC, 1977
Most Interceptions By, Both Teams, Game
7 AFC (6) vs. NFC (1), 1977

Yards Gained
Most Yards Gained, Game
78 NFC, 1986
Most Yards Gained, Both Teams, Game
99 NFC (64) vs. AFC (35), 1975

Touchdowns
Most Touchdowns, Game
1 AFC, 1973, 1990
NFC, 1984, 1986, 1990

Punting
Most Punts, Game
10 AFC, 1985
Fewest Punts, Game
0 NFC, 1989
Most Punts, Both Teams, Game
16 AFC (10) vs. NFC (6), 1985
Fewest Punts, Both Teams, Game
5 NFC (0) vs. AFC (5), 1989
AFC (2) vs. NFC (3), 1991

Average Yardage
Highest Average, Game
50.50 AFC, 1991 (2-101)

Punt Returns
Most Punt Returns, Game
7 NFC, 1985, 1987
Fewest Punt Returns, Game
0 AFC, 1984, 1989
Most Punt Returns, Both Teams, Game
11 NFC (7) vs. AFC (4), 1985
Fewest Punt Returns, Both Teams, Game
3 AFC (0) vs. NFC (3), 1984
AFC (0) vs. NFC (3), 1989
NFC (1) vs. AFC (2), 1991

Yards Gained
Most Yards Gained, Game
177 AFC, 1976
Fewest Yards Gained, Game
−1 NFC, 1991
Most Yards Gained, Both Teams, Game
263 AFC (177) vs. NFC (86), 1976
Fewest Yards Gained, Both Teams, Game
16 AFC (0) vs. NFC (16), 1984

Touchdowns
Most Touchdowns, Game
2 NFC, 1971

Kickoff Returns
Most Kickoff Returns, Game
7 AFC, 1984
Fewest Kickoff Returns, Game
1 NFC, 1971, 1984
AFC, 1988, 1991
Most Kickoff Returns, Both Teams, Game
10 AFC (5) vs. NFC (5), 1976
AFC (5) vs. NFC (5), 1986
Fewest Kickoff Returns, Both Teams, Game
5 NFC (2) vs. AFC (3), 1979
AFC (1) vs. NFC (4), 1988

Yards Gained
Most Yards Gained, Game
215 AFC, 1984
Fewest Yards Gained, Game
6 NFC, 1971
Most Yards Gained, Both Teams, Game
293 NFC (200) vs. AFC (93), 1972
Fewest Yards Gained, Both Teams, Game
99 NFC (48) vs. AFC (51), 1987

Touchdowns
Most Touchdowns, Game
None

Fumbles
Most Fumbles, Game
10 NFC, 1974
Most Fumbles, Both Teams, Game
15 NFC (10) vs. AFC (5), 1974

Recoveries
Most Fumbles Recovered, Game
10 NFC, 1974 (6 own, 4 opp)
Most Fumbles Lost, Game
4 AFC, 1974, 1988
NFC, 1974

Yards Gained
Most Yards Gained, Game
87 AFC, 1985

Touchdowns
Most Touchdowns, Game
1 AFC, 1985
NFC, 1990

Turnovers
(Number of times losing the ball on interceptions and fumbles.)
Most Turnovers, Game
8 AFC, 1974
Fewest Turnovers, Game
0 AFC, 1991
NFC, 1991
Most Turnovers, Both Teams, Game
12 AFC (8) vs. NFC (4), 1974
Fewest Turnovers, Both Teams, Game
0 AFC vs. NFC, 1991

RULES

1991 NFL Roster of Officials

Jerry Seeman, Director of Officiating
Jack Reader, Assistant Director of Officiating
Tony Veteri, Supervisor of Officials
Leo Miles, Supervisor of Officials

No.	Name	Position	College
25	Alderton, John	Line Judge	Portland State
115	Ancich, Hendi	Umpire	Harbor College
81	Anderson, Dave	Head Linesman	Salem College
34	Austin, Gerald	Referee	Western Carolina
22	Baetz, Paul	Back Judge	Heidelberg
116	Baker, Bob	Line Judge	East Texas State
91	Baker, Ken	Back Judge	Eastern Illinois
26	Baltz, Mark	Head Linesman	Ohio
55	Barnes, Tom	Line Judge	Minnesota
14	Barth, Gene	Referee	St. Louis
56	Baynes, Ron	Line Judge	Auburn
32	Bergman, Jeff	Line Judge	Robert Morris
17	Bergman, Jerry	Head Linesman	Duquesne
83	Blum, Ron	Line Judge	Marin College
90	Borgard, Mike	Side Judge	St. Louis
110	Botchan, Ron	Umpire	Occidental
101	Boylston, Bob	Umpire	Alabama
94	Carey, Mike	Side Judge	Santa Clara
39	Carlsen, Don	Side Judge	Cal State-Chico
63	Carollo, Bill	Side Judge	Wisconsin
43	Cashion, Red	Referee	Texas A&M
24	Clymer, Roy	Back Judge	New Mexico State
65	Coleman, Walt	Line Judge	Arkansas
27	Conway, Al	Umpire	Army
71	Coukart, Ed	Umpire	Northwestern
61	Creed, Dick	Side Judge	Louisville
75	Daopoulos, Jim	Back Judge	Kentucky
78	Demmas, Art	Umpire	Vanderbilt
6	Dooley, Tom	Referee	VMI
113	Dorkowski, Don	Field Judge	Cal State-Los Angeles
102	Douglas, Merrill	Side Judge	Utah
57	Fiffick, Ed	Umpire	Marquette
47	Fincken, Tom	Side Judge	Kansas State
111	Frantz, Earnie	Head Linesman	No College
50	Gereb, Neil	Umpire	California
72	Gierke, Terry	Head Linesman	Portland State
15	Glass, Bama	Line Judge	Colorado
3	Golmont, Van	Side Judge	Miami
19	Green, Scott	Field Judge	Delaware
23	Grier, Johnny	Referee	University of D.C.
40	Haggerty, Pat	Referee	Colorado State
96	Hakes, Don	Field Judge	Bradley
104	Hamer, Dale	Referee	California, Pa.
42	Hamilton, Dave	Umpire	Utah
44	Hampton, Donnie	Field Judge	Georgia
105	Hantak, Dick	Referee	Southeastern Missouri
112	Haynes, Joe	Line Judge	Alcorn State
54	Hayward, George	Head Linesman	Missouri
85	Hochuli, Ed	Back Judge	Texas-El Paso
114	Johnson, Tom	Head Linesman	Miami, Ohio
97	Jones, Nathan	Side Judge	Lewis & Clark
106	Jury, Al	Back Judge	San Bernardino Valley
107	Kearney, Jim	Back Judge	Pennsylvania
67	Keck, John	Umpire	Cornell College
108	Kemp, Stan	Referee	Michigan
86	Kukar, Bernie	Referee	St. John's
120	Lane, Gary	Side Judge	Missouri
18	Lewis, Bob	Field Judge	No College
49	Look, Dean	Side Judge	Michigan State
98	Lovett, Bill	Back Judge	Maryland
59	Luckett, Phil	Field Judge	Texas-El Paso
82	Mallette, Pat	Field Judge	Nebraska
9	Markbreit, Jerry	Referee	Illinois
38	Maurer, Bruce	Head Linesman	Ohio State
48	McCarter, Gordon	Referee	Western Reserve
95	McElwee, Bob	Referee	Navy
41	McKenzie, Dick	Line Judge	Ashland
76	Merrifield, Ed	Field Judge	Missouri
80	Millis, Tim	Back Judge	Millsaps
117	Montgomery, Ben	Umpire	Morehouse
36	Moore, Bob	Back Judge	Dayton
20	Nemmers, Larry	Referee	Upper Iowa
51	Orem, Dale	Line Judge	Louisville
77	Orr, Don	Field Judge	Vanderbilt
10	Phares, Ron	Head Linesman	Virginia Tech
79	Pointer, Aaron	Head Linesman	Pacific Lutheran
92	Poole, Jim	Back Judge	San Diego State
58	Quinby, Bill	Side Judge	Iowa
5	Quirk, Jim	Line Judge	Delaware
53	Reynolds, Bill	Line Judge	West Chester State
68	Richard, Louis	Back Judge	S.W. Louisiana
30	Riggs, Dennis	Umpire	Bellarmine
121	Rivers, Sanford	Head Linesman	Youngstown State
46	Robison, John	Field Judge	Utah
33	Roe, Howard	Referee	Wichita State
21	Schleyer, John	Head Linesman	Millersville
122	Schmitz, Bill	Field Judge	Colorado State
109	Semon, Sid	Head Linesman	Southern California
118	Sifferman, Tom	Back Judge	Seattle
73	Skelton, Bobby	Field Judge	Alabama
29	Slavin, Howard	Side Judge	Southern California
119	Spitler, Ron	Side Judge	Panhandle State
103	Stuart, Rex	Umpire	Appalachian State
4	Toole, Doug	Back Judge	Utah State
37	Upson, Larry	Field Judge	Prince George C.C.
93	Vaughan, Jack	Field Judge	Mississippi State
100	Wagner, Bob	Umpire	Penn State
28	Wedge, Don	Side Judge	Ohio Wesleyan
87	Weidner, Paul	Head Linesman	Cincinnati
89	Wells, Gordon	Umpire	Occidental
123	White, Tom	Referee	Temple
99	Williams, Banks	Back Judge	Houston
8	Williams, Dale	Head Linesman	Cal St.-Northridge
84	Wortman, Bob	Field Judge	Findlay
16	Wyant, David	Side Judge	Virginia
11	Wyant, Fred	Line Judge	West Virginia

1991 NFL Replay Officials

Bob Beeks—Twenty-two years as an NFL Line Judge. He officiated in five Super Bowls (XIV, XVI, XVIII, XXI, & XXIII). Second year as Replay Official.

Mark Burns—Worked in League office for seven years with five years in Officiating Department. He has been a game observer since 1986. Fifth year as Replay Official.

Royal Cathcart—Sixteen years as an NFL Line Judge and Side Judge. He is a former NFL player. Fifth year as Replay Official.

Bill Fette—Twenty-five years as a Field Judge in the Pac-10. Worked three Rose Bowls. Fourth year as Replay Official.

Jack Fette—Twenty-three years as an NFL Line Judge. He officiated in five Super Bowls (V, VIII, X, XII, & XXII). Fourth year as Replay Official.

Fritz Graf—Twenty-four years as an NFL Field Judge. He has been a game observer since 1984. He officiated in four Super Bowls (V, VIII, XV, & XVIII). Sixth year as Replay Official.

Dave Hawk—Eighteen years as an NFL Side Judge. Second year as Replay Official.

Chuck Heberling—Twenty-two years as an NFL Referee and Line Judge. Sixth year as Replay Official.

Dave Kamanski—Twenty-five years as NCAA Official. Referee in Pac-10 for 20 years. Worked three Rose Bowls, three East-West Shrine Games, and three Japan Bowls. Fourth year as Replay Official.

Tom Kelleher—Twenty-eight years as an NFL Back Judge. He officiated in five Super Bowls (IV, VII, XI, XV, & XIX). Fourth year as Replay Official.

Norm Kragseth—Fourteen years as an NFL Head Linesman. First year as Replay Official.

Cal Lepore—Fifteen years as an NFL Head Linesman and Referee. He officiated in Super Bowl III. Sixth year as Replay Official.

Al Sabato—Twenty years as an NFL Head Linesman. He has been a game observer since 1982. He officiated in two Super Bowls (I & VI). Sixth year as Replay Official.

George Sladky—Seventeen years as an NCAA official. Nine years with the Big Ten and eight with the Southwest Conference. He worked six bowl games. Fifth year as Replay Official.

Bill Stanley—Seventeen years as an NFL Field Judge. First year as Replay Official.

Numerical Roster

No.	Name	Position
3	Van Golmont	SJ
4	Doug Toole	BJ
5	Jim Quirk	LJ
6	Tom Dooley	R
8	Dale Williams	HL
9	Jerry Markbreit	R
10	Ron Phares	HL
11	Fred Wyant	LJ
14	Gene Barth	R
15	Bama Glass	LJ
16	David Wyant	SJ
17	Jerry Bergman	HL
18	Bob Lewis	FJ
19	Scott Green	FJ
20	Larry Nemmers	R
21	John Schleyer	HL
22	Paul Baetz	BJ
23	Johnny Grier	R
24	Roy Clymer	BJ
25	John Alderton	LJ
26	Mark Baltz	HL
27	Al Conway	U
28	Don Wedge	SJ
29	Howard Slavin	SJ
30	Dennis Riggs	U
32	Jeff Bergman	LJ
33	Howard Roe	R
34	Gerald Austin	R
36	Bob Moore	BJ
37	Larry Upson	FJ
38	Bruce Maurer	HL
39	Don Carlsen	SJ
40	Pat Haggerty	R
41	Dick McKenzie	LJ
42	Dave Hamilton	U
43	Red Cashion	R
44	Donnie Hampton	FJ
46	John Robison	FJ
47	Tom Fincken	SJ
48	Gordon McCarter	R
49	Dean Look	SJ
50	Neil Gereb	U
51	Dale Orem	LJ
53	Bill Reynolds	LJ
54	George Hayward	HL
55	Tom Barnes	LJ
56	Ron Baynes	LJ
57	Ed Fiffick	U
58	Bill Quinby	SJ
59	Phil Luckett	FJ
61	Dick Creed	SJ
63	Bill Carollo	SJ
65	Walt Coleman	LJ
67	John Keck	U
68	Louis Richard	BJ
71	Ed Coukart	U
72	Terry Gierke	HL
73	Bobby Skelton	FJ
75	Jim Daopoulos	BJ
76	Ed Merrifield	FJ
77	Don Orr	FJ
78	Art Demmas	U
79	Aaron Pointer	HL
80	Tim Millis	BJ
81	Dave Anderson	HL
82	Pat Mallette	FJ
83	Ron Blum	LJ
84	Bob Wortman	FJ
85	Ed Hochuli	BJ
86	Bernie Kukar	R
87	Paul Weidner	HL
89	Gordon Wells	U
90	Mike Borgard	SJ
91	Ken Baker	BJ
92	Jim Poole	BJ
93	Jack Vaughan	FJ
94	Mike Carey	SJ
95	Bob McElwee	R
96	Don Hakes	FJ
97	Nathan Jones	SJ
98	Bill Lovett	BJ
99	Banks Williams	BJ
100	Bob Wagner	U
101	Bob Boylston	U
102	Merrill Douglas	SJ
103	Rex Stuart	U
104	Dale Hamer	R
105	Dick Hantak	R
106	Al Jury	BJ
107	Jim Kearney	BJ
108	Stan Kemp	R
109	Sid Semon	HL
110	Ron Botchan	U
111	Earnie Frantz	HL
112	Joe Haynes	LJ
113	Don Dorkowski	FJ
114	Tom Johnson	HL
115	Hendi Ancich	U
116	Bob Baker	LJ
117	Ben Montgomery	U
118	Tom Sifferman	BJ
119	Ron Spitler	SJ
120	Gary Lane	SJ
121	Sanford Rivers	HL
122	Bill Schmitz	FJ
123	Tom White	R

1991 Officials at a Glance

Referees

Gerry Austin, No. **34,** Western Carolina, associate superintendent, county schools, 10th year.
Gene Barth, No. **14,** St. Louis, president, oil company, 21st year.
Red Cashion, No. **43,** Texas A&M, chairman, insurance company, 20th year.
Tom Dooley, No. **6,** VMI, general contractor, 14th year.
Johnny Grier, No. **23,** University of D.C., planning engineer, 11th year.
Pat Haggerty, No. **40,** Colorado State, retired educator, 27th year.
Dale Hamer, No. **104,** California (Pa.) University, vice-president, finance, 14th year.
Dick Hantak, No. **105,** Southeastern Missouri, educator, 14th year.
Stan Kemp, No. **108,** Michigan, independent insurance agent, 6th year.
Bernie Kukar, No. **86,** St. John's, owner/director, summer camp for boys, 8th year.
Jerry Markbreit, No. **9,** Illinois, trade and barter manager, 16th year.
Gordon McCarter, No. **48,** Western Reserve, sales manager, 25th year.
Bob McElwee, No. **95,** Navy, owner, heavy construction firm, 16th year.
Larry Nemmers, No. **20,** Upper Iowa, high school principal, 7th year.
Howard Roe, No. **33,** Wichita State, director, administration and finance, 8th year.
Tom White, No. **123,** Temple, president, athletic sportswear, 3rd year.

Umpires

Hendi Ancich, No. **115,** Harbor, longshoreman, 10th year.
Ron Botchan, No. **110,** Occidental, college professor, former AFL player, 12th year.
Bob Boylston, No. **101,** Alabama, stockbroker, 14th year.
Al Conway, No. **27,** Army, director of manufacturing, 23rd year.
Ed Coukart, No. **71,** Northwestern, senior vice-president, commercial bank, 3rd year.
Art Demmas, No. **78,** Vanderbilt, investments, financial planning, 24th year.
Ed Fiffick, No. **57,** Marquette, podiatrist, 13th year.
Neil Gereb, No. **50,** California, project manager, aircraft company, 11th year.
Dave Hamilton, No. **42,** Utah, assistant executive director, 17th year.
John Keck, No. **67,** Cornell College, petroleum distributor, 20th year.
Ben Montgomery, No. **117,** Morehouse, school administrator, 10th year.
Dennis Riggs, No. **30,** Bellarmine, seminary vice-president, 4th year.
Rex Stuart, No. **103,** Appalachian State, insurance agent, 8th year.
Bob Wagner, No. **100,** Penn State, executive director, cardiovascular institute, 7th year.
Gordon Wells, No. **89,** Occidental, college department chairman, 20th year.

Head Linesmen

Dave Anderson, No. **81,** Salem, insurance executive, 8th year.
Mark Baltz, No. **26,** Ohio, manufacturer's representative, 3rd year.
Jerry Bergman, No. **17,** Duquesne, executive director, pension fund, 26th year.
Earnie Frantz, No. **111,** vice-president and manager, insurance company, 11th year.
Terry Gierke, No. **72,** Portland State, real estate broker, 11th year.
George Hayward, No. **54,** Missouri, vice-president and manager, warehouse company, 1st year.
Tom Johnson, No. **114,** Miami, Ohio, teacher, executive vice-president security company, 10th year.
Bruce Maurer, No. **38,** Ohio State, administrator/associate director, recreational sports, 5th year.
Ron Phares, No. **10,** Virginia Tech, president, construction company, 7th year.
Aaron Pointer, No. **79,** Pacific Lutheran, park department administrator, 5th year.
Sanford Rivers, No. **121,** Youngstown State, assistant vice-president, school administration, 3rd year.
John Schleyer, No. **21,** Millersville, medical sales, 2nd year.
Sid Semon, No. **109,** Southern California, chairman, physical education department, 14th year.
Paul Weidner, No. **87,** Cincinnati, marketing manager, 6th year.
Dale Williams, No. **8,** Cal State-Northridge, owner, coin-operated laundromats, 12th year.

Line Judges

John Alderton, No. **25,** Portland State, vice-president, insurance, 3rd year.
Bob Baker, No. **116,** East Texas State, vocational coordinator, 5th year.
Tom Barnes, No. **55,** Minnesota, manufacturing representative, 6th year.
Ron Baynes, No. **56,** Auburn, school administrator, coach, 5th year.
Jeff Bergman, No. **32,** Robert Morris, president and chief executive officer, medical services, 1st year.
Ron Blum, No. **83,** Marin College, P.G.A. golf professional, 7th year.
Walt Coleman, No. **65,** Arkansas, president, dairy processor, 3rd year.
Bama Glass, No. **15,** Colorado, owner/manager, retail sales, 13th year.
Joe Haynes, No. **112,** Alcorn State, deputy superintendent, public schools, 8th year.
Dick McKenzie, No. **41,** Ashland, financial services, 14th year.
Dale Orem, No. **51,** Louisville, mayor, 12th year.
Jim Quirk, No. **5,** Delaware, vice-president foreign sales, government securities, 4th year.
Bill Reynolds, No. **53,** West Chester State, retired teacher, 17th year.
Fred Wyant, No. **11,** West Virginia, regional sales manager, former NFL player, 26th year.

Back Judges

Paul Baetz, No. **22,** Heidelberg, financial consultant, 14th year.
Ken Baker, No. **91,** Eastern Illinois, optician, surgical ophthalmic technician, 1st year.
Roy Clymer, No. **24,** New Mexico State, district marketing manager, gas company, 12th year.
Jim Daopoulos, No. **75,** Kentucky, mortgage broker, 3rd year.
Ed Hochuli, No. **85,** Texas-El Paso, attorney, 2nd year.
Al Jury, No. **106,** San Bernardino Valley, state traffic officer, 14th year.
Jim Kearney, No. **107,** Pennsylvania, marketing manager, 14th year.
Bill Lovett, No. **98,** Maryland, managing partner, financial sales, 2nd year.
Tim Millis, No. **80,** Millsaps, financial investigative consultant, 3rd year.
Bob Moore, No. **36,** Dayton, attorney, 8th year.
Jim Poole, No. **92,** San Diego State, college professor, 17th year.
Louis Richard, No. **68,** Southwest Louisiana, sales manager, 6th year.
Tom Sifferman, No. **118,** Seattle, manufacturer's representative, 6th year.
Doug Toole, No. **4,** Utah State, physical therapist, orthopedic and sports medicine, 4th year.
Banks Williams, No. **99,** Houston, vice-president, general sales manager, 14th year.

Side Judges

Mike Borgard, No. **90,** St. Louis, president and owner, advertising specialties, 2nd year.
Mike Carey, No. **94,** Santa Clara, marketing manager, 2nd year.
Don Carlsen, No. **39,** Cal State-Chico, budget analyst, comptroller, 3rd year.
Bill Carollo, No. **63,** Wisconsin, marketing executive, 3rd year.
Richard Creed, No. **61,** Louisville, manager, real estate, 14th year.
Merrill Douglas, No. **102,** Utah, deputy sheriff, former NFL player, 11th year.
Tom Fincken, No. **47,** Emporia State, educator, 8th year.
Van Golmont, No. **3,** Miami, regional field promotion manager, 1st year.
Nate Jones, No. **97,** Lewis and Clark, high school principal, 15th year.
Gary Lane, No. **120,** Missouri, vice-president, medical supplies, former NFL player, 10th year.
Dean Look, No. **49,** Michigan State, director, medical manufacturing, former AFL player, 19th year.
Bill Quinby, No. **58,** Iowa, athletic director, 14th year.
Howard Slavin, No. **29,** Southern California, attorney, 5th year.
Ron Spitler, No. **119,** Panhandle State, owner, service center, 10th year.
Don Wedge, No. **28,** Ohio Wesleyan, executive account manager, 20th year.
David Wyant, No. **16,** Virginia, research scientist, 1st year.

Field Judges

Don Dorkowski, No. **113,** Cal State-Los Angeles, department head, health and safety, 6th year.
Scott Green, No. **19,** Delaware, special advisor, senate judiciary committee, 1st year.
Don Hakes, No. **96,** Bradley, retired educator, 15th year.
Donnie Hampton, No. **44,** Georgia, mortgage banker, 4th year.
Bob Lewis, No. **18,** retired U.S. government specialist, 16th year.
Phil Luckett, No. **59,** Texas-El Paso, computer program analyst, federal civil services, 1st year.
Pat Mallette, No. **82,** Nebraska, real estate broker, 23rd year.
Ed Merrifield, No. **76,** Missouri, sales representative, 17th year.
Don Orr, No. **77,** Vanderbilt, mechanical contractor, 21st year.
John Robison, No. **46,** Utah, high school teacher, 4th year.
Bill Schmitz, No. **122,** Colorado State, general sales manager, 3rd year.
Bobby Skelton, No. **73,** Alabama, industrial representative, 7th year.
Larry Upson, No. **37,** Prince George City College, senior personnel management specialist, 1st year.
Jack Vaughan, No. **93,** Mississippi State, financial services, 16th year.
Bob Wortman, No. **84,** Findlay, retired supervisor, college basketball officials, 26th year.

1

TOUCHDOWN, FIELD GOAL, or SUCCESSFUL TRY
Both arms extended above head.

2

SAFETY
Palms together above head.

3

FIRST DOWN
Arm pointed toward defensive team's goal.

4

CROWD NOISE, DEAD BALL, or NEUTRAL ZONE ESTABLISHED
One arm above head with an open hand.
With fist closed: **Fourth Down.**

5

BALL ILLEGALLY TOUCHED, KICKED, OR BATTED
Fingertips tap both shoulders.

6

TIME OUT
Hands crisscrossed above head.
Same signal followed by placing one hand on top of cap: **Referee's Time Out.**
Same signal followed by arm swung at side: **Touchback.**

7

NO TIME OUT or TIME IN WITH WHISTLE
Full arm circled to simulate moving clock.

8

DELAY OF GAME, ILLEGAL SUBSTITUTION, or EXCESS TIME OUT
Folded arms.

9

FALSE START, ILLEGAL SHIFT, ILLEGAL FORMATION, or KICKOFF OR SAFETY KICK OUT OF BOUNDS
Forearms rotated over and over in front of body.

10

PERSONAL FOUL
One wrist striking the other above head.
Same signal followed by swinging leg: **Roughing Kicker.**
Same signal followed by raised arm swinging forward: **Roughing Passer.**
Same signal followed by hand striking back of calf: **Clipping.**

11

HOLDING
Grasping one wrist, the fist clenched, in front of chest.

12

ILLEGAL USE OF HANDS, ARMS, OR BODY
Grasping one wrist, the hand open and facing forward, in front of chest.

13

PENALTY REFUSED, INCOMPLETE PASS, PLAY OVER, or MISSED GOAL
Hands shifted in horizontal plane.

14

PASS JUGGLED INBOUNDS AND CAUGHT OUT OF BOUNDS
Hands up and down in front of chest (following incomplete pass signal).

15

ILLEGAL FORWARD PASS
One hand waved behind back followed by loss of down signal (23).

16

INTENTIONAL GROUNDING OF PASS
Parallel arms waved in a diagonal plane across body. Followed by loss of down signal (23).

17

INTERFERENCE WITH FORWARD PASS or FAIR CATCH
Hands open and extended forward from shoulders with hands vertical.

18

INVALID FAIR CATCH SIGNAL
One hand waved above head.

19

INELIGIBLE RECEIVER OR INELIGIBLE MEMBER OF KICKING TEAM DOWNFIELD
Right hand touching top of cap.

20

ILLEGAL CONTACT
One open hand extended forward.

21

OFFSIDE or ENCROACHING
Hands on hips.

22

ILLEGAL MOTION AT SNAP
Horizontal arc with one hand.

23

LOSS OF DOWN
Both hands held behind head.

24

CRAWLING, INTERLOCKING INTERFERENCE, PUSHING, or HELPING RUNNER
Pushing movement of hands to front with arms downward.

25

TOUCHING A FORWARD PASS OR SCRIMMAGE KICK
Diagonal motion of one hand across another.

26

UNSPORTSMANLIKE CONDUCT
Arms outstretched, palms down. (Same signal means continuous action fouls are disregarded.) Chop block.

27

ILLEGAL CUT or BLOCKING BELOW THE WAIST
Hand striking front of thigh preceded by personal foul signal (10).

28

ILLEGAL CRACKBACK
Strike of an open right hand against the right mid thigh preceded by personal foul signal (10).

29

PLAYER DISQUALIFIED
Ejection signal.

30

TRIPPING
Repeated action of right foot in back of left heel.

31

UNCATCHABLE FORWARD PASS
Palm of right hand held parallel to ground above head and moved back and forth.

NFL Digest of Rules

This Digest of Rules of the National Football League has been prepared to aid players, fans, and members of the press, radio, and television media in their understanding of the game.

It is not meant to be a substitute for the official rule book. In any case of conflict between these explanations and the official rules, the rules always have precedence.

In order to make it easier to coordinate the information in this digest the topics discussed generally follow the order of the rule book.

Officials' Jurisdictions, Positions, and Duties

Referee—General oversight and control of game. Gives signals for all fouls and is final authority for rule interpretations. Takes a position in backfield 10 to 12 yards behind line of scrimmage, favors right side (if quarterback is right-handed passer). Determines legality of snap, observes deep back(s) for legal motion. On running play, observes quarterback during and after handoff, remains with him until action has cleared away, then proceeds downfield, checking on runner and contact behind him. When runner is downed, Referee determines forward progress from wing official and, if necessary, adjusts final position of ball.

On pass plays, drops back as quarterback begins to fade back, picks up legality of blocks by near linemen. Changes to complete concentration on quarterback as defenders approach. Primarily responsible to rule on possible roughing action on passer and if ball becomes loose, rules whether ball is free on a fumble or dead on an incomplete pass.

During kicking situations, Referee has primary responsibility to rule on kicker's actions and whether or not any subsequent contact by a defender is legal.

Umpire—Primary responsibility to rule on players' equipment, as well as their conduct and actions on scrimmage line. Lines up approximately four to five yards downfield, varying position from in front of weakside tackle to strongside guard. Looks for possible false start by offensive linemen. Observes legality of contact by both offensive linemen while blocking and by defensive players while they attempt to ward off blockers. Is prepared to call rule infractions if they occur on offense or defense. Moves forward to line of scrimmage when pass play develops in order to insure that interior linemen do not move illegally downfield. If offensive linemen indicate screen pass is to be attempted, Umpire shifts his attention toward screen side, picks up potential receiver in order to insure that he will legally be permitted to run his pattern and continues to rule on action of blockers. Umpire is to assist in ruling on incomplete or trapped passes when ball is thrown overhead or short.

Head Linesman—Primarily responsible for ruling on offside, encroachment, and actions pertaining to scrimmage line prior to or at snap. Keys on closest setback on his side of the field. On pass plays, Linesman is responsible to clear this receiver approximately seven yards downfield as he moves to a point five yards beyond the line. Linesman's secondary responsibility is to rule on any illegal action taken by defenders on any delay receiver moving downfield. Has full responsibility for ruling on sideline plays on his side, e.g., pass receiver or runner in or out of bounds. Together with Referee, Linesman is responsible for keeping track of number of downs and is in charge of mechanics of his chain crew in connection with its duties.

Linesman must be prepared to assist in determining forward progress by a runner on play directed toward middle or into his side zone. He, in turn, is to signal Referee or Umpire what forward point ball has reached. Linesman is also responsible to rule on legality of action involving any receiver who approaches his side zone. He is to call pass interference when the infraction occurs and is to rule on legality of blockers and defenders on plays involving ball carriers, whether it is entirely a running play, a combination pass and run, or a play involving a kick.

Line Judge—Straddles line of scrimmage on side of field opposite Linesman. Keeps time of game as a backup for clock operator. Along with Linesman is responsible for offside, encroachment, and actions pertaining to scrimmage line prior to or at snap. Line Judge keys on closest setback on his side of field. Line Judge is to observe his receiver until he moves at least seven yards downfield. He then moves toward backfield side, being especially alert to rule on any back in motion and on flight of ball when pass is made (he must rule whether forward or backward). Line Judge has primary responsibility to rule whether or not passer is behind or beyond line of scrimmage when pass is made. He also assists in observing actions by blockers and defenders who are on his side of field. After pass is thrown, Line Judge directs attention toward activities that occur in back of Umpire. During punting situations, Line Judge remains at line of scrimmage to be sure that only the end men move downfield until kick has been made. He also rules whether or not the kick crossed line and then observes action by members of the kicking team who are moving downfield to cover the kick.

Back Judge—Operates on same side of field as Line Judge, 20 yards deep. Keys on wide receiver on his side. Concentrates on path of end or back, observing legality of his potential block(s) or of actions taken against him. Is prepared to rule from deep position on holding or illegal use of hands by end or back or on defensive infractions committed by player guarding him. Has primary responsibility to make decisions involving sideline on his side of field, e.g., pass receiver or runner in or out of bounds.

Back Judge makes decisions involving catching, recovery, or illegal touching of a loose ball beyond line of scrimmage; rules on plays involving pass receiver, including legality of catch or pass interference; assists in covering actions of runner, including blocks by teammates and that of defenders; calls clipping on punt returns; and, together with Field Judge, rules whether or not field goal attempts are successful.

Side Judge—Operates on same side of field as Linesman, 20 yards deep. Keys on wide receiver on his side. Concentrates on path of end or back, observing legality of his potential block(s) or of actions taken against him. Is prepared to rule from deep position on holding or illegal use of hands by end or back or on defensive infractions committed by player guarding him. Has primary responsibility to make decisions involving sideline on his side of field, e.g., pass receiver or runner in or out of bounds.

Side Judge makes decisions involving catching, recovery, or illegal touching of a loose ball beyond line of scrimmage; rules on plays involving pass receiver, including legality of catch or pass interference; assists in covering actions of runner, including blocks by teammates and that of defenders; and calls clipping on punt returns.

Field Judge—Takes a position 25 yards downfield. In general, favors the tight end's side of field. Keys on tight end, concentrates on his path and observes legality of tight end's potential block(s) or of actions taken against him. Is prepared to rule from deep position on holding or illegal use of hands by end or back or on defensive infractions committed by player guarding him.

Field Judge times interval between plays on 45/25-second clock plus intermission between two periods of each half; makes decisions involving catching, recovery, or illegal touching of a loose ball beyond line of scrimmage; is responsible to rule on plays involving end line; calls pass interference, fair catch infractions, and clipping on kick returns; and, together with Back Judge, rules whether or not field goals and conversions are successful.

Definitions

1. **Chucking:** Warding off an opponent who is in front of a defender by contacting him with a quick extension of arm or arms, followed by the return of arm(s) to a flexed position, thereby breaking the original contact.
2. **Clipping:** Throwing the body across the back of an opponent's leg or hitting him from the back below the waist while moving up from behind unless the opponent is a runner or the action is in close line play.
3. **Close Line Play:** The area between the positions normally occupied by the offensive tackles, extending three yards on each side of the line of scrimmage.
4. **Crackback:** Eligible receivers who take or move to a position more than two yards outside the tackle may not block an opponent below the waist if they then move back inside to block.
5. **Dead Ball:** Ball not in play.
6. **Double Foul:** A foul by each team during the same down.
7. **Down:** The period of action that starts when the ball is put in play and ends when it is dead.
8. **Encroachment:** When a player enters the neutral zone and makes contact with an opponent before the ball is snapped.
9. **Fair Catch:** An unhindered catch of a kick by a member of the receiving team who must raise one arm a full length above his head while the kick is in flight.
10. **Foul:** Any violation of a playing rule.
11. **Free Kick:** A kickoff, kick after a safety, or kick after a fair catch. It may be a placekick, dropkick, or punt, except a punt may not be used on a kickoff.
12. **Fumble:** The loss of possession of the ball.
13. **Game Clock:** Scoreboard game clock.
14. **Impetus:** The action of a player that gives momentum to the ball.
15. **Live Ball:** A ball legally free kicked or snapped. It continues in play until the down ends.
16. **Loose Ball:** A live ball not in possession of any player.
17. **Muff:** The touching of a loose ball by a player in an unsuccessful attempt to obtain possession.
18. **Neutral Zone:** The space the length of a ball between the two scrimmage lines. The offensive team and defensive team must remain behind their end of the ball.
    Exception: The offensive player who snaps the ball.
19. **Offside:** A player is offside when any part of his body is beyond his scrimmage or free kick line when the ball is snapped.
20. **Own Goal:** The goal a team is guarding.
21. **Play Clock:** 45/25 second clock.
22. **Pocket Area:** Applies from a point two yards outside of either offensive tackle and includes the tight end if he drops off the line of scrimmage to pass protect. Pocket extends longitudinally behind the line back to offensive team's own end line.
23. **Possession:** When a player controls the ball throughout the act of clearly touching both feet, or any other part of his body other than his hand(s), to the ground inbounds.
24. **Post-Possession Foul:** A foul by the receiving team that occurs after a ball is legally kicked from scrimmage prior to possession changing. The ball must cross the line of scrimmage and the receiving team must retain possession of the kicked ball.
25. **Punt:** A kick made when a player drops the ball and kicks it while it is in flight.
26. **Safety:** The situation in which the ball is dead on or behind a team's own goal if the impetus comes from a player on that team. Two points are scored for the opposing team.
27. **Shift:** The movement of two or more offensive players at the same time before the snap.
28. **Striking:** The act of swinging, clubbing, or propelling the arm or forearm in contacting an opponent.
29. **Sudden Death:** The continuation of a tied game into sudden death overtime in which the team scoring first (by safety, field goal, or touchdown) wins.
30. **Touchback:** When a ball is dead on or behind a team's own goal line, provided the impetus came from an opponent and provided it is not a touchdown or a missed field goal.

31. **Touchdown:** When any part of the ball, legally in possession of a player inbounds, is on, above, or over the opponent's goal line, provided it is not a touchback.
32. **Unsportsmanlike Conduct:** Any act contrary to the generally understood principles of sportsmanship.

Summary of Penalties

Automatic First Down

1. Awarded to offensive team on all defensive fouls with these exceptions:
   (a) Offside.
   (b) Encroachment.
   (c) Delay of game.
   (d) Illegal substitution.
   (e) Excessive time out(s).
   (f) Incidental grasp of facemask.
   (g) Prolonged, excessive or premeditated celebrations by individual players or groups of players.
   (h) Running into the kicker.

Loss of Down (No yardage)

1. Second forward pass behind the line.
2. Forward pass strikes ground, goal post, or crossbar.
3. Forward pass goes out of bounds.
4. Forward pass is first touched by eligible receiver who has gone out of bounds and returned.
5. Forward pass touches or is caught by an ineligible receiver on or behind line.
6. Forward pass thrown from behind line of scrimmage after ball once crossed the line.

Five Yards

1. Defensive holding or illegal use of hands (automatic first down).
2. Delay of game.
3. Encroachment.
4. Too many time outs.
5. False start.
6. Illegal formation.
7. Illegal shift.
8. Illegal motion.
9. Illegal substitution.
10. First onside kickoff out of bounds between goal lines and not touched.
11. Invalid fair catch signal.
12. More than 11 players on the field at snap for either team.
13. Less than seven men on offensive line at snap.
14. Offside.
15. Failure to pause one second after shift or huddle.
16. Running into kicker.
17. More than one man in motion at snap.
18. Grasping facemask of opponent.
19. Player out of bounds at snap.
20. Ineligible member(s) of kicking team going beyond line of scrimmage before ball is kicked.
21. Illegal return.
22. Failure to report change of eligibility.
23. Prolonged, excessive or premeditated celebrations by individual players or groups of players.
24. Loss of team time out(s) or five-yard penalty on the defense for excessive crowd noise.

10 Yards

1. Offensive pass interference.
2. Ineligible player downfield during passing down.
3. Holding, illegal use of hands, arms or body by offense.
4. Tripping by a member of either team.
5. Helping the runner.
6. Deliberately batting or punching a loose ball.
7. Deliberately kicking a loose ball.

15 Yards

1. Chop block.
2. Clipping below the waist.
3. Fair catch interference.
4. Illegal crackback block by offense.
5. Piling on (automatic first down).
6. Roughing the kicker (automatic first down).
7. Roughing the passer (automatic first down).
8. Twisting, turning, or pulling an opponent by the facemask.
9. Unnecessary roughness.
10. Unsportsmanlike conduct.
11. Delay of game at start of either half.
12. Illegal blocking below the waist.
13. A tackler using his helmet to butt, spear, or ram an opponent.
14. Any player who uses the top of his helmet unnecessarily.
15. A punter, placekicker, or holder who simulates being roughed by a defensive player.
16. A defender who takes a running start from beyond the line of scrimmage in an attempt to block a field goal or point after touchdown.

Five Yards and Loss of Down

1. Forward pass thrown from beyond line of scrimmage.

10 Yards and Loss of Down

1. Intentional grounding of forward pass (safety if passer is in own end zone). If foul occurs more than 10 yards behind line, play results in loss of down at spot of foul.

15 Yards and Loss of Coin Toss Option

1. Team's late arrival on the field prior to scheduled kickoff.

15 Yards (and disqualification if flagrant)

1. Striking opponent with fist.
2. Kicking or kneeing opponent.
3. Striking opponent on head or neck with forearm, elbow, or hands whether or not the initial contact is made below the neck area.
4. Roughing kicker.
5. Roughing passer.
6. Malicious unnecessary roughness.
7. Unsportsmanlike conduct.
8. Palpably unfair act. (Distance penalty determined by the Referee after consultation with other officials.)

15 Yards and Automatic Disqualification

1. Using a helmet that is not worn as a weapon.

Suspension From Game

1. Illegal equipment. (Player may return after one down when legally equipped.)

Touchdown

1. When Referee determines a palpably unfair act deprived a team of a touchdown. (Example: Player comes off bench and tackles runner apparently en route to touchdown.)

Field

1. Sidelines and end lines are out of bounds. The goal line is actually in the end zone. A player with the ball in his possession scores when the ball is on, above, or over the goal line.
2. The field is rimmed by a white border, a minimum six feet wide, along the sidelines. All of this is out of bounds.
3. The hashmarks (inbound lines) are 70 feet, 9 inches from each sideline.
4. Goal posts must be single-standard type, offset from the end line and painted bright gold. The goal posts must be 18 feet, 6 inches wide and the top face of the crossbar must be 10 feet above the ground. Vertical posts extend at least 30 feet above the crossbar. A ribbon 4 inches by 42 inches long is to be attached to the top of each post. The actual goal is the plane extending indefinitely above the crossbar and between the outer edges of the posts.
5. The field is 360 feet long and 160 feet wide. The end zones are 30 feet deep. The line used in try-for-point plays is two yards out from the goal line.
6. Chain crew members and ball boys must be uniformly identifiable.
7. All clubs must use standardized sideline markers. Pylons must be used for goal line and end line markings.
8. End zone markings and club identification at 50 yard line must be approved by the Commissioner to avoid any confusion as to delineation of goal lines, sidelines, and end lines.

Ball

1. The home club must have 24 balls available for testing by the Referee one hour before game time. In case of bad weather, a playable ball is to be substituted on request of the offensive team captain.

Coin Toss

1. The toss of coin will take place within three minutes of kickoff in center of field. The toss will be called by the visiting captain. The winner may choose one of two privileges and the loser gets the other:
   (a) Receive or kick
   (b) Goal his team will defend
2. Immediately prior to the start of the second half, the captains of both teams must inform the officials of their respective choices. The loser of the original coin toss gets first choice.

Timing

1. The stadium game clock is official. In case it stops or is operating incorrectly, the Line Judge takes over the official timing on the field.
2. Each period is 15 minutes. The intermission between the periods is two minutes. Halftime is 12 minutes, unless otherwise specified.
3. On charged team time outs, the Field Judge starts watch and blows whistle after 1 minute 50 seconds, unless television does not utilize the time for commercial. In this case the length of the time out is reduced to 40 seconds.
4. Referee may allow two minutes for injured player and three minutes for equipment repair.
5. Each team is allowed three time outs each half.
6. Time between plays will be 45 seconds from the end of a given play until the snap of the ball for the next play, or a 25-second interval after certain administrative stoppages and game delays.
7. Clock will start running when ball is snapped following all changes of team possession.
8. With the exception of the last two minutes of the first half and the last five minutes of the second half, the game clock will be restarted following a kickoff return, a player going out of bounds on a play from scrimmage, or after declined penalties when appropriate on the referee's signal.
9. Consecutive team time outs can be taken by opposing teams but the length of the second time out will be reduced to 40 seconds.
10. When, in the judgment of the Referee, the level of crowd noise prevents the offense from hearing its signals, he can institute a series of procedures which can result in a loss of team time outs or a five-yard penalty against the defensive team.

Sudden Death

1. The sudden death system of determining the winner shall prevail when score is tied at the end of the regulation playing time of all NFL games. The team scoring first during overtime play shall be the winner and the game automatically ends upon any score (by safety, field goal, or touchdown) or when a score is awarded by Referee for a palpably unfair act.
2. At the end of regulation time the Referee will immediately toss coin at center of field in accordance with rules pertaining to the usual pregame toss. The captain of the visiting team will call the toss.
3. Following a three-minute intermission after the end of the regulation game, play will be continued in 15-minute periods or until there is a score. There is a two-minute intermission between subsequent periods. The teams change goals at the start of each period. Each team has three time outs and general provisions for play in the last two minutes of a half shall prevail. Disqualified players are not allowed to return.
   Exception: In preseason and regular season games there shall be a maximum of 15 minutes of sudden death with two time outs instead of three. General provisions for play in the last two minutes of a half will be in force.

Timing in Final Two Minutes of Each Half

1. On kickoff, clock does not start until the ball has been legally touched by player of either team in the field of play. (In all other cases, clock starts with kickoff.)
2. A team cannot buy an excess time out for a penalty. However, a fourth time out is allowed without penalty for an injured player, who must be removed immediately. A fifth time out or more is allowed for an injury and a five-yard penalty is assessed if the clock was running. Additionally, if the clock was running and the score is tied or the team in possession is losing, the ball cannot be put in play for at least 10 seconds on the fourth or more time out. The half or game can end while those 10 seconds are run off on the clock.
3. If the defensive team is behind in the score and commits a foul when it has no time outs left in the final 30 seconds of either half, the offensive team can decline the penalty for the foul and have the time on the clock expire.
4. Fouls that occur in the last five minutes of the fourth quarter as well as the last two minutes of the first half will result in the clock starting on the snap.

Try-for-Point

1. After a touchdown, the scoring team is allowed a try-for-point during one scrimmage down. The ball may be spotted anywhere between the inbounds lines, two or more yards from the goal line. The successful conversion counts one point, whether by run, kick, or pass.
2. The defensive team never can score on a try-for-point. As soon as defense gets possession, or the kick is blocked, the ball is dead.
3. Any distance penalty for fouls committed by the defense that prevent the try from being attempted can be enforced on the succeeding kickoff. Any foul committed on a successful try will result in a distance penalty being assessed on the ensuing kickoff.
4. Only the fumbling player may advance a fumble during a try-for-point.

Players-Substitutions

1. Each team is permitted 11 men on the field at the snap.
2. Unlimited substitution is permitted. However, players may enter the field only when the ball is dead. Players who have been substituted for are not permitted to linger on the field. Such lingering will be interpreted as unsportsmanlike conduct.
3. Players leaving the game must be out of bounds on their own side, clearing the field between the end lines, before a snap or free kick. If player crosses end line leaving field, it is delay of game (five-yard penalty).
4. Substitutes who remain in the game must move onto the field as far as the inside of the field numerals before moving to a wide position.

Kickoff

1. The kickoff shall be from the kicking team's 35 yard line at the start of each half and after a field goal and try-for-point. A kickoff is one type of free kick.
2. Either a one-, two-, or three-inch tee may be used (no tee permitted for field goal or try-for-point plays). The ball is put in play by a placekick or dropkick.
3. If the kickoff clears the opponent's goal posts it is not a field goal.
4. A kickoff is illegal unless it travels 10 yards OR is touched by the receiving team. Once the ball is touched by the receiving team it is a free ball. Receivers may recover and advance. Kicking team may recover but NOT advance UNLESS receiver had possession and lost the ball.
5. When a kickoff goes out of bounds between the goal lines without being touched by the receiving team, the ball belongs to the receivers 30 yards from the spot of the kick or at the out-of-bounds spot unless the ball went out-of-bounds the first time an onside kick was attempted. In this case the kicking team is to be penalized five yards and the ball must be kicked again.
6. When a kickoff goes out of bounds between the goal lines and is touched last by receiving team, it is receiver's ball at out-of-bounds spot.

Free Kick

1. In addition to a kickoff, the other free kicks are a kick after a safety and a kick after a fair catch. In both cases, a dropkick, placekick, or punt may be used (a punt may not be used on a kickoff).
2. On a free kick after a fair catch, captain of receiving team has the option to put ball in play by punt, dropkick, or placekick without a tee, or by snap. If the placekick or dropkick goes between the uprights a field goal is scored.
3. On a free kick after a safety, the team scored upon puts ball in play by a punt, dropkick, or placekick without tee. No score can be made on a free kick following a safety, even if a series of penalties places team in position. (A field goal can be scored only on a play from scrimmage or a free kick after a fair catch.)

Field Goal

1. All field goals attempted and missed from scrimmage line beyond the 20 yard line will result in the defensive team taking possession of the ball at the scrimmage line. On any field goal attempted and missed from scrimmage line inside the 20 yard line, ball will revert to defensive team at the 20 yard line.

Safety

1. The important factor in a safety is impetus. Two points are scored for the opposing team when the ball is dead on or behind a team's own goal line if the impetus came from a player on that team.

Examples of Safety:

(a) Blocked punt goes out of kicking team's end zone. Impetus was provided by punting team. The block only changes direction of ball, not impetus.
(b) Ball carrier retreats from field of play into his own end zone and is downed. Ball carrier provides impetus.
(c) Offensive team commits a foul and spot of enforcement is behind its own goal line.
(d) Player on receiving team muffs punt and, trying to get ball, forces or illegally kicks it into end zone where he or a teammate recovers. He has given new impetus to the ball.

Examples of Non-Safety:

(a) Player intercepts a pass with both feet inbounds in the field of play and his momentum carries him into his own end zone. Ball is put in play at spot of interception.
(b) Player intercepts a pass in his own end zone and is downed. Impetus came from passing team, not from defense. (Touchback)
(c) Player passes from behind his own goal line. Opponent bats down ball in end zone. (Incomplete pass)

Measuring

1. The forward point of the ball is used when measuring.

Position of Players at Snap

1. Offensive team must have at least seven players on line.
2. Offensive players, not on line, must be at least one yard back at snap. (**Exception:** player who takes snap.)
3. No interior lineman may move after taking or simulating a three-point stance.
4. No player of either team may invade neutral zone before snap.
5. No player of offensive team may charge or move, after assuming set position, in such manner as to lead defense to believe snap has started.
6. If a player changes his eligibility, the Referee must alert the defensive captain after player has reported to him.
7. All players of offensive team must be stationary at snap, except one back who may be in motion parallel to scrimmage line or backward (not forward).
8. After a shift or huddle all players on offensive team must come to an absolute stop for at least one second with no movement of hands, feet, head, or swaying of body.
9. Quarterbacks can be called for a false start penalty (five yards) if their actions are judged to be an obvious attempt to draw an opponent offside.

Use of Hands, Arms, and Body

1. No player on offense may assist a runner except by blocking for him. There shall be no interlocking interference.
2. A runner may ward off opponents with his hands and arms but no other player on offense may use hands or arms to obstruct an opponent by grasping with hands, pushing, or encircling any part of his body during a block. Hands (open or closed) can be thrust forward to initially contact an opponent on or outside the opponent's frame, but the blocker must work to bring his hands on or inside the frame.
   Note: Pass blocking: Hand(s) thrust forward that slip outside the body of the defender will be legal if blocker worked to bring them back inside. Hand(s) or arm(s) that encircle a defender—i.e., hook an opponent—are to be considered illegal and officials are to call a foul for holding.
   Blocker cannot use his hands or arms to push from behind, hang onto, or encircle an opponent in a manner that restricts his movement as the play develops.
3. Hands cannot be thrust forward above the frame to contact an opponent on the neck, face or head.
   Note: The frame is defined as the part of the opponent's body below the neck that is presented to the blocker.
4. A defensive player may not tackle or hold an opponent other than a runner. Otherwise, he may use his hands, arms, or body only:
   (a) To defend or protect himself against an obstructing opponent.
   Exception: An eligible receiver is considered to be an obstructing opponent ONLY to a point five yards beyond the line of scrimmage unless the player who receives the snap clearly demonstrates no further intention to pass the ball. Within this five-yard zone, a defensive player may make contact with an eligible receiver that may be maintained as long as it is continuous and unbroken. The defensive player cannot use his hands or arms to push from behind, hang onto, or encircle an eligible receiver in a manner that restricts movement as the play develops. Beyond this five-yard limitation, a defender may use

his hands or arms ONLY to defend or protect himself against impending contact caused by a receiver. In such reaction, the defender may not contact a receiver who attempts to take a path to evade him.

(b) To push or pull opponent out of the way on line of scrimmage.

(c) In actual attempt to get at or tackle runner.

(d) To push or pull opponent out of the way in a legal attempt to recover a loose ball.

(e) During a legal block on an opponent who is not an eligible pass receiver.

(f) When legally blocking an eligible pass receiver above the waist.

Exception: Eligible receivers lined up within two yards of the tackle, whether on or immediately behind the line, may be blocked below the waist at or behind the line of scrimmage. NO eligible receiver may be blocked below the waist after he goes beyond the line.

Note: Once the quarterback hands off or pitches the ball to a back, or if the quarterback leaves the pocket area, the restrictions on the defensive team relative to the offensive receivers will end, provided the ball is not in the air.

5. A defensive player must not contact an opponent above the shoulders with the palm of his hand except to ward him off on the line. This exception is permitted only if it is not a repeated act against the same opponent during any one contact. In all other cases the palms may be used on head, neck, or face only to ward off or push an opponent in legal attempt to get at the ball.
6. Any offensive player who pretends to possess the ball or to whom a teammate pretends to give the ball may be tackled provided he is crossing his scrimmage line between the ends of a normal tight offensive line.
7. An offensive player who lines up more than two yards outside his own tackle or a player who, at the snap, is in a backfield position and subsequently takes a position more than two yards outside a tackle may not clip an opponent anywhere nor may he contact an opponent below the waist if the blocker is moving toward the ball and if contact is made within an area five yards on either side of the line.
8. A player of either team may block at any time provided it is not pass interference, fair catch interference, or unnecessary roughness.
9. A player may not bat or punch:

   (a) A loose ball (in field of play) toward his opponent's goal line or in any direction in either end zone.

   (b) A ball in player possession or attempt to get possession.

   Exception: A forward or backward pass may be batted, tipped, or deflected in any direction at any time by either the offense or the defense.

   Note: A pass in flight that is controlled or caught may only be thrown backward.
10. No player may deliberately kick any ball except as a punt, dropkick, or placekick.

Forward Pass

1. A forward pass may be touched or caught by any eligible receiver. All members of the defensive team are eligible. Eligible receivers on the offensive team are players on either end of line (other than center, guard, or tackle) or players at least one yard behind the line at the snap. A T-formation quarterback is not eligible to receive a forward pass during a play from scrimmage.

   Exception: T-formation quarterback becomes eligible if pass is previously touched by an eligible receiver.
2. An offensive team may make only one forward pass during each play from scrimmage (Loss of down).
3. The passer must be behind his line of scrimmage (Loss of down and five yards, enforced from the spot of pass).
4. Any eligible offensive player may catch a forward pass. If a pass is touched by one offensive player and touched or caught by a second eligible offensive player, pass completion is legal. Further, all offensive players become eligible once a pass is touched by an eligible receiver or any defensive player.
5. The rules concerning a forward pass and ineligible receivers:

   (a) If ball is touched accidentally by an ineligible receiver on or behind his line: loss of down.

   (b) If ineligible receiver is illegally downfield: loss of 10 yards.

   (c) If touched or caught (intentionally or accidentally) by ineligible receiver beyond the line: loss of 10 yards or loss of down.
6. The player who first controls and continues to maintain control of a pass will be awarded the ball even though his opponent later establishes joint control of the ball.
7. Any forward pass becomes incomplete and ball is dead if:

   (a) Pass hits the ground or goes out of bounds.

   (b) Hits the goal post or the crossbar of either team.

   (c) Is caught by offensive player after touching ineligible receiver.

   (d) An illegal pass is caught by the passer.
8. A forward pass is complete when a receiver clearly touches the ground with both feet inbounds while in possession of the ball. If a receiver would have landed inbounds with both feet but is carried or pushed out of bounds while maintaining possession of the ball, pass is complete at the out-of-bounds spot.
9. If an eligible receiver goes out of bounds accidentally or is forced out by a defender and returns to catch a pass, the play is regarded as a pass caught out of bounds. (Loss of down, no yardage.)
10. On a fourth down pass—when the offensive team is inside the opposition's 20 yard line—an incomplete pass results in a loss of down at the line of scrimmage.
11. If a personal foul is committed by the defense prior to the completion of a pass, the penalty is 15 yards from the spot where ball becomes dead.
12. If a personal foul is committed by the offense prior to the completion of a pass, the penalty is 15 yards from the previous line of scrimmage.

Intentional Grounding of Forward Pass

1. Intentional grounding of a forward pass is a foul: loss of down and 10 yards from previous spot if passer is in the field of play or loss of down at the spot of the foul if it occurs more than 10 yards behind the line or safety if passer is in his own end zone when ball is released.
2. It is considered intentional grounding of a forward pass when the ball strikes the ground after the passer throws, tosses, or lobs the ball to prevent a loss of yards by his team.
3. It is not intentional grounding when the defensive rushers have not put sufficient pressure on the passer to prevent him, for strategic purposes, from throwing the ball downfield in a natural and effective motion even though there is no apparent chance of completion.

Protection of Passer

1. By interpretation, a pass begins when the passer—with possession of ball—starts to bring his hand forward. If ball strikes ground after this action has begun, play is ruled an incomplete pass. If passer loses control of ball prior to his bringing his hand forward, play is ruled a fumble.
2. No defensive player may run into a passer of a legal forward pass after the ball has left his hand (15 yards). The Referee must determine whether opponent had a reasonable chance to stop his momentum during an attempt to block the pass or tackle the passer while he still had the ball.
3. No defensive player who has an unrestricted path to the quarterback may hit him flagrantly in the area of the knee(s) when approaching in any direction.
4. Officials are to blow the play dead as soon as the quarterback is clearly in the grasp and control of any tackler, and his safety is in jeopardy.

Pass Interference

1. There shall be no interference with a forward pass thrown from behind the line. The restriction for the passing team starts with the snap. The restriction on the defensive team starts when the ball leaves the passer's hand. Both restrictions end when the ball is touched by anyone.
2. The penalty for defensive pass interference is an automatic first down at the spot of the foul. If interference is in the end zone, it is first down for the offense on the defense's 1 yard line. If previous spot was inside the defense's 1 yard line, penalty is half the distance to the goal line.
3. The penalty for offensive pass interference is 10 yards from the previous spot.
4. It is pass interference by either team when any player movement beyond the offensive line significantly hinders the progress of an eligible player or such player's opportunity to catch the ball during a legal forward pass. When players are competing for position to make a play on the ball, any contact by hands, arms or body shall be considered incidental unless prohibited. Prohibited conduct shall be when a player physically restricts or impedes the opponent in such a manner that is visually evident and materially affects the opponent's opportunity to gain position or retain his position to catch the ball. If a player has gained position, he shall not be considered to have impeded or restricted his opponent in a prohibited manner if all of his actions are a bona fide effort to go to and catch the ball. Provided an eligible player is not interfered with in such a manner, the following exceptions to pass interference will prevail:

   (a) If neither player is looking for the ball and there is incidental contact in the act of moving to the ball that does not materially affect the route of an eligible player, there is no interference. If there is any question whether the incidental contact materially affects the route, the ruling shall be no interference.

   Note: Inadvertent tripping is not a foul in this situation.

   (b) Any eligible player looking for and intent on playing the ball who initiates contact, however severe, while attempting to move to the spot of completion or interception will not be called for interference.

   (c) Any eligible player who makes contact, however severe, with one or more eligible players while looking for and making a genuine attempt to catch or bat a reachable ball, will not be called for interference.

   (d) It must be remembered that defensive players have as much right to the ball as offensive eligible receivers.

   (e) Pass interference by the defense is not to be called when the forward pass is clearly uncatchable.

   (f) Note: There is no defensive pass interference behind the line.

Backward Pass

1. Any pass not forward is regarded as a backward pass or lateral. A pass parallel to the line is a backward pass. A runner may pass backward at any time. Any player on either team may catch the pass or recover the ball after it touches the ground.
2. A backward pass that strikes the ground can be recovered and advanced by offensive team.
3. A backward pass that strikes the ground can be recovered but cannot be advanced by the defensive team.
4. A backward pass caught in the air can be advanced by the defensive team.
5. A backward pass in flight may not be batted forward by an offensive player.

Fumble

1. The distinction between a fumble and a muff should be kept in mind in considering rules about fumbles. A fumble is the loss of possession of the ball. A muff is the touching of a loose ball by a player in an unsuccessful attempt to obtain possession.
2. A fumble may be advanced by any player on either team regardless of whether recovered before or after ball hits the ground.

3. A fumble that goes forward and out of bounds will return to the fumbling team at the spot of the fumble unless the ball goes out of bounds in the opponent's end zone. In this case, it is a touchback.
4. If an offensive player fumbles anywhere on the field during a fourth down play, or if a player fumbles on any down after the two-minute warning in a half, only the fumbling player is permitted to recover and/or advance the ball. If recovered by any other offensive player, the ball is dead at the spot of the fumble unless it is recovered behind the spot of the fumble. In that case, ball is dead at spot of recovery. Any defensive player may recover and/or advance any fumble.
   Exception: The fourth-down fumble rule does not apply if a player touches, but does not possess, a direct snap from center, i.e., a snap in flight as opposed to a hand-to-hand exchange.

Kicks From Scrimmage

1. Any kick from scrimmage must be made from behind the line to be legal.
2. Any punt or missed field goal that touches a goal post is dead.
3. During a kick from scrimmage, only the end men, as eligible receivers on the line of scrimmage at the time of the snap, are permitted to go beyond the line before the ball is kicked.
   Exception: An eligible receiver who, at the snap, is aligned or in motion behind the line and more than one yard outside the end man on his side of the line, clearly making him the outside receiver, REPLACES that end man as the player eligible to go downfield after the snap. All other members of the kicking team must remain at the line of scrimmage until the ball has been kicked.
4. Any punt that is blocked and does not cross the line of scrimmage can be recovered and advanced by either team. However, if offensive team recovers it must make the yardage necessary for its first down to retain possession if punt was on fourth down.
5. The kicking team may never advance its own kick even though legal recovery is made beyond the line of scrimmage. Possession only.
6. A member of the receiving team may not run into or rough a kicker who kicks from behind his line unless contact is:
   (a) Incidental to and after he had touched ball in flight.
   (b) Caused by kicker's own motions.
   (c) Occurs during a quick kick, or a kick made after a run, or after kicker recovers a loose ball. Ball is loose when kicker muffs snap or snap hits ground.
   (d) Defender is blocked into kicker.
   The penalty for running into the kicker is 5 yards. For roughing the kicker: 15 yards, an automatic first down and disqualification if flagrant.
7. If a member of the kicking team attempting to down the ball on or inside opponent's 5 yard line carries the ball into the end zone, it is a touchback.
8. Fouls during a punt are enforced from the previous spot (line of scrimmage).
   Exception: Illegal touching, illegal fair catch, invalid fair catch signal, and fouls by the receiving team during loose ball after ball is kicked.
9. While the ball is in the air or rolling on the ground following a punt or field goal attempt and receiving team commits a foul before gaining possession, receiving team will retain possession and will be penalized for its foul.
10. It will be illegal for a defensive player to jump or stand on any player, or be picked up by a teammate or to use a hand or hands on a teammate to gain additional height in an attempt to block a kick (Penalty 15 yards, unsportsmanlike conduct).
11. A punted ball remains a kicked ball until it is declared dead or in possession of either team.
12. Any member of the punting team may down the ball anywhere in the field of play. However, it is illegal touching (Official's time out and receiver's ball at spot of illegal touching). This foul does not offset any foul by receivers during the down.
13. Defensive team may advance all kicks from scrimmage (including unsuccessful field goal) whether or not ball crosses defensive team's goal line. Rules pertaining to kicks from scrimmage apply until defensive team gains possession.

Fair Catch

1. The member of the receiving team must raise one arm a full length above his head and wave it from side to side while kick is in flight. (Failure to give proper sign: receivers' ball five yards behind spot of signal.) **Note:** It is legal for the receiver to shield his eyes from the sun by raising one hand no higher than the helmet.
2. No opponent may interfere with the fair catcher, the ball, or his path to the ball. Penalty: 15 yards from spot of foul and fair catch is awarded.
3. A player who signals for a fair catch is not required to catch the ball. However, if a player signals for a fair catch, he may not block or initiate contact with any player on the kicking team until the ball touches a player. Penalty: snap 15 yards behind spot of foul.
4. If ball hits ground or is touched by member of kicking team in flight, fair catch signal is off and all rules for a kicked ball apply.
5. Any undue advance by a fair catch receiver is delay of game. No specific distance is specified for undue advance as ball is dead at spot of catch. If player comes to a reasonable stop, no penalty. For violation, five yards.
6. If time expires while ball is in play and a fair catch is awarded, receiving team may choose to extend the period with one free kick down. However, placekicker may not use tee.

Foul on Last Play of Half or Game

1. On a foul by defense on last play of half or game, the down is replayed if penalty is accepted.
2. On a foul by the offense on last play of half or game, the down is not replayed and the play in which the foul is committed is nullified.
   Exception: Fair catch interference, foul following change of possession, illegal touching. No score by offense counts.
3. On double foul on last play of half or game, down is replayed.

Spot of Enforcement of Foul

1. There are four basic spots at which a penalty for a foul is enforced:
   (a) Spot of foul: The spot where the foul is committed.
   (b) Previous spot: The spot where the ball was put in play.
   (c) Spot of snap, pass, fumble, return kick, or free kick: The spot where the act connected with the foul occurred.
   (d) Succeeding spot: The spot where the ball next would be put in play if no distance penalty were to be enforced.
   Exception: If foul occurs after a touchdown and before the whistle for a try-for-point, succeeding spot is spot of next kickoff.
2. All fouls committed by offensive team behind the line of scrimmage and in the field of play shall be penalized from the previous spot.
3. When spot of enforcement for fouls involving defensive holding or illegal use of hands by the defense is behind the line of scrimmage, any penalty yardage to be assessed on that play shall be measured from the line if the foul occurred beyond the line.

Double Foul

1. If there is a double foul during a down in which there is a change of possession, the team last gaining possession may keep the ball unless its foul was committed prior to the change of possession.
2. If double foul occurs after a change of possession, the defensive team retains the ball at the spot of its foul or dead ball spot.
3. If one of the fouls of a double foul involves disqualification, that player must be removed, but no penalty yardage is to be assessed.
4. If the kickers foul during a punt before possession changes and the receivers foul after possession changes, penalties will be offset and the down is replayed.

Penalty Enforced on Following Kickoff

1. When a team scores by touchdown, field goal, extra point, or safety and either team commits a personal foul, unsportsmanlike conduct, or obvious unfair act during the down, the penalty will be assessed on the following kickoff.

Procedures to Terminate or Temporarily Delay Completion of a Game

The National Football League holds to the position that all games should be played to their conclusion. However, if in the opinion of appropriate League authorities, it is impossible to begin or continue a game due to an emergency, or a game is deemed to be imminently threatened by any such emergency—e.g., severely inclement weather, lightning, flooding, power failure, interference by spectators, or other non-participants—then the following procedures will serve as guidelines for the Commissioner and/or his duly appointed representatives. The Commissioner will have the power to review the circumstances of each emergency and to adjust the following procedures in whatever manner he deems appropriate. If, in the Commissioner's opinion, it is reasonable to project that the resumption of an interrupted game would not change its ultimate result, he will be empowered to terminate the game.

1. The League employees vested with the authority to define emergencies under these procedures are the Commissioner, his representatives, and the game Referee. In cases where neither the Commissioner nor his representatives are present, the referee shall have sole authority, but he must make every effort to contact the Commissioner or representative for consultation. In all cases of significant delay, the League authorities will consult with the management of the participating clubs.
2. If, due to an emergency, a regular-season or postseason game is not started at its scheduled time and cannot be played at any later time that same day, the game, nevertheless, must be played on a subsequent date to be determined by the Commissioner.
3. If there is deemed to be a threat of an emergency (e.g., incoming tropical storm) that may occur during the playing of a game, the starting time of such game will not be moved to an earlier time unless there is clearly sufficient time to make an orderly change.
4. If an interrupted regular-season or postseason game cannot be completed on the same day, such game will be rescheduled by the Commissioner and resumed at that point.
5. In instances which require the Commissioner to reschedule a regular-season game, he will make every effort to set the game for no later than two days after its originally scheduled date, and if possible, at its original site. If unable to do so, he will schedule it at the nearest available facility. If it is impossible to schedule the game within two days after its original date, the Commissioner will attempt to schedule it on the Tuesday of the next calendar week in which the two involved clubs play other clubs no earlier than Sunday.
6. If an emergency interrupts a postseason game and such game cannot be resumed on that same date, the Commissioner will make every effort to arrange for its completion as soon as possible. If unable to schedule the game at the same site, he will select an appropriate alternate site. He will terminate the game short of completion only if in his judgment the continuation of the game would not be normally expected to alter the ultimate outcome.
7. In all instances where a game is resumed after interruption, the resumption will begin at the point at which the game was interrupted. The referee will call time out when it is necessary to declare an emergency interruption, and he will make a record of the team possessing the ball, position of the ball on

the field, down, distance, time remaining in the period, and any other pertinent information required for an efficient and equitable resumption of play.

Note: In recent history, only two games, both preseason, have been terminated. In 1976, the Chicago College All-Star game was terminated due to thunderstorms with the Steelers leading the All-Stars 24-0, and the 1980 Pro Football Hall of Fame Game at Canton, Ohio, was called with 5:29 remaining due to severe thunder and lightning with the Chargers and Packers tied 0-0.

NOTES

NOTES

NOTES

NOTES

NOTES

NOTES

NOTES